THE SPORTS ILLUSTRATED

1995 SPORTS ALMANAC

By the Editors of Sports Illustrated

LITTLE, BROWN AND COMPANY

Boston   New York   Toronto   London

Sports Illustrated

1995 SPORTS ALMANAC

First Edition

ISBN 0-316-80860-1

Sports Illustrated 1995 Sports Almanac was produced by Bishop Books
of New York City.

Sports Illustrated Editorial Director for Books: Joe Marshall

Front Cover Photography credits:
Ken Griffey Jr. (top): Chuck Solomon
Emmitt Smith (bottom): Rick Rickman
Back Cover Photography credits:
Larry Csonka (top): Walter Iooss Jr.
Bonnie Blair (middle): Heinz Kluetmeier
David Robinson (bottom): David E. Klutho
Title page photography credit: Jim Gund

10   9   8   7   6   5   4   3   2   1

COM

Published simultaneously in Canada by
Little, Brown & Company (Canada) Limited

PRINTED IN THE UNITED STATES OF AMERICA

CONTENTS

Expanded Contents

Expanded Contents *(Cont.)*

Expanded Contents (Cont.)

In compiling the *Sports Illustrated 1995 Sports Almanac*, the editors would again like to thank Natasha Simon and Linda Wachtel of the Sports Illustrated library for their invaluable assistance. They would also like to extend their gratitude to the media relations offices of the following organizations for their help in providing information and materials relating to their sports: Major League Baseball; the Canadian Football League; the National Football League; the National Collegiate Athletic Association; the National Basketball Association; the National Hockey League; the Association of Tennis Professionals; the World Tennis Association; the U.S. Tennis Association; the U.S. Golf Association; the Ladies Professional Golf Association; the Professional Golfers Association; Thoroughbred Racing Communications, Inc.; the U.S. Trotting Association; the Breeders' Cup; Churchill Downs; the New York Racing Association Inc.; the Maryland Jockey Club; Championship Auto Racing Teams; the National Hot Rod Association; the International Motor Sports Association; the National Association for Stock Car Auto Racing; the Professional Bowlers Association; the Ladies Professional Bowlers Tour; the American Professional Soccer League; the National Professional Soccer League; *the Fédération Internationale De Football Association*; the U.S. Soccer Federation; the U.S. Olympic Committee; USA Track & Field; U.S. Swimming; U.S. Diving; U.S. Skiing; U.S. Skating; the U.S. Chess Federation; U.S. Curling; the Iditarod Trail Committee; the International Game Fish Association; the U.S. Gymnastics Federation; the Lacrosse Foundation; the American Power Boat Association; the Professional Rodeo Cowboys Association; U.S. Rowing; the American Softball Association; the Triathlon Federation USA; the National Archery Association; USA Wrestling; the U.S. Squash Racquets Association; the U.S. Polo Association; ABC Sports and the U.S. Volleyball Association.

The following sources were consulted in gathering information:

Baseball   *The Baseball Encyclopedia*, Macmillan Publishing Co., 1990; *Total Baseball*, Warner Books, 1991; *Baseballistics*, St. Martin's Press, 1990; *The Book of Baseball Records*, Seymour Siwoff, publisher, 1991; *The Complete Baseball Record Book*, The Sporting News Publishing Co., 1992; *The Sporting News Baseball Guide*, The Sporting News Publishing Co., 1993; *The Sporting News Baseball Register*, The Sporting News Publishing Co., 1993; *National League Green Book—1994*, The Sporting News Publishing Co., 1993; *American League Red Book—1994*, The Sporting News Publishing Co., 1993; *The Scouting Report: 1993*, Stats, Inc., Harper Perennial, 1993.

Pro Football   *The Official 1993 National Football League Record & Fact Book*, The National Football League, 1993; *The Official National Football League Encyclopedia*, New American Library, 1990; *The Sporting News Football Guide*, The Sporting News Publishing Co., 1993; *The Sporting News Football Register*, The Sporting News Publishing Co., 1993; *The 1993 National Football League Record & Fact Book*, Workman Publishing, 1993; *The Football Encyclopedia,* David Neft and Richard Cohen, St. Martin's Press, 1991.

College Football   *1994 NCAA Football*, The National Collegiate Athletic Association, 1993.

Pro Basketball   *The Official NBA Basketball Encyclopedia*, Villard Books, 1989; *The Sporting News Official 1993–94 NBA Guide*, The Sporting News Publishing Co., 1993.

College Basketball   *1994 NCAA Basketball*, The National Collegiate Athletic Association, 1993.

Hockey   *The National Hockey League Official Guide & Record Book 1993-94*, The National Hockey League, 1993; *The Sporting News Complete Hockey Book,* The Sporting News Publishing Co., 1993; *The Complete Encyclopedia of Hockey,* Visible Ink Press, 1993.

Tennis   *1994 Official USTA Tennis Yearbook*, H. O. Zimman, Inc., 1994; *IBM/ATP Tour 1994 Player Guide*, Association of Tennis Professionals, 1994; *WTA Official 1994 Media Guide*, Women's Tennis Association, 1994.

Golf   *PGA Tour Book 1994*, PGA Tour Creative Services, 1994; *LPGA 1994 Player Guide*, LPGA Communications Department, 1994; *Senior PGA Tour Book 1994*, PGA Tour Creative Services, 1994; *USGA Yearbook 1994*, U.S. Golf Association, 1994.

Boxing   *The Ring 1986–87 Record Book and Boxing Encyclopedia*, The Ring Publishing Corp., 1987. (To subscribe to *The Ring* magazine, write to P.O. Box 768, Rockville Centre, New York 11571-9905; or call (516) 678-7464); *Computer Boxing Update*, Ralph Citro, Inc., 1992.

Horse Racing   *The American Racing Manual 1994*, Daily Racing Form, Inc., 1994; *1994 Directory and Record Book*, The Thoroughbred Racing Association, 1994; *The Trotting and Pacing Guide, 1994*, United States Trotting Association, 1994; *Breeders' Cup 1993 Statistics*, Breeders' Cup Limited, 1993; *NYRA Media Guide 1993*, The New York Racing Association, 1994; *The 120th Kentucky Derby Media Guide, 1994*, Churchill Downs Public Relations Dept., 1994; *The 120th Preakness Press Guide, 1994*, Maryland Jockey Club, 1994; *Harness Racing News,* Harness Racing Communications.

Motor Sports   *The Official NASCAR Yearbook and Press Guide 1994*, UMI Publications, Inc., 1994; *1994 Indianapolis 500 Media Fact Book*, Indy 500 Publications, 1994; *IMSA 1994 Yearbook*, International Motor Sports Association, 1994; *1994 Winston Drag Racing Series Media Guide*, Sports Marketing Enterprises, 1994.

Bowling   *1994 Professional Bowlers Association Press, Radio and Television Guide*, Professional Bowlers Association, Inc., 1994; *The Ladies Pro Bowlers Tour 1994 Souvenir Tour Guide*, Ladies Pro Bowlers Tour, 1994.

Soccer   *Major Soccer League Official Guide 1991–92*, Major Soccer League, Inc., 1991; *Rothmans Football Yearbook 1993–94*, Headline Book Publishing, 1993; *American Professional Soccer League 1992 Media Guide*, APSL Media Relations Department, 1992; The *European Football Yearbook*, Facer Publications Limited, 1988; *Soccer America,* Burling Communications.

NCAA Sports   *1993–94 National Collegiate Championships*, The National Collegiate Athletic Association, 1994; *1993-94 National Directory of College Athletics,* Collegiate Directories Inc., 1993.

Olympics   *The Complete Book of the Olympics*, Little, Brown and Co., 1991.

Track and Field   *American Athletics Annual 1993*, The Athletics Congress/USA, 1993.

Swimming   *6th World Swimming Championships Media Guide*, The World Swimming Championships Organizing Committee, 1991.

Skiing   *U.S. Ski Team 1994 Media Guide / USSA Directory*, U.S. Ski Association, 1993; *Ski Racing Annual Competition Guide 1993–94*, Ski Racing International, 1993; *Ski Magazine's Encyclopedia of Skiing*, Harper & Row, 1974; *Caffä Lavazza Ski World Cup Press Kit*, Biorama, 1991.

Scorecard

Auburn Shocks Florida · Nebraska Stops Kansas State

OCTOBER 24, 1994
$2.95 (CAN. $3.95)

Sports Illustrated

Penn State:
The New No. 1

Freddie Scott and the
Nittany Lions Overpower Michigan

A summary of late Fall 1994 events

AUTO RACING

A triumphant Dale Earnhardt did a lap of honor while standing on the trunk of a car on Oct. 23, the day he won the AC Delco 500 at North Carolina Motor Speedway in Rockingham, N.C. Earnhardt had good reason to celebrate: Not only had the win clinched this season's NASCAR points title with two events remaining, but that title tied Richard Petty's alltime record of seven Winston Cup titles. Earnhardt did not allow his exuberance to cloud his natural modesty. "We have seven titles," said Earnhardt, "but Richard Petty's still the King."

And on Oct. 9, 54-year-old Mario Andretti drove in his final race, the Grand Prix of Monterey, at Laguna Seca Raceway, where he finished 19th. Indeed, though it had been over a year since Andretti had last won a race, the highlights of his illustrious career were fixed firmly in the memories of the fans at Laguna Seca who cheered him during a parade lap in his

honor. In his 31-year career Andretti won 52 Indy Car races (including 29 from 1966 through '69). In 1967 he also won both the Daytona 500 and the 12 Hours of Sebring. He won the World Championship in 1978, in just his second season of F/1 racing.

BASEBALL

No doubt it's small recompense for the frustration of never learning how they might have fared in postseason play, but the Los Angeles Dodgers—who were leading the National League West by 3½ games when the strike ended the 1994 season—won their third straight Rookie of the Year Award. Raul Mondesi, the Dodgers' rightfielder, follows Mike Piazza (1993) and Eric Karros ('92) as winners of the award. Mondesi hit .306 with 16 homers and 56 RBIs in the strike-shortened season. More importantly, the 23-year-old Dominican led the major leagues with 16 putouts.

In the American League, Bob Hamelin of the Kansas City Royals became the first DH to win Rookie of the Year honors. Hamelin, who hit 24 home runs, drove in 65 runs and batted .282, garnered 25 of 28 first-place votes to outpoint Cleveland Indian outfielder Manny Ramirez.

Manager of the Year honors went to Felipe Alou of the Montreal Expos in the National League and to the New York Yankees' Buck Showalter in the American League. Under the 59-year-old Alou, the Expos improved their record from 94–68 in 1993 (.580) to 74–40 (.649), best in the majors. Showalter, the youngest manager in the majors at 38 and the first Yankee manager to win the award since its inception in 1983, led the Yankees to a 70–43 record, best in the American League.

In the National League the winners of the Cy Young and the MVP awards were both chosen unanimously. Houston Astro

Mondesi batted .306 to become the third straight Dodger to win Rookie of the Year honors.

JOHN BIEVER

first baseman Jeff Bagwell, who hit .368 with 39 homers and a major league-leading 116 RBIs, won the MVP award. Greg Maddux of the Atlanta Braves made history by claiming a third straight Cy Young Award. Maddux was clearly the best pitcher in the majors. His major league-leading ERA of 1.56 was 1.09 lower than that of runner-up Steve Ontiveros of Oakland, and his 16–6 record included 10 complete games and three shutouts.

A Cy Young Award winner by a much narrower margin was Kansas City Royal David Cone, who edged Jimmy Key of the New York Yankees, 108 points to 96. Cone had a 2.94 ERA and a record of 16–6, while Key went 17–4 with an ERA of 3.27.

Frank Thomas became the sixth American League player to win back-to-back MVP awards. The 26-year-old Chicago White Sox first baseman batted .353 with 38 home runs and 101 RBIs.

Elsewhere on the planet—in Japan to be precise—a Fall Classic was played. In the 45th edition of the Japan Series, the Yomiuri Giants, the New York Yankees of Japanese baseball, beat the crosstown rival Seibu Lions.

PRO BASKETBALL

No doubt about it: Glenn Robinson had every right to expect substantial compensation for his services to the Milwaukee Bucks in this, his rookie season. After all, the 21-year-old former Purdue forward was the top pick in last summer's NBA draft, having led the NCAA in scoring last season with 30.3 points per game. In the wake of the huge multi-year contracts signed by Derrick Coleman and Larry Johnson, to name just two, what might a potential franchise player like Robinson be worth to a struggling franchise like Milwaukee?

The answer, according to Buck general manager Mike Dunleavy: not as much as Robinson thinks. On Oct. 18 Dunleavy took the unusual step of making public the figures that were being bandied about in the club's negotiations with Robinson. The 6' 7", 240-pound rookie, it seems, was turning his nose

MARY ANN CARTER

The bucks Robinson had in mind were not the ones who picked him first in the NBA draft.

up at the Bucks' offer of a guaranteed $60 million for nine years and asking a whopping $100 for 13 years. So Dunleavy called a press conference, hoping to set the record straight for fans. "I hope at some point sanity will come into play," he said.

The NBA season was guaranteed a timely start—with or without Robinson—when NBA commissioner David Stern and players union leader Charles Grantham agreed on Oct. 27 to a no-strike, no-lockout agreement. Said Grantham, "The integrity of the game is the victor here."

BOXING

WBC welterweight champion Pernell Whitaker laid impressive claim to the title of world's best fighter, pound-for-pound, when he laid out Buddy McGirt on Oct. 1 at the Scope in Norfolk, Va. Whitaker has always resented what he saw as the excuses made by and for McGirt after their bout at Madison Square Garden in March of 1993. Whitaker had won, but he was miffed by speculation that McGirt's injured left shoulder had cost him the match.

AL TIELEMANS

Carter was averaging a healthy 7.7 yards per carry for the undefeated Nittany Lions.

In Norfolk, Whitaker danced and pranced and mugged. "We've got to put our tap shoes on," he said afterwards. "I'm an entertainer." At one point he maneuvered McGirt into a corner simply in order to wink at the row of McGirt supporters seated nearby. Throughout, he made the process of demolishing McGirt look easy.

Whatever one's opinion of Whitaker's antics, it is hard to deny that he is providing much needed thrills, especially considering the sorry state of the heavyweight ranks. That was underscored at Wembley Arena in London, on Sept. 23, when WBC heavyweight champion Lennox Lewis lost to Oliver McCall, a 5–1 underdog whose main claim to fame was having served as Mike Tyson's sparring partner. McCall, a 29-year-old from Chicago who came into the fight with a 24–5 record, knocked Lewis onto his back in the second round.

COLLEGE FOOTBALL

College football made the most of the major league baseball strike, offering fans one of the most exciting, wide-open seasons in years. Entering the final month of the regular season, a pair of teams were still in contention for the national title—with a number of others waiting in the wings in the event those two slipped up—and a plethora of exciting players was still vying for the Heisman Trophy.

On Oct. 29 Nebraska (9–0) and Penn State (7–0) each made strong claims for the top spot in the college football rankings. Nebraska, ranked No. 2, demolished No. 3-ranked Colorado 24–7, while top-ranked Penn State humiliated Ohio State, 63–14. The following Monday, the polls split on which was the better team. The Associated Press poll ranked Nebraska No. 1, with the Huskers getting 33 first-place votes to the Nittany Lions' 28. The *USA Today*/CNN poll reversed that order, with top-ranked Penn State garnering 32 first-place votes to Nebraska's 30. The two teams will not meet this year, so it's quite possible that once again the national title will be split.

The mighty fell early and often. On Oct. 15, at the Orange Bowl, the Washington Huskies overcame a 14–3 deficit to upset the Miami Hurricanes 38–20, snapping their 58-game home win streak. The following week Auburn, seething with indignation that NCAA sanctions had muted and mooted their 17-game win streak, took its frustration out on No. 1 ranked Florida, beating the Gators 36–33 in Gainesville.

Still, one moment stood out above all others. On Sept. 24, with six seconds to play and his team trailing Michigan 26–21, Colorado quarterback Kordell Stewart threw a tight spiral high above Michigan Stadium. The ball traveled 73 yards in the air, all the way to the Michigan end zone where six Michigan defenders were waiting to knock it down. It was tipped by Blake Anderson into the waiting hands of Bison wide receiver Michael Westbrook. Colorado won 27–26.

One wondered whether this miracle would do for Stewart what a similar Hail Mary had done for Doug Flutie 10 years earlier—win him the Heisman. It was the kind of memorable moment Stewart needed to distinguish himself in an exceptionally crowded race. Among the contenders:

• Stewart's own teammate, tailback Rashaan Salaam, who went into the Nebraska game leading the nation in rushing (179.4 yards per game). And on an otherwise disappointing day for Colorado, he rushed for 134 yards and his team's one TD against Nebraska.

• Penn State's talented pair, quarterback Kerry Collins and running back Ki-Jana Carter. The only teammates ever to go 1–2 in the Heisman voting were Army's Doc Blanchard and Glenn Davis in 1945, but Collins and Carter have a shot at duplicating their feat. Apart from the advantage of playing for a team that was undefeated and ranked No. 1, each has played well in games both big and small. Carter carried the ball 26 times for 165 yards against Michigan and rushed for 137 yards and four touchdowns two weeks later against Ohio State. Most impressive of all is the fact that he was averaging 7.7 yards per carry.

Against Ohio State, Collins completed 19 of 23 passes for 265 yards and two TDs; against Michigan he was 20 for 32 for 231 yards. The 6' 5", 235-pound senior also had a completion percentage of .690 and a touchdown to interception ratio of 16 to 3. Through seven games, Collins's passing efficiency rating stood at 194.75, far superior to Jim McMahon's NCAA record of 176.9.

• Finally, there's Steve McNair, who would be a shoo-in for the award if all that mattered was statistics. Unfortunately—his detractors would say fortunately—McNair plays for Alcorn State, in Division I-AA, and no player from that division has ever won the Heisman. Certainly making history would be nothing new to McNair, who posted staggering numbers week after week. On Oct. 22 McNair passed for 587 yards and four TDs and rushed for the winning touchdown in the Braves' 41–37 win over Southern. The next week he passed for 563 yards and four touchdowns and ran for two more while rallying the Braves from a 42–13 second-half deficit to a 45–45 tie. He finished the day with 13,487 career yards, breaking the I-AA record set by Neil Lomax from 1977–80. Those numbers are awesome, but will they be enough to overcome the voters' doubts about McNair's Division I-AA schedule?

PRO FOOTBALL

To everyone's surprise but their own, the team that kept its perfect record longest this year was San Diego. Coach Bobby Ross's Chargers finally lost to Denver in their seventh game. Quarterback Stan Humphries was *SI's* pick for midseason MVP, for having completing 61% of his passes, thrown only two interceptions and inspired a team that had 10 new starters. Natrone Means, frequently the Chargers' workhorse, rushed for a career high 125 yards on 19 carries against Kansas City. On Oct. 30 San Diego lost Humphries— though probably only for one game—when he dislocated his left elbow against Seattle, but the Chargers still managed to beat the Seahawks easily, 35–15, to improve their record to 7–1.

The only other team with just one loss at

With Means leading the way, San Diego charged to a 6–0 start, best in the NFL.

midseason was Dallas, which narrowly avoided losing to winless Cincinnati, edging the Bengals 23–20 on Oct. 30. If the Cowboys looked shaky it may have been because they were worried about all-pro right tackle Erik Williams, who suffered cuts, a broken rib and torn ligaments in his thumb and legs when his car crashed into a guardrail in the early morning hours of Oct. 24. It seemed possible he would miss the remainder of the season.

Humphries' main rival for midseason MVP honors was the Detroit Lions' shifty running back Barry Sanders, who had rushed for 1,039 yards in eight games, while topping 100 yards in six of them. He and Eric Dickerson are the only players ever to top 1,000 yards in their first six seasons.

Jerry Rice also reached a significant milestone on Sept. 5, when he scored three touchdowns in the 49ers' 44–14 dismantling of the L.A. Raiders. The last of those scores broke Jim Brown's record for career TDs. Rice's record 127th TD came on a 38-yard catch over cornerback Albert Lewis late in the fourth quarter.

GOLF

In recent years team events like the Ryder Cup have been generating almost as much excitement as the majors. The best of several thrilling team events this fall was the Solheim Cup, which in even years pits a team of U.S. women against a team from Europe. This year, at White Sulphur Springs, W. Va., the U.S., led by new redhead Dottie Mochrie, regained the cup with a 13–7 victory.

Mochrie, apparently unhappy with her own "dishwater blonde" hair, decided a few weeks ago to play as a redhead, and the change seems to have done wonders for her. In three matches she destroyed Sweden's Catrin Nilsmark 6 and 5, going seven-under-par through 13 holes; teamed with Brandie Burton to win a foursome match 3 and 2 against super Swedes Liselotte Neumann and Helen Alfredsson; and teamed with Burton again to beat England's Laura Davies and Alison Nicholas in better ball two and one. Though Burton also won her third match by beating Davies 2-up, it was Mochrie whose intensity seemed to propel her teammates. "This is as good as I can play," said Mochrie. It was hard to argue with her.

The surprise winner of this year's Dunhill Cup, which pitted three-man teams from countries around the world, was Canada, which beat the U.S. 2–1 in the final played on Oct. 9 at St. Andrews. The Canadiens were helped by late-match blunders by Tom Kite, who double-bogeyed the 17th in his one-stroke loss to Dave Barr, and by Fred Couples, who missed a three-foot putt on 16 in his one-stroke loss to Ray Stewart.

On that same weekend, across the English Channel in La Boulie, France,

JACQUELINE DUVOISIN

Mochrie looked a little, well ... dotty, when the U.S. women reclaimed the Solheim Cup.

Goodenow (right) has been a fierce fighter for the players throughout the negotiations.

Tiger Woods—TIGER LE TERREUR to *L'Equipe*, the French sports daily—helped the U.S. win the World Amateur Team Championship by 11 strokes over a combined team of Great Britain & Ireland. Individually, Woods finished sixth with a score of 284, leaving it to 46-year-old Allen Doyle, whose 277 won individual honors, to lead the way. In the final round Doyle proved his toughness by atoning for a bogey, triple bogey start with a six-under run over the final seven holes.

The following weekend, at the Wentworth Club in Virginia Water, England, Ernie Els beat Colin Montgomerie four and two to win the World Match Play title. That capped an astonishing week of golf by Els, whose match against a rejuvenated Seve Ballesteros must be considered one of the great matches of all time. In 35 holes, Els made two eagles and 10 birdies to beat Ballesteros, who had seven 2s and 14 birdies. "This Els is impressive," said Ballesteros, about whom the same could obviously be said.

The 1994 PGA tour could hardly have concluded on a more dramatic note. Mark McCumber won the TOUR Championship at the Olympic Club in San Francisco, by sinking a birdie putt of 40-some feet to beat Fuzzy Zoeller on the first hole of a sudden death playoff. It was McCumber's third win

of the season and was worth $540,000. Zoeller had to content himself with the knowledge that he earned $1,016,804 on the tour this year, more than anyone else has ever won without a victory.

ICE HOCKEY

Hockey fans looked on with a sense of disbelief as the season approached and labor negotiations between the NHL and its players' association yielded nothing. "It's very clear we have a wide difference of opinion," said Bob Goodenow, executive director of the NHL Players Association, on Sept. 26.

Just how far apart the two sides were became clear later that week. On Sept. 30, the day before the NHL season was scheduled to begin, league commissioner Gary Bettman announced that its start would be posponed until at least Oct. 15. And there was more bad news to come. On Oct. 24 the NHL announced that it was canceling the first four games of the season. The league indicated that some of those games might still be replayed, but this season seems truly to be on ice.

MARATHON

Defending champion Luis dos Santos of Brazil won the the Chicago Marathon on Oct. 30, in 2:11:16. Twenty-nine-year-old Kristy Johnson won the women's race in 2:31:34. Joan Benoit Samuelson, 37 and running her first marathon in 18 months, achieved her goal of meeting the 2:42

Martina Hingis was just four days past her 14th birthday when she beat Patty Fendick in Zurich.

qualifying time for the 1996 Olympic Trials, clocking 2:37:09 in sixth.

In the Beijing Marathon, also on Oct. 30, Wang Junxia led a 1-2-3 finish by Chinese women. But Wang's time of 2:31:11 was nowhere near as eye-catching as some of those she achieved last year. Qu Yunxia, the world record holder at 1500, finished third in 2:32:01.

TENNIS

Apparently undeterred by the trail of small, broken bodies lining the road to women's tennis stardom, a trio of girls joined the pro ranks this fall. First to do so was Martina Hingis of the Czech Republic, who made her debut on Oct. 4 by beating 45th-ranked Patty Fendick 6–4, 6–3 at the European Indoors championships in Zurich. "We've worked 10 years for this," said her mother, Melanie Hingis. "It's a natural development."

Following closely in Hingis's small footsteps came two American players, Venus Williams, 14, and Meilin Tu, the 16-year-old U.S. junior women's champ, who were expected to make their debuts at the Bank of the West Classic in Oakland on Nov. 1. "I'm completely against it," said Richard Williams, Venus's father, who seemed to have forgotten that while children do have rights, one of them is to be protected from their own mistakes. "I think it's insane."

Looking on with considerable dismay was the woman who is Hingis's hero and inspiration, Martina Navratilova. "I don't [approve]," she said. "But who am I?" On Nov. 15, when she is honored for her long, great career during the Virginia Slims tournament at Madison Square Garden, that question will have its resounding answer.

TRIATHLON

With five-time defending champion Mark Allen choosing not to enter the race this year, Greg Welch of Australia won the Ironman Triathlon in Kailua-Kona, Hawaii, finishing the 140.6-mile swim-bike-run in 8 hours, 20 minutes, and 27 seconds. But the best story of the long day finished right behind him in second place. Six-time Ironman champion Dave Scott, who last competed in the race five years ago, finished in 8:24:32, a faster time than any of his six wins—not bad for a 40-year-old who actually had to go out and buy his own running shoes 18 months ago when he decided to make a comeback.

Paula Newby-Fraser won her seventh women's title, finishing in 9:20:13.

Year in Sport

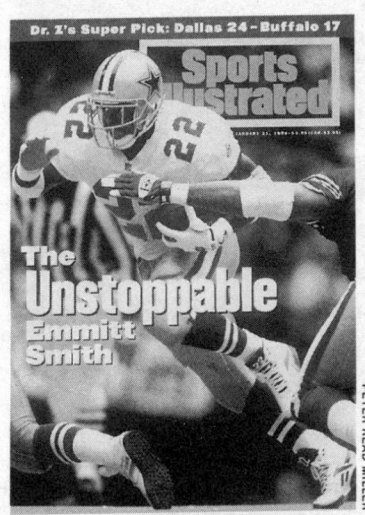

Dr. Z's Super Pick: Dallas 24 – Buffalo 17

Sports Illustrated

The Unstoppable **Emmitt Smith**

PETER READ MILLER

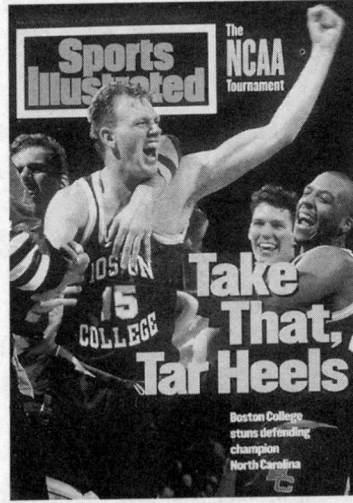

Sports Illustrated

The NCAA Tournament

Take That, Tar Heels

Boston College stuns defending champion North Carolina

MANNY MILLAN

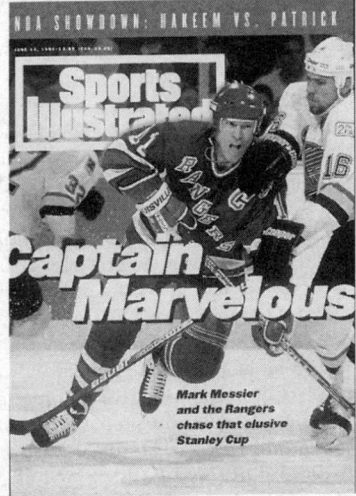

NBA SHOWDOWN: HAKEEM VS. PATRICK

Sports Illustrated

Captain Marvelous

Mark Messier and the Rangers chase that elusive Stanley Cup

DAVID E. KLUTHO

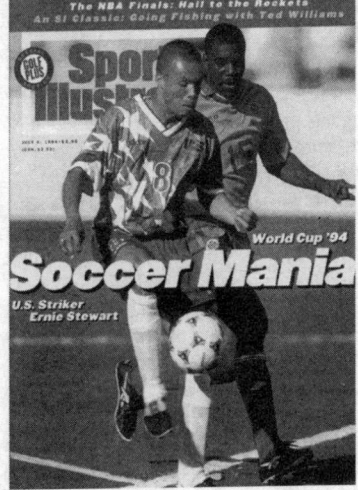

The NBA Finals: Hail to the Rockets
An SI Classic: Going Fishing with Ted Williams

Sports Illustrated

World Cup '94

Soccer Mania

U.S. Striker Ernie Stewart

CHRIS COVATTA

9

Ringing Out the Old Year

Ring the bell, wring your hands—however you ring it up, 1994 was a season to remember | by STEVE RUSHIN

YOU CAN TELL MUCH ABOUT 1994 by counting its rings. Oh, the year had the usual sporting assortment of championship rings and boxing rings and athletes in earrings, but 1994 also had Olympic rings and Simpson hearings and Capriati nose rings. Nineteen ninety-four was often a 12-ring media circus, like the 12 rings in the word *Goooooooooooooaaalll*! Which, come to think of it, looks a lot like the word *Gillooly*.

And so, we ring out the year 1994. But where to begin? With the baseball strike that canceled the World Series for the first time in 90 years? Naaahh: When the players walked out for good on Aug. 12, "I don't care if they never come back" was the knee-jerk reaction of most fans and club owners.

Speaking of knees and jerks and club owners, figure skater Nancy Kerrigan was clubbed on the right knee by a jerk named Shane Stant at the U.S. Figure Skating Championships in Detroit on Jan. 6. Stant and his bloated abettor, Shawn Eckardt, were acting in cahoots with ringleader Jeff Gillooly, and you can't spell *his* surname without the letters *o-i-l-y*. Gillooly is the ex-husband of Kerrigan's chief skating rival, Tonya Harding, who was also implicated in the botched kneecapping plot, which caused pundits worldwide to reexamine the question, "What price, glory?"

Sadly, the year taught us the dear price of *in*glory. A 27-year-old Colombian defender inadvertently scored into his own goal in a stunning 2–1 World Cup loss to the U.S. at the Rose Bowl in June. Ten days later, his team bounced from the tournament, Andres Escobar was cut down by six bullets as he left a bar at 3:30 a.m. outside his native Medellín. Escobar's alleged assassins: three men and a woman who had placed large World Cup bets in the capital of the Colombian drug trade. *Drug ring … crime ring … shots rang out.* The past year left some terrible stains, like the ring around a drained bathtub. What price, glory, indeed.

Ah, but what glory, Price. In golf, the

The peerless Price won both the British Open and the PGA.

JACQUELINE DUVOISIN

omnitalented Nick Price of Zimbabwe won the British Open and the PGA back-to-back. "It just *seems* like he wins everything he enters," said Phil Mickelson. "In reality, he onlys wins half." To be sure, the other two majors were Priceless, if not exactly priceless: 24-year-old Ernie Els of South Africa won the U.S. Open, and Spain's José Maria Olazábal was green-jacketed at Augusta.

American golfers, meanwhile, continued to emit a noxious odor on the course, with a pair of happy exceptions. Paul Azinger returned to the Tour after a successful eight-month treatment for cancer, and Tiger Woods, whose very name sounds like a golf course—or a line of oversized graphite drivers—won the U.S. Amateur at the improbable age of 18, younger even than Jack Nicklaus was when he first won the event.

Eighteen was very much the age of majority in 1994. Eighteen-year-old tennis star Jennifer Capriati was arrested on a misdemeanor charge of marijuana possession in Coral Gables, Fla., and the erstwhile prodigy appeared nose-pierced in the year's second-most jarring police mugshot. She then entered a drug and alcohol rehabilitation clinic for the second time in 12 months. Meanwhile, 18-year-old Alex Rodriguez made his major league debut at shortstop for the Seattle Mariners, the youngest kid in the bigs since 1984.

But even with a near minor in the majors, baseball's first major story was in the minors, where Michael Jordan made his professional baseball debut with the Birmingham Barons of Double A. *What's My Line?* If I'm Jordan, it's the Mendoza Line, which the ex-Bull straddled all season. Herr Air swung at more air than most shadowboxers, striking out in more than one quarter of his at bats, umpires ringing him up an astounding 114 times. But given that he hadn't played baseball since high school, his

BILL SMITH

majestic Tiger Woods, perhaps?)

The hapless Cleveland Indians also got a new park, and even some "hap," flirting with first place all summer in the inaugural season of the American League Central. Of course, second place might have sufficed for the Tribe, as two wild card teams would join the six division winners in the new '94 playoff system. But just when it was looking like autumn might be warmed by a week or two of Indian summer, the players and owners pulled the plug, leaving a ring around baseball's bathtub that may never be scoured free.

On Sept. 14, acting commissioner Bud Selig expressed his deep regret at having to cancel the remainder of the regular season, the playoffs and the World Series. But in our year of rings, the professed sorrow of the owners did not ring true. Which is to say that Selig really *was* an "acting" commissioner. Throughout the strike, owners were insisting on a salary cap, which they knew the players would never accept. As for the striking players, whose average salary was $1.2 million in 1994, they assumed that the owners would cave in during negotiations, as they had seven previous times. But the players badly miscalculated: As the other Kenny Rogers will tell you, "You never count your money while you're sittin' at the table."

Just ask members of the Louisiana Tech women's basketball team. The Lady Techsters had a two-point lead in their NCAA championship game against North Carolina, and only seven-*tenths* of a second remained on the clock. But Charlotte Smith of the Tar Heels drained a trey at the horn, giving her

final numbers were not entirely atrocious: Jordan hit .202, with three home runs, 51 RBIs and 30 stolen bases for the Chicago White Sox affiliate.

Two rungs up the ladder was the year's second-most-famous Juice, the Juiced Baseball. But even *that* could not entirely explain a major league season that was offensive in so many ways. For starters, there were *four* men threatening to make hash of Roger Maris's 33-year-old record of 61 home runs in a single season. Ken Griffey Jr. of Seattle, Frank Thomas of the White Sox, Matt Williams of San Francisco and Jeff Bagwell of Houston each had 38 or more dingers by mid-August. San Diego rightfielder Tony Gwynn, meanwhile, was hitting .394 five months into the season, a dead ringer for Ted Williams. And yet somehow, in all of this baseball-sized hail, Kenny Rogers of the Texas Rangers threw a perfect game, the line-score for the California Angels just a string of rings across the scoreboard at The Ballpark in Arlington, the new stadium that sounds more like a condominium complex. (Overlooking

team a 60–59 win and making the name Charlotte forever synonymous with North Carolina.

Indeed, while Charlotte was winning in Richmond, Arkansas was winning in Charlotte. Razorback sophomore Scotty Thurman hit his own three as the shot clock evaporated with 52 seconds remaining in the men's final, breaking a 70–70 tie with Duke and expediting a 76–72 victory. The 'Backs were backed all season by President Bill Clinton, who appeared on a March cover of *Sports Illustrated* in full Hogwear and rooted openly in the stands at the Charlotte Coliseum. In his unabashed partisanship, Clinton proved himself unique among American presidents: *Sooey generis*, you might say.

In the NBA, the Ring Trilogy ended for the Chicago Bulls, and a new league cham-

Houston's magnificent mononym led the Rockets to the NBA championship.

pion was determined in a final series that was often as painful to watch as a Wagnerian opera. The Houston Rockets beat the New York Knicks in seven unsightly games, behind their magnificent mononym at center: Hakeem. Hakeem Olajuwon was dominant as the regular-season MVP, but the NBA playoffs were so soporifically low-scoring that the league resolved to move in the three-point line and to penalize handchecks during the '94–95 season. To be sure, there were other problems: Magic Johnson coached the Lakers for 16 games but quit in disgust at the kind of athletes he found in 1994, their pagers beeping and cellular phones ringing throughout practice.

The ringers of Dream Team II won basketball's *true* world championship in Toronto in August, but if the event fails to ring a bell, fear not. Few fans noticed, perhaps because the world championship of the world's favorite sport had played out only one month earlier in North America.

Nineteen ninety-four teemed with couples we knew by first-name—Burt and Loni, Tom and Roseanne, Lisa Marie and Michael—and sports were no exception. Tonya and Nancy, O.J. and Nicole ... *Romario* and *Bebeto*? Throughout the monthlong Mardi Gras of soccer's World Cup, there was no escaping these brilliant Brazilians, these mononyms in stereo.

The XV World Cup opened in Chicago on the Friday afternoon of June 17. No sooner had the world witnessed Germany defeat Bolivia 1–0 that afternoon when its attention turned forcibly, through the Cyclops eye of television, to the surreal scenery of Los Angeles. O.J. Simpson—wanted in the murders of his ex-wife Nicole and a young man named Ron Goldman—was sitting in the back of a white Ford Bronco, pointing a gun at his own head, while being trailed slowly up the San Diego Freeway by a dozen wailing police cars, the sky at dusk chattering with helicopters, the median strips filled with cheering spectators. Simpson was charged with two counts of murder. The rest of the drama would unfold in an often ridiculous Los Angeles courtroom, one that required not so much a judge to preside but a ringmaster. TURN THE JUICE LOOSE, demanded T-shirts on sale outside the courthouse, while inside, witnesses confessed that they had already sold their stories to *The National Enquirer*.

Like many of the Simpson witnesses, the World Cup was also a sellout, but in the happier sense of that word. 3.6 million ticket holders watched players from 24 nations score spectacular goals, sport ridiculous haircuts and feign dramatic deaths in the penalty area. If Americans didn't exactly

embrace soccer, they certainly shook its unused hands, an introduction brokered by the U.S. team, which advanced to the round of 16 for the first time before succumbing to Brazil on the Fourth of July. Let freedom … ring.

Pity, though, that after a scoreless final, the world championship of "the beautiful game" (Pele's words) should be decided on penalty kicks—"a cowardly way to score" (Pele again). Justly, Pele's countrymen prevailed over Italy in the Rose Bowl shootout. The superior Brazilian side could not celebrate, however, until the last penalty kick was taken by Italy's Roberto Baggio, the world's finest player, whose shot slashed harmlessly over a wide open Brazilian goalmouth. Which was only appropriate, for Brazilian mouths were wide-open with impunity throughout the competition. Romario, the monumentally vain Brazilian forward, announced in the opening round of the World Cup, "This will be Romario's tournament." In the end, it *was*. As the musical group XTC once put it: "And all the world is football-shaped/ It's just for me to kick in space."

The victory was balm for sports fans in Brazil, who were still mourning the death of their Formula I superstar, Ayrton Senna, killed in a crash in May. So stirring was Brazilian *futbol*, in fact, that the American version of football was bound to look ersatz by comparison. Which may explain why Jimmy Johnson won a second consecutive Super Bowl ring— making good on a Romario-like guarantee—

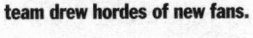
Cobi Jones (right) and the U.S. team drew hordes of new fans.

but will not be entering the Ring of Honor at Cowboy Stadium anytime soon.

The reaction to his repeat in Big D? Big *Deal*. Or so thought Dallas Cowboy owner Jerry Jones. After sending the Buffalo Bills to their—what?—38th consecutive Super Bowl defeat, Cowboy running back Emmitt Smith said dynastically, "I want to leave footprints." Johnson, though, apparently left a kind of ring-around-the-collar. Jones increasingly disdained his onetime friend, and in March parted ways with the Kevlar-coiffed coach. Erstwhile Oklahoma outlaw Barry Switzer was named the new *capo di tutti* Cowpokes, attempting to fill very large shoes indeed.

There were plenty of large, expensive, brand-new shoes to fill at Florida State. The Seminoles had been named national champions after beating Nebraska 18–16 in the Orange Bowl. FSU quarterback Charlie Ward, the superhuman super human, won the Heisman Trophy. But some of his teammates were later discovered to have taken illegal payments from sea-slug agents. Various 'Noles, likewise, were afforded lavish 100% discounts at a local Foot Locker, obviating the need for cashiers to "ring it up," as it were.

Her biological alarm clock ringing loudly, 37-year-old Martina Navratilova pressed the snooze bar at Wimbledon, making it all the way to the women's final before losing to 22-year-old Conchita Martinez of Spain. Growing up in Monzon, Martinez had practiced against a wall she named for Martina. ("Wall-Mart," perhaps?) The real Navratilova then retired from regular competition. She saw the writing on the wall, and it was in Spanish. After all, two other Spaniards won the French Open: Sergi Bruguera and Arantxa Sanchez Vicario, the latter winning the U.S. Open as well. As ever, Miguel Indurain of Spain won the Tour de France, his fourth victory in cycling's most prestigious event. Throw in Olazabal's green jacket, and 1994 saw a reign of Spain that was mainly hard to explain. Much like Andre Agassi winning the men's draw at the U.S. Open, in spite of the fact that he was unseeded.

Messier was Moses for the Rangers, leading them to their first Stanley Cup in 54 years.

Unseeded, like the fallow field tilled by the New York Rangers lo these last 54 years. Sergei Federov of Detroit was the MVP of the NHL, making goalies eat hockey pucks like Ring-Dings. But it was the Rangers who ended an exhilarating Stanley Cup playoffs by beating the Vancouver Canucks in seven games. It was the *team's* first Cup since 1940, but captain Mark Messier's sixth in 15 years. And yet, what price, glory? Buoyed by victory, coach Mike Keenan bolted town, and Messier took the advice of his agent-father and held out for millions. *Hello, fadda....*

Hello, mudda: A 9–1 long shot named Go for Gin splashed to victory on a sloppy track at Churchill Downs, winning the Kentucky Derby for trainer Nick Zito, who then presumably went for gin, rather than the traditional mint julep, to toast his second Derby victory. Good thing Zito celebrated while he could, since the thoroughbred season

ended up belonging to another horse, Holy Bull, who won eight of ten starts in 1994 including a convincing win at the Travers Stakes over Tabasco Cat, the winner of both the Preakness and Belmont.

Among fast *people*, however, American sprinter Leroy Burrell distinguished himself. The new fastest man in the world set a planetary record of 9.85 seconds in a 100-meter race in Lausanne, Switzerland. In longer distances, Noureddine Morceli of Algeria continued to run rings around the competition. And in even longer distances still, Al Unser Jr. was supreme, winning for the second time in Indianapolis, on that vaunted oval ring that evokes those oval rings in the number 500.

Which brings us, penultimately, to the ring itself. In boxing, ring star Evander Holyfield in April looked more like Ringo Starr. Or perhaps it was his opponent, a lefty named Michael Moorer, who more closely resembled Ringo. After all, it was Moorer who did the drumming, winning a 12-round decision over Holyfield for the heavyweight championship in Las Vegas. The fight affirmed both Moorer's nickname (Nasty) and the slogan on his T-shirt (U HAVE THE RIGHT 2 REMAIN VIOLENT). There was, also, this regrettable fact: that the Detroit native has a record for assault *outside* the ring, as well.

And if assault charges do not provide a natural segue into our final ringed spectacle, the 1994 Winter Olympics, what possibly could? By February, Kerrigan had recovered from the Lillehammering on her knee, and Harding had successfully litigated her way to the Games in Lillehammer, Norway, but their showdown (or throwdown) would have to wait until the end of the fortnight. One day after the opening ceremonies, a 23-year-old Alaskan skier named Tommy Moe won the men's downhill, stunning all who looked on, including His Royal Highness King Harald V of Norway, HRH Queen Sonja and HRH HRC, the American First Lady.

The first American lady ever to win five Olympic gold medals is speed skater Bonnie Blair, whose victories in the 500- and 1,000-meter events gave her one more gold than sprinter Evelyn Ashford, swimmer Janet Evans and diver Pat McCormick. But the most moving victory on the oval ring belonged to Dan Jansen. Competing in his fourth Olympics, Jansen slipped in the 500- meter race in Norway, giving him only one more chance to win a medal in memory of his sister Jane, who died of leukemia during the 1988 Games in Calgary. Naturally, Jansen not only won the 1,000 meters five days after his 500 disappointment, he set a world record. "This time," said Jansen's coach,

Jansen's redemption was the Olympics' most moving moment.

Peter Mueller, "the man upstairs took care of him."

Which left only the *Upstairs, Downstairs* melodrama of women's figure skating for God to sort out. Wearing more makeup than the collective members of Kiss ever did, Harding broke a lace, aborted her routine and skated again in the women's long program. But God and an international panel of judges had her eighth.

Kerrigan performed with near-flawless precision, but was fated to finish second— to a 16-year-old pixie named Oksana Baiul. Then Harding returned to the U.S., where she would be wooed by wrestling promoters and await the pay-per-view broadcast of her wedding-night escapades. Kerrigan went straight to Orlando and put the *dis* into Disney World, denouncing her parade there as "the most corniest thing I've ever done."

Little did we know that the rest of the year would be a Ringling Bros. circus, as well. And that long after it was over, 1994 would still be ringing in our ears.

The Year in Sport Calendar

compiled by John Bolster

Baseball

Nov 1, 1993—Cincinnati Reds owner Marge Schott returns to work after an eight month, league-imposed suspension for making racial slurs. The Reds had committed to hiring a human resources director in her absence but failed to do so, citing financial limitations.

Nov 2—Chicago White Sox righthander Jack McDowell, who won 22 games in 1993, wins the American League Cy Young Award.

Nov 3—Atlanta's Greg Maddux becomes the first pitcher since Sandy Koufax to win the National League Cy Young Award in consecutive years. He had 20 victories and a 2.36 ERA in 1993.

Nov 9—Barry Bonds wins the National League MVP award for the third time in four years. The San Francisco leftfielder, who joins a group of seven other three-time MVPs, batted .336 with 123 RBI and 46 home runs.

Nov 10—Chicago White Sox first baseman Frank Thomas, who batted .317 with 128 RBI and 41 home runs, is named the American League MVP. Other award winners include Mike Piazza of Los Angeles, NL Rookie of the Year, and Angel rightfielder Tim Salmon, AL Rookie of the Year.

Nov 16—Pittsburgh Pirate shortstop Jay Bell wins the National League Gold Glove award, supplanting Cardinal Ozzie Smith, who had won the award every year since 1979.

Nov 17—Terry Collins is named manager of the Houston Astros.

Nov 22—Free-agent first baseman Will Clark signs a five-year, $30 million contract with the Texas Rangers. The Baltimore Orioles sign free-agent lefthander Sid Fernandez to a three-year, $9 million deal.

Dec 2—The Philadelphia Phillies trade closer Mitch Williams, who failed in four of seven save opportunities in the 1993 postseason, to the Astros for reliever Doug Jones and righthander Jeff Juden. The Cleveland Indians join the free-agent spending spree, signing future Hall of Famer Eddie Murray and pitcher Dennis Martinez to one and two year deals, respectively.

MARTHA JANE STANTON

Dec 6—Citing a "financial crisis" caused by a 40% decline in television revenues, the Cincinnati Reds announce they cannot offer arbitration to veteran third baseman Chris Sabo. He later signs with Baltimore.

Dec 6—The Colorado Rockies retain first baseman Andres Galarraga, who hit .370 to win the National League batting title in 1993, for four years and $12 million plus incentives.

Dec 7—Otis Nixon signs a two-year, $7 million deal with the Boston Red Sox.

Dec 12—The Baltimore Orioles, who were in the running to sign free-agent first baseman Will Clark, reach a five-year, $30 million agreement with Rafael Palmeiro, the man Clark ousted when he signed with Texas on Nov 22.

Dec 15—Julio Franco, who won the American League batting title in 1991 while with Texas, signs a one-year, $1 million contract with the Chicago White Sox.

Dec 19—Rickey Henderson re-signs with the Oakland Athletics, who

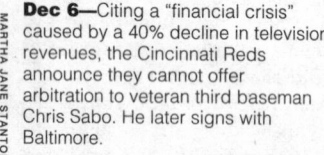

Williams made the Giants look prescient.

18   THE YEAR IN SPORT

WALTER IOOSS JR.

Jordan's switch to baseball was closely watched.

traded him to Toronto late last season, for two years and $8.6 million. The next day the New York Yankees, who had tried to sign Henderson, close a two-year deal worth $3 million with ex-Angel leadoff man Luis Polonia.

Dec 28—The San Francisco Giants sign All-Star slugger Matt Williams for five years and $30.75 million. The club now has nearly $75 million committed to Barry Bonds and Williams together.

Jan 5, 1994—The New York Mets trade Vince Coleman, who had a series of off-field problems as a Met, to the Kansas City Royals for leftfielder Kevin McReynolds.

Jan 8—Harvey Haddix, the Pittsburgh Pirate lefthander who pitched 12 perfect innings in 1959 against the Milwaukee Braves only to lose 1–0 in the 13th, dies of emphysema at the age of 68.

Jan 12—Former Philadelphia Phillie lefthander Steve Carlton is easily voted into baseball's Hall of Fame. Orlando Cepeda, former Giant and Cardinal first baseman, misses election by seven votes in his 15th and final try.

Jan 13—Retired NBA star Michael Jordan, who has been taking three hours of batting practice a day, tells the *Chicago Tribune* he wants to try to play major league baseball.

Jan 18—After a 12-hour meeting in Fort Lauderdale, Fla., owners unanimously approve a revenue-sharing plan that will enable small-market teams to remain financially competitive with large-market clubs. The agreement will not take effect unless the player's union agrees to a salary cap, a development not considered likely.

Jan 19—Club owners approve divisional realignment and an extra tier of playoffs. They fail to elect a commissioner to replace Fay Vincent, who was forced out by the owners on Sept. 7, 1992.

Jan 25—The Chicago White Sox announce they are inviting NBA legend Michael Jordan to their spring training camp in Sarasota, Fla.

Jan 30—Bo Jackson signs with the California Angels for one year and $1 million, plus incentives. Baseball's alltime save leader, Lee Smith, signs a one year, $1.5 million contract with the Baltimore Orioles.

Jan 30—Hall of Famer Mickey Mantle checks into the Betty Ford Center to receive treatment for alcoholism.

Jan 31—The Chicago White Sox now have $50 million committed to the corners of their infield as they sign third baseman Robin Ventura to a four-year, $20.6 million contract. First baseman Frank Thomas a four-year $29 million deal.

Feb 3—Ron Gant, rightfielder for the Atlanta Braves, breaks his right leg in a motorbike accident in the Atlanta suburbs.

Feb 7—The Chicago White Sox sign Michael Jordan to a minor league contract. He reports to spring training the following week.

Feb 9—Cal Ripken is honored as the shortstop with the most home runs in baseball history. He hit his 278th to top Ernie Banks last July 15 but because of a recordkeeping error which credited Banks with homers he hit as a first baseman, the milestone is not noticed until today.

Feb 10—Milwaukee Brewer Robin Yount, who has 3,142 career hits, announces his retirement.

Feb 11—From New York City, the owners release a deceptively titled missive headed "Restructuring Report Enhances Commissioner's Authority." The "restructured" powers bar the commissioner from acting unilaterally regarding business matters of the game, such as expansion, realignment and interleague play.

Feb 15—Arbitrator Thomas Roberts awards a total of $59.48 million to players as compensation for the owners' collusion against free agents. The decision covers lost salary and interest for the 1986–87 seasons and includes over $2 million for former slugger Jack Clark.

Feb 26—Former Yankee shortstop Phil Rizzuto and deceased ex-Cub manager Leo Durocher are elected to the Baseball Hall of Fame by the Veterans Committee.

Mar 1—Leonard Coleman succeeds Bill White as National League President.

Mar 17—The Atlanta Braves release outfielder Ron Gant, who broke his leg Feb. 3 in a motorbike accident, giving him $901,639.20 as 30 days' termination pay. Gant signs with Cincinnati on June 21 but sits out the season because of his injury.

Mar 31—Michael Jordan is assigned to the Class AA Birmingham Barons, the Chicago White Sox's Southern League affiliate.

Apr 3—Opening … Night! That's right, the St. Louis Cardinals defeat the Cincinnati Reds 6–4 in the first ever nighttime season opener. The season's first batter, St. Louis's Ray Lankford, hits a home run off the Reds' Jose Rijo. The next day the Cleveland Indians debut their new Jacobs Field and win an 11-inning, 4–3 thriller over Seattle. In the opener at Wrigley Field, Cub outfielder Tuffy Rhodes hits three home runs off the Mets' Dwight Gooden.

Apr 8—Atlanta's Kent Mercker pitches the first no-hitter of the year, blanking the Dodgers 6–0.

Apr 11—Philadelphia's John Kruk, who was diagnosed with testicular cancer in spring training, makes his return, going 3 for 5, with a double in his first at bat.

Apr 12—Scott Cooper of the Boston Red Sox becomes the first player since 1991 to hit for the

Rodriguez was just 18 when he joined Seattle.

CHUCK SOLOMON

cycle as the Sox outscore Kansas City 22–11.

Apr 20—Chicago's Tim Raines ties an American League record when he reaches base seven times without making an out in the White Sox's 8–6, 12-inning win over the Brewers.

April 28—Scott Erickson of the Minnesota Twins throws the second no-hitter of the season in a 6–0 victory over Milwaukee.

May 3—The Chicago Cubs lose their club-record 12th straight home game, 5–2 to the Cincinnati Reds. The following day they break the streak with a 5–2 win over the Reds.

May 13—Tim Salmon, the California rightfielder, hits two homers, two singles and a double against Seattle to give him 13 hits in his last three games, tying an American League record. The sizzling stretch raises his average from .272 to .336.

May 24—The Mariners' Ken Griffey Jr. hits his 21st home run of the year, breaking Mickey Mantle's record of 20 homers in the first two months of the season.

May 25—The Los Angeles Dodgers place Darryl Strawberry on waivers after he completes a four-week stay in a substance-abuse clinic.

May 29—The Atlanta Braves trade Deion Sanders to the Cincinnati Reds for Roberto Kelly.

May 31—The Houston Astros release Mitch Williams when he refuses to accept a new, non-closer role in the bullpen.

June 13—Chicago Cub second baseman Ryne Sandberg, who batted .289 with 245 HRs and 905 RBI in 13 years, announces his retirement.

June 14—The owners unveil their salary cap proposal, which they claim will restore economic order and competitive balance to the game. Among the elements are a 50-50 total revenue split between players and owners and the elimination of salary arbitration. Player reaction is unanimously negative; the strike threat increases.

June 28—New York Met pitcher Dwight Gooden is suspended without pay for 60 days for violating his drug aftercare program.

July 7—The San Francisco Giants activate Darryl Strawberry, who was released by the Dodgers in April after failing a drug test. They win their next nine games with Strawberry in the lineup.

July 8—Alex Rodriguez, the first pick in the 1993 amateur draft, debuts at shortstop with the Seattle Mariners. The 18-year-old is the youngest player to reach the majors since Jose Rijo joined the New York Yankees 37 days short of his 19th birthday in 1984.

July 12—At Pittsburgh's Three Rivers Stadium the National League All-Stars defeat the American

BEN VAN HOOK

Ravitch was management's tough negotiator.

League All-Stars for the first time since 1987, 8–7. Atlanta's Fred McGriff, whose ninth inning two-run homer sent the game to extra innnings, is named the MVP.

July 13—California coach Jimmie Reese, at 92 the last living roommate of Babe Ruth, dies in Santa Ana, Calif.

July 18—After a 4½-hour negotiating session in New York City, the players' union overwhelmingly rejects the owners' June 14 salary cap proposal. The players also propose a collective bargaining agreement.

July 18—Cleveland slugger Albert Belle is suspended for 10 days for using a corked bat.

July 19—Houston overcomes an 11–0 deficit to defeat St. Louis 15–12, tying the National League record for comebacks.

July 27—Richard Ravitch, chief negotiator for the owners, rejects the players' collective bargaining proposal.

July 28—The Players Association, led by Don Fehr, sets a strike deadline of Aug. 12.

July 29—In his 354th at bat for the Class AA Birmingham Barons, Michael Jordan hits his first home run.

Aug 4—Minnesota Twin first baseman Kent Hrbek retires.

Aug 9—The Cleveland Indians give five-time All-Star pitcher Jack Morris his unconditional release.

Aug 10—Jeff Bagwell is hit by a pitch and breaks his left wrist. He is batting .368 with 116 RBI at the time.

Aug 12—The players go on strike, halting what was arguably the most exciting season in 25 years, with five players on a pace to hit 50+ home runs, Tony Gwynn threatening to bat .400, Greg Maddux a sure bet to win an unprecedented third consecutive Cy Young Award and four tight pennant races.

Aug 24—Representatives for management and for the players meet in New York City. After more than eight hours of negotiations they emerge no closer to a settlement. They meet again the following day with similarly fruitless results and the strike reaches its 15th day.

Sep 2—Acting commissioner Bud Selig, also the owner of the Milwaukee Brewers, announces the season will be canceled if no settlement is reached by Sep. 9.

Sep 8—The players' union makes a last-ditch revenue-sharing proposal which the owners consider then reject. The deadline for canceling the season passes the following day without an announcement.

Sep 14—At 2:18 p.m. in New York acting commissioner Bud Selig announces the season has been canceled. For the first time since 1904, there will be no World Series.

Sep 15—The Kansas City Royals dismiss manager Hal McRae. Six days later the Red Sox fire skipper Butch Hobson.

Sep 26—The Baltimore Orioles dismiss manager Johnny Oates. Oates, 48, is not long unemployed, as the Texas Rangers hire him on Oct. 19.

Oct 17—Montreal manager Felipe Alou, whose club had the best record in baseball when the strike hit, is named National League Manager of Year. Tom Trebelhorn is dismissed after one strike-shortened season as manager of the Cubs.

Oct 18—The Yankees' Buck Showalter, at 38 the youngest manager in the majors, is named American League Manager of the Year. Showalter managed New York to a 70–43 record and first place in the AL East.

Oct 19—In Washington, D.C., players and owners meet for the first time since Sep. 9. They convene with mediator Bill Usery for 90 minutes to set ground rules for future negotiations.

Oct 19—Bob Hamelin of the Kansas City Royals becomes the first DH to win the American League Rookie of the Year Award. Hamelin, who also played 24 games at first base, batted .282 with 24 home runs and 65 RBI.

Oct 20—For the third year in a row, a Los Angeles Dodger wins the National League Rookie of the Year as rightfielder Raul Mondesi is honored. Mondesi, who batted .306 with 56 RBI

Baseball (Cont.)

and a .516 slugging average, is a unanimous selection.

Oct 24—Greg Maddux of the Atlanta Braves wins an unprecedented third consecutive National League Cy Young Award for a season in which he won 16 games with a 1.56 ERA.

Oct 25—Kansas City's David Cone wins the American League Cy Young Award, edging out New York Yankee Jimmy Key. Cone was 16–4 with an earned-run average of 2.94

Oct 26—Chicago White Sox first baseman Frank Thomas wins his second consecutive American League MVP Award. Thomas hit .353 with 38 homers and 101 RBI.

Oct 27—Jeff Bagwell of the Houston Astros wins the National League MVP Award. Bagwell, a 26-year-old first baseman, hit .368 with 39 home runs and 116 RBI in just 110 games.

Boxing

Oct 29, 1993—In Tulsa, Okla., heavyweight Tommy Morrison loses his WBO crown and a chance at the WBA/IBF titles when he is knocked out at 1:33 of the first round by unknown New Yorker Michael Bentt.

Nov 6—Evander Holyfield regains his WBA/IBF heavyweight title with a 12-round majority decision over Riddick Bowe in Las Vegas. The fight is delayed for 21 minutes in the seventh round after a parachutist lands in the ropes near Bowe's corner.

Dec 6—Oscar De La Hoya, who won the lightweight gold medal at the 1992 Olympics,

cancels his Dec. 9 Madison Square Garden bout with Jesus Vidal Concepcion amidst family squabbles and pending lawsuits between his co-managers.

Dec 18—Former IBF and WBC welterweight champion Simon Brown knocks out Terry Norris in the fourth round in Puebla, Mexico, to win the WBC super welterweight belt.

Dec 22—The IBF announces it will not sanction a proposed heavyweight title unification match between Evander Holyfield and Lennox Lewis, claiming that Holyfield is obligated to fight Michael Moorer next.

Jan 13, 1994—Michael Spinks tops a list of 14 elected to the International Boxing Hall of Fame in Canastota, N.Y. Also on the list are Jack Sharkey, 91, the oldest living heavyweight champion, and trainer Eddie Futch.

Jan 29—Frankie Randall becomes the first man ever to defeat Julio César Chávez (89-0-1) when he wins a split decision in Las Vegas to claim the WBC super lightweight title.

Feb 19—Humberto Gonzalez reclaims the WBC and IBF light flyweight titles from Michael Carbajal in a hard-fought split decision victory at the Great Western Forum in Inglewood, Calif.

Feb 26—Little known Steve Little (21-13-2) upsets Michael Nunn by split decision in London to win the WBA super middleweight title. The stunner ends plans to unify the division with a matchup between Nunn and WBC titleholder Nigel Benn.

Mar 5—The squabbling in his camp mostly behind him, Oscar De La Hoya stops Jimmi Bredahl of Denmark after the tenth round of their WBO junior lightweight title fight.

Mar 7—The Supreme Court refuses to overturn Mike Tyson's 1992 rape conviction, rejecting arguments that the former heavyweight champ was denied a fair trial.

Apr 22—The heavyweight division gets its fifth champion since 1990 when Detroit's Michael Moorer outpoints Evander Holyfield in Las Vegas.

JOHN IACONO

Whitaker: pound for pound the best in the world.

Apr 26—Evander Holyfield announces his retirement after learning he has a heart condition which prevents his left venticle from expanding properly. He later changes his mind about retiring.

May 6—Lennox Lewis defeats Phil Jackson by technical knockout in the eighth round to retain his WBC heavyweight title in Atlantic City.

May 7—Julio César Chávez wins a controversial decision in his rematch with Frankie Randall in Las Vegas. When the two fighters clash heads in the eighth round, Chávez is cut and refuses to continue. The decision goes to the scorecards where Randall has a WBC-mandated point deducted for the accidental head butt and Chavez wins a split decision.

Sep 17—Without any controversy but plenty of left hooks and overhand rights, Julio César Chávez redeems himself convincingly by stopping challenger Meldrick Taylor in the eighth round of their WBC super lightweight title fight in Las Vegas.

Sep 24—Challenger Oliver McCall, a former sparring partner for Mike Tyson, knocks out Lennox Lewis 31 seconds into the second round of their WBC heavyweight title bout.

Oct 1—Pernell (Sweet Pea) Whitaker defeats James (Buddy) McGirt in a unanimous decision in Norfolk, Va., to retain his WBC welterweight title. *Sports Illustrated* calls him "Pound for Pound the Finest Fighter in the World."

College Basketball

Nov 9, 1993—The NCAA levies sanctions against the University of Nevada-Las Vegas for 26 violations dating to the 1986 recruitment of high school star Lloyd Daniels. Among the penalties: three years probation and the loss of one scholarship each of the next two years.

Nov 21—Tennessee women's basketball coach Pat Summit gains her 500th career victory, 80–45 over Ohio State, to become the nation's second winningest active coach.

Nov 24—In New York's Madison Square Garden No. 21 UMass upsets top-ranked defending national champion North Carolina, 91–86 in overtime, to advance to the finals of the men's preseason NIT. The Minutemen lose to Kansas 86-75 in the final two days later.

Nov 29—Virginia suffers its worst ever home loss, 77–36, to Connecticut.

Nov 30—The Vermont women's team loses 96–66 to Connecticut, ending its 53-game regular-season winning streak, an NCAA record.

Dec 11—Louisville's Clifford Rozier goes 15 for 15 from the field in a 90–66 victory over Eastern Kentucky, setting an NCAA record.

Jan 24, 1994—After a week which sees 17 ranked teams lose games, UCLA finds itself atop the men's poll for the first time since Jan. 31, 1983.

Feb 15—Kentucky completes the greatest comeback in college basketball history, overcoming a 31-point second half deficit to defeat LSU, 99–95.

DAVID E. KLUTHO

Thurman was Arkansas' most reliable long-range gunner.

College Basketball (Cont.)

Feb 27—Minnesota hands Indiana its worst loss since 1905, crushing the Hoosiers 106–56 in Minneapolis.

Mar 17—Wisconsin-Green Bay, the 12th seed in the West region, upsets fifth-seeded California 61–57 in the first round of the NCAA tournament. Less than a week later, Cal point guard Jason Kidd announces he will forego his final two years of college eligibility to enter the NBA draft.

Mar 19—Tenth-seeded Maryland stuns second-seeded UMass (25-3), 95–87, in Wichita, Kan.

Mar 20— In a day of second-round upsets No. 1 seed Arkansas survives the first-half ejection of star guard Scotty Thurman to beat ninth seed Georgetown, 85–73. Leading the upset list is Boston College's 75–72 triumph over top seed North Carolina, which ends the Tar Heels string of 13 Sweet 16 appearances. In the Southeast, Marquette surprises Kentucky 75–63, while in the Midwest Tulsa overcomes a 13-point deficit to defeat fourth-seeded Oklahoma State, 82–80.

Mar 26—Duke beats top-seeded Purdue 69–60 to win the Southeast Regional and reach the Final Four for the seventh time in the past nine years. In the West Regional Final, Arizona routs Missouri 92–72 and advances to the Final Four, erasing its reputation as a tournament underachiever.

Mar 27—Florida wins the East Regional by defeating Boston College 74–66. Also advancing to the Final Four is Arkansas, which beats last year's finalist Michigan 79–68 to win the Midwest Regional.

Mar 30—Villanova beats Vanderbilt 80–73 to win the 57th National Invitational Tournament.

Apr 3—Freshman center Rashard Griffith decides to quit Wisconsin, saying he is unhappy with the Badger's guard-oriented offense.

Apr 3—In NCAA semifinal games in Charlotte, Arkansas beats Arizona 91–82 and Duke tops Florida 70–65.

Apr 3—North Carolina junior Charlotte Smith sinks a three-pointer at the buzzer to give the Tar Heels the national championship, 60–59, over Louisiana Tech in Richmond, Va.

Apr 4—Arkansas beats Duke 76–72 to win the NCAA tournament. With the score tied at 70 and 50 seconds remaining, Razorback sophomore Scotty Thurman hits a three pointer as the shot clock expires. Arkansas' Corliss Williamson, a sophomore forward who scores 23 points and grabs eight rebounds in the title game, is named the Final Four's outstanding player.

Apr 18—Michigan's Juwan Howard, a 6'10" junior center, announces he will skip his senior year to enter the NBA draft. His teammate Jalen Rose, a guard, follows suit the next day.

Apr 26—Donyell Marshall of Connecticut decides to pass up his senior year and enter the NBA draft.

Oct 14—Following a controversy over secret supplemental payments, UNLV coach Rollie Massimino accepts a $1.8 million buyout of his contract from the school. One week later, Tim Grgurich, a former assistant coach with the Seattle SuperSonics, replaces him.

College Football

Oct 30, 1993—Triumph turns to near tragedy after Wisconsin defeats Michigan for the first time in 12 years, 13–10, and fans spill out of the stands to celebrate, collapsing a railing and a chain link fence. Waves of people are forced down on top of one another and 69 are injured, six critically.

Nov 6—In a matchup of the Big Ten's top two Rose Bowl contenders, Ohio State salvages a 14–14 tie with Wisconsin when Buckeye Marlon Kerner blocks Rick Schnetzky's 32-yard field goal attempt in the final seconds. Undefeated Nebraska stops Kansas' two-point play with 52 seconds left to preserve a 21–20 victory in Lawrence, Kan.

Nov 6—LSU upsets Alabama 17–13 in Tuscaloosa, ending the defending national champion's 31-game unbeaten streak. A clash of unbeaten Ivy League teams ends with Penn defeating Princeton 30–14 behind Terrance Stokes' 272 yards rushing.

Nov 13—The No. 1 and No. 2 teams in college football meet for the 28th time and, for the 10th time, No. 2 wins, as Notre Dame upsets top-ranked, previously undefeated Florida State, 31–24, in South Bend.

Nov 20—One week after winning the "Game of the Century," Notre Dame loses 41–39 at home to Boston College. Eagle David Gordon kicks a career-best 41-yard field goal as time expires to give B.C. the win and avenge a 47-point defeat in South Bend the previous year. In Morgantown, West Virginia beats Miami 17–14 to remain undefeated.

Nov 20—Yale defeats Harvard 33–31 in the 110th game between the two schools. It is the last game in Joe Restic's 23-year career as Harvard coach. In Auburn, the Tigers complete their first season on NCAA probation with a 22–14 win over archrival Alabama and a perfect 11–0 record.

Nov 20—Florida State's Charlie Ward throws four touchdown passes and runs for one in his last home game as the Seminoles blast North Carolina State, 62–3. Needing only a tie to clinch a Rose Bowl bid, Ohio State is shut out by Michigan 28–0 in Ann Arbor.

Nov 20—Boston University beats James Madison to secure the first undefeated season in its football history, which began in 1884. At the Coliseum in Los Angeles, UCLA and USC square off with a Rose Bowl bid at stake and UCLA prevails, 27–21, intercepting the Trojans at the three-yard line with two minutes remaining.

Nov 29—Two teams, Nebraska and West Virginia, finish the regular season undefeated, with wins over Oklahoma and Boston College, respectively. In the *USA Today/CNN* coaches' poll they are ranked 1–2. Florida State (11–1) defeats sixth-ranked Florida 33–21 in Gainesville. The Associated Press poll, which determines the national title matchup, ranks Nebraska No. 1 and FSU No. 2, setting up a championship showdown in the Orange Bowl. West Virginia (11–0) opts to play Florida (9–2) in the Sugar Bowl.

Dec 4—In rainy, windy Birmingham, Ala., Florida defeats the Crimson Tide 28–13 to take the SEC title game, which is a rematch and a reversal of the previous year's contest.

Dec 5—Wisconsin, which finished 5–6 last season, clinches its first Rose Bowl berth in 31 years with a 41–20 win over Michigan State in a game played in Tokyo.

Dec 7—Marshall Faulk, San Diego State running back, who finished second in the 1992 Heisman Trophy race, announces his decision to give up his final year of eligibility and enter the 1994 NFL draft. On the following day, Jimmy Klingler, Houston quarterback, makes the same announcement.

Dec 8—Texas Tech's Byron (Bam) Morris receives the Doak Walker Award as the country's outstanding running back.

Dec 9—Auburn's Terry Bowden, the only coach ever to go 11–0 in his first year, wins the Bear Bryant Award as coach of the year.

Dec 11—Florida State's Charlie Ward wins the Heisman Trophy by the widest margin of votes (1,622 points) since O.J. Simpson won by 1,750 points in 1968. Tennessee's Heath Shuler finishes second. Nebraska's Trev Alberts receives the Butkus Award as the nation's best linebacker.

Dec 11—Northern Alabama captures the Division II national championship with a 41–34 victory over Indiana (PA) at Florence, Ala.

JOE TRAVER

Shuler left college early to join the Redskins.

Mount Union (OH) wins the Amos Alonzo Stagg bowl and the Division III national title with a 34–24 win against Rowan (NJ).

Dec 13—Idaho quarterback Doug Nussmeier wins the Walter Payton Award as the Division I-AA player of the year. Dan Allen of Boston University receives the Eddie Robinson Award as the top Division I-AA coach in 1993.

Dec 18—Youngstown State and Marshall meet for the third consecutive year to decide the Division I-AA championship, and Youngstown State wins the rubbermatch 17–5 in Huntington, W. Va.

Dec 29—Thousands of Wisconsin fans are duped in a Rose Bowl ticket scam which strands them in Pasadena with hotel and airline reservations but no tickets to the game.

Jan 1, 1994—Each of the remaining undefeated teams loses on New Year's Day as Florida State nips Nebraska 18–16 in the Orange Bowl, and Florida rips West Virginia 41–7 in the Sugar Bowl. In the Cotton Bowl Notre Dame defeats Texas A&M 24–21 on a late field goal. Wisconsin beats UCLA in the Rose Bowl, 21–16.

Jan 3—The Associated Press and the *USA Today/CNN* polls rank Florida State No. 1, giving Bobby Bowden his first national title in 28 years as a head coach. Notre Dame, which beat FSU on Nov. 13, is ranked second in both polls, and Nebraska is third.

Jan 3—Quarterback Trent Dilfer of Fresno State announces he will skip his senior year and enter the NFL draft.

Jan 5—Texas A&M is banned from television and bowl games for the 1994-95 season and placed on five year's probation by the NCAA for numerous violations, including paying student-athletes for work not performed.

Jan 9—Heath Shuler, the Tennessee quarterback who was the Heisman Trophy runner-up, announces he will forego his senior season to enter the NFL draft.

Jan 12—Wisconsin's Barry Alvarez is named Division I-A Coach of the Year by the American Football Coaches Association.

Jan 31—Two Nebraska players, redshirt freshman Ramone K. Worthy and junior Abdul Muhammad, are injured in a melee at a party in Lincoln, Neb. Worthy is treated for a stab wound to his lower back. In Newburgh, N.Y., two Army players are involved in a brawl outside a party. Running back Akili King is stabbed just below the heart and in the thighs, while former player James Ray is stabbed in the thighs and buttocks.

Feb 25—In a stunningly swift turn of events, the Southwest Conference, born in 1914, is decimated when four of its eight members—Texas, Texas A&M, Baylor and Texas Tech—accept invitations to join the Big Eight, which will change its name when the Texas contingent officially joins in 1996. Left behind are TCU, Rice, SMU and Houston.

April 25—By not declaring whether he wants to play pro football or try his luck in the NBA, former Florida State quarterback Charlie Ward becomes the first Heisman Trophy winner in 35 years not to be selected in the NFL draft. He is later picked by the New York Knicks in the first round of the NBA draft.

May 13—A *Sports Illustrated* cover story alleges that members of Florida State's national championship team took illicit cash and gifts from agents during the 1993 season.

May 16—Florida State placekicker Scott Bentley pleads no contest to illegally recording a sexual encounter with a date in St. Petersburg, Fla. He is fined $500, placed on six months' probation and sentenced to 40 hours on a road crew for the misdemeanor.

July 11—The NCAA imposes penalties on the University of Washington, adding to those already placed on the school by the Pac 10 last summer for 15 rules violations. Among the sanctions are two years' probation and a limit of four televised regular season games in one of the next two years.

Aug 5—A group of major conference commissioners and Notre Dame athletic director Dick Rosenthal select a bowl coalition which will determine the national championship format through 1997. The Fiesta, Orange, and Sugar bowls will take turns hosting the national championship game—unless the No.1 team is in the non-alliance Rose Bowl—beginning after the 1995 season.

Aug 28—Nebraska quarterback Tommie Frazier runs for touchdowns of 25, 27 and 42 yards as the Cornhuskers blank West Virginia 31–0 in the Kickoff Classic at Giants Stadium.

Aug 29—In the Disneyland Pigskin Classic in Anaheim, Calif., Ohio State downs Fresno State 34–10.

Sep 10—Florida defeats Kentucky 73–7 for its second consecutive 70-point output, having beaten New Mexico State 70–21 the previous week. Also, Michigan defeats Notre Dame 26–24 in South Bend on Remy Hamilton's 42-yard field goal with two seconds remaining.

Sep 24—Colorado shocks Michigan 27–26 in Ann Arbor on a 64-yard Hail Mary pass from Kordell Stewart to Michael Westbrook as time expires. In Miami, Washington wins 38–20, ending the Hurricanes' 58-game home winning streak.

Oct 1—Colorado's Rashaan Salaam runs himself into early contention for the Heisman Trophy, gaining 317 yards in a 34–31 win at Texas.

Oct 8—For the second straight season Boston College upsets Notre Dame, this time by 30–11 in Chestnut Hill, Mass. In Miami the Hurricanes knock off previously unbeaten Florida State 34–20, and in Tucson, 17-point underdog Colorado State (6-0) defeats sixth-ranked Arizona 21–16.

Oct 15—Auburn defeats top-ranked Florida 36–33 in Gainesville to claim their 18th straight victory and Division I-A's longest winning streak.

Golf

Woods: the youngest U.S. Amateur champ ever.

Dec 12, 1993—Simon Hobday shoots a 17-under-par 199 to win the Senior Tour Championship.

Feb 6, 1994—Forty-six-year-old Johnny Miller, who has entered only five tournaments in the 1990s, wins the AT&T Pebble Beach National Pro-Am, shooting a seven-under-par 281.

Mar 27—Greg Norman shoots 25 birdies—and a lone bogey—to win the Tour Players Championship by four strokes with a course-record, 24-under-par 264.

Mar 27—Donna Andrews wins the Nabisco Dinah Shore by one stroke over Laura Davies.

Apr 10—José María Olazábal becomes the sixth European in seven years to win the Masters, finishing two strokes ahead of Tom Lehman.

Apr 17—Raymond Floyd loses a four stroke lead down the stretch, allowing Lee Trevino to win the PGA Seniors' Championship in Palm Beach Gardens, Fla.

May 8—Back on the tour only two months after a four-month suspension, John Daly wins the Bell South Classic in Atlanta.

May 15—Britain's Laura Davies wins her second consecutive tournament, the LPGA Championship in Wilmington, Del. She has five wins in the last 13 tournaments she has played worldwide. Davies shoots a final round 68 at the LPGA and finishes 15 under par at 279.

June 5—In winning the Oldsmobile Classic in East Lansing, Mich., Beth Daniel shoots a second-round 63 and finishes with a record-tying 20-under-par 268.

June 20—Ernie Els wins the U.S. Open in a three-way sudden-death playoff with Loren Roberts and Colin Montgomerie.

June 27—David Stockton wins the Senior Players Championship in Dearborn, Mich., by six strokes while his son, Dave Jr., a 25-year-old PGA Tour rookie, ties for third at the Greater Hartford Open.

July 10—One week after being hit in the neck by a stray bullet, Kim Williams finishes tied for tenth in the Jamie Farr Toledo Classic.

July 17—With a dramatic 50-foot eagle putt at 17, Nick Price comes from behind to win the British Open at Turnberry by one stroke.

July 24—Patty Sheehan takes advantage of a collapse by Helen Alfredsson to win her second U.S. Open. Sheehan's total of 277 is seven-under-par and one stroke ahead of Tammie Green.

Aug 5—After an eight-month battle with cancer, Paul Azinger returns to play the Buick Open in Flint, Mich.

Aug 14—Nick Price shoots a final-round 67 to win the PGA Championship in Tulsa, Okla., by six strokes over Corey Pavin. Price, who won the British Open in July, becomes only the seventh player since WWII to win back-to-back majors.

Aug 28—Tiger Woods, 18, becomes the youngest winner in the history of the U.S. Amateur when he rallies from five down with 12 holes remaining to beat Trip Kuehne two up.

Aug 28—Martha Nause shoots an opening round 65 to win the du Maurier Classic at the Ottawa Hunt and Golf Club in Ottawa, Ontario. Her total of 279 puts her one stroke ahead of Michelle McGann.

Sep 11—Nick Price secures his sixth victory of the year, a one-stroke victory over Mark Calcavecchia in the Canadian Open. He becomes the first golfer since 1980 to win six times in a season.

Sep 11—Missie McGeorge rallies to win the Ping-Cellular One Championship in Portland, Ore. Her victory denies both Amy Alcott and Betsy King the win each needs to enter the LPGA Hall of Fame.

Oct 23—The United States wins eight of 10 singles matches to reclaim the Solheim Cup,13–7, from Europe. Meg Mallon wins the deciding point, defeating Pam Wright on the 18th hole.

Oct 30—Mark McCumber sinks a 40-foot birdie putt to defeat Fuzzy Zoeller on the first hole of a sudden-death playoff in the Tour Championship, the final tournament of the PGA season. For the victory, McCumber earns $540,000.

Hockey

Nov 1, 1993—Boston Bruin defenseman Ray Bourque, a four-time winner of the Norris Trophy, commits to finishing his career in Boston when he signs a five-year contract worth a reported $12 million.

Nov 11—Philadelphia center Eric Lindros suffers a tear in the medial collateral ligament of his right knee, sidelining him for four to six weeks.

Nov 15—Referees and linesmen go on strike over a dispute concerning yearly base pay increases, and the NHL uses replacement officials for scheduled games.

Nov 16—Former Montreal left wing Steve Shutt leads a class of eight into the Hockey Hall of Fame. Also inducted are Guy Lapointe, ex-Canadien left wing, and former Islander goaltender Bill Smith.

Dec 1—The 16-day-old referees' strike is settled after nine hours of negotiations in Montreal between NHL executives and members of the Officials Association.

Dec 15—Goaltender Mike Richter ties a 54-year-old New York Ranger record when he extends his unbeaten streak to 19 in a 5–2 win over the Hartford Whalers.

Dec 16—Eric Lindros returns from a knee injury to set up the game-winning goal in the Flyers' 3–2 win over the Quebec Nordiques.

Dec 26—The New York Rangers' Mike Gartner scores career goal No. 600 in an 8–3 rout of the New Jersey Devils to become the sixth player in NHL history to reach the 600-goal milestone.

Jan 22, 1994—The Eastern Conference beats the Western 9–8 in the NHL All-Star game.

Jan 27—Last season's Rookie of the Year, Winnipeg's Teemu Selanne, suffers a severed Achilles tendon and will miss at least eight weeks.

Feb 5—Washington Capital right wing Petr Bondra ties an NHL record by scoring four goals in the first period of a 6–3 victory over Tampa Bay.

Feb 12—Mario Lemieux, out since Nov. 7 with back problems, returns to the Penguin lineup and has a goal and an assist in a 9–3 loss to Dallas.

Mar 19—Boston Bruin right wing Cam Neely, who recovered from injuries to his left leg and thigh to score 50 goals in 49 games this season, suffers a torn medial collateral ligament in his right knee and is lost for the rest of the year.

Mar 23—Wayne Gretzky scores the 802nd goal of his career in a 6–3 loss to Vancouver to become the NHL's alltime leading goal scorer, passing Gordie Howe.

Mar 24—The NHL announces it will adopt an NBA-style lottery for its annual draft, beginning in 1995.

Apr 8—John Paris of Nova Scotia becomes the first black head coach in pro hockey when he accepts the job with the Atlanta Knights of the International Hockey League.

Apr 14—Los Angeles King right wing Dave Taylor announces his retirement after 17 seasons.

Apr 28—Dave Hannan scores at 5:43 of the fourth overtime to give the Buffalo Sabres a 1–0 win over the New Jersey Devils in one of the longest games in NHL history. The game ties the series at 3–3, but New Jersey wins Game 7.

DAVID E. KLUTHO

Neely's phenomenal comeback was cut short.

Apr 30—San Jose, which had a 33-35-16 regular-season record, knocks the Central Division-champion Detroit Red Wings out of the playoffs with a 3–2 victory in Game 7 of their first round series. The Sharks have never been in the playoffs before and won just 11 games the previous year.

May 8—After beating Calgary in three consecutive overtime games to win their first round series, the Vancouver Canucks make their OT record 4–0 with a 2–1 win over Dallas. The Canucks' victory gives them a 3–1 lead in the second round series.

May 19—The Hartford Whalers, who have missed the playoffs the past two years, dismiss first-year coach Pierre McGuire.

May 24—The Vancouver Canucks win the Western Conference Final four games to one and advance to the Stanley Cup championship. They clinch 4–3 in double overtime at Toronto; the win is their sixth overtime victory of the playoffs.

May 25—Mark Messier guarantees a Ranger victory prior to Game 6 of the Eastern Conference finals and then scores three third period goals to make good on his claim as New York wins 4–2 over the New Jersey Devils.

May 27—The New York Rangers defeat the New Jersey Devils 2–1 in double overtime to win the Eastern Conference final four games to three and advance to the Stanley Cup championship.

June 1—The Stanley Cup final begins, as the Vancouver Canucks beat the New York Rangers 3–2 for their seventh overtime victory of the playoffs.

June 9—With a 3–1 series lead following two victories in Vancouver, the Rangers return to Madison Square Garden looking to wrap up their first Stanley Cup since 1940. Even the local tabloids are sure of victory, with the *New York Post*'s headline screaming: TONIGHT'S THE NIGHT. Alas, tonight is not the night, as the Rangers fall 6–3. They lose two nights later in Vancouver, and the series goes to a seventh game.

June 14—The Rangers end 54 years of frustration by beating Vancouver 3–2 to claim the Stanley Cup championship. Mark Messier scores one goal and assists on another. Brian Leetch, who opened the scoring in Game 7, is awarded the Conn Smythe Trophy as the most valuable player in the playoffs.

June 28—Ed Jovanovski, a 6' 2" 207-pound defenseman, is the first player selected in the NHL draft, going to the Florida Panthers. The New York Islanders take Brett Lindros, brother of Flyer star Eric, with the ninth pick.

July 4—The St. Louis Blues trade defenseman Phil Housley to the Calgary Flames for the rights to Al MacInnis, a hard-shooting defenseman.

July 6—Unrestricted free agent Craig MacTavish, a 13-year veteran fresh from helping the Rangers win the Stanley Cup, signs with the Philadelphia Flyers for two years and $1.6 million.

July 15—Claiming the Rangers breached their contract with him by making a bonus payment one day late, coach Mike Keenan unexpectedly vacates his position in New York. Two days later he announces he has agreed to become the head coach and general manager of the St. Louis Blues. The Rangers prepare a lawsuit against him.

July 24—To avoid litigation, commissioner Gary Bettman announces a settlement in the Mike Keenan affair. He suspends Keenan for 60 days (but rules the time be served right away—which means Keenan will be back Sep. 24, before the season opens), fines him $500,000 and awards the Rangers 22-year-old center Petr Nedved in exchange for Esa Tikkanen and

Lemieux decided he needed a rest from hockey.

DAVID E. KLUTHO

Hockey (Cont.)

Doug Lidster. The commissioner also fines the Blues $250,000.

Aug 30—Mario Lemieux, who has battled Hodgkin's disease and back problems over the past four seasons, announces he will sit out the 1994-95 season with the hope of returning in 1995-96.

Sept 30—With owners and players bogged down by differences over such labor issues as revenue distribution, a rookie salary cap and salary arbitration, commissioner Gary Bettman announces a lockout that will delay the season (scheduled to begin Oct. 1) until at least Oct. 15.

Oct 11—The season is indefinitely postponed after owners unanimously reject the players' latest contract proposal.

Horse Racing

Nov 6, 1993—Arcangues, a 133–1 long shot with Jerry Bailey aboard, wins the Breeders' Cup Classic. Other Breeders' Cup winners include Kotashaan in the Turf, and Lure, with Mike Smith up, in the Mile.

Dec 15—Thoroughbred trainer Jeff Lukas, D. Wayne Lukas's son, sustains multiple skull fractures when he tries to flag down a runaway horse in the family barn in Santa Anita, Calif. The stampeding horse is Kentucky Derby candidate Tabasco Cat.

Jan 5, 1994—Staying Together, a pacer who won 11 races in a row in 1993, is named Harness Horse of the Year. The horse is trained by Bob McIntosh, whose Artsplace won the award last year.

Jan 11—Paul Mellon, who owns 1993 Kentucky Derby winner Sea Hero, wins his third Eclipse Award of Merit for his contributions to Thoroughbred racing.

Jan 13—D. Wayne Lukas announces that his son Jeff is out of a coma and has a good chance at a full recovery after being run over by Tabasco Cat on Dec. 15.

Jan 20—Mike Smith, who led the nation in earnings, wins the 1993 Eclipse Award as champion jockey. Other Eclipse winners are trainer Bobby Frankel, breeder Allen Paulsen and the 2-year-old colt Dehere.

Feb 6—Kotashaan, winner of the Breeders's Cup Turf, is named 1993 Horse of the Year.

Mar 6—Tabasco Cat, with Pat Day up, wins the San Rafael Stakes, establishing himself as a Kentucky Derby contender.

Apr 16—Holy Bull wins the Blue Grass Stakes in Lexington by 3½ lengths over Valiant Nature.

May 7—Go for Gin, with Hall-of-Famer Chris McCarron up, wins the 120th running of the Kentucky Derby by 2 lengths over Strodes Creek. The 2–1 favorite, Holy Bull, never fired on the sloppy track and finished 12th. It is the second Derby victory for McCarron and for trainer Nick Zito.

May 21—D. Wayne Lukas's Tabasco Cat, with Pat Day aboard, wins the Preakness Stakes by ¾ of a length over Kentucky Derby winner Go for Gin.

May 25—Making her first appearance since a career-threatening fall last August, Julie Krone scores a third and an eighth place finish in two starts at Belmont Park.

June 11—Tabasco Cat wins two-thirds of the Triple Crown when he takes the Belmont Stakes by two lengths over Go for Gin.

Aug 6—Victory Dream wins harness racing's most prestigious race, the $1 million Hambletonian, by 2½ lengths over Mr. Lavec.

Aug 8—The youngest jockey ever to win the Triple Crown, Steve (The Kid) Cauthen, is inducted into horse racing's Hall of Fame.

CHUCK SOLOMON

Holy Bull: a virtual lock for Horse of the Year.

Cauthen, now 34, is the only rider ever to win the Kentucky Derby and the Epsom Derby. He was *Sports Illustrated's* 1977 Sportsman of the Year.

Aug 20—Holy Bull wins the $750,000 Travers Stakes, giving the 3-year-old seven wins in nine starts on the year.

Sep 17—With Mike Smith up, Holy Bull wins the $500,000 Woodward Stakes easily, making a solid claim for 3-year-old of the Year and Horse of the Year honors.

Sep 24—Tabasco Cat runs himself back into contention for year-end honors with a 2-length victory in the Kentucky Cup Classic in Florence.

Motor Sports

Nov 7, 1993—Aryton Senna and Alain Prost finish 1–2 at the season-ending Australian Grand Prix. Prost retires after the race and Senna leaves Team McLaren to take over Prost's Williams-Renault.

Nov 27—Nigel Mansell, who won the 1992 Formula One title and the '93 IndyCar crown, is named 1993 Driver of the Year, beating out NASCAR driver Rusty Wallace by nine points.

Nov 14—With a 10th-place finish in the season-ending Atlanta 500, Dale Earnhardt clinches his sixth Winston Cup championship.

Feb 6, 1994—The Nissan team of Paul Gentilozzi, Scott Pruett, Butch Leitzinger, and Steve Millen wins the 24-Hours at Daytona with an average speed of 104.80 miles per hour over 707 laps.

Feb 11—Winston Cup veteran Neil Bonnett is killed after crashing during a practice run at Daytona. Three days later Rodney Orr, a Winston Cup rookie at 31, dies in a crash on the opposite end of the same track.

Feb 20—After 279 Winston Cup starts, veteran Sterling Marlin, 36, finally wins one as he takes the checkered flag at Daytona, beating Ernie Irvan by 0.23 seconds.

Mar 20—Michael Andretti returns to the IndyCar circuit and wins the Australian FAI Grand Prix, leading from start to finish.

Mar 27—In Sao Paulo, German Michael Schumacher wins the first Formula One race of the year, overtaking Aryton Senna during an early refueling stop.

Apr 17—Al Unser Jr wins his fifth Long Beach Grand Prix, beating reigning IndyCar champ Nigel Mansell by 39 seconds.

Apr 24—Rusty Wallace wins the second-biggest short track payoff in NASCAR history when he wins the Martinsville 500 from the pole to collect $173,675.

May 1—Three-time world driving champion Aryton Senna is killed when he crashes while leading the San Marino Grand Prix. The day before, Formula One rookie Roland Ratzenberger of Austria is killed while practicing at the same track.

May 15—Michael Schumacher wins the Monaco Grand Prix by 32.3 seconds over Martin Brundle for his fourth consecutive Formula One win.

May 29—Al Unser Jr wins the second Indy 500 of his career, defeating rookie Jacques Villeneuve by 8.6 seconds.

June 5—Team Penske scores a 1-2-3 finish as Al Unser Jr holds off teammates Emerson Fittipaldi and Paul Tracy to win the Wisconsin 200, his third straight IndyCar victory.

July 10—Al Unser Jr wins his fifth race in eight starts, taking the Grand Prix of Cleveland with an average speed of 138 mph over 85 laps.

July 24—In the Diehard 500 at Talladega (Ala.) Superspeedway, Jimmy Spencer holds off Bill Elliott to take the checkered flag, his second victory in the past four Winston Cup events.

Aug 20—While practicing at the Michigan International Speedway, veteran NASCAR driver Ernie Irvan hits a piece of debris, blows a tire and slams into the wall, suffering a fractured skull and collapsed lungs.

Aug 28—Five hours after finishing first in the Belgian Grand Prix, Formula One points leader Michael Schumacher is disqualified and stripped of the victory because the skid plate underneath his car did not meet specifications. He has also been suspended for the next two races for ignoring a black flag in the July 10 British Grand Prix.

Aug 29—Nigell Mansell announces he will leave the IndyCar circuit to return to Formula One racing.

Sep 11—Al Unser Jr finishes second in the Texaco 200 in Elkhart Lake, Wis., to clinch the 1994 IndyCar title, his second and the ninth for owner Roger Penske.

Sep 25—England's Damon Hill pulls within one point of suspended Formula One leader Michael Schumacher when he wins the Portugese Grand Prix.

Oct 9—Mario Andretti retires after the Grand Prix of Monterey, his record 407th IndyCar start.

Oct 17—Michael Schumacher returns from his two-race suspension and wins the European Grand Prix in Jerez, Spain. Damon Hill finishes second and the two are separated by five points in the standings with two races remaining.

Oct 23—Dale Earnhardt wins the AC Delco 500 to clinch his seventh Winston Cup championship, tying Richard Petty's record for career titles.

MANNY MILLAN

Golden Games: Koss won three golds, all in record time.

Nov 1, 1993—The U.S. luge team leaves Germany under tightened security after one of its members is attacked by neo-Nazi skinheads in a bar on Oct 29.

Jan 6, 1994—Nancy Kerrigan is struck on the knee with a club by an unknown assailant after a practice session in Detroit's Joe Louis Arena. No bones are broken but she will be unable to compete in the nationals, which begin the next day.

Jan 8—Tonya Harding wins the U.S. championship, her second national title, securing one of two Olympic berths in women's figure skating. The U.S. Skating Federation grants Kerrigan the other spot, citing the unusual circumstances and her previous record.

Jan 12—Tonya Harding's bodyguard, Shawn Eric Eckardt, confesses to participating in a plot to attack Kerrigan.

Jan 17—Two members of the group of skinheads that attacked U.S. luger Duncan Kennedy last Oct. are convicted of assault and sentenced to over one year in jail.

Jan 19—Tonya Harding's ex-husband Jeff Gillooly is arrested and charged with planning the attack on Nancy Kerrigan. Also charged are Derrick Smith and Shane Stant, two men hired to carry out the assault, and Eckardt, who conspired with Gillooly. All four are eventually convicted and sent to prison for terms ranging from 18 months to two years.

Jan 29—Austrian skier Ulrike Maier dies after a crash in a downhill race in Garmisch-Partenkirchen, Germany

Feb 12—The 1994 Winter Olympics begin with a dazzling opening ceremonies that lights up the night over Lillehammer, Norway. In the first competition of the Games, Finland defeats the Czech Republic 3–1 in ice hockey.

Feb 12—The U.S. Olympic Committee, under the threat of a $25 million lawsuit, announces it will drop its disciplinary hearing, clearing the way for Harding, who has not been charged in the attack on Kerrigan, to compete in Lillehammer.

Feb 13—Alaskan Tommy Moe wins the gold medal in the downhill to give the U.S. its first Olympic Alpine medal since 1984. Earlier in the day Italy's Manuela Di Centa captures the first gold of these Olympics, in the 15K freestyle cross-country ski race.

Feb 13—Johann Olav Koss of Norway wins the host country's first gold medal, setting a world record in the 5,000-meter speed skating race.

Feb 14—On a disappointing day for the U.S., luger Duncan Kennedy crashes his sled and speed skater Dan Jansen, in search of his first medal in his fourth Olympics, slips in the final turn of the 500-meter race and finishes eighth.

Feb 15—Diann Roffe-Steinrotter of the U.S. wins the women's Super G—a race in which she has never placed better than fourth in World Cup competition.

Feb 17—The U.S. hockey team ties Canada 3–3 for its third tie of the Olympic tournament. Also, Tommy Moe wins the silver medal in the men's Super G.

Feb 18—Dan Jansen ends four Olympics' worth of frustration by winning the 1,000-meter race in a world record time of 1 minute 12.43 seconds.

Feb 19—Bonnie Blair wins the gold medal in the women's 500-meter speed skating race, becoming the first U.S. athlete to win the same event in three consecutive Winter Games.

Feb 20—Norway's Johann Olav Koss wins his third gold of the Games, breaking his own 10,000-meter record by 13 seconds. The victory makes him the first to win three gold medals in world record time in one Games.

Feb 21—Legendary British skaters Jayne Torvill and Christopher Dean, gold medalists in

1984, fall short in their comeback bid, winning the bronze medal in ice dancing.

Feb 23—Bonnie Blair wins the fifth gold medal of her Olympic career, in the 1,000-meter race; she now has more golds than any other U.S. woman.

Feb 23—After the technical program in women's figure skating, Nancy Kerrigan is in first place. Ukraine's Oksana Baiul is second followed by Surya Bonaly of France. Tonya Harding is tenth.

Feb 24—Cathy Turner of the U.S. wins the 500-meter short-track speed skating race. Two days later she is disqualified from the 1,000 for cross tracking.

Feb 24—Italian cross-country skier Manuela Di Centa wins her fifth medal, the gold in the 30k classical, to become the most decorated athlete of these Winter Games.

Feb 24—Oksana Baiul overtakes Nancy Kerrigan in the free-skate program to win the gold in women's figure skating by the slightest of margins. Chen Lu of China is third. Tonya Harding finishes eighth. On July 1 she is banned for life from the U.S. Figure Skating Association and stripped of her national title.

Feb 27—Alberto Tomba of Italy captures the silver medal in the slalom, making, in his words, a "magical recovery" after a poor first run places him 12th.

Feb 27—Sweden wins the ice hockey gold medal with a tense 3–2 shootout victory over Canada in the Winter Games' final event.

Pro Basketball

Nov 1, 1993—The Seattle SuperSonics trade forward Derrick McKey and guard Gerald Paddio to the Indiana Pacers for forward Detlef Schrempf.

Nov 16—Isiah Thomas breaks a bone in his right hand when he punches Detroit teammate Bill Laimbeer during an argument in practice.

Dec 1—After 13 seasons, 202 three-pointers, two championship rings and countless on-court altercations, Detroit's Bill Laimbeer announces his retirement.

JOHN BIEVER

Dec 2—The Houston Rockets defeat the New York Knicks 94–85 at Madison Square Garden to go 15–0 and equal the 45-year-old NBA record for most wins to start a season. The next night they are denied the record by the Atlanta Hawks, who beat them 133–111.

Dec 6—The Indiana Pacers sign veteran guard Byron Scott.

Dec 12—Bobby Hurley of the Sacramento Kings suffers two collapsed lungs and various broken bones when he is ejected some 75 feet from his truck after it is struck in an intersection by a speeding car.

Jan 4, 1994—The Seattle SuperSonics take their NBA-best 23–3 record to Phoenix and emerge with a 112-106 victory over the defending Western Conference champion Suns.

Jan 7—To replace point guard Doc Rivers, lost for the season

Olajuwon drove the Rockets all the way to the NBA championship.

with a knee injury the previous month, the Knicks trade forward Tony Campbell to the Dallas Mavericks for guard Derek Harper.

Jan 10—Isiah Thomas is named to Dream Team II to replace the injured Tim Hardaway.

Jan 18—The Los Angeles Clippers and the Miami Heat make a combined 23 three-pointers in their game, won 126–124 by Los Angeles, setting an NBA record.

Jan 29—After losing an NBA-record 19 games in a row at home, the Dallas Mavericks win a home game, 108–101 over Sacramento.

Feb 6—The Houston Rockets cancel a trade of Robert Horry and Matt Bullard for the Pistons' Sean Elliott after Elliott fails his physical.

Feb 13—At the 44th All-Star Game in Minneapolis, Scottie Pippen is named MVP as he leads the East to victory, scoring 29 points and grabbing 11 rebounds.

Feb 24—The Atlanta Hawks trade forward Dominique Wilkins to the LA Clippers for forward Danny Manning. Also, the Utah Jazz acquire guard Jeff Hornacek from the Philadelphia 76ers in exchange for guard Jeff Malone and a first round draft pick.

Mar 17—In defeating the Milwaukee Bucks 105–83, the Knicks hold their opponent below 90 points for the eighth consecutive game, tying the NBA post-shot clock record.

Mar 22—The Lakers announce retired superstar Magic Johnson will replace Randy Pfund as coach of the team. Also, Moses Malone moves into third place on the alltime scoring list when he scores nine points in a game at Charlotte.

Apr 6—Dan Majerle sinks his 173rd three-pointer of the season, breaking the record Vernon Maxwell set in 1990-91.

Apr 19—Future Hall of Famer Isiah Thomas, who led Detroit to two NBA titles, injures his achilles and exits what will be his last game, a loss to the Orlando Magic. He makes his retirement official May 11.

Apr 24—San Antonio's David Robinson wins the scoring title on the last day of the regular season when he scores 71 points in a 112–97 win over the LA Clippers. He joins Wilt Chamberlain, Elgin Baylor and David Thompson as the only players to score 70 points in a game. Also, Wes Unseld retires as coach of the Washington Bullets

Apr 24—Against Houston, Mahmoud Abdul-Rauf of the Denver Nuggets has a chance to break Calvin Murphy's season free throw record of 95.8%. Murphy, who played for Houston, is sitting courtside. He calls for the

ball before Abdul-Rauf's first attempt in the third quarter, rubs it, then hands it back to the official. Abdul Rauf makes his first attempt, but misses his second—and the record.

Apr 27—The NBA Board of Governors awards a franchise to the city of Vancouver.

May 3—Chris Webber of the Golden State Warriors wins the Rookie of the Year Award by six votes over Orlando's Anfernee Hardaway.

May 4—The Dallas Mavericks dismiss first-year coach Quinn Buckner after an NBA-worst 13–69 season. Dick Motta replaces him.

May 7—The Denver Nuggets bounce the Seattle SuperSonics from the playoffs, winning the fifth game at Seattle 98–94 in overtime. It is the first time a No. 8 seed has eliminated a No.1 since the league began its current playoff format in 1984.

May 10—Former Detroit Piston coach Chuck Daly leads a class of five into the NBA Hall of Fame. Also inducted are University of Louisville coach Denny Crum and former Montclair (N.J.) State star Carol Blazejowski.

May 13—The Lakers hire Del Harris to succeed Magic Johnson as coach.

May 19—The Indiana Pacers beat the No. 1-seeded Atlanta Hawks 98–79 to win their Eastern Conference semifinal series four games to two.

May 21—After losing the first two games at home, the Houston Rockets recover to win their Western Conference semifinal series with the Phoenix Suns, taking Game 7 at home, 104–94.

May 22—The three-time defending champion Chicago Bulls are eliminated by the New York Knicks, losing Game 7 of the Eastern Conference semifinals 87–77 at Madison Square Garden.

May 26—Atlanta's Lenny Wilkens is named Coach of the Year.

May 31—The Houston Rockets dismiss Utah Jazz 94–83 and win the Western Conference finals four games to one.

June 1—Reggie Miller of the Indiana Pacers is torrid in the third quarter of Game 5 of the Eastern Conference finals against the New York Knicks. He scores 25 of his game-high 39 points in the period, including five three-pointers in six minutes, as the Pacers win 93–86 to take a three games to two lead.

June 5—After they even the series on the road, Patrick Ewing leads the Knicks to a 94–90 Game 7 win over the Pacers, slam-dunking a rebound with 27 seconds remaining to give New York the edge.

June 22—The Houston Rockets beat the New York Knicks 90–84 in Game 7 to win their first NBA title. John Starks of the Knicks shoots 2 for 18 from the field, including 0–11 from three-point range. Rocket center Hakeem Olajuwon, who averaged 26.9 points, 9.1 rebounds and 3.9 blocks per game for the series, is named MVP.

June 29—At the NBA draft in Indianapolis, the Milwaukee Bucks select Purdue's Glenn Robinson with the first pick. California's Jason Kidd is the No. 2 pick, going to the Dallas Mavericks, and Grant Hill of Duke goes third to Detroit.

July 1—The Indiana Pacers announce they have acquired point guard Mark Jackson from the LA Clippers in exchange for Pooh Richardson and Malik Sealy.

July 18—The Seattle SuperSonics trade guard Ricky Pierce, the rights to first-round draft pick Carlos Rodgers and a second-round pick in 1995 to the Golden State Warriors for guard Sarunas Marciulionis.

July 22—Unrestricted free agent Dominique Wilkins signs a three-year contract with Boston Celtics.

Aug 4—Robert Parrish, the 41-year-old center who won three NBA titles with the Boston Celtics, signs a two-year deal with the Charlotte Hornets to back up Alonzo Mourning.

Aug 14—The U.S. national team (Dream Team II) wins the World Championship of Basketball in Toronto, beating Russia 137–91.

Aug 22—Former Chicago Bull guard John Paxson retires. Five weeks later Cavs All-Star Larry Nance follows suit.

Sep 8—Accepting one fifth of his market value to fit under the Phoenix salary cap, forward Danny Manning signs with the Suns for one year and $1 million.

Sep 19—Horace Grant signs a five-year contract with the Orlando Magic. Three days later the Magic sign guard Brian Shaw.

Oct 5—The NBA announces several rules changes including a closer three point line, the elimination of hand-checking on defense, and stricter illegal-defense guidelines.

Pro Football

Oct 31—Emmitt Smith rushes for a club-record 237 yards in Dallas's 23–10 win at Philadelphia.

Nov 8—The Cleveland Browns cut Bernie Kosar after weeks of disagreement between the veteran quarterback and coach Bill Belichick. Two days later, Kosar signs with Dallas to back up Troy Aikman.

Nov 14—Miami's Don Shula earns career coaching victory number 325 in the Dolphins' 19–14 win at Philadelphia, surpassing George Halas as the NFL coach with the most victories.

Nov 25—Dallas's Leon Lett hands a Turkey Day victory to Miami when he mistakenly tries to recover a blocked 41-yard field goal attempt by the Dolphins with 15 seconds remaining and the Cowboys leading 14–13. He slides in the snow, the ball squirts out, Miami recovers at the Dallas one-yard line and gets another chance at the field goal. Pete Stoyanovich boots it through and the Dolphins win 16–14.

Nov 25—Detroit's Barry Sanders, who is leading the NFL in rushing, suffers a partial tear of his left knee ligament and is lost to the Lions for the rest of the regular season.

Nov 28—After a 1–4 start, the Houston Oilers win their sixth straight game, 23–3 over Pittsburgh, to move into first place in the AFC Central.

PETER READ MILLER

Rice became the NFL's alltime touchdown leader.

Nov 30—NFL owners vote by a 26–2 count to award the league's 30th franchise to Jacksonville, Fla. The team, called the Jaguars, will begin play in 1995 in the renovated Gator Bowl.

Dec 12—Los Angeles Ram running back Jerome Bettis rushes for 212 yards in his team's 23–20 victory over New Orleans, becoming the first rookie in six years to gain over 200 yards rushing in a game, and only the eighth rookie to do so. And in a great quarterback duel, Denver's John Elway throws for 221 yards and three touchdowns in leading Denver to a 27–21 win over the Kansas City Chiefs and Joe Montana, who throws for 237 yards and two touchdowns.

Dec 15—Jeff Alm, a defensive lineman with Houston, commits suicide by shotgun after the automobile he is driving hits a highway ramp barrier and ejects his close friend Sean Lynch, killing him.

Dec 17—The Fox Network shocks CBS by outbidding them for the rights to televise NFC football. The young network will pay $400 million per year to broadcast the games for the next four years.

Dec 23—Christmas comes two days early for Troy Aikman when the Cowboy quarterback signs the biggest contract in NFL history, an eight-year deal worth $50 million.

Jan 2, 1994—On the wild final Sunday of the regular season the Miami Dolphins lose their fifth straight, 33–27 to New England, and miss the playoffs after a 9–2 start. The Houston Oilers win their 11th straight, 24–0, against the Jets and enter the playoffs with momentum despite The Punch—an on-camera swipe taken at offensive coordinator Kevin Gilbride by defensive coordinator Buddy Ryan near the Oiler bench. The Cowboys clinch the NFC East with a 16–13 overtime defeat of the Giants, and Buffalo wins its fourth straight to secure home field advantage throughout the playoffs. The Raiders make a 17-point comeback against Denver for a 33–30 overtime win and a berth in the AFC playoffs, and Detroit beats Green Bay 30–20 in the Pontiac Silverdome to clinch NFC Central.

Jan 3—In his team's last regular season game, a 37–34 Monday night overtime loss to Philadelphia, San Francisco's Steve Young becomes the first NFL quarterback to win three consecutive passing titles and the first to lodge three consecutive passer ratings of 100 or more.

Jan 4—Atlanta's Jerry Glanville is fired as coach of the Falcons after four seasons and a 27–37 record. Dismissed as well is first-year Redskin coach Richie Petitbon, who oversaw a 4–12 season, Washington's worst in 30 years.

Jan 4—Jerome Bettis of the Los Angeles Rams is named NFC Offensive Rookie of the Year. His 1,429 yards rushing are 57 yards short of the NFL season leader, Emmitt Smith, and the sixth-best rookie total of all time.

Jan 5—The San Francisco 49ers' Dana Stubblefield receives the NFC Defensive Rookie of the Year award. Stubblefield's teammate Jerry Rice is named Offensive Player of the Year.

Jan 6—Dan Reeves is named Associated Press Coach of the Year after leading the N.Y. Giants to an 11–5 record in his first season as their coach. Pittsburgh cornerback Rod Woodson receives the AP Defensive Player of the Year award.

Jan 8—Bruce Coslet of the Jets becomes the third head coach to be dismissed in a week. He is replaced by his defensive coordinator, Pete Carroll.

Jan 8—With 1:43 remaining in the AFC wild-card game, Joe Montana throws a seven-yard, fourth-down touchdown pass to Tim Barnett, forcing overtime against Pittsburgh. Kansas City wins 27–24 on a 33-yard field goal by Nick Lowery. The following day, Green Bay's Brett Favre throws a 40-yard touchdown pass to Sterling Sharpe with 55 seconds left to give the Packers a 28–24 victory over Detroit in the NFC wild-card round.

Jan 9—The Giants grind out a 17–10 NFC wild-card victory over Minnesota behind Rodney Hampton's two touchdowns and 161 yards rushing. In the AFC Napoleon McCallum scores three touchdowns, and the Raiders revive the long-passing game to outpoint Denver 42–24.

Jan 10—Dallas Cowboy running back Emmitt Smith, who won his third straight rushing title despite missing the first two games of the season due to a contract dispute, is voted the NFL's Most Valuable Player by the media.

Jan 15—Following the Giants' 44–3 playoff loss in San Francisco, their legendary linebacker Lawrence Taylor announces his retirement. He has played 13 seasons, made 10 Pro Bowl appearances, won two Super Bowl rings, and one league MVP award.

Jan 15—Buffalo advances to the AFC championship for the fourth consecutive year with a 29–23 home victory over the Raiders as Bill Brooks scores the game-winning touchdown, a 22-yard pass from Jim Kelly.

Jan 16—Joe Montana throws three second half touchdown passes as Kansas City rallies from a 10–0 deficit to upset Houston, 28–20, and advance to the AFC title game. Dallas beats Green Bay 27–17 to reach the NFC championship against San Francisco.

Jan 20—The Fox network, which earlier outbid CBS for the right to broadcast NFC football, signs CBS's crack announcing team of John Madden and Pat Summerall.

Jan 23—A Super Bowl rematch is set for Atlanta's Georgia Dome, as the Cowboys easily dismantle the 49ers 38–21 in the NFC title game, and the Bills win the AFC championship 30–13 over Kansas City.

Jan 24—The Falcons hire offensive coordinator June Jones to replace Jerry Glanville as head coach, and the Cardinals fire coach Joe Bugel after a 7–9 season.

Jan 29—Former Dallas Cowboys Tony Dorsett and Randy White lead a class of six into the Pro Football Hall of Fame in Canton, Ohio. Also inducted are former Viking coach Bud Grant, ex-Brown running back Leroy Kelly, Jackie Smith, who played tight end for St. Louis and Dallas, and retired 49er DB Jimmy Johnson.

Jan 30—The Dallas Cowboys repeat as champions while the Buffalo Bills suffer an unprecedented fourth consecutive title game defeat, 30–13, in Super Bowl XXVIII. Running back Emmitt Smith scores two touchdowns, rushes for 132 yards, and is named the game's MVP. His rushing title, regular season MVP and Super Bowl MVP trifecta is an NFL first.

Feb 1—The Washington Redskins hire former Dallas offensive coordinator Norv Turner as head coach. Two days later Buddy Ryan signs on as head coach of the Arizona Cardinals.

Feb 20—Tom Coughlin, who coached Boston College to a 21-13-1 record over the past three years, is hired to coach the expansion Jacksonville Jaguars.

Mar 2—Michael Huyghue is hired as vice president of football operations for the Jacksonville Jaguars, making him one of the highest ranking African-Americans in the league.

Mar 6—Former Miami Dolphin backup quarterback Scott Mitchell signs a three-year deal with the Detroit Lions worth an estimated $11 million.

Mar 7—Chris Miller leaves Atlanta to sign a three-year, $9 million contract with the Los Angeles Rams. One week later, the Rams trade quarterback Jim Everett to the New Orleans Saints.

Mar 14—The Atlanta Falcons decline to match New Orleans's four-year, $10 million offer to wide receiver Michael Haynes, so the free

agent, who had been declared a "transition player," joins the Saints. Also, the Minnesota Vikings release 12-year veteran quarterback Jim McMahon.

Mar 22—The NFL undergoes its first scoring change in 75 years when owners vote, by a 23–4 margin, to institute the two-point conversion after touchdowns. Two other rules favorable to the offense are approved: kickoffs will be moved from the 35-yard line to the 30, with a one-inch tee mandatory. Possession after missed field goals will be assumed at the spot of the kick and not the line of scrimmage (a seven-yard difference).

Mar 24—The Indianapolis Colts trade disgruntled quarterback Jeff George to the Atlanta Falcons for three draft picks, including a No. 1 in the '94 draft.

Mar 29—Jimmy Johnson resigns as coach of the two-time defending champion Dallas Cowboys after a personal dispute with owner Jerry Jones. The following day he is replaced by former Oklahoma Sooner coach Barry Switzer.

Apr 13—The Houston Oilers trade quarterback Warren Moon to the Minnesota Vikings for draft picks. The following week Dallas free-agent linebacker Ken Norton signs with San Francsico for five years and $8 million.

Apr 24—At the NFL draft in New York City, the Cincinnati Bengals select Ohio State defensive tackle Dan Wilkinson with the No. 1 pick. San Diego State running back Marshall Faulk is the second pick, going to the Indianapolis Colts.

June 15—The New York Giants release 38-year-old quarterback Phil Simms.

Aug 2—The Washington Redskins sign first-round pick Heath Shuler to the largest rookie contract ever, an eight-year, $19.25 million deal.

Sep 4—Highlighting an action-packed opening day is Dan Marino's recovery from surgery on his achilles tendon to throw for 473 yards and five touchdown passes in the Dolphins' 39–35 comeback victory over New England. The Cowboys win 26–9 against Pittsburgh in their opener under new coach Barry Switzer, and rookie sensation Marshall Faulk rushes for 143 yards and scores three touchdowns in the Colts' 45–21 rout of Houston.

Sep 5—Jerry Rice scores three touchdowns—career Nos. 125, 126 and 127—in the 49ers 44–14 victory over the Raiders, passing Jim Brown to become the NFL's alltime touchdown leader.

Pro Football (Cont.)

Sep 11—In a matchup of former teammates, Joe Montana throws two touchdown passes as the Kansas City Chiefs beat Steve Young and the San Francisco 49ers, 24–17.

Sep 15—Free-agent cornerback Deion Sanders signs a one-year, $1.1 million contract with the San Francisco 49ers.

Oct 2—In the first father-son coaching duel in NFL history, Don Shula's Miami Dolphins defeat David Shula's Cincinnati Bengals 23–7.

Oct 7—Joe Montana leads the Chiefs to a last-minute, 31–28 Monday Night victory over comeback specialist John Elway and the Denver Broncos.

Oct 23—The San Diego Chargers (6–1) are the last team to fall from the ranks of the unbeaten, losing to Denver 20–15.

Soccer

Nov 17, 1993—Argentina defeats Australia 1–0 in their return match to qualify for the 1994 World Cup in the U.S. The final field of 24 is set as qualifying concludes with 12 games worldwide. France is eliminated after losing 2–1 on a last-second goal by Bulgaria. Greece, Nigeria and Saudi Arabia qualify for the first time.

Nov 23—Graham Taylor quits as England's manager after the Brits fail to qualify for the World Cup.

Nov 29—The president of the French soccer federation resigns following the Olympic Marseille bribery scandal and the national team's failure to make the World Cup.

Dec 5—By an 18–5 vote, the U.S. Soccer Federation accepts Major League Soccer's application for Division I status. The league is scheduled to begin play in April 1995.

Dec 12—Sao Paulo defeats AC Milan 3–2 to win its second straight Intercontinental Cup.

Dec 15—Roberto Baggio of Juventus is named FIFA World Footballer of the Year.

Dec 19—At the World Cup draw in Las Vegas FIFA announces teams will get three points for a victory instead of two as in previous Cups. The six groupings for the World Cup are also announced. The U.S will play against Switzerland, pre-tournament favorite Colombia and Romania in the first round.

Jan 15, 1994—The U.S national team opens its '94 schedule with a 2–1 defeat of Norway in Tempe, Ariz.

Jan 23—In a preview of their World Cup opener, the U.S. ties Switzerland 1–1 in Fullerton, Calif. The following week they tie Russia by the same score.

Feb 2—Police in Buenos Aires raid the home of Argentine superstar Diego Maradona after he fires an air rifle at reporters stationed outside.

June 2—Dominic Kinnear, Chris Henderson and Brian Bliss are the last players to be cut as U.S. coach Bora Milutinovic finalizes his 22-man roster.

After his fine World Cup, Lalas left for a soccer career in Italy.

BOB MARTIN

Soccer (Cont.)

June 4—In its final World Cup tuneup, the U.S. is impressive, beating Mexico 1–0 before 91,123 at the Rose Bowl.

June 17—The 15th World Cup opens at Chicago's Soldier Field with Germany defeating Bolivia 1–0.

June 18—Eric Wynalda scores a world-class 28-yard free kick to lift the U.S to a 1–1 tie with Switzerland. The game, played on natural grass in the Pontiac Silverdome, is the first ever indoor World Cup match.

June 18—Ireland stuns Italy 1–0 when Ray Houghton scores before a festive packed house at Giants Stadium.

June 22—In one of the greatest upsets in World Cup history the U.S. shocks Colombia 2–1 in Pasadena. The victory ranks with a 1–0 defeat of England in 1950 as the best in U.S. history.

June 28—The U.S. learns it will advance to the round of 16 for the first time since the inaugural World Cup in 1930.

June 28—Russia's Oleg Salenko sets a new Cup record, scoring five goals in his team's 6–1 pasting of Cameroon.

June 30—After testing positive for five banned substances including ephedrine, Argentina's Diego Maradona is sent home by his national team. He will miss the remainder of the tournament and is later suspended for 15 months by FIFA.

July 2—Colombian defender Andres Escobar, who scored an own goal in his team's loss to the U.S., is shot to death in Medellin. One of his alleged murderers bet heavily on Colombia to win the match.

July 4—Brazil beats the U.S. 1–0 on Bebeto's goal in the 74th minute, eliminating the host nation.

July 9—Brazil defeats the Netherlands 3–2 in the quarterfinals, with all five goals coming in a 30-minute span in the second half. Branco's sizzling 30-yard free kick in the 81st minute decides the tournament's most dramatic game.

July 10—Bulgaria knocks out defending champion Germany 2–1 at Giants Stadium.

July 13—Roberto Baggio scores goals in the 21st and 26th minutes as Italy beats Bulgaria 2–1 to reach the World Cup Final. In each of the two previous rounds Baggio has scored late game-winning goals. In the other semifinal Brazil dominates Sweden en route to a 1–0 victory.

July 18—Brazil and Italy play to a 0–0 tie after 120 minutes. Brazil becomes the first four-time World Cup winner, prevailing 3–2 on penalty kicks, when Roberto Baggio sends Italy's fifth attempt over the crossbar.

July 28—Defender Alexi Lalas signs with Padova, making him the first U.S. player in Italy's vaunted Serie A league.

Aug 7—The U.S. women's national team wins the inaugural Chiquita Cup, defeating Norway 4–1.

Aug 8—U.S. midfielder Claudio Reyna signs with Bayer Leverkusen of the German Bundesliga.

Aug 9—Nike announces it has committed $18 million to sponsorship deals with Major League Soccer and the U.S. Soccer Federation.

Sep 8—After losing a close election for U.S. Soccer president to World Cup organizer Alan Rothenberg, Richard Groff is elected commissioner of the American Professional Soccer League. The two men will be the key players in the future of pro soccer in the U.S.

Oct 18—Alexi Lalas scores in Padova's stunning 2–0 upset of European champion AC Milan.

Tennis

Nov 21, 1993—Germans sweep the season-ending events in both the mens' and womens' tours as Michael Stich upsets world No. 1 Pete Sampras to win the ATP Tour World Championships and Steffi Graf beats Arantxa Sanchez Vicario in the final of the Virginia Slims Championships.

Jan 5, 1994—Pete Sampras and Michael Stich, who begin the year ranked No. 1 and 2, lose in the early rounds of the Qatar Open. Steffi Graf begins the year atop the women's rankings.

Jan 18—Jennifer Capriati announces she is leaving the pro tour until she completes high school.

Jan 30—Pete Sampras wins his third consecutive Gand Slam, beating Todd Martin in the finals of the Australian Open 7–6 (7-4), 6–4, 6–4.

Jan 30—Steffi Graf steamrolls Arantxa Sanchez Vicario 6–0, 6–2 to win the Australian Open.

Feb 1—Monica Seles, sidelined since being stabbed in the back at a tournament in Hamburg last April, falls to No. 18 in the WTA rankings.

Mar 6—For the third straight year Steffi Graf wins the Virginia Slims of Florida, beating Arantxa Sanchez Vicario 6–3, 7–5 in the final. Graf (22–0) has not lost a set in 1994.

MANNY MILAN

Graf was unbeatable in the early going.

May 16—Jennifer Capriati is arrested in a Coral Gables, Fla., hotel on a misdemeanor charge of marijuana possession Two days later she enters a drug rehabilitation center in Miami.

May 23—Martina Navratilova, who has announced this season will be her last, is eliminated in the first round of her final French Open.

June 2—Mary Pierce upsets No. 1 Steffi Graf 6–2, 6–2 in the semifinals of the French Open.

June 4—Arantxa Sanchez Vicario beats Mary Pierce 6–4, 6–4 to win the French Open.

June 5—Spain's Sergi Bruguera successfully defends his French Open title, defeating countryman Alberto Berasategui 6–3, 7–5, 2–6, 6–1 in the final.

June 21—Unseeded Lori McNeil knocks off No. 1 seed Steffi Graf in the first round at Wimbledon.

July 2—Vying for her tenth Wimbledon singles title before she retires, Martina Navratilova falls one set short, losing to Conchita Martinez in the final 6–4, 3–6, 6–3.

July 3—Pete Sampras wins his second consecutive Wimbledon title, defeating Goran Ivanisevic in the final 7–6 (7-2), 7–6 (7-5), 6–0.

July 24—Spain wins the Federation Cup for the third time, defeating the U.S. 3–0 in the championship.

Aug 14—Michael Chang wins his second straight ATP Championship with a 6–2, 7–5 win over Stefan Edberg.

Aug 17—On his 24th birthday Jim Courier announces he is leaving the game for an indefinite period. He returns for the U.S. Open but loses in the early rounds and resumes his hiatus.

Sep 5—Unseeded Andre Agassi outlasts Michael Chang 6–1, 6–7 (3-7), 6–3, 3–6, 6–1 in three hours, five minutes to advance to the quarterfinals of the U.S. Open.

Sep 10—Arantxa Sanchez Vicario wins the U.S. Open, beating Steffi Graf 1–6, 7–6 (7-3), 6–4 in the final. It is her second Grand Slam of the season.

Sep 11—Andre Agassi completes an improbable run through the U.S. Open field, defeating Michael Stich for the title, 6–1, 7–6 (7-5), 7–5.

Sep 18—Retired pro Vitas Gerulaitis, who won 27 titles including the 1977 Australian Open, is found dead in the home of a friend in Southhampton, N.Y. The cause of death is accidental carbon monoxide poisoning from a faulty propane heater.

Sep 25—In Davis Cup play at Goteburg, Sweden rallies to defeat the U.S. 3–2, behind Magnus Larsson's win over Todd Martin in the final match. At Hamburg, Russia ousts Germany 4–1. The winners will meet Dec. 2 in Russia to decide the championship.

Other Sports

Oct 31, 1993—Mark Allen wins his fifth consecutive Ironman Triathlon World Championship in Kailua-Kona, Hawaii. Paula Newby-Fraser wins her third straight women's title and breaks nine hours for the second year in a row.

Nov 14—Andres Espinosa wins the New York City Marathon in 2:10:04. Uta Pippig wins the women's race in 2:26:24.

Nov 16—Davis Phinney, the alltime U.S leader in cycling victories with 324, announces his retirement.

Nov 21—The North Carolina women's soccer team wraps up its eighth consecutive NCAA title with a 6–0 rout of George Mason. It is the Tar Heel women's 11th championship in the past 12 years.

Nov 22—The Arkansas men win their fourth straight NCAA cross-country title while the Villanova women capture their fifth straight.

Nov 27—Lynn Jennings of New Hampshire wins her seventh consecutive national cross-country title in Missoula, Mont. Todd Williams wins the men's title.

Dec 2—Chinese women set three world short-course records and win four golds at the Short Course World Championships in Spain. The U.S. men's 400-meter medley relay team sets a world record of 3:32.57.

Dec 5—The Virginia Cavaliers win an unprecedented third consecutive NCAA men's soccer crown. Forward Nate Friends scores all five of Virginia's goals in the final four. The Cavs are anchored by Hermann Award winner Claudio Reyna, a junior who leaves school after the year to play for the U.S. national team. Reyna later signs with Bayer Leverkusen of the German Bundesliga.

Dec 5—Italy's Alberto Tomba wins the Stoneham, Quebec, World Cup slalom race, defeating Austria's Thomas Stangassinger by .12 seconds.

Dec 10—Ty Murray wins his fifth consecutive and sixth career all-around title at the National Finals Rodeo. Other winners include Deb Greenough in the bareback, Dan Mortensen in the saddle-bronc, Joe Beaver in calf roping and Steve Duhon in steer wrestling.

Jan 5, 1994—Heidi Voelker finishes third in the Giant Slalom at Morzine, France, the highest finish of the season by a U.S. woman.

Jan 6—Mary T. Meagher's 13-year-old short course world record in the 100-meter butterfly falls to Zhong Weiyue of China at the world championships in Spain. Weiyue swims 58.71, breaking Meagher's mark by two tenths of a second.

Jan 8—Jamie Astaphan, the doctor who provided steroids for sprinter Ben Johnson, is arrested on drug warrants at JFK airport.

Jan 10—Summer Sanders, the U.S. swimmer who won four medals at the 1992 Olympics, announces her retirement.

Jan 16—Austria's Anita Wachter wins the World Cup

Giant Slalom at Cortina D'Ampezzo, Italy to close ground on overall leader Pernilla Wiberg of Sweden. It is Wachter's third win of the World Cup Season.

Jan 30—U.S. speed skater Dan Jansen breaks his own 500-meter world record at the World Sprint Speed Skating Championships in Calgary. Jansen, 28, finishes in 35.76 seconds, bettering the old mark by .16 seconds.

Feb 2—Hillary Lindh becomes the first U.S. woman in eight years to win a World Cup downhill when she places first at Sierra Nevada, Spain.

Feb 6—Suzy Hamilton mistakenly stops one lap short in the mile at the Mobil Invitational in Fairfax, Va. A nine-time NCAA champion while at Wisconsin, Hamilton also misjudged the finish of the 1,500-meter race at the Goodwill Games in 1990.

Feb 6—In an important tuneup for the Lillehammer Games, Alberto Tomba wins the men's World Cup slalom at Garmisch-Partenkirchen, Germany.

Feb 12—Demer Holleran wins her sixth national title at the U.S. National Hardball Squash Rackets Championship. Roberto Rosales wins his first men's title.

Feb 15—Ila Borders of Southern California College is thought to be the first woman to pitch in an NCAA or NAIA baseball game when she throws a five-hitter in 12–1 win over Claremont-Mudd.

Feb 20—Eamonn Coghlan, whose 1983 indoor mile record still stands, becomes the first runner over 40 years old to run a sub-four-

Coghlan's sub-four-minute mile at 40: another career highlight.

CLAY McLACHLAN

minute mile when he finishes in 3:58.15 at a meet in Boston.

Mar 5—Gwen Torrence wins the 200- and 60-meter dashes at the USA/Mobil Indoor Track and Field Championships, setting a new U.S. indoor record of 22.74 in the 200.

Mar 5—David Traber wins the Pro Bowlers Association National Championship, edging his brother Dale 196–187 in the title game. Johnny Petraglia finishes third but receives a $100,000 bonus for bowling a televised 300 game.

Mar 9—Marty Stern retires as track and field coach at Villanova, where his teams won 23 Big East titles.

Mar 13—Arkansas wins the NCAA men's indoor track championship for the 11th consecutive year. Also, the Kenyon men's swimming team wins its 11th straight Division III national title.

Mar 15—Martin Buser shaves almost three hours off Jeff King's 1993 record when he wins the Iditarod Trail Sled Dog Race in 10 days 13 hours 2 minutes and 39 seconds. He receives $50,000 and a pickup truck for winning the 1,100-mile race. Rick Mackey, who won the race in 1983, finishes five hours after Buser for second place and $39,500.

Mar 17—Diann Roffe-Steinrotter, the U.S. skier who won the gold in the women's Super G at Lillehammer, closes out her career in storybook fashion by winning the World Cup Super G at Vail, Colo. After the last event of the World Cup season, Norway's Kjetil Andre Aamodt is the men's overall leader, and Vreni Schneider of Switzerland wins the women's overall. Tommy Moe of the U.S. finishes sixth in the men's Super G at Vail. That places him third in the season's Super G standings, won by Norway's Jan Einar Thorsen.

Mar 19—Pat Smith of Oklahoma State becomes the first four-time NCAA Division I wrestling champion when he outpoints Sean Bormet of Michigan 5–3 in the 158-pound title match. Oklahoma State wins the team title as well, edging Iowa.

Mar 19—Stanford, led by Jenny Thompson, wins its third consecutive NCAA Division I women's swimming title in Indianapolis. The Cardinal's score of 512 beats Texas by 91 points. Kristine Quance of USC is the meet's only three-time winner, claiming the 200 and 400 individual medleys as well as the 200 breaststroke.

Mar 22—Notre Dame storms past Penn State on the final day of competition to win the NCAA men's and women's fencing championship.

Mar 26—Stanford wins its third straight NCAA Division I men's swimming title in Minneapolis,

with 566½ points to Texas's 445. Arizona's Chad Carvin, a sophomore, sets meet and U.S. Open records in both the 500-yard freestyle (4:11.59) and the 1,650-yard freestyle (14:34.91).

Mar 24—Tommy Moe wins the men's Super G at the U.S. Alpine Ski Championships in Winter Park, Colo.

Mar 26—In an event scheduled too soon after the Olympics and therefore sorely lacking in star quality, Yuka Sato of Japan wins the women's World Figure Skating title. Surya Bonaly of France wins the silver and Germany's Tanja Szewczenko takes the bronze. On the men's side, with Viktor Petrenko, Brian Boitano and Kurt Browning absent, Canada's Elvis Stojko wins the gold, Phillippe Candeloro of France captures the silver and Viacheslav Zagorodniuk of the Ukraine wins the bronze.

Mar 26—William Sigei of Kenya wins the senior men's title at the world cross-country championships in Budapest, Hungary. Helen Chepngeno of Kenya wins the women's title.

Mar 30—Janet Evans captures her 37th national swimming title, winning the 800-meter freestyle at the U.S. Championships in Federal Way, Wash. The title moves her into second place on the alltime list, with one more than Johnny Weismuller and 11 fewer than Tracy Caulkins. She wins her 38th title three days later in the 400-meter freestyle.

Apr 2—After winning three overtime games to advance to the final for the third straight year, Lake Superior State explodes against Boston University in the NCAA Division I ice hockey final. The Lakers' 9–1 victory is the most lopsided championship game since 1961.

Apr 3—Tom Dolan, a freshman at the University of Michigan, wins the 1,500-meter freestyle in 15:18.18 at the U.S. Swimming Championships for his fourth title of the meet. He is the sixth swimmer to win four national titles in one meet. His other victories came in the 400 and 800 freestyles and the 400 individual medley.

Apr 18—Uta Pippig wins the Boston Marathon in 2:21:45, breaking Joan Benoit-Samuelson's 11-year-old course record. Cosmas N'Deti is the men's winner and also breaks the course record, finishing in 2:07:15, 36 seconds ahead of Rob de Castella's 1986 mark.

Apr 23—Norm Duke captures bowling's General Tire Tournament of Champions, defeating Eric Forkel 217–194 in the championship game.

BOB MARTIN

Indurain sped to his fourth straight Tour de France.

Apr 24—Shannon Miller of the U.S. wins her second consecutive all-around gymnastics title at the World Championships in Brisbane, Australia. Ivan Ivankov of Belarus wins the men's all-around while countryman Vitaly Scherbo takes the floor exercise, vault and horizontal bar titles.

Apr 30—At the U.S. National Wrestling Championships in Las Vegas, heavyweight Bruce Baumgartner wins his 15th national title, tying a U.S. record. Greco-Roman 150-pounder Andy Seras also ties a national record by reaching his 11th consecutive U.S. final.

May 7—Penn State beats UCLA to become the first non-California school to win the NCAA men's volleyball championship.

May 12—Anne Marie Duggan beats Wendy Macpherson-Papanos 224–177 to win the WIBC Queens bowling tournament.

May 15—Russia's Viatcheslav Ekimov edges Lance Armstrong of the U.S. by 84 seconds to win the Tour DuPont.

May 29—Princeton wins the men's NCAA Division I lacrosse title for the second time in three years, defeating Virginia 9–8 on a goal by

Kevin Lowe 42 seconds into overtime. The victory completes a sweep for the school, whose women's team won the NCAA title the week before, beating Maryland 10–7 in the final.

May 30—University of Arizona pitcher Susie Parra allows just one hit and strikes out 13 batters as the Wildcats beat Cal St-Northridge 4–0 to win the NCAA Division I softball title for the second consecutive year. Parra's season pitching record stands at 33–1.

May 31—Alberto Salazar wins South Africa's famed Comrades Marathon, covering the hilly 53.8-mile course from Durban to Pietermaritzburg in 5:38:38

June 5—Erick Walder of Arkansas wins the long and triple jumps at the outdoor NCAAs for a record 10 national titles. The Razorbacks also win their third straight team title.

June 11—The Oklahoma Sooner baseball team wins the College World Series, defeating Georgia Tech 13–5 in the championship game. Oklahoma's Chip Glass, a senior centerfielder who batted .389 with three home runs, four RBIs and three stolen bases in four games in the series, is named the Most Outstanding Player of the tournament.

June 11—At the 13th National Collegiate Rowing Championships at East Fork State Park in Cincinnati, Ohio, the men's eight from Brown and the women's eight from Princeton repeat as champions.

June 18—Scott Huffman, using his patented "Huffman Roll," sets an American record in the pole vault by clearing 19' 7" at the U.S. national championships in Knoxville, Tenn.

June 18—Alexander Popov of Russia breaks Matt Biondi's six-year-old world record in the 100-meter freestyle, clocking 48.21 in Monte Carlo.

July 4—Anne Marie Letko wins the Peachtree 10k road race in Atlanta. Her time of 31:57 easily beats runner-up Jane Omoro, who finishes in 32:28. Benson Masya leads a Kenyan sweep of the top five men's places, winning in 28:01.

July 6—Leroy Burrell sets a world record in the 100-meter dash, running 9.85 at Athletissima '94 in Lausanne.

July 8—Sonia O'Sullivan of Ireland sets the only women's track and field world record of 1994, clocking 5:25.36 for 2,000 meters in Edinburgh.

July 22—William Sigei of Kenya runs 26:52.23 for 10,000 meters at the Bislett Games in Oslo, a world record. In the 5,000, Bob Kennedy of the U.S. clocks 13:02.93, finishing a close second to Khalid Skah of Morocco.

July 24—Spain's Miguel Indurain easily wins his fourth consecutive Tour de France. He joins Jacques Anquetil of France and Eddy Merckx of Belgium as the only riders to win the prestigious event four years in a row.

July 25—Yekaterina Podkopayeva, 42, of Russia outkicks a strong field to win the 1,500 meters at the Goodwill Games, in 4:04.92.

July 31—The U.S. Lacrosse team wins its sixth world championship, defeating Australia 21–7 in Bury, England. Defender Dave Pietramala scores twice.

July 31—Shannon Miller of the U.S., who has won every major national and international all-around title since the 1992 Summer Olympics, finishes second in the all-around at the Goodwill Games. Russia's Dina Kochetkova edges Miller by 0.057 points to win the gold.

July 31—Ukrainian Sergei Bubka sets his 35th world record in the pole vault, clearing 20'1¾" at altitude in Sestriere, Italy. Bubka set his first world record a decade earlier and has now added nearly a foot to that record.

Aug 2—Noureddine Morceli, who owns the world record in the 1,500 and the mile, adds the 3,000 to his collection, running 7:25.11 in Monte Carlo.

Aug 14—Despite a broken left arm held together by seven screws and a titanium plate, Jenny Thompson wins the 100-meter freestyle at the Phillips 66 National Swimming Championships in Indianapolis.

Aug 17—Thirty-four-year-old Linford Christie of Great Britain destroys a strong field in the men's 100-meter dash at the Weltklasse meet in Zurich. His time of 10.05 easily beats runner-up Jon Drummond's 10.15. Noureddine Morceli runs his first serious 5,000, using a 52.2 final lap to run away from the field and win in 13:03.85.

Aug 23—Linford Christie runs 100 meters in 9.91, his fastest time of the year, to win the Commonwealth Games title.

Aug 27—Dominique Dawes sweeps all five events at the U.S. Gymnastics Championships; she is the first to do so since 1969.

Aug 27—Maracaibo, Venezuela becomes the first Latin American team since 1958 to win the Little League World Series when it defeats Northridge, Calif., 4–3 in the title game at Williamsport, Pa.

Aug 28—Kieren Perkins of Australia swims 1,500 meters in a world-record 14:41.66 at the Commonwealth Games in Vancouver, B.C. En route he passes 800 meters in 7:46, also a world record.

Sep 2—Evan Stewart of Zimbabwe wins the one-meter springboard at the World Diving Championships in Rome.

Sep 3—At the Mobil Grand Prix in Paris, Jackie Joyner-Kersee long jumps 23' 8" to clinch the overall season title and $100,000. Noreddine Morceli wins the overall men's title.

Sep 5—On the opening day of the World Swimming Championships in Rome, the Chinese sweep all three women's events, shattering a world record and two meet records. Le Jingyi wins the 100 free in 54.01 and Lu Bin is second in 54.15, both well under Jenny Thompson's 2-year-old world record of 54.48.

Sep 6—Tom Dolan of the U.S. sets a world record in the 400-meter individual medley at the World Championships in Rome. His time of 4:12.30 is .06 seconds faster than Tamas Darnyi's 1991 mark.

Sep 7—Chinese women continue to dominate the World Swimming Championships and to arouse suspicions about their training methods. They break another world record—by a massive 1.54 seconds, with a 3:37.91 in the 400-meter freestyle relay—and set two more meet records.

Sep 9-10—Dan O'Brien of the U.S. wins his third major decathlon title of the year at the Decastar meet in Talence, France. His total of 8,710 points easily beats Eduard Hamalainen of Belarus, who scores 8,459. Heike Drechsler of Germany, making her first serious attempt at the heptathlon, racks up the highest score of the year with 6,741 points.

Sep 27—Chad Hundeby of Irvine, Calif., sets the record for swimming the English Channel when he completes the 15½ mile swim from Dover, England to Cap Cris-Nez, France in seven hours 17 minutes. The old record of seven hours 40 minutes was set 16 years ago by Penny Lee Dean, who helped coach Hundeby for his swim.

Oct 8—Aleta Sill of Dearborn, Mich., wins the PBAA women's U.S Open, bowling a 712 three-game series en route to the title.

Oct 15—Australian Greg Welch wins the Ironman Triathlon World Championship in Kailua-Kona, Hawaii, edging out Dave Scott, 40, who was attempting a comeback after winning the race five times between 1982 and '87. Paula Newby-Fraser fails to break nine hours but nonetheless wins her fourth consecutive world championship, beating Karen Smyers of Massachusetts by eight minutes.

Baseball

A Season Lost

The first season-ending strike in the history of sport cast a pall over the national pastime | by TIM KURKJIAN

T WAS WARM AND BRIGHT IN MILWAU-kee on Sept. 14, a glorious day for baseball. The schedule said the Indians were in town; perhaps they would clinch their first post-season berth in 40 years. Maybe Albert Belle would hit a couple of home runs, intensifying his race with Frank Thomas for the Triple Crown. Instead, the only baseball news of the day was as dark as any in the history of the game. At 2:18 p.m. Brewer owner Bud Selig, the acting commissioner, announced that the season had been canceled. There would be no World Series in 1994.

The unthinkable had happened. Major league players, on strike since Aug. 12, and hard-line owners failed to reach an agreement on a new contract, wiping out the remainder of one of the most fascinating seasons of all time. The game that played through World War I, a stock market crash, Adolph Hitler, Vietnam and an earthquake, couldn't resolve its civil war, a mean, ugly, disgraceful dispute that left all sides losers. For the first time since 1904, there was no Fall Classic.

"It's almost incomprehensible," Selig said. "You ask yourself, Can this be happening?"

Sadly, it did. Even sadder, there was every indication that the strike would roar into spring training 1995 and perhaps into the regular season. There was a chance, some said, that major league baseball wouldn't be played until 1996. There was talk of the owners using minor league players next year and of major league players starting their own league. "I'm dumbfounded," said Pirate centerfielder Andy Van Slyke. "I didn't think stupidity could win ... but it did."

The season-ending strike—a first in the history of professional sports—covered 34 days and 669 games. It cost players $236 million and the owners an estimated 20 million fans and $442 million in revenue. There was great concern about how many fans would come back to baseball when-ever the games resumed.

This wasn't a strike over issues, but ide-ologies: The owners say the game is head-ed for financial ruin; the Players Associa-tion says it's a robust, thriving industry. Owners say they're losing money; players say they're lying. Owners say certain clubs will have to move to survive; players say the value of franchises are skyrocketing. Consequently the two sides never came close to reaching an agreement before the season was torched. On June 14 the own-ers made their proposal, which took 14 months and 500 computer models to for-mulate. It called for a salary cap, which

Selig's brand of hardball and the players' intransigence produced rafts of empty seats.

was designed to slow spiraling salaries and trigger a revenue-sharing system among the owners that would redistribute money from big-market teams to small-market teams. The players rejected the cap proposal, claiming—among other evils—that it restricted free agency. They vowed never to accept a cap "even if we have to stay out 92 years," said Giant pitcher Rich Monteleone.

The players, whose average salary is $1.2 million per year, walked out because they felt it was their only leverage against the owners' threat to unilaterally impose the cap after the season. From Aug. 12 through Sept. 14, there were only three major negotiating sessions. Because the sides were so far apart, there was nothing to discuss. And the negotiations that were held were mostly rancorous, galvanizing each side to its cause. The only hint of

optimism came on Sept. 8, when the players submitted a counterproposal. But, according to the owners, all it did was address revenue sharing among the clubs and did nothing to restrain rising player salaries. It was quickly rejected.

That surprised (and angered) the players' union, which clearly underestimated the resolve of the owners. In negotiations over the last 30 years the owners have always cracked, and the players have always won. The players, to the final day, expected that to happen again. It didn't. Small-market owners, who needed revenue sharing and a salary cap to compete with large-market teams, rallied around Selig. So did some of the new owners who were heavily leveraged in other businesses and couldn't afford to keep losing money. So did some of the big-market owners, mainly because they were tired of always caving in to player demands. Shockingly, the owners were almost as unified as the players.

We'll never know how close to the .400 mark Gwynn might have come in a full season.

In many ways the final announcement from Selig shouldn't have come as a surprise. Two years ago several owners and players predicted that 1994 would produce the mother of all baseball labor wars, one that would make previous bitter negotiations look tame. They were right. Don Fehr, the executive director of the Players Association, and Dick Ravitch, the chief negotiator for the owners, had a contentious relationship from their first collective bargaining session in January, and by Sept. 14 they hated each other. With no commissioner to help settle the dispute or at least to keep the sides talking, there was no hope, just chaos.

Without a contract in place, the off-season would be even more chaotic. If the owners implemented their salary cap proposal, what would become of the 192 players who were eligible for free agency? How much would salary arbitration change? Would players sign contracts if tendered? These were questions without answers.

"Lawyers," said Fehr of the off-season, "are going to bill an awful lot of hours."

The labor dispute ruined one of the most intriguing, bizarre and historic sea-sons in baseball annals. It was the first year of the new divisional realignment, creating two more playoff teams per league. That made contenders out of more teams, generating more fan interest and excitement. The season had every-thing. Tight races, home runs, no-hitters, a perfect game, retirements, releases, a corked-bat caper, juiced-ball theories, long home runs, two new ballparks, a col-lapsing stadium, incredible comebacks and tape-measure home runs.

"At the All-Star Game, I saw excite-ment that I've never seen in 13 years," said Padre outfielder Tony Gwynn. "We have an outstanding product, and it's get-ting better."

The first week set the tone for the season.

On Opening Night, the first night open-er in major league history, the first hitter of the game, St. Louis's Ray Lankford, hit a home run off Cincinnati's Jose Rijo. That should have served as an omen to pitchers that balls would be flying over fences at a record pace; from the start, pitchers complained that the ball was juiced. The following day, Opening Day, an obscure outfielder named Tuffy Rhodes of the Cubs hit three home runs, in his first three at bats—the first player in history to do that on Opening Day and the first Cub to hit three consecutive homers in a game at Wrigley Field since Adolpho Phillips in 1967. All three came off the Mets' Dwight Gooden; before that game only three players had hit three home runs in their *careers* off Gooden.

Before the first week had ended, Atlanta's Kent Mercker, the fifth man in the Braves' Fab Four rotation, pitched a no-hitter in his 12th major league start—it was his first career complete game. Detroit first baseman Cecil Fielder hit a triple after going 1,909 at bats without one. Blue Jay rookie outfielder Carlos Delgado became the first player to hit a home run off the Windows Restaurant at the SkyDome, a blast of 445 feet, but 30 feet shorter than the one hit by Twin outfielder Pedro Munoz at the Metrodome. The Dodgers introduced the first Korean-born player to play in the major leagues, pitcher Chan Ho Park, who was introduced by the public-address announcer at Dodger Stadium as *Ho Chan* Park. Toronto rightfielder Joe Carter drove in 12 runs, amazing considering that he wasn't supposed to be playing until May because of a broken left thumb.

Every week was equally wild. By August a number of records were threatening to fall.

Giant third baseman Matt Williams had 43 homers when the strike hit, wrecking his bid to break Roger Maris's single-season record of 61, as well as Hack Wilson's NL record (56) and Mike Schmidt's record for home runs by a third baseman (48). Seattle's Ken Griffey Jr. had 40 homers on Aug. 11. Houston's Jeff Bagwell had 39; the White Sox's Frank Thomas, 38; San Francisco's Barry Bonds, 37; and Cleveland's Belle, 36. Six players were on a pace to hit 50 homers. No season in history has produced more than two players with 50 home runs.

There hasn't been a Triple Crown winner since Carl Yastrzemski in 1967, but Thomas and Belle had serious shots at it. Thomas was second in homers, third in hitting (.353) and tied for third in RBIs (101). Belle was third in homers, second in hitting (.357) and tied for third in RBIs. Bagwell, who suffered a broken left wrist when hit by a pitched ball on Aug. 10, was having the best year of any major leaguer, hitting .368 and leading the league with 116 RBIs. Before the injury he was on a pace for a season bettered only by Babe Ruth.

But he wasn't going to win

In spite of the controversy, Belle uncorked a marvelous season.

the NL batting title. That belonged to Gwynn, who was hitting .394 at the strike. "I really think he could hit .400," said San Diego hitting coach Merv Rettenmund. That has not been done since Ted Williams in 1941. It wasn't just Gwynn; seemingly everyone was hitting. The AL had a batting average of .273; the last time the league hit that high was 1939. Twenty-three players had five hits in a game, two more than the total in 1993, which was a monstrous offensive season. Eight players hit three homers in a game, twice as many as in '93. The Red Sox beat Kansas City 22–11 on April 12—the AL's highest scoring game since 1978. The Twins became the first team since the 1950 Red Sox to score more than 20 runs in a game twice.

This is not to say that all pitching was bad. Mercker's no-hitter against the Dodgers on April 8 was a masterpiece, after which he said, "I watched CNN

JOHN IACONO

Maddux was nearly unhittable in '94, allowing a paltry 1.56 runs per game.

Headline News at 20 and 50 past the hour ... for seven hours ... same highlights." On April 27, Minnesota's Scott Erickson—who led the AL in losses, hits and runs in '93—no-hit the Brewers and almost smiled afterward. On July 28 the Rangers' Kenny Rogers became the 15th pitcher to throw a perfect game, stifling the Angels 4–0. The son of a berry farmer from tiny Dover, Fla., a lefthanded shortstop in high school, a 39th-round draft choice who played in the first major league game he ever saw, became the first AL lefthander ever to throw a perfecto. "My life would make a great movie," he said.

Atlanta's Greg Maddux was clearly the best pitcher in either league, tying for the league lead in wins (16) and shutouts (three), leading in ERA (1.56; the next closest was 2.74) and complete games

(10). No pitcher has ever won three straight Cy Young Awards, but Maddux was a lock (the Baseball Writers Association of America, which votes on the awards, decided at the All-Star Game that awards would be presented even if there was a strike). "He's the best pitcher in our league," said Pirate coach Rich Donnelly. "He's the second-best pitcher, too."

Maddux wasn't playing for the best team, however. That honor went to the Montreal Expos, who were a staggering 74–40 when the players walked. The Expos entered this season with the second-lowest payroll in the game ($19 million), the youngest team in baseball and, supposedly, with little chance of winning the NL's strongest division, the East, which the Braves controlled. The Expos were 54–37 on July 17, trailing Atlanta by two games, then won 20 of 23 games to take a six-game lead into the strike. "It will be a shame if we don't get to reap the benefits of this season," Montreal G.M. Kevin Malone said two weeks before the strike. A shame, indeed. The Expos, formed in 1969, have never gone to the playoffs in a full season, and they've never gotten their fans fervently interested in the team, but by the beginning of August, the people of Montreal had finally taken to the most exciting and talented team in the league. Yet by the time play is resumed, there's a good chance that the Expos will have been broken up due to financial constraints.

The closest race in baseball came in the NL Central, where Cincinnati dueled the Astros to the final day, winning by half a game. The Reds had many contributors, including centerfielder Deion Sanders, who was traded by Atlanta (for center-fielder Roberto Kelly) on May 29, but Cincinnati couldn't shake the gritty Astros. On July 18, Houston trailed the Cardinals 11–0 after three innings, then scored 15 runs in the next three innings on the way to a 15–12 victory. It tied (previously done twice) for the biggest comeback in NL history.

The least noble NL race came in the West, where the Dodgers were 58–56 at the strike, 3½ games ahead of the Giants. San Francisco, which won 103 games in '93, won their first nine games after activating outfielder Darryl Strawberry on July 7 and entered the race. Strawberry had been released by the Dodgers in April after failing a drug test. But it wasn't Strawberry who sparked the Giants, it was the tremendous play of Bonds and, to a lesser extent, Williams.

The story of the AL, if not all of baseball, was the Indians. They have not been to the playoffs since 1954. They have not finished within 10 games of first place since 1959 (with the single exception of the 1981 strike season). They have not finished closer to first place than last in 25 years—a major league record. That was all going to change this year. Playing their inaugural season at beautiful Jacobs Field, the Indians won six of their first

seven games, slowed, then took off again in mid-May, winning 18 in a row at home. At the strike they were 66–47, one game behind the White Sox in the AL Central.

They were many heroes in Cleveland, including centerfielder Kenny Lofton (the best leadoff man in the game) and two veterans, pitcher Dennis Martinez and DH Eddie Murray. But the main Indian was Belle, whose intensity as a hitter is unmatched. But that desire to hit the ball harder than anyone got him suspended. On July 15, White Sox manager Gene Lamont accused Belle of using a corked bat, and the umpires confiscated it. Before it could be examined, it was mysteriously swiped from the umps' dressing room and replaced with another bat. The real bat was later produced by the Indians and found to be corked, earning Belle a 10-day suspension, which was reduced to seven games. Still it made for great theater. Before, during and after the incident, Belle did not stop hitting.

The best-hitting team, and the best team, in the league was an unlikely one, the Yankees, who have not been to the playoffs since 1981. This was a Yankee team unlike perhaps any other in the club's rich history. It was uncontroversial, even boring, a faceless group of players, seemingly all of whom can hit—but none better than rightfielder Paul O'Neill, who was hitting .359. "A live bat and a live body at every position," said Twin hitting coach Terry Crowley about the Yankees. They were leading the league in hitting and second in runs scored, rarely made mistakes defensively and got terrific pitching, especially from Jimmy Key, whose 17–4 record was tops in the AL. On Aug. 11 the Yanks had a 6½-game lead over Baltimore.

The worst team ever to lead a division was the Rangers, who have never been to the playoffs in their 23-year existence. They also opened a new stadium—The Ballpark in Arlington—but didn't fill it with wins or enthusiasm like the Indians did theirs. Still, the Rangers led the AL

One young fan had his own bargaining ploy
to add to the contract discussions.

West by one game, despite being 10
games under .500. Fittingly, Texas lost its
last six games before the strike, helping
the A's move within one game of first
place, remarkable considering that Oakland lost 40 of its first 56 games. Seattle,
the consensus pick in spring training to
win the West, charged late to get within
two games. By that time they were strictly
a road team. On July 19 several 10-pound
tiles dislodged and fell from the roof of
the Kingdome, forcing major construction
on perhaps the worst stadium in the
game. The Mariners played their final 20
games away from home.

The roof fell on the World Series teams
from 1993, the Blue Jays and the Phillies.
Toronto, the two-time defending world
champ, got off to a sluggish start, which
included blowing a seven-run lead in the
ninth against the Angels on April 15, then
losing 14–13 in the 10th. After pulling
within 5½ games of the Yankees on June
12, the Jays lost 13 of their next 14 to fall
into last place and out of contention.
Included was a stretch in which they
scored just nine runs in eight games—the

worst eight-game stretch in club history,
worse than anything done by the wretched
'81 Jays, who started Danny Ainge at second base. "I've never been on a team that
played this badly for this long," said pitcher Dave Stewart. "And I played in Texas
['83–85]. We lost around 100 games
twice."

The Phillies were devoured by injuries,
starting midway through spring training
when first baseman John Kruk was diagnosed with testicular cancer, which kept
him out until April 11. Having taken virtually no batting practice, he went 3 for 5
in his first game back, including a double
in his first at bat. There were precious few
other highlights for the Phillies. There
were many lowlights, including the night
of May 10, when they blew a seven-run
lead in the ninth against Atlanta, then lost
9–8 in the 15th. So in the space of one
month, two teams lost games in which
they had led by seven runs entering the
ninth inning. That had happened only
twice in the previous 30 years.

The Blue Jays and the Phillies probably
wanted the strike to end their seasons, but
sadly the strike abruptly ended the careers
of several players. On Aug. 4 Twin first
baseman Kent Hrbek announced his
retirement, effective at the end of the season. On July 26, 46-year-old Marlin pitcher Charlie Hough, slowed by a painful hip
injury, said it would be the last appearance of his career. Boston DH Andre
Dawson announced a few days before the
strike that this would be his final season.
The strike didn't allow us to give these
players a proper send-off. And who knows
how many other players we saw for the
last time. Tiger shortstop Alan Trammell,
Blue Jay pitcher Stewart, Indian DH Dave
Winfield and Angel DH Bo Jackson all
possibly played their final games in August
1994. It would be a shame if their careers
ended on such a stupid, negative note.

That's what a strike can do: turn a sensational season sour and permanently
damage it.

FOR THE RECORD·1994

Final Standings

National League

EASTERN DIVISION

Team	Won	Lost	Pct	GB	Home	Away
Montreal	74	40	.649	—	32-20	42-19
Atlanta	68	46	.596	6	31-24	36-22
New York	55	58	.487	18½	23-30	32-28
Philadelphia	54	61	.470	20½	34-26	20-35
Florida	51	64	.443	23½	25-34	26-30

CENTRAL DIVISION

Team	Won	Lost	Pct	GB	Home	Away
Cincinnati	66	48	.579	—	37-22	29-26
Houston	66	49	.574	½	37-22	29-27
Pittsburgh	53	61	.465	13	32-29	21-32
St. Louis	53	61	.465	13	23-33	30-28
Chicago	49	64	.434	16½	20-39	29-25

WESTERN DIVISION

Team	Won	Lost	Pct	GB	Home	Away
Los Angeles	58	56	.509	—	33-22	24-34
San Francisco	55	60	.478	3½	29-31	26-29
Colorado	53	64	.453	6½	25-33	28-31
San Diego	47	70	.402	12½	26-31	21-39

American League

EASTERN DIVISION

Team	Won	Lost	Pct	GB	Home	Away
New York	70	43	.619	—	33-24	37-19
Baltimore	63	49	.563	6½	28-27	35-22
Toronto	55	60	.478	16	33-26	22-34
Boston	54	61	.470	17	31-33	23-28
Detroit	53	62	.461	18	34-24	19-38

CENTRAL DIVISION

Team	Won	Lost	Pct	GB	Home	Away
Chicago	67	46	.593	—	34-19	33-27
Cleveland	66	47	.584	1	35-16	31-31
Kansas City	64	51	.557	4	35-24	29-27
Minnesota	53	60	.469	14	32-27	21-33
Milwaukee	53	62	.461	15	24-32	29-30

WESTERN DIVISION

Team	Won	Lost	Pct	GB	Home	Away
Texas	52	62	.456	—	31-32	21-30
Oakland	51	63	.447	1	24-32	27-31
Seattle	49	63	.438	2	22-22	27-41
California	47	68	.409	5½	23-40	24-28

1993 Playoffs

National League Championship Series

Oct 6 ....Atlanta 3 at Philadelphia 4 (10 innnings)
Oct 7 ....Atlanta 14 at Philadelphia 3
Oct 9 ....Philadelphia 4 at Atlanta 9
Oct 10 ....Philadelphia 2 at Atlanta 1
Oct 11 ....Philadelphia 4 at Atlanta 3
Oct 13 ....Atlanta 3 at Philadelphia 6

(Philadelphia wins series 4-2.)

GAME 1

Atlanta	0	0	1	1	0	0	0	0	1	0	—3
Phila	1	0	0	1	0	1	0	0	0	1	—4

WP—Williams. **LP—**McMichael. **BS—**Williams. **E—** Philadelphia: Batiste (1). **LOB—** Atlanta 11, Philadelphia 8. **2B—** Atlanta: Nixon (1), Olson (1), Avery (1); Philadelphia: Dykstra (1), Kruk (1), Hollins (1), Chamberlain (2). **HR—** Philadelphia: Incaviglia. **S—** Atlanta: Belliard. **SF—**Atlanta: Justice. **GIDP—** Philadelphia: Hollins. **A—**62,012.
Recap: After striking out the side in the first, Curt Schilling held the Braves in check for eight innings, scattering seven hits. The Phillies' Kim Batiste made up for a ninth inning, lead-blowing error by doubling home John Kruk with the game winner.

GAME 2

Atlanta	2	0	6	0	1	0	0	4	1—14
Philadelphia	0	0	0	2	0	0	0	0	1—3

WP—Maddux. **LP—**Greene. **E—**Philadelphia: Morandini (1). Stocker (1); **LOB—**Atlanta 6, Philadelphia 8. **2B—**Atlanta: Nixon (2), Gant (2). **HR—**Atlanta: Blauser (1), McGriff (1), Pendleton (1), Berryhill (1); Philadelphia: Dykstra (1), Hollins (1). **SB—**Philadelphia: Morandini (1). **CS—**Atlanta: Nixon (1). **A—**62,436.
Recap: Atlanta shooed Tommy Greene (10–0 in 16 consecutive starts at Vet Stadium) with a six-run third that featured Damon Berryhill's three-run shot to right.

GAME 3

Philadelphia	0	0	0	1	0	1	0	1	1—4
Atlanta	0	0	0	0	5	0	4	0	x—9

WP—Glavine. **LP—**Mulholland. **E—**Philadelphia: Duncan (1). **LOB—**Philadelphia 7, Atlanta 7. **2B—**Philadelphia: Chamberlain (3), Stocker (1), Eisenreich (1); Atlanta: Blauser (1), McGriff (1) Justice (1), Lemke (1). **3B—**Philadelphia: Duncan (2), Kruk (1). **HR—**Philadelphia: Kruk (1). **SB—** Philadelphia: Hollins (1). **CS—** Atlanta: Nixon (2). **A—**52,032.
Recap: Atlanta's five-run fifth broke open a tight game and chased Philadelphia starter Terry Mulholland.

GAME 4

Philadelphia	0	0	0	2	0	0	0	0	0—2
Atlanta	0	1	0	0	0	0	0	0	0—1

WP—Jackson. **LP—**Smoltz. **S—**Williams. **E—**Philadelphia: Williams (1); Atlanta: Lemke (1). **LOB—**Philadelphia 15, Atlanta 11. **2B—** Philadelphia: Thompson (1); Atlanta: McGriff (2), Pendleton (1), Lemke (2). **CS—**Atlanta: Gant (1). **S—**Atlanta: Nixon (2). **SF—**Philadelphia: Stocker. **GIDP—**Atlanta: Gant. **A—**52,032.
Recap: Danny Jackson shut down the Atlanta offense, allowing just one run over 7⅔ innings, then provided some offense of his own, driving in what proved to be the decisive run in the fourth inning.

National League Championship Series *(Cont.)*

GAME 5

Philadelphia	1	0	0	1	0	0	0	0	1	1—4
Atlanta	0	0	0	0	0	0	0	3	0—3	

WP—Williams. **LP**—Wohlers. **S**—Andersen. **BS**—Williams. **E**—Philadelphia: Batiste (2); Atlanta: Gant (1). **LOB**—Philadelphia 5, Atlanta 6. **2B**—Philadelphia: Kruk (2). **HR**—Philadelphia: Dykstra (2), Daulton (1). **S**—Philadelphia: Schilling. **SF**—Philadelphia: Chamberlain; Atlanta: Justice. **A**—52,032.

Recap: Curt Schilling tossed eight scoreless, four-hit innings at Atlanta, only to watch his three-run lead disappear as a Kim Batiste error and ineffective pitching by Mitch Williams allowed the Braves to tie the game in the ninth. Fortunately for the Phillie faithful, Lenny Dykstra drove a ball deep into the centerfield seats in the tenth for the game-winning margin.

GAME 6

Atlanta	0	0	0	0	1	0	2	0	0—3	
Philadelphia	0	0	2	0	2	2	0	0	x—6	

WP—Greene. **LP**—Maddux. **S**—Williams. **E**—Atlanta: Justice (1), Lemke (2), Maddux (1); Philadelphia: Thompson (1). **LOB**—Atlanta 6, Philadelphia 9. **2B**—Philadelphia: Daulton (1). **3B**—Philadelphia: Morandini (1). **HR**—Atlanta: Blauser (2); Philadelphia: Hollins (2). **S**—Atlanta: Maddux (2); Philadelphia: Greene (2). **GIDP**—Atlanta: Berryhill. **A**—62,502.

Recap: Darren Daulton hit a two-run double that was fair by inches in the third, Dave Hollins homered in the fifth and, an inning later, Mickey Morandini tripled in two more. Tommy Greene atoned for his Game 2 showing with seven strong innings, and Wild Thing Williams closed with uncharacteristic ease.

American League Championship Series

GAME 1

Toronto	0	0	0	2	3	0	2	0	0—7	
Chicago	0	0	0	3	0	0	0	0	0—3	

WP—Guzman. **LP**—McDowell. **E**—Toronto: Olerud (1); Chicago: Cora (1). **LOB**—Toronto 12, Chicago 13. **2B**—Toronto: Olerud (1); Chicago: Burks (1). **3B** — Toronto: Sprague **HR**—Toronto: Molitor (1). **SB**—Chicago: Raines (1), Guillen (1). **CS**— Chicago: Raines (1). **A**—46,246.

Recap: Paul Molitor went 4-for-5 with three RBIs, John Olerud added three hits and three RBIs and Toronto starter Juan Guzman overcame his own control problems to post the win for the Blue Jays.

GAME 2

Toronto	1	0	0	2	0	0	0	0	0—3	
Chicago	1	0	0	0	0	0	0	0	0—1	

WP—Stewart. **LP**—Fernandez. **S**—D. Ward **E**—Chicago: Cora (2), Pasqua (1). **LOB**—Toronto 6, Chicago 10. **2B**—Toronto: Molitor (1); Chicago: Johnson (1). **GIDP**—Toronto: Alomar, Sprague; Chicago: Johnson. **A**—46,101.

Recap: Toronto's Dave Stewart, Mr. October of the mound, recovered from first inning wildness and cruised through the sixth, fanning five. His Chicago counterpart, Alex Fernandez, pitched well for eight, but two unearned runs made the difference.

GAME 3

Chicago	0	0	5	1	0	0	0	0	0—6	
Toronto	0	0	1	0	0	0	0	0	0—1	

WP—Alvarez. **LP**—Hentgen. **E**—Toronto: Henderson (1). **LOB**—Chicago 10, Toronto 5. **2B**—Chicago: Raines (2); Toronto: Henderson (1). **SB**—Chicago Johnson (1); Toronto Henderson (1). **CS**—Chicago: Burks (1); Toronto: White (1). **S**—Chicago: Cora. **SF**—Chicago: Ventura. **GIDP**—Toronto: Sprague, Fernandez. **A**—51,783.

Recap: Coming to the White Sox' rescue was Wilson Alvarez, who pitched a complete game, allowing just one hit and two baserunners in the last five innings.

GAME 4

Chicago	0	2	0	0	0	3	1	0	1	—7
Toronto	0	0	3	0	0	1	0	0	0	—4

WP—Belcher. **LP**—Stottlemyre. **S**—Hernandez. **LOB**—Chicago 7, Toronto 11. **2B**—Toronto: Alomar. **3B**— Toronto: White (1); Chicago: Johnson (1). **HR**—Chicago: Thomas (1), Johnson (1). **GIDP**—Chicago: Burks. **A**—51,889.

Recap: Chicago's Lance Johnson homered and drove in four runs and five different pitchers contained the Blue Jays after their three-run outburst against Chicago starter Jason Bere in the third inning.

GAME 5

Chicago	0	0	0	0	1	0	0	0	2—3	
Toronto	1	1	1	1	0	0	1	0	x—5	

WP—Guzman. **LP**—McDowell. **E**—Chicago: McDowell (1). **LOB**—Toronto 12, Chicago 3. **2B**—Toronto: Henderson (2), White (1), Molitor (1). **HR**—Chicago: Ventura (1), Burks (1). **SB**—Toronto: Henderson (2), Alomar (3) Borders (1). **CS**—Toronto: Henderson (1). **GIDP**—Toronto: Olerud, Alomar; Chicago: Guillen. **A**—51,375.

Recap: Using his tricky changeup and wicked slider, Juan Guzman kept Chicago guessing, while the Sox' Jack McDowell flopped again, allowing Toronto to win their first game at home.

GAME 6

Toronto	0	2	0	1	0	0	0	0	3—6	
Chicago	0	0	2	0	0	0	0	0	1—3	

WP—Stewart. **LP**—Fernandez. **S**—D. Ward. **E**—Chicago: Cora (3), Ventura (1), Radinsky (1). **LOB**—Toronto 10, Chicago 7. **2B**—Toronto: Borders (1); Chicago: Guillen (1). **3B**—Toronto: Molitor (1). **HR**—Toronto: White (1), Chicago: Newson (1). **SB**—Toronto: Alomar (4). **A**—45,527.

Recap: A two-run triple from Molitor, a solo HR from White and another strong performance from Dave Stewart produced Toronto's second straight AL crown.

Composite Box Scores

National League Championship Series

ATLANTA

BATTING	AB	R	H	HR	RBI	Avg
Bream............1	1	1	0	0	1.000
Cabrera..........3	0	2	0	1	.667
Avery 4	1	2	0	0	.500
McGriff 23	6	10	1	4	.435
Nixon 23	3	8	0	4	.348
Pendleton 26	4	9	1	5	.346
Olson 3	0	1	0	0	.333
Pecota 3	1	1	0	0	.333
Blauser 25	5	7	2	4	.280
Maddux 4	1	1	0	0	.250
Berryhill 19	2	4	1	3	.211
Lemke 24	2	5	0	4	.208
Gant 27	4	5	0	3	.185
Justice 21	2	3	0	4	.143
5 others 8	1	0	0	0	.000
Totals...........215	33	59	5	32	.274

PITCHING	G	IP	H	BB	SO	ERA
Smoltz 1	6⅓	8	5	10	0.00
Stanton 1	1	1	1	0	0.00
Mercker 5	5	3	2	4	1.80
Glavine 1	7	6	0	5	2.57
Avery 2	13	9	6	10	2.77
Wohlers 4	5⅓	2	3	10	3.38
Maddux 2	12⅔	11	7	11	4.97
McMichael........4	4	7	2	1	6.75
Totals................6	55	59	22	54	4.75

PHILADELPHIA

BATTING	AB	R	H	HR	RBI	Avg
Batiste 1	0	1	0	1	1.000
Chamberlain....11	1	4	0	1	.364
Dykstra 25	5	7	2	2	.280
Duncan...........15	3	4	0	0	.267
Daulton 19	2	5	1	3	.263
Jackson............4	0	1	0	1	.250
Kruk................24	4	6	1	5	.250
Morandini 16	1	4	0	2	.250
Thompson 13	2	3	0	0	.231
Hollins 20	2	4	2	4	.200
Stocker 22	0	4	0	1	.182
Incaviglia 12	2	2	1	1	.167
Eisenreich 15	0	2	0	1	.133
6 others 10	1	0	0	0	.000
Totals.............207	23	47	7	22	.227

PITCHING	G	IP	H	BB	SO	ERA
Mason 2	3	1	0	2	0.00
Jackson............1	7⅔	9	2	6	1.17
Schilling 2	16	11	5	19	1.69
Williams 4	5⅓	6	2	5	1.69
Rivera 1	2	1	1	2	4.50
Thigpen 2	1⅔	1	1	3	5.40
Mulholland........1	5	9	1	2	7.20
Greene 2	9⅓	12	7	7	9.64
West 3	2⅔	5	2	1	13.50
Andersen..........3	2⅓	4	1	3	15.43
Totals................6	55	59	22	54	4.75

Deconstructing Darryl

Darryl Strawberry was in hot water for insensitive remarks he made about last year's devastating fires in Southern California, not the first time that the Strawman has suffered from foot-in-mouth disease. However, we feel that the young millionaire, a former New York Met and Los Angeles Dodger outfielder who now plays for San Francisco, has often been misunderstood and truly wants to be, as he once said, "the type of person not to hassle things." To that end, here is our attempt to interpret a few of Darryl's more memorable lines.

• What Darryl said: "I'll punch that little redneck in the face."

What Darryl meant to say: *"I admire Wally Backman's colorful cultural background, but we have our differences."*

• What Darryl said: "Sometimes I wanted to say to those guys, 'Come on Mex, come on, Kid. Get your head out of your ass. We're in a pennant race.'"

What Darryl meant to say: *"I bow to no man in my respect for Keith Hernandez and Gary Carter. But perhaps their concentration level was not what it should have been."*

• What Darryl said: "And the manager, nobody could figure out some of the stuff he was doing all season."

What Darryl meant to say: *"Davey Johnson is a fine person, but we were not always on the same page when it came to running the Mets."*

• What Darryl said: "God brought me back home for a reason."

What Darryl meant to say: *"I love L.A."*

• What Darryl said: "Let it keep burning, because I don't live there anymore. Let it burn down."

What Darryl meant to say: *"While I have fond memories of my boyhood home, one cannot wallow in nostalgia."*

American League Championship Series

TORONTO

BATTING	AB	R	H	HR	RBI	Avg
White	27	3	12	1	2	.444
Molitor	23	7	9	1	5	.391
Olerud	23	5	8	0	3	.348
T. Fernandez	2	1	7	0	1	.318
Alomar	24	3	7	0	4	.292
Sprague	21	0	6	0	4	.286
Carter	27	2	7	0	2	.259
Borders	24	1	6	0	3	.250
Henderson	25	4	3	0	0	.120
Totals...........	216	26	65	2	24	.301

PITCHING	G	IP	H	BB	SO	ERA
Cox..................	2	5	3	2	5	0.00
Castillo	2	2	0	1	1	0.00
Eichhorn	1	2	1	1	1	0.00
Stewart	2	13⅓	8	8	8	2.03
Guzman..........	2	13	8	9	9	2.08
Leiter	2	2⅔	4	2	2	3.38
Timlin	1	2⅓	3	0	2	3.86
Ward.............	4	4⅔	4	3	8	5.79
Stottlemyre	1	6	6	4	4	7.50
Hentgen	1	3	9	2	3	18.00
Totals..............	6	54	46	32	43	3.67

CHICAGO

BATTING	AB	R	H	HR	RBI	Avg
Grebeck	1	0	1	0	0	1.000
Raines	27	5	12	0	1	.444
Thomas	17	2	6	1	3	.353
LaValliere	3	0	1	0	0	.333
Burks	23	4	7	1	3	.304
Guillen	22	4	6	0	2	.273
Johnson..........	23	2	5	1	6	.217
Ventura	20	2	4	1	5	.200
Newson	5	1	1	1	1	.200
Cora	22	1	3	0	1	.136
Karkovice	15	0	0	0	0	.000
Jackson	10	1	0	0	0	.000
Pasqua	6	1	0	0	0	.000
Totals...........	194	23	46	5	22	.237

PITCHING	G	IP	H	BB	SO	ERA
Hernandez	4	4	4	0	1	0.00
McCaskill.........	3	3⅔	3	1	3	0.00
Alvarez	1	9	7	2	6	1.00
A. Fernandez.....	2	15	15	6	10	1.80
DeLeon	2	4⅔	7	1	6	1.93
Belcher	1	3⅔	3	3	1	2.45
Radinsky	4	1⅔	3	1	1	10.80
McDowell.........	2	9	18	5	5	10.00
Bere.................	1	2⅓	5	2	3	11.57
Totals..............	6	53	65	21	36	3.57

1993 World Series

Oct 16 .... Philadelphia 5 vs. Toronto 8
Oct 17 .... Philadelphia 6 vs. Toronto 4
Oct 19 .... Toronto 10 vs. Philadelphia 3
Oct 20 .... Toronto 15 vs. Philadelphia 14
Oct. 21 .... Toronto 0 vs. Philadelphia 2
Oct. 23 .... Philadelphia 6 vs. Toronto 8

(Toronto wins series 4-2.)

GAME 1 (AT TORONTO)

Philadelphia	2	0	1	0	1	0	0	0	1—5
Toronto	0	2	1	0	1	1	3	0	x—8

WP—Leiter. **LP**—Schilling. **S**—D. Ward. **E**—Philadelphia: Thompson (1); Toronto: Alomar (1), Carter (1), Sprague (1). **LOB**—Philadelphia 11, Toronto 4. **2B**—Toronto: White (1), Alomar (1). **3B**—Philadelphia: Duncan (1). **HR**—Toronto: White (1), Olerud (1). **SB**—Philadelphia: Dykstra (1), Duncan (1); Toronto: Alomar (1). **CS**—Toronto: Fernandez (1). **GIDP**—Philadelphia: Thompson; Toronto: White. **Recap:** The offense to come in this series was foreshadowed in Game 1 as the two teams battered each other's starters early. John Olerud wristed a home run in the sixth, giving the Jays a 5–4 lead, to which they added three in the seventh. Al Leiter and Duane Ward silenced the Phillie bats in closing. **T**—3:27. **A**—52,011.

GAME 2 (AT TORONTO)

Philadelphia	0	0	5	0	0	0	1	0	0—6
Toronto	0	0	0	2	0	1	0	1	0—4

WP—Mulholland. **LP**—Stewart. **Save**—Williams. **LOB**—Philadelphia 9, Toronto 5. **2B**—Toronto: White (2), Molitor (1), Fernandez (1). **HR**—Philadelphia: Dykstra (1), Eisenreich (1); Toronto: Carter. (1) **SB**—Toronto: Molitor (1), Alomar (2). **CS**— Philadelphia: Stocker (1); Toronto: Henderson (1), Alomar (1). **Recap:** In the third inning with two men on base, Jim

Eisenreich hit an 0–2 pitch over the fence in right-center to power Philadelphia to an early 5–0 lead. Toronto chipped away until Mitch Williams allowed two baserunners in the eighth, then caught Roberto Alomar in a foolish attempt to steal third. Williams earned the save by inducing a game-ending double-play grounder from Pat Borders. **T**—3:35. **A**—52,062.

GAME 3 (AT PHILADELPHIA)

Toronto	3	0	1	0	0	1	3	0	2—10
Philadelphia	0	0	0	0	1	1	0	1	0—3

WP—Hentgen. **LP**—Jackson. **E**—Toronto: Carter (2). **LOB**—Toronto 7, Philadelphia 9. **2B**—Toronto: Henderson (1); Philadelphia: Kruk (1). **3B**— Toronto: White (1), Molitor (1), Alomar (1). **HR**—Toronto: Molitor (1); Philadelphia: Thompson (1). **SB**—Toronto: Alomar (3). **SF**—Toronto: Sprague, Fernandez, Carter. **GIDP**—Philadelphia: Hollins, Chamberlain. **Recap:** Using a total of 13 hits from six different batters, Toronto pounded the Phillies in rainy, chilly Veterans Stadium to take a 2–1 series lead. Roberto Alomar, making up for his baserunning gaffe in Game 2, went 4-for-5 with 2 RBI. **T**—3:16 (plus 1:12 rain delay in first). **A**—62,689.

1993 World Series (Cont.)

GAME 4 (AT PHILADELPHIA)

Toronto	3 0 4 0 0 2 0 6 0—15
Philadelphia	4 2 0 1 5 1 1 0 0—14

WP—Castillo; **LP**—Williams; **Save**—D. Ward. **LOB**—Toronto 10, Philadelphia 8. **2B**—Toronto: Henderson (2), White (3), Carter (1), A. Leiter (1); Philadelphia: Dykstra (1), Hollins (1), Thompson (1). **3B**— Toronto: White (2); Philadelphia: Thompson (1) **HR**—Philadelphia: Dykstra 2 (3), Daulton (1) **SB**—Toronto: Henderson (1), White (1); Philadelphia: Dykstra (2), Duncan (2).

Recap: The highest scoring game in the 532-game history of the World Series, this four-hour, 14-minute, rain-sprinkled slugfest set or tied 13 Series records. Pitchers appeared to be throwing batting practice, surrendering 31 hits, including seven doubles. Trailing 14–9 in the eighth, the Blue Jays scored half-a-dozen runs off relievers Larry Andersen and Mitch Williams to take the outrageous affair.
T—4:14. **A**—62,731.

GAME 5 (AT PHILADELPHIA)

Toronto	0 0 0 0 0 0 0 0 0—0
Philadelphia	1 1 0 0 0 0 0 0 0—2

WP—Schilling; **LP**—Guzman. **E**—Toronto: Borders (1); Philadelphia: Duncan (1). **LOB**—Toronto 6, Philadelphia 8. **2B**—Philadelphia: Daulton (1), Stocker (1); Toronto: Borders (2). **SB**—Philadelphia: Dykstra (3). **CS**—Toronto: Alomar (2). **GIDP**—Toronto: Alomar, Guzman; Philadelphia: Duncan.

Recap: Night to the previous game's day, this game saw the ever-reliable Phillie pitcher Curt Schilling put out the Toronto offensive fire with a complete game,

five-hit shutout, staving off elimination for Philadelphia.
T—2:53. **A**—62,706

GAME 6 (AT TORONTO)

Philadelphia	0 0 0 1 0 0 5 0 0—6
Toronto	3 0 0 1 1 0 0 0 3—8

WP—D. Ward; **LP**—Williams; **Blown Save**—Philadelphia: Willams, 2; Toronto: Cox,1. **E**—Toronto: Alomar (2), Sprague (2). **LOB**—Philadelphia 9, Toronto 7. **2B**—Philadelphia: Daulton (2); Toronto: Olerud (1), Alomar (2). **3B**—Toronto: Molitor (2). **HR**—Toronto: Molitor (2), Carter (2). Philadelphia: Dykstra (4). **SB**—Philadelphia: Dykstra (4), Duncan (3); **SF**—Philadelphia: Incaviglia; Toronto: Sprague, Carter.

Recap: With one out in the bottom of the ninth and the Phillies leading 6–5, Joe Carter faced Mitch Williams with Paul Molitor on first and Rickey Henderson on second, 2–2 the count. He hit a low, inside fastball over the fence in left and, with fireworks detonating in the dome, made an ecstatic, leaping tour around the bases to deliver the Jays their second straight world title. It was only the second time in the 89-year history of the Fall Classic that a series had been ended by a home run.
T—3:27. **A**—52,195.

1993 World Series Composite Box Score

TORONTO

BATTING	AB	R	H	HR	RBI	Avg
Leiter	1	0	1	0	0	1.00
Molitor	24	10	12	2	8	.500
Butler	2	1	1	0	0	.500
Alomar	25	5	12	0	6	.480
Fernandez	21	2	7	0	9	.333
Borders	23	2	7	0	1	.304
White	24	6	7	1	7	.292
Carter	25	6	7	2	8	.280
Olerud	17	5	4	1	2	.235
Henderson	22	6	5	0	2	.227
Sprague	15	0	1	0	2	.867
4 others	7	0	0	0	0	.000
Totals	206	45	64	6	45	.311

PITCHING	G	IP	H	BB	SO	ERA
Timlin	2	2⅓	2	0	4	0.00
Eichhorn	1	⅓	1	1	0	0.00
Hentgen	1	6	5	3	6	1.50
Ward	4	4⅔	3	0	7	1.93
Guzman	2	12	10	8	12	3.75
Stewart	2	12	10	8	8	6.75
Leiter	3	7	12	2	5	7.71
Castillo	2	3⅓	6	3	1	8.10
Cox	3	3⅓	6	5	6	8.10
Stottlemyre	1	2	3	4	1	27.00
Totals	6	53	58	34	50	5.77

PHILADELPHIA

BATTING	AB	R	H	HR	RBI	Avg
Greene	1	1	1	0	0	1.000
Schilling	2	0	1	0	0	.500
Dykstra	23	9	8	4	8	.348
Kruk	23	4	8	0	4	.348
Duncan	29	5	10	0	2	.345
Thompson	16	3	5	1	6	.313
Hollins	23	5	6	0	2	.261
Eisenreich	26	3	6	1	7	.231
Daulton	23	4	5	1	4	.217
Stocker	19	1	4	0	1	.211
Jordan	10	0	2	0	0	.200
Morandini	5	1	1	0	1	.200
Incaviglia	8	0	1	0	1	.125
3 others	4	0	0	0	0	.000
Totals	212	36	58	7	35	.274

PITCHING	G	IP	H	BB	SO	ERA
Thigpen	2	2⅔	1	1	0	0.00
Mason	4	7⅔	4	1	7	1.17
Schilling	2	15⅓	13	5	9	3.52
Mulholland	2	10⅔	14	3	6	6.75
Jackson	1	5	6	1	1	7.20
Andersen	4	3⅔	5	3	3	12.27
Williams	3	2⅔	5	4	1	20.25
Greene	1	2⅓	7	4	1	27.00
Rivera	1	1⅓	4	2	3	27.00
West	3	1	5	1	0	27.00
Totals	6	52⅓	64	25	30	7.57

1994 Individual Leaders

National League Batting

BATTING AVERAGE
Gwynn, SD .... .394
Bagwell, Hou .... .368
Alou, Mtl .... .399
Morris, Cin .... .335
Mitchell, Cin .... .326
Jefferies, StL .... .325
Walker, Mtl .... .322
Boone, Cin .... .320
Roberts, SD .... .320
Conine, Fla .... .319

HITS
Gwynn, SD 165
Bagwell, Hou 147
Bichette, Col 147
Morris, Cin 146
Conine, Fla 144
Alou, Mtl 143
Biggio, Hou 139
Grissom, Mon 137
Bell, Pit 135
McGriff, Atl 135

TRIPLES
Butler, LA 9
Lewis, SF 9
Three tied with eight

ON-BASE PERCENTAGE
Gwynn, SD .... .454
Bagwell, Hou .... .451
Mitchell, Cin .... .429
Justice, Atl .... .427
Bonds, SF .... .426

HOME RUNS
Williams, SF 43
Bagwell, Hou 39
Bonds, SF 37
McGriff, Atl 34
Galarraga, Col 31
Mitchell, Cin 30
Bichette, Col 27
Sheffield, Fla 27

RUNS SCORED
Bagwell, Hou 104
Grissom, Mtl 96
Bonds, SF 89
Lankford, StL 89
Biggio, Hou 88
Alou, Mtl 81
McGriff, Atl 81

TOTAL BASES
Bagwell, Hou 300
Williams, SF 270
Bichette, Col 265
McGriff, Atl 264
Bonds, SF 253
Alou, Mtl 250

STOLEN BASES
Biggio, Hou 39
D. Sanders, Atl-Cin 38
Grissom, Mtl 36
Carr, Fla 32
Lewis, SF 30
Bonds, SF 29
Butler, LA 27
DeShields, LA 27

RUNS BATTED IN
Bagwell, Hou 116
Williams, SF 96
Bichette, Col 95
McGriff, Atl 94
Piazza, LA 92
Walker, Mtl 86
Galarraga, Col 85
Conine, Fla 82

DOUBLES
Biggio, Hou 44
Walker, Mtl 44
Bell, Pitt 35
Gwynn, SD 35
Bichette, Col 33

SLUGGING PERCENTAGE
Bagwell, Hou .... .750
Mitchell, Cin .... .681
Bonds, SF .... .647
McGriff, Atl .... .623
Williams, SF .... .607
Alou, Mtl .... .592
Galarraga, Col .... .592

BASES ON BALLS
Bonds, SF 74
Justice, Atl 69
Butler, LA 68
Dykstra, Phil 68
Bagwell, Hou 65
Larkin, Cin 64

National League Pitching

EARNED RUN AVERAGE
Maddux, Atl 1.56
Saberhagen, NY 2.74
Drabek, Hou 2.84
Fassero, Mtl 2.99
Reynolds, Hou 3.05
Rijo, Cn 3.08
Jones, NY 3.15

SAVES
Franco, NY 30
Beck, SF 28
Jones, Phil 27
Wetteland, Mtl 25
McMichael, Atl 21
Myers, Chi 21

WINS
Hill, Mtl 16
Maddux, Atl 16
Saberhagen, NY 14
Jackson, Phil 14
Glavine, Atl 13
Drabek, Hou 12

GAMES PITCHED
Reed, Col 61
Bautista, Chi 58
Rojas, Mtl 58
Burba, SF 57
Munoz, Col 57

STRIKEOUTS
Benes, SD 189
Rijo, Cin 171
Maddux, Atl 156
Saberhagen, NY 143
Martinez, Mtl 142
Glavine, Atl 140
Jackson, Phil 129

INNINGS PITCHED
Maddux, Atl 202
Jackson, Phil 179⅓
Saberhagen, NY 177⅓
Benes, SD 172⅔
Rijo, Cin 172½
Martinez, LA 170

COMPLETE GAMES
Maddux, Atl 10
Drabek, Hou 6
Candiotti, LA 5

SHUTOUTS
Maddux, Atl 3
R. Martinez, LA 3
Benes, SD 2
Drabek, Hou 2

American League Batting

BATTING AVERAGE

O'Neill, NY	.359
Belle, Clev.	.357
Thomas, Chi.	.353
Lofton, Clev.	.349
Boggs, NY	.342
Molitor, Tor.	.341
Clark, Tex.	.329
Griffey, Sea	.323
Palmeiro, Balt.	.319
Franco, Chi	.319

HITS

Lofton, Cle	160
Molitor, Tor.	155
Belle, Clev.	147
Thomas, Chi.	141
Griffey, Sea	140
Ripken, Balt	140
Baerga, Cle.	139
Knoblauch, Minn.	139
Palmeiro, Balt.	139
Puckett, Min	139

TRIPLES

L. Johnson, Chi.	14
Coleman, KC	12
Lofton, Clev.	9
Diaz, Mil	7

ON-BASE PERCENTAGE

Thomas, Chi.	.487
O'Neill, NY	.460
Belle, Clev.	.438
Boggs, NY	.433
Clark, Tex.	.431

HOME RUNS

Griffey, Sea	40
Thomas, Chi.	38
Belle, Cle	36
Canseco, Tex.	31
Fielder, Det	28
Carter, Tor.	27
Davis, Cal	26
Vaughn, Bos	26

RUNS SCORED

Thomas, Chi.	106
Lofton, Cle	105
Griffey, Sea	94
Phillips, Det.	91
Belle, Clev.	90
Canseco, Tex.	88
Molitor, Tor.	86
Knoblauch, Minn.	85
Palmeiro, Balt.	82

TOTAL BASES

Belle, Clev.	294
Griffey, Sea	292
Thomas, Chi.	291
Lofton, Clev.	246
Palmeiro, Balt.	240
Canseco, Tex.	237
Puckett, Minn.	237

STOLEN BASES

Lofton, Cle	60
Coleman, KC	50
Nixon, Bos	42
Knoblauch, Minn.	35
Anderson, Balt.	31

RUNS BATTED IN

Puckett, Minn.	112
Carter, Tor.	103
Belle, Cle	101
Thomas, Chi.	101
Franco, Chi	98
Sierra, Oak.	92
Canseco, Tex.	90
Fielder, Det	90
Griffey, Sea.	90

DOUBLES

Knoblauch, Minn.	45
Belle, Clev.	35
Fryman, Det	34
Thomas, Chi.	34

SLUGGING PERCENTAGE

Thomas, Chi.	.729
Belle, Clev.	.714
Griffey, Sea	.674
O'Neill, NY	.603
Hamelin, KC	.599
Vaughn, Bos	.576

BASES ON BALLS

Thomas, Chi.	109
Tettleton, Det	97
Phillips, Det.	95
Henderson, Oak	72
O'Neill, NY	72

American League Pitching

EARNED RUN AVERAGE

Ontiveros, Oak.	2.65
Clemens, Bos	2.85
Cone, KC	2.94
Mussina, Balt	3.06
Johnson, Sea	3.19
Key, NY	3.27

SAVES

L. Smith, Balt.	33
Montgomery, KC	27
Aguilera, Minn.	23
Eckersley, Oak.	19
Ayala, Sea.	18

WINS

Key, NY	17
Cone, KC	16
Mussina, Balt	16
McDonald, Balt	14
Johnson, Sea	13
Hentgen, Tor	13
Bere, Chi	12
Alvarez, Chi	12
Guzman, Tor	12

GAMES PITCHED

Wickman, NY	53
Mesa, Clev.	51
Brewer, KC	50
Guthrie, Minn	50

STRIKEOUTS

Johnson, Sea	204
Clemens, Bos	168
Finley, Cal	148
Hentgen, Tor	147
Appier, KC	145
Cone, KC	132

INNINGS PITCHED

Finley, Cal	183⅓
McDowell, Chi	181
Eldred, Mil.	179
Martinez, Clev	176⅔
Mussina, Balt	176⅓
Hentgen, Tor	174⅔

COMPLETE GAMES

Johnson, Sea	9
Finley, Cal	7
Martinez, Clev	7

SHUTOUTS

Johnson, Sea	4
Cone, KC	3
Fernandez, Chi	3
Hentgen, Tor	3
Martinez, Clev	3
Witt, Oak	3

1994 Team Statistics

National League

TEAM BATTING	BA	AB	R	H	TB	2B	3B	HR	RBI	SB	BB	SO
Cincinnati	.286	3966	609	1135	1789	210	36	124	569	119	386	731
Montreal	.279	3971	585	1106	1735	245	30	108	542	136	377	669
Houston	.278	3920	596	1090	1745	249	25	119	568	124	389	710
Colorado	.275	3976	573	1095	1754	206	39	125	540	91	378	757
San Diego	.273	4026	471	1100	1610	199	19	91	437	79	317	754
Los Angeles	.271	3872	530	1050	1607	159	28	114	503	74	363	674
Atlanta	.265	3813	529	1011	1645	195	17	135	498	48	375	662
Florida	.265	3896	462	1031	1531	178	23	92	445	65	347	742
St Louis	.263	3873	527	1017	1594	213	26	104	498	76	432	682
Philadelphia	.262	3875	519	1017	1519	206	28	80	482	67	391	705
Chicago	.259	3918	500	1015	1583	189	26	109	464	69	364	750
Pittsburgh	.258	3830	462	990	1472	196	23	80	433	50	349	719
New York	.251	3815	505	957	1509	162	21	116	476	25	335	796
San Francisco	.249	3869	504	963	1555	159	32	123	472	114	364	719

TEAM PITCHING	ERA	W	L	Sho	CG	SV	Inn	H	R	ER	BB	SO
Montreal	3.55	74	39	8	4	46	$1028\frac{2}{3}$	959	450	406	288	799
Atlanta	3.60	67	46	7	15	26	$1017\frac{1}{3}$	926	448	407	378	861
Cincinnati	3.79	66	47	6	6	27	$1029\frac{1}{2}$	1032	488	434	336	786
Philadelphia	3.90	53	61	6	7	30	$1009\frac{1}{4}$	1019	496	437	376	688
Houston	3.93	66	48	6	9	29	$1020\frac{2}{3}$	1026	495	446	365	731
San Francisco	3.99	55	60	4	2	33	$1025\frac{1}{2}$	1014	500	454	372	655
San Diego	4.06	46	70	6	8	26	$1036\frac{2}{3}$	999	525	468	388	854
New York	4.18	55	57	3	7	35	$1008\frac{1}{3}$	1058	524	468	327	634
Los Angeles	4.21	57	56	4	13	20	1005	1034	509	470	352	725
Florida	4.46	51	63	7	5	30	$1007\frac{2}{3}$	1060	568	499	426	645
Chicago	4.47	49	64	5	5	27	$1023\frac{2}{3}$	1054	549	508	392	717
Pittsburgh	4.68	52	61	1	7	24	$996\frac{1}{3}$	1089	580	518	368	650
Colorado	5.09	53	63	5	4	28	1022	1165	625	578	446	697
St Louis	5.12	52	61	7	7	28	1011	1142	615	575	353	628

American League

TEAM BATTING	BA	AB	R	H	TB	2B	3B	HR	RBI	SB	BB	SO
New York	.291	3939	663	1146	1827	235	16	138	626	55	526	651
Cleveland	.290	4022	679	1165	1946	240	20	167	647	131	382	629
Chicago	.287	3942	633	1133	1749	175	39	121	602	77	497	568
Texas	.280	3983	613	1114	1738	198	27	124	582	82	437	730
Minnesota	.276	3952	594	1092	1686	239	23	103	556	94	359	635
Baltimore	.272	3856	589	1047	1689	185	20	139	557	69	438	655
Toronto	.269	3913	568	1052	1655	208	28	113	527	78	381	682
Kansas City	.269	3911	574	1051	1638	211	38	100	538	140	376	698
Seattle	.268	3848	561	1033	1732	210	18	151	541	47	369	646
Detroit	.265	3925	647	1039	1785	216	25	160	617	46	514	890
California	.264	3943	543	1042	1612	178	16	120	518	65	402	715
Boston	.263	3940	552	1038	1658	222	19	120	523	81	404	723
Milwaukee	.262	3940	537	1032	1602	234	21	98	502	59	413	679
Oakland	.261	3855	548	1005	1547	177	13	113	514	91	416	671

TEAM PITCHING	ERA	W	L	Sho	CG	SV	Inn	H	R	ER	BB	SO
Chicago	3.96	67	46	9	13	20	$1011\frac{1}{2}$	964	498	445	377	754
Kansas City	4.23	64	51	6	5	38	$1031\frac{2}{3}$	1018	532	485	392	717
Baltimore	4.31	63	49	4	13	37	$997\frac{2}{3}$	1005	497	478	351	666
New York	4.34	70	42	2	8	31	$1006\frac{3}{4}$	1033	526	485	392	647
Cleveland	4.36	66	47	5	17	21	$1018\frac{2}{3}$	1097	562	494	404	666
Milwaukee	4.62	52	62	3	11	23	1027	1062	581	527	415	570
Toronto	4.70	54	60	4	13	26	1012	1044	572	528	478	823
Oakland	4.77	51	62	9	12	23	$994\frac{1}{2}$	967	581	527	507	726
Boston	4.93	54	61	3	6	30	$1029\frac{1}{2}$	1104	621	564	450	729
Seattle	5.03	48	63	7	12	21	975	1047	615	545	485	748
Detroit	5.35	53	61	1	15	20	1009	1126	661	600	445	559
California	5.42	47	68	4	11	21	1027	1149	660	618	436	682
Texas	5.45	52	62	4	10	26	1023	1176	697	620	394	683
Minnesota	5.68	53	60	4	6	29	1005	1197	688	634	388	602s

Atlanta Braves

BATTING

BATTING	BA	G	AB	R	H	TB	2B	3B	HR	RBI	SB	BB	SO
McGriff, Fred	.318	113	424	81	135	264	25	1	34	94	7	50	76
Justice, David	.313	104	352	61	110	187	16	2	19	59	2	69	45
Lemke, Mark	.294	104	350	40	103	127	15	0	3	31	0	38	37
Kelly, Roberto	.293	110	434	73	127	183	23	3	9	45	19	35	71
Klesko, Ryan	.278	92	245	42	68	138	13	3	17	47	1	26	48
Kelly, Mike	.273	30	77	14	21	39	10	1	2	9	0	2	17
Tarasco, Tony	.273	87	132	16	36	57	6	0	5	19	5	9	17
Blauser, Jeff	.258	96	380	56	98	145	21	4	6	45	1	38	64
Pendleton, Terry	.252	77	309	25	78	123	18	3	7	30	2	12	57
Lopez, Javy	.245	80	277	27	68	116	9	0	13	35	0	17	61
O'Brien, Charlie	.243	51	152	24	37	72	11	0	8	28	0	15	24
Beillard, Rafael	.242	46	120	9	29	38	7	1	0	9	0	2	29
Gallagher, Dave	.224	89	152	27	34	45	5	0	2	14	0	22	17
Pecota, Bill	.214	64	112	11	24	35	5	0	2	16	1	16	16

PITCHING

PITCHING	ERA	W	L	G	GS	CG	SV	INN	H	R	ER	BB	SO
Maddux, Greg	1.56	16	6	25	25	10	0	202	150	44	35	31	156
Bedrosian, Steve	3.33	0	2	46	0	0	0	46	41	20	17	18	43
Mercker, Kent	3.45	9	4	20	17	2	0	112⅓	90	46	43	45	111
Stanton, Mike	3.55	3	1	49	0	0	3	45⅔	41	18	18	26	35
McMichael, Greg	3.84	4	6	51	0	0	21	58⅔	66	29	25	19	47
Glavine, Tom	3.97	13	9	25	25	2	0	165⅓	173	76	73	70	140
Bielecki, Mike	4.00	2	0	19	1	0	0	27	28	12	12	12	18
Avery, Steve	4.04	8	3	24	24	1	0	151⅓	127	71	68	55	122
Smoltz, John	4.14	6	10	21	21	1	0	134⅔	120	69	62	48	113
Wohlers, Mark	4.59	7	2	51	0	0	1	51	51	35	26	33	58
Olson, Gregg	9.20	0	2	16	0	0	1	14⅔	19	15	15	13	10

Chicago Cubs

BATTING

BATTING	BA	G	AB	R	H	TB	2B	3B	HR	RBI	SB	BB	SO
Sosa, Sammy	.300	105	426	59	128	232	17	6	25	70	22	25	92
Grace, Mark	.298	106	403	55	120	167	23	3	6	44	0	48	41
Hill, Glenallen	.297	89	269	48	80	124	12	1	10	38	19	29	57
Sanchez, Rey	.285	96	291	26	83	98	13	1	0	24	2	20	29
May, Derrick	.284	100	345	43	98	145	19	2	8	51	3	30	34
Dunston, Shawon	.278	88	331	38	92	144	19	0	11	35	3	16	48
Maksudian, Mike	.269	26	26	6	7	9	2	0	0	4	0	10	4
Parent, Mark	.263	44	99	8	26	39	4	0	3	16	0	13	24
Zambrano, Eddie	.259	67	116	17	30	55	7	0	6	18	2	16	29
Hernandez, Jose	.242	56	132	18	32	43	2	3	1	9	2	8	29
Buechele, Steve	.242	104	339	33	82	137	11	1	14	52	1	39	80
Rhodes, Karl	.234	95	269	39	63	104	17	0	8	19	6	33	64
Wilkins, Rick	.227	100	313	44	71	121	25	2	7	39	4	40	86
Roberson, Kevin	.218	44	55	8	12	28	4	0	4	9	0	2	14
Haney, Todd	.162	17	37	6	6	9	0	0	1	2	2	3	3

PITCHING

PITCHING	ERA	W	L	G	GS	CG	SV	INN	H	R	ER	BB	SO
Foster, Steve	2.89	3	4	13	13	0	0	81	70	31	26	35	75
Trachsel, Steve	3.21	9	7	22	22	1	0	146	133	57	52	54	108
Bullinger, Jim	3.60	6	2	33	10	1	2	100	87	43	40	34	72
Myers, Randy	3.79	1	5	38	0	0	21	40½	40	18	17	16	32
Otto, Dave	3.80	0	1	36	0	0	0	45	49	20	19	22	19
Bautista, Jose	3.89	4	5	58	0	0	1	69½	75	30	30	17	45
Castillo, Frank	4.30	2	1	4	4	1	0	23	25	13	11	5	19
Crim, Chuck	4.48	5	4	49	1	0	2	64⅓	69	36	32	24	43
Pall, Donn	4.50	0	0	2	0	0	0	4	8	2	2	1	2
Plesac, Dan	4.61	2	3	54	0	0	1	54⅔	61	30	28	13	53
Bautista, Jose	4.32	1	0	15	0	0	1	16⅔	18	9	8	9	10
Banks, Willie	5.40	8	12	23	23	1	0	138½	139	88	83	56	91
Veres, Randy	5.59	1	1	10	0	0	0	9⅔	12	6	6	2	5
Morgan, Mike	6.69	2	10	15	15	1	0	80⅔	111	65	60	35	57
Guzman, Jose	9.15	2	2	4	4	0	0	19⅔	22	20	20	13	11

Cincinnati Reds

BATTING	BA	G	AB	R	H	TB	2B	3B	HR	RBI	SB	BB	SO
Morris, Hal	.335	112	436	60	146	214	30	4	10	78	6	34	62
Mitchell, Kevin	.326	95	310	57	101	211	18	1	30	77	2	59	62
Boone, Bret	.320	108	381	59	122	187	25	2	12	68	3	24	74
Brumfield, Jacob	.311	68	122	36	38	64	10	2	4	11	6	15	18
Harris, Lenny	.310	66	100	13	31	36	3	1	0	14	7	5	13
Walton, Jerome	.309	46	68	10	21	28	4	0	1	9	1	4	12
Branson, Jeff	.284	58	109	18	31	55	4	1	6	16	0	5	16
Taubensee, Eddie	.283	66	187	29	53	89	8	2	8	21	2	15	31
Sanders, Deion	.283	92	375	58	106	143	17	4	4	28	38	32	63
Fernandez, Tony	.279	104	366	50	102	156	18	6	8	50	12	44	40
Larkin, Barry	.279	110	427	78	119	179	23	5	9	52	26	64	58
Howard, Thomas	.264	83	178	24	47	73	11	0	5	24	4	10	30
Sanders, Reggie	.263	107	400	66	105	192	20	8	17	62	21	41	114
Dorsett, Brian	.245	76	216	21	53	76	8	0	5	26	0	21	33
Hunter, Brian	.234	85	256	34	60	123	16	1	15	57	0	17	56
Oliver, Joe	.211	6	19	1	4	7	0	0	1	5	0	2	3

PITCHING	ERA	W	L	G	GS	CG	SV	INN	H	R	ER	BB	SO
Carrasco, Hector	2.24	5	6	45	0	0	6	56⅓	42	17	14	30	41
McElroy, Chuck	2.34	1	2	52	0	0	5	57⅔	52	15	15	15	38
Brantley, Jeff	2.48	6	6	50	0	0	15	65⅓	46	20	18	28	63
Rijo, Jose	3.08	9	6	26	26	2	0	172⅓	177	73	59	52	171
Ruffin, Johnny	3.09	7	2	51	0	0	1	70	57	26	24	27	44
Smiley, John	3.86	11	10	24	24	1	0	158⅔	169	80	68	37	112
Schourek, Pete	4.09	7	2	22	10	0	0	81⅓	90	39	37	29	69
Hanson, Erik	4.11	5	5	22	21	0	0	122⅓	137	60	56	23	101
Browning, Tom	4.20	3	1	7	7	2	0	40⅔	34	20	19	13	22
Fortugno, Tim	4.20	1	0	25	0	0	0	30	32	14	14	14	29
Roper, John	4.50	6	2	16	15	0	0	92	90	49	46	30	51
Jarvis, Kevin	7.13	1	1	6	3	0	0	17⅔	22	14	14	5	10

Colorado Rockies

BATTING	BA	G	AB	R	H	TB	2B	3B	HR	RBI	SB	BB	SO
Kingery, Mike	.349	105	301	56	105	160	27	8	4	41	5	30	26
Castilla, Vinny	.331	52	130	16	43	65	11	1	3	18	2	7	23
Burks, Ellis	.322	42	149	33	48	101	8	3	13	24	3	16	39
Galarraga, Andres	.319	103	417	77	133	247	21	0	31	85	8	19	93
Bichette, Dante	.304	116	484	74	147	265	33	2	27	95	21	19	70
Hayes, Charlie	.288	113	423	46	122	183	23	4	10	50	3	36	71
Hubbard, Trenidad	.280	18	25	3	7	13	1	1	1	3	0	3	4
Girardi, Joe	.276	93	330	47	91	120	9	4	4	34	3	21	48
Young, Eric	.272	90	228	37	62	98	13	1	7	30	18	38	17
Liriano, Nelson	.255	87	255	39	65	101	17	5	3	31	0	42	44
Weiss, Walt	.251	110	423	58	106	128	11	4	1	32	12	56	58
VanderWal, John	.245	91	110	12	27	47	3	1	5	15	2	16	31
Sheaffer, Danny	.218	44	110	11	24	31	4	0	1	12	0	10	11
Johnson, Howard	.211	93	227	30	48	92	10	2	10	40	11	39	73

PITCHING	ERA	W	L	G	GS	CG	SV	INN	H	R	ER	BB	SO
Freeman, Marvin	2.80	10	2	19	18	0	0	112⅓	113	39	35	23	67
Munoz, Mike	3.74	4	2	57	0	0	1	45⅔	37	22	19	31	32
Reed, Steve	3.94	3	2	61	0	0	3	64	19	33	28	26	51
Ruffin, Bruce	4.04	4	5	56	0	0	16	55⅔	55	28	25	30	65
Czajkowski, Jim	4.15	0	0	5	0	0	0	8⅔	9	4	4	6	2
Nied, David	4.80	9	7	22	22	2	0	122	137	70	65	47	74
Reynoso, Armando	4.82	3	4	9	9	1	0	52⅓	54	30	28	22	25
Ritz, Kevin	5.62	5	6	15	15	0	0	73⅔	88	49	46	35	53
Harkey, Mike	5.79	1	6	24	13	0	0	91	125	61	59	35	39
Blair, Willie	5.79	0	5	47	1	0	3	77⅔	98	57	50	39	68
Painter, Lance	6.11	4	6	15	14	0	0	73⅔	91	51	50	26	41
Holmes, Darren	6.35	0	3	29	0	0	3	28⅓	35	25	20	24	33
Harris, Greg	6.65	3	12	29	19	1	1	130	154	99	96	52	82

Florida Marlins

BATTING	BA	G	AB	R	H	TB	2B	3B	HR	RBI	SB	BB	SO
Diaz, Mario	.325	32	77	10	25	33	4	2	0	11	0	6	6
Conine, Jeff	.319	115	451	60	144	237	27	6	18	82	1	40	92
Colbrunn, Greg	.303	47	155	17	47	75	10	0	6	31	1	9	27
Barberie, Bret	.301	107	372	40	112	151	20	2	5	31	2	23	65
Browne, Jerry	.295	101	329	42	97	131	17	4	3	30	3	52	23
Sheffield, Gary	.276	87	322	61	89	188	16	1	27	78	12	51	50
Natal, Bob	.276	10	29	2	8	10	2	0	0	2	1	5	5
Magadan, Dave	.275	74	211	30	58	68	7	0	1	17	0	39	25
Santiago, Benito	.273	101	337	35	92	143	14	2	11	41	1	25	57
Carr, Chuck	.263	106	433	61	114	143	19	2	2	30	32	22	71
Carrillo, Matias	.250	80	136	13	34	41	7	0	0	9	3	9	31
Abbott, Kurt	.249	101	345	41	86	136	17	3	9	33	3	16	98
Arias, Alex	.239	59	113	4	27	32	5	0	0	15	0	9	19
Renteria, Rich	.224	28	49	5	11	17	0	0	2	4	0	1	4
Everett, Carl	.216	16	51	7	11	18	1	0	2	6	4	3	15

PITCHING	ERA	W	L	G	GS	CG	SV	INN	H	R	ER	BB	SO
Hernandez, Jeremy	2.70	3	3	21	0	0	9	23⅓	16	9	7	14	13
Nen, Robb	2.95	5	5	44	0	0	15	58	46	20	19	17	60
Hammond, Chris	3.07	4	4	13	13	1	0	73⅓	79	30	25	23	40
Scheid, Rich	3.34	1	3	8	5	0	0	32⅓	35	18	12	8	17
Mathews, Terry	3.35	2	1	24	2	0	0	43	45	16	16	9	21
Perez, Yorkis	3.54	3	0	44	0	0	0	40⅔	33	18	16	14	41
Aquino, Luis	3.73	2	1	29	1	0	0	50⅓	39	22	21	22	22
Rapp, Pat	3.85	7	8	24	23	2	0	133⅓	132	67	57	69	75
Gardner, Mark	4.87	4	4	20	14	0	0	92⅓	97	53	50	30	57
Bowen, Ryan	4.94	1	5	8	8	1	0	47⅓	50	28	26	19	32
Hough, Charlie	5.15	5	9	21	21	1	0	113⅔	118	74	65	52	65
Harvey, Bryan	5.23	0	0	12	0	0	6	10⅓	12	6	6	4	10
Weathers, Dave	5.27	8	12	24	24	0	0	135	166	84	49	59	72
Lewis, Richie	5.67	1	4	45	0	0	0	54	62	44	34	38	45
Johnstone, John	5.91	1	2	17	0	0	0	21⅓	23	20	14	16	23

Houston Astros

BATTING	BA	G	AB	R	H	TB	2B	3B	HR	RBI	SB	BB	SO
Bagwell, Jeff	.368	110	400	104	147	300	32	2	39	116	15	65	65
Bream, Sid	.344	46	61	7	21	26	5	0	0	7	0	9	9
Miller, Orlando	.325	16	40	3	13	21	0	1	2	9	1	2	12
Biggio, Craig	.318	114	437	88	139	211	44	5	6	56	39	62	58
Bass, Kevin	.310	82	203	37	63	98	15	1	6	35	2	28	24
Eusebio, Tony	.296	55	159	18	47	73	9	1	5	30	0	8	33
Caminiti, Ken	.283	111	406	63	115	201	28	2	18	75	4	43	71
Finley, Steve	.276	94	373	64	103	162	16	5	11	33	13	28	52
Thompson, Milt	.274	96	241	34	66	85	7	0	4	33	9	24	30
Gonzalez, Luis	.273	112	392	57	107	168	29	4	8	67	15	49	57
Donnels, Chris	.267	54	86	12	23	37	5	0	3	5	1	13	18
Cedeno, Andujar	.263	98	342	38	90	143	26	0	9	49	1	29	79
Stankiewicz, Andy	.259	37	54	10	14	20	3	0	1	5	1	12	12
Mouton, James	.245	99	310	43	76	93	11	0	2	16	24	27	69
Felder, Mike	.239	58	117	10	28	34	2	2	0	13	3	4	12
Servais, Scott	.195	78	251	27	49	93	15	1	9	41	0	10	44

PITCHING	ERA	W	L	G	GS	CG	SV	INN	H	R	ER	BB	SO
Powell, Ross	1.23	0	0	12	0	0	0	7⅓	6	1	1	5	5
Veres, Dave	2.41	3	3	32	0	0	1	41	39	13	11	7	28
Jones, Todd	2.72	5	2	48	0	0	5	72⅔	52	23	22	26	63
Drabek, Doug	2.84	12	6	23	23	6	0	164⅔	132	58	52	45	121
Hudek, John	2.97	0	2	42	0	0	16	39⅓	24	14	13	18	39
Reynolds, Shane	3.05	8	5	33	14	0	0	124	128	46	42	21	110
Hampton, Mike	3.70	2	1	44	0	0	0	41⅓	46	19	17	16	24
Swindell, Greg	4.37	8	9	24	24	1	0	148⅓	175	80	72	26	74
Kile, Darryl	4.57	9	6	24	24	0	0	147⅔	153	84	75	82	105
Harnisch, Pete	5.40	8	5	17	17	1	0	95	100	59	57	39	62
Williams, Brian	5.74	6	5	20	13	0	0	78⅓	112	64	50	41	49

Los Angeles Dodgers

BATTING	BA	G	AB	R	H	TB	2B	3B	HR	RBI	SB	BB	SO
Hansen, Dave	.341	40	44	3	15	18	3	0	0	5	0	5	5
Piazza, Mike	.319	107	405	64	129	219	18	0	24	92	1	33	65
Butler, Brett	.314	111	417	79	131	186	13	9	8	33	27	68	52
Mondesi, Raul	.306	112	434	63	133	224	27	8	16	56	11	16	78
Treadway, Jeff	.299	52	67	14	20	23	3	0	0	5	1	5	8
Wallach, Tim	.280	113	414	68	116	208	21	1	23	78	0	46	80
Webster, Mitch	.274	82	84	16	23	39	4	0	4	12	1	8	13
Rodriguez, Henry	.268	104	306	33	82	124	14	2	8	49	0	17	58
Gwynn, Chris	.268	58	71	9	19	28	0	0	3	13	0	7	7
Karros, Eric	.266	111	406	51	108	173	21	1	14	46	2	29	53
DeShields, Delino	.250	89	320	51	80	103	11	3	2	33	27	54	53
Snyder, Cory	.235	73	153	18	36	60	6	0	6	18	1	14	47
Bournigal, Rafael	.224	40	116	2	26	31	3	1	0	11	0	9	5
Hernandez, Carlos	.219	32	64	6	14	22	2	0	2	6	0	4	14

PITCHING	ERA	W	L	G	GS	CG	SV	INN	H	R	ER	BB	SO
Seanez, Rudy	2.66	1	1	17	0	0	0	23⅔	24	7	7	9	18
Valdes, Ismael	3.18	3	1	21	1	0	0	28⅓	21	10	10	10	28
Daal, Omar	3.29	0	0	24	0	0	0	13⅔	12	5	5	5	9
Gross, Kevin	3.60	9	7	25	23	1	1	157⅓	162	64	63	43	124
Hershiser, Orel	3.79	6	6	21	21	1	0	135⅓	146	67	57	42	72
Martinez, Ramon	3.97	12	7	24	24	4	0	170	160	83	75	56	119
Candiotti, Tom	4.12	7	7	23	22	5	0	153	149	77	70	54	102
Worrell, Todd	4.29	6	5	38	0	0	11	42	37	21	20	12	44
Astacio, Pedro	4.29	6	8	23	23	3	0	149	142	77	71	47	108
McDowell, Roger	5.23	0	3	32	0	0	0	41⅓	50	25	24	22	29
Gott, Jim	5.94	5	3	37	0	0	2	36⅓	46	24	24	20	29

Montreal Expos

BATTING	BA	G	AB	R	H	TB	2B	3B	HR	RBI	SB	BB	SO
Alou, Moises	.339	107	422	81	143	250	31	5	22	78	7	42	63
Walker, Larry	.322	103	395	76	127	232	44	2	19	86	15	47	74
Cordero, Wilfredo	.294	110	415	65	122	203	30	3	15	63	41	62	16
Grissom, Marquis	.288	110	475	96	137	203	25	4	11	45	36	41	66
Floyd, Cliff	.281	100	334	43	94	133	19	4	4	41	10	24	63
Bell, Juan	.278	38	97	12	27	37	4	0	2	10	4	15	21
White, Rondell	.278	40	97	16	27	45	10	1	2	13	1	9	18
Berry, Sean	.278	103	320	43	89	145	19	2	11	41	14	32	50
Webster, Lenny	.273	57	143	13	39	64	10	0	5	23	0	16	24
Frazier, Lou	.271	76	140	25	38	43	3	1	0	14	20	18	23
Lansing, Mike	.266	106	394	44	105	145	21	2	5	35	12	30	37
Fletcher, Scott	.260	94	285	28	74	124	18	1	10	57	0	25	23
Spehr, Tim	.250	52	36	8	9	14	3	1	0	5	2	4	11
Milligan, Randy	.232	47	82	10	19	27	2	0	2	12	0	14	21
Benavides, Freddie	.188	47	85	8	16	23	5	1	0	6	0	3	15

PITCHING	ERA	W	L	G	GS	CG	SV	INN	H	R	ER	BB	SO
Henry, Butch	2.43	8	3	24	15	0	1	107⅓	97	30	29	20	70
Scott, Tim	2.70	5	2	40	0	0	1	53⅓	51	17	16	18	37
Wetteland, John	2.83	4	6	52	0	0	25	63⅔	46	22	20	21	68
Fassero, Jeff	2.99	8	6	21	21	1	0	138⅔	119	54	46	40	119
Hill, Ken	3.32	16	5	23	23	2	0	154⅔	145	61	57	44	85
Rojas, Mel	3.32	3	2	58	0	0	16	84	71	35	31	21	84
Martinez, Pedro	3.42	11	5	24	23	1	1	144⅔	115	58	55	45	142
Heredia, Gil	3.46	6	3	39	3	0	0	75⅓	85	34	29	13	62
Shaw, Jeff	3.88	5	2	46	0	0	1	67⅓	67	32	29	15	47
Rueter, Kirk	5.17	7	3	20	20	0	0	92⅓	106	60	53	23	50
White, Gabe	6.08	1	1	7	5	0	0	23⅔	24	16	16	11	17

New York Mets

BATTING	BA	G	AB	R	H	TB	2B	3B	HR	RBI	SB	BB	SO
Brogna, Rico	.351	39	131	16	46	82	11	2	7	20	1	6	29
Kent, Jeff	.292	107	415	53	121	197	24	5	14	68	1	23	84
Bonilla, Bobby	.290	108	403	60	117	203	24	1	20	67	1	55	101
Rivera, Luis	.279	32	43	11	12	25	2	1	3	5	0	4	14
Lindeman, Jim	.270	52	137	18	37	68	8	1	7	20	0	6	35
Orsulak, Joe	.260	96	292	39	76	103	3	0	8	42	4	16	21
Vizcaino, Jose	.256	103	410	47	105	133	13	3	3	33	1	33	62
McReynolds, Kevin	.256	51	180	23	46	73	11	2	4	21	2	20	34
Stinnett, Kelly	.253	47	150	20	38	54	6	2	2	14	2	11	28
Vina, Fernando	.250	79	124	20	31	37	6	0	0	6	3	12	11
Segui, David	.241	92	336	46	81	130	17	1	10	43	0	33	43
Burnitz, Jeromy	.238	45	143	26	34	47	4	0	3	15	1	23	45
Hundley, Todd	.237	91	291	45	69	129	10	1	16	42	2	25	73
Thompson, Ryan	.225	98	334	39	75	145	14	1	18	59	1	28	94
Bogar, Timothy	.154	50	52	5	8	14	0	0	2	5	1	4	11
McKnight, Jeff	.148	31	27	1	4	5	1	0	0	2	0	4	12

PITCHING	ERA	W	L	G	GS	CG	SV	INN	H	R	ER	BB	SO
Gunderson, Eric	0.00	0	0	14	0	0	0	9	5	0	0	4	4
Manzanillo, Josias	2.66	3	2	37	0	0	2	47⅓	34	15	14	13	48
Jacome, Jason	2.67	4	3	8	8	1	0	54	54	17	16	17	30
Franco, John	2.70	1	4	47	0	0	30	50	47	20	15	19	42
Saberhagen, Bret	2.74	14	4	24	24	4	0	177⅓	169	58	54	13	143
Jones, Bobby	3.15	12	7	24	24	1	0	160	157	75	56	56	80
Mason, Roger	3.75	3	5	47	0	0	1	60	55	29	25	25	33
Linton, Doug	4.47	6	2	32	3	0	0	50⅓	74	27	25	20	29
Remlinger, Mike	4.61	1	5	10	9	0	0	54⅔	55	30	28	35	33
Gozzo, Mauro	4.83	3	5	23	8	0	0	69	86	48	37	28	33
Maddux, Mike	5.11	2	1	27	0	0	2	44	45	25	25	13	32
Smith, Pete	5.55	4	10	21	21	1	0	131⅓	145	83	81	42	62
Gooden, Dwight	6.31	3	4	7	7	0	0	41⅓	46	32	29	15	40

Philadelphia Phillies

BATTING	BA	G	AB	R	H	TB	2B	3B	HR	RBI	SB	BB	SO
Ready, Randy	.381	17	42	5	16	20	1	0	1	3	0	8	6
Kruk, John	.302	75	255	35	77	109	17	0	5	38	4	42	51
Eisenreich, Jim	.300	104	290	42	87	122	15	4	4	43	6	33	31
Daulton, Darren	.300	69	257	43	77	141	17	1	15	56	4	33	43
Morandini, Mickey	.292	87	274	40	80	112	16	5	2	26	10	34	33
Jordan, Ricky	.282	72	220	29	62	104	14	2	8	37	0	6	32
Stocker, Kevin	.273	82	271	38	74	95	11	2	2	28	2	44	41
Dykstra, Lenny	.273	84	315	68	86	137	26	5	5	24	15	68	44
Duncan, Mariano	.268	88	347	49	93	141	22	1	8	48	10	17	72
Lieberthal, Mike	.266	24	79	6	21	29	3	1	1	5	0	3	5
Hatcher, Billy	.246	43	134	15	33	46	5	1	2	13	4	6	14
Longmire, Tony	.237	69	139	10	33	44	11	0	0	17	2	10	27
Batiste, Ken	.234	64	209	17	49	58	6	0	1	13	1	1	32
Incaviglia, Pete	.230	80	244	28	56	107	10	1	13	32	1	16	71
Hollins, Dave	.222	44	162	28	36	57	7	1	4	26	1	23	32
Pratt, Todd	.196	28	102	10	20	34	6	1	2	9	0	12	29

PITCHING	ERA	W	L	G	GS	CG	SV	INN	H	R	ER	BB	SO
Jones, Doug	2.17	2	4	47	0	0	27	54	55	14	13	6	38
Borland, Toby	2.36	1	0	24	0	0	1	34⅓	31	10	9	14	26
Munoz, Bobby	2.67	7	5	21	14	1	1	104½	101	40	31	35	59
Slocumb, Heathcliff	2.86	5	1	52	0	0	0	72½	75	32	23	28	58
Valenzuela, Fernando	3.00	1	2	8	7	0	0	45	42	16	15	7	19
Jackson, Danny	3.26	14	6	25	25	4	0	179½	183	71	65	46	129
West, David	3.55	4	10	31	14	0	0	99	74	44	39	61	83
Edens, Tom	4.33	5	1	42	0	0	1	54	59	26	26	18	39
Andersen, Larry	4.41	1	2	29	0	0	0	32⅔	33	20	16	15	27
Schilling, Curt	4.48	2	8	13	13	1	0	82⅓	87	42	41	28	58
Greene, Tommy	4.54	2	0	7	7	0	0	35⅔	37	20	18	22	28
Rivera, Ben	6.87	3	4	9	7	0	0	38	40	29	29	22	19

National League Team-by-Team Statistical Leaders *(Cont.)*

Pittsburgh Pirates

BATTING	BA	G	AB	R	H	TB	2B	3B	HR	RBI	SB	BB	SO
Pegues, Steve	.361	18	36	2	13	15	2	0	0	2	1	2	5
Clark, Dave	.296	86	223	37	66	109	11	1	10	46	2	22	48
Slaught, Don	.288	76	240	21	69	82	7	0	2	21	0	34	31
Martin, Al	.286	82	276	48	79	126	12	4	9	33	15	34	56
Garcia, Carlos	.277	98	412	49	114	151	15	2	6	28	18	16	67
Bell, Jay	.276	110	424	68	117	187	35	4	9	45	2	49	82
Merced, Orlando	.272	108	386	48	105	159	21	3	9	51	4	42	58
Parrish, Lance	.270	40	126	10	34	48	5	0	3	16	1	18	28
King, Jeff	.263	94	339	36	89	127	23	0	5	42	3	30	38
Varsho, Gary	.256	67	82	15	21	33	6	3	0	5	0	4	19
Wehner, John	.250	2	4	1	1	2	1	0	0	3	0	0	1
Van Slyke, Andy	.246	105	374	41	92	134	18	3	6	30	7	52	72
Cummings, Midre	.244	24	86	11	21	28	4	0	1	12	0	4	18
McClendon, Lloyd	.239	51	92	9	22	38	4	0	4	12	0	4	11
Foley, Tom	.236	59	123	13	29	45	7	0	3	15	0	13	18
Noboa, Junior	.000	2	2	0	0	0	0	0	0	0	0	0	0

PITCHING	ERA	W	L	G	GS	CG	SV	INN	H	R	ER	BB	SO
Smith, Zane	3.27	10	8	25	24	2	0	157	162	67	57	34	57
Dewey, Mark	3.68	2	1	45	0	0	1	51⅓	61	22	21	19	30
Lieber, Jon	3.73	6	7	17	17	1	0	108⅔	116	62	45	25	71
White, Rick	3.82	4	5	43	5	0	6	75⅓	79	35	32	17	38
Manzanillo, Ravelo	4.14	4	2	46	0	0	1	50	45	30	23	42	39
Wagner, Paul	4.59	7	8	29	17	1	0	119⅔	136	69	61	50	86
Cooke, Steve	5.02	4	11	25	23	2	0	134⅓	157	79	75	46	74
Neagle, Danny	5.12	9	10	24	24	2	0	137	135	80	78	49	122
Dyer, Mike	5.87	1	1	14	0	0	4	15⅓	15	12	10	12	13
Miceli, Dan	5.93	2	1	28	0	0	2	27⅓	28	19	18	11	27
Robertson, Rich	6.89	0	0	8	0	0	0	15⅔	20	12	12	10	8

St. Louis Cardinals

BATTING	BA	G	AB	R	H	TB	2B	3B	HR	RBI	SB	BB	SO
Jefferies, Gregg	.325	103	397	52	129	194	27	1	12	55	12	45	26
Perry, Gerald	325	60	77	12	25	41	7	0	3	18	1	15	12
Young, Dmitri	.317	16	41	5	13	20	3	2	0	3	2	3	8
Whiten, Mark	.293	92	334	57	98	162	18	2	14	53	10	37	75
Alicea, Luis	.278	88	205	32	57	94	12	5	5	29	4	30	38
Pagnozzi, Tom	.272	70	243	21	66	101	12	1	7	40	0	21	39
Zeile, Todd	.267	113	415	62	111	195	25	1	19	75	1	52	56
Lankford, Ray	.267	109	416	89	111	203	25	5	19	57	11	58	113
Oquendo, Jose	.264	55	129	13	34	40	2	2	0	9	1	21	16
Smith, Ozzie	.262	98	381	51	100	133	18	3	3	30	6	38	26
Jordan, Brian	.258	53	178	14	46	73	8	2	5	15	4	16	40
Pena, Geronimo	.254	83	213	33	54	102	13	1	1	34	9	24	54
Gilkey, Bernard.	.253	105	380	52	96	138	22	1	6	45	15	39	65
McGriff, Terry	.219	42	114	10	25	31	6	0	0	13	0	13	11
Coolbaugh, Scott	.190	15	21	4	4	10	0	0	2	6	0	1	4
Pappas, Erik	.091	15	44	8	4	5	1	0	0	5	0	10	13

PITCHING	ERA	W	L	G	GS	CG	SV	INN	H	R	ER	BB	SO
Buckels, Gary	2.25	0	1	10	10	0	0	12	8	5	3	7	9
Habyan, John	3.23	1	0	52	0	0	1	47⅓	50	17	17	20	46
Arocha, Rene	4.01	4	4	45	7	1	11	83	94	42	37	21	62
Rodriguez, Rich	4.03	3	5	56	0	0	0	60⅓	62	30	27	26	43
Palacios, Bincente	4.44	3	8	31	17	1	1	117⅔	104	60	58	43	95
Eversgerd, Bryan	4.52	2	3	40	1	0	0	67⅔	75	36	34	20	47
Urbani, Tom	5.15	3	7	20	10	0	0	80⅓	98	48	46	21	43
Tewksbury, Bob	5.32	12	10	24	24	4	0	155⅔	190	97	92	22	79
Cormier, Rheal	5.45	3	2	7	7	0	0	39⅔	40	24	24	7	26
Watson, Allen	5.52	6	5	22	22	0	0	115⅔	130	73	71	53	74
Olivares, Omar	5.74	3	4	14	12	1	1	73⅔	84	53	47	37	26
Sutcliffe, Rick	6.52	6	4	16	14	0	0	67⅔	93	53	49	32	26

San Diego Padres

BATTING	BA	G	AB	R	H	TB	2B	3B	HR	RBI	SB	BB	SO
Gwynn, Tony	.394	110	419	79	165	238	35	1	12	64	5	48	19
Shipley, Craig	.333	81	240	32	80	114	14	4	4	30	6	9	28
Williams, Eddie	.331	49	175	32	58	104	11	1	11	42	0	15	26
Roberts, Bip	.320	105	403	52	129	160	15	5	2	31	21	39	57
Bell, Derek	.311	108	434	54	135	197	20	0	14	54	24	29	88
Lopez, Luis	.277	77	235	29	65	89	16	1	2	20	3	15	39
Livingstone, Scott	.272	57	180	11	49	69	12	1	2	10	2	6	22
Hyers, Tim	.254	52	118	13	30	33	3	0	0	7	3	9	15
Ausmus, Brad	.251	101	327	45	82	117	12	1	7	24	5	30	63
Johnson, Brian	.247	36	93	7	23	38	4	1	3	16	0	5	21
Gutierrez, Ricky	.240	90	275	27	66	84	11	2	1	28	2	32	54
Plantier, Phil	.220	96	341	44	75	150	21	0	18	41	3	36	91
Cianfrocco, Archi	.219	59	146	9	32	52	8	0	4	13	2	3	39
Bean, Billy	.215	84	135	7	29	36	5	1	0	14	0	7	25
Clark, Jerald	.215	61	149	14	32	53	6	0	5	20	1	5	17

PITCHING	ERA	W	L	G	GS	CG	SV	INN	H	R	ER	BB	SO
Hoffman, Trevor	2.57	4	4	47	0	0	20	56	39	16	16	20	68
Martinez, Pedro	2.90	3	2	48	1	0	3	68⅓	52	31	22	49	52
Hamilton, Joey	2.98	9	6	16	16	1	0	108⅔	98	40	36	29	61
Elliott, Donnie	3.27	0	1	30	1	0	0	33	31	12	12	21	24
Ashby, Andy	3.40	6	11	24	24	4	0	164⅓	145	75	62	43	121
Mauser, Tim	3.49	2	4	35	0	0	2	49	50	21	19	19	32
Worrell, Tim	3.68	0	1	3	3	0	0	14⅔	9	7	6	5	14
Benes, Andy	3.86	6	14	25	25	2	0	172⅓	155	82	74	51	189
Sanders, Scott	4.78	4	8	23	20	0	1	111	103	63	59	48	109
Krueger, Bill	4.83	3	2	8	7	1	0	41	42	24	22	7	30
Whitehurst, Wally	4.92	4	7	13	13	0	0	64	84	37	35	26	43
Tabaka, Jeff	5.27	3	1	39	0	0	1	41	32	29	24	27	32

San Francisco Giants

BATTING	BA	G	AB	R	H	TB	2B	3B	HR	RBI	SB	BB	SO
Leonard, Mark	.364	14	11	2	4	7	1	1	0	2	0	3	2
Bonds, Barry	.312	112	397	89	122	253	18	1	37	81	29	74	43
McGee, Willie	.282	45	156	19	44	62	3	0	5	23	3	15	24
Scarsone, Steve	.272	52	103	21	28	42	8	0	2	13	0	10	20
Carreon, Mark	.270	51	100	8	27	40	4	0	3	20	0	7	20
Williams, Matt	.267	112	445	74	119	270	16	3	43	96	1	33	87
Benzinger, Todd	.265	107	328	32	87	131	13	2	9	31	2	17	84
Benjamin, Mike	.258	38	62	9	16	26	5	1	1	9	5	5	16
Lewis, Darren	.257	114	451	70	116	161	15	9	4	29	30	53	50
Manwaring, Kirt	.250	97	316	30	79	101	17	1	1	29	1	25	50
Martinez, Dave	.247	97	235	23	58	85	9	3	4	27	3	21	22
Strawberry, Darryl	.239	29	92	13	22	39	3	1	4	17	0	19	22
Patterson, John	.238	85	240	36	57	78	10	1	3	32	13	16	43
Clayton, Royce	.236	108	385	38	91	126	14	6	3	30	23	30	74
Thompson, Robby	.209	35	129	13	27	45	8	2	2	7	3	15	32
Reed, Jeff	.175	50	103	11	18	24	3	0	1	7	0	11	21

PITCHING	ERA	W	L	G	GS	CG	SV	INN	H	R	ER	BB	SO
Jackson, Mike	1.49	3	2	36	0	0	4	42⅓	23	8	7	11	51
Beck, Rod	2.77	2	4	48	0	0	28	48⅔	49	17	15	13	39
Monteleone, Rich	3.18	4	3	39	0	0	0	45⅓	43	18	16	13	16
Swift, Bill	3.38	8	7	17	17	0	0	109⅓	109	49	41	31	62
Rogers, Kevin	3.48	0	0	9	0	0	0	10⅓	10	4	4	6	7
Van Landingham, W.	3.54	8	2	16	14	0	0	84	70	37	33	43	56
Burkett, John	3.62	6	8	25	25	0	0	159⅓	176	72	64	36	85
Gomez, Pat	3.78	0	1	26	0	0	0	33⅓	23	14	14	20	14
Portugal, Mark	3.93	10	8	21	21	1	0	137⅓	135	68	60	45	87
Burba, Dave	4.38	3	6	57	0	0	0	74	59	39	36	45	84
Black, Buddy	4.47	4	2	10	10	0	0	54½	50	31	27	16	28
Frey, Steve	4.94	1	0	44	0	0	0	31	37	17	17	15	20
Hickerson, Bryan	5.40	4	8	28	14	0	1	98½	118	60	59	38	59
Bottenfield, Kent	6.15	3	1	16	1	0	1	26⅓	33	18	18	10	15

American League Team-by-Team Statistical Leaders

Baltimore Orioles

BATTING	BA	G	AB	R	H	TB	2B	3B	HR	RBI	SB	BB	SO
Palmeiro, Rafael	.319	111	436	82	139	240	32	0	23	76	7	54	63
Ripken, Cal, Jr.	.315	112	444	71	140	204	19	3	19	75	1	32	41
Hammonds, Jeffrey	.296	68	250	45	74	120	18	2	8	31	5	17	39
Baines, Harold	.294	94	326	44	96	158	12	1	16	54	0	30	49
Smith, Dwight	.281	73	196	31	55	90	7	2	8	30	2	12	37
Gomez, Leo	.274	84	285	46	78	143	20	0	15	56	0	41	55
Anderson, Brady	.263	111	453	78	119	190	25	5	12	48	31	57	75
McLemore, Mark	.257	104	343	44	88	110	11	1	3	29	20	51	50
Sabo, Chris	.256	68	258	41	66	120	15	3	11	42	1	20	38
Hoiles, Chris	.247	99	332	45	82	149	10	0	19	53	2	63	73
Hulett, Tim	.228	36	92	11	21	31	2	1	2	15	0	12	24
Tackett, Jeffrey	.226	26	53	5	12	23	3	1	2	9	0	5	13
Smith, Lonnie	.203	35	59	13	12	15	3	0	0	2	1	11	18
Devereaux, Mike	.203	85	301	35	61	100	8	2	9	33	1	22	72

PITCHING	ERA	W	L	G	GS	CG	SV	INN	H	R	ER	BB	SO
Eichhorn, Mark	2.15	6	5	43	0	0	1	71	62	19	17	19	35
Mussina, Mike	3.06	16	5	24	24	3	0	176⅓	163	63	60	42	99
Smith, Lee	3.29	1	4	41	0	0	33	38⅓	34	16	14	11	42
Williamson, Mark	4.01	3	1	28	2	0	1	67½	75	33	30	17	28
McDonald, Ben	4.06	14	7	24	24	5	0	157⅓	151	75	71	54	94
Moyer, Jamie	4.77	5	7	23	23	0	0	149	158	81	79	38	87
Fernandez, Sid	5.15	6	6	19	19	2	0	115¾	109	66	66	46	95
Mills, Alan	5.16	3	3	47	0	0	2	45⅓	43	26	26	24	44
Bolton, Tom	5.40	1	2	22	0	0	0	23⅓	29	15	14	13	12
Rhodes, Arthur	5.81	3	5	10	10	3	0	52⅔	51	34	34	30	47
Poole, Jim	6.64	1	0	38	0	0	0	20⅓	32	15	15	11	18

Boston Red Sox

BATTING	BA	G	AB	R	H	TB	2B	3B	HR	RBI	SB	BB	SO
Valentin, John	.316	84	301	53	95	152	26	2	9	49	3	42	38
Vaughn, Mo	.310	111	394	65	122	227	25	1	26	82	4	57	112
Rodriguez, Carlos	.287	57	174	15	50	69	14	1	1	13	1	11	13
Cooper, Scott	.282	104	369	49	104	167	16	4	13	53	0	30	65
Naehring, Tim	.276	80	297	41	82	123	18	1	7	42	1	30	56
Nixon, Otis	.274	103	398	60	109	126	15	1	0	25	42	55	65
Greenwell, Mike	.269	95	327	60	88	148	25	1	11	45	2	38	26
Berryhill, Damon	.263	82	255	30	67	106	17	2	6	34	0	19	59
Chamberlain, Wes	.256	51	164	13	42	65	9	1	4	20	0	12	38
Dawson, Andre	.240	75	292	34	70	136	18	0	16	48	2	9	53
Brunansky, Tom	.234	64	205	24	48	92	12	1	10	34	0	24	57
Rowland, Rich	.229	46	118	14	27	57	3	0	9	20	0	11	35
Fletcher, Scott	.227	63	185	31	42	62	9	1	3	11	8	16	14
Tinsley, Lee	.222	78	144	27	32	42	4	0	2	14	13	19	36

PITCHING	ERA	W	L	G	GS	CG	SV	INN	H	R	ER	BB	SO
Ryan, Ken	2.44	2	3	42	0	0	13	48	46	14	13	17	32
Clemens, Roger	2.85	9	7	24	24	3	0	170⅔	124	62	54	71	168
Howard, Chris	3.63	1	0	37	0	0	1	39⅔	35	17	16	12	22
Sele, Aaron	3.83	7	2	22	22	2	0	143⅓	140	68	61	60	105
Hesketh, Joe	4.26	8	5	25	20	0	0	114	117	70	54	46	83
Bankhead, Scott	4.54	3	2	27	0	0	0	37⅔	34	21	19	12	25
Viola, Frank	4.65	1	1	6	6	0	0	31	34	17	16	17	9
Fossas, Tony	4.76	2	0	44	0	0	1	34	35	18	18	15	31
Farr, Steve	5.72	2	1	30	0	0	4	28⅓	41	21	18	18	20
Finnvold, Gar	5.94	0	4	8	8	0	0	36⅓	45	27	24	15	17
Melendez, Jose	6.06	0	1	10	0	0	0	16⅓	20	11	11	8	9
Darwin, Danny	6.30	7	5	13	13	0	0	75⅔	101	54	53	24	54
Nabholz, Chris	7.64	3	5	14	12	0	0	53	67	48	45	38	28
Trlicek, Ricky	8.06	1	1	12	1	0	0	22⅓	32	21	20	16	7
Frohwirth, Todd	10.80	0	3	22	0	0	1	26⅔	40	36	32	17	13

California Angels

BATTING	BA	G	AB	R	H	TB	2B	3B	HR	RBI	SB	BB	SO
Davis, Chili	.311	108	392	72	122	220	18	1	26	84	3	69	84
Owen, Spike	.310	82	268	30	83	113	17	2	3	37	2	49	17
Hudler, Rex	.298	56	124	17	37	69	8	0	8	20	2	6	28
Salmon, Tim	.287	100	373	67	107	198	18	2	23	70	1	54	102
Jackson, Bo	.279	75	201	23	56	102	7	0	13	43	1	20	72
Edmonds, Jim	.273	94	289	35	79	109	13	1	5	37	4	30	72
DiSarcina, Gary	.260	112	389	53	101	128	14	2	3	33	3	18	28
Curtis, Chad	.256	114	453	67	116	180	23	4	11	50	25	37	69
Myers, Greg	.246	45	126	10	31	43	6	0	2	8	0	10	27
Turner, Chris	.242	58	149	23	36	48	7	1	1	12	3	10	29
Reynolds, Harold	.232	74	207	33	48	60	10	1	0	11	10	23	18
Snow, J.T.	.220	61	223	22	49	77	4	0	8	30	0	19	48
Easley, Damion	.215	88	316	41	68	104	16	1	6	30	4	29	48
Dalesandro, Mark	.200	19	25	5	5	9	1	0	1	2	0	2	4

PITCHING	ERA	W	L	G	GS	CG	SV	INN	H	R	ER	BB	SO
Patterson, Bob	4.07	2	3	47	0	0	1	42	35	21	19	15	30
Finley, Chuck	4.32	10	10	25	25	7	0	183⅓	178	95	88	71	148
Langston, Mark	4.68	7	8	18	18	2	0	119⅓	121	67	62	54	109
Leiter, Mark	4.72	4	7	40	7	0	2	95⅓	99	56	50	35	71
Anderson, Brian	5.22	7	5	18	18	0	0	101⅔	120	63	59	27	47
Schwarz, Jeff	5.50	0	0	13	0	0	0	18	14	13	11	22	18
Springer, Russ	5.52	2	2	18	5	0	2	45⅔	53	28	28	14	28
Leftwich, Phil	5.68	5	10	20	20	1	0	114	127	75	72	42	67
Dopson, John	6.14	1	4	21	5	0	1	58⅔	67	41	40	26	33
Grahe, Joe	6.65	2	5	40	0	0	13	43½	68	33	32	18	26
Magrane, Joe	7.30	2	6	20	11	1	0	74	89	63	60	51	33
Lorraine, Andrew	10.61	0	2	4	3	0	0	18⅔	30	23	22	11	10

Chicago White Sox

BATTING	BA	G	AB	R	H	TB	2B	3B	HR	RBI	SB	BB	SO
Thomas, Frank	.353	113	399	106	141	291	34	1	38	101	2	109	61
Franco, Julio	.319	112	433	72	138	221	19	2	20	98	8	62	75
Jackson, Darrin	.312	104	369	43	115	168	17	3	10	51	7	27	56
Grebeck, Craig	.309	35	97	17	30	35	5	0	0	5	0	12	5
Guillen, Ozzie	.288	100	365	46	105	127	9	5	1	39	5	14	35
Ventura, Robin	.282	109	401	57	113	184	15	1	18	78	3	61	69
LaValliere, Mike	.281	59	139	6	39	46	4	0	1	24	0	20	15
Johnson, Lance	.277	106	412	56	114	162	11	14	3	54	26	26	23
Cora, Joey	.276	90	312	55	86	113	13	4	2	30	8	38	32
Martin, Norberto	.275	45	131	19	36	48	7	1	1	16	4	9	16
Raines, Tim	.266	101	384	80	102	157	15	5	10	52	13	61	43
Newson, Warren	.255	63	102	16	26	37	5	0	2	7	1	14	23
Pasqua, Dan	.217	11	23	2	5	13	2	0	2	4	0	0	9
Karkovice, Ron	.213	77	207	33	44	88	9	1	11	29	0	36	68
Melvin, Bob	.212	20	33	5	7	10	0	0	1	4	0	1	7
Zupcic, Bob	.196	36	92	10	18	27	4	1	1	8	0	4	17

PITCHING	ERA	W	L	G	GS	CG	SV	INN	H	R	ER	BB	SO
DeLeon, Jose	3.36	3	2	42	0	0	2	67	48	28	25	31	67
McCaskill, Kirk	3.42	1	4	40	0	0	3	52⅔	51	22	20	22	37
Alvarez, Wilson	3.45	12	8	24	24	2	0	161⅔	147	72	62	62	108
Assenmacher, Paul	3.55	1	2	44	0	0	1	33	26	13	13	13	29
Cook, Dennis	3.55	3	1	38	0	0	0	33	29	17	13	14	26
McDowell, Jack	3.73	10	9	25	25	6	0	181	186	82	75	42	127
Bere, Jason	3.81	12	2	24	24	0	0	141⅔	119	65	60	80	127
Fernandez, Alex	3.86	11	7	24	24	4	0	170⅓	163	83	73	50	122
Hernandez, Roberto	4.91	4	4	45	0	0	14	47	44	29	26	19	50
Sanderson, Scott	5.09	8	4	18	14	1	0	92	110	57	52	12	36

Cleveland Indians

BATTING	BA	G	AB	R	H	TB	2B	3B	HR	RBI	SB	BB	SO
Belle, Albert	.357	106	412	90	147	294	35	2	36	101	9	58	71
Lofton, Kenny	.349	112	459	105	160	246	32	9	12	57	60	52	56
Gonzales, Rene	.348	22	23	6	8	14	1	1	1	5	2	5	3
Baerga, Carlos	.314	103	442	81	139	232	32	2	19	80	8	10	45
Pena, Tony	.295	40	112	18	33	49	8	1	2	10	0	9	11
Kirby, Wayne	.293	78	191	33	56	77	6	0	5	23	11	13	30
Alomar, Sandy, Jr.	.288	80	292	44	84	143	15	1	14	43	8	25	31
Sorrento, Paul	.280	95	322	43	90	146	14	0	14	62	0	34	68
Vizquel, Omar	.273	69	286	39	78	93	10	1	1	33	13	23	23
Ramirez, Manny	.269	91	290	51	78	151	22	0	17	60	4	42	72
Thome, Jim	.268	98	321	58	86	168	20	1	20	52	3	46	84
Murray, Eddie	.254	108	433	57	110	184	21	1	17	76	8	31	53
Espinoza, Alvaro	.238	90	231	27	55	71	13	0	1	19	1	6	33
Amaro, Ruben	.217	26	23	5	5	12	1	0	2	5	2	2	3
Maldonado, Candy	.196	42	92	14	18	40	5	1	5	12	1	19	31

PITCHING	ERA	W	L	G	GS	CG	SV	INN	H	R	ER	BB	SO
Turner, Matt	2.13	1	0	9	0	0	1	12⅔	13	6	3	7	5
Plunk, Eric	2.54	7	2	41	0	0	3	71	61	25	20	37	73
Nagy, Charles	3.45	10	8	23	23	3	0	169⅓	175	76	65	48	108
Martinez, Dennis	3.52	11	6	24	24	7	0	176⅔	166	75	69	44	92
Clark, Dave	3.82	11	3	20	20	4	0	127⅓	133	61	54	40	60
Mesa, Jose	3.82	7	5	51	0	0	2	73	71	33	31	26	63
Lopez, Albie	4.24	1	2	4	4	1	0	17	20	11	8	6	18
Grimsley, Jason	4.57	5	2	14	13	1	0	82⅓	91	47	42	34	59
Lilliquist, Derek	4.91	1	3	36	0	0	1	29⅓	34	17	16	8	15
Russell, Jeff	5.09	1	6	42	0	0	17	40⅔	43	25	23	16	28
Morris, Jack	5.60	10	6	23	23	1	0	141⅓	163	96	88	67	100
Ogea, Chad	6.06	0	1	4	1	0	0	16⅓	21	11	11	10	11
Casian, Larry	7.35	1	5	40	0	0	1	49	73	43	40	16	20
DiPoto, Jerry	8.04	0	0	7	0	0	0	15⅔	26	14	14	10	9

Detroit Tigers

BATTING	BA	G	AB	R	H	TB	2B	3B	HR	RBI	SB	BB	SO
Samuel, Juan	.309	59	136	32	42	76	9	5	5	21	5	10	26
Felix, Junior	.306	86	301	54	92	158	25	1	13	49	1	26	76
Whitaker, Lou	.301	92	322	67	97	158	21	2	12	43	2	41	47
Phillips, Tony	.281	114	438	91	123	205	19	3	19	61	13	95	105
Gibson, Kirk	.276	98	330	71	91	181	17	2	23	72	4	42	69
Trammell, Alan	.267	76	292	38	78	121	17	1	8	28	3	16	35
Fryman, Travis	.263	114	464	66	122	220	34	5	18	85	2	45	128
Fielder, Cecil	.259	109	425	67	110	214	16	2	28	90	0	50	110
Gomez, Leo	.257	84	296	32	76	119	19	0	8	53	5	33	64
Tettleton, Mickey	.248	107	339	57	84	157	18	2	17	51	0	97	98
Cuyler, Milt	.241	48	116	20	28	36	3	1	1	11	5	13	21
Bautista, Danny	.232	31	99	12	23	41	4	1	4	15	1	3	18
Kreuter, Chad	.224	65	170	17	38	49	8	0	1	19	0	28	36
Davis, Eric	.183	37	120	19	22	35	4	0	3	13	5	18	45
Flaherty, John	.150	34	40	2	6	7	1	0	0	4	0	1	11

PITCHING	ERA	W	L	G	GS	CG	SV	INN	H	R	ER	BB	SO
Davis, Storm	3.56	2	4	35	0	0	0	48	36	23	19	34	38
Groom, Buddy	3.94	0	1	40	0	0	1	32	31	14	14	13	27
Wells, David	3.96	5	7	16	16	5	0	111½	113	54	49	24	71
Boever, Joe	3.98	9	2	46	0	0	3	81⅓	80	40	36	37	49
Gardiner, Mike	4.14	2	2	38	1	0	5	58⅔	53	35	27	23	31
Gohr, Greg	4.50	2	2	8	6	0	0	34	36	19	17	21	21
Cadaret, Greg	4.73	1	1	38	0	0	2	40	41	24	21	33	29
Henneman, Mike	5.19	1	3	30	0	0	0	34⅔	43	27	20	17	27
Moore, Mike	5.42	11	10	25	25	4	0	154⅓	152	97	93	89	62
Bergman, Sean	5.60	2	1	3	3	0	0	17⅔	22	11	11	7	12
Belcher, Tim	5.89	7	15	25	25	3	0	162	192	124	106	78	76
Gullickson, Bill	5.93	4	5	21	19	1	0	115½	156	79	76	25	65
Doherty, John	6.48	6	7	18	17	2	0	101¾	139	75	73	26	28
Harris, Gene	7.15	0	0	11	0	0	1	11⅓	13	10	9	4	10

Kansas City Royals

BATTING	BA	G	AB	R	H	TB	2B	3B	HR	RBI	SB	BB	SO
Joyner, Wally	.311	97	363	52	113	163	20	3	8	57	3	47	43
Jose, Felix	.303	99	366	56	111	174	28	1	11	55	10	35	75
Gaetti, Gary	.287	90	327	53	94	151	15	3	12	57	0	19	63
Hamelin, Bob	.282	101	312	64	88	187	25	1	24	65	4	56	62
McRae, Brian	.273	114	436	71	119	165	22	6	4	40	28	54	67
Lind, Jose	.269	85	290	34	78	101	16	2	1	31	9	16	34
Gagne, Greg	.259	107	375	39	97	147	23	3	7	51	10	27	79
Mayne, Brent	.257	46	144	19	37	50	5	1	2	20	1	14	27
Macfarlane, Mike	.255	92	314	53	80	145	17	3	14	47	1	35	71
Henderson, David	.247	56	198	27	49	80	14	1	5	31	2	16	28
Shumpert, Terry	.240	64	183	28	44	78	6	2	8	24	18	13	39
Coleman, Vince	.240	104	438	61	105	149	14	12	2	33	50	29	72
Howard, David	.229	46	83	9	19	26	4	0	1	13	3	11	23
Miller, Keith	.133	5	15	1	2	2	0	0	0	0	0	0	3

PITCHING	ERA	W	L	G	GS	CG	SV	INN	H	R	ER	BB	SO
Brewer, Billy	2.56	4	1	50	0	0	3	38⅓	28	11	11	16	25
Cone, David	2.94	16	5	23	23	4	0	171¾	130	60	56	54	132
Meacham, Rusty	3.73	3	3	36	0	0	4	50⅔	51	23	21	12	36
Appier, Kevin	3.83	7	6	23	23	1	0	155	137	68	66	63	145
Montgomery, Jeff	4.03	2	3	42	0	0	27	44¾	48	21	20	15	50
Gordon, Tom	4.35	11	7	24	24	0	0	155⅓	136	79	75	87	126
Gubicza, Mark	4.50	7	9	22	22	0	0	130	158	74	65	26	59
Magnante, Mike	4.60	2	3	36	1	0	0	47	55	27	24	16	21
DeJesus, Jose	4.73	3	1	5	4	0	0	26⅔	27	14	14	13	12
Pichardo, Hipolito	4.92	5	3	45	0	0	3	67⅔	82	42	37	24	36
Belinda, Stan	5.14	2	2	37	0	0	1	49	47	36	28	24	37

Milwaukee Brewers

BATTING	BA	G	AB	R	H	TB	2B	3B	HR	RBI	SB	BB	SO
Seitzer, Kevin	.314	80	309	44	97	140	24	2	5	49	2	30	38
Listach, Pat	.296	16	54	8	16	19	3	0	0	2	2	3	8
Harper, Brian	.291	64	251	23	73	100	15	0	4	32	0	9	18
Nilsson, Dave	.275	109	397	51	109	179	28	3	12	69	1	34	61
O'Leary, Troy	.273	27	66	9	18	27	1	1	2	7	1	5	12
Reed, Jody	.271	108	399	48	108	136	22	0	2	37	5	57	34
Hamilton, Darryl	.262	36	141	23	37	52	10	1	1	13	3	15	17
Surhoff, B.J.	.261	40	134	20	35	65	11	2	5	22	0	16	14
Mieske, Matt	.259	84	259	39	67	112	13	1	10	38	3	21	62
Vaughn, Greg	.254	95	370	59	94	177	24	1	19	55	9	51	93
Spiers, Bill	.252	73	214	27	54	66	10	1	0	17	7	19	42
Diaz, Alex	.251	79	187	17	47	69	5	7	1	17	5	10	19
Jaha, John	.241	84	291	45	70	120	14	0	12	39	3	32	75
Valentin, Jose	.239	97	285	47	68	120	19	0	11	46	12	38	75
Cirillo, Jeff	.238	39	126	17	30	48	9	0	3	12	0	11	16
Valle, Dave	.232	46	112	14	26	42	8	1	2	10	0	18	22
Ward, Turner	.232	102	367	55	85	131	15	2	9	45	6	52	68

PITCHING	ERA	W	L	G	GS	CG	SV	INN	H	R	ER	BB	SO
Mercedes, Jose	2.32	2	0	19	0	0	0	31	22	9	8	16	11
Fetters, Mike	2.54	1	4	42	0	0	17	46	41	16	13	27	31
Bones, Ricky	3.43	10	9	24	24	4	0	170⅔	166	76	65	45	57
Scanlan, Bob	4.11	2	6	30	12	0	2	103	117	53	47	28	65
Bronkey, Jeff	4.35	1	1	16	0	0	1	20⅔	20	10	10	12	13
Wegman, Bill	4.51	8	4	19	19	0	0	115⅔	140	64	58	26	59
Ignasiak, Mike	4.53	3	1	23	5	0	0	47⅔	51	25	24	13	24
Henry, Doug	4.60	2	3	25	0	0	0	31⅓	32	17	16	23	20
Eldred, Cal	4.68	11	11	25	25	6	0	179	158	96	93	84	98
Orosco, Jesse	5.08	3	1	40	0	0	0	39	32	26	22	26	36
Lloyd, Graeme	5.17	2	3	43	0	0	3	47	49	28	27	15	31
Miranda, Angel	5.28	2	5	8	8	1	0	46	39	28	27	27	24
Navarro, Jaimie	6.62	4	9	29	10	0	0	89⅔	115	71	66	35	65
Higuera, Teddy	7.06	1	5	17	12	0	0	58⅔	74	55	46	36	35

Minnesota Twins

BATTING	BA	G	AB	R	H	TB	2B	3B	HR	RBI	SB	BB	SO
Mack, Shane	.333	81	303	55	101	171	21	2	15	61	4	32	51
Puckett, Kirby	.317	108	439	79	139	237	32	3	20	112	6	28	47
Knoblauch, Chuck	.312	109	445	85	139	205	45	3	5	51	35	41	56
Cole, Alex	.296	105	345	68	102	139	15	5	4	23	29	44	60
Munoz, Pedro	.295	75	244	35	72	124	15	2	11	36	0	19	67
Hrbek, Kent	.270	81	274	34	74	115	11	0	10	53	0	37	28
Meares, Pat	.266	80	229	29	61	81	12	1	2	24	5	14	50
Hale, Chip	.263	67	118	13	31	43	9	0	1	11	0	16	14
Reboulet, Jeff	.259	74	189	28	49	71	11	1	3	23	0	18	23
Winfield, Dave	.252	77	294	35	74	125	15	3	10	43	2	31	51
Leius, Scott	.246	97	350	57	86	146	16	1	14	49	2	37	58
Walbeck, Matt	.204	97	338	31	69	96	12	0	5	35	1	17	37
Parks, Derek	.191	31	89	6	17	26	6	0	1	9	0	4	20

PITCHING	ERA	W	L	G	GS	CG	SV	INN	H	R	ER	BB	SO
Schullstrom, Erik	2.77	0	0	9	0	0	1	13	13	7	4	5	13
Campbell, Kevin	2.92	1	0	14	0	0	0	24⅔	20	8	8	5	15
Aguilera, Rick	3.63	1	4	44	0	0	23	44⅔	57	23	18	10	46
Tapani, Kevin	4.62	11	7	24	24	4	0	156	181	86	80	39	91
Mahomes, Pat	4.73	9	5	21	21	0	0	120	121	68	63	62	53
Erickson, Scott	5.44	8	11	23	23	2	0	144	173	95	87	59	104
Willis, Carl	5.92	2	4	49	0	0	3	59½	89	48	39	12	37
Pulido, Carlos	5.98	3	7	19	14	0	0	84½	87	57	56	40	32
Guthrie, Mark	6.14	4	2	50	2	0	1	51½	65	43	35	18	38
Trombley, Mike	6.33	2	0	24	0	0	0	48½	56	36	34	18	32
Stevens, Dave	6.80	5	2	24	0	0	0	45	55	35	34	23	24
Deshaies, Jim	7.39	6	12	25	25	0	0	130⅓	170	109	107	54	78

New York Yankees

BATTING	BA	G	AB	R	H	TB	2B	3B	HR	RBI	SB	BB	SO
O'Neill, Paul	.359	103	368	68	132	222	25	1	21	83	5	72	56
Boggs, Wade	.342	97	366	61	125	179	19	1	11	55	2	61	29
Polonia, Luis	.311	95	350	62	109	145	21	6	1	36	20	37	36
Mattingly, Don	.304	97	372	62	113	153	20	1	6	51	0	60	24
Stanley, Mike	.300	82	290	54	87	158	20	0	17	57	0	39	56
Nokes, Matt	.291	28	79	11	23	47	3	0	7	19	0	5	16
Williams, Gerald	.291	57	86	19	25	45	8	0	4	13	1	4	17
Williams, Bernie	.289	108	408	80	118	185	29	1	12	57	16	61	54
Kelly, Pat	.280	93	286	35	80	114	21	2	3	41	6	19	51
Velarde, Randy	.279	77	280	47	78	123	16	1	9	34	4	22	61
Leyritz, Jim	.265	75	249	47	66	129	12	0	17	58	0	35	61
Tartabull, Danny	.256	104	399	68	102	185	24	1	19	67	1	66	111
Gallego, Mike	.239	89	306	39	73	110	17	1	6	41	0	38	46
Boston, Daryl	.182	52	77	11	14	28	2	0	4	14	0	6	20
Elster, Kevin	.000	7	20	0	0	0	0	0	0	0	0	1	6

PITCHING	ERA	W	L	G	GS	CG	SV	INN	H	R	ER	BB	SO
Howe, Steve	1.80	3	0	40	0	0	15	40	28	8	8	7	18
Wickman, Bob	3.09	5	4	53	0	0	6	70	54	26	24	27	56
Key, Jimmy	3.27	17	4	25	25	1	0	168	177	68	61	52	97
Kamieniecki, Scott	3.76	8	6	22	16	1	0	117⅓	115	53	49	59	71
Perez, Melido	4.10	9	4	22	22	1	0	151⅓	134	74	69	58	109
Hitchcock, Sterling	4.20	4	1	23	5	1	2	49½	48	24	23	29	37
Abbott, Jim	4.55	9	8	24	24	2	0	160⅓	167	88	81	64	90
Gibson, Paul	4.97	1	1	30	0	0	0	29	26	17	16	17	21
Ausanio, Joe	5.17	2	1	13	0	0	0	15⅔	16	9	9	6	15
Hernandez, Xavier	5.85	4	4	31	0	0	6	40	48	27	26	21	37
Mulholland, Terry	6.49	6	7	24	19	2	0	120⅔	150	94	87	37	72
Murphy, Rob	16.20	0	0	3	0	0	0	1⅔	3	3	3	0	0

Oakland A's

BATTING	BA	G	AB	R	H	TB	2B	3B	HR	RBI	SB	BB	SO
Berroa, Geronimo	.306	96	340	55	104	165	18	2	13	65	7	41	62
Steinbach, Terry	.285	103	369	51	105	163	21	2	11	57	2	26	62
Gates, Brent	.283	64	233	29	66	85	11	1	2	24	3	21	32
Javier, Stan	.272	109	419	75	114	167	23	0	10	44	24	49	76
Sierra, Ruben	.268	110	426	71	114	206	21	1	23	92	8	23	64
Neel, Troy	.266	83	278	43	74	132	13	0	15	48	2	38	61
Henderson, Dave	.260	87	296	66	77	108	13	0	6	20	22	72	45
Bordick, Mike	.253	114	391	38	99	131	18	4	2	37	7	38	44
McGwire, Mark	.252	47	135	26	34	64	3	0	9	25	0	37	40
Matos, Francisco	.250	14	28	1	7	8	1	0	0	2	1	1	2
Sax, Steve	.250	7	24	2	6	8	0	1	0	1	0	0	2
Aldrete, Mike	.242	76	178	23	43	60	5	0	4	18	2	20	35
Brosius, Scott	.238	96	324	31	77	135	14	1	14	49	2	24	57
Hemond, Scott	.222	91	198	23	44	64	11	0	3	20	7	16	51
Cruz, Fausto	.107	17	28	2	3	3	0	0	0	0	0	4	6

PITCHING	ERA	W	L	G	GS	CG	SV	INN	H	R	ER	BB	SO
Leiper, Dave	1.93	0	0	26	0	0	1	18⅔	13	4	4	6	14
Karsay, Steve	2.57	1	1	4	4	1	0	28	26	8	8	8	15
Ontiveros, Steve	2.65	6	4	27	13	2	0	115⅓	93	39	34	26	56
Acre, Mark	3.41	5	1	34	0	0	0	34⅓	24	13	13	23	21
Taylor, Bill	3.50	1	3	41	0	0	1	46⅓	38	24	18	18	48
Vosberg, Ed	3.95	0	2	16	0	0	0	13⅔	16	7	6	5	12
Briscoe, John	4.01	4	2	37	0	0	1	49⅓	31	24	22	39	45
Reyes, Carlos	4.15	0	3	27	9	0	1	78	71	38	36	44	57
Eckersley, Dennis	4.26	5	4	45	0	0	19	44⅓	49	26	21	13	47
Darling, Ron	4.50	10	11	25	25	4	0	160	162	89	80	59	108
Horsman, Vince	4.91	0	1	33	0	0	0	29⅓	29	17	16	11	20
Witt, Bobby	5.04	8	10	24	24	5	0	135⅔	151	88	76	70	111
Van Poppel, Todd	6.09	7	10	23	23	0	0	116⅔	108	80	79	89	83
Welch, Bob	7.08	3	6	25	8	0	0	68⅔	79	56	54	43	44

Seattle Mariners

BATTING	BA	G	AB	R	H	TB	2B	3B	HR	RBI	SB	BB	SO
Jefferson, Reggie	.327	63	162	24	53	88	11	0	8	32	0	17	32
Griffey, Ken, Jr	.323	111	433	94	140	292	24	4	40	90	11	56	73
Fermin, Felix	.317	101	379	52	120	144	21	0	1	35	4	11	22
Blowers, Mike	.289	85	270	37	78	118	13	0	9	49	2	25	60
Martinez, Edgar	.285	89	326	47	93	157	23	1	13	51	6	53	42
Buhner, Jay	.279	101	358	74	100	194	23	4	21	68	0	66	63
Sojo, Luis	.277	63	213	32	59	90	9	2	6	22	2	8	25
Amaral, Rich	.263	77	228	37	60	86	10	2	4	18	5	24	28
Martinez, Tino	.261	97	329	42	86	167	21	0	20	61	1	29	52
Anthony, Eric	.237	79	262	31	62	108	14	1	10	30	6	23	66
Mitchell, Keith	.227	46	128	21	29	46	2	0	5	15	0	18	22
Lovullo, Torey	.222	36	72	9	16	27	5	0	2	7	1	9	13
Wilson, Dan	.216	91	282	24	61	88	14	2	3	27	1	10	57
Howard, Chris	.200	9	25	2	5	6	1	0	0	2	0	1	6

PITCHING	ERA	W	L	G	GS	CG	SV	INN	H	R	ER	BB	SO
Nelson, Jeff	2.76	0	0	28	0	0	0	42⅓	35	18	13	20	44
Ayala, Bobby	2.86	4	3	46	0	0	18	56⅔	42	25	18	26	76
Johnson, Randy	3.19	13	6	23	23	9	0	172	132	65	61	72	204
Risley, Bill	3.44	9	6	37	0	0	0	52⅓	31	20	20	19	61
Gossage, Goose	4.18	3	0	36	0	0	1	47⅓	44	23	22	15	29
Bosio, Chris	4.32	4	10	19	19	4	0	125	137	72	60	40	67
Cummings, John	5.63	2	4	17	8	0	0	64	66	43	40	37	33
Fleming, Dave	6.46	7	11	23	23	0	0	117	152	93	84	65	65
Hibbard, Greg	6.69	1	5	15	14	0	0	80⅓	115	78	60	31	39
Boskie, Shawn	6.75	0	1	2	1	0	0	2⅔	4	2	2	1	0
King, Kevin	7.04	0	2	19	0	0	0	15⅓	21	13	12	17	6
Salkeld, Roger	7.17	2	5	13	13	0	0	59	76	47	47	45	46
Converse, Jim	8.69	0	5	13	8	0	0	48⅔	73	49	47	40	39

Texas Rangers

BATTING

BATTING	BA	G	AB	R	H	TB	2B	3B	HR	RBI	SB	BB	SO
Clark, Will	.329	110	389	73	128	195	24	2	13	80	5	71	59
Frye, Jeff	.327	57	205	37	67	93	20	3	0	18	6	29	23
Greer, Rusty	.314	80	277	36	87	135	16	1	0	46	0	46	46
Ripken, Billy	.309	32	81	9	25	30	5	0	0	6	2	3	11
Rodriguez, Ivan	.298	99	363	56	108	177	19	1	16	57	6	31	42
Beltre, Esteban	.282	48	131	12	37	42	5	0	0	12	2	16	25
Canseco, Jose	.282	111	429	88	121	237	19	2	31	90	15	69	114
Lee, Manuel	.278	95	335	41	93	121	18	2	2	38	3	21	66
Ortiz, Junior	.276	29	76	3	21	23	2	0	0	9	0	5	11
Gonzalez, Juan	.275	107	422	57	116	199	18	4	19	85	6	30	66
Redus, Gary	.273	18	33	2	9	10	1	0	0	2	0	4	6
McDowell, Oddibe	.262	59	183	34	48	58	5	1	1	15	14	28	39
James, Chris	.256	52	133	28	34	71	8	4	7	19	0	20	38
Palmer, Dean	.246	93	342	50	84	159	14	2	19	59	3	26	89
Strange, Doug	.212	73	226	26	48	77	12	1	5	26	1	15	38

PITCHING

PITCHING	ERA	W	L	G	GS	CG	SV	INN	H	R	ER	BB	SO
Oliver, Darren	3.42	4	0	43	0	0	2	50	40	24	19	35	50
Armstrong, Jack	3.60	0	1	2	2	0	0	10	9	4	4	2	7
Henke, Tom	3.79	3	6	37	0	0	15	38	33	16	16	12	39
Dettmer, John	4.33	0	6	11	9	0	0	54	63	42	26	20	27
Rogers, Kenny	4.46	11	8	24	24	6	0	167⅓	169	93	83	52	120
Brown, Kevin	4.82	7	9	26	25	3	0	170	218	109	91	50	123
Whiteside, Matt	5.02	2	2	47	0	0	1	61	68	40	34	28	37
Carpenter, Cris	5.03	2	5	47	0	0	5	59	69	35	33	20	39
Howell, Jay	5.44	4	1	40	0	0	2	43	44	29	26	16	22
Honeycutt, Rick	7.20	1	2	42	0	0	1	25	37	21	20	9	18
Bohanon, Brian	7.23	2	2	11	5	0	0	37⅓	51	31	30	8	26
Pavlik, Roger	7.69	2	5	11	11	0	0	50⅓	61	45	43	30	31
Leary, Tim	8.14	1	1	6	3	0	0	21	26	19	19	11	9

Toronto Blue Jays

BATTING

BATTING	BA	G	AB	R	H	TB	2B	3B	HR	RBI	SB	BB	SO
Molitor, Paul	.341	115	454	86	155	235	30	4	14	75	20	55	48
Alomar, Roberto	.306	107	392	78	120	177	25	4	8	38	19	51	41
Huff, Mike	.304	80	207	31	63	93	15	3	3	25	2	27	27
Olerud, John	.297	108	384	47	114	183	29	2	12	67	1	61	53
Carter, Joe	.271	111	435	70	118	228	25	2	27	103	11	33	64
White, Devon	.270	100	403	67	109	184	24	6	13	49	11	21	80
Schofield, Dick	.255	95	325	38	83	111	14	1	4	32	7	34	62
Borders, Pat	.247	85	295	24	73	97	13	1	3	26	1	15	50
Knorr, Randy	.242	40	124	20	30	53	2	0	7	19	0	10	35
Sprague, Ed	.240	109	405	38	97	151	19	1	11	44	1	23	95
Coles, Darnell	.210	48	143	15	30	50	6	1	4	15	0	10	25
Cedeno, Domingo	.196	47	97	14	19	27	2	3	0	10	1	10	31
Butler, Rob	.176	41	74	13	13	15	0	1	0	5	0	7	8

PITCHING

PITCHING	ERA	W	L	G	GS	CG	SV	INN	H	R	ER	BB	SO
Cox, Danny	1.45	1	1	10	0	0	3	18⅔	7	3	3	7	14
Castillo, Tony	2.51	5	2	41	0	0	1	68	66	22	19	28	43
Hentgen, Pat	3.40	13	8	24	24	6	0	174⅔	158	74	66	59	147
Hall, Darren	3.41	2	3	30	0	0	17	31⅔	26	12	12	14	28
Williams, Woody	3.64	1	3	38	0	0	0	59½	44	24	24	33	56
Stottlemyre, Todd	4.22	7	7	26	19	3	1	140⅔	149	67	66	48	105
Leiter, Al	5.08	6	7	20	20	1	0	111⅔	125	68	63	65	100
Timlin, Mike	5.18	0	1	34	0	0	2	40	41	25	23	20	38
Guzman, Juan	5.68	12	11	25	25	2	0	147⅓	165	102	93	76	124
Stewart, Dave	5.87	7	8	22	22	1	0	133⅓	151	89	87	62	111
Cornett, Brad	6.68	1	3	9	4	0	0	31	40	25	23	11	22
Righetti, Dave	10.18	0	1	20	0	0	0	20½	22	23	23	19	14

The World Series

Results

1903 ....Boston (A) 5, Pittsburgh (N) 3	1949 ....New York (A) 4, Brooklyn (N) 1
1904 ....No series	1950 ....New York (A) 4, Philadelphia (N) 0
1905 ....New York (N) 4, Philadelphia (A) 1	1951 ....New York (A) 4, New York (N) 2
1906 ....Chicago (A) 4, Chicago (N) 2	1952 ....New York (A) 4, Brooklyn (N) 3
1907 ....Chicago (N) 4, Detroit (A) 0; 1 tie	1953 ....New York (A) 4, Brooklyn (N) 2
1908 ....Chicago (N) 4, Detroit (A) 1	1954 ....New York (N) 4, Cleveland (A) 0
1909 ....Pittsburgh (N) 4, Detroit (A) 3	1955 ....Brooklyn (N) 4, New York (A) 3
1910 ....Philadelphia (A) 4, Chicago (N) 1	1956 ....New York (A) 4, Brooklyn (N) 3
1911 ....Philadelphia (A) 4, New York (N) 2	1957 ....Milwaukee (N) 4, New York (A) 3
1912 ....Boston (A) 4, New York (N) 3; 1 tie	1958 ....New York (A) 4, Milwaukee (N) 3
1913 ....Philadelphia (A) 4, New York (N) 1	1959 ....Los Angeles (N) 4, Chicago (A) 2
1914 ....Boston (N) 4, Philadelphia (A) 0	1960 ....Pittsburgh (N) 4, New York (A) 3
1915 ....Boston (A) 4, Philadelphia (N) 1	1961 ....New York (A) 4, Cincinnati (N) 1
1916 ....Boston (A) 4, Brooklyn (N) 1	1962 ....New York (A) 4, San Francisco (N) 3
1917 ....Chicago (A) 4, New York (N) 2	1963 ....Los Angeles (N) 4, New York (A) 0
1918 ....Boston (A) 4, Chicago (N) 2	1964 ....St Louis (N) 4, New York (A) 3
1919 ....Cincinnati (N) 5, Chicago (A) 3	1965 ....Los Angeles (N) 4, Minnesota (A) 3
1920 ....Cleveland (A) 5, Brooklyn (N) 2	1966 ....Baltimore (A) 4, Los Angeles (N) 0
1921 ....New York (N) 5, New York (A) 3	1967 ....St Louis (N) 4, Boston (A) 3
1922 ....New York (N) 4, New York (A) 0; 1 tie	1968 ....Detroit (A) 4, St Louis (N) 3
1923 ....New York (A) 4, New York (N) 2	1969 ....New York (N) 4, Baltimore (A) 1
1924 ....Washington (A) 4, New York (N) 3	1970 ....Baltimore (A) 4, Cincinnati (N) 1
1925 ....Pittsburgh (N) 4, Washington (A) 3	1971 ....Pittsburgh (N) 4, Baltimore (A) 3
1926 ....St Louis (N) 4, New York (A) 3	1972 ....Oakland (A) 4, Cincinnati (N) 3
1927 ....New York (A) 4, Pittsburgh (N) 0	1973 ....Oakland (A) 4, New York (N) 3
1928 ....New York (A) 4, St Louis (N) 0	1974 ....Oakland (A) 4, Los Angeles (N) 1
1929 ....Philadelphia (A) 4, Chicago (N) 1	1975 ....Cincinnati (N) 4, Boston (A) 3
1930 ....Philadelphia (A) 4, St Louis (N) 2	1976 ....Cincinnati (N) 4, New York (A) 0
1931 ....St Louis (N) 4, Philadelphia (A) 3	1977 ....New York (A) 4, Los Angeles (N) 2
1932 ....New York (A) 4, Chicago (N) 0	1978 ....New York (A) 4, Los Angeles (N) 2
1933 ....New York (N) 4, Washington (A) 1	1979 ....Pittsburgh (N) 4, Baltimore (A) 3
1934 ....St Louis (N) 4, Detroit (A) 3	1980 ....Philadelphia (N) 4, Kansas City (A) 2
1935 ....Detroit (A) 4, Chicago (N) 2	1981 ....Los Angeles (N) 4, New York (A) 2
1936 ....New York (A) 4, New York (N) 2	1982 ....St Louis (N) 4, Milwaukee (A) 3
1937 ....New York (A) 4, New York (N) 1	1983 ....Baltimore (A) 4, Philadelphia (N) 1
1938 ....New York (A) 4, Chicago (N) 0	1984 ....Detroit (A) 4, San Diego (N) 1
1939 ....New York (A) 4, Cincinnati (N) 0	1985 ....Kansas City (A) 4, St Louis (N) 3
1940 ....Cincinnati (N) 4, Detroit (A) 3	1986 ....New York (N) 4, Boston (A) 3
1941 ....New York (A) 4, Brooklyn (N) 1	1987 ....Minnesota (A) 4, St Louis (N) 3
1942 ....St Louis (N) 4, New York (A) 1	1988 ....Los Angeles (N) 4, Oakland (A) 1
1943 ....New York (A) 4, St Louis (N) 1	1989 ....Oakland (A) 4, San Francisco (N) 0
1944 ....St Louis (N) 4, St Louis (A) 2	1990 ....Cincinnati (N) 4, Oakland (A) 0
1945 ....Detroit (A) 4, Chicago (N) 3	1991 ....Minnesota (A) 4, Atlanta (N) 3
1946 ....St Louis (N) 4, Boston (A) 3	1992 ....Toronto (A) 4, Atlanta (N) 2
1947 ....New York (A) 4, Brooklyn (N) 3	1993 ....Toronto (A) 4, Philadelphia (N) 2
1948 ....Cleveland (A) 4, Boston (N) 2	1994 ....Series canceled due to players' strike

Air Apparent?

Arguably the worst hitter in major league baseball history was a fellow named Michael Henry Jordan, called Mike. In 1890, his only season in the big leagues, Jordan, a Pittsburgh Pirate outfielder, had 12 hits in 125 at bats for an .096 average. The 19th-century MJ is, in fact, the only nonpitcher in baseball history with more than 100 career at bats not to hit at least .100.

Oddly, Michael Jeffrey Jordan—the one hoping to make it with the Chicago White Sox some day—was born almost exactly 100 years after Michael Henry Jordan (Michael Jeffrey: Feb. 17, 1963; Michael Henry: Feb. 7, 1863). It is not known whether Michael Henry could go to his left.

Most Valuable Players

1955	Johnny Podres, Bklyn		1976	Johnny Bench, Cin
1956	Don Larsen, NY (A)		1977	Reggie Jackson, NY (A)
1957	Lew Burdette, Mil		1978	Bucky Dent, NY (A)
1958	Bob Turley, NY (A)		1979	Willie Stargell, Pitt
1959	Larry Sherry, LA		1980	Mike Schmidt, Phil
1960	Bobby Richardson, NY (A)		1981	Ron Cey, LA
1961	Whitey Ford, NY (A)			Pedro Guerrero, LA
1962	Ralph Terry, NY (A)			Steve Yeager, LA
1963	Sandy Koufax, LA		1982	Darrell Porter, StL
1964	Bob Gibson, StL		1983	Rick Dempsey, Balt
1965	Sandy Koufax, LA		1984	Alan Trammell, Det
1966	Frank Robinson, Balt		1985	Bret Saberhagen, KC
1967	Bob Gibson, StL		1986	Ray Knight, NY (N)
1968	Mickey Lolich, Det		1987	Frank Viola, Minn
1969	Donn Clendenon, NY (N)		1988	Orel Hershiser, LA
1970	Brooks Robinson, Balt		1989	Dave Stewart, Oak
1971	Roberto Clemente, Pitt		1990	Jose Rijo, Cin
1972	Gene Tenace, Oak		1991	Jack Morris, Minn
1973	Reggie Jackson, Oak		1992	Pat Borders, Tor
1974	Rollie Fingers, Oak		1993	Paul Molitor, Tor
1975	Pete Rose, Cin		1994	Series canceled due to strike

Career Batting Leaders (Minimum 50 at bats)

GAMES

Yogi Berra	75
Mickey Mantle	65
Elston Howard	54
Hank Bauer	53
Gil McDougald	53
Phil Rizzuto	52
Joe DiMaggio	51
Frankie Frisch	50
Pee Wee Reese	44
Roger Maris	41
Babe Ruth	41

AT BATS

Yogi Berra	259
Mickey Mantle	230
Joe DiMaggio	199
Frankie Frisch	197
Gil McDougald	190
Hank Bauer	188
Phil Rizzuto	183
Elston Howard	171
Pee Wee Reese	169
Roger Maris	152

HITS

Yogi Berra	71
Mickey Mantle	59
Frankie Frisch	58
Joe DiMaggio	54
Pee Wee Reese	46
Hank Bauer	46
Phil Rizzuto	45
Gil McDougald	45
Lou Gehrig	43
Eddie Collins	42
Babe Ruth	42
Elston Howard	42

BATTING AVERAGE

Pepper Martin	.418
Paul Molitor	.418
Lou Brock	.391
Thurman Munson	.373
George Brett	.373
Hank Aaron	.364
Frank Baker	.363
Roberto Clemente	.362
Lou Gehrig	.361
Reggie Jackson	.357

HOME RUNS

Mickey Mantle	18
Babe Ruth	15
Yogi Berra	12
Duke Snider	11
Reggie Jackson	10
Lou Gehrig	10
Frank Robinson	8
Bill Skowron	8
Joe DiMaggio	8
Goose Goslin	7
Hank Bauer	7
Gil McDougald	7

RUNS BATTED IN

Mickey Mantle	40
Yogi Berra	39
Lou Gehrig	35
Babe Ruth	33
Joe DiMaggio	30
Bill Skowron	29
Duke Snider	26
Reggie Jackson	24
Bill Dickey	24
Hank Bauer	24
Gil McDougald	24

RUNS

Mickey Mantle	42
Yogi Berra	41
Babe Ruth	37
Lou Gehrig	30
Joe DiMaggio	27
Roger Maris	26
Elston Howard	25
Gil McDougald	23
Jackie Robinson	22
Gene Woodling	21
Reggie Jackson	21
Duke Snider	21
Phil Rizzuto	21
Hank Bauer	21

STOLEN BASES

Lou Brock	14
Eddie Collins	14
Frank Chance	10
Davey Lopes	10
Phil Rizzuto	10
Honus Wagner	9
Frankie Frisch	9
Johnny Evers	8
Pepper Martin	7
Joe Morgan	7
Rickey Henderson	7

TOTAL BASES

Mickey Mantle	123
Yogi Berra	117
Babe Ruth	96
Lou Gehrig	87
Joe DiMaggio	84
Duke Snider	79
Hank Bauer	75
Reggie Jackson	74
Frankie Frisch	74
Gil McDougald	72

Career Batting Leaders (Cont.)

SLUGGING AVERAGE

Reggie Jackson	.755
Paul Molitor	.636
Babe Ruth	.744
Lou Gehrig	.731
Al Simmons	.658
Lou Brock	.655
Pepper Martin	.636
Hank Greenberg	.624
Charlie Keller	.611
Jimmie Foxx	.609
Dave Henderson	.606

STRIKEOUTS

Mickey Mantle	54
Elston Howard	37
Duke Snider	33
Babe Ruth	30
Gil McDougald	29
Bill Skowron	26
Hank Bauer	25
Reggie Jackson	24
Bob Meusel	24
Frank Robinson	23
George Kelly	23
Tony Kubek	23
Joe DiMaggio	23

Career Pitching Leaders (Minimum 25 innings pitched)

GAMES

Whitey Ford	22
Rollie Fingers	16
Allie Reynolds	15
Bob Turley	15
Clay Carroll	14
Clem Labine	13
Waite Hoyt	12
Catfish Hunter	12
Art Nehf	12
Paul Derringer	11
Carl Erskine	11
Rube Marquard	11
Christy Mathewson	11
Vic Raschi	11

INNINGS PITCHED

Whitey Ford	146
Christy Mathewson	101⅔
Red Ruffing	85⅔
Chief Bender	85
Waite Hoyt	83⅔
Bob Gibson	81
Art Nehf	79
Allie Reynolds	77
Jim Palmer	65
Catfish Hunter	63

WINS

Whitey Ford	10
Bob Gibson	7
Red Ruffing	7
Allie Reynolds	7
Lefty Gomez	6
Chief Bender	6
Waite Hoyt	6
Jack Coombs	5
Three Finger Brown	5
Herb Pennock	5
Christy Mathewson	5
Vic Raschi	5
Catfish Hunter	5

LOSSES

Whitey Ford	8
Eddie Plank	5
Schoolboy Rowe	5
Joe Bush	5
Rube Marquard	5
Christy Mathewson	5

SAVES

Rollie Fingers	6
Allie Reynolds	4
Johnny Murphy	4
Roy Face	3
Herb Pennock	3
Kent Tekulve	3
Firpo Marberry	3
Will McEnaney	3
Todd Worrell	3
Tug McGraw	3

EARNED RUN AVERAGE

Jack Billingham	.36
Harry Brecheen	.83
Babe Ruth	.87
Sherry Smith	.89
Sandy Koufax	.95
Hippo Vaughn	1.00
Monte Pearson	1.01
Christy Mathewson	1.15
Babe Adams	1.29
Eddie Plank	1.32

SHUTOUTS

Christy Mathewson	4
Three Finger Brown	3
Whitey Ford	3
Bill Hallahan	2
Lew Burdette	2
Bill Dinneen	2
Sandy Koufax	2
Allie Reynolds	2
Art Nehf	2
Bob Gibson	2

COMPLETE GAMES

Christy Mathewson	10
Chief Bender	9
Bob Gibson	8
Red Ruffing	7
Whitey Ford	7
George Mullin	6
Eddie Plank	6
Art Nehf	6
Waite Hoyt	6

STRIKEOUTS

Whitey Ford	94
Bob Gibson	92
Allie Reynolds	62
Sandy Koufax	61
Red Ruffing	61
Chief Bender	59
George Earnshaw	56
Waite Hoyt	49
Christy Mathewson	48
Bob Turley	46

BASES ON BALLS

Whitey Ford	34
Allie Reynolds	32
Art Nehf	32
Jim Palmer	31
Bob Turley	29
Paul Derringer	27
Red Ruffing	27
Don Gullett	26
Burleigh Grimes	26
Vic Raschi	25

League Championship Series

National League

1969 ....New York (E) 3, Atlanta (W) 0
1970 ....Cincinnati (W) 3, Pittsburgh (E) 0
1971 ....Pittsburgh (E) 3, San Francisco (W) 1
1972 ....Cincinnati (W) 3, Pittsburgh (E) 2
1973 ....New York (E) 3, Cincinnati (W) 2
1974 ....Los Angeles (W) 3, Pittsburgh (E) 1
1975 ....Cincinnati (W) 3, Pittsburgh (E) 0
1976 ....Cincinnati (W) 3, Philadelphia (E) 0
1977 ....Los Angeles (W) 3, Philadelphia (E) 1
1978 ....Los Angeles (W) 3, Philadelphia (E) 1
1979 ....Pittsburgh (E) 3, Cincinnati (W) 0
1980 ....Philadelphia (E) 3, Houston (W) 2
1981 ....Los Angeles (W) 3, Montreal (E) 2
1982 ....St Louis (E) 3, Atlanta (W) 0
1983 ....Philadelphia (E) 3, Los Angeles (W) 1
1984 ....San Diego (W) 3, Chicago (E) 2
1985 ....St Louis (E) 4, Los Angeles (W) 2
1986 ....New York (E) 4, Houston (W) 2
1987 ....St Louis (E) 4, San Francisco (W) 3
1988 ....Los Angeles (W) 4, New York (E) 3
1989 ....San Francisco (W) 4, Chicago (E) 1
1990 ....Cincinnati (W) 4, Pittsburgh (E) 2
1991 ....Atlanta (W) 4, Pittsburgh (E) 3
1992 ....Atlanta (W) 4, Pittsburgh (E) 3
1993 ....Philadelphia (E) 4, Atlanta (W) 2
1994 ....Playoffs canceled due to players' strike

American League

1969 ....Baltimore (E) 3, Minnesota (W) 0
1970 ....Baltimore (E) 3, Minnesota (W) 0
1971 ....Baltimore (E) 3, Oakland (W) 0
1972 ....Oakland (W) 3, Detroit (E) 2
1973 ....Oakland (W) 3, Baltimore (E) 2
1974 ....Oakland (W) 3, Baltimore (E) 1
1975 ....Boston (E) 3, Oakland (W) 0
1976 ....New York (E) 3, Kansas City (W) 2
1977 ....New York (E) 3, Kansas City (W) 2
1978 ....New York (E) 3, Kansas City (W) 1
1979 ....Baltimore (E) 3, California (W) 1
1980 ....Kansas City (W) 3, New York (E) 0
1981 ....New York (E) 3, Oakland (W) 0
1982 ....Milwaukee (E) 3, California (W) 2
1983 ....Baltimore (E) 3, Chicago (W) 1
1984 ....Detroit (E) 3, Kansas City (W) 0
1985 ....Kansas City (W) 4, Toronto (E) 3
1986 ....Boston (E) 4, California (W) 3
1987 ....Minnesota (W) 4, Detroit (E) 1
1988 ....Oakland (W) 4, Boston (E) 0
1989 ....Oakland (W) 4, Toronto (E) 1
1990 ....Oakland (W) 4, Boston (E) 0
1991 ....Minnesota (W) 4, Toronto (E) 1
1992 ....Toronto (E) 4, Oakland (W) 2
1993 ....Toronto (E) 4, Chicago (W) 2
1994 ....Playoffs canceled due to players' strike

NLCS Most Valuable Player

1977 ....Dusty Baker, LA
1978 ....Steve Garvey, LA
1979 ....Willie Stargell, Pitt
1980 ....Manny Trillo, Phil
1981 ....Burt Hooton, LA
1982 ....Darrell Porter, StL
1983 ....Gary Matthews, Phil

1984 ....Steve Garvey, SD
1985 ....Ozzie Smith, StL
1986 ....Mike Scott, Hou
1987 ....Jeffrey Leonard, SF
1988 ....Orel Hershiser, LA
1989 ....Will Clark, SF

1990 ....Randy Myers, Cin
        Ron Dibble, Cin
1991 ....Steve Avery, Atl
1992 ....John Smoltz, Atl
1993 ....Curt Schilling, Phil
1994 ....Playoffs canceled

ALCS Most Valuable Player

1980 ....Frank White, KC
1981 ....Graig Nettles, NY
1982 ....Fred Lynn, Calif
1983 ....Mike Boddicker, Balt
1984 ....Kirk Gibson, Det

1985 ....George Brett, KC
1986 ....Marty Barrett, Bos
1987 ....Gary Gaetti, Minn
1988 ....Dennis Eckersley, Oak
1989 ....Rickey Henderson, Oak

1990 ....Dave Stewart, Oak
1991 ....Kirby Puckett, Minn
1992 ....Roberto Alomar, Tor
1993 ....Dave Stewart, Tor
1994 ....Playoffs canceled

The All Star Game

Results

Date	Winner	Score	Site
7-6-33	American	4-2	Comiskey Park, Chi
7-10-34	American	9-7	Polo Grounds, NY
7-8-35	American	4-1	Municipal Stadium, Clev
7-7-36	National	4-3	Braves Field, Bos
7-7-37	American	8-3	Griffith Stadium, Wash
7-6-38	National	4-1	Crosley Field, Cin
7-11-39	American	3-1	Yankee Stadium, NY
7-10-40	National	4-0	Sportsman's Park, StL
7-8-41	American	7-5	Briggs Stadium, Det
7-6-42	American	3-1	Polo Grounds, NY
7-13-43	American	5-3	Shibe Park, Phil
7-11-44	National	7-1	Forbes Field, Pitt
1945	No game due to wartime travel restrictions		
7-9-46	American	12-0	Fenway Park, Bos
7-8-47	American	2-1	Wrigley Field, Chi
7-13-48	American	5-2	Sportsman's Park, StL
7-12-49	American	11-7	Ebbets Field, Bklyn

Results *(Cont.)*

Date	Winner	Score	Site
7-11-50	National	4-3	Comiskey Park, Chi
7-10-51	National	8-3	Briggs Stadium, Det
7-8-52	National	3-2	Shibe Park, Phil
7-14-53	National	5-1	Crosley Field, Cin
7-13-54	American	11-9	Municipal Stadium, Clev
7-12-55	National	6-5	County Stadium, Mil
7-10-56	National	7-3	Griffith Stadium, Wash
7-9-57	American	6-5	Busch Stadium, StL
7-8-58	American	4-3	Memorial Stadium, Balt
7-7-59	National	5-4	Forbes Field, Pitt
8-3-59	American	5-3	Memorial Coliseum, LA
7-11-60	National	5-3	Municipal Stadium, KC
7-13-60	National	6-0	Yankee Stadium, NY
7-11-61	National	5-4	Candlestick Park, SF
7-31-61	Tie*	1-1	Fenway Park, Bos
7-10-62	National	3-1	D.C. Stadium, Wash
7-30-62	American	9-4	Wrigley Field, Chi
7-9-63	National	5-3	Municipal Stadium, Clev
7-7-64	National	7-4	Shea Stadium, NY
7-13-65	National	6-5	Metropolitan Stadium, Minn
7-12-66	National	2-1	Busch Stadium, StL
7-11-67	National	2-1	Anaheim Stadium, Anaheim
7-9-68	National	1-0	Astrodome, Hou
7-23-69	National	9-3	R.F.K. Memorial Stadium, Wash
7-14-70	National	5-4	Riverfront Stadium, Cin
7-13-71	American	6-4	Tiger Stadium, Det
7-25-72	National	4-3	Atlanta Stadium, Atl
7-24-73	National	7-1	Royals Stadium, KC
7-23-74	National	7-2	Three Rivers Stadium, Pitt
7-15-75	National	6-3	County Stadium, Mil
7-13-76	National	7-1	Veterans Stadium, Phil
7-19-77	National	7-5	Yankee Stadium, NY
7-11-78	National	7-3	Jack Murphy Stadium, SD
7-17-79	National	7-6	Kingdome, Sea
7-8-80	National	4-2	Dodger Stadium, LA
8-9-81	National	5-4	Municipal Stadium, Clev
7-13-82	National	4-1	Olympic Stadium, Mon
7-6-83	American	13-3	Comiskey Park, Chi
7-10-84	National	3-1	Candlestick Park, SF
7-16-85	National	6-1	Metrodome, Minn
7-15-86	American	3-2	Astrodome, Hou
7-14-87	National	2-0	Oakland Coliseum, Oak
7-12-88	American	2-1	Riverfront Stadium, Cin
7-11-89	American	5-3	Anaheim Stadium, Anaheim
7-10-90	American	2-0	Wrigley Field, Chi
7-9-91	American	4-2	SkyDome, Toronto
7-14-92	American	13-6	Jack Murphy Stadium
7-13-93	American	9-3	Camden Yards, Balt
7-12-94	National	8-7	Three Rivers Stadium, Pitt

*Game called because of rain after 9 innings.

Most Valuable Players

1962	Maury Wills, LA	NL
	Leon Wagner, LA	AL
1963	Willie Mays, SF	NL
1964	Johnny Callison, Phil	NL
1965	Juan Marichal, SF	NL
1966	Brooks Robinson, Balt	AL
1967	Tony Perez, Cin	NL
1968	Willie Mays, SF	NL
1969	Willie McCovey, SF	NL
1970	Carl Yastrzemski, Bos	AL
1971	Frank Robinson, Balt	AL
1972	Joe Morgan, Cin	NL
1973	Bobby Bonds, SF	NL
1974	Steve Garvey, LA	NL
1975	Bill Madlock, Chi	NL
	Jon Matlack, NY	NL
1976	George Foster, Cin	NL
1977	Don Sutton, LA	NL
1978	Steve Garvey, LA	NL
1979	Dave Parker, Pitt	NL
1980	Ken Griffey, Cin	NL
1981	Gary Carter, Mont	NL
1982	Dave Concepcion, Cin	NL
1983	Fred Lynn, Calif	AL
1984	Gary Carter, Mont	NL
1985	LaMarr Hoyt, SD	NL
1986	Roger Clemens, Bos	AL
1987	Tim Raines, Mont	NL
1988	Terry Steinbach, Oak	AL
1989	Bo Jackson, KC	AL
1990	Julio Franco, Tex	AL

Most Valuable Players (Cont.)

1991 ....Cal Ripken Jr, Balt	AL	1993 ....Kirby Puckett, Minn	AL
1992 ....Ken Griffey Jr, Sea	AL	1994 ....Fred McGriff, Atl	NL

The Regular Season

Most Valuable Players
NATIONAL LEAGUE

Year	Name and Team	Position	Noteworthy
1911 ....Wildfire Schulte, Chi	Outfield	21 HR†, 121 RBI†, .300
1912 ....*Larry Doyle, NY	Second base	10 HR, 90 RBI, .330
1913 ....Jake Daubert, Bklyn	First base	52 RBI, .350†
1914 ....*Johnny Evers, Bos	Second base	F.A. .976†, .279
1915-23 ....No selection		
1924 ....Dazzy Vance, Bklyn	Pitcher	28†-6, 2.16 ERA†, 262 K†
1925 ....Rogers Hornsby, StL	Second base, Manager	39 HR†, 143 RBI†, .403†
1926 ....*Bob O'Farrell, StL	Catcher	7 HR, 68 RBI, .293
1927 ....*Paul Waner, Pitt	Outfield	237 hits†, 131 RBI†, .380†
1928 ....*Jim Bottomley, StL	First base	31 HR†, 136 RBI†, .325
1929 ....*Rogers Hornsby, Chi	Second base	39 HR, 149 RBI, 156 runs†, .380
1930 ....No selection		
1931 ....*Frankie Frisch, StL	Second base	4 HR, 82 RBI, 28 SB†, .311
1932 ....Chuck Klein, Phil	Outfield	38 HR†, 137 RBI, 226 hits†, .348
1933 ....*Carl Hubbell, NY	Pitcher	23†-12, 1.66 ERA†, 10 SO†
1934 ....*Dizzy Dean, StL	Pitcher	30†-7, 2.66 ERA, 195 K†
1935 ....*Gabby Hartnett, Chi	Catcher	13 HR, 91 RBI, .344
1936 ....*Carl Hubbell, NY	Pitcher	26†-6, 2.31 ERA†
1937 ....Joe Medwick, StL	Outfield	31 HR‡, 154 RBI†, 111 runs†, .374†
1938 ....Ernie Lombardi, Cin	Catcher	19 HR, 95 RBI, .342†
1939 ....*Bucky Walters, Cin	Pitcher	27†-11, 2.29 ERA†, 137 K‡
1940 ....*Frank McCormick, Cin	First base	19 HR, 127 RBI, 191 hits†, .309
1941 ....*Dolph Camilli, Bklyn	First base	34 HR†, 120 RBI†, .285
1942 ....*Mort Cooper, StL	Pitcher	22†-7, 1.78 ERA†, 10 SO†
1943 ....*Stan Musial, StL	Outfield	13 HR, 81 RBI, 220 hits†, .357†
1944 ....*Marty Marion, StL	Shortstop	F.A. .972†, 63 RBI
1945 ....*Phil Cavarretta, Chi	First base	6 HR, 97 RBI, .355†
1946 ....*Stan Musial, StL	First base, Outfield	103 RBI, 124 runs†, 228 hits†, .365†
1947 ....Bob Elliott, Bos	Third base	22 HR, 113 RBI, .317
1948 ....Stan Musial, StL	Outfield	39 HR, 131 RBI†, .376†
1949 ....*Jackie Robinson, Bklyn	Second base	16 HR, 124 RBI, 37 SB†, .342†
1950 ....*Jim Konstanty, Phil	Pitcher	16-7, 22 saves†, 2.66 ERA
1951 ....Roy Campanella, Bklyn	Catcher	33 HR, 108 RBI, .325
1952 ....Hank Sauer, Chi	Outfield	37 HR‡, 121 RBI†, .270
1953 ....*Roy Campanella, Bklyn	Catcher	41 HR, 142 RBI†, .312
1954 ....*Willie Mays, NY	Outfield	41 HR, 110 RBI, 13 3B†, .345†
1955 ....*Roy Campanella, Bklyn	Catcher	32 HR, 107 RBI, .318
1956 ....*Don Newcombe, Bklyn	Pitcher	27†-7, 3.06 ERA
1957 ....*Hank Aaron, Mil	Outfield	44 HR†, 132 RBI†, .322
1958 ....Ernie Banks, Chi	Shortstop	47 HR†, 129 RBI†, .313
1959 ....Ernie Banks, Chi	Shortstop	45 HR, 143 RBI†, .304
1960 ....*Dick Groat, Pitt	Shortstop	2 HR, 50 RBI, .325†
1961 ....*Frank Robinson, Cin	Outfield	37 HR, 124 RBI, .323
1962 ....Maury Wills, LA	Shortstop	104 SB†, 208 hits, .299, GG
1963 ....*Sandy Koufax, LA	Pitcher	25‡-5, 1.88 ERA†, 306 K†
1964 ....*Ken Boyer, StL	Third Base	24 HR, 119 RBI†, .295
1965 ....Willie Mays, SF	Outfield	52 HR†, 112 RBI, .317, GG
1966 ....Roberto Clemente, Pitt	Outfield	29 HR, 119 RBI, 202 hits, .317, GG
1967 ....*Orlando Cepeda, StL	First base	25 HR, 111 RBI†, .325
1968 ....*Bob Gibson, StL	Pitcher	22-9, 1.12 ERA†, 268 K†, 13 SO†, GG
1969 ....Willie McCovey, SF	First base	45 HR†, 126 RBI†, .320
1970 ....*Johnny Bench, Cin	Catcher	45 HR†, 148 RBI†, .293, GG
1971 ....Joe Torre, StL	Third base	24 HR, 137 RBI†, .363†
1972 ....*Johnny Bench, Cin	Catcher	40 HR†, 125 RBI†, .270, GG

*Played for pennant or, after 1968, division winner. †Led league. ‡Tied for league lead.

Most Valuable Players *(Cont.)*

NATIONAL LEAGUE (Cont.)

Year	Name and Team	Position	Noteworthy
1973	*Pete Rose, Cin	Outfield	5 HR, 64 RBI, .338†, 230 hits†
1974	*Steve Garvey, LA	First base	21 HR, 111 RBI, 200 hits, .312, GG
1975	*Joe Morgan, Cin	Second base	17 HR, 94 RBI, 67 SB, .327, GG
1976	*Joe Morgan, Cin	Second base	27 HR, 111 RBI, 60 SB, .320, GG
1977	George Foster, Cin	Outfield	52 HR†, 149 RBI†, .320
1978	Dave Parker, Pitt	Outfield	30 HR, 117 RBI, .334†, GG
1979	Keith Hernandez, StL	First base	11 HR, 105 RBI, 210 hits, .344†, GG
	*Willie Stargell, Pitt	First base	32 HR, 82 RBI, .281
1980	*Mike Schmidt, Phil	Third base	48 HR†, 121 RBI†, .286, GG
1981	Mike Schmidt, Phil	Third base	31 HR†, 91 RBI†, 78 runs†, .316, GG
1982	*Dale Murphy, Atl	Outfield	36 HR, 109 RBI‡, .281, GG
1983	Dale Murphy, Atl	Outfield	36 HR, 121 RBI†, .302, GG
1984	*Ryne Sandberg, Chi	Second base	19 HR, 84 RBI, 114 runs†, .314, GG
1985	*Willie McGee, StL	Outfield	10 HR, 82 RBI, 18 3B†, .353†, GG
1986	Mike Schmidt, Phil	Third base	37 HR†, 119 RBI, .290, GG
1987	Andre Dawson, Chi	Outfield	49 HR†, 137 RBI†, .287, GG
1988	*Kirk Gibson, LA	Outfield	25 HR, 76 RBI, 106 runs, .290
1989	*Kevin Mitchell, SF	Outfield	47 HR†, 125 RBI†, .291
1990	*Barry Bonds, Pitt	Outfield	33 HR, 114 RBI, .301
1991	*Terry Pendleton, Atl	Third base	23 HR, 86 RBI, .319†
1992	Barry Bonds, SF	Outfield	34 HR, 103 RBI, .311
1993	Barry Bonds, SF	Outfield	46 HR†, 123 RBI†, .336
1994	Jeff Bagwell, Hou	First base	39 HR, 116 RBI†, .368

AMERICAN LEAGUE

Year	Name and Team	Position	Noteworthy
1911	Ty Cobb, Det	Outfield	8 HR, 144 RBI†, 24 3B†, .420†
1912	*Tris Speaker, Bos	Outfield	10 HR‡, 98 RBI, 53 2B†, .383
1913	Walter Johnson, Wash	Pitcher	36†-7, 1.09 ERA†, 11 SO†, 243 K†
1914	*Eddie Collins, Phil	Second base	2 HR, 85 RBI, 122 runs†, .344
1915-21	No selection		
1922	George Sisler, StL	First base	8 HR, 105 RBI, 246 hits†, .420†
1923	*Babe Ruth, NY	Outfield	41 HR†, 131 RBI†, .393
1924	Walter Johnson, Wash	Pitcher	23†-7, 2.72 ERA†, 158 K†
1925	*Roger Peckinpaugh, Wash	Shortstop	4 HR, 64 RBI, .294
1926	George Burns, Clev	First base	114 RBI, 216 hits‡, 64 2B†, .358
1927	*Lou Gehrig, NY	First base	47 HR, 175 RBI†, 52 2B†, .373
1928	Mickey Cochrane, Phil	Catcher	10 HR, 57 RBI, .293
1929	No selection		
1930	No selection		
1931	*Lefty Grove, Phil	Pitcher	31†-4, 2.06 ERA†, 175 K†
1932	Jimmie Foxx, Phil	First base	58 HR†, 169 RBI†, 151 runs†, .364
1933	Jimmie Foxx, Phil	First base	48 HR†, 163 RBI†, .356†
1934	*Mickey Cochrane, Det	Catcher	2 HR, 76 RBI, .320
1935	*Hank Greenberg, Det	First base	36 HR‡, 170 RBI†, 203 hits, .328
1936	*Lou Gehrig, NY	First base	49 HR†, 152 RBI, 167 runs†, .354
1937	Charlie Gehringer, Det	Second base	14 HR, 96 RBI, 133 runs, .371†
1938	Jimmie Foxx, Bos	First base	50 HR, 175 RBI†, .349†
1939	*Joe DiMaggio, NY	Outfield	30 HR, 126 RBI, .381†
1940	*Hank Greenberg, Det	Outfield	41 HR†, 150 RBI†, 50 2B†, .340
1941	*Joe DiMaggio, NY	Outfield	30 HR, 125 RBI†, .357
1942	*Joe Gordon, NY	Second base	18 HR, 103 RBI, .322
1943	*Spud Chandler, NY	Pitcher	20†-4, 1.64 ERA†, 5 SO‡
1944	Hal Newhouser, Det	Pitcher	29†-9, 2.22 ERA†, 187 K†
1945	*Hal Newhouser, Det	Pitcher	25†-9, 1.81 ERA†, 8 SO†, 212 K†
1946	*Ted Williams, Bos	Outfield	38 HR, 123 RBI, 142 runs†, .342
1947	*Joe DiMaggio, NY	Outfield	20 HR, 97 RBI, .315
1948	*Lou Boudreau, Clev	Shortstop	18 HR, 106 RBI, .355
1949	Ted Williams, Bos	Outfield	43 HR†, 159 RBI‡, 150 runs†, .343
1950	*Phil Rizzuto, NY	Shortstop	125 runs, 200 hits, .324
1951	*Yogi Berra, NY	Catcher	27 HR, 88 RBI, .294
1952	Bobby Shantz, Phil	Pitcher	24†-7, 2.48 ERA
1953	Al Rosen, Clev	Third base	43 HR†, 145 RBI†, 115 runs†, .336
1954	Yogi Berra, NY	Catcher	22 HR, 125 RBI, .307

*Played for pennant or, after 1968, division winner. †Led league. ‡Tied for league lead.

Most Valuable Players (Cont.)

AMERICAN LEAGUE (Cont.)

Year	Name and Team	Position	Noteworthy
1955	*Yogi Berra, NY	Catcher	27 HR, 108 RBI, .272
1956	*Mickey Mantle, NY	Outfield	52 HR†, 130 RBI†, 132 runs†, .353†
1957	*Mickey Mantle, NY	Outfield	34 HR, 94 RBI, 121 runs†, .365
1958	Jackie Jensen, Bos	Outfield	35 HR, 122 RBI†, .286
1959	*Nellie Fox, Chi	Second base	2 HR, 70 RBI, .306, GG
1960	*Roger Maris, NY	Outfield	39 HR, 112 RBI†, .283, GG
1961	*Roger Maris, NY	Outfield	61 HR†, 142 RBI†, .269
1962	*Mickey Mantle, NY	Outfield	30 HR, 89 RBI, .321, GG
1963	*Elston Howard, NY	Catcher	28 HR, 85 RBI, .287, GG
1964	Brooks Robinson, Balt	Third base	28 HR, 118 RBI†, .317, GG
1965	*Zoilo Versalles, Minn	Shortstop	126 runs†, 45 2B‡, 12 3B‡, GG
1966	*Frank Robinson, Balt	Outfield	49 HR‡, 122 RBI†, 122 runs†, .316†
1967	*Carl Yastrzemski, Bos	Outfield	44 HR‡, 121 RBI†, 112 runs†, .326†, GG
1968	*Denny McLain, Det	Pitcher	31†-6, 1.96 ERA, 280 K
1969	*Harmon Killebrew, Minn	Third base, First base	49 HR†, 140 RBI†, .276
1970	*Boog Powell, Balt	First base	35 HR, 114 RBI, .297
1971	*Vida Blue, Oak	Pitcher	24-8, 1.82 ERA†, 8 SO†, 301 K
1972	Dick Allen, Chi	First base	37 HR†, 113 RBI†, .308
1973	*Reggie Jackson, Oak	Outfield	32 HR†, 117 RBI†, 99 runs†, .293
1974	Jeff Burroughs, Tex	Outfield	25 HR, 118 RBI†, .301
1975	*Fred Lynn, Bos	Outfield	21 HR, 105 RBI, 103 runs†, .331, GG
1976	*Thurman Munson, NY	Catcher	17 HR, 105 RBI, .302
1977	Rod Carew, Minn	First base	100 RBI, 128 runs†, 239 hits†, .388†
1978	Jim Rice, Bos	Outfield, designated hitter	46 HR†, 139 RBI†, 213 hits†, .315
1979	*Don Baylor, Calif	Outfield, designated hitter	36 HR, 139 RBI†, 120 runs†, .296
1980	*George Brett, KC	Third base	24 HR, 118 RBI, .390†
1981	*Rollie Fingers, Mil	Pitcher	6-3, 28 saves†, 1.04 ERA
1982	*Robin Yount, Mil	Shortstop	29 HR, 114 RBI, 210 hits†, .331, GG
1983	*Cal Ripken, Balt	Shortstop	27 HR, 102 RBI, 121 runs†, 211 hits†, .318
1984	*Willie Hernandez, Det	Pitcher	9-3, 32 saves, 1.92 ERA
1985	Don Mattingly, NY	First base	35 HR, 145 RBI†, 48 2B†, .324, GG
1986	*Roger Clemens, Bos	Pitcher	24†-4, 2.48 ERA†, 238 K
1987	George Bell, Tor	Outfield	47 HR, 134 RBI†, .308
1988	*Jose Canseco, Oak	Outfield	42 HR†, 124 RBI†, 40 SB, .307
1989	Robin Yount, Mil	Outfield	21 HR, 103 RBI, 101 runs, .318
1990	*Rickey Henderson, Oak	Outfield	28 HR, 119 runs†, 65 SB†, .325
1991	Cal Ripken, Jr, Balt	Shortstop	34 HR, 114 RBI, .323
1992	Dennis Eckersley, Oak	Pitcher	7-1, 1.91 ERA, 51 saves
1993	Frank Thomas, Chi	First base	41 HR, 128 RBI, .317
1994	Frank Thomas, Chi	First base	38 HR, 101 RBI, .353

*Played for pennant or, after 1968, division winner. †Led league. ‡Tied for league lead.

Notes: 2B=doubles; 3B=triples; F.A.=fielding average; GG=won Gold Glove, award begun in 1957; K=strikeouts; SO=shutouts; SB=stolen bases.

Rookies of the Year

NATIONAL LEAGUE		AMERICAN LEAGUE	
1947*	Jackie Robinson, Bklyn (1B)	1949	Roy Sievers, StL (OF)
1948*	Alvin Dark, Bos (SS)	1950	Walt Dropo, Bos (1B)
1949	Don Newcombe, Bklyn (P)	1951	Gil McDougald, NY (3B)
1950	Sam Jethroe, Bos (OF)	1952	Harry Byrd, Phil (P)
1951	Willie Mays, NY (OF)	1953	Harvey Kuenn, Det (SS)
1952	Joe Black, Bklyn (P)	1954	Bob Grim, NY (P)
1953	Junior Gilliam, Bklyn (2B)	1955	Herb Score, Clev (P)
1954	Wally Moon, StL (OF)	1956	Luis Aparicio, Chi (SS)
1955	Bill Virdon, StL (OF)	1957	Tony Kubek, NY (OF, SS)
1956	Frank Robinson, Cin (OF)	1958	Albie Pearson, Wash (OF)
1957	Jack Sanford, Phil (P)	1959	Bob Allison, Wash (OF)
1958	Orlando Cepeda, SF (1B)	1960	Ron Hansen, Balt (SS)
1959	Willie McCovey, SF (1B)	1961	Don Schwall, Bos (P)
1960	Frank Howard, LA (OF)	1962	Tom Tresh, NY (SS)

Rookies of the Year (Cont.)

NATIONAL LEAGUE (Cont.)

1961	Billy Williams, Chi (OF)
1962	Ken Hubbs, Chi (2B)
1963	Pete Rose, Cin (2B)
1964	Dick Allen, Phil (3B)
1965	Jim Lefebvre, LA (2B)
1966	Tommy Helms, Cin (2B)
1967	Tom Seaver, NY (P)
1968	Johnny Bench, Cin (C)
1969	Ted Sizemore, LA (2B)
1970	Carl Morton, Mont (P)
1971	Earl Williams, Atl (C)
1972	Jon Matlack, NY (P)
1973	Gary Matthews, SF (OF)
1974	Bake McBride, StL (OF)
1975	John Montefusco, SF (P)
1976	Pat Zachry, Cin (P)
	Butch Metzger, SD (P)
1977	Andre Dawson, Mont (OF)
1978	Bob Horner, Atl (3B)
1979	Rick Sutcliffe, LA (P)
1980	Steve Howe, LA (P)
1981	Fernando Valenzuela, LA (P)
1982	Steve Sax, LA (2B)
1983	Darryl Strawberry, NY (OF)
1984	Dwight Gooden, NY (P)
1985	Vince Coleman, StL (OF)
1986	Todd Worrell, StL (P)
1987	Benito Santiago, SD (C)
1988	Chris Sabo, Cin (3B)
1989	Jerome Walton, Chi (OF)
1990	Dave Justice, Atl (OF)
1991	Jeff Bagwell, Hou (3B)
1992	Eric Karros, LA (1B)
1993	Mike Piazza, LA (C)
1994	Raul Mondesi, LA (OF)

AMERICAN LEAGUE (Cont.)

1963	Gary Peters, Chi (P)
1964	Tony Oliva, Minn (OF)
1965	Curt Blefary, Balt (OF)
1966	Tommie Agee, Chi (OF)
1967	Rod Carew, Minn (2B)
1968	Stan Bahnsen, NY (P)
1969	Lou Piniella, KC (OF)
1970	Thurman Munson, NY (C)
1971	Chris Chambliss, Clev (1B)
1972	Carlton Fisk, Bos (C)
1973	Al Bumbry, Balt (OF)
1974	Mike Hargrove, Tex (1B)
1975	Fred Lynn, Bos (OF)
1976	Mark Fidrych, Det (P)
1977	Eddie Murray, Balt (DH)
1978	Lou Whitaker, Det (2B)
1979	Alfredo Griffin, Tor (SS)
	John Castino, Minn (3B)
1980	Joe Charboneau, Clev (OF)
1981	Dave Righetti, NY (P)
1982	Cal Ripken, Balt (SS)
1983	Ron Kittle, Chi (OF)
1984	Alvin Davis, Sea (1B)
1985	Ozzie Guillen, Chi (SS)
1986	Jose Canseco, Oak (OF)
1987	Mark McGwire, Oak (1B)
1988	Walt Weiss, Oak (SS)
1989	Gregg Olson, Balt (P)
1990	Sandy Alomar Jr, Clev (C)
1991	Chuck Knoblauch, Minn (2B)
1992	Pat Listach, Mil (SS)
1993	Tim Salmon, Calif (OF)
1994	Bob Hamelin, Minn (DH)

*Just one selection for both leagues.

Cy Young Award

Year		W-L	Sv	ERA	Year		W-L	Sv	ERA
1956	*Don Newcombe, Bklyn (NL)	27-7	0	3.06	1962	Don Drysdale, LA (NL)	25-9	1	2.83
1957	Warren Spahn, Mil (NL)	21-11	3	2.69	1963	*Sandy Koufax, LA (NL)	25-5	0	1.88
1958	Bob Turley, NY (AL)	21-7	1	2.97	1964	Dean Chance, LA (AL)	20-9	4	1.65
1959	Early Wynn, Chi (AL)	22-10	0	3.17	1965	Sandy Koufax, LA (NL)	26-8	2	2.04
1960	Vernon Law, Pitt (NL)	20-9	0	3.08	1966	Sandy Koufax, LA (NL)	27-9	0	1.73
1961	Whitey Ford, NY (AL)	25-4	0	3.21					

NATIONAL LEAGUE

Year		W-L	Sv	ERA
1967	Mike McCormick, SF	22-10	0	2.85
1968	*Bob Gibson, StL	22-9	0	1.12
1969	Tom Seaver, NY	25-7	0	2.21
1970	Bob Gibson, StL	23-7	0	3.12
1971	Ferguson Jenkins, Chi	24-13	0	2.77
1972	Steve Carlton, Phil	27-10	0	1.97
1973	Tom Seaver, NY	19-10	0	2.08
1974	Mike Marshall, LA	15-12	21	2.42
1975	Tom Seaver, NY	22-9	0	2.38
1976	Randy Jones, SD	22-14	0	2.74
1977	Steve Carlton, Phil	23-10	0	2.64
1978	Gaylord Perry, SD	21-6	0	2.72
1979	Bruce Sutter, Chi	6-6	37	2.23
1980	Steve Carlton, Phil	24-9	0	2.34
1981	F. Valenzuela, LA	13-7	0	2.48
1982	Steve Carlton, Phil	23-11	0	3.10
1983	John Denny, Phil	19-6	0	2.37
1984	†Rick Sutcliffe, Chi	16-1	0	2.69

AMERICAN LEAGUE

Year		W-L	Sv	ERA
1967	Jim Lonborg, Bos	22-9	0	3.16
1968	*Denny McLain, Det	31-6	0	1.96
1969	Denny McLain, Det	24-9	0	2.80
	Mike Cuellar, Balt	23-11	0	2.38
1970	Jim Perry, Minn	24-12	0	3.03
1971	*Vida Blue, Oak	24-8	0	1.82
1972	Gaylord Perry, Clev	24-16	1	1.92
1973	Jim Palmer, Balt	22-9	1	2.40
1974	Catfish Hunter, Oak	25-12	0	2.49
1975	Jim Palmer, Balt	23-11	1	2.09
1976	Jim Palmer, Balt	22-13	0	2.51
1977	Sparky Lyle, NY	13-5	26	2.17
1978	Ron Guidry, NY	25-3	0	1.74
1979	Mike Flanagan, Balt	23-9	0	3.08
1980	Steve Stone, Balt	25-7	0	3.23
1981	*Rollie Fingers, Mil	6-3	28	1.04
1982	Pete Vuckovich, Mi	18-6	0	3.34
1983	LaMarr Hoyt, Chi	24-10	0	3.66

Cy Young Award (Cont.)

NATIONAL LEAGUE

Year		W-L	Sv	ERA
1985	Dwight Gooden, NY	24-4	0	1.53
1986	Mike Scott, Hou	18-10	0	2.22
1987	Steve Bedrosian, Phil	5-3	40	2.83
1988	Orel Hershiser, LA	23-8	1	2.26
1989	Mark Davis, SD	4-3	44	1.85
1990	Doug Drabek, Pitt	22-6	0	2.76
1991	Tom Glavine, Atl	20-11	0	2.55
1992	Greg Maddux, Chi	20-11	0	2.18
1993	Greg Maddux, Atl	20-10	0	2.36
1994	Greg Maddux, Atl	16-6	0	1.56

AMERICAN LEAGUE

Year		W-L	Sv	ERA
1984	*Willie Hernandez, Det	9-3	32	1.92
1985	Bret Saberhagen, KC	20-6	0	2.87
1986	*Roger Clemens, Bos	24-4	0	2.48
1987	Roger Clemens, Bos	20-9	0	2.97
1988	Frank Viola, Minn	24-7	0	2.64
1989	Bret Saberhagen, KC	23-6	0	2.16
1990	Bob Welch, Oak	27-6	0	2.95
1991	Roger Clemens, Bos	18-10	0	2.62
1992	*Dennis Eckersley, Oak	7-1	51	1.91
1993	Jack McDowell, Chi	22-10	0	3.37
1994	David Cone, KC	16-4	0	2.94

*Pitchers who won the MVP and Cy Young awards in the same season.

†NL games only. Sutcliffe pitched 15 games with Cleveland before being traded to the Cubs.

Career Individual Batting

GAMES

Pete Rose	3562
Carl Yastrzemski	3308
Hank Aaron	3298
Ty Cobb	3034
Stan Musial	3026
Willie Mays	2992
Rusty Staub	2951
Dave Winfield	2927
Brooks Robinson	2896
Robin Yount	2856
Al Kaline	2834
Eddie Collins	2826
Reggie Jackson	2820
Frank Robinson	2808
Tris Speaker	2789
Honus Wagner	2789
Tony Perez	2777
Mel Ott	2734
George Brett	2707
Eddie Murray	2706

HOME RUNS

Hank Aaron	755
Babe Ruth	714
Willie Mays	660
Frank Robinson	586
Harmon Killebrew	573
Reggie Jackson	563
Mike Schmidt	548
Mickey Mantle	536
Jimmie Foxx	534
Ted Williams	521
Willie McCovey	521
Eddie Mathews	512
Ernie Banks	512
Mel Ott	511
Lou Gehrig	493
Willie Stargell	475
Stan Musial	475
Dave Winfield	463
Eddie Murray	458
Carl Yastrzemski	452

BATTING AVERAGE

Ty Cobb	.367
Rogers Hornsby	.358
Joe Jackson	.356
Ed Delahanty	.346
Ted Williams	.344
Tris Speaker	.344
Billy Hamilton	.344
Willie Keeler	.343
Dan Brouthers	.342
Babe Ruth	.342
Harry Heilmann	.342
Pete Browning	.341
Bill Terry	.341
George Sisler	.340
Lou Gehrig	.340
Jesse Burkett	.339
Nap Lajoie	.338
Riggs Stephenson	.336
Wade Boggs	.335
Al Simmons	.334
Tony Gwynn	.334

AT BATS

Pete Rose	14053
Hank Aaron	12364
Carl Yastrzemski	11988
Ty Cobb	11429
Robin Yount	11008
Stan Musial	10972
Dave Winfield	10888
Willie Mays	10881
Brooks Robinson	10654
Honus Wagner	10441
George Brett	10349
Lou Brock	10332
Luis Aparicio	10230
Tris Speaker	10208
Eddie Murray	10167
Al Kaline	10116
Rabbit Maranville	10078
Frank Robinson	10006
Eddie Collins	9949
Reggie Jackson	9864

HITS

Pete Rose	4256
Ty Cobb	4191
Hank Aaron	3771
Stan Musial	3630
Tris Speaker	3515
Carl Yastrzemski	3419
Honus Wagner	3418
Eddie Collins	3311
Willie Mays	3283
Nap Lajoie	3244
George Brett	3154
Paul Waner	3152
Robin Yount	3142
Dave Winfield	3088
Rod Carew	3053
Lou Brock	3023
Al Kaline	3007
Roberto Clemente	3000
Cap Anson	3000
Sam Rice	2987

RUNS

Ty Cobb	2245
Babe Ruth	2174
Hank Aaron	2174
Pete Rose	2165
Willie Mays	2062
Stan Musial	1949
Lou Gehrig	1888
Tris Speaker	1881
Mel Ott	1859
Frank Robinson	1829
Eddie Collins	1818
Carl Yastrzemski	1816
Ted Williams	1798
Charlie Gehringer	1774
Jimmie Foxx	1751
Honus Wagner	1735
Willie Keeler	1727
Cap Anson	1719
Jesse Burkett	1718
Billy Hamilton	1692

Career Individual Batting *(Cont.)*

DOUBLES

Tris Speaker	792
Pete Rose	746
Stan Musial	725
Ty Cobb	724
George Brett	665
Nap Lajoie	658
Carl Yastrzemski	646
Honus Wagner	643
Hank Aaron	624
Paul Waner	603
Robin Yount	583
Charlie Gehringer	574
Harry Heilmann	542
Rogers Hornsby	541
Joe Medwick	540
Al Simmons	539
Dave Winfield	535
Lou Gehrig	535
Al Oliver	529
Cap Anson	528
Frank Robinson	528

TRIPLES

Sam Crawford	312
Ty Cobb	297
Honus Wagner	252
Jake Beckley	243
Roger Connor	233
Tris Speaker	223
Fred Clarke	220
Dan Brouthers	205
Joe Kelley	194
Paul Waner	190
Bid McPhee	188
Eddie Collins	187
Sam Rice	184
Ed Delahanty	183
Jesse Burkett	183
Edd Roush	182
Ed Konetchy	181
Buck Ewing	178
Rabbit Maranville	177
Stan Musial	177
Harry Stovey	177

BASES ON BALLS

Babe Ruth	2056
Ted Williams	2019
Joe Morgan	1865
Carl Yastrzemski	1845
Mickey Mantle	1734
Mel Ott	1708
Eddie Yost	1614
Darrell Evans	1605
Stan Musial	1599
Pete Rose	1566
Harmon Killebrew	1559
Lou Gehrig	1508
Mike Schmidt	1507
Eddie Collins	1503
Rickey Henderson	1478
Willie Mays	1463
Jimmie Foxx	1452
Eddie Mathews	1444
Frank Robinson	1420
Hank Aaron	1402

RUNS BATTED IN

Hank Aaron	2297
Babe Ruth	2211
Lou Gehrig	1990
Ty Cobb	1961
Stan Musial	1951
Jimmie Foxx	1921
Willie Mays	1903
Mel Ott	1861
Carl Yastrzemski	1844
Ted Williams	1839
Al Simmons	1827
Frank Robinson	1812
Dave Winfield	1786
Eddie Murray	1738
Honus Wagner	1732
Cap Anson	1715
Reggie Jackson	1702
Tony Perez	1652
Ernie Banks	1636

SLUGGING AVERAGE

Babe Ruth	.690
Ted Williams	.634
Lou Gehrig	.632
Jimmie Foxx	.609
Hank Greenberg	.605
Joe DiMaggio	.579
Rogers Hornsby	.577
Johnny Mize	.562
Stan Musial	.559
Willie Mays	.557
Mickey Mantle	.557
Hank Aaron	.555
Ralph Kiner	.548
Hack Wilson	.545
Chuck Klein	.543
Duke Snider	.540
Frank Robinson	.537
Al Simmons	.535
Dick Allen	.534
Earl Averill	.533
Mel Ott	.533

STOLEN BASES

Rickey Henderson	1117
Lou Brock	938
Billy Hamilton	915
Ty Cobb	892
Eddie Collins	743
Tim Raines	743
Arlie Latham	739
Max Carey	738
Honus Wagner	703
Vince Coleman	698
Joe Morgan	689
Willie Wilson	660
Tom Brown	657
Bert Campaneris	649
George Davis	616
Dummy Hoy	594
Maury Wills	586
Davey Lopes	557
Cesar Cedeno	550

PINCH HITS

Manny Mota	150
Smoky Burgess	145
Greg Gross	143
Jose Morales	123
Jerry Lynch	116
Red Lucas	114
Steve Braun	113
Terry Crowley	108
Gates Brown	107
Denny Walling	107
Mike Lum	103
Rusty Staub	100
Vic Davalillo	95
Larry Biittner	95
Jerry Hairston	94
Jim Dwyer	94
Dave Philley	93
Joel Youngblood	93
Jay Johnstone	92

TOTAL BASES

Hank Aaron	6856
Stan Musial	6134
Willie Mays	6066
Ty Cobb	5863
Babe Ruth	5793
Pete Rose	5752
Carl Yastrzemski	5539
Frank Robinson	5373
Dave Winfield	5188
Tris Speaker	5104
Lou Gehrig	5059
Mel Ott	5041
George Brett	5044
Jimmie Foxx	4956
Ted Williams	4884
Eddie Murray	4883
Honus Wagner	4868
Al Kaline	4852
Reggie Jackson	4834
Robin Yount	4730

STRIKEOUTS

Reggie Jackson	2597
Willie Stargell	1936
Mike Schmidt	1883
Tony Perez	1867
Dave Kingman	1816
Bobby Bonds	1757
Dale Murphy	1748
Lou Brock	1730
Mickey Mantle	1710
Harmon Killebrew	1699
Dwight Evans	1697
Dave Winfield	1660
Lee May	1570
Dick Allen	1556
Willie McCovey	1550
Frank Robinson	1532
Willie Mays	1526
Rick Monday	1513
Greg Luzinski	1495

Career Individual Pitching

GAMES

Hoyt Wilhelm	1070
Kent Tekulve	1050
Goose Gossage	1002
Lindy McDaniel	987
Rollie Fingers	944
Gene Garber	931
Cy Young	906
Sparky Lyle	899
Jim Kaat	898
Lee Smith	891
Don McMahon	874
Jeff Reardon	869
Phil Niekro	864
Charlie Hough	858
Dennis Eckersley	849
Roy Face	848
Tug McGraw	824
Nolan Ryan	807
Walter Johnson	801
Gaylord Perry	777

LOSSES

Cy Young	315
Pud Galvin	308
Nolan Ryan	292
Walter Johnson	279
Phil Niekro	274
Gaylord Perry	265
Jack Powell	256
Don Sutton	256
Eppa Rixey	251
Bert Blyleven	250
Robin Roberts	245
Warren Spahn	245
Early Wynn	244
Steve Carlton	244
Jim Kaat	237
Frank Tanana	236
Gus Weyhing	235
Tommy John	231
Ted Lyons	230
Bob Friend	230

EARNED RUN AVERAGE

Ed Walsh	1.82
Addie Joss	1.88
Three Finger Brown	2.06
Monte Ward	2.10
Christy Mathewson	2.13
Rube Waddell	2.16
Walter Johnson	2.17
Orval Overall	2.24
Tommy Bond	2.25
Will White	2.28
Ed Reulbach	2.28
Jim Scott	2.32
Eddie Plank	2.34
Larry Corcoran	2.36
Eddie Cicotte	2.37
George McQuillan	2.38
Ed Killian	2.38
Doc White	2.38
Nap Rucker	2.42
Jeff Tesreau	2.43

INNINGS PITCHED

Cy Young	7356
Pud Galvin	5941
Walter Johnson	5923
Phil Niekro	5403
Nolan Ryan	5386
Gaylord Perry	5351
Don Sutton	5280
Warren Spahn	5244
Steve Carlton	5217
Grover Alexander	5189
Kid Nichols	5084
Tim Keefe	5061
Bert Blyleven	4969
Mickey Welch	4802
Tom Seaver	4783
Christy Mathewson	4782
Tommy John	4708
Robin Roberts	4689
Early Wynn	4564
Tony Mullane	4540

WINNING PERCENTAGE

Bob Caruthers	.692
Dave Foutz	.690
Whitey Ford	.690
Lefty Grove	.680
Vic Raschi	.667
Christy Mathewson	.665
Larry Corcoran	.663
Sam Leever	.658
Sal Maglie	.657
Roger Clemens	.655
Sandy Koufax	.655
Johnny Allen	.654
Ron Guidry	.651
Lefty Gomez	.649
Dwight Gooden	.649
Three Finger Brown	.649
John Clarkson	.648
Dizzy Dean	.644
Grover Alexander	.642
Deacon Phillippe	.639

SHUTOUTS

Walter Johnson	110
Grover Alexander	90
Christy Mathewson	80
Cy Young	76
Eddie Plank	69
Warren Spahn	63
Nolan Ryan	61
Tom Seaver	61
Bert Blyleven	60
Don Sutton	58
Ed Walsh	57
Three Finger Brown	57
Pud Galvin	57
Bob Gibson	56
Steve Carlton	55
Jim Palmer	53
Gaylord Perry	53
Juan Marichal	52
Rube Waddell	50
Vic Willis	50

WINS

Cy Young	511
Walter Johnson	416
Christy Mathewson	373
Grover Alexander	373
Warren Spahn	363
Kid Nichols	361
Pud Galvin	361
Tim Keefe	342
Steve Carlton	329
Eddie Plank	327
John Clarkson	326
Don Sutton	324
Nolan Ryan	324
Phil Niekro	318
Gaylord Perry	314
Old Hoss Radbourn	311
Tom Seaver	311
Mickey Welch	308
Lefty Grove	300
Early Wynn	300

SAVES

Lee Smith	434
Jeff Reardon	365
Rollie Fingers	341
Goose Gossage	310
Bruce Sutter	300
Dennis Eckersley	294
John Franco	266
Tom Henke	260
Dave Righetti	252
Dan Quisenberry	244
Sparky Lyle	238
Hoyt Wilhelm	227
Gene Garber	218
Dave Smith	216
Randy Myers	205
Bobby Thigpen	201
Roy Face	193
Mitch Williams	192
Doug Jones	190
Mike Marshall	188

COMPLETE GAMES

Cy Young	750
Pud Galvin	639
Tim Keefe	557
Kid Nichols	532
Walter Johnson	531
Mickey Welch	525
Old Hoss Radbourn	489
John Clarkson	485
Tony Mullane	469
Jim McCormick	466
Gus Weyhing	448
Grover Alexander	438
Christy Mathewson	435
Jack Powell	422
Eddie Plank	412
Will White	394
Amos Rusie	392
Vic Willis	388
Warren Spahn	382
Jim Whitney	377

Career Individual Pitching (Cont.)

STRIKEOUTS		BASES ON BALLS	
Nolan Ryan	5714	Nolan Ryan	2795
Steve Carlton	4136	Steve Carlton	1833
Bert Blyleven	3701	Phil Niekro	1809
Tom Seaver	3640	Early Wynn	1775
Don Sutton	3574	Bob Feller	1764
Gaylord Perry	3534	Bobo Newsom	1732
Walter Johnson	3508	Amos Rusie	1704
Phil Niekro	3342	Charlie Hough	1665
Ferguson Jenkins	3192	Gus Weyhing	1566
Bob Gibson	3117	Red Ruffing	1541
Jim Bunning	2855	Bump Hadley	1442
Mickey Lolich	2832	Warren Spahn	1434
Cy Young	2796	Earl Whitehill	1431
Frank Tanana	2773	Tony Mullane	1409
Warren Spahn	2583	Sad Sam Jones	1396
Bob Feller	2581	Tom Seaver	1390
Jerry Koosman	2556	Gaylord Perry	1379
Tim Keefe	2527	Mike Torrez	1371
Christy Mathewson	2502	Walter Johnson	1355
Don Drysdale	2486	Don Sutton	1343

Individual Batting (Single Season)

HITS		TOTAL BASES		RUNS BATTED IN	
George Sisler, 1920	257	Babe Ruth, 1921	457	Hack Wilson, 1930	190
Bill Terry, 1930	254	Rogers Hornsby, 1922	450	Lou Gehrig, 1931	184
Lefty O'Doul, 1929	254	Lou Gehrig, 1927	447	Hank Greenberg, 1937	183
Al Simmons, 1925	253	Chuck Klein, 1930	445	Jimmie Foxx, 1938	175
Rogers Hornsby, 1922	250	Jimmie Foxx, 1932	438	Lou Gehrig, 1927	175
Chuck Klein, 1930	250	Stan Musial, 1948	429	Lou Gehrig, 1930	174
Ty Cobb, 1911	248	Hack Wilson, 1930	423	Babe Ruth, 1921	171
George Sisler, 1922	246	Chuck Klein, 1932	420	Hank Greenberg, 1935	170
Willie Keeler, 1897	243	Lou Gehrig, 1930	419	Chuck Klein, 1930	170
Babe Herman, 1930	241	Joe DiMaggio, 1937	418	Jimmie Foxx, 1932	169
Heinie Manush, 1928	241				

BATTING AVERAGE		TRIPLES		STRIKEOUTS	
Hugh Duffy, 1894	.438	Owen Wilson, 1912	36	Bobby Bonds, 1970	189
Tip O'Neill, 1887	.435	Heinie Reitz, 1894	31	Bobby Bonds, 1969	187
Willie Keeler, 1897	.432	Dave Orr, 1886	31	Rob Deer, 1987	186
Ross Barnes, 1876	.429	Perry Werden, 1893	29	Pete Incaviglia, 1986	185
Rogers Hornsby, 1924	.424	Harry Davis, 1897	28	Cecil Fielder, 1990	182
Jesse Burkett, 1895	.423	Sam Thompson, 1894	27	Mike Schmidt, 1975	180
Nap Lajoie, 1901	.422	George Davis, 1893	27	Rob Deer, 1986	179
George Sisler, 1922	.420	Jimmy Williams, 1899	27	Jose Canseco, 1986	175
Ty Cobb, 1911	.420	George Treadway, 1894	26	Dave Nicholson, 1963	175
Tuck Turner, 1894	.416	Long John Reilly, 1890	26	Gorman Thomas, 1979	175
		Joe Jackson, 1912	26	Rob Deer, 1991	175
		Sam Crawford, 1914	26		
		Kiki Cuyler, 1925	26		

DOUBLES		HOME RUNS		RUNS	
Earl Webb, 1931	67	Roger Maris, 1961	61	Billy Hamilton, 1894	196
George Burns, 1926	64	Babe Ruth, 1927	60	Babe Ruth, 1921	177
Joe Medwick, 1936	64	Babe Ruth, 1921	59	Tom Brown, 1891	177
Hank Greenberg, 1934	63	Hank Greenberg, 1938	58	Joe Kelley, 1894	167
Paul Waner, 1932	62	Jimmie Foxx, 1932	58	Tip O'Neill, 1887	167
Charlie Gehringer, 1936	60	Hack Wilson, 1930	56	Lou Gehrig, 1936	167
Tris Speaker, 1923	59	Babe Ruth, 1920	54	Billy Hamilton, 1895	166
Chuck Klein, 1930	59	Mickey Mantle, 1961	54	Willie Keeler, 1894	165
Billy Herman, 1936	57	Babe Ruth, 1928	54	Babe Ruth, 1928	163
Billy Herman, 1935	57	Ralph Kiner, 1949	54	Lou Gehrig, 1931	163
				Arlie Latham, 1887	163

Individual Batting (Single Season) *(Cont.)*

STOLEN BASES		BASES ON BALLS		SLUGGING AVERAGE	
Rickey Henderson, 1982	130	Babe Ruth, 1923	170	Babe Ruth, 1920	.847
Lou Brock, 1974	118	Ted Williams, 1947	162	Babe Ruth, 1921	.846
Vince Coleman, 1985	110	Ted Williams, 1949	162	Babe Ruth, 1927	.772
Vince Coleman, 1987	109	Ted Williams, 1946	156	Lou Gehrig, 1927	.765
Rickey Henderson, 1983	108	Eddie Yost, 1956	151	Babe Ruth, 1923	.764
Vince Coleman, 1986	107	Eddie Joost, 1949	149	Rogers Hornsby, 1925	.756
Maury Wills, 1962	104	Babe Ruth, 1920	148	Jeff Bagwell, 1994	.750
Rickey Henderson, 1980	100	Jimmy Wynn, 1969	148	Jimmie Foxx, 1932	.749
Ron LeFlore, 1980	97	Eddie Stanky, 1945	148	Babe Ruth, 1924	.739
Ty Cobb, 1915	96	Jimmy Sheckard, 1911	147	Babe Ruth, 1926	.737
Omar Moreno, 1980	96				

Individual Pitching (Single Season)

GAMES		WINS		SAVES	
Mike Marshall, 1974	106	Jack Chesbro, 1904	41	Bobby Thigpen, 1990	57
Kent Tekulve, 1979	94	Ed Walsh, 1908	40	Randy Myers, 1993	53
Mike Marshall, 1973	92	Christy Mathewson, 1908	37	Dennis Eckersley, 1992	51
Kent Tekulve, 1978	91	Walter Johnson, 1913	36	Dennis Eckersley, 1990	48
Wayne Granger, 1969	90	Jouett Meekin, 1894	36	Rod Beck, 1993	48
Mike Marshall, 1979	90	Amos Rusie, 1894	36	Lee Smith, 1991	47
Kent Tekulve, 1987	90	Joe McGinnity, 1904	35	Bryan Harvey, 1991	46
Mark Eichhorn, 1987	89	Cy Young, 1895	35	Dave Righetti, 1986	46
Wilbur Wood, 1968	88	Smoky Joe Wood, 1912	34	Bruce Sutter, 1984	45
Rob Murphy, 1987	87	Frank Killen, 1893	34	Dan Quisenberry, 1983	45
				Dennis Eckersley, 1988	45
				Jeff Montgomery, 1993	45
				Bryan Harvey, 1993	45
				Duane Ward, 1993	45

GAMES STARTED		LOSSES		EARNED RUN AVERAGE	
Amos Rusie, 1893	52	Red Donahue, 1897	33	Dutch Leonard, 1914	1.01
Jack Chesbro, 1904	51	Jim Hughey, 1899	30	Three Finger Brown, 1906	1.04
Frank Killen, 1896	50	Ted Breitenstein, 1895	30	Walter Johnson, 1913	1.09
Amos Rusie, 1894	50	Vic Willis, 1905	29	Bob Gibson, 1968	1.12
Pink Hawley, 1895	50	Bill Hart, 1896	29	Christy Mathewson, 1909	1.14
Ted Breitenstein, 1894	50	Jack Taylor, 1898	29	Jack Pfiester, 1907	1.15
Ted Breitenstein, 1895	50	Still Bill Hill, 1896	28	Addie Joss, 1908	1.16
Ed Walsh, 1908	49	Duke Esper, 1893	28	Carl Lundgren, 1907	1.17
Wilbur Wood, 1972	49	Paul Derringer, 1933	27	Grover Alexander, 1915	1.22
Joe McGinnity, 1903	48	Bill Hart, 1897	27	Cy Young, 1908	1.26
Jouett Meekin, 1894	48	George Bell, 1910	27		
Frank Killen, 1893	48	Willie Sudhoff, 1898	27		
Wilbur Wood, 1973	48	Dummy Taylor, 1901	27		
		Pink Hawley, 1894	27		

INNINGS PITCHED		WINNING PERCENTAGE		SHUTOUTS	
Amos Rusie, 1893	482	Roy Face, 1959	.947	Grover Alexander, 1916	16
Ed Walsh, 1908	464	Johnny Allen, 1937	.938	Bob Gibson, 1968	13
Jack Chesbro, 1904	455	Ron Guidry, 1978	.893	Jack Coombs, 1910	13
Ted Breitenstein, 1894	447	Freddie Fitzsimmons, 1940	.889	Grover Alexander, 1915	12
Pink Hawley, 1895	444	Lefty Grove, 1931	.886	Christy Mathewson, 1908	12
Amos Rusie, 1894	444	Bob Stanley, 1978	.882	Dean Chance, 1964	11
Joe McGinnity, 1903	434	Preacher Roe, 1951	.880	Walter Johnson, 1913	11
Frank Killen, 1896	432	Tom Seaver, 1981	.875	Sandy Koufax, 1963	11
Ted Breitenstein, 1895	430	Smoky Joe Wood, 1912	.872	Ed Walsh, 1908	11
Kid Nichols, 1893	425	David Cone, 1988	.870		

Sibling Saves

On July 1, 1994, the Manzanillos—Josias of the New York Mets and Ravelo of the Pittsburgh Pirates—became the first brothers in major league history to get saves on the same night. Josias, a righty, pitched two innings to preserve a 3–1 defeat of the San Diego Padres, while Ravelo, a southpaw, saved a 6–4 win over the Cincinnati Reds with one scoreless inning. Not bad for one family.

Then again, considering that the pitchers' father, Demetrio, fathered 38 children (according to Josias), perhaps it was inevitable.

Individual Pitching (Single Season) (Cont.)

COMPLETE GAMES		STRIKEOUTS		BASES ON BALLS	
Amos Rusie, 1893	50	Nolan Ryan, 1973	383	Amos Rusie, 1893	218
Jack Chesbro, 1904	48	Sandy Koufax, 1965	382	Cy Seymour, 1898	213
Ted Breitenstein, 1894	46	Nolan Ryan, 1974	367	Bob Feller, 1938	208
Ted Breitenstein, 1895	46	Rube Waddell, 1904	349	Nolan Ryan, 1977	204
Vic Willis, 1902	45	Bob Feller, 1946	348	Nolan Ryan, 1974	202
Amos Rusie, 1894	45	Nolan Ryan, 1977	341	Amos Rusie, 1894	200
Kid Nichols, 1893	44	Nolan Ryan, 1972	329	Bob Feller, 1941	194
Cy Young, 1894	44	Nolan Ryan, 1976	327	Bobo Newsom, 1938	192
Joe McGinnity, 1903	44	Sam McDowell, 1965	325	Ted Breitenstein, 1894	191
Pink Hawley, 1895	44	Sandy Koufax, 1966	317	Tony Mullane, 1893	189
Frank Killen, 1896	44				

Manager of the Year

NATIONAL LEAGUE		AMERICAN LEAGUE	
1983	Tommy Lasorda, LA	1983	Tony La Russa, Chi
1984	Jim Frey, Chi	1984	Sparky Anderson, Det
1985	Whitey Herzog, StL	1985	Bobby Cox, Tor
1986	Hal Lanier, Hou	1986	John McNamara, Bos
1987	Buck Rodgers, Mont	1987	Sparky Anderson, Det
1988	Tommy Lasorda, LA	1988	Tony La Russa, Oak
1989	Don Zimmer, Chi	1989	Frank Robinson, Balt
1990	Jim Leyland, Pitt	1990	Jeff Torborg, Chi
1991	Bobby Cox, Atl	1991	Tom Kelly, Minn
1992	Jim Leyland, Pitt	1992	Tony La Russa, Oak
1993	Dusty Baker, SF	1993	Gene Lamont, Chi
1994	Felipe Alou, Mont.	1994	Buck Showalter, NY

Individual Batting (Single Game)

MOST RUNS

6	Mel Ott, NY (N)	Aug 4, 1934, 2nd game
		Apr 30, 1944, 1st game
	Johnny Pesky, Bos (A)	May 8, 1946
	Frank Torre, Mil (N)	Sept 2, 1957, 2nd game
	Spike Owen, Bos (A)	Aug 21, 1986

MOST HITS

7	Rennie Stennett, Pitt	Sept 16, 1975

MOST HOME RUNS

4	Lou Gehrig, NY (A)	June 3, 1932
	Gil Hodges, Bklyn	Aug 31, 1950
	Joe Adcock, Mil (N)	July 31, 1954
	Rocky Colavito, Cle	June 10, 1959
	Willie Mays, SF	April 30, 1961

MOST HOME RUNS (Cont.)

4	Bob Horner, Atl	July 6, 1986
	Mark Whiten, StL	Sep 7, 1993

MOST GRAND SLAMS

2	Tony Lazzeri, NY (A)	May 24, 1936
	Jim Tabor, Bos (A)	July 4, 1939
	Rudy York, Bos (A)	July 27, 1946
	Jim Gentile, Balt	May 9, 1961
	Tony Cloninger, Atl	July 3, 1966
	Jim Northrup, Det	June 24, 1968
	Frank Robinson, Balt	June 26, 1970

MOST RBI

12	Jim Bottomley, StL	Sep 16, 1924
	Mark Whiten, StL	Sep 7, 1993

Individual Batting (Single Inning)

MOST RUNS

3	Sammy White, Bos (A)	June 18, 1953, 7th inning

MOST HITS

3	Gene Stephens, Bos (A)	June 18, 1953, 7th inning

MOST RBI

6	Fred Merkle, NY (N)	May 13, 1911 (RBIs not officially adopted until 1920)
	Bob Johnson, Phil (A)	Aug 29, 1937

MOST RBI (Cont.)

6	Tom McBride, Bos (A)	Aug 4, 1945
	Joe Astroth, Phil (A)	Sept 23, 1950
	Gil McDougald, NY (A)	May 3, 1951
	Sam Mele, Chi (A)	June 10, 1952
	Jim Lemon, Wash	Sept 5, 1959
	Jim Ray Hart, SF	July 8, 1970
	Andre Dawson, Mont	Sept 24, 1985
	Dale Murphy, Atl	July 27, 1989
	Carlos Quintana, Bos (A)	July 30, 1991

Individual Pitching (Single Game)

MOST INNINGS PITCHED

26 .....Leon Cadore, Bklyn   May 1, 1920, tie 1-1
         Joe Oeschger, Bos (N) May 1, 1920, tie 1-1

MOST STRIKEOUTS

20 .....Roger Clemens, Bos (A) April 29, 1986

MOST RUNS ALLOWED

24 .....Al Travers, Det   May 18, 1912 (only
                             major league game)

MOST WALKS ALLOWED

16 .....Bruno Haas, Phil (A)   June 2, 1915

MOST HITS ALLOWED

26 .....Harley Parker, Cin   June 21, 1901
         Hod Lisenbee, Phil (A) Sept 11, 1936
         Al Travers, Det   May 18, 1912 (only
                                major league game)

MOST WILD PITCHES

6 .......J.R. Richard, Hou   April 10, 1979
         Phil Niekro, Atl   Aug 14, 1979
         Bill Gullickson, Mont   April 10, 1982

Individual Pitching (Single Inning)

MOST RUNS ALLOWED

13 .....Lefty O'Doul, Bos (A)   July 7, 1923

MOST WILD PITCHES

4 ....Walter Johnson, Wash Sept 21, 1914
         Phil Niekro, Atl   Aug 14, 1979

MOST WALKS ALLOWED

8 ....Dolly Gray, Wash   Aug 28, 1909

Miscellaneous

LONGEST GAME, BY INNINGS

26 .....Brooklyn 1, Boston 1   May 1, 1920

LONGEST GAME, BY TIME

4:18 ..LA 8, SF 7   Oct 2, 1962

Note: All records after 1900. All single game hitting records for nine-inning game.

Baseball Hall of Fame

Players

	Position	Career Dates	Year Selected		Position	Career Dates	Year Selected
Hank Aaron	OF	1954-76	1982	Jack Chesbro	P	1899-1909	1946
Grover Alexander	P	1911-30	1938	Fred Clarke	OF	1894-1915	1945
Cap Anson	1B	1876-97	1939	John Clarkson	P	1882-94	1963
Luis Aparicio	SS	1956-73	1984	Roberto Clemente	OF	1955-72	1973
Luke Appling	SS	1930-50	1964	Ty Cobb	OF	1905-28	1936
Earl Averill	OF	1929-41	1975	Mickey Cochrane	C	1925-37	1947
Frank Baker	3B	1908-22	1955	Eddie Collins	2B	1906-30	1939
Dave Bancroft	SS	1915-30	1971	Jimmy Collins	3B	1895-1908	1945
Ernie Banks	SS-1B	1953-71	1977	Earle Combs	OF	1924-35	1970
Jake Beckley	1B	1888-1907	1971	Roger Connor	1B	1880-97	1976
Cool Papa Bell*	OF		1974	Stan Coveleski	P	1912-28	1969
Johnny Bench	C	1967-83	1989	Sam Crawford	OF	1899-1917	1957
Chief Bender	P	1903-25	1953	Joe Cronin	SS	1926-45	1956
Yogi Berra	C	1946-65	1972	Candy Cummings	P	1872-77	1939
Jim Bottomley	1B	1922-37	1974	Kiki Cuyler	OF	1921-38	1968
Lou Boudreau	SS	1938-52	1970	Ray Dandridge*	3B		1987
Roger Bresnahan	C	1897-1915	1945	Dizzy Dean	P	1930-47	1953
Lou Brock	OF	1961-79	1985	Ed Delahanty	OF	1888-1903	1945
Dan Brouthers	1B	1879-1904	1945	Bill Dickey	C	1928-46	1954
Three Finger Brown	P	1903-16	1949	Martin Dihigo*	P-OF		1977
Jesse Burkett	OF	1890-1905	1946	Joe DiMaggio	OF	1936-51	1955
Roy Campanella	C	1948-57	1969	Bobby Doerr	2B	1937-51	1986
Rod Carew	1B-2B	1967-85	1991	Don Drysdale	P	1956-69	1984
Max Carey	OF	1910-29	1961	Hugh Duffy	OF	1888-1906	1945
Steve Carlton	P	1965-88	1994	Johnny Evers	2B	1902-29	1939
Frank Chance	1B	1898-1914	1946	Buck Ewing	C	1880-97	1946
Oscar Charleston*	OF		1976	Red Faber	P	1914-33	1964

Note: Career dates indicate first and last appearances in the majors.
*Elected on the basis of his career in the Negro leagues.

Players (Cont.)

	Position	Career Dates	Year Selected		Position	Career Dates	Year Selected
Bob Feller	P	1936-56	1962	Joe McGinnity	P	1899-1908	1946
Rick Ferrell	C	1929-47	1984	Joe Medwick	OF	1932-48	1968
Rollie Fingers	P	1968-85	1992	Johnny Mize	1B	1936-53	1981
Elmer Flick	OF	1898-1910	1963	Joe Morgan	2B	1963-84	1990
Whitey Ford	P	1950-67	1974	Stan Musial	OF-1B	1941-63	1969
Jimmie Foxx	1B	1925-45	1951	Hal Newhouser	P	1939-55	1992
Frankie Frisch	2B	1919-37	1947	Kid Nichols	P	1890-1906	1949
Pud Galvin	P	1879-92	1965	Jim O'Rourke	OF	1876-1904	1945
Lou Gehrig	1B	1923-39	1939	Mel Ott	OF	1926-47	1951
Charlie Gehringer	2B	1924-42	1949	Satchel Paige*	P	1948-65	1971
Bob Gibson	P	1959-75	1981	Jim Palmer	P	1965-84	1990
Josh Gibson*	C		1972	Herb Pennock	P	1912-34	1948
Lefty Gomez	P	1930-43	1972	Gaylord Perry	P	1962-83	1991
Goose Goslin	OF	1921-38	1968	Eddie Plank	P	1901-17	1946
Hank Greenberg	1B	1930-47	1956	Hoss Radbourn	P	1880-91	1939
Burleigh Grimes	P	1916-34	1964	Pee Wee Reese	SS	1940-58	1984
Lefty Grove	P	1925-41	1947	Sam Rice	OF	1915-35	1963
Chick Hafey	OF	1924-37	1971	Eppa Rixey	P	1912-33	1963
Jesse Haines	P	1918-37	1970	Phil Rizzuto	SS	1941-56	1994
Billy Hamilton	OF	1888-1901	1961	Robin Roberts	P	1948-66	1976
Gabby Hartnett	C.	1922-41	1955	Brooks Robinson	3B	1955-77	1983
Harry Heilmann	OF	1914-32	1952	Frank Robinson	OF	1956-76	1982
Billy Herman	2B	1931-47	1975	Jackie Robinson	2B	1947-56	1962
Harry Hooper	OF	1909-25	1971	Edd Roush	OF	1913-31	1962
Rogers Hornsby	2B	1915-37	1942	Red Ruffing	P	1924-47	1967
Waite Hoyt	P	1918-38	1969	Amos Rusie	P	1889-1901	1977
Carl Hubbell	P	1928-43	1947	Babe Ruth	OF	1914-35	1936
Catfish Hunter	P	1965-79	1987	Ray Schalk	C	1912-29	1955
Monte Irvin*	OF	1949-56	1973	Red Schoendienst	2B	1945-63	1989
Reggie Jackson	OF	1967-87	1993	Tom Seaver	P	1967-86	1992
Travis Jackson	SS	1922-36	1982	Joe Sewell	SS	1920-33	1977
Ferguson Jenkins	P	1965-83	1991	Al Simmons	OF	1924-44	1953
Hugh Jennings	SS	1891-1918	1945	George Sisler	1B	1915-30	1939
Judy Johnson*	3B		1975	Enos Slaughter	OF	1938-59	1985
Walter Johnson	P	1907-27	1936	Duke Snider	OF	1947-64	1980
Addie Joss	P	1902-10	1978	Warren Spahn	P	1942-65	1973
Al Kaline	OF	1953-74	1980	Al Spalding	P	1871-78	1939
Tim Keefe	P	1880-93	1964	Tris Speaker	OF	1907-28	1937
Willie Keeler	OF	1892-1910	1939	Willie Stargell	OF-1B	1962-82	1988
George Kell	3B	1943-57	1983	Bill Terry	1B	1923-36	1954
Joe Kelley	OF	1891-1908	1971	Sam Thompson	OF	1885-1906	1974
George Kelly	1B	1915-32	1973	Joe Tinker	SS	1902-16	1946
King Kelly	C	1878-93	1945	Pie Traynor	3B	1920-37	1948
Harmon Killebrew	1B-3B	1954-75	1984	Dazzy Vance	P	1915-35	1955
Ralph Kiner	OF	1946-55	1975	Arky Vaughan	SS	1932-48	1985
Chuck Klein	OF	1928-44	1980	Rube Waddell	P	1897-1910	1946
Sandy Koufax	P	1955-66	1972	Honus Wagner	SS	1897-1917	1936
Nap Lajoie	2B	1896-1916	1937	Bobby Wallace	SS	1894-1918	1953
Tony Lazzeri	2B	1926-39	1991	Ed Walsh	P	1904-17	1946
Bob Lemon	P	1941-58	1976	Lloyd Waner	OF	1927-45	1967
Buck Leonard*	1B		1977	Paul Waner	OF	1926-45	1952
Fred Lindstrom	3B	1924-36	1976	Monte Ward	2B-P	1878-94	1964
Pop Lloyd*	SS-1B		1977	Mickey Welch	P	1880-92	1973
Ernie Lombardi	C	1931-47	1986	Zach Wheat	OF	1909-27	1959
Ted Lyons	P	1923-46	1955	Hoyt Wilhelm	P	1952-72	1985
Mickey Mantle	OF	1951-68	1974	Billy Williams	OF	1959-76	1987
Heinie Manush	OF	1923-39	1964	Ted Williams	OF	1939-60	1966
Rabbit Maranville	SS-2B	1912-35	1954	Hack Wilson	OF	1923-34	1979
Juan Marichal	P	1960-75	1983	Early Wynn	P	1939-63	1972
Rube Marquard	P	1908-25	1971	Carl Yastrzemski	OF	1961-83	1989
Eddie Mathews	3B	1952-68	1978	Cy Young	P	1890-1911	1937
Christy Mathewson	P	1900-16	1936	Ross Youngs	OF	1917-26	1972
Willie Mays	OF	1951-73	1979				
Tommy McCarthy	OF	1884-96	1946				
Willie McCovey	1B	1959-80	1986				

Umpires

	Year Selected
Al Barlick	1989
Jocko Conlan	1974
Tom Connolly	1953
Billy Evans	1973
Cal Hubbard	1976
Bill Klem	1953
Bill McGowan	1992

Meritorious Service

	Year Selected
Ed Barrow (manager-executive)	1953
Morgan Bulkeley (executive)	1937
Alexander Cartwright (executive)	1938
Henry Chadwick (writer-executive)	1938
Happy Chandler (commissioner)	1982
Charles Comiskey (manager-executive)	1939
Rube Foster (player-manager-executive)	1981
Ford Frick (commissioner-executive)	1970
Warren Giles (executive)	1979
Will Harridge (executive)	1972
Ban Johnson (executive)	1937
Kenesaw M. Landis (commissioner)	1944
Larry MacPhail (executive)	1978
Branch Rickey (manager-executive)	1967
Al Spalding (player-executive)	1939
Bill Veeck (owner)	1991
George Weiss (executive)	1971
George Wright (player-manager)	1937
Harry Wright (player-manager-executive)	1953
Tom Yawkey (executive)	1980

Managers

	Years Managed	Year Selected
Walt Alston	1954-76	1983
Leo Durocher	1939-73	1994
Clark Griffith	1901-20	1946
Bucky Harris	1924-56	1975
Miller Huggins	1913-29	1964
Al Lopez	1951-69	1977
Connie Mack	1894-1950	1937
Joe McCarthy	1926-50	1957
John McGraw	1899-1932	1937
Bill McKechnie	1915-46	1962
Wilbert Robinson	1902-31	1945
Casey Stengel	1934-65	1966

THEY SAID IT

Al Downing, former Los Angeles Dodger lefthander, who 20 years ago served up Henry Aaron's record-breaking 715th home run, on living with his place in history : "I never say 'seven-fifteen' anymore. I now say 'quarter after seven.'"

Notable Achievements

No-Hit Games, 9 Innings or More

NATIONAL LEAGUE

Date		Pitcher and Game
1876	July 15	George Bradley, StL vs Hart 2-0
1880	June 12	John Richmond, Wor vs Clev 1-0 (perfect game)
	June 17	Monte Ward, Prov vs Buff 5-0 (perfect game)
	Aug 19	Larry Corcoran, Chi vs Bos 6-0
	Aug 20	Pud Galvin, Buff at Wor 1-0
1882	Sep 20	Larry Corcoran, Chi vs Wor 5-0
	Sep 22	Tim Lovett, Bklyn vs NY 4-0
1883	July 25	Hoss Radbourn, Prov at Clev 8-0
	Sep 13	Hugh Daily, Clev at Phil 1-0
1884	June 27	Larry Corcoran, Chi vs Prov 6-0
	Aug 4	Pud Galvin, Buff at Det 18-0
1885	July 27	John Clarkson, Chi at Prov 4-0
	Aug 29	Charles Ferguson, Phil vs Prov 1-0
1891	July 31	Amos Rusie, NY vs Bklyn 6-0
	June 22	Tom Lovett, Bklyn vs NY 4-0
1892	Aug 6	Jack Stivetts, Bos vs Bklyn 11-0
	Aug 22	Alex Sanders, Lou vs Balt 6-2
	Oct 15	Bumpus Jones, Cin vs Pitt 7-1 (first major league game)
1893	Aug 16	Bill Hawke, Balt vs Wash 5-0

Date		Pitcher and Game
1897	Sep 18	Cy Young, Clev vs Cin 6-0
1898	Apr 22	Ted Breitenstein, Cin vs Pitt 11-0
	Apr 22	Jim Hughes, Balt vs Bos 8-0
	July 8	Frank Donahue, Phil vs Bos 5-0
	Aug 21	Walter Thornton, Chi vs Bklyn 2-0
1899	May 25	Deacon Phillippe, Lou vs NY 7-0
	Aug 7	Vic Willis, Bos vs Wash 7-1
1900	July 12	Noodles Hahn, Cin vs Phil 4-0
1901	July 15	Christy Mathewson, NY at StL 5-0
1903	Sep 18	Chick Fraser, Phil at Chi 10-0
1904	June 11	Bob Wicker, Chi at NY 1-0 (hit in 10th; won in 12th)
1905	June 13	Christy Mathewson, NY at Chi 1-0
1906	May 1	John Lush, Phil at Bklyn 6-0
	July 20	Mal Eason, Bklyn at StL 2-0
	Aug 1	Harry McIntire, Bklyn vs Pitt 0-1 (hit in 11th; lost in 13th)
1907	May 8	Frank Pfeffer, Bos vs Cin 6-0
	Sep 20	Nick Maddox, Pitt vs Bklyn 2-1
1908	July 4	George Wiltse, NY vs Phil 1-0 (10 innings)
	Sep 5	Nap Rucker, Bklyn vs Bos 6-0

No-Hit Games, 9 Innings or More *(Cont.)*

NATIONAL LEAGUE *(CONT.)*

Date	Pitcher and Game	Date	Pitcher and Game
1909......Apr 15	Leon Ames, NY vs Bklyn 0-3 (hit in 10th; lost in 13th)	1965......Aug 19	Jim Maloney, Cin at Chi 1-0 (10 innings)
1912......Sep 6	Jeff Tesreau, NY at Phil 3-0	Sep 9	Sandy Koufax, LA vs Chi 1-0 (perfect game)
1914......Sep 9	George Davis, Bos vs Phil 7-0	1967......June 18	Don Wilson, Hou vs Atl 2-0
1915......Apr 15	Rube Marquard, NY vs Bklyn 2-0	1968......July 29	George Culver, Cin at Phil 6-1
Aug 31	Jimmy Lavender, Chi at NY 2-0	Sep 17	Gaylord Perry, SF vs StL 1-0
1916......June 16	Tom Hughes, Bos vs Pitt 2-0	Sep 18	Ray Washburn, StL at SF 2-0
1917......May 2	Jim Vaughn, Chi vs Cin 0-1 (hit in 10th; lost in 10th)	1969......Apr 17	Bill Stoneman, Mont at Phil 7-0
May 2	Fred Toney, Cin at Chi 1-0 (10 innings)	Apr 30	Jim Maloney, Cin vs Hou 10-0
1919......May 11	Hod Eller, Cin vs StL 6-0	May 1	Don Wilson, Hou at Cin 4-0
1922......May 7	Jesse Barnes, NY vs Phil 6-0	Aug 19	Ken Holtzman, Chi vs Atl 3-0
1924......July 17	Jesse Haines, StL vs Bos 5-0	Sep 20	Bob Moose, Pitt at NY 4-0
1925......Sep 13	Dazzy Vance, Bklyn vs Phil 10-1	1970......June 12	Dock Ellis, Pitt at SD 2-0
1929......May 8	Carl Hubbell, NY vs Pitt 11-0	July 20	Bill Singer, LA vs Phil 5-0
1934......Sep 21	Paul Dean, StL vs Bklyn 3-0	1971......June 3	Ken Holtzman, Chi at Cin 1-0
1938......June 11	Johnny Vander Meer, Cin vs Bos 3-0	June 23	Rick Wise, Phil at Cin 4-0
June 15	Johnny Vander Meer, Cin at Bklyn 6-0	Aug 14	Bob Gibson, StL at Pitt 11-0
1940......Apr 30	Tex Carleton, Bklyn at Cin, 3-0	1972......Apr 16	Burt Hooton, Chi vs Phil 4-0
1941......Aug 30	Lon Warneke, StL at Cin 2-0	Sep 2	Milt Pappas, Chi vs SD 8-0
1944......Apr 27	Jim Tobin, Bos vs Bklyn 2-0	Oct 2	Bill Stoneman, Mont vs NY 7-0
May 15	Clyde Shoun, Cin vs Bos 1-0	1973......Aug 5	Phil Niekro, Atl vs SD 9-0
1946......Apr 23	Ed Head, Bklyn vs Bos 5-0	1975......Aug 24	Ed Halicki, SF vs NY 6-0
1947......June 18	Ewell Blackwell, Cin vs Bos 6-0	1976......July 9	Larry Dierker, Hou vs Mont 6-0
1948......Sep 9	Rex Barney, Bklyn at NY 2-0	Aug 9	John Candelaria, Pitt vs LA 2-0
1950......Aug 11	Vern Bickford, Bos vs Bklyn 7-0	Sep 29	John Montefusco, SF at Atl 9-0
1951......May 6	Cliff Chambers, Pitt at Bos 3-0	1978......Apr 16	Bob Forsch, StL vs Phil 5-0
1952......June 19	Carl Erskine, Bklyn vs Chi 5-0	June 16	Tom Seaver, Cin vs StL 4-0
1954......June 12	Jim Wilson, Mil vs Phil 2-0	1979......Apr 7	Ken Forsch, Hou vs Atl 6-0
1955......May 12	Sam Jones, Chi vs Pitt 4-0	1980......June 27	Jerry Reuss, LA at SF 8-0
1956......May 12	Carl Erskine, Bklyn vs NY 3-0	1981......May 10	Charlie Lea, Mont vs SF 4-0
Sep 25	Sal Maglie, Bklyn vs Phil 5-0	Sep 26	Nolan Ryan, Hou vs LA 5-0
1959......May 26	Harvey Haddix, Pitt at Mil 0-1 (hit in 13th; lost in 13th)	1983......Sep 26	Bob Forsch, StL vs Mont 3-0
1960......May 15	Don Cardwell, Chi vs StL 4-0	1986......Sep 25	Mike Scott, Hou vs SF 2-0
Aug 18	Lew Burdette, Mil vs Phil 1-0	1988......Sep 16	Tom Browning, Cin vs LA 1-0 (perfect game)
Sep 16	Warren Spahn, Mil vs Phil 4-0	1990......June 29	Fernando Valenzuela, LA vs StL 6-0
1961......Apr 28	Warren Spahn, Mil vs SF 1-0	1990......Aug 15	Terry Mulholland, Phil vs SF 6-0
1962......June 30	Sandy Koufax, LA vs NY 5-0	1991......May 23	Tommy Greene, Phil at Mont 2-0
1963......May 11	Sandy Koufax, LA vs SF 8-0	July 26	Mark Gardner, Mont at LA 0-1 (hit in 10th, lost in 10th)
May 17	Don Nottebart, Hou vs Phil 4-1	July 28	Dennis Martinez, Mont at LA 2-0 (perfect game)
June 15	Juan Marichal, SF vs Hou 1-0	Sep 11	Kent Mercker (6), Mark Wohlers (2), and Alejandro Pena (1), Atl at SD 1-0
1964......Apr 23	Ken Johnson, Hou vs Cin 0-1	1992......Aug 17	Kevin Gross, LA vs SF 2-0
June 4	Sandy Koufax, LA at Phil 3-0	1993......Sep 8	Darryl Kile, Hou vs NY 7-1
June 21	Jim Bunning, Phil at NY 6-0 (perfect game)	1994......Apr 8	Kent Mercker, Atl vs LA 6-0
1965......June 14	Jim Maloney, Cin vs NY 0-1 (hit in 11th; lost in 11th)		

Note: Includes the games struck from the record book on September 4, 1991, when baseball's committee on statistical accuracy voted to define no-hitters as games of 9 innings or more that end with a team getting no hits.

Opportunity Knocked

The Pittsburgh Pirates left 17 runners on base—one shy of the National League record for a nine inning game—in a 6-4 loss to the Philadelphia Phillies on May 12, 1994. "I had a lot of visitors," said Pittsburgh third base coach Rich Donnelly, "but no one went home. It was like a Monopoly game: No one would advance directly to Go. They were all stuck on some utility."

No-Hit Games, 9 Innings or More *(Cont.)*

AMERICAN LEAGUE

Date	Pitcher and Game	Date	Pitcher and Game
1901......May 9	Earl Moore, Clev vs Chi 2-4 (hit in 10th; lost in 10th)	1966......Oct 8	Don Larsen, NY (A) vs Bklyn (N) 2-0 (World Series) (perfect game)
1902......Sep 20	Jimmy Callahan, Chi vs Det 3-0	1957......Aug 20	Bob Keegan, Chi vs Wash 6-0
1904......May 5	Cy Young, Bos vs Phil 3-0 (perfect game)	1958......July 20	Jim Bunning, Det at Bos 3-0
Aug 17	Jesse Tannehill, Bos at Chi 6-0	Sep 20	Hoyt Wilhelm, Balt vs NY 1-0
1905......July 22	Weldon Henley, Phil at StL 6-0	1962......May 5	Bo Belinsky, LA vs Balt 2-0
Sep 6	Frank Smith, Chi at Det 15-0	June 26	Earl Wilson, Bos vs LA 2-0
Sep 27	Bill Dinneen, Bos vs Chi 2-0	Aug 1	Bill Monbouquette, Bos at Chi 1-0
1908......June 30	Cy Young, Bos at NY 8-0	Aug 26	Jack Kralick, Minn vs KC 1-0
Sep 18	Bob Rhoades, Clev vs Bos 2-1	1965......Sep 16	Dave Morehead, Bos vs Clev 2-0
Sep 20	Frank Smith, Chi vs Phil 1-0	1966......June 10	Sonny Siebert, Clev vs Wash 2-0
Oct 2	Addie Joss, Clev vs Chi 1-0 (perfect game)	1967......Apr 30	Steve Barber (8⅔) and Stu Miller (⅓), Balt vs Det 1-2
1910......Apr 20	Addie Joss, Clev at Chi 1-0	Aug 25	Dean Chance, Minn at Clev 2-1
May 12	Chief Bender, Phil vs Clev 4-0	Sep 10	Joel Horlen, Chi vs Det 6-0
Aug 30	Tom Hughes, NY vs Clev 0-5 (hit in 10th; lost in 11th)	1968......Apr 27	Tom Phoebus, Balt vs Bos 6-0
1911......July 29	Joe Wood, Bos vs StL 5-0	May 8	Catfish Hunter, Oak vs Minn 4-0 (perfect game)
Aug 27	Ed Walsh, Chi vs Bos 5-0	1969......Aug 13	Jim Palmer, Balt vs Oak 8-0
1912......July 4	George Mullin, Det vs StL 7-0	1970......July 3	Clyde Wright, Calif vs Oak 4-0
Aug 30	Earl Hamilton, StL at Det 5-1	Sep 21	Vida Blue, Oak vs Minn 6-0
1914......May 14	Jim Scott, Chi at Wash 0-1 (hit in 10th; lost in 10th)	1973......Apr 27	Steve Busby, KC at Det 3-0
May 31	Joe Benz, Chi vs Clev 6-1	May 15	Nolan Ryan, Calif at KC 3-0
1916......June 21	George Foster, Bos vs NY 2-0	July 15	Nolan Ryan, Calif at Det 6-0
Aug 26	Joe Bush, Phil vs Clev 5-0	July 30	Jim Bibby, Tex at Oak 6-0
Aug 30	Dutch Leonard, Bos vs StL 4-0	1974......June 19	Steve Busby, KC at Mil 2-0
1917......Apr 14	Ed Cicotte, Chi at StL 11-0	July 19	Dick Bosman, Clev vs Oak 4-0
Apr 24	George Mogridge, NY at Bos 2-1	Sep 28	Nolan Ryan, Calif vs Minn 4-0
May 5	Ernie Koob, StL vs Chi 1-0	1975......June 1	Nolan Ryan, Calif vs Balt 1-0
May 6	Bob Groom, StL vs Chi 3-0	Sep 28	Vida Blue (5), Glenn Abbott and Paul Lindblad (1), Rollie Fingers (2), Oak vs Calif 5-0
June 23	Ernie Shore, Bos vs Wash 4-0 (perfect game)	1976......July 28	John Odom (5) and Francisco Barrios (4), Chi at Oak 2-1
1918......June 3	Dutch Leonard, Bos at Det 5-0	1977......May 14	Jim Colborn, KC vs Tex 6-0
1919......Sep 10	Ray Caldwell, Clev at NY 3-0	May 30	Dennis Eckersley, Clev vs Calif 1-0
1920......July 1	Walter Johnson, Wash at Bos 1-0	Sep 22	Bert Blyleven, Tex at Calif 6-0
1922......Apr 30	Charlie Robertson, Chi at Det 2-0 (perfect game)	1981......May 15	Len Barker, Clev vs Tor 3-0 (perfect game)
1923......Sep 4	Sam Jones, NY at Phil 2-0	1983......July 4	Dave Righetti, NY vs Bos 4-0
Sep 7	Howard Ehmke, Bos at Phil 4-0	Sep 29	Mike Warren, Oak vs Chi 3-0
1926......Aug 21	Ted Lyons, Chi at Bos 6-0	1984......Apr 7	Jack Morris, Det at Chi 4-0
1931......Apr 29	Wes Ferrell, Clev vs StL 9-0	Sep 30	Mike Witt, Calif at Tex 1-0 (perfect game)
Aug 8	Bob Burke, Wash vs Bos 5-0	1986......Sep 19	Joe Cowley, Chi at Calif 7-1
1934......Sep 18	Bobo Newsom, StL vs Bos 1-2 (hit in 10th; lost in 10th)	1987......Apr 15	Juan Nieves, Mil at Balt 7-0
1935......Aug 31	Vern Kennedy, Chi vs Clev 5-0	1990......Apr 11	Mark Langston (7), Mike Witt (2), Calif vs Sea 1-0
1937......June 1	Bill Dietrich, Chi vs StL 8-0	June 2	Randy Johnson, Sea vs Det 2-0
1938......Aug 27	Monte Pearson, NY vs Clev 13-0	June 11	Nolan Ryan, Tex at Oak 5-0
1940......Apr 16	Bob Feller, Clev at Chi 1-0 (opening day)	June 29	Dave Stewart, Oak at Tor 5-0
1945......Sep 9	Dick Fowler, Phil vs StL 1-0	1990......July 1	Andy Hawkins, NY at Chi 0-4 (pitched 8 innings of 9-inning game)
1946......Apr 30	Bob Feller, Clev at NY 1-0	Sep 2	Dave Stieb, Tor at Clev 3-0
1947......July 10	Don Black, Clev vs Phil 3-0	1991......May 1	Nolan Ryan, Tex vs Tor 3-0
Sep 3	Bill McCahan, Phil vs Wash 3-0	July 13	Bob Milacki (6), Mike Flanagan (1), Mark Williamson (1), and Gregg Olson (1), Balt at Oak 2-0
1948......June 30	Bob Lemon, Clev at Det 2-0	Aug 11	Wilson Alvarez, Chi at Balt 7-0
1951......July 1	Bob Feller, Clev vs Det 2-1	Aug 26	Bret Saberhagen, KC vs Chi 7-0
July 12	Allie Reynolds, NY at Clev 1-0	1993......Apr 22	Chris Bosio, Sea vs Bos 7-0
Sep 28	Allie Reynolds, NY vs Bos 8-0	Sep 4	Jim Abbott, NY vs Clev 4-0
1952......May 15	Virgil Trucks, Det vs Wash 1-0	1994......Apr 27	Scott Erickson, Minn vs Mil 6-0
Aug 25	Virgil Trucks, Det at NY 1-0	July 28	Kenny Rogers, Texas vs Calif. 4-0 (perfect game)
1953......May 6	Bobo Holloman, StL vs Phil 6-0 (first major league start)		
1956......July 14	Mel Parnell, Bos vs Chi 4-0		

Longest Hitting Streaks

NATIONAL LEAGUE				AMERICAN LEAGUE		
Player and Team	**Year**	**G**		**Player and Team**	**Year**	**G**
Willie Keeler, Balt	1897	44		Joe DiMaggio, NY	1941	56
Pete Rose, Cin	1978	44		George Sisler, StL	1922	41
Bill Dahlen, Chi	1894	42		Ty Cobb, Det	1911	40
Tommy Holmes, Bos	1945	37		Paul Molitor, Mil	1987	39
Billy Hamilton, Phil	1894	36		Ty Cobb, Det	1917	35
Fred Clarke, Lou	1895	35		Ty Cobb, Det	1912	34
Benito Santiago, SD	1987	34		George Sisler, StL	1925	34
George Davis, NY	1893	33		John Stone, Det	1930	34
Rogers Hornsby, StL	1922	32		George McQuinn, StL	1938	34
Ed Delahanty, Phil	1899	31		Dom DiMaggio, Bos	1949	34
Willie Davis, LA	1969	31		Hal Chase, NY	1907	33
Rico Carty, Atl	1970	31		Heinie Manush, Wash	1933	33
				Nap Lajoie, Cle	1906	31
				Sam Rice, Wash	1924	31
				Ken Landreaux, Minn	1980	31

Triple Crown Hitters

NATIONAL LEAGUE					AMERICAN LEAGUE				
Player and Team	**Year**	**HR**	**RBI**	**BA**	**Player and Team**	**Year**	**HR**	**RBI**	**BA**
Paul Hines, Prov	1878	4	50	.358	Nap Lajoie, Phil	1901	14	125	.422
Hugh Duffy, Bos	1894	18	145	.438	Ty Cobb, Det	1909	9	115	.377
Heinie Zimmerman,* Chi	1912	14	103	.372	Jimmie Foxx, Phil	1933	48	163	.356
Rogers Hornsby, StL	1922	42	152	.401	Lou Gehrig, NY	1934	49	165	.363
	1925	39	143	.403	Ted Williams, Bos	1942	36	137	.356
Chuck Klein, Phil	1933	28	120	.368		1947	32	114	.343
Joe Medwick, StL	1937	31	154	.374	Mickey Mantle, NY	1956	52	130	.353
					Frank Robinson, Balt	1966	49	122	.316
					Carl Yastrzemski, Bos	1967	44	121	.326

*Zimmerman ranked first in RBIs as calculated by Ernie Lanigan, but only third as calculated by Information Concepts Inc.

Triple Crown Pitchers

NATIONAL LEAGUE						AMERICAN LEAGUE					
Player and Team	**Year**	**W**	**L**	**SO**	**ERA**	**Player and Team**	**Year**	**W**	**L**	**SO**	**ERA**
Tommy Bond, Bos	1877	40	17	170	2.11	Cy Young, Bos	1901	33	10	158	1.62
Hoss Radbourn, Prov	1884	60	12	441	1.38	Rube Waddell, Phil	1905	26	11	287	1.48
Tim Keefe, NY	1888	35	12	333	1.74	Walter Johnson, Wash	1913	36	7	303	1.09
John Clarkson, Bos	1889	49	19	284	2.73		1918	23	13	162	1.27
Amos Rusie, NY	1894	36	13	195	2.78		1924	23	7	158	2.72
Christy Mathewson, NY	1905	31	8	206	1.27	Lefty Grove, Phil	1930	28	5	209	2.54
	1908	37	11	259	1.43		1931	31	4	175	2.06
Grover Alexander, Phil	1915	31	10	241	1.22	Lefty Gomez, NY	1934	26	5	158	2.33
	1916	33	12	167	1.55		1937	21	11	194	2.33
	1917	30	13	201	1.86	Hal Newhouser, Det	1945	25	9	212	1.81
Hippo Vaughn, Chi	1918	22	10	148	1.74						
Grover Alexander, Chi	1920	27	14	173	1.91						
Dazzy Vance, Bklyn	1924	28	6	262	2.16						
Bucky Walters, Cin	1939	27	11	137	2.29						
Sandy Koufax, LA	1963	25	5	306	1.88						
	1965	26	8	382	2.04						
	1966	27	9	317	1.73						
Steve Carlton, Phil	1972	27	10	310	1.97						
Dwight Gooden, NY	1985	24	4	268	1.53						

Consecutive Games Played, 500 or More Games

Lou Gehrig	2130	Frank McCormick	652
Cal Ripken Jr.	2009*	Sandy Alomar Sr	648
Everett Scott	1307	Eddie Brown	618
Steve Garvey	1207	Roy McMillan	585
Billy Williams	1117	George Pinckney	577
Joe Sewell	1103	Steve Brodie	574
Stan Musial	895	Aaron Ward	565
Eddie Yost	829	Candy LaChance	540
Gus Suhr	822	Buck Freeman	535
Nellie Fox	798	Fred Luderus	533
Pete Rose	745	Clyde Milan	511
Dale Murphy	740	Charlie Gehringer	511
Richie Ashburn	730	Vada Pinson	508
Ernie Banks	717	Tony Cuccinello	504
Earl Averill	673	Charlie Gehringer	504
Pete Rose	678	Omar Moreno	503

*Streak in progress at the end of the 1993 season.

Unassisted Triple Plays

Player and Team	Date	Pos	Opp	Opp Batter
Neal Ball, Clev	7-19-09	SS	Bos	Amby McConnell
Bill Wambsganss, Clev	10-10-20	2B	Bklyn	Clarence Mitchell
George Burns, Bos	9-14-23	1B	Clev	Frank Brower
Ernie Padgett, Bos	10-6-23	SS	Phil	Walter Holke
Glenn Wright, Pitt	5-7-25	SS	StL	Jim Bottomley
Jimmy Cooney, Chi	5-30-27	SS	Pitt	Paul Waner
Johnny Neun, Det	5-31-27	1B	Clev	Homer Summa
Ron Hansen, Wash	7-30-68	SS	Clev	Joe Azcue
Mickey Morandini	9-20-92	2B	Pitt	Jeff King

National League

Pennant Winners

Year	Team	Manager	W	L	Pct	GA
1900	Brooklyn	Ned Hanlon	82	54	.603	4½
1901	Pittsburgh	Fred Clarke	90	49	.647	7½
1902	Pittsburgh	Fred Clarke	103	36	.741	27½
1903	Pittsburgh	Fred Clarke	91	49	.650	6½
1904	New York	John McGraw	106	47	.693	13
1905	New York	John McGraw	105	48	.686	9
1906	Chicago	Frank Chance	116	36	.763	20
1907	Chicago	Frank Chance	107	45	.704	17
1908	Chicago	Frank Chance	99	55	.643	1
1909	Pittsburgh	Fred Clarke	110	42	.724	6½
1910	Chicago	Frank Chance	104	50	.675	13
1911	New York	John McGraw	99	54	.647	7½
1912	New York	John McGraw	103	48	.682	10
1913	New York	John McGraw	101	51	.664	12½
1914	Boston	George Stallings	94	59	.614	10½
1915	Philadelphia	Pat Moran	90	62	.592	7
1916	Brooklyn	Wilbert Robinson	94	60	.610	2½
1917	New York	John McGraw	98	56	.636	10
1918	Chicago	Fred Mitchell	84	45	.651	10½
1919	Cincinnati	Pat Moran	96	44	.686	9
1920	Brooklyn	Wilbert Robinson	93	61	.604	7
1921	New York	John McGraw	94	59	.614	4
1922	New York	John McGraw	93	61	.604	7
1923	New York	John McGraw	95	58	.621	4½
1924	New York	John McGraw	93	60	.608	1½

Pennant Winners *(Cont.)*

Year	Team	Manager	W	L	Pct	GA
1925	Pittsburgh	Bill McKechnie	95	58	.621	8½
1926	St Louis	Rogers Hornsby	89	65	.578	2
1927	Pittsburgh	Donie Bush	94	60	.610	1½
1928	St Louis	Bill McKechnie	95	59	.617	2
1929	Chicago	Joe McCarthy	98	54	.645	10½
1930	St Louis	Gabby Street	92	62	.597	2
1931	St Louis	Gabby Street	101	53	.656	13
1932	Chicago	Charlie Grimm	90	64	.584	4
1933	New York	Bill Terry	91	61	.599	5
1934	St Louis	Frankie Frisch	95	58	.621	2
1935	Chicago	Charlie Grimm	100	54	.649	4
1936	New York	Bill Terry	92	62	.597	5
1937	New York	Bill Terry	95	57	.625	3
1938	Chicago	Gabby Hartnett	89	63	.586	2
1939	Cincinnati	Bill McKechnie	97	57	.630	4½
1940	Cincinnati	Bill McKechnie	100	53	.654	12
1941	Brooklyn	Leo Durocher	100	54	.649	2½
1942	St Louis	Billy Southworth	106	48	.688	2
1943	St Louis	Billy Southworth	105	49	.682	18
1944	St Louis	Billy Southworth	105	49	.682	14½
1945	Chicago	Charlie Grimm	98	56	.636	3
1946	St Louis*	Eddie Dyer	98	58	.628	2
1947	Brooklyn	Burt Shotton	94	60	.610	5
1948	Boston	Billy Southworth	91	62	.595	6½
1949	Brooklyn	Burt Shotton	97	57	.630	1
1950	Philadelphia	Eddie Sawyer	91	63	.591	2
1951	New York†	Leo Durocher	98	59	.624	1
1952	Brooklyn	Chuck Dressen	96	57	.627	4½
1953	Brooklyn	Chuck Dressen	105	49	.682	13
1954	New York	Leo Durocher	97	57	.630	5
1955	Brooklyn	Walt Alston	98	55	.641	13½
1956	Brooklyn	Walt Alston	93	61	.604	1
1957	Milwaukee	Fred Haney	95	59	.617	8
1958	Milwaukee	Fred Haney	92	62	.597	8
1959	Los Angeles‡	Walt Alston	88	68	.564	2
1960	Pittsburgh	Danny Murtaugh	95	59	.617	7
1961	Cincinnati	Fred Hutchinson	93	61	.604	4
1962	San Francisco#	Al Dark	103	62	.624	1
1963	Los Angeles	Walt Alston	99	63	.611	6
1964	St Louis	Johnny Keane	93	69	.574	1
1965	Los Angeles	Walt Alston	97	65	.599	2
1966	Los Angeles	Walt Alston	95	67	.586	1½
1967	St Louis	Red Schoendienst	101	60	.627	10½
1968	St Louis	Red Schoendienst	97	65	.599	9
1969	New York (E)††	Gil Hodges	100	62	.617	8
1970	Cincinnati (W)††	Sparky Anderson	102	60	.630	14½
1971	Pittsburgh (E)††	Danny Murtaugh	97	65	.599	7
1972	Cincinnati (W)††	Sparky Anderson	95	59	.617	10½
1973	New York (E)††	Yogi Berra	82	79	.509	1½
1974	Los Angeles (W)††	Walt Alston	102	60	.630	4
1975	Cincinnati (W)††	Sparky Anderson	108	54	.667	20
1976	Cincinnati (W)††	Sparky Anderson	102	60	.630	10
1977	Los Angeles (W)††	Tommy Lasorda	98	64	.605	10
1978	Los Angeles (W)††	Tommy Lasorda	95	67	.586	2½
1979	Pittsburgh (E)††	Chuck Tanner	98	64	.605	2
1980	Philadelphia (E)††	Dallas Green	91	71	.562	1
1981	Los Angeles (W)††	Tommy Lasorda	63	47	.573	**
1982	St Louis (E)††	Whitey Herzog	92	70	.568	3
1983	Philadelphia (E)††	Pat Corrales, Paul Owens	90	72	.556	6
1984	San Diego (W)††	Dick Williams	92	70	.568	12

*Defeated Brooklyn, two games to none, in playoff for pennant. †Defeated Brooklyn, two games to one, in playoff for pennant. ‡Defeated Milwaukee, two games to none, in playoff for pennant. #Defeated Los Angeles, two games to one, in playoff for pennant. ††Won Championship Series **First half 36-21; second half 27-26.

Pennant Winners (Cont.)

Year	Team	Manager	W	L	Pct	GA
1985	St Louis (E)††	Whitey Herzog	101	61	.623	3
1986	New York (E)††	Dave Johnson	108	54	.667	21½
1987	St Louis (E)††	Whitey Herzog	95	67	.586	3
1988	Los Angeles (W)††	Tommy Lasorda	94	67	.584	7
1989	San Francisco (W)††	Roger Craig	92	70	.568	3
1990	Cincinnati (W)††	Lou Piniella	91	71	.562	5
1991	Atlanta (W)††	Bobby Cox	94	68	.580	1
1992	Atlanta††	Bobby Cox	98	64	.605	8
1993	Philadelphia††	Jim Fregosi	97	65	.599	3
1994	Season ended Aug. 11 due to players' strike					

††Won Championship Series

Leading Batsmen

Year	Player and Team	BA	Year	Player and Team	BA
1900	Honus Wagner, Pitt	.381	1930	Bill Terry, NY	.401
1901	Jesse Burkett, StL	.382	1931	Chick Hafey, StL	.349
1902	Ginger Beaumont, Pitt	.357	1932	Lefty O'Doul, Bklyn	.368
1903	Honus Wagner, Pitt	.355	1933	Chuck Klein, Phil	.368
1904	Honus Wagner, Pitt	.349	1934	Paul Waner, Pitt	.362
1905	Cy Seymour, Cin	.377	1935	Arky Vaughan, Pitt	.385
1906	Honus Wagner, Pitt	.339	1936	Paul Waner, Pitt	.373
1907	Honus Wagner, Pitt	.350	1937	Joe Medwick, StL	.374
1908	Honus Wagner, Pitt	.354	1938	Ernie Lombardi, Cin	.342
1909	Honus Wagner, Pitt	.339	1939	Johnny Mize, StL	.349
1910	Sherry Magee, Phil	.331	1940	Debs Garms, Pitt	.355
1911	Honus Wagner, Pitt	.334	1941	Pete Reiser, Bklyn	.343
1912	Heinie Zimmerman, Chi	.372	1942	Ernie Lombardi, Bos	.330
1913	Jake Daubert, Bklyn	.350	1943	Stan Musial, StL	.357
1914	Jake Daubert, Bklyn	.329	1944	Dixie Walker, Bklyn	.357
1915	Larry Doyle, NY	.320	1945	Phil Cavarretta, Chi	.355
1916	Hal Chase, Cin	.339	1946	Stan Musial, StL	.365
1917	Edd Roush, Cin	.341	1947	Harry Walker, StL-Phil	.363
1918	Zach Wheat, Bklyn	.335	1948	Stan Musial, StL	.376
1919	Edd Roush, Cin	.321	1949	Jackie Robinson, Bklyn	.342
1920	Rogers Hornsby, StL	.370	1950	Stan Musial, StL	.346
1921	Rogers Hornsby, StL	.397	1951	Stan Musial, StL	.355
1922	Rogers Hornsby, StL	.401	1952	Stan Musial, StL	.336
1923	Rogers Hornsby, StL	.384	1953	Carl Furillo, Bklyn	.344
1924	Rogers Hornsby, StL	.424	1954	Willie Mays, NY	.345
1925	Rogers Hornsby, StL	.403	1955	Richie Ashburn, Phil	.338
1926	Bubbles Hargrave, Cin	.353	1956	Hank Aaron, Mil	.328
1927	Paul Waner, Pitt	.380	1957	Stan Musial, StL	.351
1928	Rogers Hornsby, Bos	.387	1958	Richie Ashburn, Phil	.350
1929	Lefty O'Doul, Phil	.398	1959	Hank Aaron, Mil	.355

THEY SAID IT

Ken Griffey Jr, Seattle Mariner centerfielder, on the effect of the baseball strike on the stellar seasons he and Chicago White Sox first baseman Frank Thomas were enjoying: "We picked a bad year to have a good year."

Leading Batsmen *(Cont.)*

Year	Player and Team	BA	Year	Player and Team	BA
1960	Dick Groat, Pitt	.325	1977	Dave Parker, Pitt	.338
1961	Roberto Clemente, Pitt	.351	1978	Dave Parker, Pitt	.334
1962	Tommy Davis, LA	.346	1979	Keith Hernandez, StL	.344
1963	Tommy Davis, LA	.326	1980	Bill Buckner, Chi	.324
1964	Roberto Clemente, Pitt	.339	1981	Bill Madlock, Pitt	.341
1965	Roberto Clemente, Pitt	.329	1982	Al Oliver, Mont	.331
1966	Matty Alou, Pitt	.342	1983	Bill Madlock, Pitt	.323
1967	Roberto Clemente, Pitt	.357	1984	Tony Gwynn, SD	.351
1968	Pete Rose, Cin	.335	1985	Willie McGee, StL	.353
1969	Pete Rose, Cin	.348	1986	Tim Raines, Mont	.334
1970	Rico Carty, Atl	.366	1987	Tony Gwynn, SD	.370
1971	Joe Torre, StL	.363	1988	Tony Gwynn, SD	.313
1972	Billy Williams, Chi	.333	1989	Tony Gwynn, SD	.336
1973	Pete Rose, Cin	.338	1990	Willie McGee, StL	.335
1974	Ralph Garr, Atl	.353	1991	Terry Pendleton, Atl	.319
1975	Bill Madlock, Chi	.354	1992	Gary Sheffield	.330
1976	Bill Madlock, Chi	.339	1993	Andres Galarraga, Col	.370
			1994	Tony Gwynn, SD	.394

Leaders in Runs Scored

Year	Player and Team	Runs	Year	Player and Team	Runs
1900	Roy Thomas, Phil	131	1937	Joe Medwick, StL	111
1901	Jesse Burkett, StL	139	1938	Mel Ott, NY	116
1902	Honus Wagner, Pitt	105	1939	Billy Werber, Cin	115
1903	Ginger Beaumont, Pitt	137	1940	Arky Vaughan, Pitt	113
1904	George Browne, NY	99	1941	Pete Reiser, Bklyn	117
1905	Mike Donlin, NY	124	1942	Mel Ott, NY	118
1906	Honus Wagner, Pitt	103	1943	Arky Vaughan, Bklyn	112
	Frank Chance, Chi	103	1944	Bill Nicholson, Chi	116
1907	Spike Shannon, NY	104	1945	Eddie Stanky, Bklyn	128
1908	Fred Tenney, NY	101	1946	Stan Musial, StL	124
1909	Tommy Leach, Pitt	126	1947	Johnny Mize, NY	137
1910	Sherry Magee, Phil	110	1948	Stan Musial, StL	135
1911	Jimmy Sheckard, Chi	121	1949	Pee Wee Reese, Bklyn	132
1912	Bob Bescher, Cin	120	1950	Earl Torgeson, Bos	120
1913	Tommy Leach, Chi	99	1951	Stan Musial, StL	124
	Max Carey, Pitt	99		Ralph Kiner, Pitt	124
1914	George Burns, NY	100	1952	Stan Musial, StL	105
1915	Gavvy Cravath, Phil	89		Solly Hemus, StL	105
1916	George Burns, NY	105	1953	Duke Snider, Bklyn	132
1917	George Burns, NY	103	1954	Stan Musial, StL	120
1918	Heinie Groh, Cin	88		Duke Snider, Bklyn	120
1919	George Burns, NY	86	1955	Duke Snider, Bklyn	126
1920	George Burns, NY	115	1956	Frank Robinson, Cin	122
1921	Rogers Hornsby, StL	131	1957	Hank Aaron, Mil	118
1922	Rogers Hornsby, StL	141	1958	Willie Mays, SF	121
1923	Ross Youngs, NY	121	1959	Vada Pinson, Cin	131
1924	Frankie Frisch, NY	121	1960	Bill Bruton, Mil	112
	Rogers Hornsby, StL	121	1961	Willie Mays, SF	129
1925	Kiki Cuyler, Pitt	144	1962	Frank Robinson, Cin	134
1926	Kiki Cuyler, Pitt	113	1963	Hank Aaron, Mil	121
1927	Lloyd Waner, Pitt	133	1964	Dick Allen, Phil	125
	Rogers Hornsby, NY	133	1965	Tommy Harper, Cin	126
1928	Paul Waner, Pitt	142	1966	Felipe Alou, Atl	122
1929	Rogers Hornsby, Chi	156	1967	Hank Aaron, Atl	113
1930	Chuck Klein, Phil	158		Lou Brock, StL	113
1931	Bill Terry, NY	121	1968	Glenn Beckert, Chi	98
	Chuck Klein, Phil	121	1969	Bobby Bonds, SF	120
1932	Chuck Klein, Phil	152		Pete Rose, Cin	120
1933	Pepper Martin, StL	122	1970	Billy Williams, Chi	137
1934	Paul Waner, Pitt	122	1971	Lou Brock, StL	126
1935	Augie Galan, Chi	133	1972	Joe Morgan, Cin	122
1936	Arky Vaughan, Pitt	122	1973	Bobby Bonds, SF	131

Leader in Runs Scored *(Cont.)*

Year	Player and Team	Runs	Year	Player and Team	Runs
1974	Pete Rose, Cin	110	1986	Von Hayes, Phil	107
1975	Pete Rose, Cin	112		Tony Gwynn, SD	107
1976	Pete Rose, Cin	130	1987	Tim Raines, Mont	123
1977	George Foster, Cin	124	1988	Brett Butler, SF	109
1978	Ivan DeJesus, Chi	104	1989	Howard Johnson, NY	104
1979	Keith Hernandez, StL	116		Will Clark, SF	104
1980	Keith Hernandez, StL	111		Ryne Sandberg, Chi	104
1981	Mike Schmidt, Phil	78	1990	Ryne Sandberg, Chi	116
1982	Lonnie Smith, StL	120	1991	Brett Butler, LA	112
1983	Tim Raines, Mont	133	1992	Barry Bonds, Pitt	109
1984	Ryne Sandberg, Chi	114	1993	Lenny Dykstra, Phil	143
1985	Dale Murphy, Atl	118	1994	Jeff Bagwell, Hou	104

Leaders in Hits

Year	Player and Team	Hits	Year	Player and Team	Hits
1900	Willie Keeler, Bklyn	208	1945	Tommy Holmes, Bos	224
1901	Jesse Burkett, StL	228	1946	Stan Musial, StL	228
1902	Ginger Beaumont, Pitt	194	1947	Tommy Holmes, Bos	191
1903	Ginger Beaumont, Pitt	209	1948	Stan Musial, StL	230
1904	Ginger Beaumont, Pitt	185	1949	Stan Musial, StL	207
1905	Cy Seymour, Cin	219	1950	Duke Snider, Bklyn	199
1906	Harry Steinfeldt, Chi	176	1951	Richie Ashburn, Phil	221
1907	Ginger Beaumont, Bos	187	1952	Stan Musial, StL	194
1908	Honus Wagner, Pitt	201	1953	Richie Ashburn, Phil	205
1909	Larry Doyle, NY	172	1954	Don Mueller, NY	212
1910	Honus Wagner, Pitt	178	1955	Ted Kluszewski, Cin	192
	Bobby Byrne, Pitt	178	1956	Hank Aaron, Mil	200
1911	Doc Miller, Bos	192	1957	Red Schoendienst, NY-Mil	200
1912	Heinie Zimmerman, Chi	207	1958	Richie Ashburn, Phil	215
1913	Gavvy Cravath, Phil	179	1959	Hank Aaron, Mil	223
1914	Sherry Magee, Phil	171	1960	Willie Mays, SF	190
1915	Larry Doyle, NY	189	1961	Vada Pinson, Cin	208
1916	Hal Chase, Cin	184	1962	Tommy Davis, LA	230
1917	Heinie Groh, Cin	182	1963	Vada Pinson, Cin	204
1918	Charlie Hollocher, Chi	161	1964	Roberto Clemente, Pitt	211
1919	Ivy Olson, Bklyn	164		Curt Flood, StL	211
1920	Rogers Hornsby, StL	218	1965	Pete Rose, Cin	209
1921	Rogers Hornsby, StL	235	1966	Felipe Alou, Atl	218
1922	Rogers Hornsby, StL	250	1967	Roberto Clemente, Pitt	209
1923	Frankie Frisch, NY	223	1968	Felipe Alou, Atl	210
1924	Rogers Hornsby, StL	227		Pete Rose, Cin	210
1925	Jim Bottomley, StL	227	1969	Matty Alou, Pitt	231
1926	Eddie Brown, Bos	201	1970	Pete Rose, Cin	205
1927	Paul Waner, Pitt	237		Billy Williams, Chi	205
1928	Freddy Lindstrom, NY	231	1971	Joe Torre, StL	230
1929	Lefty O'Doul, Phil	254	1972	Pete Rose, Cin	198
1930	Bill Terry, NY	254	1973	Pete Rose, Cin	230
1931	Lloyd Waner, Pitt	214	1974	Ralph Garr, Atl	214
1932	Chuck Klein, Phil	226	1975	Dave Cash, Phil	213
1933	Chuck Klein, Phil	223	1976	Pete Rose, Cin	215
1934	Paul Waner, Pitt	217	1977	Dave Parker, Pitt	215
1935	Billy Herman, Chi	227	1978	Steve Garvey, LA	202
1936	Joe Medwick, StL	223	1979	Garry Templeton, StL	211
1937	Joe Medwick, StL	237	1980	Steve Garvey, LA	200
1938	Frank McCormick, Cin	209	1981	Pete Rose, Phil	140
1939	Frank McCormick, Cin	209	1982	Al Oliver, Mont	204
1940	Stan Hack, Chi	191	1983	Jose Cruz, Hou	189
	Frank McCormick, Cin	191		Andre Dawson, Mont	189
1941	Stan Hack, Chi	186	1984	Tony Gwynn, SD	213
1942	Enos Slaughter, StL	188	1985	Willie McGee, StL	216
1943	Stan Musial, StL	220	1986	Tony Gwynn, SD	211
1944	Stan Musial, StL	197			
	Phil Cavarretta, Chi	197			

Leaders in Hits *(Cont.)*

Year	Player and Team	Hits	Year	Player and Team	Hits
1987	Tony Gwynn, SD	218	1991	Terry Pendleton, Atl	187
1988	Andres Galarraga, Mont	184	1992	Terry Pendleton, Atl	199
1989	Tony Gwynn, SD	203		Andy Van Slyke, Pitt	199
1990	Brett Butler, SF	192	1993	Lenny Dykstra, Phil	194
	Lenny Dykstra, Phil	192	1994	Tony Gwynn, SD	165

Home Run Leaders

Year	Player and Team	HR	Year	Player and Team	HR
1900	Herman Long, Bos	12	1946	Ralph Kiner, Pitt	23
1901	Sam Crawford, Cin	16	1947	Ralph Kiner, Pitt	51
1902	Tommy Leach, Pitt	6		Johnny Mize, NY	51
1903	Jimmy Sheckard, Bklyn	9	1948	Ralph Kiner, Pitt	40
1904	Harry Lumley, Bklyn	9		Johnny Mize, NY	40
1905	Fred Odwell, Cin	9	1949	Ralph Kiner, Pitt	54
1906	Tim Jordan, Bklyn	12	1950	Ralph Kiner, Pitt	47
1907	Dave Brain, Bos	10	1951	Ralph Kiner, Pitt	42
1908	Tim Jordan, Bklyn	12	1952	Ralph Kiner, Pitt	37
1909	Red Murray, NY	7		Hank Sauer, Chi	37
1910	Fred Beck, Bos	10	1953	Eddie Mathews, Mil	47
	Wildfire Schulte, Chi	10	1954	Ted Kluszewski, Cin	49
1911	Wildfire Schulte, Chi	21	1955	Willie Mays, NY	51
1912	Heinie Zimmerman, Chi	14	1956	Duke Snider, Bklyn	43
1913	Gavvy Cravath, Phil	19	1957	Hank Aaron, Mil	44
1914	Gavvy Cravath, Phil	19	1958	Ernie Banks, Chi	47
1915	Gavvy Cravath, Phil	24	1959	Eddie Mathews, Mil	46
1916	Dave Robertson, NY	12	1960	Ernie Banks, Chi	41
	Cy Williams, Chi	12	1961	Orlando Cepeda, SF	46
1917	Dave Robertson, NY	12	1962	Willie Mays, SF	49
	Gavvy Cravath, Phil	12	1963	Hank Aaron, Mil	44
1918	Gavvy Cravath, Phil	8		Willie McCovey, SF	44
1919	Gavvy Cravath, Phil	12	1964	Willie Mays, SF	47
1920	Cy Williams, Phil	15	1965	Willie Mays, SF	52
1921	George Kelly, NY	23	1966	Hank Aaron, Atl	44
1922	Rogers Hornsby, StL	42	1967	Hank Aaron, Atl	39
1923	Cy Williams, Phil	41	1968	Willie McCovey, SF	36
1924	Jack Fournier, Bklyn	27	1969	Willie McCovey, SF	45
1925	Rogers Hornsby, StL	39	1970	Johnny Bench, Cin	45
1926	Hack Wilson, Chi	21	1971	Willie Stargell, Pitt	48
1927	Hack Wilson, Chi	30	1972	Johnny Bench, Cin	40
	Cy Williams, Phil	30	1973	Willie Stargell, Pitt	44
1928	Hack Wilson, Chi	31	1974	Mike Schmidt, Phil	36
	Jim Bottomley, StL	31	1975	Mike Schmidt, Phil	38
1929	Chuck Klein, Phil	43	1976	Mike Schmidt, Phil	38
1930	Hack Wilson, Chi	56	1977	George Foster, Cin	52
1931	Chuck Klein, Phil	31	1978	George Foster, Cin	40
1932	Chuck Klein, Phil	38	1979	Dave Kingman, Chi	48
	Mel Ott, NY	38	1980	Mike Schmidt, Phil	48
1933	Chuck Klein, Phil	28	1981	Mike Schmidt, Phil	31
1934	Ripper Collins, StL	35	1982	Dave Kingman, NY	37
	Mel Ott, NY	35	1983	Mike Schmidt, Phil	40
1935	Wally Berger, Bos	34	1984	Dale Murphy, Atl	36
1936	Mel Ott, NY	33		Mike Schmidt, Phil	36
1937	Mel Ott, NY	31	1985	Dale Murphy, Atl	37
	Joe Medwick, StL	31	1986	Mike Schmidt, Phil	37
1938	Mel Ott, NY	36	1987	Andre Dawson, Chi	49
1939	Johnny Mize, StL	28	1988	Darryl Strawberry, NY	39
1940	Johnny Mize, StL	43	1989	Kevin Mitchell, SF	47
1941	Dolph Camilli, Bklyn	34	1990	Ryne Sandberg, Chi	40
1942	Mel Ott, NY	30	1991	Howard Johnson, NY	38
1943	Bill Nicholson, Chi	29	1992	Fred McGriff, SD	35
1944	Bill Nicholson, Chi	33	1993	Barry Bonds, SF	46
1945	Tommy Holmes, Bos	28	1994	Matt Williams, SF	43

Runs Batted In Leaders

Year	Player and Team	RBI	Year	Player and Team	RBI
1900	Elmer Flick, Phil	110	1947	Johnny Mize, NY	138
1901	Honus Wagner, Pitt	126	1948	Stan Musial, StL	131
1902	Honus Wagner, Pitt	91	1949	Ralph Kiner, Pitt	127
1903	Sam Mertes, NY	104	1950	Del Ennis, Phil	126
1904	Bill Dahlen, NY	80	1951	Monte Irvin, NY	121
1905	Cy Seymour, Cin	121	1952	Hank Sauer, Chi	121
1906	Jim Nealon, Pitt	83	1953	Roy Campanella, Bklyn	142
	Harry Steinfeldt, Chi	83	1954	Ted Kluszewski, Cin	141
1907	Sherry Magee, Phil	85	1955	Duke Snider, Bklyn	136
1908	Honus Wagner, Pitt	109	1956	Stan Musial, StL	109
1909	Honus Wagner, Pitt	100	1957	Hank Aaron, Mil	132
1910	Sherry Magee, Phil	123	1958	Ernie Banks, Chi	129
1911	Wildfire Schulte, Chi	121	1959	Ernie Banks, Chi	143
1912	Heinie Zimmerman, Chi	103	1960	Hank Aaron, Mil	126
1913	Gavvy Cravath, Phil	128	1961	Orlando Cepeda, SF	142
1914	Sherry Magee, Phil	103	1962	Tommy Davis, LA	153
1915	Gavvy Cravath, Phil	115	1963	Hank Aaron, Mil	130
1916	Heinie Zimmerman, Chi-NY	83	1964	Ken Boyer, StL	119
1917	Heinie Zimmerman, NY	102	1965	Deron Johnson, Cin	130
1918	Sherry Magee, Phil	76	1966	Hank Aaron, Atl	127
1919	Hi Myers, Bklyn	73	1967	Orlando Cepeda, StL	111
1920	George Kelly, NY	94	1968	Willie McCovey, SF	105
	Rogers Hornsby, StL	94	1969	Willie McCovey, SF	126
1921	Rogers Hornsby, StL	126	1970	Johnny Bench, Cin	148
1922	Rogers Hornsby, StL	152	1971	Joe Torre, StL	137
1923	Irish Meusel, NY	125	1972	Johnny Bench, Cin	125
1924	George Kelly, NY	136	1973	Willie Stargell, Pitt	119
1925	Rogers Hornsby, StL	143	1974	Johnny Bench, Cin	129
1926	Jim Bottomley, StL	120	1975	Greg Luzinski, Phil	120
1927	Paul Waner, Pitt	131	1976	George Foster, Cin	121
1928	Jim Bottomley, StL	136	1977	George Foster, Cin	149
1929	Hack Wilson, Chi	159	1978	George Foster, Cin	120
1930	Hack Wilson, Chi	190	1979	Dave Winfield, SD	118
1931	Chuck Klein, Phil	121	1980	Mike Schmidt, Phil	121
1932	Don Hurst, Phil	143	1981	Mike Schmidt, Phil	91
1933	Chuck Klein, Phil	120	1982	Dale Murphy, Atl	109
1934	Mel Ott, NY	135		Al Oliver, Mont	109
1935	Wally Berger, Bos	130	1983	Dale Murphy, Atl	121
1936	Joe Medwick, StL	138	1984	Gary Carter, Mont	106
1937	Joe Medwick, StL	154		Mike Schmidt, Phil	106
1938	Joe Medwick, StL	122	1985	Dave Parker, Cin	125
1939	Frank McCormick, Cin	128	1986	Mike Schmidt, Phil	119
1940	Johnny Mize, StL	137	1987	Andre Dawson, Chi	137
1941	Dolph Camilli, Bklyn	120	1988	Will Clark, SF	109
1942	Johnny Mize, NY	110	1989	Kevin Mitchell, SF	125
1943	Bill Nicholson, Chi	128	1990	Matt Williams, SF	122
1944	Bill Nicholson, Chi	122	1991	Howard Johnson, NY	117
1945	Dixie Walker, Bklyn	124	1992	Darren Daulton, Phi	109
1946	Enos Slaughter, StL	130	1993	Barry Bonds, SF	123
			1994	Jeff Bagwell, Hou	116

Comings and Goings	The Florida Marlins' 9–8 win over the Chicago Cubs on Aug. 3, 1994, in which Marlin reliever Robb Nen earned the save and Dave Otto worked 1⅓ innings for the Cubs, marked the first time in major league history that two palindromic pitchers appeared in the same game. Apprised afterward of the momentous event, Nen said, "Wow!"

Leading Base Stealers

Year	Player and Team	SB	Year	Player and Team	SB
1900	George Van Haltren, NY	45	1953	Bill Bruton, Mil	26
	Patsy Donovan, StL	45	1954	Bill Bruton, Mil	34
1901	Honus Wagner, Pitt	48	1955	Bill Bruton, Mil	35
1902	Honus Wagner, Pitt	43	1956	Willie Mays, NY	40
1903	Jimmy Sheckard, Bklyn	67	1957	Willie Mays, NY	38
	Frank Chance, Chi	67	1958	Willie Mays, SF	31
1904	Honus Wagner, Pitt	53	1959	Willie Mays, SF	27
1905	Billy Maloney, Chi	59	1960	Maury Wills, LA	50
	Art Devlin, NY	59	1961	Maury Wills, LA	35
1906	Frank Chance, Chi	57	1962	Maury Wills, LA	104
1907	Honus Wagner, Pitt	61	1963	Maury Wills, LA	40
1908	Honus Wagner, Pitt	53	1964	Maury Wills, LA	53
1909	Bob Bescher, Cin	54	1965	Maury Wills, LA	94
1910	Bob Bescher, Cin	70	1966	Lou Brock, StL	74
1911	Bob Bescher, Cin	80	1967	Lou Brock, StL	52
1912	Bob Bescher, Cin	67	1968	Lou Brock, StL	62
1913	Max Carey, Pitt	61	1969	Lou Brock, StL	53
1914	George Burns, NY	62	1970	Bobby Tolan, Cin	57
1915	Max Carey, Pitt	36	1971	Lou Brock, StL	64
1916	Max Carey, Pitt	63	1972	Lou Brock, StL	63
1917	Max Carey, Pitt	46	1973	Lou Brock, StL	70
1918	Max Carey, Pitt	58	1974	Lou Brock, StL	118
1919	George Burns, NY	40	1975	Davey Lopes, LA	77
1920	Max Carey, Pitt	52	1976	Davey Lopes, LA	63
1921	Frankie Frisch, NY	49	1977	Frank Taveras, Pitt	70
1922	Max Carey, Pitt	51	1978	Omar Moreno, Pitt	71
1923	Max Carey, Pitt	51	1979	Omar Moreno, Pitt	77
1924	Max Carey, Pitt	49	1980	Ron LeFlore, Mont	97
1925	Max Carey, Pitt	46	1981	Tim Raines, Mont	71
1926	Kiki Cuyler, Pitt	35	1982	Tim Raines, Mont	78
1927	Frankie Frisch, StL	48	1983	Tim Raines, Mont	90
1928	Kiki Cuyler, Chi	37	1984	Tim Raines, Mont	75
1929	Kiki Cuyler, Chi	43	1985	Vince Coleman, StL	110
1930	Kiki Cuyler, Chi	37	1986	Vince Coleman, StL	107
1931	Frankie Frisch, StL	28	1987	Vince Coleman, StL	109
1932	Chuck Klein, Phil	20	1988	Vince Coleman, StL	81
1933	Pepper Martin, StL	26	1989	Vince Coleman, StL	65
1934	Pepper Martin, StL	23	1990	Vince Coleman, StL	77
1935	Augie Galan, Chi	22	1991	Marquis Grissom, Mont	76
1936	Pepper Martin, StL	23	1992	Marquis Grissom, Mont	78
1937	Augie Galan, Chi	23	1993	Chuck Carr, Flor	58
1938	Stan Hack, Chi	16	1994	Craig Biggio, Hou	39
1939	Stan Hack, Chi	17			
	Lee Handley, Pitt	17			
1940	Lonny Frey, Cin	22			
1941	Danny Murtaugh, Phil	18			
1942	Pete Reiser, Bklyn	20			
1943	Arky Vaughan, Bklyn	20			
1944	Johnny Barrett, Pitt	28			
1945	Red Schoendienst, StL	26			
1946	Pete Reiser, Bklyn	34			
1947	Jackie Robinson, Bklyn	29			
1948	Richie Ashburn, Phil	32			
1949	Jackie Robinson, Bklyn	37			
1950	Sam Jethroe, Bos	35			
1951	Sam Jethroe, Bos	35			
1952	Pee Wee Reese, Bklyn	30			

THEY SAID IT

Kevin Seitzer, Milwaukee Brewer infielder, after being hit in the face by a pitch from New York Yankee righthander Melido Perez: "I opened my eyes to see if I was in heaven or if I was in Milwaukee."

Leading Pitchers—Winning Percentage

Year	Pitcher and Team	W	L	Pct	Year	Pitcher and Team	W	L	Pct
1900	Jesse Tannehill, Pitt	20	6	.769	1948	Harry Brecheen, StL	20	7	.741
1901	Jack Chesbro, Pitt	21	10	.677	1949	Preacher Roe, Bklyn	15	6	.714
1902	Jack Chesbro, Pitt	28	6	.824	1950	Sal Maglie, NY	18	4	.818
1903	Sam Leever, Pitt	25	7	.781	1951	Preacher Roe, Bklyn	22	3	.880
1904	Joe McGinnity, NY	35	8	.814	1952	Hoyt Wilhelm, NY	15	3	.833
1905	Sam Leever, Pitt	20	5	.800	1953	Carl Erskine, Bklyn	20	6	.769
1906	Ed Reulbach, Chi	19	4	.826	1954	Johnny Antonelli, NY	21	7	.750
1907	Ed Reulbach, Chi	17	4	.810	1955	Don Newcombe, Bklyn	20	5	.800
1908	Ed Reulbach, Chi	24	7	.774	1956	Don Newcombe, Bklyn	27	7	.794
1909	Christy Mathewson, NY	25	6	.806	1957	Bob Buhl, Mil	18	7	.720
	Howie Camnitz, Pitt	25	6	.806	1958	Warren Spahn, Mil	22	11	.667
1910	King Cole, Chi	20	4	.833		Lew Burdette, Mil	20	10	.667
1911	Rube Marquard, NY	24	7	.774	1959	Roy Face, Pitt	18	1	.947
1912	Claude Hendrix, Pitt	24	9	.727	1960	Ernie Broglio, StL	21	9	.700
1913	Bert Humphries, Chi	16	4	.800	1961	Johnny Podres, LA	18	5	.783
1914	Bill James, Bos	26	7	.788	1962	Bob Purkey, Cin	23	5	.821
1915	Grover Alexander, Phil	31	10	.756	1963	Ron Perranoski, LA	16	3	.842
1916	Tom Hughes, Bos	16	3	.842	1964	Sandy Koufax, LA	19	5	.792
1917	Ferdie Schupp, NY	21	7	.750	1965	Sandy Koufax, LA	26	8	.765
1918	Claude Hendrix, Chi	19	7	.731	1966	Juan Marichal, SF	25	6	.806
1919	Dutch Ruether, Cin	19	6	.760	1967	Dick Hughes, StL	16	6	.727
1920	Burleigh Grimes, Bklyn	23	11	.676	1968	Steve Blass, Pitt	18	6	.750
1921	Bill Doak, StL	15	6	.714	1969	Tom Seaver, NY	25	7	.781
1922	Pete Donohue, Cin	18	9	.667	1970	Bob Gibson, StL	23	7	.767
1923	Dolf Luque, Cin	27	8	.771	1971	Don Gullett, Cin	16	6	.727
1924	Emil Yde, Pitt	16	3	.842	1972	Gary Nolan, Cin	15	5	.750
1925	Bill Sherdel, StL	15	6	.714	1973	Tommy John, LA	16	7	.696
1926	Ray Kremer, Pitt	20	6	.769	1974	Andy Messersmith, LA	20	6	.769
1927	Larry Benton, Bos-NY	17	7	.708	1975	Don Gullett, Cin	15	4	.789
1928	Larry Benton, NY	25	9	.735	1976	Steve Carlton, Phil	20	7	.741
1929	Charlie Root, Chi	19	6	.760	1977	John Candelaria, Pitt	20	5	.800
1930	Freddie Fitzsimmons, NY	19	7	.731	1978	Gaylord Perry, SD	21	6	.778
1931	Paul Derringer, StL	18	8	.692	1979	Tom Seaver, Cin	16	6	.727
1932	Lon Warneke, Chi	22	6	.786	1980	Jim Bibby, Pitt	19	6	.760
1933	Ben Cantwell, Bos	20	10	.667	1981*	Tom Seaver, Cin	14	2	.875
1934	Dizzy Dean, StL	30	7	.811	1982	Phil Niekro, Atl	17	4	.810
1935	Bill Lee, Chi	20	6	.769	1983	John Denny, Phil	19	6	.760
1936	Carl Hubbell, NY	26	6	.813	1984	Rick Sutcliffe, Chi	16	1	.941
1937	Carl Hubbell, NY	22	8	.733	1985	Orel Hershiser, LA	19	3	.864
1938	Bill Lee, Chi	22	9	.710	1986	Bob Ojeda, NY	18	5	.783
1939	Paul Derringer, Cin	25	7	.781	1987	Dwight Gooden, NY	15	7	.682
1940	Freddie Fitzsimmons, Bklyn	16	2	.889	1988	David Cone, NY	20	3	.870
1941	Elmer Riddle, Cin	19	4	.826	1989	Mike Bielecki, Chi	18	7	.720
1942	Larry French, Bklyn	15	4	.789	1990	Doug Drabeck, Pitt	22	6	.786
1943	Mort Cooper, StL	21	8	.724	1991	John Smiley, Pitt	20	8	.714
1944	Ted Wilks, StL	17	4	.810		Jose Rijo, Cin	15	6	.714
1945	Harry Brecheen, StL	15	4	.789	1992	Bob Tewksbury, StL	16	5	.762
1946	Murray Dickson, StL	15	6	.714	1993	Tom Glavine, Atl	22	6	.786
1947	Larry Jansen, NY	21	5	.808	1994	Ken Hill, Mtl	16	5	.762

*1981 percentages based on 10 or more victories.

Note: Based on 15 or more victories.

Radical Stupidity

The Milwaukee Brewers last year brought in a California motivational group called Radical Reality to "motivate" their players. During a clubhouse presentation, one of the Radicals ripped a phone book in two with his bare hands.

The next day an overly motivated Steve Sparks tried to duplicate the phone book feat—and dislocated his left shoulder in the process. The rookie righthander, a nonroster player, was scratched from his next scheduled pitching appearance and later was assigned to minor league camp. Said trainer John Adam, "This is one of the freakiest injuries I've seen—and a bit annoying, because I had to look up a number later."

Leading Pitchers—Earned-Run Average

Year	Player and Team	ERA	Year	Player and Team	ERA
1900	Rube Waddell, Pitt	2.37	1948	Harry Brecheen, StL	2.24
1901	Jesse Tannehill, Pitt	2.18	1949	Dave Koslo, NY	2.50
1902	Jack Taylor, Chi	1.33	1950	Jim Hearn, StL-NY	2.49
1903	Sam Leever, Pitt	2.06	1951	Chet Nichols, Bos	2.88
1904	Joe McGinnity, NY	1.61	1952	Hoyt Wilhelm, NY	2.43
1905	Christy Mathewson, NY	1.27	1953	Warren Spahn, Mil	2.10
1906	Three Finger Brown, Chi	1.04	1954	Johnny Antonelli, NY	2.29
1907	Jack Pfiester, Chi	1.15	1955	Bob Friend, Pitt	2.84
1908	Christy Mathewson, NY	1.43	1956	Lew Burdette, Mil	2.71
1909	Christy Mathewson, NY	1.14	1957	Johnny Podres, Bklyn	2.66
1910	George McQuillan, Phil	1.60	1958	Stu Miller, SF	2.47
1911	Christy Mathewson, NY	1.99	1959	Sam Jones, SF	2.82
1912	Jeff Tesreau, NY	1.96	1960	Mike McCormick, SF	2.70
1913	Christy Mathewson, NY	2.06	1961	Warren Spahn, Mil	3.01
1914	Bill Doak, StL	1.72	1962	Sandy Koufax, LA	2.54
1915	Grover Alexander, Phil	1.22	1963	Sandy Koufax, LA	1.88
1916	Grover Alexander, Phil	1.55	1964	Sandy Koufax, LA	1.74
1917	Grover Alexander, Phil	1.83	1965	Sandy Koufax, LA	2.04
1918	Hippo Vaughn, Chi	1.74	1966	Sandy Koufax, LA	1.73
1919	Grover Alexander, Chi	1.72	1967	Phil Niekro, Atl	1.87
1920	Grover Alexander, Chi	1.91	1968	Bob Gibson, StL	1.12
1921	Bill Doak, StL	2.58	1969	Juan Marichal, SF	2.10
1922	Rosy Ryan, NY	3.00	1970	Tom Seaver, NY	2.81
1923	Dolf Luque, Cin	1.93	1971	Tom Seaver, NY	1.76
1924	Dazzy Vance, Bklyn	2.16	1972	Steve Carlton, Phil	1.98
1925	Dolf Luque, Cin	2.63	1973	Tom Seaver, NY	2.08
1926	Ray Kremer, Pitt	2.61	1974	Buzz Capra, Atl	2.28
1927	Ray Kremer, Pitt	2.47	1975	Randy Jones, SD	2.24
1928	Dazzy Vance, Bklyn	2.09	1976	John Denny, StL	2.52
1929	Bill Walker, NY	3.08	1977	John Candelaria, Pitt	2.34
1930	Dazzy Vance, Bklyn	2.61	1978	Craig Swan, NY	2.43
1931	Bill Walker, NY	2.26	1979	J.R. Richard, Hou	2.71
1932	Lon Warneke, Chi	2.37	1980	Don Sutton, LA	2.21
1933	Carl Hubbell, NY	1.66	1981	Nolan Ryan, Hou	1.69
1934	Carl Hubbell, NY	2.30	1982	Steve Rogers, Mont	2.40
1935	Cy Blanton, Pitt	2.59	1983	Atlee Hammaker, SF	2.25
1936	Carl Hubbell, NY	2.31	1984	Alejandro Pena, LA	2.48
1937	Jim Turner, Bos	2.38	1985	Dwight Gooden, NY	1.53
1938	Bill Lee, Chi	2.66	1986	Mike Scott, Hou	2.22
1939	Bucky Walters, Cin	2.29	1987	Nolan Ryan, Hou	2.76
1940	Bucky Walters, Cin	2.48	1988	Joe Magrane, StL	2.18
1941	Elmer Riddle, Cin	2.24	1989	Scott Garrelts, SF	2.28
1942	Mort Cooper, StL	1.77	1990	Danny Darwin, Hou	2.21
1943	Howie Pollet, StL	1.75	1991	Dennis Martinez, Mont	2.39
1944	Ed Heusser, Cin	2.38	1992	Bill Swift, SF	2.08
1945	Hank Borowy, Chi	2.14	1993	Greg Maddux, Atl	2.36
1946	Howie Pollet, StL	2.10	1994	Greg Maddux, Atl	1.56
1947	Warren Spahn, Bos	2.33			

Note: Based on 10 complete games through 1950, then 154 innings until National League expanded in 1962, when it became 162 innings. In strike-shortened 1981, one inning per game required.

Leading Pitchers—Strikeouts

Year	Player and Team	SO	Year	Player and Team	SO
1900	Rube Waddell, Pitt	133	1912	Grover Alexander, Phil	195
1901	Noodles Hahn, Cin	233	1913	Tom Seaton, Phil	168
1902	Vic Willis, Bos	226	1914	Grover Alexander, Phil	214
1903	Christy Mathewson, NY	267	1915	Grover Alexander, Phil	241
1904	Christy Mathewson, NY	212	1916	Grover Alexander, Phil	167
1905	Christy Mathewson, NY	206	1917	Grover Alexander, Phil	200
1906	Fred Beebe, Chi-StL	171	1918	Hippo Vaughn, Chi	148
1907	Christy Mathewson, NY	178	1919	Hippo Vaughn, Chi	141
1908	Christy Mathewson, NY	259	1920	Grover Alexander, Chi	173
1909	Orval Overall, Chi	205	1921	Burleigh Grimes, Bklyn	136
1910	Christy Mathewson, NY	190	1922	Dazzy Vance, Bklyn	134
1911	Rube Marquard, NY	237	1923	Dazzy Vance, Bklyn	197

Leading Pitchers—Strikeouts *(Cont.)*

Year	Player and Team	SO	Year	Player and Team	SO
1924	Dazzy Vance, Bklyn	262	1959	Don Drysdale, LA	242
1925	Dazzy Vance, Bklyn	221	1960	Don Drysdale, LA	246
1926	Dazzy Vance, Bklyn	140	1961	Sandy Koufax, LA	269
1927	Dazzy Vance, Bklyn	184	1962	Don Drysdale, LA	232
1928	Dazzy Vance, Bklyn	200	1963	Sandy Koufax, LA	306
1929	Pat Malone, Chi	166	1964	Bob Veale, Pitt	250
1930	Bill Hallahan, StL	177	1965	Sandy Koufax, LA	382
1931	Bill Hallahan, StL	159	1966	Sandy Koufax, LA	317
1932	Dizzy Dean, StL	191	1967	Jim Bunning, Phil	253
1933	Dizzy Dean, StL	199	1968	Bob Gibson, StL	268
1934	Dizzy Dean, StL	195	1969	Ferguson Jenkins, Chi	273
1935	Dizzy Dean, StL	182	1970	Tom Seaver, NY	283
1936	Van Lingle Mungo, Bklyn	238	1971	Tom Seaver, NY	289
1937	Carl Hubbell, NY	159	1972	Steve Carlton, Phil	310
1938	Clay Bryant, Chi	135	1973	Tom Seaver, NY	251
1939	Claude Passeau, Phil-Chi	137	1974	Steve Carlton, Phil	240
	Bucky Walters, Cin	137	1975	Tom Seaver, NY	243
1940	Kirby Higbe, Phil	137	1976	Tom Seaver, NY	235
1941	Johnny Vander Meer, Cin	202	1977	Phil Niekro, Atl	262
1942	Johnny Vander Meer, Cin	186	1978	J.R. Richard, Hou	303
1943	Johnny Vander Meer, Cin	174	1979	J.R. Richard, Hou	313
1944	Bill Voiselle, NY	161	1980	Steve Carlton, Phil	286
1945	Preacher Roe, Pitt	148	1981	Fernando Valenzuela, LA	180
1946	Johnny Schmitz, Chi	135	1982	Steve Carlton, Phil	286
1947	Ewell Blackwell, Cin	193	1983	Steve Carlton, Phil	275
1948	Harry Brecheen, StL	149	1984	Dwight Gooden, NY	276
1949	Warren Spahn, Bos	151	1985	Dwight Gooden, NY	268
1950	Warren Spahn, Bos	191	1986	Mike Scott, Hou	306
1951	Warren Spahn, Bos	164	1987	Nolan Ryan, Hou	270
	Don Newcombe, Bklyn	164	1988	Nolan Ryan, Hou	228
1952	Warren Spahn, Bos	183	1989	Jose DeLeon, StL	201
1953	Robin Roberts, Phil	198	1990	David Cone, NY	233
1954	Robin Roberts, Phil	185	1991	David Cone, NY	241
1955	Sam Jones, Chi	198	1992	John Smoltz, Atl	215
1956	Sam Jones, Chi	176	1993	Jose Rijo, Cin	227
1957	Jack Sanford, Phil	188	1994	Andy Benes, SD	189
1958	Sam Jones, StL	225			

Leading Pitchers—Saves

Year	Player and Team	SV	Year	Player and Team	SV
1947	Hugh Casey, Bklyn	18	1971	Dave Giusti, Pitt	30
1948	Harry Gumpert, Cin	17	1972	Clay Carroll, Cin	37
1949	Ted Wilks, StL	9	1973	Mike Marshall, Mont	13
1950	Jim Konstanty, Phil	22	1974	Mike Marshall, LA	21
1951	Ted Wilks, StL, Pitt	13	1975	Al Hrabosky, StL	22
1952	Al Brazle, StL	16		Rawly Eastwick, Cin	22
1953	Al Brazle, StL	18	1976	Rawly Eastwick, Cin	26
1954	Jim Hughes, Bklyn	24	1977	Rollie Fingers, SD	35
1955	Jack Meyer, Phil	16	1978	Rollie Fingers, SD	37
1956	Clem Labine, Bklyn	19	1979	Bruce Sutter, Chi	37
1957	Clem Labine, Bklyn	17	1980	Bruce Sutter, Chi	28
1958	Roy Face, Pitt	20	1981	Bruce Sutter, StL	25
1959	Lindy McDaniel, StL	15	1982	Bruce Sutter, StL	36
	Don McMahon, Mil	15	1983	Lee Smith, Chi	29
1960	Lindy McDaniel, StL	26	1984	Bruce Sutter, StL	45
1961	Stu Miller, SF	17	1985	Jeff Reardon, Mont	41
	Roy Face, Pitt	17	1986	Todd Worrell, StL	36
1962	Roy Face, Pitt	28	1987	Steve Bedrosian, Phil	40
1963	Lindy McDaniel, Chi	22	1988	John Franco, Cin	39
1964	Hal Woodeshick, Hou	23	1989	Mark Davis, SD	44
1965	Ted Abernathy, Chi	31	1990	John Franco, NY	33
1966	Phil Regan, LA	21	1991	Lee Smith, StL	47
1967	Ted Abernathy, Cin	28	1992	Lee Smith, StL	42
1968	Phil Regan, Chi, LA	25	1993	Randy Myers, Chi	53
1969	Fred Gladding, Hou	29	1994	John Franco, NY	30
1970	Wayne Granger, Cin	35			

American League

Pennant Winners

Year	Team	Manager	W	L	Pct	GA*
1901	Chicago	Clark Griffith	83	53	.610	4
1902	Philadelphia	Connie Mack	83	53	.610	5
1903	Boston	Jimmy Collins	91	47	.659	14½
1904	Boston	Jimmy Collins	95	59	.617	1½
1905	Philadelphia	Connie Mack	92	56	.622	2
1906	Chicago	Fielder Jones	93	58	.616	3
1907	Detroit	Hughie Jennings	92	58	.613	1½
1908	Detroit	Hughie Jennings	90	63	.588	½
1909	Detroit	Hughie Jennings	98	54	.645	3½
1910	Philadelphia	Connie Mack	102	48	.680	14½
1911	Philadelphia	Connie Mack	101	50	.669	13½
1912	Boston	Jake Stahl	105	47	.691	14
1913	Philadelphia	Connie Mack	96	57	.627	6½
1914	Philadelphia	Connie Mack	99	53	.651	8½
1915	Boston	Bill Carrigan	101	50	.669	2½
1916	Boston	Bill Carrigan	91	63	.591	2
1917	Chicago	Pants Rowland	100	54	.649	9
1918	Boston	Ed Barrow	75	51	.595	2½
1919	Chicago	Kid Gleason	88	52	.629	3½
1920	Cleveland	Tris Speaker	98	56	.636	2
1921	New York	Miller Huggins	98	55	.641	4½
1922	New York	Miller Huggins	94	60	.610	1
1923	New York	Miller Huggins	98	54	.645	16
1924	Washington	Bucky Harris	92	62	.597	2
1925	Washington	Bucky Harris	96	55	.636	8½
1926	New York	Miller Huggins	91	63	.591	3
1927	New York	Miller Huggins	110	44	.714	19
1928	New York	Miller Huggins	101	53	.656	2½
1929	Philadelphia	Connie Mack	104	46	.693	18
1930	Philadelphia	Connie Mack	102	52	.662	8
1931	Philadelphia	Connie Mack	107	45	.704	13½
1932	New York	Joe McCarthy	107	47	.695	13
1933	Washington	Joe Cronin	99	53	.651	7
1934	Detroit	Mickey Cochrane	101	53	.656	7
1935	Detroit	Mickey Cochrane	93	58	.616	3
1936	New York	Joe McCarthy	102	51	.667	19½
1937	New York	Joe McCarthy	102	52	.662	13
1938	New York	Joe McCarthy	99	53	.651	9½
1939	New York	Joe McCarthy	106	45	.702	17
1940	Detroit	Del Baker	90	64	.584	1
1941	New York	Joe McCarthy	101	53	.656	17
1942	New York	Joe McCarthy	103	51	.669	9
1943	New York	Joe McCarthy	98	56	.636	13½
1944	St Louis	Luke Sewell	89	65	.578	1
1945	Detroit	Steve O'Neill	88	65	.575	1½
1946	Boston	Joe Cronin	104	50	.675	12
1947	New York	Bucky Harris	97	57	.630	12
1948	Cleveland†	Lou Boudreau	97	58	.626	1
1949	New York	Casey Stengel	97	57	.630	1
1950	New York	Casey Stengel	98	56	.636	3
1951	New York	Casey Stengel	98	56	.636	5
1952	New York	Casey Stengel	95	59	.617	2
1953	New York	Casey Stengel	99	52	.656	8½
1954	Cleveland	Al Lopez	111	43	.721	8
1955	New York	Casey Stengel	96	58	.623	3
1956	New York	Casey Stengel	97	57	.630	9
1957	New York	Casey Stengel	98	56	.636	8
1958	New York	Casey Stengel	92	62	.597	10
1959	Chicago	Al Lopez	94	60	.610	5
1960	New York	Casey Stengel	97	57	.630	8
1961	New York	Ralph Houk	109	53	.673	8
1962	New York	Ralph Houk	96	66	.593	5
1963	New York	Ralph Houk	104	57	.646	10½
1964	New York	Yogi Berra	99	63	.611	1

*Games aead of second-place club

Pennant Winners (Cont.)

Year	Team	Manager	W	L	Pct	GA*
1965	Minnesota	Sam Mele	102	60	.630	7
1966	Baltimore	Hank Bauer	97	63	.606	9
1967	Boston	Dick Williams	92	70	.568	1
1968	Detroit	Mayo Smith	103	59	.636	12
1969	Baltimore (E)‡	Earl Weaver	109	53	.673	19
1970	Baltimore (E)‡	Earl Weaver	108	54	.667	15
1971	Baltimore (E)‡	Earl Weaver	101	57	.639	12
1972	Oakland (W)‡	Dick Williams	93	62	.600	5½
1973	Oakland (W)‡	Dick Williams	94	68	.580	6
1974	Oakland (W)‡	Al Dark	90	72	.556	5
1975	Boston (E)‡	Darrell Johnson	95	65	.594	4½
1976	New York (E)‡	Billy Martin	97	62	.610	10½
1977	New York (E)‡	Billy Martin	100	62	.617	2½
1978	New York (E)†‡	Billy Martin, Bob Lemon	100	63	.613	1
1979	Baltimore (E)‡	Earl Weaver	102	57	.642	8
1980	Kansas City (W)‡	Jim Frey	97	65	.599	14
1981	New York (E)‡	Gene Michael, Bob Lemon	59	48	.551	#
1982	Milwaukee (E)‡	Buck Rodgers, Harvey Kuenn	95	67	.586	1
1983	Baltimore (E)‡	Joe Altobelli	98	64	.605	6
1984	Detroit (E)‡	Sparky Anderson	104	58	.642	15
1985	Kansas City (W)‡	Dick Howser	91	71	.562	1
1986	Boston (E)‡	John McNamara	95	66	.590	5½
1987	Minnesota (W)‡	Tom Kelly	85	77	.525	2
1988	Oakland (W)‡	Tony La Russa	104	58	.642	13
1989	Oakland (W)‡	Tony La Russa	99	63	.611	7
1990	Oakland (W)‡	Tony La Russa	103	59	.636	9
1991	Minnesota (W)‡	Tom Kelly	95	67	.586	8
1992	Toronto‡	Cito Gaston	96	66	.593	4
1993	Toronto‡	Cito Gaston	95	67	.586	7
1994	Season ended Aug. 11 due to players' strike					

*Games ahead of second-place club.

†Defeated Boston in one-game playoff. ‡Won championship series.

#First half 34-22; second 25-26, in season split by strike; defeated Milwaukee in playoff for Eastern Divison title.

Leading Batsmen

Year	Player and Team	BA	Year	Player and Team	BA
1901	Nap Lajoie, Phil	.422	1925	Harry Heilmann, Det	.393
1902	Ed Delahanty, Wash	.376	1926	Heinie Manush, Det	.378
1903	Nap Lajoie, Clev	.355	1927	Harry Heilmann, Det	.398
1904	Nap Lajoie, Clev	.381	1928	Goose Goslin, Wash	.379
1905	Elmer Flick, Clev	.306	1929	Lew Fonseca, Clev	.369
1906	George Stone, StL	.358	1930	Al Simmons, Phil	.381
1907	Ty Cobb, Det	.350	1931	Al Simmons, Phil	.390
1908	Ty Cobb, Det	.324	1932	Dale Alexander, Det-Bos	.367
1909	Ty Cobb, Det	.377	1933	Jimmie Foxx, Phil	.356
1910	Nap Lajoie, Clev*	.383	1934	Lou Gehrig, NY	.363
1911	Ty Cobb, Det	.420	1935	Buddy Myer, Wash	.349
1912	Ty Cobb, Det	.410	1936	Luke Appling, Chi	.388
1913	Ty Cobb, Det	.390	1937	Charlie Gehringer, Det	.371
1914	Ty Cobb, Det	.368	1938	Jimmie Foxx, Bos	.349
1915	Ty Cobb, Det	.369	1939	Joe DiMaggio, NY	.381
1916	Tris Speaker, Clev	.386	1940	Joe DiMaggio, NY	.352
1917	Ty Cobb, Det	.383	1941	Ted Williams, Bos	.406
1918	Ty Cobb, Det	.382	1942	Ted Williams, Bos	.356
1919	Ty Cobb, Det	.384	1943	Luke Appling, Chi	.328
1920	George Sisler, StL	.407	1944	Lou Boudreau, Clev	.327
1921	Harry Heilmann, Det	.394	1945	Snuffy Stirnweiss, NY	.309
1922	George Sisler, StL	.420	1946	Mickey Vernon, Wash	.353
1923	Harry Heilmann, Det	.403	1947	Ted Williams, Bos	.343
1924	Babe Ruth, NY	.378	1948	Ted Williams, Bos	.369

Leading Batsmen *(Cont.)*

Year	Player and Team	BA	Year	Player and Team	BA
1949	George Kell, Det	.343	1972	Rod Carew, Minn	.318
1950	Billy Goodman, Bos	.354	1973	Rod Carew, Minn	.350
1951	Ferris Fain, Phil	.344	1974	Rod Carew, Minn	.364
1952	Ferris Fain, Phil	.327	1975	Rod Carew, Minn	.359
1953	Mickey Vernon, Wash	.337	1976	George Brett, KC	.333
1954	Bobby Avila, Clev	.341	1977	Rod Carew, Minn	.388
1955	Al Kaline, Det	.340	1978	Rod Carew, Minn	.333
1956	Mickey Mantle, NY	.353	1979	Fred Lynn, Bos	.333
1957	Ted Williams, Bos	.388	1980	George Brett, KC	.390
1958	Ted Williams, Bos	.328	1981	Carney Lansford, Bos	.336
1959	Harvey Kuenn, Det	.353	1982	Willie Wilson, KC	.332
1960	Pete Runnels, Bos	.320	1983	Wade Boggs, Bos	.361
1961	Norm Cash, Det	.361	1984	Don Mattingly, NY	.343
1962	Pete Runnels, Bos	.326	1985	Wade Boggs, Bos	.368
1963	Carl Yastrzemski, Bos	.321	1986	Wade Boggs, Bos	.357
1964	Tony Oliva, Minn	.323	1987	Wade Boggs, Bos	.363
1965	Tony Oliva, Minn	.321	1988	Wade Boggs, Bos	.366
1966	Frank Robinson, Balt	.316	1989	Kirby Puckett, Minn	.339
1967	Carl Yastrzemski, Bos	.326	1990	George Brett, KC	.329
1968	Carl Yastrzemski, Bos	.301	1991	Julio Franco, Tex	.341
1969	Rod Carew, Minn	.332	1992	Edgar Martinez, Sea	.343
1970	Alex Johnson, Calif	.329	1993	John Olerud, Tor	.363
1971	Tony Oliva, Minn	.337	1994	Paul O'Neill, NY	.359

*League president Ban Johnson declared Ty Cobb batting champion with a .385 average, beating Lajoie's .384. However, subsequent research has led to the revision of Lajoie's average to .383 and Cobb's to .382.

Leaders in Runs Scored

Year	Player and Team	Runs	Year	Player and Team	Runs
1901	Nap Lajoie, Phil	145	1936	Lou Gehrig, NY	167
1902	Dave Fultz, Phil	110	1937	Joe DiMaggio, NY	151
1903	Patsy Dougherty, Bos	108	1938	Hank Greenberg, Det	144
1904	Patsy Dougherty, Bos-NY	113	1939	Red Rolfe, NY	139
1905	Harry Davis, Phil	92	1940	Ted Williams, Bos	134
1906	Elmer Flick, Clev	98	1941	Ted Williams, Bos	135
1907	Sam Crawford, Det	102	1942	Ted Williams, Bos	141
1908	Matty McIntyre, Det	105	1943	George Case, Wash	102
1909	Ty Cobb, Det	116	1944	Snuffy Stirnweiss, NY	125
1910	Ty Cobb, Det	106	1945	Snuffy Stirnweiss, NY	107
1911	Ty Cobb, Det	147	1946	Ted Williams, Bos	142
1912	Eddie Collins, Phil	137	1947	Ted Williams, Bos	125
1913	Eddie Collins, Phil	125	1948	Tommy Henrich, NY	138
1914	Eddie Collins, Phil	122	1949	Ted Williams, Bos	150
1915	Ty Cobb, Det	144	1950	Dom DiMaggio, Bos	131
1916	Ty Cobb, Det	113	1951	Dom DiMaggio, Bos	113
1917	Donie Bush, Det	112	1952	Larry Doby, Clev	104
1918	Ray Chapman, Clev	84	1953	Al Rosen, Clev	115
1919	Babe Ruth, Bos	103	1954	Mickey Mantle, NY	129
1920	Babe Ruth, NY	158	1955	Al Smith, Clev	123
1921	Babe Ruth, NY	177	1956	Mickey Mantle, NY	132
1922	George Sisler, StL	134	1957	Mickey Mantle, NY	121
1923	Babe Ruth, NY	151	1958	Mickey Mantle, NY	127
1924	Babe Ruth, NY	143	1959	Eddie Yost, Det	115
1925	Johnny Mostil, Chi	135	1960	Mickey Mantle, NY	119
1926	Babe Ruth, NY	139	1961	Mickey Mantle, NY	132
1927	Babe Ruth, NY	158		Roger Maris, NY	132
1928	Babe Ruth, NY	163	1962	Albie Pearson, LA	115
1929	Charlie Gehringer, Det	131	1963	Bob Allison, Minn	99
1930	Al Simmons, Phil	152	1964	Tony Oliva, Minn	109
1931	Lou Gehrig, NY	163	1965	Zoilo Versalles, Minn	126
1932	Jimmie Foxx, Phil	151	1966	Frank Robinson, Balt	122
1933	Lou Gehrig, NY	138	1967	Carl Yastrzemski, Bos	112
1934	Charlie Gehringer, Det	134	1968	Dick McAuliffe, Det	95
1935	Lou Gehrig, NY	125	1969	Reggie Jackson, Oak	123

Leaders in Runs Scored *(Cont.)*

Year	Player and Team	Runs	Year	Player and Team	Runs
1970	Carl Yastrzemski, Bos	125	1983	Cal Ripken, Balt	121
1971	Don Buford, Balt	99	1984	Dwight Evans, Bos	121
1972	Bobby Murcer, NY	102	1985	Rickey Henderson, NY	146
1973	Reggie Jackson, Oak	99	1986	Rickey Henderson, NY	130
1974	Carl Yastrzemski, Bos	93	1987	Paul Molitor, Mil	114
1975	Fred Lynn, Bos	103	1988	Wade Boggs, Bos	128
1976	Roy White, NY	104	1989	Rickey Henderson, NY-Oak	113
1977	Rod Carew, Minn	128		Wade Boggs, Bos	113
1978	Ron LeFlore, Det	126	1990	Rickey Henderson, Oak	119
1979	Don Baylor, Calif	120	1991	Paul Molitor, Mil	133
1980	Willie Wilson, KC	133	1992	Tony Phillips, Det	114
1981	Rickey Henderson, Oak	89	1993	Rafael Palmeiro, Tex	124
1982	Paul Molitor, Mil	136	1994	Frank Thomas, Chi	106

Leaders in Hits

Year	Player and Team	Hits	Year	Player and Team	Hits
1901	Nap Lajoie, Phil	229	1943	Dick Wakefield, Det	200
1902	Piano Legs Hickman, Bos-Clev	194	1944	Snuffy Stirnweiss, NY	205
1903	Patsy Dougherty, Bos	195	1945	Snuffy Stirnweiss, NY	195
1904	Nap Lajoie, Clev	211	1946	Johnny Pesky, Bos	208
1905	George Stone, StL	187	1947	Johnny Pesky, Bos	207
1906	Nap Lajoie, Clev	214	1948	Bob Dillinger, StL	207
1907	Ty Cobb, Det	212	1949	Dale Mitchell, Clev	203
1908	Ty Cobb, Det	188	1950	George Kell, Det	218
1909	Ty Cobb, Det	216	1951	George Kell, Det	191
1910	Nap Lajoie, Clev	227	1952	Nellie Fox, Chi	192
1911	Ty Cobb, Det	248	1953	Harvey Kuenn, Det	209
1912	Ty Cobb, Det	227	1954	Nellie Fox, Chi	201
1913	Joe Jackson, Clev	197		Harvey Kuenn, Det	201
1914	Tris Speaker, Bos	193	1955	Al Kaline, Det	200
1915	Ty Cobb, Det	208	1956	Harvey Kuenn, Det	196
1916	Tris Speaker, Clev	211	1957	Nellie Fox, Chi	196
1917	Ty Cobb, Det	225	1958	Nellie Fox, Chi	187
1918	George Burns, Phil	178	1959	Harvey Kuenn, Det	198
1919	Ty Cobb, Det	191	1960	Minnie Minoso, Chi	184
	Bobby Veach, Det	191	1961	Norm Cash, Det	193
1920	George Sisler, StL	257	1962	Bobby Richardson, NY	209
1921	Harry Heilmann, Det	237	1963	Carl Yastrzemski, Bos	183
1922	George Sisler, StL	246	1964	Tony Oliva, Minn	217
1923	Charlie Jamieson, Clev	222	1965	Tony Oliva, Minn	185
1924	Sam Rice, Wash	216	1966	Tony Oliva, Minn	191
1925	Al Simmons, Phil	253	1967	Carl Yastrzemski, Bos	189
1926	George Burns, Clev	216	1968	Bert Campaneris, Oak	177
	Sam Rice, Wash	216	1969	Tony Oliva, Minn	197
1927	Earle Combs, NY	231	1970	Tony Oliva, Minn	204
1928	Heinie Manush, StL	241	1971	Cesar Tovar, Minn	204
1929	Dale Alexander, Det	215	1972	Joe Rudi, Oak	181
	Charlie Gehringer, Det	215	1973	Rod Carew, Minn	203
1930	Johnny Hodapp, Clev	225	1974	Rod Carew, Minn	218
1931	Lou Gehrig, NY	211	1975	George Brett, KC	195
1932	Al Simmons, Phil	216	1976	George Brett, KC	215
1933	Heinie Manush, Wash	221	1977	Rod Carew, Minn	239
1934	Charlie Gehringer, Det	214	1978	Jim Rice, Bos	213
1935	Joe Vosmik, Clev	216	1979	George Brett, KC	212
1936	Earl Averill, Clev	232	1980	Willie Wilson, KC	230
1937	Beau Bell, StL	218	1981	Rickey Henderson, Oak	135
1938	Joe Vosmik, Bos	201	1982	Robin Yount, Mil	210
1939	Red Rolfe, NY	213	1983	Cal Ripken, Balt	211
1940	Rip Radcliff, StL	200	1984	Don Mattingly, NY	207
	Barney McCosky, Det	200	1985	Wade Boggs, Bos	240
	Doc Cramer, Bos	200	1986	Don Mattingly, NY	238
1941	Cecil Travis, Wash	218	1987	Kirby Puckett, Minn	207
1942	Johnny Pesky, Bos	205		Kevin Seitzer, KC	207

Leaders in Hits *(Cont.)*

Year	Player and Team	Hits	Year	Player and Team	Hits
1988	Kirby Puckett, Minn	234	1992	Kirby Puckett, Minn	210
1989	Kirby Puckett, Minn	215	1993	Paul Molitor, Tor	211
1990	Rafael Palmeiro, Tex	191	1994	Kenny Lofton, Cle	160
1991	Paul Molitor, Mil	216			

Home Run Leaders

Year	Player and Team	HR	Year	Player and Team	HR
1901	Nap Lajoie, Phil	13	1951	Gus Zernial, Chi-Phil	33
1902	Socks Seybold, Phil	16	1952	Larry Doby, Clev	32
1903	Buck Freeman, Bos	13	1953	Al Rosen, Clev	43
1904	Harry Davis, Phil	10	1954	Larry Doby, Clev	32
1905	Harry Davis, Phil	8	1955	Mickey Mantle, NY	37
1906	Harry Davis, Phil	12	1956	Mickey Mantle, NY	52
1907	Harry Davis, Phil	8	1957	Roy Sievers, Wash	42
1908	Sam Crawford, Det	7	1958	Mickey Mantle, NY	42
1909	Ty Cobb, Det	9	1959	Rocky Colavito, Clev	42
1910	Jake Stahl, Bos	10		Harmon Killebrew, Wash	42
1911	Frank Baker, Phil	9	1960	Mickey Mantle, NY	40
1912	Frank Baker, Phil	10	1961	Roger Maris, NY	61
	Tris Speaker, Bos	10	1962	Harmon Killebrew, Minn	48
1913	Frank Baker, Phil	13	1963	Harmon Killebrew, Minn	45
1914	Frank Baker, Phil	9	1964	Harmon Killebrew, Minn	49
1915	Braggo Roth, Chi-Clev	7	1965	Tony Conigliaro, Bos	32
1916	Wally Pipp, NY	12	1966	Frank Robinson, Balt	49
1917	Wally Pipp, NY	9	1967	Harmon Killebrew, Minn	44
1918	Babe Ruth, Bos	11		Carl Yastrzemski, Bos	44
	Tilly Walker, Phil	11	1968	Frank Howard, Wash	44
1919	Babe Ruth, Bos	29	1969	Harmon Killebrew, Minn	49
1920	Babe Ruth, NY	54	1970	Frank Howard, Wash	44
1921	Babe Ruth, NY	59	1971	Bill Melton, Chi	33
1922	Ken Williams, StL	39	1972	Dick Allen, Chi	37
1923	Babe Ruth, NY	41	1973	Reggie Jackson, Oak	32
1924	Babe Ruth, NY	46	1974	Dick Allen, Chi	32
1925	Bob Meusel, NY	33	1975	Reggie Jackson, Oak	36
1926	Babe Ruth, NY	47		George Scott, Mil	36
1927	Babe Ruth, NY	60	1976	Graig Nettles, NY	32
1928	Babe Ruth, NY	54	1977	Jim Rice, Bos	39
1929	Babe Ruth, NY	46	1978	Jim Rice, Bos	46
1930	Babe Ruth, NY	49	1979	Gorman Thomas, Mil	45
1931	Babe Ruth, NY	46	1980	Reggie Jackson, NY	41
	Lou Gehrig, NY	46		Ben Oglivie, Mil	41
1932	Jimmie Foxx, Phil	58	1981	Tony Armas, Oak	22
1933	Jimmie Foxx, Phil	48	1981	Dwight Evans, Bos	22
1934	Lou Gehrig, NY	49		Bobby Grich, Calif	22
1935	Jimmie Foxx, Phil	36		Eddie Murray, Balt	22
	Hank Greenberg, Det	36	1982	Reggie Jackson, Calif	39
1936	Lou Gehrig, NY	49		Gorman Thomas, Mil	39
1937	Joe DiMaggio, NY	46	1983	Jim Rice, Bos	39
1938	Hank Greenberg, Det	58	1984	Tony Armas, Bos	43
1939	Jimmie Foxx, Bos	35	1985	Darrell Evans, Det	40
1940	Hank Greenberg, Det	41	1986	Jesse Barfield, Tor	40
1941	Ted Williams, Bos	37	1987	Mark McGwire, Oak	49
1942	Ted Williams, Bos	36	1988	Jose Canseco, Oak	42
1943	Rudy York, Det	34	1989	Fred McGriff, Tor	36
1944	Nick Etten, NY	22	1990	Cecil Fielder, Det	51
1945	Vern Stephens, StL	24	1991	Jose Canseco, Oak	44
1946	Hank Greenberg, Det	44		Cecil Fielder, Det	44
1947	Ted Williams, Bos	32	1992	Juan Gonzalez, Tex	43
1948	Joe DiMaggio, NY	39	1993	Juan Gonzalez, Tex	46
1949	Ted Williams, Bos	43	1994	Ken Griffey Jr, Sea	40
1950	Al Rosen, Clev	37			

American League (Cont.)

Runs Batted In Leaders

Year	Player and Team	RBI	Year	Player and Team	RBI
1907	Ty Cobb, Det	116	1951	Gus Zernial, Chi-Phil	129
1908	Ty Cobb, Det	108	1952	Al Rosen, Clev	105
1909	Ty Cobb, Det	107	1953	Al Rosen, Clev	145
1910	Sam Crawford, Det	120	1954	Larry Doby, Clev	126
1911	Ty Cobb, Det	144	1955	Ray Boone, Det	116
1912	Frank Baker, Phil	133		Jackie Jensen, Bos	116
1913	Frank Baker, Phil	126	1956	Mickey Mantle, NY	130
1914	Sam Crawford, Det	104	1957	Roy Sievers, Wash	114
1915	Sam Crawford, Det	112	1958	Jackie Jensen, Bos	122
	Bobby Veach, Det	112	1959	Jackie Jensen, Bos	112
1916	Del Pratt, StL	103	1960	Roger Maris, NY	112
1917	Bobby Veach, Det	103	1961	Roger Maris, NY	142
1918	Bobby Veach, Det	78	1962	Harmon Killebrew, Minn	126
1919	Babe Ruth, Bos	114	1963	Dick Stuart, Bos	118
1920	Babe Ruth, NY	137	1964	Brooks Robinson, Balt	118
1921	Babe Ruth, NY	171	1965	Rocky Colavito, Clev	108
1922	Ken Williams, StL	155	1966	Frank Robinson, Balt	122
1923	Babe Ruth, NY	131	1967	Carl Yastrzemski, Bos	121
1924	Goose Goslin, Wash	129	1968	Ken Harrelson, Bos	109
1925	Bob Meusel, NY	138	1969	Harmon Killebrew, Minn	140
1926	Babe Ruth, NY	145	1970	Frank Howard, Wash	126
1927	Lou Gehrig, NY	175	1971	Harmon Killebrew, Minn	119
1928	Babe Ruth, NY	142	1972	Dick Allen, Chi	113
	Lou Gehrig, NY	142	1973	Reggie Jackson, Oak	117
1929	Al Simmons, Phil	157	1974	Jeff Burroughs, Tex	118
1930	Lou Gehrig, NY	174	1975	George Scott, Mil	109
1931	Lou Gehrig, NY	184	1976	Lee May, Balt	109
1932	Jimmie Foxx, Phil	169	1977	Larry Hisle, Minn	119
1933	Jimmie Foxx, Phil	163	1978	Jim Rice, Bos	139
1934	Lou Gehrig, NY	165	1979	Don Baylor, Calif	139
1935	Hank Greenberg, Det	170	1980	Cecil Cooper, Mil	122
1936	Hal Trosky, Clev	162	1981	Eddie Murray, Balt	78
1937	Hank Greenberg, Det	183	1982	Hal McRae, KC	133
1938	Jimmie Foxx, Bos	175	1983	Cecil Cooper, Mil	126
1939	Ted Williams, Bos	145		Jim Rice, Bos	126
1940	Hank Greenberg, Det	150	1984	Tony Armas, Bos	123
1941	Joe DiMaggio, NY	125	1985	Don Mattingly, NY	145
1942	Ted Williams, Bos	137	1986	Joe Carter, Clev	121
1943	Rudy York, Det	118	1987	George Bell, Tor	134
1944	Vern Stephens, StL	109	1988	Jose Canseco, Oak	124
1945	Nick Etten, NY	111	1989	Ruben Sierra, Tex	119
1946	Hank Greenberg, Det	127	1990	Cecil Fielder, Det	132
1947	Ted Williams, Bos	114	1991	Cecil Fielder, Det	133
1948	Joe DiMaggio, NY	155	1992	Cecil Fielder, Det	124
1949	Ted Williams, Bos	159	1993	Albert Belle, Cle	129
	Vern Stephens, Bos	159	1994	Kirby Puckett, Minn	112
1950	Walt Dropo, Bos	144			
	Vern Stephens, Bos	144			

Note: Runs Batted In not compiled before 1907; officially adopted in 1920.

Leading Base Stealers

Year	Player and Team	SB	Year	Player and Team	SB
1901	Frank Isbell, Chi	48	1911	Ty Cobb, Det	83
1902	Topsy Hartsel, Phil	54	1912	Clyde Milan, Wash	88
1903	Harry Bay, Clev	46	1913	Clyde Milan, Wash	75
1904	Elmer Flick, Clev	42	1914	Fritz Maisel, NY	74
	Harry Bay, Clev	42	1915	Ty Cobb, Det	96
1905	Danny Hoffman, Phil	46	1916	Ty Cobb, Det	68
1906	Elmer Flick, Clev	39	1917	Ty Cobb, Det	55
	John Anderson, Wash	39	1918	George Sisler, StL	45
1907	Ty Cobb, Det	49	1919	Eddie Collins, Chi	33
1908	Patsy Dougherty, Chi	47	1920	Sam Rice, Wash	63
1909	Ty Cobb, Det	76	1921	George Sisler, StL	35
1910	Eddie Collins, Phil	81	1922	George Sisler, StL	51

Leading Base Stealers *(Cont.)*

Year	Player and Team	SB	Year	Player and Team	SB
1923	Eddie Collins, Chi	49	1959	Luis Aparicio, Chi	56
1924	Eddie Collins, Chi	42	1960	Luis Aparicio, Chi	51
1925	John Mostil, Chi	43	1961	Luis Aparicio, Chi	53
1926	John Mostil, Chi	35	1962	Luis Aparicio, Chi	31
1927	George Sisler, StL	27	1963	Luis Aparicio, Balt	40
1928	Buddy Myer, Bos	30	1964	Luis Aparicio, Balt	57
1929	Charlie Gehringer, Det	27	1965	Bert Campaneris, KC	51
1930	Marty McManus, Det	23	1966	Bert Campaneris, KC	52
1931	Ben Chapman, NY	61	1967	Bert Campaneris, KC	55
1932	Ben Chapman, NY	38	1968	Bert Campaneris, Oak	62
1933	Ben Chapman, NY	27	1969	Tommy Harper, Sea	73
1934	Bill Werber, Bos	40	1970	Bert Campaneris, Oak	42
1935	Bill Werber, Bos	29	1971	Amos Otis, KC	52
1936	Lyn Lary, StL	37	1972	Bert Campaneris, Oak	52
1937	Bill Werber, Phil	35	1973	Tommy Harper, Bos	54
	Ben Chapman, Wash-Bos	35	1974	Bill North, Oak	54
1938	Frank Crosetti, NY	27	1975	Mickey Rivers, Calif	70
1939	George Case, Wash	51	1976	Bill North, Oak	75
1940	George Case, Wash	35	1977	Freddie Patek, KC	53
1941	George Case, Wash	33	1978	Ron LeFlore, Det	68
1942	George Case, Wash	44	1979	Willie Wilson, KC	83
1943	George Case, Wash	61	1980	Rickey Henderson, Oak	100
1944	Snuffy Stirnweiss, NY	55	1981	Rickey Henderson, Oak	56
1945	Snuffy Stirnweiss, NY	33	1982	Rickey Henderson, Oak	130
1946	George Case, Clev	28	1983	Rickey Henderson, Oak	108
1947	Bob Dillinger, StL	34	1984	Rickey Henderson, Oak	66
1948	Bob Dillinger, StL	28	1985	Rickey Henderson, NY	80
1949	Bob Dillinger, StL	20	1986	Rickey Henderson, NY	87
1950	Dom DiMaggio, Bos	15	1987	Harold Reynolds, Sea	60
1951	Minnie Minoso, Clev-Chi	31	1988	Rickey Henderson, NY	93
1952	Minnie Minoso, Chi	22	1989	Rickey Henderson, NY-Oak	77
1953	Minnie Minoso, Chi	25	1990	Rickey Henderson, Oak	65
1954	Jackie Jensen, Bos	22	1991	Rickey Henderson, Oak	58
1955	Jim Rivera, Chi	25	1992	Kenny Lofton, Cle	66
1956	Luis Aparicio, Chi	21	1993	Kenny Lofton, Cle	70
1957	Luis Aparicio, Chi	28	1994	Kenny Lofton, Cle	60
1958	Luis Aparicio, Chi	29			

Leading Pitchers—Winning Percentage

Year	Pitcher and Team	W	L	Pct	Year	Pitcher and Team	W	L	Pct
1901	Clark Griffith, Chi	24	7	.774	1925	Stan Coveleski, Wash	20	5	.800
1902	Bill Bernhard, Phil-Clev	18	5	.783	1926	George Uhle, Clev	27	11	.711
1903	Earl Moore, Clev	22	7	.759	1927	Waite Hoyt, NY	22	7	.759
1904	Jack Chesbro, NY	41	12	.774	1928	General Crowder, StL	21	5	.808
1905	Jess Tannehill, Bos	22	9	.710	1929	Lefty Grove, Phil	20	6	.769
1906	Eddie Plank, Phil	19	6	.760	1930	Lefty Grove, Phil	28	5	.848
1907	Wild Bill Donovan, Det	25	4	.862	1931	Lefty Grove, Phil	31	4	.886
1908	Ed Walsh, Chi	40	15	.727	1932	Johnny Allen, NY	17	4	.810
1909	George Mullin, Det	29	8	.784	1933	Lefty Grove, Phil	24	8	.750
1910	Chief Bender, Phil	23	5	.821	1934	Lefty Gomez, NY	26	5	.839
1911	Chief Bender, Phil	17	5	.773	1935	Eldon Auker, Det	18	7	.720
1912	Smoky Joe Wood, Bos	34	5	.872	1936	Monte Pearson, NY	19	7	.731
1913	Walter Johnson, Wash	36	7	.837	1937	Johnny Allen, Clev	15	1	.938
1914	Chief Bender, Phil	17	3	.850	1938	Red Ruffing, NY	21	7	.750
1915	Smoky Joe Wood, Bos	15	5	.750	1939	Lefty Grove, Bos	15	4	.789
1916	Eddie Cicotte, Chi	15	7	.682	1940	Schoolboy Rowe, Det	16	3	.842
1917	Reb Russell, Chi	15	5	.750	1941	Lefty Gomez, NY	15	5	.750
1918	Sad Sam Jones, Bos	16	5	.762	1942	Ernie Bonham, NY	21	5	.808
1919	Eddie Cicotte, Chi	29	7	.806	1943	Spud Chandler, NY	20	4	.833
1920	Jim Bagby, Clev	31	12	.721	1944	Tex Hughson, Bos	18	5	.783
1921	Carl Mays, NY	27	9	.750	1945	Hal Newhouser, Det	25	9	.735
1922	Joe Bush, NY	26	7	.788	1946	Boo Ferriss, Bos	25	6	.806
1923	Herb Pennock, NY	19	6	.760	1947	Allie Reynolds, NY	19	8	.704
1924	Walter Johnson, Wash	23	7	.767	1948	Jack Kramer, Bos	18	5	.783

Leading Pitchers—Winning Percentage *(Cont.)*

Year	Pitcher and Team	W	L	Pct	Year	Pitcher and Team	W	L	Pct
1949	Ellis Kinder, Bos	23	6	.793	1972	Catfish Hunter, Oak	21	7	.750
1950	Vic Raschi, NY	21	8	.724	1973	Catfish Hunter, Oak	21	5	.808
1951	Bob Feller, Clev	22	8	.733	1974	Mike Cuellar, Balt	22	10	.688
1952	Bobby Shantz, Phil	24	7	.774	1975	Mike Torrez, Balt	20	9	.690
1953	Ed Lopat, NY	16	4	.800	1976	Bill Campbell, Minn	17	5	.773
1954	Sandy Consuegra, Chi	16	3	.842	1977	Paul Splittorff, KC	16	6	.727
1955	Tommy Byrne, NY	16	5	.762	1978	Ron Guidry, NY	25	3	.893
1956	Whitey Ford, NY	19	6	.760	1979	Mike Caldwell, Mil	16	6	.727
1957	Dick Donovan, Chi	16	6	.727	1980	Steve Stone, Balt	25	7	.781
	Tom Sturdivant, NY	16	6	.727	1981*	Pete Vuckovich, Mil	14	4	.778
1958	Bob Turley, NY	21	7	.750	1982	Pete Vuckovich, Mil	18	6	.750
1959	Bob Shaw, Chi	18	6	.750		Jim Palmer, Balt	15	5	.750
1960	Jim Perry, Clev	18	10	.643	1983	Richard Dotson, Chi	22	7	.759
1961	Whitey Ford, NY	25	4	.862	1984	Doyle Alexander, Tor	17	6	.739
1962	Ray Herbert, Chi	20	9	.690	1985	Ron Guidry, NY	22	6	.786
1963	Whitey Ford, NY	24	7	.774	1986	Roger Clemens, Bos	24	4	.857
1964	Wally Bunker, Balt	19	5	.792	1987	Roger Clemens, Bos	20	9	.690
1965	Mudcat Grant, Minn	21	7	.750	1988	Frank Viola, Minn	24	7	.774
1966	Sonny Siebert, Clev	16	8	.667	1989	Bret Saberhagen, KC	23	6	.793
1967	Joel Horlen, Chi	19	7	.731	1990	Bob Welch, Oak	27	6	.818
1968	Denny McLain, Det	31	6	.838	1991	Scott Erickson, Minn	20	8	.714
1969	Jim Palmer, Balt	16	4	.800	1992	Mike Mussina, Balt	18	5	.783
1970	Mike Cuellar, Balt	24	8	.750	1993	Jimmy Key, NY	18	6	.750
1971	Dave McNally, Balt	21	5	.808	1994	Jimmy Key, NY	17	4	.810

Note: Based on 15 or more victories.

*1981 percentages based on 10 or more victories.

Leading Pitchers—Earned-Run Average

Year	Player and Team	ERA	Year	Player and Team	ERA
1913	Walter Johnson, Wash	1.14	1948	Gene Bearden, Clev	2.43
1914	Dutch Leonard, Bos	1.01	1949	Mel Parnell, Bos	2.78
1915	Smoky Joe Wood, Bos	1.49	1950	Early Wynn, Clev	3.20
1916	Babe Ruth, Bos	1.75	1951	Saul Rogovin, Det-Chi	2.78
1917	Eddie Cicotte, Chi	1.53	1952	Allie Reynolds, NY	2.07
1918	Walter Johnson, Wash	1.27	1953	Ed Lopat, NY	2.43
1919	Walter Johnson, Wash	1.49	1954	Mike Garcia, Clev	2.64
1920	Bob Shawkey, NY	2.46	1955	Billy Pierce, Chi	1.97
1921	Red Faber, Chi	2.47	1956	Whitey Ford, NY	2.47
1922	Red Faber, Chi	2.80	1957	Bobby Shantz, NY	2.45
1923	Stan Coveleski, Clev	2.76	1958	Whitey Ford, NY	2.01
1924	Walter Johnson, Wash	2.72	1959	Hoyt Wilhelm, Balt	2.19
1925	Stan Coveleski, Wash	2.84	1960	Frank Baumann, Chi	2.68
1926	Lefty Grove, Phil	2.51	1961	Dick Donovan, Wash	2.40
1927	Wilcy Moore, NY#	2.28	1962	Hank Aguirre, Det	2.21
1928	Garland Braxton, Wash	2.52	1963	Gary Peters, Chi	2.33
1929	Lefty Grove, Phil	2.81	1964	Dean Chance, LA	1.65
1930	Lefty Grove, Phil	2.54	1965	Sam McDowell, Clev	2.18
1931	Lefty Grove, Phil	2.06	1966	Gary Peters, Chi	1.98
1932	Lefty Grove, Phil	2.84	1967	Joe Horlen, Chi	2.06
1933	Monte Pearson, Clev	2.33	1968	Luis Tiant, Clev	1.60
1934	Lefty Gomez, NY	2.33	1969	Dick Bosman, Wash	2.19
1935	Lefty Grove, Bos	2.70	1970	Diego Segui, Oak	2.56
1936	Lefty Grove, Bos	2.81	1971	Vida Blue, Oak	1.82
1937	Lefty Gomez, NY	2.33	1972	Luis Tiant, Bos	1.91
1938	Lefty Grove, Bos	3.07	1973	Jim Palmer, Balt	2.40
1939	Lefty Grove, Bos	2.54	1974	Catfish Hunter, Oak	2.49
1940	Bob Feller, Clev†	2.62	1975	Jim Palmer, Balt	2.09
1941	Thornton Lee, Chi	2.37	1976	Mark Fidrych, Det	2.34
1942	Ted Lyons, Chi	2.10	1977	Frank Tanana, Calif	2.54
1943	Spud Chandler, NY	1.64	1978	Ron Guidry, NY	1.74
1944	Dizzy Trout, Det	2.12	1979	Ron Guidry, NY	2.78
1945	Hal Newhouser, Det	1.81	1980	Rudy May, NY	2.47
1946	Hal Newhouser, Det	1.94	1981	Steve McCatty, Oak	2.32
1947	Spud Chandler, NY	2.46	1982	Rick Sutcliffe, Clev	2.96

Leading Pitchers—Earned-Run Average (Cont.)

Year	Player and Team	ERA	Year	Player and Team	ERA
1983	Rick Honeycutt, Tex	2.42	1989	Bret Saberhagen, KC	2.16
1984	Mike Boddicker, Balt	2.79	1990	Roger Clemens, Bos	1.93
1985	Dave Stieb, Tor	2.48	1991	Roger Clemens, Bos	2.62
1986	Roger Clemens, Bos	2.48	1992	Roger Clemens, Bos	2.41
1987	Jimmy Key, Tor	2.76	1993	Kevin Appier, KC	2.56
1988	Allan Anderson, Minn	2.45	1994	Steve Ontiveros, Oak	2.65

Note: Based on 10 complete games through 1950, then, 154 innings until the American League expanded in 1961, when it became 162 innings. In strike-shortened 1981, one inning per game required. Earned runs not tabulated in American League prior to 1913.

#Wilcy Moore pitched only six complete games—he started 12—in 1927, but was recognized as leader because of 213 innings pitched.

†Ernie Bonham, New York, had 1.91 ERA and 10 complete games in 1940, but appeared in only 12 games and 99 innings, and Bob Feller was recognized as leader.

Leading Pitchers—Strikeouts

Year	Player and Team	SO	Year	Player and Team	SO
1901	Cy Young, Bos	159	1948	Bob Feller, Clev	164
1902	Rube Waddell, Phil	210	1949	Virgil Trucks, Det	153
1903	Rube Waddell, Phil	301	1950	Bob Lemon, Clev	170
1904	Rube Waddell, Phil	349	1951	Vic Raschi, NY	164
1905	Rube Waddell, Phil	286	1952	Allie Reynolds, NY	160
1906	Rube Waddell, Phil	203	1953	Billy Pierce, Chi	186
1907	Rube Waddell, Phil	226	1954	Bob Turley, Balt	185
1908	Ed Walsh, Chi	269	1955	Herb Score, Clev	245
1909	Frank Smith, Chi	177	1956	Herb Score, Clev	263
1910	Walter Johnson, Wash	313	1957	Early Wynn, Clev	184
1911	Ed Walsh, Chi	255	1958	Early Wynn, Chi	179
1912	Walter Johnson, Wash	303	1959	Jim Bunning, Det	201
1913	Walter Johnson, Wash	243	1960	Jim Bunning, Det	201
1914	Walter Johnson, Wash	225	1961	Camilo Pascual, Minn	221
1915	Walter Johnson, Wash	203	1962	Camilo Pascual, Minn	206
1916	Walter Johnson, Wash	228	1963	Camilo Pascual, Minn	202
1917	Walter Johnson, Wash	188	1964	Al Downing, NY	217
1918	Walter Johnson, Wash	162	1965	Sam McDowell, Clev	325
1919	Walter Johnson, Wash	147	1966	Sam McDowell, Clev	225
1920	Stan Coveleski, Clev	133	1967	Jim Lonborg, Bos	246
1921	Walter Johnson, Wash	143	1968	Sam McDowell, Clev	283
1922	Urban Shocker, StL	149	1969	Sam McDowell, Clev	279
1923	Walter Johnson, Wash	130	1970	Sam McDowell, Clev	304
1924	Walter Johnson, Wash	158	1971	Mickey Lolich, Det	308
1925	Lefty Grove, Phil	116	1972	Nolan Ryan, Calif	329
1926	Lefty Grove, Phil	194	1973	Nolan Ryan, Calif	383
1927	Lefty Grove, Phil	174	1974	Nolan Ryan, Calif	367
1928	Lefty Grove, Phil	183	1975	Frank Tanana, Calif	269
1929	Lefty Grove, Phil	170	1976	Nolan Ryan, Calif	327
1930	Lefty Grove, Phil	209	1977	Nolan Ryan, Calif	341
1931	Lefty Grove, Phil	175	1978	Nolan Ryan, Calif	260
1932	Red Ruffing, NY	190	1979	Nolan Ryan, Calif	223
1933	Lefty Gomez, NY	163	1980	Len Barker, Clev	187
1934	Lefty Gomez, NY	158	1981	Len Barker, Clev	127
1935	Tommy Bridges, Det	163	1982	Floyd Bannister, Sea	209
1936	Tommy Bridges, Det	175	1983	Jack Morris, Det	232
1937	Lefty Gomez, NY	194	1984	Mark Langston, Sea	204
1938	Bob Feller, Clev	240	1985	Bert Blyleven, Clev-Minn	206
1939	Bob Feller, Clev	246	1986	Mark Langston, Sea	245
1940	Bob Feller, Clev	261	1987	Mark Langston, Sea	262
1941	Bob Feller, Clev	260	1988	Roger Clemens, Bos	291
1942	Bobo Newsom, Wash	113	1989	Nolan Ryan, Tex	301
	Tex Hughson, Bos	113	1990	Nolan Ryan, Tex	232
1943	Allie Reynolds, Clev	151	1991	Roger Clemens, Bos	241
1944	Hal Newhouser, Det	187	1992	Randy Johnson, Sea	241
1945	Hal Newhouser, Det	212	1993	Randy Johnson, Sea	308
1946	Bob Feller, Clev	348	1994	Randy Johnson, Sea	204
1947	Bob Feller, Clev	196			

Leading Pitchers—Saves

Year	Player and Team	SV	Year	Player and Team	SV
1947	Joe Page, NY	17	1971	Ken Sanders, Mil	31
1948	Russ Christopher, Cle	17	1972	Sparky Lyle, NY	35
1949	Joe Page, NY	29	1973	John Hiller, Det	38
1950	Mickey Harris, Wash	15	1974	Terry Forster, Chi	24
1951	Ellis Kinder, Bos	14	1975	Goose Gossage, Chi	26
1952	Harry Dorish, Chi	11	1976	Sparky Lyle, NY	23
1953	Ellis Kinder, Bos	27	1977	Bill Campbell, Bos	31
1954	Johnny Sain, NY	22	1978	Goose Gossage, NY	27
1955	Ray Narleski, Cle	19	1979	Mike Marshall, Min	32
1956	George Zuverink, Bal	16	1980	Dan Quisenberry, KC	33
1957	Bob Grim, NY	19	1981	Goose Gossage, NY	33
1958	Ryne Duren, NY	20	1982	Rollie Fingers, Mil	28
1959	Turk Lown, Chi	15	1983	Dan Quisenberry, KC	35
1960	Mike Fornieles, Bos	14	1984	Dan Quisenberry, KC	45
	Johnny Klippstein, Cle	14	1985	Dan Quisenberry, KC	37
1961	Luis Arroyo, NY	29	1986	Dave Righetti, NY	46
1962	Dick Radatz, Bos	24	1987	Tom Henke, Tor	34
1963	Stu Miller, Bal	27	1988	Dennis Eckersley, Oak	45
1964	Dick Radatz, Bos	29	1989	Jeff Russell, Tex	38
1965	Ron Kline, Wash	29	1990	Bobby Thigpen, Chi	57
1966	Jack Aker, KC	32	1991	Bryan Harvey, Cal	46
1967	Minnie Rojas, Cal	27	1992	Dennis Eckersley, Oak	51
1968	Al Worthington, Min	18	1993	Jeff Montgomery, KC	45
1969	Ron Perranoski, Min	31		Duane Ward, Tor	45
1970	Ron Perranoski, Min	34	1994	Lee Smith, Bal	33

The Commissioners of Baseball

Kenesaw Mountain Landis	Elected November 12, 1920. Served until his death on November 25, 1944.
Happy Chandler	Elected April 24, 1945. Served until July 15, 1951.
Ford Frick	Elected September 20, 1951. Served until November 16, 1965.
William Eckert	Elected November 17, 1965. Served until December 20, 1968.
Bowie Kuhn	Elected February 8, 1969. Served until September 30, 1984.
Peter Ueberroth	Elected March 3, 1984. Took office October 1, 1984. Served through March 31, 1989.
A. Bartlett Giamatti	Elected September 8, 1988. Took office April 1, 1989. Served until his death on September 1, 1989.
Francis Vincent Jr	Appointed Acting Commissioner September 2, 1989. Elected Commissioner September 13, 1989. Served through September 7, 1992.
Allan H. (Bud) Selig	Elected chairman of the executive council and given the powers of interim commissioner on September 9, 1992.

THEY SAID IT

Jim DeShaies, Minnesota Twin pitcher, on ignoring baseball tradition and changing his seat in the dugout during teammate Scott Erickson's 1994 no-hitter: "I think everybody gets caught up in superstitions. But I don't put much stock in them—knock on wood."

Pro Football

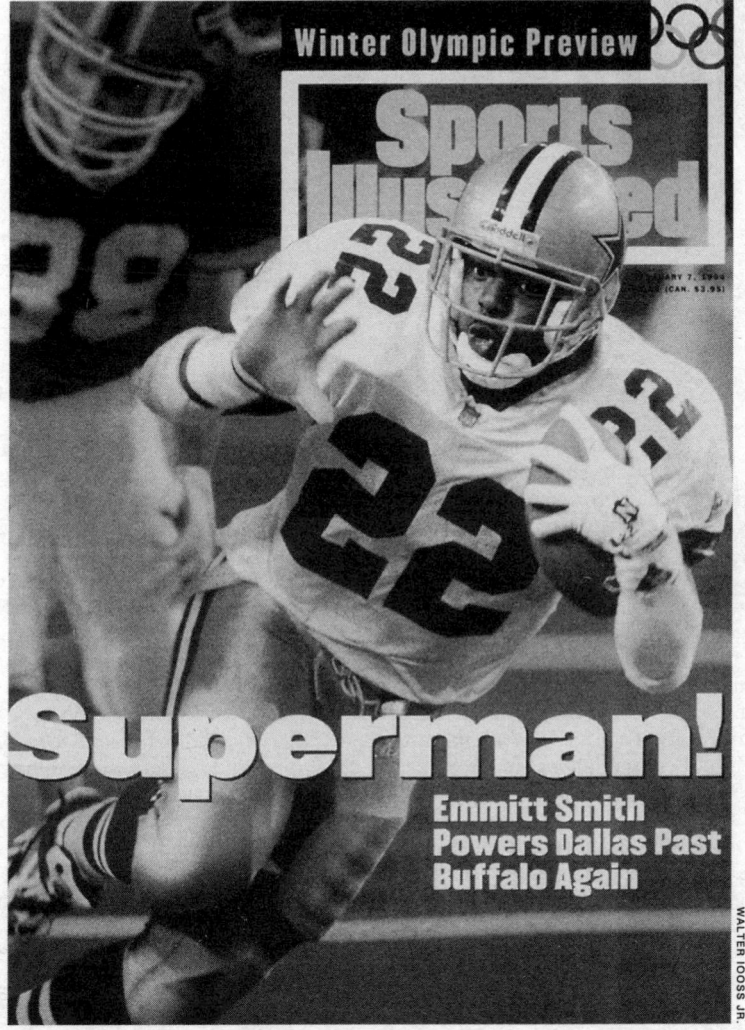

Winter Olympic Preview

Sports Illustrated

ANUARY 7, 1994
(CAN. $3.95)

Superman!

Emmitt Smith Powers Dallas Past Buffalo Again

WALTER IOOSS JR.

Big D as in Dynasty

*The mighty Cowboys rode to victory again and the murmurings
about greatness became more than talk* | by PETER KING

WE LIVE IN A TIME WHEN NOTH-
ing in sports or in society
lasts forever. Especially in
sports. No baseball team
ever looks the same, year-to-
year, in the rent-a-pennant
major leagues. Michael Jor-
dan gave the Bulls permanence, and then
he retired in mid-greatness; now pro basketball is topped by a hodgepodge of pretty
good teams. Hockey, without the back-
spasmed Mario Lemieux, is awash in parity,
and the fifth- or seventh- or ninth-best team
in the regular season could easily win the
Stanley Cup.

Which is why we may be able to find com-
fort in what is happening in the NFL these
days. In 1993, for the second straight year,
the best three teams in pro football were
Dallas, San Francisco and Buffalo, even as
the new world of free agency was chipping
away at their foundations. And nothing—
not the sudden soap-opera resignation of
Dallas coach Jimmy Johnson, not the nag-

ging inability of the 49ers to climb Mount
Dallas, not the Bills' continued mediocrity
in late January—seemed to indicate a sea-
change in the future of pro football as the
league's 75th season dawns.

Before the 1993 season began, the Cowboys lost ace backup quarterback Steve
Beuerlein to Phoenix and defensive coordinator Dave Wannstedt to Chicago, as head
coach. The 49ers lost a great defensive tackle, Pierce Holt, to Atlanta. And the Bills
lost salary flexibility because they had to
sign superstars Thurman Thomas and
Bruce Smith to huge contracts; Buffalo will
pay dearly in future years because the major
Thomas and Smith deals forced them to
lose good players like tackle Howard Ballard and cornerback Nate Odomes simply
because they couldn't afford to keep them
under the new $34.608 million salary cap
that kicked in for the 1994 season. Still,
these were the teams everybody chased in
1993, and these are the teams everyone will
be chasing for the foreseeable future.

Aikman capped a brilliant season with a convincing win over the Bills in the Super Bowl.

Dallas looked like a budding dynasty, to be sure, in the wake of their 30–13 Super Bowl victory over the Bills in Atlanta on Jan. 30, 1994. "I want to leave footprints," Dallas running back Emmitt Smith said, "and I think this team wants to leave footprints."

Why, just when free-agency is getting a toehold in pro football, does the leadership in pro football seem as settled as it's been in perhaps a generation? Look at the three best teams to see why.

1. *Dallas*. The Cowboys, 31–7 in the last two seasons, have two very important things going for them. First, they have one of the youngest teams in football, and second,

their great young players are signed into the future. Among the four previous back-to-back Super Bowl winners, only the 1975 Steelers were younger. Quarterback Troy Aikman, who in 1993 completed 69% of his passes for 3,100 yards and only six interceptions, is 27. Smith, 25, has won three straight rushing titles. Wideouts Michael Irvin and Alvin Harper, 28 and 26, respectively, are the Swann and Stallworth of this era. Franchise tackle Erik Williams is 25. Cornerbacks Kevin Smith and Larry Brown, both 24, blanketed Sterling Sharpe, Jerry Rice and Andre Reed peerlessly in last year's playoffs. Two of the Cowboys' best defensive linemen—Russell Maryland, and Leon Lett (no jokes, please, he's really good)—are both just 25 years of age.

The Cowboys were rocked by some losses to free-agency: Linebacker Ken Norton, defensive tackle Jimmie Jones and guards John Gesek and Kevin Gogan all departed, weakening the Cowboys' depth considerably. And, of course, the loss of a head coach, particularly one as effective as Jimmy Johnson—new coach Barry Switzer will have some large shoes to fill—has to affect team chemistry. But Aikman, Emmitt Smith, Kevin Smith, Lett and pass rusher Charles Haley are all

signed to long-term deals, and key left tackle Mark Tuinei is locked in until '95. "I don't think any other contender is in such good shape," owner Jerry Jones said. "I think we could be good for a long time."

2. *San Francisco.* The 49ers have some major defensive holes to fill, most notably the lack of a pass-rushing threat since the loss of Holt and Tim Harris to free-agency before last season. But quietly, in February, they rehired the respected Ray Rhodes as defensive coordinator, and coach George

The Wiliest of Foxes

The whole thing came as such a shock that even Paul Tagliabue was ashen when it happened. The unflappable NFL commissioner reacted just like fans and media mavens and NFL executives nationwide: No one in their right mind could believe that Rupert Murdoch and the upstart Fox Network had outbid CBS for the right to carry 100 National Football Conference games a year for the next four seasons.

Fox, a loose collection of 139 mostly small TV stations kept alive by its youth-oriented prime-time programming, offered the NFL some $100 million more per season than CBS did, a total of $400 million a year, to get the rights in late December. And CBS was losing money already! That's the nutty thing here.

What in the name of Bart Simpson could Fox have been thinking? And how in the world could the NFL have accepted an offer from a network that didn't even blanket the country like CBS or NBC, that didn't even have stations in some states? Fox wanted the respect the NFL could give it. The NFL wanted money. That's it.

"This was a cheap way of buying a network," said Murdoch, the Australian-born international media mogul. "Like no other sport will do, the NFL will make us

into a real network. In the future there will be 400 or 500 channels on cable, and ratings will be fragmented. But football will not fragment."

"The type of commitment they gave us was above and beyond dollars," claimed Dallas owner Jerry Jones. "They said, 'We'll take this entity, the NFC, and build a network around it.'"

But make no mistake about it, the money allowed the NFL to buttress teams against the pain of the salary cap, which was coming on March 1, 1994. The Fox bid, league sources say, allowed the NFL to raise the salary cap about $3 million higher than it would have been had the CBS bid been accepted. So the cap became $34.608 million, not the $31 million and change it might have been.

For teams struggling to fit under the cap, it was welcome relief. "Now," said Carmen Policy, president of the 49ers, "there's a light at the end of the tunnel. You can't imagine how much better we feel about things now."

The other advantage to the NFL: Fox woos kids. The traditionalists liked what CBS gave the NFL for 38 years, and the partnership was a comfortable one. Which made the parting all the more bitter. One CBS executive said, the day after Fox won the rights, "This wasn't a rights negotiation. This was a hostile takeover."

Seifert put everyone in the organization on notice that they would be better defensively in 1994, or heads would roll. Seifert, coming off his fifth double-digit winning season in five years as coach, knows what he's doing. Look at the man's record. In his first five seasons he has a better record than Bill Walsh had in his last five. Now he needs to get production out of a front seven that had only one player in 1993—rookie lineman Dana Stubblefield—with more than six sacks.

But the 49ers will continue to be threatening because, like the Cowboys, they have their stars and contributing players signed for a long time. For the third straight season, in 1993, quarterback Steve Young led the NFL in passer rating, with a 101.5. It's the first time a quarterback has had three straight 100-plus rating seasons. Young hasn't gotten the 49ers to the Super Bowl in his three seasons of starting, but don't blame him. He hasn't had the vintage defense that Bill Walsh built in the '80s. And then there's wideout

Maybe. But to say this was a negative move by the NFL is a shortsighted opinion. On the ever-changing sporting landscape, the NFL was very shy in drawing the youth of America to TV sets,

Bradshaw (left) and Summerall: two of the familiar CBS faces who moved to Fox.

JIM GUND

and into the hobby shop to buy the cards and the footballs, and into youth football programs. Go into any stadium on Sunday, and the crowd is predominantly older. There's not much of the dad, mom and two kids in NFL stadiums, unlike in baseball and basketball. The cost is so high and the tickets, in many markets, so scarce. What Fox will do, with an approach to the NFL similar to the youth-oriented approach of NBC in its coverage of the National Basketball Association, will draw younger fans to the cusp of NFL viewing. Youth-directed plans included putting some of the NFL's brightest stars into prime-time cameos on popular Fox shows like *The Simpsons* and *Melrose Place*.

And Fox, even in its debut season, wasn't going to look so unlike CBS after all. Murdoch hired the top announcing team of John Madden and Pat Summerall (for a total of $38 million over four years, astounding numbers in any league), Terry Bradshaw with his terrific studio presence and most of the behind-the-scenes CBS folk. After the emotions died down, everyone realized the games would still be on TV, Fox would do the games at least competently and the football landscape would change precious little. "We'll treat the games as a sacred trust," said David Hill, the president of Fox Sports.

Life, and football, would go on just fine.

Watters's highstepping bursts produced 950 yards in '93.

Jerry Rice, who had a classic 98-catch, 1,503-yard season; and flighty running back Ricky Watters, who rushed for 950 yards and then five touchdowns in a 44–3 playoff rout of the Giants. Obviously the defense let the 49ers down in 1993. San Francisco gave up a gaudy 23 touchdown passes and allowed opposing rushers to rip through the defense for 4.5 yards a carry. Very un-Seifertlike. But it's still clear that no team other than Dallas was stronger entering the 1994 off-season.

3. *Buffalo.* General manager John Butler was the NFL's front-office rookie of the year in 1993. He signed Smith and Thomas, staving off what would have been their probable departures after the 1994 season. And to extend contracts of 10 other valuable players, he persuaded owner Ralph Wilson to throw a total of $2 million now at players they feared losing after the 1993 season. The Bills went 12–4 in '93 (is that their record every year, or are we just imagining things?) with a typical season: 3,382 passing yards by Jim Kelly, 1,702 rushing-receiving yards from Thurman Thomas, 13.5 sacks by Bruce Smith and a special teams season par excellence by Steve Tasker.

They are the best the AFC has to offer, but let's just lay it on the line. There's some-thing missing with this team—how else can one team, year after year, dominate its division and conference and lose the Big One?—and no one can figure exactly what it is. But right here, right now, we're going to reveal the secret of the Buffalo Bills. We're going to tell you precisely why they've won the AFC four years running and yet never won a Super Bowl. It's painfully easy: The AFC East has been a soft division for five years now, with the Jets, Patriots and Colts lying passively at the Bills' feet and the Dolphins providing only the occasional challenge. Buffalo fattens up on the easy divisional meat, earning home field advantage through the playoffs. (This has happened in each Super Bowl year except 1992, when the Bills went on the road and crushed Pittsburgh and Miami to get to the Super Bowl.) Then, when teams from the AFC Central or the temperate AFC West come to the NFL's Arctic Circle, i.e., Orchard Park, N.Y., for mid-January games, the Bills have the biggest home field advantage since the one the Kennedys had in Massachusetts politics in the '60s.

At the Super Bowl the Bills have no hidden advantage and have to play a much better team than any the AFC has to offer, and so they're blown away. How is this different from the rest of the competitive football world? Teams from the NFC East, who have won four straight Super Bowls, play roughhouse, Texas death-match games (witness the Cowboys' 16–13 NFC East-deciding win on the last Sunday of the '93 regular season) during the season, toughening themselves for the playoff run. Buffalo rarely gets that consistent regular-season challenge.

But 1993 did have some shaky moments for our three premier teams. With Emmitt Smith holding out in a contract dispute, Dallas started 0–2. San Francisco opened the regular season 3–3 and finished with two straight three-point losses at home. And the Bills, during a four-game midseason stretch, lost to Pittsburgh, Kansas City and the Raiders.

Dallas, after stumbling twice to Atlanta and Miami in five days around Thanksgiving, never lost again. They won the NFC East—and a first-round playoff bye that was critical given Emmitt Smith's separated right shoulder—in week 18, beating the Giants at the Meadowlands on Eddie Murray's field goal in overtime. They looked bored in a 27–17 divisional playoff win over Green Bay. Then Johnson poked them awake with his declaration before the Dallas–San Francisco NFC Championship Game. "We will win the ballgame," Johnson told local columnist and sports talk show host Randy Galloway three nights before the game. "You can put it in three-

inch headlines. We will win the ballgame, and we're going to beat their rear ends."

"Good morning, Mr. Guarantee," was the way guard Nate Newton greeted Johnson the next day at the office. Johnson said he wanted to shake out the tightness he saw in his team. Whatever his intention, it worked quite nicely. Dallas 38, San Francisco 21.

Buffalo made the Super Bowl by outlasting the Raiders in sub-zero temperatures, then K.O.'ing Joe Montana and the Chiefs in the AFC title game. Entering the Super Bowl they felt unloved ("We're the black sheep of the NFL family," said Bill linebacker Cornelius Bennett) and super motivated. They'd turned it over nine times in a 52–17 Super Bowl XXVII loss to Dallas the previous year. If they could play a mistake-free game, they knew they could win.

For 31 minutes they did a terrific job of protecting the ball and the lead. Up 13–6, Buffalo had the ball and was driving to make it 20–6 near midfield when disaster struck. With the reliable Thomas carrying the ball

It was the same old story for Kelly: great season, great stats, disappointing finish.

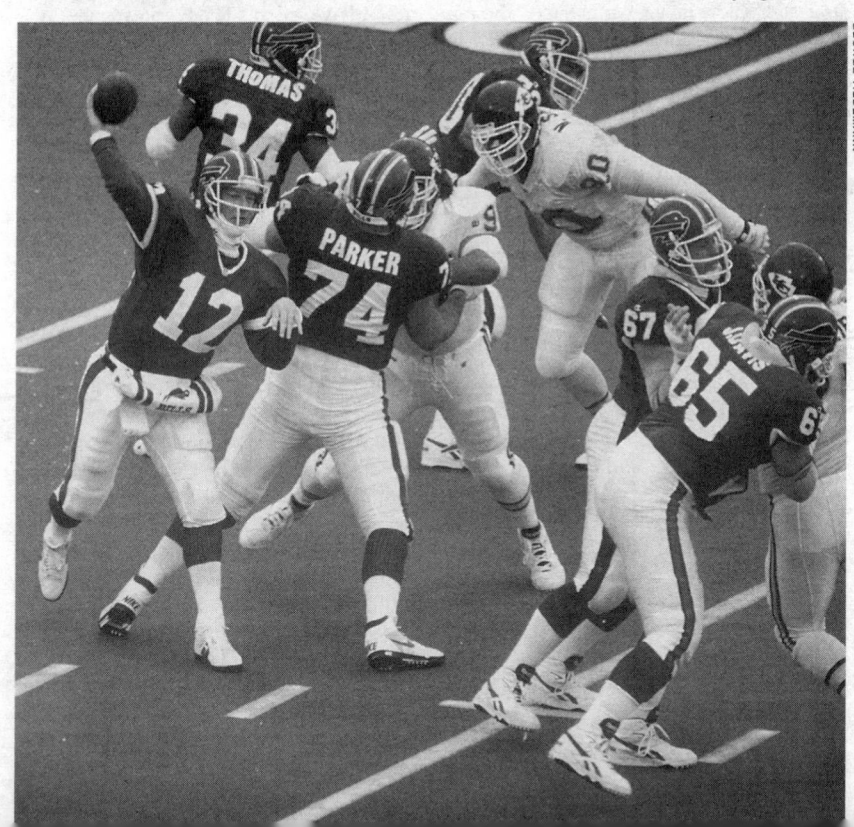

Bettis bulled his way to 1,429 yards and easy election as Rookie of the Year.

enough offensive weapons to contend, if only a pass rusher could develop. The Saints got off to a 5–0 start in 1993 but fizzled because their offense misfired constantly. In the East, pick a team. The Cardinals have new fire with new coach Buddy Ryan, who usually can find a way to get his team over .500. The Giants were a field goal behind the Cowboys for the division race thanks to superb years from Phil Simms and wise old coaching owl Dan Reeves; they may have lost too much in the 1994 free-agency season to stay competitive with Dallas, though. The Redskins have the bright young Norv Turner to try to turn their offensive horror show around.

up the middle, Lett slashed his right paw at the ball, jarring it loose. The ball bounced straight to safety James Washington, who ran it in for a 46-yard touchdown. Tie game. The pro-Dallas crowd was going bonkers, and the Bills could do nothing on their next series. "We smelled blood," said Cowboy defensive end Jim Jeffcoat. "We went into a frenzy." Dallas could do everything now. Smith ran six straight plays, for a total of 43 yards, and finished the drive a couple of minutes later with a 16-yard touchdown gallop. Dallas led 20–13. Buffalo was finished.

"If we stay together," Haley said wearily later, "we have a chance to be a dynasty. But we're not one yet."

There will be challenges. The 49ers and the Bills will stay strong. In the NFC a bunch of teams could emerge. If the Rams ever get a long-term passing companion to 1993 Rookie of the Year Jerome Bettis, who led all non-Smiths with 1,429 rushing yards, they'll rise again. The Bears, with Wannstedt rekindling a proud tradition, will soon be much better than their 7–9 record of 1993. The Falcons fired Jerry Glanville and replaced him with offensive coordinator June Jones after a 6–10 season; they have

In the AFC, New England should rise quickly, with lots of money to spend in the new salary-cap era. The Patriots, under new coach Bill Parcells, won their final two games and have one of the future's brightest quarterbacks, Drew Bledsoe. Seattle has a similarly starry quarterback, 1993 rookie Rick Mirer, who set NFL rookie records for passing yards (2,833), completions (274) and attempts (486) and seems on the verge of being a contender. Any team in the rest of the West—San Diego, with great young linebacker Junior Seau; the Raiders, with rejuvenated quarterback Jeff Hostetler; Denver, with strong-armed John Elway coming off his first 4,000-yard season; and Kansas City, with Joe Montana—could win 10 games. Houston won 11 straight games but failed against Kansas City in the '93 playoffs, setting off an exodus of coaches and players.

Such an exodus will be common in the new NFL. The Colts, millions of dollar over the 1994 cap, unceremoniously cut the AFC's leading receiver in 1993, Reggie Langhorne, after the season. "The good teams will find a way to stay good," Irvin of the Cowboys said. The good teams have already found a way.

FOR THE RECORD · 1993 - 1994

1993 NFL Final Standings

American Football Conference

EASTERN DIVISION

	W	L	T	Pct	Pts	OP
Buffalo	12	4	0	.750	329	242
Miami	9	7	0	.563	349	351
NY Jets	8	8	0	.500	270	247
New England	5	11	0	.313	238	286
Indianapolis	4	12	0	.250	189	378

CENTRAL DIVISION

	W	L	T	Pct	Pts	OP
Houston	12	4	0	.750	368	238
†Pittsburgh	9	7	0	.563	308	281
Cleveland	7	9	0	.438	304	307
Cincinnati	3	13	0	.188	187	319

WESTERN DIVISION

	W	L	T	Pct	Pts	OP
Kansas City	11	5	0	.688	328	291
†LA Raiders	10	6	0	.625	306	326
†Denver	9	7	0	.563	373	284
San Diego	8	8	0	.500	322	290
Seattle	6	10	0	.375	280	314

† Wild Card team.

National Football Conference

EASTERN DIVISION

	W	L	T	Pct	Pts	OP
Dallas	12	4	0	.750	376	229
†NY Giants	11	5	0	.688	288	205
Philadelphia	8	8	0	.500	293	315
Phoenix	7	9	0	.438	326	269
Washington	4	12	0	.250	230	345

CENTRAL DIVISION

	W	L	T	Pct	Pts	OP
Detroit	10	6	0	.625	298	292
†Minnesota	9	7	0	.563	277	290
†Green Bay	9	7	0	.563	340	282
Chicago	7	9	0	.438	236	230
Tampa Bay	5	11	0	.313	237	376

WESTERN DIVISION

	W	L	T	Pct	Pts	OP
San Francisco	10	6	0	.625	473	297
New Orleans	8	8	0	.500	317	343
Atlanta	6	10	0	.375	316	385
LA Rams	5	11	0	.313	221	367

1994 NFL Playoffs

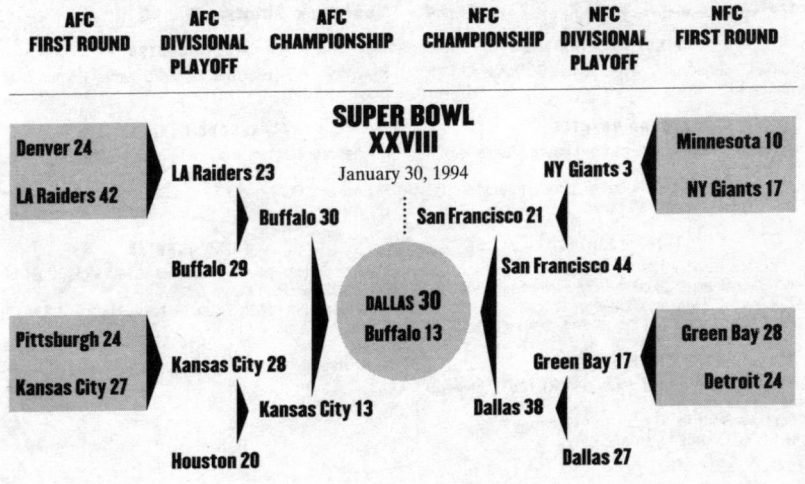

AFC FIRST ROUND	AFC DIVISIONAL PLAYOFF	AFC CHAMPIONSHIP	NFC CHAMPIONSHIP	NFC DIVISIONAL PLAYOFF	NFC FIRST ROUND

SUPER BOWL XXVIII
January 30, 1994

Denver 24 / LA Raiders 42

LA Raiders 23

Buffalo 30

Buffalo 29

DALLAS 30 / Buffalo 13

San Francisco 21

San Francisco 44

NY Giants 3

Minnesota 10 / NY Giants 17

Pittsburgh 24 / Kansas City 27

Kansas City 28

Kansas City 13

Houston 20

Dallas 38

Dallas 27

Green Bay 17

Green Bay 28 / Detroit 24

NFL Playoff Box Scores

AFC Wild-card Games

Denver	7	14	0	3—24
LA Raiders	14	7	14	7—42

FIRST QUARTER

Los Angeles: Horton 9 pass from Hostetler (Jaeger kick), 5:34. Drive: 80 yards, 7 plays.
Denver: Sharpe 23 pass from Elway (Elam kick), 8:48. Drive: 65 yards, 7 plays.
Los Angeles: Brown 65 pass from Hostetler (Jaeger kick), 12:35. Drive: 78 yards 6 plays.

SECOND QUARTER

Denver: R. Johnson 16 pass from Elway (Elam kick), 4:54. Drive: 80 yards, 12 plays.
Los Angeles: Jett 54 pass from Hostetler (Jaeger kick), 7:32. Drive: 84 yards, 5 plays.
Denver: Russell 6 pass from Elway (Elam kick), 14:28. Drive: 77 yards, 13 plays.

THIRD QUARTER

Los Angeles: McCallum 26 run (Jaeger kick), 6:52. Drive 35 yards, 3 plays.
Los Angeles: McCallum 2 run (Jaeger kick), 10:33. Drive: 52 yards, 5 plays.

FOURTH QUARTER

Denver: FG Elam 33, 2:24. Drive: 63 yards, 8 plays.
Los Angeles: McCallum 1 run (Jaeger kick), 8:17. Drive: 76 yards, 10 plays.

A: 65,314; T: 3:34.

Pittsburgh	7	10	0	7	0—24
Kansas City	7	0	3	14	3—27

FIRST QUARTER

Pittsburgh: Cooper 10 pass from O'Donnell (Anderson kick), 6:15. Drive: 66 yards, 9 plays.
Kansas City: Birden 23 pass from Krieg (Lowery kick),13:21. Drive: 75 yards, 7 plays.

SECOND QUARTER

Pittsburgh: FG Anderson 30, 5:26. Drive: 63 yards, 15 plays.
Pittsburgh: Mills 26 pass from O'Donnell (Anderson kick), 14:42. Drive 51 yards, 6 plays.

THIRD QUARTER

Kansas City: FG Lowery 23, 13:51. Drive 49 yards, 11 plays.

FOURTH QUARTER

Kansas City: Allen 2 run (Lowery kick), 6:02. Drive 80 yards, 9 plays.
Pittsburgh: Green 22 pass from O'Donnell (Anderson kick), 10:49. Drive: 74 yards, 9 plays.
Kansas City: Barnett 7 pass from Montana (Lowery kick), 13:17. Drive: 9 yards, 4 plays.

OVERTIME

Kansas City: FG Lowery 32, 11:03. Drive: 66 yards, 11 plays

A: 58,278; T: 3:05.

NFC Wild-card Games

Green Bay	0	7	14	7—28
Detroit	3	7	7	7—24

FIRST QUARTER

Detroit: FG Hanson 47, 15:00. Drive: 50 yards, 9 plays.

SECOND QUARTER

Green Bay: Sharpe 12 pass from Favre (Jacke kick), 7:04. Drive: 80 13 plays.
Detroit: Perriman 1 pass from Kramer (Hanson kick), 12:56. Drive: 94 yards, 10 plays.

THIRD QUARTER

Detroit: Jenkins 15 int return (Hanson kick), 6:40.
Green Bay: Sharpe 28 pass from Favre (Jacke kick), 10:25. Drive: 72 yards, 7 plays.
Green Bay: Teague 101 int return (Jacke kick), 13:20.

FOURTH QUARTER

Detroit: D. Moore 5 run (Hanson kick), 6:33. Drive: 89 yards, 15 plays.
Green Bay: Sharpe 40 pass from Favre (Jacke kick),14:05. Drive 71 yards, 5 plays.

A: 68,479; T: 2:53.

Minnesota	0	10	0	0—10
New York Giants	3	0	14	0—17

FIRST QUARTER

New York: FG Treadwell 26, 6:25. Drive: 48 yards, 9 plays.

SECOND QUARTER

Minnesota: C. Carter 40 pass from McMahon (Reveiz kick), 13:07. Drive: 53 yards, 4 plays.
Minnesota: FG Reveiz 52, 14:58. Drive: 2 yards, 2 plays.

THIRD QUARTER

New York: Hampton 51 run (Treadwell kick), 2:54. Drive: 63 yards, 4 plays.
New York: Hampton 2 run, (Treadwell run), 9:23. Drive: 26 yards, 8 plays.

A: 75,089; T: 3:01.

AFC Divisional Games

LA Raiders 0	17	6	0—23
Buffalo....................0	13	9	7—29

SECOND QUARTER

Los Angeles: FG Jaeger 30, 1:13. Drive: 58 yards, 11 plays.
Buffalo: Davis 1 run (kick failed), 1:30. Drive 1 yard, 1 play.
Los Angeles: McCallum 1 run (Jaeger kick), 6:50. Drive: 57 yards, 8 plays.
Los Angeles: McCallum 1 run (Jaeger kick), 13:03. Drive: 40 yards, 11 plays.
Buffalo: Thomas 8 run (Christie kick), 14:10. Drive: 76 yards, 4 plays.

THIRD QUARTER

Buffalo: Brooks 25 pass from Kelly (kick failed), 11:37. Drive: 60 yards, 5 plays.
Buffalo: FG Christie 29, 14:01. Drive: 18 yards, 5 plays.
Los Angeles: Brown 86 pass from Hostetler (kick failed), 14:30. Drive: 86 yards 2 plays.

FOURTH QUARTER

Buffalo: Brooks 22 pass from Kelly (Christie kick), 2:55. Drive: 71 yards, 9 plays.

A: 61,923; T: 3:07.

Kansas City..............0	0	7	21—28
Houston.................10	0	0	10—20

FIRST QUARTER

Houston: FG Del Greco 49, 3:50. Drive: minus-8 yards, 4 plays.
Houston: G. Brown 2 run (Del Greco kick), 13:01. Drive: 80 yards, 11 plays.

THIRD QUARTER

Kansas City: Cash 7 pass from Montana (Lowery kick), 4:41. Drive: 71 yards, 7 plays.

FOURTH QUARTER

Houston: FG Del Greco 43, 5:23. Drive: minus-1 yard, 4 plays.
Kansas City: Birden 11 pass from Montana (Lowery kick), 6:22. Drive: 71 yards, 3 plays.
Kansas City: Davis 18 pass from Montana (Lowery kick), 7:16. Drive: 12 yards, 3 plays.
Houston: Givins 7 pass from Moon (Del Greco), 11:15. Drive: 80 yards, 9 plays.
Kansas City: Allen 21 run (Lowery kick), 13:05. Drive: 79 yards, 6 plays.

A: 64,011; T: 3:13.

NFC Divisional Games

New York Giants....0	3	0	0— 3
San Francisco........9	14	14	7—44

FIRST QUARTER

San Francisco: Watters 1 run (kick failed), 4:27. Drive: 80 yards, 8 plays.
San Francisco: FG Cofer 29, 10:07. Drive: 37 yards, 7 plays.

SECOND QUARTER

San Francisco: Watters 1 run (Cofer kick), 0:02. Drive: 41 yards, 8 plays.
San Francisco: Watters 2 run (Cofer kick), 10:57. Drive: 92 yards, 8 plays.
New York: FG Treadwell 25, 15:00. Drive: 62 yards, 6 plays.

THIRD QUARTER

San Francisco: Watters 6 run (Cofer kick), 7:22. Drive: 50 yards, 7 plays.
San Francisco: Watters 2 run (Cofer kick), 13:51. Drive: 35 yards, 5 plays.

FOURTH QUARTER

San Francisco: Logan 2 run (Cofer kick), 2:34. Drive: 34 yards, 6 plays.

A: 67,143; T: 2:50.

Green Bay 3	0	7	7—17
Dallas.....................0	17	7	3—27

FIRST QUARTER

Green Bay: FG Jacke 30, 11:40. Drive: 16 yards, 7 plays.

SECOND QUARTER

Dallas: Harper 25 pass from Aikman (Murray kick), 5:53. Drive: 68 yards, 8 plays.
Dallas: FG Murray 41, 14:37. Drive: 45 yards, 10 plays.
Dallas: Novacek 6 pass from Aikman (Murray kick), 14:55. Drive: 14 yards, 2 plays.

THIRD QUARTER

Dallas:Irvin 19 pass from Aikman (Murray kick), 9:05. Drive: 69 yards, 6 plays.
Green Bay: Brooks 13 pass from Favre (Jacke kick), 13:28. Drive: 82 yards, 9 plays.

FOURTH QUARTER

Dallas: FG Murray 38, 7:22. Drive: 47 yards, 9 plays.
Green Bay: Sharpe 29 pass from Favre (Jacke kick), 14:38. Drive: 56 yards, 6 plays.

A:64,790; T: 3:00.

NFL Playoff Box Scores (Cont.)

AFC Championship

Kansas City	6	0	7	0—13
Buffalo	7	13	0	10—30

FIRST QUARTER

Buffalo: Thomas 12 run (Christie kick), 8:11. Drive: 47 yards, 6 plays.
Kansas City: FG Lowery 31, 12:46. Drive: 51 yards, 10 plays.

SECOND QUARTER

Buffalo: Thomas 3 run (Christie kick), 2:58. Drive: 80 yards, 9 plays.
Buffalo: FG Christie 23, 7:56. Drive: 41 yards, 10 plays.
Buffalo: FG Christie 25, 12:59. Drive: 56 yards, 10 plays.

THIRD QUARTER

Kansas City: Allen 1 run (Lowery kick), 11:54. Drive: 90 yards, 14 plays.

FOURTH QUARTER

Buffalo: FG Christie 18, 3:05. Drive: 79 yards, 14 plays.
Buffalo: Thomas 3 run (Christie kick), 9:30. Drive: 52 yards, 8 plays.

A: 76,642; T: 3:10.

NFC Championship

San Francisco	0	7	7	7—21
Dallas	7	21	7	3—38

FIRST QUARTER

Dallas: E. Smith 5 run (Murray kick), 6:19. Drive: 75 yards, 11 plays.

SECOND QUARTER

San Francisco: Rathman 7 pass from Young (Cofer kick), :05. Drive: 80 yards, 9 plays.
Dallas: Johnston 4 run (Murray kick), 5:12. Drive: 80 yards, 11 plays.
Dallas: E. Smith 11 pass from Aikman (Murray kick), 8:56. Drive: 24 yards, 4 plays.
Dallas: Novacek 19 pass from Aikman (Murray kick), 14:02. Drive 72 yards, 8 plays.

THIRD QUARTER

San Francisco: Watters 4 run (Cofer kick), 9:13. Drive: 43 yards, 6 plays.
Dallas: Harper 42 pass from Kosar (Murray kick), 12:36. Drive: 82 yards, 7 plays.

FOURTH QUARTER

Dallas: FG Murray 50, 5:08. Drive: 30 yards, 8 plays.
San Francisco: Young 1 run (Cofer kick), 10:54. Drive: 94 yards, 17 plays.

A: 64,902; T: 3:11.

Super Bowl Box Score

Dallas	6	0	14	10—30
Buffalo	3	10	0	0—13

FIRST QUARTER

Dallas: FG Murray 41, 2:19. Drive: 24 yards, 5 plays. Key plays: K. Williams 50-yard kickoff return to Buffalo 48; Aikman 20-yard pass to Irvin to Buffalo 28. Dallas 3, Buffalo 0.
Buffalo: FG Christie 54, 4:41. Drive: 43 yards, 8 plays. Key plays: Kelly 11-yard pass to Reed to Buffalo 23; Kelly 24-yard pass to Thomas to Dallas 39. Dallas 3, Buffalo 3.
Dallas: FG Murray 24, 11:05. Drive: 43 yards, 7 plays. Key plays: Woodson recovery of Thomas fumble at midfield; Aikman 8-yard pass to Smith to Buffalo 39; Aikman 24-yard pass to Harper to Buffalo 15. Dallas 6, Buffalo 3.

SECOND QUARTER

Buffalo: Thomas 4 run (Christie kick), 2:34. Drive: 80 yards, 17 plays. Key plays: Thomas running into the kicker penalty to Buffalo 46; K. Davis 2-yard run on 3rd-and-1 to Dallas 32; Kelly 3-yard pass to Beebe to Dallas 3. Buffalo 10, Dallas 6.
Buffalo: FG Christie 28, 15:00. Drive: 38 yards, 7 plays. Key plays: Odomes 40-yard interception return to Dallas 48; Kelly 13-yard pass to Thomas to Dallas 35; Kelly 22-yard pass to Reed to Dallas 13. Buffalo 13, Dallas 6.

THIRD QUARTER

Dallas: Washington 46 fumble return (Murray kick), 0:55. Buffalo 13, Dallas 13.
Dallas: Smith 16 run (Murray kick), 6:18. Drive: 64 yards, 8 plays. Key plays: Smith 7 carries for 62 yards. Dallas 20, Buffalo 13.

FOURTH QUARTER

Dallas: Smith 1 run (Murray kick), 5:10. Drive: 34 yards, 9 plays. Key plays: Washington 12-yard interception return to Buffalo 34; Aikman 16-yard pass to Harper on third-and-8 to Buffalo 6. Dallas 27, Buffalo 13.
Dallas: FG Murray 20, 12:10. Drive: 49 yards, 10 plays. Key plays: Aikman 4-yard pass to Novacek on third-and-2 to Buffalo 39; Aikman 35-yard pass to Harper on third-and-8 to Buffalo 1. Dallas 30, Buffalo 13.

A: 72,817; T: 3:16.

Super Bowl Box Score (*Cont.*)

Team Statistics

	Dallas	Buffalo
FIRST DOWNS	20	22
Rushing	6	6
Passing	14	15
Penalty	0	1
THIRD DOWN EFF	5–13	5–17
FOURTH DOWN EFF	1–1	2–3
TOTAL NET YARDS	341	314
Total plays	64	80
Avg gain	5.3	3.9
NET YARDS RUSHING	137	87
Rushes	35	27
Avg per rush	3.9	3.2
NET YARDS PASSING	204	227
Completed-Att.	19–27	31–50
Yards per pass	7.0	4.3
Sacked-yards lost	2–3	3–33
Had intercepted	1	1
PUNTS-Avg.	4–44	5–38
TOTAL RETURN YARDS	89	119
Punt returns	1–5	1–5
Kickoff returns	2–72	6–144
Interceptions	1–12	1–41
PENALTIES-Yds	6–50	1–10
FUMBLES-Lost	0–0	3–2
TIME OF POSSESSION	34:29	25:31

Rushing

DALLAS

	No.	Yds	Lg	TD
Smith	30	132	16	2
K. Williams	1	6	6	0
Aikman	1	3	3	0
Johnston	1	0	0	0
Kosar	1	–1	–1	0
Coleman	1	–3	–3	0

BUFFALO

	No.	Yds	Lg	TD
Davis	9	38	11	0
Thomas	16	37	6	1
Kelly	2	12	8	0

Receiving

DALLAS

	No.	Yds	Lg	TD
Irvin	5	66	20	0
Novacek	5	26	4	0
Smith	4	26	8	0
Harper	3	75	35	0
Johnston	2	14	11	0

BUFFALO

	No.	Yds	Lg	TD
Brooks	7	63	15	0
Thomas	7	52	24	0
Reed	6	75	22	0
Beebe	6	60	18	0
K. Davis	3	–5	7	0
Metzelaars	1	8	8	0
McKellar	1	7	7	0

Passing

DALLAS

	Comp	Att	Yds	Int	TD
Aikman	19	27	207	1	0

BUFFALO

	Comp	Att	Yds	Int	TD
Kelly	31	50	260	1	0

Defense

DALLAS

	Tck	Ast	Int	Sack
J. Washington	11	0	1	0
Everett	8	0	0	0
Norton	7	1	0	0
K. Smith	5	0	0	0
L. Brown	4	0	0	0
Lett	3	2	0	0
Tolbert	3	2	0	.5
J. Jones	3	0	0	0
Woodson	3	0	0	0
Casillas	2	4	0	.5
Haley	2	2	0	.5
Jeffcoat	2	1	0	1.5
Bates	2	1	0	0
Gant	2	0	0	0
Maryland	2	0	0	0
D. Smith	1	0	0	0
Fishback	1	0	0	0
Gainer	1	0	0	0
D. Thomas	1	0	0	0
Vanderbeek	1	0	0	0
E. Williams	1	0	0	0
Edwards	0	1	0	0

BUFFALO

	Tck	Ast	Int	Sack
Bennett	10	3	0	0
M. Patton	9	0	0	0
Talley	8	1	0	0
Wright	5	0	0	2
B. Smith	4	1	0	0
Odomes	3	2	1	0
H. Jones	3	0	0	0
M. Washington	3	0	0	0
Kelso	2	2	0	0
Maddox	2	0	0	0
Goganious	1	1	0	0
Lodish	1	1	0	0
Barnett	1	0	0	0
Darby	1	0	0	0
Harvey	1	0	0	0
Fina	1	0	0	0
Schulz	1	0	0	0
Tasker	1	0	0	0
Hansen	0	2	0	0

1993 Associated Press All-NFL Team

OFFENSE

Sterling Sharpe, Green Bay	Wide Receiver
Jerry Rice, San Francisco	Wide Receiver
Shannon Sharpe, Denver	Tight End
Harris Barton, San Francisco	Tackle
Erik Williams, Dallas	Tackle
Randall McDaniel, Minnesota	Guard
Steve Wisniewski, LA Raiders	Guard
Bruce Matthews, Houston	Center
Steve Young, San Francisco	Quarterback
Emmitt Smith, Dallas	Running Back
Jerome Bettis, LA Rams	Running Back

DEFENSE

Bruce Smith, Buffalo	Defensive End
Neil Smith, Kansas City	Defensive End
Cortez Kennedy, Seattle	Defensive Tackle
John Randle, Minnesota	Nose Tackle
Greg Lloyd, Pittsburgh	Outside Linebacker
Seth Joyner, Philadelphia	Outside Linebacker
Junior Seau, San Diego	Inside Linebacker
Hardy Nickerson, Tampa Bay	Inside Linebacker
Rod Woodson, Pittsburgh	Cornerback
Deion Sanders, Atlanta	Cornerback
LeRoy Butler, Green Bay	Safety
Eugene Robinson, Seattle	Safety

SPECIALISTS

Norm Johnson, Atlanta	Kicker
Greg Montgomery, Houston	Punter
Tyrone Hughes, New Orleans	Kickoff Returner
Eric Metcalf, Cleveland	Punt Returner
Steve Tasker, Buffalo	Special Teams Player

1993 AFC Team-by-Team Results

BUFFALO BILLS (12-4)			CINCINNATI BENGALS (3-13)			CLEVELAND BROWNS (7-9)		
38	NEW ENGLAND	14	14	at Cleveland	27	27	CINCINNATI	14
13	at Dallas	10	6	INDIANAPOLIS	9	23	SAN FRANCISCO	13
	OPEN DATE		7	at Pittsburgh	34	19	at LA Raiders	16
13	MIAMI	22	10	SEATTLE	19	10	at Indianapolis	23
17	NY GIANTS	14		OPEN DATE			OPEN DATE	
35	HOUSTON	7	15	at Kansas City	17	14	MIAMI	24
	OPEN DATE		17	CLEVELAND	28	28	at Cincinnati	17
19	at NY Jets	10	12	at Houston	28	28	PITTSBURGH	23
24	WASHINGTON	10		OPEN DATE			OPEN DATE	
13	at New England	10	16	PITTSBURGH	24	14	DENVER	29
0	at Pittsburgh	23	3	HOUSTON	38	5	at Seattle	22
23	INDIANAPOLIS	9	12	at NY Jets	17	20	HOUSTON	27
7	at Kansas City	23	16	LA RAIDERS	10	14	at Atlanta	17
24	LA RAIDERS	25	8	at San Francisco	21	17	NEW ORLEANS	13
10	at Philadelphia	7	2	at New England	7	17	at Houston	19
47	at Miami	34	15	LA RAMS	3	17	NEW ENGLAND	20
16	NY JETS	14	21	ATLANTA	17	42	at LA Rams	14
30	at Indianapolis	10	13	at New Orleans	20	9	at Pittsburgh	16
329		242	187		319	304		307

DENVER BRONCOS (9-7)

26	at NY Jets	20
34	SAN DIEGO	17
7	at Kansas City	15
	OPEN DATE	
35	INDIANAPOLIS	13
27	at Green Bay	30
20	LA RAIDERS	23
	OPEN DATE	
28	SEATTLE	17
29	at Cleveland	14
23	MINNESOTA	26
37	PITTSBURGH	13
17	at Seattle	9
10	at San Diego	13
27	KANSAS CITY	21
13	at Chicago	3
10	TAMPA BAY	17
30	at LA Raiders (OT)	33
373		284

HOUSTON OILERS (12-4)

21	At New Orleans	33
30	KANSAS CITY	0
17	at San Diego	18
13	LA RAMS	28
	OPEN DATE	
7	at Buffalo	35
28	at New England	14
28	CINCINNATI	12
	OPEN DATE	
24	SEATTLE	14
38	at Cincinnati	3
27	at Cleveland	20
23	PITTSBURGH	3
33	ATLANTA	17
19	CLEVELAND	17
26	at Pittsburgh	17
10	at San Francisco	7
24	NY JETS	0
368		238

INDIANAPOLIS COLTS (4-12)

20	MIAMI	24
9	at Cincinnati	6
	OPEN DATE	
23	CLEVELAND	10
13	at Denver	35
3	DALLAS	27
	OPEN DATE	
27	at Miami	41
9	NEW ENGLAND	6
24	at Washington	30
17	NY JETS	31
9	at Buffalo	23
0	SAN DIEGO	31
9	at NY Jets	6
6	at NY Giants	20
10	PHILADELPHIA	20
0	at New England	38
10	BUFFALO	30
189		378

KANSAS CITY CHIEFS (11-5)

27	at Tampa Bay	3
0	at Houston	30
15	DENVER	7
	OPEN DATE	
24	LA RAIDERS	9
17	CINCINNATI	15
17	at San Diego	14
	OPEN DATE	
10	at Miami	30
23	GREEN BAY	16
31	at LA Raiders	20
17	CHICAGO	19
23	BUFFALO	7
31	at Seattle	16
21	at Denver	27
28	SAN DIEGO	24
10	at Minnesota	30
34	SEATTLE	24
328		291

LOS ANGELES RAIDERS (10-6)

24	MINNESOTA	7
17	at Seattle	13
16	CLEVELAND	19
	OPEN DATE	
9	at Kansas City	24
24	NY JETS	20
23	at Denver	20
	OPEN DATE	
23	SAN DIEGO	30
16	at Chicago	14
20	KANSAS CITY	31
12	at San Diego	7
10	at Cincinnati	16
25	at Buffalo	24
27	SEATTLE	23
27	TAMPA BAY	20
0	at Green Bay	28
33	DENVER (OT)	30
306		326

MIAMI DOLPHINS (9-7)

24	at Indianapolis	20
14	NY JETS	24
	OPEN DATE	
22	at Buffalo	13
17	WASHINGTON	10
24	at Cleveland	14
	OPEN DATE	
41	INDIANAPOLIS	27
30	KANSAS CITY	10
10	at NY Jets	27
19	at Philadelphia	14
17	NEW ENGLAND	13
16	at Dallas	14
14	NY GIANTS	19
20	PITTSBURGH	21
34	BUFFALO	47
20	at San Diego	45
27	at New England (OT)	33
349		351

NEW ENGLAND PATRIOTS (5-11)

14	at Buffalo	38
16	DETROIT	19
14	SEATTLE	17
7	at NY Jets	45
	OPEN DATE	
23	at Phoenix	21
14	HOUSTON	28
9	at Seattle	10
6	at Indianapolis	9
10	BUFFALO	13
	OPEN DATE	
13	at Miami	17
0	NY JETS	6
14	at Pittsburgh	17
7	CINCINNATI	2
20	at Cleveland	17
38	INDIANAPOLIS	0
33	MIAMI (OT)	27
238		286

NEW YORK JETS (8-8)

20	DENVER	26
24	at Miami	14
	OPEN DATE	
45	NEW ENGLAND	7
30	PHILADELPHIA	35
20	at LA Raiders	24
	OPEN DATE	
10	BUFFALO	19
10	at NY Giants	6
27	MIAMI	10
31	at Indianapolis	27
17	CINCINNATI	12
6	At New England	0
6	INDIANAPOLIS	9
3	at Washington	0
7	DALLAS	28
14	at Buffalo	16
0	at Houston	24
270		247

PITTSBURGH STEELERS (9-7)

13	SAN FRANCISCO	24
0	at LA Rams	27
34	CINCINNATI	7
45	at Atlanta	17
	OPEN DATE	
16	SAN DIEGO	3
37	NEW ORLEANS	14
23	at Cleveland	28
	OPEN DATE	
24	at Cincinnati	16
23	BUFFALO	0
13	at Denver	37
3	at Houston	23
17	NEW ENGLAND	14
21	at Miami	20
17	HOUSTON	26
6	at Seattle	16
16	CLEVELAND	9
308		281

SAN DIEGO CHARGERS (8-8)				SEATTLE SEAHAWKS (6-10)	
18	SEATTLE	12	12	at San Diego	18
17	at Denver	34	13	LA RAIDERS	17
18	HOUSTON	17	17	at New England	14
	OPEN DATE		19	at Cincinnati	10
14	at Seattle	31	31	SAN DIEGO	14
3	at Pittsburgh	16		OPEN DATE	
14	KANSAS CITY	17	10	at Detroit	30
	OPEN DATE		10	NEW ENGLAND	9
30	at LA Raiders	23	17	at Denver	28
30	at Minnesota	17	14	at Houston	24
13	CHICAGO	16	22	Cleveland	5
7	LA RAIDERS	12		OPEN DATE	
30	at Indianapolis	0	9	DENVER	17
13	DENVER	10	16	KANSAS CITY	31
13	GREEN BAY	20	23	at LA Raiders	27
24	at Kansas City	28	27	PHOENIX	30
45	MIAMI	20	16	Pittsburgh	6
32	at Tampa Bay	17	24	at Kansas City	34
322		290	140		312

1993 NFC Team-by-Team Results

ATLANTA FALCONS (6-10)			CHICAGO BEARS (7-9)			DALLAS COWBOYS (12-4)		
13	at Detroit	30	20	NY GIANTS	26	16	at Washington	35
31	NEW ORLEANS	34	7	at Minnesota	10	10	BUFFALO	13
30	at San Francisco	37		OPEN DATE		17	at Phoenix	10
17	PITTSBURGH	45	47	TAMPA BAY	17		OPEN DATE	
0	at Chicago	6	6	ATLANTA	0	36	GREEN BAY	14
	OPEN DATE		17	at Philadelphia	6	27	at Indianapolis	3
30	LA RAMS	24		OPEN DATE		26	SAN FRANCISCO	17
26	at New Orleans	15	12	MINNESOTA	9		OPEN DATE	
24	TAMPA BAY	31	3	at Green Bay	17	23	at Philadelphia	10
	OPEN DATE		14	LA RAIDERS	16	31	NY GIANTS	9
13	at LA Rams	0	16	at San Diego	13	20	PHOENIX	15
27	DALLAS	14	19	at Kansas City	17	14	at Atlanta	27
17	CLEVELAND	14	10	at Detroit	6	14	MIAMI	16
17	at Houston	33	30	GREEN BAY	17	23	PHILADELPHIA	17
27	SAN FRANCISCO	24	10	at Tampa Bay	13	37	at Minnesota	20
17	at Washington	30	3	DENVER	13	28	at NY JETS	7
17	at Cincinnati	21	14	DETROIT	20	38	WASHINGTON	3
10	PHOENIX	27	6	at LA Rams	20	16	at NY Giants (OT)	13
316		385	236		230	376		229

DETROIT LIONS (10-6)			GREEN BAY PACKERS (9-7)			LOS ANGELES RAMS (5-11)		
30	ATLANTA	13	36	LA RAMS	6	6	at Green Bay	36
19	at New England	16	17	PHILADELPHIA	20	27	PITTSBURGH	0
3	at New Orleans	14		OPEN DATE		10	at NY Giants	20
26	PHOENIX	20	13	at Minnesota	15	28	at Houston	13
10	at Tampa Bay	27	14	at Dallas	36	6	NEW ORLEANS	37
	OPEN DATE		30	DENVER	27		OPEN DATE	
30	SEATTLE	10		OPEN DATE		24	at Atlanta	30
16	at LA Rams	13	37	at Tampa Bay	14	13	DETROIT	16
30	at Minnesota	27	17	CHICAGO	3	17	at San Francisco	40
23	TAMPA BAY	0	16	at Kansas City	23		OPEN DATE	
	OPEN DATE		19	at New Orleans	17	0	ATLANTA	13
17	at Green Bay	26	26	DETROIT	17	10	WASHINGTON	6
6	CHICAGO	10	13	TAMPA BAY	10	10	SAN FRANCISCO	35
0	MINNESOTA	13	17	at Chicago	30	10	at Phoenix	38
21	at Phoenix	14	20	at San Diego	13	23	at New Orleans	20
17	SAN FRANCISCO	55	17	MINNESOTA	21	3	at Cincinnati	15
20	at Chicago	14	28	LA RAIDERS	0	14	CLEVELAND	42
30	GREEN BAY	20	20	at Detroit	30	20	CHICAGO	6
298		292	340		282	221		367

MINNESOTA VIKINGS (9-7)

7	at LA Raiders	24
10	CHICAGO	7
	OPEN DATE	
15	GREEN BAY	13
19	at San Francisco	38
15	TAMPA BAY	0
	OPEN DATE	
19	at Chicago	12
27	DETROIT	30
17	SAN DIEGO	30
26	at Denver	23
10	at Tampa Bay	23
14	NEW ORLEANS	17
13	at Detroit	0
20	DALLAS	37
21	at Green Bay	17
30	KANSAS CITY	10
14	at Washington	9
277		**290**

NEW ORLEANS SAINTS (8-8)

33	HOUSTON	21
34	at Atlanta	31
14	DETROIT	3
16	SAN FRANCISCO	13
37	at LA Rams	6
	OPEN DATE	
14	at Pittsburgh	37
15	ATLANTA	26
20	at Phoenix	17
	OPEN DATE	
17	GREEN BAY	19
7	at San Francisco	42
17	at Minnesota	14
13	at Cleveland	17
20	LA RAMS	23
14	NY GIANTS	24
26	at Philadelphia	37
20	Cincinnati	13
317		**343**

NEW YORK GIANTS (11-5)

26	at Chicago	20
23	TAMPA BAY	7
20	LA RAMS	10
	OPEN DATE	
14	at Buffalo	17
41	at Washington	7
21	PHILADELPHIA	10
	OPEN DATE	
6	NY JETS	10
9	at Dallas	31
20	WASHINGTON	6
7	at Philadelphia	3
19	PHOENIX	17
19	at Miami	14
20	INDIANAPOLIS	6
24	at New Orleans	14
6	at Phoenix	17
13	DALLAS (OT)	16
288		**205**

PHILADELPHIA EAGLES (8-8)

23	PHOENIX	17
20	at Green Bay	17
34	WASHINGTON	31
	OPEN DATE	
35	at NY Jets	30
6	CHICAGO	17
10	at NY Giants	21
	OPEN DATE	
10	DALLAS	23
3	at Phoenix	16
14	MIAMI	19
3	NY GIANTS	7
17	at Washington	14
17	at Dallas	23
7	BUFFALO	10
20	at Indianapolis	10
37	NEW ORLEANS	26
37	at San Francisco	34
293		**315**

PHOENIX CARDINALS (7-9)

17	at Philadelphia	23
17	at Washington	10
10	DALLAS	17
20	at Detroit	26
	OPEN DATE	
21	NEW ENGLAND	23
36	WASHINGTON	6
14	at San Francisco	28
17	NEW ORLEANS	20
16	PHILADELPHIA	3
15	at Dallas	20
	OPEN DATE	
17	at NY Giants	19
30	LA RAMS	10
14	DETROIT	21
30	at Seattle	27
17	NY GIANTS	6
27	at Atlanta	10
326		**269**

SAN FRANCISCO 49ERS (10-6)

24	at Pittsburgh	13
13	at Cleveland	23
37	ATLANTA	30
13	at New Orleans	16
38	MINNESOTA	19
	OPEN DATE	
17	at Dallas	26
28	PHOENIX	14
40	LA RAMS	17
	OPEN DATE	
45	at Tampa Bay	21
42	NEW ORLEANS	7
35	at LA Rams	10
21	CINCINNATI	8
24	at Atlanta	27
55	at Detroit	17
7	HOUSTON	10
34	PHILADELPHIA	37
473		**297**

TAMPA BAY BUCCANEERS (5-11)

3	KANSAS CITY	27
7	at NY Giants	23
	OPEN DATE	
17	at Chicago	47
27	DETROIT	10
0	at Minnesota	15
	OPEN DATE	
14	GREEN BAY	37
31	at Atlanta	24
0	at Detroit	23
21	SAN FRANCISCO	45
23	MINNESOTA	10
10	at Green Bay	13
17	WASHINGTON	23
13	CHICAGO	10
20	at LA Raiders	27
17	at Denver	10
17	SAN DIEGO	32
237		**376**

WASHINGTON REDSKINS (4-12)

35	DALLAS	16
10	PHOENIX	17
31	at Philadelphia	34
	OPEN DATE	
10	at Miami	17
7	NY GIANTS	41
6	at Phoenix	36
	OPEN DATE	
10	at Buffalo	24
30	INDIANAPOLIS	24
6	at NY GIANTS	20
6	at LA RAMS	10
14	PHILADELPHIA	17
23	at Tampa Bay	17
0	NY JETS	3
30	ATLANTA	17
3	at Dallas	38
9	MINNESOTA	14
230		**345**

American Football Conference
Scoring

TOUCHDOWNS	TD	Rush	Rec	Ret	Pts	KICKING	PAT	FG	Lg	Pts
Allen, KC	15	12	3	0	90	Jaeger, Rai	27/29	35/44	53	132
Foster, Pitt	9	8	1	0	54	Del Greco, Hou	39/40	29/34	52	126
Sharpe, Den	9	0	9	0	54	Carney, SD	31/33	31/40	51	124
G. Brown, Hou	8	6	2	0	48	Elam, Den	41/42	26/35	54	119
Brown, Rai	8	0	7	1	48	Anderson, Pitt	32/32	28/30	46	116
Coates, NE	8	0	8	0	48	Stoyanovich, Mia	37/37	24/32	52	109
Delpino, Den	8	0	8	0	48	Lowery, KC	37/37	23/29	52	106
Jackson, Cle	8	0	8	0	48	Christie, Buff	36/37	23/32	59	105
Means, SD	8	8	0	0	48	Kasay, Sea	29/29	23/28	55	98
Five tied with 7 touchdowns						Biasucci, Ind	15/16	26/31	53	93

Passing

	Att	Comp	Pct Comp	Yds	Avg Gain	TD	Pct TD	Int	Pct Int	Lg	Rating Pts
Elway, Den	551	348	63.2	4030	7.31	25	4.5	10	1.8	63	92.8
Montana, KC	298	181	60.7	2144	7.19	13	4.4	7	2.3	t50	87.4
Testaverde, Cle	230	130	56.5	1797	7.81	14	6.1	9	3.9	t62	85.7
Esiason, NYJ	473	288	60.9	3421	7.23	16	3.4	11	2.3	77	84.5
Mitchell, Mia	233	133	57.1	1773	7.61	12	5.2	8	3.4	t77	84.2
Hostetler, Rai	419	236	56.3	3242	7.74	14	3.3	10	2.4	t74	82.5
Kelly, Buf	470	288	61.3	3382	7.20	18	3.8	18	3.8	t65	79.9
O'Donnell, Pitt	486	270	55.6	3208	6.60	14	2.9	7	1.4	t71	79.5
George, Ind	407	234	57.5	2526	6.21	8	2.0	6	1.5	t72	76.3
DeBerg, TB-Mia	227	136	59.9	1707	7.52	7	3.1	10	4.4	47	75.3

Pass Receiving

RECEPTIONS	No.	Yds	Avg	Lg	TD	YARDS	Yds	No.	Avg	Lg	TD
Langhorne, Ind	85	1038	12.2	t72	3	Brown, Rai	1180	80	14.8	t71	7
A. Miller, SD	84	1162	13.8	t66	7	A. Miller, SD	1162	84	13.8	t66	7
Sharpe, Den	81	995	12.3	63	9	Langhorne, Ind	1038	85	12.2	t72	3
Brown, Rai	80	1180	14.8	t71	7	Fryar, Mia	1010	64	15.8	t65	5
Blades, Sea	80	945	11.8	41	3	Sharpe, Den	995	81	12.3	63	9
Slaughter, Hou	77	904	11.7	41	5	Blades, Sea	945	80	11.8	41	3
Kirby, Mia	75	874	11.7	47	3	Green, Pitt	942	63	15.0	t71	5
Harmon, SD	73	671	9.2	37	2	Davis, KC	909	52	17.5	t66	7
Givins, Hou	68	887	13.0	t80	4	Slaughter, Hou	904	77	11.7	41	5
Metzelaars, Buf	68	609	9.0	51	4	Givins, Hou	887	68	13.0	t80	4

Rushing

	Att	Yds	Avg	Lg	TD
Thomas, Buff	355	1315	3.7	27	6
Russell, NE	300	1088	3.6	21	7
C. Warren, Sea	273	1072	3.9	t45	7
G. Brown, Hou	195	1002	5.1	26	6
J. Johnson, NYJ	198	821	4.1	t57	3
Bernstine, Den	223	816	3.7	24	4
Allen, KC	206	764	3.7	39	12
Thompson, Pitt	205	763	3.7	36	3
Butts, SD	185	746	4.0	27	4
Foster, Pitt	177	711	4.0	38	8
Potts, Ind	179	711	4.0	34	0

Total Yards from Scrimmage

	Total	Rush	Rec
Thomas, Buff	1702	1315	387
J. Johnson, NYJ	1462	821	641
Russell, NE	1333	1088	245
Kirby, Mia	1264	390	874
G. Brown, Hou	1242	1002	240
Bernstine, Den	1188	816	372
Brown, Rai	1187	7	1180
C. Warren, Sea	1171	1072	99
A. Miller, SD	1162	0	1162
Metcalf, Clev	1150	611	539

Interceptions

	No.	Yds	Lg	TD
E. Robinson, Sea	9	80	28	0
Odomes, Buff	9	65	25	0
Woodson, Pitt	8	138	t63	1
Robertson, Hou	7	137	69	0
Carrington, SD	7	104	28	0
B. Washington, NYJ	6	128	t62	1
Dishman, Hou	6	74	30	0
A. Lewis, KC	6	61	24	0

Sacks

Smith, KC	15.0
Fletcher, Den	13.5
B. Smith, Buff	13.5
S. Jones, Hou	13.0
Greene, Pitt	12.5
A. Smith, Rai	12.5
O'Neal, SD	12.0
Pleasant, Cle	11.0
Cross, Mia	10.5
Fuller, Hou	10.0

American Football Conference (*Cont.*)

Punting

	No.	Yds	Avg	Net Avg	TB	In 20	Lg	Blk	Ret	Ret Yds
Gr. Montgomery, Hou	54	2462	45.6	39.1	5	13	77	0	28	249
Rouen, Den	67	3017	45.0	37.1	8	17	62	1	33	337
Tuten, Sea	90	4007	44.5	37.3	7	21	64	1	47	475
Hansen, Clev	82	3632	44.3	35.6	10	15	72	2	48	438
L. Johnson, Cin	90	3954	43.9	36.6	12	24	60	0	47	416

Punt Returns

	No.	Yds	Avg	Lg	TD
Metcalf, Clev	36	464	12.9	t91	2
Gordon, SD	31	395	12.7	54	0
Brown, Rai	40	465	11.6	t74	1
McDuffie, Mia	28	317	11.3	t72	2
Milburn, Den	40	425	10.6	54	0

Kickoff Returns

	No.	Yds	Avg	Lg	TD
Ismail, Rai	25	605	24.2	66	0
McDuffie, Mia	32	755	23.6	48	0
Ball, Cin	23	501	21.8	45	0
Verdin, Ind	50	1050	21.0	38	0
Lewis, SD	33	684	20.7	60	0

National Football Conference

Scoring

TOUCHDOWNS	TD	Rush	Rec	Ret	Pts
Rice, SF	16	1	15	0	96
Rison, Atl	15	0	15	0	90
Sharpe, GB	11	0	11	0	66
Watters, SF	11	10	1	0	66
E. Bennett, GB	10	9	1	0	60
E. Smith, Dall	10	9	1	0	60
Williams, Phil	10	0	10	0	60
C. Carter, Minn	9	0	9	0	54
Moore, Phoe	9	9	0	0	54

Five tied with seven touchdowns.

KICKING	PAT	FG	Lg	Pts
Hanson, Det	28/28	34/43	53	130
Jacke, GB	35/35	31/37	54	128
Murray, Dall	38/38	28/33	52	122
Andersen, NO	33/33	28/35	56	117
Johnson, Atl	34/34	26/27	54	112
Cofer, SF	59/61	16/26	46	107
Reveiz, Minn	27/28	26/35	51	105
Treadwell, NYG	28/29	25/31	46	103
Butler, Chi	21/22	27/36	55	102
G. Davis, Phoe	37/37	21/28	55	100

Passing

	Att	Comp	Pct Comp	Yds	Avg Gain	TD	Pct TD	Int	Pct Int	Lg	Rating Pts
Young, SF	462	314	68.0	4023	8.71	29	6.3	16	3.5	t80	101.5
Aikman, Dall	392	271	69.1	3100	7.91	15	3.8	6	1.5	t80	99.0
Simms, NYG	400	247	61.8	3038	7.60	15	3.8	9	2.3	62	88.3
Brister, Phil	309	181	58.6	1905	6.17	14	4.5	5	1.6	58	84.9
Hebert, Atl	430	263	61.2	2978	6.93	24	5.6	17	4.0	t98	84.0
Beuerlein, Phoe	418	258	61.7	3164	7.57	18	4.3	17	4.1	t65	82.5
McMahon, Minn	331	200	60.4	1967	5.94	9	2.7	8	2.4	58	76.2
Favre, GB	522	318	60.9	3303	6.33	19	3.6	24	4.6	t66	72.2
Harbaugh, Chi	325	200	61.5	2002	6.16	7	2.2	11	3.4	48	72.1
Wilson, NO	388	221	57.0	2457	6.33	12	3.1	15	3.9	t42	70.1

Pass Receiving

RECEPTIONS	No.	Yds	Avg	Lg	TD
Sharpe, GB	112	1274	11.4	54	11
Rice, SF	98	1503	15.3	t80	15
Irvin, Dall	88	1330	15.1	t61	7
Rison, Atl	86	1242	14.4	t53	15
C. Carter, Minn	86	1071	12.5	58	9
Walker, Phil	75	610	8.1	55	3
Pritchard, Atl	74	736	9.9	34	7
Haynes, Atl	72	778	10.8	t98	4
Jones, SF	68	735	10.8	29	3

Two tied with 66 receptions.

YARDS	Yds	No.	Avg	Lg	TD
Rice, SF	1503	98	15.3	t80	15
Irvin, Dall	1330	88	15.1	t61	7
Sharpe, GB	1274	112	11.4	54	11
Rison, Atl	1242	86	14.4	t53	15
C. Carter. Minn	1071	86	12.5	58	9
E. Martin, NO	950	66	14.4	t54	3
Ellard, Rams	945	61	15.5	54	2
J. Taylor, SF	940	56	16.8	t76	5
H. Moore, Det	935	61	15.3	t93	6
Hawkins, TB	933	62	15.0	67	5

National Football Conference (Cont.)

Rushing

	Att	Yds	Avg	Lg	TD
E. Smith, Dall	283	1486	5.3	t62	9
Bettis, LA Rams	294	1429	4.9	t85	7
Pegram, Atl	292	1185	4.1	29	3
Sanders, Det	243	1115	4.6	42	3
Hampton, NYG	292	1077	3.7	20	5
Brooks, Wash	223	1063	4.8	t85	3
Moore, Phoe	263	1018	3.9	20	9
Watters, SF	208	950	4.6	39	10
Walker, Phil	174	746	4.3	35	1
Brown, NO	180	705	3.9	60	2

Total Yards from Scrimmage

	Total	Rush	Rec
E. Smith, Dall	1900	1486	414
Bettis, LA Rams	1673	1429	244
Rice, SF	1572	69	1503
Pegram, Atl	1487	1185	302
Walker, Phil	1356	746	610
Irvin, Dall	1336	6	1330
Sanders, Det	1320	1115	205
Hampton, NYG	1287	1077	210
Sharpe, GB	1282	8	1274
Watters, SF	1276	950	326

Interceptions

	No.	Yds	Lg	TD
Sanders, Atl	7	91	41	0
Allen, Phil	6	201	t94	4
Butler, GB	6	131	39	0
K. Smith, Dall	6	56	t32	1
Carter, Wash	6	54	29	0

Sacks

Trunbull, NO	13.0
White, GB	13.0
Dent, Chi	12.5
Doleman, Minn	12.5
Randle, Minn	12.5
Four tied with 11.5 sacks	

Punting

	No.	Yds	Avg	Net Avg	TB	In 20	Lg	Blk	Ret	Ret Yds
Arnold, Det	72	3207	44.5	36.8	9	15	68	0	45	377
Roby, Wash	78	3447	44.2	37.2	10	25	60	0	31	343
Camarillo, Phoe	73	3189	43.7	37.8	8	23	61	0	30	267
Barnhardt, NO	77	3356	43.6	37.5	6	26	58	0	36	348
Alexander, Atl	72	3114	43.3	37.6	3	21	75	0	41	350

Punt Returns

	No.	Yds	Avg	Lg	TD
Hughes, NO	37	503	13.6	t83	2
Carter, SF	34	411	12.1	t72	1
K. Williams, Dall	36	381	10.6	t64	2
Meggett, NYG	32	331	10.3	t75	1
Gray, Det	23	197	8.6	35	0

Kickoff Returns

	No.	Yds	Avg	Lg	TD
Brooks, GB	23	611	26.6	t95	1
Hughes, NO	30	753	25.1	t99	1
T. Smith, Atl	38	948	24.9	t97	1
Gray, Det	28	688	24.6	t95	1
Bailey, Phoe	31	699	22.5	48	0

Get the Picture

When you've played on the losing team in four straight Super Bowls, as Buffalo Bill quarterback Jim Kelly has, revenge is never far from your mind. Last spring, Kelly was one of the celebrity guests at a charity auction of sports memorabilia in Charleston, S.C., when an autographed photo of the once dynamic Dallas Cowboy duo of owner Jerry Jones and coach Jimmy Johnson went on the block. Kelly whose Bills have lost to the Cowboys the last two Super Bowls, knew what he had to do.

"I couldn't let a Dallas fan have it," said Kelly, who claimed the picture for $500. He promptly tore it into pieces.

"It was worth every penny, " said Kelly.

AFC Total Offense

	Total Yds	Yds Rush	Yds Pass	Time of Poss	Avg Pts/Game
Miami	5812	1459	4353	28:59	21.8
Houston	5658	1792	3866	31:48	23.0
Denver	5461	1693	3768	31:23	23.3
Buffalo	5260	1943	3317	27:30	20.6
Pittsburgh	5235	2003	3232	32:15	19.3
NY Jets	5212	1880	3332	32:16	16.9
New England	5065	1780	3285	29:43	14.9
LA Raiders	5014	1425	3589	30:33	19.1
San Diego	4967	1824	3143	29:52	20.1
Kansas City	4835	1655	3180	29:29	20.5
Cleveland	4740	1701	3039	29:32	19.0
Indianapolis	4705	1288	3417	27:55	11.8
Seattle	4669	2015	2654	29:02	17.5
Cincinnati	4052	1511	2541	28:58	11.7

AFC Total Defense

	Opp Total Yds	Opp Yds Rush	Opp Yds Pass	Avg PA/Game
Pittsburgh	4531	1368	3163	17.7
NY Jets	4712	1473	3239	15.4
LA Raiders	4723	1865	2858	20.4
Kansas City	4771	1620	3151	18.2
Cleveland	4778	1654	3124	19.2
New England	4796	1951	2845	17.9
Houston	4874	1273	3601	14.9
Cincinnati	5018	2220	2798	19.9
San Diego	5066	1314	3752	18.1
Denver	5149	1418	3731	17.8
Miami	5150	1665	3485	21.9
Seattle	5313	1660	3653	19.6
Buffalo	5554	1921	3633	15.1
Indianapolis	5638	2521	3117	23.6

NFC Total Offense

	Total Yds	Yds Rush	Yds Pass	Time of Poss	Avg Pts/Game
San Francisco	6435	2133	4302	30:24	29.6
Dallas	5615	2161	3454	30:56	23.5
Phoenix	5213	1809	3404	31:54	20.4
NY Giants	5145	2210	2935	32:18	18.0
Atlanta	5110	1590	3520	31:23	19.8
Philadelphia	4922	1761	3161	31:00	18.3
Minnesota	4822	1623	3199	30:27	17.3
LA Rams	4804	2014	2790	28:18	13.8
Green Bay	4750	1619	3131	30:53	21.3
New Orleans	4707	1766	2941	28:31	19.8
Detroit	4658	1944	2714	29:27	18.6
Tampa Bay	4311	1290	3021	28:38	14.8
Washington	4271	1726	2545	27:58	14.4
Chicago	3717	1677	2040	28:36	14.8

NFC Total Defense

	Opp Total Yds	Opp Yds Rush	Opp Yds Pass	Avg PA/Game
Minnesota	4404	1534	2870	18.1
Green Bay	4482	1582	2900	17.6
Chicago	4653	1835	2818	14.4
NY Giants	4663	1547	3116	12.8
Detroit	4669	1649	3020	18.3
New Orleans	4696	2090	2606	21.4
Dallas	4767	1651	3116	14.3
San Francisco	4997	1800	3197	18.6
Philadelphia	5019	2080	2939	19.7
Phoenix	5167	1861	3306	16.8
Tampa Bay	5246	1994	3252	23.5
LA Rams	5411	1851	3560	22.9
Atlanta	5421	1784	3637	24.1
Washington	5497	2111	3386	21.6

Takeaways/Giveaways

AFC

	Takeaways Int	Fum	Total	Giveaways Int	Fum	Total	Net Diff
San Diego	22	12	34	14	5	19	15
Buffalo	23	24	47	18	17	35	15
Pittsburgh	24	14	38	12	15	27	11
Kansas City	21	17	38	10	18	28	10
NY Jets	19	18	37	12	16	28	9
Seattle	22	15	37	18	13	31	6
Cincinnati	12	14	26	11	9	20	6
Denver	18	13	31	10	18	28	3
LA Raiders	14	9	23	14	11	25	-2
Houston	26	17	43	25	20	45	-2
Miami	13	14	27	18	16	34	-7
New England	13	9	22	24	10	34	-12
Indianapolis	10	11	21	15	20	35	-14
Cleveland	13	9	22	19	17	36	-14

NFC

	Takeaways Int	Fum	Total	Giveaways Int	Fum	Total	Net Diff
NY Giants	18	10	28	9	8	17	11
Minnesota	24	10	34	14	10	24	10
Dallas	14	14	28	6	16	22	6
Detroit	19	16	35	19	13	32	3
Philadelphia	20	15	35	13	21	34	1
San Francisco	19	11	30	17	13	30	0
Washington	17	14	31	21	10	31	0
Chicago	18	12	30	16	14	30	0
Green Bay	18	15	33	24	10	34	-1
New Orleans	10	20	30	21	13	34	-4
Phoenix	9	17	26	20	11	31	-5
LA Rams	11	9	20	19	11	30	-10
Tampa Bay	9	13	22	25	11	36	-14
Atlanta	13	11	24	25	17	42	-18

THEY SAID IT

Lawrence Taylor, former New York Giant linebacker, on the demands of retirement:
"The only thing I'm worried about is getting the left hand steady, then hitting it straight."

Conference Rankings

American Football Conference

	Offense			Defense		
	Total	Rush	Pass	Total	Rush	Pass
Buffalo	4	3	7	13	11	11
Cincinnati	14	11	14	8	13	1
Cleveland	11	8	12	5	7	5
Denver	3	9	3	10	4	13
Houston	2	6	2	7	1	10
Indianapolis	12	14	5	14	14	4
Kansas City	10	10	10	4	6	6
LA Raiders	8	13	4	3	10	3
Miami	1	12	1	11	9	9
New England	7	7	8	6	12	2
NY Jets	6	4	6	2	5	8
Pittsburgh	5	2	9	1	3	7
San Diego	9	5	11	9	2	14
Seattle	13	1	13	12	8	12

National Football Conference

	Offense			Defense		
	Total	Rush	Pass	Total	Rush	Pass
Atlanta	5	13	2	13	6	14
Chicago	14	10	14	3	8	2
Dallas	2	2	3	7	5	7T
Detroit	11	5	12	5	4	6
Green Bay	9	12	7	2	3	4
LA Rams	8	4	11	12	9	13
Minnesota	7	11	5	1	1	3
New Orleans	10	7	9	6	13	1
NY Giants	4	1	10	4	2	7T
Philadelphia	6	8	6	9	12	5
Phoenix	3	6	4	10	10	11
San Francisco	1	3	1	8	7	9
Tampa Bay	12	14	8	11	11	10
Washington	13	9	13	14	14	12

1993 AFC Team-by-Team Statistical Leaders

Buffalo Bills

SCORING	TD Rush	Rec	Ret	PAT	FG	S	Pts
Christie	0	0	0	36/37	23/32	0	105
K. Davis	6	0	0	0/0	0/0	0	36
Reed	0	6	0	0/0	0/0	0	36
Thomas	6	0	0	0/0	0/0	0	36
Metzelaars	0	4	0	0/0	0/0	0	24

RUSHING	No.	Yds	Avg	Lg	TD
Thomas	355	1315	3.7	27	6
K. Davis	109	391	3.6	19	6
Kelly	36	102	2.8	17	0
Gardner	20	56	2.8	8	0
Turner	11	36	3.3	10	0

PASSING	Att	Comp	Pct Comp	Yds	Avg Gain	TD	Int	Rating Pts
Kelly	470	288	61.3	3382	7.20	18	18	79.9
Reich	26	16	61.5	153	5.88	2	0	103.5

RECEIVING	No.	Yds	Avg	Lg	TD
Metzelaars	68	609	9.0	51	4
Brooks	60	714	11.9	32	5
Reed	52	854	16.4	t65	6
Thomas	48	387	8.1	37	0
Beebe	31	504	16.3	t65	3

INTERCEPTIONS: Odomes, 9

PUNTING	No.	Yds	Avg	Net Avg	TB	In 20	Lg	Blk
Mohr	74	2991	40.4	36.0	4	19	58	0

SACKS: Smith, 13.5

Cincinnati Bengals

SCORING	TD Rush	Rec	Ret	PAT	FG	S	Pts
Pelfrey	0	0	0	13/16	24/31	0	85
Pickens	0	6	0	0/0	0/0	0	36
Query	0	4	0	0/0	0/0	0	24
Six tied with 6 pts							

RUSHING	No.	Yds	Avg	Lg	TD
Green	215	589	2.7	25	0
Fenner	121	482	4.0	26	1
Klingler	41	282	6.9	29	0
Miles	22	56	2.5	15	1
Schroeder	10	41	4.1	20	0

PASSING	Att	Comp	Pct Comp	Yds	Avg Gain	TD	Int	Rating Pts
Klingler	343	190	55.4	1935	5.64	6	9	66.6
Schroeder	159	78	49.1	832	5.23	5	2	70.0

RECEIVING	No.	Yds	Avg	Lg	TD
Query	56	654	11.7	51	4
Fenner	48	427	8.9	40	0
McGee	44	525	11.9	37	0
Pickens	43	565	13.1	36	6
Green	22	115	5.2	16	0

INTERCEPTIONS: Brim, 3

PUNTING	No.	Yds	Avg	Net Avg	TB	In 20	Lg	Blk
L. Johnson	90	3954	43.9	36.6	12	24	60	0

SACKS: Stubbs, 5.0

Hit Me With Your Best Shot, Honey	To prove she is tougher than the Houston Oilers and their brawling defensive coordinator Buddy Ryan, Chief fan Chris Russert last January challenged anyone at her engagement party to trade punches. Lee Walters took the dare and knocked her backward with a punch to the right cheek. She collected herself and then broke his nose with a straight right. Lee Walters is her fiancé.

Cleveland Browns

SCORING	Rush	Rec	Ret	PAT	FG	S	Pts
			TD				
Stover	0	0	0	36/36	16/22	0	84
Jackson	0	8	0	0/0	0/0	0	48
Carrier	1	3	1	0/0	0/0	0	30
Metcalf	1	2	2	0/0	0/0	0	30

RUSHING	No.	Yds	Avg	Lg	TD
Vardell	171	644	3.8	54	3
Metcalf	129	611	4.7	55	1
Hoard	56	227	4.1	30	0
Testaverde	18	74	4.1	14	0
Baldwin	18	61	3.4	11	0

PASSING	Att	Comp	Pct Comp	Yds	Avg Gain	TD	Int	Rating Pts
Testaverde	230	130	56.5	1797	7.81	14	9	85.7
Kosar	138	79	57.2	807	5.85	5	3	77.2
Philcox	108	52	48.1	699	6.47	4	7	54.5

RECEIVING	No.	Yds	Avg	Lg	TD
Metcalf	63	539	8.6	t49	2
Carrier	43	746	17.3	55	3
Jackson	41	756	18.4	t62	8
Hoard	35	351	10.0	41	0
Kinchen	29	347	12.0	40	2

INTERCEPTIONS: Turner, 5

PUNTING	No.	Yds	Avg	Net Avg	TB	In 20	Lg	Blk
Hansen	82	3632	44.3	35.6	10	15	72	2

SACKS: Pleasant, 11

Denver Broncos

SCORING	Rush	Rec	Ret	PAT	FG	S	Pts
			TD				
Elam	0	0	0	41/42	26/35	0	119
Sharpe	0	9	0	0/0	0/0	0	54
Delpino	8	0	0	0/0	0/0	0	48
V. Johnson	0	5	0	0/0	0/0	0	30

Two tied with 24.

RUSHING	No.	Yds	Avg	Lg	TD
Bernstine	223	816	3.7	24	4
Delpino	131	445	3.4	18	8
Milburn	52	231	4.4	26	0
Elway	44	153	3.5	18	0
Rivers	15	50	3.3	14	1

PASSING	Att	Comp	Pct Comp	Yds	Avg Gain	TD	Int	Rating Pts
Elway	551	348	63.2	4030	7.31	25	10	92.8

RECEIVING	No.	Yds	Avg	Lg	TD
Sharpe	81	995	12.3	63	9
Russell	44	719	16.3	43	3
Bernstine	44	372	8.5	41	0
Milburn	38	300	7.9	50	3
V. Johnson	36	517	14.4	56	5

INTERCEPTIONS: Smith and Braxton, 3

PUNTING	No.	Yds	Avg	Net Avg	TB	In 20	Lg	Blk
Rouen	67	3017	45.0	37.1	8	17	62	1

SACKS: Fletcher, 13.5

Houston Oilers

SCORING	Rush	Rec	Ret	PAT	FG	S	Pts
			TD				
Del Greco	0	0	0	39/40	29/34	0	126
G Brown	6	2	0	0/0	0/0	0	48
Jeffires	0	6	0	0/0	0/0	0	36
Slaughter	0	5	0	0/0	0/0	0	30
Givins	0	4	0	0/0	0/0	0	24

RUSHING	No.	Yds	Avg	Lg	TD
G. Brown	195	1002	5.1	26	6
White	131	465	3.5	14	2
Moon	48	145	3.0	35	1
Tillman	9	94	10.4	34	0

PASSING	Att	Comp	Pct Comp	Yds	Avg Gain	TD	Int	Rating Pts
Moon	520	303	58.3	3485	6.70	21	21	75.2
Carlson	90	51	56.7	605	6.72	2	4	66.2

RECEIVING	No.	Yds	Avg	Lg	TD
Slaughter	77	904	11.7	41	5
Gvins	68	887	13.0	t80	4
Jeffires	66	753	11.4	t66	6
Duncan	41	456	11.1	47	3
White	34	229	6.7	20	0

INTERCEPTIONS: Robertson, 7

PUNTING	No.	Yds	Avg	Net Avg	TB	In 20	Lg	Blk
Gr. Montgomery	54	2462	45.6	39.1	5	13	77	0

SACKS: S. Jones, 13

Indianapolis Colts

SCORING	Rush	Rec	Ret	PAT	FG	S	Pts
			TD				
Biasucci	0	0	0	15/16	26/31	0	93
Culver	3	1	1	0/0	0/0	0	30
Cash	0	3	0	0/0	0/0	0	18
Langhorne	0	3	0	0/0	0/0	0	18

Five tied with 6.

RUSHING	No.	Yds	Avg	Lg	TD
Potts	179	711	4.0	34	0
Johnson	95	331	3.5	14	1
Culver	65	150	2.3	9	3
George	13	39	3.0	14	0

PASSING	Att	Comp	Pct Comp	Yds	Avg Gain	TD	Int	Rating Pts
George	407	234	57.5	2526	6.21	8	6	76.3
Trudeau	162	85	52.5	992	6.12	2	7	57.4
Majkowski	24	13	54.2	105	4.38	0	1	48.1

RECEIVING	No.	Yds	Avg	Lg	TD
Langhorne	85	1038	12.2	t72	3
Hester	64	835	13.0	58	1
Johnson	55	443	8.1	36	0
Cash	43	402	9.3	37	3
Dawkins	26	430	16.5	68	1

INTERCEPTIONS: Buchanan, 4

PUNTING	No.	Yds	Avg	Net Avg	TB	In 20	Lg	Blk
Stark	83	3595	43.3	35.9	13	18	65	0

SACKS: Hand, 5

Kansas City Chiefs

SCORING	Rush	TD Rec	Ret	PAT	FG	S	Pts
Lowery	0	0	0	37/37	23/29	0	106
Allen	12	3	0	0/0	0/0	0	90
Davis	0	7	0	0/0	0/0	0	42
Cash	0	4	0	0/0	0/0	0	24

RUSHING	No.	Yds	Avg	Lg	TD
Allen	206	764	3.7	39	12
Anders	75	291	3.9	18	0
McNair	51	278	5.5	47	2
H. Williams	42	149	3.5	19	0

PASSING	Att	Comp	Pct Comp	Yds	Avg Gain	TD	Int	Rating Pts
Montana	298	181	60.7	2144	7.19	13	7	87.4
Krieg	189	105	55.6	1238	6.55	7	3	81.4

RECEIVING	No.	Yds	Avg	Lg	TD
Davis	52	909	17.5	t66	7
Birden	51	721	14.1	t50	2
Anders	40	326	8.2	27	1
Allen	34	238	7.0	t18	3
Hayes	24	331	13.8	49	1
Cash	24	242	10.1	24	4

INTERCEPTIONS: A. Lewis, 6

PUNTING	No.	Yds	Avg	Net Avg	TB	In 20	Lg	Blk
Barker	76	3240	42.6	35.4	8	19	59	1

SACKS: Smith, 15

Miami Dolphins

SCORING	Rush	TD Rec	Ret	PAT	FG	S	Pts
Stoyanovich	0	0	0	37/37	24/32	0	109
Ingram	0	6	0	0/0	0/0	0	36
K. Jackson	0	6	0	0/0	0/0	0	36
Kirby	3	3	0	0/0	0/0	0	36
Byars	3	3	0	0/0	0/0	0	36

RUSHING	No.	Yds	Avg	Lg	TD
Higgs	186	693	3.7	31	3
Kirby	119	390	3.3	20	3
Byars	64	269	4.2	t77	3
Mitchell	21	89	4.2	32	0

PASSING	Att	Comp	Pct Comp	Yds	Avg Gain	TD	Int	Rating Pts
Mitchell	233	133	57.1	1773	7.61	12	8	84.2
DeBerg	188	113	60.1	1521	8.09	6	7	81.0
Marino	150	91	60.7	1218	8.12	8	3	95.9

RECEIVING	No.	Yds	Avg	Lg	TD
Kirby	75	874	11.7	47	3
Fryar	64	1010	15.8	t65	5
Byars	61	613	10.0	27	3
Ingram	44	707	16.1	t77	6
K. Jackson	39	613	15.7	t57	6
Martin	20	347	17.4	t80	3

INTERCEPTIONS: Brown, 5

PUNTING	No.	Yds	Avg	Net Avg	TB	In 20	Lg	Blk
Hatcher	58	2304	39.7	32.2	4	13	56	0

SACKS: Cross, 10.5

Los Angeles Raiders

SCORING	Rush	TD Rec	Ret	PAT	FG	S	Pts
Jaeger	0	0	0	27/29	35/44	0	132
Brown	0	7	1	0/0	0/0	0	42
Hostetler	5	0	0	0/0	0/0	0	30
A. Wright	0	4	0	0/0	0/0	0	24
McCallum	3	0	0	0/0	0/0	0	18
Jett	0	3	0	0/0	0/0	0	18

RUSHING	No.	Yds	Avg	Lg	TD
Robinson	156	591	3.8	16	1
Hostetler	55	202	3.7	19	5
Bell	67	180	2.7	12	1
S. Smith	47	156	3.3	13	0
McCallum	37	114	3.1	14	3

PASSING	Att	Comp	Pct Comp	Yds	Avg Gain	TD	Int	Rating Pts
Hostetler	419	236	56.3	3242	7.74	14	10	82.5
Evans	76	45	59.2	640	8.42	3	4	77.7

RECEIVING	No.	Yds	Avg	Lg	TD
Brown	80	1180	14.8	t71	7
Horton	43	467	10.9	32	1
Jett	33	771	23.4	t74	3
A. Wright	27	462	17.1	t68	4
Ismail	26	353	13.6	t43	1

INTERCEPTIONS: McDaniel, 5

PUNTING	No.	Yds	Avg	Net Avg	TB	In 20	Lg	Blk
Gossett	71	2971	41.8	35.1	9	19	61	0

SACKS: A. Smith, 12.5

New England Patriots

SCORING	Rush	TD Rec	Ret	PAT	FG	S	Pts
Bahr	0	0	0	28/29	13/18	0	67
Sisson	0	0	0	15/15	14/26	0	57
Coates	0	8	0	0/0	0/0	0	48
Russell	7	0	0	0/0	0/0	0	42

RUSHING	No.	Yds	Avg	Lg	TD
Russell	300	1088	3.6	21	7
Turner	50	231	4.6	49	0
Croom	60	198	3.3	22	1
Gash	48	149	3.1	14	1
Bledsoe	32	82	2.6	15	0

PASSING	Att	Comp	Pct Comp	Yds	Avg Gain	TD	Int	Rating Pts
Bledsoe	429	214	49.9	2494	5.81	15	15	65.0
Secules	134	75	56.0	918	6.85	2	9	54.3

RECEIVING	No.	Yds	Avg	Lg	TD
Coates	53	659	12.4	t54	8
Brisby	45	626	13.9	39	2
Timpson	42	654	15.6	48	2
Turner	39	333	8.5	26	2
Russell	26	245	9.4	69	0

INTERCEPTIONS: Hurst, 4

PUNTING	No.	Yds	Avg	Net Avg	TB	In 20	Lg	Blk
Saxon	73	3096	42.4	34.8	7	25	59	3

SACKS: Slade, 9

New York Jets

SCORING	Rush	Rec	TD Ret	PAT	FG	S	Pts
Blanchard	0	0	0	31/31	17/26	0	82
B. Baxter	7	0	0	0/0	0/0	0	42
Mitchell	0	6	0	0/0	0/0	0	36
J. Johnson	3	1	0	0/0	0/0	0	24
Burkett	0	4	0	0/0	0/0	0	24

RUSHING	No.	Yds	Avg	Lg	TD
J. Johnson	198	821	4.1	t57	3
B. Baxter	174	559	3.2	16	7
B. Thomas	59	221	3.7	24	1
Murrell	34	157	4.6	t37	1
Esiason	45	118	2.6	17	1

PASSING	Att	Comp	Pct Comp	Yds	Avg Gain	TD	Int	Rating Pts
Esiason	473	288	60.9	3421	7.23	16	11	84.5
Nagle	14	6	42.9	71	5.07	0	0	58.9

RECEIVING	No.	Yds	Avg	Lg	TD
J. Johnson	67	641	9.6	48	1
Moore	64	843	13.2	51	1
Burkett	40	531	13.3	77	4
Mitchell	39	630	16.2	t65	6
Mathis	24	352	14.7	46	0

INTERCEPTIONS: B. Washington, 6

PUNTING	No.	Yds	Avg	Net Avg	TB	In 20	Lg	Blk
Aguiar	73	2806	38.4	34.4	7	21	71	0

SACKS: Lageman, 8.5

San Diego Chargers

SCORING	Rush	Rec	TD Ret	PAT	FG	S	Pts
Carney	0	0	0	31/33	31/40	0	124
Means	8	0	0	0/0	0/0	0	48
A. Miller	0	7	0	0/0	0/0	0	42
Lewis	0	4	0	0/0	0/0	0	24
Butts	4	0	0	0/0	0/0	0	24

RUSHING	No.	Yds	Avg	Lg	TD
Butts	185	746	4.0	27	4
Means	160	645	4.0	t65	8
Harmon	46	216	4.7	19	0
Bieniemy	33	135	4.1	12	1
Jefferson	5	53	10.6	33	0

PASSING	Att	Comp	Pct Comp	Yds	Avg Gain	TD	Int	Rating Pts
Humphries	324	173	53.4	1981	6.11	12	10	71.5
Friesz	238	128	53.8	1402	5.89	6	4	72.8

RECEIVING	No.	Yds	Avg	Lg	TD
A. Miller	84	1162	13.8	t66	7
Harmon	73	671	9.2	37	2
Lewis	38	463	12.2	47	4
Jefferson	30	391	13.0	t39	2
Walker	21	212	10.1	t25	1

INTERCEPTIONS: Carrington, 7

PUNTING	No.	Yds	Avg	Net Avg	TB	In 20	Lg	Blk
Carney	4	155	38.8	34.8	0	1	46	0
Kidd	57	2431	42.6	35.9	7	16	67	0
Sullivan	13	541	41.6	39.1	0	3	50	0

SACKS: O'Neal, 12

Pittsburgh Steelers

SCORING	Rush	Rec	TD Ret	PAT	FG	S	Pts
Anderson	0	0	0	32/32	28/30	0	116
Foster	8	1	0	0/0	0/0	0	54
Green	0	5	0	0/0	0/0	0	30
Hoge	1	4	0	0/0	0/0	0	30

Three tied with 18.

RUSHING	No.	Yds	Avg	Lg	TD
Thompson	205	763	3.7	36	3
Foster	177	711	4.0	38	8
Hoge	51	249	4.9	30	1
Stone	12	121	10.1	t38	1
O'Donnell	26	111	4.3	27	0

PASSING	Att	Comp	Pct Comp	Yds	Avg Gain	TD	Int	Rating Pts
O'Donnell	486	270	55.6	3208	6.60	14	7	79.5
Tomczak	54	29	53.7	398	7.37	2	5	51.3

RECEIVING	No.	Yds	Avg	Lg	TD
Green	63	942	15.0	t71	5
Stone	41	587	14.3	44	2
Graham	38	579	15.2	51	0
Thompson	38	259	6.8	28	0
Hoge	33	247	7.5	18	4

INTERCEPTIONS: Woodson, 8

PUNTING	No.	Yds	Avg	Net Avg	TB	In 20	Lg	Blk
Royals	89	3781	42.5	34.2	3	28	61	0

SACKS: Greene, 12.5

Seattle Seahawks

SCORING	Rush	Rec	TD Ret	PAT	FG	S	Pts
Kasay	0	0	0	29/29	23/28	0	98
C. Warren	7	0	0	0/0	0/0	0	42
Martin	0	5	0	0/0	0/0	0	30
Williams	3	1	0	0/0	0/0	0	24

RUSHING	No.	Yds	Avg	Lg	TD
C. Warren	273	1072	3.9	t45	7
Williams	82	371	4.5	38	3
Mirer	68	343	5.0	33	3
Vaughn	36	153	4.3	37	0

PASSING	Att	Comp	Pct Comp	Yds	Avg Gain	TD	Int	Rating Pts
Mirer	486	274	56.4	2833	5.83	12	17	67.0

RECEIVING	No.	Yds	Avg	Lg	TD
Blades	80	945	11.8	41	3
Williams	58	450	7.8	25	1
Martin	57	798	14.0	t53	5
Edmunds	24	239	10.0	32	2
Green	23	178	7.7	20	1

INTERCEPTIONS: Robinson, 9

PUNTING	No.	Yds	Avg	Net Avg	TB	In 20	Lg	Blk
Tuten	90	4007	44.5	37.3	7	21	64	1

SACKS: Sinclair, 8

Atlanta Falcons

SCORING

	Rush	Rec	Ret	PAT	FG	S	Pts
Johnson	0	0	0	34/34	26/27	0	112
Rison	0	15	0	0/0	0/0	0	90
Pritchard	0	7	0	0/0	0/0	0	42
Haynes	0	4	0	0/0	0/0	0	24
Pegram	3	0	0	0/0	0/0	0	18

RUSHING

	No.	Yds	Avg	Lg	TD
Pegram	292	1185	4.1	29	3
Broussard	39	206	5.3	26	1
Dickerson	26	91	3.5	10	0
Hebert	24	49	2.0	14	0

PASSING

	Att	Comp	Pct Comp	Yds	Avg Gain	TD	Int	Rating Pts
Hebert	430	263	61.2	2978	6.93	24	17	84.0
Tolliver	76	39	51.3	464	6.11	3	5	56.0
Miller	66	32	48.5	345	5.23	1	3	50.4

RECEIVING

	No.	Yds	Avg	Lg	TD
Rison	86	1242	14.4	t53	15
Pritchard	74	736	9.9	34	7
Haynes	72	778	10.8	t98	4
Hill	34	384	11.3	30	0
Pegram	33	302	9.2	30	0

INTERCEPTIONS: Sanders, 7

PUNTING

	No.	Yds	Avg	Net Avg	TB	In 20	Lg	Blk
Alexander	72	3114	43.3	37.6	3	21	75	0

SACKS: Holt, 6.5

Chicago Bears

SCORING

	Rush	Rec	Ret	PAT	FG	S	Pts
Butler	0	0	0	21/22	27/36	0	102
Anderson	4	0	0	0/0	0/0	0	24
Harbaugh	4	0	0	0/0	0/0	0	24
Obee	0	3	0	0/0	0/0	0	18

Three tied with 12.

RUSHING

	No.	Yds	Avg	Lg	TD
Anderson	202	646	3.2	45	4
Worley	110	437	4.0	28	2
Harbaugh	60	277	4.6	25	4
Heyward	68	206	3.0	11	0
Conway	5	44	8.8	18	0

PASSING

	Att	Comp	Pct Comp	Yds	Avg Gain	TD	Int	Rating Pts
Harbaugh	325	200	61.5	2002	6.16	7	11	72.1
Willis	60	30	50.0	268	4.47	0	5	27.6

RECEIVING

	No.	Yds	Avg	Lg	TD
Waddle	44	552	12.5	38	1
Anderson	31	160	5.2	35	0
Obee	26	351	13.5	48	3
Conway	19	231	12.2	t38	2
Christian	16	160	10.0	36	0

INTERCEPTIONS: Carrier and Jones, 4

PUNTING

	No.	Yds	Avg	Net Avg	TB	In 20	Lg	Blk
Gardocki	80	3080	38.5	36.6	2	28	58	0

SACKS: Dent, 12.5

Dallas Cowboys

SCORING

	Rush	Rec	Ret	PAT	FG	S	Pts
Murray	0	0	0	38/38	28/33	0	122
E. Smith	9	1	0	0/0	0/0	0	60
Irvin	0	7	0	0/0	0/0	0	42
K. Williams	2	2	2	0/0	0/0	0	36
Harper	0	5	0	0/0	0/0	0	30

RUSHING

	No.	Yds	Avg	Lg	TD
E. Smith	283	1486	5.3	t62	9
Lassic	75	269	3.6	15	3
Coleman	34	132	3.9	16	2
Aikman	32	125	3.9	20	0
Johnston	24	74	3.1	11	3

PASSING

	Att	Comp	Pct Comp	Yds	Avg Gain	TD	Int	Rating Pts
Aikman	392	271	69.1	3100	7.91	15	6	99.0
Kosar	63	36	57.1	410	6.51	3	0	92.7
Garrett	19	9	47.4	61	3.21	0	0	54.9

RECEIVING

	No.	Yds	Avg	Lg	TD
Irvin	88	1330	15.1	t61	7
E. Smith	57	414	7.3	86	1
Johnston	50	372	7.4	20	1
Novacek	44	445	10.1	30	1
Harper	36	777	21.6	t80	5

INTERCEPTIONS: K. Smith, 6

PUNTING

	No.	Yds	Avg	Net Avg	TB	In 20	Lg	Blk
Jett	56	2342	41.8	37.7	3	22	59	0

SACKS: Tolbert, 7.5

Detroit Lions

SCORING

	Rush	Rec	Ret	PAT	FG	S	Pts
Hanson	0	0	0	28/28	34/43	0	130
H. Moore	0	6	0	0/0	0/0	0	36
D. Moore	3	1	0	0/0	0/0	0	24
Sanders	3	0	0	0/0	0/0	0	18

Six tied with 12.

RUSHING

	No.	Yds	Avg	Lg	TD
Sanders	243	1115	4.6	42	3
D. Moore	88	405	4.6	48	3
Lynch	53	207	3.9	15	2
Peete	45	165	3.7	28	1
Ware	7	23	3.3	8	0

PASSING

	Att	Comp	Pct Comp	Yds	Avg Gain	TD	Int	Rating Pts
Peete	252	157	62.3	1670	6.63	6	14	66.4
Kramer	138	87	63.0	1002	7.26	8	3	95.1
Ware	45	20	44.4	271	6.02	1	2	53.1

RECEIVING

	No.	Yds	Avg	Lg	TD
H. Moore	61	935	15.3	t93	6
Perriman	49	496	10.1	34	2
Sanders	36	205	5.7	17	0
Green	28	462	16.5	47	2
Holman	25	244	9.8	t28	2

INTERCEPTIONS: Swilling, 3

PUNTING

	No.	Yds	Avg	Net Avg	TB	In 20	Lg	Blk
Arnold	72	3207	44.5	36.8	9	15	68	0

SACKS: Porcher, 8.5

Green Bay Packers

SCORING

| | TD | | | | | | |
	Rush	Rec	Ret	PAT	FG	S	Pts
Jacke	0	0	0	35/35	31/37	0	128
Sharpe	0	11	0	0/0	0/0	0	66
E. Bennett	9	1	0	0/0	0/0	0	60
J. Harris	0	4	0	0/0	0/0	0	24
Thompson	3	0	0	0/0	0/0	0	18
Clayton	0	3	0	0/0	0/0	0	18

RUSHING

	No.	Yds	Avg	Lg	TD
Thompson	169	654	3.9	39	3
E. Bennett	159	550	3.5	19	9
Favre	58	216	3.7	27	1
Stephens	48	173	3.6	22	1
Brooks	3	17	5.7	21	0

PASSING

	Att	Comp	Pct Comp	Yds	Avg Gain	TD	Int	Rating Pts
Favre	522	318	60.9	3303	6.33	19	24	72.2

RECEIVING

	No.	Yds	Avg	Lg	TD
Sharpe	112	1274	11.4	54	11
E. Bennett	59	457	7.7	t39	1
J. Harris	42	604	14.4	t66	4
Clayton	32	331	10.3	32	3

INTERCEPTIONS: Butler, 6

PUNTING

	No.	Yds	Avg	Net Avg	TB	In 20	Lg	Blk
Wagner	74	3174	42.9	36.3	7	19	60	0

SACKS: White, 13

Los Angeles Rams

SCORING

| | TD | | | | | | |
	Rush	Rec	Ret	PAT	FG	S	Pts
Zendejas	0	0	0	23/25	16/23	0	71
Bettis	7	0	0	0/0	0/0	0	42
Anderson	0	4	0	0/0	0/0	0	24
Drayton	0	4	0	0/0	0/0	0	24
Three tied with 12.							

RUSHING

	No.	Yds	Avg	Lg	TD
Bettis	294	1429	4.9	t71	7
Gary	79	293	3.7	15	1
Rubley	29	102	3.5	13	0
Lester	11	74	6.7	26	0
Everett	19	38	2.0	14	0

PASSING

	Att	Comp	Pct Comp	Yds	Avg Gain	TD	Int	Rating Pts
Everett	274	135	49.3	1652	6.03	8	12	59.7
Rubley	189	108	57.1	1338	7.08	8	6	80.1

RECEIVING

	No.	Yds	Avg	Lg	TD
Ellard	61	945	15.5	54	2
Anderson	37	552	14.9	t56	4
Gary	36	289	8.0	t60	1
Drayton	27	319	11.8	27	4
Bettis	26	244	9.4	28	0

INTERCEPTIONS: Bailey, Rolling, Terrell, Lyght, 2

PUNTING

	No.	Yds	Avg	Net Avg	TB	In 20	Lg	Blk
Landeta	42	1825	43.5	32.9	7	7	66	0

SACKS: Gilbert, 10.5

Minnesota Vikings

SCORING

| | TD | | | | | | |
	Rush	Rec	Ret	PAT	FG	S	Pts
Reveiz	0	0	0	27/28	26/35	0	105
C. Carter	0	9	0	0/0	0/0	0	54
A. Carter	0	5	0	0/0	0/0	0	30
Graham	3	0	0	0/0	0/0	0	18
Three tied with 12.							

RUSHING

	No.	Yds	Avg	Lg	TD
Graham	118	487	4.1	31	3
Word	142	458	3.2	14	2
Smith	82	399	4.9	t26	2
Craig	38	119	3.1	11	1
McMahon	33	96	2.9	16	0

PASSING

	Att	Comp	Pct Comp	Yds	Avg Gain	TD	Int	Rating Pts
McMahon	331	200	60.4	1967	5.94	9	8	76.2
Salisbury	195	115	59.0	1413	7.25	9	6	84.0

RECEIVING

	No.	Yds	Avg	Lg	TD
C. Carter	86	1071	12.5	58	9
A. Carter	60	774	12.9	39	5
Jordan	56	542	9.7	53	1
Smith	24	111	4.6	12	0
Ismail	19	212	11.2	37	1
Craig	19	169	8.9	31	1

INTERCEPTIONS: Glenn, 5

PUNTING

	No.	Yds	Avg	Net Avg	TB	In 20	Lg	Blk
Newsome	90	3864	42.9	35.4	6	25	64	0

SACKS: Doleman, 12.5

New Orleans Saints

SCORING

| | TD | | | | | | |
	Rush	Rec	Ret	PAT	FG	S	Pts
Andersen	0	0	0	33/33	28/35	0	117
Early	0	6	0	0/0	0/0	0	36
Five tied with 18.							

RUSHING

	No.	Yds	Avg	Lg	TD
Brown	180	705	3.9	60	2
Wilson	31	230	7.4	44	0
Muster	64	214	3.3	18	3
Neal	21	175	8.3	t74	1
Hilliard	50	165	3.3	16	2

PASSING

	Att	Comp	Pct Comp	Yds	Avg Gain	TD	Int	Rating Pts
Wilson	388	221	57.0	2457	6.33	12	15	70.1
M. Buck	54	32	59.3	443	8.30	4	3	87.6
Walsh	38	20	52.6	271	7.13	2	3	60.3

RECEIVING

	No.	Yds	Avg	Lg	TD
E. Martin	66	950	14.4	t54	3
Early	45	670	14.9	t63	6
Hilliard	40	296	7.4	34	1
Muster	23	195	8.5	31	0
Brown	21	170	8.1	19	1

INTERCEPTIONS: Atkins, 3

PUNTING

	No.	Yds	Avg	Net Avg	TB	In 20	Lg	Blk
Barnhardt	77	3356	43.6	37.5	6	26	58	0

SACKS: Turnbull, 13

New York Giants

SCORING	Rush	Rec	Ret	PAT	FG	S	Pts
Treadwell	0	0	0	28/29	25/31	0	103
Hampton	5	0	0	0/0	0/0	0	30
Cross	0	5	0	0/0	0/0	0	30
M. Jackson	0	4	0	0/0	0/0	0	24

Three tied with 18.

RUSHING	No.	Yds	Avg	Lg	TD
Hampton	292	1077	3.7	20	5
Tillman	121	585	4.8	58	3
Meggett	69	329	4.8	23	0
Bunch	33	128	3.9	13	2

PASSING	Att	Comp	Pct Comp	Yds	Av Gain	TD	Int	Rating Pts
Simms	400	247	61.8	3038	7.60	15	9	88.3
Graham	22	8	36.4	79	3.59	0	0	47.3

RECEIVING	No.	Yds	Avg	Lg	TD
M. Jackson	58	708	12.2	t40	4
Meggett	38	319	8.4	50	0
Calloway	35	513	14.7	47	3
McCaffrey	27	335	12.4	31	2
Sherrard	24	433	18.0	t55	2

INTERCEPTIONS: Collins and G. Jackson, 4

PUNTING	No.	Yds	Avg	Net Avg	TB	In 20	Lg	Blk
Horan	44	1882	42.8	39.9	1	13	60	0
Landeta	33	1390	42.1	35.0	3	11	57	1

SACKS: Hamilton, 11.5

Philadelphia Eagles

SCORING	Rush	Rec	Ret	PAT	FG	S	Pts
Williams	0	10	0	0/0	0/0	0	60
Ruzek	0	0	0	13/16	8/10	0	37
Bavaro	0	6	0	0/0	0/0	0	36
Walker	1	3	0	0/0	0/0	0	24
Allen	0	0	4	0/0	0/0	0	64

RUSHING	No.	Yds	Avg	Lg	TD
Walker	174	746	4.3	35	1
Sherman	115	406	3.5	19	2
Hebron	84	297	3.5	33	3
Joseph	39	140	3.6	12	0

PASSING	Att	Comp	Pct Comp	Yds	Avg Gain	TD	Int	Rating Pts
Brister	309	181	58.6	1905	6.17	14	5	84.9
O'Brien	137	71	51.8	708	5.17	4	3	67.4
Cunningham	110	76	69.1	850	7.73	5	5	88.1

RECEIVING	No.	Yds	Avg	Lg	TD
Walker	75	610	8.1	55	3
Williams	60	725	12.1	t80	10
Bavaro	43	481	11.2	27	6
Bailey	41	545	13.3	58	1
Joseph	29	291	10.0	48	1

INTERCEPTIONS: Allen, 6

PUNTING	No.	Yds	Avg	Net Avg	TB	In 20	Lg	Blk
Feagles	83	3323	40.0	35.3	4	31	60	0

SACKS: Harmon, 11.5

Phoenix Cardinals

SCORING	Rush	Rec	Ret	PAT	FG	S	Pts
G. Davis	0	0	0	37/37	21/28	0	100
Moore	9	0	0	0/0	0/0	0	54
Proehl	0	7	0	0/0	0/0	0	42
R. Hill	0	4	0	0/0	0/0	0	24
Clark	0	4	0	0/0	0/0	0	24

RUSHING	No.	Yds	Avg	Lg	TD
Moore	263	1018	3.9	20	9
Hearst	76	264	3.5	57	1
Bailey	49	253	5.2	31	1
Centers	25	152	6.1	33	0

PASSING	Att	Comp	Pct Comp	Yds	Avg Gain	TD	Int	Rating Pts
Beuerlein	418	258	61.7	3164	7.57	18	4.3	82.5
Chandler	103	52	50.5	471	4.57	3	2	64.8

RECEIVING	No.	Yds	Avg	Lg	TD
Centers	66	603	9.1	29	3
Proehl	65	877	13.5	t51	7
Clark	63	818	13.0	55	4
R. Hill	35	519	14.8	t58	4
Bailey	32	243	7.6	30	0

INTERCEPTIONS: Lynch, 3

PUNTING	No.	Yds	Avg	Net Avg	TB	In 20	Lg	Blk
Camarillo	73	3189	43.7	37.8	8	23	61	0

SACKS: Harvey, 9.5

San Francisco 49ers

SCORING	Rush	Rec	Ret	PAT	FG	S	Pts
Cofer	0	0	0	59/61	16/26	0	107
Rice	1	15	0	0/0	0/0	0	96
Watters	10	1	0	0/0	0/0	0	66
Logan	7	0	0	0/0	0/0	0	42
J. Taylor	0	5	0	0/0	0/0	0	30

RUSHING	No.	Yds	Avg	Lg	TD
Watters	208	950	4.6	39	10
Young	69	407	5.9	35	2
Logan	58	280	4.8	45	7
Lee	72	230	3.2	13	1

PASSING	Att	Comp	Pct Comp	Yds	Avg Gain	TD	Int	Rating Pts
Young	462	314	68.0	4023	8.71	29	16	101.5
Bono	61	39	63.9	416	6.82	0	1	76.9

RECEIVING	No.	Yds	Avg	Lg	TD
Rice	98	1503	15.3	t80	15
Jones	68	735	10.8	29	3
J. Taylor	56	940	16.8	t76	5
Logan	37	348	9.4	24	0
Watters	31	326	10.5	t48	1

INTERCEPTIONS: McGruder, 5

PUNTING	No.	Yds	Avg	Net Avg	TB	In 20	Lg	Blk
Wilmsmeyer	42	1718	40.9	34.5	5	11	61	0

SACKS: Stubblefield, 10.5

Tampa Bay Buccaneers

SCORING	Rush	TD Rec	Ret	PAT	FG	S	Pts
Husted	0	0	0	27/27	16/22	0	75
Hawkins	0	5	0	0/0	0/0	0	30
Workman	2	2	0	0/0	0/0	0	24
Cobb	3	1	0	0/0	0/0	0	24
Copeland	0	4	0	0/0	0/0	0	24

RUSHING	No.	Yds	Avg	Lg	TD
Cobb	221	658	3.0	16	3
Workman	78	284	3.6	21	2
Royster	33	115	3.5	19	1
Erickson	26	96	3.7	15	0

PASSING	Att	Comp	Pct Comp	Yds	Avg Gain	TD	Int	Rating Pts
Erickson	457	233	51.0	3054	6.68	18	21	66.4
DeBerg	39	23	59.0	186	4.77	1	3	47.6

RECEIVING	No.	Yds	Avg	Lg	TD
Hawkins	62	933	15.0	67	5
Workman	54	411	7.6	t42	2
Copeland	30	633	21.1	t67	4
Ro. Hall	23	268	11.7	t37	1

INTERCEPTIONS: King, 3

PUNTING	No.	Yds	Avg	Net Avg	TB	In 20	Lg	Blk
Stryzinski	93	3772	40.6	35.3	3	24	57	1

SACKS: Seals, 8.5

Washington Redskins

SCORING	Rush	TD Rec	Ret	PAT	FG	S	Pts
Lohmiller	0	0	0	24/26	16/28	0	72
Sanders	0	4	0	0/0	0/0	0	24
Four tied with 18.							

RUSHING	No.	Yds	Avg	Lg	TD
Brooks	262	1063	4.8	t85	3
Mitchell	63	246	3.9	t29	3
Ervins	50	201	4.0	18	0
Byner	23	105	4.6	16	1
Gannon	21	88	4.2	12	1

PASSING	Att	Comp	Pct Comp	Yds	Avg Gain	TD	Int	Rating Pts
Rypien	319	166	52.0	1514	4.75	4	10	56.3
Gannon	125	74	59.2	704	5.63	3	7	59.6
Conklin	87	46	52.9	496	5.70	4	3	70.9

RECEIVING	No.	Yds	Avg	Lg	TD
Sanders	58	638	11.0	50	4
Monk	41	398	9.7	29	2
McGee	39	500	12.8	54	3
Byner	27	194	7.2	20	0
Middleton	24	154	6.4	18	2
Howard	23	286	12.4	27	0

INTERCEPTIONS: Carter, 6

PUNTING	No.	Yds	Avg	Net Avg	TB	In 20	Lg	Blk
Roby	78	3447	44.2	37.2	10	25	60	0

SACKS: Coleman, 6

NFL Dads: The Sequels

In early October it was David Williams, the Houston Oiler tackle, who grabbed nationwide attention when he skipped a game in New England to witness the birth of his son. In a case of better timing, Chicago Bear tackle John Wojciechowski was at his wife's bedside when she delivered a son just before noon on Saturday, Oct. 30, and by 10 p.m. he was in Green Bay for the Bears' 17–3 loss on Sunday. But a more frustrating odyssey was endured by Los Angeles Rams defensive end Fred Stokes.

Stokes was in San Francisco for a Week 9 game against the 49ers when he got a call from his wife, Regina, early Sunday morning informing him that she was going into labor. Stokes checked out of the team hotel and, after getting permission to leave from coach Chuck Knox, caught an early flight to Orange County. Stokes made it to St. Joseph Hospital, but after a few fruitless hours, doctors told him that Regina would not deliver until evening at the earliest.

So Stokes, with his wife's blessing, hired a jet for $3,300 to whisk him back to San Francisco. Alas, he arrived at Candlestick Park only minutes before the Niners completed a 40–17 rout of his Rams. Stokes expected the team to withhold his $33,333 per-game salary, just as the Oilers kept Williams's $111,111. "I chose to leave," said Stokes. "I let the team down. I felt bad. I didn't earn my money."

But he undoubtedly wasn't thinking of money late on Sunday evening when his seven-pound, five-ounce son, Landon, arrived safely with Dad in attendance. Then, on Monday afternoon, in a welcome precedent, the Rams announced that they wouldn't dock Stokes.

1994 NFL Draft

First four rounds of the 59th annual NFL Draft held April 24-25 in New York City.

First Round

	Team	Selection	Position
1.	Cincinnati	Dan Wilkinson, Ohio St	DT
2.	Indianapolis	Marshall Faulk, SD State	RB
3.	Washington	Heath Shuler, Tenn	QB
4.	New England	Willie McGinest, USC	DE
5.	Indianapolis*	Trev Alberts, Nebraska	LB
6.	Tampa Bay	Trent Dilfer, Fresno St	QB
7.	San Francisco†	Bryant Young, Notre Dame	DT
8.	Seattle	Sam Adams, Texas A&M	DE
9.	Cleveland	Antonio Langham, Ala	DB
10.	Arizona	Jamir Miller, UCLA	LB
11.	Chicago	John Thierry, Alcorn St	LB
12.	NY Jets#	Aaron Glenn, Texas A&M	DB
13.	New Orleans‡	Joe Johnson, Louisville	DE
14.	Philadelphia	Bernard Williams, Georgia	OT
15.	LA Rams**	Wayne Gandy, Auburn	OT
16.	Green Bay††	Aaron Taylor, Notre Dame	OT
17.	Pittsburgh	Charles Johnson, Colorado	WR
18.	Minnesota##	DeWayne Washington, N Carolina St	CB
19.	Minnesota	Todd Steussie, Cal	OT
20.	Miami***	Tim Bowens, Mississippi	DT
21.	Detroit	Johnnie Morton, USC	WR
22.	LA Raiders	Rob Fredrickson, Mich St	LB
23.	Dallas†††	Shante Carver, Arizona St	DE
24.	NY Giants	Thomas Lewis, Indiana	WR
25.	Kansas City	Greg Hill, Texas A&M	RB
26.	Houston	Henry Ford, Arkansas	DE
27.	Buffalo	Jeff Burris, Notre Dame	DB
28.	San Fran###	William Floyd, Florida St	RB
29.	Cleveland√	Derrick Alexander, Mich	WR

*From LA Rams †From Atlanta through Indianapolis and LA Rams #From New Orleans ‡From NY Jets **From San Diego through Miami ††From Miami ##From Denver. ‡‡From Houston. ***From Green Bay †††From San Francisco ###From Dallas. √From Philadelphia

Second Round

	Team	Selection	Position
30.	Cincinnati	Darnay Scott, SD St	WR
31.	Washington	Tre Johnson, Temple	T
32.	Indianapolis	Eric Mahlum, Cal	C
33.	LA Rams	Isaac Bruce, U of Memphis	WR
34.	Tampa Bay	Errict Rhett, Florida	RB
35.	New England	Kevin Lee, Alabama	WR
36.	Seattle	Kevin Mawae, LSU	C
37.	Philadelphia*	Bruce Walker, UCLA	DT
38.	Arizona	Chuck Levy, Arizona	RB
39.	Chicago	Marcus Spears, NW La.	T
40.	Minnesota†	David Palmer, Alabama	WR
41.	NY Jets	Ryan Yarborough, Wyoming	WR
42.	Philadelphia	Charlie Garner, Tennessee	RB
43.	San Diego	Isaac Davis, Arkansas	G
44.	New Orleans	Mario Bates, Arizona St	RB
45.	Atlanta#	Bert Emanuel, Rice	WR
46.	Dallas	Larry Allen, Sonoma St	G
47.	NY Giants	Thomas Randolph, Kansas St	DB
48.	Buffalo	Bucky Brooks, N Carolina	WR
49.	LA Rams	Toby Wright, Nebraska	DB
50.	Pittsburgh	Brentson Buckner, Clemson	DE
51.	Denver	Allen Aldridge, Houston	LB
52.	LA Raiders‡	James Folston, NE Louisiana	LB
53.	San Francisco**	Kevin Mitchell, Syarcuse	LB
54.	Miami	Aubrey Beavers, Oklahoma	LB
55.	LA Raiders	Fernando Smith, Jackson St	DE
56.	LA Rams††	Brad Ottis, Wayne St (Neb.)	DT
57.	Detroit	Van Malone, Texas	DB
58.	Kansas City	Donnell Bennett, Miami	RB
59.	NY Giants	Jason Sehorn, Southern Cal	DB
60.	Houston	Jeremy Nunley, Alabama	DE
61.	Buffalo	Lonnie Johnson, Florida St	TE
62.	San Fran##	Tyronne Drakeford, Virginia Tech	DB
63.	San Diego	Vaughn Parker, UCLA	G
64.	Buffalo	Sam Rogers, Colorado	LB
65.	Miami‡‡	Tim Ruddy, Notre Dame	C

*From Atlanta †From Cleveland through Philadelphia and Atlanta #From Minnesota. ‡From Minnesota **From Green Bay ††From San Francisco. ##From Dallas ‡‡ From Arizona

The Love of a Good Woman

New York Giant quarterback Phil Simms woke up with an inner ear infection on the morning before the Giants were to play Phoenix on Nov. 28. His wife, Diana, was all sympathy. "You better suck it up," she told Phil. "This is a big game." Simms, who played while on medication, dutifully threw for a season-high 337 yards in the Giants' win.

Final Standings

EUROPEAN DIVISION

	W	L	T	Pct	Pts/Tm	Pts/Opp
Barcelona	5	5	0	.500	104	161
Frankfurt	3	7	0	.300	150	257
London	2	7	1	.250	178	203

NORTH AMERICAN/EAST DIVISION

	W	L	T	Pct	Pts/Tm	Pts/Opp
Orlando	8	2	0	.800	247	127
NY/NJ	6	4	0	.600	284	188
Montreal	2	8	0	.200	175	274
Ohio	1	9	0	.100	132	230

NORTH AMERICAN/WEST DIVISION

	W	L	T	Pct	Pts/Tm	Pts/Opp
Sacramento	8	2	0	.800	250	152
Birmingham	7	2	1	.750	192	165
San Antonio	7	3	0	.700	195	150

Playoff Results

SEMIFINALS

Orlando 45, Birmingham 7
Sacramento 17, Barcelona 15

1992 World Bowl

June 6, 1992 at Olympic Stadium, Montreal

Sacramento	0	6	0	15—	21
Orlando	7	10	0	0 —	17

FIRST QUARTER

Orlando: Ford 10 pass from Mitchell (Bennett kick), 11:27

SECOND QUARTER

Sacramento: FG Blanchard 32, 5:16
Orlando: Davis 8 pass from Mitchell (Bennett kick), 8:12
Orlando: FG Bennett 20, 14:06
Sacramento: FG Blanchard 24, 14:59

FOURTH QUARTER

Sacramento: Green 12 pass from Archer (Stock pass from Archer), 3:33
Sacramento: Brown 2 pass from Archer (Blanchard kick), 9:16

A: 43,789.

* Note: The WLAF did not operate in 1993 or '94, but will resume play in April, 1995

WLAF Individual Leaders

PASSING

	Att	Comp	Pct Comp	Yds	Avg Gain	TD	Pct TD	Int	Pct Int	Lg	Rating Pts
Archer, Sacramento	317	194	61.2	2964	9.35	23	7.3	7	2.2	t80	107.0
Slack, NY/NJ	215	140	65.1	1898	8.83	12	5.6	7	3.3	68	98.2
Proctor, Montreal	193	113	58.5	1478	7.66	8	4.1	5	2.6	61	85.8
Perez, Frankfurt	147	86	58.5	985	6.70	6	4.1	5	3.4	46	78.2
Johnson, San Antonio	257	144	56.0	1760	6.85	8	3.1	6	2.3	63	78.0

RECEIVING

RECEPTIONS	No.	Yds	Avg	Lg	TD	YARDS	Yds	No.	Avg	Lg	TD
W. Wilson, Ohio	65	776	11.9	52	2	Brown, Sacramento	1011	48	21.1	t80	12
Bouyer, Birmingham	57	706	12.4	50	0	Ford, London	833	45	18.5	55	6
Johnson, Orlando	56	687	12.3	41	5	W. Wilson, Ohio	776	65	11.9	52	2
Garrett, London	55	509	9.3	35	1	Bouyer, Birmingham	706	57	12.4	50	0
T. Woods, Barcelona	51	546	10.7	t86	1	Johnson, Orlando	687	56	12.3	41	5

RUSHING

	Att	Yds	Avg	Lg	TD
Brown, San Antonio	166	767	4.6	54	7
Rasul, Ohio	136	572	4.2	36	4
Clack, Orlando	117	517	4.4	23	6
Pringle, Sacramento	152	507	3.3	22	6
J. Alexander, London	125	501	4.0	20	1

Other Statistical Leaders

Points (TDs)	Brown, Sacramento	72
Points (Kicking)	Doyle, Birmingham	64
Yards from Scrimmage	Brown, Sacramento	1011
Interceptions	Jones, Barcelona	9
Sacks	Lockett, London	14.0
Punting Avg.	Sullivan, San Antonio	41.6
Punt Return Avg.	D. Smith, NY/NJ	12.5
Kickoff Return Avg.	Burbage, NY/NJ	26.9

1993 Canadian Football League

EASTERN DIVISION

	W	L	T	Pts	Pct	PF	PA
Winnipeg	14	4	0	28	.778	646	421
Hamilton	6	12	0	12	.333	316	567
Ottawa	4	14	0	8	.222	387	517
Toronto	3	15	0	6	.167	330	590

WESTERN DIVISION

	W	L	T	Pts	Pct	PF	PA
Calgary	15	3	0	30	.833	646	418
Edmonton	12	6	0	24	.667	507	372
Saskatchewan	11	7	0	22	.611	511	495
B.C.	10	8	0	20	.556	574	583
Sacramento	6	12	0	12	.333	498	509

Regular Season Statistical Leaders

Points (TDs)	David Williams, Winnipeg 90
	David Sapunjis, Calgary 90
	Eddie Brown, Edmonton 90
Points (Kicking)	Mark McLoughlin, 208 Calgary
Yards (Rushing)	Mike Richardson, 925 Winnipeg
Yards (Passing)	Doug Flutie, Calgary 5092
Yards (Receiving)	David Sapunjis, Calgary 1454
Receptions	David Sapunjis, Calgary 103

1993 Playoff Results

DIVISION FINALS

Eastern: WINNIPEG 20, Hamilton 19
Western: Edmonton 29, CALGARY 15

1993 Grey Cup Championship

Nov. 28, 1993, at Calgary

Winnipeg Blue Bombers	0	10	7	6—23
Edmonton Eskimos	17	7	0	9—33

A: 50,035

Remembering the Little People

The average NFL lineman absorbs a lot of pain for little glory. Quite frequently, though, the league's leading men—quarterbacks, running backs and receivers—go out of their way to thank each member of their blue-collar supporting casts with heartfelt, and sometimes even expensive, gifts. Below is a recent sampling and two vintage examples:

Troy Aikman, QB Dallas Cowboys—Handmade cowboy boots, two roundtrip airline tickets to anywhere in the world;

Jeff Hostetler, QB LA Raiders—Set of Ping irons;

Emmitt Smith, RB Dallas Cowboys—Champagne (to everyone on the team), rolex watches and gift certificates;

Rick Mirer, QB Seattle Seahawks—Luggage;

Boomer Esiason, QB NY Jets—Leather bomber jackets, designer sunglasses, dinner every Thursday during the season;

Thurman Thomas, RB Buffalo Bills—Engraved crystal bison statues;

Jim Kelly, QB Buffalo Bills—As much as $2,500 for a sackless vistory;

Drew Bledsoe, QB New England Patriots—A bottle of Dom Perignon and a gift certificate to a big-and-tall men's store;

Dan Marino, QB Miami Dolphins—Isotoner gloves;

O.J. Simpson, RB Buffalo Bills—Gold Bracelets for his NFL-record 2,003-yard season in 1973;

John Riggins, RB Washington Redskins—Engraved Mark V Weatherby .460 Magnum elephant guns in 1983.

THEY SAID IT

Ron Wolfley, Cleveland Brown reserve fullback, on his role in the team's offense: "If you need two yards, I'll get you two. If you need four yards, I'll get you two."

FOR THE RECORD · Year by Year

The Super Bowl

Results

	Date	Winner (Share)	Loser (Share)	Score	Site (Attendance)
I	1-15-67	Green Bay ($15,000)	Kansas City ($7,500)	35-10	Los Angeles (61,946)
II	1-14-68	Green Bay ($15,000)	Oakland ($7,500)	33-14	Miami (75,546)
III	1-12-69	NY Jets ($15,000)	Baltimore ($7,500)	16-7	Miami (75,389)
IV	1-11-70	Kansas City ($15,000)	Minnesota ($7,500)	23-7	New Orleans (80,562)
V	1-17-71	Baltimore ($15,000)	Dallas ($7,500)	16-13	Miami (79,204)
VI	1-16-72	Dallas ($15,000)	Miami ($7,500)	24-3	New Orleans (81,023)
VII	1-14-73	Miami ($15,000)	Washington ($7,500)	14-7	Los Angeles (90,182)
VIII	1-13-74	Miami ($15,000)	Minnesota ($7,500)	24-7	Houston (71,882)
IX	1-12-75	Pittsburgh ($15,000)	Minnesota ($7,500)	16-6	New Orleans (80,997)
X	1-18-76	Pittsburgh ($15,000)	Dallas ($7,500)	21-17	Miami (80,187)
XI	1-9-77	Oakland ($15,000)	Minnesota ($7,500)	32-14	Pasadena (103,438)
XII	1-15-78	Dallas ($18,000)	Denver ($9,000)	27-10	New Orleans (75,583)
XIII	1-21-79	Pittsburgh ($18,000)	Dallas ($9,000)	35-31	Miami (79,484)
XIV	1-20-80	Pittsburgh ($18,000)	Los Angeles ($9,000)	31-19	Pasadena (103,985)
XV	1-25-81	Oakland ($18,000)	Philadelphia ($9,000)	27-10	New Orleans (76,135)
XVI	1-24-82	San Francisco ($18,000)	Cincinnati ($9,000)	26-21	Pontiac (81,270)
XVII	1-30-83	Washington ($36,000)	Miami ($18,000)	27-17	Pasadena (103,667)
XVIII	1-22-84	LA Raiders ($36,000)	Washington ($18,000)	38-9	Tampa (72,920)
XIX	1-20-85	San Francisco ($36,000)	Miami ($18,000)	38-16	Stanford (84,059)
XX	1-26-86	Chicago ($36,000)	New England ($18,000)	46-10	New Orleans (73,818)
XXI	1-25-87	NY Giants ($36,000)	Denver ($18,000)	39-20	Pasadena (101,063)
XXII	1-31-88	Washington ($36,000)	Denver ($18,000)	42-10	San Diego (73,302)
XXIII	1-22-89	San Francisco ($36,000)	Cincinnati ($18,000)	20-16	Miami (75,129)
XXIV	1-28-90	San Francisco ($36,000)	Denver ($18,000)	55-10	New Orleans (72,919)
XXV	1-27-91	NY Giants ($36,000)	Buffalo ($18,000)	20-19	Tampa (73,813)
XXVI	1-26-92	Washington ($36,000)	Buffalo ($18,000)	37-24	Minneapolis (63,130)
XXVII	1-31-93	Dallas ($36,000)	Buffalo ($18,000)	52-17	Pasadena (98,374)
XXVIII	1-30-94	Dallas ($38,000)	Buffalo ($23,500)	30-13	Atlanta (72,817)

Most Valuable Players

		Position
I	Bart Starr, GB	QB
II	Bart Starr, GB	QB
III	Joe Namath, NY Jets	QB
IV	Len Dawson, KC	QB
V	Chuck Howley, Dall	LB
VI	Roger Staubach, Dall	QB
VII	Jake Scott, Mia	S
VIII	Larry Csonka, Mia	RB
IX	Franco Harris, Pitt	RB
X	Lynn Swann, Pitt	WR
XI	Fred Biletnikoff, Oak	WR
XII	Randy White, Dall	DT
	Harvey Martin, Dall	DE
XIII	Terry Bradshaw, Pitt	QB
XIV	Terry Bradshaw, Pitt	QB
XV	Jim Plunkett, Oak	QB
XVI	Joe Montana, SF	QB
XVII	John Riggins, Wash	RB
XVIII	Marcus Allen, LA Raiders	RB
XIX	Joe Montana, SF	QB
XX	Richard Dent, Chi	DE
XXI	Phil Simms, NY Giants	QB
XXII	Doug Williams, Wash	QB
XXIII	Jerry Rice, SF	WR
XXIV	Joe Montana, SF	QB
XXV	Ottis Anderson, NY Giants	RB
XXVI	Mark Rypien, Washington	QB
XXVII	Troy Aikman, Dallas	QB
XXVIII	Emmitt Smith, Dallas	RB

Composite Standings

	W	L	Pct	Pts	Opp Pts
Pittsburgh Steelers	4	0	1.000	103	73
San Francisco 49ers	4	0	1.000	139	63
Green Bay Packers	2	0	1.000	68	24
NY Giants	2	0	1.000	59	39
Chicago Bears	1	0	1.000	46	10
NY Jets	1	0	1.000	16	7
Oakland/LA Raiders	3	1	.750	111	66
Washington Redskins	3	2	.600	122	103
Dallas Cowboys	4	3	.571	194	115
Baltimore Colts	1	1	.500	23	29
Kansas City Chiefs	1	1	.500	33	42
Miami Dolphins	2	3	.400	74	103
LA Rams	0	1	.000	19	31
New England Patriots	0	1	.000	10	46
Philadelphia Eagles	0	1	.000	10	27
Cincinnati Bengals	0	2	.000	37	46
Minnesota Vikings	0	4	.000	34	95
Buffalo Bills	0	4	.000	73	139
Denver Broncos	0	4	.000	50	163

THEY SAID IT

Marv Levy, Buffalo Bill coach, on meeting with his team two days after their fourth straight Super Bowl defeat: "It's too soon after the car wreck to say we're feeling better."

Career Leaders

Passing

	GP	Att	Comp	Pct Comp	Yds	Avg Gain	TD	Pct TD	Int	Pct Int	Lg	Rating Pts
Joe Montana, SF 4	122	83	68.0		1142	9.36	11	9.0	0	0.0	44	127.8
Jim Plunkett, Raiders......2	46	29	63.0		433	9.41	4	8.7	0	0.0	t80	122.8
Troy Aikman, Dall 2	57	41	71.9		480	8.42	4	7.0	1	1.8	t56	113.2
Terry Bradshaw, Pitt.......4	84	49	58.3		932	11.10	9	10.7	4	4.8	t75	112.8
Bart Starr, GB... 2	47	29	61.7		452	9.62	3	6.4	1	2.1	t62	106.0
Roger Staubach, Dall 4	98	61	62.2		734	7.49	8	8.2	4	4.1	t45	95.4
Len Dawson, KC 2	44	28	63.6		353	8.02	2	4.5	2	4.5	t46	84.8
Bob Griese, Mia 3	41	26	63.4		295	7.20	1	2.4	2	4.9	t28	72.7
Dan Marino, Mia 1	50	29	58.0		318	6.36	1	2.0	2	4.0	30	66.9
Jim Kelly, Buff 4	145	81	55.9		829	5.72	2	1.4	7	4.8	61	57.2
Joe Theismann, Wash 2	58	31	53.4		386	6.66	2	3.4	4	6.9	60	57.1

Note: Minimum 40 attempts.

Rushing

	GP	Yds	Att	Avg	Lg	TD
Franco Harris, Pitt...............4	354	101	3.5	25	4	
Larry Csonka, Mia 3	297	57	5.2	9	2	
Emmitt Smith, Dall 2	240	52	4.6	38	3	
John Riggins, Wash 2	230	64	3.6	43	2	
Timmy Smith, Wash...........1	204	22	9.3	58	2	
Thurman Thomas, Buff 4	204	52	3.9	31	4	
Roger Craig, SF.................3	198	52	3.8	18	2	
Marcus Allen, LA Raiders...1	191	20	9.6	t74	2	
Tony Dorsett, Dall..............2	162	31	5.2	29	1	
Mark van Eeghen, Oak.......2	148	36	4.1	11	0	

Receiving

	GP	No.	Yds	Avg	Lg	TD
Andre Reed, Buff 4	27	323	11.9	40	0	
Roger Craig, SF 3	20	212	10.6	40	2	
Thurman Thomas, Buff..............4	20	144	7.2	24	0	
Jerry Rice, SF............................2	18	363	20.2	44	4	
Lynn Swann, Pitt........................4	16	364	22.8	t64	3	
Chuck Foreman, Minn...............3	15	139	9.3	26	0	
Cliff Branch, Raiders.................3	14	181	12.9	50	3	
Preston Pearson, Balt-Pitt-Dall .5	12	105	8.8	14	0	
Don Beebe, Buff........................3	12	171	14.3	43	2	
Tom Novacek, Dall....................2	12	128	10.6	23	1	
Kenneth Davis, Buff...................4	12	72	6.0	19	0	

Single-Game Leaders

Scoring

	Pts
Roger Craig: XIX, San Francisco vs Miami (1 R, 2 P)	18
Jerry Rice: XXIV, San Francisco vs Denver (3 P)	18
Don Chandler: II, Green Bay vs Oakland (3 PAT, 4 FG)	15

Rushing Yards

	Yds
Timmy Smith: XXII, Washington vs Denver	204
Marcus Allen: XVIII, LA Raiders vs Washington	191
John Riggins: XVII, Washington vs Miami	166
Franco Harris: IX, Pittsburgh vs Minnesota	158
Larry Csonka: VIII, Miami vs Minnesota	145
Clarence Davis: XI, Oakland vs Minnesota	137
Thurman Thomas: XXV, Buffalo vs NY Giants	135
Emmitt Smith: XXVIII, Dallas vs Buffalo	132

Receptions

	No.
Dan Ross: XVI, Cincinnati vs San Francisco	11
Jerry Rice: XXIII, San Francisco vs Cincinnati	11
Tony Nathan: XIX, Miami vs San Francisco	10
Ricky Sanders: XXII, Washington vs Denver	9
George Sauer: III, NY Jets vs Baltimore	8
Roger Craig: XXIII, San Francisco vs Cincinnati	8
Andre Reed: XXV, Buffalo vs NY Giants	8
Andre Reed: XXVII, Buffalo vs Dallas	8

Touchdown Passes

	No.
Joe Montana: XXIV, San Francisco vs Denver	5
Terry Bradshaw: XIII, Pittsburgh vs Dallas	4
Doug Williams: XXII, Washington vs Denver	4
Troy Aikman: XXVII, Dallas vs Buffalo	4
Roger Staubach: XIII, Dallas vs Pittsburgh	3
Jim Plunkett: XV, Oakland vs Philadelphia	3
Joe Montana: XIX, San Francisco vs Miami	3
Phil Simms: XXI, NY Giants vs Denver	3

Receiving Yards

	Yds
Jerry Rice: XXIII, San Francisco vs Cincinnati	215
Ricky Sanders: XXII, Washington vs Denver	193
Lynn Swann: X, Pittsburgh vs Dallas	161
Andre Reed: XXVII, Buffalo vs Dallas	152
Jerry Rice: XXIV, San Francisco vs Denver	148
Max McGee: I, Green Bay vs Kansas City	138
George Sauer: III, NY Jets vs Baltimore	133

Passing Yards

	Yds
Joe Montana: XXIII, San Francisco vs Cincinnati	357
Doug Williams: XXII, Washington vs Denver	340
Joe Montana: XIX, San Francisco vs Miami	331
Terry Bradshaw: XIII, Pittsburgh vs Dallas	318
Dan Marino: XIX, Miami vs San Francisco	318
Terry Bradshaw: XIV, Pittsburgh vs LA Rams	309
John Elway: XXI, Denver vs NY Giants	304
Ken Anderson: XVI, Cincinnati vs San Francisco	300

1933

NFL championship   Chicago Bears 23, NY Giants 21

1934

NFL championship   NY Giants 30, Chicago Bears 13

1935

NFL championship   Detroit 26, NY Giants 7

1936

NFL championship   Green Bay 21, Boston 6

1937

NFL championship   Washington 28,
Chicago Bears 21

1938

NFL championship   NY Giants 23, Green Bay 17

1939

NFL championship   Green Bay 27, NY Giants 0

1940

NFL championship   Chicago Bears 73, Washington 0

1941

W. div playoff   Chicago Bears 33, Green Bay 14
NFL championship   Chicago Bears 37, NY Giants 9

1942

NFL championship   Washington 14, Chicago Bears 6

1943

E. div playoff   Washington 28, NY Giants 0
NFL championship   Chicago Bears 41,
Washington 21

1944

NFL championship   Green Bay 14, NY Giants 7

1945

NFL championship   Cleveland 15, Washington 14

1946

NFL championship   Chicago Bears 24, NY Giants 14

1947

E. div playoff   Philadelphia 21, Pittsburgh 0
NFL championship   Chicago Cardinals 28,
Philadelphia 21

1948

NFL championship   Philadelphia 7,
Chicago Cardinals 0

1949

NFL championship   Philadelphia 14, Los Angeles 0

1950

Am. Conf. playoff   Cleveland 8, NY Giants 3
Nat. Conf. playoff Los Angeles 24,
Chicago Bears 14
NFL championship   Cleveland 30, Los Angeles 28

1951

NFL championship   Los Angeles 24, Cleveland 17

1952

Nat. Conf. playoff Detroit 31, Los Angeles 21
NFL championship   Detroit 17, Cleveland 7

1953

NFL championship   Detroit 17, Cleveland 16

1954

NFL championship   Cleveland 56, Detroit 10

1955

NFL championship   Cleveland 38, Los Angeles 14

1956

NFL championship   NY Giants 47, Chicago Bears 7

1957

W. Conf playoff   Detroit 31, San Francisco 27
NFL championship   Detroit 59, Cleveland 14

1958

E. Conf playoff   NY Giants 10, Cleveland 0
NFL championship   Baltimore 23, NY Giants 17

1959

NFL championship   Baltimore 31, NY Giants 16

1960

NFL championship   Philadelphia 17, Green Bay 13
AFL championship   Houston 24, LA Chargers 16

1961

NFL championship   Green Bay 37, NY Giants 0
AFL championship   Houston 10, San Diego 3

1962

NFL championship   Green Bay 16, NY Giants 7
AFL championship   Dallas Texans 20, Houston 17

1963

NFL championship   Chicago 14, NY Giants 10
AFL E. div playoff Boston 26, Buffalo 8
AFL championship   San Diego 51, Boston 10

1964

NFL championship   Cleveland 27, Baltimore 0
AFL championship   Buffalo 20, San Diego 7

1965

NFL W. Conf   Green Bay 13, Baltimore 10
playoff
NFL championship   Green Bay 23, Cleveland 12
AFL championship   Buffalo 23, San Diego 0

1966

NFL championship   Green Bay 34, Dallas 27
AFL championship   Kansas City 31, Buffalo 7

1967

NFL E. Conf   Dallas 52, Cleveland 14
championship
NFL W. Conf   Green Bay 28, Los Angeles 7
championship
NFL championship   Green Bay 21, Dallas 17
AFL championship   Oakland 40, Houston 7

1968

NFL E. Conf championship	Cleveland 31, Dallas 20
NFL W. Conf championship	Baltimore 24, Minnesota 14
NFL championship	Baltimore 34, Cleveland 0
AFL W. div playoff	Oakland 41, Kansas City 6
AFL championship	NY Jets 27, Oakland 23

1969

NFL E. Conf championship	Cleveland 38, Dallas 14
NFL W. Conf championship	Minnesota 23, Los Angeles 20
NFL championship	Minnesota 27, Cleveland 7
AFL div playoffs	Kansas City 13, NY Jets 6 Oakland 56, Houston 7
AFL championship	Kansas City 17, Oakland 7

1970

AFC div playoffs	Baltimore 17, Cincinnati 0 Oakland 21, Miami 14
AFC championship	Baltimore 27, Oakland 17
NFC div playoffs	Dallas 5, Detroit 0 San Francisco 17, Minnesota 14
NFC championship	Dallas 17, San Francisco 10

1971

AFC div playoffs	Miami 27, Kansas City 24 Baltimore 20, Cleveland 3
AFC championship	Miami 21, Baltimore 0
NFC div playoffs	Dallas 20, Minnesota 12 San Francisco 24, Washington 20
NFC championship	Dallas 14, San Francisco 3

1972

AFC div playoffs	Pittsburgh 13, Oakland 7 Miami 20, Cleveland 14
AFC championship	Miami 21, Pittsburgh 17
NFC div playoffs	Dallas 30, San Francisco 28 Washington 16, Green Bay 3
NFC championship	Washington 26, Dallas 3

1973

AFC div playoffs	Oakland 33, Pittsburgh 14 Miami 34, Cincinnati 16
AFC championship	Miami 27, Oakland 10
NFC div playoffs	Minnesota 27, Washington 20 Dallas 27, Los Angeles 16
NFC championship	Minnesota 27, Dallas 10

1974

AFC div playoffs	Oakland 28, Miami 26 Pittsburgh 32, Buffalo 14
AFC championship	Pittsburgh 24, Oakland 13
NFC div playoffs	Minnesota 30, St Louis 14 Los Angeles 19, Washington 10
NFC championship	Minnesota 14, Los Angeles 10

1975

AFC div playoffs	Pittsburgh 28, Baltimore 10 Oakland 31, Cincinnati 28
AFC championship	Pittsburgh 16, Oakland 10
NFC div playoffs	Los Angeles 35, St Louis 23 Dallas 17, Minnesota 14
NFC championship	Dallas 37, Los Angeles 7

1976

AFC div playoffs	Oakland 24, New England 21 Pittsburgh 40, Baltimore 14
AFC championship	Oakland 24, Pittsburgh 7
NFC div playoffs	Minnesota 35, Washington 20 Los Angeles 14, Dallas 12
NFC championship	Minnesota 24, Los Angeles 13

1977

AFC div playoffs	Denver 34, Pittsburgh 21 Oakland 37, Baltimore 31
AFC championship	Denver 20, Oakland 17
NFC div playoffs	Dallas 37, Chicago 7 Minnesota 14, Los Angeles 7
NFC championship	Dallas 23, Minnesota 6

1978

AFC 1st-rd. playoff	Houston 17, Miami 9
AFC div playoffs	Houston 31, New England 14 Pittsburgh 33, Denver 10
AFC championship	Pittsburgh 34, Houston 5
NFC 1st-rd. playoff	Atlanta 14, Philadelphia 13
NFC div playoffs	Dallas 27, Atlanta 20 Los Angeles 34, Minnesota 10
NFC championship	Dallas 28, Los Angeles 0

1979

AFC 1st-rd. playoff	Houston 13, Denver 7
AFC div playoffs	Houston 17, San Diego 14 Pittsburgh 34, Miami 14
AFC championship	Pittsburgh 27, Houston 13
NFC 1st-rd. playoff	Philadelphia 27, Chicago 17
NFC div playoffs	Tampa Bay 24, Philadelphia 17 Los Angeles 21, Dallas 19
NFC championship	Los Angeles 9, Tampa Bay 0

1980

AFC 1st-rd. playoff	Oakland 27, Houston 7
AFC div playoffs	San Diego 20, Buffalo 14 Oakland 14, Cleveland 12
AFC championship	Oakland 34, San Diego 27
NFC 1st-rd. playoff	Dallas 34, Los Angeles 13
NFC div playoffs	Philadelphia 31, Minnesota 16 Dallas 30, Atlanta 27
NFC championship	Philadelphia 20, Dallas 7

1981

AFC 1st-rd. playoff	Buffalo 31, NY Jets 27
AFC div playoffs	San Diego 41, Miami 38 Cincinnati 28, Buffalo 21
AFC championship	Cincinnati 27, San Diego 7
NFC 1st-rd. playoff	NY Giants 27, Philadelphia 21
NFC div playoffs	Dallas 38, Tampa Bay 0 San Francisco 38, NY Giants 24
NFC championship	San Francisco 28, Dallas 27

1982

AFC 1st-rd. playoffs	Miami 28, New England 13 LA Raiders 27, Cleveland 10 NY Jets 44, Cincinnati 17 San Diego 31, Pittsburgh 28
AFC 2nd-rd. playoffs	NY Jets 17, LA Raiders 14 Miami 34, San Diego 13
AFC championship	Miami 14, NY Jets 0

1982 *(Cont.)*

NFC 1st-rd. playoffs	Washington 31, Detroit 7
	Green Bay 41, St Louis 16
	Minnesota 30, Atlanta 24
	Dallas 30, Tampa Bay 17
NFC 2nd-rd. playoffs	Washington 21, Minnesota 7
	Dallas 37, Green Bay 26
NFC championship	Washington 31, Dallas 17

1983

AFC 1st-rd. playoff	Seattle 31, Denver 7
AFC div playoffs	Seattle 27, Miami 20
	LA Raiders 38, Pittsburgh 10
AFC championship	LA Raiders 30, Seattle 14
NFC 1st-rd. playoff	LA Rams 24, Dallas 17
NFC div playoffs	San Francisco 24, Detroit 23
	Washington 51, LA Rams 7
NFC championship	Washington 24, San Francisco 21

1984

AFC 1st-rd. playoff	Seattle 13, LA Raiders 7
AFC div playoffs	Miami 31, Seattle 10
	Pittsburgh 24, Denver 17
AFC championship	Miami 45, Pittsburgh 28
NFC 1st-rd. playoff	NY Giants 16, LA Rams 13
NFC div playoffs	San Francisco 21, NY Giants 10
	Chicago 23, Washington 19
NFC championship	San Francisco 23, Chicago 0

1985

AFC 1st-rd. playoff	New England 26, NY Jets 14
AFC div playoffs	Miami 24, Cleveland 21
	New England 27, LA Raiders 20
AFC championship	New England 31, Miami 14
NFC 1st-rd. playoff	NY Giants 17, San Francisco 3
NFC div playoffs	LA Rams 20, Dallas 0
	Chicago 21, NY Giants 0
NFC championship	Chicago 24, LA Rams 0

1986

AFC 1st-rd. playoff	NY Jets 35, Kansas City 15
AFC div playoffs	Cleveland 23, NY Jets 20
	Denver 22, New England 17
AFC championship	Denver 23, Cleveland 20
NFC 1st-rd. playoff	Washington 19, LA Rams 7
NFC div playoffs	Washington 27, Chicago 13
	NY Giants 49, San Francisco 3
NFC championship	NY Giants 17, Washington 0

1987

AFC div playoffs	Cleveland 38, Indianapolis 21
	Denver 34, Houston 10
AFC championship	Denver 38, Cleveland 33
NFC 1st-rd. playoff	Minnesota 44, New Orleans 10
NFC div playoffs	Minnesota 36, San Francisco 24
	Washington 21, Chicago 17
NFC championship	Washington 17, Minnesota 10

1988

AFC 1st-rd. playoff	Houston 24, Cleveland 23
AFC div playoffs	Cincinnati 21, Seattle 13
	Buffalo 17, Houston 10
AFC championship	Cincinnati 21, Buffalo 10
NFC 1st-rd. playoff	Minnesota 28, LA Rams 17
NFC div playoffs	Chicago 20, Philadelphia 12
	San Francisco 34, Minnesota 9
NFC championship	San Francisco 28, Chicago 3

1989

AFC 1st-rd. playoff	Pittsburgh 26, Houston 23
AFC div playoffs	Cleveland 34, Buffalo 30
	Denver 24, Pittsburgh 23
AFC championship	Denver 37, Cleveland 21
NFC 1st-rd. playoff	LA Rams 21, Philadelphia 7
NFC div playoffs	LA Rams 19, NY Giants 13
	San Francisco 41, Minnesota 13
NFC championship	San Francisco 30, LA Rams 3

1990

AFC 1st-rd. playoffs	Miami 17, Kansas City 16
	Cincinnati 41, Houston 14
AFC div playoffs	Buffalo 44, Miami 34
	LA Raiders 20, Cincinnati 10
AFC championship	Buffalo 51, LA Raiders 3
NFC 1st-rd. playoffs	Chicago 16, New Orleans 6
	Washington 20, Philadelphia 6
NFC div playoffs	NY Giants 31, Chicago 3
	San Francisco 28, Washington 10
NFC championship	NY Giants 15, San Francisco 13

1991

AFC 1st-rd. playoffs	Houston 17, NY Jets 10
	Kansas City 10, LA Raiders 6
AFC div playoffs	Denver 26, Houston 24
	Buffalo 37, Kansas City 14
AFC championship	Buffalo 10, Denver 7
NFC 1st-rd. playoffs	Atlanta 27, New Orleans 20
	Dallas 17, Chicago 13
NFC div playoffs	Washington 24, Atlanta 7
	Detroit 38, Dallas 6
NFC championship	Washington 41, Detroit 10

1992

AFC 1st-rd playoffs	San Diego 17, Kansas City 0
	Buffalo 41, Houston 38 (OT)
AFC div playoffs	Buffalo 24, Pittsburgh 3
	Miami 31, San Diego 0
AFC championship	Buffalo 29, Miami 10
NFC 1st -rd playoffs	Washington 24, Minnesota 7
	Philadelphia 36, New Orleans 20
NFC div playoffs	San Francisco 20, Washington 13
	Dallas 34, Philadelphia 10
NFC championship	Dallas 30, San Francisco 20

1993

AFC 1st-rd playoffs	LA Raiders 42, Denver 24
	Kansas City 27. Pittsburgh 24 (OT)
AFC div playoffs	Buffalo 29, LA Raiders 23
	Kansas City 28, Houston 20
AFC championship	Buffalo 30, Kansas City 13
NFC 1st -rd playoffs	NY Giants 17, Minnesota 10
	Green Bay 28, Detroit 24
NFC div playoffs	San Francisco 44, NY Giants 3
	Dallas 27, Green Bay 17
NFC championship	Dallas 38, San Francisco 21

Career Leaders

Scoring

	Yrs	TD	FG	PAT	Pts
George Blanda	26	9	335	943	2002
Jan Stenerud	19	0	373	580	1699
Nick Lowery	15	0	329	486	1473
Pat Leahy	18	0	304	558	1470
Jim Turner	16	1	304	521	1439
Mark Moseley	16	0	300	482	1382
Jim Bakken	17	0	282	534	1380
Fred Cox	15	0	282	519	1365
Lou Groza	17	1	234	641	1349
Eddie Murray	16	0	277	432	1263
Jim Breech	14	0	243	517	1246
Gary Anderson	12	0	285	384	1239
Chris Bahr	14	0	241	490	1213
Matt Bahr	16	0	250	459	1209
Morten Andersen	12	0	274	380	1202
Gino Cappelletti	11	42	176	350	1130
Ray Wersching	15	0	222	456	1122
Norm Johnson	12	0	222	444	1110
Don Cockroft	13	0	216	432	1080
Garo Yepremian	14	0	210	444	1074

Cappelletti's total includes four two-point conversions.

Rushing

	Yrs	Att	Yds	Avg	Lg	TD
Walter Payton	13	3,838	16,726	4.4	76	110
Eric Dickerson	13	2,996	13,259	4.4	85	90
Tony Dorsett	12	2,936	12,739	4.3	99	77
Jim Brown	9	2,359	12,312	5.2	80	106
Franco Harris	13	2,949	12,120	4.1	75	91
John Riggins	14	2,916	11,352	3.9	66	104
O. J. Simpson	11	2,404	11,236	4.7	94	61
Ottis Anderson	16	2,562	10,273	4.0	76	81
Earl Campbell	8	2,187	9,407	4.3	81	74
Marcus Allen	12	2,296	9,309	4.1	61	91
Jim Taylor	10	1,941	8,597	4.4	84	83
Joe Perry	14	1,737	8,378	4.8	78	53
Roger Craig	11	1,991	8,189	4.1	71	56
Gerald Riggs	10	1,989	8,188	4.2	58	69
Larry Csonka	11	1,891	8,081	4.3	54	64
Freeman McNeil	12	1,798	8,074	4.5	69	38
James Brooks	12	1,685	7,962	4.7	65	49
Thurman Thomas	6	1,731	7,631	4.4	80	41
Herschel Walker	10	1,794	7,468	4.2	84	54
Mike Pruitt	11	1,844	7,378	4.0	77	51

Touchdowns

	Yrs	Rush	Pass Rec	Ret	Total TD
Jim Brown	9	106	20	0	126
Walter Payton	13	110	15	0	125
Jerry Rice	9	6	118	0	124
John Riggins	14	104	12	0	116
Marcus Allen	10	91	21	1	113
Lenny Moore	12	63	48	2	113
Don Hutson	11	3	99	3	105
Steve Largent	14	1	100	0	101
Franco Harris	13	91	9	0	100
Eric Dickerson	13	90	6	0	96

	Yrs	Rush	Pass Rec	Ret	Total TD
Jim Taylor	10	83	10	0	93
Tony Dorsett	12	77	13	1	91
Bobby Mitchell	11	18	65	8	91
Leroy Kelly	10	74	13	3	90
Charley Taylor	13	11	79	0	90
Don Maynard	15	0	88	0	88
Lance Alworth	11	2	85	0	87
Paul Warfield	13	1	85	0	86
Ottis Anderson	13	81	5	0	86
Tommy McDonald	12	0	84	1	85
Mark Clayton	11	0	85	0	85

Longest Plays

RUSHING

	Opponent	Year	Yds
Tony Dorsett, Dall	Minn	1983	99
Andy Uram, GB	Chi Cards	1939	97
Bob Gage, Pitt	Chi	1949	97
Jim Spitival, Balt	GB	1950	96
Bob Hoernschemeyer, Det	NY Yanks	1950	96

PASSING

	Opponent	Year	Yds
Frank Filchock to Andy Farkas, Washington	Pitt	1939	99
George Izo to Bobby Mitchell, Washington	Cle	1963	99
Karl Sweetan to Pat Studstill, Detroit	Balt	1966	99
Sonny Jurgensen to Gerry Allen, Washington	Chi	1968	99
Jim Plunkett to Cliff Branch, LA Raiders	Wash	1983	99
Ron Jaworski to Mike Quick, Philadelphia	Atl	1985	99

FIELD GOALS

	Opponent	Year	Yds
Tom Dempsey, NO	Det	1970	63
Steve Cox, Cle	Cin	1984	60
Morten Andersen, NO	Chi	1991	60

PUNTS

	Opponent	Year	Yds
Steve O'Neal, NY Jets	Den	1969	98
Joe Lintzenich, Chi	NY Giants	1931	94
Shawn McCarthy, NE	Buff	1991	93
Randall Cunningham, Phi	NY Giants	1989	91

THEY SAID IT

Howie Long, Los Angeles Raider defensive end, on playing against former teammate Marcus Allen, now with Kansas City: "It's kind of like watching your wife cook dinner at somebody else's house."

Career Leaders (Cont.)

Combined Yards Gained

	Yrs	Total	Rush	Rec	Int Ret	Punt Ret	Kickoff Ret	Fum Ret
Walter Payton	13	21,803	16,726	4,538	0	0	539	0
Tony Dorsett	12	16,326	12,739	3,554	0	0	0	33
Jim Brown	9	15,459	12,312	2,499	0	0	648	0
Eric Dickerson	13	15,396	13,259	2,137	0	0	0	15
James Brooks	12	14,644	7,962	3,621	0	565	2,762	0
Franco Harris	13	14,622	12,120	2,287	0	0	233	-18
O.J. Simpson	11	14,368	11,236	2,142	0	0	990	0
James Lofton	16	14,234	246	13,988	0	0	0	27
Bobby Mitchell	11	14,078	2,735	7,954	0	699	2,690	0
Marcus Allen	12	13,805	9,309	4,496	0	0	0	0
John Riggins	14	13,435	11,352	2,090	0	0	0	-7
Steve Largent	14	13,396	83	13,089	0	68	156	0
Ottis Anderson	14	13,364	10,273	3,062	0	0	0	29
Greg Pruitt	12	13,262	5,672	3,069	0	2,007	2,514	0
Roger Craig	11	13,100	8,189	4,911	0	0	0	0
Ollie Matson	14	12,884	5,173	3,285	51	595	3,746	34
Tim Brown	10	12,684	3,862	3,399	0	639	4,781	3
Lenny Moore	12	12,451	5,174	6,039	0	56	1,180	2
Don Maynard	15	12,379	70	11,834	0	132	343	0
Charlie Joiner	18	12,367	22	12,146	0	0	194	5

Passing

	Yrs	Att	Comp	Pct Comp	Yds	Avg Gain	TD	Pct TD	Int	Pct Int	Rating Pts
Joe Montana	14	4,898	3,110	63.5	37,268	7.61	257	5.3	130	2.7	93.1
Steve Young	9	1,968	1,222	62.1	15,900	8.08	105	5.3	58	3.0	92.7
Dan Marino	11	5,434	3,219	59.2	40,720	7.49	298	5.5	168	3.1	88.1
Jim Kelly	8	3,494	2,112	60.5	26,413	7.56	179	5.1	126	3.6	86.0
Roger Staubach	11	2,958	1,685	57.0	22,700	7.67	153	5.2	109	3.7	83.4
Neil Lomax	8	3,153	1,817	57.6	22,771	7.22	136	4.3	90	2.9	82.7
Sonny Jurgensen	18	4,262	2,433	57.1	32,224	7.56	255	6.0	189	4.4	82.6
Len Dawson	19	3,741	2,136	57.1	28,711	7.67	239	6.4	183	4.9	82.6
Boomer Esiason	10	3,851	2,185	56.7	29,092	7.55	190	4.9	140	3.6	82.1
Dave Krieg	14	4,178	2,431	58.2	30,485	7.30	217	5.2	163	3.9	82.1
Bernie Kosar	9	3,213	1,889	58.8	22,314	6.95	119	3.7	81	2.5	82.0
Ken Anderson	16	4,475	2,654	59.3	32,838	7.34	197	4.4	160	3.6	81.9
Danny White	13	2,950	1,761	59.7	21,959	7.44	155	5.3	132	4.5	81.7
Troy Aikman	5	1,920	1,191	62.0	13,627	7.10	69	3.6	66	3.4	81.2
Ken O'Brien	10	3,602	2,110	58.6	25,094	6.97	128	3.6	98	2.7	80.7
Bart Starr	16	3,149	1,808	57.4	24,718	7.85	152	4.8	138	4.4	80.5
Fran Tarkenton	18	6,467	3,686	57.0	47,003	7.27	342	5.3	266	4.1	80.4
Mark Rypien	6	2,207	1,244	56.4	15,928	7.22	101	4.6	75	3.4	80.3
Randall Cunningham	9	2,751	1,540	56.0	19,043	6.92	131	4.8	87	3.2	80.3
Dan Fouts	15	5,604	3,297	58.8	43,040	7.68	254	4.5	242	4.3	80.2

1,500 or more attempts. The passing ratings are based on performance standards established for completion percentage, interception percentage, touchdown percentage, and average gain. Passers are allocated points according to how their marks compare with those standards.

Receiving

	Yrs	No.	Yds	Avg	Lg	TD		Yrs	No.	Yds	Avg	Lg	TD
Art Monk	14	888	12,026	13.5	79	65	Gary Clark	9	612	9,560	15.6	84	62
Steve Largent	14	819	13,089	16.0	74	100	Henry Ellard	11	593	9,761	16.5	81	48
Charlie Joiner	18	750	12,146	16.2	87	65	Harold Carmichael	14	590	8,985	15.2	85	79
James Lofton	16	763	13,988	18.3	80	75	Fred Biletnikoff	14	589	8,974	15.2	82	76
Jerry Rice	9	708	11,776	16.6	96	118	Andre Reed	9	586	8,233	16.0	78	58
Ozzie Newsome	13	662	7,980	12.1	74	47	Mark Clayton	11	582	8,974	15.4	78	84
Charley Taylor	13	649	9,110	14.0	88	79	Harold Jackson	16	579	10,372	17.9	79	76
Drew Hill	14	634	9,831	15.5	81	60	Lionel Taylor	10	567	7,195	12.7	80	45
Don Maynard	15	633	11,834	18.7	87	88	Roger Craig	11	566	4,911	8.7	73	17
Raymond Berry	13	631	9,275	14.7	70	68	Wes Chandler	11	559	8,966	16.0	85	56

Career Leaders *(Cont.)*

Interceptions

	Yrs	No.	Yds	Avg	Lg	TD
Paul Krause	16	81	1185	14.6	81	3
Emlen Tunnell	14	79	1282	16.2	55	4
Dick (Night Train) Lane	14	68	1207	17.8	80	5
Ken Riley	15	65	596	9.2	66	5
Ronnie Lott	13	63	730	11.3	83	5

Punt Returns

	Yrs	No.	Yds	Avg	Lg	TD
George McAfee	8	112	1431	12.8	74	2
Jack Christiansen	8	85	1084	12.8	89	8
Claude Gibson	5	110	1381	12.6	85	3
Bill Dudley	9	124	1515	12.2	96	3
Rick Upchurch	9	248	3008	12.1	92	8

Punting

	Yrs	No.	Yds	Avg	Lg	Blk
Sammy Baugh	16	338	15,245	45.1	85	9
Tommy Davis	11	511	22,833	44.7	82	2
Yale Lary	11	503	22,279	44.3	74	4
Rohn Stark	12	912	40,060	43.9	72	6
Horace Gillom	7	385	16,872	43.8	80	5

Kickoff Returns

	Yrs	No.	Yds	Avg	Lg	TD
Gale Sayers	7	91	2781	30.6	103	6
Lynn Chandnois	7	92	2720	29.6	93	3
Abe Woodson	9	193	5538	28.7	105	5
Claude (Buddy) Young	6	90	2514	27.9	104	2
Travis Williams	5	102	2801	27.5	105	6

Single-Season Leaders

Scoring

POINTS

	Year	TD	PAT	FG	Pts
Paul Hornung, GB	1960	15	41	15	176
Mark Moseley, Wash.	1983	0	62	33	161
Gino Cappelletti, Bos.	1964	7	38	25	155
Chip Lohmiller, Wash.	1991	0	56	31	149
Gino Cappelletti, Bos.	1961	8	48	17	147
Paul Hornung, GB	1961	10	41	15	146
Jim Turner, NY Jets	1968	0	43	34	145
John Riggins, Wash.	1983	24	0	0	144
Kevin Butler, Chi	1985	0	51	31	144
Tony Franklin, NE	1986	0	44	32	140

Note: Cappelletti's 1964 total includes a two-point conversion.

TOUCHDOWNS

	Year	Rush	Rec	Ret	Total
John Riggins, Wash.	1983	24	0	0	24
O. J. Simpson, Buff	1975	16	7	0	23
Jerry Rice, SF	1987	1	22	0	23
Gale Sayers, Chi	1965	14	6	2	22

FIELD GOALS

	Year	Att	No.
Jeff Jaeger, LA Raiders	1993	44	35
Ali Haji-Sheikh, NY Giants	1983	42	35
Jim Turner, NY Jets	1968	46	34
Jason Hanson, Det	1993	43	34
Two tied with 33			

Rushing

YARDS GAINED

	Year	Att	Yds	Avg
Eric Dickerson, LA Rams	1984	379	2105	5.6
O. J. Simpson, Buff	1973	332	2003	6.0
Earl Campbell, Hou	1980	373	1934	5.2
Jim Brown, Clev	1963	291	1883	6.4
Walter Payton, Chi	1977	339	1852	5.5
Eric Dickerson, LA Rams	1986	404	1821	4.5
O. J. Simpson, Buff	1975	329	1817	5.5
Eric Dickerson, LA Rams	1983	390	1808	4.6
Marcus Allen, LA Raiders	1985	380	1759	4.6
Gerald Riggs, Atl	1985	397	1719	4.3
Emmitt Smith, Dall	1992	373	1713	4.6

AVERAGE GAIN

	Year	Avg
Beattie Feathers, Chi	1934	8.44
Randall Cunningham, Phil	1990	7.98
Bobby Douglass, Chi	1972	6.87

TOUCHDOWNS

	Year	No.
John Riggins, Wash	1983	24
Joe Morris, NY Giants	1985	21
Jim Taylor, GB	1962	19
Earl Campbell, Hou	1979	19
Chuck Muncie, SD	1981	19
Emmitt Smith, Dall	1992	18

Parsing Parcells

This year's Casey Stengel Memorial Award goes to New England coach Bill Parcells. After the Patriots lost to the Houston Oilers on October 17, Parcells mused: "Concentration-wise, we're having trouble crossing the line mentally from a toughness standpoint." Parcells got a head start on winning the award in training camp when he said, "I'm not a bus-station kind of guy, but there are a few players I'm not sure want to be here. They've got a brook-trout kind of look." Articulation-wise, coach Parcells has trouble crossing the line verbally from a phraseology standpoint. His listeners have a woozy kind of look.

Single-Season Leaders (Cont.)
Passing

YARDS GAINED

	Year	Att	Comp	Pct	Yds
Dan Marino, Mia	1984	564	362	64.2	5084
Dan Fouts, SD	1981	609	360	59.1	4802
Dan Marino, Mia	1986	623	378	60.7	4746
Dan Fouts, SD	1980	589	348	59.1	4715
Warren Moon, Hou	1991	655	404	61.7	4690
Warren Moon, Hou	1990	584	362	62.0	4689
Neil Lomax, StL	1984	560	345	61.6	4614
Lynn Dickey, GB	1983	484	289	59.7	4458
Dan Marino, Mia	1988	606	354	58.4	4434
Bill Kenney, KC	1983	603	346	57.4	4348
Don Majkowski, GB	1989	599	353	58.9	4318
Jim Everett, LA Rams	1989	518	304	58.7	4310

PASS RATING

	Year	Rat.
Joe Montana, SF	1989	112.4
Milt Plum, Clev	1960	110.4
Sammy Baugh, Wash	1945	109.9
Dan Marino, Mia	1984	108.9
Steve Young, SF	1992	107.0

TOUCHDOWNS

	Year	No.
Dan Marino, Mia	1984	48
Dan Marino, Mia	1986	44
George Blanda, Hou	1961	36
Y. A. Tittle, NY Giants	1963	36

Receiving

RECEPTIONS

	Year	No.	Yds
Sterling Sharpe, GB	1993	112	1274
Sterling Sharpe, GB	1992	108	1461
Art Monk, Wash	1984	106	1372
Charley Hennigan, Hou	1964	101	1546
Lionel Taylor, Den	1961	100	1176
Jerry Rice, SF	1990	100	1502
Haywood Jeffires, Hou	1991	100	1181
Todd Christensen, Rai	1986	95	1153
Johnny Morris, Chi	1964	93	1200
Al Toon, NY Jets	1988	93	1067
Michael Irvin, Dall	1991	93	1523
Andre Rison, Atl	1992	93	1121

Three tied with 92 receptions

YARDS GAINED

	Year	Yds
Charley Hennigan, Hou	1961	1746
Lance Alworth, SD	1965	1602
Jerry Rice, SF	1986	1570
Roy Green, StL	1984	1555

TOUCHDOWNS

	Year	No.
Jerry Rice, SF	1987	22
Mark Clayton, Mia	1984	18
Don Hutson, GB	1942	17
Elroy (Crazylegs) Hirsch, LA Rams	1951	17
Bill Groman, Hou	1961	17
Jerry Rice, SF	1989	17

All-Purpose Yards

	Year	Run	Rec	Ret	Total
Lionel James, SD	1985	516	1027	992	2535
Terry Metcalf, StL	1975	816	378	1268	2462
Mack Herron, NE	1974	824	474	1146	2444
Gale Sayers, Chi	1966	1231	447	762	2440
Timmy Brown, Phil	1963	841	487	1100	2428
Tim Brown, Rai	1988	50	725	1542	2317
Marcus Allen, Rai	1985	1759	555	−6	2308
Timmy Brown, Phil	1962	545	849	912	2306
Gale Sayers, Chi	1965	867	507	898	2272
Eric Dickerson, LA Rams	1984	2105	139	15	2259
O. J. Simpson, Buff	1975	1817	426	0	2243

Punting

	Year	No.	Yds	Avg
Sammy Baugh, Wash	1940	35	1799	51.4
Yale Lary, Det	1963	35	1713	48.9
Sammy Baugh, Wash	1941	30	1462	48.7
Yale Lary, Det	1961	52	2516	48.4
Sammy Baugh, Wash	1942	37	1783	48.2

Sacks

	Year	No.
Mark Gastineau, NY Jets	1984	22
Reggie White, Phil	1987	21
Chris Doleman, Minn	1989	21
Lawrence Taylor, NY Giants	1986	20.5

Interceptions

	Year	No.
Dick (Night Train) Lane, LA Rams	1952	14
Dan Sandifer, Wash	1948	13
Spec Sanders, NY Yanks	1950	13
Lester Hayes, Oak	1980	13

Kickoff Returns

	Year	Avg
Travis Williams, GB	1967	41.1
Gale Sayers, Chi	1967	37.7
Ollie Matson, Chi Cardinals	1958	35.5
Jim Duncan, Balt	1970	35.4
Lynn Chandnois, Pitt	1952	35.2

Punt Returns

	Year	Avg
Herb Rich, Balt	1950	23.0
Jack Christiansen, Det	1952	21.5
Dick Christy, NY Titans	1961	21.3
Bob Hayes, Dall	1968	20.8

Single-Game Leaders
Scoring

POINTS

	Date	Pts
Ernie Nevers, Cards vs Bears	11-28-29	40
Dub Jones, Clev vs Chi Bears	11-25-51	36
Gale Sayers, Chi Bears vs SF	12-12-65	36
Paul Hornung, GB vs Balt	10-8-61	33

On Thanksgiving Day, 1929, Nevers scored all the Cardinals' points on six rushing TDs and four PATs. The Cards defeated Red Grange and the Bears, 40-6. Jones and Sayers each rushed for four touchdowns and scored two more on returns in their teams' victories. Hornung scored four touchdowns and kicked 6 PATs and a field goal in a 45-7 win over the Colts.

FIELD GOALS

	Date	No.
Jim Bakken, StL vs Pitt	9-24-67	7
Rich Karlis, Minn vs LA Rams	11-5-89	7

Eight players tied with 6 FGs each.

Bakken was 7 for 9, Karlis 7 for 7.

TOUCHDOWNS

	Date	No.
Ernie Nevers, Cards vs Bears	11-28-29	6
Dub Jones, Clev vs Chi Bears	11-25-51	6
Gale Sayers, Chi vs SF	12-12-65	6
Bob Shaw, Chi Cards vs Balt	10-2-50	5
Jim Brown, Clev vs Balt	11-1-59	5
Abner Haynes, Dall Texans vs Oak	11-26-61	5
Billy Cannon, Hous vs NY Titans	12-10-61	5
Cookie Gilchrist, Buff vs NY Jets	12-8-63	5
Paul Hornung, GB vs Balt	12-12-65	5
Kellen Winslow, SD vs Oak	11-22-81	5
Jerry Rice, SF vs Atl	10-14-90	5

Rushing

YARDS GAINED

	Date	Yds
Walter Payton, Chi vs Minn	11-20-77	275
O. J. Simpson, Buff vs Det	11-25-76	273
O. J. Simpson, Buff vs NE	9-16-73	250
Willie Ellison, LA Rams vs NO	12-5-71	247
Cookie Gilchrist, Buff vs NY Jets	12-8-63	243

CARRIES

	Date	No.
Jamie Morris, Wash vs Cin	12-17-88	45
Butch Woolfolk, NY Giants vs Phil	11-20-83	43
James Wilder, TB vs GB	9-30-84	43
James Wilder, TB vs Pitt	10-30-83	42
Franco Harris, Pitt vs Cin	10-17-76	41
Gerald Riggs, Atl vs LA Rams	11-17-85	41

TOUCHDOWNS

	Date	No.
Ernie Nevers, Cards vs Bears	11-28-29	6
Jim Brown, Clev vs Balt	11-1-59	5
Cookie Gilchrist, Buff vs NY Jets	12-8-63	5

Passing

YARDS GAINED

	Date	Yds
Norm Van Brocklin, LA vs NY Yanks	9-28-51	554
Warren Moon, Hou vs KC	12-16-90	527
Dan Marino, Mia vs NY Jets	10-23-88	521
Phil Simms, NY Giants vs Cin	10-13-85	513
Vince Ferragamo, LA Rams vs Chi	12-26-82	509
Y. A. Tittle, NY Giants vs Wash	10-28-62	505

COMPLETIONS

	Date	No.
Richard Todd, NY Jets vs SF	9-21-80	42
Warren Moon, Hou vs Dall	11-10-91	41
Ken Anderson, Cin vs SD	12-20-82	40
Phil Simms, NY Giants vs Cin	10-13-85	40
Dan Marino, Mia vs Buff	11-16-86	39
Tommy Kramer, Minn vs Clev	12-14-80	38
Tommy Kramer, Minn vs GB	11-29-81	38
Joe Ferguson, Buff vs Mia	10-9-83	38

TOUCHDOWNS

	Date	No.
Sid Luckman, Chi Bears vs NY Giants	11-14-43	7
Adrian Burk, Phil vs Wash	10-17-54	7
George Blanda, Hou vs NY Titans	11-19-61	7
Y. A. Tittle, NY Giants vs Wash	10-28-62	7
Joe Kapp, Minn vs Balt	9-28-69	7

THEY SAID IT

Art Modell, owner of the Cleveland Browns, on the NFL's inability to reach a consensus on proposed rule changes: "The U.S. Congress can declare war with a simple majority, but we need a three-fourths majority to go to the john."

Single-Game Leaders *(Cont.)*
Receiving

YARDS GAINED

	Date	Yds
Flipper Anderson, LA Rams vs NO	11-26-89	336
Stephone Paige, KC vs SD	12-22-85	309
Jim Benton, Clev vs Det	11-22-45	303
Cloyce Box, Det vs Balt	12-3-50	302
John Taylor, SF vs LA Rams	12-11-89	286

RECEPTIONS

	Date	No.
Tom Fears, LA Rams vs GB	12-3-50	18
Clark Gaines, NY Jets vs SF	9-21-80	17
Sonny Randle, StL vs NY Giants	11-4-62	16
Rickey Young, Minn vs NE	12-16-79	15
William Andrews, Atl vs Pitt	11-15-81	15

TOUCHDOWNS

	Date	No.
Bob Shaw, Chi Cards vs Balt	10-2-50	5
Kellen Winslow, SD vs Oak	11-22-81	5
Jerry Rice, SF vs Atl	10-14-90	5

All-Purpose Yards

	Date	Yds
Billy Cannon, Hou vs NY Titans	12-10-61	373
Lionel James, SD vs LA Raiders	11-10-85	345
Timmy Brown, Phil vs StL	12-16-62	341
Gale Sayers, Chi vs Minn	12-18-66	339
Gale Sayers, Chi vs SF	12-12-65	336

Rushing

Year	Player, Team	Att.	Yards	Avg.	TD
1932	Cliff Battles, Bos	148	576	3.9	3
1933	Jim Musick, Bos	173	809	4.7	5
1934	Beattie Feathers, Chicago Bears	101	1004	9.9	8
1935	Doug Russell, Chicago Cards	140	499	3.6	0
1936	Alphonse Leemans, NY	206	830	4.0	2
1937	Cliff Battles, Wash	216	874	4.0	5
1938	Byron White, Pitt	152	567	3.7	4
1939	Bill Osmanski, Chi	121	699	5.8	7
1940	Byron White, Det	146	514	3.5	5
1941	Clarence Manders, Bklyn	111	486	4.4	5
1942	Bill Dudley, Pitt	162	696	4.3	5
1943	Bill Paschal, NY	147	572	3.9	10
1944	Bill Paschal, NY	196	737	3.8	9
1945	Steve Van Buren, Phil	143	832	5.8	15
1946	Bill Dudley, Pitt	146	604	4.1	3
1947	Steve Van Buren, Phil	217	1008	4.6	13
1948	Steve Van Buren, Phil	201	945	4.7	10
1949	Steve Van Buren, Phil	263	1146	4.4	11
1950	Marion Motley, Clev	140	810	5.8	3
1951	Eddie Price, NY	271	971	3.6	7
1952	Dan Towler, LA	156	894	5.7	10
1953	Joe Perry, SF	192	1018	5.3	10
1954	Joe Perry, SF	173	1049	6.1	8
1955	Alan Ameche, Balt	213	961	4.5	9
1956	Rick Casares, Chicago Bears	234	1126	4.8	12
1957	Jim Brown, Clev	202	942	4.7	9
1958	Jim Brown, Clev	257	1527	5.9	17
1959	Jim Brown, Clev	290	1329	4.6	14
1960	Jim Brown, Clev, NFL	215	1257	5.8	9
	Abner Haynes, Dall Texans, AFL	156	875	5.6	9
1961	Jim Brown, Clev, NFL	305	1408	4.6	8
	Billy Cannon, Hou, AFL	200	948	4.7	6
1962	Jim Taylor, GB, NFL	272	1474	5.4	19
	Cookie Gilchrist, Buff, AFL	214	1096	5.1	13
1963	Jim Brown, Clev, NFL	291	1863	6.4	12
	Clem Daniels, Oak, AFL	215	1099	5.1	3
1964	Jim Brown, Clev, NFL	280	1446	5.2	7
	Cookie Gilchrist, Buff, AFL	230	981	4.3	6
1965	Jim Brown, Clev, NFL	289	1544	5.3	17
	Paul Lowe, SD, AFL	222	1121	5.0	7
1966	Jim Nance, Bos, AFL	299	1458	4.9	11
	Gale Sayers, Chi, NFL	229	1231	5.4	8
1967	Jim Nance, Bos, AFL	269	1216	4.5	7
	Leroy Kelly, Clev, NFL	235	1205	5.1	11
1968	Leroy Kelly, Clev, NFL	248	1239	5.0	16
	Paul Robinson, Cinn, AFL	238	1023	4.3	8
1969	Gale Sayers, Chi, NFL	236	1032	4.4	8
	Dickie Post, SD, AFL	182	873	4.8	6
1970	Larry Brown, Wash, NFC	237	1125	4.7	5
	Floyd Little, Den, AFC	209	901	4.3	3
1971	Floyd Little, Den, AFC	284	1133	4.0	6
	John Brockington, GB, NFC	216	1105	5.1	4
1972	O.J. Simpson, Buff, AFC	292	1251	4.3	6
	Larry Brown, Wash, NFC	285	1216	4.3	8
1973	O.J. Simpson, Buff, AFC	332	2003	6.0	12
	John Brockington, GB, NFC	265	1144	4.3	3

Rushing *(Cont.)*

Year	Player, Team	Att.	Yards	Avg.	TD
1974	Otis Armstrong, Den, AFC	263	1407	5.3	9
	Lawrence McCutcheon, LA Rams, NFC	236	1109	4.7	3
1975	O.J. Simpson, Buff, AFC	329	1817	5.5	16
	Jim Otis, StL, NFC	269	1076	4.0	5
1976	O.J. Simpson, Buff, AFC	290	1503	5.2	8
	Walter Payton, Chi, NFC	311	1390	4.5	13
1977	Walter Payton, Chi, NFC	339	1852	5.5	14
	Mark van Eeghen, Oak, AFC	324	1273	3.9	7
1978	Earl Campbell, Hou, AFC	302	1450	4.8	13
	Walter Payton, Chi, NFC	333	1395	4.2	11
1979	Earl Campbell, Hou, AFC	368	1697	4.6	19
	Walter Payton, Chi, NFC	369	1610	4.4	14
1980	Earl Campbell, Hou, AFC	373	1934	5.2	13
	Walter Payton, Chi, NFC	317	1460	4.6	6
1981	George Rogers, NO, NFC	378	1674	4.4	13
	Earl Campbell, Hou, AFC	361	1376	3.8	10
1982	Freeman McNeil, NY Jets, AFC	151	786	5.2	6
	Tony Dorsett, Dall, NFC	177	745	4.2	5
1983	Eric Dickerson, LA Rams, NFC	390	1808	4.6	18
	Curt Warner, Sea, AFC	335	1449	4.3	13
1984	Eric Dickerson, LA Rams, NFC	379	2105	5.6	14
	Earnest Jackson, SD, AFC	296	1179	4.0	8
1985	Marcus Allen, LA Raiders, AFC	380	1759	4.6	11
	Gerald Riggs, Atl, NFC	397	1719	4.3	10
1986	Eric Dickerson, LA Rams, NFC	404	1821	4.5	11
	Curt Warner, Sea, AFC	319	1481	4.6	13
1987	Charles White, LA Rams, NFC	324	1374	4.2	11
	Eric Dickerson, Ind, AFC	223	1011	4.5	5
1988	Eric Dickerson, Ind, AFC	388	1659	4.3	14
	Herschel Walker, Dall, NFC	361	1514	4.2	5
1989	Christian Okoye, KC, AFC	370	1480	4.0	12
	Barry Sanders, Det, NFC	280	1470	5.3	14
1990	Barry Sanders, Det, NFC	255	1304	5.1	13
	Thurman Thomas, Buff, AFC	271	1297	4.8	11
1991	Emmitt Smith, Dall, NFC	365	1563	4.3	12
	Thurman Thomas, Buff, AFC	288	1407	4.9	7
1992	Emmitt Smith, Dall, NFC	373	1713	4.6	18
	Barry Foster, Pitt, AFC	390	1690	4.3	11
1993	Emmitt Smith, Dall, NFC	283	1486	5.3	9
	Thurman Thomas, Buff, AFC	355	1315	3.7	6

Passing

Year	Player, Team	Att.	Comp	Yards	TD	Int
1932	Arnie Herber, GB	101	37	639	9	9
1933	Harry Newman, NY	136	53	973	11	17
1934	Arnie Herber, GB	115	42	799	8	12
1935	Ed Danowski, NY	113	57	794	10	9
1936	Arnie Herber, GB	173	77	1239	11	13
1937	Sammy Baugh, Wash	171	81	1127	8	14
1938	Ed Danowski, NY	129	70	848	7	8
1939	Parker Hall, Clev	208	106	1227	9	13
1940	Sammy Baugh, Wash	177	111	1367	12	10
1941	Cecil Isbell, GB	206	117	1479	15	11
1942	Cecil Isbell, GB	268	146	2021	24	14
1943	Sammy Baugh, Wash	239	133	1754	23	19
1944	Frank Filchock, Wash	147	84	1139	13	9
1945	Sammy Baugh, Wash	182	128	1669	11	4
	Sid Luckman, Chi	217	117	1725	14	10
1946	Bob Waterfield, LA	251	127	1747	18	17
1947	Sammy Baugh, Wash	354	210	2938	25	15
1948	Tommy Thompson, Phi	246	141	1965	25	11
1949	Sammy Baugh, Wash	255	145	1903	18	14
1950	Norm Van Brocklin, LA	233	127	2061	18	14
1951	Bob Waterfield, LA	176	88	1566	13	10
1952	Norm Van Brocklin, LA	205	113	1736	14	17
1953	Otto Graham, Clev	258	167	2722	11	9
1954	Norm Van Brocklin, LA	260	139	2637	13	21
1955	Otto Graham, Clev	185	98	1721	15	8
1956	Ed Brown, Chi	168	96	1667	11	12
1957	Tommy O'Connell, Clev.	110	63	1229	9	8
1958	Eddie LeBaron, Wash	145	79	1365	11	10
1959	Charlie Conerly, NY	194	113	1706	14	4
1960	Milt Plum, Clev, NFL	250	151	2297	21	5
	Jack Kemp, LA, AFL	406	211	3018	20	25
1961	George Blanda, Hou, AFL	362	187	3330	36	22
	Milt Plum, Clev, NFL	302	177	2416	18	10
1962	Len Dawson, Dall, AFL	310	189	2759	29	17
	Bart Starr, GB, NFL	285	178	2438	12	9
1963	Y.A. Tittle, NY, NFL	367	221	3145	36	14
	Tobin Rote, SD, AFL	286	170	2510	20	17
1964	Len Dawson, KC, AFL	354	199	2879	30	18
	Bart Starr, GB, NFL	272	163	2144	15	4
1965	Rudy Bukich, Chi, NFL	312	176	2641	20	9
	John Hadl, SD, AFL	348	174	2798	20	21
1966	Bart Starr, GB, NFL	251	156	2257	14	3
	Len Dawson, KC, AFL	284	159	2527	26	10
1967	Sonny Jurgensen, Wash, NFL	508	288	3747	31	16
	Daryle Lamonica, Oakland, AFL	425	220	3228	30	20
1968	Len Dawson, KC, AFL	224	131	2109	17	9
	Earl Morrall, Balt, NFL	317	182	2909	26	17
1969	Sonny Jurgensen, Wash, NFL	442	274	3102	22	15
	Greg Cook, Cin, AFL	197	106	1854	15	11
1970	John Brodie, SF, NFC	378	223	2941	24	10
	Daryle Lamonica, Oak, AFC	356	179	2516	22	15
1971	Roger Staubach, Dall, NFC	211	126	1882	15	4
	Bob Griese, Mia, AFC	263	145	2089	19	9

Passing *(Cont.)*

Year	Player, Team	Att.	Comp	Yards	TD	Int
1972	Norm Snead, NY, NFC	325	196	2307	17	12
	Earl Morrall, Mia, AFC	150	83	1360	11	7
1973	Roger Staubach, Dall, NFC	286	179	2428	23	15
	Ken Stabler, Oak, AFC	260	163	1997	14	10
1974	Ken Anderson, Cin, AFC	328	213	2667	18	10
	Sonny Jurgensen, Wash, NFC	167	107	1185	11	5
1975	Ken Anderson, Cin, AFC	377	228	3169	21	11
	Fran Tarkenton, Minn, NFC	425	273	2994	25	13
1976	Ken Stabler, Oak, AFC	291	194	2737	27	17
	James Harris, LA, NFC	158	91	1460	8	6
1977	Bob Griese, Mia, AFC	307	180	2252	22	13
	Roger Staubach, Dall, NFC	361	210	2620	18	9
1978	Roger Staubach, Dall, NFC	413	231	3190	25	16
	Terry Bradshaw, Pitt, AFC	368	207	2915	28	20
1979	Roger Staubach, Dall, NFC	461	267	3586	27	11
	Dan Fouts, SD, AFC	530	332	4082	24	24
1980	Brian Sipe, Clev, AFC	554	337	4132	30	14
	Ron Jaworski, Phi, NFC	451	257	3529	27	12
1981	Ken Anderson, Cin, AFC	479	300	3754	29	10
	Joe Montana, SF, NFC	488	311	3565	19	12
1982	Ken Anderson, Cin, AFC	309	218	2495	12	9
	Joe Theismann, Wash, NFC	252	161	2033	13	9
1983	Steve Bartkowski, Atl, NFC	432	274	3167	22	5
	Dan Marino, Mia, AFC	296	173	2210	20	6
1984	Dan Marino, Mia, AFC	564	362	5084	48	17
	Joe Montana, SF, NFC	432	279	3630	28	10
1985	Ken O'Brien, NY, AFC	488	297	3888	25	8
	Joe Montana, SF, NFC	494	303	3653	27	13
1986	Tommy Kramer, Minn, NFC	372	208	3000	24	10
	Dan Marino, Mia, AFC	623	378	4746	44	23
1987	Joe Montana, SF, NFC	398	266	3054	31	13
	Bernie Kosar, Clev, AFC	389	241	3033	22	9
1988	Boomer Esiason, Cin, AFC	388	223	3572	28	14
	Wade Wilson, Minn, NFC	332	204	2746	15	9
1989	Joe Montana, SF, NFC	386	271	3521	26	8
	Boomer Esiason, Cin, AFC	455	258	3525	28	11
1990	Jim Kelly, Buffalo, AFC	346	219	2829	24	9
	Phil Simms, NY, NFC	311	184	2284	15	4
1991	Steve Young, SF, NFC	279	180	2517	17	8
	Jim Kelly, Buff, AFC	474	304	3844	33	17
1992	Steve Young, SF, NFC	402	268	3465	25	7
	Warren Moon, Hou, AFC	346	224	2521	18	12
1993	Steve Young, SF, NFC	462	314	4023	29	16
	John Elway, Den, AFC	551	348	4030	25	10

Pass Receiving

Year	Player, Team	No.	Yds	Avg	TD
1932	Ray Flaherty, NY	21	350	16.7	3
1933	John Kelly, Brooklyn	22	246	11.2	3
1934	Joe Carter, Phil	16	238	14.9	4
	Morris Badgro, NY	16	206	12.9	1
1935	Tod Goodwin, NY	26	432	16.6	4
1936	Don Hutson, GB	34	536	15.8	8
1937	Don Hutson, GB	41	552	13.5	7
1938	Gaynell Tinsley, Chi Cards	41	516	12.6	1
1939	Don Hutson, GB	34	846	24.9	6
1940	Don Looney, Phil	58	707	12.2	4
1941	Don Hutson, GB	58	738	12.7	10
1942	Don Hutson, GB	74	1211	16.4	17
1943	Don Hutson, GB	47	776	16.5	11
1944	Don Hutson, GB	58	866	14.9	9
1945	Don Hutson, GB	47	834	17.7	9
1946	Jim Benton, LA	63	981	15.6	6
1947	Jim Keane, Chi	64	910	14.2	10
1948	Tom Fears, LA	51	698	13.7	4
1949	Tom Fears, LA	77	1013	13.2	9
1950	Tom Fears, LA	84	1116	13.3	7
1951	Elroy Hirsch, LA	66	1495	22.7	17
1952	Mac Speedie, Clev	62	911	14.7	5
1953	Pete Pihos, Phil	63	1049	16.7	10
1954	Pete Pihos, Phil	60	872	14.5	10
	Billy Wilson, SF	60	830	13.8	5
1955	Pete Pihos, Phil	62	864	13.9	7
1956	Billy Wilson, SF	60	889	14.8	5
1957	Billy Wilson, SF	52	757	14.6	6
1958	Raymond Berry, Balt	56	794	14.2	9
	Pete Retzlaff, Phil	56	766	13.7	2
1959	Raymond Berry, Balt	66	959	14.5	14
1960	Lionel Taylor, Den, AFL	92	1235	13.4	12
	Raymond Berry, Baltimore, NFL	74	1298	17.5	10
1961	Lionel Taylor, Den, AFL	100	1176	11.8	4
	Jim Phillips, LA, NFL	78	1092	14.0	5
1962	Lionel Taylor, Den, AFL	77	908	11.8	4
	Bobby Mitchell, Wash, NFL	72	1384	19.2	11
1963	Lionel Taylor, Den, AFL	78	1101	14.1	10
	Bobby Joe Conrad, St. Louis, NFL	73	967	13.2	10
1964	Charley Hennigan, Houston, AFL	101	1546	15.3	8
	Johnny Morris, Chi, NFL	93	1200	12.9	10
1965	Lionel Taylor, Den, AFL	85	1131	13.3	6
	Dave Parks, SF, NFL	80	1344	16.8	12
1966	Lance Alworth, SD, AFL	73	1383	18.9	13
	Charley Taylor, Wash, NFL	72	1119	15.5	12
1967	George Sauer, NY, AFL	75	1189	15.9	6
	Charley Taylor, Wash, NFL	70	990	14.1	9

Pass Receiving *(Cont.)*

Year	Player, Team	No.	Yds	Avg	TD	Year	Player, Team	No.	Yds	Avg	TD
1968	Clifton McNeil, SF, NFL	71	994	14.0	7	1980	Kellen Winslow, SD, AFC	89	1290	14.5	9
	Lance Alworth, SD, AFL	68	1312	19.3	10		Earl Cooper, SF, NFC	83	567	6.8	4
1969	Dan Abramowicz, NO, NFL	73	1015	13.9	7	1981	Kellen Winslow, SD, AFC	88	1075	12.2	10
	Lance Alworth, SD, AFL	64	1003	15.7	4		Dwight Clark, SF, NFC	85	1105	13.0	4
1970	Dick Gordon, Chi, NFC	71	1026	14.5	13	1982	Dwight Clark, SF, NFC	60	913	15.2	5
	Marlin Briscoe, Buff, AFC	57	1036	18.2	8		Kellen Winslow, SD, AFC	54	721	13.4	6
1971	Fred Biletnikoff, Oak, AFC	61	929	15.2	9	1983	Todd Christensen, Los Angeles, AFC	92	1247	13.6	12
	Bob Tucker, NY, NFC	59	791	13.4	4		Roy Green, StL, NFC	78	1227	15.7	14
1972	Harold Jackson, Phi, NFC	62	1048	16.9	4		Charlie Brown, Wash, NFC	78	1225	15.7	8
	Fred Biletnikoff, Oak, AFC	58	802	13.8	7		Earnest Gray, NY, NFC	78	1139	14.6	5
1973	Harold Carmichael, Phi, NFC	67	1116	16.7	9	1984	Art Monk, Wash, NFC	106	1372	12.9	7
	Fred Willis, Hou, AFC	57	371	6.5	1		Ozzie Newsome, Clev, AFC	89	1001	11.2	5
1974	Lydell Mitchell, Balt, AFC	72	544	7.6	2	1985	Roger Craig, SF, NFC	92	1016	11.0	6
	Charles Young, Phi, NFC	63	696	11.0	3		Lionel James, SD, AFC	86	1027	11.9	6
1975	Chuck Foreman, Minn, NFC	73	691	9.5	9	1986	Todd Christensen, Los Angeles, AFC	95	1153	12.1	8
	Reggie Rucker, Clev, AFC	60	770	12.8	3		Jerry Rice, SF, NFC	86	1570	18.3	15
	Lydell Mitchell, Balt, AFC	60	544	9.1	4	1987	J.T. Smith, StL, NFC	91	1117	12.3	8
1976	MacArthur Lane, KC, AFC	66	686	10.4	1		Al Toon, NY, AFC	68	976	14.4	5
	Drew Pearson, Dall, NFC	58	806	13.9	6	1988	Al Toon, NY, AFC	93	1067	11.5	5
1977	Lydell Mitchell, Balt, AFC	71	620	8.7	4		Henry Ellard, LA Rams, NFC	86	1414	16.4	10
	Ahmad Rashad, Minn, NFC	51	681	13.4	2	1989	Sterling Sharpe, GB, NFC	90	1423	15.8	12
1978	Rickey Young, Minn, NFC	88	704	8.0	5		Andre Reed, Buff, AFC	88	1312	14.9	9
	Steve Largent, Sea, AFC	71	1168	16.5	8	1990	Jerry Rice, SF, NFC	100	1502	15.0	13
1979	Joe Washington, Balt, AFC	82	750	9.1	3		Haywood Jeffires, Houston, AFC	74	1048	14.2	8
	Ahmad Rashad, Minn, NFC	80	1156	14.5	9		Drew Hill, Hou, AFC	74	1019	13.8	5
						1991	Haywood Jeffires, Hou, AFC	100	1181	11.8	7
							Michael Irvin, Dall, NFC	93	1523	16.4	8
						1992	Sterling Sharpe, NFC	108	1461	13.5	13
							Haywood Jeffires, AFC	90	913	10.1	9
						1993	Sterling Sharpe, NFC	112	1274	11.4	11
							Reggie Langhorne, AFC	85	1038	12.2	3

Scoring

Year	Player, Team	TD	FG	PAT	TP	Year	Player, Team	TD	FG	PAT	TP
1932	Earl Clark, Portsmouth	6	3	10	55	1955	Doak Walker, Det	7	9	27	96
1933	Ken Strong, NY	6	5	13	64	1956	Bobby Layne, Det	5	12	33	99
	Glenn Presnell, Ports	6	6	10	64	1957	Sam Baker, Wash	1	14	29	77
1934	Jack Manders, Chi	3	10	31	79		Lou Groza, Clev	0	15	32	77
1935	Earl Clark, Det	6	1	16	55	1958	Jim Brown, Clev	18	0	0	108
1936	Earl Clark, Det	7	4	19	73	1959	Paul Hornung, GB	7	7	31	94
1937	Jack Manders, Chi	5	18	15	69	1960	Paul Hornung, GB, NFL	15	15	41	176
1938	Clarke Hinkle, GB	7	3	7	58		Gene Mingo, Den, AFL	6	18	33	123
1939	Andy Farkas, Wash	11	0	2	68	1961	Gino Cappelletti, Bos, AFL	8	17	48	147
1940	Don Hutson, GB	7	0	15	57		Paul Hornung, GB, NFL	10	15	41	146
1941	Don Hutson, GB	12	1	20	95	1962	Gene Mingo, Den, AFL	4	27	32	137
1942	Don Hutson, GB	17	1	33	138		Jim Taylor, GB, NFL	19	0	0	114
1943	Don Hutson, GB	12	3	36	117	1963	Gino Cappelletti, Bos, AFL	2	22	35	113
1944	Don Hutson, GB	9	0	31	85		Don Chandler, NY, NFL	0	18	52	106
1945	Steve Van Buren, Phil	18	0	2	110	1964	Gino Cappelletti, Bos, AFL	7	25	36	155
1946	Ted Fritsch, GB	10	9	13	100		Lenny Moore, Balt, NFL	20	0	0	120
1947	Pat Harder, Chicago Cards	7	7	39	102	1965	Gale Sayers, Chi, NFL	22	0	0	132
1948	Pat Harder, Chicago Cards	6	7	53	110		Gino Cappelletti, Bos, AFL	9	17	27	132
1949	Pat Harder, Chicago Cards	8	3	45	102	1966	Gino Cappelletti, Bos, AFL	6	16	35	119
	Gene Roberts, NY	17	0	0	102		Bruce Gossett, LA, NFL	0	28	29	113
1950	Doak Walker, Det	11	8	38	128	1967	Jim Bakken, StL, NFL	0	27	36	117
1951	Elroy Hirsch, LA	17	0	0	102		George Blanda, Oak, AFL	0	20	56	116
1952	Gordy Soltau, SF	7	6	34	94	1968	Jim Turner, NY, AFL	0	34	43	145
1953	Gordy Soltau, SF	6	10	48	114		Leroy Kelly, Clev, NFL	20	0	0	120
1954	Bobby Walston, Phil	11	4	36	114						

Scoring (Cont.)

Year	Player, Team	TD	FG	PAT	TP
1969	Jim Turner, NY, AFL	0	32	33	129
	Fred Cox, Minn, NFL	0	26	43	121
1970	Fred Cox, Minn, NFC	0	30	35	125
	Jan Stenerud, KC, AFC	0	30	26	116
1971	Garo Yepremian, Mia, AFC	0	28	33	117
	Curt Knight, Wash, NFC	0	29	27	114
1972	Chester Marcol, GB, NFC	0	33	29	128
	Bobby Howfield, NY, AFC	0	27	40	121
1973	David Ray, LA, NFC	0	30	40	130
	Roy Gerela, Pitt, AFC	0	29	36	123
1974	Chester Marcol, GB, NFC	0	25	19	94
	Roy Gerela, Pitt, AFC	0	20	33	93
1975	O.J. Simpson, Buff, AFC	23	0	0	138
	Chuck Foreman, Minn, NFC	22	0	0	132
1976	Toni Linhart, Balt, AFC	0	20	49	109
	Mark Moseley, Wash, NFC	0	22	31	97
1977	Errol Mann, Oak, AFC	0	20	39	99
	Walter Payton, Chi, NFC	16	0	0	96
1978	Frank Corral, LA, NFC	0	29	31	118
	Pat Leahy, NY, AFC	0	22	41	107
1979	John Smith, NE, AFC	0	23	46	115
	Mark Moseley, Wash, NFC	0	25	39	114
1980	John Smith, NE, AFC	0	26	51	129
	Ed Murray, Det, NFC	0	27	35	116
1981	Ed Murray, Det, NFC	0	25	46	121
	Rafael Septien, Dall, NFC	0	27	40	121
	Jim Breech, Cin, AFC	0	22	49	115
	Nick Lowery, KC, AFC	0	26	37	115

Year	Player, Team	TD	FG	PAT	TP
1982	Marcus Allen, LA, AFC	14	0	0	84
	Wendell Tyler, LA, NFC	13	0	0	78
1983	Mark Moseley, Wash, NFC	0	33	62	161
	Gary Anderson, Pitt, AFC	0	27	38	119
1984	Ray Wersching, SF, NFC	0	25	56	131
	Gary Anderson, Pitt, AFC	0	24	45	117
1985	Kevin Butler, Chi, NFC	0	31	51	144
	Gary Anderson, Pitt, AFC	0	33	40	139
1986	Tony Franklin, NE, AFC	0	32	44	140
	Kevin Butler, Chi, NFC	0	28	36	120
1987	Jerry Rice, SF, NFC	23	0	0	138
	Jim Breech, Cin, AFC	0	24	25	97
1988	Scott Norwood, Buff, AFC	0	32	33	129
	Mike Cofer, SF, NFC	0	27	40	121
1989	Mike Cofer, SF, NFC	0	29	49	136
	David Treadwell, Den, AFC	0	27	39	120
1990	Nick Lowery, KC, AFC	0	34	37	139
	Chip Lohmiller, Wash, NFC	0	30	41	131
1991	Chip Lohmiller, Wash, NFC	0	31	56	149
	Pete Stoyanovich, Mia, AFC	0	31	28	121
1992	Pete Stoyanovich, Mia, AFC	0	30	34	124
	Morten Anderson, NO, NFC	0	29	33	120
	Chip Lohmiller, Wash, NFC	0	30	30	120
1993	Jeff Jaeger, Rai, AFC	0	35	27	132
	Jason Hanson, Det, NFC	0	34	28	130

Pro Bowl Alltime Results

Date	Result
1-15-39	NY Giants 13, Pro All-Stars 10
1-14-40	Green Bay 16, NFL All-Stars 7
12-29-40	Chi Bears 28, NFL All-Stars 14
1-4-42	Chi Bears 35, NFL All-Stars 24
12-27-42	NFL All-Stars 17, Washington 14
1-14-51	A Conf 28, N Conf 27
1-12-52	N Conf 30, A Conf 13
1-10-53	N Conf 27, A Conf 7
1-17-54	East 20, West 9
1-16-55	West 26, East 19
1-15-56	East 31, West 30
1-13-57	West 19, East 10
1-12-58	West 26, East 7
1-11-59	East 28, West 21
1-17-60	West 38, East 21
1-15-61	West 35, East 31

Date	Result
1-7-62	AFL West 47, East 27
1-14-62	NFL West 31, East 30
1-13-63	AFL West 21, East 14
1-13-63	NFL East 30, West 20
1-12-64	NFL West 31, East 17
1-19-64	AFL West 27, East 24
1-10-65	NFL West 34, East 14
1-16-65	AFL West 38, East 14
1-15-66	AFL All-Stars 30, Buffalo 19
1-15-66	NFL East 36, West 7
1-21-67	AFL East 30, West 23
1-22-67	NFL East 20, West 10
1-21-68	AFL East 25, West 24
1-21-68	NFL West 38, East 20
1-19-69	AFL West 38, East 25
1-19-69	NFL West 10, East 7
1-17-70	AFL West 26, East 3
1-18-70	NFL West 16, East 13
1-24-71	NFC 27, AFC 6
1-23-72	AFC 26, NFC 13
1-21-73	AFC 33, NFC 28

Date	Result
1-20-74	AFC 15, NFC 13
1-20-75	NFC 17, AFC 10
1-26-76	NFC 23, AFC 20
1-17-77	AFC 24, NFC 14
1-23-78	NFC 14, AFC 13
1-29-79	NFC 13, AFC 7
1-27-80	NFC 37, AFC 27
2-1-81	NFC 21, AFC 7
1-31-82	AFC 16, NFC 13
2-6-83	NFC 20, AFC 19
1-29-84	NFC 45, AFC 3
1-27-85	AFC 22, NFC 14
2-2-86	NFC 28, AFC 24
2-1-87	AFC 10, NFC 6
2-7-88	AFC 15, NFC 6
1-29-89	NFC 34, AFC 3
2-4-90	NFC 27, AFC 21
2-3-91	AFC 23, NFC 21
2-2-92	NFC 21, AFC 15
2-7-93	AFC 23, NFC 20
2-6-94	NFC 17, AFC 3

Chicago All-Star Game Results

Date	Result (Attendance)
8-31-34	Chi Bears 0, All-Stars 0 (79,432)
8-29-35	Chi Bears 5, All-Stars 0 (77,450)
9-3-36	All-Stars 7, Detroit 7 (76,000)
9-1-37	All-Stars 6, Green Bay 0 (84,560)
8-31-38	All-Stars 28, Washington 16 (74,250)
8-30-39	NY Giants 9, All-Stars 0 (81,456)
8-29-40	Green Bay 45, All-Stars 28 (84,567)
8-28-41	Chi Bears 37, All-Stars 13 (98,203)
8-28-42	Chi Bears 21, All-Stars 0 (101,100)
8-25-43	All-Stars 27, Washington 7 (48,471)
8-30-44	Chi Bears 24, All-Stars 21 (48,769)
8-30-45	Green Bay 19, All-Stars 7 (92,753)
8-23-46	All-Stars 16, Los Angeles 0 (97,380)
8-22-47	All-Stars 16, Chi Bears 0 (105,840)
8-20-48	Chi Cardinals 28, All-Stars 0 (101,220)
8-12-49	Philadelphia 38, All-Stars 0 (93,780)
8-11-50	All-Stars 17, Philadelphia 7 (88,885)
8-17-51	Cleveland 33, All-Stars 0 (92,180)
8-15-52	Los Angeles 10, All-Stars 7 (88,316)
8-14-53	Detroit 24, All-Stars 10 (93,818)
8-13-54	Detroit 31, All-Stars 6 (93,470)
8-12-55	All-Stars 30, Cleveland 27 (75,000)

Date	Result (Attendance)
8-10-56	Cleveland 26, All-Stars 0 (75,000)
8-9-57	NY Giants 22, All-Stars 12 (75,000)
8-15-58	All-Stars 35, Detroit 19 (70,000)
8-14-59	Baltimore 29, All-Stars 0 (70,000)
8-12-60	Baltimore 32, All-Stars 7 (70,000)
8-4-61	Philadelphia 28, All-Stars 14 (66,000)
8-3-62	Green Bay 42, All-Stars 20 (65,000)
8-2-63	All-Stars 20, Green Bay 17 (65,000)
8-7-64	Chicago 28, All-Stars 17 (65,000)
8-6-65	Cleveland 24, All-Stars 16 (68.000)
8-5-66	Green Bay 38, All-Stars 0 (72,000)
8-4-67	Green Bay 27, All-Stars 0 (70,934)
8-2-68	Green Bay 34, All-Stars 17 (69,917)
8-1-69	NY Jets 26, All-Stars 24 (74,208)
7-31-70	Kansas City 24, All-Stars 3 (69,940)
7-30-71	Baltimore 24, All-Stars 17 (52,289)
7-28-72	Dallas 20, All-Stars 7 (54,162)
7-27-73	Miami 14, All-Stars 3 (54,103)
1974	No game
8-1-75	Pittsburgh 21, All-Stars 14 (54,103)
7-23-76	Pittsburgh 24, All-Stars 0 (52,895)

Alltime Winningest NFL Coaches

Most Career Wins

Coach	Yrs	Teams	Regular Season				Career			
			W	L	T	Pct	W	L	T	Pct
Don Shula	31	Colts, Dolphins	309	143	6	.681	327	158	6	.672
George Halas	40	Bears	319	148	31	.672	324	151	31	.672
Tom Landry	29	Cowboys	250	162	6	.605	270	178	6	.601
Curly Lambeau	33	Packers, Cardinals, Redskins	226	132	22	.623	229	134	22	.623
Chuck Noll	23	Steelers	193	148	1	.566	209	156	1	.572
Chuck Knox	21	Rams, Bills, Seahawks	182	135	1	.574	189	146	1	.563
Paul Brown	21	Browns, Bengals	166	100	6	.621	170	108	6	.609
Bud Grant	18	Vikings	158	96	5	.620	168	108	5	.607
Steve Owen	23	Giants	151	100	17	.595	153	108	17	.582
Joe Gibbs	12	Redskins	124	60	0	.674	140	65	0	.683
Hank Stram	17	Chiefs, Saints	131	97	10	.571	136	100	10	.573
Weeb Ewbank	20	Colts, Jets	130	129	7	.502	134	130	7	.507
Sid Gillman	18	Rams, Chargers, Oilers	122	99	7	.550	123	104	7	.541
Dan Reeves	13	Broncos, Giants	121	78	1	.608	128	84	1	.603
George Allen	12	Rams, Redskins	116	47	5	.705	118	54	5	.681
Don Coryell	14	Cardinals, Chargers	111	83	1	.572	114	89	1	.561
Marv Levy	13	Chiefs, Bills	110	81	0	.576	120	87	0	.580
John Madden	10	Raiders	103	32	7	.750	112	39	7	.731
Mike Ditka	11	Bears	106	62	0	.631	112	68	0	.622
Buddy Parker	15	Cardinals, Lions, Steelers	104	75	9	.577	107	76	9	.581

Top Winning Percentages

	W	L	T	Pct		W	L	T	Pct
Vince Lombardi	105	35	6	.740	George Halas	324	151	31	.671
John Madden	112	39	7	.731	Curly Lambeau	229	134	22	.623
Joe Gibbs	140	65	0	.683	Mike Ditka	112	68	0	.622
George Allen	118	54	5	.681	Bill Walsh	102	63	1	.617
Don Shula	327	158	6	.672	Paul Brown	170	108	6	.609

Alltime Number-One Draft Choices

Year	Team	Selection	Position
1936	Philadelphia	Jay Berwanger, Chicago	HB
1937	Philadelphia	Sam Francis, Nebraska	FB
1938	Cleveland	Corbett Davis, Indiana	FB
1939	Chicago Cardinals	Ki Aldrich, Texas Christian	C
1940	Chicago Cardinals	George Cafego, Tennessee	HB
1941	Chicago Bears	Tom Harmon, Michigan	HB
1942	Pittsburgh	Bill Dudley, Virginia	HB
1943	Detroit	Frank Sinkwich, Georgia	HB
1944	Boston	Angelo Bertelli, Notre Dame	QB
1945	Chicago Cardinals	Charley Trippi, Georgia	HB
1946	Boston	Frank Dancewicz, Notre Dame	QB
1947	Chicago Bears	Bob Fenimore, Oklahoma A&M	HB
1948	Washington	Harry Gilmer, Alabama	QB
1949	Philadelphia	Chuck Bednarik, Pennsylvania	C
1950	Detroit	Leon Hart, Notre Dame	E
1951	New York Giants	Kyle Rote, Southern Methodist	HB
1952	Los Angeles	Bill Wade, Vanderbilt	QB
1953	San Francisco	Harry Babcock, Georgia	E
1954	Cleveland	Bobby Garrett, Stanford	QB
1955	Baltimore	George Shaw, Oregon	QB
1956	Pittsburgh	Gary Glick, Colorado A&M	DB
1957	Green Bay	Paul Hornung, Notre Dame	HB
1958	Chicago Cardinals	King Hill, Rice	QB
1959	Green Bay	Randy Duncan, Iowa	QB
1960	Los Angeles	Billy Cannon, Louisiana St	RB
1961	Minnesota	Tommy Mason, Tulane	RB
	Buffalo (AFL)	Ken Rice, Auburn	G
1968	Minnesota	Ron Yary, Southern California	T
1969	Buffalo (AFL)	O. J. Simpson, Southern California	RB
1970	Pittsburgh	Terry Bradshaw, Louisiana Tech	QB
1971	New England	Jim Plunkett, Stanford	QB
1972	Buffalo	Walt Patulski, Notre Dame	DE
1973	Houston	John Matuszak, Tampa	DE
1974	Dallas	Ed Jones, Tennessee St	DE
1975	Atlanta	Steve Bartkowski, California	QB
1976	Tampa Bay	Lee Roy Selmon, Oklahoma	DE
1977	Tampa Bay	Ricky Bell, Southern California	RB
1978	Houston	Earl Campbell, Texas	RB
1979	Buffalo	Tom Cousineau, Ohio St	LB
1980	Detroit	Billy Sims, Oklahoma	RB
1981	New Orleans	George Rogers, South Carolina	RB
1982	New England	Kenneth Sims, Texas	DT
1983	Baltimore	John Elway, Stanford	QB
1984	New England	Irving Fryar, Nebraska	WR
1985	Buffalo	Bruce Smith, Virginia Tech	DE
1986	Tampa Bay	Bo Jackson, Auburn	RB
1987	Tampa Bay	Vinny Testaverde, Miami	QB
1988	Atlanta	Aundray Bruce, Auburn	LB
1989	Dallas	Troy Aikman, UCLA	QB
1990	Indianapolis	Jeff George, Illinois	QB
1991	Dallas	Russell Maryland, Miami	DT
1992	Indianapolis	Steve Emtman, Washington	DT
1993	New England	Drew Bledsoe, Washington St	QB
1994	Cincinnati	Dan Wilkinson, Ohio St	DT

From 1947 through 1958, the first selection in the draft was a bonus pick, awarded to the winner of a random draw. That club, in turn, forfeited its last-round draft choice. The winner of the bonus choice was eliminated from future draws. The system was abolished after 1958, by which time all clubs had received a bonus choice.

Members of the Pro Football Hall of Fame

Herb Adderley
Lance Alworth
Doug Atkins
Morris "Red" Badgro
Lem Barney
Cliff Battles
Sammy Baugh
Chuck Bednarik
Bert Bell
Bobby Bell
Raymond Berry
Charles W. Bidwill, Sr.
Fred Biletnikoff
George Blanda
Mel Blount
Terry Bradshaw
Jim Brown
Paul Brown
Roosevelt Brown
Willie Brown
Buck Buchanan
Dick Butkus
Earl Campbell
Tony Canadeo
Joe Carr
Guy Chamberlin
Jack Christiansen
Earl "Dutch" Clark
George Connor
Jimmy Conzelman
Larry Csonka
Al Davis
Willie Davis
Len Dawson
Mike Ditka
Art Donovan
Tony Dorsett
John "Paddy" Driscoll
Bill Dudley
Glen "Turk" Edwards
Weeb Ewbank
Tom Fears
Ray Flaherty
Len Ford
Dan Fortmann
Dan Fouts
Frank Gatski
Bill George
Frank Gifford
Sid Gillman
Otto Graham
Harold "Red" Grange
Bud Grant
Joe Greene
Forrest Gregg
Bob Griese
Lou Groza
Joe Guyon
George Halas

Jack Ham
John Hannah
Franco Harris
Ed Healey
Mel Hein
Ted Hendricks
Wilbur "Pete" Henry
Arnie Herber
Bill Hewitt
Clarke Hinkle
Elroy "Crazylegs" Hirsch
Paul Hornung
Ken Houston
Cal Hubbard
Sam Huff
Lamar Hunt
Don Hutson
Jimmy Johnson
John Henry Johnson
David "Deacon" Jones
Stan Jones
Sonny Jurgensen
Leroy Kelly
Walt Kiesling
Frank "Bruiser" Kinard
Earl "Curly" Lambeau
Jack Lambert
Tom Landry
Dick "Night Train" Lane
Jim Langer
Willie Lanier
Yale Lary
Dante Lavelli
Bobby Layne
Alphonse "Tuffy" Leemans
Bob Lilly
Larry Little
Vince Lombardi
Sid Luckman
Roy "Link" Lyman
John Mackey
Tim Mara
Gino Marchetti
George Preston Marshall
Ollie Matson
Don Maynard
George McAfee
Mike McCormack
Hugh McElhenny
Johnny "Blood" McNally
Mike Michalske
Wayne Millner
Bobby Mitchell
Ron Mix
Lenny Moore
Marion Motley
George Musso
Bronko Nagurski
Joe Namath

Earle "Greasy" Neale
Ernie Nevers
Ray Nitschke
Chuck Noll
Leo Nomellini
Merlin Olsen
Jim Otto
Steve Owen
Alan Page
Clarence "Ace" Parker
Jim Parker
Walter Payton
Joe Perry
Pete Pihos
Hugh "Shorty" Ray
Dan Reeves
John Riggins
Jim Ringo
Andy Robustelli
Art Rooney
Pete Rozelle
Bob St. Clair
Gale Sayers
Joe Schmidt
Tex Schramm
Art Shell
O. J. Simpson
Jackie Smith
Bart Starr
Roger Staubach
Ernie Stautner
Jan Stenerud
Ken Strong
Joe Stydahar
Fran Tarkenton
Charley Taylor
Jim Taylor
Jim Thorpe
Y. A. Tittle
George Trafton
Charley Trippi
Emlen Tunnell
Clyde "Bulldog" Turner
Johnny Unitas
Gene Upshaw
Norm Van Brocklin
Steve Van Buren
Doak Walker
Bill Walsh
Paul Warfield
Bob Waterfield
Arnie Weinmeister
Randy White
Bill Willis
Larry Wilson
Alex Wojciechowicz
Willie Wood

Champions of Other Leagues

Canadian Football League Grey Cup

Year	Results	Site	Attendance
1909	U of Toronto 26, Parkdale 6	Toronto	3,807
1910	U of Toronto 16, Hamilton Tigers 7	Hamilton	12,000
1911	U of Toronto 14, Toronto 7	Toronto	13,687
1912	Hamilton Alerts 11, Toronto 4	Hamilton	5,337
1913	Hamilton Tigers 44, Parkdale 2	Hamilton	2,100
1914	Toronto 14, U of Toronto 2	Toronto	10,500
1915	Hamilton Tigers 13, Toronto RAA 7	Toronto	2,808
1916-19	No game		
1920	U of Toronto 16, Toronto 3	Toronto	10,088
1921	Toronto 23, Edmonton 0	Toronto	9,558
1922	Queen's U 13, Edmonton 1	Kingston	4,700
1923	Queen's U 54, Regina 0	Toronto	8,629
1924	Queen's U 11, Balmy Beach 3	Toronto	5,978
1925	Ottawa Senators 24, Winnipeg 1	Ottawa	6,900
1926	Ottawa Senators 10, Toronto U 7	Toronto	8,276
1927	Balmy Beach 9, Hamilton Tigers 6	Toronto	13,676
1928	Hamilton Tigers 30, Regina 0	Hamilton	4,767
1929	Hamilton Tigers 14, Regina 3	Hamilton	1,906
1930	Balmy Beach 11, Regina 6	Toronto	3,914
1931	Montreal AAA 22, Regina 0	Montreal	5,112
1932	Hamilton Tigers 25, Regina 6	Hamilton	4,806
1933	Toronto 4, Sarnia 3	Sarnia	2,751
1934	Sarnia 20, Regina 12	Toronto	8,900
1935	Winnipeg 18, Hamilton Tigers 12	Hamilton	6,405
1936	Sarnia 26, Ottawa RR 20	Toronto	5,883
1937	Toronto 4, Winnipeg 3	Toronto	11,522
1938	Toronto 30, Winnipeg 7	Toronto	18,778
1939	Winnipeg 8, Ottawa 7	Ottawa	11,738
1940	Ottawa 12, Balmy Beach 5	Ottawa	1,700
1940	Ottawa 8, Balmy Beach 2	Toronto	4,998
1941	Winnipeg 18, Ottawa 16	Toronto	19,065
1942	Toronto RCAF 8, Winnipeg RCAF 5	Toronto	12,455
1943	Hamilton F Wild 23, Winnipeg RCAF 14	Toronto	16,423
1944	Montreal St H-D Navy 7, Hamilton F Wild 6	Hamilton	3,871
1945	Toronto 35, Winnipeg 0	Toronto	18,660
1946	Toronto 28, Winnipeg 6	Toronto	18,960
1947	Toronto 10, Winnipeg 9	Toronto	18,885
1948	Calgary 12, Ottawa 7	Toronto	20,013
1949	Montreal Als 28, Calgary 15	Toronto	20,087
1950	Toronto 13, Winnipeg 0	Toronto	27,101
1951	Ottawa 21, Saskatchewan 14	Toronto	27,341
1952	Toronto 21, Edmonton 11	Toronto	27,391
1953	Hamilton Ticats 12, Winnipeg 6	Toronto	27,313
1954	Edmonton 26, Montreal 25	Toronto	27,321
1955	Edmonton 34, Montreal 19	Vancouver	39,417
1956	Edmonton 50, Montreal 27	Toronto	27,425
1957	Hamilton 32, Winnipeg 7	Toronto	27,051
1958	Winnipeg 35, Hamilton 28	Vancouver	36,567
1959	Winnipeg 21, Hamilton 7	Toronto	33,133
1960	Ottawa 16, Edmonton 6	Vancouver	38,102
1961	Winnipeg 21, Hamilton 14	Toronto	32,651
1962	Winnipeg 28, Hamilton 27	Toronto	32,655
1963	Hamilton 21, British Columbia 10	Vancouver	36,545
1964	British Columbia 34, Hamilton 24	Toronto	32,655
1965	Hamilton 22, Winnipeg 16	Toronto	32,655
1966	Saskatchewan 29, Ottawa 14	Vancouver	36,553
1967	Hamilton 24, Saskatchewan 1	Ottawa	31,358
1968	Ottawa 24, Calgary 21	Toronto	32,655
1969	Ottawa 29, Saskatchewan 11	Montreal	33,172
1970	Montreal 23, Calgary 10	Toronto	32,669
1971	Calgary 14, Toronto 11	Vancouver	34,484
1972	Hamilton 13, Saskatchewan 10	Hamilton	33,993
1973	Ottawa 22, Edmonton 18	Toronto	36,653
1974	Montreal 20, Edmonton 7	Vancouver	34,450
1975	Edmonton 9, Montreal 8	Calgary	32,454

Canadian Football League Grey Cup (Cont.)

Year	Results	Site	Attendance
1976	Ottawa 23, Saskatchewan 20	Toronto	53,467
1977	Montreal 41, Edmonton 6	Montreal	68,318
1978	Edmonton 20, Montreal 13	Toronto	54,695
1979	Edmonton 17, Montreal 9	Montreal	65,113
1980	Edmonton 48, Hamilton 10	Toronto	54,661
1981	Edmonton 26, Ottawa 23	Montreal	52,478
1982	Edmonton 32, Toronto 16	Toronto	54,741
1983	Toronto 18, British Columbia 17	Vancouver	59,345
1984	Winnipeg 47, Hamilton 17	Edmonton	60,081
1985	British Columbia 37, Hamilton 24	Montreal	56,723
1986	Hamilton 39, Edmonton 15	Vancouver	59,621
1987	Edmonton 38, Toronto 36	Vancouver	59,478
1988	Winnipeg 22, British Columbia 21	Ottawa	50,604
1989	Saskatchewan 43, Hamilton 40	Toronto	54,088
1990	Winnipeg 50, Edmonton 11	Vancouver	46,968
1991	Toronto 36, Calgary 21	Winnipeg	51,985
1992	Calgary 24, Winnipeg 10	Toronto	45,863
1993	Edmonton 33, Winnipeg 23	Calgary	50,035

In 1909, Earl Grey, the Governor-General of Canada, donated a trophy for the Rugby Football Championship of Canada. The trophy, which subsequently became known as the Grey Cup, was originally open only to teams registered with the Canada Rugby Union. Since 1954, it has been awarded to the winner of the Canadian Football League's championship game.

AMERICAN FOOTBALL LEAGUE I

Year	Champion	Record
1926	Philadelphia Quakers	7-2

AMERICAN FOOTBALL LEAGUE II

Year	Champion	Record
1936	Boston Shamrocks	8-3
1937	LA Bulldogs	8-0

AMERICAN FOOTBALL LEAGUE III

Year	Champion	Record
1940	Columbus Bullies	8-1-1
1941	Columbus Bullies	5-1-2

ALL-AMERICAN FOOTBALL CONFERENCE

Year	Championship Game
1946	Cleveland 14, NY Yankees 9
1947	Cleveland 14, NY Yankees 3
1948	Cleveland 49, Buffalo 7
1949	Cleveland 21, San Francisco 7

WORLD FOOTBALL LEAGUE

Year	World Bowl Championship
1974	Birmingham 22, Florida 21
1975	Disbanded midseason

UNITED STATES FOOTBALL LEAGUE

Year	Championship Game
1983	Michigan 24, Philadelphia 22, at Denver
1984	Philadelphia 23, Arizona 3, at Tampa
1985	Baltimore 28, Oakland 24, at East Rutherford

Anatomy of a Rumor

The phones at the offices of the Jacksonville Jaguars, one of the two new NFL franchises, began lighting up like pinball machines one morning last February with callers asking question after question about Dallas Cowboy coach Jimmy Johnson. A local sports talk host, David Lamm of WZNS, had just reported that Wayne Weaver and David Seldin, the owner and president respectively of the Jaguars, had had a 2½ day meeting with Johnson on Weaver's boat in South Florida and that Johnson was on the verge of resigning from the Cowboys to become Jacksonville's coach–general manager. The next day the local paper, *The Florida Times Union*, reported that the Jaguars had denied the story, but the paper also said it had confirmed the Johnson meeting with what it calls "a highly reliable source."

The rumor was taken seriously. Dallas owner Jerry Jones threatened action if Jacksonville had tampered with Johnson, and the league office announced it had warned the Jags about dealing with Johnson, who had five years remaining on his contract with the Cowboys.

The thing is, it was all nonsense from the beginning. First, the only time Johnson and Seldin ever met was at a party on Dec. 6 where Johnson offered congratulations on the new franchise. Second, Seldin told *Sports Illustrated* several weeks before the rumor surfaced that Johnson had been eliminated from consideration. Finally, Johnson told *Sports Illustrated* three days before the Super Bowl that he was no longer interested in pursuing the Jacksonville posts.

How did the story surface? Well, it wouldn't be beyond Johnson, who loved tweaking Jones about his future, to have whispered about his "interest" to someone in Jacksonville, knowing that the info might then be leaked. Maybe it was just that sort of needling that helped produce the rift that caused Johnson and Jones to part company for real in March. By then, the rumors of a split were rampant, proving that sometimes when there's smoke, there really *is* fire.

College Football

Florida State, Great Debate

Florida State downed Nebraska and topped the year-end polls, but the arguments didn't end there | by AUSTIN MURPHY

I T WAS CHAOTIC, IT WAS MESSY, AND IT came down to the final second. The 1993 college football season was marked by frightening chaos at Wisconsin's Camp Randall Stadium, where students celebrating a Badger win over Michigan on Oct. 30 were crushed and trampled. It was marked by the less terrifying chaos wrought by the Associated Press (media) and *USA Today/CNN* (coaches) polls, which, taken together, formed the flawed yet powerful coalition poll, which determined the weekly rankings, which in turn determined who would be bellyaching the loudest in any given week.

His grail secured, the national championship in hand, Florida State coach Bobby Bowden strode into a press conference on the morning of Jan. 2 and announced to the gathered scribes, many of whom had voted his team No. 1, "I've been waiting a long time to say this: Men, I can't stand y'all."

That Bobby. What a kidder. He laughed,

they laughed: Everybody knew he was joking. Bowden's chummy rapport with the fourth estate became an issue in mid-November after the Seminoles were surprised in South Bend. His team had been consensus preseason favorites to win the national title, the prize that had somehow eluded him in his 27 years as a head coach. In running up nine straight wins and overwhelming their opponents by a cumulative score of 399–58, the '93 Seminoles had begun to take on mythic proportions. They had a linebacker, Derrick Brooks, who, in his first three games, outscored Florida State's opponents. Their quarterback, Charlie Ward, had the Heisman Trophy locked up by late September. One of the best teams in history—that was the word on Florida State.

The Seminoles arrived on the Notre Dame campus with a decided lack of reverence for the school's football mystique. Two made references to "Rock Knutne"; another to "the Three Horsemen." Their igno-

JOHN BIEVER

The fruits of Ward's labors: for his team, a national title; for him, the Heisman Trophy.

rance, affected or genuine, failed to protect them: The visitors found themselves trailing 21–7 at halftime. Florida State's biggest problem was up front: The Irish offensive line, anchored by future NFLers Aaron Taylor, Tim Ruddy and Todd Norman, was blowing the Seminoles D-linemen—whom they outweighed by an average of 39 pounds per man—clear off the ball.

Ward, who had been erratic most of the game, got hot in the final four minutes. Behind 31–17, he marched the team 45 yards in 99 seconds, hitting Kez McCorvey

on a fourth-down, 20-yard touchdown pass. Florida State's defense held, and Ward moved the team 49 yards to the Irish 14-yard line. On the game's last play, his desperation pass into the end zone was batted down by cornerback Shawn Wooden, and college football had a new No. 1.

For losing the season's first Game of the Century 31–24, the Seminoles were scarcely punished. The AP dropped them one measly notch, from No. 1 to No. 2. Taking particular umbrage were Nebraska and West Virginia, at Nos. 3 and 4, respectively, who despite their perfect records would apparently be denied the chance to play for the national championship, which for Florida State and no one else, apparently, had become a double-elimination tournament.

Iowa State's Jim Walden was one of many coaches who accused the AP voters of having the objectivity of Eastern bloc figure skating judges. "All of a sudden, in the last three or four years, we've gotten into a 'Let's-do-it-for-Bobby mentality,'" said Walden. "Well, Bobby got his butt beat.... I'll be glad when he finally wins one so then we can go on to something else."

Of course, the coaches who voted in the USA Today/CNN poll were not always innocent of agendas. With the regular season over, West Virginia had seven first-place votes; Florida State, 13. Yet the Mountaineers were ranked second, the Seminoles third, which means some coaches were voting Florida State fifth or sixth.

Nor was Bowden's voting record pure as the driven snow. In the euphoria following his team's win over Nebraska, Bowden declared Notre Dame to be the nation's second-best squad. Yet he admitted that when he had cast his ballot, he had

Cinderella Cheesehead

They won a school-record 10 games, rescued a dozen imperiled students, and flew 30 hours to and from Tokyo, where they secured the team's first Rose Bowl bid in 31 years.

In 1993, Cinderella was a cheesehead.

Three years had passed since Wisconsin had lost all but one of its 11 games. Though vastly improved under third-year head coach Barry Alvarez, the '93 Badgers were expected to be no more than a middle-of-the-pack squad in a Big 10 featuring Ohio State, Michigan and Penn State.

But this was no ordinary Badger team. Behind a stegosaurian offensive line, comprised of cheese-fed, in-state talent, toiled a pair of sawed-off running backs, Terrell Fletcher and Brent Moss, both 5'9", who helped Wisconsin average 251 rushing yards per game. Taking snaps was flat-topped, 22-year-old Mormon quarterback Darrell Bevell, widely believed to be the world's oldest sophomore. (He'd taken two years off school while on a two-year Mormon mission in ... Cleveland). Against Northwestern, Bevell hit 14 consecutive passes before cooling off. He

threw a single incompletion and finished 17-for-18.

After that game, a 53–14 Badgers win, Northwestern coach Gary Barnett expressed pity for Wisconsin's backups, who, he said, "didn't get to play very much."

Opponents accusing Wisconsin of running up the score—there was a switch!

Euphoria in Madison turned to nightmare on Halloween eve. After the team's 13–10 win over Michigan at Camp Randall Stadium, a surge of Wisconsin undergrads trying to storm the field resulted in a bottleneck at the bottom of the student section. Sixty-nine people were hospitalized, six in critical condition.

Moss and running mate Fletcher made sushi out of the Spartans in the Tokyo Dome.

dropped the Irish to No. 3, behind Nebraska, an egregious example of a coach using his vote to benefit his team. Small wonder the coaches refuse to reveal their votes.

Unseemly shenanigans such as these gave an immeasurable boost to the idea of a playoff system. A groundswell of support for a playoff began in December, when the NCAA announced that a "research group" had been formed to study the question. Those experts were to report their findings to a "playoff committee" of representatives from all 10 Division I-A conferences, who could then place a playoff on the agenda for the January 1995 convention, to be held in San Diego.

Not an ironclad guarantee, by any means, but not unencouraging for playoff proponents, considering the glacial pace at which most legislation moves through the bureaucratic NCAA. Said Eastern Michigan president William Shelton, a member of the Presidents Commission, "A playoff has gone from totally inconceivable to somewhat possible in a very short time."

The primary reason for a playoff, other

That there were just six critical cases, and no fatalities, was due in part to the heroics of 10 or so Badger players who waded into the trough of human limbs and pulled people to safety. "I did what I could," said offensive tackle Joe Panos. "I was just … pushing people back and picking up the ones who were unconscious and blue." Walk-on wide receiver Mike Brin performed CPR on one young woman who had stopped breathing and had no pulse. She resumed breathing, and most likely owes her life to Brin, who was recognized the following Friday as "Person of the Week" on ABC News.

Counseling was made available for traumatized players and students; calls for the players poured in from *20/20, Hard Copy, Rescue 911*—"everyone but *America's Most Wanted*" griped Alvarez, who had six days to get his team ready to host undefeated Ohio State.

Wisconsin's subsequent 14–14 tie of the Buckeyes, coupled with Ohio State's November 20th loss to Michigan, clarified things for the Badgers: If they beat Michigan State in the final game of the regular season, they would go to the Rose Bowl. Lose, and they would settle for the Thrifty Car Rental Holiday Bowl.

There was this additional wrinkle: Two years earlier, Alvarez had agreed to play the Spartans in Japan. So, in a steaming hothouse called the Tokyo Dome, Moss and Fletcher combined for 259 rushing yards as the Badgers flattened the Spartans, 41–20.

Vegas oddsmakers installed UCLA as a touchdown favorite over Wisconsin in the Rose Bowl. The Badgers had peaked, said conventional wisdom. In Pasadena, they would face a more talented Bruins team playing in its own backyard.

Why then, were the majority of the 101,000 people in the Rose Bowl wearing Badger red? UCLA fans who could not resist scalping their tickets had turned the Rose Bowl into an away game for the Bruins. Roared Alvarez to his team before the game, "Isn't Camp Randall painted up beautiful today?"

It was, indeed, a beautiful day for the Badgers to win their first Rose Bowl, behind the running of Moss, who gained 158 workmanlike yards on 36 carries, and the generosity of UCLA, which committed six turnovers. "I'm going to be sick when I watch the films," said Bruins coach Terry Donahue after the 21–16 defeat.

"When I got here, we were tenth in the league," burbled Alvarez, who was voted Coach of the Year by his peers in the American Football Coaches Association. "Now we're fifth in the country."

For her part, Cinderella kicked up her heels and had a bratwurst and a brew.

Foley engineered a dramatic last-minute drive to upset the Irish in South Bend.

than the ragged and inexact method currently in use to determine who is No. 1, is cash. A championship tournament could bring in up to $100 million. Athletic departments are cash-starved, many facing gender equity lawsuits from women demanding funds equal to the amounts budgeted for men's programs, as guaranteed by Title IX. "How are we going to pay for gender equity?" asked Shelton. "One hundred million from a playoff could help."

Arguments over the necessity of a playoff would have been much less acrimonious, of course, had Notre Dame been able to follow its upset of Florida State with a win over Boston College a week later. In that case, the coalition would have mandated a rematch: Notre Dame versus the Seminoles in the Fiesta Bowl.

But along came the Eagles to muddy the waters. Holtz warned his team that the Boston College game would be more than a "victory lap," but nobody paid much attention until a senior quarterback with a shock of red hair put a major shock in the Irish. Glenn Foley's fourth touchdown pass of the afternoon, a two-yard toss to tight end Pete Mitchell, put the Eagles up 38–17 early in the fourth quarter. Twice, however, in that same quarter, Foley fumbled center snaps, abetting a storybook comeback by the Irish:

A Kevin McDougal to Lake Dawson touchdown pass put Notre Dame on top 39–38 with just 1:09 left on the clock.

The exuberant Irish fans were apparently unfamiliar with Foley's proficiency in the two-minute drill, which had been included in virtually every Eagle practice since Tom Coughlin had taken over as BC's coach in 1991. After throwing two incompletes, Foley hit Mitchell for 12 yards, tailback Anthony Comer for six, and Mitchell, again, for 24. One timeout and an incomplete pass later, Foley found wideout Ivan Boyd on a middle-screen for nine more yards. Left-footed kicker Jeff Gordon's 41-yard field goal with :05 left on the clock knuckleballed through the uprights, sealing the season's most stunning upset and providing the highlight of Coughlin's three-year Boston College career. Three months later he would vault to the NFL, taking the head coaching job of the expansion Jacksonville Jaguars.

The Irish were but one of three Top 5 teams to tumble on this, Shakeout Saturday. No. 3 Miami was beaten by West Virginia 17–14. In Ann Arbor, No. 5 Ohio State was drubbed 28–0 by Michigan, thus preserving John Cooper's perfect record against the Wolverines: In six tries as Buckeye head coach, he has not beaten them once.

Cornhusker fans, who had been outraged to be ranked beneath a team with a loss, were calmed by the events of Shakeout Saturday. They moved up to No. 1 in the coalition poll and stayed there by beating Oklahoma to end their regular season. Thus was Nebraska assured of a crack at the national title, against Florida State in the Orange Bowl. Now it was Mountaineer head coach Don Nehlen's turn to raise a stink.

The day after the Cornhuskers beat the Sooners, West Virginia came from behind to nip Boston College 17–14. The Mountaineers had done everything possible: won 11 straight games. They had beaten the team that had beaten the team that was now ranked ahead of them, barring them from a shot at No. 1. Nehlen raised hell. Why was *his* team's 11–0 record somehow inferior to *Nebraska's* 11-0? Bobby Bowden was a fine coach and a good man, Nehlen expostulated into every live microphone he saw, but against the Irish, Bowden "didn't get it done." To exclude his Mountaineers from the title game, Nehlen said, would be "the biggest misjustice in the world."

The wronged Mountaineers took their indignation and perfect record to the Sugar Bowl, where they earned little respect from the Florida Gators, who crushed them, 41–7. Said Sugar Bowl MVP Errict Rhett, who gained 107 rushing yards and scored three touchdowns, "They're on a Vanderbilt level, with all due respect to Vanderbilt."

And to think the Mountaineers didn't even face the SEC's best team. That distinction belonged to overachieving, probation-disgraced Auburn, which was forbidden to play in a bowl. Under first year head coach Terry Bowden, the Tigers went 11–0 and finished the season ranked fourth in the AP poll.

There was a renaissance at UCLA. After beginning the season 0–2, the Bruins rattled off seven straight wins to finish 8–3. For the first time in eight seasons the Bru-

Wilkinson's ferocious play persuaded the Bengals to make him the NFL's top draft pick.

ins won the right to play in the Rose Bowl, where they would meet the Wisconsin Badgers, whose bizarre route to Pasadena had taken them through Tokyo *(see box)*.

All-America wide receiver J.J. Stokes capped a brilliant season, in which he hauled in passes good for 1,005 yards and 17 touchdowns, with a Rose Bowl–record 14 catches. Unfortunately for UCLA, the Rose Bowl turned into the equivalent of a road game. An estimated 50,000 Bruin fans could not resist selling their tickets to Wisconsin followers, for prices up to $500, transforming the Rose Bowl into a sea of Badger red. And UCLA, the team that had led the nation in takeaways, led New Year's Day in giveaways, committing six turnovers. The upstart Badgers won 21–16.

Having given away its surest claim to a national title by falling asleep against Boston College, Notre Dame went to the Cotton Bowl intent on staking another claim to the crown. An emphatic win over Texas A&M would have helped: As it was, the Irish trailed 14–7 at halftime and barely escaped with a 24–21 victory.

When the Seminoles squeaked past Nebraska, Holtz said, "Let's remember

DAMIAN STROHMEYER

three decades for a national title, he could wait another second, couldn't he?

The zebras at the Orange Bowl had decided that on the game's last play—er, rather, its *second*-to-last play—Nebraska tight end Trumane Bell's knee had touched the turf with one tick remaining on the clock. The stadium announcer intoned, "This game is *not* over."

"It seemed like some kind of cruel joke to me," Bowden said. "Really, the cruelest joke ever played on me."

But Cornhusker kicker Byron Bennett, whose 27-yarder with four minutes to play had given Nebraska a 16–15 lead, pulled this one wide left, and the Seminoles had survived underrated Nebraska—which came into the game a 17-point underdog— by the score of 18–16.

All of which delighted the Irish. In fact, when freshman kicker Scott Bentley's 22-yard field goal tumbled through the uprights with 21 seconds left, giving the Seminoles the lead, Notre Dame players watching in their Dallas hotel leaped ecstatically to their feet. Florida State's win, they assumed, would assure them at least half a national title.

No dice. In the AP poll the Seminoles earned 1,532 points, 54 more than Notre Dame. In the coaches' poll Florida State outpointed the Irish 1,523 to 1,494. "Everybody said it was the Game of the Century," said Holtz the following morning, referring to his team's November win over the national champions. "I guess it was only the Game of the Century if the right team won."

Bowden said he felt for Holtz, but he wasn't about to give up the new hardware. "That's the way the poll works," he said.

The notorious poll. It is capricious, it is inexact. It is susceptible to coaches with agendas and writers with grudges. Get used to it, though, because the coalition poll is all we have.

For now.

that the two teams that are competing for Number One have already played on the field." It was a valid point: *mano a mano* on Nov. 13, Florida State had lost to the Irish. The interesting thing about Holtz's position was that it represented a 180-degree switch—call it a Lou-turn—from his position on this same issue four years earlier. After beating Notre Dame in '89, Miami won the national title, despite Holtz's impassioned arguments that voters should weigh the *overall season* more heavily than a single game. Now he was singing a different tune, and the voters weren't listening.

In Miami a chaotic season had an appropriately sloppy conclusion, with Bowden being doused with ice water, thumped on the back and otherwise congratulated for his first national championship in 28 years, as the final seconds ticked off the Orange Bowl clock, only to be told ... Oops! Sorry Coach, we spoke too soon: You haven't won anything yet, and now Nebraska will be given a chance to kick a game-winning, 45-yard field goal.

Oh well. Bowden had waited nearly

Final Polls

Associated Press

		Record	Pts	Head Coach	SI Preseason Top 20
1	Florida St (46)	12-1-0	1532	Bobby Bowden	1
2	Notre Dame	11-1-0	1478	Lou Holtz	11
3	Nebraska	11-1-0	1418	Tom Osborne	13t
4	Auburn	11-0-0	1375	Terry Bowden	46
5	Florida	11-2-0	1307	Steve Spurrier	3
6	Wisconsin	10-1-1	1228	Barry Alvarez	22
7	West Virginia	11-1-0	1090	Don Nehlen	23
8	Penn St	10-2-0	1074	Joe Paterno	16
9	Texas A&M	10-2-0	1043	R.C. Slocum	13t
10	Arizona	10-2-0	992	Dick Tomey	12
11	Ohio St	10-1-1	971	John Cooper	30
12	Tennessee	9-2-1	870	Phil Fulmer	8
13	Boston College	9-3-0	817	Tom Coughlin	17
14	Alabama	9-3-1	685	Gene Stallings	4
15	Miami	9-3-0	611	Dennis Erickson	6
16	Colorado	8-3-1	574	Bill McCartney	5
17	Oklahoma	9-3-0	521	Gary Gibbs	18
18	UCLA	8-4-0	460	Terry Donahue	31
19	N Carolina	10-3-0	447	Mack Brown	24
20	Kansas St	9-2-1	444	Bill Snyder	51
21	Michigan	8-4-0	397	Gary Moeller	2
22	Virginia Tech	9-3-0	321	Frank Beamer	83
23	Clemson	9-3-0	164	Ken Hatfield	35
24	Louisville	9-3-0	159	H. Schnellenberger	34
25	California	9-4-0	79	Keith Gilbertson	53

Note: As voted by panel of 60 sportswriters and broadcasters following bowl games (1st-place votes in parentheses).

USA Today/CNN

		Pts	Prev Rank			Pts	Prev Rank
1	Florida St	1523	3	14	Oklahoma	636	16
2	Notre Dame	1494	4	15	Miami	604	9
3	Nebraska	1441	1	16	Colorado	586	17
4	Florida	1313	8	17	UCLA	539	13
5	Wisconsin	1271	7	18	Kansas St	523	19
6	West Virginia	1142	2	19	Michigan	496	22
7	Penn St	1132	12	20	Virginia Tech	472	20
8	Texas A&M	1107	6	21	N Carolina	452	11
9	Arizona	1094	14	22	Clemson	240	23
10	Ohio St	960	10	23	Louisville	214	25
11	Tennessee	891	5	24	California	158	—
12	Boston College	828	15	25	Southern Cal	121	—
13	Alabama	742	18				

Note: As voted by panel of 60 Division I-A head coaches; 25 points for 1st, 24 for 2nd, etc. (1st-place votes in parentheses).

Bowls and Playoffs

NCAA Division I-A Bowl Results

Date	Bowl	Result	Payout/Team ($)	Attendance
12-17-93	Las Vegas	Utah St 42, Ball St 33	228,000	15,508
12-24-92	Hancock	Oklahoma 41, Texas Tech 10	1.1 million	43,848
12-25-93	Aloha	Colorado 41, Fresno St 30	750,000	44,009
12-28-93	Liberty	Louisville 18, Michigan St 7	1 million	21,097
12-29-93	Copper	Kansas St 52, Wyoming 17	700,000	49,075
12-30-93	Holiday	Ohio St 28, Brigham Young 21	1.7 million	52,108
12-30-93	Freedom	Southern Cal 28, Utah 21	700,000	37,203

NCAA Division I-A Bowl Results

Date	Bowl	Result	Payout/Team ($)	Attendance
12-31-93	Independence	Virginia Tech 45, Indiana 20	700,000	33,819
12-31-93	Peach	Clemson 14, Kentucky 13	1.125 million	63,416
12-31-93	Gator	Alabama 24, N Carolina 10	1.5 million	67,205
1-1-94	Hall of Fame	Michigan 42, N Carolina St 7	1 million	52,649
1-1-94	Citrus	Penn St 31, Tennessee 13	2.5 million	72,456
1-1-94	Fiesta	Arizona 29, Miami 0	3 million	72,260
1-1-94	Carquest	Boston College 31, Virginia 13	1 million	38,516
1-1-94	Cotton	Notre Dame 24, Texas A&M 21	3.1 million	69,855
1-1-94	Rose	Wisconsin 21, UCLA 16	6.5 million	101,237
1-1-94	Orange	Florida St 18, Nebraska 16	4.2 million	81,536
1-1-94	Sugar	Florida 41, West Virginia 7	4.15 million	75,437

NCAA Division I-AA Championship Boxscore

Youngstown St	17	0	0	0—17
Marshall	0	0	3	2— 5

FIRST QUARTER

YSU: Darnell Clark 50 run (Jeff Wilkins kick), 14:27.
YSU: Tamron Smith 5 run (Wilkins kick), 12:21.
YSU: FG Wilkins 19, 1:53.

THIRD QUARTER

MU: FG David Merrick 27; 3:34.

FOURTH QUARTER

MU: Safety (Wilkins stepped out of end zone), 2:52.

	YSU	MU
First downs	16	16
Rushing yardage	220	49
Passing yardage	75	207
Return yardage	33	0
Passes (comp-att-int)	7-8-0	19-29-2
Punts (no.-avg)	3-47.3	3-37.0
Fumbles (no.-lost)	2-1	1-1
Penalties (no.-yards)	9-79	3-24

Att: 29,218

Small College Championship Summaries

NCAA DIVISION II

First round: North Alabama 38, Carson-Newman 28; Hampton 33, Albany St (GA) 7; Texas A&M-Kingsville 50, Portland St 15; UC-Davis 37, Fort Hayes St 34; Mankato St 34, Missouri Southern St 13; North Dakota 17, Pittsburg St 14; New Haven 48, Edinboro 28; Indiana (PA) 28, Ferris St 21.
Quarterfinals: North Alabama 45, Hampton 20; Texas A&M-Kingsville 51, UC-Davis 28; North Dakota 54, Mankato St 21; Indiana (PA) 38, New Haven 35.
Semifinals: North Alabama 27, Texas A&M-Kingsville 25; Indiana (PA) 21, North Dakota 6.
Championship: 12-11-93 Florence, AL

Indiana (PA)	0	10	14	10—34
North Alabama	7	7	0	27—41

NCAA DIVISION III

First round: Mount Union 40, Allegheny 7; Albion 41, Anderson 21; Wisconsin-La Crosse 55, Wartburg 26; St John's (Minn) 32, Coe 14; Washington & Jefferson 27, Moravian 14; Frostburg St 26, Wilkes 25; Rowan 29, Buffalo St 6; William Patterson 17, Union (NY) 7.
Quarterfinals: Mount Union 30, Albion 16; St John's (Minn) 47, Wisconsin-La Crosse 25; Washington & Jefferson 28, Frostburg St 7; Rowan 37, William Patterson 0.
Semifinals: Mount Union 56, St John's (Minn) 8; Rowan 23, Washington & Jefferson 16.
Championship: 12-11-93 Salem, VA

Rowan	9	0	15	0—24
Mount Union	7	7	7	13—34

NAIA DIVISION I PLAYOFFS

First Round: Arkansas-Monticello 26, Langston (OK) 13; Central St (OH) 58, Winona St (MN) 7; East Central (OK) 24, Western New Mexico 22; Glenville St (WV) 41, Carroll (MT) 24.
Semifinals: East Central (OK) 27, Arkansas-Monticello 0; Glenville St (WV) 13, Central St (OH) 12.
Championship: 12-11-93 Ada, OK

Glenville St (WV)	7	7	14	7—35
East Central (OK)	14	0	20	15—49

NAIA DIVISION II PLAYOFFS

First round: Baker (KS) 39, Hastings (NE) 19; Central Washington 28, Linfield (OR) 26; Doane (NB) 17, Bethany (KS) 10; Findlay (OH) 28, Tiffin (OH) 14; Hardin-Simmons (TX) 42, Evangel (MO) 21; Mary (ND) 31, Minot St (ND) 20; Pacific Lutheran (WA) 61, Cumberland (TN) 7; Westminster (PA) 20, Georgetown (KY) 13.
Quarterfinals: Baker (KS) 28, Doane (NB) 21; Hardin-Simmons (TX) 30, Mary (ND) 20; Pacific Lutheran (WA) 35, Central Washington 17; Westminster (PA) 24, Findlay (OH) 0.
Semifinals: Pacific Lutheran (WA) 52, Baker (KS) 14; Westminster (PA) 10, Hardin-Simmons (TX) 0.
Championship: 12-18-93 Portland, OR

Pacific Lutheran (WA)	14	7	7	22—50
Westminster (PA)	0	7	7	6—20

Awards

Heisman Memorial Trophy

Player/School	Class	Pos	1st	2nd	3rd	Total
Charlie Ward, Florida St.	Sr	QB	740	39	12	2,310
Heath Shuler, Tennessee	Jr	QB	10	274	110	688
David Palmer, Alabama	Jr	WR	16	78	88	292
Marshall Faulk, San Diego St	Jr	RB	7	74	81	250
Glenn Foley, Boston College	Sr	QB	5	47	71	180
LeShon Johnson, N Illinois	Sr	RB	5	51	59	176
J.J. Stokes, UCLA	Jr	WR	3	37	48	131
Tyrone Wheatley, Michigan	Jr	RB	2	31	32	100
Trent Dilfer, Fresno State	Jr	QB	2	28	29	91
Eric Zeier, Georgia	Jr	QB	0	24	37	85

Note: Former Heisman winners and the media vote, with ballots allowing for 3 names (3 points for 1st, 2 for 2nd, 1 for 3rd).

Offensive Players of the Year

Maxwell Award (Player)............................Charlie Ward, Florida St, QB
Walter Camp Player of the Year (Back) .....Charlie Ward, Florida St, QB
Davey O'Brien Award (QB) ....Charlie Ward, Florida St, QB
Doak Walker Award (RB) ....Byron Morris,Texas Tech, RB

Other Awards

Vince Lombardi/Rotary Award (Lineman) ..Aaron Taylor, Notre Dame, OT
Outland Trophy (Interior lineman) ....Rob Waldrop, Arizona,
Butkus Award (Linebacker).......................Trev Alberts, Nebraska, LB
Jim Thorpe Award (Defensive back)..........Antonio Langham, Alabama, CB
Sporting News Player of the Year ....Charlie Ward, Florida St, QB
Walter Payton Award (Div I-AA Player) ......Doug Nussmeier, Idaho, QB
Harlon Hill Trophy (Div II Player) ....Roger Graham, New Haven, RB

Coaches' Awards

Walter Camp Award ....Terry Bowden, Auburn
Eddie Robinson Award (Div I-AA) ....Dan Allen, Boston University
Bobby Dodd Award ....Barry Alvarez, Wisconsin
Bear Bryant Award ....Terry Bowden, Auburn

AFCA COACHES OF THE YEAR

DIvision I-A ....Barry Alvarez, Wisconsin
Division I-AA ....Dan Allen, Boston University
Division II and NAIA Division I....................Bobby Wallace, North Alabama
Division III and NAIA Division II..................Larry Kehres, Mount Union

Football Writers Association of America All-America Team

OFFENSE

J.J. Stokes, UCLA, Jr ....Wide receiver
Johnnie Morton, Southern Cal, Sr ....Wide receiver
Ryan Yarborough, Wyoming, Sr..........Wide receiver
Aaron Taylor, Notre Dame, Sr ....OL
Wayne Gandy, Auburn, Sr ....OL
Marcus Spears, Northwestern St (LA)Sr..OL
Mark Dickson, Virginia, Sr ....OL
Jim Pyne, Virginia Tech, Sr ....OL
Charlie Ward, Florida St, Sr.................Quarterback
Marshall Faulk, San Diego St, Jr ....Running back
LeShon Johnson, N Illinois, Sr.............Running back
John Becksvoort, Tennessee, Jr ....PK
David Palmer, Alabama, Jr ....Kick returner

DEFENSE

Dan Wilkinson, Ohio St, So..................DL
Rob Waldrop, Arizona, Sr....................DL
Derrick Alexander, Florida St, So ....DL
Shante Carver, Arizona St, Sr..............DL
Trev Alberts, Nebraska, Sr ....Linebacker
Derrick Brooks, Florida St, Jr ....Linebacker
Barron Wortham, UTEP, Sr..................Linebacker
Antonio Langham, Alabama, Sr ....Defensive back
Aaron Glenn, Texas A & M, Sr ....Defensive back
Bobby Taylor, Notre Dame, So ....Defensive back
Bracey Walker, N Carolina, Sr............Defensive back
Terry Daniel, Auburn, Jr ....Punter

Division I-A

ATLANTIC COAST CONFERENCE

	Conference			Full Season			
	W	L	T	W	L	T	Pct
Florida St	8	0	0	12	1	0	.909
N Carolina	6	2	0	10	3	0	.769
Clemson	5	3	0	9	3	0	.750
Virginia	5	3	0	7	5	0	.583
N Carolina St	4	4	0	7	5	0	.583
Georgia Tech	3	5	0	5	6	0	.455
Duke	2	6	0	3	8	0	.273
Maryland	2	6	0	2	9	0	.182
Wake Forest	1	7	0	2	9	0	.182

BIG EAST CONFERENCE

	Conference			Full Season			
	W	L	T	W	L	T	Pct
W Virginia	7	0	0	11	1	0	.917
Miami	6	1	0	9	3	0	.750
Boston College	5	2	0	9	3	0	.750
Virginia Tech	4	3	0	9	3	0	.750
Syracuse	3	4	0	6	4	1	.591
Pittsburgh	2	5	0	3	8	0	.273
Rutgers	1	6	0	4	7	0	.364
Temple	0	7	0	1	10	0	.091

BIG EIGHT CONFERENCE

	Conference			Full Season			
	W	L	T	W	L	T	Pct
Nebraska	7	0	0	11	1	0	.917
Colorado	5	1	1	8	3	1	.708
Kansas St	4	2	1	9	2	1	.792
Oklahoma	4	3	0	9	3	0	.750
Kansas	3	4	0	5	7	0	.417
Missouri	2	5	0	3	7	1	.318
Iowa St	2	5	0	3	8	0	.273
Oklahoma St	0	7	0	3	8	0	.273

BIG TEN CONFERENCE

	Conference			Full Season			
	W	L	T	W	L	T	Pct
Ohio St	6	1	1	10	1	1	.875
Wisconsin	6	1	1	10	1	1	.875
Penn St	6	2	0	10	2	0	.833
Indiana	5	3	0	8	4	0	.666
Michigan	5	3	0	8	4	0	.666
Illinois	5	3	0	5	6	0	.456
Michigan St	4	4	0	6	6	0	.500
Iowa	3	5	0	6	6	0	.500
Minnesota	3	5	0	4	7	0	.364
Northwestern	0	8	0	2	9	0	.182
Purdue	0	8	0	1	10	0	.091

BIG WEST CONFERENCE

	Conference			Full Season			
	W	L	T	W	L	T	Pct
SW Louisiana	5	1	0	8	3	0	.727
Utah St	5	1	0	7	5	0	.583
Nevada	4	2	0	7	4	0	.636
New Mexico St	3	3	0	5	6	0	.456
N Illinois	3	3	0	4	7	0	.364
Pacific	2	4	0	3	8	0	.273
UNLV	2	4	0	3	8	0	.273
La Tech	2	4	0	2	9	0	.182
San Jose St	2	4	0	2	9	0	.182
Arkansas St	1	5	0	2	8	1	.227

Division I-A (Cont.)

MID-AMERICAN CONFERENCE

	Conference			Full Season			
	W	L	T	W	L	T	Pct
Ball St	7	0	1	8	3	1	.708
W Michigan	6	1	1	7	3	1	.682
Bowling Green	5	1	2	6	3	2	.636
Cent Michigan	5	4	0	5	6	0	.455
Akron	4	4	0	5	6	0	.455
Ohio U	4	5	0	4	7	0	.364
E Michigan	3	5	0	4	7	0	.364
Toledo	3	5	0	4	7	0	.364
Miami (OH)	3	6	0	4	7	0	.364
Kent	0	9	0	0	11	0	.000

PACIFIC-10 CONFERENCE

	Conference			Full Season			
	W	L	T	W	L	T	Pct
Arizona	6	2	0	10	2	0	.833
UCLA	6	2	0	8	4	0	.667
Southern Cal	6	2	0	8	5	0	.615
Washington	5	3	0	7	4	0	.636
California	4	4	0	9	4	0	.692
Arizona St	4	4	0	6	5	0	.545
Washington St	3	5	0	5	6	0	.455
Oregon	2	6	0	5	6	0	.455
Oregon St	2	6	0	4	7	0	.364
Stanford	2	6	0	4	7	0	.364

SOUTHEASTERN CONFERENCE

	Conference			Full Season*			
East	W	L	T	W	L	T	Pct
Florida	8	1	0	11	2	0	.846
Tennessee	6	1	1	9	2	1	.792
Kentucky	4	4	0	6	6	0	.500
Georgia	2	6	0	5	6	0	.455
S Carolina	2	6	0	4	7	0	.364
Vanderbilt	1	7	0	4	7	0	.364
West							
Auburn	8	0	0	11	0	0	1.000
Alabama	5	3	1	9	3	1	.731
Arkansas	3	4	1	5	5	1	.500
Louisiana St	3	5	0	5	6	0	.455
Mississippi	3	5	0	5	6	0	.455
Mississippi St	2	5	1	3	6	2	.364

*Full season record includes SEC Championship Game in which Florida defeated Alabama, 28–13, on Dec 4. Auburn was ineligible for postsason play in 1993 due to NCAA sanctions.

SOUTHWEST ATHLETIC CONFERENCE

	Conference			Full Season			
	W	L	T	W	L	T	Pct
Texas A&M	7	0	0	10	2	0	.833
Texas Tech	5	2	0	6	6	0	.500
Texas	5	2	0	5	5	1	.500
Rice	3	4	0	6	5	0	.545
Baylor	3	4	0	5	6	0	.455
TCU	2	5	0	4	7	0	.364
SMU	1	5	1	2	7	2	.273
Houston	1	5	1	1	9	1	.136

Division I-A *(Cont.)*

WESTERN ATHLETIC CONFERENCE

	Conference				Full Season			
	W	L	T		W	L	T	Pct
Fresno St	6	2	0		8	4	0	.667
Wyoming	6	2	0		8	4	0	.667
BYU	6	2	0		6	6	0	.500
Utah	5	3	0		7	6	0	.538
Colorado St	5	3	0		5	6	0	.455
New Mexico	4	4	0		6	5	0	.500
San Diego St	4	4	0		6	6	0	.500
Hawaii	3	5	0		6	6	0	.500
Air Force	1	7	0		4	8	0	.333
UTEP	0	8	0		1	11	0	.083

INDEPENDENTS

	Full Season			
	W	L	T	Pct
Notre Dame	11	1	0	.917
Louisville	9	3	0	.750
Cincinnati	8	3	0	.727
Army	6	5	0	.546
Memphis St	6	5	0	.546
Tulsa	4	6	1	.409
Navy	4	7	0	.364
Tulane	3	9	0	.250
S Mississippi	2	8	1	.227
E Carolina	2	9	0	.182

Division I-AA

BIG SKY CONFERENCE

	Conference				Full Season			
	W	L	T		W	L	T	Pct
Montana	7	0	0		10	2	0	.833
Idaho	5	2	0		11	2	0	.846
E Washington	5	2	0		7	3	0	.700
Montana St	4	3	0		7	4	0	.636
N Arizona	3	4	0		7	4	0	.636
Weber St	3	4	0		7	4	0	.636
Boise St	1	6	0		3	8	0	.273
Idaho St	0	7	0		2	9	0	.182

GATEWAY COLLEGIATE ATHLETIC CONFERENCE

	Conference				Full Season			
	W	L	T		W	L	T	Pct
N Iowa	5	1	0		8	4	0	.667
SW Missouri St	4	2	0		7	4	0	.636
W Illinois	4	2	0		4	7	0	.364
Illinois St	2	3	1		6	4	1	.591
E Illinois	2	3	1		3	7	1	.318
Indiana St	2	4	0		4	7	0	.364
S Illinois	1	5	0		2	9	0	.182

Division I-AA *(Cont.)*

IVY GROUP

	Conference			Full Season			
	W	L	T	W	L	T	Pct
Penn	7	0	0	10	0	0	1.000
Dartmouth	6	1	0	7	3	0	.700
Princeton	5	2	0	8	2	0	.800
Brown	3	4	0	4	6	0	.400
Cornell	3	4	0	4	6	0	.400
Yale	2	5	0	3	7	0	.300
Harvard	1	6	0	3	7	0	.300
Columbia	1	6	0	2	8	0	.200

MID-EASTERN ATHLETIC CONFERENCE

	Conference			Full Season			
	W	L	T	W	L	T	Pct
Howard	6	0	0	11	1	0	.917
S Carolina St	4	2	0	8	4	0	.667
Delaware St	4	2	0	6	5	0	.545
N Carolina A&T	3	3	0	8	3	0	.727
Florida A&T	3	3	0	5	6	0	.455
Bethune-Cookman	1	5	0	3	8	0	.273
Morgan St	0	6	0	2	9	0	.182

OHIO VALLEY CONFERENCE

	Conference			Full Season			
	W	L	T	W	L	T	Pct
Eastern Kentucky	7	1	0	8	4	0	.667
Tennessee Tech	7	1	0	8	3	0	.727
Tenn-Martin	5	3	0	6	5	0	.545
Middle Tennessee St	4	4	0	5	6	0	.455
Murray St	4	4	0	4	7	0	.364
Tennessee St	4	4	0	4	7	0	.364
Morehead St	2	6	0	3	8	0	.273
SE Missouri	2	6	0	3	8	0	.273
Austin Peay	0	8	0	1	10	0	.091

PATRIOT LEAGUE

	Conference			Full Season			
	W	L	T	W	L	T	Pct
Lehigh	4	1	0	7	4	0	.636
Lafayette	3	1	1	5	4	2	.545
Bucknell	3	2	0	4	7	0	.364
Holy Cross	2	3	0	3	8	0	.273
Colgate	1	3	1	3	7	1	.318
Fordham	1	4	0	1	10	0	.091

SOUTHERN CONFERENCE

	Conference			Full Season			
	W	L	T	W	L	T	Pct
Georgia Southern	7	1	0	10	3	0	.769
Marshall	6	2	0	10	3	0	.769
W Carolina	5	3	0	6	5	0	.545
Furman	4	4	0	5	5	1	.500
Citadel	4	4	0	5	6	0	.455
Appalachian St	4	4	0	4	7	0	.364
E Tennessee St	3	5	0	5	6	0	.455
TN-Chattanooga	2	6	0	4	7	0	.364
Virginia Military	1	7	0	1	10	0	.091

Division I-AA (Cont.)

SOUTHLAND CONFERENCE

	Conference			Full Season			
	W	L	T	W	L	T	Pct
McNeese St	7	0	0	10	3	0	.769
NE Louisiana	6	1	0	9	3	0	.750
SF Austin St	5	2	0	8	4	0	.667
Northwestern (LA)	3	4	0	5	6	0	.455
North Texas	2	5	0	4	7	0	.364
Sam Houston St	2	5	0	4	7	0	.364
Nicholls St	2	5	0	3	8	0	.273
SW Texas St	1	6	0	2	9	0	.182

SOUTHWESTERN ATHLETIC CONFERENCE

	Conference			Full Season			
	W	L	T	W	L	T	Pct
Southern-BR	7	0	0	11	1	0	.917
Alcorn St	6	1	0	8	3	0	.727
Grambling	4	3	0	7	4	0	.636
Alabama St	3	3	1	5	4	1	.550
Jackson St	3	3	1	5	5	1	.500
Mississippi Valley	2	3	2	4	4	2	.500
Texas Southern	1	6	0	2	9	0	.182
Prairie View A&M	0	7	0	0	11	0	.000

YANKEE CONFERENCE

	Conference			Full Season			
	W	L	T	W	L	T	Pct
MID-ATLANTIC							
William & Mary	7	1	0	9	3	0	.750
Delaware	6	2	0	9	4	0	.692
James Madison	4	5	0	6	5	0	.545
Richmond	4	6	0	5	6	0	.455
Villanova	2	7	0	3	8	0	.273
Northeastern	2	8	0	2	9	0	.182
NEW ENGLAND							
Boston University	9	0	0	12	1	0	.923
Massachusetts	7	3	0	8	3	0	.727
Connecticut	5	3	0	6	5	0	.545
New Hampshire	5	5	0	6	5	0	.545
Maine	2	7	0	3	8	0	.273
Rhode Island	1	7	0	3	8	0	.273

INDEPENDENTS

	Full Season			
	W	L	T	Pct
Troy St	12	0	1	.962
Youngstown St	11	2	0	.846
Alabama-Birmingham	9	2	0	.818
Wagner	9	2	0	.818
Towson St	8	2	0	.800
Central Florida	8	3	0	.727
W Kentucky	8	3	0	.727
Hofstra	6	3	1	.650
St Mary's, CA	6	3	1	.650
Davidson	6	4	0	.600
Liberty	6	5	0	.545
Central Connecticut	5	5	0	.500
Marist	5	5	0	.500
Samford	5	6	0	.455
Duquesne	4	6	0	.400
St Francis, PA	3	7	0	.300
Charleston Southern	3	8	0	.273
Buffalo	1	10	0	.091

Division I-A

SCORING

	Class	GP	TD	XP	FG	Pts	Pts/Game
Byron Morris, Texas Tech	Jr	11	22	2	0	134	12.18
Marshall Faulk, San Diego St	Jr	11	24	0	0	144	12.00
Darnell Campbell, Boston Coll	Sr	11	21	0	0	126	11.45
Bryan Reeves, Nevada	Sr	11	17	0	0	102	10.20
David Small, Cincinnati	Sr	11	17	0	0	102	10.20
Lindsey Chapman, California	Sr	11	17	0	0	102	9.27
J.J. Stokes, UCLA	Jr	11	17	0	0	102	9.27
Ryan Yarborough, Wyoming	Sr	11	16	2	0	98	8.91
Calvin Jones, Nebraska	Jr	11	13	0	0	78	8.67
John Becksvoort, Tennessee	Jr	11	0	59	12	95	8.64

FIELD GOALS

	Class	GP	FGA	FG	Pct	FG/Game
Michael Proctor, Alabama	So	11	29	22	.759	1.83
Bjorn Merten, UCLA	Fr	11	25	20	.800	1.82
Nathan Morreale, Utah St.	Fr	11	27	19	.704	1.73
Kanon Parkman, Georgia	So	11	27	19	.704	1.73
Jon Baker, Arizona St.	Jr	11	26	18	.692	1.64
Tom Dallen, Cincinnati	Jr	11	22	17	.773	1.55
Tom Burke, Mississippi St	Sr	11	23	17	.739	1.55
Aaron Price, Washington St	Sr	11	31	17	.548	1.55
Tommy Thompson, Oregon	Sr	11	21	16	.762	1.45
Chris Boniol, Louisiana Tech	Sr	11	22	16	.727	1.45
Scott Szeredy, Texas	Sr	11	22	16	.727	1.45

TOTAL OFFENSE

			Rushing		Passing		Total Offense			
	Class	GP	Car	Net	Att	Yds	Yds	Yds/Play	TDR*	Yds/Game
Chris Vargas, Nevada	Sr	11	45	67	490	4265	4332	8.10	35	393.82
Mike McCoy, Utah	Jr	12	99	109	430	3860	3969	7.50	21	330.75
Eric Zeier, Georgia	Jr	11	59	-43	425	3525	3482	7.19	25	316.55
Scott Milanovich, Maryland	So	11	91	-62	431	3499	3437	6.58	29	312.45
John Walsh, Brigham Young	So	11	83	-307	397	3727	3420	7.13	31	310.91
Steve Stenstrom, Stanford	Sr	11	57	-229	455	3627	3398	6.64	27	308.91
Charlie Ward, Florida St.	Sr	11	65	339	380	3032	3371	7.58	31	306.45
Glenn Foley, Boston College	Sr	11	26	-44	363	3397	3353	8.62	25	304.82
Anthony Calvillo, Utah St.	Sr	12	89	112	469	3148	3260	5.84	23	296.36
Trent Dilfer, Fresno St.	Jr	11	36	-64	333	3276	3212	8.70	29	292.00

*Touchdowns responsible for.

RUSHING

	Class	GP	Car	Yds	Avg	TD	Yds/Game
LeShon Johnson, Northern III	Sr	11	327	1976	6.0	12	179.64
Byron Morris, Texas Tech	Jr	11	298	1752	5.9	22	159.27
Brent Moss, Wisconsin	Jr	11	276	1479	5.4	14	134.45
Ron Rivers, Fresno St.	Sr	11	216	1440	6.7	14	130.91
Marshall Faulk, San Diego St.	Jr	12	300	1530	5.1	21	127.50
Junior Smith, East Caro.	Jr	11	278	1352	4.9	9	122.91
Napoleon Kaufman, Washington	Jr	11	226	1299	5.7	14	118.09
David Small, Cincinnati	Sr	10	223	1180	5.3	17	118.00
Calvin Jones, Nebraska	Jr	9	185	1043	5.6	12	115.89
Terrell Willis, Rutgers	Fr	11	195	1261	6.5	13	114.64

Red Raider Reverse

After the Texas Tech Red Raiders lost five of their first six games, the school newspaper called for coach Spike Dykes to resign, which elicited this response from him: "The fat lady might have cleared her throat, but she hasn't sung yet." Texas Tech won its last five games and earned a trip to the John Hancock Bowl. The only singing in Lubbock these days is in praise of Dykes.

Division I-A (Cont.)

PASSING EFFICIENCY

	Class	GP	Att	Comp	Pct Comp	Yds	Yds/Att	TD	Int	Rating Pts
Trent Dilfer, Fresno St. ....Jr	11	333	217	65.16	3276	9.84	28	4	173.1
Dave Barr, California ....Jr	11	275	187	68.00	2619	9.52	21	12	164.5
Darrell Bevell, Wisconsin ....So	11	256	177	69.14	2294	8.96	19	10	161.1
Charlie Ward, Florida St. ....Sr	11	380	264	69.47	3032	7.98	27	4	157.8
Maurice DeShazo, Va. Tech.......Jr	11	230	129	56.09	2080	9.04	22	7	157.5
Heath Shuler, Tennessee ....Jr	11	285	184	64.56	2354	8.26	25	8	157.3
Glenn Foley, Boston College......Sr	11	363	222	61.16	3397	9.36	25	10	157.0
Chris Vargas, Nevada ....Sr	11	490	331	67.55	4265	8.70	34	18	156.2
John Walsh, Brigham Young .....So	11	397	244	61.46	3727	9.39	28	15	156.0
Rob Johnson, Southern Cal........Jr	12	405	278	68.64	3285	8.11	26	5	155.5

Note: Minimum 15 attempts per game.

RECEPTIONS PER GAME

	Class	GP	No.	Yds	TD	R/Game
Chris Penn, Tulsa ....Sr	11	105	1578	12	9.55
Bryan Reeves, Nevada...........Sr	10	91	1362	17	9.10
Michael Stephens, Nevada ....Sr	11	80	1062	7	7.27
Brice Hunter, Georgia ....So	11	76	970	9	6.91
Darnay Scott, San Diego St. ...Jr	11	75	1262	10	6.82

RECEIVING YARDS PER GAME

	Class	GP	No.	Yds	TD	Yds/Game
Chris Penn, Tulsa ....Sr	11	105	1578	12	143.45
Ryan Yarborough, Wyoming ....Sr	11	67	1512	16	137.45
Bryan Reeves, Nevada..........Sr	10	91	1362	17	136.20
Darnay Scott, San Diego St..............Jr	11	75	1262	10	114.73
Johnnie Morton, Southern Cal ....Sr	12	78	1373	12	114.42

ALL-PURPOSE RUNNERS

	Class	GP	Rush	Rec	PR	KOR	Yds*	Yds/Game
LeShon Johnson, Northern Ill.............Sr	11	1976	106	0	0	2082	189.27
Terrell Willis, Rutgers.........................Fr	11	1261	61	0	704	2026	184.18
Marshall Faulk, San Diego St ....Jr	11	1530	644	0	0	2174	181.17
Byron Morris, Texas Tech ....Jr	11	1752	150	0	0	1902	172.91
Mike Adams, Texas...........................So	11	68	908	256	622	1854	168.55

*Includes interceptions return yards

INTERCEPTIONS

	Class	GP	No.	Yds	TD	Int/Game
Orlanda Thomas, SW Louisiana.........Jr	11	9	84	1	.82
Anthony Bridges, Louisville................Jr	11	7	184	2	.64
Alundis Brice, Mississippi..................Jr	11	7	98	2	.64
Antonio Langham, Alabama...............Sr	11	7	67	1	.64
Troy Jensen, San Jose St..................Sr	11	7	60	0	.64

PUNTING

	Class	No.	Avg
Chris Macinnis, Air Force......................Sr	49	47.00
Terry Daniel, Auburn..............................Jr	51	46.92
Mike Nesbitt, New Mexico.....................Sr	53	45.04
Brad Faunce, Nevada-Las Vegas ....Jr	61	45.00
Pat O'Neill, Syracuse.............................Sr	44	44.32

Note: Minimum of 3.6 per game.

PUNT RETURNS

	Class	No.	Yds	TD	Avg
Aaron Glenn, Texas A&M.........Sr	17	339	2	19.94
Shawn Summers, Tennessee...So	18	255	1	14.17
Lee Gissendaner, Nwestern.....Sr	16	223	0	13.94
Scott Gumina, Mississippi St....Jr	13	180	1	13.85
Andre Coleman, Kansas St. .....Sr	27	362	1	13.41

Note: Minimum 1.2 per game.

Division I-A (Cont.)

KICKOFF RETURNS

	Class	No.	Yds	TD	Avg
Leeland McElroy, Texas A&M	Fr	15	590	3	39.33
Chris Hewitt, Cincinnati	Fr	14	441	1	31.50
Tyler Anderson, Brigham Young	Sr	19	568	1	29.89
Andre Coleman, Kansas St.	Sr	15	434	0	28.93
Jack Jackson, Florida	So	17	480	1	28.24

Note: Minimum of 1.2 per game.

Division I-A Single-Game Highs

RUSHING AND PASSING

Rushing and passing plays: 74—Tim Schade, Minnesota, Sep 4 (vs Penn St).

Rushing and passing yards: 597—John Walsh, Brigham Young, Oct 30 (vs Utah St).

Rushing plays: 46—John Leach, Wake Forest, Nov 20 (vs Maryland).

Net rushing yards: 329—John Leach, Wake Forest, Nov 20 (vs Maryland).

Passes attempted: 66—Tim Schade, Minnesota, Sep 4 (vs Penn St); Chuck Clements, Houston, Nov 13 (vs Cincinnati).

Passes completed: 38—Charlie Ward, Florida St, Nov 27 (vs Florida).

Passing yards: 619—John Walsh, Brigham Young, Oct 30 (vs Utah St).

RECEIVING AND RETURNS

Passes caught: 16—Chris Penn, Tulsa, Nov 6 (vs East Carolina).

Receiving yards: 297—Brian Oliver, Ball St, Oct 9 (vs Toledo).

Punt return yards: 136—Ray Peterson, San Diego St, Sep 4 (vs Cal St-Northridge).

Kickoff return yards: 184—Eric Scott, Northwestern, Oct 2 (vs Ohio St).

Division I-AA

SCORING

	Class	GP	TD	XP	FG	Pts	Pts/Game
Tony Vinson, Towson St	Sr	10	23	0	0	144	14.40
Keith Elias, Princeton	Sr	10	21	4	0	130	13.00
Sherriden May, Idaho	Jr	11	22	0	0	132	12.00
Richard Howell, Davidson	Sr	10	18	2	0	110	11.00
Rupert Grant, Howard	Jr	11	20	0	0	120	10.91
Anthony Russo, St John's (NY)	Sr	11	18	0	0	108	9.82

FIELD GOALS

	Class	GP	FGA	FG	Pct	FG/Game
Jose Larios, McNeese St	So	11	28	22	.786	2.00
Todd Kurz, Illinois St	Fr	11	24	18	.750	1.64
Skip Thomas, Rhode Island	Fr	11	25	17	.680	1.55
Matt Ornelaz, Cal St-Northridge	Fr	8	16	11	.688	1.38
Roger Miller, NE Louisiana	Jr	11	17	15	.882	1.36
David Merrick, Marshall	Jr	11	21	15	.714	1.36
Terry Beldon, Northern Arizona	Sr	11	23	15	.652	1.36
Mike Morello, Boston University	Jr	11	26	15	.577	1.36

Division I-AA (Cont.)

TOTAL OFFENSE

	Class	GP	Rushing				Passing		Total Offense			
			Car	Gain	Loss	Net	Att	Yds	Yds	Yds/Play	TDR*	Yds/Game
Dave Dickenson, Montana...So		11	140	612	274	338	390	3640	3978	7.51	46	361.64
Steve McNair, Alcorn St.......Jr		11	107	752	119	633	386	3197	3830	7.77	30	348.18
Tom Proudian, Iona.............So		10	81	226	272	-46	440	3368	3322	6.38	30	332.20
S. Semptimphelter, Lehigh..Sr		11	102	328	249	79	413	3449	3528	6.85	30	320.73
Doug Nussmeier, Idaho.......Sr		11	96	656	102	554	304	2960	3514	8.78	41	319.45

*Touchdowns responsible for.

RUSHING

	Class	GP	Car	Yds	Avg	TD	Yds/Game
Tony Vinson, Towson St..........................Sr		10	293	2016	6.9	23	201.60
Keith Elias, Princeton...............................Sr		10	305	1731	5.7	19	173.10
Richard Johnson, Butler ....Sr		10	322	1535	4.8	10	153.50
Irving Spikes, Northeast La ....Sr		11	246	1563	6.4	14	142.09
Anthony Russo, St. John's (NY)...............Sr		11	311	1558	5.0	16	141.64

PASSING EFFICIENCY

	Class	GP	Att	Comp	Pct Comp	Yds	Yds/Att	TD	Int	Rating Pts
Shawn Knight, William & Mary.....Jr		10	177	125	70.62	2055	11.61	22	4	204.6
Doug Nussmeier, Idaho ....Sr		11	304	185	60.86	2960	9.74	33	5	175.2
Kelvin Simmons, Troy St.............Sr		11	224	143	63.84	2144	9.57	23	6	172.8
Dave Dickenson, Montana ....So		11	390	262	67.18	3640	9.33	32	9	168.0
Dan Crowley, Towson St ....Jr		10	217	125	57.60	1882	8.67	23	4	161.7

Note: Minimum 15 attempts per game.

RECEPTIONS PER GAME

	Class	GP	No.	Yds	TD	R/Game
Dave Cecchini, Lehigh..........................Sr		11	88	1318	16	8.00
Miles Macick, Pennsylvania ....So		10	72	840	13	7.20
David Rhodes, Central Florida ....Jr		11	78	1159	12	7.09
Derrick Ingram, Alabama-Birmingham..Jr		11	76	1115	8	6.91
Todd Eckenroad, St Francis (PA)..........Sr		9	61	678	1	6.78

RECEIVING YARDS PER GAME

	Class	GP	No.	Yds	TD	Yds/Game
Dave Cecchini, Lehigh..........................Sr		11	88	1318	16	119.82
David McLeod, James Madison.............Sr		11	64	1207	6	109.73
John Hyland, Dartmouth........................Sr		10	62	1076	9	107.60
David Rhodes, Central Florida ....Jr		11	78	1159	12	105.36
David Gamble, New Hampshire............Sr		11	67	1138	13	103.45

ALL-PURPOSE RUNNERS

	Class	GP	Rush	Rec	PR	KOR	Yds*	Yds/Game
Tony Vinson, Towson St.....................Sr		10	2016	57	0	0	2073	207.30
Keith Elias, Princeton ....Sr		10	1731	193	0	15	1939	193.90
Sherriden May, Idaho.........................Jr		11	1267	331	0	296	1894	172.18
Robert Trice, Cal St-Northridge..........Sr		10	1362	157	0	139	1658	165.80
Terrance Stokes, Pennsylvania..........Jr		10	1211	284	0	162	1657	165.70

*Includes interceptions return yards

INTERCEPTIONS

	Class	GP	No.	Yds	TD	Int/Game
Chris Helon, Boston University..............Jr		11	10	42	0	.91
Zack Bronson, McNeese St...................Fr		11	9	251	1	.82
Shayne Snider, Valparaiso ....Jr		10	8	59	0	.80
Curtis Burgins, North Carolina A&T.......Sr		11	8	174	1	.73
Brent Alexander, Tennessee St............Sr		11	8	121	0	.73
Bob Jordan, New Hampshire ....Sr		11	8	52	1	.73

Division I-AA *(Cont.)*

PUNTING

	Class	No.	Avg
Terry Belden, Northern Arizona	Sr	59	45.97
Ronnie McCutchan, Furman	So	47	43.77
Craig Melograno, Lehigh	Sr	46	42.87
Josh Farrell, Sam Houston St	Jr	48	42.35
Roy Hudson, Weber St	Sr	54	41.96

Note: Minimum 3.6 per game.

Division II

SCORING

	Class	GP	TD	XP	FG	Pts	Pts/Game
Roger Graham, New Haven	Jr	10	23	0	0	138	13.8
Leonard Davis, Lenoir-Rhyne	Sr	10	21	0	0	126	12.6
Jeremy Monroe, Michigan Tech	Sr	10	19	0	0	114	11.4
Preston Jackson, UC-Davis	Sr	10	18	2	0	110	11.0
Tyree Dye, Ferris St	Jr	11	20	0	0	120	10.9

FIELD GOALS

	Class	GP	FGA	FG	Pct	FG/Game
Raul De la Flor, Humboldt St	Sr	11	26	20	76.9	1.82
Michael Geary, Indiana (PA)	Sr	10	18	15	83.3	1.50
Ryan Achilles, Ft Hays St	Fr	10	21	14	66.7	1.40
Eivind Listerud, Missouri-Rolla	Jr	10	13	12	92.3	1.20
Bryan Schewe, Savannah St	Sr	10	25	12	48.0	1.20

TOTAL OFFENSE

	Class	GP	Yds	Yds/Game
Perry Klein, LIU-CW Post	Sr	10	4052	405.2
Marty Washington, Livingston	Sr	8	3146	393.3
Brett Salisbury, Wayne St (NE)	Sr	10	3732	373.2
Jed Drenning, Glenville St	Sr	10	3593	359.3
Jamie Pass, Mankato St	Sr	11	3537	321.5

RUSHING

	Class	GP	Car	Yds	TD	Yds/Game
Keith Higdon, Cheyney	Sr	10	330	1742	17	174.2
Roger Graham, New Haven	Jr	10	182	1687	19	168.7
Preston Jackson, UC-Davis	Sr	10	244	1552	18	155.2
Joe Simmons, NC Central	Sr	11	249	1699	16	154.5
Michael Mann, Indiana (PA)	Sr	10	269	1541	16	154.1

PASSING EFFICIENCY

	Class	GP	Att	Comp	Yds	Pct Comp	TD	Int	Rating Pts
James Weir, New Haven	Jr	10	266	161	2336	60.5	31	1	172.0
Brett Salisbury, Wayne St (NE)	Sr	10	395	276	3729	69.8	29	14	166.3
Gregory Clark, Virginia St	Sr	11	380	227	3437	59.7	38	11	162.9
Perry Klein, LIU-CW Post	Sr	10	407	248	3757	60.9	38	18	160.4
Rob Hyland, North Dakota St	Fr	10	151	90	1434	59.6	12	6	157.7

Note: Minimum 15 attempts per game.

RECEPTIONS PER GAME

	Class	GP	No.	Yds	TD	C/Game
Chris George, Glenville St	Jr	10	117	1876	15	11.7
Rus Bailey, NM Highlands	Sr	10	91	1192	12	9.1
Matt Carman, Livingston	Sr	10	88	1085	14	8.8
Byron Chamberlain, Wayne St (NE)	Jr	9	78	1015	7	8.7
Damon Thomas, Wayne St (NE)	Sr	10	81	1162	12	8.1

Division II *(Cont.)*

RECEIVING YARDS PER GAME

	Class	GP	No.	Yds	TD	Yds/Game
Chris George, Glenville St	Jr	10	117	1876	15	187.6
Greg Hopkins, Slippery Rock	Jr	10	79	1229	8	122.9
Rus Bailey, NM Highlands	Sr	10	91	1192	12	119.2
T.R. McDonald, North Dakota St	Sr	10	69	1181	11	118.1
Damon Thomas, Wayne St (NE)	Sr	10	81	1162	12	116.2

INTERCEPTIONS

	Class	GP	No.	Yds	Int/Game
Troy Crissman, KY Wesleyan	So	10	9	39	.9
Tyrone Andrews, Miles	So	10	8	86	.8
Nate Gruber, Winona St	Jr	10	8	110	.8
Micky Reeves, NM Highlands	So	9	7	267	.8
Corey Bell, Morris Brown	Jr	9	7	56	.8

PUNTING

	Class	No.	Avg
Chris Carter, Henderson St	Sr	53	43.5
Shayne Boyd, E New Mexico	Sr	57	42.5
Bob Koning, NM Highlands	Jr	41	42.3
Casey Anderson, Nebraska-Kearney	So	54	42.2
Carl Lyles, Johnson Smith	Jr	38	42.2

Note: Minimum 3.6 per game.

Division III

SCORING

	Class	GP	TD	XP	FG	Pts	Pts/Game
Matt Malmberg, St John's (MN)	Jr	10	27	2	0	164	16.4
Kelvin Gladney, Millsaps	Jr	9	21	2	0	128	14.2
Jeff Robinson, Albion	Jr	9	20	0	0	120	13.3
David Kogan, Wabash	Jr	8	17	2	0	104	13.0
Carey Bender, Coe	Sr	10	21	4	0	130	13.0

FIELD GOALS

	Class	GP	FGA	FG	Pct	FG/Game
Steve Milne, Brockport St	Sr	10	16	13	81.3	1.30
Greg Brame, Wittenberg	Sr	10	22	12	54.5	1.20

Eight tied with 1.00 FG per game.

TOTAL OFFENSE

	Class	GP	Yds	Yds/Game
Jordan Poznick, Principia	Sr	8	2705	338.1
Jim Ballard, Mount Union	Sr	10	3371	337.1
Tom Stallings, St Thomas (MN)	Sr	10	3158	315.8
LeRoy Williams, Upsala	Jr	9	2604	289.3
Chris Ings, Wabash	So	9	2543	282.6

RUSHING

	Class	GP	Car	Yds	TD	Yds/Game
Carey Bender, Coe	Sr	10	261	1718	15	171.8
Heath Butler, Northwestern (WI)	Sr	8	236	1371	15	171.4
Don Dawson, Ripon	Sr	9	214	1482	16	164.7
Ronnie Howard, Bridgewater (VA)	Sr	10	281	1610	13	161.0
Rodney Bond, Jersey City St	Sr	9	275	1446	11	160.7

PASSING EFFICIENCY

	Class	GP	Att	Comp	Yds	Pct Comp	TD	Int	Rating Pts
Willie Seiler, St John's (MN)	Sr	10	205	141	2648	68.7	33	6	224.6
Jim Ballard, Mount Union	Sr	10	314	229	3304	72.9	37	11	193.2
Guy Simons, Coe	Sr	10	185	110	1979	59.4	21	9	177.1
Chris Conkling, Anderson	Sr	10	185	127	1788	68.6	12	3	168.0
Paul Bell, Allegheny	Jr	10	156	92	1467	58.9	13	5	159.0

Note: Minimum 15 attempts per game

Division III (Cont.)

RECEPTIONS PER GAME

	Class	GP	No.	Yds	TD	C/Game
Matt Newton, Principia	Sr	8	96	1080	11	12.0
Greg Lehrer, Heidelberg	Sr	10	87	1202	8	8.7
Rob Lokerson, Muhlenberg	Jr	9	76	1275	6	8.4
Sam Williams, Defiance	Jr	10	84	1209	14	8.4
Vincent Hooper, Bethel (MN)	Sr	10	79	1000	12	7.9

RECEIVING YARDS PER GAME

	Class	GP	No.	Yds	TD	Yds/Game
Rob Lokerson, Muhlenberg	Jr	9	76	1275	6	141.7
Matt Newton, Principia	Sr	8	96	1080	11	135.0
Ed Bubonics, Mount Union	Sr	10	74	1286	10	128.6
Tom Buslee, St Olaf	Sr	10	75	1281	10	128.1
Vin Moncato, FDU-Madison	Jr	10	64	1217	14	121.7

INTERCEPTIONS

	Class	GP	No.	Yds	Int/Game
Ricky Webb, Emory & Henry	Sr	8	8	56	1.0
Aaron Minor, Macalester	Sr	10	9	89	.9
Chris Nylund, Hamline	Sr	10	9	115	.9
Scott Miller, Lycoming	Jr	10	9	146	.9
Bill Palmer, Hobart	Sr	10	9	83	.9
Andy Ostrand, Carroll (WI)	Sr	9	8	49	.9
Todd Sebold, Albion	Sr	9	8	42	.9
Greg Schramm, Trinity (CN)	Jr	8	7	50	.9
Tim Schwartz, NWestern (WI)	Jr	8	7	75	.9

PUNTING

	Class	No.	Avg
Mitch Holloway, Millsaps	Sr	45	42.4
Vic Moncato, FDU-Madison	Jr	59	42.3
Brett Geijer, Illinois Benedictine	Jr	45	41.8
Jon Hardy, Wesley	Sr	51	41.2
Andy Mahle, Otterbein	Jr	54	41.1

Note: Minimum 3.6 per game

1993 NCAA Division I-A Team Leaders

Offense

SCORING

	GP	Pts	Avg
Florida St	12	518	43.2
Tennessee	11	471	42.8
Fresno St	11	437	39.7
Florida	12	472	39.3
Nebraska	11	421	38.3
Nevada	11	419	38.1
Texas Tech	11	409	37.2
Texas A&M	11	404	36.7
Notre Dame	11	403	36.6
West Va.	11	401	36.5

RUSHING

	GP	Car	Yds	Avg	TD	Yds/Game
Army	11	660	3283	5.0	35	298.5
Oregon St	11	675	3254	4.8	25	295.8
Nebraska	11	589	3167	5.4	39	287.9
Air Force	12	713	3419	4.8	29	284.9
Hawaii	12	569	3247	5.7	35	270.6
Notre Dame	11	561	2868	5.1	37	260.7
North Carolina	12	628	3036	4.8	39	253.0
Wisconsin	11	557	2759	5.0	26	250.8
West Virginia	11	542	2684	5.0	28	244.0
Virginia Tech	11	582	2671	4.6	28	242.8

TOTAL OFFENSE

	GP	Plays	Yds	Avg	TD*	Yds/Game
Nevada	11	955	6260	6.6	56	569.09
Florida St	12	939	6576	7.0	63	548.00
Fresno St	11	808	5863	7.3	53	533.00
Boston College	11	827	5570	6.7	51	506.36
Utah	12	906	5815	6.4	43	484.58
Tennessee	11	762	5286	6.9	58	480.55
Florida	12	888	5719	6.4	59	476.58
Texas Tech	11	854	5225	6.1	51	475.00
Brigham Young	11	853	5222	6.1	51	474.73
Colorado	11	841	5175	6.2	40	470.45

*Defensive and special teams TDs not included.

PASSING

	G	Att	Comp	Yds	Pct Comp	Yds/Att	TD	Int	Yds/Game
Nevada	11	516	343	4373	66.5	8.5	34	19	397.5
Brigham Young	11	458	278	4060	60.7	8.9	31	18	369.1
Maryland	11	473	302	3823	63.8	8.1	26	21	347.5
Florida	12	488	284	4072	58.2	8.3	41	21	339.3
Stanford	11	474	308	3709	65.0	7.8	27	14	337.2
Florida St	12	469	327	3909	69.7	8.3	37	6	325.8
Utah	12	433	278	3891	64.2	9.0	22	10	324.3
Georgia	11	432	272	3552	63.0	8.2	24	7	322.9
San Diego St	12	465	269	3836	57.8	8.2	28	14	319.7
Fresno St	11	350	225	3425	64.3	9.8	29	5	311.4

Single-Game Highs

Points scored: 76—Nebraska, Sep 4 (vs North Texas).
Net rushing yards: 667—Oregon St, Oct 9 (vs Pacific [CA]).
Passing yards: 619—Brigham Young, Oct 30 (vs Utah St).
Total yards: 794—Nevada, Oct 2 (vs UNLV).
Fewest total yards allowed: 31—Oklahoma , Nov 13 (vs Oklahoma St).
Passes attempted: 66—Minnesota, Sep 4 (vs Penn St); Houston Nov 13 (vs Cincinnati).
Passes completed: 38—Maryland, Nov 20 (vs Wake Forest); Florida St, Nov 27 (vs Florida)

Defense

SCORING

	GP	Pts	Avg
Florida St.	11	113	9.4
Texas A&M	11	119	10.8
Miami (FL)	11	138	12.5
Mississippi	11	142	12.9
Tennessee	11	144	13.1
Alabama	12	158	13.2
Indiana	11	152	13.8
Michigan	11	153	13.9
Arizona	11	161	14.6
West Va	11	171	15.5

TOTAL DEFENSE

	GP	Plays	Yds	Avg	Yds/Game
Mississippi	11	727	2580	3.5	234.5
Arizona	11	739	2606	3.5	236.9
Texas A&M	11	740	2724	3.7	247.6
Miami (FL)	11	723	2814	3.9	255.8
Alabama	12	738	3104	4.2	258.7
Florida St	12	773	3414	4.4	284.5
Bowling Green	11	715	3285	4.6	298.6
Washington St	11	773	3287	4.3	298.8
Ohio St.	11	744	3293	4.4	299.4
Indiana	11	747	3336	4.5	303.3

RUSHING

	GP	Car	Yds	Avg	TD	Yds/Game
Arizona	11	368	331	.9	5	30.1
Washington St	11	438	949	2.2	11	86.3
Southwestern La.	11	378	975	2.6	12	88.6
Notre Dame	11	331	985	3.0	8	89.5
Florida St	12	397	1182	3.0	6	98.5
Mississippi	11	463	1127	2.4	8	102.5
North Carolina	12	410	1230	3.0	10	102.5
Michigan	11	379	1179	3.1	6	107.2
Florida	12	417	1334	3.2	9	111.2
Illinois	11	444	1265	2.8	10	115.0

TURNOVER MARGIN

		Turnovers Gained			Turnovers Lost			Margin/
	GP	Fum	Int	Total	Fum	Int	Total	Game
UCLA	11	21	18	39	13	7	20	1.73
Fresno St	11	15	16	31	9	5	14	1.55
Cincinnati	11	13	14	27	5	7	12	1.36
Tennessee	11	15	18	33	11	9	20	1.18
Texas A&M	11	19	13	32	7	12	19	1.18
Mississippi	11	15	15	30	3	14	17	1.18
Penn St	11	11	21	32	6	13	19	1.18
Colorado	11	13	13	26	6	7	13	1.18
Notre Dame	11	10	12	22	5	5	10	1.09
Texas Tech	11	16	14	30	11	7	18	1.09

PASSING EFFICIENCY

	GP	Att	Comp	Yds	Pct Comp	Yds/Att	TD	Pct TD	Int	Pct Int	Rating Pts
Texas A&M	11	292	116	1339	39.7	4.6	5	1.7	13	4.5	75.0
Alabama	12	310	144	1539	46.5	5.0	9	2.9	22	7.1	83.5
Mississippi	11	264	117	1453	44.3	5.5	5	1.9	15	5.7	85.4
Miami (FL)	11	288	138	1517	47.9	5.3	6	2.1	17	5.9	87.2
Tennessee	11	347	167	2105	48.1	6.1	7	2.0	18	5.2	95.4
Iowa	11	291	143	1798	49.1	6.2	6	2.1	18	6.2	95.5
Central Mich	11	302	151	1730	50.0	5.7	6	2.0	13	4.3	96.1
Florida St.	12	376	181	2232	48.1	5.9	9	2.4	15	4.0	97.9
Auburn	11	349	153	2039	43.8	5.8	15	4.3	15	4.3	98.5
Cincinnati	11	315	164	1867	52.1	5.9	7	2.2	14	4.4	100.3

FOR THE RECORD·Year by Year

Year	Champion	Record	Bowl Game	Head Coach
1883	Yale	8-0-0	No bowl	Ray Tompkins (Captain)
1884	Yale	9-0-0	No bowl	Eugene L. Richards (Captain)
1885	Princeton	9-0-0	No bowl	Charles DeCamp (Captain)
1886	Yale	9-0-1	No bowl	Robert N. Corwin (Captain)
1887	Yale	9-0-0	No bowl	Harry W. Beecher (Captain)
1888	Yale	13-0-0	No bowl	Walter Camp
1889	Princeton	10-0-0	No bowl	Edgar Poe (Captain)
1890	Harvard	11-0-0	No bowl	George A. Stewart George C. Adams
1891	Yale	13-0-0	No bowl	Walter Camp
1892	Yale	13-0-0	No bowl	Walter Camp
1893	Princeton	11-0-0	No bowl	Tom Trenchard (Captain)
1894	Yale	16-0-0	No bowl	William C. Rhodes
1895	Pennsylvania	14-0-0	No bowl	George Woodruff
1896	Princeton	10-0-1	No bowl	Garrett Cochran
1897	Pennsylvania	15-0-0	No bowl	George Woodruff
1898	Harvard	11-0-0	No bowl	W. Cameron Forbes
1899	Harvard	10-0-1	No bowl	Benjamin H. Dibblee
1900	Yale	12-0-0	No bowl	Malcolm McBride
1901	Michigan	11-0-0	Won Rose	Fielding Yost
1902	Michigan	11-0-0	No bowl	Fielding Yost
1903	Princeton	11-0-0	No bowl	Art Hillebrand
1904	Pennsylvania	12-0-0	No bowl	Carl Williams
1905	Chicago	11-0-0	No bowl	Amos Alonzo Stagg
1906	Princeton	9-0-1	No bowl	Bill Roper
1907	Yale	9-0-1	No bowl	Bill Knox
1908	Pennsylvania	11-0-1	No bowl	Sol Metzger
1909	Yale	10-0-0	No bowl	Howard Jones
1910	Harvard	8-0-1	No bowl	Percy Houghton
1911	Princeton	8-0-2	No bowl	Bill Roper
1912	Harvard	9-0-0	No bowl	Percy Houghton
1913	Harvard	9-0-0	No bowl	Percy Houghton
1914	Army	9-0-0	No bowl	Charley Daly
1915	Cornell	9-0-0	No bowl	Al Sharpe
1916	Pittsburgh	8-0-0	No bowl	Pop Warner
1917	Georgia Tech	9-0-0	No bowl	John Heisman
1918	Pittsburgh	4-1-0	No bowl	Pop Warner
1919	Harvard	9-0-1	Won Rose	Bob Fisher
1920	California	9-0-0	Won Rose	Andy Smith
1921	Cornell	8-0-0	No bowl	Gil Dobie
1922	Cornell	8-0-0	No bowl	Gil Dobie
1923	Illinois	8-0-0	No bowl	Bob Zuppke
1924	Notre Dame	10-0-0	Won Rose	Knute Rockne
1925	Alabama (H)	10-0-0	Won Rose	Wallace Wade
	Dartmouth (D)	8-0-0	No bowl	Jesse Hawley
1926	Alabama (H)	9-0-1	Tied Rose	Wallace Wade
	Stanford (D)(H)	10-0-1	Tied Rose	Pop Warner
1927	Illinois	7-0-1	No bowl	Bob Zuppke
1928	Georgia Tech (H)	10-0-0	Won Rose	Bill Alexander
	Southern Cal (D)	9-0-1	No bowl	Howard Jones
1929	Notre Dame	9-0-0	No bowl	Knute Rockne
1930	Notre Dame	10-0-0	No bowl	Knute Rockne
1931	Southern Cal	10-1-0	Won Rose	Howard Jones
1932	Southern Cal (H)	10-0-0	Won Rose	Howard Jones
	Michigan (D)	8-0-0	No bowl	Harry Kipke
1933	Michigan	7-0-1	No bowl	Harry Kipke
1934	Minnesota	8-0-0	No bowl	Bernie Bierman
1935	Minnesota (H)	8-0-0	No bowl	Bernie Bierman
	Southern Meth (D)	12-1-0	Lost Rose	Matty Bell
1936	Minnesota	7-1-0	No bowl	Bernie Bierman
1937	Pittsburgh	9-0-1	No bowl	Jock Sutherland
1938	Texas Christian (AP)	11-0-0	Won Sugar	Dutch Meyer
	Notre Dame (D)	8-1-0	No bowl	Elmer Layden
1939	Southern Cal (D)	8-0-2	Won Rose	Howard Jones
	Texas A&M (AP)	11-0-0	Won Sugar	Homer Norton

Year	Champion	Record	Bowl Game	Head Coach
1940	Minnesota	8-0-0	No bowl	Bernie Bierman
1941	Minnesota	8-0-0	No bowl	Bernie Bierman
1942	Ohio St	9-1-0	No bowl	Paul Brown
1943	Notre Dame	9-1-0	No bowl	Frank Leahy
1944	Army	9-0-0	No bowl	Red Blaik
1945	Army	9-0-0	No bowl	Red Blaik
1946	Notre Dame	8-0-1	No bowl	Frank Leahy
1947	Notre Dame	9-0-0	No bowl	Frank Leahy
	Michigan*	10-0-0	Won Rose	Fritz Crisler
1948	Michigan	9-0-0	No bowl	Bennie Oosterbaan
1949	Notre Dame	10-0-0	No bowl	Frank Leahy
1950	Oklahoma	10-1-0	Lost Sugar	Bud Wilkinson
1951	Tennessee	10-1-0	Lost Sugar	Bob Neyland
1952	Michigan St	9-0-0	No bowl	Biggie Munn
1953	Maryland	10-1-0	Lost Orange	Jim Tatum
1954	Ohio St	10-0-0	Won Rose	Woody Hayes
	UCLA (UP)	9-0-0	No bowl	Red Sanders
1955	Oklahoma	11-0-0	Won Orange	Bud Wilkinson
1956	Oklahoma	10-0-0	No bowl	Bud Wilkinson
1957	Auburn	10-0-0	No bowl	Shug Jordan
	Ohio St (UP)	9-1-0	Won Rose	Woody Hayes
1958	Louisiana St	11-0-0	Won Sugar	Paul Dietzel
1959	Syracuse	11-0-0	Won Cotton	Ben Schwartzwalder
1960	Minnesota	8-2-0	Lost Rose	Murray Warmath
1961	Alabama	11-0-0	Won Sugar	Bear Bryant
1962	Southern Cal	11-0-0	Won Rose	John McKay
1963	Texas	11-0-0	Won Cotton	Darrell Royal
1964	Alabama	10-1-0	Lost Orange	Bear Bryant
1965	Alabama	9-1-1	Won Orange	Bear Bryant
	Michigan St (UPI)	10-1-0	Lost Rose	Duffy Daugherty
1966	Notre Dame	9-0-1	No bowl	Ara Parseghian
1967	Southern Cal	10-1-0	Won Rose	John McKay
1968	Ohio St	10-0-0	Won Rose	Woody Hayes
1969	Texas	11-0-0	Won Cotton	Darrell Royal
1970	Nebraska	11-0-1	Won Orange	Bob Devaney
	Texas (UPI)	10-1-0	Lost Cotton	Darrell Royal
1971	Nebraska	13-0-0	Won Orange	Bob Devaney
1972	Southern Cal	12-0-0	Won Rose	John McKay
1973	Notre Dame	11-0-0	Won Sugar	Ara Parseghian
	Alabama (UPI)	11-1-0	Lost Sugar	Bear Bryant
1974	Oklahoma	11-0-0	No bowl	Barry Switzer
	Southern Cal (UPI)	10-1-1	Won Rose	John McKay
1975	Oklahoma	11-1-0	Won Orange	Barry Switzer
1976	Pittsburgh	12-0-0	Won Sugar	Johnny Majors
1977	Notre Dame	11-1-0	Won Cotton	Dan Devine
1978	Alabama	11-1-0	Won Sugar	Bear Bryant
	Southern Cal (UPI)	12-1-0	Won Rose	John Robinson
1979	Alabama	12-0-0	Won Sugar	Bear Bryant
1980	Georgia	12-0-0	Won Sugar	Vince Dooley
1981	Clemson	12-0-0	Won Orange	Danny Ford
1982	Penn St	11-1-0	Won Sugar	Joe Paterno
1983	Miami (FL)	11-1-0	Won Orange	Howard Schnellenberger
1984	Brigham Young	13-0-0	Won Holiday	LaVell Edwards
1985	Oklahoma	11-1-0	Won Orange	Barry Switzer
1986	Penn St	12-0-0	Won Fiesta	Joe Paterno
1987	Miami (FL)	12-0-0	Won Orange	Jimmy Johnson
1988	Notre Dame	12-0-0	Won Fiesta	Lou Holtz
1989	Miami (FL)	11-1-0	Won Sugar	Dennis Erickson
1990	Colorado	11-1-1	Won Orange	Bill McCartney
	Georgia Tech (UPI)	11-0-1	Won Citrus	Bobby Ross
1991	Miami (FL)	12-0-0	Won Orange	Dennis Erickson
	Washington (CNN)	12-0-0	Won Rose	Don James
1992	Alabama	13-0-0	Won Sugar	Gene Stallings
1993	Florida St	12-1-0	Won Orange	Bobby Bowden

*The AP, which had voted Notre Dame No. 1, took a second vote, giving the national title to Michigan after its 49-0 win over Southern Cal in the Rose Bowl.

Note: Selectors: Helms Athletic Foundation (H) 1883-1935, The Dickinson System (D) 1924-40, The Associated Press (AP) 1936-present, United Press International (UPI) 1958-90, and USA Today/CNN (CNN) 1991-present.

Results of Major Bowl Games

Rose Bowl

1-1-2	Michigan 49, Stanford 0
1-1-16	Washington St 14, Brown 0
1-1-17	Oregon 14, Pennsylvania 0
1-1-18	Mare Island 19, Camp Lewis 7
1-1-19	Great Lakes 17, Mare Island 0
1-1-20	Harvard 7, Oregon 6
1-1-21	California 28, Ohio St 0
1-2-22	Washington & Jefferson 0, California 0
1-1-23	Southern Cal 14, Penn St 3
1-1-24	Navy 14, Washington 14
1-1-25	Notre Dame 27, Stanford 10
1-1-26	Alabama 20, Washington 19
1-1-27	Alabama 7, Stanford 7
1-2-28	Stanford 7, Pittsburgh 6
1-1-29	Georgia Tech 8, California 7
1-1-30	Southern Cal 47, Pittsburgh 14
1-1-31	Alabama 24, Washington St 0
1-1-32	Southern Cal 21, Tulane 12
1-2-33	Southern Cal 35, Pittsburgh 0
1-1-34	Columbia 7, Stanford 0
1-1-35	Alabama 29, Stanford 13
1-1-36	Stanford 7, Southern Meth 0
1-1-37	Pittsburgh 21, Washington 0
1-1-38	California 13, Alabama 0
1-2-39	Southern Cal 7, Duke 3
1-1-40	Southern Cal 14, Tennessee 0
1-1-41	Stanford 21, Nebraska 13
1-1-42	Oregon St 20, Duke 16
1-1-43	Georgia 9, UCLA 0
1-1-44	Southern Cal 29, Washington 0
1-1-45	Southern Cal 25, Tennessee 0
1-1-46	Alabama 34, Southern Cal 14
1-1-47	Illinois 45, UCLA 14
1-1-48	Michigan 49, Southern Cal 0
1-1-49	Northwestern 20, California 14
1-2-50	Ohio St 17, California 14
1-1-51	Michigan 14, California 6
1-1-52	Illinois 40, Stanford 7
1-1-53	Southern Cal 7, Wisconsin 0
1-1-54	Michigan St 28, UCLA 20
1-1-55	Ohio St 20, Southern Cal 7
1-2-56	Michigan St 17, UCLA 14
1-1-57	Iowa 35, Oregon St 19
1-1-58	Ohio St 10, Oregon 7
1-1-59	Iowa 38, California 12
1-1-60	Washington 44, Wisconsin 8
1-2-61	Washington 17, Minnesota 7
1-1-62	Minnesota 21, UCLA 3
1-1-63	Southern Cal 42, Wisconsin 37
1-1-64	Illinois 17, Washington 7
1-1-65	Michigan 34, Oregon St 7
1-1-66	UCLA 14, Michigan St 12
1-2-67	Purdue 14, Southern Cal 13
1-1-68	Southern Cal 14, Indiana 3
1-1-69	Ohio St 27, Southern Cal 16
1-1-70	Southern Cal 10, Michigan 3
1-1-71	Stanford 27, Ohio St 17
1-1-72	Stanford 13, Michigan 12
1-1-73	Southern Cal 42, Ohio St 17
1-1-74	Ohio St 42, Southern Cal 21
1-1-75	Southern Cal 18, Ohio St 17
1-1-76	UCLA 23, Ohio St 10
1-1-77	Southern Cal 14, Michigan 6
1-2-78	Washington 27, Michigan 20
1-1-79	Southern Cal 17, Michigan 10
1-1-80	Southern Cal 17, Ohio St 16
1-1-81	Michigan 23, Washington 6
1-1-82	Washington 28, Iowa 0
1-1-83	UCLA 24, Michigan 14
1-2-84	UCLA 45, Illinois 9
1-1-85	Southern Cal 20, Ohio St 17
1-1-86	UCLA 45, Iowa 28
1-1-87	Arizona St 22, Michigan 15
1-1-88	Michigan St 20, Southern Cal 17
1-2-89	Michigan 22, Southern Cal 14
1-1-90	Southern Cal 17, Michigan 10
1-1-91	Washington 46, Iowa 34
1-1-92	Washington 34, Michigan 14
1-1-93	Michigan 38, Washington 31
1-1-94	Wisconsin 21, UCLA 16

City: Pasadena.

Stadium: Rose Bowl.

Capacity: 104,091.

Automatic Berths: Pacific-10 champ vs Big 10 champ (since 1947).

Playing Sites: Tournament Park (1902, 1916-22), Rose Bowl (1923-41, since 1943), Duke Stadium, Durham, NC (1942).

Orange Bowl

1-1-35	Bucknell 26, Miami (FL) 0
1-1-36	Catholic 20, Mississippi 19
1-1-37	Duquesne 13, Mississippi St 12
1-1-38	Auburn 6, Michigan St 0
1-2-39	Tennessee 17, Oklahoma 0
1-1-40	Georgia Tech 21, Missouri 7
1-1-41	Mississippi St 14, Georgetown 7
1-1-42	Georgia 40, Texas Christian 26
1-1-43	Alabama 37, Boston College 21
1-1-44	Louisiana St 19, Texas A&M 14
1-1-45	Tulsa 26, Georgia Tech 12
1-1-46	Miami (FL) 13, Holy Cross 6
1-1-47	Rice 8, Tennessee 0
1-1-48	Georgia Tech 20, Kansas 14
1-1-49	Texas 41, Georgia 28
1-2-50	Santa Clara 21, Kentucky 13
1-1-51	Clemson 15, Miami (FL) 14
1-1-52	Georgia Tech 17, Baylor 14
1-1-53	Alabama 61, Syracuse 6
1-1-54	Oklahoma 7, Maryland 0
1-1-55	Duke 34, Nebraska 7
1-2-56	Oklahoma 20, Maryland 6
1-1-57	Colorado 27, Clemson 21
1-1-58	Oklahoma 48, Duke 21
1-1-59	Oklahoma 21, Syracuse 6
1-1-60	Georgia 14, Missouri 0
1-2-61	Missouri 21, Navy 14
1-1-62	Louisiana St 25, Colorado 7
1-1-63	Alabama 17, Oklahoma 0
1-1-64	Nebraska 13, Auburn 7
1-1-65	Texas 21, Alabama 17
1-1-66	Alabama 39, Nebraska 28
1-2-67	Florida 27, Georgia Tech 12
1-1-68	Oklahoma 26, Tennessee 24
1-1-69	Penn St 15, Kansas 14
1-1-70	Penn St 10, Missouri 3
1-1-71	Nebraska 17, Louisiana St 12
1-1-72	Nebraska 38, Alabama 6
1-1-73	Nebraska 40, Notre Dame 6
1-1-74	Penn St 16, Louisiana St 9
1-1-75	Notre Dame 13, Alabama 11
1-1-76	Oklahoma 14, Michigan 6
1-1-77	Ohio St 27, Colorado 10
1-2-78	Arkansas 31, Oklahoma 6

Orange Bowl (Cont.)

1-1-79..............Oklahoma 31, Nebraska 24
1-1-80..............Oklahoma 24, Florida St 7
1-1-81..............Oklahoma 18, Florida St 17
1-1-82..............Clemson 22, Nebraska 15
1-1-83..............Nebraska 21, Louisiana St 20
1-2-84..............Miami (FL) 31, Nebraska 30
1-1-85..............Washington 28, Oklahoma 17
1-1-86..............Oklahoma 25, Penn St 10
1-1-87..............Oklahoma 42, Arkansas 8
1-1-88..............Miami (FL) 20, Oklahoma 14
1-2-89..............Miami (FL) 23, Nebraska 3
1-1-90..............Notre Dame 21, Colorado 6
1-1-91..............Colorado 10, Notre Dame 9
1-1-92..............Miami 22, Nebraska 0
1-1-93..............Florida State 27, Nebraska 14
1-1-94..............Florida State 18, Nebraska 16
City: Miami.
Stadium: Orange Bowl.
Capacity: 75,500.
Automatic Berths: Big 8 champ (1954-64, since 1976).

Sugar Bowl

1-1-35..............Tulane 20, Temple 14
1-1-36..............Texas Christian 3, Louisiana St 2
1-1-37..............Santa Clara 21, Louisiana St 14
1-1-38..............Santa Clara 6, Louisiana St 0
1-2-39..............Texas Christian 15, Carnegie Tech 7
1-1-40..............Texas A&M 14, Tulane 13
1-1-41..............Boston Col 19, Tennessee 13
1-1-42..............Fordham 2, Missouri 0
1-1-43..............Tennessee 14, Tulsa 7
1-1-44..............Georgia Tech 20, Tulsa 18
1-1-45..............Duke 29, Alabama 26
1-1-46..............Oklahoma St 33, St Mary's (CA) 13
1-1-47..............Georgia 20, N Carolina 10
1-1-48..............Texas 27, Alabama 7
1-1-49..............Oklahoma 14, N Carolina 6
1-2-50..............Oklahoma 35, Louisiana St 0
1-1-51..............Kentucky 13, Oklahoma 7
1-1-52..............Maryland 28, Tennessee 13
1-1-53..............Georgia Tech 24, Mississippi 7
1-1-54..............Georgia Tech 42, W Virginia 19
1-1-55..............Navy 21, Mississippi 0
1-2-56..............Georgia Tech 7, Pittsburgh 0
1-1-57..............Baylor 13, Tennessee 7
1-1-58..............Mississippi 39, Texas 7
1-1-59..............Louisiana St 7, Clemson 0
1-1-60..............Mississippi 21, Louisiana St 0
1-2-61..............Mississippi 14, Rice 6
1-1-62..............Alabama 10, Arkansas 3
1-1-63..............Mississippi 17, Arkansas 13
1-1-64..............Alabama 12, Mississippi 7
1-1-65..............Louisiana St 13, Syracuse 10
1-1-66..............Missouri 20, Florida 18
1-2-67..............Alabama 34, Nebraska 7
1-1-68..............Louisiana St 20, Wyoming 13
1-1-69..............Arkansas 16, Georgia 2
1-1-70..............Mississippi 27, Arkansas 22
1-1-71..............Tennessee 34, Air Force 13
1-1-72..............Oklahoma 40, Auburn 22
12-31-72..........Oklahoma 14, Penn St 0
12-31-73..........Notre Dame 24, Alabama 23
12-31-74..........Nebraska 13, Florida 10
12-31-75..........Alabama 13, Penn St 6
1-1-77..............Pittsburgh 27, Georgia 3

Sugar Bowl (Cont.)

1-2-78..............Alabama 35, Ohio St 6
1-1-79..............Alabama 14, Penn St 7
1-1-80..............Alabama 24, Arkansas 9
1-1-81..............Georgia 17, Notre Dame 10
1-1-82..............Pittsburgh 24, Georgia 20
1-1-83..............Penn St 27, Georgia 23
1-2-84..............Auburn 9, Michigan 7
1-1-85..............Nebraska 28, Louisiana St 10
1-1-86..............Tennessee 35, Miami (FL) 7
1-1-87..............Nebraska 30, Louisiana St 15
1-1-88..............Syracuse 16, Auburn 16
1-2-89..............Florida St 13, Auburn 7
1-1-90..............Miami (FL) 33, Alabama 25
1-1-91..............Tennessee 23, Virginia 22
1-1-92..............Notre Dame 39, Florida 28
1-1-93..............Alabama 34, Miami 13
1-1-94..............Florida 41, West Virginia 7
City: New Orleans.
Stadium: Louisiana Superdome.
Capacity: 69,548.
Automatic Berths: Southeastern champ (since 1977).
Playing Sites: Tulane Stadium (1935-74), Superdome (1974)

Cotton Bowl

1-1-37..............Texas Christian 16, Marquette 6
1-1-38..............Rice 28, Colorado 14
1-2-39..............St. Mary's (CA) 20, Texas Tech 13
1-1-40..............Clemson 6, Boston Col 3
1-1-41..............Texas A&M 13, Fordham 12
1-1-42..............Alabama 29, Texas A&M 21
1-1-43..............Texas 14, Georgia Tech 7
1-1-44..............Texas 7, Randolph Field 7
1-1-45..............Oklahoma St 34, Texas Christian 0
1-1-46..............Texas 40, Missouri 27
1-1-47..............Arkansas 0, Louisiana St 0
1-1-48..............Southern Meth 13, Penn St 13
1-1-49..............Southern Meth 21, Oregon 13
1-2-50..............Rice 27, N Carolina 13
1-1-51..............Tennessee 20, Texas 14
1-1-52..............Kentucky 20, Texas Christian 7
1-1-53..............Texas 16, Tennessee 0
1-1-54..............Rice 28, Alabama 6
1-1-55..............Georgia Tech 14, Arkansas 6
1-2-56..............Mississippi 14, Texas Christian 13
1-1-57..............Texas Christian 28, Syracuse 27
1-1-58..............Navy 20, Rice 7
1-1-59..............Texas Christian 0, Air Force 0
1-1-60..............Syracuse 23, Texas 14
1-2-61..............Duke 7, Arkansas 6
1-1-62..............Texas 12, Mississippi 7
1-1-63..............Louisiana St 13, Texas 0
1-1-64..............Texas 28, Navy 6
1-1-65..............Arkansas 10, Nebraska 7
1-1-66..............Louisiana St 14, Arkansas 7
12-31-66..........Georgia 24, Southern Meth 9
1-1-68..............Texas A&M 20, Alabama 16
1-1-69..............Texas 36, Tennessee 13
1-1-70..............Texas 21, Notre Dame 17
1-1-71..............Notre Dame 24, Texas 11
1-1-72..............Penn St 30, Texas 6
1-1-73..............Texas 17, Alabama 13
1-1-74..............Nebraska 19, Texas 3
1-1-75..............Penn St 41, Baylor 20
1-1-76..............Arkansas 31, Georgia 10
1-1-77..............Houston 30, Maryland 21

Cotton Bowl *(Cont.)*

1-2-78..............Notre Dame 38, Texas 10
1-1-79..............Notre Dame 35, Houston 34
1-1-80..............Houston 17, Nebraska 14
1-1-81..............Alabama 30, Baylor 2
1-1-82..............Texas 14, Alabama 12
1-1-83..............Southern Meth 7, Pittsburgh 3
1-2-84..............Georgia 10, Texas 9
1-1-85..............Boston Col 45, Houston 28
1-1-86..............Texas A&M 36, Auburn 16
1-1-87..............Ohio St 28, Texas A&M 12
1-1-88..............Texas A&M 35, Notre Dame 10
1-2-89..............UCLA 17, Arkansas 3
1-1-90..............Tennessee 31, Arkansas 27
1-1-91..............Miami (FL) 46, Texas 3
1-1-92..............Florida St 10, Texas A&M 2
1-1-93..............Notre Dame 28, Texas A&M 3
1-1-94..............Notre Dame 24, Texas A&M 21

City: Dallas.

Stadium: Cotton Bowl.

Capacity: 72,032.

Automatic Berths: Southwest champ (since 1942).

Playing Sites: Fair Park Stadium (1937), Cotton Bowl (since 1938).

John Hancock Bowl

1-1-36..............Hardin-Simmons 14, New Mexico St 14
1-1-37..............Hardin-Simmons 34, UTEP 6
1-1-38..............W Virginia 7, Texas Tech 6
1-2-39..............Utah 26, New Mexico 0
1-1-40..............Catholic 0, Arizona St 0
1-1-41..............Case Reserve 26, Arizona St 13
1-1-42..............Tulsa 6, Texas Tech 0
1-1-43..............2nd Air Force 13, Hardin-Simmons 7
1-1-44..............Southwestern (TX) 7, New Mexico 0
1-1-45..............Southwestern (TX) 35, New Mexico 0
1-1-46..............New Mexico 34, Denver 24
1-1-47..............Cincinnati 18, Virginia Tech 6
1-1-48..............Miami (OH) 13, Texas Tech 12
1-1-49..............W Virginia 21, UTEP 12
1-2-50..............UTEP 33, Georgetown 20
1-1-51..............West Texas St 14, Cincinnati 13
1-1-52..............Texas St 25, Pacific 14
1-1-53..............Pacific 26, Southern Miss 7
1-1-54..............UTEP 37, Southern Miss 14
1-1-55..............UTEP 47, Florida St 20
1-2-56..............Wyoming 21, Texas Tech 14
1-1-57..............George Washington 13, UTEP 0
1-1-58..............Louisville 34, Drake 20
12-31-58..........Wyoming 14, Hardin-Simmons 6
12-31-59..........New Mexico St 28, N Texas 8
12-31-60..........New Mexico St 20, Utah St 13
12-30-61..........Villanova 17, Wichita St 9
12-31-62..........W Texas St 15, Ohio 14
12-31-63..........Oregon 21, Southern Meth 14
12-26-64..........Georgia 7, Texas Tech 0
12-31-65..........UTEP 13, Texas Christian 12
12-24-66..........Wyoming 28, Florida St 20
12-30-67..........UTEP 14, Mississippi 7
12-28-68..........Auburn 34, Arizona 10
12-20-69..........Nebraska 45, Georgia 6
12-19-70..........Georgia Tech 17, Texas Tech 9
12-18-71..........Louisiana St 33, Iowa St 15
12-30-72..........N Carolina 32, Texas Tech 28
12-29-73..........Missouri 34, Auburn 17
12-28-74..........Mississippi St 26, N Carolina 24

John Hancock Bowl *(Cont.)*

12-26-75..........Pittsburgh 33, Kansas 19
1-2-77..............Texas A&M 37, Florida 14
12-31-77..........Stanford 24, Louisiana St 14
12-23-78..........Texas 42, Maryland 0
12-22-79..........Washington 14, Texas 7
12-27-80..........Nebraska 31, Mississippi St 17
12-26-81..........Oklahoma 40, Houston 14
12-25-82..........N Carolina 26, Texas 10
12-24-83..........Alabama 28, Southern Meth 7
12-22-84..........Maryland 28, Tennessee 27
12-28-85..........Georgia 13, Arizona 13
12-25-86..........Alabama 28, Washington 6
12-25-87..........Oklahoma St 35, W Virginia 33
12-24-88..........Alabama 29, Army 28
12-30-89..........Pittsburgh 31, Texas A&M 28
12-31-90..........Michigan St 17, Southern Cal 16
12-31-91..........UCLA 6, Illinois 3
12-31-92..........Baylor 20, Arizona 15
12-24-93..........Oklahoma 41, Texas Tech 10

City: El Paso.

Stadium: Sun Bowl.

Capacity: 52,000.

Automatic Berths: None.

Name Changes: Sun Bowl (1936-86), John Hancock Sun Bowl (1987-88), John Hancock Bowl (since 1989).

Playing Sites: Kidd Field (1936-62), Sun Bowl (since 1963).

Gator Bowl

1-1-46..............Wake Forest 26, S Carolina 14
1-1-47..............Oklahoma 34, N Carolina St 13
1-1-48..............Maryland 20, Georgia 20
1-1-49..............Clemson 24, Missouri 23
1-2-50..............Maryland 20, Missouri 7
1-1-51..............Wyoming 20, Washington & Lee 7
1-1-52..............Miami (FL) 14, Clemson 0
1-1-53..............Florida 14, Tulsa 13
1-1-54..............Texas Tech 35, Auburn 13
12-31-54..........Auburn 33, Baylor 13
12-31-55..........Vanderbilt 25, Auburn 13
12-29-56..........Georgia Tech 21, Pittsburgh 14
12-28-57..........Tennessee 3, Texas A&M 0
12-27-58..........Mississippi 7, Florida 3
1-2-60..............Arkansas 14, Georgia Tech 7
12-31-60..........Florida 13, Baylor 12
12-30-61..........Penn St 30, Georgia Tech 15
12-29-62..........Florida 17, Penn St 7
12-28-63..........N Carolina 35, Air Force 0
1-2-65..............Florida St 36, Oklahoma 19
12-31-65..........Georgia Tech 31, Texas Tech 21
12-31-66..........Tennessee 18, Syracuse 12
12-30-67..........Penn St 17, Florida St 17
12-28-68..........Missouri 35, Alabama 10
12-27-69..........Florida 14, Tennessee 13
1-2-71..............Auburn 35, Mississippi 28
12-31-71..........Georgia 7, N Carolina 3
12-30-72..........Auburn 24, Colorado 3
12-29-73..........Texas Tech 28, Tennessee 19
12-30-74..........Auburn 27, Texas 3
12-29-75..........Maryland 13, Florida 0
12-27-76..........Notre Dame 20, Penn St 9
12-30-77..........Pittsburgh 34, Clemson 3
12-29-78..........Clemson 17, Ohio St 15
12-28-79..........N Carolina 17, Michigan 15
12-29-80..........Pittsburgh 37, S Carolina 9
12-28-81..........N Carolina 31, Arkansas 27
12-30-82..........Florida St 31, W Virginia 12

Results of Major Bowl Games *(Cont.)*

Gator Bowl *(Cont.)*

12-30-83 ....Florida 14, Iowa 6
12-28-84 ....Oklahoma St 21, S Carolina 14
12-30-85 ....Florida St 34, Oklahoma St 23
12-27-86 ....Clemson 27, Stanford 21
12-31-87 ....Louisiana St 30, S Carolina 13
1-1-89 ....Georgia 34, Michigan St 27
12-30-89 ....Clemson 27, W Virginia 7
1-1-91 ....Michigan 35, Mississippi 3
12-29-91 ....Oklahoma 48, Virginia 14
12-31-92 ....Florida 27, NC State 10
12-31-93 ....Alabama 24, North Carolina 10

City: Jacksonville, FL.

Stadium: Gator Bowl.

Capacity: 82,000. Automatic Berths: None.

Florida Citrus Bowl

1-1-47 ....Catawba 31, Maryville (TN) 6
1-1-48 ....Catawba 7, Marshall 0
1-1-49 ....Murray St 21, Sul Ross St 21
1-2-50 ....St Vincent 7, Emory & Henry 6
1-1-51 ....Morris Harvey 35, Emory & Henry 14
1-1-52 ....Stetson 35, Arkansas St 20
1-1-53 ....E Texas St 33, Tennessee Tech 0
1-1-54 ....E Texas St 7, Arkansas St 7
1-1-55 ....NE-Omaha 7, Eastern Kentucky 6
1-2-56 ....Juniata 6, Missouri Valley 6
1-1-57 ....W Texas St 20, Southern Miss 13
1-1-58 ....E Texas St 10, Southern Miss 9
12-27-58 ....E Texas St 26, Missouri Valley 7
1-1-60 ....Middle Tennessee St 21, Presbyterian 12
12-30-60 ....Citadel 27, Tennessee Tech 0
12-29-61 ....Lamar 21, Middle Tennessee St 14
12-22-62 ....Houston 49, Miami (OH) 21
12-28-63 ....Western Kentucky 27, Coast Guard 0
12-12-64 ....E Carolina 14, Massachusetts 13
12-11-65 ....E Carolina 31, Maine 0
12-10-66 ....Morgan St 14, West Chester 6
12-16-67 ....TN-Martin 25, West Chester 8
12-27-68 ....Richmond 49, Ohio 42
12-26-69 ....Toledo 56, Davidson 33
12-28-70 ....Toledo 40, William & Mary 12
12-28-71 ....Toledo 28, Richmond 3
12-29-72 ....Tampa 21, Kent St 18
12-22-73 ....Miami (OH) 16, Florida 7
12-21-74 ....Miami (OH) 21, Georgia 10
12-20-75 ....Miami (OH) 20, S Carolina 7
12-18-76 ....Oklahoma St 49, Brigham Young 21
12-23-77 ....Florida St 40, Texas Tech 17
12-23-78 ....N Carolina St 30, Pittsburgh 17
12-22-79 ....Louisiana St 34, Wake Forest 10
12-20-80 ....Florida 35, Maryland 20
12-19-81 ....Missouri 19, Southern Miss 17
12-18-82 ....Auburn 33, Boston Col 26
12-17-83 ....Tennessee 30, Maryland 23
12-22-84 ....Georgia 17, Florida St 17
12-28-85 ....Ohio St 10, Brigham Young 7
1-1-87 ....Auburn 16, Southern Cal 7
1-1-88 ....Clemson 35, Penn St 10
1-2-89 ....Clemson 13, Oklahoma 6
1-1-90 ....Illinois 31, Virginia 21
1-1-91 ....Georgia Tech 45, Nebraska 21
1-1-92 ....California 37, Clemson 13
1-1-93 ....Georgia 21, Ohio State 14

Florida Citrus Bowl *(Cont.)*

1-1-94 ....Penn State 31, Tennessee 13

City: Orlando, FL.

Stadium: Florida Citrus Bowl-Orlando.

Capacity: 52,300. Automatic Berths: None.

Name Change: Tangerine Bowl (1947-82), Florida Citrus Bowl (since 1983).

Playing Sites: Tangerine Bowl (1947-72, 1974-82); Florida Field, Gainesville (1973); Orlando Stadium (1983-85); Florida Citrus Bowl- Orlando (since 1986). Tangerine Bowl, Orlando Stadium and Florida Citrus Bowl-Orlando are identical site.

Liberty Bowl

12-19-59 ....Penn St 7, Alabama 0
12-17-60 ....Penn St 41, Oregon 12
12-16-61 ....Syracuse 15, Miami (FL) 14
12-15-62 ....Oregon St 6, Villanova 0
12-21-63 ....Mississippi St 16, N Carolina St
12-19-64 ....Utah 32, W Virginia 6
12-18-65 ....Mississippi 13, Auburn 7
12-10-66 ....Miami (FL) 14, Virginia Tech 7
12-16-67 ....N Carolina St 14, Georgia 7
12-14-68 ....Mississippi 34, Virginia Tech 17
12-13-69 ....Colorado 47, Alabama 33
12-12-70 ....Tulane 17, Colorado 3
12-20-71 ....Tennessee 14, Arkansas 13
12-18-72 ....Georgia Tech 31, Iowa St 30
12-17-73 ....N Carolina St 31, Kansas 18
12-16-74 ....Tennessee 7, Maryland 3
12-22-75 ....Southern Cal 20, Texas A&M 0
12-20-76 ....Alabama 36, UCLA 6
12-19-77 ....Nebraska 21, N Carolina 17
12-23-78 ....Missouri 20, Louisiana St 15
12-22-79 ....Penn St 9, Tulane 6
12-27-80 ....Purdue 28, Missouri 25
12-30-81 ....Ohio St 31, Navy 28
12-29-82 ....Alabama 21, Illinois 15
12-29-83 ....Notre Dame 19, Boston Col 18
12-27-84 ....Auburn 21, Arkansas 15
12-27-85 ....Baylor 21, Louisiana St 7
12-29-86 ....Tennessee 21, Minnesota 14
12-29-87 ....Georgia 20, Arkansas 17
12-28-88 ....Indiana 34, S Carolina 10
12-28-89 ....Mississippi 42, Air Force 29
12-27-90 ....Air Force 23, Ohio St 11
12-29-91 ....Air Force 38, Mississippi St 15
12-31-92 ....Mississippi 13, Air Force 0
12-28-93 ....Louisville 18, Michigan St 7

City: Memphis (since 1965).

Stadium: Liberty Bowl Memorial Stadium.

Capacity: 63,000.

Automatic Berths: Since 1989, winner of Commander-in-Chief's Trophy (Air Force, Army, Navy).

Playing Sites: Philadelphia (Municipal Stadium, 1959-63), Atlantic City (Convention Center, 1964), Memphis.

Peach Bowl

12-30-68 ....Louisiana St 31, Florida St 27
12-30-69 ....W Virginia 14, S Carolina 3
12-30-70 ....Arizona St 48, N Carolina 26
12-30-71 ....Mississippi 41, Georgia Tech 18

Peach Bowl *(Cont.)*

12-29-72 ....N Carolina St 49, W Virginia 13
12-28-73 ....Georgia 17, Maryland 16
12-28-74 ....Vanderbilt 6, Texas Tech 6
12-31-75 ....W Virginia 13, N Carolina St 10
12-31-76 ....Kentucky 21, N Carolina 0
12-31-77 ....N Carolina St 24, Iowa St 14
12-25-78 ....Purdue 41, Georgia Tech 21
12-31-79 ....Baylor 24, Clemson 18
1-2-81 ....Miami (FL) 20, Virginia Tech 10
12-31-81 ....W Virginia 26, Florida 6
12-31-82 ....Iowa 28, Tennessee 22
12-30-83 ....Florida St 28, N Carolina 3
12-31-84 ....Virginia 27, Purdue 24
12-31-85 ....Army 31, Illinois 29
12-31-86 ....Virginia Tech 25, N Carolina St 24
1-2-88 ....Tennessee 27, Indiana 22
12-31-88 ....N Carolina St 28, Iowa 23
12-30-89 ....Syracuse 19, Georgia 18
12-29-90 ....Auburn 27, Indiana 23
1-1-92 ....E Carolina 37, N Carolina St 34
1-2-93 ....North Carolina 21, Miss. St 17
12-31-93 ....Clemson 14, Kentucky 13

City: Atlanta.
Stadium: Atlanta Fulton County Stadium.
Capacity: 59,800.
Automatic Berths: None.
Playing Sites: Grant Field (1968-70), Atlanta Stadium (since 1971).

Fiesta Bowl

12-27-71 ....Arizona St 45, Florida St 38
12-23-72 ....Arizona St 49, Missouri 35
12-21-73 ....Arizona St 28, Pittsburgh 7
12-28-74 ....Oklahoma St 16, Brigham Young 6
12-26-75 ....Arizona St 17, Nebraska 14
12-25-76 ....Oklahoma 41, Wyoming 7
12-25-77 ....Penn St 42, Arizona St 30
12-25-78 ....Arkansas 10, UCLA 10
12-25-79 ....Pittsburgh 16, Arizona 10
12-26-80 ....Penn St 31, Ohio St 19
1-1-82 ....Penn St 26, Southern Cal 10
1-1-83 ....Arizona St 32, Oklahoma 21
1-2-84 ....Ohio St 28, Pittsburgh 23
1-1-85 ....UCLA 39, Miami (FL) 37
1-1-86 ....Michigan 27, Nebraska 23
1-2-87 ....Penn St 14, Miami (FL) 10
1-1-88 ....Florida St 31, Nebraska 28
1-2-89 ....Notre Dame 34, W Virginia 21
1-1-90 ....Florida St 41, Nebraska 17
1-1-91 ....Louisville 34, Alabama 7
1-1-92 ....Penn St 42, Tennessee 17
1-1-93 ....Syracuse 26, Colorado 22
1-1-94 ....Arizona 29, Miami 0

City: Tempe, AZ.
Stadium: Sun Devil Stadium.
Capacity: 74,000.
Automatic Berths: None.

Independence Bowl

12-13-76 ....McNeese St 20, Tulsa 16
12-17-77 ....Louisiana Tech 24, Louisville 14
12-16-78 ....E Carolina 35, Louisiana Tech 13
12-15-79 ....Syracuse 31, McNeese St 7

Independence Bowl *(Cont.)*

12-13-80 ....Southern Miss 16, McNeese St 14
12-12-81 ....Texas A&M 33, Oklahoma St 16
12-11-82 ....Wisconsin 14, Kansas St 3
12-10-83 ....Air Force 9, Mississippi 3
12-15-84 ....Air Force 23, Virginia Tech 7
12-21-85 ....Minnesota 20, Clemson 13
12-20-86 ....Mississippi 20, Texas Tech 17
12-19-87 ....Washington 24, Tulane 12
12-23-88 ....Southern Miss 38, UTEP 18
12-16-89 ....Oregon 27, Tulsa 24
12-15-90 ....Louisiana Tech 34, Maryland 34
12-29-91 ....Georgia 24, Arkansas 15
12-31-92 ....Wake Forest 39, Oregon 35
12-31-93 ....Virginia Tech 45, Indiana 20

City: Shreveport, LA.
Stadium: Independence Stadium.
Capacity: 50,560.
Automatic Berths: None.

All-American Bowl (Discontinued)

12-22-77 ....Maryland 17, Minnesota 7
12-20-78 ....Texas A&M 28, Iowa St 12
12-29-79 ....Missouri 24, S Carolina 14
12-27-80 ....Arkansas 34, Tulane 15
12-31-81 ....Mississippi St 10, Kansas 0
12-31-82 ....Air Force 36, Vanderbilt 28
12-22-83 ....W Virginia 20, Kentucky 16
12-29-84 ....Kentucky 20, Wisconsin 19
12-31-85 ....Georgia Tech 17, Michigan St 14
12-31-86 ....Florida St 27, Indiana 13
12-22-87 ....Virginia 22, Brigham Young 16
12-29-88 ....Florida 14, Illinois 10
12-28-89 ....Texas Tech 49, Duke 21
12-28-90 ....N Carolina St 31, S Mississippi 27

City: Birmingham, AL.
Stadium: Legion Field.
Capacity: 75,808.
Automatic Berths: None.
Name Change: Hall of Fame Classic (1977-84), All-American Bowl (1985-90).

Holiday Bowl

12-22-78 ....Navy 23, Brigham Young 16
12-21-79 ....Indiana 38, Brigham Young 37
12-19-80 ....Brigham Young 46, SMU 45
12-18-81 ....Brigham Young 38, Washington St 36
12-17-82 ....Ohio St 47, Brigham Young 17
12-23-83 ....Brigham Young 21, Missouri 17
12-21-84 ....Brigham Young 24, Michigan 17
12-22-85 ....Arkansas 18, Arizona St 17
12-30-86 ....Iowa 39, San Diego St 38
12-30-87 ....Iowa 20, Wyoming 19
12-30-88 ....Oklahoma St 62, Wyoming 14
12-29-89 ....Penn St 50, Brigham Young 39
12-29-90 ....Texas A&M 65, Brigham Young 14
12-30-91 ....Iowa 13, Brigham Young 13
12-30-92 ....Hawaii 27, Illinois 17
12-30-93 ....Ohio St 28, Brigham Young 21

City: San Diego.
Stadium: Jack Murphy Stadium.
Capacity: 60,750.
Automatic Berths: Western Athletic champ (except 1985).

Las Vegas Bowl

12-19-81	Toledo 27, San Jose St 25
12-18-82	Fresno St 29, Bowling Green 28
12-17-83	Northern Illinois 20, Cal St-Fullerton 13
12-15-84	NV-Las Vegas 30, Toledo 13*
12-14-85	Fresno St 51, Bowling Green 7
12-13-86	San Jose St 37, Miami (OH) 7
12-12-87	Eastern Michigan 30, San Jose St 27
12-10-88	Fresno St 35, Western Michigan 30
12-9-89	Fresno St 27, Ball St 6
12-8-90	San Jose St 48, Central Michigan 24
12-14-91	Bowling Green 28, Fresno St 21
12-18-92	Bowling Green 35, Nevada 34
12-17-93	Utah St 42, Ball St 33

* Toledo won later by forfeit.
City: Fresno, CA.
Stadium: Bulldog Stadium.
Capacity: 30,000.
Automatic Berths: Mid-American and Big West champs.
Name change: California Bowl (1981-91).

Aloha Bowl

12-25-82	Washington 21, Maryland 20
12-26-83	Penn St 13, Washington 10
12-29-84	Southern Meth 27, Notre Dame 20
12-28-85	Alabama 24, Southern Cal 3
12-27-86	Arizona 30, N Carolina 21
12-25-87	UCLA 20, Florida 16
12-25-88	Washington St 24, Houston 22
12-25-89	Michigan St 33, Hawaii 13
12-25-90	Syracuse 28, Arizona 0
12-25-91	Georgia Tech 18, Stanford 17
12-25-92	Kansas 23, Brigham Young 20
12-25-93	Colorado 41, Fresno St 30

City: Honolulu.
Stadium: Aloha Stadium.
Capacity: 50,000.
Automatic Berths: None.

Freedom Bowl

12-16-84	Iowa 55, Texas 17
12-30-85	Washington 20, Colorado 17
12-30-86	UCLA 31, Brigham Young 10
12-30-87	Arizona St 33, Air Force 28
12-29-88	Brigham Young 20, Colorado 17
12-30-89	Washington 34, Florida 7
12-29-90	Colorado St 32, Oregon 31
12-30-91	Tulsa 28, San Diego St 17
12-29-92	Fresno St 24, Southern Cal 7
12-30-93	Southern Cal 28, Utah 21

City: Anaheim.
Stadium: Anaheim Stadium.
Capacity: 70,500.
Automatic Berths: None.

Hall of Fame Bowl

12-23-86	Boston Col 27, Georgia 24
1-2-88	Michigan 28, Alabama 24
1-2-89	Syracuse 23, Louisiana St 10
1-1-90	Auburn 31, Ohio St 14
1-1-91	Clemson 30, Illinois 0
1-1-92	Syracuse 24, Ohio St 17
1-1-93	Tennessee 38, Boston College 23

Hall of Fame Bowl *(Cont.)*

1-1-94	Michigan 42, N Carolina St 7

City: Tampa.
Stadium: Tampa Stadium.
Capacity: 74,315.
Automatic Berths: None.

Copper Bowl

12-31-89	Arizona 17, N Carolina St 10
12-31-90	California 17, Wyoming 15
12-31-91	Indiana 24, Baylor 0
12-29-92	Washington St 31, Utah 28
12-29-93	Kansas St 52, Wyoming 17

City: Tucson.
Stadium: Arizona Stadium.
Capacity: 57,000.
Automatic Berths: None.

Carquest Bowl

12-28-90	Florida St 24, Penn St 17
12-28-91	Alabama 30, Colorado 25
1-1-93	Stanford 24, Penn St 3
1-1-94	Boston College 31, Virginia 13

City: Miami.
Stadium: Joe Robbie.
Capacity: 75,000. Automatic Berths: None
Name Change: Blockbuster Bowl (1990-93).

Bluebonnet Bowl (Discontinued)

12-19-59	Clemson 23, Texas Christian 7
12-17-60	Texas 3, Alabama 3
12-16-61	Kansas 33, Rice 7
12-22-62	Missouri 14, Georgia Tech 10
12-21-63	Baylor 14, LSU 7
12-19-64	Tulsa 14, Mississippi 7
12-18-65	Tennessee 27, Tulsa 6
12-17-66	Texas 19, Mississippi 0
12-23-67	Colorado 31, Miami (FL) 21
12-31-68	Southern Meth 28, Oklahoma 27
12-31-69	Houston 36, Auburn 7
12-31-70	Alabama 24, Oklahoma 24
12-31-71	Colorado 29, Houston 17
12-30-72	Tennessee 24, LSU 17
12-29-73	Houston 47, Tulane 7
12-23-74	N Carolina St 31, Houston 31
12-27-75	Texas 38, Colorado 21
12-31-76	Nebraska 27, Texas Tech 24
12-31-77	Southern Cal 47, Texas A&M 28
12-31-78	Stanford 25, Georgia 22
12-31-79	Purdue 27, Tennessee 22
12-31-80	N Carolina 16, Texas 7
12-31-81	Michigan 33, UCLA 14
12-31-82	Arkansas 28, Florida 24
12-31-83	Oklahoma St 24, Baylor 14
12-31-84	W Virginia 31, Texas Christian 14
12-31-85	Air Force 24, Texas 16
12-31-86	Baylor 21, Colorado 9
12-31-87	Texas 32, Pittsburgh 27

City: Houston.
Name change: Astro-Bluebonnet Bowl (1968-76).
Playing sites: Rice Stadium (1959-67, 1985-86),
Astrodome (1968-84, 1987).

NCAA Divisional Championships

Division I-AA

Year	Winner	Runner-Up	Score
1978	Florida A&M	Massachusetts	35-28
1979	Eastern Kentucky	Lehigh	30-7
1980	Boise St	Eastern Kentucky	31-29
1981	Idaho St	Eastern Kentucky	34-23
1982	Eastern Kentucky	Delaware	17-14
1983	Southern Illinois	Western Carolina	43-7
1984	Montana St	Louisiana Tech	19-6
1985	Georgia Southern	Furman	44-42
1986	Georgia Southern	Arkansas St	48-21
1987	NE Louisiana	Marshall	43-42
1988	Furman	Georgia Southern	17-12
1989	Georgia Southern	SF Austin St	37-34
1990	Georgia Southern	NV-Reno	36-13
1991	Youngstown St	Marshall	25-17
1992	Marshall	Youngstown St	31-28
1993	Youngstown St	Marshall	17-5

Division II

Year	Winner	Runner-Up	Score
1973	Louisiana Tech	Western Kentucky	34-0
1974	Central Michigan	Delaware	54-14
1975	Northern Michigan	Western Kentucky	16-14
1976	Montana St	Akron	24-13
1977	Lehigh	Jacksonville St	33-0
1978	Eastern Illinois	Delaware	10-9
1979	Delaware	Youngstown St	38-21
1980	Cal Poly SLO	Eastern Illinois	21-13
1981	SW Texas St	N Dakota St	42-13
1982	SW Texas St	UC-Davis	34-9
1983	N Dakota St	Central St (OH)	41-21
1984	Troy St	N Dakota St	18-17
1985	N Dakota St	N Alabama	35-7
1986	N Dakota St	S Dakota	27-7
1987	Troy St	Portland St	31-17
1988	N Dakota St	Portland St	35-21
1989	Mississippi Col	Jacksonville St	3-0
1990	N Dakota St	Indiana (PA)	51-11
1991	Pittsburg St	Jacksonville St	23-6
1992	Jacksonville St	Pittsburg St	17-13
1993	N Alabama	Indiana (PA)	41-34

Division III

Year	Winner	Runner-Up	Score
1973	Wittenberg	Juniata	41-0
1974	Central (IA)	Ithaca	10-8
1975	Wittenberg	Ithaca	28-0
1976	St John's (MN)	Towson St	31-28
1977	Widener	Wabash	39-36
1978	Baldwin-Wallace	Wittenberg	24-10
1979	Ithaca	Wittenberg	14-10
1980	Dayton	Ithaca	63-0
1981	Widener	Dayton	17-10
1982	W Georgia	Augustana (IL)	14-0
1983	Augustana (IL)	Union (NY)	21-17
1984	Augustana (IL)	Central (IA)	21-12
1985	Augustana (IL)	Ithaca	20-7
1986	Augustana (IL)	Salisbury St	31-3
1987	Wagner	Dayton	19-3
1988	Ithaca	Central (IA)	39-24
1989	Dayton	Union (NY)	17-7
1990	Allegheny	Lycoming	21-14 (OT)
1991	Ithaca	Dayton	34-20
1992	Wisconsin-LaCrosse	Washington and Jefferson	16-12
1993	Mount Union	Rowan	34-24

NAIA Divisional Championships

Division I

Year	Winner	Runner-Up	Score
1956	St Joseph's (IN) Montana State		0-0
1957	Kansas St-Pittsburg	Hillsdale (MI)	27-26
1958	Northeastern Oklahoma	Northern Arizona	19-13
1959	Texas A&I	Lenoir-Rhyne (NC)	20-7
1960	Lenoir-Rhyne	Humboldt St (CA)	15-14
1961	Kansas St-Pittsburg	Linfield (OR)	12-7
1962	Central St (OK)	Lenoir-Rhyne (NC)	28-13
1963	St John's (MN)	Prairie View (TX)	33-27
1964	Concordia-Moorhead Sam Houston		7-7
1965	St John's (MN)	Linfield (OR)	33-0
1966	Waynesburg (PA)	WI-Whitewater	42-21
1967	Fairmont St (WV)	Eastern Washington	28-21
1968	Troy St (AL)	Texas A&I	43-35
1969	Texas A&I	Concordia-Moorhead	32-7
1970	Texas A&I	Wofford (SC)	48-7
1971	Livingston (AL)	Arkansas Tech	14-12
1972	E Texas St	Carson-Newman	21-18
1973	Abilene Christian	Elon (NC)	42-14
1974	Texas A&I	Henderson St (AR)	34-23
1975	Texas A&I	Salem (WV)	37-0
1976	Texas A&I	Central Arkansas	26-0
1977	Abilene Christian	Southwestern Oklahoma	24-7
1978	Angelo St	Elon (NC)	34-14
1979	Texas A&I	Central St (OK)	20-14
1980	Elon (NC)	Northeastern Oklahoma	17-10
1981	Elon (NC)	Pittsburg St	3-0
1982	Central St (OK)	Mesa (CO)	14-11
1983	Carson-Newman (TN)	Mesa (CO)	36-28
1984	Carson-Newman (TN) Central Arkansas		19-19
1985	Central Arkansas/ Hillsdale (MI)		10-10
1986	Carson-Newman (TN)	Cameron (OK)	17-0
1987	Cameron (OK)	Carson-Newman (TN)	30-2
1988	Carson-Newman (TN)	Adams St (CO)	56-21
1989	Carson-Newman (TN)	Emporia St (KS)	34-20
1990	Central St (OH)	Mesa St (CO)	38-16
1991	Central Arkansas	Central St (OH)	19-16
1992	Central St (OH)	Gardner-Webb (NC)	19-16
1993	East Central (OK)	Glenville St (WV)	49-35

Division II

Year	Winner	Runner-Up	Score
1970	Westminster (PA)	Anderson (IN)	21-16
1971	California Lutheran	Westminster (PA)	30-14
1972	Missouri Southern	Northwestern (IA)	21-14
1973	Northwestern (IA)	Glenville St (WV)	10-3
1974	Texas Lutheran	Missouri Valley	42-0
1975	Texas Lutheran	California Lutheran	34-8
1976	Westminster (PA)	Redlands (CA)	20-13
1977	Westminster (PA)	California Lutheran	17-9
1978	Concordia-Moorhead	Findlay (OH)	7-0
1979	Findlay (OH)	Northwestern (IA)	51-6
1980	Pacific Lutheran	Wilmington	38-10
1981	Austin Coll./ Conc.-Moorhead		24-24
1982	Linfield (OR)	William Jewell (MO)	33-15
1983	Northwestern (IA)	Pacific Lutheran	25-21
1984	Linfield (OR)	Northwestern (IA)	33-22
1985	WI-La Crosse	Pacific Lutheran	24-7
1986	Linfield (OR)	Baker (KS)	17-0
1987	Pacific Lutheran	WI-Stevens Point*	16-16
1988	Westminster (PA)	WI-La Crosse	21-14
1989	Westminster (PA)	WI-La Crosse	51-30
1990	Peru St (NEB)	Westminster (PA)	17-7
1991	Georgetown (KY)	Pacific Lutheran	28-20
1992	Findlay (OH)	Linfield (OR)	26-13
1993	Pacific Lutheran (WA)	Westminster (PA)	50-20

*Forfeited 1987 season due to use of an ineligible player.

Awards

Heisman Memorial Trophy

Awarded to the best college player by the Downtown Athletic Club of New York City. The trophy is named after John W. Heisman, who coached Georgia Tech to the national championship in 1917 and later served as DAC athletic director.

Year	Winner, College, Position Winner's Season Statistics	Runner-up, College
1935	**Jay Berwanger, Chicago, HB** Rush: 119 Yds: 577 TD: 6	Monk Meyer, Army
1936	**Larry Kelley, Yale, E** Rec: 17 Yds: 372 TD: 6	Sam Francis, Nebraska
1937	**Clint Frank, Yale, HB** Rush: 157 Yds: 667 TD: 11	Byron White, Colorado
1938	**†Davey O'Brien, Texas Christian, QB** Att/Comp: 194/110 Yds: 1733 TD: 19	Marshall Goldberg, Pittsburgh
1939	**Nile Kinnick, Iowa, HB** Rush: 106 Yds: 374 TD: 5	Tom Harmon, Michigan
1940	**Tom Harmon, Michigan, HB** Rush: 191 Yds: 852 TD: 16	John Kimbrough, Texas A&M
1941	**†Bruce Smith, Minnesota, HB** Rush: 98 Yds: 480 TD: 6	Angelo Bertelli, Notre Dame
1942	**Frank Sinkwich, Georgia, HB** Att/Comp: 166/84 Yds: 1392 TD: 10	Paul Governali, Columbia
1943	**Angelo Bertelli, Notre Dame, QB** Att/Comp: 36/25 Yds: 511 TD: 10	Bob Odell, Pennsylvania
1944	**Les Horvath, Ohio State, QB** Rush: 163 Yds: 924 TD: 12	Glenn Davis, Army
1945	***†Doc Blanchard, Army, FB** Rush: 101 Yds: 718 TD: 13	Glenn Davis, Army
1946	**Glenn Davis, Army, HB** Rush: 123 Yds: 712 TD: 7	Charley Trippi, Georgia
1947	**†John Lujack, Notre Dame, QB** Att/Comp: 109/61 Yds: 777 TD: 9	Bob Chappius, Michigan
1948	***Doak Walker, Southern Methodist, HB** Rush: 108 Yds: 532 TD: 8	Charlie Justice, N Carolina
1949	**†Leon Hart, Notre Dame, E** Rec: 19 Yds: 257 TD: 5	Charlie Justice, N Carolina
1950	***Vic Janowicz, Ohio St, HB** Att/Comp: 77/32 Yds: 561 TD: 12	Hank Lauricella, Tennessee
1951	**Dick Kazmaier, Princeton, HB** Rush: 149 Yds: 861 TD: 9	Hank Lauricella, Tennessee
1952	**Billy Vessels, Oklahoma, HB** Rush: 167 Yds: 1072 TD: 17	Jack Scarbath, Maryland
1953	**John Lattner, Notre Dame, HB** Rush: 134 Yds: 651 TD: 6	Paul Geil, Minnesota
1954	**Alan Ameche, Wisconsin, FB** Rush: 146 Yds: 641 TD: 9	Kurt Burris, Oklahoma
1955	**Howard Cassady, Ohio St, HB** Rush: 161 Yds: 958 TD: 15	Jim Swink, Texas Christian
1956	**Paul Hornung, Notre Dame, QB** Att/Comp: 111/59 Yds: 917 TD: 3	Johnny Majors, Tennessee
1957	**John David Crow, Texas A&M, HB** Rush: 129 Yds: 562 TD: 10	Alex Karras, Iowa
1958	**Pete Dawkins, Army, HB** Rush: 78 Yds: 428 TD: 6	Randy Duncan, Iowa
1959	**Billy Cannon, Louisiana St, HB** Rush: 139 Yds: 598 TD: 6	Rich Lucas, Penn St
1960	**Joe Bellino, Navy, HB** Rush: 168 Yds: 834 TD: 18	Tom Brown, Minnesota
1961	**Ernie Davis, Syracuse, HB** Rush: 150 Yds: 823 TD: 15	Bob Ferguson, Ohio St
1962	**Terry Baker, Oregon St, QB** Att/Comp: 203/112 Yds: 1738 TD: 15	Jerry Stovall, Louisiana St
1963	***Roger Staubach, Navy, QB** Att/Comp: 161/107 Yds: 1474 TD: 7	Billy Lothridge, Georgia Tech
1964	**John Huarte, Notre Dame, QB** Att/Comp: 205/114 Yds: 2062 TD: 16	Jerry Rhome, Tulsa

Heisman Memorial Trophy (Cont.)

Year	Winner, College, Position Winner's Season Statistics	Runner-up, College
1965	**Mike Garrett, Southern Cal, HB** Rush: 267 Yds: 1440 TD: 16	Howard Twilley, Tulsa
1966	**Steve Spurrier, Florida, QB** Att/Comp: 291/179 Yds: 2012 TD: 16	Bob Griese, Purdue
1967	**Gary Beban, UCLA, QB** Att/Comp: 156/87 Yds: 1359 TD: 8	O.J. Simpson, Southern Cal
1968	**O.J. Simpson, Southern Cal, HB** Rush: 383 Yds: 1880 TD: 23	Leroy Keyes, Purdue
1969	**Steve Owens, Oklahoma, FB** Rush: 358 Yds: 1523 TD: 23	Mike Phipps, Purdue
1970	**Jim Plunkett, Stanford, QB** Att/Comp: 358/191 Yds: 2715 TD: 18	Joe Theismann, Notre Dame
1971	**Pat Sullivan, Auburn, QB** Att/Comp: 281/162 Yds: 2012 TD: 20	Ed Marinaro, Cornell
1972	**Johnny Rodgers, Nebraska, FL** Rec: 55 Yds: 942 TD: 17	Greg Pruitt, Oklahoma
1973	**John Cappelletti, Penn St, HB** Rush: 286 Yds: 1522 TD: 17	John Hicks, Ohio St
1974	***Archie Griffin, Ohio St, HB** Rush: 256 Yds: 1695 TD: 12	Anthony Davis, Southern Cal
1975	**Archie Griffin, Ohio St, HB** Rush: 262 Yds: 1450 TD: 4	Chuck Muncie, California
1976	**†Tony Dorsett, Pittsburgh, HB** Rush: 370 Yds: 2150 TD: 23	Ricky Bell, Southern Cal
1977	**Earl Campbell, Texas, FB** Rush: 267 Yds: 1744 TD: 19	Terry Miller, Oklahoma St
1978	***Billy Sims, Oklahoma, HB** Rush: 231 Yds: 1762 TD: 20	Chuck Fusina, Penn St
1979	**Charles White, Southern Cal, HB** Rush: 332 Yds: 1803 TD: 19	Billy Sims, Oklahoma
1980	**George Rogers, S Carolina, HB** Rush: 324 Yds: 1894 TD: 14	Hugh Green, Pittsburgh
1981	**Marcus Allen, Southern Cal, HB** Rush: 433 Yds: 2427 TD: 23	Herschel Walker, Georgia
1982	***Herschel Walker, Georgia, HB** Rush: 335 Yds: 1752 TD: 17	John Elway, Stanford
1983	**Mike Rozier, Nebraska, HB** Rush: 275 Yds: 2148 TD: 29	Steve Young, Brigham Young
1984	**Doug Flutie, Boston College, QB** Att/Comp: 396/233 Yds: 3454 TD: 27	Keith Byars, Ohio St
1985	**Bo Jackson, Auburn, HB** Rush: 278 Yds: 1786 TD: 17	Chuck Long, Iowa
1986	**Vinny Testaverde, Miami, QB** Att/Comp: 276/175 Yds: 2557 TD: 26	Paul Palmer, Temple
1987	**Tim Brown, Notre Dame, WR** Rec: 39 Yds: 846 TD: 7	Don McPherson, Syracuse
1988	***Barry Sanders, Oklahoma St, RB** Rush: 344 Yds: 2628 TD: 39	Rodney Peete, Southern Cal
1989	***Andre Ware, Houston, QB** Att/Comp: 578/365 Yds: 4699 TD: 46	Anthony Thompson, Indiana
1990	***Ty Detmer, Brigham Young, QB** Att/Comp: 562/361 Yds: 5188 TD: 41	Raghib Ismail, Notre Dame
1991	***Desmond Howard, Michigan, WR** Rec: 61 Yds: 950 TD: 23	Casey Weldon, Florida St
1992	**Gino Torretta, Miami, QB** Att/Comp: 402/228 Yds: 3060 TD: 19	Marshall Faulk, San Diego St
1993	**Charlie Ward, Florida St, QB** Att/Comp: 380/264 Yds: 3032 TD: 27	Heath Shuler, Tennessee

*Juniors (all others seniors). †Winners who played for national championship teams the same year.

Note: Former Heisman winners and national media cast votes, with ballots allowing for three names (3 points for first, 2 for second and 1 for third).

Jim Thorpe Award

Given to the best defensive back of the year, the award is presented by the Jim Thorpe Athletic Club of Oklahoma City.

Year	Player, College
1986	Thomas Everett, Baylor
1987	Bennie Blades, Miami (FL)
	Rickey Dixon, Oklahoma
1988	Deion Sanders, Florida St

Year	Player, College
1989	Mark Carrier, Southern Cal
1990	Darryl Lewis, Arizona
1991	Terrell Buckley, Florida St
1992	Deon Figures, Colorado
1993	Antonio Langham, Alabama

Outland Trophy

Given to the outstanding interior lineman, selected by the Football Writers Association of America.

Year	Player, College, Position
1946	George Connor, Notre Dame, T
1947	Joe Steffy, Army, G
1948	Bill Fischer, Notre Dame, G
1949	Ed Bagdon, Michigan St, G
1950	Bob Gain, Kentucky, T
1951	Jim Weatherall, Oklahoma, T
1952	Dick Modzelewski, Maryland, T
1953	J. D. Roberts, Oklahoma, G
1954	Bill Brooks, Arkansas, G
1955	Calvin Jones, Iowa, G
1956	Jim Parker, Ohio St, G
1957	Alex Karras, Iowa, T
1958	Zeke Smith, Auburn, G
1959	Mike McGee, Duke, T
1960	Tom Brown, Minnesota, G
1961	Merlin Olsen, Utah St, T
1962	Bobby Bell, Minnesota, T
1963	Scott Appleton, Texas, T
1964	Steve DeLong, Tennessee, T
1965	Tommy Nobis, Texas, G
1966	Loyd Phillips, Arkansas, T
1967	Ron Yary, Southern Cal, T
1968	Bill Stanfill, Georgia, T
1968	Bill Stanfill, Georgia, T

Year	Player, College, Position
1969	Mike Reid, Penn St, DT
1970	Jim Stillwagon, Ohio St, MG
1971	Larry Jacobson, Nebraska, DT
1972	Rich Glover, Nebraska, MG
1973	John Hicks, Ohio St, OT
1974	Randy White, Maryland, DE
1975	Lee Roy Selmon, Oklahoma, DT
1976	*Ross Browner, Notre Dame, DE
1977	Brad Shearer, Texas, DT
1978	Greg Roberts, Oklahoma, G
1979	Jim Ritcher, N Carolina St, C
1980	Mark May, Pittsburgh, OT
1981	*Dave Rimington, Nebraska, C
1982	Dave Rimington, Nebraska, C
1983	Dean Steinkuhler, Nebraska, G
1984	Bruce Smith, Virginia Tech, DT
1985	Mike Ruth, Boston Col, NG
1986	Jason Buck, Brigham Young, DT
1987	Chad Hennings, Air Force, DT
1988	Tracy Rocker, Auburn, DT
1989	Mohammed Elewonibi, Brigham Young, G
1990	Russell Maryland, Miami (FL), DT
1991	*Steve Emtman, Washington, DT
1992	Will Shields, Nebraska, G
1993	Rob Waldrop, Arizona, NG

*Juniors (all others seniors).

Vince Lombardi/Rotary Award

Given to the outstanding college lineman of the year, the award is sponsored by the Rotary Club of Houston.

Year	Player, College, Position
1970	Jim Stillwagon, Ohio St, MG
1971	Walt Patulski, Notre Dame, DE
1972	Rich Glover, Nebraska, MG
1973	John Hicks, Ohio St, OT
197_	Randy White, Maryland, DT
1976	Lee Roy Selmon, Oklahoma, DT
1976	Wilson Whitley, Houston, DT
1977	Ross Browner, Notre Dame, DE
1978	Bruce Clark, Penn St, DT
1979	Brad Budde, Southern Cal, G
1980	Hugh Green, Pittsburgh, DE
1981	Kenneth Sims, Texas, DT

Year	Player, College, Position
1982	Dave Rimington, Nebraska, C
1983	Dean Steinkuhler, Nebraska, G
1984	Tony Degrate, Texas, DT
1985	Tony Casillas, Oklahoma, NG
1986	Cornelius Bennett, Alabama, LB
1987	Chris Spielman, Ohio St, LB
1988	Tracy Rocker, Auburn, DT
1989	Percy Snow, Michigan St, LB
1990	Chris Zorich, Notre Dame, NG
1991	Steve Emtman, Washington, DT
1992	Marvin Jones, Florida St, LB
1993	Aaron Taylor, Notre Dame, OT

Butkus Award

Given to the top collegiate linebacker, the award was established by the Downtown Athletic Club of Orlando and named for college hall of famer Dick Butkus of Illinois.

Year	Player, College
1985	Brian Bosworth, Oklahoma
1986	Brian Bosworth, Oklahoma
1987	Paul McGowan, Florida St
1988	Derrick Thomas, Alabama

Year	Player, College
1989	Percy Snow, Michigan St
1990	Alfred Williams, Colorado
1991	Erick Anderson, Michigan
1992	Marvin Jones, Florida St
1993	Trev Alberts, Nebraska

Davey O'Brien National Quarterback Award

Given to the No. 1 quarterback in the nation by the Davey O'Brien Educational and Charitable Trust of Fort Worth. Named for Texas Christian hall of fame quarterback Davey O'Brien (1936-38).

Year	Player, College	Year	Player, College
1981	Jim McMahon, Brigham Young	1987	Don McPherson, Syracuse
1982	Todd Blackledge, Penn St	1988	Troy Aikman, UCLA
1983	Steve Young, Brigham Young	1989	Andre Ware, Houston
1984	Doug Flutie, Boston Col	1990	Ty Detmer, Brigham Young
1985	Chuck Long, Iowa	1991	Ty Detmer, Brigham Young
1986	Vinny Testaverde, Miami (FL)	1992	Gino Torretta, Miami (FL)
		1993	Charlie Ward, Florida St

Note: Originally known as the Davey O'Brien Memorial Trophy, honoring the outstanding football player in the Southwest as follows: 1977—Earl Campbell, Texas, RB; 1978—Billy Sims, Oklahoma, RB; 1979—Mike Singletary, Baylor, LB; 1980—Mike Singletary, Baylor, LB.

Maxwell Award

Given to the nation's outstanding college football player by the Maxwell Football Club of Philadelphia.

Year	Player, College, Position	Year	Player, College, Position
1937	Clint Frank, Yale, HB	1965	Tommy Nobis, Texas, LB
1938	Davey O'Brien, Texas Christian, QB	1966	Jim Lynch, Notre Dame, LB
1939	Nile Kinnick, Iowa, HB	1967	Gary Beban, UCLA, QB
1940	Tom Harmon, Michigan, HB	1968	O. J. Simpson, Southern Cal, RB
1941	Bill Dudley, Virginia, HB	1969	Mike Reid, Penn St, DT
1942	Paul Governali, Columbia, QB	1970	Jim Plunkett, Stanford, QB
1943	Bob Odell, Pennsylvania, HB	1971	Ed Marinaro, Cornell, RB
1944	Glenn Davis, Army, HB	1972	Brad Van Pelt, Michigan St, DB
1945	Doc Blanchard, Army, FB	1973	John Cappelletti, Penn St, RB
1946	Charley Trippi, Georgia, HB	1974	Steve Joachim, Temple, QB
1947	Doak Walker, Southern Meth, HB	1975	Archie Griffin, Ohio St, RB
1948	Chuck Bednarik, Pennsylvania, C	1976	Tony Dorsett, Pittsburgh, RB
1949	Leon Hart, Notre Dame, E	1977	Ross Browner, Notre Dame, DE
1950	Reds Bagnell, Pennsylvania, HB	1978	Chuck Fusina, Penn St, QB
1951	Dick Kazmaier, Princeton, HB	1979	Charles White, Southern Cal, RB
1952	John Lattner, Notre Dame, HB	1980	Hugh Green, Pittsburgh, DE
1953	John Lattner, Notre Dame, HB	1981	Marcus Allen, Southern Cal, RB
1954	Ron Beagle, Navy, E	1982	Herschel Walker, Georgia, RB
1955	Howard Cassady, Ohio St, HB	1983	Mike Rozier, Nebraska, RB
1956	Tommy McDonald, Oklahoma, HB	1984	Doug Flutie, Boston Col, QB
1957	Bob Reifsnyder, Navy, T	1985	Chuck Long, Iowa, QB
1958	Pete Dawkins, Army, HB	1986	Vinny Testaverde, Miami (FL), QB
1959	Rich Lucas, Penn St, QB	1987	Don McPherson, Syracuse, QB
1960	Joe Bellino, Navy, HB	1988	Barry Sanders, Oklahoma St, RB
1961	Bob Ferguson, Ohio St, FB	1989	Anthony Thompson, Indiana, RB
1962	Terry Baker, Oregon St, QB	1990	Ty Detmer, Brigham Young, QB
1963	Roger Staubach, Navy, QB	1991	Desmond Howard, Michigan, WR
1964	Glenn Ressler, Penn St, C	1992	Gino Torretta, Miami (FL), QB
		1993	Charlie Ward, Florida St, QB

Walter Payton Player of the Year Award

Given to the top Division I-AA football player, the award is sponsored by Sports Network and voted on by Division I-AA sports information directors.

Year	Player, College, Position
1987	Kenny Gamble, Colgate, RB
1988	Dave Meggett, Towson St, RB
1989	John Friesz, Idaho, QB
1990	Walter Dean, Grambling, RB
1991	Jamie Martin, Weber St, QB
1992	Michael Payton, Marshall, QB
1993	Doug Nussmeier, Idaho, QB

The Harlon Hill Trophy

Given to the outstanding NCAA Division II college football player, the award is sponsored by the National Harlon Hill Awards Committee, Florence, AL.

Year	Player, College, Position
1986	Jeff Bentrim, N Dakota St, QB
1987	Johnny Bailey, Texas A&I, RB
1988	Johnny Bailey, Texas A&I, RB
1989	Johnny Bailey, Texas A&I, RB
1990	Chris Simdorn, N Dakota St, QB
1991	Ronnie West, Pittsburg St, WR
1992	Ronald Moore, Pittsburg St, RB
1993	Roger Graham, New Haven, RB

Career

SCORING

Most Points Scored: 423 — Roman Anderson, Houston, 1988-91
Most Points Scored per Game: 12.1 — Marshall Faulk, San Diego St 1991-93
Most Touchdowns Scored: 65 — Anthony Thompson, Indiana, 1986-89
Most Touchdowns Scored per Game: 2.0 — Marshall Faulk, San Diego St 1991-93
Most Touchdowns Scored, Rushing: 64 — Anthony Thompson, Indiana, 1986-89
Most Touchdowns Scored, Passing: 121 — Ty Detmer, Brigham Young, 1988-91
Most Touchdowns Scored, Receiving: 43 — Aaron Turner, Pacific, 1989-92
Most Touchdowns Scored, Interception Returns: 5 — Ken Thomas, San Jose St, 1979-82; Jackie Walker, Tennessee, 1969-71
Most Touchdowns Scored, Punt Returns: 7 — Johnny Rodgers, Nebraska, 1970-72; Jack Mitchell, Oklahoma, 1946-48
Most Touchdowns Scored, Kickoff Returns: 6 — Anthony Davis, Southern Cal, 1972-74

TOTAL OFFENSE

Most Plays: 1795 — Ty Detmer, Brigham Young, 1988-91
Most Plays per Game: 48.5 — Doug Gaynor, Long Beach St, 1984-85
Most Yards Gained: 14,665 — Ty Detmer, Brigham Young, 1988-91 (15,031 passing, -366 rushing)
Most Yards Gained per Game: 318.8 — Ty Detmer, Brigham Young, 1988-91
Most 300+ Yard Games: 33 —Ty Detmer, Brigham Young, 1988-91

RUSHING

Most Rushes: 1215 — Steve Bartalo, Colorado St, 1983-86 (4813 yds)
Most Rushes per Game: 34.0 — Ed Marinaro, Cornell, 1969-71
Most Yards Gained: 6082 — Tony Dorsett, Pittsburgh, 1973-76
Most Yards Gained per Game: 174.6 — Ed Marinaro, Cornell, 1969-71
Most 100+ Yard Games: 33 — Tony Dorsett, Pittsburgh, 1973-76; Archie Griffin, Ohio St, 1972-75
Most 200+ Yard Games: 11 — Marcus Allen, Southern Cal, 1978-81

SPECIAL TEAMS

Highest Punt Return Average: 23.6 — Jack Mitchell, Oklahoma, 1946-48
Highest Kickoff Return Average: 36.2 — Forrest Hall, San Francisco, 1946-47
Highest Average Yards per Punt: 45.6 — Reggie Roby, Iowa, 1979-82

PASSING

Highest Passing Efficiency Rating: 162.7 — Ty Detmer, Brigham Young, 1988-91 (1530 attempts, 958 completions, 65 interceptions, 15,031 yards, 121 TD passes)
Most Passes Attempted: 1,530 — Ty Detmer, Brigham Young, 1988-91
Most Passes Attempted per Game: 39.6 — Mike Perez, San Jose St, 1986-87
Most Passes Completed: 958 — Ty Detmer, Brigham Young, 1988-91
Most Passes Completed per Game: 25.9 — Doug Gaynor, Long Beach St, 1984-85
Highest Completion Percentage: 65.2 — Steve Young, Brigham Young, 1981-83
Most Yards Gained: 15,031 — Ty Detmer, Brigham Young, 1988-91
Most Yards Gained per Game: 326.7 — Ty Detmer, Brigham Young, 1988-91

RECEIVING

Most Passes Caught: 266 — Aaron Turner, Pacific, 1989-92
Most Passes Caught per Game: 10.5 — Emmanuel Hazard, Houston, 1989-90
Most Yards Gained: 4,357— Ryan Yarborough, Wyoming, 1990-93
Most Yards Gained per Game: 128.6 — Howard Twilley, Tulsa, 1963-65
Highest Average Gain per Reception: 25.7 — Wesley Walker, California, 1973-75

ALL-PURPOSE RUNNING

Most Plays: 1347 — Steve Bartalo, Colorado St, 1983-86 (1215 rushes, 132 receptions)
Most Yards Gained: 7172 — Napoleon McCallum, Navy, 1981-85 (4179 rushing, 796 receiving, 858 punt returns, 1339 kickoff returns)
Most Yards Gained per Game: 237.8 — Ryan Benjamin, Pacific, 1990-92
Highest Average Gain per Play: 17.4 — Anthony Carter, Michigan, 1979-82.

INTERCEPTIONS

Most Passes Intercepted: 29 — Al Brosky, Illinois, 1950-52
Most Passes Intercepted per Game: 1.07 — Terrell Buckley, Florida St, 1989-92
Most Yards on Interception Returns: 501 — John Provost, Holy Cross, 1972-74
Highest Average Gain per Interception: 26.5 — Tom Pridemore, W Virginia, 1975-77

Single Season

SCORING
Most Points Scored: 234 — Barry Sanders, Oklahoma St, 1988
Most Points Scored per Game: 21.27 — Barry Sanders, Oklahoma St, 1988
Most Touchdowns Scored: 39 — Barry Sanders, Oklahoma St, 1988
Most Touchdowns Scored, Rushing: 37 — Barry Sanders, Oklahoma St, 1988
Most Touchdowns Scored, Passing: 54 — David Klingler, Houston, 1990
Most Touchdowns Scored, Receiving: 22 — Emmanuel Hazard, Houston, 1989
Most Touchdowns Scored, Interception Returns: 3 — by many players
Most Touchdowns Scored, Punt Returns: 4 — James Henry, Southern Miss, 1987; Golden Richards, Brigham Young, 1971; Cliff Branch , Colorado, 1971
Most Touchdowns Scored, Kickoff Returns: 3 — Leland McElroy, Texas A&M, 1993; Terance Mathis, New Mexico, 1989; Willie Gault, Tennessee, 1980; Anthony Davis, Southern Cal, 1974; Stan Brown, Purdue, 1970; Forrest Hall, San Francisco, 1946

TOTAL OFFENSE
Most Plays: 704 — David Klingler, Houston, 1990
Most Yards Gained: 5221 — David Klingler, Houston, 1990
Most Yards Gained per Game: 474.6 — David Klingler, Houston, 1990
Most 300+ Yard Games: 12 — Ty Detmer, Brigham Young, 1990

RUSHING
Most Rushes: 403 — Marcus Allen, Southern Cal, 1981
Most Rushes per Game: 39.6 — Ed Marinaro, Cornell, 1971
Most Yards Gained: 2628 — Barry Sanders, Oklahoma St, 1988
Most Yards Gained per Game: 238.9 — Barry Sanders, Oklahoma St, 1988
Most 100+ Yard Games: 11 — By nine players, most recently Barry Sanders, Oklahoma St, 1988

PASSING
Highest Passing Efficiency Rating: 176.9 — Jim McMahon, Brigham Young, 1980 (445 attempts, 284 completions, 18 interceptions, 4571 yards, 47 TD passes)
Most Passes Attempted: 643 — David Klingler, Houston, 1990
Most Passes Attempted per Game: 58.5 — David Klingler, Houston, 1990
Most Passes Completed: 374 — David Klingler, Houston, 1990
Most Passes Completed per Game: 34.0 — David Klingler, Houston, 1990
Highest Completion Percentage: 71.3 — Steve Young, Brigham Young, 1983
Most Yards Gained: (12 games)5188 — Ty Detmer, Brigham Young, 1990; (11 games) 5140 — David Klingler, Houston, 1990
Most Yards Gained per Game: 467.3 — David Klingler, Houston, 1990

RECEIVING
Most Passes Caught: 142 — Emmanuel Hazard, Houston, 1989
Most Passes Caught per Game: 13.4 — Howard Twilley, Tulsa, 1965
Most Yards Gained: 1779 — Howard Twilley, Tulsa, 1965
Most Yards Gained per Game: 177.9 — Howard Twilley, Tulsa, 1965
Highest Average Gain per Reception: 27.9 — Elmo Wright, Houston, 1968 (min. 30 receptions)

ALL-PURPOSE RUNNING
Most Plays: 432 — Marcus Allen, Southern Cal, 1981
Most Yards Gained: 3250 — Barry Sanders, Oklahoma St, 1988
Most Yards Gained per Game: 295.5 — Barry Sanders, Oklahoma St, 1988
Highest Average Gain per Play: 18.5 — Henry Bailey, UNLV, 1992

INTERCEPTIONS
Most Passes Intercepted: 14 — Al Worley, Washington, 1968
Most Yards on Interception Returns: 302 — Charles Phillips, Southern Cal, 1974
Highest Average Gain per Interception: 50.6 — Norm Thompson, Utah, 1969

SPECIAL TEAMS
Highest Punt Return Average: 25.9 — Bill Blackstock, Tennessee, 1951
Highest Kickoff Return Average: 38.2 — Forrest Hall, San Francisco, 1946
Highest Average Yards per Punt: 49.8 — Reggie Roby, Iowa, 1981

THEY SAID IT

Paul Thompson, president of Weber State College, on the possibility that his school may drop football because of financial problems: "There are more important things on this campus than football. The library is one of them."

Single Game

SCORING

Most Points Scored: 48 — Howard Griffith, Illinois, 1990 (vs Southern Illinois)
Most Field Goals: 7 — Dale Klein, Nebraska, 1985 (vs Missouri); Mike Prindle, Western Michigan, 1984 (vs Marshall)
Most Extra Points (Kick): 13 — Derek Mahoney Fresno St, 1991 (vs New Mexico); 13 — Terry Leiweke, Houston, 1968 (vs Tulsa)
Most Extra Points (2-Pts): 6 — Jim Pilot, New Mexico St, 1961 (vs Hardin-Simmons)

TOTAL OFFENSE

Most Yards Gained: 732 — David Klingler, Houston, 1990 (vs Arizona St)

RUSHING

Most Yards Gained: 396 — Tony Sands, Kansas, 1991 (vs Missouri)

RUSHING *(Cont.)*

Most Touchdowns Rushed: 8 — Howard Griffith, Illinois, 1990 (vs Southern Illinois)

PASSING

Most Passes Completed: 48 — David Klingler, Houston, 1990 (vs Southern Methodist)
Most Yards Gained: 716 — David Klingler, Houston, 1990 (vs Arizona St)
Most Touchdowns Passed: 11 — David Klingler, Houston, 1990 [vs Eastern Washington (I-AA)]

RECEIVING

Most Passes Caught: 22 — Jay Miller, Brigham Young, 1973 (vs New Mexico)
Most Yards Gained: 349 — Chuck Hughes, UTEP, 1965 (vs N Texas St)
Most Touchdown Catches: 6 — Tim Delaney, San Diego St, 1969 (vs New Mexico St)

NCAA Division I-AA Individual Records

Career

SCORING

Most Points Scored: 385 — Marty Zendejas, NV-Reno, 1984-87
Most Touchdowns Scored: 60 — Charvez Foger, NV-Reno, 1985-88
Most Touchdowns Scored, Rushing: 55 — Kenny Gamble, Colgate, 1984-87
Most Touchdowns Scored, Passing: 139 — Willie Totten, Mississippi Valley, 1982-85
Most Touchdowns Scored, Receiving: 50 — Jerry Rice, Mississippi Valley, 1981-84

PASSING

Highest Passing Efficiency Rating: 154.4 — Doug Nussmeier, Idaho, 1990-93
Most Passes Attempted: 1,606 — Neil Lomax, Portland St, 1977-80
Most Passes Completed: 938 — Neil Lomax, Portland St, 1977-80
Most Passes Completed per Game: 23.8 — Stan Greene, Boston U, 1989-90
Highest Completion Percentage: 66.9 — Jason Garrett, Princeton, 1987-88

Most Yards Gained: 13,220 — Neil Lomax, Portland St, 1977-80
Most Yards Gained per Game: 320.1 — Tom Ehrhardt, Rhode Island, 1984-85

RUSHING

Most Rushes: 963 — Kenny Gamble, Colgate, 1984-87
Most Rushes per Game: 24.5 — Keith Elias, Princeton, 1991-93
Most Yards Gained: 5,333 — Frank Hawkins, NV-Reno, 1977-80
Most Yards Gained per Game: 124.3 — Kenny Gamble, Colgate, 1984-87

RECEIVING

Most Passes Caught: 301 — Jerry Rice, Mississippi Valley, 1981-84
Most Yards Gained: 4,693 — Jerry Rice, Mississippi Valley, 1981-84
Most Yards Gained per Game: 114.5 — Jerry Rice, Mississippi Valley, 1981-84
Highest Average Gain per Reception: 24.3 — John Taylor, Delaware St, 1982-85

Single Season

SCORING

Most Points Scored: 170 — Geoff Mitchell, Weber St, 1991
Most Touchdowns Scored: 28 — Geoff Mitchell, Weber St, 1991
Most Touchdowns Scored, Rushing: 24 — Geoff Mitchell, Weber St, 1991
Most Touchdowns Scored, Passing: 56 — Willie Totten, Mississippi Valley, 1984
Most Touchdowns Scored, Receiving: 27 — Jerry Rice, Mississippi Valley, 1984

PASSING

Highest Passing Efficiency Rating: 204.6 — Shawn Knight, Wiliam & Mary, 1993
Most Passes Attempted: 518 — Willie Totten, Mississippi Valley, 1984
Most Passes Completed: 324 — Willie Totten, Mississippi Valley, 1984
Most Passes Completed per Game: 32.4 — Willie Totten, Mississippi Valley, 1984
Highest Completion Percentage: 68.2 — Jason Garrett, Princeton, 1988
Most Yards Gained: 4,557 — Willie Totten, Mississippi Valley, 1984
Most Yards Gained per Game: 455.7 — Willie Totten, Mississippi Valley, 1984

Single Season *(Cont.)*

RUSHING

Most Rushes: 351 — James Black, Akron, 1983
Most Rushes per Game: 34.0 — James Black, Akron, 1983
Most Yards Gained: 2016 — Tony Vinson, Towson St, 1993
Most Yards Gained per Game: 201.6 — Tony Vinson, Towson St, 1993

RECEIVING

Most Passes Caught: 115 — Brian Forster, Rhode Island, 1985
Most Yards Gained: 1,682 — Jerry Rice, Mississippi Valley, 1984
Most Yards Gained per Game: 168.2 — Jerry Rice, Mississippi Valley, 1984
Highest Average Gain per Reception: 26.3 — Brian Allen, Idaho, 1983 (min. 30 receptions)

Single Game

SCORING

Most Points Scored: 36 — By five players. Most recently Erwin Matthews, Richmond, 1987 (vs Massachusetts)
Most Field Goals: 8 — Goran Lingmerth, Northern Arizona, 1986 (vs Idaho)

PASSING

Most Passes Completed: 47 — Jamie Martin, Weber St, 1991 (vs Idaho St)
Most Yards Gained: 624 — Jamie Martin, Weber St, 1991 (vs Idaho St)
Most Touchdowns Passed: 9 — Willie Totten, Mississippi Valley, 1984 (vs Kentucky St)

RUSHING

Most Yards Gained: 364 — Tony Vinson, Towson St, 1993 (vs Bucknell)
Most Touchdowns Rushed: 6 — Gene Lake, Delaware St, 1984 (vs. Howard); Gill Fenerty, Holy Cross, 1983 (vs Columbia); Henry Odom, S Carolina St, 1980 (vs Morgan St)

RECEIVING

Most Passes Caught: 24 — Jerry Rice, Mississippi Valley 1983 (vs Southern-Baton Rouge)
Most Yards Gained: 370 — Michael Lerch, Princeton, 1991 (vs Brown)
Most Touchdown Catches: 5 — Rennie Benn, Lehigh, 1985 [vs Indiana (PA)]; Jerry Rice, Mississippi Valley, 1984 (vs Prairie View and vs Kentucky St)

NCAA Division II Individual Records

Career

SCORING

Most Points Scored: 464 — Walter Payton, Jackson St, 1971-74
Most Touchdowns Scored: 72 — Shawn Graves, Wofford, 1989-92
Most Touchdowns Scored, Rushing: 72 — Shawn Graves, Wofford, 1989-92
Most Touchdowns Scored, Passing: 93 — Doug Williams, Grambling, 1974-77
Most Touchdowns Scored, Receiving: 49 — Bruce Cerone, Yankton/Emporia St, 1966-69

PASSING

Highest Passing Efficiency Rating: 164.0 — Chris Petersen, UC-Davis, 1985-86
Most Passes Attempted: 1,442 — Earl Harvey, N Carolina Central, 1985-88
Most Passes Completed: 748 — Rob Tomlinson, Cal-St Chico, 1988-91
Most Passes Completed per Game: 25.0 — Tim Von Dulm, Portland St, 1969-70
Highest Completion Percentage: 69.6 — Chris Peterson, UC-Davis, 1985-86
Most Yards Gained: 10,621 — Earl Harvey, N Carolina Central, 1985-88
Most Yards Gained per Game: 298.4 — Tim Von Dulm, Portland St, 1969-70

RUSHING

Most Rushes: 1,072 — Bernie Peeters, Luther, 1968-71
Most Rushes per Game: 29.8 — Bernie Peeters, Luther, 1968-71
Most Yards Gained: 6,320 — Johnny Bailey, Texas A&I*, 1986-89
Most Yards Gained per Game: 162.1 — Johnny Bailey, Texas A&I*, 1986-89

RECEIVING

Most Passes Caught: 253 — Chris Myers, Kenyon, 1967-70
Most Yards Gained: 4,354 — Bruce Cerone, Yankton/Emporia St, 1966-69
Most Yards Gained per Game: 137.3 — Ed Bell, Idaho St, 1968-69
Highest Average Gain per Reception: 22.8 — Tyrone Johnson, Western St (CO), 1990-93

*Became Texas A&M-Kingsville in 1993

Single Season

SCORING

Most Points Scored: 178 — Terry Metcalf, Long Beach St, 1971
Most Touchdowns Scored: 29 — Terry Metcalf, Long Beach St, 1971
Most Touchdowns Scored, Rushing: 28 — Terry Metcalf, Long Beach St, 1971
Most Touchdowns Scored, Passing: 45 — Bob Toledo, San Francisco St, 1967
Most Touchdowns Scored, Receiving: 20 — Ed Bell, Idaho St, 1969

PASSING

Highest Passing Efficiency Rating: 210.1 — Boyd Crawford, College of Idaho, 1953
Most Passes Attempted: 515 — Todd Mayfield, W Texas St, 1986
Most Passes Completed: 334 — Chris Hatcher, Valdosta St, 1993
Most Passes Completed per Game: 30.4 — Chris Hatcher, Valdosta St, 1993
Highest Completion Percentage: 70.9 — Chris Hatcher, Valdosta St, 1993
Most Yards Gained: 3,757 — Perry Klein, LIU-CW Post, 1993
Most Yards Gained per Game: 357.7 — Perry Klein, LIU-CW Post,1993

RUSHING

Most Rushes: 350 — Leon Burns, Long Beach St, 1969
Most Rushes per Game: 38.6 — Mark Perkins, Hobart, 1968
Most Yards Gained: 2,011 — Johnny Bailey, Texas A&I, 1986
Most Yards Gained per Game: 182.8 — Johnny Bailey, Texas A&I, 1986

RECEIVING

Most Passes Caught: 117 — Chris George, Glenville St, 1993
Most Yards Gained: 1,876 — Chris George, Glenville St, 1993
Most Yards Gained per Game: 187.6 — Chris George, Glenville St, 1993
Highest Average Gain per Reception: 32.5 — Tyrone Johnson, Western St, 1991 (min. 30 receptions)

Single Game

SCORING

Most Points Scored: 48 — Paul Zaeske, N Park, 1968 (vs N Central); Junior Wolf, Panhandle St, 1958 [vs St Mary (KS)]
Most Field Goals: 6 — Steve Huff, Central Missouri St, 1985 (vs SE Missouri St)

PASSING

Most Passes Completed: 45 — Chris Hatcher, Valdosta St,1993 (vs W Georgia; vs.Miss.College)
Most Yards Gained: 614 — Perry Klein, LI-C.W. Post, 1993 (vs Salisbury St)
Most Touchdowns Passed: 10 — Bruce Swanson, N Park, 1968 (vs N Central)

RUSHING

Most Yards Gained: 382 — Kelly Ellis, Northern Iowa, 1979 (vs Western Illinois)
Most Touchdowns Rushed: 8 — Junior Wolf, Panhandle St, 1958 [vs St Mary (KS)]

RECEIVING

Most Passes Caught: 23 — Barry Wagner, Alabama A&M, 1989 (vs Clark Atlanta)
Most Yards Gained: 370 — Barry Wagner, Alabama A&M, 1989 (vs Clark Atlanta)
Most Touchdown Catches: 8 — Paul Zaeske, N Park, 1968 (vs N Central)

Division III Individual Records

Career

SCORING

Most Points Scored: 474 — Joe Dudek, Plymouth St, 1982-85
Most Touchdowns Scored: 79 — Joe Dudek, Plymouth St, 1982-85
Most Touchdowns Scored, Rushing: 76 — Joe Dudek, Plymouth St, 1982-85
Most Touchdowns Scored, Passing: 115 — Jim Ballard, Wilmington (OH)1990, Mt Union (OH) 91-93
Most Touchdowns Scored, Receiving: 55 — Chris Bisaillon, Illinois Wesleyan, 1989-92

RUSHING

Most Rushes: 1,152 — Antony Russo, St John's (NY) 1990-93
Most Rushes per Game: 32.7 — Chris Sizemore, Bridgewater (VA), 1972-74
Most Yards Gained: 5,834 — Antony Russo, St John's (NY) 1990-93
Most Yards Gained per Game: 154.8 — Kirk Matthieu, Maine-Maritime, 1989-93

Career *(Cont.)*

PASSING

Highest Passing Efficiency Rating: 159.5 — Jim Ballard, Wilmington (OH)1990, Mt Union (OH) 91-93

Most Passes Attempted: 1,696 — Kirk Baumgartner, WI-Stevens Point, 1986-89

Most Passes Completed: 883 — Kirk Baumgartner, WI-Stevens Point, 1986-89

Most Passes Completed per Game: 24.9 — Keith Bishop, Illinois Wesleyan, 1981; Wheaton (IL), 1983-85

Highest Completion Percentage: 62.2 — Brian Moore, Baldwin-Wallace, 1981-84

Most Yards Gained: 13,028 — Kirk Baumgartner, WI-Stevens Point, 1986-89

Most Yards Gained per Game: 317.8 — Kirk Baumgartner, WI-Stevens Point, 1986-89

RECEIVING

Most Passes Caught: 287 — Matt Newton, Principia (IL), 1990-93

Most Yards Gained: 3,846 — Dale Amos, Franklin & Marshall, 1986-89

Most Yards Gained per Game: 110.5 — Matt Newton, Principia (IL), 1990-93

Highest Average Gain per Reception: 20.0 — Marty Redlawsk, Concordia (IL), 1984-87

Single Season

SCORING

Most Points Scored: 168 — Stanley Drayton, Allegheny, 1991

Most Points Scored per Game: 16.8 — Stanley Drayton, Allegheny, 1991

Most Touchdowns Scored: 28 — Stanley Drayton, Allegheny, 1991

Most Touchdowns Scored, Rushing: 27 — Matt Malmberg, St John's (MN), 1993; Stanley Drayton, Allegheny, 1991

Most Touchdowns Scored, Passing: 39 — Kirk Baumgartner, WI-Stevens Point, 1989

Most Touchdowns Scored, Receiving: 20 — John Aromando, Trenton St, 1983

RUSHING

Most Rushes: 380 — Mike Birosak, Dickinson, 1989

Most Rushes per Game: 38.0 — Mike Birosak, Dickinson, 1989

Most Yards Gained: 2,035 — Ricky Gales, Simpson, 1989

Most Yards Gained per Game: 203.5 — Ricky Gales, Simpson, 1989

PASSING

Highest Passing Efficiency Rating: 224.6 — Willie Seiler St John's (MN), 1993

Most Passes Attempted: 527 — Kirk Baumgartner, WI-Stevens Point, 1988

Most Passes Completed: 276 — Kirk Baumgartner, WI-Stevens Point, 1988

Most Passes Completed per Game: 29.1 — Keith Bishop, Illinois Wesleyan, 1985

Highest Completion Percentage: 72.9 — Jim Ballard, Mount Union, 1993

Most Yards Gained: 3,828 — Kirk Baumgartner, WI-Stevens Point, 1988

Most Yards Gained per Game: 369.2 — Kirk Baumgartner, WI-Stevens Point, 1989

RECEIVING

Most Passes Caught: 106 — Theo Blanco, WI-Stevens Point, 1987

Most Yards Gained: 1,693 — Sean Munroe, Mass-Boston, 1992

Most Yards Gained per Game: 188.1 — Sean Munroe, Mass-Boston 1992

Highest Average Gain per Reception: 26.9 — Marty Redlawsk, Concordia (IL), 1985

Single Game

SCORING

Most Field Goals: 6 — Jim Hever, Rhodes, 1984 (vs Millsaps)

PASSING

Most Passes Completed: 50 — Tim Lynch, Hofstra, 1991 (vs Fordham)

Most Yards Gained: 602 — Tom Stallings, St Thomas (MN), 1993 (vs Bethel)

Most Touchdowns Passed: 8 — Steve Austin, Mass-Boston, 1992 (vs Framingham St); Kirk Baumgartner, WI-Stevens Point, 1989 (vs WI-Superior)

RUSHING

Most Yards Gained: 417 — Corey Bender, Coe, 1993 (vs Grinnell)

Most Touchdowns Rushed: 6 — Eric Leiser, Eureka, 1991, (vs Concordia); Rob Sinclair, Simpson, 1990 (vs Upper Iowa)

RECEIVING

Most Passes Caught: 23 — Sean Munroe, Mass-Boston, 1992 (vs Mass-Maritime)

Most Yards Gained: 332 — Sean Munroe, Mass-Boston, 1992 (vs Mass-Maritime)

Most Touchdown Catches: 5 — By 10 players. Most Recent: Sean Munroe, Mass-Boston, 1992 (vs Framingham St)

Career

Scoring

POINTS (KICKERS)	Years	Pts
Roman Anderson, Houston	1988-91	423
Carlos Huerta, Miami (FL)	1988-91	397
Jason Elam, Hawaii	1988-92	395
Derek Schmidt, Florida St	1984-87	393
Luis Zendejas, Arizona St	1981-84	368

POINTS (NON-KICKERS)	Years	Pts
Anthony Thompson, Indiana	1986-89	394
Marshall Faulk, San Diego St	1991-93	376
Tony Dorsett, Pittsburgh	1973-76	356
Glenn Davis, Army	1943-46	354
Art Luppino, Arizona	1953-56	337

POINTS PER GAME (NON-KICKERS)	Years	Pts/Game
Marshall Faulk, San Diego St	1991-93	12.1
Bob Gaiters, New Mexico St	1959-60	11.9
Ed Marinaro, Cornell	1969-71	11.8
Bill Burnett, Arkansas	1968-70	11.3
Steve Owens, Oklahoma	1967-69	11.2

Total Offense

YARDS GAINED	Years	Yds
Ty Detmer, Brigham Young	1988-91	14,665
Doug Flutie, Boston Col	1981-84	11,317
Alex Van Pelt, Pittsburgh	1989-92	10,814
Todd Santos, San Diego St	1984-87	10,513
Kevin Sweeney, Fresno St	1982-86	10,252

YARDS PER GAME	Years	Yds/Game
Ty Detmer, Brigham Young	1988-91	318.8
Mike Perez, San Jose St	1986-87	309.1
Doug Gaynor, Long Beach St	1984-85	305.0
Tony Eason, Illinois	1981-82	299.5
David Klingler, Houston	1988-91	291.5

Rushing

YARDS GAINED	Years	Yds
Tony Dorsett, Pittsburgh	1973-76	6,082
Charles White, Southern Cal	1976-79	5,598
Herschel Walker, Georgia	1980-82	5,259
Archie Griffin, Ohio St	1972-75	5,177
Darren Lewis, Texas A&M	1987-90	5,012

YARDS PER GAME	Years	Yds/Game
Ed Marinaro, Cornell	1969-71	174.6
O. J. Simpson, Southern Cal	1967-68	164.4
Herschel Walker, Georgia	1980-82	159.4
LeShon Johnson, N Illionis	1992-93	150.6
Marshall Faulk, San Diego St	1991-93	148.0

TOUCHDOWNS RUSHING	Years	TD
Anthony Thompson, Indiana	1986-89	64
Marshall Faulk, San Diego St	1991-93	57
Steve Owens, Oklahoma	1967-69	56
Tony Dorsett, Pittsburgh	1973-76	55
Ed Marinaro, Cornell	1969-71	50

Passing

PASSING EFFICIENCY	Years	Rating
Ty Detmer, Brigham Young	1988-91	162.7
Jim McMahon, Brigham Young	1977-78, 80-81	156.9
Steve Young, Brigham Young	1982, 84-86	149.8
Robbie Bosco, Brigham Young	1981-83	149.4
Chuck Long, Iowa	1981-85	148.9

Note: Minimum 500 completions.

YARDS GAINED	Years	Yds
Ty Detmer, Brigham Young	1988-91	15,031
Todd Santos, San Diego St	1984-87	11,425
Alex Van Pelt, Pittsburgh	1989-92	10,913
Kevin Sweeney, Fresno St	1982-86	10,623
Doug Flutie, Boston Col	1981-84	10,579

Note: Minimum 500 completions.

COMPLETIONS	Years	Comp
Ty Detmer, Brigham Young	1988-91	958
Todd Santos, San Diego St	1984-87	910
Brian McClure, Bowling Green	1982-85	900
Eric Wilhelm, Oregon St	1989-92	870
Alex Van Pelt, Pittsburgh	1989-92	845

Note: Minimum 500 completions.

TOUCHDOWNS PASSING	Years	TD
Ty Detmer, Brigham Young	1988-91	121
David Klingler, Houston	1988-91	92
Troy Kopp, Pacific	1989-92	87
Jim McMahon, Brigham Young	1977-78,80-81	84
Joe Adams, Tennessee St	1977-80	81

Receiving

CATCHES	Years	No.
Aaron Turner, Pacific	1989-92	266
Terance Mathis, New Mexico	1985-87, 89	263
Mark Templeton, Long Beach St	1983-86	262
Howard Twilley, Tulsa	1963-65	261
David Williams, Illinois	1983-85	245

CATCHES PER GAME	Years	No./Game
Emmanuel Hazard, Houston	1989-90	10.5
Howard Twilley, Tulsa	1963-65	10.0
Jason Phillips, Houston	1987-88	9.4
Bryan Reeves Nevada	1991-93	7.6
Two tied with 7.4 rec. per game		

YARDS GAINED	Years	Yds
Ryan Yarborough	1990-93	4,357
Aaron Turner, Pacific	1989-92	4,345
Terance Mathis, New Mexico	1985-87,89	4,254
Marc Zeno, Tulane	1984-87	3,725
Ron Sellers, Florida St	1966-68	3,598

TOUCHDOWN CATCHES	Years	TD
Aaron Turner, Pacific	1989-92	43
Ryan Yarborough, Wyoming	1990-93	42
Clarkston Hines, Duke	1986-89	38
Terance Mathis, New Mexico	1985-87,89	36
Elmo Wright, Houston	1968-70	34

Career (Cont.)

All-Purpose Running

YARDS GAINED	Years	Yds
Napoleon McCallum, Navy	1981-85	7172
Darrin Nelson, Stanford	1977-78,80-81	6885
Terance Mathis, New Mexico	1985-87,89	6691
Tony Dorsett, Pittsburgh	1973-76	6615
Paul Palmer, Temple	1983-86	6609

YARDS PER GAME	Years	Yds/Game
Ryan Benjamin, Pacific,	1990-92	237.8
Sheldon Canley, San Jose St	1988-90	205.8
Howard Stevens, Louisville	1971-72	193.7
O. J. Simpson, Southern Cal	1967-68	192.9
Ed Marinaro, Cornell	1969-71	183.0

Interceptions

PLAYER/SCHOOL	Years	Int
Al Brosky, Illinois	1950-52	29
John Provost, Holy Cross	1972-74	27
Martin Bayless, Bowling Green	1980-83	27
Tom Curtis, Michigan	1967-69	25
Tony Thurman, Boston Col	1981-84	25
Tracy Saul, Texas Tech	1989-92	25

Punting Average

PLAYER/SCHOOL	Years	Avg
Reggie Roby, Iowa	1979-82	45.6
Greg Montgomery, Michigan St	1985-87	45.4
Tom Tupa, Ohio St	1984-87	45.2
Barry Helton, Colorado	1984-87	44.9
Ray Guy, Southern Miss	1970-72	44.7

Note: At least 150 punts kicked.

Punt Return Average

PLAYER/SCHOOL	Years	Avg
Jack Mitchell, Oklahoma	1946-48	23.6
Gene Gibson, Cincinnati	1949-50	20.5
Eddie Macon, Pacific	1949-51	18.9
Jackie Robinson, UCLA	1939-40	18.8
Mike Fuller, Auburn	1972-74	17.7
Bobby Dillon, Texas	1949-51	17.7

Note: At least 1.2 punt returns per game.

Kickoff Return Average

PLAYER/SCHOOL	Years	Avg
Forrest Hall, San Francisco	1946-47	36.2
Anthony Davis, Southern Cal	1972-74	35.1
Overton Curtis, Utah St	1957-58	31.0
Fred Montgomery, New Mexico St	1991-92	30.5
Altie Taylor, Utah St	1966-68	29.3

Note: At least 1.2 kickoff returns per game.

The Envelope Please

This season's Rush Limbaugh Hot Air Award goes to … South Carolina quarterback Steve Taneyhill, who said this to Tennessee defensive end Horace Morris while returning to a huddle: "Horace, I want you to come get me." On the next play, Morris did. "The most satisfying sack of my career," he called it. The Vols won 55-3.

The 1993 Beavis and Butt-head Role Model Award is presented to … Colorado athletic Director Bill Marolt, who became so incensed at a penalty call in the Miami game on September 25 that he left his skybox and charged onto the field to confront the offending official. His display did not exactly leave him in a strong moral position when the teams engaged in a brawl later in the game.

Single Season

Scoring

POINTS	Year	Pts
Barry Sanders, Oklahoma St	1988	234
Mike Rozier, Nebraska	1983	174
Lydell Mitchell, Penn St	1971	174
Art Luppino, Arizona	1954	166
Bobby Reynolds, Nebraska	1950	157

FIELD GOALS	Year	FG
John Lee, UCLA	1984	29
Paul Woodside, W Virginia	1982	28
Luis Zendejas, Arizona St	1983	28
Fuad Reveiz, Tennessee	1982	27

Note: Three tied with 25 each.

All-Purpose Running

YARDS GAINED	Year	Yds
Barry Sanders, Oklahoma St	1988	3250
Ryan Benjamin, Pacific	1991	2995
Mike Pringle, Fullerton St	1989	2690
Paul Palmer, Temple	1986	2633
Ryan Benjamin, Pacific	1992	2597

All-Purpose Running (Cont.)

YARDS PER GAME	Years	Yds/Game
Barry Sanders, Oklahoma St	1988	295.5
Ryan Benjamin, Pacific	1991	249.6
Byron (Whizzer) White, Colorado	1937	246.3
Mike Pringle, Fullerton St	1989	244.6
Paul Palmer, Temple	1986	239.4

Total Offense

YARDS GAINED	Year	Yds
David Klingler, Houston	1990	5221
Ty Detmer, Brigham Young	1990	5022
Andre Ware, Houston	1989	4661
Jim McMahon, Brigham Young	1980	4627
Ty Detmer, Brigham Young	1989	4433

YARDS PER GAME	Year	Yds/Game
David Klingler, Houston	1990	474.6
Andre Ware, Houston	1989	423.7
Ty Detmer, Brigham Young	1990	418.5
Steve Young, Brigham Young	1983	395.1
Chris Vargas, Nevada	1993	393.8

Single Season (Cont.)

Rushing

YARDS GAINED

	Year	Yds
Barry Sanders, Oklahoma St	1988	2628
Marcus Allen, Southern Cal	1981	2342
Mike Rozier, Nebraska	1983	2148
LeShon Johnson, N Illinois	1993	1976
Tony Dorsett, Pittsburgh	1976	1948

YARDS PER GAME

	Year	Yds/Game
Barry Sanders, Oklahoma St	1988	238.9
Marcus Allen, Southern Cal	1981	212.9
Ed Marinaro, Cornell	1971	209.0
Charles White, Southern Cal	1979	180.3
Le Shon Johnson, N Illinois	1993	179.6

TOUCHDOWNS RUSHING

	Year	TD
Barry Sanders, Oklahoma St	1988	37
Mike Rozier, Nebraska	1983	29
Ed Marinaro, Cornell	1971	24
Anthony Thompson, Indiana	1988	24
Anthony Thompson, Indiana	1989	24

Passing

PASSING EFFICIENCY

	Year	Rating
Jim McMahon, Brigham Young	1980	176.9
Ty Detmer, Brigham Young	1989	175.6
Trent Dilfer, Fresno St	1993	173.1
Jerry Rhome, Tulsa	1964	172.6
Steve Young, Brigham Young	1983	168.5
Vinny Testaverde, Miami (FL)	1986	165.8

Passing (Cont.)

YARDS GAINED

	Year	Yds
Ty Detmer, Brigham Young	1990	5188
David Klingler, Houston	1990	5140
Andre Ware, Houston	1989	4699
Jim McMahon, Brigham Young	1980	4571
Ty Detmer, Brigham Young	1989	4560

COMPLETIONS

	Year	Att	Comp
David Klingler, Houston	1990	643	374
Andre Ware, Houston	1989	578	365
Ty Detmer, Brigham Young	1990	562	361
Robbie Bosco, Brigham Young 1985		511	338
Chris Vargas, Nevada	1993	490	331

Note: Minimum 15 attempts per game.

TOUCHDOWNS PASSING

	Year	TD
David Klingler, Houston	1990	54
Jim McMahon, Brigham Young	1980	47
Andre Ware, Houston	1989	46
Ty Detmer, Brigham Young	1990	41
Dennis Shaw, San Diego St	1969	39

Receiving

CATCHES

	Year	GP	No.
Emmanuel Hazard, Houston	1989	11	142
Howard Twilley, Tulsa	1965	10	134
Jason Phillips, Houston	1988	11	108
Fred Gilbert, Houston	1991	11	106
Chris Penn, Tulsa	1993	11	105

CATCHES PER GAME

	Year	No.	No./Game
Howard Twilley, Tulsa	1965	134	13.4
Emmanuel Hazard, Houston	1989	142	12.9
Jason Phillips, Houston	1988	108	9.8
Chris Penn, Tulsa	1993	105	9.6
Fred Gilbert, Houston	1991	106	9.6
Jerry Hendren, Idaho	1969	95	9.5
Howard Twilley, Tulsa	1964	95	9.5

YARDS GAINED

	Year	Yds
Howard Twilley, Tulsa	1965	1779
Emmanuel Hazard, Houston	1989	1689
Aaron Turner, Pacific	1991	1604
Chris Penn, Tulsa	1993	1578
Chuck Hughes, UTEP*	1965	1519

*UTEP was Texas Western in 1965.

TOUCHDOWN CATCHES

	Year	TD
Emmanuel Hazard, Houston	1989	22
Desmond Howard, Michigan	1991	19
Aaron Turner, Pacific	1991	18
Dennis Smith, Utah	1989	18
Tom Reynolds, San Diego St	1969	18

Single Game
Scoring

POINTS

	Opponent	Year	Pts
Howard Griffith, Illinois	Southern Illinois	1990	48
Marshall Faulk, San Diego St	Pacific	1991	44
Jim Brown, Syracuse	Colgate	1956	43
Showboat Boykin, Mississippi	Mississippi St	1951	42
Fred Wendt, UTEP*	New Mexico St	1948	42
Dick Bass, Pacific	San Diego St	1958	38

*UTEP was Texas Mines in 1948.

FIELD GOALS

	Opponent	Year	FG
Dale Klein, Nebraska	Missouri	1985	7
Mike Prindle, Western Michigan	Marshall	1984	7

Note: Klein's distances were 32-22-43-44-29-43-43.
Prindle's distances were 32-44-42-23-48-41-27.

Single Game (Cont.)

Total Offense

YARDS GAINED

	Opponent	Year	Yds
David Klingler, Houston	Arizona St	1990	732
Matt Vogler, Texas Christian	Houston	1990	696
David Klingler, Houston	Texas Christian	1990	625
Scott Mitchell, Utah	Air Force	1988	625
Jimmy Klingler, Houston	Rice	1992	612

Passing

YARDS GAINED

	Opponent	Year	Yds
David Klingler, Houston	Arizona St	1990	716
Matt Vogler, Texas Christian	Houston	1990	690
Scott Mitchell, Utah	Air Force	1988	631
Jeremy Leach, New Mexico	Utah	1989	622
Dave Wilson, Illinois	Ohio St	1980	621

COMPLETIONS

	Opponent	Year	Comp
David Klingler, Houston	Southern Methodist	1990	48
Jimmy Klingler, Houston	Rice	1992	46
Sandy Schwab, Northwestern	Michigan	1982	45
Chuck Hartlieb, Iowa	Indiana	1988	44
Jim McMahon, Brigham Young	Colorado St	1981	44

TOUCHDOWNS PASSING

	Opponent	Year	TD
David Klingler, Houston	E. Wash	1990	11

Note: Klingler's TD passes were 5-48-29-7-3-7-40-10-7-8-51.

Rushing

YARDS GAINED

	Opponent	Year	Yds
Tony Sands, Kansas	Missouri	1991	396
Marshall Faulk, San Diego St	Pacific	1991	386
Anthony Thompson, Indiana	Wisconsin	1989	377
Mike Pringle, California St-Fullerton	New Mexico St	1989	357
Rueben Mayes, Washington St	Oregon	1984	357

TOUCHDOWNS RUSHING

	Opponent	Year	TD
Howard Griffith, Illinois	Southern Illinois	1990	8

Note: Griffith's TD runs were 5-51-7-41-5-18-5-3.

Receiving

CATCHES

	Opponent	Year	No.
Jay Miller, Brigham Young	New Mexico	1973	22
Rick Eber, Tulsa	Idaho St	1967	20
Emmanuel Hazard, Houston	Texas Christian	1989	19
Emmanuel Hazard, Houston	Texas	1989	19
Ron Fair, Arizona St	Washington St	1989	19
Howard Twilley, Tulsa	Colorado St	1965	19

YARDS GAINED

	Opponent	Year	Yds
Chuck Hughes, UTEP*	N Texas St	1965	349
Rick Eber, Tulsa	Idaho St	1967	322
Harry Wood, Tulsa	Idaho St	1967	318
Jeff Evans, New Mexico St	Southern Illinois	1978	316
Tom Reynolds, San Diego St	Utah St	1971	290

*UTEP was Texas Western in 1965.

TOUCHDOWN CATCHES

	Opponent	Year	TD
Tim Delaney, San Diego St	New Mexico St	1969	6

Note: Delaney's TD catches were 2-22-34-31-30-9.

Longest Plays (since 1941)

RUSHING

	Opponent	Year	Yds
Gale Sayers, Kansas	Nebraska	1963	99
Max Anderson, Arizona St	Wyoming	1967	99
Ralph Thompson, W Texas St	Wichita St	1970	99
Kelsey Finch, Tennessee	Florida	1977	99

PASSING

	Opponent	Year	Yds
Fred Owens to Jack Ford, Portland	St Mary's (CA)	1947	99
Bo Burris to Warren McVea, Houston	Washington St	1966	99
Colin Clapton to Eddie Jenkins, Holy Cross	Boston U	1970	99
Terry Peel to Robert Ford, Houston	Syracuse	1970	99
Terry Peel to Robert Ford, Houston	San Diego St	1972	99
Cris Collinsworth to Derrick Gaffney, Florida	Rice	1977	99
Scott Ankrom to James Maness, Texas Christian	Rice	1984	99
Gino Toretta to Horace Copeland, Miami	Arkansas	1991	99

FIELD GOALS

	Opponent	Year	Yds
Steve Little, Arkansas	Texas	1977	67
Russell Erxleben, Texas	Rice	1977	67
Joe Williams, Wichita St	Southern Illinois	1978	67
Tony Franklin, Texas A&M	Baylor	1976	65
Tony Franklin, Texas A&M	Baylor	1976	64
Russell Erxleben, Texas	Oklahoma	1977	64

PUNTS

	Opponent	Year	Yds
Pat Brady, Nevada*	Loyola (CA)	1950	99
George O'Brien, Wisconsin	Iowa	1952	96
John Hadl, Kansas	Oklahoma	1959	94
Carl Knox, Texas Christian	Oklahoma St	1947	94
Preston Johnson, SMU	Pittsburgh	1940	94

*Note: Nevada was Nevada-Reno in 1950.

DIVISION I-A WINNINGEST TEAMS
Alltime Winning Percentage

	Yrs	W	L	T	Pct	GP	Bowl Record
Notre Dame	105	723	211	41	.763	975	12-6-0
Michigan	114	739	242	36	.744	1,017	12-13-0
Alabama	99	691	237	44	.734	972	26-17-3
Oklahoma	99	659	240	52	.720	951	20-10-1
Texas	101	687	273	32	.709	992	16-16-2
Southern Cal	101	630	253	52	.702	935	23-13-0
Ohio St	104	659	265	53	.702	977	13-13-0
Nebraska	104	673	290	40	.691	1,003	14-18-0
Penn St	107	674	291	41	.690	1,006	18-10-2
Tennessee	97	636	276	53	.687	965	18-16-0
Central Michigan	93	480	255	36	.646	771	3-1-0
Washington	104	562	310	49	.637	921	12-8-1
Florida St	47	315	176	16	.637	507	14-7-2
Army	104	588	327	50	.635	965	2-1-0
Miami (OH)	105	546	308	42	.633	896	5-2-0
Georgia	100	589	333	53	.631	975	15-13-3
Louisiana St	100	573	325	46	.631	944	11-16-1
Arizona St	81	444	255	24	.631	723	9-5-1
Auburn	101	558	335	46	.619	939	12-9-2
Colorado	104	557	348	36	.611	941	6-12-0
Miami (FL)	67	411	260	19	.609	690	10-10-0
Michigan St	97	521	328	43	.608	892	5-6-0
Bowling Green	75	389	243	52	.607	684	2-3-0
UCLA	75	437	280	37	.604	754	10-8-1
Minnesota	110	555	359	43	.602	957	2-3-0

Note: Includes bowl games.

Alltime Victories

Michigan	739	Georgia	589	Georgia Tech	555
Notre Dame	723	Army	588	Arkansas	550
Alabama	691	Syracuse	583	Texas A&M	549
Texas	687	Louisiana St	573	N Carolina	548
Penn St	674	Pittsburgh	566	Navy	546
Nebraska	673	Washington	562	Miami (OH)	546
Oklahoma	659	Auburn	558	Rutgers	530
Ohio St	659	Colorado	557	California	529
Tennessee	636	W Virginia	557	Clemson	525
Southern Cal	630	Minnesota	555	Michigan St	521

NUMBER ONE VS NUMBER TWO

The number 1 and number 2 teams, according to the Associated Press Poll, have met 29 times, including 10 bowl games, since the poll's inception in 1936. The number 1 teams have a 17-10-2 record in these matchups. Notre Dame (4-3-2) has played in 9 of the games.

Date	Results	Stadium
10-9-43	No. 1 Notre Dame 35, No. 2 Michigan 12	Michigan (Ann Arbor)
11-20-43	No. 1 Notre Dame 14, No. 2 Iowa Pre-Flight 13	Notre Dame (South Bend)
12-2-44	No. 1 Army 23, No. 2 Navy 7	Municipal (Baltimore)
11-10-45	No. 1 Army 48, No. 2 Notre Dame 0	Yankee (New York)
12-1-45	No. 1 Army 32, No. 2 Navy 13	Municipal (Philadelphia)
11-9-46	No. 1 Army 0, No. 2 Notre Dame 0	Yankee (New York)
1-1-63	No. 1 Southern Cal 42, No. 2 Wisconsin 37 (Rose Bowl)	Rose Bowl (Pasadena)
10-12-63	No. 2 Texas 28, No. 1 Oklahoma 7	Cotton Bowl (Dallas)
1-1-64	No. 1 Texas 28, No. 2 Navy 6 (Cotton Bowl)	Cotton Bowl (Dallas)
11-19-66	No. 1 Notre Dame 10, No. 2 Michigan St 10	Spartan (East Lansing)
9-28-68	No. 1 Purdue 37, No. 2 Notre Dame 22	Notre Dame (South Bend)
1-1-69	No. 1 Ohio St 27, No. 2 Southern Cal 16 (Rose Bowl)	Rose Bowl (Pasadena)
12-6-69	No. 1 Texas 15, No. 2 Arkansas 14	Razorback (Fayetteville)
11-25-71	No. 1 Nebraska 35, No. 2 Oklahoma 31	Owen Field (Norman)
1-1-72	No. 1 Nebraska 38, No. 2 Alabama 6 (Orange Bowl)	Orange Bowl (Miami)

NUMBER ONE VS NUMBER TWO *(Cont.)*

Date	Results	Stadium
1-1-79	No. 2 Alabama 14, No. 1 Penn St 7 (Sugar Bowl)	Sugar Bowl (New Orleans)
9-26-81	No. 1 Southern Cal 28, No. 2 Oklahoma 24	Coliseum (Los Angeles)
1-1-83	No. 2 Penn St 27, No. 1 Georgia 23 (Sugar Bowl)	Sugar Bowl (New Orleans)
10-19-85	No. 1 Iowa 12, No. 2 Michigan 10	Kinnick (Iowa City)
9-27-86	No. 2 Miami (FL) 28, No. 1 Oklahoma 16	Orange Bowl (Miami)
1-2-87	No. 2 Penn St 14, No. 1 Miami (FL) 10 (Fiesta Bowl)	Fiesta Bowl (Tempe)
11-21-87	No. 2 Oklahoma 17, No. 1 Nebraska 7	Memorial (Lincoln)
1-1-88	No. 2 Miami (FL) 20, No. 1 Oklahoma 14 (Orange Bowl)	Orange Bowl (Miami)
11-26-88	No. 1 Notre Dame 27, No. 2 Southern Cal 10	Coliseum (Los Angeles)
9-16-89	No. 1 Notre Dame 24, No. 2 Michigan 19	Michigan (Ann Arbor)
11-16-91	No. 2 Miami 17, No. 1 Florida St 16	Campbell (Tallahassee)
1-1-93	No. 2 Alabama 34, No. 1 Miami 13	Superdome (New Orleans)
11-13-93	No. 2 Notre Dame 31, No. 1 Florida St 24	Notre Dame (South Bend)
1-1-94	No. 1 Florida St 18, No. 2 Nebraska 16 (Orange Bowl)	Orange Bowl (Miami)

Longest Winning Streaks

Wins	Team	Yrs	Ended by	Score
47	Oklahoma	1953-57	Notre Dame	7-0
39	Washington	1908-14	Oregon St	0-0
37	Yale	1890-93	Princeton	6-0
37	Yale	1887-89	Princeton	10-0
35	Toledo	1969-71	Tampa	21-0
34	Pennsylvania	1894-96	Lafayette	6-4
31	Oklahoma	1948-50	Kentucky	13-7
31	Pittsburgh	1914-18	Cleveland Naval Reserve	10-9
31	Pennsylvania	1896-98	Harvard	10-0
30	Texas	1968-70	Notre Dame	24-11
29	Michigan	1901-03	Minnesota	6-6
29	Miami (FL)	1990-93	Alabama	34-13

Longest Unbeaten Streaks

No.	W	T	Team	Yrs	Ended by	Score
63	59	4	Washington	1907-17	California	27-0
56	55	1	Michigan	1901-05	Chicago	2-0
50	46	4	California	1920-25	Olympic Club	15-0
48	47	1	Oklahoma	1953-57	Notre Dame	7-0
48	47	1	Yale	1885-89	Princeton	10-0
47	42	5	Yale	1879-85	Princeton	6-5
44	42	2	Yale	1894-96	Princeton	24-6
42	39	3	Yale	1904-08	Harvard	4-0
39	37	2	Notre Dame	1946-50	Purdue	28-14
37	36	1	Oklahoma	1972-75	Kansas	23-3
37	37	0	Yale	1890-93	Princeton	6-0
35	35	0	Toledo	1969-71	Tampa	21-0
35	34	1	Minnesota	1903-05	Wisconsin	16-12
34	33	1	Nebraska	1912-16	Kansas	7-3
34	34	0	Pennsylvania	1894-96	Lafayette	6-4
34	32	2	Princeton	1884-87	Harvard	12-0
34	29	5	Princeton	1877-82	Harvard	1-0
33	30	3	Tennessee	1926-30	Alabama	18-6
33	31	2	Georgia Tech	1914-18	Pittsburgh	32-0
33	30	3	Harvard	1911-15	Cornell	10-0
32	31	1	Nebraska	1969-71	UCLA	20-17
32	30	2	Army	1944-47	Columbia	21-20
32	31	1	Harvard	1898-1900	Yale	28-0
31	30	1	Penn St	1967-70	Colorado	41-13
31	30	1	San Diego St	1967-70	Long Beach St	27-11
31	29	2	Georgia Tech	1950-53	Notre Dame	27-14
31	30	1	Alabama	1991-93	Louisiana St	17-13
31	31	0	Oklahoma	1948-50	Kentucky	13-7
31	31	0	Pittsburgh	1919-22	Cleveland Naval	10-9
31	31	0	Pennsylvania	1896-98	Harvard	10-0

Note: Includes bowl games.

Longest Losing Streaks

L		Seasons	Ended Against	Score
44	Columbia	1983-88	Princeton	16-14
34	Northwestern	1979-82	Northern Illinois	31-6
28	Virginia	1958-61	William & Mary	21-6
28	Kansas St	1945-48	Arkansas St	37-6
27	Eastern Michigan	1980-82	Kent St	9-7

Longest Series

GP	Opponents (Series Leader Listed First)	Record	First Game	GP	Opponents (Series Leader Listed First)	Record	First Game
103	Minnesota-Wisconsin	56-39-8	1890	94	Navy-Army	44-43-7	1890
102	Missouri-Kansas	48-45-9	1891	92	Penn St-Pittsburgh†	47-41-4	1893
100	Nebraska-Kansas	76-21-3	1892	91	Louisiana St-Tulane*	62-22-7	1893
100	Texas Christian-Baylor	47-46-7	1899	91	Clemson-S Carolina	54-33-4	1896
100	Texas-Texas A&M	64-31-5	1894	91	Kansas-Kansas St	61-25-5	1902
98	N Carolina-Virginia	54-40-4	1892	91	Oklahoma-Kansas	61-24-6	1903
98	Miami (OH)-Cincinnati	53-39-6	1888	91	Utah-Utah St	60-27-4	1892
97	Auburn-Georgia	46-44-7	1892	90	Auburn-Georgia Tech#	47-39-4	1892
97	Oregon-Oregon St	47-40-10	1894	90	Michigan-Ohio St	51-33-6	1897
96	Purdue-Indiana	58-32-6	1891	90	Mississippi-Miss St	52-32-6	1901
96	Stanford-California	47-38-11	1892				

†Did not meet in 1993; *Disputed series record. Tulane claims 23-60-7 record. #Have not met since 1989

NCAA Coaches' Records

ALLTIME WINNINGEST DIVISION I-A COACHES
By Percentage

Coach (Alma mater)	Colleges Coached	Yrs	W	L	T	Pct
Knute Rockne (Notre Dame '14)†	Notre Dame 1918-30	13	105	12	5	.881
Frank W. Leahy (Notre Dame '31)†	Boston Col 1939-40; Notre Dame 1941-43, 1946-53	13	107	13	9	.864
George W. Woodruff (Yale '89)†	Pennsylvania 1892-01; Illinois 1903; Carlisle 1905	12	142	25	2	.846
Barry Switzer (Arkansas '60)	Oklahoma 1973-88	16	157	29	4	.837
Percy D. Haughton (Harvard '99)†	Cornell 1899-1900; Harvard 1908-16; Columbia 1923-24	13	96	17	6	.832
Bob Neyland (Army '16)†	Tennessee 1926-34, 1936-40, 1946-52	21	173	31	12	.829
Fielding (Hurry Up) Yost (Lafayette '97)†	Ohio Wesleyan 1897; Nebraska 1898; Kansas 1899; Stanford 1900; Michigan 1901-23, 1925-26	29	196	36	12	.828
Bud Wilkinson (Minnesota '37)†	Oklahoma 1947-63	17	145	29	4	.826
Jock Sutherland (Pittsburgh '18)†	Lafayette 1919-23; Pittsburgh 1924-38	20	144	28	14	.812
Tom Osborne (Hastings '59)*	Nebraska 1973-present	21	206	47	3	.811
Bob Devaney (Alma, MI '39)†	Wyoming 1957-61; Nebraska 1962-72	16	136	30	7	.806
Frank W. Thomas (Notre Dame '23)†	Chattanooga 1925-28; Alabama 1931-42, 1944-46	19	141	33	9	.795
Joe Paterno (Brown '50)*	Penn St 1966-present	28	257	69	3	.786
Henry L. Williams (Yale '91)†	Army 1891; Minnesota 1900-21	23	141	34	12	.786
Gil Dobie (Minnesota '02)†	N Dakota St 1906-07; Washington 1908-16; Navy 1917-19; Cornell 1920-35; Boston Col 1936-38	33	180	45	15	.781
Paul W. (Bear) Bryant (Alabama '36)†	Maryland 1945; Kentucky 1946-53; Texas A&M 1954-57; Alabama 1958-82	38	323	85	17	.780

*Active coach. †Hall of Fame member.
Note: Minimum 10 years as head coach at Division I institutions; record at 4-year colleges only; bowl games included; ties computed as half won, half lost.

Top Winners by Victories

	Yrs	W	L	T	Pct		Yrs	W	L	T	Pct
Paul (Bear) Bryant	38	323	85	17	.780	*Tom Osborne	21	206	47	3	.811
Glenn (Pop) Warner	44	319	106	32	.733	Warren Woodson	31	203	95	14	.673
Amos Alonzo Stagg	57	314	199	35	.605	Vince Dooley	25	201	77	10	.715
*Joe Paterno	28	257	69	3	.786	Eddie Anderson	39	201	128	15	.606
*Bobby Bowden	28	239	78	3	.752	*Hayden Fry	32	200	152	9	.567
Woody Hayes	33	238	72	10	.759	Dana Bible	33	198	72	23	.715
Bo Schembechler	27	234	65	8	.775	Dan McGugin	30	197	55	19	.762
Jess Neely	40	207	176	19	.539	*LaVell Edwards	22	197	72	3	.730

Most Bowl Victories

	W	L	T		W	L	T
*Joe Paterno	15	8	1	Barry Switzer	8	5	0
Paul (Bear) Bryant	15	12	2	Darrell Royal	8	7	1
*Bobby Bowden	13	3	1	Vince Dooley	8	10	2
*Don James	10	5	0	*Tom Osborne	8	13	0
*Lou Holtz	10	6	2	Bob Devaney	7	3	0
John Vaught	10	8	0	Dan Devine	7	3	0
Bobby Dodd	9	4	0	Earle Bruce	7	5	0
*Johnny Majors	9	7	0	Charlie McClendon	7	6	0
*Terry Donahue	8	3	1	*Active coach.			

WINNINGEST ACTIVE DIVISION I-A COACHES
By Percentage

Coach	College Years	W	L	T	Pct*	Bowls		
						W	L	T
Tom Osborne, Nebraska	21	206	47	3	.811	8	13	0
John Robinson, Southern Cal	8	75	18	2	.800	5	1	0
Joe Paterno, Penn St	28	257	69	3	.786	15	8	1
Bobby Bowden, Florida St	28	239	78	3	.752	13	3	1
Danny Ford, Arkansas	13	101	34	5	.739	6	2	0
LaVell Edwards, Brigham Young	22	197	72	3	.730	5	12	1
Dennis Erickson, Miami (FL)	12	103	38	1	.729	4	2	0
Steve Spurrier, Florida	7	59	23	1	.717	2	2	0
Dick Sheridan, N Carolina St	16	128	56	5	.691	5	8	0
Lou Holtz, Notre Dame	23	193	84	6	.693	10	6	2

*Bowl games included.

Note: Minimum 5 years as Division I-A head coach; record at 4-year colleges only.

From Beyond the Grave

Despite having been dead for 39 years, legendary football coach Glenn (Pop) Warner won six games last season.

The NCAA, spurred by the author of a new book on Warner, credited the coach with six more victories, moving him into second place on the all-time Division I-A list. He passes Amos Alonzo Stagg with the posthumous triumphs, but still trails Paul (Bear) Bryant, who won 323 games in his 38-year career.

Five of the wins credited to Warner date back to the coach's days at Carlisle (Pa.), and one is from his tenure at the University of Pittsburgh, where he guided teams to two national championships (1916, 1918).

Warner also won 22 games at Iowa State between 1895 and 1899, but will not get credit for those victories because he coached other teams during that time and wasn't at many of the games.

His record now stands at 319-106-32, five victories ahead of Stagg.

"We want to set the record straight," said Jim Wright, the NCAA's statistics services manager.

By Victories

Joe Paterno, Penn St..............257	Bill Mallory, Indiana..............156
Bobby Bowden, Florida St..............239	Don Nehlen, W Virginia..............156
Tom Osborne, Nebraska..............206	Al Molde, W Michigan..............152
Hayden Fry, Iowa..............200	Jim Wacker, Minnesota..............150
LaVell Edwards, Brigham Young..............197	Terry Donahue, UCLA..............139
Lou Holtz, Notre Dame..............193	George Welsh, Virginia..............135
Jim Sweeney, Fresno St..............186	John Cooper, Ohio St..............126
Johnny Majors, Tennessee..............176	

WINNINGEST ACTIVE DIVISION I-AA COACHES
By Percentage

Coach, College	Yrs	W	L	T	Pct*
Eddie Robinson, Grambling	51	388	140	15	.728
Roy Kidd, Eastern Kentucky	30	247	92	8	.723
Tubby Raymond, Delaware	28	232	92	2	.715
Jimmy Satterfield, Furman	8	66	29	3	.689
Jim Tressel, Youngstown St	8	70	33	1	.678
Houston Markham, Alabama St	7	48	23	4	.666
Steve Tosches, Princeton	7	46	23	1	.664
Bill Hayes, N Carolina A&T	18	131	66	2	.663
William Collick, Delaware St	9	62	34	0	.646
Bill Davis, Tennessee St	15	104	58	1	.641

*Playoff games included.
Note: Minimum 5 years as a Division I-A and/or Division I-AA head coach; record at 4-year colleges only.

By Victories

Eddie Robinson, Grambling..............388	Willie Jeffries, S Carolina St..............132
Roy Kidd, Eastern Kentucky..............247	Bill Hayes, N Carolina A&T..............131
Tubby Raymond, Delaware..............232	Don Read, Montana..............130
Carmen Cozza, Yale..............169	James Donnelly, Middle Tennessee St..............124
Ron Randleman, Sam Houston St..............155	
Bill Bowes, New Hampshire..............142	

WINNINGEST ACTIVE DIVISION II COACHES
By Percentage

Coach, College	Yrs	W	L	T	Pct*
Rocky Hager, N Dakota St	7	66	15	1	.811
Ken Sparks, Carson-Newman	14	127	39	2	.761
Bob Cortese, Fort Hays St	14	114	38	3	.745
Peter Yetten, Bentley	6	38	13	1	.740
Joe Taylor, Hampton	11	82	32	4	.712
Dick Lowry, Hillsdale	20	152	62	3	.707
Ron Taylor, Quincy	5	35	14	2	.706
Bill Burgess, Jacksonville St	9	72	29	4	.705
Danny Hale, Bloomsburg	6	45	19	0	.703
Frank Cignetti, Indiana (PA)	12	99	42	1	.701

*Ties computed as half win, half loss. Playoff games included.
Note: Minimum 5 years as a college head coach; record at 4-year colleges only.

By Victories

Jim Malosky, MN-Duluth..............231	Claire Boroff, Kearney St..............132
Gene Carpenter, Millersville..............167	Ken Sparks, Carson-Newman..............127
Ron Harms, Texas A&M-Kingsville*..............163	Dennis Douds, E Stroudsburg..............124
Dick Lowry, Hillsdale..............152	Larry Kramer, Emporia St..............119
Douglas Porter, Fort Valley St..............141	*Formerly Texas A&I
Bud Elliott, E New Mexico St..............137	

WINNINGEST ACTIVE DIVISION III COACHES
By Percentage

Coach, College	Yrs	W	L	T	Pct*
Bob Reade, Augustana (IL)	15	138	21	1	.866
Larry Kehres, Mount Union	8	74	13	3	.839
Dick Farley, Williams	7	45	9	2	.821
Ron Schipper, Central (IA)	33	260	62	3	.805
John Luckhardt, Washington & Jefferson	12	97	25	2	.790
Bob Packard, Baldwin-Wallace	13	102	28	2	.780
Roger Harring, WI-La Crosse	25	210	60	7	.771
Rich Lackner, Carnegie Mellon	8	59	18	2	.760
John Gagliardi, St John's (MN)	45	306	96	10	.755
Rick Giancola, Montclair St	11	84	29	2	.739

*Ties computed as half win, half loss. Playoff games included.
Note: Minimum 5 years as a college head coach; record at 4-year colleges only.

By Victories

John Gagliardi, St John's (MN)	306	Frank Girardi, Lycoming	156
Ron Schipper, Central (IA)	260	Don Miller, Trinity (CT)	148
Roger Harring, WI-LaCrosse	210	Ray Smith, Hope	143
Bill Manlove, Delaware Valley	187	Joe McDaniel, Centre	142
Jim Christopherson, Concordia-Moorhead	175	Peter Mazzaferro, Bridgewater (MA)	139

NAIA Coaches' Records

WINNINGEST ACTIVE NAIA COACHES
By Percentage

Coach, College	Yrs	W	L	T	Pct*
Charlie Richard, Baker (KS)	13	117	25	1	.822
Ted Kessinger, Bethany (KS)	18	147	33	1	.815
Frosty Westering, Pacific Lutheran	27	226	72	6	.755
†Billy Joe, Central St (OH)	20	169	54	4	.753
Max Bowman, Greenville (IL)	7	44	15	1	.742
Jim Svoboda, Nebraska Wesleyan	7	51	20	0	.729
Larry Korver, Northwestern (IA)	27	202	75	6	.724
Hank Biesiot, Dickinson St (ND)	18	108	41	1	.723
Dick Strahm, Findlay (OH)	19	135	53	3	.715
†Dick Lowry, Hillsdale (MI)	19	154	62	3	.710

*Playoff games included.
†Denotes Division I coach.
Note: Minimum five years as a collegiate head coach and includes record against four-year institutions only.

By Victories

Frosty Westering, Pacific Lutheran (WA)	226	Dick Lowry, Hillsdale (MI)	154
†Jim Malosky, MN-Duluth	223	Ted Kessinger, Bethany (KS)	147
Larry Korver, Northwestern (IA)	202	Dick Strahm, Findlay (OH)	135
†Billy Joe, Central St (OH)	169	Bob Petrino, Carroll (MT)	132
Buddy Benson, Ouachita Baptist (AR)	155	Rollie Greeno, Jamestown (ND)	129

†Denotes Division I coach.

Pro Basketball

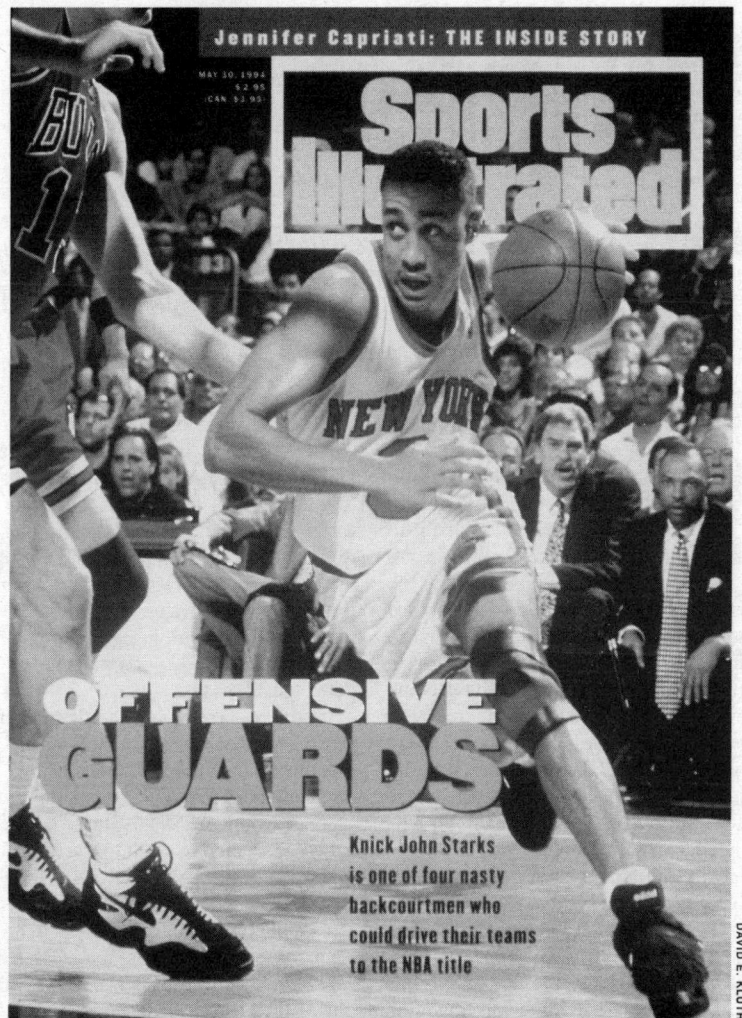

Jennifer Capriati: THE INSIDE STORY

MAY 30, 1994
$2.95
CAN $3.95

Sports Illustrated

OFFENSIVE GUARDS

Knick John Starks is one of four nasty backcourtmen who could drive their teams to the NBA title

DAVID E. KLUTHO

Baskets and Bruises

The first season of the post-Jordan era showcased nothing if not the aching absence of his Airness | by JACK McCALLUM

THE HOUSTON ROCKETS HAD WON their first NBA title less than an hour earlier, and they were now joyously passing the championship trophy around their locker room. Someone handed it to Sam Cassell, the Rockets' ebullient rookie guard, who noticed that the golden basketball at the top of the award had somehow come loose and was about to topple from its base. Cassell looked at it in surprise for a moment, then yelled to no one in particular, "Hey, who broke the trophy?"

The damaged hardware was a fitting metaphor for the NBA's turbulent season, which left the league's once golden image slightly battered. With Michael Jordan having joined Larry Bird and Magic Johnson in retirement, the NBA was suddenly without the three superstars who had defined the league over the past 15 years. Other stars did their best to fill the vacuum, most notably Charles Barkley, the Phoenix Suns' forward and quote-machine, and Shaquille O'Neal, the Orlando Magic's center-rapper-actor, who finished second to San Antonio

center David Robinson in the scoring race. And several rookies, most notably forward Chris Webber of the Golden State Warriors and point guard Anfernee Hardaway of the Orlando Magic, showed indications that they would be the league's glamorous stars in years to come. But the NBA's biggest problem was that it wasn't a player who set the tone for the league in 1993–94, it was a style of play—a bumping, grabbing, pushing, shoving style that kept scores low and tempers high all season.

It was a battling, trash-talking kind of year. There were major brawls in the playoffs during the Atlanta Hawks–Miami Heat and New York Knicks–Chicago Bulls series. Dennis Rodman, San Antonio's eccentric forward, seemed to get into a scuffle almost nightly. The New York Knicks, especially Charles Oakley, Anthony Mason and John Starks, flagrantly fouled their way to the seventh game of the NBA Finals. Even Utah Jazz owner Larry Miller made headlines during the postseason by engaging in a heated argument with a group of Denver Nugget fans. The league that once made Showtime

MANNY MILLAN

MVP Olajuwon showed that grace and athleticism could win out over Uglyball.

a household word was now beginning to do the same for the term Uglyball.

And wherever there was Uglyball, there were usually the Knicks. Even though they fell one game short of winning the championship, losing to the Rockets in the seventh game of the NBA Finals, the Knicks may have left a bigger imprint on the season than any other team. They were the biggest reason that NBA commissioner David Stern spent much of the Finals assuring fans and the media that the league planned to spend the off-season examining ways of keeping the sport from turning into one big slam-dance. To their supporters, the Knicks were

aggressive and physical. To their critics, they were dirty and dangerous. But nearly everyone agreed that the Knicks' approach was not exactly an aesthetic triumph. New York coach Pat Riley had only two players, center Patrick Ewing and guard John Starks, on whom he could depend offensively, so he emphasized stopping the other team by any means necessary, including the occasional body-slam. On offense, the Knicks' attack consisted largely of throwing up bricklike jump shots and depending on their bruising front line to grab them and put them back in.

But in the end, the Rockets and their wondrous center, Hakeem Olajuwon, reminded everyone that there was still a place for grace and athleticism and dignity in the NBA, and that place was at the top. Olaju-

Wilkens' emphasis on defense spurred the Hawks to unexpected heights.

MANNY MILLAN

won clearly established himself as the successor to Jordan as the league's preeminent player, leading the Rockets to the first championship in their history and winning the regular-season and postseason Most Valuable Player awards along the way. With his remarkable quickness and balletic moves, as well as his steadfast refusal to taunt his opponents or posture for the fans, Olajuwon proved himself fully deserving of his mantle as the NBA's new king.

To win that crown, Olajuwon had to defeat another noble aspirant to the throne— Ewing. In a confrontation of centers that recalled the great Bill Russell–Wilt Chamberlain battles of the 1960s, Olajuwon and Ewing waged a war against each other that wasn't always pretty but was unfailingly intense. Although Ewing had his moments, Olajuwon had more of them, ultimately emerging the clear victor in the individual contest as well as the team battle. The Rockets gave Olajuwon help—the Houston backcourt of Kenny Smith and Vernon Maxwell,

outplayed by the Knicks' Derek Harper and John Starks for most of the series, finally turned the tables in Game 7—but there was no question that the Rockets took the measure of the Knicks mainly because Olajuwon was able to get the better of Ewing.

It was apparent from the first game of the season that Olajuwon and the Rockets were aiming high. They tied the record for consecutive wins at the start of a season with 15, and the final victory was a win over the Knicks in New York that would prove to be a sign of things to come. The Rockets' streak finally came to an end against the Atlanta Hawks, who had a memorable season of their own. The Hawks had finished 43–39 the year before, and little more was expected of them in '93–94, but new coach Lenny Wilkens introduced them to the wonders of defense, and the result was a 57–25 regular-season record, the best in the Eastern Conference. Wilkens, who was bedeviled during his seven years with the Cleveland Cavaliers by his inability to devise a way to contain Jordan in the playoffs, apparently knew how to stop everyone else. Under his tutelage the Hawks improved from 21st in the league in team defense to fourth place.

One of the ways Wilkens made it clear to his new team that he was serious about defense was by pulling star forward Dominique Wilkins out of an early-season win over Miami twice in the first half because Wilkins was a little too shot-happy. A few months later, Wilkins was gone from the Hawks entirely, traded to the Los Angeles Clippers for forward Danny Manning in a swap of stars who would become unrestricted free agents after the season. Manning could only help the Hawks go as far as the second round of the playoffs, where they were upset by the Indiana Pacers. Wilkins finished out the season with the lowly Clippers, then bolted for the Boston Celtics during the off-season.

It seemed that nearly everyone had a long streak of some kind during the season, whether it was the 15-game winning streaks by the Rockets and the Knicks, or the 16-game losing streak by the ever-hapless Dal-

Mutombo led the Nuggets to a shocking upset of the Sonics.

las Mavericks. But for sustained excellence throughout the regular season, no team could match the Seattle SuperSonics, whose 63–19 record was the best in the league. The Sonics made two key trades during the off-season, sending underachieving forward Derrick McKey to the Indiana Pacers for versatile forward Detlef Schrempf and acquiring guard Kendall Gill from the Charlotte Hornets for forward Eddie Johnson. That gave Seattle coach George Karl two more quick, athletic players to plug into his constantly trapping, switching and gambling defense, and the result was a team that led the league in steals. The Sonics were the most exciting team in the league, thanks largely to their defense and fast-breaking style, and many of those breaks ended with point guard Gary Payton and forward Shawn Kemp teaming up for alley-oop dunks that were the stuff of highlight films. The Sonics, full of fiery, intense characters, especially Karl and Payton, played with the pedal to the metal all season, which may have been why they ran out of gas in the playoffs.

Seattle was a huge favorite in the first round of the playoffs against the young Denver Nuggets, the eighth and lowest seed in the Western Conference, and everything appeared to be going according to plan when the Sonics won the first two games at home. But then the Nuggets, led by shot-blocking center Dikembe Mutombo, recovered to tie the best-of-five series with two victories in Denver. The Nuggets then shocked the Sonics with an overtime win in Game 5 to win the series—the first time the eighth seed had eliminated the top seed since the NBA went to its current playoff format—and send Seattle into a downward

spiral that continued well into the off-season. By the middle of the summer, the Sonics had gone from being the prototype for a young, successful organization to a franchise in disarray.

Team president Bob Whitsitt, who built the team and had been voted the league's executive of the year, left the Sonics after the season in a bitter dispute with owner Barry Ackerley and resurfaced as general manager of the Portland Trail Blazers. Karl threatened to leave as well unless he received a contract extension, which Ackerley eventually gave him. After Whitsitt's departure, the Sonics traded veteran guard Ricky Pierce, who had clashed with Payton during the playoffs, to the Golden State Warriors along with draft choice Carlos Rogers for guard Sarunas Marciulionis and forward Byron Houston. Seattle also came close to a blockbuster draft day trade of Kemp for

MANNY MILLAN

It was a gratifying regular season for Pippen and all the other Bulls once known as Jordan's supporting cast. They surpassed all expectations by staying in the race for the best record in the Eastern Conference right down to the final days of the season. But a season's worth of Pippen's good work came undone in the space of 1.8 seconds in the playoffs.

In Game 3 of the Eastern Conference semifinals between the Bulls and the Knicks, New York erased a 20-point fourth-quarter deficit to tie the game. Chicago called timeout with 1.8 seconds left, and coach Phil Jackson devised a play designed to free forward Toni Kukoc for the last shot. Pippen was miffed that the play hadn't been called for him, and he was probably annoyed even further that Kukoc, a rookie from Croatia for whom Pippen could barely contain his resentment, had been chosen. When Jackson sent the team back on the floor, Pippen refused to go, taking a seat near the end of the bench. His act of selfishness didn't hurt the Bulls in the short term—Kukoc made the shot at the buzzer to give Chicago the win—but the long-term may be another story, especially for Pippen, a great player who is likely to always be remembered for that one moment in which he committed the cardinal sin of putting himself ahead of his team.

But the problems of Pippen or the Sonics or anyone else in the league seemed trivial when compared to the near-tragedy suffered by Bobby Hurley, the Sacramento Kings' rookie point guard. Hurley was driving away from the Kings' Arco Arena after a game in December when he was struck by a station wagon traveling at or near the 55 mph speed limit with its headlights off. Hurley, who was not wearing a seat belt, was thrown from his car into a ditch, where, he said later, "I thought I was going to die." But fate was kind, and help arrived quickly in the form of a passerby and Hurley's teammate Mike Peplowski. Their quick action helped save his life, but Hurley suffered several

Chicago star Scottie Pippen, but Ackerley reportedly nixed the deal at the last minute.

It would have been appropriate if Pippen had gone to Seattle, because like the Sonics, he had a wonderful year that came to a horrible conclusion. After Jordan announced his retirement just days before the start of training camp, the focus immediately shifted to Pippen. Would he be able to make the transition from second banana to leading man? For most of the season Pippen answered the question with a resounding yes. Instead of trying to replace Jordan by simply trying to score more, Pippen did a little bit of everything—scoring, passing, rebounding, defending—and he made sure to keep his teammates involved. But he also didn't hesitate to grab the spotlight for himself when the occasion called for it, as he proved by scoring 29 points in the All-Star game to win the game's Most Valuable Player award.

serious injuries to his lungs, shoulder and knee. Miraculously he was back at home in Jersey City by Christmas and was playing again in a summer league six months later, preparing for the start of the '94–'95 season.

With or without Hurley, the Kings were their usual ineffectual selves, finishing with a 28–54 record and missing the playoffs for the eighth consecutive year. They had plenty of company in their misery, as nine teams lost 50 or more games. But the worst of the worst were clearly the Dallas Mavericks, not only because their 13–69 record was the worst in the league for the second straight year, but because first-year coach Quinn Buckner and his team battled each other more intensely than they did other teams. The Dallas players all but staged a mutiny against what they considered Buckner's dictatorial style. Rookie forward Jamal Mashburn was Buckner's most outspoken critic, but nearly all the Mavericks spoke up at one time or another. The relationship between the coach and his players was so bad that owner Donald Carter fired Buckner shortly after the end of the

season even though there were four years remaining on his contract.

But Buckner's brief coaching tenure was nowhere near as short as Magic Johnson's. Los Angeles Laker owner Jerry Buss fired coach Randy Pfund and talked Johnson into taking over as coach for the final 16 games of the season, after which Johnson was to decide whether or not he wanted the job permanently. Johnson's coaching career started auspiciously enough, with the Lakers winning five of their first six games under his guidance. But it wasn't long before they returned to their undisciplined, mediocre ways. Johnson, after openly criticizing his players' work ethic, declared before the season even ended that he had no plans to return. Johnson had long made it clear that his true goal was not to coach a team but to own one, and he made a step toward that end in June, when he bought a minority share of the team from Buss, who hired former Houston and Milwaukee coach Del Harris to replace Johnson on the Laker bench.

The playoffs commenced without either the Lakers or the Boston Celtics, the first time that had happened since the Lakers joined the league, in 1948–49. And without Jordan the race for the title was as wide open as it had been in years. A long line of veteran stars who had never won a championship, including Olajuwon, Ewing, Barkley, Karl Malone and John Stockton, saw a golden opportunity to capture their first ring. All those established stars had their moments in the playoffs, but the postseason was a time for younger teams, especially the Nuggets and the Indiana

DAMIAN STROHMEYER

The Kings lost Hurley, and Hurley nearly lost his life, in an auto accident in December.

JOHN W. McDONOUGH

Pacers, to make some playoff noise as well.

The Pacers pulled off the first upset of the playoffs, sweeping O'Neal and the Magic out of the first round in three games. Then they knocked off the Hawks in six games to reach the Eastern Conference final against the Knicks. The series was tied at 2–2 when it finally hit its stride. Indiana guard Reggie Miller turned in the most spectacular individual effort of the playoffs when he scored 25 points in the fourth quarter on five three-pointers while exchanging trash talk with film director and devoted Knick fan Spike Lee the entire time. Even New York coach Pat Riley had to admit it was one of the greatest shooting displays he had ever seen, comparing Miller's effort to the best of Jordan. Miller's performance carried the Pacers to a 93–86 win and a 3–2 series lead, but the Knicks recovered to win Game 6 in Indiana and take the series with a seventh-game victory in New York.

Things were just as interesting in the West, where Phoenix and Houston met in the conference semifinals. The Rockets appeared to be doomed when the Suns won the first two games in Houston, prompting one Houston paper to print the headline, "Choke City." But the Rockets came back to win the next two games in Phoenix and ultimately eliminated the Suns in seven games. Game 7 featured the uncomfortable sight of Barkley, who had been considering retirement all season because of his back problems, limping badly up and down the court

as he gamely tried to carry the Suns through. When he was ejected near the end of the game with the Suns' defeat assured, it looked as though he might be leaving the court for the last time as an active player. But after consulting with specialists during the offseason he announced that he would return for at least another year.

The Rockets, meanwhile, moved on to face the Utah Jazz, who had finally eliminated the pesky Nuggets, in the conference finals. The Jazz had eliminated San Antonio in a bitter first round series that featured Rodman at his unpredictable, combative best. Rodman, who came to the Spurs from the Detroit Pistons in a trade for Sean Elliott before the season, had become a favorite of San Antonio fans and one of the most visible players in the league thanks to his ever-changing hair colors—he finally settled on blond for most of the season after trying red and purple—and his penchant for baiting the referees and opposing players. Against the Jazz he had run-ins with Stockton and Tom Chambers and was suspended for Game 3, which proved to be a pivotal development, as the Jazz went on to win the game and wrap up the best-of-five series in four games. But Houston had little trouble with Utah, eliminating the Jazz in five games to send the Utah stars, Malone and Stockton, home without a ring yet again.

That set up the Houston-New York matchup, in which the Knicks took a 3–2 lead going back to Houston. In Game 6, Olajuwon blocked a Starks three-point attempt at the buzzer to preserve an 86–84 Houston win and tie the series. In Game 7, the Rockets didn't need to block Starks' shots, they simply let him keep shooting. He missed 16 of his 18 shots, including all 11 of his three-point attempts, as the Rockets walked off with a 90–84 victory and the championship. It mattered little that the trophy was a touch flawed. "It's the feeling that counts," Olajuwon said after the game. "The feeling is perfect."

NBA Final Standings

Eastern Conference

ATLANTIC DIVISION

Team	W	L	Pct	GB
New York	57	25	.695	—
Orlando	50	32	.610	7
New Jersey	45	37	.549	12
Miami	42	40	.512	15
Boston	32	50	.390	25
Philadelphia	25	57	.305	32
Washington	24	58	.234	33

CENTRAL DIVISION

Team	W	L	Pct	GB
Atlanta	57	25	.695	—
Chicago	55	27	.671	2
Indiana	47	35	.573	10
Cleveland	47	35	.573	10
Charlotte	41	41	.500	16
Detroit	20	62	.244	37
Milwaukee	20	62	.244	37

Western Conference

MIDWEST DIVISION

Team	W	L	Pct	GB
Houston	58	24	.707	—
San Antonio	55	27	.671	3
Utah	53	29	.646	5
Denver	42	40	.512	16
Minnesota	20	62	.244	38
Dallas	13	69	.159	45

PACIFIC DIVISION

Team	W	L	Pct	GB
Seattle	63	19	.768	—
Phoenix	56	26	.683	7
Golden St	50	32	.610	13
Portland	47	35	.573	16
LA Lakers	33	49	.402	30
Sacramento	28	54	.341	35
LA Clippers	27	55	.329	36

1994 NBA Playoffs

EASTERN CONFERENCE

1st ROUND	SEMIFINALS	FINALS

WESTERN CONFERENCE

FINALS	SEMIFINALS	1st ROUND

NBA FINAL

HOUSTON (4-3)

Eastern bracket:
- New York / New Jersey → New York (3-1)
- Chicago / Cleveland → Chicago (3-0)
- New York (4-3) → New York (4-3)
- Atlanta / Miami → Atlanta (3-2)
- Indiana / Orlando → Indiana (3-0)
- Indiana (4-2)

Western bracket:
- Phoenix / Golden St → Phoenix (3-0)
- Portland / Houston → Houston (3-1)
- Houston (4-3)
- Houston (4-1)
- Utah / San Antonio → Utah (3-1)
- Denver / Seattle → Denver (3-2)
- Utah (4-3)

1994 NBA Playoff Results

Eastern Conference First Round

Apr 29	New Jersey	80	at New York	91
May 1	New Jersey	81	at New York	90
May 4	New York	92	at Indiana	93*
May 6	New York	102	at Indiana	92

New York won series 3-1.

Apr 28	Miami	93	at Atlanta	88
Apr 30	Miami	86	at Atlanta	104
May 3	Atlanta	86	at Miami	90
May 5	Atlanta	103	at Miami	89
May 8	Miami	91	at Atlanta	102

Atlanta won series 3-2.

Eastern Conference First Round (Cont.)

Apr 29	Cleveland	96	at Chicago	104		
May 1	Cleveland	96	at Chicago	105		
May 3	Chicago	95	at Cleveland	92*		

Chicago won series 3-0.

Apr 28	Indiana	89	at Orlando	88
Apr 30	Indiana	103	at Orlando	101
May 4	Orlando	86	at Indiana	99

Indiana won series 3-0.

Western Conference First Round

Apr 28	Denver	82	at Seattle	106
Apr 30	Denver	87	at Seattle	97
May 2	Seattle	93	at Denver	110
May 5	Seattle	85	at Denver	94*
May 7	Denver	98	at Seattle	94*

Denver won series 3-2.

Apr 29	Portland	104	at Houston	114
May 1	Portland	104	at Houston	115
May 3	Houston	115	at Portland	118
May 6	Houston	92	at Portland	89

Houston won series 3-1.

Apr 29	Golden St	104	at Phoenix	111
May 1	Golden St	111	at Phoenix	117
May 3	Phoenix	140	at Golden St	133

Phoenix won series 3-0.

Apr 28	Utah	89	at San Antonio	106
Apr 30	Utah	96	at San Antonio	84
May 3	San Antonio	72	at Utah	105
May 5	San Antonio	90	at Utah	95

Utah won series 3-1.

Eastern Conference Semifinals

May 8	Chicago	86	at New York	90
May 11	Chicago	91	at New York	96
May 13	New York	102	at Chicago	104
May 15	New York	83	at Chicago	95
May 18	Chicago	86	at New York	87
May 20	New York	79	at Chicago	93
May 22	Chicago	77	at New York	87

New York won series 4-3.

May 10	Indiana	96	at Atlanta	85
May 12	Indiana	69	at Atlanta	92
May 14	Atlanta	81	at Indiana	101
May 15	Atlanta	86	at Indiana	102
May 17	Indiana	76	at Atlanta	88
May 19	Atlanta	79	at Indiana	98

Indiana won series 4-2.

Western Conference Semifinals

May 10	Denver	91	at Utah	100
May 12	Denver	94	at Utah	104
May 14	Utah	111	at Denver	109*
May 15	Utah	82	at Denver	83
May 17	Denver	109	at Utah	101†
May 19	Utah	91	at Denver	94
May 21	Denver	81	at Utah	91

Utah won series 4-3.

May 8	Phoenix	91	at Houston	87
May 11	Phoenix	124	at Houston	117*
May 13	Houston	118	at Phoenix	102
May 15	Houston	107	at Phoenix	96
May 17	Phoenix	96	at Houston	107
May 19	Houston	86	at Phoenix	103
May 21	Phoenix	94	at Houston	104

Houston won series 4-3.

Eastern Conference Finals

May 24	Indiana	89	at New York	100
May 26	Indiana	78	at New York	89
May 28	New York	68	at Indiana	88
May 30	New York	77	at Indiana	83
June 1	Indiana	93	at New York	86
June 3	New York	98	at Indiana	91
June 5	Indiana	90	at New York	94

New York won series 4-3.

Western Conference Finals

May 23	Utah	88	at Houston	100
May 25	Utah	99	at Houston	104
May 27	Houston	86	at Utah	95
May 29	Houston	80	at Utah	78
May 31	Utah	83	at Houston	94

Houston won series 4-1.

Finals

June 8	New York	78	at Houston	85
June 10	New York	91	at Houston	83
June 12	Houston	93	at New York	89
June 15	Houston	82	at New York	91

June 17	Houston	84	at New York	91
June 19	New York	84	at Houston	86
June 22	New York	86	at Houston	90

Houston won series 4-3.

* Overtime game. †Double overtime game.

NBA Finals Composite Box Score

HOUSTON ROCKETS

Player	GP	Field Goals		3-Pt FG		Free Throws		Rebounds		A	Stl	TO	BS	Avg	Hi
		FGM	Pct	FGM	FGA	FTM	Pct	Off	Total						
Olajuwon	7	75	50.0	1	1	37	86.0	13	64	25	11	25	27	26.9	32
Maxwell	7	35	36.5	9	40	15	68.2	3	23	20	4	21	0	13.4	21
Horry	7	24	32.4	11	36	13	61.9	13	43	26	9	10	4	10.3	16
Cassell	7	19	42.2	7	16	25	92.6	6	22	20	9	18	2	10.0	15
Thorpe	7	27	51.9	0	0	11	50.0	23	79	23	6	8	0	9.3	14
Herrera	7	22	57.9	0	0	6	75.0	8	25	3	3	6	1	7.1	12

HOUSTON ROCKETS *(Cont.)*

Player	GP	Field Goals FGM	Pct	3-Pt FG FGM	FGA	Free Throws FTM	Pct	Rebounds Off	Total	A	Stl	TO	BS	Avg	Hi
K. Smith	7	14	38.9	5	14	6	100.0	2	10	22	5	14	0	5.6	11
Bullard	2	2	20.0	2	7	2	50.0	2	6	0	1	0	1	4.0	4
Elie	7	5	25.0	2	5	5	83.3	3	7	7	2	5	1	2.4	6
Cureton	1	0	—	0	0	0	—	0	0	0	0	0	0	0.0	0
Jent	3	0	00.0	0	2	0	—	0	1	0	0	1	0	0.0	0
Total	**7**	**223**	**42.6**	**37**	**121**	**120**	**75.5**	**73**	**280**	**146**	**50**	**118**	**36**	**86.1**	**93**

NEW YORK KNICKS

Player	GP	Field Goals FGM	Pct	3-Pt FG FGM	FGA	Free Throws FTM	Pct	Rebounds Off	Total	A	Stl	TO	BS	Avg	Hi
Ewing	7	58	36.3	1	5	15	71.4	32	87	12	9	22	30	18.9	25
Starks	7	39	36.8	16	50	30	76.9	3	22	41	11	17	1	17.7	27
Harper	7	42	46.7	17	39	14	82.4	7	21	42	17	12	1	16.4	23
Oakley	7	31	48.4	0	0	15	83.3	29	83	17	8	15	1	11.0	16
C. Smith	7	26	44.1	0	2	13	68.4	14	30	12	4	8	7	9.3	11
Mason	7	22	46.8	0	0	16	64.0	14	48	9	5	8	0	8.6	17
Anthony	7	10	32.3	1	8	2	100.0	3	6	17	3	4	1	3.3	7
Bonner	2	2	100.0	0	0	0	00.0	1	2	0	1	0	2	2.0	2
Davis	5	2	20.0	1	1	3	50.0	2	2	2	0	1	1	1.6	4
Williams	4	0	00.0	0	0	0	—	0	0	0	0	1	1	0.0	0
Total	**7**	**232**	**40.7**	**36**	**105**	**108**	**73.0**	**105**	**301**	**152**	**57**	**92**	**43**	**86.9**	**91**

NBA Finals Box Scores

Game 1

NEW YORK 78

NEW YORK	Min	FG M-A	FT M-A	Reb O-T	A	PF	S	TO	TP
Oakley	40	6-11	0-0	5-14	4	4	2	3	12
C. Smith	27	4-7	1-2	1-5	2	1	1	1	9
Ewing	43	10-26	3-4	2-9	2	5	2	1	23
Harper	29	3-10	0-0	1-3	5	2	1	0	8
Starks	38	3-18	3-5	0-2	3	3	2	4	11
Mason	26	1-5	3-5	2-10	2	5	2	0	5
Williams	4	0-1	0-0	0-0	0	0	0	0	0
Anthony	18	3-7	0-0	1-1	3	1	0	2	6
Davis	15	1-6	2-3	1-1	2	3	0	1	4
Totals	240	31-91	12-19	13-45	23	24	10	13	78

Percentages: FG—.341, FT—.632. 3-pt goals: 4-16, .267 (Harper 2-4, Starks 2-8, Anthony 0-1, Ewing 0-2). Team rebounds: 14. Blocked shots: 4 (Ewing 2, C. Smith, Williams).

HOUSTON 85

HOUSTON	Min	FG M-A	FT M-A	Reb O-T	A	PF	S	TO	TP
Horry	40	3-10	1-4	3-7	4	1	2	1	9
Thorpe	35	5-8	4-6	6-16	3	4	2	1	14
Olajuwon	40	10-22	8-9	0-10	1	5	3	4	28
Maxwell	38	4-16	2-5	1-3	3	1	2	3	11
K. Smith	25	1-4	0-0	0-2	5	0	1	2	3
Cassell	23	2-4	4-4	1-6	3	1	0	4	8
Herrera	20	5-6	0-2	1-3	0	4	0	0	10
Jent	4	0-1	0-0	0-1	0	2	0	1	0
Elie	15	1-3	0-0	0-1	2	3	0	1	2
Totals	240	31-74	19-30	12-49	21	21	10	17	85

Percentages: FG—.419, FT—.633. 3-pt goals: 4-16, .250 (Horry 2-6, K. Smith 1-2, Maxwell 1-6, Jent 0-1, Elie 0-1). Team rebounds: 13. Blocked shots: 4 (Olajuwon 2, Horry, Cassell). A: 16,611. Officials: Jack Madden, Dick Bavetta, Joe Crawford.

Game 2

NEW YORK 91

NEW YORK	Min	FG M-A	FT M-A	Reb O-T	A	PF	S	TO	TP
Oakley	37	5-9	0-0	2-10	4	2	2	2	10
C. Smith	28	4-8	2-2	1-4	3	5	0	1	10
Ewing	46	7-19	2-2	4-13	2	4	2	6	16
Harper	37	7-11	0-0	0-1	7	2	3	3	18
Starks	40	6-11	4-4	0-5	9	4	3	5	19
Mason	32	5-7	3-4	1-4	0	2	0	1	13
Anthony	13	2-4	0-0	0-2	3	0	0	1	4
Davis	6	0-0	1-3	0-0	0	0	0	0	1
Williams	1	0-0	0-0	0-0	0	0	0	0	0
Totals	240	36-69	12-15	9-39	28	22	10	19	91

Percentages: FG—.522, FT—.800. 3-pt goals: 7-11, .636 (Harper 4-6, Starks 3-4, Anthony 0-1) Team Rebounds: 6. Blocked shots: 10 (Ewing 6, C. Smith 3, Starks).

HOUSTON 83

HOUSTON	Min	FG M-A	FT M-A	Reb O-T	A	PF	S	TO	TP
Horry	35	4-12	1-2	3-4	2	4	1	0	11
Thorpe	42	5-8	0-0	6-12	3	5	3	1	10
Olajuwon	46	10-21	5-7	5-7	4	1	2	3	25
Maxwell	41	8-17	2-3	1-3	1	4	0	7	20
K. Smith	25	1-6	0-0	0-2	6	0	2	2	2
Bullard	14	1-7	1-2	2-5	0	0	1	0	4
Cassell	23	2-8	4-4	3-4	3	3	2	3	9
Herrera	7	1-1	0-0	1-1	1	1	0	0	2
Elie	7	0-2	0-0	0-0	0	0	0	0	0
Totals	240	32-82	13-18	17-38	20	18	11	16	83

Percentages: FG—.390, FT—.722. 3-pt goals: 6-22, .273 (Maxwell 2-6, Horry 2-7, Cassell 1-2, Bullard 1-4, Elie 0-1, K. Smith 0-2). Team Rebounds: 8. Blocked shots: 5 (Olajuwon 4, Bullard). A: 16,611. Officials: Darrell Garretson, Ed T. Rush, Hue Hollins.

Game 3

HOUSTON 93

HOUSTON	Min	FG M-A	FT M-A	Reb O-T	A	PF	S	TO	TP
Horry	43	5-11	5-6	2-8	4	3	1	4	16
Thorpe	41	3-5	3-3	3-9	2	4	0	0	9
Olajuwon	44	8-20	5-6	5-11	7	3	1	4	21
Maxwell	35	5-15	2-2	0-6	4	1	0	3	12
K. Smith	25	3-7	3-3	1-4	0	0	1	3	10
Cassell	22	4-6	4-5	1-5	1	4	0	1	15
Herrera	16	1-8	2-2	2-4	0	1	0	1	4
Elie	14	1-3	3-4	0-0	1	2	1	1	6
Totals	240	30-75	27-31	14-47	19	18	4	17	93

Percentages: FG—.400, FT—.871. 3-pt goals: 6-17, .353 (Horry 1-5, Maxwell 0-6, Smith 1-2, Cassell 3-3, Elie 1-1). Team Rebounds: 11. Blocked shots: 7 (Olajuwon 7).

NEW YORK 89

NEW YORK	Min	FG M-A	FT M-A	Reb O-T	A	PF	S	TO	TP
Oakley	40	3-8	6-10	1-5	1	5	1	1	7
C. Smith	24	3-5	3-4	2-4	2	4	0	2	9
Ewing	46	9-29	0-0	6-13	0	3	1	3	18
Harper	39	9-15	0-0	2-7	3	4	4	3	21
Starks	43	6-16	5-7	0-2	9	5	1	0	20
Mason	28	3-7	4-5	2-5	1	3	1	2	10
Anthony	9	1-5	0-0	0-0	1	1	0	0	2
Davis	6	0-1	0-0	0-0	0	0	0	0	0
Bonner	5	1-1	0-1	0-1	0	0	0	0	2
Totals	240	35-87	13-19	18-42	17	25	8	11	89

Percentages: FG—.402, FT—.684. 3-pt goals: 6-19, .316 (Ewing 0-2, Harper 3-7, Starks 3-9, Anthony 0-1). Team Rebounds: 7. Blocked shots: 9 (Ewing 7, Oakley, Davis).
A: 19,763. Officials: Jake O'Donnell, Jess Kersey, Bill Oakes.

Game 4

HOUSTON 82

HOUSTON	Min	FG M-A	FT M-A	Reb O-T	A	PF	S	TO	TP
Horry	32	3-9	2-3	1-1	3	4	1	2	10
Thorpe	40	4-7	1-3	3-10	4	5	0	1	9
Olajuwon	43	14-20	4-4	0-8	3	4	0	2	32
Maxwell	35	5-13	0-0	1-4	0	1	2	4	12
K. Smith	19	0-2	0-0	0-0	3	2	0	1	0
Cassell	30	3-11	3-3	1-4	5	4	2	5	10
Elie	13	0-4	0-0	0-1	1	0	0	0	0
Herrera	15	1-3	3-3	1-4	0	4	0	2	5
Bullard	13	1-3	1-2	0-1	0	3	0	0	4
Totals	240	31-72	14-18	7-33	19	27	5	17	82

Percentages: FG—.431, FT—.778. 3-pt goals: 6-20, .300 (Horry 2-5, Maxwell 2-6, Bullard 1-3, Cassell 1-4, k. Smith 0-2). Team Rebounds: 10. Blocked shots: 5 (Olajuwon 5).

NEW YORK 91

NEW YORK	Min	FG M-A	FT M-A	Reb O-T	A	PF	S	TO	TP
Oakley	40	5-8	6-8	9-20	3	4	1	2	16
C. Smith	27	5-15	0-0	2-3	3	3	0	1	10
Ewing	41	8-28	0-0	5-15	3	6	1	1	16
Harper	41	7-15	2-2	1-3	5	4	2	1	21
Starks	45	6-11	6-8	1-2	4	2	0	4	20
Mason	30	1-4	0-1	1-4	2	3	2	1	2
Bonner	6	1-1	0-0	1-1	0	0	0	1	2
Anthony	10	2-4	0-0	1-2	1	1	1	1	4
Totals	240	35-86	14-21	21-50	21	23	7	12	91

Percentages: FG—.407, FT—.667. 3-pt goals: 7-17, .412 (Harper 5-10, Starks 2-5, C. Smith 0-1, Anthony 0-1). Team Rebounds: 10. Blocked shots: 3 (C. Smith, Ewing, Harper).
A: 19,763. Officials: Joe Crawford, Mike Mathis, Hugh Evans.

Game 5

HOUSTON 84

HOUSTON	Min	FG M-A	FT M-A	Reb O-T	A	PF	S	TO	TP
Horry	38	2-14	1-2	4-9	6	4	0	2	7
Thorpe	46	6-14	2-4	3-13	2	1	0	2	14
Olajuwon	40	12-21	2-2	4-8	1	3	3	8	27
Maxwell	39	3-11	1-2	0-5	3	1	0	2	8
K. Smith	27	2-4	1-1	0-0	5	1	0	3	6
Herrera	18	5-8	1-1	1-3	1	3	3	0	11
Cassell	21	2-5	2-2	0-0	5	6	1	1	6
Elie	9	1-3	2-2	3-4	1	1	0	0	5
Jent	2	0-1	0-0	0-0	0	1	0	0	0
Totals	240	33-81	12-16	15-42	24	21	7	18	84

Percentages: FG—.407, FT—.750. 3-pt goals: 6-18, .333 (Horry 2-6, Olajuwon 1-1, K. Smith 1-2, Elie 1-2, Maxwell 1-4, Jent 0-1, Cassell 0-2). Team Rebounds: 6. Blocked shots: 4 (Olajuwon 2, Horry, Herrera).

NEW YORK 91

NEW YORK	Min	FG M-A	FT M-A	Reb O-T	A	PF	S	TO	TP
Oakley	43	3-8	4-4	1-6	2	4	1	3	10
C. Smith	27	1-7	4-6	4-6	1	3	3	1	6
Ewing	43	11-21	2-2	5-12	1	4	2	3	25
Harper	40	6-13	2-3	2-3	7	2	1	2	14
Starks	39	7-14	4-6	0-7	6	1	3	2	19
Mason	30	6-11	5-8	3-9	1	4	0	3	17
Davis	7	0-1	0-0	1-1	0	1	0	0	0
Anthony	10	0-4	0-0	0-1	4	0	0	0	0
Williams	1	0-0	0-0	0-0	0	0	0	0	0
Totals	240	34-79	21-29	16-45	22	19	10	14	91

Percentages: FG—.430, FT—.724. 3-pt goals: 2-9, .222 (Ewing 1-1, Starks 1-4, C. Smith 0-1, Anthony 0-1, Harper 0-2). Team Rebounds: 12. Blocked shots: 9 (Ewing 8, C. Smith).
A: 19,763. Officials: Darrell Garretson, Ed T. Rush, Dick Bavetta.

Game 6

NEW YORK 84

NEW YORK	Min	FG M-A	FT M-A	Reb O-T	A	PF	S	TO	TP
Oakley	43	5-11	2-2	1-9	0	2	1	1	12
C. Smith	27	5-10	1-1	2-3-	0	5	0	2	11
Ewing	45	6-20	5-5	6-15	3	4	0	3	17
Harper	42	2-10	5-6	1-4	10	3	4	1	10
Starks	46	9-18	4-5	1-2	8	5	2	2	27
Mason	28	3-9	1-2	3-7	1	2	0	0	6
Anthony	8	0-2	0-0	0-0	2	2	0	0	0
Williams	1	0-0	0-0	0-0	0	1	0	0	0
Totals	240	30-80	18-21	14-40	24	24	7	9	84

Percentages: FG—.375, FT—.857. 3-pt goals: 6-14, .429 (Starks 5-9, Harper 1-5). Team Rebounds: 7. Blocked shots: 5 (Ewing 4, Anthony).

HOUSTON 86

HOUSTON	Min	FG M-A	FT M-A	Reb O-T	A	PF	S	TO	TP
Horry	42	3-10	3-4	0-9	4	3	1	1	11
Thorpe	38	1-3	1-4	0-10	6	1	0	1	3
Olajuwon	43	11-21	8-8	3-10	2	5	1	2	30
Maxwell	36	4-13	1-2	0-1	5	2	0	2	10
K. Smith	27	3-6	0-0	1-1	1	2	0	1	7
Cassell	21	2-5	4-5	0-2	1	3	2	2	9
Elie	12	2-2	0-0	0-0	1	0	1	3	4
Herrera	20	6-6	0-0	1-5	1	5	0	1	12
Totals	240	32-66	17-23	5-38	21	21	5	14	86

Percentages: FG—.485, FT—.739. 3-pt goals: 5-17, .294 (Horry 2-6, K. Smith 1-2, Cassell 1-3, Maxwell 1-6). Team Rebounds: 8. Blocked shots: 6 (Olajuwon 4, Horry, Cassell).
A: 16,611. Officials: Jake O'Donnell, Jess Kersey, Jack Madden.

Game 7

NEW YORK 84

NEW YORK	Min	FG M-A	FT M-A	Reb O-T	A	PF	S	TO	TP
Oakley	42	4-9	2-2	5-14	3	6	3	0	10
C. Smith	27	4-7	2-4	2-5	1	2	0	0	10
Ewing	44	7-17	3-6	4-10	1	3	1	5	17
Harper	38	8-16	5-6	0-0	5	4	2	2	23
Starks	42	2-18	4-4	1-2	2	5	0	0	8
Mason	31	3-4	0-0	2-9	2	1	0	1	6
Anthony	12	2-5	2-2	0-0	3	1	2	0	7
Davis	4	1-2	0-0	0-0	0	1	0	0	3
Totals	240	31-78	18-24	14-40	17	23	5	11	84

Percentages: FG—.397, FT—.750. 3-pt goals: 4-20, .200 (Harper 2-5, Davis 1-1, Anthony 1-3, Starks 0-11). Team Rebounds: 13. Blocked shots: 3 (Ewing 2, C. Smith).

HOUSTON 90

HOUSTON	Min	FG M-A	FT M-A	Reb O-T	A	PF	S	TO	TP
Horry	35	4-8	0-0	0-5	3	6	3	0	8
Thorpe	35	3-7	0-2	2-9	3	3	1	2	6
Olajuwon	46	10-25	5-7	0-10	7	5	1	2	25
Maxwell	40	6-11	7-8	0-1	4	2	0	0	21
K. Smith	30	4-7	2-2	0-1	2	3	1	1	11
Herrera	25	3-6	0-0	1-5	0	3	0	2	6
Cassell	18	4-6	4-4	0-1	2	1	2	2	13
Cureton	2	0-0	0-0	0-0	0	0	0	0	0
Elie	8	0-3	0-0	0-1	1	1	0	0	0
Jent	1	0-0	0-0	0-0	0	0	0	0	0
Totals	240	34-73	18-23	3-33	22	23	8	9	90

Percentages: FG—.466, FT—.783. 3-pt goals: 4-11, .364 (Maxwell 2-6, K. Smith 1-2, Cassell 1-2, Horry 0-1). Team Rebounds: 11. Blocked shots: 5 (Olajuwon 3, Horry, Elie).
A: 16,611. Officials: Hugh Evans, Jess Crawford, Ed T. Rush.

NBA Awards

All-NBA Teams

FIRST TEAM	SECOND TEAM	THIRD TEAM
G John Stockton, Utah	Mitch Richmond, Sacramento	Mark Price, Cleveland
G Latrell Sprewell, Golden State	Kevin Johnson, Phoenix	Gary Payton, Seattle
C Hakeem Olajuwon, Houston	David Robinson, San Antonio	Shaquille O'Neal, Orlando
F Karl Malone, Utah	Charles Barkley, Phoenix	Derrick Coleman, New Jersey
F Scottie Pippen, Chicago	Shawn Kemp, Seattle	Dominique Wilkins, LA Clippers

Master Lock NBA All-Defensive Teams

FIRST TEAM	SECOND TEAM
G Gary Payton, Seattle	Nate McMillan, Seattle
G Mookie Blaylock, Atlanta	Latrell Sprewell, Golden St
C Hakeem Olajuwon, Houston	David Robinson, San Antonio
F Charles Oakley, New York	Dennis Rodman, San Antonio
F Scottie Pippen, Chicago	Horace Grant, Chicago

All-Rookie Teams
(Chosen Without Regard to Position)

FIRST TEAM	SECOND TEAM
Chris Webber, Golden St	Dino Radja, Boston
Anfernee Hardaway, Orlando	Nick Van Exel, LA Lakers
Vin Baker, Milwaukee	Shawn Bradley, Philadelphia
Jamal Mashburn, Dallas	Toni Kukoc, Chicago
Isaiah Rider, Minnesota	Lindsey Hunter, Detroit

NBA Individual Leaders

Scoring

	GP	Pts	Avg
David Robinson, SA	80	2383	29.8
Shaquille O'Neal, Orl	81	2377	29.3
Hakeem Olajuwon, Hou	80	2184	27.3
Dominique Wilkins, Atl-LA Clippers	74	1923	26.0
Karl Malone, Utah	82	2063	25.2
Patrick Ewing, NY	79	1939	24.5
Mitch Richmond, Sac	78	1823	23.4
Scottie Pippen, Chi	72	1587	22.0
Charles Barkley, Phoe	65	1402	21.6
Glenn Rice, Mia	81	1708	21.1

Rebounds

	GP	Reb	Avg
Dennis Rodman, SA	79	1367	17.3
Shaquille O'Neal, Orl	81	1072	13.2
Kevin Willis, Atl	80	963	12.0
Hakeem Olajuwon, Hou	80	955	11.9
Olden Polynice, Det-Sac	68	809	11.9
Dikembe Mutombo, Den	82	971	11.8
Charles Oakley, NY	82	965	11.8
Karl Malone Utah	82	940	11.5
Derrick Coleman, NJ	77	870	11.3
Patrick Ewing, NY	79	885	11.2

Assists

	GP	Assists	Avg
John Stockton, Utah	82	1031	12.6
Tyrone Bogues, Char	77	780	10.1
Mookie Blaylock, Atl	81	789	9.7
Kenny Anderson, NJ	82	784	9.6
Kevin Johnson, Phoe	67	637	9.5
Rod Strickland, Por	82	740	9.0
Sherman Douglas, Bos	78	683	8.8
Mark Jackson, LA Clippers	79	678	8.6
Mark Price, Clev	76	589	7.8
Michael Williams, Minn	71	512	7.2

Field-Goal Percentage

	FGA	FGM	Pct
Shaquille O'Neal, Orl	1591	953	59.9
Dikembe Mutombo, Den	365	642	56.9
Otis Thorpe, Hou	449	801	56.1
Chris Webber, GS	572	1037	55.2
Shawn Kemp, Sea	533	990	53.8
Loy Vaught, LA Clippers	695	373	53.7
Cedric Ceballos, Phoe	425	795	53.5
Rik Smits, Ind	493	923	53.4
Dale Davis, Ind	308	582	52.9
Hakeem Olajuwon, Hou	894	582	52.9
John Stockton, Utah	868	458	52.8

Free-Throw Percentage

	FTA	FTM	Pct
Mahmoud Abdul-Rauf, Den	219	229	95.6
Reggie Miller, Ind	403	444	90.8
Ricky Pierce, Sea	189	211	89.6
Sedale Threatt, LA Lakers	138	155	89.0
Mark Price, Clev	238	268	88.8
Glenn Rice, Mia	250	284	88.0
Jeff Hornacek, Phil-Utah	260	296	87.8
Scott Skiles, Orl	195	222	87.8
Terry Porter, Por	204	234	87.2
Kenny Smith, Hou	135	155	87.1

Three-Point Field-Goal Percentage

	FGA	FGM	Pct
Tracy Murray, Por	109	50	45.9
B.J. Armstrong, Chi	135	60	44.4
Reggie Miller, Ind	123	292	42.1
Steve Kerr, Chi	124	52	41.9
Scott Skiles, Orl	165	68	41.2
Eric Murdock, Mil	168	69	41.1
Mitch Richmond, Sac	312	127	40.7
Kenny Smith, Hou	220	89	40.5
Dell Curry, Char	378	152	40.2
Hubert Davis, NY	132	53	40.2

Steals

	GP	Steals	Avg
Nate McMillan, Sea	73	216	2.96
Scottie Pippen, Chi	72	211	2.93
Mookie Blaylock, Atl	81	212	2.62
John Stockton, Utah	82	199	2.43
Eric Murdock, Mil	82	197	2.40
Anfernee Hardaway, Orl	82	190	2.32
Gary Payton, Sea	82	188	2.29
Tom Gugliotta, Wash	78	172	2.21
Latrell Sprewell, GS	82	180	2.20
Dee Brown, Bos	77	156	2.03

Blocked Shots

	GP	BS	Avg
Dikembe Mutombo, Den	82	336	4.10
Hakeem Olajuwon, Hou	80	297	3.71
David Robinson, SA	80	265	3.31
Alonzo Mourning, Char	60	188	3.13
Shawn Bradley, Phil	49	147	3.00
Shaquille O'Neal, Orl	81	231	2.85
Patrick Ewing, NY	79	217	2.75
Oliver Miller, Phoe	69	156	2.26
Chris Webber, GS	76	164	2.16
Shawn Kemp, Sea	79	166	2.10

NBA Team Statistics

Offense

Team	FGM	Field Goals Pct	3FGM	3-Pt Field Goals Pct	FTM	Free Throws Pct	Off	Rebounds Total	A	Stl	Scoring Avg
Phoenix	3429	48.4	344	33.0	1674	72.8	1220	3676	2261	745	108.2
Golden State	3512	49.2	291	33.9	1529	66.4	1183	3579	2198	804	107.9
Portland	3371	45.4	272	35.3	1781	74.3	1302	3762	2070	744	107.3
Charlotte	3382	47.6	336	36.7	1632	76.4	1019	3934	2214	724	106.5
Seattle	3338	48.4	242	33.5	1769	74.5	1148	3381	2112	1053	105.9
Orlando	3341	48.5	394	34.7	1590	67.8	1177	3533	2070	683	105.7
Miami	3197	46.4	337	33.8	1744	78.5	1235	3642	1856	643	103.4
New Jersey	3169	44.5	223	32.7	1900	76.2	1300	3856	1900	696	103.2
LA Clippers	3343	46.7	252	30.3	1509	70.9	1120	3530	2169	807	103.0
Utah	3207	47.7	179	32.0	1761	74.0	1059	3444	2179	751	101.9
Atlanta	3247	46.1	268	32.3	1556	75.2	1250	3673	2056	915	101.4
Cleveland	3133	46.5	294	36.2	1736	77.0	1090	3443	2049	705	101.2
Houston	3197	47.5	429	33.4	1469	74.3	926	3545	2087	717	101.1
Sacramento	3179	45.2	257	35.3	1676	73.1	1122	3471	2029	669	101.1
Indiana	3167	48.6	184	36.8	1762	73.8	1130	3539	2055	706	101.0
Boston	3333	47.2	138	28.9	1463	73.0	1037	3417	1928	674	100.8
LA Lakers	3291	45.0	241	30.0	1410	71.7	1260	3464	1983	751	100.4
Washington	3195	46.8	221	29.7	1618	74.8	1071	3260	1823	701	100.4
Denver	3156	46.5	170	28.5	1739	71.8	1105	3662	1763	679	100.3
San Antonio	3178	47.5	249	34.9	1597	74.2	1189	3786	1896	561	100.0
New York	3098	46.0	316	34.8	1564	74.6	1175	3717	2067	752	98.5
Philadelphia	3103	45.5	318	33.8	1509	71.4	1012	3406	1827	663	98.0
Chicago	3245	47.6	233	35.4	1310	70.5	1143	3534	2102	740	98.0
Detroit	3169	45.2	358	34.4	1253	73.1	1027	3347	1767	602	96.9
Milwaukee	3044	44.7	331	32.5	1530	70.2	1126	3280	1946	800	96.9
Minnesota	2985	45.7	183	32.9	1777	77.2	990	3333	1967	600	96.7
Dallas	3055	43.2	241	31.2	1450	74.7	1271	3421	1629	767	95.1

Defense (Opponent's Statistics)

Team	FGM	Field Goals Pct	3FGM	3-Pt Field Goals Pct	FTM	Free Throws Pct	Off	Rebounds Total	Stl	Scoring Avg	Diff
New York	2783	43.1	253	30.7	1684	71.9	1016	3261	677	91.5	+7.0
San Antonio	3066	44.6	290	33.3	1349	71.6	1089	3242	632	94.8	+5.3
Chicago	3029	46.3	252	32.3	1470	74.0	985	3225	730	94.9	+3.1
Atlanta	3163	45.5	275	31.5	1285	74.2	1157	3515	641	96.2	+5.3
Houston	3152	44.0	257	30.6	1377	73.6	1138	3572	767	96.8	+4.3
Seattle	2928	45.3	326	34.5	1760	74.1	1084	3275	686	96.9	+9.1
Cleveland	3131	46.4	258	35.4	1446	73.5	1059	3394	628	97.1	+4.0
Indiana	2978	45.0	273	33.5	1768	73.0	1132	3285	826	97.5	+3.5
Utah	2973	44.8	289	29.9	1773	72.5	1100	3427	593	97.7	+4.2
Denver	3065	43.8	208	29.0	1761	75.0	1118	3449	725	98.8	+1.5
Miami	3036	45.7	295	33.1	1889	74.8	1074	3340	689	100.7	+2.7
New Jersey	3266	45.8	235	31.8	1514	74.3	1142	3670	715	101.0	+2.2
Orlando	3263	45.8	296	34.9	1525	74.5	1197	3502	756	101.8	+3.9
Phoenix	3379	47.4	283	32.8	1438	72.0	1086	3333	748	103.4	+4.8
Milwaukee	3255	49.1	286	36.2	1684	73.7	1086	3581	768	103.4	-6.5
Minnesota	3244	47.2	227	30.8	1783	72.7	1102	3398	824	103.6	-6.9
Dallas	3212	49.4	249	36.2	1841	73.7	1101	3604	782	103.8	-8.7
Portland	3311	46.9	296	35.7	1661	75.0	1016	3497	654	104.6	+2.6
LA Lakers	3337	47.6	228	31.5	1683	71.7	1284	3817	664	104.7	-4.3
Detroit	3255	47.3	272	33.4	1805	73.6	1191	3781	721	104.7	-7.8
Boston	3357	47.7	231	34.7	1673	75.4	1131	3639	690	105.1	-4.3
Philadelphia	3549	48.4	263	33.1	1297	74.4	1202	3809	806	105.6	-7.6
Golden State	3428	46.8	305	35.1	1540	73.1	1324	3732	842	106.1	+1.7
Charlotte	3463	47.1	317	34.6	1507	74.0	1217	3684	629	106.7	-0.2
Sacramento	3360	47.9	277	35.9	1767	72.2	1189	3763	746	106.9	-5.8
Washington	3569	50.8	252	34.9	1444	72.3	1119	3481	815	107.7	-7.4
LA Clippers	3512	47.3	308	34.9	1584	71.7	1348	3916	898	108.7	-5.7

NBA Team-by-Team Statistical Leaders

Atlanta Hawks

Player	GP	Min	Field Goals		3-Pt FG		Free Throws		Rebounds		A	Stl	TO	BS	Avg
			FGM	Pct	FGA	FGM	FTM	Pct	Off	Total					
Manning	68	2,520	586	48.8	17	3	228	66.9	131	465	261	99	233	82	20.6
Willis	80	2,867	627	49.9	24	9	268	71.3	335	963	150	79	188	38	19.1
Augmon	82	2,605	439	51.0	7	1	333	76.4	178	394	187	149	147	45	14.8
Blaylock	81	2,915	444	41.1	341	114	116	73.0	117	424	789	212	196	44	13.8
Ehlo	82	2,147	316	44.6	221	77	112	72.7	71	279	273	136	130	26	10.0
Ferrell	72	1,155	184	48.5	9	1	144	78.3	62	129	65	44	64	16	7.1
Lang	82	1,608	215	46.9	4	1	73	68.9	126	313	51	38	81	87	6.1
Keefe	63	763	96	45.1	0	0	81	73.0	77	201	34	20	60	9	4.3
Koncak	82	1,823	159	43.1	3	0	24	66.7	83	365	102	63	44	125	4.2
Whatley	82	1,004	120	50.8	6	0	52	78.8	22	99	181	59	78	2	3.6
Graham	21	128	21	36.8	13	3	13	76.5	4	12	13	4	5	5	2.8
Edwards	16	107	17	34.7	1	0	9	56.3	7	18	8	2	6	5	2.7
Grace	3	8	2	66.7	0	0	0	00.0	0	1	1	0	0	0	1.3
Bagley	3	13	0	00.0	0	0	2	00.0	0	1	3	0	0	2	0.7
Hawks	82	19,755	3,247	46.1	830	268	1,556	75.2	1,250	3,673	2,056	915	1,252	449	101.4
Opponents	82	19,755	3,163	45.5	872	275	1,285	74.2	1,157	3,515	1,897	641	1,465	338	96.2

Boston Celtics

Player	GP	Min	Field Goals		3-Pt FG		Free Throws		Rebounds		A	Stl	TO	BS	Avg
			FGM	Pct	FGA	FGM	FTM	Pct	Off	Total					
Brown	77	2,867	490	48.0	96	30	182	83.1	63	300	347	156	126	47	15.5
Radja	80	2,303	491	52.1	1	0	226	75.1	191	577	114	70	149	67	15.1
Douglas	78	2,789	425	46.2	56	13	177	64.1	70	193	683	89	233	11	13.3
Parish	74	1,987	356	49.1	0	0	154	74.0	141	542	82	42	108	96	11.7
Gamble	75	1,880	368	45.8	103	25	103	81.7	41	159	149	57	77	22	11.5
McDaniel	82	1,971	387	46.1	41	10	144	67.6	142	400	126	48	116	39	11.3
Fox	82	2,096	340	46.7	100	33	174	75.7	105	355	217	81	158	52	10.8
Harris	5	88	9	29.0	9	3	23	92.0	3	10	8	4	6	0	8.8
Earl	74	1,149	151	40.6	1	0	108	67.5	85	247	12	24	72	53	5.5
Pinckney	76	1,524	151	52.2	0	0	92	73.6	160	478	62	58	62	44	5.2
Abdelnaby	13	159	24	43.6	0	0	16	64.0	12	46	3	2	17	3	4.9
Oliver	44	540	89	41.6	32	13	25	75.8	8	46	33	16	21	1	4.9
Lichti	13	126	20	39.2	2	2	16	64.0	8	22	11	7	5	1	4.5
Corchiani	51	467	40	42.6	38	11	26	68.4	8	44	86	22	38	2	2.3
Wenstrom	11	37	6	60.0	0	0	6	60.0	6	12	0	0	4	2	1.6
Celtics	82	19,905	3,333	47.2	477	138	1,463	73.0	1,037	3,417	1,928	674	1,242	440	100.0
Opponents	82	19,905	3,357	47.7	665	231	1,673	75.4	1,131	3,639	2,089	690	1,273	414	105.1

Charlotte Hornets

Player	GP	Min	Field Goals		3-Pt FG		Free Throws		Rebounds		A	Stl	TO	BS	Avg
			FGM	Pct	FGA	FGM	FTM	Pct	Off	Total					
Mourning	60	2,018	427	50.5	2	0	433	76.2	177	610	86	27	199	188	21.5
L. Johnson	51	1,757	346	51.5	21	5	137	69.5	143	448	184	29	116	14	16.4
Curry	82	2,173	533	45.5	378	152	117	87.3	71	262	221	98	120	27	16.3
Hawkins	82	2,648	395	46.0	235	78	312	86.2	89	377	216	135	158	22	14.4
Brickowski	71	2,094	368	48.8	20	4	195	76.8	85	404	222	80	181	27	13.2
E. Johnson	73	1,460	339	45.9	150	59	99	78.0	80	224	125	36	84	8	11.5
Bogues	77	2,746	354	47.1	12	2	125	80.6	78	313	780	133	171	2	10.8
Gattison	77	1,644	233	52.4	0	0	126	64.6	105	358	95	59	79	46	7.7
Wingate	50	1,005	136	48.1	12	4	34	66.7	30	134	104	42	53	6	6.2
Burrell	51	767	98	41.9	6	2	46	65.7	46	132	62	37	45	16	4.8
Ellis	50	680	88	48.4	0	0	45	66.2	70	188	24	17	21	25	4.4
Robinson	31	396	55	36.2	20	6	13	44.8	6	32	63	18	43	3	4.2
Bennett	74	983	105	39.9	75	27	11	73.3	16	90	163	39	40	1	3.4
Henson	3	17	1	50.0	1	1	0	—	0	1	5	0	1	0	1.0
Hornets	82	19,830	3,382	47.6	916	336	1,632	76.4	1,019	3,494	2,214	724	1,266	394	106.5
Opponents	82	19,830	3,463	47.1	916	317	1,507	74.0	1,217	3,684	2,116	629	1,260	430	106.7

Chicago Bulls

Player	GP	Min	Field Goals		3-Pt FG		Free Throws		Rebounds		A	Stl	TO	BS	Avg
			FGM	Pct	FGA	FGM	FTM	Pct	Off	Total					
Pippen	72	2,759	627	49.1	197	63	270	66.0	173	629	403	211	232	58	22.0
Grant	70	2,570	460	52.4	6	0	137	59.6	306	769	236	74	109	84	15.1
Armstrong	82	2,770	479	47.6	135	60	194	85.5	28	170	323	80	131	9	14.8
Kukoc	75	1,808	313	43.1	118	32	156	74.3	98	297	252	81	167	33	10.9
Kerr	82	2,036	287	49.7	124	52	83	85.6	26	131	210	75	57	3	8.6
Myers	82	2,030	253	45.5	29	8	136	70.1	54	181	245	78	136	20	7.9
King	76	1,059	160	47.1	6	2	86	70.5	105	207	71	26	70	20	5.4
Williams	38	638	114	48.3	5	1	60	61.2	69	181	39	16	44	21	7.6
Wennington	76	1,371	235	48.8	2	0	72	81.8	117	353	70	43	75	29	7.1
Longley	76	1,502	219	47.1	1	0	90	72.0	129	433	109	45	119	79	6.9
Cartwright	42	780	98	51.3	0	0	39	68.4	43	152	57	8	50	8	5.6
English	36	419	56	43.4	17	8	10	47.6	9	45	38	8	36	10	3.6
Blount	67	690	76	43.7	0	0	46	61.3	76	194	56	19	52	33	3.0
Johnson	17	119	17	31.5	1	0	13	61.9	9	16	4	4	9	0	2.8
Perdue	43	397	47	42.0	1	0	23	71.9	40	126	34	8	42	11	2.7
Paxson	27	343	30	44.1	22	9	1	50.0	3	20	33	7	6	2	2.6
Bulls	**82**	**19,780**	**3,245**	**47.6**	**659**	**233**	**1,310**	**70.5**	**1,143**	**3,534**	**2,102**	**740**	**1,306**	**354**	**98.0**
Opponents	**82**	**19,780**	**3,029**	**46.3**	**780**	**252**	**1,470**	**74.0**	**985**	**3,225**	**1,840**	**730**	**1,335**	**374**	**94.9**

Cleveland Cavaliers

Player	GP	Min	Field Goals		3-Pt FG		Free Throws		Rebounds		A	Stl	TO	BS	Avg
			FGM	Pct	FGA	FGM	FTM	Pct	Off	Total					
Price	76	2,386	480	47.8	297	118	238	88.8	39	228	589	103	189	11	17.3
Daugherty	50	1,838	296	48.8	0	0	256	78.5	128	508	149	41	110	36	17.0
Wilkins	82	2,768	446	45.7	212	84	194	77.6	106	303	255	105	131	38	14.3
Williams	76	2,660	394	47.8	0	0	252	72.8	207	575	193	78	139	130	13.7
Nance	33	909	153	48.7	0	0	64	75.3	77	227	49	27	38	55	11.2
Hill	57	1,447	216	54.3	2	0	171	66.8	184	499	46	53	78	35	10.0
Mills	79	2,022	284	41.9	122	38	137	77.8	134	401	128	54	89	50	9.4
Phills	72	1,531	242	47.1	12	1	113	72.0	71	212	133	67	63	12	8.3
Brandon	73	1,548	230	42.0	32	7	139	85.8	38	159	277	84	111	16	8.3
Battle	51	814	130	47.6	19	5	73	75.3	7	39	83	22	41	1	6.6
Higgins	36	547	71	43.6	50	22	31	73.8	25	82	36	25	21	14	5.4
Ferry	70	965	149	44.6	51	14	38	88.4	47	141	74	28	41	22	5.0
Guidinger	32	131	16	500	0	0	15	71.4	15	33	3	4	16	5	1.5
Cavs	**82**	**19,855**	**3,133**	**46.5**	**813**	**294**	**1,736**	**77.0**	**1,090**	**3,443**	**2,049**	**705**	**1,136**	**426**	**101.2**
Opponents	**82**	**19,855**	**3,131**	**46.4**	**729**	**258**	**1,446**	**73.5**	**1,059**	**3,394**	**2,006**	**628**	**1,293**	**461**	**97.1**

Dallas Mavericks

Player	GP	Min	Field Goals		3-Pt FG		Free Throws		Rebounds		A	Stl	TO	BS	Avg
			FGM	Pct	FGA	FGM	FTM	Pct	Off	Total					
Jackson	82	3,066	637	44.5	60	17	285	82.1	169	388	374	87	334	25	19.2
Mashburn	79	2,896	561	40.6	299	85	306	69.9	107	353	266	89	245	14	19.2
Rooks	47	1,255	193	49.1	1	0	150	71.4	84	259	49	21	80	44	11.4
Smith	79	1,684	295	43.5	9	2	106	83.5	114	349	119	82	93	38	8.8
Campbell	63	1,214	227	44.3	28	7	94	78.3	76	186	82	50	84	15	8.8
Legler	79	1,322	131	43.8	139	52	142	84.0	36	128	120	52	60	13	8.3
Lever	81	1,947	227	40.8	74	26	75	76.5	83	283	213	159	88	15	6.9
White	18	320	45	40.2	20	6	19	57.6	30	83	11	10	18	10	6.4
Jones	81	1,773	195	47.9	1	0	78	72.9	299	605	99	61	94	31	5.8
Harris	77	1,165	162	42.1	33	7	87	73.1	45	157	106	49	78	10	5.4
Davis	15	286	24	40.7	0	0	8	66.7	30	74	6	9	5	1	3.7
Brown	1	10	1	100.0	0	0	1	100.0	0	1	0	0	0	0	3.0
Williams	38	716	49	44.5	1	0	12	42.9	95	217	25	18	22	46	2.9
Hodge	50	428	46	45.5	0	0	44	84.6	46	95	32	15	30	13	2.7
Dreiling	54	685	52	50.0	1	1	27	71.1	47	170	31	16	43	24	2.4
Wiley	16	158	9	31.0	10	3	0	—	0	10	23	15	17	0	1.3
Mavericks	**82**	**19,730**	**3,055**	**43.2**	**773**	**241**	**1,450**	**74.7**	**1,271**	**3,421**	**1,629**	**767**	**1,393**	**299**	**95.1**
Opponents	**82**	**19,730**	**3,212**	**49.4**	**688**	**249**	**1,841**	**73.7**	**1,101**	**3,604**	**1,970**	**782**	**1,428**	**507**	**103.8**

Denver Nuggets

Player	GP	Min	Field Goals		3-Pt FG		Free Throws		Rebounds		A	Stl	TO	BS	Avg
			FGM	Pct	FGA	FGM	FTM	Pct	Off	Total					
Abdul-Rauf	80	2,617	588	46.0	133	42	219	95.6	27	168	362	82	151	10	18.0
Ellis	79	2,699	483	50.2	23	7	242	67.4	220	682	167	63	172	80	15.4
R. Williams	82	2,654	418	41.2	230	64	165	73.3	98	392	300	117	163	66	13.0
Stith	82	2,853	365	45.0	9	2	291	82.9	119	349	199	116	131	16	12.5
Mutombo	82	2,853	365	56.9	1	0	256	58.3	286	971	127	59	206	336	12.0
Pack	66	1,382	223	44.3	29	6	179	75.8	25	123	356	81	204	9	9.6
Rogers	79	1,406	239	43.9	92	35	127	67.2	90	226	101	63	131	48	8.1
B. Williams	80	1,507	251	54.1	3	0	137	64.9	138	446	50	49	104	87	8.0
Hammonds	74	877	115	50.0	0	0	71	68.3	62	199	34	20	41	12	4.1
Brooks	34	190	36	36.4	23	4	9	90.0	5	21	3	0	12	2	2.5
Jordan	6	79	6	26.1	10	3	0	—	3	6	19	0	6	1	2.5
Randall	28	155	17	34.0	14	2	22	78.6	9	22	11	8	10	3	2.1
Mee	38	285	28	31.8	24	5	12	44.4	17	35	16	15	18	13	1.9
Marble	5	32	2	16.7	0	0	0	00.0	3	8	1	0	3	2	0.8
Nuggets	82	19,755	3,156	46.5	597	170	1,739	71.8	1,105	3,662	1,763	679	1,422	686	100.3
Opponents	82	19,755	3,065	43.8	717	208	1,761	75.0	1,118	3,449	1,745	725	1,245	502	98.8

Detroit Pistons

Player	GP	Min	Field Goals		3-Pt FG		Free Throws		Rebounds		A	Stl	TO	BS	Avg
			FGM	Pct	FGA	FGM	FTM	Pct	Off	Total					
Dumars	69	3,591	505	45.2	320	124	276	83.6	35	151	261	63	159	4	20.4
Mills	80	2,773	588	51.1	73	24	181	79.7	193	672	177	64	153	62	17.3
Thomas	58	1,750	318	41.7	126	39	181	70.2	46	159	399	68	202	6	14.8
Elliott	73	2,409	360	45.5	87	26	139	80.3	68	263	197	54	129	27	12.1
Hunter	82	2,172	335	37.5	207	69	104	73.2	47	189	390	121	184	10	10.3
Laimbeer	11	248	47	52.2	9	3	11	84.6	9	56	14	6	10	4	9.8
Houston	79	1,519	272	40.5	117	35	89	82.4	19	120	100	34	99	13	8.5
Anderson	77	1,624	201	54.3	3	1	88	57.1	183	571	51	55	94	68	6.4
Chilcutt	76	1,365	203	45.3	15	3	41	63.1	129	371	86	53	74	39	5.9
Wood	78	1,182	119	45.9	49	22	62	75.6	104	239	51	39	35	19	4.1
Macon	42	496	69	37.5	10	2	23	67.6	18	41	51	39	40	1	3.9
Liberty	38	285	40	32.5	28	10	19	48.7	26	61	17	11	24	4	2.9
Jones	42	877	36	46.2	1	0	19	55.9	89	235	29	14	12	43	2.2
O'Sullivan	13	56	4	33.3	0	0	9	75.0	2	10	3	0	3	0	1.3
Pistons	82	19,730	3,169	45.2	1,041	358	1,253	73.1	1,027	3,347	1,767	602	1,236	309	96.9
Opponents	82	19,730	3,255	47.3	814	272	1,805	73.6	1,191	3,781	2,097	721	1,169	368	104.7

Golden State Warriors

Player	GP	Min	Field Goals		3-Pt FG		Free Throws		Rebounds		A	Stl	TO	BS	Avg
			FGM	Pct	FGA	FGM	FTM	Pct	Off	Total					
Sprewell	82	3,533	613	43.3	391	141	353	77.4	80	401	385	180	226	76	21.0
Webber	76	2,438	572	55.2	14	0	189	53.2	305	694	272	93	206	164	17.5
Mullin	62	2,324	410	47.2	151	55	165	75.3	64	345	315	107	178	53	16.8
Owens	79	2,738	492	50.7	15	3	199	61.0	230	640	326	83	214	60	15.0
Johnson	82	2,332	356	49.2	12	0	178	70.4	41	176	433	113	172	8	10.9
Alexander	69	1,318	266	53.0	13	2	68	52.7	114	308	66	28	86	32	8.7
Gatling	82	1,296	271	58.8	1	0	129	62.0	143	397	41	40	84	63	8.2
Grayer	67	1,096	191	52.6	12	2	71	60.2	76	191	62	33	63	13	6.8
Lichti	5	58	10	35.7	2	2	9	81.8	3	10	3	0	0	0	6.2
Jennings	76	1,097	138	40.4	151	56	100	83.3	16	89	218	65	74	0	5.7
Spencer	5	63	9	50.0	0	0	3	75.0	4	12	3	1	2	2	4.2
Grant	53	382	59	40.4	61	17	22	75.9	27	89	24	18	30	8	3.0
Buechler	36	218	42	50.0	29	12	10	50.0	13	32	16	8	12	1	2.9
Houston	71	866	81	45.8	7	1	33	61.1	67	194	32	33	49	31	2.8
Demps	2	11	2	33.3	0	0	0	00.0	0	0	1	2	1	0	2.0
Murphy	9	67	6	50.0	0	0	0	0	4	10	4	2	1	0	1.7
Warriors	82	19,780	3,512	49.2	859	291	1,529	66.4	1,183	3,579	2,198	804	1,433	511	107.9
Opponents	82	19,780	3,428	46.8	869	305	1,540	73.1	1,324	3,732	2,184	842	1,426	408	106.1

Houston Rockets

Player	GP	Min	Field Goals		3-Pt FG		Free Throws		Rebounds		A	Stl	TO	BS	Avg
			FGM	Pct	FGA	FGM	FTM	Pct	Off	Total					
Olajuwon	80	3,277	894	52.8	19	8	388	71.6	229	955	287	128	271	297	27.3
Thorpe	82	2,909	449	56.1	2	0	251	65.7	271	870	189	66	185	28	14.0
Maxwell	75	2,571	380	38.9	403	120	143	74.9	42	229	380	125	185	20	13.6
Smith	78	2,209	341	48.0	220	89	135	87.1	24	138	327	59	126	4	11.6
Horry	81	2,370	322	45.9	136	44	115	73.2	128	440	231	119	137	75	9.9
Elie	67	1,606	208	44.6	167	56	154	86.0	28	181	108	50	109	8	9.3
Cassell	66	1,122	162	41.8	88	26	90	84.1	25	134	192	59	94	7	6.7
Brooks	73	1,225	142	49.1	61	23	74	87.1	10	102	149	51	55	2	5.2
Herrera	75	1,292	142	45.8	0	0	69	71.1	101	285	37	32	69	26	4.7
Robinson	6	55	10	50.0	8	2	3	37.5	4	10	6	7	10	0	4.2
Bullard	65	725	78	34.5	154	50	20	76.9	23	84	64	14	28	6	3.5
Petruska	22	92	20	43.5	15	7	6	75.0	9	31	1	2	15	3	2.4
Riley	47	219	34	48.6	1	0	20	54.1	24	59	9	5	15	9	1.9
Rockets	**82**	**19,780**	**3,197**	**47.5**	**1,285**	**429**	**1,469**	**74.3**	**926**	**3,545**	**2,087**	**717**	**1,338**	**485**	**101.1**
Opponents	**82**	**19,780**	**3,152**	**44.0**	**841**	**257**	**1,377**	**73.6**	**1,138**	**3,572**	**1,901**	**767**	**1,221**	**312**	**96.8**

Indiana Pacers

Player	GP	Min	Field Goals		3-Pt FG		Free Throws		Rebounds		A	Stl	TO	BS	Avg
			FGM	Pct	FGA	FGM	FTM	Pct	Off	Total					
Miller	79	2,638	524	50.3	292	123	403	90.8	30	212	248	119	175	24	19.9
Smits	78	2,113	493	53.4	1	0	238	79.3	135	483	156	49	151	82	15.7
McKey	76	2,613	355	50.0	31	9	192	75.6	129	402	327	111	228	49	12.0
D. Davis	66	2,292	308	52.9	1	0	155	52.7	280	718	100	48	102	106	11.7
Scott	67	1,197	256	46.7	74	27	157	80.5	19	110	133	62	103	9	10.4
Richardson	37	1,022	160	45.2	12	3	47	61.0	28	110	237	32	88	3	10.0
A. Davis	81	1,732	216	50.8	1	0	194	64.2	190	505	55	45	107	84	7.7
Workman	65	1,714	195	42.4	56	18	93	80.2	32	204	404	85	151	4	7.7
Sealy	43	623	111	40.5	16	4	59	67.8	43	118	48	31	51	8	6.6
Fleming	55	1,053	147	46.2	4	0	64	73.6	27	123	173	40	87	6	6.5
Williams	68	982	191	48.8	4	0	45	70.3	93	205	52	24	45	49	6.3
Mitchell	75	1,084	140	45.8	5	0	82	74.5	71	190	65	33	50	5	4.8
Thompson	30	282	27	35.1	0	0	16	53.3	26	75	16	10	23	8	2.3
Pacers	**82**	**19,755**	**3,167**	**48.6**	**500**	**184**	**1,762**	**73.8**	**1,130**	**3,539**	**2,055**	**706**	**1,440**	**457**	**101.0**
Opponents	**82**	**19,755**	**2,978**	**45.0**	**815**	**273**	**1,768**	**73.0**	**1,132**	**3,285**	**1,902**	**826**	**1,340**	**389**	**97.5**

Los Angeles Clippers

Player	GP	Min	Field Goals		3-Pt FG		Free Throws		Rebounds		A	Stl	TO	BS	Avg
			FGM	Pct	FGA	FGM	FTM	Pct	Off	Total					
Wilkins	74	2,635	698	44.0	295	85	442	84.7	182	481	169	92	172	30	26.0
Harper	75	2,856	569	42.6	236	71	299	71.5	129	460	344	144	242	54	20.1
Vaught	75	2,118	373	53.7	5	0	131	72.0	218	656	74	76	96	22	11.7
Jackson	79	2,711	331	45.2	127	36	167	79.1	107	348	678	120	232	6	10.9
Aguirre	39	859	163	46.8	93	37	50	69.4	28	116	104	21	70	8	10.6
Spencer	76	1,930	288	53.3	2	0	97	59.9	96	415	75	30	168	127	8.9
Ellis	49	923	159	54.5	4	0	106	71.1	94	153	31	73	43	2	8.7
Grant	78	1,533	253	44.9	62	17	65	85.5	42	142	291	119	136	12	7.5
Roberts	14	350	43	43.0	0	0	18	40.9	27	93	11	6	24	25	7.4
Outlaw	37	871	98	58.7	2	0	61	59.2	81	212	36	36	31	37	6.9
Williams	34	725	81	43.1	20	5	24	66.7	37	127	97	25	35	10	5.6
Dehere	64	759	129	37.7	57	23	61	75.3	25	68	78	28	61	3	5.3
Tolbert	49	640	74	41.8	16	6	33	73.3	36	108	30	13	39	15	3.8
Woods	40	352	49	36.8	78	27	20	57.1	13	29	71	24	34	2	3.6
James	12	75	16	38.1	18	4	5	100.0	6	14	1	2	2	0	3.4
Martin	53	535	40	45.5	0	0	31	60.8	36	117	17	8	29	33	2.1
Clippers	**82**	**19,780**	**3,343**	**46.7**	**831**	**252**	**1,509**	**70.9**	**1,120**	**3,530**	**2,169**	**807**	**1,474**	**421**	**103.0**
Opponents	**82**	**19,780**	**3,512**	**47.3**	**882**	**308**	**1,584**	**71.7**	**1,348**	**3,916**	**2,220**	**898**	**1,364**	**476**	**108.7**

Los Angeles Lakers

Player	GP	Min	Field Goals		3-Pt FG		Free Throws		Rebounds		A	Stl	TO	BS	Avg
			FGM	Pct	FGA	FGM	FTM	Pct	Off	Total					
Divac	79	2,685	453	50.6	47	9	208	68.6	282	851	307	92	191	112	14.2
Peeler	30	923	176	43.0	63	14	57	80.3	48	109	94	43	59	8	14.1
Van Exel	81	2,700	413	39.4	364	123	150	78.1	47	238	466	85	145	8	13.6
Campbell	76	2,253	373	46.2	2	0	188	68.9	167	519	86	64	98	146	12.3
Threatt	81	2,278	411	48.2	33	5	138	89.0	28	153	344	110	106	19	11.9
Christie	65	1,515	244	43.4	119	39	145	69.7	93	235	136	89	140	28	10.3
Worthy	80	1,597	340	40.6	11	32	100	74.1	48	181	154	45	97	18	10.2
Lynch	71	1,762	291	50.8	5	0	99	59.6	220	410	96	102	87	27	9.6
Bowie	25	556	75	43.6	4	1	72	86.7	27	131	47	4	43	28	8.9
Smith	73	1,617	272	44.1	50	16	85	71.4	106	195	148	59	76	14	8.8
Edwards	45	469	78	46.4	0	0	54	68.4	11	65	22	4	30	3	4.7
Rambis	50	635	59	51.8	1	0	46	64.8	84	189	32	22	26	23	3.3
Schayes	36	363	28	33.3	0	0	29	90.6	31	79	13	10	23	10	2.4
Lakers	**82**	**19,755**	**3,291**	**45.0**	**803**	**241**	**1,410**	**71.7**	**1,260**	**3,464**	**1,983**	**751**	**1,197**	**461**	**100.4**
Opponents	**82**	**19,755**	**3,337**	**47.6**	**723**	**228**	**1,683**	**71.7**	**1,284**	**3,817**	**2,163**	**664**	**1,344**	**427**	**104.7**

Miami Heat

Player	GP	Min	Field Goals		3-Pt FG		Free Throws		Rebounds		A	Stl	TO	BS	Avg
			FGM	Pct	FGA	FGM	FTM	Pct	Off	Total					
Rice	81	2,999	663	46.7	346	132	250	88.0	76	434	184	110	130	32	21.1
Smith	78	2,776	491	45.6	262	91	273	83.5	156	392	394	84	202	35	17.3
Seikaly	72	2,410	392	48.8	2	0	304	72.0	244	740	136	59	195	100	15.1
Long	69	2,201	300	44.6	6	1	187	78.6	190	495	170	89	125	26	11.4
Miner	63	1,358	254	47.7	6	4	149	82.8	75	156	95	31	95	13	10.5
Shaw	77	2,037	278	41.7	216	73	64	71.9	104	350	385	71	173	21	9.0
Coles	76	1,726	233	44.9	99	20	102	77.9	50	159	263	75	107	12	7.7
Salley	76	1,910	208	47.7	3	2	164	72.9	132	407	135	56	94	78	7.7
Geiger	72	1,199	202	57.4	5	1	116	77.9	119	303	32	36	61	29	7.2
Burton	53	697	124	43.8	15	3	120	75.9	50	136	39	18	54	20	7.0
Askins	37	319	36	40.9	21	4	9	90.0	33	82	13	11	21	1	2.3
Kessler	15	66	11	44.0	9	5	6	75.0	4	10	2	1	5	1	2.2
Bol	8	61	1	.083	3	0	0	—	1	11	0	0	5	6	0.3
Heat	**82**	**19,805**	**3,197**	**46.4**	**997**	**337**	**1,744**	**78.5**	**1,235**	**3,642**	**1,856**	**643**	**1,315**	**374**	**103.4**
Opponents	**82**	**19,805**	**3,036**	**45.7**	**892**	**295**	**1,689**	**74.8**	**1,074**	**3,340**	**1,821**	**689**	**1,314**	**438**	**100.7**

Milwaukee Bucks

Player	GP	Min	Field Goals		3-Pt FG		Free Throws		Rebounds		A	Stl	TO	BS	Avg
			FGM	Pct	FGA	FGM	FTM	Pct	Off	Total					
Murdock	82	2,533	477	46.8	168	69	234	81.3	91	261	546	197	206	12	15.3
Baker	82	2,560	435	50.1	5	1	234	56.9	277	621	163	60	162	114	13.5
Day	76	2,127	351	41.5	148	33	231	69.8	115	310	138	103	129	52	12.7
Norman	82	2,539	412	44.8	189	63	92	50.3	169	500	222	58	150	46	11.9
Edwards	82	2,322	382	47.8	106	38	151	79.9	104	329	171	83	146	27	11.6
Strong	67	1,131	141	41.3	13	3	159	77.2	109	281	48	38	61	14	6.6
Barry	72	1,242	158	41.4	115	32	97	79.5	36	146	168	102	83	17	6.2
Mayberry	82	1,472	167	41.5	119	41	58	69.0	26	101	215	46	97	4	5.3
Lohaus	67	962	102	36.3	134	46	20	69.0	33	150	62	30	58	55	4.0
Foster	3	19	4	57.1	0	0	2	100.0	0	3	0	0	1	1	3.3
Courtney	52	345	67	45.3	3	2	32	68.1	28	56	15	10	21	12	3.2
Gminski	29	309	36	35.0	0	0	14	77.8	22	74	11	13	13	16	3.0
Cook	25	203	26	48.1	1	0	10	40.0	20	56	4	3	12	14	2.5
Schayes	23	230	14	30.4	0	0	21	95.5	16	45	5	5	14	8	2.1
Bucks	**82**	**19,705**	**3,044**	**44.7**	**1,019**	**331**	**1,530**	**70.2**	**1,126**	**3,280**	**1,946**	**800**	**1,343**	**407**	**96.9**
Opponents	**82**	**19,705**	**3,255**	**49.1**	**789**	**286**	**1,684**	**73.7**	**1,086**	**3,581**	**2,092**	**768**	**1,416**	**420**	**103.4**

Minnesota Timberwolves

Player	GP	Min	FGM	Pct	FGA	FGM	FTM	Pct	Off	Total	A	Stl	TO	BS	Avg
Laettner	70	2,428	396	44.8	25	6	375	78.3	160	602	307	87	259	86	16.8
Rider	79	2,415	522	46.8	150	54	215	81.8	118	315	202	54	218	28	16.6
West	72	2,182	434	48.7	8	1	187	81.0	61	231	172	65	137	24	14.7
M. Williams	72	2,206	314	45.7	45	10	333	83.9	67	221	512	118	203	24	13.7
Person	77	2,029	356	42.2	272	100	82	75.9	55	253	185	45	121	12	11.6
King	49	1,053	146	42.8	2	0	93	68.4	90	241	58	31	83	42	7.9
Bailey	79	1,297	232	51.0	2	0	119	79.9	66	215	54	20	58	58	7.4
Smith	80	1,617	184	43.5	39	10	95	67.4	15	122	285	38	101	18	5.9
Maxey	55	626	89	53.3	2	0	70	71.4	75	199	10	16	40	33	4.5
Brown	82	1,921	167	41.5	2	0	77	65.3	119	447	72	51	75	29	3.6
Frank	67	959	67	41.9	2	0	54	71.1	83	220	57	35	49	35	2.8
Davis	68	374	40	31.7	3	1	50	73.5	21	55	22	16	19	4	1.9
T'wolves	**82**	**19,730**	**2,985**	**45.7**	**557**	**183**	**1,777**	**77.2**	**990**	**3,333**	**1,976**	**600**	**1,478**	**440**	**96.7**
Opponents	**82**	**19,730**	**3,244**	**47.2**	**738**	**227**	**1,783**	**72.7**	**1,102**	**3,398**	**2,108**	**824**	**1,164**	**549**	**103.6**

New Jersey Nets

Player	GP	Min	FGM	Pct	FGA	FGM	FTM	Pct	Off	Total	A	Stl	TO	BS	Avg
Coleman	77	2,778	541	44.7	121	38	439	77.4	262	870	262	68	208	142	20.2
Anderson	82	3,135	576	41.7	132	40	346	81.8	89	322	784	158	266	15	18.8
Edwards	82	2,727	471	45.8	99	35	167	77.0	94	281	232	120	135	34	14.0
Gilliam	82	1,969	348	51.0	1	0	274	75.9	197	500	69	38	106	61	11.8
Morris	50	1,349	203	44.7	147	53	85	72.0	91	228	83	55	52	49	10.9
Newman	81	1,697	313	47.1	90	24	182	80.9	86	180	72	69	90	37	10.3
Benjamin	77	1,817	283	48.0	0	0	152	71.0	135	499	44	35	97	90	9.3
Brown	79	1,950	167	41.5	6	1	115	75.7	188	493	93	71	72	93	5.7
Williams	70	877	125	42.7	0	0	72	60.5	109	263	26	17	35	36	4.6
Walters	48	386	60	52.2	28	14	28	82.4	6	38	71	15	30	3	3.4
Wesley	60	542	64	36.8	47	11	44	83.0	10	44	123	38	52	4	3.1
Schintzius	30	319	29	34.5	0	0	10	58.8	26	89	13	7	13	17	2.3
Mahorn	28	226	23	48.9	1	0	13	65.0	16	54	5	3	7	5	2.1
Jamerson	5	14	0	00.0	0	0	2	66.7	0	4	1	0	1	0	0.4
Nets	**82**	**19,830**	**3,169**	**44.5**	**683**	**223**	**1,900**	**76.2**	**1,300**	**3,856**	**1,900**	**696**	**1,196**	**576**	**103.2**
Opponents	**82**	**19,830**	**3,266**	**45.8**	**739**	**235**	**1,514**	**74.3**	**1,142**	**3,670**	**1,919**	**715**	**1,248**	**582**	**101.0**

New York Knickerbockers

Player	GP	Min	FGM	Pct	FGA	FGM	FTM	Pct	Off	Total	A	Stl	TO	BS	Avg
Ewing	79	2,972	745	49.6	14	4	445	76.5	219	885	179	90	260	217	24.5
Starks	59	2,057	410	42.0	337	113	187	75.4	37	185	348	95	184	6	19.0
Oakley	82	2,932	363	47.8	3	0	243	77.6	349	965	218	110	193	18	11.8
Davis	56	1,333	238	47.1	132	53	85	82.5	23	67	165	40	76	4	11.0
Smith	43	1,105	176	44.3	16	8	87	71.9	66	165	50	26	64	45	10.4
Harper	82	2,204	303	40.7	203	73	112	68.7	20	141	334	125	135	8	9.6
Anthony	80	1,994	225	39.4	160	48	130	77.4	43	189	365	114	127	13	7.9
Rivers	19	499	55	43.3	52	19	14	63.6	4	39	100	25	29	5	7.5
Blackman	55	969	161	43.6	84	30	38	90.6	23	93	76	25	44	6	7.3
Davis	50	815	110	43.8	19	6	43	79.6	13	56	83	22	45	4	5.4
Mason	73	1,903	206	47.6	1	0	116	72.0	158	427	151	31	107	9	7.2
Bonner	73	1,402	162	56.3	0	0	50	47.6	150	344	88	76	89	13	5.1
Williams	70	774	103	44.2	1	0	27	64.3	56	182	28	18	39	43	3.3
Knicks	**82**	**19,755**	**3,098**	**46.0**	**908**	**316**	**1,564**	**74.6**	**1,175**	**3,717**	**2,067**	**752**	**1,360**	**385**	**98.5**
Opponents	**82**	**19,755**	**2,783**	**43.1**	**825**	**253**	**1,684**	**71.9**	**1,016**	**3,261**	**1,677**	**677**	**1,420**	**333**	**91.5**

Orlando Magic

Player	GP	Min	Field Goals		3-Pt FG		Free Throws		Rebounds		A	Stl	TO	BS	Avg
			FGM	Pct	FGA	FGM	FTM	Pct	Off	Total					
O'Neal	81	3,224	953	59.9	2	0	471	55.4	384	1,072	195	76	222	231	29.3
Hardaway	82	3,015	509	46.6	187	50	245	74.2	192	439	544	190	292	51	16.0
Anderson	81	2,811	504	47.8	314	101	168	67.2	113	476	294	134	165	33	15.8
Scott	82	2,283	384	40.5	388	155	123	77.4	54	218	216	81	93	32	12.8
Skiles	82	2,303	276	42.9	165	68	195	87.8	42	189	503	47	193	2	9.9
Royal	74	1,357	174	50.1	2	0	199	74.0	94	248	61	50	76	16	7.4
Turner	68	1,536	199	46.7	55	18	35	77.8	79	271	60	23	75	11	6.6
Avent	74	1,371	150	37.7	0	0	89	72.4	144	338	65	33	85	31	5.3
Krystkowiak	34	682	71	48.0	1	0	31	79.5	38	123	35	14	29	4	5.1
Bowie	70	948	139	48.1	18	1	41	83.7	29	120	102	32	58	12	4.6
Green	29	126	22	38.6	4	1	28	75.7	6	12	9	6	13	1	2.5
Rollins	45	384	29	54.7	0	0	18	60.0	33	96	9	7	13	35	1.7
Kite	29	309	13	37.1	0	0	8	36.4	22	70	4	2	17	12	1.2
Tower	11	32	4	44.4	0	0	0	—	0	6	1	0	0	0	0.7
Magic	**82**	**19,730**	**3,341**	**48.5**	**1,137**	**394**	**1,590**	**67.8**	**1,177**	**3,533**	**2,070**	**683**	**1,327**	**456**	**105.7**
Opponents	**82**	**19,730**	**3,263**	**45.8**	**847**	**296**	**1,525**	**74.5**	**1,197**	**3,502**	**2,103**	**756**	**1,228**	**442**	**101.8**

Philadelphia 76ers

Player	GP	Min	Field Goals		3-Pt FG		Free Throws		Rebounds		A	Stl	TO	BS	Avg
			FGM	Pct	FGA	FGM	FTM	Pct	Off	Total					
Weatherspoon	82	3,147	602	48.3	17	4	298	69.3	254	832	192	100	195	116	18.4
J. Malone	77	2,560	525	48.6	12	7	205	83.0	51	191	125	40	85	5	16.4
Barros	81	2,519	412	46.9	354	135	116	80.0	28	196	424	107	167	5	13.3
Woolridge	74	1,955	364	47.1	14	1	208	68.9	103	298	139	41	142	56	12.7
Bradley	49	1,385	201	40.9	3	0	102	60.7	98	306	98	45	148	147	10.3
Perry	80	2,336	272	43.5	200	73	102	58.0	117	404	94	60	80	82	9.0
Dawkins	72	1,343	177	41.8	105	37	84	84.0	28	123	263	63	111	5	6.6
M. Malone	55	618	102	44.0	1	0	90	76.9	106	226	34	11	59	17	5.3
Austin	14	201	29	43.9	1	0	14	60.9	25	69	17	5	17	10	5.1
Leckner	71	1,163	139	48.1	2	0	84	64.6	75	282	86	18	86	34	5.1
Graham	70	889	122	40.0	25	2	92	83.6	21	86	66	61	65	4	4.8
Kidd	68	884	100	59.2	0	0	47	54.7	76	233	19	19	44	23	3.6
Edwards	3	44	2	11.1	5	0	2	40.0	5	14	4	3	4	1	2.0
Curry	10	43	3	21.4	2	0	3	75.0	0	1	1	1	3	0	0.9
Bol	14	116	4	21.1	3	0	0	—	3	18	1	2	5	16	0.6
76ers	**82**	**19,805**	**3,103**	**45.5**	**942**	**318**	**1,509**	**71.4**	**1,012**	**3,406**	**1,827**	**663**	**1,368**	**525**	**98.0**
Opponents	**82**	**19,805**	**3,549**	**48.4**	**795**	**263**	**1,297**	**74.4**	**1,202**	**3,809**	**2,357**	**806**	**1,190**	**385**	**105.6**

Phoenix Suns

Player	GP	Min	Field Goals		3-Pt FG		Free Throws		Rebounds		A	Stl	TO	BS	Avg
			FGM	Pct	FGA	FGM	FTM	Pct	Off	Total					
Barkley	65	2,298	518	49.5	178	48	318	70.4	198	727	296	101	206	37	21.6
K. Johnson	67	2,449	477	48.7	27	6	380	81.9	55	167	637	125	235	10	20.0
Ceballos	53	1,602	425	53.5	9	0	160	72.4	153	344	91	59	93	23	19.1
Majerle	80	3,207	476	41.8	503	192	176	73.9	120	349	275	129	137	43	16.5
Green	82	2,825	465	50.2	35	8	266	73.5	275	753	137	70	100	38	14.7
Miller	69	1,786	277	60.9	9	2	80	58.4	140	476	244	83	164	156	9.2
Ainge	68	1,555	224	41.7	244	80	78	83.0	28	131	180	57	81	8	8.9
West	82	1,236	162	56.6	0	0	58	50.0	112	295	33	31	74	109	4.7
F. Johnson	70	875	134	44.8	12	2	54	78.3	29	82	148	41	65	1	4.6
Perry	27	432	42	37.2	3	0	21	75.0	12	39	125	25	43	1	3.9
Kleine	74	848	125	48.8	11	5	30	76.9	50	193	45	14	35	19	3.9
Mustaf	33	196	30	35.7	0	0	13	59.1	20	55	8	4	10	5	2.2
Cooper	23	136	18	43.9	7	1	11	73.3	2	9	28	3	20	0	2.1
Mackey	22	69	14	37.8	2	0	4	50.0	12	24	1	0	2	3	1.5
Suns	**82**	**19,705**	**3,429**	**48.4**	**1,042**	**344**	**1,674**	**72.8**	**1,220**	**3,673**	**2,261**	**745**	**1,305**	**460**	**108.2**
Opponents	**82**	**19,705**	**3,379**	**47.4**	**863**	**283**	**1,438**	**72.0**	**1,086**	**3,333**	**2,154**	**748**	**1,254**	**437**	**103.4**

Portland Trail Blazers

Player	GP	Min	FGM	Pct	FGA	FGM	FTM	Pct	Off	Total	A	Stl	TO	BS	Avg
C. Robinson	82	2,853	641	45.7	53	13	352	76.5	164	550	159	118	169	111	20.1
Drexler	68	2,334	473	42.8	219	71	286	77.7	154	445	333	98	167	34	19.2
Strickland	82	2,889	528	48.3	10	2	353	74.9	122	370	740	147	257	24	17.2
Porter	77	2,074	348	41.6	282	110	204	87.2	45	215	401	79	166	18	13.1
Grant	77	2,112	356	46.0	7	2	84	64.1	109	351	107	70	56	49	10.4
Williams	81	2,636	291	55.5	1	0	201	67.9	315	843	80	58	111	47	9.7
Murray	66	820	167	47.0	109	50	50	69.4	43	111	31	21	37	20	6.6
Kersey	78	1,276	203	43.3	1	0	101	74.8	130	331	75	71	63	49	6.5
Bryant	79	1,441	185	48.2	1	0	72	69.2	117	315	37	32	66	29	5.6
J. Robinson	58	673	104	36.5	73	23	45	67.2	34	78	68	30	52	15	4.8
Jackson	29	187	34	39.1	6	0	12	85.7	6	17	27	4	14	2	2.8
Dudley	6	86	6	24.0	0	0	2	50.0	16	24	5	4	2	3	2.3
Smith	43	316	29	40.3	0	0	18	47.4	40	99	4	12	12	6	1.8
Thompson	14	58	6	42.9	1	0	1	50.0	7	13	3	0	5	2	0.9
Trail Blazers	**82**	**19,755**	**3,371**	**45.4**	**770**	**272**	**1,781**	**74.3**	**1,302**	**3,762**	**2,070**	**744**	**1,210**	**409**	**107.3**
Opponents	**82**	**19,755**	**3,311**	**46.9**	**830**	**296**	**1,661**	**75.0**	**1,016**	**3,497**	**2,094**	**654**	**1,391**	**393**	**104.6**

Sacramento Kings

Player	GP	Min	FGM	Pct	FGA	FGM	FTM	Pct	Off	Total	A	Stl	TO	BS	Avg
Richmond	78	2,897	635	44.5	312	127	426	83.4	70	286	313	103	216	17	23.4
Tisdale	79	2,557	552	50.1	0	215	215	80.8	159	560	139	37	124	52	16.7
Simmons	75	2,702	436	43.8	17	6	251	77.7	168	562	305	104	183	50	15.1
Webb	79	2,567	373	46.0	164	55	204	81.4	44	222	528	93	168	23	12.7
Polynice	68	2,402	346	52.3	2	0	97	50.8	299	809	41	42	78	67	11.6
Williams	57	1,356	226	39.0	132	38	148	63.5	71	235	132	52	145	23	11.2
Wilson	57	1,221	187	48.2	2	0	92	55.4	120	273	72	38	93	11	8.2
Hurley	19	499	54	37.0	16	2	24	80.0	6	34	115	13	48	1	7.1
Spencer	28	349	52	44.1	0	0	55	71.4	30	73	22	19	21	7	5.7
Smith	66	87	124	40.5	60	21	63	75.0	34	84	109	40	50	5	5.0
Brown	61	1,041	110	43.8	4	0	53	60.9	40	112	133	63	75	14	4.5
Causwell	41	674	71	51.8	0	0	40	58.8	68	186	11	19	33	49	4.4
Peplowski	55	667	76	53.9	1	0	24	54.5	49	169	24	17	34	25	3.2
Burns	23	143	22	40.0	0	0	12	52.2	13	30	9	6	7	3	2.4
Kings	**82**	**19,755**	**3,179**	**45.2**	**729**	**257**	**1,676**	**73.1**	**1,122**	**3,471**	**2,029**	**669**	**1,333**	**355**	**101.1**
Opponents	**82**	**19,755**	**3,360**	**47.9**	**771**	**277**	**1,767**	**72.2**	**1,189**	**3,763**	**2,052**	**746**	**1,341**	**498**	**106.9**

San Antonio Spurs

Player	GP	Min	FGM	Pct	FGA	FGM	FTM	Pct	Off	Total	A	Stl	TO	BS	Avg
Robinson	80	3,241	840	50.7	29	10	693	74.9	241	855	381	139	253	265	29.8
Ellis	77	2,590	478	49.4	332	131	83	77.6	70	255	80	66	75	11	15.2
Anderson	80	2,488	394	47.1	68	22	145	84.8	68	242	347	71	153	46	11.9
Del Negro	77	1,949	309	48.7	43	15	140	82.4	27	161	320	64	102	1	10.1
Knight	65	1,438	225	47.4	21	4	141	81.0	28	103	197	34	94	11	9.2
Reid	70	1,344	260	49.1	3	0	107	69.9	91	220	73	43	84	25	9.0
Cummings	59	1,133	183	42.8	2	0	63	58.9	132	297	50	31	59	13	7.3
Carr	34	465	78	48.8	1	0	42	72.4	12	51	15	9	15	22	5.8
Daniels	65	980	140	37.6	125	44	46	71.9	45	111	94	29	60	16	5.7
Rodman	79	2,989	156	53.4	24	5	53	52.0	453	1,367	184	52	138	32	4.7
Floyd	53	737	70	33.5	36	8	52	66.7	10	70	101	12	61	8	3.8
Nevitt	1	1	0	—	0	0	3	50.0	1	1	0	0	1	0	3.0
Haley	28	94	21	43.8	0	0	17	81.0	6	24	1	0	10	0	2.1
Whitney	40	339	25	30.5	30	10	12	80.0	5	29	53	11	37	1	1.8
Spurs	**82**	**19,780**	**3,178**	**47.5**	**714**	**249**	**1,597**	**74.2**	**1,189**	**3,786**	**1,896**	**561**	**1,198**	**450**	**100.0**
Opponents	**82**	**19,780**	**3,066**	**44.6**	**871**	**290**	**1,349**	**71.9**	**1,089**	**3,242**	**1,769**	**632**	**1,020**	**346**	**94.8**

Seattle SuperSonics

Player	GP	Min	Field Goals		3-Pt FG		Free Throws		Rebounds		A	Stl	TO	BS	Avg
			FGM	Pct	FGA	FGM	FTM	Pct	Off	Total					
Kemp	79	2,597	533	53.8	4	1	364	74.1	312	851	207	142	259	166	18.1
Payton	82	2,881	584	50.4	54	15	166	59.5	105	269	494	188	173	19	16.5
Schrempf	81	2,728	445	49.3	68	22	300	76.9	144	454	275	73	173	9	15.0
Pierce	51	1,022	272	47.1	32	6	189	89.6	29	83	91	42	64	5	14.5
Gill	79	2,435	429	44.3	120	38	215	78.2	91	268	275	151	143	32	14.1
Perkins	81	2,170	341	43.8	270	99	218	80.1	120	366	111	67	103	31	12.3
Askew	80	1,690	273	48.1	31	6	175	82.9	60	184	194	73	70	19	9.1
McMillan	73	1,887	177	44.7	1	0	31	56.4	50	283	387	216	126	22	6.0
Cage	82	1,708	171	54.5	1	0	36	48.6	164	444	45	77	51	38	4.6
C. King	15	86	19	39.6	7	2	15	57.7	5	15	11	4	12	0	3.7
Johnson	45	280	44	41.5	0	0	29	63.0	48	118	7	10	24	22	2.6
Scheffler	35	152	28	60.9	0	0	19	95.0	11	26	6	7	8	0	2.1
R. King	27	78	15	44.1	1	0	11	50.0	9	20	8	1	7	2	1.5
SuperSonics	**82**	**19,730**	**3,338**	**48.4**	**722**	**242**	**1,769**	**74.5**	**1,148**	**3,381**	**2,112**	**1,053**	**1,262**	**365**	**105.9**
Opponents	**82**	**19,730**	**2,928**	**45.3**	**946**	**326**	**1,760**	**74.1**	**1,084**	**3,275**	**1,808**	**686**	**1,666**	**421**	**96.9**

Utah Jazz

Player	GP	Min	Field Goals		3-Pt FG		Free Throws		Rebounds		A	Stl	TO	BS	Avg
			FGM	Pct	FGA	FGM	FTM	Pct	Off	Total					
Malone	82	3,329	772	49.7	32	8	511	69.4	235	940	328	125	234	126	25.2
Hornacek	80	2,820	472	47.0	208	70	260	87.8	60	279	419	127	171	13	15.9
Stockton	82	2,969	458	52.8	149	48	272	80.5	72	258	1,031	199	266	22	15.1
Chambers	80	1,838	329	44.0	45	14	221	78.6	87	326	79	40	89	32	11.2
Spencer	79	2,210	256	50.5	0	0	165	60.7	235	658	43	41	127	67	8.6
Corbin	82	2,149	268	45.6	29	6	117	81.3	150	389	122	99	92	24	8.0
Humphries	75	1,619	233	43.6	96	38	57	75.0	35	127	219	65	95	11	7.5
Benoit	55	1,070	139	38.5	59	12	68	77.3	89	260	23	23	37	37	6.5
Russell	67	1,121	135	48.4	22	2	62	61.4	61	181	54	68	55	19	5.0
Morningstar	23	367	39	47.6	0	0	18	60.0	31	81	15	14	19	2	4.2
Green	36	334	63	34.4	41	10	13	72.2	10	34	16	18	27	6	4.1
Bond	56	559	63	40.4	54	19	31	77.5	20	61	31	16	17	12	3.1
Crotty	45	313	45	45.5	24	11	31	86.1	11	31	77	15	27	1	2.9
Wright	15	92	8	34.8	1	0	3	75.0	6	10	0	1	6	2	1.3
Jazz	**82**	**19,830**	**3,207**	**47.7**	**559**	**179**	**1,761**	**74.0**	**1,059**	**3,444**	**2,179**	**751**	**1,191**	**364**	**101.9**
Opponents	**82**	**19,830**	**2,973**	**44.8**	**967**	**289**	**1,773**	**72.5**	**1,100**	**3,427**	**1,806**	**593**	**1,318**	**459**	**97.7**

Washington Bullets

Player	GP	Min	Field Goals		3-Pt FG		Free Throws		Rebounds		A	Stl	TO	BS	Avg
			FGM	Pct	FGA	FGM	FTM	Pct	Off	Total					
Chapman	60	2,025	431	49.8	165	64	168	81.6	57	146	185	59	117	8	18.2
MacLean	75	2,487	517	50.2	21	3	328	82.4	140	467	160	47	152	22	18.2
Gugliotta	78	2,795	540	46.6	148	40	213	68.5	189	728	276	172	247	51	17.1
Adams	70	2,337	285	40.8	191	55	224	83.0	37	183	480	96	167	6	12.1
Cheaney	65	1,604	327	47.0	23	1	124	77.0	88	190	126	63	108	10	12.0
Conlon	30	579	95	57.6	2	0	43	81.1	53	139	34	9	33	8	7.8
Ellison	47	1,178	137	46.9	3	0	70	72.2	77	242	70	25	73	50	7.3
Butler	75	1,321	207	49.5	5	0	104	57.8	106	225	77	54	87	20	6.9
Duckworth	69	1,485	184	41.7	0	0	88	66.7	103	325	56	37	101	35	6.6
Price	65	1,035	141	43.3	150	50	68	78.2	31	90	213	55	119	2	6.2
Muresan	54	650	128	54.5	0	0	48	67.6	66	192	18	28	54	48	5.6
Walker	73	1,397	132	48.2	3	0	87	69.6	118	289	33	26	44	59	4.8
Anderson	21	356	35	40.7	26	7	19	82.6	16	53	17	8	10	3	4.6
Stewart	3	35	3	37.5	0	0	7	70.0	1	7	2	2	2	1	4.3
Overton	61	749	87	40.3	11	1	43	82.7	19	69	92	21	54	1	3.6
Gaze	7	70	8	47.1	8	4	2	100.0	1	7	5	2	3	1	3.1
Paddio	18	137	22	36.7	1	0	9	56.3	5	16	11	4	6	0	2.9
Horford	3	28	0	0.00	0	0	0		1	3	0	1	1	3	0.0
Bullets	**82**	**19,705**	**3,195**	**46.8**	**744**	**221**	**1,618**	**74.8**	**1,071**	**3,260**	**1,823**	**701**	**1,403**	**321**	**100.4**
Opponents	**82**	**19,705**	**3,569**	**50.8**	**723**	**252**	**1,444**	**72.3**	**1,119**	**3,481**	**2,113**	**815**	**1,291**	**470**	**107.7**

1994 NBA Draft

First Round

1. Glenn Robinson, Milwaukee
2. Jason Kidd, Dallas
3. Grant Hill, Detroit
4. Donyell Marshall, Minnesota
5. Juwan Howard, Washington
6. Sharone Wright, Philadelphia
7. Lamond Murray, LA Clippers
8. Brian Grant, Sacramento
9. Eric Montross, Boston
10. Eddie Jones, LA Lakers
11. Carlos Rogers, Seattle
12. Khalid Reeves, Miami
13. Jalen Rose, Denver
14. Yinka Dare, New Jersey
15. Eric Piatkowski, Indiana
16. Clifford Rozier, Golden St
17. Aaron McKie, Temple
18. Eric Mobley, Milwaukee
19. Tony Dumas, Dallas
20. B.J. Tyler, Philadelphia
21. Dickey Simpkins, Chicago
22. Bill Curley, San Antonio
23. Wesley Person, Phoenix
24. Monty Williams, New York
25. Greg Minor, LA Clippers
26. Charlie Ward, New York
27. Brooks Thompson, Orlando

Second Round

28. Deon Thomas, Dallas
29. Antonio Lang, Phoenix
30. Howard Elsley, Minnesota
31. Rodney Dent, Orlando
32. Jim McIlvaine, Washington
33. Derrick Alston, Philadelphia
34. Gaylon Nickerson, Atlanta
35. Michael Smith, Sacramento
36. Andrei Fetisov, Boston (to Milwaukee)
37. Dontonio Wingfield, Seattle
38. Darrin Hancock, Charlotte
39. Anthony Miller, Golden St
40. Jeff Webster, Miami
41. William Njoku, Indiana
42. Gary Collier, Cleveland
43. Shawnelle Scott, Portland
44. Damon Bailey, Indiana
45. Dwayne Morton, Golden St
46. Voshon Lenard, Milwaukee
47. Jamie Watson, Utah
48. Jevon Crudup, Detroit
49. Kris Bruton, Chicago
50. Charles Claxton, Phoenix
51. Lawrence Funderburke, Sacramento
52. Anthony Goldwire, Phoenix
53. Albert Burditt, Houston
54. Zeljko Rebraca, Seattle

THEY SAID IT

Bob Weiss, Los Angeles Clipper Coach, on the areas in which the dethroned NBA champion Chicago Bulls missed Michael Jordan most: "Offense and defense."

Hooray for Hollywood

NBA scouting director Marty Blake was around when pro teams rode buses from arena to arena, so one can imagine his surprise when he went one-on-one with high-budget Hollywood. Blake had a minor—very minor—role in the movie *Blue Chips*, starring Nick Nolte and Shaquille O'Neal, and he was summoned last February to California to "re-loop" his scene. Blake was flown first-class from his home in Atlanta to Los Angeles, met by limousine at the airport and housed in a swank hotel. And what were those all-important lines?

"Yep," says Blake.

No, really, Marty, what were they?

"Yep," says Blake. Yep, that was his only line—yep.

Says Blake, "But I said it perfectly the second time."

NBA Champions

Season	Winner	Series	Loser	Winning Coach
1946-47	Philadelphia	4-1	Chicago	Eddie Gottlieb
1947-48	Baltimore	4-2	Philadelphia	Buddy Jeannette
1948-49	Minneapolis	4-2	Washington	John Kundla
1949-50	Minneapolis	4-2	Syracuse	John Kundla
1950-51	Rochester	4-3	New York	Les Harrison
1951-52	Minneapolis	4-3	New York	John Kundla
1952-53	Minneapolis	4-1	New York	John Kundla
1953-54	Minneapolis	4-3	Syracuse	John Kundla
1954-55	Syracuse	4-3	Ft Wayne	Al Cervi
1955-56	Philadelphia	4-1	Ft Wayne	George Senesky
1956-57	Boston	4-3	St Louis	Red Auerbach
1957-58	St Louis	4-2	Boston	Alex Hannum
1958-59	Boston	4-0	Minneapolis	Red Auerbach
1959-60	Boston	4-3	St Louis	Red Auerbach
1960-61	Boston	4-1	St Louis	Red Auerbach
1961-62	Boston	4-3	LA Lakers	Red Auerbach
1962-63	Boston	4-2	LA Lakers	Red Auerbach
1963-64	Boston	4-1	San Francisco	Red Auerbach
1964-65	Boston	4-1	LA Lakers	Red Auerbach
1965-66	Boston	4-3	LA Lakers	Red Auerbach
1966-67	Philadelphia	4-2	San Francisco	Alex Hannum
1967-68	Boston	4-2	LA Lakers	Bill Russell
1968-69	Boston	4-3	LA Lakers	Bill Russell
1969-70	New York	4-3	LA Lakers	Red Holzman
1970-71	Milwaukee	4-0	Baltimore	Larry Costello
1971-72	LA Lakers	4-1	New York	Bill Sharman
1972-73	New York	4-1	LA Lakers	Red Holzman
1973-74	Boston	4-3	Milwaukee	Tommy Heinsohn
1974-75	Golden State	4-0	Washington	Al Attles
1975-76	Boston	4-2	Phoenix	Tommy Heinsohn
1976-77	Portland	4-2	Philadelphia	Jack Ramsay
1977-78	Washington	4-3	Seattle	Dick Motta
1978-79	Seattle	4-1	Washington	Lenny Wilkens
1979-80	LA Lakers	4-2	Philadelphia	Paul Westhead
1980-81	Boston	4-2	Houston	Bill Fitch
1981-82	LA Lakers	4-2	Philadelphia	Pat Riley
1982-83	Philadelphia	4-0	LA Lakers	Billy Cunningham
1983-84	Boston	4-3	LA Lakers	K.C. Jones
1984-85	LA Lakers	4-2	Boston	Pat Riley
1985-86	Boston	4-2	Houston	K.C. Jones
1986-87	LA Lakers	4-2	Boston	Pat Riley
1987-88	LA Lakers	4-3	Detroit	Pat Riley
1988-89	Detroit	4-0	LA Lakers	Chuck Daly
1989-90	Detroit	4-1	Portland	Chuck Daly
1990-91	Chicago	4-1	LA Lakers	Phil Jackson
1991-92	Chicago	4-2	Portland	Phil Jackson
1992-93	Chicago	4-2	Phoenix	Phil Jackson
1993-94	Houston	4-3	New York	Rudy Tomjanovich

NBA Finals Most Valuable Player

1969	Jerry West, LA	1982	Magic Johnson, LA
1970	Willis Reed, NY	1983	Moses Malone, Phil
1971	Kareem Abdul-Jabbar, Mil	1984	Larry Bird, Bos
1972	Wilt Chamberlain, LA	1985	Kareem Abdul-Jabbar, LA Lakers
1973	Willis Reed, NY	1986	Larry Bird, Bos
1974	John Havlicek, Bos	1987	Magic Johnson, LA Lakers
1975	Rick Barry, GS	1988	James Worthy, LA Lakers
1976	JoJo White, Bos	1989	Joe Dumars, Det
1977	Bill Walton, Port	1990	Isiah Thomas, Det
1978	Wes Unseld, Wash	1991	Michael Jordan, Chi
1979	Dennis Johnson, Sea	1992	Michael Jordan, Chi
1980	Magic Johnson, LA	1993	Michael Jordan, Chi
1981	Cedric Maxwell, Bos	1994	Hakeem Olajuwon, Hou

NBA Most Valuable Player: Maurice Podoloff Trophy

Season	Player, Team	GP	Field Goals FGM	Pct	3-Pt FG FGM	Pct	Free Throws FTM	Pct	Rebounds Off	Total	A	Stl	BS	Avg
1955-56	Bob Pettit, StL	72	646	42.9	–	–	557	73.6	–	1,164	189	–	–	25.7
1956-57	Bob Cousy, Bos	64	478	37.8	–	–	363	82.1	–	309	478	–	–	20.6
1957-58	Bill Russell, Bos	69	456	44.2	–	–	230	51.9	–	1,564	202	–	–	16.6
1958-59	Bob Pettit, StL	72	719	43.8	–	–	667	75.9	–	1,182	221	–	–	29.2
1959-60	Wilt Chamberlain, Phil	72	1,065	46.1	–	–	577	58.2	–	1,941	168	–	–	37.6
1960-61	Bill Russell, Bos	78	532	42.6	–	–	258	55.0	–	1,868	264	–	–	16.9
1961-62	Bill Russell, Bos	76	575	45.7	–	–	286	59.5	–	1,891	341	–	–	18.9
1962-63	Bill Russell, Bos	78	511	43.2	–	–	287	55.5	–	1,843	348	–	–	16.8
1963-64	Oscar Robertson, Cin	79	840	48.3	–	–	800	85.3	–	783	868	–	–	31.4
1964-65	Bill Russell, Bos	78	429	43.8	–	–	244	57.3	–	1,878	410	–	–	14.1
1965-66	Wilt Chamberlain, Phil	79	1,074	54.0	–	–	501	51.3	–	1,943	414	–	–	33.5
1966-67	Wilt Chamberlain, Phil	81	785	68.3	–	–	386	44.1	–	1,957	630	–	–	24.1
1967-68	Wilt Chamberlain, Phil	82	819	59.5	–	–	354	38.0	–	1,952	702	–	–	24.3
1968-69	Wes Unseld, Balt	82	427	47.6	–	–	277	60.5	–	1,491	213	–	–	13.8
1969-70	Willis Reed, NY	81	702	50.7	–	–	351	75.6	–	1,126	161	–	–	21.7
1970-71	Kareem Abdul-Jabbar, Mil	82	1,063	57.7	–	–	470	69.0	–	1,311	272	–	–	31.7
1971-72	Kareem Abdul-Jabbar, Mil	81	1,159	57.4	–	–	504	68.9	–	1,346	370	–	–	34.8
1972-73	Dave Cowens, Bos	82	740	45.2	–	–	204	77.9	–	1,329	333	–	–	20.5
1973-74	Kareem Abdul-Jabbar, Mil	81	948	53.9	–	–	295	70.2	287	1,178	386	112	283	27.0
1974-75	Bob McAdoo, Buff	82	1,095	51.2	–	–	641	80.5	307	1,155	179	92	174	34.5
1975-76	Kareem Abdul-Jabbar, LA	82	914	52.9	–	–	447	70.3	272	1,383	413	119	338	37.7
1976-77	Kareem Abdul-Jabbar, LA	82	888	57.9	–	–	376	70.1	266	1,090	319	101	261	26.2
1977-78	Bill Walton, Port	58	460	52.2	–	–	177	72.0	118	766	291	60	146	18.9
1978-79	Moses Malone, Hou	82	716	54.0	–	–	599	73.9	587	1,444	147	79	119	24.8
1979-80	Kareem Abdul-Jabbar, LA	82	835	60.4	0	00.0	364	76.5	190	886	371	81	280	24.8
1980-81	Julius Erving, Phil	82	794	52.1	4	22.2	422	78.7	244	657	364	173	147	24.6
1981-82	Moses Malone, Hou	81	945	51.9	0	00.0	630	76.2	558	1,188	142	76	125	31.1
1982-83	Moses Malone, Phil	78	654	50.1	0	00.0	600	76.1	445	1,194	101	89	157	24.5
1983-84	Larry Bird, Bos	79	758	49.2	18	24.7	374	88.8	181	796	520	144	69	24.2
1984-85	Larry Bird, Bos	80	918	52.2	56	42.7	403	88.2	164	842	531	129	98	28.7
1985-86	Larry Bird, Bos	82	796	49.6	82	42.3	441	89.6	190	805	557	166	51	25.8
1986-87	Magic Johnson, LA Lakers	80	683	52.2	8	20.5	535	84.8	122	504	977	138	36	23.9
1987-88	Michael Jordan, Chi	82	1,069	53.5	7	13.2	723	84.1	139	449	485	259	131	35.0
1988-89	Magic Johnson, LA Lakers	77	579	50.9	59	31.4	513	91.1	111	607	988	138	22	22.5
1989-90	Magic Johnson, LA Lakers	79	546	48.0	106	38.4	567	89.0	128	522	907	132	34	22.3
1990-91	Michael Jordan, Chi	82	990	53.9	29	31.2	571	85.1	118	492	453	223	83	31.5
1991-92	Michael Jordan, Chi	80	943	51.9	27	27.0	491	83.2	91	511	489	182	75	30.1
1992-93	Charles Barkley, Phoe	76	716	52.0	67	30.5	445	76.5	237	928	385	119	74	25.6
1993-94	Hakeem Olajuwon, Hou	80	894	52.8	8	42.1	388	71.6	229	955	287	128	297	27.3

Coach of the Year: Arnold "Red" Auerbach Trophy

1962-63	Harry Gallatin, StL
1963-64	Alex Hannum, SF
1964-65	Red Auerbach, Bos
1965-66	Dolph Schayes, Phil
1966-67	Johnny Kerr, Chi
1967-68	Richie Guerin, StL
1968-69	Gene Shue, Balt
1969-70	Red Holzman, NY
1970-71	Dick Motta, Chi
1971-72	Bill Sharman, LA
1972-73	Tom Heinsohn, Bos
1973-74	Ray Scott, Det
1974-75	Phil Johnson, KC-Oma
1975-76	Bill Fitch, Clev
1976-77	Tom Nissalke, Hou
1977-78	Hubie Brown, Atl
1978-79	Cotton Fitzsimmons, KC
1979-80	Bill Fitch, Bos
1980-81	Jack McKinney, Ind
1981-82	Gene Shue, Wash
1982-83	Don Nelson, Mil
1983-84	Frank Layden, Utah
1984-85	Don Nelson, Mil
1985-86	Mike Fratello, Atl
1986-87	Mike Schuler, Port
1987-88	Doug Moe, Den
1988-89	Cotton Fitzsimmons, Phoe
1989-90	Pat Riley, LA Lakers
1990-91	Don Chaney, Hou
1991-92	Don Nelson, GS
1992-93	Pat Riley, NY
1993-94	Lenny Wilkens, Atl

Note: Award named after Auerbach in 1986.

NBA Rookie of the Year: Eddie Gottlieb Trophy

1952-53...Don Meineke, FW	1967-68...Earl Monroe, Balt	1981-82...Buck Williams, NJ
1953-54...Ray Felix, Balt	1968-69...Wes Unseld, Balt	1982-83...Terry Cummings, SD
1954-55...Bob Pettit, Mil	1969-70...K. Abdul-Jabbar, Mil	1983-84...Ralph Sampson, Hou
1955-56...Maurice Stokes, Roch	1970-71...Dave Cowens, Bos	1984-85...Michael Jordan, Chi
1956-57...Tom Heinsohn, Bos	Geoff Petrie, Port	1985-86...Patrick Ewing, NY
1957-58...Woody Sauldsberry, Phil	1971-72...Sidney Wicks, Port	1986-87...Chuck Person, Ind
1958-59...Elgin Baylor, Minn	1972-73...Bob McAdoo, Buff	1987-88...Mark Jackson, NY
1959-60...Wilt Chamberlain, Phil	1973-74...Ernie DiGregorio, Buff	1988-89...Mitch Richmond, GS
1960-61...Oscar Robertson, Cin	1974-75...Keith Wilkes, GS	1989-90...David Robinson, SA
1961-62...Walt Bellamy, Chi	1975-76...Alvan Adams, Phoe	1990-91...Derrick Coleman, NJ
1962-63...Terry Dischinger, Chi	1976-77...Adrian Dantley, Buff	1991-92...Larry Johnson, Char
1963-64...Jerry Lucas, Cin	1977-78...Walter Davis, Phoe	1992-93...Shaquille O'Neal, Orl
1964-65...Willis Reed, NY	1978-79...Phil Ford, KC	1993-94...Chris Webber, GS
1965-66...Rick Barry, SF	1979-80...Larry Bird, Bos	
1966-67...Dave Bing, Det	1980-81...Darrell Griffith, Utah	

NBA Defensive Player of the Year

1982-83	Sidney Moncrief, Mil
1983-84	Sidney Moncrief, Mil
1984-85	Mark Eaton, Utah
1985-86	Alvin Robertson, SA
1986-87	Michael Cooper, LA Lakers
1987-88	Michael Jordan, Chi
1988-89	Mark Eaton, Utah
1989-90	Dennis Rodman, Det
1990-91	Dennis Rodman, Det
1991-92	David Robinson, SA
1992-93	Hakeem Olajuwon, Hou
1993-94	Hakeem Olajuwon, Hou

NBA Sixth Man Award

1982-83	Bobby Jones, Phil
1983-84	Kevin McHale, Bos
1984-85	Kevin McHale, Bos
1985-86	Bill Walton, Bos
1986-87	Ricky Pierce, Mil
1987-88	Roy Tarpley, Dall
1988-89	Eddie Johnson, Phoe
1989-90	Ricky Pierce, Mil
1990-91	Detlef Schrempf, Ind
1991-92	Detlef Schrempf, Ind
1992-93	Cliff Robinson, Port
1993-94	Dell Curry, Char

J. Walter Kennedy Citizenship Award

1974-75	Wes Unseld, Wash
1975-76	Slick Watts, Sea
1976-77	Dave Bing, Wash
1977-78	Bob Lanier, Det
1978-79	Calvin Murphy, Hou
1979-80	Austin Carr, Clev
1980-81	Mike Glenn, NY
1981-82	Kent Benson, Det
1982-83	Julius Erving, Phil
1983-84	Frank Layden, Utah
1984-85	Dan Issel, Den
1985-86	Michael Cooper, LA Lakers
	Rory Sparrow, NY
1986-87	Isiah Thomas, Det
1987-88	Alex English, Den

Kennedy Citizenship Award *(Cont.)*

1988-89	Thurl Bailey, Utah
1989-90	Glenn Rivers, Atl
1990-91	Kevin Johnson, Phoe
1991-92	Magic Johnson, LA Lakers
1992-93	Terry Porter, Port
1993-94	Joe Dumars, Det

NBA Most Improved Player

1985-86	Alvin Robertson, SA
1986-87	Dale Ellis, Sea
1987-88	Kevin Duckworth, Port
1988-89	Kevin Johnson, Phoe
1989-90	Rony Seikaly, Mia
1990-91	Scott Skiles, Orl
1991-92	Pervis Ellison, Wash
1992-93	Chris Jackson, Den
1993-94	Don MacLean, Wash

NBA Executive of the Year

1972-73	Joe Axelson, KC-Oma
1973-74	Eddie Donovan, Buff
1974-75	Dick Vertlieb, GS
1975-76	Jerry Colangelo, Phoe
1976-77	Ray Patterson, Hou
1977-78	Angelo Drossos, SA
1978-79	Bob Ferry, Wash
1979-80	Red Auerbach, Bos
1980-81	Jerry Colangelo, Phoe
1981-82	Bob Ferry, Wash
1982-83	Zollie Volchok, Sea
1983-84	Frank Layden, Utah
1984-85	Vince Boryla, Den
1985-86	Stan Kasten, Atl
1986-87	Stan Kasten, Atl
1987-88	Jerry Krause, Chi
1988-89	Jerry Colangelo, Phoe
1989-90	Bob Bass, SA
1990-91	Bucky Buckwalter, Port
1991-92	Wayne Embry, Cle
1992-93	Jerry Colangelo, Phoe
1993-94	Bob Whitsitt, Seattle

Selected by *The Sporting News.*

NBA All-Time Individual Leaders

Scoring

MOST POINTS, LIFETIME

Kareem Abdul-Jabbar	38,387
Wilt Chamberlain	31,419
Moses Malone	27,360
Elvin Hayes	27,313
Oscar Robertson	26,710
John Havlicek	26,395
Alex English	25,613
Jerry West	25,192
Dominique Wilkins	24,019
Adrian Dantley	23,177

MOST POINTS, SEASON

Wilt Chamberlain, Phil	4,029	1961-62
Wilt Chamberlain, SF	3,586	1962-63
Michael Jordan, Chi	3,041	1986-87
Wilt Chamberlain, Phil	3,033	1960-61
Wilt Chamberlain, SF	2,948	1963-64
Michael Jordan, Chi	2,868	1986-87
Bob McAdoo, Buff	2,831	1974-75
Rick Barry, SF	2,775	1966-67
Michael Jordan, Chi	2,753	1989-90
Elgin Baylor, LA	2,719	1962-63

HIGHEST SCORING AVERAGE, CAREER

Michael Jordan	32.3	667 games
Wilt Chamberlain	30.1	1,045 games
Elgin Baylor	27.4	846 games
Jerry West	27.0	932 games
Dominique Wilkins	26.5	907 games
Bob Pettit	26.4	792 games
George Gervin	26.2	791 games
Karl Malone	26.1	734 games
Oscar Robertson	25.7	1,040 games
Kareem Abdul-Jabbar	24.6	1,560 games

HIGHEST SCORING AVERAGE, SEASON
(Minimum of 70 games)

Wilt Chamberlain, Phil	50.4	1961-62
Wilt Chamberlain, SF	44.8	1962-63
Wilt Chamberlain, Phil	38.4	1960-61
Wilt Chamberlain, Phil	37.6	1959-60
Michael Jordan, Chi	37.1	1986-87
Wilt Chamberlain, SF	36.9	1963-64
Rick Barry, SF	35.6	1966-67
Michael Jordan, Chi	35.0	1987-88
Elgin Baylor, LA	34.8	1960-61

MOST POINTS, GAME

	Player, Team	Opp	Date
100	Wilt Chamberlain, Phi	NY	3/2/62
78	Wilt Chamberlain, Phi	LA	12/8/61
73	Wilt Chamberlain, Phi	Chi	1/13/62
73	Wilt Chamberlain, SF	NY	11/16/62
73	David Thompson, Den	Det	4/9/78
72	Wilt Chamberlain, SF	LA	11/3/62
71	David Robinson	LAC	4/24/94
71	Elgin Baylor, LA	NY	11/15/60
70	Wilt Chamberlain, SF	Syr	3/10/63
69	Michael Jordan, Chi	Cle	3/28/90

THEY SAID IT

Shaquille O'Neal, Orlando Magic center, on the possible consequences should his respiratory ailments prove to be asthma: "I could do a Primatene Mist commercial."

Field Goal Percentage

Highest Field Goal Percentage, Career: .599—Artis Gilmore

Highest Field Goal Percentage, Season: .727—Wilt Chamberlain, LA Lakers, 1972-73 (426/586)

Free Throw Percentage

HIGHEST FREE THROW PERCENTAGE, CAREER

Mahmoud Abdul-Rauf	.921
Mark Price	.908
Rick Barry	.900
Calvin Murphy	.892
Larry Bird	.886

HIGHEST FREE THROW PERCENTAGE, SEASON

Calvin Murphy, Hou	.958	1980-81
Mahmoud Abdul-Rauf	.956	1993-94
Mark Price, Clev	.948	1992-93
Mark Price, Clev	.947	1991-92
Rick Barry, Hou	.946	1978-79

Three-Point Field Goal Percentage*

Most Three-Point Field Goals, Career: Dale Ellis—1,013

Highest Three-Point Field Goal Percentage, Career: Steve Kerr—.455

Most Three-Point Field Goals, Season: Dan Majerle, Phoe—192, 1993-94

Highest Three-Point Field Goal Percentage, Season: Jon Sundvold, Mia—.522, 1988-89

Most Three-Point Field Goals, Game: 10—Brian Shaw, Miami vs Milwaukee, 4/8/93

*First Year of Shot: 1979-80

Steals

Most Steals, Career: 2,310—Maurice Cheeks

Most Steals, Season: 301—Alvin Robertson, San Antonio, 1985-86

Most Steals, Game: 11—Larry Kenon, San Antonio vs Kansas City, 12/26/76

Rebounds

MOST REBOUNDS, CAREER

Wilt Chamberlain	23,924
Bill Russell	21,620
Kareem Abdul-Jabbar	17,440
Elvin Hayes	16,279
Moses Malone	16,166
Nate Thurmond	14,464
Walt Bellamy	14,241
Robert Parish	13,973
Wes Unseld	13,769
Jerry Lucas	12,942

MOST REBOUNDS, SEASON

Wilt Chamberlain, Phil	2,149	1960-61
Wilt Chamberlain, Phil	2,052	1961-62
Wilt Chamberlain, Phil	1,957	1966-67
Wilt Chamberlain, Phil	1,952	1967-68
Wilt Chamberlain, SF	1,946	1962-63
Wilt Chamberlain, Phil	1,943	1965-66
Wilt Chamberlain, Phil	1,941	1959-60
Bill Russell, Bos	1,930	1963-64
Bill Russell, Bos	1,878	1964-65
Bill Russell, Bos	1,868	1960-61

MOST REBOUNDS, GAME

	Player, Team	Opp	Date
55	Wilt Chamberlain, Phi	Bos	11/24/60
51	Bill Russell, Bos	Syr	2/5/60
49	Bill Russell, Bos	Phi	11/16/57
49	Bill Russell, Bos	Det	3/11/65
45	Wilt Chamberlain, Phil	Syr	2/6/60
45	Wilt Chamberlain, Phil	LA	1/21/61

Assists

MOST ASSISTS, CAREER

Magic Johnson	9,921
Oscar Robertson	9,887
John Stockton	9,383
Isiah Thomas	9,061
Maurice Cheeks	7,392

MOST ASSISTS, SEASON

John Stockton, Utah	1,164	1990-91
John Stockton, Utah	1,134	1989-90
John Stockton, Utah	1,128	1987-88
Isiah Thomas, Det	1,123	1984-85
John Stockton, Utah	1,126	1991-92

MOST ASSISTS, GAME: 30—Scott Skiles, Orlando vs Denver, 12/30/90

Blocked Shots

MOST BLOCKED SHOTS, CAREER

Kareem Abdul-Jabbar	3,189
Mark Eaton	3,064
Hakeem Olajuwon	2,741
Wayne (Tree) Rollins	2,471

MOST BLOCKED SHOTS, SEASON

Mark Eaton, Utah	456	1984-85
Manute Bol, Wash	397	1985-86
Elmore Smith, LA	393	1973-74

MOST BLOCKED SHOTS, GAME: 17—Elmore Smith, LA Lakers vs Portland, 10/28/73

NBA Season Leaders

Scoring

1946-47	Joe Fulks, Phil	1389	1971-72	Kareem Abdul-Jabber, Mil	34.8
1947-48	Max Zaslofsky, Chi	1007	1972-73	Nate Archibald, KC-Oma	34.0
1948-49	George Mikan, Minn	1698	1973-74	Bob McAdoo, Buff	30.6
1949-50	George Mikan, Minn	1865	1974-75	Bob McAdoo, Buff	34.5
1950-51	George Mikan, Minn	1932	1975-76	Bob McAdoo, Buff	31.1
1951-52	Paul Arizin, Phil	1674	1976-77	Pete Maravich, NO	31.1
1952-53	Neil Johnston, Phil	1564	1977-78	George Gervin, SA	27.2
1953-54	Neil Johnston, Phil	1759	1978-79	George Gervin, SA	29.6
1954-55	Neil Johnston, Phil	1631	1979-80	George Gervin, SA	33.1
1955-56	Bob Pettit, StL	1849	1980-81	Adrian Dantley, Utah	30.7
1956-57	Paul Arizin, Phil	1817	1981-82	George Gervin, SA	32.3
1957-58	George Yardley, Det	2001	1982-83	Alex English, Den	28.4
1958-59	Bob Pettit, StL	2105	1983-84	Adrian Dantley, Utah	30.6
1959-60	Wilt Chamberlain, Phil	2707	1984-85	Bernard King, NY	32.9
1960-61	Wilt Chamberlain, Phil	3033	1985-86	Dominique Wilkins, Atl	30.3
1961-62	Wilt Chamberlain, Phil	4029	1986-87	Michael Jordan, Chi	37.1
1962-63	Wilt Chamberlain, SF	3586	1987-88	Michael Jordan, Chi	35.0
1963-64	Wilt Chamberlain, SF	2948	1988-89	Michael Jordan, Chi	32.5
1964-65	Wilt Chamberlain, SF-Phil	2534	1989-90	Michael Jordan, Chi	33.6
1965-66	Wilt Chamberlain, Phil	2649	1990-91	Michael Jordan, Chi	31.5
1966-67	Rick Barry, SF	2775	1991-92	Michael Jordan, Chi	30.1
1967-68	Dave Bing, Det	2142	1992-93	Michael Jordan, Chi	32.6
1968-69	Elvin Hayes, SD	2327	1993-94	David Robinson, SA	29.8
1969-70	Jerry West, LA	*31.2			
1970-71	Kareem Abdul-Jabbar, Mil	31.7			

*Based on per game average since 1969-70.

Rebounding

1950-51	Dolph Schayes, Syr	1080
1951-52	Larry Foust, FW	880
	Mel Hutchins, Mil	880
1952-53	George Mikan, Minn	1007
1953-54	Harry Gallatin, NY	1098
1954-55	Neil Johnston, Phil	1085
1955-56	Bob Pettit, StL	1164
1956-57	Maurice Stokes, Roch	1256
1957-58	Bill Russell, Bos	1564
1958-59	Bill Russell, Bos	1612
1959-60	Wilt Chamberlain, Phil	1941
1960-61	Wilt Chamberlain, Phil	2149
1961-62	Wilt Chamberlain, Phil	2052
1962-63	Wilt Chamberlain, SF	1946
1963-64	Bill Russell, Bos	1930
1964-65	Bill Russell, Bos	1878
1965-66	Wilt Chamberlain, Phil	1943
1966-67	Wilt Chamberlain, Phil	1957
1967-68	Wilt Chamberlain, Phil	1952
1968-69	Wilt Chamberlain, LA	1712
1969-70	Elvin Hayes, SD	*16.9
1970-71	Wilt Chamberlain, LA	18.2
1971-72	Wilt Chamberlain, LA	19.2
1972-73	Wilt Chamberlain, LA	18.6
1973-74	Elvin Hayes, Capital	18.1
1974-75	Wes Unseld, Wash	14.8
1975-76	Kareem Abdul-Jabbar, LA	16.9
1976-77	Bill Walton, Port	14.4
1977-78	Len Robinson, NO	15.7
1978-79	Moses Malone, Hou	17.6
1979-80	Swen Nater, SD	15.0
1980-81	Moses Malone, Hou	14.8
1981-82	Moses Malone, Hou	14.7
1982-83	Moses Malone, Phil	15.3
1983-84	Moses Malone, Phil	13.4
1984-85	Moses Malone, Phil	13.1
1985-86	Bill Laimbeer, Det	13.1
1986-87	Charles Barkley, Phil	14.6
1987-88	Michael Cage, LA Clippers	13.0
1988-89	Hakeem Olajuwon, Hou	13.5
1989-90	Hakeem Olajuwon, Hou	14.0
1990-91	David Robinson, SA	13.0
1991-92	Dennis Rodman, Detroit	18.7
1992-93	Dennis Rodman, Detroit	18.3
1993-94	Dennis Rodman, San Antonio	17.3

*Based on per game average since 1969-70.

Assists

1946-47	Ernie Calverly, Prov	202
1947-48	Howie Dallmar, Phil	120
1948-49	Bob Davies, Roch	321
1949-50	Dick McGuire, NY	386
1950-51	Andy Phillip, Phil	414
1951-52	Andy Phillip, Phil	539
1952-53	Bob Cousy, Bos	547
1953-54	Bob Cousy, Bos	578
1954-55	Bob Cousy, Bos	557
1955-56	Bob Cousy, Bos	642
1956-57	Bob Cousy, Bos	478
1957-58	Bob Cousy, Bos	463
1958-59	Bob Cousy, Bos	557
1959-60	Bob Cousy, Bos	715
1960-61	Oscar Robertson, Cin	690
1961-62	Oscar Robertson, Cin	899
1962-63	Guy Rodgers, SF	825
1963-64	Oscar Robertson, Cin	868
1964-65	Oscar Robertson, Cin	861
1965-66	Oscar Robertson, Cin	847
1966-67	Guy Rodgers, Chi	908
1967-68	Wilt Chamberlain, Phil	702
1968-69	Oscar Robertson, Cin	772
1969-70	Len Wilkens, Sea	*9.1
1970-71	Norm Van Lier, Cin	10.1
1971-72	Jerry West, LA	9.7
1972-73	Nate Archibald, KC-Oma	11.4
1973-74	Ernie DiGregorio, Buff	8.2
1974-75	Kevin Porter, Wash	8.0
1975-76	Don Watts, Sea	8.1
1976-77	Don Buse, Ind	8.5
1977-78	Kevin Porter, NJ-Det	10.2
1978-79	Kevin Porter, Det	13.4
1979-80	Micheal Richardson, NY	10.1
1980-81	Kevin Porter, Wash	9.1
1981-82	Johnny Moore, SA	9.6
1982-83	Magic Johnson, LA	10.5
1983-84	Magic Johnson, LA	13.1
1984-85	Isiah Thomas, Det	13.9
1985-86	Magic Johnson, LA Lakers	12.6
1986-87	Magic Johnson, LA Lakers	12.2
1987-88	John Stockton, Utah	13.8
1988-89	John Stockton, Utah	13.6
1989-90	John Stockton, Utah	14.5
1990-91	John Stockton, Utah	14.2
1991-92	John Stockton, Utah	13.7
1992-93	John Stockton, Utah	12.0
1993-94	John Stockton, Utah	12.6

*Based on per game average since 1969-70.

Field Goal Percentage

1946-47	Bob Feerick, Wash	40.1
1947-48	Bob Feerick, Wash	34.0
1948-49	Arnie Risen, Roch	42.3
1949-50	Alex Groza, Ind	47.8
1950-51	Alex Groza, Ind	47.0
1951-52	Paul Arizin, Phil	44.8
1952-53	Neil Johnston, Phil	45.2
1953-54	Ed Macauley, Bos	48.6
1954-55	Larry Foust, FW	48.7
1955-56	Neil Johnston, Phil	45.7
1956-57	Neil Johnston, Phil	44.7
1957-58	Jack Twyman, Cin	45.2
1958-59	Ken Sears, NY	49.0
1959-60	Ken Sears, NY	47.7
1960-61	Wilt Chamberlain, Phil	50.9
1961-62	Walt Bellamy, Chi	51.9
1962-63	Wilt Chamberlain, SF	52.8
1963-64	Jerry Lucas, Cin	52.7
1964-65	Wilt Chamberlain, SF-Phil	51.0
1965-66	Wilt Chamberlain, Phil	54.0
1966-67	Wilt Chamberlain, Phil	68.3
1967-68	Wilt Chamberlain, Phil	59.5
1968-69	Wilt Chamberlain, LA	58.3
1969-70	Johnny Green, Cin	55.9

Field Goal Percentage *(Cont.)*

1970-71	Johnny Green, Cin	58.7	1982-83	Artis Gilmore, SA	62.6
1971-72	Wilt Chamberlain, LA	64.9	1983-84	Artis Gilmore, SA	63.1
1972-73	Wilt Chamberlain, LA	72.7	1984-85	James Donaldson, LA Clippers	63.7
1973-74	Bob McAdoo, Buff	54.7	1985-86	Steve Johnson, SA	63.2
1974-75	Don Nelson, Bos	53.9	1986-87	Kevin McHale, Bos	60.4
1975-76	Wes Unseld, Wash	56.1	1987-88	Kevin McHale, Bos	60.4
1976-77	Kareem Abdul-Jabbar, LA	57.9	1988-89	Dennis Rodman, Det	59.5
1977-78	Bobby Jones, Den	57.8	1989-90	Mark West, Phoe	62.5
1978-79	Cedric Maxwell, Bos	58.4	1990-91	Buck Williams, Port	60.2
1979-80	Cedric Maxwell, Bos	60.9	1991-92	Buck Williams, Port	60.4
1980-81	Artis Gilmore, Chi	67.0	1992-93	Cedric Ceballos, Phoe	57.6
1981-82	Artis Gilmore, Chi	65.2	1993-94	Shaquille O'Neal, Orl	59.9

Free Throw Percentage

1946-47	Fred Scolari, Wash	81.1	1970-71	Chet Walker, Chi	85.9
1947-48	Bob Feerick, Wash	78.8	1971-72	Jack Marin, Balt	89.4
1948-49	Bob Feerick, Wash	85.9	1972-73	Rick Barry, GS	90.2
1949-50	Max Zaslofsky, Chi	84.3	1973-74	Ernie DiGregorio, Buff	90.2
1950-51	Joe Fulks, Phil	85.5	1974-75	Rick Barry, GS	90.4
1951-52	Bob Wanzer, Roch	90.4	1975-76	Rick Barry, GS	92.3
1952-53	Bill Sharman, Bos	85.0	1976-77	Ernie DiGregorio, Buff	94.5
1953-54	Bill Sharman, Bos	84.4	1977-78	Rick Barry, GS	92.4
1954-55	Bill Sharman, Bos	89.7	1978-79	Rick Barry, Hou	94.7
1955-56	Bill Sharman, Bos	86.7	1979-80	Rick Barry, Hou	93.5
1956-57	Bill Sharman, Bos	90.5	1980-81	Calvin Murphy, Hou	95.8
1957-58	Dolph Schayes, Syr	90.4	1981-82	Kyle Macy, Phoe	89.9
1958-59	Bill Sharman, Bos	93.2	1982-83	Calvin Murphy, Hou	92.0
1959-60	Dolph Schayes, Syr	89.2	1983-84	Larry Bird, Bos	88.8
1960-61	Bill Sharman, Bos	92.1	1984-85	Kyle Macy, Phoe	90.7
1961-62	Dolph Schayes, Syr	89.6	1985-86	Larry Bird, Bos	89.6
1962-63	Larry Costello, Syr	88.1	1986-87	Larry Bird, Bos	91.0
1963-64	Oscar Robertson, Cin	85.3	1987-88	Jack Sikma, Mil	92.2
1964-65	Larry Costello, Phil	87.7	1988-89	Magic Johnson, LA Lakers	91.1
1965-66	Larry Siegfried, Bos	88.1	1989-90	Larry Bird, Bos	93.0
1966-67	Adrian Smith, Cin	90.3	1990-91	Reggie Miller, Ind	91.8
1967-68	Oscar Robertson, Cin	87.3	1991-92	Mark Price, Clev	94.7
1968-69	Larry Siegfried, Bos	86.4	1992-93	Mark Price, Clev	94.8
1969-70	Flynn Robinson, Mil	89.8	1993-94	Mahmoud Abdul-Rauf, Den	95.6

Three-Point Field Goal Percentage

1979-80	Fred Brown, Sea	44.3	1987-88	Craig Hodges, Mil-Phoe	49.1
1980-81	Brian Taylor, SD	38.3	1988-89	Jon Sundvold, Mia	52.2
1981-82	Campy Russell, NY	43.9	1989-90	Steve Kerr, Clev	50.7
1982-83	Mike Dunleavy, SA	34.5	1990-91	Jim Les, Sac	46.1
1983-84	Darrell Griffith, Utah	36.1	1991-92	Dana Barros, Sea	44.6
1984-85	Byron Scott, LA Lakers	43.3	1992-93	B.J. Armstrong, Chi	45.3
1985-86	Craig Hodges, Mil	45.1	1993-94	Tracy Murray, Por	45.9
1986-87	Kiki Vandeweghe, Por	48.1			

Steals

1973-74	Larry Steele, Por	2.68	1984-85	Micheal Richardson, NJ	2.96
1974-75	Rick Barry, GS	2.85	1985-86	Alvin Robertson, SA	3.67
1975-76	Don Watts, Sea	3.18	1986-87	Alvin Robertson, SA	3.21
1976-77	Don Buse, Ind	3.47	1987-88	Michael Jordan, Chi	3.16
1977-78	Ron Lee, Phoe	2.74	1988-89	John Stockton, Utah	3.21
1978-79	M. L. Carr, Det	2.46	1989-90	Michael Jordan, Chi	2.77
1979-80	Micheal Richardson, NY	3.23	1990-91	Alvin Robertson, Mil	3.04
1980-81	Magic Johnson, LA	3.43	1991-92	John Stockton, Utah	2.98
1981-82	Magic Johnson, LA	2.67	1992-93	Michael Jordan, Chi	2.83
1982-83	Micheal Richardson, GS-NJ	2.84	1993-94	Nate McMillan, Sea	2.96
1983-84	Rickey Green, Utah	2.65			

Blocked Shots

1973-74	Elmore Smith, LA	4.85	1984-85	Mark Eaton, Utah	5.56
1974-75	Kareem Abdul-Jabbar, Mil	3.26	1985-86	Manute Bol, Wash	4.96
1975-76	Kareem Abdul-Jabbar, LA	4.12	1986-87	Mark Eaton, Utah	4.06
1976-77	Bill Walton, Port	3.25	1987-88	Mark Eaton, Utah	3.71
1977-78	George Johnson, NJ	3.38	1988-89	Manute Bol, GS	4.31
1978-79	Kareem Abdul-Jabbar, LA	3.95	1989-90	Hakeem Olajuwon, Hou	4.59
1979-80	Kareem Abdul-Jabbar, LA	3.41	1990-91	Hakeem Olajuwon, Hou	3.95
1980-81	George Johnson, SA	3.39	1991-92	David Robinson, SA	4.49
1981-82	George Johnson, SA	3.12	1992-93	Hakeem Olajuwon, Hou	4.17
1982-83	Wayne Rollins, Atl	4.29	1993-94	Dikembe Mutombo, Den	4.10
1983-84	Mark Eaton, Utah	4.28			

NBA All-Star Game Results

Year	Result	Site	Winning Coach	Most Valuable Player
1951	East 111, West 94	Boston	Joe Lapchick	Ed Macauley, Bos
1952	East 108, West 91	Boston	Al Cervi	Paul Arizin, Phil
1953	West 79, East 75	Ft Wayne	John Kundla	George Mikan, Minn
1954	East 98, West 93 (OT)	New York	Joe Lapchick	Bob Cousy, Bos
1955	East 100, West 91	New York	Al Cervi	Bill Sharman, Bos
1956	West 108, East 94	Rochester	Charley Eckman	Bob Pettit, StL
1957	East 109, West 97	Boston	Red Auerbach	Bob Cousy, Bos
1958	East 130, West 118	St Louis	Red Auerbach	Bob Pettit, StL
1959	West 124, East 108	Detroit	Ed Macauley	Bob Pettit, StL
				Elgin Baylor, Minn
1960	East 125, West 115	Philadelphia	Red Auerbach	Wilt Chamberlain, Phil
1961	West 153, East 131	Syracuse	Paul Seymour	Oscar Robertson, Cin
1962	West 150, East 130	St Louis	Fred Schaus	Bob Pettit, StL
1963	East 115, West 108	Los Angeles	Red Auerbach	Bill Russell, Bos
1964	East 111, West 107	Boston	Red Auerbach	Oscar Robertson, Cin
1965	East 124, West 123	St Louis	Red Auerbach	Jerry Lucas, Cin
1966	East 137, West 94	Cincinnati	Red Auerbach	Adrian Smith, Cin
1967	West 135, East 120	San Francisco	Fred Schaus	Rick Barry, SF
1968	East 144, West 124	New York	Alex Hannum	Hal Greer, Phil
1969	East 123, West 112	Baltimore	Gene Shue	Oscar Robertson, Cin
1970	East 142, West 135	Philadelphia	Red Holzman	Willis Reed, NY
1971	West 108, East 107	San Diego	Larry Costello	Lenny Wilkens, Sea
1972	West 112, East 110	Los Angeles	Bill Sharman	Jerry West, LA
1973	East 104, West 84	Chicago	Tom Heinsohn	Dave Cowens, Bos
1974	West 134, East 123	Seattle	Larry Costello	Bob Lanier, Det
1975	East 108, West 102	Phoenix	K. C. Jones	Walt Frazier, NY
1976	East 123, West 109	Philadelphia	Tom Heinsohn	Dave Bing, Wash
1977	West 125, East 124	Milwaukee	Larry Brown	Julius Erving, Phil
1978	East 133, West 125	Atlanta	Billy Cunningham	Randy Smith, Buff
1979	West 134, East 129	Detroit	Lenny Wilkens	David Thompson, Den
1980	East 144, West 135 (OT)	Washington	Billy Cunningham	George Gervin, SA
1981	East 123, West 120	Cleveland	Billy Cunningham	Nate Archibald, Bos
1982	East 120, West 118	New Jersey	Bill Fitch	Larry Bird, Bos
1983	East 132, West 123	Los Angeles	Billy Cunningham	Julius Erving, Phil
1984	East 154, West 145 (OT)	Denver	K. C. Jones	Isiah Thomas, Det
1985	West 140, East 129	Indiana	Pat Riley	Ralph Sampson, Hou
1986	East 139, West 132	Dallas	K. C. Jones	Isiah Thomas, Det
1987	West 154, East 149 (OT)	Seattle	Pat Riley	Tom Chambers, Sea
1988	East 138, West 133	Chicago	Mike Fratello	Michael Jordan, Chi
1989	West 143, East 134	Houston	Pat Riley	Karl Malone, Utah
1990	East 130, West 113	Miami	Chuck Daly	Magic Johnson, LA Lakers
1991	East 116, West 114	Charlotte	Chris Ford	Charles Barkley, Phil
1992	West 153, East 113	Orlando	Don Nelson	Magic Johnson, LA Lakers
1993	West 135, East 132	Salt Lake City	Paul Westphal	Karl Malone, Utah
				John Stockton, Utah
1994	East 127, West 118	Minneapolis	Lenny Wilkens	Scottie Pippen, Chi

Members of the Basketball Hall of Fame

Contributors

Senda Abbott (1984)
Forest C. "Phog" Allen (1959)
Clair F. Bee (1967)
Walter A. Brown (1965)
John W. Bunn (1964)
Bob Douglas (1971)
Al Duer (1981)
Clifford Fagan (1983)
Harry A. Fisher (1973)
Larry Fleisher (1991)
Edward Gottlieb (1971)
Luther H. Gulick (1959)
Lester Harrison (1979)
Ferenc Hepp (1980)
Edward J. Hickox (1959)

Paul D. "Tony" Hinkle (1965)
Ned Irish (1964)
R. William Jones (1964)
J. Walter Kennedy (1980)
Emil S. Liston (1974)
John B. McLendon (1978)
Bill Mokray (1965)
Ralph Morgan (1959)
Frank Morgenweck (1962)
James Naismith (1959)
Peter F. Newell (1978)
John J. O'Brien (1961)
Larry O'Brien (1991)
Harold G. Olsen (1959)
Maurice Podoloff (1973)

H.V. Porter (1960)
William A. Reid (1963)
Elmer Ripley (1972)
Lynn W. St. John (1962)
Abe Saperstein (1970)
Arthur A. Schabinger (1961)
Amos Alonzo Stagg (1959)
Boris Stankovic (1991)
Edward Steitz (1983)
Chuck Taylor (1968)
Oswald Tower (1959)
Arthur L. Trester (1961)
Clifford Wells (1971)
Lou Wilke (1982)

Players

Nate "Tiny" Archibald (1991)
Paul J. Arizin (1977)
Thomas B. Barlow (1980)
Rick Barry (1986)
Elgin Baylor (1976)
John Beckman (1972)
Walt Bellamy (1993)
Sergei Belov (1992)
Dave Bing (1989)
Carol Blazejowski (1994)
Bennie Borgmann (1961)
Bill Bradley (1982)
Joseph Brennan (1974)
Al Cervi (1984)
Wilt Chamberlain (1978)
Charles "Tarzan" Cooper (1976)
Bob Cousy (1970)
Dave Cowens (1991)
Billy Cunningham (1985)
Bob Davies (1969)
Forrest S. DeBernardi (1961)
Dave DeBusschere (1982)
H. G. "Dutch" Dehnert (1968)
Paul Endacott (1971)
Julius Erving (1993)
Harold "Bud" Foster (1964)
Walter "Clyde" Frazier (1986)
Max "Marty" Friedman (1971)
Joe Fulks (1977)
Lauren "Laddie" Gale (1976)
Harry "the Horse" Gallatin (1991)
William Gates (1988)
Tom Gola (1975)

Hal Greer (1981)
Robert "Ace" Gruenig (1963)
Clifford O. Hagan (1977)
Victor Hanson (1960)
John Havlicek (1983)
Connie Hawkins (1992)
Elvin Hayes (1989)
Tom Heinsohn (1985)
Nat Holman (1964)
Robert J. Houbregs (1986)
Chuck Hyatt (1959)
Dan Issel (1993)
Harry (Buddy) Jeannette (1994)
William C. Johnson (1976)
D. Neil Johnston (1989)
K. C. Jones (1988)
Sam Jones (1983)
Edward "Moose" Krause (1975)
Bob Kurland (1961)
Joe Lapchick (1966)
Clyde Lovellette (1987)
Jerry Lucas (1979)
Angelo "Hank" Luisetti (1959)
C. Edward Macauley (1960)
Peter P. Maravich (1986)
Slater Martin (1981)
Branch McCracken (1960)
Jack McCracken (1962)
Bobby McDermott (1987)
Dick McGuire (1993)
Ann Meyers (1993)
George L. Mikan (1959)
Earl Monroe (1989)

Calvin Murphy (1993)
Charles "Stretch" Murphy (1960)
H. O. "Pat" Page (1962)
Bob Pettit (1970)
Andy Phillip (1961)
Jim Pollard (1977)
Frank Ramsey (1981)
Willis Reed (1981)
Oscar Robertson (1979)
John S. Roosma (1961)
Bill Russell (1974)
John "Honey" Russell (1964)
Adolph Schayes (1972)
Ernest J. Schmidt (1973)
John J. Schommer (1959)
Barney Sedran (1962)
Uljana Semjonova (1993)
Bill Sharman (1975)
Christian Steinmetz (1961)
Lusia Harris Stewart (1992)
John A. "Cat" Thompson (1962)
Nate Thurmond (1984)
Jack Twyman (1982)
Wes Unseld (1987)
Robert "Fuzzy" Vandivier (1974)
Edward A. Wachter (1961)
Bill Walton (1993)
Robert F. Wanzer (1986)
Jerry West (1979)
Nera White (1992)
Lenny Wilkens (1988)
John R. Wooden (1960)

Coaches

Harold Anderson (1984)
Red Auerbach (1968)
Sam Barry (1978)
Ernest A. Blood (1960)
Howard G. Cann (1967)
H. Clifford Carlson (1959)
Lou Carnesecca (1992)
Ben Carnevale (1969)
Everett Case (1981)
Denny Crum (1994)
Chuck Daly (1994)
Everett S. Dean (1966)

Edgar A. Diddle (1971)
Bruce Drake (1972)
Clarence Gaines (1981)
Jack Gardner (1983)
Amory T. "Slats" Gill (1967)
Marv Harshman (1984)
Edgar S. Hickey (1978)
Howard A. Hobson (1965)
Red Holzman (1985)
Hank Iba (1968)
Alvin F. "Doggie" Julian (1967)
Frank W. Keaney (1960)

George E. Keogan (1961)
Bob Knight (1991)
Ward L. Lambert (1960)
Harry Litwack (1975)
Kenneth D. Loeffler (1964)
A. C. "Dutch" Lonborg (1972)
Arad A. McCutchan (1980)
Al McGuire (1992)
Frank McGuire (1976)
Walter E. Meanwell (1959)
Raymond J. Meyer (1978)
Ralph Miller (1987)

Note: Year of election in parentheses.

Members of the Basketball Hall of Fame (Cont.)

Coaches (Cont.)

Jack Ramsay (1992)
Cesare Rubini (1994)
Adolph F. Rupp (1968)
Leonard D. Sachs (1961)

Everett F. Shelton (1979)
Dean Smith (1982)
Fred R. Taylor (1985)
Bertha Teague (1984)

Margaret Wade (1984)
Stanley H. Watts (1985)
John R. Wooden (1972)

Referees

James E. Enright (1978)
George T. Hepbron (1960)
George Hoyt (1961)
Matthew P. Kennedy (1959)
Lloyd Leith (1982)
Zigmund J. Mihalik (1985)
John P. Nucatola (1977)
Ernest C. Quigley (1961)
J. Dallas Shirley (1979)
David Tobey (1961)
David H. Walsh (1961)

Teams

Buffalo Germans (1961)
First Team (1959)
Original Celtics (1959)
Renaissance (1963)

Note: Year of election in parentheses.

ABA Champions

Year	Champion	Series	Loser	Winning Coach
1968	Pittsburgh Pipers	4-2	New Orleans Bucs	Vince Cazetta
1969	Oakland Oaks	4-1	Indiana Pacers	Alex Hannum
1970	Indiana Pacers	4-2	Los Angeles Stars	Bob Leonard
1971	Utah Stars	4-3	Kentucky Colonels	Bill Sharman
1972	Indiana Pacers	4-2	New York Nets	Bob Leonard
1973	Indiana Pacers	4-3	Kentucky Colonels	Bob Leonard
1974	New York Nets	4-1	Utah Stars	Kevin Loughery
1975	Kentucky Colonels	4-1	Indiana Pacers	Hubie Brown
1976	New York Nets	4-2	Denver Nuggets	Kevin Loughery

ABA Postseason Awards

Most Valuable Player

1967-68	Connie Hawkins, Pitt
1968-69	Mel Daniels, Ind
1969-70	Spencer Haywood, Den
1970-71	Mel Daniels, Ind
1971-72	Artis Gilmore, Ken
1972-73	Billy Cunningham, Car
1973-74	Julius Erving, NY
1974-75	Julius Erving, NY
	George McGinnis, Ind
1975-76	Julius Erving, NY

Rookie of the Year

1967-68	Mel Daniels, Minn
1968-69	Warren Armstrong, Oak
1969-70	Spencer Haywood, Den
1970-71	Charlie Scott, Vir
	Dan Issel, Ken
1971-72	Artis Gilmore, Ken
1972-73	Brian Taylor, NY
1973-74	Swen Nater, SA
1974-75	Marvin Barnes, SL
1975-76	David Thompson, Den

Coach of the Year

1967-68	Vince Cazetta, Pitt
1968-69	Alex Hannum, Oak
1969-70	Bill Sharman, LA
	Joe Belmont, Den
1970-71	Al Bianchi, Vir
1971-72	Tom Nissalke, Dall
1972-73	Larry Brown, Car
1973-74	Babe McCarthy, Ken
	Joe Mullaney, Utah
1974-75	Larry Brown, Den
1975-76	Larry Brown, Den

THEY SAID IT

Derrick Coleman, New Jersey Net forward, on why he turned down an invitation to hunt with teammate Jayson Williams: "I'm not going hunting with anyone who plays the same position as me."

ABA Season Leaders

Scoring

Year	Player	GP	Pts	Avg
1967-68	Connie Hawkins, Pitt	70	1875	26.8
1968-69	Rick Barry, Oak	35	1190	34.0
1969-70	Spencer Haywood, Den	84	2519	30.0
1970-71	Dan Issel, Ken	83	2480	29.4
1971-72	Charlie Scott, Vir	73	2524	34.6
1972-73	Julius Erving, Vir	71	2268	31.9
1973-74	Julius Erving, NY	84	2299	27.4
1974-75	George McGinnis, Ind	79	2353	29.8
1975-76	Julius Erving, NY	84	2462	29.3

Rebounds

Year	Player	Avg
1967-68	Mel Daniels, Minn	15.6
1968-69	Mel Daniels, Ind	16.5
1969-70	Spencer Haywood, Den	19.5
1970-71	Mel Daniels, Ind	18.0
1971-72	Artis Gilmore, Ken	17.8
1972-73	Artis Gilmore, Ken	17.5
1973-74	Artis Gilmore, Ken	18.3
1974-75	Swen Nater, SA	16.4
1975-76	Artis Gilmore, Ken	15.5

Assists

Year	Player	Avg
1967-68	Larry Brown, NO	6.5
1968-69	Larry Brown, Oak	7.1
1969-70	Larry Brown, Wash	7.1
1970-71	Bill Melchionni, NY	8.3
1971-72	Bill Melchionni, NY	8.4
1972-73	Bill Melchionni, NY	7.5
1973-74	Al Smith, Den	8.2
1974-75	Mack Calvin, Den	7.7
1975-76	Don Buse, Ind	8.2

Steals

Year	Player	Avg
1973-74	Ted McClain, Car	2.98
1974-75	Brian Taylor, NY	2.80
1975-76	Don Buse, Ind	4.12

Blocked Shots

Year	Player	Avg
1973-74	Caldwell Jones, SD	4.00
1974-75	Caldwell Jones, SD	3.24
1975-76	Billy Paultz, SA	3.05

*World Championship of Basketball

Year	Winner	Runner-Up	Score	Site
1950	Argentina	United States	†	Rio de Janeiro
1954	United States	Brazil	†	Rio de Janeiro
1959	Brazil	United States	†	Santiago, Chile
1963	Brazil	Yugoslavia	†	Rio de Janeiro
1967	Soviet Union	Yugoslavia	†	Montevideo, Uruguay
1970	Yugoslavia	Brazil	†	Ljubljana, Yugoslavia
1974	Soviet Union	Yugoslavia	†	San Juan
1978	Yugoslavia	Soviet Union	82-81 OT	Manila
1982	Soviet Union	United States	95-94	Cali, Colombia
1986	United States	Soviet Union	87-85	Madrid
1990	Yugoslavia	Soviet Union	92-75	Buenos Aires
1994	United States	Russia	137-91	Toronto

*U.S. professionals began competing in 1994.
†Result determined by overall record in final round of competition.

Offensive Driver

After pleading guilty last April to carrying a concealed handgun in his car, Houston Rocket guard Vernon Maxwell publicly apologized for the incident. Maxwell said he realized that he was a role model and should not be involved in anything illegal. He then said he planned to carry a shotgun in his car, since *that* is legal.

THEY SAID IT

Charles Barkley, on Tonya Harding's calling herself the Charles Barkley of figure skating: "I was going to sue her for defamation of character, but then I realized that I have no character."

College Basketball

Hog Wild

APRIL 11, 1994 $2.95 (CAN. $3.95)

RAZORBACKS
34

Corliss Williamson
Powers Arkansas to the
National Championship

JOHN W. McDONOUGH

Razorbacks Reign

A topsy-turvy season ended with a compelling title game and a crown for Arkansas | by ALEXANDER WOLFF

COLLEGE BASKETBALL SEASONS ARE usually quite simple: They begin with Midnight Madness, end with March Madness and have 19 weeks of relative sanity in between. But the 1993–94 season never had a chance to stow its straitjacket in a closet. The year was a singularly bizarre one from the moment the consensus preseason No. 1, North Carolina, lost in the semifinals of the preseason NIT until the Final Four sorted out the entire mess in Charlotte. Team after team assumed the top position in the Associated Press poll only to give it up after being upset the next week. (Over one stretch the No. 1 spot in the AP Top 25 changed hands six times in as many weeks.) In the end, Arkansas, the voters' choice in most of the weekly polls, won a stirring championship game that delighted a longtime Razorback fan and another voters' choice, President Bill Clinton.

There were other features, laudable and lamentable, marking the year:

• Glenn (Big Dog) Robinson led Purdue to a 29–5 mark, a Big Ten title and the Boilermakers' best postseason performance in six seasons. After winning virtually every national player of the year award, he decided to enter the NBA draft even though he had a year of eligibility remaining.
• The Black Coaches Association threatened a January boycott to protest a range of NCAA actions, including the college presidents' refusal to reinstate a 14th scholarship for men's basketball. A walkout was averted, and by April the two sides had reached tentative agreement on a variety of issues. The coaches won a commitment to reexamine the use of standardized tests in determining freshman eligibility, and the NCAA promised to beef up minority representation on its executive staff and committees.
• Coaches grabbed other headlines as well. John Chaney of Temple threatened to kill Massachusetts coach John Calipari following one game. At others, Xavier's Pete Gillen and Cincinnati's Bob Huggins, and

Robinson, Purdue's Big Dog all season long, couldn't resist the lure of the lucrative NBA.

Arizona's Lute Olson and California's Todd Bozeman, engaged in shouting matches. And Ricky Byrdsong of Northwestern took a leave of absence after wandering into the stands during one Wildcat game.

• Led by its fierce, cancer-survivor coach, Norm Stewart, and fearless guard Melvin Booker, Missouri came back from a 52-point December nonconference loss to the eventual NCAA champs and navigated the Big Eight season undefeated. Stewart and an old friend and in-state rival, St. Louis coach Charlie Spoonhour, received most Coach of the Year recognition.

• The Big East, derided and in decline only a season earlier, began its rehabilitation. To be sure, the six bids the league received to the NCAA tournament overstated the conference's overall strength in 1993–94. But Connecticut reached the regional semifinals with a relatively young team and All-America Donyell Marshall. Villanova won the postseason NIT. Two of the nation's top five high schoolers, Felipe Lopez and Zendon Hamilton, chose St. John's, which was heartening news for the Redmen, who suffered through a sub-.500 season for the first time in 31 years. Energetic coaches Gillen and Ralph Willard took over at Providence and Pittsburgh, respectively, while Boston College coach Jim O'Brien, thought to be on the verge of getting the boot only a few weeks before, led the Eagles to the regional final. BC's four senior starters beat Dean Smith's North Carolina Tar Heels and Bob Knight's Indiana Hoosiers back-to-back,

thus winning for their coach a contract extension.

• The elimination of the five-second closely guarded rule allowed Duke to put the ball in the hands of its wondrous senior, Grant Hill, who took his sweet time dribbling, driving, passing and shooting his Blue Devils into the NCAA title game. Duke coach Mike Krzyzewski has now guided teams to seven of the last nine Final Fours.

• Foul shooting turned most foul. Division I free throw shooters went a collective .671, the worst since 1958–59. At the same time, the three-point shot became more commonplace than ever. In 1986–87, the three-pointer's rookie season, about one in every six shots came from beyond the arc. Last season more than one in four did, a frequency that nearly caused the rules committee to move the line out from its current distance of 19' 9".

• While Charlotte, N.C., hosted a Final Four, North Carolina's Charlotte won one. The Tar Heels' Charlotte Smith, following instructions drawn up by her coach, Sylvia Hatchell, got free beyond the three-point line, took an inbounds pass and sank a three-pointer with scarcely a second left to enable UNC to beat Louisiana Tech 60–59 for the NCAA women's championship. Smith is a cousin of David Thompson, the former N.C. State star who led the Wolfpack to a national title precisely 20 years earlier, but she wore number 23, which ex–Tar Heel great Michael Jordan sported during his days in Chapel Hill. Smith's response when the pedigree of her number was pointed out to her is a measure of how far the women's game has come. "I wasn't aware [that she wore Jordan's number]," she said. "I wear the number because it's the same one my mother wore in high school."

A three-pointer of similar timeliness served the Arkansas men well. Scotty Thurman of the Razorbacks has always kept his mouth in gear, whether playing the tuba back at Ruston (La.) High, serving as president of his high school student council or playing ball. Before games he'll go up to referees and tell them straight up: "I just want you to know that I'm gonna talk. I'm gonna talk to you, I'm gonna talk to myself, and I'm gonna talk to other people. Now, I'm not going to say anything vulgar. But I'm gonna talk. That's just the way I am."

NCAA championship games are ordinarily occasions for walking it, not talking it. Yet just before halftime of the NCAA final, as the Razorbacks and their 6'6" sophomore swingman found themselves trailing Duke, Thurman complained to referee Jim Burr about the defense being applied to him by the Blue Devils' Antonio Lang.

"Just play, O.K.?" Burr barked back. "Don't be coming to me all night."

Thurman didn't utter a word in reply. He simply tossed the ball through the basket from beyond the three-point arc the next time he touched it, giving the Hogs a one-point halftime lead. When the second half reached a similar juncture—score tied at 70, with 52 seconds to play—Thurman beat a dying shot clock by sending another wordless trey whispering through the net. The shot clinched Arkansas's 76–72 victory and the Razorbacks' first NCAA title.

Having walked it, now he could talk it. "You're surprised, huh?" Thurman yelled after he bottomed out the game-winner, turning toward press row and the multitudes above and echoing the Dangerfieldian keynote his coach, Nolan Richardson, had sounded all season long.

When the major-market agenda-setters talked up other leagues, other teams, other players, Richardson took offense. "All the ratings and rankings and Sarazens and all that, they don't mean anything," he said dismissively after the Hogs won the Midwest Regional in Dallas by beating Michigan. "I've never seen a damn computer that can check a guy's heart." He meant Sagarins, as in Jeff Sagarin, whose computer rankings appear in *USA Today*, rather than anything having to do with Hall of Fame golfer Gene Sarazen. But there was no chance this was a Freudian slip. No way this man's mind was on golf.

Over the season Richardson invoked images of sledgehammers, broken-down doors, rabid dogs, prairie fires and street fights to describe the M.O. of this team. Several years back he tried for a while to get people to call the Hogs' old home, Barnhill Arena, "the Slaughterhouse," which would have presumably made the Razorbacks the Slaughterhouse Five. One gets the distinct impression that he regrets that the name never caught on.

Richardson stoked a kind of fury in the Razorbacks this year. That fury served a purpose, and he was far too intelligent not to keep the embers smoldering until he had smoked out every last doubter by reaching his ultimate goal of a title. As the Arkansas coach saw things, the dissing of his team

Thurman's long-range rainbow secured the championship for the Razorbacks.

continued at the Final Four. When tournament officials changed the time of Arkansas's 45-minute shootaround on Saturday morning before the Hogs were to play Arizona in the national semifinals, word never reached Richardson. The Razorbacks showed up late, getting only eight minutes of work in before being kicked off the floor. Motivated by the slight, they won that night.

Similarly, before the title game Richardson put a T-shirt on the locker room floor; on the shirt was printed a tournament bracket that showed Michigan having beaten Arkansas, when of course the opposite had happened. Just when you thought the Razorbacks had been accorded their due,

here was another slight to help get them through.

In Charlotte, when he met the press, Richardson kept his razored back up. "I'm in the penthouse now, but if we lose Monday, I'm in the outhouse," he said after the Hogs had gained a spot in the final against Duke, a 70–65 winner over Florida. "The headlines will be, 'He can't win the big one.'" Responding to a reporter's query in front of a roomful of journalists, Richardson said, "Did that answer your question? Because if it didn't, baby, I've got some more."

Commanding the stage, he was going to make every word count. Some of his anger at the pundits spilled over into an interview with CBS's Billy Packer, and he bristled at a TV commentator who suggested that Duke would win the title game because it

JOHN BIEVER

DAMIAN STROHMEYER

Richardson forged a national title from the fires of anger and aggrievement.

of the Southeastern Conference, the league Richardson considers to be the nation's most athletic; his leading role in the Black Coaches Association and the passionate national controversy over race, sports, education and opportunity.

But as he staggered through his first two seasons in Fayetteville—with Yvonne slipping away from him, Richardson went 31-30 using players left over from his walk-it-up predecessor, Eddie Sutton—the daggers came out. He hasn't forgotten the boosters and columnists who made his life more miserable than it already was. Of them he says, "They barbecued me every day until they ran out of sauce."

Yet he couldn't very well pity himself as he watched what Yvonne went through: the chemotherapy, the bone-marrow transplants, the time the doctors broke off a rib to get at a fungus in one of her lungs. Perhaps that's why Richardson has been able to forge something positive out of his anger. It's a system in which players with a similar sense of aggrievement and something to prove—other than the 6' 8" Williamson and 6' 11" freshman Darnell Robinson, none of the Razorbacks was a high school All-America—can thrive.

"Nobody wanted Corey Beck," Richardson says of the point guard who, more than any player he has coached, reminds Nolan of Nolan. Thurman was way back in the triple digits on those lists ranking the finest high school seniors, and he still chafes when he hears that city kids are tougher than those from backwaters such as Ruston. Frontcourt starter Dwight Stewart weighed more than 300 pounds and looked like a cartoon character when he came to Fayetteville in the fall of 1991; Richardson wound up giving him license to do virtually anything on the floor. Guard Clint McDaniel made precisely the same transformation, from scorer to defender, that Richardson made 30 earlier at Texas Western, where the Hog coach played for Don Haskins. Shooter Alex Dillard, a former high school dropout and burger flipper who earned a spot on the Razorbacks at the age

was a "smarter" team. But Richardson nodded his approval when his star, Corliss Williamson, accepted that poisonous premise for a moment and said, "If there's two guys in a fight, and one is a big, strong guy and the other's a little, smart guy, who do you think is gonna win?"

Richardson is a huge, fascinating and driven man who grew up in the polyracial but segregated town of El Paso, and as a kid spoke Spanish better than he spoke English. He and his wife, Rose, had a daughter, Yvonne, who was diagnosed with leukemia shortly after they arrived in Fayetteville. She died in January 1987. "I don't know how he's gotten through these last couple of years," said Andy Stoglin, a former assistant, six years ago, during the bleak times following Yvonne's death. "Except that everything in his life prepared him for this."

Yvonne's dying may have in turn helped prepare Richardson for the next phase of his life: the hostility of some strident Arkansans who preferred their basketball slow and their coaches white; the suspension of a few of his players in 1991 after it was alleged that they had committed sexual improprieties in an incident at a dorm; the crucible of 25, is a poster child for the opportunities his coach so often talks up. Even the team's lone white regular, Davor Rimac, relates to his coach's invocations of the rutted road. "It must have hurt him a lot," says Rimac, a Croat, of life under Jim Crow. "It's like if someone tells me I can't stay with the team because I'm not American."

Richardson took all these contributors and abolished the distinction between starters and subs, between backcourt and frontcourt. For most of the season Arkansas had only two double-figure scorers, but 10 Hogs played double-figure minutes. "We get our big guys to think they got some guard in 'em, and the little guys to think they got some post-up in 'em," the coach said.

Having so much talent baffled North Carolina's Dean Smith for much of this season. The Tar Heel coach might have learned a thing or two from watching Richardson. Again and again, at coaching clinics and press conferences, the Arkansas coach is asked how he gets his players to play so hard and how he keeps so many gifted young men so evidently happy. "I do not coach like anybody," he says. "I do not *think* like anybody. I make my teams play like I want 'em to look, and I want 'em to look so chaotic that I can't tell 'em what the keys are. Now if you get me some shooters, and this year I've got three or four who can stick it, and we hit on all cylinders, you're in *serious* trouble."

For a while Richardson called the frenzy 40 Minutes of Hell. But when he added two of the most gifted inside players in the country, he parceled out those infernal moments more judiciously, preferring by the end of

Williamson gave the Razorbacks the gifted inside player they needed.

the season a half-court game in which Williamson and Robinson could showcase their marvelous skills. That's coaching. "You don't coach X's and O's," he likes to say. "You coach people."

In the title game Richardson nearly forgot his own good advice. Leading 70–67 with more than two minutes to play, he ordered his team into a spread offense. The Razorbacks squandered that possession on a missed three-pointer by Stewart, and when Duke's Grant Hill came back with a trey of his own to tie the game, only 1:15 remained.

As if to vindicate Richardson's belief that in the end everything comes down to peo-

JOHN BIEVER

Smith's three-pointer beat the buzzer and beat Louisiana Tech for the women's title.

JIM GUND/ALLSPORT

guards Thurman in practice. "But Scotty just lets it go. He doesn't shoot after he jumps. He jumps *into* his shot."

Lang came within a hairsbreadth of tipping the ball, which air-traffic control could have picked up as it made its way hoopward. But the ball wound up nestling into the net. It wasn't a shot off some chalkboard. It was a shot a player makes.

No one left the floor more creditably than Hill, who had slung this Duke team over his shoulder like a satchel and carried it all season. He closed out four marvelous seasons with 12 points, 14 rebounds, six assists and universal approbation for his valor. But the result made Grant's mom's college roommate's husband—a guy from Hope, Ark., who lives at 1600 Pennsylvania Avenue in Washington, D.C.—teary-eyed happy.

All but two of these championship Razorbacks will be back next season. In fact, Arkansas is the first national champion since UCLA in 1967 to return all five of its starters. "I think we have half the respect we deserve," said Beck. "We have to come back and win it again next year to get the other half."

One of Beck's teammates—a high school valedictorian, an SEC All-Academic choice, an orator by nature—wasn't sure he agreed. "If we can't get respect now, I don't think we ever will," Thurman said.

But even if no one else were to offer the Razorbacks respect, the team they beat in the title game accorded them plenty. "A great team," said Krzyzewski. "All credit to Arkansas," said Lang.

"What a great shot," said the Blue Devils' Chris Collins. "The national championship, a minute left, tie game—he made a great shot."

It was a great shot, made by a pretty smart fellow. But it ended a season so discombobulated and off-form that more often than not, it made smart people look stupid.

ple and what they can do, here human nature carried the moment. First, foible: Stewart, 0-for-5 from three-point range to that point, had a notion of shooting from the top of the circle. "I was squaring up, but I fumbled it," he would say. "And I saw Scotty was open."

Then, fortitude: In the right corner Thurman knew only a second, maybe two, remained on the shot clock, and Lang, his first-half nemesis, guarded him so closely that, Thurman would say, "His whole body was in my face." As Thurman took Stewart's pass he thought of the broomstick his high school coach had asked him to shoot over long ago in a drill to develop more arc on his shot. Then he dipped his elbow and launched his regular jump shot, which is squeezed off in a trice. "People expect him to jump and shoot," said Rimac, who

NCAA Championship Game Box Score

Duke 72

DUKE	Min	FG M-A	FT M-A	Reb O-T	A	PF	TP
Hill	38	4-11	3-5	1-14	6	3	12
Lang	34	6-9	3-3	3-5	3	5	15
Parks	30	7-10	0-1	3-7	0	3	14
Capel	35	6-16	0-0	1-5	4	3	14
Collins	34	4-11	0-0	0-0	1	1	12
Clark	15	1-6	1-2	1-1	3	2	3
Meek	14	1-2	0-0	3-7	0	1	2
Totals	200	29-65	7-11	12-39	17	18	72

Percentages: FG—.446, FT—.636. 3-pt goals: 7-20, .350 (Hill 1-4, Capel 2-6, Collins 4-8, Clark 0-2). Team rebounds: 5. Blocked shots: 7 (Hill 3, Parks 2, Lang, Collins). Turnovers: 23 (Hill 9, Capel 6, Lang 5, Clark 2, Collins). Steals: 5 (Hill 3, Capel, Collins).

Arkansas 76

ARKANSAS	Min	FG M-A	FT M-A	Reb O-T	A	PF	TP
C. Williamson	35	10-24	3-5	7-8	3	3	23
Biley	3	0-0	0-0	0-0	0	1	0
Stewart	29	3-11	0-0	4-9	4	3	6
Beck	35	5-11	5-8	2-10	4	3	15
Thurman	36	6-13	0-0	1-5	1	2	15
McDaniel	32	2-5	2-4	0-2	3	2	7
Robinson	12	1-5	0-0	1-2	0	1	2
Dillard	8	1-5	1-2	1-1	0	1	4
Rimac	5	0-1	0-0	0-0	0	0	0
L. Wilson	5	2-2	0-0	1-4	0	1	4
Totals	200	30-77	11-19	17-41	15	17	76

Percentages: FG—.390, FT—.579. 3-pt goals: 5-18, .278 (Stewart 0-5, Beck 0-1, Thurman 3-5, McDaniel 1-3, Dillard 1-4). Team rebounds: 3. Blocked shots: 3 (C. Williamson 2, Rimac). Turnovers: 12 (C. Williamson 5, Beck 3, L. Wilson, McDaniel, Robinson, Stewart). Steals: 11 (Stewart 4, McDaniel 3, C. Williamson 2, Beck, Thurman). Halftime: Arkansas 34, Duke 33. A: 23,674. Officials: Burr, Silvester, Valentine.

Final AP Top 25

Poll taken before NCAA Tournament.

1. Arkansas	25-3	
2. North Carolina	27-6	
3. Connecticut	27-4	
4. Purdue	26-4	
5. Missouri	25-3	
6. Duke	23-5	
7. Massachusetts	27-6	
8. Kentucky	26-6	
9. Louisville	26-5	
10. Arizona	25-5	
11. Michigan	21-7	
12. Temple	22-7	
13. Kansas	25-7	
14. Syracuse	21-6	
15. Florida	25-7	
16. UCLA	21-6	
17. California	22-7	
18. Indiana	19-8	
19. Oklahoma State	23-9	
20. Minnesota	20-11	
21. St. Louis	23-5	
22. Marquette	22-8	
23. Alabama-Birmingham	22-7	
24. Texas	25-7	
25. Cincinnati	22-9	

National Invitation Tournament Scores

First round: Siena 76, Georgia Tech 68; Northwestern 69, DePaul 68; Xavier (OH) 80, Miami (OH) 68; Duquesne 75, NC-Charlotte 73; Bradley 66, Murray State 58; Tulane 76, Evansville 63; New Orleans 79, Texas A&M 73 OT; Vanderbilt 77, Oklahoma 67; Fresno State 79, Southern Cal 76; Clemson 96, Southern Miss 85; Old Dominion 76, Manhattan 74; West Virginia 85, Davidson 69; Villanova 103, Canisius 79; Kansas State 78, Mississippi State 67; Brigham Young 74, Arizona State 67; Gonzaga 80, Stanford 76.
Second round: Xavier (OH) 83, Northwestern 79; Clemson 96, West Virginia 79; Villanova 82, Duquesne 66; Vanderbilt 78, New Orleans 59; Siena 89, Tulane 79; Kansas State 66, Gonzaga 64; Bradley 79, Old Dominion 75; Fresno State 68, Brigham Young 66.
Third round: Villanova 76, Xavier (OH) 74; Siena 75, Bradley 62; Kansas State 115, Fresno State 77; Vanderbilt 89, Clemson 74.
Semifinals: Vanderbilt 82, Kansas State 76; Villanova 66, Siena 58.
Championship: Villanova 80, Vanderbilt 73.
Consolation game: Siena 92, Kansas State 79.

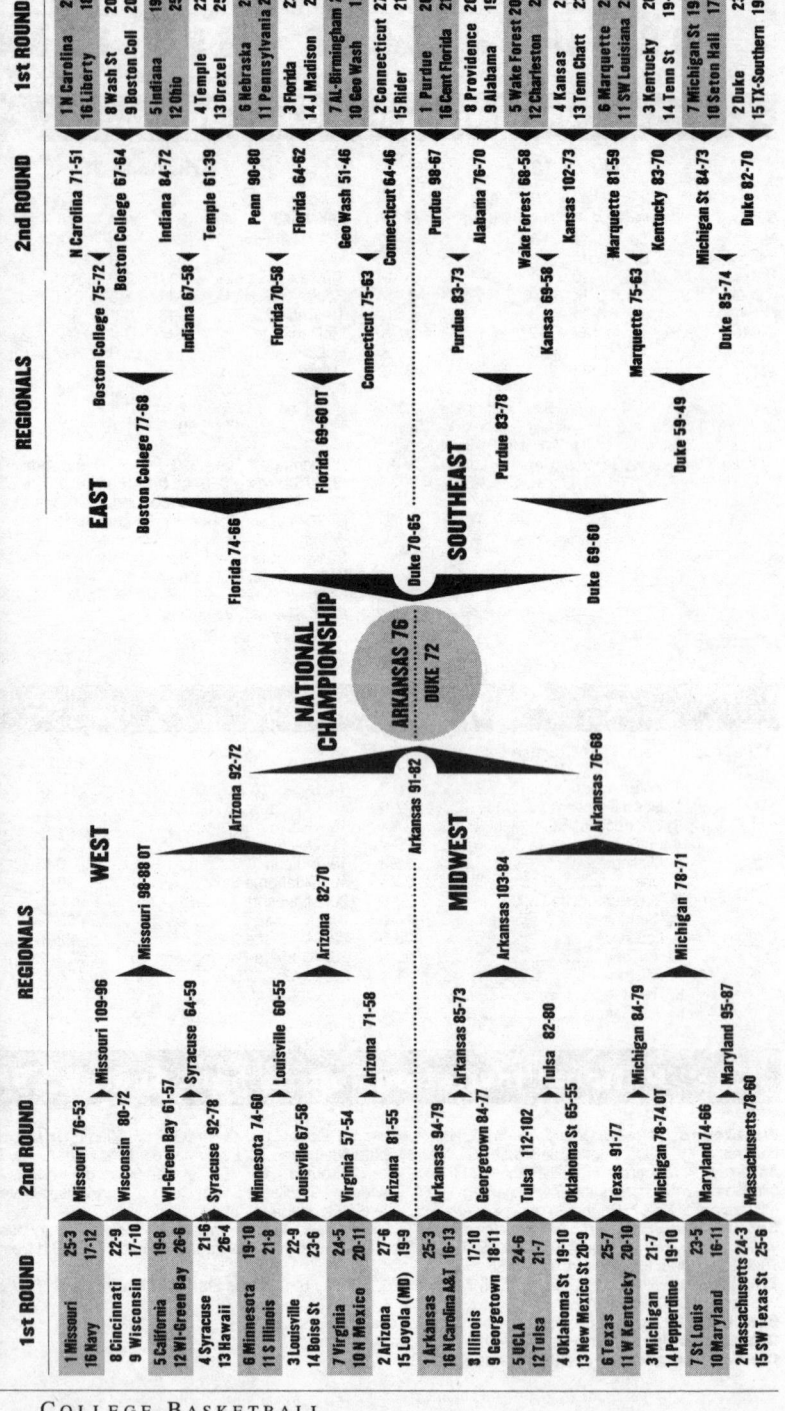

1994 NCAA Basketball Men's Division I Tournament

EAST

1st ROUND

1 N Carolina	27-6
16 Liberty	18-11
8 Wash St	20-10
9 Boston Coll	20-10
5 Indiana	19-8
12 Ohio	25-7
4 Temple	22-7
13 Drexel	25-4
6 Nebraska	20-9
11 Pennsylvania	24-2
3 Florida	23-6
14 J Madison	22-4
7 AL-Birmingham	22-7
10 Geo Wash	17-11
2 Connecticut	27-4
15 Rider	21-8

2nd ROUND
- N Carolina 71-51
- Boston College 67-64
- Indiana 84-72
- Temple 61-39
- Penn 90-80
- Florida 64-62
- Geo Wash 51-46
- Connecticut 64-46

REGIONALS
- Boston College 75-72
- Indiana 67-58
- Florida 70-58
- Connecticut 75-63
- Boston College 77-68
- Florida 69-60 OT
- Florida 74-66

SOUTHEAST

1st ROUND

1 Purdue	26-4
16 Cent Florida	21-8
8 Providence	20-9
9 Alabama	19-9
5 Wake Forest	20-11
12 Charleston	24-3
4 Kansas	25-7
13 Tenn Chatt	23-6
6 Marquette	22-8
11 SW Louisiana	22-7
3 Kentucky	26-6
14 Tenn St	19-11
7 Michigan St	19-11
10 Seton Hall	17-12
2 Duke	23-5
15 TX-Southern	19-10

2nd ROUND
- Purdue 98-67
- Alabama 76-70
- Wake Forest 68-58
- Kansas 102-73
- Marquette 81-59
- Kentucky 83-70
- Michigan St 84-73
- Duke 82-70

REGIONALS
- Purdue 83-73
- Kansas 69-58
- Marquette 75-63
- Duke 85-74
- Purdue 83-78
- Duke 59-49
- Purdue 69-60

Duke 70-65

NATIONAL CHAMPIONSHIP

ARKANSAS 76

DUKE 72

WEST

REGIONALS
- Missouri 109-96
- Syracuse 64-59
- Louisville 60-55
- Arizona 71-58
- Missouri 98-88 OT
- Arizona 82-70
- Arizona 92-72

2nd ROUND
- Missouri 76-53
- Wisconsin 80-72
- WI-Green Bay 61-57
- Syracuse 92-78
- Minnesota 74-60
- Louisville 67-58
- Virginia 57-54
- Arizona 81-55

1st ROUND

1 Missouri	25-3
16 Navy	17-12
8 Cincinnati	22-9
9 Wisconsin	17-10
5 California	19-8
12 WI-Green Bay	26-6
4 Syracuse	21-6
13 Hawaii	26-4
6 Minnesota	19-10
11 S Illinois	21-8
3 Louisville	22-9
14 Boise St	23-6
7 Virginia	24-5
10 N Mexico	20-11
2 Arizona	27-6
15 Loyola (MD)	19-9

MIDWEST

REGIONALS
- Arkansas 85-73
- Tulsa 82-80
- Michigan 84-79
- Maryland 95-87
- Arkansas 103-84
- Michigan 78-71
- Arkansas 76-68

2nd ROUND
- Arkansas 94-79
- Georgetown 84-77
- Tulsa 112-102
- Oklahoma St 65-55
- Texas 91-77
- Michigan 78-74 OT
- Maryland 74-66
- Massachusetts 78-60

1st ROUND

1 Arkansas	25-3
16 N Carolina A&T	16-13
8 Illinois	17-10
9 Georgetown	18-11
5 UCLA	24-6
12 Tulsa	21-7
4 Oklahoma St	19-10
13 New Mexico St	20-9
6 Texas	25-7
11 W Kentucky	20-10
3 Michigan	21-7
14 Pepperdine	19-10
7 St Louis	23-5
10 Maryland	16-11
2 Massachusetts	24-3
15 SW Texas St	25-6

Duke 69-60

Arkansas 91-82

Duke 85-74

Assoc. of Mid-Continent

	Conference			All Games		
	W	L	Pct	W	L	Pct
WI-Green Bay*†	15	3	.833	27	7	.794
Valparaiso	14	4	.778	20	8	.714
IL-Chicago	14	4	.778	20	9	.690
Cleveland St	9	9	.500	14	15	.483
Wright St	9	9	.500	12	18	.400
Eastern Illinois	7	11	.389	12	15	.444
Northern Illinois	7	11	.389	10	17	.370
WI-Milwaukee	7	11	.389	10	17	.370
Western Illinois	5	13	.278	7	20	.259
Youngstown St	3	15	.167	5	21	.192

Atlantic Coast

	Conference			All Games		
	W	L	Pct	W	L	Pct
Duke*	12	4	.750	28	6	.824
N Carolina†	11	5	.688	28	7	.800
Wake Forest	9	7	.563	21	11	.656
Maryland	8	8	.500	18	12	.600
Virginia	8	8	.500	18	13	.581
Georgia Tech	7	9	.438	16	13	.552
Clemson	6	10	.375	18	16	.529
Florida St	6	10	.375	13	14	.481
N Carolina St	5	11	.313	11	19	.367

Atlantic 10

	Conference			All Games		
	W	L	Pct	W	L	Pct
Massachusetts*†	14	2	.875	28	7	.800
Temple	12	4	.750	23	8	.742
Geo Washington	8	8	.500	18	12	.600
West Virginia	8	8	.500	17	12	.586
Duquesne	8	8	.500	17	13	.567
Rhode Island	7	9	.438	11	16	.407
Rutgers	6	10	.375	11	16	.407
St Joseph's (PA)	5	11	.313	14	14	.500
St Bonaventure	4	12	.250	10	17	.370

Big East

	Conference			All Games		
	W	L	Pct	W	L	Pct
Connecticut*	16	2	.889	29	5	.853
Syracuse	13	5	.722	23	7	.767
Boston College	11	7	.611	22	11	.667
Providence†	10	8	.556	20	10	.667
Georgetown	10	8	.556	17	12	.586
Villlanova	10	8	.556	20	12	.625
Seton Hall	8	10	.444	17	13	.567
Pittsburgh	7	11	.389	13	14	.481
St John's	5	13	.278	12	17	.414
Miami (FL)	0	18	.000	7	20	.259

Big Eight

	Conference			All Games		
	W	L	Pct	W	L	Pct
Missouri*	14	0	1.000	27	4	.871
Oklahoma St	10	4	.714	22	10	.688
Kansas	9	5	.643	26	8	.765
Nebraska†	7	7	.500	20	10	.667
Oklahoma	6	8	.429	15	13	.536
Kansas St	4	10	.286	20	14	.588
Iowa St	4	10	.286	14	13	.519
Colorado	2	12	.143	10	17	.370

Big Sky

	Conference			All Games		
	W	L	Pct	W	L	Pct
Weber St*	10	4	.714	20	10	.667
Idaho St	10	4	.714	18	9	.666
Idaho	9	5	.643	18	10	.643
Montana St	8	6	.571	16	11	.593
Boise St†	7	7	.500	17	13	.567
Montana	6	8	.429	19	9	.679
Northern Arizona	6	8	.429	13	13	.500
Eastern Washington	0	14	.000	5	21	.192

Big South

	Conference			All Games		
	W	L	Pct	W	L	Pct
Towson St*	16	2	.889	22	8	.733
Campbell	14	4	.778	21	8	.724
Radford	13	5	.722	20	8	.714
Liberty†	13	5	.722	18	12	.600
NC-Greensboro	11	7	.611	15	12	.556
Charleston So	8	10	.444	10	17	.370
MD-Balt. County	6	12	.333	7	20	.259
Winthrop	5	13	.278	6	21	.222
NC-Asheville	3	15	.167	5	22	.185
Coastal Carolina	1	17	.056	6	20	.231

Big Ten

	Conference			All Games		
	W	L	Pct	W	L	Pct
Purdue*	14	4	.778	29	5	.853
Michigan	13	5	.722	24	8	.750
Indiana	12	6	.667	21	9	.700
Illinois	10	8	.556	17	11	.607
Michigan St	10	8	.556	20	12	.625
Minnesota	10	8	.556	21	12	.636
Wisconsin	8	10	.444	18	11	.621
Ohio St	6	12	.333	13	16	.448
Penn St	6	12	.333	13	14	.481
Northwestern	5	13	.278	14	13	.519
Iowa	5	13	.278	11	16	.407

*Conf. champ; †Conf. tourney winner.

Big West

	Conference			All Games		
	W	L	Pct	W	L	Pct
New Mexico St*†	12	6	.667	23	8	.742
Long Beach St	11	7	.611	17	10	.630
San Jose St	11	7	.611	15	12	.556
Utah St	11	7	.611	14	13	.519
Pacific	10	8	.556	17	13	.567
UNLV	10	8	.556	15	12	.556
UC-Santa Barbara	9	9	.500	13	17	.433
Nevada	6	12	.333	11	17	.393
Cal St Fullerton	6	12	.333	8	19	.296
UC-Irvine	4	14	.222	9	19	.321

Colonial Athletic Association

	Conference			All Games		
	W	L	Pct	W	L	Pct
James Madison*†	10	4	.714	20	10	.667
Old Dominion*	10	4	.714	21	10	.677
NC-Wilmington	9	5	.643	18	10	.643
Richmond	8	6	.571	14	14	.500
E Carolina	7	7	.500	15	12	.556
George Mason	5	9	.357	10	17	.370
American	5	9	.357	8	19	.296
William & Mary	2	12	.143	4	23	.148

East Coast

	Conference			All Games		
	W	L	Pct	W	L	Pct
Troy St*	5	0	1.000	13	14	.481
NE-Illinois	4	1	.800	17	11	.607
Buffalo	3	2	.600	9	18	.333
Chicago St	2	3	.400	4	23	.148
Hofstra†	1	4	.200	9	20	.310
Central Connecticut	0	5	.000	4	21	.160

Great Midwest

	Conference			All Games		
	W	L	Pct	W	L	Pct
Marquette*	10	2	.833	24	9	.727
St Louis	8	4	.667	23	6	.793
AL-Birmingham	8	4	.667	22	8	.733
Cincinnati†	7	5	.583	22	10	.688
DePaul	4	8	.333	16	12	.571
Memphis St	4	8	.333	13	15	.464
Dayton	1	11	.083	6	21	.222

Ivy League

	Conference			All Games		
	W	L	Pct	W	L	Pct
Pennsylvania	14	0	1.000	25	3	.893
Princeton	11	3	.786	18	8	.692
Yale	7	7	.500	10	16	.385
Brown	6	8	.429	12	14	.462
Dartmouth	6	8	.429	10	16	.385
Harvard	5	9	.357	9	17	.346
Columbia	4	10	.286	6	20	.231
Cornell	3	11	.214	8	18	.308

Metro

	Conference			All Games		
	W	L	Pct	W	L	Pct
Louisville*†	10	2	.833	28	6	.824
Tulane	7	5	.583	18	11	.621
NC-Charlotte	7	5	.583	16	13	.552
Virginia Tech	6	6	.500	18	9	.667
S Mississippi	5	7	.417	14	13	.519
VCU	5	7	.417	14	13	.519
S Florida	2	10	.167	10	17	.370

Metro Atlantic

	Conference			All Games		
	W	L	Pct	W	L	Pct
Canisius*	12	2	.857	22	7	.759
Siena	10	4	.714	25	8	.758
Manhattan	10	4	.714	19	11	.633
St Peter's	8	6	.571	14	13	.519
Loyola (MD)†	6	8	.429	17	13	.567
Fairfield	4	10	.286	8	19	.296
Iona	3	11	.214	7	20	.259
Niagara	3	11	.214	6	21	.222

Mid-American

	Conference			All Games		
	W	L	Pct	W	L	Pct
Ohio University*	14	4	.778	25	8	.758
Miami (OH)	12	6	.667	19	10	.655
Bowling Green	12	6	.667	18	10	.643
Ball St	11	7	.611	16	12	.571
E Michigan	10	8	.556	15	12	.556
Toledo	10	8	.556	15	12	.556
Kent	8	10	.444	13	14	.481
W Michigan	7	11	.389	14	14	.500
Central Michigan	4	14	.222	5	21	.192
Akron	2	16	.111	8	18	.308

Mid-Eastern Athletic

	Conference			All Games		
	W	L	Pct	W	L	Pct
Coppin St*	16	0	1.000	22	8	.733
MD-Eastern Shore	10	6	.625	16	11	.593
S Carolina St	10	6	.625	15	12	.556
N Carolina A&T†	10	6	.625	16	14	.533
Bethune-Cookman	8	8	.500	9	18	.333
Howard	7	9	.438	10	17	.370
Delaware St	5	11	.313	8	19	.296
Morgan St	4	12	.250	8	20	.286
Florida A&M	2	14	.125	4	23	.148

*Conf. champ; †Conf. tourney winner.

NCAA Men's Division I Conference Standings *(Cont.)*

Midwestern Collegiate

	Conference			All Games		
	W	L	Pct	W	L	Pct
Xavier (OH)*	8	2	.800	22	9	.710
Evansville	6	4	.600	21	11	.656
Butler	6	4	.600	16	13	.552
Detroit Mercy†	5	5	.500	16	13	.552
La Salle	4	6	.400	11	16	.407
Loyola (IL)	1	9	.100	8	19	.296

Missouri Valley

	Conference			All Games		
	W	L	Pct	W	L	Pct
Tulsa*	15	3	.833	23	8	.742
S Illinois†	14	4	.778	23	7	.767
Bradley	14	4	.778	23	8	.742
Illinois St	12	6	.667	16	11	.593
N Iowa	10	8	.556	16	13	.552
SW Missouri St	7	11	.389	12	15	.444
Drake	6	12	.333	11	16	.407
Wichita St	6	12	.333	9	18	.333
Creighton	3	15	.167	7	22	.241
Indiana St	3	15	.167	4	22	.154

North Atlantic

	Conference			All Games		
	W	L	Pct	W	L	Pct
Drexel*†	12	2	.857	25	5	.833
Maine	11	3	.786	20	9	.690
Hartford	9	5	.643	16	12	.571
New Hampshire	8	6	.571	15	13	.536
Delaware	7	7	.500	14	13	.519
Boston U	4	10	.286	11	16	.407
Vermont	3	11	.214	12	15	.444
Northeastern	2	12	.143	5	22	.185

Northeast

	Conference			All Games		
	W	L	Pct	W	L	Pct
Rider*†	14	4	.778	21	9	.700
Monmouth (NJ)	13	5	.722	18	11	.621
Wagner	11	7	.611	16	12	.571
Robert Morris	11	7	.611	14	14	.500
FDU-Teaneck	10	8	.556	14	13	.519
Marist	10	8	.556	14	13	.519
Mt St Mary's	9	9	.500	14	14	.500
St Francis (PA)	9	9	.500	13	15	.464
LIU-Brooklyn	2	16	.111	3	24	.111
St Francis (NY)	1	17	.056	1	26	.037

Ohio Valley

	Conference			All Games		
	W	L	Pct	W	L	Pct
Murray St*	15	1	.938	23	6	.793
Tennessee St†	12	4	.750	19	12	.613
Austin Peay	10	6	.625	11	16	.407
E Kentucky	9	7	.563	13	14	.481
Morehead St	8	8	.500	14	14	.500
SE Missouri St	5	11	.313	10	17	.370
Tennessee Tech	5	11	.313	10	21	.323
Middle Tenn St	5	11	.313	8	19	.296
Tenn-Martin	3	13	.188	5	22	.185

Pacific-10

	Conference			All Games		
	W	L	Pct	W	L	Pct
Arizona*	14	4	.778	29	6	.829
UCLA	13	5	.722	21	7	.750
California	13	5	.722	22	8	.733
Washington St	10	8	.556	20	11	.645
Stanford	10	8	.556	17	11	.607
Arizona St	10	8	.556	15	13	.536
Southern Cal	9	9	.500	16	12	.571
Oregon	6	12	.333	10	17	.370
Washington	3	15	.167	5	22	.185
Oregon St	2	16	.111	6	21	.222

Patriot

	Conference			All Games		
	W	L	Pct	W	L	Pct
Navy*†	9	5	.643	17	13	.567
Colgate	9	5	.643	17	12	.586
Holy Cross	9	5	.643	14	14	.500
Fordham	9	5	.643	12	15	.444
Bucknell	6	8	.429	10	17	.370
Lehigh	6	8	.429	10	17	.370
Lafayette	4	10	.286	9	19	.321
Army	4	10	.286	7	20	.259

Southeastern

EAST

	Conference			All Games		
	W	L	Pct	W	L	Pct
Florida*	12	4	.750	29	8	.784
Kentucky†	12	4	.750	27	7	.794
Vanderbilt	9	7	.563	20	12	.625
Georgia	7	9	.438	14	16	.467
S Carolina	4	12	.250	9	19	.321
Tennessee	2	14	.125	5	22	.185

WEST

	Conference			All Games		
	W	L	Pct	W	L	Pct
Arkansas*	14	2	.875	30	3	.909
Alabama	12	4	.750	20	10	.667
Mississippi St	9	7	.563	18	11	.621
Mississippi	7	9	.438	14	13	.519
LSU	5	11	.313	11	16	.407
Auburn	3	13	.188	11	17	.393

*Conf. champ; †Conf. tourney winner.

Southern

	Conference			All Games		
	W	L	Pct	W	L	Pct
TN-Chattanooga*†	14	4	.778	23	7	.767
Davidson	13	5	.722	22	7	.759
E Tennessee St	13	5	.722	16	14	.533
Appalachian St	12	6	.667	16	11	.593
Georgia Southern	9	9	.500	14	14	.500
W Carolina	8	10	.444	12	16	.429
Marshall	7	11	.389	9	18	.333
The Citadel	6	12	.333	11	16	.407
Furman	6	12	.333	10	18	.357
VMI	2	16	.111	5	23	.179

Southland

	Conference			All Games		
	W	L	Pct	W	L	Pct
NE Louisiana*	15	3	.833	19	9	.679
SW Texas St†	14	4	.778	25	7	.781
Nicholls St	12	6	.667	19	9	.679
N Texas St	9	9	.500	14	15	.483
McNeese St	9	9	.500	11	16	.407
TX-San Antonio	8	10	.444	12	15	.444
Sam Houston St	7	11	.389	7	20	.259
NW Louisiana St	6	12	.333	11	15	.423
Stephen F. Austin	6	12	.333	9	18	.333
TX-Arlington	4	14	.222	7	22	.241

Southwest

	Conference			All Games		
	W	L	Pct	W	L	Pct
Texas*†	12	2	.857	26	8	.765
Texas A&M	10	4	.714	19	10	.655
Texas Tech	10	4	.714	17	11	.607
Baylor	7	7	.500	16	11	.593
Rice	6	8	.429	15	14	.517
Houston	5	9	.357	8	19	.296
Texas Christian	3	11	.214	7	20	.259
SMU	3	11	.214	6	21	.221

Southwestern Athletic

	Conference			All Games		
	W	L	Pct	W	L	Pct
Texas Southern*†	12	2	.857	19	11	.633
Jackson St	11	3	.786	18	10	.643
Alabama St	10	4	.714	19	10	.655
Southern-BR	8	6	.571	15	10	.600
Miss Valley St	6	8	.429	10	17	.370
Grambling St	4	10	.286	9	18	.233
Alcorn St	3	11	.214	3	24	.111
Prairie View	2	12	.143	5	22	.185

*Conf. champ; †Conf. tourney winner.

Sun Belt

	Conference			All Games		
	W	L	Pct	W	L	Pct
W Kentucky*	14	4	.778	20	11	.645
SW Louisiana†	13	5	.722	22	8	.733
New Orleans	12	6	.667	20	10	.667
Jacksonville	11	7	.611	17	11	.607
Arkansas St	10	8	.556	15	12	.556
TX-Pan American	9	9	.500	16	12	.571
South Alabama	9	9	.500	13	14	.481
AR-Little Rock	6	12	.333	13	15	.464
Lamar	6	12	.333	10	17	.370
Louisiana Tech	0	18	.000	2	25	.074

Trans-America

	Conference			All Games		
	W	L	Pct	W	L	Pct
Coll of Charleston*	14	2	.875	24	4	.857
Central Florida†	11	5	.688	21	9	.700
Stetson	9	7	.563	14	15	.483
Georgia St	9	7	.563	13	14	.481
Centenary	8	8	.500	16	12	.571
Florida Int'l	7	9	.438	11	16	.407
SE Louisiana	7	9	.438	10	17	.370
Samford	4	12	.250	10	18	.357
Mercer	3	13	.188	5	24	.172
Florida Atlantic	0	0	.000	3	24	.111

West Coast

	Conference			All Games		
	W	L	Pct	W	L	Pct
Gonzaga*	12	2	.857	22	8	.733
Pepperdine†	8	6	.571	19	11	.633
San Francisco	8	6	.571	17	11	.607
San Diego	7	7	.500	18	12	.600
Santa Clara	6	8	.429	13	14	.481
Portland	6	8	.429	13	17	.433
St Mary's	5	9	.357	13	14	.481
Loyola Marymount	4	10	.286	6	21	.222

Western Athletic

	Conference			All Games		
	W	L	Pct	W	L	Pct
New Mexico*	14	4	.778	23	8	.742
Fresno St	13	5	.722	21	11	.656
BYU	12	6	.667	22	10	.688
Hawaii†	11	7	.611	18	15	.545
UTEP	8	10	.444	18	12	.600
Colorado St	8	10	.444	15	13	.536
Utah	8	10	.444	14	14	.500
Wyoming	7	11	.389	14	14	.500
San Diego St	6	12	.333	12	16	429
Air Force	3	15	.167	8	18	.308

Independents

	W	L	Pct
Southern Utah St	16	11	.593
MO-Kansas City	12	17	.414
Notre Dame	12	17	.414
Cal St-Northridge	8	18	.308
Oral Roberts	6	21	.222
Cal St-Sacramento	1	26	.037

Scoring

			Field Goals			3-Pt FG		Free Throws					
	Class	GP	FGA	FG	Pct	FGA	FG	FTA	FT	Pct	Reb	Pts	Avg
Glenn Robinson, Purdue	Jr	34	762	368	48.3	208	79	270	215	79.6	344	1030	30.3
Bob Feaster, Holy Cross	Jr	28	553	261	47.2	101	42	315	221	70.2	183	785	28.0
Jervaughn Scales, Southern-BR	Sr	27	493	293	59.4	3	0	225	147	65.3	384	733	27.1
Frankie King, W Carolina	Jr	28	527	258	49.0	96	29	281	207	73.7	211	752	26.9
Tucker Neale, Colgate	Jr	29	524	249	47.5	238	95	214	178	83.2	120	771	26.6
Eddie Benton, Vermont	So	26	533	205	38.5	210	68	251	209	83.3	66	687	26.4
Doremus Bennerman, Siena	Sr	33	577	254	44.0	249	102	286	248	86.7	137	858	26.0
Tony Dumas, MO-Kansas City	Sr	29	544	229	42.1	205	74	292	221	75.7	166	753	26.0
Otis Jones, Air Force	Jr	26	461	206	44.7	201	77	226	174	77.0	93	663	25.5
Izett Buchanan, Marist	Sr	27	558	238	42.7	127	41	229	168	73.4	255	685	25.4
Gary Trent, Ohio University	So	33	536	309	57.6	33	9	291	210	72.2	377	837	25.4
Orlando Lightfoot, Idaho	Sr	28	577	263	45.6	204	71	168	113	67.3	214	710	25.4
Reggie Smith, NE Illinois	Sr	27	553	241	43.6	175	61	166	135	81.3	147	678	25.1
Donyell Marshall, Connecticut	Jr	34	599	306	51.1	132	41	266	200	75.2	302	853	25.1
Carlos Rogers, Tennessee St	Sr	31	469	288	61.4	13	4	276	179	64.9	358	759	24.5
Shawn Respert, Michigan St	Jr	32	562	272	48.4	203	92	169	142	84.0	127	778	24.3
Eric Kubel, Northwestern St	Sr	26	487	236	48.5	8	1	210	159	75.7	341	632	24.3
Lamond Murray, California	Jr	30	550	262	47.6	139	46	208	159	76.4	236	729	24.3
Sherell Ford, IL-Chicago	Jr	29	560	279	49.8	87	26	172	120	69.8	254	704	24.3
Khalid Reeves, Arizona	Sr	35	572	276	48.3	224	85	264	211	79.9	150	848	24.2
Jeff Webster, Oklahoma	Sr	28	513	264	51.5	13	3	170	132	77.6	217	663	23.7
Antoine Gillespie, UTEP	Jr	30	508	225	44.3	155	62	245	198	80.8	135	710	23.7
Tony Tolbert, Detroit Mercy	Sr	29	468	229	48.9	154	63	248	162	65.3	160	683	23.6
Mark Lueking, Army	So	25	446	172	38.6	209	77	185	156	84.3	82	577	23.1
Randy Blocker, N Iowa	Sr	28	503	239	47.5	70	26	176	141	80.1	215	645	23.0
Scott Drapeau, New Hampshire	Jr	28	498	241	48.4	71	29	189	131	69.3	277	642	22.9
Kareem Townes, La Salle	Jr	27	540	202	37.4	291	100	149	115	77.2	92	619	22.9
Gary Collier, Tulsa	Sr	31	490	254	51.8	201	93	141	109	77.3	209	710	22.9
B.J. Tyler, Texas	Sr	28	481	213	44.3	265	99	154	112	72.7	94	637	22.8
Michael Allen, SW Louisiana	Sr	30	532	220	41.4	247	80	186	162	87.1	69	682	22.7

REBOUNDS

	Class	GP	Reb	Avg
Jerome Lambert, Baylor	Jr	24	355	14.8
Jervaughn Scales, Southern-BR	Sr	27	384	14.2
Eric Kubel, Northwestern St	Sr	26	341	13.1
Kendrick Warren, VCU	Sr	27	336	12.4
Malik Rose, Drexel	So	30	371	12.4
David Vaughn, Memphis St	So	28	335	12.0
Reggie Jackson, Nicholls St	Jr	26	311	12.0
Melvin Simon, New Orleans	Sr	30	355	11.8
Kebu Stewart, UNLV	So	22	256	11.6
Carlos Rogers, Tennessee St	Sr	31	358	11.5
Michael Smith, Providence	Sr	30	334	11.5

ASSISTS

	Class	GP	A	Avg
Jason Kidd, California	So	30	272	9.1
David Edwards, Texas A&M	Sr	30	265	8.8
Tony Miller, Marquette	Jr	33	274	8.3
Eathan O'Bryant, Nevada	Jr	28	232	8.3
Abdul Abdullah, Providence	Sr	30	241	8.0
Howard Nathan, NE Louisiana	So	23	179	7.8
Orlando Smart, San Francisco	Sr	27	204	7.6
Dan Pogue, Campbell	So	28	207	7.4
Dedan Thomas, UNLV	Sr	28	205	7.3
Nelson Haggerty, Baylor	Jr	22	161	7.3

Five tied with 7.1 assists per game

3-POINT FIELD GOALS MADE PER GAME

	Class	GP	FG	Avg
Chris Brown, UC-Irvine	Jr	26	122	4.7
Keke Hicks, Coastal Carolina	Jr	26	115	4.4
Lazelle Durden, Cincinnati	Jr	25	102	4.1
Bernard Haslett, S Mississippi	Sr	30	112	3.7
Kareem Townes, La Salle	Jr	27	100	3.7
Donald Ross, George Mason	Jr	27	99	3.7
Keith Carmichael, Coppin St	Jr	30	108	3.6
B.J. Tyler, Texas	Sr	28	99	3.5
Stevin Smith, Arizona St	Sr	28	96	3.4
Josh Kohn, NC-Asheville	So	27	92	3.4
Kent Culuko, James Madison	Jr	30	101	3.4

3-POINT FIELD GOAL PERCENTAGES

	Class	GP	FGA	FG	Pct
Brent Kell, Evansville	So	29	123	62	50.4
Brian Santiago, Fresno St	Sr	32	128	64	50.0
Brandon Born, TN-Chattanooga	Jr	30	135	67	49.6
Chris Young, Canisius	So	29	109	53	48.6
Howard Eisley, Boston College	Sr	34	188	91	44.4
Marc Blucas, Wake Forest	Sr	33	109	52	47.7
Brooks Thompson, Okla St	Sr	34	233	110	47.2
Brooks Barnhard, San Diego	Sr	29	125	59	47.2
Bubba Donnelly, Robert Morris	Jr	28	138	65	47.1
Scott Neely, Campbell	Jr	29	173	81	46.8

Note: Minimum 1.5 made per game.

STEALS

	Class	GP	S	Avg
Shawn Griggs, SW Louisiana	Sr	30	120	4.0
Gerald Walker, San Francisco	So	28	109	3.9
Andre Cradle, LIU-Brooklyn	Sr	21	79	3.8
Jason Kidd, California	So	30	94	3.1
B.J. Tyler, Texas	Sr	28	87	3.1
Clarence Ceasar, LSU	Fr	27	80	3.0
Greg Black, Texas-Pan Am	Jr	28	82	2.9
Brooks Thompson, Okla St	Sr	34	99	2.9
Alex Robertson, Dayton	Sr	27	78	2.9
LaMarcus Golden, Tennessee	So	27	78	2.9
Marcus Walton, Alcorn St	Jr	22	63	2.9

BLOCKED SHOTS

	Class	GP	BS	Avg
Grady Livingston, Howard	Jr	26	115	4.4
Jim McIlvaine, Marquette	Sr	33	142	4.3
Theo Ratliff, Wyoming	Jr	28	114	4.1
David Vaughn, Memphis St	So	28	107	3.8
Tim Duncan, Wake Forest	Fr	33	124	3.8
Marcus Camby, Massachusetts	Fr	29	105	3.6
Kelvin Cato, S Alabama	So	24	85	3.5
Donyell Marshall, Connecticut	Jr	34	111	3.3
Michael McDonald, New Orleans	Sr	30	96	3.2
Pascal Fleury, MD-Baltimore County	Jr	25	80	3.2

FIELD GOAL PERCENTAGE

	Class	GP	FGA	FG	Pct
Mike Atkinson, Long Beach St	Jr	26	203	141	69.5
Lynwood Wade, SW Texas St	Sr	32	356	232	65.2
Anthony Miller, Michigan St	Sr	32	249	162	65.1
Deon Thomas, Illinois	Sr	28	327	207	63.3
Aaron Swinson, Auburn	Sr	28	371	234	63.1
Clayton Ritter, James Madison	Jr	28	366	230	62.8
Corliss Williamson, Arkansas	So	34	436	273	62.6
David Ardayfio, Army	Sr	27	289	180	62.3
Jimmy Lunsford, Alabama St	So	28	263	163	62.0
Clifford Rozier, Louisville	Jr	34	400	247	61.8

Note: Minimum 5 made per game.

FREE-THROW PERCENTAGE

	Class	GP	FTA	FT	Pct
Danny Basile, Marist	So	27	89	84	94.4
Dandrea Evans, Troy St	Sr	27	77	72	93.5
Casey Schmidt, Valparaiso	Sr	25	81	75	92.6
Matthew Hildebrand, Liberty	Sr	30	161	149	92.5
Kent Culuko, James Madison	Jr	30	127	117	92.1
Ryan Yoder, Colorado St	Sr	28	117	107	91.5
Travis Ford, Kentucky	Sr	33	113	103	91.2
Ryan Hoover, Notre Dame	So	29	84	76	90.5
Marty Cline, Morehead St	So	27	81	73	90.1
Randy Tucker, N Illinois	Sr	27	79	71	89.9

Note: Minimum 2.5 made per game.

Single-Game Highs

POINTS

62 ....Askia Jones, Kansas St, Mar 24 (vs Fresno St)
54 ....Eddie Benton, Vermont, Jan 29 (vs Drexel)
52 ....Jervaughn Scales, Southern-BR, Nov 26 (vs Patton)
51 ....Izett Buchanan, Marist, Feb 12 (vs LIU-Brooklyn)
51 ....Doremus Bennerman, Siena, Mar 30 (vs Kansas St)
50 ....Orlando Lightfoot, Idaho, Dec 21 (vs Gonzaga)

REBOUNDS

32 ....Jervaughn Scales, Southern-BR, Feb 7 (vs Grambling)
27 ....Willie Fisher, Jacksonville, Dec 4 (vs Louisiana Tech)
26 ....Eric Kubel, Northwestern St, Dec 18 (vs SE Louisiana)
26 ....Michael Smith, Providence, Jan 25 (vs Syracuse)
26 ....Jerome Lambert, Baylor, Feb 6 (vs SMU)
25 ....Jerome Lambert, Baylor, Jan 22 (vs Houston)
25 ....Jeff Clifton, Arkansas St, Jan 29 (vs AR-Little Rock)

ASSISTS

18 ....Nelson Haggerty, Baylor, Dec 20 (vs SW Louisiana)
18 ....Jason Kidd, California, Jan 20 (vs Stanford)
17 ....Danny Doyle, Iona, Feb 19 (vs Fairfield)
16 ....Arriel McDonald, Minnesota, Jan 12 (vs Wisconsin)
16 ....Eathan O'Bryant, Nevada, Jan 15 (vs UC-Irvine)
16 ....Kenny Harris, VCU, Jan 20 (vs Oklahoma)
16 ....Sean Miller, TX-Arlington, Feb 19 (vs Northwestern St)

3-POINT FIELD GOALS

14 ....Askia Jones, Kansas St, Mar 24 (vs Fresno St)
12 ....Al Dillard, Arkansas, Dec 11 (vs Delaware St)
11 ....Scott Neely, Campbell, Jan 29 (vs Coastal Carolina)
11 ....Chris Brown, UC-Irvine, Mar 13 (vs New Mexico St)
Three tied with 10

Single-Game Highs *(Cont.)*

STEALS

10 ....Brevin Knight, Stanford, Dec 20 (vs McNeese St)
10 ....Brian Bidlingmyer, Siena, Jan 15 (vs Loyola [MD])
10 ............B.J. Tyler, Texas, Jan 29 (vs Houston)
10 ....Shawn Moore, Marshall, Jan 29 (vs E Tennessee St)
Four tied with nine

BLOCKED SHOTS

11 ....Grady Livingston, Howard, Jan 13 (vs MD-Eastern Shore)
11 ....Randy Edney, Mt St Mary's (MD), Jan 15 (vs LIU-Brooklyn)
11 ....Theo Ratliff, Wyoming, Feb 3 (vs BYU)
10 ....Donyell Marshall, Connecticut, Jan 17 (vs Hartford)
10 ....Pascal Fleury, MD-Baltimore County, Jan 29 (vs Winthrop)
10 ....Cherokee Parks, Duke, Mar 11 (vs Clemson)
Nine tied with nine

NCAA Men's Division I Team Leaders

SCORING OFFENSE

	GP	W	L	Pts	Avg		GP	W	L	Pts	Avg
Southern-BR	27	16	11	2727	101.0	Arizona	35	29	6	3124	89.3
Troy St	27	13	14	2634	97.6	Nicholls St	28	19	9	2492	89.0
Arkansas	34	31	3	3176	93.4	San Francisco	28	17	11	2488	88.9
Texas	34	26	8	3119	91.7	Oklahoma	28	15	13	2477	88.5
Murray St	29	23	6	2611	90.0	George Mason	27	10	17	2385	88.3

SCORING DEFENSE

	GP	W	L	Pts	Avg		GP	W	L	Pts	Avg
Princeton	26	18	8	1361	52.3	SW Missouri St	27	12	15	1690	62.6
Temple	31	23	8	1697	54.7	Coppin St	30	22	8	1924	64.1
WI-Green Bay	34	27	7	1872	55.1	Pennsylvania	28	25	3	1799	64.3
AL-Birmingham	30	22	8	1806	60.2	Pepperdine	30	19	11	1935	64.5
Marquette	33	24	9	2040	61.8	SW Texas St	32	25	7	2070	64.7

SCORING MARGIN

	Off	Def	Mar		Off	Def	Mar
Arkansas	93.4	75.6	17.9	Kentucky	86.8	74.6	12.2
Connecticut	84.9	68.6	16.3	Kansas	80.5	68.3	12.1
Arizona	89.3	74.4	14.9	Pennsylvania	76.4	64.3	12.1
Southern-BR	101.0	87.7	13.3	Texas	91.7	79.6	12.1
N Carolina	85.6	72.4	13.2	Four tied with 11.7			

FIELD GOAL PERCENTAGE

	FGA	FG	Pct		FGA	FG	Pct
Auburn	1689	854	50.6	Bowling Green	1475	732	49.6
Michigan St	1875	955	50.3	Connecticut	2111	1045	49.5
Radford	1580	793	50.2	Southern-BR	2075	1027	49.5
James Madison	1783	890	49.9	Charleston (SC)	1574	779	49.5
N Carolina	2188	1091	49.9	Iowa St	1644	812	49.4

FIELD GOAL PERCENTAGE DEFENSE

	FGA	FG	Pct		FGA	FG	Pct
Marquette	2097	750	35.8	Manhattan	1734	671	38.7
Temple	1686	621	36.8	George Washington	1766	685	38.8
WI-Green Bay	1777	664	37.4	Drexel	1835	713	38.9
Kansas	2147	823	38.3	Charleston (SC)	1641	639	38.9
AL-Birmingham	1718	661	38.5	Mississippi St	1812	709	39.1

FREE-THROW PERCENTAGE

	FTA	FT	Pct		FTA	FT	Pct
Colgate	665	511	76.8	Indiana	776	582	75.0
WI-Green Bay	607	462	76.1	Utah	521	389	74.7
Iowa St	687	521	75.8	WI-Milwaukee	581	433	74.5
Davidson	704	529	75.1	Nebraska	690	514	74.5
Vanderbilt	742	557	75.1	Morehead St	767	567	73.9
				Wake Forest	700	517	73.9

3-POINT FIELD GOALS MADE PER GAME

	GP	FG	Avg		GP	FG	Avg
Troy St	27	262	9.7	Dayton	27	235	8.7
New Mexico	31	300	9.7	Morehead St	28	243	8.7
Vermont	27	240	8.9	Coastal Carolina	26	222	8.5
Arkansas	34	301	8.9	Coppin St	30	256	8.5
Kentucky	34	301	8.9	Utah	28	235	8.4
St Louis	29	253	8.7	Tulsa	31	254	8.2

3-POINT FIELD GOAL PERCENTAGE

	GP	FGA	FG	Pct		GP	FGA	FG	Pct
Indiana	30	401	182	45.4	Tulsa	31	628	254	40.4
Robert Morris	28	323	139	43.0	Gonzaga	30	460	186	40.4
Evansville	32	570	244	42.8	Boston College	34	579	234	40.4
Oklahoma St	34	619	258	41.7	Coppin St	30	640	256	40.0
Montana	28	369	150	40.7	Charleston (SC)	28	385	154	40.0
					NC-Asheville	27	438	175	40.0

Note: Minimum 3.0 made per game.

NCAA Women's Championship Game Box Score

North Carolina 60

North Carolina	Min	FG M-A	FT M-A	Reb O-T	A	PF	TP
Smith	40	7-19	5-7	5-23	2	2	20
Sampson	38	9-25	0-0	4-8	1	4	21
Crawley	39	4-7	6-8	0-4	1	2	14
Jones	22	0-5	2-3	1-2	3	3	2
Lawrence	40	1-2	0-0	0-4	5	1	3
Suddreth	2	0-0	0-0	0-0	0	1	0
McKee	1	0-0	0-0	0-0	0	0	0
Cooper	12	0-2	0-1	0-0	0	0	0
Gear	6	0-1	0-0	0-1	1	1	0
Totals	200	21-61	13-19	10-42	13	14	60

Percentages: FG—.344, FT—.684. 3-pt goals: 5-13, .385 (Sampson 3-7, Lawrence 1-1, Smith 1-3, Jones 0-1, Cooper 0-1). Team rebounds: 6. Blocked shots: 6 (Crawley 3, Smith 2, Jones). Turnovers: 21 (Smith 6, Crawley 6, Jones 4, Cooper 2, Sampson, Lawrence, Suddreth). Steals: 5 (Sampson 2, Crawley, Lawrence, Cooper).

Louisiana Tech 59

Louisiana Tech	Min	FG M-A	FT M-A	Reb O-T	A	PF	TP
A. Brown	13	2-6	0-0	1-2	0	3	4
Johnson	40	6-15	0-0	3-10	1	2	12
Spurlock	29	1-4	0-0	2-6	0	4	2
Thomas	24	6-14	2-2	0-4	1	3	15
Williams	27	4-19	0-1	1-6	1	0	8
Neal	26	0-3	6-8	0-2	2	2	6
Riser	3	0-0	0-0	0-1	0	0	0
Walker	20	5-7	0-0	4-5	0	0	10
L. Brown	18	1-2	0-0	1-2	0	5	2
Totals	200	25-70	8-11	12-38	5	19	59

Percentages: FG—.357, FT—.727. 3-pt goals: 1-8, .125 (Thomas 1-1, A. Brown 0-1, Johnson 0-2, Williams 0-4). Team rebounds: 6. Blocked shots: 3 (Spurlock, Neal, Riser). Turnovers: 15 (Neal 4, Johnson 3, Spurlock 2, Thomas 2, Williams 2, Walker, L. Brown). Steals: 12 (Neal 4, Spurlock 2, Thomas 2, L. Brown 2, Johnson, Williams).

Halftime: North Carolina 32, Louisiana Tech 32.
A: 11.966. Officials: Corteau, Morningstar.

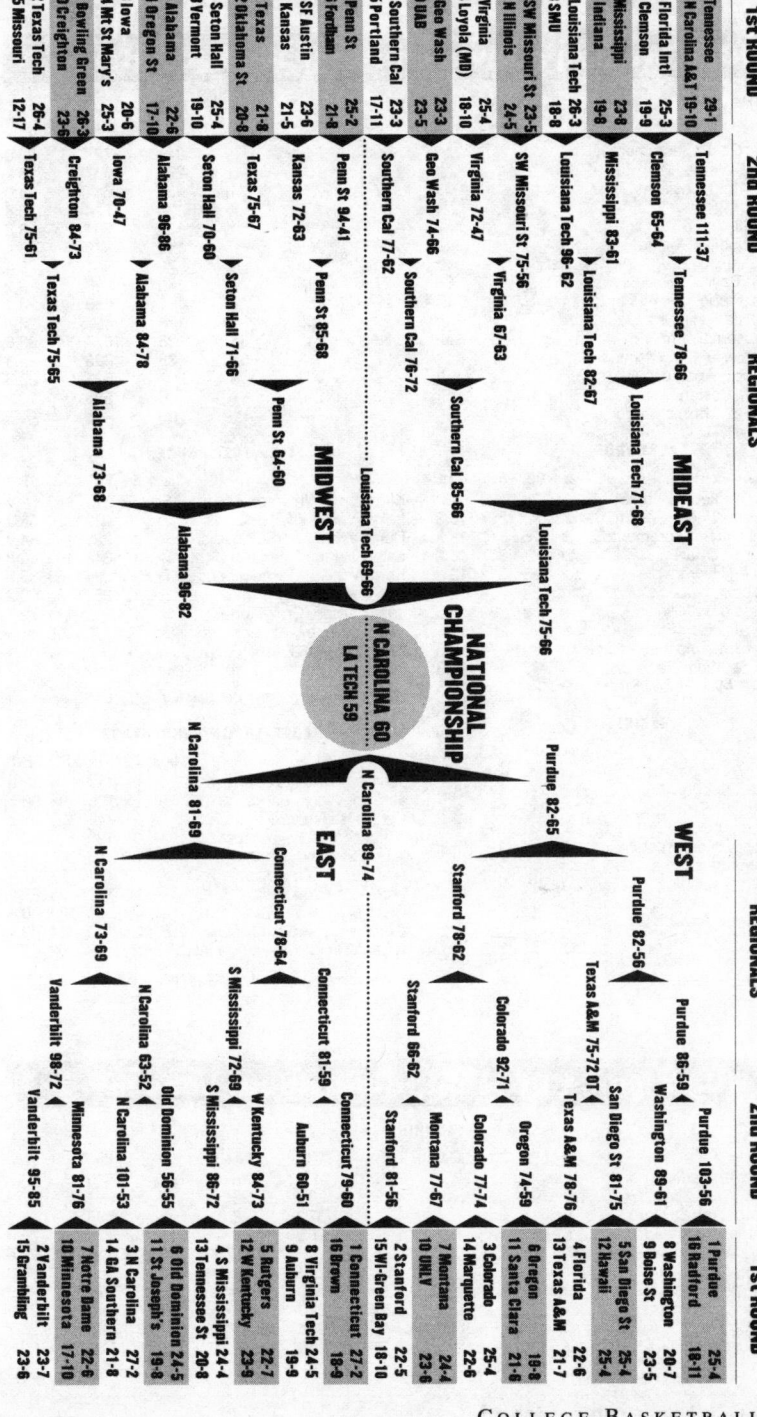

NCAA Women's Division I Individual Leaders

SCORING

	Class	GP	TFG	3FG	FT	Pts	Avg
Kristy Ryan, Cal St-Sacramento	Sr	26	240	2	245	727	28.0
Patty Stoffey, Loyola (MD)	Jr	29	263	0	231	757	26.1
Cornelia Gayden, Louisiana St	Jr	27	221	71	134	647	24.0
Sheri Turnbull, Vermont	Sr	30	257	4	196	714	23.8
Shannon Johnson, S Carolina	So	27	231	44	128	634	23.5
Carol Ann Shudlick, Minnesota	Sr	29	268	0	142	678	23.4
Natalie Williams, UCLA	Sr	24	243	0	75	561	23.4
Mary Lowry, Baylor	So	27	216	24	170	626	23.2
Trenia Tillis, Stephen F. Austin	Sr	29	267	4	131	669	23.1
Tera Sheriff, Jackson St	Jr	20	165	1	123	454	22.7
Anjinea Hopson, Grambling	Jr	30	249	84	95	677	22.6
Dawn Beachler, TX-Pan American	Sr	27	233	55	85	606	22.4
Angela Crosby, Appalachian St	Sr	28	208	0	207	623	22.3
Kerry Curren, Boston College	Sr	27	212	49	126	599	22.2

Two tied with 22.0 points per game.

REBOUNDS

	Class	GP	Reb	Avg
DeShawne Blocker, E Tenn St	Jr	26	450	17.3
Joskeen Garner, Northwestern St	So	28	387	13.8
Kristy Ryan, Cal St-Sacramento	Sr	26	347	13.3
Travesa Gant, Lamar	Sr	27	357	13.2
Tammy Butler, Harvard	Jr	26	343	13.2
Natalie Williams, UCLA	Sr	24	314	13.1
Oberon Pitterson, W Illinois	Jr	28	362	12.0
Tera Sheriff, Jackson St	Jr	20	252	12.6
Sheri Turnbull, Vermont	Sr	30	376	12.5
Lisa Leslie, Southern Cal	Sr	30	369	12.3
Donna White, Miss. Valley St	Sr	27	332	12.3

ASSISTS

	Class	GP	A	Avg
Andrea Nagy, Florida Int'l	Jr	29	298	10.3
Bozana Vidic, Oregon St	So	21	176	8.4
Sharee Mitchum, Oklahoma	Jr	30	242	8.1
Carol Madsen, Xavier (OH)	Sr	29	212	7.3
Moira Kennelly, Northwestern	Sr	27	196	7.3
Niesa Johnson, Alabama	Jr	33	237	7.2
Kelly Pilcher, Montana	Sr	30	215	7.2
Tina Robbins, SW Missouri St	Sr	30	213	7.1
Tamika Matlock, Arizona St	So	25	174	7.0
Lisa Branch, Texas A&M	So	31	214	6.9
Karen Lewis, Wichita St	Jr	27	186	6.9

FIELD GOAL PERCENTAGE

	Class	GP	FGA	FG	Pct
Kim Wood, WI-Green Bay	Sr	27	271	188	69.4
Lidiya Varbanova, Boise St	Sr	29	299	198	66.2
Deneka Knowles, SE Louisiana	So	28	225	146	64.9
Latoja Harris, Toledo	Sr	31	312	199	63.8
Kara Wolters, Connecticut	Fr	33	264	168	63.6
Kris Kugel, Creighton	Sr	31	253	160	63.2
Jenny Olson, Creighton	Jr	31	273	171	62.6
Angela Crosby, Appalachian St	Sr	28	336	208	61.9
Rushia Brown, Furman	Sr	27	394	242	61.4
DeShawn Blocker, E Tenn St	Jr	26	322	197	61.2

Note: Minimum 5 made per game.

FREE-THROW PERCENTAGE

	Class	GP	FTA	FT	Pct
Jennifer Howard, N Carolina St	Fr	27	127	118	92.9
Jennifer Clary, Idaho	Sr	25	105	95	90.5
Denise Hammersley, Fordham	Jr	30	141	125	88.7
Tiffany Woosley, Tennessee	Jr	33	125	110	88.0
Karen Stanley, Furman	Jr	28	106	93	87.7
Christie Osborne, Virginia Tech	Jr	30	111	97	87.4
Nicole Levesque, Wake Forest	Sr	27	109	95	87.2
Carol Madsen, Xavier (OH)	Sr	29	149	129	86.6
Chrissie Donahue, La Salle	Sr	28	140	121	86.4
Albena Branzova, Florida Int'l	Jr	29	108	92	85.2

Note: Minimum 2.5 made per game.

NCAA Men's Division II Individual Leaders

SCORING

	Class	GP	TFG	3FG	FT	Pts	Avg
Kwame Morton, Clarion	Sr	26	264	126	191	845	32.5
Eric Bovaird, West Liberty St	Jr	25	204	99	190	697	27.9
Eric Kline, Northern St	Jr	33	321	148	108	898	27.2
Kevin Aronson, Moorhead St	Sr	27	233	107	151	724	26.8
Jerry Meyer, MN-Duluth	Sr	27	235	98	150	718	26.6
DeCarlo Deveaux, Tampa	Sr	29	248	54	214	764	26.3
Tony Bailey, W Georgia	Sr	26	210	56	198	674	25.9
Dennis Edwards, Fort Hays St	Jr	29	326	0	97	749	25.8
Michael Aaron, Wayne St (MI)	Sr	25	256	11	120	643	25.7
Ed Wheeler, Angelo St	Sr	26	255	0	149	659	25.3

NCAA Men's Division II Individual Leaders (Cont.)

REBOUNDS

	Class	GP	Reb	Avg
Pat Armour, Jacksonville St	Jr	25	363	14.5
James Hector, American Int'l	Sr	31	435	14.0
Wayne Robertson, NH College	Sr	33	424	12.8
John Carey, Concordia (NY)	Sr	27	329	12.2
Michael Bivins, Albany St (GA)	Sr	29	349	12.0
Chris Tucker, MO Southern St	Sr	26	306	11.8
Clarence Tyson, Washburn	Sr	33	379	11.5
Dan Sandel, Le Moyne	Sr	27	310	11.5
Ed Wheeler, Angelo St	Sr	26	296	11.4
Eric Ruskiewicz, NY Tech	Sr	28	316	11.3

ASSISTS

	Class	GP	A	Avg
Ernest Jenkins, NM Highlands	Jr	27	277	10.3
Pat Chambers, Philadelphia Textile	Sr	30	290	9.7
Marcus Talbert, Colorado Christian	Jr	27	261	9.7
Darnell White, California (PA)	Sr	30	273	9.1
Mike Mitchell, Notre Dame (CA)	Sr	27	238	8.8
Tyrone Tate, S Indiana	Sr	32	270	8.4
Damon Scott, Winona St	Jr	28	220	7.9
Rob Paternostro, NH College	Jr	33	258	7.8
Tullius Pate, Coker	Jr	28	217	7.8
Donald Parrott, S Colorado	Jr	29	224	7.7
Hal Chambers, Columbus	Sr	29	222	7.7

FIELD GOAL PERCENTAGE

	Class	GP	FGA	FG	Pct
Chad Scott, California (PA)	Sr	30	245	178	72.7
Jermaine Carlton, Pfeiffer	Sr	30	341	232	68.0
Stan Gouard, S Indiana	So	31	357	242	67.8
Dennis Edwards, Fort Hays St	Jr	29	484	326	67.4
Wayne Robertson, NH College	Sr	33	407	274	67.3
Carl Johnson, Seattle Pacific	Sr	28	223	150	67.3
Roy O'Neale, W Texas A&M	Sr	30	334	221	66.2
Bill Kappel, Mesa St	Sr	29	298	197	66.1
Jared Lux, IU/PU-Indianapolis	So	27	220	144	65.5
Steve Branch, Clarion	Sr	26	214	140	65.4

Note: Minimum 5 made per game.

FREE-THROW PERCENTAGE

	Class	GP	FTA	FT	Pct
Jay Harrie, E Montana	Jr	26	92	86	93.5
Derek Chaney, N Colorado	Sr	29	105	94	89.5
Kevin Aronson, Moorhead St	Sr	27	169	151	89.3
James Moore, Wingate	Fr	26	89	79	88.8
Scott Graser, Lake Superior St	So	24	70	62	88.6
Tony Bailey, W Georgia	Sr	26	224	198	88.4
Russ Harper, Hawaii-Hilo	Sr	28	86	76	88.4
Perrell Lucas, Indianapolis	Jr	27	137	121	88.3
Kevin Burckhard, Northern St	Jr	33	99	87	87.9
Mark Meyer, West Liberty St	Jr	25	128	112	87.5

Note: Minimum 2.5 made per game.

NCAA Women's Division II Individual Leaders

SCORING

	Class	GP	TFG	3FG	FT	Pts	Avg
Tammy Greene, Philadelphia Textile	Sr	30	278	27	199	782	26.1
Nicole Collins, Angelo St	Jr	28	269	52	119	709	25.3
Kim Young, Cal St-San Bernadino	Sr	31	313	26	92	744	24.0
Lola Jones, Bluefield St	Sr	29	281	1	128	691	23.8
Iris Bethea, Pembroke St	Jr	25	210	28	146	594	23.8
Attala Young, Erskine	Jr	27	232	0	175	639	23.7
Angela Shelton, Mississippi-Women	Jr	25	215	19	140	589	23.6
Andrea Hines, E Texas St	Sr	27	241	0	154	636	23.6
Ginger Keller, Nebraska-Kearney	Sr	28	233	1	180	647	23.1
Lara Thornton, California (PA)	Sr	29	256	103	54	669	23.1

REBOUNDS

	Class	GP	Reb	Avg
Carrolyn Burke, Queens (NY)	So	25	379	15.2
Tonya Roper, Wingate	Sr	25	372	14.9
Vanessa White, Tuskegee	Jr	27	390	14.4
Lola Jones, Bluefield St	Sr	29	415	14.3
Tricia Hampton, Angelo St	Jr	29	387	13.3
Christina Hollins, Fayetteville St	So	27	351	13.0
Jen Harrington, Assumption	Sr	27	349	12.9
Sonya Cato, SC-Aiken	So	27	331	12.3
Carlita Jones, Clarion	Jr	30	364	12.1
Cynthia Bridges, Fort Valley St	Jr	27	325	12.0

ASSISTS

	Class	GP	A	Avg
Lorraine Lynch, District of Columbia	So	24	226	9.4
Joanna Bernabei, West Liberty St	Fr	27	239	8.9
Lori Richelderfer, California (PA)	Sr	28	240	8.6
Lisa Rice, Norfolk St	Jr	31	261	8.4
Lynne Liebhauser, St Michael's	Sr	27	218	8.1
Kathleen Shriver, Columbus	Sr	29	230	7.9
Cynthia Thomas, Wingate	Jr	28	209	7.5
Tammie Beckley, Cal St-San Bernadino	Jr	33	245	7.4
Jody Hill, Pace	Sr	31	221	7.1
Lori Young, Ferris St	So	21	141	6.7
Theresa Perry, Delta St	Jr	26	174	6.7

FIELD GOAL PERCENTAGE

	Class	GP	FGA	FG	Pct
Julie Szykowny, Gannon	Jr	26	233	157	67.4
Angela Watson, C Arkansas	So	27	320	214	66.9
Jackie Jackson, Mississippi College	So	24	202	129	63.9
Delaina Adams, Gardner-Webb	So	26	285	179	62.8
Cynthia Bridges, Fort Valley St	Jr	27	229	143	62.4
Tonya Foster, MO Western St	Jr	32	369	228	61.8
Angel Donley, N Kentucky	Jr	27	308	190	61.7
Shelly Havard, N Michigan	Jr	27	353	216	61.2
Jennifer Clarkson, Abilene Christian	So	30	381	233	61.2
Stacy Johnson, Delta St	Fr	25	244	149	61.1

Note: Minimum 5 made per game.

FREE-THROW PERCENTAGE

	Class	GP	FTA	FT	Pct
Sara Belanger, MN-Duluth	So	31	90	79	87.8
Kathy Murphy, Mansfield	Jr	23	88	76	86.4
Jen German, Bloomsburg	Fr	27	134	115	85.8
Kathleen Shippee, St Anselm	Jr	31	102	87	85.3
Darlene Hildebrand, Philadelphia Textile	Jr	29	128	109	85.2
Kelly Lorenz, Philadelphia Textile	Sr	30	91	77	84.6
Rhonda Matzke, Washburn	Sr	27	114	96	84.2
Esther King, Stonehill	So	32	101	85	84.2
Nicci Hays, NE Missouri St	Fr	26	91	76	83.5
Starr Ferguson, N Alabama	Jr	32	103	86	83.5

Note: Minimum 2.5 made per game.

NCAA Men's Division III Individual Leaders

SCORING

	Class	GP	TFG	3FG	FT	Pts	Avg
Steve Diekman, Grinnell	Jr	21	250	117	106	723	34.4
Moses Jean-Pierre, Plymouth St	Sr	30	257	106	243	863	28.8
Scott Fitch, Geneseo St	Sr	27	224	102	202	752	27.9
Lance Castle, Monmouth (IL)	Jr	23	218	65	131	632	27.5
Ted Berry, Christopher Newport	Sr	27	280	66	111	737	27.3
Mark Timko, Grove City	Sr	25	246	50	128	670	26.8
T.J Gondek, Colby-Sawyer	Jr	25	219	61	164	663	26.5
Rick Hughes, Thomas More	So	26	286	4	111	687	26.4
Phil Dixon, Shenandoah	So	26	230	47	158	665	25.6
Dameon Ross, Salisbury St	Sr	21	190	56	100	536	25.5

REBOUNDS

	Class	GP	Reb	Avg
Chris Sullivan, St John Fisher	Sr	23	319	13.9
Andrew South, New Jersey Tech	Jr	27	372	13.8
Blair Slattery, Occidental	Sr	24	325	13.5
Daniel Aaron, Yeshiva	Sr	19	244	12.8
Mark Walker, Upsala	Jr	27	338	12.5
Roy Jansen, Salve Regina	Sr	25	305	12.2
Larry Jones, Lehman	Fr	24	291	12.1
Jim Hoopes, Albright	Sr	25	297	11.9
Chris Eaton, Eureka	Sr	31	363	11.7
Keith Claiborne, Averett	Sr	23	268	11.7

ASSISTS

	Class	GP	A	Avg
Phil Dixon, Shenandoah	So	26	253	9.7
Stacey Ross, Fontbonne	Sr	25	214	8.6
Moses Jean-Pierre, Plymouth St	Sr	30	233	7.8
Nate Harris, Clarkson	So	24	184	7.7
Bobby Bonjean, Illinois College	Sr	22	165	7.5
Kelley McClure, Otterbein	So	28	207	7.4
Steve Evans, Union (NY)	Sr	26	192	7.4
Tres Wolf, Susquehanna	Sr	26	189	7.3
Mike Lustina, Wabash	Jr	23	166	7.2
Tom Wolfe, Salisbury St	Sr	21	151	7.2

FIELD GOAL PERCENTAGE

	Class	GP	FGA	FG	Pct
Travis Weiss, St John's (MN)	Sr	26	209	160	76.6
Dan Rush, Bridgewater (VA)	Jr	26	239	170	71.1
Greg Kemp, Aurora	Sr	25	230	159	69.1
John Wassenbergh, St Joseph's (ME)	So	26	308	210	68.2
Mike Kent, Gallaudet	So	25	310	205	66.1
Kevin Folkl, Washington (MO)	So	25	227	149	65.6
Jim South, Augsburg	So	24	189	124	65.6
Scott Lauinger, Gust Adolphus	So	23	203	132	65.0
Frank Grzywacz, Johns Hopkins	Sr	27	260	167	64.2
Abe Tubbs, Cornell College	Sr	23	333	213	64.0

Note: Minimum 5 made per game.

FREE-THROW PERCENTAGE

	Class	GP	FTA	FT	Pct
Jason Prevenost, Middlebury	Jr	22	64	60	93.8
Mark Coassolo, Elizabethtown	Sr	26	89	82	92.1
Roger Teeling, Loras	Sr	25	72	65	90.3
Gene Nolan, Washington (MO)	So	25	90	81	90.0
Scott Adams, Hanover	Sr	26	99	89	89.9
Chad Hutson, IL-Wesleyan	Jr	25	93	83	89.2
Mike Rhoades, Lebanon Valley	Jr	32	231	205	88.7
Nate Flynn, Lawrence	So	20	75	66	88.0
Scott Butcher, Emory & Henry	Sr	27	78	68	87.2
Victor Koytich, Framingham St	Jr	21	140	122	87.1

Note: Minimum 2.5 made per game.

NCAA Women's Division III Individual Leaders

SCORING

	Class	GP	TFG	3FG	FT	Pts	Avg
Emilie Hanson, Central (IA)	Jr	27	310	14	166	800	29.6
Danielle Potter, Rockford	Jr	24	261	22	138	682	28.4
Laura Williams, Principia	Sr	21	214	21	117	566	27.0
Anessa Lourensz, Utica Tech	Sr	24	210	11	178	609	25.4
Karen Barefoot, Christopher Newport	Sr	25	205	13	206	629	25.2
Kim Prewitt, Thomas More	So	25	194	107	116	611	24.4
Sybil Smith, Baruch	Jr	24	220	9	129	578	24.1
Chris Pagano, Middlebury	Sr	26	236	52	98	622	23.9
Catina Jeffries, Rust	Sr	22	195	52	80	522	23.7
Leah Onks, Maryville (TN)	Sr	27	231	42	131	635	23.5

REBOUNDS

	Class	GP	Reb	Avg
Liza Janssen, Wellesley	Sr	22	388	17.6
Naneka Brathwaite, Lincoln (PA)	So	19	311	16.4
Sybil Smith, Baruch	Jr	24	380	15.8
Giovanni Licorish, Baruch	So	24	368	15.3
Kim Roth, Salisbury St	Jr	22	335	15.2
Kiersten Schnacke, Randolph-Macon Woman's	So	23	343	14.9
Cassandra Clemons, Gaucher	Jr	24	347	14.5
Sue Burtoft, Bridgewater (MA)	Jr	22	313	14.2
Jennifer Kunz, Occidental	Jr	25	353	14.1
Vangela Crowe, Rutgers-Newark	Sr	21	287	13.7
Molly Lackman, Immaculata	Sr	23	314	13.7

ASSISTS

	Class	GP	A	Avg
Karen Barefoot, Chris. Newport	Sr	25	273	10.9
Lisa Pliskin, Blackburn	Sr	26	207	8.0
Kristie Workman, Roanoke	Sr	28	207	7.4
Leet Perez, Gallaudet	Jr	25	183	7.3
Tammy Swartzlander, E Nazarene	So	22	160	7.3
Diana Cortez, Cal Lutheran	Jr	23	161	7.0
Mary Keegan, Loras	Jr	24	164	6.8
Regan McGorry, Scranton	Sr	30	203	6.8
Patricia Frost, Upsala	Jr	25	167	6.7
Danielle Moorehead, Brockport St	Sr	26	171	6.6

FIELD GOAL PERCENTAGE

	Class	GP	FGA	FG	Pct
Kari Tufte, Luther	So	25	289	202	69.9
Katie Mans, Alma	Sr	27	311	201	64.6
Sarah Hackl, St Norbert	Jrr	22	259	160	61.8
Lanette Stephan, Franklin	So	25	241	148	61.4
Liza Janssen, Wellesley	Sr	22	329	198	60.2
Tina Kampa, St Benedict	Jr	25	220	131	59.5
Abby Dillon, Simpson	So	25	233	137	58.8
Angie Horner, Hiram	Sr	24	322	189	58.7
Katina Johnson, Ramapo	Sr	25	289	169	58.5
Sheila Retcher, Defiance	Sr	28	247	143	57.9
Pam Wubben, Calvin	Sr	25	304	176	57.9

Note: Minimum 5 made per game.

FREE-THROW PERCENTAGE

	Class	GP	FTA	FT	Pct
Stephanie Sealer, Clarkson	Jr	24	66	60	90.9
Marcy Hiner, Adrian	Jr	25	87	79	90.8
Michelle Walker, Mt Union	Jr	27	106	94	88.7
Kim Graff, Kenyon	Fr	24	76	66	86.8
Susie Young, Elizabethtown	Sr	26	79	68	86.1
Aimee Bonner, Otterbein	Jr	26	114	98	86.0
Jody Landish, WI-Whitewater	Jr	25	106	91	85.8
Michele Merten, Babson	Jr	27	110	94	85.5
Cris Shaw, Waynesburg	Sr	23	89	76	85.4
Jill Smith, Baldwin-Wallace	Fr	26	85	72	84.7

Note: Minimum 2.5 made per game.

Eureka! Cut!

President Clinton's Arkansas Razorbacks weren't the only presidentially touched team to win a title in 1994. Tiny Eureka (Ill.) College, with an enrollment of 500, won the NAIA Division II men's basketball championship on March 15 with a 98–95 overtime victory over Northern State–South Dakota. Among the faxes received by the Red Devils before their final game was one that included this inspirational message from Eureka's most famous alumnus:"I wish you all the best as you face the tough competition in the coming days. You have what it takes to be victorious; so I ask you, please go out there and win one for the Gipper."

Let's go over this one more time, Ron: The sport was football, the famous halftime speech occurred only in a movie, and you are *not* the Gipper.

NCAA Division I Men's Championship Results

NCAA Final Four Results

Year	Winner	Score	Runner-up	Third Place	Fourth Place	Winning Coach
1939	Oregon	46-33	Ohio St	*Oklahoma	*Villanova	Howard Hobson
1940	Indiana	60-42	Kansas	*Duquesne	*Southern Cal	Branch McCracken
1941	Wisconsin	39-34	Washington St	*Pittsburgh	*Arkansas	Harold Foster
1942	Stanford	53-38	Dartmouth	*Colorado	*Kentucky	Everett Dean
1943	Wyoming	46-34	Georgetown	*Texas	*DePaul	Everett Shelton
1944	Utah	42-40 (OT)	Dartmouth	*Iowa St	*Ohio St	Vadal Peterson
1945	Oklahoma St	49-45	NYU	*Arkansas	*Ohio St	Hank Iba
1946	Oklahoma St	43-40	N Carolina	Ohio St	California	Hank Iba
1947	Holy Cross	58-47	Oklahoma	Texas	CCNY	Alvin Julian
1948	Kentucky	58-42	Baylor	Holy Cross	Kansas St	Adolph Rupp
1949	Kentucky	46-36	Oklahoma St	Illinois	Oregon St	Adolph Rupp
1950	CCNY	71-68	Bradley	N Carolina St	Baylor	Nat Holman
1951	Kentucky	68-58	Kansas St	Illinois	Oklahoma St	Adolph Rupp
1952	Kansas	80-63	St John's (NY)	Illinois	Santa Clara	Forrest Allen
1953	Indiana	69-68	Kansas	Washington	Louisiana St	Branch McCracken
1954	La Salle	92-76	Bradley	Penn St	Southern Cal	Kenneth Loeffler
1955	San Francisco	77-63	La Salle	Colorado	Iowa	Phil Woolpert
1956	San Francisco	83-71	Iowa	Temple	Southern Meth	Phil Woolpert
1957	N Carolina	54-53†	Kansas	San Francisco	Michigan St	Frank McGuire
1958	Kentucky	84-72	Seattle	Temple	Kansas St	Adolph Rupp
1959	California	71-70	W Virginia	Cincinnati	Louisville	Pete Newell
1960	Ohio St	75-55	California	Cincinnati	NYU	Fred Taylor
1961	Cincinnati	70-65 (OT)	Ohio St	Vacated‡	Utah	Edwin Jucker
1962	Cincinnati	71-59	Ohio St	Wake Forest	UCLA	Edwin Jucker
1963	Loyola (IL)	60-58 (OT)	Cincinnati	Duke	Oregon St	George Ireland
1964	UCLA	98-83	Duke	Michigan	Kansas St	John Wooden
1965	UCLA	91-80	Michigan	Princeton	Wichita St	John Wooden
1966	UTEP	72-65	Kentucky	Duke	Utah	Don Haskins
1967	UCLA	79-64	Dayton	Houston	N Carolina	John Wooden
1968	UCLA	78-55	N Carolina	Ohio St	Houston	John Wooden
1969	UCLA	92-72	Purdue	Drake	N Carolina	John Wooden
1970	UCLA	80-69	Jacksonville	New Mexico St	St Bonaventure	John Wooden
1971	UCLA	68-62	Vacated‡	Vacated‡	Kansas	John Wooden
1972	UCLA	81-76	Florida St	N Carolina	Louisville	John Wooden
1973	UCLA	87-66	Memphis St	Indiana	Providence	John Wooden
1974	N Carolina St	76-64	Marquette	UCLA	Kansas	Norm Sloan
1975	UCLA	92-85	Kentucky	Louisville	Syracuse	John Wooden
1976	Indiana	86-68	Michigan	UCLA	Rutgers	Bob Knight
1977	Marquette	67-59	N Carolina	NV-Las Vegas	NC-Charlotte	Al McGuire
1978	Kentucky	94-88	Duke	Arkansas	Notre Dame	Joe Hall
1979	Michigan St	75-64	Indiana St	DePaul	Penn	Jud Heathcote
1980	Louisville	59-54	Vacated‡	Purdue	Iowa	Denny Crum
1981	Indiana	63-50	N Carolina	Virginia	Louisiana St	Bob Knight
1982	N Carolina	63-62	Georgetown	*Houston	*Louisville	Dean Smith
1983	N Carolina St	54-52	Houston	*Georgia	*Louisville	Jim Valvano
1984	Georgetown	84-75	Houston	*Kentucky	*Virginia	John Thompson
1985	Villanova	66-64	Georgetown	*St John's (NY)	Vacated‡	Rollie Massimino
1986	Louisville	72-69	Duke	*Kansas	*Louisiana St	Denny Crum
1987	Indiana	74-73	Syracuse	*NV-Las Vegas	*Providence	Bob Knight
1988	Kansas	83-79	Oklahoma	*Arizona	*Duke	Larry Brown
1989	Michigan	80-79 (OT)	Seton Hall	*Duke	*Illinois	Steve Fisher
1990	UNLV	103-73	Duke	*Arkansas	*Georgia Tech	Jerry Tarkanian
1991	Duke	72-65	Kansas	*UNLV	*N Carolina	Mike Krzyzewski
1992	Duke	71-51	Michigan	*Cincinnati	*Indiana	Mike Krzyzewski
1993	N Carolina	77-71	Michigan	*Kansas	*Kentucky	Dean Smith
1994	Arkansas	76-72	Duke	*Arizona	*Florida	Nolan Richardson

*Tied for third place.

†Three overtimes.

‡Student-athletes representing St Joseph's (PA) in 1961, Villanova in 1971 (runner-up), Western Kentucky in 1971 (third), UCLA (19 80) and Memphis State (1985) were declared ineligible subsequent to the tournament. Under NCAA rules, the teams' and ineligible student-athletes' records were deleted, and the teams' places in the standings were vacated.

NCAA Final Four MVPs

Year	Winner, School	GP	Field Goals		3-Pt FG		Free Throws		Reb	A	Stl	BS	Avg
			FGM	Pct	FGA	FGM	FTM	Pct					
1939	....None selected												
1940	....Marv Huffman, Indiana	2	7	—	—	—	4	—	—	—	—	—	9.0
1941	....John Kotz, Wisconsin	2	8	—	—	—	6	—	—	—	—	—	11.0
1942	....Howard Dallmar, Stanford	2	8	—	—	—	4	66.7	—	—	—	—	10.0
1943	....Ken Sailors, Wyoming	2	10	—	—	—	8	72.7	—	—	—	—	14.0
1944	....Arnie Ferrin, Utah	2	11	—	—	—	6	—	—	—	—	—	14.0
1945	....Bob Kurland, Oklahoma St	2	16	—	—	—	5	—	—	—	—	—	18.5
1946	....Bob Kurland, Oklahoma St	2	21	—	—	—	10	66.7	—	—	—	—	26.0
1947	....George Kaftan, Holy Cross	2	18	—	—	—	12	70.6	—	—	—	—	24.0
1948	....Alex Groza, Kentucky	2	16	—	—	—	5	—	—	—	—	—	18.5
1949	....Alex Groza, Kentucky	2	19	—	—	—	14	—	—	—	—	—	26.0
1950	....Irwin Dambrot, CCNY	2	12	42.9	—	—	4	50.0	—	—	—	—	14.0
1951	....None selected												
1952	....Clyde Lovellette, Kansas	2	24	—	—	—	18	—	—	—	—	—	33.0
1953	....*B.H.Horn, Kansas	2	17	—	—	—	17	—	—	—	—	—	25.5
1954	....Tom Gola, La Salle	2	12	—	—	—	14	—	—	—	—	—	19.0
1955	....Bill Russell, San Francisco	2	19	—	—	—	9	—	—	—	—	—	23.5
1956	....*Hal Lear, Temple	2	32	—	—	—	16	—	—	—	—	—	40.0
1957	....*Wilt Chamberlain, Kansas	2	18	51.4	—	—	19	70.4	25	—	—	—	32.5
1958	....*Elgin Baylor, Seattle	2	18	34.0	—	—	12	75.0	41	—	—	—	24.0
1959	....*Jerry West, West Virginia	2	22	66.7	—	—	22	68.8	25	—	—	—	33.0
1960	....Jerry Lucas, Ohio State	2	16	66.7	—	—	3	100.0	23	—	—	—	17.5
1961	....*Jerry Lucas, Ohio State	2	20	71.4	—	—	16	94.1	25	—	—	—	28.0
1962	....Paul Hogue, Cincinnati	2	23	63.9	—	—	12	63.2	38	—	—	—	29.0
1963	....Art Heyman, Duke	2	18	41.0	—	—	15	68.2	19	—	—	—	25.5
1964	....Walt Hazzard, UCLA	2	11	55.0	—	—	8	66.7	10	—	—	—	15.0
1965	....*Bill Bradley, Princeton	2	34	63.0	—	—	19	95.0	24	—	—	—	43.5
1966	....*Jerry Chambers, Utah	2	25	53.2	—	—	20	83.3	35	—	—	—	35.0
1967	....Lew Alcindor, UCLA	2	14	60.9	—	—	11	45.8	38	—	—	—	19.5
1968	....Lew Alcindor, UCLA	2	22	62.9	—	—	9	90.0	34	—	—	—	26.5
1969	....Lew Alcindor, UCLA	2	23	67.7	—	—	16	64.0	41	—	—	—	31.0
1970	....Sidney Wicks, UCLA	2	15	71.4	—	—	9	60.0	34	—	—	—	19.5
1971	....*Howard Porter, Villanova	2	20	48.8	—	—	7	77.8	24	—	—	—	23.5
1972	....Bill Walton, UCLA	2	20	69.0	—	—	17	73.9	41	—	—	—	28.5
1973	....Bill Walton, UCLA	2	28	82.4	—	—	2	40.0	30	—	—	—	29.0
1974	....David Thompson, NC State	2	19	51.4	—	—	11	78.6	17	—	—	—	24.5
1975	....Richard Washington, UCLA	2	23	54.8	—	—	8	72.7	20	—	—	—	27.0
1976	....Kent Benson, Indiana	2	17	50.0	—	—	7	63.6	18	—	—	—	20.5
1977	....Butch Lee, Marquette	2	11	34.4	—	—	8	100.0	6	2	1	1	15.0
1978	....Jack Givens, Kentucky	2	28	65.1	—	—	8	66.7	17	4	1	3	32.0
1979	....Earvin Johnson, Michigan St	2	17	68.0	—	—	19	86.4	17	3	0	2	26.5
1980	....Darrell Griffith, Louisville	2	23	62.2	—	—	11	68.8	7	15	0	2	28.5
1981	....Isiah Thomas, Indiana	2	14	56.0	—	—	9	81.8	4	9	3	4	18.5
1982	....James Worthy, N Carolina	2	20	74.1	—	—	2	28.6	8	9	0	4	21.0
1983	....*Akeem Olajuwon, Houston	2	16	55.2	—	—	9	64.3	40	3	2	5	20.5
1984	....Patrick Ewing, Georgetown	2	8	57.1	—	—	2	100.0	18	1	15	1	9.0
1985	....Ed Pinckney, Villanova	2	8	57.1	—	—	12	75.0	15	6	3	0	14.0
1986	....Pervis Ellison, Louisville	2	15	60.0	—	—	6	75.0	24	2	3	1	18.0
1987	....Keith Smart, Indiana	2	14	63.6	1	0	7	77.8	7	7	0	2	17.5
1988	....Danny Manning, Kansas	2	25	55.6	1	0	6	66.7	17	4	8	9	28.0
1989	....Glenn Rice, Michigan	2	24	49.0	16	7	4	100.0	16	1	0	3	29.5
1990	....Anderson Hunt, UNLV	2	19	61.3	16	9	2	50.0	4	9	1	1	24.5
1991	....Christian Laettner, Duke	2	12	54.5	1	1	21	91.3	17	2	1	2	23.0
1992	....Bobby Hurley, Duke	2	10	41.7	12	7	8	80.0	3	11	0	3	17.5
1993	....Donald Williams, N Carolina	2	15	65.2	14	10	10	100.0	4	2	2	0	25.0
1994	....Corliss Williamson, Arkansas	2	21	50.0	0	0	10	71.4	21	8	4	3	26.0

*Not a member of the championship-winning team

Best NCAA Tournament Single-Game Scoring Performances

Player and Team	Year	Round	FG	3FG	FT	TP
Austin Carr, Notre Dame vs Ohio	1970	1st	25	—	11	61
Bill Bradley, Princeton vs Wichita St.	1965	C*	22	—	14	58
Oscar Robertson, Cincinnati vs Arkansas	1958	C	21	—	14	56
Austin Carr, Notre Dame vs Kentucky	1970	2nd	22	—	8	52
Austin Carr, Notre Dame vs Texas Christian	1971	1st	20	—	12	52
David Robinson, Navy vs Michigan	1987	1st	22	0	6	50
Elvin Hayes, Houston vs Loyola (IL)	1968	1st	20	—	9	49
Hal Lear, Temple vs Southern Meth	1956	C*	17	—	14	48
Austin Carr, Notre Dame vs Houston	1971	C	17	—	13	47
Dave Corzine, DePaul vs Louisville	1978	2nd	18	—	10	46
Bob Houbregs, Washington vs Seattle	1953	2nd	20	—	5	45
Austin Carr, Notre Dame vs Iowa	1970	C	21	—	3	45
Bo Kimble, Loyola Marymount vs New Mexico St	1990	1st	17	5	6	45

C regional third place; C* third-place game.

NIT Championship Results

Year	Winner	Score	Runner-up	Year	Winner	Score	Runner-up
1938	Temple	60-36	Colorado	1966	BYU	97-84	NYU
1939	Long Island U	44-32	Loyola (IL)	1967	Southern Illinois	71-56	Marquette
1940	Colorado	51-40	Duquesne	1968	Dayton	61-48	Kansas
1941	Long Island U	56-42	Ohio U	1969	Temple	89-76	Boston College
1942	W Virginia	47-45	W Kentucky	1970	Marquette	65-53	St John's (NY)
1943	St John's (NY)	48-27	Toledo	1971	N Carolina	84-66	Georgia Tech
1944	St John's (NY)	47-39	DePaul	1972	Maryland	100-69	Niagara
1945	DePaul	71-54	Bowling Green	1973	Virginia Tech	92-91 (OT)	Notre Dame
1946	Kentucky	46-45	Rhode Island	1974	Purdue	97-81	Utah
1947	Utah	49-45	Kentucky	1975	Princeton	80-69	Providence
1948	St Louis	65-52	NYU	1976	Kentucky	71-67	NC-Charlotte
1949	San Francisco	48-47	Loyola (IL)	1977	St Bonaventure	94-91	Houston
1950	CCNY	69-61	Bradley	1978	Texas	101-93	N Carolina St
1951	BYU	62-43	Dayton	1979	Indiana	53-52	Purdue
1952	La Salle	75-64	Dayton	1980	Virginia	58-55	Minnesota
1953	Seton Hall	58-46	St John's (NY)	1981	Tulsa	86-84 (OT)	Syracuse
1954	Holy Cross	71-62	Duquesne	1982	Bradley	67-58	Purdue
1955	Duquesne	70-58	Dayton	1983	Fresno St	69-60	DePaul
1956	Louisville	93-80	Dayton	1984	Michigan	83-63	Notre Dame
1957	Bradley	84-83	Memphis St	1985	UCLA	65-62	Indiana
1958	Xavier (OH)	78-74 (OT)	Dayton	1986	Ohio St	73-63	Wyoming
1959	St John's (NY)	76-71 (OT)	Bradley	1987	Southern Miss	84-80	La Salle
1960	Bradley	88-72	Providence	1988	Connecticut	72-67	Ohio St
1961	Providence	62-59	St Louis	1989	St John's (NY)	73-65	St Louis
1962	Dayton	73-67	St John's (NY)	1990	Vanderbilt	74-72	St Louis
1963	Providence	81-66	Canisius	1991	Stanford	78-72	Oklahoma
1964	Bradley	86-54	New Mexico	1992	Virginia	81-76	Notre Dame
1965	St John's (NY)	55-51	Villanova	1993	Minnesota	62-61	Georgetown
				1994	Villanova	80-73	Vanderbilt

NCAA Division I Men's Season Leaders

Scoring Average

Year	Player and Team	Ht	Class	GP	FG	3FG	FT	Pts	Avg
1948	Murray Wier, Iowa	5-9	Sr	19	152	—	95	399	21.0
1949	Tony Lavelli, Yale	6-3	Sr	30	228	—	215	671	22.4
1950	Paul Arizin, Villanova	6-3	Sr	29	260	—	215	735	25.3
1951	Bill Mlkvy, Temple	6-4	Sr	25	303	—	125	731	29.2
1952	Clyde Lovellette, Kansas	6-9	Sr	28	315	—	165	795	28.4
1953	Frank Selvy, Furman	6-3	Jr	25	272	—	194	738	29.5
1954	Frank Selvy, Furman	6-3	Sr	29	427	—	355	1209	41.7
1955	Darrell Floyd, Furman	6-1	Jr	25	344	—	209	897	35.9
1956	Darrell Floyd, Furman	6-1	Sr	28	339	—	268	946	33.8
1957	Grady Wallace, S Carolina	6-4	Sr	29	336	—	234	906	31.2
1958	Oscar Robertson, Cincinnati	6-5	So	28	352	—	280	984	35.1

Scoring Average (Cont.)

Year	Player and Team	Ht	Class	GP	FG	3FG	FT	Pts	Avg
1959	Oscar Robertson, Cincinnati	6-5	Jr	30	331	—	316	978	32.6
1960	Oscar Robertson, Cincinnati	6-5	Sr	30	369	—	273	1011	33.7
1961	Frank Burgess, Gonzaga	6-1	Sr	26	304	—	234	842	32.4
1962	Billy McGill, Utah	6-9	Sr	26	394	—	221	1009	38.8
1963	Nick Werkman, Seton Hall	6-3	Jr	22	221	—	208	650	29.5
1964	Howard Komives, Bowling Green	6-1	Sr	23	292	—	260	844	36.7
1965	Rick Barry, Miama (FL)	6-7	Sr	26	340	—	293	973	37.4
1966	Dave Schellhase, Purdue	6-4	Sr	24	284	—	213	781	32.5
1967	Jim Walker, Providence	6-3	Sr	28	323	—	205	851	30.4
1968	Pete Maravich, Louisiana St	6-5	So	26	432	—	274	1138	43.8
1969	Pete Maravich, Louisiana St	6-5	Jr	26	433	—	282	1148	44.2
1970	Pete Maravich, Louisiana St	6-5	Sr	31	522	—	337	1381	44.5
1971	Johnny Neumann, Mississippi	6-6	So	23	366	—	191	923	40.1
1972	Dwight Lamar, Southwestern Louisiana	6-1	Jr	29	429	—	196	1054	36.3
1973	William Averitt, Pepperdine	6-1	Sr	25	352	—	144	848	33.9
1974	Larry Fogle, Canisius	6-5	So	25	326	—	183	835	33.4
1975	Bob McCurdy, Richmond	6-7	Sr	26	321	—	213	855	32.9
1976	Marshall Rodgers, TX-Pan American	6-2	Sr	25	361	—	197	919	36.8
1977	Freeman Williams, Portland St	6-4	Jr	26	417	—	176	1010	38.8
1978	Freeman Williams, Portland St	6-4	Sr	27	410	—	149	969	35.9
1979	Lawrence Butler, Idaho St	6-3	Sr	27	310	—	192	812	30.1
1980	Tony Murphy, Southern-BR	6-3	Sr	29	377	—	178	932	32.1
1981	Zam Fredrick, S Carolina	6-2	Sr	27	300	—	181	781	28.9
1982	Harry Kelly, Texas Southern	6-7	Jr	29	336	—	190	862	29.7
1983	Harry Kelly, Texas Southern	6-7	Sr	29	333	—	169	835	28.8
1984	Joe Jakubick, Akron	6-5	Sr	27	304	—	206	814	30.1
1985	Xavier McDaniel, Wichita St	6-8	Sr	31	351	—	142	844	27.2
1986	Terrance Bailey, Wagner	6-2	Jr	29	321	—	212	854	29.4
1987	Kevin Houston, Army	5-11	Sr	29	311	63	268	953	32.9
1988	Hersey Hawkins, Bradley	6-3	Sr	31	377	87	284	1125	36.3
1989	Hank Gathers, Loyola Marymount	6-7	Jr	31	419	0	177	1015	32.7
1990	Bo Kimble, Loyola Marymount	6-5	Sr	32	404	92	231	1131	35.3
1991	Kevin Bradshaw, U.S. Int'l	6-6	Sr	28	358	60	278	1054	37.6
1992	Brett Roberts, Morehead St	6-8	Sr	29	278	66	193	815	28.1
1993	Greg Guy, TX-Pan American	6-1	Jr	19	189	67	111	556	29.3
1994	Glenn Robinson, Purdue	6-8	Jr	34	368	79	215	1030	30.3

Rebounds

Year	Player and Team	Ht	Class	GP	Reb	Avg
1951	Ernie Beck, Pennsylvania	6-4	So	27	556	20.6
1952	Bill Hannon, Army	6-3	So	17	355	20.9
1953	Ed Conlin, Fordham	6-5	So	26	612	23.5
1954	Art Quimby, Connecticut	6-5	Jr	26	588	22.6
1955	Charlie Slack, Marshall	6-5	Jr	21	538	25.6
1956	Joe Holup, George Washington	6-6	Sr	26	604	†.256
1957	Elgin Baylor, Seattle	6-6	Jr	25	508	†.235
1958	Alex Ellis, Niagara	6-5	Sr	25	536	†.262
1959	Leroy Wright, Pacific	6-8	Jr	26	652	†.238
1960	Leroy Wright, Pacific	6-8	Sr	17	380	†.234
1961	Jerry Lucas, Ohio St	6-8	Jr	27	470	†.198
1962	Jerry Lucas, Ohio St	6-8	Sr	28	499	†.211
1963	Paul Silas, Creighton	6-7	Sr	27	557	20.6
1964	Bob Pelkington, Xavier (OH)	6-7	Sr	26	567	21.8
1965	Toby Kimball, Connecticut	6-8	Sr	23	483	21.0
1966	Jim Ware, Oklahoma City	6-8	Sr	29	607	20.9
1967	Dick Cunningham, Murray St	6-10	Jr	22	479	21.8
1968	Neal Walk, Florida	6-10	Jr	25	494	19.8
1969	Spencer Haywood, Detroit	6-8	So	22	472	21.5
1970	Artis Gilmore, Jacksonville	7-2	Jr	28	621	22.2
1971	Artis Gilmore, Jacksonville	7-2	Sr	26	603	23.2
1972	Kermit Washington, American	6-8	Jr	23	455	19.8
1973	Kermit Washington, American	6-8	Sr	22	439	20.0
1974	Marvin Barnes, Providence	6-9	Sr	32	597	18.7
1975	John Irving, Hofstra	6-9	So	21	323	15.4

Rebounds (Cont.)

Year	Player and Team	Ht	Class	GP	Reb	Avg
1976	Sam Pellom, Buffalo	6-8	So	26	420	16.2
1977	Glenn Mosley, Seton Hall	6-8	Sr	29	473	16.3
1978	Ken Williams, N Texas St	6-7	Sr	28	411	14.7
1979	Monti Davis, Tennessee St	6-7	Jr	26	421	16.2
1980	Larry Smith, Alcorn St	6-8	Sr	26	392	15.1
1981	Darryl Watson, Miss Valley	6-7	Sr	27	379	14.0
1982	LaSalle Thompson, Texas	6-10	Jr	27	365	13.5
1983	Xavier McDaniel, Wichita St	6-7	So	28	403	14.4
1984	Akeem Olajuwon, Houston	7-0	Jr	37	500	13.5
1985	Xavier McDaniel, Wichita St	6-8	Sr	31	460	14.8
1986	David Robinson, Navy	6-11	Jr	35	455	13.0
1987	Jerome Lane, Pittsburgh	6-6	So	33	444	13.5
1988	Kenny Miller, Loyola (IL)	6-9	Fr	29	395	13.6
1989	Hank Gathers, Loyola (CA)	6-7	Jr	31	426	13.7
1990	Anthony Bonner, St Louis	6-8	Sr	33	456	13.8
1991	Shaquille O'Neal, Louisiana St	7-1	So	28	411	14.7
1992	Popeye Jones, Murray St	6-8	Sr	30	431	14.4
1993	Warren Kidd, Middle Tenn St	6-9	Sr	26	386	14.8
1994	Jerome Lambert, Baylor	6-8	Jr	24	355	14.8

†From 1956-1962, title was based on highest individual recoveries out of total by both teams in all games.

Assists

Year	Player and Team	Class	GP	A	Avg
1984	Craig Lathen, IL-Chicago	Jr	29	274	9.45
1985	Rob Weingard, Hofstra	Sr	24	228	9.50
1986	Mark Jackson, St John's (NY)	Jr	36	328	9.11
1987	Avery Johnson, Southern-BR	Jr	31	333	10.74
1988	Avery Johnson, Southern-BR	Sr	30	399	13.30
1989	Glenn Williams, Holy Cross	Sr	28	278	9.93
1990	Todd Lehmann, Drexel	Sr	28	260	9.29
1991	Chris Corchiani, N Carolina St	Sr	31	299	9.65
1992	Van Usher, Tennessee Tech	Sr	29	254	8.76
1993	Sam Crawford, New Mex St	Sr	34	310	9.12
1994	Jason Kidd, California	So	30	272	9.06

Blocked Shots

Year	Player and Team	Class	GP	BS	Avg
1986	David Robinson, Navy	Jr	35	207	5.91
1987	David Robinson, Navy	Sr	32	144	4.50
1988	Rodney Blake, St Joseph's (PA)	Sr	29	116	4.00
1989	Alonzo Mourning, Georgetown	Fr	34	169	4.97
1990	Kenny Green, Rhode Island	Sr	26	124	4.77
1991	Shawn Bradley, Brigham Young	Fr	34	177	5.21
1992	Shaquille O'Neal, Louisiana St	Jr	30	157	5.23
1993	Theo Ratliff, Wyoming	Jr	28	124	4.43
1994	Grady Livingston, Howard	Jr	26	115	4.42

Steals

Year	Player and Team	Class	GP	S	Avg
1986	Darron Brittman, Chicago St	Sr	28	139	4.96
1987	Tony Fairley, Charleston Sou	Sr	28	114	4.07
1988	Aldwin Ware, Florida A&M	Sr	29	142	4.90
1989	Kenny Robertson, Cleveland St	Jr	28	111	3.96
1990	Ronn McMahon, E Washington	Sr	29	130	4.48
1991	Van Usher, Tennessee Tech	Jr	28	104	3.71
1992	Victor Snipes, NE Illinois	So	25	86	3.44
1993	Jason Kidd, California	Fr	29	110	3.80
1994	Shawn Griggs SW Louisiana	Sr	30	120	4.00

Single-Game Records

SCORING HIGHS VS DIVISION I OPPONENT

Pts	Player and Team vs Opponent	Date
72	Kevin Bradshaw, U.S. Int'l vs Loyola Marymount	1-5-91
69	Pete Maravich, Louisiana St vs Alabama	2-7-70
68	Calvin Murphy, Niagara vs Syracuse	12-7-68
66	Jay Handlan, Washington & Lee vs Furman	2-17-51
66	Pete Maravich, Louisiana St vs Tulane	2-10-69
66	Anthony Roberts, Oral Roberts vs N Carolina A&T	2-19-77
65	Anthony Roberts, Oral Roberts vs Oregon	3-9-77
65	Scott Haffner, Evansville vs Dayton	2-18-89
64	Pete Maravich, Louisiana St vs Kentucky	2-21-70
63	Johnny Neumann, Mississippi vs Louisiana St	1-30-71
63	Hersey Hawkins, Bradley vs Detroit	2-22-88

SCORING HIGHS VS NON-DIVISION I OPPONENT

Pts	Player and Team vs Opponent	Date
100	Frank Selvy, Furman vs Newberry	2-13-54
85	Paul Arizin, Villanova vs Philadelphia NAMC	2-12-49
81	Freeman Williams, Portland St vs Rocky Mountain	2-3-78
73	Bill Mlkvy, Temple vs Wilkes	3-3-51
71	Freeman Williams, Portland St vs Southern Oregon	2-9-77

REBOUNDING HIGHS BEFORE 1973

Reb	Player and Team vs Opponent	Date
51	Bill Chambers, William & Mary vs Virginia	2-14-53
43	Charlie Slack, Marshall vs Morris Harvey	1-12-54
42	Tom Heinsohn, Holy Cross vs Boston College	3-1-55
40	Art Quimby, Connecticut vs Boston U	1-11-55
39	Maurice Stokes, St Francis (PA) vs John Carroll	1-28-55
39	Dave DeBusschere, Detroit vs Central Michigan	1-30-60
39	Keith Swagerty, Pacific vs UC-Santa Barbara	3-5-65

REBOUNDING HIGHS SINCE 1973

Reb	Player and Team vs Opponent	Date
34	David Vaughn, Oral Roberts vs Brandeis	1-8-73
33	Robert Parish, Centenary vs Southern Miss	1-22-73
32	Jervaughn Scales, Southern-BR vs Grambling	2-7-94
32	Durand Macklin, Louisiana St vs Tulane	11-26-76
31	Jim Bradley, Northern Illinois vs WI-Milwaukee	2-19-73
31	Calvin Natt, Northeast Louisiana vs Georgia Southern	12-29-76

ASSISTS

A	Player and Team vs Opponent	Date
22	Tony Fairley, Baptist vs Armstrong St	2-9-87
22	Avery Johnson, Southern-BR vs Texas Southern	1-25-88
22	Sherman Douglas, Syracuse vs Providence	1-28-89
21	Mark Wade, NV-Las Vegas vs Navy	12-29-86
21	Kelvin Scarborough, New Mexico vs Hawaii	2-13-87
21	Anthony Manuel, Bradley vs UC-Irvine	12-19-87
21	Avery Johnson, Southern-BR vs Alabama St	1-16-88

STEALS

S	Player and Team vs Opponent	Date
13	Mookie Blaylock, Oklahoma vs Centenary	12-12-87
13	Mookie Blaylock, Oklahoma vs Loyola Marymount	12-17-88
12	Kenny Robertson, Cleveland St vs Wagner	12-3-88
12	Terry Evans, Oklahoma vs Florida A&M	1-27-93
11	Darron Brittman, Chicago St vs McKendree	2-24-86
11	Darron Brittman, Chicago St vs St Xavier	2-8-86
11	Marty Johnson, Towson St vs Bucknell	2-17-88
11	Aldwin Ware, Florida A&M vs Tuskegee	2-24-88
11	Mark Macon, Temple ve Notre Dame	1-29-89
11	Carl Thomas, E Michigan vs Chicago St	2-20-91
11	Ron Arnold, St Francis (NY) vs Mt St Mary's (MD)	2-4-93

Single-Game Records *(Cont.)*

BLOCKED SHOTS

BS	Player and Team vs Opponent	Date
14	David Robinson, Navy vs NC-Wilmington	1-4-86
14	Shawn Bradley, Brigham Young vs E Kentucky	12-7-90
13	Kevin Roberson, Vermont vs New Hampshire	1-9-92
13	Jim McIlvaine, Marquette vs Northeastern (IL)	12-9-92
12	David Robinson, Navy vs James Madison	1-9-86
12	Derrick Lewis, Maryland vs James Madison	1-28-87
12	Rodney Blake, St Joseph's (PA) vs Cleveland St	12-2-87
12	Walter Palmer, Dartmouth vs Harvard	1-9-88
12	Alan Ogg, AL-Birmingham vs Florida A&M	12-16-88
12	Dikembe Mutombo, Georgetown vs St John's (NY)	1-23-89
12	Shaquille O'Neal, Louisiana St vs Loyola Marymount	2-3-90
12	Cedric Lewis, Maryland vs S Florida	1-19-91
12	Ervin Johnson, New Orleans vs Texas A&M	12-29-92

Season Records

POINTS

Player and Team	Year	GP	FG	3FG	FT	Pts
Pete Maravich, Louisiana St	1970	31	522	—	337	1381
Elvin Hayes, Houston	1968	33	519	—	176	1214
Frank Selvy, Furman	1954	29	427	—	355	1209
Pete Maravich, Louisiana St	1969	26	433	—	282	1148
Pete Maravich, Lousiana St	1968	26	432	—	274	1138
Bo Kimble, Loyola Marymount	1990	32	404	92	231	1131
Hersey Hawkins, Bradley	1988	31	377	87	284	1125
Austin Carr, Notre Dame	1970	29	444	—	218	1106
Austin Carr, Notre Dame	1971	29	430	—	241	1101
Otis Birdsong, Houston	1977	36	452	—	186	1090

SCORING AVERAGE

Player and Team	Year	GP	FG	FT	Pts	Avg
Pete Maravich, Louisiana St	1970	31	522	337	1381	44.5
Pete Maravich, Louisiana St	1969	26	433	282	1148	44.2
Pete Maravich, Louisiana St	1968	26	432	274	1138	43.8
Frank Selvy, Furman	1954	29	427	355	1209	41.7
Johnny Neumann, Mississippi	1971	23	366	191	923	40.1
Freeman Williams, Portland St	1977	26	417	176	1010	38.8
Billy McGill, Utah	1962	26	394	221	1009	38.8
Calvin Murphy, Niagara	1968	24	337	242	916	38.2
Austin Carr, Notre Dame	1970	29	444	218	1106	38.1
Austin Carr, Notre Dame	1971	29	430	241	1101	38.0
Kevin Bradshaw, U.S. Int'l	1991	28	358	278	1054	37.6

REBOUNDS

Player and Team	Year	GP	Reb	Player and Team	Year	GP	Reb
Walt Dukes, Seton Hall	1953	33	734	Artis Gilmore, Jacksonville	1970	28	621
Leroy Wright, Pacific	1959	26	652	Tom Gola, La Salle	1955	31	618
Tom Gola, La Salle	1954	30	652	Ed Conlin, Fordham	1953	26	612
Charlie Tyra, Louisville	1956	29	645	Art Quimby, Connecticut	1955	25	611
Paul Silas, Creighton	1964	29	631	Bill Russell, San Francisco	1956	29	609
Elvin Hayes, Houston	1968	33	624	Jim Ware, Oklahoma City	1966	29	607

REBOUND AVERAGE BEFORE 1973

Player and Team	Year	GP	Reb	Avg
Charlie Slack, Marshall	1955	21	538	25.6
Leroy Wright, Pacific	1959	26	652	25.1
Art Quimby, Connecticut	1955	25	611	24.4
Charlie Slack, Marshall	1956	22	520	23.6
Ed Conlin, Fordham	1953	26	612	23.5

Season Records *(Cont.)*

REBOUND AVERAGE SINCE 1973

Player and Team	Year	GP	Reb	Avg
Kermit Washington, American	1973	22	439	20.0
Marvin Barnes, Providence	1973	30	571	19.0
Marvin Barnes, Providence	1974	32	597	18.7
Pete Padgett, NV-Reno	1973	26	462	17.8
Jim Bradley, Northern Illinois	1973	24	426	17.8

ASSISTS

Player and Team	Year	GP	A	Player and Team	Year	GP	A
Mark Wade, UNLV	1987	38	406	Sherman Douglas, Syracuse	1989	38	326
Avery Johnson, Southern-BR	1988	30	399	Sam Crawford, N Mex St	1993	34	310
Anthony Manuel, Bradley	1988	31	373	Greg Anthony, UNLV	1991	35	310
Avery Johnson, Southern-BR	1987	31	333	Reid Gettys, Houston	1984	37	309
Mark Jackson, St John's (NY)	1986	32	328	Carl Golston, Loyola (IL)	1985	33	305

ASSIST AVERAGE

Player and Team	Year	GP	A	Avg	Player and Team	Year	GP	A	Avg
Avery Johnson, Southern-BR	1988	30	399	13.3	Chris Corchiani, N Carolina St	1991	31	299	9.6
Anthony Manuel, Bradley	1988	31	373	12.0	Tony Fairley, Baptist	1987	28	270	9.6
Avery Johnson, Southern-BR	1987	31	333	10.7	Tyrone Bogues, Wake Forest	1987	29	276	9.5
Mark Wade, NV-Las Vegas	1987	38	406	10.7	Craig Neal, Georgia Tech	1988	32	303	9.5
Glenn Williams, Holy Cross	1989	28	278	9.9	Ron Weingard, Hofstra	1985	24	228	9.5

FIELD-GOAL PERCENTAGE

Player and Team	Year	GP	FG	FGA	Pct
Steve Johnson, Oregon St	1981	28	235	315	74.6
Dwayne Davis, Florida	1989	33	179	248	72.2
Keith Walker, Utica	1985	27	154	216	71.3
Steve Johnson, Oregon St	1980	30	211	297	71.0
Oliver Miller, Arkansas	1991	38	254	361	70.4
Alan Williams, Princeton	1987	25	163	232	70.3
Mark McNamara, California	1982	27	231	329	70.2
Warren Kidd, Middle Tennessee St	1991	30	173	247	70.0
Pete Freeman, Akron	1991	28	175	250	70.0
Joe Senser, West Chester	1977	25	130	186	69.9
Lee Campbell, SW Missouri St	1990	29	192	275	69.8
Stephen Scheffler, Purdue	1990	30	173	248	69.8

Based on qualifiers for annual championship.

FREE-THROW PERCENTAGE

Player and Team	Year	GP	FT	FTA	Pct
Craig Collins, Penn St	1985	27	94	98	95.9
Rod Foster, UCLA	1982	27	95	100	95.0
Danny Basile, Marist	1994	27	84	89	94.4
Carlos Gibson, Marshall	1978	28	84	89	94.4
Jim Barton, Dartmouth	1986	26	65	69	94.2
Jack Moore, Nebraska	1982	27	123	131	93.9
Dandrea Evans, Troy St	1994	27	72	77	93.5
Rob Robbins, New Mexico	1990	34	101	108	93.5
Tommy Boyer, Arkansas	1962	23	125	134	93.3
Damon Goodwin, Dayton	1986	30	95	102	93.1
Brian Magid, George Washington	1980	26	79	85	92.9
Mike Joseph, Bucknell	1990	29	144	155	92.9

Based on qualifiers for annual championship.

Season Records *(Cont.)*

THREE-POINT FIELD-GOAL PERCENTAGE

Player and Team	Year	GP	3FG	3FGA	Pct
Glenn Tropf, Holy Cross	1988	29	52	82	63.4
Sean Wightman, Western Michigan	1992	30	48	76	63.2
Keith Jennings, E Tennessee St	1991	33	84	142	59.2
Dave Calloway, Monmouth (NJ)	1989	28	48	82	58.5
Steve Kerr, Arizona	1988	38	114	199	57.3
Reginald Jones, Prairie View	1987	28	64	112	57.1
Joel Tribelhorn, Colorado St	1989	33	76	135	56.3
Mike Joseph, Bucknell	1988	28	65	116	56.0
Christian Laettner, Duke	1992	35	54	97	55.7
Reginald Jones, Prairie View	1988	27	85	155	54.8

Based on qualifiers for annual championship.

STEALS

Player and Team	Year	GP	S
Mookie Blaylock, Oklahoma	1988	39	150
Aldwin Ware, Florida A&M	1988	29	142
Darron Brittman, Chicago St	1986	28	139
Nadav Henefeld, Connecticut	1990	37	138
Mookie Blaylock, Oklahoma	1989	35	131

BLOCKED SHOTS

Player and Team	Year	GP	BS
David Robinson, Navy	1986	35	207
Shawn Bradley, BYU	1991	34	177
Alonzo Mourning, Georgetown	1989	34	169
Alonzo Mourning, Georgetown	1992	32	160
Shaquille O'Neal, Louisiana St	1992	30	157

STEAL AVERAGE

Player and Team	Year	GP	S	Avg
Darron Brittman, Chicago St	1986	28	139	4.96
Aldwin Ware, Florida A&M	1988	29	142	4.90
Ronn McMahon, E Washington	1990	29	130	4.48
Jim Paguaga, St Francis (NY)	1986	28	120	4.29
Marty Johnson, Towson St	1988	30	124	4.13

BLOCKED SHOT AVERAGE

Player and Team	Year	GP	BS	Avg
David Robinson, Navy	1986	35	207	5.91
Shaquille O'Neal, Louisiana St	1992	30	157	5.23
Shawn Bradley, BYU	1991	34	177	5.21
Cedric Lewis, Maryland	1991	28	143	5.11
Alonzo Mourning, Georgetown	1992	32	160	5.00

Career Records

POINTS

Player and Team	Ht	Final Year	GP	FG	3FG*	FT	Pts
Pete Maravich, Louisiana St	6-5	1970	83	1387	—	893	3667
Freeman Williams, Portland St	6-4	1978	106	1369	—	511	3249
Lionel Simmons, La Salle	6-7	1990	131	1244	56	673	3217
Alphonso Ford, Mississippi Valley	6-2	1993	109	1121	333	590	3165
Harry Kelly, Texas Southern	6-7	1983	110	1234	—	598	3066
Hersey Hawkins, Bradley	6-3	1988	125	1100	118	690	3008
Oscar Robertson, Cincinnati	6-5	1960	88	1052	—	869	2973
Danny Manning, Kansas	6-10	1988	147	1216	10	509	2951
Alfredrick Hughes, Loyola (IL)	6-5	1985	120	1226	—	462	2914
Elvin Hayes, Houston	6-8	1968	93	1215	—	454	2884
Larry Bird, Indiana St	6-9	1979	94	1154	—	542	2850
Otis Birdsong, Houston	6-4	1977	116	1176	—	480	2832
Kevin Bradshaw, Bethune-Cookman, U.S. Int'l	6-6	1991	111	1027	132	618	2804
Allan Houston, Tennessee	6-6	1993	128	902	346	651	2801
Hank Gathers, Southern Cal, Loyola Marymount	6-7	1990	117	1127	0	469	2723
Reggie Lewis, Northeastern	6-7	1987	122	1043	30 (1)	592	2708
Daren Queenan, Lehigh	6-5	1988	118	1024	29	626	2703
Byron Larkin, Xavier (OH)	6-3	1988	121	1022	51	601	2696
David Robinson, Navy	7-1	1987	127	1032	1	604	2669
Wayman Tisdale, Oklahoma	6-9	1985	104	1077	—	507	2661

*Listed is the number of three-pointers scored since it became the national rule in 1987; the number in the parentheses is number scored prior to 1987—these counted as three points in the game but counted as two-pointers in the national rankings. The three-pointers in the parentheses are not included in total points.

Career Records *(Cont.)*

SCORING AVERAGE

Player and Team	Final Year	GP	FG	FT	Pts	Avg
Pete Maravich, Louisiana St	1968	83	1387	893	3667	44.2
Austin Carr, Notre Dame	1971	74	1017	526	2560	34.6
Oscar Robertson, Cincinnati	1960	88	1052	869	2973	33.8
Calvin Murphy, Niagara	1970	77	947	654	2548	33.1
Dwight Lamar, Southwestern Louisiana	1973	57	768	326	1862	32.7
Frank Selvy, Furman	1954	78	922	694	2538	32.5
Rick Mount, Purdue	1970	72	910	503	2323	32.3
Darrell Floyd, Furman	1956	71	868	545	2281	32.1
Nick Werkman, Seton Hall	1964	71	812	649	2273	32.0
Willie Humes, Idaho St	1971	48	565	380	1510	31.5
William Averitt, Pepperdine	1973	49	615	311	1541	31.4
Elgin Baylor, Col. of Idaho, Seattle	1958	80	956	588	2500	31.3
Elvin Hayes, Houston	1968	93	1215	454	2884	31.0
Freeman Williams, Portland St	1978	106	1369	511	3249	30.7
Larry Bird, Indiana St	1979	94	1154	542	2850	30.3

REBOUNDS BEFORE 1973

Player and Team	Final Year	GP	Reb
Tom Gola, La Salle	1955	118	2201
Joe Holup, George Washington	1956	104	2030
Charlie Slack, Marshall	1956	88	1916
Ed Conlin, Fordham	1955	102	1884
Dickie Hemric, Wake Forest	1955	104	1802

REBOUNDS FOR CAREERS BEGINNING IN 1973 OR AFTER

Player and Team	Final Year	GP	Reb
Derrick Coleman, Syracuse	1990	143	1537
Ralph Sampson, Virginia	1983	132	1511
Pete Padgett, NV-Reno	1976	104	1464
Lionel Simmons, La Salle	1990	131	1429
Anthony Bonner, St Louis	1990	133	1424

ASSISTS

Player and Team	Final Year	GP	A
Bobby Hurley, Duke	1993	140	1076
Chris Corchiani, N Carolina St	1991	124	1038
Keith Jennings, E Tennessee St	1991	127	983
Sherman Douglas, Syracuse	1989	138	960
Greg Anthony, Portland, UNLV	1991	138	950

FIELD-GOAL PERCENTAGE

Player and Team	Final Year	FG	FGA	Pct
Stephen Scheffler, Purdue	1990	408	596	68.5
Steve Johnson, Oregon St	1981	828	1222	67.8
Murray Brown, Florida St	1980	566	847	66.8
Lee Campbell, SW Missouri St	1990	411	618	66.6
Warren Kidd, Middle Tenn St	1993	496	747	66.4

Note: Minimum 400 field goals.

FREE-THROW PERCENTAGE

Player and Team	Final Year	FT	FTA	Pct
Greg Starrick, Kentucky, Southern Illinois	1972	341	375	90.9
Jack Moore, Nebraska	1982	446	495	90.1
Steve Henson, Kansas St	1990	361	401	90.0
Steve Alford, Indiana	1987	535	596	89.8
Bob Lloyd, Rutgers	1967	543	605	89.8

Note: Minimum 300 free throws.

Career Records (Cont.)

THREE-POINT FIELD GOALS MADE

Player and Team	Final Year	GP	3FG
Doug Day, Radford	1993	117	401
Ronnie Schmitz, MO-Kansas City	1993	112	378
Mark Alberts, Akron	1993	103	375
Jeff Fryer, Loyola Marymount	1990	112	363
Dennis Scott, Georgia Tech	1990	99	351

THREE-POINT FIELD-GOAL PERCENTAGE

Player and Team	Final Year	3FG	3FGA	Pct
Tony Bennett, WI-Green Bay	1992	290	584	49.7
Keith Jennings, E Tennessee St	1991	223	452	49.3
Kirk Manns, Michigan St	1990	212	446	47.5
Tim Locum, Wisconsin	1991	227	481	47.2
David Olson, Eastern Illinois	1992	262	562	46.6

Note: Minimum 200 3-point field goals.

STEALS

Player and Team	Final Year	GP	S
Eric Murdock, Providence	1991	117	376
Michael Anderson, Drexel	1988	115	341
Kenny Robertson, New Mexico, Clev St	1990	119	341
Keith Jennings, E Tennessee St	1991	127	334
Greg Anthony, Portland, UNLV	1991	138	329

BLOCKED SHOTS

Player and Team	Final Year	GP	BS
Alonzo Mourning, Georgetown	1992	120	453
Shaquille O'Neal, Louisiana St	1992	90	412
Kevin Roberson, Vermont	1992	112	409
Rodney Blake, St Joseph's (PA)	1988	116	399
Tim Perry, Temple	1988	130	392

NCAA Division I Team Leaders

Division I Team Alltime Wins

Team	First Year	Yrs	W	L	T
N Carolina	1911	84	1598	571	0
Kentucky	1903	91	1587	513	1
Kansas	1899	96	1540	697	0
St John's (NY)	1908	87	1494	652	0
Duke	1906	89	1463	711	0
Oregon St	1902	93	1419	909	0
Temple	1895	98	1416	769	0
Pennsylvania	1902	93	1387	788	0
Syracuse	1901	93	1382	651	0
Notre Dame	1898	89	1374	718	1
Indiana	1901	94	1350	720	0
Washington	1896	92	1321	843	0
UCLA	1920	75	1315	584	0
Western Kentucky	1915	75	1304	616	0
Princeton	1901	94	1296	818	0

Note: Years in Division I only.

Division I Alltime Winning Percentage

Team	First Year	Yrs	W	L	T	Pct
NV-Las Vegas	1959	34	762	239	0	.761
Kentucky	1903	91	1587	513	1	.756
N Carolina	1911	84	1598	571	0	.737
St John's (NY)	1908	87	1494	652	0	.696
UCLA	1920	75	1315	584	0	.692
Kansas	1899	96	1540	697	0	.688
Syracuse	1901	93	1382	651	0	.680
Western Kentucky	1915	75	1304	616	0	.679
Duke	1906	89	1462	709	0	.673
DePaul	1924	71	1140	569	0	.667

Note: Minimum of 20 years in Division I.

Longest—Full Season

Team	Games	Years	Ended by
UCLA	88	1971-74	Notre Dame (71-70)
San Francisco	60	1955-57	Illinois (62-33)
UCLA	47	1966-68	Houston (71-69)
UNLV	45	1990-91	Duke (79-77)
Texas	44	1913-17	Rice (24-18)
Seton Hall	43	1939-41	LIU-Brooklyn (49-26)
LIU-Brooklyn	43	1935-37	Stanford (45-31)
UCLA	41	1968-69	Southern Cal (46-44)
Marquette	39	1970-71	Ohio St (60-59)
Cincinnati	37	1962-63	Wichita St (65-64)
N Carolina	37	1957-58	W Virginia (75-64)

Longest—Home Court

Team	Games	Years
Kentucky	129	1943-55
St Bonaventure	99	1948-61
UCLA	98	1970-76
Cincinnati	86	1957-64
Marquette	81	1967-73
Arizona	81	1945-51
Lamar	80	1978-84
Long Beach St	75	1968-74
NV-Las Vegas	72	1974-78
Arizona	71	1987-92
Cincinnati	68	1972-78

Longest—Regular Season

Team	Games	Years	Ended by
UCLA	76	1971-74	Notre Dame (71-70)
Indiana	57	1975-77	Toledo (59-57)
Marquette	56	1970-72	Detroit (70-49)
Kentucky	54	1952-55	George Tech (59-58)
San Francisco	51	1955-57	Illinois (62-33)
Pennsylvania	48	1970-72	Temple (57-52)
Ohio St	47	1960-62	Wisconsin (86-67)
Texas	44	1913-17	Rice (24-18)
UCLA	43	1966-68	Houston (71-69)
LIU-Brooklyn	43	1935-37	Stanford (45-31)
Seton Hall	42	1939-41	LIU-Brooklyn (49-26)

Active Coaches

WINS

Coach and Team	W
Dean Smith, N Carolina	802
Don Haskins, UTEP	643
Lefty Driesell, James Madison	641
Bob Knight, Indiana	640
Norm Stewart, Missouri	637
Lou Henson, Illinois	626
Gene Bartow, AL-Birmingham	617
Glenn Wilkes, Stetson	563
Gary Colson, Fresno St	548
Denny Crum Louisville,	546

Note: Minimum 5 years as a Division I head coach; includes record at 4-year colleges only.

WINNING PERCENTAGE

Coach and Team	Yrs	W	L	Pct
Dean Smith, N Carolina	33	802	230	.777
Jim Boeheim, Syracuse	18	433	140	.756
John Chaney, Temple	22	501	164	.753
Nolan Richardson, Arkansas	14	338	112	.751
Bob Knight, Indiana	29	640	223	.742
Denny Crum, Louisville	23	546	198	.734
Pete Gillen, Xavier (OH)	9	200	75	.727
John Thompson, Georgetown	23	500	190	.725
Eddie Sutton, Oklahoma St	24	522	199	.724
Lute Olsen, Arizona	21	458	179	.719

Note: Minimum 5 years as a Division I head coach; includes record at 4-year colleges only.

Alltime Winningest Division I Men's Coaches

WINS

Coach (Team)	W
Adolph Rupp (Kentucky)	875
Dean Smith (N Carolina)	802
Hank Iba (NW Missouri St, Colorado, Oklahoma St)	767
Ed Diddle (Western Kentucky)	759
Phog Allen (Baker, Kansas, Haskell, Central Missouri St, Kansas)	746
Ray Meyer (DePaul)	724
John Wooden (Indiana St, UCLA)	664
Ralph Miller (Wichita St, Iowa, Oregon St)	657
Norm Sloan (Presbyterian, Citadel, N Carolina St, Florida)	656
Don Haskins (UTEP)	643
Marv Harshman (Pacific Lutheran, Washington St, Washington)	642
Lefty Driesell (Davidson, Maryland, James Madison)	641
Bob Knight (Army, Indiana)	640
Norm Stewart (Missouri)	637

Note: Minimum 10 head coaching seasons in Division I.

NCAA Division I Winningest Men's Coaches (Cont.)

WINNING PERCENTAGE

Coach (Team)	Yrs	W	L	Pct
Jerry Tarkanian (Long Beach St 69-73, UNLV 74-92)	24	625	122	.837
Clair Bee (Rider 29-31, LIU-Brooklyn 32-45, 46-51)	21	412	87	.826
Adolph Rupp (Kentucky 31-72)	41	875	190	.822
John Wooden (Indiana St 47-48, UCLA 49-75)	29	664	162	.804
Dean Smith (N Carolina 62-)	33	802	230	.777
Harry Fisher (Columbia 07-16, Army 22-23, 25)	13	147	44	.770
Frank Keaney (Rhode Island 21-48)	27	387	117	.768
George Keogan (St Louis 16, Allegheny 19, Valparaiso 20-21, Notre Dame 24-43)	24	385	117	.767
Jack Ramsay (St Joseph's [PA] 56-66)	11	231	71	.765
Vic Bubas (Duke 60-69)	10	213	67	.761
Jim Boeheim (Syracuse 77-)	18	433	140	.756
John Chaney (Cheyney 73-82, Temple 83-)	22	501	164	.753
Nolan Richardson (Tulsa 81-85, Arkansas 86-)	14	338	112	.751
Charles "Chick" Davies (Duquesne 25-43, 47-48)	21	314	106	.748
Ray Mears (Wittenberg 57-62, Tennessee 63-77)	21	399	135	.747
Bob Knight (Army 66-71, Indiana 72-)	29	640	223	.742
Phog Allen (Baker 06-08, Kansas 08-09, Haskell 09, Cent MO St 13-19, Kansas 20-56)	48	746	264	.739
Al McGuire (Belmont Abbey 58-64, Marquette 65-77)	20	405	143	.739
Everett Chase (N Carolina St 47-64)	18	376	133	.739
Walter Meanwell (Wisconsin 12-17, 21-34; Missouri 18, 20)	22	280	101	.735

Note: Minimum 10 head coaching seasons in Division I.

NCAA Division I Women's Championship Results

Year	Winner	Score	Runner-up	Winning Coach
1982	Louisiana Tech	76-62	Cheyney	Sonja Hogg
1983	Southern Cal	69-67	Louisiana Tech	Linda Sharp
1984	Southern Cal	72-61	Tennessee	Linda Sharp
1985	Old Dominion	70-65	Georgia	Marianne Stanley
1986	Texas	97-81	Southern Cal	Jody Conradt
1987	Tennessee	67-44	Louisiana Tech	Pat Summitt
1988	Louisiana Tech	56-54	Auburn	Leon Barmore
1989	Tennessee	76-60	Auburn	Pat Summitt
1990	Stanford	88-81	Auburn	Tara VanDerveer
1991	Tennessee	70-67 (OT)	Virginia	Pat Summitt
1992	Stanford	78-62	Western Kentucky	Tara VanDerveer
1993	Texas Tech	84-82	Ohio State	Marsha Sharp
1994	N Carolina	60-59	Louisiana Tech	Sylvia Hatchell

NCAA Division I Women's Alltime Individual Leaders

Single-Game Records

SCORING HIGHS

Pts	Player and Team vs Opponent	Year
60	Cindy Brown, Long Beach St vs San Jose St	1987
58	Kim Perrot, SW Louisiana vs SE Louisiana	1990
58	Lorri Bauman, Drake vs SW Missouri St	1984
55	Patricia Hoskins, Mississippi Valley vs Southern-BR	1989
55	Patricia Hoskins, Mississippi Valley vs Alabama St	1989
54	Anjinea Hopson, Grambling vs Jackson St	1994
54	Mary Lowry, Baylor vs Texas	1994
54	Wanda Ford, Drake vs SW Missouri St	1986
53	Felisha Edwards, NE Louisiana vs Southern Mississippi	1991
53	Chris Starr, NV-Reno vs Cal St-Sacramento	1983
53	Sheryl Swoopes, Texas Tech vs Texas	1993

REBOUNDING HIGHS

Reb	Player and Team vs Opponent	Year
40	Deborah Temple, Delta St vs AL-Birmingham	1983
37	Rosina Pearson, Bethune-Cookman vs Florida Memorial	1985
33	Maureen Formico, Pepperdine vs Loyola (CA)	1985

REBOUNDING HIGHS *(Cont.)*

Reb	Player and Team vs Opponent	Year
31	Darlene Beale, Howard vs S Carolina St	1987
30	Cindy Bonforte, Wagner vs Queens (NY)	1983
29	Gail Norris, Alabama St vs Texas Southern	1992
29	Joy Kellogg, Oklahoma City vs Oklahoma Christian	1984
29	Joy Kellogg, Oklahoma City vs UTEP	1984

Six tied with 28

ASSISTS

A	Player and Team vs Opponent	Year
23	Michelle Burden, Kent St vs Ball St	1991
22	Shawn Monday, Tennessee Tech vs Morehead St	1988
22	Veronica Pettry, Loyola (IL) vs Detroit	1989
22	Tine Freil, Pacific vs Wichita St	1991
21	Tine Freil, Pacific vs Fresno St	1992
21	Amy Bauer, Wisconsin vs Detroit	1989
21	Neacole Hall, Alabama St vs Southern-BR	1989
20	Anja Bordt, St Mary's (CA) vs Loyola (CA)	1991
20	Gaynor O'Donnell, E Carolina vs NC-Asheville	1992
20	Ira Fuquay, Alcorn St vs Grambling	1993

Season Records

POINTS

Player and Team	Year	GP	FG	3FG	FT	Pts
Cindy Brown, Long Beach St	1987	35	362	—	250	974
Genia Miller, Cal St-Fullerton	1991	33	376	0	217	969
Sheryl Swoopes, Texas Tech	1993	34	356	32	211	955
Andrea Congreaves, Mercer	1992	28	353	77	142	925
Wanda Ford, Drake	1986	30	390	—	139	919
Barbara Kennedy, Clemson	1982	31	392	—	124	908
Patricia Hoskins, Mississippi Valley	1989	27	345	13	205	908
LaTaunya Pollard, Long Beach St	1983	31	376	—	155	907
Tina Hutchinson, San Diego St	1984	30	383	—	132	898
Jan Jensen, Drake	1991	30	358	6	166	888

SEASON SCORING AVERAGE

Player and Team	Year	GP	FG	3FG	FT	Pts	Avg
Patricia Hoskins, Mississippi Valley	1989	27	345	13	205	908	33.6
Andrea Congreaves, Mercer	1992	28	353	77	142	925	33.0
Deborah Temple, Delta St	1984	28	373	—	127	873	31.2
Andrea Congreaves, Mercer	1993	26	302	51	150	805	31.0
Wanda Ford, Drake	1986	30	390	—	139	919	30.6
Anucha Browne, Northwestern	1985	28	341	—	173	855	30.5
LeChandra LeDay, Grambling	1988	28	334	36	146	850	30.4
Kim Perrot, Southwestern Louisiana	1990	28	308	95	128	839	30.0
Tina Hutchinson, San Diego St	1984	30	383	—	132	898	29.9
Jan Jensen, Drake	1991	30	358	6	166	888	29.6
Genia Miller, Cal St-Fullerton	1991	33	376	0	217	969	29.4
Barbara Kennedy, Clemson	1982	31	392	—	124	908	29.3
LaTaunya Pollard, Long Beach St	1983	31	376	—	155	907	29.3
Lisa McMullen, Alabama St	1991	28	285	126	119	815	29.1
Tresa Spaulding, BYU	1987	28	347	—	116	810	28.9
Hope Linthicum, Central Conn St	1987	23	282	—	101	665	28.9

Season Records *(Cont.)*

REBOUNDS

Player and Team	Year	GP	Reb	Player and Team	Year	GP	Reb
Wanda Ford, Drake	1985	30	534	Rosina Pearson, Beth-Cookman	1985	26	480
Wanda Ford, Drake	1986	30	506	Patricia Hoskins, Miss Valley	1987	28	476
Anne Donovan, Old Dominion	1983	35	504	Cheryl Miller, Southern Cal	1985	30	474
Darlene Jones, Miss Valley	1983	31	487	Darlene Beale, Howard	1987	29	459
Melanie Simpson, Okla City	1982	37	481	Olivia Bradley, W Virginia	1985	30	458

REBOUND AVERAGE

Player and Team	Year	GP	Reb	Avg
Rosina Pearson, Bethune-Cookman	1985	26	480	18.5
Wanda Ford, Drake	1985	30	534	17.8
Katie Beck, E Tennessee St	1988	25	441	17.6
DeShawne Blocker, E Tenn St	1994	26	450	17.3
Patricia Hoskins, Mississippi Valley	1987	28	476	17.0
Wanda Ford, Drake	1986	30	506	16.9
Patricia Hoskins, Mississippi Valley	1989	27	440	16.3
Joy Kellogg, Oklahoma City	1984	23	373	16.2
Deborah Mitchell, Miss Col	1983	28	447	16.0

FIELD-GOAL PERCENTAGE

Player and Team	Year	GP	FG	FGA	Pct
Renay Adams, Tennessee Tech	1991	30	185	258	71.7
Regina Days, Georgia Southern	1986	27	234	332	70.5
Kim Wood, WI-Green Bay	1994	27	188	271	69.4
Kelly Lyons, Old Dominion	1990	31	308	444	69.4
Trina Roberts, Georgia Southern	1982	31	189	277	68.2
Lidiya Varbanova, Boise St	1991	22	128	188	68.1
Sharon McDowell, NC-Wilmington	1987	28	170	251	67.7
Lidiya Varbanova, Boise St	1992	29	228	338	67.5
Mary Raese, Idaho	1986	31	254	380	66.8
Lydia Sawney, Tennessee Tech	1983	27	167	250	66.8

Based on qualifiers for annual championship.

FREE-THROW PERCENTAGE

Player and Team	Year	GP	FT	FTA	Pct
Ginny Doyle, Richmond	1992	29	96	101	95.0
Linda Cyborski, Delaware	1991	29	74	79	93.7
Jennifer Howard, N Carolina St	1994	27	118	127	92.9
Keely Feeman, Cincinnati	1986	30	76	82	92.7
Amy Slowikowski, Kent St	1989	27	112	121	92.6
Lea Ann Parsley, Marshall	1990	28	96	104	92.3
Chris Starr, NV-Reno	1986	25	119	129	92.2
DeAnn Craft, Central Florida	1987	24	94	102	92.2
Tracey Sneed, La Salle	1988	30	151	165	91.5

Based on qualifiers for annual championship.

THEY SAID IT

Frank Kerns, Georgia Southern basketball coach, analyzing himself and his Eagles after an 80–76 loss to Cornell: "I am the worst coach of the worst Division I basketball team in the country."

Career Records

POINTS

Player and Team	Yrs	GP	Pts
Patricia Hoskins, Mississippi Valley	1985-89	110	3122
Lorri Bauman, Drake	1981-84	120	3115
Cheryl Miller, Southern Cal	1983-86	128	3018
Valorie Whiteside, Appalachian St	1984-88	116	2944
Joyce Walker, Louisiana St	1981-84	117	2906
Sandra Hodge, New Orleans	1981-84	107	2860
Andrea Congreaves, Mercer	1989-93	108	2796
Karen Pelphrey, Marshall	1983-86	114	2746
Cindy Brown, Long Beach St	1983-87	128	2696
Carolyn Thompson, Texas Tech	1981-84	121	2655
Sue Wicks, Rutgers	1984-88	125	2655

SCORING AVERAGE

Player and Team	Yrs	GP	FG	3FG	FT	Pts	Avg
Patricia Hoskins, Mississippi Valley	1985-89	110	1196	24	706	3122	28.4
Sandra Hodge, New Orleans	1981-84	107	1194	—	472	2860	26.7
Lorri Bauman, Drake	1981-84	120	1104	—	907	3115	26.0
Andrea Congreaves, Mercer	1989-93	108	1107	153	429	2796	25.9
Valorie Whiteside, Appalachian St	1984-88	116	1153	0	638	2944	25.4
Joyce Walker, Louisiana St	1981-84	117	1259	—	388	2906	24.8
Tarcha Hollis, Grambling	1988-91	85	904	3	247	2058	24.2
Karen Pelphrey, Marshall	1983-86	114	1175	—	396	2746	24.1
Erma Jones, Bethune-Cookman	1982-84	87	961	—	173	2095	24.1
Cheryl Miller, Southern Cal	1983-86	128	1159	—	700	3018	23.6
Chris Starr, Nevada-Reno	1983-86	101	881	—	594	2356	23.3

NCAA Division II Men's Championship Results

Year	Winner	Score	Runner-up	Third Place	Fourth Place
1957	Wheaton (IL)	89-65	Kentucky Wesleyan	Mount St Mary's (MD)	Cal St-Los Angeles
1958	S Dakota	75-53	St Michael's	Evansville	Wheaton (IL)
1959	Evansville	83-67	SW Missouri St	N Carolina A&T	Cal St-Los Angeles
1960	Evansville	90-69	Chapman	Kentucky Wesleyan	Cornell College
1961	Wittenberg	42-38	SE Missouri St	S Dakota St	Mount St Mary's (MD)
1962	Mount St Mary's (MD)	58-57 (OT)	Cal St-Sacramento	Southern Illinois	Nebraska Wesleyan
1963	S Dakota St	44-42	Wittenberg	Oglethorpe	Southern Illinois
1964	Evansville	72-59	Akron	N Carolina A&T	Northern Iowa
1965	Evansville	85-82 (OT)	Southern Illinois	N Dakota	St Michael's
1966	Kentucky Wesleyan	54-51	Southern Illinois	Akron	N Dakota
1967	Winston-Salem	77-74	SW Missouri St	Kentucky Wesleyan	Illinois St
1968	Kentucky Wesleyan	63-52	Indiana St	Trinity (TX)	Ashland
1969	Kentucky Wesleyan	75-71	SW Missouri St	†Vacated	Ashland
1970	Philadelphia Textile	76-65	Tennessee St	UC-Riverside	Buffalo St
1971	Evansville	97-82	Old Dominion	†Vacated	Kentucky Wesleyan
1972	Roanoke	84-72	Akron	Tennessee St	Eastern Mich
1973	Kentucky Wesleyan	78-76 (OT)	Tennessee St	Assumption	Brockport St
1974	Morgan St	67-52	SW Missouri St	Assumption	New Orleans
1975	Old Dominion	76-74	New Orleans	Assumption	TN-Chattanooga
1976	Puget Sound	83-74	TN-Chattanooga	Eastern Illinois	Old Dominion
1977	TN-Chattanooga	71-62	Randolph-Macon	N Alabama	Sacred Heart
1978	Cheyney	47-40	WI-Green Bay	Eastern Illinois	Central Florida
1979	N Alabama	64-50	WI-Green Bay	Cheyney	Bridgeport
1980	Virginia Union	80-74	New York Tech	Florida Southern	N Alabama
1981	Florida Southern	73-68	Mount St Mary's (MD)	Cal Poly-SLO	WI-Green Bay
1982	District of Columbia	73-63	Florida Southern	Kentucky Wesleyan	Cal St-Bakersfield
1983	Wright St	92-73	District of Columbia	*Cal St-Bakersfield	*Morningside
1984	Central Missouri St	81-77	St Augustine's	*Kentucky Wesleyan	*N Alabama
1985	Jacksonville St	74-73	S Dakota St	*Kentucky Wesleyan	*Mount St Mary's (MD)
1986	Sacred Heart	93-87	SE Missouri St	*Cheyney	*Florida Southern
1987	Kentucky Wesleyan	92-74	Gannon	*Delta St	*Eastern Montana

NCAA Division II Men's Championship Results *(Cont.)*

Year	Winner	Score	Runner-up	Third Place	Fourth Place
1988	Lowell	75-72	AK-Anchorage	Florida Southern	Troy St
1989	N Carolina Central	73-46	SE Missouri St	UC-Riverside	Jacksonville St
1990	Kentucky Wesleyan	93-79	Cal St-Bakersfield	N Dakota	Morehouse
1991	N Alabama	79-72	Bridgeport (CT)	*Cal St-Bakersfield	*Virginia Union
1992	Virginia Union	100-75	Bridgeport (CT)	*Cal St-Bakersfield	*California (PA)
1993	Cal St-Bakersfield	85-72	Troy St (AL)	*New Hampshire Coll	*Wayne St (MI)
1994	Cal St-Bakersfield	92-86	Southern Indiana	*New Hampshire Coll	*Washburn

*Indicates tied for third. †Student-athletes representing American International in 1969 and Southwestern Louisiana in 1971 were declared ineligible subsequent to the tournament. Under NCAA rules, the teams' and ineligible student-athletes' records were deleted, and the teams' places in t he final standings were vacated.

NCAA Division II Men's Alltime Individual Leaders

SINGLE-GAME SCORING HIGHS

Pts	Player and Team vs Opponent	Date
113	Bevo Francis, Rio Grande vs Hillsdale	1954
84	Bevo Francis, Rio Grande vs Alliance	1954
82	Bevo Francis, Rio Grande vs Bluffton	1954
80	Paul Crissman, Southern Cal Col vs Pacific Christian	1966
77	William English, Winston-Salem vs Fayetteville St	1968

Season Records

SCORING AVERAGE

Player and Team	Year	GP	FG	FT	Pts	Avg
Bevo Francis, Rio Grande	1954	27	444	367	1255	46.5
Earl Glass, Mississippi Industrial	1963	19	322	171	815	42.9
Earl Monroe, Winston-Salem	1967	32	509	311	1329	41.5
John Rinka, Kenyon	1970	23	354	234	942	41.0
Willie Shaw, Lane	1964	18	303	121	727	40.4

REBOUND AVERAGE

Player and Team	Year	GP	Reb	Avg
Tom Hart, Middlebury	1956	21	620	29.5
Tom Hart, Middlebury	1955	22	649	29.5
Frank Stronczek, American Int'l	1966	26	717	27.6
R.C. Owens, College of Idaho	1954	25	677	27.1
Maurice Stokes, St Francis (PA)	1954	26	689	26.5

ASSISTS

Player and Team	Year	GP	A
Steve Ray, Bridgeport	1989	32	400
Steve Ray, Bridgeport	1990	33	385
Tony Smith, Pfeiffer	1992	35	349
Jim Ferrer, Bentley	1989	31	309
Brian Gregory, Oakland	1989	28	300

ASSIST AVERAGE

Player and Team	Year	GP	A	Avg
Steve Ray, Bridgeport	1989	32	400	12.5
Steve Ray, Bridgeport	1990	33	385	11.7
Demetri Beekman, Assumption	1993	23	264	11.5
Brian Gregory, Oakland	1989	28	300	10.7
Ernest Jenkins, NM Higlands	1994	27	277	10.3

FIELD-GOAL PERCENTAGE

Player and Team	Year	Pct
Todd Linder, Tampa	1987	75.2
Maurice Stafford, N Alabama	1984	75.0
Matthew Cornegay, Tuskegee	1982	74.8
Brian Moten, W Georgia	1992	73.4
Ed Phillips, Alabama A&M	1968	73.3

FREE-THROW PERCENTAGE

Player and Team	Year	Pct
Billy Newton, Morgan St	1976	94.4
Kent Andrews, McNeese St	1968	94.4
Mike Sanders, Northern Colorado	1987	94.3
Jay Harrie, E Montana	1994	93.5
Joe Cullen, Hartwick	1969	93.2

Career Records

POINTS

Player and Team	Yrs	Pts
Travis Grant, Kentucky St	1969-72	4045
Bob Hopkins, Grambling	1953-56	3759
Tony Smith, Pfeiffer	1989-92	3350
Earnest Lee, Clark Atlanta	1984-87	3298
Joe Miller, Alderson-Broaddus	1954-57	3294

CAREER SCORING AVERAGE

Player and Team	Yrs	GP	Pts	Avg
Travis Grant, Kentucky St	1969-72	121	4045	33.4
John Rinka, Kenyon	1967-70	99	3251	32.8
Florindo Vieira, Quinnipiac	1954-57	69	2263	32.8
Willie Shaw, Lane	1961-64	76	2379	31.3
Mike Davis, Virginia Union	1966-69	89	2758	31.0

REBOUND AVERAGE

Player and Team	Yrs	GP	Reb	Avg
Tom Hart, Middlebury	1953, 55-56	63	1738	27.6
Maurice Stokes, St Francis (PA)	1953-55	72	1812	25.2
Frank Stronczek, American Intl	1965-67	62	1549	25.0
Bill Thieben, Hofstra	1954-56	76	1837	24.2
Hank Brown, Lowell Tech	1965-67	49	1129	23.0

ASSISTS

Player and Team	Yrs	A
Demetri Beekman, Assumption	1990-93	1044
Gallagher Driscoll, St Rose	1989-92	878
Tony Smith, Pfeiffer	1989-92	828
Steve Ray, Bridgeport	1989-90	785
Charles Jordan, Erskine	1989-92	727

ASSIST AVERAGE

Player and Team	Yrs	GP	A	Avg
Steve Ray, Bridgeport	1989-90	65	785	12.1
Demetri Beekman, Assumption	1990-93	119	1044	8.8
Mark Benson, Texas A&I	1989-91	86	674	7.8
Pat Madden, Jacksonville St	1989-91	88	688	7.8

Note: Minimum 550 Assists

FIELD-GOAL PERCENTAGE

Player and Team	Yrs	Pct
Todd Linder, Tampa	1984-87	70.8
Tom Schurfranz, Bellarmine	1989-92	70.2
Chad Scott, California (PA)	1991-94	70.0
Ed Phillips, Alabama, A&M	1968-71	68.9
Otis Evans, Wayne St (MI)	1989-92	67.7

Note: Minimum 400 FGM

FREE-THROW PERCENTAGE

Player and Team	Yrs	Pct
Kent Andrews, McNeese St	1967-69	91.6
Jon Hagen, Mankato St	1963-65	90.0
Dave Reynolds, Davis & Elkins	1986-89	89.3
Terry Gill, New Orleans	1972-74	88.2
Tony Budzik, Mansfield	1989-92	88.2

Note: Minimum 250 FTM

NCAA Division III Men's Championship Results

Year	Winner	Score	Runner-up	Third Place	Fourth Place
1975	LeMoyne-Owen	57-54	Glassboro St	Augustana (IL)	Brockport St
1976	Scranton	60-57	Wittenberg	Augustana (IL)	Plattsburgh St
1977	Wittenberg	79-66	Oneonta St	Scranton	Hamline
1978	North Park	69-57	Widener	Albion	Stony Brook
1979	North Park	66-62	Potsdam St	Franklin & Marshall	Centre
1980	North Park	83-76	Upsala	Wittenberg	Longwood
1981	Potsdam St	67-65 (OT)	Augustana (IL)	Ursinus	Otterbein
1982	Wabash	83-62	Potsdam St	Brooklyn	Cal St Stanislaus
1983	Scranton	64-63	Wittenberg	Roanoke	WI-Whitewater
1984	WI-Whitewater	103-86	Clark (MA)	DePauw	Upsala
1985	North Park	72-71	Potsdam St	Nebraska Wesleyan	Widener
1986	Potsdam St	76-73	LeMoyne-Owen	Nebraska Wesleyan	Jersey City St
1987	North Park	106-100	Clark (MA)	Wittenberg	Stockton St
1988	Ohio Wesleyan	92-70	Scranton	Nebraska Wesleyan	Hartwick
1989	WI-Whitewater	94-86	Trenton St	Southern Maine	Centre
1990	Rochester	43-42	DePauw	Washington (MD)	Calvin
1991	WI-Platteville	81-74	Franklin & Marshall	Otterbein	Ramapo (NJ)
1992	Calvin	62-49	Rochester	WI-Platteville	Jersey City St
1993	Ohio Northern	71-68	Augustana	Mass-Dartmouth	Rowan
1994	Lebanon Valley Coll	66-59 (OT)	New York University	Wittenberg	St Thomas (MN)

NCAA Division III Men's Alltime Individual Leaders

SINGLE-GAME SCORING HIGHS

Pts	Player and Team vs Opponent	Year
63	Joe DeRoche, Thomas vs St Joseph's (ME)	1988
62	Shannon Lilly, Bishop vs Southwest Assembly of God	1983
61	Steve Honderd, Calvin vs Kalamazoo	1993
61	Dana Wilson, Husson vs Ricker	1974
60	Steve Diekmann, Grinnell vs Coe	1994

Season Records

SCORING AVERAGE

Player and Team	Year	GP	FG	FT	Pts	Avg
Rickey Sutton, Lyndon St	1976	14	207	93	507	36.2
Shannon Lilly, Bishop	1983	26	345	218	908	34.9
Dana Wilson, Husson	1974	20	288	122	698	34.9
Rickey Sutton, Lyndon St	1977	16	223	112	558	34.9
Steve Diekmann, Grinnell	1994	21	250	106	723	34.4

REBOUND AVERAGE

Player and Team	Year	GP	Reb	Avg
Joe Manley, Bowie St	1976	29	579	20.0
Fred Petty, New Hampshire Col	1974	22	436	19.8
Larry Williams, Pratt	1977	24	457	19.0
Charles Greer, Thomas	1977	17	318	18.7
Larry Parker, Plattsburgh St	1975	23	430	18.7

ASSISTS

Player and Team	Year	GP	A
Robert James, Kean	1989	29	391
Ricky Spicer, WI-Whitewater	1989	31	295
Ron Torgalski, Hamilton	1989	26	275
Albert Kirchner, Mt St Vincent	1990	24	267
Steve Artis, Chris. Newport	1991	29	262

ASSIST AVERAGE

Player and Team	Year	GP	A	Avg
Robert James, Kean	1989	29	391	13.5
Albert Kirchner, Mt St Vincent	1990	24	267	11.1
Ron Torgalski, Hamilton	1989	26	275	10.6
Louis Adams, Rust	1989	22	227	10.3
Eric Johnson, Coe	1991	24	238	9.9

FIELD-GOAL PERCENTAGE

Player and Team	Year	Pct
Travis Weiss, St John's (MN)	1994	76.6
Pete Metzelaars, Wabash	1982	75.3
Tony Rychlec, Mass Maritime	1981	74.9
Tony Rychlec, Mass Maritime	1982	73.1
Russ Newnan, Menlo	1991	73.0

FREE-THROW PERCENTAGE

Player and Team	Year	Pct
Andy Enfield, Johns Hopkins	1991	95.3
Yudi Teichman, Yeshiva	1989	95.2
Chris Carideo, Widener	1992	95.2
Mike Scheib, Susquehanna	1977	94.1
Jason Prevenost, Middlebury	1994	93.8

Career Records

POINTS

Player and Team	Yrs	Pts
Andre Foreman, Salisbury St	1989-92	2940
Dwain Govan, Bishop	1972-75	2796
Dave Russell, Shepherd	1972-75	2761
Lamont Strothers, Chris Newport	1988-91	2709
Matt Hancock, Colby	1987-90	2678

CAREER SCORING AVERAGE

Player and Team	Yrs	GP	Avg
Rickey Sutton, Lyndon St	1976-79	80	29.7
John Atkins, Knoxville	1976-78	70	28.7
Jeff deLaveaga, Cal Lutheran	1989-92	80	28.1
Steve Peknik, Windham	1974-77	76	27.6
Matt Hancock, Colby	1987-90	102	26.3

REBOUND AVERAGE

Player and Team	Yrs	GP	Reb	Avg
Larry Parker, Plattsburgh St	1975-78	85	1482	17.4
Charles Greer, Thomas	1975-77	58	926	16.0
Willie Parr, LeMoyne-Owen	1974-76	76	1182	15.6
Michael Smith, Hamilton	1989-92	107	1632	15.2
Dave Kufeld, Yeshiva	1977-80	81	1222	15.1

ASSIST AVERAGE

Player and Team	Yrs	Avg
Steve Artis, Chris. Newport	1990-93	8.1
Kevin Root, Eureka	1989-91	7.1
Dennis Jacobi, Bowdoin	1989-92	7.1
Eric Johnson, Coe	1989-92	7.1
Pat Skerry, Tufts	1989-92	6.6

Hockey

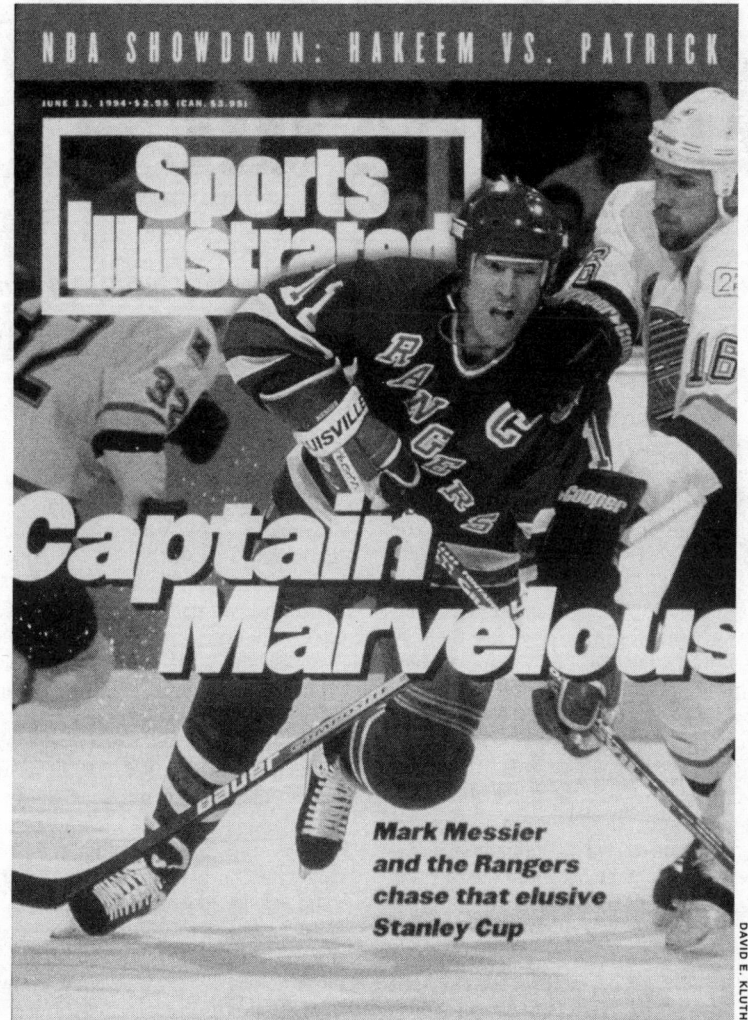

NBA SHOWDOWN: HAKEEM VS. PATRICK

JUNE 13, 1994 • $2.95 (CAN. $3.95)

Sports Illustrated

Captain Marvelous

Mark Messier and the Rangers chase that elusive Stanley Cup

DAVID E. KLUTHO

Curses Ended And Begun

The New York Rangers won their first Stanley Cup in 54 years, but lost their troubled coach to St. Louis | by AUSTIN MURPHY

THE SEASON BEGAN AND ENDED with news of Mike Keenan. The mustachioed mercenary banished one curse, only to become the object of numerous others.

After last season Keenan was hired by the increasingly desperate New York Rangers to coach them to their first Stanley Cup in 54 years. Miracle of miracles, he delivered. Barely four weeks after Manhattan's first Stanley Cup celebrations since LaGuardia was a mayor and not an airport, Keenan scrammed, claiming that the Rangers had breached their contract with him. The alleged malfeasance: They had been a day late with a bonus payment. A day later he accepted the position of coach and G.M. of the St. Louis Blues *(see sidebar)*. *The New York Post* dubbed him Benedict Arnold.

The season had begun on a less dramatic note, as the NHL made headlines for scab zebras and stultifying play. When league officials went on strike early in the season, Gary Bettman replaced them with minor leaguers. During the 17 days the strike lasted, the quality of games indisputably suffered.

Indeed, the 1993–94 regular season had threatened to go down as the Year of the Yawn. A cartoon in *The Hockey News* depicted a doctor leaning over a surgery-bound patient, asking, "General anesthetic? Or do you want to see some video of the neutral-zone trap?" With the league's five newest teams employing versions of the trap, scoring—and artistry—decreased. Alarmed, the owners voted in February to instruct officials to be more vigilant in calling restraining fouls.

That ruling coincided with a February fade by the Florida Panthers, the most successful expansion team in NHL history. But only an out-and-out collapse in the final eight games, in which they went 0-4-4, kept Las Panteras, as they became known in Miami, out of the playoffs. Still, the Panthers set records for most points (83) by an expansion team and longest unbeaten streak (nine games). Under first-year coach Kevin Constantine, the San Jose Sharks had the most dramatic one-year improvement in league history, in just their third season. The Sharks finished the regular season 57 points better than the 1992–93 Sad Jose Sharks—and went on to bounce the vastly more talented Detroit Red Wings in the first round of the playoffs.

At least the Red Wings *made* the playoffs. After earning 104 points the year before, the Quebec Nordiques plummeted to 76. The once-proud Philadelphia Flyers missed the postseason for the fifth straight year. After reaching the Cup finals a year earlier, the Los Angeles Kings did not even qualify for the playoffs, a failure that was particularly painful for owner Bruce McNall, who needed the cash.

In the off-season McNall sold 72% of the Kings to communications mavens Jeffrey Sudikoff and Joseph Cohen. Even after the sale three banks still claimed McNall owed them $162 million. In August, McNall reportedly negotiated a plea agreement with federal prosecutors, who were conducting a criminal investigation into his banking practices.

Providing the Kings with one of their few highlights was Wayne Gretzky, 33, whose power-play goal against the Vancouver Canucks on March 23 gave him 802 for his career, surpassing Gordie Howe on the NHL's alltime goal scoring list. It took Howe 1,767 games to reach 801; it took Gretzky just 1,117 to top him. The feat was all the more remarkable considering every-

Four weeks after hoisting the Cup, Keenan had an angry parting with the Rangers.

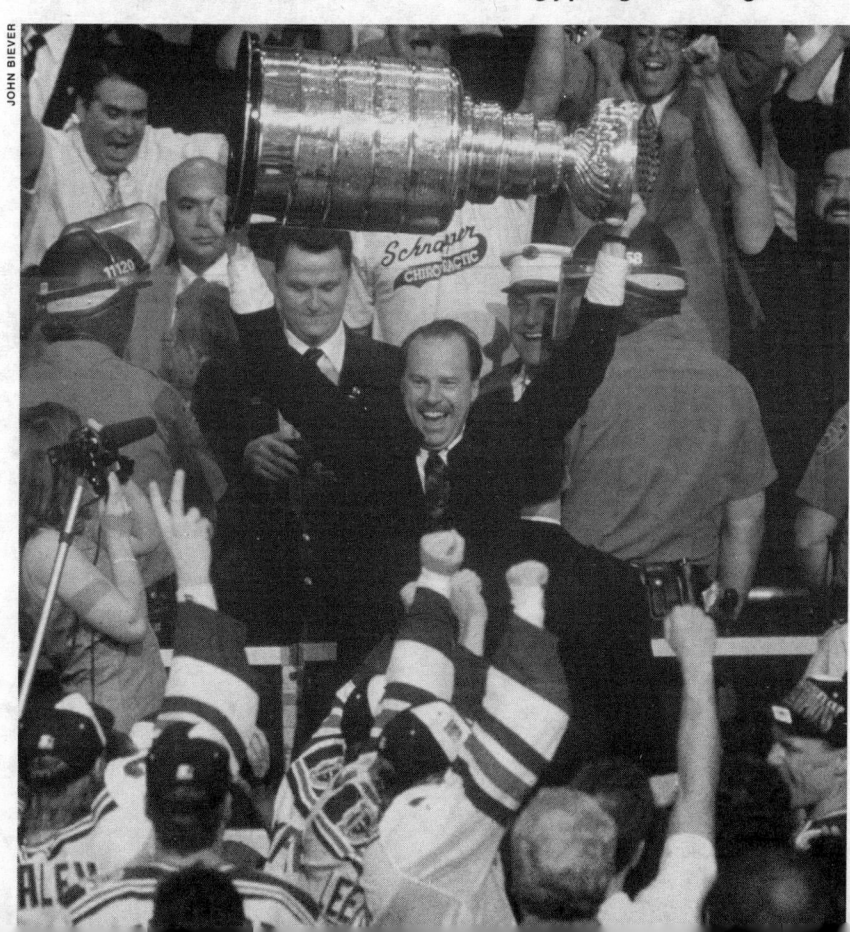

thing the six-foot, 170-pound center lacks: size, speed, a hard shot—"You could wear driving gloves and catch one of his shots, and it wouldn't hurt," said former NHL goalie Chico Resch—an aptitude for finishing breakaways, a selfish bone in his body.

Gretzky was the league's leading scorer, with 130 points—nearly doubling his team's total. Puny and shallow, the Kings could muster just 66 points on the season, finishing next to last in the Pacific Division,

behind the expansion Mighty Ducks and the Sharks. As the Sharks were captivating the Bay Area, the Mighty Ducks and the Panthers were selling out half their games, and the second-year Tampa Bay Lightning were averaging more than 21,000 a game. Even though they crapped out of the playoffs in the second round, the Dallas, né Minnesota, Stars were an unqualified success in their first season in the Lone Star State. At long last hockey was shedding its

St. Loopy Blues

They may not be be one of the NHL's most successful teams, but they are certainly among its most entertaining. How fitting that the club to which Mike Keenan made his dramatic midsummer escape was the St. Louis Blues. Over the years the Blues have been in the thick of so many blockbuster deals, they have become the Forrest Gump of the NHL. Little happens that the Blues do not somehow have a hand in.

What was it Forrest's mother used to say? *Stupid is as stupid does.* The Vancouver Canucks made their playoff push—which ended a win shy of the Stanley Cup—after a welcome infusion of talent from the Blues, who were themselves swept from the playoffs in four games. On March 3, St. Louis signed 22-year-old restricted free agent Petr Nedved to a three-year, $4.05 million contract, approximately twice his worth, according to one NHL G.M. This earned Blues president Jack Quinn and general manager Ron Caron a fresh burst of opprobrium from their colleagues around the league. Ever since they signed Brett Hull to a then-staggering four-year, $7.1 million deal in the summer of 1990, followed a month later by the signing of free-agent Scott Stevens to a four-year, $5.1 million contract, the Blues have been on the

cutting edge of discombobulating the NHL's salary structure.

In return for Nedved, according to the league's free agency policy, penned apparently before the Magna Carta, the Blues owed equitable compensation to his former team, the Canucks. But the teams couldn't agree on that compensation, so an arbitrator awarded Blues center Craig Janney to Vancouver. But Janney had just bought a house in St. Louis and refused to report, so on March 21, St. Louis sent defensemen Jeff Brown and Bret Hedican, and forward Nathan Lafayette, who played so well for their new team they were generally credited with getting the Canucks to the Stanley Cup finals.

The Blues made an early playoff exit. On Jan. 23 a trio of elderly but popular St. Louis muckers, Garth Butcher, Bob Bassen and Ron Sutter, were dealt to Quebec for Steve Duchesne, a flashy, puck-rushing defenseman. "We don't want our players to die before we trade them," cracked Caron. Stripped of their grit, the Blues were swept in the first round by the Dallas Stars, who physically dominated them. Nedved was invisible in the series.

Amends would be made! To make the team tougher, the intrepid Blues brain trust forked over $16 million for a four year contract for Al MacInnis, the label as a regional sport. "We're not just a cold weather sport," Bettman said. "We're getting a national footprint."

On the ice those multi-player brawls, for so many years a blight on the league, were all but eliminated, due to stringent penalties adopted by the NHL. Though a problem during the regular season, fighting virtually disappeared during the playoffs, which crackled with upsets, outstanding goaltending and suspense: 18 games went into overtime; six went into multiple overtimes.

One game threatened to go into the next month. On April 27 and 28, it took four overtimes for the Buffalo Sabres to beat the New Jersey Devils in Game 5 of the Eastern Conference quarterfinals. In that game Buffalo goalie Dominik (the Dominator) Hasek stopped all 70 Devil shots. It was a fitting capstone for Hasek's incredible season. After replacing Grant

DAVID E. KLUTHO

First the Blues sacrificed the season for Nedved, then sacrificed him to get Keenan.

Calgary Flame rear guard with one of the league's most feared slap shots. The same week they signed New Jersey Devil captain Scott Stevens to an offer sheet. When the Devils matched their offer and the Blues lost Stevens, it was the second time in three years they had lost him. (In September '91, shortly after the Blues signed Brendan Shanahan, then a restricted free agent with the Devils, an arbitrator gave the Devils Stevens.)

Rather than dwell on their failure to recover Stevens, the Blues hurled themselves into their next mission: replacing coach Bob Berry and Caron. To get Keenan, they sacrificed Nedved, the player for whom they sacrificed, essentially, the 1993–94 season. Easy come, easy go.

The acquisition of the shrewd Keenan as general manager could signal an end to the loopy personnel decisions for which the Blues have become known. Alas, while Keenan will undoubtedly make the Blues better, he may also make them less entertaining.

BILL FRAKES

The Blank Czech was brilliant in a losing cause during the Buffalo-New Jersey series.

Fuhr, who suffered a knee injury on Nov. 26, Hasek proceeded to become the first NHL goalie in 20 years to give up fewer than two goals a game. Hasek, a native of the Czech Republic, finished the season with a 30-20-6 record, a 1.95 goals-against average and seven shutouts, which earned him a second moniker, the Blank Czech.

Goalies were the story in the early rounds of the playoffs. Out West, a diminutive Latvian named Arturs Irbe was minding the nets for the Sharks and thoroughly frustrating the Red Wing big guns. The Sabres lost their series with the Devils in part because Hasek's counterpart, Martin Brodeur, a rangy rookie in the Ken Dryden mold, had allowed just five goals in the series' last three games. In New York, Mike Richter stopped 88 of 91 shots and threw a *pair* of bagels at the Islanders as the Rangers swept their opening-round series.

After next dispatching the Capitals in five games, the Rangers faced the Devils, their rivals across the river, whom they had beaten six times in six tries in the regular season. This one would be a cinch, right? Hardly. Devil forward Stéphane Richer's goal in the second overtime of Game 1 set the tone for what would be a dramatic seven-game series. The Rangers won easily in Game 2, and with immense difficulty in Game 3, when recently acquired forward Stéphane Matteau scored in double OT.

The Rangers were listless and lousy in losing Games 4 and 5. With the season bleeding away, captain Mark Messier did what he had been imported to New York to do. He guaranteed victory in Game 6, then backed up the audacious promise with a natural hat trick in the third period. After the first 60 minutes of Game 7—the Devils had tied the score with 7.7 seconds to play—Messier talked to the squad about what a great opportunity they had: If they could weather this adversity and go on to win the Cup, he told them, think how much sweeter it would be!

Twenty scoreless minutes later, they were back in the dressing room. Matteau approached Eddie Olczyk, a Ranger player who had not dressed for the game, and said, "Come on, Eddie, give me some luck." Olczyk kissed his stick, and Matteau went out and, at 4:24 of the second overtime, somehow swept the puck off Brodeur's stick and into the net, ending a truly epic series.

While the Devils and the Rangers hogged the hockey spotlight, the Vancouver Canucks were dominating the Toronto Maple Leafs, winning the Western Conference finals in five games. The most dramatic development in Vancouver had been the second-half detonation of Pavel Bure, a.k.a. the Russian Rocket, who scored 45 goals in his last 45 games to finish the season with 60 for the second time in two years. Whereas the 23-year-old right wing had been erased in his two previous play-

offs, this spring he was on fire, coming into the Cup finals with 13 goals.

But Bure had but one meager assist through the first two games, which the teams split. He scored early in Game 3 on a breathtaking breakaway, then killed whatever momentum he'd given his team when he drove the shaft of his stick into the face of New York's Jay Wells, breaking the defenseman's nose and opening a four-stitch trench under his left eye. Referee Andy Van Hellemond unhesitatingly awarded the Rangers a five-minute major penalty and ejected Bure from the game. Glenn Anderson's game-winning goal—New York would pile on three more in the 5–1 laugher—came 58 seconds after Bure got the thumb.

Brian Leetch owned the Pacific Coliseum two nights later, scoring once and setting up three other goals. With the series at 3–1 in favor of the Rangers and headed back to New York, preparations began for

a metropolis-wide bash: David Letterman planned to have some of the Rangers on his show; Mayor Rudy Giuliani invited them over to Gracie Mansion for a weekend barbecue. Abandoning their usual restraint, the city's tabloids also found themselves caught up in the excitement: THE CUP STOPS HERE! prophesied the front-page headline of the *New York Post*; its back-page head proclaimed TONIGHT'S THE NIGHT!

Indeed, the Cup did stop at the Garden ... for 12 hours. Indeed, it *was* the night ... to add another tear-jerking chapter to the Rangers' lugubrious postseason history.

Following the team's 6–3 loss, Keenan pointed a finger at his interviewers. The team's success had "seduced" the media, whose euphoric predictions had "rubbed off on the club." Of the distraction created by rampant rumors that he had already agreed to be the coach and G.M. of the

Detroit Red Wings next season, Keenan made no mention.

These rumors foreshadowed the circus that broke out five weeks later, when Keenan bolted to St. Louis. His bailout came as no surprise. The worst-kept secret in the Big Apple last season was the simmering hostility between Keenan and Ranger general manager Neil Smith. The Rangers sued Keenan for breaching his contract with them, which said he owed the club another four years. In a partial admission of their culpability, the Blues agreed to send Nedved to the Rangers in exchange for a pair of fading veterans, Doug Lidster and Esa Tikkanen, and the rights to Keenan.

Bettman summoned both parties to New York to dispense some justice of his own. Keenan was suspended for 60 days and forced to return $400,000 of his $500,000 signing bonus to the Rangers; the Blues were fined $250,000 for signing Keenan when he was still under contract to the Rangers. Even the Rangers and the Detroit Red Wings got $25,000 slaps on the wrist. However, this unseemly backbiting still

Bure came out flying in Game 6, nailing Leetch early with a ferocious but clean check.

could not remove the luster from their dream season for Ranger fans.

The dream had its scary parts. Bure set the tone in the third minute of Game 6, ramming Leetch into the end boards with a ferocious, clean check. The Canucks jumped all over the Rangers, outshooting them 16–7 in the first period and taking a 1–0 lead, which they parlayed into a dominant, 4–1 win.

Asked if he cared to make any predictions for Game 7, Messier would only say, "We know what we have to do." The old warhorse wasn't kidding. Messier scored the Cup-winning goal in the Rangers' 3–2 win over the Canucks.

Leetch, who opened the scoring for the Rangers, wasn't just the best player in the postseason—he also got off the best line. After sheepishly accepting the Conn Smythe Trophy, he took a call from President Bill Clinton, who said, "Congrats, man!"

They gabbed like old friends. Leetch waited until Clinton was off the line, then said, "Was that Dana Carvey?"

"I just talked to him—it's like he's in a dream," said Jack Leetch of his 26-year-old son. "He won't be down for a week."

For Ranger fans, delivered at last after 54 years, it would take longer than that.

DAVID E. KLUTHO

FOR THE RECORD·1993-1994

NHL Final Team Standings

Western Conference

CENTRAL DIVISION

	GP	W	L	T	GF	GA	Pts
Detroit	84	46	30	8	356	275	100
Toronto	84	43	29	12	280	243	98
Dallas	84	42	29	13	286	265	97
St Louis	84	40	33	11	270	283	91
Chicago	84	39	36	9	254	240	87
Winnipeg	84	24	51	9	245	344	57

PACIFIC DIVISION

	GP	W	L	T	GF	GA	Pts
Calgary	84	42	29	13	302	257	97
Vancouver	84	41	40	3	279	276	85
San Jose	84	33	35	16	252	265	81
Anaheim	84	33	46	5	229	251	71
Los Angeles	84	27	45	12	294	322	66
Edmonton	84	25	45	14	261	305	64

Eastern Conference

NORTHEAST DIVISION

	GP	W	L	T	GF	GA	Pts
Pittsburgh	84	44	27	13	299	285	101
Boston	84	42	29	13	289	252	97
Montreal	84	41	29	14	283	248	96
Buffalo	84	43	32	9	282	218	95
Quebec	84	34	42	8	275	284	76
Hartford	84	27	48	9	227	288	63
Ottawa	84	14	61	9	201	391	37

ATLANTIC DIVISION

	GP	W	L	T	GF	GA	Pts
NY Rangers	84	52	24	8	299	231	112
New Jersey	84	47	25	12	306	220	106
Washington	84	39	35	10	277	263	88
NY Islanders	84	36	36	12	282	264	84
Florida	84	33	34	17	233	233	83
Philadelphia	84	35	39	10	294	314	80
Tampa Bay	84	30	43	11	224	251	71

1994 Stanley Cup Playoffs

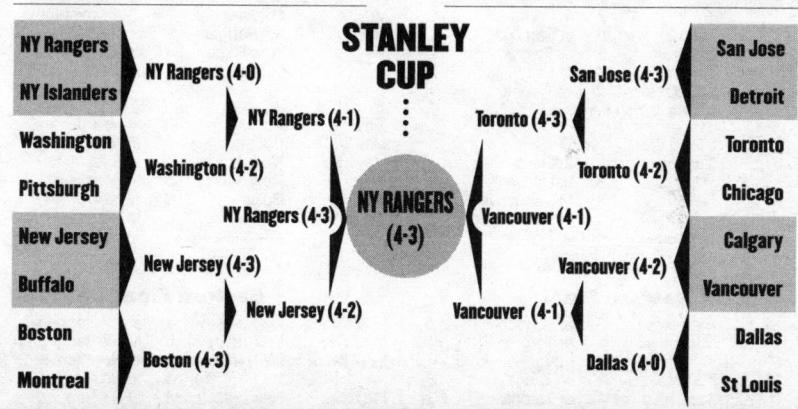

Stanley Cup Playoff Results

Conference Quarterfinals

EASTERN CONFERENCE

Apr 17	NY Islanders	0	at NY Rangers	6
Apr 18	NY Islanders	0	at NY Rangers	6
Apr 21	NY Rangers	5	at NY Islanders	1
Apr 24	NY Rangers	5	at NY Islanders	2

NY Rangers won series 4-0.

Apr 17	Washington	5	at Pittsburgh	3
Apr 19	Washington	1	at Pittsburgh	2
Apr 21	Pittsburgh	0	at Washington	2
Apr 23	Pittsburgh	1	at Washington	4
Apr 25	Washington	2	at Pittsburgh	3
Apr 27	Pittsburgh	3	at Washington	6

Washington won series 4-2.

Conference Quarterfinals *(Cont.)*

EASTERN CONFERENCE *(CONT.)*

Apr 16	Montreal	2	at Boston	3	Apr 17	Buffalo	2	at New Jersey	0
Apr 18	Montreal	3	at Boston	2	Apr 19	Buffalo	1	at New Jersey	2
Apr 21	Boston	6	at Montreal	3	Apr 21	New Jersey	2	at Buffalo	1
Apr 23	Boston	2	at Montreal	5	Apr 23	New Jersey	3	at Buffalo	5
Apr 25	Montreal	2	at Boston	1*	Apr 25	Buffalo	3	at New Jersey	5
Apr 27	Boston	3	at Montreal	2	Apr 27	New Jersey	0	at Buffalo	1#
Apr 29	Montreal	3	at Boston	5	Apr 29	Buffalo	1	at New Jersey	2

Boston won series 4-3. New Jersey won series 4-3.

WESTERN CONFERENCE

Apr 17	St Louis	3	at Dallas	5	Apr 18	Chicago	1	at Toronto	5
Apr 20	St Louis	2	at Dallas	4	Apr 20	Chicago	0	at Toronto	1*
Apr 22	Dallas	5	at St Louis	4*	Apr 23	Toronto	4	at Chicago	5
Apr 24	Dallas	2	at St Louis	1	Apr 24	Toronto	3	at Chicago	4*
					Apr 26	Chicago	0	at Toronto	1
					Apr 28	Toronto	1	at Chicago	0

Dallas won series 4-0. Toronto won series 4-2.

Apr 18	Vancouver	5	at Calgary	0	Apr 18	San Jose	5	at Detroit	4
Apr 20	Vancouver	5	at Calgary	7	Apr 20	San Jose	0	at Detroit	4
Apr 22	Calgary	4	at Vancouver	2	Apr 22	Detroit	3	at San Jose	2
Apr 24	Calgary	3	at Vancouver	2	Apr 23	Detroit	3	at San Jose	4
Apr 26	Vancouver	2	at Calgary	1*	Apr 26	San Jose	6	at Detroit	4
Apr 28	Calgary	2	at Vancouver	3*	Apr 28	Detroit	7	at San Jose	1
Apr 30	Vancouver	4	at Calgary	3†	Apr 30	San Jose	3	at Detroit	2

Vancouver won series 4-3. San Jose won series 4-3.

Conference Semifinals

WESTERN CONFERENCE

May 2	San Jose	3	at Toronto	2
May 4	San Jose	1	at Toronto	5
May 6	Toronto	2	at San Jose	5
May 8	Toronto	8	at San Jose	3
May 10	San Jose	5	at Toronto	2
May 12	Toronto	3	at San Jose	2*
May 14	San Jose	2	at Toronto	4

Toronto won series 4-3.

May 2	Vancouver	6	at Dallas	4
May 4	Vancouver	3	at Dallas	0
May 6	Dallas	4	at Vancouver	3
May 8	Dallas	1	at Vancouver	2*
May 11	Vancouver	4	at Dallas	2

Vancouver won series 4-1.

EASTERN CONFERENCE

May 1	Washington	3	at NY Rangers	6
May 3	Washington	2	at NY Rangers	5
May 5	NY Rangers	3	at Washington	0
May 7	NY Rangers	2	at Washington	4
May 9	Washington	3	at NY Rangers	4

NY Rangers won series 4-1.

May 1	Boston	2	at New Jersey	1
May 3	Boston	6	at New Jersey	5*
May 5	New Jersey	4	at Boston	2
May 7	New Jersey	5	at Boston	4*
May 9	Boston	0	at New Jersey	2
May 11	New Jersey	5	at Boston	3

New Jersey won series 4-2.

Western Final

May 16	Vancouver	2	at Toronto	3*
May 18	Vancouver	4	at Toronto	3
May 20	Toronto	0	at Vancouver	4
May 22	Toronto	0	at Vancouver	2
May 24	Vancouver	4	at Toronto	3†

Vancouver won series 4-1.

Eastern Final

May 15	New Jersey	4	at NY Rangers	3†
May 17	New Jersey	0	at NY Rangers	4
May 19	NY Rangers	3	at New Jersey	2†
May 21	NY Rangers	1	at New Jersey	3
May 23	New Jersey	4	at NY Rangers	1
May 25	NY Rangers	4	at New Jersey	3
May 27	New Jersey	1	at NY Rangers	2†

NY Rangers won series 4-3.

Stanley Cup Championship

June 1	Vancouver	3	at NY Rangers	2*	June 9	Vancouver	6	at NY Rangers	3
June 3	Vancouver	1	at NY Rangers	3	June 11	NY Rangers	1	at Vancouver	4
June 5	NY Rangers	5	at Vancouver	1	June 14	Vancouver	2	at NY Rangers	3
June 7	NY Rangers	4	at Vancouver	2					

NY Rangers won series 4-3.

*Overtime game. †Double overtime game. #Quadruple overtime game.

Stanley Cup Championship Box Scores

Game 1

Vancouver	0	0	2	1—3
NY Rangers	1	0	1	0—2

FIRST PERIOD

Scoring: 1, NY, Larmer 6 (Kovalev, Leetch) 3:32. Penalties: Wells, NY (cross-checking), 1:47; Linden, Van (tripping), 2:26; McIntyre, Van (roughing), 8:05; Lowe, NY (roughing), 8:05; Craven, Van (slashing), 10:35; Beukeboom, NY (interference),15:54.

SECOND PERIOD

Scoring: None. Penalties: Messier, NY (hooking), :20; Lidster, NY (tripping), 8:49; Courtnall, Van (interference), 13:18; Momesso, Van (goalie interference), 16:15; Beukeboom, NY (high-sticking), 19:34.

THIRD PERIOD

Scoring: 2, Van, Hedican 1 (Adams, Lumne), 5:45. 3, NY, Kovalev 6 (Leetch, Zubov), 8:29. 4, Van, Gelinas 5 (Ronning, Momesso), 19:00. Penalties: None.

OVERTIME

Scoring: 5, Van, Adams 6 (Bure, Ronning), 19:26. Penalties: Momesso, Van (roughing), 9:31; Gilbert, NY (roughing), 9:31.

Shots on goal: Van—10-5-7-9—31. NY—15-9-13-17—54. Power-play opportunities: Van 0-of-5; NY 0-of-4. Goalies: Van, McLean (54 shots, 52 saves). NY, Richter (31 shots, 28 saves). A: 18,200.
Referee: Gregson. Linesmen: Mitton, Scapinello.

Game 2

Vancouver	1	0	0—1
NY Rangers	1	1	1—3

FIRST PERIOD

Scoring: 1, NY, Lidster 1, 6:22. 2, Van, Momesso 3 (Ronning, Hedican), 14:04. Penalties: Craven, Van (tripping), 2:03; Lidster, NY (interference), 7:44; Hunter, Van (roughing), 10:21; Hunter, Van (misconduct),15:26; Anderson, NY (interference), 16:55.

SECOND PERIOD

Scoring: 3, NY, Anderson 2 (shorthanded) (Messier), 11:42. Penalties: Brown, Van (hooking), 4:27; Matteau, NY (hooking), 6:12; Graves, NY (tripping), 10:35; Antoski, Van (roughing),13:58; Tikkanen, NY (goalie interference), 17:08.

THIRD PERIOD

Scoring: 4, NY, Leetch 7 (empty net), 19:56. Penalties: Lidster, NY (interference), 1:43; Diduck, Van (high-sticking), 4:32; Kovalev, NY (high-sticking), 4:32; Brown, Van (roughing), 15:29; Gilbert, NY (roughing), 15:29.

Shots on goal: Van—10-6-13—29. NY—14-13-13—40. Power-play opportunities: Van 0-of-6; NY 0-of-4. Goalies: Van, McLean (39 shots, 37 saves). NY, Richter (29 shots, 28 saves). A: 18,200.
Referee: McCreary. Linesmen: Collins, Gauthier.

Game 3

NY Rangers	2	1	2—5
Vancouver	1	0	0—1

FIRST PERIOD

Scoring: 1, Van, Bure 14 (Linden, Adams), 1:03. 2, NY, Leetch 8, 13:39. 3, NY, Anderson 3 (Nemchinov, Beukeboom), 19:19 Penalties: Wells, NY (tripping), 2:54; Anderson, NY (roughing), 5:42; Lumme, Van (holding), 9:57; MacTavish, NY (holding), 15:40; Leetch, NY (tripping), 17:56; Lowe, NY (high-sticking), 18:12; Momesso, Van (roughing), 18:12; Bure, Van (major-game misconduct) (high-sticking), 18:21.

SECOND PERIOD

Scoring: 4, NY, Leetch 9 (Tikkanen, Beukeboom), 18:32. Penalties: Lowe, NY (roughing), 5:34; Antoski, Van (roughing), 16:28; Messier, NY (roughing), 16:28.

THIRD PERIOD

Scoring: 5, NY, Larmer 7, :25. 6, NY, Kovalev 7 (Graves, Messier), 13:03 (pp). Penalties: Tikkanen, NY (hooking), 3:13; Hedican, Van (holding), 5:34; McIntyre, Van (holding), 9:46; Momesso, Van (cross-checking), 11:42; Gelinas, Van (roughing), 16:35; Antoski, Van (double minor) (cross-checking, roughing), 19:19.

Shots on goal: NY—9-10-6—25. Van—11-5-9—25. Power-play opportunities: NY 1-of-7; Van 0-of-6. Goalies: NY, Richter (25 shots, 24 saves); Van, McLean (25 shots, 20 saves). A: 16,150.

Referee: Andy vanHellemond. Linesmen: Ray Scapinello, Randy Mitton

Game 4

NY Rangers	0	2	2—4
Vancouver	2	0	0—2

FIRST PERIOD

Scoring: 1,Van, Linden 10 (pp) (Lumme, Brown), 13:25. 2, Van, Ronning 5 (Bure, Craven), 16:19. Penalties: Courtnall, Van (elbowing), 3:11; Beukeboom, NY (high-sticking), 6:35; Graves, NY (holding),13:02; Messier, NY (boarding major), 14:17; Linden, Van (holding stick.), 15:07; Courtnall, Van (int), 17:54; Tikkanen, NY (roughing), 18:45.

SECOND PERIOD

Scoring: 3, NY, Leetch 10 (MacTavish, Gilbert), 4:03. 4, NY, Zubov 5 (pp) (Messier, Leetch), 19:44. Penalties: Lidster, NY (holding), 1:13; Brown, Van (tripping), 7:19; Lidster, NY (holding), 16:58; Adams, Van (boarding), 18:55.

THIRD PERIOD

Scoring: 5, NY, Kovalev 8 (pp) (Leetch, Zubov), 15:05. 6, NY, Larmer 8 (Zubov, Leetch), 17:56. Penalties: NY bench, served by Kocur (too many men), 3:53; Lumme, Van (holding), 4:48; Tikkanen, NY (roughing), 10:42; Diduck, Van (roughing) 10:42; Messier, NY (slashing), 11:29; Gelinas, Van (roughing), 14:31.

Shots on goal: NY—8-8-11—27. Van—8-12-10—30. Power-play opportunities: NY 2-of-9,Van 1-of-10. Goalies: NY, Richter (30 shots, 28 saves).Van, McLean (27 shots, 23 saves). A: 16,150.
Referee: Gregson. Linesmen: Collins, Gauthier.

Game 5

Vancouver........0	**1**	**5——6**	
NY Rangers......0	**0**	**3——3**	

FIRST PERIOD

Scoring: None. Penalties: Hunter, Van (elbowing), :49; Momesso, Van (slashing, fighting major), 10:06; Ronning, Van (roughing), 10:06; Beukeboom, NY (instigator, fighting major, game misconduct), 10:06; Wells, NY (high-sticking), 10:06; Matteau, NY (roughing), 10:06; Hunter, Van (roughing), 13:02; Wells, NY (roughing), 13:02; Ronning, Van (holding), 17:20; Larmer, NY (holding), 17:20; Nemchinov, NY (elbowing), 19:42.

SECOND PERIOD

Scoring: 1, Van, Brown 4 (Ronning, Antoski), 8:10. Penalties: Courtnall, Van (elbowing major), 10:13; Messier NY (hooking), 18:19.

THIRD PERIOD

Scoring: 2, Van, Courtnall 6 (Lafayette, Hedican), :26. 3, Van, Bure 15 (Craven), 2:48. 4, NY, Lidster 2 (Kovalev), 3:27. 5, NY, Larmer 9 (Matteau, Nemchinov), 6:20. 6, NY, Messier 11 (Anderson, Graves), 9:02. 7, Van, Babych 3 (Bure), 9:31. 8, Van, Courtnall 7 (Lafayette, Lumme), 12:20. 9, Van, Bure 16 (Ronning, Hedican), 13:04. Penalty: Kocur, NY (slashing), 18:41.

Shots on goal: Van—12-8-17—37. NY—10-13-15—38. Power-play opportunities: Van 0-of-4; NY 0-of-2. Goalies: Van, McLean, (38 shots, 35 saves); NY, Richter (37 shots, 31 saves). A: 18,200.

Referee: vanHellemond. Linesmen: Mitton, Scapinello.

Game 6

NY Rangers......0	**1**	**0——1**	
Vancouver........1	**1**	**2——4**	

FIRST PERIOD

Scoring: 1, Van, Brown 5, (Linden), 9:42 (pp). Penalties: Beukeboom, NY (interference), 9:39.

SECOND PERIOD

Scoring: 2, Van, Courtnall 8 (Lumme, Bure), 12:29. 3, NY, Kovalev 9 (Messier, Leetch), 14:42 (pp). Penalties: Momesso, Van. (interference), 2:26; Diduck, Van. (tripping), 7:27; McIntyre, Van (goalie interference), 13:23.

THIRD PERIOD

Scoring: 4, Van., Brown 6, 8:35. 5, Van, Courtnall 9 (Layfayette, Diduck), 18:28. Penalties: None.

Shots on goal: NY—7-12-10—29. Van—16-8-7—31. Power-play opportunities: NY 1-of-3; Van 1-of-2. Goalies: NY, Richter (31 shots, 27 saves); Van, McLean (29 shots, 28 saves). A: 16,150.

Referee: Bill McCreary. Linesmen: Kevin Collins, Gerard Gauthier.

Game 7

Vancouver........0	**1**	**1——2**	
NY Rangers......2	**1**	**0——3**	

FIRST PERIOD

Scoring: 1, NY, Leetch 11, (Zubov, Messier), 11:02. 2, NY, Graves 10 (pp) (Kovalev, Zubov), 14:45. Penalties:Lumme, Van. (cross-checking), 14:03; Hedican, Van. (roughing), 18:50; Tikkanen, NY (roughing), 18:50.

SECOND PERIOD

Scoring: 3, Van., Linden 11 (shorthanded) (Glynn, Bure), 5:21. 4, NY, Messier 12 (pp) (Graves, Noonan), 13:29. Penalties: Brown, Van. (interference), 4:39; Babych, Van.

(tripping), 12:46; Messier, NY (hooking), 16:39.

THIRD PERIOD

Scoring: 5, Van., Linden 12 (pp) (Courtnall, Ronning), 4:50. Penalties: Tikkanen, NY (hooking), 4:16; Linden, Van (roughing), 10:55; MacTavish, NY (roughing), 10:55.

Shots on goal: Van—9-12-9—30. NY—12-14-9—35. Power-play opportunities: Van. 1-of-2; NY 2-of-3. Goalies: Van., McLean (35 shots, 32 saves); NY, Richter (30 shots, 28 saves). A: 18,200.

Referee: Gregson. Linesmen: Collins, Scapinello.

Individual Playoff Leaders

Scoring

POINTS

Player and Team	GP	G	A	Pts	+/-	PM
Brian Leetch, NYR 23	11	23	34	19	6	
Pavel Bure, Van 24	16	14	30	7	40	
Mark Messier, NYR 23	12	18	30	14	33	
Doug Gilmour, Tor 18	6	22	28	3	42	
Trevor Linden, Van 24	12	13	25	3	18	
Alexei Kovalev, NYR 23	9	12	21	5	18	
Geoff Courtnall, Van 24	9	10	19	10	51	
Sergei Zubov, NYR........22	5	14	19	10	0	

Player and Team	GP	G	A	Pts	+/-	PM
Claude Lemieux, NJ 20	7	11	18	4	44	
Igor Larionov, SJ 14	5	13	18	1-	10	
Dave Ellett, Tor 18	3	15	18	1	31	
Adam Graves, NYR 23	10	7	17	12	24	
Wendel Clark, Tor..........18	9	7	16	0	24	
Steve Larmer, NYR 23	9	7	16	8	14	
John MacLean, NJ 20	6	10	16	2-	22	

* Rookie.

GOALS

Player and Team	GP	G
Pavel Bure, Van	24	16
Mark Messier, NYR	23	12
Trevor Linden, Van	24	12
Brian Leetch, NYR	23	11
Adam Graves, NYR	23	10

POWER PLAY GOALS

Player and Team	GP	PP
Dmitri Mironov, Tor	16	6
Doug Gilmour, Tor	18	5
Alexei Kovalev, NYR	23	5
Trevor Linden, Van	24	5
Brian Leetch, NYR	23	4

GAME WINNING GOALS

Player and Team	GP	GW
Brian Leetch, NYR	23	4
Mark Messier, NYR	23	4
Mike Gartner, Tor	18	3
Geoff Courtnall, Van	24	3
Shawn Burr, Det	7	2

SHORT HANDED GOALS

Player and Team	GP	SH
Mark Osborne, Tor	18	2
Kevin Miller, StL	3	1
Kris Draper, Det	7	1
Micklas Lidstrom, Det	7	1
Mike Sullivan, Cal	7	1

ASSISTS

Player and Team	GP	A
Brian Leetch, NYR	23	23
Doug Gilmour, Tor	18	22
Mark Messier, NYR	23	18
Dave Ellett, Tor	18	15
Sergei Zubov, NYR	22	14
Pavel Bure, Van	24	14

PLUS/MINUS

Player and Team	GP	+/−
Brian Leetch, NYR	23	19
Mark Messier, NYR	23	14
Adam Graves, NYR	23	12
Three Players tied at 10.		

Goaltending (Minimum 420 minutes)

GOALS AGAINST AVERAGE

Player and Team	GP	Mins	GA	Avg
Dominik Hasek, Buff	7	484	13	1.61
*Martin Brodeur, NJ	17	1171	38	1.95
Mike Richter, NYR	23	1417	49	2.07
Kirk McLean, Van	24	1544	59	2.29
Chris Osgood, Det	8	307	12	2.35

SAVE PERCENTAGE

Player and Team	GP	Mins	GA	SA	Pct	W	L
Dominik Hasek, Buff	7	484	13	261	.950	3	4
Patrick Roy, Mtl	6	375	16	220	.930	3	3
Kirk McLean, Van	24	1544	59	820	.928	15	9
*Martin Brodeur, NJ	17	1171	38	531	.926	8	9
Mike Richter, NYR	23	1417	49	623	.921	16	7
Ed Belfour, Chi	6	360	15	191	.921	2	4

NHL Awards

Award	Player and Team
Hart Trophy (MVP)	Sergei Fedorov, Det
Calder Trophy (top rookie)	Martin Brodeur, NJ
Vezina Trophy (top goaltender)	Dominik Hasek, Buff
Norris Trophy (top defenseman)	Ray Borque, Bos
Lady Byng Trophy (for gentlemanly play)	Wayne Gretzky, LA
Selke Trophy (top defensive forward)	Sergei Fedorov, Det

Award	Player and Team
Adams Award (top coach)	Jacques Lemaire, NJ
Jennings Trophy (goaltenders on club allowing fewest goals)	Dominik Hasek and Grant Fuhr, Buff
Conn Smythe Trophy (playoff MVP)	Brian Leetch, NYR

NHL Individual Leaders

Scoring

POINTS

Player and Team	GP	G	A	Pts	+/−	PM
Wayne Gretzky, LA	81	38	92	130	−25	20
Sergei Fedorov, Det	82	56	64	120	48	34
Adam Oates, Bos	77	32	80	112	10	45
Doug Gilmour, Tor	83	27	84	111	25	105
Pavel Bure, Van	76	60	47	107	1	86
Jeremy Roenick, Chi	84	46	61	107	21	126
Mark Recchi, Phil	84	40	67	107	−2	46
Brendan Shanahan, StL	81	52	50	102	−9	211
Jaromir Jagr, Pitt	80	32	67	99	15	61
Dave Andreychuk, Tor	83	53	45	98	22	98

GOALS

Player and Team	GP	G
Pavel Bure, Van	76	60
Brett Hull, StL	81	57
Sergei Fedorov, Det	82	56
Dave Andreychuk, Tor	83	53
Brendan Shanahan, StL	81	52

POWER PLAY GOALS

Player and Team	GP	PP
Pavel Bure, Van	76	25
Brett Hull, StL	81	25
Luc Robitaille, LA	83	24
Jeremy Roenick, Chi	84	24
Keith Tkachuk, Win	84	22

* Rookie.

GAME WINNING GOALS

Player and Team	GP	GW
Cam Neely, Bos	49	13
Sergei Fedorov, Det	82	10
V. Damphousse, Mtl	84	10
Five tied with nine.		

SHORT HANDED GOALS

Player and Team	GP	SHG
Brendan Shanahan, StL	81	7
Eight tied with five.		

ASSISTS

Player and Team	GP	A
Wayne Gretzky, LA	81	92
Doug Gilmour, Tor	83	84
Adam Oates, Bos	77	80
Sergei Zubov, NYR	78	77
Ray Bourque, Bos	72	71

PLUS/MINUS

Player and Team	GP	+/−
Scott Stevens, NJ	83	53
Sergei Fedorov, Det	82	48
Nicklas Lidstrom, Det	84	43
Frank Musil, Cal	75	38
Gary Roberts, Cal	73	37

Goaltending
(Minimum 25 games)

GOALS AGAINST AVERAGE

Player and Team	GP	Mins	GA	Avg
Dominik Hasek, Buff	58	3358	109	1.95
*Martin Brodeur, NJ	47	2625	105	2.40
Patrick Roy, Mtl	68	3867	161	2.50
John Vanbiesbrouck, Fla	57	3440	145	2.53
Mike Richter, NYR	68	3710	159	2.57

WINS

Player and Team	GP	Mins	W	L	T
Mike Richter, NYR	68	3710	42	12	6
Ed Belfour, Chi	70	3998	37	24	6
Curtis Joseph, StL	71	4127	36	23	11
Patrick Roy, Mtl	68	3867	35	17	11
Felix Potvin, Tor	66	3883	34	22	9

SAVE PERCENTAGE

Player and Team	GP	GA	SA	Pct	W	L
Dominik Hasek, Buff	58	109	1552	.930	30	20 6
J Vanbiesbrouck, Fla	57	145	1912	.924	21	25 11
Patrick Roy, Mtl	68	161	1956	.918	35	17 11
*Martin Brodeur, NJ	47	105	1238	.915	27	11 8
Mark Fitzpatrick, Fla	28	73	844	.913	12	8 6

SHUTOUTS

Player and Team	GP	Mins	SO	W	L	T
Dominik Hasek, Buff	58	3358	7	30	20	6
Patrick Roy, Mtl	68	3867	7	35	17	11
Ed Belfour, Chi	70	3998	7	37	24	6
Ron Hextall, NYI	65	3581	5	27	26	6
Mike Richter, NYR	68	3710	5	42	12	6

NHL Team-by-Team Statistical Leaders

Anaheim Mighty Ducks
SCORING

Player	GP	G	A	Pts	+/–	PM
Terry Yake, C	82	21	31	52	2	44
Bob Corkum, C, R	76	23	28	51	4	18
Garry Valk, L, R	78	18	27	45	8	100
Tim Sweeney, L	78	16	27	43	3	49
Bill Houlder, D	80	14	25	39	-18	40
Joe Sacco, L	84	19	18	37	-11	61
Peter Douris, R	74	12	22	34	-5	21
Shaun Van Allen	80	8	25	33	0	64
Anatoli Semenov, L, C	49	11	19	30	-4	12
Sean Hill, D	68	7	20	27	-12	78
Stephan Lebeau, C	56	15	11	26	-4	22
*Patrik Carnback, L	73	12	11	23	-8	54
Bobby Dollas, D	77	9	11	20	20	55
David Williams, D	56	5	15	20	8	42
Troy Loney, L	62	13	6	19	-5	88
Todd Ewen, R	76	9	9	18	-7	272
Don McSween, D	32	3	9	12	4	39
Steven King, R	36	8	3	11	-7	44
Randy Ladouceur, D	81	1	9	10	7	74
Jarrod Skalde, C	20	5	4	9	-3	10
Mark Ferner, D	50	3	5	8	-16	30
*John Lilley, C	13	1	6	7	1	8
Stu Grimson, L	77	1	5	6	-6	199

GOALTENDING

Player	GP	Mins	Avg	W	L	T	SO
Mikhail Shtalenkov	10	543	2.65	3	4	1	0
Guy Hebert	52	2991	2.83	20	27	3	2
Ron Tugnutt	28	1520	3.00	10	15	1	1
Team total	84	5079	2.97	33	46	5	3

Boston Bruins
SCORING

Player	GP	G	A	Pts	+/–	PM
Adam Oates, C	77	32	80	112	10	45
Ray Bourque, D	72	20	71	91	26	58
Cam Neely, R	49	50	24	74	12	54
Al Iafrate, D	79	15	43	58	16	163
Glen Wesley, D	81	14	44	58	1	64
Ted Donato, C	84	22	32	54	0	59
*Bryan Smolinski, C	83	31	20	51	4	82
Glen Murray, R	81	18	13	31	-1	48
Brent Hughes, L	77	13	11	24	10	143
*Jozef Stumpel, R	59	8	15	23	4	14
Dave Reid, L	83	6	17	23	10	25
Stephen Heinze, R	77	10	11	21	-2	32
Don Sweeney, D	75	6	15	21	29	50
Dmitri Kvartalnov, L	39	12	7	19	-9	10
Stephen Leach, R	42	5	10	15	-10	74
Daniel Marois, R	22	7	3	10	-4	18
Paul Stanton, D	71	3	7	10	-7	54
David Shaw, D	55	1	9	10	-11	85
*Cameron Stewart, C	57	3	6	9	-6	66
Glen Featherstone, D	58	1	8	9	-5	152
Gord Roberts, D	59	1	6	7	-13	40
*Fred Knipscheer, L	11	3	2	5	3	14
*Sergei Zholtok, R	24	2	1	3	-7	2

GOALTENDING

Player	GP	Mins	Avg	W	L	T	SO
Jon Casey	57	3192	2.88	30	15	9	4
John Blue	18	944	2.99	5	8	3	0
Vince Riendeau	18	976	3.07	7	6	1	1
Team total	84	5116	2.96	42	29	13	5

*Rookie

Buffalo Sabres

SCORING

Player	GP	G	A	Pts	+/−	PM
Dale Hawerchuk, C	81	35	51	86	10	91
Alexander Mogilny, R	66	32	47	79	8	22
Donald Audette, R	77	29	30	59	2	41
Yuri Khmylev, L	72	27	31	58	13	49
*Derek Plante, C	77	21	35	56	4	24
Brad May, L	84	18	27	45	-6	171
Richard Smehlik, D	84	14	27	41	22	69
Doug Bodger, D	75	7	32	39	8	76
Randy Wood, L	84	22	16	38	11	71
Wayne Presley, R	65	17	8	25	18	103
Bob Sweeney, C, R	60	11	14	25	3	94
Ken Sutton, D	78	4	20	24	-6	71
Pat LaFontaine, C	16	5	13	18	-4	2
Craig Simpson, L	22	8	8	16	-3	8
Petr Svoboda	60	2	14	16	11	89
*Phillippe Boucher, D	38	6	8	14	-1	29
Craig Muni, D	82	2	12	14	31	66
*Jason Dawe, L	32	6	7	13	1	12
Randy Moller, D	78	2	11	13	-5	154
Rob Ray, L	82	3	4	7	2	274
*Matthew Barnaby, R	35	2	4	6	-7	106
James Black, C	15	2	3	5	-4	2
*Scott Thomas, R	32	2	2	4	-6	8

GOALTENDING

Player	GP	Mins	Avg	W	L	T	SO
Dominik Hasek	53	3358	1.95	30	20	6	7
Grant Fuhr	32	1726	3.68	13	12	3	2
Team total	84	5097	2.57	43	32	9	9

Calgary Flames

SCORING

Player	GP	G	A	Pts	+/−	PM
Robert Reichel, C	84	40	53	93	20	58
Theoren Fleury, C	83	40	45	85	30	186
Gary Roberts, L	73	41	43	84	37	145
Al Macinnis, D	75	28	54	82	35	95
Joe Nieuwendyk, C	64	36	39	75	19	51
Mikael Nylander, C	73	13	42	55	8	30
Zarley Zalapski, D	69	10	37	47	-6	74
German Titov, C	76	27	18	45	20	28
Wes Walz, C	53	11	27	38	20	16
James Patrick, D	68	10	25	35	-5	40
Kelly Kisio, C	51	7	23	30	-6	28
Ronnie Stern, R	71	9	20	29	6	243
Joel Otto, C	81	11	12	23	-17	92
Michel Petit, D	63	2	21	23	5	110
Dan Keczmer, D	69	1	21	22	-8	60
Trent Yawney, D	58	6	15	21	21	60
Chris Dahlquist, D	77	1	11	12	5	52
Paul Kruse, L	68	3	8	11	-6	185
*Sandy McCarthy, R	79	5	5	10	-3	173
Mike Sullivan, C	45	4	5	9	-1	10
Frantisek Musil, D	75	1	8	9	38	50
Brad Schlegel, D	26	1	6	7	-4	4
Guy Larose, C, L	17	1	3	4	-5	14
Kevin Dahl, D	33	0	3	3	-2	23

GOALTENDING

Player	GP	Mins	Avg	W	L	T	SO
*Andrei Trefilov	11	623	2.50	3	4	2	2
Mike Vernon	48	2798	2.81	26	17	5	3
*Trevor Kidd	31	1614	3.16	13	7	6	0
Jeff Reese	1	13	4.62	0	0	0	0
*Jason Muzzatti	1	60	8.00	0	1	0	0
Team Total	84	5124	3.00	42	29	13	5

Chicago Blackhawks

SCORING

Player	GP	G	A	Pts	+/−	PM
Jeremy Roenick, C	84	46	61	107	21	125
Joe Murphy, R	81	31	39	70	1	111
Chris Chelios, D	76	16	44	60	12	212
Tony Amonte, R	79	17	25	42	0	37
Brent Sutter, C	73	9	29	38	17	43
Paul Ysebaert, L	71	14	21	35	-7	26
Dirk Graham, R	67	15	18	33	13	45
Michel Goulet, L	56	16	14	30	1	26
Christian Ruuttu, C	54	9	20	29	-4	68
Patrick Poulin, L	67	14	14	28	-8	51
Eric Weinrich, D	62	4	24	28	1	35
Steve Smith, D	57	5	22	27	-5	174
Brent Sutter, C	83	12	14	26	-8	108
Randy Cunneyworth, L	79	13	11	24	-1	100
Gary Suter, D	41	6	12	18	-12	38
*Jeff Shantz, C	52	3	13	16	-14	30

Player	GP	G	A	Pts	+/−	PM
Keith Carney, D	37	4	8	12	14	39
Neil Wilkinson, D	72	3	9	12	2	114
*Steve Dubinsky, C	27	2	6	8	1	16
Cam Russell, D	67	1	7	8	10	200
Darin Kimble, R	65	4	2	6	2	133
Robert Dirk, D	71	2	3	5	18	131
Greg Smyth, D	61	1	1	2	-4	183

GOALTENDING

Player	GP	Mins	Avg	W	L	T	SO
*Christian Soucy	1	3	0.00	0	0	0	0
Ed Belfour	70	3998	2.67	37	24	6	7
Jeff Hackett	22	1084	3.43	2	12	3	0
Team total	84	5099	2.82	39	36	9	7

* Rookie.

Dallas Stars

SCORING

Player	GP	G	A	Pts	+/–	PM
Mike Modano, R	76	50	43	93	-8	54
Russ Courtnall, R	84	23	57	80	6	59
Dave Gagner, C	76	32	29	61	13	83
Neal Broten, C	79	17	35	52	10	62
Grant Ledyard, D	84	9	37	46	7	42
Paul Cavallini, D	74	11	33	44	13	82
Dean Evason, C	80	11	33	44	-12	66
Trent Klatt, R	61	14	24	38	13	30
Mike Craig, R	72	13	24	37	-14	139
Michael McPhee, L	79	20	15	35	8	36
Brent Gilchrist, C	76	17	14	31	0	31
Derian Hatcher, D	83	12	19	31	19	211
Paul Broten, R	64	12	12	24	18	30
Mark Tinordi, D	61	6	18	24	6	143
Pelle Eklund, C	53	3	17	20	-2	10
Craig Ludwig, D	84	1	13	14	-1	123
Shane Churla, R	69	6	7	13	-8	333
Alan May, L	51	5	7	12	-3	115
Dave Barr, R	20	2	5	7	-6	21
*Jarrko Varvio, R	8	2	3	5	1	4
Doug Zmolek, D	75	1	4	5	-8	133
Chris Tancill, C	12	1	3	4	-7	8
Richard Matvichuk, D	25	0	3	3	1	22
Mike Lalor, D	35	0	3	3	-10	14

GOALTENDING

Player	GP	Mins	Avg	W	L	T	SO
Darcy Wakaluk	36	2000	2.64	18	9	6	3
Andy Moog	55	3121	3.27	24	20	7	2
Team total	84	5132	3.10	42	29	13	5

Detroit Red Wings

SCORING

Player	GP	G	A	Pts	+/–	PM
Sergei Fedorov, C	82	56	64	120	48	34
Ray Sheppard, R	82	52	41	93	13	26
Steve Yzerman, C	58	24	58	82	11	36
Paul Coffey, D	80	14	63	77	28	106
Vyacheslav Kozlov, C	77	34	39	73	27	50
Keith Primeau, L	78	31	42	73	34	173
Dino Ciccarelli, R	66	28	29	57	10	73
Nicklas Lidstrom, D	84	10	46	56	43	26
Steve Chiasson, D	82	13	33	46	17	122
Vlad Konstantinov, D	80	12	21	33	30	138
Mike Sillinger, C	62	8	21	29	2	10
*Darren McCarty, R	67	9	17	26	12	181
Mark Howe, D	44	4	20	24	16	8
Shawn Burr, C	51	10	12	22	12	31
Bob Probert, R	66	7	10	17	-1	275
*Greg Johnson, C	52	6	11	17	-7	22
*Martin Lapointe, D	50	8	8	16	7	55
Sheldon Kennedy, R	61	6	7	13	-2	30
Kris Draper, C	39	5	8	13	11	31
*Micah Aivazoff, C	59	4	4	8	-1	38
Terry Carkner, D	68	1	6	7	13	130
Sergei Bautin, D	60	0	7	7	-12	78
Bob Halkidis, D	28	1	4	5	-1	93
*Jason York, D	7	1	2	3	0	2

GOALTENDING

Player	GP	Mins	Avg	W	L	T	S
Bob Essensa	13	778	2.62	4	7	2	1
*Chris Osgood	41	2206	2.86	23	8	5	2
Tim Cheveldae	30	1572	3.47	16	9	1	1
Vince Riendeau	8	345	4.00	2	4	0	0
Peter Ing	3	170	5.29	1	2	0	0
Team total	84	5094	3.24	46	30	8	4

Edmonton Oilers

SCORING

Player	GP	G	A	Pts	+/–	PM	Player	GP	G	A	Pts	+/–	PM
Doug Weight, C	84	24	50	74	-22	47	*Brent Grieve, L	27	13	5	18	4	21
*Jason Arnott, C	78	33	35	68	1	104	Scott Thornton, C	61	4	7	11	-15	104
Zdeno Ciger, L	84	22	35	57	-11	8	Louie Debrusk, L	48	4	6	10	-9	185
Shayne Corson, L,	64	25	29	54	118	11	*Adam Bennett, D	48	3	6	9	-8	49
Igor Kravchuk, D	81	12	38	50	-12	16	*Peter White, L	26	3	5	8	1	2
Bob Beers, D	82	11	32	43	-22	86	Shjon Podein, C	28	3	5	8	3	8
Scott Pearson, L	72	19	18	37	-4	165	Luke Richardson, D	69	2	6	8	-13	131
Fredrik Olausson, D	73	11	24	35	-7	30							
Steve Rice, R	63	17	15	32	-10	36							
*Boris Mironov, D	79	7	24	31	-33	110							
Ilya Byakin, D	44	8	20	28	-3	30							
*Dean McAmmond, C	45	6	21	27	12	16							
Mike Stapleton, C	81	12	13	25	-5	46							
Kelly Buchberger, L,	84	3	18	21	-20	199							
*Kirk Maltby, R	68	11	8	19	-2	74							
Vladimir Vujtek, L	40	4	15	19	-7	14							

GOALTENDING

Player	GP	Mins	Avg	W	L	T	SO
Wayne Cowley	1	57	3.16	0	1	0	0
Bill Ranford	71	4070	3.48	22	34	11	1
*Fred Brathwaite	19	982	3.54	3	10	3	0
Team total	84	5121	3.57	25	45	14	1

* Rookie.

Florida Panthers

SCORING

Player	GP	G	A	Pts	+/–	PM
Bob Kudelski, C	86	40	30	70	-33	24
Scott Mellanby, R	80	30	30	60	0	149
*Jesse Belanger, C	70	17	33	50	-4	16
Andrei Lomakin, L	76	19	28	47	1	26
Gord Murphy, D	84	14	29	43	-11	71
Brian Skrudland, C	79	15	25	40	13	136
Dave Lowry, L	80	15	22	37	-4	64
Tom Fitzgerald, R	83	18	14	32	-3	54
Brian Benning, D	73	6	24	30	-7	107
Mike Hough, L	78	6	23	29	3	62
Jody Hull, R	69	13	13	26	6	8
*Rob Niedermayer, D	65	9	17	26	-11	51
Bill Lindsay, L	84	6	6	12	-2	97
Keith Brown, Tk	51	4	8	12	11	60
Brent Severyn, D	67	4	7	11	-1	156
Joe Cirella, D	63	1	9	10	8	99
Mike Foligno, R	43	4	5	9	7	53
Geoff Smith, L	77	1	8	9	-13	50
Jeff Daniels, L	70	3	5	8	-1	20

GOALTENDING

Player	GP	Mins	Avg	W	L	T	SO
J Vanbiesbrouck	57	3440	2.53	21	25	11	1
Mark Fitzpatrick	28	1603	2.73	12	8	6	1
Eldon Reddick	2	80	6.00	0	1	0	0
Team total	84	5144	2.72	33	34	17	2

Hartford Whalers

SCORING

Player	GP	G	A	Pts	+/–	PM
Pat Verbeek, R	84	37	38	75	-15	177
Geoff Sanderson, C	82	41	26	67	-13	42
Andrew Cassels, C	79	16	42	58	-21	37
Robert Kron, L	77	24	26	50	0	8
*Chris Pronger, D	81	5	25	30	-3	113
Brian Propp, L	65	12	17	29	3	44
Jocelyn Lemieux, R	82	18	9	27	-3	82
Paul Ranheim, L	82	10	17	27	-18	22
Alexander Godynyuk, D	69	3	19	22	13	75
Frantisek Kucera, D	76	5	16	21	-3	48
Darren Turcotte, C	32	4	15	19	-13	17
*Ted Drury, C	50	6	12	18	-15	36
Adam Burt, D	63	1	17	18	-4	75
*Jim Storm, L	68	6	10	16	4	27
Igor Chibirev, C	37	4	11	15	7	2
Bryan Marchment,	55	4	11	15	-14	166
Mark Janssens, C, L	84	2	10	12	-13	137
Robert Petrovicky, C	33	6	5	11	-1	39
Jim Sandlak, R	27	6	2	8	6	32
Brad McCrimmon, D	65	1	5	6	-7	72
*Kevin Smyth, L	21	3	2	5	-1	10
Marc Potvin, R	54	2	3	5	-8	272
*Ted Crowley, D	21	1	2	3	-1	10

GOALTENDING

Player	GP	Mins	Avg	W	L	T	SO
*Mike Lenarduzzi	1	21	2.86	0	0	0	0
Sean Burke	47	2750	2.99	17	24	5	2
Jeff Reese	19	1066	3.09	5	9	3	1
Frank Pietrangelo	19	964	3.60	5	11	1	0
Mario Gosselin	7	239	5.27	0	4	0	0
Team total	84	5099	3.39	27	48	9	3

* Rookie.

Los Angeles Kings

SCORING

Player	GP	G	A	Pts	+/–	PM
Wayne Gretzky, C	81	38	92	130	-25	20
Luc Robitaille, L	83	44	42	86	-20	86
Jari Kurri, L	81	31	46	77	-24	48
Rob Blake, D	84	20	48	68	-7	137
Alexei Zhitnik, D	81	12	40	52	-11	101
Mike Donnelly, L	81	21	21	42	2	34
Darryl Sydor, D	84	8	27	35	-9	94
John Druce, R	55	14	17	31	16	50
Marty McSorley, D	65	7	24	31	-12	194
Rob Blake, D	76	16	43	59	18	152
Pat Conacher, L	77	15	13	28	0	71
Kevin Todd, C	47	8	14	22	-3	24
Tony Granato, L	50	7	14	21	-2	150
Warren Rychel, L	80	10	9	19	-19	322
*Robert Lang, C	32	9	10	19	7	10
Charlie Huddy, D	79	5	13	18	4	71
Dixon Ward, R	67	12	3	15	-22	82
Timothy Watters, D	60	1	9	10	-11	67
Donald Dufresne, D	60	2	6	8	-7	58
Doug Houda, D	61	2	6	8	-19	188
Dave Taylor, R	33	4	3	7	-1	28
Gary Schuchuk, R	56	3	4	7	-8	30
Jim Paek, D	59	1	5	6	-8	18

GOALTENDING

Player	GP	Mins	Avg	W	L	T	SO
Rick Knickle	4	174	3.10	1	2	0	0
Robb Stauber	22	1144	3.41	4	11	5	1
Kelly Hrudey	64	3713	3.68	22	31	7	1
*Dave Goverde	1	60	7.00	0	1	0	0
Team total	84	5124	3.77	27	45	12	2

Montreal Canadiens

SCORING

Player	GP	G	A	Pts	+/–	PM
Vincent Damphousse, L	84	40	51	91	0	75
Brian Bellows, L	77	33	38	71	9	36
Kirk Muller, L	76	23	34	57	-1	96
Mathieu Schneider, D	75	20	32	52	15	62
Mike Keane, R	80	16	30	46	6	119
Gilbert Dionne, L	74	19	26	45	-9	31
John LeClair, L	74	19	24	43	17	32
Lyle Odelein, D	79	11	29	40	8	276
Guy Carbonneau, C	79	14	24	38	16	48
Eric Desjardins, C	84	12	23	35	-1	97
Paul DiPietro, C	70	13	20	33	-2	37
Benoit Brunet, L	71	10	20	30	14	20
*Oleg Petrov, R	55	12	15	27	7	2
Patrice Brisebois, D	53	2	21	23	5	63
Gary Leeman, R	31	4	11	15	5	17
Ed Ronan, R	61	6	8	14	3	42
*Peter Popovic, D	47	2	12	14	10	26
J.J. Daigneault, D	68	2	12	14	16	73
Kevin Haller, D	68	4	9	13	3	118
Ron Wilson, C	48	2	10	12	-2	12
*Pierre Sevigny, L	43	4	5	9	6	42

GOALTENDING

Player	GP	Mins	Avg	W	L	T	SO
Patrick Roy	66	3867	2.50	35	17	11	7
*Les Kuntar	6	302	3.18	2	2	0	0
Ron Tugnutt	8	378	3.81	2	3	1	0
Andre Racicot	11	500	4.44	2	6	2	0
*Frederic Chabot	1	60	5.00	0	1	0	0
Team total	84	5122	2.91	41	29	14	7

New Jersey Devils

SCORING

Player	GP	G	A	Pts	+/–	PM
Scott Stevens, D	83	18	60	78	53	112
Stephane Richer, R	80	36	36	72	31	16
John MacLean, R	80	37	33	70	30	95
Valeri Zelepukin	82	26	31	57	36	70
Corey Millen, C	78	20	30	50	24	52
Bernie Nicholls, C	61	19	27	46	24	86
Scott Niedermayer, D	81	10	36	46	34	42
Bill Guerin, C	81	25	19	44	14	101
Claude Lemieux, R	79	18	26	44	13	86
Tom Chorske, R	76	21	20	41	14	32
Bobby Holik, C	70	13	20	33	28	72
Bobby Carpenter, L	76	10	23	33	7	51
Bruce Driver, D	66	8	24	32	29	63
Alexander Semak, C	54	12	17	29	6	22
Randy McKay, R	78	12	15	27	24	244
Mike Peluso, L	69	4	16	20	19	238
Tommy Albelin, D	62	2	17	19	20	36
*Jaroslav Modry, D	41	2	15	17	10	18
*Jim Dowd, C	15	5	10	15	8	0
Viacheslav Fetisov, D	52	1	14	15	14	30
*David Emma, C	15	5	5	10	0	2
Ken Daneyko, D	78	1	9	10	27	176
*Jason Smith, D	41	0	5	5	7	43

GOALTENDING

Player	GP	Mins	Avg	W	L	T	SO
*Martin Brodeur	47	2625	2.40	27	11	8	3
Chris Terreri	44	2340	2.72	20	11	4	2
Peter Sidorkiewicz	3	130	2.77	0	3	0	0
Team total	84	5104	2.59	47	25	12	5

New York Islanders

SCORING

Player	GP	G	A	Pts	+/–	PM
Pierre Turgeon, C	69	38	56	94	14	18
Steve Thomas, L	78	42	33	75	-9	139
Derek King, L	78	30	40	70	18	59
Benoit Hogue, C	83	36	33	69	-7	73
Vladimir Malakhov, D	76	10	47	57	29	80
Marty McInnis, C	81	25	31	56	31	24
Ray Ferraro, C	82	21	32	53	1	83
Patrick Flatley, R	64	12	30	42	12	40
Travis Green, R	83	18	22	40	16	44
Tom Kurvers, D	66	9	31	40	7	47
Brad Dalgarno, R	73	11	19	30	14	62
Uwe Krupp, D	41	7	14	21	11	30
David Volek, L	32	5	9	14	0	10
Scott LaChance, D	74	3	11	14	-5	70
Dennis Vaske, D	65	2	11	13	21	76
Darius Kasparaitis, D	76	1	10	11	-6	142
Keith Acton, C	77	2	7	9	-5	71
David Maley, C	56	0	6	6	-7	104
Richard Pilon, D	28	1	4	5	-4	75
Mick Vukota, R	72	3	1	4	-5	237
Christopher Luongo, D	17	1	3	4	-1	13
Dean Chynoweth, D	39	0	4	4	3	122

GOALTENDING

Player	GP	Mins	Avg	W	L	T	SO
*Jamie McLennan	22	1287	2.84	8	7	6	0
Ron Hextall	65	3581	3.08	27	26	6	5
Tom Draper	7	227	4.23	1	3	0	0
Team total	84	5119	3.09	36	36	12	5

*Rookie.

New York Rangers

SCORING

Player	GP	G	A	Pts	+/–	PM
Sergei Zubov, D	78	12	77	89	20	39
Mark Messier, C	76	26	58	84	25	76
Adam Graves, C	84	52	27	79	27	127
Brian Leetch, D	84	23	56	79	28	67
Steve Larmer, R	68	21	39	60	14	41
Alexei Kovalev, R	76	23	33	56	18	154
Esa Tikkanen, L	83	22	32	54	5	114
Sergei Nemchinov, C	76	22	27	49	13	36
Glenn Anderson, R	85	21	20	41	-5	62
Brian Noonan, C, R	76	18	23	41	7	69
Stephane Matteau, L	77	19	19	38	15	57
Craig MacTavish, C	78	20	13	33	-14	91
Kevin Lowe, D	71	5	14	19	4	70
*A. Karpovtsev, D	67	3	15	18	12	58
Jeff Beukeboom, D	68	8	8	16	18	170
Greg Gilbert, L	76	4	11	15	-3	29
Mike Hudson, C, L	48	4	7	11	-5	47
Jay Wells, D	79	2	7	9	4	110
Ed Olczyk, C, L	37	3	5	8	-1	28
Nick Kypreos, L	56	3	5	8	-16	139
Joey Kocur, R	71	2	1	3	-9	129

GOALTENDING

Player	GP	Mins	Avg	W	L	T	SO
Glenn Healy	29	1368	3.03	10	12	2	2
Mike Richter	68	3710	2.57	42	12	2	5
Team total	84	5089	2.72	52	24	8	7

Ottawa Senators

SCORING

Player	GP	G	A	Pts	+/–	PM
*Alexei Yashin, C	83	30	49	79	-49	22
*Alexandre Daigle, C	84	20	31	51	-45	20
David McLlwain, C	66	17	26	43	-40	48
Sylvain Turgeon, L	47	11	15	26	-25	52
Troy Mallette, C, L	82	7	16	23	-33	166
Brad Shaw, D	66	4	19	23	-41	59
Norm Maciver, D	53	3	20	23	-26	26
Gord Dineen, D	77	0	21	21	-52	89
Evgeny Davydov, L, R	64	7	13	20	-9	46
Andrew McBain, R	55	11	8	19	-41	64
*Scott Levins, R	62	8	11	19	-26	162
Dave Archibald, C, L	33	10	8	18	-7	14
Vladimir Ruzicka, C	42	5	13	18	-21	14
Kerry Huffman, D	62	4	14	18	-28	40
Darren Rumble, D	70	6	9	15	-50	116
Dan Quinn, C, R	13	7	0	7	0	6
Brad Lauer, R	30	2	5	7	-15	6
Dennis Vial, D	55	2	5	7	-9	214
Phil Borque, L	27	2	4	6	-4	8
Troy Murray, C	27	2	4	6	2	10
Jarmo Kekalainen, C	28	1	5	6	-8	14
Robert Burakowski, R	23	2	3	5	-7	6
*Dimitri Filiminov, D	30	1	4	5	-10	18

GOALTENDING

Player	GP	Mins	Avg	W	L	T	SO
*Darrin Madeley	32	1583	4.36	3	18	5	0
Craig Billington	63	3319	4.59	11	41	4	0
Mark Laforest	5	182	5.60	0	2	0	0
Daniel Berthiaume	1	1	20.00	0	0	0	0
Team total	84	5105	4.67	14	61	9	0

Philadelphia Flyers

SCORING

Player	GP	G	A	Pts	+/-	PM
Mark Recchi, R	84	40	67	107	-2	46
Eric Lindros, C	65	44	53	97	16	103
Rod Brind'Amour, C	84	35	62	97	-9	85
*Mikael Renberg, L	83	38	44	82	8	36
Garry Galley, D	81	10	60	70	-11	91
Yves Racine, D	67	9	43	52	-11	48
Josef Beranek, C	80	28	21	49	-2	85
Kevin Dineen, R	71	19	23	42	-9	113
Brent Fedyk, R	72	20	18	38	-14	74
Mark Lamb, C	85	12	24	36	-44	72
Dimitri Yushkevich, D	75	5	25	30	-8	86
Rob DiMaio, C	53	11	12	23	-4	46
Dave Tipppett, C, L	73	4	11	15	-20	38
*Andre Faust, C	37	8	5	13	-1	10
Jeff Finley, D	55	1	8	9	16	24
Allan Conroy, C	62	4	3	7	-12	65
Rob Zettler, D	75	0	7	7	-26	134
*Jason Bowen, L	56	1	5	6	12	87
Dave Brown, R	71	1	4	5	-12	137
*Bob Wilkie, D	10	1	3	4	-2	8
Ryan McGill, D	50	1	3	4	-5	112
*Stewart Malgunas, D	67	1	3	4	2	86

GOALTENDING

Player	GP	Mins	Avg	W	L	T	SO
Dominic Roussel	60	3285	3.34	29	20	5	3
Tommy Soderstrom	34	1736	4.01	6	18	4	7
Frederic Chabot	4	70	4.29	0	1	1	0
Team total	84	5102	3.69	35	39	10	10

Pittsburgh Penguins

SCORING

Player	GP	G	A	Pts	+/-	PM
Jaromir Jagr, R	80	32	67	99	15	61
Ron Francis, C	82	27	66	93	-3	62
Kevin Stevens, L	83	41	47	88	-24	155
Larry Murphy, D	84	17	56	73	10	44
Joe Mullen, R	84	38	32	70	9	41
Martin Straka, C	84	30	34	64	24	24
Tomas Sandstrom, R	78	23	35	58	-7	83
Doug Brown, R	77	18	37	55	19	18
Shawn McEachern, C	76	20	22	42	14	34
Rick Tocchet, R	51	14	26	40	-15	134
Mario Lemieux, C	22	17	20	37	-2	32
Greg Hawgood, D	64	6	28	34	9	36
Ulf Samuelsson, D	80	5	24	29	23	199
Bryan Trottier, C	41	4	11	15	-12	36
Peter Taglianetti, D	60	2	12	14	5	142
Kjell Samuelsson, D	59	5	8	13	18	118
*Markus Naslund, R	71	4	7	11	-3	27
Greg Brown, D	36	3	8	11	1	28
Jim McKenzie, L	71	3	5	8	-7	146
Grant Jennings, D	61	2	4	6	-10	126

GOALTENDING

Player	GP	Mins	Avg	W	L	T	SO
Roberto Romano	2	125	1.44	1	0	1	0
Tom Barrasso	44	2482	3.36	22	15	5	2
Ken Wregget	42	2456	3.37	21	12	7	1
Rob Dopson	2	45	4.00	0	0	0	0
Team total	84	5118	3.34	44	27	13	3

Quebec Nordiques

SCORING

Player	GP	G	A	Pts	+/-	PM
Joe Sakic, C	84	28	64	92	-8	18
Mats Sundin, R	84	32	53	85	1	60
Valeri Kamensky, L	76	28	37	65	12	42
Mike Ricci, C	83	30	21	51	-9	113
Scott Young, D	76	26	25	51	-4	14
Ron Sutter, C	73	15	25	40	2	90
*Iain Fraser, C	60	17	20	37	-5	23
Andrey Kovalenko, R	58	16	17	33	-5	46
Martin Rucinsky, L	60	9	23	32	4	58
Bob Bassen, C	83	13	15	28	-17	99
Claude Lapointe, C	59	11	17	28	2	70
Alexei Gusarov, D	76	5	20	25	3	38
Curtis Leschyshyn, D	72	5	17	22	-2	65
Garth Butcher, D	77	4	15	19	-7	143
*David Karpa, D	60	5	12	17	0	148
Steven Finn, D	80	4	13	17	-9	159
Craig Wolanin, D	63	6	10	16	16	80

Player	GP	G	A	Pts	+/-	PM
*Mike McKee, L	48	3	12	15	5	41
Chris Lindberg, L	37	6	8	14	-1	12
Tommy Sjodin, D	29	1	11	12	4	22
Brad Werenka, D	26	0	11	11	3	22
*Chris Simon, L	37	4	4	8	-2	132
Adam Foote, D	45	2	6	8	3	67
*Reggie Savage, C	17	3	4	7	3	16
Paul MacDermid, R	44	2	3	5	-3	35
Owen Nolan, R	6	2	2	4	2	8

GOALTENDING

Player	GP	Mins	Avg	W	L	T	SO
Jacques Cloutier	14	475	3.03	3	2	1	0
*Jocelyn Thibault	29	1504	3.31	8	13	3	0
Stephane Fiset	50	2798	3.39	20	25	4	2
*Garth Snow	5	279	3.44	3	2	0	0
Team total	84	5080	3.45	34	42	8	2

* Rookie.

St Louis Blues

SCORING

Player	GP	G	A	Pts	+/-	PM
Brendan Shanahan, R	81	52	50	102	-9	211
Brett Hull, R	81	57	40	97	-3	38
Craig Janney, C	69	16	68	84	-14	24
Kevin Miller, L	75	23	25	48	6	83
Steve Duchesne, D	36	12	19	31	1	14
Vitali Prokhorov, L	55	15	10	25	-6	20
Philippe Bozon, C	80	9	16	25	4	42
Alexei Kasatonov, D	63	4	20	24	-3	62
Phil Housley, D	26	7	15	22	-5	12
*Vitali Karamnov, L	59	9	12	21	-3	51
Petr Nedved, C	19	6	14	20	2	8
*Jim Montgomery, C	67	6	14	20	-1	44
Igor Koroloev, R	73	6	10	16	-12	40
Peter Stastny, C	17	5	11	16	-2	4
Murray Baron, D	77	5	9	14	-14	123
Tony Hrkac, C	36	6	5	11	-11	8
Rick Zombo, D	74	2	8	10	-15	85
Doug Crossman, D	50	2	7	9	1	10
Tom Tilley, D	48	1	7	8	3	32
Kelly Chase, R	68	2	5	7	-5	278
Dave Mackey, L	30	2	3	5	-4	56
*Dan Laperriere, D	20	1	3	4	-1	8

GOALTENDING

Player	GP	Mins	Avg	W	L	T	SO
Curtis Joseph	71	4127	3.10	36	23	11	1
Jim Hrivnak	23	970	4.27	4	10	0	0
Team total	84	5107	3.32	40	33	11	1

San Jose Sharks

SCORING

Player	GP	G	A	Pts	+/-	PM
Ulf Dahlen, R	78	25	44	69	-1	10
Sergei Makarov, R	80	30	38	68	11	78
Todd Elik, C	79	25	41	66	-3	95
Sandis Ozolnich, D	81	26	38	64	16	24
Igor Larionov, C	60	18	38	56	20	40
Pat Falloon, R	83	22	31	53	-3	18
Johan Garpenlov, L	80	18	35	53	9	28
Ray Whitney, D	61	14	26	40	2	14
Jeff Norton, D	64	7	33	40	16	36
Rob Gaudreau, R	84	15	20	35	-10	28
Bob Errey, L	64	12	18	30	-11	126
Gaetan Duchesne, L	84	12	18	30	8	28
Tom Pederson, D	74	6	19	25	3	31
Vyatcheslav Butsayev, C	59	12	11	23	0	68
Jeff Odgers, L	81	13	8	21	-13	222
Jamie Baker, C	65	12	5	17	2	38
*Mike Rathje, D	47	1	9	10	-9	59
Dale Craigwell, C	58	3	6	9	-13	16
Jay More, D	49	1	6	7	-5	63
*Jaroslav Otevrel, L	9	3	2	5	-5	2
*Michal Sykora, D	22	1	4	5	-4	14
*Vlastimil Kroupa, D	27	1	3	4	-6	20

GOALTENDING

Player	GP	Mins	Avg	W	L	T	SO
Arturs Irbe	74	4412	2.84	30	28	16	3
Jimmy Waite	15	697	4.30	3	7	0	0
Team total	84	5125	3.10	33	35	16	3

Tampa Bay Lightning

SCORING

Player	GP	G	A	Pts	+/-	PM
Brian Bradley, C	78	24	40	64	-8	56
Petr Klima, L, R	75	28	27	55	-15	76
Denis Savard, C	74	18	28	46	-1	106
Danton Cole, R	81	20	23	43	7	32
*Chris Gratton, C	84	13	29	42	-25	123
Chris Tucker, C	66	17	23	40	9	28
Shawn Chambers, D	66	11	23	34	-6	23
Chris Joseph, D	76	11	20	31	-21	136
Pat Elynuik, R	67	13	15	28	-21	64
Mikael Andersson, L	76	13	12	25	8	23
Roman Hamrlik, D	64	3	18	21	-14	135
Adam Creighton, C	53	10	10	20	-7	37
Marc Bergevin, D	83	1	15	16	-5	87
Marc Bureau, C	75	8	7	15	-9	30

Player	GP	G	A	Pts	+/-	PM
Gerard Gallant, L	51	4	9	13	-6	74
Rob Zamuner, L, C	59	6	6	12	-9	42
Rudy Poeschek, D	71	3	6	9	3	118
Bill McDougall, C	22	3	3	6	-4	8
*Chris Lipuma, D	27	0	4	4	1	77
*Brent Gretzky, C	10	1	2	3	0	2
*Jim Cummins, R	26	1	2	3	-1	84

GOALTENDING

Player	GP	Mins	Avg	W	L	T	SO
Wendell Young	9	480	2.50	2	3	1	1
Darren Puppa	63	3653	2.71	22	33	6	4
J.C. Bergeron	3	134	3.13	1	1	0	0
Pat Jablonski	15	834	3.88	5	6	3	0
Team total	84	5116	2.94	30	43	11	5

* Rookie.

Toronto Maple Leafs

SCORING

Player	GP	G	A	Pts	+/-	PM
Doug Gilmour, C	83	27	84	111	25	105
D. Andreychuk, L	83	53	45	98	22	98
Wendel Clark, L	64	46	30	76	10	115
Mike Gartner, C	81	34	30	64	20	62
Dave Ellett, D	68	7	36	43	6	42
Dimitri Mironov, D	76	9	27	36	5	78
Nikolai Borschevsky, R	45	14	21	35	6	10
John Cullen, C	53	13	17	30	-2	67
Rob Pearson, R	67	12	18	30	-6	189
Jamie Macoun, D	82	3	27	30	-5	115
Todd Gill, D	45	4	23	27	8	44
Mark Osborne, L	73	9	16	25	2	145
Bill Berg, L	83	8	11	19	-3	93
Mike Eastwood, C	54	8	10	18	2	28
Peter Zezel, C	41	8	8	16	5	19
Kent Manderville, L	67	7	9	16	5	63
Bob Rouse, D	63	5	11	16	8	101
Mark Greig, R	44	6	7	13	-5	41
Mike Krushelnyski, C	54	5	6	11	-5	28
Sylvain Lefebvre, D	84	2	9	11	33	79
Drake Berehowsky, D	49	2	8	10	-3	63
Ken Baumgartner, D	64	4	4	8	-6	185
*Yanic Perreault, C	13	3	3	6	1	0

GOALTENDING

Player	GP	Mins	Avg	W	L	T	SO
*Damian Rhodes	22	1213	2.62	9	7	3	0
Felix Potvin	66	3883	2.89	34	22	9	3
Team total	84	5115	2.85	43	29	12	3

Vancouver Canucks

SCORING

Player	GP	G	A	Pts	+/-	PM
Pavel Bure, L	76	60	47	107	1	86
Geoff Courtnall, L	82	26	44	70	15	123
Cliff Ronning, C	76	25	43	68	7	42
Jeff Brown, D	74	14	52	66	-11	56
Trevor Linden, R	84	32	29	61	6	73
Murray Craven, C	78	15	40	55	5	30
Jyrki Lumme, D	83	13	42	55	3	50
Jiri Slegr, D	78	5	33	38	0	86
Greg Adams, L	68	13	24	37	-1	20
Dave Babych, D	73	4	28	32	0	52
Gino Odjick, L	76	16	13	29	13	271
Martin Gelinas, L	64	14	14	28	-8	34
Jimmy Carson, D	59	11	17	28	-15	24
Sergio Momesso, L	68	14	13	27	-2	149
Dana Murzyn, D	80	6	14	20	4	109
Brian Glynn, D	64	2	13	15	-19	53
S Charbonneau, R	30	7	7	14	-3	49
Bret Hedican, D	69	0	12	12	-7	64
Gerald Diduck, D	55	1	10	11	2	72
Adrien Plavsic, D	47	1	9	10	-5	6
John McIntyre, C	62	3	6	9	-9	38
*Nathan Lafayette, C	49	3	4	7	-7	18
Tim Hunter, R	56	3	4	7	-7	171
*Dane Jackson, R	12	5	1	6	3	9
*Dan Kesa, R	19	2	4	6	-3	14
*Yevgeny Namestnikov,D	17	0	5	5	-2	10

GOALTENDING

Player	GP	Mins	Avg	W	L	T	SO
Kirk McLean	52	3128	2.99	23	26	3	3
Kay Whitmore	32	1921	3.53	18	14	0	0
Team total	84	5070	3.27	41	40	3	3

Washington Capitals

SCORING

Player	GP	G	A	Pts	+/-	PM
Joe Juneau, C	74	19	66	85	11	41
Mike Ridley, C	81	26	44	70	15	24
Dimitri Khristich, C	83	29	29	58	-2	73
Sylvain Cote, D	84	16	35	51	30	66
Michal Pivonka, C	82	14	36	50	2	38
Peter Bondra, R	69	24	19	43	22	40
Randy Burridge, L	78	25	17	42	-1	73
Calle Johansson, D	84	9	33	42	3	59
Kevin Hatcher, D	72	16	24	40	-13	106
Kelly Miller, L	84	14	25	39	8	32
Dale Hunter, C	52	9	29	38	-4	131
Keith Jones, R	68	16	19	35	4	149
Todd Krygier, L	66	12	18	30	-4	60
*Pat Peake, C	49	11	18	29	1	39
Steve Konowalchuk, C	62	12	14	26	9	33
Dave Poulin, C	63	6	19	25	-1	52
Joe Reekie, D	84	1	16	17	15	156
*John Slaney, D	47	7	9	16	3	27
Craig Berube, L	84	7	7	14	-4	305
Tim Bergland, R	54	5	6	11	-15	10
Shawn Anderson, D	50	0	9	9	-1	12
Jim Johnson, D	61	0	7	7	-7	63
*Kevin Kaminski, C	13	0	5	5	2	87

GOALTENDING

Player	GP	Mins	Avg	W	L	T	SO
Don Beaupre	53	2853	2.84	24	16	8	2
R. Tabaracci	32	1770	3.06	13	14	2	2
*Byron Dafoe	5	230	3.39	2	2	0	0
*Olaf Kolzig	7	224	5.36	0	3	0	0
Team total	84	5099	3.09	39	35	10	4

* Rookie.

Winnipeg Jets

SCORING

Player	GP	G	A	Pts	+/−	PM
Keith Tkachuk, R	84	41	40	81	-12	255
Nelson Emerson, C	83	33	41	74	-38	80
Alexei Zhamnov, C	61	26	45	71	-20	62
Darrin Shannon, L	77	21	37	58	-18	87
Teemu Selanne, R	51	25	29	54	-23	22
Thomas Steen, C	76	19	32	51	-38	32
Dallas Drake, C	62	13	27	40	-1	49
Stephane Quintal, D	81	8	18	26	-25	119
Teppo Numminen, D	57	5	18	23	-23	28
Dave Manson, D	70	4	17	21	-14	191
Tie Domi, R	81	8	11	19	-8	347
Luciano Borsato, C	75	5	13	18	-11	28
Igor Ulanov, D	74	0	17	17	-11	165
Wayne McBean, D	50	3	13	16	-34	40
Randy Gilhen, C	60	7	7	14	-12	50

Player	GP	G	A	Pts	+/−	PM
Russ Romaniuk, L	24	4	8	12	-11	6
Mike Eagles, C	73	4	8	12	-20	96
Kris King, L	83	4	8	12	-22	205
Dean Kennedy, D	76	2	8	10	-22	164
John LeBlanc, L, R	17	6	2	8	-2	2
*Dave Tomlinson, C	31	1	3	4	-12	24
Darryl Shannon, D	20	0	4	4	-6	18

GOALTENDING

Player	GP	Mins	Avg	W	L	T	SO
Bob Essensa	56	3136	3.85	19	30	6	1
Tim Cheveldae	14	788	3.96	5	8	1	1
*Mike O'Neill	17	738	4.15	0	9	1	0
S. Beauregard	13	418	4.88	0	4	1	0
Team total	84	5098	4.05	24	51	9	2

* Rookie.

NHL All-Star Game

Western	4	2	2—8
Eastern	3	2	4—9

First Period: Scoring—1, West, Roenick 1 (Nieuwendyk, Blake), 7:31; 2, East, Kudelski 1 (Turgeon, Bourque), 9:46; 3, West, Fedorov 1 (Bure, Ozolinsh), 10:20; 4, East, Lindros 1 (unassisted), 11:00; 5, West, Shanahan 1 (Gretzky, Hull), 13:21; 6, East, Yashin 1 (Sakic, Turgeon), 14:29; 7, West, Andreychuk 1 (MacInnis, Fedorov), 15:10. Penalties—None.

Second Period: Scoring—8, East, S. Stevens 1 (Oates, Sanderson), 10:37; 9, West, Coffey 1 (Andreychuk, Gilmour), 12:36; 10, West, Ozolinsh 1 (Taylor, Roenick), 14:39; 11, East, Messier 1 (Mullen, Graves), 15:05. Penalties—None.

Third Period: Scoring—12, West, Ozolinsh 2 (Bure), :55; 13, East, Mullen 1 (Graves, Messier), 1:28; 14, West, Shanahan 2 (Gretzky, Chelios), 7:40; 15, East, Sakic 1 (Trugeon, S. Stevens), 10:41; 16, East, Kudelski 2 (Messier), 13:59; 17, East, Yashin 2 (Sakic, Turgeon), 16:18. Penalties—None.

SHOTS ON GOAL

	1	2	3	Tot
Western	17	21	8	46
Eastern	19	18	19	56

GOALTENDERS

	Time	SA	GA	ENG	Dec
Western, Potvin	20:00	16	3	0	
Western, Joseph	20:00	15	4	0	
Western, Irbe	20:00	16	2	0	L
Eastern, Roy	20:00	13	4	0	
Eastern, Vanbiesbrouck	20:00	6	2	0	
Eastern, Richter	20:00	19	2	0	W

PP Conversions: West 0 for 0; East 0 for 0.
Referee: McCreary. Linesmen: Brobeker, Dapuzzo.
Attendance: 18,200 (at Madison Square Garden).
All-Star Game MVP: Mike Richter, NYR (East).

1994 NHL Draft

First Round

The opening round of the 1994 NHL draft was held in Hartford on June 28.

Team	Selection	Position
1.....Florida	Ed Jovanovski, Windsor	D
2.....Anaheim	Oleg Tverdovsky, Sov. Wing	D
3.....Ottawa	Radek Bonk, Las Vegas	C
4.....Edmonton	Jason Bonsignore, Niagara Falls	C
5.....Hartford	Jeff O'Neill, Guelph	C
6.....Edmonton	Ryan Smyth, Moose Jaw	L
7.....Los Angeles	Jamie Storr, Owen Sound	G
8.....Tampa Bay	Jason Weimer, Portland	L
9.....NY Islanders	Brett Lindros, Kingston	R
10...Washington	Nolan Baumgartner, Kamloops	D
11...San Jose	Jeff Friesen, Regina	C
12...Quebec	Wade Belak, Saskatoon	D
13...Vancouver	Mattais Ohlund, Pitea	D

Team	Selection	Position
14....Chicago	Ethan Moreau, Niagara Falls	L
15...Washington	Alexander Kharlamov, CSKA	L
16...Toronto	Eric Fichaud, Chicoutimi	G
17...Buffalo	Wayne Primeau, Owen Sound	C
18...Montreal	Brad Brown, North Bay	D
19...Calgary	Chris Dingman, Brandon	L
20...Dallas	Jason Botterill, U. of Michigan	L
21...Boston	Yevgeni Ryabchikov, Molot Perm	G
22...Quebec	Jeff Kealty, Cath. Memorial HS	D
23...Detroit	Yan Golubovsky, CSKA	D
24...Pittsburgh	Chris Wells, Seattle	C
25...New Jersey	Vadim Sharifjanov, R	R
26...NY Rangers	Dan Cloutier, Sault Ste. Marie	G

FOR THE RECORD·Year by Year

The Stanley Cup

Awarded annually to the team that wins the NHL's best-of-seven final-round playoffs. The Stanley Cup is the oldest trophy competed for by professional athletes in North America. It was donated in 1893 by Frederick Arthur, Lord Stanley of Preston.

Results

WINNERS PRIOR TO FORMATION OF NHL IN 1917

1892-93	Montreal A.A.A.
1893-94	Montreal A.A.A.
1894-95	Montreal Victorias
1895-96	Winnipeg Victorias (Feb)
1895-96	Montreal Victorias (Dec)
1896-97	Montreal Victorias
1897-98	Montreal Victorias
1898-99	Montreal Victorias (Feb)
1898-99	Montreal Shamrocks (Mar)
1899-1900	Montreal Shamrocks
1900-01	Winnipeg Victorias
1901-02	Winnipeg Victorias (Jan)
1901-02	Montreal A.A.A. (Mar)
1902-03	Montreal A.A.A. (Feb)
1902-03	Ottawa Silver Seven (Mar)
1903-04	Ottawa Silver Seven
1904-05	Ottawa Silver Seven
1905-06	Ottawa Silver Seven (Feb)
1905-06	Montreal Wanderers (Mar)
1906-07	Kenora Thistles (Jan)
1906-07	Montreal Wanderers (Mar)
1907-08	Montreal Wanderers
1908-09	Ottawa Senators
1909-10	Montreal Wanderers
1910-11	Ottawa Senators
1911-12	Quebec Bulldogs
1912-13	Quebec Bulldogs
1913-14	Toronto Blueshirts
1914-15	Vancouver Millionaires
1915-16	Montreal Canadiens
1916-17	Seattle Metropolitans

NHL WINNERS AND FINALISTS

Season	Champion	Finalist	GP in Final
1917-18	Toronto Arenas	Vancouver Millionaires	5
1918-19	No decision*	No decision*	5
1919-20	Ottawa Senators	Seattle Metropolitans	5
1920-21	Ottawa Senators	Vancouver Millionaires	5
1921-22	Toronto St Pats	Vancouver Millionaires	5
1922-23	Ottawa Senators	Vancouver Millionaires, Edmonton	3, 2
1923-24	Montreal Canadiens	Vancouver Millionaires, Calgary	2, 2
1924-25	Victoria Cougars	Montreal Canadiens	4
1925-26	Montreal Maroons	Victoria Cougars	4
1926-27	Ottawa Senators	Boston Bruins	4
1927-28	New York Rangers	Montreal Maroons	5
1928-29	Boston Bruins	New York Rangers	2
1929-30	Montreal Canadiens	Boston Bruins	2
1930-31	Montreal Canadiens	Chicago Blackhawks	5
1931-32	Toronto Maple Leafs	New York Rangers	3
1932-33	New York Rangers	Toronto Maple Leafs	4
1933-34	Chicago Blackhawks	Detroit Red Wings	4
1934-35	Montreal Maroons	Toronto Maple Leafs	3
1935-36	Detroit Red Wings	Toronto Maple Leafs	4
1936-37	Detroit Red Wings	New York Rangers	5
1937-38	Chicago Blackhawks	Toronto Maple Leafs	4
1938-39	Boston Bruins	Toronto Maple Leafs	5
1939-40	New York Rangers	Toronto Maple Leafs	6
1940-41	Boston Bruins	Detroit Red Wings	4
1941-42	Toronto Maple Leafs	Detroit Red Wings	7
1942-43	Detroit Red Wings	Boston Bruins	4
1943-44	Montreal Canadiens	Chicago Blackhawks	4
1944-45	Toronto Maple Leafs	Detroit Red Wings	7
1945-46	Montreal Canadiens	Boston Bruins	5
1946-47	Toronto Maple Leafs	Montreal Canadiens	6
1947-48	Toronto Maple Leafs	Detroit Red Wings	4
1948-49	Toronto Maple Leafs	Detroit Red Wings	4
1949-50	Detroit Red Wings	New York Rangers	7
1950-51	Toronto Maple Leafs	Montreal Canadiens	5
1951-52	Detroit Red Wings	Montreal Canadiens	4
1952-53	Montreal Canadiens	Boston Bruins	5
1953-54	Detroit Red Wings	Montreal Canadiens	7

The Stanley Cup (Cont.)

NHL WINNERS AND FINALISTS (Cont.)

1954-55	Detroit Red Wings	Montreal Canadiens	7
1955-56	Montreal Canadiens	Detroit Red Wings	5
1956-57	Montreal Canadiens	Boston Bruins	5
1957-58	Montreal Canadiens	Boston Bruins	6
1958-59	Montreal Canadiens	Toronto Maple Leafs	5
1959-60	Montreal Canadiens	Toronto Maple Leafs	4
1960-61	Chicago Blackhawks	Detroit Red Wings	6
1961-62	Toronto Maple Leafs	Chicago Blackhawks	6
1962-63	Toronto Maple Leafs	Detroit Red Wings	5
1963-64	Toronto Maple Leafs	Detroit Red Wings	7
1964-65	Montreal Canadiens	Chicago Blackhawks	7
1965-66	Montreal Canadiens	Detroit Red Wings	6
1966-67	Toronto Maple Leafs	Montreal Canadiens	6
1967-68	Montreal Canadiens	St Louis Blues	4
1968-69	Montreal Canadiens	St Louis Blues	4
1969-70	Boston Bruins	St Louis Blues	4
1970-71	Montreal Canadiens	Chicago Blackhawks	7
1971-72	Boston Bruins	New York Rangers	6
1972-73	Montreal Canadiens	Chicago Blackhawks	6
1973-74	Philadelphia Flyers	Boston Bruins	6
1974-75	Philadelphia Flyers	Buffalo Sabres	6
1975-76	Montreal Canadiens	Philadelphia Flyers	4
1976-77	Montreal Canadiens	Boston Bruins	4
1977-78	Montreal Canadiens	Boston Bruins	6
1978-79	Montreal Canadiens	New York Rangers	5
1979-80	New York Islanders	Philadelphia Flyers	6
1980-81	New York Islanders	Minnesota North Stars	5
1981-82	New York Islanders	Vancouver Canucks	4
1982-83	New York Islanders	Edmonton Oilers	4
1983-84	Edmonton Oilers	New York Islanders	5
1984-85	Edmonton Oilers	Philadelphia Flyers	5
1985-86	Montreal Canadiens	Calgary Flames	6
1986-87	Edmonton Oilers	Philadelphia Flyers	7
1987-88	Edmonton Oilers	Boston Bruins	4
1988-89	Calgary Flames	Montreal Canadiens	6
1989-90	Edmonton Oilers	Boston Bruins	5
1990-91	Pittsburgh Penguins	Minnesota North Stars	6
1991-92	Pittsburgh Penguins	Chicago Black Hawks	4
1992-93	Montreal Canadiens	Los Angeles Kings	5
1993-94	New York Rangers	Vancouver Canucks	7

*In 1919 the Montreal Canadiens traveled to meet Seattle, the PCHL champions. After 5 games had been played—the teams were tied at 2 wins and 1 tie—the series was called off by the local Department of Health because of the influenza epidemic and the death of Canadian defenseman Joe Hall from influenza.

Conn Smythe Trophy

Awarded to the Most Valuable Player of the Stanley Cup playoffs, as selected by the Professional Hockey Writers Association. The trophy is named after the former coach, general manager, president and owner of the Toronto Maple Leafs.

1965	Jean Beliveau, Mtl	1980	Bryan Trottier, NYI
1966	Roger Crozier, Det	1981	Butch Goring, NYI
1967	Dave Keon, Tor	1982	Mike Bossy, NYI
1968	Glenn Hall, StL	1983	Bill Smith, NYI
1969	Serge Savard, Mtl	1984	Mark Messier, Edm
1970	Bobby Orr, Bos	1985	Wayne Gretzky, Edm
1971	Ken Dryden, Mtl	1986	Patrick Roy, Mtl
1972	Bobby Orr, Bos	1987	Ron Hextall, Phil
1973	Yvan Cournoyer, Mtl	1988	Wayne Gretzky, Edm
1974	Bernie Parent, Phil	1989	Al MacInnis, Calg
1975	Bernie Parent, Phil	1990	Bill Ranford, Edm
1976	Reggie Leach, Phil	1991	Mario Lemieux, Pitt
1977	Guy Lafleur, Mtl	1992	Mario Lemieux, Pitt
1978	Larry Robinson, Mtl	1993	Patrick Roy, Mtl
1979	Bob Gainey, Mtl	1994	Brian Leetch, NYR

Alltime Stanley Cup Playoff Leaders

Points

	Yrs	GP	G	A	Pts
*Wayne Gretzky, Edm, LA	15	180	110	236	346
*Mark Messier, Edm, NYR	14	200	99	160	259
*Jari Kurri, Edm, LA	13	174	102	120	222
*Glenn Anderson,Edm,Tor,NYR	13	208	91	116	207
*Bryan Trottier, NYI, Pitt	17	221	71	113	184
Jean Beliveau, Mtl	17	162	79	97	176
Denis Potvin, NYI	14	185	56	108	164
Mike Bossy, NYI	10	129	85	75	160
Gordie Howe, Det, Har	20	157	68	92	160
*Bobby Smith, Minn, Mtl	13	184	64	96	160
*Denis Savard, Chi, Mtl	14	137	58	94	152
Stan Mikita, Chi	18	155	59	91	150
*Brian Propp, Phil, Bos, Minn	15	160	64	84	148

	Yrs	GP	G	A	Pts
*Larry Robinson, Mtl, LA	20	227	28	116	144
Jacques Lemaire, Mtl	11	145	61	78	139
Phil Esposito, Chi, Bos, NYR	15	130	61	76	137
*Ray Bourque, Bos	15	152	33	103	136
*Paul Coffey,Edm,Pitt,LA,Det	10	123	44	92	136
Guy Lafleur, Mtl, NYR	14	128	58	76	134
Bobby Hull, Chi, Hart	14	119	62	67	129
Henri Richard, Mtl	18	180	49	80	129
Yvon Cournoyer, Mtl	12	147	64	63	127
Maurice Richard, Mtl	15	133	82	44	126

*Active player.

Goals

	Yrs	GP	G
*Wayne Gretzky, Edm, LA	15	180	110
*Jari Kurri, Edm, LA	13	174	102
*Mark Messier, Edm, NYR	14	200	99
*Glenn Anderson, Edm, Tor,NYR	13	208	91
Mike Bossy, NYI	10	129	85
Maurice Richard, Mtl	15	133	82
Jean Beliveau, Mtl	17	162	79
*Bryan Trottier, NYI, Pitt	17	221	75
Gordie Howe, Det, Hart	20	157	68
Yvon Cournoyer, Mtl	12	147	64
*Brian Propp, Phil, Bos, Minn	15	160	64

*Active player.

Assists

	Yrs	GP	A
*Wayne Gretzky, Edm, LA	15	180	236
*Mark Messier, Edm, NYR	14	200	160
*Jari Kurri, Edm, LA	12	174	120
*Glenn Anderson, Edm, Tor, NYR	13	208	116
*Larry Robinson, Mtl, LA	20	227	116
*Bryan Trottier, NYI, Pitt	17	221	113
Denis Potvin, NYI	14	185	108
*Ray Bourque, Bos	15	152	103
Jean Beliveau, Mtl	17	162	97
*Bobby Smith, Minn, Mtl	13	184	96

*Active player.

Goaltending

WINS	W	L	Pct
Billy Smith	88	36	.709
Ken Dryden	80	32	.714
*Grant Fuhr	77	36	.681
Jacques Plante	71	37	.657
Patrick Roy	67	39	.632
Andy Moog	59	41	.590
Turk Broda	58	42	.580
Terry Sawchuk	54	48	.529
Glenn Hall	49	65	.429
Gerry Cheevers	47	35	.573

SHUTOUTS	GP	W	SO
Clint Benedict	48	25	15
Jacques Plante	112	71	15
Turk Broda	101	58	13
Terry Sawchuk	106	54	12
Ken Dryden	112	80	10

GOALS AGAINST AVG	Avg
George Hainsworth	1.93
Turk Broda	1.98
Jacques Plante	2.17
Ken Dryden	2.40
Bernie Parent	2.43

Note: At least 50 games played.

Alltime Stanley Cup Standings

TEAM	W	L	Pct
Montreal	374	235	.614
Boston	226	234	.491
Toronto	197	213	.481
Chicago	170	199	.461
Detroit	168	182	.480
NY Rangers	165	177	.483
NY Islanders	128	90	.587
Edmonton	120	60	.667
Philadelphia	116	107	.520
St Louis	93	117	.443
Dallas*	85	90	.486

TEAM	W	L	Pct
Pittsburgh	69	56	.552
Calgary	66	79	.455
Buffalo	61	77	.442
Los Angeles	55	87	.387
Vancouver	48	59	.449
Washington	47	56	.456
Hartford	34	41	.453
Quebec	33	41	.446
New Jersey	31	36	.463
Winnipeg	17	39	.304

*Minnesota North Stars 1967-93

Note: Teams ranked by playoff victories.

Stanley Cup Coaching Records

Coach	Team	Yrs	Series	Series W	Series L	Games G	Games W	L	T	Cups	Pct
Toe Blake	Mtl	13	23	18	5	119	82	37	0	8	.689
Glen Sather	Edm	11	30	23	7	*142	97	45	0	4	.683
Scott Bowman	Five teams	20	40	26	14	226	140	86	0	6	.620
Hap Day	Tor	9	14	10	4	80	49	31	0	5	.613
Al Arbour	StL, NYI	16	42	30	12	209	123	86	0	4	.589
Mike Keenan	Phil, Chi, NYR	9	25	17	8	140	81	59	0	1	.579
Fred Shero	Phil, NYR	8	21	15	6	108	61	47	0	2	.565
Jacques Demers	Que, StL, Det, Mtl	8	19	12	7	98	55	43	0	1	.561
Lester Patrick	NYR	12	24	14	10	65	31	26	8	2	.538
Tommy Ivan	Det	7	12	8	4	67	36	31	0	3	.537

*Does not include suspended game, May 24, 1988.
Note: Coaches ranked by winning percentage. Minimum: 65 games.

The 10 Longest Overtime Games

Date	Scorer	OT	Results	Series	Series Winner
3-24-36	Mud Bruneteau	116:30	Det 1 vs Mtl M 0	SF	Det
4-3-33	Ken Doraty	104:46	Tor 1 vs Bos 0	SF	Tor
3-23-43	Jack McLean	70:18	Tor 3 vs Det 2	SF	Det
3-28-30	Gus Rivers	68:52	Mtl 2 vs NYR 1	SF	Mtl
4-18-87	Pat LaFontaine	68:47	NYI 3 vs Wash 2	DSF	NYI
3-27-51	Maurice Richard	61:09	Mtl 3 vs Det 2	SF	Mtl
3-26-32	Fred Cook	59:32	NYR 4 vs Mtl 3	SF	NYR
3-21-39	Mel Hill	59:25	Bos 2 vs NYR 1	SF	Bos
5-15-90	Petr Klima	55:13	Edm 3 vs Bos 2	F	Edm
4-9-31	Cy Wentworth	53:50	Chi 3 vs Mtl 2	F	Mtl

NHL Awards

Hart Memorial Trophy

Awarded annually "to the player adjudged to be the most valuable to his team." The original trophy was donated by Dr. David A. Hart, father of Cecil Hart, former manager-coach of the Montreal Canadiens. In the decade of the 1980s Wayne Gretzky won the award nine of 10 times.

	Winner	Key Statistics	Runner-Up
1924	Frank Nighbor, Ott	10 goals, 3 assists in 20 games	Sprague Cleghorn, Mtl
1925	Billy Burch, Ham	20 goals, 4 assists in 27 games	Howie Morenz, Mtl
1926	Nels Stewart, Mtl M	42 points in 36 games	Sprague Cleghorn, Mtl
1927	Herb Gardiner, Mtl	12 points in 44 games on defense	Bill Cook, NYR
1928	Howie Morenz, Mtl	33 goals, 18 assists	Roy Worters, Pitt
1929	Roy Worters, NYA	1.21 goals against, 13 shutouts	Ace Bailey, Tor
1930	Nels Stewart, Mtl M	39 games, 16 assists	Lionel Hitchman, Bos
1931	Howie Morenz, Mtl	28 games, 23 assists	Eddie Shore, Bos
1932	Howie Morenz, Mtl	24 games, 25 assists	Ching Johnson, NYR
1933	Eddie Shore, Bos	27 assists in 48 games as defense	Bill Cook, NYR
1934	Aurel Joliat, Mtl	27 points	Lionel Conacher, Chi
1935	Eddie Shore, Bos	26 assists in 48 games as defense	Charlie Conacher, Tor
1936	Eddie Shore, Bos	16 assists in 46 games as defense	Hooley Smith, Mtl M
1937	Babe Siebert, Mtl	28 points	Lionel Conacher, Mtl M
1938	Eddie Shore, Bos	17 points in 47 games as defense	Paul Thompson, Chi
1939	Toe Blake, Mtl	led NHL with 47 points	Syl Apps, Tor
1940	Ebbie Goodfellow, Det	28 points	Syl Apps, Tor
1941	Bill Cowley, Bos	led NHL with 45 assists and 62 points	Dit Clapper, Bos
1942	Tom Anderson, Bos	41 points in his final year	Syl Apps, Tor
1943	Bill Cowley, Bos	led NHL with 45 assists	Doug Bentley, Chi
1944	Babe Pratt, Tor	57 points in 50 games	Bill Cowley, Bos
1945	Elmer Lach, Mtl	led NHL with 54 assists and 80 points	Maurice Richard, Mtl
1946	Max Bentley, Chi	61 points in 47 games	Gaye Stewart, Tor
1947	Maurice Richard, Mtl	45 games, 26 assists	Milt Schmidt, Bos
1948	Buddy O'Connor, NYR	60 points in 60 games	Frank Brimsek, Bos
1949	Sid Abel, Det	28 games, 26 assists	Bill Durnan, Mtl

Hart Memorial Trophy (Cont.)

	Winner	Key Statistics	Runner-Up
1950	Charlie Rayner, NYR	6 shutouts	Ted Kennedy, Tor
1951	Milt Schmidt, Bos	61 points in 62 games	Maurice Richard, Mtl
1952	Gordie Howe, Det	led NHL in games (47) and points (86)	Elmer Lach, Mtl
1953	Gordie Howe, Det	tops in G (49), A (46), PTS (95)	Al Rollins, Chi
1954	Al Rollins, Chi	3960 minutes	Ted Kelly, Det
1955	Ted Kennedy, Tor	52 points	Harry Lumley, Tor
1956	Jean Beliveau, Mtl	led NHL in goals (47) and points (88)	Tod Sloan, Tor
1957	Gordie Howe, Det	led NHL in games (44) and points (89)	Jean Beliveau, Mtl
1959	Andy Bathgate, NYR	40 games, 48 assists	Gordie Howe, Det
1960	Gordie Howe, Det	45 assists, 73 points	Bobby Hull, Chi
1961	Bernie Geoffrion, Mtl	50 goals, 95 points	Johnny Bower, Tor
1962	Jacques Plante, Mtl	42 wins, 2.37 goals against	Doug Harvey, NYR
1963	Gordie Howe, Det	47 assists, 73 points	Stan Mikita, Chi
1964	Jean Beliveau, Mtl	50 assists, 78 points	Bobby Hull, Chi
1965	Bobby Hull, Chi	39 goals, 32 assists	Norm Ullman, Det
1966	Bobby Hull, Chi	led NHL with 54 goals, 97 points	Jean Beliveau, Mtl
1967	Stan Mikita, Chi	led NHL with 62 assists, 97 points	Ed Giacomin, NYR
1968	Stan Mikita, Chi	40 goals, 47 assists	Jean Beliveau, Mtl
1969	Phil Esposito, Bos	led NHL with 77 assists, 126 points	Jean Beliveau, Mtl
1970	Bobby Orr, Bos	led NHL with 87 assists, 120 points	Tony Esposito, Chi
1971	Bobby Orr, Bos	102 assists, 139 points	Tony Esposito, Chi
1972	Bobby Orr, Bos	80 assists, 117 points	Ken Dryden, Mtl
1973	Bobby Clarke, Phil	67 goals, 104 points	Phil Esposito, Bos
1974	Phil Esposito, Bos	led NHL with 68 goals, 105 points	Bernie Parent, Phil
1975	Bobby Clarke, Phil	89 assists, 116 points	Rogatien Vachon, LA
1976	Bobby Clarke, Phil	89 assists, 119 points	Denis Potvin, NYI
1977	Guy Lafleur, Mtl	led NHL with 80 assists, 136 points	Bobby Clarke, Phil
1978	Guy Lafleur, Mtl	led NHL with 60 goals, 132 points	Bryan Trottier, NYI
1979	Bryan Trottier, NYI	led NHL with 87 assists, 134 points	Guy Lafleur, Mtl
1980	Wayne Gretzky, Edm	led NHL with 86 assists, 137 points	Marcel Dionne, LA
1981	Wayne Gretzky, Edm	led NHL with 109 assists, 164 points	Mike Liut, StL
1982	Wayne Gretzky, Edm	led NHL in G (71), A (120), PTS (212)	Bryan Trottier, NYI
1983	Wayne Gretzky, Edm	led NHL in G (71), A (125), PTS (196)	Pete Peeters, Bos
1984	Wayne Gretzky, Edm	led NHL in G (87), A (118), PTS (205)	Rod Langway, Was
1985	Wayne Gretzky, Edm	led NHL in G (73), A (135), PTS (208)	Dale Hawerchuk, Win
1986	Wayne Gretzky, Edm	set NHL record in A (163), PTS (215)	Mario Lemieux, Pitt
1987	Wayne Gretzky, Edm	led NHL in G (62), A (121), PTS (183)	Ray Bourque, Bos
1988	Mario Lemieux, Pitt	led NHL in G (70), PTS (168)	Grant Fuhr, Edm
1989	Wayne Gretzky, LA	114 assists, 168 points	Mario Lemieux, Pitt
1990	Mark Messier, Edm	84 assists, 129 points	Ray Bourque, Bos
1991	Brett Hull, StL	86 goals, 131 points	Wayne Gretzky, LA
1992	Mark Messier, NYR	72 assists, 107 points	Patrick Roy, Mtl
1993	Mario Lemieux, Pitt	69 goals, 91 assists in 60 games	Doug Gilmour, Toronto
1994	Sergei Fedorov, Det	56 goals, 64 assists	Dominik Hasek, Buffalo

Art Ross Trophy

Awarded annually "to the player who leads the league in scoring points at the end of the regular season." The trophy was presented to the NHL in 1947 by Arthur Howie Ross, former manager-coach of the Boston Bruins. The tie-breakers, in order, are as follows: (1) player with most goals, (2) player with fewer games played, (3) player scoring first goal of the season. Bobby Orr is the only defenseman in NHL history to win this trophy, and he won it twice (1970 and 1975).

	Winner	Pts		Winner	Pts
1919	Newsy Lalonde, Mtl	44	1927	Bill Cook, NYR	42
1920	Joe Malone, Que	30	1928	Howie Morenz, Mtl	37
1921	Newsy Lalonde, Mtl	48	1929	Ace Bailey, Tor	51
1922	Punch Broadbent, Ott	41	1930	Cooney Weiland, Bos	32
1923	Babe Dye, Tor	46	1931	Howie Morenz, Mtl	73
1924	Cy Denneny, Ott	37	1932	Harvey Jackson, Tor	51
1925	Babe Dye, Tor	23	1933	Bill Cook, NYR	53
1926	Nels Stewart, Mtl M	44	1934	Charlie Conacher, Tor	50

Note: Listing is for scoring leader prior to inception of Art Ross Trophy in 1947-48.

Art Ross Trophy (Cont.)

Winner	Pts	Winner	Pts
1935 ...Charlie Conacher, Tor	57	1965 ...Stan Mikita, Chi	87
1936 ...Sweeney Schriner, NYA	45	1966 ...Bobby Hull, Chi	97
1937 ...Sweeney Schriner, NYA	46	1967 ...Stan Mikita, Chi	97
1938 ...Gordie Drillon, Tor	52	1968 ...Stan Mikita, Chi	87
1939 ...Toe Blake, Mtl	47	1969 ...Phil Esposito, Bos	126
1940 ...Milt Schmidt, Bos	52	1970 ...Bobby Orr, Bos	120
1941 ...Bill Cowley, Bos	62	1971 ...Phil Esposito, Bos	152
1942 ...Bryan Hextall, NYR	56	1972 ...Phil Esposito, Bos	133
1943 ...Doug Bentley, Chi	73	1973 ...Phil Esposito, Bos	130
1944 ...Herb Cain, Bos	82	1974 ...Phil Esposito, Bos	145
1945 ...Elmer Lach, Mtl	80	1975 ...Bobby Orr, Bos	135
1946 ...Max Bentley, Chi	61	1976 ...Guy Lafleur, Mtl	125
1947 ...*Max Bentley, Chi	72	1977 ...Guy Lafleur, Mtl	136
1948 ...Elmer Lach, Mtl	61	1978 ...Guy Lafleur, Mtl	132
1949 ...Roy Conacher, Chi	68	1979 ...Bryan Trottier, NYI	134
1950 ...Ted Lindsay, Det	78	1980 ...Marcel Dionne, LA	137
1951 ...Gordie Howe, Det	86	1981 ...Wayne Gretzky, Edm	164
1952 ...Gordie Howe, Det	86	1982 ...Wayne Gretzky, Edm	212
1953 ...Gordie Howe, Det	95	1983 ...Wayne Gretzky, Edm	196
1954 ...Gordie Howe, Det	81	1984 ...Wayne Gretzky, Edm	205
1955 ...Bernie Geoffrion, Mtl	75	1985 ...Wayne Gretzky, Edm	208
1956 ...Jean Beliveau, Mtl	88	1986 ...Wayne Gretzky, Edm	215
1957 ...Gordie Howe, Det	89	1987 ...Wayne Gretzky, Edm	183
1958 ...Dickie Moore, Mtl	84	1988 ...Mario Lemieux, Pitt	168
1959 ...Dickie Moore, Mtl	96	1989 ...Mario Lemieux, Pitt	199
1960 ...Bobby Hull, Chi	81	1990 ...Wayne Gretzky, LA	142
1961 ...Bernie Geoffrion, Mtl	95	1991 ...Wayne Gretzky, LA	163
1962 ...Bobby Hull, Chi	84	1992 ...Mario Lemieux, Pitt	131
1963 ...Gordie Howe, Det	86	1993 ...Mario Lemieux, Pitt	160
1964 ...Stan Mikita, Chi	89	1994 ...Wayne Gretzky, LA	130

Lady Byng Memorial Trophy

Awarded annually "to the player adjudged to have exhibited the best type of sportsmanship and gentlemanly conduct combined with a high standard of playing ability." Lady Byng, who first presented the trophy in 1925, was the wife of Canada's Governor-General. She donated a second trophy in 1936 after the first was given permanently to Frank Boucher of the New York Rangers, who won it seven times in eight seasons. Stan Mikita, one of the league's most penalized players during his early years in the NHL, won the trophy twice late in his career (1967 and 1968).

1925 ...Frank Nighbor, Ott	1949 ...Bill Quackenbush, Det	1973 ...Gilbert Perreault, Buff
1926 ...Frank Nighbor, Ott	1950 ...Edgar Laprade, NYR	1974 ...John Bucyk, Bos
1927 ...Billy Burch, NYA	1951 ...Red Kelly, Det	1975 ...Marcel Dionne, Det
1928 ...Frank Boucher, NYR	1952 ...Sid Smith, Tor	1976 ...Jean Ratelle, NYR-Bos
1929 ...Frank Boucher, NYR	1953 ...Red Kelly, Det	1977 ...Marcel Dionne, LA
1930 ...Frank Boucher, NYR	1954 ...Red Kelly, Det	1978 ...Butch Goring, LA
1931 ...Frank Boucher, NYR	1955 ...Sid Smith, Tor	1979 ...Bob MacMillan, Atl
1932 ...Joe Primeau, Tor	1956 ...Earl Reibel, Det	1980 ...Wayne Gretzky, Edm
1933 ...Frank Boucher, NYR	1957 ...Andy Hebenton, NYR	1981 ...Rick Kehoe, Pitt
1934 ...Frank Boucher, NYR	1958 ...Camille Henry, NYR	1982 ...Rick Middleton, Bos
1935 ...Frank Boucher, NYR	1959 ...Alex Delvecchio, Det	1983 ...Mike Bossy, NYI
1936 ...Doc Romnes, Chi	1960 ...Don McKenney, Bos	1984 ...Mike Bossy, NYI
1937 ...Marty Barry, Det	1961 ...Red Kelly, Tor	1985 ...Jari Kurri, Edm
1938 ...Gordie Drillon, Tor	1962 ...Dave Keon, Tor	1986 ...Mike Bossy, NYI
1939 ...Clint Smith, NYR	1963 ...Dave Keon, Tor	1987 ...Joe Mullen, Calg
1940 ...Bobby Bauer, Bos	1964 ...Ken Wharram, Chi	1988 ...Mats Naslund, Mtl
1941 ...Bobby Bauer, Bos	1965 ...Bobby Hull, Chi	1989 ...Joe Mullen, Calg
1942 ...Syl Apps, Tor	1966 ...Alex Delvecchio, Det	1990 ...Brett Hull, StL
1943 ...Max Bentley, Chi	1967 ...Stan Mikita, Chi	1991 ...Wayne Gretzky, LA
1944 ...Clint Smith, Chi	1968 ...Stan Mikita, Chi	1992 ...Wayne Gretzky, LA
1945 ...Billy Mosienko, Chi	1969 ...Alex Delvecchio, Det	1993 ...Pierre Turgeon, NYI
1946 ...Toe Blake, Mont	1970 ...Phil Goyette, StL	1994 ...Wayne Gretzky, LA
1947 ...Bobby Bauer, Bos	1971 ...John Bucyk, Bos	
1948 ...Buddy O'Connor, NYR	1972 ...Jean Ratelle, NYR	

James Norris Memorial Trophy

Awarded annually "to the defense player who demonstrates throughout the season the greatest all-around ability in the position." James Norris was the former owner-president of the Detroit Red Wings. Bobby Orr holds the record for most consecutive times winning the award (eight, 1968-1975).

1954 ....Red Kelly, Det	1968 ....Bobby Orr, Bos	1982 ....Doug Wilson, Chi
1955 ....Doug Harvey, Mtl	1969 ....Bobby Orr, Bos	1983 ....Rod Langway, Wash
1956 ....Doug Harvey, Mtl	1970 ....Bobby Orr, Bos	1984 ....Rod Langway, Wash
1957 ....Doug Harvey, Mtl	1971 ....Bobby Orr, Bos	1985 ....Paul Coffey, Edm
1958 ....Doug Harvey, Mtl	1972 ....Bobby Orr, Bos	1986 ....Paul Coffey, Edm
1959 ....Tom Johnson, Mtl	1973 ....Bobby Orr, Bos	1987 ....Ray Bourque, Bos
1960 ....Doug Harvey, Mtl	1974 ....Bobby Orr, Bos	1988 ....Ray Bourque, Bos
1961 ....Doug Harvey, Mtl	1975 ....Bobby Orr, Bos	1989 ....Chris Chelios, Mtl
1962 ....Doug Harvey, NYR	1976 ....Denis Potvin, NYI	1990 ....Ray Bourque, Bos
1963 ....Pierre Pilote, Chi	1977 ....Larry Robinson, Mtl	1991 ....Ray Bourque, Bos
1964 ....Pierre Pilote, Chi	1978 ....Denis Potvin, NYI	1992 ....Brian Leetch, NYR
1965 ....Pierre Pilote, Chi	1979 ....Denis Potvin, NYI	1993 ....Chris Chelios, Chi
1966 ....Jacques Laperriere, Mtl	1980 ....Larry Robinson, Mtl	1994 ....Ray Bourque, Bos
1967 ....Harry Howell, NYR	1981 ....Randy Carlyle, Pitt	

Calder Memorial Trophy

Awarded annually "to the player selected as the most proficient in his first year of competition in the National Hockey League." Frank Calder was a former NHL president. Sergei Makarov, who won the award in 1989-1990, was the oldest recipient of the trophy, at 31. Players are no longer eligible for the award if they are 26 or older as of September 15th of the season in question.

1933 ....Carl Voss, Det	1954 ....Camille Henry, NYR	1975 ....Eric Vail, Atl
1934 ....Russ Blinko, Mtl M	1955 ....Ed Litzenberger, Chi	1976 ....Bryan Trottier, NYI
1935 ....Dave Schriner, NYA	1956 ....Glenn Hall, Det	1977 ....Willi Plett, Atl
1936 ....Mike Karakas, Chi	1957 ....Larry Regan, Bos	1978 ....Mike Bossy, NYI
1937 ....Syl Apps, Tor	1958 ....Frank Mahovlich, Tor	1979 ....Bobby Smith, Minn
1938 ....Cully Dahlstrom, Chi	1959 ....Ralph Backstrom, Mtl	1980 ....Ray Bourque, Bos
1939 ....Frank Brimsek, Bos	1960 ....Bill Hay, Chi	1981 ....Peter Stastny, Que
1940 ....Kilby MacDonald, NYR	1961 ....Dave Keon, Tor	1982 ....Dale Hawerchuk, Winn
1941 ....Johnny Quilty, Mtl	1962 ....Bobby Rousseau, Mtl	1983 ....Steve Larmer, Chi
1942 ....Grant Warwick, NYR	1963 ....Kent Douglas, Tor	1984 ....Tom Barrasso, Buff
1943 ....Gaye Stewart, NYR	1964 ....Jacques Laperriere, Mtl	1985 ....Mario Lemieux, Pitt
1944 ....Gus Bodnar, Tor	1965 ....Roger Crozier, Det	1986 ....Gary Suter, Calg
1945 ....Frank McCool, Tor	1966 ....Brit Selby, Tor	1987 ....Luc Robitaille, LA
1946 ....Edgar Laprade, NYR	1967 ....Bobby Orr, Bos	1988 ....Joe Nieuwendyk, Calg
1947 ....Howie Meeker, Tor	1968 ....Derek Sanderson, Bos	1989 ....Brian Leetch, NYR
1948 ....Jim McFadden, Det	1969 ....Danny Grant, Minn	1990 ....Sergei Makarov, Calg
1949 ....Pentti Lund, NYR	1970 ....Tony Esposito, Chi	1991 ....Ed Belfour, Chi
1950 ....Jack Gelineau, Bos	1971 ....Gilbert Perreault, Buff	1992 ....Pavel Bure, Van
1951 ....Terry Sawchuk, Det	1972 ....Ken Dryden, Mtl	1993 ....Teemu Selanne, Winn
1952 ....Bernie Geoffrion, Mtl	1973 ....Steve Vickers, NYR	1994 ....Martin Brodeur, NJ
1953 ....Gump Worsley, NYR	1974 ....Denis Potvin, NYI	

Vezina Trophy

Awarded annually "to the goalkeeper adjudged to be the best at his position." The trophy is named after Georges Vezina, an outstanding goalie for the Montreal Canadiens who collapsed during a game on November 28, 1925, and died a few months later of tuberculosis. The general managers of the 21 NHL teams vote on the award.

1927 ....George Hainsworth, Mtl	1940 ....Dave Kerr, NYR	1953 ....Terry Sawchuk, Det
1928 ....George Hainsworth, Mtl	1941 ....Turk Broda, Tor	1954 ....Harry Lumley, Tor
1929 ....George Hainsworth, Mtl	1942 ....Frank Brimsek, Bos	1955 ....Terry Sawchuk, Det
1930 ....Tiny Thompson, Bos	1943 ....Johnny Mowers, Det	1956 ....Jacques Plante, Mtl
1931 ....Roy Worters, NYA	1944 ....Bill Durnan, Mtl	1957 ....Jacques Plante, Mtl
1932 ....Charlie Gardiner, Chi	1945 ....Bill Durnan, Mtl	1958 ....Jacques Plante, Mtl
1933 ....Tiny Thompson, Bos	1946 ....Bill Durnan, Mtl	1959 ....Jacques Plante, Mtl
1934 ....Charlie Gardiner, Chi	1947 ....Bill Durnan, Mtl	1960 ....Jacques Plante, Mtl
1935 ....Lorne Chabot, Chi	1948 ....Turk Broda, Tor	1961 ....Johnny Bower, Tor
1936 ....Tiny Thompson, Bos	1949 ....Bill Durnan, Mtl	1962 ....Jacques Plante, Mtl
1937 ....Normie Smith, Det	1950 ....Bill Durnan, Mtl	1963 ....Glenn Hall, Chi
1938 ....Tiny Thompson, Bos	1951 ....Al Rollins, Tor	1964 ....Charlie Hodge, Mtl
1939 ....Frank Brimsek, Bos	1952 ....Terry Sawchuk, Det	

Vezina Trophy (Cont.)

1965	Terry Sawchuk, Tor	
	Johnny Bower, Tor	
1966	Gump Worsley, Mtl	
	Charlie Hodge, Mtl	
1967	Glenn Hall, Chi	
	Rogie Vachon, Mtl	
1969	Jacques Plante, StL	
	Glenn Hall, StL	
1970	Tony Esposito, Chi	
1971	Ed Giacomin, NYR	
	Gilles Villemure, NYR	
1972	Tony Esposito, Chi	
	Gary Smith, Chi	
1973	Ken Dryden, Mtl	
1974	Bernie Parent, Phil	
	Tony Esposito, Chi	

1975	Bernie Parent, Phil
1976	Ken Dryden, Mtl
1977	Ken Dryden, Mtl
	Michel Larocque, Mtl
1978	Ken Dryden, Mtl
	Michel Larocque, Mtl
1979	Ken Dryden, Mtl
	Michel Larocque, Mtl
1980	Bob Sauve, Buff
	Don Edwards, Buff
1981	Richard Sevigny, Mtl
	Denis Herron, Mtl
	Michel Larocque, Mtl
1982	Bill Smith, NYI
1983	Pete Peeters, Bos
1984	Tom Barrasso, Buff

1985	Pelle Lindbergh, Phil
1986	John Vanbiesbrouck, NYR
1987	Ron Hextall, Phil
1988	Grant Fuhr, Edm
1989	Patrick Roy, Mtl
1990	Patrick Roy, Mtl
1991	Ed Belfour, Chi
1992	Patrick Roy, Mtl
1993	Ed Belfour, Chi
1994	Dominik Hasek, Buff

Selke Trophy

Awarded annually "to the forward who best excels in the defensive aspects of the game." The trophy is named after Frank J. Selke, the architect of the Montreal Canadians dynasty that won five consecutive Stanley Cups in the late '50s. The winner is selected by a vote of the Professional Hockey Writers Association.

1978	Bob Gainey, Mtl	
1979	Bob Gainey, Mtl	
1980	Bob Gainey, Mtl	
1981	Bob Gainey, Mtl	
1982	Steve Kasper, Bos	
1983	Bobby Clarke, Phi	

1984	Doug Jarvis, Wash
1985	Craig Ramsay, Buf
1986	Troy Murray, Chi
1987	Dave Poulin, Phil
1988	Guy Carbonneau, Mtl
1989	Guy Carbonneau, Mtl

1990	Rick Meagher, StL
1991	Dirk Graham, Chi
1992	Guy Carbonneau, Mtl
1993	Doug Gilmour, Tor
1994	Sergei Fedorov, Det

Adams Award

Awarded annually "to the NHL coach adjudged to have contributed the most to his team's success." The trophy is named in honor of Jack Adams, longtime coach and general manager of the Detroit Red Wings. The winner is selected by a vote of the National Hockey League Broadcasters' Association.

1974	Fred Shero, Phil	
1975	Bob Pulford, LA	
1976	Don Cherry, Bos	
1977	Scott Bowman, Mtl	
1978	Bobby Kromm, Det	
1979	Al Arbour, NYI	
1980	Pat Quinn, Phi	

1981	Red Berenson, StL
1982	Tom Watt, Win
1983	Orval Tessier, Chi
1984	Bryan Murray, Wash
1985	Mike Keenan, Phil
1986	Glen Sather, Edm
1987	Jacques Demers, Det

1988	Jacques Demers, Det
1989	Pat Burns, Mtl
1990	Bob Murdoch, Winn
1991	Brian Sutter, StL
1992	Pat Quinn, Van
1993	Pat Burns, Tor
1994	Jacques Lemaire, NJ

NHL Lock-In

There are certain ins and outs that first-year NHL commissioner Gary Bettman has yet to master. Bettman traveled to Los Angeles March 23rd in anticipation of Wayne Gretzky's record-breaking 802nd NHL goal. Late in the first intermission of the game at the Forum between Gretzky's Kings and the Vancouver Canucks, Bettman ducked into the visitors' dressing room to use the facilities. When the Canucks left to start the second period, equipment manager Patty O'Neill, thinking he was the last man out, closed the dressing-room door and padlocked it from the outside. A desperate Bettman had to bang on the door and shout before an attendant finally heard him.

Fortuitously, Gretzky waited until 14:47 of the second period, by which time the commish was back in his seat, to score the historic goal.

Career Records

Alltime Point Leaders

	Player	Yrs	GP	G	A	Pts	Pts/game
1.	*Wayne Gretzky, Edm, LA	15	1125	803	1655	2458	2.185
2.	Gordie Howe, Det, Hart	26	1767	801	1049	1850	1.047
3.	Marcel Dionne, Det, LA, NYR	18	1348	731	1040	1771	1.314
4.	Phil Esposito, Chi, Bos, NYR	18	1282	717	873	1590	1.240
5.	Stan Mikita, Chi	22	1394	541	926	1467	1.052
6.	*Bryan Trottier, NYI, Pitt	18	1279	524	901	1425	1.114
7.	John Bucyk, Det, Bos	23	1540	556	813	1369	.889
8.	Guy Lafleur, Mtl, NYR, Que	17	1126	560	793	1353	1.201
9.	Gilbert Perreault, Buff	17	1191	512	814	1326	1.113
10.	*Mark Messier, Edm, NYR	15	1081	478	838	1316	1.217
11.	Alex Delvecchio, Det	24	1549	456	825	1281	.827
12.	Jean Ratelle, NYR, Bos	21	1281	491	776	1267	.989
13.	Norm Ullman, Det, Tor	20	1410	490	739	1229	.872
14.	Jean Beliveau, Mtl	20	1125	507	712	1219	1.084
15.	Bobby Clarke, Phil	15	1144	358	852	1210	1.058

*Active player.

Alltime Goal-Scoring Leaders

	Player	Yrs	GP	G	G/game
1.	*Wayne Gretzky, Edm, LA	15	1125	803	.714
2.	Gordie Howe, Det, Hart	26	1767	801	.453
3.	Marcel Dionne, Det, LA, NYR	18	1348	731	.542
4.	Phil Esposito, Chi, Bos, NYR	18	1282	717	.559
5.	*Mike Gartner, Wash, Minn, NYR, Tor	15	1170	617	.527
6.	Bobby Hull, Chi, Winn, Hart	16	1063	610	.574
7.	Mike Bossy, NYI	10	752	573	.762
8.	Guy Lafleur, Mtl, NYR, Que	17	1126	560	.497
9.	John Bucyk, Det, Bos	23	1540	556	.361
10.	Maurice Richard, Mtl	18	978	544	.556

*Active player.

Alltime Assist Leaders

	Player	Yrs	GP	A	A/game
1.	*Wayne Gretzky, Edm, LA	15	1125	1655	1.471
2.	Gordie Howe, Det, Hart	26	1767	1049	.594
3.	Marcel Dionne, Det, LA, NYR	18	1348	1040	.772
4.	Stan Mikita, Chi	22	1394	926	.664
5.	*Bryan Trottier, NYI, Pitt	18	1279	901	.705
6.	Phil Esposito, Chi, Bos, NYR	18	1282	873	.681
7.	Bobby Clarke, Phil	15	1144	852	.745
8.	Alex Delvecchio, Det	24	1549	825	.533
9.	Gilbert Perreault, Buff	17	1191	814	.683
10.	John Bucyk, Det, Bos	23	1540	813	.528

*Active player.

Alltime Penalty Minutes Leaders

	Player	Yrs	GP	PIM	Min/game
1.	Dave Williams, 5 teams	13	962	3966	4.12
2.	Chris Nilan, Mtl, NYR, Bos	13	688	3043	4.42
3.	*Dale Hunter, Que, Wash	13	1054	3003	2.85
4.	*Tim Hunter, Cal, Que, Van	13	675	2769	4.10
5.	Willi Plett, 4 teams	12	834	2572	3.08
6.	*Marty McSorley, Edm, LA	10	666	2640	3.96
7.	Dave Schultz, 4 teams	9	535	2294	4.29
8.	Laurie Boschman, 5 teams	14	1009	2265	2.24
9.	Bryan Watson, 6 teams	16	878	2212	2.52
10.	Terry O'Reilly, Bos	14	891	2095	2.35

*Active player.

Goaltending Records

ALLTIME WIN LEADERS

Goaltender	W	L	T	Pct
Terry Sawchuk	435	337	188	.551
Jacques Plante	434	246	137	.615
Tony Esposito	423	307	151	.566
Glenn Hall	407	327	165	.544
Rogie Vachon	355	291	115	.542
Gump Worsley	335	353	150	.489
Harry Lumley	332	324	143	.505
Billy Smith	305	233	105	.556
*Andy Moog	303	148	64	.651
Turk Broda	302	224	101	.562

*Active player.

ACTIVE GOALTENDING LEADERS

Goaltender	W	L	T	Pct
Andy Moog, Edm, Bos	303	148	64	.651
Patrick Roy, Mtl	260	146	59	.623
Mike Vernon, Cal	239	143	46	.612
Grant Fuhr, Edm, Tor	287	185	68	.594
Tom Barrasso, Buff, Pitt	266	196	60	.567
Kelly Hrudey, NYI, LA	230	197	66	.534
Don Beaupre, Minn, Wash	254	221	72	.530

Note: Ranked by winning percentage; minimum 250 games played.

ALLTIME SHUTOUT LEADERS

Goaltender	Team	Yrs	GP	SO
Terry Sawchuk	Det, Bos, Tor, LA, NYR	21	971	103
George Hainsworth	Mtl, Tor	11	464	94
Glenn Hall	Det, Chi, StL	18	906	84
Jacques Plante	Mtl, NYR, StL, Tor, Bos	18	837	82
Tiny Thompson	Bos, Det	12	553	81
Alex Connell	Ott, Det, NYA, Mtl M	12	417	81
Tony Esposito	Mtl, Chi	16	886	76
Lorne Chabot	NYR, Tor, Mtl, Chi, Mtl M, NYA	11	411	73
Harry Lumley	Det, NYR, Chi, Tor, Bos	16	804	71
Roy Worters	Pitt Pir, NYA, *Mtl	12	484	66

*Played 1 game for Canadiens in 1929-30, not a shutout.

Coaching Records

Coach	Team	Seasons	W	L	T	Pct*
Scott Bowman	five teams	1967–	878	410	234	.654
Toe Blake	Mtl	1955-68	500	255	159	.634
Glen Sather	Edm	1979-89	442	241	99	.629
Fred Shero	Phil, NYR	1971-81	390	225	119	.612
Tommy Ivan	Det, Chi	1947-54, 56-58	302	196	112	.587
Emile Francis	NYR, StL	1965-77, 81-83	393	273	112	.577
Bryan Murray	Wash, Det	1981-92	420	309	106	.576
Billy Reay	Tor, Chi	1957-59, 63-77	542	385	175	.571
Al Arbour	StL, NYI	1970-86, 88-94	781	577	248	.564
Dick Irvin	Chi, Tor, Mtl	1930-56	690	521	226	.559

*Percentage arrived at by dividing possible points into actual points.
Note: Minimum 600 regular-season games. Ranked by %.

Single-Season Records

Points per Game

Player	Season	GP	Pts	Avg
Wayne Gretzky, Edm	1985-86	80	215	2.69
Mario Lemieux, Pitt	1992-93	60	160	2.66
Wayne Gretzky, Edm	1981-82	80	212	2.65
Mario Lemieux, Pitt	1988-89	76	199	2.62
Wayne Gretzky, Edm	1984-85	80	208	2.60
Wayne Gretzky, Edm	1982-83	80	196	2.45
Wayne Gretzky, Edm	1987-88	64	149	2.33
Wayne Gretzky, Edm	1986-87	79	183	2.32
Mario Lemieux, Pitt	1987-88	77	168	2.18
Wayne Gretzky, LA	1988-89	78	168	2.15

Player	Season	GP	Pts	Avg
Wayne Gretzky, LA	1990-91	78	163	2.08
Mario Lemieux, Pitt	1989-90	59	123	2.08
Wayne Gretzky, Edm	1980-81	80	164	2.05
Bill Cowley, Bos	1943-44	36	71	1.97
Phil Esposito, Bos	1970-71	78	152	1.95
Wayne Gretzky, LA	1989-90	73	142	1.95
Steve Yzerman, Det	1988-89	80	155	1.94
Bernie Nicholls, LA	1988-89	79	150	1.90
Phil Esposito, Bos	1973-74	78	145	1.86

Goals per Game

Player	Season	GP	G	Avg
Joe Malone, Mtl	1917-18	20	44	2.20
Cy Denneny, Ott	1917-18	22	36	1.64
Newsy Lalonde, Mtl	1917-18	14	23	1.64
Joe Malone, Que	1919-20	24	39	1.63
Newsy Lalonde, Mtl	1919-20	23	36	1.57
Joe Malone, Ham	1920-21	20	30	1.50
Babe Dye, Ham, Tor	1920-21	24	35	1.46
Cy Denneny, Ott	1920-21	24	34	1.42
Reg Noble, Tor	1917-18	20	28	1.40
Newsy Lalonde, Mtl	1920-21	24	33	1.38

Note: Minimum 20 goals in one season.

Assists per Game

Player	Season	GP	A	Avg
Wayne Gretzky, Edm	1985-86	80	163	2.04
Wayne Gretzky, Edm	1987-88	64	109	1.70
Wayne Gretzky, Edm	1984-85	80	135	1.69
Wayne Gretzky, Edm	1983-84	74	118	1.59
Wayne Gretzky, Edm	1982-83	80	125	1.56
Wayne Gretzky, LA	1990-91	78	122	1.56
Wayne Gretzky, Edm	1986-87	79	121	1.53
Mario Lemieux, Pitt	1992-93	60	91	1.52
Wayne Gretzky, Edm	1981-82	80	120	1.50
Mario Lemieux, Pitt	1988-89	76	114	1.50
Adam Oates, StL	1990-91	60	90	1.50

Shutout Leaders

	Season	SO	Length of Schedule
George Hainsworth, Mtl	1928-29	22	44
Alex Connell, Ott	1925-26	15	36
Alex Connell, Ott	1927-28	15	44
Hal Winkler, Bos	1927-28	15	44
Tony Esposito, Chi	1969-70	15	76
George Hainsworth, Mtl	1926-27	14	44
Clint Benedict, Mtl M	1926-27	13	44
Alex Connell, Ott	1926-27	13	44
George Hainsworth, Mtl	1927-28	13	44
Roy Worters, NYA	1927-28	13	44
John Roach, NYR	1928-29	13	44
Roy Worters, NYA	1928-29	13	44
Harry Lumley, Tor	1953-54	13	70
Tiny Thompson, Bos	1928-29	12	44
Lorne Chabot, Tor	1928-29	12	44
Chuck Gardiner, Chi	1930-31	12	44
Terry Sawchuk, Det	1951-52	12	70
Terry Sawchuk, Det	1953-54	12	70
Terry Sawchuk, Det	1954-55	12	70
Glenn Hall, Det	1955-56	12	70

	Season	SO	Length of Schedule
Bernie Parent, Phil	1973-74	12	78
Bernie Parent, Phil	1974-75	12	80
Lorne Chabot, NYR	1927-28	11	44
Harry Holmes, Det	1927-28	11	44
Clint Benedict, Mtl M	1928-29	11	44
Joe Miller, Pitt Pirates	1928-29	11	44
Tiny Thompson, Bos	1932-33	11	48
Terry Sawchuk, Det	1950-51	11	70
Lorne Chabot, NYR	1926-27	10	44
Roy Worters, Pitt Pirates	1927-28	10	44
Clarence Dolson, Det	1928-29	10	44
John Roach, Det	1932-33	10	48
Chuck Gardiner, Chi	1933-34	10	48
Tiny Thompson, Bos	1935-36	10	48
Frank Brimsek, Bos	1938-39	10	48
Bill Durnan, Mtl	1948-49	10	60
Gerry McNeil, Mtl	1952-53	10	70
Harry Lumley, Tor	1952-53	10	70
Tony Esposito, Chi	1973-74	10	78
Ken Dryden, Mtl	1976-77	10	80

Single-Game Records

Goals

	Date	G
Joe Malone, Que vs Tor	1-31-20	7
Newsy Lalonde, Mtl vs Tor	1-10-20	6
Joe Malone, Que vs Ott	3-10-20	6
Corb Denneny, Tor vs Ham	1-26-21	6
Cy Denneny, Ott vs Ham	3-7-21	6
Syd Howe, Det vs NYR	2-3-44	6
Red Berenson, StL vs Phil	11-7-68	6
Darryl Sittler, Tor vs Bos	2-7-76	6

Assists

	Date	A
Billy Taylor, Det vs Chi	3-16-47	7
Wayne Gretzky, Edm vs Wash	2-15-80	7
Wayne Gretzky, Edm vs Chi	12-11-85	7
Wayne Gretzky, Edm vs Que	2-14-86	7

Note: 19 tied with 6.

Points

	Date	G	A	Pts
Darryl Sittler, Tor vs Bos	2-7-76	6	4	10
Maurice Richard, Mtl vs Det	12-28-44	5	3	8
Bert Olmstead, Mtl vs Chi	1-9-54	4	4	8
Tom Bladon, Phil vs Clev	12-11-77	4	4	8
Bryan Trottier, NYI vs NYR	12-23-78	5	3	8
Peter Stastny, Que vs Wash	2-22-81	4	4	8
Anton Stastny, Que vs Wash	2-22-81	3	5	8
Wayne Gretzky, Edm vs NJ	11-19-83	3	5	8
Wayne Gretzky, Edm vs Minn	1-4-84	4	4	8
Paul Coffey, Edm vs Det	3-14-86	2	6	8
Mario Lemieux, Pitt vs StL	10-15-88	2	6	8
Bernie Nicholls, LA vs Tor	12-1-88	2	6	8
Mario Lemieux, Pitt vs NJ	12-31-88	5	3	8

Points

Season	Player and Club	Pts	Season	Player and Club	Pts
1917-18	Joe Malone, Mtl	44*	1956-57	Gordie Howe, Det	89
1918-19	Newsy Lalonde, Mtl	30	1957-58	Dickie Moore, Mtl	84
1919-20	Joe Malone, Que	48	1958-59	Dickie Moore, Mtl	96
1920-21	Newsy Lalonde, Mtl	41	1959-60	Bobby Hull, Chi	81
1921-22	Punch Broadbent, Ott	46	1960-61	Bernie Geoffrion, Mtl	95
1922-23	Babe Dye, Tor	37	1961-62	Andy Bathgate, NY	84
1923-24	Cy Denneny, Ott	23		Bobby Hull, Chi	84
1924-25	Babe Dye, Tor	44	1962-63	Gordie Howe, Det	86
1925-26	Nels Stewart, Mtl M	42	1963-64	Stan Mikita, Chi	89
1926-27	Bill Cook, NY	37	1964-65	Stan Mikita, Chi	87
1927-28	Howie Morenz, Mtl	51	1965-66	Bobby Hull, Chi	97
1928-29	Ace Bailey, Tor	32	1966-67	Stan Mikita, Chi	97
1929-30	Cooney Weiland, Bos	73	1967-68	Stan Mikita, Chi	87
1930-31	Howie Morenz, Mtl	51	1968-69	Phil Esposito, Bos	126
1931-32	Harvey Jackson, Tor	53	1969-70	Bobby Orr, Bos	120
1932-33	Bill Cook, NY	50	1970-71	Phil Esposito, Bos	152
1933-34	Charlie Conacher, Tor	52	1971-72	Phil Esposito, Bos	133
1934-35	Charlie Conacher, Tor	57	1972-73	Phil Esposito, Bos	130
1935-36	Sweeney Schriner, NYA	45	1973-74	Phil Esposito, Bos	145
1936-37	Sweeney Schriner, NYA	46	1974-75	Bobby Orr, Bos	135
1937-38	Gord Drillon, Tor	52	1975-76	Guy Lafleur, Mtl	125
1938-39	Hector Blake, Mtl	47	1976-77	Guy Lafleur, Mtl	136
1939-40	Milt Schmidt, Bos	52	1977-78	Guy Lafleur, Mtl	132
1940-41	Bill Cowley, Bos	62	1978-79	Bryan Trottier, NYI	134
1941-42	Bryan Hextall, NY	54	1979-80	Marcel Dionne, LA	137
1942-43	Doug Bentley, Chi	73		Wayne Gretzky, Edm	137
1943-44	Herb Cain, Bos	82	1980-81	Wayne Gretzky, Edm	164
1944-45	Elmer Lach, Mtl	80	1981-82	Wayne Gretzky, Edm	212
1945-46	Max Bentley, Chi	61	1982-83	Wayne Gretzky, Edm	196
1946-47	Max Bentley, Chi	72	1983-84	Wayne Gretzky, Edm	205
1947-48	Elmer Lach, Mtl	61	1984-85	Wayne Gretzky, Edm	208
1948-49	Roy Conacher, Chi	68	1985-86	Wayne Gretzky, Edm	215
1949-50	Ted Lindsay, Det	78	1986-87	Wayne Gretzky, Edm	183
1950-51	Gordie Howe, Det	86	1987-88	Mario Lemieux, Pitt	168
1951-52	Gordie Howe, Det	86	1988-89	Mario Lemieux, Pitt	199
1952-53	Gordie Howe, Det	95	1989-90	Wayne Gretzky, LA	142
1953-54	Gordie Howe, Det	81	1990-91	Wayne Gretzky, LA	163
1954-55	Bernie Geoffrion, Mtl	75	1991-92	Mario Lemieux, Pitt	131
1955-56	Jean Beliveau, Mtl	88	1992-93	Mario Lemieux, Pitt	160
			1993-94	Wayne Gretzky, LA	130

Goals

Season	Player and Club	G	Season	Player and Club	G
1917-18	Joe Malone, Mtl	44	1936-37	Larry Aurie, Det	23
1918-19	Odie Cleghorn, Mtl	23		Nels Stewart, Bos, NYA	23
1919-20	Joe Malone, Que	39	1937-38	Gord Drill, Tor	26
1920-21	Babe Dye, Ham, Tor	35	1938-39	Roy Conacher, Bos	26
1921-22	Punch Broadbent, Ott	32	1939-40	Bryan Hextall, NY	24
1922-23	Babe Dye, Tor	26	1940-41	Bryan Hextall, NY	26
1923-24	Cy Denneny, Ott	22	1941-42	Lynn Patrick, NY	32
1924-25	Babe Dye, Tor	38	1942-43	Doug Bentley, Chi	43
1925-26	Nels Stewart, Mtl M	34	1943-44	Doug Bentley, Chi	38
1926-27	Bill Cook, NY	33	1944-45	Maurice Richard, Mtl	50
1927-28	Howie Morenz, Mtl	33	1945-46	Gaye Stewart, Tor	37
1928-29	Ace Bailey, Tor	22	1946-47	Maurice Richard, Mtl	45
1929-30	Cooney Weiland, Bos	43	1947-48	Ted Lindsay, Det	33
1930-31	Bill Cook, NY	30	1948-49	Sid Abel, Det	28
1931-32	Charlie Conacher, Tor	34	1949-50	Maurice Richard, Mtl	43
	Bill Cook, NY	34	1950-51	Gordie Howe, Det	43
1932-33	Bill Cook, NY	28	1951-52	Gordie Howe, Det	47
1933-34	Charlie Conacher, Tor	32	1952-53	Gordie Howe, Det	49
1934-35	Charlie Conacher, Tor	36	1953-54	Maurice Richard, Mtl	37
1935-36	Charlie Conacher, Tor	23	1954-55	Bernie Geoffrion, Mtl	38
	Bill Thoms, Tor	23		Maurice Richard, Mtl	38

Goals (Cont.)

Season	Player and Club	G	Season	Player and Club	G
1955-56	Jean Beliveau, Mtl	47	1975-76	Guy Lafleur, Mtl	56
1956-57	Gordie Howe, Det	44	1976-77	Steve Shutt, Mtl	60
1957-58	Dickie Moore, Mtl	36	1977-78	Guy Lafleur, Mtl	60
1958-59	Jean Beliveau, Mtl	45	1978-79	Mike Bossy, NYI	69
1959-60	Bobby Hull, Chi	39	1979-80	Charlie Simmer, LA	56
	Bronco Horvath, Bos	39		Blaine Stoughton, Hart	56
1960-61	Bernie Geoffrion, Mtl	50	1980-81	Mike Bossy, NYI	68
1961-62	Bobby Hull, Chi	50	1981-82	Wayne Gretzky, Edm	92
1962-63	Gordie Howe, Det	38	1982-83	Wayne Gretzky, Edm	71
1963-64	Bobby Hull, Chi	43	1983-84	Wayne Gretzky, Edm	87
1964-65	Norm Ullman, Det	42	1984-85	Wayne Gretzky, Edm	73
1965-66	Bobby Hull, Chi	54	1985-86	Jari Kurri, Edm	68
1966-67	Bobby Hull, Chi	52	1986-87	Wayne Gretzky, Edm	62
1967-68	Bobby Hull, Chi	44	1987-88	Mario Lemieux, Pitt	70
1968-69	Bobby Hull, Chi	58	1988-89	Mario Lemieux, Pitt	85
1969-70	Phil Esposito, Bos	43	1989-90	Brett Hull, Chi	72
1970-71	Phil Esposito, Bos	76	1990-91	Brett Hull, Chi	78
1971-72	Phil Esposito, Bos	66	1991-92	Brett Hull, Chi	70
1972-73	Phil Esposito, Bos	55	1992-93	Alexander Mogilny, Buff	76
1973-74	Phil Esposito, Bos	68		Teemu Selanne, Winn	76
1974-75	Phil Esposito, Bos	61	1993-94	Pavel Bure, Van	60

Assists

Season	Player and Club	A	Season	Player and Club	A
1917-18	statistic not kept		1957-58	Henri Richard, Mtl	52
1918-19	Newsy Lalonde, Mtl	9	1958-59	Dickie Moore, Mtl	55
1919-20	Corbett Denneny, Tor	12	1959-60	Bobby Hull, Chi	42
1920-21	Louis Berlinquette, Mtl	9	1960-61	Jean Beliveau, Mtl	58
1921-22	Punch Broadbench, Ott	14	1961-62	Andy Bathgate, NY	56
1922-23	Babe Dye, Tor	11	1962-63	Henri Richard, Mtl	50
1923-24	Billy Boucher, Mtl	6	1963-64	Andy Bathgate, NY, Tor	58
1924-25	Cy Denneny, Ott	15	1964-65	Stan Mikita, Chi	59
1925-26	Cy Denneny, Ott	12	1965-66	Stan Mikita, Chi	48
1926-27	Dick Irvin, Chi	18		Bobby Rousseau, Mtl	48
1927-28	Howie Morenz, Mtl	18		Jean Beliveau, Mtl	48
1928-29	Frank Boucher, NY	16	1966-67	Stan Mikita, Chi	62
1929-30	Frank Boucher, NY	36	1967-68	Phil Esposito, Bos	49
1930-31	Joe Primeau, Tor	36	1968-69	Phil Esposito, Bos	77
1931-32	Joe Primeau, Tor	37	1969-70	Bobby Orr, Bos	87
1932-33	Frank Boucher, NY	28	1970-71	Bobby Orr, Bos	102
1933-34	Joe Primeau, Tor	32	1971-72	Bobby Orr, Bos	80
1934-35	Art Chapman, NYA	28	1972-73	Phil Esposito, Bos	75
1935-36	Art Chapman, NYA	28	1973-74	Bobby Orr, Bos	89
1936-37	Syl Apps, Tor	29	1974-75	Bobby Clarke, Phil	89
1937-38	Syl Apps, Tor	29		Bobby Orr, Bos	89
1938-39	Bill Cowley, Bos	34	1975-76	Bobby Clarke, Phil	89
1939-40	Milt Schmidt, Bos	30	1976-77	Guy Lafleur, Mtl	80
1940-41	Bill Cowley, Bos	45	1977-78	Bryan Trottier, NYI	77
1941-42	Phil Watson, NY	37	1978-79	Bryan Trottier, NYI	87
1942-43	Bill Cowley, Bos	45	1979-80	Wayne Gretzky, Edm	86
1943-44	Clint Smith, Chi	49	1980-81	Wayne Gretzky, Edm	109
1944-45	Elmer Lach, Mtl	54	1981-82	Wayne Gretzky, Edm	120
1945-46	Elmer Lach, Mtl	34	1982-83	Wayne Gretzky, Edm	125
1946-47	Billy Taylor, Det	46	1983-84	Wayne Gretzky, Edm	118
1947-48	Doug Bentley, Chi	37	1984-85	Wayne Gretzky, Edm	135
1948-49	Doug Bentley, Chi	43	1985-86	Wayne Gretzky, Edm	163
1949-50	Ted Lindsay, Det	55	1986-87	Wayne Gretzky, Edm	121
1950-51	Gordie Howe, Det	43	1987-88	Wayne Gretzky, Edm	109
	Ted Kennedy, Tor	43	1988-89	Wayne Gretzky, LA	114
1951-52	Elmer Lach, Mtl	50		Mario Lemieux, Pitt	114
1952-53	Gordie Howe, Det	46	1989-90	Wayne Gretzky, LA	102
1953-54	Gordie Howe, Det	48	1990-91	Wayne Gretzky, LA	122
1954-55	Bert Olmstead, Mtl	48	1991-92	Wayne Gretzky, LA	90
1955-56	Bert Olmstead, Mtl	56	1992-93	Adam Oates, Bos	97
1956-57	Ted Lindsay, Det	55	1993-94	Wayne Gretzky, LA	92

Goals Against Average

Season	Goaltender and Club	GP	Min	GA	SO	Avg
1917-18	Georges Vezina, Mtl	21	1282	84	1	3.93
1918-19	Clint Benedict, Ott	18	1113	53	2	2.86
1919-20	Clint Benedict, Ott	24	1444	64	5	2.66
1920-21	Clint Benedict, Ott	24	1457	75	2	3.09
1921-22	Clint Benedict, Ott	24	1508	84	2	3.34
1922-23	Clint Benedict, Ott	24	1478	54	4	2.19
1923-24	Georges Vezina, Mtl	24	1459	48	3	1.97
1924-25	Georges Vezina, Mtl	30	1860	56	5	1.81
1925-26	Alex Connell, Ott	36	2251	42	15	1.12
1926-27	Clint Benedict, Mtl M	43	2748	65	13	1.42
1927-28	George Hainsworth, Mtl	44	2730	48	13	1.05
1928-29	George Hainsworth, Mtl	44	2800	43	22	0.92
1929-30	Tiny Thompson, Bos	44	2680	98	3	2.19
1930-31	Roy Worters, NYA	44	2760	74	8	1.61
1931-32	Chuck Gardiner, Chi	48	2989	92	4	1.85
1932-33	Tiny Thompson, Bos	48	3000	88	11	1.76
1933-34	Wilf Cude, Det, Mtl	30	1920	47	5	1.47
1934-35	Lorne Chabot, Chi	48	2940	88	8	1.80
1935-36	Tiny Thompson, Bos	48	2930	82	10	1.68
1936-37	Normie Smith, Det	48	2980	102	6	2.05
1937-38	Tiny Thompson, Bos	48	2970	89	7	1.80
1938-39	Frank Brimsek, Bos	43	2610	68	10	1.56
1939-40	Dave Kerr, NYR	48	3000	77	8	1.54
1940-41	Turk Broda, Tor	48	2970	99	5	2.00
1941-42	Frank Brimsek, Bos	47	2930	115	3	2.35
1942-43	Johnny Mowers, Det	50	3010	124	6	2.47
1943-44	Bill Durnan, Mtl	50	3000	109	2	2.18
1944-45	Bill Durnan, Mtl	50	3000	121	1	2.42
1945-46	Bill Durnan, Mtl	40	2400	104	4	2.60
1946-47	Bill Durnan, Mtl	60	3600	138	4	2.30
1947-48	Turk Broda, Tor	60	3600	143	5	2.38
1948-49	Bill Durnan, Mtl	60	3600	126	10	2.10
1949-50	Bill Durnan, Mtl	64	3840	141	8	2.20
1950-51	Al Rollins, Tor	40	2367	70	5	1.77
1951-52	Terry Sawchuk, Det	70	4200	133	12	1.90
1952-53	Terry Sawchuk, Det	63	3780	120	9	1.90
1953-54	Harry Lumley, Tor	69	4140	128	13	1.86
1954-55	Harry Lumley, Tor	69	4140	134	8	1.94
	Terry Sawchuk, Det	68	4060	132	12	1.94
1955-56	Jacques Plante, Mtl	64	3840	119	7	1.86
1956-57	Jacques Plante, Mtl	61	3660	123	9	2.02
1957-58	Jacques Plante, Mtl	57	3386	119	9	2.11
1958-59	Jacques Plante, Mtl	67	4000	144	9	2.16
1959-60	Jacques Plante, Mtl	69	4140	175	3	2.54
1960-61	Johnny Bower, Tor	58	3480	145	2	2.50
1961-62	Jacques Plante, Mtl	70	4200	166	4	2.37
1962-63	Jacques Plante, Mtl	56	3320	138	5	2.49
1963-64	Johnny Bower, Tor	51	3009	106	5	2.11
1964-65	Johnny Bower, Tor	34	2040	81	3	2.38
1965-66	Johnny Bower, Tor	35	1998	75	3	2.25
1966-67	Glenn Hall, Chi	32	1664	66	2	2.38
1967-68	Gump Worsley, Mtl	40	2213	73	6	1.98
1968-69	Jacques Plante, StL	37	2139	70	5	1.96
1969-70	Ernie Wakely, StL	30	1651	58	4	2.11
1970-71	Jacques Plante Tor	40	2329	73	4	1.88
1971-72	Tony Esposito, Chi	48	2780	82	9	1.77
1972-73	Ken Dryden, Mtl	54	3165	119	6	2.26
1973-74	Bernie Parent, Phil	73	4314	136	12	1.89
1974-75	Bernie Parent, Phil	68	4041	137	12	2.03
1975-76	Ken Dryden, Mtl	62	3580	121	8	2.03
1976-77	Michael Larocque, Mtl	26	1525	53	4	2.09
1977-78	Ken Dryden, Mtl	52	3071	105	5	2.05
1978-79	Ken Dryden, Mtl	47	2814	108	5	2.30
1979-80	Bob Sauve, Buff	32	1880	74	4	2.36
1980-81	Richard Sevigny, Mtl	33	1777	71	2	2.40
1981-82	Denis Herron, Mtl	27	1547	68	3	2.64

Goals Against Average *(Cont.)*

Season	Goaltender and Club	GP	Min	GA	SO	Avg
1982-83	Pete Peeters, Bos	62	3611	142	8	2.36
1983-84	Pat Riggin, Wash	41	2299	102	4	2.66
1984-85	Tom Barrasso, Buff	54	3248	144	5	2.66
1985-86	Bob Froese, Phil	51	2728	116	5	2.55
1986-87	Brian Hayward, Mtl	37	2178	102	1	2.81
1987-88	Pete Peeters, Wash	35	1896	88	2	2.78
1988-89	Patrick Roy, Mtl	48	2744	113	4	2.47
1989-90	Patrick Roy, Mtl	54	3173	134	3	2.53
	Mike Liut, Hart, Wash	37	2161	91	4	2.53
1990-91	Ed Belfour, Chi	74	4127	170	4	2.47
1991-92	Patrick Roy, Mtl	67	3935	155	5	2.36
1992-93	*Felix Potvin, Tor	48	2781	116	2	2.50
1993-94	Dominik Hasek, Buff	58	3358	109	7	1.95

*Rookie.

Penalty Minutes

Season	Player and Club	GP	PIM	Season	Player and Club	GP	PIM
1918-19	Joe Hall, Mtl	17	85	1956-57	Gus Mortson, Chi	70	147
1919-20	Cully Wilson, Tor	23	79	1957-58	Lou Fontinato, NYR	70	152
1920-21	Bert Corbeau, Mtl	24	86	1958-59	Ted Lindsay, Chi	70	184
1921-22	S Cleghorn, Mtl	24	63	1959-60	Carl Brewer, Tor	67	150
1922-23	Billy Boucher, Mtl	24	52	1960-61	Pierre Pilote, Chi	70	165
1923-24	Bert Corbeau, Mtl	24	55	1961-62	Lou Fontinato, Mtl	54	167
1924-25	Billy Boucher, Mtl	30	92	1962-63	Howie Young, Det	64	273
1925-26	Bert Corbeau, Tor	36	121	1963-64	Vic Hadfield, NYR	69	151
1926-27	Nels Stewart, Mtl M	44	133	1964-65	Carl Brewer, Tor	70	177
1927-28	Eddie Shore, Bos	44	165	1965-66	R Fleming, Bos, NYR	69	166
1928-29	Red Dutton, Mtl M	44	139	1966-67	John Ferguson, Mtl	67	177
1929-30	Joe Lamb, Ott	44	119	1967-68	Barclay Plager, StL	49	153
1930-31	Harvey Rockburn, Det	42	118	1968-69	F Kennedy, Phi, Tor	77	219
1931-32	Red Dutton, NYA	47	107	1969-70	Keith Magnuson, Chi	76	213
1932-33	Red Horner, Tor	48	144	1970-71	Keith Magnuson, Chi	76	291
1933-34	Red Horner, Tor	42	126	1971-72	Brian Watson, Pitt	75	212
1934-35	Red Horner, Tor	46	125	1972-73	Dave Schultz, Phil	76	259
1935-36	Red Horner, Tor	43	167	1973-74	Dave Schultz, Phil	73	348
1936-37	Red Horner, Tor	48	124	1974-75	Dave Schultz, Phil	76	472
1937-38	Red Horner, Tor	47	82	1975-76	S Durbano, Pitt, KC	69	370
1938-39	Red Horner, Tor	48	85	1976-77	Dave Williams, Tor	77	338
1939-40	Red Horner, Tor	30	87	1977-78	Dave Schultz, LA, Pitt	74	405
1940-41	Jimmy Orlando, Det	48	99	1978-79	Dave Williams, Tor	77	298
1941-42	Jimmy Orlando, Det	48	81	1979-80	Jimmy Mann, Winn	72	287
1942-43	Jimmy Orlando, Det	40	89	1980-81	Dave Williams, Van	77	343
1943-44	Mike McMahon, Mtl	42	98	1981-82	Paul Baxter, Pitt	76	409
1944-45	Pat Egan, Bos	48	86	1982-83	Randy Holt, Wash	70	275
1945-46	Jack Stewart, Det	47	73	1983-84	Chris Nilan, Mtl	76	338
1946-47	Gus Mortson, Tor	60	133	1984-85	Chris Nilan, Mtl	77	358
1947-48	Bill Barilko, Tor	57	147	1985-86	Joey Kocur, Det	59	377
1948-49	Bill Ezinicki, Tor	52	145	1986-87	Tim Hunter, Cal	73	361
1949-50	Bill Ezinicki, Tor	67	144	1987-88	Bob Probert, Det	74	398
1950-51	Gus Mortson, Tor	60	142	1988-89	Tim Hunter, Cal	75	375
1951-52	Gus Kyle, Bos	69	127	1989-90	Basil McRae, Minn	66	351
1952-53	Maurice Richard, Mtl	70	112	1990-91	Bob Ray, Buff	66	350
1953-54	Gus Mortson, Chi	68	132	1991-92	Mike Peluso, Chi	63	408
1954-55	Fern Flaman, Bos	70	150	1992-93	Marty McSorley, LA	81	399
1955-56	Lou Fontinato, NYR	70	202	1993-94	Tie Domi, Winn	81	347

NHL All-Star Game

First played in 1947, this game was scheduled before the start of the regular season and used to match the defending Stanley Cup champions against a squad made up of league All-Stars from other teams. In 1966 the games were moved to mid-season, although there was no game that year. The format changed to a conference versus conference showdown in 1969.

Results

Year	Site	Score	MVP	Attendance
1947	Toronto	All-Stars 4, Toronto 3	None named	14,169
1948	Chicago	All-Stars 3, Toronto 1	None named	12,794
1949	Toronto	All-Stars 3, Toronto 1	None named	13,541
1950	Detroit	Detroit 7, All-Stars 1	None named	9,166
1951	Toronto	1st team 2, 2nd team 2	None named	11,469
1952	Detroit	1st team 1, 2nd team 1	None named	10,680
1953	Montreal	All-Stars 3, Montreal 1	None named	14,153
1954	Detroit	All-Stars 2, Detroit 2	None named	10,689
1955	Detroit	Detroit 3, All-Stars 1	None named	10,111
1956	Montreal	All-Stars 1, Montreal 1	None named	13,095
1957	Montreal	All-Stars 5, Montreal 3	None named	13,003
1958	Montreal	Montreal 6, All-Stars 3	None named	13,989
1959	Montreal	Montreal 6, All-Stars 1	None named	13,818
1960	Montreal	All-Stars 2, Montreal 1	None named	13,949
1961	Chicago	All-Stars 3, Chicago 1	None named	14,534
1962	Toronto	Toronto 4, All-Stars 1	Eddie Shack, Tor	14,236
1963	Toronto	All-Stars 3, Toronto 3	Frank Mahovlich, Tor	14,034
1964	Toronto	All-Stars 3, Toronto 2	Jean Beliveau, Mtl	14,232
1965	Montreal	All-Stars 5, Montreal 2	Gordie Howe, Det	13,529
1967	Montreal	Montreal 3, All-Stars 0	Henri Richard, Mtl	14,284
1968	Toronto	Toronto 4, All-Stars 3	Bruce Gamble, Tor	15,753
1969	Montreal	East 3, West 3	Frank Mahovlich, Det	16,260
1970	St Louis	East 4, West 1	Bobby Hull, Chi	16,587
1971	Boston	West 2, East 1	Bobby Hull, Chi	14,790
1972	Minnesota	East 3, West 2	Bobby Orr, Bos	15,423
1973	NY Rangers	East 5, West 4	Greg Polis, Pitt	16,986
1974	Chicago	West 6, East 4	Garry Unger, StL	16,426
1975	Montreal	Wales 7, Campbell 1	Syl Apps Jr, Pitt	16,080
1976	Philadelphia	Wales 7, Campbell 5	Pete Mahovlich, Mtl	16,436
1977	Vancouver	Wales 4, Campbell 3	Rick Martin, Buff	15,607
1978	Buffalo	Wales 3, Campbell 2 (OT)	Billy Smith, NYI	16,433
1980	Detroit	Wales 6, Campbell 3	Reg Leach, Phil	21,002
1981	Los Angeles	Campbell 4, Wales 1	Mike Liut, StL	15,761
1982	Washington	Wales 4, Campbell 2	Mike Bossy, NYI	18,130
1983	NY Islanders	Campbell 9, Wales 3	Wayne Gretzky, Edm	15,230
1984	NJ Devils	Wales 7, Campbell 6	Don Maloney, NYR	18,939
1985	Calgary	Wales 6, Campbell 4	Mario Lemieux, Pitt	16,825
1986	Hartford	Wales 4, Campbell 3 (OT)	Grant Fuhr, Edm	15,100
1988	St Louis	Wales 6, Campbell 5 (OT)	Mario Lemieux, Pitt	17,878
1989	Edmonton	Campbell 9, Wales 5	Wayne Gretzky, LA	17,503
1990	Pittsburgh	Wales 12, Campbell 7	Mario Lemieux, Pitt	16,236
1991	Chicago	Campbell 11, Wales 5	Vince Damphousse, Tor	18,472
1992	Philadelphia	Campbell 10, Wales 6	Brett Hull, StL	17,380
1993	Montreal	Wales 16, Campbell 6	Mike Gartner, NYR	17,137
1994	NY Rangers	East 9, West 8	Mike Richter, NYR	18,200

Note: The Challenge Cup, a series between the NHL All-Stars and the Soviet Union, was played instead of the All-Star Game in 1979. Eight years later, Rendez-Vous '87, a two-game series matching the Soviet Union and the NHL All-Stars, replaced the All-Star Game.

THEY SAID IT

Boston Bruin wing Cam Neely, after overcoming knee surgery to score 50 goals in 44 games, third-fastest in league history:"I wasn't sure about 50 shifts, let alone 50 goals."

Located in Toronto, the Hockey Hall of Fame was officially opened on August 26, 1961. The current president is Ian "Scotty" Morrison, a former NHL referee. There are, at present, 281 members of the Hockey Hall of Fame—192 players, 77 "Builders," and 12 on-ice officials. To be eligible, player and referee/linesman candidates should have been out of the game for three years, but the Hall's Board of Directors can make exceptions.

Players

Sid Abel (1969)
Jack Adams (1959)
Charles "Syl" Apps (1961)
George Armstrong (1975)
Irvine "Ace" Bailey (1975)
Donald H. "Dan" Bain (1945)
Hobey Baker (1945)
Bill Barber (1990)
Marty Barry (1965)
Andy Bathgate (1978)
Jean Beliveau (1972)
Clint Benedict (1965)
Douglas Bentley (1964)
Max Bentley (1966)
Hector "Toe" Blake (1966)
Leo Boivin (1986)
Dickie Boon (1952)
Mike Bossy (1991)
Emile "Butch" Bouchard (1966)
Frank Boucher (1958)
George "Buck" Boucher (1960)
Johnny Bower (1976)
Russell Bowie (1945)
Frank Brimsek (1966)
Harry L. "Punch" Broadbent (1962)
Walter "Turk" Broda (1967)
John Bucyk (1981)
Billy Burch (1974)
Harry Cameron (1962)
Gerry Cheevers (1985)
Francis "King" Clancy (1958)
Aubrey "Dit" Clapper (1947)
Bobby Clarke (1987)
Sprague Cleghorn (1958)
Neil Colville (1967)
Charlie Conacher (1961)
Alex Connell (1958)
Bill Cook (1952)
Arthur Coulter (1974)
Yvan Cournoyer (1982)
Bill Cowley (1968)
Samuel "Rusty" Crawford (1962)
Jack Darragh (1962)
Allan M. "Scotty" Davidson (1950)
Clarence "Hap" Day (1961)
Alex Delvecchio (1977)
Cy Denneny (1959)
Marcel Dionne (1992)
Gordie Drillon (1975)
Charles Drinkwater (1950)
Ken Dryden (1983)

Woody Dumart (1992)
Thomas Dunderdale (1974)
Bill Durnan (1964)
Mervyn A. "Red" Dutton (1958)
Cecil "Babe" Dye (1970)
Phil Esposito (1984)
Tony Esposito (1988)
Arthur F. Farrell (1965)
Ferdinand "Fern" Flaman (1990)
Frank Foyston (1958)
Frank Frederickson (1958)
Bill Gadsby (1970)
Bob Gainey (1992)
Chuck Gardiner (1945)
Herb Gardiner (1958)
Jimmy Gardner (1962)
Bernie "Boom Boom" Geoffrion (1972)
Eddie Gerard (1945)
Ed Giacomin (1987)
Rod Gilbert (1982)
Hamilton "Billy" Gilmour (1962)
Frank "Moose" Goheen (1952)
Ebenezer R. "Ebbie" Goodfellow (1963)
Mike Grant (1950)
Wilfred "Shorty" Green (1962)
Si Griffis (1950)
George Hainsworth (1961)
Glenn Hall (1975)
Joe Hall (1961)
Doug Harvey (1973)
George Hay (1958)
William "Riley" Hern (1962)
Bryan Hextall (1969)
Harry "Hap" Holmes (1972)
Tom Hooper (1962)
George "Red" Horner (1965)
Miles "Tim" Horton (1977)
Gordie Howe (1972)
Syd Howe (1965)
Harry Howell (1979)
Bobby Hull (1983)
John "Bouse" Hutton (1962)
Harry M. Hyland (1962)
James "Dick" Irvin (1958)
Harvey "Busher" Jackson (1971)
Ernest "Moose" Johnson (1952)
Ivan "Ching" Johnson (1958)
Tom Johnson (1970)
Aurel Joliat (1947)

Gordon "Duke" Keats (1958)
Leonard "Red" Kelly (1969)
Ted "Teeder" Kennedy (1966)
Dave Keon (1986)
Elmer Lach (1966)
Guy Lafleur (1988)
Edouard "Newsy" Lalonde (1950)
Jacques Laperriere (1987)
Guy LaPointe (1993)
Edgar Laprade (1993)
Jean "Jack" Laviolette (1962)
Hugh Lehman (1958)
Jacques Lemaire (1984)
Percy LeSueur (1961)
Herbert A. Lewis (1989)
Ted Lindsay (1966)
Harry Lumley (1980)
Lanny McDonald (1992)
Frank McGee (1945)
Billy McGimsie (1962)
George McNamara (1958)
Duncan "Mickey" MacKay (1952)
Frank Mahovlich (1981)
Joe Malone (1950)
Sylvio Mantha (1960)
Jack Marshall (1965)
Fred G. "Steamer" Maxwell (1962)
Stan Mikita (1983)
Dicky Moore (1974)
Patrick "Paddy" Moran (1958)
Howie Morenz (1945)
Billy Mosienko (1965)
Frank Nighbor (1947)
Reg Noble (1962)
Herbert "Buddy" O'Connor (1988)
Harry Oliver (1967)
Bert Olmstead (1985)
Bobby Orr (1979)
Bernie Parent (1984)
Brad Park (1988)
Lester Patrick (1947)
Lynn Patrick (1980)
Gilbert Perreault (1990)
Tommy Phillips (1945)
Pierre Pilote (1975)
Didier "Pit" Pitre (1962)
Jacques Plante (1978)
Denis Potvin (1991)
Walter "Babe" Pratt (1966)

Players *(Cont.)*

Joe Primeau (1963)
Marcel Pronovost (1978)
Bob Pulford (1991)
Harvey Pulford (1945)
Hubert "Bill" Quackenbush (1976)
Frank Rankin (1961)
Jean Ratelle (1985)
Claude "Chuck" Rayner (1973)
Kenneth Reardon (1966)
Henri Richard (1979)
Maurice "Rocket" Richard (1961)
George Richardson (1950)
Gordon Roberts (1971)
Art Ross (1945)
Blair Russel (1965)
Ernest Russell (1965)
Jack Ruttan (1962)
Serge Savard (1986)
Terry Sawchuk (1971)
Fred Scanlan (1965)
Milt Schmidt (1961)
Dave "Sweeney" Schriner (1962)
Earl Seibert (1963)
Oliver Seibert (1961)
Eddie Shore (1947)
Steve Shutt (1993)
Albert C. "Babe" Siebert (1964)
Harold "Bullet Joe" Simpson (1962)
Daryl Sittler (1989)
Alfred E. Smith (1962)
Billy Smith (1993)
Reginald "Hooley" Smith (1972)
Thomas Smith (1973)
Allan Stanley (1981)
Russell "Barney" Stanley (1962)
John "Black Jack" Stewart (1964)
Nels Stewart (1962)
Bruce Stuart (1961)
Hod Stuart (1945)
Frederic "Cyclone" (O.B.E.) Taylor (1947)
Cecil R. "Tiny" Thompson (1959)
Vladislav Tretiak (1989)
Harry J. Trihey (1950)
Norm Ullman (1982)
Georges Vezina (1945)
Jack Walker (1960)
Marty Walsh (1962)
Harry E. Watson (1962)
Ralph "Cooney" Weiland (1971)
Harry Westwick (1962)
Fred Whitcroft (1962)
Gordon "Phat" Wilson (1962)
Lorne "Gump" Worsley (1980)
Roy Worters (1969)

Builders

Charles Adams (1960)
Weston W. Adams (1972)
Thomas "Frank" Ahearn (1962)
John "Bunny" Ahearne (1977)
Montagu Allan (C.V.O.) (1945)
Harold Ballard (1977)
David Bauer (1989)
John Bickell (1978)
Scott Bowman (1991)
George V. Brown (1961)
Walter A. Brown (1962)
Frank Buckland (1975)
Jack Butterfield (1980)
Frank Calder (1947)
Angus D. Campbell (1964)
Clarence Campbell (1966)
Joe Cattarinich (1977)
Joseph "Leo" Dandurand (1963)
Francis Dilio (1964)
George S. Dudley (1958)
James A. Dunn (1968)
Alan Eagleson (1989)
Emile Francis (1982)
Jack Gibson (1976)
Tommy Gorman (1963)
Frank Griffiths (1993)
William Hanley (1986)
Charles Hay (1974)
James C. Hendy (1968)
Foster Hewitt (1965)
William Hewitt (1947)
Fred J. Hume (1962)
George "Punch" Imlach (1984)
Tommy Ivan (1974)
William M. Jennings (1975)
Gordon W. Juckes (1979)
John Kilpatrick (1960)
Seymour Knox III (1993)
George Leader (1969)
Robert LeBel (1970)
Thomas F. Lockhart (1965)
Paul Loicq (1961)
Frederic McLaughlin (1963)
John Mariucci (1985)
John "Jake" Milford (1984)
Hartland Molson (1973)
Francis Nelson (1947)
Bruce A. Norris (1969)
James Norris, Sr. (1958)
James D. Norris (1962)
William M. Northey (1947)
John O'Brien (1962)
Frank Patrick (1958)
Fred Page (1993)
Allan W. Pickard (1958)
Rudy Pilous (1985)
Norman "Bud" Poile (1990)
Samuel Pollock (1978)
Donat Raymond (1958)
John Robertson (1947)
Claude C. Robinson (1947)

Builders *(Cont.)*

Philip D. Ross (1976)
Frank J. Selke (1960)
Harry Sinden (1983)
Frank D. Smith (1962)
Conn Smythe (1958)
Edward M. Snider (1988)
Lord Stanley of Preston (G.C.B.) (1945)
James T. Sutherland (1947)
Anatoli V. Tarasov (1974)
Lloyd Turner (1958)
William Tutt (1978)
Carl Potter Voss (1974)
Fred C. Waghorn (1961)
Arthur Wirtz (1971)
Bill Wirtz (1976)
John A. Ziegler, Jr. (1987)

Referees/Linesmen

John Ashley (1981)
William L. Chadwick (1964)
John D'Amico (1993)
Chaucer Elliott (1961)
George Hayes (1988)
Robert W. Hewitson (1963)
Fred J. "Mickey" Ion (1961)
Matt Pavelich (1987)
Mike Rodden (1962)
J. Cooper Smeaton (1961)
Roy "Red" Storey (1967)
Frank Udvari (1973)

Note: Year of election to the Hall of Fame is in parentheses after the member's name.

Tennis

Buddy Ryan: The NFL's Mystery Man

Sports Illustrate

JULY 11, 1994·$2.95 (CAN.$3.95)

Pistol Pete

Wimbledon King
Pete Sampras

BILL FRAKES

Break Point For Tennis

Injuries, retirements and flameouts highlighted a season of crisis and change | by SALLY JENKINS

TENNIS IS A PERSONALITY-DRIVEN game. Whatever is going on in the players' lives is directly reflected in the sport. In the 1994 season, judging by top-ranked Pete Sampras's bad ankle and Steffi Graf's stiff back, tennis was ailing. Injuries, absences and a Spanish wave were some of the trends. Perennial lady-in-waiting Arantxa Sanchez Vicario somehow won two Grand Slam titles while Graf was alternately hurt and bored. Sampras was the Australian and Wimbledon champion and a clear-cut No. 1, but faded in the stretch and ended the year by retiring during his second match in the U.S.'s loss to Sweden in the Davis Cup semifinals.

Events off the court were as significant as those on, and unfortunately some of them involved sadness and loss. Jennifer Capriati, 18, the once-effervescent girl who was supposed to be the next Chris Evert, instead became the game's latest flameout, a victim of too much too soon. Martina Navratilova, 37, finally retired after reaching one last, miraculous Wimbledon final, losing to Conchita Martinez, a 22-year-old from Barcelona. Monica Seles remained inactive a full year after being stabbed on the court by an attacker in Hamburg, Germany. And Vitas Gerulaitis suffered an untimely death at 40. But there were also some things to celebrate, such as the birth of Boris Becker's first child and Andre Agassi's triumphant U.S. Open victory and love affair with model Brooke Shields, marking a happy return to form after career-threatening wrist surgery ruined most of '93 for him.

Capriati was on an indefinite sabbatical from the tour, supposedly to finish high school, when she was arrested in May for possession of marijuana in a seedy motel room in Coral Gables, Fla. While her peers on the tour were preparing for the French Open, where just three years earlier she had become one of the youngest semifinalists in history, Capriati was enjoying a lost weekend. With Capriati were two companions arrested for possession of crack cocaine and heroin. Capriati, overweight and with a ring through her nose, entered a drug rehabilitation center in Miami for a month of voluntary treatment. When she resurfaced in the fall she and her family had moved from the

Tampa area to Palm Springs, Calif., where she announced her intention to play again and launched a comeback bid for 1995.

Capriati's self-destructive behavior was not a tragedy, although some labeled it so. That became clear when real tragedy struck just after the U.S. Open in September. Gerulaitis, one of the most affable and charismatic stars in the history of the sport, was found dead in a Southhampton, N.Y. cottage where he was a weekend guest during a charity tournament appearance. Gerulaitis, a former Wimbledon and U.S. Open finalist raised on the public courts of Queens, N.Y., died of carbon monoxide poisoning when a faulty propane heater leaked noxious fumes as he took an afternoon nap. Gerulaitis had overcome a substance-abuse problem, which he acknowledged shortened his career, and was building a second career as a TV analyst for ESPN. His Long Island funeral drew scores of tennis luminaries, including Jimmy Connors, Bjorn Borg, John McEnroe, Evert and Billie Jean King.

One of those particularly affected by the death of Gerulaitis was Sampras, the 23-year-old champion with whom he had

Sanchez Vicario didn't miss many in '94, winning both the French and the U.S. Opens.

become close friends. It was Gerulaitis who comforted Sampras when he lay on the floor of the referee's office at the U.S. Open after failing to defend his title, upset in the fourth round by Jaime Yzaga of Peru. Sampras suffered from tendinitis in his ankle for much of the summer and was not fit to go five sets. After losing the match, Sampras collapsed in the small office, exhausted and with feet so badly blistered they were bloody, and ordered everybody out of the room except Gerulaitis. The former player gently removed Sampras's shirt and shoes and later carried his racket bag back to the locker room for him. "Vitas was the kind of guy I could tell anything to," Sampras said. "We were getting closer and closer."

The deterioration of Sampras's health was a pity after an absolutely dominant performance for much of the season. Second-ranked Goran Ivanisevic wasn't even close to matching Sampras's exquisite form, and neither was anyone else. Sampras captured the Australian Open to start the year, won

A tuft of grass: Wimbledon memento for a great champion.

ground strokes and steady nerves. He won seven of eight tiebreakers as he worked his way through the draw to Sampras.

Sampras, meanwhile, was working up to a shockingly easy defeat of two-time defending champion Jim Courier, 6–3, 6–4, 6–4, in the semifinals. It marked the sixth time in seven meetings that Sampras beat former No. 1 Courier. Sampras's dominance may have accounted for the workmanlike Courier's bout of depression in '94, as he gradually fell in the rankings, first out of the Top 5 and then out of the Top 10 by year's end. Asked what he could do to interrupt Sampras's roll, Courier said, "Maybe break his leg on a changeover."

In the final against Martin, his good golfing buddy, Sampras was almost flaw-

the Italian Open in the spring, was defeated in the French Open quarterfinals and then glided to a second straight Wimbledon victory. However, he turned an ankle during the fortnight at the All England Club, and then developed tendinitis. Wimbledon represented his last good tennis of the year. Sampras's Australian title came over unheralded Todd Martin, playing in his first Grand Slam final, 7–6, 6–4, 6–4. The 6'6" Martin, 23, is an example of the new wealth of talent that exists in the U.S. only a few years after it seemed that no one would replace McEnroe and Connors. Barely ranked in the Top 100 at the start of '93, Martin rose to the Top 10 by the end of '94. In reaching the Australian final he displayed a 120 mph serve, lashing

less. Sampras, who has been labeled boring because he prefers to let his racket do the talking, had once again proved that you can be a great player and a nice guy at the same time. "I'm not going to apologize for trying to do this right," he said during the tournament, after former Australian great John Newcombe blasted him for not being more charismatic.

Sampras's all-court excellence gives him, in the minds of many observers, the best chance to accomplish a Grand Slam sweep in a calendar year since Rod Laver did it in 1969. Thus, no sooner had Sampras won the Australian than people were speculating on his chances at the French Open. But Sampras has never advanced beyond the quarters in Roland Garros, and he was stopped this time by Courier, who got a small measure of revenge. But Courier's victory was short-lived. He fell a day later himself to eventual champion Sergi Bruguera, who then won an all-Spanish final over countryman Alberto Berasategui in a hypnotically boring final, 6–3, 7–5, 2–6, 6–1.

The French was a far more interesting tournament on the women's side of the draw, where for two weeks 19-year-old Mary Pierce inspired the Parisian crowds to jubilant chants of "Mah-ree, Mah-ree!" with her sledgehammer game. Pierce lost just six games in her first five matches and stunned Graf in the semifinals 6–2, 6–2, to reach the first Grand Slam final of her career. It was almost unprecedented to see Graf outhit to such an extent. Although her loss to Sanchez Vicario in the final, 6–4, 6–4, was disappointing, Pierce, a young woman with three passports, a French mother and a home in Florida, had established herself as a beloved daughter of France and a new star. She had also proved that she should no longer be known as the abused daughter of Jim Pierce but simply as a fine tennis player. Over the last 12 months Pierce grew from a battered victim who obtained restraining orders to keep her father, formerly her coach, at bay, into a self-possessed young person. Jim Pierce has often made news with his disruptive outbursts and threatening behavior, which caused him to be banned from the tour. "I'm finally becoming Mary Pierce the player," Mary said later. "The true me is finally coming out."

Wimbledon was the exclusive property of Navratilova, which was as it should have been. Navratilova owns a record nine singles titles and is quite simply the greatest player in the history of the tournament, man or woman. If there was any doubt about that Navratilova promptly proved it once again by nearly adding a 10th title in her last singles performance at the All England Club.

It was as if fate made way for Navratilova, who entered the tournament uncertain of her chances after a first-round loss at the French. Graf, the three-time defending champion and winner of five of the last six Wimbledons, had the uncommon bad luck of drawing 22nd-ranked unseeded Lori McNeil as her first-round opponent. McNeil is an uneven but undeniably talented player who had beaten Graf in a previous meeting—at the 1992 Virginia Slims Championships—and also had a defeat of Evert to her credit in reaching the 1987 U.S. Open semifinals. Her lapses in concentration, however, had prevented her from cracking the Top 10. At Wimbledon, McNeil showed new resolve, no matter how late in her career it may be for a breakthrough. McNeil had learned some profound lessons as she struggled all year to cope with grief over the suicide in January of her father, Charlie, a former All Pro defensive back for the San Diego Chargers in the 1960s. "I was able to handle it better than I would have four or five years ago," McNeil said after her 7–5, 7–6 victory over Graf.

With Graf dispatched, Navratilova's remarkable progress became the centerpiece of the tournament. No one expected her to make the final, and Jana Novotna of Czechoslovakia even dared to speak of her as a thing of the past. "Her will is there, but the body just can't do it anymore," Novotna said. Right. That was before Navratilova dismissed Novotna in a three-set quarterfinal. Navratilova, of course, was the overwhelming sentimental favorite. But her opponent was a young Spaniard with inexhaustible legs and fresh ambition. As a girl Martinez had named the wall she practiced against "Martina." In the final she unfeelingly passed the legend with an array of laser ground strokes. But after Martinez completed her 6–4, 3–6, 6–3 victory, Navratilova had to hold her up, such was the shock of her first Grand Slam title over such a decorated opponent. Fittingly, Martinez was just one year older than Navratilova had been when she won her first Wimbledon, in 1978. As Navratilova left Centre Court for the last time, she stooped and pulled a tuft of grass from the court. "It's enough," she said. Later she reflected on the place she regards as her spiritual home. "It's like a relation-

Agassi charged back to prominence with a win in the U.S. Open.

ship where you love that person more and more," she said. "It gets deeper. And you know, it's been reciprocated. I feel this place in my bones."

Navratilova's appearance in the Wimbledon final, inspiring as it was, revealed a fascinating lack of order in the women's game. Were it not for Martinez and countrywoman Sanchez Vicario, Graf would have no consistent competition in the Top 5. Fortunately, Spain has filled the void.

At the U.S. Open no one could call Sanchez Vicario a handmaiden to Graf after she won what was possibly the best women's final of the last 10 years, 1–6, 7–6, 6–4. "Nobody can take away what I did," she said. She was right. Unthinkably Graf, with her back ailing and her enthusiasm flagging at the age of 25, had lost three straight Grand Slams in '94.

In the men's game Sampras was better able to maintain his hold on the rank and file. In his straight-set beheading of Ivanisevic in the Wimbledon final, Sampras established himself as the preeminent player of his generation. He became the first man since Becker in 1985 and '86 to win back-to-back Wimbledon titles, and he collected his fourth major championship in five events. He lost just one set in the entire tournament and dropped his serve just three times. His lead over Ivanisevic in the ATP rankings was already the largest in the history of the tour computer. With a total of five Grand Slam titles to his credit, Sampras showed that he is capable of reaching his ultimate goal, equaling idol Rod Laver's 11. "I'm getting there," he said. "I've proved to myself and other people I can go down in the record books." Sampras even showed a little *joie de vivre* when he took off his shirt and tossed it into the crowd. It was just unfortunate that Sampras's body betrayed him going into the U.S. Open, when the sore ankle prevented him from playing so much as a single warmup match. That he reached the round of 16 was a testament to his natural ability.

With Sampras gimpy, the Open belonged to that far more experienced shirt tosser, Andre Agassi. But then Agassi has always been a man of gestures rather than accomplishments. Last year it was Barbra Streisand causing a sensation as his courtside companion. This year it was Shields the supermodel. But Agassi hadn't won much outside of romance, sidelined by surgery and struggling to recuperate. Throughout his career, in fact, Agassi has been dangerously close to underachieving; his only major championship was the 1992 Wimbledon title. Agassi entered the Open unseeded and with five seeded players in his way. He defeated them all, including Michael Stich in the straight-set final, 6–1, 7–6, 7–5. Agassi unraveled Stich in the way a far more concentrated player, such as Sampras, would have. Was it a harbinger of consistency to come? Everyone hoped so, none more ardently than Agassi himself. "I feel I should have about four or five Grand Slam titles by now," he said. "It will be disappointing if I can't accomplish the things I'm capable of."

1994 Grand Slam Champions

Australian Open

Men's Singles

	Winner	Finalist	Score
Quarterfinals	Pete Sampras (1)	Magnus Gustaffson (10)	7-6 (7-4), 2-6, 6-3, 7-6 (7-4)
	Jim Courier (3)	Goran Ivanisevic (5)	7-6 (9-7), 6-4, 6-2
	Stefan Edberg (4)	Thomas Muster (6)	6-2, 6-3, 6-4
	Todd Martin (9)	MaliVai Washington	6-2, 7-6 (7-4), 7-6 (7-5)
Semifinals	Pete Sampras	Jim Courier	6-3, 6-4, 6-4
	Todd Martin	Stefan Edberg	3-6, 7-6 (9-7), 7-6 (9-7), 7-6 (7-4)
Final	Pete Sampras	Todd Martin	7-6 (7-4), 6-4, 6-4

Women's Singles

	Winner	Finalist	Score
Quarterfinals	Steffi Graf (1)	Lindsay Davenport	6-3, 6-2
	Arantxa Sanchez Vicario (2)	Manuela Maleeva (8)	7-6 (7-3), 6-4
	Gabriela Sabatini (4)	Jana Novotna (5)	6-3, 6-4
	Kimiko Date (10)	Conchita Martinez (3)	6-2, 4-6, 6-3
Semifinals	Steffi Graf	Kimiko Date	6-3, 6-3
	Arantxa Sanchez Vicario	Gabriela Sabatini	6-1, 6-2
Final	Steffi Graf	Arantxa Sanchez Vicario	6-0, 6-2

Doubles

	Winner	Finalist	Score
Men's Final	Jacco Eltingh/ Paul Haarhuis (3)	Byron Black/ Jonathan Stark (2)	6-7 (7-3), 6-3, 6-4, 6-3
Women's Final	Gigi Fernandez/ Natalia Zvereva (1)	Patty Fendick/ Meredith McGrath (7)	6-3, 4-6, 6-4
Mixed Final	Andrei Olhovskiy/ Larisa Neiland (6)	Todd Woodbridge/ Helena Sukova (1)	7-5, 6-7 (0-7), 6-2

French Open

Men's Singles

	Winner	Finalist	Score
Quarterfinals	Jim Courier (7)	Pete Sampras (1)	6-4, 5-7, 6-4, 6-4
	Sergi Bruguera (6)	Andrei Medvedev (4)	6-3, 6-2, 7-5
	Alberto Berasategui	Goran Ivanisevic (5)	6-4, 6-3, 6-3
	Magnus Larsson	Hendrik Dreekmann	3-6, 6-7 (7-1), 7-6 (7-3), 6-0, 6-1
Semifinals	Sergi Bruguera	Jim Courier	6-3, 5-7, 6-3, 6-3
	Alberto Berasategui	Magnus Larsson	6-3, 6-4, 6-1
Final	Sergi Bruguera	Alberto Berasategui	6-3, 7-5, 2-6, 6-1

Women's Singles

	Winner	Finalist	Score
Quarterfinals	Mary Pierce (12)	Petra Ritter	6-0, 6-2
	Steffi Graf (1)	Gorro Chategui	6-4, 6-1
	Conchita Martinez (3)	Sabine Hack (16)	2-6, 6-0, 6-2
	Arantxa Sanchez Vicario (2)	Julie Halard	6-1, 7-6 (8-6)
Semifinals	Mary Pierce	Steffi Graf	6-2, 6-2
	Arantxa Sanchez Vicario	Conchita Martinez	6-3, 6-1
Final	Arantxa Sanchez Vicario	Mary Pierce	6-4, 6-4

Note: Seedings in parentheses.

French Open *(Cont.)*

Doubles

	Winner	Finalist	Score
Men's Final	Byron Black/ Jonathan Stark (2)	Jan Apelle/ Jonas Bjorkman (12)	6-4, 7-6 (7-5)
Women's Final	Gigi Fernandez/ Natalia Zvereva (1)	Lindsay Davenport/ Lisa Raymond (11)	6-2, 6-2
Mixed Final	Kristie Boogert/ Menno Oosting	Larisa Neiland/ Andrei Olhovskiy (7)	7-5, 3-6, 7-5

Wimbledon

Men's Singles

	Winner	Finalist	Score
Quarterfinals	Pete Sampras (1)	Michael Chang (10)	6-4, 6-1, 6-3
	Boris Becker (7)	Christian Bergstrom	7-6 (7-5), 6-4, 6-3
	Goran Ivanisevic (4)	Guy Forget	7-6 (7-3), 7-6 (7-3), 6-4
	Todd Martin (6)	Wayne Ferreira	6-3, 6-2, 3-6, 5-7, 7-5
Semifinals	Pete Sampras	Todd Martin	6-4, 6-4, 3-6, 6-3
	Goran Ivanisevic	Boris Becker	6-2, 7-6 (8-6), 6-4
Final	Pete Sampras	Goran Ivanisevic	7-6 (7-2), 7-6 (7-5), 6-0

Women's Singles

	Winner	Finalist	Score
Quarterfinals	Lori McNeil	Larisa Neiland	6-3, 6-4
	Martina Navratilova (4)	Jana Novotna (5)	5-7, 6-0, 6-1
	Conchita Martinez (3)	Lindsay Davenport (9)	6-2, 6-7 (4-7), 6-3
	Gigi Fernandez	Zina Garrison-Jackson (13)	6-4, 6-4
Semifinals	Martina Navratilova	Gigi Fernandez	6-4, 7-6 (8-6)
	Conchita Martinez	Lori McNeil	3-6, 6-2, 7-6 (10-8)
Final	Conchita Martinez	Martina Navratilova	6-4, 3-6, 6-3

Doubles

	Winner	Finalist	Score
Men's Final	Todd Woodbridge/ Mark Woodforde (5)	Grant Connell/ Patrick Galbraith (2)	7-6 (7-3), 6-3, 6-1
Women's Final	Gigi Fernandez/ Natalia Zvereva (1)	Arantxa Sanchez Vicario/ Jana Novotna (2)	6-4, 6-1
Mixed Final	Todd Woodbridge/ Helena Sukova (4)	T.J. Middleton/ Lori McNeil	3-6, 7-5, 6-3

U.S. Open

Men's Singles

	Winner	Finalist	Score
Quarterfinals	Karel Novacek	Jaime Yzaga	6-2, 6-7 (9-7), 6-1, 5-7, 6-3
	Michael Stich (4)	Jonas Bjorkman	3-6, 6-3, 6-2, 6-7 (7-3), 6-3
	Andre Agassi	Thomas Muster (13)	7-6 (7-5), 6-3, 6-0
	Todd Martin (9)	Bernd Karbacher	6-2, 4-6, 6-3, 6-2
Semifinals	Michael Stich	Karel Novacek	7-5, 6-3, 7-6 (7-4)
	Andre Agassi	Todd Martin	6-3, 4-6, 6-2, 6-3
Final	Andre Agassi	Michael Stich	6-1, 7-6 (7-5), 7-5

Note: Seedings in parentheses.

Grand Slam Champions *(Cont.)*

U.S. Open *(Cont.)*

Women's Singles

	Winner	Finalist	Score
Quarterfinals	Steffi Graf (1)	Amanda Coetzer (11)	6-0, 6-2
	Jana Novotna (7)	Mary Pierce	6-4, 6-0
	Arantxa Sanchez Vicario(2)	Kimiko Date (5)	6-3, 6-0
	Gabriela Sabatini	Gigi Fernandez	6-2, 7-5
Semifinals	Arantxa Sanchez Vicario	Gabriela Sabatini	6-1, 7-6 (8-6)
	Steffi Graf	Jana Novotna	6-3, 7-5
Final	Arantxa Sanchez Vicario	Steffi Graf	1-6, 7-6 (7-3), 6-4

Doubles

	Winner	Finalist	Score
Men's Final	Jacco Eltingh/ Paul Haarhuis (3)	Todd Woodbridge/ Mark Woodforde (4)	6-3, 7-6 (7-1)
Women's Final	Jana Novotna/ Arantxa Sanchez-Vicario (2)	Katerina Maleeva/ Robin White	6--3, 6-3
Mixed Final	Elna Reinach/ Patrick Galbraith (8)	Jana Novotna/ Todd Woodbridge	6-2, 6-4

Note: Seedings in parentheses.

Major Tournament Results

Men's Tour (Late 1993)

Date	Tournament	Site	Winner	Finalist	Score
Sep 27-Oct 3	Swiss Indoors	Basel	Michael Stich	Stefan Edberg	6-4, 6-7 (7-5), 6-3, 6-2
Oct 4-10	Australian Indoor	Sydney	Jaime Yzaga	Petr Korda	6-4, 4-6, 7-6, 7-6
Oct 11-17	Seiko Super Tennis	Tokyo	Ivan Lendl	Todd Martin	6-4, 6-4
Oct 18-24	Grand Prix de Tennis	Lyon	Pete Sampras	Cedric Pioline	7-6, 1-6, 7-5
Oct 25-31	Stockholm Open	Stockholm	Michael Stich	Goran Ivanisevic	4-6, 7-6, 7-6, 6-2
Nov 1-7	Open de Paris	Paris	Goran Ivanisevic	Andrei Medvedev	6-4, 6-2, 7-6
Nov 8-14	European Community Championship	Antwerp, Belgium	Pete Sampras	Magnus Gustafsson	6-1, 6-4

Men's Tour (through September 11, 1994)

Date	Tournament	Site	Winner	Finalist	Score
Jan 17-30	Australian Open	Melbourne	Pete Sampras	Todd Martin	7-6 (7-4), 6-4, 6-4
Jan 31-Feb 6	Dubai Tennis Open	Dubai, United Arab Emirates	Magnus Gustafsson	Sergi Bruguera	6-4, 6-2
Feb 7-13	Muratti Time Indoor	Milan	Boris Becker	Petr Korda	6-2, 3-6, 6-3
Feb 14-20	Eurocard Open	Stuttgart	Stefan Edberg	Goran Ivanisevic	4-6, 6-4, 6-2, 6-2
Feb 28-Mar 6	Newsweek Champions Cup	Indian Wells, CA	Pete Sampras	Petr Korda	4-6, 6-3, 3-6, 6-3, 6-2
Mar 11-20	Lipton Intl Players Championships	Key Biscayne	Pete Sampras	Andre Agassi	5-7, 6-3, 6-3
Apr 4-10	Japan Open Tennis Championship	Tokyo	Pete Sampras	Michael Chang	6-4, 6-2
Apr 18-24	Volvo Monte Carlo Open	Monte Carlo	Andrei Medvedev	Sergi Bruguera	7-5, 6-1, 6-3
May 2-8	Panasonic German Open	Hamburg	Andrei Medvedev	Yevgeny Kafelnikov	6-4, 6-4, 3-6, 6-3
May 9-15	Mercedes Italian Open	Rome	Pete Sampras	Boris Becker	6-1, 6-2, 6-2
May 23-Jun 5	French Open	Paris	Sergi Bruguera	Alberto Berasategui	6-3, 7-5, 2-6, 6-1
Jun 20-July 3	Wimbledon Championships	Wimbledon	Pete Sampras	Goran Ivanisevic	7-6 (7-2), 7-6 (7-5), 6-0
July 18-24	Mercedes Cup	Stuttgart	Alberto Berasategui	Andrea Gaudenzi	7-5, 6-3, 7-6(5)

Men's Tour (through September 11) *(Cont.)*

Date	Tournament	Site	Winner	Finalist	Score
July 25-31	Canadian Open	Montreal	Andre Agassi	Jason Stoltenberg	6-4, 6-4
Aug 8-14	Thriftway ATP Championship	Cincinnati	Michael Chang	Stefan Edberg	6-2, 7-5
Aug 15-21	RCA/US Men's Hardcourt Championships	Indianapolis	Wayne Ferreira	Olivier Delaitre	6-2, 6-1
Aug 15-21	Volvo Intl Tennis Tournament	New Haven	Boris Becker	Marc Rosset	6-3, 7-5
Aug 29-Sep 11	US Open	New York	Andre Agassi	Michael Stich	6-1, 7-6 (7-5), 7-5

Women's Tour (Late 1993)

Date	Tournament	Site	Winner	Finalist	Score
Oct 4-10	Barilla Indoors	Zurich	Manuela Maleeva-Fragniere	Martina Navratilova	6-3, 7-6 (7-1)
Oct 11-17	Porsche Tennis Grand Prix	Filderstadt, Germany	Mary Pierce	Natalia Zvereva	6-3, 6-3
Oct 19-24	Autoglass Classic	Brighton, England	Jana Novotna	Anke Huber	6-2, 6-4
Oct 26-31	Nokia Grand Prix	Essen, Germany	Natalia Medvedeva	Conchita Martinez	6-7 (4-7), 7-5, 6-4
Nov 1-7	Bank of the West Classic	Oakland	Martina Navratilova	Zina Garrison-Jackson	6-2, 7-6 (7-1)
Nov 8-14	Virginia Slims of Philadelphia	Philadelphia	Conchita Martinez	Steffi Graf	6-3, 6-3
Nov 15-21	Virginia Slims Championships	New York	Steffi Graf	Arantxa Sanchez Vicario	6-1, 6-4, 3-6, 6-1

Women's Tour (through September 11, 1994)

Date	Tournament	Site	Winner	Finalist	Score
Jan 3-9	Danone Australian Hardcourt Championships	Brisbane	Lindsay Davenport	Florencia Labat	6-1, 2-6, 6-3
Jan 10-16	Peters NSW Open	Sydney	Kimiko Date	Mary Joe Fernandez	6-4, 6-2
Jan 17-30	Ford Australian Open	Melbourne	Steffi Graf	Arantxa Sanchez Vicario	6-0, 6-2
Feb 1-6	Toray Pan Pacific Open	Tokyo	Steffi Graf	Martina Navratilova	6-2, 6-4
Feb 7-13	Virginia Slims of Chicago	Chicago	Natalia Zvereva	Chanda Rubin	6-3, 7-5
Feb 15-20	Open Gaz de France	Paris	Martina Navratilova	Julie Halard	7-5, 6-3
Feb 28-Mar 6	Virginia Slims of Florida	Delray Beach	Steffi Graf	Arantxa Sanchez Vicario	6-3, 7-5
Mar 11-20	Lipton Intl Players Championships	Key Biscayne	Steffi Graf	Natalia Zvereva	4-6, 6-1, 6-2
Mar 21-27	Virginia Slims of Houston	Houston	Sabine Hack	Mary Pierce	7-5, 6-4
Mar 28-Apr 3	Family Circle Magazine Cup	Hilton Head Island, SC	Conchita Martinez	Natalia Zvereva	6-4, 6-0
Apr 4-10	Bausch & Lomb Championships	Amelia Island, FL	Arantxa Sanchez Vicario	Gabriela Sabatini	6-1, 6-4
Apr 19-24	International Championships of Spain	Barcelona	Arantxa Sanchez Vicario	Iva Majoli	6-0, 6-2
Apr 25-May 1	Citizen Cup	Hamburg	Arantxa Sanchez Vicario	Steffi Graf	4-6, 7-6 (7-3) 7-6 (8-6)
May 2-8	Italian Open	Rome	Conchita Martinez	Martina Navratilova	7-6 (7-5), 6-4

Women's Tour *(Cont.)*

Date	Tournament	Site	Winner	Finalist	Score
May 9-15	German Open	Berlin	Steffi Graf	Brenda Schultz	7-6 (8-6), 6-4
May 23-Jun 5	French Open	Paris	Arantxa Sanchez Vicario	Mary Pierce	6-4, 6-4
June 13-18	Volkswagen Cup	Eastbourne, England	Meredith McGrath	Linda Harvey-Wild	6-2, 6-4
Jun 20-July 3	Wimbledon Championships	Wimbledon	Conchita Martinez	Martina Navratilova	6-4, 3-6, 6-3
July 25-31	US Hardcourts	Stratton Mt, Vermont	Conchita Martinez	Arantxa Sanchez Vicario	4-6, 6-3, 6-4
Aug 1-7	Toshiba Tennis Classic	San Diego	Steffi Graf	Arantxa Sanchez Vicario	6-2, 6-1
Aug 8-14	Virginia Slims of L.A.	Manhattan Beach	Amy Frazier	Ann Grossman	6-1, 6-3
Aug 15-21	Canadian Open	Montreal	Arantxa Sanchez Vicario	Steffi Graf	7-5, 1-6, 7-6 (7-4)
Aug 29-Sep 11	US Open	New York	Arantxa Sanchez Vicario	Steffi Graf	1-6, 7-6 (7-3), 6-4

1993 Singles Leaders

Men

Rank	Player	Tournament Wins	Match Record	Earnings ($)
1	Pete Sampras	8	83–15	3,648,075
2	Michael Stich	6	73–24	2,936,521
3	Jim Courier	5	58–17	3,584,321
4	Sergi Bruguera	5	64–24	1,447,484
5	Stefan Edberg	1	59–25	2,309,509
6	Andrei Medvedev	3	57–24	1,301,143
7	Goran Ivanisevic	3	54–21	1,818,897
8	Michael Chang	6	65–20	1,743,524
9	Thomas Muster	7	77–20	805,066
10	Cedric Pioline	0	51–26	841,239
11	Boris Becker	2	41–19	1,765,839
12	Petr Korda	0	50–23	1,517,229
13	Todd Martin	1	45–22	642,108
14	Magnus Gustaffson	1	52–30	605,490
15	Richard Krajicek	1	35–22	729,753
16	Marc Rosset	3	49–22	622,733
17	Karel Novacek	2	43–25	682,306
18	Alexander Volkov	1	44–29	568,300
19	Ivan Lendl	2	33–23	1,075,876
20	Arnaud Boetsch	2	46–26	532,831

Note: Compiled by the Association of Tennis Professionals (ATP).

Women

Rank	Player	Tournament Wins	Match Record	Earnings ($)
1	Steffi Graf	10	76–6	2,809,012
2	Arantxa Sanchez Vicario	4	77–14	1,653,602
3	Martina Navratilova	5	46–8	925,722
4	Conchita Martinez	5	71–13	1,145,313
5	Gabriela Sabatini	0	51–18	955,471
6	Jana Novotna	2	47–17	669,192
7	Mary Joe Fernandez	1	34–13	543,306
8	Monica Seles*	2	17–2	437,589
9	Jennifer Capriati	1	29–11	354,214
10	Anke Huber	1	42–15	440,326
11	Manuela Maleeva-Fragniere	2	36–16	505,484
12	Mary Pierce	1	38–15	334,903
13	Kimiko Date	1	24–11	210,449
14	Zina Garrison-Jackson	2	43–19	318,386
15	Amanda Coetzer	2	42–19	352,417
16	Magdalena Maleeva	0	38–16	256,991
17	Helena Sukova	0	26–16	406,929
18	Nathalie Tauziat	1	44–19	299,514
19	Natalia Zvereva	0	37–19	323,994
20	Lindsay Davenport	1	38–6	170,944

Note: Compiled by the Women's Tennis Association (WTA).

*Injured April 30. Missed rest of season.

1993 Davis Cup

FINALS

Germany d. Australia 4-1 at Dusseldorf, Germany
Michael Stich (Ger) d. Jason Stoltenberg (Aus) 6-7, 6-3, 6-1, 6-3
Richard Fromberg (Aus) d. Marc Goellner (Ger) 3-6, 5-7, 7-6 (9-7), 6-2, 9-7
M Stich and P Kuhnen (Ger) d. T Woodbridge and M Woodforde (Aus) 7-6, 4-6, 6-3, 7-6
Michael Stich (Ger) d. Richard Fromberg (Aus) 6-4, 6-2, 6-2
Marc Goellner d Jason Stoltenberg 6-1, 6-7 (2-7), 7-6 (7-3)

1994 Davis Cup

FIRST ROUND

United States d. India 5-0.
Netherlands d. Belgium 5-0.
Sweden d. Denmark 5-0.
France d. Hungary 4-1.
Czech Republic d. Israel 4-1.
Russia d. Australia 4-1.
Italy d. Spain 4-1.
Austria d. Germany 3-2.

QUARTER FINAL ROUND

United States d. Netherlands 3-2.
Sweden d. France 3-2.
Russia d. Czech Republic 3-2.
Germany d. Spain 3-2.

FINAL: Russia versus Sweden to be held Dec.2-4 in Russia.

SEMIFINALS

Sweden d. United States 3-2 at Goteburg, Sweden.
Todd Martin (U.S.) d. Stefan Edberg (Swe)
Pete Sampras (U.S.) d. Magnus Larsson (Swe)
Jan Apell and Jonas Bjorkman (Swe) d. Jared Palmer and Jonathan Stark (U.S.)
Stefan Edberg (Swe) d. Pete Sampras (U.S.)(RET)
Magnus Larsson (Swe) d. Todd Martin (U.S)

Russia d. Germany 4-1 at Hamburg Germany
Yevgeny Kafelnikov (Rus) d. Bernd Karbacher (Ger)
Alexander Volkov (Rus) d. Michael Stich (Ger)
Yevgeny Kafelnikov and Andrei Olhovskiy (Rus) d. Michael Stich and Kaarsten Braasch
Yevgeny Kafelnikov (Rus) d. Michael Stich (Ger)
Bernd Karbacher (Ger) d. Alexander Volkov (Rus)

1994 Federation Cup

FIRST ROUND

Spain d. Chile 3-0
Argentina d. Cuba 3-0
Sweden d. Belgium 2-1
Japan d. China 2-1
Germany d. Colombia 3-0
Slovak Republic d. Finland 2-1
South Africa d. Paraguay 3-0
The Netherlands d. Belarus 2-1
Bulgaria d. Croatia 2-1
Indonesia d. Chinese Taipei 2-1
Italy d. Denmark 2-1
France d. North Korea 3-0
Austria d. Poland 2-1
Australia d. Latvia 2-1
Canada d. Switzerland 3-0
United States d. Czech Republic 3-0

SECOND ROUND

Spain d. Argentina 3-0
Japan d. Sweden 3-0
Germany d. Slovak Republic 2-1
South Africa d. The Netherlands 2-1
Bulgaria d. Indonesia 3-0
France d. Italy 3-0
Austria d. Australia 2-1
United States d. Canada 3-0

QUARTERFINALS

Spain d. Japan 3-0
Germany d. South Africa 3-0
France d. Bulgaria 2-1
United States d. Austria 3-0

SEMIFINALS

Spain d. Germany 2-1
Sabine Hack (Ger) d. Conchita Martinez (Spain) 2-6, 7-5, 6-4
Arantxa Sanchez Vicario (Spain) d. Anke Huber (Ger) 4-6, 6-0, 7-5
C. Martinez and A. Sanchez-Vicario (Spain) d. B. Rittner and C. Singer (Ger) 7-5, 6-1.

United States d. France 3-0
Mary Joe Fernandez (U.S.) d. Julie Halard (Fra) 6-1, 6-3
Lindsay Davenport (U.S.) d. Mary Pierce (Fra) 5-7, 6-2, 6-2
Gigi Fernandez and Zina Garrison-Jackson (U.S.) d. Julie Halard and Nathalie Tauziat (Fra) 3-6, 6-1, 6-2

FINALS

Spain d. United States 3-0
Conchita Martinez (Spain) d. Mary Joe Fernandez (U.S.) 6-2, 6-2
Arantxa Sanchez Vicario (Spain) d. Lindsay Davenport (U.S.) 6-2, 6-1
Arantxa Sanchez Vicario and Conchita Martinez (Spain) d. Gigi Fernandez and Mary Joe Fernandez (U.S.) 6-3, 6-4.

Note: Held at Frankfurt, Germany, July 18-24, 1994

FOR THE RECORD·Year by Year

Grand Slam Tournaments

MEN
Australian Championships

Year	Winner	Finalist	Score
1905	Rodney Heath	A. H. Curtis	4-6, 6-3, 6-4, 6-4
1906	Tony Wilding	H. A. Parker	6-0, 6-4, 6-4
1907	Horace M. Rice	H. A. Parker	6-3, 6-4, 6-4
1908	Fred Alexander	A. W. Dunlop	3-6, 3-6, 6-0, 6-2, 6-3
1909	Tony Wilding	E. F. Parker	6-1, 7-5, 6-2
1910	Rodney Heath	Horace M. Rice	6-4, 6-3, 6-2
1911	Norman Brookes	Horace M. Rice	6-1, 6-2, 6-3
1912	J. Cecil Parke	A. E. Beamish	3-6, 6-3, 1-6, 6-1, 7-5
1913	E. F. Parker	H. A. Parker	2-6, 6-1, 6-2, 6-3
1914	Pat O'Hara Wood	G. L. Patterson	6-4, 6-3, 5-7, 6-1
1915	Francis G. Lowe	Horace M. Rice	4-6, 6-1, 6-1, 6-4
1916-18	No tournament		
1919	A. R. F. Kingscote	E. O. Pockley	6-4, 6-0, 6-3
1920	Pat O'Hara Wood	Ron Thomas	6-3, 4-6, 6-8, 6-1, 6-3
1921	Rhys H. Gemmell	A. Hedeman	7-5, 6-1, 6-4
1922	Pat O'Hara Wood	Gerald Patterson	6-0, 3-6, 3-6, 6-3, 6-2
1923	Pat O'Hara Wood	C. B. St John	6-1, 6-1, 6-3
1924	James Anderson	R. E. Schlesinger	6-3, 6-4, 3-6, 5-7, 6-3
1925	James Anderson	Gerald Patterson	11-9, 2-6, 6-2, 6-3
1926	John Hawkes	J. Willard	6-1, 6-3, 6-1
1927	Gerald Patterson	John Hawkes	3-6, 6-4, 3-6, 18-16, 6-3
1928	Jean Borotra	R. O. Cummings	6-4, 6-1, 4-6, 5-7, 6-3
1929	John C. Gregory	R. E. Schlesinger	6-2, 6-2, 5-7, 7-5
1930	Gar Moon	Harry C. Hopman	6-3, 6-1, 6-3
1931	Jack Crawford	Harry C. Hopman	6-4, 6-2, 2-6, 6-1
1932	Jack Crawford	Harry C. Hopman	4-6, 6-3, 3-6, 6-3, 6-1
1933	Jack Crawford	Keith Gledhill	2-6, 7-5, 6-3, 6-2
1934	Fred Perry	Jack Crawford	6-3, 7-5, 6-1
1935	Jack Crawford	Fred Perry	2-6, 6-4, 6-4, 6-4
1936	Adrian Quist	Jack Crawford	6-2, 6-3, 4-6, 3-6, 9-7
1937	Vivian B. McGrath	John Bromwich	6-3, 1-6, 6-0, 2-6, 6-1
1938	Don Budge	John Bromwich	6-4, 6-2, 6-1
1939	John Bromwich	Adrian Quist	6-4, 6-1, 6-3
1940	Adrian Quist	Jack Crawford	6-3, 6-1, 6-2
1941-45	No tournament		
1946	John Bromwich	Dinny Pails	5-7, 6-3, 7-5, 3-6, 6-2
1947	Dinny Pails	John Bromwich	4-6, 6-4, 3-6, 7-5, 8-6
1948	Adrian Quist	John Bromwich	6-4, 3-6, 6-3, 2-6, 6-3
1949	Frank Sedgman	Ken McGregor	6-3, 6-3, 6-2
1950	Frank Sedgman	Ken McGregor	6-3, 6-4, 4-6, 6-1
1951	Richard Savitt	Ken McGregor	6-3, 2-6, 6-3, 6-1
1952	Ken McGregor	Frank Sedgman	7-5, 12-10, 2-6, 6-2
1953	Ken Rosewall	Mervyn Rose	6-0, 6-3, 6-4
1954	Mervyn Rose	Rex Hartwig	6-2, 0-6, 6-4, 6-2
1955	Ken Rosewall	Lew Hoad	9-7, 6-4, 6-4
1956	Lew Hoad	Ken Rosewall	6-4, 3-6, 6-4, 7-5
1957	Ashley Cooper	Neale Fraser	6-3, 9-11, 6-4, 6-2
1958	Ashley Cooper	Mal Anderson	7-5, 6-3, 6-4
1959	Alex Olmedo	Neale Fraser	6-1, 6-2, 3-6, 6-3
1960	Rod Laver	Neale Fraser	5-7, 3-6, 6-3, 8-6, 8-6
1961	Roy Emerson	Rod Laver	1-6, 6-3, 7-5, 6-4
1962	Rod Laver	Roy Emerson	8-6, 0-6, 6-4, 6-4
1963	Roy Emerson	Ken Fletcher	6-3, 6-3, 6-1
1964	Roy Emerson	Fred Stolle	6-3, 6-4, 6-2
1965	Roy Emerson	Fred Stolle	7-9, 2-6, 6-4, 7-5, 6-1
1966	Roy Emerson	Arthur Ashe	6-4, 6-8, 6-2, 6-3
1967	Roy Emerson	Arthur Ashe	6-4, 6-1, 6-1
1968	Bill Bowrey	Juan Gisbert	7-5, 2-6, 9-7, 6-4
1969*	Rod Laver	Andres Gimeno	6-3, 6-4, 7-5
1970	Arthur Ashe	Dick Crealy	6-4, 9-7, 6-2
1971	Ken Rosewall	Arthur Ashe	6-1, 7-5, 6-3

Australian Championships *(Cont.)*

Year	Winner	Finalist	Score
1972	Ken Rosewall	Mal Anderson	7-6, 6-3, 7-5
1973	John Newcombe	Onny Parun	6-3, 6-7, 7-5, 6-1
1974	Jimmy Connors	Phil Dent	7-6, 6-4, 4-6, 6-3
1975	John Newcombe	Jimmy Connors	7-5, 3-6, 6-4, 7-5
1976	Mark Edmondson	John Newcombe	6-7, 6-3, 7-6, 6-1
1977 (Jan)	Roscoe Tanner	Guillermo Vilas	6-3, 6-3, 6-3
1977 (Dec)	Vitas Gerulaitis	John Lloyd	6-3, 7-6, 5-7, 3-6, 6-2
1978	Guillermo Vilas	John Marks	6-4, 6-4, 3-6, 6-3
1979	Guillermo Vilas	John Sadri	7-6, 6-3, 6-2
1980	Brian Teacher	Kim Warwick	7-5, 7-6, 6-3
1981	Johan Kriek	Steve Denton	6-2, 7-6, 6-7, 6-4
1982	Johan Kriek	Steve Denton	6-3, 6-3, 6-2
1983	Mats Wilander	Ivan Lendl	6-1, 6-4, 6-4
1984	Mats Wilander	Kevin Curren	6-7, 6-4, 7-6, 6-2
1985 (Dec)	Stefan Edberg	Mats Wilander	6-4, 6-3, 6-3
1987 (Jan)	Stefan Edberg	Pat Cash	6-3, 6-4, 3-6, 5-7, 6-3
1988	Mats Wilander	Pat Cash	6-3, 6-7, 3-6, 6-1, 8-6
1989	Ivan Lendl	Miloslav Mecir	6-2, 6-2, 6-2
1990	Ivan Lendl	Stefan Edberg	4-6, 7-6, 5-2 ret
1991	Boris Becker	Ivan Lendl	1-6, 6-4, 6-4, 6-4
1992	Jim Courier	Stefan Edberg	6-3, 3-6, 6-4, 6-2
1993	Jim Courier	Stefan Edberg	6-2, 6-1, 2-6, 7-5
1994	Pete Sampras	Todd Martin	7-6 (7-4), 6-4, 6-4

*Became Open (amateur and professional) in 1969.

French Championships

Year	Winner	Finalist	Score
1925†	Rene Lacoste	Jean Borotra	7-5, 6-1, 6-4
1926	Henri Cochet	Rene Lacoste	6-2, 6-4, 6-3
1927	Rene Lacoste	Bill Tilden	6-4, 4-6, 5-7, 6-3, 11-9
1928	Henri Cochet	Rene Lacoste	5-7, 6-3, 6-1, 6-3
1929	Rene Lacoste	Jean Borotra	6-3, 2-6, 6-0, 2-6, 8-6
1930	Henri Cochet	Bill Tilden	3-6, 8-6, 6-3, 6-1
1931	Jean Borotra	Claude Boussus	2-6, 6-4, 7-5, 6-4
1932	Henri Cochet	Giorgio de Stefani	6-0, 6-4, 4-6, 6-3
1933	Jack Crawford	Henri Cochet	8-6, 6-1, 6-3
1934	Gottfried von Cramm	Jack Crawford	6-4, 7-9, 3-6, 7-5, 6-3
1935	Fred Perry	Gottfried von Cramm	6-3, 3-6, 6-1, 6-3
1936	Gottfried von Cramm	Fred Perry	6-0, 2-6, 6-2, 2-6, 6-0
1937	Henner Henkel	Henry Austin	6-1, 6-4, 6-3
1938	Don Budge	Roderick Menzel	6-3, 6-2, 6-4
1939	Don McNeill	Bobby Riggs	7-5, 6-0, 6-3
1940	No tournament		
1941‡	Bernard Destremau	n/a	n/a
1942‡	Bernard Destremau	n/a	n/a
1943‡	Yvon Petra	n/a	n/a
1944‡	Yvon Petra	n/a	n/a
1945‡	Yvon Petra	Bernard Destremau	7-5, 6-4, 6-2
1946	Marcel Bernard	Jaroslav Drobny	3-6, 2-6, 6-1, 6-4, 6-3
1947	Joseph Asboth	Eric Sturgess	8-6, 7-5, 6-4
1948	Frank Parker	Jaroslav Drobny	6-4, 7-5, 5-7, 8-6
1949	Frank Parker	Budge Patty	6-3, 1-6, 6-1, 6-4
1950	Budge Patty	Jaroslav Drobny	6-1, 6-2, 3-6, 5-7, 7-5
1951	Jaroslav Drobny	Eric Sturgess	6-3, 6-3, 6-3
1952	Jaroslav Drobny	Frank Sedgman	6-2, 6-0, 3-6, 6-4
1953	Ken Rosewall	Vic Seixas	6-3, 6-4, 1-6, 6-2
1954	Tony Trabert	Arthur Larsen	6-4, 7-5, 6-1
1955	Tony Trabert	Sven Davidson	2-6, 6-1, 6-4, 6-2
1956	Lew Hoad	Sven Davidson	6-4, 8-6, 6-3
1957	Sven Davidson	Herbie Flam	6-3, 6-4, 6-4
1958	Mervyn Rose	Luis Ayala	6-3, 6-4, 6-4
1959	Nicola Pietrangeli	Ian Vermaak	3-6, 6-3, 6-4, 6-1
1960	Nicola Pietrangeli	Luis Ayala	3-6, 6-3, 6-4, 4-6, 6-3
1961	Manuel Santana	Nicola Pietrangeli	4-6, 6-1, 3-6, 6-0, 6-2
1962	Rod Laver	Roy Emerson	3-6, 2-6, 6-3, 9-7, 6-2

French Championships *(Cont.)*

Year	Winner	Finalist	Score
1963	Roy Emerson	Pierre Darmon	3-6, 6-1, 6-4, 6-4
1964	Manuel Santana	Nicola Pietrangeli	6-3, 6-1, 4-6, 7-5
1965	Fred Stolle	Tony Roche	3-6, 6-0, 6-2, 6-3
1966	Tony Roche	Istvan Gulyas	6-1, 6-4, 7-5
1967	Roy Emerson	Tony Roche	6-1, 6-4, 2-6, 6-2
1968*	Ken Rosewall	Rod Laver	6-3, 6-1, 2-6, 6-2
1969	Rod Laver	Ken Rosewall	6-4, 6-3, 6-4
1970	Jan Kodes	Zeljko Franulovic	6-2, 6-4, 6-0
1971	Jan Kodes	Ilie Nastase	8-6, 6-2, 2-6, 7-5
1972	Andres Gimeno	Patrick Proisy	4-6, 6-3, 6-1, 6-1
1973	Ilie Nastase	Nikki Pilic	6-3, 6-3, 6-0
1974	Bjorn Borg	Manuel Orantes	6-7, 6-0, 6-1, 6-1
1975	Bjorn Borg	Guillermo Vilas	6-2, 6-3, 6-4
1976	Adriano Panatta	Harold Solomon	6-1, 6-4, 4-6, 7-6
1977	Guillermo Vilas	Brian Gottfried	6-0, 6-3, 6-0
1978	Bjorn Borg	Guillermo Vilas	6-1, 6-1, 6-3
1979	Bjorn Borg	Victor Pecci	6-3, 6-1, 6-7, 6-4
1980	Bjorn Borg	Vitas Gerulaitis	6-4, 6-1, 6-2
1981	Bjorn Borg	Ivan Lendl	6-1, 4-6, 6-2, 3-6, 6-1
1982	Mats Wilander	Guillermo Vilas	1-6, 7-6, 6-0, 6-4
1983	Yannick Noah	Mats Wilander	6-2, 7-5, 7-6
1984	Ivan Lendl	John McEnroe	3-6, 2-6, 6-4, 7-5, 7-5
1985	Mats Wilander	Ivan Lendl	3-6, 6-4, 6-2, 6-2
1986	Ivan Lendl	Mikael Pernfors	6-3, 6-2, 6-4
1987	Ivan Lendl	Mats Wilander	7-5, 6-2, 3-6, 7-6
1988	Mats Wilander	Henri Leconte	7-5, 6-2, 6-1
1989	Michael Chang	Stefan Edberg	6-1, 3-6, 4-6, 6-4, 6-2
1990	Andres Gomez	Andre Agassi	6-3, 2-6, 6-4, 6-4
1991	Jim Courier	Andre Agassi	3-6, 6-4, 2-6, 6-1, 6-4
1992	Jim Courier	Petr Korda	7-5, 6-2, 6-1
1993	Sergi Bruguera	Jim Courier	6-4, 2-6, 6-2, 3-6, 6-3
1994	Sergi Bruguera	Alberto Berasategui	6-3, 7-5, 2-6, 6-1

†1925 was the first year that entries were accepted from all countries.
‡From 1941 to 1945 the event was called Tournoi de France and was closed to all foreigners.
*Became Open (amateur and professional) in 1968 but closed to contract professionals in 1972.

Wimbledon Championships

Year	Winner	Finalist	Score
1877	Spencer W. Gore	William C. Marshall	6-1, 6-2, 6-4
1878	P. Frank Hadow	Spencer W. Gore	7-5, 6-1, 9-7
1879	John T. Hartley	V. St Leger Gould	6-2, 6-4, 6-2
1880	John T. Hartley	Herbert F. Lawford	6-0, 6-2, 2-6, 6-3
1881	William Renshaw	John T. Hartley	6-0, 6-2, 6-1
1882	William Renshaw	Ernest Renshaw	6-1, 2-6, 4-6, 6-2, 6-2
1883	William Renshaw	Ernest Renshaw	2-6, 6-3, 6-3, 4-6, 6-3
1884	William Renshaw	Herbert F. Lawford	6-0, 6-4, 9-7
1885	William Renshaw	Herbert F. Lawford	7-5, 6-2, 4-6, 7-5
1886	William Renshaw	Herbert F. Lawford	6-0, 5-7, 6-3, 6-4
1887	Herbert F. Lawford	Ernest Renshaw	1-6, 6-3, 3-6, 6-4, 6-4
1888	Ernest Renshaw	Herbert F. Lawford	6-3, 7-5, 6-0
1889	William Renshaw	Ernest Renshaw	6-4, 6-1, 3-6, 6-0
1890	William J. Hamilton	William Renshaw	6-8, 6-2, 3-6, 6-1, 6-1
1891	Wilfred Baddeley	Joshua Pim	6-4, 1-6, 7-5, 6-0
1892	Wilfred Baddeley	Joshua Pim	4-6, 6-3, 6-3, 6-2
1893	Joshua Pim	Wilfred Baddeley	3-6, 6-1, 6-3, 6-2
1894	Joshua Pim	Wilfred Baddeley	10-8, 6-2, 8-6
1895	Wilfred Baddeley	Wilberforce V. Eaves	4-6, 2-6, 8-6, 6-2, 6-3
1896	Harold S. Mahoney	Wilfred Baddeley	6-2, 6-8, 5-7, 8-6, 6-3
1897	Reggie F. Doherty	Harold S. Mahoney	6-4, 6-4, 6-3
1898	Reggie F. Doherty	H. Laurie Doherty	6-3, 6-3, 2-6, 5-7, 6-1
1899	Reggie F. Doherty	Arthur W. Gore	1-6, 4-6, 6-2, 6-3, 6-3
1900	Reggie F. Doherty	Sidney H. Smith	6-8, 6-3, 6-1, 6-2
1901	Arthur W. Gore	Reggie F. Doherty	4-6, 7-5, 6-4, 6-4
1902	H. Laurie Doherty	Arthur W. Gore	6-4, 6-3, 3-6, 6-0

Wimbledon Championship (Cont.)

Year	Winner	Finalist	Score
1903	H. Laurie Doherty	Frank L. Riseley	7-5, 6-3, 6-0
1904	H. Laurie Doherty	Frank L. Riseley	6-1, 7-5, 8-6
1905	H. Laurie Doherty	Norman E. Brookes	8-6, 6-2, 6-4
1906	H. Laurie Doherty	Frank L. Riseley	6-4, 4-6, 6-2, 6-3
1907	Norman E. Brookes	Arthur W. Gore	6-4, 6-2, 6-2
1908	Arthur W. Gore	H. Roper Barrett	6-3, 6-2, 4-6, 3-6, 6-4
1909	Arthur W. Gore	M. J. G. Ritchie	6-8, 1-6, 6-2, 6-2, 6-2
1910	Anthony F. Wilding	Arthur W. Gore	6-4, 7-5, 4-6, 6-2
1911	Anthony F. Wilding	H. Roper Barrett	6-4, 4-6, 2-6, 6-2 ret
1912	Anthony F. Wilding	Arthur W. Gore	6-4, 6-4, 4-6, 6-4
1913	Anthony F. Wilding	Maurice E. McLoughlin	8-6, 6-3, 10-8
1914	Norman E. Brookes	Anthony F. Wilding	6-4, 6-4, 7-5
1915-18	No tournament		
1919	Gerald L. Patterson	Norman E. Brookes	6-3, 7-5, 6-2
1920	Bill Tilden	Gerald L. Patterson	2-6, 6-3, 6-2, 6-4
1921	Bill Tilden	Brian I. C. Norton	4-6, 2-6, 6-1, 6-0, 7-5
1922	Gerald L. Patterson	Randolph Lycett	6-3, 6-4, 6-2
1923	Bill Johnston	Francis T. Hunter	6-0, 6-3, 6-1
1924	Jean Borotra	Rene Lacoste	6-1, 3-6, 6-1, 3-6, 6-4
1925	Rene Lacoste	Jean Borotra	6-3, 6-3, 4-6, 8-6
1926	Jean Borotra	Howard Kinsey	8-6, 6-1, 6-3
1927	Henri Cochet	Jean Borotra	4-6, 4-6, 6-3, 6-4, 7-5
1928	Rene Lacoste	Henri Cochet	6-1, 4-6, 6-4, 6-2
1929	Henri Cochet	Jean Borotra	6-4, 6-3, 6-4
1930	Bill Tilden	Wilmer Allison	6-3, 9-7, 6-4
1931	Sidney B. Wood Jr	Francis X. Shields	walkover
1932	Ellsworth Vines	Henry Austin	6-4, 6-2, 6-0
1933	Jack Crawford	Ellsworth Vines	4-6, 11-9, 6-2, 2-6, 6-4
1934	Fred Perry	Jack Crawford	6-3, 6-0, 7-5
1935	Fred Perry	Gottfried von Cramm	6-2, 6-4, 6-4
1936	Fred Perry	Gottfried von Cramm	6-1, 6-1, 6-0
1937	Don Budge	Gottfried von Cramm	6-3, 6-4, 6-2
1938	Don Budge	Henry Austin	6-1, 6-0, 6-3
1939	Bobby Riggs	Elwood Cooke	2-6, 8-6, 3-6, 6-3, 6-2
1940-45	No tournament		
1946	Yvon Petra	Geoff E. Brown	6-2, 6-4, 7-9, 5-7, 6-4
1947	Jack Kramer	Tom P. Brown	6-1, 6-3, 6-2
1948	Bob Falkenburg	John Bromwich	7-5, 0-6, 6-2, 3-6, 7-5
1949	Ted Schroeder	Jaroslav Drobny	3-6, 6-0, 6-3, 4-6, 6-4
1950	Budge Patty	Frank Sedgman	6-1, 8-10, 6-2, 6-3
1951	Dick Savitt	Ken McGregor	6-4, 6-4, 6-4
1952	Frank Sedgman	Jaroslav Drobny	4-6, 6-3, 6-2, 6-3
1953	Vic Seixas	Kurt Nielsen	9-7, 6-3, 6-4
1954	Jaroslav Drobny	Ken Rosewall	13-11, 4-6, 6-2, 9-7
1955	Tony Trabert	Kurt Nielsen	6-3, 7-5, 6-1
1956	Lew Hoad	Ken Rosewall	6-2, 4-6, 7-5, 6-4
1957	Lew Hoad	Ashley Cooper	6-2, 6-1, 6-2
1958	Ashley Cooper	Neale Fraser	3-6, 6-3, 6-4, 13-11
1959	Alex Olmedo	Rod Laver	6-4, 6-3, 6-4
1960	Neale Fraser	Rod Laver	6-4, 3-6, 9-7, 7-5
1961	Rod Laver	Chuck McKinley	6-3, 6-1, 6-4
1962	Rod Laver	Martin Mulligan	6-2, 6-2, 6-1
1963	Chuck McKinley	Fred Stolle	9-7, 6-1, 6-4
1964	Roy Emerson	Fred Stolle	6-4, 12-10, 4-6, 6-3
1965	Roy Emerson	Fred Stolle	6-2, 6-4, 6-4
1966	Manuel Santana	Dennis Ralston	6-4, 11-9, 6-4
1967	John Newcombe	Wilhelm Bungert	6-3, 6-1, 6-1
1968*	Rod Laver	Tony Roche	6-3, 6-4, 6-2
1969	Rod Laver	John Newcombe	6-4, 5-7, 6-4, 6-4
1970	John Newcombe	Ken Rosewall	5-7, 6-3, 6-2, 3-6, 6-1
1971	John Newcombe	Stan Smith	6-3, 5-7, 2-6, 6-4, 6-4
1972	Stan Smith	Ilie Nastase	4-6, 6-3, 6-3, 4-6, 7-5
1973	Jan Kodes	Alex Metreveli	6-1, 9-8, 6-3
1974	Jimmy Connors	Ken Rosewall	6-1, 6-1, 6-4
1975	Arthur Ashe	Jimmy Connors	6-1, 6-1, 5-7, 6-4
1976	Bjorn Borg	Ilie Nastase	6-4, 6-2, 9-7

Wimbledon Championships *(Cont.)*

Year	Winner	Finalist	Score
1977	Bjorn Borg	Jimmy Connors	3-6, 6-2, 6-1, 5-7, 6-4
1978	Bjorn Borg	Jimmy Connors	6-2, 6-2, 6-3
1979	Bjorn Borg	Roscoe Tanner	6-7, 6-1, 3-6, 6-3, 6-4
1980	Bjorn Borg	John McEnroe	1-6, 7-5, 6-3, 6-7, 8-6
1981	John McEnroe	Bjorn Borg	4-6, 7-6, 7-6, 6-4
1982	Jimmy Connors	John McEnroe	3-6, 6-3, 6-7, 7-6, 6-4
1983	John McEnroe	Chris Lewis	6-2, 6-2, 6-2
1984	John McEnroe	Jimmy Connors	6-1, 6-1, 6-2
1985	Boris Becker	Kevin Curren	6-3, 6-7, 7-6, 6-4
1986	Boris Becker	Ivan Lendl	6-4, 6-3, 7-5
1987	Pat Cash	Ivan Lendl	7-6, 6-2, 7-5
1988	Stefan Edberg	Boris Becker	4-6, 7-6, 6-4, 6-2
1989	Boris Becker	Stefan Edberg	6-0, 7-6, 6-4
1990	Stefan Edberg	Boris Becker	6-2, 6-2, 3-6, 3-6, 6-4
1991	Michael Stich	Boris Becker	6-4, 7-6, 6-4
1992	Andre Agassi	Goran Ivanisevic	6-7, 6-4, 6-4, 1-6, 6-4
1993	Pete Sampras	Jim Courier	7-6 (7-3), 7-6 (8-6), 3-6, 6-3
1994	Pete Sampras	Goran Ivanisevic	7-6 (7-2), 7-6 (7-5), 6-0

*Became Open (amateur and professional) in 1968 but closed to contract professionals in 1972.

Note: Prior to 1922 the tournament was run on a challenge-round system. The previous year's winner "stood out" of an All Comers event, which produced a challenger to play him for the title.

United States Championships

Year	Winner	Finalist	Score
1881	Richard D. Sears	W. E. Glyn	6-0, 6-3, 6-2
1882	Richard D. Sears	C. M. Clark	6-1, 6-4, 6-0
1883	Richard D. Sears	James Dwight	6-2, 6-0, 9-7
1884	Richard D. Sears	H. A. Taylor	6-0, 1-6, 6-0, 6-2
1885	Richard D. Sears	G. M. Brinley	6-3, 4-6, 6-0, 6-3
1886	Richard D. Sears	R. L. Beeckman	4-6, 6-1, 6-3, 6-4
1887	Richard D. Sears	H. W. Slocum Jr	6-1, 6-3, 6-2
1888‡	H. W. Slocum Jr	H. A. Taylor	6-4, 6-1, 6-0
1889	H. W. Slocum Jr	Q. A. Shaw	6-3, 6-1, 4-6, 6-2
1890	Oliver S. Campbell	H. W. Slocum Jr	6-2, 4-6, 6-3, 6-1
1891	Oliver S. Campbell	Clarence Hobart	2-6, 7-5, 7-9, 6-1, 6-2
1892	Oliver S. Campbell	Frederick H. Hovey	7-5, 3-6, 6-3, 7-5
1893‡	Robert D. Wrenn	Frederick H. Hovey	6-4, 3-6, 6-4, 6-4
1894	Robert D. Wrenn	M. F. Goodbody	6-8, 6-1, 6-4, 6-4
1895	Frederick H. Hovey	Robert D. Wrenn	6-3, 6-2, 6-4
1896	Robert D. Wrenn	Frederick H. Hovey	7-5, 3-6, 6-0, 1-6, 6-1
1897	Robert D. Wrenn	Wilberforce V. Eaves	4-6, 8-6, 6-3, 2-6, 6-2
1898‡	Malcolm D. Whitman	Dwight F. Davis	3-6, 6-2, 6-2, 6-1
1899	Malcolm D. Whitman	J. Parmly Paret	6-1, 6-2, 3-6, 7-5
1900	Malcolm D. Whitman	William A. Larned	6-4, 1-6, 6-2, 6-2
1901‡	William A. Larned	Beals C. Wright	6-2, 6-8, 6-4, 6-4
1902	William A. Larned	Reggie F. Doherty	4-6, 6-2, 6-4, 8-6
1903	H. Laurie Doherty	William A. Larned	6-0, 6-3, 10-8
1904‡	Holcombe Ward	William J. Clothier	10-8, 6-4, 9-7
1905	Beals C. Wright	Holcombe Ward	6-2, 6-1, 11-9
1906	William J. Clothier	Beals C. Wright	6-3, 6-0, 6-4
1907‡	William A. Larned	Robert LeRoy	6-2, 6-2, 6-4
1908	William A. Larned	Beals C. Wright	6-1, 6-2, 8-6
1909	William A. Larned	William J. Clothier	6-1, 6-2, 5-7, 1-6, 6-1
1910	William A. Larned	Thomas C. Bundy	6-1, 5-7, 6-0, 6-8, 6-1
1911	William A. Larned	Maurice E. McLoughlin	6-4, 6-4, 6-2
1912†	Maurice E. McLoughlin	Bill Johnson	3-6, 2-6, 6-2, 6-4, 6-2
1913	Maurice E. McLoughlin	Richard N. Williams	6-4, 5-7, 6-3, 6-1
1914	Richard N. Williams	Maurice E. McLoughlin	6-3, 8-6, 10-8
1915	Bill Johnston	Maurice E. McLoughlin	1-6, 6-0, 7-5, 10-8
1916	Richard N. Williams	Bill Johnston	4-6, 6-4, 0-6, 6-2, 6-4
1917#	R. L. Murray	N. W. Niles	5-7, 8-6, 6-3, 6-3
1918	R. L. Murray	Bill Tilden	6-3, 6-1, 7-5
1919	Bill Johnston	Bill Tilden	6-4, 6-4, 6-3
1920	Bill Tilden	Bill Johnston	6-1, 1-6, 7-5, 5-7, 6-3

United States Championships *(Cont.)*

Year	Winner	Finalist	Score
1921	Bill Tilden	Wallace F. Johnson	6-1, 6-3, 6-1
1922	Bill Tilden	Bill Johnston	4-6, 3-6, 6-2, 6-3, 6-4
1923	Bill Tilden	Bill Johnston	6-4, 6-1, 6-4
1924	Bill Tilden	Bill Johnston	6-1, 9-7, 6-2
1925	Bill Tilden	Bill Johnston	4-6, 11-9, 6-3, 4-6, 6-3
1926	Rene Lacoste	Jean Borotra	6-4, 6-0, 6-4
1927	Rene Lacoste	Bill Tilden	11-9, 6-3, 11-9
1928	Henri Cochet	Francis T. Hunter	4-6, 6-4, 3-6, 7-5, 6-3
1929	Bill Tilden	Francis T. Hunter	3-6, 6-3, 4-6, 6-2, 6-4
1930	John H. Doeg	Francis X. Shields	10-8, 1-6, 6-4, 16-14
1931	Ellsworth Vines	George M. Lott Jr	7-9, 6-3, 9-7, 7-5
1932	Ellsworth Vines	Henri Cochet	6-4, 6-4, 6-4
1933	Fred Perry	Jack Crawford	6-3, 11-13, 4-6, 6-0, 6-1
1934	Fred Perry	Wilmer L. Allison	6-4, 6-3, 1-6, 8-6
1935	Wilmer L. Allison	Sidney B. Wood Jr	6-2, 6-2, 6-3
1936	Fred Perry	Don Budge	2-6, 6-2, 8-6, 1-6, 10-8
1937	Don Budge	Gottfried von Cramm	6-1, 7-9, 6-1, 3-6, 6-1
1938	Don Budge	Gene Mako	6-3, 6-8, 6-2, 6-1
1939	Bobby Riggs	Welby van Horn	6-4, 6-2, 6-4
1940	Don McNeill	Bobby Riggs	4-6, 6-8, 6-3, 6-3, 7-5
1941	Bobby Riggs	Francis Kovacs II	5-7, 6-1, 6-3, 6-3
1942	Ted Schroeder	Frank Parker	8-6, 7-5, 3-6, 4-6, 6-2
1943	Joseph R. Hunt	Jack Kramer	6-3, 6-8, 10-8, 6-0
1944	Frank Parker	William F. Talbert	6-4, 3-6, 6-3, 6-3
1945	Frank Parker	William F. Talbert	14-12, 6-1, 6-2
1946	Jack Kramer	Tom P. Brown	9-7, 6-3, 6-0
1947	Jack Kramer	Frank Parker	4-6, 2-6, 6-1, 6-0, 6-3
1948	Pancho Gonzales	Eric W. Sturgess	6-2, 6-3, 14-12
1949	Pancho Gonzales	Ted Schroeder	16-18, 2-6, 6-1, 6-2, 6-4
1950	Arthur Larsen	Herbie Flam	6-3, 4-6, 5-7, 6-4, 6-3
1951	Frank Sedgman	Vic Seixas	6-4, 6-1, 6-1
1952	Frank Sedgman	Gardnar Mulloy	6-1, 6-2, 6-3
1953	Tony Trabert	Vic Seixas	6-3, 6-2, 6-3
1954	Vic Seixas	Rex Hartwig	3-6, 6-2, 6-4, 6-4
1955	Tony Trabert	Ken Rosewall	9-7, 6-3, 6-3
1956	Ken Rosewall	Lew Hoad	4-6, 6-2, 6-3, 6-3
1957	Mal Anderson	Ashley J. Cooper	10-8, 7-5, 6-4
1958	Ashley J. Cooper	Mal Anderson	6-2, 3-6, 4-6, 10-8, 8-6
1959	Neale Fraser	Alex Olmedo	6-3, 5-7, 6-2, 6-4
1960	Neale Fraser	Rod Laver	6-4, 6-4, 9-7
1961	Roy Emerson	Rod Laver	7-5, 6-3, 6-2
1962	Rod Laver	Roy Emerson	6-2, 6-4, 5-7, 6-4
1963	Rafael Osuna	Frank Froehling III	7-5, 6-4, 6-2
1964	Roy Emerson	Fred Stolle	6-4, 6-2, 6-4
1965	Manuel Santana	Cliff Drysdale	6-2, 7-9, 7-5, 6-1
1966	Fred Stolle	John Newcombe	4-6, 12-10, 6-3, 6-4
1967	John Newcombe	Clark Graebner	6-4, 6-4, 8-6
1968**	Arthur Ashe	Bob Lutz	4-6, 6-3, 8-10, 6-0, 6-4
1968*	Arthur Ashe	Tom Okker	14-12, 5-7, 6-3, 3-6, 6-3
1969**	Stan Smith	Bob Lutz	9-7, 6-3, 6-1
1969*	Rod Laver	Tony Roche	7-9, 6-1, 6-3, 6-2
1970	Ken Rosewall	Tony Roche	2-6, 6-4, 7-6, 6-3
1971	Stan Smith	Jan Kodes	3-6, 6-3, 6-2, 7-6
1972	Ilie Nastase	Arthur Ashe	3-6, 6-3, 6-7, 6-4, 6-3
1973	John Newcombe	Jan Kodes	6-4, 1-6, 4-6, 6-2, 6-3
1974	Jimmy Connors	Ken Rosewall	6-1, 6-0, 6-1
1975	Manuel Orantes	Jimmy Connors	6-4, 6-3, 6-3
1976	Jimmy Connors	Bjorn Borg	6-4, 3-6, 7-6, 6-4
1977	Guillermo Vilas	Jimmy Connors	2-6, 6-3, 7-6, 6-0
1978	Jimmy Connors	Bjorn Borg	6-4, 6-2, 6-2
1979	John McEnroe	Vitas Gerulaitis	7-5, 6-3, 6-3
1980	John McEnroe	Bjorn Borg	7-6, 6-1, 6-7, 5-7, 6-4
1981	John McEnroe	Bjorn Borg	4-6, 6-2, 6-4, 6-3
1982	Jimmy Connors	Ivan Lendl	6-3, 6-2, 4-6, 6-4
1983	Jimmy Connors	Ivan Lendl	6-3, 6-7, 7-5, 6-0
1984	John McEnroe	Ivan Lendl	6-3, 6-4, 6-1

United States Championships *(Cont.)*

Year	Winner	Finalist	Score
1985	Ivan Lendl	John McEnroe	7-6, 6-3, 6-4
1986	Ivan Lendl	Miloslav Mecir	6-4, 6-2, 6-0
1987	Ivan Lendl	Mats Wilander	6-7, 6-0, 7-6, 6-4
1988	Mats Wilander	Ivan Lendl	6-4, 4-6, 6-3, 5-7, 6-4
1989	Boris Becker	Ivan Lendl	7-6, 1-6, 6-3, 7-6
1990	Pete Sampras	Andre Agassi	6-4, 6-3, 6-2
1991	Stefan Edberg	Jim Courier	6-2, 6-4, 6-0
1992	Stefan Edberg	Pete Sampras	3-6, 6-4, 7-6, 6-2
1993	Pete Sampras	Cédric Pioline	6-4, 6-4, 6-3
1994	Andre Agassi	Michael Stich	6-1, 7-6 (7-5), 7-5

*Became Open (amateur and professional) in 1968; †Challenge round abolished; ‡No challenge round played.
#National Patriotic Tournament; **Amateur event held.

WOMEN
Australian Championships

Year	Winner	Finalist	Score
1922	Margaret Molesworth	Esna Boyd	6-3, 10-8
1923	Margaret Molesworth	Esna Boyd	6-1, 7-5
1924	Sylvia Lance	Esna Boyd	6-3, 3-6, 6-4
1925	Daphne Akhurst	Esna Boyd	1-6, 8-6, 6-4
1926	Daphne Akhurst	Esna Boyd	6-1, 6-3
1927	Esna Boyd	Sylvia Harper	5-7, 6-1, 6-2
1928	Daphne Akhurst	Esna Boyd	7-5, 6-2
1929	Daphne Akhurst	Louise Bickerton	6-1, 5-7, 6-2
1930	Daphne Akhurst	Sylvia Harper	10-8, 2-6, 7-5
1931	Coral Buttsworth	Margorie Crawford	1-6, 6-3, 6-4
1932	Coral Buttsworth	Kathrine Le Messurier	9-7, 6-4
1933	Joan Hartigan	Coral Buttsworth	6-4, 6-3
1934	Joan Hartigan	Margaret Molesworth	6-1, 6-4
1935	Dorothy Round	Nancye Wynne Bolton	1-6, 6-1, 6-3
1936	Joan Hartigan	Nancye Wynne Bolton	6-4, 6-4
1937	Nancye Wynne Bolton	Emily Westacott	6-3, 5-7, 6-4
1938	Dorothy Bundy	D. Stevenson	6-3, 6-2
1939	Emily Westacott	Nell Hopman	6-1, 6-2
1940	Nancye Wynne Bolton	Thelma Coyne	5-7, 6-4, 6-0
1941-45	No tournament		
1946	Nancye Wynne Bolton	Joyce Fitch	6-4, 6-4
1947	Nancye Wynne Bolton	Nell Hopman	6-3, 6-2
1948	Nancye Wynne Bolton	Marie Toomey	6-3, 6-1
1949	Doris Hart	Nancye Wynne Bolton	6-3, 6-4
1950	Louise Brough	Doris Hart	6-4, 3-6, 6-4
1951	Nancye Wynne Bolton	Thelma Long	6-1, 7-5
1952	Thelma Long	H. Angwin	6-2, 6-3
1953	Maureen Connolly	Julia Sampson	6-3, 6-2
1954	Thelma Long	J. Staley	6-3, 6-4
1955	Beryl Penrose	Thelma Long	6-4, 6-3
1956	Mary Carter	Thelma Long	3-6, 6-2, 9-7
1957	Shirley Fry	Althea Gibson	6-3, 6-4
1958	Angela Mortimer	Lorraine Coghlan	6-3, 6-4
1959	Mary Carter-Reitano	Renee Schuurman	6-2, 6-3
1960	Margaret Smith	Jan Lehane	7-5, 6-2
1961	Margaret Smith	Jan Lehane	6-1, 6-4
1962	Margaret Smith	Jan Lehane	6-0, 6-2
1963	Margaret Smith	Jan Lehane	6-2, 6-2
1964	Margaret Smith	Lesley Turner	6-3, 6-2
1965	Margaret Smith	Maria Bueno	5-7, 6-4, 5-2 ret
1966	Margaret Smith	Nancy Richey	Default
1967	Nancy Richey	Lesley Turner	6-1, 6-4
1968	Billie Jean King	Margaret Smith	6-1, 6-2
1969*	Margaret Smith Court	Billie Jean King	6-4, 6-1
1970	Margaret Smith Court	Kerry Melville Reid	6-3, 6-1
1971	Margaret Smith Court	Evonne Goolagong	2-6, 7-6, 7-5
1972	Virginia Wade	Evonne Goolagong	6-4, 6-4

Australian Championships *(Cont.)*

Year	Winner	Finalist	Score
1973	Margaret Smith Court	Evonne Goolagong	6-4, 7-5
1974	Evonne Goolagong	Chris Evert	7-6, 4-6, 6-0
1975	Evonne Goolagong	Martina Navratilova	6-3, 6-2
1976	Evonne Goolagong Cawley	Renata Tomanova	6-2, 6-2
1977 (Jan)	Kerry Melville Reid	Dianne Balestrat	7-5, 6-2
1977 (Dec)	Evonne Goolagong Cawley	Helen Gourlay	6-3, 6-0
1978	Chris O'Neil	Betsy Nagelsen	6-3, 7-6
1979	Barbara Jordan	Sharon Walsh	6-3, 6-3
1980	Hana Mandlikova	Wendy Turnbull	6-0, 7-5
1981	Martina Navratilova	Chris Evert Lloyd	6-7, 6-4, 7-5
1982	Chris Evert Lloyd	Martina Navratilova	6-3, 2-6, 6-3
1983	Martina Navratilova	Kathy Jordan	6-2, 7-6
1984	Chris Evert Lloyd	Helena Sukova	6-7, 6-1, 6-3
1985 (Dec)	Martina Navratilova	Chris Evert Lloyd	6-2, 4-6, 6-2
1987 (Jan)	Hana Mandlikova	Martina Navratilova	7-5, 7-6
1988	Steffi Graf	Chris Evert	6-1, 7-6
1989	Steffi Graf	Helena Sukova	6-4, 6-4
1990	Steffi Graf	Mary Joe Fernandez	6-3, 6-4
1991	Monica Seles	Jana Novotna	5-7, 6-3, 6-1
1992	Monica Seles	Mary Joe Fernandez	6-2, 6-3
1993	Monica Seles	Steffi Graf	4-6, 6-3, 6-2
1994	Steffi Graf	Arantxa Sanchez Vicario	6-0, 6-2

*Became Open (amateur and professional) in 1969.

French Championships

Year	Winner	Finalist	Score
1925†	Suzanne Lenglen	Kathleen McKane	6-1, 6-2
1926	Suzanne Lenglen	Mary K. Browne	6-1, 6-0
1927	Kea Bouman	Irene Peacock	6-2, 6-4
1928	Helen Wills	Eileen Bennett	6-1, 6-2
1929	Helen Wills	Simone Mathieu	6-3, 6-4
1930	Helen Wills Moody	Helen Jacobs	6-2, 6-1
1931	Cilly Aussem	Betty Nuthall	8-6, 6-1
1932	Helen Wills Moody	Simone Mathieu	7-5, 6-1
1933	Margaret Scriven	Simone Mathieu	6-2, 4-6, 6-4
1934	Margaret Scriven	Helen Jacobs	7-5, 4-6, 6-1
1935	Hilde Sperling	Simone Mathieu	6-2, 6-1
1936	Hilde Sperling	Simone Mathieu	6-3, 6-4
1937	Hilde Sperling	Simone Mathieu	6-2, 6-4
1938	Simone Mathieu	Nelly Landry	6-0, 6-3
1939	Simone Mathieu	Jadwiga Jedrzejowska	6-3, 8-6
1940-45	No tournament		
1946	Margaret Osborne	Pauline Betz	1-6, 8-6, 7-5
1947	Patricia Todd	Doris Hart	6-3, 3-6, 6-4
1948	Nelly Landry	Shirley Fry	6-2, 0-6, 6-0
1949	Margaret Osborne duPont	Nelly Adamson	7-5, 6-2
1950	Doris Hart	Patricia Todd	6-4, 4-6, 6-2
1951	Shirley Fry	Doris Hart	6-3, 3-6, 6-3
1952	Doris Hart	Shirley Fry	6-4, 6-4
1953	Maureen Connolly	Doris Hart	6-2, 6-4
1954	Maureen Connolly	Ginette Bucaille	6-4, 6-1
1955	Angela Mortimer	Dorothy Knode	2-6, 7-5, 10-8
1956	Althea Gibson	Angela Mortimer	6-0, 12-10
1957	Shirley Bloomer	Dorothy Knode	6-1, 6-3
1958	Zsuzsi Kormoczi	Shirley Bloomer	6-4, 1-6, 6-2
1959	Christine Truman	Zsuzsi Kormoczi	6-4, 7-5
1960	Darlene Hard	Yola Ramirez	6-3, 6-4
1961	Ann Haydon	Yola Ramirez	6-2, 6-1
1962	Margaret Smith	Lesley Turner	6-3, 3-6, 7-5
1963	Lesley Turner	Ann Haydon Jones	2-6, 6-3, 7-5
1964	Margaret Smith	Maria Bueno	5-7, 6-1, 6-2
1965	Lesley Turner	Margaret Smith	6-3, 6-4
1966	Ann Jones	Nancy Richey	6-3, 6-1
1967	Francoise Durr	Lesley Turner	4-6, 6-3, 6-4

French Championships *(Cont.)*

Year	Winner	Finalist	Score
1968*	Nancy Richey	Ann Jones	5-7, 6-4, 6-1
1969	Margaret Smith Court	Ann Jones	6-1, 4-6, 6-3
1970	Margaret Smith Court	Helga Niessen	6-2, 6-4
1971	Evonne Goolagong	Helen Gourlay	6-3, 7-5
1972	Billie Jean King	Evonne Goolagong	6-3, 6-3
1973	Margaret Smith Court	Chris Evert	6-7, 7-6, 6-4
1974	Chris Evert	Olga Morozova	6-1, 6-2
1975	Chris Evert	Martina Navratilova	2-6, 6-2, 6-1
1976	Sue Barker	Renata Tomanova	6-2, 0-6, 6-2
1977	Mima Jausovec	Florenza Mihai	6-2, 6-7, 6-1
1978	Virginia Ruzici	Mima Jausovec	6-2, 6-2
1979	Chris Evert Lloyd	Wendy Turnbull	6-2, 6-0
1980	Chris Evert Lloyd	Virginia Ruzici	6-0, 6-3
1981	Hana Mandlikova	Sylvia Hanika	6-2, 6-4
1982	Martina Navratilova	Andrea Jaeger	7-6, 6-1
1983	Chris Evert Lloyd	Mima Jausovec	6-1, 6-2
1984	Martina Navratilova	Chris Evert Lloyd	6-3, 6-1
1985	Chris Evert Lloyd	Martina Navratilova	6-3, 6-7, 7-5
1986	Chris Evert Lloyd	Martina Navratilova	2-6, 6-3, 6-3
1987	Steffi Graf	Martina Navratilova	6-4, 4-6, 8-6
1988	Steffi Graf	Natalia Zvereva	6-0, 6-0
1989	Arantxa Sanchez Vicario	Steffi Graf	7-6, 3-6, 7-5
1990	Monica Seles	Steffi Graf	7-6, 6-4
1991	Monica Seles	Arantxa Sanchez Vicario	6-3, 6-4
1992	Monica Seles	Steffi Graf	6-2, 3-6, 10-8
1993	Steffi Graf	Mary Joe Fernandez	4-6, 6-2, 6-4
1994	Arantxa Sanchez Vicario	Mary Pierce	6-4, 6-4

*Became Open (amateur and professional) in 1968 but closed to contract professionals in 1972.

†1925 was the first year that entries were accepted from all countries.

Wimbledon Championships

Year	Winner	Finalist	Score
1884	Maud Watson	Lilian Watson	6-8, 6-3, 6-3
1885	Maud Watson	Blanche Bingley	6-1, 7-5
1886	Blanche Bingley	Maud Watson	6-3, 6-3
1887	Charlotte Dod	Blanche Bingley	6-2, 6-0
1888	Charlotte Dod	Blanche Bingley Hillyard	6-3, 6-3
1889	Blanche Bingley Hillyard		
1890	Lena Rice		
1891	Charlotte Dod		
1892	Charlotte Dod	Blanche Bingley Hillyard	6-1, 6-1
1893	Charlotte Dod	Blanche Bingley Hillyard	6-8, 6-1, 6-4
1894	Blanche Bingley Hillyard		
1895	Charlotte Cooper		
1896	Charlotte Cooper	Mrs. W. H. Pickering	6-2, 6-3
1897	Blanche Bingley Hillyard	Charlotte Cooper	5-7, 7-5, 6-2
1898	Charlotte Cooper		
1899	Blanche Bingley Hillyard	Charlotte Cooper	6-2, 6-3
1900	Blanche Bingley Hillyard	Charlotte Cooper	4-6, 6-4, 6-4
1901	Charlotte Cooper Sterry	Blanche Bingley Hillyard	6-2, 6-2
1902	Muriel Robb	Charlotte Cooper Sterry	7-5, 6-1
1903	Dorothea Douglass		
1904	Dorothea Douglass	Charlotte Cooper Sterry	6-0, 6-3
1905	May Sutton	Dorothea Douglass	6-3, 6-4
1906	Dorothea Douglass	May Sutton	6-3, 9-7
1907	May Sutton	Dorothea Douglass Lambert Chambers	6-1, 6-4
1908	Charlotte Cooper Sterry		
1909	Dora Boothby		
1910	Dorothea Douglass Lambert Chambers	Dora Boothby	6-2, 6-2
1911	Dorothea Douglass Lambert Chambers	Dora Boothby	6-0, 6-0
1912	Ethel Larcombe		

Wimbledon Championships *(Cont.)*

Year	Winner	Finalist	Score
1913	Dorothea Douglass Lambert Chambers		
1914	Dorothea Douglass Lambert Chambers	Ethel Larcombe	7-5, 6-4
1915-18	No tournament		
1919	Suzanne Lenglen	Dorothea Douglass Lambert Chambers	10-8, 4-6, 9-7
1920	Suzanne Lenglen	Dorothea Douglass Lambert Chambers	6-3, 6-0
1921	Suzanne Lenglen	Elizabeth Ryan	6-2, 6-0
1922	Suzanne Lenglen	Molla Mallory	6-2, 6-0
1923	Suzanne Lenglen	Kathleen McKane	6-2, 6-2
1924	Kathleen McKane	Helen Wills	4-6, 6-4, 6-2
1925	Suzanne Lenglen	Joan Fry	6-2, 6-0
1926	Kathleen McKane Godfree	Lili de Alvarez	6-2, 4-6, 6-3
1927	Helen Wills	Lili de Alvarez	6-2, 6-4
1928	Helen Wills	Lili de Alvarez	6-2, 6-3
1929	Helen Wills	Helen Jacobs	6-1, 6-2
1930	Helen Wills Moody	Elizabeth Ryan	6-2, 6-2
1931	Cilly Aussem	Hilde Kranwinkel	7-5, 7-5
1932	Helen Wills Moody	Helen Jacobs	6-3, 6-1
1933	Helen Wills Moody	Dorothy Round	6-4, 6-8, 6-3
1934	Dorothy Round	Helen Jacobs	6-2, 5-7, 6-3
1935	Helen Wills Moody	Helen Jacobs	6-3, 3-6, 7-5
1936	Helen Jacobs	Hilde Kranwinkel Sperling	6-2, 4-6, 7-5
1937	Dorothy Round	Jadwiga Jedrzejowska	6-2, 2-6, 7-5
1938	Helen Wills Moody	Helen Jacobs	6-4, 6-0
1939	Alice Marble	Kay Stammers	6-2, 6-0
1940-45	No tournament		
1946	Pauline Betz	Louise Brough	6-2, 6-4
1947	Margaret Osborne	Doris Hart	6-2, 6-4
1948	Louise Brough	Doris Hart	6-3, 8-6
1949	Louise Brough	Margaret Osborne duPont	10-8, 1-6, 10-8
1950	Louise Brough	Margaret Osborne duPont	6-1, 3-6, 6-1
1951	Doris Hart	Shirley Fry	6-1, 6-0
1952	Maureen Connolly	Louise Brough	6-4, 6-3
1953	Maureen Connolly	Doris Hart	8-6, 7-5
1954	Maureen Connolly	Louise Brough	6-2, 7-5
1955	Louise Brough	Beverly Fleitz	7-5, 8-6
1956	Shirley Fry	Angela Buxton	6-3, 6-1
1957	Althea Gibson	Darlene Hard	6-3, 6-2
1958	Althea Gibson	Angela Mortimer	8-6, 6-2
1959	Maria Bueno	Darlene Hard	6-4, 6-3
1960	Maria Bueno	Sandra Reynolds	8-6, 6-0
1961	Angela Mortimer	Christine Truman	4-6, 6-4, 7-5
1962	Karen Hantze Susman	Vera Sukova	6-4, 6-4
1963	Margaret Smith	Billie Jean Moffitt	6-3, 6-4
1964	Maria Bueno	Margaret Smith	6-4, 7-9, 6-3
1965	Margaret Smith	Maria Bueno	6-4, 7-5
1966	Billie Jean King	Maria Bueno	6-3, 3-6, 6-1
1967	Billie Jean King	Ann Haydon Jones	6-3, 6-4
1968*	Billie Jean King	Judy Tegart	9-7, 7-5
1969	Ann Haydon Jones	Billie Jean King	3-6, 6-3, 6-2
1970	Margaret Smith Court	Billie Jean King	14-12, 11-9
1971	Evonne Goolagong	Margaret Smith Court	6-4, 6-1
1972	Billie Jean King	Evonne Goolagong	6-3, 6-3
1973	Billie Jean King	Chris Evert	6-0, 7-5
1974	Chris Evert	Olga Morozova	6-0, 6-4
1975	Billie Jean King	Evonne Goolagong Cawley	6-0, 6-1
1976	Chris Evert	Evonne Goolagong Cawley	6-3, 4-6, 8-6
1977	Virginia Wade	Betty Stove	4-6, 6-3, 6-1
1978	Martina Navratilova	Chris Evert	2-6, 6-4, 7-5
1979	Martina Navratilova	Chris Evert Lloyd	6-4, 6-4
1980	Evonne Goolagong Cawley	Chris Evert Lloyd	6-1, 7-6
1981	Chris Evert Lloyd	Hana Mandlikova	6-2, 6-2
1982	Martina Navratilova	Chris Evert Lloyd	6-1, 3-6, 6-2

Wimbledon Championships *(Cont.)*

Year	Winner	Finalist	Score
1983	Martina Navratilova	Andrea Jaeger	6-0, 6-3
1984	Martina Navratilova	Chris Evert Lloyd	7-6, 6-2
1985	Martina Navratilova	Chris Evert Lloyd	4-6, 6-3, 6-2
1986	Martina Navratilova	Hana Mandlikova	7-6, 6-3
1987	Martina Navratilova	Steffi Graf	7-5, 6-3
1988	Steffi Graf	Martina Navratilova	5-7, 6-2, 6-1
1989	Steffi Graf	Martina Navratilova	6-2, 6-7, 6-1
1990	Martina Navratilova	Zina Garrison	6-4, 6-1
1991	Steffi Graf	Gabriela Sabatini	6-4, 3-6, 8-6
1992	Steffi Graf	Monica Seles	6-2, 6-1
1993	Steffi Graf	Jana Novotna	7-6 (8-6), 1-6, 6-4
1994	Conchita Martinez	Martina Navratilova	6-4, 3-6, 6-3

*Became Open (amateur and professional) in 1968 but closed to contract professionals in 1972.

Note: Prior to 1922 the tournament was run on a challenge round system. The previous year's winner "stood out" of an All Comers event, which produced a challenger to play her for the title.

United States Championships

Year	Winner	Finalist	Score
1887	Ellen Hansell	Laura Knight	6-1, 6-0
1888	Bertha L. Townsend	Ellen Hansell	6-3, 6-5
1889	Bertha L. Townsend	Louise Voorhes	7-5, 6-2
1890	Ellen C. Roosevelt	Bertha L. Townsend	6-2, 6-2
1891	Mabel Cahill	Ellen C. Roosevelt	6-4, 6-1, 4-6, 6-3
1892	Mabel Cahill	Elisabeth Moore	5-7, 6-3, 6-4, 4-6, 6-2
1893	Aline Terry	Alice Schultze	6-1, 6-3
1894	Helen Hellwig	Aline Terry	7-5, 3-6, 6-0, 3-6, 6-3
1895	Juliette Atkinson	Helen Hellwig	6-4, 6-2, 6-1
1896	Elisabeth Moore	Juliette Atkinson	6-4, 4-6, 6-2, 6-2
1897	Juliette Atkinson	Elisabeth Moore	6-3, 6-3, 4-6, 3-6, 6-3
1898	Juliette Atkinson	Marion Jones	6-3, 5-7, 6-4, 2-6, 7-5
1899	Marion Jones	Maud Banks	6-1, 6-1, 7-5
1900	Myrtle McAteer	Edith Parker	6-2, 6-2, 6-0
1901	Elisabeth Moore	Myrtle McAteer	6-4, 3-6, 7-5, 2-6, 6-2
1902**	Marion Jones	Elisabeth Moore	6-1, 1-0 retired
1903	Elisabeth Moore	Marion Jones	7-5, 8-6
1904	May Sutton	Elisabeth Moore	6-1, 6-2
1905	Elisabeth Moore	Helen Homans	6-4, 5-7, 6-1
1906	Helen Homans	Maud Barger-Wallach	6-4, 6-3
1907	Evelyn Sears	Carrie Neely	6-3, 6-2
1908	Maud Barger-Wallach	Evelyn Sears	6-3, 1-6, 6-3
1909	Hazel Hotchkiss	Maud Barger-Wallach	6-0, 6-1
1910	Hazel Hotchkiss	Louise Hammond	6-4, 6-2
1911	Hazel Hotchkiss	Florence Sutton	8-10, 6-1, 9-7
1912†	Mary K. Browne	Eleanora Sears	6-4, 6-2
1913	Mary K. Browne	Dorothy Green	6-2, 7-5
1914	Mary K. Browne	Marie Wagner	6-2, 1-6, 6-1
1915	Molla Bjurstedt	Hazel Hotchkiss Wightman	4-6, 6-2, 6-0
1916	Molla Bjurstedt	Louise Hammond Raymond	6-0, 6-1
1917‡	Molla Bjurstedt	Marion Vanderhoef	4-6, 6-0, 6-2
1918	Molla Bjurstedt	Eleanor Goss	6-4, 6-3
1919	Hazel Hotchkiss Wightman	Marion Zinderstein	6-1, 6-2
1920	Molla Bjurstedt Mallory	Marion Zinderstein	6-3, 6-1
1921	Molla Bjurstedt Mallory	Mary K. Browne	4-6, 6-4, 6-2
1922	Molla Bjurstedt Mallory	Helen Wills	6-3, 6-1
1923	Helen Wills	Molla Bjurstedt Mallory	6-2, 6-1
1924	Helen Wills	Molla Bjurstedt Mallory	6-1, 6-3
1925	Helen Wills	Kathleen McKane	3-6, 6-0, 6-2
1926	Molla Bjurstedt Mallory	Elizabeth Ryan	4-6, 6-4, 9-7
1927	Helen Wills	Betty Nuthall	6-1, 6-4
1928	Helen Wills	Helen Jacobs	6-2, 6-1
1929	Helen Wills	Phoebe Holcroft Watson	6-4, 6-2
1930	Betty Nuthall	Anna McCune Harper	6-1, 6-4
1931	Helen Wills Moody	Eileen Whitingstall	6-4, 6-1
1932	Helen Jacobs	Carolin Babcock	6-2, 6-2

United States Championship *(Cont.)*

Year	Winner	Finalist	Score
1933	Helen Jacobs	Helen Wills Moody	8-6, 3-6, 3-0 retired
1934	Helen Jacobs	Sarah Palfrey	6-1, 6-4
1935	Helen Jacobs	Sarah Palfrey Fabyan	6-2, 6-4
1936	Alice Marble	Helen Jacobs	4-6, 6-3, 6-2
1937	Anita Lizane	Jadwiga Jedrzejowska	6-4, 6-2
1938	Alice Marble	Nancye Wynne	6-0, 6-3
1939	Alice Marble	Helen Jacobs	6-0, 8-10, 6-4
1940	Alice Marble	Helen Jacobs	6-2, 6-3
1941	Sarah Palfrey Cooke	Pauline Betz	7-5, 6-2
1942	Pauline Betz	Louise Brough	4-6, 6-1, 6-4
1943	Pauline Betz	Louise Brough	6-3, 5-7, 6-3
1944	Pauline Betz	Margaret Osborne	6-3, 8-6
1945	Sarah Palfrey Cooke	Pauline Betz	3-6, 8-6, 6-4
1946	Pauline Betz	Patricia Canning	11-9, 6-3
1947	Louise Brough	Margaret Osborne	8-6, 4-6, 6-1
1948	Margaret Osborne duPont	Louise Brough	4-6, 6-4, 15-13
1949	Margaret Osborne duPont	Doris Hart	6-4, 6-1
1950	Margaret Osborne duPont	Doris Hart	6-4, 6-3
1951	Maureen Connolly	Shirley Fry	6-3, 1-6, 6-4
1952	Maureen Connolly	Doris Hart	6-3, 7-5
1953	Maureen Connolly	Doris Hart	6-2, 6-4
1954	Doris Hart	Louise Brough	6-8, 6-1, 8-6
1955	Doris Hart	Patricia Ward	6-4, 6-2
1956	Shirley Fry	Althea Gibson	6-3, 6-4
1957	Althea Gibson	Louise Brough	6-3, 6-2
1958	Althea Gibson	Darlene Hard	3-6, 6-1, 6-2
1959	Maria Bueno	Christine Truman	6-1, 6-4
1960	Darlene Hard	Maria Bueno	6-4, 10-12, 6-4
1961	Darlene Hard	Ann Haydon	6-3, 6-4
1962	Margaret Smith	Darlene Hard	9-7, 6-4
1963	Maria Bueno	Margaret Smith	7-5, 6-4
1964	Maria Bueno	Carole Graebner	6-1, 6-0
1965	Margaret Smith	Billie Jean Moffitt	8-6, 7-5
1966	Maria Bueno	Nancy Richey	6-3, 6-1
1967	Billie Jean King	Ann Haydon Jones	11-9, 6-4
1968*	Virginia Wade	Billie Jean King	6-4, 6-4
1968#	Margaret Smith Court	Maria Bueno	6-2, 6-2
1969*	Margaret Smith Court	Nancy Richey	6-2, 6-2
1969#	Margaret Smith Court	Virginia Wade	4-6, 6-3, 6-0
1970	Margaret Smith Court	Rosie Casals	6-2, 2-6, 6-1
1971	Billie Jean King	Rosie Casals	6-4, 7-6
1972	Billie Jean King	Kerry Melville	6-3, 7-5
1973	Margaret Smith Court	Evonne Goolagong	7-6, 5-7, 6-2
1974	Billie Jean King	Evonne Goolagong	3-6, 6-3, 7-5
1975	Chris Evert	Evonne Goolagong Cawley	5-7, 6-4, 6-2
1976	Chris Evert	Evonne Goolagong Cawley	6-3, 6-0
1977	Chris Evert	Wendy Turnbull	7-6, 6-2
1978	Chris Evert	Pam Shriver	7-6, 6-4
1979	Tracy Austin	Chris Evert Lloyd	6-4, 6-3
1980	Chris Evert Lloyd	Hana Mandlikova	5-7, 6-1, 6-1
1981	Tracy Austin	Martina Navratilova	1-6, 7-6, 7-6
1982	Chris Evert Lloyd	Hana Mandlikova	6-3, 6-1
1983	Martina Navratilova	Chris Evert Lloyd	6-1, 6-3
1984	Martina Navratilova	Chris Evert Lloyd	4-6, 6-4, 6-4
1985	Hana Mandlikova	Martina Navratilova	7-6, 1-6, 7-6
1986	Martina Navratilova	Helena Sukova	6-3, 6-2
1987	Martina Navratilova	Steffi Graf	7-6, 6-1
1988	Steffi Graf	Gabriela Sabatini	6-3, 3-6, 6-1
1989	Steffi Graf	Martina Navratilova	3-6, 6-4, 6-2
1990	Gabriela Sabatini	Steffi Graf	6-2, 7-6
1991	Monica Seles	Martina Navratilova	7-6, 6-1
1992	Monica Seles	Arantxa Sanchez Vicario	6-3, 6-2
1993	Steffi Graf	Helena Sukova	6-3, 6-3
1994	Arantxa Sanchez Vicario	Steffi Graf	1-6, 7-6 (7-3), 6-4

*Became Open (amateur and professional) in 1968; †Challenge round abolished.
‡National Patriotic Tournament; #Amateur event held; **Five-set final abolished.

Singles

Don Budge, 1938
Maureen Connolly, 1953
Rod Laver, 1962, 1969
Margaret Smith Court, 1970
Steffi Graf, 1988

Doubles

Frank Sedgman and Ken McGregor, 1951
Martina Navratilova and Pam Shriver, 1984
Maria Bueno and two partners: Christine Truman
    (Australian), Darlene Hard (French, Wimbledon
    and U.S. Championships), 1960

Mixed Doubles

Margaret Smith and Ken Fletcher, 1963
Owen Davidson and two partners: Lesley Turner
    (Australian), Billie Jean King (French, Wimbledon
    and U.S. Championships), 1967

The Alltime Grand Slam Champions

MEN

Player	Aus. S-D-M	French S-D-M	Wim. S-D-M	U.S. S-D-M	Total
Roy Emerson	6-3-0	2-6-0	2-3-0	2-4-0	28
John Newcombe	2-5-0	0-3-0	3-6-0	2-3-1	25
Frank Sedgman	2-2-2	0-2-2	1-3-2	2-2-2	22
Bill Tilden	*	0-0-1	3-1-0	7-5-4	21
Rod Laver	3-4-0	2-1-1	4-1-2	2-0-0	20
Jean Borotra	1-1-1	2-6-2	2-3-1	0-0-1	20
Fred Stolle	0-3-1	1-2-0	0-2-3	1-3-2	18
Ken Rosewall	4-3-0	2-2-0	0-2-0	2-2-1	18
Neale Fraser	0-3-1	0-3-0	1-2-0	2-3-3	18
Adrian Quist	3-10-0	0-1-0	0-2-0	0-1-0	17
John Bromwich	2-8-1	0-0-0	0-2-2	0-1-1	17
John McEnroe	0-0-0	0-0-1	3-4-0	4-5-0	17
H.L. Doherty	*	*	5-8-0	1-2-0	16
Henri Cochet	*	4-3-2	2-2-0	1-0-1	15
Vic Seixas	0-1-0	0-2-1	1-0-4	1-2-3	15
Jack Crawford	4-4-1	1-1-1	1-1-1	0-0-0	15
Bob Hewitt	0-2-1	0-1-2	0-5-2	0-1-1	15

WOMEN

Player	Aus. S-D-M	French S-D-M	Wim. S-D-M	U.S. S-D-M	Total
Margaret Court	11-8-2	5-4-4	3-2-5	5-5-8	62
Martina Navratilova	3-8-0	2-7-2	9-7-1	4-9-2	54
Billie Jean King	1-0-1	1-1-2	6-10-4	4-5-4	39
Margaret duPont	*	2-3-0	1-5-1	3-13-9	37
Louise Brough	1-1-0	0-3-0	4-5-4	1-12-4	35
Doris Hart	1-1-2	2-5-3	1-4-5	2-4-5	35
Helen Wills Moody	*	4-2-0	8-3-1	7-4-2	30
Elizabeth Ryan	*	0-4-0	0-12-7	0-1-2	26
Suzanne Lenglen	*	6-2-2	6-6-3	0-0-0	25
Pam Shriver	0-7-0	0-4-1	0-5-0	0-5-0	22
Chris Evert	2-0-0	7-2-0	3-1-0	6-0-0	21
Maria Bueno	0-1-0	0-1-1	3-5-0	4-5-0	20
Darlene Hard	*	1-2-2	0-4-3	2-6-0	20
Sarah Palfrey Cooke	*	0-0-1	0-2-0	2-9-4	18
Alice Marble	*	*	1-2-3	4-4-4	18

*Did not compete.

National Team Competition

Davis Cup

Started in 1900 as the International Lawn Tennis Challenge Trophy by America's Dwight Davis, the runner-up in the 1898 U.S. Championships. A Davis Cup meeting between two countries is known as a tie and is a three-day event consisting of two singles matches, followed by one doubles match and then two more singles matches. The United States boasts the greatest number of wins (30), followed by Australia (20).

Year	Winner	Finalist	Site	Score
1900	United States	Great Britain	Boston	3-0
1901	No tournament			

Davis Cup *(Cont.)*

Year	Winner	Finalist	Site	Score
1902	United States	Great Britain	New York	3-2
1903	Great Britain	United States	Boston	4-1
1904	Great Britain	Belgium	Wimbledon	5-0
1905	Great Britain	United States	Wimbledon	5-0
1906	Great Britain	United States	Wimbledon	5-0
1907	Australasia	Great Britain	Wimbledon	3-2
1908	Australasia	United States	Melbourne	3-2
1909	Australasia	United States	Sydney	5-0
1910	No tournament			
1911	Australasia	United States	Christchurch, NZ	5-0
1912	Great Britain	Australasia	Melbourne	3-2
1913	United States	Great Britain	Wimbledon	3-2
1914	Australasia	United States	New York	3-2
1915-18	No tournament			
1919	Australasia	Great Britain	Sydney	4-1
1920	United States	Australasia	Auckland, NZ	5-0
1921	United States	Japan	New York	5-0
1922	United States	Australasia	New York	4-1
1923	United States	Australasia	New York	4-1
1924	United States	Australia	Philadelphia	5-0
1925	United States	France	Philadelphia	5-0
1926	United States	France	Philadelphia	4-1
1927	France	United States	Philadelphia	3-2
1928	France	United States	Paris	4-1
1929	France	United States	Paris	3-2
1930	France	United States	Paris	4-1
1931	France	Great Britain	Paris	3-2
1932	France	United States	Paris	3-2
1933	Great Britain	France	Paris	3-2
1934	Great Britain	United States	Wimbledon	4-1
1935	Great Britain	United States	Wimbledon	5-0
1936	Great Britain	Australia	Wimbledon	3-2
1937	United States	Great Britain	Wimbledon	4-1
1938	United States	Australia	Philadelphia	3-2
1939	Australia	United States	Philadelphia	3-2
1940-45	No tournament			
1946	United States	Australia	Melbourne	5-0
1947	United States	Australia	New York	4-1
1948	United States	Australia	New York	5-0
1949	United States	Australia	New York	4-1
1950	Australia	United States	New York	4-1
1951	Australia	United States	Sydney	3-2
1952	Australia	United States	Adelaide	4-1
1953	Australia	United States	Melbourne	3-2
1954	United States	Australia	Sydney	3-2
1955	Australia	United States	New York	5-0
1956	Australia	United States	Adelaide	5-0
1957	Australia	United States	Melbourne	3-2
1958	United States	Australia	Brisbane	3-2
1959	Australia	United States	New York	3-2
1960	Australia	Italy	Sydney	4-1
1961	Australia	Italy	Melbourne	5-0
1962	Australia	Mexico	Brisbane	5-0
1963	United States	Australia	Adelaide	3-2
1964	Australia	United States	Cleveland	3-2
1965	Australia	Spain	Sydney	4-1
1966	Australia	India	Melbourne	4-1
1967	Australia	Spain	Brisbane	4-1
1968	United States	Australia	Adelaide	4-1
1969	United States	Romania	Cleveland	5-0
1970	United States	West Germany	Cleveland	5-0
1971	United States	Romania	Charlotte, NC	3-2
1972	United States	Romania	Bucharest	3-2
1973	Australia	United States	Cleveland	5-0
1974	South Africa	India	*	walkover
1975	Sweden	Czechoslovakia	Stockholm	3-2

Davis Cup (Cont.)

Year	Winner	Finalist	Site	Score
1976	Italy	Chile	Santiago	4-1
1977	Australia	Italy	Sydney	3-1
1978	United States	Great Britain	Palm Springs	4-1
1979	United States	Italy	San Francisco	5-0
1980	Czechoslovakia	Italy	Prague	4-1
1981	United States	Argentina	Cincinnati	3-1
1982	United States	France	Grenoble	4-1
1983	Australia	Sweden	Melbourne	3-2
1984	Sweden	United States	Gothenburg	4-1
1985	Sweden	West Germany	Munich	3-2
1986	Australia	Sweden	Melbourne	3-2
1987	Sweden	India	Gothenburg	5-0
1988	West Germany	Sweden	Gothenburg	4-1
1989	West Germany	Sweden	Stuttgart	3-2
1990	United States	Australia	St Petersburg	3-2
1991	France	United States	Lyon	3-1
1992	United States	Switzerland	Fort Worth, TX	3-1
1993	Germany	Australia	Dusseldorf	4-1

*India refused to play the final in protest over South Africa's governmental policy of apartheid.
Note: Prior to 1972 the challenge-round system was in effect, with the previous year's winner "standing out" of the competition until the finals. A straight 16-nation tournament has been held since 1981.

Federation Cup

The women's equivalent of the Davis Cup, this competition was started in 1963 by the International Lawn Tennis Federation (now the ITF). Unlike the Davis Cup, though, all entrants gather at one site at one time for a tournament that is concluded within one week. Matches consist of two singles and one doubles. The United States boasts the greatest number of wins (14), followed by Australia (7).

Year	Winner	Finalist	Site	Score
1963	United States	Australia	London	2-1
1964	Australia	United States	Philadelphia	2-1
1965	Australia	United States	Melbourne	2-1
1966	United States	West Germany	Turin	3-0
1967	United States	Great Britain	West Berlin	2-0
1968	Australia	Netherlands	Paris	3-0
1969	United States	Australia	Athens	2-1
1970	Australia	Great Britain	Freiburg	3-0
1971	Australia	Great Britain	Perth	3-0
1972	South Africa	Great Britain	Johannesburg	2-1
1973	Australia	South Africa	Bad Homburg	3-0
1974	Australia	United States	Naples	2-1
1975	Czechoslovakia	Australia	Aix-en-Provence	3-0
1976	United States	Australia	Philadelphia	2-1
1977	United States	Australia	Eastbourne	2-1
1978	United States	Australia	Melbourne	2-1
1979	United States	Australia	Madrid	3-0
1980	United States	Australia	West Berlin	3-0
1981	United States	Great Britain	Nagoya	3-0
1982	United States	West Germany	Santa Clara	3-0
1983	Czechoslovakia	West Germany	Zurich	2-1
1984	Czechoslovakia	Australia	Sao Paulo	2-1
1985	Czechoslovakia	United States	Tokyo	2-1
1986	United States	Czechoslovakia	Prague	3-0
1987	West Germany	United States	Vancouver	2-1
1988	Czechoslovakia	USSR	Melbourne	2-1
1989	United States	Spain	Tokyo	3-0
1990	United States	USSR	Atlanta	2-1
1991	Spain	United States	Nottingham	2-1
1992	Germany	Spain	Frankfurt	2-1
1993	Spain	Australia	Frankfurt	3-0
1994	Spain	United States	Frankfurt	3-0

ATP Computer Year-End Top 10

1973

Ilie Nastase
John Newcombe
Jimmy Connors
Tom Okker
Stan Smith
Ken Rosewall
Manuel Orantes
Rod Laver
Jan Kodes
Arthur Ashe

1974

Jimmy Connors
John Newcombe
Bjorn Borg
Rod Laver
Guillermo Vilas
Tom Okker
Arthur Ashe
Ken Rosewall
Stan Smith
Ilie Nastase

1975

Jimmy Connors
Guillermo Vilas
Bjorn Borg
Arthur Ashe
Manuel Orantes
Ken Rosewall
Ilie Nastase
John Alexander
Roscoe Tanner
Rod Laver

1976

Jimmy Connors
Bjorn Borg
Ilie Nastase
Manuel Orantes
Raul Ramirez
Guillermo Vilas
Adriano Panatta
Harold Solomon
Eddie Dibbs
Brian Gottfried

1977

Jimmy Connors
Guillermo Vilas
Bjorn Borg
Vitas Gerulaitis
Brian Gottfried
Eddie Dibbs
Manuel Orantes
Raul Ramirez
Ilie Nastase
Dick Stockton

1978

Jimmy Connors
Bjorn Borg
Guillermo Vilas
John McEnroe
Vitas Gerulaitis
Eddie Dibbs
Brian Gottfried
Raul Ramirez
Harold Solomon
Corrado Barazzutti

1979

Bjorn Borg
Jimmy Connors
John McEnroe
Vitas Gerulaitis
Roscoe Tanner
Guillermo Vilas
Arthur Ashe
Harold Solomon
Jose Higueras
Eddie Dibbs

1980

Bjorn Borg
John McEnroe
Jimmy Connors
Gene Mayer
Guillermo Vilas
Ivan Lendl
Harold Solomon
Jose-Luis Clerc
Vitas Gerulaitis
Eliot Teltscher

1981

John McEnroe
Ivan Lendl
Jimmy Connors
Bjorn Borg
Jose-Luis Clerc
Guillermo Vilas
Gene Mayer
Eliot Teltscher
Vitas Gerulaitis
Peter McNamara

1982

John McEnroe
Jimmy Connors
Ivan Lendl
Guillermo Vilas
Vitas Gerulaitis
Jose-Luis Clerc
Mats Wilander
Gene Mayer
Yannick Noah
Peter McNamara

1983

John McEnroe
Ivan Lendl
Jimmy Connors
Mats Wilander
Yannick Noah
Jimmy Arias
Jose Higueras
Jose-Luis Clerc
Kevin Curren
Gene Mayer

1984

John McEnroe
Jimmy Connors
Ivan Lendl
Mats Wilander
Andres Gomez
Anders Jarryd
Henrik Sundstrom
Pat Cash
Eliot Teltscher
Yannick Noah

Able with Cane

Mercifully, the Michael Fay and/or caning stories have all but ceased in the U.S., but two books about Singapore's celebrated crime and punishment incident hit that country's bookstores late last summer. One, *The Caning of Michael Fay* by Dr. Gopal Baratham, provides the unsettling revelation that like baseball and tennis players, each Singapore caner has his own swinging style.

"There were those who twirled and those who ... took careful aim," writes Baratham. "There were those who took three steps forward and those who stood absolutely still ... some played a serve-and-volley game and some preferred to play from the baseline, some used a lot of topspin, others preferred the quick smash."

Topspin?

ATP Computer Year-End Top 10 (Cont.)

1985

Ivan Lendl
John McEnroe
Mats Wilander
Jimmy Connors
Stefan Edberg
Boris Becker
Yannick Noah
Anders Jarryd
Miloslav Mecir
Kevin Curren

1986

Ivan Lendl
Boris Becker
Mats Wilander
Yannick Noah
Stefan Edberg
Henri Leconte
Joakim Nystrom
Jimmy Connors
Miloslav Mecir
Andres Gomez

1987

Ivan Lendl
Stefan Edberg
Mats Wilander
Jimmy Connors
Boris Becker
Miloslav Mecir
Pat Cash
Yannick Noah
Tim Mayotte
John McEnroe

1988

Mats Wilander
Ivan Lendl
Andre Agassi
Boris Becker
Stefan Edberg
Kent Carlsson
Jimmy Connors
Jakob Hlasek
Henri Leconte
Tim Mayotte

1989

Ivan Lendl
Boris Becker
Stefan Edberg
John McEnroe
Michael Chang
Brad Gilbert
Andre Agassi
Aaron Krickstein
Alberto Mancini
Jay Berger

1990

Stefan Edberg
Boris Becker
Ivan Lendl
Andre Agassi
Pete Sampras
Andres Gomez
Thomas Muster
Emilio Sanchez
Goran Ivanisevic
Brad Gilbert

1991

Stefan Edberg
Jim Courier
Boris Becker
Michael Stich
Ivan Lendl
Pete Sampras
Guy Forget
Karel Novacek
Petr Korda
Andre Agassi

1992

Jim Courier
Stefan Edberg
Pete Sampras
Goran Ivanisevic
Boris Becker
Michael Chang
Petr Korda
Ivan Lendl
Andre Agassi
Richard Krajicek

1993

Pete Sampras
Michael Stich
Jim Courier
Sergi Bruguera
Stefan Edberg
Andrei Medvedev
Goran Ivanisevic
Michael Chang
Thomas Muster
Cedric Pioline

WTA Computer Year-End Top 10

1973

Margaret Smith Court
Billie Jean King
Evonne Goolagong
Chris Evert
Rosie Casals
Virginia Wade
Kerry Reid
Nancy Gunter
Julie Heldman
Helga Masthoff

1974

Billie Jean King
Evonne Goolagong
Chris Evert
Virginia Wade
Julie Heldman
Rosie Casals
Kerry Reid
Olga Morozova
Lesley Hunt
Francoise Durr

1975

Chris Evert
Billie Jean King
Evonne Goolagong Cawley
Martina Navratilova
Virginia Wade
Margaret Smith Court
Olga Morozova
Nancy Gunter
Francoise Durr
Rosie Casals

1976

Chris Evert
Evonne Goolagong Cawley
Virginia Wade
Martina Navratilova
Sue Barker
Betty Stove
Dianne Balestrat
Mima Jausovec
Rosie Casals
Francoise Durr

1977

Chris Evert
Billie Jean King
Martina Navratilova
Virginia Wade
Sue Barker
Rosie Casals
Betty Stove
Dianne Balestrat
Wendy Turnbull
Kerry Reid

1978

Martina Navratilova
Chris Evert
Evonne Goolagong Cawley
Virginia Wade
Billie Jean King
Tracy Austin
Wendy Turnbull
Kerry Reid
Betty Stove
Dianne Balestrat

WTA Computer Year-End Top 10 (Cont.)

1979

Martina Navratilova
Chris Evert Lloyd
Tracy Austin
Evonne Goolagong Cawley
Billie Jean King
Dianne Balestrat
Wendy Turnbull
Virginia Wade
Kerry Reid
Sue Barker

1980

Chris Evert Lloyd
Tracy Austin
Martina Navratilova
Hana Mandlikova
Evonne Goolagong Cawley
Billie Jean King
Andrea Jaeger
Wendy Turnbull
Pam Shriver
Greer Stevens

1981

Chris Evert Lloyd
Tracy Austin
Martina Navratilova
Andrea Jaeger
Hana Mandlikova
Sylvia Hanika
Pam Shriver
Wendy Turnbull
Bettina Bunge
Barbara Potter

1982

Martina Navratilova
Chris Evert Lloyd
Andrea Jaeger
Tracy Austin
Wendy Turnbull
Pam Shriver
Hana Mandlikova
Barbara Potter
Bettina Bunge
Sylvia Hanika

1983

Martina Navratilova
Chris Evert Lloyd
Andrea Jaeger
Pam Shriver
Sylvia Hanika
Jo Durie
Bettina Bunge
Wendy Turnbull
Tracy Austin
Zina Garrison

1984

Martina Navratilova
Chris Evert Lloyd
Hana Mandlikova
Pam Shriver
Wendy Turnbull
Manuela Maleeva
Helena Sukova
Claudia Kohde-Kilsch
Zina Garrison
Kathy Jordan

1985

Martina Navratilova
Chris Evert Lloyd
Hana Mandlikova
Pam Shriver
Claudia Kohde-Kilsch
Steffi Graf
Manuela Maleeva
Zina Garrison
Helena Sukova
Bonnie Gadusek

1986

Martina Navratilova
Chris Evert Lloyd
Steffi Graf
Hana Mandlikova
Helena Sukova
Pam Shriver
Claudia Kohde-Kilsch
Manuela Maleeva
Kathy Rinaldi
Gabriela Sabatini

1987

Steffi Graf
Martina Navratilova
Chris Evert
Pam Shriver
Hana Mandlikova
Gabriela Sabatini
Helena Sukova
Manuela Maleeva
Zina Garrison
Claudia Kohde-Kilsch

Sportin' Bands

The link between the world of sports and the world of pop music continues. Tim McGraw, a son of former big league reliever Tug, tops the country charts with his brazenly un-P.C. hit *Indian Outlaw*. The cloyingly catchy song, which includes such lyrics as "You can find me in my wigwam/ I'll be beating on my tom-tom," has drawn heavy criticism from Native American groups, but McGraw, whose father was known for his irrepressible enthusiasm, says that he's "flabbergasted" by all the attention and that he means no disrespect with the song. He actually said that some of his best friends are Native Americans.

Drawing less controversy—and fewer sales— is Bud Collins, a Frank Zappaesque band from the University of Connecticut named, for no apparent reason, after the smooth-pated tennis commentator. Also from courtside: Bettie Serveert, an Amsterdam-based quartet whose name derives, with a little topspin, from that of former Dutch tennis star Betty Stove. Stove has an instructional TV series airing in Holland that's entitled *Bettie Serveert*, which means "Betty Serves" in Dutch. Says drummer Berend Dubbe of the band's name, "It's very stupid, but it is too late to change it."

And there's still another tennis connection: A German band with the unsavory name of Run-Over Schoolchildren was recently ordered to pay Steffi Graf $35,000 in damages for using lyrics suggesting that she had an incestuous relationship with her father. A court in Karlsruhe, Germany, threw out an appeal by the four-member band of a ruling in Graf's favor last year. The offending lyrics were included in the song (which was later banned in Germany) called *I Wanna Make Love with Steffi Graf*.

Of much gentler stuff is the homage paid by two other bands to a pair of former New York Mets. Yo La Tengo, which is not a mariachi band but a Hoboken, N.J.-based alternative-rock group popular with college audiences, takes its name from Elio Chacon, the shortstop for the original 1962 Mets, who was given to shouting, *"Yo la tengo"* (Spanish for "I got it!") whenever he prepared to catch a pop-up. And a four-member rock group is named after Chacon's lovably incompetent teammate at first base. If you're ever in Cincinnati, we urge you to check out Throneberry.

WTA Computer Year-End Top 10 *(Cont.)*

1988

Steffi Graf
Martina Navratilova
Chris Evert
Gabriela Sabatini
Pam Shriver
Manuela Maleeva-Fragniere
Natalia Zvereva
Helena Sukova
Zina Garrison
Barbara Potter

1989

Steffi Graf
Martina Navratilova
Gabriela Sabatini
Zina Garrison
Arantxa Sanchez Vicario
Monica Seles
Conchita Martinez
Helena Sukova
Manuela Maleeva-Fragniere
*Chris Evert

1990

Steffi Graf
Monica Seles
Martina Navratilova
Mary Joe Fernandez
Gabriela Sabatini
Katerina Maleeva
Arantxa Sanchez Vicario
Jennifer Capriati
Manuela Maleeva-Fragniere
Zina Garrison

1991

Monica Seles
Steffi Graf
Gabriela Sabatini
Martina Navratilova
Arantxa Sanchez Vicario
Jennifer Capriati
Jana Novotna
Mary Joe Fernandez
Conchita Martinez
Manuela Maleeva-Fragniere

1992

Monica Seles
Steffi Graf
Gabriela Sabatini
Arantxa Sanchez Vicario
Martina Navratilova
Mary Joe Fernandez
Jennifer Capriati
Conchita Martinez
Manuela Maleeva-Fragniere
Jana Novotna

1993

Steffi Graf
Arantxa Sanchez Vicario
Martina Navratilova
Conchita Martinez
Gabriela Sabatini
Jana Novotna
Mary Joe Fernandez
Monica Seles
Jennifer Capriati
Anke Huber

*When Chris Evert announced her retirement at the 1989 United States Open, she was ranked 4 in the world. That was her last official series tournament.

Prize Money

Top 25 Men's Career Prize Money Leaders

	Earnings ($)
Ivan Lendl	20,248,503
Stefan Edberg	16,749,270
Boris Becker	14,272,504
John McEnroe	12,227,622
Pete Sampras	10,311,612
Jim Courier	9,061,864
Jimmy Connors	8,498,820
Mats Wilander	7,422,048
Andre Agassi	6,865,338
Michael Stich	6,546,115
Goran Ivanisevic	5,694,858
Michael Chang	5,268,440
Guillermo Vilas	4,923,452
Anders Jarryd	4,817,454
Sergi Bruguera	4,518,716
Emilio Sanchez	4,409,660
Andres Gomez	4,284,725
Brad Gilbert	4,251,914
Petr Korda	4,182,013
Guy Forget	3,906,071
Jakob Hlasek	3,822,072
Tomas Smid	3,699,738
Bjorn Borg	3,655,751
Yannick Noah	3,295,395
John Fitzgerald	2,971,076

Note: From arrival of Open tennis in 1968 through September 26, 1994.

Top 25 Women's Career Prize Money Leaders

	Earnings ($)
Martina Navratilova	19,957,777
Steffi Graf	14,615,990
Chris Evert	8,896,195
Gabriela Sabatini	7,439,422
Arantxa Sanchez Vicario	7,429,016
Monica Seles	7,408,981
Pam Shriver	5,259,482
Helena Sukova	5,197,811
Zina Garrison Jackson	4,205,531
Jana Novotna	4,121,422
Natalia Zvereva	3,871,556
Conchita Martinez	3,486,832
Hana Mandlikova	3,340,959
Manuela Maleeva-Fragniere	3,244,811
Gigi Fernandez	3,132,702
Mary Joe Fernandez	3,049,213
Wendy Turnbull	2,769,024
Lori McNeil	2,667,578
Larisa Neiland	2,379,076
Claudia Kohde-Kilsch	2,225,837
Katerina Maleeva	2,077,255
Tracy Austin	1,992,380
Billie Jean King	1,966,487
Nathalie Tauziat	1,804,398
Ros Nideffer	1,613,282

Note: From arrival of Open tennis in 1968 through September 26, 1994.

Open Era Overall Wins

Men's Career Leaders—Tournaments Won

The top tournament-winning men from the institution of Open tennis in 1968 through September 26, 1994.

	W		W
Jimmy Connors	109	Arthur Ashe	33
Ivan Lendl	94	Mats Wilander	33
John McEnroe	77	John Newcombe	32
Bjorn Borg	62	Manuel Orantes	32
Guillermo Vilas	61	Ken Rosewall	32
Ilie Nastase	57	Tom Okker	31
Rod Laver	47	Pete Sampras	29
Boris Becker	41	Vitas Gerulaitis	27
Stefan Edberg	40	Jose-Luis Clerc	25
Stan Smith	39	Brian Gottfried	25

Women's Career Leaders—Tournaments Won

The top tournament-winning women from the institution of Open tennis in 1968 through September 26, 1994.

	W		W
Martina Navratilova	167	Hana Mandlikova	27
Chris Evert	157	Nancy Richey	25
Evonne Goolagong Cawley	88	Gabriela Sabatini	25
Steffi Graf	86	Kerry Melville Reid	22
Margaret Court	79	Sue Barker	21
Billie Jean King	71	Pam Shriver	21
Virginia Wade	55	Julie Heldman	20
Helga Masthoff	37	Conchita Martinez	20
Monica Seles	32	Dianne Fromholtz Balestrat	19
Olga Morozova	31	Manuela Maleeva Fragniere	19
Tracy Austin	29	Arantxa Sanchez Vicario	19

Annual ATP/WTA Champions

Men's ATP Tour—World Championship

Year	Player	Year	Player
1970	Stan Smith	1982	Ivan Lendl
1971	Ilie Nastase	1983	Ivan Lendl
1972	Ilie Nastase	1984	John McEnroe
1973	Ilie Nastase	1985	John McEnroe
1974	Guillermo Vilas	1986	Ivan Lendl
1975	Ilie Nastase	1986	Ivan Lendl
1976	Manuel Orantes	1987	Ivan Lendl
1977	Not held	1988	Boris Becker
1978	Jimmy Connors	1989	Stefan Edberg
1979	John McEnroe	1990	Andre Agassi
1980	Bjorn Borg	1991	Pete Sampras
1981	Bjorn Borg	1992	Boris Becker
		1993	Michael Stich

Note: Event held twice in 1986.

THEY SAID IT

Jim Courier, the former world's No. 1-ranked tennis player, on his current slump: "At the moment, my best surface is my bed."

Women—Virginia Slims Championship

Year	Player	Year	Player
1972	Chris Evert	1983	Martina Navratilova
1973	Chris Evert	1984	Martina Navratilova
1974	Evonne Goolagong	1985	Martina Navratilova
1975	Chris Evert	1986	Martina Navratilova
1976	Evonne Goolagong	1986	Martina Navratilova
1977	Chris Evert	1987	Steffi Graf
1978	Martina Navratilova	1988	Gabriela Sabatini
1979	Martina Navratilova	1989	Steffi Graf
1980	Tracy Austin	1990	Monica Seles
1981	Martina Navratilova	1991	Monica Seles
1982	Sylvia Hanika	1992	Monica Seles
		1993	Steffi Graf

Note: Virginia Slims Championship held twice in 1986.

Net Loss Net Gain

The woes that bedevil tennis came to surface in two very different ways last August. As Jim Courier, citing a lack of desire, walked away from the game at a tournament in Indianapolis, the Association of Tennis Professionals (ATP), in hopes of reviving fan interest, unleashed an assortment of what it called "eye and ear candy" during a tournament in New Haven, Conn.

Courier, who turned 24 on the first day of a hiatus that he said might last "one week, one month, one year, or 10 years," portended his departure last November at the ATP Tour World Championship in Germany, where he took advantage of a changeover to catch up on some reading. The signal was clear: His motivational fires were burning out. Sure enough, by July he was out of the Top 10. And last August, following a second round loss in Indianapolis, Courier called it quits (he returned to play the U.S. Open, where he lost in the second round and then resumed his exile from the game).

Meanwhile, in New Haven, the ATP began its quest for greater fan appeal. First, before each match, the competitors were introduced, one at a time, to a song they had requested (Andre Agassi, for instance, chose soulmate Barbra Streisand's *The Way We Were*). Second, a disc jockey played music during warmups and changeovers, with selections ranging from Frank Sinatra to Pearl Jam. Finally, after some matches the winners stayed on court to field questions from fans.

Agassi was one of many players who decried the playing of music during changeovers, using words like *joke, embarrassment* and *circus* to describe the environment during a second-round loss.

But the feeling here is that the ATP has hit on something, at least with the musical introductions and postmatch interviews. Indeed, an exit poll showed that 77% enjoyed the postmatch interview while only 44% found the match more enjoyable because of music during the changeovers.

Even no-frills immortal Rod Laver liked the introductions and the postmatch interviews. "We thought tiebreakers were the greatest mess of all time, but we adjusted," said Laver. "As long as the music stops when the players are walking onto the court, they'll get used to it."

International Tennis Hall of Fame

Pauline Betz Addie (1965)
George T. Adee (1964)
Fred B. Alexander (1961)
Wilmer L. Allison (1963)
Manuel Alonso (1977)
Arthur Ashe (1985)
Juliette Atkinson (1974)
Tracy Austin (1992)
Lawrence A. Baker (1975)
Maud Barger-Wallach (1958)
Angela Mortimer Barrett (1993)
Karl Behr (1969)
Mallory Molla Bjurstedt (1958)
Bjorn Borg (1987)
Jean Borotra (1976)
Maureen Connolly Brinker(1968)
John Bromwich (1984)
Norman Everard Brookes (1977)
Mary K. Browne (1957)
Jacques Brugnon (1976)
J. Donald Budge (1964)
Maria E. Bueno (1978)
May Sutton Bundy (1956)
Mabel E. Cahill (1976)
Oliver S. Campbell (1955)
Malcom Chace (1961)
Dorothea Douglass Lambert
  Chambers (1981)
Philippe Chatrier (1992)
Louise Brough Clapp (1967)
Clarence Clark (1983)
Joseph S. Clark (1955)
William J. Clothier (1956)
Henri Cochet (1976)
Bud Collins (1994)
Ashley Cooper (1991)
Margaret Smith Court (1979)
Gottfried von Cramm (1977)
John H. Crawford (1979)
Joseph F. Cullman III (1990)
Allison Danzig (1968)
Sarah Palfrey Danzig (1963)
Dwight F. Davis (1956)
Charlotte Dod (1983)
John H. Doeg (1962)
Laurie Doherty (1980)
Reggie Doherty (1980)
Jaroslav Drobny (1983)
Margaret Osborne duPont
  (1967)
James Dwight (1955)
Roy Emerson (1982)
Pierre Etchebaster (1978)
Robert Falkenburg (1974)
Neale Fraser (1984)
Charles S. Garland (1969)
Althea Gibson (1971)

Kathleen McKane Godfree
  (1978)
Richard A. Gonzales (1968)
Evonne Goolagong Cawley
  (1988)
Bryan M. Grant Jr (1972)
David Gray (1985)
Clarence Griffin (1970)
King Gustaf V of Sweden
  (1980)
Harold H. Hackett (1961)
Ellen Forde Hansell (1965)
Darlene R. Hard (1973)
Doris J. Hart (1969)
Gladys M. Heldman (1979)
W. E. "Slew" Hester Jr (1981)
Bob Hewitt (1992)
Lew Hoad (1980)
Harry Hopman (1978)
Fred Hovey (1974)
Joseph R. Hunt (1966)
Lamar Hunt (1993)
Francis T. Hunter (1961)
Shirley Fry Irvin (1970)
Helen Hull Jacobs (1962)
William Johnston (1958)
Ann Haydon Jones (1985)
Perry Jones (1970)
Billie Jean King (1987)
Jan Kodes (1990)
John A. Kramer (1968)
Rene Lacoste (1976)
Al Laney (1979)
William A. Larned (1956)
Arthur D. Larsen (1969)
Rod G. Laver (1981)
Suzanne Lenglen (1978)
Dorothy Round Little (1986)
George M. Lott Jr (1964)
Gene Mako (1973)
Hana Mandlikova (1994)
Alice Marble (1964)
Alastair B. Martin (1973)
William McChesney Martin (1982)
Chuck McKinley (1986)
Maurice McLoughlin (1957)
Frew McMillan (1992)
W. Donald McNeill (1965)
Elisabeth H. Moore (1971)
Gardnar Mulloy (1972)
R. Lindley Murray (1958)
Julian S. Myrick (1963)
Ilie Nastase (1991)
John D. Newcombe (1986)
Arthur C. Nielsen Sr (1971)
Betty Nuthall (1977)
Alex Olmedo (1987)

Rafael Osuna (1979)
Mary Ewing Outerbridge (1981)
Frank A. Parker (1966)
Gerald Patterson (1989)
Budge Patty (1977)
Theodore R. Pell (1967)
Fred Perry (1975)
Tom Pettitt (1982)
Nicola Pietrangeli (1986)
Adrian Quist (1984)
Dennis Ralston (1987)
Ernest Renshaw (1983)
Willie Renshaw (1983)
Vincent Richards (1961)
Robert L. Riggs (1967)
Helen Wills Moody Roark
  (1959)
Anthony D. Roche (1986)
Ellen C. Roosevelt (1975)
Ken Rosewall (1980)
Elizabeth Ryan (1972)
Manuel Santana (1984)
Richard Savitt (1976)
Frederick R. Schroeder (1966)
Eleonora Sears (1968)
Richard D. Sears (1955)
Frank Sedgman (1979)
Pancho Segura (1984)
Vic Seixas Jr (1971)
Francis X. Shields (1964)
Henry W. Slocum Jr (1955)
Stan Smith (1987)
Fred Stolle (1985)
William F. Talbert (1967)
Bill Tilden (1959)
Lance Tingay (1982)
Ted Tinling (1986)
Bertha Townsend Toulmin
  (1974)
Tony Trabert (1970)
James H. Van Alen (1965)
John Van Ryn (1963)
Guillermo Vilas (1991)
Ellsworth Vines (1962)
Virginia Wade (1989)
Marie Wagner (1969)
Holcombe Ward (1956)
Watson Washburn (1965)
Malcolm D. Whitman (1955)
Hazel Hotchkiss Wightman
  (1957)
Anthony Wilding (1978)
Richard Norris Williams II
  (1957)
Sidney B. Wood (1964)
Robert D. Wrenn (1955)
Beals C. Wright (1956)

Note: Years in parentheses are dates of induction.

Golf

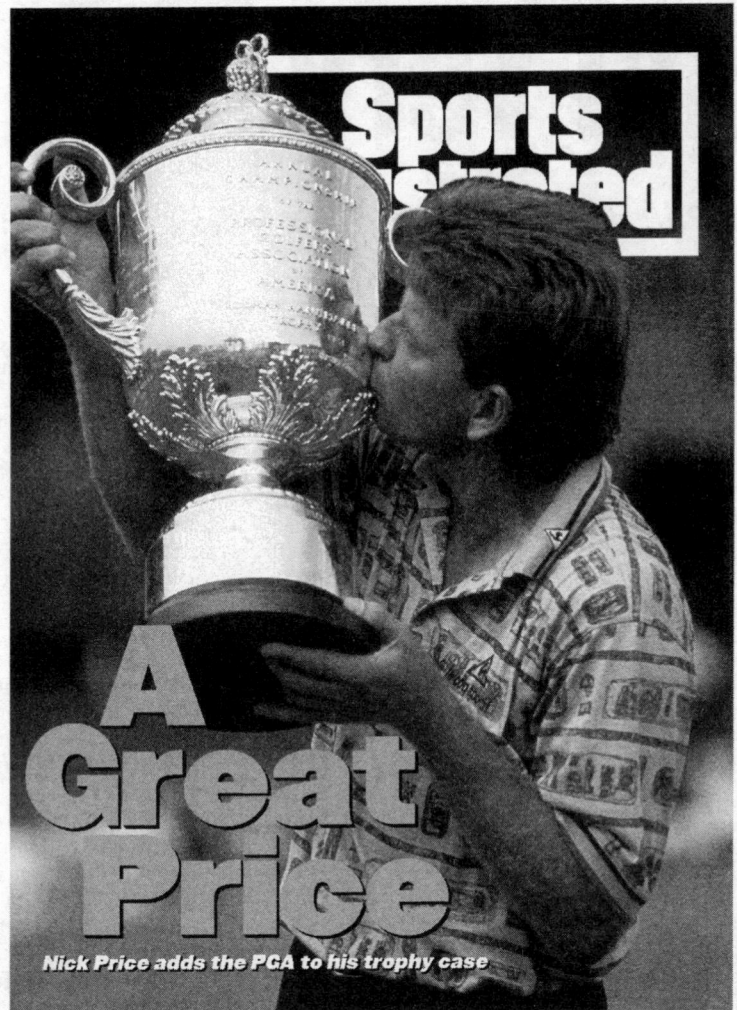

Sports Illustrated

A Great Price

Nick Price adds the PGA to his trophy case

BOB GOMEL

Red, White and Very Blue

Nick Price dominated a golf season in which American men failed to win a single major title | by RICK REILLY

OLF GOT ITS GREEN CARD IN 1994, with three majors going to players from Africa, one to a Spaniard and the U.S. Amateur to a kid from another planet.

His name is Tiger Woods, and the fact that he: a) came from further behind than anybody in U.S. Amateur history and b) was, at 18, the youngest player ever to win it, younger even than Fat Jack Nicklaus, at 19, and c) is the first black to ever hold the title—all that was big, almost as big as the fact that he was actually, incredibly, preposterously an American.

For until Woods and his monster follow-through came along, it had been the worst year for American golf since they rationed rubber. It was the Year of the Guy with the Funny Accent and the Thick Passport and the Thin Cigarettes. Actually, it had mostly been the year of Nick Price, the Popeye-armed Orlando resident with the Vanilla Ice haircut and the steel-blue eyes. He not only became the first golfer to win back-to-back majors in 12 years—he won the British and the PGA Championship—but also won an astounding six times on the

Tour, the most since Watson won six times in 1980.

That wouldn't have been so maddening—Americans had never lost the first *three* majors before, never mind the whole enchilada—if Price hadn't been such an annoying *gentleman* about the whole thing. Week after week he would appear at the top of the leader boards and then come into the press tents smiling and shaking hands and answering questions for an hour or more. And each day when the press figured they had him plumb wore out, he would just throw another 67 at them and be back for more. *Now, Nick, if we could just have a few more details on those preschool years.*

In one ungodly stretch he won the Western Open in Chicago, went straight to the British Open and won, tying Watson's all-time Turnberry record of 268, then flew back across the pond, took two weeks off, finished fourth at Memphis and then came to the PGA at Southern Hills in Tulsa, where he simply stepped on the neck of everybody there, hog-tying the field and shooting 269 to win by six shots and an

Oklahoma county. It was only the lowest score in an American major in history is all. If you're keeping track, that's winning three out of four, which made you think you fell asleep and woke up in 1945 and Byron Nelson was winning everything but the war. At least that's what it made Ben Crenshaw think. "I don't know if anybody's hit it this good since Hogan or Nelson," he said.

The 37-year-old Price not only had the Year of the Year, he also had the Putt of the Year, and it gave him the major he'd come so achingly close to winning twice before only to lose both times—the British. He canned an impossible double-break, three-day-camel-ride, 50-foot job that allowed him to eagle the par-5 17th on Sunday. Of course, that putt should only have tied it for him, except for the brain freeze that 29-year-old Jesper Parnevik of Sweden had the hole before. Parnevik is the man who wears his golf hat turned upward to allow a logo not only on the front of the hat but also, eureka, on the underside of the bill. Unfortunately, this method seems to cut off circulation to the cerebellum. Parnevik came to the 18th that day at Turnberry with a two-shot lead, but he *thought* he trailed by one. He wasn't sure who he trailed or why, since, for some reason, he stopped looking at the scoreboards on the 11th.

Olazabal drove well, but it was his uncanny short game that won him the Masters.

So with a very nice lie on the 18th, he decided he needed to fly his wedge right at the pin, a dangerous little idea. It came up short in some nasty rough. Parnevik chopped out and two-putted for a bogey. That put Price within one, and when he made that Loch Ness monster of a putt, he suddenly had it won. "I guess I screwed up," said Parnevik.

The only consolation for Parnevik was that he got his first big endorsement out of the deal. "I've had a little trouble with numbers lately," he could be seen saying a month later in an ad for an American hotel chain. "But here's one I won't forget: 1-800. ..." It was the phone number of the chain, and it was plastered all over the room.

You wouldn't think a scoreboard would be that hard to miss—Uh, fellas, they're those giant things with *your name* written on them—but Ernie Els did the same exact thing a month before at the U.S. Open at Oakmont outside sizzling Pittsburgh. Els, a 24-year-old South African with the sweetest swing in golf, had himself a one-shot lead at maybe the hardest course in the country as he came to the last hole. Again, he led by one, over unknown Loren

Roberts of the U.S. and pudgy Brit Colin Montgomerie, but he didn't know it, since he hadn't looked at a scoreboard since the 15th. Els must have been in Parnevik's class at the Chris Webber Institute of Mathematics because for some reason Els too thought he was one *behind* instead of one ahead. He figured he needed a birdie standing there on the short 18th and tried to hit a driver to Philadelphia.

Instead, he hit it toward Harrisburg, so far left that it ended up just in front of the 15th tee. Jailed, looking at an impossible shot under a tee sign and a bunker and yet over a hillock to an uphill green, Els was actually about to go for it when his caddie told him, "Hold back a minute. Five under would still lead." *Now you tell me.* Els chipped out and made a bogey, forcing a three-way tie. "I'm kicking my backside over that one," Els said that Sunday night. So were American golf fans, since that brain lock foisted upon them the worst

extra day of golf since the Boise Country Club Fall Trophy four-ball.

Lifeless, anticlimactic and boring Monday playoffs are, of course, what the USGA deserves for sticking to its Flintstone-era 18-hole next-day playoff instead of the thrilling one-hole or four-hole playoff every other major uses. But this Monday playoff was even worse. This Monday playoff was uglier than a sack of navels.

The first five holes almost killed the golf boom by themselves. In those first five the new Three Stooges hit four greens. Total. Montgomerie chunked three chips. They made three bogeys, three doubles and a triple, tying a record Nellie Fox once set. The 2nd hole alone was comical in its hackishness. Els hit his second shot into a bush, had to take a drop *on the 3rd tee box*, bladed that one over the green, chili-

Woods and his assortment of miracle shots promise a few U.S. victories in the future.

MICHAEL O'BRYON

dipped on and two-putted for a triple-bogey seven. Montgomerie, meanwhile, was laying two near the green and butchered his way to a six. Roberts won the hole with a bogey. Sorry, Loren, our group doesn't pay bogey skins.

Finally, on the 20th playoff hole of the day—Oakmont's 11th—Roberts swiped his drive right and made bogey. The extra-large Els was settled by then, finally realizing he could hit two-irons and still beat this bunch. He did just that, parred the hole and won the U.S. Open.

Still, the first 3¾ days Els played were beautiful, and don't forget, he won at the place where Nicklaus kick-started his career, where Johnny Miller was most brilliant and where Arnold Palmer's dad took him as a boy. Els became only the fifth player since World War II to win a major before the age of 25. "I think I just played with the next god," said Curtis Strange of Els.

If the young Els used 1994 to prove he has the prettiest long game in golf, then the young (28) Jose Maria Olazabal (oh-luh-THAH-bull) proved he has the prettiest—and most deadly—short one. The Spaniard tied tongues all over Augusta in April by winning the Masters, where chairman Jack Stephens was stuck with the job of pronouncing his name at the awards ceremony: "Uh … Jose … Muh-rie … Ohlay … bozzul." Ollie, as Augustans will probably start calling him, is the son of a Spanish greenskeeper and grew up knocking little white balls into little dark cups on the putting green 30 feet from his front door. In the end, it was Olazabal's uncanny chipping and putting that whipped the lone American chasing him, journeyman pro Tom Lehman, who had never won a Tour event, much less the classiest tournament in the world. Ollie was the sixth foreigner to win the Masters in the last seven years. He went on to win the World Series—half a major—just for good measure.

And that is how the large bagel happened, oh-for-the-year for the red, white and very blue, an unprecedented under-achievement. Among the vanquished glamour Yanks lying in a pile at the end of the year were these:

• Watson, who never hit the ball sweeter in all his 44 years, according to his long time caddie, Bruce Edwards, but putted like a piano mover. He had a chance to win at Augusta and lost. He had the lead for two days at the British and made 38 putts on Sunday—38!—to lose. He hovered around the lead at the U.S. Open and putted himself into an alsoplaying. Through it all Watson refused to change styles, grips or stances. "I lived by this sword," he said of his glory years. "Now I'm dying by it." R.I.P.

• Fred Couples, who blew out his back sky-diving … er, no, hang gliding … well, no … motocross racing … well, actually, hitting a few practice balls before his round early in the spring at Doral, allowing him time to go home and build on the relationship with his new love—ESPN2.

• Payne Stewart, who nearly completed the Reverse Slam (missing the cut at every major). He finally made one: the PGA, by one shot. Stewart switched balls and clubs this season—to Top-Flight—and let's hope he got good money because he immediately started missing cuts. Said one Oklahoman, watching him flail away at the practice range, "I don't think he likes his new bats." It was also possible that Stewart missed having his best buddy around, Paul Azinger, who came back from cancer at the end of the year. Azinger was diagnosed with lymphoma in the shoulder blade two weeks after winning the 1993 PGA at Toledo and yet vowed to make it to Tulsa to defend his title. That he missed the cut there meant nothing. That he played at all was a victory. The cancer is said to have completely left his body. The smile has not.

• John Daly, who might consider for 30 seconds what Azinger's been through, had a typically tumultuous year. Daly, a.k.a. the Human Incident, finished serving his second PGA Tour suspension (nobody we can think of ever had even one) in time for the

JACQUELINE DUVOISIN

With his win at the U.S. Open, Els proved that he had the prettiest long game in golf.

spring Florida swing and seemed to play well. He actually led the British on Friday until he lost a ball on the 10th and proceeded to lose interest. He made a triple bogey there and then four-putted the par-3 11th from not more than 20 feet, raking his last three putts carelessly until one happened to go in. He finished dead last. Two months later he got into a parking lot throwdown at the World Series of Golf with the parents of little-known pro Jeff Roth. Witnesses said Daly had hit into Roths' group twice. At press time a third suspension was possible.

• American ski instructors. Three good American players fell to skiing accidents and missed goodly parts of the year—Phil Mickelson, Brad Faxon and Mark Wiebe. In fact, when another non-American, Greg Norman, was breaking every TPC scoring record in March on his way to a colossal 24-under-par win, Faxon strolled up to a reporter and offered a good way to slow him down. "Let's take him skiing," he said.

O.K., so there were some U.S.A. bright spots. Lehman rebounded from his two-shot Masters loss and went on to win the Memorial a month later, putting up four straight 67s, which is nice anytime you can get it and also blew away the old record at Muirfield Village. And 46-year-old Johnny Miller took off his NBC blazer and took out his seven-wood and his jab putting stroke and beat—who else?—Watson in a miraculous victory at the Pebble Beach AT&T Pro-Am to start the year. Get this: It was the only tournament Miller had

planned on entering all year. "Congratulations," said Watson. "Now get back in the booth."

And, O.K., American women had a good year, especially after Swedish superstar Helen Alfredsoon yakked up her seven-shot lead on Saturday at the U.S. Open in Lake Orion, Mich., and let Patty Sheehan reel her in to win her second open and 32nd LPGA victory. It's only fair. Sheehan once lost an Open after leading by nine.

The Shot of the Year, though, had to be the one that went into Kim Williams's neck the week of the LPGA's Youngstown-Warren (Ohio) Classic. Walking into a drugstore, she was hit by a stray bullet from a semi-automatic weapon. She spent two days in the hospital, played the next weekend at the Jamie Farr Toledo Classic and finished, quite remarkably, 10th. The bullet remains in her still.

And then a dervish named Tiger Woods showed up at the TPC course in Ponte Vedra in August for the amateur and gave golf a taste of what might be some unforgettable things to come. If Els and Ollie are young and great, Woods is younger and might someday be greater. He has not yet blinked in the face of his potential, and his bag comes equipped with miracle shots. At the amateur, he was tied with 22-year-old Trip Kuehne (whose sister Kelli won the '94 USGA Girls) when he came to the par-3 island-green 17th. Woods's nine-iron headed right of the pin, started to fade, had alligator written all over it, hit three feet from the edge of the water, bounced once and checked up *left*, rejecting every possible law of physics. Bigger yet, he made the 15-foot gagger from the fringe to take the lead for good. And all this *before* entering Stanford.

Hang tough, American golf fans. Tiger Woods is coming, even if the foreigners don't know it yet. Or *him* yet. Somebody asked England's Sandy Lyle what he thought of Tiger Woods. "Sorry," said Lyle. "Never played there."

FOR THE RECORD·1993-1994

Men's Majors

The Masters

Augusta National GC; Augusta, GA
(par 72; 6,905 yds) April 7-10

Player	Score	Earnings ($)
José María Olazabal	74-67-69-69—279	360,000
Tom Lehman	70-70-69-72—281	216,000
Larry Mize	68-71-72-71—282	136,000
Tom Kite	69-72-71-71—283	96,000
Jay Haas	72-72-72-69—285	73,000
Jim McGovern	72-70-71-72—285	73,000
Loren Roberts	75-68-72-70—285	73,000
Corey Pavin	71-72-73-70—286	60,000
Ernie Els	74-67-74-71—286	60,000
John Huston	72-72-74-69—287	50,000
Ian Baker-Finch	71-71-71-74—287	50,000
Ray Floyd	70-74-71-72—287	50,000
Tom Watson	70-71-73-74—288	42,000
Dan Forsman	74-66-76-73—289	38,000
Mark O'Meara	75-70-76-70—291	34,000
Brad Faxon	71-73-73-74—291	34,000
Chip Beck	71-71-75-74—291	34,000
Seve Ballesteros	70-76-75-71—292	24,343
Ben Crenshaw	74-73-73-72—292	24,343
Hale Irwin	73-68-79-72—292	24,343
Bill Glasson	72-73-75-72—292	24,343
Lanny Wadkins	73-74-73-72—292	24,343
David Edwards	73-72-73-74—292	24,343
Greg Norman	70-70-75-77—292	24,343

U.S. Open

Oakmont Country Club; Oakmont PA
(par 71; 6,946 yds) June 16-20

Player	Score	Earnings ($)
Ernie Els*	69-71-66-73—279	320,000
Loren Roberts	76-69-64-70—279	141,827
C. Montgomerie**	71-65-73-70—279	141,827
Curtis Strange	70-70-70-70—280	108,655
John Cook	73-65-73-71—282	75,728
Clark Dennis	71-71-70-71—283	54,839
Greg Norman	71-71-69-72—283	54,839
Tom Watson	68-73-68-74—283	54,839
Frank Nobilo	69-71-68-76—284	40,133
Duffy Waldorf	74-68-73-69—284	40,133
Jeff Maggert	71-68-75-70—284	40,133
Jeff Sluman	72-69-72-71—284	40,133
Jim McGovern	73-69-74-69—285	31,582
Scott Hoch	72-72-70-71—285	31,582
David Edwards	73-65-75-72—285	31,582
Fred Couples	72-71-69-74—286	27,300
Steve Lowery	71-71-68-76—286	27,300
Hale Irwin	69-69-71-78—287	23,825
Seve Ballesteros	72-72-70-73—287	23,825
Scott Verplank	70-72-75-70—287	23,825
Sam Torrance	72-71-76-69—288	20,593
Steve Pate	74-66-71-77—288	20,593

* Won on second hole of sudden death playoff.

** Eliminated after 18 playoff holes.

British Open

Turnberry; Turnberry, Scotland
(par 70; 6,957 yds) July 14-17

Player	Score	Earnings ($)
Nick Price	69-66-67-66—268	178,200
Jesper Parnevik	68-66-68-67—269	142,560
Fuzzy Zoeller	71-66-64-70—271	119,880
Mark James	72-67-66-68—273	82,080
Dave Feherty	68-69-66-70—273	82,080
Anders Forsbrand	72-71-66-64—273	82,080
Brad Faxon	69-65-67-73—274	58,320
Nick Faldo	75-66-70-64—275	48,600
Tom Kite	71-69-66-69—275	48,600
Colin Montgomerie	72-69-65-69—275	48,600
Larry Mize	73-69-64-70—276	31,320
Russell Claydon	72-71-68-65—276	31,320
Mark McNulty	71-70-68-67—276	31,320
Frank Nobilo	69-67-72-68—276	31,320
Jonathan Lomas	66-70-72-68—276	31,320
Mark Calcavecchia	71-70-67-68—276	31,320
Greg Norman	71-67-69-69—276	31,320
Tom Watson	68-65-69-74—276	31,320
Ronan Rafferty	71-66-65-74—276	31,320
Vijay Singh	70-68-69-70—277	20,250
Mark Brooks	74-64-71-68—277	20,250
Greg Turner	65-71-70-71—277	20,250
Peter Senior	68-71-67-71—277	20,250

PGA Championship

Southern Hills CC; Tulsa, OK
(par 70; 6,834 yds) August 11-14

Player	Score	Earnings ($)
Nick Price	67-65-70-67—269	310,000
Corey Pavin	70-67-69-69—275	160,000
Phil Mickelson	68-71-67-70—276	110,000
Nick Faldo	73-67-71-66—277	76,667
Greg Norman	71-69-67-70—277	76,667
John Cook	71-67-69-70—277	76,667
Steve Elkington	73-70-66-69—278	57,500
José María Olazabal	72-66-70-70—278	57,500
Tom Kite	72-68-69-70—279	41,000
Tom Watson	69-72-67-71—279	41,000
Loren Roberts	69-72-67-71—279	41,000
Ben Crenshaw	70-67-70-72—279	41,000
Ian Woosnam	68-72-73-66—279	41,000
Jay Haas	71-66-68-75—280	32,000
Kirk Triplett	71-69-71-70—281	27,000
Larry Mize	72-72-67-70—281	27,000
Mark McNulty	72-68-70-71—281	27,000
Glen Day	70-69-70-72—281	27,000
Craig Parry	70-69-70-73—282	18,666
Craig Stadler	70-70-74-68—282	18,666
Mark McCumber	73-70-71-68—282	18,666
Fuzzy Zoeller	69-71-72-70—282	18,666
Bill Glasson	71-73-68-70—282	18,666
Curtis Strange	73-71-68-70—282	18,666

Men's Tour Results

Late 1993 PGA Tour Events

Tournament	Final Round	Winner	Score/ Under Par	Earnings ($)
Kapalua International	Nov 7	Fred Couples	274/-18	180,000
World Cup of Golf	Nov 14	Fred Couples/Davis Love	556/-20	130,000 each
JC Penney Classic	Dec 5	Mike Springer/Melissa McNamara	265/-19	120,000 each

1994 PGA Tour Events

Tournament	Final Round	Winner	Score/ Under Par	Earnings ($)
Mercedes Championships	Jan 9	Phil Mickelson**	276/-12	180,000
United Airlines Hawaiian Open	Jan 16	Brett Ogle	269/-19	216,000
Northern Telecom Open	Jan 23	Andrew Magee	270/-18	198,000
Phoenix Open	Jan 30	Bill Glasson	268/-16	216,000
AT&T Pebble Beach National Pro-Am	Feb 6	Johnny Miller	281/-7	225,000
Los Angeles Open	Feb 13	Corey Pavin	271/-13	180,000
Bob Hope Chrysler Classic	Feb 20	Scott Hoch	334/-26	198,000
Buick Invitational	Feb 27	Craig Stadler	268–20	198,000
Doral Ryder Open	Mar 6	John Huston	274/-14	252,000
Honda Classic	Mar 13	Nick Price	276/-8	198,000
Nestle Invitational	Mar 20	Loren Roberts	275/-13	216,000
Tour Players Championship	Mar 27	Greg Norman	264/-24	450,000
Freeport-McMoRan Classic	Apr 3	Ben Crenshaw	273/-15	216,000
The Masters	Apr 10	José María Olazábal	279/-9	360,000
MCI Heritage Classic	Apr 17	Hale Irwin	266/-18	225,000
K Mart Greater Greensboro Open	Apr 24	Mike Springer	275/-13	270,000
Shell Houston Open	May 1	Mike Heinen	272/-16	234,000
BellSouth Classic	May 8	John Daly	274/-14	216,000
GTE Byron Nelson Classic	May 15	Neal Lancaster	132/-11	216,000
Memorial Tournament	May 22	Tom Lehman	268/-20	270,000
Southwestern Bell Colonial	May 30	Nick Price*	266/-14	252,000
Kemper Open	June 5	Mark Brooks	271/-13	234,000
Buick Classic	June 12	Lee Janzen	268/-16	216,000
U.S. Open	June 19	Ernie Els	279/-5	320,000
Greater Hartford Open	June 26	David Frost	268/-12	216,000
Motorola Western Open	July 3	Nick Price	277/-11	216,000
Anheuser-Busch Classic	July 10	Mark McCumber	267/-17	198,000
British Open	July 17	Nick Price	268/-12	178,200
New England Classic	July 24	Kenny Perry	268/-16	180,000
St. Jude Classic	July 31	Dicky Pride*	267/-17	225,000
Buick Open	Aug 7	Fred Couples	270/-18	198,000
PGA Championship	Aug 14	Nick Price	269/-11	310,000
The International	Aug 21	Steve Lowery	+35 ‡	252,000
NEC World Series of Golf	Aug 28	José María Olazábal	269/-11	360,000
Greater Milwaukee Open	Sept 4	Mike Springer	268/-16	180,000
Canadian Open	Sept 11	Nick Price	275/-13	234,000
B.C. Open	Sept 18	Mike Sullivan	266/-18	162,000
Hardees Classic	Sept 25	Mark McCumber	265/-15	180,000
Buick Southern Open#	Oct 2	Steve Elkington	200/-16	144,000
Walt Disney World/Oldsmobile Classic	Oct 9	Rick Fehr	269/-19	198,000
Texas Open	Oct 16	Bob Estes	265/-19	180,000
Las Vegas Invitational	Oct 23	Bruce Lietzke	332/-28	270,000
TOUR Championship	Oct 30	Mark McCumber*	274/-10	540,000

*Won on 1st playoff hole.

**Won on 2nd playoff hole.

‡Revised Stableford scoring.

#Tournament shortened by rain.

Women's Majors

Nabisco Dinah Shore

Mission Hills CC; Rancho Mirage, CA
(par 72; 6,446 yds) March 24–27

Player	Score	Earnings ($)
Donna Andrews	70-69-67-70—276	105,000
Laura Davies	70-68-69-70—277	65,165
Tammie Green	70-72-69-68—279	47,553
Jan Stephenson	70-69-70-71—280	36,985
Michelle McGann	70-68-70-73—281	29,940
Gail Graham	73-71-71-68—283	21,251
Kelly Robbins	73-70-69-71—283	21,251
Brandie Burton	73-73-65-72—283	21,251
Hollis Stacy	72-72-70-70—284	15,674
Nancy Lopez	68-72-73-71—284	15,674
Meg Mallon	72-75-69-69—285	12,064
L. Neumann	76-71-68-70—285	12,064
Dana Dormann	73-71-70-71—285	12,064
Dale Eggeling	71-71-71-72—285	12,064
Kris Monaghan	70-76-70-70—286	9,862
Vicki Fergon	69-74-72-71—286	9,862
Lauri Merten	74-74-71-68—287	9,862
Nancy Scranton	75-70-69-73—287	9,862

LPGA Championship

DuPont Country Club; Wilmington, DE
(par 71; 6,386 yds) May 12–15

Player	Score	Earnings ($)
Laura Davies	70-72-69-68—279	165,000
Alice Ritzman	68-73-71-70—282	102,402
Elaine Crosby	76-71-69-67—283	54,660
Pat Bradley	73-73-70-67—283	54,660
Hiromi Kobayashi	72-73-71-67—283	54,660
Liselotte Neumann	74-73-67-69—283	54,660
Sherri Steinhauer	75-70-72-68—285	27,676
Amy Alcott	71-75-70-69—285	27,676
Beth Daniel	72-74-68-71—285	27,676
Patty Sheehan	72-68-72-73—285	27,676
Dottie Mochrie	68-78-70-70—286	20,203
Meg Mallon	71-71-69-75—286	20,203
Val Skinner	74-69-72-72—287	18,266
Juli Inkster	69-76-74-69—288	16,051
Dana Dormann	71-76-71-70—288	16,051
Chris Johnson	70-74-73-71—288	16,051
Barb Mucha	73-74-75-67—289	12,257
Nanci Bowen	73-75-73-68—289	12,257
Tammie Green	71-76-74-68—289	12,257
Donna Andrews	73-76-69-71—289	12,257
Betsy King	74-73-71-71—289	12,257
Missie McGeorge	75-71-70-73—289	12,257
Kris Monaghan	72-72-72-73—289	12,257
Mardi Lunn	70-75-70-74—289	12,257
Robin Walton	70-70-75-74—289	12,257

U.S. Women's Open

Indianwood G & CC, Lake Orion, MI
(par 71; 6,244 yds) July 21-24

Player	Score	Earnings ($)
Patty Sheehan	66-71-69-71—277	155,000
Tammie Green	66-72-69-71—278	85,000
L. Neumann	69-72-71-69—281	47,752
Tania Abitbol	72-68-73-70—283	31,133
Alicia Dibos	69-68-73-73—283	31,133
Amy Alcott	71-67-77-69—284	21,487
Meg Mallon	70-72-73-69—284	21,487
Betsy King	69-71-72-72—284	21,487
Kelly Robbins	71-72-70-72—285	16,466
Donna Andrews	67-72-70-76—285	16,466
Helen Alfredsson	63-69-76-77—285	16,446
Lauri Merten	74-68-75-69—286	12,805
Dottie Mochrie	72-72-71-71—286	12,805
Lisa Grimes	72-73-69-72—286	12,805
Michelle Estill	69-68-75-74—286	12,805
Judy Dickinson	66-73-73-74—286	12,805
Laura Davies	68-68-75-75—286	12,805
Michelle McGann	71-70-77-69—287	10,203
Juli Inkster	75-72-69-71—287	10,203
Beth Daniel	69-74-71-73—287	10,203
Joan Pitcock	74-72-67-74—287	10,203
Stephanie Maynor	73-70-76-69—288	9,012
Lisa Walters	72-73-72-71—288	9,012
Sherri Steinhauer	68-72-74-74—288	9,012

du Maurier Ltd. Classic

Ottawa Hunt and GC; Ottawa, Ontario
(par 72; 6,340 yds) August 25-28

Player	Score	Earnings ($)
Martha Nause	65-71-72-71—279	120,000
Michelle McGann	66-71-71-72—280	74,474
L. Neumann	70-67-71-73—281	54,346
Jane Geddes	74-67-70-72—283	34,888
Meg Mallon	70-72-68-73—283	34,888
Betsy King	67-69-74-73—283	34,888
Dawn Coe-Jones	72-70-71-71—284	20,128
Marianne Moore	69-72-70-73—284	20,128
Judy Dickinson	72-68-70-74—284	20,128
Kelly Robbins	66-70-73-75—284	20,128
Vicki Fergon	72-68-75-70—285	14,223
Sherri Steinhauer	68-72-73-72—285	14,223
Patty Sheehan	71-71-68-75—285	14,223
Amy Alcott	73-70-72-71—286	12,076
Dottie Mochrie	67-74-72-73—286	12,076
Jane Crafter	71-74-75-67—287	9,862
Page Dunlap	72-69-75-71—287	9,862
Alice Ritzman	76-70-68-73—287	9,862
Rosie Jones	73-70-70-74—287	9,862
Jenny Lidback	70-72-71-74—287	9,862
Alicia Dibos	71-71-70-75—287	9,862

Women's Tour Results

Late 1993 LPGA Tour Events

Tournament	Final Round	Winner	Score/ Under Par	Earnings ($)
JC Penney Classic	Dec 5	M. McNamara/M. Springer	265/–19	110,000 each

1994 LPGA Tour Events

Tournament	Final Round	Winner	Score/ Under Par	Earnings ($)
HealthSouth Palm Beach Classic	Feb 6	Dawn Coe-Jones	201/–15	60,000
Hawaiian Ladies Open	Feb 20	Marta Figueras-Dotti	209/–7	75,000
Tournament of Champions	Mar 6	Dottie Mochrie	287/–1	115,000
Ping/Welch's Championship	Mar 13	Donna Andrews	276/–12	63,750
Standard Register Ping	Mar 20	Laura Davies	277/–15	105,000
Nabisco Dinah Shore	Mar 27	Donna Andrews	276/–12	105,000
Atlanta Women's Championship	Apr 17	Val Skinner	206/–10	97,500
Sprint Championship	May 1	Sherri Steinhauer	273/–15	180,000
Sara Lee Classic	May 8	Laura Davies	203/–13	78,750
McDonald's LPGA Championship	May 15	Laura Davies	279/–15	165,000
Lady Keystone Open	May 22	Elaine Crosby	211/–5	60,000
LPGA Corning Classic	May 29	Beth Daniel	278/–10	75,000
Oldsmobile Classic	June 5	Beth Daniel	268/–20	90,000
Minnesota Classic	June 12	Liselotte Neumann	205/–11	75,000
Rochester International	June 19	Tammie Green	276/–12	75,000
ShopRite LPGA Classic	June 26	Donna Andrews	207/–6	75,000
Youngstown-Warren Classic	July 3	Tammie Green	206/–10	82,500
Jamie Farr Toledo Classic	July 10	Kelly Robbins*	204/–9	75,000
Big Apple Classic	July 17	Beth Daniel*	276/–8	97,500
U.S. Women's Open	July 24	Patty Sheehan	277/–7	155,000
Ping/Welch's Championship	July 31	Helen Alfredsson	274/–14	67,500
McCall's Classic	Aug 7	Carolyn Hill	275/–13	75,000
Children's Medical Center Classic	Aug 14	Maggie Will	210/–6	52,500
Chicago Challenge	Aug 21	Jane Geddes	272/–16	75,000
du Maurier Ltd. Classic	Aug 28	Martha Nause	279/–9	120,000
Rail Classic	Sept 4	Barb Mucha	203/–13	78,750
Ping-Cellular One Championship	Sept 11	Missie McGeorge	207/–9	75,000
Safeco Classic	Sept 18	Deb Richard	276/–12	75,000
Heartland Classic	Oct 2	Liselotte Neumann	278/–10	75,000
LPGA Women's Championship	Oct 16	Beth Daniel	274/-14	105,000

* Won on first hole of playoff.

Senior Men's Tour Results

Late 1993 Senior Tour Events

Tournament	Final Round	Winner	Score/ Under Par	Earnings ($)
PING Kaanapali Classic	Oct 31	George Archer*	199/–14	82,500
Senior TOUR Championship	Dec 12	Simon Hobday	199/–17	150,000

1994 Senior Tour Events

Tournament	Final Round	Winner	Score/ Under Par	Earnings ($)
Mercedes Championship	Jan 9	Jack Nicklaus	279/–9	100,000
Royal Caribbean Classic	Feb 6	Lee Trevino††	205/–8	120,000
GTE Suncoast Classic	Feb 13	Rocky Thompson	201/–12	105,000
IntelliNet Challenge	Feb 20	Mike Hill	201/–15	75,000
Chrysler Cup	Feb 27	George Archer*	203/–13	55,000
GTE West Classic	Mar 6	Jay Sigel	198/–12	82,500
Vantage at the Dominion	Mar 13	Jim Albus	208/–8	97,500
Doug Sanders Celebrity Classic	Mar 27	Tom Wargo	209/–7	75,000

1994 Senior Tour Events *(Cont.)*

Tournament	Final Round	Winner	Score/ Under Par	Earnings ($)
Fuji Grandslam	Mar 28	Lee Trevino	207/–9	77,600
The Tradition	Apr 3	Ray Floyd*	271/–17	127,500
PGA Seniors' Championship	Apr 17	Lee Trevino	279/–9	115,000
Dallas Reunion Pro-Am	Apr 24	Larry Gilbert	202/–8	75,000
Las Vegas Classic	May 1	Ray Floyd	203/–13	135,000
Liberty Mutual Legends of Golf	May 8	D. Douglass/Charles Coody	188/–28	200,000
Paine Webber Invitational	May 15	Lee Trevino	203/–13	112,500
Cadillac NFL Classic	May 22	Ray Floyd	206/–10	135,000
Bell Atlantic Classic	May 30	Lee Trevino	206/–4	105,000
Bruno's Memorial Classic	June 5	Jim Dent	201/–15	150,000
Nationwide Championship	June 12	Dave Stockton	198/–18	172,000
Bell South Senior Classic	June 19	Lee Trevino	199/–17	157,500
Ford Senior Players Championship	June 27	David Stockton	271/–17	210,000
U.S. Senior Open	July 3	Simon Hobday	274/–10	145,000
Kroger Classic	July 10	Jim Colbert	199/–14	127,500
Ameritech Senior Open	July 17	John Paul Cain	202/–14	112,500
Southwestern Bell Senior	July 24	Jim Colbert	196/–14	105,000
Northville Long Island Classic	July 31	Lee Trevino	200/–16	97,500
Bank of Boston Senior Golf Classic	Aug 7	Jim Albus	203/–13	112,500
First of America Classic	Aug 14	Tony Jacklin	136/–8	97,500
Burnet Classic	Aug 21	Dave Stockton	203/–13	157,500
Franklin Quest	Aug 28	Tom Weiskopf	204/–12	75,000
GTE Northwest Classic	Sept 4	Simon Hobday†	209/–7	82,500
Quicksilver Seniors	Sept 11	Dave Eichelberger	209/–7	157,500
Bank One Classic	Sept 18	Isao Aoki	202/–14	82,500
Brickyard Crossing Championship	Sept 25	Isao Aoki	133/–11	105,000
Vantage Championship	Oct 2	Larry Gilbert	198/–18	225,000
The Transamerica	Oct 9	Kermit Zarley*	204/–12	90,000
Gold Rush	Oct 16	Bob Murphy*	208/–8	97,500
Ralph's Senior Classic	Oct 23	Jack Kiefer	197/–16	112,500
Kaanapali Classic	Oct 30	Bob Murphy	195/–18	82,500

*Won on 1st playoff hole. † Won on 3rd playoff hole. †† Won on fourth playoff hole.

Amateur Results

Tournament	Final Round	Winner	Score	Runner-Up
Junior Amateur	July 30	Terry Noe	2 up	Andy Barnes
Girls' Junior	July 16	Kelli Kuehne	5 & 3	Molly Cooper
Women's Amateur	Aug 13	Wendy Ward	2 & 1	Jill McGill
Men's Amateur	Aug 28	Tiger Woods	2 up	Trip Kuehne
Women's Mid-Amateur	Sep 15	Sarah Ingram	2 & 1	Marla Jemsek
Men's Mid-Amateur	Sep 22	Tim Jackson	1-up	Tommy Brennan
Senior Women	Sep 23	Marlene Streit	1-up	Nancy Fitzgerald
Senior Men	Sep 24	O. Gordon Brewer	5 & 4	Bob Hollander

International Results

Tournament	Final Round	Winner	Score	Runner-Up
World Cup	Nov 14,1993	United States	556	Zimbabwe
Curtis Cup Matches	July 31	Great Britain/Ireland	9–9	United States
Presidents Cup	Sep 18	United States	20–12	Int'l Team
Solheim Cup	Oct 23	United States	13–7	Europe
World Amateur Team Championship	Oct 9	United States	629	GB/Ireland

PGA Tour Final 1994 Money Leaders

Name	Events	Best Finish	Scoring Average	Money ($)
Nick Price	19	1 (6)	69.39	1,499,927
Greg Norman	16	1	68.81	1,330,307
Mark McCumber	20	1 (3)	69.56	1,208,209
Tom Lehman	23	1	69.46	1,031,144
Fuzzy Zoeller	19	2 (5)	69.89	1,016,804
Loren Roberts	22	1	69.61	1,015,671
José María Olazábal	8	1 (2)	68.87	969,900
Corey Pavin	20	1	69.63	906,305
Jeff Maggert	26	2 (2)	70.25	814,475
Hale Irwin	22	1	69.72	814,436

LPGA Tour Final 1993 Money Leaders

Name	Events	Best Finish	Scoring Average	Money ($)
Betsy King	27	1	70.85	595,992
Patty Sheehan	21	1	71.04	540,547
Brandie Burton	26	1 (3)	71.02	517,741
Dottie Mochrie	25	1	71.09	429,118
Helen Alfredsson	22	1	71.40	402,685
Lauri Merten	23	1	72.03	394,744
Tammie Green	23	1 (2)	71.46	356,579
Hiromi Kobayashi	24	1 (2)	71.78	347,060
Donna Andrews	23	2	71.54	334,285
Trish Johnson	16	1 (2)	71.64	331,745

Senior Tour Final 1993 Money Leaders

Name	Events	Best Finish	Scoring Average	Money ($)
Dave Stockton	34	1 (5)	69.71	1,175,944
Bob Charles	29	1 (3)	69.59	1,046,823
George Archer	32	1 (4)	69.86	963,124
Lee Trevino	25	1 (3)	70.00	956,591
Chi Chi Rodriguez	32	1	70.41	798,857
Mike Hill	29	1 (2)	69.97	798,116
Jim Colbert	31	1 (2)	70.57	779,889
Bob Murphy	27	1 (2)	70.24	768,743
Ray Floyd	14	1 (2)	69.67	713,168
Simon Hobday	34	1 (2)	71.40	670,417

Play It As It Flies

It was the best drive he had hit all day, but never did Randall Kemp imagine his ball would go as far as it did. Playing last summer with four friends at the Highlands Golf Course in Bella Vista, Ark., Kemp, a 31-year-old physician from Wetumka, Okla., drove his tee shot on the 14th hole 250 yards down the middle of the fairway. Next up, George Miles sliced his drive into the woods.

That was when the black helicopter flew in low and fast over the trees and landed on the narrow fairway at the spot where Kemp's drive had come to rest. As the golfers looked on in amazement, a man none of them had ever seen before jumped out of the copter, plucked Kemp's ball from the grass and climbed back in as the chopper took off and zoomed away. "It was a regular old ball," says the still baffled Kemp. "I don't know why anyone would take it."

Kemp and his buddies reported the inexplicable ball-snatching to the course manager, who, after satisfying himself that none of the golfers had been drinking, called the cops. A foursome following Kemp's group also reported seeing the helicopter. The Bella Vista sheriff's department checked with every airport in the area, but none had any record of a helicopter either taking off or landing that day. So far, the mystery chopper has not been seen again.

Still, the incident didn't ruin the hole for Kemp. "After going over the rule book," he says, "the guys let me drop a ball without a penalty stroke."

Men's Golf

THE MAJOR TOURNAMENTS
The Masters

Year	Winner	Score	Runner-Up
1934	Horton Smith	284	Craig Wood
1935	Gene Sarazen* (144)	282	Craig Wood (149) (only 36-hole playoff)
1936	Horton Smith	285	Harry Cooper
1937	Byron Nelson	283	Ralph Guldahl
1938	Henry Picard	285	Ralph Guldahl, Harry Cooper
1939	Ralph Guldahl	279	Sam Snead
1940	Jimmy Demaret	280	Lloyd Mangrum
1941	Craig Wood	280	Byron Nelson
1942	Byron Nelson* (69)	280	Ben Hogan (70)
1943-45	No tournament		
1946	Herman Keiser	282	Ben Hogan
1947	Jimmy Demaret	281	Byron Nelson, Frank Stranahan
1948	Claude Harmon	279	Cary Middlecoff
1949	Sam Snead	282	Johnny Bulla, Lloyd Mangrum
1950	Jimmy Demaret	283	Jim Ferrier
1951	Ben Hogan	280	Skee Riegel
1952	Sam Snead	286	Jack Burke, Jr
1953	Ben Hogan	274	Ed Oliver, Jr
1954	Sam Snead* (70)	289	Ben Hogan (71)
1955	Cary Middlecoff	279	Ben Hogan
1956	Jack Burke, Jr	289	Ken Venturi
1957	Doug Ford	282	Sam Snead
1958	Arnold Palmer	284	Doug Ford, Fred Hawkins
1959	Art Wall, Jr	284	Cary Middlecoff
1960	Arnold Palmer	282	Ken Venturi
1961	Gary Player	280	Charles R. Coe, Arnold Palmer
1962	Arnold Palmer* (68)	280	Gary Player (71), Dow Finsterwald (77)
1963	Jack Nicklaus	286	Tony Lema
1964	Arnold Palmer	276	Dave Marr, Jack Nicklaus
1965	Jack Nicklaus	271	Arnold Palmer, Gary Player
1966	Jack Nicklaus* (70)	288	Tommy Jacobs (72), Gay Brewer, Jr (78)
1967	Gay Brewer, Jr	280	Bobby Nichols
1968	Bob Goalby	277	Roberto DeVicenzo
1969	George Archer	281	Billy Casper, George Knudson, Tom Weiskopf
1970	Billy Casper* (69)	279	Gene Littler (74)
1971	Charles Coody	279	Johnny Miller, Jack Nicklaus
1972	Jack Nicklaus	286	Bruce Crampton, Bobby Mitchell, Tom Weiskopf
1973	Tommy Aaron	283	J. C. Snead
1974	Gary Player	278	Tom Weiskopf, Dave Stockton
1975	Jack Nicklaus	276	Johnny Miller, Tom Weiskopf
1976	Ray Floyd	271	Ben Crenshaw
1977	Tom Watson	276	Jack Nicklaus
1978	Gary Player	277	Hubert Green, Rod Funseth, Tom Watson
1979†	Fuzzy Zoeller* (4-3)	280	Ed Sneed (4-4), Tom Watson (4-4)
1980	Seve Ballesteros	275	Gibby Gilbert, Jack Newton
1981	Tom Watson	280	Johnny Miller, Jack Nicklaus
1982	Craig Stadler* (4)	284	Dan Pohl (5)
1983	Seve Ballesteros	280	Ben Crenshaw, Tom Kite
1984	Ben Crenshaw	277	Tom Watson
1985	Bernhard Langer	282	Curtis Strange, Seve Ballesteros, Ray Floyd
1986	Jack Nicklaus	279	Greg Norman, Tom Kite
1987	Larry Mize* (4-3)	285	Seve Ballesteros (5), Greg Norman (4-4)
1988	Sandy Lyle	281	Mark Calcavecchia
1989	Nick Faldo* (5-3)	283	Scott Hoch (5-4)
1990	Nick Faldo* (4-4)	278	Ray Floyd (4-x)
1991	Ian Woosnam	277	José María Olazabal
1992	Fred Couples	275	Ray Floyd
1993	Bernhard Langer	277	Chip Beck
1994	José María Olazábal	279	Tom Lehman

*Winner in playoff. Playoff scores are in parentheses. †Playoff cut from 18 holes to sudden death.

Note: Played at Augusta National Golf Club, Augusta, GA.

United States Open Championship

Year	Winner	Score	Runner-Up	Site
1895	Horace Rawlins	†173	Willie Dunn	Newport GC, Newport, RI
1896	James Foulis	†152	Horace Rawlins	Shinnecock Hills GC, Southampton, NY
1897	Joe Lloyd	†162	Willie Anderson	Chicago GC, Wheaton, IL
1898	Fred Herd	328	Alex Smith	Myopia Hunt Club, Hamilton, MA
1899	Willie Smith	315	George Low	Baltimore CC, Baltimore
			Val Fitzjohn	
			W. H. Way	
1900	Harry Vardon	313	John H. Taylor	Chicago GC, Wheaton, IL
1901	Willie Anderson* (85)	331	Alex Smith (86)	Myopia Hunt Club, Hamilton, MA
1902	Laurie Auchterlonie	307	Stewart Gardner	Garden City GC, Garden City, NY
1903	Willie Anderson* (82)	307	David Brown (84)	Baltusrol GC, Springfield, NJ
1904	Willie Anderson	303	Gil Nicholls	Glen View Club, Golf, IL
1905	Willie Anderson	314	Alex Smith	Myopia Hunt Club, Hamilton, MA
1906	Alex Smith	295	Willie Smith	Onwentsia Club, Lake Forest, IL
1907	Alex Ross	302	Gil Nicholls	Philadelphia Cricket Club, Chestnut Hill, PA
1908	Fred McLeod* (77)	322	Willie Smith (83)	Myopia Hunt Club, Hamilton, MA
1909	George Sargent	290	Tom McNamara	Englewood GC, Englewood, NJ
1910	Alex Smith* (71)	298	John McDermott (75)	Philadelphia Cricket Club, Chestnut Hill, PA
			Macdonald Smith (77)	
1911	John McDermott* (80)	307	Mike Brady (82)	Chicago GC, Wheaton, IL
			George Simpson (85)	
1912	John McDermott	294	Tom McNamara	CC of Buffalo, Buffalo
1913	Francis Ouimet* (72)	304	Harry Vardon (77)	The Country Club, Brookline, MA
			Edward Ray (78)	
1914	Walter Hagen	290	Chick Evans	Midlothian CC, Blue Island, IL
1915	Jerry Travers	297	Tom McNamara	Baltusrol GC, Springfield, NJ
1916	Chick Evans	286	Jock Hutchison	Minikahda Club, Minneapolis
1917-18	No tournament			
1919	Walter Hagen* (77)	301	Mike Brady (78)	Brae Burn CC, West Newton, MA
1920	Edward Ray	295	Harry Vardon	Inverness CC, Toledo
			Jack Burke	
			Leo Diegel	
			Jock Hutchison	
1921	Jim Barnes	289	Walter Hagen	Columbia CC, Chevy Chase, MD
			Fred McLeod	
1922	Gene Sarazen	288	John L. Black	Skokie CC, Glencoe, IL
			Bobby Jones	
1923	Bobby Jones* (76)	296	Bobby Cruickshank (78)	Inwood CC, Inwood, NY
1924	Cyril Walker	297	Bobby Jones	Oakland Hills CC, Birmingham, MI
1925	W. MacFarlane* (75-72)	291	Bobby Jones (75-73)	Worcester CC, Worcester, MA
1926	Bobby Jones	293	Joe Turnesa	Scioto CC, Columbus, OH
1927	Tommy Armour* (76)	301	Harry Cooper (79)	Oakmont CC, Oakmont, PA
1928	Johnny Farrell* (143)	294	Bobby Jones (144)	Olympia Fields CC, Matteson, IL
1929	Bobby Jones* (141)	294	Al Espinosa (164)	Winged Foot GC, Mamaroneck, NY
1930	Bobby Jones	287	Macdonald Smith	Interlachen CC, Hopkins, MN
1931	Billy Burke* (149-148)	292	George Von Elm	Inverness Club, Toledo
			(149-149)	
1932	Gene Sarazen	286	Phil Perkins	Fresh Meadows CC, Flushing, NY
			Bobby Cruickshank	
1933	Johnny Goodman	287	Ralph Guldahl	North Shore CC, Glenview, IL
1934	Olin Dutra	293	Gene Srazen	Merion Cricket Club, Ardmore, PA
1935	Sam Parks, Jr	299	Jimmy Thompson	Oakmont CC, Oakmont, PA
1936	Tony Manero	282	Harry Cooper	Baltusrol GC (Upper Course), Springfield, NJ
1937	Ralph Guldahl	281	Sam Snead	Oakland Hills CC, Birmingham, MI
1938	Ralph Guldahl	284	Dick Metz	Cherry Hills CC, Denver, CO
1939	Byron Nelson* (68-70)	284	Craig Wood (68-73)	Philadelphia CC, Philadelphia
			Denny Shute (76)	
1940	Lawson Little* (70)	287	Gene Sarazen (73)	Canterbury GC, Cleveland
1941	Craig Wood	284	Denny Shute	Colonial Club, Fort Worth
1942-45	No tournament			
1946	Lloyd Mangrum* (72-72)	284	Vic Ghezzi (72-73)	Canterbury GC, Cleveland
			Byron Nelson (72-73)	
1947	Lew Worsham* (69)	282	Sam Snead (70)	St Louis CC, Clayton, MO
1948	Ben Hogan	276	Jimmy Demaret	Riviera CC, Los Angeles

United States Open Championship *(Cont.)*

Year	Winner	Score	Runner-Up	Site
1949	Cary Middlecoff	286	Sam Snead Clayton Heafner	Medinah CC, Medinah, IL
1950	Ben Hogan* (69)	287	Lloyd Mangrum (73) George Fazio (75)	Merion GC, Ardmore, PA
1951	Ben Hogan	287	Clayton Heafner	Oakland Hills CC, Birmingham, MI
1952	Julius Boros	281	Ed Oliver	Northwood CC, Dallas
1953	Ben Hogan	283	Sam Snead	Oakmont CC, Oakmont, PA
1954	Ed Furgol	284	Gene Littler	Baltusrol GC (Lower Course), Springfield, NJ
1955	Jack Fleck* (69)	287	Ben Hogan (72)	Olympic Club (Lake Course), San Francisco
1956	Cary Middlecoff	281	Ben Hogan Julius Boros	Oak Hill CC, Rochester, NY
1957	Dick Mayer* (72)	282	Cary Middlecoff (79)	Inverness Club, Toledo
1958	Tommy Bolt	283	Gary Player	Southern Hills CC, Tulsa
1959	Billy Casper	282	Bob Rosburg	Winged Foot GC, Mamaroneck, NY
1960	Arnold Palmer	280	Jack Nicklaus	Cherry Hills CC, Denver
1961	Gene Littler	281	Bob Goalby Doug Sanders	Oakland Hills CC, Birmingham, MI
1962	Jack Nicklaus* (71)	283	Arnold Palmer (74)	Oakmont CC, Oakmont, PA
1963	Julius Boros* (70)	293	Jacky Cupit (73) Arnold Palmer (76)	The Country Club, Brookline, MA
1964	Ken Venturi	278	Tommy Jacobs	Congressional CC, Washington, DC
1965	Gary Player* (71)	282	Kel Nagle (74)	Bellerive CC, St Louis
1966	Billy Casper* (69)	278	Arnold Palmer (73)	Olympic Club (Lake Course), San Francisco
1967	Jack Nicklaus	275	Arnold Palmer	Baltusrol GC (Lower Course), Springfield, NJ
1968	Lee Trevino	275	Jack Nicklaus	Oak Hill CC, Rochester, NY
1969	Orville Moody	281	Deane Beman Al Geiberger Bob Rosburg	Champions GC (Cypress Creek Course), Houston
1970	Tony Jacklin	281	Dave Hill	Hazeltine GC, Chaska, MN
1971	Lee Trevino* (68)	280	Jack Nicklaus (71)	Merion GC (East Course), Ardmore, PA
1972	Jack Nicklaus	290	Bruce Crampton	Pebble Beach GL, Pebble Beach, CA
1973	Johnny Miller	279	John Schlee	Oakmont CC, Oakmont, PA
1974	Hale Irwin	287	Forrest Fezler	Winged Foot GC, Mamaroneck, NY
1975	Lou Graham* (71)	287	John Mahaffey (73)	Medinah CC, Medinah, IL
1976	Jerry Pate	277	Tom Weiskopf Al Geiberger	Atlanta Athletic Club, Duluth, GA
1977	Hubert Green	278	Lou Graham	Southern Hills CC, Tulsa
1978	Andy North	285	Dave Stockton J. C. Snead	Cherry Hills CC, Denver
1979	Hale Irwin	284	Gary Player Jerry Pate	Inverness Club, Toledo
1980	Jack Nicklaus	272	Isao Aoki	Baltusrol GC (Lower Course), Springfield, NJ
1981	David Graham	273	George Burns Bill Rogers	Merion GC, Ardmore, PA
1982	Tom Watson	282	Jack Nicklaus	Pebble Beach GL, Pebble Beach, CA
1983	Larry Nelson	280	Tom Watson	Oakmont CC, Oakmont, PA
1984	Fuzzy Zoeller* (67)	276	Greg Norman (75)	Winged Foot GC, Mamaroneck, NY
1985	Andy North	279	Dave Barr T. C. Chen Denis Watson	Oakland Hills CC, Birmingham, MI
1986	Ray Floyd	279	Lanny Wadkins Chip Beck	Shinnecock Hills GC, Southampton, NY
1987	Scott Simpson	277	Tom Watson	Olympic Club (Lake Course), San Francisco
1988	Curtis Strange* (71)	278	Nick Faldo (75)	The Country Club, Brookline, MA
1989	Curtis Strange	278	Chip Beck Mark McCumber Ian Woosnam	Oak Hill CC, Rochester, NY
1990	Hale Irwin* (74) (3)	280	Mike Donald (74) (4)	Medinah CC, Medinah, IL
1991	Payne Stewart (75)	282	Scott Simpson (77)	Hazeltine GC, Chaska, MN
1992	Tom Kite	285	Jeff Sluman	Pebble Beach GL, Pebble Beach, CA
1993	Lee Janzen	272	Payne Stewart	Baltusrol GC, Springfield, NJ
1994	Ernie Els*	279	Loren Roberts Colin Montgomerie	Oakmont CC, Oakmont, PA

*Winner in playoff. Playoff scores are in parentheses. The 1990 playoff went to one hole of sudden death after an 18-hole playoff. In the 1994 playoff, Montgomerie was eliminated after 18 playoff holes, and Els beat Roberts on the 20th.
†Before 1898, 36 holes. From 1898 on, 72 holes.

British Open

Year	Winner	Score	Runner-Up	Site
1860†	Willie Park	174	Tom Morris, Sr	Prestwick, Scotland
1861‡	Tom Morris, Sr	163	Willie Park	Prestwick, Scotland
1862	Tom Morris, Sr	163	Willie Park	Prestwick, Scotland
1863	Willie Park	168	Tom Morris, Sr	Prestwick, Scotland
1864	Tom Morris, Sr	160	Andrew Strath	Prestwick, Scotland
1865	Andrew Strath	162	Willie Park	Prestwick, Scotland
1866	Willie Park	169	David Park	Prestwick, Scotland
1867	Tom Morris, Sr	170	Willie Park	Prestwick, Scotland
1868	Tom Morris, Jr	154	Tom Morris, Sr	Prestwick, Scotland
1869	Tom Morris, Jr	157	Tom Morris, Sr	Prestwick, Scotland
1870	Tom Morris, Jr	149	David Strath Bob Kirk	Prestwick, Scotland
1871	No tournament			
1872	Tom Morris, Jr	166	David Strath	Prestwick, Scotland
1873	Tom Kidd	179	Jamie Anderson	St Andrews, Scotland
1874	Mungo Park	159	No record	Musselburgh, Scotland
1875	Willie Park	166	Bob Martin	Prestwick, Scotland
1876	Bob Martin#	176	David Strath	St Andrews, Scotland
1877	Jamie Anderson	160	Bob Pringle	Musselburgh, Scotland
1878	Jamie Anderson	157	Robert Kirk	Prestwick, Scotland
1879	Jamie Anderson	169	Andrew Kirkaldy James Allan	St Andrews, Scotland
1880	Robert Ferguson	162	No record	Musselburgh, Scotland
1881	Robert Ferguson	170	Jamie Anderson	Prestwick, Scotland
1882	Robert Ferguson	171	Willie Fernie	St Andrews, Scotland
1883	Willie Fernie*	159	Robert Ferguson	Musselburgh, Scotland
1884	Jack Simpson	160	Douglas Rolland Willie Fernie	Prestwick, Scotland
1885	Bob Martin	171	Archie Simpson	St Andrews, Scotland
1886	David Brown	157	Willie Campbell	Musselburgh, Scotland
1887	Willie Park, Jr	161	Bob Martin	Prestwick, Scotland
1888	Jack Burns	171	Bernard Sayers David Anderson	St Andrews, Scotland
1889	Willie Park, Jr* (158)	155	Andrew Kirkaldy (163)	Musselburgh, Scotland
1890	John Ball	164	Willie Fernie	Prestwick, Scotland
1891	Hugh Kirkaldy	166	Andrew Kirkaldy Willie Fernie	St Andrews, Scotland
1892	Harold Hilton	**305	John Ball Hugh Kirkaldy	Muirfield, Scotland
1893	William Auchterlonie	322	John E. Laidlay	Prestwick, Scotland
1894	John H. Taylor	326	Douglas Rolland	Royal St George's, England
1895	John H. Taylor	322	Alexander Herd	St Andrews, Scotland
1896	Harry Vardon* (157)	316	John H. Taylor (161)	Muirfield, Scotland
1897	Harold Hilton	314	James Braid	Hoylake, England
1898	Harry Vardon	307	Willie Park, Jr	Prestwick, Scotland
1899	Harry Vardon	310	Jack White	Royal St George's, England
1900	John H. Taylor	309	Harry Vardon	St Andrews, Scotland
1901	James Braid	309	Harry Vardon	Muirfield, Scotland
1902	Alexander Herd	307	Harry Vardon	Hoylake, England
1903	Harry Vardon	300	Tom Vardon	Prestwick, Scotland
1904	Jack White	296	John H. Taylor	Royal St George's, England
1905	James Braid	318	John H. Taylor Rolland Jones	St Andrews, Scotland
1906	James Braid	300	John H. Taylor	Muirfield, Scotland
1907	Arnaud Massy	312	John H. Taylor	Hoylake, England
1908	James Braid	291	Tom Ball	Prestwick, Scotland
1909	John H. Taylor	295	James Braid Tom Ball	Deal, England
1910	James Braid	299	Alexander Herd	St Andrews, Scotland
1911	Harry Vardon	303	Arnaud Massy	Royal St George's, England
1912	Ted Ray	295	Harry Vardon	Muirfield, Scotland
1913	John H. Taylor	304	Ted Ray	Hoylake, England
1914	Harry Vardon	306	John H. Taylor	Prestwick, Scotland
1915-19	No tournament			
1920	George Duncan	303	Alexander Herd	Deal, England

British Open *(Cont.)*

Year	Winner	Score	Runner-Up	Site
1921	Jock Hutchison* (150)	296	Roger Wethered (159)	St Andrews, Scotland
1922	Walter Hagen	300	George Duncan	Royal St George's, England
			Jim Barnes	
1923	Arthur G. Havers	295	Walter Hagen	Troon, Scotland
1924	Walter Hagen	301	Ernest Whitcombe	Hoylake, England
1925	Jim Barnes	300	Archie Compston	Prestwick, Scotland
			Ted Ray	
1926	Bobby Jones	291	Al Watrous	Royal Lytham and St Annes GC, St Anne's-on-the-Sea, England
1927	Bobby Jones	285	Aubrey Boomer	St Andrews, Scotland
1928	Walter Hagen	292	Gene Sarazen	Royal St George's, England
1929	Walter Hagen	292	Johnny Farrell	Muirfield, Scotland
1930	Bobby Jones	291	Macdonald Smith	Hoylake, England
			Leo Diegel	
1931	Tommy Armour	296	Jose Jurado	Carnoustie, Scotland
1932	Gene Sarazen	283	Macdonald Smith	Prince's, England
1933	Denny Shute* (149)	292	Craig Wood (154)	St Andrews, Scotland
1934	Henry Cotton	283	Sidney F. Brews	Royal St George's, England
1935	Alfred Perry	283	Alfred Padgham	Muirfield, Scotland
1936	Alfred Padgham	287	James Adams	Hoylake, England
1937	Henry Cotton	290	Reginald A. Whitcombe	Carnoustie, Scotland
1938	Reginald A. Whitcombe	295	James Adams	Royal St George's, England
1939	Richard Burton	290	Johnny Bulla	St Andrews, Scotland
1940-45	No tournament			
1946	Sam Snead	290	Bobby Locke	St Andrews, Scotland
			Johnny Bulla	
1947	Fred Daly	293	Reginald W. Horne	Hoylake, England
			Frank Stranahan	
1948	Henry Cotton	294	Fred Daly	Muirfield, Scotland
1949	Bobby Locke* (135)	283	Harry Bradshaw (147)	Royal St George's, England
1950	Bobby Locke	279	Roberto DeVicenzo	Troon, Scotland
1951	Max Faulkner	285	Tony Cerda	Portrush, Ireland
1952	Bobby Locke	287	Peter Thomson	Royal Lytham, England
1953	Ben Hogan	282	Frank Stranahan	Carnoustie, Scotland
			Dai Rees	
			Peter Thomson	
			Tony Cerda	
1954	Peter Thomson	283	Sidney S. Scott	Royal Birkdale, England
			Dai Rees	
			Bobby Locke	
1955	Peter Thomson	281	John Fallon	St Andrews, Scotland
1956	Peter Thomson	286	Flory Van Donck	Hoylake, England
1957	Bobby Locke	279	Peter Thomson	St Andrews, Scotland
1958	Peter Thomson* (139)	278	Dave Thomas (143)	Royal Lytham, England
1959	Gary Player	284	Fred Bullock	Muirfield, Scotland
			Flory Van Donck	
1960	Kel Nagle	278	Arnold Palmer	St Andrews, Scotland
1961	Arnold Palmer	284	Dai Rees	Royal Birkdale, England
1962	Arnold Palmer	276	Kel Nagle	Troon, Scotland
1963	Bob Charles* (140)	277	Phil Rodgers (148)	Royal Lytham, England
1964	Tony Lema	279	Jack Nicklaus	St Andrews, Scotland
1965	Peter Thomson	285	Brian Huggett	Southport, England
			Christy O'Connor	
1966	Jack Nicklaus	282	Doug Sanders	Muirfield, Scotland
			Dave Thomas	
1967	Robert DeVicenzo	278	Jack Nicklaus	Hoylake, England
1968	Gary Player	289	Jack Nicklaus	Carnoustie, Scotland
			Bob Charles	
1969	Tony Jacklin	280	Bob Charles	Royal Lytham, England
1970	Jack Nicklaus* (72)	283	Doug Sanders (73)	St Andrews, Scotland
1971	Lee Trevino	278	Lu Liang Huan	Royal Birkdale, England
1972	Lee Trevino	278	Jack Nicklaus	Muirfield, Scotland
1973	Tom Weiskopf	276	Johnny Miller	Troon, Scotland
1974	Gary Player	282	Peter Oosterhuis	Royal Lytham, England
1975	Tom Watson* (71)	279	Jack Newton (72)	Carnoustie, Scotland

British Open (Cont.)

Year	Winner	Score	Runner-Up	Site
1976	Johnny Miller	279	Jack Nicklaus	Royal Birkdale, England
			Seve Ballesteros	
1977	Tom Watson	268	Jack Nicklaus	Turnberry, Scotland
1978	Jack Nicklaus	281	Ben Crenshaw	St Andrews, Scotland
			Tom Kite	
			Ray Floyd	
			Simon Owen	
1979	Seve Ballesteros	283	Ben Crenshaw	Royal Lytham, England
			Jack Nicklaus	
1980	Tom Watson	271	Lee Trevino	Muirfield, Scotland
1981	Bill Rogers	276	Bernhard Langer	Royal St George's, England
1982	Tom Watson	284	Nick Price	Royal Troon, Scotland
			Peter Oosterhuis	
1983	Tom Watson	275	Andy Bean	Royal Birkdale, England
1984	Seve Ballesteros	276	Tom Watson	St Andrews, Scotland
			Bernhard Langer	
1985	Sandy Lyle	282	Payne Stewart	Royal St George's, England
1986	Greg Norman	280	Gordon Brand	Turnberry, Scotland
1987	Nick Faldo	279	Paul Azinger	Muirfield, Scotland
			Rodger Davis	
1988	Seve Ballesteros	273	Nick Price	Royal Lytham, England
1989††	Mark Calcavecchia* (4-3-3-3)	275	Wayne Grady (4-4-4-4) Greg Norman (3-3-4-x)	Royal Troon, Scotland
1990	Nick Faldo	270	Payne Stewart	St Andrews, Scotland
			Mark McNulty	
1991	Ian Baker-Finch	272	Mike Harwood	Royal Birkdale, England
1992	Nick Faldo	272	John Cook	Muirfield, Scotland
1993	Greg Norman	267	Nick Faldo	Royal St George's, England
1994	Nick Price	268	Jesper Parnevik	Turnberry, Scotland

*Winner in playoff. Playoff scores are in parentheses. †The first event was open only to professional golfers.
‡The second annual open was open to amateurs and pros. #Tied, but refused playoff.
**Championship extended from 36 to 72 holes. ††Playoff cut from 18 holes to 4 holes.

PGA Championship

Year	Winner	Score	Runner-Up	Site
1916	Jim Barnes	1 up	Jock Hutchison	Siwanoy CC, Bronxville, NY
1917-18	No tournament			
1919	Jim Barnes	6 & 5	Fred McLeod	Engineers CC, Roslyn, NY
1920	Jock Hutchison	1 up	J. Douglas Edgar	Flossmoor CC, Flossmoor, IL
1921	Walter Hagen	3 & 2	Jim Barnes	Inwood CC, Far Rockaway, NY
1922	Gene Sarazen	4 & 3	Emmet French	Oakmont CC, Oakmont, PA
1923	Gene Sarazen	1 up 38 holes	Walter Hagen	Pelham CC, Pelham, NY
1924	Walter Hagen	2 up	Jim Barnes	French Lick CC, French Lick, IN
1925	Walter Hagen	6 & 5	William Mehlhorn	Olympia Fields CC, Olympia Fields, IL
1926	Walter Hagen	5 & 3	Leo Diegel	Salisbury GC, Westbury, NY
1927	Walter Hagen	1 up	Joe Turnesa	Cedar Crest CC, Dallas
1928	Leo Diegel	6 & 5	Al Espinosa	Five Farms CC, Baltimore
1929	Leo Diegel	6 & 4	Johnny Farrell	Hillcrest CC, Los Angeles
1930	Tommy Armour	1 up	Gene Sarazen	Fresh Meadow CC, Flushing, NY
1931	Tom Creavy	2 & 1	Denny Shute	Wannamoisett CC, Rumford, RI
1932	Olin Dutra	4 & 3	Frank Walsh	Keller GC, St Paul
1933	Gene Sarazen	5 & 4	Willie Goggin	Blue Mound CC, Milwaukee
1934	Paul Runyan	1 up	Craig Wood	Park CC, Williamsville, NY
1935	Johnny Revolta	5 & 4 38 holes	Tommy Armour	Twin Hills CC, Oklahoma City
1936	Denny Shute	3 & 2	Jimmy Thomson	Pinehurst CC, Pinehurst, NC
1937	Denny Shute	1 up 37 holes	Harold McSpaden	Pittsburgh FC, Aspinwall, PA
1938	Paul Runyan	8 & 7	Sam Snead	Shawnee CC, Shawnee-on-Delaware, PA
1939	Henry Picard	1 up 37 holes	Byron Nelson	Pomonok CC, Flushing, NY
1940	Byron Nelson	1 up	Sam Snead	Hershey CC, Hershey, PA
1941	Vic Ghezzi	1 up 38 holes	Byron Nelson	Cherry Hills CC, Denver

$5,000.00
IS UP FOR GRABS!

Here's your chance to win $5,000 in cash.
Just answer these short questions and return this card today!

1. Who is your favorite NFL team? _____

2. What is your favorite sport to watch? _____

3. What is your favorite sport to play? _____

4. Do you play golf?   Yes ☐   No ☐
   (If YES, please complete questions 5-6.)

5. How many rounds of golf do you play per year?
   ☐ 26+   ☐ 9-25   ☐ 0-8

6. What is your handicap?
   ☐ 0-9   ☐ 10-18   ☐ 19+

Please fill in your address:

_____
NAME

_____
ADDRESS

_____
CITY   STATE   ZIP

☐ Check here if you would like to receive SI's Insider Authentics Catalog.

4RSICS-PCR648

 **GET INTO IT!**

NBD2

PGA Championship *(Cont.)*

Year	Winner	Score	Runner-Up	Site
1942	Sam Snead	2 & 1	Jim Turnesa	Seaview CC, Atlantic City
1943	No tournament			
1944	Bob Hamilton	1 up	Byron Nelson	Manito G & CC, Spokane, WA
1945	Byron Nelson	4 & 3	Sam Byrd	Morraine CC, Dayton
1946	Ben Hogan	6 & 4	Ed Oliver	Portland GC, Portland, OR
1947	Jim Ferrier	2 & 1	Chick Harbert	Plum Hollow CC, Detroit
1948	Ben Hogan	7 & 6	Mike Turnesa	Norwood Hills CC, St Louis
1949	Sam Snead	3 & 2	Johnny Palmer	Hermitage CC, Richmond
1950	Chandler Harper	4 & 3	Henry Williams, Jr	Scioto CC, Columbus, OH
1951	Sam Snead	7 & 6	Walter Burkemo	Oakmont CC, Oakmont, PA
1952	Jim Turnesa	1 up	Chick Harbert	Big Spring CC, Louisville
1953	Walter Burkemo	2 & 1	Felice Torza	Birmingham CC, Birmingham, MI
1954	Chick Harbert	4 & 3	Walter Burkemo	Keller GC, St Paul
1955	Doug Ford	4 & 3	Cary Middlecoff	Meadowbrook CC, Detroit
1956	Jack Burke	3 & 2	Ted Kroll	Blue Hill CC, Boston
1957	Lionel Hebert	2 & 1	Dow Finsterwald	Miami Valley CC, Dayton
1958	Dow Finsterwald	276	Billy Casper	Llanerch CC, Havertown, PA
1959	Bob Rosburg	277	Jerry Barber	Minneapolis GC, St Louis Park, MN
			Doug Sanders	
1960	Jay Hebert	281	Jim Ferrier	Firestone CC, Akron
1961	Jerry Barber* (67)	277	Don January (68)	Olympia Fields CC, Olympia Fields, IL
1962	Gary Player	278	Bob Goalby	Aronimink GC, Newton Square, PA
1963	Jack Nicklaus	279	Dave Ragan, Jr	Dallas Athletic Club, Dallas
1964	Bobby Nichols	271	Jack Nicklaus	Columbus CC, Columbus, OH
			Arnold Palmer	
1965	Dave Marr	280	Billy Casper	Laurel Valley CC, Ligonier, PA
			Jack Nicklaus	
1966	Al Geiberger	280	Dudley Wysong	Firestone CC, Akron
1967	Don January* (69)	281	Don Massengale (71)	Columbine CC, Littleton, CO
1968	Julius Boros	281	Bob Charles	Pecan Valley CC, San Antonio
			Arnold Palmer	
1969	Ray Floyd	276	Gary Player	NCR CC, Dayton
1970	Dave Stockton	279	Arnold Palmer	Southern Hills CC, Tulsa
			Bob Murphy	
1971	Jack Nicklaus	281	Billy Casper	PGA Natl GC, Palm Beach Gardens, FL
1972	Gary Player	281	Tommy Aaron	Oakland Hills CC, Birmingham, MI
			Jim Jamieson	
1973	Jack Nicklaus	277	Bruce Crampton	Canterbury GC, Cleveland
1974	Lee Trevino	276	Jack Nicklaus	Tanglewood GC, Winston-Salem, NC
1975	Jack Nicklaus	276	Bruce Crampton	Firestone CC, Akron
1976	Dave Stockton	281	Ray Floyd	Congressional CC, Bethesda, MD
			Don January	
1977†	Lanny Wadkins* (4-4-4)	282	Gene Littler (4-4-5)	Pebble Beach GL, Pebble Beach, CA
1978	John Mahaffey* (4-3)	276	Jerry Pate (4-4)	Oakmont CC, Oakmont, PA
			Tom Watson (4-5)	
1979	David Graham* (4-4-2)	272	Ben Crenshaw (4-4-4)	Oakland Hills CC, Birmingham, MI
1980	Jack Nicklaus	274	Andy Bean	Oak Hill CC, Rochester, NY
1981	Larry Nelson	273	Fuzzy Zoeller	Atlanta Athletic Club, Duluth, GA
1982	Raymond Floyd	272	Lanny Wadkins	Southern Hills CC, Tulsa
1983	Hal Sutton	274	Jack Nicklaus	Riviera CC, Pacific Palisades, CA
1984	Lee Trevino	273	Gary Player	Shoal Creek, Birmingham, AL
			Lanny Wadkins	
1985	Hubert Green	278	Lee Trevino	Cherry Hills CC, Denver
1986	Bob Tway	276	Greg Norman	Inverness CC, Toledo
1987	Larry Nelson* (4)	287	Lanny Wadkins (5)	PGA Natl GC, Palm Beach Gardens, FL
1988	Jeff Sluman	272	Paul Azinger	Oak Tree GC, Edmond, OK
1989	Payne Stewart	276	Mike Reid	Kemper Lakes GC, Hawthorn Woods, IL
1990	Wayne Grady	282	Fred Couples	Shoal Creek, Birmingham, AL
1991	John Daly	276	Bruce Lietzke	Crooked Stick GC, Carmel, IN
1992	Nick Price	278	Jim Gallagher Jr	Bellerive CC, St. Louis
1993	Paul Azinger* (4-4)	272	Greg Norman (4-5)	Inverness CC, Toldeo, OH
1994	Nick Price	269	Corey Pavin	Southern Hills CC, Tulsa, OK

*Winner in playoff. Playoff scores are in parentheses.

†Playoff changed from 18 holes to sudden death.

THE PGA TOUR
Season Money Leaders

	Earnings ($)			Earnings ($)
1934 ......Paul Runyan	6,767.00		1966 ......Billy Casper	121,944.92
1935 ......Johnny Revolta	9,543.00		1967 ......Jack Nicklaus	188,998.08
1936 ......Horton Smith	7,682.00		1968 ......Billy Casper	205,168.67
1937 ......Harry Cooper	14,138.69		1969 ......Frank Beard	164,707.11
1938 ......Sam Snead	19,534.49		1970 ......Lee Trevino	157,037.63
1939 ......Henry Picard	10,303.00		1971 ......Jack Nicklaus	244,490.50
1940 ......Ben Hogan	10,655.00		1972 ......Jack Nicklaus	320,542.26
1941 ......Ben Hogan	18,358.00		1973 ......Jack Nicklaus	308,362.10
1942 ......Ben Hogan	13,143.00		1974 ......Johnny Miller	353,021.59
1943 ......No statistics compiled			1975 ......Jack Nicklaus	298,149.17
1944 ......Byron Nelson (war bonds)	37,967.69		1976 ......Jack Nicklaus	266,438.57
1945 ......Byron Nelson (war bonds)	63,335.66		1977 ......Tom Watson	310,653.16
1946 ......Ben Hogan	42,556.16		1978 ......Tom Watson	362,428.93
1947 ......Jimmy Demaret	27,936.83		1979 ......Tom Watson	462,636.00
1948 ......Ben Hogan	32,112.00		1980 ......Tom Watson	530,808.33
1949 ......Sam Snead	31,593.83		1981 ......Tom Kite	375,698.84
1950 ......Sam Snead	35,758.83		1982 ......Craig Stadler	446,462.00
1951 ......Lloyd Mangrum	26,088.83		1983 ......Hal Sutton	426,668.00
1952 ......Julius Boros	37,032.97		1984 ......Tom Watson	476,260.00
1953 ......Lew Worsham	34,002.00		1985 ......Curtis Strange	542,321.00
1954 ......Bob Toski	65,819.81		1986 ......Greg Norman	653,296.00
1955 ......Julius Boros	63,121.55		1987 ......Curtis Strange	925,941.00
1956 ......Ted Kroll	72,835.83		1988 ......Curtis Strange	1,147,644.00
1957 ......Dick Mayer	65,835.00		1989 ......Tom Kite	1,395,278.00
1958 ......Arnold Palmer	42,607.50		1990 ......Greg Norman	1,165,477.00
1959 ......Art Wall	53,167.60		1991 ......Corey Pavin	979,430.00
1960 ......Arnold Palmer	75,262.85		1992 ......Fred Couples	1,344,188.00
1961 ......Gary Player	64,540.45		1993 ......Nick Price	1,478,557.00
1962 ......Arnold Palmer	81,448.33		1994 ......Nick Price	1,499,927.00
1963 ......Arnold Palmer	128,230.00			
1964 ......Jack Nicklaus	113,284.50			
1965 ......Jack Nicklaus	140,752.14			

Note: Total money listed from 1968 through 1974. Official money listed from 1975 on.

Career Money Leaders‡

	Earnings ($)		Earnings ($)		Earnings ($)
1. Tom Kite	9,159,418	18. Ray Floyd	5,129,013	35. Lee Trevino	3,478,449
2. Greg Norman	7,937,869	19. David Frost	5,100,514	36. Peter Jacobsen	3,472,507
3. Fred Couples	6,889,149	20. Mark Calcavecchia	5,023,163	37. David Edwards	3,420,417
4. Paul Azinger	6,774,728	21. Fuzzy Zoeller	4,748,065	38. Joey Sindelar	3,362,503
5. Tom Watson	6,751,328	22. Gil Morgan	4,735,868	39. Tim Simpson	3,348,787
6. Nick Price	6,726,418	23. Scott Hoch	4,673,254	40. Jeff Sluman	3,296,749
7. Payne Stewart	6,523,260	24. Jay Haas	4,604,562	41. Larry Nelson	3,273,248
8. Curtis Strange	6,433,442	25. Davis Love III	4,511,891	42. Steve Elkington	3,271,135
9. Ben Crenshaw	6,107,759	26. Mark McCumber	4,423,778	43. Andy Bean	3,243,075
10. Lanny Wadkins	5,931,370	27. Larry Mize	4,294,710	44. Ken Green	3,174,225
11. Corey Pavin	5,835,444	28. John Cook	4,274,977	45. Loren Roberts	3,131,398
12. Hale Irwin	5,654,063	29. Wayne Levi	4,191,292	46. Tom Purtzer	3,130,116
13. Craig Stadler	5,606,436	30. Scott Simpson	3,973,159	47. John Huston	3,113,443
14. Chip Beck	5,585,763	31. Hal Sutton	3,931,853	48. D.A. Weibring	3,095,307
15. Bruce Lietzke	5,440,868	32. John Mahaffey	3,671,400	49. Brad Faxon	3,065,652
16. Jack Nicklaus	5,372,176	33. Steve Pate	3,571,833	50. Mike Reid	3,029,011
17. Mark O'Meara	5,212,337	34. Jim Gallagher, Jr	3,526,698		

Top Single-Season Earnings‡

	Earnings ($)	Year		Earnings ($)	Year
Nick Price	1,499,927	1994	Greg Norman	1,330,307	1994
Nick Price	1,478,557	1993	Mark McCumber	1,208,209	1994
Paul Azinger	1,458,456	1993	Payne Stewart	1,201,301	1989
Tom Kite	1,395,278	1989	Greg Norman	1,165,477	1990
Greg Norman	1,359,653	1993	Curtis Strange	1,147,644	1988
Fred Couples	1,344,188	1992	Jim Gallagher, Jr	1,078,870	1993

‡Through 12/31/94.

Most Career Wins‡

	Wins		Wins		Wins
Sam Snead	81	Billy Casper	51	Horton Smith	32
Jack Nicklaus	70	Walter Hagen	40	Tom Watson	32
Ben Hogan	63	Cary Middlecoff	40	Harry Cooper	31
Arnold Palmer	60	Gene Sarazen	38	Jimmy Demaret	31
Byron Nelson	52	Lloyd Mangrum	36	Leo Diegel	30

‡Statistics through 10/31/94

Year by Year Statistical Leaders

SCORING AVERAGE

1980	Lee Trevino	69.73
1981	Tom Kite	69.80
1982	Tom Kite	70.21
1983	Raymond Floyd	70.61
1984	Calvin Peete	70.56
1985	Don Pooley	70.36
1986	Scott Hoch	70.08
1987	David Frost	70.09
1988	Greg Norman	69.38
1989	Payne Stewart	69.485†
1990	Greg Norman	69.10
1991	Fred Couples	69.59
1992	Fred Couples	69.38
1993	Greg Norman	68.90
1994	Greg Norman	68.81

Note: Scoring average per round, with adjustments made at each round for the field's course scoring average.

DRIVING DISTANCE

		Yds
1980	Dan Pohl	274.3
1981	Dan Pohl	280.1
1982	Bill Calfee	275.3
1983	John McComish	277.4
1984	Bill Glasson	276.5
1985	Andy Bean	278.2
1986	Davis Love III	285.7
1987	John McComish	283.9
1988	Steve Thomas	284.6
1989	Ed Humenik	280.9
1990	Tom Purtzer	279.6
1991	John Daly	288.9
1992	John Daly	283.4
1993	John Daly	288.9
1994	Davis Love III	283.8

Note: Average computed by charting distance of two tee shots on a predetermined par-four or par-five hole (one on front nine, one on back nine).

DRIVING ACCURACY

1980	Mike Reid	79.5
1981	Calvin Peete	81.9
1982	Calvin Peete	84.6
1983	Calvin Peete	81.3
1984	Calvin Peete	77.5
1985	Calvin Peete	80.6
1986	Calvin Peete	81.7
1987	Calvin Peete	83.0
1988	Calvin Peete	82.5
1989	Calvin Peete	82.6
1990	Calvin Peete	83.7

DRIVING ACCURACY (Cont.)

1991	Hale Irwin	78.3
1992	Doug Tewell	82.3
1993	Doug Tewell	82.5
1994	David Edwards	81.6

Note: Percentage of fairways hit on number of par-four and par-five holes played; par-three holes excluded.

GREENS IN REGULATION

1980	Jack Nicklaus	72.1
1981	Calvin Peete	73.1
1982	Calvin Peete	72.4
1983	Calvin Peete	71.4
1984	Andy Bean	72.1
1985	John Mahaffey	71.9
1986	John Mahaffey	72.0
1987	Gil Morgan	73.3
1988	John Adams	73.9
1989	Bruce Lietzke	72.6
1990	Doug Tewell	70.9
1991	Bruce Lietzke	73.8
1992	Tim Simpson	74.0
1993	Fuzzy Zoeller	73.6
1994	Bill Glasson	73.0

Note: Average of greens reached in regulation out of total holes played; hole is considered hit in regulation if any part of the ball rests on the putting surface in two shots less than the hole's-five hit in two shots is one green in regulation.

PUTTING

1980	Jerry Pate	28.81
1981	Alan Tapie	28.70
1982	Ben Crenshaw	28.65
1983	Morris Hatalsky	27.96
1984	Gary McCord	28.57
1985	Craig Stadler	28.627†
1986	Greg Norman	1.736
1987	Ben Crenshaw	1.743
1988	Don Pooley	1.729
1989	Steve Jones	1.734
1990	Larry Rinker	1.7467†
1991	Jay Don Blake	1.7326†
1992	Mark O'Meara	1.731
1993	David Frost	1.739
1994	Loren Roberts	1.737

Note: Average number of putts taken on greens reached in regulation; prior to 1986, based on average number of putts per 18 holes.

ALL-AROUND

1987	Dan Pohl	170
1988	Payne Stewart	170
1989	Paul Azinger	250
1990	Paul Azinger	162
1991	Scott Hoch	283
1992	Fred Couples	256
1993	Gil Morgan	252
1994	Bob Estes	227

Note: Addition of the places of standing from the other nine statistical categories; the player with the number closest to zero leads.

SAND SAVES

1980	Bob Eastwood	65.4
1981	Tom Watson	60.1
1982	Isao Aoki	60.2
1983	Isao Aoki	62.3
1984	Peter Oosterhuis	64.7
1985	Tom Purtzer	60.8
1986	Paul Azinger	63.8
1987	Paul Azinger	63.2
1988	Greg Powers	63.5
1989	Mike Sullivan	66.0
1990	Paul Azinger	67.2
1991	Ben Crenshaw	64.9
1992	Mitch Adcock	66.9
1993	Ken Green	64.4
1994	Corey Pavin	65.4

Note: Percentage of up-and-down efforts from greenside sand traps only; fairway bunkers excluded.

PAR BREAKERS

1980	Tom Watson	.213
1981	Bruce Lietzke	.225
1982	Tom Kite	.2154†
1983	Tom Watson	.211
1984	Craig Stadler	.220
1985	Craig Stadler	.218
1986	Greg Norman	.248
1987	Mark Calcavecchia	.221
1988	Ken Green	.236
1989	Greg Norman	.224
1990	Greg Norman	.219

Note: Average based on total birdies and eagles scored out of total holes played. Discontinued as an official category after 1990.

† Number had to be carried to extra decimal place to determine winner.

Year by Year Statistical Leaders (Cont.)

EAGLES			BIRDIES		
1980	Dave Eichelberger	16	1980	Andy Bean	388
1981	Bruce Lietzke	12	1981	Vance Heafner	388
1982	Tom Weiskopf	10	1982	Andy Bean	392
	J. C. Snead	10	1983	Hal Sutton	399
	Andy Bean	10	1984	Mark O'Meara	419
1983	Chip Beck	15	1985	Joey Sindelar	411
1984	Gary Hallberg	15	1986	Joey Sindelar	415
1985	Larry Rinker	14	1987	Dan Forsman	409
1986	Joey Sindelar	16	1988	Dan Forsman	465
1987	Phil Blackmar	20	1989	Ted Schulz	415
1988	Ken Green	21	1990	Mike Donald	401
1989	Lon Hinkle	14	1991	Scott Hoch	446
	Duffy Waldorf	14	1992	Jeff Sluman	417
1990	Paul Azinger	14	1993	John Huston	426
1991	Andy Bean	15	1994	Brad Bryant	397
1992	Dan Forsman	18			
1993	Davis Love III	15			
1994	Davis Love III	18			

Note: Total of eagles scored.

Note: Total of birdies scored.

PGA Player of the Year Award

1948	Ben Hogan	1964	Ken Venturi	1980	Tom Watson
1949	Sam Snead	1965	Dave Marr	1981	Bill Rogers
1950	Ben Hogan	1966	Billy Casper	1982	Tom Watson
1951	Ben Hogan	1967	Jack Nicklaus	1983	Hal Sutton
1952	Julius Boros	1968	Not awarded	1984	Tom Watson
1953	Ben Hogan	1969	Orville Moody	1985	Lanny Wadkins
1954	Ed Furgol	1970	Billy Casper	1986	Bob Tway
1955	Doug Ford	1971	Lee Trevino	1987	Paul Azinger
1956	Jack Burke	1972	Jack Nicklaus	1988	Curtis Strange
1957	Dick Mayer	1973	Jack Nicklaus	1989	Tom Kite
1958	Dow Finsterwald	1974	Johnny Miller	1990	Wayne Levi
1959	Art Wall	1975	Jack Nicklaus	1991	Fred Couples
1960	Arnold Palmer	1976	Jack Nicklaus	1992	Fred Couples
1961	Jerry Barber	1977	Tom Watson	1993	Nick Price
1962	Arnold Palmer	1978	Tom Watson		
1963	Julius Boros	1979	Tom Watson		

Vardon Trophy: Scoring Average

Year	Winner	Avg	Year	Winner	Avg	Year	Winner	Avg
1937	Harry Cooper	*500	1959	Art Wall	70.35	1977	Tom Watson	70.32
1938	Sam Snead	520	1960	Billy Casper	69.95	1978	Tom Watson	70.16
1939	Byron Nelson	473	1961	Arnold Palmer	69.85	1979	Tom Watson	70.27
1940	Ben Hogan	423	1962	Arnold Palmer	70.27	1980	Lee Trevino	69.73
1941	Ben Hogan	494	1963	Billy Casper	70.58	1981	Tom Kite	69.80
1942-46	No award		1964	Arnold Palmer	70.01	1982	Tom Kite	70.21
1947	Jimmy Demaret	69.90	1965	Billy Casper	70.85	1983	Raymond Floyd	70.61
1948	Ben Hogan	69.30	1966	Billy Casper	70.27	1984	Calvin Peete	70.56
1949	Sam Snead	69.37	1967	Arnold Palmer	70.18	1985	Don Pooley	70.36
1950	Sam Snead	69.23	1968	Billy Casper	69.82	1986	Scott Hoch	70.08
1951	Lloyd Mangrum	70.05	1969	Dave Hill	70.34	1987	Don Pohl	70.25
1952	Jack Burke	70.54	1970	Lee Trevino	70.64	1988	Chip Beck	69.46
1953	Lloyd Mangrum	70.22	1971	Lee Trevino	70.27	1989	Greg Norman	69.49
1954	E. J. Harrison	70.41	1972	Lee Trevino	70.89	1990	Greg Norman	69.10
1955	Sam Snead	69.86	1973	Bruce Crampton	70.57	1991	Fred Couples	69.59
1956	Cary Middlecoff	70.35	1974	Lee Trevino	70.53	1992	Fred Couples	69.38
1957	Dow Finsterwald	70.30	1975	Bruce Crampton	70.51	1993	Nick Price	69.11
1958	Bob Rosburg	70.11	1976	Don January	70.56			

*Point system used, 1937-41.

Note: As of 1988, based on minimum of 60 rounds per year.

Alltime PGA Tour Records*

Scoring

90 HOLES

325—(67-67-64-65-62) by Tom Kite, at four courses, La Quinta, CA, in winning the 1993 Bob Hope Classic (35 under par).

72 HOLES

257—(60-68-64-65) by Mike Souchak, at Brackenridge Park GC, San Antonio, to win 1955 Texas Open (27 under par).

54 HOLES

Opening rounds

191—(66-64-61) by Gay Brewer, at Pensacola CC, Pensacola, FL, in winning the 1967 Pensacola Open.

Consecutive rounds

189—(63-63-63) by Chandler Harper in the last three rounds to win the 1954 Texas Open at Brackenridge Park GC, San Antonio.

36 HOLES

Opening rounds

126—(64-62) by Tommy Bolt, at Cavalier Yacht & CC, Virginia Beach, VA, in 1954 Virginia Beach Open.

126—(64-62) by Paul Azinger, at Oak Hills CC, San Antonio, in 1989 Texas Open.

Consecutive rounds

125—(64-61) by Gay Brewer in the middle rounds of the 1967 Pensacola Open, which he won, at Pensacola CC, Pensacola, FL.

125—(63-62) by Ron Streck in the last two rounds to win the 1978 Texas Open at Oak Hills CC, San Antonio.

125—(62-63) by Blaine McCallister in the middle two rounds in winning the 1988 Hardee's Golf Classic at Oakwood CC, Coal Valley, IL.

18 HOLES

59—by Al Geiberger, at Colonial Country Club, Memphis, in second round in winning 1977 Memphis Classic.

59—by Chip Beck, at Sunrise Golf Club, Las Vegas, in third round of the 1991 Las Vegas Invitational.

9 HOLES

27—by Mike Souchak, at Brackenridge Park GC, San Antonio, on par-35 second nine of first round in 1955 Texas Open.

27—by Andy North at En-Joie GC, Endicott, NY, on par-34 second nine of first round in 1975 BC Open.

MOST CONSECUTIVE ROUNDS UNDER 70

19—Byron Nelson in 1945.

MOST BIRDIES IN A ROW

8—Bob Goalby at Pasadena GC, St Petersburg, FL, during fourth round in winning the 1961 St Petersburg Open.

8—Fuzzy Zoeller, at Oakwood CC, Coal Valley, IL, during first round of 1976 Quad Cities Open.

8—Dewey Arnette, Warwick Hills GC, Grand Blanc, MI, during first round of the 1987 Buick Open.

Scoring (Cont.)

MOST BIRDIES IN A ROW TO WIN

5—Jack Nicklaus to win 1978 Jackie Gleason Inverrary Classic (last 5 holes).

Wins

MOST CONSECUTIVE YEARS WINNING AT LEAST ONE TOURNAMENT

17—Jack Nicklaus, 1962-78.

17—Arnold Palmer, 1955-71.

16—Billy Casper, 1956-71.

MOST CONSECUTIVE WINS

11—Byron Nelson, from Miami Four Ball, March 8-11, 1945, through Canadian Open, August 2-4, 1945.

MOST WINS IN A SINGLE EVENT

8—Sam Snead, Greater Greensboro Open, 1938, 1946, 1949, 1950, 1955, 1956, 1960, and 1965.

MOST CONSECUTIVE WINS IN A SINGLE EVENT

4—Walter Hagen, PGA Championships, 1924-27.

MOST WINS IN A CALENDAR YEAR

18—Byron Nelson, 1945.

MOST YEARS BETWEEN WINS

12—Howard Twitty, 1980–93.

MOST YEARS FROM FIRST WIN TO LAST

29—Sam Snead, 1936-65.

29—Ray Floyd, 1963-92.

YOUNGEST WINNERS

John McDermott, 19 years and 10 months, 1911 US Open.

OLDEST WINNER

Sam Snead, 52 years and 10 months, 1965 Greater Greensboro Open.

WIDEST WINNING MARGIN: STROKES

16—Bobby Locke, 1948 Chicago Victory National Championship.

Putting

FEWEST PUTTS, ONE ROUND

18—Andy North, at Kingsmill GC, in second round of 1990 Anheuser Busch Golf Classic.

18—Kenny Knox, at Harbour Town GL, in first round of 1989 MCI Heritage Classic.

18—Mike McGee, at Colonial CC, in first round of 1987 Federal Express St Jude Classic.

18—Sam Trahan, at Whitemarsh Valley CC, in final round of 1979 IVB Philadelphia Golf Classic.

18—Jim McGovern, at TPC at Southwind, in second round of 1992 Federal Express St. Jude Classic.

FEWEST PUTTS, FOUR ROUNDS

93—Kenny Knox, in 1989 MCI Heritage Classic at Harbour Town GL.

*Through 10/31/94.

THE MAJOR TOURNAMENTS

LPGA Championship

Year	Winner	Score	Runner-Up	Site
1955	Beverly Hanson† (4 and 3)	220	Louise Suggs	Orchard Ridge CC, Ft Wayne, IN
1956	Marlene Hagge* (5)	291	Patty Berg (6)	Forest Lake CC, Detroit
1957	Louise Suggs	285	Wiffi Smith	Churchill Valley CC, Pittsburgh
1958	Mickey Wright	288	Fay Crocker	Churchill Valley CC, Pittsburgh
1959	Betsy Rawls	288	Patty Berg	Sheraton Hotel CC, French Lick, IN
1960	Mickey Wright	292	Louise Suggs	Sheraton Hotel CC, French Lick, IN
1961	Mickey Wright	287	Louise Suggs	Stardust CC, Las Vegas
1962	Judy Kimball	282	Shirley Spork	Stardust CC, Las Vegas
1963	Mickey Wright	294	Mary Lena Faulk Mary Mills Louise Suggs	Stardust CC, Las Vegas
1964	Mary Mills	278	Mickey Wright	Stardust CC, Las Vegas
1965	Sandra Haynie	279	Clifford A. Creed	Stardust CC, Las Vegas
1966	Gloria Ehret	282	Mickey Wright	Stardust CC, Las Vegas
1967	Kathy Whitworth	284	Shirley Englehorn	Pleasant Valley CC, Sutton, MA
1968	Sandra Post* (68)	294	Kathy Whitworth (75)	Pleasant Valley CC, Sutton, MA
1969	Betsy Rawls	293	Susie Berning Carol Mann	Concord GC, Kiamesha Lake, NY
1970	Shirley Englehorn* (74)	285	Kathy Whitworth (78)	Pleasant Valley CC, Sutton, MA
1971	Kathy Whitworth	288	Kathy Ahern	Pleasant Valley CC, Sutton, MA
1972	Kathy Ahern	293	Jane Blalock	Pleasant Valley CC, Sutton, MA
1973	Mary Mills	288	Betty Burfeindt	Pleasant Valley CC, Sutton, MA
1974	Sandra Haynie	288	JoAnne Carner	Pleasant Valley CC, Sutton, MA
1975	Kathy Whitworth	288	Sandra Haynie	Pine Ridge GC, Baltimore
1976	Betty Burfeindt	287	Judy Rankin	Pine Ridge GC, Baltimore
1977	Chako Higuchi	279	Pat Bradley Sandra Post Judy Rankin	Bay Tree Golf Plantation, N. Myrtle Beach, SC
1978	Nancy Lopez	275	Amy Alcott	Jack Nicklaus GC, Kings Island, OH
1979	Donna Caponi	279	Jerilyn Britz	Jack Nicklaus GC, Kings Island, OH
1980	Sally Little	285	Jane Blalock	Jack Nicklaus GC, Kings Island, OH
1981	Donna Caponi	280	Jerilyn Britz Pat Meyers	Jack Nicklaus GC, Kings Island, OH
1982	Jan Stephenson	279	JoAnne Carner	Jack Nicklaus GC, Kings Island, OH
1983	Patty Sheehan	279	Sandra Haynie	Jack Nicklaus GC, Kings Island, OH
1984	Patty Sheehan	272	Beth Daniel Pat Bradley	Jack Nicklaus GC, Kings Island, OH
1985	Nancy Lopez	273	Alice Miller	Jack Nicklaus GC, Kings Island, OH
1986	Pat Bradley	277	Patty Sheehan	Jack Nicklaus GC, Kings Island, OH
1987	Jane Geddes	275	Betsy King	Jack Nicklaus GC, Kings Island, OH
1988	Sherri Turner	281	Amy Alcott	Jack Nicklaus GC, Kings Island, OH
1989	Nancy Lopez	274	Ayako Okamoto	Jack Nicklaus GC, Kings Island, OH
1990	Beth Daniel	280	Rosie Jones	Bethesda CC, Bethesda, MD
1991	Meg Mallon	274	Pat Bradley Ayako Okamoto	Bethesda CC, Bethesda, MD
1992	Betsy King	267	Karen Noble	Bethesda CC, Bethesda, MD
1993	Patty Sheehan	275	Lauri Merten	Bethesda CC, Bethesda, MD
1994	Laura Davies	279	Alice Ritzman	DuPont CC, Wilmington, DE

*Won in playoff. Playoff scores are in parentheses. 1956 was sudden death; 1968 and 1970 were 18-hole playoffs.
†Won match play final.

U.S. Women's Open

Year	Winner	Score	Runner-Up	Site
1946	Patty Berg	5 & 4	Betty Jameson	Spokane CC, Spokane, WA
1947	Betty Jameson	295	Sally Sessions Polly Riley	Starmount Forest CC, Greensboro, NC
1948	Babe Zaharias	300	Betty Hicks	Atlantic City CC, Northfield, NJ
1949	Louise Suggs	291	Babe Zaharias	Prince George's G & CC, Landover, MD
1950	Babe Zaharias	291	Betsy Rawls	Rolling Hills CC, Wichita, KS
1951	Betsy Rawls	293	Louise Suggs	Druid Hills GC, Atlanta

U.S. Women's Open (Cont.)

Year	Winner	Score	Runner-Up	Site
1952	Louise Suggs	284	Marlene Bauer	Bala GC, Philadelphia
			Betty Jameson	
1953	Betsy Rawls* (71)	302	Jackie Pung (77)	CC of Rochester, Rochester, NY
1954	Babe Zaharias	291	Betty Hicks	Salem CC, Peabody, MA
1955	Fay Crocker	299	Mary Lena Faulk	Wichita CC, Wichita, KS
			Louise Suggs	
1956	Kathy Cornelius* (75)	302	Barbara McIntire (82)	Northland CC, Duluth, MN
1957	Betsy Rawls	299	Patty Berg	Winged Foot GC, Mamaroneck, NY
1958	Mickey Wright	290	Louise Suggs	Forest Lake CC, Detroit
1959	Mickey Wright	287	Louise Suggs	Churchill Valley CC, Pittsburgh
1960	Betsy Rawls	292	Joyce Ziske	Worcester CC, Worcester, MA
1961	Mickey Wright	293	Betsy Rawls	Baltusrol GC (Lower Course), Springfield, NJ
1962	Murle Breer	301	Jo Ann Prentice	Dunes GC, Myrtle Beach, SC
			Ruth Jessen	
1963	Mary Mills	289	Sandra Haynie	Kenwood CC, Cincinnati
			Louise Suggs	
1964	Mickey Wright* (70)	290	Ruth Jessen (72)	San Diego CC, Chula Vista, CA
1965	Carol Mann	290	Kathy Cornelius	Atlantic City CC, Northfield, NJ
1966	Sandra Spuzich	297	Carol Mann	Hazeltine Natl GC, Chaska, MN
1967	Catherine LaCoste	294	Susie Berning	Hot Springs GC (Cascades Course),
			Beth Stone	Hot Springs, VA
1968	Susie Berning	289	Mickey Wright	Moslem Springs GC, Fleetwood, PA
1969	Donna Caponi	294	Peggy Wilson	Scenic Hills CC, Pensacola, FL
1970	Donna Caponi	287	Sandra Haynie	Muskogee CC, Muskogee, OK
			Sandra Spuzich	
1971	JoAnne Carner	288	Kathy Whitworth	Kahkwa CC, Erie, PA
1972	Susie Berning	299	Kathy Ahern	Winged Foot GC, Mamaroneck, NY
			Pam Barnett	
			Judy Rankin	
1973	Susie Berning	290	Gloria Ehret	CC of Rochester, Rochester, NY
			Shelley Hamlin	
1974	Sandra Haynie	295	Carol Mann	La Grange CC, La Grange, IL
			Beth Stone	
1975	Sandra Palmer	295	JoAnne Carner	Atlantic City CC, Northfield, NJ
			Sandra Post	
			Nancy Lopez	
1976	JoAnne Carner* (76)	292	Sandra Palmer (78)	Rolling Green CC, Springfield, PA
1977	Hollis Stacy	292	Nancy Lopez	Hazeltine Natl GC, Chaska, MN
1978	Hollis Stacy	289	JoAnne Carner	CC of Indianapolis, Indianapolis
			Sally Little	
1979	Jerilyn Britz	284	Debbie Massey	Brooklawn CC, Fairfield, CT
			Sandra Palmer	
1980	Amy Alcott	280	Hollis Stacy	Richland CC, Nashville
1981	Pat Bradley	279	Beth Daniel	La Grange CC, La Grange, IL
1982	Janet Anderson	283	Beth Daniel	Del Paso CC, Sacramento
			Sandra Haynie	
			Donna White	
			JoAnne Carner	
1983	Jan Stephenson	290	JoAnne Carner	Cedar Ridge CC, Tulsa
			Patty Sheehan	
1984	Hollis Stacy	290	Rosie Jones	Salem CC, Peabody, MA
1985	Kathy Baker	280	Judy Dickinson	Baltusrol GC (Upper Course), Springfield, NJ
1986	Jane Geddes* (71)	287	Sally Little (73)	NCR GC, Dayton
1987	Laura Davies* (71)	285	Ayako Okamoto (73)	Plainfield CC, Plainfield, NJ
			JoAnne Carner (74)	
1988	Liselotte Neumann	277	Patty Sheehan	Baltimore CC, Baltimore
1989	Betsy King	278	Nancy Lopez	Indianwood G & CC, Lake Orion, MI
1990	Betsy King	284	Patty Sheehan	Atlanta Athletic Club, Duluth, GA
1991	Meg Mallon	283	Pat Bradley	Colonial Club, Fort Worth
1992	Patty Sheehan* (72)	280	Juli Inkster	Oakmont CC, Oakmont, PA
1993	Lauri Merten	280	Donna Andrew	Crooked Stick, Carmel, IN
			Helen Alfredsson	
1994	Patty Sheehan	277	Tammie Green	Indianwood G & CC, Lake Orion, MI

*Winner in playoff. 18-hole playoff scores are in parentheses.

Women's Golf (Cont.)

Dinah Shore

Year	Winner	Score	Runner-Up
1972	Jane Blalock	213	Carol Mann, Judy Rankin
1973	Mickey Wright	284	Joyce Kazmierski
1974	Jo Ann Prentice*	289	Jane Blalock, Sandra Haynie
1975	Sandra Palmer	283	Kathy McMullen
1976	Judy Rankin	285	Betty Burfeindt
1977	Kathy Whitworth	289	JoAnne Carner, Sally Little
1978	Sandra Post*	283	Penny Pulz
1979	Sandra Post	276	Nancy Lopez
1980	Donna Caponi	275	Amy Alcott
1981	Nancy Lopez	277	Carolyn Hill
1982	Sally Little	278	Hollis Stacy, Sandra Haynie
1983	Amy Alcott	282	Beth Daniel, Kathy Whitworth
1984	Juli Inkster*	280	Pat Bradley
1985	Alice Miller	275	Jan Stephenson
1986	Pat Bradley	280	Val Skinner
1987	Betsy King*	283	Patty Sheehan
1988	Amy Alcott	274	Colleen Walker
1989	Juli Inkster	279	Tammie Green, JoAnne Carner
1990	Betsy King	283	Kathy Postlewait, Shirley Furlong
1991	Amy Alcott	273	Dottie Mochrie
1992	Dottie Mochrie*	279	Juli Inkster
1993	Helen Alfredsson	284	Amy Benz, Tina Barrett, Betsy King
1994	Donna Andrews	276	Laura Davies

*Winner in sudden-death playoff.

Note: Designated fourth major in 1983.

Played at Mission Hills CC, Rancho Mirage, CA.

du Maurier Classic

Year	Winner	Score	Runner-Up	Site
1973	Jocelyne Bourassa*	214	Sandra Haynie Judy Rankin	Montreal GC, Montreal
1974	Carole Jo Callison	208	JoAnne Carner	Candiac GC, Montreal
1975	JoAnne Carner*	214	Carol Mann	St George's CC, Toronto
1976	Donna Caponi*	212	Judy Rankin	Cedar Brae G & CC, Toronto
1977	Judy Rankin	214	Pat Meyers Sandra Palmer	Lachute G & CC, Montreal
1978	JoAnne Carner	278	Hollis Stacy	St George's CC, Toronto
1979	Amy Alcott	285	Nancy Lopez	Richelieu Valley CC, Montreal
1980	Pat Bradley	277	JoAnne Carner	St George's CC, Toronto
1981	Jan Stephenson	278	Nancy Lopez Pat Bradley	Summerlea CC, Dorion, Quebec
1982	Sandra Haynie	280	Beth Daniel	St George's CC, Toronto
1983	Hollis Stacy	277	JoAnne Carner Alice Miller	Beaconsfield GC, Montreal
1984	Juli Inkster	279	Ayako Okamoto	St George's G & CC, Toronto
1985	Pat Bradley	278	Jane Geddes	Beaconsfield CC, Montreal
1986	Pat Bradley*	276	Ayako Okamoto	Board of Trade CC, Toronto
1987	Jody Rosenthal	272	Ayako Okamoto	Islesmere GC, Laval, Quebec
1988	Sally Little	279	Laura Davies	Vancouver GC, Coquitlam, British Columbia
1989	Tammie Green	279	Pat Bradley Betsy King	Beaconsfield GC, Montreal
1990	Cathy Johnston	276	Patty Sheehan	Westmount G & CC, Kitchener, Ontario
1991	Nancy Scranton	279	Debbie Massey	Vancouver GC, Coquitlam, British Columbia
1992	Sherri Steinhauer	277	Judy Dickinson	St. Charles CC, Winnipeg, Manitoba
1993	Brandie Burton	277	Betsy King	London Hunt and CC, London, Ontario
1994	Martha Nause	279	Michelle McGann	Ottawa Hunt and GC, Ottawa, Ont.

*Winner in sudden-death playoff.

Note: Designated third major in 1979.

THE LPGA TOUR

Season Money Leaders

		Earnings ($)			Earnings ($)
1950	Babe Zaharias	14,800	1972	Kathy Whitworth	65,063
1951	Babe Zaharias	15,087	1973	Kathy Whitworth	82,864
1952	Betsy Rawls	14,505	1974	JoAnne Carner	87,094
1953	Louise Suggs	19,816	1975	Sandra Palmer	76,374
1954	Patty Berg	16,011	1976	Judy Rankin	150,734
1955	Patty Berg	16,492	1977	Judy Rankin	122,890
1956	Marlene Hagge	20,235	1978	Nancy Lopez	189,814
1957	Patty Berg	16,272	1979	Nancy Lopez	197,489
1958	Beverly Hanson	12,639	1980	Beth Daniel	231,000
1959	Betsy Rawls	26,774	1981	Beth Daniel	206,998
1960	Louise Suggs	16,892	1982	JoAnne Carner	310,400
1961	Mickey Wright	22,236	1983	JoAnne Carner	291,404
1962	Mickey Wright	21,641	1984	Betsy King	266,771
1963	Mickey Wright	31,269	1985	Nancy Lopez	416,472
1964	Mickey Wright	29,800	1986	Pat Bradley	492,021
1965	Kathy Whitworth	28,658	1987	Ayako Okamoto	466,034
1966	Kathy Whitworth	33,517	1988	Sherri Turner	350,851
1967	Kathy Whitworth	32,937	1989	Betsy King	654,132
1968	Kathy Whitworth	48,379	1990	Beth Daniel	863,578
1969	Carol Mann	49,152	1991	Pat Bradley	763,118
1970	Kathy Whitworth	30,235	1992	Dottie Mochrie	693,335
1971	Kathy Whitworth	41,181	1993	Betsy King	595,992

Career Money Leaders*

	Earnings ($)		Earnings ($)		Earnings ($)
1. Pat Bradley	4,535,841.03	11. Rosie Jones	2,069,365,97	21. Deb Richard	1,417,730.00
2. Betsy King	4,502,634.50	12. Jane Geddes	1,995,654.30	22. Donna Caponi	1,387,919.73
3. Patty Sheehan	4,131,837.01	13. Juli Inkster	1,956,589.23	23. Kathy Postlewait	1,373,199.27
4. Nancy Lopez	3,866,850.83	14. Hollis Stacy	1,908,963.99	24. Chris Johnson	1,345,438.50
5. Beth Daniel	3,832,665.80	15. Colleen Walker	1,850,123.71	25. Sandra Palmer	1,330,436.86
6. Amy Alcott	2,910,706.14	16. Judy Dickinson	1,743,928.92	26. Dawn Coe-Jones	1,298,787.57
7. JoAnne Carner	2,784,597.63	17. Kathy Whitworth	1,722,440.01	27. Tammie Green	1,296,894.00
8. Ayako Okamoto	2,683,360.85	18. D. Ammaccapane	1,569,872.00	28. Jane Blalock	1,290,943.62
9. Jan Stephenson	2,175,309.00	19. Sally Little	1,550,095.80	29. Cindy Rarick	1,263,785.50
10. Dottie Mochrie	2,099,753.00	20. Meg Mallon	1,508,674.00	30. Debbie Massey	1,246,674.13

*Through 12/31/93.

LPGA Player of the Year

1966	Kathy Whitworth	1980	Beth Daniel
1967	Kathy Whitworth	1981	JoAnne Carner
1968	Kathy Whitworth	1982	JoAnne Carner
1969	Kathy Whitworth	1983	Patty Sheehan
1970	Sandra Haynie	1984	Betsy King
1971	Kathy Whitworth	1985	Nancy Lopez
1972	Kathy Whitworth	1986	Pat Bradley
1973	Kathy Whitworth	1987	Ayako Okamoto
1974	JoAnne Carner	1988	Nancy Lopez
1975	Sandra Palmer	1989	Betsy King
1976	Judy Rankin	1990	Beth Daniel
1977	Judy Rankin	1991	Pat Bradley
1978	Nancy Lopez	1992	Dottie Mochrie
1979	Nancy Lopez	1993	Betsy King

Water Hazard

Over the years the Japanese government has taken a lot of heat for its defiance of international whaling regulations. But rest assured that Japan is plenty strict when it comes to other sorts of marine abuse. Recently Japan slapped one citizen with a misdemeanor charge, punishable by a fine of as much as $306, for polluting the seas. It seems that the man, frustrated by the shortness of local driving ranges, hit more than 2,000 golf balls into Tokyo Bay.

Vare Trophy: Best Scoring Average

		Avg				Avg				Avg
1953	Patty Berg	75.00	1967	Kathy Whitworth	72.74	1981	JoAnne Carner	71.75
1954	Babe Zaharias	75.48	1968	Carol Mann	72.04	1982	JoAnne Carner	71.49
1955	Patty Berg	74.47	1969	Kathy Whitworth	72.38	1983	JoAnne Carner	71.41
1956	Patty Berg	74.57	1970	Kathy Whitworth	72.26	1984	Patty Sheehan	71.40
1957	Louise Suggs	74.64	1971	Kathy Whitworth	72.88	1985	Nancy Lopez	70.73
1958	Beverly Hanson	74.92	1972	Kathy Whitworth	72.38	1986	Pat Bradley	71.10
1959	Betsy Rawls	74.03	1973	Judy Rankin	73.08	1987	Betsy King	71.14
1960	Mickey Wright	73.25	1974	JoAnne Carner	72.87	1988	Colleen Walker	71.26
1961	Mickey Wright	73.55	1975	JoAnne Carner	72.40	1989	Beth Daniel	70.38
1962	Mickey Wright	73.67	1976	Judy Rankin	72.25	1990	Beth Daniel	70.54
1963	Mickey Wright	72.81	1977	Judy Rankin	72.16	1991	Pat Bradley	70.76
1964	Mickey Wright	72.46	1978	Nancy Lopez	71.76	1992	Dottie Mochrie	70.80
1965	Kathy Whitworth	72.61	1979	Nancy Lopez	71.20	1993	Nancy Lopez	70.83
1966	Kathy Whitworth	72.60	1980	Amy Alcott	71.51			

Most Career Wins*

	Wins		Wins		Wins
Kathy Whitworth	88	JoAnne Carner	42	Jane Blalock	29
Mickey Wright	82	Sandra Haynie	42	Amy Alcott	29
Patty Berg	57	Carol Mann	38	Betsy King	29
Betsy Rawls	55	Babe Zaharias	31	Beth Daniel	27
Louise Suggs	50	Patty Sheehan	31	Judy Rankin	26
Nancy Lopez	47	Pat Bradley	30		

*Through 12/31/93.

Alltime LPGA Tour Records*

Scoring

72 HOLES

268—(66-67-69-66) by Nancy Lopez to win at the Willow Creek GC, High Point, NC, in the 1985 Henredon Classic (20 under par).

54 HOLES

197—(67-65-65) by Pat Bradley to win at the Rail GC, Springfield, Ill., in the 1991 Rail Charity Golf Classic (19 under par).

36 HOLES

129—(64-65) by Judy Dickinson at Pasadena Yacht & CC, St Petersburg, in the 1985 S&H Golf Classic (15 under par).

18 HOLES

62—by Mickey Wright at Hogan Park GC, Midland, TX, in the first round in winning the 1964 Tall City Open (9 under par).

62—by Vicki Fergon at Almaden G & CC, San Jose, CA, in the second round of the 1984 San Jose Classic (11 under par).

62—by Laura Davies at the Rail Golf Club, Springfield, Ill., in the first round of the 1991 Rail Charity Golf Classic (10 under par).

62—by Hollis Stacy at Meridian Valley Country Club, Seattle, WA, in the second round of the 1992 Safeco Classic (10 under par).

9 HOLES

28—by Mary Beth Zimmerman at Rail GC, 1984 Rail Charity Golf Classic, Springfield, IL (par 36). Zimmerman shot 64.

28—by Pat Bradley at Green Gables CC, Denver, 1984 Columbia Savings Classic (par 35). Bradley shot 65.

Scoring (Cont.)

9 HOLES (Cont.)

28—by Muffin Spencer-Devlin at Knollwood CC, Elmsford, NY, in winning the 1985 MasterCard International Pro-Am (par 35). Spencer-Devlin shot 64.

28—by Peggy Kirsch at Squaw Creek CC, Vienna, OH, in the 1991 Phar-Mor (7 under par).

MOST CONSECUTIVE ROUNDS UNDER 70

9—Beth Daniel, in 1990.

MOST BIRDIES IN A ROW

8—Mary Beth Zimmerman at Rail GC in Springfield, IL, in the second round of the 1984 Rail Charity Classic. Zimmerman shot 64 (8 under par).

Wins

MOST CONSECUTIVE WINS IN SCHEDULED EVENTS

4—Mickey Wright, in 1962.
4—Mickey Wright, in 1963.
4—Kathy Whitworth, in 1969.

MOST CONSECUTIVE WINS IN ENTERED TOURNAMENTS

5—Nancy Lopez, in 1987.

MOST WINS IN A CALENDAR YEAR

13—Mickey Wright, in 1963.

WIDEST WINNING MARGIN, STROKES

14—Louise Suggs, 1949 US Women's Open.
14—Cindy Mackey, 1986 MasterCard Int'l Pro-Am.

*Through 12/31/93.

Senior Golf

U.S. Senior Open

Year	Winner	Score	Runner-Up	Site
1980	Roberto DeVicenzo	285	William C. Campbell	Winged Foot GC, Mamaroneck, NY
1981	Arnold Palmer* (70)	289	Bob Stone (74)	Oakland Hills CC, Birmingham, MI
			Billy Casper (77)	
1982	Miller Barber	282	Gene Littler	Portland GC, Portland, OR
			Dan Sikes, Jr	
1983	Billy Casper* (75) (3)	288	Rod Funseth (75) (4)	Hazeltine GC, Chaska, MN
1984	Miller Barber	286	Arnold Palmer	Oak Hill CC, Rochester, NY
1985	Miller Barber	285	Roberto DeVicenzo	Edgewood Tahoe GC, Stateline, NV
1986	Dale Douglass	279	Gary Player	Scioto CC, Columbus, OH
1987	Gary Player	270	Doug Sanders	Brooklawn CC, Fairfield, CT
1988	Gary Player* (68)	288	Bob Charles (70)	Medinah CC, Medinah, IL
1989	Orville Moody	279	Frank Beard	Laurel Valley GC, Ligonier, PA
1990	Lee Trevino	275	Jack Nicklaus	Ridgewood CC, Paramus, NJ
1991	Jack Nicklaus (65)	282	Chi Chi Rodriguez (69)	Oakland Hills CC, Birmingham, MI
1992	Larry Laoretti	275	Jim Colbert	Saucon Valley CC, Bethlehem, PA
1993	Jack Nicklaus	278	Tom Weiskopf	Cherry Hills CC, Englewood, CO
1994	Simon Hobday	274	Jim Albus	Pinehurst Resort & CC, Pinehurst, NC

*Winner in playoff. Playoff scores are in parentheses. The 1983 playoff went to one hole of sudden death after an 18-hole playoff.

SENIOR TOUR

Season Money Leaders*

Year	Winner	Earnings ($)	Year	Winner	Earnings ($)
1980	Don January	44,100	1987	Chi Chi Rodriguez	509,145
1981	Miller Barber	83,136	1988	Bob Charles	533,929
1982	Miller Barber	106,890	1989	Bob Charles	725,887
1983	Don January	237,571	1990	Lee Trevino	1,190,518
1984	Don January	328,597	1991	Mike Hill	1,065,657
1985	Peter Thomson	386,724	1992	Lee Trevino	1,027,002
1986	Bruce Crampton	454,299	1993	Dave Stockton	1,175,944

Career Money Leaders*

#	Player	Earnings ($)	#	Player	Earnings ($)
1.	Bob Charles	4,689,368	17.	Walter Zembriski	2,127,658
2.	Chi Chi Rodriguez	4,539,124	18.	Dave Hill	2,009,502
3.	Mike Hill	3,973,978	19.	Jim Ferree	2,006,183
4.	Lee Trevino	3,906,533	20.	Gene Littler	1,978,399
5.	George Archer	3,634,508	21.	Dave Stockton	1,845,366
6	Dale Douglass	3,569,491	22.	Rocky Thompson	1,766,631
7.	Bruce Crampton	3,500,675	23.	Don Bies	1,764,168
8.	Miller Barber	3,267,325	24.	Gibby Gilbert	1,657,360
9.	Gary Player	3,156,251	25.	Billy Casper	1,581,204
10.	Al Geiberger	3,028,331	26.	Bobby Nichols	1,505,966
11.	Orville Moody	2,848,834	27.	Arnold Palmer	1,500,776
12.	Harold Henning	2,815,179	28.	Gay Brewer	1,471,330
13.	Don January	2,679,215	29.	Larry Mowry	1,460,547
14.	Jim Dent	2,667,715	30.	Simon Hobday	1,421,454
15.	Jim Colbert	2,486,406			
16.	Charles Coody	2,472,733		*Through 12/31/93.	

Most Career Wins*

Player	Wins	Player	Wins
Miller Barber	24	Gary Player	17
Don January	22	Mike Hill	15
Chi Chi Rodriguez	22	George Archer	15
Bob Charles	21	Peter Thomson	11
Bruce Crampton	19	Orville Moody	11
Lee Trevino	18		

* Through 12/31/93.

MAJOR MEN'S AMATEUR CHAMPIONSHIPS

U.S. Amateur

Year	Winner	Score	Runner-Up	Site
1895	Charles B. Macdonald	12 & 11	Charles E. Sands	Newport GC, Newport, RI
1896	H. J. Whigham	8 & 7	J.G Thorp	Shinnecock Hills GC, Southampton, NY
1897	H. J. Whigham	8 & 6	W. Rossiter Betts	Chicago GC, Wheaton, IL
1898	Findlay S. Douglas	5 & 3	Walter B. Smith	Morris County GC, Morristown, NJ
1899	H. M. Harriman	3 & 2	Findlay S. Douglas	Onwentsia Club, Lake Forest, IL
1900	Walter Travis	2 up	Findlay S. Douglas	Garden City GC, Garden City, NY
1901	Walter Travis	5 & 4	Walter E. Egan	CC of Atlantic City, NJ
1902	Louis N. James	4 & 2	Eben M. Byers	Glen View Club, Golf, Ill.
1903	Walter Travis	5 & 4	Eben M. Byers	Nassau CC, Glen Cove, NY
1904	H. Chandler Egan	8 & 6	Fred Herreshoff	Baltusrol GC, Springfield, NJ
1905	H. Chandler Egan	6 & 5	D.E. Sawyer	Chicago GC, Wheaton, IL
1906	Eben M. Byers	2 up	George S. Lyon	Englewood GC, Englewood, NJ
1907	Jerry Travers	6 & 5	Archibald Graham	Euclid Club, Cleveland, OH
1908	Jerry Travers	8 & 7	Max H. Behr	Garden City GC, Garden City, NY
1909	Robert A. Gardner	4 & 3	H. Chandler Egan	Chicago GC, Wheaton, IL
1910	William C. Fownes, Jr	4 & 3	Warren K. Wood	The Country Club, Brookline, MA
1911	Harold Hilton	1 up	Fred Herreshoff	The Apawamis Club, Rye, NY
1912	Jerry Travers	7 & 6	Charles Evans, Jr.	Chicago GC, Wheaton, IL
1913	Jerry Travers	5 & 4	John G. Anderson	Garden City GC, Garden City, NY
1914	Francis Ouimet	6 & 5	Jerry Travers	Ekwanok CC, Manchester, VT
1915	Robert A. Gardner	5 & 4	John G. Anderson	CC of Detroit, Grosse Pt. Farms, MI
1916	Chick Evans	4 & 3	Robert A. Gardner	Merion Cricket Club, Haverford, PA
1917-18	No tournament			
1919	S. Davidson Herron	5 & 4	Bobby Jones	Oakmont CC, Oakmont, PA
1920	Chick Evans	7 & 6	Francis Ouimet	Engineers' CC, Roslyn, NY
1921	Jesse P. Guilford	7 & 6	Robert A. Gardner	St. Louis CC, Clayton, MO
1922	Jess W. Sweetser	3 & 2	Chick Evans	The Country Club, Brookline, MA
1923	Max R. Marston	1 up	Jess W. Sweetser	Flossmoor CC, Flossmoor, IL
1924	Bobby Jones	9 & 8	George Von Elm	Merion Cricket Club, Ardmore, PA
1925	Bobby Jones	8 & 7	Watts Gunn	Oakmont CC, Oakmont, PA
1926	George Von Elm	2 & 1	Bobby Jones	Baltusrol GC, Springfield, NJ
1927	Bobby Jones	8 & 7	Chick Evans	Minikahda Club, Minneapolis
1928	Bobby Jones	10 & 9	T. Phillip Perkins	Brae Burn CC, West Newton, MA
1929	Harrison R. Johnston	4 & 3	Dr. O.F. Willing	Del Monte G & CC, Pebble Beach, CA
1930	Bobby Jones	8 & 7	Eugene V. Homans	Merion Cricket Club, Ardmore, PA
1931	Francis Ouimet	6 & 5	Jack Westland	Beverly CC, Chicago, IL
1932	C. Ross Somerville	2 & 1	John Goodman	Baltimore CC, Timonium, MD
1933	George T. Dunlap, Jr	6 & 5	Max R. Marston	Kenwood CC, Cincinnati, OH
1934	Lawson Little	8 & 7	David Goldman	The Country Club, Brookline, MA
1935	Lawson Little	4 & 2	Walter Emery	The Country Club, Cleveland, OH
1936	John W. Fischer	1 up	Jack McLean	Garden City GC, Garden City, NY
1937	John Goodman	2 up	Raymond E. Billows	Alderwood CC, Portland, OR
1938	William P. Turnesa	8 & 7	B. Patrick Abbott	Oakmont CC, Oakmont, PA
1939	Marvin H. Ward	7 & 5	Raymond E. Billows	North Shore CC, Glenview, IL
1940	Richard D. Chapman	11 & 9	W. McCullough, Jr	Winged Foot GC, Mamaroneck, NY
1941	Marvin H. Ward	4 & 3	B. Patrick Abbott	Omaha Field Club, Omaha, NE
1942-45	No tournament			
1946	Ted Bishop	1 up	Smiley L. Quick	Baltusrol GC, Springfield, NJ
1947	Skee Riegel	2 & 1	John W. Dawson	Del Monte G & CC, Pebble Beach, CA
1948	William P. Turnesa	2 & 1	Raymond E. Billows	Memphis CC, Memphis, TN
1949	Charles R. Coe	11 & 10	Rufus King	Oak Hill CC, Rochester, NY
1950	Sam Urzetta	1 up	Frank Stranahan	Minneapolis GC, Minneapolis, MN
1951	Billy Maxwell	4 & 3	Joseph F. Gagliardi	Saucon Valley CC, Bethlehem, PA
1952	Jack Westland	3 & 2	Al Mengert	Seattle GC, Seattle, WA
1953	Gene Littler	1 up	Dale Morey	Oklahoma City G & CC, Oklahoma City
1954	Arnold Palmer	1 up	Robert Sweeny	CC of Detroit, Grosse Pt. Farms, MI
1955	E. Harvie Ward, Jr	9 & 8	Wm. Hyndman III	CC of Virginia, Richmond, VA
1956	E. Harvie Ward, Jr	5 & 4	Charles Kocsis	Knollwood Club, Lake Forest, IL
1957	Hillman Robbins, Jr	5 & 4	Dr. Frank M. Taylor	The Country Club, Brookline, MA
1958	Charles R. Coe	5 & 4	Tommy Aaron	Olympic Club, San Francisco, CA
1959	Jack Nicklaus	1 up	Charles R. Coe	Broadmoor GC, Colorado Springs, CO
1960	Deane Beman	6 & 4	Robert W. Gardner	St. Louis CC, Clayton, MO
1961	Jack Nicklaus	8 & 6	H. Dudley Wysong	Pebble Beach GL, Pebble Beach, CA

U.S. Amateur *(Cont.)*

Year	Winner	Score	Runner-Up	Site
1962	Labron E. Harris, Jr	1 up	Downing Gray	Pinehurst CC, Pinehurst, NC
1963	Deane Beman	2 & 1	Richard H. Sikes	Wakonda Club, Des Moines, IA
1964	William C. Campbell	1 up	Edgar M. Tutwiler	Canterbury GC, Cleveland, OH
1965	Robert J. Murphy, Jr	291	Robert B. Dickson	Southern Hills, CC, Tulsa, OK
1966	Gary Cowan	285-75	Deane Beman	Merion GC, Ardmore, PA
1967	Robert B. Dickson	285	Marvin Giles III	Broadmoor GC, Colorado Springs, CO
1968	Bruce Fleisher	284	Marvin Giles III	Scioto CC, Columbus, OH
1969	Steven N. Melnyk	286	Marvin Giles III	Oakmont CC, Oakmont, PA
1970	Lanny Wadkins	279	Tom Kite	Waverley CC, Portland, OR
1971	Gary Cowan	280	Eddie Pearce	Wilmington CC, Wilmington DE
1972	Marvin Giles, III	285	two tied	Charlotte CC, Charlotte, NC
1973	Craig Stadler	6 & 5	David Strawn	Inverness Club, Toledo, OH
1974	Jerry Pate	2 & 1	John P. Grace	Ridgewood CC, Ridgewood, NJ
1975	Fred Ridley	2 up	Keith Fergus	CC of Virginia, Richmond, VA
1976	Bill Sander	8 & 6	C. Parker Moore, Jr	Bel Air CC, Los Angeles, CA
1977	John Fought	9 & 8	Doug Fischesser	Aronimink GC, Newton Square, PA
1978	John Cook	5 & 4	Scott Hoch	Plainfield CC, Plainfield, NJ
1979	Mark O'Meara	8 & 7	John Cook	Canterbury GC, Cleveland, OH
1980	Hal Sutton	9 & 8	Bob Lewis	CC of North Carolina, Pinehurst, NC
1981	Nathaniel Crosby	1 up	Brian Lindley	Olympic Club, San Francisco, CA
1982	Jay Sigel	8 & 7	David Tolley	The Country Club, Brookline, MA
1983	Jay Sigel	8 & 7	Chris Perry	North Shore CC, Glenviedw IL
1984	Scott Verplank	4 & 3	Sam Randolph	Oak Tree GC, Edmond, OK
1985	Sam Randolph	1 up	Peter Persons	Montclair GC, West Orange, NJ
1986	Buddy Alexander	5 & 3	Chris Kite	Shoal Creek, Shoal Creek AL
1987	Bill Mayfair	4 & 3	Eric Rebmann	Jupiter Hills Club, Jupiter, FL
1988	Eric Meeks	7 & 6	Danny Yates	Va. Hot Springs G & CC, VA
1989	Chris Patton	3 & 1	Danny Green	Merion GC, Ardmore, PA
1990	Phil Mickelson	5 & 4	Manny Zerman	Cherry Hills CC, Englewood, CO
1991	Mitch Voges	7 & 6	Manny Zerman	The Honors Course, Ooltewah, TN
1992	Justin Leonard	8 & 7	Tom Scherrer	Muirfield Village GC, Dublin, OH
1993	John Harris	5 & 3	Danny Ellis	Champions GC, Houston, TX
1994	Tiger Woods	2 up	Trip Kuehne	TPC-Sawgrass, Ponte Vedre, FL

Note: All stroke play from 1965 to 1972.

U.S. Junior Amateur

1948 .... Dean Lind	1964 .... Johnny Miller	1980 .... Eric Johnson
1949 .... Gay Brewer	1965 .... James Masserio	1981 .... Scott Erickson
1950 .... Mason Rudolph	1966 .... Gary Sanders	1982 .... Rich Marik
1951 .... Tommy Jacobs	1967 .... John Crooks	1983 .... Tim Straub
1952 .... Don Bisplinghoff	1968 .... Eddie Pearce	1984 .... Doug Martin
1953 .... Rex Baxter	1969 .... Aly Trompas	1985 .... Charles Rymer
1954 .... Foster Bradley	1970 .... Gary Koch	1986 .... Brian Montgomery
1955 .... William Dunn	1971 .... Mike Brannan	1987 .... Brett Quigley
1956 .... Harlan Stevenson	1972 .... Bob Byman	1988 .... Jason Widener
1957 .... Larry Beck	1973 .... Jack Renner	1989 .... David Duval
1958 .... Buddy Baker	1974 .... David Nevatt	1990 .... Mathew Todd
1959 .... Larry Lee	1975 .... Brett Mullin	1991 .... Tiger Woods
1960 .... Bill Tindall	1976 .... Madden Hatcher, III	1992 .... Tiger Woods
1961 .... Charles McDowell	1977 .... Willie Wood, Jr	1993 .... Tiger Woods
1962 .... Jim Wiechers	1978 .... Don Hurter	1994 .... Terry Noe
1963 .... Gregg McHatton	1979 .... Jack Larkin	

Note: Event is for amateur golfers younger than 18 years of age.

Mid-Amateur Championship

1981 .... Jim Holtgrieve	1986 .... Bill Loeffler	1991 .... Jim Stuart
1982 .... William Hoffer	1987 .... Jay Sigel	1992 .... Danny Yates
1983 .... Jay Sigel	1988 .... David Eger	1993 .... Jeff Thomas
1984 .... Mike Podolak	1989 .... James Taylor	1994 .... Tim Jackson
1985 .... Jay Sigel	1990 .... Jim Stuart	

Note: Event is for amateur golfers at least 25 years of age.

British Amateur

1887 ....H. G. Hutchinson	1924 .............E.W.E. Holderness	1962 ....R. Davies
1888 ....John Ball	1925 ....R. Harris	1963 ....M. Lunt
1889 .............J.E. Laidlay	1926 ....Jess Sweetser	1964 ....C. Clark
1890 ....John Ball	1927 ....Dr. W. Tweddell	1965 ....M. Bonallack
1891 .............J.E. Laidlay	1928 .............T.P. Perkins	1966 .............C.R. Cole
1892 ....John Ball	1929 .............C.J.H. Tolley	1967 ....R. Dickson
1893 ....Peter Anderson	1930 ....Robert T. Jones, Jr.	1968 ....M. Bonallack
1894 ....John Ball	1931 ....E. Martin Smith	1969 ....M. Bonallack
1895 .............L.M.B. Melville	1932 ....J. DeForest	1970 ....M. Bonallack
1896 .............F.G. Tait	1933 ....M. Scott	1971 ....Steve Melnyk
1897 .............A.J.T. Allan	1934 ....W. Lawson Little	1972 ....Trevor Homer
1898 .............F.G. Tait	1935 ....W. Lawson Little	1973 ....R. Siderowf
1899 ....John Ball	1936 ....H. Thomson	1974 ....Trevor Homer
1900 .............H.H. Hilton	1937 ....R. Sweeney, Jr.	1975 ....M. Giles
1901 .............H.H. Hilton	1938 .............C.R. Yates	1976 ....R. Siderowf
1902 ....C. Hutchings	1939 .............A.T. Kyle	1977 ....P. McEvoy
1903 ....R. Maxwell	1940-45... not held	1978 ....P. McEvoy
1904 .............W.J. Travis	1946 ....J. Bruen	1979 ....J. Sigel
1905 .............A.G. Barry	1947 ....Willie D. Turnesa	1980 ....D. Evans
1906 ....James Robb	1948 ....Frank R. Stranahan	1981 ....P. Ploujoux
1907 ....John Ball	1949 .............S.M. McReady	1982 ....M. Thompson
1908 .............E.A. Lassen	1950 ....Frank R. Stranahan	1983 ....A. Parkin
1909 ....R. Maxwell	1951 ....Richard D. Chapman	1984 .............J.M. Olazabal
1910 ....John Ball	1952 .............E.H. Ward	1985 ....G. McGimpsey
1911 .............H.H. Hilton	1953 .............J.B. Carr	1986 ....D. Curry
1912 ....John Ball	1954 .............D.W. Bachli	1987 ....P. Mayo
1913 .............H.H. Hilton	1955 .............J.W. Conrad	1988 ....C. Hardin
1914 .............J.L.C. Jenkins	1956 .............J.C. Beharrel	1989 ....S. Dodd
1915-19......not held	1957 ....R. Reid Jack	1990 ....R. Muntz
1920 .............C.J.H. Tolley	1958 .............J.B. Carr	1991 ....G. Wolstenholme
1921 .............W.I. Hunter	1959 ....Deane Beman	1992 ....S. Dundas
1922 .............E.W.E. Holderness	1960 .............J.B. Carr	1993 ....I. Pyman
1923 .............R.H. Wethered	1961 ....M. Bonallack	1994 ....L. James

Amateur Public Links

1922 ....Edmund R. Held	1948 ....Michael R. Ferentz	1972 ....Bob Allard
1923 ....Richard J. Walsh	1949 ....Kenneth J. Towns	1973 ....Stan Stopa
1924 ....Joseph Coble	1950 ....Stanley Bielat	1974 ....Charles Barenaba
1925 ....Raymond J. McAuliffe	1951 ....Dave Stanley	1975 ....Randy Barenaba
	1952 ....Omer L. Bogan	1976 ....Eddie Mudd
1926 ....Lester Bolstad	1953 ....Ted Richards, Jr.	1977 ....Jerry Vidovic
1927 ....Carl F. Kauffmann	1954 ....Gene Andrews	1978 ....Dean Prince
1928 ....Carl F. Kauffmann	1955 ....Sam D. Kocsis	1979 ....Dennis Walsh
1929 ....Carl F. Kauffmann	1956 ....James H. Buxbaum	1980 ....Jodie Mudd
1930 ....Robert E. Wingate	1957 ....Don Essig III	1981 ....Jodie Mudd
1931 ....Charles Ferrera	1958 ....Daniel D. Sikes, Jr.	1982 ....Billy Tuten
1932 .............R.L. Miller	1959 ....William A. Wright	1983 ....Billy Tuten
1933 ....Charles Ferrera	1960 ....Verne Callison	1984 ....Bill Malley
1934 ....David A. Mitchell	1961 ....Richard H. Sikes	1985 ....Jim Sorenson
1935 ....Frank Strafaci	1962 ....Richard H. Sikes	1986 ....Bill Mayfair
1936 ....B. Patrick Abbott	1963 ....Robert Lunn	1987 ....Kevin Johnson
1937 ....Bruce N. McCormick	1964 ....William McDonald	1988 ....Ralph Howe, III
1938 ....Al Leach	1965 ....Arne Dokka	1989 ....Tim Hobby
1939 ....Andrew Szwedko	1966 ....Lamont Kaser	1990 ....Michael Combs
1940 ....Robert C. Clark	1967 ....Verne Callison	1991 ....David Berganio, Jr.
1941 ....William M. Welch, Jr.	1968 ....Gene Towry	1992 ....Warren Schulte
1942-45........not held	1969 ....John M. Jackson, Jr.	1993 ....David Berganio, Jr.
1946 ....Smiley L. Quick	1970 ....Robert Risch	1994 ....Guy Yamamoto
1947 ....Wilfred Crossley	1971 ....Fred Haney	

U.S. Senior Golf

1955 ....J. Wood Platt	1969 ....Curtis Person, Sr	1983 ....William Hyndman, III
1956 ....Frederick J. Wright	1970 ....Gene Andrews	1984 ....Bob Rawlins
1957 ....J. Clark Espie	1971 ....Tom Draper	1985 ....Lewis W. Oehmig
1958 ....Thomas C. Robbins	1972 ....Lewis W. Oehmig	1986 ....Bo Williams
1959 ....J. Clark Espie	1973 ....William Hyndman, III	1987 ....John Richardson
1960 ....Michael Cestone	1974 ....Dale Morey	1988 ....Clarence Moore
1961 ....Dexter H. Daniels	1975 ....William F. Colm	1989 ....Bo Williams
1962 ....Merrill L. Carlsmith	1976 ....Lewis W. Oehmig	1990 ....Jackie Cummings
1963 ....Merrill L. Carlsmith	1977 ....Dale Morey	1991 ....Bill Bosshard
1964 ....William D. Higgins	1978 ....K. K. Compton	1992 ....Clarence Moore
1965 ....Robert B. Kiersky	1979 ....William C. Campbell	1993 ....Joe Ungvary
1966 ....Dexter H. Daniels	1980 ....William C. Campbell	1994 ....O. Gordon Brewer
1967 ....Ray Palmer	1981 ....Ed Updegraff	
1968 ....Curtis Person, Sr	1982 ....Alton Duhon	

Event is for golfers at least 55 years of age.

MAJOR WOMEN'S AMATEUR CHAMPIONSHIPS

U.S. Women's Amateur

Year	Winner	Score	Runner-Up	Site
1895 ....Mrs. Charles S. Brown		132	Nellie Sargent	Meadow Brook Club, Hempstead, NY
1896 ....Beatrix Hoyt		2 & 1	Mrs. Arthur Turnure	Morris Couty GC, Morristown, NJ
1897 ....Beatrix Hoyt		5 & 4	Nellie Sargent	Essex County Club, Manchester, MA
1898 ....Beatrix Hoyt		5 & 3	Maude Wetmore	Ardsley Club, Ardsley-on-Hudson, NY
1899 ....Ruth Underhill		2 & 1	Margaret Fox	Philadelphia CC, Philadelphia, PA
1900 ....Frances C. Griscom		6 & 5	Margaret Curtis	Shinnecock Hills GC, Shinnecock Hills, NY
1901 ....Genevieve Hecker		5 & 3	Lucy Herron	Baltusrol GC, Springfield, NJ
1902 ....Genevieve Hecker		4 & 3	Louisa A. Wells	The Country Club, Brookline, MA
1903 ....Bessie Anthony		7 & 6	J. Anna Carpenter	Chicago GC, Wheaton, IL
1904 ....Georgianna M. Bishop		5 & 3	Mrs. E.F. Sanford	Merion Cricket Club, Haverford, PA
1905 ....Pauline Mackay		1 up	Margaret Curtis	Morris County GC, Convent, NJ
1906 ....Harriot S. Curtis		2 & 1	Mary B. Adams	Brae Burn CC, West Newton, MA
1907 ....Margaret Curtis		7 & 6	Harriot S. Curtis	Midlothian CC, Blue Island, IL
1908 ....Katherine C. Harley		6 & 5	Mrs. T.H. Polhemus	Chevy Chase Club, Chevy Chase, MD
1909 ....Dorothy I. Campbell		3 & 2	Nonna Barlow	Merion Cricket Club, Haverford, PA
1910 ....Dorothy I. Campbell		2 & 1	Mrs. G.M. Martin	Homewood CC, Flossmoor, IL
1911 ....Margaret Curtis		5 & 3	Lillian B. Hyde	Baltusrol GC, Springfield, NJ
1912 ....Margaret Curtis		3 & 2	Nonna Barlow	Essex County Club, Manchester, MA
1913 ....Gladys Ravenscroft		2 up	Marion Hollins	Wilmington CC, Wilmington, DE
1914 ....Katherine Harley		1 up	Elaine V. Rosenthal	Nassau CC, Glen Cove, NY
1915 ....Florence Vanderbeck		3 & 2	Margaret Gavin	Onwentsia Club, Lake Forest, IL
1916 ....Alexa Stirling		2 & 1	Mildred Caverly	Belmont Springs CC, Waverley, MA
1917-18 ......No tournament				
1919...........Alexa Stirling		6 & 5	Margaret Gavin	Shawnee CC, Shawnee-on Delaware, PA
1920 ....Alexa Stirling		5 & 4	Dorothy Campbell	Mayfield CC, Cleveland, OH
1921 ....Marion Hollins		5 & 4	Alexa Stirling	Hollywood GC, Deal, NJ
1922 ....Glenna Collett		5 & 4	Margaret Gavin	Greenbriar GC, White Sulphur Springs, W. Va.
1923 ....Edith Cummings		3 & 2	Alexa Stirling	Westchester-Biltmore CC, Rye, NY
1924 ....Dorothy Campbell		7 & 6	Mary K. Browne	Rhode Island CC, Nyatt, RI
1925 ....Glenna Collett		9 & 8	Alexa Stirling	St. Louis CC, Clayton, MO
1926 ....Helen Stetson		3 & 1	Elizabeth Goss	Merion Cricket Club, Ardmore, PA
1927 ....Miiriam Burns Horn		5 & 4	Maureen Orcutt	Cherry Valley Club, Garden City, NY
1928 ....Glenna Collett		13 & 12	Virginia Van Wie	Va. Hot Springs G & TC, Hot Springs, VA
1929 ....Glenna Collett		4 & 3	Leona Pressler	Oakland Hills CC, Birmingham, MI
1930 ....Glenna Collett		6 & 5	Virginia Van Wie	Los Angeles CC, Beverly Hills, CA
1931 ....Helen Hicks		2 & 1	Glenna Collet Vare	CC of Buffalo, Williamsville, NY
1932 ....Virginia Van Wie		10 & 8	Glenna Collet Vare	Salem CC, Peabody, MA
1933 ....Virginia Van Wie		4 & 3	Helen Hicks	Exmoor CC, Highland Park, IL
1934 ....Virginia Van Wie		2 & 1	Dorothy Traung	Whitemarsh Valley CC, Chestnut Hill, PA
1935 ....Glenna Collett Vare		3 & 2	Patty Berg	Interlachen CC, Hopkins, MN
1936 ....Pamela Barton		4 & 3	Maureen Orcutt	Canoe Brook CC, Summit, NJ

U.S. Women's Amateur (Cont.)

Year	Winner	Score	Runner-Up	Site
1937	Estelle Lawson	7 & 6	Patty Berg	Memphis CC, Memphis, TN
1938	Patty Berg	6 & 5	Estelle Lawson	Westmoreland CC, Wilmette, IL
1939	Betty Jameson	3 & 2	Dorothy Kirby	Wee Burn Club, Darien, CT
1940	Betty Jameson	6 & 5	Jane S. Cothran	Del Monte G & CC, Pebble Beach, CA
1941	Elizabeth Hicks	5 & 3	Helen Sigel	The Country Club, Brookline, MA
1942-45	No tournament			
1946	Babe Zaharias	11 & 9	Clara Sherman	Southern Hills CC, Tulsa, OK
1947	Louise Suggs	2 up	Dorothy Kirby	Franklin Hills CC, Franklin, MI
1948	Grace S. Lenczyk	4 & 3	Helen Sigel	Del Monte G & CC, Pebble Beach, CA
1949	Dorothy Porter	3 & 2	Dorothy Kielty	Merion GC, Ardmore, PA
1950	Beverly Hanson	6 & 4	Mae Murray	Atlanta AC, Atlanta, GA
1951	Dorothy Kirby	2 & 1	Claire Doran	Town & CC, St. Paul, MN
1952	Jacqueline Pung	2 & 1	Shirley McFedters	Waverley CC, Portland, OR
1953	Mary Lena Faulk	3 & 2	Polly Riley	Rhode Island CC, West Barrington, RI
1954	Barbara Romack	4 & 2	Miickey Wright	Allegheny CC, Sewickley, PA
1955	Patricia A. Lesser	7 & 6	Jane Nelson	Myers Park CC, Charlotte, NC
1956	Marlene Stewart	2 & 1	JoAnne Gunderson	Meridian Hills CC, Indianapolis, IN
1957	JoAnne Gunderson	8 & 6	Ann Casey Johnstone	Del Paso CC, Sacramento, CA
1958	Anne Quast	3 & 2	Barbara Romack	Wee Burn CC, Darien, CT
1959	Barbara McIntire	4 & 3	Joanne Goodwin	Congressional CC, Washington, D.C.
1960	JoAnne Gunderson	6 & 5	Jean Ashley	Tulsa CC, Tulsa, OK
1961	Anne Quast Sander	14 & 13	Phyllis Preuss	Tacoma G & CC, Tacoma, WA
1962	JoAnne Gunderson	9 & 8	Anne Baker	CC of Rochester, Rochester, NY
1963	Anne Quast Sander	2 & 1	Peggy Conley	Taconic GC, Williamstown, MA
1964	Barbara McIntire	3 & 2	JoAnne Gunderson	Prairie Dunes CC, Hutchinson, KS
1965	Jean Ashley	5 & 4	Anne Quast Sander	Lakewood CC, Denver, CO
1966	JoAnne Gunderson	1 up	Marlene Stewart Streit	Sewickley Heights GC, Sewickley, PA
1967	Mary Lou Dill	•5 & 4	Jean Ashley	Annandale GC, Pasadena, CA
1968	JoAnne Gunderson Carner	5 & 4	Anne Quast Sander	Birmingham CC, Birmingham, MI
1969	Catherine Lacoste	3 & 2	Shelley Hamling	Las Colinas CC, Irving, TX
1970	Martha Wilkinson	3 & 2	Cynthia Hall	Wee Burn CC, Darien, CT
1971	Laura Baugh	1 up	Beth Barry	Atlanta CC, Atlanta, GA
1972	Mary Budke	5 & 4	Cynthia Hill	St. Louis CC, St. Louis, MO
1973	Carol Semple	1 up	Anne Quast Sander	Montclair GC, Montclair, NJ
1974	Cynthia Hill	5 & 4	Carol Semple	Broadmoor GC, Seattle, WA
1975	Beth Daniel	3 & 2	Donna Horton	Brae Burn CC, West Newton, MA
1976	Donna Horton	2 & 1	Marianne Bretton	Del Paso CC, Sacramento, CA
1977	Beth Daniel	3 & 1	Cathy Sherk	Cincinnati CC, Cincinnati, OH
1978	Cathy Sherk	4 & 3	Judith Oliver	Sunnybrook GC, Plymouth Meeting, PA
1979	Carolyn Hill	7 & 6	Patty Sheehan	Memphis CC, Memphis, TN
1980	Juli Inkster	2 up	Patti Rizzo	Prairie Dunes CC, Hutchinson, KS
1981	Juli Inkster	1 up	Lindy Goggin	Waverley CC, Portland, OR
1982	Juli Inkster	4 & 3	Cathy Hanlon	Broadmoor GC, Colorado Springs, CO
1983	Joanne Pacillo	2 & 1	Sally Quinlan	Canoe Brook CC, Summit, NJ
1984	Deb Richard	1 up	Kimberly Williams	Broadmoor GC, Seattle, WA
1985	Michiko Hattori	5 & 4	Cheryl Stacy	Fox Chapel CC, Pittsburgh, PA
1986	Kay Cockerill	9 & 7	Kathleen McCarthy	Pasatiempo GC, Santa Cruz, CA
1987	Kay Cockerill	3 & 2	Tracy Kerdyk	Rhode Island CC, Barrington, RI
1988	Pearl Sinn	6 & 5	Karen Noble	Minikahda Club, Miinneapolis, MN
1989	Vicki Goetze	4 & 3	Brandie Burton	Pinehurst CC (No. 2), Pinehurst, NC
1990	Pat Hurst	37 holes	Stephanie Davis	Canoe Brook CC, Summit, NJ
1991	Amy Fruhwirth	5 & 4	Heidi Voorhees	Prairie Dunes CC, Hutchinson, KN
1992	Vicki Goetz	1-up	Annika Sorensteam	Kemper Lakes GC, Hawthorne Hills, IL
1993	Jill McGill	1-up	Sarah Ingram	San Diego CC, Chula Vista, CA
1994	Wendy Ward	2 & 1	Jill McGill	The Homestead, Hot Springs, WV

Girls' Junior Championship

1949 Marlene Bauer	1965 Gail Sykes	1981 Kay Cornelius
1950 Patricia Lesser	1966 Claudia Mayhew	1982 Heather Farr
1951 Arlene Brooks	1967 Elizabeth Story	1983 Kim Saiki
1952 Mickey Wright	1968 Peggy Harmon	1984 Cathy Mockett
1953 Millie Meyerson	1969 Hollis Stacy	1985 Dana Lofland
1954 Margaret Smith	1970 Hollis Stacy	1986 Pat Hurst
1955 Carole Jo Kabler	1971 Hollis Stacy	1987 Michelle McGann
1956 JoAnne Gunderson	1972 Nancy Lopez	1988 Jamille Jose
1957 Judy Eller	1973 Amy Alcott	1989 Brandie Burton
1958 Judy Eller	1974 Nancy Lopez	1990 Sandrine Mendiburu
1959 Judy Rand	1975 Dayna Benson	1991 Emilee Klein
1960 Carol Sorenson	1976 Pilar Dorado	1992 Jamie Koizumi
1961 Mary Lowell	1977 Althea Tome	1993 Kellee Booth
1962 Mary Lou Daniel	1978 Lori Castillo	1962 Maureen Orcutt
1963 Janis Ferraris	1979 Penny Hammel	1963 Sis Choate
1964 Peggy Conley	1980 Laurie Rinker	1994 Kelli Kuehne

Women's British Amateur

1893 Lady Margaret Scott	1927 Miss Thion de la Chaume	1960 B. McIntyre
1894 Lady Margaret Scott	1928 Miss N. Le Blan	1961 M. Spearman
1895 Lady Margaret Scott	1929 Miss J. Wethered	1962 M. Spearman
1896 Miss Pascoe	1930 Miss D. Fishwick	1963 B. Varangot
1897 Miss E.C. Orr	1931 Miss E. Wilson	1964 C. Sorenson
1898 Miss L. Thomson	1932 Miss E. Wilson	1965 B. Varangot
1899 Miss M. Hezlet	1933 Miss E. Wilson	1966 E. Chadwick
1900 Miss Adair	1934 Mrs. A.M. Holm	1967 E. Chadwick
1901 Miss Graham	1935 Miss W. Morgan	1968 B. Varangot
1902 Miss M. Hezlet	1936 Miss P. Barton	1975 C. Lacoste
1903 Miss Adair	1937 Miss J. Anderson	1976 D. Oxley
1904 Miss L. Dod	1938 Mrs. A.M. Holm	1977 A. Uzielli
1905 Miss B. Thompson	1939 Miss P. Barton	1978 E. Kennedy
1906 Mrs. Kennon	1940–45 not held	1979 M. Madill
1907 Miss M. Hezlet	1946 G.W. Hetherington	1980 A. Quast
1908 Miss M. Titterton	1947 B. Zaharias	1981 I.C. Robertson
1909 Miss D. Campbell	1948 L. Suggs	1982 K. Douglas
1910 Miss Grant Suttie	1949 F. Stephens	1983 J. Thornhill
1911 Miss D. Campbell	1950 Vicomtesse de Saint Sauveur	1984 J. Rosenthal
1912 Miss G. Ravenscroft	1951 P.J. MacCann	1985 L. Beman
1913 Miss M. Dodd	1952 M. Paterson	1986 M. McGuire
1914 Miss C. Leitch	1953 M. Stewart	1987 J. Collingham
1915–19 not held	1954 F. Stephens	1988 J. Furby
1920 Miss C. Leitch	1955 J. Valentine	1989 H. Dobson
1921 Miss C. Leitch	1956 M. Smith	1990 J. Hall
1922 Miss J. Wethered	1957 P. Garvey	1991 V. Michaud
1923 Miss D. Chambers	1958 J. Valentine	1992 P. Pedersen
1924 Miss J. Wethered	1959 E. Price	1993 Catriona Lambert
1925 Miss J. Wethered		1994 Emma Duggleby
1926 Miss C. Leitch		

Women's Amateur Public Links

1977 Kelly Fuiks	1984 Heather Farr	1990 Cathy Mockett
1978 Kelly Fuiks	1985 Danielle Ammaccapane	1991 Tracy Hanson
1979 Lori Castillo	1986 Cindy Schreyer	1992 Amy Fruhwirth
1980 Lori Castillo	1987 Tracy Kerdyk	1993 Connie Masterson
1981 Mary Enright	1988 Pearl Sinn	1994 Jill McGill
1982 Nancy Taylor	1989 Pearl Sinn	
1983 Kelli Antolock		

U.S. Senior Women's Amateur

1964 ....Loma Smith	1975 ....Alberta Bower	1986 ....Connie Guthrie
1965 ....Loma Smith	1976 ....Cecile H. Maclaurin	1987 ....Anne Sander
1966 ....Maureen Orcutt	1977 ....Dorothy Porter	1988 ....Lois Hodge
1967 ....Marge Mason	1978 ....Alice Dye	1989 ....Anne Sander
1968 ....Carolyn Cudone	1979 ....Alice Dye	1990 ....Anne Sander
1969 ....Carolyn Cudone	1980 ....Dorothy Porter	1991 ....Phyllis Preuss
1970 ....Carolyn Cudone	1981 ....Dorothy Porter	1992 ....Rosemary Thompson
1971 ....Carolyn Cudone	1982 ....Edean Ihlanfeldt	1993 ....Anne Sander
1972 ....Carolyn Cudone	1983 ....Dorothy Porter	1994 ....Marlene Streit
1973 ....Gwen Hibbs	1984 ....Constance Guthrie	
1974 ....Justine Cushing	1985 ....Marlene Streit	

Women's Mid-Amateur Championship

1987	Cindy Scholefield
1988	Martha Lang
1989	Robin Weiss
1990	Carol Semple Thompson
1991	Sarah LeBrun Ingram
1992	Marion Mamey-McInerney
1993	Sarah Ingram
1994	Sarah Ingram

International Golf

Ryder Cup Matches

Year	Results	Site
1927	United States 9½, Great Britain 2½	Worcester CC, Worcester, MA
1929	Great Britain 7, United States 5	Moortown GC, Leeds, England
1931	United States 9, Great Britain 3	Scioto CC, Columbus, OH
1933	Great Britain 6½, United States 5½	Southport and Ainsdale Courses, Southport, England
1935	United States 9, Great Britain 3	Ridgewood CC, Ridgewood, NJ
1937	United States 8, Great Britain 4	Southport and Ainsdale Courses, Southport, England
1939-1945	No tournament	
1947	United States 11, Great Britain 1	Portland GC, Portland, OR
1949	United States 7, Great Britain 5	Ganton GC, Scarborough, England
1951	United States 9½, Great Britain 2½	Pinehurst CC, Pinehurst, NC
1953	United States 6½, Great Britain 5½	Wentworth Club, Surrey, England
1955	United States 8, Great Britain 4	Thunderbird Ranch & CC, Palm Springs, CA
1957	Great Britain 7½, United States 4½	Lindrick GC, Yorkshire, England
1959	United States 8½, Great Britain 3½	Eldorado CC, Palm Desert, CA
1961	United States 14½, Great Britain 9½	Royal Lytham & St Anne's GC, St Anne's-on-the-Sea, England
1963	United States 23, Great Britain 9	East Lake CC, Atlanta
1965	United States 19½, Great Britain 12½	Royal Birkdale GC, Southport, England
1967	United States 23½, Great Britain 8½	Champions GC, Houston
1969	United States 16, Great Britain 16	Royal Birkdale GC, Southport, England
1971	United States 18½, Great Britain 13½	Old Warson CC, St Louis
1973	United States 19, Great Britain 13	Hon Co of Edinburgh Golfers, Muirfield, Scotland
1975	United States 21, Great Britain 11	Laurel Valley GC, Ligonier, PA
1977	United States 12½, Great Britain 7½	Royal Lytham & St Anne's GC, St Anne's-on-the-Sea, England
1979	United States 17, Europe 11	Greenbrier, White Sulphur Springs, WV
1981	United States 18½, Europe 9½	Walton Heath GC, Surrey, England
1983	United States 14½, Europe 13½	PGA National GC, Palm Beach Gardens, FL
1985	Europe 16½, United States 11½	Belfry GC, Sutton Coldfield, England
1987	Europe 15, United States 13	Muirfield GC, Dublin, OH
1989	Europe 14, United States 14	Belfry GC, Sutton Coldfield, England
1991	United States 14½, Europe 13½	Ocean Course, Kiawah Island, SC
1993	United States 15, Europe 13	Belfry GC, Sutton Coldfield, England

Team matches held every odd year between US professionals and those of Great Britain/Europe (since 1979, prior to which was US vs GB). Team members selected on basis of finishes in PGA and European tour events.

International Golf *(Cont.)*

Walker Cup Matches

Year	Results	Site
1922	United States 8, Great Britain 4	Nat. Golf Links of America, Southampton, NY
1923	United States 6, Great Britain 5	St. Andrews, Scotland
1924	United States 9, Great Britain 3	Garden City GC, Garden City, NY
1926	United States 6, Great Britain 5	St. Andrews, Scotland
1928	United States 11, Great Britain 1	Chicago GC, Wheaton, IL
1930	United States 10, Great Britain 2	Royal St. George GC, Sandwich, England
1932	United States 8, Great Britain 1	The Country Club, Brookline, MA
1934	United States 9, Great Britain 2	St. Andrews, Scotland
1936	United States 9, Great Britain 0	Pine Valley GC, Clementon, NJ
1938	Great Britain 7, United States 4	St. Andrews, Scotland
1940-46	No tournament	
1947	United States 8, Great Britain 4	St. Andrews, Scotland
1949	United States 10, Great Britain 2	Winged Foot GC, Mamaroneck, NY
1951	United States 6, Great Britain 3	Birkdale GC, Southport, England
1953	United States 9, Great Britain 3	The Kittansett Club, Marion, MA
1955	United States 10, Great Britain 2	St. Andrews, Scotland
1957	United States 8, Great Britain 3	Minikahda Club, Minneapolis, MN
1959	United States 9, Great Britain 3	Muirfield, Scotland
1961	United States 11, Great Britain 1	Seattle GC, Seattle, WA
1963	United States 12, Great Britain 8	Ailsa Course, Turnberry, Scotland
1965	Great Britain 11, United States 11	Baltimore CC, Five Farms, Baltimore, MD
1967	United States 13, Great Britain 7	Royal St. George's GC, Sandwich, England
1969	United States 10, Great Britain 8	Milwaukee CC, Milwaukee, WI
1971	Great Britain 13, United States 11	St. Andrews, Scotland
1973	United States 14, Great Britain 10	The Country Club, Brookline, MA
1975	United States 15½, Great Britain 8½	St. Andrews, Scotland
1977	United States 16, Great Britain 8	Shinnecock Hills GC, Southampton, NY
1979	United States 15½, Great Britain 8½	Muirfield, Scotland
1981	United States 15, Great Britain 9	Cypress Point Club, Pebble Beach, CA
1983	United States 13½, Great Britain 10½	Royal Liverpool GC, Hoylake, England
1985	United States 13, Great Britain 11	Pine Valley GC, Pine Valley, NJ
1987	United States 16½, Great Britain 7½	Sunningdale GC, Berkshire, England
1989	Great Britain 12½, United States 11½	Peachtree Golf Club, Atlanta, GA
1991	United States 14, Great Britain 10	Portmarnock GC, Dublin, Ireland
1993	United States 19, Great Britain 5	Interlachen CC, Edina, MN

Men's amateur team competition every other year between United States and Great Britain. US team members selected by USGA.

Curtis Cup Matches

Year	Results	Site
1932	United States 5½, British Isles 3½	Wentworth GC, Wentworth, England
1934	United States 6½, British Isles 2½	Chevy Chase Club, Chevy Chase, MD
1936	United States 4½, British Isles 4½	King's Course, Gleneagles, Scotland
1938	United States 5½, British Isles 3½	Essex CC, Manchester, MA
1940-46	No tournament	
1948	United States 6½, British Isles 2½	Birkdale GC, Southport, England
1950	United States 7½, British Isles 1½	CC of Buffalo, Williamsville, NY
1952	British Isles 5, United States 4	Muirfield, Scotland
1954	United States 6, British Isles 3	Merion GC, Ardmore, PA
1956	British Isles 5, United States 4	Prince's GC, Sandwich Bay, England
1958	British Isles 4½, United States 4½	Brae Burn CC, West Newton, Mass.
1960	United States 6½, British Isles 2½	Lindrick GC, Worksop, England
1962	United States 8, British Isles 1	Broadmoor CG, Colorado Springs,CO
1964	United States 10½, British Isles 7½	Royal Porthcawl GC, Porthcawl, South Wales
1966	United States 13, British Isles 5	Va. Hot Springs G & TC, Hot Springs, VA
1968	United States 10½, British Isles 7½	Royal County Down GC, Newcastle, N. Ire.
1970	United States 11½, British Isles 6½	Brae Burn CC, West Newton, MA
1972	United States 10, British Isles 8	Western Gailes, Ayrshire, Scotland
1974	United States 13, British Isles 5	San Francisco GC, San Francisco, CA
1976	United States 11½, British Isles 6½	Royal Lytham & St. Annes GC, England

Curtis Cup Matches (Cont.)

Year	Results	Site
1978	United States 12, British Isles 6	Apawamis Club, Rye, NY
1980	United States 13, British Isles 5	St. Pierre G & CC, Chepstow, Wales
1982	United States 14½, British Isles 3½	Denver CC, Denver, CO
1984	United States 9½, British Isles 8½	Muirfield, Scotland
1986	British Isles 13, United States 5	Prairie Dunes CC, Hutchinson, KS
1988	British Isles 11, United States 7	Royal St. George's GC, Sandwich, England
1990	United States 14, British Isles 4	Somerset Hills CC, Bernardsville, NJ
1992	Great Britain/Ireland 10, United States 8	Royal Liverpool GC, Hoylake, England
1994	Great Britain/Ireland 9, United States 9	The Honors Course, Ooltewah, TN

Women's amateur team competition every other year between the United States and Great Britain. US team members selected by USGA.

Masters' Universe

The Masters, perhaps the most important golf tournament in the world, has once again established itself as the most self-important. In early September the pooh-bahs at the Augusta National Golf Club got CBS commentator Gary McCord booted off the Masters, which he'd covered for the last nine years. The lords of Augusta whistled, and the executives at CBS scooped up their bags. And they say the caddie system is dying.

McCord's transgression was treating the Masters as if it were a sporting event, an attitude that doesn't make the cut along the sun-dappled, azalea-adorned links of Augusta. Specifically, McCord got the boot for joking that the greens were so slick that they seemed to have been groomed "with bikini wax" and for describing a piece of bumpy ground as looking "suspiciously like body bags."

Borderline tasteless? Yes. Grounds for dismissal? Hardly. Nonetheless, the CBS caddies tripped over themselves to do the bidding of their masters at the Masters. Economics played a part in the network's compliance, of course. With an evaporating sports schedule, the network could hardly afford to lose a top live event that has been on its schedule since 1956.

Then again, CBS has been bowing and scraping before the Masters for so long that it has become a way of life. In 1966 the network execs established their own parameters for free speech when, at Augusta's behest, they removed commentator Jack Whitaker (whose urbane commentary and sonorous tones would seem to play well at Augusta) because he described a surging gallery as a mob. Sniffed Masters president Clifford Roberts: "We don't have mobs at Augusta."

The McCord affair harks back to Dallas Cowboy owner Jerry Jones's firing of radio announcer Brad Sham. Sham had the temerity to defend his colleague, color commentator Dale Hansen, for daring to ask coach Barry Switzer in public about reports of dissension on the coaching staff. Explained Jones: "We want our broadcasts to be positive." We don't expect the tyrannical Jones to be embarrassed by his actions. But we hope CBS execs are by theirs.

THEY SAID IT

Greg Norman after finishing one over par to win the 1993 Grand Slam of Golf: "It was like a mackerel in the moonlight—shiny one minute, smelly the next."

Boxing

Boxing Blahs

A shallow talent pool and a marquee heavyweight still in jail
made for another dull year in the ring | by RICHARD HOFFER

JULIO CESAR CHAVEZ, ALL THAT'S left of boxing's royalty, arrested his descent into mortality with a fairly conclusive knockout at year's end. Except for that win over a faded Meldrick Taylor, in a rematch that came four years too late, the game might have foundered entirely. New stars were reluctant to emerge, and in 1994 even the old ones seemed spent.

It was another year in limbo, the shallow talent pool stagnant, perhaps even drained a bit more. It began in disaster, as Chávez, officially undefeated in 90 fights, took on a 32-year-old challenger in defense of his super lightweight title. There was no question that Chávez, himself going on 32, was no longer what he once was. His fight with Pernell Whitaker on Sept. 11, 1993, a roundly derided draw, seemed to signal the end of his reign. But once Frankie Randall decisioned him in a January bout, it became popular to ask what exactly Chávez once was. The greatest boxer of his era or a cultural phenomenon whose popularity accounted for as much success as his fists? His legend was not exactly bolstered by the whining that accompanied the loss. He complained bitterly of referee Richard Steele, who

deducted critical points for low blows in that fight. Chávez saw little irony in the fact that Steele had saved him in a 1990 bout with Taylor, stopping a fight Chávez was losing with only two seconds left.

But the revisionist historians really began to gather after his Cinco de Mayo rematch with Randall. Even though Chávez reached out to veteran trainer Emanuel Steward to correct his decline, he could do no better than score a technical decision over Randall in regaining his title. Chávez was leading on the scorecards when he suffered an unintentional head butt and refused to come out for the ninth round. This was not the rugged warrior that Mexico had come to celebrate. Steward said the fighter may have panicked in the ring. Less kindly fans agreed he quit. Perhaps because of that 1990 bout with Taylor, which had marinated in controversy all these years, Chávez was never really able to capture the North American fan base. But, more tragic now, he was losing the Mexicans. The man who had been called upon to give his blessing to a presidential candidate, was now being booed at public events.

Finally, in September, in a match that not even the MGM Grand was wild to have (it forced promoter Don King to

lower his site fee if he insisted on the bout), Chávez was allowed to face Taylor, whose career had nose-dived after the first Chávez fight. Taylor was considered damaged goods, when he was considered at all, but he at least retained the cachet of a Chávez nemesis. But not for long.

Though Taylor danced impressively and piled up points, the stolid Chávez finally hurt him in the sixth round and then stopped him in the eighth. A Mexican Independence Day crowd quickly returned Chávez to their little pantheon of heroes. For now.

While all this was going on, boxing's undercard was having trouble firming up. The career of Michael Carbajal, for example, took a detour when Humberto Gonzalez took his light flyweight title in a February bout. Carbajal, who had beaten the 5'1'' Gonzalez the year before to unify the championship, was becoming a star attraction, generating an unthought

Chávez and his apparent return to form was one of the few bright spots for boxing in '94.

of $1 million purse for himself. And then Gonzalez, bloodied, stretched the undefeated champion the entire 12 rounds and came away with a decision. A third match between the two may be even more problematic than a third Chávez-Randall fight. Negotiations may have been complicated by Carbajal's arrest on felony charges involving gunshots at a neighborhood party. Carbajal denied any gang involvement, but his Olympic Games stature was certainly diminished by that incident as much as by his only defeat.

The heavyweight division was no more stable than the lighter weights. It had its moments but, for yet another year, it took a penologist to report them. Mike Tyson, the last man to lend big-boy boxing some excitement, spent another season of his prime in prison even though he might not have had to. Apparently the former champion would have been sprung if only he could have mustered a sincere enough apology for his rape of Desiree Washington three years earlier. Instead, he told the judge at a sentence-reduction hearing, "I've committed no crime" and said he was "going to stick with that to my grave. I never violated anyone's chastity."

Tyson wasn't learning anything, not his lesson and, as it turned out, not his reading and writing either. It took two tries before he softened his unrepentance (in a later letter to the court) and passed his GED (after failing his first test by one point). The judge might ultimately be impressed enough with this rehabilitation to shorten Tyson's sentence by as much as three months, which would put him back in the heavyweight mix by February 1995.

There was boxing without him. Some of the fights were satisfying and others just ridiculous. One fight that incorporated both elements was Evander Holyfield's upset of young Riddick Bowe. Holyfield, a worthy if unmemorable champion in the post-Tyson years, had been retired by Bowe in late 1992. But, the division being what it was—Bowe and Lennox Lewis continued to avoid each other and delay the unification of the title—it was only a year to the week before the stolid Holyfield returned and was rematched with his more colorful counterpart. It wasn't all that eagerly awaited. Holyfield had looked horrible in his one tune-up fight, so this rematch didn't figure to remind anyone of the Thrilla in Manila. In fact, Bowe spoke for all of boxing when he said he was afraid that Holyfield had "talked himself into a serious ass-whupping."

But, in another down year for boxing, it was all the division could produce in the way of entertainment. And indeed there was something for everybody. Most people will remember only the paraglider who tried to drop into the ring but instead got entangled in the ropes and was pulled away by Bowe's handlers and badly beat-

en on the spot. Too bad. Because the most impressive show of the evening was the last half of the bout, when the 217-pound Holyfield backed the 246-pound Bowe against the ropes, closed the champion's left eye and gathered enough points to win a close but uncontroversial decision.

Realizing his promotional engine had just thrown a rod, Bowe quietly disappeared for a costly rebuilding job. The deeply religious Holyfield, meanwhile, revealed God's plan to the rest of the boxing world: He was to keep fighting until the 1996 Olympics, to be held in his hometown, Atlanta, where he would meet the released and rehabilitated Tyson in the biggest fight of all time. "God meant for me to be in there until Tyson comes out," he reported.

This was terrific news for boxing. The pairing of a guy who signs chapter and verse after his autograph with a convicted rapist—a fight that could never have been made during their prime—ought to satisfy everyone's need for drama. Until then, Holyfield needed only to pick off the mandatory challenger, a Sonny Liston wannabe named Michael Moorer, and then beat Lennox Lewis to unify the division. After his Bowe upset, this seemed like small work indeed. Moorer seemed the smallest work of all. True, he was 34–0 and had a well documented thirst for violence. His brawls back in Pennsylvania were legend. But he was considered to be something of a head case, reluctant to train and ever apt to just freeze in the

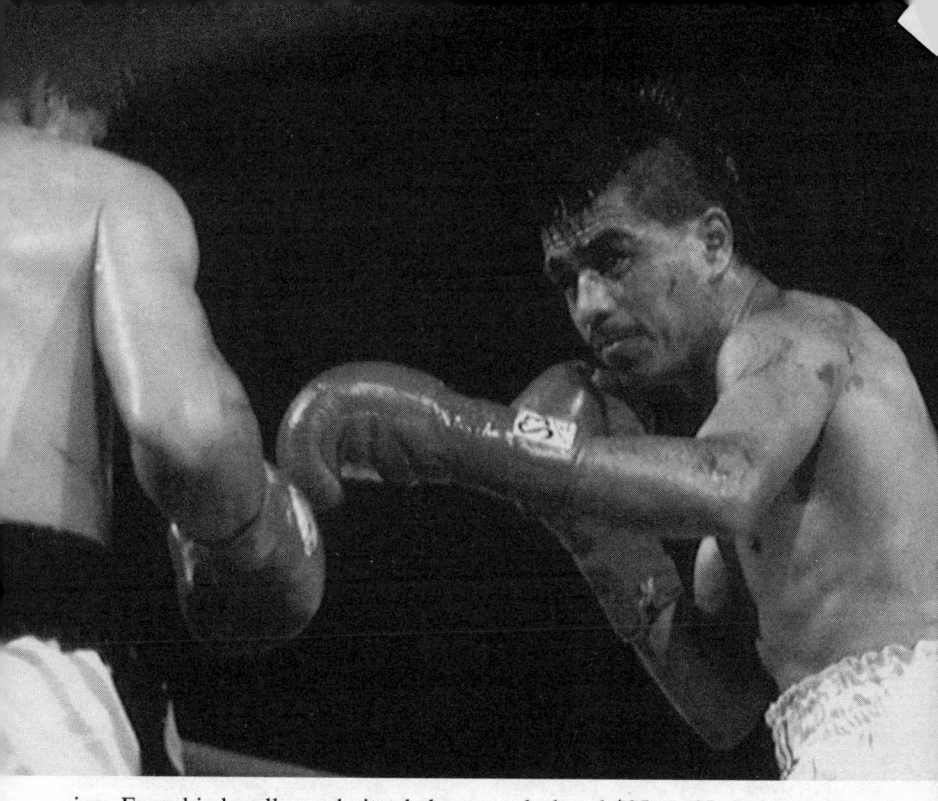

ring. Even his handlers admitted they couldn't count on him to perform in any predictable way whatsoever. His training camp was made especially tense by the arrival of trainer Teddy Atlas, a Cus D'Amato disciple who had been in on the creation of the Tyson monster. Atlas was kind of a poor man's Anthony Robbins, part motivator and part psychologist. He was also absolutely fearless. As manager John Davimos warned Moorer, notoriously fractious with his trainers, "Michael, he put a gun to Tyson's head! He'll shoot *you* for sure!" There were, from both Atlas's and Moorer's accounts, scary moments as Atlas drilled the young fighter, but it never came to gunplay. As the fight approached, though, not even Atlas knew which way to bet. In fact, he lay awake one night the week of the Las Vegas fight, waiting for a sign. Which sounded right, he wondered, 34–1 or 35–0? He got up, crept down to the casino's roulette table

and placed $25 on 35. Before he could even think about what he had done, the croupier was sliding $875 his way. Holyfield wasn't the only one getting visions that week.

There was nothing very supernatural about the fight, though. Moorer, a southpaw, prodded Holyfield with the jab all night. Lou Duva, who had been associated with both fighters, was shocked. "It was like this was the first he knew of Moorer being lefthanded." Holyfield ate so much of the jab that in the fifth round he began to bleed from a cut above his left eye.

Still, it was a close fight, and it may have taken the timely bullying of Atlas to win his fighter the decision, close as it was. When Moorer returned to his corner after the eighth round, Atlas refused to relinquish the stool. "You don't want to do what it takes to become champion," he told an astonished Moorer, "let me do it."

Not surprisingly Moorer went on to jab his way to a decision. There was a weird aftermath to that fight. Holyfield went to the hospital because of a shoulder injured in the bout and received the news that he had a cardiac condition that would prevent him from ever fighting again. At first the 31-year-old Holyfield took it with characteristic equanimity; he retired immediately and began appearing at evangelical events, where he participated in the laying on of hands. But later, citing a miracle faith healing, he pronounced himself fit enough to resume boxing. He was even defiant about it. "If they don't license me in this country," he said, "I'll go overseas." Having almost as much trouble getting a fight was the new champion. Moorer, taking on a money-making bout, agreed to fight 45-year-old George Foreman, who hadn't fought since losing to an increasingly suspect Tommy Morrison more than a year before. It looked like nobody really wanted the fight, though, particularly the WBA, which refused to sanction the bout. But then the dispute moved to Nevada courts and a decision there paved the way for the two to fight in Las Vegas in November. It may prove to be a fight only a state judge could love.

Moorer's jab was his most effective weapon in a surprising win over Holyfield.

Bowe was also having trouble proceeding with his career. A bout with Larry Donald, scheduled for the summer, was postponed until later in the year after Bowe injured his back in training. And the one time he did get back into the ring, in an August bout with Buster Mathis Jr., the results were less than satisfactory. Bowe was easily beating Buster when, in the fourth round, Mathis dropped to one knee. Bowe hit him anyway—nearly took his head off—and the judges had to rule it "no contest." More or less, nothing happened.

That was pretty much the story of 1994: Nothing happened. Yet, as the year drew to a close there was some hope for boxing, and it didn't necessarily involve the early release of Mike Tyson. Besides the excitement that the smaller guys were creating, there was the anticipated November fight between undefeated champions Roy Jones and James Toney, for Toney's IBF super middleweight title. The winner of that fight could emerge as the latter-day Sugar Ray Leonard. And the middle divisions, if you throw in WBC middleweight champ Gerald McClellan, could once again become boxing's hot spot.

Mostly, though, it was one more year of waiting, waiting for Chávez to be retired, waiting for Tyson to return, waiting for something to happen. For one more year, nothing good ever did.

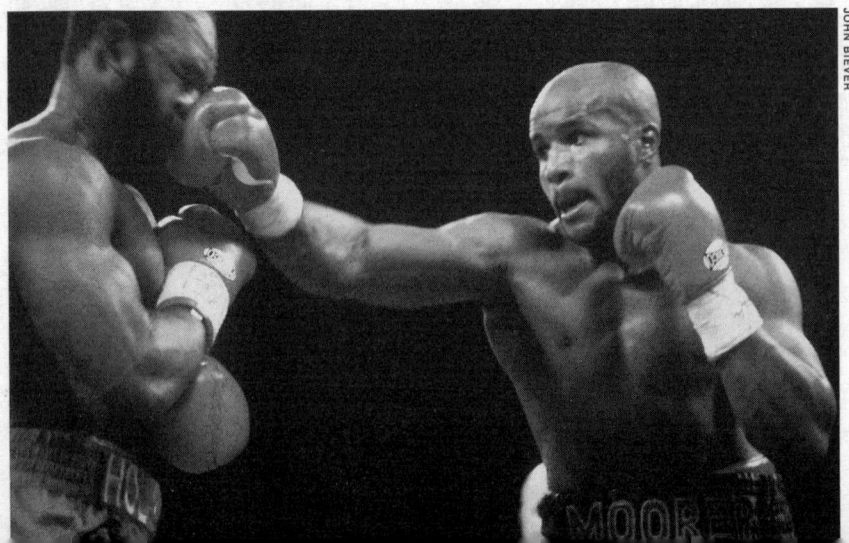

FOR THE RECORD·1993-1994

Current Champions

Division	Weight Limit	WBC Champion	WBA Champion	IBF Champion
Heavyweight	None	Lennox Lewis	Michael Moorer	Michael Moorer
Cruiserweight	190	Anaclet Wamba	Orlin Norris	Alfred Cole
Light heavyweight	175	Jeff Harding	Virgil Hill	Henry Maske
Super middleweight	168	Nigel Benn	Frank Liles	James Toney
Middleweight	160	Gerald McClellan	Jorge Castro	Roy Jones
Junior middleweight	154	Terry Norris	Julio César Vasquez	Vincent Pettway
Welterweight	147	Pernell Whitaker	Ike Quartey	Felix Trinidad
Junior welterweight	140	Julio César Chávez	Frankie Randall	Jake Rodriguez
Lightweight	135	Miguel Gonzalez	Orzubek Nazarov	Rafael Ruelas
Junior lightweight	130	Jesse James Leija	Genaro Hernandez	Juan Molina
Featherweight	126	Kevin Kelly	Eloy Rojas	Tom Johnson
Junior featherweight	122	Hector Acero	Wilfredo Vasquez	Vuyani Bungu
Bantamweight	118	Yasuei Yakushiji	Daorung Chuvatana	Orlando Canizales
Junior bantamweight	115	Hiroshi Kawashima	Lee Hung-Chul	Harold Grey
Flyweight	112	Yuri Arbachakov	Saen Sow Ploenchit	Pinchit Sithbangprachan
Junior flyweight	108	Humberto Gonzalez	Leo Gamez	Humberto Gonzalez
Strawweight	105	Ricardo Lopez	Chana Porpaoin	Ratanaapol Vorapin

Note: WBC = World Boxing Council; WBA = World Boxing Association; IBF = International Boxing Federation

Championship and Major Fights of 1993 and 1994

Abbreviations: WBC=World Boxing Council; WBA= World Boxing Association; IBF=International Boxing Federation; KO=knockout; TKO=technical knockout; Dec=decision; Split=split decision; Disq=disqualification.

Heavyweight

Date	Winner	Loser	Result	Title	Site
Oct 2	Lennox Lewis	Frank Bruno	KO 7	WBC	London
Nov 6	Evander Holyfield	Riddick Bowe	Dec 12	WBA, IBF	Las Vegas
Apr 22	Michael Moorer	Evander Holyfield	Dec 12	WBA, IBF	Las Vegas
May 6	Lennox Lewis	Phil Jackson	TKO 8	WBC	Atlantic City, N.J.

Cruiserweight

Date	Winner	Loser	Result	Title	Site
Nov 6	Orlin Norris	Marcelo Figueroa	TKO 6	WBA	Paris
Mar 4	Orlin Norris	Arthur Williams	Split 12	WBA	Las Vegas
July 2	Orlin Norris	Arthur Williams	TKO 3	WBA	Las Vegas
July 14	Anaclet Wamba	Adolpho Washington	Draw	WBC	Monte Carlo
July 23	Alfred Cole	Nate Miller	Dec 12	IBF	Bismarck, N. Dak.

Light Heavyweight

Date	Winner	Loser	Result	Title	Site
Nov 9	Virgil Hill	Saul Montana	TKO 10	WBA	Fargo, N. Dak.
Dec 11	Henry Maske	David Vedder	Dec 12	IBF	Dusseldorf, Germany
Dec 17	Virgil Hill	Guy Waters	Dec 12	WBA	Minot, N. Dak.
Mar 26	Henry Maske	Ernie Magdaleno	TKO 9	IBF	Dortmund, Germany
June 4	Henry Maske	Andrea Magi	Dec 12	IBF	Dortmund, Germany
July 23	Jeff Harding	Mike McCallum	Dec 12	WBC	Bismarck, N. Dak.
July 23	Virgil Hill	Frank Tate	Dec 12	WBA	Bismarck, N. Dak.

Super Middleweight

Date	Winner	Loser	Result	Title	Site
Dec 18	Michael Nunn	Merqui Sosa	Dec 12	WBA	Puebla, Mexico
Feb 26	Nigel Benn	Henry Wharton	Dec 12	WBC	London
Feb 26	Steve Little	Michael Nunn	Split 12	WBA	London
Mar 5	James Toney	Tim Littles	TKO 4	IBF	Los Angeles
Aug 12	Frank Liles	Steve Little	Dec 12	WBA	Tucuman, Argentina
Sep 10	Nigel Benn	Juan Carlos Gimenez	Dec 12	WBC	Birmingham, England

Middleweight

Date	Winner	Loser	Result	Title	Site
Mar 4	Gerald McClellan	Gilbert Baptist	TKO 1	WBC	Las Vegas
May 7	Gerald McClellan	Julian Jackson	TKO 1	WBC	Las Vegas
May 27	Roy Jones	Thomas Tate	TKO 2	IBF	Las Vegas
Aug 12	Jorge Castro	Reggie Johnson	Split 12	WBA	Tucuman, Argentina

Junior Middleweight (Super Welterweight)

Date	Winner	Loser	Result	Title	Site
Jan 22	Julio César Vasquez	Juan Ramon Medina	Dec 12	WBA	Alma Ata, Kazakhstan
Jan 29	Simon Brown	Troy Waters	Dec 12	WBC	Las Vegas
Mar 4	Julio César Vasquez	Arman Picar	TKO 2	WBA	Las Vegas
Mar 4	Gianfranco Rosi	Vincent Pettway	Draw	IBF	Las Vegas
Apr 8	Julio César Vasquez	Ricardo Nunez	Dec 12	WBA	Tucuman, Argentina
May 7	Terry Norris	Simon Brown	Dec 12	WBC	Las Vegas
May 21	Julio César Vasquez	Ahmet Dottuev	TKO 10	WBA	Belfast
Aug 21	Julio César Vasquez	Ronald Wright	Dec 12	WBA	St Jean de Luz, France
Sep 17	Vincent Pettway	Gianfranco Rosi	KO 4	IBF	Las Vegas

Welterweight

Date	Winner	Loser	Result	Title	Site
Jan 29	Felix Trinidad	Hector Camacho	Dec 12	IBF	Las Vegas
Apr 9	Pernell Whitaker	Santos Cardona	Dec 12	WBC	Norfolk, Virginia
Jun 4	Ike Quartey	Crisanto Espana	TKO 11	WBA	Levallois-Perret, France
Sep 17	Felix Trinidad	Yori Boy Campas	TKO 4	IBF	Las Vegas

Junior Welterweight (Super Lightweight)

Date	Winner	Loser	Result	Title	Site
Nov 19	Charles Murray	Courtney Hooper	TKO 5	IBF	Atlantic City, N.J.
Dec 17	Juan Martin Coggi	Eder Gonzalez	TKO 7	WBA	Tucuman, Argentina
Dec 18	Julio César Chávez	Andy Holligan	TKO 5	WBC	Puebla, Mexico
Jan 29	Frankie Randall	Julio César Chávez	Split 12	WBC	Las Vegas
Feb 13	Jake Rodriguez	Charles Murray	Dec 12	IBF	Atlantic City, N.J.
Mar 18	Juan Martin Coggi	Eder Gonzalez	TKO 3	WBA	Las Vegas
Apr 21	Jake Rodriguez	Ray Oliveira	Dec 12	IBF	Ledyard, Conn.
May 7	Julio César Chávez	Frankie Randall	Tech dec.	WBC	Las Vegas
Aug 27	Jake Rodriguez	George Scott	TKO 9	IBF	Bushkill, Penn.
Sep 17	Julio César Chávez	Meldrick Taylor	TKO 8	WBC	Las Vegas
Sep 17	Frankie Randall	Juan Martin Coggi	Dec 12	WBA	Las Vegas

Lightweight

Date	Winner	Loser	Result	Title	Site
Oct 30	Orzubek Nazarov	Dingaan Thobela	Dec 12	WBA	Johannesburg, S Africa
Nov 27	Miguel Gonzalez	Wilfredo Rocha	TKO 11	WBC	Mexico City
Feb 19	Rafael Ruelas	Freddie Pendleton	Dec 12	IBF	Inglewood, Calif.
Mar 19	Orzubek Nazarov	Dingaan Thobela	Dec 12	WBA	Temba, Bophuthatswana
Mar 29	Miguel Gonzalez	Jean-Baptiste Mendy	TKO 5	WBC	Levallois-Perret, France
May 7	Rafael Ruelas	Mike Evgen	TKO 3	IBF	Las Vegas
Aug 6	Miguel Gonzalez	Leavander Johnson	TKO 8	WBC	Ciudad Jaurez, Mexico

Junior Lightweight (Super Featherweight)

Date	Winner	Loser	Result	Title	Site
Jan 22	Juan Molina	Floyd Havard	TKO 6	IBF	Cardiff, Wales
Jan 31	Genaro Hernandez	Jorge Ramirez	TKO 8	WBA	Inglewood, Calif.
Apr 22	Juan Molina	Gregorio Vargas	Dec 12	IBF	Las Vegas
May 7	James Leija	Azumah Nelson	Dec 12	WBC	Las Vegas
Sep 17	James Leija	Gabriel Ruelas	Dec 12	WBC	Las Vegas

Featherweight

Date	Winner	Loser	Result	Title	Site
Nov 30	Tom Johnson	Stephane Haccoun	TKO 9	IBF	Marseilles, France
Dec 4	Kevin Kelley	Gregorio Vargas	Dec 12	WBC	Reno, Nev.
Dec 4	Eloy Rojas	Park Yung-Kyun	Split 12	WBA	Kwang Myung, S Korea
Feb 12	Tom Johnson	Orlando Soto	Dec 12	IBF	St Louis
Mar 19	Eloy Rojas	Seiji Asakawa	TKO 5	WBA	Kobe, Japan
May 6	Kevin Kelley	Jesse Benavides	Dec 12	WBC	Atlantic City, N.J.
Sep 11	Eloy Rojas	Samart Payakaroon	KO 8	WBA	Trang, Thailand

Junior Featherweight (Super Bantamweight)

Date	Winner	Loser	Result	Title	Site
Nov 18	Wilfredo Vasquez	Hiroaki Yokota	Dec 12	WBA	Tokyo
Feb 19	Kennedy McKinney	Jose Rincones	KO 5	IBF	Temba, South Africa
Mar 2	Wilfredo Vasquez	Yuichi Kasai	TKO 1	WBA	Tokyo
Apr 9	Tracy Patterson	Richard Duran	Dec 12	WBC	Reno, Nev.
Apr 16	Kennedy McKinney	Welcome Ncita	Dec 12	IBF	South Padre Isl., Tex.
July 2	Wilfredo Vasquez	Choi Jae-Won	TKO 2	WBA	Las Vegas
Aug 20	Vuyani Bungu	Kennedy McKinney	Dec 12	IBF	Temba, South Africa
Aug 26	Hector Acero	Tracy Patterson	Split 12	WBC	Atlantic City, N.J.

Bantamweight

Date	Winner	Loser	Result	Title	Site
Nov 20	Orlando Canizales	Juvenal Berrio	Dec 12	IBF	Temba, South Africa
Dec 23	Yasuei Yakushiji	Byun Jung-Il	Split 12	WBC	Nagoya, Japan
Jan 8	Junior Jones	Elvis Alvarez	Dec 12	WBA	Catskill, N.Y.
Feb 26	Orlando Canizales	Gerardo Martinez	TKO 4	IBF	San Jose, Calif.
Apr 16	Yasuei Yakushiji	Josefino Suarez	KO 10	WBC	Nagoya, Japan
Apr 22	John M. Johnson	Junior Jones	TKO 11	WBA	Las Vegas
Jun 7	Orlando Canizales	Orlando Bohol	TKO 5	IBF	South Padre Isl., Tex.
July 17	Daorung Chuvatana	John M. Johnson	TKO 1	WBA	Uttaradit, Thailand
July 31	Yasuei Yakushiji	Byun Jung-Il	TKO 11	WBC	Nagoya, Japan

Junior Bantamweight (Super Flyweight)

Date	Winner	Loser	Result	Title	Site
Nov 5	Katsuya Onizuka	Khaoyai Mahasarakan	Dec 12	WBA	Tokyo
Nov 13	Jose Luis Bueno	Moon Sung-Kil	Split 12	WBC	Pohang, S Korea
Nov 26	Julio Cesar Borboa	Rolando Pascua	TKO 5	IBF	Hermosillo, Mexico
Apr 3	Katsuya Onizuka	Lee Seung-Koo	Dec 12	WBA	Tokyo
Apr 25	Julio Cesar Borboa	Jorge Roman	TKO 4	IBF	Inglewood, Calif.
May 4	Hiroshi Kawashima	Jose Luis Bueno	Dec 12	WBC	Yokahama, Japan
May 21	Julio Cesar Borboa	Jaji Sibali	TKO 9	IBF	Temba, South Africa
Aug 7	Hiroshi Kawashima	Carlos Salazar	Dec 12	WBC	Tokyo
Aug 29	Harold Grey	Julio Cesar Borboa	Split 12	IBF	Inglewood, Calif.
Sep 18	Lee Hyung-Chul	Katsuya Onizuka	TKO 9	WBA	Tokyo

Flyweight

Date	Winner	Loser	Result	Title	Site
Dec 13	Yuri Arbachakov	Cha Nam-Hoon	Dec 12	WBC	Kyoto, Japan
Jan 23	Pinchit Sithbangprachan	Arthur Johnson	Dec 12	IBF	Surat Thani, Thailand
Feb 13	Saen Sow Ploenchit	David Griman	Dec 12	WBA	Chachoengsao, Thailand
Apr 10	Saen Sow Ploenchit	Jesus Rojas	Dec 12	WBA	Samutprakan, Thailand
May 8	Pinchit Sithbangprachan	Jose Luis Zepeda	Split 12	IBF	Rajaburi, Thailand
Jun 12	Saen Sow Ploenchit	Achilles Guzman	Dec 12	WBA	Wattananakhon, Thailand
Aug 1	Yuri Arbachakov	Hugo Soto	KO 8	WBC	Tokyo

Junior Flyweight

Date	Winner	Loser	Result	Title	Site
Feb 5	Leo Gamez	Juan Antonio Torres	TKO 7	WBA	Panama City
Feb 19	Humberto Gonzalez	Michael Carbajal	Split 12	WBC, IBF	Inglewood, Calif.
Jun 27	Leo Gamez	Hadow CP Gym	Split 12	WBA	Bangkok
Sep 10	Humberto Gonzalez	Juan D. Cordoba	KO 7	WBC	Lake Tahoe, Nev.

Strawweight (Mini Flyweight)

Date	Straw/minifly Winner	Loser	Result	Title	Site
Nov 28	Chana Porpaoin	Rafael Torres	KO 4	WBA	Phichit, Thailand
Dec 10	Ratanapal Sow Voraphin	Felix Naranjo	TKO 2	IBF	Supan Buri, Thailand
Dec 18	Ricardo Lopez	Manny Melchor	KO 11	WBC	Lake Tahoe, Nev.
Feb 27	Ratanapol Sow Voraphin	Ronnie Magramo	Dec 12	IBF	Bangmulnak, Thailand
Mar 26	Chana Porpaoin	Carlos Murillo	Dec 12	WBA	Chonburi, Thailand
May 7	Ricardo Lopez	Kermin Guardia	Dec 12	WBC	Las Vegas
May 14	Ratanapol Sow Voraphin	Roger Espanola	TKO 6	IBF	Saraburi, Thailand
Aug 20	Ratanapol Sow Voraphin	Marcelino Bolivar	TKO 4	IBF	Burium, Thailand
Sep 3	Chana Porpaoin	Kang Keum-Young	Dec 12	WBA	Phatthalung, Thailand
Sep 17	Ricardo Lopez	Y Saengmorokot	TKO 1	WBC	Las Vegas

Arms Traders

Inspired by recent turn-in-your-gun-for-money programs in other cities, former heavyweight champion Riddick Bowe and his manager, Rock Newman, offered $100 in cash for each gun brought to the Union Temple Baptist church in southeast Washington, D.C., last January. "In our wildest estimations, we thought 1,000 guns would be the max," says Newman. "We grossly miscalculated."

Despite temperatures dipping toward zero, more than 2,000 people lined up outside the church, some for as many as five hours, to turn in their weapons. By midnight Bowe and Newman had collected 3,600 guns—and paid out $360,000.

"We'd brought $75,000 in cash in a shopping bag," says Newman, who together with Bowe circulated among the crowd shaking hands and signing autographs throughout the day. "But by midafternoon that was gone. So we started writing checks. We'd made a commitment to get as many guns as we could."

Says Bowe, "This city is one of the worst in the nation for murders. Maybe what we did can help turn that around."

World Champions

Sanctioning bodies include the National Boxing Association (NBA), the New York State Athletic Commission (NY), the World Boxing Association (WBA), the World Boxing Council (WBC), and the International Boxing Federation (IBF).

Heavyweights
(Weight: Unlimited)

Champion	Reign	Champion	Reign	Champion	Reign
John L. Sullivan	1885-92	Floyd Patterson	1956-59	Michael Dokes* WBA	1982-83
James J. Corbett	1892-97	Ingemar Johansson	1959-60	Gerrie Coetzee* WBA	1983-84
Bob Fitzsimmons	1897-99	Floyd Patterson	1960-62	Tim Witherspoon* WBC	1984
James J. Jeffries	1899-1905†	Sonny Liston	1962-64	Pinklon Thomas* WBC	1984-86
Marvin Hart	1905-06	Muhammad Ali		Greg Page* WBA	1984-85
Tommy Burns	1906-08	(Cassius Clay)	1964-70	Michael Spinks	1985-87
Jack Johnson	1908-15	Ernie Terrell* WBA	1965-67	Tim Witherspoon* WBA	1986
Jess Willard	1915-19	Joe Frazier* NY	1968-70	Trevor Berbick* WBC	1986
Jack Dempsey	1919-26	Jimmy Ellis* WBA	1968-70	Mike Tyson* WBC	1986-87
Gene Tunney	1926-28	Joe Frazier	1970-73	James Bonecrusher	
Max Schmeling	1930-32	George Foreman	1973-74	Smith* WBA	1986-87
Jack Sharkey	1932-33	Muhammad Ali	1974-78	Tony Tucker* IBF	1987
Primo Carnera	1933-34	Leon Spinks	1978	Mike Tyson	1987-90
Max Baer	1934-35	Ken Norton* WBC	1978	Buster Douglas	1990
James J. Braddock	1935-37	Larry Holmes* WBC	1978-80	Evander Holyfield	1990-92
Joe Louis	1937-49†	Muhammad Ali	1978-79†	Lennox Lewis* WBC	1993-
Ezzard Charles	1949-51	John Tate* WBA	1979-80	Riddick Bowe	1992-93
Jersey Joe Walcott	1951-52	Mike Weaver* WBA	1980-82	Evander Holyfield	1993-94
Rocky Marciano	1952-56†	Larry Holmes	1980-85	Michael Moorer	1994-

Cruiserweights
(Weight Limit: 190 pounds)

Champion	Reign	Champion	Reign	Champion	Reign
Marvin Camel* WBC	1980	Carlos De Leon* WBC	1986-88	Glenn McCrory* IBF	1989-90
Carlos De Leon* WBC	1980-82	Evander Holyfield		Jeff Lampkin* IBF	1990
Ossie Ocasio* WBA	1982-84	* WBA	1986-88	Massimiliano	
S.T. Gordon* WBC	1982-83	Ricky Parkey* IBF	1986-87	Duran* WBC	1990-91
Carlos De Leon* WBC	1983-85	Evander Holyfield		Bobby Czyz*† WBA	1991-92
Marvin Camel* IBF	1983-84	* WBA/IBF	1987-88	Anaclet Wamba* WBC	1991-
Lee Roy Murphy* IBF	1984-86	Evander Holyfield		James Pritchard* IBF	1991
Piet Crous* WBA	1984-85	WBA/IBF/WBC	1988†	James Warring* IBF	1991-92
Alfonso Ratliff* WBC	1985	Toufik Belbouli* WBA	1989	Alfred Cole* IBF	1992-
Dwight Braxton* WBA	1985-86	Robert Daniels* WBA	1989-91	Orlin Norris* WBA	1993-
Bernard Benton* WBC	1985-86	Carlos De Leon* WBC	1989-90		

Note: Division called Junior Heavyweights by the WBA.

Light Heavyweights
(Weight Limit: 175 pounds)

Champion	Reign	Champion	Reign	Champion	Reign
Jack Root	1903	Bob Olin	1934-35	Victor Galindez* WBA	1974-78
George Gardner	1903	John Henry Lewis	1935-38	Miguel A. Cuello* WBC	1977-78
Bob Fitzsimmons	1903-05	Melio Bettina	1939	Mate Parlov* WBC	1978
Philadelphia Jack		Billy Conn	1939-40†	Mike Rossman* WBA	1978-79
O'Brien	1905-12†	Anton Christoforidis	1941	Marvin Johnson* WBC	1978-79
Jack Dillon	1914-16	Gus Lesnevich	1941-48	Matthew Saad	
Battling Levinsky	1916-20	Freddie Mills	1948-50	Muhammad* WBC	1979-81
Georges Carpentier	1920-22	Joey Maxim	1950-52	Marvin Johnson* WBA	1979-80
Battling Siki	1922-23	Archie Moore	1952-62†	Eddie Mustapha	
Mike McTigue	1923-25	Harold Johnson* NBA	1961	Muhammad* WBA	1980-81
Paul Berlenbach	1925-26	Harold Johnson	1962-63	Michael Spinks* WBA	1981-83
Jack Delaney	1926-27†	Willie Pastrano	1963-65	Dwight Muhammad	
Jimmy Slattery* NBA	1927	Jose Torres	1965-66	Qawi* WBC	1981-83
Tommy Loughran	1927-29	Dick Tiger	1966-68	Michael Spinks	1983-85†
Maxie Rosenbloom	1930-34	Bob Foster	1968-74†	J. B. Williamson* WBC	1985-86
George Nichols* NBA	1932	Vicente Rondon* WBA	1971-72	Slobodan Kacar* IBF	1985-86
Bob Godwin* NBA	1933	John Conteh* WBC	1974-77	Marvin Johnson* WBA	1986-87

*Champion not generally recognized. †Champion retired or relinquished title.

Light Heavyweights *(Cont.)*

Champion	Reign
Dennis Andries* WBC	...1986-87
Bobby Czyz* IBF	...1986-87
Leslie Stewart* WBA	1987
Virgil Hill* WBA	1987
Prince Charles Williams* IBF	1987-

Champion	Reign
Thomas Hearns* WBC	...1987†
Donny Lalonde* WBC	...1987-88
Sugar Ray Leonard* WBC	1988
Dennis Andries* WBC	...1989
Jeff Harding* WBC	1989-90
Dennis Andries* WBC	...1990-91

Champion	Reign
Thomas Hearns* WBA	..1991-92
Jeff Harding* WBA	1991-
Iran Barkley* WBA	1992
Henry Maske* IBF	1993-
Virgil Hill* WBA	1992-

Super Middleweights
(Weight Limit: 168 pounds)

Champion	Reign
Murray Sutherland* IBF	.1984
Chong-Pal Park* IBF	1984-87
Chong-Pal Park* WBA	...1987-88
Graciano Rocchigiani* IBF	1988-89
Fulgencio Obelmejias* WBA	1988-89

Champion	Reign
Sugar Ray Leonard* WBC	.............1988-90†
In-Chul Baek* WBA	1989-90
Lindell Holmes* IBF	1990-91
Christopher Tiozzo* WBA	1990-91
Mauro Galvano* WBC	...1990-
Victor Cordova* WBA	1991

Champion	Reign
Darrin Van Horn* IBF	1991-92
Iran Barkley *WBA	1992
Nigel Benn* WBC	1992-
James Toney* IBF	1992-
Michael Nunn* WBA	1992-94
Steve Little* WBA	1994
Frank Liles* WBA	1994-

Middleweights
(Weight Limit: 160 pounds)

Champion	Reign
Jack Dempsey	1884-91
Bob Fitzsimmons	1891-97
Kid McCoy	1897-98
Tommy Ryan	1898-1907
Stanley Ketchel	1908
Billy Papke	1908
Stanley Ketchel	1908-10
Frank Klaus	1913
George Chip	1913-14
Al McCoy	1914-17
Mike O'Dowd	1917-20
Johnny Wilson	1920-23
Harry Greb	1923-26
Tiger Flowers	1926
Mickey Walker	...............1926-31†
Gorilla Jones	1931-32
Marcel Thil	1932-37
Fred Apostoli	1937-39
Al Hostak* NBA	1938
Solly Krieger* NBA	1938-39
Al Hostak* NBA	1939-40
Ceferino Garcia	1939-40
Ken Overlin	1940-41
Tony Zale* NBA	1940-41
Billy Soose	1941

Champion	Reign
Tony Zale	1941-47
Rocky Graziano	1947-48
Tony Zale	1948
Marcel Cerdan	1948-49
Jake La Motta	1949-51
Sugar Ray Robinson	1951
Randy Turpin	1951
Sugar Ray Robinson	1951-52
Bobo Olson	1953-55
Sugar Ray Robinson	1955-57
Gene Fullmer	1957
Sugar Ray Robinson	1957
Carmen Basilio	1957-58
Sugar Ray Robinson	1958-60
Gene Fullmer* NBA	1959-62
Paul Pender	1960-61
Terry Downes	1961-62
Paul Pender	1962-63
Dick Tiger* WBA	1962-63
Dick Tiger	1963
Joey Giardello	1963-65
Dick Tiger	1965-66
Emile Griffith	1966-67
Nino Benvenuti	1967
Emile Griffith	1967-68

Champion	Reign
Nino Benvenuti	1968-70
Carlos Monzon	..........1970-77†
Rodrigo Valdez* WBC	...1974-76
Rodrigo Valdez	1977-78
Hugo Corro	1978-79
Vito Antuofermo	1979-80
Alan Minter	1980
Marvin Hagler	1980-87
Sugar Ray Leonard	1987
Frank Tate* IBF	1987-88
Sumbu Kalambay* WBA	1987-89
Thomas Hearns* WBC	..1987-88
Iran Barkley* WBC	1988-89
Michael Nunn* IBF	1988-91
Roberto Duran* WBC	1989-90
Mike McCallum* WBA	...1989-91
Julian Jackson* WBC	1990-
James Toney* IBF	1991-
Reggie Johnson* WBA	.1992-94
Roy Jones* IBF	1993-
Gerald McClellan* WBC	1993-
Jorge Castro* WBA	1994-

Junior Middleweights
(Weight Limit: 154 pounds)

Champion	Reign
Emile Griffith (EBU)	1962-63
Dennis Moyer	1962-63
Ralph Dupas	1963
Sandro Mazzinghi	1963-65
Nino Benvenuti	1965-66
Ki-Soo Kim	1966-68
Sandro Mazzinghi	1968
Freddie Little	1969-70
Carmelo Bossi	1970-71
Koichi Wajima	1971-74
Oscar Albarado	1974-75
Koichi Wajima	1975

Champion	Reign
Miguel de Oliveira* WBC	1975-76
Jae-Do Yuh	1975-76
Elisha Obed* WBC	1975-76
Koichi Wajima	1976
Jose Duran	1976
Eckhard Dagge* WBC	..1976-77
Miguel Angel Castellini	.1976-77
Eddie Gazo	1977-78
Rocky Mattioli* WBC	1977-79
Masashi Kudo	1978-79
Maurice Hope* WBC	1979-81
Ayub Kalule	1979-81

Champion	Reign
Wilfred Benitez* WBC	...1981-82
Sugar Ray Leonard	1981-82
Tadashi Mihara* WBA	...1981-82
Davey Moore* WBA	1982-83
Thomas Hearns* WBC	..1982-84
Roberto Duran* WBA	...1983-84
Mark Medal* IBF	1984
Thomas Hearns	1984-86
Mike McCallum* WBA	...1984-87
Carlos Santos* IBF	1984-86
Buster Drayton* IBF	1986-87
Duane Thomas* WBC	...1986-87

*Champion not generally recognized. †Champion retired or relinquished title.

Junior Middleweights (Cont.)

Champion	Reign	Champion	Reign	Champion	Reign
Matthew Hilton* IBF	1987-88	Darrin Van Horn* IBF	1989	Vinny Pazienza* WBA	1991-92
Lupe Aquino* WBC	1987	Rene Jacquot* WBC	1989	Julio C. Vasquez* WBA	1992-
Gianfranco Rosi* WBC	1987-88	John Mugabi* WBC	1989-90	Simon Brown* WBC	1994
Julian Jackson* WBA	1987-90	Gianfranco Rosi* IBF	1989-94	Terry Norris *WBC	1994
Donald Curry* WBC	1988-89	Terry Norris* WBC	1990-94	Vincent Pettway* IBF	1994-
Robert Hines* IBF	1988-89	Gilbert Dele* WBA	1991		

Note: Division called Super Welterweight by the WBC.

Welterweights
(Weight Limit: 147 pounds)

Champion	Reign	Champion	Reign	Champion	Reign
Paddy Duffy	1888-90	Young Corbett III	1933	John H. Stracey	1975-76
Mysterious Billy Smith	1892-94	Jimmy McLarnin	1933-34	Carlos Palomino	1976-79
Tommy Ryan	1894-98	Barney Ross	1934	Pipino Cuevas* WBA	1976-80
Mysterious Billy Smith	1898-1900	Jimmy McLarnin	1934-35	Wilfredo Benitez	1979
Rube Ferns	1900	Barney Ross	1935-38	Sugar Ray Leonard	1979-80
Matty Matthews	1900-01	Henry Armstrong	1938-40	Roberto Duran	1980
Rube Ferns	1901	Fritzie Zivic	1940-41	Thomas Hearns* WBA	1980-81
Joe Walcott	1901-04	Red Cochrane	1941-46	Sugar Ray Leonard	1980-82
The Dixie Kid	1904-05	Marty Servo	1946	Donald Curry* WBA	1983-85
Honey Mellody	1906-07	Sugar Ray Robinson	1946-51†	Milton McCrory* WBC	1983-85
Twin Sullivan	1907-08	Johnny Bratton	1951	Donald Curry	1985-86
Jimmy Gardner	1908	Kid Gavilan	1951-54	Lloyd Honeyghan	1986-87
Jimmy Clabby	1910-11	Johnny Saxton	1954-55	Jorge Vaca WBC	1987-88
Waldemar Holberg	1914	Tony DeMarco	1955	Lloyd Honeyghan WBC	1988-89
Tom McCormick	1914	Carmen Basilio	1955-56	Mark Breland* WBA	1987
Matt Wells	1914-15	Johnny Saxton	1956	Marlon Starling* WBA	1987-88
Mike Glover	1915	Carmen Basilio	1956-57	Tomas Molinares* WBA	1988-89
Jack Britton	1915	Virgil Akins	1958	Simon Brown* IBF	1988-91
Ted "Kid" Lewis	1915-16	Don Jordan	1958-60	Mark Breland* WBA	1989-90
Jack Britton	1916-17	Kid Paret	1960-61	Marlon Starling* WBC	1989-90
Ted "Kid" Lewis	1917-19	Emile Griffith	1961	Aaron Davis* WBA	1990-91
Jack Britton	1919-22	Kid Paret	1961-62	Maurice Blocker* WBC	1990-91
Mickey Walker	1922-26	Emile Griffith	1962-63	Meldrick Taylor* WBA	1991-1992
Pete Latzo	1926-27	Luis Rodriguez	1963	Simon Brown* WBC	1991
Joe Dundee	1927-29	Emile Griffith	1963-66	Buddy McGirt* WBC	1991-1993
Jackie Fields	1929-30	Curtis Cokes	1966-69	Felix Trinidad* IBF	1992-
Young Jack Thompson	1930	Jose Napoles	1969-70	Pernell Whitaker WBC	1993-
Tommy Freeman	1930-31	Billy Backus	1970-71	Crisanto Espana* WBA	1992-94
Young Jack Thompson	1931	Jose Napoles	1971-75	Ike Quartey* WBA	1994-
Lou Brouillard	1931-32	Hedgemon Lewis* NY	1972-73		
Jackie Fields	1932-33	Angel Espada* WBA	1975-76		

Junior Welterweight
(Weight Limit: 140 pounds)

Champion	Reign	Champion	Reign	Champion	Reign
Pinkey Mitchell	1922-25	Carlos Hernandez	1965-66	Antonio	
Red Herring	1925	Sandro Lopopolo	1966-67	Cervantes* WBA	1977-80
Mushy Callahan	1926-30	Paul Fujii	1967-68	Sang-Hyun Kim* WBC	1978-80
Jack (Kid) Berg	1930-31	Nicolino Loche	1968-72	Saoul Mamby* WBC	1980-82
Tony Canzoneri	1931-32	Pedro Adigue* WBC	1968-70	Aaron Pryor* WBA	1980-83
Johnny Jadick	1932-33	Bruno Arcari* WBC	1970-74	Leroy Haley* WBC	1982-83
Sammy Fuller*	1932-33	Alfonso Frazer	1972	Aaron Pryor* IBF	1983-85
Battling Shaw	1933	Antonio Cervantes	1972-76	Bruce Curry* WBC	1983-84
Tony Canzoneri	1933	Perico		Johnny	
Barney Ross	1933-35	Fernandez* WBC	1974-75	Bumphus* WBA	1984
Tippy Larkin	1946	Saensak		Bill Costello* WBC	1984-
Carlos Ortiz	1959-60	Muangsurin* WBC	1975-76	Gene Hatcher* WBA	1984-85
Duilio Loi	1960-62	Wilfred Benitez	1976-79	Ubaldo Sacco* WBA	1985-86
Eddie Perkins	1962	Miguel Velasquez* WBC	1976	Lonnie Smith* WBC	1985-86
Duilio Loi	1962-63	Saensak		Patrizio Oliva* WBA	1986-87
Roberto Cruz* WBA	1963	Muangsurin* WBC	1976-78	Gary Hinton* IBF	1986
Eddie Perkins	1963-65			Rene Arredondo* WBC	1986

*Champion not generally recognized. †Champion retired or relinquished title.

Junior Welterweights (Cont.)

Champion	Reign
Tsuyoshi Hamada* WBC	1986-87
Joe Louis Manley* IBF	1986-87
Terry Marsh* IBF	1987
Juan Martin Coggi* WBA	1987-90
Rene Arredondo* WBC	1987
Roger Mayweather* WBC	1987-89

Champion	Reign
James McGirt* IBF	1988
Meldrick Taylor* IBF	1988-90
Julio César Chávez* WBC	1989-94
Julio César Chávez* IBF	1990-91
Loreto Garza* WBA	1990-91
Juan Coggi* WBA	1991
Edwin Rosario* WBA	1991-92

Champion	Reign
Rafael Pineda* IBF	1991-92
Akinobu Hiranaka* WBA	1992
Pernell Whitaker*† IBF	1992-93
Charles Murray* IBF	1993-94
Jake Rodriguez* IBF	1994-
Juan Coggi* WBA	1993-94
Frankie Randall* WBA	1994
Frankie Randall* WBA	1994-
Julio César Chávez WBC	1994-

Lightweights
(Weight Limit: 135 pounds)

Champion	Reign
Jack McAuliffe	1886-94
Kid Lavigne	1896-99
Frank Erne	1899-1902
Joe Gans	1902-04
Jimmy Britt	1904-05
Battling Nelson	1905-06
Joe Gans	1906-08
Battling Nelson	1908-10
Ad Wolgast	1910-12
Willie Ritchie	1912-14
Freddie Welsh	1915-17
Benny Leonard	1917-25†
Jimmy Goodrich	1925
Rocky Kansas	1925-26
Sammy Mandell	1926-30
Al Singer	1930
Tony Canzoneri	1930-33
Barney Ross	1933-35†
Tony Canzoneri	1935-36
Lou Ambers	1936-38
Henry Armstrong	1938-39
Lou Ambers	1939-40
Sammy Angott* NBA	1940-41
Lew Jenkins	1940-41
Sammy Angott	1941-42†
Beau Jack* NY	1942-43
Bob Montgomery* NY	1943
Sammy Angott* NBA	1943-44
Beau Jack* NY	1943-44
Bob Montgomery* NY	1944-47
Juan Zurita* NBA	1944-45
Ike Williams	1947-51
James Carter	1951-52

Champion	Reign
Lauro Salas	1952
James Carter	1952-54
Paddy DeMarco	1954
James Carter	1954-55
Wallace Smith	1955-56
Joe Brown	1956-62
Carlos Ortiz	1962-65
Ismael Laguna	1965
Carlos Ortiz	1965-68
Carlos Teo Cruz	1968-69
Mando Ramos	1969-70
Ismael Laguna	1970
Ken Buchanan	1970-72
Roberto Duran	1972-79†
Chango Carmona* WBC	1972
Rodolfo Gonzalez* WBC	1972-74
Ishimatsu Suzuki* WBC	1974-76
Estaban DeJesus* WBC	1976-78
Jim Watt* WBC	1979-81
Ernesto Espana* WBA	1979-80
Hilmer Kenty* WBA	1980-81
Sean O'Grady* WBA	1981
Claude Noel* WBA	1981
Alexis Arguello* WBC	1981-82
Arturo Frias* WBA	1981-82
Ray Mancini* WBA	1982-84
Alexis Arguello	1982-83
Edwin Rosario* WBC	1983-84
Choo Choo Brown* IBF	1984

Champion	Reign
Livingstone Bramble* WBA	1984-86
Jose Luis Ramirez* WBC	1984-85
Harry Arroyo* IBF	1984-85
Jimmy Paul* IBF	1985-86
Hector Camacho* WBC	1985-86
Greg Haugen* IBF	1986-87
Edwin Rosario* WBA	1986-87
Julio César Chavez* WBA	1987-88
Jose Luis Ramirez* WBC	1987-88
Julio César Chavez	1988-89
Vinny Pazienza* IBF	1987-88
Greg Haugen* IBF	1988-89
Pernell Whitaker* WBC, IBF	1989-90
Edwin Rosario* WBA	1989-90, 1991-92
Juan Nazario* WBA	1990
Pernell Whitaker* WBA, WBC	1990-92
Pernell Whitaker* IBF	1991-92
Julio César Chávez* IBF	1990-91
Julio César Chávez* WBC	1990-92
Miguel Gonzalez* WBC	1992-
Joey Gamache* WBA	1992-93
Dingaan Thobela* WBA	1993
Fred Pendleton* IBF	1993-94
Orzubek Nazarov* WBA	1994-
Rafael Ruelas* IBF	1994-

Junior Lightweights
(Weight Limit: 130 pounds)

Champion	Reign
Johnny Dundee	1921-23
Jack Bernstein	1923
Johnny Dundee	1923-24
Steve (Kid) Sullivan	1924-25
Mike Ballerino	1925
Tod Morgan	1925-29
Benny Bass	1929-31
Kid Chocolate	1931-33
Frankie Klick	1933-34
Sandy Saddler	1949-50
Harold Gomes	1959-60
Gabriel (Flash) Elorde	1960-67

Champion	Reign
Yoshiaki Numata	1967
Hiroshi Kobayashi	1967-71
Rene Barrientos* WBC	1969-70
Yoshiaki Numata* WBC	1970-71
Alfredo Marcano	1971-72
Richardo Arredondo* WBC	1971-74
Ben Villaflor	1972-73
Kuniaki Shibata	1973
Ben Villaflor	1973-76
Kuniaki Shibata* WBC	1974-75
Alfredo Escalera* WBC	1975-78

Champion	Reign
Samuel Serrano	1976-80
Alexis Arguello* WBC	1978-80
Yasutsune Uehara	1980-81
Rafael (Bazooka) Limon* WBC	1980-81
Cornelius Boza-Edwards* WBC	1981
Samuel Serrano	1981-83
Rolando Navarrete* WBC	1981-82
Rafael (Bazooka) Limon* WBC	1982

Note: Division called Super Featherweight by the WBC.

*Champion not generally recognized. †Champion retired or relinquished title.

Junior Lightweights (Cont.)

Champion	Reign
Bobby Chacon* WBC	1982-83
Roger Mayweather	1983-84
Hector Camacho* WBC	1983-84
Rocky Lockridge	1984-85
Hwan-Kil Yuh* IBF	1984-85
Julio Cesar Chavez* WBC	1984-87
Lester Ellis* IBF	1985-

Champion	Reign
Wilfredo Gomez	1985-86
Barry Michael* IBF	1985-87
Alfredo Layne* WBA	1986
Brian Mitchell* WBA	1986-91
Rocky Lockridge* IBF	1987-88
Azumah Nelson* WBC	1988-94
Tony Lopez* IBF	1988-89
Juan Molina* IBF	1989-90

Champion	Reign
Tony Lopez* IBF	1990-91
Joey Gamache, WBA	1991
Brian Mitchell* IBF	1991
Genaro Hernandez* WBA	1991-
James Leija* WBC	1994-
Juan Molina* IBF	1991-

Featherweights
(Weight Limit: 126 pounds)

Champion	Reign
Torpedo Billy Murphy	1890
Young Griffo	1890-92
George Dixon	1892-97
Solly Smith	1897-98
Dave Sullivan	1898
George Dixon	1898-1900
Terry McGovern	1900-01
Young Corbett II	1901-04
Jimmy Britt	1904
Brooklyn Tommy Sullivan	1904-05
Abe Attell	1906-12
Johnny Kilbane	1912-23
Eugene Criqui	1923
Johnny Dundee	1923-24
Kid, Kaplan	1925-26
Benny Bass	1927-28
Tony Canzoneri	1928
Andre Routis	1928-29
Battling Battalino	1929-32
Tommy Paul* NBA	1932-33
Kid Chocolate* NY	1932-33
Freddie Miller* NBA	1933-36
Mike Beloise* NY	1936-37
Petey Sarron* NBA	1936-37
Maurice Holtzer	1937-38
Henry Armstrong	1937-38
Joey Archibald* NY	1938-39
Leo Rodak* NBA	1938-39
Joey Archibald	1939-40
Petey Scalzo* NBA	1940-41

Champion	Reign
Harry Jeffra	1940-41
Joey Archibald	1941
Richie Lamos* NBA	1941
Chalky Wright	1941-42
Jackie Wilson* NBA	1941-43
Willie Pep	1942-48
Jackie Callura* NBA	1943
Phil Terranova* NBA	1943-44
Sal Bartolo* NBA	1944-46
Sandy Saddler	1948-49
Willie Pep	1949-50
Sandy Saddler	1950-57†
Kid Bassey	1957-59
Davey Moore	1959-63
Sugar Ramos	1963-64
Vicente Saldivar	1964-67†
Paul Rojas* WBA	1968
Jose Legra* WBC	1968-69
Shozo Saijyo* WBA	1968-71
Johnny Famechon* WBC	1969-70
Vicente Saldivar* WBC	1970
Kuniaki Shibata WBC	1970-72
Antonio Gomez* WBA	1971-72
Clemente Sanchez WBC	1972
Ernesto Marcel* WBA	1972-74
Jose Legra WBC	1972-73
Eder Jofre WBC	1973-74
Ruben Olivares* WBA	1974
Bobby Chacon* WBC	1974-75

Champion	Reign
Alexis Arguello WBA	1974-76
Ruben Olivares* WBC	1975
Poison Kotey* WBC	1975-76
Danny Lopez WBC	1976-80
Rafael Ortega* WBA	1977
Cecilio Lastra* WBA	1977-78
Eusebio Pedroza* WBA	1978-85
Salvador Sanchez WBC	1980-82
Juan LaPorte* WBC	1982-84
Wilfredo Gomez* WBC	1984
Min-Keun Oh* IBF	1984-85
Azumah Nelson* WBC	1984-88
Barry McGuigan* WBA	1985-86
Ki Young Chung* IBF	1985-86
Steve Cruz* WBA	1986-87
Antonio Rivera* IBF	1986-88
Antonio Esparragoza* WBA	1987-91
Calvin Grove* IBF	1988
Jorge Paez* IBF	1988-91
Jeff Fenech* WBC	1988-90†
Marcos Villasana* WBC	1990-91
Paul Hodkinson* WBC	1991-
Troy Dorsey* IBF	1991
Manuel Medina* IBF	1991-
Yung Kyun Park* WBA	1991-93
Gregorio Vargas* WBC	1993
Tom Johnson* IBF	1993-
Eloy Rojas* WBA	1993-
Kevin Kelley* WBC	1993-

Junior Featherweights
(Weight Limit: 122 pounds)

Champion	Reign
Jack (Kid) Wolfe*	1922-23
Carl Duane*	1923-24
Rigoberto Riasco* WBC	1976
Royal Kobayashi* WBC	1976
Dong-Kyun Yum* WBC	1976-77
Wilfredo Gomez* WBC	1977-83
Soo-Hwan Hong* WBA	1977-78
Ricardo Cardona* WBA	1978-80
Leo Randolph* WBA	1980
Sergio Palma* WBA	1980-82
Leonardo Cruz* WBA	1982-84
Jaime Garza* WBC	1983
Bobby Berna* IBF	1983-84
Loris Stecca* WBA	1984
Seung-Il Suh* IBF	1984-85

Champion	Reign
Victor Callejas* WBA	1984-86
Juan (Kid) Meza* WBC	1984-85
Ji-Won Kim* IBF	1985-86
Lupe Pintor* WBC	1985-86
Samart Payakaroon* WBC	1986-87
Seung-Hoon Lee* IBF	1987-88
Louie Espinoza* WBA	1987
Jeff Fenech* WBC	1987
Julio Gervacio* WBA	1987-88
Daniel Zaragoza* WBC	1988-90
Jose Sanabria* IBF	1988-89
Bernardo Pinango* WBA	1988
Juan Jose Estrada* WBA	1988-89

Champion	Reign
Fabrice Benichou* IBF	1989-90
Jesus Salud* WBA	1989-90
Welcome Ncita* IBF	1990-
Paul Banke* WBC	1990
Luis Mendoza* WBA	1990-91
Rual Perez* WBA	1992-
Pedro Decima* WBC	1990-91
Kiyoshi Hatanaka* WBC	1991
Daniel Zaragoza* WBC	1991-92
Tracy Patterson* WBC	1992-94
Kennedy McKinney* IBF	1993-94
Wilfredo Vasquez* WBA	1992-
Vuyani Bungu* IBF	1994-
Hector Acero* WBC	1994-

Note: Division called Super Bantamweight by the WBC.

*Champion not generally recognized. †Champion retired or relinquished title.

Bantamweights
(Weight Limit: 118 pounds)

Champion	Reign
Spider Kelly	1887
Hughey Boyle	1887-88
Spider Kelly	1889
Chappie Moran	1889-90
George Dixon	1890-91
Pedlar Palmer*	1895-99
Terry McGovern	1899-1900
Harry Harris	1901-2
Harry Forbes	1902-3
Frankie Neil	1903-4
Joe Bowker	1904-5
Jimmy Walsh	1905-6
Owen Moran	1907-8
Monte Attell*	1909-10
Frankie Conley	1910-11
Johnny Coulon	1911-14
Kid Williams	1914-17
Kewpie Ertle*	1915
Pete Herman	1917-20
Joe Lynch	1920-21
Pete Herman	1921
Johnny Buff	1921-22
Joe Lynch	1922-24
Abe Goldstein	1924
Cannonball Martin	1924-25
Phil Rosenberg	1925-27
Bud Taylor NBA	1927-28
Bushy Graham* NY	1928-29
Panama Al Brown	1929-35
Sixto Escobar* NBA	1934-35
Baltazar Sangchilli	1935-36
Lou Salica* NBA	1935
Sixto Escobar* NBA	1935-36

Champion	Reign
Tony Marino	1936
Sixto Escobar	1936-37
Harry Jeffra	1937-38†
Sixto Escobar	1938-39
Georgie Pace NBA	1939-40
Lou Salica	1940-42
Manuel Ortiz	1942-47
Harold Dade	1947
Manuel Ortiz	1947-50
Vic Toweel	1950-52
Jimmy Carruthers	1952-54†
Robert Cohen	1954-56
Paul Macias* NBA	1955-57
Mario D'Agata	1956-57
Alphonse Halimi	1957-59
Joe Becerra	1959-60†
Eder Jofre	1961-65
Fighting Harada	1965-68
Lionel Rose	1968-69
Ruben Olivares	1969-70
Chucho Castillo	1970-71
Ruben Olivares	1971-72
Rafael Herrera	1972
Enrique Pinder	1972-73
Romeo Anaya	1973
Rafael Herrera* WBC	1973-74
Soo-Hwan Hong	1974-75
Rodolfo Martinez* WBC	1974-76
Alfonso Zamora	1975-77
Carlos Zarate* WBC	1976-79
Jorge Lujan	1977-80
Lupe Pintor* WBC	1979-83
Julian Solis	1980

Champion	Reign
Jeff Chandler	1980-84
Albert Davila* WBC	1983-85
Richard Sandoval	1984-86
Satoshi Shingaki* IBF	1984-85
Jeff Fenech* IBF	1985
Daniel Zaragoza* WBC	1985
Miguel Lora* WBC	1985-88
Gaby Canizales	1986
Bernardo Pinango	1986-87
Wilfredo Vasquez* WBA	1987-88
Kevin Seabrooks* IBF	1987-88
Kaokor Galaxy* WBA	1988
Moon Sung-Kil* WBA	1988-89
Kaokor Galaxy* WBA	1989
Raul Perez* WBC	1988-91
Orlando Canizales* IBF	1988-
Luisito Espinosa* WBA	1989-91
Israel Contreras* WBA	1991-92
Eddie Cook* WBA	1992-
Greg Richardson* WBC	1991
Joichiro Tatsuyoshi, WBC	1991-92
Victor Rabanales* WBC	1992-93
Jung-Il Byun* WBC	1993
Jorge Julio WBA	1993
Yasuei Yakushiji* WBC	1993-
Junior Jones* WBA	1994
John M. Johnson* WBA	1994
Daorung Chuvatana* WBA	1994-

Junior Bantamweights
(Weight Limit: 115 pounds)

Champion	Reign
Rafael Orono* WBC	1980-81
Chul-Ho Kim* WBC	1981-82
Gustavo Ballas* WBA	1981
Rafael Pedroza* WBA	1981-82
Jiro Watanabe* WBA	1982-84
Rafael Orono* WBC	1982-83
Payao Poontarat* WBC	1983-84
Joo-Do Chun* IBF	1983-85
Jiro Watanabe	1984-86
Kaosai Galaxy* WBA	1984

Champion	Reign
Ellyas Pical* IBF	1985-86
Cesar Polanco* IBF	1986
Gilberto Roman* WBC	1986-87
Ellyas Pical* IBF	1986
Santos Laciar* WBC	1987
Tae-Il Chang* IBF	1987
Sugar Rojas* WBC	1987-88
Ellyas Pical* IBF	1987-89
Giberto Roman* WBC	1988-89
Juan Polo Perez* IBF	1989-90

Champion	Reign
Nana Konadu* WBC	1989-90
Sung-Kil Moon* WBC	1990-93
Robert Quiroga* IBF	1990-93
Julio Borboa* IBF	1993-94
Katsuya Onizuka* WBA	1993-94
Lee Hyung-Chul* WBA	1994-
Jose Luis Bueno* WBC	1993-94
Hiroshi Kawashima* WBC	1994-
Harold Grey* IBF	1994-

Note: Division called Super Flyweight by the WBC.

Flyweights
(Weight Limit: 112 pounds)

Champion	Reign
Sid Smith	1913
Bill Ladbury	1913-14
Percy Jones	1914
Joe Symonds	1914-16
Jimmy Wilde	1916-23
Pancho Villa	1923-25
Fidel LaBarba	1925-27†
Frenchy Belanger NBA	1927-28
Corporal Izzy Schwartz NY	1927-29
Frankie Genaro NBA	1928-29

Champion	Reign
Spider Pladner NBA	1929
Frankie Genaro NBA	1929-31
Midget Wolgast* NY	1930-35
Young Perez NBA	1931-32
Jackie Brown NBA	1932-35
Benny Lynch	1935-38
Small Montana* NY	1935-37
Peter Kane	1938-43
Little Dado* NY	1938-40
Jackie Paterson	1943-48
Rinty Monaghan	1948-50

Champion	Reign
Terry Allen	1950
Dado Marino	1950-52
Yoshio Shirai	1953-54
Pascual Perez	1954-60
Pone Kingpetch	1960-62
Masahiko Harada	1962-63
Pone Kingpetch	1963
Hiroyuki Ebihara	1963-64
Pone Kingpetch	1964-65
Salvatore Burrini	1965-66

*Champion not generally recognized. †Champion retired or relinquished title.

Flyweights (Cont.)

Champion	Reign
Horacio Accavallo* WBA	1966-68
Walter McGowan	1966
Chartchai Chionoi	1966-69
Efren Torres	1969-70
Hiroyuki Ebihara* WBA	1969
Bernabe Villacampo* WBA	1969-70
Chartchai Chionoi	1970
Berkrerk Chartvanchai* WBA	1970
Masao Ohba* WBA	1970-73
Erbito Salavarria	1970-73
Betulio Gonzalez* WBA	1972
Venice Borkorsor* WBC	1972-73
Venice Borkorsor	1973
Chartchai Chionoi* WBA	1973-74
Betulio Gonzalez* WBA	1973-74
Shoji Oguma* WBC	1974-75
Susumu Hanagata* WBA	1974-75
Miguel Canto* WBC	1975-79
Erbito Salavarria* WBA	1975-76

Champion	Reign
Alfonso Lopez* WBA	1976
Gustavo Espadas* WBA	1976-78
Betulio Gonzalez* WBA	1978-79
Chan-Hee Park* WBC	1979-80
Luis Ibarra* WBA	1979-80
Tae-Shik Kim* WBA	1980
Shoji Oguma* WBC	1980-81
Peter Mathebula* WBA	1980-81
Santos Laciar* WBA	1981
Antonio Avelar* WBC	1981-82
Luis Ibarra* WBA	1981
Juan Herrera* WBA	1981-82
Prudencio Cardona* WBC	1982
Santos Laciar* WBA	1982-85
Freddie Castillo* WBC	1982
Eleoncio Mercedes* WBC	1982-83
Charlie Magri* WBC	1983
Frank Cedeno* WBC	1983-84
Soon-Chun Kwon* IBF	1983-85
Koji Kobayashi* WBC	1984
Gabriel Bernal* WBC	1984
Sot Chitalada* WBC	1984-88
Hilario Zapate* WBA	1985-87

Champion	Reign
Chong-Kwan Chung* IBF	1985-86
Bi-Won Chung* IBF	1986
Hi-Sup Shin* IBF	1986-87
Dodie Penalosa* IBF	1987
Fidel Bassa* WBA	1987-89
Choi-Chang Ho* IBF	1987-88
Rolando Bohol* IBF	1988
Yong-Kang Kim* WBC	1988-89
Duke McKenzie* IBF	1988-89
Sot Chitalada* WBC	1989-91
Dave McAuley* IBF	1989-92
Jesus Rojas* WBA	1989-90
Yul-Woo Lee* WBA	1990
Leopard Tamakuma* WBA	1990-91
Muangchai Kittikasem* WBC	1991-92
Yuri Arbachakov* WBC	1992-
Yong Kang Kim* WBA	1991-92
Rodolfo Blanco* IBF	1992-93
Pinchit Sithbangprachan* IBF	1993-
David Griman* WBA	1992-94
Saen Sow Ploenchit* WBA	1994-

Junior Flyweights
(Weight Limit: 108 pounds)

Champion	Reign
Franco Udella* WBC	1975
Jaime Rios* WBA	1975-76
Luis Estaba* WBC	1975-78
Juan Guzman* WBA	1976
Yoko Gushiken* WBA	1976-81
Freddy Castillo* WBC	1978
Netrnoi Vorasingh* WBC	1978
Sung-Jun Kim* WBC	1978-80
Shigeo Nakajima* WBC	1980
Hilario Zapata* WBC	1980-82
Pedro Flores* WBA	1981
Hwan-Jin Kim* WBA	1981
Katsuo Tokashiki* WBA	1981-83
Amado Urzua* WBC	1982

Champion	Reign
Tadashi Tomori* WBC	1982
Hilario Zapata* WBC	1982-83
Jung-Koo Chang* WBC	1983-88
Lupe Madera* WBA	1983-84
Dodie Penalosa* IBF	1983-86
Francisco Quiroz* WBA	1984-85
Joey Olivo* WBA	1985
Myung-Woo Yuh* WBA	1985-91
Jum-Hwan Choi* IBF	1986-88
Tacy Macalos* IBF	1988-89
German Torres* WBC	1988-89
Yul-Woo Lee* WBC	1989
Muangchai Kittikasem* IBF	1989-90

Champion	Reign
Humberto Gonzalez* WBC	1989-90
Michael Carbajal* IBF	1990-94
Rolando Pascua* WBC	1990
Melchor Cob Castro* WBC	1991
Humberto Gonzalez* WBC	1991-93
Hirokia Ioka* WBA	1991-92
Michael Carbajal, WBC	1993-94
Myung-Woo Yuh* WBA	1993
Leo Gamez* WBA	1993-
Humberto GonzalezIBF	1994-

Note: Division called Light Flyweight by the WBC.

Strawweights
(Weight Limit: 105 pounds)

Champion	Reign
Franco Udella* WBC	1975
Jaime Rios* WBA	1975-76
Luis Estaba* WBC	1975-78
Juan Guzman* WBA	1976
Yoko Gushiken* WBA	1976-81
Freddy Castillo* WBC	1978
Netrnoi Vorasingh* WBC	1978
Sung-Jun Kim* WBC	1978-80
Shigeo Nakajima* WBC	1980
Hilario Zapata* WBC	1980-82
Pedro Flores* WBA	1981
Hwan-Jin Kim* WBA	1981
Katsuo Tokashiki* WBA	1981-83

Champion	Reign
Amado Urzua* WBC	1982
Tadashi Tomori* WBC	1982
Hilario Zapata* WBC	1982-83
Jung-Koo Chang* WBC	1983-88
Lupe Madera* WBA	1983-84
Dodie Penalosa* IBF	1983-86
Francisco Quiroz* WBA	1984-85
Joey Olivo* WBA	1985
Myung-Woo Yuh* WBA	1985-93
Jum-Hwan Choi* IBF	1986-88
Tacy Macalos* IBF	1988-89
German Torres* WBC	1988-89
Yul-Woo Lee* WBC	1989

Champion	Reign
Muangchai Kittikasem* IBF	1989-90
Humberto Gonzalez* WBC	1989-90
Michael Carbajal* IBF	1990
Rolando Pascua* WBC	1990
Melchor Cob Castro* WBC	1991
Ricardo Lopez* WBC	1990-
Ratanapol Voraphin* IBF	1992-
Chana Porpaoin* WBA	1993-

*Champion not generally recognized. Note: Division called Light Flyweight by the WBC.

Alltime Career Leaders

TOTAL BOUTS

Name	Years Active	Bouts
Len Wickwar	1928-47	463
Jack Britton	1905-30	350
Johnny Dundee	1910-32	333
Billy Bird	1920-48	318
George Marsden	1928-46	311
Maxie Rosenbloom	1923-39	299
Harry Greb	1913-26	298
Young Stribling	1921-33	286
Battling Levinsky	1910-29	282
Ted (Kid) Lewis	1909-29	279

Note: Based on records in *The Ring Record Book* and *Boxing Encyclopedia.*

MOST KNOCKOUTS

Name	Years Active	KOs
Archie Moore	1936-63	130
Young Stribling	1921-33	126
Billy Bird	1920-48	125
George Odwell	1930-45	114
Sugar Ray Robinson	1940-65	110
Sandy Saddler	1944-56	103
Sam Langford	1902-26	102
Henry Armstrong	1931-45	100
Jimmy Wilde	1911-23	98
Len Wickwar	1928-47	93

Note: Based on records in *The Ring Record Book* and *Boxing Encyclopedia.*

World Heavyweight Championship Fights

Date	Winner	Wgt	Loser	Wgt	Result	Site
Sep 7, 1892	James J. Corbett*	178	John L. Sullivan	212	KO 21	New Orleans
Jan 25, 1894	James J. Corbett	184	Charley Mitchell	158	KO 3	Jacksonville, FL
Mar 17, 1897	Bob Fitzsimmons*	167	James J. Corbett	183	KO 14	Carson City, NV
June 9, 1899	James J. Jeffries*	206	Bob Fitzsimmons	167	KO 11	Coney Island, NY
Nov 3, 1899	James J. Jeffries	215	Tom Sharkey	183	Ref 25	Coney Island, NY
Apr 6, 1900	James J. Jeffries	n/a	Jack Finnegan	n/a	KO 1	Detroit
May 11, 1900	James J. Jeffries	218	James J. Corbett	188	KO 23	Coney Island, NY
Nov 15, 1901	James J. Jeffries	211	Gus Ruhlin	194	TKO 6	San Francisco
July 25, 1902	James J. Jeffries	219	Bob Fitzsimmons	172	KO 8	San Francisco
Aug 14, 1903	James J. Jeffries	220	James J. Corbett	190	KO 10	San Francisco
Aug 25, 1904	James J. Jeffries	219	Jack Munroe	186	TKO 2	San Francisco
July 3, 1905	Marvin Hart*	190	Jack Root	171	KO 12	Reno
Feb 23, 1906	Tommy Burns*	180	Marvin Hart	188	Ref 20	Los Angeles
Oct 2, 1906	Tommy Burns	n/a	Jim Flynn	n/a	KO 15	Los Angeles
Nov 28, 1906	Tommy Burns	172	Jack O'Brien	163½	Draw 20	Los Angeles
May 8, 1907	Tommy Burns	180	Jack O'Brien	167	Ref 20	Los Angeles
Jul 4, 1907	Tommy Burns	181	Bill Squires	180	KO 1	Colma, CA
Dec 2, 1907	Tommy Burns	177	Gunner Moir	204	KO 10	London
Feb 10, 1908	Tommy Burns	n/a	Jack Palmer	n/a	KO 4	London
Mar 17, 1908	Tommy Burns	n/a	Jem Roche	n/a	KO 1	Dublin
Apr 18, 1908	Tommy Burns	n/a	Jewey Smith	n/a	KO 5	Paris
June 13, 1908	Tommy Burns	184	Bill Squires	183	KO 8	Paris
Aug 24, 1908	Tommy Burns	181	Bill Squires	184	KO 13	Sydney
Sep 2, 1908	Tommy Burns	183	Bill Lang	187	KO 6	Melbourne
Dec 26, 1908	Jack Johnson*	192	Tommy Burns	168	TKO 14	Sydney
Mar 10, 1909	Jack Johnson	n/a	Victor McLaglen	n/a	ND 6	Vancouver
May 19, 1909	Jack Johnson	205	Jack O'Brien	161	ND 6	Philadelphia
June 30, 1909	Jack Johnson	207	Tony Ross	214	ND 6	Pittsburgh
Sep 9, 1909	Jack Johnson	209	Al Kaufman	191	ND 10	San Francisco
Oct 16, 1909	Jack Johnson	205½	Stanley Ketchel	170¼	KO 12	Colma, CA
July 4, 1910	Jack Johnson	208	James J. Jeffries	227	KO 15	Reno
July 4, 1912	Jack Johnson	195½	Jim Flynn	175	TKO 9	Las Vegas
Dec 19, 1913	Jack Johnson	n/a	Jim Johnson	n/a	Draw 10	Paris
June 27, 1914	Jack Johnson	221	Frank Moran	203	Ref 20	Paris
Apr 5, 1915	Jess Willard*	230	Jack Johnson	205½	KO 26	Havana
Mar 25, 1916	Jess Willard	225	Frank Moran	203	ND 10	New York
July 4, 1919	Jack Dempsey*	187	Jess Willard	245	TKO 4	Toledo, OH
Sep 6, 1920	Jack Dempsey	185	Billy Miske	187	KO 3	Benton Harbor, MI
Dec 14, 1920	Jack Dempsey	188¼	Bill Brennan	197	KO 12	New York
July 2, 1921	Jack Dempsey	188	Georges Carpentier	172	KO 4	Jersey City
July 4, 1923	Jack Dempsey	188	Tommy Givvons	175½	Ref 15	Shelby, MT
Sep 14, 1923	Jack Dempsey	192½	Luis Firpo	216½	KO 2	New York
Sep 23, 1926	Gene Tunney*	189½	Jack Dempsey	190	UD 10	Philadelphia
Sep 22, 1927	Gene Tunney	189½	Jack Dempsey	192½	UD 10	Chicago
July 26, 1928	Gene Tunney	192	Tom Heeney	203½	TKO 11	New York
June 12, 1930	Max Schmeling*	188	Jack Sharkey	197	Foul 4	New York
July 3, 1931	Max Schmeling	189	Young Stribling	186½	TKO 15	Cleveland
June 21, 1932	Jack Sharkey*	205	Max Schmeling	188	Split 15	Long Island City
June 29, 1933	Primo Carnera*	260½	Jack Sharkey	201	KO 6	Long Island City

Date	Winner	Wgt	Loser	Wgt	Result	Site
Oct 22, 1933	Primo Carnera	259½	Paulino Uzcudun	229¼	UD 15	Rome
Mar 1, 1934	Primo Carnera	270	Tommy Loughran	184	UD 15	Miami
June 14, 1934	Max Baer*	209½	Primo Carnera	263¼	TKO 11	Long Island City
June 13, 1935	James J. Braddock*	193¾	Max Baer	209½	UD 15	Long Island City
June 22, 1937	Joe Louis	197¼	James J. Braddock	197	KO 8	Chicago
Aug 30, 1937	Joe Louis	197	Tommy Farr	204¼	UD 15	New York
Feb 23, 1938	Joe Louis	200	Nathan Mann	193½	KO 3	New York
Apr 1, 1938	Joe Louis	202½	Harry Thomas	196	KO 5	Chicago
June 22, 1938	Joe Louis	198¼	Max Schmeling	193	KO 1	New York
Jan 25, 1939	Joe Louis	200¼	John Henry Lewis	180¾	KO 1	New York
Apr 17, 1939	Joe Louis	201¼	Jack Roper	204¾	KO 1	Los Angeles
June 28, 1939	Joe Louis	200¾	Tony Galento	233¾	TKO 4	New York
Sep 20, 1939	Joe Louis	200	Bob Pastor	183	KO 11	Detroit
Feb 9, 1940	Joe Louis	203	Arturo Godoy	202	Split 15	New York
Mar 29, 1940	Joe Louis	201½	Johnny Paychek	187½	KO 2	New York
June 20, 1940	Joe Louis	199	Arturo Godoy	201¼	TKO 8	New York
Dec 16, 1940	Joe Louis	202¼	Al McCoy	180¾	TKO 6	Boston
Jan 31, 1941	Joe Louis	202½	Red Burman	188	KO 5	New York
Feb 17, 1941	Joe Louis	203½	Gus Dorazio	193½	KO 2	Philadelphia
Mar 21, 1941	Joe Louis	202	Abe Simon	254½	TKO 13	Detroit
Apr 8, 1941	Joe Louis	203½	Tony Musto	199½	TKO 9	St Louis
May 23, 1941	Joe Louis	201½	Buddy Baer	237½	Disq 7	Washington, DC
June 18, 1941	Joe Louis	199½	Billy Conn	174	KO 13	New York
Sep 29, 1941	Joe Louis	202¼	Lou Nova	202½	TKO 6	New York
Jan 9, 1942	Joe Louis	206¾	Buddy Baer	250	KO 1	New York
Mar 27, 1942	Joe Louis	207½	Abe Simon	255½	KO 6	New York
June 9, 1946	Joe Louis	207	Billy Conn	187	KO 8	New York
Sep 18, 1946	Joe Louis	211	Tami Mauriello	198½	KO 1	New York
Dec 5, 1947	Joe Louis	211½	Jersey Joe Walcott	194½	Split 15	New York
June 25, 1948	Joe Louis	213½	Jersey Joe Walcott	194¾	KO 11	New York
June 22, 1949	Ezzard Charles*	181¾	Jersey Joe Walcott	195½	UD 15	Chicago
Aug 10, 1949	Ezzard Charles	180	Gus Lesnevich	182	TKO 8	New York
Oct 14, 1949	Ezzard Charles	182	Pat Valentino	188½	KO 8	San Francisco
Aug 15, 1950	Ezzard Charles	183¼	Freddie Beshore	184½	TKO 14	Buffalo
Sep 27, 1950	Ezzard Charles	184½	Joe Louis	218	UD 15	New York
Dec 5, 1950	Ezzard Charles	185	Nick Barone	178½	KO 11	Cincinnati
Jan 12, 1951	Ezzard Charles	185	Lee Oma	193	TKO 10	New York
Mar 7, 1951	Ezzard Charles	186	Jersey Joe Walcott	193	UD 15	Detroit
May 30, 1951	Ezzard Charles	182	Joey Maxim	181½	UD 15	Chicago
July 18, 1951	Jersey Joe Walcott*	194	Ezzard Charles	182	KO 7	Pittsburgh
June 5, 1952	Jersey Joe Walcott	196	Ezzard Charles	191½	UD 15	Philadelphia
Sep 23, 1952	Rocky Marciano*	184	Jersey Joe Walcott	196	KO 13	Philadelphia
May 15, 1953	Rocky Marciano	184½	Jersey Joe Walcott	197¾	KO 1	Chicago
Sep 24, 1953	Rocky Marciano	185	Roland LaStarza	184¾	TKO 11	New York
June 17, 1954	Rocky Marciano	187½	Ezzard Charles	185½	UD 15	New York
Sep 17, 1954	Rocky Marciano	187	Ezzard Charles	192½	KO 8	New York
May 16, 1955	Rocky Marciano	189	Don Cockell	205	TKO 9	San Francisco
Sep 21, 1955	Rocky Marciano	188¼	Archie Moore	188	KO 9	New York
Nov 30, 1956	Floyd Patterson*	182¼	Archie Moore	187¾	KO 5	Chicago
July 29, 1957	Floyd Patterson	184	Tommy Jackson	192½	TKO 10	New York
Aug 22, 1957	Floyd Patterson	187¼	Pete Rademacher	202	KO 6	Seattle
Aug 18, 1958	Floyd Patterson	184½	Roy Harris	194	TKO 13	Los Angeles
May 1, 1959	Floyd Patterson	182½	Brian London	206	KO 11	Indianapolis
June 26, 1959	Ingemar Johansson*	196	Floyd Patterson	182	TKO 3	New York
June 20, 1960	Floyd Patterson*	190	Ingemar Johansson	194¾	KO 5	New York
Mar 13, 1961	Floyd Patterson	194¾	Ingemar Johansson	206½	KO 6	Miami Beach
Dec 4, 1961	Floyd Patterson	188½	Tom McNeeley	197	KO 4	Toronto
Sep 25, 1962	Sonny Liston*	214	Floyd Patterson	189	KO 1	Chicago
July 22, 1963	Sonny Liston	215	Floyd Patterson	194½	KO 1	Las Vegas
Feb 25, 1964	Cassius Clay	210½	Sonny Liston	218	TKO 7	Miami Beach
Mar 5, 1965	Ernie Terrell WBA*	199	Eddie Machen	192	UD 15	Chicago
May 25, 1965	Muhammad Ali	206	Sonny Liston	215¼	KO 1	Lewiston, ME
Nov 1, 1965	Ernie Terrell WBA*	206	George Chuvalo	209	UD 15	Toronto
Nov 2, 1965	Muhammad Ali	210	Floyd Patterson	196¾	TKO 12	Las Vegas
Mar 29, 1966	Muhammad Ali	214½	George Chuvalo	216	UD 15	Toronto
May 21, 1966	Muhammad Ali	201½	Henry Cooper	188	TKO 6	London
June 28, 1966	Ernie Terrell WBA*	209½	Doug Jones	187½	UD 15	Houston
Aug 6, 1966	Muhammad Ali	209½	Brian London	201½	KO 3	London

World Heavyweight Championship Fights *(Cont.)*

Date	Winner	Wgt	Loser	Wgt	Result	Site
Sep 10, 1966	Muhammad Ali	203½	Karl Mildenberger	194¼	TKO 12	Frankfurt
Nov 14, 1966	Muhammad Ali	212¾	Cleveland Williams	210½	TKO 3	Houston
Feb 6, 1967	Muhammad Ali	212¼	Ernie Terrell WBA	212½	UD 15	Houston
Mar 22, 1967	Muhammad Ali	211½	Zora Folley	202½	KO 7	New York
Mar 4, 1968	Joe Frazier*	204½	Buster Mathis	243½	TKO 11	New York
Apr 27, 1968	Jimmy Ellis*	197	Jerry Quarry	195	Maj 15	Oakland
June 24, 1968	Joe Frazier NY*	203½	Manuel Ramos	208	TKO 2	New York
Aug 14, 1968	Jimmy Ellis WBA*	198	Floyd Patterson	188	Ref 15	Stockholm
Dec 10, 1968	Joe Frazier NY*	203	Oscar Bonavena	207	UD 15	Philadelphia
Apr 22, 1969	Joe Frazier NY*	204½	Dave Zyglewicz	190½	KO 1	Houston
June 23, 1969	Joe Frazier NY*	203½	Jerry Quarry	198½	TKO 8	New York
Feb 16, 1970	Joe Frazier NY*	205	Jimmy Ellis WBA	201	TKO 5	New York
Nov 18, 1970	Joe Frazier*	209	Bob Foster	188	KO 2	Detroit
Mar 8, 1971	Joe Frazier*	205½	Muhammad Ali	215	UD 15	New York
Jan 15, 1972	Joe Frazier	215½	Terry Daniels	195	TKO 4	New Orleans
May 26, 1972	Joe Frazier	217½	Ron Stander	218	TKO 5	Omaha
Jan 22, 1973	George Foreman*	217½	Joe Frazier	214	TKO 2	Kingston, Jam.
Sep 1, 1973	George Foreman	219½	Jose Roman	196½	KO 1	Tokyo
Mar 26, 1974	George Foreman	224¼	Ken Norton	212¼	TKO 2	Caracas
Oct 30, 1974	Muhammad Ali*	216-½	George Foreman	220	KO 8	Kinshasa, Zaire
Mar 24, 1975	Muhammad Ali	223½	Chuck Wepner	225	TKO 15	Cleveland
May 16, 1975	Muhammad Ali	224½	Ron Lyle	219	TKO 11	Las Vegas
July 1, 1975	Muhammad Ali	224½	Joe Bugner	230	UD 15	Kuala Lumpur, Malaysia
Oct 1, 1975	Muhammad Ali	224½	Joe Frazier	215	TKO 15	Manila
Feb 20, 1976	Muhammad Ali	226	Jean Pierre Coopman	206	KO 5	San Juan
Apr 30, 1976	Muhammad Ali	230	Jimmy Young	209	UD 15	Landover, MD
May 24, 1976	Muhammad Ali	230	Richard Dunn	206½	TKO 5	Munich
Sep 28, 1976	Muhammad Ali	221	Ken Norton	217½	UD 15	New York
May 16, 1977	Muhammad Ali	221¼	Alfredo Evangelista	209¼	UD 15	Landover, MD
Sep 29, 1977	Muhammad Ali	225	Earnie Shavers	211¼	UD 15	New York
Feb 15, 1978	Leon Spinks*	197¼	Muhammad Ali	224¼	Split 15	Las Vegas
June 9, 1978	Larry Holmes*	209	Ken Norton WBC	220	Split 15	Las Vegas
Sep 15, 1978	Muhammad Ali*	221	Leon Spinks	201	UD 15	New Orleans
Nov 10, 1978	Larry Holmes WBC*	214	Alfredo Evangelista	208¼	KO 7	Las Vegas
Mar 23, 1979	Larry Holmes WBC*	214	Osvaldo Ocasio	207	TKO 7	Las Vegas
June 22, 1979	Larry Holmes WBC*	215	Mike Weaver	202	TKO 12	New York
Sep 28, 1979	Larry Holmes WBC*	210	Earnie Shavers	211	TKO 11	Las Vegas
Oct 20, 1979	John Tate*	240	Gerrie Coetzee	222	UD 15	Pretoria
Feb 3, 1980	Larry Holmes WBC*	213½	Lorenzo Zanon	215	TKO 6	Las Vegas
Mar 31, 1980	Mike Weaver*	232	John Tate WBA	232	KO 15	Knoxville
Mar 31, 1980	Larry Holmes WBC*	211	Leroy Jones	254½	TKO 8	Las Vegas
July 7, 1980	Larry Holmes WBC*	214¼	Scott LeDoux	226	TKO 7	Minneapolis
Oct 2, 1980	Larry Holmes WBC*	211¼	Muhammad Ali	217½	TKO 11	Las Vegas
Oct 25, 1980	Mike Weaver WBA*	210	Gerrie Coetzee	226½	KO 13	Sun City
Apr 11, 1981	Larry Holmes	215	Trevor Berbick	215½	UD 15	Las Vegas
June 12, 1981	Larry Holmes	212¼	Leon Spinks	200¼	TKO 3	Detroit
Oct 3, 1981	Mike Weaver WBA*	215	James Quick Tillis	209	UD 15	Rosemont, IL
Nov 6, 1981	Larry Holmes	213¼	Renaldo Snipes	215¾	TKO 11	Pittsburgh
June 11, 1982	Larry Holmes	212½	Gerry Cooney	225½	TKO 13	Las Vegas
Nov 26, 1982	Larry Holmes	217½	Tex Cobb	234¼	UD 15	Houston
Dec 10, 1982	Michael Dokes*	216	Mike Weaver WBA	209¾	TKO 1	Las Vegas
Mar 27, 1983	Larry Holmes	221	Lucien Rodriguez	209	UD 12	Scranton
May 20, 1983	Michael Dokes WBA*	223	Mike Weaver	218½	Draw 15	Las Vegas
May 20, 1983	Larry Holmes	213	Tim Witherspoon	219½	Split 12	Las Vegas
Sep 10, 1983	Larry Holmes	223	Scott Frank	211¼	TKO 5	Atlantic City
Sep 23, 1983	Gerrie Coetzee*	215	Michael Dokes WBA	217	KO 10	Richfield, OH
Nov 25, 1983	Larry Holmes	219	Marvis Frazier	200	TKO 1	Las Vegas
Mar 9, 1984	Tim Witherspoon	220¼	Greg Page	239½	Maj 12	Las Vegas
Aug 31, 1984	Pinklon Thomas*	216	Tim Witherspoon WBC	217	Maj 12	Las Vegas
Nov 9, 1984	Larry Holmes IBF	221½	James Smith	227	TKO 12	Las Vegas
Dec 1, 1984	Greg Page*	236½	Gerrie Coetzee WBA	218	KO 8	Sun City
Mar 15, 1985	Larry Holmes	223½	David Bey	233¼	TKO 10	Las Vegas
Apr 29, 1985	Tony Tubbs*	229	Greg Page WBA	239½	UD 15	Buffalo
May 20, 1985	Larry Holmes	224¼	Carl Williams	215	UD 15	Las Vegas
June 15, 1985	Pinklon Thomas*	220¼	Mike Weaver	221¼	KO 8	Las Vegas
Sep 21, 1985	Michael Spinks*	200	Larry Holmes IBF	221½	UD 15	Las Vegas
Jan 17, 1986	Tim Witherspoon	227	Tony Tubbs WBA	229	Maj 15	Atlanta

World Heavyweight Championship Fights (Cont.)

Date	Winner	Wgt	Loser	Wgt	Result	Site
Mar 22, 1986	Trevor Berbick*	218½	Pinklon Thomas WBC	222¾	UD 15	Las Vegas
Apr 19, 1986	Michael Spinks	205	Larry Holmes	223	Split 15	Las Vegas
July 19, 1986	Tim Witherspoon*	234¾	Frank Bruno	228	TKO 11	Wembley, Eng.
Sep 6, 1986	Michael Spinks	201	Steffen Tangstad	214¾	TKO 4	Las Vegas
Nov 22, 1986	Mike Tyson*	221¼	Trevor Berbick WBC	218½	TKO 2	Las Vegas
Dec 12, 1986	James Smith*	228½	Tim Witherspoon WBA	233½	TKO 1	New York
Mar 7, 1987	Mike Tyson WBC*	219	James Smith WBA	233	UD 12	Las Vegas
May 30, 1987	Mike Tyson*	218¾	Pinklon Thomas	217¾	TKO 6	Las Vegas
May 30, 1987	Tony Tucker	222¼	Buster Douglas	227¼	TKO 10	Las Vegas
June 15, 1987	Michael Spinks	208¾	Gerry Cooney	238	TKO 5	Atlantic City
Aug 1, 1987	Mike Tyson*	221	Tony Tucker IBF	221	UD 12	Las Vegas
Oct 16, 1987	Mike Tyson*	216	Tyrell Biggs	228¾	TKO 7	Atlantic City
Jan 22, 1988	Mike Tyson*	215¾	Larry Holmes	225¾	TKO 4	Atlantic City
Mar 20, 1988	Mike Tyson*	216¼	Tony Tubbs	238¼	KO 2	Tokyo
June 27, 1988	Mike Tyson*	218¼	Michael Spinks	212¼	KO 1	Atlantic City
Feb 25, 1989	Mike Tyson	218	Frank Bruno	228	TKO 5	Las Vegas
July 21, 1989	Mike Tyson	219¼	Carl Williams	218	TKO 1	Atlantic City
Feb 10, 1990	Buster Douglas*	231½	Mike Tyson	220½	KO 10	Tokyo
Oct 25, 1990	Evander Holyfield	208	Buster Douglas	246	KO 3	Las Vegas
Apr 19, 1991	Evander Holyfield	212	George Foreman	257	UD 12	Atlantic City
Nov 23, 1991	Evander Holyfield	210	Bert Cooper	215	TKO 7	Atlanta
June 19, 1992	Evander Holyfield	210	Larry Holmes	233	UD 12	Las Vegas
Nov 13, 1992	Riddick Bowe	235	Evander Holyfield	205	UD 12	Las Vegas
Feb 6, 1993	Riddick Bowe	243	Michael Dokes	244	KO 1	New York City
May 8, 1993	Lennox Lewis	235	Tony Tucker	235	UD 12	Las Vegas
May 22, 1993	Riddick Bowe	244	Jesse Ferguson	224	KO 2	Washington, D.C.
Oct 2, 1993	Lennox Lewis	229	Frank Bruno	233	KO 7	London
Nov 6, 1993	Evander Holyfield	217	Riddick Bowe	246	Split 12	Las Vegas
Apr 22, 1994	Michael Moorer	214	Evander Holyfield	214	Split 12	Las Vegas
May 6, 1994	Lennox Lewis	235	Phil Jackson	218	TKO 8	Atlantic City

*Champion not generally recognized.

KO=knockout; TKO=technical knockout; UD=unanimous decision; Split=split decision; Ref=referee's decision; Disq=disqualification; ND=no decision.

Ring Magazine Fighter and Fight of the Year

Year	Fighter	Fight	Winner	Site
1928	Gene Tunney	Award not given until 1945		
1929	Tommy Loughran	Award not given until 1945		
1930	Max Schmeling	Award not given until 1945		
1931	Tommy Loughran	Award not given until 1945		
1932	Jack Sharkey	Award not given until 1945		
1933	No award	Award not given until 1945		
1934	Tony Canzoneri	Award not given until 1945		
	Barney Ross	Award not given until 1945		
1935	Barney Ross	Award not given until 1945		
1936	Joe Louis	Award not given until 1945		
1937	Henry Armstrong	Award not given until 1945		
1938	Joe Louis	Award not given until 1945		
1939	Joe Louis	Award not given until 1945		
1940	Billy Conn	Award not given until 1945		
1941	Joe Louis	Award not given until 1945		
1942	Ray Robinson	Award not given until 1945		
1943	Fred Apostoli	Award not given until 1945		
1944	Beau Jack	Award not given until 1945		
1945	Willie Pep	Rocky Graziano-Cochrane	Rocky Graziano	New York City
1946	Tony Zale	Tony Zale-Rocky Graziano	Tony Zale	New York City
1947	Gus Lesnevich	Rocky Graziano-Tony Zale	Rocky Graziano	Chicago
1948	Ike Williams	Marcel Cerdan-Tony Zale	Marcel Cerdan	Jersey City
1949	Ezzard Charles	Willie Pep-Sandy Saddler	Willie Pep	New York City
1950	Ezzard Charles	Jake LaMotta-Laurent Dauthuille	Jake LaMotta	Detroit
1951	Ray Robinson	Jersey Joe Walcott-Ezzard Charles	Jersey Joe Walcott	Pittsburgh
1952	Rocky Marciano	Rocky Marciano-Jersey Joe Walcott	Rocky Marciano	Philadelphia
1953	Carl Olson	Rocky Marciano-Roland LaStarza	Rocky Marciano	New York City
1954	Rocky Marciano	Rocky Marciano-Ezzard Charles	Rocky Marciano	New York City
1955	Rocky Marciano	Carmen Basilio-Tony DeMarco	Carmen Basilio	Boston

Year	Fighter	Fight	Winner	Site
1956	Floyd Patterson	Carmen Basilio-Johnny Saxton	Carmen Basilio	Syracuse
1957	Carmen Basilio	Carmen Basilio-Ray Robinson	Carmen Basilio	New York City
1958	Ingemar Johansson	Ray Robinson-Carmen Basilio	Ray Robinson	Chicago
1959	Ingemar Johansson	Gene Fullmer-Carmen Basilio	Gene Fullmer	San Francisco
1960	Floyd Patterson	Floyd Patterson-Ingemar Johansson	Floyd Patterson	New York City
1961	Joe Brown	Joe Brown-Dave Charnley	Joe Brown	London
1962	Dick Tiger	Joey Giardello-Henry Hank	Joey Giardello	Philadelphia
1963	Cassius Clay	Cassius Clay-Doug Jones	Cassius Clay	New York City
1964	Emile Griffith	Cassius Clay-Sonny Liston	Cassius Clay	Miami Beach
1965	Dick Tiger	Floyd Patterson-George Chuvalo	Floyd Patterson	New York City
1966	No award	Jose Torres-Eddie Cotton	Jose Torres	Las Vegas
1967	Joe Frazier	Nino Benvenuti-Emile Griffith	Nino Benvenuti	New York City
1968	Nino Benvenuti	Dick Tiger-Frank DePaula	Dick Tiger	New York City
1969	Jose Napoles	Joe Frazier-Jerry Quarry	Joe Frazier	New York City
1970	Joe Frazier	Carlos Monzon-Nino Benvenuti	Carlos Monzon	Rome
1971	Joe Frazier	Joe Frazier-Muhammed Ali	Joe Frazier	New York City
1972	Muhammed Ali Carlos Monzon	Bob Foster-Chris Finnegan	Bob Foster	London
1973	George Foreman	George Foreman-Joe Frazier	George Foreman	Kingston, Jam.
1974	Muhammed Ali	Muhammed Ali-George Foreman	Muhammed Ali	Kinshasa
1975	Muhammed Ali	Muhammed Ali-Joe Frazier	Muhammed Ali	Manila
1976	George Foreman	George Foreman-Ron Lyle	George Foreman	Las Vegas
1977	Carlos Zarate	Joe Young-George Foreman	Joe Young	San Juan
1978	Muhammed Ali	Leon Spinks-Muhammed Ali	Leon Spinks	La Vegas
1979	Ray Leonard	Danny Lopez-Tony Ayala	Danny Lopez	San Antonio
1980	Thomas Hearns	Saad Muhammed-Danny Lopez	Saad Muhammed	McAfee, NJ
1981	Ray Leonard Salvador Sanchez	Ray Leonard-Tonny Hearns	Ray Leonard	Las Vegas
1982	Larry Holmes	Bobby Chacon-Rafael Limon	Bobby Chacon	Sacramento
1983	Marvin Hagler	Bobby Chacon-Cornelius Boza-Edwards	Bobby Chacon	Las Vegas
1984	Thomas Hearns	Jose Luis Ramirez-Edwin Rosario	Jose Luis Ramirez	San Juan
1985	Donald Curry Marvin Hagler	Marvin Hagler-Tommy Hearns	Marvin Hagler	Las Vegas
1986	Mike Tyson	Stevie Cruz-Barry McGuigan	Stevie Cruz	Las Vegas
1987	Evander Holyfield	Ray Leonard-Marvin Hagler	Ray Leonard	Las Vegas
1988	Mike Tyson	Tony Lopez-Rocky Lockridge	Tony Lopez	Inglewood, CA
1989	Pernell Whitaker	Roberto Duran-Iran Barkley	Roberto Duran	Atlantic City
1990	Julio César Chávez	Julio César Chávez-Meldrick Taylor	Julio César Chávez	Las Vegas
1991	James Toney	Robert Quiroga-Kid Akeem Anifowoshe	Robert Quiroga	San Antonio
1992	Riddick Bowe	Riddick Bowe-Evander Holyfield	Riddick Bowe	Las Vegas
1993	Michael Carbajal	Michael Carbajal-Humberto Gonzalez	Michael Carbajal	Las Vegas

U.S. Olympic Gold Medalists

LIGHT FLYWEIGHT

1984	Paul Gonzales

FLYWEIGHT

1904	George Finnegan
1920	Frank Di Gennara
1024	Fidel LaBarba
1952	Nathan Brooks
1976	Leo Randolph
1984	Steve McCrory

BANTAMWEIGHT

1904	Oliver Kirk
1988	Kennedy McKinney

FEATHERWEIGHT

1904	Oliver Kirk
1924	John Fields
1984	Meldrick Taylor

LIGHTWEIGHT

1904	Harry Spanger
1920	Samuel Mosberg
1968	Ronald W. Harris

LIGHTWEIGHT (Cont.)

1976	Howard Davis
1984	Pernell Whitaker
1992	Oscar De La Hoya

LIGHT WELTERWEIGHT

1952	Charles Adkins
1972	Ray Seales
1976	Ray Leonard
1984	Jerry Page

WELTERWEIGHT

1904	Albert Young
1932	Edward Flynn
1960	Wilbert McClure
1984	Mark Breland
1984	Frank Tate

MIDDLEWEIGHT

1904	Charles Mayer
1932	Carmen Bath
1952	Floyd Patterson
1960	Edward Crook
1976	Michael Spinks

LIGHT HEAVYWEIGHT

1920	Eddie Eagan
1952	Norvel Lee
1956	James Boyd
1960	Cassius Clay
1976	Leon Spinks
1988	Andrew Maynard

HEAVYWEIGHT

1984	Henry Tillman
1988	Ray Mercer

SUPER HEAVYWEIGHT

1904	Samuel Berger
1952	H. Edward Sanders
1956	T. Peter Rademacher
1964	Joe Frazier
1968	George Foreman
1984	Tyrell Biggs

Horse Racing

Sports Illustrated

BULL MARKET

A victory in the Blue Grass makes Holy Bull the colt to watch

JOHN W. McDONOUGH

A Year Full Of Bull

The season came down to a much awaited showdown
between Tabasco Cat and Holy Bull | by WILLIAM F. REED

O N THE SUNNY AFTERNOON OF Saturday, Aug. 20, before a restless crowd of 46,395 at venerable Saratoga in upstate New York, the two most compelling story lines of the 1994 thoroughbred racing year converged in the 125th running of the Travers Stakes.

The favorite was Holy Bull, the big gray colt that had been bequeathed to veteran trainer Jimmy Croll by the late Rachel Carpenter, his longtime patron. Known for his powerful front-running style, the Bull had captured five of his previous six starts by a combined total of almost 18 lengths. His only slip had come in the Kentucky Derby, where he disappointed his backers by finishing a mysterious 12th in a race won by Go for Gin.

His main challenger in the Travers figured to be Tabasco Cat, who had rebounded from a sixth-place finish in the Derby to win the Preakness and the Belmont Stakes, the other two legs of the sport's Triple Crown. The Cat's performance provided a badly needed boost to the career of trainer D. Wayne Lukas, who had slumped horribly in the '90s after setting new national standards for earnings and victories in the previous

decade. Ironically, Tabasco Cat had almost killed Jeff Lukas, Wayne's son and top assistant, in a stable accident on Dec. 15, 1993, at Santa Anita in California.

To make sure that Holy Bull wouldn't be able to get an easy lead, Lukas decided to use a "rabbit," which in racing parlance means a horse whose sole duty is to try to lure a front-runner into a suicidal speed duel in order to set up a winning finishing kick by his stablemate. In the Travers, the rabbit would be a fast horse named Commanche Trail.

When the starting gate sprung open, Commanche Trail, breaking from the outside post position, went hell-bent for the lead, which he briefly seized. With Commanche Trail on his flank, Holy Bull was under constant pressure. Although Holy Bull wrested the lead from Commanche Trail on the backstretch and drew off to a clear advantage, nobody, including Croll, was certain how much the Bull would have left coming out of the final turn and heading down the stretch. "I was a little concerned," admitted Croll later.

Concern, in fact, was the dominant emotion in the industry, however brave a face its leaders put on. At least the sport had a new

BILL FRAKES

leader in J. Brian McGrath, who was named the first commissioner of the Thoroughbred Racing Association, a coalition of most of the leading tracks in North America. McGrath, who came to racing with a strong background in international marketing and television, said he foresaw a bright future for racing. "This is not a business that's going out of business," said McGrath, ignoring reports that pari-mutuel betting dropped by $64 million in 1993 and that thoroughbred racing had lost 1.3% of its fan base.

Nevertheless, the news in 1994 was mostly good for the sport, at least as far as racing itself was concerned. For example:

• Popular jockey Julie Krone made a successful comeback from the serious injuries she had sustained during a 1993 racing accident at Saratoga.

• Older horses Lure and Paradise Creek staged a riveting rivalry in turf races.

• A pair of outstanding mares, Sky Beauty and Flawlessly, continued to dominate their competition in New York and California, respectively.

Tabasco Cat (left) was able to drive past Derby winner Go for Gin in the Preakness.

• And at Keeneland in July, a daughter of Mr. Prospector, out of Winning Colors, who in 1988 became only the third filly to win the Kentucky Derby, sold for $1.1 million, the top price in the track's annual yearling sales.

As usual, however, the focus was on the 3-year-olds who would compete in the Triple Crown. As the year began, Dehere and Brocco were virtually cofavorites to win the Kentucky Derby. Despite losing to Brocco last fall in the $1 million Breeders' Cup Juvenile at Santa Anita, Dehere was voted the 2-year-old championship by virtue of his five victories in seven starts. His other loss was to Holy Bull in the Belmont Futurity.

Dehere's owner, Robert Brennan, who also was chairman of the Board of Regents at Seton Hall University, named the colt for Terry Dehere, a former star guard for the Pirates' nationally prominent basketball team. After Dehere, the colt, had won three starts in August 1993, at Saratoga, Brennan

BILL FRAKES

With McCarron up, it was thumbs up for Go for Gin, an upset victor in the Derby.

eighth to Secretariat in 1973, and Bet Twice, who was second to Alysheba in 1987. "I just didn't want to go unless I had a real chance," Croll said. That was no bull, either, and the case of Al Hattab proves it. Many observers regarded that colt as a Derby contender in 1969, but Croll believed the Derby distance would be too much for the colt. When Croll told that to Carpenter, the colt's owner, she simply said, "Don't go."

Croll's prudence was rewarded in a surprising way. Years later Al Hattab sired a filly, Sharon Brown, who became a broodmare despite winning only three of 32 starts. Her fifth foal, born at Bonnie Heath Farm in Florida in 1991, was named Holy Bull, reportedly a tribute to his sire, Great Above, and to New York Yankee broadcaster Phil Rizzuto, whom Carpenter admired and whose trademark expression is "Holy cow!" Indeed, had he been born a filly, Holy Bull would have been Holy Cow.

Carpenter, a somewhat eccentric heiress to the A&P grocery fortune, hired Croll in 1957 and stayed with him until she died on Aug. 14, 1993, at 78. On the very day that Carpenter died, Holy Bull won his first start at Monmouth Park in New Jersey. After another win, he caught the racing world's attention in the Belmont Futurity by handing Dehere his first loss. "From then on," said Croll, "he just kept getting better."

Heading into the 1994 Kentucky Derby, the only blemish on Holy Bull's record was an off-the-board finish in the Fountain of Youth that was won by Dehere. However, he had an excuse that was no bull. After looming into contention at the top of the stretch, the Bull sustained a breathing problem, known as a "flipped palate," that ended his chances. But Croll made corrections and, in Dehere's absence, Holy Bull won the Florida Derby by a whopping 5¾ lengths. When he followed that with a 3½-length victory in the Blue Grass Stakes at Keeneland, he became the East's best hope to win the Kentucky Derby, far ahead of Go for Gin, who had finished second to Irgun in the Wood Memorial at Aqueduct in New York.

Tabasco Cat's route to the Derby had

held a press conference to announce that every penny of the colt's earnings would go into a new foundation to inspire inner-city youths to surrender their guns. Alas for Brennan and his noble cause, however, Dehere didn't make the Triple Crown races because of a leg injury he sustained between the Fountain of Youth Stakes, which he won, and the Florida Derby.

Croll, who turned 74 three days before Holy Bull's romp in the Florida Derby, took out his trainer's license in 1940. Although he had trained 59 stakes winners heading into 1994, he had run only two horses in the Kentucky Derby—Royal and Regal, who finished been overshadowed by tragedy. On the morning of Dec. 15, 1993, Lukas was standing outside his office when he heard a lot of commotion and then the thud he'll never forget. Tabasco Cat had gotten loose after a workout and had run over Jeff. As he bent over Jeff's crumpled body, Wayne initially thought his son was dead. "He never moved or moaned," Wayne said. When the paramedics arrived, the first thought was to take Jeff to a nearby hospital by ambulance. But one of the paramedics insisted it would be better to call a helicopter. "It landed right next to the barn," Wayne said. "If they'd used the ambulance, we would have lost him. As it was, we barely saved him."

For weeks Jeff, 36, was in a coma, his condition critical because of multiple injuries that included fractures at the base of his skull. When he finally woke up on Jan. 11, his dad was well on his way toward getting Tabasco Cat to the Kentucky Derby. Indeed, the colt went into the April 9 Santa Anita Derby off back-to-back victories in the El Camino Real at Bay Meadows and the San Rafael at Santa Anita. Although the Cat finished second in the Santa Anita Derby, just behind Brocco, Wayne Lukas shipped the colt to Churchill Downs with high hopes.

As it turned out, the 1994 Triple Crown did not settle much of anything. The Derby went to Go for Gin because of his ability to handle the sloppy surface at Churchill Downs, along with trainer Nick Zito's ability to get a colt at his best on the first Saturday in May. Only three years after getting his first Derby win with Strike the Gold, Zito did it again, with a big assist from the weatherman. Owned by Bill Condren and Joe Cornacchia, Go for Gin took the lead soon after the start and splashed to a two-length win over Strodes Creek. Brocco, Tabasco Cat and Holy Bull finished fourth, sixth and 12th, respectively.

On the Wednesday before the Preakness, Lukas arrived at Pimlico in Baltimore without the swagger of years past. A year earlier his colt Union City had broken a leg and had had to be destroyed, beginning what Lukas would come to think of as the Year from Hell. In the wake of the Preakness,

BILL FRAKES

Croll's 54-year career as a trainer was finally rewarded by the talented Holy Bull.

some turf writers accused him of knowingly running a lame horse. His critics said he was desperate to make a big score because his business empire was collapsing. Although Lukas eventually admitted that he had indeed suffered some financial setbacks, he went on the counterattack against those who intimated that he cared more about his finances than he did about his horses.

The Preakness field didn't include Brocco, who was being pointed toward the Belmont Stakes, or Holy Bull, who had embarked on a non–Triple Crown path that would enable him to regain much of his pre-Derby luster with victories in the Metropolitan, Dwyer and Haskell. As Holy Bull's victories piled up, his Derby peformance looked more puzzling. Unfortunately, the Churchill Downs stewards had failed to order postrace tests on Holy Bull, which would have eliminated the possiblility that somebody had given him a tranquilizer to affect his performance. Yet Bernie Hettel, chief steward in Kentucky, insisted he didn't think he needed to test the $2.20–$1 Derby favorite. "Holy Bull wasn't a prohibitive favorite, so I wasn't overly concerned about testing him," said Hettel.

In the Preakness, Tabasco Cat and jockey

Horse racing fans everywhere cheered Krone's return to the track.

who had unaccountably upset Tabasco Cat two weeks earlier in the Jim Dandy, and Concern, the Arkansas Derby winner who seemed to be coming to hand for trainer Dick Small.

As the race unfolded, Holy Bull's challenger after he had put away Commanche Trail wasn't Tabasco Cat, who didn't seem to like the track, but Concern, who, coming out of the turn for home, seemed to close a lot of ground in only a couple of strides. Mike Smith, riding Holy Bull, became so concerned that he began tapping his colt with the whip, a rare occurrence for the big, long-striding gray. After hanging for a few strides, Concern came on again inside the 16th pole, closing ground to the point that the stewards needed to see a photo before confirming Holy Bull as winner by a neck in the time of 2:02 on a track that was still sticky from hard rains on Thursday. Incredibly, Tabasco Cat never fired—Lukas blamed the track conditions—and finished third, 17 lengths back of the leaders.

In holding on, the Bull answered the critics who questioned his breeding and his ability to handle pressure. "He did what he had to do," said Croll, who had been inducted into racing's Hall of Fame only 12 days earlier. "They tried all ways to beat him, set the pace, everything. I was a little concerned at the eighth pole, but he dug in and held [Concern] off. In my heart I thought he would react O.K."

On the morning after the Travers, the last word belonged to Bob Coffey, who grooms Holy Bull for Croll. "He came and stomped the Cat and chewed up the rabbit," Coffey said before putting Holy Bull on a van for the return trip to his home base at Monmouth Park. "Now it's time to go home."

Pat Day came from off the pace to take a ¾-length victory over the gritty Go for Gin, giving Lukas his first victory in a Grade I race since October 1991. "It was an absolute script, just the way I wanted it to be," said Lukas, who refused the opportunity to lash out at his media critics. An hour after the race, as Lukas stood in the gathering twilight at Pimlico, a traffic helicopter flew low over the barn from which Tabasco Cat was being led out to graze. "I hate that noise," said Lukas, his smile momentarily becoming a frown. "Every time I hear it, I think about what happened to Jeff, and it makes me a little sick."

Tabasco Cat's subsequent victory in the Belmont—Go for Gin again was second—established him as the king of the 1994 Triple Crown, but it left open the question of whether he was better than Holy Bull, who had looked invincible since leaving Churchill Downs. Their showdown came in the Travers. The presence of the rabbit Commanche Trail added a new dimension. The only other horses in the field were Unaccounted For,

FOR THE RECORD·1993–1994

THOROUGHBRED RACING

The Triple Crown

120th Kentucky Derby

May 7, 1994. Grade I, 3-year-olds; 8th race, Churchill Downs, Louisville. All 126 lbs. Distance: 1¼ miles. Stakes value: $878,000; Winner: $628,800; Second: $145,000; Third: $70,000; Fourth: $35,000. Track: Cloudy and sloppy. Off: 5:34 p.m. Winner: Go for Gin (B c by Cormorant-Never Knock by Stage Door Johnny); Times: 0:22⅘, 0:47⅕, 1:11⅘, 1:37⅗; 2:03⅗. Won: Driving. Breeder: Darmstadt Pamela Du Pont.

Horse	Finish-PP	Margin	Jockey/Owner
Go for Gin	1-8	2	Chris McCarron/ Joseph Cornacchia and William Condren
Strodes Creek	2-7	2½	Eddie Delahoussaye/ Arthur Hancock et. al.
Blumin Affair	3-13	¾	Jerry Bailey/ Leroy Bowman and Art Vogel
Brocco	4-10	1¼	Gary Stevens / Mr. and Mrs. Albert Broccoli
Soul of the Matter	5-1	2½	Kent Desormeaux/ Burt Bacharach
Tabasco Cat	6-9	1¼	Pat Day/ Overbrook Farm and David Reynolds
Southern Rhythm	7-12	1½	Garrett Gomez/ Heiligbrodt, Keefer, New
Powis Castle	8-3	2	Chris Antley/ Vistas Stable
Mahogany Hall	9-6	½	Willie Martinez/ Robert Hoeweler
Smilin Singin Sam	10-11	2	Larry Melancon/ Dogwood Stable
Meadow Flight	11-14	2	Shane Sellers/ Aliyuee Ben J. Stable
Holy Bull	12-4	2	Mike Smith/ Jimmy Croll Jr.
Valiant Nature	13-2	15	Laffit Pincay Jr./ V H W Stable
Ulises	14-5	—	Jorge Chavez/ Robert Perez

119th Preakness Stakes

May 21, 1994. Grade I, 3-year-olds; 10th race, Pimlico Race Course, Baltimore. All 126 lbs. Distance: 1 3/16 miles; Stakes value: $686, 800; Winner: $447, 720; Second: $137,760; Third: $68,880; Fourth: $34,440. Track: Fast. Off: 5:32 p.m. Winner: Tabasco Cat (Ch C-Storm Cat-Barbicue Sauce by Sauce Boat); Times: 0:23⅗, 0:47⅖, 1:11⅘, 1:37, 1:56⅖. Won: Driving. Breeder: Overbrook Farm & Reynolds David (Ky).

Horse	Finish-PP	Margin	Jockey/Owner
Tabasco Cat	1-1	1¾	Pat Day/ Overbrook Farm and David Reynolds
Go for Gin	2-2	6	Chris McCarron/ William Condren and Joseph Cornacchia
*Concern	3-3	½	Garrett Gomez/ Robert E. Meyerhoff
Kandaly	4-7	1¾	Craig Perret/ R. Cole, R. Lamarque, L. Roussel
Numerous	5-10	½	Pat Valenzuela/ Howard B. Keck
Blumin Affair	6-6	2	Jerry Bailey/ Arthur Vogel and Leroy Bowman
*Looming	7-9	½	Andrea Seefeldt/ Robert E. Meyerhoff
Silver Goblin	8-4	¾	Dale Cordova/ Al J. Horton
Powis Castle	9-5	11	Brent Bartram/ Vistas Stable
Polar Expedition	10-8	—	Kurt Bourque/ James B. Cody

126th Belmont Stakes

June 11, 1994. Grade I, 3-year-olds; 9th race, Belmont Park, Elmont, NY. All 126 lbs. Distance: 1½ miles. Stakes purse: $653,800; Winner: $392,280; Second: $143, 836; Third: $78,456; Fourth: $39,228. Track: Fast. Off: 5:31 p.m. Winner: Tabasco Cat (Ch C, 3, Storm Cat-Barbicue Sauce by Sauce Boat); Times: 0:23⅘, 0:42⅖, 1:11⅕, 1:35⅖, 2:00⅘, 2:26⅘. Won: Driving. Breeder: Overbrook Farm and David Reynolds.

Horse	Finish-PP	Margin	Jockey/Owner
Tabasco Cat	1-2	2	Pat Day/ Overbrook Farm and David Reynolds
Go for Gin	2-1	½	Chris McCarron/ William Condren and Joseph Cornacchia
Strodes Creek	3-6	3½	Jerry Bailey/ Arthur Hancock
Signal Tap	4-3	5	Jose Santos/ Centennial Farm
Amathos	5-4	35	Mike Smith/ Mohammed al Maktoum
Ulises	6-5	—	Craig Perret/Robert Perez

Major Stakes Races

Late 1993

Date	Race	Track	Distance	Winner	Jockey/Trainer	Purse ($)
Sep 15 ....Del Mar Futura	Del Mar	7 furlongs	Winning Pact	Corey Nakatani/ Gary Jones	250,000
Sep 18 ....Man O' War Stakes	Belmont	1⅜ miles	Star of Cozzene	Jose Santos/ Mark Hennig	400,000
Sep 18 ....Woodward Stakes	Belmont	1⅛ miles	Bertrando	Gary Stevens/ Robert Frankel	500,000
Sep 19 ....Molson Export Million	Woodbine	1⅛ miles	Peteski	Craig Perret/ Roger Attfield	1,000,000
Oct 2.......Super Derby XIV	Louisiana	1¼ miles	Wallenda	Herb McCauley/ F. Alexander	750,000
Oct 3.......Prix De L'Arc De Triomphe	Longchamp	1½ miles	Urban Sea	Eric Saint-Martin/ J. Lesbordes	1,519,205
Oct 9.......Turf Classic	Belmont	1½ miles	Apple Tree	Mike Smith/ Andre Fabre	500,000
Oct 10.....Oak Tree Invitational	Santa Anita	1½ miles	Kotashaan	Kent Desormeaux/ R. Madella	400,000
Oct 15.....Meadowlands Cup	Meadowlands	1⅛ miles	Marquetry	Kent Desormeaux/ Robert Frankel	500,000
Oct 16.....Jockey Club Gold Cup	Belmont	1¼ miles	Miner's Mark	Chris McCarron/ Claude McGaughey	850,000
Oct 16.....Champagne Stakes	Belmont	1 mile	Dehere	Chris McCarron/ R. Nobles	500,000
Oct 17.....Rothmans International	Woodbine	1½ miles	Husband	C. Asmussen/ J. Fellows	1,038,500
Oct 23.....Washington D.C. Int'l.	Laurel	1 mile	Buckhar	Jean Cruguet/ W. Freeman	600,000
Nov 6 ......Breeders' Cup Classic	Santa Anita	1¼	Arcangues	Jerry Bailey/ Andre Fabre	3,000,000
Nov 6 ......Breeders' Cup Sprint	Santa Anita	6 furlongs	Cardmania	Eddie Delahoussaye/ D. Meredith	1,000,000
Nov 6 ......Breeders' Cup Juvenile Fillies	Santa Anita	1¹⁄₁₆ miles	Phone Chatter	Laffit Pincay/ R. Madella	1,000,000
Nov 6 ......Breeders' Cup Distaff	Santa Anita	1⅛ miles	Hollywood Wildcat	Eddie Delahoussaye/Nell Drysdale	1,000,000
Nov 6 ......Breeders' Cup Mile	Santa Anita	1 mile	Lure	Mike Smith/ Claude McGaughey	1,000,000
Nov 6 ......Breeders' Cup Juvenile	Santa Anita	1¹⁄₁₆ miles	Brocco	Gary Stevens/ R. Winick	2,000,000
Nov 6 ......Breeders' Cup Turf	Santa Anita	1½ miles	Kotashaan	Kent Desormeaux/ R. Mandella	2,000,000
Nov. 28 ...Matriarch Stakes	Hollywood Park	1⅛ miles	Flawlessly	Chris McCarron/ Charlie Whittingham	400,000
Nov 28 ....Japan Cup	Tokyo	1½ miles	Legacy World	Kent Desormeaux/ H. Mori	3,123,779
Dec 12....Hollywood Turf Cup	Hollywood Park	1½ miles	Fraise	Chris McCarron/ William Mott	500,000
Dec 19....Hollywood Futurity	Hollywood Park	1¹⁄₁₆ miles	Valiant Nature	Laffit Pincay, Jr/ Ron McAnally	500,000

1994 (Through August 29)

Date	Race	Track	Distance	Winner	Jockey/Trainer	Purse ($)
Feb 5 ......Donn Handicap	Gulfstream	1⅛ miles	Pistols and Roses	Herberto Castillo/ George Gianos	300,000
Feb 6 ......Charles H. Strub Stakes	Santa Anita	1¼ miles	Diazo	Laffit Pincay, Jr/ Bill Shoemaker	500,000
Feb 13 ....San Antonio Handicap	Santa Anita	1⅛ miles	The Wicked North	Kent Desormeaux/ D. Bernstein	268,000
Feb 20 ....Fountain of Youth Stakes	Gulfstream	1¹⁄₁₆ miles	Dehere	Craig Perret/ R. Nobles	200,000
Feb 21 ....San Luis Obispo Handicap	Santa Anita	1½ miles	Fanmore	Kent Desormeaux/ Robert Frankel	200,000
Mar 5 ......Santa Anita Handicap	Santa Anita	1¼ miles	Stuka	Chris Antley/ Gary Jones	1,000,000
Mar 6 ......Gulfstream Park Handicap	Gulfstream	1¼ miles	Scuffleburg	Craig Perret/ William Mott	500,000

1994 (Through August 29) *(Cont.)*

Date	Race	Track	Distance	Winner	Jockey/Trainer	Purse ($)
Mar 6	Santa Margarita Handicap	Santa Anita	1⅛ miles	Paseana	Chris McCarron/ Ron McAnally	300,000
Mar 12	Florida Derby	Gulfstream	1⅛ miles	Holy Bull	Mike Smith/ Jimmy Croll	500,000
Mar 13	Santa Anita Oaks	Santa Anita	1¹⁄₁₆ miles	Lakeway	Kent Desormeaux/ Gary Jones	200,000
Mar 13	Pan American Handicap	Gulfstream	1½ miles	Fraise	Mike Smith/ William Mott	300,000
Mar 19	Louisiana Derby	Fairgrounds	1¹⁄₁₆ miles	Kandaly	Craig Perret/ L. Roussel	326,250
Mar 26	Gotham Stakes	Aqueduct	1 mile	Irgun	Jerry Bailey/ S. Young	250,000
Apr 2	Jim Beam Stakes	Turfway Park	1⅛ miles	Polar Expedition	Curt Bourque/ H. Robertson	600,000
Apr 9	Santa Anita Derby	Santa Anita	1⅛ miles	Brocco	Gary Stevens/ R. Winick	500,000
Apr 9	Remington Park Derby	Remington Park	1¹⁄₁₆ miles	Smilin Singin Sam	Larry Melcancon/ N. O'Calllaghan	300,000
Apr 16	Wood Memorial Stakes	Aqueduct	1⅛ miles	Irgun	Gary Stevens/ S. Young	500,000
Apr 16	Oaklawn Handicap	Oaklawn Park	1⅛ miles	The Wicked North	Kent Desormeaux/ D. Bernstein	750,000
Apr 16	Blue Grass Stakes	Keeneland	1⅛ miles	Holy Bull	Mike Smith/ Jimmy Croll	500,000
Apr 17	Fantasy Stakes	Oaklawn Park	1¹⁄₁₆ miles	Two Altazano	Kirk LeBlanc/ M. Stidham	250,000
Apr 22	Apple Blossom Handicap	Oaklawn Park	1¹⁄₁₆ miles	Nine Keys	Mike Smith/ A. Penna, Jr.	500,000
Apr 23	Arkansas Derby	Oaklawn Park	1⅛ miles	Concern	Garrett Gomez/ Richard Small	500,000
Apr 30	Illinois Derby	Sportsmen Park	1⅛ miles	Rustic Light	Early Fires/ R. Hale	500,000
May 7	Kentucky Derby	Churchill Downs	1¼ miles	Go for Gin	Chris McCarron/ Nick Zito	878,800
May 14	Pimlico Special Handicap	Pimlico	1³⁄₁₆ miles	As Indicated	Robbie Davis/ Rick Schosberg	600,000
May 15	Preakness Stakes	Pimlico	1³⁄₁₆ miles	Tabasco Cat	Pat Day/ D. Wayne Lukas	688,800
May 30	Hollywood Turf Handicap	Hollywood Park	1¼ miles	Grand Flotilla	Gary Stevens/ J. Sahadi	500,000
May 30	Metropolitan Handicap	Belmont	1 mile	Holy Bull	Mike Smith/ Jimmy Croll	500,000
June 1	Ever Ready (Epsom) Derby	Epsom Downs	1½ miles	Erhaab	Willie Carson/ J. Dunlop	1,172,174
June 5	Californian Stakes	Hollywood Park	1⅛ miles	The Wicked North	Kent Desormeaux/ D. Berstein	300,000
June 11	Belmont Stakes	Belmont	1½ miles	Tabasco Cat	Pat Day/ D. Wayne Lukas	500,000
June 26	Caesars International	Atlantic City	1³⁄₁₆ miles	Lure	Mike Smith/ Claude McGaughey	500,000
June 27	Budweiser Irish Derby	The Curragh	1½ miles	Balanchine	L. Dettori/ H. Ibrahim	900,900
July 2	Hollywood Gold Cup	Hollywood Park	1¼ miles	Slew of Damascus	Gary Stevens/ C. Roberts	750,000
July 3	Beverly Hills Handicap	Hollywood Park	1⅛ miles	Corrazona	Gary Stevens/ Richard Mandella	323,400
July 3	Arlington Classic	Arlington	1⅛ miles	Eagle Eye	Corey Nakatani/ Robert Frankel	300,000
July 4	Suburban Handicap	Belmont	1¼ miles	Devil His Due	Mike Smith/ Allen Jerkens	350,000
July 10	Queen's Plate	Woodbine	1¼ miles	Basqueian	Jim Lauzon/ D. Vella	396,000
July 24	Vanity Invitational Handicap	Hollywood Park	1⅛ miles	Potridee	Alex Solis/ Ron McNally	300,000

Major Stakes Races (Cont.)

1994 (Through August 29) (Cont.)

Date	Race	Track	Distance	Winner	Jockey/Trainer	Purse ($)
July 31	Haskell Invitational	Monmouth	1⅛ miles	Holy Bull	Mike Smith/ Jimmy Croll	500,000
Aug 6	Ramona Handicap	Del Mar	1⅛ miles	Flawlessly	Chris McCarron/ Charlie Whittingham	300,000
Aug 13	Pacific Classic	Del Mar	1¼ miles	Tinners Way	Eddie Delahous-saye/Robert Frankel	1,000,000
Aug 20	Travers Stakes	Saratoga	1¼ miles	Holy Bull	Mike Smith/ Jimmy Croll	750,000
Aug 27	Whitney Handicap	Saratoga	1⅛ miles	Colonial Affair	Jose Santos/ Scotty Schulhofer	350,000
Aug 27	Beverly D Stakes	Arlington	1$^{3}/_{16}$ miles	Hatoof	Walter Swinburn/ C. Head	300,000
Aug 28	Secretariat Stakes	Arlington	1¼ miles	Vaudeville	Gary Stevens/ F. Fierce	400,000
Aug 28	Arlington Million	Arlington	1¼ miles	Paradise Creek	Pat Day/ William Mott	1,000,000
Aug 28	The Hopeful	Saratoga	7 furlongs	Wild Escapade	Jorge Chevez/ L. O'Brien	200,000
Aug 29	The Spinaway	Saratoga	7 furlongs	Flanders	Pat Day/ D. Wayne Lukas	200,000

1993 Statistical Leaders

Horses

Horse	Starts	1st	2nd	3rd	Purses ($)
Kotashaan	10	6	3	0	2,619,014
Sea Hero	9	2	0	2	2,484,190
Bertrando	9	3	4	1	2,227,800
Devil His Due	11	4	2	1	1,939,120
Star of Cozzene	12	6	4	0	1,776,071
Arcangues	1	1	0	0	1,560,000
Prairie Bayou	8	5	2	0	1,405,521
Kissin Kris	12	2	4	2	1,341,292
Peteski	10	7	2	1	1,287,150
Lure	8	6	2	0	1,212,323

Jockeys

Jockey	Mounts	1st	2nd	3rd	Purses ($)	Win Pct	$ Pct*
Mike Smith	1,510	343	235	214	14,008,148	.23	.53
Kent Desormeaux	1,214	279	208	162	13,206,031	.23	.54
Jerry Bailey	1,104	209	163	148	12,360,114	.19	.47
Chris McCarron	963	157	168	157	11,673,795	.16	.50
Gary Stevens	1,236	248	223	177	11,598,946	.20	.52
Eddie Delahoussaye	1,213	228	190	169	10,315,419	.19	.48
Pat Day	1,049	263	209	152	8,901,194	.25	.60
Jose Santos	1,169	191	188	158	8,729,705	.16	.46
C.S. Nakatani	1,226	206	182	155	8,210,269	.17	.44
Laffit Pincay, Jr	1,222	166	172	169	6,743,689	.14	.42

*Percentage in the Money (1st, 2nd, and 3rd)

Bonne Chance

The French colt Arcangues was the longest shot in the field of 13 at the Breeders' Cup Classic last November in Arcadia, Calif. The infield tote board couldn't even reflect how long a shot Arcangues was because the boards numbers only go as high as 99-1, and the horse's odds were 133-1. The 5-year-old, trained by Fenchman Andre Fabre, is by Sagace and is out of the Irish River mare Albertine. Carrying Jockey Jerry Bailey in the Classic, Arcangues miraculously came home a winner in 2:00⅗. The winning payoff on a $2 bet was $269.20, the biggest in the ten year history of the Breeders' Cup.

Trainers

Trainer	Starts	1st	2nd	3rd	Purses ($)	Win Pct	$ Pct*
Robert Frankel	346	79	55	40	8,883,252	.23	.50
Richard E. Mandella	344	65	66	51	6,586,592	.19	.53
Claude McGaughey	95	25	17	11	4,519,338	.26	.56
Roger L. Attfield	101	27	15	9	3,414,880	.27	.50
Ronald McNally	117	17	19	25	3,359,384	.15	.52
Allen H. Jerkens	66	18	12	7	3,350,682	.27	.56
Mark Hennig	97	19	24	11	3,243,565	.20	.56
Gary F. Jones	96	23	12	16	3,237,942	.24	.53
MacKenzie Miller	25	7	2	4	3,001,724	.28	.52
William L. Mott	104	18	20	23	2,736,224	.17	.59

*Percentage in the Money (1st, 2nd, and 3rd)

Owners

Owner	Starts	1st	2nd	3rd	Purses ($)	Stable Leader
John Franks	1,077	176	176	140	5,682,786	Kissin Kris
Golden Eagle Farm	608	101	108	65	3,613,066	Best Pal
Rokeby Stable	119	27	20	18	3,596,335	Sea Hero
Loblolly Stable	204	50	28	32	3,301,307	Prairie Bayou
Frank Stronach	384	73	63	60	3,012,898	Explosive Red
Allen E. Paulson	374	65	49	51	2,664,813	Cleone
Juddmonte Farms	186	33	34	25	2,354,384	Toussaud
Team Valor	100	23	24	8	2,264,985	Star of Cozzene
La Presle Farms	16	7	2	0	2,640,864	Kotashaan
Lion Crest Stable	17	6	3	3	1,998,800	Devil His Due

Note: 1993 statistical leaders courtesy of *Daily Racing Form*.

HARNESS RACING

Major Stakes Races (late 1993)

Date	Race	Location	Winner	Driver/Trainer	Purse ($)
Oct 8	Kentucky Futurity	Lexington Red Mile	Pine Chip	John Campbell/ Chuck Sylvester	141,300
Oct 8	BC Three-Year-Old Filly/Mare Pace	Mohawk	Swing Back	Kelly Sheppard/ Tod Sheppard	330,675
Oct 8	BC Three-Year-Old Mare Trot	Mohawk	Lifetime Dream	Paul MacDonnell/ George Elliott	330,675
Oct 8	BC Aged Horse/ Gelding Pace	Mohawk	Staying Together	Bill O'Donnell/ Bob McIntosh	396,810
Oct 8	BC Aged Horse/ Gelding Trot	Mohawk	Earl	Chris Christoforou,Jr/ Chris Christoforou	396,810
Oct 23	BC Two-Year-Old Colt/Gelding Pace	Freehold	Expensive Scooter	Jack Moiseyev/ Bill Robinson	300,000
Oct 23	BC Two-Year-Old Filly Pace	Freehold	Electric Slide	Mike LaChance/ Bob McIntosh	300,000
Oct 23	BC Three-Year-Old Colt/Gelding Pace	Freehold	Life Sign	John Campbell/ Gene Riegle	300,000
Oct 23	BC Three-Year-Old Filly Pace	Freehold	Immortality	John Campbell/ Bob McIntosh	300,000
Oct 29	BC Two-Year-Old Colt/Gelding Trot	Pompano Harness	Westgate Crown	John Campbell/ Raz McKenzie	300,000
Oct 29	BC Three-Year-Old Colt/Gelding Trot	Pompano Harness	Pine Chip	John Campbell/ Chuck Sylvester	300,000
Oct 29	BC Three-Year-Old Filly Trot	Pampano Harness	Expressway Hanover	Per Henriksen/ Per Henriksen	300,000
Oct 29	Two-Year-Old Filly Trot	Pompano	Gleam	Jimmy Takter/ Jimmy Takter	300,000
Nov 20	Governor's Cup	Garden State	Magical Mike	John Campbell/ Tom Haughton	550,000

1994 (Through September 3)

Date	Race	Location	Winner	Driver/Trainer	Purse ($)
June 25	North America Cup	Woodbine	Cam's Card Shark	John Campbell/ Bill Robinson	1,000,000
July 2	Messenger Stakes	Rosecraft	Cam's Card Shark	John Campbell/ Bill Robinson	342,595
July 9	Yonkers Trot	Yonkers Raceway	Bullville Victory	Cat Manzi/ Per Eriksson	381,280
July 16	Meadowlands Pace	Meadowlands	Cam's Card Shark	John Campbell/ Bill Robinson	1,000,000
Aug 2	Peter Haughton Memorial	Meadowlands	Donerail	John Campbell/ Stanley Dark	564,750
Aug 3	Merrie Annabelle	Meadowlands	Cr Kay Suzie	Carl Allen/ Carl Allen	385,500
Aug 6	Hambletonian	Meadowlands	Victory Dream	Mike LaChance Ron Gurfein	1,200,000
Aug 6	Hambletonian Oaks	Meadowlands	Gleam	Malvern Burroughs/ Jimmy Takter	375,000
Aug 13	Woodrow Wilson	Meadowlands	Dontgetinmyway	John Campbell/ Bill Robinson	774,750
Aug 13	Sweetheart	Meadowlands	Efishnc	Ron Waples/ Bruce Hickel	567,500
Aug 14	Adios	Meadows	Cam's Card Shark	John Campbell/ Bill Robinson	427,520
Aug 27	Cane Pace	Yonkers Raceway	Falcons Future	Ken Holliday/ Lonnie McIntosh	391,780
Sep 3	World Trotting Derby	DuQuoin	Bullville Victory	William Fahy/ Per Eriksson	650,000

Major Races

The Hambletonian

Horse	Driver	PP	¼	½	¾	Stretch	Finish
Victory Dream	Michel LaChance	1	2	1	1	1-2½	1-2¾
Mr. Lavec	Jimmy Takter	3	1	2	2	2-2½	2-2¾
Bye Tsem	Joe Hudon, Jr	10	6	6	4	4-4¼	3-4
Smasher	Bill O'Donnell	4	7	7	6	5-5¼	4-4¾
Federal Yankee	D.R. Ackerman	5	9	8	8	6-7¾	5-6¾
Bullville Victory	John Campbell	2	3	3	5	3-2¾	6-7¾
Bosphorus	Ron Waples	8	8	4	3	7-8	7-14
Call Upson	Cat Manzi	7	4	5	7	8-9¼	8-15
Space Probe	William Fahy	9	10	10	9	9-dis	9-30
Gum Ball	Mickey McNichol	6	5	9	10	10-dis	10-46

Time: :26.3; :56.1; 1:25.4; 1:54.1; Fast

The Little Brown Jug*

Horse	Driver	PP	¼	½	¾	Stretch	Finish
Life Sign	John Campbell	2	4	3	2	2	1-½
Riyadh	Jim Morrill	1	1	1	1	1	2-½
Presidential Ball	Jack Moiseyev	3	2	2	3	3	3-¾
Ready To Rumble	Joe Pavia Jr.	4	3	4	5	4	4-½
Getting Personal	J. Stark	7	7	6	6	6	5-3
Captain Pantastic	Walter Case	6	6	5	4	5	6-4
Native Born	Bill O'Donnell	5	5	7	7	7	7-4¾
Incoreyable Big	K. O'Donnell	8	8	8	8	8	8

Time: :27.0; :56.0; 1:23.4; 1:52.0; Fast

*1993 result

1993 Statistical Leaders

1993 Leading Moneywinners by Age, Sex and Gait

Division	Horse	Starts	1st	2nd	3rd	Earnings ($)
2-Year-Old Pacing Colts	Magical Mike	16	13	1	0	769,408
2-Year-Old Pacing Fillies	Freedom's Friend	11	6	3	0	600,412
3-Year-Old Pacing Colts	Presidential Ball	25	17	5	2	2,222,166
3-Year-Old Pacing Fillies	Ellamony	20	16	1	2	581,335
Aged Pacing Horses	Staying Together	26	21	1	0	1,169,155
Aged Pacing Mares	Shady Daisy	32	13	7	4	500,605
2-Year-Old Trotting Colts	Westgate Crown	8	7	0	1	766,626
2-Year-Old Trotting Fillies	Armbro Monarch	11	8	2	1	441,071
3-Year-Old Trotting Colts	Pine Chip	24	16	3	1	1,363,483
3-Year-Old Trotting Fillies	Winky's Goal	19	10	3	1	525,105
Aged Trotting Horses	Earl	18	12	2	1	502,753
Aged Trotting Mares	Lifetime Dream	18	4	2	4	218,587

Drivers

Driver	Earnings ($)	Driver	Earnings ($)
John Campbell	9,926,482	Dave Magee	4,020,128
Jack Moiseyev	8,202,270	Michel Lachance	3,912,458
Ron Pierce	4,940,990	Ron Waples	3,858,663
Cat Manzi	4,727,416	Stev Condren	3,212,218
Doug Brown	4,446,467	Bill O'Donnell	3,210,542

Back on Track

Johnny Longden, 87, is the tenth winningest jockey of all time and a member of the horse racing Hall of Fame. After losing his wife of 52 years to breast cancer in 1989, Johnny, who was known as the Pumper during his riding days for his hard driving style, moved to a retirement community in Banning, Calif. There his days became increasingly lonely. An hour and a half from the track at Santa Anita, Longden's new home offered no diversion. Anguished by any reminder of the track, he boxed up his trophies and other mementos and sent them off to an auction house. Fortunately his son Vance, 67, intervened before any of the relics were sold.

Vance also suggested his father get back into racing as an owner. The two began going to horse auctions, driving up and down the California coast looking at yearlings and unraced 2-year-olds. Longden spotted Our Blue Michael at a sale in Pomona, Calif. in 1993. "That's a good looking colt," he told his son. "If I buy him, will you train him?" "Done," Vance replied. At the drop of a gavel Longden was back in the horse business. Suddenly he was alive again. He planted orchids in his tiny garden. He was on the phone daily to Vance—unless he was at the track monitoring Blue's workouts. And after the workouts he would head over to the kitchen to play gin rummy with the backstretch workers. Although Our Blue Michael has done much to regenerate Longden, the same cannot be said of Longden's effect on Blue. In 13 starts the colt has won once and finished in the money three other times. But to see Longden watching one of Blues' races, his knuckles white from gripping his cane, is to see Johnny become the Pumper, once more.

THEY SAID IT

Nick Zito, trainer of Kentucky Derby winner Go for Gin, on the importance of consistent workouts: "A lot of horses get distracted. It's just human nature"

FOR THE RECORD · Year by Year

THOROUGHBRED RACING

Kentucky Derby

Run at Churchill Downs, Louisville, KY, on the first Saturday in May.

Year	Winner (Margin)	Jockey	Second	Third	Time
1875	Aristides (1)	Oliver Lewis	Volcano	Verdigris	2:37¾
1876	Vagrant (2)	Bobby Swim	Creedmoor	Harry Hill	2:38¼
1877	Baden-Baden (2)	William Walker	Leonard	King William	2:38
1878	Day Star (2)	Jimmie Carter	Himyar	Leveler	2:37¼
1879	Lord Murphy (1)	Charlie Shauer	Falsetto	Strathmore	2:37
1880	Fonso (1)	George Lewis	Kimball	Bancroft	2:37½
1881	Hindoo (4)	Jimmy McLaughin	Lelex	Alfambra	2:40
1882	Apollo (½)	Babe Hurd	Runnymede	Bengal	2:40¼
1883	Leonatus (3)	Billy Donohue	Drake Carter	Lord Raglan	2:43
1884	Buchanan (2)	Isaac Murphy	Loftin	Audrain	2:40¼
1885	Joe Cotton (Neck)	Erskine Henderson	Bersan	Ten Booker	2:37¼
1886	Ben Ali (½)	Paul Duffy	Blue Wing	Free Knight	2:36½
1887	Montrose (2)	Isaac Lewis	Jim Gore	Jacobin	2:39¼
1888	MacBeth II (1)	George Covington	Gallifet	White	2:38¼
1889	Spokane (Nose)	Thomas Kiley	Proctor Knott	Once Again	2:34½
1890	Riley (2)	Isaac Murphy	Bill Letcher	Robespierre	2:45
1891	Kingman (1)	Isaac Murphy	Balgowan	High Tariff	2:52¼
1892	Azra (Nose)	Alonzo Clayton	Huron	Phil Dwyer	2:41½
1893	Lookout (5)	Eddie Kunze	Plutus	Boundless	2:39¼
1894	Chant (2)	Frank Goodale	Pearl Song	Sigurd	2:41
1895	Halma (3)	Soup Perkins	Basso	Laureate	2:37½
1896	Ben Brush (Nose)	Willie Simms	Ben Eder	Semper Ego	2:07¼
1897	Typhoon II (Head)	Buttons Garner	Ornament	Dr. Catlett	2:12½
1898	Plaudit (Neck)	Willie Simms	Lieber Karl	Isabey	2:09
1899	Manuel (2)	Fred Taral	Corsini	Mazo	2:12
1900	Lieut. Gibson (4)	Jimmy Boland	Florizar	Thrive	2:06¼
1901	His Eminence (2)	Jimmy Winkfield	Sannazarro	Driscoll	2:07¾
1902	Alan-a-Dale (Nose)	Jimmy Winkfield	Inventor	The Rival	2:08¾
1903	Judge Himes (¾)	Hal Booker	Early	Bourbon	2:09
1904	Elwood (½)	Frankie Prior	Ed Tierney	Brancas	2:08½
1905	Agile (3)	Jack Martin	Ram's Horn	Layson	2:10¾
1906	Sir Huon (2)	Roscoe Troxler	Lady Navarre	James Reddick	2:08 ⅕
1907	Pink Star (2)	Andy Minder	Zal	Ovelando	2:12⅗
1908	Stone Street (1)	Arthur Pickens	Sir Cleges	Dunvegan	2:15⅕
1909	Wintergreen (4)	Vincent Powers	Miami	Dr. Barkley	2:08⅕
1910	Donau (½)	Fred Herbert	Joe Morris	Fighting Bob	2:06⅖
1911	Meridian (¾)	George Archibald	Governor Gray	Colston	2:05
1912	Worth (Neck)	Carroll H. Schilling	Duval	Flamma	2:09⅖
1913	Donerail (½)	Roscoe Goose	Ten Point	Gowell	2:04⅘
1914	Old Rosebud (8)	John McCabe	Hodge	Bronzewing	2:03⅖
1915	Regret (2)	Joe Notter	Pebbles	Sharpshooter	2:05⅖
1916	George Smith (Neck)	Johnny Loftus	Star Hawk	Franklin	2:04
1917	Omar Khayyam (2)	Charles Borel	Ticket	Midway	2:04⅗
1918	Exterminator (1)	William Knapp	Escoba	Viva America	2:10⅘
1919	Sir Barton (5)	Johnny Loftus	Billy Kelly	Under Fire	2:09⅘
1920	Paul Jones (Head)	Ted Rice	Upset	On Watch	2:09
1921	Behave Yourself (Head)	Charles Thompson	Black Servant	Prudery	2:04⅕
1922	Morvich (½)	Albert Johnson	Bet Mosie	John Finn	2:04⅗
1923	Zev (1½)	Earl Sande	Martingale	Vigil	2:05⅖
1924	Black Gold (½)	John Mooney	Chilhowee	Beau Butler	2:05⅕
1925	Flying Ebony (1½)	Earl Sande	Captain Hal	Son of John	2:07⅗
1926	Bubbling Over (5)	Albert Johnson	Bagenbaggage	Rock Man	2:03⅘
1927	Whiskery (Head)	Linus McAtee	Osmond	Jock	2:06
1928	Reigh Count (3)	Chick Lang	Misstep	Toro	2:10⅖
1929	Clyde Van Dusen (2)	Linus McAtee	Naishapur	Panchio	2:10⅘
1930	Gallant Fox (2)	Earl Sande	Gallant Knight	Ned O.	2:07⅗

Kentucky Derby (Cont.)

Year	Winner (Margin)	Jockey	Second	Third	Time
1931	Twenty Grand (4)	Charles Kurtsinger	Sweep All	Mate	2:01⅘
1932	Burgoo King (5)	Eugene James	Economic	Stepenfetchit	2:05⅕
1933	Brokers Tip (Nose)	Don Meade	Head Play	Charley O.	2:06⅘
1934	Cavalcade (2½)	Mack Garner	Discovery	Agrarian	2:04
1935	Omaha (1½)	Willie Saunders	Roman Soldier	Whiskolo	2:05
1936	Bold Venture (Head)	Ira Hanford	Brevity	Indian Broom	2:03⅗
1937	War Admiral (1¾)	Charles Kurtsinger	Pompoon	Reaping Reward	2:03⅕
1938	Lawrin (1)	Eddie Arcaro	Dauber	Can't Wait	2:04⅘
1939	Johnstown (8)	James Stout	Challedon	Heather Broom	2:03⅗
1940	Gallahadion (1½)	Carroll Bierman	Bimelech	Dit	2:05
1941	Whirlaway (8)	Eddie Arcaro	Staretor	Market Wise	2:01⅖
1942	Shut Out (2½)	Wayne Wright	Alsab	Valdina Orphan	2:04⅖
1943	Count Fleet (3)	John Longden	Blue Swords	Slide Rule	2:04
1944	Pensive (4½)	Conn McCreary	Broadcloth	Stir Up	2:04⅕
1945	Hoop Jr. (6)	Eddie Arcaro	Pot o' Luck	Darby Dieppe	2:07
1946	Assault (8)	Warren Mehrtens	Spy Song	Hampden	2:06⅗
1947	Jet Pilot (Head)	Eric Guerin	Phalanx	Faultless	2:06⅘
1948	Citation (3½)	Eddie Arcaro	Coaltown	My Request	2:05⅖
1949	Ponder (3)	Steve Brooks	Capot	Palestinian	2:04⅕
1950	Middleground (1¼)	William Boland	Hill Prince	Mr. Trouble	2:01⅗
1951	Count Turf (4)	Conn McCreary	Royal Mustang	Ruhe	2:02⅗
1952	Hill Gail (2)	Eddie Arcaro	Sub Fleet	Blue Man	2:01⅗
1953	Dark Star (Head)	Hank Moreno	Native Dancer	Invigorator	2:02
1954	Determine (1½)	Ray York	Hasty Road	Hasseyampa	2:03
1955	Swaps (1½)	Bill Shoemaker	Nashua	Summer Tan	2:01⅘
1956	Needles (¾)	Dave Erb	Fabius	Come On Red	2:03⅖
1957	Iron Liege (Nose)	Bill Hartack	Gallant Man	Round Table	2:02⅕
1958	Tim Tam (½)	Ismael Valenzuela	Lincoln Road	Noureddin	2:05
1959	Tomy Lee (Nose)	Bill Shoemaker	Sword Dancer	First Landing	2:02⅕
1960	Venetian Way (3½)	Bill Hartack	Bally Ache	Victoria Park	2:02⅖
1961	Carry Back (¾)	John Sellers	Crozier	Bass Clef	2:04
1962	Decidedly (2¼)	Bill Hartack	Roman Line	Ridan	2:00⅖
1963	Chateaugay (1¼)	Braulio Baeza	Never Bend	Candy Spots	2:01⅘
1964	Northern Dancer (Neck)	Bill Hartack	Hill Rise	The Scoundrel	2:00
1965	Lucky Debonair (Neck)	Bill Shoemaker	Dapper Dan	Tom Rolfe	2:01⅕
1966	Kauai King (½)	Don Brumfield	Advocator	Blue Skyer	2:02
1967	Proud Clarion (1)	Bobby Ussery	Barbs Delight	Damascus	2:00⅗
1968	Forward Pass (Disq.)	Ismael Valenzuela	Francie's Hat	T.V. Commercial	2:02⅕
1969	Majestic Prince (Neck)	Bill Hartack	Arts and Letters	Dike	2:01⅘
1970	Dust Commander (5)	Mike Manganello	My Dad George	High Echelon	2:03⅖
1971	Canonero II (3¾)	Gustavo Avila	Jim French	Bold Reason	2:03⅕
1972	Riva Ridge (3¼)	Ron Turcotte	No Le Hace	Hold Your Peace	2:01⅘
1973	Secretariat (2-½)	Ron Turcotte	Sham	Our Native	1:59⅖
1974	Cannonade (2¼)	Angel Cordero Jr	Hudson County	Agitate	2:04
1975	Foolish Pleasure (1¾)	Jacinto Vasquez	Avatar	Diabolo	2:02
1976	Bold Forbes (1)	Angel Cordero Jr	Honest Pleasure	Elocutionist	2:01⅗
1977	Seattle Slew (1¾)	Jean Cruguet	Run Dusty Run	Sanhedrin	2:02⅕
1978	Affirmed (1¼)	Steve Cauthen	Alydar	Believe It	2:01⅕
1979	Spectacular Bid (2¾)	Ronald J. Franklin	General Assembly	Golden Act	2:02⅖
1980	Genuine Risk (1)	Jacinto Vasquez	Rumbo	Jaklin Klugman	2:02
1981	Pleasant Colony (¾)	Jorge Velasquez	Woodchopper	Partez	2:02
1982	Gato Del Sol (2½)	Eddie Delahoussaye	Laser Light	Reinvested	2:02⅕
1983	Sunny's Halo (2)	Eddie Delahoussaye	Desert Wine	Caveat	2:02⅕
1984	Swale (3¼)	Laffit Pincay Jr	Coax Me Chad	At the Threshold	2:02⅖
1985	Spend A Buck (5)	Angel Cordero Jr	Stephan's Odyssey	Chief's Crown	2:00⅕
1986	Ferdinand (2¼)	Bill Shoemaker	Bold Arrangement	Broad Brush	2:02⅘
1987	Alysheba (¾)	Chris McCarron	Bet Twice	Avies Copy	2:03⅖
1988	Winning Colors (Neck)	Gary Stevens	Forty Niner	Risen Star	2:02⅕
1989	Sunday Silence (2½)	Pat Valenzuela	Easy Goer	Awe Inspiring	2:05
1990	Unbridled (3½)	Craig Perret	Summer Squall	Pleasant Tap	2:02
1991	Strike the Gold (1¾)	Chris Antley	Best Pal	Mane Minister	2:03
1992	Lil E. Tee (1)	Pat Day	Casual Lies	Dance Floor	2:03
1993	Sea Hero (2½)	Jerry Bailey	Prairie Bayou	Wild Gale	2:02⅖
1994	Go for Gin (2½)	Chris McCarron	Strodes Creek	Blumin Affair	2:03⅗

Note: Distance: 1½ miles (1875-95), 1¼ miles (1896-present).

Preakness

Run at Pimlico Race Course, Baltimore, Md., two weeks after the Kentucky Derby.

Year	Winner (Margin)	Jockey	Second	Third	Time
1873	Survivor (10)	G. Barbee	John Boulger	Artist	2:43
1874	Culpepper (¾)	W. Donohue	King Amadeus	Scratch	2:56½
1875	Tom Ochiltree (2)	L. Hughes	Viator	Bay Final	2:43½
1876	Shirley (4)	G. Barbee	Rappahannock	Algerine	2:44¾
1877	Cloverbrook (4)	C. Holloway	Bombast	Lucifer	2:45½
1878	Duke of Magenta (6)	C. Holloway	Bayard	Albert	2:41¾
1879	Harold (3)	L. Hughes	Jericho	Rochester	2:40½
1880	Grenada (¾)	L. Hughes	Oden	Emily F.	2:40½
1881	Saunterer (½)	T. Costello	Compensation	Baltic	2:40½
1882	Vanguard (Neck)	T. Costello	Heck	Col Watson	2:44½
1883	Jacobus (4)	G. Barbee	Parnell		2:42½
1884	Knight of Ellerslie (2)	S. Fisher	Welcher		2:39½
1885	Tecumseh (2)	Jim McLaughlin	Wickham	John C.	2:49
1886	The Bard (3)	S. Fisher	Eurus	Elkwood	2:45
1887	Dunboyne (1)	W. Donohue	Mahoney	Raymond	2:39½
1888	Refund (3)	F. Littlefield	Judge Murray	Glendale	2:49
1889	Buddhist (8)	W. Anderson	Japhet		2:17½
1890*	Montague (3)	W. Martin	Philosophy	Barrister	2:36¾
1894	Assignee (3)	Fred Taral	Potentate	Ed Kearney	1:49¼
1895	Belmar (1)	Fred Taral	April Fool	Sue Kittie	1:50½
1896	Margrave (1)	H. Griffin	Hamilton II	Intermission	1:51
1897	Paul Kauvar (1½)	C. Thorpe	Elkins	On Deck	1:51¼
1898	Sly Fox (2)	C. W. Simms	The Huguenot	Nuto	1:49⅗
1899	Half Time (1)	R. Clawson	Filigrane	Lackland	1:47
1900	Hindus (Head)	H. Spencer	Sarmation	Ten Candles	1:48⅖
1901	The Parader (2)	F. Landry	Sadie S.	Dr. Barlow	1:47⅕
1902	Old England (Nose)	L. Jackson	Major Daingerfield	Namtor	1:45⅘
1903	Flocarline (½)	W. Gannon	Mackey Dwyer	Rightful	1:44⅘
1904	Bryn Mawr (1)	E. Hildebrand	Wotan	Dolly Spanker	1:44⅕
1905	Cairngorm (Head)	W. Davis	Kiamesha	Coy Maid	1:45⅘
1906	Whimsical (4)	Walter Miller	Content	Larabie	1:45
1907	Don Enrique (1)	G. Mountain	Ethon	Zambesi	1:45⅖
1908	Royal Tourist (4)	E. Dugan	Live Wire	Robert Cooper	1:46⅖
1909	Effendi (1)	Willie Doyle	Fashion Plate	Hilltop	1:39⅗
1910	Layminster (½)	R. Estep	Dalhousie	Sager	1:40⅗
1911	Watervale (1)	E. Dugan	Zeus	The Nigger	1:51
1912	Colonel Holloway (5)	C. Turner	Bwana Tumbo	Tipsand	1:56⅗
1913	Buskin (Neck)	J. Butwell	Kleburne	Barnegat	1:53⅖
1914	Holiday (¾)	A. Schuttinger	Brave Cunarder	Defendum	1:53⅘
1915	Rhine Maiden (1½)	Douglas Hoffman	Half Rock	Runes	1:58
1916	Damrosch (1½)	Linus McAtee	Greenwood	Achievement	1:54⅘
1917	Kalitan (2)	E. Haynes	Al M. Dick	Kentucky Boy	1:54⅖
1918	War Cloud (¾)	Johnny Loftus	Sunny Slope	Lanius	1:53⅗
1918	Jack Hare, Jr (2)	C. Peak	The Porter	Kate Bright	1:53⅖
1919	Sir Barton (4)	Johnny Loftus	Eternal	Sweep On	1:53
1920	Man o' War (1½)	Clarence Kummer	Upset	Wildair	1:51⅗
1921	Broomspun (¾)	F. Coltiletti	Polly Ann	Jeg	1:54⅕
1922	Pillory (Head)	L. Morris	Hea	June Grass	1:51⅗
1923	Vigil (1¼)	B. Marinelli	General Thatcher	Rialto	1:53⅗
1924	Nellie Morse (1½)	J. Merimee	Transmute	Mad Play	1:57⅕
1925	Coventry (4)	Clarence Kummer	Backbone	Almadel	1:59
1926	Display (Head)	J. Maiben	Blondin	Mars	1:59⅘
1927	Bostonian (½)	A. Abel	Sir Harry	Whiskery	2:01⅗
1928	Victorian (Nose)	Sonny Workman	Toro	Solace	2:00⅕
1929	Dr. Freeland (1)	Louis Schaefer	Minotaur	African	2:01⅗
1930	Gallant Fox (¾)	Earl Sande	Crack Brigade	Snowflake	2:00⅗
1931	Mate (1½)	G. Ellis	Twenty Grand	Ladder	1:59
1932	Burgoo King (Head)	E. James	Tick On	Boatswain	1:59⅘
1933	Head Play (4)	Charles Kurtsinger	Ladysman	Utopian	2:02
1934	High Quest (Nose)	R. Jones	Cavalcade	Discovery	1:58⅕
1935	Omaha (6)	Willie Saunders	Firethorn	Psychic Bid	1:58⅖
1936	Bold Venture (Nose)	George Woolf	Granville	Jean Bart	1:59

Preakness (Cont.)

Year	Winner (Margin)	Jockey	Second	Third	Time
1937	War Admiral (Head)	Charles Kurtsinger	Pompoon	Flying Scot	1:58⅖
1938	Dauber (7)	M. Peters	Cravat	Menow	1:59⅘
1939	Challedon (1¼)	George Seabo	Gilded Knight	Volitant	1:59⅘
1940	Bimelech (3)	F. A. Smith	Mioland	Gallahadion	1:58⅗
1941	Whirlaway (5½)	Eddie Arcaro	King Cole	Our Boots	1:58⅘
1942	Alsab (1)	B. James	Requested Sun Again	(dead heat for second)	1:57
1943	Count Fleet (8)	Johnny Longden	Blue Swords	Vincentive	1:57⅖
1944	Pensive (¾)	Conn McCreary	Platter	Stir Up	1:59⅕
1945	Polynesian (2½)	W. D. Wright	Hoop Jr	Darby Dieppe	1:58⅘
1946	Assault (Neck)	Warren Mehrtens	Lord Boswell	Hampden	2:01⅖
1947	Faultless (1¼)	Doug Dodson	On Trust	Phalanx	1:59
1948	Citation (5½)	Eddie Arcaro	Vulcan's Forge	Boyard	2:02⅖
1949	Capot (Head)	Ted Atkinson	Palestinian	Noble Impulse	1:56
1950	Hill Prince (5)	Eddie Arcaro	Middleground	Dooley	1:59⅕
1951	Bold (7)	Eddie Arcaro	Counterpoint	Alerted	1:56⅖
1952	Blue Man (3½)	Conn McCreary	Jampol	One Count	1:57⅖
1953	Native Dancer (Neck)	Eric Guerin	Jamie K.	Royal Bay Gem	1:57⅘
1954	Hasty Road (Neck)	Johnny Adams	Correlation	Hasseyampa	1:57⅖
1955	Nashua (1)	Eddie Arcaro	Saratoga	Traffic Judge	1:54⅗
1956	Fabius (¾)	Bill Hartack	Needles	No Regrets	1:58⅖
1957	Bold Ruler (2)	Eddie Arcaro	Iron Liege	Inside Tract	1:56⅕
1958	Tim Tam (1½)	I. Valenzuela	Lincoln Road	Gone Fishin'	1:57⅕
1959	Royal Orbit (4)	William Harmatz	Sword Dancer	Dunce	1:57
1960	Bally Ache (4)	Bobby Ussery	Victoria Park	Celtic Ash	1:57⅗
1961	Carry Back (¾)	Johnny Sellers	Globemaster	Crozier	1:57⅗
1962	Greek Money (Nose)	John Rotz	Ridan	Roman Line	1:56⅕
1963	Candy Spots (3½)	Bill Shoemaker	Chateaugay	Never Bend	1:56⅕
1964	Northern Dancer (2¼)	Bill Hartack	The Scoundrel	Hill Rise	1:56⅘
1965	Tom Rolfe (Neck)	Ron Turcotte	Dapper Dan	Hail to All	1:56⅕
1966	Kauai King (1¾)	Don Brumfield	Stupendous	Amberoid	1:55⅖
1967	Damascus (2¼)	Bill Shoemaker	In Reality	Proud Clarion	1:55⅕
1968	Forward Pass (6)	I. Valenzuela	Out of the Way	Nodouble	1:56⅘
1969	Majestic Prince (Head)	Bill Hartack	Arts and Letters	Jay Ray	1:55⅗
1970	Personality (Neck)	Eddie Belmonte	My Dad George	Silent Screen	1:56⅕
1971	Canonero II (1½)	Gustavo Avila	Eastern Fleet	Jim French	1:54
1972	Bee Bee Bee (1¼)	Eldon Nelson	No Le Hace	Key to the Mint	1:55⅗
1973	Secretariat (2½)	Ron Turcotte	Sham	Our Native	1:54⅖
1974	Little Current (7)	Miguel Rivera	Neapolitan Way	Cannonade	1:54⅗
1975	Master Derby (1)	Darrel McHargue	Foolish Pleasure	Diabolo	1:56⅖
1976	Elocutionist (3)	John Lively	Play the Red	Bold Forbes	1:55
1977	Seattle Slew (1½)	Jean Cruguet	Iron Constitution	Run Dusty Run	1:54⅖
1978	Affirmed (Neck)	Steve Cauthen	Alydar	Believe It	1:54⅖
1979	Spectacular Bid (5½)	Ron Franklin	Golden Act	Screen King	1:54⅕
1980	Codex (4¾)	Angel Cordero Jr	Genuine Risk	Colonel Moran	1:54⅕
1981	Pleasant Colony (1)	Jorge Velasquez	Bold Ego	Paristo	1:54⅗
1982	Aloma's Ruler (½)	Jack Kaenel	Linkage	Cut Away	1:55⅖
1983	Deputed Testamony (2¾)	Donald Miller Jr	Desert Wine	High Honors	1:55⅖
1984	Gate Dancer (1½)	Angel Cordero Jr	Play On	Fight Over	1:53⅗
1985	Tank's Prospect (Head)	Pat Day	Chief's Crown	Eternal Prince	1:53⅖
1986	Snow Chief (4)	Alex Solis	Ferdinand	Broad Brush	1:54⅘
1987	Alysheba (½)	Chris McCarron	Bet Twice	Cryptoclearance	1:55⅘
1988	Risen Star (1¼)	E. Delahoussaye	Brian's Time	Winning Colors	1:56⅕
1989	Sunday Silence (Nose)	Pat Valenzuela	Easy Goer	Rock Point	1:53⅘
1990	Summer Squall (2¼)	Pat Day	Unbridled	Mister Frisky	1:53⅗
1991	Hansel (Head)	Jerry Bailey	Corporate Report	Mane Minister	1:54
1992	Pine Bluff (¾)	Chris McCarron	Alydeed	Casual Lies	1:55⅗
1993	Prairie Bayou (½)	Mike Smith	Cherokee Run	El Bakan	1:56⅗
1994	Tabasco Cat (¾)	Pat Day	Go For Gin	Concern	1:56⅖

*Preakness was not run 1891-1893. In 1918, it was run in two divisions.

Note: Distance: 1½ miles (1873-88), 1¼ miles (1889), 1½ miles (1890), 1 1/16 miles (1894-1900), 1 mile and 70 yards (1901-1907), 1 1/16 miles (1908), 1 mile (1909-10), 1⅛ miles (1911-24), 1 3/16 miles (1925-present).

Belmont

Run at Belmont Park, Elmont, NY, three weeks after the Preakness Stakes. Held previously at two locations in the Bronx, NY: Jerome Park (1867—1889) and Morris Park (1890—1904).

Year	Winner (Margin)	Jockey	Second	Third	Time
1867	Ruthless (Head)	J. Gilpatrick	De Courcy	Rivoli	3:05
1868	General Duke (2)	R. Swim	Northumberland	Fannie Ludlow	3:02
1869	Fenian (Unknown)	C. Miller	Glenelg	Invercauld	3:04¼
1870	Kingfisher (½)	E. Brown	Foster	Midday	2:59½
1871	Harry Bassett (3)	W. Miller	Stockwood	By-the-Sea	2:56
1872	Joe Daniels (¾)	James Rowe	Meteor	Shylock	2:58¼
1873	Springbok (4)	James Rowe	Count d'Orsay	Strachino	3:01¾
1874	Saxon (Neck)	G. Barbee	Grinstead	Aaron Pennington	2:39½
1875	Calvin (2)	R. Swim	Aristides	Milner	2:40¼
1876	Algerine (Head)	W. Donahue	Fiddlestick	Barricade	2:40½
1877	Cloverbrook (1)	C. Holloway	Loiterer	Baden-Baden	2:46
1878	Duke of Magenta (2)	L. Hughes	Bramble	Sparta	2:43½
1879	Spendthrift (5)	S. Evans	Monitor	Jericho	2:42¾
1880	Grenada (½)	L. Hughes	Ferncliffe	Turenne	2:47
1881	Saunterer (Neck)	T. Costello	Eole	Baltic	2:47
1882	Forester (5)	James McLaughlin	Babcock	Wyoming	2:43
1883	George Kinney (2)	James McLaughlin	Trombone	Renegade	2:42½
1884	Panique (½)	James McLaughlin	Knight of Ellerslie	Himalaya	2:42
1885	Tyrant (3½)	Paul Duffy	St Augustine	Tecumseh	2:43
1886	Inspector B (1)	James McLaughlin	The Bard	Linden	2:41
1887	Hanover (28-32)	James McLaughlin	Oneko		2:43½
1888	Sir Dixon (12)	James McLaughlin	Prince Royal		2:40¼
1889	Eric (Head)	W. Hayward	Diable	Zephyrus	2:47
1890	Burlington (1)	S. Barnes	Devotee	Padishah	2:07¾
1891	Foxford (Neck)	E. Garrison	Montana	Laurestan	2:08¾
1892	Patron (Unknown)	W. Hayward	Shellbark		2:17
1893	Comanche (Head)(21)	Willie Simms	Dr. Rice	Rainbow	1:53¼
1894	Henry of Navarre (2-4)	Willie Simms	Prig	Assignee	1:56½
1895	Belmar (Head)	Fred Taral	Counter Tenor	Nanki Pooh	2:11½
1896	Hastings (Neck)	H. Griffin	Handspring	Hamilton II	2:24½
1897	Scottish Chieftain (1)	J. Scherrer	On Deck	Octagon	2:23¼
1898	Bowling Brook (8)	P. Littlefield	Previous	Hamburg	2:32
1899	Jean Bereaud (Head)	R. R. Clawson	Half Time	Glengar	2:23
1900	Ildrim (Head)	N. Turner	Petrucio	Missionary	2:21½
1901	Commando (½)	H. Spencer	The Parader	All Green	2:21
1902	Masterman (2)	John Bullmann	Ranald	King Hanover	2:22½
1903	Africander (2)	John Bullmann	Whorler	Red Knight	2:23⅕
1904	Delhi (3½)	George Odom	Graziallo	Rapid Water	2:06⅗
1905	Tanya (1/2)	E. Hildebrand	Blandy	Hot Shot	2:08
1906	Burgomaster (4)	L. Lyne	The Quail	Accountant	2:20
1907	Peter Pan (1)	G. Mountain	Superman	Frank Gill	Unknown
1908	Colin (Head)	Joe Notter	Fair Play	King James	Unknown
1909	Joe Madden (8)	E. Dugan	Wise Mason	Donald MacDonald	2:21⅗
1910*	Sweep (6)	J. Butwell	Duke of Ormonde		2:22
1913	Prince Eugene (½)	Roscoe Troxler	Rock View	Flying Fairy	2:18
1914	Luke McLuke (8)	M. Buxton	Gainer	Charlestonian	2:20
1915	The Finn (4)	G. Byrne	Half Rock	Pebbles	2:18⅖
1916	Friar Rock (3)	E. Haynes	Spur	Churchill	2:22
1917	Hourless (10)	J. Butwell	Skeptic	Wonderful	2:17⅘
1918	Johren (2)	Frank Robinson	War Cloud	Cum Sah	2:20⅖
1919	Sir Barton (5)	Johnny Loftus	Sweep On	Natural Bridge	2:17⅖
1920	Man o' War (20)	Clarence Kummer	Donnacona		2:14⅕
1921	Grey Lag (3)	Earl Sande	Sporting Blood	Leonardo II	2:16⅘
1922	Pillory (2)	C. H. Miller	Snob II	Hea	2:18⅘
1923	Zev (1½)	Earl Sande	Chickvale	Rialto	2:19
1924	Mad Play (2)	Earl Sande	Mr. Mutt	Modest	2:18⅘
1925	American Flag (8)	Albert Johnson	Dangerous	Swope	2:16⅘
1926	Crusader (1)	Albert Johnson	Espino	Haste	2:32⅕
1927	Chance Shot (1½)	Earl Sande	Bois de Rose	Flambino	2:32⅖

Belmont (Cont.)

Year	Winner (Margin)	Jockey	Second	Third	Time
1928	Vito (3)	Clarence Kummer	Genie	Diavolo	2:33⅕
1929	Blue Larkspur (¾)	Mack Garner	African	Jack High	2:32⅘
1930	Gallant Fox (3)	Earl Sande	Whichone	Questionnaire	2:31⅗
1931	Twenty Grand (10)	Charles Kurtsinger	Sun Meadow	Jamestown	2:29⅗
1932	Faireno (1½)	T. Malley	Osculator	Flag Pole	2:32⅘
1933	Hurryoff (1½)	Mack Garner	Nimbus	Union	2:32⅗
1934	Peace Chance (6)	W. D. Wright	High Quest	Good Goods	2:29⅕
1935	Omaha (1½)	Willie Saunders	Firethorn	Rosemont	2:30⅗
1936	Granville (Nose)	James Stout	Mr. Bones	Hollyrood	2:30
1937	War Admiral (3)	Charles Kurtsinger	Sceneshifter	Vamoose	2:28⅗
1938	Pasteurized (Neck)	James Stout	Dauber	Cravat	2:29⅖
1939	Johnstown (5)	James Stout	Belay	Gilded Knight	2:29⅗
1940	Bimelech (¾)	F. A. Smith	Your Chance	Andy K	2:29⅗
1941	Whirlaway (2½)	Eddie Arcaro	Robert Morris	Yankee Chance	2:31
1942	Shut Out (2)	Eddie Arcaro	Alsab	Lochinvar	2:29⅕
1943	Count Fleet (25)	Johnny Longden	Fairy Manhurst	Deseronto	2:28⅕
1944	Bounding Home (½)	G. L. Smith	Pensive	Bull Dandy	2:32⅕
1945	Pavot (5)	Eddie Arcaro	Wildlife	Jeep	2:30⅕
1946	Assault (3)	Warren Mehrtens	Natchez	Cable	2:30⅘
1947	Phalanx (5)	R. Donoso	Tide Rips	Tailspin	2:29⅖
1948	Citation (8)	Eddie Arcaro	Better Self	Escadru	2:28⅕
1949	Capot (½)	Ted Atkinson	Ponder	Palestinian	2:30⅕
1950	Middleground (1)	William Boland	Lights Up	Mr. Trouble	2:28⅗
1951	Counterpoint (4)	D. Gorman	Battlefield	Battle Morn	2:29
1952	One Count (2½)	Eddie Arcaro	Blue Man	Armageddon	2:30⅕
1953	Native Dancer (Neck)	Eric Guerin	Jamie K.	Royal Bay Gem	2:38⅗
1954	High Gun (Neck)	Eric Guerin	Fisherman	Limelight	2:30⅘
1955	Nashua (9)	Eddie Arcaro	Blazing Count	Portersville	2:29
1956	Needles (Neck)	David Erb	Career Boy	Fabius	2:29⅘
1957	Gallant Man (8)	Bill Shoemaker	Inside Tract	Bold Ruler	2:26⅗
1958	Cavan (6)	Pete Anderson	Tim Tam	Flamingo	2:30⅕
1959	Sword Dancer (¾)	Bill Shoemaker	Bagdad	Royal Orbit	2:28⅖
1960	Celtic Ash (5½)	Bill Hartack	Venetian Way	Disperse	2:29⅗
1961	Sherluck (2¼)	Braulio Baeza	Globemaster	Guadalcanal	2:29⅕
1962	Jaipur (Nose)	Bill Shoemaker	Admiral's Voyage	Crimson Satan	2:28⅘
1963	Chateaugay (2½)	Braulio Baeza	Candy Spots	Choker	2:30⅕
1964	Quadrangle (2)	Manuel Ycaza	Roman Brother	Northern Dancer	2:28⅖
1965	Hail to All (Neck)	John Sellers	Tom Rolfe	First Family	2:28⅖
1966	Amberold (2½)	William Boland	Buffle	Advocator	2:29⅗
1967	Damascus (2½)	Bill Shoemaker	Cool Reception	Gentleman James	2:28⅘
1968	Stage Door Johnny (1¼)	Hellodoro Gustines	Forward Pass	Call Me Prince	2:27⅕
1969	Arts and Letters (5½)	Braulio Baeza	Majestic Prince	Dike	2:28⅘
1970	High Echelon (¾)	John L. Rotz	Needles N Pins	Naskra	2:34
1971	Pass Catcher (¾)	Walter Blum	Jim French	Bold Reason	2:30⅖
1972	Riva Ridge (7)	Ron Turcotte	Ruritania	Cloudy Dawn	2:28
1973	Secretariat (31)	Ron Turcotte	Twice a Prince	My Gallant	2:24
1974	Little Current (7)	Miguel A. Rivera	Jolly Johu	Cannonade	2:29⅕
1975	Avatar (Neck)	Bill Shoemaker	Foolish Pleasure	Master Derby	2:28⅕
1976	Bold Forbes (Neck)	Angel Cordero Jr	McKenzie Bridge	Great Contractor	2:29
1977	Seattle Slew (4)	Jean Cruguet	Run Dusty Run	Sanhedrin	2:29⅗
1978	Affirmed (Head)	Steve Cauthen	Alydar	Darby Creek Road	2:26⅘
1979	Coastal (3¼)	Ruben Hernandez	Golden Act	Spectacular Bid	2:28⅗
1980	Temperence Hill (2)	Eddie Maple	Genuine Risk	Rockhill Native	2:29⅘
1981	Summing (Neck)	George Martens	Highland Blade	Pleasant Colony	2:29
1982	Conquistador Cielo (14½)	Laffit Pincay, Jr	Gato Del Sol	Illuminate	2:28⅕
1983	Caveat (3½)	Laffit Pincay, Jr	Slew o'Gold	Barberstown	2:27⅘
1984	Swale (4)	Laffit Pincay, Jr	Pine Circle	Morning Bob	2:27⅕
1985	Creme Fraiche (½)	Eddie Maple	Stephan's Odyssey	Chief's Crown	2:27
1986	Danzig Connection (1¼)	Chris McCarron	Johns Treasure	Ferdinand	2:29⅘

Belmont (Cont.)

Year	Winner (Margin)	Jockey	Second	Third	Time
1987	Bet Twice (14)	Craig Perret	Cryptoclearance	Gulch	2:28⅕
1988	Risen Star (14¾)	Eddie Delahoussaye	Kingpost	Brian's Time	2:26⅖
1989	Easy Goer (8)	Pat Day	Sunday Silence	Le Voyageur	2:26
1990	Go and Go (8¼)	Michael Kinane	Thirty Six Red	Baron de Vaux	2:27⅕
1991	Hansel (Head)	Jerry Bailey	Strike the Gold	Mane Minister	2:28
1992	A.P. Indy (¾)	Eddie Delahoussaye	My Memoirs	Pine Bluff	2:26
1993	Colonial Affair	Julie Krone	Kissin Kris	Wild Gale	2:29⅘
1994	Tabasco Cat	Pat Day	Go For Gin	Strodes Creek	2:26⅘

*Race not held in 1911-1912.

Note: Distance: 1 mile 5 furlongs (1867-89), 1¼ miles (1890-1905), 1⅜ miles (1906-25), 1½ miles (1926-present).

Triple Crown Winners

Year	Horse	Jockey	Owner	Trainer
1919	Sir Barton	John Loftus	J. K. L. Ross	H. G. Bedwell
1930	Gallant Fox	Earle Sande	Belair Stud	James Fitzsimmons
1935	Omaha	William Saunders	Belair Stud	James Fitzsimmons
1937	War Admiral	Charles Kurtsinger	Samuel D. Riddle	George Conway
1941	Whirlaway	Eddie Arcaro	Calumet Farm	Ben Jones
1943	Count Fleet	John Longden	Mrs J. D. Hertz	Don Cameron
1946	Assault	Warren Mehrtens	King Ranch	Max Hirsch
1948	Citation	Eddie Arcaro	Calumet Farm	Jimmy Jones
1973	Secretariat	Ron Turcotte	Meadow Stable	Lucien Laurin
1977	Seattle Slew	Jean Cruguet	Karen L. Taylor	William H. Turner Jr
1978	Affirmed	Steve Cauthen	Harbor View Farm	Laz Barrera

Just Say Neigh

Did you hear about the huge outdoor concert in New York that really shook up the neighbors? No, we're not talking about Woodstock. We mean the Lollapalooza music festival held Aug. 2 at the Saratoga trotting track.

The nine hour concert, featuring such alternative bands as the Beastie Boys, Smashing Pumpkins and the Breeders (who have nothing to do with the cup of the same name), was so raucous that several racehorses stabled nearby had to be tranquilized, and at least two were scratched from races the next day.

"All I know is it was very, very loud," says trainer Richard Schosberg of the music that rendered his stable anything but stable. "Everything was vibrating."

Schosberg says that three of his horses were upset by the din but that 4-year-old filly Personal Bid took it the hardest. "She was bug-eyed, tearing around the stall, charging the webbing, spinning and kicking the walls," he says.

Dude, sounds like she was in the mood to mosh.

Horse of the Year

Year	Horse	Owner	Trainer	Breeder
1936	Granville	Belair Stud	James Fitzsimmons	Belair Stud
1937	War Admiral	Samuel D. Riddle	George Conway	Mrs. Samuel D. Riddle
1938	Seabiscuit	Charles S. Howard	Tom Smith	Wheatley Stable
1939	Challedon	William L. Brann	Louis J. Schaefer	Branncastle Farm
1940	Challedon	William L. Brann	Louis J. Schaefer	Branncastle Farm
1941	Whirlaway	Calumet Farm	Ben Jones	Calumet Farm
1942	Whirlaway	Calumet Farm	Ben Jones	Calumet Farm
1943	Count Fleet	Mrs. John D. Hertz	Don Cameron	Mrs. John D. Hertz
1944	Twilight Tear	Calumet Farm	Ben Jones	Calumet Farm
1945	Busher	Louis B. Mayer	George Odom	Idle Hour Stock Farm
1946	Assault	King Ranch	Max Hirsch	King Ranch
1947	Armed	Calumet Farm	Jimmy Jones	Calumet Farm
1948	Citation	Calumet Farm	Jimmy Jones	Calumet Farm
1949	Capot	Greentree Stable	John M. Gaver Sr	Greentree Stable
1950	Hill Prince	C. T. Chenery	Casey Hayes	C. T. Chenery
1951	Counterpoint	C. V. Whitney	Syl Veitch	C. V. Whitney
1952	One Count	Mrs. W. M. Jeffords	O. White	W. M. Jeffords
1953	Tom Fool	Greentree Stable	John M. Gaver Sr	D. A. Headley
1954	Native Dancer	A. G. Vanderbilt	Bill Winfrey	A. G. Vanderbilt
1955	Nashua	Belair Stud	James Fitzsimmons	Belair Stud
1956	Swaps	Ellsworth-Galbreath	Mesh Tenney	R. Ellsworth
1957	Bold Ruler	Wheatley Stable	James Fitzsimmons	Wheatley Stable
1958	Round Table	Kerr Stables	Willy Molter	Claiborne Farm
1959	Sword Dancer	Brookmeade Stable	Elliott Burch	Brookmeade Stable
1960	Kelso	Bohemia Stable	C. Hanford	Mrs. R. C. duPont
1961	Kelso	Bohemia Stable	C. Hanford	Mrs. R. C. duPont
1962	Kelso	Bohemia Stable	C. Hanford	Mrs. R. C. duPont
1963	Kelso	Bohemia Stable	C. Hanford	Mrs. R. C. duPont
1964	Kelso	Bohemia Stable	C. Hanford	Mrs. R. C. duPont
1965	Roman Brother	Harbor View Stable	Burley Parke	Ocala Stud
1966	Buckpasser	Ogden Phipps	Eddie Neloy	Ogden Phipps
1967	Damascus	Mrs. E. W. Bancroft	Frank Y. Whiteley Jr	Mrs. E. W. Bancroft
1968	Dr. Fager	Tartan Stable	John A. Nerud	Tartan Farms
1969	Arts and Letters	Rokeby Stable	Elliott Burch	Paul Mellon
1970	Fort Marcy	Rokeby Stable	Elliott Burch	Paul Mellon
1971	Ack Ack	E. E. Fogelson	Charlie Whittingham	H. F. Guggenheim
1972	Secretariat	Meadow Stable	Lucien Laurin	Meadow Stud
1973	Secretariat	Meadow Stable	Lucien Laurin	Meadow Stud
1974	Forego	Lazy F Ranch	Sherrill W. Ward	Lazy F Ranch
1975	Forego	Lazy F Ranch	Sherrill W. Ward	Lazy F Ranch
1976	Forego	Lazy F Ranch	Frank Y. Whiteley Jr	Lazy F Ranch
1977	Seattle Slew	Karen L. Taylor	Billy Turner Jr	B. S. Castleman
1978	Affirmed	Harbor View Farm	Laz Barrera	Harbor View Farm
1979	Affirmed	Harbor View Farm	Laz Barrera	Harbor View Farm
1980	Spectacular Bid	Hawksworth Farm	Bud Delp	Mmes. Gilmore and Jason
1981	John Henry	Dotsam Stable	Ron McAnally and Lefty Nickerson	Golden Chance Farm
1982	Conquistador Cielo	H. de Kwiatkowski	Woody Stephens	L. E. Landoli
1983	All Along	Daniel Wildenstein	P. L. Biancone	Dayton
1984	John Henry	Dotsam Stable	Ron McAnally	Golden Chance Farm
1985	Spend a Buck	Hunter Farm	Cam Gambolati	Irish Hill Farm & R. W. Harper
1986	Lady's Secret	Mr. & Mrs. Eugene Klein	D. Wayne Lukas	R. H. Spreen
1987	Ferdinand	Mrs. H. B. Keck	Charlie Whittingham	H. B. Keck

Horse of the Year *(Cont.)*

Year	Horse	Owner	Trainer	Breeder
1988	Alysheba	D. & P. Scharbauer	Jack Van Berg	Preston Madden
1989	Sunday Silence	Gaillard, Hancock, & Whittingham	Charlie Whittingham	Oak Cliff Thoroughbreds
1990	Criminal Type	Calumet Farm	D. Wayne Lukas	Calumet Farm
1991	Black Tie Affair	Jeffrey Sullivan	Ernie Poulos	Stephen D. Peskoff
1992	A.P. Indy	Tomonori Tsurumaki	Neil Drysdale	W.S. Farish & W.S. Kilroy
1993	Kotashaan	La Presle Farm	Richard Mandella	La Presle Farm

Note: From 1936 to 1970, the *Daily Racing Form* annually selected a "Horse of the Year." In 1971 the *Daily Racing Form*, with the Thoroughbred Racing Association and the National Turf Writers Association, jointly created the Eclipse Awards.

Eclipse Award Winners

2-YEAR-OLD COLT

1971	Riva Ridge
1972	Secretariat
1973	Protagonist
1974	Foolish Pleasure
1975	Honest Pleasure
1976	Seattle Slew
1977	Affirmed
1978	Spectacular Bid
1979	Rockhill Native
1980	Lord Avie
1981	Deputy Minister
1982	Roving Boy
1983	Devil's Bag
1984	Chief's Crown
1985	Tasso
1986	Capote
1987	Forty Niner
1988	Easy Goer
1989	Rhythm
1990	Fly So Free
1991	Arazi
1992	Gilded Time
1993	Dehere

2-YEAR-OLD FILLY

1971	Numbered Account
1972	La Prevoyante
1973	Talking Picture
1974	Ruffian
1975	Dearly Precious
1976	Sensational
1977	Lakeville Miss
1978	Candy Eclair
	It's in the Air
1979	Smart Angle
1980	Heavenly Cause
1981	Before Dawn
1982	Landaluce
1983	Althea
1984	Outstandingly
1985	Family Style
1986	Brave Raj
1987	Epitome
1988	Open Mind
1989	Go for Wand
1990	Meadow Star
1991	Pleasant Stage
1992	Eliza
1993	Phone Chatter

3-YEAR-OLD COLT

1971	Canonero II
1972	Key to the Mint
1973	Secretariat
1974	Little Currant
1975	Wajima
1976	Bold Forbes
1977	Seattle Slew
1978	Affirmed
1979	Spectacular Bid
1980	Temperence Hill
1981	Pleasant Colony
1982	Conquistador Cielo
1983	Slew o' Gold
1984	Swale
1985	Spend A Buck
1986	Snow Chief
1987	Alysheba
1988	Risen Star
1989	Sunday Silence
1990	Unbridled
1991	Hansel
1992	A.P. Indy
1993	Prairie Bayou

3-YEAR-OLD FILLY

1971	Turkish Trousers
1972	Susan's Girl
1973	Desert Vixen
1974	Chris Evert
1975	Ruffian
1976	Revidere
1977	Our Mims
1978	Tempest Queen
1979	Davona Dale
1980	Genuine Risk
1981	Wayward Lass
1982	Christmas Past
1983	Heartlight No. One
1984	Life's Magic
1985	Mom's Command
1986	Tiffany Lass
1987	Sacahuista
1988	Winning Colors
1989	Open Mind
1990	Go for Wand
1991	Dance Smartly
1992	Saratoga Dew
1993	Hollywood Wildcat

OLDER COLT, HORSE OR GELDING

1971	Ack Ack (5)
1972	Autobiography (4)
1973	Riva Ridge (4)
1974	Forego (4)
1975	Forego (5)
1976	Forego (6)
1977	Forego (7)
1978	Seattle Slew (4)
1979	Affirmed (4)
1980	Spectacular Bid (4)
1981	John Henry (6)
1982	Lemhi Gold (4)
1983	Bates Motel (4)
1984	Slew o'Gold (4)
1985	Vanlandingham (4)
1986	Turkoman (4)
1987	Ferdinand (4)
1988	Alysheba (4)
1989	Blushing John (4)
1990	Criminal Type (5)
1991	Black Tie Affair (5)
1992	Pleasant Tap (5)
1993	Bertrando (4)

CHAMPION TURF HORSE

1971	Run the Gantlet (3)
1972	Cougar II (6)
1973	Secretariat (3)
1974	Dahlia (4)
1975	Snow Knight (4)
1976	Youth (3)
1977	Johnny D (3)
1978	Mac Diarmida (3)

Eclipse Awards (Cont.)

STEEPLECHASE OR HURDLE HORSE

1971.....Shadow Brook (7)
1972.....Soothsayer (5)
1973.....Athenian Idol (5)
1974.....Gran Kan (8)
1975.....Life's Illusion (4)
1976.....Straight & True (6)
1977.....Cafe Prince (7)
1978.....Cafe Prince (8)
1979.....Martie's Anger (4)
1980.....Zaccio (4)
1981.....Zaccio (5)
1982.....Zaccio (6)
1983.....Flatterer (4)
1984.....Flatterer (5)
1985.....Flatterer (6)
1986.....Flatterer (7)
1987.....Inlander (6)
1988.....Jimmy Lorenzo (6)
1989.....Highland Bud (4)
1990.....Morley Street (7)
1991.....Morley Street (8)
1992.....Lonesome Glory (4)
1993.....Lonesome Glory (5)

OLDER FILLY OR MARE

1971.....Shuvee (5)
1972.....Typecast (6)
1973.....Susan's Girl (4)
1974.....Desert Vixen (4)
1975.....Susan's Girl (6)
1976.....Proud Delta (4)
1977.....Cascapedia (4)
1978.....Late Bloomer (4)
1979.....Waya (5)
1980.....Glorious Song (4)
1981.....Relaxing (5)
1982.....Track Robbery (6)
1983.....Ambassador of Luck (4)
1984.....Princess Rooney (4)
1985.....Life's Magic (4)
1986.....Lady's Secret (4)
1987.....North Sider (5)
1988.....Personal Ensign (4)
1989.....Bayakoa (5)
1990.....Bayakoa (6)
1991.....Queena (5)
1992.....Paseana (5)
1993.....Paseana (6)

CHAMPION MALE TURF HORSE

1979.....Bowl Game (5)
1980.....John Henry (5)
1981.....John Henry (6)
1982.....Perrault (4)
1983.....John Henry (8)
1984.....John Henry (9)
1985.....Cozzene (4)
1986.....Manila (3)
1987.....Theatrical (5)
1988.....Sunshine Forever (3)
1989.....Steinlen (6)

CHAMPION MALE TURF HORSE (Cont.)

1990.....Itsallgreektome (3)
1991.....Tight Spot (4)
1992.....Sky Classic (5)
1993.....Kotashaan (5)

OUTSTANDING OWNER

1971.....Mr. & Mrs. E. E. Fogleson
1974.....Dan Lasater
1975.....Dan Lasater
1976.....Dan Lasater
1977.....Maxwell Gluck
1978.....Harbor View Farm
1979.....Harbor View Farm
1980.....Mr. & Mrs. Bertram Firestone
1981.....Dotsam Stable
1982.....Viola Sommer
1983.....John Franks
1984.....John Franks
1985.....Mr. & Mrs. Eugene Klein
1986.....Mr. & Mrs. Eugene Klein
1987.....Mr. & Mrs. Eugene Klein
1988.....Ogden Phipps
1989.....Ogden Phipps
1990.....Frances Genter
1991.....Sam-Son Farm
1992.....Juddmonte Farms
1993.....John Franks

SPRINTER

1971.....Ack Ack (5)
1972.....Chou Croute (4)
1973.....Shecky Greene (3)
1974.....Forego (4)
1975.....Gallant Bob (3)
1976.....My Juliet (4)
1977.....What a Summer (4)
1978.....Dr. Patches (4)
         J. O. Tobin (4)
1979.....Star de Naskra (4)
1980.....Plugged Nickel (3)
1981.....Guilty Conscience (5)
1982.....Gold Beauty (4)
1983.....Chinook Pass (4)
1984.....Eillo (4)
1985.....Precisionist (4)
1986.....Smile (4)
1987.....Groovy (4)
1988.....Gulch (4)
1989.....Safely Kept (3)
1990.....Housebuster (3)
1991.....Housebuster (4)
1992.....Rubiano (5)
1993.....Cardmania (7)

CHAMPION FEMALE TURF HORSE

1979.....Trillion (5)
1980.....Just a Game II (4)
1981.....De La Rose (3)
1982.....April Run (4)

CHAMPION FEMALE TURF HORSE (Cont.)

1983.....All Along (4)
1984.....Royal Heroine (4)
1985.....Pebbles (4)
1986.....Estrapade (6)
1987.....Miesque (3)
1988.....Miesque (4)
1989.....Brown Bess (7)
1990.....Laugh and Be Merry (5)
1991.....Miss Alleged (4)
1992.....Flawlessly (4)
1993.....Flawlessly (5)

OUTSTANDING TRAINER

1971.....Charlie Whittingham
1972.....Lucien Laurin
1973.....H. Allen Jerkens
1974.....Sherrill Ward
1975.....Steve DiMauro
1976.....Lazaro Barrera
1977.....Lazaro Barrera
1978.....Lazaro Barrera
1979.....Lazaro Barrera
1980.....Bud Delp
1981.....Ron McAnally
1982.....Charlie Whittingham
1983.....Woody Stephens
1984.....Jack Van Berg
1985.....D. Wayne Lukas
1986.....D. Wayne Lukas
1987.....D. Wayne Lukas
1988.....Claude R. McGaughey III
1989.....Charlie Whittingham
1990.....Carl Nafzger
1991.....Ron McAnally
1992.....Ron McAnally
1993.....Bobby Frankel

OUTSTANDING JOCKEY

1971.....Laffit Pincay Jr
1972.....Braulio Baeza
1973.....Laffit Pincay Jr
1974.....Laffit Pincay Jr
1975.....Braulio Baeza
1976.....Sandy Hawley
1977.....Steve Cauthen
1978.....Darrel McHargue
1979.....Laffit Pincay Jr
1980.....Chris McCarron
1981.....Bill Shoemaker
1982.....Angel Cordero Jr
1983.....Angel Cordero Jr
1984.....Pat Day
1985.....Laffit Pincay Jr
1986.....Pat Day
1987.....Pat Day
1988.....Jose Santos
1989.....Kent Desormeaux
1990.....Craig Perret
1991.....Pat Day
1992.....Kent Desormeaux
1993.....Mike Smith

Note: Number in parentheses is horse's age.

Awards (Cont.)

Eclipse Awards (Cont.)

OUTSTANDING APPRENTICE JOCKEY

1971.....Gene St. Leon
1972.....Thomas Wallis
1973.....Steve Valdez
1974.....Chris McCarron
1975.....Jimmy Edwards
1976.....George Martens
1977.....Steve Cauthen
1978.....Ron Franklin
1979.....Cash Asmussen
1980.....Frank Lovato Jr
1981.....Richard Migliore
1982.....Alberto Delgado
1983.....Declan Murphy
1984.....Wesley Ward
1985.....Art Madrid Jr
1986.....Allen Stacy
1987.....Kent Desormeaux
1988.....Steve Capanas
1989.....Michael Luzzi
1990.....Mark Johnston
1991.....Mickey Walls
1992.....Jesus A. Bracho
1993.....Juan Umana

SPECIAL AWARD

1971.....Robert J. Kleberg
1974.....Charles Hatton
1976.....Bill Shoemaker
1980.....John T. Landry
Pierre E. Bellocq (Peb)
1984.....C. V. Whitney
1985.....Arlington Park
1987.....Anheuser-Busch
1988.....Edward J. DeBartolo Sr
1989.....Richard Duchossois

OUTSTANDING BREEDER

1974.....John W. Galbreath
1975.....Fred W. Hooper
1976.....Nelson Bunker Hunt
1977.....Edward Plunket Taylor
1978.....Harbor View Farm
1979.....Claiborne Farm
1980.....Mrs. Henry D. Paxson
1981.....Golden Chance Farm
1982.....Fred W. Hooper
1983.....Edward Plunket Taylor
1984.....Claiborne Farm
1985.....Nelson Bunker Hunt

OUTSTANDING BREEDER *(Cont.)*

1986.....Paul Mellon
1987.....Nelson Bunker Hunt
1988.....Ogden Phipps
1989.....North Ridge Farm
1990.....Calumet Farm
1991.....John and Betty Mabee
1992.....William S. Farish III
1993.....Allen Paulson

AWARD OF MERIT

1976.....Jack J. Dreyfus
1977.....Steve Cauthen
1978.....Ogden Phipps
1979.....Frank E. Kilroe
1980.....John D. Schapiro
1981.....Bill Shoemaker
1984.....John Gaines
1985.....Keene Daingerfield
1986.....Herman Cohen
1987.....J. B. Faulconer
1988.....John Forsythe
1989.....Michael P. Sandler
1991.....Fred W. Hooper

Note: Special Award and Award of Merit not presented annually. For long-term and/or outstanding service to the industry.

Breeders' Cup

Location: Hollywood Park (CA) 1984, 1987; Aqueduct Racetrack (NY) 1985; Santa Anita Park (CA) 1986, 1993; Churchill Downs (KY) 1988, 1991; Gulfstream Park (FL) 1989, 1992; Belmont Park (NY) 1990.

Juveniles

Year	Winner (Margin)	Jockey	Second	Third	Time
1984	Chief's Crown (¾)	Don MacBeth	Tank's Prospect	Spend a Buck	1:36⅕
1985	Tasso (Nose)	Laffit Pincay Jr	Storm Cat	Scat Dancer	1:36⅕
1986	Capote (1¼)	Laffit Pincay Jr	Qualify	Alysheba	1:43⅘
1987	Success Express (1¾)	Jose Santos	Regal Classic	Tejano	1:35⅕
1988	Is It True (1¼)	Laffit Pincay Jr	Easy Goer	Tagel	1:46⅗
1989	Rhythm (2)	Craig Perret	Grand Canyon	Slavic	1:43⅗
1990	Fly So Free (3)	Jose Santos	Take Me Out	Lost Mountain	1:43⅖
1991	Arazi (4¾)	Pat Valenzuela	Bertrando	Snappy Landing	1:44⅗
1992	Gilded Time (¾)	Chris McCarron	It'sali'lknownfact	River Special	1:43⅖
1993	Brocco (5)	Gary Stevens	Blumin Affair	Tabasco Cat	1:42⅘

Note: One mile (1984–85, 87); 1 1/16 miles (1986 and since 1988).

Juvenile Fillies

Year	Winner (Margin)	Jockey	Second	Third	Time
1984	Outstandingly*	Walter Guerra	Dusty Heart	Fine Spirit	1:37⅘
1985	Twilight Ridge (1)	Jorge Velasquez	Family Style	Steal a Kiss	1:35⅘
1986	Brave Raj (5½)	Pat Valenzuela	Tappiano	Saros Brig	1:43⅕
1987	Epitome (Nose)	Pat Day	Jeanne Jones	Dream Team	1:36⅖
1988	Open Mind (1¾)	Angel Cordero Jr	Darby Shuffle	Lea Lucinda	1:46⅗
1989	Go for Wand (2¾)	Randy Romero	Sweet Roberta	Stella Madrid	1:44⅕
1990	Meadow Star (5)	Jose Santos	Private Treasure	Dance Smartly	1:44
1991	Pleasant Stage (Neck)	Eddie Delahoussaye	La Spia	Cadillac Women	1:46⅖
1992	Eliza (1½)	Pat Valenzuela	Educated Risk	Boots 'n Jackie	1:42⅘
1993	Phone Chatter (Head)	Laffit Pincay	Sardula	Heavenly Prize	1:43

*In 1984, winner Fran's Valentine was disqualified for interference in the stretch and placed 10th.
Note: One mile (1984—85, 87); 1 1/16 miles (1986 and since 1988).

Breeders' Cup (Cont.)

Sprint

Year	Winner (Margin)	Jockey	Second	Third	Time
1984	Eillo (Nose)	Craig Perret	Commemorate	Fighting Fit	1:10⅕
1985	Precisionist (¾)	Chris McCarron	Smile	Mt. Livermore	1:08⅖
1986	Smile (1¼)	Jacinto Vasquez	Pine Tree Lane	Bedside Promise	1:08⅖
1987	Very Subtle (4)	Pat Valenzuela	Groovy	Exclusive Enough	1:08⅘
1988	Gulch (¾)	Angel Cordero Jr	Play the King	Afleet	1:10⅖
1989	Dancing Spree (Neck)	Angel Cordero Jr	Safely Kept	Dispersal	1:09
1990	Safely Kept (Neck)	Craig Perret	Dayjur	Black Tie Affair	1:09⅗
1991	Sheikh Albadou (Neck)	Pat Eddery	Pleasant Tap	Robyn Dancer	1:09⅕
1992	Thirty Slews (Neck)	Eddie Delahoussaye	Meafara	Rubiano	1:08⅕
1993	Cardmania (Neck)	Eddie Delahoussaye	Meafara	Gilded Time	1:08⅗

Note: Six furlongs (since 1984).

Mile

Year	Winner (Margin)	Jockey	Second	Third	Time
1984	Royal Heroine (1½)	Fernando Toro	Star Choice	Cozzene	1:32⅗
1985	Cozzene (2¼)	Walter Guerra	Al Mamoon*	Shadeed	1:35
1986	Last Tycoon (Head)	Yves St-Martin	Palace Music	Fred Astaire	1:35⅕
1987	Miesque (3½)	Freddie Head	Show Dancer	Sonic Lady	1:32⅘
1988	Miesque (4)	Freddie Head	Steinlen	Simply Majestic	1:38⅗
1989	Steinlen (¾)	Jose Santos	Sabona	Most Welcome	1:37⅕
1990	Royal Academy (Neck)	Lester Piggott	Itsallgreektome	Priolo	1:35⅕
1991	Opening Verse (2¼)	Pat Valenzuela	Val de Bois	Star of Cozzene	1:37⅖
1992	Lure (3)	Mike Smith	Paradise Creek	Brief Truce	1:32⅘
1993	Lure (2¼)	Mike Smith	Ski Paradise	Fourstars Allstar	1:33⅖

*2nd place finisher Palace Music was disqualified for interference and placed 9th.

Distaff

Year	Winner (Margin)	Jockey	Second	Third	Time
1984	Princess Rooney (7)	Eddie Delahoussaye	Life's Magic	Adored	2:02⅖
1985	Life's Magic (6¼)	Angel Cordero Jr	Lady's Secret	Dontstop Themusic	2:02
1986	Lady's Secret (2½)	Pat Day	Fran's Valentine	Outstandingly	2:01⅕
1987	Sacahuista (2¼)	Randy Romero	Clabber Girl	Oueee Bebe	2:02⅘
1988	Personal Ensign (Nose)	Randy Romero	Winning Colors	Goodbye Halo	1:52
1989	Bayakoa (1½)	Laffit Pincay Jr	Gorgeous	Open Mind	1:47⅖
1990	Bayakoa (6¾)	Laffit Pincay Jr	Colonial Waters	Valay Maid	1:49⅕
1991	Dance Smarty (½)	Pat Day	Versailles Treaty	Brought to Mind	1:50⅘
1992	Paseana (4)	Chris McCarron	Versailles Treaty	Magical Maiden	1:48
1993	Hollywood Wildcat	Eddie Delahoussaye	Paseana	Re Toss	1:48⅕

Note: 1¼ miles (1984-87); 1⅛ miles (since 1988).

Turf

Year	Winner (Margin)	Jockey	Second	Third	Time
1984	Lashkari (Neck)	Yves St-Martin	All Along	Raami	2:25⅕
1985	Pebbles (Neck)	Pat Eddery	Strawberry Rd II	Mourjane	2:27
1986	Manila (Neck)	Jose Santos	Theatrical	Estrapade	2:25⅖
1987	Theatrical (½)	Pat Day	Trempolino	Village Star II	2:24⅖
1988	Great Communicator (½)	Ray Sibille	Sunshine Forever	Indian Skimmer	2:35⅕
1989	Prized (Head)	Eddie Delahoussaye	Sierra Roberta	Star Lift	2:28
1990	In the Wings (½)	Gary Stevens	With Approval	El Senor	2:29⅗
1991	Miss Alleged (2)	Eric Legrix	Itsallgreektome	Quest for Fame	2:30⅘
1992	Fraise (Nose)	Pat Valenzuela	Sky Classic	Quest For Fame	2:24
1993	Kotashaan	Kent Desormeaux	Bien Bien	Luazar	2:25

Note: 1½ miles.

Classic

Year	Winner (Margin)	Jockey	Second	Third	Time
1984	Wild Again (Head)	Pat Day	Slew o' Gold*	Gate Dancer	2:03⅖
1985	Proud Truth (Head)	Jorge Velasquez	Gate Dancer	Turkoman	2:00⅘

Breeders' Cup *(Cont.)*

Classic *(Cont.)*

Year	Winner (Margin)	Jockey	Second	Third	Time
1986	Skywalker (1-¼)	Laffit Pincay Jr	Turkoman	Precisionist	2:00⅖
1987	Ferdinand (Nose)	Bill Shoemaker	Alysheba	Judge Angelucci	2:01⅗
1988	Alysheba (Nose)	Chris McCarron	Seeking the Gold	Waquoit	2:04⅘
1989	Sunday Silence (½)	Chris McCarron	Easy Goer	Blushing John	2:00⅕
1990	Unbridled (1)	Pat Day	Ibn Bey	Thirty Six Red	2:02⅕
1991	Black Tie Affair	Jerry Bailey	Twilight Agenda	Unbridled	2:02⅘
1992	A.P. Indy (2)	Eddie Delahoussaye	Pleasant Tap	Jolypha	2:00⅕
1993	Arcangues	Jerry Bailey	Bertrando	Kissin Kris	2:00⅘

*2nd place finisher Gate Dancer was disqualified for interference and placed 3rd.
Note: 1¼ miles.

England's Triple Crown Winners

England's Triple Crown consists of the Two Thousand Guineas, held at Newmarket; the Epsom Derby, held at Epsom Downs; and the St. Leger Stakes, held at Doncaster.

Year	Horse	Owner
1853	West Australian	Mr. Bowes
1865	Gladiateur	F. DeLagrange
1866	Lord Lyon	R. Sutton
1886	*Ormonde	Duke of Westminster
1891	Common	†F. Johnstone
1893	Isinglass	H. McCalmont
1897	Galtee More	J. Gubbins
1899	Flying Fox	Duke of Westminster
1900	Diamond Jubilee	Prince of Wales
1903	*Rock Sand	J. Miller
1915	Pommern	S. Joel
1917	Gay Crusader	Mr. Fairie
1918	Gainsborough	Lady James Douglas
1935	*Bahram	Aga Khan
1970	‡Nijinsky II	C. W. Engelhard

*Imported into United States. †Raced in name of Lord Alington in Two Thousand Guineas. ‡Canadian-bred.

Annual Leaders

Horse—Money Won

Year	Horse	Age	Starts	1st	2nd	3rd	Winnings ($)
1919	Sir Barton	3	13	8	3	2	88,250
1920	Man o'War	3	11	11	0	0	166,140
1921	Morvich	2	11	11	0	0	115,234
1922	Pillory	3	7	4	1	1	95,654
1923	Zev	3	14	12	1	0	272,008
1924	Sarzen	3	12	8	1	1	95,640
1925	Pompey	2	10	7	2	0	121,630
1926	Crusader	3	15	9	4	0	166,033
1927	Anita Peabody	2	7	6	0	1	111,905
1928	High Strung	2	6	5	0	0	153,590
1929	Blue Larkspur	3	6	4	1	0	153,450
1930	Gallant Fox	3	10	9	1	0	308,275
1931	Gallant Flight	2	7	7	0	0	219,000
1932	Gusto	3	16	4	3	2	145,940
1933	Singing Wood	2	9	3	2	2	88,050
1934	Cavalcade	3	7	6	1	0	111,235
1935	Omaha	3	9	6	1	2	142,255
1936	Granville	3	11	7	3	0	110,295
1937	Seabiscuit	4	15	11	2	2	168,580
1938	Stagehand	3	15	8	2	3	189,710
1939	Challedon	3	15	9	2	3	184,535
1940	Bimelech	3	7	4	2	1	110,005
1941	Whirlaway	3	20	13	5	2	272,386
1942	Shut Out	3	12	8	2	0	238,872
1943	Count Fleet	3	6	6	0	0	174,055
1944	Pavot	2	8	8	0	0	179,040
1945	Busher	3	13	10	2	1	273,735
1946	Assault	3	15	8	2	3	424,195
1947	Armed	6	17	11	4	1	376,325
1948	Citation	3	20	19	1	0	709,470

Note: Annual leaders on pages 460-465 courtesy of *The American Racing Manual*, a publication of Daily Racing Form, Inc.

Horse—Money Won *(Cont.)*

Year	Horse	Age	Starts	1st	2nd	3rd	Winnings ($)
1949	Ponder	3	21	9	5	2	321,825
1950	Noor	5	12	7	4	1	346,940
1951	Counterpoint	3	15	7	2	1	250,525
1952	Crafty Admiral	4	16	9	4	1	277,225
1953	Native Dancer	3	10	9	1	0	513,425
1954	Determine	3	15	10	3	2	328,700
1955	Nashua	3	12	10	1	1	752,550
1956	Needles	3	8	4	2	0	440,850
1957	Round Table	3	22	15	1	3	600,383
1958	Round Table	4	20	14	4	0	662,780
1959	Sword Dancer	3	13	8	4	0	537,004
1960	Bally Ache	3	15	10	3	1	445,045
1961	Carry Back	3	16	9	1	3	565,349
1962	Never Bend	2	10	7	1	2	402,969
1963	Candy Spots	3	12	7	2	1	604,481
1964	Gun Bow	4	16	8	4	2	580,100
1965	Buckpasser	2	11	9	1	0	568,096
1966	Buckpasser	3	14	13	1	0	669,078
1967	Damascus	3	16	12	3	1	817,941
1968	Forward Pass	3	13	7	2	0	546,674
1969	Arts and Letters	3	14	8	5	1	555,604
1970	Personality	3	18	8	2	1	444,049
1971	Riva Ridge	2	9	7	0	0	503,263
1972	Droll Role	4	19	7	3	4	471,633
1973	Secretariat	3	12	9	2	1	860,404
1974	Chris Evert	3	8	5	1	2	551,063
1975	Foolish Pleasure	3	11	5	4	1	716,278
1976	Forego	6	8	6	1	1	401,701
1977	Seattle Slew	3	7	6	0	1	641,370
1978	Affirmed	3	11	8	2	0	901,541
1979	Spectacular Bid	3	12	10	1	1	1,279,334
1980	Temperence Hill	3	17	8	3	1	1,130,452
1981	John Henry	6	10	8	0	0	1,798,030
1982	Perrault	5	8	4	1	2	1,197,400
1983	All Along	4	7	4	1	1	2,138,963
1984	Slew o'Gold	4	6	5	1	0	2,627,944
1985	Spend A Buck	3	7	5	1	1	3,552,704
1986	Snow Chief	3	9	6	1	1	1,875,200
1987	Alysheba	3	10	3	3	1	2,511,156
1988	Alysheba	4	9	7	1	0	3,808,600
1989	Sunday Silence	3	9	7	2	0	4,578,454
1990	Unbridled	3	11	4	3	2	3,718,149
1991	Dance Smartly	3	8	8	0	0	2,876,821
1992	A.P. Indy	3	7	5	0	1	2,622,560
1993	Kotashaan	3	10	6	3	0	2,619,014

Trainer—Money Won

Year	Trainer	Wins	Winnings ($)	Year	Trainer	Wins	Winnings ($)
1908	James Rowe, Sr	50	284,335	1925	G. R. Tompkins	30	199,245
1909	Sam Hildreth	73	123,942	1926	Scott P. Harlan	21	205,681
1910	Sam Hildreth	84	148,010	1927	W. H. Bringloe	63	216,563
1911	Sam Hildreth	67	49,418	1928	John F. Schorr	65	258,425
1912	John F. Schorr	63	58,110	1929	James Rowe, Jr	25	314,881
1913	James Rowe, Sr	18	45,936	1930	Sunny Jim Fitzsimmons	47	397,355
1914	R. C. Benson	45	59,315	1931	Big Jim Healey	33	297,300
1915	James Rowe, Sr	19	75,596	1932	Sunny Jim Fitzsimmons	68	266,650
1916	Sam Hildreth	39	70,950	1933	Humming Bob Smith	53	135,720
1917	Sam Hildreth	23	61,698	1934	Humming Bob Smith	43	249,938
1918	H. Guy Bedwell	53	80,296	1935	Bud Stotler	87	303,005
1919	H. Guy Bedwell	63	208,728	1936	Sunny Jim Fitzsimmons	42	193,415
1920	L. Feustal	22	186,087	1937	Robert McGarvey	46	209,925
1921	Sam Hildreth	85	262,768	1938	Earl Sande	15	226,495
1922	Sam Hildreth	74	247,014	1939	Sunny Jim Fitzsimmons	45	266,205
1923	Sam Hildreth	75	392,124	1940	Silent Tom Smith	14	269,200
1924	Sam Hildreth	77	255,608	1941	Plain Ben Jones	70	475,318

Trainer—Money Won *(Cont.)*

Year	Trainer	Wins	Winnings ($)	Year	Trainer	Wins	Winnings ($)
1942	John M. Gaver Sr	48	406,547	1968	Eddie Neloy	52	1,233,101
1943	Plain Ben Jones	73	267,915	1969	Elliott Burch	26	1,067,936
1944	Plain Ben Jones	60	601,660	1970	Charlie Whittingham	82	1,302,354
1945	Silent Tom Smith	52	510,655	1971	Charlie Whittingham	77	1,737,115
1946	Hirsch Jacobs	99	560,077	1972	Charlie Whittingham	79	1,734,020
1947	Jimmy Jones	85	1,334,805	1973	Charlie Whittingham	85	1,865,385
1948	Jimmy Jones	81	1,118,670	1974	Pancho Martin	166	2,408,419
1949	Jimmy Jones	76	978,587	1975	Charlie Whittingham	93	2,437,244
1950	Preston Burch	96	637,754	1976	Jack Van Berg	496	2,976,196
1951	John M. Gaver Sr	42	616,392	1977	Laz Barrera	127	2,715,848
1952	Plain Ben Jones	29	662,137	1978	Laz Barrera	100	3,307,164
1953	Harry Trotsek	54	1,028,873	1979	Laz Barrera	98	3,608,517
1954	Willie Molter	136	1,107,860	1980	Laz Barrera	99	2,969,151
1955	Sunny Jim Fitzsimmons	66	1,270,055	1981	Charlie Whittingham	74	3,993,302
1956	Willie Molter	142	1,227,402	1982	Charlie Whittingham	63	4,587,457
1957	Jimmy Jones	70	1,150,910	1983	D. Wayne Lukas	78	4,267,261
1958	Willie Molter	69	1,116,544	1984	D. Wayne Lukas	131	5,835,921
1959	Willie Molter	71	847,290	1985	D. Wayne Lukas	218	11,155,188
1960	Hirsch Jacobs	97	748,349	1986	D. Wayne Lukas	259	12,345,180
1961	Jimmy Jones	62	759,856	1987	D. Wayne Lukas	343	17,502,110
1962	Mesh Tenney	58	1,099,474	1988	D. Wayne Lukas	318	17,842,358
1963	Mesh Tenney	40	860,703	1989	D. Wayne Lukas	305	16,103,998
1964	Bill Winfrey	61	1,350,534	1990	D. Wayne Lukas	267	14,508,871
1965	Hirsch Jacobs	91	1,331,628	1991	D. Wayne Lukas	289	15,942,223
1966	Eddie Neloy	93	2,456,250	1992	D. Wayne Lukas	230	9,806,436
1967	Eddie Neloy	72	1,776,089	1993	Robert Frankel	79	8,883,252

Jockey—Money Won

Year	Jockey	Mts	1st	2nd	3rd	Pct	Winnings ($)
1919	John Loftus	177	65	36	24	.37	252,707
1920	Clarence Kummer	353	87	79	48	.25	292,376
1921	Earl Sande	340	112	69	59	.33	263,043
1922	Albert Johnson	297	43	57	40	.14	345,054
1923	Earl Sande	430	122	89	79	.28	569,394
1924	Ivan Parke	844	205	175	121	.24	290,395
1925	Laverne Fator	315	81	54	44	.26	305,775
1926	Laverne Fator	511	143	90	86	.28	361,435
1927	Earl Sande	179	49	33	19	.27	277,877
1928	Pony McAtee	235	55	43	25	.23	301,295
1929	Mack Garner	274	57	39	33	.21	314,975
1930	Sonny Workman	571	152	88	79	.27	420,438
1931	Charles Kurtsinger	519	93	82	79	.18	392,095
1932	Sonny Workman	378	87	48	55	.23	385,070
1933	Robert Jones	471	63	57	70	.13	226,285
1934	Wayne D. Wright	919	174	154	114	.19	287,185
1935	Silvio Coucci	749	141	125	103	.19	319,760
1936	Wayne D. Wright	670	100	102	73	.15	264,000
1937	Charles Kurtsinger	765	120	94	106	.16	384,202
1938	Nick Wall	658	97	94	82	.15	385,161
1939	Basil James	904	191	165	105	.21	353,333
1940	Eddie Arcaro	783	132	143	112	.17	343,661
1941	Don Meade	1164	210	185	158	.18	398,627
1942	Eddie Arcaro	687	123	97	89	.18	481,949
1943	John Longden	871	173	140	121	.20	573,276
1944	Ted Atkinson	1539	287	231	213	.19	899,101
1945	John Longden	778	180	112	100	.23	981,977
1946	Ted Atkinson	1377	233	213	173	.17	1,036,825
1947	Douglas Dodson	646	141	100	75	.22	1,429,949
1948	Eddie Arcaro	726	188	108	98	.26	1,686,230
1949	Steve Brooks	906	209	172	110	.23	1,316,817
1950	Eddie Arcaro	888	195	153	144	.22	1,410,160
1951	Bill Shoemaker	1161	257	197	161	.22	1,329,890
1952	Eddie Arcaro	807	188	122	109	.23	1,859,591
1953	Bill Shoemaker	1683	485	302	210	.29	1,784,187

Jockey—Money Won (Cont.)

Year	Jockey	Mts	1st	2nd	3rd	Pct	Winnings ($)
1954	Bill Shoemaker	1251	380	221	142	.30	1,876,760
1955	Eddie Arcaro	820	158	126	108	.19	1,864,796
1956	Bill Hartack	1387	347	252	184	.25	2,343,955
1957	Bill Hartack	1238	341	208	178	.28	3,060,501
1958	Bill Shoemaker	1133	300	185	137	.26	2,961,693
1959	Bill Shoemaker	1285	347	230	159	.27	2,843,133
1960	Bill Shoemaker	1227	274	196	158	.22	2,123,961
1961	Bill Shoemaker	1256	304	186	175	.24	2,690,819
1962	Bill Shoemaker	1126	311	156	128	.28	2,916,844
1963	Bill Shoemaker	1203	271	193	137	.22	2,526,925
1964	Bill Shoemaker	1056	246	147	133	.23	2,649,553
1965	Braulio Baeza	1245	270	200	201	.22	2,582,702
1966	Braulio Baeza	1341	298	222	190	.22	2,951,022
1967	Braulio Baeza	1064	256	184	127	.24	3,088,888
1968	Braulio Baeza	1089	201	184	145	.18	2,835,108
1969	Jorge Velasquez	1442	258	230	204	.18	2,542,315
1970	Laffit Pincay Jr	1328	269	208	187	.20	2,626,526
1971	Laffit Pincay Jr	1627	380	288	214	.23	3,784,377
1972	Laffit Pincay Jr	1388	289	215	205	.21	3,225,827
1973	Laffit Pincay Jr	1444	350	254	209	.24	4,093,492
1974	Laffit Pincay Jr	1278	341	227	180	.27	4,251,060
1975	Braulio Baeza	1190	196	208	180	.16	3,674,398
1976	Angel Cordero Jr	1534	274	273	235	.18	4,709,500
1977	Steve Cauthen	2075	487	345	304	.23	6,151,750
1978	Darrel McHargue	1762	375	294	263	.21	6,188,353
1979	Laffit Pincay Jr	1708	420	302	261	.25	8,183,535
1980	Chris McCarron	1964	405	318	282	.20	7,666,100
1981	Chris McCarron	1494	326	251	207	.22	8,397,604
1982	Angel Cordero Jr	1838	397	338	227	.22	9,702,520
1983	Angel Cordero Jr	1792	362	296	237	.20	10,116,807
1984	Chris McCarron	1565	356	276	218	.23	12,038,213
1985	Laffit Pincay Jr	1409	289	246	183	.21	13,415,049
1986	Jose Santos	1636	329	237	222	.20	11,329,297
1987	Jose Santos	1639	305	268	208	.19	12,407,355
1988	Jose Santos	1867	370	287	265	.20	14,877,298
1989	Jose Santos	1459	285	238	220	.20	13,847,003
1990	Gary Stevens	1504	283	245	202	.19	13,881,198
1991	Chris McCarron	1440	265	228	206	.18	14,441,083
1992	Kent Desormeaux	1568	361	260	208	.23	14,193,006
1993	Mike Smith	1,510	343	235	214	.23	14,008,148

Jockey—Races Won

Year	Jockey	Mts	1st	2nd	3rd	Pct
1895	J. Perkins	762	192	177	129	.25
1896	J. Scherrer	1093	271	227	172	.24
1897	H. Martin	803	173	152	116	.21
1898	T. Burns	973	277	213	149	.28
1899	T. Burns	1064	273	173	266	.26
1900	C. Mitchell	874	195	140	139	.23
1901	W. O'Connor	1047	253	221	192	.24
1902	J. Ranch	1069	276	205	181	.26
1903	G.C. Fuller	918	229	152	122	.25
1904	E. Hildebrand	1169	297	230	171	.25
1905	D. Nicol	861	221	143	136	.26
1906	W. Miller	1384	388	300	199	.28
1907	W. Miller	1194	334	226	170	.28
1908	V. Powers	1260	324	204	185	.26
1909	V. Powers	704	173	121	114	.25
1910	G. Garner	947	200	188	153	.20
1911	T. Koerner	813	162	133	112	.20
1912	P. Hill	967	168	141	129	.17
1913	M. Buxton	887	146	131	136	.16
1914	J. McTaggart	787	157	132	106	.20
1915	M. Garner	775	151	118	90	.19
1916	F. Robinson	791	178	131	124	.23

Jockey—Races Won (Cont.)

Year	Jockey	Mts	1st	2nd	3rd	Pct
1917	W. Crump	803	151	140	101	.19
1918	F. Robinson	864	185	140	108	.21
1919	C. Robinson	896	190	140	126	.21
1920	J. Butwell	721	152	129	139	.21
1921	C. Lang	696	135	110	105	.19
1922	M. Fator	859	188	153	116	.22
1923	I. Parke	718	173	105	95	.24
1924	I. Parke	844	205	175	121	.24
1925	A. Mortensen	987	187	145	138	.19
1926	R. Jones	1172	190	163	152	.16
1927	L. Hardy	1130	207	192	151	.18
1928	J. Inzelone	1052	155	152	135	.15
1929	M. Knight	871	149	132	133	.17
1930	H.R. Riley	861	177	145	123	.21
1931	H. Roble	1174	173	173	155	.15
1932	J. Gilbert	1050	212	144	160	.20
1933	J. Westrope	1224	301	235	166	.25
1934	M. Peters	1045	221	179	147	.21
1935	C. Stevenson	1099	206	169	146	.19
1936	B. James	1106	245	195	161	.22
1937	J. Adams	1265	260	186	177	.21
1938	J. Longden	1150	236	168	171	.21
1939	D. Meade	1284	255	221	180	.20
1940	E. Dew	1377	287	201	180	.21
1941	D. Meade	1164	210	185	158	.18
1942	J. Adams	1120	245	185	150	.22
1943	J. Adams	1069	228	159	171	.21
1944	T. Atkinson	1539	287	231	213	.19
1945	J.D. Jessop	1085	290	182	168	.27
1946	T. Atkinson	1377	233	213	173	.17
1947	J. Longden	1327	316	250	195	.24
1948	J. Longden	1197	319	233	161	.27
1949	G. Glisson	1347	270	217	181	.20
1950	W. Shoemaker	1640	388	266	230	.24
1951	C. Burr	1319	310	232	192	.24
1952	A. DeSpirito	1482	390	247	212	.26
1953	W. Shoemaker	1683	485	302	210	.29
1954	W. Shoemaker	1251	380	221	142	.30
1955	W. Hartack	1702	417	298	215	.25
1956	W. Hartack	1387	347	252	184	.25
1957	W. Hartack	1238	341	208	178	.28
1958	W. Shoemaker	1133	300	185	137	.26
1959	W. Shoemaker	1285	347	230	159	.27
1960	W. Hartack	1402	307	247	190	.22
1961	J. Sellers	1394	328	212	227	.24
1962	R. Ferraro	1755	352	252	226	.20
1963	W. Blum	1704	360	286	215	.21
1964	W. Blum	1577	324	274	170	.21
1965	J. Davidson	1582	319	228	190	.20
1966	A. Gomez	996	318	173	142	.32
1967	J. Velasquez	1939	438	315	270	.23
1968	A. Cordero Jr.	1662	345	278	219	.21
1969	L. Snyder	1645	352	290	243	.21
1970	S. Hawley	1908	452	313	265	.24
1971	L Pincay Jr.	1627	380	288	214	.23
1972	S. Hawley	1381	367	269	200	.27
1973	S. Hawley	1925	515	336	292	.27
1974	C.J. McCarron	2199	546	392	297	.25
1975	C.J. McCarron	2194	458	389	305	.21
1976	S. Hawley	1637	413	245	201	.25
1977	S. Cauthen	2075	487	345	304	.23
1978	E. Delahoussaye	1666	384	285	238	.23
1979	D. Gall	2146	479	396	326	.22
1980	C.J. McCarron	1964	405	318	282	.20
1981	D. Gall	1917	376	305	297	.20

Jockey—Races Won (Cont.)

Year	Jockey	Mts	1st	2nd	3rd	Pct
1982	P. Day	1870	399	326	255	.21
1983	P. Day	1725	454	321	251	.26
1984	P. Day	1694	399	296	259	.24
1985	C.W. Antley	2335	469	371	288	.20
1986	P. Day	1417	429	246	202	.30
1987	K. Desormeaux	2207	450	370	294	.28
1988	K. Desormeaux	1897	474	295	276	.25
1989	K. Desormeaux	2312	598	385	309	.25
1990	P. Day	1421	364	265	222	.26
1991	P. Day	1405	430	256	213	.31
1992	R.A. Baze	1691	433	296	237	.25
1993	R.A. Baze	1,579	410	297	225	.26

Leading Jockeys—Career Records Through 1993

Jockey	Years Riding	Mts	1st	2nd	3rd	Win Pct	Winnings ($)
Shoemaker, W. (1990)	42	40,350	8,833	6,136	4,987	.219	123,375,524
Pincay, L. Jr.	28	38,695	8,054	6,379	5,344	.208	177,153,172
Cordero, A. Jr.	31	38,646	7,057	6,136	6,359	.183	164,526,217
Velasquez, J.	31	39,234	6,625	5,970	5,557	.169	122,957,325
Gall, D.	37	36,321	6,396	5,132	3,553	.176	19,493,195
Snyder, L.	34	35,557	6,385	5,015	3,418	.180	47,121,556
Gambardella, C.	38	38,484	6,263	5,866	5,279	.163	27,664,070
Day, P.	21	27,891	6,105	4,729	3,864	.219	138,465,865
Hawley, S.	27	29,098	6,051	4,487	3,823	.208	79,349,842
Longden, J. (1966)	40	32,413	6,032	4,914	4,273	.186	24,665,800
McCarron, C. J.	19	28,124	5,924	4,653	3,851	.211	167,628,755
E. Fires	29	37,694	5,562	4,702	4,500	.148	63,584,818
Delahoussaye, E.	24	31,654	5,192	4,555	4,359	.164	130,000,052
Vasquez, J.	34	36,577	5,157	4,616	4,416	.142	78,421,248
Arcaro E. (1961)	31	24,092	4,779	3,807	3,302	.198	30,039,543
Brumfield, D. (1989)	37	33,223	4,573	4,076	3,758	.138	48,567,861
Brooks, S. (1975)	34	30,330	4,451	4,219	3,658	.147	18,239,817
Blum, W. (1975)	22	28,673	4,382	3,913	3,350	.153	26,497,189
Baze, R. A.	20	24,189	4,334	3,693	3,299	.179	63,093,078
Hartack, W. (1974)	22	21,535	4,272	3,370	2,871	.198	26,466,758
Maple, E.	26	31,245	4,116	4,177	4,020	.131	94,236,829
Gomez, A. (1980)	34	17,028	4,081	2,947	2,405	.240	11,777,297
Dittfach, H. (1989)	33	33,905	4,000	4,092	6,113	.118	13,506,052
Atkinson, D. (1959)	22	23,661	3,795	3,300	2,913	.160	17,449,360
Whited, D. E.	36	27,930	3,784	3,592	3,356	.135	25,067,466

Note: Records include available statistics for races ridden in foreign countries. Figures in parentheses after jockey's name indicate last year in which he rode.

Leading jockeys courtesy of *The American Racing Manual*, a publication of Daily Racing Form, Inc.

National Museum of Racing Hall of Fame

HORSES

Ack Ack (1986, 1966)
Affectionately (1989, 1960)
Affirmed (1980, 1975)
All Along (1990, 1979)
Alsab (1976, 1939)
Alydar (1989, 1975)
American Eclipse (1970, 1814)
Armed (1963, 1941)
Artful (1956, 1902)

Arts and Letters (1993, 1966)
Assault (1964, 1943)
Battleship (1969, 1927)
Bed o'Roses (1976, 1947)
Beldame (1956, 1901)
Ben Brush (1955, 1893)
Bewitch (1977, 1945)
Bimelech (1990, 1937)
Black Gold (1989, 1921)

Black Helen (1991, 1932)
Blue Larkspur (1957, 1926)
Bold Ruler (1973, 1954)
Bon Nouvel (1976, 1960)
Boston (1955, 1833)
Broomstick (1956, 1901)
Buckpasser (1970, 1963)
Busher (1964, 1942)
Bushranger (1967, 1930)

HORSES *(Cont.)*

Cafe Prince (1985, 1970)
Carry Back (1975, 1958)
Challedon (1977, 1936)
Chris Evert (1988, 1971)
Cicada (1967, 1959)
Citation (1959, 1945)
Coaltown (1983, 1945)
Colin (1956, 1905)
Commando (1956, 1898)
Count Fleet (1961, 1940)
Dahlia (1981, 1970)
Damascus (1974, 1964)
Dark Mirage (1974, 1965)
Davona Dale (1985, 1976)
Desert Vixen (1979, 1970)
Devil Diver (1980, 1939)
Discovery (1969, 1931)
Domino (1955, 1891)
Dr. Fager (1971, 1964)
Eight Thirty (1993, 1938)
Elkridge (1966, 1938)
Emperor of Norfolk (1988, 1885)
Equipoise (1957, 1928)
Exterminator (1957, 1915)
Fairmount (1985, 1921)
Fair Play (1956, 1905)
Fashion (1980, 1837)
Firenze (1981, 1884)
Flatterer (1993, 1980)
Forego (1979, 1970)
Gallant Bloom (1977, 1966)
Gallant Fox (1957, 1927)
Gallant Man (1987, 1954)
Gallorette (1962, 1942)
Gamely (1980, 1964)
Genuine Risk (1986, 1977)
Good and Plenty (1956, 1900)

Grey Lag (1957, 1918)
Hamburg (1986, 1895)
Hanover (1955, 1884)
Henry of Navarre (1985, 1891)
Hill Prince (1991, 1947)
Hindoo (1955, 1878)
Imp (1965, 1894)
Jay Trump (1971, 1957)
John Henry (1990, 1975)
Johnstown (1992, 1982)
Jolly Roger (1965, 1922)
Kelso (1967, 1957)
Kentucky (1983, 1861)
Kingston (1955, 1884)
Lady's Secret (1992, 1982)
L'Escargot (1977, 1963)
Lexington (1955, 1850)
Longfellow (1971, 1867)
Luke Blackburn (1956, 1877)
Majestic Prince (1988, 1966)
Man o'War (1957, 1917)
Miss Woodford (1967, 1880)
Myrtlewood (1979, 1932)
Nashua (1965, 1952)
Native Dancer (1963, 1950)
Native Diver (1978, 1959)
Neji (1966, 1950)
Northern Dancer (1976, 1961)
Oedipus (1978, 1946)
Old Rosebud (1968, 1911)
Omaha (1965, 1932)
Pan Zareta (1972, 1910)
Parole (1984, 1879)
Peter Pan (1956, 1904)
Princess Doreen (1982, 1921)
Princess Rooney (1991, 1980)
Real Delight (1987, 1949)

Regret (1957, 1912)
Reigh Count (1978, 1925)
Roamer (1981, 1911)
Roseben (1956, 1901)
Round Table (1972, 1954)
Ruffian (1976, 1972)
Ruthless (1975, 1864)
Salvator (1955, 1886)
Sarazen (1957, 1921)
Seabiscuit (1958, 1933)
Searching (1978, 1952)
Seattle Slew (1981, 1974)
Secretariat (1974, 1970)
Shuvee (1975, 1966)
Silver Spoon (1978, 1956)
Sir Archy (1955, 1805)
Sir Barton (1957, 1916)
Slew o' Gold (1992, 1980)
Spectacular Bid (1982, 1976)
Stymie (1975, 1941)
Susan's Girl (1976, 1969)
Swaps (1966, 1952)
Sword Dancer (1977, 1956)
Sysonby (1956, 1902)
Ta Wee (1993, 1967)
Ten Broeck (1982, 1872)
Tim Tam (1985, 1955)
Tom Fool (1960, 1949)
Top Flight (1966, 1929)
Tosmah (1984, 1961)
Twenty Grand (1957, 1928)
Twilight Tear (1963, 1941)
Two Lea (1982, 1946)
War Admiral (1958, 1934)
Whirlaway (1959, 1938)
Whisk Broom II (1979, 1907)
Zev (1983, 1920)

Note: Years of election and foaling in parentheses.

HARNESS RACING

Major Races

Hambletonian

Year	Winner	Driver	Year	Winner	Driver
1926	Guy McKinney	Nat Ray	1944	Yankee Maid	Henry Thomas
1927	Iosola's Worthy	Marvin Childs	1945	Titan Hanover	H. Pownall Sr
1928	Spenser	W. H. Leese	1946	Chestertown	Thomas Berry
1929	Walter Dear	Walter Cox	1947	Hoot Mon	Sep Palin
1930	Hanover's Bertha	Tom Berry	1948	Demon Hanover	Harrison Hoyt
1931	Calumet Butler	R. D. McMahon	1949	Miss Tilly	Fred Egan
1932	The Marchioness	William Caton	1950	Lusty Song	Del Miller
1933	Mary Reynolds	Ben White	1951	Mainliner	Guy Crippen
1934	Lord Jim	Doc Parshall	1952	Sharp Note	Bion Shively
1935	Greyhound	Sep Palin	1953	Helicopter	Harry Harvey
1936	Rosalind	Ben White	1954	Newport Dream	Del Cameron
1937	Shirley Hanover	Henry Thomas	1955	Scott Frost	Joe O'Brien
1938	McLin Hanover	Henry Thomas	1956	The Intruder	Ned Bower
1939	Peter Astra	Doc Parshall	1957	Hickory Smoke	J. Simpson Sr
1940	Spencer Scott	Fred Egan	1958	Emily's Pride	Flave Nipe
1941	Bill Gallon	Lee Smith	1959	Diller Hanover	Frank Ervin
1942	The Ambassador	Ben White	1960	Blaze Hanover	Joe O'Brien
1943	Volo Song	Ben White	1961	Harlan Dean	James Arthur

Hambletonian (Cont.)

Year	Winner	Driver	Year	Winner	Driver
1962	A. C.'s Viking	Sanders Russell	1979	Legend Hanover	George Sholty
1963	Speedy Scot	Ralph Baldwin	1980	Burgomeister	Bill Haughton
1964	Ayres	J. Simpson, Sr	1981	Shiaway St. Pat	Ray Remmen
1965	Egyptian Candor	Del Cameron	1982	Speed Bowl	Tom Haughton
1966	Kerry Way	Frank Ervin	1983	Duenna	Stanley Dancer
1967	Speedy Streak	Del Cameron	1984	Historic Freight	Ben Webster
1968	Nevele Pride	Stanley Dancer	1985	Prakas	Bill O'Donnell
1969	Lindy's Pride	H. Beissinger	1986	Nuclear Kosmos	Ulf Thoresen
1970	Timothy T.	J. Simpson, Jr	1987	Mack Lobell	John Campbell
1971	Speedy Crown	H. Beissinger	1988	Armbro Goal	John Campbell
1972	Super Bowl	Stanley Dancer	1989	Park Avenue Joe*	Ron Waples
1973	Flirth	Ralph Baldwin		Probe*	Bill Fahy
1974	Christopher T.	Bill Haughton	1990	Harmonious	John Campbell
1975	Bonefish	Stanley Dancer	1991	Giant Victory	Jack Moiseyev
1976	Steve Lobell	Bill Haughton	1992	Alf Palema	Mickey McNichol
1977	Green Speed	Bill Haughton	1993	American Winner	Ron Pierce
1978	Speedy Somolli	H. Beissinger	1994	Victory Dream	Mike LaChance

*Park Avenue Joe and Probe dead-heated for win. Park Avenue Joe finished first in the summary 2-1-1 to Probe's 1-9-1 finish.

Note: Run at 1 mile since 1947.

Little Brown Jug

Year	Winner	Driver	Year	Winner	Driver
1946	Ensign Hanover	Wayne Smart	1970	Most Happy Fella	Stanley Dancer
1947	Forbes Chief	Del Cameron	1971	Nansemond	Herve Filion
1948	Knight Dream	Frank Safford	1972	Strike Out	Keith Waples
1949	Good Time	Frank Ervin	1973	Melvin's Woe	Joe O'Brien
1950	Dudley Hanover	Del Miller	1974	Armbro Omaha	Bill Haughton
1951	Tar Heel	Del Cameron	1975	Seatrain	Ben Webster
1952	Meadow Rice	Wayne Smart	1976	Keystone Ore	Stanley Dancer
1953	Keystoner	Frank Ervin	1977	Governor Skipper	John Chapman
1954	Adios Harry	Morris MacDonald	1978	Happy Escort	William Popfinger
1955	Quick Chief	Bill Haughton	1979	Hot Hitter	Herve Filion
1956	Noble Adios	John Simpson Sr	1980	Niatross	Clint Galbraith
1957	Torpid	John Simpso Sr	1981	Fan Hanover	Glen Garnsey
1958	Shadow Wave	Joe O'Brien	1982	Merger	John Campbell
1959	Adios Butler	Clint Hodgins	1983	Ralph Hanover	Ron Waples
1960	Bullet Hanover	John Simpson Sr	1984	Colt Fortysix	Chris Boring
1961	Henry T. Adios	Stanley Dancer	1985	Nihilator	Bill O'Donnell
1962	Lehigh Hanover	Stanley Dancer	1986	Barberry Spur	Bill O'Donnell
1963	Overtrick	John Patterson	1987	Jaguar Spur	Dick Stillings
1964	Vicar Hanover	Bill Haughton	1988	B. J. Scoot	Michel Lachance
1965	Bret Hanover	Frank Ervin	1989	Goalie Jeff	Michel Lachance
1966	Romeo Hanover	George Sholty	1990	Beach Towel	Ray Remmen
1967	Best of All	James Hackett	1991	Precious Bunny	Jack Moiseye
1968	Rum Customer	Bill Haughton	1992	Fake Left	Ron Waples
1969	Laverne Hanover	Bill Haughton	1993	Life Sign	John Campbell

Breeders' Crown

1984

Div	Winner	Driver
2PC	Dragon's Lair	Jeff Mallet
2PF	Amneris	John Campbell
3PC	Troublemaker	Bill O'Donnell
3PF	Naughty But Nice	Tommy Haughton
2TC	Workaholic	Berndt Lindstedt
2TF	Conifer	George Sholty
3TC	Baltic Speed	Jan Nordin
3TF	Fancy Crown	Bill O'Donnell

1985

Div	Winner	Driver
2PC	Robust Hanover	John Campbell
2PF	Caressable	Herve Filion
3PC	Nihilator	Bill O'Donnell
3PF	Stienam	Buddy Gilmour
2TC	Express Ride	John Campbell
2TF	JEF's Spice	Mickey McNichol
3TC	Prakas	John Campbell
3TF	Armbro Devona	Bill O'Donnell
AP	Division Street	Michel Lachance
AT	Sandy Bowl	John Campbell

1986

Div	Winner	Driver
2PC	Sunset Warrior	Bill Gale
2PF	Halcyon	Ray Remmen
3PC	Masquerade	Richard Silverman
3PF	Glow Softly	Ron Waples
2TC	Mack Lobell	John Campbell
2TF	Super Flora	Ron Waples
3TC	Sugarcane Hanover	Ron Waples
3TF	JEF's Spice	Bill O'Donnell
APM	Samshu Bluegrass	Michel Lachance
ATM	Grades Singing	Herve Filion
APH	Forrest Skipper	Lucien Fontaine
ATH	Nearly Perfect	Mickey McNichol

1987

Div	Winner	Driver
2PC	Camtastic	Bill O'Donnell
2PF	Leah Almahurst	Bill Fahy
3PC	Call For Rain	Clint Galbraith
3PF	Pacific	Tom Harmer
2TC	Defiant One	Howard Beissinger
2TF	Nan's Catch	Berndt Lindstedt
3TC	Mack Lobell	John Campbell
3TF	Armbro Fling	George Sholty
APM	Follow My Star	John Campbell
ATM	Grades Singing	Olle Goop
APH	Armbro Emerson	Walter Whelan
ATH	Sugarcane Hanover	Ron Waples

1988

Div	Winner	Driver
2PC	Kentucky Spur	Dick Stillings
2PF	Central Park West	John Campbell
3PC	Camtastic	Bill O'Donnell
3PF	Sweet Reflection	Bill O'Donnell
2TC	Valley Victory	Bill O'Donnell
2TF	Peace Corps	John Campbell
3TC	Firm Tribute	Mark O'Mara

1988 *(Cont.)*

Div	Winner	Driver
3TF	Nalda Hanover	Mickey McNichol
APM	Anniecrombie	Dave Magee
ATM	Armbro Flori	Larry Walker
APH	Call For Rain	Clint Galbraith
ATH	Mack Lobell	John Campbell

1989

Div	Winner	Driver
2PC	Till We Meet Again	Mickey McNichol
2PF	Town Pro	Doug Brown
3PC	Goalie Jeff	Michel Lachance
3PF	Cheery Hello	John Campbell
2TC	Royal Troubador	Carl Allen
2TF	Delphi's Lobell	Ron Waples
3TC	Esquire Spur	Dick Stillings
3TF	Pace Corps	John Campbell
APM	Armbro Feather	John Kopas
ATM	Grades Singing	Olle Goop
APH	Matt's Scooter	Michel Lachance
ATH	Delray Lobell	John Campbell

1990

Div	Winner	Driver
2PC	Artsplace	John Campbell
2PF	Miss Easy	John Campbell
3PC	Beach Towel	Ray Remmen
3PF	Town Pro	Doug Brown
2TC	Crysta's Best	Dick Richardson Jr
2TF	Jean Bi	Jan Nordin
3TC	Embassy Lobell	Michel Lachance
3TF	Me Maggie	Berndt Lindstedt
APM	Caesar's Jackpot	Bill Fahy
ATM	Peace Corps	Stig Johansson
APH	Bay's Fella	Paul MacDonell
ATH	No Sex Please	Ron Waples

1991

Div	Winner	Driver
2PC	Digger Almahurst	Doug Brown
2PF	Hazleton Kay	John Campbell
3PC	Three Wizzards	Bill Gale
3PF	Miss Easy	John Campbell
2TC	King Conch	Bill Gale
2TF	Armbro Keepsake	John Campbell
3TC	Giant Victory	Ron Pierce
3TF	Twelve Speed	Ron Waples
APM	Delinquent Account	Bill O'Donnell
ATM	Me Maggie	Berndt Lindstedt
APH	Camluck	Michel Lachance
ATH	Billyjojimbob	Paul MacDonell

1992

Div	Winner	Driver
2PC	Village Jiffy	Ron Waples
2PF	Immortality	John Campbell
3PC	Kingsbridge	Roger Mayotte
3PF	So Fresh	John Campbell
2TC	Giant Chill	John Patterson, Jr
2TF	Winky's Goal	Cat Manzi
3TC	Baltic Striker	Michel Lachance
3TF	Imperfection	Michel Lachance

Note: 2=Two-year-old; T=Trotter; C=Colt; 3=Three-year-old; P=Pacer; F=Filly; A=Aged; H=Horse; M=Mare.

Breeders' Crown *(Cont.)*

1992 *(Cont.)*

Div	Winner	Driver
APM	.........Shady Daisy	Ron Pierce
ATM	.........Peace Corps	Torbjorn Jansson
APH	...........Artsplace	John Campbell
ATH	...........No Sex Please	Ron Waples

1993

Div	Winner	Driver
2PC	..........Expensive Scooter	Jack Moiseyev
2PF	............Electric Scooter	Mike LaChance
3PC	...........Life Sign	John Campbell

1993 *(Cont.)*

Div	Winner	Driver
3PF	............Immortality	John Campbell
2TC	..........Westgate Crown	John Campbell
2TF	...........Gleam	Jimmy Takter
3TC	...........Pine Chip	John Campbell
3TF	............Expressway Hanover	Per Henriksen
APM	.........Swing Back	Kelly Sheppard
ATM	.........Lifetime Dream	Paul MacDonnell
APH	..........Staying Together	Bill O'Donnell
ATH	...........Earl	Chris Christoforou Jr

Note: 2=Two-year-old; T=Trotter; C=Colt; 3=Three-year-old; P=Pacer; F=Filly; A=Aged; H=Horse; M=Mare.

Triple Crown Winners

Trotting

Trotting's Triple Crown consists of the Hambletonian (first run in 1926), the Kentucky Futurity (first run in 1893), and the Yonkers Trot (known as the Yonkers Futurity when it began in 1955).

Year	Horse	Owner	Breeder	Trainer & Driver
1955	......Scott Frost	S.A. Camp Farms	Est of W. N. Reynolds	Joe O'Brien
1963	......Speedy Scot	Castleton Farms	Castleton Farms	Ralph Baldwin
1964	......Ayres	Charlotte Sheppard	Charlotte Sheppard	John Simpson Sr
1968	......Nevele Pride	Nevele Acres & Lou Resnick	Mr & Mrs E. C. Quin	Stanley Dancer
1969	......Lindy's Pride	Lindy Farm	Hanover Shoe Farms	Howard Beissinger
1972	......Super Bowl	Rachel Dancer & Rose Hild Breeding Farm	Stoner Creek Stud	Stanley Dancer

Pacing

Pacing's Triple Crown consists of the Cane Pace (called the Cane Futurity when it began in 1955), the Little Brown Jug (first run in 1946), and the Messenger Stake (first run in 1956).

Year	Horse	Owner	Breeder	Trainer/Driver
1959	...Adios Butler	Paige West & Angelo Pelillo	R. C. Carpenter	Paige West/Clint Hodgins
1965	...Bret Hanover	Richard Downing	Hanover Shoe Farms	Frank Ervin
1966	...Romeo Hanover	Lucky Star Stables & Morton Finder	Hanover Shoe Farms	Jerry Silverman/ William Meyer (Cane) & George Sholty (Jug & Messenger)
1968	...Rum Customer	Kennilworth Farms & L. C. Mancuso	Mr. & Mrs. R. C. Larkin	Bill Haughton
1970	...Most Happy Fella	Egyptian Acres Stable	Stoner Creek Stud	Stanley Dancer
1980	...Niatross	Niagara Acres, C. Galbraith & Niatross Stables	Niagara Acres	Clint Galbraith
1983	...Ralph Hanover	Waples Stable, Pointsetta Stable, Grant's Direct Stable & P. J. Baugh	Hanover Shoe Farms	Stew Firlotte/Ron Waples

Awards

Horse of the Year

Year	Horse	Gait	Owner	Year	Horse	Gait	Owner
1947	...Victory Song	T	Castleton Farm	1952	...Good Time	P	William Cane
1948	...Rodney	T	R. H. Johnston	1953	...Hi Lo's Forbes	P	Mr. and Mrs. Earl Wagner
1949	...Good Time	P	William Cane	1954	...Stenographer	T	Max Hempt
1950	...Proximity	T	Ralph and Gordon Verhurst	1955	...Scott Frost	T	S. A. Camp Farms
1951	...Pronto Don	T	Hayes Fair Acres Stable	1956	...Scott Frost	T	S. A. Camp Farms
				1957	...Torpid	P	Sherwood Farm

Horse of the Year (Cont.)

Year	Horse	Gait	Owner
1958	Emily's Pride	T	Walnut Hall and Castleton Farms
1959	Bye Bye Byrd	P	Mr. and Mrs. Rex Larkin
1960	Adios Butler	P	Adios Butler Syndicate
1961	Adios Butler	P	Adios Butler Syndicate
1962	Su Mac Lad	T	I. W. Berkemeyer
1963	Speedy Scot	T	Castleton Farm
1964	Bret Hanover	P	Richard Downing
1965	Bret Hanover	P	Richard Downing
1966	Bret Hanover	P	Richard Downing
1967	Nevele Pride	T	Nevele Acres
1968	Nevele Pride	T	Nevele Acres, Louis Resnick
1969	Nevele Pride	T	Nevele Acres, Louis Resnick
1970	Fresh Yankee	T	Duncan MacDonald
1971	Albatross	P	Albatross Stable
1972	Albatross	P	Amicable Stable
1973	Sir Dalrae	P	A La Carte Racing Stable
1974	Delmonica Hanover	T	Delvin Miller, W. Arnold Hanger
1975	Savoir	T	Allwood Stable
1976	Keystone Ore	P	Mr. and Mrs. Stanley Dancer, Rose Hild Farms, Robert Jones
1977	Green Speed	T	Beverly Lloyds
1978	Abercrombie	P	Shirley Mitchell, L. Keith Bulen
1979	Niatross	P	Niagara Acres, Clint Galbraith
1980	Niatross	P	Niatross Syndicate, Niagara Acres, Clint Galbraith
1981	Fan Hanover	P	Dr. J. Glen Brown
1982	Cam Fella	P	Norm Clements, Norm Faulkner
1983	Cam Fella	P	JEF's Standardbred, Norm Clements, Norm Faulkner
1984	Fancy Crown	T	Fancy Crown Stable
1985	Nihilator	P	Wall Street-Nihilator Syndicate
1986	Forrest Skipper	P	Forrest L. Bartlett
1987	Mack Lobell	T	One More Time Stable and Fair Wind Farm
1988	Mack Lobell	T	John Erik Magnusson
1989	Matt's Scooter	P	Gordon and Illa Rumpel, Charles Jurasvinski
1990	Beach Towel	P	Uptown Stables
1991	Precious Bunny	P	R. Peter Heffering
1992	Artsplace	P	George Segal
1993	Staying Together	P	Robert Hamather

Note: Balloting is conducted by the U.S Trotting Association and U.S. Harness Writers Association.

Leading Drivers—Money Won

Year	Driver	Winnings ($)	Year	Driver	Winnings ($)
1946	Thomas Berry	121,933	1970	Herve Filion	1,647,837
1947	H. C. Fitzpatrick	133,675	1971	Herve Filion	1,915,945
1948	Ralph Baldwin	153,222	1972	Herve Filion	2,473,265
1949	Clint Hodgins	184,108	1973	Herve Filion	2,233,303
1950	Del Miller	306,813	1974	Herve Filion	3,474,315
1951	John Simpson Sr	333,316	1975	Carmine Abbatiello	2,275,093
1952	Bill Haughton	311,728	1976	Herve Filion	2,278,634
1953	Bill Haughton	374,527	1977	Herve Filion	2,551,058
1954	Bill Haughton	415,577	1978	Carmine Abbatiello	3,344,457
1955	Bill Haughton	599,455	1979	John Campbell	3,308,984
1956	Bill Haughton	572,945	1980	John Campbell	3,732,306
1957	Bill Haughton	586,950	1981	Bill O'Donnell	4,065,608
1958	Bill Haughton	816,659	1982	Bill O'Donnell	5,755,067
1959	Bill Haughton	771,435	1983	John Campbell	6,104,082
1960	Del Miller	567,282	1984	Bill O'Donnell	9,059,184
1961	Stanley Dancer	674,723	1985	Bill O'Donnell	10,207,372
1962	Stanley Dancer	760,343	1986	John Campbell	9,515,055
1963	Bill Haughton	790,086	1987	John Campbell	10,186,495
1964	Stanley Dancer	1,051,538	1988	John Campbell	11,148,565
1965	Bill Haughton	889,943	1989	John Campbell	9,738,450
1966	Stanley Dancer	1,218,403	1990	John Campbell	11,620,878
1967	Bill Haughton	1,305,773	1991	Jack Moiseyev	9,568,468
1968	Bill Haughton	1,654,463	1992	John Campbell	8,202,108
1969	Del Insko	1,635,463	1993	John Campbell	9,926,482

Motor Sports

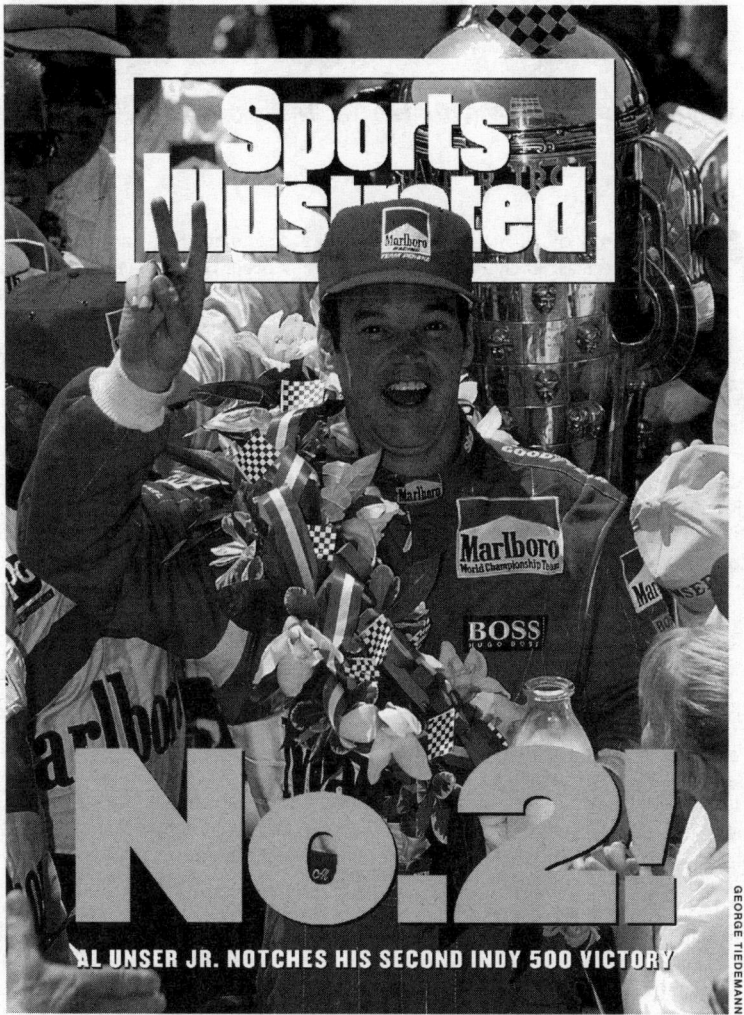

Sports Illustrated

NO. 2!

AL UNSER JR. NOTCHES HIS SECOND INDY 500 VICTORY

GEORGE TIEDEMANN

Family Affairs

The racing family and the families in racing had a season of big wins—and tragic losses | by BRUCE NEWMAN

O
N THE FACE OF IT, AUTO RACING seems the least likely of sports to run in families. Its dangers are well known even to outsiders, and keenly felt in the paddock of any racetrack, where it is rare to find someone who has never had a friend killed in some high-speed calamity. Given the collective—and therefore self-protective—nature of families, it would seem the more recognizable the danger, the less likely a father would be to encourage his son to try it.

And yet, it has always been that way with racing. Fathers and sons, boys and their toys. (That this phenomenon rarely applies to fathers and daughters is, as they say, no accident.) The Andrettis, the Pettys, the Mears gang, the Unsers: Each of these clans has members who are deaf, limping around on shattered feet or moldering in the grave because of racing, and yet they cannot seem to stop.

This year the Andrettis lost their racing patriarch with the retirement of Mario, but his seat will ably be filled next season by his son Michael. Al Unser Sr., whose oldest brother, Jerry, was killed while practicing for the Indianapolis 500 in 1959 and whose younger brother, Bobby, won the race three times, also retired this year. Big Al, who had won the Indy 500 four times, announced

that at 55 the end had come, when he couldn't get a decent car to qualify at Indianapolis this year. Two weeks later his son went out and won the race.

Little Al had trailed his Penske teammate Emerson Fittipaldi most of the race, and with 16 laps to go it was all he could do to hold Fittipaldi off from lapping him. But Fittipaldi, who comes from a Brazilian racing family himself, got a few inches too low on the track, and this slight deviation pitched his car up into the wall and out of the race. In victory circle, Unser was surrounded by Big Al and his own 11-year-old son, whose official nickname is Just Al.

"I've heard Al say that after he won the [1990 Indy Car points] championship, his dad and his uncle told him, 'You ain't nothin' till you've won Indy," said Paul Tracy, the third driver on the Penske team. "And then he won Indy two years ago, and they said, 'You still ain't much—we've won it seven times.' That's a lot to live up to."

Little Al had no trouble living up to the family legacy in 1994, winning seven more races and the driving title as the lead driver for Roger Penske. Unser had been advised so often by his father and uncle to follow in their tire tracks at Team Penske if he ever got the chance that, he said, "all Roger had to do was breathe in my direction." The heavy breathing propelled Unser to equal

GEORGE TIEDEMANN

Michael Andretti's record for most victories in a season, as well as to spearhead a flying wedge of Penskes that finished 1-2-3 in four different races.

But even with all these outsized accomplishments, Unser didn't want the world to stop calling him Little Al. "I've always been proud of my father to the point that I'm really happy to be known as 'son of,'" Junior explained. "When I first started driving a sprint car, my dad told me he didn't care what I did as long as I put everything I had into it. So the pressure of being an Unser instantly went away. I don't mind being Little Al, because it means I'm still young. Besides, we've got Just Al waiting in the wings." You could tell by the way he said it that Unser

had pride of authorship, that there would be nothing Just about this Al, any more than there was Little about his father.

Stock car racing, already at the peak of its popularity, found a way to reinvent itself in '94 by putting on a new race in an old place. The Brickyard 400 had its inaugural running at the Indianapolis Motor Speedway on Aug. 6, ending that track's proud 86-year-old tradition of systematically excluding races of every creed and naturally aspirated religion other than the Indianapolis 500 from its sacred grounds.

The Brickyard 400 and the Daytona 500 now form the yin-and-yang "thang" of the NASCAR season, and their results were emblematic of their different faces. Daytona was won by Sterling Marlin—son of Coo Coo, loser of 166 straight NASCAR races—who had hung in through 17 years and 278 consecutive losses on the NASCAR circuit before becoming a very good old boy. The Brickyard was won by 23-year-old Jeff Gordon, who was in his second full season as a NASCAR driver, but was no stranger to success. Gordon raced sprint cars while growing up in nearby Pittsboro, Ind., and had won countless races before he was old enough to have a regular driver's license. If Gordon can continue to perform with the verve that he displayed in his charge to the checkered flag in the Brickyard, his victory may signal the start of two new eras, one NASCAR's and the other his own.

Daytona is both the first race on the schedule and the sport's traditional showcase, but this year it was the first in a series of grim reminders that racing, with all its

JOE PICCIOLO

Gordon (right) had to hold off a late challenge from Irvan at the Brickyard.

zoomy thrills, is still too often attended by death. During the first week of practice Neil Bonnett, who was attempting to come back from a career in broadcasting, went head-on into a wall and died at the age of 47. Some drivers felt he was not up to the job anymore and couldn't understand why defending Winston Cup champion Dale Earnhardt had allowed Bonnett to test one of his backup cars. "Nobody in this garage wanted to see Neil back driving," said driver Morgan Shepherd. "I don't know why Earnhardt and them helped him like they did."

Earnhardt said he was simply helping out an old friend. "Racing was everything to him," Earnhardt said. "He wasn't happy when he couldn't race. It really meant something to him for somebody to ... talk to him instead of ignoring him because he wasn't a race car driver. He had a lot of people ignore him who he thought were his friends, and that hurt."

Rodney Orr was just 31 when his car went into the wall at Daytona only hours before the funeral service for Bonnett began in Alabama. The effect of the two sudden deaths was so traumatic that driver Rusty Wallace, who had cartwheeled his own car at Daytona and Talladaga the year before, stood up in the drivers meetings before every race that week and pleaded for caution. "He's been flying around here, so he ought to know," said driver Geoff Bodine.

Bodine would eventually do some flying around of his own at the Brickyard, and the launching pad, amazingly enough, was the front bumper of his brother Brett's car. Geoff and Brett Bodine had worked their way into the lead on the race's 99th lap when they began patting each other on the behind, as brothers sometimes will, first Geoff tapping Brett, then Brett ramming Geoff into the wall at 150 mph. As brothers sometimes will. "We've been having some family problems, and he just took it out on me on the racetrack," Geoff said.

Gordon stayed out in front most of the way after that but had to withstand a dramatic late charge by Ernie Irvan, who pulled alongside him with 10 laps to go and wouldn't let go for the next five laps. Irvan had worked his way up from the 17th qualifying position to the lead of the most important race of the year—just as he had done in the season points race—and then as the cars emerged from Turn 2 doorhandle-to-doorhandle, Irvan's right front tire went flat. And so did his chances.

At the time the incident seemed only a cruel disappointment, but it would prove oddly premonitory to an event later that month that would drastically change not only Irvan's life but also the course of the season championship race. During a practice session for the Michigan 400, Irvan's right front tire again went flat, this time sending him head-on into the retaining wall. With serious head and lung injuries, Irvan remained on life-support systems for a week, then gradually began to show signs of recovery. With Irvan out for the year (and possibly for his career), the driving championship fell once again into the lap of Earnhardt, who had won it six times before.

If Earnhardt represented the old guard, in Formula One, Michael Schumacher represented the vanguard of a new generation of talented young drivers. That turned out to be both a blessing and a curse, for in the absence of established stars, and with the onset of regulations slowing everyone down, the sport seemed diminished.

It was a season that will one day be most happily forgotten by everybody, up to and including Schumacher, in Formula One, or as they may have to start calling it, Formula Wane. Schumacher convincingly won almost all the races in which he was given a fair chance to compete—seven victories in all—but he lost the British Grand Prix when he repeatedly ignored a black flag given him by the race stewards for passing Britain's Damon Hill on the *warmup* lap.

That penalty then led to a two-race suspension of Schumacher just as he was about to clinch the driving title and allowed Hill to pull to within 11 points with just four races to go. It didn't help that Schumacher won the Belgian Grand Prix and was then disqualified because a piece of plywood on the bottom of his Benneton-Ford, which was sheared away during a spinout in a gravel trap, was judged too thin to be within the newly tightened rules. With its most absorbing action taking place away from the track, the once supreme-

Earnhart won the seventh NASCAR driving championship of his illustrious career.

ly glamorous F/1 went from being merely boring to an event bordering on irrelevance.

Schumacher's emergence as the sport's preeminent driver had been expected to come in due course, but no one—not even the confident young German himself—could have foreseen that it would come so suddenly, and at the expense of the one driver to whom Schumacher, and all his lessers, humbly deferred. After six seasons in which he had won three world championships with Team McLaren, Senna had accepted a contract worth a reported $20 million to switch to the Williams team, whose cars won the past two championships, first with Nigel Mansell and then Alain Prost.

"I have been waiting for it so long … to start this new life," Senna said before the racing began. But when it did, he was never able to start his new life, first spinning out at his home race in Brazil, then being knocked off the circuit in the first turn at Japan. Senna arrived at the Grand Prix of San Marino in Imola with no points in the world championship race that had once been practically conceded to him. Schumacher's Benneton-Ford won both of those races and would win again at Imola, but Senna had once again demonstrated the primacy of his will by bettering Schumacher's qualifying lap by nearly half a second. It was the 65th pole of Senna's F/1 career—more than twice as many as any other driver in the history of Grand Prix rac-

MIKE SCULLY

spread through the Brazilian slums and soccer stadiums, where Senna was the source of an almost incalculable national pride. One soccer match was transfigured by the announcement of Senna's death into an impromptu wake, when a crowd of nearly 100,000 people stood and clapped their hands in unison, mournfully chanting, "Ole-oleleo la, Sen-na, Sen-na."

The deaths of Senna and Ratzenberger, and another accident at Monaco a fortnight later, which left Karl Wendlinger of Austria in a coma, brought an immediate transformation in the design of the cars

ing—but this one would be his last.

The death of Austrian rookie Roland Ratzenberger the day before the race had already roiled the Formula One paddock, for there had been no racing-related fatalities in the sport for a decade. Senna was so distraught that after the final qualifying session he rode out to the spot where Ratzenberger's car had left the track at nearly 200 mph, and as he stood there alone he began to weep. He was still shaken following the pre-race warmup the next morning, telling reporters, "Today was not typical. My car is very difficult to drive."

A violent crash on the starting grid caused the first six laps to be run under caution, but when the cars returned to racing, Senna was leading as he approached the sweeping left-hand turn known as Tamburello. "He looked nervous from the very first lap," said Schumacher, who had followed Senna into the turn. "The car touched with the rear skids, went a bit sideways, and he just lost it." In the Williams garages, where engineers were monitoring telemetry screens of data being transmitted from Senna's car every few 100ths of a second, the lovely blooms of color suddenly went flat.

When a brain scan later produced the same flat line telemetry, word quickly

that, in turn, slowed them down and presumably made the racing safer. Some purists felt that the loss of horsepower and aerodynamic downforce turned F/1 into F/½, but this whining was rarely heard from the drivers. "Something needed to be done," said Jordan driver Eddie Irvine. "Everyone got very complacent. They didn't realize what speeds these cars were doing and how bad the conditions at some circuits were."

They certainly weren't bad enough to discourage the return to Formula One of Nigel Mansell, the reigning Indy Car champion whose rancorous departure from F/1 two years ago set in motion the order of succession that led Senna to drive for Williams. When the same team that had once spurned Mansell's contract demands suddenly hugged him to its clammy English bosom, Mansell jumped back into its arms—for $1 million a race. After finishing his expatriate days without a win, Mansell prepared for his return to F/1 by driving in three largely meaningless races for Williams at the end of the season.

Mansell had tried for two years to leave his racing family, but now he was going back because it was where he belonged. It's easy enough, even for the best drivers, to lose their way on a racetrack. But they never lose sight of where home is.

FOR THE RECORD·1993-1994

CART Racing

Indianapolis 500

Results of the 78th running of the Indianapolis 500 and 4th round of the 1994 Indy Car season. Held Sunday, May 29, at the 2.5-mile Indianapolis Motor Speedway in Speedway, IN.

Distance, 500 miles; starters, 33; time of race, 3:06:29; average speed, 160.872 mph; margin of victory, 8.6 seconds; caution flags, 7 for 43 laps; lead changes, 10 among 3 drivers; attendance, 450,000.

TOP 10 FINISHERS

Pos	Driver (start pos.)	Car	Qual. Speed	Laps	Status
1	Al Unser Jr (1)	Penske-Mercedes	228.011	200	running
2	*Jacques Villeneuve (4)	Reynard-Ford	226.259	200	running
3	Bobby Rahal (28)	Penske-limor	220.178	199	running
4	Jimmy Vasser (16)	Reynard-Ford	222.262	199	running
5	Robby Gordon (19)	Lola-Ford	221.293	199	running
6	Michael Andretti (5)	Reynard-Ford	226.205	198	running
7	Teo Fabi (24)	Reynard-limor	223.394	198	running
8	Eddie Cheever (11)	Lola-Menard	223.163	197	running
9	*Bryan Herta (22)	Lola-Ford	220.992	197	running
10	John Andretti (10)	Lola-Ford	223.263	196	running

1994 Indy Car Results

Date	Track/Distance	Winner (start pos.)	Car	Avg Speed
Mar 20	Australian Grand Prix	Michael Andretti (2)	Ford-Cosworth XB	80.994
Apr 10	Slick 50 200	Emerson Fittipaldi (6)	Penske-limor V8	107.437
Apr 17	Long Beach Grand Prix	Al Unser Jr (2)	Penske-limor V8	99.283**
May 29	Indianapolis 500	Al Unser Jr (1)	Penske-Mercedes	160.872
June 5	Miller Genuine Draft 200	Al Unser Jr (11)	Penske-limor V8	118.804
June 12	Detroit Grand Prix	Paul Tracy (3)	Penske-limor V8	86.245**
June 26	Portland 200	Al Unser Jr (1)	Penske-limor V8	107.777**
July 10	Cleveland Grand Prix	Al Unser Jr (1)	Penske-limor V8	138.026**
July 17	Indy Toronto	Michael Andretti (8)	Ford-Cosworth XB	96.673
July 31	Michigan 500	Scott Goodyear (12)	Ford-Cosworth XB	159.800
Aug 14	Mid-Ohio 200	Al Unser Jr (1)	Penske-limor V8	110.387
Aug 21	New Hampshire 200	Al Unser Jr (10)	Penske-limor V8	122.635
Sep 4	Indy Vancouver	Al Unser Jr (8)	Penske-limor V8	89.166**
Sep 11	Wisconsin 200	*Jacques Villeneuve (2)	Ford-Cosworth XB	116.922
Sep 18	Nazareth 200	Paul Tracy (2)	Penske-limor V8	131.141
Oct 9	Monterey Grand Prix	Paul Tracy (1)	Penske-limor V8	92.978

*Rookie

**Track Record

Note: Distances are in miles.

Championship Standings

Driver	Starts	Wins	Pts
Al Unser Jr	16	8	225
Emerson Fittipaldi	16	1	178
Paul Tracy	16	3	152
Michael Andretti	16	2	118
Robby Gordon	16	0	104
Jacques Villeneuve	15	1	94
Raul Boesel	16	0	90
Nigel Mansell	16	0	88
Teo Fabi	16	0	79
Bobby Rahal	16	0	59

NASCAR Racing

Daytona 500

Results of the opening round of the 1994 Winston Cup series. Held Sunday, February 20, at the 2.5-mile high-banked Daytona International Speedway.

Distance, 500 miles; starters, 42; time of race, 3:11:10; average speed, 156.931 mph; margin of victory, .23 seconds; caution flags, 4 for 22 laps; lead changes, 33 among 14 drivers; attendence, 120,000.

TOP 10 FINISHERS

Pos	Driver (start pos.)	Car	Laps	Winnings ($)
1	Sterling Marlin (4)	Chevrolet	200	258,275
2	Ernie Irvan (3)	Ford	200	190,750
3	Terry Labonte (9)	Chevrolet	200	138,475
4	Jeff Gordon (6)	Chevrolet	200	112,525
5	Morgan Shepherd (12)	Ford	200	92,805
6	Greg Sacks (31)	Ford	200	70,480
7	Dale Earnhardt (2)	Chevrolet	200	110,340
8	Ricky Rudd (20)	Ford	200	56,465
9	Bill Elliott (8)	Ford	200	65,615
10	Ken Schrader (13)	Chevrolet	200	59,565

Late 1993 NASCAR Results

Date	Track/Distance	Winner (start pos.)	Car	Avg Speed	Winnings ($)
Oct 24	Rockingham 500	Rusty Wallace	Pontiac	114.036	52,850
Oct 31	Phoenix 500	Mark Martin (3)	Ford	100.375	67,034
Nov 14	Atlanta 500	Rusty Wallace (20)	Pontiac	125.221	92,100

Note: Distances are in miles unless followed by * (laps) or K (kilometers).

1994 NASCAR Results (through October 23)

Date	Track/Distance	Winner (start pos.)	Car	Avg Speed	Winnings ($)
Feb 20	Daytona 500	Sterling Marlin (4)	Chevrolet	156.931	258,275
Feb 27	Rockingham 500	Rusty Wallace (15)	Ford	125.239	52,885
Mar 6	Richmond 400*	Ernie Irvan (7)	Ford	98.334	71,175
Mar 13	Atlanta 500	Ernie Irvan (7)	Ford	146.136	86,100
Mar 27	Darlington 400	Dale Earnhardt (9)	Chevrolet	132.432	70,190
Apr 10	Bristol 500*	Dale Earnhardt (24)	Chevrolet	89.647	72,570
Apr 17	N Wilkesboro 400*	Terry Labonte	Chevrolet	95.816	61,640
Apr 24	Martinsville 500*	Rusty Wallace (1)	Ford	76.700	173,675
May 1	Talladega 500	Dale Earnhardt (4)	Chevrolet	157.478	94,865
May 15	Sonoma 300K	Ernie Irvan (1)	Ford	77.458	78,810
May 29	Charlotte 600	Jeff Gordon (1)	Chevrolet	139.445	196,500
June 5	Dover Downs 500	Rusty Wallace (6)	Ford	102.529	70,605
June 12	Pocono 500	Rusty Wallace (1)	Ford	128.801	84,525
June 19	Michigan 400	Rusty Wallace (5)	Ford	125.022	66,980
July 2	Daytona 400	Jimmy Spencer (3)	Ford	155.558	75,880
July 10	New Hampshire 300*	Ricky Rudd (3)	Ford	87.599	91,875
July 17	Pocono 500	Geoff Bodine (1)	Ford	136.075	103,270
July 24	Talladega 500	Jimmy Spencer (2)	Ford	163.217	81,450
Aug 6	Brickyard 400	Jeff Gordon (3)	Chevrolet	131.977	613,000
Aug 14	Watkins Glen 90*	Mark Martin (1)	Ford	93.752	85,100
Aug 21	Michigan 400	Geoff Bodine (1)	Ford	139.914	89,595
Sep 4	Southern 500	Bill Elliott (9)	Ford	127.952	68,330
Sept 10	Richmond 400*	Terry Labonte (3)	Chevrolet	104.156	67,765
Sept 18	Dover Downs 500	Rusty Wallace (10)	Ford	112.556	55,055
Sept 25	Martinsville 500	Rusty Wallace (7)	Ford	77.145	69,125
Oct 3	N Wilkesboro 400*	Geoff Bodine	Ford	96.522	61,440
Oct 10	Charlotte 500	Dale Jarrett (22)	Chevy	145.920	106,800
Oct 23	Rockingham 500	Dale Earnhardt (20)	Chevy	126.407	60,600

*Distance in laps.

Note: Distances are in miles unless followed by K (kilometers)

1993 Winston Cup Standings

Driver	Car	Starts	Wins	Pts
Dale Earnhardt	Chevy	30	6	4526
Rusty Wallace	Pontiac	30	10	4446
Mark Martin	Ford	30	5	4150
Dale Jarrett	Chevy	30	1	4000
Kyle Petty	Pontiac	30	1	3960
Ernie Irvan	Ford	30	3	3834
Morgan Shepherd	Ford	30	1	3807
Bill Elliott	Ford	30	0	3774
Ken Schrader	Chevy	30	0	3715
Ricky Rudd	Chevy	30	1	3644

1993 Winston Cup Driver Winnings

Driver	Winnings ($)
Dale Earnhardt	3,353,789
Rusty Wallace	1,702,154
Mark Martin	1,657,662
Ernie Irvan	1,400,468
Dale Jarrett	1,242,394
Bill Elliott	955,859
Ken Schrader	952,748
Kyle Petty	914,652
Geoff Bodine	783,762
Morgan Shepherd	782,523

Formula One/Grand Prix Racing

1994 Formula One Results (through October 16)

Date	Grand Prix	Winner	Car	Avg Speed
Mar 27	Brazil	Michael Schumacher	Benetton-Ford	119.7
Apr 17	Pacific	Michael Schumacher	Benetton-Ford	114.8
May 1	San Marino	Michael Schumacher	Benetton-Ford	122.88
May 15	Monaco	Michael Schumacher	Benetton-Ford	88.061
May 28	Spain	Damon Hill	Williams-Renault	119.556
June 12	Canada	Michael Schumacher	Benetton-Ford	109.536
July 3	France	Michael Schumacher	Benetton-Ford	115.74
July 10	Britain	Damon Hill	Williams-Renault	125.609
July 31	Germany	Gerhard Berger	Ferrari	137.635
Aug 14	Hungary	Michael Schumacher	Benetton-Ford	105.237
Aug 28	Belgium	Damon Hill	Williams-Renault	129.379
Sept 11	Italy	Damon Hill	Williams-Renault	146.520
Sept 25	Portugal	Damon Hill	Williams-Renault	114.743
Oct 16	Spain	Michael Schumacher	Benetton-Ford	113.43

1993 World Championship Standings

Drivers compete in Grand Prix races for the title of World Driving Champion. Below are the top 10 results from the 1993 season. Points are awarded for places 1-6 as follows: 10-6-4-3-2-1.

Driver, Country	Starts	Wins	Car	Pts
Alain Prost, France	16	7	Williams-Renault	99
Ayrton Senna, Brazil	16	5	McLaren-Ford	73
Damon Hill, Great Britain	16	3	Williams-Renault	69
Michael Schumacher, Germany	16	1	Benetton-Ford	52
Riccardo Patrese, Italy	16	0	Benetton-Ford	20
Jean Alesi, France	16	0	Ferrari	16
Martin Brundle, Great Britain	16	0	Ligier-Renault	13
Gerhard Berger, Germany	16	0	Ferrari	12
Johnny Herbert, Great Britain	16	0	Lotus-Ford	11
Mark Blundell, Great Britain	16	0	Ligier-Renault	10

IMSA Racing

The 24 Hours of Daytona

Held at the Daytona International Speedway on February 5-6, 1994, the 24 Hours of Daytona annually serves as the opening round for the International Motor Sports Association sports car season.

Place	Drivers	Car	Distance
1	Paul Gentilozzi, Scott Pruett, Butch Leitzinger Steve Millen	Nissan 300 ZX	707 laps (104.80 mph)
2	Dominique Dupuy, Bob Wollek, Jack Leconte, Jesus Pareja	Porsche 911	683 laps
3	Dirk Ebeling, Karl Wlazik, Ulrich Richter, Gunter Doebler	Porsche 911	671 laps
4	Mark Sandridge, Harold Grohs, Bernd Maylaender Frank Katthoefer	Porsche 911	670 laps
5	Irv Hoerr, Tommy Riggins, R.K. Smith, Darin Brassfield Price Cobb	Olds Cutlass	665 laps

1994 World Sports Car Championship Results

Date	Race	Winner(s)	Car (Class)	Avg Speed
Feb 5-6	24 Hours of Daytona	Gentilozzi/Pruett/Leitzinger Millen	Nissan 300 ZX (GTS)	104.80
Mar 19	12 Hours of Sebring	Steve Millen/John Morton/ Johnny O'Connell	Nissan 300 ZX (GTS)	100.633
Apr 17	Road Atlanta	Jay Cochran	Ferrari (WSC)	116.04
May 30	Lime Rock GP	Gianpiero Moretti	Ferrari (WSC)	101.24
June 26	Watkins Glen	Gianpiero Moretti/ Eliseo Salazar	Ferrari (WSC)	108.59
July 10	Indianapolis	Gianpiero Moretti/ Eliseo Salazar	Ferrari (WSC)	102.26
July 24	Laguna Seca	Fermin Velez/Andy Evans	Ferrari (WSC)	90.165
Aug 7	Portland	Jeremy Dale	Oldsmobile (WSC)	86.343
Oct 1	Phoenix	Jeremy Dale	Oldsmobile (WSC)	87.637

1994 Supreme GT Series Results

Date	Race	Winner(s)	Car (Class)	Avg Speed
Apr 17	Road Atlanta	Steve Millen	Nissan (GTS)	113.49
May 30	Lime Rock GP	Irv Hoerr	Oldsmobile (GTS)	100.52
July 10	Indianapolis	Irv Hoerr	Oldsmobile (GTS)	93.414
July 24	Laguna Seca	Johnny O'Connell	Nissan (GTS)	89.314
Aug 7	Portland	Steve Millen	Nissan (GTS)	86.917
Oct 1	Phoenix	Johnny O'Connell	Nissan (GTS)	83.744

Note: Supreme GT for IMSA GTS/GTO/GTU cars

1994 World Sports Car Championship Standings

Driver	Pts
Wayne Taylor	190
Jeremy Dale	187
Jim Downing	178
Andy Evans	169
Bob Schader	160
Eliseo Salazar	158
James Weaver	127
Fermin Velez	108
Paul Debban	100
Hugh Fuller	96

FIA World Sports Car Racing

The 24 Hours of LeMans

Held at LeMans, France, on June 18-19, 1994, the 24 Hours of LeMans is the most prestigious event in the FIA World Sports Car Championship.

Place	Drivers	Car	Distance
1	Yannick Dalmas, Hurley Haywood, Mauro Baldi	Porsche 962	344 laps (121.33)
2	Eddie Irvine, Mauro Martini, Jeff Krosnoff	Toyota 94CV	343 laps

The 24 Hours of LeMans (Cont.)

Place	Drivers	Car	Distance
3	Hans Stuck, Danny Sullivan, Thierry Boutsen	Porsche 962	343 laps
4	Steven Andskar, George Fouche, Bob Wollek	Toyota 94CV	328 laps
5	Steve Millen, Johnny O'Connell, John Morton	Nissan 300 ZX	317 laps
6	Derek Bell, Robin Donovan, Jurgen Laessig	Porsche K8	316 laps
7	Jean-Louis Ricci, Andy Evans, Phillipe Olczyk	Porsche C32LM	310 laps
8	Dominique Dupuy, Carlos Palau, Jesus Pareja	Porsche Carrera RSR	307 laps
9	Enzo Calderari, Lilian Bryner, Renato Mastropietro	Porsche Carrera RSR	299 laps
10	Tomlje Matjaz, Patrick Huisman, Cor Euser	Porsche Carrera RSR	295 laps

Drag Racing

National Hot Rod Association

1994 Results (through September 18)

TOP FUEL

Date	Race, Site	Winner	Time	Speed
Feb 6	Winternationals, Pomona, CA	Shelly Anderson	5.464	178.74
Feb 20	Arizona Nationals, Phoenix	Cory McClenathan	4.985	268.17
March 6	Slick 50 Nationals, Houston	Don Prudhomme	4.881	294.50
March 20	Gatornationals, Gainesville, FL	Connie Kalitta	4.794	290.79
April 24	Southern Nationals, Atlanta	Connie Kalitta	4.875	290.62
May 15	Mid-South Nationals, Memphis	Tommy Johnson Jr	4.883	296.63
May 22	Mopar Nationals, Englishtown N.J.	Pat Austin	4.882	282.30
June 12	Springnationals, Columbus, OH	Scott Kalitta	4.952	252.10
June 26	Western Auto Nationals, Topeka, KS	Scott Kalitta	4.824	299.40
July 24	Mile-High Nationals, Denver	Scott Kalitta	5.070	270.43
July 31	California Nationals, Sonoma, CA	Scott Kalitta	4.802	298.11
Aug 7	Northwest Nationals, Seattle	Joe Amato	4.859	295.08
Aug 22	Champion Auto Nationals, Brainerd, MN	Don Prudhomme	4.798	294.88
Sept 5	US Nationals, Indianapolis	Connie Kalitta	4.806	301.60
Sept 18	Keysone Nationals, Reading, PA	Scott Kalitta	4.751	304.87

FUNNY CAR

Date	Race, Site	Winner	Time	Speed
Feb 6	Winternationals, Pomona, CA	K.C. Spurlock	5.128	284.00
Feb 20	Arizona Nationals, Phoenix	John Force	5.184	288.83
March 6	Slick 50 Nationals, Houston	Al Hoffman	5.171	287.44
March 20	Gatornationals, Gainesville, FL	John Force	5.347	263.00

Dave at the Brickyard

Maybe you saw the news that David Letterman, a longtime fan of auto racing, is thinking about financing his own Indy Car racing team. We know we shouldn't attempt this. We know it has been overdone. We know we'll never make it as funny as Dave would. But we can't resist presenting...

The Top 10 Reasons Dave Is Thinking About Buying an Indy Team:

10) Leno has his Harleys—we want something that makes even more noise!

9) Need some big-time prize money to pay for speeding tickets incurred on drives home to Connecticut.

8) Stupid Pit-Crew Tricks.

7) Strapping Paul Shaffer into a four-wheel death missile loaded with highly flammable fuel and sending him down the straightaway at 235 mph just seems like the thing to do.

6) Figure it's the easiest way to meet Miss Crankshaft '94.

5) Golly! A chance to hear Jim Nabors sing *Back Home Again in Indiana* in person.

4) *Late Show* female staffers would really like "to get to know" Danny Sullivan.

3) Hey, look what it did for Paul Newman.

2) Nothing to do on Memorial Day weekend since Cher canceled the cookout.

1) Decals! Decals! Decals!

National Hot Rod Association (Cont.)

FUNNY CAR (Cont.)

Date	Race, Site	Winner	Time	Speed
April 24	Southern Nationals, Atlanta	John Force	5.223	287.81
May 15	Mid-South Nationals, Memphis	Gordie Bonin	5.337	288.55
May 22	Mopar Nationals, Englishtown N.J.	Mark Oswald	5.169	288.16
June 12	Springnationals, Columbus, OH	Gordie Bonin	5.232	282.92
June 26	Western Auto Nationals, Topeka, KS	John Force	5.106	292.11
July 24	Mile High Nationals, Denver	John Force	5.256	282.30
July 31	California Nationals, Sonoma, CA	John Force	5.147	290.97
Aug 8	Northwest Nationals, Seattle	John Force	5.036	291.82
Aug 22	Champion Auto Nationals, Brainerd, MN	John Force	5.136	291.16
Sept 5	US Nationals, Indianapolis	Cruz Pedregon	5.135	288.73
Sept 18	Keystone Nationals, Reading, PA	John Force	5.010	302.11

PRO STOCK

Date	Race, Site	Winner	Time	Speed
Feb 6	Winternationals, Pomona, CA	Warren Johnson	7.095	195.52
Feb 20	Arizona Nationals, Phoenix	Scott Geoffrion	7.117	194.25
March 6	Slick 50 Nationals Houston	Warren Johnson	7.071	196.20
March 20	Gatornationals, Gainesville, FL	Warren Johnson	7.136	195.14
April 24	Southern Nationals, Atlanta	Scott Geoffrion	7.090	194.93
May 15	Mid-South Nationals, Memphis	Darrell Alderman	7.141	192.71
May 22	Mopar Nationals, Englishtown N.J.	Larry Morgan	7.134	194.04
June 13	Springnationals, Columbus, OH	Scott Geoffrion	7.227	192.14
June 26	Western Auto Nationals, Topeka, KS	Scott Geoffrion	7.153	194.21
July 24	Mile-High Nationals, Denver	Darrell Alderman	7.519	182.33
July 31	California Nationals, Sonoma, CA	Darrell Alderman	7.046	195.77
Aug 8	Northwest Nationals, Seattle	Steve Schmidt	7.132	193.05
Aug 22	Champion Auto Nationals, Brainerd, MN	Jim Yates	7.225	190.51
Sept 5	US Nationals, Indianapolis	Warren Johnson	7.132	193.96
Sept 18	Keystone Nationals, Reading, PA	Darrell Alderman	7.027	195.06

1993 Standings

TOP FUEL

Driver	Wins	Pts
Eddie Hill	6	12,798
Scott Kalitta	2	11,542
Kenny Bernstein	2	11,064
Mike Dunn	1	10,064
Rance McDaniel	0	9,730
Cory McClenathan	0	9,066
Joe Amato	2	8,844
Ed McCulloch	1	8,652
Doug Herbert	1	8,424
Tommy Johnson Jr	1	8,196

FUNNY CAR

Driver	Wins	Pts
John Force	10	18,074
Chuck Etchells	3	12,320
Cruz Pedregon	2	11,850
Al Hoffmann	1	11,496
Tom Hoover	1	8,672

FUNNY CAR (Cont.)

Driver	Wins	Pts
Kenji Okazaki	0	7,332
Jim Epler	0	7,252
Gordon Mineo	0	6,812
Gary Bolger	0	6,372
Whit Bazemore	0	6,290

PRO STOCK

Driver	Wins	Pts
Warren Johnson	9	17,008
Kurt Johnson	3	13,502
Scott Geoffrion	1	11,668
Larry Morgan	1	10,330
Mark Pawuk	1	8,532
Bob Glidden	2	8,506
Bruce Allen	0	7,444
Rickie Smith	1	7,130
Jerry Eckman	0	6,590
David Rampy	0	5,996

CART Racing

Indianapolis 500

First held in 1911, the Indy 500——200 laps of the 2.5-mile Indianapolis Motor Speedway Track (called the Brickyard in honor of its original pavement)——has grown to become the most famous auto race in the world. Held on Memorial Day weekend, it annually draws the largest crowd of any sporting event in the world.

Year	Winner (Start Position)	Car	Avg MPH	Pole Winner	MPH
1911	Ray Harroun (28)	Marmon Wasp	74.590	Lewis Strang	Awarded pole
1912	Joe Dawson (7)	National	78.720	Gil Anderson	Drew pole
1913	Jules Goux (7)	Peugeot	75.930	Caleb Bragg	Drew pole
1914	Rene Thomas (15)	Delage	82.470	Jean Chassagne	Drew pole
1915	Ralph DePalma (2)	Mercedes	89.840	Howard Wilcox	98.90
1916	Dario Resta (4)	Peugeot	84.000	John Aitken	96.69
1917-18	No race				
1919	Howard Wilcox (2)	Peugeot	88.050	Rene Thomas	104.78
1920	Gaston Chevrolet (6)	Monroe	88.620	Ralph DePalma	99.15
1921	Tommy Milton (20)	Frontenac	89.620	Ralph DePalma	100.75
1922	Jimmy Murphy (1)	Murphy Special	94.480	Jimmy Murphy	100.50
1923	Tommy Milton (1)	H.C.S. Special	90.950	Tommy Milton	108.17
1924	L. L. Corum Joe Boyer (21)	Duesenberg Special	98.230	Jimmy Murphy	108.037
1925	Peter DePaolo (2)	Duesenberg Special	101.130	Leon Duray	113.196
1926	Frank Lockhart (20)	Miller Special	95.904	Earl Cooper	111.735
1927	George Souders (22)	Duesenberg	97.545	Frank Lockhart	120.100
1928	Louis Meyer (13)	Miller Special	99.482	Leon Duray	122.391
1929	Ray Keech (6)	Simplex Piston Ring Special	97.585	Cliff Woodbury	120.599
1930	Billy Arnold (1)	Miller Hartz Special	100.448	Billy Arnold	113.268
1931	Louis Schneider (13)	Bowes Seal-Fast Special	96.629	Russ Snowberger	112.796
1932	Fred Frame (27)	Miller Hartz Special	104.144	Lou Moore	117.363
1933	Louis Meyer (6)	Tydol Special	104.162	Bill Cummings	118.524
1934	Bill Cummings (10)	Boyle Products Special	104.863	Kelly Petillo	119.329
1935	Kelly Petillo (22)	Gilmore Speedway Special	106.240	Rex Mays	120.736
1936	Louis Meyer (28)	Ring-Free Special	109.069	Rex Mays	119.664
1937	Wilbur Shaw (2)	Shaw-Gilmore Special	113.580	Bill Cummings	123.343
1938	Floyd Roberts (1)	Burd Piston Ring Special	117.200	Floyd Roberts	125.681
1939	Wilbur Shaw (3)	Boyle Special	115.035	Jimmy Snyder	130.138
1940	Wilbur Shaw (2)	Boyle Special	114.277	Rex Mays	127.850
1941	Floyd Davis Mauri Rose (17)	Noc-Out Hose Clamp Special	115.117	Mauri Rose	128.691
1942-45	No race				
1946	George Robson (15)	Thorne Engineering Special	114.820	Cliff Bergere	126.471
1947	Mauri Rose (3)	Blue Crown Spark Plug Special	116.338	Ted Horn	126.564
1948	Mauri Rose (3)	Blue Crown Spark Plug Special	119.814	Rex Mays	130.577
1949	Bill Holland (4)	Blue Crown Spark Plug Special	121.327	Duke Nalon	132.939
1950	Johnnie Parsons (5)	Wynn's Friction Proofing	124.002	Walt Faulkner	134.343
1951	Lee Wallard (2)	Belanger Special	126.244	Duke Nalon	136.498
1952	Troy Ruttman (7)	Agajanian Special	128.922	Fred Agabashian	138.010
1953	Bill Vukovich (1)	Fuel Injection Special	128.740	Bill Vukovich	138.392
1954	Bill Vukovich (19)	Fuel Injection Special	130.840	Jack McGrath	141.033
1955	Bob Sweikert (14)	John Zink Special	128.209	Jerry Hoyt	140.045
1956	Pat Flaherty (1)	John Zink Special	128.490	Pat Flaherty	145.596
1957	Sam Hanks (13)	Belond Exhaust Special	135.601	Pat O'Connor	143.948
1958	Jim Bryan (7)	Belond AP Parts Special	133.791	Dick Rathmann	145.974
1959	Rodger Ward (6)	Leader Card 500 Roadster	135.857	Johnny Thomson	145.908
1960	Jim Rathmann (2)	Ken-Paul Special	138.767	Eddie Sachs	146.592
1961	A. J. Foyt (7)	Bowes Seal-Fast Special	139.130	Eddie Sachs	147.481
1962	Rodger Ward (2)	Leader Card 500 Roadster	140.293	Parnelli Jones	150.370
1963	Parnelli Jones (1)	Agajanian-Willard Special	143.137	Parnelli Jones	151.153
1964	A. J. Foyt (5)	Sheraton-Thompson Special	147.350	Jim Clark	158.828
1965	Jim Clark (2)	Lotus Ford	150.686	A. J. Foyt	161.233
1966	Graham Hill (15)	American Red Ball Special	144.317	Mario Andretti	165.899
1967	A. J. Foyt (4)	Sheraton-Thompson Special	151.207	Mario Andretti	168.982
1968	Bobby Unser (3)	Rislone Special	152.882	Joe Leonard	171.559
1969	Mario Andretti (2)	STP Oil Treatment Special	156.867	A. J. Foyt	170.568
1970	Al Unser (1)	Johnny Lightning 500 Special	155.749	Al Unser	170.221

Indianapolis 500 (Cont.)

Year	Winner (Start Position)	Car	Avg MPH	Pole Winner	MPH
1971	Al Unser (5)	Johnny Lightning Special	157.735	Peter Revson	178.696
1972	Mark Donohue (3)	Sunoco McLaren	162.962	Bobby Unser	195.940
1973	Gordon Johncock (11)	STP Double Oil Filters	159.036	Johnny Rutherford	198.413
1974	Johnny Rutherford (25)	McLaren	158.589	A. J. Foyt	191.632
1975	Bobby Unser (3)	Jorgensen Eagle	149.213	A. J. Foyt	193.976
1976	Johnny Rutherford (1)	Hy-Gain McLaren/Goodyear	148.725	Johnny Rutherford	188.957
1977	A. J. Foyt (4)	Gilmore Racing Team	161.331	Tom Sneva	198.884
1978	Al Unser (5)	FNCTC Chaparral Lola	161.361	Tom Sneva	202.156
1979	Rick Mears (1)	The Gould Charge	158.899	Rick Mears	193.736
1980	Johnny Rutherford (1)	Pennzoil Chaparral	142.862	Johnny Rutherford	192.256
1981	Bobby Unser (1)	Norton Spirit Penske PC-9B	139.084	Bobby Unser	200.546
1982	Gordon Johncock (5)	STP Oil Treatment	162.026	Rick Mears	207.004
1983	Tom Sneva (4)	Texaco Star	162.117	Teo Fabi	207.395
1984	Rick Mears (3)	Pennzoil Z-7	163.612	Tom Sneva	210.029
1985	Danny Sullivan (8)	Miller American Special	152.982	Pancho Carter	212.583
1986	Bobby Rahal (4)	Budweiser/Truesports/March	170.722	Rick Mears	216.828
1987	Al Unser (20)	Cummins Holset Turbo	162.175	Mario Andretti	215.390
1988	Rick Mears (1)	Penske-Chevrolet	144.809	Rick Mears	219.198
1989	Emerson Fittipaldi (3)	Penske-Chevrolet	167.581	Rick Mears	223.885
1990	Arie Luyendyk (3)	Domino's Pizza Chevrolet	185.981*	Emerson Fittipaldi	225.301†
1991	Rick Mears (1)	Penske-Chevrolet	176.457	Rick Mears	224.113
1992	Al Unser Jr (12)	G92-Chevrolet	134.477	Roberto Guerrero	232.482
1993	Emerson Fittipaldi (9)	Penske-Chevrolet	157.207	Arie Luyendyk	223.967
1994	Al Unser Jr. (1)	Penske-Mercedes	160.872	Al Unser Jr.	228.011

*Track record, winning time. †Track record, qualifying time.

Indianapolis 500 Rookie of the Year Award

1952 ....Art Cross	1967 ....Denis Hulme	1982 ....Jim Hickman
1953 ....Jimmy Daywalt	1968 ....Billy Vukovich	1983 ....Teo Fabi
1954 ....Larry Crockett	1969 ....Mark Donohue*	1984 ....Michael Andretti
1955 ....Al Herman	1970 ....Donnie Allison	Roberto Guerrero
1956 ....Bob Veith	1971 ....Denny Zimmerman	1985 ....Arie Luyendyk
1957 ....Don Edmunds	1972 ....Mike Hiss	1986 ....Randy Lanier
1958 ....George Amick	1973 ....Graham McRae	1987 ....Fabrizio Barbazza
1959 ....Bobby Grim	1974 ....Pancho Carter	1988 ....Billy Vukovich III
1960 ....Jim Hurtubise	1975 ....Bill Puterbaugh	1989 ....Bernard Jourdain
1961 ....Parnelli Jones*	1976 ....Vern Schuppan	Scott Pruett
Bobby Marshman	1977 ....Jerry Sneva	1990 ....Eddie Cheever
1962 ....Jimmy McElreath	1978 ....Rick Mears*	1991 ....Jeff Andretti
1963 ....Jim Clark*	Larry Rice	1992 ....Lyn St. James
1964 ....Johnny White	1979 ....Howdy Holmes	1993 ....Nigel Mansell
1965 ....Mario Andretti*	1980 ....Tim Richmond	1994 ....Jacques Villeneuve
1966 ....Jackie Stewart	1981 ....Josele Garza	*Future winner of Indy 500.

Indy Car Champions

From 1909 to 1955, this championship was awarded by the American Automobile Association (AAA), and from 1956 to 1979 by United States Auto Club (USAC). Since 1979, Championship Auto Racing Teams (CART) has conducted the championship.

1909 ....George Robertson	1925 ....Peter DePaolo	1941 ....Rex Mays
1910 ....Ray Harroun	1926 ....Harry Hartz	1942-45 ......No racing
1911 ....Ralph Mulford	1927 ....Peter DePaolo	1946 ....Ted Horn
1912 ....Ralph DePalma	1928 ....Louis Meyer	1947 ....Ted Horn
1913 ....Earl Cooper	1929 ....Louis Meyer	1948 ....Ted Horn
1914 ....Ralph DePalma	1930 ....Billy Arnold	1949 ....Johnnie Parsons
1915 ....Earl Cooper	1931 ....Louis Schneider	1950 ....Henry Banks
1916 ....Dario Resta	1932 ....Bob Carey	1951 ....Tony Bettenhausen
1917 ....Earl Cooper	1933 ....Louis Meyer	1952 ....Chuck Stevenson
1918 ....Ralph Mulford	1934 ....Bill Cummings	1953 ....Sam Hanks
1919 ....Howard Wilcox	1935 ....Kelly Petillo	1954 ....Jimmy Bryan
1920 ....Tommy Milton	1936 ....Mauri Rose	1955 ....Bob Sweikert
1921 ....Tommy Milton	1937 ....Wilbur Shaw	1956 ....Jimmy Bryan
1922 ....Jimmy Murphy	1938 ....Floyd Roberts	1957 ....Jimmy Bryan
1923 ....Eddie Hearne	1939 ....Wilbur Shaw	1958 ....Tony Bettenhausen
1924 ....Jimmy Murphy	1940 ....Rex Mays	1959 ....Rodger Ward

Indy Car Champions (Cont.)

1960 ....A. J. Foyt	1972 ....Joe Leonard	1983 ....Al Unser
1961 ....A. J. Foyt	1973 ....Roger McCluskey	1984 ....Mario Andretti
1962 ....Rodger Ward	1974 ....Bobby Unser	1985 ....Al Unser
1963 ....A. J. Foyt	1975 ....A. J. Foyt	1986 ....Bobby Rahal
1964 ....A. J. Foyt	1976 ....Gordon Johncock	1987 ....Bobby Rahal
1965 ....Mario Andretti	1977 ....Tom Sneva	1988 ....Danny Sullivan
1966 ....Mario Andretti	1978 ....Tom Sneva	1989 ....Emerson Fittipaldi
1967 ....A. J. Foyt	1979 ....A. J. Foyt	1990 ....Al Unser Jr
1968 ....Bobby Unser	1979 ....Rick Mears	1991 ....Michael Andretti
1969 ....Mario Andretti	1980 ....Johnny Rutherford	1992 ....Bobby Rahal
1970 ....Al Unser	1981 ....Rick Mears	1993 ....Nigel Mansell
1971 ....Joe Leonard	1982 ....Rick Mears	1994 ....Al Unser Jr.

Alltime Indy Car Leaders

WINS		WINNINGS ($)		POLE POSITIONS	
A. J. Foyt	67	Al Unser Jr*	13,871,093	Mario Andretti*	66
Mario Andretti*	52	Bobby Rahal*	12,654,491	A. J. Foyt	53
Al Unser	39	Emerson Fittipaldi*	12,346,625	Bobby Unser	49
Bobby Unser	35	Mario Andretti*	11,279,654	Rick Mears	40
Rick Mears	29	Rick Mears	11,050,807	Michael Andretti*	27
Michael Andretti*	29	Michael Andretti*	10,774,566	Al Unser*	27
Johnny Rutherford	27	Danny Sullivan	8,254,673	Johnny Rutherford	23
Al Unser Jr*	27	Arie Luyendyk*	6,844,771	Gordon Johncock	20
Rodger Ward	26	Al Unser	6,740,843	Danny Sullivan	19
Gordon Johncock	25	A. J. Foyt	5,357,589	Rex Mays	19
Ralph DePalma	24	Raul Boesel*	4,819,834	Bobby Rahal*	18
Bobby Rahal*	24	Scott Brayton*	4,500,711	Emerson Fittipaldi*	17
Tommy Milton	23	Tom Sneva	4,392,993	Don Branson	15
Earl Cooper	21	Roberto Guerrero*	4,275,163	Tom Sneva*	14
Emerson Fittipaldi*	21	Johnny Rutherford	4,209,232	Tony Bettenhausen	14
Tony Bettenhausen	21	Teo Fabi*	3,860,048	Parnelli Jones	12
Jimmy Murphy	19	Scott Goodyear*	3,860,048	Danny Ongais	11
Jimmy Bryan	19	Gordon Johncock	3,431,414	Rodger Ward	11
Ralph Mulford	17	Kevin Cogan	3,202,106		
Danny Sullivan	17	John Andretti*	3,175,374	Three tied with 10	

*Active driver.

Note: Leaders through September 11, 1994.

NASCAR Racing

Stock Car Racing's Major Events

Winston offers a $1 million bonus to any driver to win 3 of NASCAR's top 4 events in the same season. These races are the richest (Daytona 500), the fastest (Winston 500 at Talladega), the longest (Coca-Cola 600 at Charlotte) and the oldest (Heinz Southern 500 at Darlington). These events form the backbone of NASCAR racing. Only 3 drivers, LeeRoy Yarbrough (1969), David Pearson (1976) and Bill Elliott (1985), have scored the 3-track hat trick.

Daytona 500

Year	Winner	Car	Avg MPH	Pole Winner	MPH
1959	Lee Petty	Oldsmobile	135.520	Cotton Owens	143.198
1960	Junior Johnson	Chevrolet	124.740	Fireball Roberts	151.556
1961	Marvin Panch	Pontiac	149.601	Fireball Roberts	155.709
1962	Fireball Roberts	Pontiac	152.529	Fireball Roberts	156.995
1963	Tiny Lund	Ford	151.566	Johnny Rutherford	165.183
1964	Richard Petty	Plymouth	154.345	Paul Goldsmith	174.910
1965	Fred Lorenzen	Ford	141.539	Darel Dieringer	171.151
1966	Richard Petty	Plymouth	160.627	Richard Petty	175.165
1967	Mario Andretti	Ford	149.926	Curtis Turner	180.831
1968	Cale Yarborough	Mercury	143.251	Cale Yarborough	189.222
1969	LeeRoy Yarbrough	Ford	157.950	David Pearson	190.029
1970	Pete Hamilton	Plymouth	149.601	Cale Yarborough	194.015
1971	Richard Petty	Plymouth	144.462	A. J. Foyt	182.744

Daytona 500 (Cont.)

Year	Winner	Car	Avg MPH	Pole Winner	MPH
1972	A. J. Foyt	Mercury	161.550	Bobby Isaac	186.632
1973	Richard Petty	Dodge	157.205	Buddy Baker	185.662
1974	Richard Petty	Dodge	140.894	David Pearson	185.017
1975	Benny Parsons	Chevrolet	153.649	Donnie Allison	185.827
1976	David Pearson	Mercury	152.181	A. J. Foyt	185.943
1977	Cale Yarborough	Chevrolet	153.218	Donnie Allison	188.048
1978	Bobby Allison	Ford	159.730	Cale Yarborough	187.536
1979	Richard Petty	Oldsmobile	143.977	Buddy Baker	196.049
1980	Buddy Baker	Oldsmobile	177.602*	A. J. Foyt	195.020
1981	Richard Petty	Buick	169.651	Bobby Allison	194.624
1982	Bobby Allison	Buick	153.991	Benny Parsons	196.317
1983	Cale Yarborough	Pontiac	155.979	Ricky Rudd	198.864
1984	Cale Yarborough	Chevrolet	150.994	Cale Yarborough	201.848
1985	Bill Elliott	Ford	172.265	Bill Elliott	205.114
1986	Geoff Bodine	Chevrolet	148.124	Bill Elliott	205.039
1987	Bill Elliott	Ford	176.263	Bill Elliott	210.364†
1988	Bobby Allison	Buick	137.531	Ken Schrader	193.823
1989	Darrell Waltrip	Chevrolet	148.466	Ken Schrader	196.996
1990	Derrike Cope	Chevrolet	165.761	Ken Schrader	196.515
1991	Earnie Irvan	Chevrolet	148.148	Davey Allison	195.955
1992	Davey Allison	Ford	160.256	Sterling Marlin	192.213
1993	Dale Jarrett	Chevrolet	154.972	Kyle Petty	189.426
1994	Sterling Marlin	Chevrolet	156.931	Loy Allen Jr.	190.158

*Track record, winning time. †Track record, qualifying time.

Note: The Daytona 500, held annually in February, now opens the NASCAR season with 200 laps around the high-banked Daytona, FL, superspeedway.

World 600

Year	Winner	Car	Avg MPH	Pole Winner
1960	Joe Lee Johnson	Chevy	107.752	J.L. Johnson
1961	David Pearson	Pontiac	111.634	Richard Petty
1962	Nelson Stacy	Ford	125.552	Fireball Roberts
1963	Fred Lorenzen	Ford	132.418	Junior Johnson
1964	Jim Paschal	Plymouth	125.772	Junior Johnson
1965	Fred Lorenzen	Ford	121.772	Fred Lorenzon
1966	Marvin Panch	Plymouth	135.042	Paul Goldsmith
1967	Jim Paschal	Plymouth	135.832	Cale Yarborough
1968	Buddy Baker	Dodge	104.207	Donnie Allison
1969	Lee Yarbrough	Mercury	134.631	Donnie Allison
1970	Donnie Allison	Ford	129.680	Bobby Isaac
1971	Bobby Allison	Mercury	140.442	Charlie Glotzbach
1972	Buddy Baker	Dodge	142.255	Bobby Allison
1973	Buddy Baker	Dodge	134.890	Buddy Baker
1974	David Pearson	Mercury	135.720	David Pearson
1975	Richard Petty	Dodge	145.327	David Pearson
1976	David Pearson	Mercury	137.352	David Pearson
1977	Richard Petty	Dodge	137.636	David Pearson
1978	Darrell Waltrip	Chevy	138.355	David Pearson
1979	Darrell Waltrip	Chevy	136.674	Neil Bonnet
1980	Benny Parsons	Chevy	119.265	Cale Yarborough
1981	Bobby Allison	Buick	129.326	Neil Bonnet
1982	Neil Bonnett	Ford	130.508	David Pearson
1983	Neil Bonnett	Chevy	140.406	Buddy Baker
1984	Bobby Allison	Buick	129.233	Harry Gant
1985	Darrell Waltrip	Chevy	141.807	Bill Elliott
1986	Dale Earnhardt	Chevy	140.406	Geoff Bodine
1987	Kyle Petty	Ford	131.483	Bill Elliott
1988	Darrell Waltrip	Chevy	124.460	Davey Allison
1989	Darrell Waltrip	Chevy	144.077	Alan Kulwicki
1990	Rusty Wallace	Pontiac	137.650	Ken Schrader
1991	Davey Allison	Ford	138.951	Mark Martin
1992	Dale Earnhardt	Chevy	132.980	Bill Elliott
1993	Dale Earnhardt	Chevy	145.504	Ken Schrader
1994	Jeff Gordon	Chevy	139.445	Jeff Gordon

Note: Held at the 1.5-mile Charlotte, NC, Motor Speedway on Memorial Day weekend.

Talladega 500

Year	Winner	Car	Avg MPH	Pole Winner	MPH
1969	Richard Brickhouse	Dodge	153.778	Charlie Glotzbach	199.466
1970	Pete Hamilton	Plymouth	158.517	Bobby Isaac	186.834
1971	Bobby Allison	Mercury	145.945	Davey Allison	187.323
1972	James Hylton	Mercury	148.728	Bobby Isaac	190.677
1973	Dick Brooks	Plymouth	145.454	Bobby Allison	187.064
1974	Richard Petty	Dodge	148.637	David Pearson	184.926
1975	Buddy Baker	Ford	130.892	Dave Marcis	191.340
1976	Dave Marcis	Dodge	157.547	Dave Marcis	190.651
1977	Davey Allison	Chevy	162.524	Benny Parsons	192.682
1978	Lennie Pond	Olds	174.700	Cale Yarborough	192.917
1979	Darrell Waltrip	Olds	161.229	Neil Bonnet	193.600
1980	Neil Bonnet	Mercury	166.894	Buddy Baker	198.545
1981	Ron Bouchard	Buick	156.737	Harry Gant	195.897
1982	Darrell Waltrip	Buick	168.157	Geoff Bodine	199.400
1983	Dale Earnhardt	Ford	170.611	Cale Yarborough	201.744
1984	Dale Earnhardt	Chevy	155.485	Cale Yarborough	202.474
1985	Cale Yarborough	Ford	148.772	Bill Elliott	207.578
1986	Bobby Hillin	Buick	151.552	Bill Elliott	209.005
1987	Bill Elliott	Ford	171.293	Bill Elliott	203.827
1988	Ken Schrader	Chevy	154.505	Darrell Waltrip	196.274
1989	Terry Labonte	Ford	157.354	Mark Martin	194.800
1990	Dale Earnhardt	Chevy	174.430	Dale Earnhardt	192.513
1991	Harry Gant	Olds	165.620	Sterling Marlin	192.085
1992	Ernie Irvan	Chevy	176.309	Sterling Marlin	190.586
1993	Dale Earnhardt	Chevy	153.858	Bill Elliott	192.397
1994	Jimmy Spencer	Ford	163.217	Dale Earnhardt	193.470

Note: Held at the 2.66-mile high-banked Talladega, AL, Superspeedway on the last weekend in July.

Southern 500

Year	Winner	Car	Avg MPH	Pole Winner
1950	Johnny Mantz	Plymouth	76.260	Wally Campbell
1951	Herb Thomas	Hudson	76.900	Marshall Teague
1952	Fonty Flock	Olds	74.510	Dick Rathman
1953	Buck Baker	Olds	92.780	Fonty Flock
1954	Herb Thomas	Hudson	94.930	Buck Baker
1955	Herb Thomas	Chevy	92.281	Tim Flock
1956	Curtis Turner	Ford	95.067	Buck Baker
1957	Speedy Thompson	Chevy	100.100	Paul Goldsmith
1958	Fireball Roberts	Chevy	102.590	Fireball Roberts
1959	Jim Reed	Chevy	111.836	Fireball Roberts
1960	Buck Baker	Pontiac	105.901	Cotton Owens
1961	Nelson Stacy	Ford	117.880	Fireball Roberts
1962	Larry Frank	Ford	117.965	Fireball Roberts
1963	Fireball Roberts	Ford	129.784	Fireball Roberts
1964	Buck Baker	Dodge	117.757	Richard Petty
1965	Ned Jarrett	Ford	115.924	Junior Johnson
1966	Darel Dieringer	Mercury	114.830	Lee Yarborough
1967	Richard Petty	Plymouth	131.933	David Pearson
1968	Cale Yarborough	Mercury	126.132	Charlie Glotzbach
1969	Lee Yarbrough	Ford	105.612	Cale Yarborough
1970	Buddy Baker	Dodge	128.817	David Pearson
1971	Bobby Allison	Mercury	131.398	Bobby Allison
1972	Bobby Allison	Chevy	128.124	David Pearson
1973	Cale Yarborough	Chevy	134.033	David Pearson
1974	Cale Yarborough	Chevy	111.075	Richard Petty
1975	Bobby Allison	Matador	116.825	David Pearson
1976	David Pearson	Mercury	120.534	David Pearson
1977	David Pearson	Mercury	106.797	Darrell Waltrip
1978	Cale Yarborough	Olds	116.828	David Pearson
1979	David Pearson	Chevy	126.259	Bobby Allison
1980	Terry Labonte	Chevy	115.210	Darrell Waltrip
1981	Neil Bonnett	Ford	126.410	Harry Gant
1982	Cale Yarborough	Buick	126.703	David Pearson
1983	Bobby Allison	Buick	123.343	Neil Bonnett
1984	Harry Gant	Chevy	128.270	Harry Gant

Southern 500 *(Cont.)*

Year	Winner	Car	Avg MPH	Pole Winner
1985	Bill Elliott	Ford	121.254	Bill Elliott
1986	Tim Richmond	Chevy	121.068	Tim Richmond
1987	Dale Earnhardt	tChevy	115.520	Davey Allison
1988	Bill Elliott	Ford	128.297	Bill Elliott
1989	Dale Earnhardt	Chevy	135.462	Alan Kulwicki
1990	Dale Earnhardt	Chevy	123.141	Dale Earnhardt
1991	Harry Gant	Olds	133.508	Davey Allison
1992	Darrell Waltrip	Chevy	129.114	Sterling Marlin
1993	Mark Martin	Ford	137.932	Ken Schrader
1994	Bill Elliott	Ford	127.915	Geoff Bodine

Note: Held at the 1.366-mile Darlington, SC, International Raceway on Labor Day weekend.

Winston Cup NASCAR Champions

Year	Driver	Car	Wins	Poles	Winnings ($)
1949	Red Byron	Oldsmobile	2	0	5,800
1950	Bill Rexford	Oldsmobile	1	0	6,175
1951	Herb Thomas	Hudson	7	4	18,200
1952	Tim Flock	Hudson	8	4	20,210
1953	Herb Thomas	Hudson	11	10	27,300
1954	Lee Petty	Dodge	7	3	26,706
1955	Tim Flock	Chrysler	18	19	33,750
1956	Buck Baker	Chrysler	14	12	29,790
1957	Buck Baker	Chevy	10	5	24,712
1958	Lee Petty	Olds	7	4	20,600
1959	Lee Petty	Plymouth	10	2	45,570
1960	Rex White	Chevy	6	3	45,260
1961	Ned Jarrett	Chevy	1	4	27,285
1962	Joe Weatherly	Pontiac	9	6	56,110
1963	Joe Weatherly	Mercury	3	6	58,110
1964	Richard Petty	Plymouth	9	8	98,810
1965	Ned Jarrett	Ford	13	9	77,966
1966	David Pearson	Dodge	14	7	59,205
1967	Richard Petty	Plymouth	27	18	130,275
1968	David Pearson	Ford	16	12	118,824
1969	David Pearson	Ford	11	14	183,700
1970	Bobby Isaac	Dodge	11	13	121,470
1971	Richard Petty	Plymouth	21	9	309,225
1972	Richard Petty	Plymouth	8	3	227,015
1973	Benny Parsons	Chevy	1	0	114,345
1974	Richard Petty	Dodge	10	7	299,175
1975	Richard Petty	Dodge	13	3	378,865
1976	Cale Yarborough	Chevy	9	2	387,173
1977	Cale Yarborough	Chevy	9	3	477,499
1978	Cale Yarborough	Oldsmobile	10	8	530,751
1979	Richard Petty	Chevy	5	1	531,292
1980	Dale Earnhardt	Chevy	5	0	588,926
1981	Darrell Waltrip	Buick	12	11	693,342
1982	Darrell Waltrip	Buick	12	7	873,118
1983	Bobby Allison	Buick	6	0	828,355
1984	Terry Labonte	Chevy	2	2	713,010
1985	Darrell Waltrip	Chevy	3	4	1,318,735
1986	Dale Earnhardt	Chevy	5	1	1,783,880
1987	Dale Earnhardt	Chevy	11	1	2,099,243
1988	Bill Elliott	Ford	6	6	1,574,639
1989	Rusty Wallace	Pontiac	6	4	2,247,950
1990	Dale Earnhardt	Chevy	9	4	3,083,056
1991	Dale Earnhardt	Chevy	4	0	2,396,685
1992	Alan Kulwicki	Ford	2	6	2,322,561
1993	Dale Earnhardt	Chevy	6	2	1,508,740

Alltime NASCAR Leaders

WINS		WINNINGS ($)		POLE POSITIONS	
Richard Petty	200	Dale Earnhardt*	20,711,924	Richard Petty	127
David Pearson	105	Bill Elliott*	14,241,694	David Pearson	113
Bobby Allison	84	Darrell Waltrip*	13,333,393	Cale Yarborough	70
Darrell Waltrip*	84	Rusty Wallace*	10,524,646	Darrell Waltrip*	58
Cale Yarborough	83	Terry Labonte*	8,536,645	Bobby Allison	57
Dale Earnhardt*	62	Harry Gant*	8,340,334	Bobby Isaac	51
Lee Petty	54	Ricky Rudd*	8,210,310	Junior Johnson	47
Junior Johnson	50	Geoff Bodine*	8,115,643	Bill Elliott*	46
Ned Jarrett	50	Richard Petty	7,757,964	Buck Baker	44
Herb Thomas	49	Mark Martin*	7,346,979	Buddy Baker	40
Buck Baker	46	Bobby Allison	7,102,233	Herb Thomas	38
Tim Flock	40	Ken Schrader*	6,383,948	Tim Flock	37
Bill Elliott*	40	Kyle Petty*	6,303,968	Fireball Roberts	37
Rusty Wallace*	38	Davey Allison	6,210,589	Ned Jarrett	36
Bobby Isaac	37	Ernie Irvan*	5,427,804	Rex White	36
Fireball Roberts	32	Morgan Shepherd*	5,333,972	Geoff Bodine	35

*Active drivers.

Note: NASCAR Leaders through September 18, 1994.

Formula One/Grand Prix Racing

World Driving Champions

Year	Winner	Car	Year	Winner	Car
1950	Guiseppe Farina, Italy	Alfa Romeo	1969	Jackie Stewart, Scotland	Matra-Ford
1951	Juan-Manuel Fangio, Argentina	Alfa Romeo	1970	Jochen Rindt, Austria*	Lotus-Ford
1952	Alberto Ascari, Italy	Ferrari	1971	Jackie Stewart, Scotland	Tyrell-Ford
1953	Alberto Ascari, Italy	Ferrari	1972	Emerson Fittipaldi, Brazil	Lotus-Ford
1954	Juan-Manuel Fangio, Argentina	Maserati/Mercedes	1973	Jackie Stewart, Scotland	Tyrell-Ford
1955	Juan-Manuel Fangio, Argentina	Mercedes	1974	Emerson Fittipaldi, Brazil	McLaren-Ford
			1975	Niki Lauda, Austria	Ferrari
1956	Juan-Manuel Fangio, Argentina	Ferrari	1976	James Hunt, England	McLaren-Ford
			1977	Niki Lauda, Austria	Ferrari
1957	Juan-Manuel Fangio, Argentina	Maserati	1978	Mario Andretti, U.S.	Lotus-Ford
			1979	Jody Scheckter, S Africa	Ferrari
1958	Mike Hawthorne, England	Ferrari	1980	Alan Jones, Australia	Williams-Ford
1959	Jack Brabham, Australia	Cooper-Climax	1981	Nelson Piquet, Brazil	Brabham-Ford
1960	Jack Brabham, Australia	Cooper-Climax	1982	Keke Rosberg, Finland	Williams-Ford
1961	Phil Hill, United States	Ferrari	1983	Nelson Piquet, Brazil	Brabham-BMW
1962	Graham Hill, England	BRM	1984	Niki Lauda, Austria	McLaren-Porsche
1963	Jim Clark, Scotland	Lotus-Climax	1985	Alain Prost, France	McLaren-Porsche
1964	John Surtees, England	Ferrari	1986	Alain Prost, France	McLaren-Porsche
1965	Jim Clark, Scotland	Lotus-Climax	1987	Nelson Piquet, Brazil	Williams-Honda
1966	Jack Brabham, Australia	Brabham-Climax	1988	Ayrton Senna, Brazil	McLaren-Honda
1967	Denis Hulme, New Zealand	Brabham-Repco	1989	Alain Prost, France	McLaren-Honda
			1990	Ayrton Senna, Brazil	McLaren-Honda
			1991	Ayrton Senna, Brazil	McLaren-Honda
1968	Graham Hill, England	Lotus-Ford	1992	Nigel Mansell, Britain	Williams-Renault
			1993	Alain Prost, France	Williams-Renault

*The championship was awarded after Rindt was killed in practice for the Italian Grand Prix.

Alltime Grand Prix Winners

Driver	Wins	Driver	Wins
Alain Prost, France	51	Juan-Manuel Fangio, Argentina	24
Ayrton Senna, Brazil	41	Nelson Piquet, Brazil*	20
Jackie Stewart, Scotland	27	Stirling Moss, England	16
Nigel Mansell, England*	28	Jack Brabham, Australia	14
Jim Clark, Scotland	25	Graham Hill, England	14
Niki Lauda, Austria	25	Emerson Fittipaldi, Brazil*	14

*Active driver.

Note: Grand Prix Winners through September 18, 1994.

Alltime Grand Prix Pole Winners

Driver	Poles	Driver	Poles
Ayrton Senna, Brazil	65	Mario Andretti, United States*	18
Alain Prost, France	41	Jackie Stewart, Scotland	17
Jim Clark, Scotland	33	Stirling Moss, England	16
Juan-Manuel Fangio, Argentina	28	Alberto Ascari, Italy	14
Niki Lauda, Austria	24	Ronnie Peterson, Sweden	14
Nelson Piquet, Brazil*	24	James Hunt, England	14

*Active driver. Note: Pole Winners through 1993 season.

IMSA Racing

The 24 Hours of Daytona

Year	Winner	Car	Avg Speed	Distance
1962	Dan Gurney	Lotus 19-Class SP11	104.101 mph	3 hrs (312.42 mi)
1963	Pedro Rodriguez	Ferrari-Class 12	102.074 mph	3 hrs (308.61 mi)
1964	Pedro Rodriguez/Phil Hill	Ferrari 250 LM	98.230 mph	2,000 km
1965	Ken Miles/Lloyd Ruby	Ford	99.944 mph	2,000 km
1966	Ken Miles/Lloyd Ruby	Ford Mark II	108.020 mph	24 hrs (2,570.63 mi)
1967	Lorenzo Bandini/Chris Amon	Ferrari 330 P4	105.688 mph	24 hrs (2,537.46 mi)
1968	Vic Elford/Jochen Neerpasch	Porsche 907	106.697 mph	24 hrs (2,565.69 mi)
1969	Mark Donohue/Chuck Parsons	Chevy Lola	99.268 mph	24 hrs (2,383.75 mi)
1970	Pedro Rodriguez/Leo Kinnunen	Porsche 917	114.866 mph	24 hrs (2,758.44 mi)
1971	Pedro Rodriguez/Jackie Oliver	Porsche 917K	109.203 mph	24 hrs (2,621.28 mi)
1972*	Mario Andretti/Jacky Ickx	Ferrari 312/P	122.573 mph	6 hrs (738.24 mi)
1973	Peter Gregg/Hurley Haywood	Porsche Carrera	106.225 mph	24 hrs (2,552.7 mi)
1974	(No race)			
1975	Peter Gregg/Hurley Haywood	Porsche Carrera	108.531 mph	24 hrs (2,606.04 mi)
1976†	Peter Gregg/Brian Redman/ John Fitzpatrick	BMW CSL	104.040 mph	24 hrs (2,092.8 mi)
1977	John Graves/Hurley Haywood/ Dave Helmick	Porsche Carrera	108.801 mph	24 hrs (2,615 mi)
1978	Rolf Stommelen/ Antoine Hezemans/Peter Gregg	Porsche Turbo	108.743 mph	24 hrs (2,611.2 mi)
1979	Ted Field/Danny Ongais/ Hurley Haywood	Porsche Turbo	109.249 mph	24 hrs (2,626.56 mi)
1980	Volkert Meri/Rolf Stommelen/ Reinhold Joest	Porsche Turbo	114.303 mph	24 hrs
1981	Bob Garretson/Bobby Rahal/ Brian Redman	Porsche Turbo	113.153 mph	24 hrs
1982	John Paul, Jr/John Paul, Sr/ Rolf Stommelen	Porsche Turbo	114.794 mph	24 hrs
1983	Preston Henn/Bob Wollek/ Claude Ballot-Lena/A. J. Foyt	Porsche Turbo	98.781 mph	24 hrs
1984	Sarel van der Merwe/ Graham Duxbury/Tony Martin	Porsche March	103.119 mph	24 hrs (2,476.8 mi)
1985	A. J. Foyt/Bob Wollek/ Al Unser, Sr/Thierry Boutsen	Porsche 962	104.162 mph	24 hrs (2,502.68 mi)
1986	Al Holbert/Derek Bell/Al Unser Jr	Porsche 962	105.484 mph	24 hrs (2,534.72 mi)
1987	Chip Robinson/Derek Bell/ Al Holbert/Al Unser Jr	Porsche 962	111.599 mph	24 hrs (2,680.68 mi)
1988	Martin Brundle/John Nielsen/ Raul Boesel	Jaguar XJR-9	107.943 mph	24 hrs (2,591.68 mi)
1989	John Andretti/Derek Bell/ Bob Wollek	Porsche 962	92.009 mph	24 hrs (2,210.76 mi)
1990	Davy Jones/Jan Lammers/ Andy Wallace	Jaguar XJR-12	112.857 mph	24 hrs (2,709.16 mi)
1991	Hurley Haywood/John Winter/ Frank Jelinski/Henri Pescarolo/ Bob Wollek	Porsche 962C	106.633 mph	24 hrs (2,559.64 mi)
1992	Massahiro Hasemi/ Kazuoyshi Hoshino/Toshio Suzuki/Anders Olofsson	Nissan R91CP	112.987	24 hrs (2,712.72 mi)
1993	P.J. Jones/Mark Dismore/ Rocky Moran	Toyota Eagle MK III	103.537	24 hrs (2,484.88 mi)

The 24 Hours of Daytona (Cont.)

Year	Winner	Car	Avg Speed	Distance
1994	Paul Gentilozzi/ Scott Pruett/ Butch Leitzinger/ Steve Millen	Nissan 300 ZX	104.80	24 hrs (2693.67)

*Race shortened due to fuel crisis.
†Course lengthened from 3.81 miles to 3.84 miles.

World Champions

Year	Winner	Car	Year	Winner	Car
1971	Peter Gregg/ Hurley Haywood	Porsche 914	1982	John Paul Jr	Chevy Lola
			1983	Al Holbert	Chevy March
1972	Hurley Haywood	Porsche 911	1984	Randy Lanier	Chevy March
1973	Peter Gregg	Porsche Carrera	1985	Al Holbert	Porsche 962
1974	Peter Gregg	Porsche Carrera	1986	Al Holbert	Porsche 962
1975	Peter Gregg	Porsche Carrera	1987	Chip Robinson	Porsche 962
1976	Al Holbert	Chevy Monza	1988	Geoff Brabham	Nissan GTP
1977	Al Holbert	Chevy Monza	1989	Geoff Brabham	Nissan GTP
1978	Peter Gregg	Porsche 935	1990	Geoff Brabham	Nissan GTP
1979	Peter Gregg	Porsche 935	1991	Geoff Brabham	Nissan NPT
1980	John Fitzpatrick	Porsche 935	1992	Juan Fangio II	Toyota EGL MKIII
1981	Brian Redman	Chevy Lola	1993	Juan Fangio II	Toyota EGL MKIII

Alltime IMSA Leaders

WINS

Al Holbert	49
Peter Gregg	41
Hurley Haywood	28
Geoff Brabham	26
Gene Felton	25
Irv Hoerr	25
Don Devendorf	22
Jim Downing	22
Jack Baldwin	21
Tommy Riggins	21
Amos Johnson	20
Bob Earl	20

FASTEST QUALIFIERS

Peter Gregg	37
Al Holbert	27
Geoff Brabham	26
John Paul Jr	19
John Fitzpatrick	12
Sarel Van der Merwe	11
Chip Robinson	11
Davy Jones	10
Danny Ongais	10
David Hobbs	9
Klaus Ludwig	9
John Greenwood	8
Hans Stuck	8
Bill Whittington	7

Note: Leaders through 1993 season.

FIA World Sports Car Racing

The 24 Hours of LeMans

Year	Winning Drivers	Car
1923	André Lagache/René Léonard	Chenard & Walker
1924	John Duff/Francis Clement	Bentley 3-litre
1925	Gérard de Courcelles/André Rossignol	La Lorraine
1926	Robert Bloch/André Rossignol	La Lorraine
1927	J. Dudley Benjafield/Sammy Davis	Bentley 3-litre
1928	Woolf Barnato/Bernard Rubin	Bentley 4½
1929	Woolf Barnato/Sir Henry Birkin	Bentley Speed Six
1930	Woolf Barnato/Glen Kidston	Bentley Speed Six
1931	Earl Howe/Sir Henry Birkin	Alfa Romeo 8C-2300 sc
1932	Raymond Sommer/Luigi Chinetti	Alfa Romeo 8C-2300 sc
1933	Raymond Sommer/Tazio Nuvolari	Alfa Romeo 8C-2300 sc
1934	Luigi Chinetti/Philippe Etancelin	Alfa Romeo 8C-2300 sc

The 24 Hours of LeMans (Cont.)

Year	Winning Drivers	Car
1935	John Hindmarsh/Louis Fontés	Lagonda M45R
1936	Race cancelled	
1937	Jean-Pierre Wimille/Robert Benoist	Bugatti 57G sc
1938	Eugene Chaboud/Jean Tremoulet	Delahaye 135M
1939	Jean-Pierre Wimille/Pierre Veyron	Bugatti 57G sc
1940-48	Races cancelled	
1949	Luigi Chinetti/Lord Selsdon	Ferrari 166MM
1950	Louis Rosier/Jean-Louis Rosier	Talbot-Lago
1951	Peter Walker/Peter Whitehead	Jaguar C
1952	Hermann Lang/Fritz Reiss	Mercedes-Benz 300 SL
1953	Tony Rolt/Duncan Hamilton	Jaguar C
1954	Froilan Gonzales/Maurice Trintignant	Ferrari 375
1955	Mike Hawthorn/Ivor Bueb	Jaguar D
1956	Ron Flockhart/Ninian Sanderson	Jaguar D
1957	Ron Flockhart/Ivor Buab	Jaguar D
1958	Olivier Gendebien/Phil Hill	Ferrari 250 TR58
1959	Carroll Shelby/Roy Salvadori	Aston Martin DBR1
1960	Olivier Gendebien/Paul Fräre	Ferrari 250 TR59/60
1961	Olivier Gendebien/Phil Hill	Ferrari 250 TR61
1962	Olivier Gendebien/Phil Hill	Ferrari 250P
1963	Lodovico Scarfiotti/Lorenzo Bandini	Ferrari 250P
1964	Jean Guichel/Nino Vaccarella	Ferrari 275P
1965	Jochen Rindt/Masten Gregory	Ferrari 250LM
1966	Chris Amon/Bruce McLaren	Ford Mk2
1967	Dan Gurney/A. J. Foyt	Ford Mk4
1968	Pedro Rodriguez/Lucien Bianchi	Ford GT40
1969	Jacky Ickx/Jackie Oliver	Ford GT40
1970	Hans Herrmann/Richard Attwood	Porsche 917
1971	Helmut Marko/Gijs van Lennep	Porsche 917
1972	Henri Pescarolo/Graham Hill	Matra-Simca MS670
1973	Henri Pescarolo/Gérard Larrousse	Matra-Simca MS670B
1974	Henri Pescarolo/Gérard Larrousse	Matra-Simca MS670B
1975	Jacky Ickx/Derek Bell	Mirage-Ford MB
1976	Jacky Ickx/Gijs van Lennep	Porsche 936
1977	Jacky Ickx/Jurgen Barth/Hurley Haywood	Porsche 936
1978	Jean-Pierre Jaussaud/Didier Pironi	Renault-Alpine A442
1979	Klaus Ludwig/Bill Whttington/Don Whittington	Porsche 935
1980	Jean-Pierre Jaussaud/Jean Rondeau	Rondeau-Ford M379B
1981	Jacky Ickx/Derek Bell	Porsche 936-81
1982	Jacky Ickx/Derek Bell	Porsche 956
1983	Vern Schuppan/Hurley Haywood/Al Holbert	Porsche 956-83
1984	Klaus Ludwig/Henri Pescarolo	Porsche 956B
1985	Klaus Ludwig/Paolo Barilla/John Winter	Porsche 956B
1986	Derek Bell/Hans-Joachim Stuck/Al Holbert	Porsche 962C
1987	Derek Bell/Hans-Joachim Stuck/Al Holbert	Porsche 962C
1988	Jan Lammers/Johnny Dumfries/Andy Wallace	Jaguar XJR9LM
1989	Jochen Mass/Manuel Reuter/Stanley Dickens	Sauber-Mercedes C9-88
1990	John Nielsen/Price Cobb/Martin Brundle	TWR Jaguar XJR-12
1991	Volker Weidler/Johnny Herbert/Bertrand Gachof	Mazda 787B
1992	Derek Warwick/Yannick Dalmas/Mark Blundell	Peugeot 905B
1993	Geoff Brabham/Christophe Bouchut/Eric Helary	Peugeot 905
1994	Yannick Dalmas/Hurley Haywood/Mauro Baldi	Porsche 962

Drag Racing: Milestone Performances

Top Fuel

ELAPSED TIME

9.00	Jack Chrisman	Feb 18, 1961	Pomona, CA
8.97	Jack Chrisman	May 20, 1961	Empona, VA
7.96	Bobby Vodnick	May 16, 1964	Bayview, MD
6.97	Don Johnson	May 7, 1967	Carlsbad, CA
5.97	Mike Snively	Nov 17, 1972	Ontario, CA
5.78	Don Garlits	Nov 18, 1973	Ontario, CA
5.698	Gary Beck	Oct 10, 1975	Ontario, CA
5.636	Don Garlits	Oct 10, 1975	Ontario, CA
5.573	Gary Beck	Oct 18, 1981	Irvine, CA
5.484	Gary Beck	Sep 6, 1982	Clermont, IN
5.391	Gary Beck	Oct 1, 1983	Fremont, CA
5.280	Darrell Gwynn	Sep 25, 1986	Ennis, TX
5.176	Darrell Gwynn	April 4, 1987	Ennis, TX
5.090	Joe Amato	Oct 1, 1987	Ennis, TX
4.990	Eddie Hill	April 9, 1988	Ennis, TX
4.936	Eddie Hill	Oct 9, 1988	Baytown, TX
4.919	Gary Ormsby	Oct 7, 1989	Ennis, TX
4.881	Gary Ormsby	Sep 29, 1990	Topeka, KS
4.801	Eddie Hill	March 22, 1992	Gainesville, FL

SPEED

180.36	Connie Kalitta	Sep 3, 1962	Clermont, IN
190.26	Don Garlits	Sep 21, 1963	East Haddam, CT
201.34	Don Garlits	Aug 1, 1964	Great Meadows, NJ
226.12	John Edmunds	May 7, 1967	Carlsbad, CA
232.55	Larry Hendrickson	July 11, 1970	Vancouver, WA
243.24	Don Garlits	March 18, 1973	Gainesville, FL
250.69	Don Garlits	Oct 11, 1975	Ontario, CA
260.11	Joe Amato	March 18, 1984	Gainesville, FL
272.56	Don Garlits	March 23, 1986	Gainesville, FL
282.13	Joe Amato	Sep 5, 1987	Clermont, IN
291.54	Connie Kalitta	Feb 11, 1989	Pomona, CA
294.88	Michael Brotherton	Oct 7, 1989	Ennis, TX
294.88	Gary Ormsby	Oct 8, 1989	Ennis, TX
296.05	Gary Ormsby	Sep 29, 1990	Topeka, KS
297.12	Mike Dunn	March 8, 1992	Baytown, TX
301.70	Kenny Bernstein	March 20, 1992	Gainesville, FL
303.6	Pat Austin	April 25, 1993	Atlanta, GA

Funny Car

ELAPSED TIME

6.92	Leroy Goldstein	Sep 3, 1970	Clermont, IN
5.987	Don Prudhomme	Oct 12, 1975	Ontario, CA
5.868	Raymond Beadle	July 16, 1981	Englishtown, NJ
5.799	Tom Anderson	Sep 3, 1982	Clermont, IN
5.637	Don Prudhomme	Sep 4, 1982	Clermont, IN
5.588	Rick Johnson	Feb 3, 1985	Pomona, CA
5.425	Kenny Bernstein	Sep 26, 1986	Ennis, TX
5.397	Kenny Bernstein	April 5, 1987	Ennis, TX
5.255	Ed McCulloch	April 17, 1988	Ennis, TX
5.193	Don Prudhomme	March 2, 1989	Baytown, TX
5.132	Ed McCulloch	Oct 7, 1989	Ennis, TX
5.102	Cruz Pedregon	March 8, 1992	Baytown, TX

SPEED

200.44	Gene Snow	August, 1968	Houston, TX
250.00	Don Prudhomme	May 23, 1982	Erwinville, LA
260.11	Kenny Bernstein	March 18, 1984	Gainesville, FL

Funny Car (Cont.)

SPEED (Cont.)

271.41.................Kenny Bernstein	Aug 30, 1986	Clermont, IN
280.72.................Mike Dunn	Oct 2, 1987	Ennis, TX
283.28.................Mark Oswald	Oct 29, 1989	Pomona, CA
284.18.................Mark Oswald	Oct 11, 1990	Ennis, TX
289.94.................Jim White	Sept 15, 1991	Mohnton, PA
290.13.................Jim White	Oct 11, 1991	Ennis TX
291.82.................Jim White	Oct 25, 1991	Pomona, CA
300.40.................Jim Epler	Oct 3, 1993	Topeka, KS

Pro Stock

ELAPSED TIME

7.778...................Lee Shepherd	March 12, 1982	Gainesville, FL
7.655...................Lee Shepherd	Oct 1, 1982	Fremont, CA
7.557...................Bob Glidden	Feb 2, 1985	Pomona, CA
7.497...................Bob Glidden	Sep 13, 1985	Maple Grove, PA
7.377...................Bob Glidden	Aug 28, 1986	Clermont, IN
7.294...................Frank Sanchez	Oct 7, 1988	Baytown, TX
7.256...................Bob Glidden	March 11, 1989	Baytown, TX
7.184...................Darrell Alderman	Oct 12, 1990	Ennis, TX
7.127...................Warren Johnson	July 31, 1992	Sonoma, CA

SPEED

181.08.................Warren Johnson	Oct 1, 1982	Fremont, CA
190.07.................Warren Johnson	Aug 29, 1986	Clermont, IN
191.32.................Bob Glidden	Sep 4, 1987	Clermont, IN
192.18.................Warren Johnson	Oct 13, 1990	Ennis, TX
193.21.................Bob Glidden	July 28, 1991	Sonoma, CA
194.46.................Warren Johnson	March 20, 1992	Gainesville, FL
194.51.................Warren Johnson	July 31, 1992	Sonoma, CA

Alltime Drag Racing Leaders

NATIONAL EVENT WINS		BEST WON-LOST RECORD (WINNING PCT)	
Bob Glidden	84	John Myers	128-28 (821)
Don Prudhomme	48	Bob Glidden	761-171 (.817)
Warren Johnson	47	David Schultz	161-42 (.793)
Kenny Bernstein	41	Joe Amato	333-131 (.703)
John Force	41	Warren Johnson	370-165 (.693)
Don Garlits	35	John Force	314-147 (.681)
Joe Amato	34	Kenny Bernstein	343-163 (.678)
David Schultz	33	Cruz Pedregon	74-36 (.673)
Lee Shepherd	26	Don Prudhomme	357-184 (.659)
Terry Vance	24	Mark Oswald	245-149 (.623)

Note: Drag Racing Leaders through September 20, 1994.

THEY SAID IT

Jay Cochran, assessing his Ferrari's performance after winning the Road Atlanta World Sports Car race last April: "The car was beautiful, flawless—and it was red."

Bowling

Sports Illustrated

HAVING A BALL

Norm Duke: bowling's man on a roll

Hollywood Spares

*New venues, rowdy crowds, and a nod from Hollywood
gave bowling new life and a new 'tude* | by KELLI ANDERSON

THE WORDS *BOWLING* AND *HIP* ARE rarely uttered in the same breath, but 1994 brought the two concepts startlingly close together. It was the first full year of the PBA's relaxed standards on facial fuzz and hair length, which spawned at least two ponytails and numerous beards, and it was the year Hollywood gave a nod to bowling in the movie *Greedy* by featuring Michael J. Fox as a pro bowler (albeit an anachronistically clean-shaven one). But 1994 may be best remembered as the year that saw the age-old stepladder format for televised finals break out of the confines of a bowling center and enter a new arena—one that reverberated with, of all things, the rhythm of rap.

On April 2, just as grass and flowers were poking through the ground outside the Erie (Pa.) Civic Center, 28-year-old Dennis Horan was experiencing a rejuvenation of his own inside. Before a foot-stomping, hand-clapping, sign-waving, rap-chanting record PBA crowd of 4,200, Horan beat Brian Voss 267–235 in the PBA's SplitFire Spark Plug Open on four lanes set up on the convention center floor. It was a milestone for Horan, who had never won a PBA event, but more significantly, it was a shot in the arm for pro bowling. Spectators, many of whom had begun the afternoon with tailgate parties in the parking lot, compared the event's atmosphere to a basketball game, a boxing match, a football game—even, if one took into consideration the autograph hounds hanging over the rail, a baseball game. It was, in other words, like anything but a typical polite and buttoned-up televised bowling final.

"The energy was overwhelming," said Horan, who months later was still basking in the memory of rolling strikes to chants of "Whoomp! There it is!" a line the crowd borrowed from the rap group Tag Team. "I felt totally relaxed out there. I remember thinking, This is cool, this is totally free and uninhibited—this is where I'm supposed to be."

It is where finalists in at least six events will be in 1995. But even as pro bowling tested out a new finals format, one of the major stories of 1994 was about coming to grips with the old. Thirty-year-old Norm Duke, an elfin, Texas-bred bowling prodigy who joined the tour at age 18 and beat Earl Anthony on national TV in his first finals, had failed to win another title for the next eight years because he could not perform under the glare of television lights. After reading and rereading motivational books such as *See You at the Top* and *In the Mind's Eye: Enhancing Human Performance*, Duke won two titles in 1991 and another in '93. In 1994 he put an emphatic end to his TV woes by winning four titles in as many months.

Duke's fourth title came at the inaugural General Tire Tournament of Champions, in Fairlawn, Ohio, in April, an event christened by a bizarre stepladder finals disfigured by 14 open frames, 11 splits, two gutter balls, one foot fault and one *winning* score of 159. In the last game Duke, sporting a newly legal beard, beat top qualifier Eric Forkel 217–184 and went home to Oklahoma $65,000 richer. Although Duke took most of the summer off to recuperate from surgery on his right foot, as of September he was the favorite for Bowler of the Year honors.

Last season's Bowler of the Year, Walter Ray Williams, who won seven titles in 1993, had won just one through the first eight months of '94. On the other hand, he regained his form in horseshoe pitching, winning his sixth world title at Spearfish, N. Dak., in August.

Hall of Famer Johnny Petraglia, who hadn't won a tournament since 1980, partially compensated for 14 years of titledrought by rolling a 300 in the second game of the nationally televised PBA championship in Toledo in March. The perfect game netted him $100,000 in addition to his $8,000 check for third place. The battle for first was left to Dave and Dale Traber, who became the first brothers in PBA history to bowl against each other in a tournament final. Joked Dave after beating his older sibling 196–187, "I love my brother, but I'll be damned if I'm going to lose to him. If he had beaten me, I'd have had to kill him."

Just about as competitive was the Ladies Pro Bowlers Tour, which received a welcome

DAVID LIAM KYLE

Duke overcame his stage fright to win four titles in four months in '94.

financial boost from Sam's Town Casino, the tour's new umbrella sponsor. One player benefiting from the infusion of cash was Anne Marie Duggan, whose $113,000 in prize money as of September put her on pace to break the LPBT's single-season earnings record. Using a collection of 20 balls which she compares to "a set of golf clubs," Duggan dominated the first half of 1994 by winning three titles—including the major WIBC Queens—grabbing second twice and cashing in all 14 events before the summer break.

In the interests of streamlining, bowling moved toward a consolidation of its many acronyms—including the PBA, BPAA, LBPT, WIBC, ABC and SPBA—into something a little more monolithic. Of course, a new logo will give bowling another chance to show its new 'tude, which raises a burning question: Will the old red, white and blue give way to purple, black and teal?

FOR THE RECORD·1993-1994

The Majors

MEN

PBA National Championship

CHAMPIONSHIP ROUND

Bowler	Games	Total	Earnings ($)
David Traber	1	196	27,000
Dale Traber	2	380	14,000
Johnny Petraglia	3	725	8,000*
Walter Ray Williams	1	194	6,000
Erik Forkel	1	181	5,000

Playoff Results: Petraglia def. Forkel, 237-181; Petraglia def. Williams, 300-194; Dale Traber def. Petraglia, 193-188; David Traber def. Dale Traber, 196-187.
* Petraglia received $100,000 bonus from True Value for televised 300 game.

Held at Ducat's Imperial Lanes, Toledo, Ohio, Feb 27-March 5, 1994.

BPAA United States Open

CHAMPIONSHIP ROUND

Bowler	Games	Total	Earnings ($)
Justin Hromek	1	267	46,000
Parker Bohn III	4	869	24,000
Eric Forkel	1	202	14,000
Brian Voss	1	180	10,500
Jess Stayrook	1	179	8,500

Playoff Results: Bohn def. Stayrook, 219-179; Bohn def. Voss, 192-180; Bohn defeated Forkel, 228-202; Hromek def. Bohn, 267-230.

Held at Bowl One, Troy, MI, April 3-9, 1994.

General Tire Tournament of Champions

CHAMPIONSHIP ROUND

Bowler	Games	Total	Earnings ($)
Norm Duke	2	422	65,000
Eric Forkel	1	194	35,000
Randy Pedersen	2	410	26,000
Pete Weber	2	365	19,000
Steve Jaros	1	158	13,000

Playoff Results: Weber def. Jaros, 159-158; Pedersen def. Weber, 224-206; Duke def. Pedersen, 205-186; Duke def. Forkel, 217-194.

Held at Riviera Lanes, Fairlawn, Ohio, April 19-23, 1994.

ABC Masters Tournament

CHAMPIONSHIP ROUND

Bowler	Games	Total	Earnings ($)
Hobo Boothe	1	194	38,000
Rich Moores	4	878	23,000
Ron Winger	1	199	16,500
Mike Berlin	1	206	11,000
Gary Dickinson	1	211	7,000

Playoff Results: Moores def. Dickinson, 256-211; Moores def. Berlin, 217-206; Moores def. Winger, 221-199; Boothe def. Moores, 194-184.

Held at Greenacres Bowl, Greenacres, Fl, March 24-30, 1994.

WOMEN

Sam's Town Invitational

CHAMPIONSHIP ROUND

Bowler	Games	Total	Earnings ($)
Robin Romeo	1	194	20,000
Tammy Turner	2	419	10,000
Dana Miller-Mackie	2	438	5,000
Kim Couture	2	386	4,500
Wendy Macpherson	1	194	4,000

Playoff Results: Couture def. Macpherson, 196-194; Miller-Mackie def. Couture, 234-190; Turner def. Miller-Mackie, 228-204; Romeo def. Turner, 194-191.

Held at Sam's Town Bowling Center, Las Vegas, NV, Nov. 13-20, 1993.

WIBC Queens

CHAMPIONSHIP ROUND

Bowler	Games	Total	Earnings ($)
Anne Marie Duggan	4	913	12,510
Aleta Sill	1	218	6,385
Dede Davidson	1	191	3,875
Regi Jonak	1	161	2,755
Wendy Macpherson-Papanos	1	177	2,085

Playoff Results: Duggan def. Macpherson-Papanos 224-177; Duggan def. Jonak, 248-161; Duggan def. Davidson, 203-191; Duggan def. Sill, 238-218.

Held at Ritz Bowl Classic, Salt Lake City, UT, May 8-12, 1994.

BPAA United States Open

CHAMPIONSHIP ROUND

Bowler	Games	Total	Earnings ($)
Aleta Sill	3	712	18,000
Anne Marie Duggan	1	170	9,000
Marianne DiRupo	1	183	7,000
Carolyn Dorin	2	503	5,000
Tish Johnson	1	218	4,000

Playoff Results: Dorin def. Johnson 245-216; Sill def. Dorin 279-258; Sill def. DiRupo 204-183; Sill def. Duggan 229-170.

Held at Northrock Lanes, Wichita, KS, Oct 1-8, 1994.

Nothing to Spare

"It was like the four-minute mile being broken for the first time." That's how Eric Cornell, director of the monthly king-of-the-hill tournament at Riverbend Bowl in Corunna, Mich., put it after watching Troy Ockerman roll three straight 300 games in the finals of the December 1993 event. The American Bowling Congress did not certify the games as a 900 series because they occurred in separate portions of a 'multiple event tournament', but they are the only three consecutive perfect games in history. The 26-year-old Ockerman, a video game serviceman from Owoso, Mich., and now the Roger Bannis-ter of the alleys, was, by all accounts, remarkably relaxed. "People were talking, and he was joking back," says Cornell.

But in the end Ockerman, who has a 216 average, showed that he felt pressure. After letting his 36th ball go, he turned away and dropped to one knee, afraid to look. "But then I lifted my head and saw the pins go down," says Ockerman. "I screamed, 'Yes!'" He was then carried triumphantly around the lanes on the shoulders of spectators. "It was incredible," he says. "It's not just once in a lifetime. It's once in history."

PBA Tour Results

1993 Fall Tour

Date	Event	Winner	Earnings ($)	Runner-Up
Oct 7-10	Oronamin C Japan Cup	Pete Weber	39,000	Brian Voss
Oct 16-20	Rochester Open	Roger Bowker	23,000	Dave Ferraro
Oct 23-27	Greater Detroit Open	Norm Duke	23,000	Walter Ray Williams, Jr
Oct 30-Nov 3	Touring Players Championship	Jason Couch	27,000	Parker Bohn III
Nov 4-10	Brunswick Memorial World Open	Dave Husted	46,440	Brian Voss

1994 Winter Tour

Date	Event	Winner	Earnings ($)	Runner-Up
Jan 18-22	AC-Delco Classic	Norm Duke	44,000	Robert Smith
Jan 23-29	Showboat Invitational	Walter Ray Williams, Jr	37,000	Pete Weber
Feb 1-5	Quaker State Open	Steve Hoskins	41,000	Pete Weber
Feb 6-12	Choice Hotels Classic	Norm Duke	38,000	Walter Ray Williams, Jr
Feb 15-19	Bud Light Hall of Fame Championship	Andy Neuer	30,000	Walter Ray Williams, Jr
Feb 22-26	True Value Open	Bryan Goebel	43,000	Norm Duke
Feb 27-Mar 5	PBA National Championship	David Traber	27,000	Dale Traber
Mar 8-12	Brunswick Johnny Petraglia Open	Norm Duke	34,000	Bryan Goebel
Mar 15-19	Leisure's Long Island Open	Amleto Monacelli	24,000	Steve Wilson
Mar 22-26	Tums Classic	Harry Sullins	23,000	Jess Stayrook
Mar 29-Apr 2	Splitfire Spark Plug Open	Dennis Horan	39,000	Brian Voss
Apr 3-9	BPAA U.S. Open	Justin Hromek	46,000	Parker Bohn III
Apr 11-16	IOF Foresters Bowling for Miracles Open	Mike Edwards	43,000	Pete Weber
Apr 19-23	General Tire Tournament of Champions	Norm Duke	65,000	Eric Forkel

1994 Spring/Summer Tour

Date	Event	Winner	Earnings ($)	Runner-Up
June 24-28	Northwest Classic	Dave Husted	16,000	Walter Ray Williams, Jr
July 1-5	Oregon Open	Dave D'Entremont	16,000	Joe Firpo
July 8-12	Hilton Hotels Classic	John Mazza	27,000	Walter Ray Williams, Jr
July 15-19	Active West Open	Bryan Goebel	14,000	Steve Hoskins
July 22-26	Tucson Open	Steve Hoskins	14,000	Walter Ray Williams, Jr
Aug 12-16	Sherwin-Williams Classic	Dave Husted	27,000	George Branham III
Aug 19-23	Greater Harrisburg Open	Randy Pedersen	16,000	Bob Vespi
Aug 26-30	Greater Lexington Classic	Amleto Monacelli	20,000	Brian Voss

1993 Senior Fall Tour

Date	Event	Winner	Earnings ($)	Runner-Up
Aug 8-11	Springfield Senior Open	Darrel Curtis	6,000	Barry Gurney
Oct 1-6	Hammer Senior Open	Gary Dickinson	12,000	John Hricsina
Oct 9-13	St Petersburg/Clearwater Senior Open	John Handegard	12,000	Gary Dickinson
Oct 16-20	Don Carter PBA Senior Classic	Frankie May	12,000	Dave Davis
Nov 9-15	Ebonite Senior Championship	Gene Stus	25,000	Gary Dickinson

1994 Senior Tour (through Aug 13)

Date	Event	Winner	Earnings ($)	Runner-Up
May 29-June 2	Lansing Senior Open	Dave Davis	7,500	Lon Marshall
June 5-8	Greater Providence Senior Open	Rich Holden	6,500	Tommy Evans
June 12-16	Canadian Senior Open	Mel Wolf	6,500	Gene Stus
June 19-23	Wyoming Valley Senior Open	Sam Flanagan	9,000	John Handegard
Aug 2-6	Rocky Mountain Senior Open	John Handegard	8,000	Gene Stus
Aug 9-13	Showboat Senior Invitational	Tommy Evans	24,000	Frankie May

LPBT Tour Results

1993 Fall Tour

Date	Event	Winner	Earnings ($)	Runner-Up
Oct 5-10	Columbia 300 Delaware Open	Kim Berke	10,800	Leanne Barrette
Oct 12-17	Hammer Eastern Open	Sandra Jo Shiery	9,000	Diana Teeters
Oct 19-24	Three Rivers Open	Marianne Dirupo	9,000	Cheryl Daniels
Oct 26-31	Brunswick Open	Michelle Mullen	9,000	Carol Gianotti
Nov 3-7	Hammer Midwest Open	Lisa Wagner	9,000	Debbie McMullen
Nov 13-20	Sam's Town Invitational	Robin Romeo	20,000	Tammy Turner

1994 Winter Tour

Date	Event	Winner	Earnings ($)	Runner-Up
Feb 6-10	Lady Ebonite Classic	Carolyn Dorin	12,600	Aleta Sill
Feb 12-17	Alexandria Louisiana Open	Leanne Barrette	5,000	Jeanne Naccarato
Feb 20-24	New Orleans Classic	Debbie McMullen	9,000	Marianne DiRupo
Feb 26-Mar 3	Claremore Classic	Tammy Turner	5,000	Michelle Mullen
Mar 6-10	AMF Ninja Challenge	Kim Couture	10,800	Darris Street
Mar 13-17	Texas Border Shootout	Anne Marie Duggan	9,000	Tammy Turner

1994 Spring Tour

Date	Event	Winner	Earnings ($)	Runner-Up
Apr 24-28	Greater San Diego Classic	Sandra Jo Shiery	9,000	Aleta Sill
May 1-5	Santa Maria Classic	Anne Marie Duggan	9,000	Aleta Sill
May 8-12	WIBC Queens	Anne Marie Duggan	12,510	Aleta Sill
May 15-19	Omaha Classic	Marianne DiRupo	9,000	Kim Couture
May 15-19	Arlington Heights Open	Cheryl Daniels	9,000	Anne Marie Duggan
June 5-9	Hammond Open	Cheryl Daniels	9,000	Kim Couture
June 12-16	Rocket City Challenge	Aleta Sill	9,000	Robin Romeo
June 19-23	Sam's Town Tunica Classic	Dana Miller-Mackie	9,000	Tish Johnson

Triumphant Trios

When Marge Rubinski of suburban Cleveland bowled a perfect 300 in a league game last January, her family earned a place in the American Bowling Congress record books. Her husband Tom and son Dan have also rolled perfect games, making the Rubinski's the third mother-father-son trio known to have accomplished the feat. The other families who have achieved the perfecta trifecta are the Hills of Lawton, Okla. (1976), and the Ervins from Indianapolis (1984).

PBA

MONEY LEADERS

Name	Titles	Tournaments	Earnings ($)
Walter Ray Williams, Jr	7	33	294,370
Parker Bohn III	2	30	174,528
Pete Weber	2	30	159,480
Brian Voss	1	27	147,735
Ron Williams	2	34	147,235

AVERAGE

Name	Games	Pinfall	Average
Walter Ray Williams, Jr	1300	289,885	222.98
Brian Voss	902	198,516	220.08
Amleto Monacelli	932	205,048	220.01
Dave Arnold	1221	268,436	219.85
Dave Ferraro	959	209,185	218.14

Seniors

MONEY LEADERS

Name	Titles	Tournaments	Earnings ($)
Gary Dickinson	2	13	78,250
Gene Stus	1	14	75,565
John Handegard	2	13	67,123
Frankie May	1	13	50,128
John Hricsina	2	14	46,559

AVERAGE

Name	Games	Pinfall	Average
Gary Dickinson	573	125,130	218.38
John Handegard	509	110,829	217.73
Gene Stus	576	124,596	216.31
Dennis Torgerson	297	63,963	215.36
John Hricsina	508	109,117	214.80

LPBT

MONEY LEADERS

Name	Titles	Tournaments	Earnings ($)
Aleta Sill	2	16	57,995.00
Tish Johnson	0	17	57,824.00
Lisa Wagner	2	17	51,663.00
Wendy Macpherson	1	16	50,511.00
Dana Miller-Mackie	1	17	49,755.00

AVERAGE

Name	Games	Pinfall	Average
Tish Johnson	672	144,744	215.39
Wendy Macpherson	657	141,344	215.14
Leanne Barrette	630	135,261	214.70
Kim Couture	704	150,549	213.85
Dana Miller-Mackie	624	133,380	213.75

FOR THE RECORD·Year by Year

BPAA United States Open

Year	Winner	Score	Runner-Up	Site
1942	John Crimmins	265.09-262.33	Joe Norris	Chicago
1943	Connie Schwoegler	not available	Frank Benkovic	Chicago
1944	Ned Day	315.21-298.21	Paul Krumske	Chicago
1945	Buddy Bomar	304.46-296.16	Joe Wilman	Chicago
1946	Joe Wilman	310.27-305.37	Therman Gibson	Chicago
1947	Andy Varipapa	314.16-308.04	Allie Brandt	Chicago
1948	Andy Varipapa	309.23-309.06	Joe Wilman	Chicago
1949	Connie Schwoegler	312.31-307.27	Andy Varipapa	Chicago
1950	Junie McMahon	318.37-307.17	Ralph Smith	Chicago
1951	Dick Hoover	305.29-304.07	Lee Jouglard	Chicago
1952	Junie McMahon	309.29-305.41	Bill Lillard	Chicago
1953	Don Carter	304.17-297.36	Ed Lubanski	Chicago
1954	Don Carter	308.02-307.25	Bill Lillard	Chicago
1955	Steve Nagy	307.17-303.34	Ed Lubanski	Chicago
1956	Bill Lillard	304.30-304.22	Joe Wilman	Chicago
1957	Don Carter	308.49-305.45	Dick Weber	Chicago
1958	Don Carter	311.03-308.09	Buzz Fazio	Minneapolis
1959	Billy Welu	311.48-310.26	Ray Bluth	Buffalo
1960	Harry Smith	312.24-308.12	Bob Chase	Omaha
1961	Bill Tucker	318.49-309.11	Dick Weber	San Bernadino
1962	Dick Weber	299.34-297.38	Roy Lown	Miami Beach
1963	Dick Weber	642-591	Billy Welu	Kansas City, MO
1964	Bob Strampe	714-616	Tommy Tuttle	Dallas
1965	Dick Weber	608-586	Jim St. John	Philadelphia
1966	Dick Weber	684-681	Nelson Burton Jr	Lansing, MI
1967	Les Schissler	613-610	Pete Tountas	St. Ann, MO
1968	Jim Stefanich	12,401-12,104	Billy Hardwick	Garden City, NY
1969	Billy Hardwick	12,585-11,463	Dick Weber	Miami
1970	Bobby Cooper	12,936-12,307	Billy Hardwick	Northbrook, IL
1971	Mike Limongello	397 (2 games)	Teata Semiz	St. Paul, MN
1972	Don Johnson	233 (1 game)	George Pappas	New York City
1973	Mike McGrath	712 (3 games)	Earl Anthony	New York City
1974	Larry Laub	749 (3 games)	Dave Davis	New York City
1975	Steve Neff	279 (1 game)	Paul Colwell	Grand Prairie, TX
1976	Paul Moser	226 (1 game)	Jim Frazier	Grand Prairie, TX
1977	Johnny Petraglia	279 (1 game)	Bill Spigner	Greensboro, NC
1978	Nelson Burton Jr	873 (4 games)	Jeff Mattingly	Greensboro, NC
1979	Joe Berardi	445 (2 games)	Earl Anthony	Windsor Locks, CT
1980	Steve Martin	930 (4 games)	Earl Anthony	Windsor Locks, CT
1981	Marshall Holman	684 (3 games)	Mark Roth	Houston, TX
1982	Dave Husted	1011 (4 games)	Gil Sliker	Houston, TX
1983	Gary Dickinson	214 (1 game)	Steve Neff	Oak Lawn, IL
1984	Mark Roth	244 (1 game)	Guppy Troup	Oak Hill, IL
1985	Marshall Holman	233 (1 game)	Wayne Webb	Venice, FL
1986	Steve Cook	467 (2 games)	Frank Ellenburg	Venice, FL
1987	Del Ballard Jr	525 (2 games)	Pete Weber	Tacoma, WA
1988	Pete Weber	929 (4 games)	Marshall Holman	Atlantic City, NJ
1989	Mike Aulby	429 (2 games)	Jim Pencak	Edmond, OK
1990	Ron Palombi Jr	269 (1 game)	Amleto Monacelli	Indianapolis, IN
1991	Pete Weber	956 (4 games)	Mark Thayer	Indianapolis, IN
1992	Robert Lawrence	667 (3 games)	Scott Devers	Canandaigua, NY
1993	Del Ballard, Jr	505 (2 games)	Walter Ray Williams,	Canandaigua, NY
1994	Justin Hromek	267 (1 game)	Parker Bohn III	Troy, MI

Note: From 1942 to 1970, the tournament was called the BPAA All-Star. Peterson scoring was used from 1942 through 1962. Under this system, the winner of an individual match game gets one point, plus one point for each 50 pins knocked down. From 1963 through 1967, a three-game championship was held between the two top qualifiers. From 1968 through 1970 total pinfall determined the winner. From 1971 to the present, five qualifiers compete for the championship.

PBA National Championship

Year	Winner	Score	Runner-Up	Site
1960	Don Carter	6512 (30 games)	Ronnie Gaudern	Memphis, TN
1961	Dave Soutar	5792 (27 games)	Morrie Oppenheim	Cleveland, OH
1962	Carmen Salvino	5369 (25 games)	Don Carter	Philadelphia, PA
1963	Billy Hardwick	13,541 (61 games)	Ray Bluth	Long Island, NY
1964	Bob Strampe	13,979 (61 games)	Ray Bluth	Long Island, NY
1965	Dave Davis	13,895 (61 games)	Jerry McCoy	Detroit, MI
1966	Wayne Zahn	14,006 (61 games)	Nelson Burton Jr	Long Island, NY
1967	Dave Davis	421 (2 games)	Pete Tountas	New York City
1968	Wayne Zahn	14,182 (60 games)	Nelson Burton Jr	New York City
1969	Mike McGrath	13,670 (60 games)	Bill Allen	Garden City, NY
1970	Mike McGrath	660 (3 games)	Dave Davis	Garden City, NY
1971	Mike Limongello	911 (4 games)	Dave Davis	Paramus, NJ
1972	Johnny Guenther	12,986 (56 games)	Dick Ritger	Rochester, NY
1973	Earl Anthony	212 (1 game)	Sam Flanagan	Oklahoma City, OK
1974	Earl Anthony	218 (1 game)	Mark Roth	Downey, CA
1975	Earl Anthony	245 (1 game)	Jim Frazier	Downey, CA
1976	Paul Colwell	191 (1 game)	Dave Davis	Seattle, WA
1977	Tommy Hudson	206 (1 game)	Jay Robinson	Seattle, WA
1978	Warren Nelson	453 (2 games)	Joseph Groskind	Reno, NV
1979	Mike Aulby	727 (3 games)	Earl Anthony	Las Vegas, NV
1980	Johnny Petraglia	235 (1 game)	Gary Dickinson	Sterling Heights, MI
1981	Earl Anthony	242 (1 game)	Ernie Schlegel	Toledo, OH
1982	Earl Anthony	233 (1 game)	Charlie Tapp	Toledo, OH
1983	Earl Anthony	210 (1 game)	Mike Durbin	Toledo, OH
1984	Bob Chamberlain	961 (4 games)	Dan Eberl	Toledo, OH
1985	Mike Aulby	476 (2 games)	Steve Cook	Toledo, OH
1986	Tom Crites	190 (1 game)	Mike Aulby	Toledo, OH
1987	Randy Pedersen	759 (3 games)	Amleto Monacelli	Toledo, OH
1988	Brian Voss	246 (1 game)	Todd Thompson	Toledo, OH
1989	Pete Weber	221 (1 game)	Dave Ferraro	Toledo, OH
1990	Jim Pencak	900 (4 games)	Chris Warren	Toledo, OH
1991	Mike Miller	450 (2 games)	Norm Duke	Toledo, OH
1992	Eric Forkel	833 (4 games)	Bob Vespi	Toledo, OH
1993	Ron Palombi Jr	237 (1 game)	Eugene McCune	Toledo, OH
1994	David Traber	196 (1 game)	Dale Traber	Toledo, OH

Note: Totals from 1963-66, 1968-69 and 1972 include bonus pins.

General Tire Tournament of Champions

Year	Winner	Score	Runner-Up	Site
1965	Billy Hardwick	484 (2 games)	Dick Weber	Akron, OH
1966	Wayne Zahn	595 (3 games)	Dick Weber	Akron, OH
1967	Jim Stefanich	227 (1 game)	Don Johnson	Akron, OH
1968	Dave Davis	213 (1 game)	Don Johnson	Akron, OH
1969	Jim Godman	266 (1 game)	Jim Stefanich	Akron, OH
1970	Don Johnson	299 (1 game)	Dick Ritger	Akron, OH
1971	Johnny Petraglia	245 (1 game)	Don Johnson	Akron, OH
1972	Mike Durbin	775 (3 games)	Tim Harahan	Akron, OH
1973	Jim Godman	451 (2 games)	Barry Asher	Akron, OH
1974	Earl Anthony	679 (3 games)	Johnny Petraglia	Akron, OH
1975	Dave Davis	448 (2 games)	Barry Asher	Akron, OH
1976	Marshall Holman	441 (2 games)	Billy Hardwick	Akron, OH
1977	Mike Berlin	434 (2 games)	Mike Durbin	Akron, OH
1978	Earl Anthony	237 (1 game)	Teata Semiz	Akron, OH
1979	George Pappas	224 (1 game)	Dick Ritger	Akron, OH
1980	Wayne Webb	750 (3 games)	Gary Dickinson	Akron, OH
1981	Steve Cook	287 (1 game)	Pete Couture	Akron, OH
1982	Mike Durbin	448 (2 games)	Steve Cook	Akron, OH
1983	Joe Berardi	865 (4 games)	Henry Gonzalez	Akron, OH
1984	Mike Durbin	950 (4 games)	Mike Aulby	Akron, OH
1985	Mark Williams	616 (3 games)	Bob Handley	Akron, OH
1986	Marshall Holman	233 (1 game)	Mark Baker	Akron, OH
1987	Pete Weber	928 (4 games)	Jim Murtishaw	Akron, OH
1988	Mark Williams	237 (1 game)	Tony Westlake	Fairlawn, OH

General Tire Tournament of Champions (Cont.)

Year	Winner	Score	Runner-Up	Site
1989	Del Ballard Jr	490 (2 games)	Walter Ray Williams Jr	Fairlawn, OH
1990	Dave Ferraro	226 (1 game)	Tony Westlake	Fairlawn, OH
1991	David Ozio	476 (2 games)	Amleto Monacelli	Fairlawn, OH
1992	Marc McDowell	471 (2 games)	Don Genalo	Fairlawn, OH
1993	George Branham III	227 (1 game)	Parker Bohn III	Fairlawn, OH
1994	Norm Duke	422 (2 games)	Eric Forkel	Fairlawn, OH

Note: Called Firestone Tournament of Champions 1965-93.

ABC Masters Tournament

Year	Winner	Scoring Avg	Runner-Up	Site
1951	Lee Jouglard	201.8	Joe Wilman	St. Paul, MN
1952	Willard Taylor	200.32	Andy Varipapa	Milwaukee, WI
1953	Rudy Habetler	200.13	Ed Brosius	Chicago, IL
1954	Eugene Elkins	205.19	W. Taylor	Seattle, WA
1955	Buzz Fazio	204.13	Joe Kristof	Ft. Wayne, IN
1956	Dick Hoover	209.9	Ray Bluth	Rochester, NY
1957	Dick Hoover	216.39	Bill Lillard	Ft. Worth, TX
1958	Tom Hennessy	209.15	Lou Frantz	Syracuse, NY
1959	Ray Bluth	214.26	Billy Golembiewski	St. Louis, MO
1960	Billy Golembiewski	206.13	Steve Nagy	Toledo, OH
1961	Don Carter	211.18	Dick Hoover	Detroit, MI
1962	Billy Golembiewski	223.12	Ron Winger	Des Moines, IA
1963	Harry Smith	219.3	Bobby Meadows	Buffalo, NY
1964	Billy Welu	227	Harry Smith	Oakland, CA
1965	Billy Welu	202.12	Don Ellis	St. Paul, MN
1966	Bob Strampe	219.80	Al Thompson	Rochester, NY
1967	Lou Scalia	216.9	Bill Johnson	Miami Beach, FL
1968	Pete Tountas	220.15	Buzz Fazio	Cincinnati, OH
1969	Jim Chestney	223.2	Barry Asher	Madison, WI
1970	Don Glover	215.10	Bob Strampe	Knoxville, TN
1971	Jim Godman	229.8	Don Johnson	Detroit, MI
1972	Bill Beach	220.27	Jim Godman	Long Beach, CA
1973	Dave Soutar	218.61	Dick Ritger	Syracuse, NY
1974	Paul Colwell	234.17	Steve Neff	Indianapolis, IN
1975	Eddie Ressler	213.51	Sam Flanagan	Dayton, OH
1976	Nelson Burton Jr	220.79	Steve Carson	Oklahoma City
1977	Earl Anthony	218.21	Jim Godman	Reno, NV
1978	Frank Ellenburg	200.61	Earl Anthony	St. Louis, MO
1979	Doug Myers	202.9	Bill Spigner	Tampa, FL
1980	Neil Burton	206.69	Mark Roth	Louisville, KY
1981	Randy Lightfoot	218.3	Skip Tucker	Memphis, TN
1982	Joe Berardi	207.12	Ted Hannahs	Baltimore, MD
1983	Mike Lastowski	212.65	Pete Weber	Niagara Falls, NY
1984	Earl Anthony	212.5	Gil Sliker	Reno, NV
1985	Steve Wunderlich	210.4	Tommy Kress	Tulsa, OK
1986	Mark Fahy	206.5	Del Ballard Jr	Las Vegas, NV
1987	Rick Steelsmith	210.7	Brad Snell	Niagara Falls, NY
1988	Del Ballard Jr	219.1	Keith Smith	Jacksonville, FL
1989	Mike Aulby	218.5	Mike Edwards	Wichita, KS
1990	Chris Warren	231.6	David Ozio	Reno, NV
1991	Doug Kent	226.8	George Branham III	Toledo, OH
1992	Ken Johnson	230.0	Dave D'Entremont	Corpus Christi, TX
1993	Phil Ware	238.0	Frankie May	Tulsa, OK
1994	Hobo Boothe	194.0	Rich Moores	Greenacres, Fl

Laub Lays it on

PBA Hall of Famer Larry Laub set a Senior Tour record for margin of victory when he bowled the only perfect game in June's Chicagoland Senior Open, defeating Jim Moore 300-149 in the 10th game of match play. It seems Laub has a knack for the rout—he holds the same record on the PBA Tour for his 290-118 drubbing of Mark Estes in 1975.

Women's Majors

BPAA United States Open

Year	Winner	Score	Runner-Up	Site
1949	Marion Ladewig	113.26-104.26	Catherine Burling	Chicago
1950	Marion Ladewig	151.46-146.06	Stephanie Balogh	Chicago
1951	Marion Ladewig	159.17-148.03	Sylvia Wene	Chicago
1952	Marion Ladewig	154.39-142.05	Shirley Garms	Chicago
1953	Not held			
1954	Marion Ladewig	148.29-143.01	Sylvia Wene	Chicago
1955	Sylvia Wene	142.30-141.11	Sylvia Fanta	Chicago
1955	Anita Cantaline	144.40-144.13	Doris Porter	Chicago
1956	Marion Ladewig	150.16-145.41	Marge Merrick	Chicago
1957	Not held			
1958	Merle Matthews	145.09-143.14	Marion Ladewig	Minneapolis
1959	Marion Ladewig	149.33-143.00	Donna Zimmerman	Buffalo
1960	Sylvia Wene	144.14-143.26	Marion Ladewig	Omaha
1961	Phyllis Notaro	144.13-143.12	Hope Riccilli	San Bernadino
1962	Shirley Garms	138.44-135.49	Joy Abel	Miami Beach
1963	Marion Ladewig	586-578	Bobbie Shaler	Kansas City, MO
1964	LaVerne Carter	683-609	Evelyn Teal	Dallas
1965	Ann Slattery	597-550	Sandy Hooper	Philadelphia
1966	Joy Abel	593-538	Bette Rockwell	Lansing, MI
1967	Gloria Bouvia	578-516	Shirley Garms	St. Ann, MO
1968	Dotty Fothergill	9,000-8,187	Doris Coburn	Garden City, NY
1969	Dotty Fothergill	8,284-8,258	Kayoka Suda	Miami
1970	Mary Baker	8,730-8,465	Judy Cook	Northbrook, IL
1971	Paula Carter	5,660-5,650	June Llewellyn	Kansas City, MO
1972	Lorrie Nichols	5,272-5,189	Mary Baker	Denver
1973	Millie Martorella	5,553-5,294	Patty Costello	Garden City, NY
1974	Patty Costello	219-216	Betty Morris	Irving, TX
1975	Paula Carter	6,500-6,352	Lorrie Nichols	Toledo, OH
1976	Patty Costello	11,341-11,281	Betty Morris	Tulsa, OK
1977	Betty Morris	10,511-10,358	Virginia Norton	Milwaukee, WI
1978	Donna Adamek	236-202	Vesma Grinfelds	Miami
1979	Diana Silva	11,775-11,718	Bev Ortner	Phoenix
1980	Pat Costello	223-199	Shinobu Saitoh	Rockford, IL
1981	Donna Adamek	201-190	Nikki Gianulias	Rockford, IL
1982	Shinobu Saitoh	12,184-12,028	Robin Romeo	Hendersonville, TN
1983	Dana Miller-Mackie	247-200	Aleta Sill	St. Louis
1984	Karen Ellingsworth	236-217	Lorrie Nichols	St. Louis
1985	Pat Mercatani	214-178	Nikki Gianulias	Topeka, KS
1986	Wendy Macpherson	265-179	Lisa Wagner	Topeka, KS
1987	Carol Norman	206-179	Cindy Coburn	Mentor, OH
1988	Lisa Wagner	226-218	Lorrie Nichols	Winston-Salem, NC
1989	Robin Romeo	187-163	Michelle Mullen	Addison, IL
1990	Dana Miller-Mackie	190-189	Tish Johnson	Dearborn Heights, MI
1991	Anne Marie Duggan	196-185	Leanne Barrette	Fountain Valley, CA
1992	Tish Johnson	216-213	Aleta Sill	Fountain Valley, CA
1993	Dede Davidson	213-194	Dana Miller-Mackie	Garland, TX
1994	Aleta Sill	229-170	Anne Marie Duggan	Wichita, KS

Note: From 1942 to 1970, the tournament was called the BPAA All-Star. Peterson scoring was used from 1949 through 1962. Under this system, the winner of an individual match game gets one point, plus one point for each 50 pins knocked down. From 1963 through 1967, a three-game championship was held between the two top qualifiers. From 1968 through 1973, 1975-77, 1979 and 1982, total pinfall determined the winner. In the other years, five qualifiers competed in a playoff for the championship, with the final match listed above.

Strikes In Stereo

The second longest-running live sports series on network television is—surprise—"The Professional Bowlers Tour". The ABC telecast, which has been on the air for 34 years, trails only the broadcast of college football in that department and is inked with the network through 1995. The latest feature of the telecast is *stereo*. Rest easy, t.v. viewers, that's not an earthquake in your backyard, it's just pinfall—in sensaround.

WIBC Queens

Year	Winner	Score	Runner-Up	Site
1961	Janet Harman	794-776	Eula Touchette	Fort Wayne, IN
1962	Dorothy Wilkinson	799-794	Marion Ladewig	Phoenix, AZ
1963	Irene Monterosso	852-803	Georgette DeRosa	Memphis, TN
1964	D. D. Jacobson	740-682	Shirley Garms	Minneapolis, MN
1965	Betty Kuczynski	772-739	LaVerne Carter	Portland, OR
1966	Judy Lee	771-742	Nancy Peterson	New Orleans, LA
1967	Millie Ignizio	840-809	Phyllis Massey	Rochester, NY
1968	Phyllis Massey	884-853	Marian Spencer	San Antonio, TX
1969	Ann Feigel	832-765	Millie Ignizio	San Diego, CA
1970	Millie Ignizio	807-797	Joan Holm	Tulsa, OK
1971	Millie Ignizio	809-778	Katherine Brown	Atlanta, GA
1972	Dotty Fothergill	890-841	Maureen Harris	Kansas City, MO
1973	Dotty Fothergill	804-791	Judy Soutar	Las Vegas, NV
1974	Judy Soutar	939-705	Betty Morris	Houston, TX
1975	Cindy Powell	758-674	Patty Costello	Indianapolis, IN
1976	Pam Buckner	214-178	Shirley Sjostrom	Denver, CO
1977	Dana Stewart	175-167	Vesma Grinfelds	Milwaukee, WI
1978	Loa Boxberger	197-176	Cora Fiebig	Miami, FL
1979	Donna Adamek	216-181	Shinobu Saitoh	Tucson, AZ
1980	Donna Adamek	213-165	Cheryl Robinson	Seattle, WA
1981	Katsuko Sugimoto	166-158	Virginia Norton	Baltimore, MD
1982	Katsuko Sugimoto	160-137	Nikki Gianulias	St. Louis, MO
1983	Aleta Sill	214-188	Dana Miller-Mackie	Las Vegas, NV
1984	Kazue Inahashi	248-222	Aleta Sill	Niagara Falls, NY
1985	Aleta Sill	279-192	Linda Graham	Toledo, OH
1986	Cora Fiebig	223-177	Barbara Thorberg	Orange County, CA
1987	Cathy Almeida	850-817	Lorrie Nichols	Hartford, CT
1988	Wendy Macpherson	213-199	Leanne Barrette	Reno/Carson City, NV
1989	Carol Gianotti	207-177	Sandra Jo Shiery	Bismarck-Mandan, ND
1990	Patty Ann	207-173	Vesma Grinfelds	Tampa, FL
1991	Dede Davidson	231-159	Jeanne Maiden	Cedar Rapids, IA
1992	Cindy Coburn-Carroll	184-170	Dana Miller-Mackie	Lansing, MI
1993	Jan Schmidt	201-163	Pat Costello	Baton Rouge, LA
1994	Anne Marie Duggan	224-177	Wendy Macpherson-Papanos	Salt Lake City, UT

Sam's Town Invitational

Year	Winner	Score	Runner-Up	Site
1984	Aleta Sill	238 (1 game)	Cheryl Daniels	Las Vegas, NV
1985	Patty Costello	236 (1 game)	Robin Romeo	Las Vegas, NV
1986	Aleta Sill	238 (1 game)	Dina Wheeler	Las Vegas, NV
1987	Debbie Bennett	880 (4 games)	Lorrie Nichols	Las Vegas, NV
1988	Donna Adamek	634 (3 games)	Robin Romeo	Las Vegas, NV
1989	Tish Johnson	210 (1 game)	Dede Davidson	Las Vegas, NV
1990	Wendy Macpherson	900 (4 games)	Jeanne Maiden	Las Vegas, NV
1991	Lorrie Nichols	469 (2 games)	Dana Miller-Mackie	Las Vegas, NV
1992	Tish Johnson	279 (1 game)	Robin Romeo	Las Vegas, NV
1993	Robin Romeo	194 (1 game)	Tammy Turner	Las Vegas, NV

PWBA Championships

Year	Winner	Year	Winner
1960	Marion Ladewig	1971	Patty Costello
1961	Shirley Garms	1972	Patty Costello
1962	Stephanie Balogh	1973	Betty Morris
1963	Janet Harman	1974	Pat Costello
1964	Betty Kuczynski	1975	Pam Buckner
1965	Helen Duval	1976	Patty Costello
1966	Joy Abel	1977	Vesma Grinfelds
1967	Betty Mivalez	1978	Toni Gillard
1968	Dotty Fothergill	1979	Cindy Coburn
1969	Dotty Fothergill	1980	Donna Adamek
1970	Bobbe North		

Men's Awards

BWAA Bowler of the Year

1942 ....Johnny Crimmins	1961 ....Dick Weber	1978 ....Mark Roth
1943 ....Ned Day	1962 ....Don Carter	1979 ....Mark Roth
1944 ....Ned Day	1963 ....Dick Weber,	1980 ....Wayne Webb
1945 ....Buddy Bomar	............Billy Hardwick (PBA)*	1981 ....Earl Anthony
1946 ....Joe Wilman	1964 ....Billy Hardwick,	1982 ....Earl Anthony
1947 ....Buddy Bomar	............Bob Strampe (PBA)*	1983 ....Earl Anthony
1948 ....Andy Varipapa	1965 ....Dick Weber	1984 ....Mark Roth
1949 ....Connie Schwoegler	1966 ....Wayne Zahn	1985 ....Mike Aulby
1950 ....Junie McMahon	1967 ....Dave Davis	1986 ....Walter Ray Williams, Jr
1951 ....Lee Jouglard	1968 ....Jim Stefanich	1987 ....Marshall Holman
1952 ....Steve Nagy	1969 ....Billy Hardwick	1988 ....Brian Voss
1953 ....Don Carter	1970 ....Nelson Burton Jr	1989 ....Mike Aulby,
1954 ....Don Carter	1971 ....Don Johnson	............Amleto Monacelli (PBA)*
1955 ....Steve Nagy	1972 ....Don Johnson	1990 ....Amleto Monacelli
1956 ....Bill Lillard	1973 ....Don McCune	1991 ....David Ozio
1957 ....Don Carter	1974 ....Earl Anthony	1992 ....Dave Ferraro
1958 ....Don Carter	1975 ....Earl Anthony	1993 ....Walter Ray Williams, Jr
1959 ....Ed Lubanski	1976 ....Earl Anthony	
1960 ....Don Carter	1977 ....Mark Roth	

*The PBA began selecting a player of the year in 1963. Its selection has been the same as the BWAA's in all but three years.

Women's Awards

BWAA Bowler of the Year

1948 ....Val Mikiel	1965 ....Betty Kuczynski	1982 ....Nikki Gianulias
1949 ....Val Mikiel	1966 ....Joy Abel	1983 ....Lisa Wagner
1950 ....Marion Ladewig	1967 ....Millie Martorella	1984 ....Aleta Sill
1951 ....Marion Ladewig	1968 ....Dotty Fothergill	1985 ....Aleta Sill,
1952 ....Marion Ladewig	1969 ....Dotty Fothergill	............Patty Costello (LPBT)*
1953 ....Marion Ladewig	1970 ....Mary Baker	1986 ....Lisa Wagner,
1954 ....Marion Ladewig	1971 ....Paula Sperber Carter	............Jeanne Madden (LPBT)*
1955 ....Marion Ladewig	1972 ....Patty Costello	1987 ....Betty Morris
1956 ....Sylvia Martin	1973 ....Judy Soutar	1988 ....Lisa Wagner
1957 ....Anita Cantaline	1974 ....Betty Morris	1989 ....Robin Romeo
1958 ....Marion Ladewig	1975 ....Judy Soutar	1990 ....Tish Johnson,
1959 ....Marion Ladewig	1976 ....Patty Costello	............Leanne Barrette (LPBT)*
1960 ....Sylvia Martin	1977 ....Betty Morris	1991 ....Leanne Barrette
1961 ....Shirley Garms	1978 ....Donna Adamek	1992 ....Tish Johnson
1962 ....Shirley Garms	1979 ....Donna Adamek	1993 ....Lisa Wagner
1963 ....Marion Ladewig	1980 ....Donna Adamek	
1964 ....LaVerne Carter	1981 ....Donna Adamek	

*The LPBT began selecting a player of the year in 1983. Its selection has been the same as the BWAA's in all but three years.

Career Leaders

Earnings

MEN		WOMEN	
Pete Weber $1,684,307		Aleta Sill $597,871	
Marshall Holman $1,629,928		Lisa Wagner................................$565,517	
Mike Aulby $1,427,763		Donna Adamek $533,472	
Mark Roth.......................................$1,422,763		Nikki Gianulias $496,063	
Walter Ray Williams, Jr $1,377,779		Lorrie Nichols..............................$479,444	

Titles

MEN		WOMEN	
Earl Anthony......................................41		Lisa Wagner................................28	
Mark Roth..33		*Patty Costello..25	
Don Johnson 26		Aleta Sill..20	
Dick Weber 26		*Donna Adamek......................................19	
Mike Aulby 22		Nikki Gianulias 18	
		Tish Johnson 18	

Soccer

Pro Football Returns to Baltimore

Sports Illustrated

JULY 25, 1994 · $2.95 (CAN.$2.95)

Viva! Brazil!

SIMON BRUTY

Cup Classic

Defying the skeptics, the U.S. hosted one of the most exciting and successful World Cups in history | by **HANK HERSCH**

OW WILL IT BE CATALOGED IN THE annals of soccer, the 1994 World Cup? As the Summer of Love, when the United States, opening its arms and its stadiums to a sport it had never tightly embraced, entered into a monthlong clinch that peaked with the upstart Yanks taking the field on July 4? Under 52 Pickup, that being the number of colorful, fierce and relatively high-scoring matches that attracted a gate of 3.6 million people, generated some $4 billion in domestic revenues and sent the Nielsen ratings soaring like a goalkeeper's punt? Or by the Witching Half Hour, the length of the scoreless overtime that followed scoreless regulation play in the Cup final, forcing Brazil and Italy to decide the championship in the capricious manner of penalty kicks?

In the end, how Cup '94 will be remembered is less important than *that* it will be remembered in the globe's last pocket of soccerphobes, the heretofore recalcitrant States. From June 17 to July 17, from shoreline to shoreline, through brave headers and even braver hairdos, the sport secured here, if you will, a foothold. It was Oprah Winfrey who kicked off the opening ceremonies at Soldier Field in Chicago, the nation's premier purveyor of the unusual introducing yet another rare act. And by the finale at the Rose Bowl in Pasadena, the ponytailed Roberto Baggio of

Italy had become as familiar to viewers as Oprah's curios as he stood poised over the ball and took point-blank aim at the Brazilian goal, the hopes of two nations in the balance.

The Cup's grip on its home audience began on its second day. In the afternoon, at Giants Stadium in East Rutherford, N.J., Ireland beat Italy 1–0 in a wonderfully hard-fought match. But the play was not the thing; the crowd was. Packed with Americans whose ancestors hailed from one country or the other, the stands were awash in proud colors, from the Azzurri's blue to the Gaels' more predominant green, white and orange. Flags waved. Bagpipes blew. Seats rattled. The Irish fans chanted nonstop, singing, to the tune of *He's Got the Whole World in His Hands*, lyrics that went, "You've got the best footballers in the world/ But they look like Sophia Loren." The Italians raged at their players and the fates. The scene was lovely pandemonium, and even a distracted channel surfer could feel it.

Still more important, June 18 also marked the home team's debut against Switzerland at the Silverdome in Detroit and the locals' turn to funnel their own patriotism onto the pitch. As the host nation the U.S. received an automatic berth in the 24-team field and a top seeding in one of the six groups. Skeptics, both foreign and domestic, who wondered if the country could stage the Cup with proper regard for its sanctity had even greater

A perfectly placed patriot missile from Wynalda (far right) tied the Swiss.

doubts about the worthiness of a U.S. squad that had been outscored 8–2 in Italy a quadrennium ago. Before its opener the team was asked endlessly whether its performance would augur the Cup's success or the sport's growth here, and endlessly its members tried to acknowledge the pressure without assuming too much of it. "It is very important we put on a good game, an attractive game," said U.S. assistant coach Timo Liekoski. "It is also important to get a good result."

In the hopes of motivating all the entries to play more aggressive soccer, Cup '94 CEO Alan Rothenberg had persuaded the sport's governing body, the Fédération Internationale de Football Associations (FIFA), to award three points rather than two for a victory during the first round. (There would still be one point for a tie and none for a loss.) Given the national team's inability to score goals in warmup matches, some thought Rothenberg's

rule would end up undermining his own pre-Cup pledge that the U.S. would reach the knockout round of 16. Coach Bora Milutinovic gave his troops mystical *Chimayo* dirt from New Mexico to sprinkle on their shoes for luck before the match, but when they fell behind the organized and experienced Swiss 1–0 in the 39th minute, their dreams of advancement seemed in danger of turning to dust.

Just before halftime the Swiss committed a foul 28 yards from their goal. U.S. midfielders Tab Ramos, Eric Wynalda and John Harkes—the nucleus of the '90 team, each now an established pro in Europe—discussed briefly who would take the free kick. Wynalda decided he would, even though he was suffering from a mysterious case of hives that had swollen his hands and arms and turned much of his anatomy red. He launched a patriot's missile, a gorgeous curling shot that cleared the wall of defenders and found the upper left corner of the net: a world-class goal. "You really have to hit it perfect for it to work," Eric the Red said, "and that's what happened."

The 1–1 tie gave the U.S. players a vital point. But in all likelihood a win would still be required to advance, and the host's next opponent, on June 22 in Pasadena, was a pretournament favorite, Colombia. With mop-topped midfielder Carlos Valderrama at the controls, the Colombians had no peers in the wonders of the one-touch attack, each connection eliciting an "Olé" from the faithful. To combat the Colombians' affinity for tidy passing up the gut, Bora had defenders Paul Caligiuri, Marcelo Balboa, Alexi Lalas and Fernando Clavijo clog the middle of the pitch and concede the wings. The tactic bamboozled the Colombians, who had other worries as well. Before the match the team received a fax at its hotel in Fullerton, Calif., that threatened the homes, families and persons of coach Francisco Maturana and midfielder Gabriel Gomez if Gomez played. He didn't.

The team's discombobulation reached its zenith in the 35th minute. Harkes sent a cross in from the left wing, hoping Ernie Stewart would run onto it. But before Stewart could, Colombian defender Andres Escobar stuck his leg backward in an attempt to clear the ball and accidentally directed it past his own keeper, Oscar Cordoba. Stewart got his own goal, taking a chipped pass from Ramos in the second half to put the U.S. up by a deuce. Tony Meola stood tall in the U.S. nets, making 14 saves and allowing only a last-minute goal. And when the 2–1 win was in the books, the star-spangled U.S. players pranced around the roaring Rose Bowl wearing American flags like capes; they were superheroes who had accomplished the unimaginable.

Before the match Bora had asked assistant coach Steve Sampson to write some words of wisdom on the team's blackboard, and he chose three: SEIZE THE MOMENT. The U.S. did, even though Bora, a native Serbian uncomfortable with the English language, would wonder about the phrase later. "What is this 'size' the moment?" he asked. The answer, Bora, was huge. With the shocker of Colombia, the Cup had officially caught on. The U.S. would now move onto the second round, even after a 1–0 loss to Romania. Through the first 36 games, attendance at the vast stadiums was averaging 96% of capacity. Scoring would increase to 2.69 goals a game, up 22% from the '90 average. And each U.S. match was drawing a larger and larger TV audience, with the Romania game winning its time period, period. "Making soccer history" was the Cup '94 slogan, and so far, the future looked bright.

Just as the passion of soccer was spreading, however, its ugliest manifestation cast a dark cloud. Though there would be no major incidents of violence in the States, as many had feared, there would be one in *futbol*-mad Colombia. On July 2, outside a bar near Medellín, three men and a woman accosted Escobar, who had returned home when Colombia failed to advance. The assailants insulted Escobar about the own goal, calling him *hijueputa*—son of a whore. Then one of the men pulled out a gun and began to fire, striking Escobar with six bullets.

Four days before Escobar had ended a guest column in the daily *El Tiempo* by writing, "Please, let's not let the defeat affect our respect for the sport and the team. See you later, because life goes on." Not for the 27-year-old defender, who was taken to a hospital and pronounced dead.

Back in the U.S., a minor storm was brewing. On June 30, FIFA announced it was suspending the most famous—and infamous—name in soccer, Diego Maradona of Argentina, from the rest of the tournament after he tested positive for five banned substances. At that point the 33-year-old Maradona, having shed 26 pounds, was shaping up as a heartwarming comeback story. He was flashing his old form, his team was 2–0, and he was poised to set a record by appearing in his 22nd Cup match. Some 57.6% Argentines polled believed that Maradona's ouster was the result of a conspiracy against him, but it seemed more likely that he was victimized by a weight-loss regimen that included over-the-counter stimulants. Without Maradona, Argentina bowed out meekly to Romania in the second round.

By then, though, other characters had emerged, among them Romario, Brazil's relentless attacker. Leading his nation's quest for the coveted *tetra*, or fourth World Cup

PETER READ MILLER

U.S. midfielder Cobi Jones, "except for the ending."

For the survivors much remained to be writ. There was a dazzling quarterfinal at the Cotton Bowl in Dallas, where all the scoring in Brazil's 3–2 victory over the Netherlands took place in a 30-minute span in the second half. And the Bulgarians' stunning 2–1 upset of Germany, the defending champion, in the quarterfinals, when first Hristo Stoichkov's magical left foot and then Yordan Lechkov's bald noggin delivered the death blows. And the bulging eyes of Sweden's keeper, Thomas Ravelli, who stymied Romania on penalty kicks before succumbing to Romario and

title, Romario was living up to his own billing as the planet's foremost player. Brazil's distinctive playing style, set to the rhythms of the samba, was enchanting U.S. fans old and new, who found in it both order and artistry. There was one problem: The Brazilians would be the Yanks' next foe, on July 4 at Stanford Stadium. "If we lose, that is what we are supposed to do," Lalas said before the match. "But if Brazil loses. ..."

Alas, Brazil didn't. The U.S. had to do without three of its midfielders: Claudio Reyna, who had a pulled hamstring; Harkes, who had picked up a second yellow card against Romania; and Ramos, who was elbowed brutally by the defender Leonardo late in the first half and suffered a fractured skull. Still, the 1–0 verdict didn't reflect the Brazilians' dominance, even as they played a man short after Leonardo's ejection. In the 74th minute Romario set up the decisive goal, eluding a sliding tackle outside the penalty area and laying the ball off elegantly to Bebeto, who beat Meola without breaking stride. "It was a great script," said

Co. in the final four. And the sudden emergence of Baggio, the '93 Player of the Year, whose scoring spree spelled defeat for Spain in the quarters and Bulgaria in the semis.

Unfortunately, though, the Cup final provided another objectionable ending. After 120 minutes of gutty soccer played by two of the sport's most favored nations, a pair of Italy's more fabled players failed to deliver on their penalty kicks. First it was Franco Baresi, the 34-year-old sweeper, who had soldiered on bravely despite a bum knee, blasting his shot high over the bar. Then it was Baggio, also ailing, with a sore hamstring, kicking fifth with his team down 3–2. He sent his attempt sailing over Brazil's keeper, Claudio Taffarel, to end the match and the Cup.

"We have to accept the rules with great calmness and serenity," said Italy's coach, Arrigo Sacchi. Making it even more palatable was the brilliance of the Brazilians, who had dominated all but the scoreboard. The right team had triumphed—and so, in the U.S., had the sport.

World Cup 1994

Group Standings

GROUP A

Country	GP	W	L	T	G	GA	Pts
†Romania	3	2	1	0	5	5	6
†Switzerland	3	1	1	1	5	4	4
†United States	3	1	1	1	3	3	4
Colombia	3	1	2	0	4	5	3

GROUP D

Country	GP	W	L	T	G	GA	Pts
†Nigeria	3	2	1	0	6	2	6
†Bulgaria	3	2	1	0	6	3	6
†Argentina	3	2	1	0	6	3	6
Greece	3	0	3	0	0	8	0

GROUP B

Country	GP	W	L	T	G	GA	Pts
†Brazil	3	2	0	1	6	1	7
†Sweden	3	1	0	2	6	4	5
Russia	3	1	2	0	7	6	3
Cameroon	3	0	2	1	3	11	1

GROUP E

Country	GP	W	L	T	G	GA	Pts
†Mexico	3	1	1	1	3	3	4
†Ireland	3	1	1	1	2	2	4
†Italy	3	1	1	1	2	2	4
Norway	3	1	1	1	1	1	4

GROUP C

Country	GP	W	L	T	G	GA	Pts
†Germany	3	2	0	1	5	3	7
†Spain	3	1	0	2	6	4	5
S Korea	3	0	1	2	4	5	2
Bolivia	3	0	2	1	1	4	1

GROUP F

Country	GP	W	L	T	G	GA	Pts
†N'lands	3	2	1	0	4	3	6
†S. Arabia	3	2	1	0	4	3	6
†Belgium	3	2	1	0	2	1	6
Morocco	3	0	3	0	2	5	0

†Advanced to second round.

Note: In the first round, teams are awarded three points for a victory, one for a tie. The top two in each group, plus the four third place teams with the best records, advance to the round of 16.

First Round Group Scores

GROUP A
U.S. 2, Colombia 1
U.S. 1, Switzerland 1
Romania 1, U.S. 0
Romania 3, Colombia 1
Switzerland 4, Romania 1
Colombia 2, Switzerland 0

GROUP B
Cameroon 2, Sweden 2
Brazil 2, Russia 0
Brazil 3, Cameroon 0

GROUP B *(Cont.)*
Sweden 3, Russia 1
Russia 6, Cameroon 1
Brazil 1, Sweden 1

GROUP C
Germany 1, Bolivia 0
Spain 2, South Korea 2
Germany 1, Spain 1
South Korea 0, Bolivia 0
Germany 3, South Korea 2
Spain 3, Bolivia 1

GROUP D
Argentina 4, Greece 0
Nigeria 3, Bulgaria 0
Argentina 2, Nigeria 1
Bulgaria 4, Greece 0
Nigeria 2, Greece 0
Bulgaria 2, Argentina 0

GROUP E
Ireland 1, Italy 0
Norway 1 Mexico 0
Italy 1, Norway 0

GROUP E *(Cont.)*
Mexico 2, Ireland 1
Ireland 0, Norway 0
Italy 1, Mexico 1

GROUP F
Belgium 1, Morocco 0
Netherlands 2, S. Arabia 1
Belgium 1, Netherlands 0
Saudi Arabia 2, Morocco 1
Netherlands 2, Morocco 1
Saudi Arabia 1, Belgium 0

World Cup Tournament

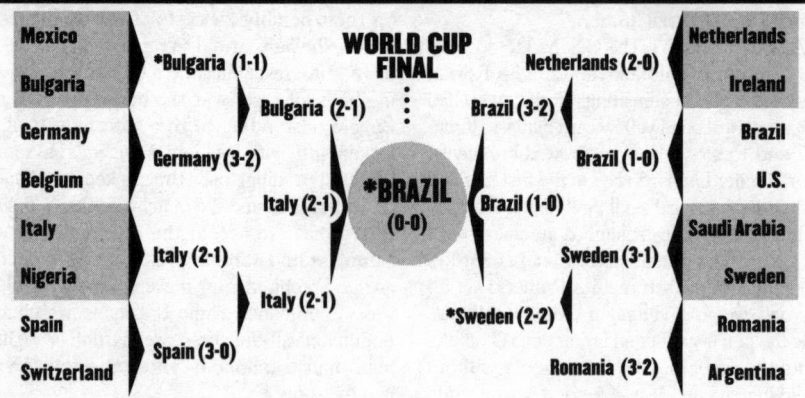

Mexico
Bulgaria — *Bulgaria (1-1)
Bulgaria (2-1)
Germany
Belgium — Germany (3-2)
Italy — Italy (2-1)
Nigeria — Italy (2-1)
Spain — Spain (3-0)
Italy (2-1)

WORLD CUP FINAL
*BRAZIL (0-0)

Netherlands — Netherlands (2-0)
Ireland
Brazil — Brazil (3-2)
U.S. — Brazil (1-0)
Brazil (1-0)
Saudi Arabia — Sweden (3-1)
Sweden — *Sweden (2-2)
Romania — Romania (3-2)
Argentina

*Won tie-breaking shootout.

U.S. Men's National Team Results

Date	Opponent	Site	Result	U.S. Goals
Jan 15	Norway	Tempe	2-1 W	Balboa, Jones
Jan 22	Switzerland	Fullerton, Calif.	1-1 T	Own Goal
Jan 29	Russia	Seattle	1-1 T	Lalas
Feb 10	Denmark	Hong Kong	0-0 (2-4)	none
Feb 13	Romania	Hong Kong	2-1 L	Balboa
Feb 18	Bolivia	Miami	1-1 T	Jones
Feb 20	Sweden	Miami	3-1 L	Perez
March 12	South Korea	Fullerton, Calif.	1-1 T	Balboa
March 26	Bolivia	Dallas	2-2 T	Perez (2)
April 16	Moldova	Jacksonville, Fla.	1-1 T	Sorber
April 20	Moldova	Davidson, N.C.	3-0 W	Klopas, Lapper, Reyna
April 24	Iceland	San Diego	2-1 L	Klopas
April 30	Chile	Albuquerque, N.M.	0-2 L	none
May 7	Estonia	Fullerton, Calif.	4-0 W	Klopas, Reyna, Balboa, Moore
May 15	Armenia	Fullerton, Calif.	1-0 W	Klopas
May 25	Saudi Arabia	Piscataway, N.J.	0-0 T	none
May 28	Greece	New Haven, Conn.	1-1 T	Klopas
June 4	Mexico	Pasadena, Calif.	1-0 W	Wegerle
June 18†	Switzerland	Pontiac, Mich	1-1 T	Wynalda
June 22†	Colombia	Pasadena, Calif.	2-1 W	Own Goal, Stewart
June 26†	Romania	Pasadena, Calif.	1-0 L	none
July 4†	Brazil	Pasadena, Calif.	1-0 L	none

†World Cup match

U.S. Women's National Team

Date	Opponent	Site	Result	U.S. Goals
March 16	Portugal	Silves, Portugal	5-0 W	Gabarra (2), Lilly, Milbrett, Foudy
March 18	Sweden	V.R. Sta. Antonio, Port.	1-0 W	Hamm
March 20	Norway	Faro, Portugal	1-0 L	none
April 10	Trinidad & Tobago	Scarborough, Tobago	3-1 W	Lilly, Foudy, Roberts
April 14	Canada	San Fernando, Trinidad	4-1 W	Akers-Stahl (2), Gabarra (2)
April 17	Canada	Port of Spain, Trinidad	3-0 W	Venturini, Akers-Stahl, MacMillan
July 31	Germany	Washington, D.C.	2-1 W	Hamm, Akers-Stahl
August 3	China	Piscataway, N.J.	1-0 W	Foudy
August 7	Norway	Worcester, Mass.	4-1 W	Own Goal, Akers-Stahl, Hamm (2)
August 13	Mexico*	Montreal	9-0 W	Lilly (2), Venturini, Hamm, Akers-Stahl (2), Robers, Lalor, Gabarra
August 17	Trinidad & Tobago*	Montreal	11-1 W	Hamm (4), Gabarra (2), Venturini (2) Akers-Stahl, Lilly, Cromwell
August 19	Jamaica*	Montreal	10-0 W	Akers-Stahl (2), Lilly (2), Overbeck (2) Roberts, Gabarra, Rafanelli, Milbrett
August 21	Canada*	Montreal	6-0 W	Hamm, Own Goal, Roberts, Gabarra Foudy, Akers-Stahl

*CONCACAF qualifying match.

Cover Up

Television viewers in Iran who tuned in to the Germany-Bolivia World Cup match in Chicago must have wondered why, with the players wilting in the heat, spectators at Soldier Field were wearing hats, gloves and fur coats. That inexplicable scene, which was repeated on subsequent World Cup telecasts, was not a sign of American insanity but the result of some sleight of hand by Iranian television.

With Cup matches being broadcast in Iran for the first time since the 1979 Islamic revolution, fundamentalist authorities were concerned about Iranian viewers' seeing shots of decadent Western fans—particularly female fans—in shorts and revealing tops. To avoid that, producers in Tehran, using a several second electronic delay, simply spliced in footage of heavily clad spectators from winter matches in all scenes in which the crowd appeared. "The correction of un-Islamic scenes is not a problem," said a spokesman for Iranian TV, who clearly hadn't checked a U.S weather map.

1993 Toyota Cup Final

Competition between winners of European Cup and Libertadores Cup.

TOKYO: DEC 12, 1993

Sao Paulo (Brazil) 1   2 —3
A.C. Milan (Italy) 1   1 —2

Goals: Palhinha (20), Massaro (48), Cerezo (59), Papin (82), Muller (86).

Att: 60,000

Sao Paulo: Zetti, Cafu, Valber, Ronaldo, Andre, Cerezo, Doriva, Leonardo, Dinho, Palhinha (Juninho 64), Muller.
A.C. Milan: Rossi, Panucci, Costacurta, Baresi, Maldini, Donadoni, Desailly, Albertini (Tassotti 79), Massaro, Raducioiu (Orlando 79), Papin.

European Cup

League champions of the countries belonging to UEFA (Union of European Football Associations).

ATHENS: MAY 18, 1994

A.C. Milan (Italy) 2   2 —4
Barcelona (Spain) 0   0 —0

Goals: Massaro (22,45), Savicevic (47), Desailly (58).

Att: 70,000

A.C. Milan: Rossi, Tassotti, Galli, Maldini (Nava 85), Panucci, Boban, Albertini, Desailly, Donadoni, Savicevic, Massaro.
Barcelona: Zubizarreta, Ferrer, Koeman, Nadal, Beguiristain (Eusebio 51), Bakero, Guardiola, Amor, Sergi (Quique 72) Stoitchkov, Romario.

European Cup-Winners' Cup

Cup winners of countries belonging to UEFA.

COPENHAGEN: MAY 4, 1994

Arsenal (England) 1   0 —1
Parma (Italy) 0   0 —0

Goals: Smith (19).

Att: 33,765

Arsenal: Seaman, Dixon, Winterburn, Bould, Adams, Selley, Davis, Morrow, Campbell, Smith, Merrson (McGoldrick 86).
Parma: Bucci, Bennarivo, Apollini, Minotti, Di Chiara, Sensini, Pin (Melli 70), Crippa, Brolin, Zola, Asprilla.

UEFA Cup

Competition between teams other than league champions and cup-winners from UEFA.

(SECOND LEG) MILAN: MAY 11, 1994

Internazionale (Italy) 0   1 —1
Salzburg (Austria) 0   0 —0

Goals: Jonk (62) (aggregate: 2–0).

Att: 80,326

Internazionale: Zenga, A. Paganin, Fontolan (R. Farri 67), Jonk, Bergomi, Battistini, Orlando, Manicone, Berti, Bergkamp (M.Paganin 89), Sosa.
Salzburg: Konrad, Lainer, Weber, Winklhofer (Amerhauser 67), Fuerstaller, Aigner, Jurcevic, Artner (Steiner 75), Marquinho, Felersinger, Huetter.

Libertadores Cup

Competition between champion clubs and runners-up of 10 South American National Associations.

(FIRST LEG) SAO PAULO: MAY 19, 1993

Sao Paulo (Brazil) 2   3 —5
Univ. Catolica (Chile)......0   1 —1

Goals: own (31), Vitor (41), Gilmar (55), Rai (60) Muller (65); Almada, PK, (80) (Sao Paulo wins 5–3 on aggregate).

Att: 94,629

Sao Paulo: Zetti, Vitor, Valber, Gilmar, Ronaldo, Luis (Andre), Cafu, Rai, Pintado, Dinho, Palhinha, Muller.
Univ. Catolica: Wirth, Romero, Vazquez, Lopez (Barrera), Contreras, Parraguaz, Lepe, Tupper, Lunari, Almada, Perez (Reinoso).

THEY SAID IT

Legendary soccer star Pelé, on Switzerland coach Roy Hodgson's edict to his team that it abstain from sex during the World Cup: "Generally, I think normal sex is not a problem."

National Club Champions—Europe

Country	League Champion	League Scoring Leader, Club	Cup Winner
Albania	Partizani	Dosti, Partizani	Partizani
Austria	FK Austria	Danek, Tirol	Tirol
Belgium	Anderlecht	Weber, Cercle Brugge	Standard Liege
Bulgaria	Levski Sofia	Guetov, Levski Sofia	CSKA Sofia
Belarus	Dynamo Minsk	Baranouski, Dynamo Minsk	Neman Grodno
		Romachenko, Dnepr	
Croatia	Zagreb Croatia	Vlaovic, C. Zagreb	Hajduk Split
Cyprus	Omonia	Scepovic, Apollon	Apoel Nicosia
Denmark	FC Copenhagen	Moller, Aalborg	Odense BK
England	Manchester United	Sheringham, Tottenham	Arsenal
Estonia	Norma Tallinn	Bragin, Norma Tallinn	Nikol Tallinn
Faroe Isles	B68 Tofta	Justinssen, GI	HB Havnar
Finland	HJK Helsinki	Antonio, Jazz Pori	My Pa
France	Olympique Marseille	Boksix, Marseille	Paris St. Germaine

National Club Champions—Europe *(Cont.)*

Country	League Champion	League Scoring Leader, Club	Cup Winner
Georgia	Dynamo Tbilisi	Melgreladze, Samgurali	Dynamo Tbilisi
Germany	Werder Bremen	Yeboah, Eintracht Frankfurt	Leverkusen
Greece	AEK Athens	Dimitriadis, AEK Athens	Panathinaikos
Holland	Feyenoord	Bergkamp, Ajax Amsterdam	Ajax Amsterdam
Hungary	Honved Kispest	Rapasi, Vac	Ferencuaros
Iceland	IA Akranes	Gunnlauggson, IA Akranes	Valur
Ireland	Cork City	Morley, Cork City	Shelbourne
Italy	AC Milan	Signori, Lazio	Torino
Latvia	Skonto Riga	Jevnerovich, VEF	RAF Jelgava
Lithuania	Ekranas	Shlekis, Ekranas	Zal Vilnius
Luxembourg	Union	Krings, Avenir Beggen	Avenir Beggen
Malta	Floriana	Zacchau, Hibernians	Floriana
Northern Ireland	Linfield	Cowans, Portadown	Bangor
Norway	Rosenborg	Kaasa, Kongsvinger	Rosenborg
Poland	Leggia Warsaw	Podbrozny, Lech Poznan	Katowice
		Sliwowski, Liggia Warsaw	
Portugal	FC Porto	Cadete, Sporting	Benefica
Romania	Stegua Bucharest	Dumitrescu, Stegua Bucharest	Uni Craiova
Russia	Spartak Moscow	Kasumov, Spartak Moscow	Torpedo Moscow
San Marino	Tre Fiori	Bernardini, Libertas	Tre Fiori
Scotland	Rangers	McCoist, Rangers	Rangers
Slovenia	Olimpija Ljubljana	Udovic, Slovan Mavrica	Olimpija Ljubljana
Spain	Barcelona	Bebeto, La Coruna	Real Madrid
Sweden	IAK Stockholm	Eklund, Osters	Degefors
Switzerland	Aarau	Anderson, Sion	Lugano
Turkey	Galatasaray	Tanju, Fenerbahce	Galatasaray
Ukraine	Dynamo Kiev	Gusev, Chernomorets	Dynamo Kiev
Wales	Cwmbran Town	Woods, Ebbw Vale	Cardiff City
Yugoslavia	Partizan Belgrade	Mihajlovic, Vojvodina	Red Star Belgrade
		Drobrnjak, Red Star Belgrade	

National Professional Soccer League

Final Standings

American	W	L	Pct	GB	PF	PA	National	W	L	Pct	GB	PF	PA
Baltimore	26	14	.650	—	594	553	St Louis	25	15	.625	—	676	566
Cleveland	23	17	.575	3.0	717	613	Detroit	24	16	.600	1.0	575	577
Buffalo	19	21	.475	7.0	499	515	Wichita	22	18	.550	3.0	598	572
Harrisburg	19	21	.475	7.0	557	585	Milwaukee	20	20	.500	5.0	496	486
Canton	18	22	.450	8.0	537	584	Chicago	15	25	.375	10.0	501	616
Dayton	15	25	.375	11.0	644	665	Kansas City	14	26	.350	11.0	566	628

Playoff Results (Semi-Finals)

HARRISBURG VS CLEVELAND

Date	Results	Attendance
Apr 13	Harrisburg 14 vs Cleveland 13	3,808
Apr 15	Cleveland 15 vs Harrisburg 10	5,891
Apr 17	Cleveland 21 vs Harrisburg 10	5,712

(Cleveland wins series 2–1)

ST LOUIS VS DETROIT

Date	Results	Attendance
Apr 14	St Louis 16 vs Detroit 7	2,210
Apr 15	St Louis 15 vs Detroit 10	6,124

(St Louis wins series 2–0)

CHAMPIONSHIP SERIES

Date	Results	Attendance
Apr 21	St Louis 26 vs Cleveland 6	5,791
Apr 23	Cleveland 21 vs St Louis 14	10,322
Apr 24	Cleveland 29 vs St Louis 8	9,107
Apr 27	Cleveland 17 vs St Louis 15 (2 OT)	11,162

(Cleveland wins series 3–1)

Statistical Leaders

SCORING

Rank	Player	3PG	2PG	1PG	Assists	Points
1	Zoran Karic, Clev	9	60	16	104	267
2	Hector Marinaro, Clev	6	85	22	43	253
3	Andy Chapman, Det	1	62	20	31	178
4	David Doyle, StL	5	48	22	42	175
5	Gino DiFlorio, Can	2	57	8	31	159

THREE-POINT GOALS

Player	Team	Games	3PG
1	Zoran Karic	Clev	36	9
2	Hector Marinaro	Clev	37	6
3	Michael Richardson	Chi	40	6
4	David Doyle	StL	38	5
4	Jon Parry	KC	40	5
4	Paul Wright	Balt	35	5

ASSISTS

Player	Team	Games	Assists
1	Zoran Karic	Clev	36	104
2	Pato Margetic	Chi	39	71
3	Franklin McIntosh	Har	39	55
4	Drago	Det	29	53
5	Michael King	Mil	39	46

GOALKEEPING LEADERS (Minimum 1410 minutes)

Player	Team	GP	Min	Shots	Svs	GA	PAA	W	L
1	Victor Nogueira	Mil	38	2170:50	708	496	212	11.17	20	18
2	Jamie Swanner	Buf	39	2202:37	871	644	227	11.90	19	19
3	Cris Vaccaro	Balt	32	1780:37	628	434	194	12.23	23	7
4	P.J. Johns	Can	30	1597:44	589	403	186	13.52	13	14
5	Kris Peat	Wich	39	2099:11	709	450	259	13.63	19	16

American Professional Soccer League

1993 Final Standings

	W	L	GF	GA	Pts	Home	Road
Vancouver Eighty-Sixers	15	9	43	35	126	9-3	6-6
Colorado Foxes	15	9	40	34	121	8-4	7-5
Tampa Bay Rowdies	12	12	53	47	118	6-6	6-6
Los Angeles Salsa	12	12	41	37	109	8-4	4-8
Toronto Blizzard	10	14	35	41	96	9-3	1-11
Ft Lauderdale Strikers	9	15	39	52	93	6-6	3-9
Montreal Impact	11	13	28	33	90	7-5	4-8

Point system—six points for each victory in regulation or overtime; four points for a Shootout win; two points for a Shootout loss; one bonus point for each goal in regulation up to a maximun of three (regardless of whether team wins or loses

Playoff Results: Four teams—Vancouver, Colorado, Tampa Bay, and Los Angeles—qualified for the playoffs. Los Angeles beat Vancouver 3-2, Colorado defeated Tampa Bay 1-0, in the Semis; Colorado defeated Los Angeles 3-1 in the finals for the APSL championship.

SCORING LEADERS

Paulinho, Los Angeles	37
Paul Wright, Los Angeles	33
Paul Dougherty, Tampa Bay	27
Zico Doe, Ft Lauderdale	26
Hector Marinaro, Toronto	26

ASSISTS LEADERS

Hector Marinaro, Toronto	12
Paul Dougherty, Tampa Bay	11
Ivor Evans, Vancouver	8
Dale Mitchell, Vancouver	8
Four tied with seven	

GOALS LEADERS

Paulinho, Los Angeles	15
Paul Wright, Los Angeles	13
Zico Doe, Ft Lauderdale	12
Scott Benedetti, Colorado	10
Taifour Diane, Colorado	10
Domenic Mobilio, Vancouver	10

GOALS-AGAINST-AVERAGE LEADERS

Jim St Andre, Colorado	1.19
Pat Harrington, Montreal	1.35
Brett Phillips, Tampa Bay	1.39
Ian Feuer, Los Angeles	1.40
Paul Dolan, Vancouver	1.42

The World Cup

Results

Year	Champion	Score	Runner-Up	Winning Coach
1930	Uruguay	4-2	Argentina	Alberto Supicci
1934	Italy	2-1	Czechoslovakia	Vittorio Pozzo
1938	Italy	4-2	Hungary	Vittorio Pozzo
1950	Uruguay	2-1	Brazil	Juan Lopez
1954	West Germany	3-2	Hungary	Sepp Herberger
1958	Brazil	5-2	Sweden	Vicente Feola
1962	Brazil	3-1	Czechoslovakia	Aymore Moreira
1966	England	4-2	West Germany	Alf Ramsey
1970	Brazil	4-1	Italy	Mario Zagalo
1974	West Germany	2-1	Netherlands	Helmut Schoen
1978	Argentina	3-1	Netherlands	Cesar Menotti
1982	Italy	3-1	West Germany	Enzo Bearzot
1986	Argentina	3-2	West Germany	Carlos Bilardo
1990	West Germany	1-0	Argentina	Franz Beckenbauer
1994	Brazil	0-0 (3-2)	Italy	Carlos Alberto Parreira

Alltime World Cup Participation

Of the 58 nations which have taken part in the World Cup, only Brazil has competed in each of the 15 tournaments held to date. West Germany or an undivided Germany (1934 , '38 and '94) have played in 14 World Cups.

	Matches	Wins	Ties	Losses	Goals For	Goals Against
Brazil	73	49	13	11	159	68
*Germany	73	42	16	15	154	97
Italy	61	35	14	12	97	59
Argentina	52	26	9	17	90	65
England	41	18	12	11	55	38
†Russia	34	16	6	12	60	40
Uruguay	37	15	8	14	61	52
France	34	15	5	14	71	56
Yugoslavia	33	15	5	13	55	42
Hungary	32	15	3	14	87	57
Spain	37	15	9	13	53	44
Poland	25	13	5	7	39	29
Sweden	37	13	7	17	62	60
Austria	26	12	2	12	40	43
Czechoslovakia	30	11	5	14	44	45
Netherlands	25	11	6	8	43	29
Belgium	29	9	4	16	37	53
Mexico	33	7	8	18	31	68
Chile	21	7	3	11	26	32
Portugal	9	6	0	3	19	12
Romania	17	6	4	7	26	29
Switzerland	22	6	3	13	33	51
United States	14	4	1	9	17	33
Scotland	20	4	6	10	23	35
Peru	15	4	3	8	19	31
Bulgaria	22	3	7	12	21	42
Northern Ireland	13	3	5	5	13	23
Paraguay	11	3	4	4	16	25
Cameroon	11	3	4	4	11	21
Denmark	4	3	0	1	10	6
Nigeria	4	2	0	2	7	4
East Germany	6	2	2	2	5	5
Costa Rica	4	2	0	2	4	6
Saudi Arabia	4	2	0	2	5	6
Colombia	10	2	2	6	13	20
Algeria	6	2	1	3	6	10
Wales	5	1	3	1	4	4
Morocco	7	1	3	3	5	8
Republic of Ireland	9	1	5	3	4	7
Tunisia	3	1	1	1	3	2
North Korea	4	1	1	2	5	9
Cuba	3	1	1	1	5	12
Turkey	3	1	0	2	10	11
Norway	4	1	1	2	2	3
Israel	3	1	0	2	1	3
Honduras	3	0	2	1	2	3
Egypt	4	0	2	2	3	6
Kuwait	3	0	1	2	2	6
Australia	3	0	1	2	0	5
Iran	3	0	1	2	2	8
South Korea	11	0	3	8	9	34
Dutch East Indies	1	0	0	1	0	6
Iraq	3	0	0	3	1	4
Canada	3	0	0	3	0	5
United Arab Emirates	3	0	0	3	2	11
New Zealand	3	0	0	3	2	12
Haiti	3	0	0	3	2	14
Zaire	3	0	0	3	0	14
Bolivia	6	0	1	5	1	20
El Salvador	6	0	0	6	1	22
Greece	3	0	0	3	0	8

Note: Matches decided by penalty kicks are shown as drawn games.

*Includes West Germany 1950-90.

†Includes USSR 1930-1990

World Cup Final Box Scores

URUGUAY 1930

Uruguay	1	3	—	4
Argentina	2	0	—	2

FIRST HALF

Scoring: 1, Uruguay, Dorado (12); 2, Argentina, Peucelle (20); 3, Argentina, Stabile (37).

SECOND HALF

Scoring: 4, Uruguay, Cea (57); 5, Uruguay, Iriarte (68); 6, Uruguay, Castro (89).

Argentina: Botosso, Della Toree, Paternoster, Evaristo, J., Monti, Suarez, Peucelle, Varallo, Stabile, Ferreira, Evaristo, M.

Uruguay: Ballesteros, Nasazzi, Mascheroni, Andrade, Fernandez, Gestido, Dorado, Scarone, Castro, Cea, Iriarte.

Referee: Langenus (Belgium).

FRANCE 1938

Italy	3	1	—	4
Hungary	1	1	—	2

FIRST HALF

Scoring: 1, Italy, Colaussi (5); 2, Hungary, Titkos (7); Italy Piola (16); 4, Italy, Piola (35).

SECOND HALF

Scoring: 5, Hungary, Sarosi (70); 6, Italy, Colaussi (82).

Italy: Olivieri, Foni, Rava, Serantoni, Andreolo, Locatelli, Biavati, Meazza, Piola, Ferrari, Colaussi.

Hungary: Szabo; Polger, Biro, Szalay, Szucs, Lazar, Sas, Vincze, Sarosi, Zsengeller, Titkos.

Referee: Capdeville (France).

SWITZERLAND 1954

W Germany	2	1	—	3
Hungary	2	0	—	2

FIRST HALF

Scoring: 1, Hungary, Puskas (6); 2, Hungary, Czibor (8); 3, W Germ, Morlock (10); 4, W Germ, Rahn (18).

SECOND HALF

Scoring: 5, W Germ, Rahn (84).

West Germany: Turek; Posipal, Kohlmeyer, Eckel, Liebrich, Mai, Rahn, Morlock, Walter, O., Walter, F., Schaefer.

Hungary: Grosics; Buzansky, Lantos, Bozsik, Lorant, Zakarias, Czibor, Kocsis, Hidegkuti, Puskas, Toth.

Referee: Ling (England).

ITALY 1934

Italy	0	1	1	—	2
Czechoslovakia	0	1	0	—	1

SECOND HALF

Scoring: 1, Czech., Puc (70); 2, Italy, Orsi (80).

OVERTIME

Scoring: 3, Italy, Schiavio (95).

Italy: Combi, Monzeglio, Allemandi, Ferraris Monti, Monti, Bertolini, Guaita, Meazza, Schiavio, Ferrari, Orsi.

Czechoslovakia: Planicka, Zenisek, Ctyroky, Kostalek, Cambal, Cambal, Krcil, Junek, Svoboda, Sobotka, Nejedly, Puc.

Referee: Eklind (Sweden).

BRAZIL 1950

Uruguay	0	2	—	2
Brazil	0	1	—	1

SECOND HALF

Scoring: 1, Brazil, Friaca (47); 2, Uruguay, Schiaffino (66); 3, Uruguay Ghiggia (79).

Uruguay: Maspoli, Gonzales, Tejera, Gambretta, Varela, Andrade, Ghiggia, Perez, Miguez, Schiffiano, Moran

Brazil: Barbosa, Augusto, Juvenal, Bauer, Banilo, Bigode, Friaca, Zizinho, Ademir, Jair, Chico.

Referee: Reader (England).

SWEDEN 1958

Brazil	2	3	—	5
Sweden	1	1	—	2

FIRST HALF

Scoring:1, Sweden, Liedholm (3); 2, Brazil, Vava (9); 3, Brazil, Vava (32).

SECOND HALF

Scoring: 4, Brazil, Péle (55); 5, Brazil, Zagalo (68); 6, Sweden Simonsson (80); 7, Brazil, Pele (90).

Brazil: Glymar, Santos, D., Santos, N., Zito, Bellini, Orlando, Garrincha, Didi, Vava, Péle, Zagalo.

Sweden: Svensson, Bergmark, Axbom, Boerjesson, Gustavsson, Parling, Hamrin, Gren, Simonsson, Liedholm, Skoglund.

Referee: Guigue (France).

CHILE 1962

Brazil	1	2	—	3
Czechoslovakia	1	0	—	1

FIRST HALF

Scoring: 1, Czech, Masopust (15); 2, Brazil, Amarildo (17).

SECOND HALF

Scoring: 3, Brazil, Zito (68); 4, Brazil, Vava (77).

Brazil: Glymar; Santos, D., Santos, N., Zito, Mauro, Zozimo, Garrincha, Didi, Vava, Amarildo, Zagalo.

Czechoslovakia: Schroiff, Tichy, Novak, Pluskal, Popluhar, Masopust, Pospichal, Scherer, Kvasnak, Kadraba, Jelinek.

Referee: Latychev (USSR).

World Cup Final Box Scores *(Cont.)*

ENGLAND 1966

England............1	1	2——4
W. Germany........1	1	0——2

FIRST HALF

Scoring: 1, Germany, Haller (12); 2, England, Hurst, (18).

SECOND HALF

Scoring: 3, England, Peters (78); 4, Germany, Weber (90).

OVERTIME

Scoring: 5, England, Hurst (101); 6, England, Hurst (120).

England: Banks, Cohen, Wilson, Stiles, Charlton, J., Moore, Ball, Hurst, Hunt, Charlton, R., Peters.

W. Germnay: Tilkowski, Hottges, Schmellinger, Beckenbauer, Schulz, Weber, Held, Haller, Seeler, Overath, Emmerich.

Referee: Dienst (Switzerland).

W. GERMANY 1974

W. Germany.....2	0 ——2
Netherlands.....1	0 ——1

FIRST HALF

Scoring: 1, The Netherlands, Neeskens, PK, (1) 2, W. Germany, Breitner, PK, (26); 3, W. Germany, Muller, (44).

W. Germany: Maier, Vogts, Beckenbauer, Schwarzenbeck, Breitner, Hoeness, Bonhof, Overath, Grabowski, Muller, Holzenbein.

The Netherlands: Jongbloed, Suurbier, Rijsbergen (de Jong), Haan, Krol, Jansen, Neeskens, van Hanagem, Cruyff, Rensenbrink (van der Kerkhof).

Referee: Taylor (England).

ITALY 1982

Italy.................0	3 ——3
W. Germany.....0	1 ——1

SECOND HALF

Scoring: 1, Italy, Rossi (57); 2, Italy, Tardelli (68); 3, Italy, Altobelli (81); 4, Germany, Breitner (83).

Italy: Zoff, Bergomi, Scirea, Collovati, Cabrini, Oriali, Gentile, Tardelli, Conti, Rossi, Graziani (Altobelli, Causio).

W. Germany: Schumacher, Kaltz, Stielike, Foerster, K., Foerster, B., Dremmler (Hrubesch), Breitner, Briegel, Rummenigge (Mueller), Fishcher (Littbrarski).

Referee: Coelho (Brazil).

MEXICO 1970

Brazil.................1	3 ——4
Italy...................1	0 ——1

FIRST HALF

Scoring: 1, Brazil, Péle (18); 2, Italy, Boninsegna (32).

SECOND HALF

Scoring: 3, Brazil, Gerson (65); 4, Brazil, Jairzinho (70); 5, Brazil, Alberto (86).

Brazil: Feliz, Alberto, Brito, Wilson, Piazza, Everaldo, Clodoaldo, Gerson, Jairzinho, Tostao, Péle, Rivelino.

Italy: Albertosi, Burgnich, Cera, Rosato, Facchetti, Bertini (Juliano), Mazzola, De Sisti, Domenghini, Boninsegna (Rivera), Riva.

Referee: Glockner (E. Germany).

ARGENTINA 1978

Argentina.........1	0	2——3
Netherlands.....0	1	0——1

FIRST HALF

Scoring: 1, Argentina, Kempes (38).

SECOND HALF

Scoring: 2, The Netherlands , Nanninga (81).

OVERTIME

Scoring: 3, Arg., Kempes (104); 4, Arg., Bertoni (114).

Argentina: Fillol, Olguin, Galvan, Passarella, Tarantini, Ardiles (Larrosa), Gallego, Kempes, Bertoni, Luque, Ortiz (Houseman).

The Netherlands: Jongbloed, Jansen (Suurbier), Krol, Brandts, Poortvliet, Neeskens, Haan, van der Kerkhoff, W., van der Kerkhoff, R., Rep (Nanninga), Rensenbrink.

Referee: Gonella (Italy).

MEXICO 1986

Argentina.........1	2 ——3
W. Germany.....0	2 ——2

FIRST HALF

Scoring: 1, Argentina, Brown (22).

SECOND HALF

Scoring: 2, Arg., Valdano (55); 3, W. Germ., Rummenigge (73) 4, W. Germ., Voller (81); 5, Arg., Burruchaga (83).

Argentina: Pumpido, Brown, Cuciuffo, Ruggeri, Olarticoecha, Bastista, Giusti, Burruchaga (90, Trobbiani), Enrique, Maradona, Valdona.

W. Germany: Schumacher, Jakobs, Forster, Eder, Brehme, Matthaus, Berthold, Magath (62 Hoeness), Briegel, Rummenigge, Allofs (46 Voller).

Referee: Filho (Brazil).

World Cup Final Box Scores (Cont.)

ITALY 1990

W Germany	0	1—1
Argentina	0	0—0

UNITED STATES 1994

Italy	0	0	0—0
Brazil	0	0	0—0

SECOND HALF

Scoring: 1, W. Germany, Brehme, PK, (84).

W. Germany: Illgner, Brehme, Kohler, Augenthaler, Buchwald, Berthold (Reuter), Littbarski, Haessler, Mattaeus, Voeller, Klinsmann.

Argentina: Goychoechea, Lorenzo, Serrizuela, Sensini, Ruggeri (Monzon), Simon, Basualdo, Burruchag (Calderon), Maradona, Troglio, Dezottir.

Referee: Coelho (Brazil).

Scoring: None. Shootout goals: Italy—2: Albertini, Evani; Brazil—3: Romario, Branco, Dunga

Italy: Pagliuca, Benarrivo, Maldini, Baresi, Mussi (Apolloni 35), Albertini, D. Baggio (Evani 95), Berti, Donadoni, Baggio, Massaro,

Brazil: Taffarel, Jorginho (Cafu 21), Branco, Aldair, Santos, Silva, Dunga, Zinho (Viola 106), Mazinho, Bebeto, Romario

Referee: Sandor Puhl (Hungary).

Alltime Leaders

GOALS

Player, Nation	Tournaments	Goals	Player, Nation	Tournaments	Goals
Gerd Muller, West Germany	1970, '74	14	Ademir, Brazil	1950	9
Just Fontaine, France	1958	13	Eusebio, Portugal	1966	9
Pelé, Brazil	1958, '62, '66, '70	12	Jairzinho, Brazil	1970, '74	9
Sandor Kocsis, Hungary	1954	11	Paolo Rossi, Italy	1982, '86	9
Teofilo Cubillas, Peru	1970, '78	10	Karl-Heinz Rummenigge,		
Gregorz Lato, Poland	1974, '78, '82	10	W. Germany	1978, '82, '86	9
Helmut Rahn, West Germany	1954, '58	10	Uwe Seeler, West Germany	1958, '62, '66, '70	9
Gary Lineker, England	1986, '90	10	Vava, Brazil	1958, '62	9

LEADING SCORER, CUP BY CUP

Year	Player/Nation	Goals	Year	Player/Nation	Goals
1930	Guillermo Stabile, Argentina	8	1962	Leonel Sanchez, Chile	4
1934	Oldrich Nejedly, Czechoslovakia	5		Vava, Brazil	
1938	Leonidas da Silva, Brazil	8	1966	Eusebio Ferreira, Portugal	9
1950	Ademir de Menenzes, Brazil	9	1970	Gerd Mueller, West Germany	10
1954	Sandor Kocsis, Hungary	11	1974	Gregorz Lato, Poland	7
1958	Just Fontaine, France	13	1978	Mario Kempes, Argentina	6
1962	Florian Albert, Hungary	4	1982	Paolo Rossi, Italy	6
	Valentin Ivanov, USSR		1986	Gary Lineker, England	6
	Garrincha, Brazil		1990	Salvatore Schillaci, Italy	6
	Drazan Jerkovic, Yugoslavia		1994	Hristo Stoitchkov, Bulgaria	6
				Oleg Salenko, Russia	

Most Goals, Individual, One Game

Goals	Player, Nation	Score	Date
5	Oleg Salenko, Russia	Russia-Cameroon, 6-1	6-28-94
4	Leonidas, Brazil	Brazil-Poland, 6-5	6-5-38
4	Ernest Willimowski, Poland	Brazil-Poland, 6-5	6-5-38
4	Gustav Wetterstrîm, Sweden	Sweden-Cuba, 8-0	6-12-38
4	Juan Alberto Schiaffino, Uruguay	Uruguay-Bolivia, 8-0	7-2-50
4	Ademir, Brazil	Brazil-Sweden, 7-1	7-9-50
4	Sandor Kocsis, Hungary	Hungary-West Germany, 8-3	6-20-54
4	Just Fontaine, France	France-West Germany, 6-3	6-28-58
4	Eusebio, Portugal	Portugal-No. Korea, 5-3	7-23-66
4	Emilio Butragueño, Spain	Spain-Denmark, 5-1	6-18-86

Note: 30 players have scored 31 World Cup hat tricks. Gerd Muller of West Germany is the only man to have two World Cup hat tricks, both in 1970. The last hat tricks were 6-23-90, Tomas Skuhravy (Czech) vs. Costa Rica and Michel (Spain) vs. So. Korea, 6-17-90.

Attendance and Goal Scoring, Year by Year

Year	Site	No. of Games	Goals	Goals/Game	Attendance	Avg Att
1930	Uruguay	18	70	3.89	434,500	24,139
1934	Italy	17	70	4.12	395,000	23,235
1938	France	18	84	4.67	483,000	26,833
1950	Brazil	22	88	4.00	1,337,000	60,773
1954	Switzerland	26	140	5.38	943,000	36,269
1958	Sweden	35	126	3.60	868,000	24,800
1962	Chile	32	89	2.78	776,000	24,250
1966	England	32	89	2.78	1,614,677	50,459
1970	Mexico	32	95	2.97	1,673,975	52,312
1974	West Germany	38	97	2.55	1,774,022	46,685
1978	Argentina	38	102	2.68	1,610,215	42,374
1982	Spain	52	146	2.80	1,856,277	35,698
1986	Mexico	52	132	2.54	2,441,731	46,956
1990	Italy	52	115	2.21	2,514,443	48,354
1994	United States	52	140	2.69	3,567,415	68,604
Totals		516	1583	3.07	22,289,255	43,196

The United States in the World Cup

URUGUAY 1930: FINAL COMPETITION

Date	Opponent	Result	Scoring
7-13-30	Belgium	3-0 W	US: McGhee 2, Patenaude
7-17-30	Paraguay	3-0 W	US: Patenaude 2, Florie
7-26-30	Argentina	1-6 L	ARG: Monti 2, Scopelli 2, Stabile 2 US: Brown.

BRAZIL 1950: FINAL COMPETITION

Date	Opponent	Result	Scoring
6-25-50	Spain	1-3 L	US: Pariani SPN: Igoa, Basora, Zarra
6-29-50	England	1-0 W	US: Gaetjens.
7-2-50	Chile	2-5 L	US: Wallace, Maca CHL: Robledo, Cremaschi 3, Prieto

ITALY 1934: FINAL COMPETITION

Date	Opponent	Result	Scoring
5-27-34	Italy	1-7 L	US: Donelli ITA: Schiavio 3, Orsi 2, Meazza, Ferrari

ITALY 1990: FINAL COMPETITION

Date	Opponent	Result	Scoring
6-10-90	Czechoslovakia	1-5 L	US: Caligiuri Czech: Skuhravy 2, Hasek, Bilek, Luhovy
6-14-90	Italy	0-1 L	Italy: Giannini
6-19-90	Austria	1-2 L	US: Murray Austria: Rodax, Ogris

UNITED STATES 1994: FINAL COMPETITION

Date	Opponent	Result	Scoring
6-18-94	Switzerland	1-1 T	US: Wynalda Sui: Bregy
6-22-94	Colombia	2-1 W	US: Escobar (own goal), Stewart Colombia: Valencia
6-26-94	Romania	1-0 L	Romania: Petrescu
7-4-94	Brazil	1-0 L	Brazil: Bebeto

International Competition

European Championship

Official name: the European Football Championship. Held every four years since 1960.

Year	Champion	Score	Runner-up	Year	Champion	Score	Runner-up
1960	USSR	2-1	Yugoslavia	1980	West Germany	2-1	Belgium
1964	Spain	2-1	USSR	1984	France	2-0	Spain
1968	Italy	2-0	Yugoslavia	1988	Holland	2-0	USSR
1972	West Germany	3-0	USSR	1992	Denmark	2-0	Germany
1976	Czechoslovakia*	2-2	West Germany				

*Won on penalty kicks.

Under-20 World Championship

Year	Host	Champion	Runner-Up
1977	Tunisia	USSR	Mexico
1979	Japan	Argentina	USSR
1981	Australia	W. Germany	Qatar
1983	Mexico	Brazil	Argentina
1985	USSR	Brazil	Spain
1987	Chile	Yugoslavia	W. Germany
1989	Saudi Arabia	Portugal	Nigeria
1991	Portugal	Portugal	Brazil
1993	Australia	Brazil	Ghana

Under-17 World Championship

1985	Nigeria
1987	USSR
1989	Saudi Arabia

Under-17 *(Cont.)*

1991	Ghana
1993	Nigeria

Pan American Games

1951	Argentina
1955	Argentina
1959	Argentina
1963	Brazil
1967	Mexico
1971	Argentina
1975	Brazil-Mexico (tie)
1979	Brazil
1983	Uruguay
1987	Brazil
1991	United States

South American Championship (Copa America)

Year	Champion	Host	Year	Champion	Host
1916	Uruguay	Argentina	1947	Argentina	Ecuador
1917	Uruguay	Uruguay	1949	Brazil	Brazil
1919	Brazil	Brazil	1953	Paraguay	Peru
1920	Uruguay	Chile	1955	Argentina	Chile
1921	Argentina	Argentina	1956	Uruguay	Uruguay
1922	Brazil	Brazil	1957	Argentina	Peru
1923	Uruguay	Uruguay	1958	Argentina	Argentina
1924	Uruguay	Uruguay	1959	Uruguay	Ecuador
1925	Argentina	Argentina	1963	Bolivia	Bolivia
1926	Uruguay	Chile	1967	Uruguay	Uruguay
1927	Argentina	Peru	1975	Peru	Various sites
1929	Argentina	Argentina	1979	Paraguay	Various sites
1935	Uruguay	Peru	1983	Uruguay	Various sites
1937	Argentina	Argentina	1987	Uruguay	Argentina
1939	Peru	Peru	1989	Brazil	Brazil
1941	Argentina	Chile	1990	Brazil	Argentina
1942	Uruguay	Uruguay	1991	Argentina	Chile
1945	Argentina	Chile	1993	Argentina	Ecuador
1946	Argentina	Argentina			

Awards

European Footballer of the Year

Year	Player	Team	Year	Player	Team
1956	Stanley Matthews	Blackpool	1973	Johan Cruyff	Barcelona
1957	Alfredo Di Stefano	Real Madrid	1974	Johan Cruyff	Barcelona
1958	Raymond Kopa	Real Madrid	1975	Oleg Blokhin	Dynamo Kiev
1959	Alfredo Di Stefano	Real Madrid	1976	Franz Beckenbauer	Bayern Munich
1960	Luis Suarez	Barcelona	1977	Allan Simonsen	Borussia Moenchengladbach
1961	Omar Sivori	Juventus			
1962	Josef Masopust	Dukla Prague	1978	Kevin Keegan	SV Hamburg
1963	Lev Yashin	Moscow Dynamo	1979	Kevin Keegan	SV Hamburg
1964	Denis Law	Manchester United	1980	Karl-Heinz Rummenigge	Bayern Munich
1965	Eusebio	Benfica			
1966	Bobby Charlton	Manchester United	1981	Karl-Heinz Rummenigge	Bayern Munich
1967	Florian Albert	Ferencvaros			
1968	George Best	Manchester United	1982	Paolo Rossi	Juventus
1969	Gianni Rivera	AC Milan	1983	Michel Platini	Juventus
1970	Gerd Mueller	Bayern Munich	1984	Michel Platini	Juventus
1971	Johan Cruyff	Ajax	1985	Michel Platini	Juventus
1972	Franz Beckenbauer	Bayern Munich	1986	Igor Belanov	Dynamo Kiev

European Footballer of the Year *(Cont.)*

1987	Ruud Gullit	AC Milan	1991	Jean-Pierre Papin	Olympique Marseille
1988	Marco Van Basten	AC Milan	1992	Marco Van Basten	AC Milan
1989	Marco Van Basten	AC Milan	1993	Roberto Baggio	Juventus
1990	Lothar Matthaeus	Inter Milan			

African Footballer of the Year

Year	Player	Team	Year	Player	Team
1970	Salif Keita	Mali	1983	Mahmoud Al-Khatib	Egypt
1971	Ibrahim Sunday	Ghana	1984	ThÇophile Abega	Cameroon
1972	Chérif Souleyman	Guinea	1985	Mohamed Timoumi	Morocco
1973	Tshimimu Bwanga	Zaire	1986	Badou Zaki	Morocco
1974	Paul Moukila	Congo	1987	Rabah Madjer	Algeria
1975	Ahmed Faras	Morocco	1988	Kalusha Bwalya	Zambia
1976	Roger Milla	Cameroon	1989	George Weah	Liberia
1977	Dhiab Tarak	Tunisia	1990	Roger Milla	Cameroon
1978	Abdul Razak	Ghana	1991	Abedi Pele	Ghana
1979	Thomas Nkono	Cameroon	1992	Abedi Pele	Ghana
1980	Jean Manga Onguene	Cameroon	1993	Rashidi Yekini	Nigeria
1981	Lakhdar Belloumi	Algeria		Selected by *France Football*.	
1982	Thomas Nkono	Cameroon			

South American Player of the Year

Year	Player	Team	Year	Player	Team
1971	Tostao	Cruzeiro	1983	Socrates	Corinthians
1972	Teofilo Cubillas	Alianza Lima	1984	Enzo Francescoli	River Plate
1973	Pelé	Santos	1985	Julio Cesar Romero	Fluminense
1974	Elias Figueroa	Internacional	1986	Antonio Alzamendi	River Plate
1975	Elias Figueroa	Internacional	1987	Carlos Valderrama	Deportivo Cali
1976	Elias Figueroa	Internacional	1988	Ruben Paz	Racing Buenos Aires
1977	Zico	Flamengo	1989	Bebeto	Vasco da Gama
1978	Mario Kempes	Valencia	1990	Raul Amarilla	Olimpia
1979	Diego Maradona	Argentinos Juniors	1991	Oscar Ruggeri	Velez Sarsfield
1980	Diego Maradona	Boca Juniors	1992	Rai	Sao Paulo
1981	Zico	Flamengo	1993	Carlos Valderrama	Junior Barranquilla
1982	Zico	Flamengo			

Club Competition

Toyota Cup

Competition between winners of European Champion Clubs' Cup and Libertadores Cup.

1960...Real Madrid, Spain	1972...Ajax, Holland	1984...Independiente, Argentina
1961...Penarol, Uruguay	1973...Independiente, Argentina	1985...Juventus, Italy
1962...Santos, Brazil	1974...Atletico de Madrid, Spain	1986...River Plate, Argentina
1963...Santos, Brazil	1975...No tournament	1987...Porto, Portugal
1964...Inter, Italy	1976...Bayern Munich	1988...Nacional, Uruguay
1965...Inter, Italy	1977...Boca Juniors, Argentina	1989...Milan, Italy
1966...Penarol, Uruguay	1978...No tournament	1990...Milan, Italy
1967...Racing Club, Argentina	1979...Olimpia, Paraguay	1991...Red Star Belgrade,
1968...Estudiantes, Argentina	1980...Nacional, Uruguay	Yugoslavia
1969...Milan, Italy	1981...Flamengo, Brazil	1992...Sao Paulo, Brazil
1970...Feyenoord, Netherlands	1982...Penarol, Uruguay	1993...Sao Paulo, Brazil
1971...Nacional, Uruguay	1983...Gremio, Brazil	

Note: Until 1968 a best-of-three-games format decided the winner. After that a two-game/total-goal format was used until Toyota became the sponsor in 1980, moved the game to Tokyo, and switched the format to a one game championship. The European Cup runner-up substituted for the winner in 1971, 1973, 1974, and 1979.

European Cup

1956...Real Madrid, Spain	1961...Benfica, Portugal	1966...Real Madrid, Spain
1957...Real Madrid, Spain	1962...Benfica, Portugal	1967...Celtic, Scotland
1958...Real Madrid, Spain	1963...A.C. Milan, Italy	1968...Manchester United,
1959...Real Madrid, Spain	1964...Inter-Milan, Italy	England
1960...Real Madrid, Spain	1965...Inter-Milan, Italy	1969...A.C. Milan, Italy

European Cup (Cont.)

1970...Feyenoord, Netherlands	West Germany	1985...Juventus, Italy
1971...Ajax Amsterdam, Netherlands	1977...Liverpool, England	1986...Steaua Bucharest, Romania
1972...Ajax Amsterdam, Netherlands	1978...Liverpool, England	1987...Porto, Portugal
1973...Ajax Amsterdam, Netherlands	1979...Nottingham Forest, England	1988...P.S.V. Eindhoven, Netherlands
1974...Bayern Munich, West Germany	1980...Nottingham Forest, England	1989...A.C. Milan, Italy
1975...Bayern Munich, West Germany	1981...Liverpool, England	1990...A.C. Milan, Italy
1976...Bayern Munich,	1982...Aston Villa, England	1991...Red Star, Belgrade
	1983...SV Hamburg, West Germany	1992...Barcelona, Spain
	1984...Liverpool, England	1993...Olympique Marseille, France
		1994...A.C. Milan, Italy

Note: On four occasions the European Cup winner has refused to play in the Intercontinental Cup (now Toyota Cup) and has been replaced by the runner-up: Panathinaikos (Greece) in 1971, Juventus (Italy) in 1973, Atletico Madrid (Spain) in 1974, and Malmo (Sweden) in 1979.

Libertadores Cup

Competition between champion clubs and runners-up of 10 South American National Associations.

1960...Penarol, Uruguay	1972...Independiente, Argentina	1984...Independiente, Argentina
1961...Penarol, Uruguay	1973...Independiente, Argentina	1985...Argentinos Juniors, Argentina
1962...Santos, Brazil	1974...Independiente, Argentina	1986...River Plate, Argentina
1963...Santos, Brazil	1975...Independiente, Argentina	1987...Penarol, Uruguay
1964...Independiente, Argentina	1976...Cruzeiro, Brazil	1988...Nacional, Uruguay
1965...Independiente, Argentina	1977...Boca Juniors, Argentina	1989...Atletico Nacional, Colombia
1966...Penarol, Uruguay	1978...Boca Juniors, Argentina	1990...Olimpia, Paraguay
1967...Racing Club, Argentina	1979...Olimpia, Paraguay	1991...Colo Colo, Chile
1968...Estudiantes, Argentina	1980...Nacional, Uruguay	1992...Sao Paulo, Brazil
1969...Estudiantes, Argentina	1981...Flamengo, Brazil	1993...Sao Paulo, Brazil
1970...Estudiantes, Argentina	1982...Penarol, Uruguay	
1971...Nacional, Uruguay	1983...Gremio, Brazil	

UEFA Cup

Competition between teams other than league champions and cup winners from the Union of European Football Associations.

1958...Barcelona, Spain	1972...Tottenham Hotspur, England	1982...I.F.K. Gothenburg, Sweden
1959...No tournament	1973...Liverpool, England	1983...Anderlecht, Belgium
1960...Barcelona, Spain	1974...Feyenoord, Netherlands	1984...Tottenham Hotspur, England
1961...AS Roma, Italy	1975...Borussia Moenchengladbach, West Germany	1985...Real Madrid, Spain
1962...Valencia, Spain	1976...Liverpool, England	1986...Real Madrid, Spain
1963...Valencia, Spain	1977...Juventus, Italy	1987...I.F.K. Gothenburg, Sweden
1964...Real Zaragoza, Spain	1978...P.S.V. Eindhoven, Netherlands	1988...Bayer Leverkusen, West Germany
1965...Ferencvaros, Hungary	1979...Borussia Moenchengladbach, West Germany	1989...Naples, Italy
1966...Barcelona, Spain	1980...Eintracht Frankfurt, West Germany	1990...Juventus, Italy
1967...Dynamo Zagreb, Yugoslavia	1981...Ipswich Town, England	1991...Inter-Milan, Italy
1968...Leeds United, England		1992...Torino, Italy
1969...Newcastle United, England		1993...Juventus, Italy
1970...Arsenal, England		1994...Internazionale, Italy
1971...Leeds United, England		

European Cup-Winners' Cup

Competition between cup winners of countries belonging to UEFA.

1961...A.C. Fiorentina, Italy	1968...A.C. Milan, Italy	1976...Anderlecht, Belgium
1962...Atletico Madrid, Spain	1969...Slovan Bratislava, Czechoslovakia	1977...S.V. Hamburg, West Germany
1963...Tottenham Hotspur, England	1970...Manchester City, England	1978...Anderlecht, Belgium
1964...Sporting Lisbon, Portugal	1971...Chelsea, England	1979...Barcelona, Spain
1965...West Ham United, England	1972...Glasgow Rangers, Scotland	1980...Valencia, Spain
1966...Borussia Dortmund, West Germany	1973...A.C. Milan, Italy	1981...Dynamo Tbilisi, USSR
1967...Bayern Munich, West Germany	1974...Magdeburg, East Germany	1982...Barcelona, Spain
	1975...Dynamo Kiev, USSR	1983...Aberdeen, Scotland
		1984...Juventus, Italy

European Cup-Winners' Cup *(Cont.)*

1985...Everton, England
1986...Dynamo Kiev, USSR
1987...Ajax Amsterdam,
     Netherlands

1988...Mechelen, Belgium
1989...Barcelona, Spain
1990...Sampdoria, Italy
1991...Manchester United, England

1992...Werder Bremen, Germany
1993...Parma, Italy
1994...Arsenal, England

Major Soccer League

Results

Called the Major Indoor Soccer League from 1979-90.

	Champion	Series	Runner-Up	Championship Series Most Valuable Player
1979	NY Arrows	2-0	Philadelphia	Shep Messing, NY
1980	NY Arrows	7-4	Houston	Steve Zungul, NY
1981	NY Arrows	6-5	St Louis	Steve Zungul, NY
1982	NY Arrows	3-2	St Louis	Steve Zungul, NY
1983	San Diego	3-2	Baltimore	Juli Veee, SD
1984	Baltimore	4-1	St Louis	Scott Manning, Balt
1985	San Diego	4-1	Baltimore	Steve Zungul, SD
1986	San Diego	4-3	Minnesota	Brian Quinn, SD
1987	Dallas	4-3	Tacoma	Tatu, Dall
1988	San Diego	4-0	Cleveland	Hugo Perez, SD
1989	San Diego	4-3	Baltimore	Victor Nogueira, SD
1990	San Diego	4-2	Baltimore	Brian Quinn, SD
1991	San Diego	4-2	Cleveland	Ben Collins, SD
1992	San Diego	4-2	Dallas	Thomas Usiyan, SD

Championship format: 1979, best-of-three-games series; 1980-81, one-game championship; 1982-83, best-of-five-games series; 1984 to present, best-of-seven-games series.

Statistical Leaders

SCORING

Year	Player/Team	Points
1978-79	Fred Grgurev, Phil	74
1979-80	Steve Zungul, NY	136
1980-81	Steve Zungul, NY	152
1981-82	Steve Zungul, NY	163
1982-83	Steve Zungul, NY	122
1983-84	Stan Stamenkovic, Balt	97
1984-85	Steve Zungul, SD	136
1985-86	Steve Zungul, Tac	115
1986-87	Tatu, Dall	111
1987-88	Erik Rasmussen, Wich	112
1988-89	Preci, Tac	104
1989-90	Tatu, Dall	113
1990-91	Tatu, Dall	144
1991-92	Zoran Karic, Clev	102

GOALS

Year	Player/Team	Goals
1978-79	Fred Grgurev, Phil	46
1979-80	Steve Zungul, NY	90
1980-81	Steve Zungul, NY	108
1981-82	Steve Zungul, NY/GB	103
1982-83	Steve Zungul, NY/GB	75
1983-84	Mark Liveric, NY	58
1984-85	Steve Zungul, SD	68
1985-86	Erik Rasmussen, Wich	67
1986-87	Tatu, Dall	73
1987-88	Hector Marinaro, Minn	58
1988-89	Preki, Tac	51
1989-90	Tatu, Dall	64
1990-91	Tatu, Dall	78
1991-92	Hector Marinaro, Clev	53

ASSISTS

Year	Player/Team	Assists
1978-79	Fred Grgurev, Phil	28
1979-80	Steve Zungul, NY	46
1980-81	Jorgen Kristensen, Wich	52
1981-82	Steve Zungul, NY	60
1982-83	Stan Stamenkovic, Mem	65
1983-84	Stan Stamenkovic, Balt	63
1984-85	Steve Zungul, SD	68
1985-86	Steve Zungul, Tac	60
1986-87	Kai Haaskivi, Clev	55
1987-88	Preki, Tac	58
1988-89	Preki, Tac	53
1989-90	Jan Goossens, KC	55
1990-91	Tatu, Dall	66
1991-92	Zoran Karic, Clev	63

TOP GOALKEEPERS

Year	Player/Team	Goals Agst Avg
1978-79	Paul Hammond, Hous	4.16
1979-80	Sepp Gantenhammer, Hous	4.42
1980-81	Enzo DiPede, Chi	4.06
1981-82	Slobo Lijjevski, StL	3.85*
1982-83	Zoltan Toth, NY	4.01
1983-84	Slobo Lijjevski, StL	3.67
1984-85	Scott Manning, Balt	3.89
1985-86	Keith Van Eron, Balt	3.66
1986-87	Tino Lettieri, Minn	3.38
1987-88	Zoltan Toth, SD	2.94
1988-89	Victor Nogueira, SD	2.86
1989-90	Joe Papaleo, Dall	3.34
1990-91	Victor Nogueira, SD	4.37
1991-92	Victor Nogueira, SD	4.60

North American Soccer League

Formed in 1968 by the merger of the National Professional Soccer League and the USA League, both of which had begun operations a year earlier. The NPSL's lone champion was the Oakland Clippers. The USA League, which brought entire teams in from Europe, was won in 1967 by the LA Wolves, who were the English League's Wolverhampton Wanderers.

Year	Champion	Score	Runner-Up	Regular Season MVP
1968	Atlanta	0-0, 3-0	San Diego	John Kowalik, Chi
1969	Kansas City	No game	Atlanta	Cirilio Fernandez, KC
1970	Rochester	3-0,1-3	Washington	Carlos Metidieri, Roch
1971	Dallas	1-2, 4-1, 2-0	Atlanta	Carlos Metidieri, Roch
1972	NY	2-1	St Louis	Randy Horton, NY
1973	Philadelphia	2-0	Dallas	Warren Archibald, Mia
1974	Los Angeles	4-3*	Miami	Peter Silvester, Balt
1975	Tampa Bay	2-0	Portland	Steve David, Miami
1976	Toronto	3-0	Minnesota	Pelé, NY
1977	NY	2-1	Seattle	Franz Beckenbauer, NY
1978	NY	3-1	Tampa Bay	Mike Flanagan, NE
1979	Vancouver	2-1	Tampa Bay	Johan Cruyff, LA
1980	NY	3-0	Ft Lauderdale	Roger Davies, Sea
1981	Chicago	1-0*	NY	Giorgio Chinaglia, NY
1982	NY	1-0	Seattle	Peter Ward, Sea
1983	Tulsa	2-0	Toronto	Roberto Cabanas, NY
1984	Chicago	2-1, 3-2	Toronto	Steve Zungul, SJ

Shootout.

Championship Format: 1968 & 1970: Two games/total goals. 1971 & 1984: Best-of-three game series. 1972-1983: One game championship. Title in 1969 went to the regular season champion.

Statistical Leaders

SCORING

Year	Player/Team	Pts	Year	Player/Team	Pts
1968	John Kowalik, Chi	69	1977	Steven David, LA	58
1969	Kaiser Motaung, Atl	36	1978	Giorgio Chinaglia, NY	79
1970	Kirk Apostolidis, Dall	35	1979	Oscar Fabbiani, Tampa Bay	58
1971	Carlos Metidieri, Roch	46	1980	Giorgio Chinaglia, NY	77
1972	Randy Horton, NY	22	1981	Giorgio Chinaglia, NY	74
1973	Kyle Rote, Dall	30	1982	Giorgio Chinaglia, NY	55
1974	Paul Child, San Jose	36	1983	Roberto Cabanas, NY	66
1975	Steven David, Miami	52	1984	Slavisa Zungul, Golden Bay	50
1976	Giorgio Chinaglia, NY	49			

American Professional Soccer League

Year	Champion	Score	Runner-Up	Regular Season MVP
1991	San Francisco	1-3, 2-0 (1-0 on penalty kicks)	Albany	Jean Harbor, MD
1992	Colorado	1-0	Tampa Bay	Taifour Diane, CO
1993	Colorado	3-1 (OT)	Los Angeles	Taifour Diane, CO

NCAA Sports

Sports Illustrated

FLYING HIGH

Oklahoma knocks off Georgia Tech for the NCAA baseball title

CHUCK SOLOMON

Objects of Desire

An odd assortment of lucky charms inspired the NCAA
champions in soccer, hockey and baseball | by HANK HERSCH

N OLD BRIEFCASE FILLED WITH oddments, a torn picture of a fabled work of art, a five-foot stretch of rope. Found in an attic or washed up on a shoreline, these artifacts would hardly seem to have any meaningful connection. But during the 1993–94 NCAA championships, each one served as a talisman that bound a team together, and they all now carry the same whiff of victory.

SOCCER
During recent NCAA tournaments, Virginia coach Bruce Arena has carried an attaché case that contains everything from Japanese charms to an inspirational letter from a former player to a coveted award known as the golden jock. He began his rare collection in 1989, the year the Cavaliers won their first national championship. And after they defeated South Carolina 2–0 on Dec. 5 at Davidson, N.C., to win their third straight title, Arena added another item to his mini-warehouse: a removable fiberglass cast worn all season by forward Nate Friends.

The first three-peat champion in the 35 years of the NCAA men's tournament, Virginia got all five of its goals from Friends, a 6' 2", 185-pound junior who grew up in McLean, Va. In the semifinals against Princeton, Friends used his speed to get behind the Tigers' zone defense and scored a hat trick in the 3–1 win. Then two days later, in the title match, he used his head and his foot, nodding in Mike Fisher's corner kick from the far post in the 40th minute and driving home a seven-yard volley off Fisher's indirect kick in the 86th.

After the game, while the rest of the Cavs celebrated their historic win in a pileup, Friends calmly did a TV interview and wished his brother, Jason, a quick recovery from the flu. Nate himself had coped all season with a broken wrist, which he injured while training in August. But his five-goal onslaught in the Final Four—an output two shy of his total for the entire season—hardly had him turning cartwheels, even if he could have. "I wanted to win, and I really didn't care who scored," Friends said. "But if I had to score, that was O.K., too."

Arena called the rugged final a "blue-collar game," which made it an odd fit for

Friends. His father, Nate Sr., is a corporate vice president and general counsel for a division of AT&T. Nate Jr. didn't have to sweat getting a scholarship, but he did have to choose between soccer and basketball, and he considered attending some Division I schools that would have allowed him to suit up for each season. His heart, though, belonged to soccer. "He's very similar playing both sports—the quick first step and the jumping ability—and he's just really tenacious," said Nate Sr.

The same could be said for the Cavaliers. Their approach is similar to the "total soccer" favored by the Netherlands in the 1970s, when players celebrated their skills by filling any role at any given time. Even the color of their jerseys is a collegiate echo of Holland's Clockwork Orange. Of course, any concept is more effective when it is being executed by nine former high school All-Americas under the orchestration of a midfielder like junior Claudio Reyna, the nonpareil passer who would wind up winning the Missouri Athletic Club college player of the year award for the second straight season.

But by the sheer volume of his goal scoring, the unassuming Friends upstaged even Reyna. His season-long struggle to find the net had prompted Arena to jokingly promise Friends a warmup suit if he scored in the ACC tournament. Friends did, so Arena continued with his imaginary incentives. After notching another goal in the finals, Friends was supposed to receive a van. "All this couldn't happen to a better kid," Arena said. "But don't misunderstand me—Nate's not getting the van."

So Arena snapped his case shut on yet another NCAA title, his fourth in five years. And now, from the star of the '93 champions, his collection includes the supporting cast.

HOCKEY
Before skating onto the ice for the national title game on April 2 in St. Paul, Lake

Friends (20) contributed five goals and a new item for Arena's lucky collection.

Superior State goalie Blaine Lacher took a page torn from a humanities textbook and zipped it inside the lining of his blocker. The paper carried a picture of Michelangelo's statue of David, the slingshot whiz whom Lacher and the rest of the team had taken to their hearts as the archetypal underdog. A small school (enrollment: 3,400) from Sault Ste. Marie in Michigan's distant Upper Peninsula—a.k.a. "The Land Above the Bridge" or home of the "Yoopers"—Lake State was about to face another giant in Boston University, and the players wanted all the ammunition they could get.

BOB DONNAN

"It's kind of our little thing," Lacher explained. "[David's] the man."

Thus armed, the Soo Lakers secured a triumph of biblical proportions. Propelled by five smooth goals in the second period, Lake State housebroke the Terriers 9–1 in the biggest championship game blowout since 1961. Right wing Rob Valicevic scored two goals and set up two more, center Gerald Tallaire racked up four assists, and 12 Lakers recorded a point. "The difference in effort and discipline between the two teams was remarkable," Boston coach Jack Parker said. Added Soo Laker coach Jeff Jackson, "I find it unbelievable. We just had so much jump."

Jackson has influenced his team's choice of iconography. At his house he has four one-foot-tall statues of David that he bought on a trip to Italy several years ago, one of which made the trip to St. Paul and the rounds at the post-victory party. The casual observer might think Jackson's collection a mite excessive; the rest of collegiate hockey would find it wholly misleading. Despite a roster without any high school All-Americas, the Lakers became the first team to appear in three straight finals since Wisconsin from 1981 to '83, and the title was their second in three years.

Lacher was on the team during its '92 championship run, but not on the ice. He had come to Sault Ste. Marie from Medicine Hat, Alberta, and the bright lights of what was, relatively speaking, the big city blinded him. He was arrested one night for disorderly conduct, and while the charges were dropped, he did serve a two-game suspension imposed by Jackson. After being reinstated he was lit up for 15 goals in a two-game series against lowly Ohio State. Lacher's ledger over the remaining 10 games of his freshman season: four minutes, two saves.

"I was scared," he recalls. "I was a mental case. I really believed that I wasn't good enough." Lacher went to see Jackson at the end of the season. "[Blaine] wouldn't even look me in the eye," Jackson says. "He was sobbing uncontrollably. It was then, I think,

DAVID E. KLUTHO

With Michelangelo's David in his blocker, Lacher turned in a masterpiece of his own.

that he realized how desperate he was for the sport."

Over his sophomore season Lacher rebuilt his confidence; as a junior he razed the opposition's. He emerged as the top goaltender in the nation, leading college hockey in goals-against average (2.02) and save percentage (.916), while setting a Division I record by going more than 375 minutes without allowing a goal. He battled a torn hamstring that caused him to miss 10 games, and he sat out two more with chicken pox. Then he deployed all his wiles and guts in three white-knuckle overtime victories leading up to the final.

Seeded fourth in the West regional, the Soo Lakers first came back from a one-goal

deficit in the third period and squeezed past Northwestern 6–5. Then they upended Michigan—a team they had lost to *four times* during the season—on a blast by Valicevic, 5–4. Finally, in the semis, Lake State nipped Harvard 3–2 on a spectacular snatch-and-score by Clayton Beddoes. Gloving a high pass at center ice from Sean Tallaire, the tournament's Most Outstanding Player, Beddoes set the puck down in stride, zoomed in on net and slipped a shot past Aaron Israel at 4:16 in OT.

The Soo Lakers were due a breather in the finals, and they got one thanks to Lacher, who made 25 saves. "We keep playing these big, bad schools," he said. "And here we are, this little Lake Superior that always seems to come up big—like David." So big that the Lakers may deserve to be considered Goliaths.

BASEBALL

The question posed to the Oklahoma baseball team at its first spring workout was this: If you were hanging from a cliff and holding onto a rope, who would you want at the other end of the line? "Who would hold that rope?" assistant coach Sunny Golloway asked. "Who would go over the edge trying to help you rather than let you fall?"

The responses varied: fathers, girlfriends, roommates. But the answer Golloway and coach Larry Cochell wanted from the Sooners was a teammate, any teammate. After that bit of instruction, Cochell and Co. kept a five-foot piece of rope in a prominent place in the dugout throughout the season to remind the troops of the need for cohesion and camaraderie. At those times when the club hit a lull, pitcher Kenny Gajewski would grab the

Oklahoma's Glass hit three ropes out of the park in the College World Series.

cord and drag it from one end of the bench to the other. "Let's hear it," Gajewski would shout. "C'mon. Twenty-five guys pulling on the same rope."

But no matter how tightly the rope bound the team together, Oklahoma needed a bungee-sized stretch to do what it eventually did: knock off a talent-rich Georgia Tech team 13–5 in the championship game and become only the fifth team in 44 years to go unbeaten in both the regional tournament and the double-elimination College World Series. The Sooners were unranked in each of the three preseason polls, and even when they reached No. 13 at the end of the regular year, they were the lowest-rated team of the final eight at Omaha. "We said there's only one way to earn that respect: to do it with their bats and their gloves and show them the way we can play," Cochell said.

Oklahoma's stunning roll provided the Big Eight with its first baseball title since 1959 and gave Cochell, a 28-year veteran who had guided three schools to the series, a ring at last. Fittingly, it was a player known for hitting ropes—senior center-

fielder Chip Glass—who pulled the Sooners to the summit by hitting .389 and belting three home runs, as many as he muscled in 227 at bats during the season. No matter that Glass's grip resembled a Little Leaguer's. "People think when you choke high up that you're not going to have as much power," he said. "But it doesn't matter as long as you hit the sweet spot."

The Sooners needed all the might they could muster against Tech. While Oklahoma had only one player selected in the first six rounds of the major league draft—Jerry Whittaker, who was taken in the second round by the Chicago White Sox—the Yellow Jackets had four of the top 40 picks, including catcher Jason Varitek, *Baseball America's* Player of the Year, who was chosen 14th by the Seattle Mariners. Varitek was in the middle of the game's pivotal moment, a moment he shared with Glass.

The Sooners had taken a 2–0 lead in the first, which Tech equaled on home runs by Varitek and Nomar Gaciaparra. But Oklahoma blew the game open in the fourth after Glass singled and stole to put runners on second and third. M.J. Mariani then rapped a base hit to center, sending Glass roaring around third and past Cochell, who had signaled for him to stop. "I didn't see Coach put up his hands until I was going by him," Glass said. Varitek made a sweep tag at the plate, and on a close call Glass was safe, prompting a heated dispute by the Yellow Jackets and igniting a five-run inning for the Sooners. "It was a turning point," Varitek said. "But you can't blame the whole game on one call. We self-destructed after that."

Damon Minor launched a three-run homer while Glass added a solo shot in the sixth, and the hottest-hitting team in the tournament set a record for runs scored in a series finale. "If you had seen us six weeks ago, we might not have been the best," said second baseman Ricky Guttierez. "But we played the best when we had to and won the national championship." Allowing Oklahoma to stand alone, together, at the top of college baseball.

FOR THE RECORD·1993-1994

NCAA Team Champions

Fall 1993

Cross-Country

MEN

	Champion	Runner-Up
Division I:	Arkansas	Brigham Young
Division II:	Adams St	Edinboro
Division III:	North Central	WI-La Crosse

WOMEN

	Champion	Runner-Up
Division I:	Villanova	Arkansas
Division II:	Adams St	Cal Poly-San Luis Obispo
Division III:	Cortland St	Calvin

Field Hockey

WOMEN

	Champion	Runner-Up
Division I:	Maryland	N Carolina
Division II	Bloomsburg	Lock Haven
Division III:	Cortland St	Mary Washington

Football

MEN

	Champion	Runner-Up
Division I-A:	Florida St	
Division I-AA:	Youngstown St	Marshall
Division II:	N Alabama	Indiana (PA)
Division III:	Mount Union	Rowan

Soccer

MEN

	Champion	Runner-Up
Division I:	Virginia	S Carolina
Division II:	Seattle Pacific	Southern Connecticut St
Division III:	UC San Diego	Williams

WOMEN

	Champion	Runner-Up
Division I:	N Carolina	George Mason
Division II:	Barry	Cal Poly-San Luis Obispo
Division III:	Trenton St	Plymouth St

Volleyball

WOMEN

	Champion	Runner-Up
Division I:	Long Beach St	Penn St
Division II:	N Michigan	Cal St-Bakersfield
Division III:	Washington (MO)	Juniata

Water Polo

MEN

Champion	Runner-Up
Stanford	Southern Cal

NCAA Team Champions (Cont.)

Winter 1993-1994

Basketball

MEN

	Champion	Runner-Up
Division I:	Arkansas	Duke
Division II:	Cal St-Bakersfield	Southern Indiana
Division III:	Lebanon Valley	New York University

WOMEN

	Champion	Runner-Up
Division I:	N Carolina	Louisiana Tech
Division II:	N Dakota St	Cal St-San Bernardino
Division III:	Capital (OH)	Washington (MO)

Fencing

Champion	Runner-Up
Notre Dame	Penn St

Gymnastics

MEN

Champion	Runner-Up
Nebraska	Stanford

WOMEN

Champion	Runner-Up
Utah	Alabama

Ice Hockey

MEN

	Champion	Runner-Up
Division I:	Lake Superior St	Boston University
Division II:	Bernidji St	AL-Huntsville
Division III:	WI-River Falls	WI-Superior

Rifle

Champion	Runner-Up
AK-Fairbanks	West Virginia

Skiing

Champion	Runner-Up
Vermont	Utah

Swimming and Diving

MEN

	Champion	Runner-Up
Division I:	Stanford	Texas
Division II:	Oakland	Cal St-Bakersfield
Division III:	Kenyon	UC-San Diego

WOMEN

	Champion	Runner-Up
Division I:	Stanford	Texas
Division II:	Oakland	Air Force
Division III:	Kenyon	Hope

Wrestling

MEN

	Champion	Runner-Up
Division I:	Oklahoma St	Iowa
Division II:	Central Oklahoma	Mankato St
Division III:	Ithaca	Wartburg

Winter 1993-1994 *(Cont.)*

Indoor Track

MEN

	Champion	Runner-Up
Division I:	Arkansas	Tennessee
Division II:	Abilene Christian	St Augustine's
Division III:	WI-La Crosse	Nebraska Wesleyan

WOMEN

	Champion	Runner-Up
Division I:	Louisiana St	Alabama
Division II:	Abilene Christian	Norfolk St
Division III:	WI-Oshkosh	Christopher Newport

Spring 1994

Baseball

MEN

	Champion	Runner-Up
Division I:	Oklahoma	Georgia Tech
Division II:	Central Missouri St	Florida Southern
Division III:	WI-Oshkosh	Wesleyan (CT)

Golf

MEN

	Champion	Runner-Up
Division I:	Stanford	Texas
Division II:	Columbus	N Florida
Division III:	Methodist	UC San Diego

WOMEN

Champion	Runner-Up
Arizona St	Southern Cal

Lacrosse

MEN

	Champion	Runner-Up
Division I:	Princeton	Virginia
Division II:	Springfield	New York Tech
Division III:	Salisbury St	Hobart

WOMEN

	Champion	Runner-Up
Division I:	Princeton	Maryland
Division III:	Trenton St	William Smith

Softball

WOMEN

	Champion	Runner-Up
Division I:	Arizona	Cal St-Northridge
Division II:	Merrimack	Humboldt St
Division III:	Trenton St	Bridgewater St (MA)

Tennis

MEN

	Champion	Runner-Up
Division I:	Southern Cal	Stanford
Division II:	Lander (SC)	Hampton
Division III:	Washington (MD)	Claremont-M-S

WOMEN

	Champion	Runner-Up
Division I:	Georgia	Stanford
Division II:	N Florida	Cal Poly Pomona
Division III:	UC-San Diego	Williams

Spring 1994 (Cont.)
Outdoor Track
MEN

	Champion	Runner-Up
Division I:	Arkansas	UTEP
Division II:	St Augustine's	Abilene Christian
Division III:	North Central	WI-La Crosse

WOMEN

Division I:	Louisiana St	Texas
Division II:	Alabama A&M	Abilene Christian
Division III:	Christopher Newport	WI-Oshkosh

Volleyball
MEN

Champion	Runner-Up
Penn St	UCLA

NCAA Division I Individual Champions

Fall 1993
Cross-Country
MEN

Champion	Runner-Up
Josephat Kapkory, Washington St	Jason Bunston, Arkansas

WOMEN

Champion	Runner-Up
Carole Zajac, Villanova	Jennifer Rhines, Villanova

Winter 1993-1994
Fencing
MEN

	Champion	Runner-Up
Sabre	Thomas Strzalkowski, Penn St	Beran Rose, Yale
Foil	Kwame van Leeuwen, Harvard	Andy Gearhart, Penn St
Épée	Harald Winkmann, Princeton	Ben Millett, Penn St

WOMEN

Foil	Olga Kalinovskaya, Penn St	Olga Chernyak, Penn St

Gymnastics
MEN

	Champion	Runner-Up
All-around	Dennis Harrison, Nebraska	Josh Stein, Stanford
Vault	Steve McCain, UCLA	Dennis Harrison, Nebraska
		Doug Macey, UCLA
Parallel bars	Richard Grace, Nebraska	Burkett Powell, Nebraska
		Steve McCain, UCLA
Horizontal bar	Jim Foody, UCLA	Dennis Harrison, Nebraska
Floor exercise	Mark Booth, Stanford	Blaine Wilson, Ohio St
		Dennis Harrison, Nebraska
		Jay Thornton, Iowa
		Greg Umphrey, UCLA
Pommel horse	Jason Bertram, California	Josh Stein, Stanford
Rings	Chris LaMorte, New Mexico	Garry Denk, Iowa

Gymnastics (Cont.)

WOMEN

	Champion	Runner-Up
All-around	Jenny Hansen, Kentucky	Agina Simpkins, Georgia
Balance beam	Jenny Hansen, Kentucky	Beth Wymer, Michigan
Uneven bars	Sandy Woolsey, Utah	Kim Kelly, Alabama
	Beth Wymer, Michigan	
	Lori Strong, Georgia	
Floor exercise	Hope Spivey-Sheeley, Georgia	Kim Kelly, Alabama
Vault	Jenny Hansen, Kentucky	Suzann Metz, Utah

Skiing

MEN

	Champion	Runner-Up
Slalom	Louis-Francois Gagnon, Utah	Mattais Erlandsson, New Mexico
Giant slalom	Erik Roland, Denver	Brett Grabowski, Vermont
Freestyle cross country	Niklas Skoglund, New Mexico	Pete Vordenberg, Michigan Tech
Classical cross country	Harvard Solbakken, Utah	Trond Nystad, Vermont

WOMEN

	Champion	Runner-Up
Slalom	Gibson LaFountaine, Vermont	Narcisa Sehovic, Denver
Giant slalom	Christl Hager, Utah	Kirsten Rogers, Middlebury
Freestyle cross country	Nina Hamilton, Vermont	Karianne Opgard, Vermont
Classical cross country	Mina Turvo, AK-Anchorage	Leanne Lubta, N Michigan

Wrestling

	Champion	Runner-Up
118 lb	Sam Henson, Clemson	Eric Akin, Iowa St
126 lb	David Hirsch, Cornell	Jody Staylor, Old Dominion
134 lb	T.J. Jaworsky, N Carolina	Babak Mohammadi, Oregon St
142 lb	Alan Fried, Oklahoma St	Gerry Abas, Fresno St
150 lb	Lincoln McIlravy, Iowa	Brian Harper, Michigan
158 lb	Pat Smith, Oklahoma St	Sean Bormet, Michigan
167 lb	Mark Branch, Oklahoma St	Laszlo Molnar, Cal St-Fullerton
177 lb	Dean Morrison, West Virginia	Reese Andy, Wyoming
190 lb	Joel Sharratt, Iowa	Andy Foster, Oklahoma
Heavyweight	Kerry McCoy, Penn St	Justin Greenlee, Northern Iowa

Swimming

MEN

	Champion	Time	Runner-Up	Time
50-yard freestyle	Brian Retterer, Stanford	19.45	Gustavo Borges, Michigan	19.50
100-yard freestyle	Gustavo Borges, Michigan	42.46	Joe Hudepohl, Stanford	42.91
200-yard freestyle	Gustavo Borges, Michigan	1:34.31	Joe Hudepohl, Stanford	1:34.69
			Ugur Taner, California	1:34.69
500-yard freestyle	Chad Carvin, Arizona	4:11.59*	Tom Dolan, Michigan	4:12.30
1650-yard freestyle	Chad Carvin, Arizona	14:34.91*	Matt Hooper, Texas	14:42.02
100-yard backstroke	Brian Retterer, Stanford	46.07	Derek Weatherford, Stanford	46.75
200-yard backstroke	Derek Weatherford, Stanford	1:42.18	Royce Sharp, Michigan	1:42.45
100-yard breaststroke	Tyler Mayfield, Stanford	53.73	Travis Myers, Alabama	53.93
200-yard breaststroke	Kurt Grote, Stanford	1:56.79	Tyler Mayfield, Stanford	1:57.67
100-yard butterfly	Rafal Szukala, Iowa	47.43	Stephen Clarke, Florida	47.47
200-yard butterfly	Ugur Taner, California	1:44.54	Ray Carey, Stanford	1:44.74
200-yard IM	Greg Burgess, Florida	1:43.66	Paul Nelson, Minnesota	1:45.33
400-yard IM	Greg Burgess, Florida	3:40.64*	Tom Dolan, Michigan	3:43.79

	Champion	Pts	Runner-Up	Pts
1-meter diving†	Chemi Gil, Miami (FL)	562.50	Brian Earley, Southern Cal	562.45
3-meter diving†	Evan Stewart, Tennessee	614.65	Brian Earley, Southern Cal	609.25
Platform†	Brian Earley, Southern Cal	817.90	Tom Caruso, Arkansas	687.30

*Meet Record.

†Scoring based on 22 dives

Swimming (Cont.)

WOMEN

	Champion	Time	Runner-Up	Time
50-yard freestyle	Amy Van Dyken, Colorado St	21.77*	Jenny Thompson, Stanford	22.26
100-yard freestyle	Jenny Thompson, Stanford	47.74	Nicole Haislett, Florida	48.29
			Amy Van Dyken, Colorado St	48.29
200-yard freestyle	Nicole Haislett, Florida	1:44.51	Whitney Hedgepeth, Texas	1:45.90
500-yard freestyle	Nicole Haislett, Florida	4:43.36	Leslie Mix, Tennessee	4:43.41
1650-yard freestyle	Tobie Smith, Texas	16:07.26	Leslie Mix, Tennessee	16:14.16
100-yard backstroke	Lea Loveless, Stanford	53.51	Janie Wagstaff, Florida	53.67
200-yard backstroke	Whitney Hedgepeth, Texas	1:53.05	Lea Loveless, Stanford	1:54.21
100-yard breaststroke	Beata Kaszuba, Arizona St	1:00.46*	Penelope Heyns, Nebraska	1:01.43
200-yard breaststroke	Kristine Quance, Southern Cal	2:10.69*	Beata Kaszuba, Arizona St	2:10.86
100-yard butterfly	Jenny Thompson, Stanford	51.81	Amy Van Dyken, Colorado St	52.07
200-yard butterfly	Berit Puggaard, SMU	1:57.99	Becky Crowe, Stanford	1:58.66
200-yard IM	Kristine Quance, Southern Cal	1:58.89	Lea Loveless, Stanford	1:59.14
400-yard IM	Kristine Quance, Southern Cal	4:08.71	Anne Kampfe, Michigan	4:13.93

	Champion	Pts	Runner-Up	Pts
1-meter diving#	Vanessa Thelin, BYU	449.80	Cheril Santini, SMU	436.20
3-meter diving†	Robin Carter, Texas	522.10	Kristen Kane, Indiana	515.25
Platform†	Susie Ryan, Louisiana St	584.65	Kathy Carboy, Louisiana St	572.60

*Meet Record
#Scoring based on 20 dives
†Scoring based on 22 dives

Indoor Track

MEN

	Champion	Mark	Runner-Up	Mark
55-meter dash	Greg Saddler, Mississippi	6.11	Tim Harden, Kentucky	6.13
55-meter hurdles	Robert Foster, Fresno St	7.11	Philip Riley, Florida St	7.18
200-meter dash	Chris Nelloms, Ohio St	20.60	Andrew Tynes, UTEP	20.85
400-meter dash	Calvin Davis, Arkansas	46.18	Chris Jones, Rice	46.37
800-meter run	Jose Parrilla, Tennessee	1:47.77	Marko Koers, Illinois	1:48.30
Mile run	Niall Bruton, Arkansas	3:59.34	Andrew Keith, Providence	4:00.55
3000-meter run	Josephat Kapkory, Wash St	7:50.90*	Jim Svenoy, UTEP	7:51.24
5000-meter run	Jason Bunston, Arkansas	13:48.07	Sean Found, Colorado	13:51.11
High jump	Randy Jenkins, Tennessee	7 ft 7 in	Ray Doakes, Arkansas	7 ft 6 in
Long jump	Erick Walder, Arkansas	27 ft 8 in	Kareem Streete-Thompson, Rice	26 ft 8¼ in
Triple jump	Erick Walder, Arkansas	56 ft 6¾ in	Jerome Romain, Arkansas	55 ft 2¼ in
Shot put	John Godina, UCLA	65 ft 8¾ in	Brent Noon, Georgia	64 ft 8½ in
Pole vault	Lawrence Johnson, Tenn	19 ft 1½ in*	Nick Hysong, Arizona St	18 ft ½ in
35-pound wt throw	Ron Willis, S Carolina	71 ft 11 in	Brian Murer, SMU	71 ft 8¾ in

WOMEN

	Champion	Mark	Runner-Up	Mark
55-meter dash	Holli Hyche, Indiana St	6.70	Cheryl Taplin, Louisiana St	6.72
55-meter hurdles	Dionne Rose, Middle Tenn St	7.60	Tonya Williams, Illinois	7.76
200-meter dash	Holli Hyche, Indiana St	22.90*	Flirtisha Harris, Seton Hall	23.11
400-meter dash	Flirtisha Harris, Seton Hall	52.11	Janeen Jones, Georgia Tech	52.71
800-meter run	Amy Wickus, Wisconsin	2:02.05*	Karen Bennett, Arizona	2:04.27
Mile run	Amy Rudolph, Providence	4:37.64	Candace Lessmeister, Rice	4:41.41
3000-meter run	Kay Gooch, Oklahoma	8:58.85	Tonya Todd, Brigham Young	9:20.68
5000-meter run	Brenda Sleeuwenhoek, Ariz	16:46.54	Louise Watson, Stanford	16:50.55
High jump	Amy Acuff, UCLA	6 ft 2¼ in	Sherry Gould, Virginia	6 ft 1½ in
			J.C. Broughton, Arizona	6 ft 1½ in
Long jump	Daphnie Saunders, LSU	22 ft 1 in*	Dedra Davis, Tennessee	22 ft ¼ in
Triple jump	Telisa Young, Texas	43 ft 3¾ in	Nicola Martial, Nebraska	43 ft 1 in
Shot put	Eileen Vanisi, Texas	58 ft 1¾ in	Danyel Mitchell, Louisiana St	55 ft 10 ¼ in

*Meet record

Rifle

	Champion	Pts	Runner-Up	Pts
Smallbore	Cory Brunetti, AK-Fairbanks	1173	Jean Foster, West Virginia	1173
Air rifle	Nancy Napolski, Kentucky	391	Robin Orth, Air Force	389

NCAA Division I Individual Champions *(Cont.)*

Golf

MEN

Champion	Score	Runner-Up	Score
Justin Leonard, Texas	271	Alan Bratton, Oklahoma St	276

WOMEN

Champion	Score	Runner-Up	Score
Emilee Klein, Arizona St	286	Wendy Ward, Arizona St	288

Outdoor Track

MEN

	Champion	Mark	Runner-Up	Mark
100-meter dash	Sam Jefferson	10.12w	Tim Harden, Kentucky	10.13w
200-meter dash	Andrew Tynes, UTEP	20.20w	Aki Bradley, Mississippi St	20.27w
400-meter dash	Derek Mills, Georgia Tech	45.06	Chris Jones, Rice	45.11
800-meter run	Jose Parilla, Tennessee	1:46.01	Marko Koers, Illinois	1:46.44
1,500-meter run	Graham Hood, Arkansas	3:42.10	Erik Nedeau, Northeastern	3:42.44
3,000-met. steeplech.	Jim Svenoy, UTEP	8:41.22	Mark Johansen, BYU	8:45.58
5,000-meter run	Brian Baker, Arkansas	14:22.09	Jason Bunston, Arkansas	14:25.27
10,000-meter run	Teddy Mitchell, Arkansas	29:39.54	Josephat Kapkory, Wash St	29:45.25
110-meter hurdles	Robert Foster, Fresno St	13.53	Jeff Jackson, Baylor	13.56
400-meter hurdles	Octavius Terry, Georgia Tech	49.85	Mitchel Francis, Clemson	49.86
High jump	Randy Jenkins, Tennessee	7 ft 7 in	Steve Smith, Indiana	7 ft 7 in
Pole vault	Nick Hysong, Arizona St	18 ft 8¼ in	Bill Deering, Miami (FL)	18 8¼ in
Long jump	Erick Walder, Arkansas	27 ft 4 ½in	Roland McGhee, Midd TN St	27 ft 4 ½in
Triple jump	Erick Walder, Arkansas	55 ft 5¾ in	Jerome Romain, Arkansas	55 ft 1 in
Shot put	Brent Noon, Georgia	67 ft 9¾ in	Kjell Ove Hauge, UTEP	65 ft 10¼ in
Discus throw	John Godina, UCLA	198 ft 5 in	Gregg Hart, Indiana	190 ft 10 in
Hammer throw	Balazs Kiss, Southern Cal	245 ft 6 in	Alex Papadimitriou, UTEP	237 ft 7 in
Javelin throw	Todd Reich, Fresno St	266 ft 9in*	Derek Trafas, Florida	258 ft 1 in
Decathlon	Enoch Borozinski, Nevada	7870	Robert Pendergist, Mt St Mary's	7837

WOMEN

	Champion	Mark	Runner-Up	Mark
100-meter dash	Holli Hyche, Indiana St	11.23	Cheryl Taplin, Louisiana St	11.25
200-meter dash	Merlene Frazer, Texas	22.49w	Holli Hyche, Indiana St	22.76w
400-meter dash	Flirtisha Harris, Seton Hall	51.65	Janeen Jones, Georgia Tech	52.11
800-meter run	Inez Turner, SW Texas St	2:01.50	Amy Wickus, Wisconsin	2:02.70
1,500-meter run	Amy Rudolph, Providence	4:17.99	Amy Wickus, Wisconsin	4:18.83
3,000-meter run	Karen Hecox, UCLA	9:22.63	Kay Gooch, Oklahoma	9:27.07
5,000-meter run	Jen Rhines, Villanova	16:21.60	Carole Zajac, Villanova	16:26.19
10,000-meter run	Carole Zajac, Villanova	33:32.36	Liz Scanlon, Oklahoma	34:11.47
100-meter hurdles	Gillian Russell, Miami (FL)	12.97	Kim Carson, Louisiana St	13.37
400-meter hurdles	Debbie Parris, Louisiana St	55.54	Keisha Marvin, UCLA	56.62
High jump	Gai Kapernick, Louisiana St	6 ft 2¼ in	Amy Acuff, UCLA	6 ft 2¼ in
Long jump	Dedra Davis, Tennessee	22 ft 5¾ inw	Marion Jones, N Carolina	22 ft 1¾ in
Triple jump	Nicola Martial, Nebraska	44 ft 11¾ in	Telisa Young, Texas	44 ft 4¾ in
Shot put	Eileen Vanisi, Texas	58 ft 2 ½ in*	Valeyta Althouse, UCLA	57 ft 6¼in
Discus throw	Danyel Mitchell, Louisiana St	193 ft 10 in	Alana Preston, Tennessee	173 ft 7 in
Javelin throw	Valerie Tulloch, Rice	187 ft 7 in	Jen McCormick, Stanford	172 ft 1 in
Heptathlon	Diane Guthrie, George Mason	6032	Kelly Blair, Oregon	5877

*Meet Record. w=wind-aided.

Tennis

MEN

	Champion	Score	Runner-Up
Singles	Mark Merklein, Florida	(6-2, 6-7, 6-4)	Wayne Black, Southern Cal
Doubles	Laurent Miquelard & Joe Simmons, MIss St	(7-6, 2-6, 6-3)	Wayne Black & Jon Leach, Southern Cal

WOMEN

	Champion	Score	Runner-Up
Singles	Angela Lettiere, Georgia	(7-6, 6-2)	Keri Phebus, UCLA
Doubles	Rebecca Jensen & Nora Koves, Kansas	(6-4, 7-5)	Marie-Laure Bougnol & Pascale Piquemal, Mississippi

FOR THE RECORD·Year by Year

CHAMPIONSHIP RESULTS

Baseball

Men

DIVISION I

Year	Champion	Coach	Score	Runner-Up	Most Outstanding Player
1947	California*	Clint Evans	8-7	Yale	No award
1948	Southern Cal	Sam Barry	9-2	Yale	No award
1949	Texas*	Bibb Falk	10-3	Wake Forest	Charles Teague, Wake Forest, 2B
1950	Texas	Bibb Falk	3-0	Washington St	Ray VanCleef, Rutgers, CF
1951	Oklahoma*	Jack Baer	3-2	Tennnessee	Sidney Hatfield, Tennessee, P-1B
1952	Holy Cross	Jack Barry	8-4	Missouri	James O'Neill, Holy Cross, P
1953	Michigan	Ray Fisher	7-5	Texas	J. L. Smith, Texas, P
1954	Missouri	John "Hi" Simmons	4-1	Rollins	Tom Yewcic, Michigan St, C
1955	Wake Forest	Taylor Sanford	7-6	Western Michigan	Tom Borland, Oklahoma St, P
1956	Minnesota	Dick Siebert	12-1	Arizona	Jerry Thomas, Minnesota, P
1957	California*	George Wolfman	1-0	Penn St	Cal Emery, Penn St, P-1B
1958	Southern Cal	Rod Dedeaux	8-7†	Missouri	Bill Thom, Southern Cal, P
1959	Oklahoma St	Toby Greene	5-3	Arizona	Jim Dobson, Oklahoma St, 3B
1960	Minnesota	Dick Siebert	2-1‡	Southern Cal	John Erickson, Minnesota, 2B
1961	Southern Cal*	Rod Dedeaux	1-0	Oklahoma St	Littleton Fowler, Oklahoma St, P
1962	Michigan	Don Lund	5-4	Santa Clara	Bob Garibaldi, Santa Clara, P
1963	Southern Cal	Rod Dedeaux	5-2	Arizona	Bud Hollowell, Southern Cal, C
1964	Minnesota	Dick Siebert	5-1	Missouri	Joe Ferris, Maine, P
1965	Arizona St	Bobby Winkles	2-1#	Ohio St	Sal Bando, Arizona St, 3B
1966	Ohio St	Marty Karow	8-2	Oklahoma St	Steve Arlin, Ohio St, P
1967	Arizona St	Bobby Winkles	11-2	Houston	Ron Davini, Arizona St, C
1968	Southern Cal*	Rod Dedeaux	4-3	Southern Illinois	Bill Seinsoth, Southern Cal, 1B
1969	Arizona St	Bobby Winkles	10-1	Tulsa	John Dolinsek, Arizona St, LF
1970	Southern Cal	Rod Dedeaux	2-1	Florida St	Gene Ammann, Florida St, P
1971	Southern Cal	Rod Dedeaux	7-2	Southern Illinois	Jerry Tabb, Tulsa, P
1972	Southern Cal	Rod Dedeaux	1-0	Arizona St	Russ McQueen, Southern Cal, P
1973	Southern Cal*	Rod Dedeaux	4-3	Arizona St	Dave Winfield, Minnesota, P-OF
1974	Southern Cal	Rod Dedeaux	7-3	Miami (FL)	George Milke, Southern Cal, P
1975	Texas	Cliff Gustafson	5-1	S Carolina	Mickey Reichenbach, Texas, 1B
1976	Arizona	Jerry Kindall	7-1	Eastern Michigan	Steve Powers, Arizona, P-DH
1977	Arizona St	Jim Brock	2-1	S Carolina	Bob Horner, Arizona St, 3B
1978	Southern Cal*	Rod Dedeaux	10-3	Arizona St	Rod Boxberger, Southern Cal, P
1979	Cal St-Fullerton	Augie Garrido	2-1	Arkansas	Tony Hudson, Cal St-Fullerton, P
1980	Arizona	Jerry Kindall	5-3	Hawaii	Terry Francona, Arizona, LF
1981	Arizona St	Jim Brock	7-4	Oklahoma St	Stan Holmes, Arizona St, LF
1982	Miami (FL)*	Ron Fraser	9-3	Wichita St	Dan Smith, Miami (FL), P
1983	Texas*	Cliff Gustafson	4-3	Alabama	Calvin Schiraldi, Texas, P
1984	Cal St-Fullerton	Augie Garrido	3-1	Texas	John Fishel, Cal St-Fullerton, LF
1985	Miami (FL)	Ron Fraser	10-6	Texas	Greg Ellena, Miami (FL), DH
1986	Arizona	Jerry Kindall	10-2	Florida St	Mike Senne, Arizona, LF
1987	Stanford	Mark Marquess	9-5	Oklahoma St	Paul Carey, Stanford, RF
1988	Stanford	Mark Marquess	9-4	Arizona St	Lee Plemel, Stanford, P
1989	Wichita St	Gene Stephenson	5-3	Texas	Greg Brummett, Wichita St, P
1990	Georgia	Steve Webber	2-1	Oklahoma St	Mike Rebhan, Georgia, P
1991	Louisiana St	Skip Bertman	6-3	Wichita St	Gary Hymel, Louisiana St, C
1992	Pepperdine	Andy Lopez	3-2	Cal St-Fullerton	Phil Nevin, Cal St-Fullerton, 3B
1993	Louisiana St	Skip Bertman	8-0	Wichita St	Todd Walker, Louisiana St, 2B
1994	Oklahoma	Larry Cochell	13-5	Georgia Tech	Chip Glass, Oklahoma, CF

*Undefeated teams in College World Series play. †12 innings. ‡10 innings. #15 innings.

DIVISION II

Year	Champion	Year	Champion	Year	Champion	Year	Champion
1968	Chapman*	1975	Florida Southern	1982	UC-Riverside*	1989	Cal Poly-SLO
1969	Illinois St*	1976	Cal Poly-Pomona	1983	Cal Poly-Pomona*	1990	Jacksonville St
1970	Cal St-Northridge	1977	UC-Riverside	1984	Cal St-Northridge	1991	Jacksonville St
1971	Florida Southern	1978	Florida Southern	1985	Florida Southern*	1992	Tampa*
1972	Florida Southern	1979	Valdosta St	1986	Troy St	1993	Tampa
1973	UC-Irvine*	1980	Cal Poly-Pomona*	1987	Troy St*	1994	Central Missouri St
1974	UC-Irvine	1981	Florida Southern*	1988	Florida Southern*		

*Undefeated teams.

DIVISION III

Year	Champion	Year	Champion	Year	Champion
1976	Cal St-Stanislaus	1982	Eastern Connecticut St	1989	NC Wesleyan
1977	Cal St-Stanislaus	1983	Marietta	1990	Eastern Connecticut St
1978	Glassboro St	1984	Ramapo	1991	Southern Maine
1979	Glassboro St	1985	WI-Oshkosh	1992	William Patterson
1980	Ithaca	1986	Marietta	1993	Montclair St
1981	Marietta	1987	Montclair St	1994	WI-Oshkosh
		1988	Ithaca		

Cross-Country

Men

DIVISION I

Year	Champion	Coach	Pts	Runner-Up	Pts	Individual Champion	Time
1938	Indiana	Earle Hayes	51	Notre Dame	61	Greg Rice, Notre Dame	20:12.9
1939	Michigan St	Lauren Brown	54	Wisconsin	57	Walter Mehl, Wisconsin	20:30.9
1940	Indiana	Earle Hayes	65	Eastern Michigan	68	Gilbert Dodds, Ashland	20:30.2
1941	Rhode Island	Fred Tootell	83	Penn St	110	Fred Wilt, Indiana	20:30.1
1942	Indiana	Earle Hayes	57			Oliver Hunter, Notre Dame	20:18.0
	Penn St	Charles Werner	57				
1943	No meet						
1944	Drake	Bill Easton	25	Notre Dame	64	Fred Feiler, Drake	21:04.2
1945	Drake	Bill Easton	50	Notre Dame	65	Fred Feiler, Drake	21:14.2
1946	Drake	Bill Easton	42	NYU	98	Quentin Brelsford, Ohio Wesleyan	20:22.9
1947	Penn St	Charles Werner	60	Syracuse	72	Jack Milne, N Carolina	20:41.1
1948	Michigan St	Karl Schlademan	41	Wisconsin	69	Robert Black, Rhode Island	19:52.3
1949	Michigan St	Karl Schlademan	59	Syracuse	81	Robert Black, Rhode Island	20:25.7
1950	Penn St	Charles Werner	53	Michigan St	55	Herb Semper Jr, Kansas	20:31.7
1951	Syracuse	Robert Grieve	80	Kansas	118	Herb Semper Jr, Kansas	20:09.5
1952	Michigan St	Karl Schlademan	65	Indiana	68	Charles Capozzoli, Georgetown	19:36.7
1953	Kansas	Bill Easton	70	Indiana	82	Wes Santee, Kansas	19:43.5
1954	Oklahoma St	Ralph Higgins	61	Syracuse	118	Allen Frame, Kansas	19:54.2
1955	Michigan St	Karl Schlademan	46	Kansas	68	Charles Jones, Iowa	19:57.4
1956	Michigan St	Karl Schlademan	28	Kansas	88	Walter McNew, Texas	19:55.7
1957	Notre Dame	Alex Wilson	121	Michigan St	127	Max Truex, Southern Cal	19:12.3
1958	Michigan St	Francis Dittrich	79	Western Michigan	104	Crawford Kennedy, Michigan State	20:07.1
1959	Michigan St	Francis Dittrich	44	Houston	120	Al Lawrence, Houston	20:35.7
1960	Houston	John Morriss	54	Michigan St	80	Al Lawrence, Houston	19:28.2
1961	Oregon St	Sam Bell	68	San Jose St	82	Dale Story, Oregon St	19:46.6
1962	San Jose St	Dean Miller	58	Villanova	69	Tom O'Hara, Loyola (IL)	19:20.3
1963	San Jose St	Dean Miller	53	Oregon	68	Victor Zwolak, Villanova	19:35.0
1964	Western Miichigan	George Dales	86	Oregon	116	Elmore Banton, Ohio	20:07.5
1965	Western Miichigan	George Dales	81	Northwestern	114	John Lawson, Kansas	29:24.0
1966	Villanova	James Elliott	79	Kansas St	155	Gerry Lindgren, Washington St	29:01.4
1967	Villanova	James Elliott	91	Air Force	96	Gerry Lindgren, Washington St	30:45.6
1968	Villanova	James Elliott	78	Stanford	100	Michael Ryan, Air Force	29:16.8
1969	UTEP	Wayne Vandenburg	74	Villanova	88	Gerry Lindgren, Washington St	28:59.2
1970	Villanova	James Elliott	85	Oregon	86	Steve Prefontaine, Oregon	28:00.2
1971	Oregon	Bill Dellinger	83	Washington St	122	Steve Prefontaine, Oregon	29:14.0
1972	Tennessee	Stan Huntsman	134	E Tennessee St	148	Neil Cusack, E Tennessee St	28:23.0
1973	Oregon	Bill Dellinger	89	UTEP	157	Steve Prefontaine, Oregon	28:14.0
1974	Oregon	Bill Dellinger	77	Western Kentucky	110	Nick Rose, Western Kentucky	29:22.0
1975	UTEP	Ted Banks	88	Washington St	92	Craig Virgin, Illinois	28:23.3

Men (Cont.)

Year	Champion	Coach	Pts	Runner-Up	Pts	Individual Champion	Time
1976	UTEP	Ted Banks	62	Oregon	117	Henry Rono, Washington St	28:06.6
1977	Oregon	Bill Dellinger	100	UTEP	105	Henry Rono, Washington St	28:33.5
1978	UTEP	Ted Banks	56	Oregon	72	Alberto Salazar, Oregon	29:29.7
1979	UTEP	Ted Banks	86	Oregon	93	Henry Rono, Washington St	28:19.6
1980	UTEP	Ted Banks	58	Arkansas	152	Suleiman Nyambui, UTEP	29:04.0
1981	UTEP	Ted Banks	17	Providence	109	Mathews Motshwarateu, UTEP	28:45.6
1982	Wisconsin	Dan McClimon	59	Providence	138	Mark Scrutton, Colorado	30:12.6
1983	Vacated			Wisconsin	164	Zakarie Barie, UTEP	29:20.0
1984	Arkansas	John McDonnell	101	Arizona	111	Ed Eyestone, Brigham Young	29:28.8
1985	Wisconsin	Martin Smith	67	Arkansas	104	Timothy Hacker, Wisconsin	29:17.88
1986	Arkansas	John McDonnell	69	Dartmouth	141	Aaron Ramirez, Arizona	30:27.53
1987	Arkansas	John McDonnell	87	Dartmouth	119	Joe Falcon, Arkansas	29:14.97
1988	Wisconsin	Martin Smith	105	Northern Arizona	160	Robert Kennedy, Indiana	29:20.0
1989	Iowa St	Bill Bergan	54	Oregon	72	John Nuttall, Iowa St	29:30.55
1990	Arkansas	John McDonnell	68	Iowa St	96	Jonah Koech, Iowa St	29:05.0
1991	Arkansas	John McDonnell	52	Iowa St	114	Sean Dollman, Western Ky	30:17.1
1992	Arkansas	John McDonnell	46	Wisconsin	87	Bob Kennedy, Indiana	30:15.3
1993	Arkansas	John McDonnell	31	Brigham Young	153	Josephat Kapkory, Wash St	29:32.4

DIVISION II

Year	Champion	Year	Champion
1958	Northern Illinois	1976	UC-Irvine
1959	S Dakota St	1977	Eastern Illinois
1960	Central St (OH)	1978	Cal Poly-SLO
1961	Southern Illinois	1979	Cal Poly-SLO
1962	Central St (OH)	1980	Humboldt St
1963	Emporia St	1981	Millersville
1964	Kentucky St	1982	Eastern Washington
1965	San Diego St	1983	Cal Poly-Pomona
1966	San Diego St	1984	SE Missouri St
1967	San Diego St	1985	S Dakota St
1968	Eastern Illinois	1986	Edinboro
1969	Eastern Illinois	1987	Edinboro
1970	Eastern Michigan	1988	Edinboro/ Mankato St
1971	Cal St-Fullerton	1989	S Dakota St
1972	N Dakota St	1990	Edinboro
1973	S Dakota St	1991	MA-Lowell
1974	SW Missouri St	1992	Adams St
		1993	Adams St

DIVISION III

Year	Champion	Year	Champion
1973	Ashland	1983	Brandeis
1974	Mount Union	1984	St Thomas (MN)
1975	North Central	1985	Luther
1976	North Central	1986	St Thomas (MN)
1977	Occidental	1987	North Central
1978	North Central	1988	WI-Oshkosh
1979	North Central	1989	WI-Oshkosh
1980	Carleton	1990	WI-Oshkosh
1981	North Central	1991	Rochester
1982	North Central	1992	North Central
		1993	North Central

Women
DIVISION I

Year	Champion	Coach	Pts	Runner-Up	Pts	Individual Champion	Time
1981	Virginia	John Vasvary	36	Oregon	83	Betty Springs, N Carolina St	16:19.0
1982	Virginia	Martin Smith	48	Stanford	91	Lesley Welch, Virginia	16:39.7
1983	Oregon	Tom Heinonen	95	Stanford	98	Betty Springs, N Carolina St	16:30.7
1984	Wisconsin	Peter Tegen	63	Stanford	89	Cathy Branta, Wisconsin	16:15.6
1985	Wisconsin	Peter Tegen	58	Iowa St	98	Suzie Tuffey, N Carolina St	16:22.5
1986	Texas	Terry Crawford	62	Wisconsin	64	Angela Chalmers, N Arizona	16:55.49

Cross Country (Cont.)

Women (Cont.)

DIVISION I (Cont.)

Year	Champion	Coach	Pts	Runner-Up	Pts	Individual Champion	Time
1987	Oregon	Tom Heinonen	97	N Carolina St	99	Kimberly Betz, Indiana	16:10.85
1988	Kentucky	Don Weber	75	Oregon	128	Michelle Dekkers, Indiana	16:30.0
1989	Villanova	Marty Stern	99	Kentucky	168	Vicki Huber, Villanova	15:59.86
1990	Villanova	Marty Stern	82	Providence	172	Sonia O'Sullivan, Villanova	16:06.0
1991	Villanova	Marty Stern	85	Arkansas	168	Sonia O'Sullivan, Villanova	16:30.3
1992	Villanova	Marty Stern	123	Arkansas	130	Carole Zajac, Villanova	17:01.9
1993	Villanova	Marty Stern	66	Arkansas	71	Carole Zajac, Villanova	16:40.3

DIVISION II

Year	Champion	Year	Champion	Year	Champion
1981	S Dakota St	1985	Cal Poly-SLO	1989	Cal Poly-SLO
1982	Cal Poly-SLO	1986	Cal Poly-SLO	1990	Cal Poly-SLO
1983	Cal Poly-SLO	1987	Cal Poly-SLO	1991	Cal Poly-SLO
1984	Cal Poly-SLO	1988	Cal Poly-SLO	1992	Adams St
				1993	Adams St

DIVISION III

Year	Champion	Year	Champion	Year	Champion
1981	Central (IA)	1986	St Thomas (MN)	1990	Cortland St
1982	St Thomas (MN)	1987	St Thomas (MN)	1991	WI-Oshkosh
1983	WI-La Crosse		WI-Oshkosh	1992	Cortland St
1984	St Thomas (MN)	1988	WI-Oshkosh	1993	Cortland St
1985	Franklin & Marshall	1989	Cortland St		

Fencing

Men

TEAM CHAMPIONS

Year	Champion	Coach	Pts	Runner-Up	Pts
1941	Northwestern	Henry Zettleman	28½	Illinois	27
1942	Ohio St	Frank Riebel	34	St John's (NY)	33½
1943-1946	No tournament				
1947	NYU	Martinez Castello	72	Chicago	50½
1948	CCNY	James Montague	30	Navy	28
1949	Army	Servando Velarde	63		
	Rutgers	Donald Cetrulo	63		
1950	Navy	Joseph Fiems	67½	NYU	66½
				Rutgers	66½
1951	Columbia	Servando Velarde	69	Pennsylvania	64
1952	Columbia	Servando Velarde	71	NYU	69
1953	Pennsylvania	Lajos Csiszar	94	Navy	86
1954	Columbia	Irving DeKoff	61		
	NYU	Hugo Castello	61		
1955	Columbia	Irving DeKoff	62	Cornell	57
1956	Illinois	Maxwell Garret	90	Columbia	88
1957	NYU	Hugo Castello	65	Columbia	64
1958	Illinois	Maxwell Garret	47	Columbia	43
1959	Navy	Andre Deladrier	72	NYU	65
1960	NYU	Hugo Castello	65	Navy	57
1961	NYU	Hugo Castello	79	Princeton	68
1962	Navy	Andre Deladrier	76	NYU	74
1963	Columbia	Irving DeKoff	55	Navy	50
1964	Princeton	Stan Sieja	81	NYU	79
1965	Columbia	Irving DeKoff	76	NYU	74
1966	NYU	Hugo Castello	5-0	Army	5-2
1967	NYU	Hugo Castello	72	Pennsylvania	64
1968	Columbia	Louis Bankuti	92	NYU	87
1969	Pennsylvania	Lajos Csiszar	54	Harvard	43
1970	NYU	Hugo Castello	71	Columbia	63
1971	NYU	Hugo Castello	68		
	Columbia	Louis Bankuti	68		

TEAM CHAMPIONS (Cont.)

Year	Champion	Coach	Pts	Runner-Up	Pts
1972	Detroit	Richard Perry	73	NYU	70
1973	NYU	Hugo Castello	76	Pennsylvania	71
1974	NYU	Hugo Castello	92	Wayne St (MI)	87
1975	Wayne St (MI)	Istvan Danosi	89	Cornell	83
1976	NYU	Herbert Cohen	79	Wayne St (MI)	77
1977	Notre Dame	Michael DeCicco	114*	NYU	114
1978	Notre Dame	Michael DeCicco	121	Pennsylvania	110
1979	Wayne St (MI)	Istvan Danosi	119	Notre Dame	108
1980	Wayne St (MI)	Istvan Danosi	111	Pennsylvania	106
				MIT	106
1981	Pennsylvania	Dave Micahnik	113	Wayne St (MI)	111
1982	Wayne St (MI)	Istvan Danosi	85	Clemson	77
1983	Wayne St (MI)	Aladar Kogler	86	Notre Dame	80
1984	Wayne St (MI)	Gil Pezza	69	Penn St	50
1985	Wayne St (MI)	Gil Pezza	141	Notre Dame	140
1986	Notre Dame	Michael DeCicco	151	Columbia	141
1987	Columbia	George Kolombatovich	86	Pennsylvania	78
1988	Columbia	George Kolombatovich Aladar Kogler	90	Notre Dame	83
1989	Columbia	George Kolombatovich Aladar Kogler	88	Penn St	85
1990	Penn St	Emmanuil Kaidanov	36	Columbia-Barnard	35
1991	Penn St	Emmanuil Kaidanov	4700	Columbia-Barnard	4200
1992	Columbia-Barnard	George Kolombatovich/ Aladar Kogler	4150	Penn St	3646
1993	Columbia-Barnard	George Kolumbatovich Aladar Kogler	4525	Penn St	4500
1994	Notre Dame	Michael DeCicco	4350	Penn St	4075

*Tie broken by a fence-off.

Note: Beginning in 1990, men's and women's combined teams competed for the national championship.

INDIVIDUAL CHAMPIONS

Foil	Sabre	Épée
1941....Edward McNamara, Northwestern	William Meyer, Dartmouth	G. H. Boland, Illinois
1942....Byron Kreiger, Wayne St (MI)	Andre Deladrier, St John's (NY)	Ben Burtt, Ohio St
1947....Abraham Balk, NYU	Oscar Parsons, Temple	Abraham Balk, NYU
1948....Albert Axelrod, CCNY	James Day, Navy	William Bryan, Navy
1949....Ralph Tedeschi, Rutgers	Alex Treves, Rutgers	Richard C. Bowman, Army
1950....Robert Nielsen, Columbia	Alex Treves, Rutgers	Thomas Stuart, Navy
1951....Robert Nielsen, Columbia	Chamberless Johnston, Princeton	Daniel Chafetz, Columbia
1952....Harold Goldsmith, CCNY	Frank Zimolzak, Navy	James Wallner, NYU
1953....Ed Nober, Brooklyn	Robert Parmacek, Pennsylvania	Jack Tori, Pennsylvania
1954....Robert Goldman, Pennsylvania	Steve Sobel, Columbia	Henry Kolowrat, Princeton
1955....Herman Velasco, Illinois	Barry Pariser, Columbia	Donald Tadrawski, Notre Dame
1956....Ralph DeMarco, Columbia	Gerald Kaufman, Columbia	Kinmont Hoitsma, Princeton
1957....Bruce Davis, Wayne St (MI)	Bernie Balaban, NYU	James Margolis, Columbia
1958....Bruce Davis, Wayne St (MI)	Art Schankin, Illinois	Roland Wommack, Navy
1959....Joe Paletta, Navy	Al Morales, Navy	Roland Wommack, Navy
1960....Gene Glazer, NYU	Mike Desaro, NYU	Gil Eisner, NYU
1961....Herbert Cohen, NYU	Israel Colon, NYU	Jerry Halpern, NYU
1962....Herbert Cohen, NYU	Barton Nisonson, Columbia	Thane Hawkins, Navy
1963....Jay Lustig, Columbia	Bela Szentivanyi, Wayne St (MI)	Larry Crum, Navy
1964....Bill Hicks, Princeton	Craig Bell, Illinois	Paul Pesthy, Rutgers
1965....Joe Nalven, Columbia	Howard Goodman, NYU	Paul Pesthy, Rutgers
1966....Al Davis, NYU	Paul Apostol, NYU	Bernhardt Hermann, Iowa
1967....Mike Gaylor, NYU	Todd Makler, Pennsylvania	George Masin, NYU
1968....Gerard Esponda, San Francisco	Todd Makler, Pennsylvania	Don Sieja, Cornell
1969....Anthony Kestler, Columbia	Norman Braslow, Pennsylvania	James Wetzler, Pennsylvania
1970....Walter Krause, NYU	Bruce Soriano, Columbia	John Nadas, Case Reserve

INDIVIDUAL CHAMPIONS (Cont.)

Foil	Sabre	Épée
1971....Tyrone Simmons, Detroit	Bruce Soriano, Columbia	George Szunyogh, NYU
1972....Tyrone Simmons, Detroit	Bruce Soriano, Columbia	Ernesto Fernandez, Pennsylvania
1973....Brooke Makler, Pennsylvania	Peter Westbrock, NYU	Risto Hurme, NYU
1974....Greg Benko, Wayne St (MI)	Steve Danosi, Wayne St (MI)	Risto Hurme, NYU
1975....Greg Benko, Wayne St (MI)	Yuri Rabinovich, Wayne St (MI)	Risto Hurme, NYU
1976....Greg Benko, Wayne St (MI)	Brian Smith, Columbia	Randy Eggleton, Pennsylvania
1977....Pat Gerard, Notre Dame	Mike Sullivan, Notre Dame	Hans Wieselgren, NYU
1978....Ernest Simon, Wayne St (MI)	Mike Sullivan, Notre Dame	Bjorne Vaggo, Notre Dame
1979....Andrew Bonk, Notre Dame	Yuri Rabinovich, Wayne St (MI)	Carlos Songini, Cleveland St
1980....Ernest Simon, Wayne St (MI)	Paul Friedberg, Pennsylvania	Gil Pezza, Wayne St (MI)
1981....Ernest Simon, Wayne St (MI)	Paul Friedberg, Pennsylvania	Gil Pezza, Wayne St (MI)
1982....Alexander Flom, George Mason	Neil Hick, Wayne St (MI)	Peter Schifrin, San Jose St
1983....Demetrios Valsamis, NYU	John Friedberg, North Carolina	Ola Harstrom, Notre Dame
1984....Charles Higgs-Coulthard, Notre Dame	Michael Lofton, NYU	Ettore Bianchi, Wayne St (MI)
1985....Stephan Chauvel, Wayne St (MI)	Michael Lofton, NYU	Ettore Bianchi, Wayne St (MI)
1986....Adam Feldman, Penn St	Michael Lofton, NYU	Chris O'Loughlin, Pennsylvania
1987....William Mindel, Columbia	Michael Lofton, NYU	James O'Neill, Harvard
1988....Marc Kent, Columbia	Robert Cottingham, Columbia	Jon Normile, Columbia
1989....Edward Mufel, Penn St	Peter Cox, Penn St	Jon Normile, Columbia
1990....Nick Bravin, Stanford	David Mandell, Columbia	Jubba Beshin, Notre Dame
1991....Ben Atkins, Columbia	Vitali Nazlimov, Penn St	Marc Oshima, Columbia
1992....Nick Bravin, Stanford	Tom Strzalkowski, Penn St	Harald Bauder, Wayne St
1993....Nick Bravin, Stanford	Tom Strzalkowski, Penn St	Ben Atkins, Columbia
1994....Kwame van Leeuwen, Harvard	Tom Strzalkowski, Penn St	Harald Winkman, Princeton

Women

TEAM CHAMPIONS

Year	Champion	Coach	Rec	Runner-Up	Rec
1982	Wayne St (MI)	Istvan Danosi	7-0	San Jose St	6-1
1983	Penn St	Beth Alphin	5-0	Wayne St (MI)	3-2
1984	Yale	Henry Harutunian	3-0	Penn St	2-1
1985	Yale	Henry Harutunian	3-0	Pennsylvania	2-1
1986	Pennsylvania	David Micahnik	3-0	Notre Dame	2-1
1987	Notre Dame	Yves Auriol	3-0	Temple	2-1
1988	Wayne St (MI)	Gil Pezza	3-0	Notre Dame	2-1
1989	Wayne St (MI)	Gil Pezza	3-0	Columbia-Barnard	2-1

Note: Beginning in 1990, men's and women's combined teams competed for the national championship.

INDIVIDUAL CHAMPIONS

1982.................Joy Ellingson, San Jose St	1989.................Yasemin Topcu, Wayne St (MI)
1983.................Jana Angelakis, Penn St	1990.................Tzu Moy, Columbia-Barnard
1984.................Mary Jane O'Neill, Pennsylvania	1991.................Heidi Piper, Notre Dame
1985.................Caitlin Bilodeaux, Columbia-Barnard	1992.................Olga Cheryak, Penn St
1986.................Molly Sullivan, Notre Dame	1993.................Olga Kalinovskaya, Penn St
1987.................Caitlin Bilodeaux, Columbia-Barnard	1994.................Olga Kalinovskaya, Penn St
1988.................Molly Sullivan, Notre Dame	

Field Hockey

Women

DIVISION I

Year	Champion	Coach	Score	Runner-Up
1981	Connecticut	Diane Wright	4-1	Massachusetts
1982	Old Dominion	Beth Anders	3-2	Connecticut
1983	Old Dominion	Beth Anders	3-1 (3 OT)	Connecticut
1984	Old Dominion	Beth Anders	5-1	Iowa
1985	Connecticut	Diane Wright	3-2	Old Dominion
1986	Iowa	Judith Davidson	2-1 (2 OT)	New Hampshire
1987	Maryland	Sue Tyler	2-1 (OT)	N Carolina
1988	Old Dominion	Beth Anders	2-1	Iowa

DIVISION I (Cont.)

Year	Champion	Coach	Score	Runner-Up
1989	N Carolina	Karen Shelton	2-1 (3 OT)*	Old Dominion
1990	Old Dominion	Beth Anders	5-0	N Carolina
1991	Old Dominion	Beth Anders	2-0	N Carolina
1992	Old Dominion	Beth Anders	4-0	Iowa
1993	Maryland	Missy Meharg	2-1 (3 OT)*	N Carolina

*Penalty strokes.

DIVISION II (DISCONTINUED, THEN RENEWED)

Year	Champion	Coach	Score	Runner-Up
1981	Pfeiffer	Ellen Briggs	5-3	Bentley
1982	Lock Haven	Sharon E. Taylor	4-1	Bloomsburg
1983	Bloomsburg	Jan Hutchinson	1-0	Lock Haven
1992	Lock Haven	Sharon E. Taylor	3-1	Bloomsburg
1993	Bloomsburg	Jan Hutchison	2-1 (2 OT)	Lock Haven

DIVISION III

Year	Champion	Year	Champion	Year	Champion
1981	Trenton St	1986	Salisbury St	1991	Trenton St
1982	Ithaca	1987	Bloomsburg	1992	William Smith
1983	Trenton St	1988	Trenton St	1993	Cortland St
1984	Bloomsburg	1989	Lock Haven		
1985	Trenton St	1990	Trenton St		

Golf

Men

DIVISION I

Results, 1897-1938

Year	Champion	Site	Individual Champion
1897	Yale	Ardsley Casino	Louis Bayard Jr, Princeton
1898	Harvard (spring)		John Reid Jr, Yale
1898	Yale (fall)		James Curtis, Harvard
1899	Harvard		Percy Pyne, Princeton
1900	No tournament		
1901	Harvard	Atlantic City	H. Lindsley, Harvard
1902	Yale (spring)	Garden City	Charles Hitchcock Jr, Yale
1902	Harvard (fall)	Morris County	Chandler Egan, Harvard
1903	Harvard	Garden City	F. O. Reinhart, Princeton
1904	Harvard	Myopia	A. L. White, Harvard
1905	Yale	Garden City	Robert Abbott, Yale
1906	Yale	Garden City	W. E. Clow Jr, Yale
1907	Yale	Nassau	Ellis Knowles, Yale
1908	Yale	Brae Burn	H. H. Wilder, Harvard
1909	Yale	Apawamis	Albert Seckel, Princeton
1910	Yale	Essex County	Robert Hunter, Yale
1911	Yale	Baltusrol	George Stanley, Yale
1912	Yale	Ekwanok	F. C. Davison, Harvard
1913	Yale	Huntingdon Valley	Nathaniel Wheeler, Yale
1914	Princeton	Garden City	Edward Allis, Harvard
1915	Yale	Greenwich	Francis Blossom, Yale
1916	Princeton	Oakmont	J. W. Hubbell, Harvard
1917-18	No tournament		
1919	Princeton	Merion	A. L. Walker Jr, Columbia
1920	Princeton	Nassau	Jess Sweetster, Yale
1921	Dartmouth	Greenwich	Simpson Dean, Princeton
1922	Princeton	Garden City	Pollack Boyd, Dartmouth
1923	Princeton	Siwanoy	Dexter Cummings, Yale
1924	Yale	Greenwich	Dexter Cummings, Yale
1925	Yale	Montclair	Fred Lamprecht, Tulane
1926	Yale	Merion	Fred Lamprecht, Tulane
1927	Princeton	Garden City	Watts Gunn, Georgia Tech
1928	Princeton	Apawamis	Maurice McCarthy, Georgetown

Men (Cont.)

Results, 1897-1938 (Cont.)

Year	Champion	Site	Individual Champion
1929	Princeton	Hollywood	Tom Aycock, Yale
1930	Princeton	Oakmont	G. T. Dunlap Jr, Princeton
1931	Yale	Olympia Fields	G. T. Dunlap Jr, Princeton
1932	Yale	Hot Springs	J. W. Fischer, Michigan
1933	Yale	Buffalo	Walter Emery, Oklahoma
1934	Michigan	Cleveland	Charles Yates, Georgia Tech
1935	Michigan	Congressional	Ed White, Texas
1936	Yale	North Shore	Charles Kocsis, Michigan
1937	Princeton	Oakmont	Fred Haas Jr, Louisiana St
1938	Stanford	Louisville	John Burke, Georgetown

Results, 1939-1994

Year	Champion	Coach	Score	Runner-Up	Score	Host or Site	Individual Champion
1939	Stanford	Eddie Twiggs	612	Northwestern	614	Wakonda	Vincent D'Antoni, Tulane
				Princeton	614		
1940	Princeton	Walter Bourne	601			Ekwanok	Dixon Brooke, Virginia
	Louisiana St	Mike Donahue	601				
1941	Stanford	Eddie Twiggs	580	Louisiana St	599	Ohio St	Earl Stewart, Louisiana St
1942	Louisiana St	Mike Donahue	590			Notre Dame	Frank Tatum Jr
	Stanford	Eddie Twiggs	590				
1943	Yale	William Neale Jr	614	Michigan	618	Olympia Fields	Wallace Ulrich, Carleton
1944	Notre Dame	George Holderith	311	Minnesota	312	Inverness	Louis Lick, Minnesota
1945	Ohio St	Robert Kepler	602	Northwestern	621	Ohio St	John Lorms, Ohio St
1946	Stanford	Eddie Twiggs	619	Michigan	624	Princeton	George Hamer, Georgia
1947	Louisiana St	T. P. Heard	606	Duke	614	Michigan	Dave Barclay, Michigan
1948	San Jose St	Wilbur Hubbard	579	Louisiana St	588	Stanford	Bob Harris, San Jose St
1949	N Texas	Fred Cobb	590	Purdue	600	Iowa St	Harvie Ward, N Carolina
				Texas	600		
1950	N Texas	Fred Cobb	573	Purdue	577	New Mexico	Fred Wampler, Purdue
1951	N Texas	Fred Cobb	588	Ohio St	589	Ohio St	Tom Nieporte, Ohio St
1952	N Texas	Fred Cobb	587	Michigan	593	Purdue	Jim Vickers, Oklahoma
1953	Stanford	Charles Finger	578	N Carolina	580	Broadmoor	Earl Moeller, Oklahoma St
1954	Southern Meth	Graham Ross	572	N Texas	573	Houston, Rice	Hillman Robbins, Memphis St
1955	Louisiana St	Mike Barbato	574	N Texas	583	Tennessee	Joe Campbell, Purdue
1956	Houston	Dave Williams	601	N Texas	602	Ohio St	Rick Jones, Ohio St
				Purdue	602		
1957	Houston	Dave Williams	602	Stanford	603	Broadmoor	Rex Baxter Jr, Houston
1958	Houston	Dave Williams	570	Oklahoma St	582	Williams	Phil Rodgers, Houston
1959	Houston	Dave Williams	561	Purdue	571	Oregon	Dick Crawford, Houston
1960	Houston	Dave Williams	603	Purdue	607	Broadmoor	Dick Crawford, Houston
				Oklahoma St	607		
1961	Purdue	Sam Voinoff	584	Arizona St	595	Lafayette	Jack Nicklaus, Ohio St
1962	Houston	Dave Williams	588	Oklahoma St	598	Duke	Kermit Zarley, Houston
1963	Oklahoma St	Labron Harris	581	Houston	582	Wichita St	R. H. Sikes, Ark.
1964	Houston	Dave Williams	580	Oklahoma St	587	Broadmoor	Terry Small, San Jose St

Men (Cont.)

Results, 1939-1994 (Cont.)

Year	Champion	Coach	Score	Runner-Up	Score	Host or Site	Individual Champion
1965 ....Houston	Dave Williams	577	Cal St-LA	587	Tennessee	Marty Fleckman, Houston
1966 ....Houston	Dave Williams	582	San Jose St	586	Stanford	Bob Murphy, Florida
1967 ....Houston	Dave Williams	585	Florida	588	Shawnee, PA	Hale Irwin, Colorado
1968 ....Florida	Buster Bishop	1154	Houston	1156	New Mexico St	Grier Jones, Oklahoma St
1969 ....Houston	Dave Williams	1223	Wake Forest	1232	Broadmoor	Bob Clark, Cal St-LA
1970 Houston	Dave Williams	1172	Wake Forest	1182	Ohio St	John Mahaffey, Houston
1971 ....Texas	George Hannon	1144	Houston	1151	Arizona	Ben Crenshaw, Texas
1972 ....Texas	George Hannon	1146	Houston	1159	Cape Coral	Ben Crenshaw, Texas Tom Kite, Texas
1973 ....Florida	Buster Bishop	1149	Oklahoma St	1159	Oklahoma St	Ben Crenshaw, Texas
1974 ....Wake Forest	Jess Haddock	1158	Florida	1160	San Diego St	Curtis Strange, Wake Forest
1975 ....Wake Forest	Jess Haddock	1156	Oklahoma St	1189	Ohio St	Jay Haas, Wake Forest
1976 ....Oklahoma St	Mike Holder	1166	Brigham Young	1173	New Mexico	Scott Simpson, Southern Cal
1977 ....Houston	Dave Williams	1197	Oklahoma St	1205	Colgate	Scott Simpson, Southern Cal
1978 ....Oklahoma St	Mike Holder	1140	Georgia	1157	Oregon	David Edwards, Oklahoma St
1979 ....Ohio St	James Brown	1189	Oklahoma St	1191	Wake Forest	Gary Hallberg, Wake Forest
1980 ....Oklahoma St	Mike Holder	1173	Brigham Young	1177	Ohio St	Jay Don Blake, Utah St
1981 ....Brigham Young	Karl Tucker	1161	Oral Roberts	1163	Stanford	Ron Commans, Southern Cal
1982 ....Houston	Dave Williams	1141	Oklahoma St	1151	Pinehurst	Billy Ray Brown, Houston
1983 ....Oklahoma St	Mike Holder	1161	Texas	1168	Fresno St	Jim Carter, Arizona St
1984 ....Houston	Dave Williams	1145	Oklahoma St	1146	Houston	John Inman, N Carolina
1985 ....Houston	Dave Williams	1172	Oklahoma St	1175	Florida	Clark Burroughs, Ohio St
1986 ....Wake Forest	Jess Haddock	1156	Oklahoma St	1160	Wake Forest	Scott Verplank, Oklahoma St
1987 ....Oklahoma St	Mike Holder	1160	Wake Forest	1176	Ohio St	Brian Watts, Oklahoma St
1988 ....UCLA	Eddie Merrins	1176	UTEP Oklahoma Oklahoma St	1179 1179 1179	Southern Cal	E. J. Pfister, Oklahoma St
1989 ....Oklahoma	Gregg Grost	1139	Texas	1158	Oklahoma Oklahoma St	Phil Mickelson, Arizona St
1990 ....Arizona St	Steve Loy	1155	Florida	1157	Florida	Phil Mickelson, Arizona St
1991 ....Oklahoma St	Mike Holder	1161	N Carolina	1168	San Jose St	Warren Schutte, UNLV
1992 ....Arizona	Rick LaRose	1129	Arizona St	1136	New Mexico	Phil Mickelson, Arizona St
1993 ....Florida	Buddy Alexander	1145	Georgia Tech	1146	Kentucky	Todd Demsey, Arizona St
1994 ....Stanford	Wally Goodwin	1129	Texas	1133	McKinney, TX	Justin Leonard, Texas

Notes: Match play, 1897-1964; par-70 tournaments held in 1969, 1973 and 1989; par-71 tournaments held in 1968, 1981 and 1988; all other championships par-72 tournaments. Scores are based on 4 rounds instead of 2 after 1967.

Golf (Cont.)

Men (Cont.)

DIVISION II

Year	Champion
1963	SW Missouri St
1964	Southern Illinois
1965	Middle Tennessee St
1966	Cal St-Chico
1967	Lamar
1968	Lamar
1969	Cal St-Northridge
1970	Rollins
1971	New Orleans
1972	New Orleans
1973	Cal St-Northridge
1974	Cal St-Northridge
1975	UC-Irvine
1976	Troy St
1977	Troy St
1978	Columbus
1979	UC-Davis
1980	Columbus
1981	Florida Southern
1982	Florida Southern
1983	SW Texas St
1984	Troy St
1985	Florida Southern
1986	Florida Southern
1987	Tampa
1988	Tampa
1989	Columbus
1990	Florida Southern
1991	Florida Southern
1992	Columbus
1993	Abilene Christian
1994	Columbus

DIVISION III

Year	Champion
1975	Wooster
1976	Cal St-Stanislaus
1977	Cal St-Stanislaus
1978	Cal St-Stanislaus
1979	Cal St-Stanislaus
1980	Cal St-Stanislaus
1981	Cal St-Stanislaus
1982	Ramapo
1983	Allegheny
1984	Cal St-Stanislaus
1985	Cal St-Stanislaus
1986	Cal St-Stanislaus
1987	Cal St-Stanislaus
1988	Cal St-Stanislaus
1989	Cal St-Stanislaus
1990	Methodist (NC)
1991	Methodist (NC)
1992	Methodist (NC)
1993	UC-San Diego
1994	UC-San Diego

Note: All championships par-72 except for 1986 and 1988, which were par-71; fourth round of 1975 championships canceled as a result of bad weather, first round of 1988 championships canceled as a result of rain.

Women

Year	Champion	Coach	Score	Runner-Up	Score	Individual Champion
1982	Tulsa	Dale McNamara	1191	Texas Christian	1227	Kathy Baker, Tulsa
1983	Texas Christian	Fred Warren	1193	Tulsa	1196	Penny Hammel, Miami (FL)
1984	Miami (FL)	Lela Cannon	1214	Arizona St	1221	Cindy Schreyer, Georgia
1985	Florida	Mimi Ryan	1218	Tulsa	1233	Danielle Ammaccapane, Arizona St
1986	Florida	Mimi Ryan	1180	Miami (FL)	1188	Page Dunlap, Florida
1987	San Jose St	Mark Gale	1187	Furman	1188	Caroline Keggi, New Mexico
1988	Tulsa	Dale McNamara	1175	Georgia Arizona	1182 1182	Melissa McNamara, Tulsa
1989	San Jose St	Mark Gale	1208	Tulsa	1209	Pat Hurst, San Jose St
1990	Arizona St	Linda Vollstedt	1206	UCLA	1222	Susan Slaughter, Arizona
1991	UCLA*	Jackie Steinmann	1197	San Jose St	1197	Annika Sorenstam, Arizona
1992	San Jose St	Mark Gale	1171	Arizona	1175	Vicki Goetze, Georgia
1993	Arizona St	Linda Vollstedt	1187	Texas	1189	Charlotta Sorenstam, Texas
1994	Arizona St	Linda Vollstedt	1189	Southern Cal	1205	Emilee Klein, Arizona St

*Won sudden death playoff. Note: Par-74 tournaments held in 1983 and 1988; par-72 tournament held in 1990; all other championships par-73 tournaments.

Gymnastics

Men
Team Champions

Year	Champion	Coach	Pts	Runner-Up	Pts
1938 ....Chicago	Dan Hoffer	22	Illinois	18
1939 ....Illinois	Hartley Price	21	Army	17
1940 ....Illinois	Hartley Price	20	Navy	17
1941 ....Illinois	Hartley Price	68.5	Minnesota	52.5
1942 ....Illinois	Hartley Price	39	Penn St	30
1943-47 ....No tournament				
1948 ....Penn St	Gene Wettstone	55	Temple	34.5
1949 ....Temple	Max Younger	28	Minnesota	18
1950 ....Illinois	Charley Pond	26	Temple	25
1951 ....Florida St	Hartley Price	26	Illinois	23.5
			Southern Cal	23.5
1952 ....Florida St	Hartley Price	89.5	Southern Cal	75
1953 ....Penn St	Gene Wettstone	91.5	Illinois	68
1954 ....Penn St	Gene Wettstone	137	Illinois	68
1955 ....Illinois	Charley Pond	82	Penn St	69
1956 ....Illinois	Charley Pond	123.5	Penn St	67.5
1957 ....Penn St	Gene Wettstone	88.5	Illinois	80
1958 ....Michigan St	George Szypula	79		
	Illinois	Charley Pond	79		
1959 ....Penn St	Gene Wettstone	152	Illinois	87.5
1960 ....Penn St	Gene Wettstone	112.5	Southern Cal	65.5
1961 ....Penn St	Gene Wettstone	88.5	Southern Illinois	80.5
1962 ....Southern Cal	Jack Beckner	95.5	Southern Illinois	75
1963 ....Michigan	Newton Loken	129	Southern Illinois	73
1964 ....Southern Illinois	Bill Meade	84.5	Southern Cal	69.5
1965 ....Penn St	Gene Wettstone	68.5	Washington	51.5
1966 ....Southern Illinois	Bill Meade	187.200	California	185.100
1967 ....Southern Illinois	Bill Meade	189.550	Michigan	187.400
1968 ....California	Hal Frey	188.250	Southern Illinois	188.150
1969 ....Iowa	Mike Jacobson	161.175	Penn St	160.450
	Michigan*	Newton Loken		Colorado St	
1970 ....Michigan	Newton Loken	164.150	Iowa St	164.050
			New Mexico St	
1971 ....Iowa St	Ed Gagnier	319.075	Southern Illinois	316.650
1972 ....Southern Illinois	Bill Meade	315.925	Iowa St	312.325
1973 ....Iowa St	Ed Gagnier	325.150	Penn St	323.025
1974 ....Iowa St	Ed Gagnier	326.100	Arizona St	322.050
1975 ....California	Hal Frey	437.325	Louisiana St	433.700
1976 ....Penn St	Gene Wettstone	432.075	Louisiana St	425.125
1977 ....Indiana St	Roger Counsil	434.475		
	Oklahoma	Paul Ziert	434.475		
1978 ....Oklahoma	Paul Ziert	439.350	Arizona St	437.075
1979 ....Nebraska	Francis Allen	448.275	Oklahoma	446.625
1980 ....Nebraska	Francis Allen	563.300	Iowa St	557.650
1981 ....Nebraska	Francis Allen	284.600	Oklahoma	281.950
1982 ....Nebraska	Francis Allen	285.500	UCLA	281.050
1983 ....Nebraska	Francis Allen	287.800	UCLA	283.900
1984 ....UCLA	Art Shurlock	287.300	Penn St	281.250
1985 ....Ohio St	Michael Willson	285.350	Nebraska	284.550
1986 ....Arizona St	Don Robinson	283.900	Nebraska	283.600
1987 ....UCLA	Art Shurlock	285.300	Nebraska	284.750
1988 ....Nebraska	Francis Allen	288.150	Illinois	287.150
1989 ....Illinois	Yoshi Hayasaki	283.400	Nebraska	282.300
1990 ....Nebraska	Francis Allen	287.400	Minnesota	287.300
1991 ....Oklahoma	Greg Buwick	288.025	Penn St	285.500
1992 ....Stanford	Sadao Hamada	289.575	Nebraska	288.950
1993 ....Stanford	Sadao Hamada	276.500	Nebraska	275.500
1994 ....Nebraska	Francis Allen	288.250	Stanford	285.925

*Trampoline.

Men *(Cont.)*
Individual Champions

ALL-AROUND

1938 .....Joe Giallombardo, Illinois
1939 .....Joe Giallombardo, Illinois
1940 .....Joe Giallombardo, Illinois
        Paul Fina, Illinois
1941 .....Courtney Shanken, Chicago
1942 .....Newt Loken, Minnesota
1948 .....Ray Sorenson, Penn St
1949 .....Joe Kotys, Kent
1950 .....Joe Kotys, Kent
1951 .....Bill Roetzheim, Florida St
1952 ....Jack Beckner, Southern Cal
1953 ....Jean Cronstedt, Penn St
1954 .....Jean Cronstedt, Penn St
1955 .....Karl Schwenzfeier, Penn St
1956 .....Don Tonry, Illlnois
1957 .....Armando Vega, Penn St
1958 .....Abie Grossfeld, Illinois
1959 .....Armando Vega, Penn St
1960 .....Jay Werner, Penn St
1961 .....Gregor Weiss, Penn St
1962 .....Robert Lynn, Southern Cal
1963 .....Gil Larose, Michigan
1964 .....Ron Barak, Southern Cal
1965 .....Mike Jacobson, Penn St
1966 .....Steve Cohen, Penn St
1967 .....Steve Cohen, Penn St
1968 .....Makoto Sakamoto, USC
1969 .....Mauno Nissinen, Wash
1970 .....Yoshi Hayasaki, Wash
1971 .....Yoshi Hayasaki, Wash
1972 .....Steve Hug, Stanford
1973 .....Steve Hug, Stanford
        Marshall Avener, Penn St.
1974 .....Steve Hug, Stanford
1975 .....Wayne Young, BYU
1976   Peter Kormann, Southern
        Conn St
1977 .....Kurt Thomas, Indiana St
1978 .....Bart Conner, Oklahoma
1979 .....Kurt Thomas, Indiana St
1980 .....Jim Hartung, Nebraska
1981 .....Jim Hartung, Nebraska
1982 .....Peter Vidmar, UCLA
1983 .....Peter Vidmar, UCLA
1984 .....Mitch Gaylord, UCLA
1985 .....Wes Suter, Nebraska
1986 .....Jon Louis, Stanford
1987 ....Tom Schlesinger, Nebraska
1988 .....Vacated†
1989 .....Patrick Kirsey, Nebraska
1990 .....Mike Racanelli, Ohio St
1991 .....John Roethlisberger, Minn
1992 .....John Roethlisberger, Minn
1993 .....John Roethlisberger, Minn
1994 .....Dennis Harrison, Nebraska

HORIZONTAL BAR

1938 .....Bob Sears, Army
1939 .....Adam Walters, Temple
1940 .....Norm Boardman, Temple
1941 .....Newt Loken, Minnesota
1942 .....Norm Boardman, Temple
1948 .....Joe Calvetti, Illinois
1949 .....Bob Stout, Temple

1950 .....Joe Kotys, Kent
1951 .....Bill Roetzheim, Florida St
1952 .....Charles Simms, USC
1953 .....Hal Lewis, Navy
1954 .....Jean Cronstedt, Penn St
1955 .....Carlton Rintz, Michigan St
1956 .....Ronnie Amster, Florida St
1957 .....Abie Grossfeld, Illinois
1958 .....Abie Grossfeld, Illinois
1959 .....Stanley Tarshis, Mich St
1960 .....Stanley Tarshis, Mich St
1961 .....Bruno Klaus, Southern Ill
1962 .....Robert Lynn, USC
1963 .....Gil Larose, Michigan
1964 .....Ron Barak, USC
1965 .....Jim Curzi, Michigan St
        Mike Jacobsen, Penn St
1966 .....Rusty Rock, Cal St-
        Northridge
1967 .....Rich Grigsby, Cal St-
        Northridge
1968 .....Makoto Sakamoto, USC
1969 .....Bob Manna, New Mexico
1970 .....Yoshi Hayasaki, Wash
1971 .....Brent Simmons, Iowa St
1972 .....Tom Lindner, Souhern Ill
1973 .....Jon Aitken, New Mexico
1974 .....Rick Banley, Indiana St
1975 .....Rich Larsen, Iowa St
1976 .....Tom Beach, California
1977 .....John Hart, UCLA
1978 .....Mel Cooley, Washington
1979 .....Kurt Thomas, Indiana St
1980 .....Philip Cahoy, Nebraska
1981 .....Philip Cahoy, Nebraska
1982 .....Peter Vidmar, UCLA
1983 .....Scott Johnson, Nebraska
1984 .....Charles Lakes, Illinois
1985 .....Dan Hayden, Arizona St
        Wes Suter, Nebraska
1986 .....Dan Hayden, Arizona St
1987 .....David Moriel, UCLA
1988 .....Vacated†
1989 .....Vacated†
1990 .....Chris Waller, UCLA
1991 .....Luis Lopez, New Mexico
1992 .....Jair Lynch, Stanford
1993 .....Steve McCain, UCLA
1994 .....Jim Foody, UCLA

PARALLEL BARS

1938 .....Erwin Beyer, Chicago
1939 .....Bob Sears, Army
1940 .....Bob Hanning, Minnesota
1941 .....Caton Cobb, Illinois
1942 .....Hal Zimmerman, Penn St
1948 .....Ray Sorenson, Penn St
1949 .....Joe Kotys, Kent
        Mel Stout, Michigan St
1950 .....Joe Kotys, Kent
1951 .....Jack Beckner, USC
1952 .....Jack Beckner, USC
1953 .....Jean Cronstedt, Penn St
1954 .....Jean Cronstedt, Penn St
1955 .....Carlton Rintz, Michigan St
1956 .....Armando Vega, Penn St

1957 .....Armando Vega, Penn St
1958 .....Tad Muzyczko, Mich St
1959 .....Armando Vega, Penn St
1960 .....Robert Lynn, Southern Cal
1961 .....Fred Tijerina, Southern Ill
        Jeff Cardinalli, Springfield
1962 .....Robert Lynn, Southern Cal
1963 .....Arno Lascari, Michigan
1964 .....Ron Barak, Southern Cal
1965 .....Jim Curzi, Michigan St
1966 .....Jim Curzi, Michigan St
1967 .....Makoto Sakamoto, USC
1968 .....Makoto Sakamoto, USC
1969 .....Ron Rapper, Michigan
1970 .....Ron Rapper, Michigan
1971 .....Brent Simmons, Iowa St
        Tom Dunn, Penn St
1972 .....Dennis Mazur, Iowa St
1973 .....Steve Hug, Stanford
1974 .....Steve Hug, Stanford
1975 .....Yoichi Tomita, Long
        Beach St
1976 .....Gene Whelan, Penn St
1977 .....Kurt Thomas, Indiana St
1978 .....John Corritore, Michigan
1979 .....Kurt Thomas, Indiana St
1980 .....Philip Cahoy, Nebraska
1981 .....Philip Cahoy, Nebraska
        Peter Vidmar, UCLA
        Jim Hartung, Nebraska
1982 .....Jim Hartung, Nebraska
1983 .....Scott Johnson, Nebraska
1984 .....Tim Daggett, UCLA
1985 .....Dan Hayden, Arizona St
        Noah Riskin, Ohio St
        Seth Riskin, Ohio St
1986 .....Dan Hayden, Arizona St
1987 .....Kevin Davis, Nebraska
        Tom Schlesinger, Nebraska
1988 .....Kevin Davis, Nebraska
1989 .....Vacated†
1990 .....Patrick Kirksey, Nebraska
1991 .....Scott Keswick, UCLA
        John Roethlisberger, Minn
1992 .....Dom Minicucci, Temple
1993 .....Jair Lynch, Stanford
1994 .....Richard Grace, Nebraska

LONG HORSE VAULT

1938 .....Erwin Beyer, Chicago
1939 .....Marv Forman, Illinois
1940 .....Earl Shanken, Chicago
1941 .....Earl Shanken, Chicago
1942 .....Earl Shanken, Chicago
1948 .....Jim Peterson, Minnesota
1962 .....Bruno Klaus, Southern Ill
1963 .....Gil Larose, Michigan
1964 .....Sidney Oglesby, Syracuse
1965 .....Dan Millman, California
1966 .....Frank Schmitz, S Illinois
1967 .....Paul Mayer, S Illinois
1968 .....Bruce Colter, Cal St-Los
        Angeles
1969 .....Dan Bowles, California
        Jack McCarthy, Illinois
1970 .....Doug Boger, Arizona

Men (Cont.)
Individual Champions (Cont.)

1971.....Pat Mahoney, Cal St-
          Northridge
1972.....Gary Morava, Southern Ill
1973.....John Crosby, S Conn St
1974.....Greg Goodhue, Oklahoma
1975.....Tom Beach, California
1976.....Sam Shaw, Cal St-
          Fullerton
1977.....Steve Wejmar, Wash
1978.....Ron Galimore, Louisiana St
1979.....Leslie Moore, Oklahoma
1980.....Ron Galimore, Iowa St
1981.....Ron Galimore, Iowa St
1982.....Randall Wickstrom, Cal
          Steve Elliott, Nebraska
1983.....Chris Riegel, Nebraska
          Mark Oates, Oklahoma
1984.....Chris Riegel, Nebraska
1985.....Derrick Cornelius,
          Cortland St
1986.....Chad Fox, New Mexico
1987.....Chad Fox, New Mexico
1988.....Chad Fox, New Mexico
1989.....Chad Fox, New Mexico
1990.....Brad Hayashi, UCLA
1991.....Adam Carton, Penn St
1992.....Jason Hebert, Syracuse
1993.....Steve Wiegel, N Mexico
1994.....Steve McCain, UCLA

SIDE HORSE

1938.....Erwin Beyer, Chicago
1939.....Erwin Beyer, Chicago
1940.....Harry Koehnemann, Illinois
1941.....Caton Cobb, Illinois
1942.....Caton Cobb, Illinois
1948.....Steve Greene, Penn St
1949.....Joe Berenato, Temple
1950.....Gene Rabbitt, Syracuse
1951.....Joe Kotys, Kent
1952.....Frank Bare, Illinois
1953.....Carlton Rintz, Michigan St
1954.....Robert Lawrence, Penn St
1955.....Carlton Rintz, Michigan St
1956.....James Brown, Cal St-
          Los Angeles
1957.....John Davis, Illinois
1958.....Bill Buck, Iowa
1959.....Art Shurlock, California
1960.....James Fairchild, California
1961.....James Fairchild, California
1962.....Mike Aufrecht, Illinois
1963.....Russ Mills, Yale
1964.....Russ Mills, Yale
1965.....Bob Elsinger, Springfield
1966.....Gary Hoskins, Cal St-
          Los Angeles
1967.....Keith McCanless, Iowa
1968.....Jack Ryan, Colorado
1969.....Keith McCanless, Iowa
1970.....Russ Hoffman, Iowa St
          John Russo, Wisconsin
1971.....Russ Hoffman, Iowa St

1972.....Russ Hoffman, Iowa St
1973.....Ed Slezak, Indiana St
1974.....Ted Marcy, Stanford
1975.....Ted Marcy, Stanford
1976.....Ted Marcy, Stanford
1977.....Chuck Walter, New Mexico
1978.....Mike Burke, Northern Ill
1979.....Mike Burke, Northern Ill
1980.....David Stoldt, Illinois
1981.....Mark Bergman, California
          Steve Jennings, New Mexico
1982.....Peter Vidmar, UCLA
          Steve Jennings, New Mexico
1983.....Doug Kieso, Northern Ill
1984.....Tim Daggett, UCLA
1985.....Tony Pineda, UCLA
1986.....Curtis Holdsworth, UCLA
1987.....Li Xiao Ping, Cal St-
          Fullerton
1988.....Vacated†
          Mark Sohn, Penn St
1989.....Mark Sohn, Penn St
          Chris Waller, UCLA
1990.....Mark Sohn, Penn St
1991.....Mark Sohn, Penn St
1992.....Che Bowers, Nebraska
1993.....John Roethlisberger, Minn
1994.....Jason Bertram, California

FLOOR EXERCISE

1941.....Lou Fina, Illinois
1953.....Bob Sullivan, Illinois
1954.....Jean Cronstedt, Penn St
1955.....Don Faber, Illinois
1956.....Jamile Ashmore, Florida St
1957.....Norman Marks, Cal St-
          Los Angeles
1958.....Abie Grossfeld, Illinois
1959.....Don Tonry, Illinois
1960.....Ray Hadley, Illinois
1961.....Robert Lynn, Southern Cal
1962.....Robert Lynn, Southern Cal
1963.....Tom Seward, Penn St
          Mike Henderson, Michigan
1964.....Rusty Mitchell, S Illinois
1965.....Frank Schmitz, S Illinois
1966.....Frank Schmitz, S Illinois
1967.....Dave Jacobs, Michigan
1968.....Toby Towson, Michigan St
1969.....Toby Towson, Michigan St
1970.....Tom Proulx, Colorado St
1971.....Stormy Eaton, New Mexico
1972.....Odessa Lovin, Oklahoma
1973.....Odessa Lovin, Oklahoma
1974.....Doug Fitzjarrell, Iowa St
1975.....Kent Brown, Arizona St
1976.....Bob Robbins, Colorado St
1977.....Ron Galimore, Louisiana St
1978.....Curt Austin, Iowa St
1979.....Mike Wilson, Oklahoma
          Bart Conner, Oklahoma
1980.....Steve Elliott, Nebraska
1981.....James Yuhashi, Oregon

1982.....Steve Elliott, Nebraska
1983.....Scott Johnson, Nebraska
          David Branch, Arizona St
          Donnie Hinton, Arizona St
1984.....Kevin Ekburg, Northern Ill
1985.....Wes Suter, Nebraska
1986.....Jerry Burrell, Arizona St
          Brian Ginsberg, UCLA
1987.....Chad Fox, New Mexico
1988.....Chris Wyatt, Temple
1989.....Jody Newman, Arizona St
1990.....Mike Racanelli, Ohio St
1991.....Brad Hayashi, UCLA
1992.....Brian Winkler, Michigan
1993.....Richard Grace, Nebraska
1994.....Mark Booth, Stanford

RINGS

1959.....Armando Vega, Penn St
1960.....Sam Garcia, Southern Cal
1961.....Fred Orlofsky, Southern Ill
1962.....Dale Cooper, Michigan St
1963.....Dale Cooper, Michigan St
1964.....Chris Evans, Arizona St
1965.....Glenn Gailis, Iowa
1966.....Ed Gunny, Michigan St
1967.....Josh Robison, California
1968.....Pat Arnold, Arizona
1969.....Paul Vexler, Penn St
          Ward Maythaler, Iowa St
1970.....Dave Seal, Indiana St
1971.....Charles Ropiequet, S Illinois
1972.....Dave Seal, Indiana St
1973.....Bob Mahorney, Indiana St
1974.....Keith Heaver, Iowa St
1975.....Keith Heaver, Iowa St
1976.....Doug Wood, Iowa St
1977.....Doug Wood, Iowa St
1978.....Scott McEldowney, Oregon
1979.....Kirk Mango, Northern Ill
1980.....Jim Hartung, Nebraska
1981.....Jim Hartung, Nebraska
1982.....Jim Hartung, Nebraska
1983.....Alex Schwartz, UCLA
1984.....Tim Daggett, UCLA
1985.....Mark Diab, Iowa St
1986.....Mark Diab, Iowa St
1987.....Paul O'Neill, Houst Baptist
1988.....Paul O'Neill, New Mexico
1989.....Vacated†
          Paul O'Neill, New Mexico
1990.....Wayne Cowden, Penn St
1991.....Adam Carton, Penn St
1992.....Scott Keswick, UCLA
1993.....Chris LaMorte, N Mexico
1994.....Chris LaMorte, N Mexico

† Championships won by Miguel
Rubio (All Around, 1988; Horizontal
Bar, 1988-89) and Alfonso Rodriguez
(Pommel Horse, 1988; Rings, 1989;
Parallel Bars, 1989) were vacated by
action of the NCAA Committee on
Infractions

Gymnastics (Cont.)

Men (Cont.)

DIVISION II (DISCONTINUED)

Year	Champion	Coach	Pts	Runner-Up	Pts
1968	Cal St-Northridge	Bill Vincent	179.400	Springfield	178.050
1969	Cal St-Northridge	Bill Vincent	151.800	Southern Connecticut St	145.075
1970	Northwestern Louisiana	Armando Vega	160.250	Southern Connecticut St	159.300
1971	Cal St-Fullerton	Dick Wolfe	158.150	Springfield	156.987
1972	Cal St-Fullerton	Dick Wolfe	160.550	Southern Connecticut St	153.050
1973	Southern Connecticut St	Abe Grossfeld	160.750	Cal St-Northridge	158.700
1974	Cal St-Fullerton	Dick Wolfe	309.800	Southern Connecticut St	309.400
1975	Southern Connecticut St	Abe Grossfeld	411.650	IL-Chicago	398.800
1976	Southern Connecticut St	Abe Grossfeld	419.200	IL-Chicago	388.850
1977	Springfield	Frank Wolcott	395.950	Cal St-Northridge	381.250
1978	IL-Chicago	C. Johnson/A. Gentile	406.850	Cal St-Northridge	400.400
1979	IL-Chicago	Clarence Johnson	418.550	WI-Oshkosh	385.650
1980	WI-Oshkosh	Ken Allen	260.550	Cal St-Chico	256.050
1981	WI-Oshkosh	Ken Allen	209.500	Springfield	201.550
1982	WI-Oshkosh	Ken Allen	216.050	East Stroudsburg	211.200
1983	East Stroudsburg	Bruno Klaus	258.650	WI-Oshkosh	257.850
1984	East Stroudsburg	Bruno Klaus	270.800	Cortland St	246.350

Women
Team Champions

Year	Champion	Coach	Pts	Runner-Up	Pts
1982	Utah	Greg Marsden	148.60	Cal St-Fullerton	144.10
1983	Utah	Greg Marsden	184.65	Arizona St	183.30
1984	Utah	Greg Marsden	186.05	UCLA	185.55
1985	Utah	Greg Marsden	188.35	Arizona St	186.60
1986	Utah	Greg Marsden	186.95	Arizona St	186.70
1987	Georgia	Suzanne Yoculan	187.90	Utah	187.55
1988	Alabama	Sarah Patterson	190.05	Utah	189.50
1989	Georgia	Suzanne Yoculan	192.65	UCLA	192.60
1990	Utah	Greg Marsden	194.900	Alabama	194.575
1991	Alabama	Sarah Patterson	195.125	Utah	194.375
1992	Utah	Greg Marsden	195.650	Georgia	194.600
1993	Georgia	Suzanne Yoculan	198.000	Alabama	196.825
1994	Utah	Greg Marsden	196.400	Alabama	196.350

Individual Champions

ALL-AROUND

1982.....Sue Stednitz, Utah
1983.....Megan McCunniff, Utah
1984.....Megan McCunniff-Marsden, Utah
1985.....Penney Hauschild, Alabama
1986.....Penney Hauschild, Alabama
Jackie Brummer, Arizona St
1987.....Kelly Garrison-Steves, Oklahoma
1988.....Kelly Garrison-Steves, Oklahoma
1989.....Corrinne Wright, Georgia
1990.....Dee Dee Foster, Alabama
1991.....Hope Spivey, Georgia
1992.....Missy Marlowe, Utah
1993.....Jenny Hansen, Kentucky
1994.....Jenny Hansen, Kentucky

VAULT

1982.....Elaine Alfano, Utah
1983.....Elaine Alfano, Utah
1984.....Megan Marsden, Utah
1985.....Elaine Alfano, Utah
1986.....Kim Neal, Arizona St
Pam Loree, Penn St
1987.....Yumi Mordre, Washington
1988.....Jill Andrews, UCLA
1989.....Kim Hamilton, UCLA
1990.....Michele Bryant, Nebraska
1991.....Anna Basaldva, Arizona
1992.....Tammy Marshall, Massachusetts
Heather Stepp, Georgia
Kristein Kenoyer, Utah
1993.....Heather Stepp, Georgia
1994.....Jenny Hansen, Kentucky

BALANCE BEAM

1982.....Sue Stednitz, Utah
1983.....Julie Goewey, Cal St-Fullerton
1984.....Heidi Anderson, Oregon St
1985.....Lisa Zeis, Arizona St
1986.....Jackie Brummer, Arizona St
1987.....Yumi Mordre, Washington
1988.....Kelly Garrison-Steves, Oklahoma
1989.....Jill Andrews, UCLA
Joy Selig, Oregon St
1990.....Joy Selig, Oregon St
1991.....Missy Marlowe, Utah
1992.....Missy Marlowe, Utah
Dana Dobransky, Alabama
1993.....Dana Dobransky, Alabama
1994.....Jenny Hansen, Kentucky

FLOOR EXERCISE

1982.....Mary Ayotte-Law, Oregon St
1983.....Kim Neal, Arizona St
1984.....Maria Anz, Florida
1985.....Lisa Mitzel, Utah
1986.....Lisa Zeis, Arizona St
Penney Hauschild, Alabama
1987.....Kim Hamilton, UCLA
1988.....Kim Hamilton, UCLA
1989.....Corrinne Wright, Georgia
Kim Hamilton, UCLA
1990.....Joy Selig, Oregon St
1991.....Hope Spivey, Georgia
1992.....Missy Marlowe, Utah
1993.....Heather Stepp, Georgia
Tammy Marshall, Massachusetts
Amy Durham, Oregon St
1994.....Hope Spivey-Sheeley, Georgia

Women (Cont.)
Individual Champions (Cont.)

UNEVEN BARS

1982....Lisa Shirk, Pittsburgh
1983....Jeri Cameron, Arizona St
1984....Jackie Brummer,
     Arizona St
1985....Penney Hauschild,
     Alabama
1986....Lucy Wener, Georgia

1987....Lucy Wener, Georgia
1988....Kelly Garrison-Steves,
     Oklahoma
1989....Lucy Wener, Georgia
1990....Marie Roethlisberger,
     Minnesota
1991....Kelly Macy, Georgia

1992....Missy Marlowe, Utah
1993....Agina Simpkins, Georgia
     Beth Wymer, Michigan
1994....Sandy Woolsey, Utah
     Beth Wymer, Michigan
     Lori Strong, Georgia

DIVISION II (DISCONTINUED)

Year	Champion	Coach	Pts	Runner-Up	Pts
1982	Cal St-Northridge	Donna Stuart	138.10	Jacksonville St	134.05
1983	Denver	Dan Garcia	174.80	Cal St-Northridge	174.35
1984	Jacksonville St	Robert Dillard	173.40	SE Missouri St	171.45
1985	Jacksonville St	Robert Dillard	176.85	SE Missouri St	173.95
1986	Seattle Pacific	Laurel Tindall	175.80	Jacksonville St	175.15

Ice Hockey

DIVISION I

Year	Champion	Coach	Score	Runner-Up	Most Outstanding Player
1948	Michigan	Vic Heyliger	8-4	Dartmouth	Joe Riley, Dartmouth, F
1949	Boston Col	John Kelley	4-3	Dartmouth	Dick Desmond, Dartmouth, G
1950	Colorado Col	Cheddy Thompson	13-4	Boston U	Ralph Bevins, Boston U, G
1951	Michigan	Vic Heyliger	7-1	Brown	Ed Whiston, Brown, G
1952	Michigan	Vic Heyliger	4-1	Colorado Col	Kenneth Kinsley, Colorado Col, G
1953	Michigan	Vic Heyliger	7-3	Minnesota	John Matchefts, Michigan, F
1954	Rensselaer	Ned Harkness	5-4 (OT)	Minnesota	Abbie Moore, Rensselaer, F
1955	Michigan	Vic Heyliger	5-3	Colorado Col	Philip Hilton, Colorado Col, Def
1956	Michigan	Vic Heyliger	7-5	Michigan Tech	Lorne Howes, Michigan, G
1957	Colorado Col	Thomas Bedecki	13-6	Michigan	Bob McCusker, Colorado Col, F
1958	Denver	Murray Armstrong	6-2	N Dakota	Murray Massier, Denver, F
1959	N Dakota	Bob May	4-3 (OT)	Michigan St	Reg Morelli, N Dakota, F
1960	Denver	Murray Armstrong	5-3	Michigan Tech	Bob Marquis, Boston U, F
1961	Denver	Murray Armstrong	12-2	St Lawrence	Barry Urbanski, Boston U, G
1962	Michigan Tech	John MacInnes	7-1	Clarkson	Louis Angotti, Michigan Tech, F
1963	N Dakota	Barney Thorndycraft	6-5	Denver	Al McLean, N Dakota, F
1964	Michigan	Allen Renfrew	6-3	Denver	Bob Gray, Michigan, G
1965	Michigan Tech	John MacInnes	8-2	Boston Col	Gary Milroy, Michigan Tech, F
1966	Michigan St	Amo Bessone	6-1	Clarkson	Gaye Cooley, Michigan St, G
1967	Cornell	Ned Harkness	4-1	Boston U	Walt Stanowski, Cornell, Def
1968	Denver	Murray Armstrong	4-0	N Dakota	Gerry Powers, Denver, G
1969	Denver	Murray Armstrong	4-3	Cornell	Keith Magnuson, Denver, Def
1970	Cornell	Ned Harkness	6-4	Clarkson	Daniel Lodboa, Cornell, Def
1971	Boston U	Jack Kelley	4-2	Minnesota	Dan Brady, Boston U, G
1972	Boston U	Jack Kelley	4-0	Cornell	Tim Regan, Boston U, G
1973	Wisconsin	Bob Johnson	4-2	Denver	Dean Talafous, Wisconsin, F
1974	Minnesota	Herb Brooks	4-2	Michigan Tech	Brad Shelstad, Minnesota, G
1975	Michigan Tech	John MacInnes	6-1	Minnesota	Jim Warden, Michigan Tech, G
1976	Minnesota	Herb Brooks	6-4	Michigan Tech	Tom Vanelli, Minnesota, F
1977	Wisconsin	Bob Johnson	6-5 (OT)	Michigan	Julian Baretta, Wisconsin, G
1978	Boston U	Jack Parker	5-3	Boston Col	Jack O'Callahan, Boston U, Def
1979	Minnesota	Herb Brooks	4-3	N Dakota	Steve Janaszak, Minnesota, G
1980	N Dakota	John Gasparini	5-2	Northern Michigan	Doug Smail, N Dakota, F
1981	Wisconsin	Bob Johnson	6-3	Minnesota	Marc Behrend, Wisconsin, G
1982	N Dakota	John Gasparini	5-2	Wisconsin	Phil Sykes, N Dakota, F
1983	Wisconsin	Jeff Sauer	6-2	Harvard	Marc Behrend, Wisconsin, G
1984	Bowling Green	Jerry York	5-4 (OT)	MN-Duluth	Gary Kruzich, Bowling Green, G
1985	Rensselaer	Mike Addesa	2-1	Providence	Chris Terreri, Providence, G
1986	Michigan St	Ron Mason	6-5	Harvard	Mike Donnelly, Michigan St, F
1987	N Dakota	John Gasparini	5-3	Michigan St	Tony Hrkac, N Dakota, F
1988	Lake Superior St	Frank Anzalone	4-3 (OT)	St Lawrence	Bruce Hoffort, Lake Superior St, G
1989	Harvard	Bill Cleary	4-3 (OT)	Minnesota	Ted Donato, Harvard, F
1990	Wisconsin	Jeff Sauer	7-3	Colgate	Chris Tancill, Wisconsin, F
1991	N Michigan	Rick Comley	8-7 (3OT)	Boston U	Scott Beattie, N Michigan, F

DIVISION I (Cont.)

Year	Champion	Coach	Score	Runner-Up	Most Outstanding Player
1992	Lake Superior St	Jeff Jackson	4-2	Wisconsin	Paul Constantin, Lake Superior St, F
1993	Maine	Shawn Walsh	5-4	Lake Superior St	Jim Montgomery, Maine
1994	Lake Superior St	Jeff Jackson	9-1	Boston U	Sean Tallaire, Lake Superior St

DIVISION II (DISCONTINUED, THEN RENEWED)

Year	Champion	Coach	Score	Runner-Up
1978	Merrimack	Thom Lawler	12-2	Lake Forest
1979	Lowell	Bill Riley Jr	6-4	Mankato St
1980	Mankato St	Don Brose	5-2	Elmira
1981	Lowell	Bill Riley Jr	5-4	Plattsburgh St
1982	Lowell	Bill Riley Jr	6-1	Plattsburgh St
1983	Rochester Inst	Brian Mason	4-2	Bemidji St
1984	Bemidji St	R.H. (Bob) Peters	14-4*	Merrimack
1993	Bemidji St	R.H. (Bob) Peters	15-6*	Mercyhurst
1994	Bemidji St	R.H. (Bob) Peters	7-6*	AL-Huntsville

*Two-game, total-goal series.

DIVISION III

Year	Champion	Coach	Score	Runner-Up
1984	Babson	Bob Riley	8-0	Union (NY)
1985	Rochester Inst	Bruce Delventhal	5-1	Bemidji St
1986	Bemidji St	R.H. (Bob) Peters	8-5	Vacated
1987	Vacated			Oswego St
1988	WI-River Falls	Rick Kozuback	7-1, 3-5, 3-0	Elmira
1989	WI-Stevens Point	Mark Mazzoleni	3-3, 3-2	Rochester Inst
1990	WI-Stevens Point	Mark Mazzoleni	10-1, 3-6, 1-0	Plattsburgh St
1991	WI-Stevens Point	Mark Mazzoleni	6-2	Mankato St
1992	Plattsburgh St	Bob Emery	7-3	WI-Stevens Point
1993	WI-Stevens Point	Joe Baldarotta	4-3	WI-River Falls
1994	WI-River Falls	Dean Talafous	6-4	WI-Superior

Lacrosse

Men

DIVISION I

Year	Champion	Coach	Score	Runner-Up
1971	Cornell	Richie Moran	12-6	Maryland
1972	Virginia	Glenn Thiel	13-12	Johns Hopkins
1973	Maryland	Bud Beardmore	10-9 (2 OT)	Johns Hopkins
1974	Johns Hopkins	Bob Scott	17-12	Maryland
1975	Maryland	Bud Beardmore	20-13	Navy
1976	Cornell	Richie Moran	16-13 (OT)	Maryland
1977	Cornell	Richie Moran	16-8	Johns Hopkins
1978	Johns Hopkins	Henry Ciccarone	13-8	Cornell
1979	Johns Hopkins	Henry Ciccarone	15-9	Maryland
1980	Johns Hopkins	Henry Ciccarone	9-8 (2 OT)	Virginia
1981	N Carolina	Willie Scroggs	14-13	Johns Hopkins
1982	N Carolina	Willie Scroggs	7-5	Johns Hopkins
1983	Syracuse	Roy Simmons Jr	17-16	Johns Hopkins
1984	Johns Hopkins	Don Zimmerman	13-10	Syracuse
1985	Johns Hopkins	Don Zimmerman	11-4	Syracuse
1986	N Carolina	Willie Scroggs	10-9 (OT)	Virginia
1987	Johns Hopkins	Don Zimmerman	11-10	Cornell
1988	Syracuse	Roy Simmons Jr	13-8	Cornell
1989	Syracuse	Roy Simmons Jr	13-12	Johns Hopkins
1990	Syracuse	Roy Simmons Jr	21-9	Loyola (MD)
1991	N Carolina	Dave Klarmann	18-13	Towson St
1992	Princeton	Bill Tierney	10-9	Syracuse
1993	Syracuse	Roy Simmons Jr	13-12	N Carolina
1994	Princeton	Bill Tierney	9-8 (OT)	Virginia

DIVISION II (DISCONTINUED, THEN RENEWED)

Year	Champion	Coach	Score	Runner-Up
1974	Towson St	Carl Runk	18-17 (OT)	Hobart
1975	Cortland St	Chuck Winters	12-11	Hobart

Lacrosse (Cont.)

Men (Cont.)

DIVISION II (Cont.) (EVENT DISCONTINUED, THEN RENEWED)

Year	Champion	Coach	Score	Runner-Up
1976	Hobart	Jerry Schmidt	18-9	Adelphi
1977	Hobart	Jerry Schmidt	23-13	Washington (MD)
1978	Roanoke	Paul Griffin	14-13	Hobart
1979	Adelphi	Paul Doherty	17-12	MD-Baltimore County
1980	MD-Baltimore County	Dick Watts	23-14	Adelphi
1981	Adelphi	Paul Doherty	17-14	Loyola (MD)
1993	Adelphi	Kevin Sheehan	11-7	LIU-C.W. Post
1994	Springfield	Keith Bugbee	15-12	New York Tech

DIVISION III

Year	Champion	Coach	Score	Runner-Up
1980	Hobart	Dave Urick	11-8	Cortland St
1981	Hobart	Dave Urick	10-8	Cortland St
1982	Hobart	Dave Urick	9-8 (OT)	Washington (MD)
1983	Hobart	Dave Urick	13-9	Roanoke
1984	Hobart	Dave Urick	12-5	Washington (MD)
1985	Hobart	Dave Urick	15-8	Washington (MD)
1986	Hobart	Dave Urick	13-10	Washington (MD)
1987	Hobart	Dave Urick	9-5	Ohio Wesleyan
1988	Hobart	Dave Urick	18-9	Ohio Wesleyan
1989	Hobart	Dave Urick	11-8	Ohio Wesleyan
1990	Hobart	B. J. O'Hara	18-6	Washington (MD)
1991	Hobart	B. J. O'Hara	12-11	Salisbury St
1992	Nazareth (NY)	Scott Nelson	13-12	Hobart
1993	Hobart	B.J. O'Hara	16-10	Ohio Wesleyan
1994	Salisbury St	Jim Berkman	15-9	Hobart

Women

DIVISION I

Year	Champion	Coach	Score	Runner-Up
1982	Massachusetts	Pamela Hixon	9-6	Trenton St
1983	Delaware	Janet Smith	10-7	Temple
1984	Temple	Tina Sloan Green	6-4	Maryland
1985	New Hampshire	Marisa Didio	6-5	Maryland
1986	Maryland	Sue Tyler	11-10	Penn St
1987	Penn St	Susan Scheetz	7-6	Temple
1988	Temple	Tina Sloan Green	15-7	Penn St
1989	Penn St	Susan Scheetz	7-6	Harvard
1990	Harvard	Carole Kleinfelder	8-7	Maryland
1991	Virginia	Jane Miller	8-6	Maryland
1992	Maryland	Cindy Timchal	11-10	Harvard
1993	Virginia	Jane Miller	8-6 (OT)	Princeton
1994	Princeton	Chris Sailer	10-7	Virginia

DIVISION III

Year	Champion	Score	Runner-Up	Year	Champion	Score	Runner-Up
1985	Trenton St	7-4	Ursinus	1990	Ursinus	7-6	St Lawrence
1986	Ursinus	12-10	Trenton St	1991	Trenton St	7-6	Ursinus
1987	Trenton St	8-7 (OT)	Ursinus	1992	Trenton St	5-3	William Smith
1988	Trenton St	14-11	William Smith	1993	Trenton St	10-9	William Smith
1989	Ursinus	8-6	Trenton St	1994	Trenton St	29-11	William Smith

Rifle

Men's and Women's Combined

Year	Champion	Coach	Score	Runner-Up	Score	Individual Champion Air Rifle	Individual Champion Smallbore
1980	Tennessee Tech	James Newkirk	6201	W Virginia	6150	Rod Fitz-Randolph, Tennessee Tech	Rod Fitz-Randolph, Tennessee Tech
1981	Tennessee Tech	James Newkirk	6139	W Virginia	6136	John Rost, W Virginia	Kurt Fitz-Randolph, Tennessee Tech
1982	Tennessee Tech	James Newkirk	6138	W Virginia	6136	John Rost, W Virginia	Kurt Fitz-Randolph, Tennessee Tech

Men's and Women's Combined (Cont.)

Year	Champion	Coach	Score	Runner-Up	Score	Individual Champion Air Rifle	Smallbore
1983	W Virginia	Edward Etzel	6166	Tennessee Tech	6148	Ray Slonena, Tennessee Tech	David Johnson, W Virginia
1984	W Virginia	Edward Etzel	6206	East Tennessee St	6142	Pat Spurgin, Murray St	Bob Broughton, W Virginia
1985	Murray St	Elvis Green	6150	W Virginia	6149	Christian Heller, W Virginia	Pat Spurgin, Murray St
1986	W Virginia	Edward Etzel	6229	Murray St	6163	Marianne Wallace, Murray St	Mike Anti, W Virginia
1987	Murray St	Elvis Green	6205	W Virginia	6203	Rob Harbison, TN-Martin	Web Wright, W Virginia
1988	W Virginia	Greg Perrine	6192	Murray St	6183	Deena Wigger, Murray St	Web Wright, W Virginia
1989	W Virginia	Edward Etzel	6234	S Florida	6180	Michelle Scarborough, S Florida	Deb Sinclair, AK-Fairbanks
1990	W Virginia	Marsha Beasley	6205	Navy	6101	Gary Hardy, W Virginia	Michelle Scarborough S Florida
1991	W Virginia	Marsha Beasley	6171	Alaska-Fairbanks	6110	Ann Pfiffner, W Virginia	Soma Dutta, UTEP
1991	W Virginia	Marsha Beasley	6171	Alaska-Fairbanks	6110	Ann Pfiffner, W Virginia	Soma Dutta, UTEP
1992	W Virginia	Marsha Beasley	6214	Alaska-Fairbanks	6166	Ann Pfiffner, W Virginia	Tim Manges, W Virginia
1993	W Virginia	Marsha Beasley	6179	Alaska-Fairbanks	6169	Trevor Gathman, W Virginia	Eric Uptagrafft, W Virginia
1994	AK-Fairbanks	Randy Pitney	6194	W Virginia	6187	Nancy Napolski, Kentucky	Cory Brunetti, AK-Fairbanks

Men's and Women's Combined

Year	Champion	Coach	Pts	Runner-Up	Pts	Host or Site
1954	Denver	Willy Schaeffler	384.0	Seattle	349.6	NV-Reno
1955	Denver	Willy Schaeffler	567.05	Dartmouth	558.935	Norwich
1956	Denver	Willy Schaeffler	582.01	Dartmouth	541.77	Winter Park
1957	Denver	Willy Schaeffler	577.95	Colorado	545.29	Ogden Snow Basin
1958	Dartmouth	Al Merrill	561.2	Denver	550.6	Dartmouth
1959	Colorado	Bob Beattie	549.4	Denver	543.6	Winter Park
1960	Colorado	Bob Beattie	571.4	Denver	568.6	Bridger Bowl
1961	Denver	Willy Schaeffler	376.19	Middlebury	366.94	Middlebury
1962	Denver	Willy Schaeffler	390.08	Colorado	374.30	Squaw Valley
1963	Denver	Willy Schaeffler	384.6	Colorado	381.6	Solitude
1964	Denver	Willy Schaeffler	370.2	Dartmouth	368.8	Franconia Notch
1965	Denver	Willy Schaeffler	380.5	Utah	378.4	Crystal Mountain
1966	Denver	Willy Schaeffler	381.02	Western Colorado	365.92	Crested Butte
1967	Denver	Willy Schaeffler	376.7	Wyoming	375.9	Sugarloaf Mountain
1968	Wyoming	John Cress	383.9	Denver	376.2	Mount Werner
1969	Denver	Willy Schaeffler	388.6	Dartmouth	372.0	Mount Werner
1970	Denver	Willy Schaeffler	386.6	Dartmouth	378.8	Cannon Mountain
1971	Denver	Peder Pytte	394.7	Colorado	373.1	Terry Peak
1972	Colorado	Bill Marolt	385.3	Denver	380.1	Winter Park
1973	Colorado	Bill Marolt	381.89	Wyoming	377.83	Middlebury
1974	Colorado	Bill Marolt	176	Wyoming	162	Jackson Hole
1975	Colorado	Bill Marolt	183	Vermont	115	Fort Lewis
1976	Colorado Dartmouth	Bill Marolt Jim Page	112 112			Bates
1977	Colorado	Bill Marolt	179	Wyoming	154.5	Winter Park
1978	Colorado	Bill Marolt	152.5	Wyoming	121.5	Cannon Mountain
1979	Colorado	Tim Hinderman	153	Utah	130	Steamboat Springs
1980	Vermont	Chip LaCasse	171	Utah	151	Lake Placid and Stowe
1981	Utah	Pat Miller	183	Vermont	172	Park City
1982	Colorado	Tim Hinderman	461	Vermont	436.5	Lake Placid
1983	Utah	Pat Miller	696	Vermont	650	Bozeman

Skiing (Cont.)

Men's and Women's Combined (Cont.)

Year	Champion	Coach	Pts	Runner-Up	Pts	Host or Site
1984	Utah	Pat Miller	750.5	Vermont	684	New Hampshire
1985	Wyoming	Tim Ameel	764	Utah	744	Bozeman
1986	Utah	Pat Miller	612	Vermont	602	Vermont
1987	Utah	Pat Miller	710	Vermont	627	Anchorage
1988	Utah	Pat Miller	651	Vermont	614	Middlebury
1989	Vermont	Chip LaCasse	672	Utah	668	Jackson Hole
1990	Vermont	Chip LaCasse	671	Utah	571	Vermont
1991	Colorado	Richard Rokos	713	Vermont	682	Park City
1992	Vermont	Chip LaCasse	693.5	New Mexico	642.5	New Hampshire
1993	Utah	Pat Miller	783	Vermont	700.5	Steamboat Springs
1994	Vermont	Chip LaCasse	688	Utah	667	Sugarloaf, ME

Soccer

Men

DIVISION I

Year	Champion	Coach	Score	Runner-Up
1959	St Louis	Bob Guelker	5-2	Bridgeport
1960	St Louis	Bob Guelker	3-2	Maryland
1961	West Chester	Mel Lorback	2-0	St Louis
1962	St Louis	Bob Guelker	4-3	Maryland
1963	St Louis	Bob Guelker	3-0	Navy
1964	Navy	F. H. Warner	1-0	Michigan St
1965	St Louis	Bob Guelker	1-0	Michigan St
1966	San Francisco	Steve Negoesco	5-2	LIU-Brooklyn
1967	Michigan St	Gene Kenney	0-0	Game called
	St Louis	Harry Keough		due to inclement weather
1968	Maryland	Doyle Royal	2-2 (2 OT)	
	Michigan St	Gene Kenney		
1969	St Louis	Harry Keough	4-0	San Francisco
1970	St Louis	Harry Keough	1-0	UCLA
1971	Vacated		3-2	St Louis
1972	St Louis	Harry Keough	4-2	UCLA
1973	St Louis	Harry Keough	2-1 (OT)	UCLA
1974	Howard	Lincoln Phillips	2-1 (4 OT)	St Louis
1975	San Francisco	Steve Negoesco	4-0	SIU-Edwardsville
1976	San Francisco	Steve Negoesco	1-0	Indiana
1977	Hartwick	Jim Lennox	2-1	San Francisco
1978	Vacated		2-0	Indiana
1979	SIU-Edwardsville	Bob Guelker	3-2	Clemson
1980	San Francisco	Steve Negoesco	4-3 (OT)	Indiana
1981	Connecticut	Joe Morrone	2-1 (OT)	Alabama A&M
1982	Indiana	Jerry Yeagley	2-1 (8 OT)	Duke
1983	Indiana	Jerry Yeagley	1-0 (2 OT)	Columbia
1984	Clemson	I. M. Ibrahim	2-1	Indiana
1985	UCLA	Sigi Schmid	1-0 (8 OT)	American
1986	Duke	John Rennie	1-0	Akron
1987	Clemson	I. M. Ibrahim	2-0	San Diego St
1988	Indiana	Jerry Yeagley	1-0	Howard
1989	Santa Clara	Steve Sampson	1-1 (2 OT)	
	Virginia	Bruce Arena		
1990	UCLA	Sigi Schmid	1-0 (OT)	Rutgers
1991	Virginia	Bruce Arena	0-0*	Santa Clara
1992	Virginia	Bruce Arena	2-0	San Diego
1993	Virginia	Bruce Arena	2-0	S Carolina

*Under a rule passed in 1991, the NCAA determined that when a score is tied after regulation and overtime, and the championship is determined by penalty kicks, the official score will be 0-0.

DIVISION II

Year	Champion	Year	Champion	Year	Champion
1972	SIU-Edwardsville	1975	Baltimore	1978	Seattle Pacific
1973	MO-St Louis	1976	Loyola (MD)	1979	Alabama A&M
1974	Adelphi	1977	Alabama A&M	1980	Lock Haven

Soccer (Cont.)

Men's (Cont.)

DIVISION II (Cont.)

Year	Champion	Year	Champion	Year	Champion
1981	Tampa	1986	Seattle Pacific	1991	Florida Tech
1982	Florida Intl	1987	Southern Connecticut St	1992	Southern Connecticut St
1983	Seattle Pacific	1988	Florida Tech	1993	Seattle Pacific
1984	Florida Intl	1989	New Hampshire Col		
1985	Seattle Pacific	1990	Southern Connecticut St		

DIVISION III

Year	Champion	Year	Champion	Year	Champion
1974	Brockport St	1981	Glassboro St	1988	UC-San Diego
1975	Babson	1982	NC-Greensboro	1989	Elizabethtown
1976	Brandeis	1983	NC-Greensboro	1990	Glassboro St
1977	Lock Haven	1984	Wheaton (IL)	1991	UC-San Diego
1978	Lock Haven	1985	NC-Greensboro	1992	Kean
1979	Babson	1986	NC-Greensboro	1993	UC-San Diego
1980	Babson	1987	NC-Greensboro		

Women

DIVISION I

Year	Champion	Coach	Score	Runner-Up
1982	N Carolina	Anson Dorrance	2-0	Central Florida
1983	N Carolina	Anson Dorrance	4-0	George Mason
1984	N Carolina	Anson Dorrance	2-0	Connecticut
1985	George Mason	Hank Leung	2-0	N Carolina
1986	N Carolina	Anson Dorrance	2-0	Colorado Col
1987	N Carolina	Anson Dorrance	1-0	Massachusetts
1988	N Carolina	Anson Dorrance	4-1	N Carolina St
1989	N Carolina	Anson Dorrance	2-0	Colorado Col
1990	N Carolina	Anson Dorrance	6-0	Connecticut
1991	N Carolina	Anson Dorrance	3-1	Wisconsin
1992	N Carolina	Anson Dorrance	9-1	Duke
1993	N Carolina	Anson Dorrance	6-0	George Mason

DIVISION II

Year	Champion
1988	Cal St-Hayward
1989	Barry
1990	Sonoma St
1991	Cal St-Dominguez Hills
1992	Barry
1993	Barry

DIVISION III

Year	Champion
1986	Rochester
1987	Rochester
1988	William Smith
1989	UC-San Diego
1990	Ithaca
1991	Ithaca
1992	Cortland St
1993	Trenton St

Softball

Women
DIVISION I

Year	Champion	Coach	Score	Runner-Up
1982	UCLA*	Sharron Backus	2-0†	Fresno St
1983	Texas A&M	Bob Brock	2-0‡	Cal St-Fullerton
1984	UCLA	Sharron Backus	1-0#	Texas A&M
1985	UCLA	Sharron Backus	2-1**	Nebraska
1986	Cal St-Fullerton*	Judi Garman	3-0	Texas A&M
1987	Texas A&M	Bob Brock	4-1	UCLA
1988	UCLA	Sharron Backus	3-0	Fresno St
1989	UCLA*	Sharron Backus	1-0	Fresno St
1990	UCLA	Sharron Backus	2-0	Fresno St
1991	Arizona	Mike Candrea	5-1	UCLA
1992	UCLA*	Sharron Backus	2-0	Arizona
1993	Arizona	Mike Candrea	1-0	UCLA
1994	Arizona	Mike Candrea	4-0	Cal St-Northridge

*Undefeated teams in final series. †8 innings. ‡12 innings. #13 innings. **9 innings.

Softball (Cont.)

Women (Cont.)

DIVISION II			DIVISION III	
Year	Champion		Year	Champion
1982	Sam Houston St		1982	Eastern Connecticut St*
1983	Cal St-Northridge		1983	Trenton St
1984	Cal St-Northridge		1984	Buena Vista*
1985	Cal St-Northridge		1985	Eastern Connecticut St
1986	SF Austin St		1986	Eastern Connecticut St
1987	Cal St-Northridge		1987	Trenton St*
1988	Cal St-Bakersfield		1988	Central (IA)
1989	Cal St-Bakersfield		1989	Trenton St*
1990	Cal St-Bakersfield		1990	Eastern Connecticut St
1991	Augustana (SD)		1991	Central (IA)
1992	Missouri Southern		1992	Trenton St
1993	Florida Southern		1993	Central (IA)
1994	Merrimack		1994	Trenton St

*Undefeated teams in final series.

Swimming

Men

DIVISION I

Year	Champion	Coach	Pts	Runner-Up	Pts
1937	Michigan	Matt Mann	75	Ohio St	39
1938	Michigan	Matt Mann	46	Ohio St	45
1939	Michigan	Matt Mann	65	Ohio St	58
1940	Michigan	Matt Mann	45	Yale	42
1941	Michigan	Matt Mann	61	Yale	58
1942	Yale	Robert J. H. Kiphuth	71	Michigan	39
1943	Ohio St	Mike Peppe	81	Michigan	47
1944	Yale	Robert J. H. Kiphuth	39	Michigan	38
1945	Ohio St	Mike Peppe	56	Michigan	48
1946	Ohio St	Mike Peppe	61	Michigan	37
1947	Ohio St	Mike Peppe	66	Michigan	39
1948	Michigan	Matt Mann	44	Ohio St	41
1949	Ohio St	Mike Peppe	49	Iowa	35
1950	Ohio St	Mike Peppe	64	Yale	43
1951	Yale	Robert J. H. Kiphuth	81	Michigan St	60
1952	Ohio St	Mike Peppe	94	Yale	81
1953	Yale	Robert J. H. Kiphuth	96½	Ohio St	73½
1954	Ohio St	Mike Peppe	94	Michigan	67
1955	Ohio St	Mike Peppe	90	Yale	51
				Michigan	51
1956	Ohio St	Mike Peppe	68	Yale	54
1957	Michigan	Gus Stager	69	Yale	61
1958	Michigan	Gus Stager	72	Yale	63
1959	Michigan	Gus Stager	137½	Ohio St	44
1960	Southern Cal	Peter Daland	87	Michigan	73
1961	Michigan	Gus Stager	85	Southern Cal	62
1962	Ohio St	Mike Peppe	92	Southern Cal	46
1963	Southern Cal	Peter Daland	81	Yale	77
1964	Southern Cal	Peter Daland	96	Indiana	91
1965	Southern Cal	Peter Daland	285	Indiana	278½
1966	Southern Cal	Peter Daland	302	Indiana	286
1967	Stanford	Jim Gaughran	275	Southern Cal	260
1968	Indiana	James Counsilman	346	Yale	253
1969	Indiana	James Counsilman	427	Southern Cal	306
1970	Indiana	James Counsilman	332	Southern Cal	235
1971	Indiana	James Counsilman	351	Southern Cal	260
1972	Indiana	James Counsilman	390	Southern Cal	371
1973	Indiana	James Counsilman	358	Tennessee	294
1974	Southern Cal	Peter Daland	339	Indiana	338
1975	Southern Cal	Peter Daland	344	Indiana	274
1976	Southern Cal	Peter Daland	398	Tennessee	237

Men *(Cont.)*
DIVISION I *(Cont.)*

Year	Champion	Coach	Pts	Runner-Up	Pts
1977	Southern Cal	Peter Daland	385	Alabama	204
1978	Tennessee	Ray Bussard	307	Auburn	185
1979	California	Nort Thornton	287	Southern Cal	227
1980	California	Nort Thornton	234	Texas	220
1981	Texas	Eddie Reese	259	UCLA	189
1982	UCLA	Ron Ballatore	219	Texas	210
1983	Florida	Randy Reese	238	Southern Meth	227
1984	Florida	Randy Reese	287½	Texas	277
1985	Stanford	Skip Kenney	403½	Florida	302
1986	Stanford	Skip Kenney	404	California	335
1987	Stanford	Skip Kenney	374	Southern Cal	296
1988	Texas	Eddie Reese	424	Southern Cal	369½
1989	Texas	Eddie Reese	475	Stanford	396
1990	Texas	Eddie Reese	506	Southern Cal	423
1991	Texas	Eddie Reese	476	Stanford	420
1992	Stanford	Skip Kenney	632	Texas	356
1993	Stanford	Skip Kenney	520½	Michigan	396
1994	Stanford	Skip Kenney	566½	Texas	445

DIVISION II

Year	Champion	Year	Champion
1964	Bucknell	1980	Oakland
1965	San Diego St	1981	Cal St-Northridge
1966	San Diego St	1982	Cal St-Northridge
1967	UC-Santa Barbara	1983	Cal St-Northridge
1968	Long Beach St	1984	Cal St-Northridge
1969	UC-Irvine	1985	Cal St-Northridge
1970	UC-Irvine	1986	Cal St-Bakersfield
1971	UC-Irvine	1987	Cal St-Bakersfield
1972	Eastern Michigan	1988	Cal St-Bakersfield
1973	Cal St-Chico	1989	Cal St-Bakersfield
1974	Cal St-Chico	1990	Cal St-Bakersfield
1975	Cal St-Northridge	1991	Cal St-Bakersfield
1976	Cal St-Chico	1992	Cal St-Bakersfield
1977	Cal St-Northridge	1993	Cal St-Bakersfield
1978	Cal St-Northridge	1994	Oakland
1979	Cal St-Northridge		

DIVISION III

Year	Champion	Year	Champion
1975	Cal St-Chico	1985	Kenyon
1976	St Lawrence	1986	Kenyon
1977	Johns Hopkins	1987	Kenyon
1978	Johns Hopkins	1988	Kenyon
1979	Johns Hopkins	1989	Kenyon
1980	Kenyon	1990	Kenyon
1981	Kenyon	1991	Kenyon
1982	Kenyon	1992	Kenyon
1983	Kenyon	1993	Kenyon
1984	Kenyon	1994	Kenyon

Women
DIVISION I

Year	Champion	Coach	Pts	Runner-Up	Pts
1982	Florida	Randy Reese	505	Stanford	383
1983	Stanford	George Haines	418½	Florida	389½
1984	Texas	Richard Quick	392	Stanford	324
1985	Texas	Richard Quick	643	Florida	400
1986	Texas	Richard Quick	633	Florida	586
1987	Texas	Richard Quick	648½	Stanford	631½
1988	Texas	Richard Quick	661	Florida	542½
1989	Stanford	Richard Quick	610½	Texas	547
1990	Texas	Mark Schubert	632	Stanford	622½
1991	Texas	Mark Schubert	746	Stanford	653
1992	Stanford	Richard Quick	735½	Texas	651

Women (Cont.)

DIVISION I (Cont.)

Year	Champion	Coach	Pts	Runner-Up	Pts
1993	Stanford	Richard Quick	649½	Florida	421
1994	Stanford	Richard Quick	512	Texas	421

	DIVISION II		DIVISION III	
Year	Champion	Year		Champion
1982	Cal St-Northridge	1982		Williams
1983	Clarion	1983		Williams
1984	Clarion	1984		Kenyon
1985	S Florida	1985		Kenyon
1986	Clarion	1986		Kenyon
1987	Cal St-Northridge	1987		Kenyon
1988	Cal St-Northridge	1988		Kenyon
1989	Cal St-Northridge	1989		Kenyon
1990	Oakland (MI)	1990		Kenyon
1991	Oakland (MI)	1991		Kenyon
1992	Oakland (MI)	1992		Kenyon
1993	Oakland (MI)	1993		Kenyon
1994	Oakland (MI)	1994		Kenyon

Tennis

Men

INDIVIDUAL CHAMPIONS 1883-1945

Year	Champion	Year	Champion
1883	Joesph Clark, Harvard (spring)	1914	George Church, Princeton
1883	Howard Taylor, Harvard (fall)	1915	Richard Williams II, Harvard
1884	W. P. Knapp, Yale	1916	G. Colket Caner, Harvard
1885	W. P. Knapp, Yale	1917-18	No tournament
1886	G. M. Brinley, Trinity (CT)	1919	Charles Garland, Yale
1887	P. S. Sears, Harvard	1920	Lascelles Banks, Yale
1888	P. S. Sears, Harvard	1921	Philip Neer, Stanford
1889	R. P. Huntington, Jr, Yale	1922	Lucien Williams, Yale
1890	Fred Hovey, Harvard	1923	Carl Fischer, Philadelphia Osteo
1891	Fred Hovey, Harvard	1924	Wallace Scott, Washington
1892	William Larned, Cornell	1925	Edward Chandler, California
1893	Malcolm Chace, Brown	1926	Edward Chandler, California
1894	Malcolm Chace, Yale	1927	Wilmer Allison, Texas
1895	Malcolm Chace, Yale	1928	Julius Seligson, Lehigh
1896	Malcolm Whitman, Harvard	1929	Berkeley Bell, Texas
1897	S. G. Thompson, Princeton	1930	Clifford Sutter, Tulane
1898	Leo Ware, Harvard	1931	Keith Gledhill, Stanford
1899	Dwight Davis, Harvard	1932	Clifford Sutter, Tulane
1900	Raymond Little, Princeton	1933	Jack Tidball, UCLA
1901	Fred Alexander, Princeton	1934	Gene Mako, Southern Cal
1902	William Clothier, Harvard	1935	Wilbur Hess, Rice
1903	E. B. Dewhurst, Pennsylvania	1936	Ernest Sutter, Tulane
1904	Robert LeRoy, Columbia	1937	Ernest Sutter, Tulane
1905	E. B. Dewhurst, Pennsylvania	1938	Frank Guernsey, Rice
1906	Robert LeRoy, Columbia	1939	Frank Guernsey, Rice
1907	G. Peabody Gardner, Jr, Harvard	1940	Donald McNeil, Kenyon
1908	Nat Niles, Harvard	1941	Joseph Hunt, Navy
1909	Wallace Johnson, Pennsylvania	1942	Frederick Schroeder, Jr, Stanford
1910	R. A. Holden, Jr, Yale	1943	Pancho Segura, Miami (FL)
1911	E. H. Whitney, Harvard	1944	Pancho Segura, Miami (FL)
1912	George Church, Princeton	1945	Pancho Segura, Miami (FL)
1913	Richard Williams II, Harvard		

DIVISION I

Year	Champion	Coach	Pts	Runner-Up	Pts	Individual Champion
1946	Southern Cal	William Moyle	9	William & Mary	6	Robert Falkenburg, Southern Cal
1947	William & Mary	Sharvey G. Umbeck	10	Rice	4	Gardner Larned, William & Mary
1948	William & Mary	Sharvey G. Umbeck	6	San Francisco	5	Harry Likas, San Francisco

Men (Cont.)

DIVISION I (Cont.)

Year	Champion	Coach		Runner-Up		Individual Champion
1949	San Francisco	Norman Brooks	7	Rollins/Tulane/	4	Jack Tuero, Tulane
				Washington		
1950	UCLA	William Ackerman	11	California	5	Herbert Flam, UCLA
				Southern Cal	5	
1951	Southern Cal	Louis Wheeler	9	Cincinnati	7	Tony Trabert, Cincinnati
1952	UCLA	J. D. Morgan	11	California	5	Hugh Stewart, Southern Cal
				Southern Cal	5	
1953	UCLA	J. D. Morgan	11	California	6	Hamilton Richardson, Tulane
1954	UCLA	J. D. Morgan	15	Southern Cal	10	Hamilton Richardson, Tulane
1955	Southern Cal	George Toley	12	Texas	7	Jose Aguero, Tulane
1956	UCLA	J. D. Morgan	15	Southern Cal	14	Alejandro Olmedo, Southern Cal
1957	Michigan	William Murphy	10	Tulane	9	Barry MacKay, Michigan
1958	Southern Cal	George Toley	13	Stanford	9	Alejandro Olmedo, Southern Cal
1959	Notre Dame	Thomas Fallon	8			Whitney Reed, San Jose St
	Tulane	Emmet Pare	8			
1960	UCLA	J. D. Morgan	18	Southern Cal	8	Larry Nagler, UCLA
1961	UCLA	J. D. Morgan	17	Southern Cal	16	Allen Fox, UCLA
1962	Southern Cal	George Toley	22	UCLA	12	Rafael Osuna, Southern Cal
1963	Southern Cal	George Toley	27	UCLA	19	Dennis Ralston, Southern Cal
1964	Southern Cal	George Toley	26	UCLA	25	Dennis Ralston, Southern Cal
1965	UCLA	J. D. Morgan	31	Miami (FL)	13	Arthur Ashe, UCLA
1966	Southern Cal	George Toley	27	UCLA	23	Charles Pasarell, UCLA
1967	Southern Cal	George Toley	28	UCLA	23	Bob Lutz, Southern Cal
1968	Southern Cal	George Toley	31	Rice	23	Stan Smith, Southern Cal
1969	Southern Cal	George Toley	35	UCLA	23	Joaquin Loyo-Mayo, Southern Cal
1970	UCLA	Glenn Bassett	26	Trinity (TX)	22	Jeff Borowiak, UCLA
				Rice	22	
1971	UCLA	Glenn Bassett	35	Trinity (TX)	27	Jimmy Connors, UCLA
1972	Trinity (TX)	Clarence Mabry	36	Stanford	30	Dick Stockton, Trinity (TX)
1973	Stanford	Dick Gould	33	Southern Cal	28	Alex Mayer, Stanford
1974	Stanford	Dick Gould	30	Southern Cal	25	John Whitlinger, Stanford
1975	UCLA	Glenn Bassett	27	Miami (FL)	20	Bill Martin, UCLA
1976	Southern Cal	George Toley	21			Bill Scanlon, Trinity (TX)
	UCLA	Glenn Bassett	21			
1977	Stanford	Dick Gould		Trinity (TX)		Matt Mitchell, Stanford
1978	Stanford	Dick Gould		UCLA		John McEnroe, Stanford
1979	UCLA	Glenn Bassett		Trinity (TX)		Kevin Curren, Texas
1980	Stanford	Dick Gould		California		Robert Van't Hof, Southern Cal
1981	Stanford	Dick Gould		UCLA		Tim Mayotte, Stanford
1982	UCLA	Glenn Bassett		Pepperdine		Mike Leach, Michigan
1983	Stanford	Dick Gould		Southern Meth		Greg Holmes, Utah
1984	UCLA	Glenn Bassett		Stanford		Mikael Pernfors, Georgia
1985	Georgia	Dan Magill		UCLA		Mikael Pernfors, Georgia
1986	Stanford	Dick Gould		Pepperdine		Dan Goldie, Stanford
1987	Georgia	Dan Magill		UCLA		Andrew Burrow, Miami (FL)
1988	Stanford	Dick Gould		Louisiana St		Robby Weiss, Pepperdine
1989	Stanford	Dick Gould		Georgia		Donni Leaycraft, Louisiana St
1990	Stanford	Dick Gould		Tennessee		Steve Bryan, Texas
1991	Southern Cal	Dick Leach		Georgia		Jared Palmer, Stanford
1992	Stanford	Dick Gould		Notre Dame		Alex O'Brien, Stanford
1993	Southern Cal	Dick Leach		Georgia		Chris Woodruff, Tennessee
1994	Southern Cal	Dick Leach		Stanford		Mark Merklein, Florida

Note: Prior to 1977, individual wins counted in the team's total points. In 1977, a dual-match single-elimination team championship was initiated, eliminating the point system.

DIVISION II

Year	Champion	Year	Champion	Year	Champion
1963	Cal St-LA	1971	UC-Irvine	1979	SIU-Edwardsville
1964	Cal St-LA/ S Illinois	1972	UC-Irvine/ Rollins	1980	SIU-Edwardsville
1965	Cal St-LA	1973	UC-Irvine	1981	SIU-Edwardsville
1966	Rollins	1974	San Diego	1982	SIU-Edwardsville
1967	Long Beach St	1975	UC-Irvine/ San Diego	1983	SIU-Edwardsville
1968	Fresno St	1976	Hampton		
1969	Cal St-Northridge	1977	UC-Irvine		
1970	UC-Irvine	1978	SIU-Edwardsville		

Tennis (Cont.)

Men (Cont.)

DIVISION II (Cont.)

Year	Champion	Year	Champion	Year	Champion
1984	SIU-Edwardsville	1988	Chapman	1992	UC-Davis
1985	Chapman	1989	Hampton	1993	Lander (SC)
1986	Cal Poly-SLO	1990	Cal Poly-SLO	1994	Lander (SC)
1987	Chapman	1991	Rollins		

DIVISION III

Year	Champion	Year	Champion	Year	Champion
1976	Kalamazoo	1982	Gustavus Adolphus	1989	UC-Santa Cruz
1977	Swarthmore	1983	Redlands	1990	Swarthmore
1978	Kalamazoo	1984	Redlands	1991	Kalamazoo
1979	Redlands	1985	Swarthmore	1992	Kalamazoo
1980	Gustavus Adolphus	1986	Kalamazoo	1993	Kalamazoo
1981	Claremont-M-S	1987	Kalamazoo	1994	Washington (MD)
	Swarthmore	1988	Washington & Lee		

Women

DIVISION I

Year	Champion	Coach	Runner-Up	Individual Champion
1982	Stanford	Frank Brennan	UCLA	Alycia Moulton, Stanford
1983	Southern Cal	Dave Borelli	Trinity (TX)	Beth Herr, Southern Cal
1984	Stanford	Frank Brennan	Southern Cal	Lisa Spain, Georgia
1985	Southern Cal	Dave Borelli	Miami (FL)	Linda Gates, Stanford
1986	Stanford	Frank Brennan	Southern Cal	Patty Fendick, Stanford
1987	Stanford	Frank Brennan	Georgia	Patty Fendick, Stanford
1988	Stanford	Frank Brennan	Florida	Shaun Stafford, Florida
1989	Stanford	Frank Brennan	UCLA	Sandra Birch, Stanford
1990	Stanford	Frank Brennan	Florida	Debbie Graham, Stanford
1991	Stanford	Frank Brennan	UCLA	Sandra Birch, Stanford
1992	Florida	Andy Brandi	Texas	Lisa Raymond, Florida
1993	Texas	Jeff Moore	Stanford	Lisa Raymond, Florida
1994	Georgia	Jeff Wallace	Stanford	Angela Lettiere, Georgia

DIVISION II

Year	Champion	Year	Champion	Year	Champion
1982	Cal St-Northridge	1987	SIU-Edwardsville	1992	Cal Poly-Pomona
1983	TN-Chattanooga	1988	SIU-Edwardsville	1993	UC-Davis
1984	TN-Chattanooga	1989	SIU-Edwardsville	1994	N Florida
1985	TN-Chattanooga	1990	UC-Davis		
1986	SIU-Edwardsville	1991	Cal Poly-Pomona		

DIVISION III

Year	Champion	Year	Champion	Year	Champion
1982	Occidental	1987	UC-San Diego	1992	Pomona-Pitzer
1983	Principia	1988	Mary Washington	1993	Kenyon
1984	Davidson	1989	UC-San Diego	1994	UC San Diego
1985	UC-San Diego	1990	Gustavus Adolphus		
1986	Trenton St	1991	Mary Washington		

Indoor Track and Field

Men

DIVISION I

Year	Champion	Coach	Pts	Runner-Up	Pts
1965	Missouri	Tom Botts	14	Oklahoma St	12
1966	Kansas	Bob Timmons	14	Southern Cal	13
1967	Southern Cal	Vern Wolfe	26	Oklahoma	17
1968	Villanova	Jim Elliott	35	Southern Cal	25
1969	Kansas	Bob Timmons	41½	Villanova	33
1970	Kansas	Bob Timmons	27½	Villanova	26
1971	Villanova	Jim Elliott	22	UTEP	19¼
1972	Southern Cal	Vern Wolfe	19	Bowling Green/ Mich St	18
1973	Manhattan	Fred Dwyer	18	Kansas/Kent St/UTEP	12
1974	UTEP	Ted Banks	19	Colorado	18

Indoor Track and Field *(Cont.)*

Men *(Cont.)*

DIVISION I *(Cont.)*

Year	Champion	Coach	Pts	Runner-Up	Pts
1975	UTEP	Ted Banks	36	Kansas	17½
1976	UTEP	Ted Banks	23	Villanova	15
1977	Washington St	John Chaplin	25½	UTEP	25
1978	UTEP	Ted Banks	44	Auburn	38
1979	Villanova	Jim Elliott	52	UTEP	51
1980	UTEP	Ted Banks	76	Villanova	42
1981	UTEP	Ted Banks	76	Southern Meth	51
1982	UTEP	John Wedel	67	Arkansas	30
1983	Southern Meth	Ted McLaughlin	43	Villanova	32
1984	Arkansas	John McDonnell	38	Washington St	28
1985	Arkansas	John McDonnell	70	Tennessee	29
1986	Arkansas	John McDonnell	49	Villanova	22
1987	Arkansas	John McDonnell	39	Southern Meth	31
1988	Arkansas	John McDonnell	34	Illinois	29
1989	Arkansas	John McDonnell	34	Florida	31
1990	Arkansas	John McDonnell	44	Texas A&M	36
1991	Arkansas	John McDonnell	34	Georgetown	27
1992	Arkansas	John McDonnell	53	Clemson	46
1993	Arkansas	John McDonnell	66	Clemson	30
1994	Arkansas	John McDonnell	83	UTEP	45

DIVISION II

Year	Champion	Year	Champion	Year	Champion
1985	SE Missouri St	1989	St Augustine's	1993	Abilene Christian
1987	St Augustine's	1990	St Augustine's	1994	Abilene Christian
1988	Abilene Christian	1991	St Augustine's		
	St Augustine's	1992	St Augustine's		

DIVISION III

Year	Champion	Year	Champion	Year	Champion
1985	St Thomas (MN)	1989	North Central	1993	WI-La Crosse
1986	Frostburg St	1990	Lincoln (PA)	1994	WI-La Crosse
1987	WI-La Crosse	1991	WI-La Crosse		
1988	WI-La Crosse	1992	WI-La Crosse		

Women

DIVISION I

Year	Champion	Coach	Pts	Runner-Up	Pts
1983	Nebraska	Gary Pepin	47	Tennessee	44
1984	Nebraska	Gary Pepin	59	Tennessee	48
1985	Florida St	Gary Winckler	34	Texas	32
1986	Texas	Terry Crawford	31	Southern Cal	26
1987	Louisiana St	Loren Seagrave	49	Tennessee	30
1988	Texas	Terry Crawford	71	Villanova	52
1989	Louisiana St	Pat Henry	61	Villanova	34
1990	Texas	Terry Crawford	50	Wisconsin	26
1991	Louisiana St	Pat Henry	48	Texas	39
1992	Florida	Bev Kearney	50	Stanford	26
1993	Louisiana St	Pat Henry	49	Wisconsin	44
1994	Louisiana St	Pat Henry	48	Alabama	29

DIVISION II

Year	Champion	Year	Champion	Year	Champion
1985	St Augustine's	1989	Abilene Christian	1992	Alabama A&M
1987	St Augustine's	1990	Abilene Christian	1993	Abilene Christian
1988	Abilene Christian	1991	Abilene Christian	1994	Abilene Christian

DIVISION III

Year	Champion	Year	Champion	Year	Champion
1985	MA-Boston	1989	Christopher Newport	1993	Lincoln (PA)
1986	MA-Boston	1990	Christopher Newport	1994	WI-Oshkosh
1987	MA-Boston	1991	Cortland St		
1988	Christopher Newport	1992	Christopher Newport		

Outdoor Track and Field

Men

DIVISION I

Year	Champion	Coach	Pts	Runner-Up	Pts
1921	Illinois	Harry Gill	20†	Notre Dame	16†
1922	California	Walter Christie	28†	Penn St	19†
1923	Michigan	Stephen Farrell	29†	Mississippi St	16
1924	No meet				
1925	Stanford*	R. L. Templeton	31†		
1926	Southern Cal*	Dean Cromwell	27†		
1927	Illinois*	Harry Gill	35†		
1928	Stanford	R. L. Templeton	72	Ohio St	31
1929	Ohio St	Frank Castleman	50	Washington	42
1930	Southern Cal	Dean Cromwell	55†	Washington	40
1931	Southern Cal	Dean Cromwell	77†	Ohio St	31†
1932	Indiana	Billy Hayes	56	Ohio St	49†
1933	Louisiana St	Bernie Moore	58	Southern Cal	54
1934	Stanford	R. L. Templeton	63	Southern Cal	54†
1935	Southern Cal	Dean Cromwell	74†	Ohio St	40†
1936	Southern Cal	Dean Cromwell	103†	Ohio St	73
1937	Southern Cal	Dean Cromwell	62	Stanford	50
1938	Southern Cal	Dean Cromwell	67†	Stanford	38
1939	Southern Cal	Dean Cromwell	86	Stanford	44†
1940	Southern Cal	Dean Cromwell	47	Stanford	28†
1941	Southern Cal	Dean Cromwell	81†	Indiana	50
1942	Southern Cal	Dean Cromwell	85†	Ohio St	44†
1943	Southern Cal	Dean Cromwell	46	California	39
1944	Illinois	Leo Johnson	79	Notre Dame	43
1945	Navy	E. J. Thomson	62	Illinois	48†
1946	Illinois	Leo Johnson	78	Southern Cal	42†
1947	Illinois	Leo Johnson	59†	Southern Cal	34†
1948	Minnesota	James Kelly	46	Southern Cal	41†
1949	Southern Cal	Jess Hill	55†	UCLA	31
1950	Southern Cal	Jess Hill	49†	Stanford	28
1951	Southern Cal	Jess Mortenson	56	Cornell	40
1952	Southern Cal	Jess Mortenson	66†	San Jose St	24†
1953	Southern Cal	Jess Mortenson	80	Illinois	41
1954	Southern Cal	Jess Mortenson	66†	Illinois	31†
1955	Southern Cal	Jess Mortenson	42	UCLA	34
1956	UCLA	Elvin Drake	55†	Kansas	51
1957	Villanova	James Elliott	47	California	32
1958	Southern Cal	Jess Mortenson	48†	Kansas	40†
1959	Kansas	Bill Easton	73	San Jose St	48
1960	Kansas	Bill Easton	50	Southern Cal	37
1961	Southern Cal	Jess Mortenson	65	Oregon	47
1962	Oregon	William Bowerman	85	Villanova	40†
1963	Southern Cal	Vern Wolfe	61	Stanford	42
1964	Oregon	William Bowerman	70	San Jose St	40
1965	Oregon	William Bowerman	32		
	Southern Cal	Vern Wolfe	32		
1966	UCLA	Jim Bush	81	Brigham Young	33
1967	Southern Cal	Vern Wolfe	86	Oregon	40
1968	Southern Cal	Vern Wolfe	58	Washington St	57
1969	San Jose St	Bud Winter	48	Kansas	45
1970	Brigham Young	Clarence Robison	35		
	Kansas	Bob Timmons	35		
	Oregon	William Bowerman	35		
1971	UCLA	Jim Bush	52	Southern Cal	41
1972	UCLA	Jim Bush	82	Southern Cal	49
1973	UCLA	Jim Bush	56	Oregon	31
1974	Tennessee	Stan Huntsman	60	UCLA	56
1975	UTEP	Ted Banks	55	UCLA	42
1976	Southern Cal	Vern Wolfe	64	UTEP	44
1977	Arizona St	Senon Castillo	64	UTEP	50
1978	UCLA/UTEP	Jim Bush/Ted Banks	50		
1979	UTEP	Ted Banks	64	Villanova	48
1980	UTEP	Ted Banks	69	UCLA	46
1981	UTEP	Ted Banks	70	Southern Meth	57
1982	UTEP	John Wedel	105	Tennessee	94
1983	Southern Meth	Ted McLaughlin	104	Tennessee	102

Men (Cont.)

DIVISION I (Cont.)

Year	Champion	Coach	Pts	Runner-Up	Pts
1984	Oregon	Bill Dellinger	113	Washington St	94½
1985	Arkansas	John McDonnell	61	Washington St	46
1986	Southern Meth	Ted McLaughlin	53	Washington St	52
1987	UCLA	Bob Larsen	81	Texas	28
1988	UCLA	Bob Larsen	82	Texas	41
1989	Louisiana St	Pat Henry	53	Texas A&M	51
1990	Louisiana St	Pat Henry	44	Arkansas	36
1991	Tennessee	Doug Brown	51	Washington St	42
1992	Arkansas	John McDonnell	60	Tennessee	46½
1993	Arkansas	John McDonnell	69	LSU/Ohio St	45
1994	Arkansas	John McDonnell	83	UTEP	45

*Unofficial championship. †Fraction of a point.

DIVISION II

Year	Champion	Year	Champion	Year	Champion
1963	MD-Eastern Shore	1974	Eastern Illinois	1984	Abilene Christian
1964	Fresno St		Norfolk St	1985	Abilene Christian
1965	San Diego St	1975	Cal St-Northridge	1986	Abilene Christian
1966	San Diego St	1976	UC-Irvine	1987	Abilene Christian
1967	Long Beach St	1977	Cal St-Hayward	1988	Abilene Christian
1968	Cal Poly-SLO	1978	Cal St-LA	1989	St Augustine's
1969	Cal Poly-SLO	1979	Cal Poly-SLO	1990	St Augustine's
1970	Cal Poly-SLO	1980	Cal Poly-SLO	1991	St Augustine's
1971	Kentucky St	1981	Cal Poly-SLO	1992	St Augustine's
1972	Eastern Michigan	1982	Abilene Christian	1993	St Augustine's
1973	Norfolk St	1983	Abilene Christian	1994	St Augustine's

DIVISION III

Year	Champion	Year	Champion	Year	Champion
1974	Ashland	1981	Glassboro St	1988	WI-La Crosse
1975	Southern-N Orleans	1982	Glassboro St	1989	North Central
1976	Southern-N Orleans	1983	Glassboro St	1990	Lincoln (PA)
1977	Southern-N Orleans	1984	Glassboro St	1991	WI-La Crosse
1978	Occidental	1985	Lincoln (PA)	1992	WI-La Crosse
1979	Slippery Rock	1986	Frostburg St	1993	WI-La Crosse
1980	Glassboro St	1987	Frostburg St	1994	North Central

Women

DIVISION I

Year	Champion	Coach	Pts	Runner-Up	Pts
1982	UCLA	Scott Chisam	153	Tennessee	126
1983	UCLA	Scott Chisam	116½	Florida St	108
1984	Florida St	Gary Winckler	145	Tennessee	124
1985	Oregon	Tom Heinonen	52	Florida St/LSU	46
1986	Texas	Terry Crawford	65	Alabama	55
1987	Louisiana St	Loren Seagrave	62	Alabama	53
1988	Louisiana St	Loren Seagrave	61	UCLA	58
1989	Louisiana St	Pat Henry	86	UCLA	47
1990	Louisiana St	Pat Henry	53	UCLA	46
1991	Louisiana St	Pat Henry	78	Texas	67
1992	Louisiana St	Pat Henry	87	Florida	81
1993	Louisiana St	Pat Henry	93	Wisconsin	44
1994	Louisiana St	Pat Henry	86	Texas	43

DIVISION II

Year	Champion	Year	Champion	Year	Champion
1982	Cal Poly-SLO	1987	Abilene Christian	1992	Alabama A&M
1983	Cal Poly-SLO	1988	Abilene Christian	1993	Alabama A&M
1984	Cal Poly-SLO	1989	Cal Poly-SLO	1994	Alabama A&M
1985	Abilene Christian	1990	Cal Poly-SLO		
1986	Abilene Christian	1991	Cal Poly-SLO		

DIVISION III

Year	Champion	Year	Champion	Year	Champion
1982	Central (IA)	1987	Chris. Newport	1992	Chris. Newport
1983	WI-La Crosse	1988	Chris. Newport	1993	Lincoln (PA)
1984	WI-La Crosse	1989	Chris. Newport	1994	Chris. Newport
1985	Cortland St	1990	WI-Oshkosh		
1986	MA-Boston	1991	WI-Oshkosh		

Volleyball

Men

Year	Champion	Coach	Score	Runner-Up	Most Outstanding Player
1970	UCLA	Al Scates	3-0	Long Beach St	Dane Holtzman, UCLA
1971	UCLA	Al Scates	3-0	UC-Santa Barbara	Kirk Kilgore, UCLA
					Tim Bonynge, UC-Santa Barbara
1972	UCLA	Al Scates	3-2	San Diego St	Dick Irvin, UCLA
1973	San Diego St	Jack Henn	3-1	Long Beach St	Duncan McFarland, San Diego St
1974	UCLA	Al Scates	3-2	UC-Santa Barbara	Bob Leonard, UCLA
1975	UCLA	Al Scates	3-1	UC-Santa Barbara	John Bekins, UCLA
1976	UCLA	Al Scates	3-0	Pepperdine	Joe Mika, UCLA
1977	Southern Cal	Ernie Hix	3-1	Ohio St	Celso Kalache, Southern Cal
1978	Pepperdine	Marv Dunphy	3-2	UCLA	Mike Blanchard, Pepperdine
1979	UCLA	Al Scates	3-1	Southern Cal	Sinjin Smith, UCLA
1980	Southern Cal	Ernie Hix	3-1	UCLA	Dusty Dvorak, Southern Cal
1981	UCLA	Al Scates	3-2	Southern Cal	Karch Kiraly, UCLA
1982	UCLA	Al Scates	3-0	Penn St	Karch Kiraly, UCLA
1983	UCLA	Al Scates	3-0	Pepperdine	Ricci Luyties, UCLA
1984	UCLA	Al Scates	3-1	Pepperdine	Ricci Luyties, UCLA
1985	Pepperdine	Marv Dunphy	3-1	Southern Cal	Bob Ctvrtlik, Pepperdine
1986	Pepperdine	Rod Wilde	3-2	Southern Cal	Steve Friedman, Pepperdine
1987	UCLA	Al Scates	3-0	Southern Cal	Ozzie Volstad, UCLA
1988	Southern Cal	Bob Yoder	3-2	UC-Santa Barbara	Jen-Kai Liu, Southern Cal
1989	UCLA	Al Scates	3-1	Stanford	Matt Sonnichsen, UCLA
1990	Southern Cal	Jim McLaughlin	3-1	Long Beach St	Bryan Ivie, Southern Cal
1991	Long Beach St	Ray Ratelle	3-1	Southern Cal	Brent Hilliard, Long Beach St
1992	Pepperdine	Marv Dunphy	3-0	Stanford	Alon Grinberg, Pepperdine
1993	UCLA	Al Skates	3-0	Cal St-Northridge	Mike Sealy/Jeff Nygaard, UCLA
1994	Penn St	Tom Peterson	3-2	UCLA	Ramon Hernandez, Penn St

Women

DIVISION I

Year	Champion	Coach	Score	Runner-Up
1981	Southern Cal	Chuck Erbe	3-2	UCLA
1982	Hawaii	Dave Shoji	3-2	Southern Cal
1983	Hawaii	Dave Shoji	3-0	UCLA
1984	UCLA	Andy Banachowski	3-2	Stanford
1985	Pacific	John Dunning	3-1	Stanford
1986	Pacific	John Dunning	3-0	Nebraska
1987	Hawaii	Dave Shoji	3-1	Stanford
1988	Texas	Mick Haley	3-0	Hawaii
1989	Long Beach St	Brian Gimmillaro	3-0	Nebraska
1990	UCLA	Andy Banachowski	3-0	Pacific
1991	UCLA	Andy Banachowski	3-2	Long Beach St
1992	Stanford	Don Shaw	3-1	UCLA
1993	Long Beach St	Brian Gimmillaro	3-1	Penn St

DIVISION II

Year	Champion	Year	Champion	Year	Champion
1981	Cal St-Sacramento	1986	UC-Riverside	1991	West Texas St
1982	UC-Riverside	1987	Cal St-Northridge	1992	Portland St
1983	Cal St-Northridge	1988	Portland St	1993	Northern Michigan
1984	Portland St	1989	Cal St-Bakersfield		
1985	Portland St	1990	West Texas St		

DIVISION III

Year	Champion	Year	Champion	Year	Champion
1981	UC-San Diego	1986	UC-San Diego	1991	Washington (MO)
1982	La Verne	1987	UC-San Diego	1992	Washington (MO)
1983	Elmhurst	1988	UC-San Diego	1993	Washington (MO)
1984	UC-San Diego	1989	Washington (MO)		
1985	Elmhurst	1990	UC-San Diego		

Water Polo

Men

Year	Champion	Coach	Score	Runner-Up
1969	UCLA	Bob Horn	5-2	California
1970	UC-Irvine	Ed Newland	7-6 (3 OT)	UCLA
1971	UCLA	Bob Horn	5-3	San Jose St
1972	UCLA	Bob Horn	10-5	UC-Irvine
1973	California	Pete Cutino	8-4	UC-Irvine
1974	California	Pete Cutino	7-6	UC-Irvine
1975	California	Pete Cutino	9-8	UC-Irvine
1976	Stanford	Art Lambert	13-12	UCLA
1977	California	Pete Cutino	8-6	UC-Irvine
1978	Stanford	Dante Dettamanti	7-6 (3 OT)	California
1979	UC-Santa Barbara	Pete Snyder	11-3	UCLA
1980	Stanford	Dante Dettamanti	8-6	California
1981	Stanford	Dante Dettamanti	17-6	Long Beach St
1982	UC-Irvine	Ed Newland	7-4	Stanford
1983	California	Pete Cutino	10-7	Southern Cal
1984	California	Pete Cutino	9-8	Stanford
1985	Stanford	Dante Dettamanti	12-11 (2 OT)	UC-Irvine
1986	Stanford	Dante Dettamanti	9-6	California
1987	California	Pete Cutino	9-8 (OT)	Southern Cal
1988	California	Pete Cutino	14-11	UCLA
1989	UC-Irvine	Ed Newland	9-8	California
1990	California	Steve Heaston	8-7	Stanford
1991	California	Steve Heaston	7-6	UCLA
1992	California	Steve Heaston	12-11	Stanford
1993	Stanford	Dante Dettamanti	11-9	Southern Cal

Wrestling

Division I

Year	Champion	Coach	Pts	Runner-Up	Pts	Most Outstanding Wrestler
1928	Oklahoma St*	E. C. Gallagher				
1929	Oklahoma St	E. C. Gallagher	26	Michigan	18	
1930	Oklahoma St*	E. C. Gallagher	27	Illinois	14	
1931	Oklahoma St*	E. C. Gallagher		Michigan		
1932	Indiana*	W. H. Thom		Oklahoma St		Edwin Belshaw, Indiana
1933	Oklahoma St*	E. C. Gallagher				Allan Kelley, Oklahoma St
	Iowa St*	Hugo Otopalik				Pat Johnson, Harvard
1934	Oklahoma St	E. C. Gallagher	29	Indiana	19	Ben Bishop, Lehigh
1935	Oklahoma St	E. C. Gallagher	36	Oklahoma	18	Ross Flood, Oklahoma St
1936	Oklahoma	Paul Keen	14	Central St (OK)	10	Wayne Martin, Oklahoma
				Oklahoma St	10	
1937	Oklahoma St	E. C. Gallagher	31	Oklahoma	13	Stanley Henson, Oklahoma St
1938	Oklahoma St	E. C. Gallagher	19	Illinois	15	Joe McDaniels, Oklahoma St
1939	Oklahoma St	E. C. Gallagher	33	Lehigh	12	Dale Hanson, Minnesota
1940	Oklahoma St	E. C. Gallagher	24	Indiana	14	Don Nichols, Michigan
1941	Oklahoma St	Art Griffith	37	Michigan St	26	Al Whitehurst, Oklahoma St
1942	Oklahoma St	Art Griffith	31	Michigan St	26	David Arndt, Oklahoma St
1943-45	No tournament					
1946	Oklahoma St	Art Griffith	25	Northern Iowa	24	Gerald Leeman, Northern Iowa
1947	Cornell	Paul Scott	32	Northern Iowa	19	William Koll, Northern Iowa
1948	Oklahoma St	Art Griffith	33	Michigan St	28	William Koll, Northern Iowa
1949	Oklahoma St	Art Griffith	32	Northern Iowa	27	Charles Hetrick, Oklahoma St
1950	Northern Iowa	David McCuskey	30	Purdue	16	Anthony Gizoni, Waynesburg
1951	Oklahoma	Port Robertson	24	Oklahoma St	23	Walter Romanowski, Cornell
1952	Oklahoma	Port Robertson	22	Northern Iowa	21	Tommy Evans, Oklahoma
1953	Penn St	Charles Speidel	21	Oklahoma	15	Frank Bettucci, Cornell
1954	Oklahoma St	Art Griffith	32	Pittsburgh	17	Tommy Evans, Oklahoma
1955	Oklahoma St	Art Griffith	40	Penn St	31	Edward Eichelberger, Lehigh
1956	Oklahoma St	Art Griffith	65	Oklahoma	62	Dan Hodge, Oklahoma
1957	Oklahoma	Port Robertson	73	Pittsburgh	66	Dan Hodge, Oklahoma
1958	Oklahoma St	Myron Roderick	77	Iowa St	62	Dick Delgado, Oklahoma
1959	Oklahoma St	Myron Roderick	73	Iowa St	51	Ron Gray, Iowa St
1960	Oklahoma	Thomas Evans	59	Iowa St	40	Dave Auble, Cornell

Wrestling (Cont.)

DIVISION I (Cont.)

Year	Champion	Coach	Pts	Runner-Up	Pts	Most Outstanding Wrestler
1961	Oklahoma St	Myron Roderick	82	Oklahoma	63	E. Gray Simons, Lock Haven
1962	Oklahoma St	Myron Roderick	82	Oklahoma	45	E. Gray Simons, Lock Haven
1963	Oklahoma	Thomas Evans	48	Iowa St	45	Mickey Martin, Oklahoma
1964	Oklahoma St	Myron Roderick	87	Oklahoma	58	Dean Lahr, Colorado
1965	Iowa St	Harold Nichols	87	Oklahoma St	86	Yojiro Uetake, Oklahoma St
1966	Oklahoma St	Myron Roderick	79	Iowa St	70	Yojiro Uetake, Oklahoma St
1967	Michigan St	Grady Peninger	74	Michigan	63	Rich Sanders, Portland St
1968	Oklahoma St	Myron Roderick	81	Iowa St	78	Dwayne Keller, Oklahoma St
1969	Iowa St	Harold Nichols	104	Oklahoma	69	Dan Gable, Iowa St
1970	Iowa St	Harold Nichols	99	Michigan St	84	Larry Owings, Washington
1971	Oklahoma St	Tommy Chesbro	94	Iowa St	66	Darrell Keller, Oklahoma St
1972	Iowa St	Harold Nichols	103	Michigan St	72½	Wade Schalles, Clarion
1973	Iowa St	Harold Nichols	85	Oregon St	72½	Greg Strobel, Oregon St
1974	Oklahoma	Stan Abel	69½	Michigan	67	Floyd Hitchcock, Bloomsburg
1975	Iowa	Gary Kurdelmeier	102	Oklahoma	77	Mike Frick, Lehigh
1976	Iowa	Gary Kurdelmeier	123½	Iowa St	85¾	Chuch Yagla, Iowa
1977	Iowa St	Harold Nichols	95½	Oklahoma St	88¾	Nick Gallo, Hofstra
1978	Iowa	Dan Gable	94½	Iowa St	94	Mark Churella, Michigan
1979	Iowa	Dan Gable	122½	Iowa St	88	Bruce Kinseth, Iowa
1980	Iowa	Dan Gable	110¾	Oklahoma St	87	Howard Harris, Oregon St
1981	Iowa	Dan Gable	129¾	Oklahoma	100¼	Gene Mills, Syracuse
1982	Iowa	Dan Gable	131¾	Iowa St	111	Mark Schultz, Oklahoma
1983	Iowa	Dan Gable	155	Oklahoma St	102	Mike Sheets, Oklahoma St
1984	Iowa	Dan Gable	123¾	Oklahoma St	98	Jim Zalesky, Iowa
1985	Iowa	Dan Gable	145¼	Oklahoma	98½	Barry Davis, Iowa
1986	Iowa	Dan Gable	158	Oklahoma	84¼	Marty Kistler, Iowa
1987	Iowa St	Jim Gibbons	133	Iowa	108	John Smith, Oklahoma St
1988	Arizona St	Bobby Douglas	93	Iowa	85½	Scott Turner, N Carolina St
1989	Oklahoma St	Joe Seay	91¼	Arizona St	70½	Tim Krieger, Iowa St
1990	Oklahoma St	Joe Seay	117¾	Arizona St	104¾	Chris Barnes, Oklahoma St
1991	Iowa	Dan Gable	157	Oklahoma St	108¾	Jeff Prescott, Penn St
1992	Iowa	Dan Gable	149	Oklahoma St	100½	Tom Brands, Iowa
1993	Iowa	Dan Gable	123¾	Penn St	87½	Terry Steiner, Iowa
1994	Oklahoma St	John Smith	94¾	Iowa	76½	Pat Smith, Oklahoma St

*Unofficial champions.

DIVISION II

Year	Champion
1963	Western St (CO)
1964	Western St (CO)
1965	Mankato St
1966	Cal Poly-SLO
1967	Portland St
1968	Cal Poly-SLO
1969	Cal Poly-SLO
1970	Cal Poly-SLO
1971	Cal Poly-SLO
1972	Cal Poly-SLO
1973	Cal Poly-SLO
1974	Cal Poly-SLO
1975	Northern Iowa
1976	Cal St-Bakersfield
1977	Cal St-Bakersfield
1978	Northern Iowa
1979	Cal St-Bakersfield
1980	Cal St-Bakersfield
1981	Cal St-Bakersfield
1982	Cal St-Bakersfield
1983	Cal St-Bakersfield
1984	SIU-Edwardsville
1985	SIU-Edwardsville
1986	SIU-Edwardsville
1987	Cal St-Bakersfield
1988	N Dakota St
1989	Portland St
1990	Portland St
1991	NE-Omaha
1992	Central Oklahoma
1993	Central Oklahoma
1994	Central Oklahoma

DIVISION III

Year	Champion
1974	Wilkes
1975	John Carroll
1976	Montclair St
1977	Brockport St
1978	Buffalo
1979	Trenton St
1980	Brockport St
1981	Trenton St
1982	Brockport St
1983	Brockport St
1984	Trenton St
1985	Trenton St
1986	Montclair St
1987	Trenton St
1988	St Lawrence
1989	Ithaca
1990	Ithaca
1991	Augsburg
1992	Brockport
1993	Augsburg
1994	Ithaca

INDIVIDUAL CHAMPIONSHIP
RECORDS

Swimming and Diving

Men

Event	Time	Record Holder	Date
50-yard freestyle	19.14	David Fox, N Carolina St	3-25-93
100-yard freestyle	41.80	Matt Biondi, California	4-4-87
200-yard freestyle	1:33.03	Matt Biondi, California	4-3-87
500-yard freestyle	4:11.59	Chad Carvin, Arizona	3-24-94
1650-yard freestyle	14:34.91	Chad Carvin, Arizona	3-26-94
100-yard backstroke	46.12	Jeff Rouse, Stanford	3-28-92
200-yard backstroke	1:40.64	Jeff Rouse, Stanford	3-28-92
100-yard breaststroke	52.48	Steve Lundquist, Southern Meth	3-25-83
200-yard breaststroke	1:53.77	Mike Barrowman, Michigan	3-24-90
100-yard butterfly	46.26	Pablo Morales, Stanford	4-4-86
200-yard butterfly	1:41.78	Melvin Stewart, Tennessee	3-30-91
200-yard individual medley	1:43.52	Greg Burgess, Florida	3-25-93
400-yard individual medley	3:40.64	Greg Burgess, Florida	3-26-94

Women

Event	Time	Record Holder	Date
50-yard freestyle	21.77	Amy Van Dyken, Colorado St	3-18-94
100-yard freestyle	47.61	Jenny Thompson, Stanford	3-21-92
200-yard freestyle	1:43.28	Nicole Haislett, Florida	3-20-92
500-yard freestyle	4:34.39	Janet Evans, Stanford	3-15-90
1650-yard freestyle	15:39.14	Janet Evans, Stanford	3-17-90
100-yard backstroke	53.98	Betsy Mitchell, Texas	3-21-92
200-yard backstroke	1:52.98	Whitney Hedgepeth, Texas	3-21-87
100-yard breaststroke	1:00.46	Beata Kaszuba, Arizona St	3-19-94
200-yard breaststroke	2:10.69	Kristine Quance, Southern Cal	3-19-94
100-yard butterfly	51.75	Crissy Ahmann-Leighton, Arizona	3-20-92
200-yard butterfly	1:53.42	Summer Sanders, Stanford	3-21-92
200-yard individual medley	1:55.54	Summer Sanders, Stanford	3-20-92
400-yard individual medley	4:02.28	Summer Sanders, Stanford	3-20-92

Indoor Track and Field

Men

Event	Mark	Record Holder	Date
55-meter dash	6.00	Lee McRae, Pittsburgh	3-14-86
55-meter hurdles	7.07	Allen Johnson, N Carolina	3-13-92
200-meter dash	20.59	Michael Johnson, Baylor	3-10-89
400-meter dash	45.79	Gabriel Luke, Rice	3-10-90
500-meter run	59.82	Roddie Haley, Arkansas	3-15-86
800-meter run	1:46.19	George Kersh, Mississippi	3-9-91
1000-meter run	2:18.74	Freddie Williams, Abilene Christian	3-15-86
1500-meter run	3:43.48	Paul Donovan, Arkansas	3-9-85
3000-meter run	7:50.90	Josephat Kapkory, Wash St	3-11-94
5000-meter run	13:37.94	Jonah Koech, Iowa St	3-9-90
High jump	7 ft 9¼ in	Hollis Conway, Southwestern Louisiana	3-11-89
Pole vault	19 ft 1½ in	Lawrence Johnson, Tennessee	3-12-94
Long jump	27 ft 10 in	Carl Lewis, Houston	3-13-81
Triple jump	56 ft 9½ in	Keith Connor, Southern Meth	3-13-81
Shot put	69 ft 8½ in	Michael Carter, SMU	3-13-81
		Soren Tallhem, Brigham Young	3-9-85
35-pound weight throw	76 ft 5½ in	Robert Weir, SMU	3-11-83

Women

Event	Mark	Record Holder	Date
55-meter dash	6.56	Gwen Torrence, Georgia	3-14-87
55-meter hurdles	7.44	Lynda Tolbert, Arizona St	3-9-90
200-meter dash	22.90	Holly Hyche, Indiana St	3-11-94
400-meter dash	51.05	Maicel Malone, Arizona St	3-9-91
500-meter run	1:08.89	Linetta Wilson, Nebraska	3-14-87
800-meter run	2:02.05	Amy Wickus, Wisconsin	3-11-94
1000-meter run	2:41.08	Trena Hull, NV-Las Vegas	3-14-87
1500-meter run	4:17.85	Tina Krebs, Clemson	3-9-85
3000-meter run	8:54.98	Stephanie Herbst, Wisconsin	3-15-86
5000-meter run	15:48.17	Valerie McGovern, Kentucky	3-9-90
High jump	6 ft 3½ in	J.C. Broughton, Arizona	3-14-93
Long jump	22 ft 1 in	Daphne Saunders, Louisiana St	3-12-94
Triple jump	45 ft 9 in	Sheila Hudson, California	3-10-90
Shot put	57 ft 11¾ in	Regina Cavanaugh, Rice	3-14-86

Outdoor Track and Field

Men

Event	Mark	Record Holder	Date
100-meter dash	10.03	Stanley Floyd, Houston	6-5-82
		Joe DeLoach, Houston	6-4-88
200-meter dash	19.87	Lorenzo Daniel, Mississippi St	6-3-88
400-meter dash	44.00	Quincy Watts, Southern Cal	6-6-92
800-meter run	1:44.70	Mark Everett, Florida	6-1-90
1500-meter run	3:35.30	Sydney Maree, Villanova	6-6-81
3000-meter steeplechase	8:12.39	Henry Rono, Washington St	6-1-78
5000-meter run	13:20.63	Sydney Maree, Villanova	6-2-79
10000-meter run	28:01.30	Suleiman Nyambui, UTEP	6-1-79
110-meter high hurdles	13.22	Greg Foster, UCLA	6-2-78
400-meter intermediate hurdles	47.85	Kevin Young, UCLA	6-3-88
High jump	7 ft 9¾ in	Hollis Conway, Southwestern Louisiana	6-3-89
Pole vault	19 ft ¼ in	Istvan Bagyula, George Mason	5-31-91
Long jump	28 ft	Erick Walder, Arkansas	6-3-93
Triple jump	57 ft 7¾ in	Keith Connor, Southern Meth	6-5-82
Shot put	71 ft 11 in	John Brenner, UCLA	6-2-84
Discus throw	220 ft	Karny Keshmiri, Nevada	6-5-92
Hammer throw	257 ft 0 in	Ken Flax, Oregon	6-6-86
Javelin throw	266 ft 9 in	Todd Riech, Fresno St	6-3-94
Decathlon	8279 pts	Tito Steiner, Brigham Young	6-2/3-81

Women

Event	Mark	Record Holder	Date
100-meter dash	10.78	Dawn Sowell, Louisiana St	6-3-89
200-meter dash	22.04	Dawn Sowell, Louisiana St	6-2-89
400-meter dash	50.18	Pauline Davis, Alabama	6-3-89
800-meter run	1:59.11	Suzy Favor, Wisconsin	6-1-90
1500-meter run	4:08.26	Suzy Favor, Wisconsin	6-2-90
3000-meter run	8:47.35	Vicki Huber, Villanova	6-3-88
5000-meter run	15:38.47	Annette Hand, Oregon	6-4-88
10000-meter run	32:28.57	Sylvia Mosqueda, Cal St-LA	6-1-88
100-meter hurdles	12.70	Tananjalyn Stanley, Louisiana St	6-3-89
400-meter hurdles	54.64	Latanya Sheffield, San Diego St	5-31-85
High jump	6 ft 4¼ in	Katrena Johnson, Arizona	6-1-85
Long jump	22 ft 9¼ in	Sheila Echols, Louisiana St	6-5-87
Triple jump	46 ft ¾ in	Sheila Hudson, California	6-2-90
Shot put	58 ft 2½ in	Eileen Vanisi, Texas	6-3-94
Discus throw	209 ft 10 in	Leslie Deniz, Arizona St	6-4-83
Javelin throw	206 ft 9 in	Karin Smith, Cal Poly-SLO	6-4-82
Heptathlon	6365 pts	Jackie Joyner, UCLA	5-30/31-83

Olympic

"Nearly Perfect"

Doom and gloom turned to sunshine as the Winter Games proved to be a huge success | by WILLIAM OSCAR JOHNSON

AT THE CLOSING CEREMONIES FOR the 1994 Winter Olympic Games, an exuberant Juan Antonio Samaranch, the ever optimistic, ever ongoing president of the IOC, gushed that these had been the "best ever" Olympics of winter and urged the burghers of Lillehammer to bid for the Games again in 2010 because they had been "so nearly perfect."

It is all part of Olympic lore now, but "nearly perfect" was about the last thing anyone would have predicted before the Lillehammer Games began. In fact, the success of this Olympics was uncertain from the moment Samaranch mispronounced the name as "Lily-Yammer" when he announced the award in Seoul in September '88. No sooner had the home folks heard that they had won than they began worrying that they had bitten off way too much for a small, rural Norwegian town to chew. Letters appeared in the local paper asking, "Can't we just give these Games back?"

But that wasn't allowed, so they plowed worriedly ahead and ultimately the project took off with a phenomenal infusion of about $1 billion from the Norwegian government. Venues were completed well ahead of schedule, and they were built to meet such strict and enlightened environmental standards that the IOC has said it will incorporate Lillehammer thinking into all future Olympic construction.

Moreover, the facilities received unprecedented waves of raves from athletes who used them in pre-Olympic competitions. A serious exception was the wimpy women's downhill in Hafjell, which caused 12 of 15 top-seed racers to boycott the final training run before a World Cup race in early March 1993. After some civilized debate, the Norwegian hosts transplanted the event to the tougher mountain in Kvitfjell, where the men's downhill had already been declared "a super course" by the racers.

However, as the Games drew closer,

doubts again were raised around town. There was the question of potential transportation snafus—à la the infamous Lake Placid bus-system breakdowns of '80. Lillehammer had never dealt with such multitudinous crowds or with such complex travel logistics. Due to an extreme shortage of hotel rooms in the vicinity, every morning of the 16-day Olympics, roughly 100,000 spectators had to travel 110 miles from Oslo to Lillehammer and every night they had to go back.

Trains—some as close as 10 minutes apart—running over a single-track railroad, which could be shut down both ways by common emergencies ranging from blizzards to broken-down equipment to moose floundering out of deep snow onto the track, were the major mode of transportation for those masses. In the two weeks before the Olympics were to open, moose suddenly became the central source of fear and anxiety. Unusually heavy snowfalls in the wilderness had cut food supplies there

Blair became the winningest American woman in Olympic history with her fifth gold.

and caused 10 times the normal number of moose to flock in to feed in the vicinity of the railroad. Indeed, no fewer than 78 moose had already been hit by Oslo-Lillehammer trains in the weeks before the Games. A moose-disrupted Olympics seemed inevitable. What to do? In the end the moose herd's threat to the Olympics was thwarted by wildlife experts who spread an anti-moose dose of wolf urine beside the track and also established a series of pro-moose feeding lots at locations far from the railroad. De-moosed, the trains ran on time, as did all other forms of transportation.

A more abstract—but potentially more pernicious—threat to the Lillehammer Games dealt with a matter of potential disruption and dark shadows cast by events occurring beyond the borders of Norway. To Olympic organizers' horror, *Time*

The 1,000 brought redemption at last for Jansen.

JOHN BIEVER

Along with this list of star-crossed events, the magazine brought in the death two weeks before Lillehammer of Ulrike Maier, 26, an immensely popular and talented Austrian Olympic Alpine ski racer who suffered a massive head injury after a fall in a downhill in Garmisch, Germany, as well as the terrible fate of the battered city of Sarajevo, which had given the world an unforgettably harmonious Olympics in 1984 and now, with the 10th anniversary of those gentle Games at hand, had been turned into a human slaughterhouse.

magazine published a cover story the week the Games began with a dire headline: THE STAR-CROSSED OLYMPICS. Inside, the story declared these Games to be "painfully ill-starred" because they were cursed by events ranging "from murder to mayhem to medical peril...." To arrive at these desperate definitions, *Time*'s editors had woven together a mixed bag of troubles and tragedies that could be connected to the Lillehammer Olympics one way or another. They included the recent murder of an American Olympic ice dancer's father, a terrible accident back in December on the Lillehammer luge run in which a German luge coach lost a leg in a collision with a U.S. athlete, the sacrifice by a U.S. speed skater of her place on the Olympic team when she contributed bone-marrow to her ill brother, the strange loss in an Arctic storm of the brother of Norway's greatest Olympic cross-country ski hero, Vegard Ulvang, who was to take the athletes' oath at the opening ceremonies.

Certainly all these bleak things together cast a pre-Games pall over Lillehammer, if not the whole world, but even more threatening to the Olympic soul was what *Time* labeled "The Slippery Saga of Tonya Harding." This, of course, involved two rival American figure skaters—Harding and Nancy Kerrigan— and a brutal assault on Kerrigan in January that was meant to cripple her knee and prevent her from competing in the Lillehammer Games *(page 676)*. Ultimately, Harding's husband confessed to planning the crime, Kerrigan recovered from what proved to be a minor injury to win the silver, and Harding finished eighth, admitting later that she had known about the plot after the fact but didn't participate in the brutal act. All these tawdry goings-on created such a large and sordid media circus that early on it seemed possible that Lillehammer might be forever remembered as the place where the world's first tabloid Olympics took place.

Indeed, the drumbeat of sensationalism

certainly didn't hurt the TV ratings: CBS averaged 27.8 for the Olympic duration and had the sixth highest prime-time rating in history, 48.5, 126.6 million people, on Feb. 23, the night that Harding and Kerrigan competed in the short program.

But in fact, when these Games finally got going, they produced a flood of stories of quite a different sort—bedtime stories, children's hour stories, heartwarming, soul-satisfying, *upbeat* stories, which no right-minded scandal-mongering tabloid editor would touch with a 235-centimeter downhill racing ski. As fate would have it, the most inspiring of these was a slippery saga, too, and it happened to star the most hopelessly star-crossed Olympian in recent memory: the American speed skater Dan Jansen. For much of the past decade, he has been consistently the greatest non-Olympic sprinter on earth, world champion and world-record breaker again and again. However, four times in four Olympic races, first in Calgary in '88 and then Albertville in '92, he had failed. Lillehammer was his last try. The 500 meters, his best event, was run on Valentine's Day, but no hearts or flowers for him: For the fifth straight time Dan Jansen flunked an Olympic test, touching the ice with his left hand on the final turn, losing the fragment of a second that left him eighth. "Why, God?" cried his wife, Robin. "Why again?"

There was one more chance, in the 1,000 three days later, but no one had much hope, least of all a deeply discouraged Jansen. Later he said, "I went in with such low expectations because I didn't want to set myself up for disappointment." He skated the race of his life—except!—in the next-to-last turn his left hand grazed the ice again, and the horror of a sixth straight Olympic screw-up was upon him. "For some reason I was calm about it," he said later, and he finished in a lifetime best time of 1:12.43. It wasn't only Americans who celebrated, for everyone felt great compassion for this eminently likable, profoundly unlucky fellow. In return for the world's cheers he gave Norwegians the loveliest possible signature image for their Olympics when he skated his victory lap with his blue-eyed baby girl, Jane, cradled in his arm.

The bedtime stories kept coming—a surprising number starring Americans. Most familiar was Bonnie Blair, the homespun speed skater supreme who made winning Olympic races seem as easy as Dan Jansen made it seem difficult. In Lillehammer she won her fourth and fifth gold medals over three Olympics, and when she was told this total made her the winningest American female Olympian in history, she blurted in genuine surprise, "Is *that* what it is?"

Downhill racer Tommy Moe, an unsung Alaskan who had long been a competitor of high hopes but unfulfilled promise, slammed down the gorgeous men's downhill course in Kvitfjell to win the gold, repeating the feat achieved by the cocky, one-time juvenile delinquent Bill Johnson in Sarajevo. Moe, too, had had minor delinquency problems in his teenage years and when he was asked to compare himself to the mouthy Johnson, Moe said coolly, "Billy is Billy. His achievements are what I want to copy, not his personality." Four days later Moe went out and bested Johnson's record by winning a completely unexpected silver medal in the Super G.

And in the women's Super G there was yet another American heart-warmer: Diann Roffe-Steinrotter won the gold to cap her 11th season as a World Cup racer. Hers had been a flawed, pain-racked career full of extremes: In 1985, at 17, she became the second-youngest person to win a world championship, getting gold in the giant slalom at Bormio, Italy. Until Lillehammer, Roffe-Steinrotter had won exactly one World Cup race and suffered a rash of savage injuries that kept her out of two full seasons and countless individual races. With classic true grit, she kept coming back. "I didn't want to cop out on my own potential," she said. And after the Lillehammer victory, she crowed, "I have no regrets at all about my life to this point."

Short-track racer Cathy Turner, 31, fresh from a career with the Ice Capades, won a

Norway's Koss, who won three gold medals, was as generous as he is talented.

ty who is also a cross-country skier, won five medals in all—two golds, two silvers and a bronze. Though a Milan tabloid ran a picture during the Olympics of her topless on a beach, Di Centa's Lillehammer story proved to be one of inspiration instead of titillation. Now 31, *la bella Manuela* had fought off male chauvinist coaches and blood doping on her team in the early '80s and rebounded bravely to world-class competition after a long hospitalization in 1992 due to a debilitating thyroid ailment. Her success in Lillehammer was doubly gratifying in that it symbolized far more than the mere medals she won: "I want little girls to be inspired by seeing that a woman who is not like a man can win in sport," she said. "I think my medals touch all women."

Indeed, as the Lillehammer Olympics went on, more and more people were touched by the Norwegian ambience. Even the weather was *nice* beyond belief with brilliant sunshine day after day, accompanied by temperatures so cold that the pillowy snow didn't melt, and all of the Olympic venues remained as pretty as illustrations in a children's book. Thousands of happy, hardy Norwegians camped in the fairy-tale woods above the town so they could line the cross-country ski racing trails—100,000 strong—to roar *Heiah! Heiah!* as their local heroes raced by. The amazing Norwegian sportsmen even *heiah*-ed over the success of their opponents, including the Italian 4x10 relay team which eked out an astonishing eye-blink victory over the favored Norwegians, and the indominable king of Kazakhstan, Vladimir Smirnov, 29, who held off powerful Norwegians to win the classic 50-kilometer men's cross-country ski race, his first Olympic gold in an eight-year career.

As it turned out, of course, the Norwegians had plenty to *heiah* about on their own. When the flags were finally furled after the closing ceremonies, the Norwegians had triumphed beyond their wildest hopes. Their No. 1 medal count among the

gold in '92 and another in Lillehammer in this odd, rough young Olympic sport, but she did wind up with some definite regrets. After she won the gold in the 500-meter race, she was a favorite in the 1,000—until she was summarily disqualified in the semifinals for allegedly interfering with an opponent. She denied it, but the ruling stood. Turner quit on the spot, saying, "I have a husband and a life; I'm going home. I don't want to be around these people." Though this didn't fit the happy-ending mode of the Jansen/Moe/Blair/Roffe-Steinrotter sagas, neither did it do anything to tarnish the bright narrative these Games were spinning out.

The U.S. won 13 medals, a Winter Olympics record for the country but a paltry take when compared to Norway's 26, Germany's 24 and Russia's 23. Surprisingly, the most successful individual medal winner was not from any of the nations above: Manuela Di Centa, an Italian beau-

80 nations competing was 10 gold, 11 silver, five bronze. The total of 26 didn't break the all time Winter Olympics record of 29 medals, won by the Soviet Union in 1988, but it was still the third highest total ever. And at the end, when individual Norwegians stacked up their medals like poker chips, it was the speed skater, Johann Olav Koss, 25, who had the richest, if not the highest pile. Koss won three gold medals and set three world records, including in the 10,000-meter race, where he shattered his own three-year-old mark by 12.99 seconds, an eternity. A dedicated medical student in real life, he announced that he would donate a $30,000 victory check from the Norwegian government to aid Sarajevo, and he gave his winning skates to a charity auction where they brought $80,000. There was talk of putting up a statue of Koss, and a headline in a local paper called him simply SUPERMAN! A Dutch rival, Rintje Ritsma, said in flat admiration, "He is from another star."

The rest of the Norwegian gold rush was contributed by people on various kinds of skis. The most-popular medallist: cross-country skier Bjorn Daehle, a rangy, humorous redhead who won two golds and two silvers to go with three golds and one silver he won in Albertville. The most welcome: Espen Bredesen won gold in the normal hill ski jump—Norway's first Olympic ski jumping victory in 30 years.

The most exotic: Stine Lise Hattestad won gold in the women's freestyle moguls event, a jazzy glamour event not of the ilk usually attempted by self-effacing Norwegians. The most overwhelming: In the Alpine combined event Norwegians swept the medals—gold (Lasse Kjus), silver (Kjetil Andre Aamodt) and bronze (Harald Christian Strand Nilsen)—and in a laughter-filled press conference, Kjus summarized the race in six little words that served also to define the essence of what transpired in Lillehammer over those 16 lovely days: "It was perfect for us Norwegians."

And what was perfect for them was also perfect for us—and presumably could be again in 2010. Or any other year they would like to do it.

Daehle, with two golds and two silvers, was one of the Games' most popular winners.

SCANFOTO/TERJE BRINGEDAL

FOR THE RECORD·1992 Games

TRACK AND FIELD

Men

100 METERS
1. ..Linford Christie, Great Britain — 9.96
2. ..Frank Fredericks, Namibia — 10.02
3. ..Dennis Mitchell, United States — 10.04

200 METERS
1. ..Mike Marsh, United States — 20.01
2. ..Frank Fredericks, Namibia — 20.13
3. ..Michael Bates, United States — 20.38

400 METERS
1. ..Quincy Watts, United States — 43.50OR
2. ..Steve Lewis, United States — 44.21
3. ..Samson Kitur, Kenya — 44.24

800 METERS
1. ..William Tanui, Kenya — 1:43.66
2. ..Nixon Kiprotich, Kenya — 1:43.70
3. ..Johnny Gray, United States — 1:43.97

1500 METERS
1. ..Fermin Cacho, Spain — 3:40.12
2. ..Rachid El-Basir, Morocco — 3:40.62
3. ..Mohamed Ahmed Sulaiman, Qatar — 3:40.69

5000 METERS
1. ..Dieter Baumann, Germany — 13:12.52
2. ..Paul Bitok, Kenya — 13:12.71
3. ..Fita Bayisa, Ethiopia — 13:13.03

10,000 METERS
1. ..Khalid Skah, Morocco — 27:46.70
2. ..Richard Chelimo, Kenya — 27:47.72
3. ..Addis Abebe, Ethiopia — 28.00.07

MARATHON
1. ..Hwang Young-Cho, South Korea — 2:13:23
2. ..Koichi Morishita, Japan — 2:13:45
3. ..Stephan Freigang, Germany — 2:14:00

110-METER HURDLES
1. ..Mark McKoy, Canada — 13.12
2. ..Tony Dees, United States — 13.24
3. ..Jack Pierce, United States — 13.26

400-METER HURDLES
1. ..Kevin Young, United States — 46.78WR
2. ..Winthrop Graham, Jamaica — 47.66
3. ..Kriss Akabusi, Great Britain — 47.82

3000-METER STEEPLECHASE
1. ..Mathew Birir, Kenya — 8:08.84
2. ..Patrick Sang, Kenya — 8:09.55
3. ..William Mutwol, Kenya — 8:10.74

4 X 100 METER RELAY
1. ..United States: Mike Marsh, Leroy Burrell, Dennis Mitchell, Carl Lewis — 37.40WR
2. ..Nigeria — 37.98
3. ..Cuba — 38.00

4 X 400 METER RELAY
1. ..United States: Andrew Valmon, Quincy Watts, Michael Johnson, Steve Lewis — 2:55.74 WR
2. ..Cuba — 2:59.51
3. ..Great Britain — 2:59.73

20-KILOMETER WALK
1. ..Daniel Plaza, Spain — 1:21:45
2. ..Guillaume Leblanc, France — 1:22:25
3. ..Giovanni De Benedictis, Italy — 1:23:11

50-KILOMETER WALK
1. ..Andrey Perlov, Unified Team — 3:50:13
2. ..Carlos Mercenario, Mexico — 3:52:09
3. ..Ronald Weigel, Germany — 3:53:45

HIGH JUMP
1. ..Javier Sotomayor, Cuba — 7 ft 8 in
2. ..Patrik Sjoberg, Sweden — 7 ft 8 in
3. ..Artur Partyka, Poland — 7 ft 8 in
3. ..Timothy Forsythe, Australia — 7 ft 8 in
3. ..Hollis Conway, United States — 7 ft 8 in

POLE VAULT
1. ..Maksim Tarasov, Unified Team — 19 ft ¼ in
2. ..Igor Trandenkov, Unified Team — 19 ft ¼ in
3. ..Javier Garcia, Spain — 18 ft 10¼ in

LONG JUMP
1. ..Carl Lewis, United States — 28 ft 5½ in
2. ..Mike Powell, United States — 28 ft 4¼ in
3. ..Joe Greene, United States — 27 ft 4½in

TRIPLE JUMP
1. ..Mike Conley, United States — 59 ft 7½ in
2. ..Charles Simpkins, United States — 57 ft 9 in
3. ..Frank Rutherford, Bahamas — 56 ft 11½in

SHOT PUT
1. ..Mike Stulce, United States — 71 ft 2½in
2. ..Jim Doehring, United States — 68 ft 9¼ in
3. ..Vyacheslav Lykho, Unified Team — 68 ft 8½in

DISCUS THROW
1. ..Romas Ubartas, Lithuania — 213 ft 8 in.
2. ..Jürgen Schult, Germany — 213 ft 1 in
3. ..Roberto Moya, Cuba — 210 ft 4 in

HAMMER THROW
1. ..Andrey Abduvaliyev, Unified Team — 270 ft 9 in
2. ..Igor Astapkovich, Unified Team — 268 ft 11 in
3. ..Igor Nikulin, Unified Team — 267 ft

JAVELIN
1. ..Jan Zelezny, Czechoslovakia — 294 ft 2 in OR
2. ..Seppo Räty, Finland — 284 ft 1 in
3. ..Steve Backley, Great Britain — 273 ft 7 in

DECATHLON

	Pts
1. ..Robert Zmelik, Czechoslovakia	8611
2. ..Antonio Peñalver, Spain	8412
3. ..Dave Johnson, United States	8309

Note: OR=Olympic record. WR=world record. EOR=equals Olympic record. EWR=equals world record

TRACK AND FIELD *(Cont.)*

Women

100 METERS

1. ..Gail Devers, United States — 10.82
2. ..Juliet Cuthbert, Jamaica — 10.83
3. ..Irina Privalova, Unified Team — 10.84

200 METERS

1. ..Gwen Torrence, United States — 21.81
2. ..Juliet Cuthbert, Jamaica — 22.02
3. ..Merlene Ottey, Jamaica — 22.09

400 METERS

1. ..Marie-Jose Péréc, France — 48.83
2. ..Olga Bryzgina, Unified Team — 49.05
3. ..Ximena Restrepo, Colombia — 49.64

800 METERS

1. ..Ellen Van Langen, The Netherlands — 1:55.54
2. ..Lilia Nurutdinova, Unified Team — 1:55.99
3. ..Ana Fidelia Quirot, Cuba — 1:56.80

1500 METERS

1. ..Hassiba Boulmerka, Algeria — 3:55.30
2. ..Lyudmila Rogacheva, Unified Team — 3:56.91
3. ..Qu Yunxia, China — 3:57.08

3000 METERS

1. ..Elena Romanova, Unified Team — 8:46.04
2. ..Tatiana Dorovskikh, Unified Team — 8:46.85
3. ..Angela Chalmers, Canada — 8:47.22

10,000 METERS

1. ..Derartu Tulu, Ethiopia — 31:06.02
2. ..Elana Meyer, South Africa — 31:11.75
3. ..Lynn Jennings, United States — 31:19.89

MARATHON

1. ..Valentina Yegorova, Unified Team — 2:32:41
2. ..Yuko Arimori, Japan — 2:32:49
3. ..Lorraine Moller, New Zealand — 2:33:59

100-METER HURDLES

1. ..Paraskevi Patoulidou, Greece — 12.64
2. ..LaVonna Martin, United States — 12.69
3. ..Yordanka Donkova, Bulgaria — 12.70

400-METER HURDLES

1. ..Sally Gunnell, Great Britain — 53.23
2. ..Sandra Farmer-Patrick, United States — 53.69
3. ..Janeene Vickers, United States — 54.31

4 X 100 METER RELAY

1. ..United States: Evelyn Ashford, Esther Jones, Carlette Guidry, Gwen Torrence — 42.11
2. ..Unified Team — 42.16
3. ..Nigeria — 42.81

4 X 400 METER RELAY

1. ..Unified Team: Yelena Ruzina, Lioudmila Dzhigalova, Olga Nazarova, Olga Bryzgina — 3:20.20
2. ..United States: Natasha Kaiser, Gwen Torrence, Jearl Miles, Rochelle Stevens — 3:20.92
3. ..Great Britain — 3:24.23

HIGH JUMP

1. ..Heike Henkel, Germany — 6 ft 7½ in
2. ..Galina Astafei, Romania — 6 ft 6¾ in
3. ..Joanet Quintero, Cuba — 6 ft 5½ in

LONG JUMP

1. ..Heike Drechsler, Germany — 23 ft 5¼ in
2. ..Inessa Kravets, Unified Team — 23 ft 4½ in
3. ..Jackie Joyner-Kersee, United States — 23 ft 2½ in

SHOT PUT

1. ..Svetlana Kriveleva, Unified Team — 69 ft 1¼ in
2. ..Huang Zhihong, China — 67 ft 2 in
3. ..Kathrin Neimke, Germany — 64 ft 10¾ in

DISCUS THROW

1. ..Maritza Martén, Cuba — 229 ft 10 in
2. ..Tzvetanka Mintcheva Khristova, Unified Team — 222 ft 4 in
3. ..Daniela Costian, Australia — 217 ft 4 in

JAVELIN

1. ..Silke Renk, Germany — 224 ft 2 in
2. ..Natalia Shikolenka, Unified Team — 223 ft 11 in
3. ..Karen Forkel, Germany — 219 ft 4 in

HEPTATHLON

	Pts
1. ..Jackie Joyner-Kersee, United States	7044
2. ..Irina Belova, Unified Team	6845
3. ..Sabine Braun, Germany	6649

BADMINTON

Men

SINGLES

1. ..Allan Budikusuma, Indonesia
2. ..Ardy B. Wiranata, Indonesia
3. ..Hermawan Susanto, Indonesia
3. ..Thomas Stuer-Lauridsen, Denmark

DOUBLES

1. ..Park Joo-Bong & Kim Moon Soo, South Korea
2. ..Rudy Gunawan & Eddy Hrtona, Indonesia
3. ..Razif Sidek & Jalani Sidek, Malaysia
3. ..Li Yongbo & Tian Bingyi, China

Women

SINGLES

1. ..Susi Susanti, Indonesia
2. ..Bang Soo Hyun, South Korea
3. ..Huang Hua, China
3. ..Tang Jiuhong, China

DOUBLES

1. ...Hwang Hye Young & Chung So Young, South Korea
2. ..Guan Weizhen & Nong Qunhua, China
3. ..Lin Yanfen & Yao Fen, China
3. ..Young Ah Gil & Eun Jung Shim, South Korea

BASEBALL

1. .... Cuba
2. .... Taiwan
3. .... Japan

CANOE/KAYAK

Men

C-1 FLATWATER 500 METERS

1....Nikolai Boukhalov, Bulgaria	1:51.14
2....Mikhail Slivinski, Unfied Team	1:51.40
3....Olaf Heukrodt, Germany	1:53.00

C-1 FLATWATER 1000 METERS

1....Nikolai Boukhalov, Bulgaria	4:05.92
2....Ivana Klementzjeve, Latvia	4:06.60
3....Gyorgy Zala, Hungary	4:07.35

C-2 FLATWATER 500 METERS

1....A. Maccekov & D. Dovgalenok, Unified Team	1:41.54
2....U. Papke & I. Spelly, Germany	1:41.68
3....M. Marinov & B. Stoyanov, Bulgaria	1:41.94

C-2 FLATWATER 1000 METERS

1....U. Papke & I. Spelly, Germany	3:37.42
2....A. Nielsson & C. Frederiksen, Denmark	3:39.26
3....D. Hoyer & O. Bolvin, France	3:39.51

C-1 WHITEWATER SLALOM

	Pts
1....Lukos Pollerr, Czechoslovakia	113.69
2....Gareth John Marriott, Great Britain	116.48
3....Jacky Avril, France	117.18

C-2 WHITEWATER SLALOM

	Pts
1....S. Strausbaugh & J, Jacobi, U.S.	122.41
2....M. Simek & J. Rohan, Czechosolvakia	124.25
3....F. Adisson & W. Forgues, France	124.38

K-1 FLATWATER 500 METERS

1....Mikko Kolehmainen, Finland	1:40.34
2....Zaolt Gyulay, Hungary	1:40.64
3....Knut Hofmann, Norway	1:40.71

K-1 FLATWATER 1000 METERS

1....Clint Robinson, Australia	3:37.26
2....Knut Hofmann, Norway	3:37.50
3....Greg Barton, United States	3:37.93

Men *(Cont.)*

K-2 FLATWATER 500 METERS

1....K. Bluhm & T. Gutsche, Germany	1:28.27
2....M. Freimut & W. Kurpiewski, Poland	1:29.84
3....A. Rossi & B. Dreossi, Italy	1:30.00

K-2 FLATWATER 1000 METERS

1....K. Bluhm & T. Gutsche, Germany	3:16.10
2....G. Olsson & K. Sundqvist, Sweden	3:17.70
3....G. Kotowicz & D. Bielkowski, Poland	3:18.86

K-4 FLATWATER 1000 METERS

1....Germany	2:54.18
2....Hungary	2:54.82
3....Australia	2:56.97

Women

K-1 WHITEWATER SLALOM

	Pts
1....Pierpaolo Ferrazzi, Italy	106.89
2....Sylvain Curiruer, France	107.06
3....Jochen Lettmann, Germany	108.52

K-1 FLATWATER 500 METERS

1....Birgit Schmidt, Germany	1:51.60
2....Rita Koban, Hungary	1:51.96
3....Izabella Dylewska, Poland	1:52.36

K-2 FLATWATER 500 METERS

1....R. Portwich & A. Von Seck, Germany	1:40.29
2....S. Gunnarsson & A. Andersson, Sweden	1:40.41
3....R. Koban & E. Donusz, Hungary	1:40.81

K-4 FLATWATER 500 METERS

1....Hungary	1:38.32
2....Germany	1:38.47
3....Sweden	1:39.79

K-1 WHITEWATER SLALOM

	Pts
1....Elizabeth Micheler, Germany	126.41
2....Danielle Woodward, Australia	128.27
3....Dana Chladek, United States	131.75

BASKETBALL

Men

Final: United States 117, Croatia 85
Lithuania (3rd)
United States: Christian Laettner, David Robinson, Patrick Ewing, Larry Bird, Scottie Pippen, Michael Jordan, Clyde Drexler, Karl Malone, John Stockton, Chris Mullin, Charles Barkley, Earvin Johnson

Women

Final: Unified Team 76, China 66
United States (3rd):
Teresa Edwards, Daedra Charles, Clarissa Davis, Tammy Jackson, Teresa Weatherspoon, Vickie Orr, Victoria Bullett, Carolyn Jones, Katrina McClain, Medina Dixon, Cynthia Cooper, Suzanne McConnell

BOXING

LIGHT FLYWEIGHT (106 LB)

1. ....Rogelio Marcelo, Cuba
2. ....Daniel Bojinov, Bulgaria
3. ....Jan Quast, Germany
3. ....Roel Velasco, Philippines

FLYWEIGHT (112 LB)

1. ....Su Choi Choi, North Korea
2. ....Raul Gonzalez, Cuba
3. ....Timothy Austin, United States
3. ....Istvan Kovacs, Hungary

BANTAMWEIGHT (119 LB)

1. ....Joel Casamayor, Cuba
2. ....Wayne McCullough, Ireland
3. ....Li Gwang Sik, North Korea
3. ....Mohamed Achik, Morocco

FEATHERWEIGHT (125 LB)

1. ....Andreas Tews, Germany
2. ....Faustino Reyes, Spain
3. ....Hocine Soltani, Algeria
3. ....Ramazi Paliani, Unified Team

LIGHTWEIGHT (132 LB)

1. ....Oscar De La Hoya, United States
2. ....Marco Rudolph, Germany
3. ....Hong Sung Sik, North Korea
3. ....Namjil Bayarsaikhan, Mongolia

LIGHT WELTERWEIGHT (139 LB)

1. ....Hector Vinent, Cuba
2. ....Mark Leduc, Canada
3. ....Jyri Kjall, Finland
3. ....Leonard Doroftei, Romania

WELTERWEIGHT (147 LB)

1. ....Michael Carruth, Ireland
2. ....Juan Hernandez, Cuba
3. ....Aniibal Acevedo Santiago, Puerto Rico
3. ....Arkom Chenglai, Thailand

LIGHT MIDDLEWEIGHT (156 LB)

1. ....Juan Lemus, Cuba
2. ....Orhan Delibas, Netherlands
3. ....Gyorgy Mizsei, Hungary
3. ....Robin Reid, Great Britain

MIDDLEWEIGHT (165 LB)

1. ....Ariel Hernandez, Cuba
2. ....Chris Byrd, United States
3. ....Chris Johnson, Canada
3. ....Lee Seung Bae, South Korea

LIGHT HEAVYWEIGHT (178 LB)

1. ....Torsten May, Germany
2. ....Rostislav Zaoulitchnyi, Unified Team
3. ....Zoltan Beres, Hungary
3. ....Wojciech Bartnik, Poland

HEAVYWEIGHT (201 LB)

1. ....Felix Savon, Cuba
2. ....David Izonritei, Nigeria
3. ....Arnold Van Der Lijde, The Netherlands
3. ....David Tua, New Zealand

SUPERHEAVYWEIGHT (201+ LB)

1. ....Roberto Balado, Cuba
2. ....Richard Igbineghu, Nigeria
3. ....Brian Nielsen, Denmark
3. ....Svilen Roussinov, Bulgaria

GYMNASTICS

Men

ALL-AROUND

		Pts
1.	Vitaly Scherbo, Unified Team	59.025
2.	Grigory Misiutin, Unified Team	58.925
3.	Valery Belenki, Unified Team	58.625

HORIZONTAL BAR

		Pts
1.	Trent Dimas, United States	9.875
1.	Grigory Misiutin, Unified Team	9.837
3.	Andreas Wecker, Germany	9.837

PARALLEL BARS

		Pts
1.	Vitaly Scherbo, Unified Team	9.900
2.	Li Jing, China	9.812
3.	Guo Linyao, China	9.800
3.	Igor Korobchinski, Unified Team	9.800
3.	Masayuki Matsunaga, Japan	9.800

VAULT

		Pts
1.	Vitaly Scherbo, Unified Team	9.856
2.	Grigory Misiutin, Unified Team	9.781
3.	Yoo Ok Ryul, South Korea	9.762

Women

ALL-AROUND

		Pts
1.	Tatiana Gutsu, Unified Team	39.737
2.	Shannon Miller, United States	39.725
3.	Lavinia Milosovici, Romania	39.687

VAULT

		Pts
1.	Henrietta Onodi, Hungary	9.925
1.	Lavinia Milosovici, Romania	9.925
3.	Tatiana Lisenko, Unified Team	9.912

UNEVEN BARS

		Pts
1.	Lu Li, China	10.000
2.	Tatiana Gutsu, Unified Team	9.975
3.	Shannon Miller, United States	9.962

BALANCE BEAM

		Pts
1.	Tatiana Lisenko, Unified Team	9.975
2.	Lu Li, China	9.912
2.	Shannon Miller, United States	9.912

GYMNASTICS (Cont.)

Men

POMMEL HORSE

	Pts
1. ....Vitaly Scherbo, Unified Team	9.925
1. ....Pae Gil Su, North Korea	9.925
3. ....Andreas Wecker, Germany	9.887

RINGS

	Pts
1. ....Vitaly Scherbo, Unified Team	9.937
1. ....Li Jing, China	9.875
3. ....Li Xiaosahuang, China	9.862
3. ....Andreas Wecker, Germany	9.862

FLOOR EXERCISE

	Pts
1. ....Li Xizosahuang, China	9.925
2. ....Grigory Misiutin, Unified Team	9.787
2. ....Yukio Iketani, Japan	9.787

TEAM COMBINED EXERCISES

	Pts
1. ....Unified Team	585.450
2. ....China	580.375
3. ....Japan	578.250

Women

FLOOR EXERCISE

	Pts
1. ....Lavinia Milosovici, Romania	10.000
2. ....Henrietta Onodi, Hungary	9.950
3. ....Shannon Miller, United States	9.912
3. ....Cristina Bontas, Romania	9.912
3. ....Tatiana Gutsu, Unified Team	9.912

TEAM COMBINED EXERCISES

	Pts
1. ....Unified Team	395.666
2. ....Romania	395.079
3. ....United States	394.704

RHYTHMIC ALL-AROUND

	Pts
1. ....Aleksandra Timoshenko, Unified Team	59.037
2. ....Carolina Pascual Gracia, Spain	58.100
3. ....Oksana Skaldina, Unified Team	57.912

SWIMMING

Men

50-METER FREESTYLE

1. ..Aleksandr Popov, Unified Team	21.91 OR
2. ..Matt Biondi, United States	22.09
3. ..Tom Jager, Unified States	22.30

100-METER FREESTYLE

1. ..Aleksandr Popov, Unified Team	49.02
2. ..Gustavo Borges, Brazil	49.43
3. ..Stephan Caron, France	49.50

200-METER FREESTYLE

1. ..Evgueni Sadovyi, Unified Team	1:46.70 OR
2. ..Anders Holmertz, Sweden	1:46.86
3. ..Antti Kasvio, Finland	1:47.63

400-METER FREESTYLE

1. ..Evgueni Sadovyi, Unified Team	3:45.00 WR
2. ..Kieren Perkins, Australia	3:45.16
3. ..Anders Holmertz, Sweden	3:46.77

1500-METER FREESTYLE

1. ..Kieren Perkins, Australia	14:43.48 WR
2. ..Glen Housman, Australia	14:55.29
3. ..Jörg Hoffmann, Germany	15:02.29

100-METER BACKSTROKE

1. ..Mark Tewksbury, Canada	53.98 WR
2. ..Jeff Rouse, United States	54.04
3. ..David Berkoff, United States	54.78

100-METER BACKSTROKE

1. ..Martin Zubero-Lopez, Spain	1:58.47 OR
2. ..Vladimir Selkov, Unified Team	1:58.87
3. ..Stefano Battistelli, Italy	1:59.40

100-METER BREASTSTROKE

1. ..Nelson Diebel, United States	1:01.50 OR
2. ..Norbert Rozsa, Hungary	1:01.68
3. ..Philip Rogers, Australia	1:01.76

200-METER BREASTSTROKE

1. ..Mike Barrowman, United States	2:10.16 WR
2. ..Norbert Rozsa, Hungary	2:11.23
3. ..Nick Gillingham, Great Britain	2:11.29

100-METER BUTTERFLY

1. ..Pablo Morales, United States	53.32
2. ..Rafal Szukala, Poland	53.35
3. ..Anthony Nesty, Surinam	53.41

200-METER BUTTERFLY

1. ..Melvin Stewart, United States	1:56.26
2. ..Danyon Loader, New Zealand	1:57.93
3. ..Franck Esposito, France	1:58.51

200-METER INDIVIDUAL MEDLEY

1. ..Tamas Darnyi, Hungary	2:00.76
2. ..Greg Burgess, United States	2:00.97
3. ..Attila Czene, Hungary	2:01.00

400-METER INDIVIDUAL MEDLEY

1. ..Tamas Darnyi, Hungary	4:14.23 OR
2. ..Eric Namesnik, United States	4:15.57
3. ..Luca Sacchi, Italy	4:16.34

4 X 100 METER MEDLEY RELAY

1. ..United States: Jeff Rouse, Nelson Diebel, Pablo Morales, Jon Olsen	3:36.93 WR
2. ..Unified Team	3:38.56
3. ..Canada	3:39.66

Note: OR=Olympic record. WR=world record. EOR=equals Olympic record. EWR=equals world record

SWIMMING (Cont.)

Men (Cont.)

4 X 100 METER FREESTYLE RELAY

1. ..United States: Joe Hudepohl, Matt Biondi, Tom Jager, Jon Olsen	3:16.74	
2. ..Unified Team	3:17.56	
3. ..Germany	3:17.90	

4 X 200 METER FREESTYLE RELAY

1. ..Unified Team: Dimitri Lepikov, Vladimir Pychenko, Veniamin Taianovitch, Evgueni Sadovyi	7:11.95 WR	
2. ..Sweden	7:15.51	
3. ..United States	7:16.23	

Women

50-METER FREESTYLE

1. ..Yang Wenyi, China	24.79 WR	
2. ..Zhuang Yong, China	25.08	
3. ..Angel Martino, United States	25.23	

100-METER FREESTYLE

1. ..Zhuang Yong, China	54.64 OR	
2. ..Jenny Thompson, United States	54.84	
3. ..Franziska Van Almsick, Germany	54.94	

200-METER FREESTYLE

1. ..Nicole Haislett, United States	1:57.90	
2. ..Franziska Van Almsick, Germany	1:58.00	
3. ..Kerstin Kielgass, Germany	1:59.67	

400-METER FREESTYLE

1. ..Dagmar Hase, Germany	4:07.18	
2. ..Janet Evans, United States	4:07.37	
3. ..Hayley Lewis, Australia	4:11.22	

800-METER FREESTYLE

1. ..Janet Evans, United States	8:25.52	
2. ..Hayley Lewis, Australia	8:30.34	
3. ..Jana Henke, Germany	8:30.99	

100-METER BACKSTROKE

1. ..Krisztina Egerszegi, Hungary	1:00.68 OR	
2. ..Tunde Szabo, Hungary	1:01.14	
3. ..Lea Loveless, United States	1:01.43	

200-METER BACKSTROKE

1. ..Krisztina Egerszegi, Hungary	2:07.06	
2. ..Dagmar Hase, Germany	2:09.46	
3. ..Nicole Stevenson, Australia	2:10.20	

100-METER BREASTSTROKE

1. ..Elena Roudkovskaia, Unified Team	1:08.00	
2. ..Anita Nall, United States	1:08.17	
3. ..Samantha Riley, Australia	1:09.25	

200-METER BREASTSTROKE

1. ..Kyoko Iwasaki, Japan	2:26.65 OR	
2. ..Lin Li, China	2:26.85	
3. ..Anita Nall, United States	2:26.88	

100-METER BUTTERFLY

1. ..Qian Hong, China	58.62 OR	
2. ..Crissy Ahmann-Leighton, United States	58.74	
3. ..Catherine Plewinski, France	59.01	

200-METER BUTTERFLY

1. ..Summer Sanders, United States	2:08.67	
2. ..Wang Ziaohong, China	2:09.01	
3. ..Susan O'Neill, Australia	2:09.03	

200-METER INDIVIDUAL MEDLEY

1. ..Lin Li, China	2:11.65 WR	
2. ..Summer Sanders, United States	2:11.91	
3. ..Daniela Hunger, Germany	2:13.92	

400-METER INDIVIDUAL MEDLEY

1. ..Krisztina Egerszegi, Hungary	4:36.54	
2. ..Lin Li, China	4:36.73	
3. ..Summer Sanders, United States	4:37.58	

4 X 100 METER MEDLEY RELAY

1. ..United States: Lea Loveless, Anita Nall, Crissy Ahmann-Leighton, Jenny Thompson	4:02.54 WR	
2. ..Germany	4:05.19	
3. ..Unified Team	4:06.44	

4 X 100 METER FREESTYLE RELAY

1. ..United States: Nicole Haislett, Dara Torres, Angel Martino, Jenny Thompson	3:39.46 WR	
2. ..China	3:40.12	
3. ..Germany	3:41.60	

DIVING

Men

SPRINGBOARD

		Pts
1. ....Mark Lenzi, United States		676.53
2. ....Tan Liangde, China		645.57
3. ....Dmitri Saoutine, Unified Team		627.78

PLATFORM

		Pts
1. ....Sun Shuwei, China		677.31
2. ....Scott Donie, United States		633.63
3. ....Xiong Ni, China		600.15

Women

SPRINGBOARD

		Pts
1. ....Gao Min, China		572.40
2. ....Irina Lachko, Unified Team		514.14
3. ....Brita Pia Baldus, Germany		503.07

PLATFORM

		Pts
1. ....Fu Mingxia, China		461.43
2. ....Yelena Mirochina, Unified Team		411.63
3. ....Mary Ellen Clark, United States		401.91

Note: OR=Olympic record. WR=world record. EOR=equals Olympic record. EWR=equals world record

INDIVIDUAL ARCHERY

Men

1. ....Sebastien Flute, France
2. ....Chung Jae Hun, South Korea
3. ....Simon Terry, Great Britain

Women

1. ....Cho Youn Jeong, South Korea
2. ....Kim Soo Nyung, South Korea
3. ....Natalia Valeeva, Unified Team

CYCLING

Men

100 KM TEAM TIME TRIAL

1. ..Germany: Bernd Dittert,   2:01:39
   Christian Meyer, Uwe Peschel,
   Michael Rich
2. ..Italy   2:02:39
3. ..France   2:05:25

1 KM TIME TRIAL

1. ..Jose Moreno, Spain   1:03.342 OR
2. ..Shane Kelly, Australia   1:04.288
3. ..Erin Hartwell, United States   1:04.753

4000 METER INDIVIDUAL PURSUIT

1. ..Chris Boardman, Great Britain
2. ..Jens Lehmann, Germany
3. ..Gary Anderson, New Zealand

4000 METER TEAM PURSUIT

1. ..Germany: M. Gloeckner,   4:08.791
   Jens Lehmann, Stefan Steinweg,
   Guido Fulst
2. ..Australia   4:10.218
3. ..Denmark   4:15.860

POINTS RACE

1. ..Giovanni Lombardi, Italy   44
2. ..Leon Van Bon, The Netherlands   43
3. ..Cedric Mathy, Belgium   41

INDIVIDUAL ROAD RACE

1. ..Fabio Casartelli, Italy   4:35.21
2. ..Erik Dekker, The Netherlands   4:35.22
3. ..Dainis Ozols, Latvia   4:35.24

Women

SPRINT

1. ......Erika Saloumiae, Estonia
2. ......Annett Neumann, Germany
3. ......Ingrid Haringa, The Netherlands

ROAD RACE

1. ..Kathryn Watt, Australia   2:04.42
2. ..Jeannie Longo-Ciprelli, France   2:05.02
3. ..Monique Knol, The Netherlands   2:05.03

EQUESTRIAN

3-DAY TEAM

1. ......Australia: David Green,   288.60
   Gillian Rolton, Andrew Hoy
   Matthew Ryan
2. ......New Zealand   290.80
3. ......Germany   300.30

3-DAY INDIVIDUAL

1. ......Matthew Ryan, Australia   70.00
2. ......Herbert Blocker, Germany   81.30
3. ......Blyth Tait, New Zealand   87.60

TEAM DRESSAGE

1. ......Germany: Isabelle Werth,   5224
   Klaus Balkenhol,
   Monica Theodorescu, Nicole Uphoff
2. ......The Netherlands   4742
3. ......United States   4643

INDIVIDUAL DRESSAGE

1. ......Nicole Uphoff, Germany   1768
2. ......Isabelle Werth, Germany   1762
3. ......Klaus Balkenhol, Germany   1694

TEAM JUMPING

1. ......The Netherlands: Piet Raymakers,   12.00
   Bert Romp, Jan Tops, Jos Lansink
2. ......Austria   16.75
3. ......France   24.75

INDIVIDUAL JUMPING

1. ......Ludger Beerbaum, Germany   0.00
2. ......Piet Raymakers, The Netherlands   .25
3. ......Norman Dello Joio, United States   4.75

Note: OR=Olympic record. WR=world record. EOR=equals Olympic record. EWR=equals world record

INDIVIDUAL FENCING

Men

FOIL

1. ....Philippe Omnes, France
2. ....Sergei Goloubitski, Unified Team
3. ....Elvis Gregory Gil, Cuba

SABRE

1. ....Bence Szabo, Hungary
2. ....Marco Marin, Italy
3. ....Jean-Francois Lamour, France

Men *(Cont.)*

EPEE

1. ....Eric Srecki, France
2. ....Pavel Kolobkov, Unified Team
3. ....Jean-Michel Henry, France

Women

FOIL

1. ....Giovanna Trillini, Italy
2. ....Wang Huifeng, China
3. ....Tatiana Sadovskaia, Unified Team

FIELD HOCKEY

Men

1. ....Germany
2. ....Australia
3. ....Pakistan

Women

1. ....Spain
2. ....Germany
3. ....Great Britain

TEAM HANDBALL

Men

1. ....Unified Team
2. ....Sweden
3. ....France

Women

1. ....South Korea
2. ....Norway
3. ....Unified Team

JUDO

EXTRA-LIGHTWEIGHT

1. ....Nazim Guseinov, Unified Team
2. ....Yoon Hyun, South Korea
3. ....Tadanori Koshino, Japan
3. ....Richard Trautmann, Germany

HALF-LIGHTWEIGHT

1. ....Rogerio Sampaio Cardoso, Brazil
2. ....Josef Czak, Hungary
3. ....Udo Quellmalz, Germany
3. ....Israel Hernandez Planas, Cuba

LIGHTWEIGHT

1. ....Toshihiko Koga, Japan
2. ....Bertalan Hajtos, Hungary
3. ....Chung Hoon, South Korea
3. ....Shay Oren Smadga, Israel

HALF-MIDDLEWEIGHT

1. ....Hidehiko Yoshida, Japan
2. ....Jason Morris, United States
3. ....Bertrand Domaisin, France
3. ....Kím Byung Joo, South Korea

MIDDLEWEIGHT

1. ....Waldemar Legien, Poland
2. ....Pascal Tayot, France
3. ....Hirotaka Okada, Japan
3. ....Nicolas Gill, Canada

HALF-HEAVYWEIGHT

1. ....Antal Kovacs, Hungary
2. ....Raymond Stevens, Great Britain
3. ....Dmitri Sergeev, Unified Team
3. ....Theo Meijer, The Netherlands

HEAVYWEIGHT

1. ....David Khakaleshvili, Unified Team
2. ....Naoya Ogowa, Japan
3. ....David Douillet, France
3. ....Imre Csosz, Hungary

MODERN PENTATHLON

TEAM

1. ....Poland
2. ....Unified Team
3. ....Italy

INDIVIDUAL

1. ....Arkadiusz Skrzypaszek, Poland
2. ....Attila Mizser, Hungary
3. ....Eduard Zenovka, Unified Team

ROWING

Men

SINGLE SCULLS
1. ..Thomas Lange, Germany 6:51.40
2. ..Vaclav Chalupa, Czechoslovakia 6:52.93
3. ..Kajetan Broniewski, Poland 6:56.82

DOUBLE SCULLS
1. ..Australia 6:17.32
2. ..Austria 6:18.42
3. ..The Netherlands 6:22.82

COXLESS PAIR
1. ..Great Britain 6:27.72
2. ..Germany 6:32.68
3. ..Slovenia 6:33.43

COXED FOUR
1. ..Romania 5:59.37
2. ..Germany 6:00.34
3. ..Poland 6:03.27

COXED PAIR
1. ..Great Britain 6:49.83
2. ..Italy 6:50.98
3. ..Romania 6:51.58

QUADRUPLE SCULLS
1. ..Germany 5:45.17
2. ..Norway 5:47.09
3. ..Italy 5:47.33

COXLESS FOUR
1. ..Australia 5:55.04
2. ..United States 5:56.68
3. ..Slovenia 5:58.24

EIGHT-OARS
1. ..Canada 5:29.53
2. ..Romania 5:29.67
3. ..Germany 5:31.00

Women

SINGLE SCULLS
1. ..Elisabeta Lipa, Romania 7:25.54
2. ..Annelies Bredael, Belgium 7:26.64
3. ..Silken Suzette Laumann, Canada 7:28.85

DOUBLE SCULLS
1. ..Germany 6:49.00
2. ..Romania 6:51.47
3. ..China 6:55.16

COXLESS PAIR
1. ..Canada 7:06.22
2. ..Germany 7:07.96
3. ..United States 7:08.12

COXLESS FOUR
1. ..Canada 6:30.85
2. ..United States 6:31.86
3. ..Germany 6:32.34

QUADRUPLE SCULLS
1. ..Germany 6:20.18
2. ..Romania 6:24.34
3. ..Unified Team 6:25.07

EIGHT-OARS
1. ..Canada 6:02.62
2. ..Romania 6:06.26
3. ..Germany 6:07.80

SOCCER

1. ....Spain
2. ....Poland
3. ....Ghana

SYNCHRONIZED SWIMMING

SOLO
	Pts
1. ....Kristen Babb-Sprague, United States	191.848
2. ....Sylvie Frechette, Canada	191.717
3. ....Fumiko Okuno, Japan	187.056

DUET
	Pts
1. ....Karen & Sarah Josephson, United States	192.175
2. ....Penny & Vicky Vilagos, Canada	189.394
3. ....Fumiko Okuno & Aki Takayama, Japan	186.868

SHOOTING

Men

THREE-POSITION RIFLE
	Pts
1. .....Gracha Petikian, Unified Team	1267.4
2. .....Bob Foth, United States	1266.6
3. .....Ryohei Koba, Japan	1265.9

AIR RIFLE
	Pts
1. .....Jury Fedkin, Unified Team	695.3
2. .....Franck Badiou, France	691.9
3. .....Johann Riederer, Germany	691.7

FREE RIFLE PRONE
	Pts
1. .....Eun-Chul Lee, South Korea	702.5
2. .....Harald Stenvaag, Norway	701.4
3. .....Stevan Pletikosic, Independent Team	701.1

FREE PISTOL
	Pts
1. .....Konstantine Loukachik, Unified Team	658
2. .....Yifu Wang, China	657
3. .....Ragnar Skanaker, Sweden	657

SHOOTING

Men

RAPID-FIRE PISTOL

	Pts
1......Ralf Schumann, Germany	885
2......Afanasij Kusmin, Latvia	882
3......Vladimir Vokhmianin, Unified Team	882

AIR PISTOL

	Pts
1......Yifu Wang, China	684.8
2......Sergei Pyzhianov, Unified Team	684.1
3......Sorin Babii, Romania	684.1

RUNNING TARGET

	Pts
1......Michael Jakosits, Germany	673
2......Anatolij Asrabaev, Unified Team	672
3......Lubos Racansky, Czechoslovakia	670

TRAP

	Pts
1......Petr Hrdlicka, Czechoslovakia	219
2......Kazumi Watanabe, Japan	219
3......Marco Venturini, Italy	218

SKEET

	Pts
1......Shan Zhang, China	223
2......Juan Giah, Peru	222
3......Bruno Rossetti, Italy	222

Women

THREE-POSITION RIFLE

	Pts
1......Launi Meili, United States	684.3
2......Nonca Matova, Bulgaria	682.7
3......Malgorzata Ksiazkiewicz, Poland	681.5

AIR RIFLE

	Pts
1......Kab-Soon Yeo, South Korea	498.2
2......Vessela Letcheva, Bulgaria	495.3
3......Aranka Binder, Independent Team	495.1

AIR PISTOL

	Pts
1......Marina Logvinenko, Unified Team	486.4
2......Jasna Sekaric, Independent Team	486.4
3......Maria Grousdeva, Bulgaria	481.6

SPORT PISTOL

	Pts
1......Marina Logvinenko, Unified Team	684
2......Duihong Li, China	680
3......Dorisuren Monchbajar, Mongolia	679

TABLE TENNIS

Men

SINGLES

1. ....Jan-Ove Waldner, Sweden
2. ....Jean Gatien, France
3. ....Kim Taek Soo, South Korea
3. ....Ma Wenge, China

DOUBLES

1. ....Lu Lin & Wang Tao, China
2. ....Steffan Fetzner & Jorg Rosskopf, Germany
3. ....Kang Hee Chan & Lee Chul Seung, South Korea
3. ....Kim Taek Soo & Yoo Nam Kyu, South Korea

Women

SINGLES

1. ....Deng Yaping, China
2. ....Qiao Hong, China
3. ....Hyun Jung Hwa, South Korea
3. ....Li Bun Hui, North Korea

DOUBLES

1. ....Deng Yaping & Qiao Hong, China
2. ....Chen Zihe & Gao Jun, China
3. ....Li Bun Hui & Yu Sun Bok, North Korea
3. ....Hong Cha Ok & Hyun Jung Hwa, South Korea

TENNIS

Men

SINGLES

1. ....Marc Rosset, Switzerland
2. ....Jordi Arrese, Spain
3. ....Goran Ivanisevic, Croatia
3. ....Andrei Cherkasov, Unified Team

DOUBLES

1. ....Boris Becker & Michael Stich, Germany
2. ....Wayne Ferreira & Piet Norval, South Africa
3. ....Goran Ivanisevic & Goran Prpic, Croatia
3. ....Javier Frana & Christian Carlos Miniussi, Argentina

Women

SINGLES

1. ....Jennifer Capriati, United States
2. ....Steffi Graf, Germany
3. ....Aranxta Sanchez Vicario, Spain
3. ....Mary Joe Fernandez, United States

DOUBLES

1. ....Gigi Fernandez & Mary Joe Fernandez, United States
2. ....Conchita Martinez & Aranxta Sanchez Vicario, Spain
3. ....Natalya Zvereva & Leila Meskhi, Unified Team
3. ....Rachel McQuillan & Nicole Provis, Australia

VOLLEYBALL

Men

1. ....Brazil
2. ....The Netherlands
3. ....United States: Bob Ctvrtlik, Doug Partie, Steve Timmons, Scott Fortune, Jeff Stork, Eric Sato, Dan Hanan, Dan Greenbaum, Uvaldo Acosta, Bryan Ivie, Bob Samuelson, Javier Gaspar, Trevor Schirman, Carlos Briceno, Nick Becker, Brent Hilliard, Mark Arnold, Allen Allen

Women

1. ....Cuba
2. ....Unified Team
3. ....United States: Tee Sanders, Yoko Zetterlund, Ann Schirman, Kim Oden, Lori Endicott, Paula Weishoff, Caren Kemner, Tammy Liley, Elaina Oden, Daiva Tomkus, Deitre Collins, Janet Cobbs, Tara Battle, Liane Sato, Ruth Lawanson, Bev Oden

WATER POLO

1. ....Italy
2. ....Spain
3. ....Unified Team

WEIGHTLIFTING

114 POUNDS

1. ....Ivan Ivanov, Bulgaria	584 lb
2. ....Lin Qisheng, China	579 lb
3. ....Traian Ciharean, Romania	557 lb

123 POUNDS

1. ....Chun Byun Kwan, South Korea	634 lb
2. ....Liu Shoubin, China	612 lb
3. ....Luo Jianming, China	612 lb

132 POUNDS

1. ....Naim Suleymanoglu, Turkey	705 lb
2. ....Nikolai Peshalov, Unified Team	672 lb
3. ....He Yingqiang, China	650 lb

148.5 POUNDS

1. ....Israel Militossian, Unified Team	744 lb
2. ....Yoto Yotov, Bulgaria	722 lb
3. ....Andreas Behm, Germany	706 lb

165 POUNDS

1. ....Fedor Kassapu, Unified Team	788 lb
2. ....Pablo Lara Rodriguez, Cuba	788 lb
3. ....Kim Myong Nam, North Korea	777 lb

181.5 POUNDS

1. ....Pyrros Dimas, Greece	816 lb
2. ....Krzysztof Siemion, Poland	816 lb
3. ....Ibragim Samadov, Unified Team	816 lb

198 POUNDS

1. ....Kakhi Kakhiachveili, Unified Team	910 lb OR
2. ....Sergei Sirtsov, Unified Team	910 lb OR
3. ....Sergivsz Wolczanjecki, Poland	865 lb

220 POUNDS

1. ....Victor Tregoubov, Unified Team	904 lb
2. ....Timour Taimazov, Unified Team	887 lb
3. ....Waldemar Malak, Poland	882 lb

243 POUNDS

1. ....Ronny Weller, Germany	953 lb
2. ....Artur Akoev, Unified Team	948 lb
3. ....Stefan Botev, Bulgaria	920 lb

243+ POUNDS

1. ....Aleksandr Kurlovich, Unified Team	992 lb
2. ....Leonid Taranenko, Unified Team	937 lb
3. ....Manfred Nerlinger, Germany	909 lb

FREESTYLE WRESTLING

106 POUNDS

1. ....Kim Il, North Korea
2. ....Kim Jong, South Korea
3. ....Vougar Oroudjov, Unified Team

115 POUNDS

1. ....Li Hak Son, North Korea
2. ....Zeke Jones, United States
3. ....Valentin Jordanov, Bulgaria

126 POUNDS

1. ....Alejandro Puerto Diaz, Cuba
2. ....Serguei Smal, Unified Team
3. ....Kim Yong Sik, North Korea

137 POUNDS

1. ....John Smith, United States
2. ....Asgari Mohammadian, Iran
3. ....Lazaro Reinoso, Cuba

150 POUNDS

1. ....Arsen Fadzaev, Unified Team
2. ....Valentin Getzov, Bulgaria
3. ....Kosei Akaishi, Japan

163 POUNDS

1. ....Park Jang-Soon, South Korea
2. ....Kenny Monday, United States
3. ....Amir Khadem, Iran

181 POUNDS

1. ....Kevin Jackson, United States
2. ....Elmadi Jabraijlov, Unified Team
3. ....Rasul Khadem, Iran

198 POUNDS

1. ....Makharbek Khadartsev, Unified Team
2. ....Kenan Simsek, Turkey
3. ....Chris Campbell, United States

220 POUNDS

1. ....Leri Khabelov, Unified Team
2. ....Heiko Balz, Germany
3. ....Ali Kayali, Turkey

286 POUNDS

1. ....Bruce Baumgartner, United States
2. ....Jeffrey Thue, Canada
3. ....David Gobedjichvili, Unified Team

Note: OR=Olympic record. WR=world record. EOR=equals Olympic record. EWR=equals world record

GRECO-ROMAN WRESTLING

106 POUNDS
1. ....Oleg Koutcherenko, Unified Team
2. ....Vincenzo Maenza, Italy
3. ....Wilber Sanchez, Cuba

115 POUNDS
1. ....Jon Ronningen, Norway
2. ....Alfred Ter-Mkrtychan, Unified Team
3. ....Min Kyung, South Korea

126 POUNDS
1. ....An Han-Bong, South Korea
2. ....Rifat Yildiz, Germany
3. ....Sheng Zetian, China

137 POUNDS
1. ....Akif Pirim, Turkey
2. ....Sergei Martynov, Unified Team
3. ....Juan Maren, Cuba

150 POUNDS
1. ....Attila Repka, Hungary
2. ....Islam Duguchiev, Unified Team
3. ....Rodney Smith, United States

163 POUNDS
1. ....Mnatsakan Iskandarian, Unified Team
2. ....Josef Tracz, Poland
3. ....Torbjoern Korbakk, Sweden

181 POUNDS
1. ....Peter Farkas, Hungary
2. ....Piotr Stepien, Poland
3. ....Daulet Tourlykhanov, Unified Team

198 POUNDS
1. ....Maik Bullmann, Germany
2. ....Hakki Basar, Turkey
3. ....Gogi Kogouachvili, Unified Team

220 POUNDS
1. ....Hector Millian, Cuba
2. ....Dennis Koslowski, United States
3. ....Sergei Demyashkevich, Unified Team

286 POUNDS
1. ....Aleksandr Karelin, Unified Team
2. ....Tomas Johansson, Sweden
3. ....Ioan Grigoras, Romania

YACHTING

SOLING CLASS
1. ....Denmark
2. ....United States
3. ....Great Britain

STAR CLASS
1. ....United States
2. ....New Zealand
3. ....Canada

FLYING DUTCHMAN CLASS
1. ....Spain
2. ....United States
3. ....Denmark

FINN CLASS
1. ....Jose Van Der Ploeg, Spain
2. ....Brian Ledbetter, United States
3. ....Craig Monk, New Zealand

TORNADO CLASS
1. ....France
2. ....United States
3. ....Australia

EUROPE CLASS
1. ....Linda Andersen, Norway
2. ....Natalia Via Dufresne, Spain
3. ....Julia Trotman, United States

MEN'S 470 CLASS
1. ....Spain
2. ....United States
3. ....Estonia

WOMEN'S 470 CLASS
1. ....Spain
2. ....New Zealand
3. ....United States

1994 Winter Games

BIATHLON

Men

10 KILOMETERS
1. ..Sergei Tchepikov, Russia 28:07.0
2. ..Ricco Gross, Germany 28:13.0
3. ..Sergei Tarasov, Russia 28:27.4

20 KILOMETERS
1. ..Sergei Tarasov, Russia 57:25.3
2. ..Frank Luck, Germany 57:28.7
3. ..Sven Fischer, Germany 57:41.9

4 X 7.5 KILOMETER RELAY
1. ....Germany 1:30:22.1
2. ....Russia 1:31:23.6
3. ....France 1:32:31.3

Women

7.5 KILOMETERS
1. ..Myriam Bedard, Canada 26:08.8
2. ..Svetlana Paramygina, Belarus 26:09.9
3. ..Valentyna Tserbe, Ukraine 26:10.0

15 KILOMETERS
1. ..Myriam Bedard, Canada 52:06.6
2. ..Anne Briand, France 52:53.3
3. ..Ursula Disl, Germany 53:15.3

3 X 7.5 KILOMETER RELAY
1. ....Russia 1:47:19.5
2. ....Germany 1:51:16.5
3. ....France 1:52:28.3

BOBSLED

4-MAN BOB

1.	Germany II	3:27.78
2.	Switzerland	3:27.84
3.	Germany	3:28.01

2-MAN BOB

1.	Switzerland	3:30.81
2.	Switzerland II	3:30.86
3.	Italy	3:31.01

ICE HOCKEY

1.	Sweden
2.	Canada
3.	Finland

LUGE

Men

SINGLES

1.	Georg Hackl, Germany	3:21.571
2.	Markus Prock, Austria	3:21.584
3.	Armin Zoggeler, Italy	3:21.833

DOUBLES

1.	K. Brugger and W. Huber, Italy	1:36.720
2.	H. Raffl and N. Huber, Italy	1:36.769
3.	S. Krausse and J. Behrendt, Ger.	1:36.945

Women

SINGLES

1.	Gerda Weissensteiner, Italy	3:15.517
2.	Susi Erdmann, Germany	3:16.276
3.	Andrea Tagwerker, Austria	3:16.652

FIGURE SKATING

Men

1.	Alexei Urmanov, Russia
2.	Elvis Stojko, Canada
3.	Philippe Candeloro, France

Pairs

1.	Ekaterina Gordeeva and Sergei Grinkov, Russia
2.	Natalia Mishkutienok and Artur Dmitriev, Russia
3.	Isabella Brasseur and Lloyd Eisler, Canada

Women

1.	Oksana Baiul, Ukraine
2.	Nancy Kerrigan, United States
3.	Chen Lu, China

Ice Dancing

1.	Oksana Gritschuk and Evgeni Platov, Russia
2.	Maia Usova and Alexander Zhulin, Russia
3.	Jayne Torvill and Christopher Dean, Great Britain

SPEED SKATING

Men

500 METERS

1.	Aleksandr Golubev, Russia	36.33 OR
2.	Sergei Klevchenya, Russia	36.39
3.	Manabu Horii, Japan	36.53

1000 METERS

1.	Dan Jansen, United States	1:12.43 WR
2.	Igor Zhelezovsky, Belarus	1:12.72
3.	Sergei Klevchenya, Russia	1:12.85

1500 METERS

1.	Johann Olav Koss, Norway	1:51.29 WR
2.	Rintje Ritsma, The Netherlands	1:54.85
3.	Falko Zandstra, The Netherlands	1:54.90

Women

500 METERS

1.	Bonnie Blair, United States	39.25
2.	Susan Auch, Canada	39.61
3.	Franziska Schenk, Germany	39.70

1000 METERS

1.	Bonnie Blair, United States	1:18.74
2.	Anke Baier, Germany	1:20.12
3.	Qiaobo Ye, China	1:20.22

1500 METERS

1.	Emese Hunyady, Austria	2:02.19
2.	Svetlana Fedotkina, Russia	2:02.69
3.	Seiko Hashimoto, Japan	2:06.88

Note: OR=Olympic Record; WR=World Record; EOR=Equals Olympic Record; EWR=Equals World Record; WB=World Best.

SPEED SKATING (Cont.)

Men (Cont.)

5000 METERS

1. ..Johann Olav Koss, Norway	6:34.96 WR
2. ..Kjell Storelid, Norway	6:42.68
3. ..Rintje Ritsma, Netherlands	6:43.94

10,000 METERS

1. ..Johann Olav Koss, Norway	13:30.55 WR
2. ..Kjell Storelid, Norway	13:49.25
3. ..Bart Veldkamp, The Netherlands	13:56.73

Women (Cont.)

3000 METERS

1. ..Gunda Niemann, Germany	4:19.90
2. ..Heike Warnicke, Germany	4:22.88
3. ..Emese Hunyady, Austria	4:24.64

5000 METERS

1. ..Gunda Niemann, Germany	7:31.57
2. ..Heike Warnicke, Germany	7:37.59
3. ..Claudia Pechstein, Germany	7:39.80

SHORT TRACK SPEED SKATING

Men

500 METERS

1. ..Chae Ji-Hoon, South Korea	43.45
2. ..Mirko Vuillermin, Italy	43.47
3. ..Nicholas Gooch, Great Britain	43.68

1000 METERS

1. ....Ki-Hoon Kim, South Korea	1:34.57
2. ..Ji-Hoon Chae, South Korea	1:34.92
3. ..Marc Gagnon, Canada	DNF

5000-METER RELAY

1. ....Italy	7:11.74 OR
2. ..United States	7:13.37
3. ..Australia	7:13.68

Women

500 METERS

1. ..Cathy Turner, United States	45.98 OR
2. ..Yanmei Zhang, China	46.44
3. ..Amy Peterson, United States	46.76

1000 METERS

1. ..Chun Lee-Kyung, South Korea	1:36.87
2. ..Nathalie Lambert, Canada	1:36.97
3. ..Kim So-Hee, South Korea	1:37.09

3000-METER RELAY

1. ....South Korea	4:26.64 OR
2. ..Canada	4:32.04
3. ..United States	4:39.34

ALPINE SKIING

Men

DOWNHILL

1. ..Tommy Moe, United States	1:45.75
2. ..Kjetil Andre Aamodt, Norway	1:45.79
3. ..Edward Podivinsky, Canada	1:45.87

SUPER GIANT SLALOM

1. ..Markus Wasmeier, Germany	1:32.53
2. ..Tommy Moe, United States	1:32.61
3. ..Kjetil Andre Aamodt, Norway	1:32.93

GIANT SLALOM

1. ..Markus Wasmeier, Germany	2:52.46
2. ..Urs Kaelin, Switzerland	2:52.48
3. ..Christian Mayer, Austria	2:52.58

SLALOM

1. ..Thomas Stangassinger, Austria	2:02.02
2. ..Alberto Tomba, Italy	2:02.17
3. ..Jure Kosir, Slovenia	2:02.53

COMBINED

	Pts
1. ..Lasse Kjus, Norway	3:17.53
2. ..Kjell Andre Aamodt, Norway	3:18.55
3. ..Harald Strand Nilsen, Norway	3:19.14

Women

DOWNHILL

1. ..Katja Seizinger, Germany	1:35.93
2. ..Picabo Street, United States	1:36.59
3. ..Isolde Kostner, Italy	1:36.85

SUPER GIANT SLALOM

1. ..Diann Roffe-Steinrotter, U.S.	1:22.15
2. ..Svetlana Gladischeva, Russia	1:22.44
3. ..Isolde Kostner, Italy	1:22.45

GIANT SLALOM

1. ..Deborah Compagnoni, Italy	2:30.97
2. ..Martina Ertl, Germany	2:32.19
2. ..Vreni Schneider, Switzerland	2:32.97

SLALOM

1. ..Vreni Schneider, Switzerland	1:56.01
2. ..Elfriede Eder, Austria	1:56.35
3. ..Katja Koren, Slovenia	1:56.61

COMBINED

1. ..Pernilla Wiberg, Sweden	3:05.16
2. ..Vreni Schneider, Switzerland	3:05.29
3. ..Alenka Dovzan, Slovenia	3:06.64

Note: OR=Olympic Record; WR=World Record; EOR=Equals Olympic Record; EWR=Equals World Record; WB=World Best; DNF=Did Not Finish.

ALPINE SKIING *(Cont.)*

FREESTYLE SKIING

Men		Women	
MOGUL		**MOGUL**	
	Pts		Pts
1. ..Jean-Luc Brassard, Canada	27.24	1. ..Stine Lise Hattestad, Norway	25.97
2. ..Sergei Shoupletsov, Russia	26.90	2. ..Liz McIntyre, United States	25.89
3. ..Edgar Grospiron, France	26.64	3. ..Elizaveta Kojevnikova, Russia	25.81
AERIAL		**AERIAL**	
	Pts		Pts
1. ..Andreas Schoenbaechler, Switz.	234.67	1. ..Lina Cherjazova, Uzbekistan	166.84
2. ..Philippe Laroche, Canada	228.63	2. ..Marie Lindgren, Sweden	165.88
3. ..Lloyd Langlois, Canada	222.44	3. ..Hilde Synnove Lid, Norway	164.13

NORDIC SKIING

Men

10 KILOMETERS (CLASSICAL)

1. ..Bjorn Daehlie, Norway — 24:20.1
2. ..Vladimir Smirnov, Russia — 24:38.3
3. ..Marco Albarello, Italy — 24:42.3

30 KILOMETERS (CLASSICAL)

1. ..Thomas Alsgaard, Norway — 1:12:26.4
2. ..Bjorn Daehlie, Norway — 1:13:13.6
3. ..Myka Myllyla, Finland — 1:14:14.5

50 KILOMETERS (FREESTYLE)

1. ..Vladimir Smirnov, Kazakhstan — 2:07:20.3
2. ..Myka Myllyla, Finland — 2:08:41.9
3. ..Sture Sivertsen, Norway — 2:08:49.0

15 KILOMETERS (FREESTYLE)

1. ..Bjorn Daehlie, Norway — 1:00.08.8
2. ..Vladimir Smirnov, Kazakhstan — 1:00:38.0
3. ..Silvio Fauner, Italy — 1:01:48.6

4 X 10 KILOMETER RELAY (MIXED)

1. ....Italy — 1:41:15.0
2. ....Norway — 1:41:15.4
3. ....Finland — 1:42:15.6

SKI JUMPING (NORMAL HILL)

		Pts
1. ..Espen Bredesen, Norway		282.0
2. ..Lasse Ottesen, Norway		268.0
3. ..Dieter Thoma, Germany		260.5

SKI JUMPING (LARGE HILL)

		Pts
1. ..Jens Weisflogg, Germany		274.5
2. ..Espen Bredesen, Norway		266.5
3. ..Andreas Goldberger, Austria		255.0

TEAM SKI JUMPING

		Pts
1. ....Germany		970.1
2. ....Japan		956.9
3. ....Austria		918.9

NORDIC COMBINED

1. ....Fred B. Lundberg, Norway — 457.970
2. ....Takanori Kono, Japan — 446.345
3. ....Bjarte Engen Vik, Norway — 446.175

TEAM COMBINED

1. ....Japan — 1368.860
2. ....Norway — 1310.940
3. ....Switzerland — 1275.240

Women

5 KILOMETERS (CLASSICAL)

1. ..Lyubov Egorova, Russia — 14:08.8
2. ..Manuela Di Centa, Italy — 14:28.3
3. ..Marja-Liisa Kirvesniemi, Finland — 14:36.0

15 KILOMETERS (FREESTYLE)

1. ..Manuela Di Centa, Italy — 39:44.5
2. ..Lyubov Egorova, Russia — 41:03.0
3. ..Nina Gavriluk, Russia — 41:10.4

10 KILOMETERS (FREESTYLE)

1. ..Lyubov Egorova, Russia — 41:38.1
2. ..Maunela Di Centa, Italy — 41:46.4
3. ..Stefania Belmondo, Italy — 42:21.1

30 KILOMETERS (CLASSICAL)

1. ..Manuela Di Centa, Italy — 1:25:41.6
2. ..Marit Wold, Norway — 1:25:57.8
3. ..Marja-Liisa Kirvesniemi, Finland — 1:26:13.6

4 X 5 KILOMETER RELAY (MIXED)

1. ....Russia — 57:12.5
2. ....Norway — 57:42.6
3. ....Italy — 58:42.6

FOR THE RECORD·Year by Year

Olympic Games Locations and Dates

Summary... Summer

	Year	Site	Dates	Men	Women	Nations	Most Medals	US Medals
I	1896	Athens, Greece	Apr 6-15	311	0	13	Greece (10-19-18—47)	11-6-2—19 (2nd)
II	1900	Paris, France	May 20-Oct 28	1319	11	22	France (29-41-32—102)	20-14-19—53 (2nd)
III	1904	St Louis, United States	July 1-Nov 23	681	6	12	United States (80-86-72—238)	
—	1906	Athens, Greece	Apr 22-May 28	77	7	20	France (15-9-16—40)	12-6-5—23 (4th)
IV	1908	London, Great Britain	Apr 27-Oct 31	1999	36	23	Britain (56-50-39—145)	23-12-12—47 (2nd)
V	1912	Stockholm, Sweden	May 5-July 22	2490	57	28	Sweden (24-24-17—65)	23-19-19—61 (2nd)
VI	1916	Berlin, Germany	Cancelled because of war					
VII	1920	Antwerp, Belgium	Apr 20-Sep 12	2543	64	29	United States (41-27-28—96)	
VIII	1924	Paris, France	May 4-July 27	2956	136	44	United States (45-27-27—99)	
IX	1928	Amsterdam, Netherlands	May 17-Aug 12	2724	290	46	United States (22-18-16—56)	
X	1932	Los Angeles, United States	July 30-Aug 14	1281	127	37	United States (41-32-31—104)	
XI	1936	Berlin, Germany	Aug 1-16	3738	328	49	Germany (33-26-30—89)	24-20-12—56 (2nd)
XII	1940	Tokyo, Japan	Cancelled because of war					
XIII	1944	London, Great Britain	Cancelled because of war					
XIV	1948	London, Great Britain	July 29-Aug 14	3714	385	59	United States (38-27-19—84)	
XV	1952	Helsinki, Finland	July 19-Aug 3	4407	518	69	United States (40-19-17—76)	
XVI	1956	Melbourne, Australia*	Nov 22-Dec 8	2958	384	67	USSR (37-29-32—98)	32-25-17—74 (2nd)
XVII	1960	Rome, Italy	Aug 25-Sep 11	4738	610	83	USSR (43-29-31—103)	34-21-16—71 (2nd)
XVIII	1964	Tokyo, Japan	Oct 10-24	4457	683	93	United States (36-26-28—90)	
XIX	1968	Mexico City, Mexico	Oct 12-27	4750	781	112	United States (45-28-34—107)	
XX	1972	Munich, West Germany	Aug 26-Sep 10	5848	1299	122	USSR (50-27-22—99)	33-31-30—94 (2nd)
XXI	1976	Montreal, Canada	July 17-Aug 1	4834	1251	92†	USSR (49-41-35—125)	34-35-25—94 (3rd)
XXII	1980	Moscow, USSR	July 19-Aug 3	4265	1088	81‡	USSR (80-69-46—195)	Did not compete
XXIII	1984	Los Angeles, United States	July 28-Aug 12	5458	1620	141#	United States (83-61-30—174)	
XXIV	1988	Seoul, South Korea	Sep 17-Oct 2	7105	2476	160	USSR (55-31-46—132)	36-31-27—94 (3rd)
XXV	1992	Barcelona, Spain	July 25-Aug. 9	7555	3008	172	Unified Team (45-38-29—112)	37-34-37—108 (2nd)

*The equestrian events were held in Stockholm, Sweden, June 10-17, 1956.

†This figure includes Cameroon, Egypt, Morocco, and Tunisia, countries that boycotted the 1976 Olympics after some of their athletes had already competed.

‡The US was among 65 countries that refused to participate in the 1980 Summer Games in Moscow.

#The USSR, East Germany, and 14 other countries skipped the Summer Games in Los Angeles.

Winter

	Year	Site	Dates	Men	Women	Nations	Most Medals	US Medals
I	1924	Chamonix, France	Jan 25-Feb 4	281	13	16	Norway (4-7-6—17)	1-2-1—4 (3rd)
II	1928	St Moritz, Switzerland	Feb 11-19	468	27	25	Norway (6-4-5—15)	2-2-2—6 (2nd)
III	1932	Lake Placid, United States	Feb 4-15	274	32	17	United States (6-4-2—12)	
IV	1936	Garmisch-Partenkirchen, Germany	Feb 6-16	675	80	28	Norway (7-5-3—15)	1-0-3—4 (T-5th)
—	1940	Garmisch-Partenkirchen, Germany	Cancelled because of war					
—	1944	Cortina d'Ampezzo, Italy	Cancelled because of war					
V	1948	St Moritz, Switzerland	Jan 30-Feb 8	636	77	28	Norway (4-3-3—10) Sweden (4-3-3—10) Switzerland (3-4-3—10)	3-4-2—9 (4th)
VI	1952	Oslo, Norway	Feb 14-25	623	109	30	Norway (7-3-6—16)	4-6-1—11 (2nd)
VII	1956	Cortina d'Ampezzo, Italy	Jan 26-Feb 5	686	132	32	USSR (7-3-6—16)	2-3-2—7 (T-4th)
VIII	1960	Squaw Valley, United States	Feb 18-28	521	144	30	USSR (7-5-9—21)	3-4-3—10 (2nd)
IX	1964	Innsbruck, Austria	Jan 29-Feb 9	986	200	36	USSR (11-8-6—25)	1-2-3—6 (7th)
X	1968	Grenoble, France	Feb 6-18	1081	212	37	Norway (6-6-2—14)	1-5-1—7 (T-7th)
XI	1972	Sapporo, Japan	Feb 3-13	1015	217	35	USSR (8-5-3—16)	3-2-3—8 (6th)
XII	1976	Innsbruck, Austria	Feb 4-15	900	228	37	USSR (13-6-8—27)	3-3-4—10 (T-3rd)
XIII	1980	Lake Placid, United States	Feb 14-23	833	234	37	USSR (10-6-6—22)	6-4-2—12 (3rd)
XIV	1984	Sarajevo, Yugoslavia	Feb 7-19	1002	276	49	USSR (6-10-9—25)	4-4-0—8 (T-5th)
XV	1988	Calgary, Canada	Feb 13-28	1128	317	57	USSR (11-9-9—29)	2-1-3—6 (T-8th)
XVI	1992	Albertville, France	Feb 8-23	1318	490	65	Germany (10-10-6—26)	5-4-2—11 (6th)
XVII	1994	Lillehammer, Norway	Feb 11-27	1302	542		Norway (10-11-5—26)	6-5-2—13 (T-5th)

Summer Games Champions

TRACK AND FIELD

Men

100 METERS

1896	Thomas Burke, United States	12.0		
1900	Frank Jarvis, United States	11.0		
1904	Archie Hahn, United States	11.0		
1906	Archie Hahn, United States	11.2		
1908	Reginald Walker, South Africa	10.8 OR		
1912	Ralph Craig, United States	10.8		
1920	Charles Paddock, United States	10.8		
1924	Harold Abrahams, Great Britain	10.6 OR		
1928	Percy Williams, Canada	10.8		
1932	Eddie Tolan, United States	10.3 OR		
1936	Jesse Owens, United States	10.3		
1948	Harrison Dillard, United States	10.3		

1952	Lindy Remigino, United States	10.4
1956	Bobby Morrow, United States	10.5
1960	Armin Hary, West Germany	10.2 OR
1964	Bob Hayes, United States	10.0 EWR
1968	Jim Hines, United States	9.95 WR
1972	Valery Borzov, USSR	10.14
1976	Hasely Crawford, Trinidad	10.06
1980	Allan Wells, Great Britain	10.25
1984	Carl Lewis, United States	9.99
1988	Carl Lewis, United States*	9.92 WR
1992	Linford Christie, Great Britain	9.96

*Ben Johnson, Canada, disqualified.

TRACK AND FIELD *(Cont.)*

Men *(Cont.)*

200 METERS

1900	John Walter Tewksbury, United States	22.2
1904	Archie Hahn, United States	21.6 OR
1906	Not held	
1908	Robert Kerr, Canada	22.6
1912	Ralph Craig, United States	21.7
1920	Allen Woodring, United States	22.0
1924	Jackson Scholz, United States	21.6
1928	Percy Williams, Canada	21.8
1932	Eddie Tolan, United States	21.2 OR
1936	Jesse Owens, United States	20.7 OR
1948	Mel Patton, United States	21.1
1952	Andrew Stanfield, United States	20.7
1956	Bobby Morrow, United States	20.6 OR
1960	Livio Berruti, Italy	20.5 EWR
1964	Henry Carr, United States	20.3 OR
1968	Tommie Smith, United States	19.83 WR
1972	Valery Borzov, USSR	20.00
1976	Donald Quarrie, Jamaica	20.23
1980	Pietro Mennea, Italy	20.19
1984	Carl Lewis, United States	19.80 OR
1988	Joe DeLoach, United States	19.75 OR
1992	Mike Marsh, United States	20.01

400 METERS

1896	Thomas Burke, United States	54.2
1900	Maxey Long, United States	49.4 OR
1904	Harry Hillman, United States	49.2 OR
1906	Paul Pilgrim, United States	53.2
1908	Wyndham Halswelle, Great Britain	50.0
1912	Charles Reidpath, United States	48.2 OR
1920	Bevil Rudd, South Africa	49.6
1924	Eric Liddell, Great Britain	47.6 OR
1928	Ray Barbuti, United States	47.8
1932	William Carr, United States	46.2 WR
1936	Archie Williams, United States	46.5
1948	Arthur Wint, Jamaica	46.2
1952	George Rhoden, Jamaica	45.9
1956	Charles Jenkins, United States	46.7
1960	Otis Davis, United States	44.9 WR
1964	Michael Larrabee, United States	45.1
1968	Lee Evans, United States	43.86 WR
1972	Vincent Matthews, United States	44.66
1976	Alberto Juantorena, Cuba	44.26
1980	Viktor Markin, USSR	44.60
1984	Alonzo Babers, United States	44.27
1988	Steve Lewis, United States	43.87
1992	Quincy Watts, United States	43.50 OR

800 METERS

1896	Edwin Flack, Australia	2:11
1900	Alfred Tysoe, Great Britain	2:01.2
1904	James Lightbody, United States	1:56 OR
1906	Paul Pilgrim, United States	2:01.5
1908	Mel Sheppard, United States	1:52.8 WR
1912	James Meredith, United States	1:51.9 WR
1920	Albert Hill, Great Britain	1:53.4
1924	Douglas Lowe, Great Britain	1:52.4
1928	Douglas Lowe, Great Britain	1:51.8 OR

800 METERS *(Cont.)*

1932	Thomas Hampson, Great Britain	1:49.8 WR
1936	John Woodruff, United States	1:52.9
1948	Mal Whitfield, United States	1:49.2 OR
1952	Mal Whitfield, United States	1:49.2 EOR
1956	Thomas Courtney, United States	1:47.7 OR
1960	Peter Snell, New Zealand	1:46.3 OR
1964	Peter Snell, New Zealand	1:45.1 OR
1968	Ralph Doubell, Australia	1:44.3 EWR
1972	Dave Wottle, United States	1:45.9
1976	Alberto Juantorena, Cuba	1:43.50 WR
1980	Steve Ovett, Great Britain	1:45.40
1984	Joaquim Cruz, Brazil	1:43.00 OR
1988	Paul Ereng, Kenya	1:43.45
1992	William Tanui, Kenya	1:43.66

1500 METERS

1896	Edwin Flack, Australia	4:33.2
1900	Charles Bennett, Great Britain	4:06.2 WR
1904	James Lightbody, United States	4:05.4 WR
1906	James Lightbody, United States	4:12.0
1908	Mel Sheppard, United States	4:03.4 OR
1912	Arnold Jackson, Great Britain	3:56.8 OR
1920	Albert Hill, Great Britain	4:01.8
1924	Paavo Nurmi, Finland	3:53.6 OR
1928	Harry Larva, Finland	3:53.2 OR
1932	Luigi Beccali, Italy	3:51.2 OR
1936	Jack Lovelock, New Zealand	3:47.8 WR
1948	Henri Eriksson, Sweden	3:49.8
1952	Josef Barthel, Luxemburg	3:45.1 OR
1956	Ron Delany, Ireland	3:41.2 OR
1960	Herb Elliott, Australia	3:35.6 WR
1964	Peter Snell, New Zealand	3:38.1
1968	Kipchoge Keino, Kenya	3:34.9 OR
1972	Pekkha Vasala, Finland	3:36.3
1976	John Walker, New Zealand	3:39.17
1980	Sebastian Coe, Great Britain	3:38.4
1984	Sebastian Coe, Great Britain	3:32.53 OR
1988	Peter Rono, Kenya	3:35.96
1992	Fermin Cacho, Spain	3:40.12

5000 METERS

1912	Hannes Kolehmainen, Finland	14:36.6 WR
1920	Joseph Guillemot, France	14:55.6
1924	Paavo Nurmi, Finland	14:31.2 OR
1928	Villie Ritola, Finland	14:38
1932	Lauri Lehtinen, Finland	14:30 OR
1936	Gunnar Hickert, Finland	14:22.2 OR
1948	Gaston Reiff, Belgium	14:17.6 OR
1952	Emil Zatopek, Czechoslovakia	14:06.6 OR
1956	Vladimir Kuts, USSR	13:39.6 OR
1960	Murray Halberg, New Zealand	13:43.4
1964	Bob Schul, United States	13:48.8
1968	Mohamed Gammoudi, Tunisia	14:05.0
1972	Lasse Viren, Finland	13:26.4 OR
1976	Lasse Viren, Finland	13:24.76
1980	Miruts Yifter, Ethiopia	13:21.0
1984	Said Aouita, Morocco	13:05.59 OR
1988	John Ngugi, Kenya	13:11.70
1992	Dieter Baumann, Germany	13:12.52

Note: OR=Olympic Record; WR=World Record; EOR=Equals Olympic Record; EWR=Equals World Record; WB=World Best.

TRACK AND FIELD (Cont.)

Men (Cont.)

10,000 METERS

1912	Hannes Kolehmainen, Finland	31:20.8
1920	Paavo Nurmi, Finland	31:45.8
1924	Vilho (Ville) Ritola, Finland	30:23.2 WR
1928	Paavo Nurmi, Finland	30:18.8 OR
1932	Janusz Kusocinski, Poland	30:11.4 OR
1936	Ilmari Salminen, Finland	30:15.4
1948	Emil Zatopek, Czechoslovakia	29:59.6 OR
1952	Emil Zatopek, Czechoslovakia	29:17.0 OR
1956	Vladimir Kuts, USSR	28:45.6 OR
1960	Pyotr Bolotnikov, USSR	28:32.2 OR
1964	Billy Mills, United States	28:24.4 OR
1968	Naftali Temu, Kenya	29:27.4
1972	Lasse Viren, Finland	27:38.4 WR
1976	Lasse Viren, Finland	27:40.38
1980	Miruts Yifter, Ethiopia	27:42.7
1984	Alberto Cova, Italy	27:47.54
1988	Brahim Boutaib, Morocco	27:21.46 OR
1992	Khalid Skah, Morocco	27:46.70

MARATHON

1896	Spiridon Louis, Greece	2:58:50
1900	Michel Theato, France	2:59:45
1904	Thomas Hicks, United States	3:28:53
1906	William Sherring, Canada	2:51:23.6
1908	John Hayes, United States	2:55:18.4 OR
1912	Kenneth McArthur, South Africa	2:36:54.8
1920	Hannes Kolehmainen, Finland	2:32:35.8 WB
1924	Albin Stenroos, Finland	2:41:22.6
1928	Boughera El Ouafi, France	2:32:57
1932	Juan Zabala, Argentina	2:31:36 OR
1936	Kijung Son, Japan (Korea)	2:29:19.2 OR
1948	Delfo Cabrera, Argentina	2:34:51.6
1952	Emil Zatopek, Czechoslovakia	2:23:03.2 OR
1956	Alain Mimoun O'Kacha, France	2:25:00.0
1960	Abebe Bikila, Ethiopia	2:15:16.2 WB
1964	Abebe Bikila, Ethiopia	2:12:11.2 WB
1968	Mamo Wolde, Ethiopia	2:20:26.4
1972	Frank Shorter, United States	2:12:19.8
1976	Waldemar Cierpinski, East Germany	2:09:55 OR
1980	Waldemar Cierpinski, East Germany	2:11:03.0
1984	Carlos Lopes, Portugal	2:09:21.0 OR
1988	Gelindo Bordin, Italy	2:10:32
1992	Hwang Young-Cho, S Korea	2:13:23

Note: Marathon distances: 1896, 1904—40,000 meters; 1900—40,260 meters; 1906—41,860 meters; 1912—40,200 meters; 1920—42,750 meters; 1908 and since 1924—42,195 meters (26 miles, 385 yards).

110-METER HURDLES

1896	Thomas Curtis, United States	17.6
1900	Alvin Kraenzlein, United States	15.4 OR
1904	Frederick Schule, United States	16.0
1906	Robert Leavitt, United States	16.2
1908	Forrest Smithson, United States	15.0 WR
1912	Frederick Kelly, United States	15.1
1920	Earl Thomson, Canada	14.8 WR
1924	Daniel Kinsey, United States	15.0
1928	Sydney Atkinson, South Africa	14.8
1932	George Saling, United States	14.6
1936	Forrest Towns, United States	14.2
1948	William Porter, United States	13.9 OR
1952	Harrison Dillard, United States	13.7 OR
1956	Lee Calhoun, United States	13.5 OR
1960	Lee Calhoun, United States	13.8
1964	Hayes Jones, United States	13.6
1968	Willie Davenport, United States	13.3 OR
1972	Rod Milburn, United States	13.24 EWR
1976	Guy Drut, France	13.30
1980	Thomas Munkelt, East Germany	13.39
1984	Roger Kingdom, United States	13.20 OR
1988	Roger Kingdom, United States	12.98 OR
1992	Mark McKoy, Canada	13.12

400-METER HURDLES

1900	John Walter Tewksbury, United States	57.6
1904	Harry Hillman, United States	53.0
1906	Not held	
1908	Charles Bacon, United States	55.0 WR
1912	Not held	
1920	Frank Loomis, United States	54.0 WR
1924	F. Morgan Taylor, United States	52.6
1928	David Burghley, Great Britain	53.4 OR
1932	Robert Tisdall, Ireland	51.7
1936	Glenn Hardin, United States	52.4
1948	Roy Cochran, United States	51.1 OR
1952	Charles Moore, United States	50.8 OR
1956	Glenn Davis, United States	50.1 EOR
1960	Glenn Davis, United States	49.3 EOR
1964	Rex Cawley, United States	49.6
1968	Dave Hemery, Great Britain	48.12 WR
1972	John Akii-Bua, Uganda	47.82 WR
1976	Edwin Moses, United States	47.64 WR
1980	Volker Beck, East Germany	48.70
1984	Edwin Moses, United States	47.75
1988	Andre Phillips, United States	47.19 OR
1992	Kevin Young, United States	46.78 WR

THEY SAID IT

Rick Gentile, the senior vice president of CBS Sports, on host Greg Gumbel's Olympic performance at the Lillehammer Winter Games: "He filled the Greg Gumbel role very well."

TRACK AND FIELD *(Cont.)*

Men *(Cont.)*

3000-METER STEEPLECHASE

1920	Percy Hodge, Great Britain	10:00.4 OR
1924	Vilho (Ville) Ritola, Finland	9:33.6 OR
1928	Toivo Loukola, Finland	9:21.8 WR
1932	Volmari Iso-Hollo, Finland	10:33.4*
1936	Volmari Iso-Hollo, Finland	9:03.8 WR
1948	Thore Sjöstrand, Sweden	9:04.6
1952	Horace Ashenfelter, United States	8:45.4 WR
1956	Chris Brasher, Great Britain	8:41.2 OR
1960	Zdzislaw Krzyszkowiak, Poland	8:34.2 OR
1964	Gaston Roelants, Belgium	8:30.8 OR
1968	Amos Biwott, Kenya	8:51
1972	Kipchoge Keino, Kenya	8:23.6 OR
1976	Anders Gärderud, Sweden	8:08.2 WR
1980	Bronislaw Malinowski, Poland	8:09.7
1984	Julius Korir, Kenya	8:11.8
1988	Julius Kariuki, Kenya	8:05.51 OR
1992	Matthew Birir, Kenya	8:08.84

*About 3450 meters; extra lap by error.

4 X 100-METER RELAY

1912	Great Britain	42.4 OR
1920	United States	42.2 WR
1924	United States	41.0 EWR
1928	United States	41.0 EWR
1932	United States	40.0 EWR
1936	United States	39.8 WR
1948	United States	40.6
1952	United States	40.1
1956	United States	39.5 WR
1960	West Germany	39.5 EWR
1964	United States	39.0 WR
1968	United States	38.2 WR
1972	United States	38.19 EWR
1976	United States	38.33
1980	USSR	38.26
1984	United States	37.83 WR
1988	USSR	38.19
1992	United States	37.40 WR

4 X 400-METER RELAY

1908	United States	3:29.4
1912	United States	3:16.6 WR
1920	Great Britain	3:22.2
1924	United States	3:16.0 WR
1928	United States	3:14.2 WR
1932	United States	3:08.2 WR
1936	Great Britain	3:09.0
1948	United States	3:10.4 WR
1952	Jamaica	3:03.9 WR
1956	United States	3:04.8
1960	United States	3:02.2 WR
1964	United States	3:00.7 WR
1968	United States	2:56.16 WR
1972	Kenya	2:59.8
1976	United States	2:58.65
1980	USSR	3:01.1
1984	United States	2:57.91
1988	United States	2:56.16 EWR
1992	United States	2:55.74 WR

20-KILOMETER WALK

1956	Leonid Spirin, USSR	1:31:27.4
1960	Vladimir Golubnichiy, USSR	1:33:07.2
1964	Kenneth Mathews, Great Britain	1:29:34.0 OR
1968	Vladimir Golubnichiy, USSR	1:33:58.4
1972	Peter Frenkel, East Germany	1:26:42.4 OR
1976	Daniel Bautista, Mexico	1:24:40.6 OR
1980	Maurizio Damilano, Italy	1:23:35.5 OR
1984	Ernesto Canto, Mexico	1:23:13.0 OR
1988	Jozef Pribilinec, Czechoslovakia	1:19:57.0 OR
1992	Daniel Plaza, Spain	1:21:45.0

50-KILOMETER WALK

1932	Thomas Green, Great Britain	4:50:10
1936	Harold Whitlock, Great Britain	4:30:41.4 OR
1948	John Ljunggren, Sweden	4:41:52
1952	Giuseppe Dordoni, Italy	4:28:07.8 OR
1956	Norman Read, New Zealand	4:30:42.8
1960	Donald Thompson, Great Britain	4:25:30 OR
1964	Abdon Parnich, Italy	4:11:12.4 OR
1968	Christoph Höhne, East Germany	4:20:13.6
1972	Bernd Kannenberg, West Germany	3:56:11.6 OR
1980	Hartwig Gauder, East Germany	3:49:24.0 OR
1984	Raul Gonzalez, Mexico	3:47:26.0 OR
1988	Viacheslav Ivanenko, USSR	3:38:29.0 OR
1992	Andrey Perlov, Unified Team	3:50:13

HIGH JUMP

1896	Ellery Clark, United States	5 ft 11¼ in
1900	Irving Baxter, United States	6 ft 2¾ in OR
1904	Samuel Jones, United States	5 ft 11 in
1906	Cornelius Leahy, Great Britain/Ireland	5 ft 10 in
1908	Harry Porter, United States	6 ft 3 in OR
1912	Alma Richards, United States	6 ft 4 in OR
1920	Richmond Landon, United States	6 ft 4 in OR
1924	Harold Osborn, United States	6 ft 6 in OR
1928	Robert W. King, United States	6 ft 4½ in
1932	Duncan McNaughton, Canada	6 ft 5½ in
1936	Cornelius Johnson, United States	6 ft 8 in OR
1948	John L. Winter, Australia	6 ft 6 in
1952	Walter Davis, United States	6 ft 8½ in OR
1956	Charles Dumas, United States	6 ft 11½ in OR
1960	Robert Shavlakadze, USSR	7 ft 1 in OR
1964	Valery Brumel, USSR	7 ft 1¾ in OR
1968	Dick Fosbury, United States	7 ft 4¼ in OR
1972	Yuri Tarmak, USSR	7 ft 3¾ in
1976	Jacek Wszola, Poland	7 ft 4½ in OR
1980	Gerd Wessig, East Germany	7 ft 8¾ in WR
1984	Dietmar Mögenburg, West Germany	7 ft 8½ in
1988	Gennadiy Avdeyenko, USSR	7 ft 9¾ in OR
1992	Javier Sotomayor, Cuba	7 ft 8 in.

Note: OR=Olympic Record; WR=World Record;
EOR=Equals Olympic Record; EWR=Equals World Record;
WB=World Best.

TRACK AND FIELD (Cont.)

Men (Cont.)

POLE VAULT

1896	William Hoyt, United States	10 ft 10 in
1900	Irving Baxter, United States	10 ft 10 in
1904	Charles Dvorak, United States	11 ft 5¾ in
1906	Fernand Gonder, France	11 ft 5¾ in
1908	Alfred Gilbert, United States Edward Cooke, Jr, United States	12 ft 2 in OR
1912	Harry Babcock, United States	12 ft 11½ in OR
1920	Frank Foss, United States	13 ft 5 in WR
1924	Lee Barnes, United States	12 ft 11½ in
1928	Sabin Carr, United States	13 ft 9¼ in OR
1932	William Miller, United States	14 ft 1¾ in OR
1936	Earle Meadows, United States	14 ft 3¼ in OR
1948	Guinn Smith, United States	14 ft 1¼ in
1952	Robert Richards, United States	14 ft 11 in OR
1956	Robert Richards, United States	14 ft 11½ in OR
1960	Don Bragg, United States	15 ft 5 in OR
1964	Fred Hansen, United States	16 ft 8¾ in OR
1968	Bob Seagren, United States	17 ft 8½ in OR
1972	Wolfgang Nordwig, East Germany	18 ft ½ in OR
1976	Tadeusz Slusarski, Poland	18 ft ½ in EOR
1980	Wladyslaw Kozakiewicz, Poland	18 ft 11½ in WR
1984	Pierre Quinon, France	18 ft 10¼ in
1988	Sergei Bubka, USSR	19 ft 9¼ in OR
1992	Maksim Tarasov, Unified Team	19 ft ¼ in

LONG JUMP

1896	Ellery Clark, United States	20 ft 10 in
1900	Alvin Kraenzlein, United States	23 ft 6¾ in OR
1904	Meyer Prinstein, United States	24 ft 1 in OR
1906	Meyer Prinstein, United States	23 ft 7½ in
1908	Frank Irons, United States	24 ft 6½ in OR
1912	Albert Gutterson, United States	24 ft 11¼ in OR
1920	William Peterssen, Sweden	23 ft 5½ in
1924	DeHart Hubbard, United States	24 ft 5 in
1928	Edward B. Hamm, United States	25 ft 4½ in OR
1932	Edward Gordon, United States	25 ft ¾ in
1936	Jesse Owens, United States	26 ft 5½ in OR
1948	William Steele, United States	25 ft 8 in
1952	Jerome Biffle, United States	24 ft 10 in
1956	Gregory Bell, United States	25 ft 8¼ in
1960	Ralph Boston, United States	26 ft 7¾ in OR
1964	Lynn Davies, Great Britain	26 ft 5¾ in
1968	Bob Beamon, United States	29 ft 2½ in WR

LONG JUMP (Cont.)

1972	Randy Williams, United States	27 ft ½ in
1976	Arnie Robinson, United States	27 ft 4¾ in
1980	Lutz Dombrowski, East Germany	28 ft ¼ in
1984	Carl Lewis, United States	28 ft ¼ in
1988	Carl Lewis, United States	28 ft 7½ in
1992	Carl Lewis, United States	28 ft 5½ in

TRIPLE JUMP

1896	James Connolly, United States	44 ft 11¾ in
1900	Meyer Prinstein, United States	47 ft 5¾ in OR
1904	Meyer Prinstein, United States	47 ft 1 in
1906	Peter O'Connor, Great Britain/Ireland	46 ft 2¼ in
1908	Timothy Ahearne, Great Britain/Ireland	48 ft 11¼ in OR
1912	Gustaf Lindblom, Sweden	48 ft 5¼ in
1920	Vilho Tuulos, Finland	47 ft 7 in
1924	Anthony Winter, Australia	50 ft 11¼ in WR
1928	Mikio Oda, Japan	49 ft 11 in
1932	Chuhei Nambu, Japan	51 ft 7 in WR
1936	Naoto Tajima, Japan	52 ft 6 in WR
1948	Arne Ahman, Sweden	50 ft 6¼ in
1952	Adhemar da Silva, Brazil	53 ft 2¾ in WR
1956	Adhemar da Silva, Brazil	53 ft 7¾ in OR
1960	Jozef Schmidt, Poland	55 ft 2 in
1964	Jozef Schmidt, Poland	55 ft 3½ in OR
1968	Viktor Saneyev, USSR	57 ft ¾ in WR
1972	Viktor Saneyev, USSR	56 ft 11¾ in
1976	Viktor Saneyev, USSR	56 ft 8¾ in
1980	Jaak Uudmae, USSR	56 ft 11¼ in
1984	Al Joyner, United States	56 ft 7½ in
1988	Khristo Markov, Bulgaria	57 ft 9½ in OR
1992	Mike Conley, United States	59 ft 7½ in

SHOT PUT

1896	Robert Garrett, United States	36 ft 9¾ in
1900	Richard Sheldon, United States	46 ft 3¼ in OR
1904	Ralph Rose, United States	48 ft 7 in WR
1906	Martin Sheridan, United States	40 ft 5¼ in
1908	Ralph Rose, United States	46 ft 7½ in
1912	Pat McDonald, United States	50 ft 4 in OR
1920	Ville Porhola, Finland	48 ft 7¼ in
1924	Clarence Houser, United States	49 ft 2¼ in
1928	John Kuck, United States	52 ft ¾ in WR
1932	Leo Sexton, United States	52 ft 6 in OR
1936	Hans Woellke, Germany	53 ft 1¾ in OR
1948	Wilbur Thompson, United States	56 ft 2 in OR
1952	Parry O'Brien, United States	57 ft ½ in OR
1956	Parry O'Brien, United States	60 ft 11¼ in OR
1960	William Nieder, United States	64 ft 6¾ in OR

TRACK AND FIELD *(Cont.)*

Men *(Cont.)*

SHOT PUT *(Cont.)*

1964	Dallas Long, United States	66 ft 8½ in OR
1968	Randy Matson, United States	67 ft 4¾ in
1972	Wladyslaw Komar, Poland	69 ft 6 in OR
1976	Udo Beyer, East Germany	69 ft ¾ in
1980	Vladimir Kiselyov, USSR	70 ft ½ in OR
1984	Alessandro Andrei, Italy	69 ft 9 in
1988	Ulf Timmermann, East Germany	73 ft 8¾ in OR
1992	Mike Stulce, United States	71 ft 2½ in

DISCUS THROW

1896	Robert Garrett, United States	95 ft 7½ in
1900	Rudolf Bauer, Hungary	118 ft 3 in OR
1904	Martin Sheridan, United States	128 ft 10½ in OR
1906	Martin Sheridan, United States	136 ft
1908	Martin Sheridan, United States	134 ft 2 in OR
1912	Armas Taipele, Finland	148 ft 3 in OR
1920	Elmer Niklander, Finland	146 ft 7 in
1924	Clarence Houser, United States	151 ft 4 in OR
1928	Clarence Houser, United States	155 ft 3 in OR
1932	John Anderson, United States	162 ft 4 in OR
1936	Ken Carpenter, United States	165 ft 7 in OR
1948	Adolfo Consolini, Italy	173 ft 2 in OR
1952	Sim Iness, United States	180 ft 6 in OR
1956	Al Oerter, United States	184 ft 11 in OR
1960	Al Oerter, United States	194 ft 2 in OR
1964	Al Oerter, United States	200 ft 1 in OR
1968	Al Oerter, United States	212 ft 6 in OR
1972	Ludvik Danek, Czechoslovakia	211 ft 3 in
1976	Mac Wilkins, United States	221 ft 5 in OR
1980	Viktor Rashchupkin, USSR	218 ft 8 in
1984	Rolf Dannenberg, West Germany	218 ft 6 in
1988	Jürgen Schult, East Germany	225 ft 9 in OR
1992	Romas Ubartas, Lithuania	213 ft 8 in

HAMMER THROW

1900	John Flanagan, United States	163 ft 1 in
1904	John Flanagan, United States	168 ft 1 in OR
1906	Not held	
1908	John Flanagan, United States	170 ft 4 in OR
1912	Matt McGrath, United States	179 ft 7 in OR
1920	Pat Ryan, United States	173 ft 5 in
1924	Fred Tootell, United States	174 ft 10 in
1928	Patrick O'Callaghan, Ireland	168 ft 7 in
1932	Patrick O'Callaghan, Ireland	176 ft 11 in
1936	Karl Hein, Germany	185 ft 4 in
1948	Imre Nemeth, Hungary	183 ft 11 in
1952	Jozsef Csermak, Hungary	197 ft 11 in WR
1956	Harold Connolly, United States	207 ft 3 in OR
1960	Vasily Rudenkov, USSR	220 ft 2 in OR

HAMMER THROW *(Cont.)*

1964	Romuald Klim, USSR	228 ft 10 in OR
1968	Gyula Zsivotsky, Hungary	240 ft 8 in OR
1972	Anatoli Bondarchuk, USSR	247 ft 8 in OR
1976	Yuri Sedykh, USSR	254 ft 4 in OR
1980	Yuri Sedykh, USSR	268 ft 4 in WR
1984	Juha Tiainen, Finland	256 ft 2 in
1988	Sergei Litvinov, USSR	278 ft 2 in OR
1992	Andrey Abduvaliyev, Unified Team	270 ft 9 in

JAVELIN

1908	Erik Lemming, Sweden	179 ft 10 in
1912	Erik Lemming, Sweden	198 ft 11 in WR
1920	Jonni Myyrä, Finland	215 ft 10 in OR
1924	Jonni Myyrä, Finland	206 ft 6 in
1928	Eric Lundkvist, Sweden	218 ft 6 in OR
1932	Matti Jarvinen, Finland	238 ft 6 in OR
1936	Gerhard Stöck, Germany	235 ft 8 in
1948	Kai Rautavaara, Finland	228 ft 10½ in
1952	Cy Young, United States	242 ft 1 in OR
1956	Egil Danielson, Norway	281 ft 2¼ in WR
1960	Viktor Tsibulenko, USSR	277 ft 8 in
1964	Pauli Nevala, Finland	271 ft 2 in
1968	Janis Lusis, USSR	295 ft 7 in OR
1972	Klaus Wolfermann, West Germany	296 ft 10 in OR
1976	Miklos Nemeth, Hungary	310 ft 4 in WR
1980	Dainis Kuta, USSR	299 ft 2⅜ in
1984	Arto Härkönen, Finland	284 ft 8 in
1988	Tapio Korjus, Finland	276 ft 6 in
1992	Jan Zelezny, Czechoslovakia	294 ft 2 in OR

DECATHLON

		Pts
1904	Thomas Kiely, Ireland	6036
1912	Jim Thorpe, United States*	8412 WR
1920	Helge Lövland, Norway	6803
1924	Harold Osborn, United States	7711 WR
1928	Paavo Yrjölä, Finland	8053.29 WR
1932	James Bausch, United States	8462 WR
1936	Glenn Morris, United States	7900 WR
1948	Robert Mathias, United States	7139
1952	Robert Mathias, United States	7887 WR
1956	Milton Campbell, United States	7937 OR
1960	Rafer Johnson, United States	8392 OR
1964	Willi Holdorf, West Germany	7887
1968	Bill Toomey, United States	8193 OR
1972	Nikolai Avilov, USSR	8454 WR
1976	Bruce Jenner, United States	8617 WR
1980	Daley Thompson, Great Britain	8495
1984	Daley Thompson, Great Britain	8798 EWR
1988	Christian Schenk, East Germany	8488
1992	Robert Zmelik, Czechoslovakia	8611

*In 1913, Thorpe was disqualified for having played professional baseball in 1910. His record was restored in 1982.

Note: OR=Olympic Record; WR=World Record;

EOR=Equals Olympic Record; EWR=Equals World Record; WB=World Best.

TRACK AND FIELD (Cont.)

Women

100 METERS

1928 ...Elizabeth Robinson, United States	12.2 EWR	
1932 ...Stella Walsh, Poland	11.9 EWR	
1936 ...Helen Stephens, United States	11.5	
1948 ....Francina Blankers-Koen, Netherlands	11.9	
1952 ...Marjorie Jackson, Australia	11.5 EWR	
1956 ...Betty Cuthbert, Australia	11.5 EWR	
1960 ...Wilma Rudolph, United States	11.0	
1964 ...Wyomia Tyus, United States	11.4	
1968 ...Wyomia Tyus, United States	11.0 WR	
1972 ...Renate Stecher, East Germany	11.07	
1976 ...Annegret Richter, West Germany	11.08	
1980 ...Lyudmila Kondratyeva, USSR	11.06	
1984 ...Evelyn Ashford, United States	10.97 OR	
1988 ...Florence Griffith Joyner, United States	10.54	
1992 ...Gail Devers, United States	10.82	

200 METERS

1948...Francina Blankers-Koen, Netherlands	24.4	
1952 ..Marjorie Jackson, Australia	23.7	
1956 ..Betty Cuthbert, Australia	23.4 EOR	
1960 ..Wilma Rudolph, United States	24.0	
1964 ..Edith McGuire, United States	23.0 OR	
1968 ..Irena Szewinska, Poland	22.5 WR	
1972 ..Renate Stecher, East Germany	22.40 EWR	
1976 ..Bärbel Eckert, East Germany	22.37 OR	
1980 ..Bärbel Wöckel (Eckert), East Germany	22.03 OR	
1984...Valerie Brisco-Hooks, United States	21.81 OR	
1988 ..Florence Griffith Joyner, United States	21.34 WR	
1992 ..Gwen Torrence, United States	21.81	

400 METERS

1964 ...Betty Cuthbert, Australia	52.0 OR	
1968 ...Colette Besson, France	52.0 EOR	
1972 ...Monika Zehrt, East Germany	51.08 OR	
1976 ...Irena Szewinska, Poland	49.29 WR	
1980 ...Marita Koch, East Germany	48.88 OR	
1984 ...Valerie Brisco-Hooks, United States	48.83 OR	
1988 ...Olga Bryzgina, USSR	48.65 OR	
1992 ...Marie-José Pérec, France	48.83	

800 METERS

1928 ....Lina Radke, Germany	2:16.8 WR	
1932....Not held 1932-1956		
1960 ....Lyudmila Shevtsova, USSR	2:04.3 EWR	
1964 ....Ann Packer, Great Britain	2:01.1 OR	
1968 ....Madeline Manning, United States	2:00.9 OR	
1972 ....Hildegard Falck, West Germany	1:58.55 OR	
1976 ....Tatyana Kazankina, USSR	1:54.94 WR	
1980 ....Nadezhda Olizarenko, USSR	1:53.42 WR	
1984 ....Doina Melinte, Romania	1:57.6	
1988 ....Sigrun Wodars, East Germany	1:56.10	
1992 ....Ellen Van Langen, the Netherlands	1:55.54	

1500 METERS

1972 ....Lyudmila Bragina, USSR	4:01.4 WR	
1976 ....Tatyana Kazankina, USSR	4:05.48	
1980 ....Tatyana Kazankina, USSR	3:56.6 OR	
1984 ....Gabriella Dorio, Italy	4:03.25	

1500 METERS (Cont.)

1988 ....Paula Ivan, Romania	3:53.96 OR	
1992 ....Hassiba Boulmerka, Algeria	3:55.30	

3000 METERS

1984 ....Maricica Puica, Romania	8:35.96 OR	
1988 ....Tatyana Samolenko, USSR	8:26.53 OR	
1992 ....Elena Romanova, Unified Team	8:46.04	

10,000 METERS

1988 ....Olga Bondarenko, USSR	31:05.21 OR	
1992 ....Derartu Tulu, Ethiopia	31:06.02	

MARATHON

1984 ....Joan Benoit, United States	2:24:52	
1988 ....Rosa Mota, Portugal	2:25:40	
1992 ....Valentin Yegorova, Unified Team	2:32:41	

80-METER HURDLES

1932 ..Babe Didrikson, United States	11.7 WR	
1936 ..Trebisonda Valla, Italy	11.7	
1948 ..Francina Blankers-Koen, Netherlands	11.2 OR	
1952 ..Shirley Strickland, Australia	10.9 WR	
1956 ..Shirley Strickland, Australia	10.7 OR	
1960 ..Irina Press, USSR	10.8	
1964 ..Karin Balzer, East Germany	10.5	
1968 ..Maureen Caird, Australia	10.3 WR	

- 100-METER HURDLES

1972 ....Annelie Ehrhardt, East Germany	12.59 WR	
1976 ....Johanna Schaller, East Germany	12.77	
1980 ....Vera Komisova, USSR	12.56 OR	
1984 ....Benita Fitzgerald-Brown, United States	12.84	
1988 ....Yordanka Donkova, Bulgaria	12.38 OR	
1992 ....Paraskevi Patoulidou, Greece	12.64	

400-METER HURDLES

1984 ....Nawal el Moutawakel, Morocco	54.61 OR	
1988 ....Debra Flintoff-King, Australia	53.17 OR	
1992 ....Sally Gunnell, Great Britain	53.23	

4 X 100-METER RELAY

1928 ....Canada	48.4 WR	
1932 ....United States	46.9 WR	
1936 ....United States	46.9	
1948 ....Netherlands	47.5	
1952 ....United States	45.9 WR	
1956 ....Australia	44.5 WR	
1960 ....United States	44.5	
1964 ....Poland	43.6	
1968 ....United States	42.8 WR	
1972 ....West Germany	42.81 EWR	
1976 ....East Germany	42.55 OR	
1980 ....East Germany	41.60 WR	
1984 ....United States	41.65	
1988 ....United States	41.98	
1992 ....United States	42.11	

Note: OR=Olympic Record; WR=World Record; EOR=Equals Olympic Record; EWR=Equals World Record; WB=World Best.

Summer Games Champions (Cont.)

TRACK AND FIELD (Cont.)

Women (Cont.)

4 X 400-METER RELAY

1972	East Germany	3:23 WR
1976	East Germany	3:19.23 WR
1980	USSR	3:20.02
1984	United States	3:18.29 OR
1988	USSR	3:15.18 WR
1992	Unified Team	3:20.20

HIGH JUMP

1928	Ethel Catherwood, Canada	5 ft 2½ in
1932	Jean Shiley, United States	5 ft 5¼ in WR
1936	Ibolya Csak, Hungary	5 ft 3 in
1948	Alice Coachman, United States	5 ft 6 in OR
1952	Esther Brand, South Africa	5 ft 5¾ in
1956	Mildred L. McDaniel, United States	5 ft 9¼ in WR
1960	Iolanda Balas, Romania	6 ft ¾ in OR
1964	Iolanda Balas, Romania	6 ft 2¾ in OR
1968	Miloslava Reskova, Czechoslovakia	5 ft 11½ in
1972	Ulrike Meyfarth, West Germany	6 ft 3½ in EWR
1976	Rosemarie Ackermann, East Germany	6 ft 4 in OR
1980	Sara Simeoni, Italy	6 ft 5½ in OR
1984	Ulrike Meyfarth, West Germany	6 ft 7½ in OR
1988	Louise Ritter, United States	6 ft 8 in OR
1992	Heike Henkel, Germany	6 ft 7½ in

LONG JUMP

1948	Olga Gyarmati, Hungary	18 ft 8¼ in
1952	Yvette Williams, New Zealand	20 ft 5¾ in OR
1956	Elzbieta Krzeskinska, Poland	20 ft 10 in EWR
1960	Vyera Krepkina, USSR	20 ft 10¾ in OR
1964	Mary Rand, Great Britain	22 ft 2¼ in WR
1968	Viorica Viscopoleanu, Romania	22 ft 4½ in WR
1972	Heidemarie Rosendahl, West Germany	22 ft 3 in
1976	Angela Voigt, East Germany	22 ft ¾ in
1980	Tatyana Kolpakova, USSR	23 ft 2 in OR
1984	Anisoara Stanciu, Romania	22 ft 10 in
1988	Jackie Joyner-Kersee, United States	24 ft 3½ in OR
1992	Heike Drechsler, Germany	23 ft 5¼ in

SHOT PUT

1948	Micheline Ostermeyer, France	45 ft 1½ in
1952	Galina Zybina, USSR	50 ft 1¾ in WR
1956	Tamara Tyshkevich, USSR	54 ft 5 in OR
1960	Tamara Press, USSR	56 ft 10 in OR
1964	Tamara Press, USSR	59 ft 6¼ in OR
1968	Margitta Gummel, East Germany	64 ft 4 in WR
1972	Nadezhda Chizhova, USSR	69 ft WR
1976	Ivanka Hristova, Bulgaria	69 ft 5¼ in OR
1980	Ilona Slupianek, East Germany	73 ft 6¼ in
1984	Claudia Losch, West Germany	67 ft 2¼ in

SHOT PUT (Cont.)

1988	Natalya Lisovskaya, USSR	72 ft 11¾ in
1992	Svetlana Kriveleva, Unified Team	69 ft 1¼ in

DISCUS THROW

1928	Helena Konopacka, Poland	129 ft 11¾ in WR
1932	Lillian Copeland, United States	133 ft 2 in OR
1936	Gisela Mauermayer, Germany	156 ft 3 in OR
1948	Micheline Ostermeyer, France	137 ft 6 in
1952	Nina Romaschkova, USSR	168 ft 8 in OR
1956	Olga Fikotova, Czechoslovakia	176 ft 1 in OR
1960	Nina Ponomaryeva, USSR	180 ft 9 in OR
1964	Tamara Press, USSR	187 ft 10 in OR
1968	Lia Manoliu, Romania	191 ft 2 in OR
1972	Faina Melnik, USSR	218 ft 7 in OR
1976	Evelin Schlaak, East Germany	226 ft 4 in OR
1980	Evelin Jahl (Schlaak), East Germany	229 ft 6 in OR
1984	Ria Stalman, Netherlands	214 ft 5 in
1988	Martina Hellmann, East Germany	237 ft 2 in OR
1992	Maritza Martén, Cuba	229 ft 10 in

JAVELIN THROW

1932	Babe Didrikson, United States	143 ft 4 in OR
1936	Tilly Fleischer, Germany	148 ft 3 in OR
1948	Herma Bauma, Austria	149 ft 6 in
1952	Dana Zatopkova, Czechoslovakia	165 ft 7 in
1956	Inese Jaunzeme, USSR	176 ft 8 in
1960	Elvira Ozolina, USSR	183 ft 8 in OR
1964	Mihaela Penes, Romania	198 ft 7 in
1968	Angela Nemeth, Hungary	198 ft
1972	Ruth Fuchs, East Germany	209 ft 7 in OR
1976	Ruth Fuchs, East Germany	216 ft 4 in OR
1980	Maria Colon, Cuba	224 ft 5 in OR
1984	Tessa Sanderson, Great Britain	228 ft 2 in OR
1988	Petra Felke, East Germany	245 ft OR
1992	Silke Renk, Germany	224 ft 2 in

PENTATHLON

		Pts
1964	Irina Press, USSR	5246 WR
1968	Ingrid Becker, West Germany	5098
1972	Mary Peters, Great Britain	4801 WR*
1976	Siegrun Siegl, East Germany	4745
1980	Nadezhda Tkachenko, USSR	5083 WR

*In 1971, 100-meter hurdles replaced 80-meter hurdles, necessitating a change in scoring tables.

HEPTATHLON

		Pts
1984	Glynis Nunn, Australia	6390 OR
1988	Jackie Joyner-Kersee, United States	7291 WR
1992	Jackie Joyner-Kersee, United States	7044

BASKETBALL

Men

1936

Final: United States 19, Canada 8
United States: Ralph Bishop, Joe Fortenberry, Carl Knowles, Jack Ragland, Carl Shy, William Wheatley, Francis Johnson, Samuel Balter, John Gibbons, Frank Lubin, Arthur Mollner, Donald Piper, Duane Swanson, Willard Schmidt

1948

Final: United States 65, France 21
United States: Cliff Barker, Don Barksdale, Ralph Beard, Lewis Beck, Vince Boryla, Gordon Carpenter, Alex Groza, Wallace Jones, Bob Kurland, Ray Lumpp, Robert Pitts, Jesse Renick, Bob Robinson, Ken Rollins

1952

Final: United States 36, USSR 25
United States: Charles Hoag, Bill Hougland, Melvin Dean Kelley, Bob Kenney, Clyde Lovellette, Marcus Freiberger, Victor Wayne Glasgow, Frank McCabe, Daniel Pippen, Howard Williams, Ronald Bontemps, Bob Kurland, William Lienhard, John Keller

1956

Final: United States 89, USSR 55
United States: Carl Cain, Bill Hougland, K. C. Jones, Bill Russell, James Walsh, William Evans, Burdette Haldorson, Ron Tomsic, Dick Boushka, Gilbert Ford, Bob Jeangerard, Charles Darling

1960

Final: United States 90, Brazil 63
United States: Jay Arnette, Walt Bellamy, Bob Boozer, Terry Dischinger, Jerry Lucas, Oscar Robertson, Adrian Smith, Burdette Haldorson, Darrall Imhoff, Allen Kelley, Lester Lane, Jerry West

1964

Final: United States 73, USSR 59
United States: Jim Barnes, Bill Bradley, Larry Brown, Joe Caldwell, Mel Counts, Richard Davies, Walt Hazzard, Lucius Jackson, John McCaffrey, Jeff Mullins, Jerry Shipp, George Wilson

1968

Final: United States 65, Yugoslavia 50
United States: John Clawson, Ken Spain, Jo-Jo White, Michael Barrett, Spencer Haywood, Charles Scott, William Hosket, Calvin Fowler, Michael Silliman, Glynn Saulters, James King, Donald Dee

1972

Final: USSR 51, United States 50
United States: Kenneth Davis, Doug Collins, Thomas Henderson, Mike Bantom, Bobby Jones, Dwight Jones, James Forbes, James Brewer, Tom Burleson, Tom McMillen, Kevin Joyce, Ed Ratleff

1976

Final: United States 95, Yugoslavia 74
United States: Phil Ford, Steve Sheppard, Adrian Dantley, Walter Davis, Quinn Buckner, Ernie Grunfeld, Kenny Carr, Scott May, Michel Armstrong, Tom La Garde, Phil Hubbard, Mitch Kupchak

1980

Final: Yugoslavia 86, Italy 77
U.S. participated in boycott.

1984

Final: United States 96, Spain 65
United States: Steve Alford, Leon Wood, Patrick Ewing, Vern Fleming, Alvin Robertson, Michael Jordan, Joe Kleine, Jon Koncak, Wayman Tisdale, Chris Mullin, Sam Perkins, Jeff Turner

1988

Final: USSR 76, Yugoslavia 63
United States (3rd): Mitch Richmond, Charles E. Smith, IV, Vernell Coles, Hersey Hawkins, Jeff Grayer, Charles D. Smith, Willie Anderson, Stacey Augmon, Dan Majerle, Danny Manning, J. R. Reid, David Robinson

1992

Final: United States 117, Croatia 85
United States: David Robinson, Christian Laettner, Patrick Ewing, Larry Bird, Scottie Pippen, Michael Jordan, Clyde Drexler, Karl Malone, John Stockton, Chris Mullin, Charles Barkley, Earvin Johnson

Women

1976

Gold USSR; Silver, United States*
United States: Cindy Brogdon, Susan Rojcewicz, Ann Meyers, Lusia Harris, Nancy Dunkle, Charlotte Lewis, Nancy Lieberman, Gail Marquis, Patricia Roberts, Mary Anne O'Connor, Patricia Head, Julienne Simpson

*In 1976 the women played a round-robin tournament, with the gold medal going to the team with the best record. The USSR won with a 5-0 record, and the USA, with a 3-2 record, was given the silver by virtue of a 95-79 victory over Bulgaria, which was also 3-2.

1980

Final: USSR 104, Bulgaria 73
U.S. participated in boycott.

1984

Final: United States 85, Korea 55
United States: Teresa Edwards, Lea Henry, Lynette Woodard, Anne Donovan, Cathy Boswell, Cheryl Miller, Janice Lawrence, Cindy Noble, Kim Mulkey, Denise Curry, Pamela McGee, Carol Menken-Schaudt

BASKETBALL (Cont.)

Women (Cont.)

1988

Final: United States 77, Yugoslavia 70
United States: Teresa Edwards, Mary Ethridge, Cynthia Brown, Anne Donovan, Teresa Weatherspoon, Bridgette Gordon, Victoria Bullett, Andrea Lloyd, Katrina McClain, Jennifer Gillom, Cynthia Cooper, Suzanne McConnell

1992

Final: Unified Team 76, China 66
United States (3rd): Teresa Edwards, Teresa Weatherspoon, Victoria Bullett, Katrina McClain, Cynthia Cooper, Suzanne McConnell, Daedra Charles, Clarissa Davis, Tammy Jackson, Vickie Orr, Carolyn Jones, Medina Dixon

BOXING

LIGHT FLYWEIGHT (106 LB)

1968	Francisco Rodriguez, Venezuela
1972	Gyorgy Gedo, Hungary
1976	Jorge Hernandez, Cuba
1980	Shamil Sabyrov, USSR
1984	Paul Gonzalez, United States
1988	Ivailo Hristov, Bulgaria
1992	Rogelio Marcelo, Cuba

FLYWEIGHT (112 LB)

1904	George Finnegan, United States
1906-1912	Not held
1920	Frank Di Gennara, United States
1924	Fidel LaBarba, United States
1928	Antal Kocsis, Hungary
1932	Istvan Enekes, Hungary
1936	Willi Kaiser, Germany
1948	Pascual Perez, Argentina
1952	Nathan Brooks, United States
1956	Terence Spinks, Great Britain
1960	Gyula Torok, Hungary
1964	Fernando Atzori, Italy
1968	Ricardo Delgado, Mexico
1972	Georgi Kostadinov, Bulgaria
1976	Leo Randolph, United States
1980	Peter Lessov, Bulgaria
1984	Steve McCrory, United States
1988	Kim Kwang Sun, South Korea
1992	Su Choi Chol, North Korea

BANTAMWEIGHT (119 LB)

1904	Oliver Kirk, United States
1906	Not held
1908	A. Henry Thomas, Great Britain
1912	Not held
1920	Clarence Walker, South Africa
1924	William Smith, South Africa
1928	Vittorio Tamagnini, Italy
1932	Horace Gwynne, Canada
1936	Ulderico Sergo, Italy
1948	Tibor Csik, Hungary
1952	Pentti Hamalainen, Finland
1956	Wolfgang Behrendt, East Germany
1960	Oleg Grigoryev, USSR
1964	Takao Sakurai, Japan
1968	Valery Sokolov, USSR
1972	Orlando Martinez, Cuba
1976	Yong Jo Gu, North Korea
1980	Juan Hernandez, Cuba
1984	Maurizio Stecca, Italy
1988	Kennedy McKinney, United States
1992	Joel Casamayor, Cuba

FEATHERWEIGHT (125 LB)

1904	Oliver Kirk, United States
1906	Not held
1908	Richard Gunn, Great Britain
1912	Not held
1920	Paul Fritsch, France
1924	John Fields, United States
1928	Lambertus van Klaveren, Netherlands
1932	Carmelo Robledo, Argentina
1936	Oscar Casanovas, Argentina
1948	Ernesto Formenti, Italy
1952	Jan Zachara, Czechoslovakia
1956	Vladimir Safronov, USSR
1960	Francesco Musso, Italy
1964	Stanislav Stephashkin, USSR
1968	Antonio Roldan, Mexico
1972	Boris Kousnetsov, USSR
1976	Angel Herrera, Cuba
1980	Rudi Fink, East Germany
1984	Meldrick Taylor, United States
1988	Giovanni Parisi, Italy
1992	Andreas Tews, Germany

LIGHTWEIGHT (132 LB)

1904	Harry Spanger, United States
1906	Not held
1908	Frederick Grace, Great Britain
1912	Not held
1920	Samuel Mosberg, United States
1924	Hans Nielsen, Denmark
1928	Carlo Orlandi, Italy
1932	Lawrence Stevens, South Africa
1936	Imre Harangi, Hungary
1948	Gerald Dreyer, South Africa
1952	Aureliano Bolognesi, Italy
1956	Richard McTaggart, Great Britain
1960	Kazimierz Pazdzior, Poland
1964	Jozef Grudzien, Poland
1968	Ronald Harris, United States
1972	Jan Szczepanski, Poland
1976	Howard Davis, United States
1980	Angel Herrera, Cuba
1984	Pernell Whitaker, United States
1988	Andreas Zuelow, East Germany
1992	Oscar De La Hoya, United States

LIGHT WELTERWEIGHT (139 LB)

1952	Charles Adkins, United States
1956	Vladimir Yengibaryan, USSR
1960	Bohumil Nemecek, Czechoslovakia
1964	Jerzy Kulej, Poland
1968	Jerzy Kulej, Poland
1972	Ray Seales, United States
1976	Ray Leonard, United States

BOXING *(Cont.)*

LIGHT WELTERWEIGHT *(Cont.)*

1980 ....Patrizio Oliva, Italy
1984 ....Jerry Page, United States
1988 ....Viatcheslav Janovski, USSR
1992 ....Hector Vinent, Cuba

WELTERWEIGHT (147 LB)

1904 ....Albert Young, United States
1906-1912 ......Not held
1920 ....Albert Schneider, Canada
1924 ....Jean Delarge, Belgium
1928 ....Edward Morgan, New Zealand
1932 ....Edward Flynn, United States
1936 ....Sten Suvio, Finland
1948 ....Julius Torma, Czechoslovakia
1952 ....Zygmunt Chychla, Poland
1956 ....Nicolae Linca, Romania
1960 ....Giovanni Benvenuti, Italy
1964 ....Marian Kasprzyk, Poland
1968 ....Manfred Wolke, East Germany
1972 ....Emilio Correa, Cuba
1976 ....Jochen Bachfeld, East Germany
1980 ....Andres Aldama, Cuba
1984 ....Mark Breland, United States
1988 ....Robert Wangila, Kenya
1992 ....Michael Carruth, Ireland

LIGHT MIDDLEWEIGHT (156 LB)

1952 ....Laszlo Papp, Hungary
1956 ....Laszlo Papp, Hungary
1960 ....Wilbert McClure, United States
1964 ....Boris Lagutin, USSR
1968 ....Boris Lagutin, USSR
1972 ....Dieter Kottysch, West Germany
1976 ....Jerzy Rybicki, Poland
1980 ....Armando Martinez, Cuba
1984 ....Frank Tate, United States
1988 ....Park Si-Hun, South Korea
1992 ....Juan Lemus, Cuba

MIDDLEWEIGHT (165 LB)

1904 ....Charles Mayer, United States
1908 ....John Douglas, Great Britain
1912 ....Not held
1920 ....Harry Mallin, Great Britain
1924 ....Harry Mallin, Great Britain
1928 ....Piero Toscani, Italy
1932 ....Carmen Barth, United States
1936 ....Jean Despeaux, France
1948 ....Laszlo Papp, Hungary
1952 ....Floyd Patterson, United States
1956 ....Gennady Schatkov, USSR
1960 ....Edward Crook, United States
1964 ....Valery Popenchenko, USSR
1968 ....Christopher Finnegan, Great Britain
1972 ....Vyacheslav Lemechev, USSR
1976 ....Michael Spinks, United States

MIDDLEWEIGHT *(Cont.)*

1980 ....Jose Gomez, Cuba
1984 ....Shin Joon Sup, South Korea
1988 ....Henry Maske, East Germany
1992 ....Ariel Hernandez, Cuba

LIGHT HEAVYWEIGHT (178 LB)

1920 ....Edward Eagan, United States
1924 ....Harry Mitchell, Great Britain
1928 ....Victor Avendano, Argentina
1932 ....David Carstens, South Africa
1936 ....Roger Michelot, France
1948 ....George Hunter, South Africa
1952 ....Norvel Lee, United States
1956 ....James Boyd, United States
1960 ....Cassius Clay, United States
1964 ....Cosimo Pinto, Italy
1968 ....Dan Poznyak, USSR
1972 ....Mate Parlov, Yugoslavia
1976 ....Leon Spinks, United States
1980 ....Slobodan Kacer, Yugoslavia
1984 ....Anton Josipovic, Yugoslavia
1988 ....Andrew Maynard, United States
1992 ....Torsten May, Germany

HEAVYWEIGHT (OVER 201 LB)

1904 ....Samuel Berger, United States
1906 ....Not held
1908 ....Albert Oldham, Great Britain
1912 ....Not held
1920 ....Ronald Rawson, Great Britain
1924 ....Otto von Porat, Norway
1928 ....Arturo Rodriguez Jurado, Argentina
1932 ....Santiago Lovell, Argentina
1936 ....Herbert Runge, Germany
1948 ....Rafael Inglesias, Argentina
1952 ....H. Edward Sanders, United States
1956 ....T. Peter Rademacher, United States
1960 ....Franco De Piccoli, Italy
1964 ....Joe Frazier, United States
1968 ....George Foreman, United States
1972 ....Teofilo Stevenson, Cuba
1976 ....Teofilo Stevenson, Cuba
1980 ....Teofilo Stevenson, Cuba

HEAVYWEIGHT (201* LB)

1984 ....Henry Tillman, United States
1988 ....Ray Mercer, United States
1992 ....Felix Savon, Cuba

SUPER HEAVYWEIGHT (UNLIMITED)

1984 ....Tyrell Biggs, United States
1988 ....Lennox Lewis, Canada
1992 ....Roberto Balado, Cuba

*Until 1984 the heavyweight division was unlimited. With the addition of the super heavyweight division, a limit of 201 pounds was imposed.

SWIMMING

Men

50-METER FREESTYLE

1904	Zoltan Halmay, Hungary (50 yds)	28.0
1988	Matt Biondi, United States	22.14 WR
1992	Aleksandr Popov, Unified Team	22.30

100-METER FREESTLYE

1896	Alfred Hajos, Hungary	1:22.2 OR
1904	Zoltan Halmay, Hungary (100 yds)	1:02.8
1906	Charles Daniels, United States	1:13.4
1908	Charles Daniels, United States	1:05.6 WR
1912	Duke Kahanamoku, United States	1:03.4
1920	Duke Kahanamoku, United States	1:00.4 WR
1924	John Weissmuller, United States	59.0 OR
1928	John Weissmuller, United States	58.6 OR
1932	Yasuji Miyazaki, Japan	58.2
1936	Ferenc Csik, Hungary	57.6
1948	Wally Ris, United States	57.3 OR
1952	Clarke Scholes, United States	57.4
1956	Jon Henricks, Australia	55.4 OR
1960	John Devitt, Australia	55.2 OR
1964	Don Schollander, United States	53.4 OR
1968	Mike Wenden, Australia	52.2 WR
1972	Mark Spitz, United States	51.22 WR
1976	Jim Montgomery, United States	49.99 WR
1980	Jörg Woithe, East Germany	50.40
1984	Rowdy Gaines, United States	49.80 OR
1988	Matt Biondi, United States	48.63 OR
1992	Aleksandr Popov, Unified Team	49.02

200-METER FREESTYLE

1900	Frederick Lane, Australia	2:25.2 OR
1904	Charles Daniels, United States	2:44.2
1906	Not held 1906-1964	
1968	Michael Wenden, Australia	1:55.2 OR
1972	Mark Spitz, United States	1:52.78 WR
1976	Bruce Furniss, United States	1:50.29 WR
1980	Sergei Kopliakov, USSR	1:49.81 OR
1984	Michael Gross, West Germany	1:47.44 WR
1988	Duncan Armstrong, Australia	1:47.25 WR
1992	Evgueni Sadovyi, Unified Team	1:46.70

400-METER FREESTYLE

1896	Paul Neumann, Austria (500 yds)	8:12.6
1904	Charles Daniels, U.S. (440 yds)	6:16.2
1906	Otto Scheff, Austria (440 yds)	6:23.8
1908	Henry Taylor, Great Britain	5:36.8
1912	George Hodgson, Canada	5:24.4
1920	Norman Ross, United States	5:26.8
1924	John Weissmuller, United States	5:04.2 OR
1928	Albert Zorilla, Argentina	5:01.6 OR
1932	Buster Crabbe, United States	4:48.4 OR
1936	Jack Medica, United States	4:44.5 OR
1948	William Smith, United States	4:41.0 OR
1952	Jean Boiteux, France	4:30.7 OR
1956	Murray Rose, Australia	4:27.3 OR
1960	Murray Rose, Australia	4:18.3 OR
1964	Don Schollander, United States	4:12.2 WR
1968	Mike Burton, United States	4:09.0 OR
1972	Brad Cooper, Australia	4:00.27 OR
1976	Brian Goodell, United States	3:51.93 WR
1980	Vladimir Salnikov, USSR	3:51.31 OR
1984	George DiCarlo, United States	3:51.23 OR
1988	Uwe Dassler, East Germany	3:46.95 WR
1992	Evgueni Sadovyi, Unified Team	3:45.00 WR

1500-METER FREESTYLE

1908	Henry Taylor, Great Britain	22:48.4 WR
1912	George Hodgson, Canada	22:00.0 WR
1920	Norman Ross, United States	22:23.2
1924	Andrew Charlton, Australia	20:06.6 WR
1928	Arne Borg, Sweden	19:51.8 OR
1932	Kusuo Kitamura, Japan	19:12.4 OR
1936	Noboru Terada, Japan	19:13.7
1948	James McLane, United States	19:18.5
1952	Ford Konno, United States	18:30.3 OR
1956	Murray Rose, Australia	17:58.9
1960	John Konrads, Australia	17:19.6 OR
1964	Robert Windle, Australia	17:01.7 OR
1968	Mike Burton, United States	16:38.9 OR
1972	Mike Burton, United States	15:52.58 OR
1976	Brian Goodell, United States	15:02.40 WR
1980	Vladimir Salnikov, USSR	14:58.27 WR
1984	Michael O'Brien, United States	15:05.20
1988	Vladimir Salnikov, USSR	15:00.40
1992	Kieren Perkins, Australia	14:43.48 WR

100-METER BACKSTROKE

1904	Walter Brack, Germany (100 yds)	1:16.8
1908	Arno Bieberstein, Germany	1:24.6 WR
1912	Harry Hebner, United States	1:21.2
1920	Warren Kealoha, United States	1:15.2
1924	Warren Kealoha, United States	1:13.2 OR
1928	George Kojac, United States	1:08.2 WR
1932	Masaji Kiyokawa, Japan	1:08.6
1936	Adolph Kiefer, United States	1:05.9 OR
1948	Allen Stack, United States	1:06.4
1952	Yoshi Oyakawa, United States	1:05.4 OR
1956	David Thiele, Australia	1:02.2 OR
1960	David Thiele, Australia	1:01.9 OR
1964	Not held	
1968	Roland Matthes, East Germany	58.7 OR
1972	Roland Matthes, East Germany	56.58 OR
1976	John Naber, United States	55.49 WR
1980	Bengt Baron, Sweden	56.33
1984	Rick Carey, United States	55.79
1988	Daichi Suzuki, Japan	55.05
1992	Mark Tewksbury, Canada	53.98 WR

200-METER BACKSTROKE

1900	Ernst Hoppenberg, Germany	2:47.0
1904	Not held 1904-1960	
1964	Jed Graef, United States	2:10.3 WR
1968	Roland Matthes, East Germany	2:09.6 OR
1972	Roland Matthes, East Germany	2:02.82 EWR
1976	John Naber, United States	1:59.19 WR
1980	Sandor Wladar, Hungary	2:01.93
1984	Rick Carey, United States	2:00.23
1988	Igor Polianski, USSR	1:59.37
1992	Martin Lopez-Zubero, Spain	1:58.47 OR

100-METER BREASTSTROKE

1968	Don McKenzie, United States	1:07.7 OR
1972	Nobutaka Taguchi, Japan	1:04.94 WR
1976	John Hencken, United States	1:03.11 WR
1980	Duncan Goodhew, Great Britain	1:03.44
1984	Steve Lundquist, United States	1:01.65 WR
1988	Adrian Moorhouse, Great Britain	1:02.04
1992	Nelson Diebel, United States	1:01.50 OR

SWIMMING (Cont.)

Men (Cont.)

200-METER BREASTSTROKE

1908	Frederick Holman, Great Britain	3:09.2 WR
1912	Walter Bathe, Germany	3:01.8 OR
1920	Haken Malmroth, Sweden	3:04.4
1924	Robert Skelton, United States	2:56.6
1928	Yoshiyuki Tsuruta, Japan	2:48.8 OR
1932	Yoshiyuki Tsuruta, Japan	2:45.4
1936	Tetsuo Hamuro, Japan	2:41.5 OR
1948	Joseph Verdeur, United States	2:39.3 OR
1952	John Davies, Australia	2:34.4 OR
1956	Masura Furukawa, Japan	2:34.7 OR
1960	William Mulliken, United States	2:37.4
1964	Ian O'Brien, Australia	2:27.8 WR
1968	Felipe Munoz, Mexico	2:28.7
1972	John Hencken, United States	2:21.55 WR
1976	David Wilkie, Great Britain	2:15.11 WR
1980	Robertas Zhulpa, USSR	2:15.85
1984	Victor Davis, Canada	2:13.34 WR
1988	Jozsef Szabo, Hungary	2:13.52
1992	Mike Barrowman, United States	2:10.16 WR

100-METER BUTTERFLY

1968	Doug Russell, United States	55.9 OR
1972	Mark Spitz, United States	54.27 WR
1976	Matt Vogel, United States	54.35
1980	Pär Arvidsson, Sweden	54.92
1984	Michael Gross, West Germany	53.08 WR
1988	Anthony Nesty, Suriname	53.00 OR
1992	Pablo Morales, United States	53.32

200-METER BUTTERFLY

1956	William Yorzyk, United States	2:19.3 OR
1960	Michael Troy, United States	2:12.8 WR
1964	Kevin Berry, Australia	2:06.6 WR
1968	Carl Robie, United States	2:08.7
1972	Mark Spitz, United States	2:00.70 WR
1976	Mike Bruner, United States	1:59.23 WR
1980	Sergei Fesenko, USSR	1:59.76
1984	Jon Sieben, Australia	1:57.04 WR
1988	Michael Gross, West Germany	1:56.94 OR
1992	Melvin Stewart, United States	1:56.26 OR

200-METER INDIVIDUAL MEDLEY

1968	Charles Hickcox, United States	2:12.0 OR
1972	Gunnar Larsson, Sweden	2:07.17 WR
1984	Alex Baumann, Canada	2:01.42 WR
1988	Tamas Darnyi, Hungary	2:00.17 WR
1992	Tamas Darnyi, Hungary	2:00.76

400-METER INDIVIDUAL MEDLEY

1964	Richard Roth, United States	4:45.4 WR
1968	Charles Hickcox, United States	4:48.4
1972	Gunnar Larsson, Sweden	4:31.98 OR
1976	Rod Strachan, United States	4:23.68 WR
1980	Aleksandr Sidorenko, USSR	4:22.89 OR
1984	Alex Baumann, Canada	4:17.41 WR
1988	Tamas Darnyi, Hungary	4:14.75 WR
1992	Tamas Darnyi, Hungary	4:14.23 WR

4 X 100-METER MEDLEY RELAY

1960	United States	4:05.4 WR
1964	United States	3:58.4 WR
1968	United States	3:54.9 WR
1972	United States	3:48.16 WR
1976	United States	3:42.22 WR
1980	Australia	3:45.70
1984	United States	3:39.30 WR
1988	United States	3:36.93 WR
1992	United States	3:36.93 EWR

4 X 100-METER FREESTYLE RELAY

1964	United States	3:32.2 WR
1968	United States	3:31.7 WR
1972	United States	3:26.42 WR
1976-1980	Not held	
1984	United States	3:19.03 WR
1988	United States	3:16.53 WR
1992	United States	3:16.74

4 X 200-METER FREESTYLE RELAY

1906	Hungary (1000 m)	16:52.4
1908	Great Britain	10:55.6
1912	Australia/New Zealand	10:11.6 WR
1920	United States	10:04.4 WR
1924	United States	9:53.4 WR
1928	United States	9:36.2 WR
1932	Japan	8:58.4 WR
1936	Japan	8:51.5 WR
1948	United States	8:46.0 WR
1952	United States	8:31.1 OR
1956	Australia	8:23.6 WR
1960	United States	8:10.2 WR
1964	United States	7:52.1 WR
1968	United States	7:52.33
1972	United States	7:35.78 WR
1976	United States	7:23.22 WR
1980	USSR	7:23.50
1984	United States	7:15.69 WR
1988	United States	7:12.51 WR
1992	Unified Team	7:11.95 WR

Women

50-METER FREESTYLE

1988	Kristin Otto, East Germany	25.49 OR
1992	Yang Wenyi, China	24.79 WR

100-METER FREESTYLE

1912	Fanny Durack, Australia	1:22.2
1920	Ethelda Bleibtrey, United States	1:13.6 WR
1924	Ethel Lackie, United States	1:12.4
1928	Albina Osipowich, United States	1:11.0 OR

100-METER FREESTYLE (Cont.)

1932	Helene Madison, United States	1:06.8 OR
1936	Hendrika Mastenbroek, Netherlands	1:05.9 OR
1948	Greta Andersen, Denmark	1:06.3
1952	Katalin Szöke, Hungary	1:06.8
1956	Dawn Fraser, Australia	1:02.0 WR
1960	Dawn Fraser, Australia	1:01.2 OR
1964	Dawn Fraser, Australia	59.5 OR
1968	Jan Henne, United States	1:00.0

SWIMMING *(Cont.)*

Women *(Cont.)*

100-METER FREESTYLE *(Cont.)*

1972	Sandra Neilson, United States	58.59 OR
1976	Kornelia Ender, East Germany	55.65 WR
1980	Barbara Krause, East Germany	54.79 WR
1984	Carrie Steinseifer, United States	55.92
	Nancy Hogshead, United States	55.92
1988	Kristin Otto, East Germany	54.93
1992	Zhuang Yong, China	54.64 OR

200-METER FREESTYLE

1968	Debbie Meyer, United States	2:10.5 OR
1972	Shane Gould, Australia	2:03.56 WR
1976	Kornelia Ender, East Germany	1:59.26 WR
1980	Barbara Krause, East Germany	1:58.33 OR
1984	Mary Wayte, United States	1:59.23
1988	Heike Friedrich, East Germany	1:57.65 OR
1992	Nicole Haislett, United States	1:57.90

400-METER FREESTYLE

1924	Martha Norelius, United States	6:02.2 OR
1928	Martha Norelius, United States	5:42.8 WR
1932	Helene Madison, United States	5:28.5 WR
1936	Hendrika Mastenbroek, Netherlands	5:26.4 OR
1948	Ann Curtis, United States	5:17.8 OR
1952	Valeria Gyenge, Hungary	5:12.1 OR
1956	Lorraine Crapp, Australia	4:54.6 OR
1960	Chris von Saltza, United States	4:50.6 OR
1964	Virginia Duenkel, United States	4:43.3 OR
1968	Debbie Meyer, United States	4:31.8 OR
1972	Shane Gould, Australia	4:19.44 WR
1976	Petra Thümer, East Germany	4:09.89 WR
1980	Ines Diers, East Germany	4:08.76 WR
1984	Tiffany Cohen, United States	4:07.10 OR
1988	Janet Evans, United States	4:03.85 WR
1992	Dagmar Hase, Germany	4:07.18

800-METER FREESTYLE

1968	Debbie Meyer, United States	9:24.0 OR
1972	Keena Rothhammer, United States	8:53.68 WR
1976	Petra Thümer, East Germany	8:37.14 WR
1980	Michelle Ford, Australia	8:28.90 OR
1984	Tiffany Cohen, United States	8:24.95 OR
1988	Janet Evans, United States	8:20.20 OR
1992	Janet Evans, United States	8:25.52

100-METER BACKSTROKE

1924	Sybil Bauer, United States	1:23.2 OR
1928	Marie Braun, Netherlands	1:22.0
1932	Eleanor Holm, United States	1:19.4
1936	Dina Senff, Netherlands	1:18.9
1948	Karen Harup, Denmark	1:14.4 OR
1952	Joan Harrison, South Africa	1:14.3
1956	Judy Grinham, Great Britain	1:12.9 OR
1960	Lynn Burke, United States	1:09.3 OR
1964	Cathy Ferguson, United States	1:07.7 WR
1968	Kaye Hall, United States	1:06.2 WR
1972	Melissa Belote, United States	1:05.78 OR
1976	Ulrike Richter, East Germany	1:01.83 OR
1980	Rica Reinisch, East Germany	1:00.86 WR
1984	Theresa Andrews, United States	1:02.55
1988	Kristin Otto, East Germany	1:00.89
1992	Krisztina Egerszegi, Hungary	1:00.68 OR

200-METER BACKSTROKE

1968	Pokey Watson, United States	2:24.8 OR
1972	Melissa Belote, United States	2:19.19 WR
1976	Ulrike Richter, East Germany	2:13.43 OR
1980	Rica Reinisch, East Germany	2:11.77 WR
1984	Jolanda De Rover, Netherlands	2:12.38
1988	Krisztina Egerszegi, Hungary	2:09.29 OR
1992	Krisztina Egerszegi, Hungary	2:07.06

100-METER BREASTSTROKE

1968	Djurdjica Bjedov, Yugoslavia	1:15.8 OR
1972	Catherine Carr, United States	1:13.58 WR
1976	Hannelore Anke, East Germany	1:11.16
1980	Ute Geweniger, East Germany	1:10.22
1984	Petra Van Staveren, Netherlands	1:09.88 OR
1988	Tania Dangalakova, Bulgaria	1:07.95 OR
1992	Elena Roudkovskaia, Unified Team	1:08.00

200-METER BREASTSTROKE

1924	Lucy Morton, Great Britain	3:33.2 OR
1928	Hilde Schrader, Germany	3:12.6
1932	Clare Dennis, Australia	3:06.3 OR
1936	Hideko Maehata, Japan	3:03.6
1948	Petronella Van Vliet, Netherlands	2:57.2
1952	Eva Szekely, Hungary	2:51.7 OR
1956	Ursula Happe, West Germany	2:53.1 OR
1960	Anita Lonsbrough, Great Britain	2:49.5 WR
1964	Galina Prozumenshikova, USSR	2:46.4 OR
1968	Sharon Wichman, United States	2:44.4 OR
1972	Beverly Whitfield, Australia	2:41.71 OR
1976	Marina Koshevaia, USSR	2:33.35 WR
1980	Lina Kaciusyte, USSR	2:29.54 OR
1984	Anne Ottenbrite, Canada	2:30.38
1988	Silke Hoerner, East Germany	2:26.71 WR
1992	Kyoko Iwasaki, Japan	2:26.65 OR

100-METER BUTTERFLY

1956	Shelley Mann, United States	1:11.0 OR
1960	Carolyn Schuler, United States	1:09.5 OR
1964	Sharon Stouder, United States	1:04.7 WR
1968	Lynn McClements, Australia	1:05.5
1972	Mayumi Aoki, Japan	1:03.34 WR
1976	Kornelia Ender, East Germany	1:00.13 EWR
1980	Caren Metschuck, East Germany	1:00.42
1984	Mary T. Meagher, United States	59.26
1988	Kristin Otto, East Germany	59.00 OR
1992	Qian Hong, China	58.62 OR

200-METER BUTTERFLY

1968	Ada Kok, Netherlands	2:24.7 OR
1972	Karen Moe, United States	2:15.57 WR
1976	Andrea Pollack, East Germany	2:11.41 OR
1980	Ines Geissler, East Germany	2:10.44 OR
1984	Mary T. Meagher, United States	2:06.90 OR
1988	Kathleen Nord, East Germany	2:09.51
1992	Summer Sanders, United States	2:08.67

200-METER INDIVIDUAL MEDLEY

1968	Claudia Kolb, United States	2:24.7 OR
1972	Shane Gould, Australia	2:23.07 WR
1976	Not held 1976-1980	
1984	Tracy Caulkins, United States	2:12.64 OR

SWIMMING (Cont.)

Women (Cont.)

200-METER INDIVIDUAL MEDLEY *(Cont.)*

1988 ....Daniela Hunger, East Germany	2:12.59 OR
1992 ....Lin Li, China	2:11.65 WR

400-METER INDIVIDUAL MEDLEY

1964 ....Donna de Varona, United States	5:18.7 OR
1968 ....Claudia Kolb, United States	5:08.5 OR
1972 ....Gail Neall, Australia	5:02.97 WR
1976 ....Ulrike Tauber, East Germany	4:42.77 WR
1980 ....Petra Schneider, East Germany	4:36.29 WR
1984 ....Tracy Caulkins, United States	4:39.24
1988 ....Janet Evans, United States	4:37.76
1992 ....Krisztina Egerszegi, Hungary	4:36.54

4 X 100-METER MEDLEY RELAY

1960 ....United States	4:41.1 WR
1964 ....United States	4:33.9 WR
1968 ....United States	4:28.3 OR
1972 ....United States	4:20.75 WR
1976 ....East Germany	4:07.95 WR
1980 ....East Germany	4:06.67 WR
1984 ....United States	4:08.34
1988 ....East Germany	4:03.74 OR
1992 ....United States	4:02.54 WR

4 X 100-METER FREESTYLE RELAY

1912 ....Great Britain	5:52.8 WR
1920 ....United States	5:11.6 WR
1924 ....United States	4:58.8 WR
1928 ....United States	4:47.6 WR
1932 ....United States	4:38.0 WR
1936 ....Netherlands	4:36.0 OR
1948 ....United States	4:29.2 OR
1952 ....Hungary	4:24.4 WR
1956 ....Australia	4:17.1 WR
1960 ....United States	4:08.9 WR
1964 ....United States	4:03.8 WR
1968 ....United States	4:02.5 OR
1972 ....United States	3:55.19 WR
1976 ....United States	3:44.82 WR
1980 ....East Germany	3:42.71 WR
1984 ....United States	3:43.43
1988 ....East Germany	3:40.63 OR
1992 ....United States	3:39.46 WR

Note: OR=Olympic Record; WR=World Record; EOR=Equals Olympic Record; EWR=Equals World Record; WB=World Best.

DIVING

Men

SPRINGBOARD

	Pts
1908 .....Albert Zürner, Germany	85.5
1912 .....Paul Günther, Germany	79.23
1920 .....Louis Kuehn, United States	675.40
1924 .....Albert White, United States	97.46
1928 .....Pete DesJardins, United States	185.04
1932 .....Michael Galitzen, United States	161.38
1936 .....Richard Degener, United States	163.57
1948 .....Bruce Harlan, United States	163.64
1952 .....David Browning, United States	205.29
1956 .....Robert Clotworthy, United States	159.56
1960 .....Gary Tobian, United States	170.00
1964 .....Kenneth Sitzberger, United States	159.90
1968 .....Bernie Wrightson, United States	170.15
1972 .....Vladimir Vasin, USSR	594.09
1976 .....Phil Boggs, United States	619.05
1980 .....Aleksandr Portnov, USSR	905.02
1984 .....Greg Louganis, United States	754.41
1988 .....Greg Louganis, United States	730.80
1992 .....Mark Lenzi, United States	676.53

PLATFORM

	Pts
1904 .....George Sheldon, United States	12.66
1906 .....Gottlob Walz, Germany	156.0
1908 .....Hjalmar Johansson, Sweden	83.75
1912 .....Erik Adlerz, Sweden	73.94
1920 .....Clarence Pinkston, United States	100.67
1924 .....Albert White, United States	97.46
1928 .....Pete DesJardins, United States	98.74
1932 .....Harold Smith, United States	124.80
1936 .....Marshall Wayne, United States	113.58
1948 .....Sammy Lee, United States	130.05
1952 .....Sammy Lee, United States	156.28
1956 .....Joaquin Capilla, Mexico	152.44
1960 .....Robert Webster, United States	165.56
1964 .....Robert Webster, United States	148.58
1968 .....Klaus Dibiasi, Italy	164.18
1972 .....Klaus Dibiasi, Italy	504.12
1976 .....Klaus Dibiasi, Italy	600.51
1980 .....Falk Hoffmann, East Germany	835.65
1984 .....Greg Louganis, United States	710.91
1988 .....Greg Louganis, United States	638.61
1992 .....Sun Shuwei, China	677.31

Women

SPRINGBOARD

	Pts
1920 .....Aileen Riggin, United States	539.90
1924 .....Elizabeth Becker, United States	474.50
1928 .....Helen Meany, United States	78.62
1932 .....Georgia Coleman, United States	87.52
1936 .....Marjorie Gestring, United States	89.27
1948 .....Victoria Draves, United States	108.74

SPRINGBOARD *(Cont.)*

	Pts
1952 ....Patricia McCormick, United States	147.30
1956 ....Patricia McCormick, United States	142.36
1960 .....Ingrid Krämer, East Germany	155.81
1964 .....Ingrid Engel Krämer, East Germany	145.00
1968 ....Sue Gossick, United States	150.77

DIVING *(Cont.)*

Women *(Cont.)*

SPRINGBOARD *(Cont.)*

		Pts
1972	Micki King, United States	450.03
1976	Jennifer Chandler, United States	506.19
1980	Irina Kalinina, USSR	725.91
1984	Sylvie Bernier, Canada	530.70
1988	Gao Min, China	580.23
1992	Gao Min, China	572.40

PLATFORM

		Pts
1912	Greta Johansson, Sweden	39.90
1920	Stefani Fryland-Clausen, Denmark	34.60
1924	Caroline Smith, United States	33.20
1928	Elizabeth B. Pinkston, United States	31.60

PLATFORM *(Cont.)*

		Pts
1932	Dorothy Poynton, United States	40.26
1936	Dorothy Poynton Hill, United States	33.93
1948	Victoria Draves, United States	68.87
1952	Patricia McCormick, United States	79.37
1956	Patricia McCormick, United States	84.85
1960	Ingrid Krämer, East Germany	91.28
1964	Lesley Bush, United States	99.80
1968	Milena Duchkova, Czechoslovakia	109.59
1972	Ulrika Knape, Sweden	390.00
1976	Elena Vaytsekhovskaya, USSR	406.59
1980	Martina Jäschke, East Germany	596.25
1984	Zhou Jihong, China	435.51
1988	Xu Yanmei, China	445.20
1992	Fu Mingxia, China	461.43

GYMNASTICS

Men

ALL-AROUND

		Pts
1900	Gustave Sandras, France	302
1904	Julius Lenhart, Austria	69.80
1906	Pierre Paysse, France	97
1908	Alberto Braglia, Italy	317.0
1912	Alberto Braglia, Italy	135.0
1920	Giorgio Zampori, Italy	88.35
1924	Leon Stukelj, Yugoslavia	110.340
1928	Georges Miez, Switzerland	247.500
1932	Romeo Neri, Italy	140.625
1936	Alfred Schwarzmann, Germany	113.100
1948	Veikko Huhtanen, Finland	229.70
1952	Viktor Chukarin, USSR	115.70
1956	Viktor Chukarin, USSR	114.25
1960	Boris Shakhlin, USSR	115.95
1964	Yukio Endo, Japan	115.95
1968	Sawao Kato, Japan	115.90
1972	Sawao Kato, Japan	114.65
1976	Nikolai Andrianov, USSR	116.65
1980	Aleksandr Dityatin, USSR	118.65
1984	Koji Gushiken, Japan	118.70
1988	Vladimir Artemov, USSR	119.125
1992	Vitaly Scherbo, Unified Team	59.025

HORIZONTAL BAR

		Pts
1896	Hermann Weingärtner, Germany	—
1900	Not held	
1904	Anton Heida, United States	40
1908-20	Not held	
1924	Leon Stukelj, Yugoslavia	19.73
1928	Georges Miez, Switzerland	19.17
1932	Dallas Bixler, United States	18.33
1936	Aleksanteri Saarvala, Finland	19.367
1948	Josef Stalder, Switzerland	19.85
1952	Jack Günthard, Switzerland	19.55
1956	Takashi Ono, Japan	19.60
1960	Takashi Ono, Japan	19.60
1964	Boris Shakhlin, USSR	19.625
1968	Akinori Nakayama, Japan	19.55
1972	Mitsuo Tsukahara, Japan	19.725

HORIZONTAL BAR *(Cont.)*

		Pts
1976	Mitsuo Tsukahara, Japan	19.675
1980	Stoyan Deltchev, Bulgaria	19.825
1984	Shinji Morisue, Japan	20.00
1988	Vladimir Artemov, USSR	19.90
1992	Trent Dimas, United States	9.875

PARALLEL BARS

		Pts
1896	Alfred Flatow, Germany	—
1900	Not held	
1904	George Eyser, United States	44
1908-20	Not held	
1924	August Güttinger, Switzerland	21.63
1928	Ladislav Vacha, Czechoslovakia	18.83
1932	Romeo Neri, Italy	18.97
1936	Konrad Frey, Germany	19.067
1948	Michael Reusch, Switzerland	19.75
1952	Hans Eugster, Switzerland	19.65
1956	Viktor Chukarin, USSR	19.20
1960	Boris Shakhlin, USSR	19.40
1964	Yukio Endo, Japan	19.675
1968	Akinori Nakayama, Japan	19.475
1972	Sawao Kato, Japan	19.475
1976	Sawao Kato, Japan	19.675
1980	Aleksandr Tkachyov, USSR	19.775
1984	Bart Conner, United States	19.95
1988	Vladimir Artemov, USSR	19.925
1992	Vitaly Scherbo, Unified Team	9.900

LONG HORSE VAULT

		Pts
1896	Karl Schumann, Germany	—
1900	Not held	
1904	George Eyser, United States	36
1908-20	Not held	
1924	Frank Kriz, United States	9.98
1928	Eugen Mack, Switzerland	9.58
1932	Savino Guglielmetti, Italy	18.03
1936	Alfred Schwarzmann, Germany	19.20
1948	Paavo Aaltonen, Finland	19.55

GYMNASTICS (Cont.)

Men (Cont.)

LONG HORSE VAULT (Cont.)

		Pts
1952	Viktor Chukarin, USSR	19.20
1956	Helmut Bantz, Germany	18.85
1960	Takashi Ono, Japan	19.35
1964	Haruhiro Yamashita, Japan	19.60
1968	Mikhail Voronin, USSR	19.00
1972	Klaus Köste, East Germany	18.85
1976	Nikolai Andrianov, USSR	19.45
1980	Nikolai Andrianov, USSR	19.825
1984	Lou Yun, China	19.95
1988	Lou Yun, China	19.875
1992	Vitaly Scherbo, Unified Team	9.856

SIDE HORSE

		Pts
1896	Louis Zutter, Switzerland	—
1900	Not held	
1904	Anton Heida, United States	42
1908-20	Not held	
1924	Josef Wilhelm, Switzerland	21.23
1928	Hermann Hänggi, Switzerland	19.75
1932	Istvan Pelle, Hungary	19.07
1936	Konrad Frey, Germany	19.333
1948	Paavo Aaltonen, Finland	19.35
1952	Viktor Chukarin, USSR	19.50
1956	Boris Shakhlin, USSR	19.25
1960	Eugen Ekman, Finland	19.375
1964	Miroslav Cerar, Yugoslavia	19.525
1968	Miroslav Cerar, Yugoslavia	19.325
1972	Viktor Klimenko, USSR	19.125
1976	Zoltan Magyar, Hungary	19.70
1980	Zoltan Magyar, Hungary	19.925
1984	Li Ning, China	19.95
1988	Dmitri Bilozerchev, USSR	19.95
1992	Vitaly Scherbo, Unified Team	9.925

RINGS

		Pts
1896	Ioannis Mitropoulos, Greece	—
1900	Not held	
1904	Hermann Glass, United States	45
1908-20	Not held	
1924	Francesco Martino, Italy	21.553
1928	Leon Stukelj, Yugoslavia	19.25
1932	George Gulack, United States	18.97
1936	Alois Hudec, Czechoslovakia	19.433
1948	Karl Frei, Switzerland	19.80
1952	Grant Shaginyan, USSR	19.75
1956	Albert Azaryan, USSR	19.35
1960	Albert Azaryan, USSR	19.725
1964	Takuji Haytta, Japan	19.475
1968	Akinori Nakayama, Japan	19.45

RINGS (Cont.)

		Pts
1972	Akinori Nakayama, Japan	19.35
1976	Nikolai Andrianov, USSR	19.65
1980	Aleksandr Dityatin, USSR	19.875
1984	Koji Gushiken, Japan	19.85
1988	Holger Behrendt, East Germany	19.925
1992	Vitaly Scherbo, Unified Team	9.937

FLOOR EXERCISES

		Pts
1896-28	Not held	
1932	Istvan Pelle, Hungary	9.60
1936	Georges Miez, Switzerland	18.666
1948	Ferenc Pataki, Hungary	19.35
1952	K. William Thoresson, Sweden	19.25
1956	Valentin Muratov, USSR	19.20
1960	Nobuyuki Aihara, Japan	19.45
1964	Franco Menichelli, Italy	19.45
1968	Sawao Kato, Japan	19.475
1972	Nikolai Andrianov, USSR	19.175
1976	Nikolai Andrianov, USSR	19.45
1980	Roland Brückner, East Germany	19.75
1984	Li Ning, China	19.925
1988	Sergei Kharkov, USSR	19.925
1992	Li Xiaosahuang, China	9.925

TEAM COMBINED EXERCISES

		Pts
1896-00	Not held	
1904	Turngemeinde Philadelphia	374.43
1906	Norway	19.00
1908	Sweden	438
1912	Italy	265.75
1920	Italy	359.855
1924	Italy	839.058
1928	Switzerland	1718.625
1932	Italy	541.850
1936	Germany	657.430
1948	Finland	1358.30
1952	USSR	574.40
1956	USSR	568.25
1960	Japan	575.20
1964	Japan	577.95
1968	Japan	575.90
1972	Japan	571.25
1976	Japan	576.85
1980	USSR	598.60
1984	United States	591.40
1988	USSR	593.35
1992	Unified Team	585.45

GYMNASTICS (Cont.)

Women

ALL-AROUND

		Pts
1952	Maria Gorokhovskaya, USSR	76.78
1956	Larissa Latynina, USSR	74.933
1960	Larissa Latynina, USSR	77.031
1964	Vera Caslavska, Czechoslovakia	77.564
1968	Vera Caslavska, Czechoslovakia	78.25
1972	Lyudmila Tousischeva, USSR	77.025
1976	Nadia Comaneci, Romania	79.275
1980	Yelena Davydova, USSR	79.15
1984	Mary Lou Retton, United States	79.175
1988	Yelena Shushunova, USSR	79.662
1992	Tatiana Gutsu, Unified Team	39.737

SIDE HORSE VAULT

		Pts
1952	Yekaterina Kalinchuk, USSR	19.20
1956	Larissa Latynina, USSR	18.833
1960	Margarita Nikolayeva, USSR	19.316
1964	Vera Caslavska, Czechoslovakia	19.483
1968	Vera Caslavska, Czechoslovakia	19.775
1972	Karin Janz, East Germany	19.525
1976	Nelli Kim, USSR	19.80
1980	Natalya Shaposhnikova, USSR	19.725
1984	Ecaterina Szabo, Romania	19.875
1988	Svetlana Boginskaya, USSR	19.905
1992	Henrietta Onodi, Hungary	9.925
	Lavinia Milosovici, Romania	9.925

UNEVEN BARS

		Pts
1952	Margit Korondi, Hungary	19.40
1956	Agnes Keleti, Hungary	18.966
1960	Polina Astakhova, USSR	19.616
1964	Polina Astakhova, USSR	19.332
1968	Vera Caslavska, Czechoslovakia	19.65
1972	Karin Janz, East Germany	19.675
1976	Nadia Comaneci, Romania	20.00
1980	Maxi Gnauck, East Germany	19.875
1984	Ma Yanhong, China	19.95
1988	Daniela Silivas, Romania	20.00
1992	Lu Li, China	10.00

BALANCE BEAM

		Pts
1952	Nina Bocharova, USSR	19.22
1956	Agnes Keleti, Hungary	18.80
1960	Eva Bosakova, Czechoslovakia	19.283

BALANCE BEAM (Cont.)

		Pts
1964	Vera Caslavska, Czechoslovakia	19.449
1968	Natalya Kuchinskaya, USSR	19.65
1972	Olga Korbut, USSR	19.40
1976	Nadia Comaneci, Romania	19.95
1980	Nadia Comaneci, Romania	19.80
1984	Simona Pauca, Romania	19.80
1988	Daniela Silivas, Romania	19.924
1992	Tatiana Lisenko, Unified Team	9.975

FLOOR EXERCISES

		Pts
1952	Agnes Keleti, Hungary	19.36
1956	Agnes Keleti, Hungary	18.733
1960	Larissa Latynina, USSR	19.583
1964	Larissa Latynina, USSR	19.599
1968	Vera Caslavska, Czechoslovakia	19.675
1972	Olga Korbut, USSR	19.575
1976	Nelli Kim, USSR	19.85
1980	Nadia Comaneci, Romania	19.875
1984	Ecaterina Szabo, Romania	19.975
1988	Daniela Silivas, Romania	19.937
1992	Lavinia Milosovici, Romania	10.00

TEAM COMBINED EXERCISES

		Pts
1928	Holland	316.75
1932	Not held	
1936	Germany	506.50
1948	Czechoslovakia	445.45
1952	USSR	527.03
1956	USSR	444.800
1960	USSR	382.320
1964	USSR	280.890
1968	USSR	382.85
1972	USSR	380.50
1976	USSR	466.00
1980	USSR	394.90
1984	Romania	392.02
1988	USSR	395.475
1992	Unified Team	395.666

RHYTHMIC ALL-AROUND

		Pts
1984	Lori Fung, Canada	57.95
1988	Marina Lobach, USSR	60.00
1992	Aleksandra Timoshenko, UTeam	59.037

Sic Transit Gloria

The sad story of luge champion Gerda Weissensteiner only went from bad to worse. Within days of her gold-medal performance in the women's singles event at Lillehammer, the newly celebrated Italian star learned that her brother had been killed in a motorcycle accident. Then, while she was attending his funeral, her house was burglarized and her gold medal stolen.

BIATHLON

Men

10 KILOMETERS

1980....Frank Ullrich, East Germany	32:10.69
1984....Eirik Kvalfoss, Norway	30:53.8
1988....Frank-Peter Rötsch, W Germany	25:08.1
1992....Mark Kirchner, Germany	26:02.3
1994....Sergei Tchepikov, Russia	28:07.0

20 KILOMETERS

1960....Klas Lestander, Sweden	1:33:21.6
1964....Vladimir Melyanin, Soviet Union	1:20:26.8
1968....Magnar Solberg, Norway	1:13:45.9
1972....Magnar Solberg, Norway	1:15:55.5
1976....Nikolay Kruglov, Soviet Union	1:14:12.26
1980....Anatoliy Alyabiev, Soviet Union	1:08:16.31
1984....Peter Angerer, W Germany	1:11:52.7

20 KILOMETERS (Cont.)

1988....Frank-Peter Rötsch, W Germany	56:33.3
1992....Evgueni Redkine, Unified Team	57:34.4
1994....Sergei Tarasov, Russia	57:25.3

4 X 7.5-KILOMETER RELAY

1968 ....Soviet Union	2:13:02.4
1972 ....Soviet Union	1:51:44.92
1976 ....Soviet Union	1:57:55.64
1980 ....Soviet Union	1:34:03.27
1984 ....Soviet Union	1:38:51.7
1988 ....Soviet Union	1:22:30.0
1992 ....Germany	1:24:43.5
1994 ....Germany	1:30:22.1

Women

7.5 KILOMETERS

1992....Antissa Restzova, Unified Team	24:29.2
1994....Myriam Bedard, Canada	26:08.8

15 KILOMETERS

1992....Antje Misersky, Germany	51:47.2
1994....Myriam Bedard, Canada	52:06.6

3 X 7.5-KILOMETER RELAY

1992....France	1:15:55.6
1994....Russia	1:47:19.5

BOBSLED

4-MAN BOB

1924....Switzerland (Eduard Scherrer)	5:45.54
1928....United States (William Fiske) (5-man)	3:20.50
1932....United States (William Fiske)	7:53.68
1936....Switzerland (Pierre Musy)	5:19.85
1948....United States (Francis Tyler)	5:20.10
1952....Germany (Andreas Ostler)	5:07.84
1956....Switzerland (Franz Kapus)	5:10.44
1960....Not held	
1964....Canada (Victor Emery)	4:14.46
1968....Italy (Eugenio Monti) (2 runs)	2:17.39
1972....Switzerland (Jean Wicki)	4:43.07
1976....East Germany (Meinhard Nehmer)	3:40.43
1980....East Germany (Meinhard Nehmer)	3:59.92
1984....East Germany (Wolfgang Hoppe)	3:20.22
1988....Switzerland (Ekkehard Fasser)	3:47.51
1992....Austria (Ingo Appelt)	3:53.90
1994....Germany (Harold Czudaj)	3:27.78

Note: Driver in parentheses.

2-MAN BOB

1932....United States (Hubert Stevens)	8:14.74
1936....United States (Ivan Brown)	5:29.29
1948....Switzerland (Felix Endrich)	5:29.20
1952....Germany (Andreas Ostler)	5:24.54
1956....Italy (Lamberto Dalla Costa)	5:30.14
1960....Not held	
1964....Great Britain (Anthony Nash)	4:21.90
1968....Italy (Eugenio Monti)	4:41.54
1972....West Germany (Wolfgang Zimmerer)	4:57.07
1976....East Germany (Meinhard Nehmer)	3:44.42
1980....Switzerland (Erich Schärer)	4:09.36
1984....East Germany (Wolfgang Hoppe)	3:25.56
1988....USSR (Janis Kipours)	3:53.48
1992....Switzerland (Gustav Weder)	4:03.26
1994....Switzerland (Gustav Weder)	3:30.81

Note: Driver in parentheses.

ICE HOCKEY

1920* ....Canada, United States, Czechoslovakia	
1924 .....Canada, United States, Great Britain	
1928 .....Canada, Sweden, Switzerland	
1932 .....Canada, United States, Germany	
1936 .....Great Britain, Canada, United States	
1948 .....Canada, Czechoslovakia, Switzerland	
1952 .....Canada, United States, Sweden	
1956 .....USSR, United States, Canada	
1960 .....United States, Canada, USSR	
1964 .....USSR, Sweden, Czechoslovakia	
1968 .....USSR, Czechoslovakia, Canada	
1972 .....USSR, United States, Czechoslovakia	
1976 .....USSR, Czechoslovakia, West Germany	
1980 .....United States, USSR, Sweden	
1984 .....USSR, Czechoslovakia, Sweden	
1988 .....USSR, Finland, Sweden	
1992 .....Unified Team, Canada, Czechoslovakia	
1994 .....Sweden, Canada, Finland	

*Competition held at summer games in Antwerp.
Note: Gold, silver, and bronze medals.

LUGE

Men

	SINGLES			DOUBLES	
1964	Thomas Köhler, East Germany	3:26.77	1964	Austria	1:41.62
1968	Manfred Schmid, Austria	2:52.48	1968	East Germany	1:35.85
1972	Wolfgang Scheidel, W Germany	3:27.58	1972	East Germany	1:28.35
1976	Detlef Guenther, West Germany	3:27.688	1976	East Germany	1:25.604
1980	Bernhard Glass, West Germany	2:54.796	1980	East Germany	1:19.331
1984	Paul Hildgartner, Italy	3:04.258	1984	West Germany	1:23.620
1988	Jens Müller, West Germany	3:05.548	1988	East Germany	1:31.940
1992	Georg Hackl, Germany	3:02.363	1992	Germany	1:32.053
1994	Georg Hackl, Germany	3:21.571	1994	Italy	1:36.720

Women

	SINGLES			SINGLES (Cont.)	
1964	Ortrun Enderlein, Germany	3:24.67	1984	Steffi Martin, East Germany	2:46.570
1968	Erica Lechner, Italy	2:28.66	1988	Steffi Walter (Martin) E Germany	3:03.973
1972	Anna-Maria Müller, East Germany	2:59.18	1992	Doris Neuner, Austria	3:06.696
1976	Margit Schumann, East Germany	2:50.621	1994	Gerda Weissensteiner, Italy	3:15.517
1980	Vera Zozulya, USSR	2:36.537			

FIGURE SKATING

Men

	SINGLES		SINGLES (Cont.)
1908*	Ulrich Salchow, Sweden	1968	Wolfgang Schwarz, Austria
1920†	Gillis Grafström, Sweden	1972	Ondrej Nepela, Czechoslovakia
1924	Gillis Grafström, Sweden	1976	John Curry, Great Britain
1928	Gillis Grafström, Sweden	1980	Robin Cousins, Great Britain
1932	Karl Schäfer, Austria	1984	Scott Hamilton, United States
1936	Karl Schäfer, Austria	1988	Brian Boitano, United States
1948	Dick Button, United States	1992	Victor Petrenko, Unified Team
1952	Dick Button, United States	1994	Alexei Urmanov, Russia
1956	Hayes Alan Jenkins, United States		
1960	David Jenkins, United States	*Competition held at summer games in London	
1964	Manfred Schnelldorfer, West Germany	†Competition held at summer games in Antwerp	

Women

	SINGLES		SINGLES (Cont.)
1908*	Madge Syers, Great Britain	1968	Peggy Fleming, United States
1920†	Magda Julin, Sweden	1972	Beatrix Schuba, Austria
1924	Herma Szabo-Planck, Austria	1976	Dorothy Hamill, United States
1928	Sonja Henie, Norway	1980	Anett Pötzsch, East Germany
1932	Sonja Henie, Norway	1984	Katarina Witt, East Germany
1936	Sonja Henie, Norway	1988	Katarina Witt, East Germany
1948	Barbara Ann Scott, Canada	1992	Kristi Yamaguchi, United States
1952	Jeanette Altwegg, Great Britain	1994	Oksana Baiul, Ukraine
1956	Tenley Albright, United States		
1960	Carol Heiss, United States	*Competition held at summer games in London	
1964	Sjoukje Dijkstra, Netherlands	†Competition held at summer games in Antwerp	

FIGURE SKATING (Cont.)

Mixed

PAIRS

1908* ..Anna Hübler & Heinrich Burger, Germany
1920#..Ludovika & Walter Jakobsson, Finland
1924....Helene Engelmann & Alfred Berger, Austria
1928....Andree Joly & Pierre Brunet, France
1932....Andree Brunet (Joly) & Pierre Brunet, France
1936....Maxi Herber & Ernst Baier, Germany
1948....Micheline Lannoy & Pierre Baugniet, Belgium
1952....Ria Falk and Paul Falk, West Germany
1956....Elisabeth Schwartz & Kurt Oppelt, Austria
1960....Barbara Wagner & Robert Paul, Canada
1964....Lyudmila Beloussova & Oleg Protopopov, USSR
1968....Lyudmila Beloussova & Oleg Protopopov, USSR
1972....Irina Rodnina & Alexei Ulanov, USSR
1976....Irina Rodnina & Aleksandr Zaitzev, USSR
1980....Irina Rodnina & Aleksandr Zaitzev, USSR
1984....Elena Valova & Oleg Vasiliev, USSR
1988....Ekaterina Gordeeva & Sergei Grinkov, USSR

PAIRS (Cont.)

1992....Natalia Michkouteniok & Artour Dmitriev, Unified Team
1994....Ekaterina Gordeeva and Sergei Grinkov, Russia

ICE DANCING

1976....Lyudmila Pakhomova & Aleksandr Gorshkov, USSR
1980....Natalia Linichuk & Gennadi Karponosov, USSR
1984....Jayne Torvill & Christopher Dean, Great Britain
1988....Natalia Bestemianova & Andrei Bukin, USSR
1992....Marina Klimova & Sergei Ponomarenko, Unified Team
1994....Oksana Gritschuk and Evgeni Platov, Russia

*Competition held at summer games in London.
#Competition held at summer games in Antwerp.

SPEED SKATING

Men

500 METERS

1924....Charles Jewtraw, United States	44.0	
1928....Clas Thunberg, Finland	43.4 OR	
Bernt Evensen, Norway	43.4 OR	
1932....John Shea, United States	43.4 EOR	
1936....Ivar Ballangrud, Norway	43.4 EOR	
1948....Finn Helgesen, Norway	43.1 OR	
1952....Kenneth Henry, United States	43.2	
1956....Yevgeny Grishin, USSR	40.2 EWR	
1960....Yevgeny Grishin, USSR	40.2 EWR	
1964....Terry McDermott, United States	40.1 OR	
1968....Erhard Keller, West Germany	40.3	
1972....Erhard Keller, West Germany	39.44 OR	
1976....Yevgeny Kulikov, USSR	39.17 OR	
1980....Eric Heiden, United States	38.03 OR	
1984....Sergei Fokichev, USSR	38.19	
1988....Uwe-Jens Mey, East Germany	36.45 WR	
1992....Uwe-Jens Mey, East Germany	37.14	
1994....Aleksandr Golubev, Russia	36.33	

1000 METERS

1976....Peter Mueller, United States	1:19.32
1980....Eric Heiden, United States	1:15.18 OR
1984....Gaetan Boucher, Canada	1:15.80
1988....Nikolai Gulyaev, USSR	1:13.03 OR
1992....Olaf Zinke, Germany	1:14.85
1994....Dan Jansen, United States	1:12.43 WR

1500 METERS

1924....Clas Thunberg, Finland	2:20.8
1928....Clas Thunberg, Finland	2:21.1
1932....John Shea, United States	2:57.5
1936....Charles Mathisen, Norway	2:19.2 OR
1948....Sverre Farstad, Norway	2:17.6 OR

1500 METERS (Cont.)

1952....Hjalmar Andersen, Norway	2:20.4
1956....Yevgeny Grishin, USSR	2:08.6 WR
Yuri Mikhailov, USSR	2:08.6 WR
1960....Roald Aas, Norway	2:10.4
Yevgeny Grishin, USSR	2:10.4
1964....Ants Anston, USSR	2:10.3
1968....Cornelis Verkerk, Netherlands	2:03.4 OR
1972....Ard Schenk, Netherlands	2:02.96 OR
1976....Jan Egil Storholt, Norway	1:59.38 OR
1980....Eric Heiden, United States	1:55.44 OR
1984....Gaetan Boucher, Canada	1:58.36
1988....Andre Hoffmann, East Germany	1:52.06 WR
1992....Johann Olav Koss, Norway	1:54.81
1994....Johann Olav Koss, Norway	1:51.29 WR

5000 METERS

1924....Clas Thunberg, Finland	8:39.0
1928....Ivar Ballangrud, Norway	8:50.5
1932....Irving Jaffee, United States	9:40.8
1936....Ivar Ballangrud, Norway	8:19.6 OR
1948....Reidar Liaklev, Norway	8:29.4
1952....Hjalmar Andersen, Norway	8:10.6 OR
1956....Boris Shilkov, USSR	7:48.7 OR
1960....Viktor Kosichkin, USSR	7:51.3
1964....Knut Johannesen, Norway	7:38.4 OR
1968....Fred Anton Maier, Norway	7:22.4 WR
1972....Ard Schenk, Netherlands	7:23.61
1976....Sten Stensen, Norway	7:24.48
1980....Eric Heiden, United States	7:02.29 OR
1984....Sven Tomas Gustafson, Sweden	7:12.28
1988....Tomas Gustafson, Sweden	6:44.63 WR
1992....Geir Karlstad, Norway	6:59.97
1994....Johann Olav Koss, Norway	6:34.96 WR

Note: OR=Olympic Record; WR=World Record; EOR=Equals Olympic Record; EWR=Equals World Record; WB=World Best.

SPEED SKATING (Cont.)

Men (Cont.)

10,000 METERS

1924	Julius Skutnabb, Finland	18:04.8
1928	Not held, thawing of ice	
1932	Irving Jaffee, United States	19:13.6
1936	Ivar Ballangrud, Norway	17:24.3 OR
1948	Ake Seyffarth, Sweden	17:26.3
1952	Hjalmar Andersen, Norway	16:45.8 OR
1956	Sigvard Ericsson, Sweden	16:35.9 OR
1960	Knut Johannesen, Norway	15:46.6 WR
1964	Jonny Nilsson, Sweden	15:50.1

10,000 METERS (Cont.)

1968	Johnny Höglin, Sweden	15:23.6 OR
1972	Ard Schenk, Netherlands	15:01.35 OR
1976	Piet Kleine, Netherlands	14:50.59 OR
1980	Eric Heiden, United States	14:28.13 WR
1984	Igor Malkov, USSR	14:39.90
1988	Tomas Gustafson, Sweden	13:48.20 WR
1992	Bart Veldkamp, The Netherlands	14:12.12
1994	Johann Olav Koss, Norway	13:30.55 WR

Women

500 METERS

1960	Helga Haase, East Germany	45.9
1964	Lydia Skoblikova, USSR	45.0 OR
1968	Lyudmila Titova, USSR	46.1
1972	Anne Henning, United States	43.33 OR
1976	Sheila Young, United States	42.76 OR
1980	Karin Enke, East Germany	41.78 OR
1984	Christa Rothenburger, East Germany	41.02 OR
1988	Bonnie Blair, United States	39.10 WR
1992	Bonnie Blair, United States	40.33
1994	Bonnie Blair, United States	39.25

1000 METERS

1960	Klara Guseva, USSR	1:34.1
1964	Lydia Skoblikova, USSR	1:33.2 OR
1968	Carolina Geijssen, Netherlands	1:32.6 OR
1972	Monika Pflug, West Germany	1:31.40 OR
1976	Tatiana Averina, USSR	1:28.43 OR
1980	Natalya Petruseva, USSR	1:24.10 OR
1984	Karin Enke, East Germany	1:21.61 OR
1988	Christa Rothenburger, East Germany	1:17.65 WR
1992	Bonnie Blair, United States	1:21.90
1994	Bonnie Blair, United States	1:18.74

1500 METERS

1960	Lydia Skoblikova, USSR	2:25.2 WR
1964	Lydia Skoblikova, USSR	2:22.6 OR
1968	Kaija Mustonen, Finland	2:22.4 OR
1972	Dianne Holum, United States	2:20.85 OR
1976	Galina Stepanskaya, USSR	2:16.58 OR
1980	Anne Borckink, Netherlands	2:10.95 OR
1984	Karin Enke, East Germany	2:03.42 WR
1988	Yvonne van Gennip, Netherlands	2:00.68 OR
1992	Jacqueline Boerner, Germany	2:05.87
1994	Emese Hunyady, Austria	2:02.19

3000 METERS

1960	Lydia Skoblikova, USSR	5:14.3
1964	Lydia Skoblikova, USSR	5:14.9
1968	Johanna Schut, Netherlands	4:56.2 OR
1972	Christina Baas-Kaiser, Netherlands	4:52.14 OR
1976	Tatiana Averina, USSR	4:45.19 OR
1980	Bjorg Eva Jensen, Norway	4:32.13 OR
1984	Andrea Schöne, East Germany	4:24.79 OR
1988	Yvonne van Gennip, Netherlands	4:11.94 WR
1992	Gunda Niemann, Germany	4:19.90
1994	Svetlana Bazhanova, Russia	4:17.43

5000 METERS

1988	Yvonne van Gennip, Netherlands	7:14.13 WR
1992	Gunda Niemann, Germany	7:31.57
1994	Claudia Pechstein, Germany	7:14.37

SHORT TRACK SPEED SKATING

Men

500 METERS

1994	Chae Ji-Hoon, South Korea	43.54

1000 METERS

1992	Kim Ki-Hoon, South Korea	1:30.76 WR
1994	Kim Ki-Hoon, South Korea	1:34.57

5000-METER RELAY

1992	Korea	7:14.02 WR
1994	Italy	7:11.74 OR

Women

500 METERS

1992	Cathy Turner, United States	47.04
1994	Cathy Turner, United States	45.98 OR

1000 METERS

1994	Chun Lee-Kyung, South Korea	1:36.87

3000-METER RELAY

1992	Canada	4:36.62
1994	South Korea	4:26.64 OR

ALPINE SKIING

Men

DOWNHILL

1948	Henri Oreiller, France	2:55.0
1952	Zeno Colo, Italy	2:30.8
1956	Anton Sailer, Austria	2:52.2
1960	Jean Vuarnet, France	2:06.0
1964	Egon Zimmermann, Austria	2:18.16
1968	Jean-Claude Killy, France	1:59.85
1972	Bernhard Russi, Switzerland	1:51.43
1976	Franz Klammer, Austria	1:45.73
1980	Leonhard Stock, Austria	1:45.50
1984	Bill Johnson, United States	1:45.59
1988	Pirmin Zurbriggen, Switzerland	1:59.63
1992	Patrick Ortlieb, Austria	1:50.37
1994	Tommy Moe, United States	1:45.75

SUPER GIANT SLALOM

1988	Franck Piccard, France	1:39.66
1992	Kjetil Andre Aamodt, Norway	1:13.04
1994	Markus Wasmeier, Germany	1:32.53

GIANT SLALOM

1952	Stein Eriksen, Norway	2:25.0
1956	Anton Sailer, Austria	3:00.1
1960	Roger Staub, Switzerland	1:48.3
1964	Francois Bonlieu, France	1:46.71
1968	Jean-Claude Killy, France	3:29.28
1972	Gustav Thöni, Italy	3:09.62
1976	Heini Hemmi, Switzerland	3:26.97
1980	Ingemar Stenmark, Sweden	2:40.74
1984	Max Julen, Switzerland	2:41.18
1988	Alberto Tomba, Italy	2:06.37
1992	Alberto Tomba, Italy	2:06.98
1994	Markus Wasmeier, Germany	2:52.46

SLALOM

1948	Edi Reinalter, Switzerland	2:10.3
1952	Othmar Schneider, Austria	2:00.0
1956	Anton Sailer, Austria	3:14.7
1960	Ernst Hinterseer, Austria	2:08.9
1964	Josef Stiegler, Austria	2:11.13
1968	Jean-Claude Killy, France	1:39.73
1972	Francisco Fernandez Ochoa, Spain	1:49.27
1976	Piero Gros, Italy	2:03.29
1980	Ingemar Stenmark, Sweden	1:44.26
1984	Phil Mahre, United States	1:39.41
1988	Alberto Tomba, Italy	1:39.47
1992	Finn Christian Jagge, Norway	1:44.39
1994	Thomas Stangassinger, Austria	2:02.02

*COMBINED

		Pts
1936	Franz Pfnür, Germany	99.25
1948	Henri Oreiller, France	3.27
1988	Hubert Strolz, Austria	36.55
1992	Josef Polig, Italy	14.58
1994	Lasse Kjus, Norway	3:17.53

*Beginning in 1994, scoring was based on time.

Women

DOWNHILL

1948	Hedy Schlunegger, Switzerland	2:28.3
1952	Trude Jochum-Beiser, Austria	1:47.1
1956	Madeleine Berthod, Switzerland	1:40.7
1960	Heidi Biebl, West Germany	1:37.6
1964	Christl Haas, Austria	1:55.39
1968	Olga Pall, Austria	1:40.87
1972	Marie-Theres Nadig, Switzerland	1:36.68
1976	Rosi Mittermaier, West Germany	1:46.16
1980	Annemarie Moser-Pröll, Austria	1:37.52
1984	Michela Figini, Switzerland	1:13.36
1988	Marina Kiehl, West Germany	1:25.86
1992	Kerrin Lee-Gartner, Canada	1:52.55
1994	Katja Seizinger, Germany	1:35.93

SUPER GIANT SLALOM

1988	Sigrid Wolf, Austria	1:19.03
1992	Deborah Compagnoni, Italy	1:21.22
1994	Diann Rolfe-Steinrotter	1:22.15

GIANT SLALOM

1952	Andrea Mead Lawrence, United States	2:06.8
1956	Ossi Reichert, West Germany	1:56.5
1960	Yvonne Rüegg, Switzerland	1:39.9
1964	Marielle Goitschel, France	1:52.24
1968	Nancy Greene, Canada	1:51.97
1972	Marie-Theres Nadig, Switzerland	1:29.90
1976	Kathy Kreiner, Canada	1:29.13
1980	Hanni Wenzel, Liechtenstein (2 runs)	2:41.66
1984	Debbie Armstrong, United States	2:20.98
1988	Vreni Schneider, Switzerland	2:06.49
1992	Pernilla Wiberg, Sweden	2:12.74
1994	Deborah Compagnoni, Italy	2:30.97

SLALOM

1948	Gretchen Fraser, United States	1:57.2
1952	Andrea Mead Lawrence, United States	2:10.6
1956	Renee Colliard, Switzerland	1:52.3
1960	Anne Heggtveigt, Canada	1:49.6
1964	Christine Goitschel, France	1:29.86
1968	Marielle Goitschel, France	1:25.86
1972	Barbara Cochran, United States	1:31.24
1976	Rosi Mittermaier, West Germany	1:30.54
1980	Hanni Wenzel, Liechtenstein	1:25.09
1984	Paoletta Magoni, Italy	1:36.47
1988	Vreni Schneider, Switzerland	1:36.69
1992	Petra Kronberger, Austria	1:32.68
1994	Vreni Schneider, Switzerland	1:56.01

*COMBINED

		Pts
1988	Anita Wachter, Austria	29.25
1992	Petra Kronberger, Austria	2.55
1994	Pernilla Wiberg, Sweden	3:05.16

NORDIC SKIING

Men

15 KILOMETERS (CLASSICAL)

*1924 ..Thorlief Haug, Norway	1:14:31.0
†1928..Johan Gröttumsbraaten, Norway	1:37:01.0
‡1932..Sven Utterström, Sweden	1:23:07.0
*1936 ..Erik-August Larsson, Sweden	14:38.0
*1948 ..Martin Lundström, Sweden	13:50.0
*1952 ..Hallgeir Brenden, Norway	1:34.0
1956....Hallgeir Brenden, Norway	49:39.0
1960....Haakon Brusveen, Norway	51:55.5
1964....Eero Mantyränta, Finland	50:54.1
1968....Harald Grönningen, Norway	47:54.2
1972....Sven-Ake Lundback, Sweden	45:28.24
1976....Nikolay Bajukov, Unified Team	43:58.47
1980....Thomas Wassberg, Sweden	41:57.63
1984....Gunde Swan, Sweden	41:25.6
1988....Michael Deviatyarov, USSR	41:18.9
**1992.Vegard Ulvang, Norway	27:36.0
**1994.Bjorn Daehlie, Norway	24:20.1

*distance was 18 km; †distance was 19.7 km.;
‡distance was 18.2 km; **distance was 10 km.

30 KILOMETERS (CLASSICAL)

1956....Veikko Hakulinen, Finland	1:44:06.0
1960....Sixten Jernberg, Sweden	1:51:03.9
1964....Eero Mantyränta, Finland	1:30:50.7
1968....Franco Nones, Italy	1:35:39.2
1972....Viaceslav Vedenine, USSR	1:36:31.2
1976....Sergei Savelyev, USSR	1:30:29.38
1980....Nikolai Simyatov, USSR	1:27:02.80
1984....Nikolai Simyatov, USSR	1:28:56.3
1988....Alexey Prokororov, USSR	1:24:26.3
1992....Vegard Ulvang, Norway	1:22:27.8
1994....Thomas Alsgaard, Norway	1:12:26.4

50 KILOMETERS (FREESTYLE)

1924....Thorlief Haug, Norway	3:44:32.0
1928....Per Erik Hedlund, Sweden	4:52:03.0
1932....Veli Saarinen, Finland	4:28:00.0
1936....Elis Wiklund, Sweden	3:30:11.0
1948....Nils Karlsson, Sweden	3:47:48.0
1952....Veikko Hakulinen, Finland	3:33:33.0
1956....Sixten Jernberg, Sweden	2:50:27.0
1960....Kalevi Hämäläinen, Finland	2:59:06.3
1964....Sixten Jernberg, Sweden	2:43:52.6
1968....Olle Ellefsaeter, Norway	2:28:45.8
1972....Paal Tyldrum, Norway	2:43:14.75
1976....Ivar Formo, Norway	2:37:30.50
1980....Nikolai Simyatov, USSR	2:27:24.60
1984....Thomas Wassberg, Sweden	2:15:55.8
1988....Gunde Svan, Sweden	2:04:30.9
1992....Bjorn Dählie, Norway	2:03:41.5
1994....Vladimir Smirnov, Kazakhstan	2:07:20.3

15 KILOMETERS (FREESTYLE)

1992....Bjorn Daehlie, Norway	1:05:37.9
1994....Bjorn Daehlie, Norway	1:00:08.8

4 X 10 KILOMETER RELAY

1936	Finland	2:41:33.0
1948	Sweden	2:32:80.0
1952	Finland	2:20:16.0
1956	USSR	2:15:30.0
1960	Finland	2:18:45.6
1964	Sweden	2:18:34.6
1968	Norway	2:08:33.5
1972	USSR	2:04:47.94
1976	Finland	2:07:59.72
1980	USSR	1:57:03.46
1984	Sweden	1:55:06.3
1988	Sweden	1:43:58.6
1992	Norway	1:39:26.0
1994	Italy	1:41:15.0

SKI JUMPING (NORMAL HILL)

		Pts
1964....Veikko Kankkonen, Finland	229.90
1968....Jiri Raska, Czechoslovakia	216.5
1972....Yukio Kasaya, Japan	244.2
1976....Hans-Georg Aschenbach, East Germany	252.0
1980....Toni Innauer, Austria	266.3
1984....Jens Weissflog, East Germany	215.2
1988....Matti Nykänen, Finland	229.1
1992....Ernst Vettori, Austria	222.8
1994....Espen Bredesen, Norway	282.0

SKI JUMPING (LARGE HILL)

		Pts
1924....Jacob Tullin Thams, Norway	18.960
1928....Alf Andersen, Norway	19.208
1932....Birger Ruud, Norway	228.1
1936....Birger Ruud, Norway	232.0
1948....Petter Hugsted, Norway	228.1
1952....Arnfinn Bergmann, Norway	226.0
1956....Antti Hyvärinen, Finland	227.0
1960....Helmut Recknagel, East Germany	227.2
1964....Toralf Engan, Norway	230.70
1968....Vladimir Beloussov, USSR	231.3
1972....Wojciech Fortuna, Poland	219.9
1976....Karl Schnabl, Austria	234.8
1980....Jouko Tormanen, Finland	271.0
1984....Matti Nykänen, Finland	231.2
1988....Matti Nykänen, Finland	224.0
1992....Toni Nieminen, Finland	239.5
1994....Jens Weissflog, Germany	274.5

TEAM SKI JUMPING

		Pts
1988....Finland	634.4
1992....Finland	644.4
1994....Germany	970.1

NORDIC COMBINED

		Pts
*1924 ..Thorleif Haug, Norway	18.906
*1928 ..Johan Gröttumsbraaten, Norway	17.833
1932....Johan Gröttumsbraaten, Norway	446.0
1936....Oddbjörn Hagen, Norway	430.30

NORDIC SKIING *(Cont.)*

Men *(Cont.)*

NORDIC COMBINED *(Cont.)*

	Pts
1948....Heikki Hasu, Finland	448.80
1952....Simon Slattvik, Norway	451.621
1956....Sverre Stenersen, Norway	455.0
1960....Georg Thoma, West Germany	457.952
1964....Tormod Knutsen, Norway	469.28
1968....Frantz Keller, West Germany	449.04
1972....Ulrich Wehling, East Germany	413.34
1976....Ulrich Wehling, East Germany	423.39
1980....Ulrich Wehling, East Germany	432.20
1984....Tom Sandberg, Norway	422.595
1988....Hippolyt Kempf, Switzerland	432.230
1992....Fabrice Guy, France	426.47
1994....Fred B. Lundberg, Norway	457.970

TEAM NORDIC COMBINED

1988....West Germany
1992....Japan
1994....Japan

*Different scoring system; 1924-1952 distance was 18 km.; 1952-present, 15 km.

Women

5 KILOMETERS (CLASSICAL)

1964....Klaudia Boyarskikh, USSR	17:50.5
1968....Toini Gustafsson, Sweden	16:45.2
1972....Galina Kulakova, USSR	17:00.50
1976....Helena Takalo, Finland	15:48.69
1980....Raisa Smetanina, USSR	15:06.92
1984....Marja-Liisa Hamalainen, Finland	17:04.0
1988....Marjo Matikainen, Finland	15:04.0
1992....Marjut Lukkarinen, Finland	14:13.8
1994....Lyubova Egorova, Russia	14:08.8

10 KILOMETERS (CLASSICAL)

1952....Lydia Widemen, Finland	41:40.0
1956....Lyubov Kosyryeva, USSR	38:11.0
1960....Maria Gusakova, USSR	39:46.6
1964....Klaudia Boyarskikh, USSR	40:24.3
1968....Toini Gustafsson, Sweden	36:46.5
1972....Galina Kulakova, USSR	34:17.8
1976....Raisa Smetanina, USSR	30:13.41
1980....Barbara Petzold, East Germany	30:31.54
1984....Marja-Lissa Hamalainen, Finland	31:44.2
1988....Vida Ventsene, USSR	30:08.3

15 KILOMETERS (CLASSICAL)

1992....Lyubov Egorova, Unified Team	42:20.8
1994....Manuela Di Centa, Italy	39:44.5

20 KILOMETERS (FREESTYLE)

1984....Marja-Liisa Hamalainen, Finland	1:01:45.0
1988....Tamara Tikhonova, USSR	55:53.6

30 KILOMETERS (FREESTYLE)

1992....Stefania Belmondo, Italy	1:22:30.1
1994....Manuela Di Centa, Italy	1:25:41.6

10 KILOMETERS FREESTYLE PURSUIT

1992....Lyubov Egorova, Unified Team	40:07.7
1994....Lyubov Egorova, Russia	41:38.1

4 X 5-KILOMETER RELAY

1956....Finland	1:9:01.0
1960....Sweden	1:4:21.4
1964....USSR	59:20.0
1968....Norway	57:30.0
1972....USSR	48:46.15
1976....USSR	1:07:49.75
1980....East Germany	1:02:11.10
1984....Norway	1:06:49.7
1988....USSR	59:51.1
1992....Unified Team	59:34.8
1994....Russia	57:12.5

Note: 10 km. (classical) changed to 15 km. (classical) in 1992; 20 km. (freestyle) changed to 30 km. (freestyle).

FREESTYLE SKIING

Men

MOGUL

	Pts
1992....Edgar Grospiron, France	25.81
1994....Jean-Luc Brassard, Canada	27.24

AERIAL

	Pts
1994....Andreas Schoenbaechler, SWI	234.67

Women

MOGUL

	Pts
1992....Donna Weinbrecht, United States	23.69
1994....Stine Lise Hattestad, Norway	25.97

AERIAL

	Pts
1994....Lina Cherjazova, Uzbekistan	166.84

Track and Field

9.85!

Leroy Burrell sprints to a new world record in the 100-meter dash

JEAN-BERNARD SIEBER/AGENCE DE PRESSE ARC/REUTER

A Dashing Year

The men's 100-meter dash was the scene of most of the year's action, on and off the track | by MERRELL NODEN

NASTY, BRUTISH AND SHORT. THAT'S how English philosopher Thomas Hobbes described human life three centuries ago, and that's how track and field's most riveting event, the men's 100, came to look in the summer of 1994. With Olympic champion Linford Christie reaching the ripe old age of 34 and world-record holder Carl Lewis not much younger at 33, the jockeying to become the next "world's fastest man" was ferocious, producing a world record, a slew of great races and one extremely ugly incident. Among the contenders were three Americans: Lewis's burly training partner Leroy Burrell; scowling Dennis Mitchell, a.k.a. the Green Machine for the lime-green bodysuit he wears; and onetime boy preacher Jon Drummond, green-eyed and intense.

Burrell struck first. On July 6 in Lausanne, Switzerland, he destroyed a strong field in 9.85. That snipped .01 off Lewis's three-year-old world record, but Burrell was not impressed. "Everyone thinks this [record] will be broken a few more times this year,"

he said. "I feel like I've been handed a hot piece of gold." Determined not to be greedy, he ran one more race, then headed home to Houston to train for the Goodwill Games and the Weltklasse meet in Zurich.

In Burrell's absence, Mitchell quickly emerged as the summer's most consistent sprinter. He ran fast and he ran often, clocking 9.97 in Stockholm and 9.94 in Oslo. A notoriously quick starter, Mitchell is also renowned for his antics at the starting line, where he scowls and poses, turning 90 degrees to sight menacingly along his shoulder in the direction of the finish line.

Mitchell's scowl grew even fiercer when it seemed, as the Goodwill Games approached, that he was not going to be invited to join Lewis, Christie and Burrell in the most hyped 100 of the year. Whatever luster the race lost when Christie pulled out with an injury, it gained when Mitchell was included at the last moment. When he ran 10.07 into a strong headwind, Mitchell made his point. Lewis then pulled out of the Goodwill Games long jump, where he was to face Mike Powell, and spent several weeks fighting a stomach virus he says he picked up in St. Petersburg. He came back to run poorly in two late-season races, leaving one to wonder about his future. As Christie helpfully pointed out, it has been three years since Lewis broke 10 seconds for the 100.

Even without Lewis the men's 100 at the Weltklasse meet three weeks later shaped up as a tantalizing race. Christie's fitness was the only question mark; he pulled a hamstring in losing to Drummond in London on July 15. When the weather turned rotten in Zurich, with high winds and cold rain, many believed the old man would tighten up. Not so. Christie splashed to a huge win, his 10.05 easily beating Drummond, who finished second in 10.15. Mitchell was fourth (10.23) and Burrell seventh (10.39).

The macho posturing that characterizes the sprints turned ugly later that night, when Mitchell encountered Nigerian sprinter Olapade Adeniken in the lobby of Zurich's Nova-Park Hotel. In the past Mitchell's barks have always seemed more threatening than his bites. That changed dramatically. Mitchell is alleged to have kicked Adeniken in the head while two other men held him down, but not before Adeniken delivered several karate kicks to Mitchell's head. The fight, which grew out of a minor dispute at a car rental counter in Durham, N.C., the week before, left bloodstains on the lobby carpet. "Sprinters are very aggressive people," said Christie the next day. "Hurdlers, for example, can talk to each other; sprinters cannot."

Next stop for Christie was the Commonwealth Games in Vancouver, where he won easily in 9.91. Back in Europe, he lost twice to Drummond, but he is clearly not going to surrender his world and Olympic crowns without a good fight.

With no world or Olympic title to focus on, many track and field athletes either aimed for records or tried new events. Sergei Bubka vaulted 20' 1¾" in Sestriere, Italy, to set his 35th world record, but most of the year's records fell in the longer track events. Haile Gebresilasie of Ethiopia snipped 1.43 seconds off Said Aouita's 5,000 record, running 12:56.96. World cross-country champion

Christie may be a bit long in the tooth at 34, but he showed he can still compete.

William Sigei of Kenya set a world 10,000 record of 26:52.23. Sonia O'Sullivan of Ireland set a world record for 2,000 meters (5:25.36) and ran 8:21.64 for 3,000, fastest by a non-Chinese woman. Indeed, the Chinese women's absence in 1994 was almost as eye-catching as their presence had been in '93. And for the first time in a decade an American man actually looked capable of beating the Africans. Recent Indiana University grad Bob Kennedy, 23, set an American record in the 3,000 (7:35.33) and ran 13:02.93 in the 5,000.

But the year's most impressive record went to world mile-record-holder Noureddine Morceli of Algeria, who, incredible as it seems, is only 24. On a warm night in Monte Carlo, Morceli ran 7:25.11 for 3,000 meters, hacking almost four seconds off Moses Kiptanui's world mark. Morceli's time looked all the more awesome in this, the 40th anniversary of Roger Bannister's first sub-four-minute mile, since it is the equivalent of *two* four-minute miles. In a summer of trash-talking and violence, the boldest statement came, refreshingly, from the soft-spoken Morceli, Sir Roger's worthy heir.

FOR THE RECORD·1993-1994

U.S. Outdoor Track and Field Championships

Knoxville, Tenn., June 14-18, 1994

Men

100 METERS

1.	Dennis Mitchell, Mazda TC	10.13
2.	Jon Drummond, Nike LA	10.14
3.	Vince Henderson, U. of Arkansas	10.27

200 METERS

1.	Ron Clark, Prime Time Sports	20.77
2.	Bryan Bridgewater, Nike LA	20.85
3.	Dino Napier, U.S. Army	20.89

400 METERS

1.	Antonio Pettigrew, Reebok	44.43
2.	Jason Rouser, Nike LA	45.19
3.	Calvin Davis, U. of Arkansas	45.20

800 METERS

1.	Mark Everett, JD	1:46.08
2.	Stanley Redwine, Foot Locker AC	1:47.45
3.	Jose Parrilla, Adidas	1:47.78

1500 METERS

1.	Terrance Herrington, adidas	3:37.77
2.	Jason Pyrah, unattached	3:38.20
3.	Erik Nedeau, Northeastern	3:38.31

STEEPLECHASE

1.	Mark Croghan, Nike Intl	8:23.47
2.	Marc Davis, Nike Intl	8:30.86
3.	Danny Lopez, adidas	8:31.86

5000 METERS

1.	Matt Giusto, Foot Locker AC	14:04.30
2.	Reuben Reina, Foot Locker AC	14:04.35
3.	Ronnie Harris, Reebok East	14:04.72

10,000 METERS

1.	Tom Ansberry, Nike	29:01.84
2.	Steve Plasencia, Asics	29:03.54
3.	Jim Westphal, Nike North	29:14.49

110-METER HURDLES

1.	Mark Crear, Reebok RC	13.36
2.	Robert Reading, Accusplit	13.37
3.	Allen Johnson, Nike Atlantic	13.41

400-METER HURDLES

1.	Derrick Adkins, Reebok RC	48.41
2.	Octavius Terry, Georgia Tech	49.03
3.	Torrance Zellner, Asics	49.07

20-KILOMETER WALK

1.	Allen James, Athletes in Action	1:28:35.9
2.	Jonathan Matthews, GGW	1:29:02.3
3.	Andrzej Chylinski, NYAC	1:30:04.6

HIGH JUMP

1.	Hollis Conway, Reebok RC	7 ft 5¾ in
2T.	Tony Barton, adidas	7 ft 4½ in
2T.	Steve Smith, Indiana St	7 ft 4½ in

POLE VAULT

1.	Scott Huffman, Foot Locker RC	19 ft 7 in
2.	Dean Starkey, Reebok RC	18 ft 8¼ in
3.	Brent Burns, Reebok RC	18 ft 8¼ in

LONG JUMP

1.	Mike Powell, Foot Locker AC	28 ft 5¾ in w
2.	Kareem Streete-Thompson, Reebok RC	28 ft 4¼ inw
3.	Dion Bentley, U. of Florida	26 ft 5½ inw

TRIPLE JUMP

1.	Mike Conley, Foot Locker AC	57 ft 5½ in
2.	Kenny Harrison, Mizuno TC	56 ft 3 in
3.	Reggie Jones, adidas	55 ft 7 ¾in

SHOT PUT

1.	C.J. Hunter, USW	68 ft 3¾ in
2.	Randy Barnes, Goldwin	68 ft 1½ in
3.	Brent Noon, Georgia	67 ft 3¼ in

DISCUS THROW

1.	Mike Gravelle, unattached	201 ft 4 in
2.	Randy Heisler, Nike Indiana	197 ft 8 in
3.	Carlos Scott, Prime Time Sports	194 ft 7 in

HAMMER THROW

1.	Lance Deal, NYAC	270 ft 8 in AR
2.	Jim Driscoll, unat	240 ft 6 in
3.	Kevin McMahon, Georgetown	235 ft 4 in

JAVELIN THROW

1.	Todd Riech, Fresno St	255 ft 5 in
2.	Tom Pukstys, adidas	253 ft 9 in
3.	Ed Kaminski, SSTC	252 ft 8 in

DECATHLON

1.	Dan O'Brien, Foot Locker AC	8707 pts.
2.	Steve Fritz, Accusplit SC	8548 pts.
3.	Kip Janvrin, VISA TC	8287 pts.

*Meet record. w=wind aided. AR=American Record.

Women

100 METERS

1.	Gail Devers, Nike Intl	11.12
2.	Carlette Guidry, adidas	11.15
3.	Cheryl Taplin, LSU	11.26

200 METERS

1.	Carlette Guidry, adidas	22.71
2.	Dannette Young, Reebok RC	22.81
3.	Chryste Gaines, Mizuno	23.33

400 METERS

1.	Natasha Kaiser-Brown, Foot Locker AC	50.53
2.	Maicel Malone, Asics	50.77
3.	Jearl Miles, Reebok RC	50.78

800 METERS

1.	Joetta Clark, Foot Locker AC	2:00.41
2.	Amy Wickus, U. of Wisconsin	2:00.60
3.	Meredith Rainey, Foot Locker AC	2:00.65

1500 METERS

1.	Regina Jacobs, Mizuno	4:07.71
2.	Suzy Hamilton, Reebok RC	4:08.15
3.	Kathey Franey, Reebok RC	4:08.79

3,000 METERS

1.	Annette Peters, Nike Intl	9:01.69
2.	Libbie Johnson, Mizuno	9:07.25
3.	Joan Nesbit, New Balance	9:14.74

5,000 METERS

1.	Ceci St. Geme, Asics	15:57.71
2.	Jen Rhines, Villanova	16:04.02
3.	Misti Demko, Asics	16:10.85

10,000 METERS

1.	Olga Appell, Reebok	32:23.76
2.	Gwyn Coogan, adidas	32:24.81
3.	Anne Marie Letko, Nike RR	32:41.67

10,000 METER WALK

1.	Teresa Vaill, unattached	45:01.46AR
2.	Michelle Rohl, PAC	45:07.58
3.	Deb Van Orden, unattached	47:00.30

*Meet record. w=wind aided. AR=American Record.

100-METER HURDLES

1.	Jackie Joyner-Kersee, Honda	12.88
2.	LaVonna Martin-Floreal, Reebok RC	13.06
3.	Cheryl Dickey, Nike South	13.25

400-METER HURDLES

1.	Kim Batten, Reebok RC	54.51
2.	Tonja Buford, Nike Intl	55.87
3.	Trevaia Williams, Atoms	56.55

HIGH JUMP

1.	Angela Bradburn, unattached	6 ft 3½ in
2.	Tisha Waller, Goldwin	6 ft 2¼ in
3.	Karol Damon, Goldwin	6 ft 1¼ in

LONG JUMP

1.	Jackie Joyner-Kersee, Honda	23 ft 5¼ in w
2.	Sheila Echols, Goldwin	21 ft 7 ½ in
3.	Terri Turner-Hairston, Mizuno	21 ft 6¾ in w

TRIPLE JUMP

1.	Sheila Hudson-Strudwick, Reebok RC	45 ft 8¼ in AR
2.	Diana Orrange, Prime Time Sp	46 ft ½ in
3.	Carla Shannon, unattached	44 ft 10¾ in

SHOT PUT

1.	Connie Price-Smith, Nike Coast	64 ft 3¾ in
2.	Ramona Pagel, Nike Coast	58 ft 9¼ in
3.	Dawn Dumble, unattached	57 ft 3¾ in

DISCUS THROW

1.	Connie Price-Smith, Nike Coast	195 ft 1 in
2.	Lacy Barnes, Nike	193 ft 7 in
3.	Kris Kuehl, unattached	188 ft 2 in

JAVELIN

1.	Donna Mayhew, Nike Coast	193 ft 4 in
2.	Nicole Carroll, Santa Monica TC	185 ft 4 in
3.	Lynda Lipson, KK	182 ft 3 in

HEPTATHLON

1.	Kym Carter, Nike West	6371 pts.
2.	Jamie McNeair, PATC	6323 pts.
3.	DeDe Nathan, Nike Indiana	6189 pts.

Not Counting on This

Suzy Hamilton had already begun to celebrate her defeat of Olympic 1500 champion Hassiba Boulmerka in the mile at last February's Mobil One Invitational when she began to get the sickening feeling that something was wrong. As the rest of the field sped past her, it dawned on Hamilton that she must have miscounted laps in the eight lap race and launched her kick a lap early. Hamilton did not rejoin the race.

"I can't blame anyone but myself," said Hamilton, who thought she saw a sign saying there was one lap to go when, in fact, there were two. "It's one of those things that happen. Luckily this isn't the Olympic Trials, or it would be a disaster. I'll take this as a learning experience."

In fact, Hamilton suffered a similar lapse in concentration once before. In the 1990 Goodwill Games she misjudged the location of the finish line in another tight race, thereby losing a chance at a medal.

If it's any consolation, Suzy, Boulmerka ran the Millrose Games mile two nights earlier with her shorts on backwards.

IAAF World Track and Field Championships

Stuttgart, Germany, August 14-22, 1993

Men

100 METERS

1.	Linford Christie, Great Britain	9.87
2.	Andre Cason, United States	9.92
3.	Dennis Mitchell, United States	9.99

200 METERS

1.	Frank Fredericks, Namibia	19.85*
2.	John Regis, Great Britain	19.94
3.	Carl Lewis, United States	19.99

400 METERS

1.	Michael Johnson, United States	43.65*
2.	Butch Reynolds, United States	44.13
3.	Samson Kitur, Kenya	44.54

800 METERS

1.	Paul Ruto, Kenya	1:44.71
2.	Guiseppie D'Urso, Italy	1:44.86
3.	Billy Konchellah, Kenya	1:44.89

1,500 METERS

1.	Nourredine Morceli, Algeria	3:34.24
2.	Fermin Cacho, Spain	3:35.56
3.	Abdi Bile, Somalia	3:35.96

STEEPLECHASE

1.	Moses Kiptanui, Kenya	8:06.36*
2.	Patrick Sang, Kenya	8:07.53
3.	Alesandro Lambruschini, Italy	8:08.78

5,000 METERS

1.	Ismael Kirui, Kenya	13:02.75*
2.	Haile Gebresilasie, Ethiopia	13:03.17
3.	Fita Bayesa, Ethiopia	13:05.40

10,000 METERS

1.	Haile Gebresilasie, Ethiopia	27:46.02
2.	Moses Tanui, Kenya	27:46.54
3.	Richard Chelimo, Kenya	28:06.02

MARATHON

1.	Mark Plaatjes, United States	2:13:57
2.	Lucketz Swartbooi, Namibia	2:14:11
3.	Bert Van Vlaanderen, Holland	2:15:12

110-METER HURDLES

1.	Colin Jackson, Great Britain	12.91†
2.	Tony Jarrett, Great Britain	13.00
3.	Jack Pierce, United States	13.06

400-METER HURDLES

1.	Kevin Young, United States	47.18*
2.	Samuel Matete, Zambia	47.60
3.	Winthrop Graham, Jamaica	47.62

20-KILOMETER WALK

1.	Valentin Massana, Spain	1:22:31
2.	Giovanni De Benedictis, Italy	1:23:06
3.	Danie Plaza, Spain	1:23:18

50-KILOMETER WALK

1.	Jesus Angel Garcia, Spain	3:41:41
2.	Valentin Kononen, Finland	3:42:02
3.	Valery Spitsyn, Russia	3:42:50

4 X 100 METER RELAY

1.	United States	37.48
2.	Great Britain	37.77
3.	Canada	37.83

4 X 400 METER RELAY

1.	United States	2:54.29†
2.	Kenya	2:59.82
3.	Germany	2:59.99

HIGH JUMP

1.	Javier Sotomayor, Cuba	7 ft 10½ in*
2.	Artur Partyka, Poland	7 ft 9¼ in
3.	Steve Smith, Great Britain	7 ft 9¼ in

POLE VAULT

1.	Sergei Bubka, Ukraine	19 ft 8¼ in*
2.	Grigoriy Yegerov, Kazakhstan	19 ft 4½ in
3.	Maksim Tarasov, Russia	19 ft ½ in

LONG JUMP

1.	Mike Powell, United States	28 ft 2¼ in
2.	Stanislav Tarasenko, Russia	26 ft 9¼ in
3.	Vitaliy Kirilenko, Ukraine	26 ft 9 in

TRIPLE JUMP

1.	Mike Conley, United States	58 ft 7¼
2.	Leonid Voloshin, Russia	57 ft 11 in
3.	Jonathan Edwards, Gr Britain	57 ft 2¾ in

SHOT PUT

1.	Werner Guenthor, Switzerland	72 ft 1 in
2.	Randy Barnes, United States	71 ft 6¼ in
3.	Mike Stulce, United States	68 ft 8½ in

DISCUS

1.	Lars Reidel, Germany	222 ft 2 in
2.	Dmitry Shevchenko, Russia	219 ft 6 in
3.	Juergen Schult, Germany	216 ft 11 in

HAMMER

1.	Andrey Abduvaliyev, Tajikistan	267 ft 10 in
2.	Igor Astapkovich, Belarus	262 ft 1 in
3.	Tibor Gecsek, Hungary	260 ft 11 in

JAVELIN

1.	Jan Zelezny, Czech Republic	282 ft 1 in
2.	Kimmo Kinnunen, Finland	278 ft 2 in
3.	Dmitriy Polyunin, Uzbekistan	273 ft 7 in

DECATHLON

1.	Dan O'Brien, United States	8817 pts
2.	Eduard Hamalainen, Belarus	8724 pts
3.	Paul Meier, Germany	8548 pts

*Meet record. †World record

Stuttgart, Germany

Women

100 METERS

1. Gail Devers, United States — 10.82*
2. Merlene Ottey, Jamaica — 10.82
3. Gwen Torrence, United States — 10.89

200 METERS

1. Merlene Ottey, Jamaica — 21.98
2. Gwen Torrence, United States — 22.00
3. Irina Privalova, Russia — 22.13

400 METERS

1. Jearl Miles, United States — 49.82
2. Natasha Kaiser-Brown, U.S. — 50.17
3. Sandie Richards, Jamaica — 50.44

800 METERS

1. Maria Mutola, Mozambique — 1:55.43
2. Lyubov Gurina, Russia — 1:57.10
3. Ella Kovacs, Romania — 1:57.92

1,500 METERS

1. Dong Liu, China — 4:00.50
2. Sonia O'Sullivan, Ireland — 4:03.48
3. Hassiba Boulmerka, Algeria — 4:04.29

3,000 METERS

1. Yunxia Qu, China — 8:28.71*
2. Linli Zhang, China — 8:29.25
3. Liron Zhang, China — 8:31.95

10,000 METERS

1. Wang Junxia, China — 30:49.30*
2. Huandi Zhong, China — 31:12.55
3. Tecla Lorupe, Kenya — 31:29.91

MARATHON

1. Junko Asari, Japan — 2:30:03
2. Manuela Machado, Portugal — 2:30:54
3. Tomoe Abe, Japan — 2:31:01

100-METER HURDLES

1. Gail Devers, United States — 12.46**
2. Marina Azyabina, Russia — 12.60
3. Lynda Tolbert, United States — 12.67

400-METER HURDLES

1. Sally Gunnell, Great Britain — 52.74†
2. Sandra Farmer-Patrick, U.S. — 52.79**
3. Margarita Ponomaryova, Russia — 53.48

10-KILOMETER WALK

1. Sari Essayah, Finland — 42:59
2. Ileana Salvador, Italy — 43:08
3. Encamacion Granados, Spain — 43:26

4 X 100 METER RELAY

1. Russia — 41.49
2. United States — 41.49
3. Jamaica — 41.94

4 X 400 METER RELAY

1. United States — 3:16.71
2. Russia — 3:18.38
3. Great Britain — 3:23.41

HIGH JUMP

1. Ioamnet Quintero, Cuba — 6 ft 6¼ in
2. Silvia Costa, Cuba — 6 ft 5½ in
3. Sigrid Kirchmann, Austria — 6 ft 5½ in

LONG JUMP

1. Heike Drechsler, Germany — 23 ft 4 in
2. Larisa Berezhnaya, Ukraine — 22 ft 10¾ in
3. Renata Nielsen, Denmark — 22 ft 2¼ in

TRIPLE JUMP

1. Ana Biryukova, Russia — 49 ft 6¼ in†
2. Yolanda Chen, Russia — 48 ft 2¾ in
3. Iva Prandzheva, Bulgaria — 46 ft 8¼ in

SHOT PUT

1. Zhihong Huang, China — 67 ft 6 in
2. Svetlana Krivelyova, Russia — 65 ft 6¼ in
3. Kathrin Neimke, Germany — 64 ft 8 in

DISCUS

1. Olga Burova, Russia — 221 ft 1 in
2. Daniela Costian, Australia — 214 ft 5 in
3. Chunfeng Min, China — 214 ft 1 in

JAVELIN

1. Trine Hattestad, Finland — 227 ft 0 in
2. Karen Forkel, Germany — 215 ft 10 in
3. Natalya Shikolenko, Belarus — 215 ft 4 in

HEPTATHLON

1. Jackie Joyner-Kersee, U.S. — 6837 pts
2. Sabine Braun, Germany — 6797 pts
3. Svetlana Buraga, Belarus — 6635 pts

*Meet record. **American record. †World record.

Use Your Head!

A surprisingly large number of entrants in the 1993 New York City Marathon fell ill after the race. According to New York *Newsday*, the cause was not just the heat and humidity, which soared to record levels on race day, but also because the runners had taken far more than the recommended dosage of the painkiller Advil, which they had received in their entry packets. The painkiller was one of the marathon's sponsors.

IAAF World Cross-Country Championships

Budapest, March 26, 1994

MEN (12,200 METERS; 7.58 MILES)

1. ....William Sigei, Kenya — 34:29
2. ....Simon Chemwoyo, Kenya — 34:30
3. ....Haile Gebresilasie, Ethiopia — 34:32

WOMEN (6,200 METERS; 3.85 MILES)

1. ....Helen Chepngeno, Kenya — 20:45
2. ....Catherina McKiernan, Ireland — 20:52
3. ....Conceiçao Ferreira, Portugal — 20:52

Major Marathons

New York City: November 14, 1993

MEN

1. ....Andres Espinosa, Mexico — 2:10:04
2. ....Bob Kempainen, United States — 2:11:03
3. ....Arturo Barrios, Mexico — 2:12:21

WOMEN

1. ....Uta Pippig, Germany — 2:26:24
2. ....Olga Appell, Mexico — 2:28:56
3. ....Nadia Prasad, France — 2:30:16

Tokyo: November 21, 1993

WOMEN ONLY

1. ....Valentina Yegorova, Russia — 2:26:40
2. ....Mari Tanigawa, Japan — 2:28:22
3. ....Katrin Dörre, Germany — 2:28:52

Fukuoka, Japan: December 5, 1993

MEN ONLY

1. ....Dionicio Ceron, Mexico — 2:08:51
2. ....Gert Thys, South Africa — 2:09:31
3. ....Valdenor dos Santos, Brazil — 2:10:20

Honolulu: December 12, 1993

MEN

1. ....Bong Ju-lee, South Korea — 2:13:16
2. ....Cosmas N'Deti, Kenya — 2:13:40
3. ....Josphat N'Deti, Kenya — 2:13:48

WOMEN

1. ....Carla Beurskens, Netherlands — 2:32:20
2. ....Amy Legacki, United States — 2:43:39
3. ....Madeline Tormoen, United States — 2:45:25

Los Angeles: March 6, 1994

MEN

1. ....Paul Pilkington, United States — 2:12:13
2. ....Luca Barzaghi, Italy — 2:12:52
3. ....Andrzej Krzyscin, Poland — 2:13:21

WOMEN

1. ....Olga Appell, United States — 2:28:12
2. ....Emma Scaunich, Italy — 2:37:05
3. ....Sylvia Mosqueda, United States — 2:40:12

Rotterdam: April 17, 1994

MEN

1. ....Vincent Rousseau, Belgium — 2:07:51
2. ....Willie Mtolo, South Africa — 2:10:17
3. ....Hu Gangjun, China — 2:10:28

WOMEN

1. ....Miyoka Asahina, Japan — 2:25:52
2. ....Ritva Lemettingen, Finland — 2:29:16
3. ....Carla Beurskens, Netherlands — 2:29:43

London: April 17, 1994

MEN

1. ....Dionicio Ceron, Mexico — 2:08:53
2. ....Abebe Mekonnen, Ethiopia — 2:09:17
3. ....German Silva, Mexico — 2:09:18

WOMEN

1. ....Katrin Dörre, Germany — 2:32:34
2. ....Lisa Ondieki, Australia — 2:33:17
3. ....Janet Mayal, Brazil — 2:34:21

Boston: April 18, 1994

MEN

1. ....Cosmas N'Deti, Kenya — 2:07:15
2. ....Andres Espinosa, Mexico — 2:07:19
3. ....Jackson Kipngok, Kenya — 2:08:08

WOMEN

1. ....Uta Pippig, Germany — 2:21:45
2. ....Valentina Yegorova, Russia — 2:23:33
3. ....Elana Meyer, South Africa — 2:25:15

FOR THE RECORD·Year by Year

TRACK AND FIELD

World Records

As of September 20, 1994. World outdoor records are recognized by the International Amateur Athletics Federation (IAAF).

Men

Event	Mark	Record Holder	Date	Site
100 meters	9.85	Leroy Burrell, United States	7-6-94	Lausanne, Switzerland
200 meters	19.72	Pietro Mennea, Italy	9-12-79	Mexico City
400 meters	43.29	Butch Reynolds, United States	8-17-88	Zurich
800 meters	1:41.73	Sebastian Coe, Great Britain	6-10-81	Florence
1,000 meters	2:12.18	Sebastian Coe, Great Britain	7-11-81	Oslo
1,500 meters	3:28.86	Noureddine Morceli, Algeria	9-6-92	Rieti, Italy
Mile	3:44.29	Noureddine Morceli, Algeria	9-5-93	Rieti, Italy
2,000 meters	4:50.81	Said Aouita, Morocco	7-16-87	Paris
3,000 meters	7:25.11	Noureddine Morceli, Algeria	8-2-94	Monte Carlo
Steeplechase	8:02.08	Moses Kiptanui, Kenya	8-19-92	Zurich
5,000 meters	12:56.96	Haile Gebresilasie, Ethiopia	6-4-94	Hengelo, Netherlands
10,000 meters	26:52.23	William Sigei, Kenya	7-22-94	Oslo
20,000 meters	56:55.6	Arturo Barrios, Mexico	3-30-91	La Flâche, France
Hour	21,101 meters	Arturo Barrios, Mexico	3-30-91	La Flâche, France
25,000 meters	1:13:55.8	Toshihiko Seko, Japan	3-22-81	Christchurch, New Zealand
30,000 meters	1:29:18.8	Toshihiko Seko, Japan	3-22-81	Christchurch, New Zealand
Marathon	2:06:50	Belayneh Densimo, Ethiopia	4-17-88	Rotterdam
110-meter hurdles	12.91	Colin Jackson, Great Britain	8-20-93	Stuttgart, Germany
400-meter hurdles	46.78	Kevin Young, United States	8-6-92	Barcelona
20 kilometer walk	1:17:26	Bernardo Segura, Mexico	5-7-94	Softeland, Norway
30 kilometer walk	2:01:44.1	Maurizio Damilano, Italy	10-3-92	Cuneo, Italy
50 kilometer walk	3:41:38.4 ˙	Raul Gonzalez, Mexico	5-25-79	Bergen, Norway
4x100-meter relay	37.40	United States (Mike Marsh, Leroy Burrell, Dennis Mitchell, Carl Lewis)	8-8-92	Barcelona
		United States (Jon Drummond, Andre Cason, Dennis Mitchell, Leroy Burrell)	8-22-93	Stuttgart, Germany
4x200-meter relay	1:18.68	Santa Monica TC (Mike Marsh, Leroy Burrell, Floyd Heard, Carl Lewis)	4-17-94	Walnut, California
4x400-meter relay	2:54.29	United States (Andrew Valmon, Quincy Watts, Butch Reynolds, Michael Johnson)	8-22-93	Barcelona
4x800-meter relay	7:03.89	Great Britain (Peter Elliott, Garry Cook, Steve Cram, Sebastian Coe)	8-30-82	London
4x1500-meter relay	14:38.8	West Germany (Thomas Wessinghage, Harald Hudak, Michael Lederer, Karl Fleschen)	8-17-77	Cologne
High jump	8 ft ½ in	Javier Sotomayor, Cuba	7-27-93	Salamanca, Spain
Pole vault	20 ft 1¾ in	Sergei Bubka, Ukraine	7-31-94	Sestriere, Italy
Long jump	29 ft 4½ in	Mike Powell, United States	8-30-91	Tokyo
Triple jump	58 ft 11½ in	Willie Banks, United States	6-16-85	Indianapolis
Shot put	75 ft 10¼ in	Randy Barnes, United States	5-20-90	Westwood, CA
Discus throw	243 ft 0 in	Jürgen Schult, East Germany	6-6-86	Neubrandenburg, Germany
Hammer throw	284 ft 7 in	Yuri Syedikh, USSR	8-30-86	Stuttgart
Javelin throw	313 ft 10 in	Jan Zelezny, Czech Republic	8-29-93	Sheffield, England
Decathlon	8891 pts	Dan O'Brien, United States	9-4/5-92	Talence, France

Note: The decathlon consists of 10 events——the 100 meters, long jump, shot put, high jump and 400 meters on the first day; the 110-meter hurdles, discus, pole vault, javelin and 1500 meters on the second.

Women

Event	Mark	Record Holder	Date	Site
100 meters	10.49	Florence Griffith Joyner, United States	7-16-88	Indianapolis
200 meters	21.34	Florence Griffith Joyner, United States	9-29-88	Seoul
400 meters	47.60	Marita Koch, East Germany	10-6-85	Canberra, Australia
800 meters	1:53.28	Jarmila Kratochvílová, Czechoslovakia	7-26-83	Munich
1,000 meters	2:30.67	Christine Wachtel, East Germany	8-17-90	Berlin
1,500 meters	3:50.46	Qu Yunxia, China	9-11-93	Beijing
Mile	4:15.61	Paula Ivan, Romania	7-10-89	Nice
2,000 meters	5:25.36	Sonia O'Sullivan, Ireland	7-8-94	Edinburgh
3,000 meters	8:06.11	Wang Junxia, China	9-13-93	Beijing
5,000 meters	14:37.33	Ingrid Kristiansen, Norway	8-5-86	Stockholm
10,000 meters	29:31.78	Wang Junxia, China	9-8-93	Beijing
25,000 meters	1:29:29.2	Karolina Szabó, Hungary	4-22-88	Budapest
30,000 meters	1:49:05.6	Karolina Szabó, Hungary	4-22-88	Budapest
Marathon	2:21:06	Ingrid Kristiansen, Norway	4-21-85	London
100-meter hurdles	12.21	Yordanka Donkova, Bulgaria	8-20-88	Stara Zagora, Bulgaria
400-meter hurdles	52.74	Sally Gunnell, Great Britain	8-19-93	Stuttgart, Germany
5-kilometer walk	20:17.19	Kerry Junna-Saxby, Australia	1-14-90	Sydney, Australia
10-kilometer walk	41:56.23	Nadezhda Ryashkina, USSR	7-24-90	Seattle
4x100-meter relay	41.37	East Germany (Silke Gladisch, Sabine Reiger, Ingrid Auerswald, Marlies Göhr)	10-6-85	Canberra, Australia
4x200-meter relay	1:28.15	East Germany (Marlies Göhr, Romy Müller, Bärbel Wöckel, Marita Koch)	8-9-80	Jena, East Germany
4x400-meter relay	3:15.17	USSR (Tatyana Ledovskaya, Olga Nazarova, Maria Pinigina, Olga Bryzgina)	10-1-88	Seoul
4x800-meter relay	7:50.17	USSR (Nadezhda Olizarenko, Lyubov Gurina, Lyudmila Borisova, Irina Podyalovskaya)	8-5-84	Moscow
High jump	6 ft 10¼ in	Stefka Kostadinova, Bulgaria	8-30-87	Rome
Long jump	24 ft 8¼ in	Galina Chistyakova, USSR	6-11-88	Leningrad
Triple Jump	49 ft 6¼ in	Ana Biryukova, Russia	8-21-93	Stuttgart, Germany
Shot put	74 ft 3 in	Natalya Lisovskaya, USSR	6-7-87	Moscow
Discus throw	252 ft 0 in	Gabriele Reinsch, East Germany	7-9-88	Neubrandenburg, Germany
Javelin throw	262 ft 5 in	Petra Felke, East Germany	9-9-88	Berlin
Heptathlon	7291 pts	Jackie Joyner-Kersee, United States	9-23/24-88	Seoul

Note: The heptathlon consists of 7 events—the 100-meter hurdles, high jump, shot put and 200 meters on the first day; the long jump, javelin and 800 meters on the second.

A Renaissance Runner, Indeed

There were echoes from the past everywhere on January 22, 1994, at the Legends Mile in Miami. To celebrate the 40th anniversary of Roger Bannister's historic first sub-four-minute mile, the race organizer's had assembled a field that included former world mile record holders Peter Snell, Jim Ryun and Steve Cram). As it turned out, former No.1-ranked 1,500-meter runner Marty Liquori outkicked his onetime rival Kip Keino, the 1968 Olympic 1,500 champion, both runners clocking 5:23.6

Presiding over all of this as starter—and looking slightly out of place in his blue blazer and gray wool trousers amid the throng of roller bladers and halter tops—was Bannister himself. He does not dwell in the past but will wax eloquent on it when called upon to do so. "When I went up to Oxford, I wanted to take part in sport," said Sir Roger. "I was too light for rowing, and I wasn't skilled enough for rugby. But I knew I could run."

On a drizzly May afternoon in 1954, at the Iffley Road track in Oxford, he ran the 3:59.4 mile that changed track forever. "I suppose people will remember me for that," he said. "But my life has other strands."

Indeed. *The Four Minute Mile*, which Bannister wrote in six weeks as a 26-year-old medical student, remains one of the best sports books you'll ever read. As chairman of the British Sports Council, he instituted track's first drug-testing program, in 1973. Bannister retired last October after eight years as Master of Oxford's Pembroke College, but he hardly plans to be inactive: He will edit medical journals and revise the third edition of his *Disorders of the Autonomic Nervous System*. He's 65 now and walks with a cane after breaking his right ankle in a car accident in 1975. But he still gets exercise, by cycling.

"He's delightful," says Ryun simply, summing up the feelings of his fellow legends.

As of September 20, 1994. American outdoor records are recognized by USA Track and Field (USATF). WR=world record.

Men

Event	Mark	Record Holder	Date	Site
100 meters	9.85 WR	Leroy Burrell	7-6-94	Lausanne
200 meters	19.73	Mike Marsh	8-5-92	Barcelona
400 meters	43.29 WR	Butch Reynolds	8-17-88	Zurich
800 meters	1:42.60	Johnny Gray	8-28-85	Koblenz, Germany
1,000 meters	2:13.9	Rick Wohlhuter	7-30-74	Oslo
1,500 meters	3:29.77	Sydney Maree	8-25-85	Cologne
Mile	3:47.69	Steve Scott	7-7-82	Oslo
2,000 meters	4:52.44	Jim Spivey	9-15-87	Lausanne
3,000 meters	7:35.33	Bob Kennedy	7-18-94	Nice, France
Steeplechase	8:09.17	Henry Marsh	8-28-85	Koblenz, Germany
5,000 meters	13:01.15	Sydney Maree	7-27-85	Oslo
10,000 meters	27:20.56	Mark Nenow	9-5-86	Brussels
20,000 meters	58:25.0	Bill Rodgers	8-9-77	Boston
Hour	20,547 meters	Bill Rodgers	8-9-77	Boston
25,000 meters	1:14:11.8	Bill Rodgers	2-21-79	Saratoga, CA
30,000 meters	1:31:49	Bill Rodgers	2-21-79	Saratoga, CA
Marathon	2:10:04	Pat Petersen	4-23-89	London
110-meter hurdles	12.92	Roger Kingdom	8-16-89	Zurich
400-meter hurdles	46.78 WR	Kevin Young	8-6-92	Barcelona
20-kilometer walk	1:24:50	Tim Lewis	5-7-88	Seattle
30-kilometer walk	2:21:40	Herm Nelson	9-7-91	Bellevue, WA
50-kilometer walk	4:04:23.8	Herm Nelson	10-29-89	Seattle
4x100-meter relay	37.40 WR	United States (Mike Marsh, Leroy Burrell, Dennis Mitchell, Carl Lewis)	8-8-92	Barcelona
		United States (Jon Drummond, Andre Cason, Dennis Mitchell, Leroy Burrell)	8-22-93	Stuttgart, Germany
4x200-meter relay	1:18.68 WR	Santa Monica Track Club (Mike Marsh, Leroy Burrell, Floyd Heard, Carl Lewis)	4-17-94	Walnut, CA
4x400-meter relay	2:54.29 WR	United States (Andrew Valmon, Quincy Watts, Butch Reynolds, Michael Johnson)	8-22-93	Stuttgart, Germany
4x800-meter relay	7:06.5	Santa Monica Track Club (James Robinson, David Mack, Earl Jones, Johnny Gray)	4-26-86	Walnut, CA
4x1500-meter relay	14:46.3	National Team (Dan Aldredge, Andy Clifford, Todd Harbour, Tom Duits)	6-24-79	Bourges, France
High jump	7 ft 10½ in	Charles Austin	8-15-91	Zurich
Pole vault	19 ft 7 in	Scott Huffman	6-18-94	Knoxville
Long jump	29 ft 4½ in WR	Mike Powell	8-30-91	Tokyo
Triple jump	58 ft 11½ in WR	Willie Banks	6-16-85	Indianapolis
Shot put	75 ft 10¼ in WR	Randy Barnes	5-20-90	Westwood, CA
Discus throw	237 ft 4 in	Ben Plucknett	7-7-81	Stockholm
Hammer throw	270 ft 8 in	Lance Deal	6-17-94	Knoxville
Javelin throw	281 ft 2 in	Tom Pukstys	6-26-93	Kuortane, Finland
Decathlon	8891 pts WR	Dan O'Brien	9-4/5-92	Talence, France

Women

Event	Mark	Record Holder	Date	Site
100 meters	10.49 WR	Florence Griffith Joyner	7-16-88	Indianapolis
200 meters	21.34 WR	Florence Griffith Joyner	9-29-88	Seoul
400 meters	48.83	Valerie Brisco-Hooks	8-6-84	Los Angeles
800 meters	1:56.90	Mary Slaney	8-16-85	Bern, Switzerland
1,500 meters	3:57.12	Mary Slaney	7-26-83	Stockholm
Mile	4:16.71	Mary Slaney	8-21-85	Zurich
2,000 meters	5:32.7	Mary Slaney	8-3-84	Eugene, Ore.
3,000 meters	8:25.83	Mary Slaney	9-7-85	Rome
5,000 meters	14:56.07	Annette Peters	8-27-93	Berlin
10,000 meters	31:19.89	Lynn Jennings	8-7-92	Barcelona
Marathon	2:21:21	Joan Samuelson	10-20-85	Chicago
100-meter hurdles	12.46	Gail Devers	8-20-93	Stuttgart, Germany
400-meter hurdles	52.79	Sandra Farmer-Patrick	8-19-93	Stuttgart, Germany
5,000 meter walk	21:28.17	Teresa Vaill	4-24-93	Philadelphia
10,000 meter walk	44:41.9	Michelle Rohl	7-26-94	Moscow
10-kilometer walk road	44:42	Debbi Lawrence	5-16-92	Kenosha, Wisconsin
4x100-meter relay	41.49	National Team (Michelle Finn, Gwen Torrence, Wenda Vereen, Gail Devers)	8-22-93	Stuttgart, Germany
4x200-meter relay	1:32.57	Louisiana State (Tananjalyn Stanley, Sylvia Brydson, Esther Jones, Dawn Sowell)	4-28-89	Des Moines
4x400-meter relay	3:15.51	Olympic Team (Denean Howard, Diane Dixon, Valerie Brisco, Florence Griffith Joyner)	10-1-88	Seoul
4x800-meter relay	8:17.09	Athletics West (Sue Addison, Lee Arbogast, Mary Decker, Chris Mullen)	4-24-83	Walnut, Calif.
High jump	6 ft 8 in	Louise Ritter	7-8-88	Austin
		Louise Ritter	9-30-88	Seoul
Long jump	24 ft 7 in	Jackie Joyner-Kersee	5-22-94	New York City
			7-31-94	Sestriere, Italy
Triple jump	46 ft 8¼ in	Sheila Hudson	6-20-92	New Orleans
			6-16-94	Knoxville
Shot put	66 ft 2½ in	Ramona Pagel	6-25-88	San Diego
Discus throw	216 ft 10 in	Carol Cady	5-31-86	San Jose
Javelin throw	227 ft 5 in	Kate Schmidt	9-10-77	Fürth, West Germany
Heptathlon	7291 pts WR	Jackie Joyner-Kersee	9-23/24-88	Seoul

World and American Indoor Records

Men

As of September 20, 1994. American indoor records are recognized by USA Track and Field. World Indoor records are recognized by the International Amateur Athletics Federation (IAAF).

Event	Mark	Record Holder	Date	Site
50 meters	5.61	Manfred Kokot, East Germany (W)	2-4-73	Berlin
	5.61	James Sanford (W, A)	2-20-81	San Diego
55 meters*	6.00	Lee McRae (A)	3-14-86	Oklahoma City
60 meters	6.41	Andre Cason (W, A)	2-14-92	Madrid
200 meters	20.36	Bruno Marie-Rose, France (W)	2-22-72	Liévin, France
	20.55	Michael Johnson (A)	1-26-91	Liévin, France
400 meters	45.02	Danny Everett (W, A)	2-2-92	Stuttgart
800 meters	1:44.84	Paul Ereng, Kenya (W)	3-4-89	Budapest
	1:45.00	Johnny Gray (A)	3-8-92	Sindelfingen, Germany
1,000 meters	2:15.26	Noureddine Morceli, Algeria (W)	2-22-92	Birmingham, England
	2:18.19	Ocky Clark (A)	2-12-89	Stuttgart
1,500 meters	3:34.16	Noureddine Morceli, Algeria (W)	2-28-91	Seville
	3:38.12	Jeff Atkinson (A)	3-5-89	Budapest
Mile	3:49.78	Eamonn Coughlan, Ireland (W)	2-27-83	East Rutherford, NJ
	3:51.8	Steve Scott (A)	2-20-81	San Diego

Men (Cont.)

Event	Mark	Record Holder	Date	Site
3,000 meters	7:37.31	Moses Kiptanui, Kenya (W)	2-20-92	Seville
	7:39.94	Steve Scott (A)	2-10-89	East Rutherford, NJ
5,000 meters	13:20.4	Suleiman Nyambui, Tanzania (W)	2-6-81	New York City
	13:20.55	Doug Padilla (A)	2-12-82	Rosemont, Illinois
50-meter hurdles	6.25	Mark McKoy, Canada (W)	3-3-86	Kobe, Japan
	6.35	Greg Foster (A)	1-27-85	Rosemont, Illinois
	6.35	Greg Foster (A)	1-31-87	Ottawa, Ontario
55-meter hurdles*	6.82	Renaldo Nehemiah (A)	1-30-82	Dallas
60-meter hurdles	7.30	Colin Jackson, Great Britain (W)	3-6-94	Sindelfingen, Germany
	7.36	Greg Foster (A)	1-16-87	Los Angeles
5,000-meter walk	18:15.25	Grigori Kornev, CIS	2-7-92	Karlsruhe, Germany
4x200-meter relay	1:22.11	Great Britain (W) (Linford Christie, Darren Braithwaite, Ade Mafe, John Regis)	3-3-91	Glasgow
	1:22.71	National Team (Thomas Jefferson, Raymond Pierre, Antonio McKay, Kevin Little)	3-3-91	Glasgow
4x400-meter relay	3:03.05	Germany (W) (Rico Lieder, Jens Carlowitz, Klaus Just, Thomas Schönlebe)	3-10-91	Seville
	3:03.24	National Team (A) (Raymond Pierre, Chip Jenkins, Andrew Valmon, Antonio McKay)	3-10-91	Seville
4x800-meter relay	7:17.8	Soviet Union (W) (Valeriy Taratynov, Stanislav Meshcherskikh, Aleksey Taranov, Viktor Semyashkin)	3-14-71	Sofia
	7:18.23	University of Florida (A) (Dedric Jones, Lewis Lacy, Stephen Adderly, Scott Peters)	3-14-92	Sindelfingen, Germany
High jump	7 ft 11½ in	Javier Sotomayor, Cuba (W)	3-4-89	Budapest
	7 ft 10½ in	Hollis Conway (A)	3-10-91	Seville
Pole vault	20 ft 2 in	Sergei Bubka, Ukraine (W)	2-21-93	Donetsk, Ukraine
	19 ft 3¾ in	Billy Olsen (A)	1-25-86	Albuquerque
Long jump	28 ft 10½ in	Carl Lewis (W, A)	1-27-84	New York City
Triple jump	58 ft 3¾ in	Leonid Voloshin (W)	2-6-94	Grenoble, France
Shot put	74 ft 4¼ in	Randy Barnes (W, A)	1-20-89	Los Angeles
Weight Throw*	81 ft 6 in	Lance Deal (A)	2-26-93	Princeton, N.J.
Pentathlon	4440 pts	Christian Plaziat, France (W)	2-25-90	Toronto
	4399 pts	Bruce Reid (A)	2-25-89	Baton Rouge
Heptathlon	6476 pts	Dan O'Brien (W, A)	3-13/14-93	Toronto

*No recognized world record

Amazing Ana

In the course of her career, Cuban middle distance star Ana Fidelia Quirot has won an Olympic bronze medal and four Pan-Am Games gold medals and run the third-fastest women's 800 meters in history, 1:54.44. Yet, those performances pale beside the 2:05.22 she ran on November 28, 1993, to place second in the 800 at the Central American and Caribbean Games in Ponce, Puerto Rico.

It was Quirot's first race since she suffered near-fatal burns when a stove exploded at her home in Havana in January of 1993. She was seven months pregnant at the time, and her child, born prematurely, died soon after. Despite her injuries Quirot resumed training within weeks of the accident, jogging the hospital stairs, all the while insisting she would be back.

She proved it in Ponce, completing a recovery that her doctor termed "incredible." Still, Quirot suggested she was not satisfied and is determined to compete in the 1995 Pan-Am Games and the 1996 Olympics. Who would bet against her?

Women

Event	Mark	Record Holder	Date	Site
50 meters	6.00	Merlene Ottey, Jamaica (W)	2-4-94	Moscow
	6.10	Gail Devers (A)	2-20-93	Los Angeles
55 meters*	6.56	Gwen Torrence (A)	3-14-87	Oklahoma City
60 meters	6.92	Irina Privalova, Russia (W)	2-11-93	Madrid
	6.95	Gail Devers (A)	3-12-93	Toronto
200 meters	21.87	Merlene Ottey, Jamaica (W)	2-13-93	Lievin, France
	22.74	Gwen Torrence (A)	3-5-94	Atlanta
400 meters	49.59	Jarmila Kratochvilová, Czech.	3-7-82	Milan
	50.64	Diane Dixon (A)	3-10-91	Seville
800 meters	1:56.40	Christine Wachtel, E Germany (W)	2-14-88	Vienna
	1:58.9	Mary Slaney (A)	2-22-80	San Diego
1,000 meters	2:34.67	Lilia Nurutdinova, CIS (W)	2-7-92	Moscow
	2:34.67	Lyubov Kremlyova, Russia (W)	2-13-93	Lievin, France
	2:37.60	Mary Slaney (A)	1-21-89	Portland
1,500 meters	4:00.27	Doina Melinte, Romania (W)	2-9-90	East Rutherford, NJ
	4:00.80	Mary Slaney (A)	2-8-80	New York City
Mile	4:17.14	Doina Melinte, Romania (W)	2-9-90	East Rutherford, NJ
	4:20.5	Mary Slaney (A)	2-19-82	San Diego
3,000 meters	8:33.82	Elly van Hulst, Netherlands (W)	3-4-89	Budapest
	8:40.45	Lynn Jennings (A)	2-23-90	New York City
5,000 meters	15:03.17	Liz McColgan, Scotland (W)	2-22-92	Birmingham, England
	15:22.64	Lynn Jennings (A)	1-7-90	Hanover, NH
50-meter hurdles	6.58	Cornelia Oschkenat, E Germany (W)	2-20-88	Berlin
	6.84	Kim McKenzie (A)	1-20-89	Ottaway
	6.84	Jackie Joyner-Kersee (A)	2-20-93	Los Angeles
55-meter hurdles*	7.37	Jackie Joyner-Kersee (A)	2-3-89	New York City
60-meter hurdles	7.69	Lyudmila Narozhilenko, Russia (W)	2-4-90	Chelyabinsk, Russia
	7.81	Jackie Joyner-Kersee (A)	2-5-89	Fairfax, VA
3,000 meter walk	11:44.00	Yelena Ivanova, CIS (W)	2-7-92	Moscow
	12:20.42	Debbi Lawrence (A)	3-12-93	Toronto
4x200-meter relay	1:32.55	SC Eintracht Hamm, W Gemany (W) (Helga Arendt, Silke-Beate Knoll, Mechthild Kluth, Gisela Kinzel)	2-20-88	Dortmund, W Germany
	1:34.97	National Team (A) (Wenda Vereen, Kim Graham, Angela Williams, Terri Dendy)	2-13-93	Birmingham, England
4x400-meter relay	3:27.22	Germany (W) (Sandra Seuser, Annett Hesselbarth, Katrin Schreiter, Grit Breuer)	3-10-91	Seville
	3:29.00	National Team (A) (Terri Dendy, Lillie Leatherwood, Jearl Miles, Diane Dixon)	3-10-91	Seville
4x800-meter relay	8:18.71	Russia (Natalya Zaytseva, Olga Kuvnetsova, Yelena Afanasyeva, Yekaterina Podkopayeva)	2-4-94	Moscow
High jump	6 ft 9½ in	Heike Henkel, Germany (W)	2-8-92	Karlsruhe, Germany
	6 ft 6¾ in	Coleen Sommer (A)	2-13-82	Ottawa
Long jump	24 ft 2¼ in	Heike Drechsler, E Germany (W)	2-14-88	Vienna
	23 ft 4¼ in	Jackie Joyner-Kersee (A)	3-5-94	Atlanta
Triple jump	48 ft 10¾ in	Inna Lasovskaya, Russia (W)	2-13-94	Liévin, France
	45 ft 9 in	Sheila Hudson (A)	3-10-90	Indianapolis
Shot put	73 ft 10 in	Helena Fibingerová, Czech. (W)	2-19-77	Jablonec, Czech.
	65 ft ¾ in	Ramona Pagel (A)	2-20-87	Inglewood, California
Weight Throw*	62 ft 10 in	Sonja Fitts (unatt)	2-28-92	Princeton, N.J.
Pentathlon	4991 pts	Irina Byelova, CIS (W)	2-14/15-92	Berlin
	4566 pts	Kym Carter (A)	3-12-93	Toronto

*No recognized world record

World Track and Field Championships

Historically, the Olympics have served as the outdoor world championships for track and field. In 1983 the International Amateur Athletic Federation (IAAF) instituted a separate World Championship meet, to be held every 4 years between the Olympics. The first was held in Helsinki in 1983, the second in Rome in 1987, the third in Tokyo in 1991. In 1993 the IAAF began to hold the meet on a biennial basis.

HELSINKI 1983

Men

TRACK EVENTS

Event	Winner	Time
100 meters	Carl Lewis, United States	10.07
200 meters	Calvin Smith, United States	20.14
400 meters	Bert Cameron, Jamaica	45.05
800 meters	Willi Wulbeck, West Germany	1:43.65
1,500 meters	Steve Cram, Great Britain	3:41.59
Steeplechase	Patriz Ilg, West Germany	8:15.06
5,000 meters	Eamonn Coghlan, Ireland	13:28.53
10,000 meters	Alberto Cova, Italy	28:01.04
Marathon	Rob de Castella, Australia	2:10:03
110-meter hurdles	Greg Foster, United States	13.42
400-meter hurdles	Edwin Moses, United States	47.50
20 kilometer walk	Ernesto Canto, Mexico	1:20:49
50 kilometer walk	Ronald Weigel, East Germany	3:43:08
4x100 meter relay	United States (Emmit King, Willie Gault, Calvin Smith, Carl Lewis)	37.86
4x400 meters	USSR (Sergei Lovachev, Alecksandr Troschilo, Nikolay Chernyetski, Viktor Markin)	3:00.79

FIELD EVENTS

Event	Winner	Mark
High jump	Gennadi Avdeyenko, USSR	7 ft 7¼ in
Pole vault	Sergei Bubka, USSR	18 ft 8¼ in
Long jump	Carl Lewis, United States	28 ft 3/4 in
Triple jump	Zdzislaw Hoffmann, Poland	57 ft 2 in
Shot put	Edward Sarul, Poland	70 ft 2¼ in
Discus throw	Imrich Bugar, Czechoslovakia	222 ft 2 in
Hammer throw	Sergei Litvinov, USSR	271 ft 3 in
Javelin throw	Detlef Michel, East Germany	293 ft 7 in

DECATHLON

Event	Winner	Pts
Decathlon	Daley Thompson, Great Britain	8666 pts.

Women

TRACK EVENTS

Event	Winner	Time
100 meters	Marlies Gohr, East Germany	10.97
200 meters	Marita Koch, East Germany	22.13
400 meters	Jarmila Kratochvilova, Czechoslovakia	47.99
800 meters	Jarmila Kratochvilova, Czechoslovakia	1:54.68
1,500 meters	Mary Slaney, United States	4:00.90
3,000 meters	Mary Slaney, United States	8:34.62
Marathon	Grete Waitz, Norway	2:28:09
100-meter hurdles	Bettine Jahn, East Germany	12.35
400-meter hurdles	Yekaterina Fesenko, USSR	54.14
4x100 meter relay	East Germany (Silke Gladisch, Marita Koch, Averswald, Marlies Gohr)	41.76
4x400 meter relay	East Germany (Kerstin Walther, Sabine Busch, Marita Koch, Dagmar Rubsam)	3:19.73

FIELD EVENTS

Event	Winner	Mark
High jump	Tamara Bykova, USSR	6 ft 7 in
Long jump	Heike Daute, East Germany	23 ft 10¼ in
Shot put	Helena Fibingerova, Czechoslovakia	69 ft ¾ in
Discus throw	Martina Opitz, East Germany	226 ft 2 in
Javelin throw	Tiina Lillak, Finland	232 ft 4 in

HEPTATHLON

Event	Winner	Pts
Heptathlon	Ramona Neubert, East Germany	6714

ROME 1987

Men

TRACK EVENTS

Event	Winner	Time
100 meters*	Carl Lewis, United States	9.93WR
200 meters	Calvin Smith, United States	20.16
400 meters	Thomas Schoenlebe, East Germany	44.33
800 meters	Billy Konchellah, Kenya	1:43.06
1,500 meters	Abdi Bile, Somalia	3:36.80
Steeplechase	Francesco Panetta, Italy	8:08.57
5,000 meters	Said Aouita, Morocco	13:26.44
10,000 meters	Paul Kipkoech, Kenya	27:38.63
Marathon	Douglas Wakiihuri, Kenya	2:11:48
110-meter hurdles	Greg Foster, United States	13.21
400-meter hurdles	Edwin Moses, United States	47.46
20 kilometer walk	Maurizio Damilano, Italy	1:20:45
50 kilometer walk	Hartwig Gauder, East Germany	3:40:53
4x100 meter relay	United States (Lee McRae, Lee McNeil, Harvey Glance, Carl Lewis)	37.90
4x400 meter relay	United States (Danny Everett, Rod Haley, Antonio McKay, Butch Reynolds)	2:57.29

FIELD EVENTS

Event	Winner	Mark
High jump	Patrik Sjoberg, Sweden	7 ft 9¾ in
Pole vault	Sergei Bubka, USSR	19 ft 2¼ in
Long jump	Carl Lewis, United States	28 ft 5¼ in
Triple jump	Khristo Markov, Bulgaria	58 ft 9½ in
Shot put	Werner Gunthor, Switzerland	72 ft 11¼ in
Discus throw	Juergen Schult, East Germany	225 ft 6 in
Hammer throw	Sergei Litvinov, USSR	272 ft 6 in
Javelin throw	Seppo Räty, Finland	274 ft 1 in

DECATHLON

Event	Winner	Pts
Decathlon	Torsten Voss, East Germany	8680

Women

TRACK EVENTS

Event	Winner	Time
100 meters	Silke Gladisch, East Germany	10.90
200 meters	Silke Gladisch, East Germany	21.74
400 meters	Olga Bryzgina, USSR	49.38
800 meters	Sigrun Wodars, East Germany	1:55.26
1,500 meters	Tatyana Samolenko, USSR	3:58.56
3,000 meters	Tatyana Samolenko, USSR	8:38.73
10,000 meters	Ingrid Kristiansen, Norway	31:05.85
Marathon	Rosa Mota, Portugal	2:25:17
100-meter hurdles	Ginka Zagorcheva, Bulgaria	12.34
400-meter hurdles	Sabine Busch, East Germany	53.62
10 kilometer walk	Irina Strakhova, USSR	44:12
4x100 meter relay	United States (Alice Brown, Diane Williams, Florence Griffith, Pam Marshall)	41.58
4x400 meter relay	East Germany (Dagmar Neubauer, Kirsten Emmelmann, Petra Müller, Sabine Busch)	3:18.63

FIELD EVENTS

Event	Winner	Mark
High jump	Stefka Kostadinova, Bulgaria	6 ft 10¼ in
Long jump	Jackie Joyner-Kersee, United States	24 ft 1¾ in
Shot put	Natalya Lisovskaya, USSR	69 ft 8¼ in
Discus throw	Martina Hellmann, East Germany	235 ft 0 in
Javelin throw	Fatima Whitbread, Great Britain	251 ft 5 in

HEPTATHLON

Event	Winner	Pts
Heptathlon	Jackie Joyner-Kersee, United States	7128

WR=World record.

*Ben Johnson, Canada, disqualified

TOKYO 1991

Men

TRACK EVENTS

Event	Winner	Time
100 meters	Carl Lewis, US	9.86 WR
200 meters	Michael Johnson, US	20.01
400 meters	Antonio Pettigrew, US	44.57
800 meters	Billy Konchellah, Kenya	1:43.99
1,500 meters	Noureddine Morceli, Algeria	3:32.84
Steeplechase	Moses Kiptanui, Kenya	8:12.59
5,000 meters	Yobes Ondieki, Kenya	13:14.45
10,000 meters	Moses Tanui, Kenya	27:38.74
Marathon	Hiromi Taniguchi, Japan	2:14:57
110-meter hurdles	Greg Foster, US	13.06
400-meter hurdles	Samuel Matete, Zambia	47.64
20-kilometer walk	Maurizio Damilano, Italy	1:19:37
50-kilometer walk	Aleksandr Potashov, USSR	3:53:09
4x100-meter relay	United States (Andre Cason, Leroy Burrell, Dennis Mitchell, Carl Lewis)	37.50 WR
4x400-meter relay	Great Britain (Roger Black, Derek Redmond, John Regis, Kriss Akabusi)	2:57.53

FIELD EVENTS

Event	Winner	Mark
High jump	Charles Austin, United States	7 ft 9¾ in
Pole vault	Sergei Bubka, USSR	19 ft 6¼ in
Long jump	Mike Powell, United States	29 ft 4 ½ in WR
Triple jump	Kenny Harrison, United States	58 ft 4 in
Shot put	Werner Gunthor, Switzerland	71 ft 1¼ in
Discus	Lars Riedel, Germany	217 ft 2 in
Hammer	Yuriy Sedykh, USSR	268 ft
Javelin	Kimmo Kinnunen, Finland	297 ft 11 in

DECATHLON

Event	Winner	Pts
Decathlon	Dan O'Brien, US	8812

Women

TRACK EVENTS

Event	Winner	Time
100 meters	Katrin Krabbe, Germany	10.99
200 meters	Katrin Krabbe, Germany	22.09
400 meters	Marie-Jose Perec, France	49.13
800 meters	Lilia Nurutdinova, USSR	1:57.50
1,500 meters	Hassiba Boulmerka, Algeria	4:02.21
3,000 meters	Tatyana Dorovskikh, USSR	8:35.82
10,000 meters	Liz McColgan, Great Britain	31:14.31
Marathon	Wanda Panfil, Poland	2:29:53
100-meter hurdles	Lyudmila Narozhilenko, USSR	12.59
400-meter hurdles	Tatyana Ledovskaya, USSR	53.11
10-kilometer walk	Alina Ivanova, USSR	42:57
4x100-meter relay	Jamaica (Dahlia Duhaney, Juliet Cuthbert, Beverley McDonald, Merlene Ottey)	41.94
4x400-meter relay	USSR (Tatyana Ledovskaya, Lyudmila Dzhigalova, Olga Nazarova, Olga Bryzgina)	3:18.43

FIELD EVENTS

Event	Winner	Mark
High jump	Heike Henkel, Germany	6 ft 8¾ in
Long jump	Jackie Joyner-Kersee, United States	24 ft ¼ in
Shot put	Zhihong Huang, China	68 ft 4¼ in
Discus	Tsvetanka Khristova, Bulgaria	233 ft
Javelin	Demei Xu, China	225 ft 8 in

HEPTATHLON

Event	Winner	Pts
Heptathlon	Sabine Braun, Germany	6672 pts

WR=World record.

Track & Field News Athlete of the Year

Each year (since 1959 for men and since 1974 for women) Track & Field News has chosen the outstanding athlete in the sport.

Men

Year	Athlete	Event
1959	Martin Lauer, West Germany	110-meter hurdles/Decathlon
1960	Rafer Johnson, United States	Decathlon
1961	Ralph Boston, United States	Long jump
1962	Peter Snell, New Zealand	800/1500 meters
1963	C. K. Yang, Taiwan	Decathlon/Pole vault
1964	Peter Snell, New Zealand	800/1500 meters
1965	Ron Clarke, Australia	5,000/10,000 meters
1966	Jim Ryun, United States	800/1500 meters
1967	Jim Ryun, United States	1500 meters
1968	Bob Beamon, United States	Long jump
1969	Bill Toomey, United States	Decathlon
1970	Randy Matson, United States	Shot put
1971	Rod Milburn, United States	110-meter hurdles
1972	Lasse Viren, Finland	5,000/10,000 meters
1973	Ben Jipcho, Kenya	1500/5000 meters/Steeplechase
1974	Rick Wohlhuter, United States	800/1500 meters
1975	John Walker, New Zealand	800/1500 meters
1976	Alberto Juantorena, Cuba	400/800 meters
1977	Alberto Juantorena, Cuba	400/800 meters
1978	Henry Rono, Kenya	5,000/10,000 meters/Steeplechase
1979	Sebastian Coe, Great Britain	800/1500 meters
1980	Edwin Moses, United States	400-meter hurdles
1981	Sebastian Coe, Great Britain	800/1500 meters
1982	Carl Lewis, United States	100/200 meters/Long jump
1983	Carl Lewis, United States	100/200 meters/Long jump
1984	Carl Lewis, United States	100/200 meters/Long jump
1985	Said Aouita, Morocco	1500/5000 meters
1986	Yuri Syedikh, USSR	Hammer throw
1987	Ben Johnson, Canada	100 meters
1988	Sergei Bubka, USSR	Pole vault
1989	Roger Kingdom, United States	110-meter hurdles
1990	Michael Johnson, United States	200/400 meters
1991	Sergei Bubka, CIS	Pole vault
1992	Kevin Young, United States	400-meter hurdles
1993	Noureddine Morceli	1500/3000/mile

Women

Year	Athlete	Event
1974	Irena Szewinska, Poland	100/200/400 meters
1975	Faina Melnik, USSR	Shot put/Discus
1976	Tatyana Kazankina, USSR	800/1500 meters
1977	Rosemarie Ackermann, East Germany	High jump
1978	Marita Koch, East Germany	100/200/400 meters
1979	Marita Koch, East Germany	100/200/400 meters
1980	Ilona Briesenick, East Germany	Shot put
1981	Evelyn Ashford, United States	100/200 meters
1982	Marita Koch, East Germany	100/200/400 meters
1983	Jarmila Kratochvilova, Czechoslovakia	200/400/800 meters
1984	Evelyn Ashford, United States	100 meters
1985	Marita Koch, East Germany	100/200/400 meters
1986	Jackie Joyner-Kersee, United States	Long jump/Heptathlon
1987	Jackie Joyner-Kersee, United States	100-meter hurdles/Long jump/Heptathlon
1988	Florence Griffith Joyner, United States	100/200 meters
1989	Ana Quirot, Cuba	400/800 meters
1990	Merlene Ottey, Jamaica	100/200 meters
1991	Heike Henkel, Germany	High jump
1992	Heike Drechsler, Germany	Long Jump
1993	Wang Junxia, China	1500/3000/10,000/marathon

MARATHON

World Record Progression

Men

Record Holder	Time	Date	Site
John Hayes, United States	2:55:18.4	7-24-08	Shepherd's Bush, London
Robert Fowler, United States	2:52:45.4	1-1-09	Yonkers, NY
James Clark, United States	2:46:52.6	2-12-09	New York City
Albert Raines, United States	2:46:04.6	5-8-09	New York City
Frederick Barrett, Great Britain	2:42:31	5-26-09	Shepherd's Bush, London
Harry Green, Great Britain	2:38:16.2	5-12-13	Shepherd's Bush, London
Alexis Ahlgren, Sweden	2:36:06.6	5-31-13	Shepherd's Bush, London
Johannes Kolehmainen, Finland	2:32:35.8	8-22-20	Antwerp, Belgium
Albert Michelsen, United States	2:29:01.8	10-12-25	Port Chester, NY
Fusashige Suzuki, Japan	2:27:49	3-31-35	Tokyo
Yasuo Ikenaka, Japan	2:26:44	4-3-35	Tokyo
Kitei Son, Japan	2:26:42	11-3-35	Tokyo
Yun Bok Suh, Korea	2:25:39	4-19-47	Boston
James Peters, Great Britain	2:20:42.2	6-14-52	Chiswick, England
James Peters, Great Britain	2:18:40.2	6-13-53	Chiswick, England
James Peters, Great Britain	2:18:34.8	10-4-53	Turku, Finland
James Peters, Great Britain	2:17:39.4	6-26-54	Chiswick, England
Sergei Popov, USSR	2:15:17	8-24-58	Stockholm
Abebe Bikila, Ethiopia	2:15:16.2	9-10-60	Rome
Toru Terasawa, Japan	2:15:15.8	2-17-63	Beppu, Japan
Leonard Edelen, United States	2:14:28	6-15-63	Chiswick, England
Basil Heatley, Great Britain	2:13:55	6-13-64	Chiswick, England
Abebe Bikila, Ethiopia	2:12:11.2	6-21-64	Tokyo
Morio Shigematsu, Japan	2:12:00	6-12-65	Chiswick, England
Derek Clayton, Australia	2:09:36.4	12-3-67	Fukuoka, Japan
Derek Clayton, Australia	2:08:33.6	5-30-69	Antwerp, Belgium
Rob de Castella, Australia	2:08:18	12-6-81	Fukuoka, Japan
Steve Jones, Great Britain	2:08:05	10-21-84	Chicago
Carlos Lopes, Portugal	2:07:12	4-20-85	Rotterdam, Netherlands
Belayneh Densimo, Ethiopia	2:06:50	4-17-88	Rotterdam, Netherlands

Women

Record Holder	Time	Date	Site
Dale Greig, Great Britain	3:27:45	5-23-64	Ryde, England
Mildred Simpson, New Zealand	3:19:33	7-21-64	Auckland, New Zealand
Maureen Wilton, Canada	3:15:22	5-6-67	Toronto
Anni Pede-Erdkamp, West Germany	3:07:26	9-16-67	Waldniel, West Germany
Caroline Walker, United States	3:02:53	2-28-70	Seaside, OR
Elizabeth Bonner, United States	3:01:42	5-9-71	Philadelphia
Adrienne Beames, Australia	2:46:30	8-31-71	Werribee, Australia
Chantal Langlace, France	2:46:24	10-27-74	Neuf Brisach, France
Jacqueline Hansen, United States	2:43:54.5	12-1-74	Culver City, CA
Liane Winter, West Germany	2:42:24	4-21-75	Boston
Christa Vahlensieck, West Germany	2:40:15.8	5-3-75	Dülmen, West Germany
Jacqueline Hansen, United States	2:38:19	10-12-75	Eugene, OR
Chantal Langlace, France	2:35:15.4	5-1-77	Oyarzun, France
Christa Vahlensieck, West Germany	2:34:47.5	9-10-77	West Berlin, West Germany
Grete Waitz, Norway	2:32:29.9	10-22-78	New York City
Grete Waitz, Norway	2:27:32.6	10-21-79	New York City
Grete Waitz, Norway	2:25:41.3	10-26-80	New York City
Grete Waitz, Norway	2:25:29	4-17-83	London
Joan Benoit Samuelson, United States	2:22:43	4-18-83	Boston
Ingrid Kristiansen, Norway	2:21:06	4-21-85	London

Boston Marathon

The Boston Marathon began in 1897 as a local Patriot's Day event. Run every year but 1918 since then, it has grown into one of the world's premier marathons.

Men

Year	Winner	Time	Year	Winner	Time
1897	John J. McDermott, United States	2:55:10	1946	Stylianos Kyriakides, Greece	2:29:27
1898	Ronald J. McDonald, United States	2:42:00	1947	Yun Bok Suh, Korea	2:25:39
1899	Lawrence J. Brignolia, United States	2:54:38	1948	Gerard Cote, Canada	2:31:02
1900	James J. Caffrey, Canada	2:39:44	1949	Karl Gosta Leandersson, Sweden	2:31:50
1901	James J. Caffrey, Canada	2:29:23	1950	Kee Yong Ham, Korea	2:32:39
1902	Sammy Mellor, United States	2:43:12	1951	Shigeki Tanaka, Japan	2:27:45
1903	John C. Lorden, United States	2:41:29	1952	Doroteo Flores, Guatemala	2:31:53
1904	Michael Spring, United States	2:38:04	1953	Keizo Yamada, Japan	2:18:51
1905	Fred Lorz, United States	2:38:25	1954	Veikko Karvonen, Finland	2:20:39
1906	Timothy Ford, United States	2:45:45	1955	Hideo Hamamura, Japan	2:18:22
1907	Tom Longboat, Canada	2:24:24	1956	Antti Viskari, Finland	2:14:14
1908	Thomas Morrissey, United States	2:25:43	1957	John J. Kelley, United States	2:20:05
1909	Henri Renaud, United States	2:53:36	1958	Franjo Mihalic, Yugoslavia	2:25:54
1910	Fred Cameron, Canada	2:28:52	1959	Eino Oksanen, Finland	2:22:42
1911	Clarence H. DeMar, United States	2:21:39	1960	Paavo Kotila, Finland	2:20:54
1912	Mike Ryan, United States	2:21:18	1961	Eino Oksanen, Finland	2:23:39
1913	Fritz Carlson, United States	2:25:14	1962	Eino Oksanen, Finland	2:23:48
1914	James Duffy, Canada	2:25:01	1963	Aurele Vandendriessche, Belgium	2:18:58
1915	Edouard Fabre, Canada	2:31:41	1964	Aurele Vandendriessche, Belgium	2:19:59
1916	Arthur Roth, United States	2:27:16	1965	Morio Shigematsu, Japan	2:16:33
1917	Bill Kennedy, United States	2:28:37	1966	Kenji Kimihara, Japan	2:17:11
1918	No race		1967	David McKenzie, New Zealand	2:15:45
1919	Carl Linder, United States	2:29:13	1968	Amby Burfoot, United States	2:22:17
1920	Peter Trivoulidas, Greece	2:29:31	1969	Yoshiaki Unetani, Japan	2:13:49
1921	Frank Zuna, United States	2:18:57	1970	Ron Hill, England	2:10:30
1922	Clarence H. DeMar, United States	2:18:10	1971	Alvaro Mejia, Colombia	2:18:45
1923	Clarence H. DeMar, United States	2:23:37	1972	Olavi Suomalainen, Finland	2:15:39
1924	Clarence H. DeMar, United States	2:29:40	1973	Jon Anderson, United States	2:16:03
1925	Chuck Mellor, United States	2:33:00	1974	Neil Cusack, Ireland	2:13:39
1926	John C. Miles, Canada	2:25:40	1975	Bill Rodgers, United States	2:09:55
1927	Clarence H. DeMar, United States	2:40:22	1976	Jack Fultz, United States	2:20:19
1928	Clarence H. DeMar, United States	2:37:07	1977	Jerome Drayton, Canada	2:14:46
1929	John C. Miles, Canada	2:33:08	1978	Bill Rodgers, United States	2:10:13
1930	Clarence H. DeMar, United States	2:34:48	1979	Bill Rodgers, United States	2:09:27
1931	James "Hinky" Henigan, United States	2:46:45	1980	Bill Rodgers, United States	2:12:11
1932	Paul de Bruyn, Germany	2:33:36	1981	Toshihiko Seko, Japan	2:09:26
1933	Leslie Pawson, United States	2:31:01	1982	Alberto Salazar, United States	2:08:52
1934	Dave Komonen, Canada	2:32:53	1983	Gregory A. Meyer, United States	2:09:00
1935	John A. Kelley, United States	2:32:07	1984	Geoff Smith, England	2:10:34
1936	Ellison M. "Tarzan" Brown, United States	2:33:40	1985	Geoff Smith, England	2:14:05
1937	Walter Young, Canada	2:33:20	1986	Rob de Castella, Australia	2:07:51
1938	Leslie Pawson, United States	2:35:34	1987	Toshihiko Seko, Japan	2:11:50
1939	Ellison M. "Tarzan" Brown, United States	2:28:51	1988	Ibrahim Hussein, Kenya	2:08:43
1940	Gerard Cote, Canada	2:28:28	1989	Abebe Mekonnen, Ethiopia	2:09:06
1941	Leslie Pawson, United States	2:30:38	1990	Gelindo Bordin, Italy	2:08:19
1942	Bernard Joseph Smith, United States	2:26:51	1991	Ibrahim Hussein, Kenya	2:11:06
1943	Gerard Cote, Canada	2:28:25	1992	Ibrahim Hussein, Kenya	2:08.14
1944	Gerard Cote, Canada	2:31:50	1993	Cosmas N'Deti, Kenya	2:09:33
1945	John A. Kelley, United States	2:30:40	1994	Cosmas N'Deti, Kenya	2:07:15

Women

Year	Winner	Time	Year	Winner	Time
1966	Roberta Gibb, United States	3:21:40*	1976	Kim Merritt, United States	2:47:10
1967	Roberta Gibb, United States	3:27:17*	1977	Miki Gorman, United States	2:48:33
1968	Roberta Gibb, United States	3:30:00*	1978	Gayle Barron, United States	2:44:52
1969	Sara Mae Berman, United States	3:22:46*	1979	Joan Benoit, United States	2:35:15
1970	Sara Mae Berman, United States	3:05:07*	1980	Jacqueline Gareau, Canada	2:34:28
1971	Sara Mae Berman, United States	3:08:30*	1981	Allison Roe, New Zealand	2:26:46
1972	Nina Kuscsik, United States	3:10:36	1982	Charlotte Teske, West Germany	2:29:33
1973	Jacqueline A. Hansen, United States	3:05:59	1983	Joan Benoit, United States	2:22:43
1974	Miki Gorman, United States	2:47:11	1984	Lorraine Moller, New Zealand	2:29:28
1975	Liane Winter, West Germany	2:42:24	1985	Lisa Larsen Weidenbach, United States	2:34:06

Women (Cont.)

Year	Winner	Time	Year	Winner	Time
1986	Ingrid Kristiansen, Norway	2:24:55	1991	Wanda Panfil, Poland	2:24:18
1987	Rosa Mota, Portugal	2:25:21	1992	Olga Markova, Russia	2:23:43
1988	Rosa Mota, Portugal	2:24:30	1993	Olga Markova, Russia	2:25:27
1989	Ingrid Kristiansen, Norway	2:24:33	1994	Uta Pippig, Germany	2:21:45
1990	Rosa Mota, Portugal	2:25:24	*Unofficial.		

Note: Over the years the Boston course has varied in length. The distances have been 24 miles, 1232 yards (1897-1923); 26 miles, 209 yards (1924-1926); 26 miles 385 yards (1927-1952); and 25 miles, 958 yards (1953-1956). Since 1957, the course has been certified to be the standard marathon distance of 26 miles, 385 yards.

New York City Marathon

From 1970 through 1975 the New York City Marathon was a small local race run in the city's Central Park. In 1976 it was moved to the streets of New York's 5 boroughs. It has since become one of the biggest and most prestigious marathons in the world.

Men

Year	Winner	Time	Year	Winner	Time
1970	Gary Muhrcke, United States	2:31:38	1982	Alberto Salazar, United States	2:09:29
1971	Norman Higgins, United States	2:22:54	1983	Rod Dixon, New Zealand	2:08:59
1972	Sheldon Karlin, United States	2:27:52	1984	Orlando Pizzolato, Italy	2:14:53
1973	Tom Fleming, United States	2:21:54	1985	Orlando Pizzolato, Italy	2:11:34
1974	Norbert Sander, United States	2:26:30	1986	Gianni Poli, Italy	2:11:06
1975	Tom Fleming, United States	2:19:27	1987	Ibrahim Hussein, Kenya	2:11:01
1976	Bill Rodgers, United States	2:10:10	1988	Steve Jones, Great Britain	2:08:20
1977	Bill Rodgers, United States	2:11:28	1989	Juma Ikangaa, Tanzania	2:08:01
1978	Bill Rodgers, United States	2:12:12	1990	Douglas Wakiihuri, Kenya	2:12:39
1979	Bill Rodgers, United States	2:11:42	1991	Salvador Garcia, Mexico	2:09:28
1980	Alberto Salazar, United States	2:09:41	1992	Willie Mtolo, South Africa	2:09:29
1981	Alberto Salazar, United States	2:08:13	1993	Andres Espinosa, Mexico	2:10:04

Women

Year	Winner	Time	Year	Winner	Time
1970	No finisher		1982	Grete Waitz, Norway	2:27:14
1971	Beth Bonner, United States	2:55:22	1983	Grete Waitz, Norway	2:27:00
1972	Nina Kuscsik, United States	3:08:41	1984	Grete Waitz, Norway	2:29:30
1973	Nina Kuscsik, United States	2:57:07	1985	Grete Waitz, Norway	2:28:34
1974	Katherine Switzer, United States	3:07:29	1986	Grete Waitz, Norway	2:28:06
1975	Kim Merritt, United States	2:46:14	1987	Priscilla Welch, Great Britain	2:30:17
1976	Miki Gorman, United States	2:39:11	1988	Grete Waitz, Norway	2:28:07
1977	Miki Gorman, United States	2:43:10	1989	Ingrid Kristiansen, Norway	2:25:30
1978	Grete Waitz, Norway	2:32:30	1990	Wanda Panfiil, Poland	2:30:45
1979	Grete Waitz, Norway	2:27:33	1991	Liz McColgan, Scotland	2:27:23
1980	Grete Waitz, Norway	2:25:41	1992	Lisa Ondieki, Australia	2:24:40
1981	Allison Roe, New Zealand	2:25:29	1993	Uta Pippig, Germany	2:26:24

CROSS COUNTRY

World Cross-Country Championships

Conducted by the International Amateur Athletic Federation (IAAF), this meet annually brings together the best runners in the world at every distance from the mile to the marathon to compete in the same cross-country race.

Men

Year	Winner	Winning Team	Year	Winner	Winning Team
1973	Pekka Paivarinta, Finland	Belgium	1977	Leon Schots, Belgium	Belgium
1974	Eric DeBeck, Belgium	Belgium	1978	John Treacy, Ireland	France
1975	Ian Stewart, Scotland	New Zealand	1979	John Treacy, Ireland	England
1976	Carlos Lopes, Portugal	England	1980	Craig Virgin, United States	England

Men (Cont.)

Year	Winner	Winning Team	Year	Winner	Winning Team
1981	Craig Virgin, United States	Ethiopia	1988	John Ngugi, Kenya	Kenya
1982	Mohammed Kedir, Ethiopia	Ethiopia	1989	John Ngugi, Kenya	Kenya
1983	Bekele Debele, Ethiopia	Ethiopia	1990	Khalid Skah, Morocco	Kenya
1984	Carlos Lopes, Portugal	Ethiopia	1991	Khalid Skah, Morocco	Kenya
1985	Carlos Lopes, Portugal	Ethiopia	1992	John Ngugi, Kenya	Kenya
1986	John Ngugi, Kenya	Kenya	1993	William Sigei, Kenya	Kenya
1987	John Ngugi, Kenya	Kenya	1994	William Sigei, Kenya	Kenya

Women

Year	Winner	Winning Team	Year	Winner	Winning Team
1973	Paola Cacchi, Italy	England	1984	Maricica Puica, Romania	United States
1974	Paola Cacchi, Italy	England	1985	Zola Budd, England	United States
1975	Julie Brown, United States	United States	1986	Zola Budd, England	England
1976	Carmen Valero, Spain	USSR	1987	Annette Sergent, France	United States
1977	Carmen Valero, Spain	USSR	1988	Ingrid Kristiansen, Norway	USSR
1978	Grete Waitz, Norway	Romania	1989	Annette Sergent, France	USSR
1979	Grete Waitz, Norway	United States	1990	Lynn Jennings, United States	USSR
1980	Grete Waitz, Norway	USSR	1991	Lynn Jennings, United States	Kenya
1981	Grete Waitz, Norway	USSR	1992	Lynn Jennings, United States	Kenya
1982	Maricica Puica, Romania	USSR	1993	Albertina Dias, Portugal	Kenya
1983	Grete Waitz, Norway	United States	1994	Helen Chepngeno, Kenya	Portugal

Notable Achievements

Longest Winning Streaks

MEN

Event	Name and Nationality	Streak	Years
100-meter dash	Bob Hayes, United States	49	1962-64
200-meter dash	Manfred Gemar, Germany	41	1956-60
400-meter run	Ardalion Ignatyev, USSR	29	1952-56
800-meter run	Mal Whitffield, United States	40	1951-54
1500-meter run	Josy Barthel, Luxembourg	17	1952
1500-meter run/mile	Steve Ovett, Great Britain	45	1977-80
Mile	Herb Elliott, Australia	35	1957-60
Steeplechase	Gaston Roelants, Belgium	45	1961-66
5000-meter run	Emil Zátopek, Czechoslovakia	48	1949-52
10,000-meter run	Emil Zátopek, Czechoslovakia	38	1948-54
Marathon	Frank Shorter, United States	6	1971-73
110-meter hurdles	Jack Davis, United States	44	1952-55
400-meter hurdles	Edwin Moses, United States	107	1977-87
High Jump	Ernie Shelton, United States	46	1953-55
Pole Vault	Bob Richards, United States	50	1950-52
Long Jump	Carl Lewis, United States	65	1981-91
Triple Jump	Adhemar da Silva, Brazil	60	1950-56
Shot Put	Parry O'Brien, United States	116	1952-56
Discus Throw	Ricky Bruch, Sweden	54	1972-73
Hammer Throw	Imre Nemeth, Hungary	73	1946-50
Javelin Throw	Janis Lusis, USSR	41	1967-70
Decathlon	Bob Mathias, United States	11	1948-56

WOMEN

Event	Name and Nationality	Streak	Years
100-meter dash	Merlene Ottey, Jamaica	56	1987-91
200-meter dash	Irena Szewinska, Poland	38	1973-75
400-meter run	Irena Szewinska, Poland	36	1973-78
800-meter run	Ana Fidelia Quirot, Cuba	36	1987-90
1500-meter run	Paula Ivan, Romania	15	1988-91
1500-meter run/mile	Paula Ivan, Romania	19	1988-90
3000-meter run	Mary Slaney, United States	10	1982-84
10,000-meter run	Ingrid Kristiansen, Norway	5	1985-87

Longest Winning Streaks (Cont.)

WOMEN (Cont.)

Event	Name and Nationality	Streak	Years
Marathon	Katrin Dörre, East Germany	10	1982-86
100-meter hurdles	Annelie Ernhardt, East Germany	44	1972-75
400-meter hurdles	Ann-Louise Skoglund, Sweden	18	1981-83
High Jump	Iolanda Balas, Romania	140	1956-67
Long Jump	Tatyana Shchelkanova, USSR	19	1964-66
Shot Put	Nadezhda Chizhova, USSR	57	1969-73
Discus Throw	Gisela Mauermeyer, Germany	65	1935-42
Javelin Throw	Ruth Fuchs, East Germany	30	1972-73
Multi	Heide Rosendahl, West Germany	15	1969-72

Most Consecutive Years Ranked No. 1 in the World

MEN

No.	Name and Nationality	Event	Years
9	Victor Saneyev, USSR	Triple Jump	1968-76
8	Bob Richards, United States	Pole Vault	1949-56
8	Ralph Boston, United States	Long Jump	1960-67
7	Emil Zátopek (Czech)	10,000-meter run	1948-54

WOMEN

No.	Name and Nationality	Event	Years
9	Iolanda Balas, Romania	High Jump	1958-66
8	Ruth Fuchs, East Germany	Javelin Throw	1972-79
7	Faina Melnick, USSR	Discus Throw	1971-77

Major Barrier Breakers

MEN

Event	Mark	Name and Nationality	Date	Site
sub 10-second 100-meter dash	9.95	Jim Hines, United States	Oct. 14, 1968	Mexico City
sub 20-second 200-meter dash	19.83	Tommie Smith, United States	Oct. 16, 1968	Mexico City
sub 45-second 400-meter run	44.9	Otis Davis, United States	Sept. 6, 1960	Rome.
sub 1:45 800-meter run	1:44.3	Peter Snell, New Zealand	Feb. 3, 1962	Christchurch, New Zealand
sub four minute mile	3:59.4	Roger Bannister, Great Britain	May 6, 1954	Oxford
sub 3:50 mile	3:49.4	John Walker, New Zealand	Aug. 12, 1975	Goteborg
sub 13-minute 5,000-meter run	12:58.39	Said Aouita, Morocco	July 22, 1986	Rome
sub 27:00 10,000-meter run	26:58.38	Yobes Ondieki, Kenya	July 10, 1993	Oslo
sub 13-second 110-meter hurdles	12.93	Renaldo Nehemiah, United States	Aug. 19, 1981	Zurich
sub 50-second 400-meter hurdles	49.5	Glenn Davis, United States	June 29, 1956	Los Angeles
7' high jump	7' ⅝"	Charles Dumas, United States	June 29, 1956	Los Angeles
8' high jump	8'	Javier Sotomayor, Cuba	July 29, 1989	San Juan
20' pole vault	20'	Sergei Bubka, USSR	March 15, 1991	San Sebastian, Spain
70' shot put	70' 7¼"	Randy Matson, United States	May 5, 1965	College Station, Texas
200' discus throw	200' 5"	Al Oerter, United States	May 18, 1962	Los Angeles
300' (new) javelin	300' 1"	Steve Backley, Great Britain	Jan. 25, 1992	Auckland, New Zealand

WOMEN

Event	Mark	Name and Nationality	Date	Site
sub 11-second 100-meter dash	10.88	Marlies Oelsner, East Germany	July 1, 1977	Dresden
sub 22-second 200-meter dash	21.71	Marita Koch, East Germany	June 10, 1979	Karl Marx Stadt
sub 50-second 400-meter run	49.9	Irena Szewinska, Poland	June 22, 1974	Warsaw
sub 2:00 800-meter run	1:59.1	Shin Geum Dan, North Korea	Nov. 12, 1963	Djakarta
sub 4:00 1500-meter run	3:56.0	Tatyana Kazankina, USSR	June 28, 1976	Podolsk, USSR

Major Barrier Breakers *(Cont.)*
WOMEN *(Cont.)*

Event	Mark	Name and Nationality	Date	Site
sub 4:20 mile	4:17.55	Mary Decker, United States	Feb. 16, 1980	Houston
sub 15:00 5,000-meter run	14:58.89	Ingrid Kristiansen, Norway	June 28, 1984	Oslo
sub 30:00 10,000-meter run	29:31.78	Wang Junxia, China	Sept. 8, 1993	Beijing
sub 2:30 marathon	2:27:33	Grete Waitz, Norway	Oct. 21, 1979	New York City
sub 13-second 100-meter hurdles	12.9	Karin Balzer, East Germany	Sept. 5, 1969	Berlin
6' high jump	6'	Iolanda Balas, Romania	Oct. 18, 1958	Budapest
70' shot put	70' 4½"	Nadyezhda Chizhova, USSR	Sept. 29, 1973	Varna, Bulgaria
200' discus throw	201'	Liesel Westermann, West Germany	Nov. 5, 1967	Sao Paulo
200' javelin throw	201' 4"	Elvira Ozolina, USSR	Aug. 27, 1964	Kiev
first 7,000-point heptathlon	7,148	Jackie Joyner-Kersee, United States	July 6-7, 1986	Moscow

Olympic Accomplishments

Oldest Olympic gold medalist—Patrick (Babe) McDonald, United States, 42 years, 26 days, 56-pound weight throw, 1920

Oldest Olympic medalist—Tebbs Lloyd Johnson, Great Britain, 48 years, 115 days, 1948 (bronze), 50K walk

Youngest Olympic gold medalist—Barbara Jones, United States, 15 years 123 days, 1952, 4 x 100 relay

Youngest gold medalist in individual event—Ulrike Meyfarth, West Germany, 16 years, 123 days, 1972, high jump

World Record Accomplishments*

Most world records equaled or set in a day—6, Jesse Owens, United States, 5/25/35, (9.4 100-yard dash; 26' 8¼" long jump; 20.3 200-meter dash and 220-yard dash; and 22.6 220-yard hurdles and 200-meter hurdles

Most records in a year—10, Gunder Hägg, Sweden, 1941-42, 1500 to 5,000 meters

Most records in a career—35, Sergei Bubka, 1983-94, pole vault indoors and out

Longest span of record setting—11 years, 20 days, Irena Szewinska, Poland, 1965-76, 200-meter dash

Youngest person to set a set world record—Carolina Gisolf, Holland, 15 years, 5 days, 1928, high jump , 5' 3⅜"

Youngest man to set a world record—John Thomas, United States, 17 years, 355 days, 1959, high jump, 7' 1¼"

Oldest person to set world record—Carlos Lopes, Portugal, 38 years, 59 days, marathon, 2:07:12

Greatest percentage improvement—6.59, Bob Beamon, United States, 1968, long jump

Longest lasting record—long jump, 26' 8¼", Jesse Owens, United States, 25 years, 79 days (1935-60)

Highest clearance over head, men—23¼", Franklin Jacobs United States (5' 8"), 1978

Highest over head by a woman—12¾", Yolanda Henry, United States (5' 6"), 1990

*Marks sanctioned by the IAAF

Four for the Ages

On February 20, 1994, at the Massachusetts state high school indoor meet, as 3,000 high school athletes screamed themselves hoarse, Eamonn Coghlan ran his 41-year-old legs into track history. In a specially organized masters mile on Harvard's speedy 220-yard banked-board oval track, Coghlan followed his rabbit, half-miler Stanley Redwine, through the half in 1:59.76 and the three quarters in 2:59.21. Redwine then dropped out, leaving Coghlan to run a deafening gauntlet. He stopped the clock in 3:58.15, making him the first runner 40 or older to break the four-minute barrier. Fittingly, Coghlan's feat came 40 years after Roger Bannister first broke four minutes.

The preparation for his landmark effort took a heavy toll on Coghlan, 11 years removed from his still-standing world indoor record of 3:49.78. In early December he flew to Gainesville, Fla., to train while his wife, Yvonne, and their four children stayed home in Dublin. "I missed by son's

rugby season," Coghlan said wistfully earlier this winter. "I missed his soccer season." When his chronically sore left leg began to hurt, Coghlan stepped up his physical-therapy regimen to two hours a day, six days a week and regained some of his speed.

Coghlan had originally planned to use the Harvard race as a tune-up, with his big effort to follow at the USA/Mobil Indoor Championships in Atlanta in early March. But he was finally persuaded not to waste an opportunity on a track as famously fast as Harvard's. "That rekindled my gut feeling to go for it every time," said Coghlan.

It's hard to say whether other 40-year-olds will soon match or better Coghlan's standard, much as the four-minute floodgates opened after Bannister's feat. After all, the financial incentives—Coghlan got a reported $100,000 for his mile—were only for the first 40-year-old to run under four minutes. But *this* 3:58.15 will always be a wondrous mark to behold.

Swimming

Le Jingyi and the Chinese woman's team destroy the competition at the Worlds— but are they for real?

Sports Illustrated

SPLASH SMASH

BOB MARTIN

A Tidal Wave Of Doubt

The Chinese women lowered records and raised suspicions
at the world championships in Rome | by LEIGH MONTVILLE

THE SENSE OF DOOM COULD NOT BE avoided. What to do next? What to say? It was the next-to-last day of the 1994 world swimming championships at the Foro Italico pool in Rome in the second week of September, and an entire sport was in competitive trouble.

"Someone asked me if I think we have a chance in the 400-meter medley relay tonight," Richard Quick, coach of the United States' women's team, said. "I said, 'Well, a Chinese swimmer set a world record in the 100 freestyle. In the backstroke and the butterfly, Chinese swimmers set meet records. In the breaststroke a Chinese swimmer was second. Do we have a chance? Maybe if someone plants a bomb in the Chinese lane, we have a chance, but otherwise ....' "

China. China. China. In a performance reminiscent of East Germany's dominance of women's events through the '70s and '80s, another totalitarian country had unveiled a staggering number of world-class swimmers to leave everyone else in their wake. Their medley relay victory—no bomb appeared in the pool that night—started with a world-record split of 1:00.16 in the backstroke by He Cihong and ended with a world-record 53.81 freestyle split by Le Jingyi for an overall, eye-widening 4:01.67 world record that was an exclamation point to all that they did.

How good were they? They broke five world records in the meet and won 12 of 16 women's events. Le, 19, was the meet's outstanding performer, with four gold medals and world records in both the 50- and the 100-meter freestyles. The most amazing fact was that none of the five Chinese swimmers, nicknamed the Five Golden Flowers, who had won four gold medals and five silver in the 1992 Olympics in Barcelona, had any part in this. These were different swimmers, new swimmers.

It all seemed too good to be ... well, true. Charges of drug use, unsubstantiated by any hard evidence, were everywhere. "The sport is under a cloud," Quick said. "It gets so you can't believe what you see in front of you. Isn't that a shame? That you're immediately

BOB MARTIN

suspicious of anything good that happens? Something has to be done to bring in competent drug testing. If that doesn't happen, we're going to go off in a direction that I, frankly, don't want to be a part of."

Detractors pointed out the similarity in the Chinese performance to the East German success: a large number of female swimmers suddenly performing amazing feats without any accompanying rise in performance by male swimmers. The East Germans, after the collapse of the Berlin Wall, admitted drug use and mostly faded from the scene. Weren't the Chinese taking their place? A position statement from 18 countries asked the sport's governing body, FINA, to use "financial resources, manpower and technology" to resolve "the potentially devastating problem" of "the extensive use of performance-enhancing drugs."

Chinese coach Chen Yunpeng denied all doping charges and invited the West to visit China and see what his swimmers were doing in training. Assistant coach Zhou Ming said China had merged training theories of the West with the theories of the old Eastern bloc to create new approaches to swimming. Both coaches mentioned the phrase "sour grapes" about the drug controversy, but it promised only to grow larger as the 1996 Olympics in Atlanta neared.

"For 20 years our entire sport kept quiet about the Germans because we couldn't

Lu Bin, who won the 200-meter individual medley, was just one of many Chinese stars.

prove anything," Quick said. "For 20 years our kids were cheated out of things they should have won, and we just sat still. Well, we're not sitting still now."

The men's competition, where no Chinese swimmer even qualified for a final, was much quieter. The U.S. standout was 19-year-old Tom Dolan of Arlington, Va., who overcame a severe asthma condition to set a world record in the 400-meter individual medley at 4:12.30. Distance swimmer Kieren Perkins of Australia set a world record of 3:43.80 in the 400-meter freestyle and also captured the 1,500, where earlier in the summer he had broken his own world record by swimming 14:41.66 at the Commonwealth Games. Alexander Popov, of Russia, taking control of the events Matt Biondi once owned, captured both the 50 and the 100 free in Rome, having broken Biondi's world record in the 100 in June. Jani Sievinen of Finland set a world record of 1:58.16 in the 200 IM.

"This meet was a good test for us," U.S. men's coach Jon Urbanchek said. "It gave us a good idea of where we are and what we have to do to get ready for Atlanta. We have some young swimmers, and this was a good experience for them. I'm encouraged."

The U.S. women, alas, had much different thoughts.

FOR THE RECORD·1993-1994

World Swimming and Diving Championships

Rome; September 1–11

Men

50-METER FREESTYLE

1. ....Alexander Popov, Russia — 22.17
2. ....Gary Hall, United States — 22.44
3. ....Raimundas Mazuolis, Lithuania — 22.52

100-METER FREESTYLE

1. ....Alexander Popov, Russia — 49.12
2. ....Gary Hall, United States — 49.41
3. ....Gustavo Borges, Brazil — 49.52

200-METER FREESTYLE

1. ....Antti Kasvio, Finland — 1:47.32
2. ....Anders Holmertz, Sweden — 1:48.24
3. ....Danyon Loader, New Zealand — 1:48.24

400-METER FREESTYLE

1. ....Kieran Perkins, Australia — 3:43.80*
2. ....Antti Kasvio, Finland — 3:48.55
3. ....Danyon Loader, New Zealand — 3:48.62

1500-METER FREESTYLE

1. ....Kieran Perkins, Australia — 14:50.52
2. ....Daniel Kowalski, Australia — 14:53.42
3. ....Steffen Zesner, Germany — 15:09.20

100-METER BACKSTROKE

1. ....Martin Lopez Zubero, Spain — 55.17
2. ....Jeff Rouse, United States — 55.51
3. ....Tamas Deutsch, Germany — 55.69

200-METER BACKSTROKE

1. ....Vladimir Selkov, Russia — 1:57.42‡
2. ....Martin Lopez-Zubero — 1:58.75
3. ....Royce Sharp, United States — 1:58.86

100-METER BREASTSTROKE

1. ....Norbert Rozsa, Hungary — 1:01.24‡
2. ....Karoly Guttler, Hungary — 1:01.44
3. ....Frederic Deburghgraeve, Belgium — 1:01.79

200-METER BREASTSTROKE

1. ....Norbert Rozsa, Hungary — 2:12.81
2. ....Eric Wunderlich, United States — 2:12.87
3. ....Karoly Guttler, Hungary — 2:14.12

100-METER BUTTERFLY

1. ....Rafal Szukala, Poland — 53.51
2. ....Lars Frolander, Sweden — 53.65
3. ....Denis Pankratov, Russia — 53.68

200-METER BUTTERFLY

1. ....Denis Pankratov, Russia — 1:56.54
2. ....Danyon Loader, New Zealand — 1:57.99
3. ....Chris-Carol Bremer, Germany — 1:58.11

200-METER INDIVIDUAL MEDLEY

1. ....Jani Sievin, Finland — 1:58.16*
2. ....Greg Burgess, United States — 2:00.86
3. ....Attila Czena, Hungary — 2:01.84

400-METER INDIVIDUAL MEDLEY

1. ....Tom Dolan, United States — 4:12.30*
2. ....Jani Sievinen, Finland — 4:13.29
3. ....Eric Namesnik, United States — 4:15.69

400-METER MEDLEY RELAY

1. ....United States (Jeff Rouse, — 3:37.74
Eric Wunderlich,
Mark Henderson, Gary Hall)
2. ....Russia — 3:38.28
3. ....Hungary — 3:39.47

400-METER FREESTYLE RELAY

1. ....United States (Jon Olsen, — 3:16.90‡
Josh Davis, Ugur Taner,
Gary Hall)
2. ....Russia — 3:18.12
3. ....Brazil — 3:19.35

800-METER FREESTYLE RELAY

1. ....Sweden (Christer Waller, — 7:17.34
Tommy Werner, Lars Frolander,
Anders Holmertz)
2. ....Russia — 7:18.13
3. ....Germany — 7:19.10

ONE-METER SPRINGBOARD

1. ....Evan Stewart, Zimbabwe — 382.14
2. ....Lan Wei, China — 375.96
3. ....Brian Earley, United States — 361.59

THREE-METER SPRINGBOARD

1. ....Yu Zhuocheng, China — 655.44
2. ....Dmitry Sautin, Russia — 646.59
3. ....Wang Tianling, China — 638.22

10-METER PLATFORM

1. ....Dmitry Sautin, Russia — 634.71
2. ....Sun Shuwei, China — 630.03
3. ....Vladimir Timoshinin, Russia — 607.32

WATER POLO

1. ....Italy
2. ....Spain
3. ....Russia

Note: Italy d. Spain 10-6; Russia d. Croatia 14-13.

*World Record; ‡Meet Record.

Women

50-METER FREESTYLE

1. ....Le Jingyi, China — 24.51*
2. ....Natalia Mesheryakova, Russia — 25.10
3. ....Amy van Dyken, United States — 25.18

100-METER FREESTYLE

1. ....Le Jingyi, China — 54.01*
2. ....Lu Bin, China — 54.15
3. ....Franziska Van Almsick, Germany — 54.77

200-METER FREESTYLE

1. ....Franziska Van Almsick, Germany — 1:56.78*
2. ....Lu Bin, China — 1:56.89
3. ....Claudia Poll, Costa Rica — 1:57.61

400-METER FREESTYLE

1. ....Yang Aihua, China — 4:09.64
2. ....Christina Teuscher, United States — 4:10.21
3. ....Claudia Poll, Costa Rica — 4:10.61

800-METER FREESTYLE

1. ....Janet Evans, United States — 8:29.85
2. ....Hayley Lewis, Australia — 8:29.94
3. ....Brooke Bennett, United States — 8:31.30

100-METER BACKSTROKE

1. ....He Cihong, China — 1:00.57‡
2. ....Nina Zhivanevskaya, Russia — 1:00.83
3. ....Barbara Bedford, United States — 1:01.32

200-METER BACKSTROKE

1. ....He Cihong, China — 2:07.40‡
2. ....Krisztina Egerszegi, Hungary — 2:09.10
3. ....Lorenza Vigarani, Italy — 2:10.92

100-METER BREASTSTROKE

1. ....Samantha Riley, Australia — 1:07.69*
2. ....Dai Guohong, China — 1:09.26
3. ....Yuan Yuan, China — 1:10.19

200-METER BREASTSTROKE

1. ....Samantha Riley, Australia — 2:26.87‡
2. ....Yuan Yuan, China — 2:27.38
3. ....Brigitte Becue, Belgium — 2:28.85

100-METER BUTTERFLY

1. ....Liu Limin, China — 58.98‡
2. ....Qu Yun, China — 59.69
3. ....Susan O'Neill, Australia — 1:00.11

200-METER BUTTERFLY

1. ....Liu Limin, China — 2:07.25‡
2. ....Qu Yun, China — 2:07.42
3. ....Susan O'Neill, Australia — 2:09.54

*World Record; ‡Meet Record.

200-METER INDIVIDUAL MEDLEY

1. ....Lu Bin, China — 2:12.34
2. ....Allison Wagner, United States — 2:14.40
3. ....Elli Overton, Australia — 2:15.26

400-METER INDIVIDUAL MEDLEY

1. ....Dai Guohong, China — 4:39.14
2. ....Allison Wagner, United States — 4:39.98
3. ....Kristine Quance, United States — 4:42.21

400-METER MEDLEY RELAY

1. ....China (He Cihong, Dai Guohong, Liu Limin, Le Jingyi) — 4:01.67*
2. ....United States — 4:06.53
3. ....Russia — 4:06.70

400-METER FREESTYLE RELAY

1. ....China (Le Jingyi, Shan Ying, Le Ying, Lu Bin) — 3:37.91*
2. ....United States — 3:39.46
3. ....Germany — 3:42.94

800-METER FREESTYLE RELAY

1. ....China (Le Ying, Yang Alhua, Zhou Guabin, Lu Bin) — 7:57.96‡
2. ....Germany — 8:01.37
3. ....United States — 8:03.16

ONE-METER SPRINGBOARD

1. ....Chen Lixia, China — 279.30
2. ....Tan Shuping, China — 276.00
3. ....Annie Pelletier, Canada — 273.84

THREE-METER SPRINGBOARD

1. ....Tan Shuping, China — 548.49
2. ....Vera Ilyina, Russia — 498.60
3. ....Claudia Bockner, Germany — 480.15

TEN-METER PLATFORM

1. ....Fu Minxia, China — 434.04
2. ....,Chi Bin, China — 420.24
3. ....Maria Jose Alcala, Mexico — 396.48

WATER POLO

1. ....Hungary
2. ....Netherlands
3. ....Italy

Note: Hungary d. the Netherlands 7–5; Italy d. the U.S. 14–9.

1994 Major Competitions

Men   Women

Men	Women
50 free ....Mark Foster, Great Britain, 21.84	Le Jingyi, China, 24.23*
100 free.......Fernando De Quariroz, Brazil, 48.38	Le Jingyi, China, 53.01*
200 free......Antti Kasvio, Finland, 1:45.21	Karen Pickering, Great Britain, 1:56.25
400 free........Daniel Kowalski, Australia, 3:42.95	Janet Evans, United States, 4:05.64
800 free	Janet Evans, United States, 8:22.43
1500 free......Daniel Kowalski, Australia, 14:42.04	
100 back......Tripp Schwenk, United States, 52.98	Angel Martino, United States, 58.50*
200 back......Tripp Schwenk, United States, 1:54.19	He Cihong, China, 2:06.09
100 breast.... Philip Rogers, Australia, 59.56	Dai Guohong, China, 1:06.58*
200 breast....Nick Gillingham, Great Britain, 2:07.91	Dai Guohong, China, 2:21.99*
100 fly.........Milos Milosevic, Croatia, 52.79	Susan O'Neill, Australia, 59.19
200 fly.........Franck Esposito, France, 1:55.42	Liu Limin, China, 2:08.51
200 IM.........Christian Keller, Germany, 1:56.80	Allison Wagner, United States, 2:07.79*
400 IM.........Curtis Myden, Canada, 4:10.41	Dai Guohong, China, 4:29.00*
400 m relay ..United States, 3:32.57	China, 3:57.73*
400 f relay ....Brazil, 3:12.11	China, 3:35.97*
800 f relay ....Sweden, 7:05.92	China, 7:52.45*

Men	Women
50 free ....Tom Jager, unattached, 22.33	Amy Van Dyken, unattached, 25.37
100 free.......Gary Hall, Phoenix Swim Club, 49.31	Jenny Thompson, Stanford Swimming, 55.50
200 free.......Chad Carvin, Hilldenbrand Aquatics, 1:49.19	Christina Teuscher, Badger Swim Club, 1:59.71
400 free.......Chad Carvin, Hilldenbrand Aquatics, 3:49.83	Janet Evans, Trojan Swim Club, 4:08.78
800 free.......Tom Dolan, Curl-Burke, 8:04.34	Janet Evans, Trojan Swim Club, 8:30.82
1500 free......Carlton Bruner, Club Wolverine, 15:12.37	Janet Evans, Trojan Swim Club, 16:24.24
100 back.....Jeff Rouse, Stanford Swimming, 54.79	Lea Loveless, Stanford Swimming, 1:01.73
200 back.....Brad Bridgewater, Texas Aquatics,. 1:59.21	Barbara Bedford, Florida Aquatics, 2:11.29
100 breast...Seth Van Neerden, Ft Lauderdale Swim T, 1:01.40	Kelli King-Bednar, Hilldenbrand Aquatics, 1:10.46
200 breast...Seth Van Neerden, Ft Lauderdale Swim T, 2:13.27	Allison Wagner, Florida Aquatics, 2:28.86
100 fly.........Mark Henderson, Curl-Burke, 53.60	Jenny Thompson, Stanford Swimming, 1:00.34
200 fly.........Ugur Taner, Chinook Aquatics Club, 1:59.04	Whitney Phelps, North Baltimore Aquatics, 2:11.04
200 IM.........Greg Burgess, Florida Aquatics, 2:00.90	Allison Wagner, Florida Aquatics, 2:13.88
400 IM ....Eric Namesnik, Club Wolverine, 4:14.41	Allison Wagner, Florida Aquatics, 4:40.27
1-m sp*........Chris Devine, Penn State Diving, 583.59	Melisa Moses, unattached, 461.28
3-m sp*.......Mark Bradshaw, Ohio State Diving, 655.68	Melisa Moses, unattached, 474.96
Platform*......Bryan Gillooly, Team Orlando, 580.53 points	Becky Ruehl, Cincinnati Stingrays, 409.14

* Phillips 66 National Diving Championships held in Moultrie, Ga., Aug 17–21.

World and American Records set in 1994

Men

Event	Mark	Record Holder	Date	Site
100 freestyle	48.21	Alexander Popov, Russia (W)	6-18-94	Monte Carlo
400 freestyle	3:43.80	Kieran Perkins, Australia (W)	9-9-94	Rome
800 freestyle	7:46.00	Kieran Perkins, Australia (W)	8-24-94	Vancouver, BC
1500 freestyle	14:41.66	Kieran Perkins, Australia (W)	8-24-94	Vancouver, BC
100 breast	1:00.40	Seth Van Neerden (A)	8-14-94	Indianapolis
200 IM	1:58.16	Jani Sievinen, Finland (W)	9-11-94	Rome
400 IM	4:12.30	Tom Dolan (W,A)	9-6-94	Rome

Women

Event	Mark	Record Holder	Date	Site
50 freestyle	24.51	Le Jingyi, China (W)	9-11-94	Rome
	25.18	Amy Van Dyken (A)	9-11-94	Rome
100 freestyle	54.01	Le Jingyi, China (W)	9-5-94	Rome
200 freestyle	1:56.78	F. Van Almsick, Germany (W)	9-6-94	Rome
100 back	1:00.16	He Cihong, China (W)	9-10-94	Rome
100 breast	1:07.69	Samantha Riley, Australia (W)	9-9-94	Rome
200 breast	2:24.76	Rebecca Brown, Australia (W)	3-16-94	Queensland, Aus.
400 medley relay	4:01.67	China (He Cihong, Dai Guohong, Liu Limin, Le Jingyi) (W)	9-10-94	Rome
400 freestyle relay	3:37.91	China (Le Jingyi, Ying Shan, Le Ying, Lu Bin) (W)	9-7-94	Rome

MEN
Freestyle

Event	Time
50 meters	21.81
100 meters	48.42
200 meters	1:46.69
	1:47.72
400 meters	3:43.80
	3:48.06
800 meters	7:46.00
	7:52.45
1500 meters	14:41.66
	15:01.51

Record Holder	Date	Site
Tom Jager (W,A)	3-24-90	Nashville
Alexander Popov, Russia (W)	6-18-94	Monte Carlo
Matt Biondi (A)	8-10-88	Austin
Giorgio Lamberti, Italy (W)	8-15-89	Bonn
Matt Biondi (A)	8-8-88	Austin
Kieran Perkins, Australia (W)	9-9-94	Rome
Matt Cetlinski (A)	8-11-88	Austin
Kieran Perkins, Australia (W)	8-24-94	Vancouver, B.C.
Sean Killion (A)	7-27-87	Clovis, CA
Kieran Perkins, Australia (W)	8-24-94	Vancouver, B.C.
George DiCarlo (A)	6-30-84	Indianapolis

Backstroke

Event	Time
100 meters	53.86*
200 meters	1:56.57
	1:58.66

*Set on first leg of relay.

Record Holder	Date	Site
Jeff Rouse (W,A)	7-31-92	Barcelona
Martin Zubero, Spain (W)	11-23-91	Tuscaloosa
Royce Sharp (A)	3-3-92	Indianapolis

Breaststroke

Event	Time
100 meters	1:00.95
	1:01.40
	1:01.40
200 meters	2:10.16

Record Holder	Date	Site
Karoly Guttler, Hungary (W)	8-5-93	Sheffield, England
Nelson Diebel (A)	3-1-92	Indianapolis
Seth Van Neerden (A)	8-14-94	Indianapolis
Mike Barrowman (W,A)	7-29-92	Barcelona

Butterfly

Event	Time
100 meters	52.84
200 meters	1:55.69

Record Holder	Date	Site
Pablo Morales (W,A)	6-23-86	Orlando, FL
Melvin Stewart (W,A)	1-12-91	Perth, Australia

Individual Medley

Event	Time
200 meters	1:59.36
	2:00.11
400 meters	4:12.30

Record Holder	Date	Site
Jani Sievinen, Finland (W)	9-11-94	Rome
Dave Wharton (A)	8-20-89	Tokyo
Tom Dolan (W,A)	9-6-94	Rome

Relays

Event	Time
400-meter medley	3:36.93
	3:36.93
400-meter freestyle	3:16.53
800-meter freestyle	7:11.95
	7:12.51

Record Holder	Date	Site
United States (David Berkoff, Rich Schroeder, Matt Biondi, Chris Jacobs) (W,A)	9-23-88	Seoul
United States (Jeff Rouse, Nelson Diebel, Pablo Morales, Jon Olsen), (W, A)	7-31-92	Barcelona
United States (Chris Jacobs, Troy Dalbey, Tom Jager, Matt Biondi) (W,A)	9-23-88	Seoul
EUN (Dmitri Lepikov, Vladimir Taianovitch Veniamin Taianovitch, Yevgeny Sadovyi) (W)	7-27-92	Barcelona
United States (Troy Dalbey, Matt Cetlinski, Doug Gjertsen, Matt Biondi) (A)	9-21-88	Seoul

WOMEN

Freestyle

Event	Time	Record Holder	Date	Site
50 meters	24.51	Li Jingyi, China (W)	9-11-94	Rome
	25.18	Amy Van Dyken, (A)	9-11-94	Rome
100 meters	54.01	Li Jingyi, China (W)	9-5-94	Rome
	54.48	Jenny Thompson (A)	3-1-92	Indianapolis
200 meters	1:57.55	Franziska Van Almsick, Germany (W)	9-6-94	Rome
	1:57.90	Nicole Haislett (A)	7-27-92	Barcelona
400 meters	4:03.85	Janet Evans (W,A)	9-22-88	Seoul
800 meters	8:16.22	Janet Evans (W,A)	8-20-89	Tokyo
1500 meters	15:52.10	Janet Evans (W,A)	3-26-88	Orlando, FL

Backstroke

Event	Time	Record Holder	Date	Site
100 meters	1:00.16	He Cihong, China (W)	9-10-94	Rome
	1:00.82†	Lea Loveless (A)	7-30-92	Barcelona
200 meters	2:06.62	Krisztina Egerszegi, Hungary (W)	8-26-91	Athens, Greece
	2:08.60	Betsy Mitchell (A)	6-27-86	Orlando, FL

Breaststroke

Event	Time	Record Holder	Date	Site
100 meters	1:07.69	Samantha Riley, Australia (W)	9-9-94	Rome
	1:08.17	Anita Nall (A)	7-29-92	Barcelona
200 meters	2:24.76	Rebecca Brown (W)	3-16-94	Queensland, Aus.
	2:25.35	Anita Nall (A)	3-2-92	Indianapolis

Butterfly

Event	Time	Record Holder	Date	Site
100 meters	57.93	Mary T. Meagher (W,A)	8-16-81	Brown Deer, WI
200 meters	2:05.96	Mary T. Meagher (W,A)	8-13-81	Brown Deer, WI

Individual Medley

Event	Time	Record Holder	Date	Site
200 meters	2:11.65	Lin Li, China (W)	7-30-92	Barcelona
	2:11.91	Summer Sanders (A)	7-30-92	Barcelona
400 meters	4:36.10	Petra Schneider, East Germany (W)	8-1-82	Guayaquil, Ecuador
	4:37.58	Summer Sanders (A)	7-26-92	Barcelona

Relays

Event	Time	Record Holder	Date	Site
400-meter medley	4:01.67	China (He Cihong, Dai Guohong, Liu Limin, Le Jingyi) (W)	9-10-94	Rome
	4:02.54	United States (Lea Loveless, Anita Nall, Crissy Ahmann-Leighton, Jenny Thompson) (A)	7-30-92	Barcelona
400-meter freestyle	3:37.91	China (Le Jingyi, Ying Shan, Le Ying, Lu Bin) (W)	9-7-94	Rome
	3:39.46	United States (Nicole Haislett, Dara Torres Angel Martino, Jenny Thompson) (A)	7-28-92	Barcelona
800-meter freestyle	7:55.47	East Germany (Manuela Stellmach, Astrid Strauss, Anke Mohring, Heike Friedrich) (W)	8-18-87	Strasbourg, France
	8:02.12	United States (Betsy Mitchell, Mary T. Meagher, Kim Brown, Mary Wayte) (A)	8-22-86	Madrid

†Time swum on leadoff leg of 400-meter medley relay.

Venues: Belgrade, Sep 4-9, 1973; Cali, Colombia, July 18-27, 1975; West Berlin, Aug 20-28, 1978; Guayaquil, Equador, Aug 1-7, 1982; Madrid, Aug 17-22, 1986; Perth, Australia, Jan 7-13, 1991; Rome, Sep 1-11, 1994.

MEN

50-meter Freestyle

1986	Tom Jager, United States	22.49‡
1991	Tom Jager, United States	22.16‡
1994	Alexander Popov, Russia	22.17

100-meter Freestyle

1973	Jim Montgomery, United States	51.70
1975	Andy Coan, United States	51.25
1978	David McCagg, United States	50.24
1982	Jorg Woithe, East Germany	50.18
1986	Matt Biondi, United States	48.94
1991	Matt Biondi, United States	49.18
1994	Alexander Popov, Russia	49.12

200-meter Freestyle

1973	Jim Montgomery, United States	1:53.02
1975	Tim Shaw, United States	1:52.04‡
1978	Billy Forrester, United States	1:51.02‡
1982	Michael Gross, West Germany	1:49.84
1986	Michael Gross, West Germany	1:47.92
1991	Giorgio Lamberti, Italy	1:47.27‡
1994	Antti Kasvio, Finland	1:47.32

400-meter Freestyle

1973	Rick DeMont, United States	3:58.18‡
1975	Tim Shaw, United States	3:54.88‡
1978	Vladimir Salnikov, USSR	3:51.94‡
1982	Vladimir Salnikov, USSR	3:51.30‡
1986	Rainer Henkel, West Germany	3:50.05
1991	Joerg Hoffman, Germany	3:48.04‡
1994	Kieran Perkins, Australia	3:43.80*

1500-meter Freestyle

1973	Stephen Holland, Australia	15:31.85
1975	Tim Shaw, United States	15:28.92‡
1978	Vladimir Salnikov, USSR	15:03.99‡
1982	Vladimir Salnikov, USSR	15:01.77‡
1986	Rainer Henkel, West Germany	15:05.31
1991	Joerg Hoffman, Germany	14:50.36*
1994	Kieran Perkins, Australia	14:50.52

100-meter Backstroke

1973	Roland Matthes, East Germany	57.47
1975	Roland Matthes, East Germany	58.15
1978	Bob Jackson, United States	56.36‡
1982	Dirk Richter, East Germany	55.95
1986	Igor Polianski, USSR	55.58‡
1991	Jeff Rouse, United States	55.23‡
1994	Martin Lopez Zubero, Spain	55.17‡

200-meter Backstroke

1973	Roland Matthes, East Germany	2:01.87†
1975	Zoltan Varraszto, Hungary	2:05.05
1978	Jesse Vassallo, United States	2:02.16
1982	Rick Carey, United States	2:00.82‡
1986	Igor Polianski, USSR	1:58.78‡
1991	Martin Zubero, Spain	1:59.52
1994	Vladimir Selkov, Russia	1:57.42‡

100-meter Breaststroke

1973	John Hencken, United States	1:04.02†
1975	David Wilkie, Great Britain	1:04.26‡
1978	Walter Kusch, West Germany	1:03.56‡
1982	Steve Lundquist, United States	1:02.75‡
1986	Victor Davis, Canada	1:02.71
1991	Norbert Rozsa, Hungary	1:01.45*
1994	Norbert Rozsa, Hungary	1:01.24‡

200-meter Breaststroke

1973	David Wilkie, Great Britain	2:19.28†
1975	David Wilkie, Great Britain	2:18.23‡
1978	Nick Nevid, United States	2:18.37
1982	Victor Davis, Canada	2:14.77*
1986	Jozsef Szabo, Hungary	2:14.27‡
1991	Mike Barrowman, United States	2:11.23*
1994	Norbert Rozsa, Hungary	2:12.81

100-meter Butterfly

1973	Bruce Robertson, Canada	55.69
1975	Greg Jagenburg, United States	55.63
1978	Joe Bottom, United States	54.30
1982	Matt Gribble, United States	53.88‡
1986	Pablo Morales, United States	53.54‡
1991	Anthony Nesty, Suriname	53.29‡
1994	Rafal Szukala, Poland	53.51

200-meter Butterfly

1973	Robin Backhaus, United States	2:03.32
1975	Bill Forrester, United States	2:01.95‡
1978	Mike Bruner, United States	1:59.38‡
1982	Michael Gross, East Germany	1:58.85‡
1986	Michael Gross, East Germany	1:56.53‡
1991	Melvin Stewart, United States	1:55.69*
1994	Denis Pankratov, Russia	1:56.54

200-meter Individual Medley

1973	Gunnar Larsson, Sweden	2:08.36
1975	Andras Hargitay, Hungary	2:07.72
1978	Graham Smith, Canada	2:03.65*
1982	Alexander Sidorenko, USSR	2:03.30‡
1986	Tamás Darnyi, Hungary	2:01.57‡
1991	Tamás Darnyi, Hungary	1:59.36*
1994	Jani Sievin, Finland	1:58.16*

400-meter Individual Medley

1973	Andras Hargitay, Hungary	4:31.11
1975	Andras Hargitay, Hungary	4:32.57
1978	Jesse Vassallo, United States	4:20.05*
1982	Ricardo Prado, Brazil	4:19.78*
1986	Tamás Darnyi, Hungary	4:18.98‡
1991	Tamás Darnyi, Hungary	4:12.36*
1994	Tom Dolan, United States	4:12.30*

* World record; ‡Meet record.

MEN *(Cont.)*

400-meter Medley Relay

1973.....United States (Mike Stamm, John Hencken, Joe Bottom, Jim Montgomery)	3:49.49
1975.....United States (John Murphy, Rick Colella, Greg Jagenburg, Andy Coan)	3:49.00
1978.....United States (Robert Jackson, Nick Nevid, Joe Bottom, David McCagg)	3:44.63
1982.....United States (Rick Carey, Steve Lundquist, Matt Gribble, Rowdy Gaines)	3:40.84*
1986.....United States (Dan Veatch, David Lundberg, Pablo Morales, Matt Biondi)	3:41.25
1991.....United States (Jeff Rouse, Eric Wunderlich, Mark Henderson Matt Biondi)	3:39.66‡
1994 United States (Jeff Rouse, Eric Wunderlich, Mark Henderson, Gary Hall)	3:37.74‡

400-meter Freestyle Relay

1973.....United States (Mel Nash, Joe Bottom, Jim Montgomery, John Murphy)	3:27.18
1975.....United States (Bruce Furniss, Jim Montgomery, Andy Coan, John Murphy)	3:24.85
1978.....United States (Jack Babashoff, Rowdy Gaines, Jim Montgomery, David McCagg)	3:19.74
1982.....United States (Chris Cavanaugh, Robin Leamy, David McCagg, Rowdy Gaines)	3:19.26*
1986.....United States (Tom Jager, Mike Heath, Paul Wallace, Matt Biondi)	3:19.89
1991.....United States (Tom Jager, Brent Lang, Doug Gjertsen, Matt Biondi)	3:17.15‡
1994.....United States (Jon Olsen, Josh Davis, Ugur Taner, Gary Hall)	3:16.90‡

800-meter Freestyle Relay

1973.....United States (Kurt Krumpholz, Robin Backhaus, Rick Klatt, Jim Montgomery)	7:33.22*
1975....West Germany (Klaus Steinbach, Werner Lampe, Hans Joachim Geisler, Peter Nocke)	7:39.44
1978.....United States (Bruce Furniss, Billy Forrester, Bobby Hackett, Rowdy Gaines)	7:20.82
1982.....United States (Rich Saeger, Jeff Float, Kyle Miller, Rowdy Gaines)	7:21.09
1986.....East Germany (Lars Hinneburg, Thomas Flemming, Dirk Richter, Sven Lodziewski)	7:15.91‡
1991.....Germany (Peter Sitt, Steffan Zesner, Stefan Pfeiffer, Michael Gross)	7:13.50‡
1994.....Sweden (Christer Waller, Tommy Werner, Lars Frolander, Anders Holmertz)	7:17.34

WOMEN

50-meter Freestyle

1986....Tamara Costache, Romania	25.28*
1991....Zhuang Yong, China	25.47
1994....Le Jingyi, China	24.51*

100-meter Freestyle

1973....Kornelia Ender, East Germany	57.54
1975....Kornelia Ender, East Germany	56.50
1978....Barbara Krause, East Germany	55.68‡
1982....Birgit Meineke, East Germany	55.79
1986....Kristin Otto, East Germany	55.05‡
1991....Nicole Haislett, United States	55.17
1994....Le Jingyi, China	54.01*

200-meter Freestyle

1973....Keena Rothhammer, United States	2:04.99
1975....Shirley Babashoff, United States	2:02.50
1978....Cynthia Woodhead, United States	1:58.53*
1982....Annemarie Verstappen, Netherlands	1:59.53†
1986....Heike Friedrich, East Germany	1:58.26‡
1991....Hayley Lewis, Australia	2:00.48
1994....Franziska Van Almsick, Germany	1:56.78*

400-meter Freestyle

1973.....Heather Greenwood, United States	4:20.28
1975....Shirley Babashoff, United States	4:22.70
1978....Tracey Wickham, Australia	4:06.28*
1982....Carmela Schmidt, East Germany	4:08.98
1986....Heike Friedrich, East Germany	4:07.45
1991....Janet Evans, United States	4:08.63
1994....Yang Aihua, China	4:09.64

800-meter Freestyle

1973....Novella Calligaris, Italy	8:52.97
1975....Jenny Turrall, Australia	8:44.75‡
1978....Tracey Wickham, Australia	8:24.94‡
1982....Kim Linehan, United States	8:27.48
1986....Astrid Strauss, East Germany	8:28.24
1991....Janet Evans, United States	8:24.05‡
1994....Janet Evans, United States	8:29.85

100-meter Backstroke

1973....Ulrike Richter, East Germany	1:05.42
1975....Ulrike Richter, East Germany	1:03.30‡
1978....Linda Jezek, United States	1:02.55‡

* World record; ‡Meet record.

WOMEN *(Cont.)*

100-meter Backstroke *(Cont.)*

1982....Kristin Otto, East Germany — 1:01.30‡
1986....Betsy Mitchell, United States — 1:01.74
1991....Krisztina Egerszegi, Hungary — 1:01.78
1994....He Cihong, China — 1:00.57

200-meter Backstroke

1973....Melissa Belote, United States — 2:20.52
1975....Birgit Treiber, East Germany — 2:15.46*
1978....Linda Jezek, United States — 2:11.93*
1982....Cornelia Sirch, East Germany — 2:09.91*
1986....Cornelia Sirch, East Germany — 2:11.37
1991....Krisztina Egerszegi, Hungary — 2:09.15‡
1994....He Cihong, China — 2:07.40

100-meter Breaststroke

1973....Renate Vogel, East Germany — 1:13.74
1975....Hannalore Anke, East Germany — 1:12.72
1978....Julia Bogdanova, USSR — 1:10.31*
1982....Ute Geweniger, East Germany — 1:09.14‡
1986....Sylvia Gerasch, East Germany — 1:08.11*
1991....Linley Frame, Australia — 1:08.81
1994....Samantha Riley, Australia — 1:07.96*

200-meter Breaststroke

1973....Renate Vogel, East Germany — 2:40.01
1975....Hannalore Anke, East Germany — 2:37.25‡
1978....Lina Kachushite, USSR — 2:31.42*
1982....Svetlana Varganova, USSR — 2:28.82‡
1986....Silke Hoerner, East Germany — 2:27.40*
1991....Elena Volkova, USSR — 2:29.53
1994....Samantha Riley, Australia — 2:26.87‡

100-meter Butterfly

1973....Kornelia Ender, East Germany — 1:02.53
1975....Kornelia Ender, East Germany — 1:01.24*
1978....Joan Pennington, United States — 1:00.20‡
1982....Mary T. Meagher, United States — 59.41‡
1986....Kornelia Gressler, East Germany — 59.51
1991....Qian Hong, China — 59.68
1994....Liu Limin, China — 58.98‡

200-meter Butterfly

1973....Rosemarie Kother, East Germany — 2:13.76†
1975....Rosemarie Kother, East Germany — 2:15.92
1978....Tracy Caulkins, United States — 2:09.87*
1982....Ines Geissler, East Germany — 2:08.66‡
1986....Mary T. Meagher, United States — 2:08.41‡
1991....Summer Sanders, United States — 2:09.24
1994....Liu Limin, China — 2:07.25‡

200-meter Individual Medley

1973....Andrea Huebner, East Germany — 2:20.51
1975....Kathy Heddy, United States — 2:19.80
1978....Tracy Caulkins, United States — 2:14.07*
1982....Petra Schneider, East Germany — 2:11.79
1986....Kristin Otto, East Germany — 2:15.56
1991....Li Lin, China — 2:13.40
1994....Lu Bin, China — 2:12.34‡

* World record; ‡Meet record

400-meter Individual Medley

1973....Gudrun Wegner, East Germany — 4:57.71
1975....Ulrike Tauber, East Germany — 4:52.76‡
1978....Tracy Caulkins, United States — 4:40.83*
1982....Petra Schneider, East Germany — 4:36.10*
1986....Kathleen Nord, East Germany — 4:43.75
1991....Lin Li, China — 4:41.45
1994....Dai Guohong, China — 4:39.14

400-meter Medley Relay

1973....East Germany (Ulrike Richter, — 4:16.84
Renate Vogel, Rosemarie Kother,
Kornelia Ender)
1975....East Germany (Ulrike Richter, — 4:14.74
Hannelore Anke, Rosemarie Kother,
Kornelia Ender)
1978....United States (Linda Jezek, — 4:08.21‡
Tracy Caulkins, Joan Pennington,
Cynthia Woodhead)
1982....East Germany (Kristin Otto, — 4:05.8*
Ute Gewinger, Ines Geissler,
Birgit Meineke)
1986....East Germany (Kathrin — 4:04.82
Zimmermann, Sylvia Gerasch,
Kornelia Gressler, Kristin Otto)
1991....United States (Janie Wagstaff, — 4:06.51
Tracey McFarlane, Crissy
Ahmann-Leighton, Nicole Haislett)
1994....China (He Cihong, Dai Guohong, — 4:01.67*
Liu Limin, Lu Bin)

400-meter Freestyle Relay

1973....East Germany (Kornelia Ender, — 3:52.45
Andrea Eife, Andrea Huebner,
Sylvia Eichner)
1975....East Germany (Kornelia Ender, — 3:49.37
Barbara Krause, Claudia Hempel,
Ute Bruckner)
1978....United States (Tracy Caulkins, — 3:43.43*
Stephanie Elkins, Joan Pennington,
Cynthia Woodhead)
1982....East Germany (Birgit Meineke, — 3:43.97
Susanne Link, Kristin Otto,
Caren Metschuk)
1986....East Germany (Kristin Otto, — 3:40.57*
Manuela Stellmach, Sabine
Schulze, Heike Friedrich)
1991....United States (Nicole Haislett, — 3:43.26
Julie Cooper, Whitney Hedgepeth,
Jenny Thompson)
1994....China (Le Jingyi, Ying Shan, — 3:37.91*
Le Ying, Lu Bin)

800-meter Freestyle Relay

1986....East Germany (Manuela — 7:59.33*
Stellmach, Astrid Strauss,
Nadja Bergknecht, Heike Friedrich)
1991....Germany (Kerstin Kielgass, — 8:02.56
Manuela Stellmach, Dagmar Hase,
Stephanie Ortwig)
1994....China (Le Ying, Yang Alhua, — 7:57.96
Zhou Guabin, Lu Bin)

World Diving Championships

MEN

1-meter Springboard

		Pts
1991	Edwin Jongejans, Holland	588.51
1994	Evan Stewart, Zimbabwe	382.14

3-meter Springboard

		Pts
1973	Phil Boggs, United States	618.57
1975	Phil Boggs, United States	597.12
1978	Phil Boggs, United States	913.95
1982	Greg Louganis, United States	752.67
1986	Greg Louganis, United States	750.06
1991	Kent Ferguson, United States	650.25
1994	Wu Zhuocheng, China	655.44

Platform

		Pts
1973	Klaus Dibiasi, Italy	559.53
1975	Klaus Dibiasi, Italy	547.98
1978	Greg Louganis, United States	844.11
1982	Greg Louganis, United States	634.26
1986	Greg Louganis, United States	668.58
1991	Sun Shuwei, China	626.79
1994	Dmitry Sautin, Russia	634.71

WOMEN

1-meter Springboard

		Pts
1991	Gao Min, China	478.26
1994	Chen Lixia, China	279.30

3-meter Springboard

		Pts
1973	Christa Koehler, East Germany	442.17
1975	Irina Kalinina, USSR	489.81
1978	Irina Kalinina, USSR	691.43
1982	Megan Neyer, United States	501.03
1986	Gao Min, China	582.90
1991	Gao Min, China	539.01
1994	Tan Shuping, China	548.49

Platform

		Pts
1973	Ulrike Knape, Sweden	406.77
1975	Janet Ely, United States	403.89
1978	Irina Kalinina, USSR	412.71
1982	Wendy Wyland, United States	438.79
1986	Chen Lin, China	449.67
1991	Fu Mingxia, China	426.51
1994	Fu Mingxia, China	434.04

Yucky

Many visitors bring bottled water to Russia. But last weekend, as the Goodwill Games opened in St. Petersburg, members of the U.S. swim team filled jugs with pool water to take home as souvenirs. The Red Army Pools filtration system had turned the pool Gatorade-green.

Problems began a week before the Games, when a pool attendant forgot to bag the charcoal for putting it in the filter. With the water as black as India ink, scuba divers swept silt from the pool bottom while workers dumped in chemicals. Though by Saturday the water had taken on a more palatable avocado tint, the squeamish Swedish swimmers withdrew and flew back to Stockholm.

When the U.S. contingent got its first peek at the pool that night, one trainer asked where the frogs and lily pads were. "I felt like an Easter egg in dye," said U.S. backstroker Barbara Bedford. "I didn't know what color I'd come out."

The scheduled two-day swimming competition was consolidated and held Sunday. But not before the murky water had stained, at least etmporarily, the reputation of these games.

U.S. Olympic Champions

Men

50-METER FREESTYLE

1988	Matt Biondi	22.14*

100-METER FREESTLYE

1906	Charles Daniels	1:13.4
1908	Charles Daniels	1:05.6*
1912	Duke Kahanamoku	1:03.4
1920	Duke Kahanamoku	1:00.4
1924	John Weissmuller	59.0‡
1928	John Weissmuller	58.6‡
1948	Wally Ris	57.3‡
1952	Clarke Scholes	57.4
1964	Don Schollander	53.4‡
1972	Mark Spitz	51.22*
1976	Jim Montgomery	49.99*
1984	Rowdy Gaines	49.80‡
1988	Matt Biondi	48.63‡

200-METER FREESTYLE

1904	Charles Daniels	2:44.2
1906	Not held 1906-1964	
1972	Mark Spitz	1:52.78*
1976	Bruce Furniss	1:50.29*

400-METER FREESTYLE

1904	Charles Daniels (440 yds)	6:16.2
1920	Norman Ross	5:26.8
1924	John Weissmuller	5:04.2‡
1932	Buster Crabbe	4:48.4‡
1936	Jack Medica	4:44.5‡
1948	William Smith	4:41.0‡
1964	Don Schollander	4:12.2*
1968	Mike Burton	4:09.0‡
1976	Brian Goodell	3:51.93*
1984	George DiCarlo	3:51.23‡

1500-METER FREESTYLE

1920	Norman Ross	22:23.2
1948	James McLane	19:18.5
1952	Ford Konno	18:30.3‡
1968	Mike Burton	16:38.9‡
1972	Mike Burton	15:52.58‡
1976	Brian Goodell	15:02.40*
1984	Michael O'Brien	15:05.20

100-METER BACKSTROKE

1912	Harry Hebner	1:21.2
1920	Warren Kealoha	1:15.2
1924	Warren Kealoha	1:13.2‡
1928	George Kojac	1:08.2*
1936	Adolph Kiefer	1:05.9‡
1948	Allen Stack	1:06.4
1952	Yoshi Oyakawa	1:05.4‡
1976	John Naber	55.49*
1984	Rick Carey	55.79

200-METER BACKSTROKE

1964	Jed Graef	2:10.3*
1976	John Naber	1:59.19*
1984	Rick Carey	2:00.23

100-METER BREASTSTROKE

1968	Donald McKenzie	1:07.7‡
1976	John Hencken	1:03.11*
1984	Steve Lundquist	1:01.65 *
1992	Nelson Diebel	1:01.50‡

200-METER BREASTSTROKE

1924	Robert Skelton	2:56.6
1948	Joseph Verdeur	2:39.3‡
1960	William Mulliken	2:37.4
1972	John Hencken	2:21.55
1992	Mike Barrowman	2:10.16*

100-METER BUTTERFLY

1968	Douglas Russell	55.9‡
1972	Mark Spitz	54.27*
1976	Matt Vogel	54.35
1992	Pablo Morales	53.32

200-METER BUTTERFLY

1956	William Yorzyk	2:19.3‡
1960	Michael Troy	2:12.8*
1968	Carl Robie	2:08.7
1972	Mark Spitz	2:00.70*
1976	Mike Bruner	1:59.23*
1992	Melvin Stewart	1:56.26

200-METER INDIVIDUAL MEDLEY

1968	Charles Hickcox	2:12.0‡

400-METER INDIVIDUAL MEDLEY

1964	Richard Roth	4:45.4*
1968	Charles Hickcox	4:48.4
1976	Rod Strachan	4:23.68*

3-METER SPRINGBOARD DIVING

1920	Louis Kuehn	675.4 points
1924	Albert White	696.4
1928	Pete Desjardins	185.04
1932	Michael Galitzen	161.38
1936	Richard Degener	163.57
1948	Bruce Harlan	163.64
1952	David Browning	205.29
1956	Robert Clotworthy	159.56
1960	Gary Tobian	170.00
1964	Kenneth Sitzberger	159.90
1968	Bernard Wrightson	170.15
1976	Philip Boggs	619.05
1984	Greg Louganis	754.41
1988	Greg Louganis	730.80

PLATFORM DIVING

1904	George Sheldon	12.66
1920	Clarence Pinkston	100.67
1924	Albert White	97.46
1928	Pete Desjardins	98.74
1932	Harold Smith	124.80
1936	Marshall Wayne	113.58
1948	Sammy Lee	130.05
1952	Sammy Lee	156.28
1960	Robert Webster	165.56
1964	Robert Webster	148.58
1984	Greg Louganis	576.99
1988	Greg Louganis	638.61

* World record; ‡Meet (Olympic) record.

Women

100-METER FREESTLYE

1920	Ethelda Bleibtrey	1:13.6*
1924	Ethel Lackie	1:12.4
1928	Albina Osipowich	1:11.0‡
1932	Helene Madison	1:06.8‡
1968	Jan Henne	1:00.0
1972	Sandra Neilson	58.59‡
1984	Carrie Steinseifer	55.92
	Nancy Hogshead	55.92

200-METER FREESTYLE

1968	Debbie Meyer	2:10.5‡
1984	Mary Wayte	1:59.23
1992	Nicole Haislett	1:57.90

400-METER FREESTYLE

1924	Martha Norelius	6:02.2‡
1928	Martha Norelius	5:42.8*
1932	Helene Madison	5:28.5*
1948	Ann Curtis	5:17.8‡
1960	Chris von Saltza	4:50.6
1964	Virginia Duenkel	4:43.3‡
1968	Debbie Meyer	4:31.8‡
1984	Tiffany Cohen	4:07.10‡
1988	Janet Evans	4:03.85*

800-METER FREESTYLE

1968	Debbie Meyer	9:24.0‡
1972	Keena Rothhammer	8:53.86*
1984	Tiffany Cohen	8:24.95‡
1988	Janet Evans	8:20.20‡
1992	Janet Evans	8:25.52

100-METER BACKSTROKE

1924	Sybil Bauer	1:23.2‡
1932	Eleanor Holm	1:19.4
1960	Lynn Burke	1:09.3‡
1964	Cathy Ferguson	1:07.7*
1968	Kaye Hall	1:06.2*
1972	Melissa Belote	1:05.78‡
1984	Theresa Andrews	1:02.55

200-METER BACKSTROKE

1968	Pokey Watson	2:24.8‡
1972	Melissa Belote	2:19.19*

100-METER BREASTSTROKE

1972	Catherine Carr	1:13.58*

200-METER BREASTSTROKE

1968	Sharon Wichman	2:44.4‡

100-METER BUTTERFLY

1956	Shelley Mann	1:11.0‡
1960	Carolyn Schuler	1:09.5‡
1964	Sharon Stouder	1:04.7*
1984	Mary T. Meagher	59.26

200-METER BUTTERFLY

1972	Karen Moe	2:15.57*
1984	Mary T. Meagher	2:06.90‡
1992	Summer Sanders	2:08.67

200-METER INDIVIDUAL MEDLEY

1968	Sharon Wichman	2:44.4‡
1984	Tracy Caulkins	2:12.64‡

400-METER INDIVIDUAL MEDLEY

1964	Donna De Varona	5:18.7‡
1968	Claudia Kolb	5:08.5‡
1984	Tracy Caulkins	4:39.24
1988	Janet Evans	4:37.76

3-METER SPRINGBOARD DIVING

1920	Aileen Riggin	539.9 points
1924	Elizabeth Becker	474.5
1928	Helen Meany	78.62
1932	Georgia Coleman	87.52
1936	Marjorie Gestring	89.27
1948	Victoria Draves	108.74
1952	Patricia McCormick	147.30
1956	Patricia McCormick	142.36
1968	Sue Gossick	150.77
1972	Micki King	450.03
1976	Jennifer Chandler	506.19

PLATFORM DIVING

1924	Caroline Smith	33.2
1928	Elizabeth Becker Pinkston	31.6
1932	Dorothy Poynton	40.26
1936	Dorothy Poynton Hill	33.93
1948	Victoria Draves	68.87
1952	Patricia McCormick	79.37
1956	Patricia McCormick	84.85
1964	Lesley Bush	99.80

* World record; ‡ Meet (Olympic) record.

Notable Achievements

Barrier Breakers

MEN

Event	Barrier	Athlete and Nation	Time	Date
100 Freestyle	1:00	Johnny Weissmuller, United States	58.6	7-9-22
100 Freestyle	:50	James Montgomery, United States	49.99	7-25-76
200 Freestyle	2:00	Don Schollander, United States	1:58.8	7-27-63
200 Freestyle	1:50	Sergei Kopliakov, USSR	1:49.83	4-7-79
400 Freestyle	4:00	Rick DeMont, United States	3:58.18	9-6-73
400 Freestyle	3:50	Vladimir Salnikov, USSR	3:49.57	3-12-82
800 Freestyle	8:00	Vladimir Salnikov, USSR	7:56.49	3-23-79
1500 Freestyle	15:00	Vladimir Salnikov, USSR	14:58.27	7-22-80
100 Backstroke	1:00	Thompson Mann, United States	59.6	10-16-64
200 Backstroke	2:00	John Naber, United States	1:59.19	7-24-76
200 Breaststroke	2:30	Chester Jastremski, United States	2:29.6	8-19-61
100 Butterfly	1:00	Lance Larson, United States	59.0	6-29-60
200 Butterfly	2:00	Roger Pyttel, East Germany	1:59.63	6-3-76

WOMEN

Event	Barrier	Athlete and Nation	Time	Date
100 Freestyle	1:00	Dawn Fraser, Australia	59.9	10-27-62
200 Freestyle	2:00	Kornelia Ender, East Germany	1:59.78	6-2-76
400 Freestyle	4:30	Debbie Meyer, United States	4:29.0	8-18-67
800 Freestyle	10:00	Jane Cederqvist, Sweden	9:55.6	8-17-60
800 Freestyle	9:00	Ann Simmons, United States	8:59.4	9-10-71
1500 Freestyle	20:00	Ilsa Konrads, Australia	19:25.7	1-14-60
	16:00	Janet Evans, United States	15:52.10	3-26-88
200 Backstroke	2:30	Satoko Tanaka, Japan	2:29.6	2-10-63
100 Butterfly	1:00	Christiane Knacke, East Germany	59.78	8-28-77
400 Individual Medley	5:00	Gudrun Wegner, East Germany	4:57.51	9-6-73

Olympic Achievements

MOST INDIVIDUAL GOLDS IN SINGLE OLYMPICS

MEN

No.	Athlete and Nation	Olympic Year	Events
4	Mark Spitz, United States	1972	100, 200 Free; 100, 200 Fly

WOMEN

No.	Athlete and Nation	Olympic Year	Events
4	Kristin Otto, East Germany	1988	50, 100 Free; 100 Back; 100 Fly
3	Debbie Meyer, United States	1968	200, 400, 800 Free
3	Shane Gould, Australia	1972	200, 400 Free; 200 IM
3	Kornelia Ender, East Germany	1976	100, 200 Free; 100 Fly
3	Janet Evans, United States	1988	400, 800 Free; 400 IM
3	Krisztina Egerszegi, Hungary	1992	100, 200 Back; 400 IM

Olympic Achievements *(Cont.)*

MOST INDIVIDUAL OLYMPIC GOLD MEDALS, CAREER

MEN

No.	Athlete and Nation	Olympic Years and Events
4..................Charles Meldrum Daniels, United States		1904 (220, 440 Free); 1906 (100 Free,) 1908 (100 Free)
4..................Roland Matthes, East Germany		1968 (100, 200 Back); 1972 (100, 200 Back)
4..................Mark Spitz, United States		1972 (100, 200 Free; 100, 200 Fly)

WOMEN

4..................Kristin Otto, East Germany		1988 (50 Free; 100 Free, Back and Fly)

Most Olympic Gold Medals in a Single Olympics, Men—7, Mark Spitz, United States, 1972, 100, 200 Free; 100, 200 Fly; 4 x 100, 4 x 200 Free Relays; 4 x 100 Medley
Most Olympic Gold Medals in a Single Olympics, Women—6, Kristin Otto, East Germany, 1988, 50, 100 Free; 100 Back; 100 Fly; 4 x 100 Free Relay; 4 x 100 Medley Relay
Most Olympic Medals in a Career, Men—
11, Matt Biondi, United States:1984 (one gold), '88 (five gold, one silver, one bronze), 92 (two gold, one silver)
11, Mark Spitz, United States: 1968 (two gold, one silver, one bronze), 1972 (seven gold)
Most Olympic Medals in Career, Women—
8, Dawn Fraser, Australia: 1956 (two gold, one silver), '60 (one gold, two silver), '64 (one gold, one silver)
8, Kornelia Ender, East Germany: 1972 (three silver), '76 (four gold, one silver)
8, Shirley Babashoff, United States: 1972 (one gold, two silver), '76 (one gold, four silver)
Winner, Same Event, Three Consecutive Olympics—Dawn Fraser, Australia, 100 Freestyle, 1956, '60, '64.
Youngest Person to Win an Olympic Diving Gold—Marjorie Gestring, United States, 1936, 13 years, 9 months, springboard diving
Youngest Person to Win Olympic Swimming Gold—Krisztina Egerszegi, Hungary, 1988, 14 years, one month, 200 backstroke

World Record Achievements

Most World Records, Career, Women—42, Ragnhild Hveger, Denmark, 1936-42
Most World Records, Career, Men—32, Arne Borg, Sweden, 1921-29
Most Freestyle Records Held Concurrently—
5, Helene Madison, United States, 1931-33.
5, Shane Gould, Australia, 1972.
Most Consecutive Lowerings of a Record—10, Kornelia Ender, East Germany, 100 Freestyle, 7-13-73 to 7-19-76.
Longest Duration of World Record—19 years, 359 days, 1:04.6 in 100 Free, Willy den Ouden , the Netherlands

Skiing

The Winter Olympics

Sports Illustrated

FEBRUARY 21, 1994
$2.95 (CAN. $3.95)

USA

Golden Boy

**Downhill Champion
Tommy Moe**

JOHN BIEVER

Surprises in the Snow

Brilliant performances and stirring upsets made for an unforgettable ski season | by **WILLIAM OSCAR JOHNSON**

ORLD-CLASS ALPINE SKI RACING was blessed with two unforgettable major events in a single season—a nearly flawless 16-day Winter Olympics in Lillehammer, Norway, and a smashing, sun-drenched week in Vail, Colo., where eight World Cup races were scheduled over four days to bring the 1993–94 season to an end on a rhapsodic high note.

Fittingly enough the best performer in both of these superb competitions was the sport's best racer of the moment: the ineffably sweet Swiss slalomist, Vreni Schneider. Now 29 and in her tenth year of competition, Schneider won the gold in the Lillehammer slalom, the silver in the combined and the bronze in the giant slalom. She had already won double gold in Calgary in '88, in the slalom and the GS, and the total of three gold medals plus the silver and the bronze made her the most-decorated woman skier in Olympic history.

"My medals give me so much joy and confidence," she said after Lillehammer, "that I can ski with great momentum for the rest of the season." Sure enough, in Vail, Schneider out-momentumed everyone—men and women alike—with a magnificent week of World Cup results, which included a victory in the slalom (her 51st World Cup career win), a second in the giant slalom, an eighth in the Super G and a phenomenal third in the downhill, a race she rarely enters and even more rarely masters.

This staggering performance gave her an unprecedented 272-point accumulation over those four races in Vail. She wound up with the World Cup slalom title (her fifth) and overwhelmed Pernilla Wiberg of Sweden 1,656 to 1,343, for the overall World Cup title (her second). She had said before the Vail triumph that there was "a 50-50 chance" she would retire after this season. After Vail, however, even this modest, sensible mountain girl from the back-valley village of Elm couldn't resist the heady joys of

CARL YARBROUGH

From season's start, through its finish in Vail, Schneider flew past the competition.

victory. "I don't want to think about any retirement now," she said with a smile. "I will sit down and consider the options with my family, but the way I feel on my skis, I cannot imagine I will end my career now."

The Alpine ski triumphs at the Norwegian Olympics were multi-faceted and multinational *(page 576)*, but the most surprising team performance was produced by Americans—the unheralded Alaskan Tommy Moe, 24, previously winless on the World Cup circuit, got a gold in the downhill and a silver in the Super G; Diann Roffe-Steinrotter, 26, whose last World Cup victory was in 1985, got a gold in the Super G; and Picabo Street, 22, a winsome but still winless superstar-in-the-making, got a silver in the downhill. Interestingly enough, many U.S. skiers attributed their team success in part to their furious reaction to a searingly negative story in SI, which referred to the U.S.

ski team as a bunch of "lead-footed snow plows," and to an editorial in *Ski Racing*, which called U.S. ski results "pathetic."

The most unexpected individual performance among Olympic Alpine skiers was by the venerable German Markus Wasmeier, 30, who had never finished better than fourth in three previous Olympics but this time won gold in both the Super G and the giant slalom. In doing so, he defeated the definitive supermen of Alpine skiing—Norway's brilliant young all-arounder, Kjetil André Aamodt, 21, who had won the Super G gold in Albertville in '92 as well as three more medals (none gold) in the Lillehammer Games; and Italy's rock-star slalomist, Alberto Tomba, 26, who had won golds in the Olympic GS in both '88 and '92 but went off course in Lillehammer. Tomba did manage to win the silver in the slalom, and this put him in the history books as the only Alpine skier ever to win medals in three different Winter Olympics.

As thrilling as the Olympic competitions

Roffe-Steinrotter took the Super G at both the Olympics and the World Cup finale in Vail.

were, a dark shadow lay over the pistes of Lillehammer. Two weeks before the Games began, Ulrike Maier, 26, a popular two-time world champion and the only mother actively racing in World Cup competition, died after a fall in a downhill in Garmisch, Germany. Her friends from the women's World Cup circuit were devastated. After Italy's Deborah Campagnoni won the gold in the giant slalom, she dedicated her victory to Maier, saying, "This was her race." Campagnoni then sobbed for almost a full minute on worldwide TV before she regained her composure. Austrian skiers, both men and women, were obviously jolted by the tragedy: The entire team won just three Olympic medals, a gold, a silver and a bronze—fewer than the American "snowplows." However, by the time the season-ending Vail spectacular rolled around, the memory of Ulrike Maier was working as an inspiration: Her Austrian teammates, Anita Wachter and Christian Mayer, both won World Cups for the giant slalom in their respective divisions.

As for other noteworthy World Cups: The brilliant German speed demon, Katja Seizinger, 22, wrapped up her third straight downhill title and her first Super G World Cup; Tomba won the slalom World Cup for the fourth time; the ageless but peerless Marc Girardelli won the men's downhill World Cup—his 13th title in 15 years, and Aamodt brought home his first overall men's World Cup even though he had won only three regular-season races in '93–94. Someone asked him if this was his best season. "It's difficult to say," he said. "I had more victories last year, but this year I'm the world's best skier. Last year I was second-best overall, so this must be my best season. I really don't know."

Of all the celebrations during Vail's season finisher, the one most enjoyed by all followed Roffe-Steinrotter's stunning victory in the Super G. She had declared this to be her last World Cup race after an 11-year career. No one expected her to win, but when she did, the crowd roared as if for a favorite daughter, and her fellow racers covered her with congratulatory kisses. Beaming an incandescent smile, Roffe-Steinrotter said, "I don't want to stop racing, but I have to because I said I would. And why not? Everyone keeps yelling 'Fairy tale! Fairy tale!' and what better way to quit than with a fairy-tale ending?"

Many felt that Vail's festive finale had provided a similar ending to a World Cup season that had had some violent ups and downs.

FOR THE RECORD·1993-1994

World Cup Season Race Results

Men

Date	Event	Site	Winner
10-30-93	Giant Slalom	Soelden, Austria	Franck Piccard, France
11-27-93	Giant Slalom	Park City, Utah	Guenther Mader, Austria
11-28-93	Slalom	Park City, Utah	Thomas Stangassinger, Austria
12-5-93	Slalom	Stoneham, Quebec	Alberto Tomba, Italy
12-12-93	Super G	Val d'Isere, France	Guenther Mader, Austria
12-13-93	Giant Slalom	Val d'Isere, France	Christian Mayer, Austria
12-14-93	Slalom	Sestriere, Italy	Alberto Tomba, Italy
12-17-93	Downhill	Val Gardena, Italy	Markus Foser, Liechtenstein
12-18-93	Downhill	Val Gardena, Italy	Patrick Ortlieb, Austria
12-19-93	Giant Slalom	Alta Badia, Italy	Steve Locher, Switzerland
12-20-93	Slalom	Madonna di Compiglio, Italy	Jure Kosir, Slovenia
12-22-93	Super G	Lech, Austria	Hannes Trinkl, Austria
12-29-93	Downhill	Bormio, Italy	Hannes Trinkl, Austria
1-6-94	Downhill	Saalbach, Austria	Ed Podivinsky, Canada
1-8-94	Giant Slalom	Kranjska Gora, Slovenia	Fredrik Nyberg, Sweden
1-9-94	Slalom	Kranjska Gora, Slovenia	Finn Christian Jagge, Norway
1-11-94	Giant Slalom	Hinterstoder, Austria	Kjetil André Aamodt, Norway
1-15-94	Downhill	Kitzbuehel, Austria	Patrick Ortlieb, Austria
1-16-94	Slalom	Kitzbuehel, Austria	Thomas Stangassinger, Austria
1-15/16-94	Combined	Kitzbuehel, Austria	Lasse Kjus, Norway
1-18-94	Giant Slalom	Crans-Montana, Switzerland	Jan Einar Thorsen, Norway
1-22-94	Downhill	Wengen, Switzerland	William Besse, Switzerland
1-23-94	Super G	Wengen, Switzerland	Marc Girardelli, Luxembourg
1-29-94	Downhill	Chamonix, France	Kjetil André Aamodt, Norway
1-30-94	Slalom	Chamonix, France	Alberto Tomba, Italy
1-29/30-94	Combined	Chamonix, France	Kjetil André Aamodt, Norway
2-6-94	Slalom	Garmisch-Partenkirchen, Germany	Alberto Tomba, Italy
3-4-94	Downhill	Aspen, Colorado	Hannes Trinkl, Austria
3-5-94	Downhill	Aspen, Colorado	Cary Mullen, Canada
3-6-94	Giant Slalom	Aspen, Colorado	Fredrik Nyberg, Sweden
3-12-94	Downhill	Whistler Mountain, B.C.	Atle Skaardal, Norway
3-13-94	Super G	Whistler Mountain, B.C.	Tommy Moe, United States
3-16-94	Downhill	Vail, Colorado	William Besse, Switzerland
3-17-94	Super G	Vail, Colorado	Jan Einar Thorsen, Norway
3-19-94	Giant Slalom	Vail, Colorado	Kjetil André Aamodt, Norway

Women

Date	Event	Site	Winner
10-31-93	Giant Slalom	Soelden, Austria	Anita Wachter, Austria
11-26-93	Giant Slalom	Santa Caterina, Italy	Anita Wachter, Austria
11-27-93	Giant Slalom	Santa Caterina, Italy	Ulrike Maier, Austria
11-28-93	Slalom	Santa Caterina, Italy	Vreni Schneider, Switzerland
12-4-93	Downhill	Tignes, France	Kate Pace, Canada
12-5-93	Giant Slalom	Tignes, France	Deborah Compagnoni, Italy
12-11-93	Giant Slalom	Veysonnaz, Switzerland	Deborah Compagnoni, Italy
12-12-93	Slalom	Veysonnaz, Switzerland	Pernilla Wiberg, Sweden
12-18-93	Downhill	St Anton, Austria	Anja Haas, Austria
12-19-93	Slalom	St Anton, Austria	Vreni Schneider, Switzerland
12-18/19-93	Combined	St Anton, Austria	Renate Goetschl, Austria
12-22-93	Super G	Flachau, Austria	Katja Koren, Slovenia
1-5-94	Giant Slalom	Morzine, France	Deborah Compagnoni, Italy
1-6-94	Slalom	Morzine, France	Pernilla Wiberg, Sweden
1-9-94	Slalom	Altenmarkt, Austria	Vreni Schneider, Switzerland
1-14-94	Downhill	Cortina d'Ampezzo, Italy	Katja Seizinger, Germany
1-15-94	Super G	Cortina d'Ampezzo, Italy	Katja Seizinger, Germany
1-16-94	Giant Slalom	Cortina d'Ampezzo, Italy	Anita Wachter, Austria
1-17-94	Super G	Cortina d'Ampezzo, Italy	Alenka Dovzan, Slovenia and Pernilla Wiberg, Sweden
1-21-94	Giant Slalom	Maribor, Slovenia	Ulrike Maier, Austria
1-22-94	Slalom	Maribor, Slovenia	Urska Hrovat, Slovenia
1-23-94	Slalom	Maribor, Slovenia	Vreni Schneider, Switzerland
1-29-94	Downhill	Garmisch-Partenkirchen	Isolde Kostner, Italy

Women *(Cont.)*

2-2-94	Downhill	Sierra-Nevada, Spain	Hilary Lindh, United States
2-5-94	Slalom	Sierra-Nevada, Spain	Vreni Schneider, Switzerland
2-5/6-94	Combined	Sierra Nevada, Spain	Pernilla Wiberg, Sweden
3-6-94	Downhill	Whistler Mountain, B.C.	Katja Seizinger, Germany
3-9-94	Super G	Mammouth Mountain, Calif.	Katja Seizinger, Germany
3-10-94	Slalom	Mammouth Mountain, Calif.	Vreni Schneider, Switzerland
3-16-94	Downhill	Vail, Colorado	Katja Seizinger, Germany
3-17-94	Super G	Vail, Colorado	Diann Roffe-Steinrotter, U.S.A.
3-19-94	Giant Slalom	Vail, Colorado	Martina Ertl, Germany
3-20-94	Slalom	Vail, Colorado	Vreni Schneider, Switzerland

World Cup Standings

Men

OVERALL

	Pts
Kjetil André Aamodt, Norway	1392
Marc Girardelli, Luxembourg	1007
Alberto Tomba, Italy	822
Günther Mader, Austria	821
Hannes Trinkl, Austria	701
Jan Einar Thorsen, Norway	657
Lasse Kjus, Norway	651
Tommy Moe, United States	650

DOWNHILL

	Pts
Marc Girardelli, Luxembourg	556
Hannes Trinkl, Austria	530
Patrick Ortlieb, Austria	487
Cary Mullen, Canada	461
William Besse, Switzerland	446
Atle Skaardal, Norway	399
Ed Podivinsky, Canada	313
Tommy Moe, United States	308

SLALOM

	Pts
Alberto Tomba, Italy	540
Thomas Stangassinger, AUT	452
Jure Kosir, Slovenia	421
Finn Christian Jagge, Norway	389
Tomas Fogdoe, Sweden	352
Bernhard Gstrein, Austria	268
Thomas Sykora, Austria	268
Peter Roth, Germany	248

GIANT SLALOM

	Pts
Christian Mayer, Austria	496
Kjetil André Aamodt, Norway	494
Franck Piccard, France	414
Fredrik Nyberg, Sweden	384
Steve Locher, Switzerland	356
Michael Von Gruenigen, Switzerland	351
Tobias Barnerssoi, Germany	308
Guenther Mader, Austria	295

SUPER G

	Pts
Jan Einar Thorsen, Norway	280
Marc Girardelli, Luxembourg	275
Tommy Moe, United States	242
Kjetil André Aamodt, Norway	207
Günther Mader, Austria	202
Atle Skaardal, Norway	202
Lasse Kjus, Norway	194
Hannes Trinkl, Austria	165

Women

OVERALL

	Pts
Vreni Schneider, SUI	1656
Pernilla Wiberg, Sweden	1343
Katja Seizinger, Germany	1195
Anita Wachter, Austria	1057
Martina Ertl, Germany	933
Deborah Compagnoni, Italy	841
Ulrike Maier, Austria	711
Bibiana Perez, Italy	666

DOWNHILL

	Pts
Katja Seizinger, Germany	482
Kate Pace, Canada	398
Melanie Suchet, France	258
Isolde Kostner, Italy	236
Hilary Lindh, United States	214
Veronika Stallmaier, Austria	183
Warwara Zelenskaja, Russia	178
Picabo Street, United States	175

SLALOM

	Pts
Vreni Schneider, Switzerland	860
Pernilla Wiberg, Sweden	620
Urska Hrovat, Slovenia	386
Martina Ertl, Germany	303
Morena Gallizio, Italy	286
Marianne Kjoerstad, Norway	279
Christine vonGruenigen, SUI	244
Patricia Chauvet, France	234

GIANT SLALOM

	Pts
Anita Wachter, Austria	635
Vreni Schneider, Switzerland	516
Deborah Compagnoni, Italy	515
Ulrike Maier, Austria	432
Martina Ertl, Germany	360
Katja Seizinger, Germany	258
Heidi Voelker, United States	251
Carole Merle, France	242

SUPER G

	Pts
Katja Seizinger, Germany	416
Bibiana Perez, Italy	266
Hilde Gerg, Germany	200
Alenka Dovzan, Slovenia	198
Pernilla Wiberg, Sweden	189
Katja Koren, Slovenia	180
Ulrike Maier, Austria	160
Heidi Zurbriggen, Switzerland	159

FOR THE RECORD·Year by Year

Event Descriptions

Downhill: A speed event entailing a single run on a course with a minimum vertical drop of 500 meters (800 for Men's World Cup) and very few control gates.
Slalom: A technical event in which times for runs on 2 courses are totaled to determine the winner. Skiers must make many quick, short turns through a combination of gates (55-75 gates for men, 40-60 for women) over a short course (140-220-meter vertical drop for men, 120-180 for women).

Giant Slalom: A faster technical event with fewer, more broadly spaced gates than in the slalom. Times for runs on 2 courses with vertical drops of 250-400 meters (250-300 for women) are combined to determine the winner.
Super G: A speed event that is a cross between the downhill and the giant slalom.
Combined: An event in which scores from designated slalom and downhill races are combined to determine finish order.

FIS World Championships

Sites

1931	Mürren, Switzerland
1932	Cortina d'Ampezzo, Italy
1933	Innsbruck, Austria
1934	St Moritz, Switzerland
1935	Mürren, Switzerland
1936	Innsbruck, Austria
1937	Chamonix, France
1938	Engelberg, Switzerland
1939	Zakopane, Poland

Men

DOWNHILL

1931	Walter Prager, Switzerland
1932	Gustav Lantschner, Austria
1933	Walter Prager, Switzerland
1934	David Zogg, Switzerland
1935	Franz Zingerle, Austria
1936	Rudolf Rominger, Switzerland
1937	Émile Allais, France
1938	James Couttet, France
1939	Hans Lantschner, Germany

SLALOM

1931	David Zogg, Switzerland
1932	Friedrich Dauber, Germany
1933	Anton Seelos, Austria
1934	Franz Pfnür, Germany
1935	Anton Seelos, Austria
1936	Rudi Matt, Austria
1937	Émile Allais, France
1938	Rudolf Rominger, Switzerland
1939	Rudolf Rominger, Switzerland

Women

DOWNHILL

1931	Esme Mackinnon, Great Britain
1932	Paola Wiesinger, Italy
1933	Inge Wersin-Lantschner, Austria
1934	Anni Rüegg, Switzerland
1935	Christel Cranz, Germany
1936	Evie Pinching, Great Britain
1937	Christel Cranz, Germany
1938	Lisa Resch, Germany
1939	Christel Cranz, Germany

SLALOM

1931	Esme Mackinnon, Great Britain
1932	Rösli Streiff, Switzerland
1933	Inge Wersin-Lantschner, Austria
1934	Christel Cranz, Germany
1935	Anni Rüegg, Switzerland
1936	Gerda Paumgarten, Austria
1937	Christel Cranz, Germany
1938	Christel Cranz, Germany
1939	Christel Cranz, Germany

FIS World Alpine Ski Championships

Sites

1950............Aspen, Colorado	1978............Garmisch-Partenkirchen, West Germany
1954............Are, Sweden	1982............Schladming, Austria
1958............Badgastein, Austria	1985............Bormio, Italy
1962............Chamonix, France	1987............Crans-Montana, Switzerland
1966............Portillo, Chile	1989............Vail, Colorado
1970............Val Gardena, Italy	1991............Saalbach-Hinterglemm, Austria
1974............St Moritz, Switzerland	1993............Morioka-Shizukuishi, Japan

Men

DOWNHILL

1950............Zeno Colo, Italy	1978............Josef Walcher, Austria
1954............Christian Pravda, Austria	1982............Harti Weirather, Austria
1958............Toni Sailer, Austria	1985............Pirmin Zurbriggen, Switzerland
1962............Karl Schranz, Austria	1987............Peter Müller, Switzerland
1966............Jean-Claude Killy, France	1989............Hansjörg Tauscher, West Germany
1970............Bernard Russi, Switzerland	1991............Franz Heinzer, Switzerland
1974............David Zwilling, Austria	1993............Urs Lehmann, Switzerland

SLALOM

1950............Georges Schneider, Switzerland	1978............Ingemar Stenmark, Sweden
1954............Stein Eriksen, Norway	1982............Ingemar Stenmark, Sweden
1958............Josl Rieder, Austria	1985............Jonas Nilsson, Sweden
1962............Charles Bozon, France	1987............Frank Wörndl, West Germany
1966............Carlo Senoner, Italy	1989............Rudolf Nierlich, Austria
1970............Jean-Noël Augert, France	1991............Marc Girardelli, Luxembourg
1974............Gustavo Thoeni, Italy	1993............Kjetil André Aamodt, Norway

GIANT SLALOM

1950............Zeno Colo, Italy	1978............Ingemar Stenmark, Sweden
1954............Stein Eriksen, Norway	1982............Steve Mahre, United States
1958............Toni Sailer, Austria	1985............Markus Wasmaier, West Germany
1962............Egon Zimmermann, Austria	1987............Pirmin Zurbriggen, Switzerland
1966............Guy Périllat, France	1989............Rudolf Nierlich, Austria
1970............Karl Schranz, Austria	1991............Rudolf Nierlich, Austria
1974............Gustavo Thoeni, Italy	1993............Kjetil André Aamodt, Norway

COMBINED

1982............Michel Vion, France	1989............Marc Girardelli, Luxembourg
1985............Pirmin Zurbriggen, Switzerland	1991............Stefan Eberharter, Austria
1987............Marc Girardelli, Luxembourg	1993............Lasse Kjus, Norway

SUPER G

1987............Pirmin Zurbriggen, Switzerland	1991............Stefan Eberharter, Austria
1989............Martin Hangl, Switzerland	1993............Cancelled due to weather

Women

DOWNHILL

1950............Trude Beiser-Jochum, Austria	1978............Annemarie Moser-Pröll, Austria
1954............Ida Schopfer, Switzerland	1982............Gerry Sorensen, Canada
1958............Lucile Wheeler, Canada	1985............Michela Figini, Switzerland
1962............Christl Haas, Austria	1987............Maria Walliser, Switzerland
1966............Erika Schinegger, Austria	1989............Maria Walliser, Switzerland
1970............Annerösli Zryd, Switzerland	1991............Petra Kronberger, Austria
1974............Annemarie Moser-Pröll, Austria	1993............Kate Pace, Canada

SLALOM

1950............Dagmar Rom, Austria	1978............Lea Sölkner, Austria
1954............Trude Klecker, Austria	1982............Erika Hess, Switzerland
1958............Inger Bjornbakken, Norway	1985............Perrine Pelen, France
1962............Marianne Jahn, Austria	1987............Erika Hess, Switzerland
1966............Annie Famose, France	1989............Mateja Svet, Yugoslavia
1970............Ingrid Lafforgue, France	1991............Vreni Schneider, Switzerland
1974............Hanni Wenzel, Liechtenstein	1993............Karin Buder, Austria

Women (Cont.)

GIANT SLALOM

1950 ....Dagmar Rom, Austria	1978 ....Maria Epple, West Germany
1954 ....Lucienne Schmith-Couttet, France	1982 ....Erika Hess, Switzerland
1958 ....Lucile Wheeler, Canada	1985 ....Diann Roffe, United States
1962 ....Marianne Jahn, Austria	1987 ....Vreni Schneider, Switzerland
1966 ....Marielle Goitschel, France	1989 ....Vreni Schneider, Switzerland
1970 ....Betsy Clifford, Canada	1991 ....Pernilla Wiberg, Sweden
1974 ....Fabienne Serrat, France	1993 ....Carole Merle, France

COMBINED

1982 ....Erika Hess, Switzerland	1989 ....Tamara McKinney, United States
1985 ....Erika Hess, Switzerland	1991 ....Chantal Bournissen, Switzerland
1987 ....Erika Hess, Switzerland	1993 ....Miriam Vogt, Germany

SUPER G

1987 ....Maria Walliser, Switzerland	1991 ....Ulrike Maier, Austria
1989 ....Ulrike Maier, Austria	1993 ....Katja Seizinger, Germany

World Cup Season Title Holders

Men
OVERALL

1967 ....Jean-Claude Killy, France	1981 ....Phil Mahre, United States
1968 ....Jean-Claude Killy, France	1982 ....Phil Mahre, United States
1969 ....Karl Schranz, Austria	1983 ....Phil Mahre, United States
1970 ....Karl Schranz, Austria	1984 ....Pirmin Zurbriggen, Switzerland
1971 ....Gustavo Thoeni, Italy	1985 ....Marc Girardelli, Luxembourg
1972 ....Gustavo Thoeni, Italy	1986 ....Marc Girardelli, Luxembourg
1973 ....Gustavo Thoeni, Italy	1987 ....Pirmin Zurbriggen, Switzerland
1974 ....Piero Gros, Italy	1988 ....Pirmin Zurbriggen, Switzerland
1975 ....Gustavo Thoeni, Italy	1989 ....Marc Girardelli, Luxembourg
1976 ....Ingemar Stenmark, Sweden	1990 ....Pirmin Zurbriggen, Switzerland
1977 ....Ingemar Stenmark, Sweden	1991 ....Marc Girardelli, Luxembourg
1978 ....Ingemar Stenmark, Sweden	1992 ....Paul Accola, Switzerland
1979 ....Peter Lüscher, Switzerland	1993 ....Marc Girardelli, Luxembourg
1980 ....Andreas Wenzel, Liechtenstein	1994 ....Kjetil André Aamodt, Norway

DOWNHILL

1967 ....Jean-Claude Killy, France	1981 ....Harti Weirather, Austria
1968 ....Gerhard Nenning, Austria	1982 ....Steve Podborski, Canada
1969 ....Karl Schranz, Austria	Peter Müller, Switzerland
1970 ....Karl Schranz, Austria	1983 ....Franz Klammer, Austria
Karl Cordin, Austria	1984 ....Urs Raber, Switzerland
1971 ....Bernhard Russi, Switzerland	1985 ....Helmut Höflehner, Austria
1972 ....Bernhard Russi, Switzerland	1986 ....Peter Wirnsberger, Austria
1973 ....Roland Collumbin, Switzerland	1987 ....Pirmin Zurbriggen, Switzerland
1974 ....Roland Collumbin, Switzerland	1988 ....Pirmin Zurbriggen, Switzerland
1975 ....Franz Klammer, Austria	1989 ....Marc Girardelli, Luxembourg
1976 ....Franz Klammer, Austria	1990 ....Helmut Höflehner, Austria
1977 ....Franz Klammer, Austria	1991 ....Franz Heinzer, Switzerland
1978 ....Franz Klammer, Austria	1992 ....Franz Heinzer, Switzerland
1979 ....Peter Müller, Switzerland	1993 ....Franz Heinzer, Switzerland
1980 ....Peter Müller, Switzerland	1994 ....Marc Girardelli, Luxembourg

SLALOM

1967 ....Jean-Claude Killy, France	1974 ....Gustavo Thoeni, Italy
1968 ....Domeng Giovanoli, Switzerland	1975 ....Ingemar Stenmark, Sweden
1969 ....Jean-Noël Augert, France	1976 ....Ingemar Stenmark, Sweden
1970 ....Patrick Russel and Alain Penz, France	1977 ....Ingemar Stenmark, Sweden
1971 ....Jean-Noël Augert, France	1978 ....Ingemar Stenmark, Sweden
1972 ....Jean-Noël Augert, France	1979 ....Ingemar Stenmark, Sweden
1973 ....Gustavo Thoeni, Italy	1980 ....Ingemar Stenmark, Sweden

Men (Cont.)

SLALOM (Cont.)

1981	Ingemar Stenmark, Sweden		1988	Alberto Tomba, Italy
1982	Phil Mahre, United States		1989	Armin Bittner, West Germany
1983	Ingemar Stenmark, Sweden		1990	Armin Bittner, West Germany
1984	Marc Girardelli, Luxembourg		1991	Marc Girardelli, Luxembourg
1985	Marc Girardelli, Luxembourg		1992	Alberto Tomba, Italy
1986	Rok Petrovic, Yugoslavia		1993	Tomas Fogdof, Sweden
1987	Bojan Krizaj, Yugoslavia		1994	Alberto Tomba, Italy

GIANT SLALOM

1967	Jean-Claude Killy, France		1982	Phil Mahre, United States
1968	Jean-Claude Killy, France		1983	Phil Mahre, United States
1969	Karl Schranz, Austria		1984	Ingemar Stenmark, Sweden
1970	Gustavo Thoeni, Italy			Pirmin Zurbriggen, Switzerland
1971	Patrick Russel, France		1985	Marc Girardelli, Luxembourg
1972	Gustavo Thoeni, Italy		1986	Joël Gaspoz, Switzerland
1973	Hans Hinterseer, Austria		1987	Joël Gaspoz, Switzerland
1974	Piero Gros, Italy			Pirmin Zurbriggen, Switzerland
1975	Ingemar Stenmark, Sweden		1988	Alberto Tomba, Italy
1976	Ingemar Stenmark, Sweden		1989	Pirmin Zurbriggen, Switzerland
1977	Heini Hemmi, Switzerland		1990	Ole-Cristian Furuseth, Norway
	Ingemar Stenmark, Sweden			Günther Mader, Austria
1978	Ingemar Stenmark, Sweden		1991	Alberto Tomba, Italy
1979	Ingemar Stenmark, Sweden		1992	Alberto Tomba, Italy
1980	Ingemar Stenmark, Sweden		1993	Kjetil André Aamodt, Norway
1981	Ingemar Stenmark, Sweden		1994	Christian Mayer, Austria

SUPER G

1986	Markus Wasmeier, West Germany		1991	Franz Heinzer, Switzerland
1987	Pirmin Zurbriggen, Switzerland		1992	Paul Accola, Switzerland
1988	Pirmin Zurbriggen, Switzerland		1993	Kjetil André Aamodt, Norway
1989	Pirmin Zurbriggen, Switzerland		1994	Jan Einar Thorsen, Norway
1990	Pirmin Zurbriggen, Switzerland			

COMBINED

1979	Andreas Wenzel, Liechtenstein		1987	Pirmin Zurbriggen, Switzerland
1980	Andreas Wenzel, Liechtenstein		1988	Hubert Strolz, Austria
1981	Phil Mahre, United States		1989	Marc Girardelli, Luxembourg
1982	Phil Mahre, United States		1990	Pirmin Zurbriggen, Switzerland
1983	Phil Mahre, United States		1991	Marc Girardelli, Luxembourg
1984	Andreas Wenzel, Liechtenstein		1992	Paul Accola, Switzerland
1985	Andreas Wenzel, Liechtenstein		1993	Marc Girardelli, Luxembourg
1986	Markus Wasmaier, West Germany		1994	Kjetil-André Aamodt, Norway

Women

OVERALL

1967	Nancy Greene, Canada		1981	Marie-Thérèse Nadig, Switzerland
1968	Nancy Greene, Canada		1982	Erika Hess, Switzerland
1969	Gertrud Gabl, Austria		1983	Tamara McKinney, United States
1970	Michèle Jacot, France		1984	Erika Hess, Switzerland
1971	Annemarie Pröll, Austria		1985	Michela Figini, Switzerland
1972	Annemarie Pröll, Austria		1986	Maria Walliser, Switzerland
1973	Annemarie Pröll, Austria		1987	Maria Walliser, Switzerland
1974	Annemarie Moser-Pröll, Austria		1988	Michela Figini, Switzerland
1975	Annemarie Moser-Pröll, Austria		1989	Vreni Schneider, Switzerland
1976	Rosi Mitermaier, West Germany		1990	Petra Kronberger, Austria
1977	Lise-Marie Morerod, Switzerland		1991	Petra Kronberger, Austria
1978	Hanni Wenzel, Liechtenstein		1992	Petra Kronberger, Austria
1979	Annemarie Moser-Pröll, Austria		1993	Anita Wachter, Austria
1980	Hanni Wenzel, Liechtenstein		1994	Vreni Schneider, Switzerland

Women *(Cont.)*

DOWNHILL

1967	Marielle Goitschel, France	1981	Marie-Thérèse Nadig, Switzerland
1968	Isabelle Mir, France	1982	Marie-Cecile Gros-Gaudenier, France
	Olga Pall, Austria	1983	Doris De Agostini, Switzerland
1969	Wiltrud Drexel, Austria	1984	Maria Walliser, Switzerland
1970	Isabelle Mir, France	1985	Michela Figini, Switzerland
1971	Annemarie Pröll, Austria	1986	Maria Walliser, Switzerland
1972	Annemarie Pröll, Austria	1987	Michela Figini, Switzerland
1973	Annemarie Pröll, Austria	1988	Michela Figini, Switzerland
1974	Annemarie Moser-Pröll, Austria	1989	Michela Figini, Switzerland
1975	Annemarie Moser-Pröll, Austria	1990	Katrin Gutensohn-Knopf, Germany
1976	Brigitte Totschnig, Austria	1991	Chantal Bournissen, Switzerland
1977	Brigitte Totschnig-Habersatter, Austria	1992	Katja Seizinger, Germany
1978	Annemarie Moser-Pröll, Austria	1993	Katja Seizinger, Germany
1979	Annemarie Moser-Pröll, Austria	1994	Katja Seizinger, Germany
1980	Marie-Thérèse Nadig, Switzerland		

SLALOM

1967	Marielle Goitschel, France	1982	Erika Hess, Switzerland
1968	Marielle Goitschel, France	1983	Erika Hess, Switzerland
1969	Gertrud Gabl, Austria	1984	Tamara McKinney, United States
1970	Ingrid Lafforgue, France	1985	Erika Hess, Switzerland
1971	Britt Lafforgue, France	1986	Roswitha Steiner, Austria
1972	Britt Lafforgue, France		Erika Hess, Switzerland
1973	Patricia Emonet, France	1987	Corrine Schmidhauser, Switzerland
1974	Christa Zechmeister, West Germany	1988	Roswitha Steiner, Austria
1975	Lise-Marie Morerod, Switzerland	1989	Vreni Schneider, Switzerland
1976	Rosi Mittermaier, West Germany	1990	Vreni Schneider, Switzerland
1977	Lise-Marie Morerod, Switzerland	1991	Petra Kronberger, Austria
1978	Hanni Wenzel, Liechtenstein	1992	Vreni Schneider, Switzerland
1979	Regina Sackl, Austria	1993	Vreni Schneider, Switzerland
1980	Perrine Pelen, France	1994	Vreni Schneider, Switzerland
1981	Erika Hess, Switzerland		

GIANT SLALOM

1967	Nancy Greene, Canada	1982	Irene Epple, West Germany
1968	Nancy Greene, Canada	1983	Tamara McKinney, United States
1969	Marilyn Cochran, United States	1984	Erika Hess, Switzerland
1970	Michèle Jacot, France	1985	Maria Keihl, West Germany
	Françoise Macchi, France		Michela Figini, Switzerland
1971	Annemarie Pröll, Austria	1986	Vreni Schneider, Switzerland
1972	Annemarie Pröll, Austria	1987	Vreni Schneider, Switzerland
1973	Monika Kaserer, Austria		Maria Walliser, Switzerland
1974	Hanni Wenzel, Liechtenstein	1988	Mateja Svet, Yugoslavia
1975	Annemarie Moser-Pröll, Austria	1989	Vreni Schneider, Switzerland
1976	Lise-Marie Morerod, France	1990	Anita Wachter, Austria
1977	Lise-Marie Morerod, France	1991	Vreni Schneider, Switzerland
1978	Lise-Marie Morerod, France	1992	Carole Merle, France
1979	Christa Kinshofer, West Germany	1993	Carole Merle, France
1980	Hanni Wenzel, Liechtenstein	1994	Anita Wachter, Austria
1981	Marie-Thérèse Nadig, Switzerland		

SUPER G

1986	Maria Keihl, West Germany	1991	Carole Merle, France
1987	Maria Walliser, Switzerland	1992	Carole Merle, France
1988	Michela Figini, Switzerland	1993	Katja Seizinger, Germany
1989	Carole Merle, France	1994	Katja Seizinger, Germany
1990	Carole Merle, France		

COMBINED

1979	Annemarie Moser-Pröll, Austria	1983	Hanni Wenzel, Liechtenstein
	Hanni Wenzel, Liechtenstein	1984	Erika Hess, Switzerland
1980	Hanni Wenzel, Liechtenstein	1985	Brigitte Oertli, Switzerland
1981	Marie-Thérèse Nadig, Switzerland	1986	Maria Walliser, Switzerland
1982	Irene Epple, West Germany	1987	Brigitte Oertli, Switzerland

World Cup Season Title Holders (Cont.)

Women (Cont.)

COMBINED (Cont.)

1988	Brigitte Oertli, Switzerland	1992	Sabine Ginther, Austria
1989	Brigitte Oertli, Switzerland	1993	Anita Wachter, Austria
1990	Anita Wachter, Austria	1994	Pernilla Wiberg, Sweden
1991	Sabine Ginther, Austria		

World Cup Career Victories

Men

DOWNHILL

25	Franz Klammer, Austria
19	Peter Müller, Switzerland
14	Franz Heinzer, Switzerland*

SLALOM

37	Ingemar Stenmark, Sweden
20	Alberto Tomba, Italy*
17	Marc Girardelli, Luxembourg*

GIANT SLALOM

44	Ingemar Stenmark, Sweden
11	Pirmin Zurbriggen, Switzerland
10	Gustavo Thoeni, Italy
	Alberto Tomba, Italy*

SUPER G

7	Marc Girardelli, Luxembourg*
6	Markus Wasmeier, Germany*
4	Pirmin Zurbriggen, Switzerland

COMBINED

11	Phil Mahre, United States
8	Pirmin Zurbriggen, Switzerland
5	Marc Girardelli, Luxembourg*
	Andreas Wenzel, Lichtenstein

*still active

Women

DOWNHILL

33	Annemarie Moser-Pröll, Austria
17	Michela Figini, Switzerland
14	Maria Walliser, Switzerland

SLALOM

28	Vreni Schneider, Switzerland*
21	Erika Hess, Switzerland
14	Perrine Pelen, France

GIANT SLALOM

19	Vreni Schneider, Switzerland*
16	Annemarie Moser-Pröll, Austria
12	Hanni Wenzel, Lichtenstein

SUPER G

12	Carole Merle, France*
4	Katja Seizinger, Germany*
3	Maria Kiehl, Germany
	Maria Walliser, Switzerland
	Sigrid Wolf, Austria

COMBINED

8	Hanni Wenzel, Lichtenstein
7	Annemarie Moser-Pröll, Austria
6	Brigitte Oertli, Switzerland

*still active

U.S. Olympic Gold Medalists

Men

Year	Winner	Event
1980	Phil Mahre	Combined
1984	Bill Johnson	Downhill
1984	Phil Mahre	Slalom
1994	Tommy Moe	Downhill

Women

Year	Winner	Event
1948	Gretchen Fraser	Slalom
1952	Andrea Mead Lawrence	Slalom
1952	Andrea Mead Lawrence	Giant Slalom
1972	Barbara Ann Cochran	Slalom
1984	Debbie Armstrong	Giant Slalom
1994	Diann Roffe-Steinrotter	Super G

Figure Skating

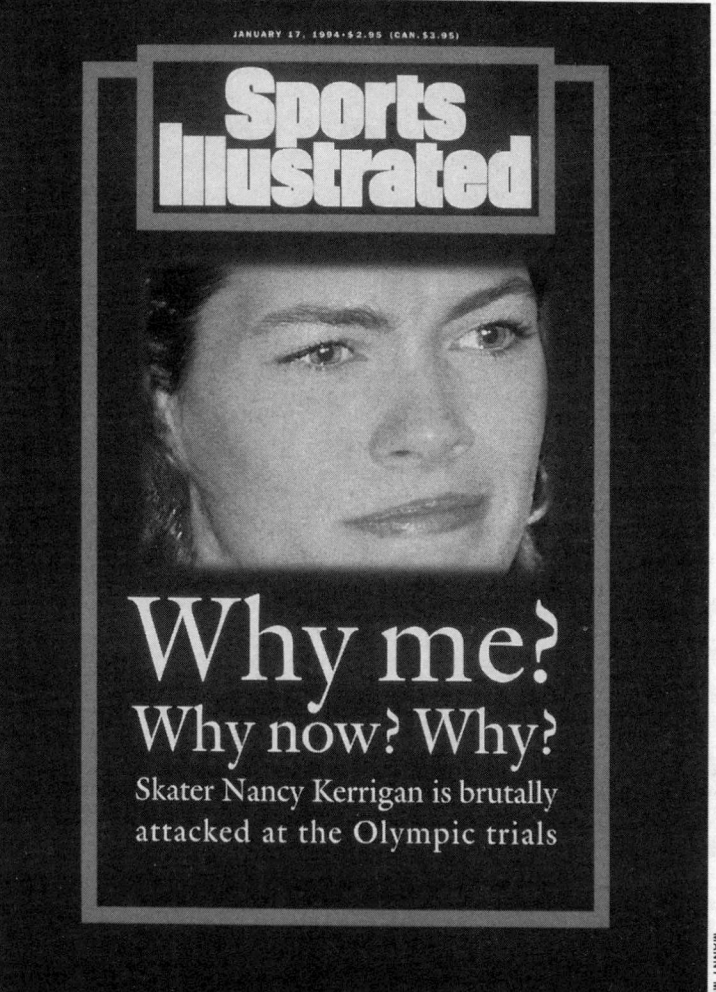

A Sport Soiled

The once genteel world of figure skating was badly sullied by the Harding-Kerrigan affair | by E.M. SWIFT

T WAS, UNFORTUNATELY, UNFORGET-table. 1994 was a year like no other in figure skating, a year this once genteel sport would hope never to see the likes of again. The troubles began on Jan. 6, when Nancy Kerrigan, the defending ladies champion, was savagely attacked in Detroit on the eve of the U.S. Nationals. Struck on the knee by a metal baton by a then unknown assailant, Kerrigan captured the attention and sympathy of the nation with her pained and plaintive query: "Why me? Why now? Why?" Before the winter was over, U.S. skating and Olympic officials, frustrated in their attempts to throw Tonya Harding off the U.S. Olympic team, must have been asking themselves the same questions.

The attack on Kerrigan remained front-page news for weeks, titillating the entire country with its bizarre twists. It was soon discovered that the assault was planned and carried out by four men with close ties to 24-year-old Harding, the 1991 U.S. champion whose off-ice behavior had long been a source of concern and embarrassment to the U.S. Figure Skating Association. Among those implicated: Harding's live-in ex-husband, Jeff Gillooly, who fingered Harding as a co-conspirator in the planning and cover-up of the attack. All four men eventually pleaded guilty to charges relating to the assault and received prison sentences of 18 months. On March 16 Harding struck a deal in which she pleaded guilty to a felony charge of "conspiring to hinder prosecution" in connection with the attack. Harding avoided jail time but was placed on three years probation, assessed $110,000 in fines and sentenced to 500 hours of community service. She was also forced to resign as a member of the USFSA, losing her spot in the world championships.

Harding's lawyers had been able, however, to keep her on the Olympic team, for which she qualified by winning the Nationals after Kerrigan's forced withdrawal. Faced with the threat of a $25 million lawsuit should they proceed with a disciplinary hearing against Harding, the USOC backed down on the eve of the Lillehammer Games. Kerrigan, who completely recovered from her knee injury, was awarded the other Olympic spot, which set up a Snow White vs. the wicked stepmother showdown that promised to send the television ratings for the ladies competition through the Nielson's roof. CBS wasn't disappointed. The night of the Kerrigan-Harding short-program shoot-out proved to be the third-most watched sports event in U.S. television history. But if viewers were expecting the two Americans to battle it out in the mud for the gold, they were disappointed. The out

Baiul's scrappy style vaulted her past Kerrigan by a razor-thin margin.

BILL EPPRIDGE

of shape Harding, dressed like an elephant trainer who'd been on a cheeseburger binge, wallowed home 10th in the short program and eighth overall.

The showdown turned out to be between the elegant Kerrigan, who never skated better than she did in Lillehammer, and the defending world champion, 16-year-old Oksana Baiul of Ukraine. Baiul, an ingenue seeking to replace Norway's own Sonja Henie as the youngest Olympic champion ever, was hobbled by an injury of her own. In practice the day before the ladies finals, Baiul crashed into another skater in a collision that left her with a badly bruised back and three stitches in her right calf.

Uncertain whether she would be able to compete until minutes before she took the ice the final night, Baiul proved to be as scrappy as she is beguiling, landing every jump she tried, then doing a bit of freelancing at the end of her program to beef up her technical marks. She needed every one of them, beating Kerrigan by the slimmest of margins, five judges to four.

Nearly lost amid the drama and seamy intrigue of the ladies competition was the fact that 1994 marked the first year that professionals were allowed to return to the amateur ranks. Many of them wondered why they had bothered after competing in Lillehammer. British ice dancing legends Jane Torvill and Christopher Dean of England, unbeaten in competition since 1981, finished third in the Olympics (a much-criticized placement) as Oksana Gritschuk and Evgeny Platov of Russia came away with the gold medal. In the men's competition, which was generally disappointing in both quality and excitement, there was an outright changing of the generational guard. The big three—1988 gold medalist Brian Boitano, 1992 gold medalist Viktor Petrenko and four-time world champion Kurt Browning—finished sixth, fourth and fifth, respectively. All three butchered their short programs. Consequently gold, silver and bronze in Lillehammer went to Russia's Alexei Urmanov, Canada's Elvis Stojko and Phillipe Candelero of France.

Among the returning pros only the enchanting Russian husband and wife team of Ekaterina Gordeeva and Sergei Grinkov, who won their first gold medal in Calgary in 1988, skated to form. In what was widely hailed as the finest pairs competition ever held, G & G edged out compatriots Natalia Mishkutienok and Artur Dmitriev, who had been the 1992 gold medalists in Albertville.

Of the 12 medalists from Lillehammer, only five chose to compete in the world championships in Nagano, Japan, in March, reducing that event to a highfalutin' exhibition. The troubled '94 season came to a tragic close when 1976 gold medalist John Curry of England died of AIDS on April 15. Curry, who was 44, will be remembered for seamlessly melding athleticism with artistry, for skating classical ballet on a stage of ice.

In the end, though, 1994 will be remembered for its seaminess, not its seamlessness; for the 10 weeks when thuggery, deceit and legal maneuverings were superimposed over an icy Olympic stage, soiling an entire sport.

FOR THE RECORD·1993-1994

World Champions

Women

1........Yuka Sato, Japan
2........Surya Bonaly, France
3........Tanja Szewczenko, Germany

Men

1........Elvis Stojko, Canada
2........Phillippe Candeloro, France
3........Viacheslav Zagorodniuk, Ukraine

Pairs

1........Evgenia Shishkova and Vadim Naumov, Russia
2........Isabelle Brasseur and Lloyd Eisler, Canada
3........Marina Eltsova and Bushkov, Russia

Dance

1........Oksana Gritschuk and Evgeny Platov, Russia
2........Sophie Moniotte and Pascal Lavanchy, France
3........Susanna Rahkamo and Petri Kokko, Finland

World Figure Skating Championships Medal Table

Chiba, Japan, March 22–27

Country	Gold	Silver	Bronze	Total
Russia	2	0	1	3
France	0	3	0	3
Canada	1	1	0	2
Japan	1	0	0	1
Germany	0	0	1	1
Ukraine	0	0	1	1
Finland	0	0	1	1

Champions of the United States

Detroit, Michigan, January 4–8

Women

1........Tonya Harding, Portland, OR
2........Michelle Kwan, Torrance, CA
3........Nicole Bobek, Chicago, IL

Men

1........Scott Davis, Broadmoor SC
2........Brian Boitano, The Peninsula FSC
3........Aren Nielson, Winterhurst FSC

Pairs

1........Jenni Meno and Todd Sand, Winterhurst FSC/Los Angeles FSC
2........Kyoko Ina and Jason Dungjen, SC of New York/ SC of New York
3........Karen Courtland and Todd Reynolds, U of Delaware FSC/Houston FSC

Dance

1........Elizabeth Punsalan and Jerod Swallow, Broadmoor SC/Detroit SC
2........Susan Wynne and Russ Witherby, Skokie Valley SC/Phila SC & HS
3........Amy Webster and Ron Kravette, SC of Boston/Los Angeles FSC

Special Achievements

Women successfully landing a triple Axel in competition:
Midori Ito, Japan, 1988 free-skating competition at Aichi, Japan.
Tonya Harding, United States, 1991 U.S. Figure Skating Championship.

1-900-Two- Bums

There were many low points reached in the aftermath of the attack on Nancy Kerrigan, but perhaps the lowest was the $4.99-per-minute Opinion Line of Derrick Smith and Shane Stant, the "muscle" behind the operation. Paying listeners were treated to the recorded voices of the two cons running down a point-by-point account of the fiasco and, using their incisive brand of reasoning, implying the guilt of Tonya Harding. The tape ends with a sales pitch for such must-own items as "miniature baton key rings (only $29.95!), and autographed souvenir memorabilia." Six minutes of this drivel cost $30.

Skating Terminology*

Basic Skating Terms

Edges: The two sides of the skating blade, on either side of the grooved center. There is an inside edge, on the inner side of the leg; and an outside edge, on the outer side of the leg.

Free Foot, Hip, Knee, Side, Etc.: The foot a skater is not skating on at any one time is the free foot; everything on that side of the body is then called "free." (See also "skating foot.")

Free Skating (Freestyle): A 4- or 5-minute competition program of free-skating components, choreographed to music, with no set elements. Skating moves include jumps, spins, steps and other linking movements.

Skating Foot, Hip, Knee, Side, Etc.: Opposite of the free foot, hip, knee, side, etc. The foot a skater is skating on at any one time is the skating foot; everything on that side of the body is then called "skating."

Toe Picks (Toe Rakes): The teeth at the front of the skate blade, used primarily for certain jumps and spins.

Trace, Tracing: The line left on the ice by the skater's blade.

Jumps

Waltz: A beginner's jump, involving half a revolution in the air, taken from a forward outside edge and landed on the back outside edge of the other foot.

Toe Loop: A one-revolution jump taken off from and landed on the same back outside edge. This jump is similar to the loop jump except that the skater kicks the toe pick of the free leg into the ice upon takeoff, providing added power.

Toe Walley: A jump similar to the toe loop, except that the takeoff is from the inside edge.

Flip: A jump taken off with the toe pick of the free leg from a back inside edge and landed on a back outside edge, with one in-air revolution.

Lutz: A toe jump similar to the flip, taken off with the toe pick of the free leg from a backwrd outside edge. The skater enters the jump skating in one direction, and concludes the jump skating in the opposite direction. Usually performed in the corners of the rink. Named after founder Alois Lutz, who first completed the jump in Vienna, 1918.

Salchow: A one-, two- or three-revolution jump. The skater takes off from the back inside edge of one foot and lands backwards on the outside edge of the right foot, the opposite foot from which the skater took off. Named for its originator and first Olympic champion (1908), Sweden's Ulrich Salchow.

Axel: A combination of the waltz and loop jumps, including one-and-a-half revolutions. The only jump begun from a forward outside edge, the axel is landed on the back outside edge of the opposite foot. Named for its inventor, Norway's Axel Paulsen.

Spins

Spin: The rotation of the body in one place on the ice. Various spins are the back, fast or scratch, sit, camel, butterfly and layback.

Camel Spin: A spin with the skater in an arabesque position (the free leg at right angles to the leg on the ice).

Flying Camel Spin: A jump spin ending in the camel-spin position.

Flying Sit Spin: A jump spin in which the skater leaps off the ice, assumes a sitting position at the peak of the jump, lands and spins in a similar sitting position.

Pair Movements/Techniques

Death Spiral: One of the most dramatic moves in figure skating. The man, acting as the center of a circle, holds tightly to the hand of his partner and pulls her around him. The woman, gliding on one foot, achieves a position almost horizontal to the ice.

Lifts: The most spectacular moves in pairs skating. They involve any maneuver in which the man lifts the woman off the ice. The man often holds his partner above his head with one hand.

Throws: The man lifts the woman into the air and throws her away from him. She spins in the air and lands on one foot.

Twist: The man throws the woman into the air. She spins in the air (either a double- or triple-twist), and he catches her at the landing.

*Compiled by the United States Figure Skating Assocation.

World Champions

Women

Women *(Cont.)*

1956	Carol Heiss, United States
1957	Carol Heiss, United States
1958	Carol Heiss, United States
1959	Carol Heiss, United States
1960	Carol Heiss, United States
1961	No competition
1962	Sjoukje Dijkstra, Netherlands
1963	Sjoukje Dijkstra, Netherlands
1964	Sjoukje Dijkstra, Netherlands
1965	Petra Burka, Canada
1966	Peggy Fleming, United States
1967	Peggy Fleming, United States
1968	Peggy Fleming, United States
1969	Gabriele Seyfert, East Germany
1970	Gabriele Seyfert, East Germany
1971	Beatrix Schuba, Austria
1972	Beatrix Schuba, Austria
1973	Karen Magnussen, Canada
1974	Christine Errath, East Germany
1975	Dianne DeLeeuw, Netherlands
1976	Dorothy Hamill, United States
1977	Linda Fratianne, United States
1978	Annett Poetzsch, East Germany
1979	Linda Fratianne, United States
1980	Annett Poetzsch, East Germany
1981	Denise Biellmann, Switzerland
1982	Elaine Zayak, United States
1983	Rosalynn Sumners, United States
1984	Katarina Witt, East Germany
1985	Katarina Witt, East Germany
1986	Debi Thomas, United States
1987	Katarina Witt, East Germany
1988	Katarina Witt, East Germany
1989	Midori Ito, Japan
1990	Jill Trenary, United States
1991	Kristi Yamaguchi, United States
1992	Kristi Yamaguchi, United States
1993	Oksana Baiul, Ukraine
1994	Yuka Sato, Japan

Men

1896	Gilbert Fuchs, Germany
1897	Gustav Hugel, Austria
1898	Henning Grenander, Sweden
1899	Gustav Hugel, Austria
1900	Gustav Hugel, Austria
1901	Ulrich Salchow, Sweden
1902	Ulrich Salchow, Sweden
1903	Ulrich Salchow, Sweden
1904	Ulrich Salchow, Sweden
1905	Ulrich Salchow, Sweden
1906	Gilbert Fuchs, Germany
1907	Ulrich Salchow, Sweden
1908	Ulrich Salchow, Sweden
1909	Ulrich Salchow, Sweden
1910	Ulrich Salchow, Sweden
1911	Ulrich Salchow, Sweden
1912	Fritz Kachler, Austria
1913	Fritz Kachler, Austria
1914	Gosta Sandhal, Sweden
1915-21	No competition
1922	Gillis Grafstrom, Sweden
1923	Fritz Kachler, Austria
1924	Gillis Grafstrom, Sweden
1925	Willy Bockl, Austria
1926	Willy Bockl, Austria
1927	Willy Bockl, Austria
1928	Willy Bockl, Austria
1929	Gillis Grafstrom, Sweden
1930	Karl Schafer, Austria
1931	Karl Schafer, Austria
1932	Karl Schafer, Austria
1933	Karl Schafer, Austria
1934	Karl Schafer, Austria
1935	Karl Schafer, Austria
1936	Karl Schafer, Austria
1937	Felix Kaspar, Austria
1938	Felix Kaspar, Austria
1939	Graham Sharp, Great Britain
1940-46	No competition
1947	Hans Gerschwiler, Switzerland
1948	Dick Button, United States
1949	Dick Button, United States
1950	Dick Button, United States
1951	Dick Button, United States
1952	Dick Button, United States
1953	Hayes Alan Jenkins, United States
1954	Hayes Alan Jenkins, United States
1955	Hayes Alan Jenkins, United States
1956	Hayes Alan Jenkins, United States
1957	David W. Jenkins, United States
1958	David W. Jenkins, United States
1959	David W. Jenkins, United States
1960	Alan Giletti, France
1961	No competition
1962	Donald Jackson, Canada
1963	Donald McPherson, Canada
1964	Manfred Schneldorfer, W Germany
1965	Alain Calmat, France
1966	Emmerich Danzer, Austria
1967	Emmerich Danzer, Austria
1968	Emmerich Danzer, Austria
1969	Tim Wood, United States
1970	Tim Wood, United States
1971	Andrej Nepela, Czechoslovakia
1972	Andrej Nepela, Czechoslovakia
1973	Andrej Nepela, Czechoslovakia
1974	Jan Hoffmann, East Germany
1975	Sergei Volkov, USSR
1976	John Curry, Great Britain
1977	Vladimir Kovalev, USSR
1978	Charles Tickner, United States
1979	Vladimir Kovalev, USSR
1980	Jan Hoffmann, East Germany
1981	Scott Hamilton, United States
1982	Scott Hamilton, United States
1983	Scott Hamilton, United States
1984	Scott Hamilton, United States
1985	Aleksandr Fadeev, USSR
1986	Brian Boitano, United States
1987	Brian Orser, Canada
1988	Brian Boitano, United States
1989	Kurt Browning, Canada
1990	Kurt Browning, Canada
1991	Kurt Browning, Canada
1992	Viktor Petrenko, CIS
1993	Kurt Browning, Canada
1994	Elvis Stojko, Canada

Pairs

1908..................Anna Hubler, Heinrich Burger, Germany	1958..................Barbara Wagner, Robert Paul, Canada
1909..................Phyllis Johnson, James H. Johnson, Great Britain	1959..................Barbara Wagner, Robert Paul, Canada
1910..................Anna Hubler, Heinrich Burger, Germany	1960..................Barbara Wagner, Robert Paul, Canada
1911..................Ludowika Eilers, Walter Jakobsson, Germany/Finland	1961..................No competition
	1962..................Maria Jelinek, Otto Jelinek, Canada
1912..................Phyllis Johnson, James H. Johnson, Great Britain	1963..................Marika Kilius, Hans-Jurgen Baumler, West Germany
1913..................Helene Engelmann, Karl Majstrik, Germany	1964..................Marika Kilius, Hans-Jurgen Baumler, West Germany
1914..................Ludowika Jakobsson-Eilers, Walter Jakobsson-Eilers, Finland	1965..................Ljudmila Protopopov, Oleg Protopopov, USSR
1915-21..............No competition	1966..................Ljudmila Protopopov, Oleg Protopopov, USSR
1922..................Helene Engelmann, Alfred Berger, Germany	1967..................Ljudmila Protopopov, Oleg Protopopov, USSR
1923..................Ludowika Jakobsson-Eilers, Walter Jakobsson-Eilers, Finland	1968..................Ljudmila Protopopov, Oleg Protopopov, USSR
1924..................Helene Engelmann, Alfred Berger, Germany	1969..................Irina Rodnina, Alexsei Ulanov, USSR
1925..................Herma Jaross-Szabo, Ludwig Wrede, Austria	1970..................Irina Rodnina, Alexsei Ulanov, USSR
	1971..................Irina Rodnina, Sergei Ulanov, USSR
1926..................Andree Joly, Pierre Brunet, France	1972..................Irina Rodnina, Sergei Ulanov, USSR
1927..................Herma Jaross-Szabo, Ludwig Wrede, Austria	1973..................Irina Rodnina, Aleksandr Zaitsev, USSR
1928..................Andree Joly, Pierre Brunet, France	1974..................Irina Rodnina, Aleksandr Zaitsev, USSR
1929..................Lilly Scholz, Otto Kaiser, Austria	1975..................Irina Rodnina, Aleksandr Zaitsev, USSR
1930..................Andree Brunet-Joly, Pierre Brunet-Joly, France	1976..................Irina Rodnina, Aleksandr Zaitsev, USSR
1931..................Emilie Rotter, Laszlo Szollas, Hungary	1977..................Irina Rodnina, Aleksandr Zaitsev, USSR
1932..................Andree Brunet-Joly, Pierre Brunet-Joly, France	1978..................Irina Rodnina, Aleksandr Zaitsev, USSR
1933..................Emilie Rotter, Laszlo Szollas, Hungary	1979..................Tai Babilonia, Randy Gardner, United States
1934..................Emilie Rotter, Laszlo Szollas, Hungary	1980..................Maria Cherkasova, Sergei Shakhrai, USSR
1935..................Emilie Rotter, Laszlo Szollas, Hungary	1981..................Irina Vorobieva, Igor Lisovsky, USSR
1936..................Maxi Herber, Ernst Bajer, Germany	1982..................Sabine Baess, Tassilio Thierbach, East Germany
1937..................Maxi Herber, Ernst Bajer, Germany	1983..................Elena Valova, Oleg Vasiliev, USSR
1938..................Maxi Herber, Ernst Bajer, Germany	1984..................Barbara Underhill, Paul Martini, Canada
1939..................Maxi Herber, Ernst Bajer, Germany	
1940-46..............No competition	1985..................Elena Valova, Oleg Vasiliev, USSR
1947..................Micheline Lannoy, Pierre Baugniet, Belgium	1986..................Yekaterina Gordeeva, Sergei Grinkov, USSR
1948..................Micheline Lannoy, Pierre Baugniet, Belgium	1987..................Yekaterina Gordeeva, Sergei Grinkov, USSR
1949..................Andrea Kekessy, Ede Kiraly, Hungary	1988..................Elena Valova, Oleg Vasiliev, USSR
1950..................Karol Kennedy, Peter Kennedy, United States	1989..................Yekaterina Gordeeva, Sergei Grinkov, USSR
1951..................Ria Baran, Paul Falk, West Germany	1990..................Yekaterina Gordeeva, Sergei Grinkov, USSR
1952..................Ria Baran Falk, Paul Falk, West Germany	1991..................Natalia Mishkutienok, Artur Dmitriev, USSR
1953..................Jennifer Nicks, John Nicks, Great Britain	1992..................Natalia Mishkutienok, Artur Dmitriev CIS
1954..................Frances Dafoe, Norris Bowden, Canada	1993..................Isabelle Brasseur, Lloyd Eisler, Canada
1955..................Frances Dafoe, Norris Bowden, Canada	1994..................Evgenia Shishkova, Vadim Naumov, Russia
1956..................Sissy Schwarz, Kurt Oppelt, Austria	
1957..................Barbara Wagner, Robert Paul, Canada	

Dance

1950	Lois Waring, Michael McGean, U.S.
1951	Jean Westwood, Lawrence Demmy, Great Britain
1952	Jean Westwood, Lawrence Demmy, Great Britain
1953	Jean Westwood, Lawrence Demmy, Great Britain
1954	Jean Westwood, Lawrence Demmy, Great Britain
1955	Jean Westwood, Lawrence Demmy, Great Britain
1956	Pamela Wieght, Paul Thomas, Great Britain
1957	June Markham, Courtney Jones, Great Britain
1958	June Markham, Courtney Jones, Great Britain
1959	Doreen D. Denny, Courtney Jones, Great Britain
1960	Doreen D. Denny, Courtney Jones, Great Britain
1961	No competition
1962	Eva Romanova, Pavel Roman, Czechoslovakia
1963	Eva Romanova, Pavel Roman, Czechoslovakia
1964	Eva Romanova, Pavel Roman, Czechoslovakia
1965	Eva Romanova, Pavel Roman, Czechoslovakia
1966	Diane Towler, Bernard Ford, Great Britain
1967	Diane Towler, Bernard Ford, Great Britain
1968	Diane Towler, Bernard Ford, Great Britain
1969	Diane Towler, Bernard Ford, Great Britain
1970	Ljudmila Pakhomova, Aleksandr Gorshkov, USSR
1971	Ljudmila Pakhomova, Aleksandr Gorshkov, USSR
1972	Ljudmila Pakhomova, Aleksandr Gorshkov, USSR
1973	Ljudmila Pakhomova, Aleksandr Gorshkov, USSR
1974	Ljudmila Pakhomova, Aleksandr Gorshkov, USSR
1975	Irina Moiseeva, Andreij Minenkov, USSR
1976	Ljudmila Pakhomova, Aleksandr Gorshkov, USSR
1977	Irina Moiseeva, Andreij Minenkov, USSR
1978	Natalia Linichuk, Gennadi Karponosov, USSR
1979	Natalia Linichuk, Gennadi Karponosov, USSR
1980	Krisztina Regoeczy, Andras Sallai, Hungary
1981	Jayne Torvill, Christopher Dean, Great Britain
1982	Jayne Torvill, Christopher Dean, Great Britain
1983	Jayne Torvill, Christopher Dean, Great Britain
1984	Jayne Torvill, Christopher Dean, Great Britain
1985	Natalia Bestemianova, Andrei Bukin, USSR
1986	Natalia Bestemianova, Andrei Bukin, USSR
1987	Natalia Bestemianova, Andrei Bukin, USSR
1988	Natalia Bestemianova, Andrei Bukin, USSR
1989	Marina Klimova, Sergei Ponomarenko, USSR
1990	Marina Klimova, Sergei Ponomarenko, USSR
1991	Isabelle Duchesnay, Paul Duchesnay, France
1992	Marina Klimova, Sergei Ponomarenko , CIS
1993	Renee Roca, Gorsha Sur, Broadmoor SC, United States
1994	Oksana Gritschuk, Evgeny Platov, Russia

Champions of the United States

The championships held in 1914, 1918, 1920 and 1921 under the auspices of the International Skating Union of America were open to Canadians, although they were considered to be United States championships. Beginning in 1922, the championships have been held under the auspices of the United States Figure Skating Association.

Women

1914	Theresa Weld, SC of Boston
1915-17	No competition
1918	Rosemary S. Beresford, New York SC
1919	No competition
1920	Theresa Weld, SC of Boston
1921	Theresa Weld Blanchard, SC of Boston
1922	Theresa Weld Blanchard, SC of Boston
1923	Theresa Weld Blanchard, SC of Boston
1924	Theresa Weld Blanchard, SC of Boston
1925	Beatrix Loughran, New York SC
1926	Beatrix Loughran, New York SC
1927	Beatrix Loughran, New York SC
1928	Maribel Y. Vinson, SC of Boston
1929	Maribel Y. Vinson, SC of Boston
1930	Maribel Y. Vinson, SC of Boston
1931	Maribel Y. Vinson, SC of Boston
1932	Maribel Y. Vinson, SC of Boston
1933	Maribel Y. Vinson, SC of Boston
1934	Suzanne Davis, SC of Boston
1935	Maribel Y. Vinson, SC of Boston
1936	Maribel Y. Vinson, SC of Boston
1937	Maribel Y. Vinson, SC of Boston
1938	Joan Tozzer, SC of Boston
1939	Joan Tozzer, SC of Boston

Women *(Cont.)*

1940	Joan Tozzer, SC of Boston
1941	Jane Vaughn, Philadelphia SC & HS
1942	Jane Vaughn Sullivan, Philadelphia SC & HS
1943	Gretchen Van Zandt Merrill, SC of Boston
1944	Gretchen Van Zandt Merrill, SC of Boston
1945	Gretchen Van Zandt Merrill, SC of Boston
1946	Gretchen Van Zandt Merrill, SC of Boston
1947	Gretchen Van Zandt Merrill, SC of Boston
1948	Gretchen Van Zandt Merrill, SC of Boston
1949	Yvonne Claire Sherman, SC of New York
1950	Yvonne Claire Sherman, SC of New York
1951	Sonya Klopfer, Junior SC of New York
1952	Tenley E. Albright, SC of Boston
1953	Tenley E. Albright, SC of Boston
1954	Tenley E. Albright, SC of Boston
1955	Tenley E. Albright, SC of Boston
1956	Tenley E. Albright, SC of Boston
1957	Carol E. Heiss, SC of New York
1958	Carol E. Heiss, SC of New York
1959	Carol E. Heiss, SC of New York
1960	Carol E. Heiss, SC of New York
1961	Laurence R. Owen, SC of Boston
1962	Barbara Roles Pursley, Arctic Blades FSC
1963	Lorraine G. Hanlon, SC of Boston
1964	Peggy Fleming, Arctic Blades FSC
1965	Peggy Fleming, Arctic Blades FSC
1966	Peggy Fleming, City of Colorado Springs
1967	Peggy Fleming, Broadmoor SC
1968	Peggy Fleming, Broadmoor SC
1969	Janet Lynn, Wagon Wheel FSC
1970	Janet Lynn, Wagon Wheel FSC
1971	Janet Lynn, Wagon Wheel FSC
1972	Janet Lynn, Wagon Wheel FSC
1973	Janet Lynn, Wagon Wheel FSC
1974	Dorothy Hamill, SC of New York
1975	Dorothy Hamill, SC of New York
1976	Dorothy Hamill, SC of New York
1977	Linda Fratianne, Los Angeles FSC
1978	Linda Fratianne, Los Angeles FSC
1979	Linda Fratianne, Los Angeles FSC
1980	Linda Fratianne, Los Angeles FSC
1981	Elaine Zayak, SC of New York
1982	Rosalynn Sumners, Seattle SC
1983	Rosalynn Sumners, Seattle SC
1984	Rosalynn Sumners, Seattle SC
1985	Tiffany Chin, San Diego FSC
1986	Debi Thomas, Los Angeles FSC
1987	Jill Trenary, Broadmoor SC
1988	Debi Thomas, Los Angeles FSC
1989	Jill Trenary, Broadmoor SC
1990	Jill Trenary, Broadmoor SC
1991	Tonya Harding, Carousel FSC
1992	Kristi Yamaguchi, St Moritz ISC
1993	Nancy Kerrigan, Colonial FSC
1994	Tonya Harding, Portland FSC

Men

1914	Norman M. Scott, WC of Montreal
1915-17	No competition
1918	Nathaniel W. Niles, SC of Boston
1919	No competition
1920	Sherwin C. Badger, SC of Boston
1921	Sherwin C. Badger, SC of Boston
1922	Sherwin C. Badger, SC of Boston
1923	Sherwin C. Badger, SC of Boston
1924	Sherwin C. Badger, SC of Boston
1925	Nathaniel W. Niles, SC of Boston
1926	Chris I. Christenson, Twin City FSC
1927	Nathaniel W. Niles, SC of Boston
1928	Roger F. Turner, SC of Boston
1929	Roger F. Turner, SC of Boston
1930	Roger F. Turner, SC of Boston
1931	Roger F. Turner, SC of Boston
1932	Roger F. Turner, SC of Boston
1933	Roger F. Turner, SC of Boston
1934	Roger F. Turner, SC of Boston
1935	Robin H. Lee, SC, New York
1936	Robin H. Lee, SC, New York
1937	Robin H. Lee, SC, New York
1938	Robin H. Lee, Chicago FSC
1939	Robin H. Lee, St Paul FSC
1940	Eugene Turner, Los Angeles FSC
1941	Eugene Turner, Los Angeles FSC
1942	Robert Specht, Chicago FSC
1943	Arthur R. Vaughn, Jr, Philadelphia SC & HS
1944-45	No competition
1946	Dick Button, Philadelphia SC & HS
1947	Dick Button, Philadelphia SC & HS
1948	Dick Button, Philadelphia SC & HS
1949	Dick Button, Philadelphia SC & HS
1950	Dick Button, SC of Boston
1951	Dick Button, SC of Boston
1952	Dick Button, SC of Boston
1953	Hayes Alan Jenkins, Cleveland SC
1954	Hayes Alan Jenkins, Broadmoor SC
1955	Hayes Alan Jenkins, Broadmoor SC
1956	Hayes Alan Jenkins, Broadmoor SC
1957	David Jenkins, Broadmoor SC
1958	David Jenkins, Broadmoor SC
1959	David Jenkins, Broadmoor SC
1960	David Jenkins, Broadmoor SC
1961	Bradley R. Lord, SC of Boston
1962	Monty Hoyt, Broadmoor SC
1963	Thomas Litz, Hershey FSC
1964	Scott Ethan Allen, SC of New York
1965	Gary C. Visconti, Detroit SC
1966	Scott Ethan Allen, SC of New York
1967	Gary C. Visconti, Detroit SC
1968	Tim Wood, Detroit SC
1969	Tim Wood, Detroit SC
1970	Tim Wood, City of Colorado Springs
1971	John Misha Petkevich, Great Falls FSC
1972	Kenneth Shelley, Arctic Blades FSC
1973	Gordon McKellen, Jr, SC of Lake Placid
1974	Gordon McKellen, Jr, SC of Lake Placid
1975	Gordon McKellen, Jr, SC of Lake Placid
1976	Terry Kubicka, Arctic Blades FSC
1977	Charles Tickner, Denver FSC
1978	Charles Tickner, Denver FSC
1979	Charles Tickner, Denver FSC
1980	Charles Tickner, Denver FSC
1981	Scott Hamilton, Philadelphia SC & HS
1982	Scott Hamilton, Philadelphia SC & HS
1983	Scott Hamilton, Philadelphia SC & HS
1984	Scott Hamilton, Philadelphia SC & HS
1985	Brian Boitano, Peninsula FSC

Men *(Cont.)*

1986 ......Brian Boitano, Peninsula FSC	1991 ......Todd Eldredge, Los Angeles FSC
1987 ......Brian Boitano, Peninsula FSC	1992 ......Christopher Bowman, Los Angeles FSC
1988 ......Brian Boitano, Peninsula FSC	1993 ......Scott Davis, Broadmoor SC
1989 ......Christopher Bowman, Los Angeles FSC	1994 ......Scott Davis, Broadmoor SC
1990 ......Todd Eldredge, Los Angeles FSC	

Pairs

1914 ......Jeanne Chevalier, Norman M. Scott, WC of Montreal	1947 ......Yvonne Claire Sherman, Robert J. Swenning, SC of New York
1915-17 .No competition	1948 ......Karol Kennedy, Peter Kennedy, Seattle SC
1918 ......Theresa Weld, Nathaniel W. Niles, SC of Boston	1949 ......Karol Kennedy, Peter Kennedy, Seattle SC
1919 ......No competition	1950 ......Karol Kennedy, Peter Kennedy, Broadmoor SC
1920 ......Theresa Weld, Nathaniel W. Niles, SC of Boston	1951 ......Karol Kennedy, Peter Kennedy, Broadmoor SC
1921 ......Theresa Weld Blanchard, Nathaniel W. Niles,SC of Boston	1952 ......Karol Kennedy, Peter Kennedy, Broadmoor SC
1922 ......Theresa Weld Blanchard, Nathaniel W. Niles, SC of Boston	1953 ......Carole Ann Ormaca, Robin Greiner, SC of Fresno
1923 ......Theresa Weld Blanchard, Nathaniel W. Niles, SC of Boston	1954 ......Carole Ann Ormaca, Robin Greiner, SC of Fresno
1924 ......Theresa Weld Blanchard, Nathaniel W. Niles, SC of Boston	1955 ......Carole Ann Ormaca, Robin Greiner, St Moritz ISC
1925 ......Theresa Weld Blanchard, Nathaniel W. Niles, SC of Boston	1956 ......Carole Ann Ormaca, Robin Greiner, St Moritz ISC
1926 ......Theresa Weld Blanchard, Nathaniel W. Niles SC of Boston	1957 ......Nancy Rouillard Ludington, Ronald Ludington, Commonwealth FSC/ SC of Boston
1927 ......Theresa Weld Blanchard, Nathaniel W. Niles, SC of Boston	1958 ......Nancy Rouillard Ludington, Ronald Ludington, Commonwealth FSC/ SC of Boston
1928 ......Maribel Y. Vinson, Thornton L. Coolidge, SC of Boston	1959 ......Nancy Rouillard Ludington, Ronald Ludington, Commonwealth FSC
1929 ......Maribel Y. Vinson, Thornton L. Coolidge, SC of Boston	1960 ......Nancy Rouillard Ludington, Ronald Ludington, Commonwealth FSC
1930 ......Beatrix Loughran, Sherwin C. Badger, SC of New York	1961 ......Maribel Y. Owen, Dudley S. Richards, SC of Boston
1931 ......Beatrix Loughran, Sherwin C. Badger, SC of New York	1962 ......Dorothyann Nelson, Pieter Kollen, Village of Lake Placid
1932 ......Beatrix Loughran, Sherwin C. Badger, SC of New York	1963 ......Judianne Fotheringill, Jerry J. Fotheringill, Broadmoor SC
1933 ......Maribel Y. Vinson, George E. B. Hill, SC of Boston	1964 ......Judianne Fotheringill, Jerry J. Fotheringill, Broadmoor SC
1934 ......Grace E. Madden, James L. Madden, SC of Boston	1965 ......Vivian Joseph, Ronald Joseph, Chicago FSC
1935 ......Maribel Y. Vinson, George E. B. Hill, SC of Boston	1966 ......Cynthia Kauffman, Ronald Kauffman, Seattle SC
1936 ......Maribel Y. Vinson, George E. B. Hill, SC of Boston	1967 ......Cynthia Kauffman, Ronald Kauffman, Seattle SC
1937 ......Maribel Y. Vinson, George E. B. Hill, SC of Boston	1968 ......Cynthia Kauffman, Ronald Kauffman, Seattle SC
1938 ......Joan Tozzer, M. Bernard Fox, SC of Boston	1969 ......Cynthia Kauffman, Ronald Kauffman, Seattle SC
1939 ......Joan Tozzer, M. Bernard Fox, SC of Boston	1970 ......Jo Jo Starbuck, Kenneth Shelley, Arctic Blades FSC
1940 ......Joan Tozzer, M. Bernard Fox, SC of Boston	1971 ......Jo Jo Starbuck, Kenneth Shelley, Arctic Blades FSC
1941 ......Donna Atwood, Eugene Turner, Mercury FSC/Los Angeles FSC	1972 ......Jo Jo Starbuck, Kenneth Shelley, Arctic Blades FSC
1942 ......Doris Schubach, Walter Noffke, Springfield Ice Birds	1973 ......Melissa Militano, Mark Militano, SC of New York
1943 ......Doris Schubach, Walter Noffke, Springfield Ice Birds	1974 ......Melissa Militano, Johnny Johns, SC of New York/Detroit SC
1944 ......Doris Schubach, Walter Noffke, Springfield Ice Birds	1975 ......Melissa Militano, Johnny Johns, SC of New York/Detroit SC
1945 ......Donna Jeanne Pospisil, Jean-Pierre Brunet, SC of New York	
1946 ......Donna Jeanne Pospisil, Jean-Pierre Brunet, SC of New York	

Pairs *(Cont.)*

1976 ......Tai Babilonia, Randy Gardner,
Los Angeles FSC
1977 ......Tai Babilonia, Randy Gardner,
Los Angeles FSC
1978 ......Tai Babilonia, Randy Gardner,
Los Angeles FSC/Santa Monica FSC
1979 ......Tai Babilonia, Randy Gardner,
Los Angeles FSC/Santa Monica FSC
1980 ......Tai Babilonia, Randy Gardner,
Los Angeles FSC/Santa Monica FSC
1981 ......Caitlin Carruthers, Peter Carruthers,
SC of Wilmington
1982 ......Caitlin Carruthers, Peter Carruthers,
SC of Wilmington
1983 ......Caitlin Carruthers, Peter Carruthers,
SC of Wilmington
1984 ......Caitlin Carruthers, Peter Carruthers,
SC of Wilmington
1985 ......Jill Watson, Peter Oppegard,
Los Angeles FSC

1986 ......Gillian Wachsman, Todd Waggoner,
SC of Wilmington
1987 ......Jill Watson, Peter Oppegard,
Los Angeles FSC
1988 ......Jill Watson, Peter Oppegard,
Los Angeles FSC
1989 ......Kristi Yamaguchi, Rudi Galindo,
St Moritz ISC
1990 ......Kristi Yamaguchi, Rudi Galindo,
St Moritz ISC
1991 ......Natasha Kuchiki, Todd Sand,
Los Angeles FSC
1992 ......Calla Urbanski, Rocky Marval,
U of Delaware FSC/SC of New York
1993 ......Calla Urbanski, Rocky Marval,
U of Delaware FSC/SC of New York
1994 ......Jenni Meno,Todd Sand,
Winterhurst FSC/Los Angeles FSC

Dance

1914 ......Waltz
Theresa Weld, Nathaniel W. Niles,
SC of Boston
1915-19.No competition
1920 ......Waltz
Theresa Weld, Nathaniel W. Niles, SC Boston
Fourteenstep
Gertrude Cheever Porter, Irving Brokaw,NYSC
1921 ......Waltz and Fourteenstep
Theresa Weld Blanchard, Nathaniel W.
Niles, SC of Boston
1922 ......Waltz
Beatrix Loughran, Edward M. Howland,
New York SC/SC of Boston
Fourteenstep
Theresa Weld Blanchard, Nathaniel W.
Niles, SC of Boston
1923 ......Waltz
Mr. & Mrs. Henry W. Howe, New York SC
Fourteenstep
Sydney Goode, James B. Greene, NYSC
1924 ......Waltz
Rosaline Dunn, Frederick Gabel
New York SC
Fourteenstep
Sydney Goode, James B. Greene,
New York SC
1925 ......Waltz and Fourteenstep
Virginia Slattery, Ferrier T. Martin,
New York SC
1926 ......Waltz
Rosaline Dunn, Joseph K. Savage,
New York SC
Fourteenstep
Sydney Goode, James B. Greene,
New York SC
1927 ......Waltz and Fourteenstep
Rosaline Dunn, Joseph K. Savage,
New York SC
1928 ......Waltz
Rosaline Dunn, Joseph K. Savage,
New York SC
Fourteenstep
Ada Bauman Kelly, George T. Braakman,
New York SC

1929 ......Waltz and Original Dance combined
Edith C. Secord, Joseph K. Savage,
SC of New York
1930 ......Waltz
Edith C. Secord, Joseph K. Savage,
SC of New York
Original
Clara Rotch Frothingham, George E. B. Hill,
SC of Boston
1931 ......Waltz
Edith C. Secord, Ferrier T. Martin,
SC of New York
Original
Theresa Weld Blanchard, Nathaniel W.
Niles, SC of Boston
1932 ......Waltz
Edith C. Secord, Joseph K. Savage,
SC of New York
Original
Clara Rotch Frothingham, George E. B. Hill,
SC of Boston
1933 ......Waltz
Ilse Twaroschk, Frederick F. Fleishmann,
Brooklyn FSC
Original
Suzanne Davis, Frederick Goodridge,
SC of Boston
1934 ......Waltz
Nettie C. Prantel, Roy Hunt, SC of New York
Original
Suzanne Davis, Frederick Goodridge,
SC of Boston
1935 ......Waltz
Nettie C. Prantel, Roy Hunt, SC of New York
1936 ......Marjorie Parker, Joseph K. Savage,
SC of New York
1937 ......Nettie C. Prantel, Harold Hartshorne,
SC of New York
1938 ......Nettie C. Prantel, Harold Hartshorne,
SC, of New York
1939 ......Sandy Macdonald, Harold Hartshorne,
SC of New York
1940 ......Sandy Macdonald, Harold Hartshorne,
SC of New York
1941 ......Sandy Macdonald, Harold Hartshorne, SCNY

Dance *(Cont.)*

1942 ......Edith B. Whetstone, Alfred N. Richards, Jr,
Philadelphia SC & HS

1943 ......Marcella May, James Lochead, Jr,
Skate & Ski Club

1944 ......Marcella May, James Lochead, Jr,
Skate & Ski Club

1945 ......Kathe Mehl Williams, Robert J. Swenning,
SC of New York

1946 ......Anne Davies, Carleton C. Hoffner, Jr,
Washington FSC

1947 .....Lois Waring, Walter H. Bainbridge, Jr,
Baltimore FSC/Washigton FSC

1948 .....Lois Waring, Walter H. Bainbridge, Jr,
Baltimore FSC/Washington FSC

1949 .....Lois Waring, Walter H. Bainbridge, Jr,
Baltimore FSC/Washington FSC

1950 ......Lois Waring, Michael McGean, Baltimore FSC

1951 ......Carmel Bodel, Edward L. Bodel,
St Moritz ISC

1952 ......Lois Waring, Michael McGean,
Baltimore FSC

1953 ......Carol Ann Peters, Daniel C. Ryan,
Washington FSC

1954 ......Carmel Bodel, Edward L. Bodel, St Moritz ISC

1955 ......Carmel Bodel, Edward L. Bodel,
St Moritz ISC

1956 ......Joan Zamboni, Roland Junso,
Arctic Blades FSC

1957 ......Sharon McKenzie, Bert Wright,
Los Angeles FSC

1958 ......Andree Anderson, Donald Jacoby,
Buffalo SC

1959 ......Andree Anderson Jacoby, Donald Jacoby,
Buffalo SC

1960 ......Margie Ackles, Charles W. Phillips, Jr,
Los Angeles FSC/Arctic Blades FSC

1961 ......Diane C. Sherbloom, Larry Pierce,
Los Angeles FSC/WC of Indianapolis

1962 ......Yvonne N. Littlefield, Peter F. Betts,
Arctic Blades FSC/ Paramount, CA

1963 ......Sally Schantz, Stanley Urban,
SC of Boston/Buffalo SC

1964 ......Darlene Streich, Charles D. Fetter, Jr,
WC of Indianapolis

1965 ......Kristin Fortune, Dennis Sveum,
Los Angeles FSC

1966 ......Kristin Fortune, Dennis Sveum,
Los Angeles FSC

1967 ......Lorna Dyer, John Carrell, Broadmoor SC

1968 ......Judy Schwomeyer, James Sladky,
WC of Indianapolis/Genesee FSC

1969 ......Judy Schwomeyer, James Sladky,
WC of Indianapolis/Genesee FSC

1970 ......Judy Schwomeyer, James Sladky,
WC of Indianapolis/Genesee FSC

1971 ......Judy Schwomeyer, James Sladky,
WC of Indianapolis/Genesee FSC

1972 ......Judy Schwomeyer, James Sladky,
WC of Indianapolis/Genesee FSC

1973 ......Mary Karen Campbell, Johnny Johns,
Lansing SC/Detroit SC

1974 ......Colleen O'Connor, Jim Millns,
Broadmoor SC/City of Colorado Springs

1975 ......Colleen O'Connor, Jim Millns,
Broadmoor SC

1976 ......Colleen O'Connor, Jim Millns,
Broadmoor SC

1977 ......Judy Genovesi, Kent Weigle,
SC of Hartford/Charter Oak FSC

1978 ......Stacey Smith, John Summers,
SC of Wilmington

1979 ......Stacey Smith, John Summers,
SC of Wilmington

1980 ......Stacey Smith, John Summers,
SC of Wilmington

1981 ......Judy Blumberg, Michael Seibert,
Broadmoor SC/ISC of Indianapolis

1982 ......Judy Blumberg, Michael Seibert,
Broadmoor SC/ISC of Indianapolis

1983 ......Judy Blumberg, Michael Seibert,
Pittsburgh FSC

1984 ......Judy Blumberg, Michael Seibert,
Pittsburgh FSC

1985 ......Judy Blumberg, Michael Seibert,
Pittsburgh FSC

1986 ......Renee Roca, Donald Adair,
Genesee FSC/Academy FSC

1987 ......Suzanne Semanick, Scott Gregory,
U of Delaware SC

1988 ......Suzanne Semanick, Scott Gregory,
U of Delaware SC

1989 ......Susan Wynne, Joseph Druar,
Broadmoor SC/Seattle SC

1990 ......Susan Wynne, Joseph Druar,
Broadmoor SC/Seattle SC

1991 ......Elizabeth Punsalan, Jerod Swallow,
Broadmoor SC

1992 ......April Sargent, Russ Witherby,
Ogdensburg FSC/U of Delaware FSC

1993 ......Renee Roca, Gorsha Sur, Broadmoor SC

1994 ......Elizabeth Punsalan, Jerod Swallow,
Broadmoor SC/Detroit SC

U.S. Olympic Gold Medalists

Women

1956 ....Tenley Albright	1976 ....Dorothy Hamill
1960 ....Carol Heiss	1992 ....Kristi Yamaguchi
1968 ....Peggy Fleming	

Men

1948 ....Richard Button	1960 ....David W. Jenkins
1952 ....Richard Button	1984 ....Scott Hamilton
1956 ....Hayes Alan Jenkins	1988 ....Brian Boitano

Miscellaneous Sports

Sports Illustrated

Little Big Man

Justin Gentile leads Northridge (Calif.) into the
Little League World Series

Earthquake Kids

Little Leaguers from earthquake-ravaged Northridge,
California reached the World Series | by KELLY WHITESIDE

MOTHER NATURE WAS TERRI-bly cruel to the state of California in 1994, even tormenting a group of 12-year-old boys from North-ridge—dubbed the Earth-quake Kids—who were playing Maracaibo, Venezuela, in the championship game of the Little League World Series in Williamsport, Pa., last August. With some help from a thunder-storm, Venezuela won 4–3 to become the first Latin American team since 1958 to capture the Little League title. Even the winning pitcher, Cesar Hidalgo, credited the nasty weather and not his nasty fast-ball. "I think it was rain from God that made it turn out so well," he said.

That afternoon, as the clouds rolled over the Allegheny Mountains and darkened the ballpark, TV cameramen put little yel-low slickers over their cameras, the grounds crew inched closer to a large spool of blue tarp, and some fidgety Little League officials delivered the afternoon's forecast to each other over walkie-talkies:

"The storm is now five miles away ... four ... three ..." Venezuela, the tournament favorite, was expected to soundly thrash the Quake Kids, but at the top of the third inning, the game was still scoreless. With two outs and a full count on Effinson Mora, Venezuela's ninth batter, North-ridge pitcher Justin Gentile glanced up at the heavens as if to plead, Why now?

For the next hour, booms of thunder replaced the pings of aluminum, and the players went back to their dormitories to wait out what would be a three-hour rain delay, the longest in the 48 years of the world series. The field, at the bottom of a natural amphitheater, filled with a foot and a half of water in the left- and rightfield corners. During the lengthy wait, thoughts drifted from the game.... Hidalgo imagined what it might be like to slide down the hill just beyond the outfield fence that a group of kids had turned into a muddy luge run. Northridge centerfielder Michael Nesbit wondered whether the tarp covering the infield could double as a giant Slip N' Slide. Northridge manager Larry Baca decided to

His baseballs took a hit, but Gordon did some hitting of his own.

lie down for a moment, and he fell asleep.

Once the skies cleared and the water was pumped from the field with a fire hose, the game resumed. But a storm cloud hovered over Northridge. Mora stepped back into the box with the count full and smacked a double to rightfield. At times Northridge's play was as sloppy as the field conditions. Gentile threw five wild pitches, all which paved the way for a Venezuelan run, and gave up seven hits after the intermission. Venezuela, a team that committed two errors in the first inning, returned to the field more composed. "After the rain delay their pitcher started to throw harder," said Northridge shortstop Matt Fisher. "We had the momentum, then lost it."

Though the Northridge players left Williamsport as the runner-ups, they returned home as heroes. Baseball in Northridge mattered more so than in any other year as the game took on added significance. "Everything changed after the earthquake," says Tim Cunningham, an actor and the father of Matt, the team's catcher. "The aftershocks were scary, so we wanted our kids to check in fairly often so we knew where they were. I felt safe when Matt was playing baseball, because out on a field nothing can happen to you. No roof can fall on you."

Baseball became an escape from the wreckage, a diversion from dealing with insurance companies and federal agencies; it was the town's best news during a very difficult year. "At home we're reminded of the earthquake every day. This helped us forget how bad it was," said Matt Cassel, the team's first baseman.

Most of the team's families lived in tents, cars and rental houses after the 6.8 temblor shook the town on Jan. 17, and four families were still displaced as of August. Much was damaged, from small sentimental items such as rightfielder Spencer Gordon's prized baseballs signed by Willie Mays and Nolan Ryan, which were scuffed and cut when a dresser fell on them, to large businesses such as a new restaurant, Ravioli's, that was located next to the Little League field and owned by Justin's father, John Gentile. The restaurant, which opened only five days before the quake hit, was forced to close after losing $80,000 worth of equipment and $20,000 worth of wine.

At the world series, seven months after the quake, 2,800 miles away from the fault line, a shiver of panic ran down the spine of Shirley Tuber, mother of leftfielder Peter, whenever she heard a plate break or a door slam. "It's silly. I have to remind myself that I'm in the middle of Pennsylvania. There are no earthquakes here," she said. After all, at the championship game in Williamsport, it's comforting to know that the worst thing that can happen is finishing second best.

FOR THE RECORD · Year by Year

Archery

National Men's Champions

1879 ......Will H. Thompson	1916 .....Dr. Robert Elmer	1959 ......Wilbert Vetrovsky
1880 ......L. L. Pedinghaus	1919 .....Dr. Robert Elmer	1960 ......Robert Kadlec
1881 ......F. H. Walworth	1920 .....Dr. Robert Elmer	1961 ......Clayton Sherman
1882 ......D. H. Nash	1921 .....James Jiles	1962 ......Charles Sandlin
1883 ......Col. Robert Williams	1922 .....Dr. Robert Elmer	1963 ......Dave Keaggy, Jr.
1884 ......Col. Robert Williams	1923 .....Bill Palmer	1964 ......Dave Keaggy, Jr.
1885 ......Col. Robert Williams	1924 .....James Jiles	1965 ......George Slinzer
1886 ......W. A. Clark	1925 .....Dr. Paul Crouch	1966 ......Hardy Ward
1887 ......W. A. Clark	1926 .....Stanley Spencer	1967 ......Ray Rogers
1888 ......Lewis Maxson	1927 .....Dr. Paul Crouch	1968 ......Hardy Ward
1889 ......Lewis Maxson	1928 .....Bill Palmer	1969 ......Ray Rogers
1890 ......Lewis Maxson	1929 .....Dr. E. K. Roberts	1970 ......Joe Thornton
1891 ......Lewis Maxson	1930 .....Russ Hoogerhyde	1971 ......John Williams
1892 ......Lewis Maxson	1931 .....Russ Hoogerhyde	1972 ......Kevin Erlandson
1893 ......Lewis Maxson	1932 .....Russ Hoogerhyde	1973 ......Darrell Pace
1894 ......Lewis Maxson	1933 .....Ralph Miller	1974 ......Darrell Pace
1895 ......W. B. Robinson	1934 .....Russ Hoogerhyde	1975 ......Darrell Pace
1896 ......Lewis Maxson	1935 .....Gilman Keasey	1976 ......Darrell Pace
1897 ......W. A. Clark	1936 .....Gilman Keasey	1977 ......Rick McKinney
1898 ......Lewis Maxson	1937 .....Russ Hoogerhyde	1978 ......Darrell Pace
1899 ......M. C. Howell	1938 .....Pat Chambers	1979 ......Rick McKinney
1900 ......A. R. Clark	1939 .....Pat Chambers	1980 ......Rick McKinney
1901 ......Will H. Thompson	1940 .....Russ Hoogerhyde	1981 ......Rick McKinney
1902 ......Will H. Thompson	1941 .....Larry Hughes	1982 ......Rick McKinney
1903 ......Will H. Thompson	1946 .....Wayne Thompson	1983 ......Rick McKinney
1904 ......George Bryant	1947 ......Jack Wilson	1984 ......Darrell Pace
1905 ......George Bryant	1948 .....Larry Hughes	1985 ......Rick McKinney
1906 ......Henry Richardson	1949 .....Russ Reynolds	1986 ......Rick McKinney
1907 ......Henry Richardson	1950 .....Stan Overby	1987 ......Rick McKinney
1908 ......Will H. Thompson	1951 .....Russ Reynolds	1988 ......Jay Barrs
1909 ......Geroge Bryant	1952 .....Robert Larson	1989 ......Ed Eliason
1910 ......Henry Richardson	1953 .....Bill Glackin	1990 ......Ed Eliason
1911 ......Dr. Robert Elmer	1954 .....Robert Rhode	1991 ......Ed Eliason
1912 ......George Bryant	1955 .....Joe Fries	1992 ......Alan Rasor
1913 ......George Bryant	1956 .....Joe Fries	1993 ......Jay Barrs
1914 ......Dr. Robert Elmer	1957 .....Joe Fries	1994 ......Jay Barrs
1915 ......Dr. Robert Elmer	1958 ......Robert Bitner	

National Women's Champions

1879 ......Mrs. S. Brown	1903 ......Mrs. M. C. Howell	1929 ......Audrey Grubbs
1880 ......Mrs. T. Davies	1904 ......Mrs. M. C. Howell	1930 ......Audrey Grubbs
1881 ......Mrs. Gibbes	1905 ......Mrs. M. C. Howell	1931 ......Doroth Cummings
1882 ......Mrs. A. H. Gibbes	1906 ......Mrs. E. C. Cook	1932 ......Ilda Hanchette
1883 ......Mrs. M. C. Howell	1907 ......Mrs. M. C. Howell	1933 ......Madelaine Taylor
1884 ......Mrs. H. Hall	1908 ......Harriet Case	1934 ......Desales Mudd
1885 ......Mrs. M. C. Howell	1909 ......Harriet Case	1935 ......Ruth Hodgert
1886 ......Mrs. M. C. Howell	1910 ......J. V. Sullivan	1936 ......Gladys Hammer
1887 ......Mrs. A. M. Phillips	1911 ......Mrs. J. S. Taylor	1937 ......Gladys Hammer
1888 ......Mrs. A. M. Phillips	1912 ......Mrs. Witwer Tayler	1938 ......Jean Tenney
1889 ......Mrs. A. M. Phillips	1913 ......Mrs. P. Fletcher	1939 ......Belvia Carter
1890 ......Mrs. M. C. Howell	1914 ......Mrs. B. P. Gray	1940 ......Ann Weber
1891 ......Mrs. M. C. Howell	1915 .....Cynthia Wesson	1941 ......Ree Dillinger
1892 ......Mrs. M. C. Howell	1916 .....Cynthia Wesson	1946 ......Ann Weber
1893 ......Mrs. M. C. Howell	1919 .....Dorothy Smith	1947 ......Ann Weber
1894 ......Mrs. Albert Kern	1920 .....Cynthia Wesson	1948 ......Jean Lee
1895 ......Mrs. M. C. Howell	1921 .....Mrs. L. C. Smith	1949 ......Jean Lee
1896 ......Mrs. M. C. Howell	1922 .....Dorothy Smith	1950 ......Jean Lee
1897 ......Mrs. J. S. Baker	1923 .....Norma Pierce	1951 ......Jean Lee
1898 ......Mrs. M. C. Howell	1924 .....Dorothy Smith	1952 ......Ann Weber
1899 ......Mrs. M. C. Howell	1925 .....Dorothy Smith	1953 ......Ann Weber
1900 ......Mrs. M. C. Howell	1926 .....Dorothy Smith	1954 ......Luarette Young
1901 ......Mrs. C. E. Woodruff	1927 ......Mrs. R. Johnson	1955 ......Ann Clark
1902 ......Mrs. M. C. Howell	1928 ......Beatrice Hodgson	1956 ......Carole Meinhart

National Women's Champions (Cont.)

1957 .....Carole Meinhart	1970 .....Nancy Myrick	1983 .....Nancy Myrick
1958 .....Carole Meinhart	1971 .....Doreen Wilber	1984 .....Ruth Rowe
1959 .....Carole Meinhart	1972 .....Ruth Rowe	1985 .....Terri Pesho
1960 .....Ann Clark	1973 .....Doreen Wilber	1986 .....Debra Ochs
1961 .....Victoria Cook	1974 .....Doreen Wilber	1987 .....Terry Quinn
1962 .....Nancy Vonderheide	1975 .....Irene Lorensen	1988 .....Debra Ochs
1963 .....Nancy Vonderheide	1976 .....Luann Ryon	1989 .....Debra Ochs
1964 .....Victoria Cook	1977 .....Luann Ryon	1990 .....Denise Parker
1965 .....Nancy Pfeiffer	1978 .....Luann Ryon	1991 .....Denise Parker
1966 .....Helen Thornton	1979 .....Lynette Johnson	1992 .....Sherry Block
1967 .....Ardelle Mills	1980 .....Judi Adams	1993 .....Denise Parker
1968 .....Victoria Cook	1981 .....Debra Metzger	1994 .....Judy Adams
1969 .....Doreen Wilber	1982 .....Luann Ryon	

Chess

World Champions

1866-94..................Wilhelm Steinitz, Austria	1961-63...................Mikhail Botvinnik, USSR
1894-1921...............Emanuel Lasker, Germany	1963-69...................Tigran Petrosian, USSR
1921-27..................Jose Capablanca, Cuba	1969-72...................Boris Spassky, USSR
1927-35..................Alexander Alekhine, France	1972-75...................Bobby Fischer, United States
1935-37..................Max Euwe, Holland	1975-85...................Anatoly Karpov, USSR
1937-47..................Alexander Alekhine, France	1985-93...................*Garry Kasparov, USSR
1948-57..................Mikhail Botvinnik, USSR	1993.......................vacant
1957-58..................Vassily Smyslov, USSR	1994.......................Anatoly Karpov, Russia
1958-59..................Mikhail Botvinnik, USSR	*Kasparov stripped of title by FIDE in 1993
1960-61..................Mikhail Tal, USSR	

United States Champions

1857-71..................Paul Morphy	1968-69...................Larry Evans
1871-76..................George Mackenzie	1969-72...................Samuel Reshevsky
1876-80..................James Mason	1972-73...................Robert Byrne
1880-89..................George Mackenzie	1973-74...................Lubomir Kavalek/ John Grefe
1889-90..................Samuel Lipschutz	1974-77...................Walter Browne
1890......................Jackson Showalter	1978-80...................Lubomir Kavalek
1890-91..................Max Judd	1980-81...................Larry Evans
1891-92..................Jackson Showalter	Larry Christiansen
1892-94..................Samuel Lipschutz	Walter Browne
1894......................Jackson Showalter	1981-83...................Walter Browne/ Yasser Seirawan
1894-95..................Albert Hodges	1983.......................Roman Dzindzichashvili
1895-97..................Jackson Showalter	Larry Christiansen
1897-1906...............Harry Pillsbury	Walter Browne
1906-09..................Vacant	1984-85...................Lev Alburt
1909-36..................Frank Marshall	1986.......................Yasser Seirawan
1936-44..................Samuel Reshevsky	1987.......................Joel Benjamin/ Nick DeFirmian
1944-46..................Arnold Denker	1988.......................Michael Wilder
1946-48..................Samuel Reshevsky	1989.......................Roman Dzindzichashvili
1948-51..................Herman Steiner	Stuart Rachels
1951-54..................Larry Evans	Yasser Seirawan
1954-57..................Arthur Bisguier	1990.......................Lev Alburt
1957-61..................Bobby Fischer	1991.......................Gata Kamski
1961-62..................Larry Evans	1992.......................Patrick Wolf
1962-68..................Bobby Fischer	1993.......................A. Yermolinsky/ A. Shabalov

Curling

World Champions

Year	Country, Skip	Year	Country, Skip
1972	Canada, Crest Melesnuk	1977	Sweden, Ragnar Kamp
1973	Sweden, Kjell Oscarius	1978	United States, Bob Nichols
1974	United States, Bud Somerville	1979	Norway, Kristian Soerum
1975	Switzerland, Otto Danieli	1980	Canada, Rich Folk
1976	United States, Bruce Roberts	1981	Switzerland, Jurg Tanner

World Champions (Cont.)

Year	Country, Skip	Year	Country, Skip
1982	Canada, Al Hackner	1988	Norway, Eigil Ramsfjell
1983	Canada, Ed Werenich	1989	Canada, Pat Ryan
1984	Norway, Eigil Ramsfjell	1990	Canada, Ed Werenich
1985	Canada, Al Hackner	1991	Scotland, David Smith
1986	Canada, Ed Luckowich	1992	Switzerland, Markus Eggler
1987	Canada, Russ Howard	1993	Canada, Russ Howard
		1994	Canada, Rick Folk

U.S. Men's Champions

Year	Site	Winning Club	Skip
1957	Chicago, IL	Hibbing, MN	Harold Lauber
1958	Milwaukee, WI	Detroit, MI	Douglas Fisk
1959	Green Bay, WI	Hibbing, MN	Fran Kleffman
1960	Chicago, IL	Grafton, ND	Orvil Gilleshammer
1961	Grand Forks, ND	Seattle, WA	Frank Crealock
1962	Detroit, MI	Hibbing, MN	Fran Kleffman
1963	Duluth, MN	Detroit, MI	Mike Slyziuk
1964	Utica, NY	Duluth, MN	Robert Magle, Jr.
1965	Seattle, WA	Superior, WI	Bud Somerville
1966	Hibbing, MN	Fargo, ND	Joe Zbacnik
1967	Winchester, MA	Seattle, WA	Bruce Roberts
1968	Madison, WI	Superior, WI	Bud Somerville
1969	Grand Forks, ND	Superior, WI	Bud Somerville
1970	Ardsley, NY	Grafton, ND	Art Tallackson
1971	Duluth, MN	Edmore, ND	Dale Dalziel
1972	Wilmette, IL	Grafton, ND	Robert Labonte
1973	Colorado Springs, CO	Winchester, MA	Charles Reeves
1974	Schenectady, NY	Superior, WI	Bud Somerville
1975	Detroit, MI	Seattle, WA	Ed Risling
1976	Wausau, WI	Hibbing, MN	Bruce Roberts
1977	Northbrook, IL	Hibbing, MN	Bruce Roberts
1978	Utica, NY	Superior, WI	Bob Nichols
1979	Superior, WI	Bemidji, MN	Scott Baird
1980	Bemidji, MN	Hibbing, MN	Paul Pustovar
1981	Fairbanks, AK	Superior, WI	Bob Nichols
1982	Brookline, MA	Madison, WI	Steve Brown
1983	Colorado Springs, CO	Colorado Springs, CO	Don Cooper
1984	Hibbing, MN	Hibbing, MN	Bruce Roberts
1985	Mequon, WI	Wilmette, IL	Tim Wright
1986	Seattle, WA	Madison, WI	Steve Brown
1987	Lake Placid, NY	Seattle, WA	Jim Vukich
1988	St. Paul, MN	Seattle, WA	Doug Jones
1989	Detroit, MI	Seattle, WA	Jim Vukich
1990	Superior, WI	Seattle, WA	Doug Jones
1991	Utica, NY	Madison, WI	Steve Brown
1992	Grafton, ND	Seattle	Doug Jones
1993	St Paul, MN	Bemidji, MN	Scott Baird
1994	Duluth, MN	Bemidji, MN	Scott Baird

U.S. Women's Champions

Year	Site	Winning Club	Skip
1977	Wilmette, IL	Hastings, NY	Margaret Smith
1978	Duluth, MN	Wausau, WI	Sandy Robarge
1979	Winchester, MA	Seattle, WA	Nancy Langley
1980	Seattle, WA	Seattle, WA	Sharon Kozal
1981	Kettle Moraine, WI	Seattle, WA	Nancy Langley
1982	Bowling Green, OH	Oak Park, IL	Ruth Schwenker
1983	Grafton, ND	Seattle, WA	Nancy Langley
1984	Wauwatosa, WI	Duluth, MN	Amy Hatten
1985	Hershey, PA	Fairbanks, AK	Bev Birklid
1986	Chicago, IL	St. Paul, MN	Gerri Tilden
1987	St. Paul, MN	Seattle, WA	Sharon Good
1988	Darien, CT	Seattle, WA	Nancy Langley
1989	Detroit, MI	Rolla, ND	Jan Lagasse

Curling (Cont.)

U.S. Women's Champions (Cont.)

1990	Superior, WI	Denver, CO	Bev Behnke
1991	Utica, NY	Houston, TX	Maymar Gemmell
1992	Grafton, ND	Madison, WI	Lisa Schoeneberg
1993	St Paul, MN	Denver, CO	Bev Behnke
1994	Duluth, MN	Denver, CO	Bev Behnke

Cycling

Professional Road Race World Champions

1927 ....Alfred Binda, Italy
1928 ....George Ronsse, Belgium
1929 ....George Ronsse, Belgium
1930 ....Alfred Binda, Italy
1931 ....Learco Guerra, Italy
1932 ....Alfred Binda, Italy
1933 ....George Speicher, France
1934 ....Karel Kaers, Belgium
1935 ....Jean Aerts, Belgium
1936 ....Antonio Magne, France
1937 ....Elio Meulenberg, Belgium
1938 ....Marcel Kint, Belgium
1939 ....No competition
1940 ....No competition
1941 ....No competition
1942 ....No competition
1943 ....No competition
1944 ....No competition
1945 ....No competition
1946 ....Hans Knecht, Switzerland
1947 ....Theo. Middelkamp, Holland
1948 ....Alberic Schotte, Belgium
1949 ....Henri Van Steenbergen, Belgium
1950 ....Alberic Schotte, Belgium

1951 ....Ferdinand Kubler, Switzerland
1952 ....Heinz Mueller, Germany
1953 ....Fausto Coppi, Italy
1954 ....Louison Bobet, France
1955 ....Stan Ockers, Belgium
1956 ....Rik Van Steenbergen, Belgium
1957 ....Rik Van Steenbergen, Belgium
1958 ....Ercole Baldini, Italy
1959 ....Andre Darrigade, France
1960 ....Rik van Looy, Belgium
1961 ....Rik van Looy, Belgium
1962 ....Jean Stablenski, France
1963 ....Bennoni Beheyt, Belgium
1964 ....Jan Janssen, Holland
1965 ....Tommy Simpson, England
1966 ....Rudi Altig, West Germany
1967 ....Eddy Merckx, Belgium
1968 ....Vittorio Adorni, Italy
1969 ....Harm Ottenbros, Netherlands
1970 ....J.P. Monseré, Belgium
1971 ....Eddy Merckx, Belgium
1972 ....Marino Basso, Italy

1973 ....Felice Gimondi, Italy
1974 ....Eddy Merckx, Belgium
1975 ....Hennie Kuiper, Holland
1976 ....Freddy Maertens, Belgium
1977 ....Francesco Moser, Italy
1978 ....Gerri Knetemann, Holland
1979 ....Jan Raas, Holland
1980 ....Bernard Hinault, France
1981 ....Freddy Maertens, Belgium
1982 ....Giuseppe Saronni, Italy
1983 ....Greg LeMond, United States
1984 ....Claude Criquielion, Belgium
1985 ....Joop Zoetemelk, Holland
1986 ....Moreno Argentin, Italy
1987 ....Stephen Roche, Ireland
1988 ....Maurizio Fondriest, Italy
1989 ....Greg LeMond, United States
1990 ....Rudy Dhaenene, Belgium
1991 ....Gianni Bugno, Italy
1992 ....Gianni Bugno, Italy
1993 ....Lance Armstrong, United States
1994   Luc LeBlanc, France

Tour DuPont Winners

Year	Winner	Time
1989	Dag Otto Lauritzen, Norway	33 hrs, 28 min, 48 sec
1990	Raul Alcala, Mexico	45 hrs, 20 min, 9 sec
1991	Erik Breukink, Holland	48 hrs, 56 min, 53 sec
1992	Greg LeMond, United States	44 hrs, 27 min, 43 sec
1993	Raul Alcala, Mexico	46 hrs, 42 min, 52 sec
1994	Viatcheslav Ekimov, Russia	47 hrs, 14 min, 29 sec

Tour de France Winners

Year	Winner	Time
1903	Maurice Garin, France	94 hrs, 33 min
1904	Henri Cornet, France	96 hrs, 5 min, 56 sec
1905	Louis Trousselier, France	110 hrs, 26 min, 58 sec
1906	Rene Pottier, France	Not available
1907	Lucien Petit-Breton, France	158 hrs, 54 min, 5 sec
1908	Lucien Petit-Breton, France	Not available
1909	Francois Faber, Luxembourg	157 hrs, 1 min, 22 sec
1910	Octave Lapize, France	162 hrs, 41 min, 30 sec
1911	Gustave Garrigou, France	195 hrs, 37 min
1912	Odile Defraye, Belgium	190 hrs, 30 min, 28 sec
1913	Philippe Thys, Belgium	197 hrs, 54 min
1914	Philippe Thys, Belgium	200 hrs, 28 min, 48 sec
1915-18	No race	
1919	Firmin Lambot, Belgium	231 hrs, 7 min, 15 sec
1920	Philippe Thys, Belgium	228 hrs, 36 min, 13 sec
1921	Leon Scieur, Belgium	221 hrs, 50 min, 26 sec
1922	Firmin Lambot, Belgium	222 hrs, 8 min, 6 sec

Tour de France Winners (Cont.)

Year	Winner	Time
1923	Henri Pelissier, France	222 hrs, 15 min, 30 sec
1924	Ottavio Bottechia, Italy	226 hrs, 18 min, 21 sec
1925	Ottavio Bottechia, Italy	219 hrs, 10 min, 18 sec
1926	Lucien Buysse, Belgium	238 hrs, 44 min, 25 sec
1927	Nicolas Frantz, Luxembourg	198 hrs, 16 min, 42 sec
1928	Nicolas Frantz, Luxembourg	192 hrs, 48 min, 58 sec
1929	Maurice Dewaele, Belgium	186 hrs, 39 min, 16 sec
1930	Andre Leducq, France	172 hrs, 12 min, 16 sec
1931	Antonin Magne, France	177 hrs, 10 min, 3 sec
1932	Andre Leducq, France	154 hrs, 12 min, 49 sec
1933	Georges Speicher, France	147 hrs, 51 min, 37 sec
1934	Antonin Magne, France	147 hrs, 13 min, 58 sec
1935	Romain Maes, Belgium	141 hrs, 32 min
1936	Sylvere Maes, Belgium	142 hrs, 47 min, 32 sec
1937	Roger Lapebie, France	138 hrs, 58 min, 31 sec
1938	Gino Bartali, Italy	148 hrs, 29 min, 12 sec
1939	Sylvere Maes, Belgium	132 hrs, 3 min, 17 sec
1940-46	No race	
1947	Jean Robic, France	148 hrs, 11 min, 25 sec
1948	Gino Bartali, Italy	147 hrs, 10 min, 36 sec
1949	Fausto Coppi, Italy	149 hrs, 40 min, 49 sec
1950	Ferdi Kubler, Switzerland	145 hrs, 36 min, 56 sec
1951	Hugo Koblet, Switzerland	142 hrs, 20 min, 14 sec
1952	Fausto Coppi, Italy	151 hrs, 57 min, 20 sec
1953	Louison Bobet, France	129 hrs, 23 min, 25 sec
1954	Louison Bobet, France	140 hrs, 6 min, 5 sec
1955	Louison Bobet, France	130 hrs, 29 min, 26 sec
1956	Roger Walkowiak, France	124 hrs, 1 min, 16 sec
1957	Jacques Anquetil, France	129 hrs, 46 min, 11 sec
1958	Charly Gaul, Luxembourg	116 hrs, 59 min, 5 sec
1959	Federico Bahamontes, Spain	123 hrs, 46 min, 45 sec
1960	Gastone Nencini, Italy	112 hrs, 8 min, 42 sec
1961	Jacques Anquetil, France	122 hrs, 1 min, 33 sec
1962	Jacques Anquetil, France	114 hrs, 31 min, 54 sec
1963	Jacques Anquetil, France	113 hrs, 30 min, 5 sec
1964	Jacques Anquetil, France	127 hrs, 9 min, 44 sec
1965	Felice Gimondi, Italy	116 hrs, 42 min, 6 sec
1966	Lucien Aimar, France	117 hrs, 34 min, 21 sec
1967	Roger Pingeon, France	136 hrs, 53 min, 50 sec
1968	Jan Janssen, Netherlands	133 hrs, 49 min, 32 sec
1969	Eddy Merckx, Belgium	116 hrs, 16 min, 2 sec
1970	Eddy Merckx, Belgium	119 hrs, 31 min, 49 sec
1971	Eddy Merckx, Belgium	96 hrs, 45 min, 14 sec
1972	Eddy Merckx, Belgium	108 hrs, 17 min, 18 sec
1973	Luis Ocana, Spain	122 hrs, 25 min, 34 sec
1974	Eddy Merckx, Belgium	116 hrs, 16 min, 58 sec
1975	Bernard Thevenet, France	114 hrs, 35 min, 31 sec
1976	Lucien Van Impe, Belgium	116 hrs, 22 min, 23 sec
1977	Bernard Thevenet, France	115 hrs, 38 min, 30 sec
1978	Bernard Hinault, France	108 hrs, 18 min
1979	Bernard Hinault, France	103 hrs, 6 min, 50 sec
1980	Joop Zoetemelk, Netherlands	109 hrs, 19 min, 14 sec
1981	Bernard Hinault, France	96 hrs, 19 min, 38 sec
1982	Bernard Hinault, France	92 hrs, 8 min, 46 sec
1983	Laurent Fignon, France	105 hrs, 7 min, 52 sec
1984	Laurent Fignon, France	112 hrs, 3 min, 40 sec
1985	Bernard Hinault, France	113 hrs, 24 min, 23 sec
1986	Greg LeMond, United States	110 hrs, 35 min, 19 sec
1987	Stephen Roche, Ireland	115 hrs, 27 min, 42 sec
1988	Pedro Delgado, Spain	84 hrs, 27 min, 53 sec
1989	Greg LeMond, United States	87 hrs, 38 min, 35 sec
1990	Greg LeMond, United States	90 hrs, 43 min, 20 sec
1991	Miguel Induráin, Spain	101 hrs, 1 min, 20 sec
1992	Miguel Induráin, Spain	100 hrs, 49 min, 30 sec
1993	Miguel Induráin, Spain	95 hrs, 57 min, 9 sec
1994	Miguel Induráin, Spain	103 hrs, 38 min, 38 sec

Sled Dog Racing

Iditarod

Year	Winner	Time	Year	Winner	Time
1973	Dick Wilmarth	20 days, 00:49:41	1984	Dean Osmar	12 days, 15:07:33
1974	Carl Huntington	20 days, 15:02:07	1985	Libby Riddles	18 days, 00:20:17
1975	Emmitt Peters	14 days, 14:43:45	1986	Susan Butcher	11 days, 15:06:00
1976	Gerald Riley	18 days, 22:58:17	1987	Susan Butcher	11 days, 02:05:13
1977	Rick Swenson	16 days, 16:27:13	1988	Susan Butcher	11 days, 11:41:40
1978	Dick Mackey	14 days, 18:52:24	1989	Joe Runyan	11 days, 05:24:34
1979	Rick Swenson	15 days, 10:37:47	1990	Susan Butcher	11 days, 01:53:23
1980	Joe May	14 days, 07:11:51	1991	Rick Swenson	12 days, 16:34:39
1981	Rick Swenson	12 days, 08:45:02	1992	Martin Buser	10 days, 19:17:15
1982	Rick Swenson	16 days, 04:40:10	1993	Jeff King	10 days, 15:38:15
1983	Dick Mackey	12 days, 14:10:44	1994	Martin Buser	10 days, 13:02:39

Fishing

Saltwater Fishing Records

Species	Weight	Where Caught	Date	Angler
Albacore	88 lb 2 oz	Port Mogan, Canary Islands	Nov 19, 1977	Siegfried Dickemann
Amberjack, greater	155 lb 10 oz	Challenger Bank, Bermuda	June 24, 1981	Joseph Dawson
Amberjack, Pacific	104 lb	Baja California, Mexico	July 4, 1984	Richard Cresswell
Barracuda, great	85 lb	Christmas Island, Kiribati	April 11, 1992	John W. Helfrich
Barracuda, Mexican	21 lb	Phantom Isle, Costa Rica	Mar 27, 1987	E. Greg Kent
Barracuda, pickhandle	58 lb 6 oz	Mission Beach, Australia	Nov 7, 1993	Bruce Shepherd
Bass, barred sand	13 lb 3 oz	Huntington Beach, CA	Aug 29, 1988	Robert Halaj
Bass, black sea	9 lb 8 oz	Virginia Beach, VA	Jan 9, 1987	Joe Mizelle, Jr
Bass, European	20 lb 11 oz	Stes Maries de la Mer, France	May 6, 1986	Jean Baptiste Bayle
Bass, giant sea	563 lb 8 oz	Anacapa Island, CA	Aug 20, 1968	James D. McAdam, Jr
Bass, striped	78 lb 8 oz	Atlantic City, NJ	Sep 21, 1982	Albert McReynolds
Bluefish	31 lb 12 oz	Hatteras Inlet, NC	Jan 30, 1972	James M. Hussey
Bonefish	19 lb	Zululand, South Africa	May 26, 1962	Brian W. Batchelor
Bonito, Atlantic	18 lb 4 oz	Fayal Island, Azores	July 8, 1953	D. G. Higgs
Bonito, Pacific	14 lb 12 oz	Baja California, Mexico	Oct. 12, 1980	Jerome H. Rilling
Cabezon	23 lb	Juan De Fuca Strait, WA	Aug 4, 1990	Wesley Hunter
Cobia	135 lb 9 oz	Shark Bay, Australia	July 9, 1985	Peter W. Goulding
Cod, Atlantic	98 lb 12 oz	Isle of Shoals, NH	June 8, 1969	Alphonse Bielevich
Cod, Pacific	30 lb	Andrew Bay, AK	June 7, 1984	Donald Vaughn
Conger	110 lb 8 oz	Plymouth, England	Aug. 20, 1991	Hans C. Clausen
Dolphin	87 lb	Papagallo Gulf, Costa Rica	Sep 25, 1976	Manual Salazar
Drum, black	113 lb 1 oz	Lewes, DE	Sep 15, 1975	Gerald Townsend
Drum, red	94 lb 2 oz	Avon, NC	Nov 7, 1984	David Deuel
Eel, marbled	36 lb 1 oz	Durban, South Africa	June 10, 1984	Ferdie van Nooten
Eel, American	8 lb 8 oz	Brewster, MA	May 17, 1992	Gerald G. Lapierre, Sr
Flounder, southern	20 lb 9 oz	Nassau Sound, FL	Dec 23, 1983	Larenza Mungin
Flounder, summer	22 lb 7 oz	Montauk, NY	Sep 15, 1975	Charles Nappi
Grouper, Warsaw	436 lb 12 oz	Destin, FL	Dec 22, 1985	Steve Haeusler
Halibut, Atlantic	255 lb 4 oz	Gloucester, MA	July 28, 1989	Sonny Manley
Halibut, California	53 lb 4 oz	Santa Rosa Island, CA	July 7, 1988	Russell Harmon
Halibut, Pacific	368 lb	Gustavus, AK	July 5, 1991	Celia H. Dueitt
Jack, crevalle	57 lb 5 oz	Barra do Kwanza, Angola	Oct 10, 1992	Cam Nicolson
Jack, horse-eye	24 lb 8 oz	Miami, FL	Dec 20, 1982	Tilo Schnau
Jack, Pacific, crevalle	29 lb. 8 oz	Playa Zancudo, Costa Rica	Jan 1, 1991	Ronald C. Snody
Jewfish	680 lb	Fernandina Beach, FL	May 20, 1961	Lynn Joyner
Kawakawa	29 lb	NSW, Australia	Dec 17, 1986	Ronald Nakamura
Lingcod	69 lb	Langara Island, B.C.	June 16, 1992	Murray M. Romer
Mackerel, cero	17 lb 2 oz	Islamorada, FL	Apr 5, 1986	G. Michael Mills
Mackerel, king	90 lb	Key West, FL	Feb 16, 1976	Norton Thomton
Mackerel, Spanish	13 lb	Ocracoke Inlet, NC	Nov 4, 1987	Robert Cranton
Marlin, Atlantic blue	1402 lb	Vitoria, Brazil	Feb. 29, 1992	Paulo R.A. Amorim
Marlin, black	1560 lb	Cabo Blanco, Peru	Aug 4, 1953	A. C. Glassell, Jr
Marlin, Pacific blue	1376 lb	Kaaiwa Point, HI	May 31, 1982	J. W. deBeaubien
Marlin, striped	494 lb	Tutukaka, New Zealand	Jan 16, 1986	Bill Boniface
Marlin, white	181 lb 14 oz	Vitoria, Brazil	Dec 8, 1979	Evandro Luiz Caser
Permit	53 lb 4 oz	Lake Worth, FL	Mar 25, 1994	Roy Brooker
Pollock	46 lb 10 oz	Ogunquit, ME	Oct. 24, 1990	Linda Paul

Fishing (Cont.)

Saltwater Fishing Records (Cont.)

Species	Weight	Where Caught	Date	Angler
Pompano, African	50 lb 8 oz	Daytona Beach, FL	Apr 21, 1990	Tom Sargent
Roosterfish	114 lb	La Paz, Mexico	June 1, 1960	Abe Sackheim
Runner, blue	8 lb 4 oz	Bimini, Bahamas	Sep 9, 1990	Brent Rowland
Runner, rainbow	37 lb 9 oz	Isla Clarion, Mexico	Nov. 21, 1991	Tom Pfleger
Sailfish, Atlantic	135 lb 5 oz	Lagos, Nigeria	Nov. 10, 1991	Ron King
Sailfish, Pacific	221 lb	Santa Cruz Island, Ecuador	Feb 12, 1947	C. W. Stewart
Seabass, white	83 lb 12 oz	San Felipe, Mexico	Mar 31, 1953	L. C. Baumgardner
Seatrout, spotted	16 lb	Mason's Beach, VA	May 28, 1977	William Katko
Shark, blue	437 lb	Catherine Bay, NSW, Australia	Oct 2, 1976	Peter Hyde
Shark, Greenland	1708 lb 9 oz	Trondheim, Norway	Oct 18, 1987	Terje Nordtvedt
Shark, hammerhead	991 lb	Sarasota, FL	May 30, 1982	Allen Ogle
Shark, white	2664 lb	Ceduna, Australia	Apr 21, 1959	Alfred Dean
Shark, mako	1115 lb	Black River, Mauritius	Nov 16, 1988	Patrick Guillanton
Shark, porbeagle	507 lb	Caithness, Scotland	Mar 9, 1993	Christopher Bennet
Shark, thresher	802 lb	Tutukaka, New Zealand	Feb 8, 1981	Dianne North
Shark, tiger	1780 lb	Cherry Grove, SC	June 14, 1964	Walter Maxwell
Skipjack, black	26 lb	Baja California, Mexico	Oct. 23, 1991	Clifford K. Hamaishi
Snapper, cubera	121 lb 8 oz	Cameron, LA	July 5, 1982	Mike Hebert
Snook	53 lb 10 oz	Costa Rica	Oct 18, 1978	Gilbert Ponzi
Spearfish	90 lb 13 oz	Madeira Island, Portugal	June 2, 1980	Joseph Larkin
Swordfish	1182 lb	Iquique, Chile	May 7, 1953	L. Marron
Tanguigue	99 lb	Natal, South Africa	Mar 14, 1982	Michael J. Wilkinson
Tarpon	283 lb 4 oz	Sherbor Island, Sierre Leone	April 16, 1991	Yvon Victor Sebag
Tautog	24 lb	Wachapreagee, VA	Aug 25, 1987	Gregory Bell
Tope	72 lb 12 oz	Parengarenga Harbor, New Zealand	Dec 19, 1986	Melanie Feldman
Trevally, bigeye	15 lb 8 oz	Waianae, HI	Mar 6, 1992	Darryl R. Bailey
Trevally, giant	145 lb 8 oz	Maui, HI	Mar 28, 1991	Russell Mori
Tuna, Atlantic bigeye	375 lb 8 oz	Ocean City, MD	Aug 26, 1977	Cecil Browne
Tuna, blackfin	42 lb	Bermuda	June 2, 1978	Alan J. Card
		Challenger Bank, Bermuda	July 18, 1989	Gilbert C. Pearman
Tuna, bluefin	1496 lb	Aulds Cove, Nova Scotia	Oct 26, 1979	Ken Fraser
Tuna, longtail	79 lb 2 oz	Montague Island, NSW, Australia	Apr 12, 1982	Tim Simpson
Tuna, Pacific bigeye	435 lb	Cabo Blanco, Peru	Apr 17, 1957	Russel Lee
Tuna, skipjack	41 lb 14 oz	Mauritius	Nov 12, 1985	Edmund Heinzen
Tuna, southern bluefin	348 lb 5 oz	Whakatane, New Zealand	Jan 16, 1981	Rex Wood
Tuna, yellowfin	388 lb 12 oz	San Benedicto Is, Mexico	Apr 1, 1977	Curt Wiesenhutter
Tunny, little	35 lb 2 oz	Cape de Garde, Algeria	Dec 14, 1988	Jean Yves Chatard
Wahoo	155 lb 8 oz	San Salvador, Bahamas	Apr 3, 1990	William Bourne
Weakfish	19 lb 2 oz	Jones Beach Inlet, NY	Oct 11, 1984	Dennis Rooney
		Delaware Bay, Delaware	May 20, 1989	William E. Thomas
Yellowtail, California	79 lb 4 oz	Baja California, Mexico	July 2, 1991	Robert I. Welker
Yellowtail, southern	114 lb 10 oz	Tauranga, New Zealand	Feb 5, 1984	Mike Godfrey

Freshwater Fishing Records

Species	Weight	Where Caught	Date	Angler
Barramundi	63 lb 2 oz	Queensland, Australia	April 28, 1991	Scott Barnsley
Bass, largemouth	22 lb 4 oz	Montgomery Lake, GA	June 2, 1932	George W. Perry
Bass, peacock	26 lb 8 oz	Matevini River, Colombia	Jan 26, 1982	Rod Neubert
Bass, redeye	8 lb 3 oz	Flint River, GA	Oct 23, 1977	David A. Hubbard
Bass, rock	3 lb	York River, Ontario	Aug 1, 1974	Peter Gulgin
Bass, smallmouth	11 lb 15 oz	Dale Hollow Lake, KY	July 9, 1955	David L. Hayes
Bass, Suwannee	3 lb 14 oz	Suwannee River, FL	Mar 2, 1985	Ronnie Everett
Bass, white	6 lb 13 oz	Orange, VA	July 31, 1989	Ronald Sprouse
Bass, whiterock	24 lb 3 oz	Leesville Lake, VA	May 12, 1989	David Lambert
Bass, yellow	2 lb 4 oz	Lake Monroe, IN	Mar 27, 1977	Donald L. Stalker
Bluegill	4 lb 12 oz	Ketona Lake, AL	Apr 9, 1950	T. S. Hudson
Bowfin	21 lb 8 oz	Florence, SC	Jan 29, 1980	Robert Harmon
Buffalo, bigmouth	70 lb 5 oz	Bastrop, LA	Apr 21, 1980	Delbert Sisk
Buffalo, black	55 lb 8 oz	Cherokee Lake, TN	May 3, 1984	Edward McLain
Buffalo, smallmouth	68 lb 8 oz	Lake Hamilton, AR	May 16, 1984	Jerry Dolezal
Bullhead, brown	5 lb 8 oz	Veal Pond, GA	May 22, 1975	Jimmy Andrews
Bullhead, yellow	4 lb 4 oz	Mormon Lake, AZ	May 11, 1984	Emily Williams
Burbot	18 lb 4 oz	Pickford, MI	Jan 31, 1980	Thomas Courtemanche

Freshwater Fishing Records (Cont.)

Species	Weight	Where Caught	Date	Angler
Carp	75 lb 11 oz	Lac de St Cassien, France	May 21, 1987	Leo van der Gugten
Catfish, blue	109 lb 4 oz	Moncks Corner, SC	Mar 14, 1991	George A. Lijewski
Catfish, channel	58 lb	Santee-Cooper Reservoir, SC	July 7, 1964	W. B. Whaley
Catfish, flathead	91 lb 4 oz	Lake Lewisville, TX	Mar 28, 1982	Mike Rogers
Catfish, white	18 lb 14 oz	Inverness, FL	Sept. 21, 1991	Jim Miller
Char, Arctic	32 lb 9 oz	Tree River, Canada	July 30, 1981	Jeffrey Ward
Crappie, white	5 lb 3 oz	Enid Dam, MS	July 31, 1957	Fred L. Bright
Dolly Varden	18 lb 9 oz	Mashutuk River, AK	July 13, 1993	Richard B. Evans
Dorado	51 lb 5 oz	Corrientes, Argentina	Sep 27, 1984	Armando Giudice
Drum, freshwater	54 lb 8 oz	Nickajack Lake, TN	Apr 20, 1972	Benny E. Hull
Gar, alligator	279 lb	Rio Grande River, TX	Dec 2, 1951	Bill Valverde
Gar, Florida	21 lb 3 oz	Boca Raton, FL	June 3, 1981	Jeff Sabol
Gar, longnose	50 lb 5 oz	Trinity River, TX	July 30, 1954	Townsend Miller
Gar, shortnose	5 lb	Sally Jones Lake, OK	Apr 26, 1985	Buddy Croslin
Gar, spotted	8 lb 12 oz	Tennessee River, AL	Aug 26, 1987	Winston Baker
Grayling, Arctic	5 lb 15 oz	Katseyedie River, Northwest Territories	Aug 16, 1967	Jeanne P. Branson
Inconnu	53 lb	Pah River, AK	Aug 20, 1986	Lawrence Hudnall
Kokanee	9 lb 6 oz	Okanagan Lake, Vernon, BC	June 18, 1988	Norm Kuhn
Muskellunge	65 lb	Lake Huron	Oct 15, 1988	Ken J. O'Brien
Muskellunge, tiger	51 lb 3 oz	Lac Vieux-Desert, WI, MI	July 16, 1919	John Knobla
Perch, Nile	191 lb 8 oz	Lake Victoria, Kenya	Sept. 5, 1991	Andy Davison
Perch, white	4 lb 12 oz	Messalonskee Lake, ME	June 4, 1949	Mrs Earl Small
Perch, yellow	4 lb 3 oz	Bordentown, NJ	May 1865	C. C. Abbot
Pickerel, chain	9 lb 6 oz	Homerville, GA	Feb 17, 1961	Baxley McQuaig, Jr
Pike, northern	55 lb 1 oz	Lake of Grefeern, West Germany	Oct 16, 1986	Lothar Louis
Redhorse, greater	9 lb 3 oz	Salmon River, Pulaski, NY	May 11, 1985	Jason Wilson
Redhorse, silver	11 lb 7 oz	Plum Creek, WI	May 29, 1985	Neal Long
Salmon, Atlantic	79 lb 2 oz	Tana River, Norway	1928	Henrik Henriksen
Salmon, chinook	97 lb 4 oz	Kenai River, AK	May 17, 1985	Les Anderson
Salmon, chum	32 lb	Behm Canal, AK	June 7, 1985	Fredrick Thynes
Salmon, coho	33 lb 4 oz	Pulaski, NY	Sept 27, 1989	Jerry Lifton
Salmon, pink	13 lb 1 oz	Ontario, Canada	Sept. 23, 1992	Ray Higaki
Salmon, sockeye	15 lb 3 oz	Kenai River, AK	Aug 9, 1987	Stan Roach
Sauger	8 lb 12 oz	Lake Sakakawea, ND	Oct 6, 1971	Mike Fischer
Shad, American	11 lb 4 oz	Connecticut River, MA	May 19, 1986	Bob Thibodo
Sturgeon, white	468 lb	Benicia, CA	July 9, 1983	Joey Pallotta III
Sunfish, green	2 lb 2 oz	Stockton Lake, MO	June 18, 1971	Paul M. Dilley
Sunfish, redbreast	1 lb 12 oz	Suwannee River, FL	May 29, 1984	Alvin Buchanan
Sunfish, redear	4 lb 13 oz	Marianna, FL	Mar 13, 1986	Joey Floyd
Tigerfish, giant	97 lb	Zaire River, Kinshasa, Zaire	July 9, 1988	Raymond Houtmans
Tilapia	6 lb	Clewiston, FL	June 24, 1989	Joseph Tucker
Trout, Apache	5 lb 3 oz	Apache Reservation, AZ	May 29, 1991	John Baldwin
Trout, brook	14 lb 8 oz	Nipigon River, Ontario	July 1916	W. J. Cook
Trout, brown	40 lb 4 oz	Heber Springs, AR	May 9, 1992	Howard L. Collins
Trout, bull	32 lb	Lake Pend Oreille, ID	Oct 27, 1949	N. L. Higgins
Trout, cutthroat	41 lb	Pyramid Lake, NV	Dec 1925	J. Skimmerhorn
Trout, golden	11 lb	Cook's Lake, WY	Aug 5, 1948	Charles S. Reed
Trout, lake	66 lb 8 oz	Great Bear Lake, Northwest Territories	July 19, 1991	Rodney Harback
Trout, rainbow	42 lb 2 oz	Bell Island, AK	June 22, 1970	David Robert White
Trout, tiger	20 lb 13 oz	Lake Michigan, WI	Aug 12, 1978	Pete Friedland
Walleye	25 lb	Old Hickory Lake, TN	Aug 1, 1960	Mabry Harper
Warmouth	2 lb 7 oz	Yellow River, Holt, FL	Oct 19, 1985	Tony D. Dempsey
Whitefish, lake	14 lb 6 oz	Meaford, Ontario	May 21, 1984	Dennis Laycock
Whitefish, mountain	5 lb 6 oz	Rioh River, Saskatchewan, Canada	June 15, 1988	John Bell
Whitefish, broad	9 lb	Tozitna River, Alaska	July 17, 1989	Al Mathews
Whitefish, round	6 lb	Putahow River, Manitoba	June 14, 1984	Allen Ristori
Zander	25 lb 2 oz	Trosa, Sweden	June 12, 1986	Harry Lee Tennison

Greyhound Racing

Annual Greyhound Race of Champions Winners

Year	Winner (Sex)	Affiliation/Owner	Year	Winner	Affiliation/Owner
1982	DD's Jackie (F)	Wonderland Park/R.H. Walters, Jr.	1988	BB's Old Yellow (M)	Supplemental (Southland)/ Margie Bonita Hyers
1983	Comin' Attraction (F)	Rocky Mt Greyhound Park/ Bob Riggin	1989	Osh Kosh Juliet (F)	Tampa Greyhound Track/ William F. Pollard
1984	Fallon (F)	Tampa Greyhound Track/ E.J. Alderson	1990	Daring Don (M)	Interstate Kennel Club/ Perry Padrta
1985	Lady Delight (F)	Lincoln Greyhound Park/ Julian A. Gay	1991	Mo Kick (M)	Flagler Greyhound Track/ Eric M. Kennon
1986	Ben G Speedboat (M)	Multnomah Kennel Club/ Louis Bennett	1992	Dicky Vallie (M)	Dairyland Greyhound Track/ George Benjamin
1987	ET's Pesky (F)	Supplemental (Flagler)/ Emil Tanis	1993	Mega Morris (M)	Jacksonville Kennel Club/ Ferrell's Kennel

Gymnastics

World Champions

MEN

All-Around

Year	Champion and Nation	Year	Champion and Nation
1903	Joseph Martinez, France	1958	Boris Shaklin, Soviet Union
1905	Marcel Lalue, France	1962	Yuri Titov, Soviet Union
1907	Joseph Czada, Czechoslovakia	1966	Mikhail Voronin, Soviet Union
1909	Marcos Torres, France	1970	Eizo Kenmotsu, Japan
1911	Ferdinand Steiner, Czechoslovakia	1974	Shigeru Kasamatsu, Japan
1913	Marcos Torres, France	1978	Nikolai Andrianov, Soviet Union
1922	Peter Sumi, Yugoslavia	1979	Alexander Ditiatin, Soviet Union
	Frantisek Pechacek, Czech	1981	Yuri Korolev, Soviet Union
1926	Peter Sumi, Yugoslavia	1983	Dimitri Bilozertchev, Soviet Union
1930	Josip Primozic, Yugoslavia	1985	Yuri Korolev, Soviet Union
1934	Eugene Mack, Switzerland	1987	Dimitri Bilozertchev, Soviet Union
1938	Jan Gajdos, Czechoslovakia	1989	Igor Korobchinsky, Soviet Union
1950	Walter Lehmann, Switzerland	1991	Grigori Misutin, CIS
1954	Valentin Mouratov, Soviet Union	1993	Vitaly Scherbo, Belarus
	Victor Chukarin, Soviet Union	1994	Ivan Ivankov, Belarus

Pommel Horse

Year	Champion and Nation	Year	Champion and Nation
1930	Josip Primozic, Yugoslavia	1981	Michael Mikolai,E Germ/Li Xiaoping, Chi
1934	Eugene Mack, Switzerland	1983	Dmitri Bilozertchev, Soviet Union
1938	Michael Reusch, Switzerland	1985	Valentin Moguilny, Soviet Union
1950	Josef Stalder, Switzerland	1987	Zsolt Borkai, Hungary
1954	Grant Chaguinjan, Soviet Union		Dmitri Bilozertchev, Soviet Union
1958	Boris Shaklin, Soviet Union	1989	Valentin Moguilny, Soviet Union
1962	Miroslav Cerar, Yugoslavia	1991	Valeri Belenki, Soviet Union
1966	Miroslav Cerar, Yugoslavia	1992	Pae Gil Su, North Korea
1970	Miroslav Cerar, Yugoslavia		Vitaly Scherbo, CIS
1974	Zoltan Magyar, Hungary		Li Jing, China
1978	Zoltan Magyar, Hungary	1993	Pae Gil Su, North Korea
1979	Zoltan Magyar, Hungary	1994	Marius Urzica, Romania

Floor Exercise

Year	Champion and Nation	Year	Champion and Nation
1930	Josip Primozic, Yugoslavia	1970	Akinori Nakayama, Japan
1934	Georges Miesz, Switzerland	1974	Shigeru Kasamatsu, Japan
1938	Jan Gajdos, Czechoslovakia	1978	Kurt Thomas, United States
1950	Josef Stalder, Switzerland	1979	Kurt Thomas, United States
1954	Valentin Mouratov, Soviet Union		Roland Brucker, GDR
	Masao Takemoto, Japan	1981	Yuri Korolev, Sov. Union/Li Yuejui, Chi
1958	Masao Takemoto, Japan	1983	Tong Fei, China
1962	Nobuyuki Aihara, Japan	1985	Tong Fei, China
	Yukio Endo, Japan	1987	Lou Yun, China
1966	Akinori Nakayama, Japan	1989	Igor Korobchinsky, Soviet Union

Gymnastics (Cont.)

World Champions (Cont.)

MEN (Cont.)

Floor Exercise (Cont.)

Year	Champion and Nation	Year	Champion and Nation
1991	Igor Korobchinsky, Soviet Union	1993	Grigori Misutin, Ukraine
1992	Igor Korobchinsky, CIS	1994	Vitaly Scherbo, Belarus

Rings

Year	Champion and Nation	Year	Champion and Nation
1930	Emanuel Loffler, Czechoslovakia	1978	Nikolai Andrianov, Soviet Union
1934	Alois Hudec, Czechoslovakia	1979	Alexander Ditiatin, Soviet Union
1938	Alois Hudec, Czechoslovakia	1981	Alexander Ditiatin, Soviet Union
1950	Walter Lehmann, Switzerland	1983	Dimitri Bilozertchev, Soviet Union
1954	Albert Azarian, Soviet Union	1985	Li Ning, China/Yuri Korolev, Sov Union
1958	Albert Azarian, Soviet Union	1987	Yuri Korolev, Soviet Union
1962	Yuri Titov, Soviet Union	1989	Andreas Aguilar, West Germany
1966	Mikhail Voronin, Soviet Union	1991	Grigory Misutin, Soviet Union
1970	Akinori Nakayama, Japan	1992	Vitaly Scherbo, CIS
1974	Nikolai Andrianov, Soviet Union	1993	Yuri Chechi, Italy
	Danut Grecu, Romania	1994	Yuri Chechi, Italy

Parallel Bars

Year	Champion and Nation	Year	Champion and Nation
1930	Josip Primozic, Yugoslavia	1983	Vladimir Artemov, Soviet Union
1934	Eugene Mack, Switzerland		Lou Yun, China
1938	Michael Reusch, Switzerland	1985	Sylvio Kroll, East Germany
1950	Hans Eugster, Switzerland		Valentin Moguilny, Soviet Union
1954	Victor Chukarin, Soviet Union	1987	Vladimir Artemov, Soviet Union
1958	Boris Shaklin, Soviet Union	1989	Li Jing, China
1962	Miroslav Cerar, Yugoslavia		Vladimir Artemov, Soviet Union
1966	Sergei Diamidov, Soviet Union	1991	Li Jing, China
1970	Akinori Nakayama, Japan	1992	Li Jin, China
1974	Eizo Kenmotsu, Japan		Alexei Voropaev, CIS
1978	Eizo Kenmotsu, Japan	1993	Vitaly Scherbo, Belarus
1979	Bart Conner, United States	1994	Huang Liping, China
1981	Koji Gushiken, Japan		
	Alexandr Ditiatin, Soviet Union		

High Bar

Year	Champion and Nation	Year	Champion and Nation
1930	Istvan Pelle, Hungary	1979	Kurt Thomas, United States
1934	Ernst Winter, Germany	1981	Alexander Takchev, Soviet Union
1938	Michael Reusch, Switzerland	1983	Dimitri Bilozertchev, Soviet Union
1950	Paavo Aaltonen, Finland	1985	Tong Fei, China
1954	Valentin Mouratov, Soviet Union	1987	Dimitri Bilozertchev, Soviet Union
1958	Boris Shaklin, Soviet Union	1989	Li Chunyang, China
1962	Takashi Ono, Japan	1991	Li Chunyang, China
1966	Akinori Nakayama, Japan		Ralf Buechner, Germany
1970	Eizo Kenmotsu, Japan	1992	Grigori Misutin, CIS
1974	Eberhard Gienger, West Germany	1993	Sergei Kharkov, Russia
1978	Shigeru Kasamatsu, Japan	1994	Vitaly Scherbo, Belarus

Vault

Year	Champion and Nation	Year	Champion and Nation
1934	Eugene Mack, Switzerland	1981	Ralf-Peter Hemmann, East Germany
1938	Eugene Mack, Switzerland	1983	Arthur Akopian, Soviet Union
1950	Ernst Gebendinger, Switzerland	1985	Yuri Korolev, Soviet Union
1954	Leo Sotornik, Czechoslovakia	1987	Lou Yun, China
1958	Yuri Titov, Soviet Union		Sylvio Kroll, East Germany
1962	Premysel Krbec, Czechoslovakia	1989	Joreg Behrend, East Germany
1966	Haruhiro Yamashita, Japan	1991	Yoo Ok Youl, South Korea
1970	Mitsuo Tsukahara, Japan	1992	Yoo Ok Youl, South Korea
1974	Shigeru Kasamatsu, Japan	1993	Vitaly Scherbo, Belarus
1978	Junichi Shimizu, Japan	1994	Vitaly Scherbo, Belarus
1979	Alexander Ditiatin, Soviet Union		

World Champions (Cont.)

WOMEN

All-Around

Year	Champion and Nation	Year	Champion and Nation
1934	Vlasta Dekanova, Czechoslovakia	1979	Nelli Kim, Soviet Union
1938	Vlasta Dekanova, Czechoslovakia	1981	Olga Bicherova, Soviet Union
1950	Helena Rakoczy, Poland	1983	Natalia Yurchenko, Soviet Union
1954	Galina Roudiko, Soviet Union	1985	Elena Shoushounova, Soviet Union
1958	Larissa Latynina, Soviet Union		Oksana Omeliantchik, Soviet Union
1962	Larissa Latynina, Soviet Union	1987	Aurelia Dobre, Romania
1966	Vera Caslavska, Czechoslovakia	1989	Svetlana Bouguinskaia, Soviet Union
1970	Ludmilla Tourischeva, Soviet Union	1991	Kim Zmeskal, United States
1974	Ludmilla Tourischeva, Soviet Union	1993	Shannon Miller, United States
1978	Elena Mukhina, Soviet Union	1994	Shannon Miller, United States

Floor Exercise

Year	Champion and Nation	Year	Champion and Nation
1950	Helena Rakoczy, Poland	1983	Ecaterina Szabo, Romania
1954	Tamara Manina, Soviet Union	1985	Oksana Omeliantchik, Soviet Union
1958	Eva Bosakava, Czechoclovakia	1987	Elena Shoushounova, Soviet Union
1962	Larissa Latynina, Soviet Union		Daniela Silivas, Romania
1966	Natalia Kuchinskaya, Soviet Union	1989	Svetlana Bouguinskaia, Soviet Union
1970	Ludmilla Tourischeva, Soviet Union		Daniela Silivas, Romania
1974	Ludmilla Tourischeva, Soviet Union	1991	Cristina Bontas, Romania
1978	Nelli Kim, Soviet Union		Oksana Tchusovitina, Soviet Union
	Elena Mukhina, Soviet Union	1992	Kim Zmeskal, United States
1979	Emilia Eberle, Romania	1993	Shannon Miller, United States
1981	Natalia Ilenko, Soviet Union	1994	Dina Kochetkova, Russia

Uneven Bars

Year	Champion and Nation	Year	Champion and Nation
1950	Gertchen Kolar, Austria	1981	Maxi Gnauck, East Germany
	Anna Pettersson, Sweden	1983	Maxi Gnauck, East Germany
1954	Agnes Keleti, Hungary	1985	Gabriele Fahrnich, East Germany
1958	Larissa Latynina, Soviet Union	1987	Daniela Silivas, Romania
1962	Irina Pervuschina, Soviet Union		Doerte Thuemmler, East Germany
1966	Natalia Kuchinskaya, Soviet Union	1989	Fan Di, China
1970	Karin Janz, East Germany		Daniela Silivas, Romania
1974	Annelore Zinke, East Germany	1991	Gwang Suk Kim, North Korea
1978	Marcia Frederick, United States	1992	Lavinia Milosivici, Romania
1979	Ma Yanhong, China	1993	Shannon Miller, United States
	Maxi Gnauck, East Germany	1994	Luo Li, China

Balance Beam

Year	Champion and Nation	Year	Champion and Nation
1950	Helena Rakoczy, Poland	1981	Maxi Gnauck, East Germany
1954	Keiko Tanaka, Japan	1983	Olga Mostepanova, Soviet Union
1958	Larissa Latynina, Soviet Union	1985	Daniela Silivas, Romania
1962	Eva Bosakova, Czechoslovakia	1987	Aurelia Dobre, Romania
1966	Natalia Kuchinskaya, Soviet Union	1989	Daniela Silivas, Romania
1970	Erika Zuchold, East Germany	1991	Svetlana Boguinskaia, Soviet Union
1974	Ludmilla Tourischeva, Soviet Union	1992	Kim Zmeskal, United States
1978	Nadia Comaneci, Romania	1993	Lavinia Milosovici, Romania
1979	Vera Cerna, Czechoslovakia	1994	Shannon Miller, United States

Vault

Year	Champion and Nation	Year	Champion and Nation
1950	Helena Rakoczy, Poland	1981	Maxi Gnauck, East Germany
1954	T Manina, Sov Union/A Pettersson, Swe	1983	Boriana Stoyanova, Bulgaria
1958	Larissa Latynina, Soviet Union	1985	Elena Shoushounova, Soviet Union
1962	Vera Caslavska, Czechoslovakia	1987	Elena Shoushounova, Soviet Union
1966	Vera Caslavska, Czechoslovakia	1989	Olesia Durnik, Soviet Union
1970	Erika Zuchold, East Germany	1991	Lavinia Milosovici, Romania
1974	Olga Korbut, Soviet Union	1992	Henrietta Onodi, Hungary
1978	Nelli Kim, Soviet Union	1993	Elena Piskun, Belarus
1979	Dumitrita Turner, Romania	1994	Gina Gogean, Romania

National Champions

MEN

All-Around

Year	Champion	Year	Champion	Year	Champion
1963	Art Shurlock	1974	John Crosby	1985	Brian Babcock
1964	Rusty Mitchell	1975	Tom Beach	1986	Tim Daggett
1965	Rusty Mitchell		Bart Conner	1987	Scott Johnson
1966	Rusty Mitchell	1976	Kurt Thomas	1988	Dan Hayden
1967	Katsuzoki Kanzaki	1977	Kurt Thomas	1989	Tim Ryan
1968	Yoshi Hayasaki	1978	Kurt Thomas	1990	John Roethlisberger
1969	Steve Hug	1979	Bart Conner	1991	Chris Waller
1970	Makoto Sakamoto	1980	Peter Vidmar	1992	John Roethlisberger
	Mas Watanabe	1981	Jim Hartung	1993	John Roethlisberger
1971	Yoshi Takei	1982	Peter Vidmar	1994	Scott Keswick
1972	Yoshi Takei	1983	Mitch Gaylord		
1973	Marshall Avener	1984	Mitch Gaylord		

Floor Exercise

Year	Champion	Year	Champion	Year	Champion
1963	Tom Seward	1973	John Crosby	1986	Robert Sundstrom
1964	Rusty Mitchell	1974	John Crosby	1987	John Sweeney
1965	Rusty Mitchell	1975	Peter Korman	1988	Mark Oates
1966	Dan Millman	1977	Ron Galimore		Charles Lakes
1967	Katsuzoki Kanzaki	1978	Kurt Thomas	1989	Mike Racanelli
	Ron Aure	1979	Ron Galimore	1990	Bob Stelter
1968	Katsuzoki Kanzaki	1980	Ron Galimore	1991	Mike Racanelli
1969	Steve Hug	1981	Jim Hartung	1992	Gregg Curtis
	Dave Thor	1982	Jim Hartung	1993	Kerry Huston
1970	Makoto Sakamoto	1983	Mitch Gaylord	1994	Jeremy Killen
1971	John Crosby	1984	Peter Vidmar		
1972	Yoshi Takei	1985	Mark Oates		

Pommel Horse

Year	Champion	Year	Champion	Year	Champion
1963	Larry Spiegel	1973	Marshall Avener	1985	Phil Cahoy
1964	Sam Bailie	1974	Marshall Avener	1986	Phil Cahoy
1965	Jack Ryan	1975	Bart Conner	1987	Tim Daggett
1966	Jack Ryan	1977	Gene Whelan	1988	Kevin Davis
1967	Paul Mayer	1978	Jim Hartung	1989	Kevin Davis
	Dave Doty	1979	Bart Conner	1990	Patrick Kirksey
1968	Katsuoki Kanzaki	1980	Jim Hartung	1991	Chris Waller
1969	Dave Thor	1981	Jim Hartung	1992	Chris Waller
1970	Mas Watanabe	1982	Jim Hartung	1993	Chris Waller
1971	Leonard Caling	1983	Bart Conner	1994	Mihai Begiu
1972	Sadao Hamada	1984	Tim Daggett		

Rings

Year	Champion	Year	Champion	Year	Champion
1963	Art Shurlock	1973	Jim Ivicek	1985	Dan Hayden
1964	Glen Gailis	1974	Tom Weeden	1986	Dan Hayden
1965	Glen Gailis	1975	Tom Beach	1987	Scott Johnson
1966	Glen Gailis	1977	Kurt Thomas	1988	Dan Hayden
1967	Fred Dennis	1978	Mike Silverstein	1989	Scott Keswick
	Don Hatch	1979	Bart Conner	1990	Scott Keswick
1968	Yoshi Hayasaki	1980	Jim Hartung	1991	Scott Keswick
1969	Fred Dennis	1981	Jim Hartung	1992	Tim Ryan
	Bob Emery	1982	Jim Hartung	1993	John Roethlisberger
1970	Makoto Sakamoto		Peter Vidmar	1994	Scott Keswick
1971	Yoshi Takei	1983	Mitch Gaylord		
1972	Yoshi Takei	1984	Jim Hartung		

National Champions (Cont.)

MEN (Cont.)

Vault

Year	Champion	Year	Champion	Year	Champion
1963	Art Shurlock	1974	John Crosby	1985	Scott Johnson
1964	Gary Hery	1975	Tom Beach		Mark Oates
1965	Brent Williams	1977	Ron Galimore	1986	Scott Wilbanks
1966	Dan Millman	1978	Jim Hartung	1987	John Sweeney
1967	Jack Kenan	1979	Ron Galimore	1988	John Sweeney
	Sid Jensen	1980	Ron Galimore		Bill Paul
1968	Rich Scorza	1981	Ron Galimore	1989	Bill Roth
1969	Dave Butzman	1982	Jim Hartung	1990	Lance Ringnald
1970	Makoto Sakamoto		Jim Mikus	1991	Scott Keswick
1971	Gary Morava	1983	Chris Reigel	1992	Trent Dimas
1972	Mike Kelley	1984	Chris Reigel	1993	Bill Roth
1973	Gary Morava			1994	Keith Wiley

Parallel Bars

Year	Champion	Year	Champion	Year	Champion
1963	Tom Seward	1975	Bart Conner	1985	Tim Daggett
1964	Rusty Mitchell	1977	Kurt Thomas	1986	Tim Daggett
1965	Glen Gailis	1978	Bart Conner	1987	Scott Johnson
1966	Ray Hadley	1979	Bart Conner	1988	Dan Hayden
1967	Katsuzoki Kanzaki	1980	Phil Cahoy		Kevin Davis
	Tom Goldsborough		Larry Gerard	1989	Conrad Voorsanger
1968	Yoshi Hayasaki	1981	Bart Conner	1990	Trent Dimas
1969	Steve Hug	1982	Peter Vidmar	1991	Scott Keswick
1970	Makoto Sakamoto	1983	Mitch Gaylord	1992	Jair Lynch
1971	Brent Simmons	1984	Peter Vidmar	1993	Chainey Umphrey
1972	Yoshi Takei		Mitch Gaylord	1994	Steve McCain
1973	Marshall Avener		Tim Daggett		
1974	Jim Ivicek				

High Bars

Year	Champion	Year	Champion	Year	Champion
1963	Art Shurlock	1974	Brent Simmons	1985	Dan Hayden
1964	Glen Gailis	1975	Tom Beach	1986	Dan Hayden
1965	Rusty Mitchell	1977	Kurt Thomas		David Moriel
1966	Katsuzoki Kanzaki	1978	Kurt Thomas	1987	David Moriel
1967	Katsuzoki Kanzaki	1979	Yoichi Tomita	1988	Dan Hayden
	Jerry Fontana	1980	Jim Hartung	1989	Tim Ryan
1968	Yoshi Hayasaki	1981	Bart Conner	1990	Trent Dimas
1969	Rich Grisby	1982	Mitch Gaylord		Lance Ringnald
1970	Makoto Sakamoto	1983	Mario McCutcheon	1991	Lance Ringnald
1971	Yoshi Takei	1984	Peter Vidmar	1992	Jair Lynch
1972	Tom Lindner		Tim Daggett	1993	Steve McCain
1973	John Crosby		Mitch Gaylord	1994	Scott Keswick

WOMEN

All-Around

Year	Champion	Year	Champion	Year	Champion
1963	Donna Schanezer	1973	Joan Moore Gnat	1985	Sabrina Mar
1965	Gail Daley	1974	Joan Moore Gnat	1986	Jennifer Sey
1966	Donna Schanezer	1975	Tammy Manville	1987	Kristie Phillips
1968	Linda Scott	1976	Denise Cheshire	1988	Phoebe Mills
1969	Joyce Tanac	1977	Donna Turnbow	1989	Brandy Johnson
	Schroeder	1978	Kathy Johnson	1990	Kim Zmeskal
1970	Cathy Rigby McCoy	1979	Leslie Pyfer	1991	Kim Zmeskal
1971	Joan Moore Gnat	1980	Julianne McNamara	1992	Kim Zmeskal
	Linda Metheny	1981	Tracee Talavera	1993	Shannon Miller
	Mulvihill	1982	Tracee Talavera	1994	Dominique Dawes
1972	Joan Moore Gnat	1983	Dianne Durham		
	Cathy Rigby McCoy	1984	Mary Lou Retton		

Gymnastics (Cont.)

National Champions (Cont.)

WOMEN (Cont.)

Vault

Year	Champion	Year	Champion	Year	Champion
1963	Donna Schanezer	1974	Dianne Dunbar	1985	Yolanda Mavity
1965	Gail Daley	1975	Kolleen Casey	1986	Joyce Wilborn
1966	Donna Schanezer	1976	Debbie Wilcox	1987	Rhonda Faehn
1968	Terry Spencer	1977	Lisa Cawthron	1988	Rhonda Faehn
1969	Joyce Tanac Schroeder	1978	Rhonda Schwandt Sharon Shapiro	1989	Brandy Johnson
	Cleo Carver	1979	Christa Canary	1990	Brandy Johnson
1970	Cathy Rigby McCoy	1980	Julianne McNamara	1991	Kerri Strug
1971	Joan Moore Gnat Adele Gleaves		Beth Kline	1992	Kerri Strug
1972	Cindy Eastwood	1981	Kim Neal	1993	Dominique Dawes
1973	Roxanne Pierce Mancha	1982	Yumi Mordre	1994	Dominique Dawes
		1983	Dianne Durham		
		1984	Mary Lou Retton		

Uneven Bars

Year	Champion	Year	Champion	Year	Champion
1963	Donna Schanezer	1973	Roxanne Pierce Mancha	1984	Julianne McNamara
1965	Irene Haworth	1974	Diane Dunbar	1985	Sabrina Mar
1966	Donna Schanezer	1975	Leslie Wolfsberger	1986	Marie Roethlisberger
1968	Linda Scott	1976	Leslie Wolfsberger	1987	Melissa Marlowe
1969	Joyce Tanac Schroeder	1977	Donna Turnbow	1988	Chelle Stack
	Lisa Nelson	1978	Marcia Frederick	1989	Chelle Stack
1970	Roxanne Pierce Mancha	1979	Marcia Frederick	1990	Sandy Woolsey
1971	Joan Moore Gnat	1980	Marcia Frederick	1991	Elisabeth Crandall
1972	Cathy Rigby McCoy	1981	Julianne McNamara	1992	Dominique Dawes
		1982	Marie Roethlisberger	1993	Shannon Miller
		1983	Julianne McNamara	1994	Dominique Dawes

Balance Beam

Year	Champion	Year	Champion	Year	Champion
1963	Leissa Krol	1974	Joan Moore Gnat	1985	Kelly Garrison-Steves
1965	Gail Daley	1975	Kyle Gayner	1986	Angie Denkins
1966	Irene Haworth Linda Scott	1976	Carrie Englert	1987	Kristie Phillips
1968	Linda Scott	1977	Donna Turnbow	1988	Kelly Garrison-Steves
1969	Lonna Woodward	1978	Christa Canary	1989	Brandy Johnson
1970	Joyce Tanac Schroeder	1979	Heidi Anderson	1990	Betty Okino
1971	Linda Metheny Mulvihill	1980	Kelly Garrison-Steves	1991	Shannon Miller
1972	Kim Chace	1981	Tracee Talavera	1992	Kerri Strug Kim Zmeskal
1973	Nancy Thies Marshall	1982	Julianne McNamara	1993	Dominique Dawes
		1983	Dianne Durham	1994	Dominique Dawes
		1984	Pam Bileck Tracee Talavera		

Floor Exercise

Year	Champion	Year	Champion	Year	Champion
1963	Donna Schanezer	1975	Kathy Howard	1986	Yolanda Mavity
1965	Gail Daley	1976	Carrie Englert	1987	Kristie Phillips
1966	Donna Schanezer	1977	Kathy Johnson	1988	Phoebe Mills
1968	Linda Scott	1978	Kathy Johnson	1989	Brandy Johnson
1970	Cathy Rigby McCoy	1979	Heidi Anderson	1990	Brandy Johnson
1971	Joan Moore Gnat Linda Metheny Mulvihill	1980	Beth Kline	1991	Kim Zmeskal Dominique Dawes
		1981	Michelle Goodwin	1992	Kim Zmeskal
1972	Joan Moore Gnat	1982	Amy Koopman	1993	Shannon Miller
1973	Joan Moore Gnat	1983	Dianne Durham	1994	Dominique Dawes
1974	Joan Moore Gnat	1984	Mary Lou Retton		
		1985	Sabrina Mar		

Handball

National Four-Wall Champions

1919.....Bill Ranft	1938.....Joe Platak	1957.....Jimmy Jacobs	1976.....Fred Lewis
1920.....Max Gold	1939.....Joe Platak	1958.....John Sloan	1977.....Naty Alvarado
1921.....Carl Haedge	1940.....Joe Platak	1959.....John Sloan	1978.....Fred Lewis
1922.....Art Shinners	1941.....Joe Platak	1960.....Jimmy Jacobs	1979.....Naty Alvarado
1923.....Joe Murray	1942.....Jack Clemente	1961.....John Sloan	1980.....Naty Alvarado
1924.....Maynard Lasw	1943.....Joe Platak	1962.....Oscar Obert	1981.....Fred Lewis
1925.....Maynard Lasw	1944.....Frank Coyle	1963.....Oscar Obert	1982.....Naty Alvarado
1926.....Maynard Laswe	1945.....Joe Platak	1964.....Jimmy Jacobs	1983.....Naty Alvarado
1927.....George Nelson	1946.....Angelo Trutio	1965.....Jimmy Jacobs	1984.....Naty Alvarado
1928.....Joe Griffin	1947.....Gus Lewis	1966.....Paul Haber	1985.....Naty Alvarado
1919.....Al Banuet	1948.....Gus Lewis	1967.....Paul Haber	1986.....Naty Alvarado
1930.....Al Banuet	1949.....Vic Hershkovitz	1968.....Stuffy Singer	1987.....Naty Alvarado
1931.....Al Banuet	1950.....Ken Schneider	1969.....Paul Haber	1988.....Naty Alvarado
1932.....Angelo Trutio	1951.....Walter Plakan	1970.....Paul Haber	1989.....Poncho Monreal
1933.....Sam Atcheson	1952.....Vic Hershkowitz	1971.....Paul Haber	1990.....Naty Alvarado
1934.....Sam Atcheson	1953.....Bob Brady	1972.....Fred Lewis	1991.....John Bike
1935.....Joe Platak	1954.....Vic Hershkowitz	1973.....Terry Muck	1992.....Octavio Silveyra
1936.....Joe Platak	1955.....Jimmy Jacobs	1974.....Fred Lewis Pro	1993.....David Chapman
1937.....Joe Platak	1956.....Jimmy Jacobs	1975.....Fred Lewis	1994.....Octavio Silveyra

National Three-Wall Champions

1950.....Vic Hershkowitz	1962.....Oscar Obert	1974.....Fred Lewis	1986.....Vern Roberts
1951.....Vic Hershkowitz	1963.....Marty Decatur	1975.....Lou Russo	1987.....Vern Roberts
1952.....Vic Hershkowitz	1964.....Marty Decatur	1976.....Lou Russo	1988.....Jon Kendler
1953.....Vic Herskkowitz	1965.....Carl Obert	1977.....Fred Lewis	1989.....John Bike
1954.....Vic Hershkowitz	1966.....Marty Decatur	1978.....Fred Lewis	1990.....Vince Munoz
1955.....Vic Hershkowitz	1967.....Carl Obert	1979.....Naty Alvarado	1991.....John Bike
1956.....Vic Hershkowitz	1968.....Marty Decatur	1980.....Lou Russo	1992.....John Bike
1957.....Vic Hershkowitz	1969.....Marty Decatur	1981.....Naty Alvarado	1993.....Eric Klarman
1958.....Vic Hershkowitz	1970.....Steve August	1982.....Naty Alvarado	1994.....David Chapman
1959.....Jimmy Jacobs	1971.....Lou Russo	1983.....Naty Alvarado	
1960.....Jimmy Jacobs	1972.....Lou Russo	1984.....Naty Alvarado	
1961.....Jimmy Jacobs	1973.....Paul Haber	1985.....Vern Roberts	

World Four-Wall Champions

1984....................Merv Deckert, Canada	1991....................Pancho Monreal, United States
1986....................Vern Roberts, United States	1994....................David Chapman, United States
1988....................Naty Alvarado, United States	

Lacrosse

United States Club Lacrosse Association Champions

1960....................Mt Washington Club	1978....................Long Island Athletic Club
1961....................Baltimore Lacrosse Club	1979....................Maryland Lacrosse Club
1962....................Mt Washington Club	1980....................Long Island Athletic Club
1963....................University Club	1981....................Long Island Athletic Club
1964....................Mt Washington Club	1982....................Maryland Lacrosse Club
1965....................Mt Washington Club	1983....................Maryland Lacrosse Club
1966....................Mt Washington Club	1984....................Maryland Lacrosse Club
1967....................Mt Washington Club	1985....................Long Island-Hofstra Lacrosse Club
1968....................Long Island Athletic Club	1986....................Long Island-Hofstra Lacrosse Club
1969....................Long Island Athletic Club	1987....................Long Island-Hofstra Lacrosse Club
1970....................Long Island Athletic Club	1988....................Maryland Lacrosse Club
1971....................Long Island Athletic Club	1989....................Long Island-Hofstra Lacrosse Club
1972....................Carling	1990....................Mt Washington Club
1973....................Long Island Athletic Club	1991....................Mt Washington Club
1974....................Long Island Athletic Club	1992....................Maryland Lacrosse Club
1975....................Mt Washington Club	1993....................Mt Washington Club
1976....................Mt Washington Club	1994....................Long Island-Hofstra Lacrosse Club
1977....................Mt Washington Club	

Little League Baseball

Little League World Series Champions

Year	Champion	Runner-Up	Score	Year	Champion	Runner-Up	Score
1947	Williamsport, PA.	Lock Haven, PA.	16-7	1971	Tainan, Taiwan	Gary, IN	12-3
1948	Lock Haven, PA	St. Petersburg, FL	6-5	1972	Taipei, Taiwan	Hammond, IN	6-0
1949	Hammonton, NJ	Pensacola, FL	5-0	1973	Tainan City, Taiwan	Tucson, AZ	12-0
1950	Houston, TX	Bridgeport, CT	2-1	1974	Kao Hsiung, Taiwan	El Cajun, CA	7-2
1951	Stamford, CT	Austin, TX	3-0	1975	Lakewood, NJ	Tampa, FL	4-3
1952	Norwalk, CT	Monongahela, PA	4-3	1976	Tokyo, Japan	Campbell, CA	10-3
1953	Birmingham, AL	Schenectady, NY	1-0	1977	Kao Hsiung, Taiwan	El Cajun, CA	7-2
1954	Schenectady, NY	Colton, CA	7-5	1978	Pin-Tung, Taiwan	Danville, CA	11-1
1955	Morrisville, PA	Merchantville, NJ	4-3	1979	Hsien, Taiwan	Campbell, CA	2-1
1956	Roswell, NM	Merchantville, NJ	3-1	1980	Hua Lian, Taiwan	Tampa, FL	4-3
1957	Monterrrey, Mex.	LaMesa, CA	4-0	1981	Tai-Chung, Taiwan	Tampa, FL	4-2
1958	Monterrey, Mex.	Kankakee, IL	10-1	1982	Kirkland, WA	Hsien, Taiwan	6-0
1959	Hamtramck, MI	Auburn, CA	12-0	1983	Marietta, GA	Barahona, D.Rep.	3-1
1960	Levittown, PA	Ft. Worth, TX	5-0	1984	Seoul, S. Korea	Altamonte Sgs, FL	6-2
1961	El Cajon, CA	El Campo, TX	4-2	1985	Seoul, S. Korea	Mexicali, Mex.	7-1
1962	San Jose, CA	Kankakee, IL	3-0	1986	Tainan Park, Taiwan	Tucson, AZ	12-0
1963	Granada Hills, CA	Stratford, CT	2-1	1987	Hua Lian, Taiwan	Irvine, CA	21-1
1964	Staten Island, NY	Monterrey, Mex.	4-0	1988	Tai-Chung, Taiwan	Pearl City, HI	10-0
1965	Windsor Locks, CT	Stoney Creek, Can.	3-1	1989	Trumbull, CT	Kaohsiung, Taiwan	5-2
1966	Houston, TX	W.New York, NJ	8-2	1990	Taipei, Taiwan	Shippensburg, PA	9-0
1967	West Tokyo, Japan	Chicago, IL	4-1	1991	Tai-Chung, Taiwan	San Ramon Vly, CA	11-0
1968	Osaka, Japan	Richmond, VA	1-0	1992*	Long Beach, CA	Zamboanga, Phil.	6-0
1969	Taipei, Taiwan	Santa Clara, CA	5-0	1993	Long Beach, CA	David Chiriqui, Pan.	3-2
1970	Wayne, NJ	Campbell, CA	2-0	1994	Maracaibo, Venez	Northridge, Calif.	4-3

*Long Beach declared a 6-0 winner after the international tournament committee determined that Zamboanga City had used players that were not within its city limits.

Motor Boat Racing

American Power Boat Association Gold Cup Champions

Year	Boat	Driver	Avg MPH	Year	Boat	Driver	Avg MPH
1904	Standard (June)	Carl Riotte	23.160	1930	Hotsy Totsy	Vic Kliesrath	52.673
1904	Vingt-et-Un II (Sep)	W. Sharpe Kilmer	24.900	1931	Hotsy Totsy	Vic Kliesrath	53.602
1905	Chip I	J. Wainwright	15.000	1932	Delphine IV	Bill Horn	57.775
1906	Chip II	J. Wainwright	25.000	1933	El Lagarto	George Reis	56.260
1907	Chip II	J. Wainwright	23.903	1934	El Lagarto	George Reis	55.000
1908	Dixie II	E. J. Schroeder	29.938	1935	El Lagarto	George Reis	55.056
1909	Dixie II	E. J. Schroeder	29.590	1936	Impshi	Kaye Don	45.735
1910	Dixie III	F. K. Burnham	32.473	1937	Notre Dame	Clell Perry	63.675
1911	MIT II	J. H. Hayden	37.000	1938	Alagi	Theo Rossi	64.340
1912	P.D.Q. II	A. G. Miles	39.462	1939	My Sin	Z. G. Simmons, Jr	66.133
1913	Ankle Deep	Cas Mankowski	42.779	1940	Hotsy Totsy III	Sidney Allen	48.295
1914	Baby Speed Demon II	Jim Blackton & Bob Edgren	48.458	1941	My Sin	Z. G. Simmons, Jr	52.509
				1942-45	No race		
1915	Miss Detroit	Johnny Milot & Jack Beebe	37.656	1946	Tempo VI	Guy Lombardo	68.132
				1947	Miss Peps V	Danny Foster	57.000
1916	Miss Minneapolis	Bernard Smith	48.860	1948	Miss Great Lakes	Danny Foster	46.845
1917	Miss Detroit II	Gar Wood	54.410	1949	My Sweetie	Bill Cantrell	73.612
1918	Miss Detroit II	Gar Wood	51.619	1950	Slo-Mo-Shun IV	Ted Jones	78.216
1919	Miss Detroit III	Gar Wood	42.748	1951	Slo-Mo-Shun IV	Lou Fageol	90.871
1920	Miss America I	Gar Wood	62.022	1952	Slo-Mo-Shun IV	Stan Dollar	79.923
1921	Miss America I	Gar Wood	52.825	1953	Slo-Mo-Shun IV	Joe Taggart & Lou Fageol	99.108
1922	Packard Chriscraft	J. G. Vincent	40.253				
1923	Packard Chriscraft	Caleb Bragg	43.867	1954	Slo-Mo-Shun IV	Joe Taggart & Lou Fageol	92.613
1924	Baby Bootlegger	Caleb Bragg	45.302				
1925	Baby Bootlegger	Caleb Bragg	47.240	1955	Gale V	Lee Schoenith	99.552
1926	Greenwich Folly	George Townsend	47.984	1956	Miss Thriftaway	Bill Muncey	96.552
				1957	Miss Thriftaway	Bill Muncey	101.787
1927	Greenwich Folly	George Townsend	47.662	1958	Hawaii Kai III	Jack Regas	103.000
				1959	Maverick	Bill Stead	104.481
1928	No race			1960	No race		
1929	Imp	Richard Hoyt	48.662	1961	Miss Century 21	Bill Muncey	99.678

American Power Boat Association Gold Cup Champions *(Cont.)*

Year	Boat	Driver	Avg MPH	Year	Boat	Driver	Avg MPH
1962	Miss Century 21	Bill Muncey	100.710	1979	Atlas Van Lines	Bill Muncey	100.765
1963	Miss Bardahl	Ron Musson	105.124	1980	Miss Budweiser	Dean Chenoweth	106.932
1964	Miss Bardahl	Ron Musson	103.433				
1965	Miss Bardahl	Ron Musson	103.132	1981	Miss Budweiser	Dean Chenoweth	116.932
1966	Tahoe Miss	Mira Slovak	93.019				
1967	Miss Bardahl	Bill Shumacher	101.484	1982	Atlas Van Lines	Chip Hanauer	120.050
1968	Miss Bardahl	Bill Shumacher	108.173	1983	Atlas Van Lines	Chip Hanauer	118.507
1969	Miss Budweiser	Bill Sterett	98.504	1984	Atlas Van Lines	Chip Hanauer	130.175
1970	Miss Budweiser	Dean Chenoweth	99.562	1985	Miller American	Chip Hanauer	120.643
				1986	Miller American	Chip Hanauer	116.523
1971	Miss Madison	Jim McCormick	98.043	1987	Miller American	Chip Hanauer	127.620
1972	Atlas Van Lines	Bill Muncey	104.277	1988	Miss Circus Circus	Chip Hanauer & Jim Prevost	123.756
1973	Miss Budweiser	Dean Chenoweth	99.043	1989	Miss Budweiser	Tom D'Eath	131.209
				1990	Miss Budweiser	Tom D'Eath	143.176
1974	Pay 'n Pak	George Henley	104.428	1991	Winston Eagle	Mark Tate	137.771
1975	Pay 'n Pak	George Henley	108.921	1992	Miss Budweiser	Chip Hanauer	136.282
1976	Miss U.S.	Tom D'Eath	100.412	1993	Miss Budweiser	Chip Hanauer	141.195
1977	Atlas Van Lines	Bill Muncey	111.822	1994	Smokin' Joe Camel	Mark Tate	145.260
1978	Atlas Van Lines	Bill Muncey	111.412				

American Power Boat Association Annual Champion Drivers

Year	Driver	Boats	Wins	Year	Driver	Boats	Wins
1947	Danny Foster	Miss Peps V	6	1971	Dean Chenoweth	Miss Budweiser	2
1948	Dan Arena	Such Crust	2	1972	Bill Muncey	Atlas Van Lines	6
1949	Bill Cantrell	My Sweetie	7	1973	Mickey Remund	Pay 'n Pack	4
1950	Dan Foster	Such Crust/DaphneX	2	1974	George Henley	Pay 'n Pack	7
1951	Chuck Thompson	Miss Pepsi	5	1975	Billy Schumacher	Weisfield's	2
1952	Chuck Thompson	Miss Pepsi	3	1976	Bill Muncey	Atlas/Mt. Everelt	5
1953	Lee Schoenith	Gale II	1	1977	Mickey Remund	Miss Budweiser	3
1954	Lee Schoenith	Gale V	4	1978	Bill Muncey	Atlast Van Lines	6
1955	Lee Schoenith	Gale V/Wha Hoppen	1	1979	Bill Muncey	Atlas Van Lines	7
1956	Russ Schleeh	Shanty I	3	1980	Dean Chenoweth	MIss Budweiser	5
1957	Jack Regas	Hawaii Kai III	5	1981	Dean Chenoweth	Miss Budweiser	6
1958	Mira Slovak	Bardah/Miss Buren	3	1982	Chip Hanauer	Atlas Van Lines	5
1959	Bill Stead	Maverick	5	1983	Chip Hanauer	Atlas Van Lines	3
1960	Bill Muncey	Miss Thriftway	4	1984	Jim Kropfeld	Miss Budweiser	4
1961	Bill Muncey	Miss Century 21	4	1985	Chip Hanauer	Miller American	5
1962	Bill Muncey	Miss Century 21	5	1986	Jim Kropfeld	Miss Budweiser	3
1963	Bill Cantrell	Gale V	0	1987	Jim Kropfeld	Miss Budweiser	5
1964	Ron Musson	Miss Bardahl	4	1988	Tom D'Eath	Miss Budweiser	4
1965	Ron Musson	Miss Bardahl	4	1989	Chip Hanauer	Miss Circus Circus	3
1966	Mira Slovak	Tahoe Miss	4	1990	Chip Hanauer	Miss Circus Circus	6
1967	Bill Schumacher	Miss Bardahl	6	1991	Mark Tate	Winston/Oberto	3
1968	Bill Schumacher	Miss Bardahl	4	1992	Chip Hanauer	Miss Budweiser	7
1969	Bill Sterett, Sr.	Miss Budweiser	4	1993	Chip Hanauer	Miss Budweiser	7
1970	Dean Chenoweth	Miss Budweiser	4				

American Power Boat Association Annual Champion Boats

Year	Boat	Owner	Wins	Year	Boat	Owner	Wins
1970	Miss Budweiser	Little-Friedkin	4	1982	Atlas Van Lines	Fran Muncey	5
1971	Miss Budweiser	Little-Friedkin	2	1983	Atlas Van Lines	Muncey-Lucero	3
1972	Atlas Van Lines	Joe Schoenith	6	1984	Miss Budweiser	Bernie Little	6
1973	Pay 'n Pak	Dave Heerensperger	4	1985	Miller American	Muncey-Lucero	5
1974	Pay 'n Pak	Dave Heerensperger	7	1986	Miss Budweiser	Bernie Little	3
1975	Pay 'n Pak	Dave Heerensperger	5	1987	Miss Budweiser	Bernie Little	5
1976	Atlas Van Lines	Bill Muncey	5	1988	Miss Budweiser	Bernie Little	4
1977	Miss Budweiser	Bernie Little	3	1989	Miss Budweiser	Bernie Little	4
1978	Atlas Van Lines	Bill Muncey	6	1990	Circus Circus	Bill Bennett	6
1979	Atlas Van Lines	Bill Muncey	7	1991	Miss Budweiser	Bernie Little	4
1980	Miss Budweiser	Bernie Little	5	1992	Miss Budweiser	Bernie Little	7
1981	Miss Budweiser	Bernie Little	6	1993	Miss Budweiser	Bernie Little	7

Polo

United States Open Polo Champions

1904 ......Wanderers	1937 ......Old Westbury	1967 ......Bunntyco——Oak Brook
1905-09 .Not contested	1938 ......Old Westbury	1968 ......Midland
1910 ......Ranelagh	1939 ......Bostwick Field	1969 ......Tulsa Greenhill
1911 ......Not contested	1940 ......Aknusti	1970 ......Tulsa Greenhill
1912 ......Cooperstown	1941 ......Gulf Stream	1971 ......Oak Brook
1913 ......Cooperstown	1942-45 .Not contested	1972 ......Milwaukee
1914 ......Meadow Brook Magpies	1946 ......Mexico	1973 ......Oak Brook
1915 ......Not contested	1947 ......Old Westbury	1974 ......Milwaukee
1916 ......Meadow Brook	1948 ......Hurricanes	1975 ......Milwaukee
1917-18 .Not contested	1949 ......Hurricanes	1976 ......Willow Bend
1919 ......Meadow Brook	1950 ......Bostwick	1977 ......Retama
1920 ......Meadow Brook	1951 ......Milwaukee	1978 ......Abercrombie & Kent
1921 ......Great Neck	1952 ......Beverly Hills	1979 ......Retama
1922 ......Argentine	1953 ......Meadow Brook	1980 ......Southern Hills
1923 ......Meadow Brook	1954 ......C.C.C.—Meadow Brook	1981 ......Rolex A & K
1924 ......Midwick	1955 ......C.C.C.	1982 ......Retama
1925 ......Orange County	1956 ......Brandywine	1983 ......Ft. Lauderdale
1926 ......Hurricanes	1957 ......Detroit	1984 ......Retama
1927 ......Sands Point	1958 ......Dallas	1985 ......Carter Ranch
1928 ......Meadow Brook	1959 ......Circle F	1986 ......Retama II
1929 ......Hurricanes	1960 ......Oak Brook C.C.C.	1987 ......Aloha
1930 ......Hurricanes	1961 ......Milwaukee	1988 ......Les Diables Bleus
1931 ......Santa Paula	1962 ......Santa Barbara	1989 ......Les Diables Bleus
1932 ......Templeton	1963 ......Tulsa	1990 ......Les Diables Bleus
1933 ......Aurora	1964 ......Concar Oak Brook	1991 ......Grant's Farm Manor
1934 ......Templeton	1965 ......Oak Brook—Santa	1992 ......Hanalei Bay
1935 ......Greentree	Barbara	1993 ......Gehache
1936 ......Greentree	1966 ......Tulsa	1994 ......Aspen

Top-Ranked Players

The United States Polo Association ranks its registered players from minus 2 to plus 10 goals, with 10 Goal players being the game's best. At present, the USPA recognizes eleven 10-Goal and eight 9-Goal players:

10-GOAL

Michael Vincen Azzaro (San Antonio)
Carlos Gracida (San Antonio)
Bautista Heguy (Palm Beach)
Alberto Heguy Jr (Palm Beach)
Juan Ignacio Merlos (Palm Beach)
Ernesto Trotz (Palm Beach)
Adolfo Cambiaso (Palm Beach)
Guillermo Gracida Jr (Palm Beach)
Eduardo Heguy (Palm Beach)
Christian LaPrida (Palm Beach)
Gonzalo Pieres (Palm Beach)

9-GOAL

Mariano Aguerre (Greenwich)
Benjamin Araya (Palm Beach)
Esteban Panelo (Hidden Pond)
Owen Rinehart (Palm Beach)
A.D. Alberdi (El Dorado)
Hector Juni Crotto (Palm Beach)
Alfonso Pieres (Palm Beach)
Martin Zubia (Palm Beach)

Rodeo

All-Around

1929....Earl Thode	1947....Todd Whatley	1963....Dean Oliver	1979....Tom Ferguson
1930....Clay Carr	1948....Gerald Roberts	1964....Dean Oliver	1980....Paul Tierney
1931....John Schneider	1949....Jim Shoulders	1965....Dean Oliver	1981....Jimmie Cooper
1932....Donald Nesbit	1950....Bill Linderman	1966....Larry Mahan	1982....Chris Lybbert
1933....Clay Carr	1951....Casey Tibbs	1967....Larry Mahan	1983....Roy Cooper
1934....Leonard Ward	1952....Harry Tompkins	1968....Larry Mahan	1984....Dee Picket
1935....Everett Bowman	1953....Bill Linderman	1969....Larry Mahan	1985....Lewis Feild
1936....John Bowman	1954....Buck Rutherford	1970....Larry Mahan	1986....Lewis Feild
1937....Everett Bowman	1955....Casey Tibbs	1971....Phil Lyne	1987....Lewis Feild
1938....Burel Mulkey	1956....Jim Shoulders	1972....Phil Lyne	1988....Dave Appleton
1939....Paul Carney	1957....Jim Shoulders	1973....Larry Mahan	1989....Ty Murray
1940....Fritz Truan	1958....Jim Shoulders	1974....Tom Ferguson	1990....Ty Murray
1941....Homer Pettigrew	1959....Jim Shoulders	1975....Tom Ferguson	1991....Ty Murray
1942....Gerald Roberts	1960....Harry Tompkins	1976....Tom Ferguson	1992....Ty Murray
1943....Louis Brooks	1961....Benny Reynolds	1977....Tom Ferguson	1993....Ty Murray
1944....Louis Brooks	1962....Tom Nesmith	1978....Tom Ferguson	

Rodeo Champions

Saddle Bronc Riding

1929....Earl Thode	1947....Carl Olson	1963....Guy Weeks	1979....Bobby Berger
1930....Clay Carr	1948....Gene Pruett	1964....Marty Wood	1980....Clint Johnson
1931....Earl Thode	1949....Casey Tibbs	1965....Shawn Davis	1981....B. Gjermundson
1932....Peter Knight	1950....Bill Linderman	1966....Marty Wood	1982....Monty Henson
1933....Peter Knight	1951....Casey Tibbs	1967....Shawn Davis	1983....B. Gjermundson
1934....Leonard Ward	1952....Casey Tibbs	1968....Shawn Davis	1984....B. Gjermundson
1935....Peter Knight	1953....Casey Tibbs	1969....Bill Smith	1985....B. Gjermundson
1936....Peter Knight	1954....Casey Tibbs	1970....Dennis Reiners	1986....Bud Munroe
1937....Burel Mulkey	1955....DebCopenhaver	1971....Bill Smith	1987....Clint Johnson
1938....Burel Mulkey	1956....DebCopenhaver	1972....Mel Hyland	1988....Clint Johnson
1939....Fritz Truan	1957....Alvin Nelson	1973....Bill Smith	1989....Clint Johnson
1940....Fritz Truan	1958....Marty Wood	1974....John McBeth	1990....Robert Etbauer
1941....Doff Aber	1959....Casey Tibbs	1975....Monty Henson	1991....Robert Etbauer
1942....Doff Aber	1960....Enoch Walker	1976....Monty Henson	1992....Billy Etbauer
1943....Louis Brooks	1961....Winston Bruce	1977....Bobby Berger	1993....Dan Mortensen
1944....Louis Brooks	1962....Kenny McLean	1978....Joe Marvel	

Bareback Riding

1932....Smoky Snyder	1949....Jack Buschbom	1964....Jim Houston	1979....Bruce Ford
1933....Nate Waldrum	1950....Jim Shoulders	1965....Jim Houston	1980....Bruce Ford
1934....Leonard Ward	1951....Casey Tibbs	1966....Paul Mayo	1981....J.C. Trujillo
1935....Frank Schneider	1952....Harry Tompkins	1967....Clyde Vamvoras	1982....Bruce Ford
1936....Smoky Snyder	1953....Eddy Akridge	1968....Clyde Vamvoras	1983....Bruce Ford
1937....Paul Carney	1954....Eddy Akridge	1969....Gary Tucker	1984....Larry Peabody
1938....Pete Grubb	1955....Eddy Adridge	1970....Paul Mayo	1985....Lewis Feild
1939....Paul Carney	1956....Jim Shoulders	1971....Joe Alexander	1986....Lewis Feild
1940....Carl Dossey	1957....Jim Shoulders	1972....Joe Alexander	1987....Bruce Ford
1941....George Mills	1958....Jim Shoulders	1973....Joe Alexander	1988....Marvin Garrett
1942....Louis Brooks	1959....Jack Buschbom	1974....Joe Alexander	1989....Marvin Garrett
1943....Bill Linderman	1960....Jack Buschbom	1975....Joe Alexander	1990....Chuck Logue
1944....Louis Brooks	1961....Eddy Akridge	1976....Joe Alexander	1991....Clint Corey
1947....Larry Finley	1962....Ralph Buell	1977....Joe Alexander	1992....Wayne Herman
1948....Sonny Tureman	1963....John Hawkins	1978....Bruce Ford	1993....Deb Greenough

Bull Riding

1929....John Schneider	1944....Ken Roberts	1963....Bill Kornell	1980....Don Gay
1930....John Schneider	1947....Wag Blessing	1964....Bob Wegner	1981....Don Gay
1931....Smokey Snyder	1948....Harry Tompkins	1965....Larry Mahan	1982....Charles Sampson
1932....John Schneider	1949....Harry Tompkins	1966....Ronnie Rossen	1983....Cody Snyder
1932....Smokey Snyder	1950....Harry Tompkins	1967....Larry Mahan	1984....Don Gay
John Schneider	1951....Jim Shoulders	1968....George Paul	1985....Ted Nuce
1933....Frank Schneider	1952....Harry Tompkins	1969....Doug Brown	1986....Tuff Hedeman
1934....Frank Schneider	1953....Todd Whatley	1970....Gary Leffew	1987....Lane Frost
1935....Smokey Snyder	1954....Jim Shoulders	1971....Bill Nelson	1988....Jim Sharp
1936....Smokey Snyder	1955....Jim Shoulders	1972....John Quintana	1989....Tuff Hedeman
1937....Smokey Snyder	1956....Jim Shoulders	1973....Bobby Steiner	1990....Jim Sharp
1938....Kid Fletcher	1957....Jim Shoulders	1974....Don Gay	1991....Tuff Hedeman
1939....Dick Griffith	1958....Jim Shoulders	1975....Don Gay	1992....Cody Custer
1940....Dick Griffith	1959....Jim Shoulders	1976....Don Gay	1993....Ty Murray
1941....Dick Griffith	1960....Harry Tompkins	1977....Don Gay	
1942....Dick Griffith	1961....Ronnie Rossen	1978....Don Gay	
1943....Ken Roberts	1962....Freckles Brown	1979....Don Gay	

Calf Roping

1929....Everett Bowman	1939....Toots Mansfield	1950....Toots Mansfield	1960....Dean Oliver
1930....Jake McClure	1940....Toots Mansfield	1951....Don McLaughlin	1961....Dean Oliver
1931....Herb Meyers	1941....Toots Mansfield	1952....Don McLaughlin	1962....Dean Oliver
1932....Richard Merchant	1942....Clyde Burk	1953....Don McLaughlin	1963....Dean Oliver
1933....Bill McFarlane	1943....Toots Mansfield	1954....Don McLaughlin	1964....Dean Oliver
1934....Irby Mundy	1944....Clyde Burk	1955....Dean Oliver	1965....Glen Franklin
1935....Everett Bowman	1945-46 No champ.	1956....Ray Wharton	1966....Junior Garrison
1936....Clyde Burk	1947....Troy Fort	1957....Don McLaughlin	1967....Glen Franklin
1937....Everett Bowman	1948....Toots Mansfield	1958....Dean Oliver	1968....Glen Franklin
1938....Burel Mulkey	1949....Troy Fort	1959....Jim Bob Altizer	1969....Dean Oliver

Rodeo Champions (Cont.)

Calf Roping (Cont.)

1970....Junior Garrison	1976....Roy Cooper	1982....Roy Cooper	1988....Joe Beaver
1971....Phil Lyne	1977....Roy Cooper	1983....Roy Cooper	1989....Rabe Rabon
1972....Phil Lyne	1978....Roy Cooper	1984....Roy Cooper	1990....Troy Pruitt
1973....Ernie Taylor	1979....Paul Tierney	1985....Joe Beaver	1991....Fred Whitfield
1974....Tom Ferguson	1980....Roy Cooper	1986....Chris Lybbert	1992....Joe Beaver
1975....Jeff copenhaver	1981....Roy Cooper	1987....Joe Beaver	1993....Joe Beaver

Steer Wrestling

1929....Gene Ross	1945-46 No champ.	1962....Tom Nesmith	1978....Byron Walker
1930....Everett Bowman	1947....Todd Whatley	1963....Jim Bynum	1979....Stan Williamson
1931....Gene Ross	1948....Homer Pettigrew	1964....C.R. Boucher	1980....Butch Myers
1932....Hugh Bennett	1949....Bill McGuire	1965....Harley May	1981....Byron Walker
1933....Everett Bowman	1950....Bill Linderman	1966....Jack Roddy	1982....Stan Williamson
1934....Shorty Ricker	1951....Dub Phillips	1967....Roy Duvall	1983....Joel Edmondson
1935....Everett Bowman	1952....Harley May	1968....Jack Roddy	1984....John W. Jones
1936....Jack Kerschner	1953....Ross Dollarhide	1969....Roy Duvall	1985....Ote Berry
1937....Gene Ross	1954....James Bynum	1970....John W. Jones	1986....Steve Duhon
1938....Everett Bowman	1955....Benny Combs	1971....Billy Hale	1987....Steve Duhon
1939....Harry Hart	1956....Harley May	1972....Roy Duvall	1988....John W. Jones
1940....Homer Pettigrew	1957....Clark McEntire	1973....Bob Marshall	1989....John W. Jones
1941....Hub Whiteman	1958....James Bynum	1974....Tommy Puryear	1990....Ote Berry
1942....Homer Pettigrew	1959....Harry Charters	1975....F. Shepperson	1991....Ote Berry
1943....Homer Pettigrew	1960....Bob A. Robinson	1976....Tom Ferguson	1992....Mark Roy
1944....Homer Pettigrew	1961....Jim Bynum	1977....Larry Ferguson	1993....Steve Duhon

Team Roping

1929....Charles Maggini	1944....Murphy Chaney	1963....Les Hirdes	1980....Tee Woolman
1930....Norman Cowan	1947....Jim Brister	1964....Bill Hamilton	1981....Walt Woodard
1931....Arthur Beloat	1948....Joe Glenn	1965....Jim RodriguezJr.	1982....Tee Woolman
1932....Ace Gardner	1949....Ed Yanez	1966....Ken Luman	1983....Leo Camarillo
1933....Roy Adams	1950....Buck Sorrels	1967....Joe Glenn	1984....Dee Pickett
1934....Andy Jauregui	1951....Olan Sims	1968....Art Arnold	1985....Jake Barnes
1935....Lawrence Conltk	1952....Asbury Schell	1969....Jerold Camarillo	1986....Clay O. Cooper
1936....John Rhodes	1953....Ben Johnson	1970....John Miller	1987....Clay O. Cooper
1937....Asbury Schell	1954....Eddie Schell	1971....John Miller	1988....Jake Barnes
1938....John Rhodes	1955....Vern Castro	1972....Leo Camarillo	1989....Jake Barnes
1939....Asbury Schell	1956....Dale Smith	1973....Leo Camarillo	1990....Allen Bach
1940....Pete Grubb	1957....Dale Smith	1974....H.P. Evetts	1991....Bob Harris
1941....Jim Hudson	1958....Ted Ashworth	1975....Leo Camarillo	1992....Clay O. Cooper
1942....Verne Castro	1959....Jim RodriguezJr.	1976....Leo Camarillo	1993....Bobby Hurley
........Vic Castro	1960....Jim RodriguezJr.	1977....Jerold Camarillo	
1943....Mark Hull	1961....Al Hooper	1978....Doyle Gellerman	
........Leonard Block	1962....Jim RodriguezJr.	1979....Allen Bach	

Steer Roping

1929....Charles Maggini	1946....Everett Shaw	1963....Don McLaughlin	1980....Guy Allen
1930....Clay Carr	1947....Ike Rude	1964....Sonny Davis	1981....Arnold Felts
1931....Andy Jauregui	1948....Everett Shaw	1965....Sonney Wright	1982....Guy Allen
1932....George Weir	1949....Shoat Webster	1966....Sonny Davis	1983....Roy Cooper
1933....John Bowman	1950....Shoat Webster	1967....Jim Bob Altizer	1984....Guy Allen
1934....John McEntire	1951....Everett Shaw	1968....Sonny Davis	1985....Jim Davis
1935....Richard Merchant	1952....Buddy Neal	1969....Walter Arnold	1986....Jim Davis
1936....John Bowman	1953....Ike Rude	1970....Don McLaughlin	1987....Shaun Burchett
1937....Everett Bowman	1954....Shoat Webster	1971....Olin Young	1988....Shaun Burchett
1938....Hugh Bennett	1955....Shoat Webster	1972....Allen Keller	1989....Guy Allen
1939....Dick Truitt	1956....Jim Snively	1973....Roy Thompson	1990....Phil Lyne
1940....Clay Carr	1957....Clark McEntire	1974....Olin Young	1991....Guy Allen
1941....Ike Rude	1958....Clark McEntire	1975....Roy Thompson	1992....Guy Allen
1942....King Merrit	1959....Everett Shaw	1976....Marvin Cantrell	1993....Guy Allen
1943....Tom Rhodes	1960....Don McLaughlin	1977....Buddy Cockrell	
1944....Tom Rhodes	1961....Clark McEntire	1978....Sonny Worrell	
1945....Everett Shaw	1962....Everett Shaw	1979....Gary Good	

Rowing

National Collegiate Rowing Champions

MEN'S EIGHT

1982 ....Yale	1987 ....Harvard	1992 ....Harvard
1983 ....Harvard	1988 ....Harvard	1993 ....Brown
1984 ....Washington	1989 ....Harvard	1994 ....Brown
1985 ....Harvard	1990 ....Wisconsin	
1986 ....Wisconsin	1991 ....Pennsylvania	

WOMEN'S EIGHT

1979 ....Yale	1985 ....Washington	1991 ....Boston University
1980 ....California	1986 ....Wisconsin	1992 ....Boston University
1981 ....Washington	1987 ....Washington	1993 ....Princeton
1982 ....Washington	1988 ....Washington	1994 ....Princeton
1983 ....Washington	1989 ....Cornell	
1984 ....Washington	1990 ....Princeton	

Rugby

National Men's Club Championship

Year	Winner	Runner-Up	Year	Winner	Runner-Up
1979	Old Blues (Calif.)	St Louis Falcons	1987	Old Blues (Calif.)	Pittsburgh
1980	Old Blues (Calif.)	St. Louis Falcons	1988	Old Mission Beach AC	Milwaukee
1981	Old Blues (Calif.)	Old Blue (NY)	1989	Old Mission Beach AC	Philly/Whitemarsh
1982	Old Blues (Calif.)	Denver Barbos	1990	Denver Barbos	Old Blues (CA)
1983	Old Blues (Calif.)	Dallas Harlequins	1991	Old Mission Beach AC	Washington
1984	Dallas Harlequins	Los Angeles	1992	Old Blues (Calif.)	Mystic River (MA)
1985	Milwaukee	Denver Barbos	1993	Old Mission Beach AC	Milwaukee
1986	Old Blues (Calif.)	Old Blue (NY)	1994	Old Mission Beach AC	Life College (GA)

National Men's Collegiate Championship

Year	Winner	Runner-Up	Year	Winner	Runner-Up
1980	California	Air Force	1987	San Diego State	Air Force
1981	California	Harvard	1988	California	Dartmouth
1982	California	Life College	1989	Air Force	Long Beach
1983	California	Air Force	1990	Air Force	Army
1984	Harvard	Colorado	1991	California	Army
1985	California	Maryland	1992	California	Army
1986	California	Dartmouth	1993	California	Air Force
			1994	California	Navy

World Cup Championship

Year	Winner	Runner-Up	Year	Winner	Runner-Up
1987	New Zealand	France	1991	Australia	England

Sailing

America's Cup Champions

SCHOONERS AND J-CLASS BOATS

Year	Winner	Skipper	Series	Loser	Skipper
1851	America	Richard Brown			
1870	Magic	Andrew Comstock	1-0	Cambria, Great Britain	J. Tannock
1871	Columbia (2-1)	Nelson Comstock	4-1	Livonia, Great Britain	J. R. Woods
	Sappho (2-0)	Sam Greenwood			
1876	Madeleine	Josephus Williams	2-0	Countess of Dufferin, Canada	J. E. Ellsworth
1881	Mischief	Nathanael Clock	2-0	Atalanta, Canada	Alexander Cuthbert
1885	Puritan	Aubrey Crocker	2-0	Genesta, Great Britain	John Carter
1886	Mayflower	Martin Stone	2-0	Galatea, Great Britain	Dan Bradford
1887	Volunteer	Henry Haff	2-0	Thistle, Great Britain	John Barr
1893	Vigilant	William Hansen	3-0	Valkyrie II, Great Britain	William Granfield
1895	Defender	Henry Haff	3-0	Valkyrie III, Great Britain	William Granfield
1899	Columbia	Charles Barr	3-0	Shamrock I, Great Britain	Archie Hogarth
1901	Columbia	Charles Barr	3-0	Shamrock II, Great Britain	E. A. Sycamore
1903	Reliance	Charles Barr	3-0	Shamrock III, Great Britain	Bob Wringe

America's Cup Champions (Cont.)

SCHOONERS AND J-CLASS BOATS (Cont.)

Year	Winner	Skipper	Series	Loser	Skipper
1920	Resolute	Charles F. Adams	3-2	Shamrock IV, Great Britain	William Burton
1930	Enterprise	Harold Vanderbilt	4-0	Shamrock V, Great Britain	Ned Heard
1934	Rainbow	Harold Vanderbilt	4-2	Endeavour, Great Britain	T. O. M. Sopwith
1937	Ranger	Harold Vanderbilt	4-0	Endeavour II, Great Britain	T. O. M. Sopwith

12-METER BOATS

Year	Winner	Skipper	Series	Loser	Skipper
1958	Columbia	Briggs Cunningham	4-0	Sceptre, Great Britain	Graham Mann
1962	Weatherly	Bus Mosbacher	4-1	Gretel, Australia	Jock Sturrock
1964	Constellation	Bob Bavier & Eric Ridder	4-0	Sovereign, Australia	Peter Scott
1967	Intrepid	Bus Mosbacher	4-0	Dame Pattie, Australia	Jock Sturrock
1970	Intrepid	Bill Ficker	4-1	Gretel II, Australia	Jim Hardy
1974	Courageous	Ted Hood	4-0	Southern Cross, Australia	John Cuneo
1977	Courageous	Ted Turner	4-0	Australia	Noel Robins
1980	Freedom	Dennis Conner	4-1	Australia	Jim Hardy
1983	Australia II	John Bertrand	4-3	Liberty, United States	Dennis Conner
1987	Stars & Stripes	Dennis Conner	4-0	Kookaburra III, Australia	Iain Murray

60-FOOT CATAMARAN VS 133-FOOT MONOHULL

Year	Winner	Skipper	Series	Loser	Skipper
1988	Stars & Stripes	Dennis Conner	2-0	New Zealand	David Barnes

75-FOOT MONOHULL (IACC)

Year	Winner	Skipper	Series	Loser	Skipper
1992	America[3]	Bill Koch	4-1	Il Moro di Vinezia, Italy	Paul Cayard

Note: Winning entry was from the United States every year but 1983, when an Australian vessel won.

Shooting World Champions

Men

50M FREE RIFLE PRONE

1947 .....O. Sannes, Norway
1949 .....A.C. Jackson, United States
1952 .....A.C. Jackson, United States
1954 .....G. Boa, Canada
1958 .....M. Nordquist
1962 .....K. Wenk, West Germany
1966 .....D. Boyd, United States
1970 .....M. Fiess, S. Africa
1974 .....K. Bulan, Czech.
1978 .....A. Allan, Great Britain
1982 .....V. Danilschenko, Soviet Union
1986 .....S. Bereczky, Hungary
1990 .....V. Bochkarev, Sov Union
1994 .....Venjie Li, China

AIR RIFLE

1966 .....G. Kümmet, W. Germany
1970 .....G. Kusterman, W. Germ.
1974 .....E. Pedzisz, Poland
1978 .....O. Schlipf, W. Germany
1979 .....K. Hillenbrand
1981 .....F. Bessy, France
1982 .....F. Rettkowski, E. Germ.
1983 .....P. Heberle, France
1985 .....P. Heberle, France
1986 .....H. Riederer, W. Germany

AIR RIFLE (Cont.)

1987 .....K. Ivanov, Soviet Union
1989 .....J. P. Amet, France
1990 .....H. Riederer, W. Germany
1994 .....Boris Polak, Israel

MEN'S TRAP

1929 .....De Lumniczer, Hungary
1930 .....M. Arie, United States
1931 .....Kiszkurno, Poland
1933 .....De Lumniczer, Hungary
1934 .....A. Montagh, Hungary
1935 .....R. Sack, W. Germany
1936 .....Kiszkurno, Poland
1937 .....K. Huber, Finland
1938 .....I. Strassburger, Hungary
1939 .....De Lumniczer, Hungary
1947 .....H. Liljedahl, Sweden
1949 .....F. Rocchi, Argentina
1950 .....C. Sala, Italy
1952 .....P.J. Grossi, Argentina
1954 .....C. Merlo, Italy
1958 .....F. Eisenlauer, United States
1959 .....H. Badravi, Egypt
1961 .....E. Mattarelli, Italy
1962 .....W. Zimenko, Soviet Union
1965 .....J.E. Lire, Chile
1966 .....K. Jones, United States
1967 .....G. Rennard, Belgium
1969 .....E. Mattarelli, Italy

MEN'S TRAP (Cont.)

1970 .....M. Carrega, France
1971 .....M. Carrega, France
1973 .....A. Andrushkin, Soviet Union
1974 .....M. Carrega, France
1975 .....J. Primrose, Canada
1977 .....E. Azkue, Spain
1978 .....E. Vallduvi, Spain
1979 .....M. Carrega, France
1981 .....A. Asanov, Soviet Union
1982 .....L. Giovonnetti, Italy
1983 .....J. Primrose, Canada
1985 .....M. Bednarik, Czech.
1986 .....M. Benarik, Czech.
1987 .....D. Monakov, Soviet Union
1989 .....M. Venturini, Italy
1990 .....J. Damne, E. Germany
1994 .....Dmitriy Monakov, Ukraine

THREE POSITION RIFLE

1929 .....O. Ericsson, Sweden
1930 .....Petersen, Denmark
1931 .....Amundson, Norway
1933 .....De Lisle, France
1935 .....Leskinnen, Finland
1937 .....Mazoyer, France
1939 .....Steigelmann, Germany
1947 .....I. H. Erben, Sweden
1949 .....P. Janhonen, Finland
1952 .....Kongshaug, Norway

Men *(Cont.)*

THREE POSITION RIFLE *(Cont.)*

1954 .....A. Bugdanov,
   Soviet Union
1958 .....Itkis, Soviet Union
1962 .....G. Anderson,
   United States

THREE POSITION RIFLE *(Cont.)*

1966 .....G. Anderson,
   United States
1970 .....Parkhimovitch,
   Soviet Union
1974 .....L. Wigger, United States

THREE POSITION RIFLE *(Cont.)*

1978 .....E. Svensson, Sweden
1982 .....K. Ivanov, Soviet Union
1986 .....P. Heinz, W. Germany
1990 .....E. C. Lee, S. Korea
1994 .....Petr Kurka, Czech Republic

Women

THREE POSITION RIFLE

1966 .....M. Thompson,
   United States
1970 .....M. Thompson Murdock,
   United States
1974 .....A. Pelova, Bulgaria
1978 .....W. Oliver, United States
1982 .....M. Helbig, E. Germany
1986 .....V. Letcheva, Bulgaria
1990 .....V. Letcheva, Bulgaria
1994 .....A. Maloukhina, Russia

AIR RIFLE

1970 ....V. Cherkasque, Soviet Union
1974 .....T. Ratkinova, Soviet Union
1978 .....W. Oliver, United States
1979 .....K. Monez, United States
1981 .....S. Romaristova,
   Soviet Union

AIR RIFLE *(Cont.)*

1982 .....S. Lang, W. Germany
1983 .....M. Helbig, E. Germany
1985 .....E. Forian, Hungary
1986 .....V. Letcheva, Bulgaria
1987 .....V. Letcheva, Bulgaria
1989 .....V. Letcheva, Bulgaria
1990 .....E.Joc, Hungary
1994 .....S. Pfeilschifter, Germany

SPORT PISTOL

1966 .....N. Rasskazova,
   Soviet Union
1970 .....N. Stoljarova, Soviet Union
1974 .....N. Stoljarova, Soviet Union
1978 .....K. Dyer, United States
1982 .....P. Balogh, Hungary
1986 .....M. Dobrantcheva,
   Soviet Union

SPORT PISTOL *(Cont.)*

1990 .....M. Logvinenko, Sov Union
1994 .....Soon Hee Boo, S. Korea

AIR PISTOL

1970 .....S. Carroll, United States
1974 .....Z. Simonian, Soviet Union
1978 .....K. Hansson, Sweden
1979 .....R. Fox, United States
1981 .....N. Kalinina, Soviet Union
1982 .....M. Dobrantcheva,
   Soviet Union
1983 .....K. Bodin, Sweden
1985 .....M. Dobrantcheva, Sov Union
1986 .....A. Völker, E. Germany
1987 .....J. Brajkovic, Yugoslavia
1989 .....N. Salukvadse,
   Soviet Union
1990 .....Jasna Sekaric, Yugoslavia
1994 .....Jasna Sekaric, IOP

Softball

Men

MAJOR FAST PITCH

Year	Champion
1933	J. L. Gill Boosters, Chicago
1934	Ke-Nash-A, Kenosha, WI
1935	Crimson Coaches, Toledo, OH
1936	Kodak Park, Rochester, NY
1937	Briggs Body Team, Detroit
1938	The Pohlers, Cincinnati
1939	Carr's Boosters, Covington, KY
1940	Kodak Park, Rochester, NY
1941	Bendix Brakes, South Bend, IN
1942	Deep Rock Oilers, Tulsa
1943	Hammer Air Field, Fresno
1944	Hammer Air Field, Fresno
1945	Zollner Pistons, Fort Wayne, IN
1946	Zollner Pistons, Fort Wayne, IN
1947	Zollner Pistons, Fort Wayne, IN
1948	Briggs Beautyware, Detroit
1949	Tip Top Tailors, Toronto
1950	Clearwater (FL) Bombers
1951	Dow Chemical, Midland, MI
1952	Briggs Beautyware, Detroit
1953	Briggs Beautyware, Detroit
1954	Clearwater (FL) Bombers
1955	Raybestos Cardinals, Stratford, CT
1956	Clearwater (FL) Bombers
1957	Clearwater (FL) Bombers
1958	Raybestos Cardinals, Stratford, CT
1959	Sealmasters, Aurora, IL
1960	Clearwater (FL) Bombers
1961	Sealmasters, Aurora, IL
1962	Clearwater (FL) Bombers
1963	Clearwater (FL) Bombers
1964	Burch Tool, Detroit
1965	Sealmasters, Aurora, IL
1966	Clearwater (FL) Bombers
1967	Sealmasters, Aurora, IL
1968	Clearwater (FL) Bombers
1969	Raybestos Cardinals, Stratford, CT
1970	Raybestos Cardinals, Stratford, CT
1971	Welty Way, Cedar Rapids, IA
1972	Raybestos Cardinals, Stratford, CT
1973	Clearwater (FL) Bombers
1974	Gianella Bros, Santa Rosa, CA
1975	Rising Sun Hotel, Reading, PA
1976	Raybestos Cardinals, Stratford, CT
1977	Billard Barbell, Reading, PA
1978	Billard Barbell, Reading, PA
1979	McArdle Pontiac/Cadillac, Midland, MI
1980	Peterbilt Western, Seattle
1981	Archer Daniels Midland, Decatur, IL
1982	Peterbilt Western, Seattle
1983	Franklin Cardinals, Stratford, CT
1984	California Kings, Merced, CA
1985	Pay'n Pak, Seattle
1986	Pay'n Pak, Seattle
1987	Pay'n Pak, Seattle
1988	TransAire, Elkhart, IN
1989	Penn Corp, Sioux City, IA
1990	Penn Corp, Sioux City, IA
1991	Guanella Brothers, Rohnert Park, CA
1992	Natl Health Care Disc, Sioux City, IA
1993	Natl Health Care Disc, Sioux City, IA
1994	Decatur Pride, Decatur IL

Men (Cont.)

SUPER SLOW PITCH

1981...............Howard's/Western Steer, Denver, NC	1988................Starpath, Monticello, KY
1982................Jerry's Catering, Miami, Fla.	1989................Ritch's Salvage, Harrisburg, NC
1983...............Howard's/Western Steer, Denver, NC	1990................Steele's Silver Bullets, Grafton, OH
1984...............Howard's/Western Steer, Denver, NC	1991................Sunbelt/Worth, Centerville, GA
1985...............Steele's Sports, Grafton, OH	1992................Ritch's/Superior, Windsor Locks, CT
1986...............Steele's Sports, Grafton, OH	1993................Ritch's/Superior, Windsor Locks, CT
1987...............Steele's Sports, Grafton, OH	1994................Bell Corp, Tampa, Fla.

MAJOR SLOW PITCH

1953...............Shields Construction, Newport, KY	1974..........Howard's Furniture, Denver, NC
1954...............Waldneck's Tavern, Cincinnati	1975..........Pyramid Cafe, Lakewood, OH
1955...............Lang Pet Shop, Covington, KY	1976..........Warren Motors, Jacksonville, FL
1956...............Gatliff Auto Sales, Newport, KY	1977..........Nelson Painting, Oklahoma City
1957...............Gatliff Auto Sales, Newport, KY	1978..........Campbell Carpets, Concord, CA
1958...............East Side Sports, Detroit	1979..........Nelco Mfg Co, Oklahoma City
1959...............Yorkshire Restaurant, Newport, KY	1980..........Campbell Carpets, Concord, CA
1960...............Hamilton Tailoring, Cincinnati	1981..........Elite Coating, Gordon, CA
1961...............Hamilton Tailoring, Cincinnati	1982..........Triangle Sports, Minneapolis
1962...............Skip Hogan A.C., Pittsburgh	1983..........No. 1 Electric & Heating, Gastonia, NC
1963...............Gatliff Auto Sales, Newport, KY	1984..........Lilly Air Systems, Chicago
1964...............Skip Hogan A.C., Pittsburgh	1985..........Blanton's, Fayetteville, NC
1965...............Skip Hogan A.C., Pittsburgh	1986..........Non-Ferrous Metals, Cleveland
1966...............Michael's Lounge, Detroit	1987..........Starpath, Monticello, KY
1967...............Jim's Sport Shop, Pittsburgh	1988..........Bell Corp/FAF, Tampa, FL
1968...............County Sports, Levittown, NY	1989..........Ritch's Salvage, Harrisburg, NC
1969...............Copper Hearth, Milwaukee	1990..........New Construction, Shelbyville, IN
1970...............Little Caesar's, Southgate, MI	1991..........Riverside Paving, Louisville, KY
1971...............Pile Drivers, Virginia Beach, VA	1992..........Vernon's, Jacksonville, FL
1972...............Jiffy Club, Louisville, KY	1993..........Back Porch/Destin Roofing, Destin, FL
1973...............Howard's Furniture, Denver, NC	1994..........Riverside RAM/Taylor Bros., Louisville, KY

Women

MAJOR FAST PITCH

1933..........Great Northerns, Chicago	1964..........Erv Lind Florists, Portland, OR
1934..........Hart Motors, Chicago	1965..........Orange (CA) Lionettes
1935..........Bloomer Girls, Cleveland	1966..........Raybestos Brakettes, Stratford, CT
1936..........Nat'l Screw & Mfg, Cleveland	1967..........Raybestos Brakettes, Stratford, CT
1937..........Nat'l Screw & Mfg, Cleveland	1968..........Raybestos Brakettes, Stratford, CT
1938..........J. J. Krieg's, Alameda, CA	1969..........Orange (CA) Lionettes
1939..........J. J. Krieg's, Alameda, CA	1970..........Orange (CA) Lionettes
1940..........Arizona Ramblers, Phoenix	1971..........Raybestos Brakettes, Stratford, CT
1941..........Higgins Midgets, Tulsa	1972..........Raybestos Brakettes, Stratford, CT
1942..........Jax Maids, New Orleans	1973..........Raybestos Brakettes, Stratford, CT
1943..........Jax Maids, New Orleans	1974..........Raybestos Brakettes, Stratford, CT
1944..........Lind & Pomeroy, Portland, OR	1975..........Raybestos Brakettes, Stratford, CT
1945..........Jax Maids, New Orleans	1976..........Raybestos Brakettes, Stratford, CT
1946..........Jax Maids, New Orleans	1977..........Raybestos Brakettes, Stratford, CT
1947..........Jax Maids, New Orleans	1978..........Raybestos Brakettes, Stratford, CT
1948..........Arizona Ramblers, Phoenix	1979..........Sun City (AZ) Saints
1949..........Arizona Ramblers, Phoenix	1980..........Raybestos Brakettes, Stratford, CT
1950..........Orange (CA) Lionettes	1981..........Orlando (FL) Rebels
1951..........Orange (CA) Lionettes	1982..........Raybestos Brakettes, Stratford, CT
1952..........Orange (CA) Lionettes	1983..........Raybestos Brakettes, Stratford, CT
1953..........Betsy Ross Rockets, Fresno	1984..........Los Angeles Diamonds
1954..........Leach Motor Rockets, Fresno	1985..........Hi-Ho Brakettes, Stratford, CT
1955..........Orange (CA) Lionettes	1986..........Southern California Invasion, Los Angeles
1956..........Orange (CA) Lionettes	1987..........Orange County Majestics, Anaheim, CA
1957..........Hacienda Rockets, Fresno	1988..........Hi-Ho Brakettes, Stratford, CT
1958..........Raybestos Brakettes, Stratford, CT	1989..........Whittier (CA) Raiders
1959..........Raybestos Brakettes, Stratford, CT	1990..........Raybestos Brakettes, Stratford, CT
1960..........Raybestos Brakettes, Stratford, CT	1991..........Raybestos Brakettes, Stratford, CT
1961..........Gold Sox, Whittier, CA	1992..........Raybestos Brakettes, Stratford, CT
1962..........Orange (CA) Lionettes	1993..........Redding Rebels, Redding, CA
1963..........Raybestos Brakettes, Stratford, CT	1994..........Redding Rebels, Redding, CA

Women *(Cont.)*

MAJOR SLOW PITCH

1959.........Pearl Laundry, Richmond, VA	1977.........Fox Valley Lassies, St Charles, IL
1960.........Carolina Rockets, High Pt, NC	1978.........Bob Hoffman's Dots, Miami
1961.........Dairy Cottage, Covington, KY	1979.........Bob Hoffman's Dots, Miami
1962.........Dana Gardens, Cincinnati	1980.........Howard's Rubi-Otts, Graham, NC
1963.........Dana Gardens, Cincinnati	1981.........Tifton (GA) Tomboys
1964.........Dana Gardens, Cincinnati	1982.........Richmond (VA) Stompers
1965.........Art's Acres, Omaha	1983.........Spooks, Anoka, MN
1966.........Dana Gardens, Cincinnati	1984.........Spooks, Anoka, MN
1967.........Ridge Maintenance, Cleveland	1985.........Key Ford Mustangs, Pensacola, FL
1968.........Escue Pontiac, Cincinnati	1986.........Sur-Way Tomboys, Tifton, GA
1969.........Converse Dots, Hialeah, FL	1987.........Key Ford Mustangs, Pensacola, FL
1970.........Rutenschruder Floral, Cincinnati	1988.........Spooks, Anoka, MN
1971.........Gators, Ft Lauderdale, FL	1989.........Canaan's Illusions, Houston
1972.........Riverside Ford, Cincinnati	1990.........Spooks, Anoka, MN
1973.........Sweeney Chevrolet, Cincinnati	1991.........Kannan's Illusions, San Antonio, TX
1974.........Marks Brothers Dots, Miami	1992.........Universal Plastics, Cookeville, TN
1975.........Marks Brothers Dots, Miami	1993.........Universal Plastics, Cookeville, TN
1976.........Sorrento's Pizza, Cincinnati	1994.........Universal Plastics, Cookeville, TN

Speedskating

All World Champions
MEN

1891.....Joseph F. Donoghue, US	1932.....Ivar Ballangrud, Norway	1967.....Kees Verkerk, Holland
1893.....Jaap Eden, Holland	1933.....Hans Engnestangen, Nor	1968.....Fred Anton Maier, Nor.
1895.....Jaap Eden, Holland	1934.....Bernt Evensen, Norway	1969.....Dag Fornaes, Norway
1896.....Jaap Eden, Holland	1935.....Michael Staksrud, Nor.	1970.....Ard Schenk, Holland
1897.....Jack K. McCulloch, Can.	1936.....Ivar Ballangrud, Norway	1971.....Ard Schenk, Holland
1898.....Peder Ostlund, Norway	1937.....Michael Staksrud, Nor.	1972.....Ard Schenk, Holland
1899.....Peder Ostlund, Norway	1938.....Ivar Ballangrud, Norway	1973.....Göran Claeson, Sweden
1900.....Edvard Engelsaas, Nor.	1939.....Birger Wasenius, Finland	1974.....Sten Stensen, Norway
1901.....Franz F. Wathan, Finland	1947.....Lassi Parkkinen, Finland	1975.....Harm Kuipers, Holland
1904.....Sigurd Mathisen, Norway	1948.....Odd Lundberg, Norway	1976.....Piet Kleine, Holland
1905.....C. Coen de Koning, Holl.	1949.....Kornel Pajor, Hungary	1977.....Eric Heiden, USA
1908.....Oscar Mathisen, Norway	1950.....Hjalmar Andersen, Nor.	1978.....Eric Heiden, USA
1909.....Oscar Mathisen, Norway	1951.....Hjalmar Andersen, Nor.	1979.....Eric Heiden, USA
1910.....Nikolai Strunnikov, Russia	1952.....Hjalmar Andersen, Nor.	1980.....Hilbert van der Duin, Holl.
1911.....Nikolai Strunnikov, Russia	1953.....Oleg Goncharenko, Sov U	1981.....Amund Sjobrand, Norway
1912.....Oscar Mathisen, Norway	1954.....Boris Shilkov, Sov U	1982.....Hilbert van der Duin, Holl
1913.....Oscar Mathisen, Norway	1955.....Sigvard Ericsson, Swe.	1983.....Rolf Falk-Larssen, Nor.
1914.....Oscar Mathisen, Norway	1956.....Oleg Goncharenko, Sov U	1984.....Oleg Bozhev, Sov U
1922.....Harald Strom, Norway	1957.....Knut Johannesen, Nor.	1985.....Hein Vergeer, Holland
1923.....Klas Thunberg, Finland	1958.....Oleg Goncharenko, Sov U	1986.....Hein Vergeer, Holland
1924.....Roald Larsen, Norway	1959.....Juhani Järvinen, Finland	1987.....Nikolai Guliaev, Sov U
1925.....Klas Thunberg, Finland	1960.....Boris Stenin, Sov U	1988.....Eric Flaim, USA
1926.....Ivar Ballangrud, Norway	1961.....Henk van der Grift, Holl.	1989.....Leo Visser, Holland
1927.....Bernt Evensen, Norway	1962.....Viktor Kosichkin, Sov U	1990.....Johann Olav Koss, Nor.
1928.....Klas Thunberg, Finland	1963.....Jonny Nilsson, Sweden	1991.....Johann Olav Koss, Nor.
1929.....Klas Thunberg, Finland	1964.....Knut Johannesen, Nor.	1992.....Roberto Sighel, Italy
1930.....Michael Staksrud, Nor.	1965.....Per Ivar Moe, Norway	1993.....Falko Zandstra, Holland
1931.....Klas Thunberg, Finland	1966.....Kees Verkerk, Holland	1994.....Johann Olav Koss, Nor.

WOMEN

1936.....Kit Klein, USA	1953.....Khalida Shchegoleeva, Soviet Union	1962.....Inga Artamonova, Sov U
1937.....Laila Schou Nilsen, Nor.	1954.....Lidia Selikhova, Sov U	1963.....Lidia Skoblikova, Sov U
1938.....Laila Schou Nilsen, Nor.	1955.....Rimma Zhukova, Sov U	1964.....Lidia Skoblikova, Sov U
1939.....Verné Lesche, Finland	1956.....Sofia Kondakova, Sov U	1965.....Inga Artamonova, Sov U
1947.....Verné Lesche, Finland	1957.....Inga Artamonova, Sov U	1966.....Valentina Stenina, Sov U
1948.....Maria Isakova, Sov U	1958.....Inga Artamonova, Sov U	1967.....Stien Kaiser, Holland
1949.....Maria Isakova, Sov U	1959.....Tamara Rylova, Sov U	1968.....Stien Kaiser, Holland
1950.....Maria Isakova, Sov U	1960.....Valentina Stenina, Sov U	1969.....Lasma Kauniste, Sov U
1951.....Eevi Huttunen, Finland	1961.....Valentina Stenina, Sov U	1970.....Atje Keulen-Deelstra, Holl.
1952.....Lidia Selikhova, Sov U		1971.....Nina Statkevich, Sov U

Speedskating (Cont.)

All World Champions (Cont.)

WOMEN (Cont.)

1972 .....Atje Keulen-Deelstra, Holl.	1980 .....Natalia Petruseva, Sov U	1988 .....Karin Kania, GDR
1973 .....Atje Keulen-Deelstra, Holl.	1981 .....Natalia Petruseva, Sov U	1989 .....Constanze Moser, GDR
1974 .....Atje Keulen-Deelstra, Holl.	1982 .....Karin Busch, GDR	1990 .....Jacqueline Börner, GDR
1975 .....Karin Kessow, GDR	1983 .....Andrea Schöne, GDR	1991 .....Gunda Kleemann, Ger.
1976 .....Sylvia Burka, Canada	1984 .....Karin Enke-Busch, GDR	1992 .....Gunda Niemann-
1977 .....Vera Bryndzej, Sov U	1985 .....Andrea Schöne, GDR	.............Kleemann, Germany
1978 .....Tatiana Averina, Sov U	1986 .....Karin Kania-Enke, GDR	1993 ......Gunda Niemann, Germany
1979 .....Beth Heiden, USA	1987 .....Karin Kania, GDR	1994 .....Emese Hunyady, Austria

Squash

National Men's Champions

Year	Champion, Hometown	Year	Champion, Hometown
1907 ....John A. Miskey, Philadelphia		1952 ....Harry B. Conlon, Buffalo	
1908 ....John A. Miskey, Philadelphia		1953 ....Ernest Howard, Toronto	
1909 ....William L. Freeland, Philadelphia		1954 ....G. Diehl Mateer Jr., Philadelphia	
1910 ....John A. Miskey, Philadelphia		1955 ....Henri R. Salaun, Hartford, CT	
1911 ....Francis S. White, Philadelphia		1956 ....G. Diehl Mateer Jr., Philadelphia	
1912 ....Constantine Hutchins, Boston		1957 ....Henri R. Salaun, Boston	
1913 ....Morton L. Newhall, Philadelphia		1958 ....Henri R. Salaun, Boston	
1914 ....Constantine Hutchins, Boston		1959 ....Benjamin H. Heckscher, Philadelphia	
1915 ....Stanley W. Pearson, Philadelphia		1960 ....G. Diehl Mateer Jr., Philadelphia	
1916 ....Stanley W. Pearson, Philadelphia		1961 ....Henri R. Salaun, Hartford, CT	
1917 ....Stanley W. Pearson, Philadelphia		1962 ....Samuel P. Howe III, Philadelphia	
1918-19....No tournament		1963 ....Benjamin H. Heckscher, Philadelphia	
1920 ....Charles C. Peabody, Boston		1964 ....Ralph E. Howe, New York	
1921 ....Stanley W. Pearson, Philadelphia		1965 ....Stephen T. Vehslage, New York	
1922 ....Stanley W. Pearson, Philadelphia		1966 ....Victor Niederhoffer, Chicago	
1923 ....Stanley W. Pearson, Philadelphia		1967 ....Samuel P. Howe III, Philadelphia	
1924 ....Gerald Roberts, England		1968 ....Colin Adair, Montreal	
1925 ....W. Palmer Dixon, New York		1969 ....Anil Nayar, Boston	
1926 ....W. Palmer Dixon, New York		1970 ....Anil Nayar, Boston	
1927 ....Myles Baker, Boston		1971 ....Colin Adair, Montreal	
1928 ....Herbert N. Rawlins Jr., New York		1972 ....Victor Niederhoffer, New York	
1929 ....J. Lawrence Pool New York		1973 ....Victor Niederhoffer, New York	
1930 ....Herbert N. Rawlins Jr., New York		1974 ....Victor Niederhoffer, New York	
1931 ....J. Lawrence Pool, New York		1975 ....Victor Niederhoffer, New York	
1932 ....Beckman H. Pool, New York		1976 ....Peter Briggs, New York	
1933 ....Beckman H. Pool, New York		1977 ....Thomas E. Page, Philadelphia	
1934 ....Neil J. Sullivan II, Philadelphia		1978 ....Michael Desaulniers, Montreal	
1935 ....Donald Strachan, Philadelphia		1979 ....Mario Sanchez, Mexico	
1936 ....Germain G. Glidden, New York		1980 ....Michael Desaulniers, Montreal	
1937 ....Germain G. Glidden, New York		1981 ....Mark Alger, Tacoma, WA	
1938 ....Germain G. Glidden, New York		1982 ....John Nimick, Narberth, PA	
1939 ....Donald Strachan, Philadelphia		1983 ....Kenton Jernigan, Newport, RI	
1940 ....A. Willing Patterson, Philadelphia		1984 ....Kenton Jernigan, Newport, RI	
1941 ....Charles M. P. Britton, Philadelphia		1985 ....Kenton Jernigan, Newport, RI	
1942 ....Charles M. P. Britton, Philadelphia		1986 ....Hugh LaBossier, Seattle	
1943-45....No tournament		1987 ....Frank J. Stanley IV, Princeton, NJ	
1946 ....Charles M. P. Britton, Philadelphia		1988 ....Scott Dulmage, Toronto	
1947 ....Charles M. P. Britton, Philadelphia		1989 ....Rodolfo Rodriquez, Mexico	
1948 ....Stanley W. Pearson Jr., Philadelphia		1990 ....Hector Barragan, Mexico	
1949 ....H. Hunter Lott Jr., Philadelphia		1991 ....Hector Barragan, Mexico	
1950 ....Edward J. Hahn, Detroit		1992 ....Hector Barragan, Mexico	
1951 ....Edward J. Hahn, Detroit		1993 ....Hector Barragan, Mexico	
		1994 ....Roberto Rosales, Mexico	

Squash *(Cont.)*

National Women's Champions

Year	Champion, Hometown	Year	Champion, Hometown
1928	Eleanora Sears, Boston	1963	Margaret Varner, Wilmington, DE
1929	Margaret Howe, Boston	1964	Ann Wetzel, Philadelphia
1930	Hazel Wightman, Boston	1965	Joyce Davenport, Philadelphia
1931	Ruth Banks, Philadelphia	1966	Betty Meade, Philadelphia
1932	Margaret Howe, Boston	1967	Betty Meade, Philadelphia
1933	Susan Noel, England	1968	Betty Meade, Philadelphia
1934	Margaret Howe, Boston	1969	Joyce Davenport, Philadelphia
1935	Margot Lumb, England	1970	Nina Moyer, Princeton, NJ
1936	Anne Page, Philadelphia	1971	Carol Thesieres, Philadelphia
1937	Anne Page, Philadelphia	1972	Nina Moyer, Princeton, NJ
1938	Cecile Bowes, Philadelphia	1973	Gretchen Spruance, Wilmington, DE
1939	Anne Page, Philadelphia	1974	Gretchen Spruance, Wilmington, DE
1940	Cecile Bowes, Philadelphia	1975	Ginny Akabane, Rochester, NY
1941	Cecile Bowes, Philadelphia	1976	Gretchen Spruance, Wilmington, DE
1942-46	No tournament	1977	Gretchen Spruance, Wilmington, DE
1947	Anne Page Homer, Philadelphia	1978	Gretchen Spruance, Wilmington, DE
1948	Cecile Bowes, Philadelphia	1979	Heather McKay, Toronto
1949	Janet Morgan, England	1980	Barbara Maltby, Philadelphia
1950	Betty Howe, New Haven, CT	1981	Barbara Maltby, Philadelphia
1951	Jane Austin, Philadelphia	1982	Alicia McConnell, New York
1952	Margaret Howe, Boston	1983	Alicia McConnell, New York
1953	Margaret Howe, Boston	1984	Alicia McConnell, New York
1954	Lois Dilks, Philadelphia	1985	Alicia McConnell, New York
1955	Janet Morgan, England	1986	Alicia McConnell, Bala Cynwyd, PA
1956	Betty Howe Constable, Princeton, NJ	1987	Alicia McConnell, New York
1957	Betty Howe Constable, Princeton, NJ	1988	Alicia McConnell, New York
1958	Betty Howe Constable, Princeton, NJ	1989	Demer Holleran, Hanover, NH
1959	Betty Howe Constable, Princeton, NJ	1990	Demer Holleran, Hanover, NH
1960	Margaret Varner, Wilmington, DE	1991	Demer Holleran, Hanover, NH
1961	Margaret Varner, Wilmington, DE	1992	Demer Holleran, Hanover, NH
1962	Margaret Varner, Wilmington, DE	1993	Demer Holleran, Hanover, NH
		1994	Demer Holleran, Hanover, NH

Triathlon

Ironman Championship

MEN

Date	Winner	Time	Site
1978	Gordon Haller	11:46	Waikiki Beach
1979	Tom Warren	11:15:56	Waikiki Beach
1980	Dave Scott	9:24:33	Ala Moana Park
1981	John Howard	9:38:29	Kailua-Kona
1982	Scott Tinley	9:19:41	Kailua-Kona
1982	Dave Scott	9:08:23	Kailua-Kona
1983	Dave Scott	9:05:57	Kailua-Kona
1984	Dave Scott	8:54:20	Kailua-Kona
1985	Scott Tinley	8:50:54	Kailua-Kona
1986	Dave Scott	8:28:37	Kailua-Kona
1987	Dave Scott	8:34:13	Kailua-Kona
1988	Scott Molina	8:31:00	Kailua-Kona
1989	Mark Allen	8:09:15	Kailua-Kona
1990	Mark Allen	8:28:17	Kailua-Kona
1991	Mark Allen	8:18:32	Kailua-Kona
1992	Mark Allen	8:09:09	Kailua-Kona
1993	Mark Allen	8:07:46	Kailua-Kona

WOMEN

Date	Winner	Time	Site
1978	No finishers		
1979	Lyn Lemaire	12:55	Waikiki Beach
1980	Robin Beck	11:21:24	Ala Moana Park
1981	Linda Sweeney	12:00:32	Kailua-Kona
1982	Kathleen McCartney	11:09:40	Kailua-Kona
1982	Julie Leach	10:54:08	Kailua-Kona

Ironman Championship *(Cont.)*

WOMEN *(Cont.)*

Date	Winner	Time	Site
1983	Sylviane Puntous	10:43:36	Kailua-Kona
1984	Sylviane Puntous	10:25:13	Kailua-Kona
1985	Joanne Ernst	10:25:22	Kailua-Kona
1986	Paula Newby-Fraser	9:49:14	Kailua-Kona
1987	Erin Baker	9:35:25	Kailua-Kona
1988	Paula Newby-Fraser	9:01:01	Kailua-Kona
1989	Paula Newby-Fraser	9:00:56	Kailua-Kona
1990	Erin Baker	9:13:42	Kailua-Kona
1991	Paula Newby-Fraser	9:07:52	Kailua-Kona
1992	Paula Newby-Fraser	8:55:29	Kailua-Kona
1993	Paula Newby-Fraser	8:58:23	Kailua-Kona

Note: The Ironman Championship was contested twice in 1982.

Volleyball

World Champions

MEN

Year	Winner	Runnerup	Site
1949	Soviet Union	Czechoslovakia	Prague, Czechoslovakia
1952	Soviet Union	Czechoslovakia	Moscow, Soviet Union
1956	Czechoslovakia	Soviet Union	Paris, France
1960	Soviet Union	Czechoslovakia	Rio de Janeiro, Brazil
1962	Soviet Union	Czechoslovakia	Moscow, Soviet Union
1966	Czechoslovakia	Romania	Prague, Czechoslovakia
1970	East Germany	Bulgaria	Sofia, Bulgaria
1974	Poland	Soviet Union	Mexico City
1978	Soviet Union	Italy	Rome, Italy
1982	Soviet Union	Brazil	Buenos Aires, Argentina
1986	United States	Soviet Union	Paris, France
1990	Italy	Cuba	Rio de Janeiro, Brazil
1994	Italy	Netherlands	Athens, Greece

WOMEN

Year	Winner	Runnerup	Site
1952	Soviet Union	Poland	Moscow, Soviet Union
1956	Soviet Union	Romania	Paris, France
1960	Soviet Union	Japan	Rio de Janeiro, Brazil
1962	Japan	Soviet Union	Moscow, Soviet Union
1966	Japan	United States	Prague, Czechoslovakia
1970	Soviet Union	Japan	Sofia, Bulgaria
1974	Japan	Soviet Union	Mexico City
1978	Cuba	Japan	Rome, Italy
1982	China	Peru	Lima, Peru
1986	China	Cuba	Prague, Czechoslovakia
1990	Soviet Union	China	Beijing, China

U.S. Men's Open Champions—Gold Division

Year	Site	Year	Site
1928	Germantown, PA YMCA	1942	North Ave. YMCA, IL
1929	Hyde Park YMCA, IL	1943-44	No Championships
1930	Hyde Park YMCA, IL	1945	North Ave. YMCA, IL
1931	San Antonio, TX YMCA	1946	Pasadena, CA YMCA
1932	San Antonio, TX YMCA	1947	North Ave. YMCA, IL
1933	Houston, TX YMCA	1948	Hollywood, CA YMCA
1934	Houston, TX YMCA	1949	Downtown YMCA, CA
1935	Houston, TX YMCA	1950	Long Beach, CA YMCA
1936	Houston, TX YMCA	1951	Hollywood, CA YMCA
1937	Duncan YMCA, IL	1952	Hollywood, CA YMCA
1938	Houston, TX YMCA	1953	Hollywood, CA YMCA
1939	Houston, TX YMCA	1954	Stockton, CA YMCA
1940	Los Angeles AC, CA	1955	Stockton, CA YMCA
1941	North Ave. YMCA, IL	1956	Hollywood, CA YMCA Stars

U.S. Men's Open Champions—Gold Division *(Cont.)*

1957	Hollywood, CA YMCA Stars	1976	Maliabu, L.A., CA
1958	Hollywood, CA YMCA Stars	1977	Chuck's, Santa Barbara
1959	Hollywood, CA YMCA Stars	1978	Chuck's, Los Angeles
1960	Westside JCC, CA	1979	Nautilus, Long Beach
1961	Hollywood, CA YMCA	1980	Olympic Club, San Francisco
1962	Hollywood, CA YMCA	1981	Nautilus, Long Beach
1963	Hollywood, CA YMCA	1982	Chuck's, Los Angeles
1964	Hollywood, CA YMCA Stars	1983	Nautilus Pacifica, CA
1965	Westside JCC, CA	1984	Nautilus Pacifica, CA
1966	Sand & Sea Club, CA	1985	Molten/SSI Torrance, CA
1967	Fresno, CA VBC	1986	Molten, Torrance, CA
1968	Westside JCC, L.A., CA	1987	Molten, Torrance, CA
1969	Los Angeles, CA YMCA	1988	Molten, Torrance, CA
1970	Chart House, San Diego	1989	Not held
1971	Santa Monica, CA YMCA	1990	Nike, Carson, CA
1972	Chart House, San Diego	1991	Offshore, Woodland Hills, CA
1973	Chuck's Steak, L.A., CA	1992	Creole Six Pack, Elmhurst, NY
1974	Un of CA Santa Barbara	1993	Asics, Huntington Beach, CA
1975	Chart House, San Diego	1994	Asics/Paul Mitchell, Hunt. Beach, CA

U.S. Women's Open Champions—Gold Division

1949	Eagles, Houston TX	1972	E Pluribus Unum, Houston
1950	Voit #1, Santa Monica, CA	1973	E Pluribus Unum, Houston
1951	Eagles, Houston, TX	1974	Renegades, Los Angeles, CA
1952	Voit #1, Santa Monica, CA	1975	Adidas, Norwalk, CA
1953	Voit #1, Los Angeles, CA	1976	Pasadena, TX
1954	Houstonettes, Houston, TX	1977	Spoilers, Hermosa, CA
1955	Mariners, Santa Monica, CA	1978	Nick's, Los Angeles, CA
1956	Mariners, Santa Monica, CA	1979	Mavericks, Los Angeles, CA
1957	Mariners, Santa Monica, CA	1980	NAVA, Fountain Valley, CA
1958	Mariners, Santa Monica, CA	1981	Utah State, Logan, UT
1959	Mariners, Santa Monica, CA	1982	Monarchs, Hilo, HI
1960	Mariners, Santa Monica, CA	1983	Syntex, Stockton, CA
1961	Breakers, Long Beach, CA	1984	Chrysler, Palo Alto, CA
1962	Shamrocks, Long Beach, CA	1985	Merrill Lynch, Arizona
1963	Shamrocks, Long Beach, CA	1986	Merrill Lynch, Arizona
1964	Shamrocks, Long Beach, CA	1987	Chrysler, Pleasanton, CA
1965	Shamrocks, Long Beach, CA	1988	Chrysler, Hayward, CA
1966	Renegades, Los Angeles, CA	1989	Plymouth, Hayward, CA
1967	Shamrocks, Long Beach, CA	1990	Plymouth, Hayward, CA
1968	Shamrocks, Long Beach, CA	1991	Fitness, Champaign, IL
1969	Shamrocks, Long Beach, CA	1992	Nick's Kronies, Chicago, IL
1970	Shamrocks, Long Beach, CA	1993	Nick's Fishmarket, Chicago, IL
1971	Renegades, Los Angeles, CA	1994	Nick's Fishmarket, Chicago, IL

Wrestling

United States National Champions
1983

FREESTYLE		FREESTYLE *(Cont.)*		GRECO-ROMAN *(Cont.)*	
105.5	Rich Salamone	220	Greg Gibson	149.5	Jim Martinez
114.5	Joe Gonzales	Hvy	Bruce Baumgartner	163	James Andre
125.5	Joe Corso	Team	Sunkist Kids	180.5	Steve Goss
136.5	Rich Dellagatta*			198	Steve Fraser*
149.5	Bill Hugent	**GRECO-ROMAN**		220	Dennis Koslowski
163	Lee Kemp	105.5	T. J. Jones	Hvy	No champion
180.5	Chris Campbell	114.5	Mark Fuller	Team	Minnesota Wrestling
198	Pete Bush	125.5	Rob Hermann		Club
		136.5	Dan Mello		

*Outstanding wrestler

United States National Champions (Cont.)

1984

FREESTYLE

105.5	Rich Salamone
114.5	Charlie Heard
125.5	Joe Corso
136.5	Rick Dellagatta
149.5	Andre Metzger
163	Dave Schultz*
180.5	Mark Schultz
198	Steve Fraser

FREESTYLE (Cont.)

220	Harold Smith
Hvy	Bruce Baumgartner
Team	Sunkist Kids

GRECO-ROMAN

105.5	T. J. Jones
114.5	Mark Fuller
125.5	Frank Famiano

GRECO-ROMAN (Cont.)

136.5	Dan Mello
149.5	Jim Martinez*
163	John Matthews
180.5	Tom Press
198	Mike Houck
220	No champion
Hvy	No champion
Team	Adirondack Three-Style, WA

1985

FREESTYLE

105.5	Tim Vanni
114.5	Jim Martin
125.5	Charlie Heard
136.5	Darryl Burley
149.5	Bill Nugent*
163	Kenny Monday
180.5	Mike Sheets
198	Mark Schultz

FREESTYLE (Cont.)

220	Greg Gibson
286	Bruce Baumgartner
Team	Sunkist Kids

GRECO-ROMAN

105.5	T. J. Jones
114.5	Mark Fuller
125.5	Eric Seward*

GRECO-ROMAN (Cont.)

136.5	Buddy Lee
149.5	Jim Martinez
163	David Butler
180.5	Chris Catallo
198	Mike Houck
220	Greg Gibson
286	Dennis Koslowski
Team	U.S. Marine Corps

1986

FREESTYLE

105.5	Rich Salamone
114.5	Joe Gonzales
125.5	Kevin Darkus
136.5	John Smith
149.5	Andre Metzger*
163	Dave Schultz
180.5	Mark Schultz
198	Jim Scherr
220	Dan Severn

FREESTYLE (Cont.)

286	Bruce Baumgartner
Team	Sunkist Kids (Div. I)
	Hawkeye Wrestling
	Club (Div. II)

GRECO-ROMAN

105.5	Eric Wetzel
114.5	Shawn Sheldon
125.5	Anthony Amado

GRECO-ROMAN (Cont.)

136.5	Frank Famiano
149.5	Jim Martinez
163	David Butler*
180.5	Darryl Gholar
198	Derrick Waldroup
220	Dennis Koslowski
286	Duane Koslowski
Team	U.S. Marine Corps (Div. I)
	U.S. Navy (Div. II)

1987

FREESTYLE

105.5	Takashi Irie
114.5	Mitsuru Sato
125.5	Barry Davis
136.5	Takumi Adachi
149.5	Andre Metzger
163	Dave Schultz*
180.5	Mark Schultz
198	Jim Scherr
220	Bill Scherr

FREESTYLE (Cont.)

286	Bruce Baumgartner
Team	Sunkist Kids (Div. I)
	Team Foxcatcher (Div. II)

GRECO-ROMAN

105.5	Eric Wetzel
114.5	Shawn Sheldon
125.5	Eric Seward
136.5	Frank Famiano

GRECO-ROMAN (Cont.)

149.5	Jim Martinez
163	David Butler
180.5	Chris Catallo
198	Derrick Waldroup*
220	Dennis Koslowski
286	Duane Koslowski
Team	U.S. Marine Corp (Div. I)
	U.S. Army (Div. II)

1988

FREESTYLE

105.5	Tim Vanni
114.5	Joe Gonzales
125.5	Kevin Darkus
136.5	John Smith*
149.5	Nate Carr
163	Kenny Monday
180.5	Dave Schultz
198	Melvin Douglas III
220	Bill Scherr

FREESTYLE (Cont.)

286	Bruce Baumgartner
Team	Sunkist Kids (Div. I)
	Team Foxcatcher (Div. II)

GRECO-ROMAN

105.5	T. J. Jones
114.5	Shawn Sheldon
125.5	Gogi Parseghian*
136.5	Dalen Wasmund

GRECO-ROMAN (Cont.)

149.5	Craig Pollard
163	Tony Thomas
180.5	Darryl Gholar
198	Mike Carolan
220	Dennis Koslowski
286	Duane Koslowski
Team	U.S. Marine Corps (Div. I)
	Sunkist Kids (Div. II)

1989

FREESTYLE

105.5	Tim Vanni
114.5	Zeke Jones
125.5	Brad Penrith
136.5	John Smith
149.5	Nate Carr
163	Rob Koll

FREESTYLE (Cont.)

180.5	Rico Chiapparelli
198	Jim Scherr*
220	Bill Scherr
286	Bruce Baumgartner
Team	Sunkist Kids (Div. I)
	Team Foxcatcher (Div. II)

GRECO-ROMAN

105.5	Lew Dorrance
114.5	Mark Fuller
125.5	Gogi Parseghian
136.5	Isaac Anderson
149.5	Andy Seras*
163	David Butler

1989 (Cont.)

GRECO-ROMAN (Cont.)

180.5 ......John Morgan
198 ....Michial Foy

GRECO-ROMAN (Cont.)

220 ....Steve Lawson
286 ....Craig Pittman

GRECO-ROMAN (Cont.)

Team ......U.S. Marine Corps (Div. I)
Jets USA (Div. II)

1990

FREESTYLE

105.5 ......Rob Eiter
114.5 ......Zeke Jones
125.5 ......Joe Melchiore
136.5 ......John Smith
149.5 ......Nate Carr
163 ....Rob Koll
180.5 ......Royce Alger
198 ....Chris Campbell*

FREESTYLE (Cont.)

220 ....Bill Scherr
286 ....Bruce Baumgartner
Team ......Sunkist Kids (Div. I)
Team Foxcatcher (Div. II)

GRECO-ROMAN

105.5 ......Lew Dorrance
114.5 ......Sam Henson
125.5 ......Mark Pustelnik

GRECO-ROMAN (Cont.)

136.5 ......Isaac Anderson
149.5 ......Andy Seras
163 ....David Butler
180.5 ......Derrick Waldroup
198 ....Randy Coutre*
220 ....Chris Tironi
286 ....Matt Ghaffari
Team ......Jets USA (Div. I)
California Jets (Div. II)

1991

FREESTYLE

105.5 ......Tim Vanni
114.5 ......Zeke Jones
125.5 ......Brad Penrith
136.5 ......John Smith*
149.5 ......Townsend Saunders
163 ....Kenny Monday
180.5 ......Kevin Jackson
198 ....Chris Campbell

FREESTYLE (Cont.)

220 ....Mark Coleman
286 ....Bruce Baumgartner
Team ......Sunkist Kids (Div. I)
Jets USA (Div. II)

GRECO-ROMAN

105.5 ......Eric Wetzel
114.5 ......Shawn Sheldon
125.5 ......Frank Famiano

GRECO-ROMAN (Cont.)

136.5 ......Buddy Lee
149.5 ......Andy Seras
163 ....Gordy Morgan
180.5 ......John Morgan*
198 ....Michial Foy
220 ....Dennis Koslowski
286 ....Craig Pittman
Team ......Jets USA (Div. I)
Sunkist Kids (Div. II)

1992

FREESTYLE

105.5 ......Rob Elter
114.5 ......Jack Griffin
125.5 ......Kendall Cross*
136.5 ......John Fisher
149.5 ......Matt Demaray
163 ....Greg Elinsky
180.5 ......Royce Alger
198 ....Dan Chaid
220 ....Bill Scherr

FREESTYLE (Cont.)

286 ....Bruce Baumgartner
Team ......Sunkist Kids (Div. I)
Team Foxcatcher (Div. II)

GRECO-ROMAN

105.5 ......Eric Wetzel
114.5 ......Mark Fuller
125.5 ......Dennis Hall
136.5 ......Buddy Lee*

GRECO-ROMAN (Cont.)

149.5 ......Rodney Smith
163 ....Travis West
180.5 ......John Morgan
198 ....Michial Foy
220 ....Dennis Koslowski
286 ....Matt Ghaffari
Team ......NY Athletic Club (Div. I)
Sunkist Kids (Div. II)

1993

FREESTYLE

105.5 ......Rob Elter
114.5 ......Zeke Jones
125.5 ......Brad Penrith
136.5 ......Tom Brands
149.5 ......Matt Demaray
163 ....Dave Schultz*
180.5 ......Kevin Jackson
198 ....Melvin Douglas
220 ....Kirk Trost

FREESTYLE (Cont.)

286 ....Bruce Baumgartner
Team ......Sunkist Kids (Div. I)
Team Foxcatcher (Div. II)

GRECO-ROMAN

105.5 ......Eric Wetzel
114.5 ......Shawn Sheldon
125.5 ......Dennis Hall*
136.5 ......Shon Lewis

GRECO-ROMAN (Cont.)

149.5 ......Andy Seras
163 ....Gordy Morgan
180.5 ......Dan Henderson
198 ....Randy Couture
220 ....James Johnson
286 ....Matt Ghaffari
Team ......NY Athletic Club (Div. I)
Sunkist Kids (Div. II)

1994

FREESTYLE

105.5 ......Tim Vanni
114.5 ......Zeke Jones
125.5 ......Terry Brands
136.5 ......Tom Brands
149.5 ......Matt Demaray
163 ....Dave Schultz
180.5 ......Royce Alger
198 ....Melvin Douglas
220 ....Mark Kerr

FREESTYLE (Cont.)

286 ....Bruce Baumgartner*
Team ......Sunkist Kids (Div. I)
Team Foxcatcher (Div. II)

GRECO-ROMAN

105.5 ......Isaac Ramaswamy
114.5 ......Shawn Sheldon
125.5 ......Dennis Hall
136.5 ......Shon Lewis

GRECO-ROMAN (Cont.)

149.5 ......Andy Seras*
163 ....Gordy Morgan
180.5 ......Dan Henderson
198 ....Derrick Waldroup
220 ....James Johnson
286 ....Matt Ghaffari
Team ......Armed Forces (Div. I)
NY Athletic Club (Div. II)

*Outstanding wrestler

The Sports Market

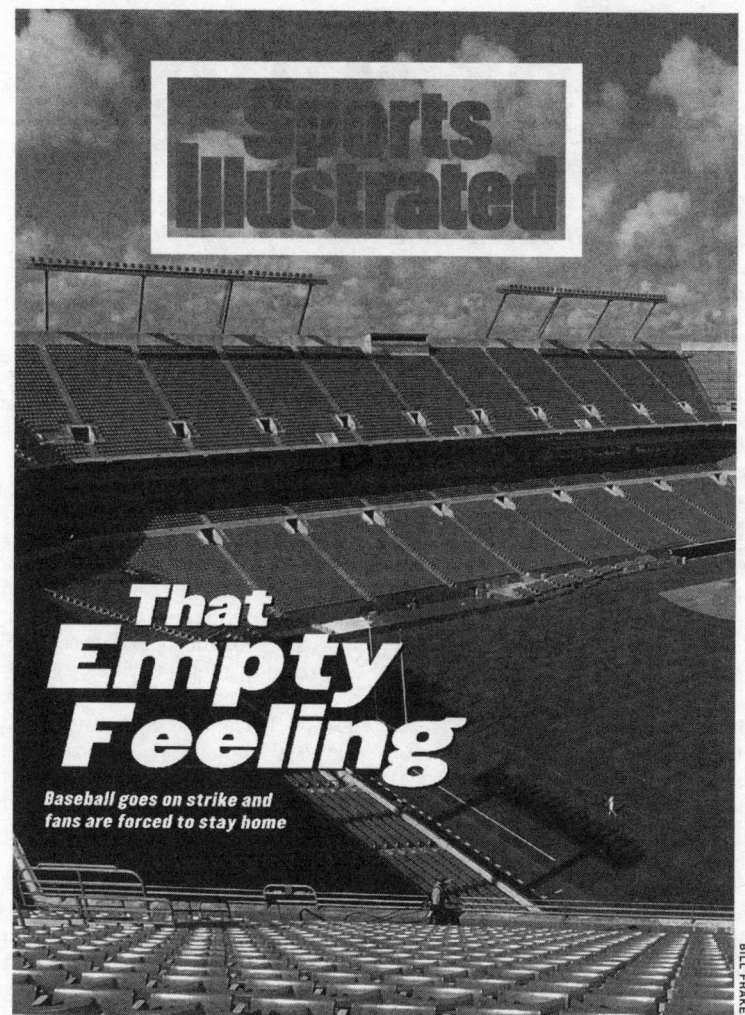

Sports Illustrated

That Empty Feeling

Baseball goes on strike and fans are forced to stay home

BILL FRAKES

Major League Labor Pains

Bitter conflict between owners and players threatened
the very survival of their sports | by JOHN STEINBREDER

THERE WAS AS MUCH ACTION AT THE bargaining table and in the courtroom last year as there was on the playing field as team owners and players in the major sports leagues haggled incessantly over salary caps, revenue sharing programs, complicated tax plans and collective bargaining agreements. The divisions in Major League Baseball were so great that its 770-odd players went out on strike August 12, and with talks still stalled a month later, the owners decided to call off the playoffs and World Series. The start of the 1994-95 National Hockey League season was threatened when commissioner Gary Bettman announced that the owners, who have been operating without a collective bargaining agreement with their players for more than a year, would shut down the league if a new contract was not signed by the beginning of the regular season. And the National Basketball Association, which had been relatively free of labor strife the past decade, found itself embroiled in a heated legal battle with a players associa-

tion that wants the league to scrap its cherished salary cap and give the players more freedom to move from team to team.

Nowhere was the fighting bloodier than in Major League Baseball, which saw postseason play canceled for the first time since 1904. The seeds for that dispiriting move were sown last winter when team owners, seeking to bridge what they said was a widening economic gap between the big- and small-market franchises, agreed to a revenue-sharing program. But implementation of that plan was contingent on the players accepting a salary cap and the owners' claims that they were in financial trouble. The players, led by union chief Donald Fehr, believed that by agreeing to a cap they would, in effect, be giving back many of the benefits they had wrested from the owners in hard-fought labor battles over the previous two decades. They also felt that the owners, who at one point said that 19 of baseball's 28 franchises—including the New York Mets and Los Angeles Dodgers—were losing money, were not being honest with their financial numbers

Fehr (right) and owners' rep Richard Ravitch found little to shake hands about.

and wanted the players to make concessions because they could not manage their teams better and control their often reckless spending habits. The two sides tried to find some middle ground, but when the owners refused to take the cap off the table, the players went out on strike. The players and owners met several times after the games had stopped, but to no avail. And with talks still at a standstill in mid-September, acting commissioner Bud Selig announced that the rest of the season as well as the League Championship playoffs and the World Series would not be held.

Those moves are proving costly. The owners lost an estimated $442 million for a season that ended 52 days and 669 games early, and the players $229 million. And that's not including revenues and pay they would have taken in from the playoffs and World Series. Clubs have laid off dozens of workers in their front offices, and countless local merchants, who earn money doing everything from seating fans to parking cars, were suddenly unemployed. Sales of baseball-related licensed merchandise have

fallen, and according to a survey of 22 teams by the U.S. Conference of Mayors, local economies lost an average $1.16 million in economic activity for each game that was not played in their towns. The Baseball Network, the joint broadcasting venture between baseball, NBC and ABC, is expected to lose an estimated $30 million from unplayed regular season games and another $100 million from the canceled playoffs and World Series games.

And while there is no telling how the strike will affect baseball in the future, it's safe to say that the game is entering a time of great uncertainty. As long as there isn't a collective bargaining agreement, ball clubs won't be trading players and signing free agents with their usual vigor this winter. It will be difficult for franchises to woo advertisers—many of whom are so discouraged with baseball that they are already looking to put their sports marketing dollars elsewhere—for their game programs, stadium

Bettmann was the second league head to announce that his sport would be put on hold.

billboards and television broadcasts. Teams will also have a hard time convincing season ticket holders to ante up for another year after pulling the rug out from under them in '94. And what right-minded fan would shell out hundreds of dollars for a pair of box seats when there is serious concern that the 1995 campaign may not start on time or be canceled altogether? In fact, baseball may have a hard time getting many of its fans—who have endured eight work stoppages in 23 years—back to the ball park, and that could further damage a sport—often heralded as America's national pastime—that has been steadily losing ground to basketball, football and hockey.

Baseball is also in danger of losing its anti-trust exemption, and once again there is rumbling on Capitol Hill about overturning the sport's unique legal status and giving players the right to sue the owners over anti-trust violations. Congress has made noise about doing this in the past, but the current talk seems more serious than ever before. "If the strike is still going when we reconvene in January, there is going to be some very strong momentum to do something about the anti-trust exemption," says former major league

pitcher Jim Bunning, now a Republican representative from Kentucky. Adds Ohio Senator Howard Metzenbaum: "Don't think for a moment that Congress will forget the sorry spectacle we have witnessed in the summer of 1994."

This should be the best of times for hockey. One of its flagship franchises, the New York Rangers, won the Stanley Cup for the first time in 54 years, and the Cup finals drew record television audiences. ESPN posted a 5.2 cable rating for the deciding game seven, the highest ever for a hockey game on cable, and ratings for the entire final series were up 19 percent from the previous year. Four of the NHL's newest teams—the Florida Panthers, Tampa Bay Lightning, San Jose Sharks and the Anaheim Mighty Ducks—consistently sold out their arenas and helped boost the sport's popularity in the Sunbelt to new heights. Licensed merchandise sales for the entire league have soared from $100 million in 1989 to $800 million last year and an estimated $3 billion for 1994. The sport has also nurtured something of a hip image: Brent Hull shot pucks with David Letterman on his *Late Show*, Mark Messier was the only professional athlete to appear at the MTV Awards ceremony, style-conscious magazines such as *Vibe* and *Details* took feature-length looks at the sport and

724   SPORTS MARKET

advertisers began seeing hockey players as more than stick-swinging goons and started employing them more frequently in marketing campaigns. And in September, the Fox Network agreed to pay the league a record $155 million over five years for the right to broadcast NHL games beginning with the 1995 All-Star game while ESPN extended its cable rights package an additional two seasons.

But it's not certain that Fox or ESPN will have any games to show its viewers. NHL team owners and players have been operating without a collective bargaining agreement for more than a year, and just two weeks before the scheduled start of the 1994-95 season, commissioner Gary Bettman said he would postpone the beginning of regular season play if a new agreement had not been struck rather than face the same sort of mid-season walkout that Major League baseball players undertook. The major issues separating the two sides involves revenue-sharing and some form of taxation linked to salaries, and while it's not clear who will prevail, one thing is for sure: With hockey enjoying new-found cachet, everyone associated with the NHL will lose if the league misses this opportunity to build on its recent gains.

Talk of a lockout also surfaced in the NBA as it got ready to open the 1994-95 season. The league's collective bargaining agreement expired last June, and rather than try to settle their disputes at the negotiating table, the players and owners have spent most of their time fighting each other in court. The owners won the first round last summer when a district court judge dismissed the players' claims of antitrust violations and urged the two to work out an agreement on their own. The players moved to appeal that decision, and with only two weeks left before the start of training camp, neither side had moved off of their position. And with talks more or less at an impasse, the owners began talking about shutting down the league in November if no bargaining agreement had been reached by then. They, too, don't want to work through most of the season without a contract and have the players walk, a la baseball, just before the postseason begin.

The primary issue in this dispute is the salary cap. Eleven years ago, the NBA became the first major sports league to adopt the cap, and the league has flourished with that device in place. But while the owners would like to keep the current cap structure—or one with some modifications—the players feel it has outlived its usefulness and want to see it scrapped. They would also like to see the draft abolished and the so-called right of first refusal, which enables teams to prevent player defections by matching higher offers, rescinded.

The NFL is the only one of the four major sports leagues to be operating with some semblance of labor peace, its owners and players having signed a seven-year pact

JOHN BIEVER

Can there be any doubt that Simms' release was related to the salary cap?

two years ago that included, among other things, a salary cap. But while there haven't been any threats of strikes or lockouts, there has been plenty of controversy, mainly because many teams have had to either waive high-priced veterans or slash their salaries to get under the cap. Consider what happened to the New York Giants' Phil Simms. After leading his ballclub to an improbable 11-5 record and a playoff spot in 1993, Simms and his $2.5 million salary were unceremoniously dropped from the team a month before training camp was scheduled to start. And several stalwart players are now earning far less than they did a year ago. Cardinal receiver Gary Clark saw his pay drop from $3.4 million to just under $1 million, and Browns linebacker Carl Banks went from $2.1 million to $225,000.

Still, most observers believe the new system is working well. Clubs are turning over 64 percent of their projected revenue to the players and benefits are vastly improved over the previous accord. And the 262 players who were unrestricted free agents and changed teams this past year saw their average-per-year salary jump 37 percent.

The salary cap certainly hasn't done anything to hurt the league's popularity and fiscal health. A recent Harris poll reports that 24 percent of all respondents say pro football is their favorite sport. The 1993 season had the highest total (13,966,843) and per-game (62,352) attendance in history, and the Super Bowl last January between the Dallas Cowboys and the Buffalo Bills was the most-watched television progam in U.S. history. In addition, Fox Broadcasting gave NFL owners and players plenty of money to play with by agreeing to pay a staggering $1.58 billion for the television rights to NFC games for the next four years.

Soccer will never enjoy the wealth and popularity that pro football does in this country, but the World Cup tournament, which was held with great success in the U.S. last summer, demonstrated that it is a powerful sport. Some 3.6 million fans attended the games—by far the most in

No one shied away from the World Cup, which drew some very respectable ratings.

Cup history—and television ratings were double and triple what sponsors, who pumped an estimated $300 million into the tournament, expected. The Cup's final match between Brazil and Italy, for example, posted a 12.4 overnight Nielsen rating, the largest ever for a soccer match in the U.S.

Professional golf continues to thrive, but the sport got a bit of bad news in 1994 when PGA commissioner Deane Beman stepped down after 20 years at the helm. Though he was a somewhat controversial commish, few can argue that golf isn't much better off than it was when Beman, a former player, began running the PGA in 1974. That year, the primary PGA tour

consisted of 43 main tournaments and 14 satellite events, with players competing for $8.1 million in purses. Today, the three tours conducted by the PGA—the regular Tour, the Seniors Tour and the Nike Tour—have a total of 123 events and more than $100 million in prize money.

Then there were the Olympics. Bidding only against itself, CBS paid a record $375 million for the American television rights to the 1998 Winter Games in Nagano, Japan. Some observers thought the price was too high, but CBS had been stung by the loss of the NFC rights to Fox only weeks before and didn't want to lose Nagano as well. And perhaps the hefty fee did not seem so out-of-line when the ratings for the Lillehammer Games came in a month later. Thanks in large part to the Tonya Harding/Nancy Kerrigan soap opera,

they were the most watched in Olympic history, averaging a 27.8 Nielsen rating, some 14% above the previous record set in Munich in the summer of 1972. The much-anticipated meeting between Harding and Kerrigan in the women's free skating program produced a remarkable 48.5 rating, making it the third-highest rated sports event in U.S. history.

Those are numbers that the powers in baseball, basketball and hockey only dream about, and if they ever hope to achieve such audiences themselves, they are going to have to stop bickering and start playing their games. It would also help if they came up with better ways of marketing their products. A good place to start would be to halt all this talk about capping players' salaries and consider putting a limit on lawyers instead.

Baseball Directory

Major League Baseball
Address: 350 Park Avenue
New York, NY 10022
Telephone: (212) 339-7800
Commissioner: TBA
Chairmam of the Executive Council: Bud Selig

Major League Baseball Players Association
Address: 12 East 49th Street 24th Floor
New York, NY 10017
Telephone: (212) 826-0808
Executive Director: Donald Fehr
Director of Marketing: Judy Heeter

American League

American League Office
Address: 350 Park Avenue
New York, NY 10022
Telephone: (212) 339-7600
President: Dr. Gene Budig
Director of Public Relations: Phyllis Merhige

Baltimore Orioles
Address: Oriole Park at Camden Yards
333 W Camden Street
Baltimore, MD 21201
Telephone: (410) 685-9800
Stadium (Capacity): Camden Yards (48,262)
Managing Partner/Owner: Peter G. Angelos
Vice President: Roland Hemond
Manager: TBA
Director of Community and Media Relations: Charles Steinberg

Boston Red Sox
Address: 4 Yawkey Way
Fenway Park
Boston, MA 02215
Telephone: (617) 267-9440
Stadium (Capacity): Fenway Park (33,871)
Majority Owner/Chairman of the Board: John Harrington
Executive VP of Baseball Operations: Lou Gorman
Executive VP and GM: Daniel F. Duquette
Manager: TBA
Vice President, Public Relations: Dick Bresciani

California Angels
Address: P.O. Box 2000
Anaheim Stadium
Anaheim, CA 92803
Telephone: (714) 937-7200 or (213) 625-1123
Stadium (Capacity): Anaheim Stadium (64,573)
Chairman of the Board: Gene Autry
General Manager: Bill Bavasi
Manager: Marcel Lachemann
Assistant VP of Media Relations: John Sevano

Chicago White Sox
Address: Comiskey Park
Chicago, IL 60616
Telephone: (312) 924-1000
Stadium (Capacity): Comiskey Park (44,321)
Chairman: Jerry Reinsdorf
General Manager: Ron Schueler
Manager: Gene Lamont
Director of Publc Relations: Doug Abel

Cleveland Indians
Address: Jacobs Field
2401 Ontario Street
Cleveland, OH 44115-4003
Telephone: (216) 861-1200
Stadium (Capacity): Jacobs Field (74,483)
Chairman of the Board and CEO: Richard Jacobs
Executive VP and General Manager: John Hart
Manager: Mike Hargrove
Vice President, Public Relations: Bob DiBiasio

Detroit Tigers
Address: 2121 Trumbull
Tiger Stadium
Detroit, MI 48216
Telephone: (313) 962-4000
Stadium (Capacity): Tiger Stadium (52,416)
Owner, Chairman and President: Mike Ilitch
President and Chief Operating Officer: TBA
Manager: Sparky Anderson
Vice President, Media and Public Relations: Dan Ewald

Kansas City Royals
Address: P.O. Box 419969
Kansas City, MO 64141
Telephone: (816) 921-2200
Stadium (Capacity): Kauffman Stadium (40,625)
Chairman of the Board and CEO: David D. Glass
General Manager: Herk Robinson
Manager: TBA
Vice President, Public Relations: Dean Vogelaar

Milwaukee Brewers
Address: Milwaukee County Stadium
Milwaukee, WI 53214
Telephone: (414) 933-4114
Stadium (Capacity): Milwaukee County Stadium (53,192)
President and Chief Executive Officer: Bud Selig
Senior VP, Baseball Operations: Sal Bando
Manager: Phil Garner
Director of Publicity: TBA

Minnesota Twins
Address: 501 Chicago Avenue South
Hubert H. Humphrey Metrodome
Minneapolis, MN 55415
Telephone: (612) 375-1366
Stadium (Capacity): Hubert H. Humphrey Metrodome (56,144)
Owner: Carl Pohlad
General Manager: Terry Ryan
Manager: Tom Kelly
Director of Media Relations: Rob Antony

New York Yankees
Address: Yankee Stadium
Bronx, NY 10451
Telephone: (718) 293-4300
Stadium (Capacity): Yankee Stadium (57,545)
Majority Owner: George Steinbrenner
Managing General Partner: Joseph Molloy
General Manager: Gene Michael
Manager: Buck Showalter
Director of Media Relations and Publicity: Rob Butcher

American League *(Cont.)*

Oakland Athletics
Address: Oakland-Alameda County Coliseum
         Oakland, CA 94621
Telephone: (510) 638-4900
Stadium (Capacity): Oakland-Alameda County
  Coliseum (46,990)
Owner/Managing General Partner: Walter Haas
President and General Manager: Sandy Alderson
Manager: Tony LaRussa
Director of Baseball Information: Jay Alves

Seattle Mariners
Address: P.O. Box 4100
         Seattle, WA 98104
Telephone: (206) 628-3555
Stadium (Capacity): The Kingdome (59,166)
Chairman: John Ellis
General Manager: Woody Woodward
Manager: Lou Piniella
Director of Public Relations: Dave Aust

Texas Rangers
Address: P.O. Box 90111
         Arlington, TX 76004
Telephone: (817) 273-5222
Stadium (Capacity): The Ballpark in Arlington (49,292)
General Partners: George W. Bush, Rusty Rose
Acting General Manager: Sandy Johnson
Manager: Kevin Kennedy
Vice President, Public Relations: John Blake

Toronto Blue Jays
Address: SkyDome
         1 Blue Jays Way, Suite 3200
         Toronto, Ontario, Canada M5V 1J1
Telephone: (416) 341-1000
Stadium (Capacity): SkyDome (50,516)
Chairman of the Board: Peter N.T. Widdrington
President and CEO: Paul Beeston
Executive VP of Baseball Operations: Pat Gillick
Manager: Cito Gaston
Director of Public Relations: Howard Starkman

National League

National League Office
Address: 350 Park Avenue
         New York, NY 10022
Telephone: (212) 339-7700
President: Leonard Coleman
Director of Public Relations: Ricky Clemons

Atlanta Braves
Address: P.O. Box 4064
         Atlanta, GA 30302
Telephone: (404) 522-7630
Stadium (Capacity): Atlanta-Fulton County Stadium
  (52,007)
Owner: Ted Turner
General Manager: John Schuerholz
Manager: Bobby Cox
Director of Public Relations: Jim Schultz

Chicago Cubs
Address: 1060 West Addison
         Wrigley Field
         Chicago, IL 60613
Telephone: (312) 404-2827
Stadium (Capacity): Wrigley Field (38,765)
Chairman of the Board: Stanton R. Cook
Executive VP of Baseball Operations: Larry Himes
Manager: Tom Trebelhorn
Director of Media Relations: Sharon Panozzo

Cincinnati Reds
Address: 100 Riverfront Stadium
         Cincinnati, OH 45202
Telephone: (513) 421-4510
Stadium (Capacity): Riverfront Stadium (52,952)
General Partner: Marge Schott
General Manager: James G. Bowden
Manager: Davey Johnson
Publicity Director: Jon Braude

Colorado Rockies
Address: 1700 Broadway, Suite 2100
         Denver, CO 80290
Telephone: (303) 292-0200
Stadium (Capacity): Coors Field (52,000)
President: Jerry McMorris
Executive VP of Baseball Operations: John McHale
Manager: Don Baylor
Director of Public Relations: Mike Swanson

Florida Marlins
Address: 2267 N.W. 199th Street
         Miami, FL 33056
Telephone: (305) 626-7400
Stadium (Capacity): Joe Robbie Stadium (45,706)
Owner: H. Wayne Huizenga
Vice President and General Manager: David
  Dombrowski
Manager: Rene Lachemann
Director of Media Relations: Chuck Pool

Houston Astros
Address: P.O. Box 288
         Houston, TX 77001
Telephone: (713) 799-9500
Stadium (Capacity): Astrodome (54,313)
Chairman: Drayton McLane Jr.
General Manager: Bob Watson
Manager: Terry Collins
Director of Media Relations: Rob Matwick

Los Angeles Dodgers
Address: 1000 Elysian Park Avenue
         Los Angeles, CA 90012
Telephone: (213) 224-1500
Stadium (Capacity): Dodger Stadium (56,000)
President: Peter O'Malley
Executive Vice President: Fred Claire
Manager: Tom Lasorda
Director of Publicity: Jay Lucas

Montreal Expos
Address: P.O. Box 500
         Station M
         Montreal
         Quebec, Canada H1V 3P2
Telephone: (514) 253-3434
Stadium (Capacity): Olympic Stadium (46,500)
President: Claude Brochu
General Manager: Kevin Malone
Manager: Felipe Alou
Director, Media Relations: Rich Griffin

National League *(Cont.)*

New York Mets
Address: Shea Stadium
            Flushing, NY 11368
Telephone: (718) 507-6387
Stadium (Capacity): Shea Stadium (55,601)
Chairman: Nelson Doubleday
President and CEO: Fred Wilpon
Executive VP of Baseball Operations: Joe McIlvaine
Manager: Dallas Green
Director of Media Relations: Jay Horwitz

Philadelphia Phillies
Address: P.O. Box 7575
            Philadelphia, PA 19101
Telephone: (215) 463-6000
Stadium (Capacity): Veterans Stadium (62,382)
President: Bill Giles
General Manager: Lee Thomas
Manager: Jim Fregosi
Vice President, Public Relations: Larry Shenk

Pittsburgh Pirates
Address: P.O. Box 7000
            Pittsburgh, PA 15212
Telephone: (412) 323-5000
Stadium (Capacity): Three Rivers Stadium (58,729)
President and CEO: Mark Sauer
General Manager: Cam Bonifay
Manager: Jim Leyland
Director of Media Relations: Jim Trdinich

St. Louis Cardinals
Address: 250 Stadium Plaza
            Busch Stadium
            St. Louis, MO 63102
Telephone: (314) 421-3060
Stadium (Capacity): Busch Stadium (57,001)
Chairman of the Board: August A. Busch III
General Manager: Dal Maxvill
Manager: Joe Torre
Director of Public Relations: Brian Bartow

San Diego Padres
Address: P.O. Box 2000
            San Diego, CA 92112
Telephone: (619) 283-7294
Stadium (Capacity): San Diego/Jack Murphy Stadium
(60,000)
Chairman: Tom Werner
General Manager: Randy Smith
Manager: Jim Riggleman
Director of Media Relations: TBA

San Francisco Giants
Address: Candlestick Park
            San Francisco, CA 94124
Telephone: (415) 468-3700
Stadium (Capacity): Candlestick Park (63,000)
Chairman: Peter Magowan
General Manager: Bob Quinn
Manager: Dusty Baker
Director of Public Relations: Bob Rose

Pro Football Directory

National Football League
Address: 410 Park Avenue
            New York, New York 10022
Telephone: (212) 758-1500
Commissioner: Paul Tagliabue
Director of Communications: Greg Aiello

National Football League Players Association
Address: 2021 L Street, N.W.
            Washington, D.C. 20036
Telephone: (202) 463-2200
Executive Director: Gene Upshaw
Director, Public Relations: Frank Woschitz

National Conference

Arizona Cardinals
Address: P.O. Box 888
            Phoenix, AZ 85001
Telephone: (602) 379-0101
Stadium (Capacity): Sun Devil Stadium (73,377)
President: Bill Bidwill
Coach and General Manager: Buddy Ryan
Vice President: Larry Wilson
Director of Public Relations: Paul Jensen

Atlanta Falcons
Address: 2745 Burnette Road
            Suwanee, GA 30174
Telephone: (404) 945-1111
Stadium (Capacity): Georgia Dome (71,500)
Chairman of the Board: Rankin M. Smith Sr.
President: Taylor W. Smith
Director of Player Personnel: Ken Herock
Coach: June Jones
Publicity Director: Charlie Taylor

Chicago Bears
Address: 250 N. Washington Road
            Lake Forest, IL 60045
Telephone: (708) 295-6600
Stadium (Capacity): Soldier Field (66,946)
President: Michael McCaskey
Coach: Dave Wannstedt
Director of Public Relations: Bryan Harlan

Dallas Cowboys
Address: One Cowboys Parkway
            Irving, TX 75063
Telephone: (214) 556-9900
Stadium (Capacity): Texas Stadium (65,024)
Owner, President, and General Manager: Jerry Jones
Coach: Barry Switzer
Public Relations Director: Rich Dalrymple

National Conference *(Cont.)*

Detroit Lions
Address: 1200 Featherstone Road
             Pontiac, MI 48342
Telephone: (313) 335-4131
Stadium (Capacity): Pontiac Silverdome (80,500)
President and Owner: William Clay Ford
Executive Vice President: Chuck Schmidt
Coach: Wayne Fontes
Media Relations Director: Mike Murray

Green Bay Packers
Address: 1265 Lombardi Avenue
             Green Bay, WI 54304
Telephone: (414) 496-5700
Stadium (Capacity): Lambeau Field (59,543),
  Milwaukee County Stadium (56,051)
President: Bob Harlan
General Manager: Ron Wolf
Coach: Mike Holmgren
Public Relations Director: Lee Remmel

Los Angeles Rams
Address: 2327 W. Lincoln Avenue
             Anaheim, CA 92801
Telephone: (714) 535-7267
Stadium (Capacity): Anaheim Stadium (69,008)
President: Georgia Frontiere
Executive VP: John Shaw
Vice President and Coach: Chuck Knox
Director of Public Relations: Rick Smith

Minnesota Vikings
Address: 9520 Viking Drive
             Eden Prairie, MN 55344
Telephone: (612) 828-6500
Stadium (Capacity): HHH Metrodome (63,000)
President: Roger L. Hendrick
VP of Administrative and Team Operations: Jeff Diamond
Coach: Dennis Green
Public Relations Director: David Pelletier

New Orleans Saints
Address: 6928 Saints Drive
             Metairie, LA 70003
Telephone: (504) 733-0255
Stadium (Capacity): Louisiana Superdome (69,065)
Owner: Tom Benson
VP of Football Operations: Bill Kuharich
Executive VP of Administration: Jim Miller
VP/Head Coach: Jim Mora
Director of Media Relations: Rusty Kasmiersky

New York Giants
Address: Giants Stadium
             East Rutherford, NJ 07073
Telephone: (201) 935-8111
Stadium (Capacity): Giants Stadium (77,311)
President and co-CEO: Wellington T. Mara
Chairman and co-CEO: Preston Robert Tisch
General Manager: George Young
Coach: Dan Reeves
Director of Public Relations: Pat Hanlon

Philadelphia Eagles
Address: Veterans Stadium
             Broad Street and Pattison Avenue
             Philadelphia, PA 19148
Telephone: (215) 463-2500
Stadium (Capacity): Veterans Stadium (65,178)
Owner: Jeffrey Lurie
President and COO: Harry Gamble
Coach: Rich Kotite
Director of Public Relations: Ron Howard

San Francisco 49ers
Address: 4949 Centennial Boulevard
             Santa Clara, CA 95054
Telephone: (408) 562-4949
Stadium (Capacity): Candlestick Park (66,455)
Owner: Edward J. DeBartolo Jr.
General Manager: John McVay
Coach: George Seifert
Public Relations Director: Rodney Knox

Tampa Bay Buccaneers
Address: One Buccaneer Place
             Tampa, FL 33607
Telephone: (813) 870-2700
Stadium (Capacity): Tampa Stadium (74,321)
Owner: Hugh F. Culverhouse
Director of Football Operations and Coach: Sam
  Wyche
Director of Public Relations: Rick Odioso

Washington Redskins
Address: Redskin Park Drive
             Ashburn, VA 22011
Telephone: (703) 478-8900
Stadium (Capacity): RFK Memorial Stadium (55,683)
Owner: Jack Kent Cooke
General Manager: Charley Casserly
Coach: Norv Turner
Director of Communications: Rick Vaughn

American Conference

Buffalo Bills
Address: One Bills Drive
             Orchard Park, NY 14127
Telephone: (716) 648-1800
Stadium (Capacity): Rich Stadium (80,290)
President: Ralph C. Wilson Jr.
Executive VP/General Manager: John Butler
Coach: Marv Levy
Director of Media Relations: Scott Berchtold

Cincinnati Bengals
Address: 200 Riverfront Stadium
             Cincinnati, OH 45202
Telephone: (513) 621-3550
Stadium (Capacity): Riverfront Stadium (60,389)
President: John Sawyer
General Manager: Mike Brown
Coach: Dave Shula
Director of Public Relations: Allan Heim

American Conference *(Cont.)*

Cleveland Browns
Address: 80 First Avenue
          Berea, OH 44017
Telephone: (216) 891-5000
Stadium (Capacity): Cleveland Stadium (78,512)
President: Art Modell
Coach: Bill Belichick
VP and Director of Public Relations: Kevin Byrne

Denver Broncos
Address: 13665 Broncos Parkway
          Englewood, CO 80112
Telephone: (303) 649-9000
Stadium (Capacity): Mile High Stadium (76,273)
President/CEO: Pat Bowlen
General Manager: John Beake
Coach: Wade Phillips
Director of Media Relations: Jim Saccomano

Houston Oilers
Address: 6910 Fannin Street
          Houston, TX 77030
Telephone: (713) 797-9111
Stadium (Capacity): Astrodome (62,021)
President: K. S. (Bud) Adams Jr.
General Manager: Floyd Reese
Coach: Jack Pardee
Director of Media Relations: Chip Namias

Indianapolis Colts
Address: P.O. Box 535000
          Indianapolis, IN 46253
Telephone: (317) 297-2658
Stadium (Capacity): Hoosier Dome (60,129)
Owner: Robert Irsay
VP and General Manager: Jim Irsay
Coach: Ted Marchibroda
Public Relations Director: Craig Kelley

Kansas City Chiefs
Address: One Arrowhead Drive
          Kansas City, MO 64129
Telephone: (816) 924-9300
Stadium (Capacity): Arrowhead Stadium (77,622)
Founder: Lamar Hunt
President and General Manager: Carl Peterson
Coach: Marty Schottenheimer
Public Relations Director: Bob Moore

Los Angeles Raiders
Address: 332 Center Street
          El Segundo, CA 90245
Telephone: (310) 322-3451
Stadium (Capacity): Los Angeles Memorial Coliseum
(92,516)
President and General Partner: Al Davis
Coach: Art Shell
Executive Assistant: Al LoCasale

Miami Dolphins
Address: Joe Robbie Stadium
          7500 S.W. 30th Street
          Davie, FL 33314
Telephone: (305) 452-7000
Stadium (Capacity): Joe Robbie Stadium (74,916)
Chairman of the Board/Owner: H. Wayne Huizenga
Executive VP/General Manager: Eddie J. Jones
Coach: Don Shula
Media Relations Director: Harvey Greene

New England Patriots
Address: Foxboro Stadium
          Route 1
          Foxboro, MA 02035
Telephone: (508) 543-8200
Stadium (Capacity): Foxboro Stadium (60,794)
President and CEO: Robert K. Kraft
VP Owners Representative: Jonathan Kraft
VP Business Operations: Andy Wasynczuk
Coach: Bill Parcells
Dir. of Public and Community Relations: Donald Lowery

New York Jets
Address: 1000 Fulton Avenue
          Hempstead, NY 11550
Telephone: (516) 538-6600
Stadium (Capacity): Giants Stadium (76,891)
Chairman of the Board: Leon Hess
General Manager: Dick Steinberg
Coach: Pete Carroll
Director of Public Relations: Frank Ramos

Pittsburgh Steelers
Address: Three Rivers Stadium
          300 Stadium Circle
          Pittsburgh, PA 15212
Telephone: (412) 323-1200
Stadium (Capacity): Three Rivers Stadium (59,600)
President: Dan Rooney
Director of Football Operations: Tom Donahoe
Coach: Bill Cowher
Public Relations Coordinator: Dan Edwards

San Diego Chargers
Address: San Diego Jack Murphy Stadium
          P.O. Box 609609
          San Diego, CA 92160
Telephone: (619) 280-2111
Stadium (Capacity): San Diego Jack Murphy Stadium
(61,863)
Chairman of the Board/President: Alex G. Spanos
General Manager: Bobby Beathard
Coach: Bobby Ross
Director of Public Relations: Bill Johnston

Seattle Seahawks
Address: 11220 N.E. 53rd Street
          Kirkland, WA 98033
Telephone: (206) 827-9777
Stadium (Capacity): The Kingdome (66,400)
Owner: Ken Behring
President: David Behring
GM and Coach: Tom Flores
VP of Administration and Public Relations: Gary Wright

Pro Football Directory (Cont.)

Other Leagues

Canadian Football League
Address: 110 Eglinton Avenue West, 5th floor
             Toronto, Ontario M4R 1A3, Canada
Telephone: (416) 322-9650
Commissioner: Larry Smith
Communications Director: Michael Murray

World League of American Football
Address: 540 Madison Avenue
             New York, NY 10022
Telephone: (212) 758-1500
Chief Operating Officer: Tom Spock

Pro Basketball Directory

National Basketball Association
Address: 645 Fifth Avenue
             New York, NY 10022
Telephone: (212) 826-7000
Commissioner: David Stern
Deputy Commissioner: Russell Granik
Vice President, Public Relations: Brian McIntyre

National Basketball Association Players Association
Address: 1775 Broadway
             Suite 2401
             New York, NY 10019
Telephone: (212) 333-7510
Executive Director: Charles Grantham

Atlanta Hawks
Address: One CNN Center, South Tower
             Suite 405
             Atlanta, GA 30303
Telephone: (404) 827-3800
Arena (Capacity): The Omni (16,510)
Owner: Ted Turner
President: Stan Kasten
General Manager: Pete Babcock
Coach: Lenny Wilkens
Director of Media Relations: Arthur Triche

Boston Celtics
Address: 151 Merrimac Street
             Boston, MA 02114
Telephone: (617) 523-6050
Arena (Capacity): Boston Garden (14,890)
Owner and Chairman of the Board: Paul Gaston
President: Arnold (Red) Auerbach
General Manager: Jan Volk
Coach: Chris Ford
Director of Public Relations: R. Jeffrey Twiss

Charlotte Hornets
Address: 100 Hive Drive
             Charlotte, NC 28217
Telephone: (704) 357-0252
Arena (Capacity): Charlotte Coliseum (23,698)
Owner: George Shinn
President: Spencer Stolpen
Coach: Allan Bristow
Director of Media Relations: Harold Kaufman

Chicago Bulls
Address: 1901 W. Madison
             Chicago, IL 60612
Telephone: (312) 455-4000
Arena (Capacity): United Center (21,500)
Chairman: Jerry Reinsdorf
General Manager: Jerry Krause
Coach: Phil Jackson
Director of Media Services: Tim Hallam

Cleveland Cavaliers
Address: One Center Court
             Cleveland, OH 44115
Telephone: (216) 420-2262
Arena (Capacity): Gund Arena (20,562)
Chairman of the Board: Gordon Gund
President/COO, Team Division: Wayne Embry
Coach: Mike Fratello
Director of Public Relations: Bob Price

Dallas Mavericks
Address: Reunion Arena
             777 Sports Street
             Dallas, TX 75207
Telephone: (214) 748-1808
Arena (Capacity): Reunion Arena (17,502)
Owner and President: Donald Carter
General Manager: Norm Sonju
Coach: Dick Motta
Director of Public Relations: Kevin Sullivan

Denver Nuggets
Address: McNichols Sports Arena
             1635 Clay Street
             Denver, CO 80204
Telephone: (303) 893-6700
Arena (Capacity): McNichols Sports Arena (17,171)
Owners: Comsat Corporation
General Manager: Bernie Bickerstaff
Coach: Dan Issel
Media Relations Director: Tommy Sheppard

Detroit Pistons
Address: The Palace of Auburn Hills
             Two Championship Drive
             Auburn Hills, MI 48326
Telephone: (810) 377-0100
Arena (Capacity): The Palace of Auburn Hills (21,454)
Owner: William M. Davidson
VP of Basketball Operations: Bill McKinney
Coach: Don Chaney
VP, Public Relations: Matt Dobek

Golden State Warriors
Address: 7000 Coliseum Way
              Oakland Coliseum Arena
              Oakland, CA 94621
Telephone: (510) 638-6300
Arena (Capacity): Oakland Coliseum Arena (15,025)
Chairman: James F. Fitzgerald
Coach and General Manager: Don Nelson
Media Relations Director: Julie Marvel

Houston Rockets
Address: The Summit
              Ten Greenway Plaza
              Houston, TX 77046
Telephone: (713) 627-0600
Arena (Capacity): The Summit (16,279)
Owner: Leslie Alexander
President: John Thomas
General Manager: Bob Weinhauer
Coach: Rudy Tomjanovich
Director of Media Information: Rose Pietrzak

Indiana Pacers
Address: 300 E. Market Street
              Indianapolis, IN 46204
Telephone: (317) 263-2100
Arena (Capacity): Market Square Arena (16,530)
Owners: Melvin Simon and Herbert Simon
President: Donnie Walsh
Coach: Larry Brown
Media Relations Director: David Benner

Los Angeles Clippers
Address: L.A. Memorial Sports Arena
              3939 S. Figueroa Street
              Los Angeles, CA 90037
Telephone: (213) 748-8000
Arena (Capacity): L.A. Memorial Sports Arena (16,021)
Owner: Donald T. Sterling
VP of Basketball Operations: Elgin Baylor
Coach: Bill Fitch
VP of Communications: Joe Safety

Los Angeles Lakers
Address: Great Western Forum
              3900 West Manchester Boulevard
              Inglewood, CA 90306
Telephone: (310) 419-3100
Arena (Capacity): The Great Western Forum (17,505)
Owner: Dr. Jerry Buss
General Manager: Jerry West
Coach: Del Harris
Director of Public Relations: John Black

Miami Heat
Address: The Miami Arena
              Miami, FL 33136
Telephone: (305) 577-4328
Arena (Capacity): Miami Arena (15,200)
Managing Partner: Lewis Schaffel
Executive VP: Pauline Winick
Coach: Kevin Loughery
Director of Public Relations: Mark Pray

Milwaukee Bucks
Address: The Bradley Center
              1001 N. Fourth Street
              Milwaukee, WI 53203
Telephone: (414) 227-0500
Arena (Capacity): The Bradley Center (18,633)
Owner: Herb Kohl
Coach and VP of Bask. Operations: Mike Dunleavy
Public Relations Director: Bill King II

Minnesota Timberwolves
Address: 600 First Avenue North
              Minneapolis, MN 55403
Telephone: (612) 673-1600
Arena (Capacity): Target Center (19,006)
Owners: Glen Taylor
General Manager and Director of Player Personnel:
  Jack McCloskey
Coach: Bill Blair
Director of Media Relations: Kent Wipf

New Jersey Nets
Address: 405 Murray Hill Parkway
              East Rutherford, NJ 07073
Telephone: (201) 935-8888
Arena (Capacity): Meadowlands Arena (20,029)
Chairman/CEO: Alan L. Aufzien
General Manager: Willis Reed
Coach: Butch Beard
Director of Public Relations: John Mertz

New York Knickerbockers
Address: Madison Square Garden
              Two Pennsylvania Plaza
              New York, NY 10121
Telephone: (212) 465-6499
Arena (Capacity): Madison Square Garden (19,763)
Owner: ITT/Sheraton and Cablevision
President: David Checketts
General Manager: Ernie Grunfeld
Coach: Pat Riley
Vice President, Public Relations: John Cirillo

Orlando Magic
Address: P.O. Box 76
              Orlando, FL 32802
Telephone: (407) 649-3200
Arena (Capacity): Orlando Arena (15,151)
Owner: Rich DeVos
General Manager: Pat Williams
Coach: Brian Hill
Director of Publicity/Media Relations: Alex Martins

Philadelphia 76ers
Address: Veterans Stadium
              P.O. Box 25040
              Broad Street and Pattison Avenue
              Philadelphia, PA 19147
Telephone: (215) 339-7600
Arena (Capacity): The Spectrum (18,168)
Owner and President: Harold Katz
General Manager:and Coach: John Lucas
Public Relations Director: Joe Favorito

Phoenix Suns
Address: P.O. Box 1369
              Phoenix, AZ 85001
Telephone: (602) 379-7867
Arena (Capacity): America West Arena (19,023)
Owner: Jerry Colangelo
Coach: Paul Westphal
Media Relations Director: Julie Fie

Pro Basketball Directory (Cont.)

Portland Trail Blazers
Address: 700 N.E. Multnomah Street
                Suite 600
                Portland, OR 97232
Telephone: (503) 234-9291
Arena (Capacity): Memorial Coliseum (12,888)
Chairman of the Board: Paul Allen
President and GM of Blazers Basketball, Inc.: Bob Whitsitt
President of Trailblazers, Inc.: Marshall Glickman
Coach: P.J. Carlesimo
Director of Basketball Information: John Christiansen
Director of Sports Communication: John Lashway

Sacramento Kings
Address: One Sports Parkway
                Sacramento, CA 95834
Telephone: (916) 928-0000
Arena (Capacity): ARCO Arena (17,317)
Managing General Partner: Jim Thomas
VP of Basketball Operations: Geoff Petrie
Coach: Garry St. Jean
Director of Media Relations: Travis Stanley

San Antonio Spurs
Address: AlamoDome
                100 Montana
                San Antonio, TX 78203
Telephone: (210) 554-7787
Arena (Capacity): AlamoDome (20,662)
Chairman: General Robert McDermott
President and CEO: John C. Diller
Coach: Bob Hill
Director of Public Relations: Tom James

Seattle Supersonics
Address: 190 Queen Anne Avenue North
                Suite 200
                Seattle, WA 98109
Telephone: (206) 281-5800
Arena (Capacity): The Tacoma Dome (16,225)
Owner: Barry Ackerley
President and General Manager: Wally Walker
Coach: George Karl
Director of Public/Media Relations: Cheri White

Utah Jazz
Address: 301 West So. Temple
                Salt Lake City, UT 84101
Telephone: (801) 575-7800
Arena (Capacity): Delta Center (19,911)
Owner: Larry H. Miller
General Manager: R. Tim Howells
Coach: Jerry Sloan
Director of Media Services/Special Events: Kim Turner

Washington Bullets
Address: One Harry S. Truman Drive
                Landover, MD 20785
Telephone: (301) 773-2255
Arena (Capacity): USAir Arena (18,756)
Owner: Abe Pollin
General Manager: John Nash
Coach: Jim Lynam
Director of Communications: Matt Williams

Other League

Continental Basketball Association
Address: 701 Market Street, Suite 140
                St. Louis, MO 63101
Telephone: (314) 621-7222
Commissioner: Tom Valdiserri
Director of Media Relations: Brett Meister

Hockey Directory

National Hockey League
Address: 1251 Avenue of Americas
                47th floor
                New York, NY 10020-1198
Telephone: (212) 789-2000
Commissioner: Gary Bettman
Senior VP and Chief Operating Officer: Steven Solomon
Vice President, Public Relations: Arthur Pincus

National Hockey League Players Association
Address: One Dundas Street West
                Suite 2300
                Toronto, Ontario
                Canada M5G 1Z3
Telephone: (416) 408-4040
Executive Director: Bob Goodenow

Mighty Ducks of Anaheim
Address: 2695 Katella Avenue
                P.O. Box 61077
                Anaheim, CA 92806
Telephone: (714) 704-2700
Arena (Capacity): Arrowhead Pond of Anaheim (17,174)
Owner: Disney Sports Enterprises
General Manager: Jack Ferreira
Coach: Ron Wilson
Director of Media Relations: Bill Robertson

Boston Bruins
Address: Boston Garden
                150 Causeway Street
                Boston, MA 02114
Telephone: (617) 227-3206
Arena (Capacity): Boston Garden (14,448)
Owner and Governor: Jeremy M. Jacobs
Alternative Governor, President and General Manager: Harry Sinden
Coach: Brian Sutter
Director of Media Relations: Heidi Holland

Buffalo Sabres
Address: Memorial Auditorium
                Buffalo, NY 14202
Telephone: (716) 856-7300
Arena (Capacity): Memorial Auditorium (16,284)
Chairman of the Board and President: Seymour H. Knox III
General Manager and Coach: John Muckler
Director of Public Relations: Steve Rossi

Calgary Flames

Address: Olympic Saddledome
              P.O. Box 1540, Station M
              Calgary, Alberta T2P 3B9
Telephone: (403) 261-0475
Arena (Capacity): Olympic Saddledome (20,230)
Owners: Grant A. Bartlett, Harley N. Hotchkiss, N.
  Murray Edwards, Ronald V. Joyce, Alvin G. Libin,
  Allan P. Markin, J.R. McCaig, Byron J. Seaman, and
  Daryl K. Seaman
President and Governor: William Hay
Director of Hockey Operations: Al MacNeil
General Manager: Doug Risebrough
Coach: Dave King
Director of Public Relations: Rick Skaggs

Chicago Blackhawks

Address: United Center
              1901 W. Madison Street
              Chicago, IL 60612
Telephone: (312) 733-5300
Arena (Capacity): United Center (20,500)
President: William W. Wirtz
General Manager: Robert Pulford
Coach: Darryl Sutter
Public Relations Director: Jim DeMaria

Dallas Stars

Address: 901 Main Street
              Suite 2301
              Dallas, TX 75202
Telephone: (214) 712-2890
Arena (Capacity): Reunion Arena (16,914)
Owner: Norman N. Green
General Manager and Coach: Bob Gainey
Director of Public Relations: Larry Kelly

Detroit Red Wings

Address: Joe Louis Sports Arena
              600 Civic Center Drive
              Detroit, MI 48226
Telephone: (313) 396-7544
Arena (Capacity): Joe Louis Sports Arena (19,275)
Senior Vice President: Jim Devellano
Director of Player Personnel and Head Coach: Scott
  Bowman
Assistant General Manager: Ken Holland
Director of Public Relations: Bill Jamieson

Edmonton Oilers

Address: Edmonton Coliseum
              Edmonton, Alberta T5B 4M9
Telephone: (403) 474-8561
Arena (Capacity): Edmonton Coliseum
  (under renovation)
Owner and Governor: Peter Pocklington
General Manager: Glen Sather
Coach: George Burnett
Director of Public Relations: Bill Tuele

Florida Panthers

Address: 100 Northeast Third Avenue, 10th floor
              Fort Lauderdale, FL 33301
Telephone: (305) 768-1900
Arena (Capacity): Miami Arena (14,503)
Owner: H. Wayne Huizenga
General Manager: Bryan Murray
Coach: Roger Neilson
Director of Media Relations: Greg Bouris

Hartford Whalers

Address: 242 Trumbull Street, 8th floor
              Hartford, CT 06103
Telephone: (203) 728-3366
Arena (Capacity): Hartford Civic Center Coliseum
  (15,635)
Owner: KTR Hockey Ltd. Partnership
President and General Manager: Jim Rutherford
Assistant General Manager: Terry McDonnell
Coach: Paul Holmgren
Director of Public Relations: John Forslund

Los Angeles Kings

Address: The Great Western Forum
              3900 West Manchester Boulevard
              P.O. Box 17013
              Inglewood, CA 90308
Telephone: (310) 419-3160
Arena (Capacity): The Great Western Forum (16,005)
Governor: Bruce McNall
General Manager: Sam McMaster
Coach: Barry Melrose
Media Relations: Rick Minch

Montreal Canadiens

Address: Montreal Forum
              2313 St. Catherine Street West
              Montreal, Quebec H3H 1N2
Telephone: (514) 932-2582
Arena (Capacity): Montreal Forum (16,259; standing:
  1,700)
Chairman of the Board, President and Governor:
  Ronald Corey
General Manager: Serge A. Savard
Coach: Jacques Demers
Director of Communications: Donald Beauchamp

New Jersey Devils

Address: Byrne Meadowlands Arena
              P.O. Box 504
              East Rutherford, NJ 07073
Telephone: (201) 935-6050
Arena (Capacity): Byrne Meadowlands Arena
  (19,040)
Chairman: John J. McMullen
President and General Manager: Lou Lamoriello
Coach: Jacques Lemaire
Director of Media Relations: Mike Levine

New York Islanders

Address: Nassau Veterans' Memorial Coliseum
              Uniondale, NY 11553
Telephone: (516) 794-4100
Arena (Capacity): Nassau Veterans' Memorial
  Coliseum (16,297)
Co-Chairmen: Robert Rosenthal, Stephen Walsh
General Manager: Don Maloney
Coach: Lorne Henning
Media Relations Director: Ginger Killian

New York Rangers

Address: Madison Square Garden
              4 Pennsylvania Plaza
              New York, NY 10001
Telephone: (212) 465-6000
Arena (Capacity): Madison Square Garden (18,200)
Owner: ITT Cablevision
President and General Manager: Neil Smith
Coach: Colin Campbell
Director of Communications: Barry Watkins

Ottawa Senators

Address: 301 Moodie Drive
              Suite 200
              Nepean, Ontario K2H 9C4
Telephone: (613) 721-0115
Arena (Capacity): Ottawa Civic Centre (10,500)
Founder: Bruce M. Firestone
Chairman and Governor: Rod Bryden
General Manager: Randy Sexton
Coach: Rick Bowness
Director, Media Relations: Laurent Benoit

Philadelphia Flyers

Address: The Spectrum
              Pattison Place
              Philadelphia, PA 19148
Telephone: (215) 465-4500
Arena (Capacity): The Spectrum (17,380)
Majority Owners: Ed Snider and family
Limited Partners: Sylvan and Fran Tobin
President and General Manager: Bob Clarke
Coach: Terry Murray
Vice President of Public Relations: Mark Piazza

Pittsburgh Penguins

Address: Civic Arena
              300 Auditorium Place
              Pittsburgh, PA 15219
Telephone: (412) 642-1800
Arena (Capacity): Civic Arena (17,537)
Ownership: Howard Baldwin, Morris Belzberg,
  Thomas Ruta
General Manager: Craig Patrick
Coach: Eddie Johnston
Director of Media Relations: Harry Sanders

Quebec Nordiques

Address: Colisée de Québec
              2205 Ave de Colisée
              Quebec City, Quebec G1L 4W7
Telephone: (418) 529-8441
Arena (Capacity): Colisée de Québec (15,399)
President and Governor: Marcel Aubut
General Manager: Pierre Lacroix
Coach: Marc Crawford
Director of Press Relations: Jean Martineau

St. Louis Blues

Address: Kiel Center
              P.O. Box 66792
              St. Louis, MO 63166-6792
Telephone: (314) 622-2500
Arena (Capacity): Kiel Center (19,260)
Chairman: Michael F. Shanahan
General Manager and Coach: Mike Keenan
Director, Public Relations: Susie Mathieu

San Jose Sharks

Address: 525 West Santa Clara Street
              San Jose, CA 95113
Telephone: (408) 287-7070
Arena (Capacity): San Jose Arena (17,190)
Owner: George and Gordon Gund
VP and Director of Hockey Operations: Dean
  Lombardi
Coach: Kevin Constantine
Director of Media Relations: Ken Arnold

Tampa Bay Lightning

Address: 501 East Kennedy Boulvard
              Suite 175
              Tampa, FL 33602
Telephone: (813) 229-2658
Arena (Capacity): The Thunderdome (27,000)
President: Yoshio Nakamura
General Manager and President: Phil Esposito
Coach: Terry Crisp
Media Relations Manager: Gerry Helper

Toronto Maple Leafs

Address: Maple Leaf Gardens
              60 Carlton Street
              Toronto, Ontario M5B 1L1
Telephone: (416) 977-1641
Arena (Capacity): Maple Leaf Gardens (15,720)
Chairman: Steve A. Stavro
General Manager: Cliff Fletcher
Coach: Pat Burns
Director of Business Operations and Communications:
  Bob Stellick

Vancouver Canucks

Address: Pacific Coliseum
              100 North Renfrew Street
              Vancouver, B.C. V5K 3N7
Telephone: (604) 254-5141
Arena (Capacity): Pacific Coliseum (16,150)
Board of Directors: (Northwest Sports Enterprises
  Ltd.) J. Lawrence Dampier, Arthur R. Griffiths
  (Chairman and CEO), Frank W. Griffiths, Emily
  Griffiths-Hamilton, Doug Holtby, Michael J.
  Korenberg (Vice-Chair and COO), Coleman E. Hall,
  Senator Edward M. Lawson, W. L. McEwen,
  Senator Ray Perrault, Peter Paul Saunders, Andrew
  E. Saxton, Peter W. Webster, Sydney W. Welsh,
  David A. Williams, D. Alexander Farac (Sec.)
President and General Manager: Pat Quinn
Coach: Rick Lee
Director of Public and Media Relations: Steve
  Tambellini

Washington Capitals

Address: USAir Arena
              Landover, MD 20785
Telephone: (301) 386-7000
Arena (Capacity): USAir Arena (18,130)
Board of Directors: Abe Pollin, David P. Binderman,
  Stewart L. Binderman, James E. Cafritz, A. James
  Clark, Albert Cohen, J. Martin Irving, James T.
  Lewis, R. Robert Linowes, Arthur K. Mason, Dr.
  Jack Meshel, David M. Osnos, Richard M. Patrick
VP and General Manager: Dave Poile
Coach: Jim Schoenfeld
VP of Communications: Ed Quinlan

Winnipeg Jets

Address: Winnipeg Arena
              15–1430 Maroons Road
              Winnipeg, Manitoba R3G 0L5
Telephone: (204) 982-5387
Arena (Capacity): Winnipeg Arena (15,393)
President and Governor: Barry L. Shenkarow
Alternate Governor: Bill Davis
Board of Directors: Barry L. Shenkarow, Dick Archer,
  Barry McQueen, Marvin Shenkarow, Steve
  Bannatyne, Harvey Secter, Bill Davis
General Manager and Coach: John Paddock
Director of Communications: Richard Nairn

NATIONAL COLLEGIATE ATHLETIC ASSOCIATION (NCAA)
Address: 6201 College Boulevard
             Overland Park, KS 66211
Telephone: (913) 339-1906
Executive Director: Cedric Dempsey
Director of Public Information: Kathryn Reith

ATLANTIC COAST CONFERENCE
Address: P.O. Drawer ACC
             Greensboro, NC 27419-6999
Telephone: (910) 854-8787
Commissioner: Eugene F. Corrigan
Director of Media Relations: Brian Morrison

Clemson University
Address: Clemson, SC 29633
Nickname: Tigers
Telephone: (803) 656-2114
Football Stadium (Capacity): Clemson Memorial
  Stadium (81,473)
Basketball Arena (Capacity): Littlejohn Coliseum (11,020)
Acting President: Phil Prince
Athletic Director: Bobby Robinson
Football Coach: Tommy West
Basketball Coach: Rick Barnes
Sports Information Director: Tim Bourret

Duke University
Address: Durham, NC 27708
Nickname: Blue Devils
Telephone: (919) 684-2633
Football Stadium (Capacity): Wallace Wade Stadium
  (33,941)
Basketball Arena (Capacity): Cameron Indoor
  Stadium (9,314)
President: Nan Keohane
Athletic Director: Tom Butters
Football Coach: Fred Goldsmith
Basketball Coach: Mike Krzyzewski
Sports Information Director: Mike Cragg

Florida State University
Address: P.O. Box 2195
             Tallahassee, FL 32316
Nickname: Seminoles
Telephone: (904) 644-1403
Football Stadium (Capacity): Doak S. Campbell
  Stadium (75,000)
Basketball Arena (Capacity): Leon County Civic
  Center (12,500)
President: Sandy D'Alemberte
Interim Athletic Director: Wayne Hogan
Football Coach: Bobby Bowden
Basketball Coach: Pat Kennedy
Sports Information Director: Rob Wilson

Georgia Tech
Address: 150 Bobby Dodd Way
             Atlanta, GA 30332
Nickname: Yellow Jackets
Telephone: (404) 894-2000
Football Stadium (Capacity): Bobby Dodd
  Stadium/Grant Field (46,000)
Basketball Arena (Capacity): Alexander Memorial
  Coliseum (10,000)
President: G. Wayne Clough
Athletic Director: Dr. Homer Rice
Football Coach: Bill Lewis
Basketball Coach: Bobby Cremins
Sports Information Director: Mike Finn

University of Maryland
Address: P.O. Box 295
             College Park, MD 20740
Nickname: Terrapins
Telephone: (301) 314-7064
Football Stadium (Capacity): Byrd Stadium (45,000)
Basketball Arena (Capacity): Cole Fieldhouse
  (14,500)
President: Dr. William E. Kirwin
Athletic Director: Deborah Yow
Football Coach: Mark Duffner
Basketball Coach: Gary Williams
Sports Information Director: Herb Hartnett

University of North Carolina
Address: P.O. Box 2126
             Chapel Hill, NC 27514
Nickname: Tar Heels
Telephone: (919) 962-2123
Football Stadium (Capacity): Kenan Memorial
  Stadium (52,000)
Basketball Arena (Capacity): Dean E. Smith Center
  (21,572)
Chancellor: Paul Hardin
Athletic Director: John Swofford
Football Coach: Mack Brown
Basketball Coach: Dean Smith
Sports Information Director: Rick Brewer

North Carolina State University
Address: Box 8501
             Raleigh, NC 27695
Nickname: Wolfpack
Telephone: (919) 515-2102
Football Stadium (Capacity): Carter-Finley Stadium
  (51,500)
Basketball Arena (Capacity): Reynolds Coliseum
  (12,400)
Chancellor: Dr. Larry K. Monteith
Athletic Director: Todd Turner
Football Coach: Mike O'Cain
Basketball Coach: Les Robinson
Sports Information Director: Mark Bockelman

University of Virginia
Address: P.O. Box 3785
             Charlottesville, VA 22903
Nickname: Cavaliers
Telephone: (804) 982-5151
Football Stadium (Capacity): Scott Stadium (42,000)
Basketball Arena (Capacity): University Hall (8,500)
President: John Casteen III
Athletic Director: Jim Copeland, Jr.
Football Coach: George Welsh
Basketball Coach: Jeff Jones
Sports Information Director: Rich Murray

Wake Forest University
Address: P.O. Box 7426
             Winston-Salem, NC 27109
Nickname: Demon Deacons
Telephone: (910) 759-5640
Football Stadium (Capacity): Groves Stadium
  (31,500)
Basketball Arena (Capacity): Lawrence Joel
  Memorial Coliseum (14,407)
President: Dr. Thomas K. Hearn Jr.
Athletic Director: Ron Wellman
Football Coach: Jim Caldwell
Basketball Coach: Dave Odom
Sports Information Director: John Justus

College Sports Directory (Cont.)

BIG EAST CONFERENCE
Address: 56 Exchange Terrace, fifth floor
             Providence, RI 02903
Telephone: (401) 272-9108
Commissioner: Michael A. Tranghese
Ass't Commissioner for Public Relations: John
  Paquette

Boston College
Address: Chestnut Hill, MA 02167
Nickname: Eagles
Telephone: (617) 552-2628
Football Stadium (Capacity): Alumni Stadium (44,500)
Basketball Arena (Capacity): Silvio O. Conte Forum
  (8,604)
President: Rev. J. Donald Monan, S.J.
Athletic Director: Chet Gladchuk
Football Coach: Dan Henning
Basketball Coach: Jim O'Brien
Sports Information Director: Reid Oslin

University of Connecticut
Address: 2095 Hillside Road
             Storrs, CT 06269-3078
Nickname: Huskies
Telephone: (203) 486-2725
Football Stadium (Capacity): Memorial Stadium
  (16,200)
Basketball Arena (Capacity): Gampel Pavilion (8,241)
President: Dr. Harry J. Hartley
Athletic Director: Lew Perkins
Football Coach: Skip Holtz
Basketball Coach: Jim Calhoun
Sports Information Director: Tim Tolokan

Note: Division I-AA football

Georgetown University
Address: 37th & O Street, NW
             Washington, DC 20057
Nickname: Hoyas
Telephone: (202) 687-2435
Football Stadium (Capacity): Kehoe Field (2,000)
Basketball Arena (Capacity): USAir Arena (19,035)
President: Rev. Leo J. O'Donovan, S.J.
Senior Athletic Director: Francis X. Rienzo
Athletic Director: Joseph Lang
Football Coach: Robert Benson
Basketball Coach: John Thompson
Sports Information Director: Bill Shapland (basketball),
  Bill Hurd

Note: Division I-AA football

University of Miami
Address: One Hurricane Drive
             Coral Gables, FL 33146
Nickname: Hurricanes
Telephone: (305) 284-3244
Football Stadium (Capacity): Orange Bowl (74,476)
Basketball Arena (Capacity): Miami Arena (16,500)
President: Edward Foote II
Athletic Director: Paul T. Dee
Football Coach: Dennis Erickson
Basketball Coach: Leonard Hamilton
Sports Information Director: John Hahn

University of Pittsburgh
Address: Dept. of Athletics, P.O. Box 7436
             Pittsburgh, PA 15213
Nickname: Panthers
Telephone: (412) 648-8240
Football Stadium (Capacity): Pitt Stadium (56,500)
Basketball Arena (Capacity): Fitzgerald Field House
  (6,798), Pittsburgh Civic Arena (16,798)
Chancellor: J. Dennis O'Connor
Athletic Director: Oval Jaynes
Football Coach: Johnny Majors
Basketball Coach: Ralph Willard
Sports Information Director: Ron Wall

Providence College
Address: River Avenue
             Providence, RI 02918
Nickname: Friars
Telephone: (401) 865-2265
Basketball Arena (Capacity): Providence Civic Center
  (13,410)
President: Rev. Philip A. Smith, O.P.
Athletic Director: John Marinatto
Basketball Coach: Pete Gillen
Sports Information Director: Gregg Burke

Note: No football program

Rutgers University
Address: P.O. Box 1149
             Piscataway, NJ 08855-1149
Nickname: Scarlet Knights
Telephone: (908) 445-4200
Football Stadium (Capacity): Rutgers Stadium
  (42,000), Giants Stadium (76,000)
Basketball Arena (Capacity): Louis Brown Athletic
  Center (9,000)
President: Dr. Francis L. Lawrence
Athletic Director: Frederick Gruninger
Football Coach: Doug Graber
Basketball Coach: Bob Wenzel
Sports Information Director: Peter Kowalski

Note: Plays football in Big East, basketball in Atlantic 10
Conference.

St. John's University
Address: 8000 Utopia Parkway
             Jamaica, NY 11439
Nickname: Red Storm
Telephone: (718) 990-6367
Football Stadium (Capacity): St. John's Stadium (3,000)
Basketball Arena (Capacity): Alumni Hall (6,008),
  Madison Square Garden (19,576)
President: Very Rev. Donald J. Harrington, C.M.
Athletic Director: John W. Kaiser
Football Coach: Bob Ricca
Basketball Coach: Brian Mahoney
Sports Information Director: Frank Racaniello

Note: Division I-AA football

Seton Hall University
Address: 400 South Orange Avenue
             South Orange, NJ 07079
Nickname: Pirates
Telephone: (201) 761-9497
Basketball Arena (Capacity): Walsh Auditorium
  (3,200), The Meadowlands (20,029)
President: Rev. Thomas R. Peterson
Athletic Director: Larry Keating
Basketball Coach: George Blaney
Sports Information Director: John Wooding

Note: No football program

Syracuse University

Address: Manley Field House
              Syracuse, NY 13244-5020
Nickname: Orangemen
Telephone: (315) 443-2608
Football Stadium (Capacity): Carrier Dome (50,000)
Basketball Arena (Capacity): Carrier Dome (33,000)
Chancellor: Dr. Kenneth Shaw
Athletic Director: Jake Crouthamel
Football Coach: Paul Pasqualoni
Basketball Coach: Jim Boeheim
Sports Information Director: Larry Kimball

Temple University

Address: McGonigle Hall
              Philadelphia, PA 19122
Nickname: Owls
Telephone: (215) 204-7445
Football Stadium (Capacity): Veterans Stadium
  (66,592)
Basketball Arena (Capacity): McGonigle Hall (3,900)
President: Peter J. Liacouras
Athletic Director: R. C. Johnson
Football Coach: Ron Dickerson
Basketball Coach: John Chaney
Sports Information Director: Al Shrier

Note: Plays football in Big East, basketball in Atlantic 10 Conference.

Villanova University

Address: Lancaster Avenue
              Villanova, PA 19085
Nickname: Wildcats
Telephone: (215) 519-4110
Football Stadium (Capacity): Villanova Stadium (13,400)
Basketball Arena (Capacity): duPont Pavilion (6,500),
  The Spectrum (18,497)
President: Rev. Edmund Dobbin, O.S.A.
Athletic Director: Gene DeFilippo
Football Coach: Andy Talley
Basketball Coach: Steve Lappas
Sports Information Director: Jim DeLorenzo

Note: Division I-AA football

Virginia Tech

Address: Jamerson Athletic Center
              Blacksburg, VA 24061
Nickname: Hokies
Telephone: (703) 231-6726
Football Stadium (Capacity): Lane Stadium/Worsham
  Field (51,000)
Basketball Arena (Capacity): Cassell Coliseum (9,971)
President: Dr. Paul Torgersen
Athletic Director: Dave Braine
Football Coach: Frank Beamer
Basketball Coach: Bill Foster
Sports Information Director: Dave Smith

Note: Plays football in Big East, basketball in Metro Conference.

West Virginia University

Address: P.O. Box 0877
              Morgantown, WV 26507-0877
Nickname: Mountaineers
Telephone: (304) 293-2821
Football Stadium (Capacity): Mountaineer Field
  (63,500)
Basketball Arena (Capacity): WVU Coliseum (14,000)
President: Dr. Neil Bucklew
Athletic Director: Ed Pastilong
Football Coach: Don Nehlen
Basketball Coach: Gale Catlett
Sports Information Director: Shelley Poe

Note: Plays football in Big East, basketball in Atlantic 10 Conference.

BIG EIGHT CONFERENCE

Address: 104 West Ninth Street, Suite 408
              Kansas City, MO 64105
Telephone: (816) 471-5088
Commissioner: Carl C. James
Publicity Director: Jeff Bollig

University of Colorado

Address: Campus Box 357
              Boulder, CO 80309
Nickname: Buffaloes
Telephone: (303) 492-5626
Football Stadium (Capacity): Folsom Field (51,748)
Basketball Arena (Capacity): Coors Event Center
  (11,199)
President: Dr. Judith Albino
Athletic Director: Bill Marolt
Football Coach: Bill McCartney
Basketball Coach: Joe Harrington
Sports Information Director: David Plati

Iowa State University

Address: 1802 S. Fourth
              Olsen Annex
              Ames, IA 50011
Nickname: Cyclones
Telephone: (515) 294-3372
Football Stadium (Capacity): Cyclone Stadium-Trice
  Field (50,000)
Basketball Arena (Capacity): Hilton Coliseum
  (14,020)
President: Dr. Martin C. Jischke
Athletic Director: Gene Smith
Football Coach: Jim Walden
Basketball Coach: Tim Floyd
Sports Information Director: Tom Kroeschell

University of Kansas

Address: Allen Field House, Room 104
              Lawrence, KS 66045
Nickname: Jayhawks
Telephone: (913) 864-3417
Football Stadium (Capacity): Memorial Stadium
  (50,250)
Basketball Arena (Capacity): Allen Field House
  (15,800)
Interim Chancellor: Dr. Del Shankel
Athletic Director: Dr. Bob Fredrick
Football Coach: Glen Mason
Basketball Coach: Roy Williams
Sports Information Director: Doug Vance

Kansas State University
Address: Manhattan, KS 66502
Nickname: Wildcats
Telephone: (913) 532-6011
Football Stadium (Capacity): KSU Stadium (45,000)
Basketball Arena (Capacity): Bramlage Coliseum
  (13,500)
President: Dr. Jon Wefald
Athletic Director: Max Urick
Football Coach: Bill Snyder
Basketball Coach: Dana Altman
Sports Information Director: Ben Boyle

University of Missouri
Address: P.O. Box 677
              Columbia, MO 65205
Nickname: Tigers
Telephone: (314) 882-3241
Football Stadium (Capacity): Faurot Field (62,000)
Basketball Arena (Capacity): Hearnes Center (13,349)
Chancellor: Dr. Charles Kiesler
Athletic Director: Joe Castiglione
Football Coach: Larry Smith
Basketball Coach: Norm Stewart
Sports Information Director: Bob Brendel

University of Nebraska
Address: 116 South Stadium
              Lincoln, NE 68588
Nickname: Cornhuskers
Telephone: (402) 472-2263
Football Stadium (Capacity): Memorial Stadium
  (73,650)
Basketball Arena (Capacity): Bob Devaney Sports
  Center (14,302)
President: L. Dennis Smith
Athletic Director: Bill Byrne
Football Coach: Tom Osborne
Basketball Coach: Danny Nee
Sports Information Director: Chris Anderson

University of Oklahoma
Address: 180 W. Brooks, Room 235
              Norman, OK 73019
Nickname: Sooners
Telephone: (405) 325-8231
Football Stadium (Capacity): Owen Field (74,993)
Basketball Arena (Capacity): Lloyd Noble Center
  (10,861)
President: David Boren
Athletic Director: Donnie Duncan
Football Coach: Gary Gibbs
Basketball Coach: Calvin Samson
Sports Information Director: Mike Prusinski

Oklahoma State University
Address: 202 Gallagher-Iba Arena
              Stillwater, OK 74078
Nickname: Cowboys
Telephone: (405) 744-5749
Football Stadium (Capacity): Lewis Field (50,614)
Basketball Arena (Capacity): Gallagher-Iba Arena
  (6,381)
President: Dr. James Halligan
Interim Athletic Director: Dave Martin
Football Coach: Pat Jones
Basketball Coach: Eddie Sutton
Sports Information Director: Steve Buzzard

BIG TEN CONFERENCE
Address: 1500 West Higgins Road
              Park Ridge, IL 60068
Telephone: (708) 696-1010
Commissioner: James E. Delany
Assistant Commissioner: Mark Rudner

University of Illinois
Address: 1817 S. Neil Street, Suite 201
              Champaign, IL 61820
Nickname: Fighting Illini
Telephone: (217) 333-1390
Football Stadium (Capacity): Memorial Stadium (72,292)
Basketball Arena (Capacity): Assembly Hall (16,153)
President: Stanley O. Ikenberry
Athletic Director: Ronald Guenther
Football Coach: Lou Tepper
Basketball Coach: Lou Henson
Sports Information Director: Mike Pearson

Indiana University
Address: 17th Street and Fee Lane/Assembly Hall
              Bloomington, IN 47405
Nickname: Hoosiers
Telephone: (812) 855-2421
Football Stadium (Capacity): Memorial Stadium
  (52,354)
Basketball Arena (Capacity): Assembly Hall (17,357)
President: Myles Brand
Athletic Director: Clarence Doninger
Football Coach: Bill Mallory
Basketball Coach: Bob Knight
Sports Information Director: Kit Klingelhoffer

University of Iowa
Address: 205 Carver-Hawkeye Arena
              Iowa City, IA 52242
Nickname: Hawkeyes
Telephone: (319) 335-9411
Football Stadium (Capacity): Kinnick Stadium (70,397)
Basketball Arena (Capacity): Carver-Hawkeye Arena
  (15,500)
President: Hunter R. Rawlings III
Athletic Director: Robert Bowlsby
Football Coach: Hayden Fry
Basketball Coach: Tom Davis
Sports Information Director: Phil Haddy

University of Michigan
Address: 1000 S. State Street
              Ann Arbor, MI 48109
Nickname: Wolverines
Telephone: (313) 763-4423
Football Stadium (Capacity): Michigan Stadium
  (102,501)
Basketball Arena (Capacity): Crisler Arena (13,562)
President: James Duderstadt
Athletic Director: Dr. Joseph Roberson
Football Coach: Gary Moeller
Basketball Coach: Steve Fisher
Sports Information Director: Bruce Madej

Michigan State University

Address: East Lansing, MI 48824
Nickname: Spartans
Telephone: (517) 355-2271
Football Stadium (Capacity): Spartan Stadium (72,027)
Basketball Arena (Capacity): Jack Breslin Student
  Events Center (15,138)
President: M. Peter McPherson
Athletic Director: Merrily Dean Baker
Football Coach: George Perles
Basketball Coach: Jud Heathcote
Sports Information Director: Ken Hoffman

University of Minnesota

Address: 516 15th Avenue S.E.
  Minneapolis, MN 55455
Nickname: Golden Gophers
Telephone: (612) 625-4090
Football Stadium (Capacity): Hubert H. Humphrey
  Metrodome (64,669)
Basketball Arena (Capacity): Williams Arena (14,300)
President: Nils Hasselmo
Athletic Director: McKinley Boston
Football Coach: Jim Wacker
Basketball Coach: Clem Haskins
Sports Information Director: Marc Ryan

Northwestern University

Address: 1501 Central Street
  Evanston, IL 60208
Nickname: Wildcats
Telephone: (708) 491-3205
Football Stadium (Capacity): Dyche Stadium (49,256)
Basketball Arena (Capacity): Welsh-Ryan Arena (8,117)
President: Henry S. Bienen
Athletic Director: Rick Taylor
Football Coach: Gary Barnett
Basketball Coach: Ricky Birdsong
Director of Media Services: Greg Shea

Ohio State University

Address: 410 Woody Hayes Drive
  Columbus, OH 43210
Nickname: Buckeyes
Telephone: (614) 292-6861
Football Stadium (Capacity): Ohio Stadium (91,470)
Basketball Arena (Capacity): St. John Arena (13,276)
President: Dr. E. Gordon Gee
Athletic Director: Andy Geiger
Football Coach: John Cooper
Basketball Coach: Randy Ayers
Sports Information Director: Steve Snapp

Penn State University

Address: Recreation Building
  University Park, PA 16802
Nickname: Nittany Lions
Telephone: (814) 865-1757
Football Stadium (Capacity): Beaver Stadium (93,967)
Basketball Arena (Capacity): Recreation Hall (6,846)
President: Dr. Joab Thomas
Athletic Director: Tim Curley
Football Coach: Joe Paterno
Basketball Coach: Bruce Parkhill
Sports Information Director: Jeff Nelson
Associate Athletic Director: Thalman

Purdue University

Address: Mackey Arena
  West Lafayette, IN 47907
Nickname: Boilermakers
Telephone: (317) 494-3200
Football Stadium (Capacity): Ross-Ade Stadium
  (67,861)
Basketball Arena (Capacity): Mackey Arena (14,123)
President: Dr. Steven C. Beering
Athletic Director: Morgan Burke
Football Coach: Jim Colletto
Basketball Coach: Gene Keady
Sports Information Director: Mark Adams

University of Wisconsin

Address: 1440 Monroe Street
  Madison, WI 53711
Nickname: Badgers
Telephone: (608) 262-1811
Football Stadium (Capacity): Camp Randall Stadium
  (77,745)
Basketball Arena (Capacity): UW Fieldhouse (11,895)
Chancellor: David Ward
Athletic Director: Pat Richter
Football Coach: Barry Alvarez
Basketball Coach: Stan Van Gundy
Sports Information Director: Steve Malchow

BIG WEST CONFERENCE

Address: 2 Corporate Park
  Suite 206
  Irvine, CA 92714
Telephone: (714) 261-2525
Commissioner: Dennis Farrell
Publicity Director: Dennis Bickmeyer

California State University–Fullerton

Address: 800 North State College Boulevard
  P.O. Box 34080
  Fullerton, CA 92634-9480
Nickname: Titans
Telephone: (714) 773-2677
Basketball Arena (Capacity): Titan Gym (4,000)
President: Dr. Milton A. Gordon
Athletic Director: John Easterbrook
Interim Basketball Coach: Bob Hawking
Sports Information Director: Mel Franks

Note: No football program in 1994.

Fresno State University

Address: 5305 N. Campus Drive
  Fresno, CA 93740-0027
Nickname: Bulldogs
Telephone: (209) 278-2643
Football Stadium (Capacity): Bulldog Stadium
  (41,031)
Basketball Arena (Capacity): Selland Arena (10,159)
President: Dr. John Welty
Athletic Director: Dr. Gary Cunningham
Football Coach: Jim Sweeney
Basketball Coach: Gary Colson
Sports Information Director: Scott Johnson

Long Beach State University
Address: 1250 Bellflower Boulevard
Long Beach, CA 90840
Nickname: 49ers
Telephone: (310) 985-4655
Basketball Arena (Capacity): The Pyramid (5,000)
President: Dr. Robert C. Maxson
Acting Athletic Director: David O'Brien
Basketball Coach: Seth Greenberg
Sports Information Director: Scott Cathcart

University of Nevada at Las Vegas
Address: 4505 Maryland Parkway
Las Vegas, NV 89154
Nickname: Runnin' Rebels
Telephone: (702) 895-3207
Football Stadium (Capacity): Sam Boyd Stadium
(32,000)
Basketball Arena (Capacity): Thomas and Mack
Center (18,500)
Interim President: Kenny Guinn
Athletic Director: Jim Weaver
Football Coach: Jeff Horton
Basketball Coach: Tim Grgurich
Sports Information Director: Chris Johnson

New Mexico State University
Address: Box 3145
Las Cruces, NM 88003
Nickname: Aggies
Telephone: (505) 646-4126
Football Stadium (Capacity): Aggie Memorial Stadium
(30,343)
Basketball Arena (Capacity): Pan American Center
(13,007)
Interim President: William B. Conroy
Athletic Director: Al Gonzales
Football Coach: Jim Hess
Basketball Coach: Neil McCarthy
Sports Information Director: Steve Shutt

University of the Pacific
Address: 3601 Pacific Avenue
Stockton, CA 95211
Nickname: Tigers
Telephone: (209) 946-2479
Football Stadium (Capacity): Amos Alonzo Stagg
Memorial Stadium (30,000)
Basketball Arena (Capacity): A.G. Spanos Center
(6,150)
President: Dr. Bill Atchley
Athletic Director: Bob Lee
Football Coach: Chuck Shelton
Basketball Coach: Bob Thomason
Sports Information Director: Kevin Messenger

San Jose State University
Address: One Washington Square
San Jose, CA 95192-0062
Nickname: Spartans
Telephone: (408) 924-1200
Football Stadium (Capacity): Spartan Stadium
(31,218)
Basketball Arena (Capacity): Event Center (4,600)
President: J. Handel Evans
Athletic Director: Dr. Tom Brennan
Football Coach: John Ralston
Basketball Coach: Stan Morrison
Sports Information Director: Lawrence Fan

Utah State University
Address: Logan, UT 84322-7400
Nickname: Aggies
Telephone: (801) 797-1850
Football Stadium (Capacity): Romney Stadium
(30,000)
Basketball Arena (Capacity): The Smith Spectrum
(10,200)
President: George Emert
Athletic Director: Chuck Bell
Football Coach: Charlie Weatherbie
Basketball Coach: Larry Eustachy
Sports Information Director: John Lewandowski

IVY LEAGUE
Address: 120 Alexander Street
Princeton, NJ 08544
Telephone: (609) 258-6426
Commissioner: Jeff Orleans
Publicity Director: Chuck Yrigoyen

Brown University
Address: Hope Street
Providence, RI 02912
Nickname: Bears
Telephone: (401) 863-2211
Football Stadium (Capacity): Brown Stadium (20,000)
Basketball Arena (Capacity): Paul Bailey Pizzitola
Memorial Sports Center (2,500)
President: Vartan Gregorian
Athletic Director: David Roach
Football Coach: Mark Whipple
Basketball Coach: Franklin Dobbs
Sports Information Director: Christopher Humm

Columbia University
Address: Dodge Physical Fitness Center
New York, NY 10027
Nickname: Lions
Telephone: (212) 854-2538
Football Stadium (Capacity): Lawrence A. Wien
Stadium at Baker Field (17,000)
Basketball Arena (Capacity): Levien Gymnasium
(3,400)
President: Dr. George Rupp
Athletic Director: Dr. John Reeves
Football Coach: Ray Tellier
Basketball Coach: Jack Rohan
Sports Information Director: William C. Steinman

Cornell University
Address: Teagle Hall, Campus Road
Ithaca, NY 14853
Nickname: Big Red
Telephone: (607) 255-5220
Football Stadium (Capacity): Schoellkopf Field (27,000)
Basketball Arena (Capacity): Alberding Fieldhouse
(4,750)
President: Frank Rhodes
Athletic Director: Charles Moore
Football Coach: Jim Hofher
Basketball Coach: Al Walker
Sports Information Director: Dave Wohlhueter

Dartmouth College
Address: 6083 Alumni Gym
             Hanover, NH 03755
Nickname: Big Green
Telephone: (603) 646-2465
Football Stadium (Capacity): Memorial Field (20,416)
Basketball Arena (Capacity): Leede Arena
  (2,100)
President: James Freedman
Athletic Director: Richard G. Jaeger
Football Coach: John Lyons
Basketball Coach: Dave Faucher
Sports Information Director: Kathy Slattery

Harvard University
Address: 60 John F. Kennedy St.
             Cambridge, MA 02138
Nickname: Crimson
Telephone: (617) 495-2204
Football Stadium (Capacity): Harvard Stadium
  (37,967)
Basketball Arena (Capacity): Briggs Athletic Center
  (3,000)
President: Neil L. Rudentsine
Athletic Director: William J. Cleary, Jr. '56
Football Coach: Tim Murphy
Basketball Coach: Frank Sullivan
Sports Information Director: John Veneziano

University of Pennsylvania
Address: Weightman Hall North
             235 South 33rd Street
             Philadelphia, PA 19104-6322
Nickname: Quakers
Telephone: (215)898-6121
Football Stadium (Capacity): Franklin Field (60,546)
Basketball Arena (Capacity): Palestra Arena (8,700)
President: Dr. Judith Rodin
Athletic Director: Steven Bilsky
Football Coach: Al Bagnoli
Basketball Coach: Fran Dunphy
Director, Media Relations: Gail Stasulli Zachary
Director, Athletic Communications: Brad Hurlbut

Princeton University
Address: P.O. Box 71
             Jadwin Gym
             Princeton, NJ 08544
Nickname: Tigers
Telephone: (609) 258-3568
Football Stadium (Capacity): Palmer Stadium (45,725)
Basketball Arena (Capacity): Jadwin Gym (7,550)
President: Harold Shapiro
Athletic Director: Gary D. Walters
Football Coach: Steve Tosches
Basketball Coach: Pete Carril
Sports Information Director: Kurt Kehl

Yale University
Address: Box 208216
             New Haven, CT 06520
Nickname: Bulldogs, Elis
Telephone: (203) 432-1456
Football Stadium (Capacity): Yale Bowl (70,896)
Basketball Arena (Capacity): Payne Whitney Gym
  (3,100)
President: Richard C. Levin
Athletic Director: Tom Beckett
Football Coach: Carmen Cozza
Basketball Coach: Dick Kuchen
Sports Information Director: Steve Conn

MID-AMERICAN CONFERENCE
Address: Four Seagate, Suite 102
             Toledo, OH 43604
Telephone: (419) 249-7177
Commissioner: Jerry Ippoliti
Publicity Director: Sue Wagner

Ball State University
Address: 2000 University Avenue
             Muncie, IN 47306
Nickname: Cardinals
Telephone: (317) 285-8225
Football Stadium (Capacity): Ball State University
  Stadium (16,319)
Basketball Arena (Capacity): University Arena
  (11,500)
President: Dr. John E. Worthen
Athletic Director: Don Purvis
Football Coach: Paul Schudel
Basketball Coach: Ray McCallum
Sports Information Director: Joe Hernandez

Bowling Green University
Address: Bowling Green, OH 43403
Nickname: Falcons
Telephone: (419) 372-2401
Football Stadium (Capacity): Doyt L. Perry Stadium
  (30,599)
Basketball Arena (Capacity): Anderson Arena (5,000)
President: Dr. Paul Olscamp
Athletic Director: Ron Zwierlein
Football Coach: Gary Blackney
Basketball Coach: Jim Larranga
Sports Information Director: Steve Barr

Central Michigan University
Address: Rose Center
             Mount Pleasant, MI 48859
Nickname: Chippewas
Telephone: (517) 774-3041
Football Stadium (Capacity): Kelly/Shorts Stadium
  (20,083)
Basketball Arena (Capacity): Rose Arena (6,000)
President: Leonare Plachta
Athletic Director: Herb Deromedi
Football Coach: Dick Flynn
Basketball Coach: Leonard Drake
Sports Information Director: Fred Stabley, Jr.

Eastern Michigan University
Address: Bowen Fieldhouse
             Ypsilanti, MI 48197
Nickname: Eagles
Telephone: (313) 487-1050
Football Stadium (Capacity): Rynearson Stadium
  (30,200)
Basketball Arena (Capacity): Bowen Arena (5,600)
President: Dr. William Shelton
Athletic Director: Tim Weiser
Football Coach: Ron Cooper
Basketball Coach: Ben Braun
Sports Information Director: James Streeter

Kent University

Address: Kent, OH 44242
Nickname: Golden Flashes
Telephone: (216) 672-3120
Football Stadium (Capacity): Dix Stadium (30,520)
Basketball Arena (Capacity): Memorial Athletic and
  Convocation Center (6,034)
President: Dr. Carol A. Cartwright
Athletic Director: Laing Kennedy
Football Coach: Jim Corrigall
Basketball Coach: Dave Grube
Sports Information Director: Dale Gallagher

Miami University

Address: Millett Hall
             Oxford, OH 45056
Nickname: Redskins
Telephone: (513) 529-3113
Football Stadium (Capacity): Yager Stadium (25,183)
Basketball Arena (Capacity): Millett Hall (9,200)
President: Dr. Paul G. Risser
Interim Athletic Director: Darrell Hedric
Football Coach: Randy Walker
Basketball Coach: Herb Sendek
Sports Information Director: TBA

Ohio University

Address: P.O. Box 689
             Convocation Center
             Athens, OH 45701-2979
Nickname: Bobcats
Telephone: (614) 593-1174
Football Stadium (Capacity): Don Peden Stadium
  (20,000)
Basketball Arena (Capacity): Convocation Center
  (13,000)
President: Dr. Robert Glidden
Athletic Director: Harold McElhaney
Football Coach: Tom Lichtenberg
Basketball Coach: Larry Hunter
Associate Media Relations Director: Pam Fronko

University of Toledo

Address: 2801 W. Bancroft St.
             Toledo, OH 43606
Nickname: Rockets
Telephone: (419) 537-4184
Football Stadium (Capacity): Glass Bowl (26,248)
Basketball Arena (Capacity): Savage Hall (9,000)
President: Dr. Frank E. Horton
Athletic Director: Dr. Allen R. Bohl
Football Coach: Gary Pinkel
Basketball Coach: Larry Gipson
Sports Information Director: Rod Brandt

Western Michigan University

Address: Kalamazoo, MI 49008
Nickname: Broncos
Telephone: (616) 387-4104
Football Stadium (Capacity): Waldo Stadium (30,062)
Basketball Arena (Capacity): University Arena (5,800)
President: Dr. D. H. Haenicke
Athletic Director: Dan Meinert
Football Coach: Al Molde
Basketball Coach: Bob Donewald
Sports Information Director: John Beatty

PACIFIC-10 CONFERENCE

Address: 800 S. Broadway, Suite 400
             Walnut Creek, CA 94596
Telephone: (510) 932-4411
Commissioner: Thomas C. Hansen
Publicity Director: Jim Muldoon

University of Arizona

Address: McHale Center
             Tuscon, AZ 85721
Nickname: Wildcats
Telephone: (602) 621-2211
Football Stadium (Capacity): Arizona Stadium (56,167)
Basketball Arena (Capacity): McHale Center (13,447)
President: Dr. Manuel Pacheco
Athletic Director: Jim Livengood
Football Coach: Dick Tomey
Basketball Coach: Lute Olson
Sports Information Director: Butch Henry

Arizona State University

Address: Tempe, AZ 85287
Nickname: Sun Devils
Telephone: (602) 965-6592
Football Stadium (Capacity): Sun Devil Stadium (74,865)
Basketball Arena (Capacity): University Activity
  Center (14,287)
President: Lattie Coor
Athletic Director: Charles Harris
Football Coach: Bruce Snyder
Basketball Coach: Bill Frieder
Sports Information Director: Mark Brand

University of California

Address: Berkeley, CA 94720
Nickname: Golden Bears
Telephone: (510) 642-5363
Football Stadium (Capacity): Memorial Stadium (75,662)
Basketball Arena (Capacity): Harmon Gym (6,578),
  Oakland-Alameda County Coliseum Arena (15,039)
Chancellor: Chang-Lin Tien
Athletic Director: John Kasser
Football Coach: Keith Gilbertson
Basketball Coach: Todd Bozeman
Sports Information Director: Kevin Reneau

University of California at Los Angeles

Address: 405 Hilgard Avenue
             Los Angeles, CA 90024
Nickname: Bruins
Telephone: (310) 206-6831
Football Stadium (Capacity): Rose Bowl (102,083)
Basketball Arena (Capacity): Pauley Pavilion (12,819)
Chancellor: Dr. Charles Young
Athletic Director: Peter T. Dalis
Football Coach: Terry Donahue
Basketball Coach: Jim Harrick
Sports Information Director: Marc Dellins

University of Oregon

Address: Len Casanova Athletic Center
             2727 Leo Harris Parkway
             Eugene, OR 97401
Nickname: Ducks
Telephone: (503) 346-4481
Football Stadium (Capacity): Autzen Stadium (41,698)
Basketball Arena (Capacity): McArthur Court (10,063)
President: David Fronmayer
Interim Athletic Director: Dan Williams
Football Coach: Rich Brooks
Basketball Coach: Jerry Green
Sports Information Director: Steve Hellyer

Oregon State University

Address: Gill Coliseum
                Corvallis, OR 97331
Nickname: Beavers
Telephone: (503) 737-3720
Football Stadium (Capacity): Parker Stadium (36,345)
Basketball Arena (Capacity): Gill Coliseum (10,400)
President: Dr. John V. Bryne
Athletic Director: Dutch Baughman
Football Coach: Jerry Pettibone
Basketball Coach: Jim Anderson
Sports Information Director: Hal Cowan

University of Southern California

Address: Los Angeles, CA 90089
Nickname: Trojans
Telephone: (213) 740-8480
Football Stadium (Capacity): Los Angeles Memorial
  Coliseum (94,159)
Basketball Arena (Capacity): Los Angeles Memorial
  Sports Arena (15,509)
President: Dr. Steven Sample
Athletic Director: Mike Garrett
Football Coach: John Robinson
Basketball Coach: George Raveling
Sports Information Director: Tim Tessalone

Stanford University

Address: Stanford, CA 94305
Nickname: Cardinal
Telephone: (415) 723-4418
Football Stadium (Capacity): Stanford Stadium (86,019)
Basketball Arena (Capacity): Maples Pavilion (7,500)
President: Gerhard Casper
Athletic Director: Dr. Ted Leland
Football Coach: Bill Walsh
Basketball Coach: Mike Montgomery
Sports Information Director: Gary Migdol

University of Washington

Address: 202 Graves Building
                Seattle, WA 98195
Nickname: Huskies
Telephone: (206) 543-2230
Football Stadium (Capacity): Husky Stadium (72,500)
Basketball Arena (Capacity): Hec Edmundson
  Pavilion (8,000)
President: Dr. William P. Gerberding
Athletic Director: Barbara Hedges
Football Coach: Jim Lambright
Basketball Coach: Bob Bender
Sports Information Director: Jim Daves

Washington State University

Address: 107 Bohler Gym
                Pullman, WA 99164-1610
Nickname: Cougars
Telephone: (509) 335-0270
Football Stadium (Capacity): Martin Stadium (40,000)
Basketball Arena (Capacity): Friel Court (12,058)
President: Dr. Samuel H. Smith
Athletic Director: Rick Dickson
Football Coach: Mike Price
Basketball Coach: Kevin Eastman
Sports Information Director: Rod Commons

SOUTHEASTERN CONFERENCE

Address: 2201 Civic Center Boulevard
                Birmingham, AL 35203
Telephone: (205) 458-3000
Commissioner: Roy Kramer
Publicity Director: Mark Whitworth

University of Alabama

Address: P.O. Box 870323
                Paul Bryant Drive
                Tuscaloosa, AL 35487
Nickname: Crimson Tide
Telephone: (205) 348-3600
Football Stadium (Capacity): Bryant-Denny Stadium
(70,123)
Basketball Arena (Capacity): Coleman Coliseum
(15,043)
President: Dr. Roger Sayers
Athletic Director: Cecil (Hootie) Ingram
Football Coach: Gene Stallings
Basketball Coach: David Hobbs
Sports Information Director: Larry White

University of Arkansas

Address: Broyles Athletic Center
                Fayetteville, AR 72701
Nickname: Razorbacks
Telephone: (501) 575-2751
Football Stadium (Capacity): Razorback Stadium
(52,968)
Basketball Arena (Capacity): Bud Walton Arena
(19,002)
Chancellor: Dr. Dan Ferritor
Athletic Director: Frank Broyles
Football Coach: Danny Ford
Basketball Coach: Nolan Richardson
Sports Information Director: Rick Schaeffer

Auburn University

Address: P.O. Box 351
                Auburn, AL 36831-0351
Nickname: Tigers
Telephone: (205) 844-9800
Football Stadium (Capacity): Jordan Hare Stadium
(85,214)
Basketball Arena (Capacity): Beard-Eaves Memorial
  Coliseum (13,500)
President: Dr. William V. Muse
Athletic Director: David Housel
Football Coach: Terry Bowden
Basketball Coach: Cliff Elles
Sports Information Director: Kent Partridge

University of Florida

Address: P.O. Box 14485
                Gainesville, FL 32604
Nickname: Gators
Telephone: (904) 375-4683
Football Stadium (Capacity): Ben Hill Griffin Stadium
  at Florida Field (83,000)
Basketball Arena (Capacity): Stephen C. O'Connell
  Center (12,000)
President: Dr. John Lombardi
Athletic Director: Jeremy Foley
Football Coach: Steve Spurrier
Basketball Coach: Lon Kruger
Sports Information Director: John Humenik

College Sports Directory *(Cont.)*

University of Georgia
Address: P.O. Box 1472
Athens, GA 30613-1472
Nickname: Bulldogs
Telephone: (706) 542-1621
Football Stadium (Capacity): Sanford Stadium (86,117)
Basketball Arena (Capacity): The Coliseum (10,512)
President: Dr. Charles Knapp
Athletic Director: Vince Dooley
Football Coach: Ray Goff
Basketball Coach: Hugh Durham
Sports Information Director: Claude Felton

University of Kentucky
Address: Memorial Coliseum
Lexington, KY 40506
Nickname: Wildcats
Telephone: (606) 257-3838
Football Stadium (Capacity): Commonwealth Stadium (57,800)
Basketball Arena (Capacity): Rupp Arena (23,000)
President: Dr. Charles Wethington Jr.
Athletic Director: C. M. Newton
Football Coach: Bill Curry
Basketball Coach: Rick Pitino
Sports Information Director: Tony Neeley

Louisiana State University
Address: Baton Rouge, LA 70894
Nickname: Fighting Tigers
Telephone: (504) 388-8226
Football Stadium (Capacity): Tiger Stadium (80,150)
Basketball Arena (Capacity): Pete Maravich Assembly Center (14,164)
Chancellor: Dr. William E. Davis
Athletic Director: Joe Dean
Football Coach: Curley Hallman
Basketball Coach: Dale Brown
Sports Information Director: Herb Vincent

University of Mississippi
Address: P.O. Box 217
University, MS 38677
Nickname: Rebels
Telephone: (601) 232-7522
Football Stadium (Capacity): Vaught-Hemingway Stadium (42,577)
Basketball Arena (Capacity): C. M. (Tad) Smith Coliseum (8,135)
Chancellor: Dr. R. Gerald Turner
Interim Athletic Director: Robert Khayat
Interim Football Coach: Joe Lee Dunn
Basketball Coach: Robert Evans
Sports Information Director: Langston Rogers

Mississippi State University
Address: P.O. Drawer 5308
Mississippi St., MS 39762
Nickname: Bulldogs
Telephone: (601) 325-2703
Football Stadium (Capacity): Scott Field (41,200)
Basketball Arena (Capacity): Humphrey Coliseum (9,149)
President: Dr. Donald Zacharias
Athletic Director: Larry Templeton
Football Coach: Jackie Sherrill
Basketball Coach: Richard Williams
Sports Information Director: Mike Nemeth

University of South Carolina
Address: Rex Enright Athletic Center
1300 Rosewood Drive
Columbia, SC 29208
Nickname: Gamecocks
Telephone: (803) 777-5204
Football Stadium (Capacity): Williams-Brice Stadium (72,400)
Basketball Arena (Capacity): Frank McGuire Arena (12,401)
President: Dr. John Palms
Athletic Director: Dr. Mike McGee
Football Coach: Brad Scott
Basketball Coach: Eddie Fogler
Sports Information Director: Kerry Tharp

University of Tennessee
Address: P.O. Box 15016
Knoxville, TN 37901
Nickname: Volunteers
Telephone: (615) 974-1212
Football Stadium (Capacity): Neyland Stadium (91,902)
Basketball Arena (Capacity): Thompson Boling Arena and Assembly Center (24,535)
President: Dr. Joseph E. Johnson
Athletic Director: Doug Dickey
Football Coach: Phillip Fulmer
Basketball Coach: Kevin O'Neill
Sports Information Director: Bud Ford

Vanderbilt University
Address: P.O. Box 120158
Nashville, TN 37212
Nickname: Commodores
Telephone: (615) 322-4121
Football Stadium (Capacity): Vanderbilt Stadium (41,000)
Basketball Arena (Capacity): Memorial Gym (15,309)
Chancellor: Joe B. Wyatt
Athletic Director: Paul Hoolahan
Football Coach: Gerry DiNardo
Basketball Coach: Jan Van Breda Kolff
Sports Information Director: Rod Williamson

SOUTHWEST ATHLETIC CONFERENCE
Address: P.O. Box 569420
Dallas, TX 75356
Telephone: (214) 634-7353
Commissioner and Sports Information Director: Steve Hatchell

Baylor University
Address: 3031 Dutton
Waco, TX 76711
Nickname: Bears
Telephone: (817) 755-1234
Football Stadium (Capacity): Floyd Casey Stadium (48,500)
Basketball Arena (Capacity): Ferrell Center (10,080)
President: Dr. Herbert H. Reynolds
Athletic Director: Dr. Dick Ellis
Football Coach: Chuck Reedy
Basketball Coach: Darrel Johnson
Sports Information Director: Maxey Parrish

University of Houston
Address:　3855 Holman
　　　　　Houston, TX 77204-5121
Nickname: Cougars
Telephone: (713) 743-9370
Football Stadium (Capacity): Astrodome (65,000)
Basketball Arena (Capacity): Hofheinz Pavilion
　(10,060)
President: Dr. James Pickering
Athletic Director: William C. Carr
Football Coach: Kim Helton
Basketball Coach: Alvin Brooks
Sports Information Director: Ted Nance

Rice University
Address:　MS548, 6100 S. Main
　　　　　Houston, TX 77005-1892
Nickname: Owls
Telephone: (713) 527-4034
Football Stadium (Capacity): Rice Stadium (70,000)
Basketball Arena (Capacity): Autry Court (5,000)
President: Malcolm Gillis
Athletic Director: Bobby May
Football Coach: Ken Hatfield
Basketball Coach: Willis Wilson
Sports Information Director: Bill Cousins

Southern Methodist University
Address:　SMU Box 216
　　　　　Dallas, TX 75275
Nickname: Mustangs
Telephone: (214) 768-2883
Football Stadium (Capacity): Ownby Stadium (23,783)
Basketball Arena (Capacity): Moody Coliseum (9,007)
President: TBA
Athletic Director: TBA
Football Coach: Tom Rossley
Basketball Coach: John Shumate
Sports Information Director: Ed Wisneski

University of Texas
Address:　P.O. Box 7399
　　　　　Austin, TX 78713
Nickname: Longhorns
Telephone: (512) 471-7437
Football Stadium (Capacity): Memorial Stadium
　(77,809)
Basketball Arena (Capacity): Erwin Special Events
　Center (16,231)
Chancellor: Dr. William Cunningham
Athletic Director: DeLoss Dodds
Football Coach: John Mackovic
Basketball Coach: Tom Penders
Sports Information Director: Bill Little

Texas A&M University
Address:　John Koldus Building
　　　　　College Station, TX 77843
Nickname: Aggies
Telephone: (409) 845-3218
Football Stadium (Capacity): Kyle Field (72,387)
Basketball Arena (Capacity): G. Rollie White
　Coliseum (7,800)
President: Dr. Ray Bowen
Athletic Director: Wally Groff
Football Coach: R. C. Slocum
Basketball Coach: Tony Barone
Sports Information Director: Alan Cannon

Texas Christian University
Address:　P.O. Box 32924
　　　　　Fort Worth, TX 76129
Nickname: Horned Frogs
Telephone: (817) 921-7969
Football Stadium (Capacity): Amon G. Carter Stadium
　(46,000)
Basketball Arena (Capacity): Daniel-Meyer Coliseum
　(7,166)
Chancellor: Dr. William E. Tucker
Athletic Director: Frank Windegger
Football Coach: Pat Sullivan
Basketball Coach: Billy Tubbs
Sports Information Director: Glen Stone

Texas Tech University
Address:　Box 43021
　　　　　Lubbock, TX 79409
Nickname: Red Raiders
Telephone: (806) 742-2770
Football Stadium (Capacity): Jones Stadium (50,500)
Basketball Arena (Capacity): Lubbock Municipal
　Coliseum (8,196)
President: Dr. Robert Lawless
Athletic Director: Bob Bockrath
Football Coach: Spike Dykes
Basketball Coach: James Dickey
Sports Information Director: Joe Hornaday

WESTERN ATHLETIC CONFERENCE
Address:　14 West Dry Creek Circle
　　　　　Littleton, CO 80120
Telephone: (303) 795-1962
Commissioner: Karl Benson
Publicity Director: Jeff Hurd

Air Force
Address: Colorado Springs, CO 80840-5461
Nickname: Falcons
Telephone: (719) 472-4008
Football Stadium (Capacity): Falcon Stadium (52,153)
Basketball Arena (Capacity): Clune Arena (6,007)
President: Lt. Gen. Paul E. Stein
Athletic Director: Col. Kenneth L. Schweitzer
Football Coach: Fisher DeBerry
Basketball Coach: Reggie Minton
Sports Information Director: David Kellogg

Brigham Young University
Address:　30 Smith Field House
　　　　　Provo, UT 84602
Nickname: Cougars
Telephone: (801) 378-4911
Football Stadium (Capacity): Cougar Stadium
　(65,000)
Basketball Arena (Capacity): Marriott Center (23,000)
President: Rex Lee
Athletic Director: Clayne Jensen
Football Coach: LaVell Edwards
Basketball Coach: Roger Reid
Sports Information Director: Ralph Zobell

Colorado State University

Address: Moby Arena
Fort Collins, CO 80523
Nickname: Rams
Telephone: (303) 491-5300
Football Stadium (Capacity): Hughes Stadium (30,000)
Basketball Arena (Capacity): Moby Arena (9,001)
President: Dr. Albert C. Yates
Athletic Director: Tom Jurich
Football Coach: Sonny Lubick
Basketball Coach: Stew Morrill
Sports Information Director: Gary Ozello

University of Hawaii

Address: 1335 Lower Campus Road
Honolulu, HI 96822-2370
Nickname: Rainbow Warriors
Telephone: (808) 956-8111
Football Stadium (Capacity): Aloha Stadium (50,000)
Basketball Arena (Capacity): Special Events Arena (7,575)
President: Dr. Kenneth Mortimer
Athletic Director: Hugh Yoshida
Football Coach: Bob Wagner
Basketball Coach: Riley Wallace
Sports Information Director: Ed Inouye

University of New Mexico

Address: 1414 University S.E.
Albuquerque, NM 87131
Nickname: Lobos
Telephone: (505) 277-6375
Football Stadium (Capacity): University Stadium (30,646)
Basketball Arena (Capacity): University Arena—The Pit (18,100)
President: Dr. Richard Peck
Athletic Director: Rudy Davalos
Football Coach: Dennis Franchione
Basketball Coach: Dave Bliss
Sports Information Director: Greg Remington

San Diego State University

Address: San Diego, CA 92182
Nickname: Aztecs
Telephone: (619) 594-5163
Football Stadium (Capacity): San Diego Jack Murphy Stadium (61,104)
Basketball Arena (Capacity): Peterson Gym (3,668)
President: Dr. Thomas B. Day
Athletic Director: Dr. Fred Miller
Football Coach: Ted Tollner
Basketball Coach: Fred Trenkle
Sports Information Director: John Rosenthal

University of Texas at El Paso

Address: 201 Baltimore
El Paso, TX 79902
Nickname: Miners
Telephone: (915) 747-5347
Football Stadium (Capacity): Sun Bowl (53,000)
Basketball Arena (Capacity): Special Events Center (12,222)
President: Dr. Diana Natalicio
Athletic Director: John Thompson
Football Coach: Charlie Bailey
Basketball Coach: Don Haskins
Sports Information Director: Eddie Mullens

University of Utah

Address: Huntsman Center
Salt Lake City, UT 84112
Nickname: Utes
Telephone: (801) 581-8171
Football Stadium (Capacity): Rice Stadium (35,000)
Basketball Arena (Capacity): Huntsman Center (15,000)
President: Dr. Arthur K. Smith
Athletic Director: Dr. Chris Hill
Football Coach: Ron McBride
Basketball Coach: Rick Majerus
Sports Information Director: Bruce Woodbury

University of Wyoming

Address: P.O. Box 3414
Laramie, WY 82071-3414
Nickname: Cowboys
Telephone: (307) 766-2292
Football Stadium (Capacity): War Memorial Stadium (33,500)
Basketball Arena (Capacity): Arena-Auditorium (15,028)
President: Dr. Terry Roark
Athletic Director: Paul Roach
Football Coach: Joe Tiller
Basketball Coach: Joby Wright
Sports Information Director: Kevin McKinney

INDEPENDENTS

Army

Address: West Point, NY 10996
Nickname: Cadets/Black Knights
Telephone: (914) 938-3303
Football Stadium (Capacity): Michie Stadium (39,929)
Basketball Arena (Capacity): Cristl Arena (5,043)
Superintendent: Lt. Gen. Howard D. Graves
Athletic Director: Al Vanderbush
Football Coach: Bob Sutton
Basketball Coach: Dino Gaudio
Sports Information Director: Bob Kinney

Note: Plays football as independent, basketball in Patriot League.

University of Cincinnati

Address: Cincinnati, OH 45221-0021
Nickname: Bearcats
Telephone: (513) 556-5601
Football Stadium (Capacity): Nippert Stadium (35,500)
Basketball Arena (Capacity): Myrl Shoemaker Center (13,176)
President: Dr. Joseph A. Steger
Athletic Director: Gerald O'Dell
Football Coach: Rick Minter
Basketball Coach: Bob Huggins
Sports Information Director: Tom Hathaway

Note: Plays football as independent, basketball in Great Midwest Conference.

East Carolina University

Address: Greenville, NC 27858-4353
Nickname: Pirates
Telephone: (919) 328-4600
Football Stadium (Capacity): Dowdy-Ficklen Stadium (35,000)
Basketball Arena (Capacity): Williams Arena (7,500)
Chancellor: Dr. Richard R. Eakin
Athletic Director: David R. Hart, Jr.
Football Coach: Steve Logan
Basketball Coach: Eddie Payne
Sports Information Director: Charles Bloom

College Sports Directory (Cont.)

University of Louisville
Address: Louisville, KY 40292
Nickname: Cardinals
Telephone: (502) 852-5732
Football Stadium (Capacity): Cardinal Stadium (37,500)
Basketball Arena (Capacity): Freedom Hall (19,000)
President: Dr. Donald Swain
Athletic Director: William Olsen
Football Coach: Howard Schnellenberger
Basketball Coach: Denny Crum
Sports Information Director: Kenny Klein

Note: Plays football as independent, basketball in Metro Conference.

Navy
Address: 566 Brownson Road, Ricketts Hall
Annapolis, MD 21402
Nickname: Midshipmen
Telephone: (410) 268-6220
Football Stadium (Capacity): Navy-Marine Corps Memorial Stadium (30,000)
Basketball Arena (Capacity): Alumni Hall (5,710)
Superintendent: Adm. Charles A. Larson, USN
Athletic Director: Jack Lengyel
Football Coach: George Chaump
Basketball Coach: Don DeVoe
Sports Information Director: Thomas Bates

Note: Plays football as independent, basketball in the Patriot League.

The University of Memphis
Address: Memphis, TN 38152
Nickname: Tigers
Telephone: (901) 678-2337
Football Stadium (Capacity): Liberty Bowl Memorial Stadium/Rex Dockery Field (62,380)
Basketball Arena (Capacity): The Pyramid (20,142)
President: Dr. V. Lane Rawlins
Athletic Director: Charles Cavagnaro
Football Coach: Chuck Stobart
Basketball Coach: Larry Finch
Sports Information Director: Bob Winn

University of Notre Dame
Address: Notre Dame, IN 46556
Nickname: Fighting Irish
Telephone: (219) 631-6107
Football Stadium (Capacity): Notre Dame Stadium (59,075)
Basketball Arena (Capacity): Joyce Athletic and Convocation Center (11,418)
President: Rev. Edward A. Malloy, CSC
Athletic Director: Richard Rosenthal
Football Coach: Lou Holtz
Basketball Coach: John MacLeod
Sports Information Director: John Heisler

University of Southern Mississippi
Address: Box 5017
Hattiesburg, MS 39406
Nickname: Golden Eagles
Telephone: (601) 266-4503
Football Stadium (Capacity): M. M. Roberts Stadium (33,000)
Basketball Arena (Capacity): Green Coliseum (8,095)
President: Dr. Aubrey K. Lucas
Athletic Director: Bill McLellan
Football Coach: Jeff Bower
Basketball Coach: M. K. Turk
Sports Information Director: Regiel Napier

Note: Plays football as independent, basketball in Metro Conference.

Tulane University
Address: James Wilson Jr. Center for Intercollegiate Athletics
New Orleans, LA 70118
Nickname: Green Wave
Telephone: (504) 865-5501
Football Stadium (Capacity): Louisiana Superdome (71,000)
Basketball Arena (Capacity): Fogelman Arena (5,000)
President: Dr. Eamon Kelly
Athletic Director: Dr. Kevin White
Football Coach: Eugene (Buddy) Teevens
Basketball Coach: Perry Clark
Sports Information Director: Lenny Vangilder

Note: Plays football as independent, basketball in Metro Conference.

University of Tulsa
Address: 600 S. College
Tulsa, OK 74104
Nickname: Golden Hurricane
Telephone: (918) 631-2395
Football Stadium (Capacity): Skelley Stadium (40,385)
Basketball Arena (Capacity): Tulsa Convention Center (8,659)
President: Dr. Robert H. Donaldson
Athletic Director: Rick Dickson
Football Coach: Dave Rader
Basketball Coach: Orlando (Tubby) Smith
Sports Information Director: Don Tomkalski

THEY SAID IT

Jason Kidd, former Cal-Berkeley guard and No. 1 draft pick of the Dallas Mavericks, on the Mavs's prospects: "Now that I'm here, we'll turn the program around 360 degrees."

Olympic Sports Directory

United States Olympic Committee
Address: Olympic House
            1 Olympic Plaza
            Colorado Springs, CO 80909
Telephone: (719) 632-5551
Executive Director: John Krimsky, Jr.
Director of Plans and Programs: Jeff Cravens

U.S. Olympic Training Center
Address: 1 Olympic Plaza
            Colorado Springs, CO 80909
Telephone: (719) 578-4500
Director: Mike Moran

U.S. Olympic Training Center
Address: 421 Old Military Road
            Lake Placid, NY 12946
Telephone: (518) 523-2600
Director: Gloria Chadwick

International Olympic Committee
Address: Chateau de Vidy
            CH-1007 Lausanne
            Switzerland
Telephone: (41.21) 25 3271/3272
President: Juan Antonio Samaranch
Director General: Francois Carrard
Public Relations Officer: Michele Verdier

Atlanta Olympic Organizing Committee
Address: Suite 6000
            250 Williams St.
            Atlanta, GA 30301-1996
Telephone: (404) 224-1996
Co-Chairman: Hon. Andrew Young
President: William Porter Payne
Executive Director: Doug Gatlin
(Games of the XXVIth Olympiad; Tentative Dates:
July 20—August 4, 1996)

U.S. Olympic Organizations

Archery

National Archery Association (NAA)
Address: 1 Olympic Plaza
            Colorado Springs, CO 80909
Telephone: (719) 578-4576
President: Tom Stevenson, Jr.
Executive Director: Christine McCartney

Athletics (Track & Field)

USA Track & Field (formerly TAC)
Address: P.O. Box 120
            Indianapolis, IN 46206
Telephone: (317) 261-0500
President: Larry Ellis
Executive Director: Ollan Cassell
Press Information Director: Pete Cava

Badminton

U.S. Badminton Association (USBA)
Address: 1 Olympic Plaza
            Colorado Springs, CO 80909
Telephone: (719) 578-4808
President: Cynthia Kelly
Executive Director: Jim Hadley

Baseball

U.S. Baseball Federation (USBF)
Address: 2160 Greenwood Avenue
            Trenton, NJ 08609
Telephone: (609) 586-2381
President: Mark Marquess
Executive Director: Richard Case
Communications Director: TBA

Basketball

USA Basketball
Address: 5465 Mark Dabling Blvd.
            Colorado Springs, CO 80918
Telephone: (719) 590-4800
President: C.M. Newton
Executive Director: Warren Brown
Assistant Executive Director for Public Relations:
  Craig Miller

Biathlon

U.S. Biathlon Association (USBA)
Address: 421 Old Military Road
            Lake Placid, NY 12946
Telephone: (518) 523-3836
President: Don Edwards
Executive Director: Dusty Johnstone

Bobsled

U.S. Bobsled and Skeleton Federation
Address: P.O. Box 828
             Lake Placid, NY 12946
Telephone: (518) 523-1842
President: Jim Morris
Executive Director: Matt Roy
Marketing and Communications Director: Terry Kent

Bowling

U.S. Tenpin Bowling Federation
Address: 5301 South 76th Street
             Greendale, WI 53129
Telephone: (414) 421-9008
President: Max Skelton
Executive Director: Gerald Koenig
Communications Director: Christine Krebs

Boxing

USA Boxing
Address: 1 Olympic Plaza
             Colorado Springs, CO 80909
Telephone: (719) 578-4506
President: Jerry Dusenberry
Executive Director: Bruce Mathis
Director of Communications: Kurt Stenerson

Canoe/Kayak

U.S. Canoe and Kayak Team
Address: Pan American Plaza, Suite 610
             201 South Capitol Avenue
             Indianapolis, IN 46225
Telephone: (317) 237-5690
Chairman: Eric Haught
Executive Director: Chuck Wielgus
Director of Comm. and Marketing: Craig Bohnert

Cycling

U.S. Cycling Federation (USCF)
Address: 1 Olympic Plaza
             Colorado Springs, CO 80909
Telephone: (719) 578-4581
President: Mike Fraysse
Executive Director: Lisa Voight
Media and Public Relations Director: Steve Penny

Diving

United States Diving, Inc. (USD)
Address: Pan American Plaza, Suite 430
             201 South Capitol Avenue
             Indianapolis, IN 46225
Telephone: (317) 237-5252
President: Steve McFarland
Executive Director: Todd Smith
Director of Communications: Dave Shatkowski

Equestrian

U.S. Equestrian Team (USET)
Address: Gladstone, NJ 07934
Telephone: (908) 234-0155
Chairman of the Board and President: Robert C.
 Standish
Director of Public Relations: Marty Bauman

Fencing

U.S. Fencing Association (USFA)
Address: 1 Olympic Plaza
             Colorado Springs, CO 80909
Telephone: (719) 578-4511
President: Stephen Sobel
Executive Director: Carla-Mae Richards
Media Relations Director: Colleen Walker-Mar

Field Hockey

**U.S. Field Hockey Association (USFHA)
(Women)**
Address: 1 Olympic Plaza
             Colorado Springs, CO 80909
Telephone: (719) 578-4567
President: Jenepher Shillingford
Executive Director: Carrie Haag
Director of Public Relations: Mark Whitney

Figure Skating

U.S. Figure Skating Association (USFSA)
Address: 20 First Street
             Colorado Springs, CO 80906
Telephone: (719) 635-5200
President: Claire Ferguson
Executive Director: Jerry Lace
Communications Director: Kristin Matta

Gymnastics

U.S. Gymnastics Federation (USGF)
Address: Pan American Plaza, Suite 300
             201 South Capitol Avenue
             Indianapolis, IN 46225
Telephone: (317) 237-5050
Chairman of the Board: Sandy Knapp
President: Kathy Scanlan
Director of Public Relations: Luan Peszek

Hockey

USA Hockey
Address: 4965 North 30th Street
             Colorado Springs, CO 80919
Telephone: (719) 599-5500
President: Walter Bush
Executive Director: Dave Ogrean
Public Relations Coordinator: Darryl Sibel

Judo

United States Judo, Inc. (USJ)
Address: P.O. Box 10013
             El Paso, TX 79991
Telephone: (915) 565-8754
President and Media Contact: Frank Fullerton

Luge

U.S. Luge Association (USLA)
Address: P.O. Box 651
          Lake Placid, NY 12946
Telephone: (518) 523-2071
President: Dwight Bell
Executive Director: Ron Rossi
Public Relations and Media Coordinator:
  Dmitri Feld

Modern Pentathlon

U.S. Modern Pentathlon Association (USMPA)
Address: 530 McCullough Avenue, Suite 619
          San Antonio, TX 78215
Telephone: (210) 246-3000
President: Robert Marbut
Executive Director: W. Dean Billick

Racquetball

American Amateur Racquetball Association (AARA)
Address: 1685 West Uintah
          Colorado Springs, CO 80904
Telephone: (719) 635-5396
President: Van Dubolsky
Executive Director: Luke St. Onge
Public Relations Director: Linda Mojer

Roller Skating

U.S. Amateur Confederation of Roller Skating (USAC/RS)
Address: 4730 South Street
          P.O. Box 6579
          Lincoln, NE 68506
Telephone: (402) 483-7551
President: Betty Ann Danna
Executive Director: George H. Pickard
Sports Information Director: Andy Seeley

Rowing

U.S. Rowing Association (USRA)
Address: Pan American Plaza, Suite 400
          201 South Capitol Avenue
          Indianapolis, IN 46225
Telephone: (317) 237-5656
President: Frank Coyle
Executive Director: Sandra Hughes
Director of Communications: Maureen Merhoff

Shooting

USA Shooting Association
Address: 1 Olympic Plaza
          Colorado Springs, CO 80909
Telephone: (719) 578-4670
Chairman: Sandra Baldwin
Director of Communications: Nancy Moore
Program Administrator: Stephen Ducoff

Skiing

U.S. Skiing
Address: P.O. Box 100
          Park City, UT 84060
Telephone: (801) 649-9090
Chairman: Nick Badami
President and CEO: Mike Jacki
Vice-Chairman: Serge Lussi
President, U.S. Ski Team Foundation:
  Vinton Sommerville
Director of Communications: Tom Kelly
Media Services Coordinator: Deborah Engen Clouse

Soccer

U.S. Soccer Federation (USSF)
Address: 1801-1811 South Prairie Avenue
          Chicago, IL 60616
Telephone: (312) 808-1300
President: Alan Rothenberg
Executive Director: Hank Steinbrecher
Director of Communications: Tom Lang

Softball

Amateur Softball Association (ASA)
Address: 2801 N.E. 50th Street
          Oklahoma City, OK 73111
Telephone: (405) 424-5266
President: Wayne Myers
Executive Director: Don Porter
Director of Communications: Ron Babb

Speedskating

U.S. International Speedskating Association (USISA)
Address: P.O. Box 16157
          Rocky River, OH 44116
Telephone: (216) 899-0128
President: Bill Cushman
Executive Director: Katie Marquand
Media Contact: Susan Polakoff-Shaw

Swimming

U.S. Swimming, Inc. (USS)
Address: 1 Olympic Plaza
          Colorado Springs, CO 80909
Telephone: (719) 578-4578
President: Carol Zaleski
Executive Director: Ray Essick
Communication Director: Charlie Snyder

Synchronized Swimming

U.S. Synchronized Swimming, Inc. (USSS)
Address: Pan American Plaza, Suite 510
          201 South Capitol Avenue
          Indianapolis, IN 46225
Telephone: (317) 237-5700
President: Nancy Wichtman
Executive Director: Debbie Hesse
Membership and Communications: Laura LaMarca

Table Tennis

U.S. Table Tennis Association (USTTA)
Address: 1 Olympic Plaza
Colorado Springs, CO 80909
Telephone: (719) 578-4583
Executive Director: Paul Montville
President: Dan Seemiller
Deputy Executive Director: Linda Gleeson

Taekwondo

U.S. Taekwondo Union (USTU)
Address: 1 Olympic Plaza, Suite 405
Colorado Springs, CO 80909
Telephone: (719) 578-4632
President: Hwa Chong
Executive Director: Robert Fujimura

Team Handball

U.S. Team Handball Federation (USTHF)
Address: 1 Olympic Plaza
Colorado Springs, CO 80909
Telephone: (719) 578-4582
President: Dr. Peter Buehning
Executive Director: Michael D. Cavanaugh
Media Contact: Evelyn Anderson

Tennis

U.S. Tennis Association
Address: 70 West Red Oak Lane
White Plains, NY 10604
Telephone: (914) 696-7000
President: Jay Howard Frazier
Executive Director: M. Marshall Happer III
Director of Communications: Page Crosland

Volleyball

U.S. Volleyball Association (USVBA)
Address: 3595 East Fountain Boulevard, Suite I-2
Colorado Springs, CO 80910-1740
Telephone: (719) 637-8300
President: Jerry Sherman
Executive Director: John Carroll

Water Polo

United States Water Polo (USWP)
Address: Pan American Plaza, Suite 520
201 South Capitol Avenue
Indianapolis, IN 46225
Telephone: (317) 237-5599
President: Richard Foster
Executive Director: Bruce J. Wigo
Director of Media and Public Relations: Eileen Sexton

Weightlifting

U.S. Weightlifting Federation (USWF)
Address: 1 Olympic Plaza
Colorado Springs, CO 80909
Telephone: (719) 578-4508
President: Jim Schmitz
Executive Director: George Greenway
Communications Director: John Halpin

Wrestling

USA Wrestling
Address: 6155 Lehman
Colorado Springs, CO 80918
Telephone: (719) 598-8181
President: Larry Sciacchetano
Executive Director: Jim Scherr
Director of Communications: Gary Abbott

Yachting

U.S. Yacht Racing Union (USYRU)
Address: P.O. Box 209
Newport, RI 02840
Telephone: (401) 849-5200
President: David Irish
Executive Director: Terry Hopper
Communications Director: Dana Marane
Olympic Yachting Director: Jonathan R. Harley

Affiliated Sports Organizations

Amateur Athletic Union (AAU)
Address: 3400 West 86th Street
P.O. Box 68207
Indianapolis, IN 46268
Telephone: (317) 872-2900
President: Bobby Dodd
Executive Director: Dr. Lou Marciani

Curling

U.S. Curling Association (USCA)
Address: 1100 Center Point Drive
Box 866
Stevens Point, WI 54481
Telephone: (715) 344-1199
President: Denis Fox
Executive Director: David Garber

Affiliated Sports Organizations (Cont.)

Karate

USA Karate Federation
Address: 1300 Kenmore Boulevard
             Akron, OH 44314
Telephone: (216) 753-3114
President: George Anderson

Orienteering

U.S. Orienteering Federation
Address: P.O. Box 1444
             Forest Park, GA 30051
Telephone: (404) 363-2110
President: Larry Pedersen
Executive Director: Robin Shannonhouse
Media and Publicity Contact: John Nash
Publicity telephone: (914) 941-0896

Squash

U.S. Squash Racquets Association
Address: 23 Cynwyd Road
             P.O. Box 1216
             Bala Cynwyd, PA 19004
Telephone: (215) 667-4006
President: Alan Fox
Executive Director: Craig Brand

Trampoline and Tumbling

American Trampoline and Tumbling Association
Address: 400 West Broadway, Suite 207
             or P.O. Box 306
             Brownfield, TX 79316-0306
Telephone: (806) 637-8670
President: Connie Mara
Executive Director: Ann Sims

Triathlon

Triathlon Federation USA
Address: 3595 East Fountain Boulevard, Suite F-1
             Colorado Springs, CO 80910
Telephone: (719) 597-9090
President and Executive Director: Steve Locke
Deputy Director and Media Contact: Tim Yount

Underwater Swimming

Underwater Society of America
Address: 849 West Orange Avenue
             No. 1002
             South San Francisco, CA 94080
Telephone: (415) 583-8492
President: George Rose

Water Skiing

American Water Ski Association
Address: 799 Overlook Drive, S.E.
             Winter Haven, FL 33884
Telephone: (813) 324-4341
President: Harold Hill
Executive Director: Duke Waldrop
Public Relations Manager: Don Cullimore

Miscellaneous Sports Directory

American Professional Soccer League
Address: 3702 Pender Dr., Suite 210
             Fairfax, VA 22030
Telephone: (703) 273-7767
Chairman of the Board: Dr. William De La Peña
Commissioner: Richard Groff
Director of Operations: Emily Ballus

Continental Indoor Soccer League
Address: 16027 Ventura Boulevard, Suite 605
             Encino, CA 91436
Telephone: (818) 906-7627
Commissioner: Ron Weinstein
Director of Public Relations: Dan Courtemanchi

National Professional Soccer League
Address: 229 Third Street NW
             Canton, OH 44702
Telephone: (216) 455-4625
Commissioner: Steve Paxos
Director of Operations: Paul Luchowski

Ladies Professional Golf Association
Address: 2570 W International Speedway
             Boulevard, Suite B
             Daytona Beach, FL 32114
Telephone: (904) 254-8800
Commissioner: Charles S. Mechem Jr.
Director of Communications: Elaine Scott

Professional Golfers Association
Address: 112 TPC Boulevard
             Ponte Vedra, FL 32082
Telephone: (904) 285-3700
Commissioner: Ken Finchem
Director of Public Relations: John Morris

United States Golf Association
Address: P.O. Box 708, Golf House
             Liberty Corner Road
             Far Hills, NJ 07931-0708
Telephone: (908) 234-2300
President: Reg Murphy

Association of Tennis Professionals Tour
Address: 200 ATP Tour Boulevard
             Ponte Vedra Beach, FL 32082
Telephone: (904) 285-8000
Chief Executive Officer: Mark Miles
Director of Communications: Pete Alfano

Women's Tennis Association
Address: 133 First Street N.E.
             St. Petersburg, FL 33701
Telephone: (813) 895-5000
Chief Executive Officer: Anne Person-Worcester
President: Martina Navratilova
Director of Public Relations: Ana Leaird

United States Tennis Association
Address: 70 West Red Oak Lane
             White Plains, NY 10604
Telephone: (914) 696-7000
President: Jay Howard Frazier
Executive Director: M. Marshall Happer III
Director of Communications: Page Crosland

National Association for Stock Car Auto Racing (NASCAR)
Address: P.O. Box 2875, 1801 W International
             Speedway Boulevard
             Daytona Beach, FL 32120
Telephone: (904) 253-0611
President: Bill France Jr.
Manager of Public Relations: Andy Hall

Championship Auto Racing Teams (CART)
Address: 390 Enterprise Court
             Bloomfield Hills, MI 48302
Telephone: (810) 334-8500
President/CEO: Andrew Craig
Director of Publicity: TBA

National Hot Rod Association
Address: 2035 East Financial Way
             Glendora, CA 91741
Telephone: (818) 914-4761
President: Dallas Gardner
Director of Communications: Denny Darnell

International Motor Sports Association
Address: 3502 Henderson Boulevard
             Tampa, FL 33609
Telephone: (813) 877-4672
President: Al Kelley, Jr.
Media Director: Lynn Myfelt

Professional Rodeo Cowboys Association
Address: 101 Pro Rodeo Drive
             Colorado Springs, CO 80919
Telephone: (719) 593-8840
Commissioner: Lewis Cryer
Director of Communications: Steve Fleming

Thoroughbred Racing Associations of America
Address: 420 Fair Hill Drive, Suite 1
             Elkton, MD 21921
Telephone: (410) 392-9200
President: Christopher Scherf
Director of Service Bureau: Conrad Sobkoviak

Thoroughbred Racing Communications, Inc.
Address: 40 East 52nd Street
             New York, NY 10022
Telephone: (212) 371-5910
Executive Director: Tom Merritt
Director of Media Relations and Development:
  Bob Curran

Breeders' Cup Limited
Address: 2525 Harrodsburg Road
             Lexington, KY 40504-3359
Telephone: (606) 223-5444
President: James Bassett
Media Relations Directors: James Gluckson and
  Ben Metzger

The Jockeys' Guild, Inc.
Address: 250 West Main Street
             Lexington, KY 40507
Telephone: (606) 259-3211
President: Jerry Bailey
National Manager/Secretary: John Giovanni

United States Trotting Association
Address: 750 Michigan Avenue
             Columbus, OH 43215
Telephone: (614) 224-2291
President: Corwin Nixon
Publicity Department: John Pawlak

Professional Bowlers Association
Address: 1720 Merriman Road, P.O. Box 5118
             Akron, OH 44334-0118
Telephone: (216) 836-5568
Commissioner: Michael Connor
Public Relations Director: Kevin Shippy

Ladies Pro Bowlers Tour
Address: 7171 Cherryvale Boulevard
             Rockford, IL 61112
Telephone: (815) 332-5756
Executive Tournament Director: Rick Hudson
Media Director: Lennie Gessler

Women's International Bowling Congress
Address: 5301 South 76th Street
             Greendale, WI 53129-1191
Telephone: (414) 421-9000
President: Joyce Deitch
Public Relations Manager: Karen Sytsma

American Bowling Congress
Address: 5301 South 76th Street
             Greendale, WI 53129
Telephone: (414) 421-6400
President: Larry Schafer
Communications Executive: Steve James

Association of Volleyball Professionals
Address: 15260 Ventura Blvd., Suite #2250
             Sherman Oaks, CA 91403
Telephone: (818) 386-2486
President: Jon Stevenson
Public Relations: Alison Canfield

U.S. Chess Federation
Address: 186 Route 9W
             New Windsor, NY 12553
Telephone: (914) 562-8350
Executive Director: Al Lawrence
Director of Operations: George Fillippone

Iditarod Trail Committee
Address: P.O. Box 870800
             Wasilla, AK 99687
Telephone: (907) 376-5155
Executive Director: Stan Hooley
Race Director: Joanne Potts

International Game Fish Association
Address: 1301 East Atlantic Boulevard
             Pompano Beach, FL 33060
Telephone: (305) 941-3474
President: Mike Leech

American Greyhound Track Operators Association
Address: 1065 Northeast 125th Street, Suite 219
             North Miami, FL 33161
Telephone: (305) 893-2101
President: Fred Havenick
Secretary/Executive Director: George D. Johnson Jr.

U.S. Handball Association
Address: 2333 North Tucson Boulevard
             Tucson, AZ 85716
Telephone: (602) 795-0434
Executive Director: Vern Roberts
Director of Public Relations: Cheri Morden

U.S. Club Lacrosse Association
Address: c/o Lacrosse Foundation
             113 W University Parkway
             Baltimore, MD 21210
Telephone: (410) 235-6882
Executive Director: Steven B. Stenersen

Little League Baseball, Inc.
Address: P.O. Box 3485
             Williamsport, PA 17701
Telephone: (717) 326-1921
President: Dr. Creighton Hale
Communications Director: Dennis Sullivan

American Powerboating Association
Address: P.O. Box 377
             East Pointe, MI 48021
Telephone: (810) 773-9700
Executive Administrator: Gloria Urbin

U.S. Polo Association
Address: 4059 Iron Works Pike
             Lexington, KY 40511
Telephone: (606) 255-0593
Interim Executive Director: George Alexander, Jr.

U.S. Rugby Football Union
Address: 3595 East Fountain Boulevard
             Colorado Springs, CO 80910
Telephone: (719) 637-1022
Executive Director: TBA

MINOR LEAGUES

Baseball (AAA)

American Association
Address: 6801 Miama Ave., Suite 3
             Cincinnati, OH 45243
Telephone: (513) 271-4800
President: Branch B. Rickey

International League
Address: 55 South High Street, Suite 202
             Dublin, OH 43017
Telephone: (614) 791-9300
President: Randy Mobley

Mexican League
Address: Angela Pola #16
             Col. Periodista, C.P. 11220
             Mexico D.F.
Telephone: (905) 587-10-07
President: Petro Cisneros

Pacific Coast League
Address: 2345 South Alma School Rd., Suite 110
             Mesa, AZ 85210
Telephone: (602) 838-2171
President: Bill Cutler

Hockey

American Hockey League
Address: 425 Union Street
             West Springfield, MA 01089
Telephone: (413) 781-2030
President: David Andrews
Senior VP of Hockey Operations: Gordon Anziano

International Hockey League
Address: 1577 North Woodward Ave., Suite 212
             Bloomfield Hills, MI 48304
Telephone: (810) 258-0580
Commissioner: Robert P. Ufer
VP of Public Relations: Tim Bryant

Hall of Fame Directory

National Baseball Hall of Fame And Museum
Address: P.O. Box 590
              Cooperstown, NY 13326
Telephone: (607) 547-9114
President: Donald C. Marr, Jr.
Director of Public Relations: Bill Guilfoile

Naismith Memorial Basketball Hall of Fame
Address: 1150 West Columbus Avenue
              Springfield, Mass. 01101
Telephone: (413) 781-6500
President: Joseph O'Brien
Director of Public Relations: Robin Deutsch

National Bowling Hall of Fame And Museum
Address: 111 Stadium Plaza
              St Louis, MO 63102
Telephone: (314) 231-6340
Executive Director: Gerald Baltz
Director of Marketing: Raleigh Ragan

National Boxing Hall of Fame
Address: 1 Hall of Fame Drive
              Canastota, NY 13032
Telephone: (315) 697-7095
President: Donald Ackerman
Executive Director: Edward Brophy

Professional Football Hall of Fame
Address: 2121 George Halas Drive NW
              Canton, OH 44708
Telephone: (216) 456-8207
Executive Director: Pete Elliott
Vice President, Public Relations: Don Smith

LPGA Hall of Fame
Address: 2570 West International Speedway
              Boulevard, Suite B
              Daytona Beach, FL 32114
Telephone: (904) 254-8800
Commissioner: Charles S. Mechem
Communications Director: Elaine Scott

Note: PGA Hall of Fame is closed until at least 1995.

Professional Hockey Hall of Fame
Address: 30 Young Street BCE Place
              Toronto, Ontario Canada M5E 1X8
Telephone: (416) 360-7735
President: David Taylor
Director of Marketing: Phil Denyes

National Museum of Racing and Hall of Fame
Address: 191 Union Avenue
              Saratoga Springs, NY 12866
Telephone: (518) 584-0400
Executive Director: Peter Hammell
Assistant Director: Catherine Maguire

National Soccer Hall of Fame
Address: 5-11 Ford Avenue
              Oneonta, N.Y. 13820
Telephone: (607) 432-3351
Executive Director: Albert Colone
External Affairs: Will Lunn

International Swimming Hall of Fame
Address: 1 Hall of Fame Drive
              Fort Lauderdale, FL 33316
Telephone: (305) 462-6536
President: Dr. Samuel J. Freas
Director of Marketing: Michelle Mitchell-Rocha

International Tennis Hall of Fame
Address: 194 Bellevue Avenue
              Newport, R.I. 02840
Telephone: (401) 849-3990
Executive Director: Mark Stenning
Director of Public Relations: Linda Johnson

National Track & Field Hall of Fame
Address: P.O. Box 120
              Indianapolis, IN 46206
Telephone: (317) 261-0500
Curator: Marty Weiss
Director of Media Relations: Pete Cava

FOR THE RECORD·Year by Year

Athlete Awards

Sports Illustrated Sportsman of the Year

1954	Roger Bannister, Track
1955	Johnny Podres, Baseball
1956	Bobby Morrow, Track
1957	Stan Musial, Baseball
1958	Rafer Johnson, Track
1959	Ingemar Johansson, Boxing
1960	Arnold Palmer, Golf
1961	Jerry Lucas, Basketball
1962	Terry Baker, Football
1963	Pete Rozelle, Pro Football
1964	Ken Venturi, Golf
1965	Sandy Koufax, Baseball
1966	Jim Ryun, Track
1967	Carl Yastrzemski, Baseball
1968	Bill Russell, Pro Basketball
1969	Tom Seaver, Baseball
1970	Bobby Orr, Hockey
1971	Lee Trevino, Golf
1972	Billie Jean King, Tennis
	John Wooden, Basketball
1973	Jackie Stewart, Auto Racing
1974	Muhammad Ali, Boxing
1975	Pete Rose, Baseball
1976	Chris Evert, Tennis
1977	Steve Cauthen, Horse Racing
1978	Jack Nicklaus, Golf
1979	Terry Bradshaw, Pro Football
	Willie Stargell, Baseball
1980	US Olympic Hockey Team
1981	Sugar Ray Leonard, Boxing
1982	Wayne Gretzky, Hockey
1983	Mary Decker, Track
1984	Mary Lou Retton, Gymnastics
	Edwin Moses, Track
1985	Kareem Abdul-Jabbar, Pro Basketball
1986	Joe Paterno, Football
1987	Athletes Who Care
	Bob Bourne, Hockey
	Kip Keino, Track
	Judi Brown King, Track
	Dale Murphy, Baseball
	Chip Rives, Football
	Patty Sheehan, Golf
	Rory Sparrow, Pro Basketball
	Reggie Williams, Pro Football
1988	Orel Hershiser, Baseball
1989	Greg LeMond, Cycling
1990	Joe Montana, Pro Football
1991	Michael Jordan, Pro Basketball
1992	Arthur Ashe
1993	Don Shula, Pro Football

Associated Press Athletes of the Year

	MEN	WOMEN
1931	Pepper Martin, Baseball	Helene Madison, Swimming
1932	Gene Sarazen, Golf	Babe Didrikson, Track
1933	Carl Hubbell, Baseball	Helen Jacobs, Tennis
1934	Dizzy Dean, Baseball	Virginia Van Wie, Golf
1935	Joe Louis, Boxing	Helen Wills Moody, Tennis
1936	Jesse Owens, Track	Helen Stephens, Track
1937	Don Budge, Tennis	Katherine Rawls, Swimming
1938	Don Budge, Tennis	Patty Berg, Golf
1939	Nile Kinnick, Football	Alice Marble, Tennis
1940	Tom Harmon, Football	Alice Marble, Tennis
1941	Joe DiMaggio, Baseball	Betty Hicks Newell, Golf
1942	Frank Sinkwich, Football	Gloria Callen, Swimming
1943	Gunder Haegg, Track	Patty Berg, Golf
1944	Byron Nelson, Golf	Ann Curtis, Swimming
1945	Bryon Nelson, Golf	Babe Didrikson Zaharias, Golf
1946	Glenn Davis, Football	Babe Didrikson Zaharias, Golf
1947	Johnny Lujack, Football	Babe Didrikson Zaharias, Golf
1948	Lou Boudreau, Baseball	Fanny Blankers-Koen, Track
1949	Leon Hart, Football	Marlene Bauer, Golf
1950	Jim Konstanty, Baseball	Babe Didrikson Zaharias, Golf
1951	Dick Kazmaier, Football	Maureen Connolly, Tennis
1952	Bob Mathias, Track	Maureen Connolly, Tennis
1953	Ben Hogan, Golf	Maureen Connolly, Tennis
1954	Willie Mays, Baseball	Babe Didrikson Zaharias, Golf
1955	Hopalong Cassidy, Football	Patty Berg, Golf
1956	Mickey Mantle, Baseball	Pat McCormick, Diving
1957	Ted Williams, Baseball	Althea Gibson, Tennis
1958	Herb Elliott, Track	Althea Gibson, Tennis
1959	Ingemar Johansson, Boxing	Maria Bueno, Tennis
1960	Rafer Johnson, Track	Wilma Rudolph, Track
1961	Roger Maris, Baseball	Wilma Rudolph, Track
1962	Maury Wills, Baseball	Dawn Fraser, Swimming
1963	Sandy Koufax, Baseball	Mickey Wright, Golf
1964	Don Schollander, Swimming	Mickey Wright, Golf

Associated Press Athletes of the Year *(Cont.)*

	MEN	WOMEN
1965	Sandy Koufax, Baseball	Kathy Whitworth, Golf
1966	Frank Robinson, Baseball	Kathy Whitworth, Golf
1967	Carl Yastrzemski, Baseball	Billie Jean King, Tennis
1968	Denny McLain, Baseball	Peggy Fleming, Skating
1969	Tom Seaver, Baseball	Debbie Meyer, Swimming
1970	George Blanda, Pro Football	Chi Cheng, Track
1971	Lee Trevino, Golf	Evonne Goolagong, Tennis
1972	Mark Spitz, Swimming	Olga Korbut, Gymnastics
1973	O. J. Simpson, Pro Football	Billie Jean King, Tennis
1974	Muhammad Ali, Boxing	Chris Evert, Tennis
1975	Fred Lynn, Baseball	Chris Evert, Tennis
1976	Bruce Jenner, Track	Nadia Comaneci, Gymnastics
1977	Steve Cauthen, Horse Racing	Chris Evert, Tennis
1978	Ron Guidry, Baseball	Nancy Lopez, Golf
1979	Willie Stargell, Baseball	Tracy Austin, Tennis
1980	US Olympic Hockey Team	Chris Evert Lloyd, Tennis
1981	John McEnroe, Tennis	Tracy Austin, Tennis
1982	Wayne Gretzky, Hockey	Mary Decker, Track
1983	Carl Lewis, Track	Martina Navratilova, Tennis
1984	Carl Lewis, Track	Mary Lou Retton, Gymnastics
1985	Dwight Gooden, Baseball	Nancy Lopez, Golf
1986	Larry Bird, Pro Basketball	Martina Navratilova, Tennis
1987	Ben Johnson, Track	Jackie Joyner-Kersee, Track
1988	Orel Hershiser, Baseball	Florence Griffith Joyner, Track
1989	Joe Montana, Pro Football	Steffi Graf, Tennis
1990	Joe Montana, Pro Football	Beth Daniel, Golf
1991	Michael Jordan, Pro Basketball	Monica Seles, Tennis
1992	Michael Jordan, Pro Basketball	Monica Seles, Tennis
1993	Michael Jordan, Pro Basketball	Sheryl Swoopes, College Basketball

James E. Sullivan Award

Presented annually by the Amateur Athletic Union to the athlete who "by his or her performance, example and influence as an amateur, has done the most during the year to advance the cause of sportsmanship."

1930	Bobby Jones, Golf	1960	Rafer Johnson, Track
1931	Barney Berlinger, Track	1961	Wilma Rudolph, Track
1932	Jim Bausch, Track	1962	Jim Beatty, Track
1933	Glenn Cunningham, Track	1963	John Pennel, Track
1934	Bill Bonthron, Track	1964	Don Schollander, Swimming
1935	Lawson Little, Golf	1965	Bill Bradley, Basketball
1936	Glenn Morris, Track	1966	Jim Ryun, Track
1937	Don Budge, Tennis	1967	Randy Matson, Track
1938	Don Lash, Track	1968	Debbie Meyer, Swimming
1939	Joe Burk, Rowing	1969	Bill Toomey, Track
1940	Greg Rice, Track	1970	John Kinsella, Swimming
1941	Leslie MacMitchell, Track	1971	Mark Spitz, Swimming
1942	Cornelius Warmerdam, Track	1972	Frank Shorter, Track
1943	Gilbert Dodds, Track	1973	Bill Walton, Basketball
1944	Ann Curtis, Swimming	1974	Rich Wohlhuter, Track
1945	Doc Blanchard, Football	1975	Tim Shaw, Swimming
1946	Arnold Tucker, Football	1976	Bruce Jenner, Track
1947	John B. Kelly, Jr, Rowing	1977	John Naber, Swimming
1948	Bob Mathias, Track	1978	Tracy Caulkins, Swimming
1949	Dick Button, Skating	1979	Kurt Thomas, Gymnastics
1950	Fred Wilt, Track	1980	Eric Heiden, Speed Skating
1951	Bob Richards, Track	1981	Carl Lewis, Track
1952	Horace Ashenfelter, Track	1982	Mary Decker, Track
1953	Sammy Lee, Diving	1983	Edwin Moses, Track
1954	Mal Whitfield, Track	1984	Greg Louganis, Diving
1955	Harrison Dillard, Track	1985	Joan B. Samuelson, Track
1956	Pat McCormick, Diving	1986	Jackie Joyner-Kersee, Track
1957	Bobby Morrow, Track	1987	Jim Abbott, Baseball
1958	Glenn Davis, Track	1988	Florence Griffith Joyner, Track
1959	Parry O'Brien, Track	1989	Janet Evans, Swimming

James E. Sullivan Award (Cont.)

1990	John Smith, Wrestling	1993	Charlie Ward, College Football,
1991	Mike Powell, Track		Basketball
1992	Bonnie Blair, Speed Skating		

The Sporting News Man of the Year

1968	Denny McLain, Baseball	1982	Whitey Herzog, Baseball
1969	Tom Seaver, Baseball	1983	Bowie Kuhn, Baseball
1970	John Wooden, Basketball	1984	Peter Ueberroth, LA Olympics
1971	Lee Trevino, Golf	1985	Pete Rose, Baseball
1972	Charles O. Finley, Baseball	1986	Larry Bird, Pro Basketball
1973	O. J. Simpson, Pro Football	1987	No award
1974	Lou Brock, Baseball	1988	Jackie Joyner-Kersee, Track
1975	Archie Griffin, Football	1989	Joe Montana, Pro Football
1976	Larry O'Brien, Pro Basketball	1990	Nolan Ryan, Baseball
1977	Steve Cauthen, Horse Racing	1991	Michael Jordan, Pro Basketball
1978	Ron Guidry, Baseball	1992	Mike Krzyzewski, College
1979	Willie Stargell, Baseball		Basketball Coach
1980	George Brett, Baseball	1993	Pat Gillick and Cito Gaston,
1981	Wayne Gretzky, Hockey		Baseball

United Press International Male and Female Athlete of the Year

	MEN	WOMEN
1974	Muhammad Ali, Boxing	Irena Szewinska, Track and Field
1975	Joao Oliveira, Track and Field	Nadia Comaneci, Gymnastics
1976	Alberto Juantorena, Track and Field	Nadia Comaneci, Gymnastics
1977	Alberto Juantorena, Track and Field	Rosie Ackermann, Track and Field
1978	Henry Rono, Track and Field	Tracy Caulkins, Swimming
1979	Sebastian Coe, Track and Field	Marita Koch, Track and Field
1980	Eric Heiden, Speed Skating	Hanni Wenzel, Alpine Skiing
1981	Sebastian Coe, Track and Field	Chris Evert Lloyd, Tennis
1982	Daley Thompson, Track and Field	Marita Koch, Track and Field
1983	Carl Lewis, Track and Field	Jarmila Kratochvilova, Track and Field
1984	Carl Lewis, Track and Field	Martina Navratilova, Tennis
1985	Steve Cram, Track and Field	Mary Decker Slaney, Track and Field
1986	Diego Maradona, Soccer	Heike Drechsler, Track and Field
1987	Ben Johnson, Track and Field	Steffi Graf, Tennis
1988	Matt Biondi, Swimming	Florence Griffith Joyner, Track and Field
1989	Boris Becker, Tennis	Steffi Graf, Tennis
1990	Stefan Edberg, Tennis	Merlene Ottey, Track and Field
1991	Michael Jordan, Pro Basketball	Monica Seles, Tennis
1992	Mario Lemieux, Hockey	Monica Seles, Tennis
1993	Michael Jordan, Pro Basketball	Steffi Graf, Tennis

Dial Award

Presented annually by the Dial Corporation to the male and female national high school athlete/scholar of the year.

	MEN	WOMEN
1979	Herschel Walker, Football	No award
1980	Bill Fralic, Football	Carol Lewis, Track
1981	Kevin Willhite, Football	Cheryl Miller, Basketball
1982	Mike Smith, Basketball	Elaine Zayak, Skating
1983	Chris Spielman, Football	Melanie Buddemeyer, Swimming
1984	Hart Lee Dykes, Football	Nora Lewis, Basketball
1985	Jeff George, Football	Gea Johnson, Track
1986	Scott Schaffner, Football	Mya Johnson, Track
1987	Todd Marinovich, Football	Kristi Overton, Water Skiing
1988	Carlton Gray, Football	Courtney Cox, Basketball
1989	Robert Smith, Football	Lisa Leslie, Basketball
1990	Derrick Brooks, Football	Vicki Goetze, Golf
1991	Jeff Buckey, Football, Track	Katie Smith, Basketball, Volleyball, Track
1992	Jacque Vaughn, Basketball	Amanda White, Track, Swimming
1993	Tiger Woods, Golf	Kristin Folkl, Basketball

Profiles

A Memorable Masters

Sports Illustrated

APRIL 18, 1994 · $2.95 (CAN. $3.95)

'I WAS KILLING MYSELF'
My Life as
An Alcoholic
By Mickey Mantle

MICHAEL O'NEILL

Henry Aaron (b. 2-5-34): Baseball OF. "Hammerin' Hank." Alltime leader in HR (755) and RBI (2,297); third in hits (3,771). 1957 MVP. Led league in HR and RBI 4 times each, runs scored 3 times, hits and batting average 2 times. No. 44, he had 44 homers 4 times. Had 40+ HR 8 times; 100+ RBI 11 times; .300+ average 14 times. 24-time All-Star. Career span 1954–76; jersey number retired by Atlanta and Milwaukee.

Kareem Abdul-Jabbar (b. 4-16-47): Born Lew Alcindor. Basketball C. All-time leader points scored (38,387), field goals attempted (28,307), field goals made (15,837), blocked shots (3,189), games played (1,560), and years played (20); third all-time rebounds (17,440). Won 6 MVP awards (1971–72, 1974, 1976–77, 1980). Career scoring average was 24.6, rebounding average 11.2. 10-time All-Star, All-Defensive team 5 times. 1970 Rookie of the Year. Played on 6 championship teams; was playoff MVP in 1971, 1985. Career span 1969–88 with Milwaukee, Los Angeles. Also played on 3 NCAA championship teams with UCLA; tournament MVP 1967–69; Player of the Year 2 times.

Affirmed (b. 2-21-75): Thoroughbred race horse. Triple Crown winner in 1978 with jockey Steve Cauthen aboard. Trained by Laz Barrera.

Troy Aikman (b. 11-21-66): Football QB. MVP of Super Bowl XXVII, in which he completed 22 of 30 passes for 273 yards and four TDs with no interceptions. Led Cowboys to Super Bowl XXVIII victory. Career span since 1989 with Dallas Cowboys.

Tenley Albright (b. 7-18-35): Figure skater. Gold medalist at 1956 Olympics, silver medalist at 1952 Olympics. World champion 2 times (1953, 1955) and U.S. champion 5 consecutive years (1952–56).

Grover Cleveland Alexander (b. 2-26-1887, d. 11-4-50): Baseball RHP. Third alltime most wins (373), second most shutouts (90). Won 30+ games 3 times, 20+ games 6 other times. Set rookie record with 28 wins in 1911. Career span 1911–30 with Philadelphia (NL), Chicago (NL), St Louis (NL).

Vasili Alexeyev (b. 1942): Soviet weightlifter. Gold medalist at 2 consecutive Olympics in 1972, 1976. World champion 8 times.

Muhammad Ali (b. 1-17-42): Born Cassius Clay. Boxer. Heavyweight champion 3 times (1964–67, 1974–78, 1978–79). Stripped of title in 1967 because he refused to serve in the Vietnam War. Career record 56–5 with 37 KOs. Defended title 19 times. Also light heavyweight gold medalist at 1960 Olympics.

Phog Allen (b. 11-18-1885, d. 9-16-74): College baskeball coach. Fifth alltime most wins (746); .739 career winning percentage. Won 1952 NCAA championship. Most of career, 1920–56, with Kansas.

Bobby Allison (b. 12-3-37): Auto racer. Third all-time in NASCAR victories (84) at the time of his retirement. Won Daytona 500 3 times (1978, 1982, 1988). Also NASCAR champion in 1983.

Naty Alvarado (b. 7-25-55): Mexican-born handball player. "El Gato (The Cat)". Won a record 11 U.S. pro four-wall handball titles starting in 1977.

Lance Alworth (b. 8-3-40): Football WR. "Bambi" led NFL in receiving in 1966, '68 and '69. 200+ yards in a game 5 times in career, a record. Gained 100+ yards

in game 41 times. In 1965 gained 1,602 yards, still second highest seasonal yardage ever. Career span 1962–70 with San Diego and 1971–72 with Dallas. Elected to Pro Football Hall of Fame 1978.

Sparky Anderson (b. 2-22-34): Baseball manager. Only manager to win World Series in both leagues (Detroit, 1984, Cincinnati, 1975–76); only manager to win 100 games in both leagues.

Willie Anderson (b. 1880, d. 1910): Scottish golfer. Won U.S. Open 4 times (1901 and an unmatched three straight, 1903–05). Also won 4 Western Opens between 1902 and 1909.

Mario Andretti (b. 2-28-40): Auto racer. The only driver in history to win Daytona 500 (1967), Indy 500 (1969) and Formula One world championship (1978). Second alltime in CART victories (52 as of retirement in Oct. 1994). Also 12 career Formula One victories. USAC/CART champion 4 times (consecutively 1965–66, 1969, 1984). Named Indy 500 Rookie of the Year in 1965.

Earl Anthony (b. 4-27-38): Bowler. Won PBA National Championship 6 times, more than any other bowler (consecutively 1973–75, 1981–83) and Tournament of Champions 2 times (1974, 1978). First bowler to top $1 million in career earnings. Bowler of the Year 6 times (consecutively 1974–76, 1981–83). Has won 45 career PBA titles since 1970.

Said Aouita (b. 11-2-60): Track and field. Moroccan set world records in 2,000 meters (4:50.81 in 1987), and 5,000 meters (12:58.39 in 1987). 1984 Olympic champion in 5,000; 1988 Olympic third place in 800.

Al Arbour (b. 11-1-32): Hockey D-coach. Led NY Islanders to 4 consecutive Stanley Cup championships (1980–83). Also played on 3 Stanley Cup champions: Detroit, Chicago and Toronto, from 1953 to 1971.

Eddie Arcaro (b. 2-19-16): Horse racing jockey. The only jockey to win the Triple Crown 2 times (aboard Whirlaway in 1941, Citation in 1948). Rode Preakness Stakes winner (1941, 1948, consecutively 1950–51, 1955, 1957) and Belmont Stakes winner (consecutively 1941–42, 1945, 1948, 1952, 1955) 6 times each and Kentucky Derby winner 5 times (1938, 1941, 1945, 1948, 1952). 4,779 career wins.

Nate Archibald (b. 9-2-48): Basketball player. "Tiny" only by NBA standards at 6' 1", 160 pounds. Drafted by Cincinnati in 1970. Averaged 34 points per game for K.C.-Omaha in 1972–73. Led NBA in scoring (34.0) and assists (910) in 1972–73. First team, all-NBA in 1973, '75 and '76. MVP of NBA All Star game in 1981. Retired in 1984.

Alexis Arguello (b. 4-19-52): Nicaraguan Boxer. Won world titles in three weight classes— featherweight, super featherweight and lightweight. Won first title, WBA featherweight, on 11-23-74 when he KO'd Ruben Olivares in 13. Won last title, vacant WBC lightweight, on 5-22-82 when he KO'd Andrew Ganigan in 5. Career record: 86 bouts; won 65 by KO, 15 by decision; lost 6, three by KO.

Henry Armstrong (b. 12-12-12): Boxer. Champion in 3 different weight classes: featherweight (1937— relinquished 1938), welterweight (1938–40) and lightweight (1938–39). Career record 145-20-9 with 98 KOs (27 consecutively, 1937–38) from 1931 to 1945.

Arthur Ashe (b. 7-10-43; d. 2-6-93): Tennis player. First black man to win U.S. Open (1968, as an amateur), Australian Open (1970) and Wimbledon singles titles (1975). 33 career tournament victories. Member of Davis Cup team 1963–78; captain 1980–85. Died of AIDS-related pneumonia.

Assault (b. 1943): Thoroughbred race horse. Horse of the Year for 1946; won Triple Crown that year. Won Kentucky Derby by 8 lengths; Preakness by a neck over Lord Boswell; and the Belmont by 3 lengths from Natchez. Trained by Max Hirsch.

Red Auerbach (b. 9-20-17): Basketball coach-executive. All-time leader in wins (938). Coached Boston from 1946 to 1965, winning 9 championships, 8 consecutively. Had .662 career winning percentage, with 50+ wins 8 consecutive seasons. Also won 7 championships as general manager.

Hobey Baker (b. 1-15-1892, d. 12-21-18): Sportsman. Member of both college football and hockey Halls of Fame. College hockey and football star with Princeton, 1911–14. Fighter pilot in World War I, died in plane crash. College hockey Player of the Year award named in his honor.

Seve Ballesteros (b. 4-9-57): Spanish golfer. Notorious scrambler. Won British Opens in 1979, '84 and '88. Won Masters in 1980 and '83.

Ernie Banks (b. 1-31-31): Baseball SS-1B. "Mr. Cub." Won 2 consecutive MVP awards, in 1958–59. 512 career HR. League leader in HR, RBI 2 times each; career batting average of .274; 40+ HR 5 times; 100+ RBI 8 times. Most HR by a shortstop with 47 in 1958. Career span 1953–71 with Chicago.

Roger Bannister (b. 3-23-29): Track and field. British runner broke the 4-minute mile barrier, running 3:59.4 on May 6, 1954.

Red Barber (b. 2-17-08, d. 10-22-92): Sportscaster. TV-radio baseball announcer was the voice of Cincinnati, Brooklyn and NY Yankees. His expressions, such as "sitting in the catbird seat," "pea patch" and "rhubarb" captivated audiences from 1934 to 1966.

Charles Barkley (b. 2-20-63): Basketball F. Five-time first-team All-Star. All-Rookie team, 1985. Led NBA in rebounding, 1987. Averaged 20+ points in seven of 8 seasons with Philadelphia. 1992 Olympic team leading scorer. Traded to Phoenix before 1992-93 season. League MVP for 1992-93 season.

Rick Barry (b. 3-28-44): Basketball F. Only player in history to win scoring titles in NBA (San Francisco, 1967) and ABA (Oakland, 1969). Third alltime highest free throw percentage (.900). Career scoring average 23.2. Led league in free throw percentage 6 times, steals and scoring 1 time each. Averaged 30+ points 2 times, 20+ points 6 other times. 5-time All-Star. 1975 playoff MVP with Golden State. 1966 Rookie of the Year. Career span 1967–79.

Carmen Basilio (b. 4-2-27): Boxer. Won titles in two weight classes, welter and middle. Lost first welter title bid to Kid Gavilan on 9-18-53. Won world welter title by TKO of Tony DeMarco in 12 rounds on 6-10-55. Lost, regained and retained welter title in three fights with Johnny Saxton. Won and then lost middleweight title in two 15 round fights with Ray Robinson. Made three unsucccessful bids to regain middle title. *The Ring* Fighter of the Year for 1957. Career record: 78 bouts; won 26 by KO and 29 by decision; drew 7; lost 16, two by KO. Elected to Boxing Hall of Fame in 1969.

Sammy Baugh (b. 3-17-14): Football QB-P. Set records by leading league in passing 6 times and punting 4 times. Also holds record for highest career punting average (45.1) and highest season average (51.0 in 1940). Career span 1937–52 with Washington. Also All-America with Texas Christian 3 consecutive seasons.

Elgin Baylor (b. 9-16-34): Basketball F. Third alltime highest scoring average (27.4), scored 23,149 points. Averaged 30+ points 3 consecutive seasons, 20+ points 8 other times. 10-time All-Star. 1962 Rookie of the Year. Played in 8 finals without winning championship. Career span 1958–71 with Los Angeles. Also 1958 MVP in NCAA tournament with Seattle.

Bob Beamon (b. 8-29-46): Track and field. Gold medalist in long jump at 1968 Olympics with world record jump of 29' 2½" that stood until 1991.

Franz Beckenbauer (b. 1945): West German soccer player. Captain of 1974 World Cup champions and coach of 1990 champions. Also played for NY Cosmos from 1977 to 1980.

Boris Becker (b. 11-22-67): German tennis player. The youngest male player to win a Wimbledon singles title at age 17 in 1985. Has won 3 Wimbledon titles (consecutively 1985–86, 1989), 1 U.S. Open (1989) and 1 Australian Open title (1991). Led West Germany to 2 consecutive Davis Cup victories (1988–89).

Chuck Bednarik (b. 5-1-25): Football C-LB. Last of the great two-way players, was named All-Pro at both center and linebacker. Missed only 3 games in 14 seasons with Philadelphia from 1949–62. Also All-America 2 times at Pennsylvania.

Clair Bee (b. 3-2-1896, d. 5-20-83): Basketball coach. Originated 1-3-1 defense, helped develop three-second rule, 24-second clock. Won 82.7 percent of games as coach for Rider College and Long Island University. Coach Baltimore Bullets, 1952–54. Author, 23-volume Chip Hilton series for children, 21 nonfiction sports books.

Jean Beliveau (b. 8-31-31): Hockey C. Won MVP award 2 times (1956, 1964), playoff MVP in 1965. Led league in assists 3 times, goals 2 times and points 1 time. 507 career goals, 712 assists. All-Star 6 times. Played on 10 Stanley Cup champions with Montreal from 1950 to 1971.

Bert Bell (b. 2-25-1895, d. 10-11-59): Football executive. Second NFL commissioner (1946–59). Also owner of Philadelphia (1933–40) and Pittsburgh (1941–46). Proposed the first college draft in 1936.

James "Cool Papa" Bell (b. 5-17-03): Baseball OF. Legendary foot speed—according to Satchel Paige could flip light switch and be in bed before room was dark. Hit .392 in games against white major leaguers. Career span 1922–46 with many teams of the Negro Leagues, including the Pittsburgh Crawfords and the Homestead Grays. Inducted in the Hall of Fame in 1974.

Lyudmila Belousova/Oleg Protopov (no dates of birth available): Soviet figure skaters. Won Olympic gold medal in pairs competition in 1964 and 1968. Won four consecutive World and European championships (1965–68) and eight consecutive Soviet titles (1961–68).

Deane Beman (b. 4-22-38): Commissioner of the PGA Tour 1974–94. Won British Amateur title in 1959 and U.S. Amateur titles in 1960 and 1963.

Johnny Bench (b. 12-7-47): Baseball C. MVP in 1970, 1972; World Series MVP in 1976; Rookie of the Year in 1968. 389 career HR. League leader in HR 2 times, RBI 3 times. Career span 1967–83 with Cincinnati.

Patty Berg (b. 2-13-18): Golfer. Alltime women's leader in major championships (16), third alltime in career wins (57). Won Titleholders Championship (1937–39, 1948, 1953–54, 1957) and Western Open (1941, 1943, 1948, 1951, 1955, 1957–58) 7 times each, the most of any golfer. Also won U.S. Women's Amateur (1938) and U.S. Women's Open (1946).

Yogi Berra (b. 5-12-25): Baseball C. Played on 10 World Series winners. All-time Series leader in games, at bats, hits and doubles. MVP in 1951 and consecutively 1954–55. 358 career HR. Career span 1946–65. Also managed pennant-winning Yankees (1964) and NY Mets (1973).

Jay Berwanger (b. 3-19-14): College football RB. Won the first Heisman Trophy and named All-America with Chicago in 1935.

Raymond Berry (b. 2-27-33): Football E. Led NFL in receiving 1958–60. In 13-season career, caught 631 passes, 68 for TDs. Career span 1955–67, all with Baltimore Colts. Later coached New England Patriots from 1984–89 with 51–41 record.

George Best (b. 5-22-46): Irish soccer player. Led Manchester United to European Cup title in 1968. Named England's and Europe's Player of the Year in 1968. Played in North American Soccer League for Los Angeles (1976–78), Fort Lauderdale (1978–79) and San Jose (1980–81). Frequent troubles with alcohol and gambling overshadowed career.

Abebe Bikila (b. 8-7-32, d. 10-25-73): Track and field. Ethiopian barefoot runner won consecutive gold medals in the marathon at Olympics, in 1960 and 1964.

Fred Biletnikoff (b. 2-23-43): Football WR. In 14 pro seasons caught 589 passes for 8,974 yards and 76 TDs. In 1961 led NFL receivers with 61 catches; in '62 led AFC with 58. Career span 1965–78, all with Raiders. Elected to Pro Football Hall of Fame in 1988.

Dmitri Bilozerchev (b. 12-22-66): Soviet gymnast. Won 3 gold medals at 1988 Olympics. Made comeback after shattering his left leg into 44 pieces in 1985. Two-time world champion (1983, 1987). At 16, became youngest to win all-around world championship title in 1983.

Dave Bing (b. 11-24-43): Basketball G. Averaged 24.8 points a game in four years at Syracuse. NBA Rookie of Year in 1967. Led NBA in scoring (27.1) in 1968. MVP NBA All Star game in 1976. In 12 year career from 1967–78, most of it with Detroit Pistons, averaged 20.3 points.

Matt Biondi (b. 10-8-65): Swimmer. Winner of 5 gold medals, 1 silver medal and 1 bronze medal at 1988 Olympics. Won one gold and one silver at 1992 Olympics.

Larry Bird (b. 12-7-56): Basketball F. Won 3 consecutive MVP awards (1984–86) and 2 playoff MVP awards (1984, 1986). Also Rookie of the Year (1980) and All-Star 9 consecutive seasons. Has led league in free throw percentage 4 times. Averaged 20+ points 10 times. Career span 1979-1992 with Boston. Named College Player of the Year in 1979 with Indiana State.

Bonnie Blair (b. 3-18-64): Speed skater. Won gold medal in 500 meters and bronze medal in 1,000 meters

at 1988 Olympics and gold medals in both events in 1992 and '94. Also 1989 World Sprint champion. Winner of 1992 Sullivan Award.

Toe Blake (b. 8-21-12): Hockey LW and coach. Second alltime highest winning percentage (.640) and fifth in wins (582). Led Montreal to 8 Stanley Cup championships from 1955 to 1968 (consecutively 1956–60, 1965–66, 1968). Also MVP and scoring leader in 1939. Played on 2 Stanley Cup champions with Montreal from 1932 to 1948.

Doc Blanchard (b. 12-11-24): College football FB. "Mr. Inside." Teamed with Glenn Davis to lead Army to 3 consecutive undefeated seasons (1944–46) and 2 consecutive national championships (1944–45). Won Heisman Trophy and Sullivan Award in 1945. Also All-America 3 times.

George Blanda (b. 9-17-27): Football QB-K. Alltime leader in seasons played (26), games played (340), points scored (2,002) and points after touchdown (943); third in field goals (335). Also passed for 26,920 career yards and 236 touchdowns. Tied record with 7 touchdown passes on Nov. 19, 1961. Player of the Year 2 times (1961, 1970). Retired at age 48, the oldest to ever play. Career span 1949–75 with Chicago, Houston, Oakland.

Fanny Blankers-Koen (b. 4-26-18): Track and field. Dutch athlete won four gold medals at 1948 Olympics, in 100-meters; 200 meters; 80-meter hurdles; and 400-meter relay. Versatile, she also set world records in high jump (5' 7-1/4" in 1943), long jump (20' 6" in 1943) and pentathlon (4,692 points in 1951).

Wade Boggs (b. 6-15-58): Baseball 3B. Won 5 batting titles (1983, consecutively 1985–88); has had .350+ average 5 times, 200+ hits 7 times. Career span 1982–92 with Boston, 1993- with New York Yankees.

Nick Bollettieri (b. 7-31-31): Tennis coach. Since 1976, has run Nick Bollettieri Tennis Academy in Bradenton, Fla. Former residents of the academy include Andre Agassi, Monica Seles and Jim Courier.

Barry Bonds (b. 7-24-64): Baseball OF. Three-time National League MVP (1990, '92, '93). Career span 1986 to '92, with Pirates; 1993- with Giants.

Bjorn Borg (b. 6-6-56): Swedish tennis player. Second alltime men's leader in Grand Slam singles titles (11—tied with Rod Laver). Set modern record by winning 5 consecutive Wimbledon titles (1976–80). Won 6 French Open titles (consecutively 1974–75, 1978–81). Reached U.S. Open final 4 times, but title eluded him. 65 career tournament victories. Led Sweden to Davis Cup win in 1975.

Julius Boros (b. 3-3-20): Golfer. Won US. Opens in 1952 at Northwood CC in Dallas and in 1963 at The Country Club in Brookline, Mass. Also won 1968 PGA Championship at Pecan Valley CC, San Antonio, when 48 years old, making him oldest winner of a major ever. Led PGA money list in 1952 and '55.

Mike Bossy (b. 1-22-57): Hockey RW. In 1978 set NHL rookie scoring record of 54 goals, broken in 1993. Scored 50 or more each of first nine seasons, totaling 573 goals and 1,126 points in 10 seasons (1977–78 through 1986–87) with New York Islanders. Elected to Hall of Fame in 1991.

Ralph Boston (b. 5-9-39): Track and field. Long jumper won medals at 3 consecutive Olympics; gold in 1960, silver in 1964, bronze in 1968.

Ray Bourque (b. 12-28-60): Hockey D. Won Norris

Trophy as NHL's top defenseman five times. Career span since 1979 with Boston Bruins.

Scotty Bowman (b. 9-18-33): Hockey coach. Entered 1994–95 season with Detroit as alltime leader in regular season wins (878) and in regular season winning percentage (.654). Also alltime leader in playoff wins (140). Led Montreal to 5 Stanley Cups, and has also coached St Louis and Buffalo. Won Jack Adams Award, Coach of the Year, 1976–77.

Bill Bradley (b. 7-28-43): Basketball F. Played on 2 NBA championship teams with New York from 1967 to 1977. Player of the Year and NCAA tournament MVP in 1965 with Princeton; All-America 3 times; Sullivan Award winner in 1965. Rhodes scholar. U.S. Senator (D-NJ) since 1979.

Terry Bradshaw (b. 9-2-48): Football QB. Played on 4 Super Bowl champions (consecutively 1974–75, 1978–79); named Super Bowl MVP 2 consecutive seasons (1978–79). 212 career touchdown passes; 27,989 yards passing. Player of the Year in 1978. Career span 1970–83 with Pittsburgh.

George Brett (b. 5-15-53): Baseball 3B-1B. MVP in 1980 with .390 batting average; 3 batting titles, in 1976, 1980, 1990; and .300+ average 11 times. Led league in hits and triples 3 times. Reached 3,000-hit mark in 1992. Career span 1973–93, with Kansas City. Career totals: 3,153 hits; 317 HR; 1,595 RBIs; batting average .305.

Bret Hanover (b. 5-19-62): Horse. Son of Adios. Won 62 of 68 harness races and earned $922,616. Undefeated as two-year-old. From total of 1,694 foals, he sired winners of $61 million and 511 horses which have recorded sub-2:00 performances.

Lou Brock (b. 6-18-39): Baseball OF. Second alltime most stolen bases (938); second most season steals (118). Led league in steals 8 times, with 50+ steals 12 consecutive seasons. Alltime World Series leader in steals (14—tied with Eddie Collins); third in Series batting average (.391). 3,023 career hits. Career span 1961–79 with St Louis.

Jim Brown (b. 2-17-36): Football FB. Second alltime in touchdowns (126); and fourth in yards rushing (12,312). Led league in rushing a record 8 times. His 5.22-yards per carry average is also the best ever. Player of the Year 4 times (consecutively 1957–58, 1963, 1965) and Rookie of the Year in 1957. Rushed for 1,000+ yards in 7 seasons, 200+ yards in 4 games, 100+ yards in 54 other games. Career span 1957–65 with Cleveland; never missed a game. Also All-America with Syracuse.

Paul Brown (b. 9-7-08, d. 8-5-91): Football coach. Led Cleveland to 10 consecutive championship games. Won 4 consecutive AAFC titles (1946–49) and 3 NFL titles (1950, consecutively 1954–55). Coached Cleveland from 1946 to 1962; became first coach of Cincinnati, 1968–75, and then general manager. Career coaching record 222-113-9. Also won national championship with Ohio State in 1942.

Avery Brundage (b. 9-28-1887, d. 5-5-75): Amateur sports executive. President of International Olympic Committee 1952–72. Served as president of U.S. Olympic Committee 1929–53. Also president of Amateur Athletic Union 1928–35. Member of 1912 U.S. Olympic track and field team.

Paul "Bear" Bryant (b. 9-11-13, d. 1-26-83): College football coach. Alltime Division I-A leader in wins (323). Won 6 national championships (1961, consecutively 1964–65, 1973, consecutively 1978–79)

with Alabama. Career record 323–85–17, including 4 undefeated seasons. Also won 15 bowl games. Career span 1945–82 with Maryland, Kentucky, Texas A&M, Alabama.

Sergei Bubka (b. 12-4-63): Track and field. Ukrainian pole vaulter was gold medalist at 1988 Olympics. Only four-time world outdoor champion in any event (1983, 1987, 1991, 1993). First man to vault 20 feet, set world indoor record of 20' 2" on 2-21-93 and world outdoor record of 20' 1½", set on 9-20-92.

Buck Buchanan (b. 9-10-40): Football DT. Career span 1963–75 with Kansas City Chiefs. Elected to Pro Football Hall of Fame 1990.

Don Budge (b. 6-13-15): Tennis player. First player to achieve the Grand Slam, in 1938. Won 2 consecutive Wimbledon and U.S. singles titles (1937–38), 1 French and 1 Australian title (1938).

Dick Butkus (b. 12-9-42): Football LB. Recovered 25 opponents' fumbles, second most in history. Selected for Pro Bowl 8 times. Career span 1965–73 with Chicago. Also All-America 2 times with Illinois. Award recognizing the outstanding college linebacker named in his honor.

Dick Button (b. 7-18-29): Figure skater. Gold medalist at 2 consecutive Olympics in 1948, 1952. World champion 5 consecutive years (1948–52) and U.S. champion 7 consecutive years (1946–52). Sullivan Award winner in 1949.

Walter Byers (b. 3-13-22): Amateur sports executive. First executive director of NCAA, served from 1952 to 1987.

Frank Calder (b. 11-17-1877, d. 2-4-43): Hockey executive. First commissioner of NHL, served from 1917 to 1943. Rookie of the Year award named in his honor.

Walter Camp (b. 4-7-1859, d. 3-14-25): Football pioneer. Played for Yale in its first football game vs. Harvard on Nov. 17, 1876. Proposed rules such as 11 men per side, scrimmage line, center snap, yards and downs. Founded the All-America selections in 1889.

Roy Campanella (b. 11-19-21; d. 6-26-93): Baseball C. Career span 1948–57, ended when paralyzed in car crash. MVP in 1951, 1953, 1955. Played on 5 pennant winners; 1955 World Series winner with Brooklyn Dodgers.

Earl Campbell (b. 3-29-55): Football RB. Tenth alltime yards rushing (9,407); third alltime season yards rushing (1,934 in 1980) and touchdowns rushing (19 in 1979). Led league in rushing 3 consecutive seasons. Rushed for 1,000+ yards in 5 seasons. Scored 74 career touchdowns. Player of the Year 2 consecutive seasons (1978–79). Rookie of the Year in 1978. Career span 1978–85 with Houston, New Orleans. Won Heisman Trophy with Texas in 1977.

John Campbell (b. 4-8-55): Canadian harness racing driver. Alltime leading money winner with over $100 million in earnings. Leading money winner 1986–90. Has more than 5,500 career wins.

Billy Cannon (b. 2-8-37): Football RB. Led Louisiana State to national championship in 1958 and won Heisman Trophy in 1959. Signed contract in both NFL (Los Angeles) and AFL (Houston). Houston won lawsuit for his services. Played in 6 AFL championship games with Houston, Oakland, Kansas City. Career span 1960–70. Served three-year jail term for 1983 conviction on counterfeiting charges.

Jose Canseco (b. 7-2-64): Baseball OF. Only player to top 40 homers (42) and 40 (40) steals in same season (1988). AL MVP in 1988, when he also batted .307 with 124 RBIs. Career span 1985–1992 with Oakland and since 1992 with Texas Rangers.

Harry Caray (b. 3-1-17): Sportscaster. TV-radio baseball announcer since 1945 with St Louis (NL), Oakland, Chicago (AL) and Chicago (NL). Achieved celebrity status on Cubs' superstation WGN by singing "Take Me Out to the Ballgame" with Wrigley Field fans.

Rod Carew (b. 10-1-45): Baseball 2B-1B. Won 7 batting titles (1969, consecutively 1972–75, 1977–78). Had .328 career average, 3,053 career hits, and .300+ average 15 times. 1967 Rookie of the Year. Career span 1967–85; jersey number (29) retired by Minnesota and California.

Steve Carlton (b. 12-22-44): Baseball LHP. Second alltime most strikeouts (4,136). 4 Cy Young awards (1972, 1977, 1980, 1982). 329 career wins; won 20+ games 6 times. League leader in wins 4 times, innings pitched and strikeouts 5 times each. Struck out 19 batters in 1 game in 1969. Career span 1965–88 with St. Louis, Philadelphia and four other teams in last two years.

JoAnne Carner (b. 4-21-39): Golfer. Won 42 titles, including US Women's Opens in 1971 and '76 and du Maurier Classic in 1975 and '78. LPGA top earner in 1974 and 1982–83. LPGA Player of the Year in 1974 and 1981–82. Won five Vare Trophies (1974–75 and 1981–83).

Joe Carr (b. 10-22-1880; d. 5-20-39): Football administrator. Instrumental in forming American Professional Football Association in 1920. President of AAFA from 1922 to '39.

Don Carter (b. 7-29-26): Bowler. Won All-Star Tournament 4 times (1952, 1954, 1956, 1958) and PBA National Championship in 1960. Voted Bowler of the Year 6 times (consecutively 1953–54, 1957–58, 1960, 1962).

Alexander Cartwright (b. 4-17-1820, d. 7-12-1892): Baseball pioneer. Organized the first baseball game on June 19, 1846, and set the basic rules of bases 90 feet apart, 9 men per side, 3 strikes per out and 3 outs per inning. In that first game his New York Knickerbockers lost to the New York Nine 23–1 at Elysian Fields in Hoboken, NJ.

Billy Casper (b. 6-24-31): Golfer. Famed putter. Won 51 PGA tournaments. PGA Player of Year in both 1966 and '70. Won Vardon Trophy in 1960, '63, '64, '65 and '68. Won the US Open twice, in 1959 at Winged Foot in Mamaronek, New York, and in 1966 in 18-hole playoff over Arnold Palmer at Olympic Club, San Francisco. Beat Gene Littler in 18 hole playoff to win 1970 Masters.

Tracy Caulkins (b. 1-11-63): Swimmer. Won 3 gold medals at 1984 Olympics. Won 48 U.S. national titles, more than any other swimmer, from 1978 to 1984. Also won Sullivan Award in 1978.

Steve Cauthen (b. 5-1-60): Jockey. In 1978 became youngest jockey to win Triple Crown, aboard Affirmed. First jockey to top $6 million in season earnings (1977). *Sports Illustrated* Sportsman of Year for 1977. Moved to England in 1979. Among the 1,389 winners he had ridden in England through end of 1990 were two winners of Epsom Derby—Slip Anchor in 1985 and Reference Point in 1987.

Evonne Goolagong Cawley (b. 7-31-51): Tennis. Won 4 Australian Open titles from 1974 through '77; won '71 French Open; Wimbledon in 1971 and '80, Runnerup four straight years at U.S. Open (1973–76) which she never won.

Bill Chadwick (b. 10-10-15): Hockey referee. Spent 16 years as a referee despite vision in only one eye. Developed hand signals to signify penalties. Also former television announcer for the New York Rangers.

Wilt Chamberlain (b. 8-21-36): Basketball C. Alltime leader in rebounds (23,924) and rebounding average (22.9). Alltime season leader in points scored (4,029 in 1962), scoring average (50.4 in 1962), rebounding average (27.2 in 1961) and field goal percentage (.727 in 1973). Alltime single-game most points scored (100 in 1962) and most rebounds (55 in 1960). Second alltime most points scored (31,419) and most field goals made (12,681). 4 MVP awards (1960, consecutively 1966–68); playoff MVP in 1972 and 1960 Rookie of the Year. 7-time All-Star. 30.1 career scoring average. Career span 1959–72 with Philadelphia, Los Angeles. Also named College Player of the Year in 1957 at Kansas.

Colin Chapman (b. 1928, d. 12-16-83): Auto racing engineer. Founded Lotus race and street cars, designing the first Lotus racer in 1948. Introduced the monocoque design for Formula One cars in 1962 and ground effects in 1978. Four of his drivers, including Mario Andretti, won Formula One world championships.

Julio Cesar Chavez (b. 7-12-62): Boxer. Through 10-1-94 the current WBC junior welterweight champion has a career record of 91-1-1. But many thought he lost fight against Pernell Whitaker on 9-10-93 in Alamodome which ended officially as a "majority draw". Also won titles as super featherweight (1984–87) and lightweight (1987–89).

Gerry Cheevers (b. 12-7-40): Hockey goalie. Goaltender for Stanley Cup-winning Boston Bruins teams of 1970 and '72. In 12 seasons with Boston had 230-94-74 record with a goals against average of 2.89. Also coached Bruins from 1980–84, with 204-126-46 record. Elected to Hall of Fame 1985.

Citation (b. 4-11-45, d. 8-8-70): Thoroughbred race horse. Triple Crown winner in 1948 with jockey Eddie Arcaro aboard. Trained by Ben A. Jones.

King Clancy (b. 2-25-03, d. 11-6-86): Hockey D. Four-time All-Star. Coach, Montreal Maroons, Toronto. Referee. Trophy named in his honor, recognizing leadership qualities and contribution to community.

Jim Clark (b. 3-4-36, d. 4-7-68): Scottish auto racer. Fifth alltime in Formula 1 victories (25—tied with Niki Lauda). Formula 1 champion 2 times (1963, 1965). Won Indy 500 1 time (1965). Named Indy 500 Rookie of the Year in 1963. Killed during competition in 1968 at age 32.

Bobby Clarke (b. 8-13-49): Hockey C. Won MVP award 3 times (1973, consecutively 1975–76). 358 career goals, 852 assists. Led league in assists 2 consecutive seasons and scored 100+ points 3 times. Played on 2 consecutive Stanley Cup champions (1974–75) with Philadelphia. Career span 1969 to 1984. Also general manager with Philadelphia from 1984 to 1990, Minnesota 1991-92, Florida 1993-94, and Philadelphia since 1994.

Roger Clemens (b. 8-4-62): Baseball RHP. Record 20 strikeouts in 1 game. Won 2 consecutive Cy Young

Awards in 1986, 1987. Also 1986 MVP. League leader in ERA 4 times, wins and strikeouts 2 times each. Career span since 1984 with Boston.

Roberto Clemente (b. 8-18-34, d. 12-31-72): Baseball OF. Killed in plane crash while still an active player. Had 3,000 hits and .317 career average. 4 batting titles; .300+ average 13 times. 1966 MVP; 1971 World Series MVP. 12 consecutive Gold Gloves; led league in assists 5 times. Career span 1955–72 with Pittsburgh.

Ty Cobb (b. 12-18-1886, d. 7-17-61): Baseball OF. Alltime leader in batting average (.367) and runs scored (2,245); second most hits (4,191); fourth most stolen bases (892). 1911 MVP and 1909 Triple Crown winner. 12 batting titles. Had .400+ average 3 times, .350+ average 13 other times; 200+ hits 9 times. Led league in hits 7 times, steals 6 times and runs scored 5 times. Career span 1905–28 with Detroit.

Mickey Cochrane (b. 4-6-03, d. 6-28-62): Baseball C. Alltime highest career batting average among catchers (.320). MVP in 1928, 1934. Had .300+ average 8 times. Career span 1925–37 with Philadelphia, Detroit.

Sebastian Coe (b. 9-29-56): Track and field. British runner was gold medalist in 1,500 meters and silver medalist in 800 meters at 2 consecutive Olympics in 1980, 1984. World record holder in 800 meters (1:41.73 set in 1981) and 1,000 meters (2:12.18 set in 1981). Now a member of parliament.

Eddie Collins (b. 5-2-1887, d. 3-25-51): Baseball 2B. Alltime leader among 2nd basemen in games, chances and assists; led league in fielding 9 times. 3,311 career hits; .333 career average; .330+ average 12 times. Fifth alltime most stolen bases (743—tied with Tim Raines); alltime most World Series steals (14—tied with Lou Brock); alltime leader in single-game steals (6, twice). 1914 MVP. Career span 1906–30 with Philadelphia, Chicago.

Nadia Comaneci (b. 11-12-61): Romanian gymnast. First ever to score a perfect 10 at Olympics (on uneven parallel bars in 1976). Won 3 gold, 2 silver and 1 bronze medal at 1976 Olympics. Also won 2 gold and 2 silver medals at 1980 Olympics.

Dennis Conner (b. 9-16-42): Sailing. Captain of America's Cup winner 3 times (1980, '87, '88).

Maureen Connolly (b. 9-17-34, d. 6-21-69): Tennis player. "Little Mo" first woman to achieve the Grand Slam, in 1953. Won the U.S. singles title in 1951 at age 16. Thereafter lost only 4 matches before retiring in 1954 because of a broken leg caused by a riding accident. Was never beaten in singles at Wimbledon, winning 3 consecutive titles (1952–54). Won 3 consecutive U.S. singles titles (1951–53) and 2 consecutive French titles (1953–54). Also won 1 Australian title (1953).

Jimmy Connors (b. 9-2-52): Tennis player. Alltime men's leader in tournament victories (109). Held men's #1 ranking a record 159 consecutive weeks, July 29, 1974 through Aug. 16, 1977. Won 5 U.S. Open singles titles on 3 different surfaces (grass 1974, clay 1976, hard 1978, consecutively 1982–83). Won 2 Wimbledon singles titles (1974, 1982) farther apart than anyone since Bill Tilden. Also won 1974 Australian Open title. Reached Grand Slam final 7 other times.

Jim Corbett (b. 9-1-1866, d. 2-18-33): Boxer. "Gentleman Jim". Invented jab. Fight with Australian Peter Jackson on 5-21-91 ruled no contest when neither could continue into 62nd round. Won heavyweight title on 9-7-92 with a KO of John Sullivan in 21 rounds; it was first heavyweight title fight using gloves. Retained title with KO of British champ Charley Mitchell. Lost title when KO'd by Bob Fitzsimmons in 14 on 3-17-1897, then lost two bids to regain it against Jim Jeffries. Career record: 19 fights; won 7 by KO and 4 by decision; drew 2; lost 4; 2 no decision. Elected to Boxing Hall of Fame in 1954.

Angel Cordero (b. 11-8-42): Jockey. At end of 1993 third alltime in wins (7,057) and earnings ($164,526,217). Led yearly earnings three times, in 1976 and 1982–83, winning Eclipse Awards in the last two years.

Howard Cosell (b. 3-25-18): Sportscaster. Lawyer turned TV-radio sports commentator in 1953. Best known for his work on "Monday Night Football." His nasal voice and "tell it like it is" approach made him a controversial figure.

James "Doc" Counsilman (b. 12-28-20): Swimming coach. Coached Indiana from 1957 to 1990. Won 6 consecutive NCAA championships (1968–73). Career record 287–36–1. Coached U.S. men's team at Olympics in 1964, 1976. Also oldest person to swim English Channel (58 in 1979).

Count Fleet (b. 3-24-40, d. 12-3-73): Thoroughbred race horse. Triple Crown winner in 1943 with jockey Johnny Longden aboard. Trained by Don Cameron.

Yvan Cournoyer (b. 11-22-43): Hockey RW. "The Roadrunner" had 428 goals and 435 assists during his 15 season career with the Montreal Canadiens. Had 25 or more goals in 12 straight seasons. Played on 10 Stanley Cup championship teams. Elected to Hall of Fame in 1982.

Margaret Smith Court (b. 7-16-42): Australian tennis player. Alltime leader in Grand Slam singles titles (26) and total Grand Slam titles (66). Achieved Grand Slam in 1970 and mixed doubles Grand Slam in 1963 with Ken Fletcher. Won 11 Australian singles titles (consecutively 1960–66, 1969–71, 1973), 5 French titles (1962, 1964, consecutively 1969–70, 1973), 5 U.S. titles (1962, 1965, consecutively 1969–70, 1973) and 3 Wimbledon titles (1963, 1965, 1970). Also won 19 Grand Slam doubles titles and 19 mixed doubles titles.

Bob Cousy (b. 8-9-28): Basketball G. Seventh alltime most assists (6,955), second alltime most assists in a game (28 in 1958). League leader in assists 8 consecutive seasons. Averaged 18+ points and named to All-Star team 10 consecutive seasons. 1957 MVP. Played on 6 championship teams with Boston from 1950 to 1969. Also played on NCAA championship team in 1947 with Holy Cross.

Dave Cowens (b. 10-25-48): Basketball C. After college career at Florida State, NBA co-Rookie of Year in 1971. NBA MVP for 1973. All-Star game MVP in 1973. Career span 1970–71 through 1982–83, all but the last year with the Boston Celtics. Elected to Hall of Fame in 1991.

Ben Crenshaw (b. 1-11-52): Golfer. Legendary putter. Won 1984 Masters.

Larry Csonka (b. 12-25-46): Football RB. In 11 seasons rushed 1,891 times for 8,081 yards (4.3 per carry) and 64 TDs. MVP of Super Bowl VIII, when he rushed 33 times for a then Super Bowl record 145 yards in Miami's 24–7 defeat of Minnesota. Career span 1968–74, 1979 with Miami Dolphins; 1976–78 with New York Giants. Elected to Hall of Fame in 1987.

Billy Cunningham (b. 6-3-43): Basketball player and coach. Averaged 24.8 points a game at North Carolina. In nine seasons (1965–66 through 1975–76) with Philadelphia 76ers, averaged 20.8 points per game. All NBA first team 1969, '70 and '71. In 8 seasons as Sixer coach went 454–196 in season, 66–39 in playoffs and won NBA title in 1983. Elected to Hall of Fame in 1985.

Chuck Daly (b. 7-20-30): Basketball coach. Won 2 consecutive championships with Detroit (1989–90). Won 50+ games 4 consecutive seasons. Coach of 1992 Olympic team. Career span as pro coach 1983–92 with Pistons; 1992–94 with New Jersey Nets.

Damascus (b. 1964): Thoroughbred race horse. After finishing 3rd in 1967 Kentucky Derby, won the Preakness, the Belmont, the Dwyer, the American Derby, the Travers, the Woodward and others—12 of 16 starts. Unanimous Horse of the Year for 1967.

Stanley Dancer (b. 7-25-27): Harness racing driver. Only driver to win the Trotting Triple Crown 2 times (Nevele Pride in 1968, Super Bowl in 1972). Also won Pacing Triple Crown driving Most Happy Fella in 1970. Won The Hambletonian 4 times (1968, 1972, 1975, 1983). Driver of the Year in 1968.

Tamas Darnyi (b. 6-3-67): Hungarian swimmer. Gold medalist in 200-meter and 400-meter individual medleys at 1988 and 1992 Olympics. Also won both events at World Championships in 1986 and 1991. Set world records in these events at 1991 Championships (1:59.36 and 4:12.36).

Al Davis (b. 7-4-29): Football executive. Owner and general manager of Oakland-LA Raiders since 1963. Built winningest franchise in sports history (304-185-11—a .619 winning percentage entering the 1994 season). Team has won 3 Super Bowl championships (1976, 1980, 1983). Also served as AFL commissioner in 1966, helped negotiate AFL–NFL merger.

Ernie Davis (b. 12-14-39, d. 5-18-63): Football RB. Won Heisman Trophy in 1961, the first black man to win the award. All-America 3 times at Syracuse. First selection in 1962 NFL draft, but became fatally ill with leukemia and never played professionally.

Glenn Davis (b. 12-26-24): College football HB. "Mr. Outside." Teamed with Doc Blanchard to lead Army to 3 consecutive undefeated seasons (1944–46) and 2 consecutive national championships (1944–45). Won Heisman Trophy in 1946. Also named All-America 3 times.

John Davis (b. 1-12-21, d. 7-13-84): Weightlifter. Gold medalist at 2 consecutive Olympics in 1948, 1952. World champion 6 times.

Pete Dawkins (b. 3-8-38): Football RB. Starred at Army 1956–58. Won Heisman Trophy 1958. Was first captain of cadets, class president, top 5 percent of class academically, and football team captain; first man to do all four at West Point. Did not play pro football. Attended Oxford on Rhodes scholarship, won two Bronze Stars in Vietnam, rose to brigadier general before leaving Army to become investment banker. Made unsuccessful run for Senate from New Jersey in 1988.

Len Dawson (b. 6-20-35): Football QB. Completed 2,136 of 3,741 pass attempts with 239 TDs. In first Super Bowl threw for one TD in 35–10 loss to Green Bay. MVP of Super Bowl IV, which Kansas City won 23–7 over Minnesota. Career span 1957–75, the last 13 seasons with Kansas City Chiefs. Elected to Hall of Fame in 1987.

Dizzy Dean (b. 1-16-11, d. 7-17-74): Baseball RHP. 1934 MVP with 30 wins. League leader in strikeouts, complete games 4 times each. 150 career wins. Arm trouble shortened career after 134 wins by age 26. Career span 1930–41 and 1947 with St Louis and Chicago Cubs.

Dave DeBusschere (b. 10-16-40): Basketball F. NBA First Team Defense six straight seasons, 1969–74. Member of NBA champion New York Knicks in 1970 and '73. Career span 1962–63 through middle of 1968–69 season with Detroit Pistons; through 1973–74 with Knicks. Youngest coach (24) in NBA history. Elected to NBA Hall of Fame in 1982.

Pierre de Coubertin (b. 1-1-1863, d. 9-2-37): Frenchman called the father of the Modern Olympics. President of International Olympic Committee from 1896 to 1925.

Jack Dempsey (b. 6-24-1895, d. 5-31-83): Boxer. Heavyweight champion (1919–26), lost title to Gene Tunney and rematch in the famous "long count" bout in 1927. Career record 62-6-10 with 49 KOs from 1914 to 1928.

Gail Devers (b. 11-19-66): Track and field sprinter/hurdler. Won 100 at 1992 Olympics; leading 100 hurdles when she tripped over final hurdle and finished fifth. Successfully completed same double at 1993 World Championships, winning 100 in 10.82 and 100 hurdles in American record 12.46. Also won world indoor title in 60 (6.95). Battled Graves Disease.

Klaus Dibiasi (b. 10-6-47): Italian diver. Gold medalist in platform at 3 consecutive Olympics (1968, 1972, 1976) and silver medalist at 1964 Olympics.

Eric Dickerson (b. 9-2-60): Football RB. Alltime season leader in yards rushing (2,105 in 1984), second alltime most career yards rushing (13,259). Rushed for 1,000+ yards a record 7 consecutive seasons; 100+ yards in 61 games, including a record 12 times in 1984. Led league in rushing 4 times. Rookie of the Year in 1983. Career span 1983–93 with Los Angeles Rams, Indianapolis, L.A. Raiders and Atlanta Falcons.

Bill Dickey (b. 6-6-07): Baseball C. Lifetime average .313. Hit 202 career home runs. Played on 11 AL All-Star teams. In eight World Series, hit five homers and 24 RBIs. Career span 1928–43 and 1946, all with the New York Yankees. Inducted to Hall of Fame 1954.

Harrison Dillard (b. 7-8-23): Track and field. Only man to win Olympic gold medal in sprint (100 meters in 1948) and hurdles (110 meters in 1952). Sullivan Award winner in 1955.

Joe DiMaggio (b. 11-25-14): Baseball OF. Voted baseball's greatest living player. Record 56-game hitting streak in 1941. MVP in 1939, 1941, 1947. Had .325 career batting average; .300+ average 11 times; 100+ RBI 9 times. League leader in batting average, HR, and RBI 2 times each. Played on 10 World Series winners with NY Yankees. Career span 1936–51.

Mike Ditka (b. 10-18-39): Football TE-Coach. NFL Rookie of the Year in 1961. Named to Pro Bowl five times. Made 427 catches for 5,812 yards and 43 TDs. Career span 1961 to '72 with Bears, Eagles and Cowboys. Coach of Bears from 1982–92 with 112–68 overall record. Coach of Bear team that won Super Bowl XX, 46–10 over New England. Elected to Hall of Fame 1988.

Tony Dorsett (b. 4-7-54): Football RB. Third alltime in yards rushing (12,739), fourth in attempts (2,936).

Rushed for 1,000+ yards in 8 seasons. Set record for longest run from scrimmage with 99-yard touchdown run on January 3, 1983. Scored 91 career touchdowns. Named Rookie of the Year in 1977. Career span 1977–88 with Dallas, Denver. Also won Heisman Trophy in 1976, leading Pittsburgh to national championship. Alltime NCAA leader in yards rushing and only man to break 6,000-yard barrier (6,082).

Abner Doubleday (b. 6-26-1819, d. 1-26-1893): Civil War hero incorrectly credited as the inventor of baseball in Cooperstown, New York, in 1839. More recent research calls Alexander Cartwright the true father of the game.

Clyde Drexler (b. 6-22-62): Basketball G. Nicknamed "The Glide" for his smooth play. Member of U.S. "Dream Team" that won 1992 Olympic gold medal. Career span since 1984 with Portland Trail Blazers.

Don Drysdale (b. 7-23-36, d. 7-3-93): Baseball RHP. Led NL three times in strikeouts (1959, '60, '62) and once in wins (1962). Won 1962 Cy Young Award with 25–9 mark. In 1968 pitched six straight shutouts en route to major league record—broken in 1988 by Orel Hershiser—of 58 consecutive scoreless innings. Career record of 209–166, with 2,484 K's and ERA of 2.95. Career span 1956–69, all with Dodgers. Inducted into Hall of Fame 1984.

Ken Dryden (b. 8-8-47): Hockey G. Goaltender of the Year 5 times (1973, consecutively 1976–79). Playoff MVP as a rookie in 1971, maintained rookie status and named Rookie of the Year in 1972. Led league in goals against average 4 times, wins and shutouts 4 times each. Career record 258-57-74, including 46 shutouts. Career 2.24 goals against average is the modern record. Second alltime in playoff wins (80). Tied record of 4 playoff shutouts in 1977. Played on 6 Stanley Cup champions with Montreal from 1970 to 1979.

Roberto Duran (b. 6-16-51): Panamanian boxer. Champion in 3 different weight classes: lightweight (1972–79), welterweight (1980, lost rematch to Sugar Ray Leonard in famous "no mas" bout) and junior middleweight (1983–84). Career record 90–9 with 62 KOs since 1967.

Leo Durocher (b. 7-27-05, d. 10-7-91): Baseball manager. "Leo the Lip." Said "Nice guys finish last." Managed 3 pennant winners and 1954 World Series winner. Won 2,008 games in 24 years. Led Brooklyn 1939–48; New York 1948–55; Chicago 1966–72; and Houston 1972–73.

Eddie Eagan (b. 4-26-1898, d. 6-14-67): Only American athlete to win gold medal at Summer and Winter Olympic Games (boxing 1920, bobsled 1932).

Alan Eagleson (b. 4-24-33): Hockey labor leader. Founder of NHL Players' Association and its executive director from 1967–92.

Dale Earnhardt (b. 4-29-52): Auto racer. NASCAR champion 5 times (1980, 1986–87, 1990–91). 62 career NASCAR victories through 9-18-94.

Stefan Edberg (b. 1-19-66): Swedish tennis player. Has won 2 Wimbledon singles titles (1988, 1990), 2 Australian Open titles (1985, 1987) and 2 U.S. Open titles (1991, 1992). Led Sweden to 3 Davis Cup victories (consecutively 1984–85, 1987).

Gertrude Ederle (b. 10-23-06): Swimmer. First woman to swim the English Channel, in 1926. Swam 21 miles from England to France in 14:39. Also won 3 medals at the 1924 Olympics.

Herb Elliott (b. 2-25-38): Track and field. Australian runner was gold medalist in 1960 Olympic 1,500 meters in world record 3:35.6. Also set world mile record of 3:54.5 in 1958. Undefeated at 1500 meters/mile in international competition. Retired at 21.

John Elway (b. 6-28-60): Football QB. First player taken in 1983 NFL draft. Topped 3,000 yards passing every season from 1985–91. Through '93 season had thrown for 34,246 yards, 183 TDs. Famous for last minute drives, 32 of which won games in fourth quarter. Career span since 1983 with Denver Broncos.

Roy Emerson (b. 11-3-36): Australian tennis player. Alltime men's leader in Grand Slam singles titles (12). Won 6 Australian titles, 5 consecutively (1961, 1963–67), 2 consecutive Wimbledon titles (1964–65), 2 U.S. titles (1961, 1964) and 2 French titles (1963, 1967). Also won 13 Grand Slam doubles titles.

Kornelia Ender (b. 10-25-58): East German swimmer. Won 4 gold medals at 1976 Olympics and 3 silver medals at 1972 Olympics.

Julius Erving (b. 2-22-50): "Dr. J." Basketball F. Third alltime most points scored for combined ABA and NBA career (30,026). 24.2 scoring average. Averaged 20+ points 14 consecutive seasons. 4 MVP awards, consecutively 1974–76, 1981; playoff MVP 1974, 1976. All-Star 9 times. Led league in scoring 3 times. Played on 3 championship teams, with New York (ABA) and Philadelphia (NBA). Career span 1971 to 1986.

Phil Esposito (b. 2-20-42): Hockey C. "Espo." First to break the 100-point barrier (126 in 1969). Fourth alltime in points (1,590) and goals (717), sixth in assists (873). Led league in goals 6 consecutive seasons, points 5 times and assists 3 times. Won MVP award 2 times (1969, 1974). Scored 30+ goals 13 consecutive seasons and 100+ points 6 times. All-Star 6 times. Career span 1963–81 with Chicago, Boston, NY Rangers. Also general manager of NY Rangers from 1986 to 1989. Currently general manager of Tampa Bay.

Tony Esposito (b. 4-23-43): Hockey goalie. Brother of Phil. A five-time All Star during 16-season NHL career, almost all of it with the Chicago Blackhawks. In 886 games gave up 2,563 goals, an average of 2.92 per game. Won or shared Vezina Trophy three times. Elected to Hall of Fame in 1988.

Janet Evans (b. 8-28-71): Swimmer. Won 3 gold medals at 1988 Olympics and 1 at 1992 Olympics. Set world record in 400-meter freestyle (4:03.85 in 1988), 800-meter freestyle (8:16.22 in 1989) and 1,500-meter freestyle (15:52.10 in 1988). Sullivan Award winner in 1989.

Lee Evans (b. 2-25-47): Track and field. Gold medalist in 400 meters at 1968 Olympics with world record time of 43.86 that stood until 1988.

Chris Evert (b. 12-21-54): Also Chris Evert Lloyd. Tennis player. Second alltime in tournament victories (157). Third alltime in women's Grand Slam singles titles (18—tied with Martina Navratilova). Won at least 1 Grand Slam singles title every year from 1974 to 1986. Won 7 French Open titles (1974–75, 1979–1980, 1983, 1985–86), 6 U.S. Open titles (1975–77, 1978, 1980, 1982), 3 Wimbledon titles (1974, 1976, 1981) and 2 Australian Open titles (1982, 1984). Reached Grand Slam finals 16 other times. Reached semifinals at 52 of her last 56 Grand Slam tournaments.

Weeb Ewbank (b. 5-6-07): Football coach. Only coach to win titles in both the NFL and AFL. Coached Baltimore Colts to classic overtime defeat of New York Giants in 1958 and New York Jets to their stunning 16–7 win over Baltimore in Super Bowl III. Career record of 134-130-7. Career span 1954–62 with Colts and 1963–73 with Jets. Elected to Hall of Fame in 1978.

Patrick Ewing (b. 8-5-62): Basketball C. 1986 Rookie of the Year with New York. 20+ points average in all 9 seasons with Knicks. All-NBA first team 1990. Nine-season career scoring average of 23.8 through start of 1994–95 season. Played on 3 NCAA final teams with Georgetown (1982, 1984–85); tournament MVP in 1984. All-America 3 times.

Nick Faldo (b. 7-18-57): British golfer. Winner of the Masters 2 consecutive years (1989–90) and British Open 3 times (1987, 1990, 1992).

Juan Manuel Fangio (b. 6-24-11): Argentinian auto racer. Seventh all-time in Formula 1 victories (24, but in just 51 starts). Formula 1 champion 5 times, the most of any driver (1951, consecutively 1954–57). Retired in 1958.

Bob Feller (b. 11-3-18): Baseball RHP. League leader in wins 6 times, strikeouts 7 times, innings pitched 5 times. Pitched 3 no-hitters and 12 one-hitters. 266 career wins; 2,581 career strikeouts. Won 20+ games 6 times. Served 4 years in military during career. Career span 1936–41, 1945–56 with Cleveland.

Tom Ferguson (b. 12-20-50): Rodeo. First to top $1 million in career earnings. All-Around champion 6 consecutive years (1974–79).

Enzo Ferrari (b. 2-8-1898, d. 8-14-88): Auto racing engineer. Team owner since 1929, he built first Ferrari race car in Italy in 1947 and continued to preside over Ferrari race and street cars until his death. In 61 years of competition, Ferrari's cars have won over 5,000 races.

Mark Fidrych (b. 8-14-54): Baseball RHP. "The Bird." Rookie of the Year in 1976 with Detroit. Had 19–9 record with league-best 2.39 ERA and 24 complete games. Habit of talking to the ball on the mound made him a cult hero. Arm injuries curtailed career.

Cecil Fielder (b. 9-21-63): Baseball 1B. The last man to hit 50+ HR (51 in 1990). Has led the major leagues in HR twice and RBI 3 consecutive seasons (1990–92) after spending 1989 season in Japanese league. Career span since 1985 with Toronto, Detroit.

Herve Filion (b. 2-1-40): Harness racing driver. Alltime leader in career wins (more than 13,000). Driver of the Year 10 times, more than any other driver (consecutively 1969–74, 1978, 1981, 1989).

Rollie Fingers (b. 8-25-46): Baseball RHP. Third alltime in saves (341); third in relief wins (107); fifth in appearances (944). 1981 Cy Young and MVP winner; 1974 World Series MVP. Alltime Series leader in saves (6). Career span 1968–85 with Oakland, San Diego, Milwaukee.

Bobby Fischer (b. 3-9-43): Chess. World champion from 1972 to 1975, the only American to hold title. Never played competitive chess during his reign. Forfeited title to Anatoly Karpov by refusing to play him.

Carlton Fisk (b. 12-26-47): Baseball C. Alltime HR leader among catchers (352) and second in games caught (2,226). 376 career HR, including a record 75 after age 40. Rookie of the Year in 1972 and All-Star 11 times. Hit dramatic 12th-inning HR to win Game 6 of

1975 World Series. Career span 1969-93 with Boston, Chicago (AL).

Emerson Fittipaldi (b. 12-12-46): Brazilian auto racer. Won Indy 500 in 1989 and '93. Won CART championship in 1989. Currently 21 career CART victories and 14 career Formula 1 victories. Formula 1 champion 2 times (1972, 1974).

James Fitzsimmons (b. 7-23-1874, d. 3-11-66): Horse racing trainer. "Sunny Jim." Trained Triple Crown winner 2 times (Gallant Fox in 1930, Omaha in 1935). Trained Belmont Stakes winner 6 times (1930, 1932, consecutively 1935–36, 1939, 1955), Preakness Stakes winner 4 times (1930, 1935, 1955, 1957) and Kentucky Derby winner 3 times (1930, 1935, 1939).

Peggy Fleming (b. 7-27-48): Figure skater. Gold medalist at 1968 Olympics. World champion 3 consecutive years (1966–68) and U.S. champion 5 consecutive years (1964–68).

Curt Flood (b. 1-18-38): Baseball OF. Won 7 consecutive Gold Gloves from 1963 to 1969. Career batting average of .293. Refused to be traded after 1969 season, challenging baseball's reserve clause. Supreme Court rejected his plea, but baseball was eventually forced to adopt free agency system. Career span 1956–69 with St. Louis.

Whitey Ford (b. 10-21-26): Baseball LHP. All-time World Series leader in wins, losses, games started, innings pitched, hits allowed, walks and strikeouts. 236 career wins, 2.75 ERA. Third alltime best career winning percentage (.690). Led league in wins and winning percentage 3 times each; ERA, shutouts, innings pitched 2 times each. 1961 Cy Young winner and World Series MVP. Career span 1950, 1953–67 with New York Yankees.

Forego (b. 1970): Thoroughbred race horse. Horse of the Year in 1974 (won 8 of 13 starts); '75 (won 6 of 9); and '76 (won 6 of 8). Finished fourth in 1973 Kentucky Derby. Over six years won 34 of 57 starts and $1,938,957.

George Foreman (b. 1-22-48): Boxer. Heavyweight champion (1973–74). Retired in 1977, but returned to the ring in 1987. Lost 12–round decision to champion Evander Holyfield in 1991. Retired after losing to Tommy Morrison 6-7-93. Career record 72–4 with 67 KOs since 1969. Also heavyweight gold medalist at 1968 Olympics.

Dick Fosbury (b. 3-6-47): Track and field. Gold medalist in high jump at 1968 Olympics. Introduced back-to-the-bar style of high jumping, called the "Fosbury Flop."

Jimmie Foxx (b. 10-22-07, d. 7-21-67): Baseball 1B. Won 3 MVP awards, consecutively 1932–33, 1938. Fourth alltime highest slugging average (.609), with 534 career HR; hit 30+ HR 12 consecutive seasons, 100+ RBI 13 consecutive seasons. Won Triple Crown in 1933. Led league in HR 4 times, batting average 2 times. Career span 1925–45 with Philadelphia, Boston.

A. J. Foyt (b. 1-16-35): Auto racer. Alltime leader in Indy Car victories (67). Won Indy 500 4 times (1961, 1964, 1967, 1977), Daytona 500 1 time (1972), 24 Hours of Daytona 2 times (1983, 1985) and 24 Hours of LeMans 1 time (1967). USAC champion 7 times, more than any other driver (consecutively 1960–61, 1963–64, 1967, 1975, 1979).

William H. G. France (b. 9-26-09): Auto racing executive. Founder of NASCAR and president from

1948 to 1972, succeeded by his son Bill Jr. Builder of Daytona and Talladega speedways.

Dawn Fraser (b. 9-4-37): Australian swimmer. Only swimmer to win gold medal in same event at 3 consecutive Olympics (100-meter freestyle in 1956, 1960, 1964). First woman to break the 1-minute barrier at 100 meters (59.9 in 1962).

Joe Frazier (b. 1-12-44): Boxer. "Smokin' Joe." Heavyweight champion (1970–73). Best known for his 3 epic bouts with Muhammad Ali. Career record 32-4-1 with 27 KOs from 1965 to 1976. Also heavyweight gold medalist at 1964 Olympics.

Walt Frazier (b. 3-29-45): Basketball G. Point guard on championship Knick teams of 1970 and '73. First team All Star in 1970, '72, '74 and '75. First team All Defense every year from 1969–1975. Averaged 18.9 points per game in 13-season NBA career. Elected to Hall of Fame in 1986.

Frankie Frisch (b. 9-9-98, d. 3-12-73): Baseball IN. "The Fordham Flash." Led NL in hits in 1923 (223). Hit over .300 13 seasons. Scored 100+ runs 7 times. Drove in 100+ runs three times. Career .316 batting average. Career span 1919–36, with New York Giants and 1927–37 with St. Louis Cardinals "Gashouse Gang." NL MVP in 1931. Elected to Hall of Fame in 1947.

Dan Gable (b. 10-25-48): Wrestler. Gold medalist in 149–pound division at 1972 Olympics. Also NCAA champion 2 times (in 1968 at 130 pounds, in 1969 at 137 pounds). Career record 118–1. Coached Iowa to NCAA championship 12 years (consecutively 1978–86 and 1991–93).

Clarence Gaines (b. 5-21-23): College basketball coach. "Bighouse." Retired after 1992-93 season with 828 career wins in 46 seasons at Division II Winston-Salem State since 1947.

John Galbreath (b. 8-10-1897, d. 7-20-88): Horse racing owner. Owner of Darby Dan Farms from 1935 until his death and of baseball's Pittsburgh Pirates from 1946 to 1985. Only man to breed and own winners of both the Kentucky Derby (Chateaugay in 1963 and Proud Clarion in 1967) and the Epsom Derby (Roberto in 1972).

Gallant Fox (b. 3-23-27, d. 11-13-54): Thoroughbred race horse. Triple Crown winner in 1930 with jockey Earle Sande aboard. Trained by James Fitzsimmons. The only Triple Crown winner to sire another Triple Crown winner (Omaha in 1935).

Don Garlits (b. 1-14-32): Auto racer. "Big Daddy." Has won 35 National Hot Rod Association top fuel events. Sixth on alltime NHRA national event win list. Won 3 NHRA top fuel points titles (1975, 1985–86). First top fuel driver to surpass 190 mph (1963), 200 mph (1964), 240 mph (1973), 250 mph (1975) and 270 mph (1986). Credited with developing rear engine dragster.

Lou Gehrig (b. 6-19-03, d. 6-2-41): Baseball 1B. "The Iron Horse." All-time leader in consecutive games played (2,130) and grand slam HR (23), third in RBI (1,990) and slugging average (.632). MVP in 1927, 1936; won Triple Crown in 1934. .340 career average; 493 career HR. 100+ RBI 13 consecutive seasons. Led league in RBI 5 times and HR 3 times. Played on 7 World Series winners with New York Yankees. Died of disease since named for him. Career span 1923–39.

Bernie Geoffrion (b. 2-16-31): Hockey RW. "Boom Boom" for his powerful slapshot. Won Hart Memorial

Trophy for 1960–61. Scored 393 goals and 429 assists in 16 seasons (1950–51 through 1967–68), the first 14 with the Montreal Canadiens, the final two with the New York Rangers. Elected to Hall of Fame 1972.

Eddie Giacomin (b. 6-6-39): Hockey goalie. "Fast Eddie" led NHL goalies in games won for three straight seasons. Shared Vezina Trophy for 1970–71. In 610 games gave up 1,675 goals, a goals against average of 2.82. Career span 1965–75 with the New York Rangers and 1975–78 with Detroit Red Wings.

Althea Gibson (b. 8-25-27): Tennis player. Won 2 consecutive Wimbledon and U.S. singles titles (1957–58), the first black player to win these tournaments. Also won 1 French title (1956).

Bob Gibson (b. 11-9-35): Baseball RHP. 1968 Cy Young and MVP award winner with alltime National League best in ERA (1.12) and second most shutouts (13). Also 1970 Cy Young award winner. Record holder for most strikeouts in a World Series game (17); Series MVP in 1964, 1967. Won 20+ games 5 times. 251 career wins; 3,117 strikeouts. Pitched no-hitter in 1971. Career span 1959–75 with St. Louis.

Josh Gibson (b. 12-21-11, d. 1-20-47): Baseball C in Negro leagues. "The Black Babe Ruth." Couldn't play in major leagues because of color. Credited with 950 HR (75 in 1931, 69 in 1934) and .350 batting average. Had .400+ average 2 times. Career span 1930–46 with Homestead Grays, Pittsburgh Crawfords.

Kirk Gibson (b. 5-28-57): Baseball OF. Played on 2 World Series champions (Detroit in 1984 and Los Angeles in 1988). Hit dramatic pinch-hit HR in 9th inning to win Game 1 of 1988 series. MVP in 1988. Career span since 1979, currently with Detroit. Also starred in baseball and football at Michigan State.

Frank Gifford (b. 8-16-30): Football RB. NFL Player of Year in 1956 when he rushed for 819 yards and caught 51 passes. Played in seven Pro Bowls. Retired for one season after ferocious hit by Chuck Bednarik. Career span 1952–60 and 1962–64, all with New York Giants. Elected to Hall of Fame in 1977.

Rod Gilbert (b. 7-1-41): Hockey RW. Played 16 seasons, all with the New York Rangers (1960–61 through 1977–78), and had 406 goals and 615 assists. Elected to Hall of Fame 1982.

Sid Gillman (b. 10-26-11): Football coach. Developed wide-open, pass-oriented style of offense, introduced techniques for situational player substitutions and the study of game films. Won one division title with Los Angeles Rams and five division titles and one AFL championship (1963) with Los Angeles/San Diego Chargers. Career span 1955–59 Los Angeles Rams; 1960 Los Angeles Chargers; 1961–69 San Diego; 1973–74 Houston. Lifetime record 124-101-7. Also general manager in San Diego and Houston.

Pancho Gonzales (b. 5-9-28): Tennis player. Won 2 consecutive U.S. singles titles (1948–49). In 1969, at age 41, beat Charlie Pasarell 22–24, 1–6, 16–14, 6–3, 11–9 in longest Wimbledon match ever (5:12).

Shane Gould (b. 11-23-56): Australian swimmer. Won 3 gold medals, 1 silver and 1 bronze at 1972 Olympics. Set 11 world records over 23-month period beginning in 1971. Held world record in 5 freestyle distances ranging from 100 meters to 1,500 meters in late 1971 and 1972. Retired at age 16.

Steffi Graf (b. 6-14-69): German tennis player. Achieved the Grand Slam in 1988. Has won 3

Australian Open singles titles (1988–90), 5 Wimbledon titles (1988–89, 1991–93), 3 French Open titles (1987–88 and '93) and 3 U.S. Open titles (1988–89 and '93). Held the #1 ranking a record 186 weeks; Aug. 17, 1987 through March 10, 1991. Also, gold medalist at 1988 Olympics.

Otto Graham (b. 12-6-21): Football QB. Led Cleveland to 10 championship games in his 10-year career. Played on 4 consecutive AAFC champions (1946–49) and 3 NFL champions (1950, consecutively 1954–55). Combined league totals: 23,584 yards passing, 174 touchdown passes. Player of the Year 2 times (1953, 1955). Led league in passing 6 times. Career span 1946–55.

Red Grange (b. 6-13-03, d. 1-28-91): Football HB. "The Galloping Ghost." All-America 3 consecutive seasons with Illinois (1923–25), scoring 31 touchdowns in 20-game collegiate career. Signed by George Halas of Chicago in 1925, attracted sellout crowds across the country. Established the first AFL with manager C. C. Pyle in 1926, but league folded after 1 year. Career span 1925–34 with Chicago, New York.

Rocky Graziano (b. 6-7-22, d. 5-22-90): Boxer. Middleweight champion from 1947 to 1948. Career record 67–13. Endured 3 brutal title fights against Tony Zale, with Zale winning by KO in 1946 and 1948, and Graziano winning by KO in 1947.

Hank Greenberg (b. 1-1-11, d. 9-4-86): Baseball 1B. 331 career HR (58 in 1938). MVP in 1935, 1940. League leader in HR and RBI 4 times each. Fifth alltime highest slugging average (.605). 100+ RBI 7 times. Career span 1933-41, 1945-47 with Detroit, Pittsburgh.

Joe Greene (b. 9-24-46): Football DT. "Mean Joe." Anchored Pittsburgh's famed "Steel Curtain" defense. Selected for Pro Bowl 10 times. Played on 4 Super Bowl champions (consecutively 1974-75, 1978-79). Career span 1969 to 1981.

Forrest Gregg (b. 10-18-33): Football OT/G. Played in then-record 188 straight games from 1956 through 1971. Named all-NFL eight straight years starting in 1960. Career span 1956–71, most of it with Green Bay Packers. Played on winning Packer team in first two Super Bowls. Inducted into Hall of Fame in 1977.

Wayne Gretzky (b. 1-26-61): Hockey C. "The Great One." Most dominant player in history. Alltime scoring leader in points (2,458), assists (1,655), and goals (803). Alltime single season scoring leader in points (215 in 1986), goals (92 in 1982) and assists (163 in 1986). Has won MVP award 9 times, more than any other player (consecutively 1980-87, 1989). Led league in assists 14 times, scoring 11 times, goals 5 times. Scored 200+ points 4 times, 100+ points 9 other times; 70+ goals 4 consecutive seasons, 50+ goals 5 other times; 100+ assists 11 consecutive seasons. Also alltime playoff scoring leader in points (346), goals (110) and assists (236). Playoff MVP 2 times (1985, 1988). All-Star 8 times. Played on 5 Stanley Cup champions with Edmonton from 1978 to 1988. Traded to Los Angeles on Aug. 9, 1988.

Bob Griese (b. 2-3-45): Football QB. Career span 1967–80 with Miami Dolphins. Played in three straight Super Bowls, 1971–73. Quarterback of 1972 Dolphin team that went 17–0. Won Super Bowl VII and VIII. In 14 seasons completed 1,926 passes for 25,092 yards and 192 TDs. Elected to Hall of Fame in 1990.

Archie Griffin (b. 8-21-54): College football RB. Only player to win the Heisman Trophy 2 times

(consecutively 1974-75), with Ohio State. Fourth alltime NCAA most yards rushing (5,177), his 6.13 yards per carry is the collegiate record. Professional career span 1976-83 with Cincinnati; totaled 2,808 yards rushing and 192 receptions.

Lefty Grove (b. 3-6-00, d. 5-22-75): Baseball LHP. 300 career wins and fourth alltime highest winning percentage (.680). League leader in ERA 9 times, strikeouts 7 consecutive seasons. Won 20+ games 8 times. 1931 MVP. Career span 1925-41 with Philadelphia, Boston.

Tony Gwynn (b. 5-9-60): Baseball OF. 5 batting titles (1984, consecutively 1987-89, '94). League leader in hits 5 times, with .300+ average 10 times, 200+ hits 4 times. Career span since 1982 with San Diego.

Walter Hagen (b. 12-21-1892, d. 10-5-69): Golfer. Third alltime leader in major championships (11). Won PGA Championship 5 times (1921, consecutively 1924-27), British Open 4 times (1922, 1924, consecutively 1928-29) and U.S. Open 2 times (1914, 1919). Won 40 career tournaments.

Marvin Hagler (b. 5-23-54): Boxer. "Marvelous." Middleweight champion (1980-87). Career record 62-3-2 with 52 KOs from 1973 to 1987. Defended title 13 times.

George Halas (b. 2-2-1895, d. 10-31-83): Football owner and coach. "Papa Bear." Alltime leader in seasons coaching (40) and second in wins (324). Career record 324-151-31 intermittently from 1920 to 1967. Remained as owner until his death. Chicago won a record 7 NFL championships during his tenure.

Glenn Hall (b. 10-3-31): Hockey goalie. "Mr. Goalie" was an All-Star goalie in 11 of his 18 seasons. Set record for consecutive games by a goaltender, with 502, and ended career with goals against average of 2.51. Won or shared Vezina Trophy three times. Career span 1952–53 through 1970–71.

Arthur B. "Bull" Hancock (b. 1-24-10, d. 9-14-72): Horse racing owner. Owner of Claiborne Farm and arguably the greatest breeder in history. For 15 straight years, from 1955 to 1969, a Claiborne stallion led the sire list. Foaled at Claiborne Farm were 4 Horses of the Year (Kelso, Round Table, Bold Ruler and Nashua).

Tom Harmon (b. 9-28-19, d. 3-17-90): Football RB. Won Heisman Trophy in 1940 with Michigan. Triple-threat back led nation in scoring and named All-America 2 consecutive seasons (1939-40). Awarded Silver Star and Purple Heart in World War II. Played in NFL with Los Angeles (1946-47).

Franco Harris (b. 3-7-50): Football RB. Fifth alltime most rushing yards (12,120) and fifth in rushing touchdowns (91). Rushed for 1,000+ yards in 8 seasons, 100+ yards in 47 games. Scored 100 career touchdowns. Selected for Pro Bowl 9 times. Rookie of the Year in 1972. Played on 4 Super Bowl champions (consecutively 1974-75, 1978-79) with Pittsburgh. Super Bowl MVP in 1974. Holds Super Bowl record for most rushing yards (354) and most rushing touchdowns (4). Made the "Immaculate Reception" to win 1972 playoff game against Oakland. Career span 1972-83 with Pittsburgh.

Leon Hart (b. 11-2-28): Football DE. Won Heisman Trophy in 1949, the last lineman to win the award. Played on 3 national champions with Notre Dame (consecutively 1946-47, 1949) and the Irish went undefeated during his 4 years (36-0-2). Also played on 3 NFL champions with Detroit. Career span 1950-57.

Bill Hartack (b. 12-9-32): Horse racing jockey. Rode Kentucky Derby winner 5 times (1957, 1960, 1962, 1964, 1969), Preakness Stakes winner 3 times (1956, 1964, 1969) and Belmont Stakes winner 1 time (1960).

Doug Harvey (b. 12-19-24, d. 12-26-90): Hockey D. Defensive Player of the Year 7 times (consecutively 1954-57, 1959-61). Led league in assists in 1954. All-Star 10 times. Played on 6 Stanley Cup champions with Montreal from 1947 to 1968.

Billy Haughton (b. 11-2-23, d. 7-15-86): Harness racing driver. Won the Pacing Triple Crown driving Rum Customer in 1968. Won The Hambletonian 4 times (1974, consecutively 1976-77, 1980).

John Havlicek (b. 4-8-40): Basketball F/G. Member of Ohio State team that won 1960 NCAA title. "Hondo" averaged 20.8 points per game over 16-season NBA career, all with Boston. First team NBA All Star in 1971, '72, '73 and '74. Member of eight Celtic teams that won NBA title. Playoff MVP 1974. Elected to Hall of Fame in 1983.

Elvin Hayes (b. 11-17-45): Basketball C. 1968 *Sporting News* College Player of Year as Houston senior. Averaged 21.0 points per game over 16-season NBA career. Led NBA in scoring (28.4) in 1969 and in rebounding in 1970 (16.9 per game) and '74 (18.1). First team All NBA in 1975, '77 and '79. Elected to Hall of Fame in 1989.

Woody Hayes (b. 2-14-13, d. 3-12-87): College football coach. Sixth alltime in wins (238). Won national championship 3 times (1954, 1957, 1968) and Rose Bowl 4 times. Career record 238-72-10, including 4 undefeated seasons, with Ohio State from 1951 to 1978. Forced to resign after striking an opposing player during 1978 Gator Bowl.

Marques Haynes (b. 10-3-26): Basketball G. Known as "The World's Greatest Dribbler." Since 1946 has barnstormed more than 4 million miles throughout 97 countries for the Harlem Globetrotters, Harlem Magicians, Meadowlark Lemon's Bucketeers, Harlem Wizards.

Thomas Hearns (b. 10-18-58): Boxer. "Hit Man." Champion in 5 different weight classes: junior middleweight, light heavyweight, middleweight, super middleweight, and light heavyweight.

Eric Heiden (b. 6-14-58): Speed skater. Won 5 gold medals at 1980 Olympics. World champion 3 consecutive years (1977-79). Also won Sullivan Award in 1980.

Carol Heiss (b. 1-20-40): Figure skater. Gold medalist at 1960 Olympics, silver medalist at 1956 Olympics. World champion 5 consecutive years (1956-60) and U.S. champion 4 consecutive years (1957-60). Married 1956 gold medalist Hayes Jenkins.

Rickey Henderson (b. 12-25-57): Baseball OF. Alltime career stolen base leader (1117); alltime season stolen base record holder (130) in 1982. Led league in steals 11 times. Scored 100+ runs 11 times. 1990 MVP. Alltime most HR leading off game. Career span since 1979 with Oakland, New York and Toronto.

Sonja Henie (b. 4-8-12, d. 10-12-69): Norwegian figure skater. Gold medalist at 3 consecutive Olympics (1928, 1932, 1936). World champion 10 consecutive years (1927-36).

Orel Hershiser (b. 9-16-58): Baseball RHP. Alltime leader most consecutive scoreless innings pitched (59 in 1988). Cy Young Award winner in 1988 and World Series MVP. Career span since 1983 with Los Angeles.

Foster Hewitt (b. 11-21-02, d. 4-22-85): Hockey sportscaster. In 1923, aired one of hockey's first radio broadcasts. Became the voice of hockey in Canada on radio and later television. Famous for the phrase, "He shoots ... he scores!"

Tommy Hitchcock (b. 2-11-00, d. 4-19-44): Polo. 10-goal rating 18 times in his 19-year career from 1922 to 1940. Killed in plane crash in World War II.

Lew Hoad (b. 11-23-34): Australian tennis player. Won 2 consecutive Wimbledon singles titles (1956-57). Also won French title and Australian title in 1956, but failed to achieve the Grand Slam when defeated at Forest Hills by countryman Ken Rosewall.

Ben Hogan (b. 8-13-12): Golfer. Third alltime in career wins (63). Won U.S. Open 4 times (1948, consecutively 1950-51, 1953), the Masters (1951, 1953) and PGA Championship (1946, 1948) 2 times each and British Open once (1953). PGA Player of the Year 4 times (1948, consecutively 1950-51, 1953).

Marshall Holman (b. 9-29-54): Bowler. Won 21 PBA titles between 1975 and 1988. Had leading average in 1987 (213.54) and was named PBA Bowler of the Year.

Nat Holman (b. 10-18-1896): College basketball coach. Only coach in history to win NCAA and NIT championships in same season in 1950 with CCNY. 423 career wins, a .689 winning percentage.

Larry Holmes (b. 11-3-49): Boxer. Heavyweight champion (1978-85). Career record 53–3 with 37 KOs from 1973 to 1991. Defended title 21 times.

Lou Holtz (b. 1-6-37): Football coach. Coached Notre Dame to national championship in 1988 with 12–0 record and a 34–21 win over West Virginia in Fiesta Bowl. At start of '94 season had 193-84-6 career record. 10-6-2 career record in bowl games. Career span 1969–71 at William & Mary (13–20); 1972–75 at N.C. State (33-12-3); 1977–83 at Arkansas (60-21-2); 1984–85 at Minnesota 10–12); and since 1986 at Notre Dame (77-19-1).

Evander Holyfield (b. 10-19-62): Boxer. Won heavyweight crown Oct. 25, 1990 when he beat James "Buster" Douglas in Las Vegas. Lost title to Riddick Bowe in Las Vegas on 11-13-92, regained it from Bowe one year later, then lost to Michael Moorer on 4-22-94. Career record 30-2-0.

Red Holzman (b. 8-10-20): Basketball coach. Led New York Knicks to NBA title in 1970 and '73. NBA coach of the Year in 1970. Member of Rochester team that won NBA title in both 1946 (in NBL) and '51. After two-year coaching stints with Milwaukee and St. Louis, coached New York Knicks from 1968–82. Elected to Hall of Fame in 1985.

Harry Hopman (b. 8-12-06, d. 12-27-85): Australian tennis coach. As nonplaying captain, led Australia to 15 Davis Cup titles between 1950 and 1969. Mentor to Lew Hoad, Ken Rosewall, Rod Laver and John Newcombe.

Willie Hoppe (b. 10-11-1887, d. 2-1-59): Billiards. Won 51 world championship matches from 1904 to 1952.

Rogers Hornsby (b. 4-27-1896, d. 1-5-63): Baseball 2B. Second all-time highest career batting average (.358) and 7 batting titles, including .424 average in 1924. 200+ hits 7 times; .400+ average 3 times and .300+ average 12 other times. Led league in slugging average 9 times. Triple Crown winner in 1922, 1925; MVP award winner in 1925, 1929. Career span 1915-37 with St Louis (NL), New York (NL), Boston, Chicago (NL).

Paul Hornung (b. 12-23-35): Football RB-K. Led league in scoring 3 consecutive seasons, including a record 176 points in 1960 (15 touchdowns, 15 field goals, 41 extra points). Player of the Year in 1961. Career span 1957-66 with Green Bay. Suspended for 1963 season by Pete Rozelle for gambling. Also won Heisman Trophy in 1956 with Notre Dame.

Gordie Howe (b. 3-31-28): Hockey RW. Second alltime in goals (801), first in years played (26) and games (1,767). Second alltime in points (1,850) and assists (1,049). Won MVP award 6 times (consecutively 1952-53, 1957-58, 1960, 1963). Led league in scoring 6 times, goals 5 times and assists 3 times. Scored 40+ goals 5 times, 30+ goals 13 other times, 100+ points 3 times. All-Star 12 times. Played on 4 Stanley Cup champions with Detroit from 1946 to 1971. Teamed with sons Mark and Marty in the WHA with Houston and New England from 1973 to 1979, in NHL with Hartford in 1980.

Carl Hubbell (b. 6-22-03, d. 11-21-88): Baseball LHP. 253 career wins. MVP in 1933, 1936. League leader in wins and ERA 3 times each. Won 24 consecutive games from 1936 to 1937. Struck out Ruth, Gehrig, Foxx, Simmons and Cronin consecutively in 1934 All-Star game. Pitched no-hitter in 1929. Career span 1928-43 with New York.

Sam Huff (b. 10-4-34): Football LB. Made 30 interceptions. Career span 1956-69 with New York Giants and Washington Redskins. Elected to Hall of Fame in 1982.

Bobby Hull (b. 1-3-39): Hockey LW. "The Golden Jet." Sixth alltime in goals scored (610). Led league in goals 7 times and points 3 times. Scored 50+ goals 5 times, 30+ goals 8 other times. Won MVP award 2 consecutive seasons (1965-66). Son Brett won MVP award in 1991, the only father and son to be so honored. All-Star 10 times. Career span 1957-72 with Chicago, 1973-80 with Winnipeg of WHA.

Brett Hull (b. 8-9-64): Hockey RW. Son of Bobby Hull. Won Hart Memorial Trophy for 1990–91 season. Career span 1986–87 with Calgary Flames; since 1987 with St. Louis Blues.

Jim "Catfish" Hunter (b. 4-8-46): Baseball RHP. 1974 Cy Young award winner. Won 20+ games 5 consecutive seasons. Led league in wins and winning percentage 2 times each, ERA 1 time. 250+ innings pitched 8 times. Pitched perfect game in 1968. Member of 5 World Series champions for Oakland and New York Yankees. Career span 1965-79.

Don Hutson (b. 1-31-13): Football WR. Third alltime in touchdown receptions (99). Led league in pass receptions 8 times, receiving yards 7 times and scoring 5 consecutive seasons. Caught at least 1 pass in 95 consecutive games. Player of the Year 2 consecutive seasons (1941-42). Career span 1935-45 with Green Bay.

Hank Iba (b. 8-6-04; d. 1-15-93): College basketball coach. Coached Oklahoma A&M (which became Oklahoma State) from 1934 to 1970. Team won NCAA titles in 1945 and '46. 767 career wins is third alltime behind Adolph Rupp and Dean Smith.

Jackie Ickx (b. 1-1-45): Belgian auto racer. Won the 24 Hours of LeMans a record six times (1969, consecutively 1975-77, 1981-82) before retiring in 1985.

Punch Imlach (b. 3-15-18, d. 12-1-87): Hockey

coach. Seventh alltime in wins (467). With Toronto from 1958 to 1969. Won 4 Stanley Cup championships (consecutively 1962-64, 1967).

Bo Jackson (b. 11-30-62): Baseball OF and Football RB. Only person in history to be named to baseball All-Star game and football Pro Bowl game. 1985 Heisman Trophy winner at Auburn. First pick in 1986 NFL draft by Tampa Bay, but opted to play baseball at Kansas City. 1989 All-Star game MVP. Signed with football's LA Raiders in 1988. Sustained football injury in 1990, released from baseball contract by KC, signed by Chicago and returned from injury in early September 1991, but comeback failed at first. Had hip replacement surgery and hit homer in first at bat afterwards.

Joe Jackson (b. 7-16-1889, d. 12-5-51): Baseball OF. "Shoeless Joe." Third alltime highest career batting average (.356), with .300+ average 11 times. One of the "8 men out" banned from baseball for throwing 1919 World Series. Career span 1908-20 with Cleveland, Chicago.

Reggie Jackson (b. 5-18-46): Baseball OF. "Mr. October." Alltime leader in World Series slugging average (.755). 1977 Series MVP, hit 3 HR in final game on 3 consecutive pitches. 563 career HR total is sixth best alltime. Led league in HR 4 times. 1973 MVP. Alltime strikeout leader (2,597). In a 12-year period played on 10 first-place teams, 5 World Series winners. Career span 1967-87 with Oakland, New York, California. Inducted to baseball Hall of Fame in 1993.

Bruce Jenner (b. 10-28-49): Track and Field. Set world decathlon record (8,634) in winning gold medal at 1976 Olympics. Sullivan Award winner in 1976.

John Henry (b. 1975): Thoroughbred race horse. Sold as yearling for $1,100, the gelding was Horse of the Year in 1981 and in 1984 and retired with then-record $6,597,947 in winnings.

Ben Johnson (b. 12-30-61): Track and field. Canadian sprinter set world record in 100 meters (9.83 in 1987). Won event at 1988 Olympics in 9.79, but gold medal revoked for failing drug test. Both world records revoked for steroid usage. Suspended for life after testing positive for elevated testosterone level at an indoor meet in Montreal on 1-17-93.

Earvin "Magic" Johnson (b. 8-14-59): Basketball G. Sat out the 1991-92 season after being diagnosed with HIV, the virus that causes AIDS. Alltime leader in assists (9,921); alltime playoff leader in assists (2,320) and steals (358). MVP award 3 times (1987, consecutively 1989-90) and playoff MVP 1980, 1982, 1987. Played on 5 championship teams with Los Angeles since 1979. All-Star 8 consecutive seasons. League leader in assists 4 times, steals 2 times, free throw percentage 1 time. Also won NCAA championship and named tournament MVP in 1979 with Michigan State.

Jack Johnson (b. 3-31-1878, d. 6-10-46): Boxer. First black heavyweight champion (1908-15). Career record 78-8-12 with 45 KOs from 1897 to 1928.

Jimmy Johnson (b. 7-16-43): Football coach. Led the Cowboys from 1–15 in 1989, his first season in Dallas, to a 52–17 win over the Buffalo Bills in the Super Bowl XXVII just four seasons later. Also coached Super Bowl XXVIII champion Cowboys before resigning because of a dispute with owner Jerry Jones. Head coach at Oklahoma State from 1979–83 and Univ. of Miami 1984–88 with career collegiate record of

81-34-3. Johnson's Hurricanes won national championship in 1987.

Michael Johnson (b. 9-13-67): Track and field sprinter. Only person ever to break 44 seconds for 400 (best of 43.65) and 20 seconds for 200 (19.79). Won 200 at 1991 World Championships and 400 at 1993 World Championships. Anchored US 4 x 400 team at 1993 World Championship to world record of 2:54.29 with fastest ever relay carry of 42.97.

Walter Johnson (b. 11-6-1887, d. 12-10-46): Baseball RHP. "Big Train." Alltime leader in shutouts (110), second in wins (416), fourth in losses (279) and third in innings pitched (5,923). His 2.17 career ERA and 3,508 career strikeouts are seventh best alltime. MVP in 1913, 1924. Won 20+ games 12 times. League leader in strikeouts 12 times, ERA 5 times, wins 6 times. Pitched no-hitter in 1920. Career span 1907-27 with Washington.

Ben A. Jones (b. 12-31-1882, d. 6-13-61): Horse racing trainer. Trained Triple Crown winner 2 times (Whirlaway in 1941, Citation in 1948). Trained Kentucky Derby winner 6 times, more than any other trainer (1938, 1941, 1944, consecutively 1948-49, 1952), Preakness Stakes winner 2 times (1941, 1944) and Belmont Stakes winner 1 time (1941).

Bobby Jones (b. 3-17-02, d. 12-18-71): Golfer. Achieved golf's only recognized Grand Slam in 1930. Second alltime in major championships (13). Won U.S. Amateur 5 times, more than any golfer (consecutively 1924-25, 1927-28, 1930), U.S. Open 4 times (1923, 1926, consecutively 1929-30), British Open 3 times (consecutively 1926-27, 1930) and British Amateur (1930). Also designed Augusta National course, site of the Masters, and founded the tournament. Winner of Sullivan Award in 1930.

K.C. Jones (b. 5-25-32): Basketball G-coach. Member of 8 straight NBA-championship Boston Celtic teams in his nine season career from 1958–59 through 1966–67. Averaged 7.4 points and 4.3 assists per game. Coached Celtics from 1983–84 through 1987–88, with 308–102 regular season record and 65–37 playoff record with NBA titles in 1984 and '86.

Robert Trent Jones (b. 6-20-06): English-born golf course architect designed or remodelled over 400 courses, including Baltusrol, Hazeltine, Oak Hill and Winged Foot. In the mid-60s five straight U.S. Opens were played on courses designed or remodelled by Jones.

Sam Jones (b. 6-24-33): Basketball G. Played 12 seasons with Boston Celtics (1958–69) and made the playoffs every year, winning NBA title every year from 1959–66 plus 1968 and '69. Averaged 17.7 points per game for career. Elected to Hall of Fame in 1983.

Michael Jordan (b. 2-17-63): Basketball G. "Air." After 1992-93 season, alltime highest regular season scoring average (32.3) and most points scored in a playoff game (63 in 1986). Led league in scoring 7 consecutive seasons, steals 3 times. MVP in 1988, 1991-92; playoff MVP in 1991-93; Rookie of the Year in 1985. All-Star team 6 consecutive seasons, All-Defensive team 5 consecutive seasons. Career span since 1984–93 with Chicago. Announced retirement on 10-6-93. Also College Player of the Year in 1984. Played on NCAA championship team with North Carolina in 1982. Member of gold medal-winning 1984 and '92 Olympic teams.

Florence Griffith Joyner (b. 12-21-59): Track and field. Won 3 gold medals (100 meters, 200 meters, 4x100-meter relay) at 1988 Olympics; silver medalist at 1984 Olympics. Women's world record holder in 100 meters (10.49 set in 1988) and 200 meters (21.34 set at 1988 Olympics). Sullivan Award winner in 1988.

Jackie Joyner-Kersee (b. 3-3-62): Track and field. Gold medalist in heptathlon and long jump at 1988 Olympics and in the former at the 1992 Olympics. Heptathlon world record holder (7,291 points set at 1988 Olympics). Also won silver medal in heptathlon at 1984 Olympics and bronze in long jump at 1992 Olympics. Sullivan Award winner in 1986.

Alberto Juantorena (b. 3-12-51): Track and field. Cuban was gold medalist in 400 meters and 800 meters at 1976 Olympics.

Sonny Jurgensen (b. 8-23-34): Football QB. In 18 seasons completed 2,433 of 4,262 pass attempts for 32,224 yards and 255 TDs. Led NFL in passing both 1967 and '69. Career span 1957–1974 with Philadelphia Eagles and Washington Redskins. Elected to Hall of Fame in 1983.

Duke Kahanamoku (b. 8-24-1890, d. 1-22- 68): Swimmer. Won a total of 5 medals (3 gold and 2 silver) at 3 Olympics in 1912, 1920, 1924. Introduced the crawl stroke to America. Surfing pioneer and water polo player. Later sheriff of Honolulu.

Al Kaline (b. 12-19-34): Baseball OF. 3,007 career hits and 399 career HR. Youngest player to win batting title with .340 average as a 20-year-old in 1955. Had .300+ average 9 times. Played in 18 All-Star games. Career span 1953-74 with Detroit.

Anatoly Karpov (b. 5-23-61): Soviet chess player. First world champion to receive title by default, in 1975, when Bobby Fischer chose not to defend his crown. Champion until 1985 when beaten by Gary Kasparov. Recognized by FIDE as champion in 1994.

Gary Kasparov (b. 4-13-63): Born Harry Weinstein. Chess player. World champion from 1985 to 1993 when stripped of title by FIDE.

Kip Keino (b. 1-17-40): Track and field. Kenyan was gold medalist in 1,500 meters at 1968 Olympics and in steeplechase at 1972 Olympics.

Jim Kelly (b. 2-14-60): Football QB. Led NFL in passing in 1990 (219 of 346 for 2,829 yards and 24 TDs). Led AFC in passing in 1991. In eight seasons through '93 completed 2,112 of 3,494 attempts for 26,413 yards and 179 TDs. Career span 1983–85 with New Jersey Generals (USFL), since 1986 with Buffalo Bills. Led Bills to four straight Super Bowls, all losses.

Kelso (b. 1957, d. 1983): Thoroughbred race horse. Gelding was Horse of the Year 5 straight years (1960-64). Finished in the money in 53 of 63 races. Career earnings $1,977,896.

Harmon Killebrew (b. 6-29-36): Baseball 3B-1B. 573 career HR total is fifth most alltime. 100+ RBI 9 times, 40+ HR 8 times. League leader in HR 6 times and RBI 4 times. 1969 MVP. 100+ walks and strikeouts 7 times each. Career span 1954-75 with Washington, Minnesota.

Jean Claude Killy (b. 8-30-43): French skier. Won 3 gold medals at 1968 Olympics. World Cup overall champion 2 consecutive years (1967-68).

Ralph Kiner (b. 10-27-22): Baseball OF. Second to Babe Ruth in alltime HR frequency (7.1 HR every 100 at bats). 369 career HR. Led league in HR 7 consecutive seasons, with 50+ HR 2 times; 100+ RBI and runs scored in same season 6 times; 100+ walks 6 times. Career span 1946-55 with Pittsburgh.

Billie Jean King (b. 11-22-43): Tennis player. Won a record 20 Wimbledon titles, including 6 singles titles (consecutively 1966-68, 1972-73, 1975). Won 4 U.S. singles titles (1967, consecutively 1971-72, 1974), and singles titles at Australian Open (1968) and French Open (1972). Won 27 Grand Slam doubles titles—total of 39 Grand Slam titles is third alltime. Helped found the women's pro tour in 1970, serving as president of the Women's Tennis Association 2 times. Helped form Team Tennis.

Nile Kinnick (b. 7-9-18, d. 6-2-43): College football RB. Won the Heisman Trophy in 1939 with Iowa. Premier runner, passer and punter was killed in plane crash during routine Navy training flight. Stadium in Iowa City named in his honor.

Tom Kite (b. 12-9-49): Golfer. PGA alltime money leader, with $8,500,729 through end of '93 season. Led PGA in scoring average in 1981 (69.80) and '82 (70.21). PGA Player of Year in 1989, when he won a then-record $1,395,278. Shook reputation for failing to win the big ones by winning 1992 US Open at windy Pebble Beach.

Franz Klammer (b. 12-3-54): Austrian alpine skier. Greatest downhiller ever. Gold medalist in downhill at 1976 Olympics. Also won four World Cup downhill titles (1975-78).

Bob Knight (b. 10-25-40): College basketball coach. Won 3 NCAA championships with Indiana in 1976, 1981, 1987. Coached U.S. Olympic team to gold medal in 1984. 640 career wins and .742 career winning percentage entering 1994-95 season. Career span since 1966.

Olga Korbut (b. 5-16-55): Soviet gymnast. First ever to complete backward somersault on balance beam. Won 3 gold medals at 1972 Olympics.

Sandy Koufax (b. 12-30-35): Baseball LHP. Cy Young Award winner 3 times (1963, consecutively 1965-66); and MVP in 1963; World Series MVP in 1963, 1965. Pitched 1 perfect game, 3 no-hitters. League leader in ERA 5 consecutive seasons, strikeouts 4 times. Won 25+ games 3 times. Career record 165-87, with 2.76 ERA. Career span 1955-66 with Brooklyn/Los Angeles.

Jack Kramer (b. 8-1-21): Tennis player. Won 2 consecutive U.S. singles titles (1946-47) and 1 Wimbledon title (1947). Also won 6 Grand Slam doubles titles. Served as executive director of Association of Tennis Professionals from 1972 to 1975.

Ingrid Kristiansen (b. 3-21-56): Track and field. Norwegian runner is only person—male or female—to hold world records in 5,000 meters (14:37.33 set in 1986), 10,000 meters (30:13.74 set in 1986) and marathon (2:21:06 set in 1985). Also won Boston Marathon 2 times (1986, 1989).

Bob Kurland (b. 12-23-24): College basketball player. 6' 10¼" center on Oklahoma A&M teams that won NCAA titles in 1945 and '46. Consensus All America and NCAA tournament MVP in both 1945 and '46. Led nation in scoring in '46. His habit of swatting shots off rim led to creation of goaltending rule in 1945. Won gold medals in both 1948 and '52 Olympics. Turned down lucrative pro offers, playing instead for Phillips 66 Oilers AAU team.

Rene Lacoste (b. 7-2-05): French tennis player. "The Crocodile." One of France's "Four Musketeers" of the 1920s. Won 3 French singles titles (1925, 1927, 1929), 2 consecutive U.S. titles (1926-27) and 2 Wimbledon titles (1925, 1928). Also designed casual shirt with embroidered crocodile that bears his name.

Marion Ladewig (b. 10-30-14): Bowler. Won All-Star Tournament 8 times (consecutively 1949-52, 1954, 1956, 1959, 1963) and WPBA National Championship once (1960). Also voted Bowler of the Year 9 times, more than any other bowler (consecutively 1950-54, 1957-59, 1963).

Guy Lafleur (b. 9-20-51): Hockey RW. Won MVP award 2 consecutive seasons (1977-78), playoff MVP in 1977. Scored 50+ goals and 100+ points 6 consecutive seasons. Led league in points scored 3 consecutive seasons, goals and assists 1 time each. 560 career goals, 793 assists. Played on 5 Stanley Cup champions with Montreal from 1971 to 1985.

Curly Lambeau (b. 4-9-1898; d. 6-1-65): Football Q and coach. Quarterback for Packer team in early 20's. Record of 212-106-21 in his 29 seasons (1921–49) as Packer coach, winning three NFL titles in 1929–31.

Jack Lambert (b. 7-8-52): Football LB. Anchored Pittsburgh's famed "Steel Curtain" defense. Selected for Pro Bowl 9 times. Played on 4 Super Bowl champions (consecutively 1974-75, 1978-79) with Pittsburgh from 1974 to 1984.

Jake LaMotta (b. 7-10-21): Boxer. "The Bronx Bull." Subject of *Raging Bull*, movie by Martin Scorcese, starring Robert DeNiro. Won middleweight title by knocking out Marcel Cerdan in 10 on 6-16-49. Lost title to Ray Robinson, who KO'd him in 13 on 2-13-51. Career record: 106 bouts; won 30 by KO and 53 by decision; drew 4; and lost 19, 4 by KO.

Kenesaw Mountain Landis (b. 11-20-1866, d. 11-25-44): Baseball's first and most powerful commissioner from 1920 to 1944. By banning the 8 "Black Sox" involved in the fixing of the 1919 World Series, he restored public confidence in the integrity of baseball.

Tom Landry (b. 9-11-24): Football coach. Third alltime in wins (270). The first coach in Dallas history, from 1960 to 1988. Led team to 13 division titles, 7 championship games and 5 Super Bowls. Won 2 Super Bowl championships (1971, 1977). Career record 270-178-6.

Dick "Night Train" Lane (b. 4-16-28): Football DB. Third alltime in interceptions (68) and second in interception yardage (1,207). Set record with 14 interceptions as a rookie in 1952. Career span 1952-65 with Los Angeles, Chicago Cardinals, Detroit.

Joe Lapchick (b. 4-12-00, d. 8-10-70): Basketball C-coach. One of the first big men in basketball, member of New York's Original Celtics. Coached St. John's (1936-47, 1956-65) winning four NIT Tournaments. Coached New York Knicks, 1947-56.

Steve Largent (b. 9-28-54): Football WR. Second alltime in pass receptions (819) and TD receptions (100), and alltime leader in consecutive games with reception (177), seasons with 50+ receptions (10), and seasons with 1,000+ yards receiving (8). Career span 1976-89 with Seattle.

Don Larsen (b. 8-7-29): Baseball RHP. Pitched only perfect game in World Series history for the NY Yankees on Oct. 8, 1956, beating the Dodgers 2-0; named World Series MVP. Career span 1953-67 for many teams.

Tommy Lasorda (b. 9-22-27): Baseball manager. Has spent nearly his entire minor and major league career in the Dodgers organization as a pitcher, coach and manager. Has managed Dodgers since 1977, winning 4 pennants and 2 World Series (1981, 1988).

Rod Laver (b. 8-9-38): Australian tennis player. "Rocket." Only player to achieve the Grand Slam twice (as an amateur in 1962 and as a pro in 1969). Second alltime in men's Grand Slam singles titles (11—tied with Bjorn Borg). Won 4 Wimbledon titles (consecutively 1961-62, 1968-69), 3 Australian titles (1960, 1962, 1969), 2 U.S. titles (1962, 69) and 2 French titles (1962, 1969). Also won 8 Grand Slam doubles titles. First player to earn $1 million in prize money. 47 career tournament victories. Member of undefeated Australian Davis Cup team from 1959 to 1962.

Andrea Mead Lawrence (b. 4-19-32): Skier. Gold medalist in slalom and giant slalom at 1952 Olympics.

Bobby Layne (b. 12-19-26; d. 12-1-86): Football QB. Led Detroit Lions to NFL championships in both 1952 and '53. In 1952 led NFL in every passing category. Career span 1948–62, most with the Detroit Lions. Elected to Hall of Fame in 1967.

Sammy Lee (b. 8-1-20): Diver. Gold medalist at 2 consecutive Olympics (highboard in 1948, 1952); bronze medalist in springboard at 1948 Olympics. Won the 1953 Sullivan Award. Also 1960 U.S. Olympic diving coach.

Jacques Lemaire (b. 9-7-45): Hockey C-Coach. As center for Montreal Canadiens from 1967–68 through 1978–79 was part of eight Stanley Cup winning teams. Over 12 seasons, all with Montreal, scored 366 goals and had 469 assists. Elected to Hall of Fame in 1984. Coached Canadiens 1983-85 and N.J. Devils since 1993.

Mario Lemieux (b. 10-5-65): Hockey C. Won MVP award in 1988, playoff MVP in 1991. Led league in most points 4 seasons and goals scored 2 consecutive seasons, assists 1 season. Scored 40+ goals and 100+ points 6 consecutive seasons, including 85 goals and 199 points in 1989. Rookie of the Year in 1985. Won 1992-93 scoring title despite sitting out six weeks to receive treatment for Hodgkin's disease, a form of cancer. Career span since 1984 with Pittsburgh.

Greg LeMond (b. 6-26-61): Cyclist. Only American to win Tour de France; won event 3 times (1986, consecutively 1989-90). Recovered from hunting accident to win in 1989.

Ivan Lendl (b. 3-7-60): Tennis player. Second alltime men's most career tournament victories (94). Won 3 consecutive U.S. Open singles titles (1985-87) and 3 French Open titles (1984, consecutively 1985-86). Also won 2 consecutive Australian Open titles (1989-90). Reached Grand Slam final 9 other times. Alltime leader in prize money, with more than $20 million.

Suzanne Lenglen (b. 5-24-1899, d. 7-4-38): French tennis player. Lost only 1 match from 1919 to her retirement in 1926. Won 6 Wimbledon singles and doubles titles (consecutively 1919-23, 1925). Won 6 French singles and doubles titles (consecutively 1920-23, 1925-26).

Sugar Ray Leonard (b. 5-17-56): Boxer. Champion in 5 different weight classes: welterweight, junior middleweight, middleweight, light heavyweight and super middleweight. Career record 36-2-1 with 25 KOs from 1977 to 1991. Also light welterweight gold medalist at 1976 Olympics.

Carl Lewis (b. 7-1-61): Track and field. Held world record for 100 meters 9.86; set on 8-25-91 at World Championships in Tokyo. Duplicated Jesse Owens's feat by winning 4 gold medals at 1984 Olympics (100 and 200 meters, 4x100-meter relay and long jump). Also won 2 gold medals (100 meters, long jump) and 1 silver (200 meters) at 1988 Olympics and two gold medals (long jump, 4x100 relay) at 1992 Olympics. Sullivan Award winner in 1981.

Nancy Lieberman (b. 7-1-58): Basketball G. Three-time All-America at Old Dominion. Player of the Year (1979, 1980). Olympian, 1976, and selected for 1980 team, but quit because of Moscow boycott. Promoter of women's basketball, played in WPBL, WABA. First woman to play basketball in a men's professional league (USBL) in 1986.

Bob Lilly (b. 7-26-39): Football DT. Dallas Cowboys' first ever draft pick, first Pro Bowl player and first all-NFL choice. Made all-NFL eight times. Career span 1961–74, all with Cowboys. Elected to Hall of Fame in 1980.

Sonny Liston (b. 5-8-32, d. 12-30-70): Boxer. Heavyweight champion from 1962 to 1964. Won title by KO of Floyd Patterson on 9-25-62. Lost title when TKO'd by Cassius Clay (Muhammad Ali) on 2-25-64 and then lost rematch on 5-25-65 when KO'd in first round. Career record: 54 fights; won 39 by KO and 11 by decision; lost 4, three by KO.

Vince Lombardi (b. 6-11-13, d. 9-3-70): Football coach. Alltime highest winning percentage (.740). Career record 105-35-6. Won 5 NFL championships and 2 consecutive Super Bowl titles with Green Bay from 1959 to 1967. Coached Washington in 1969. Super Bowl trophy named in his honor.

Johnny Longden (b. 2-14-07): Horse racing jockey. Rode Triple Crown winner Count Fleet in 1943. Tenth alltime most wins (6,032).

Nancy Lopez (b. 1-6-57): Golfer. LPGA Player of the Year 4 times (consecutively 1978-79, 1985, 1988). Winner of LPGA Championship 3 times (1978, 1985, 1989). Youngest member of the LPGA Hall of Fame.

Greg Louganis (b. 1-29-60): Diver. Gold medalist in platform and springboard at 2 consecutive Olympics in 1984, 1988. World champion 5 times (platform in 1978, 1982, 1986; springboard in 1982, 1986). Also Sullivan Award winner in 1984.

Joe Louis (b. 5-13-14, d. 4-12-81): Boxer. "The Brown Bomber." Longest title reign of any heavyweight champion (11 years, 9 months) from June 1937 through March 1949. Career record 63-3 with 49 KOs from 1934 to 1951. Defended title 25 times.

Jerry Lucas (b. 3-30-40): Basketball F. Star at Ohio State. *Sporting News* College Player of Year in both 1961 and '62. In 1960 member of both NCAA championship team and gold-medal winning U.S. Olympic team. Averaged over 20 points and 20 rebounds a game for college career. NBA Rookie of Year in 1964. In 11 NBA seasons averaged 17 points a game. Elected to Hall of Fame in 1979.

Sid Luckman (b. 11-21-16): Football QB. Played on 4 NFL champions (consecutively 1940-41, 1943, 1946) with Chicago. Player of the Year in 1943. Tied record with 7 touchdown passes on Nov. 14, 1943. All-Pro 6 times. 137 career touchdown passes. Career span 1939-50. Also All-America with Columbia.

Jon Lugbill (b. 5-27-61): White water canoe racer. Won 5 world singles titles from 1979 to 1989.

Hank Luisetti (b. 6-16-16): Basketball F. The first player to use the one-handed shot. All-America at Stanford 3 consecutive years from 1936-38.

D. Wayne Lukas (b. 9-2-35): Horse racing trainer. Former college basketball coach and quarter horse trainer takes mass production approach with stables at most major tracks around country. Trained two Horses of the Year, Lady's Secret in 1986 and Criminal Type in 1990. Won 1988 Kentucky Derby with a filly, Winning Colors. Won 1994 Preakness and Belmont with Tabasco Cat.

Connie Mack (b. 2-22-1862, d. 2-8-56): Born Cornelius McGillicuddy. Baseball manager. Managed Philadelphia for 50 years (1901-50) until age 87. All-time leader in games (7,755), wins (3,731) and losses (3,948). Won 9 pennants and 5 World Series (1910-11, 1913, 1929-30).

Larry Mahan (b. 11-21-43): Rodeo. All-Around champion 6 times (consecutively 1966-70, 1973).

Frank Mahovlich (b. 1-10-38): Hockey LW. Winner of Calder Trophy for top rookie for 1957–58 season. In 18 NHL seasons with Toronto Maple Leafs, Detroit Red Wings and Montreal Canadiens, had 533 goals and 570 assists. Played for six Stanley Cup winners. Elected to Hall of Fame 1981.

Phil Mahre (b. 5-10-57): Skier. Gold medalist in slalom at 1984 Olympics (twin brother Steve won silver medal). World Cup champion 3 consecutive years (1981-83).

Joe Malone (b. 2-28-1890, d. 5-15-69): Hockey F. "Phantom Joe." Led the NHL in its first season, 1917-18, with 44 goals in 20 games with Montreal. Led league in scoring 2 times (1918, 1920). Holds NHL record with most goals scored, single game (7) in 1920.

Karl Malone (b. 7-24-63): Basketball F. "The Mailman." Five-time first-team All-Star. All-Star MVP, 1989. All-Rookie team, 1986. Scored 20+ points per game in seven of eight seasons with Utah. Member of 1992 Olympic team. Career span since 1987 with Utah.

Moses Malone (b. 3-23-55): Basketball C. Entering 1994-95 season alltime leader free throws made (8,509), fifth in rebounds (16,166) and third in points scored (27,360). 3 MVP awards in 1979, consecutively 1982-83; playoff MVP in 1983. 4-time All-Star. Led league in rebounding 6 times, 5 consecutively. Career span since 1976 with Houston, Philadelphia, Washington, Atlanta, Milwaukee.

Man o' War (b. 1917, d. 1947): Thoroughbred race horse. Won 20 of 21 races from 1919 to 1920. Only loss was in 1919 in Sanford Stakes to Upset. Passed up Derby but won both Preakness and Belmont. Winner of $249,465. Sire of War Admiral, 1937 Triple Crown winner.

Mickey Mantle (b. 10-20-31): Baseball OF. Won 3 MVP awards, consecutively 1956-57 and 1962; won Triple Crown in 1956. 536 career HR. Greatest switch hitter in history. Played in 20 All-Star games. Alltime World Series leader in HR (18), RBI (40) and runs scored (42). No. 7 was a member of 7 World Series winners with NY Yankees. Career span 1951-68.

Diego Maradona (b. 10-30-60): Argentine soccer player. Led Argentina to 1986 World Cup victory and to 1990 World Cup finals. Led Naples to Italian League titles (1987, 1990), Italian Cup (1987) and to

European Champion Clubs' Cup title (1989). Throughout 1980s often acknowledged as best player in the world. Tested positive for cocaine and suspended by FIFA and Italian Soccer Federation for 15 months in March 1991. Also failed drug test in 1994 World Cup and suspended before second round.

Pete Maravich (b. 6-22-47, d. 1-5-88): Basketball G. "Pistol Pete." Alltime NCAA leader in points scored (3,667), scoring average (44.2) and games scoring 50+ points (28, including then Division I record 69 points in 1970). Alltime season leader in points scored (1,381) and scoring average (44.5) in 1970. College Player of the Year in 1970. NCAA scoring leader and All-America 3 consecutive seasons from 1968 to 1970 with Louisiana State. Also led NBA in scoring in 1977. Averaged 20+ points 8 times. All-Star 2 times. Career span 1970-79 with Atlanta, New Orleans/Utah, Boston.

Gino Marchetti (b. 1-2-27): Football DE. Played in Pro Bowl every year from 1955 to '65, except 1958 when he broke right ankle tackling Frank Gifford in Colts' 23–17 win over the Giants. Career span 1952–66, almost all with Baltimore Colts. Inducted into Hall of Fame in 1972.

Rocky Marciano (b. 9-1-23, d. 8-31-69): Boxer. Heavyweight champion (1952-56). Career record 49-0 with 43 KOs from 1947 to 1956. Retired as undefeated champion.

Juan Marichal (b. 10-24-37): Baseball RHP. 243 career wins, 2.89 career ERA. Won 20+ games 6 times; 250+ innings pitched 8 times; 200+ strikeouts 6 times. Pitched no-hitter in 1963. Career span 1960-75, mostly with San Francisco.

Dan Marino (b. 9-15-61): Football QB. Set alltime season record for yards passing (5,084) and touchdown passes (48) in 1984. Prior to 1994-95 season had passed for 4,000+ yards 4 other seasons and 400+ yards a record 10 games. Player of the Year in 1984. Career totals through 1993-94 season: 40,720 yards passing, 298 touchdown passes. Career span since 1983 with Miami.

Roger Maris (b. 9-10-34, d. 12-14-85): Baseball OF. Broke Babe Ruth's alltime season HR record with 61 in 1961. Won consecutive MVP awards and led league in RBI 1960-61. Career span 1957-68 with Kansas City, New York (AL), St Louis.

Billy Martin (b. 5-16-28, d. 12-25-89): Baseball 2B-manager. Volatile manager was hired and fired by Minnesota, Detroit, Texas, New York Yankees (5 times!) and Oakland from 1969 to 1988. Won World Series with Yankees as manager in 1977 and as player 4 times.

Eddie Mathews (b. 10-13-31): Baseball 3B. 512 career HR and 30+ HR 9 consecutive seasons. League leader in HR 2 times, walks 4 times. Career span 1952-68 with Milwaukee.

Christy Mathewson (b. 8-12-1880, d. 10-7-25): Baseball RHP. Third alltime most wins (373) and shutouts (80); fifth alltime best ERA (2.13). Led league in wins 5 times; won 30+ games 4 times and 20+ games 9 other times. Led league in ERA and strikeouts 5 times each. 300+ innings pitched 11 times. Pitched 2 no-hitters. Pitched 3 shutouts in 1905 World Series. Career span 1900-16 with New York.

Bob Mathias (b. 11-17-30): Track and field. At age 17, youngest to win gold medal in decathlon at 1948 Olympics. First decathlete to win gold medal at consecutive Olympics (1948, 1952). Also won Sullivan Award in 1948.

Ollie Matson (b. 5-1-30): Football RB. Versatile runner totalled 12,884 combined yards rushing, receiving and kick returning. Scored 73 career touchdowns, including a 105-yard kickoff return on Oct. 14, 1956, the second longest ever. Career span 1952-66 with Chicago Cardinals, Los Angeles, Detroit, Philadelphia. Also won bronze medal in 400-meters at 1952 Olympics.

Roland Matthes (b. 11-17-50): German swimmer. Gold medalist in 100-meter and 200-meter backstroke at 2 consecutive Olympics (1968, 1972). Set 16 world records from 1967 to 1973.

Don Maynard (b. 1-25-37): Football WR. Retired in 1973 as the NFL's alltime leading receiver. In 15 seasons, 10 with the New York Jets, caught 633 passes for 11,834 yards and 88 TDs. Averaged 18.7 yards per catch for career. In 1967 and '68 led AFL with average of 20.2 and 22.8 yards per catch. Elected to Hall of Fame in 1987.

Willie Mays (b. 5-6-31): Baseball OF. "Say Hey Kid." MVP in 1954, 1965; Rookie of the Year in 1951. Third alltime most HR (660), with 50+ HR 2 times, 30+ HR 9 other times. Led league in HR 4 times. 100+ RBI 10 times; 100+ runs scored 12 consecutive seasons. 3,283 career hits. Led league in stolen bases 4 consecutive seasons. 30 HR and 30 steals in same season 2 times and first man in history to hit 300+ HR and steal 300+ bases. Won 11 consecutive Gold Gloves; set record for career putouts by an outfielder and league record for total chances. His catch in the 1954 World Series off the bat of Vic Wertz called the greatest ever. Career span 1951-73 with New York and San Francisco Giants, New York Mets.

Bill Mazeroski (b. 9-5-36): Baseball 2B. Hit dramatic 9th-inning home run in Game 7 to win 1960 World Series, first of only two Series' to end on a home run. Also a great fielder, won Gold Glove 8 times. Led league in assists 9 times, double plays 8 times and putouts 5 times.

Joe McCarthy (b. 4-21-1887, d. 1-3-78): Baseball manager. Alltime highest winning percentage among managers for regular season (.615) and World Series (.763). First manager to win pennants in both leagues (Chicago (NL), 1929, New York (AL), 1932). From 1926 to 1950 his teams won 7 World Series and 9 pennants.

Mark McCormack (b. 11-6-30): Sports marketing agent. Founded International Management Group in 1962. Also author of best-selling business advice books.

Pat McCormick (b. 5-12-30): Diver. Gold medalist in platform and springboard at 2 consecutive Olympics (1952, 1956). Also won Sullivan Award in 1956.

Willie McCovey (b. 1-10-38): Baseball 1B. Led NL in homers three times (1963, '68, '69) and in RBIs twice (1968–69). 521 career homers. .270 career batting average. Hit 18 grand slams, a NL record. Rookie of Year 1959. NL MVP in 1969. Career span 1959–73 and 1977–80 with San Francisco Giants, 1974–76 with San Diego Padres and 1976 with Oakland A's. Elected to Hall of Fame in 1986.

John McEnroe (b. 2-26-59): Tennis player. Has won 4 U.S. Open singles titles (consecutively 1979-81, 1984) and 3 Wimbledon titles (1981, consecutively 1983-84). Also won 8 Grand Slam doubles titles. Third

alltime men's most career tournament victories (77). Led U.S. to 5 Davis Cup victories (1978-79, 1981-82, 1992).

John McGraw (b. 4-7-1873, d. 2-25-34): Baseball manager. Second alltime most games (4,801) and wins (2,784). Guided New York Giants to 3 World Series titles and 10 pennants from 1902 to 1932.

Denny McLain (b. 3-29-44): Baseball RHP. Last pitcher to win 30+ games in a season (Detroit, 1968); won 20+ games 2 other times. Won 2 consecutive Cy Young Awards (1968-69). Led league in innings pitched 2 times. Served 2½-year jail term for 1985 conviction of extortion, racketeering and drug possession. Career span 1963-72.

Mary T. Meagher (b. 10-27-64): Swimmer. "Madame Butterfly." Won 3 gold medals at 1984 Olympics (100-meter butterfly, 200-meter butterfly and 400-medley relay). World record holder in 100-meter butterfly (57.93 set in 1981) and 200-meter butterfly (2:05.96 set in 1981).

Rick Mears (b. 12-3-51): Auto racer. Has won Indy 500 4 times (1979, 1984, 1988, 1991). Fifth alltime in CART victories (29 as of 10-1-94) and CART champion 3 times (1979, consecutively 1981-82). Named Indy 500 Rookie of the Year in 1978.

Cary Middlecoff (b. 1-6-21): Golfer. Also a dentist. Won 40 PGA tournaments, including 1955 Masters and US Opens in 1949 and '56. Won 1956 Vardon Trophy.

George Mikan (b. 6-18-24): Basketball C. Averaged 20+ points per game and named to All-Star team 6 consecutive seasons. Led league in scoring 3 times, rebounding 1 time. Played on 5 championship teams in 6 years (1949-54) with Minneapolis. Also played on 1945 NIT championship team with DePaul. All-America 3 times. Served as ABA Commissioner from 1968 to 1969.

Stan Mikita (b. 5-20-40): Hockey C. Won MVP award 2 consecutive seasons (1967-68). Fourth alltime in assists (926); fifth alltime in points (1,467). Led league in assists 4 consecutive seasons and points 4 times. 541 career goals. All-Star 6 times. Career span 1958-80 with Chicago.

Del Miller (b. 7-5-13): Harness racing driver. Has raced in 8 decades since 1929, the longest career of any athlete. Won The Hambletonian in 1950. As of 10-17-94 has won 2,442 career races.

Marvin Miller (b. 4-14-17): Labor negotiator. Union chief of Major League Baseball Players Association from 1966 to 1984. Led strikes in 1972 and 1981. Negotiated 5 labor contracts with owners that increased minimum salary and pension fund, allowed for agents and arbitration, and brought about the end of the reserve clause and the beginning of free agency.

Art Monk (b. 12-5-57): Football WR. Caught more passes than anyone in NFL history (888 for 12,026 and 79 TDs through end of 1993-94 season). 106 catches in 1984 was NFL single season record. Twice caught 13 passes in single game. Career span 1980–93 with Redskins, since 1993 with New York Jets.

Earl Monroe (b. 11-21-44): Basketball G. "The Pearl" played 13 seasons (1968–80) with the Baltimore Bullets and New York Knicks. NBA Rookie of Year in 1968. Member of 1973 NBA championship Knicks team. Averaged 18.8 points a game. Elected to Hall of Fame 1989.

Joe Montana (b. 6-11-56): Football QB. Entering 1994 season alltime highest-rated passer (93.1), fourth in completions (3,110), fifth in passing yards (37,268) and fourth in touchdown passes (257). Has won 4 Super Bowl championships (1981, 1984, consecutively 1988-89) with San Francisco since 1979. Named Super Bowl MVP 3 times (1981, 1984, 1989). Player of the Year in 1989. Also led Notre Dame to national championship in 1977. Traded to Kansas City in 1993.

Carlos Monzon (b. 8-7-42): Argentine boxer. Longest title reign of any middleweight champion (6 years, 9 months) from Nov. 1970 through Aug. 1977. Career record 89-3-9 with 61 KOs from 1963 to 1977. Won 82 consecutive bouts from 1964 to 1977. Defended title 14 times. Retired as champion.

Helen Wills Moody (b. 10-6-05): Tennis player. Second alltime most women's Grand Slam singles titles (19). Her 8 Wimbledon titles are second most alltime (consecutively 1927-30, 1932-33, 1935, 1938). Won 7 U.S. titles (consecutively 1923-25, 1927-29, 1931) and 4 French titles (consecutively 1928-30, 1932). Also won 12 Grand Slam doubles titles.

Archie Moore (b. 12-13-16): Boxer. Longest title reign of any light heavyweight champion (9 years, 1 month) from Dec. 1952 through Feb. 1962. Career record 199-26-8 with an alltime record 145 KOs from 1935 to 1965. Retired at age 52.

Davey Moore (b. 11-1-33; d. 3-23-63): Boxer. Won featherweight title by KO of Kid Bassey in 13 on 3-18-59. Five successful defenses of title, before losing it on 3-21-63 to Sugar Ramos who KO'd him in 10. Died two days after fight of brain damage suffered during fight. Career record: 67 bouts; won 30 by KO, 28 by decision, 1 because of foul; drew 1; lost 7, two by KO.

Noureddine Morceli (b. 2-20-70). Algerian track and field middle distance runner. Set world record for mile (3:44.39) in Rieti, Italy, on 9-5-93. Set world record for 1,500 (3:28.86) on 9-5-92. World champion at 1,500 in both 1991 and '93. Finished a shocking seventh at 1992 Olympics. Only man ever to rank first in the world at 1,500/mile four straight years (1990-93).

Joe Morgan (b. 9-19-43): Baseball 2B. Won 2 consecutive MVP awards in 1975-76. Third alltime most walks (1,865), tenth most stolen bases (689). Led league in walks 4 times. 100+ walks and runs scored 8 times each; 40+ stolen bases 9 times. Won 5 Gold Gloves. Second alltime most games played by 2nd baseman (2,527). Career span 1963-84 with Houston, Cincinnati.

Willie Mosconi (b. 6-27-13; d. 9-16-93): Pocket billiards player. Won world title a record 15 straight times between 1941 and 1957. Once pocketed 526 balls without a miss.

Edwin Moses (b. 8-31-55): Track and field. Gold medalist in 400-meter hurdles at 2 Olympics, in 1976, 1984 (U.S. boycotted 1980 Games); bronze medalist at 1988 Olympics. Set four world records in 400-meter hurdles (best of 47.02 set on 8-31-83). Now second alltime in 400 hurdles to Kevin Young's world record 46.78. Also won 122 consecutive races from 1977 to 1987. Won Sullivan Award in 1983.

Marion Motley (b. 6-5-20): Football FB. All-time AAFC leader in yards rushing (3,024). Also led NFL in rushing 1 time. Combined league totals: 4,712 yards rushing, 39 touchdowns. Played on 4 consecutive AAFC champions (1946-49), 1 NFL champion (1950) with Cleveland from 1946 to 1953.

Shirley Muldowney (b. 6-19-40): Drag racer. First woman to win the Top Fuel championship, which she won 3 times (1977, 1980, 1982).

Anthony Munoz (b. 8-19-58): Football OT. Probably the greatest tackle ever. Made Pro Bowl a record-tying 11 times. Career span 1980-92 with the Cincinnati Bengals.

Isaac Murphy (b. 4-16-1861, d. 2-12-1896): Horse racing jockey. Top jockey of his era, Murphy, who was black, won 3 Kentucky Derbys (aboard Buchanan in 1884, Riley in 1890 and Kingman in 1891).

Eddie Murray (b. 2-24-56): Baseball 1B. 100+ RBIs 6 seasons and 30+ HRs five seasons. Through '94 season had 2,930 hits, 458 HRs and 1,738 RBI. Alltime leader in RBI by switch hitter. Career span 1977-88 with Baltimore Orioles; 1989-91 with LA Dodgers; 1992-93 with New York Mets, since 1994 with Cleveland Indians.

Jim Murray (b. 12-29-19): Sportswriter. Won Pulitzer Prize in 1990. Named Sportswriter of the Year 14 times. Columnist for *Los Angeles Times* since 1961.

Ty Murray (b. 10-11-69): Rodeo cowboy. All-Around world champion, 1989-93. Set single-season earnings record, 1990 ($213,771). Rookie of the Year, 1988. At 20 in 1989, became youngest man ever to win national all-around title.

Stan Musial (b. 11-21-20): Baseball OF-1B. "Stan the Man." Had .331 career batting average and 475 career HR. MVP award winner 1943, 1946, 1948. Fourth alltime in hits (3,630) and third in doubles (725). Won 7 batting titles. Led league in hits 6 times, slugging average 5 times, doubles 8 times. Had .300+ batting average 17 times, 200+ hits 6 times, 100+ RBI 10 times, and 100+ runs scored 11 times. 24-time All-Star. Career span 1941-63 with St. Louis.

John Naber (b. 1-20-56): Swimmer. Won 4 gold medals and 1 silver medal at 1976 Olympics. Sullivan Award winner in 1977.

Bronko Nagurski (b. 11-3-08, d. 1-7-90): Football FB. Punishing runner played on 3 NFL champions (consecutively 1932-33, 1943) with Bears. Rushed for 2,778 career yards, 1930-37 and 1943 with Chicago. Also All-America with Minnesota.

James Naismith (b. 11-6-1861, d. 11-28-39): Invented basketball in 1891 while an instructor at YMCA Training School in Springfield, Mass. Refined the game while a professor at Kansas from 1898 to 1937. Hall of Fame is named in his honor.

Joe Namath (b. 5-31-43): Football QB. "Broadway Joe." Super Bowl MVP in 1968 after he guaranteed victory for AFL. 173 career touchdown passes. Led league in yards passing 3 times, including 4,007 yards in 1967. Player of the Year in 1968, Rookie of the Year in 1965. Career span 1965-77 with NY Jets, LA Rams.

Ilie Nastase (b. 7-19-46): Romanian tennis player. "Nasty" for his unruly deportment on court. Beat Arthur Ashe to win 1972 US Open title. Won 1973 French Open. Twice Wimbledon runnerup (to Stan Smith in 1972 and Bjorn Borg in '76).

Martina Navratilova (b. 10-18-56): Tennis player. Third alltime most women's Grand Slam singles titles (18—tied with Chris Evert). Won a record 9 Wimbledon titles, including 6 consecutively (1978-79, 1982-87, 1990). Won 4 U.S. Open titles (consecutively 1983-84, 1986-87), 3 Australian Open titles (1981, 1983, 1985) and 2 French Open titles (1982, 1984). Reached Grand

Slam final 13 other times. Also won 36 Grand Slam doubles titles. Her total of 54 Grand Slam titles is second alltime to Margaret Court's. Completed a non-calendar year Grand Slam in 1984-85. Set mark for longest winning streak with 74 matches in 1984. Also won the doubles Grand Slam in 1984 with Pam Shriver. Won 109 consecutive matches with Shriver from 1983 to 1985. Retired after 1994 season.

Byron Nelson (b. 2-14-12): Golfer. Won the Masters (1937, 1942) and PGA Championship (1940, 1945) 2 times and U.S. Open once (1939). Won 52 career tournaments, including 11 consecutively in 1945.

Ernie Nevers (b. 6-11-03, d. 5-3-76): Football FB. Set alltime pro single game record for points scored (40) and touchdowns (6) on Nov. 28, 1929. Career span 1926-31 with Duluth, Chicago. Also a pitcher with St. Louis, surrendered 2 of Babe Ruth's 60 HR in 1927. All-America at Stanford, earned 11 letters in 4 sports.

John Newcombe (b. 5-23-44): Australian tennis player. Won 3 Wimbledon singles titles (1967, consecutively 1970-71), 2 U.S. titles (1967, 1973) and 2 Australian Open titles (1973, 1975). Also won 17 Grand Slam doubles titles.

Pete Newell (b. 8-31-15): College basketball coach. Despite coaching only 13 seasons, 1947 through 1960, was first coach to win NIT, NCAA and Olympic crowns. Led Univ. of San Francisco to 1949 NIT title, Cal to 1959 NCAA title, and the 1960 U.S. Olympic basketball team that included Jerry Lucas, Oscar Robertson and Jerry West to gold medal. Overall collegiate coaching record of 234–123.

Jack Nicklaus (b. 1-21-40): Golfer. "The Golden Bear." Alltime leader in major championships (20). Second alltime in career wins (70). Winner of the Masters 6 times, more than any golfer (1963, consecutively 1965-66, 1972, 1975, 1986—at age 46, the oldest player to win event), PGA Championship 5 times (1963, 1971, 1973, 1975, 1980), U.S. Open 4 times (1962, 1967, 1972, 1980), British Open 3 times (1966, 1970, 1978) and U.S. Amateur 2 times (1959, 1961). PGA Player of the Year 5 times (1967, consecutively 1972-73, 1975-76). Also NCAA champion with Ohio State in 1961.

Ray Nitschke (b. 12-29-36): Football LB. Defensive signal caller for the great Packer teams of the '60s. Voted Packer MVP by teammates after 1967 season. MVP of the 1962 NFL title game. Career span 1958–72 with Green Bay Packers.

Greg Norman (b. 2-10-55): Golfer. "The Shark" led PGA in winnings in 1986 and '90. Won Vardon Trophy twice, 1989–90. Won two British Opens—in 1986 at Turnberry and in '93 at Royal St. George's—but is almost as famous for his heartbreaking misses. Beaten at the 1986 PGA when Bob Tway holed out a sand shot and at the 1987 Masters when Larry Mize chipped in from a tough downhill lie.

James D. Norris (b. 11-6-06, d. 2-25-66): Hockey executive. Owner of Detroit from 1933 to 1943 and Chicago from 1946 to 1966. Teams won 4 Stanley Cup championships (consecutively 1936-37, 1943, 1961). Defensive Player of the Year award named in his honor. Also a boxing promoter, operated International Boxing Club from 1949 to 1958.

Paavo Nurmi (b. 6-13-1897, d. 10-2-73): Track and field. Finnish middle- and long-distance runner won a total of 9 gold medals at 3 Olympics in 1920, 1924, 1928

Matti Nykänen (b. 7-17-63): Finnish ski jumper. Three-time Olympic gold medalist. Won 90-meter jump (1984, 1988) and 70-meter jump (1988). World champion on 90-meter jump in 1982. Won four World Cups (1983, 1985, 1986, 1988).

Dan O'Brien (b. 7-18-66): Track and field decathlete. Won world decathlon title in 1991 and 1993. Set world decathlon record of 8,891 in Talence, France, on 9-4 and 5-92. Heavily favored to win 1992 Olympic decathlon but missed making U.S. team when he no heighted in pole vault at U.S. Olympic Trials.

Parry O'Brien (b. 1-28-32): Track and field. Shot putter who revolutionized the event with his "glide" technique and won Olympic gold medals in 1952 and 1956, silver in 1960. Set 10 world records from 1953 to 1959, topped by a put of 63' 4" in 1959. Sullivan Award winner in 1959.

Al Oerter (b. 8-19-36): Track and field. Gold medalist in discus at 4 consecutive Olympics (1956, 1960, 1964, 1968), setting Olympic record each time. First to break the 200-foot barrier, throwing 200' 5" in 1962.

Sadaharu Oh (b. 5-20-40): Baseball 1B in Japanese league. 868 career HR in 22 seasons for the Tokyo Giants. Led league in HR 15 times, RBI 13 times, batting 5 times and runs 13 consecutive seasons. Awarded MVP 9 times; won 2 consecutive Triple Crowns and 9 Gold Gloves.

Hakeem Olajuwon (b. 1-21-63): Basketball C. From Nigeria. As part of the University of Houston's "Phi Slamma Jamma" his senior year led NCAA in field goal percentage, rebounding and blocked shots in 1984. All-NBA First Team 1987, '88, '89, '93, 94. Led NBA in rebounding in both 1989 (13.5 per game) and '90 (14.0). League MVP in 1994 as he led Houston to NBA title. Career span since1985 with the Rockets.

Merlin Olsen (b. 9-15-40): Fooball DT. Part of L.A. Rams "Fearsome Foursome" defensive line. Named to Pro Bowl 14 straight times. Career span 1962–76, all with L.A. Rams. Elected to Hall of Fame 1982.

Omaha (b. 1932): Thoroughbred race horse. In 1935 third horse to win Triple Crown. Won Kentucky Derby by 1½ lengths over Roman Soldier; Preakness by 6 over Firethorn; and the Belmont by 1½ from Firethorn. Trained by Sunny Jim Fitzsimmons.

Shaquille O'Neal (b. 3-6-72): Basketball C. As LSU junior led NCAA in blocked shots in 1992, with 5.23 a game, and averaged 4.58 over his 90-game, three-year career. Top pick of Orlando Magic in 1992 NBA draft. Almost unanimous NBA Rookie of the Year 1993. Averaged 23.4 points, 13.9 rebounds and 3.5 blocked shots in first NBA season. Led Magic to first ever playoff appearance in 1994.

Bobby Orr (b. 3-20-48): Hockey D. Defensive Player of the Year more than any other player, 8 consecutive seasons (1968-75). Won MVP award 3 consecutive seasons (1970-72), playoff MVP 2 times (1970, 1972). Also Rookie of the Year in 1967. Led league in assists 5 times and scoring 2 times. Career span 1966-77 with Boston.

Mel Ott (b. 3-2-09, d. 11-21-58): Baseball OF. 511 career HR, 1,861 RBI, .304 batting average. League leader in HR and walks 6 times each. 100+ RBI 9 times and 100+ walks 10 times. Career span 1926-47 with New York.

Jim Otto (b. 1-5-38): Football C. Number 00 started every game (308) in his 15 year career (1960–74) with the Oakland Raiders. Inducted into Hall of Fame in 1980.

Kristin Otto (b. 1966): German swimmer. Won 6 gold medals for East Germany at 1988 Olympics.

Jesse Owens (b. 9-12-13, d. 3-31-80): Track and field. Gold medalist in 4 events (100 meters and 200 meters; 4x100-meter relay and long jump) at 1936 Olympics. At the 1935 Big 10 championship set or equaled 4 world record in 70 minutes, including 100 yards, long jump, 220-yard low hurdles and 220 dash.

Alan Page (b. 8-7-45): Football DT. First defensive player to be named NFL Player of the Year, in 1972. Career span 1967–78 with Minnesota Vikings and 1978–81 with Chicago Bears. Now sits on Minnesota Supreme Court.

Satchel Paige (b. 7-7-06, d. 6-8-82): Baseball RHP. Alltime greatest black pitcher, didn't pitch in major leagues until 1948 at age 42 with Cleveland. Oldest pitcher in major league history at age 59 with Kansas City in 1965. Pitched in the Negro leagues from 1926 to 1950 with Birmingham Black Barons, Pittsburgh Crawfords and Kansas City Monarchs. Estimated career record is 2,000 wins, 250 shutouts, 30,000 strikeouts, 45 no-hitters. Said "Don't look back. Something may be gaining on you."

Arnold Palmer (b. 9-10-29): Golfer. Fourth alltime in career wins (60). Won the Masters 4 times (1958, 1960, 1962, 1964), British Open 2 consecutive years (1961-62) and U.S. Open (1960) and U.S. Amateur (1954) once each. PGA Player of the Year 2 times (1960, 1962). The first golfer to surpass $1 million in career earnings. Also won Seniors Championship 2 times (1980, 1984) and U.S. Senior Open once (1981). 10 career seniors titles as of 10-1-94.

Jim Palmer (b. 10-15-45): Baseball RHP. 268 career wins, 2.86 ERA. Won 3 Cy Young Awards (1973, consecutively 1975-76). Won 20+ games 8 times. Led league in wins 3 times, innings pitched 4 times, ERA 2 times. Never allowed a grand slam HR. Pitched on 6 World Series teams with Baltimore, including shutout at 20 years old in 1966. Pitched no-hitter in 1969. Jockey underwear pitchman. Career span 1965-84.

Bernie Parent (b. 4-3-45): Hockey G. Alltime leader for wins in a season (47 in 1974). Goaltender of the Year, playoff MVP, league leader in wins, goals against average and shutouts 2 consecutive seasons (1974-75). Career record 270-197-121, including 55 shutouts. Career 2.55 goals against average. Tied record of 4 playoff shutouts in 1975. Played on 2 consecutive Stanley Cup champions (1974-75). Career span 1965 to 1979 with Philadelphia. Also the first NHL player to sign with the WHA in 1972, with Philadelphia.

Brad Park (b. 7-6-48): Hockey D. Seven-time All Star. In 17 seasons with the New York Rangers, Boston Bruins and Detroit Red Wings (1968–69 through 1984–85) scored 213 goals and had 683 assists. Elected to Hall of Fame 1988.

Jim Parker (b. 4-3-34): Football T/G. Winner of 1956 Outland Trophy as Ohio State senior. Blocked for Johnny Unitas. All-NFL four times at guard, four times at tackle. Career span 1957–67, all with Baltimore Colts. Inducted into Hall of Fame in 1973.

Joe Paterno (b. 12-21-26): College football coach. Fourth alltime in wins in Division I-A (257—the most of any active coach at that level). Has won 2 national championships (1982, 1986) with Penn State since 1966. Career record 257-69-3, including 4 undefeated seasons. Has also won 15 bowl games.

Lester Patrick (b. 12-30-1883, d. 6-1-60): Hockey coach. Led NY Rangers to three Stanley Cup championships (1928, 1933, 1940). Originated the NHL's farm system and developed playoff format.

Floyd Patterson (b. 1-4-35): Boxer. Heavyweight champion 2 times (1956-59, 1960-62). First heavyweight to regain title, in rematch with Ingemar Johansson. Career record 55-8-1 with 40 KOs from 1952 to 1972. Also middleweight gold medalist at 1952 Olympics.

Walter Payton (b. 7-25-54): Football RB. Alltime leader in yards rushing (16,726), rushing attempts (3,838), games gaining 100+ yards rushing (77), seasons gaining 1,000+ yards rushing (10) and rushing touchdowns (110). His 125 total touchdowns rank third. Rushed for a record 275 yards on Nov. 20, 1977. Selected for Pro Bowl 9 times. Player of the Year 2 times (1977, 1985). Led league in rushing 5 consecutive seasons. Career span 1975-87 with Chicago.

Pele (b. 10-23-40): Born Edson Arantes do Nascimento. Brazilian soccer player. Soccer's great ambassador. Played on 3 World Cup winners with Brazil (1958, 1962, 1970). Helped promote soccer in U.S. by playing with NY Cosmos from 1975 to 1977. Scored 1,281 goals in 22 years.

Willie Pep (b. 9-19-22): Boxer. Featherweight champion 2 times (1942-48, 1949-50). Lost title to Sandy Saddler, won it back in rematch, then lost it to Saddler again. Career record 230-11-1 with 65 KOs from 1940 to 1966. Won 73 consecutive bouts from 1940 to 1943. Defended title 9 times.

Gil Perreault (b. 11-13-50): Hockey C. Won Calder Trophy as NHL's top rookie for 1970–71 season. Played 17 seasons (1970–71 through 1986–87), all with Buffalo Sabres. Scored 512 goals and had 814 assists in career. Elected to Hall of Fame in 1990.

Fred Perry (b. 5-18-09): British tennis player. Won 3 consecutive Wimbledon singles titles (1934-36), the last British man to win the tournament. Also won 3 U.S. titles (consecutively 1933-34, 1936), 1 French title (1935) and 1 Australian title (1934).

Gaylord Perry (b. 9-15-38): Baseball RHP. Only pitcher to win Cy Young Award in both leagues (Cleveland 1972, San Diego 1978). 314 career wins, 3,534 strikeouts. 20+ wins 5 times; 200+ strikeouts 8 times; 250+ innings pitched 12 times. Pitched no-hitter in 1968. Admitted to throwing a spitter. Career span 1962-83 with San Francisco, Cleveland, San Diego.

Bob Pettit (b. 12-12-32): Basketball F. First player in history to break 20,000-point barrier (20,880 career points scored). Sixth alltime highest scoring average (26.4) and seventh most free throws made (6,182). Also grabbed 12,849 rebounds for 16.2 average. MVP in 1956, 1959. Rookie of the Year in 1955. All-Star 10 consecutive seasons. Led league in scoring 2 times, rebounding 1 time. Career span 1954-64 with St Louis.

Richard Petty (b. 7-2-37): Auto racer. Alltime leader in NASCAR victories (200). Daytona 500 winner (1964, 1966, 1971, consecutively 1973-74, 1979, 1981) and NASCAR champion (1964, 1967, consecutively 1971-72, 1974-75, 1979) 7 times each, the most of any driver. First stock car racer to reach $1 million in earnings. Son of Lee Petty, 3-time NASCAR champion (1954, consecutively 1958-59). Retired after 1992 season.

Laffit Pincay Jr. (b. 12-29-46): Jockey. Through 1993 had won more money than any other jockey

($177,153,172) and was second only to Bill Shoemaker in wins, with 8,054. Won 5 Eclipse Awards as outstanding jockey. Rode 3 Kentucky Derby winners; 2 Preakness winners; and 1 Belmont winner.

Jacques Plante (b. 1-17-29, d. 2-27-86): Hockey G. First goalie to wear a mask. Second alltime in wins (434) and second lowest modern goals against average (2.38). Goaltender of the Year 7 times, more than any other goalie (consecutively 1955-59, 1961, 1968). Won MVP award in 1961. Led league in goals against average 8 times, wins 6 times and shutouts 4 times. Was on 6 Stanley Cup champions with Montreal from 1952 to 1962 and played for 4 other teams until retirement in 1972.

Gary Player (b. 11-1-35): South African golfer. Won the Masters (1961, 1974, 1978) and British Open (1959, 1968, 1974) 3 times each, PGA Championship 2 times (1962, 1972) and U.S. Open (1965). Also won Seniors Championship 3 times (1986, 1988, 1990) and U.S. Senior Open 2 consecutive years (1987-88).

Sam Pollock (b. 12-15-25): Hockey executive. As general manager of Montreal from 1964 to 1978 won 9 Stanley Cup championships (1965-66, 1968-69, 1971, 1973, 1976-78).

Denis Potvin (b. 10-29-53): Hockey D. Seven time All Star during 15 season career (1973–74 through 1987–88), all with New York Islanders. Won Calder Trophy for 1973–74 season. Won Norris Trophy three times. Captained Islanders to four Stanley Cup championships. Elected to Hall of Fame in 1991.

Mike Powell (b. 11-10-63): Track and field. Long jumper broke Bob Beamon's 23-year-old world record at 1991 World Championships in Tokyo with a jump of 29' 4½".

Annemarie Moser-Pröll (b. 3-27-53): Austrian skier. Gold medalist in downhill at 1980 Olympics. World Cup overall champion 6 times, more than any other skier (consecutively 1971-75, 1979).

Alain Prost (b. 2-24-55): French auto racer. Alltime leader in Formula 1 victories. Formula 1 champion 4 times (consecutively 1985-86, 1989, 1993).

Jack Ramsay (b. 2-21-25): Basketball coach. Never played in NBA. Coached 11 seasons at St. Joseph's University, with 234–72 record. Overall record of 864–783 as NBA coach. Coach of NBA champion 1977 Portland Trail Blazers. Elected to Hall of Fame 1992.

Jean Ratelle (b. 10-3-40): Hockey C. In 21 season career (1960–61 through 1980–81) with the New York Rangers and Boston Bruins, scored 491 goals and had 776 assists. Twice won Lady Bing Trophy. Elected to Hall of Fame in 1985.

Willis Reed (b. 6-25-42): Basketball C. Played 10 seasons (1965–74), all with the New York Knicks. Career average of 18.7 points a game. NBA Rookie of Year in 1965. Playoff MVP of both Knick championship teams, in 1970 and '73. NBA MVP in 1970. Elected to Hall of Fame in 1970.

Harold Henry "Pee Wee" Reese (b. 7-23-18): Baseball SS. Played for 7 pennant-winning Dodger teams. Led NL in runs scored in 1949, with 132. Elected to Hall of Fame in 1984.

Mary Lou Retton (b. 1-24-68): Gymnast. Won 1 gold, 1 silver and 2 bronze medals at 1984 Olympics.

Grantland Rice (b. 11-1-1880, d. 7-13-54): Sportswriter. Legendary figure during sport's Golden Age of the 1920s. Wrote "When the Last Great Scorer comes / To mark against your name, / He'll write not 'won' or 'lost' / But how you played the game." Also named the 1924-25 Notre Dame backfield the "Four Horsemen."

Jerry Rice (b. 10-13-62): Football WR. Alltime leader in touchdowns (127th on 9-5-94), touchdown receptions (120) and in consecutive games with a TD reception (13 in 1988). Player of the Year in 1987 and led league in scoring (138 points on 23 touchdowns). Super Bowl MVP in 1989 with record 215 receiving yards on 11 catches. Also set Super Bowl record with 3 touchdown receptions in 1990. Career span since 1985 with San Francisco 49ers.

Henri Richard (b. 2-29-36): Hockey C. "The Pocket Rocket." Played on 11 Stanley Cup champions with Montreal. Four-time All-Star. Career span from 1955 to 1975.

Maurice Richard (b. 8-4-21): Hockey RW. "The Rocket." First player ever to score 50 goals in a season, in 1945. Led league in goals 5 times. 544 career goals. Won MVP award in 1947. All-Star 8 times. Tied playoff game record for most goals (5 on March 23, 1944). Played on 8 Stanley Cup champions with Montreal from 1942 to 1959.

Bob Richards (b. 2-2-26): Track and field. The only pole vaulter to win gold medal at 2 consecutive Olympics (1952, 1956). Also won Sullivan Award in 1951.

Branch Rickey (b. 12-20-1881, d. 12-9-65): Baseball executive. Integrated major league baseball in 1947 by signing Jackie Robinson to contract with Brooklyn Dodgers. Conceived minor league farm system in 1919 at St Louis; instituted batting cage and sliding pit.

Pat Riley (b. 3-20-45): Basketball coach. Going into 1994-95 season most playoff wins (131). Coached Los Angeles to 4 championships, 2 consecutively, from 1981 to 1989. 60+ wins 6 times (4 times consecutively), 50+ wins 4 other times. Led New York Knicks to NBA Finals in 1994.

Cal Ripken Jr (b. 8-24-60): Baseball SS. Ended 1994 season with second longest consecutive game streak (2,009 since May 29, 1982). Set record for consecutive errorless games by a shortstop (95 in 1990). MVP in 1983 and Rookie of the Year in 1982. Has hit 20+ HRs in 11 consecutive seasons and started in 10 consecutive All-Star games.

Glenn "Fireball" Roberts (b. 1-20-31, d. 7-2-64): Auto racer. Won 34 NASCAR races. Died as a result of fiery accident in World 600 at Charlotte Motor Speedway in May 1964. At time of his death had won more major races than any other driver in NASCAR history.

Oscar Robertson (b. 11-24-38): Basketball G. "The Big O." Second alltime most assists (9,887), second most free throws made (7,694), fifth most points scored (26,710), sixth most field goals made (9,508) and ninth highest scoring average (25.7). MVP in 1964, All-Star 9 consecutive seasons and 1961 Rookie of the Year. Led league in assists 6 times, free throw percentage 2 times. Averaged 30+ points 6 times in 7 seasons, 20+ points 4 other times. Only player in history to average a season triple-double (1961). Career span 1960-72 with Cincinnati, Milwaukee. Also College Player of the Year, All-America and NCAA scoring leader 3 consecutive seasons from 1958 to 1960 with Cincinnati. Third alltime NCAA highest scoring average (33.8); sixth most points scored (2,973).

Brooks Robinson (b. 5-18-37): Baseball 3B. Alltime leader in assists, putouts, double plays and fielding average among 3rd baseman. Won 16 consecutive Gold Gloves. Led league in fielding average a record 11 times. MVP in 1964—led league in RBI—and MVP in 1970 World Series. Career span 1955-77 with Baltimore.

David Robinson (b. 8-6-65): Basketball C. *Sporting News* Player of the Year for 1987. Led college players in 1986 in both rebounding (13.0) and blocked shots (5.91, a record that still stands). NBA Rookie of Year in 1990. Led NBA in rebounding 1991 (13.0) and in blocked shots in 1992, when he was named Defensive Player of the Year.

Eddie Robinson (b. 2-13-19): College football coach. Has had alltime college record 388 career wins at Division I-AA Grambling State since 1941.

Frank Robinson (b. 8-31-35): Baseball OF-manager. Only player to win MVP awards in both leagues (Cincinnati, 1961, Baltimore, 1966). Won Triple Crown and World Series MVP in 1966. Rookie of the Year in 1956. Fourth alltime most HR (586). 30+ HR 11 times; 100+ RBI 6 times; 100+ runs scored 8 times (led league 3 times). Had .300+ batting average 9 times. Became first black manager in major leagues, with Cleveland in 1975. Career span as player 1956-76. Career span as manager 1975-77 with Cleveland; 1981-84 with San Francisco; 1988-91 with Baltimore.

Jackie Robinson (b. 1-13-19, d. 10-24-72): Baseball 2B. Broke the color barrier as first black player in major leagues in 1947 with Brooklyn Dodgers. 1947 Rookie of the Year; 1949 MVP with .342 batting average to lead league. Had .311 career batting average. Led league in stolen bases 2 times; stole home 19 times. Played on 6 pennant winners in 10 years with Brooklyn.

Larry Robinson (b. 6-2-51): Hockey D. Twice won Norris Trophy as NHL's top defenseman. Career span 1972–73 through 1991–92, all but the last three with the Montreal Canadiens. Member of six Montreal teams that won Stanley Cup. Awarded Conn Smythe Trophy as MVP of 1978 Stanley Cup.

Sugar Ray Robinson (b. 5-3-21, d. 4-12-89): Born Walker Smith, Jr. Boxer. Called best pound-for-pound boxer in history. Welterweight champion (1946-51) and middleweight champion 5 times. Career record 174-19-6 with 109 KOs from 1940 to 1965. Won 91 consecutive bouts from 1943 to 1951. 15 of his 19 losses came after age 35. Retired at age 45.

Knute Rockne (b. 3-4-1888, d. 3-31-31): College football coach. Won national championship 3 times (1924, consecutively 1929-30). Alltime highest winning percentage (.881). Career record 105-12-5, including 5 undefeated seasons, with Notre Dame from 1918 to 1930.

Bill Rodgers (b. 12-23-47): Track and field. Won the Boston and New York City marathons 4 times each between 1975 and 1980.

Chi Chi Rodriguez (b. 10-23-35): Golfer. Puerto Rican had won 22 Senior tour events through 1993 season. Led senior money list for 1987 ($509,145). Won 8 events during PGA career that began in 1960.

Art Rooney (b. 1-27-01; d. 8-25-88): Owner of Pittsburgh Steelers. Bought team in 1933 and ran it until his death in 1988. Elected to Hall of Fame in 1964.

Murray Rose (b. 1-6-39) Australian swimmer. Won 3 gold medals (including 400- and 1500-meter freestyle) at 1956 Olympics. Also won 1 gold, 1 silver and 1 bronze medal at 1960 Olympics.

Pete Rose (b. 4-14-41): Baseball OF-IF. "Charlie Hustle." Alltime leader in hits (4,256), games played (3,562) and at bats (14,053); second in doubles (746); fourth in runs scored (2,165). Had .303 career average and won 3 batting titles. Averaged .300+ 15 times, 200+ hits and 100+ runs scored each 10 times. Led league in hits 7 times, runs scored 4 times, doubles 5 times. 1963 Rookie of the Year; 1973 MVP; 1975 World Series MVP. Had 44-game hitting streak in 1978. Played in 17 All-Star games, starting at 5 different positions. Career span 1963-86 with Cincinnati, Philadelphia. Manager of Cincinnati from 1984 to 1989. Banned from baseball for life by Commissioner Bart Giamatti in 1989 for betting activities. Served 5-month jail term for tax evasion in 1990. Ineligible for Hall of Fame.

Ken Rosewall (b. 11-2-34): Australian tennis player. Won Grand Slam singles titles at ages 18 and 35. Won 4 Australian titles (1953, 1955, consecutively 1971-72), 2 French titles (1953, 1968) and 2 U.S. titles (1956, 1970). Reached 4 Wimbledon finals, but title eluded him.

Art Ross (b. 1-13-1886, d. 8-5-64): Hockey D-coach. Improved design of puck and goal net. Manager-coach of Boston, 1924-45, won Stanley Cup, 1938-39. The Art Ross Trophy is awarded to the NHL scoring champion.

Donald Ross (b. 1873, d. 4-26-48): Scottish-born golf course architect. Trained at St. Andrews under Old Tom Morris. Designed over 500 courses, including Pinehurst No. 2 course and Oakland Hills.

Patrick Roy (b. 10-5-65): Hockey G. Won Vezina Trophy as NHL's top goalie three times. Won Conn Smythe Trophy as MVP of 1993 Stanley Cup. Career span since 1984 with Montreal.

Pete Rozelle (b. 3-1-26): Football executive. Fourth NFL commissioner, served from 1960 to 1989. During his term, league expanded from 12 to 28 teams. Created Super Bowl in 1966 and negotiated merger with AFL. Devised plan for revenue sharing of lucrative TV monies among owners. Presided during players' strikes of 1982, 1987.

Wilma Rudolph (b. 6-23-40): Track and field. Gold medalist in 3 events (100-, 200- and 4x100-meter relay) at 1960 Olympics. Also won Sullivan Award in 1961.

Adolph Rupp (b. 9-2-01, d. 12-10-77): College basketball coach. Alltime NCAA leader in wins (875) and third highest winning percentage (.822). Won 4 NCAA championships: consecutively 1948-49, 1951, 1958. Career span 1930-72 with Kentucky.

Amos Rusie (b. 5-3-1871, d. 12-6-42): Baseball RHP. Fastball was so intimidating that in 1893 the pitching mound was moved back 5' 6" to its present distance of 60' 6" Led league in strikeouts and walks 5 times each. Career record 246-174, 3.07 ERA with New York (NL) from 1889-1901.

Bill Russell (b. 2-12-34): Basketball C. Won MVP award 5 times (1958, consecutively 1961-63, 1965). Played on 11 championship teams, 8 consecutively, with Boston (1957, 1959-66, 1968-69). Player-coach 1968-69 (league's first black coach). Second alltime most rebounds (21,620) and second highest rebounding average (22.5); second most rebounds in a game (51 in 1960). Led league in rebounding 4 times. Also played on 2 consecutive NCAA championship teams with San

Francisco in 1955-56; tournament MVP in 1955. Member of gold medal-winning 1956 Olympic team.

Babe Ruth (b. 2-6-1895, d. 8-16-48): Born George Herman Ruth. Baseball P-OF. Most dominant player in history. Alltime leader in slugging average (.690), HR frequency (8.5 HR every 100 at bats) and walks (2,056); second alltime most HR (714), RBI (2,211) and runs scored (2,174). Holds season record highest slugging average (.847 in 1920). 1923 MVP. Had .342 career batting average and 2,873 hits. 60 HR in 1927, 50+ HR 3 other times and 40+ HR 7 other times; 100+ RBI and 100+ walks 13 times each; 100+ runs scored 12 times. Second alltime most World Series HR (15), including his "called shot" off Charlie Root in 1932. Began career as a pitcher for Boston Red Sox: 94 career wins and 2.28 ERA. Won 20+ games 2 times; ERA leader in 1916. Played on 10 pennant winners, 7 World Series winners (3 with Boston, 4 with New York). Sold to Yankees in 1920 (Boston hasn't won World Series since). Career span 1914-35.

Nolan Ryan (b. 1-31-47): Baseball RHP. Pitched record 7th no hitter on May 1, 1991. Alltime leader in strikeouts (5,714), walks (2,795). League leader in strikeouts 11 times, walks 8 times, shutouts 3 times, ERA 2 times. 300+ strikeouts 6 times, including season record of 383 in 1973. 324 career wins. Career span 1966–93 with New York (NL), California, Houston, Texas.

Jim Ryun (b. 4-29-47): Track and field. Youngest ever to run under four minutes for the mile (3:59.0 at 17 years, 37 days). Set two world records in mile (3:51.3 in 1966 and 3:51.1 in 1967) and one in 1,500 (3:33.1 in 1967). Plagued by bad luck at Olympics; won silver medal in 1968 1,500 meters despite mononucleosis; was bumped and fell in 1972. Won Sullivan Award in 1967.

Toni Sailer (b. 11-17-35): Austrian skier. Won gold medals in 1956 Olympics in slalom, giant slalom and downhill, the first skier to accomplish the feat.

Juan Antonio Samaranch (b. 7-17-20): Amateur sports executive. Spaniard served as president of International Olympic Committee from 1980-1993.

Joan Benoit Samuelson (b. 5-16-57): Track and field. Gold medalist in first ever women's Olympic marathon (1984). Won Boston Marathon 2 times (1979, 1983). Sullivan Award winner in 1985.

Barry Sanders (b. 7-16-68): Football RB. Alltime NCAA season leader in yards rushing (2,628 in 1988). Won Heisman Trophy in 1988 at Oklahoma State. Entered NFL in 1989 with Detroit and named Rookie of the Year. Gained 1,000+ yards rushing and named to Pro Bowl each of his first 5 seasons. Led league in rushing in 1990.

Gene Sarazen (b. 2-27-02): Golfer. Won PGA Championship 3 times (consecutively 1922-23, 1933), U.S. Open 2 times (1922, 1932), British Open once (1932) and the Masters once (1935). His win at the Masters included golf's most famous shot, a double eagle on the 15th hole of the final round to tie Craig Wood (Sarazen then won the playoff). Won 38 career tournaments. Also won Seniors Championship 2 times (1954, 1958). Pioneered the sand wedge in 1930.

Glen Sather (b. 9-2-43): Hockey coach and general manager. As coach, fourth alltime highest winning percentage (.634) and sixth in regular season wins (442). Led Edmonton to 4 Stanley Cup championships (consecutively 1984-85, 1987-88) from 1979 to 1989.

Relinquished coaching duties in 1989. Also played for 6 teams from 1966 to 1976.

Terry Sawchuk (b. 12-28-29): Hockey G. All-time leader in wins (435) and shutouts (103). Career 2.52 goals against average. Goaltender of the Year 4 times (consecutively 1951-52, 1954, 1964). Led league in wins and shutouts 3 times and goals against average 2 times. Rookie of the Year in 1950. Tied record of 4 playoff shutouts in 1952. Played on 4 Stanley Cup champions with Detroit and Toronto from 1949 to 1969.

Gale Sayers (b. 5-30-43): Football RB. Alltime leader in kickoff return average (30.6). Scored 56 career touchdowns, including a rookie record 22 in 1965. Led league in rushing and gained 1,000+ yards rushing 2 times. Averaged 5 yards per carry, third best in history. Rookie of the Year in 1965. Tied record with 6 rushing touchdowns on Dec. 12, 1965. Career span 1965-71 with Chicago cut short due to knee injury. Also All-America 2 times while at Kansas.

Dolph Schayes (b. 5-19-28): Basketball player. College star at NYU. In 1960 became first NBA player to reach 15,000 career points. Also first NBA player to play in 1,000 games. Led NBA in free throw percentage three times, and averaged .843 for his career. Over stretch of 10 years played in 706 consecutive games. Elected to Hall of Fame 1972.

Bo Schembechler (b. 4-1-29): Football coach. In 21 seasons at Michigan from 1969–89, had a 194-48-5 record. Overall college coaching record 234-65-8.

Mike Schmidt (b. 9-27-49): Baseball 3B. Won 3 MVP awards (consecutively 1980-81, 1986). 548 career HR. Led league in HR 8 times, slugging average 5 times and RBI, walks and strikeouts 4 times each. 40+ HR 3 times, 30+ HR 10 other times; 100+ RBI 9 times, 100+ runs scored 7 times, 100+ strikeouts 12 times and third alltime most strikeouts (1,883). 100+ walks 7 times. Won 10 Gold Gloves. Career span 1972-89 with Philadelphia.

Don Schollander (b. 4-30-46): Swimmer. Won 4 gold medals (including 100- and 400-meter freestyle) at 1964 Olympics; won 1 gold and 1 silver medal at 1968 Olympics. Also won Sullivan Award in 1964.

Dick Schultz (b. 9-5-29): Amateur sports executive. Second executive director of the NCAA, served from 1987 to '93. Also served as athletic director at Cornell (1976-81) and Virginia (1981-87).

Seattle Slew (b. 1974): Thoroughbred race horse. Horse of the Year for 1977, when he won the Triple Crown, winning the Kentucky Derby by 1¾ lengths; the Preakness by 1½; and the Belmont by 4. In three year career from 1976–78, won 14 of 17 starts.

Tom Seaver (b. 11-17-44): Baseball RHP. "Tom Terrific." 311 career wins, 2.86 ERA. Cy Young Award winner 3 times (1969, 1973, 1975) and Rookie of the Year 1967. Fourth alltime most strikeouts (3,640). Led league in strikeouts 5 times, winning percentage 4 times and wins and ERA 3 times each. Won 20+ games 5 times; 200+ strikeouts 10 times. Struck out 19 batters in 1 game in 1970, including the final 10 in succession. Pitched no-hitter in 1978. Career span 1967-86 with New York (NL), Cincinnati, Chicago (AL), Boston.

Secretariat (b. 3-30-70, d. 10-4-89): Thoroughbred race horse. Triple Crown winner in 1973 with jockey Ron Turcotte aboard. Trained by Lucien Laurin.

Monica Seles (b. 12-2-73): Tennis player. Has won 3 consecutive French Open singles titles (1990-92), 3 Australian Open titles (1991-93) and 2 U.S. Open titles (1991-92). Seles' 1993 season ended on 4-30 when she was stabbed in the back by Gunther Parche while seated during a changeover in a tournament in Hamburg, Germany; also missed 1994 season.

Bill Sharman (b. 5-25-26): Basketball G. First team All Star four straight years 1956–59. Led NBA in free throw percentage every year from 1953–57, and in 1959 and '61. All Star Game MVP in 1955. NBA Coach of the Year in 1972, when his Lakers won NBA title. Elected to Hall of Fame in 1974.

Wilbur Shaw (b. 10-31-02, d. 10-30-54): Auto racer. Won Indy 500 3 times in 4 years (1937, consecutively 1939-40). AAA champion 2 times (1937, 1939). Also pioneered the use of the crash helmet after suffering skull fracture in 1923 crash.

Patty Sheehan (b. 10-27-57): Golfer. Won back-to-back LPGA championships, 1983–84. Won 1992 US Women's Open. 1983 LPGA Player of Year. Vare Trophy winner in 1984. Through '92 season, 29 career wins on LPGA tour; fourth alltime in earnings, with $3,562,370.01.

Fred Shero (b. 10-23-25, d. 11-24-90): Hockey coach. Fourth all-time highest winning percentage (.612, regular season). Led Philadelphia to 2 Stanley Cup championships (1974-75). Also coached NY Rangers. Played defense for NY Rangers, 1947-50.

Bill Shoemaker (b. 8-19-31): Horse racing jockey. Alltime leader in wins (8,833). Rode Belmont Stakes winner 5 times (1957, 1959, 1962, 1967, 1975), Kentucky Derby winner 4 times (1955, 1959, 1965, 1986--at age 54, the oldest jockey to win Derby) and Preakness Stakes winner 2 times (1963, 1967). Also won Eclipse Award in 1981.

Eddie Shore (b. 11-25-02, d. 3-16-85): Hockey D. Won MVP award 4 times (1933, consecutively 1935-36, 1938). All-Star 7 times. Played on 2 Stanley Cup champions with Boston from 1926 to 1940.

Frank Shorter (b. 10-31-47): Track and field. Gold medalist in marathon at 1972 Olympics, the first American to win the event since 1908. Olympic silver medalist in 1976 marathon. Sullivan Award winner in 1972.

Jim Shoulders (b. 5-13-28): Rodeo. Alltime leader in career titles (16). All-Around champion 5 times (1949, consecutively 1956-59).

Don Shula (b. 1-4-30): Football coach. Alltime leader in wins (327). Won 2 consecutive Super Bowl championships (1972-73) with Miami, including NFL's only undefeated season in 1972. Also reached Super Bowl 4 other times. Career span since 1963 with Baltimore and Miami.

Al Simmons (b. 5-22-02; d. 5-26-56): Baseball OF. "Bucketfoot Al" for hitting stance. Named AL MVP for 1929, when he led league 157 RBIs. Led league in batting average in 1930 (.381) and '31 (.390). Lifetime average of .334 with 307 homers. Career span 1924–44 with a variety of teams, but mostly Philadelphia A's. Elected to Hall of Fame in 1953.

O. J. Simpson (b. 7-9-47): Given name Orenthal James. Football RB. Seventh alltime in yards rushing (11,236). Gained 1,000+ yards rushing 5 consecutive seasons, including then-record 2,003 yards in 1973. Player of the Year 3 times (consecutively 1972-73, 1975). Led league in rushing 4 times. Gained 200+

yards rushing in a game a record 6 times, including 273 yards on Nov. 25, 1976. Scored 61 career touchdowns, including 23 in 1975. Also won Heisman Trophy with USC in 1968.

Sir Barton (b. 1916): Thoroughbred race horse. In 1919, before they were linked to the Triple Crown, became first horse to win the Kentucky Derby, the Preakness and the Belmont Stakes. Won 8 of 13 starts as 3-year-old.

George Sisler (b. 3-24-1893, d. 3-26-73): Baseball 1B. Alltime most hits in a season (257 in 1920). League leader in hits 2 times, with 200+ hits 6 times. Won 2 batting titles, including .420 average in 1922; averaged .400+ 2 times and .300+ 11 other times. Had 2,812 career hits and .340 average. Career span 1915-30 with St Louis.

Mary Decker Slaney (b. 8-4-58): Track and field. American record holder in 5 events ranging from 800 to 3,000 meters. Won 1,500 and 3,000 meters at World Championships in 1983. Lost chance for medal at 1984 Olympics when she tripped and fell after contact with Zola Budd. Won Sullivan Award in 1982.

Dean Smith (b. 2-28-31): College basketball coach. Entered 1994-95 season second alltime in wins (802), the most among active coaches; fifth alltime highest winning percentage (.777). Alltime most NCAA tournament appearances (24), reached Final Four 9 times. Won NCAA championship in 1982 and '93. Coached 1976 Olympic team to gold medal. Career span since 1962 with North Carolina.

Emmitt Smith (b. 5-15-69): Football RB. Led NFL in rushing in 1991 (1,563 yards) and '92 (1,713 and 18 TDs). Rushed for 108 yards in 52–17 Cowboy win over Bills in Super Bowl XXVII. Rushed for 132 yards and named MVP of Super Bowl XXVIII, a 30–13 Dallas victory over Buffalo. Career span since 1990 with Cowboys.

Ozzie Smith (b. 12-26-54): Baseball SS. "The Wizard of Oz." May be the best defensive shortstop in history. Holds alltime record for most assists in a season among shortstops (621 in 1980). 10 consecutive starts in All-Star game. Won 13 consecutive Gold Gloves. Career span since 1978 with San Diego, St Louis.

Red Smith (b. 9-25-05, d. 1-15-82): Sportswriter. Won Pulitzer Prize in 1976. After Grantland Rice, the most widely syndicated sports columnist. His literate essays appeared in the *NY Herald Tribune* from 1945 to 1971 and the *NY Times* from 1971 to 1982.

Stan Smith (b. 12-14-46): Tennis. Won 39 tournaments in career, including 1972 Wimbledon in 5 sets over Ilie Nastase. Won 1971 US Open over Jan Kodes and amateur version of U.S. Open in 1969. 1970 won inaugural Grand Prix Masters. Inducted to Tennis Hall of Fame in 1987.

Tommy Smith (b. 6-5-44): Track and field. Sprinter won 1968 Olympic 200 meters in world record of 19.83, then was expelled from Olympic Village, along with bronze medalist John Carlos, for raising black-gloved fist and bowing head during playing of national anthem to protest racism in U.S.

Conn Smythe (b. 2-1-1895, d. 11-18-80): Hockey executive. As general manager with Toronto from 1929 to 1961 won 7 Stanley Cup championships (1932, 1942, 1945, consecutively 1947-49, 1951). Award for playoff MVP named in his honor.

Sam Snead (b. 5-27-12): Golfer. Alltime leader in career wins (81). Won the Masters (1949, 1952, 1954) and PGA Championship (1942, 1949, 1951) 3 times each and British Open (1946). Runner-up at U.S. Open 4 times, but title eluded him. PGA Player of the Year in 1949. Won Seniors Championship 6 times, more than any golfer (1964-65, 1967, 1970, 1972-73).

Peter Snell (b. 12-17-38): Track and field. New Zealand runner was gold medalist in 800 meters at 2 consecutive Olympics in 1960, 1964. Also gold medalist in 1,500 meters at 1964 Olympics. Twice broke world mile record; broke world 800 record once.

Duke Snider (b. 9-19-26): Baseball OF. Career .295 average, 407 HR and 1,333 RBIs. Hit 40+ HR 5 consecutive seasons and 100+ RBIs 6 times. Also led league in runs scored 3 consecutive seasons. Played on 6 pennant winners with the Brooklyn Dodgers. World Series total of 11 HR and 26 RBIs are NL best. Career span from 1947-64.

Javier Sotomayor (b. 10-13-67): Track and field. Cuban high jumper broke the 8-foot barrier with world record jump of 8' 0" in 1989. Set current record of 8' ½" in 7-27-93 in Salamanca, Spain.

Warren Spahn (b. 4-23-21): Baseball LHP. Alltime leader in games won for a lefthander (363). 20+ wins 13 times. League leader in wins 8 times (5 seasons consecutively), complete games 9 times (7 seasons consecutively), strikeouts 4 consecutive seasons, innings pitched 4 times and ERA 3 times. 1957 Cy Young award. 63 career shutouts. Pitched 2 no-hitters after age 39. Career span 1942-65, all but last year with Boston (NL), Milwaukee.

Tris Speaker (b. 4-4-1888, d. 12-8-58): Baseball OF. Alltime leader in doubles (792), fifth in hits (3,514) and fifth in batting average (.345). 1 batting title (.386 in 1916), but .375+ average 6 times and .300+ average 12 other times. League leader in doubles 8 times, hits 2 times and HR and RBI 1 time each. 200+ hits 4 times, 40+ doubles 10 times and 100+ runs scored 7 times. MVP in 1912. Alltime leader among outfielders in assists and double plays, second in putouts. Career span 1907-28 with Boston, Cleveland.

Michael Spinks (b. 7-13-56): Boxer. 1976 Olympic middleweight champion. Brother Leon was heavyweight champ. Won world light heavyweight title by decision over Mustafa Muhammad on 7-18-81. Defended it 5 times and then consolidated light heavy titles with decision over Dwight Braxton on 3-18-83. Defended four more times. Won heavyweight title on 9-22-85 in decision over Larry Holmes. Lost title to Mike Tyson in 91 seconds on 6-27-88.

Mark Spitz (b. 2-10-50): Swimmer. Won a record 7 gold medals (2 in freestyle, 2 in butterfly, 3 in relays) at 1972 Olympics, setting world record in each event. Also won 2 gold medals and 1 silver and 1 bronze medal at 1968 Olympics. Sullivan Award winner in 1971.

Amos Alonzo Stagg (b. 8-16-1862, d. 3-17-65): College football coach. Third alltime in wins (314). Won national championship with Chicago in 1905. Coach of the Year with Pacific in 1943 at age 81. Career record 314-199-35, including 5 undefeated seasons, from 1892 to 1946. Only person elected to both college football and basketball Halls of Fame. Played in the first basketball game in 1891.

Willie Stargell (b. 3-6-40): Baseball OF/1B. "Pops" achieved a 1979 MVP triple crown, winning NL regular season, playoff and World Series MVP awards. Led NL in homers in 1971 and '73. Only person to hit ball out of Dodger Stadium and he did it twice. Hit 475 career homers. Drove in 1,540 runs. Had .282 career batting average. Played all 21 seasons with the Pirates. Elected to Hall of Fame in 1988.

Bart Starr (b. 1-9-34): Football QB. Played on 3 NFL champions (consecutively 1961-62, 1965) and first two Super Bowl champions (1966-67) with Green Bay. Also named MVP of first two Super Bowls. Player of the Year in 1966. Led league in passing 3 times. Also coached Green Bay to 53-77-3 record from 1975 to 1983.

Roger Staubach (b. 2-5-42): Football QB. Won Heisman Trophy with Navy as a junior in 1963. Served 4-year military obligation before turning pro. Led Dallas to 6 NFC Championships, 4 Super Bowls and 2 Super Bowl titles (1971, 1977). Player of the Year and Super Bowl MVP in 1971. Also led league in passing 4 times. Career span 1969-79.

Jan Stenerud (b. 11-26-42): Football K. Second to George Blanda on NFL scoring list, with 1,699 points. Converted an NFL record 373 field goals in 558 attempts. Career span 1967–79 with Kansas City Chiefs, 1980–83 with Green Bay Packers and 1984–85 with Minnesota Vikings. First pure kicker inducted to Hall of Fame 1991.

Casey Stengel (b. 7-30-1890, d. 9-29-75): Baseball manager. "The Ol' Perfesser." Managed New York Yankees to 10 pennants and 7 World Series titles (5 consecutively) in 12 years from 1949 to 1960. Alltime leader in World Series games (63) and wins (37), second in winning percentage (.587) and losses (26). Platoon system was his trademark strategy, Stengelese his trademark language ("You could look it up"). Managed New York Mets from 1962 to 1965. Jersey number (37) retired by Yankees and Mets.

Ingemar Stenmark (b. 3-18-56): Swedish skier. Gold medalist in slalom and giant slalom at 1980 Olympics. World Cup overall champion 3 consecutive years (1976-78).

Woody Stephens (b. 9-1-13): Horse racing trainer. Trained 2 Kentucky Derby winners (Cannonade, who won the 100th Derby in 1974 and Swale in 1984) and an incredible 5 straight Belmont winners from 1982-86, starting with 1982 Horse of the Year Conquistador Cielo.

David Stern (b. 9-22-42): Fourth NBA commissioner. Served since 1984. Average worth of a franchise has tripled from $20 million to $65 million. Owners rewarded him with 5-year, $27.5 million contract extension in 1990.

Jackie Stewart (b. 6-11-39): Scottish auto racer. Fourth alltime in Formula 1 victories (27); Formula 1 champion 3 times (1969, 1971, 1973). Also Indy 500 Rookie of the Year in 1966. Retired in 1973.

John L. Sullivan (b. 10-15-1858, d. 2-2-18): Boxer. Last bare knuckle champion. Heavyweight title holder (1882-92), lost to Jim Corbett. Career record 38-1-3 with 33 KOs from 1878 to 1892.

Paul Tagliabue (b. 11-24-40): Football executive. Fifth NFL commissioner, has served since 1989.

Anatoli Tarasov (b. 1918): Hockey coach. Orchestrated Soviet Union's emergence as a hockey power. Won 9 consecutive world amateur championships (1963-71) and 3 Olympic gold medals in 1964, 1968, 1972.

Fran Tarkenton (b. 2-3-40): Football QB. Alltime leader in touchdown passes (342), yards passing (47,003), pass attempts (6,467) and pass completions (3,686). Player of the Year in 1975. Career span 1961-78 with Minnesota, NY Giants.

Lawrence Taylor (b. 2-4-59): Football LB. Revolutionized the linebacker position. Ended 1993 season as the alltime leader in sacks. Also named to Pro Bowl a record 10 consecutive seasons. Player of the Year in 1986. Has played on 2 Super Bowl champions with New York Giants (1986, 1990). Career span 1981-93 with Giants.

Isiah Thomas (b. 4-30-61): Basketball G. Member of Indiana University team that won 1981 NCAA title. Point guard for Detroit Pistons 1982–94. All-NBA First Team 1984, '85 and '86. NBA All Star Game MVP both 1984 and '86. Led NBA in assists (13.9) in 1984–85. Third alltime in assists (8,662). Member of Piston team that won NBA title in both 1989 and '90.

Thurman Thomas (b. 5-15-66): Football RB. Led AFC in rushing both 1990 (1,297 yards) and '91 (1,407). Career span since 1988 with Buffalo Bills.

Daley Thompson (b. 7-30-58): Track and field. British decathlete was gold medalist at 2 consecutive Olympics in 1980, 1984. At 1984 Olympics set world record (8,847 points) that lasted eight years.

John Thompson (b. 9-2-41): College basketball coach. From 1973 to present, head coach at Georgetown, where he taught Patrick Ewing, Alonzo Mourning and Dikembe Mutombo to play center. Won NCAA title in 1984, beating Houston 84–75. NCAA runnerup in 1982 and '85. Overall record in 21 years as college coach 500–190.

Bobby Thomson (b. 10-25-23): Baseball OF. Hit dramatic 9th-inning playoff home run to win NL pennant for New York Giants on Oct. 3, 1951. The Giants came from 13½ games behind the Brooklyn Dodgers on Aug. 11 to win the pennant on Thomson's 3-run homer off Ralph Branca in the final game of the 3-game playoff.

Jim Thorpe (b. 5-28-1888, d. 3-28-53): Sportsman. Gold medalist in decathlon and pentathlon at 1912 Olympics. Played pro baseball with New York (NL) and Cincinnati from 1913 to 1919, and pro football with several teams from 1919 to 1926. Also All-America 2 times with Carlisle.

Dick Tiger (b. 8-14-29; d. 12-14-71): Nigerian Boxer. Born Richard Ihetu. Won middleweight title by decision over Gene Fullmer on 10-23-62. Lost middle title to Joey Giardello on 12-7-63, then regained it from Giardello on 10-21-65. Won world light heavyweight title by decision over Jose Torres on 12-16-66, then lost it when KO'd by Bob Foster in 4 on 5-24-68. *The Ring* Fighter of the Year for 1962 and '65. Career record: 61-17-3. Elected to Boxing Hall of Fame 1974.

Bill Tilden (b. 2-10-1893, d. 6-5-53): Tennis player. "Big Bill." Won 7 U.S. singles titles, 6 consecutively (1920-25, 1929) and 3 Wimbledon titles (consecutively 1920-21, 1930). Also won 6 Grand Slam doubles titles. Led U.S. to 7 consecutive Davis Cup victories (1920-26).

Ted Tinling (b. 6-23-10, d. 5-23-90): British tennis couturier. The premier source on women's tennis from Suzanne Lenglen to Steffi Graf. Also designed tennis clothes, most notably the frilled lace panties worn by Gorgeous Gussy Moran at Wimbledon in 1949.

Y.A. Tittle (b. 10-24-26): Football QB. Threw 33 TD passes in 1962 and in '63 led league in passing, completing 221 of 367 attempts for 3,145 yards and 36 TDs. Career span 1948–64, mostly with San Francisco 49ers and New York Giants. Inducted into Hall of Fame 1971.

Jayne Torvill/Christopher Dean (b. 10-7-57/ b. 7-27-58): British figure skaters. Won 4 consecutive ice dancing world championships (1981-84) and Olympic ice dancing gold medal (1984). Won world professional championships in 1985. Won Olympic ice dancing bronze in 1994.

Vladislav Tretiak (b. 4-25-52): Hockey G. Led Soviet Union to 3 gold medals at Olympics in 1972, 1976, 1984. Played on 13 world amateur champions from 1970 to 1984.

Lee Trevino (b. 12-1-39): Golfer. Won U.S. Open (1968, 1971), British Open (consecutively 1971-72) and PGA Championship (1974, 1984) 2 times each. PGA Player of the Year in 1971. Also won U.S. Senior Open in 1990. First Senior $1 million season.

Emlen Tunnell (b. 3-29-25, d. 7-23-75): Football S. Alltime leader in interception yardage (1,282) and second in interceptions (79). All-Pro 9 times. Career span 1948-61 with New York Giants and Green Bay.

Gene Tunney (b. 5-25-1897, d. 11-7-78): Boxer. Heavyweight champion (1926-28). Defeated Jack Dempsey 2 times, including famous "long count" bout. Career record 65-2-1 with 43 KOs from 1915 to 1928. Retired as champion.

Ted Turner (b. 11-19-38): Sportsman. Skipper who successfully defended the America's Cup in 1977. Also owner of the Atlanta Braves since 1976 and Hawks since 1977. Founded the Goodwill Games in 1986.

Mike Tyson (b. 6-30-66): Boxer. Youngest heavyweight champion at 19 years old in 1986. Held title until knocked out by James "Buster" Douglas in Tokyo on Feb. 10, 1990. Career record as of 10-1-93 41–1 with 36 KOs since 1985. Convicted of rape in 1992, currently serving sentence.

Johnny Unitas (b. 5-7-33): Football QB. Alltime leader for consecutive games throwing touchdown pass (47, 1956-60), third alltime touchdown passes (290), fourth alltime yards passing (40,239). Led league in touchdown passes a record 4 consecutive seasons. Player of the Year 3 times (1959, 1964, 1967). Career span 1956-72 with Baltimore, San Diego.

Al Unser Sr. (b. 5-29-39): Auto racer. Won Indy 500 4 times (consecutively 1970-71, 1978, 1987). Third alltime in CART victories (39). USAC/CART champion 3 times (1970, 1983, 1985). Brother of Bobby.

Bobby Unser (b. 2-20-34): Auto racer. Won Indy 500 3 times (1968, 1975, 1981). Fourth alltime in CART victories (35). USAC champion 2 times (1968, 1974). Brother of Al, Sr.

Harold S. Vanderbilt (b. 7-6-1884, d. 7-4-70): Sailer. Owner and skipper who successfully defended the America's Cup 3 consecutive times (1930, 1934, 1937).

Glenna Collett Vare (b. 6-20-03, d. 2-2-89): Golfer. Won U.S. Women's Amateur 6 times, more than any golfer (1922, 1925, consecutively 1928-30, 1935).

Bill Veeck (b. 2-9-14, d. 1-2-86): Baseball owner. From 1946 to 1980, owned ballclubs in Cleveland, St Louis (AL), Chicago (AL). In 1948, Cleveland became baseball's first team to draw 2 million in attendance.

That year Veeck integrated AL by signing Larry Doby and then Satchel Paige. A brilliant promoter, Veeck sent midget Eddie Gaedel up to bat for St Louis in 1951. Brought exploding scoreboard to stadiums and put players' names on uniforms.

Guillermo Vilas (b. 8-17-52): Tennis. Argentine won 50 straight matches in 1977. In '77 won French Open, where he beat Brian Gottfried, and the U.S. Open, where he beat Jimmy Connors. Also won Australian Open twice, 1978–79.

Lasse Viren (b. 7-22-49): Track and field. Finnish runner was gold medalist in 5,000 and 10,000 meters at 2 consecutive Olympics (1972, 1976).

Virginia Wade (b. 7-10-45): Tennis. Beloved in Britain, Wade won four major titles, most notably Wimbledon in 1977, its centenary year, where she triumphed over Betty Stove. Also won 1968 U.S. Open and '72 Australian Open.

Honus Wagner (b. 2-24-1874, d. 12-6-55): Baseball SS. Had .327 career batting average, 3,415 hits and 8 batting titles. Averaged .300+ 15 consecutive seasons. Led league in RBI 4 times, with 100+ RBI 9 times. Third alltime in triples (252) and league leader in doubles 8 times. Ninth alltime in stolen bases (703) and league leader 5 times. Career span 1897-1917 with Pittsburgh.

Grete Waitz (b. 10-1-53): Track and field. Norwegian runner has won New York City Marathon a record 9 times (consecutively 1978-80, 1982-86, 1988). Won the women's marathon at the 1983 World Championship.

Jersey Joe Walcott (b. 10-31-14): Boxer. Heavyweight champion from 1951 to 1952. Won title at age 37 on fifth attempt before surrendering it to Rocky Marciano. Later became sheriff of Camden, NJ.

Doak Walker (b. 1-1-27): Football HB. Led league in scoring 2 times, his first and final seasons. All-Pro 5 times. Played on 2 consecutive NFL champions (1952-53) with Detroit. Career span 1950 to 1955. Also won Heisman Trophy as a junior in 1948. All-America 3 consecutive seasons with SMU.

Herschel Walker (b. 3-3-62): Football RB. Won Heisman Trophy in 1982 with Georgia. Turned pro by entering USFL with New Jersey. Gained 7,000+ rushing yards and scored 61 touchdowns in 3 seasons before league folded. Entered NFL in 1986 with Dallas and led league in rushing yards (1,514 in 1988). Currently with Philadelphia.

Bill Walsh (b. 11-30-31): Football coach. Led the San Francisco 49ers to four Super Bowl wins, after the 1981, '84, '88 and '89 seasons. Career record with 49ers 102-63-1. Developed short-passing game. Returned to Stanford University for 1992 season.

Bill Walton (b. 11-5-52): Basketball C. MVP in 1978, playoff MVP in 1977. Led league in rebounding and blocks in 1977. Career span 1974-86 with Portland, San Diego, Boston. Also College Player of the Year 3 consecutive seasons (1972-74). Played on 2 consecutive NCAA championship teams (1972-73) with UCLA; tournament MVP twice (1972-73). Sullivan Award winner in 1973.

Junxia Wang (b. 1963): Chinese distance runner. Broke four existing world records over six days in Sept. 1993. Broke 10,000 (29:31.78) on 9-8; ran 1500 in 3:51.92 in finishing second to countrywoman Qu Yunxia's world record of 3:50.46 on 9-11; ran 3,000 record of 8:12.19 in heats on 9-12 and lowered it to 8:06.11 on 9-13.

War Admiral (b. 1934): Thoroughbred race horse. A son of Man o' War, won Triple Crown and Horse of the Year honors in 1937.

Paul Warfield (b. 11-28-42): Football WR. Caught 427 passes for 8,565 yards and 85 TDs. Played on two Super Bowl-winning Miami Dolphin teams. Career span 1964–74, all with Cleveland Browns except for 1970–74 with Miami Dolphins. Inducted to Hall of Fame 1983.

Glenn "Pop" Warner (b. 4-5-1871, d. 9-7-54): College football coach. Second alltime in wins (319). Won 3 national championships with Pittsburgh (1916, 1918) and Stanford (1926). Career record 319-106-32 with 6 teams from 1896 to 1938.

Tom Watson (b. 9-4-49): Golfer. Winner of British Open 5 times (1975, 1977, 1980, consecutively 1982-83), the Masters 2 times (1977, 1981) and U.S. Open once (1982). PGA Player of the Year 6 times, more than any golfer (consecutively 1977-80, 1982, 1984).

Dick Weber (b. 12-23-29): Bowler. Won All-Star Tournament 4 times (consecutively 1962-63, 1965-66). Voted Bowler of the Year 3 times (1961, 1963, 1965). Won 31 career PBA titles.

Johnny Weismuller (b. 6-2-04, d. 1-21-84): Swimmer. Won 3 gold medals (including 100- and 400-meter freestyle) at 1924 Olympics and 2 gold medals at 1928 Olympics. Also played Tarzan in the movies.

Jerry West (b. 5-28-38): Basketball G. 10 time All-Star; All-Defensive Team 4 times; 1969 playoff MVP. Set season record for most free throws made (840 in 1966). Led league in assists and scoring 1 time each. Career span 1960-72 with Los Angeles. Currently general manager. Also NCAA tournament MVP in 1959. All-America 2 times with West Virginia. Played on 1960 gold medal-winning Olympic team.

Whirlaway (b. 4-2-38, d. 4-6-53): Thoroughbred race horse. Triple Crown winner in 1941 with jockey Eddie Arcaro aboard. Trained by Ben A. Jones.

Byron "Whizzer" White (b. 6-8-17): Football RB. Led NFL in rushing 2 times (Pittsburgh in 1938, Detroit in 1940). Led NCAA in scoring and rushing with Colorado in 1937; named All-America. Supreme Court justice from 1962 to '93.

Reggie White (b. 12-19-62): Football DE. Entering the 1993 season only player to have as many sacks (137) as games (137). Winner in new era of free agency, signed with Packers for $17 million over four years. Career span: 1984 with Memphis Showboats, 1985–92 with Philadelphia Eagles and since 1993 with Green Bay.

Charles Whittingham (b. 4-13-13): Thoroughbred race horse trainer. "Bald Eagle" after losing hair to tropical disease in World War II. In 1986 became the oldest trainer to win Kentucky Derby, with Ferdinand. Led yearly earnings list for trainers from 1970–73 consecutively; in 1975; and in 1981–82 consecutively. Won three Eclipse Awards and trained two Horses of the Year (Ack Ack in 1971 and Ferdinand in 1987).

Kathy Whitworth (b. 9-27-39): Golfer. Alltime LPGA leader with 88 tour victories, including six majors. Won LPGA Championship in 1967, '71 and '75. Won 1977 Dinah Shore. Won Titleholders Championship (extinct major) in 1965 and '66. Won Western Open (extinct major) in 1967. Won Vare Trophy every year from 1965–72, except 1968. LPGA Player of Year from 1966–69 and 1971–73.

Hoyt Wilhelm (b. 7-26-23): Baseball RHP. Only relief pitcher in Hall of Fame. Threw knuckleball until age 48. Alltime pitching leader in games (1,070) and relief wins (124). Career record: 143-122, 2.52 ERA, 227 saves. Hit home run in his first at bat (never hit another) and pitched no-hitter in 1958. Career span with 9 teams from 1952-72.

Bud Wilkinson (b. 4-23-15 d. 2-9-94): Football coach. Alltime NCAA leader in consecutive wins (47, 1953-57). Won 3 national championships (1950, consecutively 1955-56) with Oklahoma, where he coached from 1947 to 1963. Won Orange Bowl 4 times and Sugar Bowl 2 times. Career record 145-29-4, including 4 undefeated seasons. Also coached with St Louis of NFL in 1978-79.

Billy Williams (b. 6-15-38): Baseball OF. Nicknamed "Sweet Swinging". NL Rookie of the Year for 1961. Hit 426 career home runs. Drove in 1,475 runs. Lifetime averge of .290. Named to six NL All Star teams. Career span 1959-74 with Chicago Cubs, 1975-76 with Oakland A's. Elected to Hall of Fame in 1987.

Ted Williams (b. 8-30-18): Baseball OF. "The Splendid Splinter." Last player to hit .400 (.406 in 1941). MVP in 1946, 1949 and Triple Crown winner in 1942, 1947. Sixth alltime highest batting average (.344), second most walks (2,019) and second highest slugging average (.634). Tied for tenth career HR (521); 11th in career RBI (1,839). League leader in batting average and runs scored 6 times each, RBI and HR 4 times each, walks 8 times and doubles 2 times. Had .300+ average 15 consecutive seasons; 100+ RBI and runs scored 9 times each; 30+ HR 8 times; and 100+ walks 11 times. Lost nearly 5 seasons to military service. Career span 1939-42 and 1946-60 with Boston.

Hack Wilson (b. 4-26-00; d. 11-23-48): Baseball OF. Stood 5' 6" but weighed 210. Had five incredible seasons 1926-30. Best was 1930 when he hit .356, scored 146 runs, hit a NL record 56 homers and drove in 190, which is still the major league record. Declined through drinking. Career span 1923-34 with several teams. Elected to Hall of Fame in 1979.

Dave Winfield (b. 10-3-51): Baseball OF. Also drafted out of Univ. of Minnesota for both pro basketball and football. Led NL in RBIs in 1979 (118). In 1992, first 40-year-old to get 100+ RBIs, with 108. Had clutch double to win 1992 World Series. Got 3,000th hit, off Dennis Eckersley, on 9-16-93. Career span 1973-80 with San Diego; 1981-90 with Yankees; 1990-91 with California; 1992 with Toronto; and since 1993 with Minnesota.

Major W. C. Wingfield (b. 19-16-1833, d. 4-18-12): British tennis pioneer. Credited with inventing the game of tennis, which he called "Sphairistike" or "sticky" and patented in February 1874.

Colonel Matt Winn (b. 6-30-1861, d. 10-6-49): As general manager of Churchill Downs from 1904 until his death, promoted the Kentucky Derby into the premier race in the country.

Katarina Witt (b. 12-3-65): East German figure skater. Gold medalist at 2 consecutive Olympics in 1984, 1988. Also world champion 4 times (consecutively 1984-85, 1987-88).

John Wooden (b. 10-14-10): College basketball coach. Only member of basketball Hall of Fame as coach and player. Coached UCLA to 10 NCAA championships in 12 years (consecutively 1964-65, 1967-73, 1975). Alltime winning streak 88 games

(1971-74). 664 career wins and fourth alltime highest winning percentage (.804). Career span 1949-75 with UCLA. Also 1932 College Player of the Year at Purdue.

Mickey Wright (b. 2-14-35): Golfer. Second alltime in career wins (82) and major championships (13—tied with Louise Suggs). Won U.S. Open 4 times (consecutively 1958-59, 1961, 1964), LPGA Championship 4 times, more than any golfer (1958, consecutively 1960-61, 1963), Western Open 3 times (consecutively 1962-63, 1966) and Titleholders Championship twice (1961-62).

Cale Yarborough (b. 3-27-40): Auto racer. Won Daytona 500 4 times (1968, 1977, consecutively 1983-84). Fifth alltime in NASCAR victories (83). Also NASCAR champion 3 consecutive years (1976-78).

Carl Yastrzemski (b. 8-22-39): Baseball OF. "Yaz." 3,419 career hits, 452 HR. 1967 MVP and Triple Crown winner. 3 batting titles, including .301 in 1968, the lowest ever to win. Second alltime in games played (3,308) and fourth in walks (1,845). Holds league record for most times intentionally walked (190) and seasons leading in outfield assists (6). Career span 1961-83 with Boston.

Cy Young (b. 3-29-1867, d. 11-4-55): Baseball RHP. Alltime leader in wins (511), losses (315), innings pitched (7,354.2) and complete games (749); fourth in shutouts (76). Had 2.63 career ERA. Pitched 3 no-hitters, including a perfect game in 1904. Pitching award named in his honor. Career span 1890-1911 with Cleveland, Boston.

Robin Yount (b. 9-16-55): Baseball OF/SS. Became Brewer shortstop at 18. Landslide winner of 1982 AL MVP in 1982 when he hit .331 with 29 homers. Hit .414 in Brewers' 1982 Series loss to Cardinals. 3,142 hits. Shoulder injury made Yount move to outfield in 1984. Career span 1974-93, all with the Brewers.

Babe Didrikson Zaharias (b. 6-26-14, d. 9-27-56): Sportswoman. The greatest female athlete. Gold medalist in 80-meter hurdles and javelin throw at 1932 Olympics; also won silver medal in high jump (her gold medal jump was disallowed for using the then-illegal western roll). Became a golfer in 1935 and won 12 major titles, including U.S. Open 3 times (1948, 1950, 1954—a year after cancer surgery). Also helped found the LPGA in 1949.

Tony Zale (b. 5-29-13): Boxer. Born Anthony Zaleski. "The Man of Steel." Won vacant middleweight title by decision over Georgie Abrams on 11-28-41. Lost title to Billy Conn on 2-13-42. Spent almost 4 years in Navy. In sensational 3 fight series with Rocky Graziano, retained title with KO in 6 on 9-27-46; lost it to Graziano by KO in 6 on 7-17-47; and then reclaimed it by KOing Graziano in 3 on 6-10-48. Lost title to Marcel Cerdan, who KO'd him in 12 on 9-21-48. Career record: 88 bouts; won 46 by KO and 24 by decision; drew 2; lost 16, 4 by KO. Elected to Boxing Hall of Fame 1958.

Emil Zatopek (b. 9-19-22): Track and field. Czechoslovakian runner became only athlete to win gold medal in 5,000 and 10,000 meters and marathon, at 1952 Olympics. Also gold medalist in 10,000 meters at 1948 Olympics.

Obituaries

Vitas Gerulaitis
1954-1994

MANNY MILLAN

Obituaries

Jeff Alm, 25, football player. A defensive end for the Houston Oilers, Alm committed suicide after an automobile accident in which his friend, Sean Lynch, was killed. Alm was the second round draft pick out of Notre Dame in 1990 for the Oilers. In Houston, of self-inflicted gunshot wounds, December 14, 1993.

Ray Arcel, 94, boxing trainer. Arcel trained some of boxing's best-known figures during a career that spanned 70 years. His 20 world champions included Benny Leonard, Barney Ross, Ezzard Charles, Larry Holmes and Roberto Duran. Red Smith described the courteous and well-spoken Arcel as "the first gentleman of fistfighting." Arcel himself, who learned his trade in the long-gone gyms and fight clubs of New York City, said that "boxing is brain over brawn." In New York City, of natural causes, March 7.

Verlon Biggs, 51, football player. A defensive star with the New York Jets, Biggs helped Joe Namath make good on his promise to defeat the Baltimore Colts in Super Bowl III. In Moss Point, Miss., of leukemia, June 7.

Lewis Billups, 30, football player. Billups was a Cincinnati Bengal defensive back from 1986 through 1988 and played in Super Bowl XXIII. He was killed when he lost control of his car while trying to avoid another vehicle changing lanes. In Orlando, of injuries sustained in the crash, April 9.

Neil Bonnett, 47, auto racer. Bonnett was attempting a comeback after a three-year absence when he became, with Rodney Orr, the second driver to die in a four-day period at Daytona International Speedway. Bonnett, who had pulled Davey Allison out of his deadly helicopter crash in June 1993, was the third member of racing's "Alabama Gang" to die in 18 months. In Daytona Beach, Fla., of head injuries sustained in the crash, February 11.

Ray (Muscles) Bray Sr., 76, football player. Bray, a guard, played in three NFL championships for George Halas's Chicago Bears (1940, 1941 and 1946). The Bears 73–0 defeat of the Redskins in 1940 was the most decisive victory in NFL history. In Mesa, Ariz., of natural causes, December 26, 1993.

Jim Brock, 57, baseball coach. With 1,100 wins in 23 years at Arizona State, Brock was one of college baseball's winningest coaches. During his tenure, the Sun Devils made it to the College World Series 13 times, winning two World Series titles and finishing second four times. Named Coach of the Year in 1977 and 1981, Brock sent 64 players to the big leagues, including Barry Bonds and Hubie Brooks. In Mesa, Az., of cancer, June 12.

Lee Roy Caffey, 53, football player. Caffey was an all-pro linebacker for Vince Lombardi's champion Green Bay Packer teams and played in the 1971 Super Bowl for the Dallas Cowboys. In Houston, of cancer, January 18.

Hugh Culverhouse, 75, football team owner. Dressed in white pants, orange-and-white shirt, orange-striped tie and matching saddle oxfords, the owner of the Tampa Bay Buccaneers cut a stylish figure at home games, adding a note of color to the otherwise gray gloom of the Buc's unbroken string of losing seasons since 1981. Culverhouse, who made his money in Florida real estate and his law practice, purchased the Bucs in 1974 and won NFC Central titles in 1979–81 behind quarterback Doug Williams. Culverhouse also served as chairman of the NFL's finance committee during the 1982 and '87 player strikes. In New Orleans, of lung cancer, August 25.

John Curry, 44, skater. The 1976 Olympic and world figure skating champion, known as the Nureyev of skating, Curry died of an AIDS-related heart attack seven years after learning he was HIV-positive. He had spoken openly about his illness and his homosexuality since '91. "My whole circle of friends died [of AIDS]," he told the London *Daily Mail*. "I don't mean just lovers, but I'm talking about pals and people you go to the theater or to dinner with. I think the more open people are, the easier it gets for everybody else because it demystifies [AIDS]....I want people to understand the importance of safe sex. After all, no one is immune." Curry, an elegant and courageous man who seamlessly melded athleticism and artistry, was praised by Dick Button as "the finest and most intelligent all-around skater I've ever seen." In Stratford-upon-Avon, England, of an AIDS-related heart attack, April 22.

Easy Goer, 8, thoroughbred race horse. The champion two-year-old of 1988, Easy Goer's rivalry with Sunday Silence excited the horse racing world in 1989, when Easy Goer won the Belmont and placed second to Sunday Silence in the Kentucky Derby and Preakness. A son of Alydar, Easy Goer won 14 of 20 starts, with five seconds and one third, and retired in 1990 with earnings of $4,873,770. At Claiborne Farm, of natural causes, May 12.

Heather Farr, 28, golfer. National junior golf champion and an All-America at Arizona State University, Farr never won an LPGA event, but she earned the respect of many for her fight against cancer and her gutsy personality. In Scottsdale, Ariz., of cancer, November 20, 1993.

Charles S. (Chub) Feeney, 72, baseball manager. President of the National League from 1970–86, Feeney hailed from an old baseball family. His grandfather bought the New York Giants in 1919 and ran the ball club until his death in 1936, when his son, Horace, took over. Chub joined in 1946 and spent 24 years with the Giants, moving with them from New York to San Francisco. As the de-facto general manager (he never held the title) of the team, Feeney was one of the first managers to hire black and Latin players, and he helped make the Giants the National League champions in 1962. On his popular radio show, *Ask Chub Feeney*, he fielded calls from opinionated fans with wit and style. He retired from baseball in 1988 after briefly serving as president of the San Diego Padres. In San Francisco, of a heart attack, January 10.

Jim Finks, 66, football general manager. When Finks joined the New Orleans Saints in January 1986 as president and general manager, the "Aints" had gone 19 years without a winning season. By 1991, New Orleans won the conference with an 11–5 mark. Finks also had success in baseball, helping lead the Chicago Cubs to the NL East title in 1984—their first since 1945. Finks nearly became NFL commisioner in 1989, but was able to get only 18 of 21 votes needed from the 28 owners. As a player, Finks entered the NFL with the Pittsburgh Steelers in 1949, first as a defensive back and then as quarterback. He made the Pro Bowl in 1952. In New Orleans, of lung cancer, May 8.

Alonzo Smith (Jake) Gaither, 90, football coach. Between 1945 and '69, the character-building Gaither won more football games than just about any other coach in the country. In the days of segregation, he put together powerhouse teams at the predominantly black Florida A&M, where he had three unbeaten seasons and an overall record of 203-36-4. He sent 42 players to the NFL, including Bob Hayes and Willie Galimore. Famous for his "I like my players mobile, agile and hostile" comment, Gaither was in fact revered for his quiet, eloquent manner, and often counseled Florida governor LeRoy Collins during civil rights turmoils in the '50s and '60s. In Tallahassee, of natural causes, February 18.

Vitas Gerulaitis, 40, tennis player. An engaging, gregarious player who won the Australian Open in 1977, attained the No. 3 ranking in 1978, and reached the finals of the 1979 U.S. Open and the 1980 French Open, Gerulaitis's accidental death from carbon monoxide poisoning shocked the tennis world.

Sally Jenkins writes:

"Vitas Gerulaitis was a man who moved between various eras of tennis as smoothly as he once moved from baseline to net. He chatted amiably in his television work with oldies but goodies like Tony Trabert and Fred Stolle, he jammed on the guitar with John McEnroe, he gave counsel to young superstar Pete Sampras. When Gerulaitis was found dead at the home of an acquaintance in Southampton, N.Y., the tennis world lost a free spirit and a shaggy-haired ambassador.

"Despite a career in which he ranked among the top five players in the world in four different years, Gerulaitis was better known for his Studio 54 lifestyle. He was one of the few athletes who admitted using cocaine, in the late 1970s and early '80s, and also acknowledged that his penchant for partying had hurt him on the court. He was reportedly treated for substance abuse in 1983 and was implicated, though never charged, in a cocaine-dealing conspiracy that same year.

"But by all indications Gerulaitis had pulled his life together. He did commentary for CBS during the U.S. Open (his native Brooklynese accent was part of his charm), he played on the masters circuit and, most of all, he kept up relations with the myriad friends he made in the game....

"Gerulaitis's flamboyance and penchant for high living masked the fact that he was a tenacious competitor with nonpareil quickness and a variety of shots hatched on New York City's public courts. What he lacked was the one big weapon that would have pushed him ahead of his more successful contemporaries—Bjorn Borg, Jimmy Connors, and good buddy John McEnroe, who beat him in the final of the '79 U.S. Open. But he will be remembered as a man who wrestled with his personal demons and hung around to do some good."

In Southampton, N.Y., of accidental carbon monoxide poisoning, September 18.

George Gregory, 88, basketball player. Gregory, who played for Columbia University, was the first black All-America basketball player when he was selected in 1931. In New York City, of cancer, May 21.

Alton Grizzard, 24, football player. Navy quarterback from 1987-90, Grizzard was the school's alltime career total offense leader with 5,666 yards rushing and passing. With his friend Kerryn O'Neill, he was shot at the U.S. Naval Amphibious Base at Coronado, Calif., by a fellow officer who then committed suicide. In Coronado, Calif., of gunshot wounds, December 1, 1993.

Harvey Haddix, 68, baseball player. Haddix pitched 12 innings of perfect baseball for the Pittsburgh Pirates on May 26, 1959, arguably the best-pitched game in history. The lefthander eventually lost his game 1–0 to Milwaukee on a home run in the 13th. Over his career, Haddix pitched for five teams and was an All-Star three times. He once said: "Every single day I put on a uniform for the rest of my life, I was asked about the perfect game. Every single day." In Springfield, Ohio, of emphysema, January 8.

Ron Hansen, jockey. Hansen's decomposed body was found in the mud flats of the San Francisco Bay in January 1994, nearly five months after he disappeared following an accident on the San Mateo Bridge. While driving his Jaguar over the bridge at perhaps 100 mph, Hansen smashed into another car, which skidded against the guardrail and flipped. Hansen had nearly 3,700 wins and earned purses worth $36.6 million. In San Francisco, cause unknown, October 1.

Larry Klein, 42, sailor. The U.S.'s best hope for 1996 Olympic gold in the soling class, Klein died in the choppy, icy waters near Alcatraz Island during the San Francisco Big Boat series. He was a world champion in three classes (soling, etchells and J/24s) between 1989 and 1991, and was named Rolex Yachtsman of the Year in 1989. Off Alcatraz Island, Calif., from drowning, September 17.

Fred Lebow, 62, New York Marathon Race Director. The man responsible for turning the New York City marathon into the largest in the world, an international spectacle involving 25,000 runners, Lebow was a promotional machine extraordinaire and often received more attention than his elite runners. With Frank Shorter and Bill Rodgers, he sparked the running boom in the U.S. Lebow's beard, cycling cap and sweatsuit were his trademarks; the marathon and the 31,000-member New York Road Runners Club his legacies. In New York City, of brain cancer, October 9.

Bobby Lewis, 63, boxing coach. The U.S. Olympic boxing coach in 1972, Lewis also trained George Foreman and Ron Lyle. In Aurora, Colo., of heart disease, November 13.

Ulrike Maier, 26, skier. Winner of the Super G at the world championships in 1989 (when she was three months pregnant) and 1991, Maier was a strong contender for the gold in the 1994 Olympics, after which she planned to retire. But in a World Cup downhill race just two weeks before the Olympics, she caught an edge with her right ski on a patch of ice, swerved out of control and broke her neck in the crash. In Murnau, Germany, of a broken neck, January 29.

Bob Matheson, 49, football player. Linebacker for the Miami Dolphins, Matheson, who wore number 53, became associated with the "53 defense," an innovative defensive tactic which had Matheson changing positions from defensive end to linebacker depending on the alignment. In Durham, N.C., of Hodgkin's disease, September 5.

Frank McGuire, 80, basketball coach. The stylishly dressed, quick-tongued McGuire coached two schools to the NCAA men's basketball championships, North Carolina in 1957 (where the 31–0 Tar Heels beat Wilt Chamberlain's Kansas team in triple overtime 54–53) and his alma mater St. John's in 1952 (an 80–63 loss to Kansas). During his years at North Carolina,

1953–61, he helped create the state's mania for basketball and hired now-legendary coach Dean Smith. McGuire coached South Carolina from 1965–80 and had a school-record 283 wins. In West Columbia, S.C., of a stroke, October 11.

Wangila Napunyi, 26, boxer. Napunyi earned his 1988 Olympic gold in the first welterweight final to be decided by a knockout (after 16 decisions). He was also the first black African boxer to win an Olympic championship. He died from a head injury suffered during a 10-round bout with David Gonzales of Houston. In Las Vegas, of head injuries, July 22.

Kerryn O'Neill, 21, runner. A Navy track star who set three academy records—in cross country, the indoor 5,000 meters and outdoor 5,000 meters—and earned 12 varsity letters, O'Neill, with Alton Grizzard, was shot on a U.S. naval base by her former boyfriend. In Coronado, Calif., of gunshot wounds, December 1, 1993.

Rodney Orr, 31, auto racer. Orr's death in the crash of his Ford in a practice race at Daytona International Speedway was the second in a four-day period, following the death of Neil Bonnett. In Daytona Beach, Fla., of head injuries sustained in the crash, February 14.

Jimmie Reese, 92, baseball coach. A beloved conditioning coach for the California Angels, Reese was the last living roommate of Babe Ruth. He was in baseball for 78 years and was known as the best fungo-hitting coach in the majors. Among his closest friends were Reggie Jackson, Jim Abbott and Nolan Ryan. In Santa Ana, Calif., of natural causes, July 13.

Ayrton Senna, 34, auto racer. The three-time world champion and winner of 41 Grand Prix races (second only to Alain Prost) over a ten-year career, Senna's death at the San Marino Grand Prix was a stunning blow to the racing world.

Bruce Newman writes:

"In the end, in the sudden, final instant of his life, Ayrton Senna could not have known what hit him. He could not have seen what, in the next moment, would kill him. This was not possible, not even for Senna. When his Williams-Renault FW16 failed to negotiate the sweeping left turn called Tamburello at the San Marino Grand Prix in Imola, Italy, Senna's car rocketed off the circuit and into a concrete retaining wall, an impact so instantaneous at 186 mph that he could not have shifted his eyes from the open track ahead in time to see it.

"The penetrating brown eyes of Ayrton Senna da Silva were always fixed firmly upon the prize, and last weekend they had brought him to the pole position for the 65th time in his Formula One career, more than twice as many times as any other driver in the history of the sport. ...

"Last week in Imola, Senna had plainly seen something—or felt something—on the track that was beyond his ability to comprehend, and it frightened him. But what was it? During Friday's time trials, a fellow Brazilian, Rubens Barrichello, had suffered a slight concussion when his Jordan-Hart became airborne and crashed hard. On Saturday, after Austrian rookie Roland Ratzenberger, driving for the Simtek team, had lost control of his car and flown off the track to his death at nearly 200 mph during qualifying, Senna refused to take his car out of the garage for more laps. Ratzenberger's was the first death in Formula One racing in 12 years, and when word reached the paddock, Senna was said to have had the unmistakable look of someone who had just seen his own shadow....

"He was still so shaken on Sunday morning that he refused to speak to reporters after the warmup session, except to tersely say, 'Today was not typical. My car is very difficult to drive.'...

"Senna transcended the tiresome debate about whether race drivers are really athletes, because he was something far rarer in this world than an athlete—he was a genius. Senna could take an 1,100-pound racing car and transform it into a living, breathing thing, a throbbing dance partner in his dangerous pas de deux. Michael Andretti, the American who was Senna's teammate with McLaren last year, once tried to explain what separated Senna from other Formula One drivers. 'It's confidence,' Andretti said. 'When he goes into the corner, he knows the car's going to stick for him. He just drives through [mechanical] problems. I need the car to be working for me to have a chance. He doesn't.'

"Former world champion Niki Lauder said simply, 'He was the best driver who ever lived.'...

"In Brazil, Senna was seen as an almost godlike figure, commuting to races from his ranch in a private jet. TV Globo, the nation's largest network, assigned a crew just to follow Senna from race to race....

"As the news of his death began to spread, people gathered outside Senna's apartment building in Sao Paulo and wept. Brazil's president, Itamar Franco, declared three days of mourning and offered the family the use of the presidential plane to bring the body home. In Rio's Maracana Stadium nearly 100,000 fans who had been watching a soccer match between Flamengo and Vasco stood and clapped their hands in unison, chanting 'Ole-oleleo la, Sen-na, Sen-na.' The scene was repeated in every stadium in which a game was played in Brazil that afternoon."

In Imola, Italy, of injuries sustained in the crash, May 1.

Jack Sharkey, 91, boxer. Sharkey won the heavyweight boxing championship on June 21, 1932 in a fight against Max Schmeling and lost it the following year to Primo Carnera. His career record was 38-13-3 with one no decision. Before his death, Sharkey was inducted into the International Boxing Hall of Fame, in January 1994. In Beverly, Mass., of natural causes, August 17.

Eric Show, 37, baseball player. The winningest—and most paranoid—pitcher in San Diego Padre history, Show won 101 games during his 11-year major league career and helped the Padres win the 1984 National League pennant, but as Franz Lidz writes, Show made more enemies than friends:

"While Show accused presidents from Kennedy to Reagan of leftist leanings, teammates questioned his cavalier attitude toward the game. He routinely showed up late at the ballpark. Pat Dobson, who was San Diego's pitching coach from 1988 to '90, once said Show couldn't pitch well unless the 'moons of Remulak were aligned.' Indeed, Show, an accomplished jazz guitarist, seemed at peace only while strumming his Gibson....

"In 1985 he surrendered Pete Rose's 4,192nd career hit and then sat on the mound with his arms folded as the crowd saluted Rose for having broken Ty Cobb's record....

"The Padres released him after the [1990] season, and he signed with the Oakland A's. He showed up for spring training with both hands bandaged. He had cut them on barbed wire, Show explained, while fleeing two assailants outside a convenience store. The A's sent him home.

"Show spent the next two years in and out of rehab centers. Last July, San Diego police found him strung out on crystal methadrine and had to subdue him with pepper gas. Show said people were out to kill him and begged the cops to kill him.

"The autopsy report did not give a cause of death, and officials say it will be at least four weeks until they know for sure what killed Show. Whatever the final cause, it was something that had been coming on for a long time. Though Show was estranged from the Padres at the time of his death, the team no doubt had a special place in his troubled heart. 'We were a family,' he once said. 'A dysfunctional family, but a family just the same.' "

At a drug rehabilitation center in Dulzura, Calif., from an overdose of heroin and cocaine, March 16.

Roy Simmons, 94, lacrosse coach. Simmons, who coached Jim Brown in football and lacrosse, built Syracuse into a lacrosse powerhouse, compiling a record of 251-130-1 over 38 years, and guided the school to its only national football title in 1959. In Syracuse, N.Y., of a stroke-induced coma, August 19.

Helen Stephens, 75, runner. Stephens was a double gold medalist in track (in the 100 meters and the 4 x 100 relay) at the 1936 Olympic games in Berlin. In St. Louis, from a stroke, January 17.

Earl Strom, 66, basketball referee. One of the best known of the NBA's referees, Strom's sound judgment and passion for the game earned him the respect of players and coaches alike from his first call in 1957. Strom was a colorful, demonstrative referee, and at his retirement from the NBA after the 1989-90 season, he was rated the No. 1 pro hoops referee in everyone's poll. Strom had the distinction of officiating Game 7 in all of his era's nine seven-game NBA Finals. In Pottstown, Penn., of brain cancer, July 10.

Chuck Taylor, 74, football coach. A participant in the Rose Bowl first as a Stanford player and then as coach and athletic director, Taylor led Stanford to one of its best years ever, a 9-1 record and No. 7 national ranking in 1951.

Hank Thomson, 86, horseman. Thomson, publisher of the *The Delaware* (Ohio) *Gazette*, co-founded the Little Brown Jug, one of harness racing's Triple Crown races for 3-year old pacers, with lawyer Joseph Neville Jr. in the 1940s. Thomson also was senior vice president of the Grand Circuit and a founder of Pacing's Triple Crown. In Delaware, Ohio, of cancer, January 24.

Marvin Eugene Throneberry, 60, baseball player. Given his initials, it was only fitting that Marvelous Marv came to symbolize the amazin'ly inept 1962 Mets, the team that lost 120 games. While Throneberry had his best year in '62, hitting .244 with 16 homers, in one particularly horrendous June game he cost New York six runs in one inning. But the New York faithful loved him, and at the New York Baseball Writers dinner after the season, he was given the Good Guy award for his self-deprecating demeanor. "They told me not to stand up here too long holding this plaque," said Marvelous Marv. "I might drop it."

He became a star again in the late 1970s and early '80s as a result of his appearances in the Miller Lite TV commercials, uttering the line, "I still don't know why they asked me to do this commercial."
In Collierville, Tenn., of cancer, July 23.

Ellsworth Vines, 82, tennis player. A two-time U.S. national champion (in 1931 and '32), Vines won Wimbledon in 1931 and was the runner-up in '32. He was inducted into the International Tennis Hall of Fame in 1962. In Palm Springs, of kidney disease, March 18.

Jersey Joe Walcott, 80, boxer. Walcott didn't fight for a championship title until his 17th year as a fighter, but when he finally captured the title at 36 years, 6 months, he was the oldest man to do so. Walcott held the title from 1951 until 1952, when Rocky Marciano knocked him out in the 13th round. His first title bid was thwarted by Joe Louis in 1947, a bout many—including Louis—though Walcott won. "Joe [Louis] thought he had lost and started leaving the ring," said trainer Eddie Futch. Walcott later became sheriff of Camden, New Jersey. In Camden, from natural causes, February 25.

Bud Wilkinson, 77, football coach. From 1948-'58, Wilkinson's teams at Oklahoma amassed a record of 107-8-2, including three national championships and a stunning, NCAA-record 47 consecutive victories (1953-57). His teams won four Orange Bowls and two Sugar Bowls. Oklahoma's Gridiron Galahad, as one journalist called him, was a creative, organized coach who ran a no-huddle, high-powered offense. A star quarterback at the University of Minnesota (he led the College All-Stars to a win in 1937 over the professional champions, the Green Bay Packers), Wilkinson earned a master's degree in English from Syracuse with the intention of becoming a professor, but got sidetracked into football. He eventually left Oklahoma to enter politics, winning the Republican nomination in the 1964 U.S. Senate race but losing the general election. The graceful, dignified Wilkinson gained access to President Nixon's inner circle as a consultant in 1969 but quit after he found himself sealed off by Nixon aides Bob Haldeman and John Ehrlichman. After ten years of college football broadcasting, he accepted the St. Louis Cardinal coaching job at age 61, but was axed at the end of his second, losing season.

Former Sooner running back Prentice Gautt, whom Wilkinson recruited in 1957 as the first black athlete at Oklahoma, paid tribute to Wilkinson: "I place him completely above words like *pettiness* and *prejudice*. Those things weren't in him."
In St. Louis, of congestive heart failure, February 9.

Ike Williams, 71, boxer. Lightweight boxing champion from 1947-'51, Williams was *Ring* magazine's fighter of the year in 1948. He was 123-25-5 with 60 knockouts when he retired in 1955. In Los Angeles, of natural causes, September 6.

Bob Woolf, 65, attorney-agent. A pioneering attorney-agent to the stars, Woolf represented such athletes as Julius Erving, Rocket Ismail, and Thurman Munson. His first client was Red Sox pitcher Earl Wilson, who hired him in 1965. Known for maintaining his pleasant manner even in the toughest negotiations, Woolf signed Boston sports legends Larry Bird and Carl Yastrzemski and negotiated for rock stars New Kids on the Block and journalist Larry King. On Fisher Island, Fla., of a heart attack, November 30, 1993.

Cliff Young, 29, baseball player. The third Cleveland Indian pitcher to die in a year, Young was killed when the truck he was driving crashed into a tree. He was 3-3 with one save and a 4.62 ERA before elbow surgery ended his 1993 season in August. In Willis, Tex., of injuries sustained in the crash, November 4, 1993.